Tolley's
VAT C
200

GW00722730

Sixteenth Edition

by
Alan Dolton MA (Oxon)
and
Robert Wareham BSc (Econ) FCA

Tolley Publishing

First Edition	March 1982
Second Edition	March 1984
Third Edition	March 1988
Fourth Edition	August 1989
Fifth Edition	June 1990
Sixth Edition	April 1991
Seventh Edition	April 1992
Eighth Edition	April 1993
Ninth Edition	April 1994
Tenth Edition	April 1995
Eleventh Edition	April 1996
Twelfth Edition	April 1997
Thirteenth Edition	May 1998
Fourteenth Edition	April 1999
Fifteenth Edition	April 2000
Sixteenth Edition	April 2001

Published by
Tolley
2 Addiscombe Road
Croydon, Surrey CR9 5AF, England
020 8686 9141

Typeset by Kerrypress Ltd
Luton, Beds.

Printed in Great Britain by
The Bath Press, Somerset

Reed Elsevier (UK) Ltd 2001
ISBN 07545 1159–6

About This Book

VAT was introduced in the UK in 1973. The thousands of appeal decisions form an essential commentary on many aspects of the legislation. They also show the impact of the tax on an increasing range of business and private circumstances.

This edition of Tolley's VAT Cases contains entries for more than 3,500 cases, comprising public VAT tribunal decisions and court decisions (High Court, Court of Session and above), decided up to 1 January 2001, which are relevant to current VAT legislation. The book is one of the Tolley annuals and is updated to 1 January each year. Where possible, 'postscripts' have been added where later decisions bear directly on relevant entries.

The digest of decisions is in 65 chapters arranged alphabetically by subject, together with an introductory survey of the leading decisions reached in 2000. Tables of cases, statutes, statutory instruments and European Community Directives and a detailed subject index are provided.

Most of the cases in this edition relate to periods before *Value Added Tax Act 1994* came into force. References marked with an asterisk (*) are to legislation which has replaced that involved in the case summarised.

A database containing full transcripts of most of the cases summarised in this book is available in CD-ROM format from Butterworths Tolley. Individual transcripts of tribunal decisions are available from the Combined Tax Tribunal, 15/19 Bedford Avenue, London WC1B 3A5 (telephone 020 7631 4242).

The summaries of cases are published with kind permission of the VAT Tribunal Headquarters.

The first two editions of this book were published under the title Grout's Value Added Tax Cases, and the summaries of decisions were prepared by the late Victor Grout CBE LLB. Summaries of cases for the third and fourth editions were prepared by VATAX Advisory Services Ltd.

Tolley Publishing

How to Use This Book

Each case summary is identified by the number of the chapter containing it and its entry number in that chapter. Thus, 13.1 is *New Ash Green Village Association Ltd*, entry number 1 in chapter 13 CLUBS, ASSOCIATIONS AND ORGANISATIONS. Summaries are indexed in the alphabetical table of cases near the end of the book.

If it is desired to refer to a particular case, the parties to which are not known, or to cases dealing with a particular subject, the book provides three ways of obtaining the information required. Firstly, there is the Contents list at the beginning of the book, which lists the chapters and the main headings in them. The longer chapters are also headed by their own contents lists, which contain any subheadings as well as the main headings.

Secondly, after the alphabetical table of names of parties there is a table of statutes. In accordance with the method of citing legislation described at the head of Abbreviations and References (to which particular attention is drawn), the cases are listed by reference to current legislation where the legislation in force at the time of the case has been replaced.

Thirdly, there is an extensive general subject index at the end of the book.

Contents

Contents

Contents

Contents

Contents

Contents

Contents

Abbreviations and References

References throughout the book to numbered sections and schedules are to the Value Added Tax Act 1994 unless otherwise stated. An asterisk (*) added to a statutory reference indicates that it has replaced, but is similar or identical to, the relevant legislation involved in the case. References to Tribunals Rules, VAT Regulations and Special Provisions Order are respectively to The Value Added Tax Tribunals Rules 1986 (SI 1986 No 590), The Value Added Tax Regulations 1995 (SI 1995 No 2518) and The Value Added Tax (Special Provisions) Order 1995 (SI 1995 No 1268). A reference to Notice No 700 is to HM Customs & Excise Notice No 700 and similarly for other numbered Notices. Certain of these Notices, or parts of them, have statutory force.

ABBREVIATIONS

Art	=	Article
C & E	=	Customs & Excise
CA	=	Court of Appeal
Ch D	=	Chancery Division
CIR	=	Commissioners of Inland Revenue
CJEC	=	Court of Justice of the European Communities
col.	=	column
Commissioners	=	Commissioners of C & E
Commrs	=	Commissioners of C & E
CS	=	Court of Session (Scotland)
DC	=	Divisional Court
EC	=	European Community
ECHR	=	European Court of Human Rights
EEC	=	European Economic Community
ex p.	=	ex parte
FA	=	Finance Act
F(No 2)A	=	Finance (No 2) Act
FC(A)	=	Federal Court (Australia)
HL	=	House of Lords
ICAEW	=	Institute of Chartered Accountants in England and Wales
ICTA	=	Income and Corporation Taxes Act
KB	=	King's Bench Division
NI	=	Northern Ireland
oao	=	on the application of
p	=	page
PC	=	Privy Council
PCC	=	Parochial Church Council
PCTA	=	Provisional Collection of Taxes Act 1968
QB	=	Queen's Bench Division
r	=	rule
Reg	=	Regulation
RSC	=	Rules of the Supreme Court
s	=	section
Sch	=	Schedule
Sec	=	Section
SI	=	Statutory Instrument
t/a	=	trading as
VATA	=	Value Added Tax Act

Abbreviations and References

REFERENCES (*denotes a series accredited for citation in court)

AC	=	*Law Reports, Appeal Cases, (Incorporated Council of Law Reporting for England and Wales, 3, Stone Buildings, Lincoln's Inn, WC2A 3XN)
AEECR	=	All England Law Reports: European Cases, (Butterworths, Halsbury House, 35 Chancery Lane, London WC2A 1EL).
All ER	=	*All England Law Reports, (Butterworths, as above).
All ER (D)	=	All England Reporter Direct, (Butterworths, as above).
ALR	=	Argus Law Reports, Victoria.
BCLC	=	Butterworth's Company Law Cases, (Butterworths, as above).
BTC	=	British Tax Cases, (CCH Editions Ltd, Telford Road, Bicester, Oxon OX6 0XD).
BVC	=	British Value Added Tax Cases, (CCH Editions Ltd, as above).
CBNS	=	Common Bench New Series Reports.
Ch	=	*Law Reports, Chancery Division.
CMLR	=	Common Market Law Reports (European Law Centre, South Quay Plaza, 183 Marsh Wall, London E14 9FT).
Cr AR	=	Criminal Appeal Reports.
D	=	Session Cases, 2nd Series (Dunlop).
DLR	=	Dominion Law Reports.
E & E	=	Ellis & Ellis's Reports.
ECCD	=	European Commission Collection of Decisions.
ECDR	=	European Commission Decisions and Reports.
ECR	=	European Community Reports.
EG	=	Estates Gazette.
EHRR	=	European Human Rights Reports.
FCR	=	Federal Court Reports (Australia).
H & N	=	*Hurlstone & Norman's Reports.
ICR	=	Industrial Cases Reports.
ITLR	=	International Tax Law Reports, (Butterworths, as above).
LR Ind App	=	*Law Reports, Indian Appeals.
LTR	=	*Law Times Reports.
OJ	=	Official Journal of the European Communities.
SC	=	Court of Session Cases.
SCLR	=	Scottish Civil Law Reports.
STC	=	*Simon's Tax Cases, (Butterworths, as above).
STI	=	Simon's Tax Intelligence, (Butterworths, as above).
TC	=	*Official Reports of Tax Cases, (HM Stationery Office, 49 High Holborn, WC1V 6HB).
TTC	=	Tolley's Tax Cases, (Butterworths Tolley, 2 Addiscombe Road, Croydon CR9 5AF).
VATDR	=	Value Added Tax and Duties Reports, (HM Stationery Office, as above).
VATTR	=	Value Added Tax Tribunal Reports, (HM Stationery Office, as above).
VTD	=	VAT Tribunal Decision, (VAT and Duties Tribunals Headquarters, 15-19 Bedford Avenue, London WC1B 3AS).
WLR	=	*Weekly Law Reports, (Incorporated Council of Law Reporting, as above).

Court cases. The first number in the citation refers to the volume, and the second to the page, so that [1985] 1 All ER 15 means that the report is to be found on page fifteen of the first volume of the All England Law Reports for 1985. Where no volume number is given, only one volume was produced in that year. Citation where appropriate is of Simon's Tax Cases, one set of the official series (i.e. either the Law Reports or the Weekly Law Reports), and the All England Reports. For CJEC cases, the official case reference is given together with citations for the Common Market Law Reports, the European Community Reports, and (where appropriate) Simon's Tax Cases and the All England Reports. Only in default of these are other series referred to. The citation is preceded by the Court and the month and year of the decision.

Tribunal cases. Where a decision is reported in the Value Added Tax Tribunals Reports (VATTR) or Value Added Tax and Duties Reports (VATDR) published by HM Stationery Office by the direction of the President of the VAT and Duties Tribunals, the citation is the VATTR or VATDR reference followed by the number assigned to the decision by the VAT Tribunals Headquarters [e.g. *[1989] VATTR 199 (VTD 4137)*].

In other cases the citation is the tribunal centre reference followed by the number assigned to the decision by the VAT and Duties Tribunals Headquarters [e.g. *MAN/77/247 (VTD 537)*]. The letters in the tribunal centre reference are the first three letters of the tribunal [e.g. EDN = Edinburgh, LON = London, MAN = Manchester]. In all tribunal cases only the appellant or applicant is named.

Where legal decisions are very recent and in the lower courts or the VAT tribunal, it must be remembered that they may be reversed on appeal.

Glossary of Latin & Old French Phrases

acte claire	=	so obvious as to leave no scope for any reasonable doubt.
causa causans	=	the immediate cause; the last link in the chain of causation.
causa sine qua non	=	an essential link in the chain of causation, but not the immediate cause.
certiorari	=	a writ commanding a lower court to certify a matter to the High Court.
eiusdem generis	=	of the same type.
estoppel	=	rule of evidence which stops a person from denying the truth of a statement previously made by him to, and relied on by, another person.
estoppel per rem judicatum	=	rule of evidence which stops a person from contesting an issue decided by the Court in previous litigation between the same parties.
ex gratia	=	voluntarily, without accepting legal liability.
ex parte	=	an application made to the court by one party without giving notice to the other party.
in re	=	in the matter of, concerning.
inter alia	=	among other things.
mandamus	=	a writ ordering the performance of a specific duty.
obiter dictum / obiter dicta	=	opinion(s) expressed by a judge in passing, on issues which do not form part of the essential reasoning of the decision in the case (and thus carry little authority as precedents).
per incuriam	=	where a court overlooks relevant authorities (so that the decision may be considered doubtful or unreliable).
prima facie	=	at first sight.
ratio decidendi	=	reason for deciding; the principle of law on which a case is decided.
re	=	in the matter of; concerning.
res judicata	=	an issue which a court has decided in an action between parties and cannot be questioned in a later action between the same parties.
sic	=	thus (used, for example, to show that a grammatical mistake was that of the original authority being cited, and is not a mistake made by the editor or typesetter).
sine die	=	indefinitely.
sub nomine	=	under the name of.
sui generis	=	of its own type.
ultra vires	=	outside the powers recognised by law as belonging to the person or body in question; without authority.

Survey of Leading Decisions in 2000

There follows a numerical analysis and outline narrative survey of the court decisions reached in 2000 and included in this book. The numerical analysis is confined to decisions in UK courts, and thus excludes decisions of the CJEC and ECHR. 'Other' decisions are those in which Customs were not a party and neutral as to the outcome, or those which were not wholly or substantially in favour of either party. The figures in brackets are the averages of the corresponding figures for the years 1990–1999 inclusive.

Court	Number of decisions			
	TOTAL	For Customs	For taxpayer	Others
High Court and Court of Session (Outer House)	32 *(18.6)*	19 *(11.1)*	7 *(5.8)*	6 *(1.7)*
Court of Appeal, CA(NI) and Court of Session (Inner House)	6 *(7.7)*	2 *(3.9)*	4 *(3.1)*	–*(0.7)*
House of Lords	–*(1.0)*	–*(0.6)*	–*(0.3)*	–*(0.1)*
Total for all courts	38 *(27.3)*	21 *(15.6)*	11 *(9.2)*	6 *(2.5)*

The enactment of the *Human Rights Act 1998* has drawn many practitioners' attention to the potential importance of the European Convention on Human Rights. In *Georgiou*, 32.1 HUMAN RIGHTS, the European Court of Human Rights upheld the validity of a penalty imposed under *VATA 1994, s 60*.

The Court of Justice of the European Communities has again delivered a significant number of decisions which affect UK VAT law. One interesting decision came in the case of *Ampafrance SA v Directeur des Services Fiscaux de Maine-et-Loire*, 21.235 EUROPEAN COMMUNITY LAW, where the Court held that a derogation issued by the EC Council was invalid. For a more detailed discussion of the case, see De Voil Indirect Tax Intelligence, October 2000.

The European Commission again brought infraction proceedings against the UK, and four other Member States, in the cases noted at 21.80 to 21.82 EUROPEAN COMMUNITY LAW. To the anger of several MPs, the CJEC held that the UK should subject certain road tolls to VAT, and should account to the Commission for the tax which should have been levied, with interest from 1994.

In *Tullihallitus v Salumets & Others*, 21.56 EUROPEAN COMMUNITY LAW, the CJEC held that VAT was chargeable on sales of ethyl alcohol which had been smuggled into the EU. The interpretation of *Article 4(1)* of the *EC Sixth Directive* was considered in *Staatssecretaris van Financien v Heerma*, 21.62 EUROPEAN COMMUNITY LAW. In *Finanzamt Goslar v Breitsohl*, 21.71 EUROPEAN COMMUNITY LAW, the CJEC upheld the principle that an election to waive exemption cannot be limited to buildings alone, and has to include the land on which the buildings stood. The application of *Article 4(5)* of the *Sixth Directive* was considered in *Fazenda Pública v Câmara Municipal do Porto*, 21.83 EUROPEAN COMMUNITY LAW. In *Dotter v Willimaier*, 21.145 EUROPEAN COMMUNITY LAW, the CJEC held that certain services supplied by an Austrian doctor did not qualify for exemption under *Article 13A1(c)* of the *EC Sixth Directive*.

In *Amengual Far v Amengual Far*, 21.170 EUROPEAN COMMUNITY LAW, the CJEC held that *Article 13B(b)* of the *EC Sixth Directive* allowed Member States 'to subject to VAT lettings of immovable property and, by way of exception, to exempt only lettings of immovable property to be used for dwelling purposes'. In *Midland Bank plc*, 21.193 EUROPEAN COMMUNITY LAW,

Survey of Leading Decisions in 2000

the CJEC confirmed the established principle that input tax was only deductible if there was a direct and immediate link between a particular input transaction and a particular output transaction, and held that it was for the national court to apply the 'direct and immediate link' test to the facts of each particular case. In *Grundstückgemeinschaft Schloßstraße GbR v Finanzamt Paderborn*, 21.194 EUROPEAN COMMUNITY LAW, the CJEC held that certain retrospective German legislation was a breach of the Community law principle of legitimate expectation.

In *Schmeink & Cofreth AG & Co KG v Finanzamt Borken*, 21.202 EUROPEAN COMMUNITY LAW, the CJEC held that it was for Member States 'to lay down the procedures to apply as regards the adjustment of improperly invoiced VAT'. Adjustments could be made conditional on the issuer of the invoice having 'in sufficient time wholly eliminated the risk of any loss in tax revenues'. In *Floridienne SA v Belgian State*, 21.213 EUROPEAN COMMUNITY LAW, the CJEC gave some slightly Delphic guidance on the interpretation of *Article 19* of the *Sixth Directive*. The effect of *Article 28(3)(b)* of the *EC Sixth Directive* was considered in *Idéal Tourisme SA v Belgium*, 21.239 EUROPEAN COMMUNITY LAW. The refund provisions of the *Eighth Directive* were considered in *Ministre du Budget v Société Monte Dei Paschi Di Siena*, 21.249 EUROPEAN COMMUNITY LAW.

The CA decision in *Plantiflor Ltd*, 23.2 EXEMPTIONS: MISCELLANEOUS, clearly did not please Customs, who swiftly appealed to the House of Lords. As Ian Somerville has pointed out in 'Croner's VAT Briefing', the decision 'has significant potential implications in view of the current explosion in Internet retailing. Even if the VAT on each individual transaction is only a few pence, Customs must be daunted by the overall cost of losing this case ... (and) may well seek a change in the legislation'. Michael Conlon wrote in 'VAT Intelligence' that 'it is difficult to regard Parcelforce as making a supply direct to the customer. The necessary legal relationship, involving reciprocal obligations, is lacking. The House of Lords decision, which may extend wider than the treatment of postage, is awaited with interest.' Similarly, Ian Roxan observed in 'British Tax Review' that Ward LJ's judgment can be read as suggesting that 'commercial agreements where promises are exchanged but no money passes do not involve any supplies of services'. Such an approach would appear to 'offer fascinating opportunities for companies to exchange services without incurring uncreditable input tax'.

Customs also suffered a high-profile defeat in *FDR Ltd*, 26.3 FINANCE. The case was decided on the wording of *VATA 1994, Sch 9, Group 5* before the introduction of *Notes 2A* and *2B*, which were introduced by *VAT (Finance) Order 1999 (SI 1999 No 594)* with effect from 10 March 1999. The change to the legislation was intended 'to clarify ... that third party credit management is not exempt'. However, the judgment of Laws LJ suggests that, notwithstanding this change to the UK legislation, the company's supplies would still be held to be exempt from VAT by virtue of *Article 13B(d)(3)* of the *EC Sixth Directive*. Customs have applied to the House of Lords for leave to appeal against the CA decision, on the grounds that it 'challenges the UK's interpretation of European law'.

The case of *Century Life plc*, 36.11 FINANCE, proceeded with unusual speed, being decided by both the QB and the CA during 2000. The QB allowed the company's appeal, holding that the supplies in question qualified for exemption, and the CA upheld this decision. In *R v C & E Commrs (ex p. Building Societies Ombudsman Co Ltd)*, 45.24 PAYMENT OF TAX, the CA allowed the company's appeal against the QB decision. Rix LJ held that the introduction of the retrospective three-year time limit did not 'permit the Commissioners to use their new clawback powers so as to override a judicial decision which pre-dates 4 December 1996'.

Customs had only two victories in the Court of Appeal in 2000. These were the cases of *Pegasus Birds Ltd*, 3.46 ASSESSMENT, and *Co-Operative Wholesale Society Ltd*, 16.4 DEATH.

The High Court decision in *R v C & E Commrs (ex p. F & I Services Ltd)*, 2.232 APPEALS, is an interesting, although not decisive, examination of the consequences when a VAT officer gives an assurance which is inaccurate. The company claimed that, following an assurance by an officer (Miss Sellick), it had spent more than £350,000 in preparing for the launch of the scheme, and contended that the decision to withdraw her ruling was an abuse of power. Alternatively, the company contended that it should be entitled to damages for negligence, as 'Miss Sellick's unequivocal rulings were made carelessly and without any regard to the Commissioners' settled policy'.

Carnwath J reviewed the evidence in detail and held that there was no legal basis for any claim for compensation, but that, as this was 'a developing area of the law', the company's claim for damages for negligence should 'continue as though begun by writ'. Carnwath J observed that, applying *dicta* of Lord Browne-Wilkinson in *R v CIR (ex p. Matrix Securities Ltd), HL [1994] STC 272*, 'the test is one of fairness, not only to the taxpayer, but also to the Customs and to the general body of taxpayers'. Accordingly, 'the legitimate expectation is not that the clearance will be treated as binding come what may, but that, if there is a change in the understanding of the legal position, it will not be treated as retrospective'. Carnwath J observed that the effect of the original ruling 'was not simply to lift a VAT burden from one group of taxpayers (the car dealers), but to impose it on another (the participating retailers)'. On the evidence, the officer who had made the ruling had had all the necessary information, and had made her ruling 'without making sure that it was in accordance with the Customs' current view of the law. Had she taken the precaution of consulting Policy Division or more senior officers, she would not have given the advice she did.'

It will be interesting to see how the claim for damages is finally resolved. There is a very clear distinction between the *F & I* case and the *Matrix* case to which Carnwath J referred in his judgment. There are obvious similarities, as the inspector in the *Matrix* case and Miss Sellick in the *F & I* case both appear to have been out of their depth and to have given assurances which would not have been given by an 'ordinarily competent inspector' (to use the standard adopted by the House of Lords in the well-known case of *Olin Energy Systems Ltd v Scorer, HL [1985] STC 218*). However, in the *Matrix* case, the courts were unanimous in holding that the information submitted by the company had been 'inaccurate and misleading'. Lord Jauncey observed that 'the proposed sale by the receiver of the property for £8m was a card of critical importance in the exercise which the applicant asked the Revenue to carry out and was never placed on the table'. The Revenue were therefore entitled to withdraw the clearance. Lord Browne-Wilkinson and Lord Griffiths observed that the applicant had been aware that the Revenue required applications for clearance to be made to its Financial Institutions Division, so that a clearance by a local inspector was not to be treated as binding. By contrast, in the *F & I* case, the affidavit submitted by the Policy Adviser for the relevant directorate in Customs clearly accepted that, on 3 March 1998, when Miss Sellick gave her ruling, she 'was in possession of sufficient facts to enable her to reach a correct conclusion as to the VAT consequences of the scheme. Unfortunately she did not.'

Needless to say, the case raises important issues of policy. Discussing the question in 'British Tax Review', Jeremy Woolf has concluded that 'there are powerful public policy reasons for considering that it is inappropriate to impose a duty of care on the Commissioners or, if a duty is to be imposed, that the duty should only be of a limited nature'.

One noteworthy development during 2000 was that appeals from VAT tribunals were transferred from the Queen's Bench to the Chancery Division. The change seems to be a sensible one, for, as Clare Mainprice had written in 'Tolley's VAT Planning', the previous arrangements had meant that a considerable number of VAT appeals had been heard by judges of the Queen's Bench Division 'who had little or no experience in taxation matters'.

Survey of Leading Decisions in 2000

Notwithstanding this change, Customs have, as usual, won the majority of their cases in the High Court. In *Henderson*, 3.11 ASSESSMENT, the Ch D upheld backdated assessments on the proprietor of a fish and chip shop. Assessments on a company in the construction industry were upheld in *McNicholas Construction Co Ltd*, 3.77 ASSESSMENT. In *Lex Services plc*, 9.72 CARS, the Ch D upheld the tribunal decision that output tax was chargeable on the agreed sale prices of second-hand cars. The decision here is in line with the decision which the CS reached in the 1999 case of *North Anderson Cars Ltd*, 63.73 VALUATION (which dealt with new cars rather than second-hand cars). In *City of London Magistrates' Court and Others*, 14.83 COLLECTION AND ENFORCEMENT, the QB held that applications for access orders under *VATA 1994, Sch 11 para 11* were civil proceedings rather than criminal proceedings. In *Mirror Group Newspapers Ltd*, 26.30 FINANCE, the QB upheld the tribunal decision that input tax relating to a share issue was directly attributable to exempt supplies.

Normally, when the CJEC delivers judgment, that is the last which the public hear of a particular case. The case of *Kuwait Petroleum (GB) Ltd*, 21.90 EUROPEAN COMMUNITY LAW, proved to be an exception, because despite the seemingly decisive nature of the decision which the CJEC reached in 1999 (see 21.89 EUROPEAN COMMUNITY LAW), the company continued to fight on. Not surprisingly, its appeals were dismissed both by the tribunal and by the Ch D.

Over the years of VAT, there have many cases concerning the provisions for zero-rating certain types of food. In *Fluff Ltd*, 27.81 FOOD, the QB upheld the tribunal decision that sales of maggots did not qualify for zero-rating. In *Meschia's Frozen Foods*, 27.97 FOOD, the Ch D held that soft frozen yoghurt failed to qualify for zero-rating.

In *R v HM Treasury (ex p. Service Authority for the National Crime Squad and Others)*, 40.3 LOCAL AUTHORITIES AND STATUTORY BODIES, the Chancellor of the Exchequer had personally rejected a VAT refund claim by the Service Authority for the National Crime Squad. The Service Authority applied for judicial review, but the QB rejected the application. Moses J observed that the Home Secretary, who had written to the Chancellor in support of the claim, had 'wanted a word with the Chancellor of the Exchequer before any final decision was made. It is a matter of disappointment that the words which were exchanged have not been revealed in these proceedings.' An application for judicial review was also rejected in *R v C & E Commrs (ex p. Greater Manchester Police Authority)*, 40.4 LOCAL AUTHORITIES AND STATUTORY BODIES.

Appeals against penalties were dismissed in *Akbar*, 47.49 PENALTIES: EVASION OF TAX, and *Stuttard*, 47.71 PENALTIES: EVASION OF TAX. In *Gray*, 53.36 REGISTRATION, the Ch D upheld Customs' interpretation of *Sch 1 para 1(3)*. In *Church Schools Foundation Ltd*, 58.33 SUPPLY, the Ch D held that output tax was chargeable on a payment made by a charity to an associated charity.

Following the notorious shooting at a school in Dunblane, a company surrendered a substantial number of guns, and was paid more than £500,000 as compensation. In *Parker Hale Ltd*, 58.118 SUPPLY, the QB upheld the tribunal decision that VAT was chargeable on this payment. In *Peninsular & Oriental Steam Navigation Company*, 58.366 SUPPLY, the QB upheld the tribunal decision that VAT was chargeable on goods sold on a ferry travelling from Portsmouth to Spain. In *Higher Education Statistics Agency Ltd*, 61.76 TRANSFERS OF GOING CONCERNS, the QB upheld Customs' interpretation of *Article 5* of the *Special Provisions Order*.

In *Littlewoods Organisation plc*, 63.31 VALUATION, the Ch D upheld an assessment on supplies of goods to agents of a mail order company. In *Kingfisher plc*, 63.44 VALUATION, the Ch D approved the 1975 tribunal decision in *Davies*, 63.43 VALUATION, and upheld Customs' interpretation of the VAT treatment of 'Provident vouchers'.

In *R v C & E Commrs (ex p. British Sky Broadcasting Group plc)*, 2.233 APPEALS, the QB granted a late application for judicial review, holding on the evidence that the company had a 'reasonably arguable claim' which should be considered in detail.

The case of *Cheeseman*, 3.68 ASSESSMENT, is an interesting discussion of the difference between making an assessment (form VAT 641) and notifying that assessment (form VAT 655). In *Appleby Bowers*, 5.46 BOOKS, ETC., the Ch D held that leaflets, supplied with promotional services, qualified for zero-rating. In *Barclays Bank plc*, 30.15 GROUPS OF COMPANIES, the Ch D upheld the tribunal decision that a company had ceased to be a member of the relevant VAT group in February 1995 rather than July 1995.

The Ch D allowed the company's appeal in *Royal & Sun Alliance Group plc*, 43.129 PARTIAL EXEMPTION, holding that the company was entitled to make an adjustment under *VAT Regulations 1995 (SI 1995 No 2518), reg 109*. In *First Choice Holidays plc*, 59.11 TOUR OPERATORS AND TRAVEL AGENTS, the Ch D upheld the tribunal decision that 'where a customer is charged a reduced price for a holiday, the difference between the published list price and the reduced price should not be taken into account when assessing the margin'.

In *Eastwood Care Homes (Ilkeston) Ltd*, 2.138 APPEALS, Lightman J allowed an application for a late appeal against a tribunal decision. The case of *Cantrell*, 15.82 CONSTRUCTION OF BUILDINGS, ETC. concerned the interpretation of *VATA 1994, Sch 8, Group 5, Note 16*, and might therefore be considered to be a question of law rather than one of fact. Nevertheless, Lightman J held on the evidence that he had no alternative but to remit the case to a new tribunal for rehearing. Another case to be remitted to a new tribunal was *Hodges*, 58.236 SUPPLY (concerning the VAT status of apprentice jockeys). The case of *Keeping Newcastle Warm*, 63.96 VALUATION, was referred to the CJEC for a ruling on *Article 11A1(a)* of the *EC Sixth Directive*.

RAP Group plc, 43.32 PARTIAL EXEMPTION, is an interesting case where input tax was reclaimed on professional fees. The tribunal had rejected the company's claim, but the Ch D drew a distinction between the work done by stockbrokers, accountants and solicitors. The solicitors had provided a detailed invoice analysing their services, and the court held that, in view of this, part of the tax shown on their invoice was attributable to taxable supplies.

As always, the Commissioners won the majority of tribunal appeals. One case which they will be very pleased to have won was *RBS Leasing & Services (No 1) Ltd*, 63.2 VALUATION. The tribunal upheld a direction under *VATA 1994, Sch 6 para 1*, observing that the bank involved in the case had 'deliberately implemented a scheme for VAT avoidance'.

The case of *Upton*, 9.108 CARS, turned on somewhat unusual facts, but was noteworthy for the strong criticisms made by the tribunal chairman, Mr. de Voil, of the Commissioners' failure to draw relevant precedents to the attention of the tribunal. He observed that the tribunal 'had to bring the *Martinez* case to the attention of both parties ourselves. This really will not do. The *Martinez* decision – the weightiest and most important tribunal decision yet, if we may respectfully say so, in a field where there are far too many apparently conflicting tribunal decisions and, as yet, no High Court judgment to guide us – was released on 21 October 1999, six months ago, and has found its way into the printed reports of VAT & Duties Tribunal cases. As we said in another case recently, one might expect the Commissioners to keep abreast of recent decisions, particularly in a minefield as tricky as this one, and to ensure that those they instruct are equally up-to-date.'

The Commissioners were also strongly criticised by the Tribunal President, Mr. Oliver, in the case of *London Federation of Clubs for Young People*, 2.345 APPEALS. He awarded costs against the Commissioners and strongly criticised the conduct of Customs' Solicitors' Office, observing that 'taxpayers must not be prejudiced by official delays' and that 'a proper standard of efficiency is demanded from the Commissioners'.

As usual, the tribunal has had to consider the application of VAT to a wide range of economic activities. In *Casson*, 7.105 BUSINESS, it discussed the sale of horse manure, while in *Rudd*, 58.253 SUPPLY, it had to rule on the VAT liability of different types of massage. For details of other tribunal cases decided during the year, the reader will have to wade through the book.

1   Agents

The cases in this chapter are arranged under the following headings.

DEFINITION OF AGENT

1.1   In a case concerning zero-rating provisions in *FA 1972*, which have since been superseded, the Commissioners issued an assessment on a woman who had organised educational holidays. She appealed, contending that she was acting as an agent of overseas organisations, so that she was not required to account for VAT under the law then in force. The tribunal accepted this contention but the QB remitted the case to the tribunal for rehearing. Woolf J held that the tribunal had erred in law, and defined agency as 'the relationship which exists between two persons, one of whom expressly or impliedly consents that the other should represent him or act on his behalf and the other of whom similarly consents to represent the former or so to act'. *C & E Commrs v E Johnson, QB [1980] STC 624*. (*Note*. There was no further public hearing of the appeal.)

WHETHER ACTING AS AGENT OR PRINCIPAL

Note. With effect from 1 June 1995, where an agent acts in his or her own name in relation to a supply of goods, the goods are treated as having been supplied to and by the agent. See *VATA 1994, s 47(2A)*, introduced by *FA 1995, s 23*. If the goods are eligible second-hand goods, the 'margin scheme' may be used provided that the conditions of the scheme are met. Cases relating to periods before 1 June 1995 should be read in the light of the subsequent change in the law.

Cases held to constitute an agency

1.2   **Art dealers.** A partnership which carried on business as art dealers was approached by a potential customer who wished to purchase an oil painting. They sought advice from a specialist dealer who recommended a painting which he had in stock, which he suggested that they could sell for between £3,000 and £5,000. The partners agreed a price with their customer of £3,300, and received this sum in cash before they had actually purchased the painting from the specialist dealer. They subsequently paid him £2,700 for the painting. The Commissioners issued an assessment on the partners, charging output tax on the full price of £3,300 paid by the customer. They appealed, contending that they had undertaken the transaction as agents for the specialist dealer, and that they should only be required to account for tax on their profit of £600. The tribunal accepted this contention and allowed their appeal. *JNS Bagshawe & CAE Walker, LON/84/163 (VTD 1762)*.

1.3 Agents

1.3 **Building company.** A building contractor (D) was also the controlling shareholder of a company carrying on a similar business. D recruited subcontractors to work for the company when required. The Commissioners assessed the company on the basis that it had supplied the services of some of these subcontractors to D for work which he had undertaken as a contractor. The company appealed, contending that it had merely acted as an agent for D and had not made any supplies to D as an independent principal. The tribunal accepted this contention and allowed the company's appeal. *WF Dickinson (Dorset) Ltd, LON/87/327 (VTD 2778).*

1.4 **Meals delivered by taxi—whether proprietor of delivery service acting as agent or principal.** A trader (N) operated a delivery service, whereby food was delivered from restaurants to consumers by taxi. Customers contacted N with orders for food, following which N contacted the restaurant and a taxi driver, and the taxi driver collected the meal and paid for it either by cash or by a voucher debiting the cost to N. The driver received payment from the customer, including a delivery charge, and N received a payment described as an 'agency fee' from the restaurant. Where a customer wished to pay by credit card, N claimed the amounts in question from the credit card company. N only accounted for output tax on the 'agency fees'. The Commissioners issued an assessment charging output tax on the full amounts paid by the consumers, including the prices of the meals and the delivery charges paid to the drivers. The tribunal allowed N's appeal, holding that the meals were purchased by the taxi drivers rather than by N, and that N was acting as an agent rather than as a principal. *Dr R Nader (t/a Try Us), LON/89/1395Y (VTD 4927).* (*Note.* For a subsequent application for costs, see 2.265 APPEALS.)

1.5 **Company providing catering services for charity at residential homes.** A charity which operated a number of residential homes engaged a company (P) to provide catering services at the homes. P was paid a management fee, and also retained discounts which it obtained on the bulk purchase of food. It accounted for VAT on the management fee, but did not account for VAT on the discounts. The Commissioners issued an assessment charging output tax on the discounts, on the basis that P was acting as an agent of the charity and that the discounts were part of the consideration for P's services. The tribunal dismissed P's appeal, holding on the evidence that there was a single supply of catering services, and that P was acting as an agent of the charity when it made its purchases of food. Accordingly, the discounts which P retained constituted consideration for P's services, and P was required to account for output tax on them. *PBK Catering Ltd, LON/91/2688Y (VTD 11426).*

1.6 **Sales of craft pottery.** A partnership sold craft pottery from a retail shop. The partners purchased some items for resale, but other items were deposited with them by individual potters. In such cases, the partners considered that they were acting as agents for the potters, and only accounted for VAT on their agreed commission. The Commissioners issued an assessment on the basis that the partners were selling the pottery as principals, and should account for VAT on the full sale price. The QB allowed the partners' appeal, holding that the legal relationship between the partners and the potters depended on the conditions of sale actually agreed between them. On the evidence, the only reasonable conclusion was that the partnership was selling the pottery as agents of the individual potters. *J K Hill & S J Mansell (t/a J K Hill & Co) v C & E Commrs, QB [1988] STC 424.* (*Note.* For another issue in this case, not taken to the QB, see 34.106 INPUT TAX.)

1.7 **Second-hand musical equipment.** A company owned seven shops trading in second-hand musical equipment. It accepted and paid for goods brought into its shops by members of the public, but in such cases it gave the vendors a notice stating that 'these goods are accepted for sale on your behalf by the company acting as your agent ... the goods will remain your property until sold'. The Commissioners issued an assessment to the company, charging output tax on the full sale price of the goods. The company appealed, contending that it was acting as an agent and should only be assessed on its margin. The tribunal accepted this contention and allowed the appeal, holding that the terms of the contract agreed between the company and the vendors made it clear that the company was acting as an agent rather than as a principal. The QB upheld this decision. Although the fact that the company sometimes repaired the goods which it sold was unusual in a contract of agency, this practice did not displace the clear terms of the contract. *C & E Commrs v Music & Video Exchange Ltd, QB [1992] STC 220.*

1.8   **Company investing money deposited by clients.**   A company received money from members of the public and invested it in options and futures. Since the company was not itself entitled to deal on the London, Chicago and New York exchanges, it dealt through brokers. The Commissioners assessed the company on the basis that it was acting as a principal when buying and selling options and futures. The company appealed, contending that it was acting as the agent of its clients. The tribunal allowed the company's appeal, holding on the evidence that the company was acting as the agent of its investors and not as a principal on its own account. *Cornhill Management Ltd, [1991] VATTR 1 (VTD 5444).*

1.9   **'Party plan' hostesses.**   See the cases noted at 1.74 to 1.76 below.

1.10   **Musical tuition at universities.**   See *Alberni String Quartet,* 20.2 EDUCATION.

1.11   **Export of goods.**   See *Geistlich Sons Ltd,* 24.25 EXPORTS.

1.12   **Import of goods.**   See *Angela Walker,* 33.16 IMPORTS.

1.13   **Input tax reclaimed by company managing pop group.**   A company carried on the business of managing the affairs of performers in the entertainment industry. In 1983 it managed a European tour by an Australian pop group. In the course of arranging the tour, the company entered into various contracts, some of which were in its own name and some in the name of the group. It reclaimed input tax in respect of the supplies made under these contracts. The Commissioners rejected the claim and the tribunal dismissed the company's appeal, holding that the company was acting as an agent for the group rather than as a principal, and that the supplies under the contracts were made to the group rather than to the company. *World Chief Ltd, LON/87/350 (VTD 2582).*

1.14   **Input tax claimed on purchase of paper.**   A company (L), which carried on business as an advertising agency, reclaimed input tax in respect of the purchase of a large quantity of paper. The Commissioners rejected the claim, considering that L had acquired the paper as agent for a US company, rather than as a principal. The tribunal upheld the Commissioners' contentions and dismissed L's appeal. *LS & A International Ltd, LON/88/598X (VTD 3717).*

1.15   **Company paying employees on behalf of parent company.**   See *British United Shoe Machinery Co Ltd,* 38.71 INVOICES.

1.16   **Nursing agency.**   See *British Nursing Co-Operation Ltd,* 31.5 HEALTH AND WELFARE; *Reed Personnel Services Ltd,* 31.6 HEALTH AND WELFARE; *Sheffield & Rotherham Nursing Agency,* 31.7 HEALTH AND WELFARE; *Fairburn,* 31.10 HEALTH AND WELFARE; *BUPA Nursing Services Ltd,* 58.227 SUPPLY, and *South Hams Nursing Agency,* 58.228 SUPPLY.

1.17   **Company dealing in vehicle registration numberplates.**   See *Tayside Numbers Ltd,* 45.9 PAYMENT OF TAX.

1.18   **Auctioneers.**   See *Jocelyn Feilding Fine Arts Ltd,* 56.5 SECOND-HAND GOODS.

1.19 Agents

1.19 **Charity sharing office accommodation with associated company.** See *Durham Aged Mineworkers' Homes Association*, 58.40 SUPPLY.

1.20 **Driving instructors.** See the cases noted at 58.180 to 58.188 SUPPLY.

1.21 **Taxi and car hire businesses.** See *Triumph & Albany Car Service*, 58.189 SUPPLY; *Hussain*, 58.190 SUPPLY, and *Carless*, 58.191 SUPPLY.

1.22 **Taxi drivers.** See *Hamiltax*, 58.194 SUPPLY; *Knowles*, 58.195 SUPPLY, and *Snaith*, 58.196 SUPPLY.

1.23 **Escort agency.** See *Marlow & Hind*, 63.80 VALUATION.

1.24 **Company trading as pawnbroker.** A company which traded as a pawnbroker sold quantities of gold coins. The Commissioners formed the opinion that it had sold the coins as a principal and should have accounted for output tax on the full sale price. They issued an assessment accordingly. The company appealed, contending that it had sold the coins as an agent of the members of the public who provided the coins, rather than as an independent principal, and was therefore only required to account for output tax on its profit. The tribunal allowed the company's appeal, holding on the evidence that 'on the true construction of the contract notes the appellant acted as the seller's agent in the transactions in question'. *Music & Video Exchange Ltd*, 1.7 above, applied. *Lombard Guildhouse plc, MAN/93/1417 (VTD 12974).*

1.25 **Motorcycle courier service.** A company operated a motorcycle courier service. It had about 150 accounts customers. Where work was carried out for such customers, the company retained 40% of the receipts and paid the other 60% to the couriers. The company also received occasional requests from people other than accounts customers. In such cases, it allowed the riders who worked for it to accept the work and retain the whole of the payments which they received. It did not account for output tax on such payments. The Commissioners issued an assessment to recover the tax and the tribunal dismissed the company's appeal, holding that the couriers were acting as agents of the company, even though the company made no profit from the cash customers. The tribunal observed that the company had an interest in allowing the couriers to keep sums received for cash work, since 'this meant that the riders could rely on immediate cash receipts to meet their cash needs for such items as petrol and personal expenses'. *Triumph & Albany Car Service*, 58.189 SUPPLY, and *Camberwell Cars Ltd*, 58.200 SUPPLY, distinguished. *Prontobikes Ltd, LON/94/1198A (VTD 13213).*

1.26 **Company providing parking control services—whether agent of landowner.** A company provided parking control services, under an agreement with a landowner. The landowner paid the company a fixed fee of £200 pa plus VAT, and the company placed a notice on the site, warning that vehicles parked without authority would be clamped and that the charge for removing the clamp was £58.75. The company retained such fees and did not account for tax on them. The Commissioners issued an assessment charging output tax. The company appealed, contending that the charges represented damages for trespass which were paid to it as an independent principal and were outside the scope of VAT. The tribunal rejected this contention and dismissed the appeal, holding on the evidence that the company was acting an agent of the landowner, applying *Arthur v Anker, CA 1996, [1997] QB 564; [1996] 3 All ER 783*. By allowing the company to retain the fees, the landowner had effectively paid the fees back to the company 'as a fee for carrying out its services to the landowner of carrying out parking control'. The fees were therefore consideration for a standard-rated supply of services. *Seagar Enterprises Ltd (t/a Ace Security Services), LON/97/1190 (VTD 15432).*

Cases held not to constitute an agency

1.27　**Sale of taxis—whether supplier acting as agent for customer.**　A trader (F) obtained black taxicabs from London to sell in Blackpool and accounted for tax only on his profit. The Commissioners assessed him on the full sale price and he appealed, contending that he was acting as agent for the purchasers of the vehicles and that tax should be payable only on his commission. The tribunal rejected this contention, holding that there were two separate sales and that F was acting as an independent principal. *D Flitcroft, MAN/86/328 (VTD 2328).*

1.28　**Proprietor of taxi business—whether acting as independent principal.**　See *Hussain*, 58.190 SUPPLY.

1.29　**Taxi drivers—whether acting as independent principals.**　See *Jivelynn Ltd*, 58.198 SUPPLY, and *Kearns*, 58.199 SUPPLY.

1.30　**Refreshments sold by hostesses on buses.**　A company which operated long-distance express bus and coach services arranged for refreshments to be sold by hostesses or stewards to passengers during the journey. The hostesses were required to purchase the food for sale as refreshments out of their own money, and were entitled to retain any profits made. The Commissioners assessed the company on the basis that the hostesses were acting as agents, and that the company was liable to account for output tax on the full amounts paid by the passengers. The company appealed, contending that the hostesses were acting as independent principals, and that it was only liable to account for tax on the amounts which it received from the hostesses. The tribunal accepted this contention and allowed the appeal. *National Bus Company, LON/86/622 (VTD 2530).*

1.31　**Chiropractor.**　A doctor (M) carried on a practice as a chiropractor. He entered into an agreement with another chiropractor (C), whereby C provided chiropractic services at M's premises, using M's equipment. The fees from the patients treated by C were divided equally between C and M. The Commissioners issued an assessment on the basis that the effect of the agreement was that C was treating patients as an agent of M, so that M was accountable for VAT on the whole of the fees charged, and not merely on the 50% which he retained. The tribunal allowed M's appeal, finding that 'none of the provisions in the agreement points conclusively towards the relationship of principal and agent', and holding that C was supplying services to the patients as a principal, rather than as M's agent. Accordingly, M was only required to account for output tax on the amounts which he actually received from C. *Dr SGP Middleton, MAN/90/588 (VTD 6034, 11208).*

1.32　**Dealer in industrial mouldings.**　A trader acted as exclusive distributor of a type of polyurethane mouldings manufactured by a German company. The Commissioners issued a ruling that he was acting as an agent of the German company, so that his commission was standard-rated. He appealed, contending that he was an independent principal and that the amounts which he received from the manufacturer were zero-rated under the legislation then in force. The tribunal accepted his evidence and allowed his appeal, applying *dicta* in *Potter*, 1.73 below. *MC Linham, LON/92/1651A (VTD 11359).*

1.33　**Goods sold at auction organised by fund-raising committee.**　A committee was established to raise funds to aid blood sports, such as stag-hunting and fox-hunting. It organised an auction in connection with a horse-race meeting, at which it sold goods which had been donated to it by supporters of its activities. It did not account for output tax on the sales made at the auction. The Commissioners issued an assessment charging tax on the sales, and the committee appealed, contending that it was selling the goods as agents for the donors. The tribunal rejected this contention and dismissed the appeal, holding that the committee was selling the goods as independent principals rather than as agents. *Hill & Mansell*, 1.6 above, distinguished. *The Cheltenham Countryside Race Day, LON/93/2877A (VTD 12460)*.

1.34   **Auctioneers.**   A company traded as auctioneers. In cases where a successful bidder failed to pay the amount promised, the company paid the vendor as if it had received the amount in question, and subsequently offered the goods for sale again, but did not account for output tax on the proceeds of this sale. The Commissioners issued an assessment charging tax on the proceeds, and the company appealed, contending that it was selling such goods as agents for the original vendor. The tribunal rejected this contention and dismissed the appeal, holding on the evidence that in such cases the company was selling the goods as an independent principal rather than as an agent, and was obliged to account for output tax. *Athol Street Auctioneers Ltd v Isle of Man Treasury, MAN/93/375 (VTD 12478)*. (*Note*. Compare *Jocelyn Feilding Fine Arts Ltd*, 56.5 SECOND-HAND GOODS.)

1.35   **Mail broker.**   A company carried on business as a mail broker. It only accounted for output tax on 20% of the payments which it received from two major clients, treating the remaining 80% as disbursements. The Commissioners issued an assessment charging tax on the payments, and the company appealed, contending that it was acting as an agent and had accounted for tax on the correct basis. The tribunal rejected this contention and dismissed the appeal, holding that the company was trading as an independent principal and was required to account for output tax on the full amount of the payments which it received. *Music & Video Exchange Ltd*, 1.7 above, distinguished. *Mail Brokers International Ltd, LON/94/1939A (VTD 14188)*.

1.36   **Company providing staff for clients.**   A company (H) provided temporary accountancy and banking staff for client companies. It accounted for PAYE in accordance with *ICTA 1988, s 134*, and until 1994 it accounted for VAT on the basis that it was acting as an independent principal. In 1995 its accountants formed the opinion that it should only have accounted for VAT on its commission, and not on the amounts which it passed to the temps as wages. They wrote to the Commissioners requesting permission to issue credit notes on this basis. The Commissioners rejected the claim, and H appealed. The tribunal dismissed the appeal, holding on the evidence that H had been acting as an independent principal and had been supplying temporary staff for 'a unitary charge', rather than merely introducing staff in return for commission. *Reed Personnel Services Ltd*, 31.6 HEALTH AND WELFARE, distinguished. *Hays Personnel Services Ltd, LON/95/2610 (VTD 14882)*.

1.37   **Partnership providing live-in carers—whether acting as principal or agent.**   A partnership provided live-in carers. The Commissioners issued an assessment charging tax on the charges which the partnership made to its clients. The partnership appealed, contending that it was acting as an agent rather than as a principal, and should only be required to account for tax on the commission which it retained. The tribunal rejected this contention and dismissed the appeal, holding that the partnership was acting as an independent principal and that VAT was due on the whole of its takings. *Hays Personnel Services Ltd*, 1.36 above, applied; *Reed Personnel Services Ltd*, 31.6 HEALTH AND WELFARE, distinguished. The tribunal observed that the carers could not be treated as independently carrying out economic activities, within *Article 4(1)* of the *EC Sixth Directive*. *Clarina Live-In Care Service, LON/99/96 (VTD 16434)*.

1.38   **Input tax reclaimed on supplies for property development.**   A company (D) which carried on a property development business became aware of two sites which were suitable for development, but did not have the resources to finance the work. It entered into arrangements with a larger company (C) whereby C acquired the freehold interest in one site and the leasehold interest in the other (the freehold of the latter site being retained by the local County Council). D was to build large office buildings on the sites and to receive payment from C to meet the costs of the work. At the completion of the work, C was to pay D the excess of the value of the buildings over their cost. D reclaimed input tax on the expenditure incurred on the work, and the Commissioners issued assessments to recover the tax, considering that D was acting as an agent for C, rather than as an independent principal. The tribunal allowed D's appeal. On the evidence, D 'undertook all responsibility and liability for the development work'. The work was a joint venture which was intended to result in an investment for C and a profit for D. The supplies made to D were made to it as a principal. *Drexlodge Ltd, MAN/88/705 (VTD 5614)*.

1.39   **Magazine distribution company.**   A company carried on business as a distributor of magazines. The Commissioners issued assessments on the basis that the company supplied the magazines as an agent of the publishers, and that since it never took possession of the magazines, the consideration which it received was for making supplies of marketing and distribution services to the publishers, which were standard-rated. The company appealed, contending that, under its contracts, it purchased the magazines from the publishers for an agreed percentage of the cover price and sold them to wholesalers. Its supplies were supplies of the magazines to wholesalers, and were zero-rated under what is now *VATA 1994, Sch 8, Group 3, Item 2*. The tribunal accepted this contention and allowed the company's appeal. Although the company did not take physical possession of the magazines, on the evidence it clearly purchased the magazines from the publishers, and supplied them to wholesalers as principal. It incurred the costs of transporting the magazines, and also incurred the risk of their loss in transit. The sale of the magazines was, therefore, within the zero-rating provisions of *Group 3, Item 2. Odhams Distribution Pergamon Holdings Ltd, LON/90/1546Y (VTD 6295)*.

1.40   See also *Keesing (UK) Ltd*, 5.75 BOOKS, ETC.

1.41   **Company placing orders for magazines with publishers.**   A company (N) obtained orders for magazines from students and staff at universities and schools, and placed these orders with the publishers. The subscribers paid their subscriptions to N, which paid lesser amounts to the publishers, retaining part of the amounts paid. The publishers sent the magazines directly to the subscribers. N did not account for VAT, considering that it was supplying the magazines, which were zero-rated goods within what is now *VATA 1994, Sch 8, Group 3*, to the subscribers. The Commissioners issued an assessment on the basis that the magazines were supplied by the publishers to the subscribers, that N was dealing with the subscribers' orders merely as an agent of the publishers, and that N was making a standard-rated supply of services to the publishers. The tribunal allowed N's appeal, holding that N was acting as a principal and that the magazines were supplied by the publishers to N and by N to the subscribers. Accordingly, N's supplies were zero-rated. *Nordic Subscription Service UK Ltd, MAN/90/892 (VTD 10705)*.

1.42   **Nursing agency.**   See *Allied Medicare Nursing Services Ltd*, 31.4 HEALTH AND WELFARE, and *Parkinson*, 31.9 HEALTH AND WELFARE.

1.43   **Tupperware sub-distributors.**   See *Potter*, 1.73 below.

1.44   **'Door-to-door' salesmen.**   See *Betterware Products Ltd*, 1.78 below, and *Kelly*, 1.79 below.

1.45   **Property conveyancing business.**   See *Culverhouse*, 53.142 REGISTRATION.

1.46   **Association of taxi drivers.** See *Eastbourne Town Radio Cars Association*, 58.31 SUPPLY.

1.47   **Hairstylists at salon.** See *Ashmore*, 58.213 SUPPLY.

1.48   **Hostesses at night club.** See *Leapmagic Ltd*, 58.278 SUPPLY.

1.49   **Launderette staff providing 'service washes'.** See *Ivychain Ltd*, 58.226 SUPPLY.

1.50   **School photographs supplied by photographer to school for resale to parents.** A photographer supplied school photographs to schools which resold the photographs to parents at prices recommended by the photographer. The school retained an agreed percentage of the payments and paid the balance to the photographer. The Commissioners issued an assessment on the basis that the school was acting as an agent and that the photographer was liable to account for VAT on the amounts paid by the parents to the school, rather than just the amounts received by him from the school. The tribunal allowed the photographer's appeal, holding that the schools had not entered into an agency agreement and that the photographer's customers were the schools rather than the parents. The QB upheld the tribunal decision, holding that the schools had not been authorised to create contractual agreements between the photographer and the parents. *C & E Commrs v PLA Paget, QB [1989] STC 773.*

1.51   **Supply of facilities for taking school photographs—whether school acting as agent of local education authority.** See *Lancashire County Council*, 58.279 SUPPLY.

1.52   **Company arranging for delivery of plants by Post Office—whether acting as agent of customers.** See *Plantiflor Ltd*, 23.2 EXEMPTIONS: MISCELLANEOUS.

1.53   **Admission to Council playground including miniature railway operated by independent contractor—whether Council acting as agent of contractor.** See *Hemsworth Town Council*, 58.251 SUPPLY.

1.54   **Company purchasing building from development company and arranging for renovation to be carried out by associated building company—whether building company acting as agent for development company.** See *Lonsdale Travel Ltd*, 58.419 SUPPLY.

1.55   **Tenant of bomb-damaged building arranging for repairs—whether acting as principal or as agent of landlord.** See *Commercial Union Assurance Co plc*, 34.49 INPUT TAX.

1.56   **Company operating travel club.** See *The UK Travel Agent Ltd*, 62.10 TRANSPORT.

1.57   **Amount paid to finance company under sales promotion scheme—whether vendor acting as agent of finance company.** See *Classic Driveways (UK) Ltd*, 63.37 VALUATION.

SUPPLIES THROUGH AGENTS ACTING IN OWN NAME (VATA 1994, s 47(2A, 3))

1.58   In a case where the facts were complex and unusual, the Commissioners issued an assessment on the basis that a company had purchased goods as an agent for another company, within what is now *VATA 1994, s 47(3)*, and should therefore have accounted for output tax. The tribunal allowed the company's appeal, holding that the goods had been purchased as an independent principal. As a result, *s 47(3)* was not applicable and the basis of the assessment was untenable. (The tribunal declined to consider the alternative argument that the amount of the assessment would have been the same if the Commissioners had based their assessment on the company having acted as an independent principal.) *Halroy Products Ltd, MAN/79/80 (VTD 1010)*.

1.59   A borough council had engaged contractors to carry out building and engineering work. Subsequently the council entered into an agreement with a finance company, whereby the finance company became the contractor and appointed the council as its agent. The subcontractors who performed the work were paid by the council, which was reimbursed by the finance company. (Additionally, the finance company agreed to pay the contractors amounts outstanding under the contracts and the council agreed to reimburse the company for this.) The council reclaimed the input tax charged to it by the contractors, but did not account for output tax on its deemed supplies of building services to the company. The Commissioners issued an assessment on the basis that, by virtue of what is now *VATA 1994, s 47(3)*, the council should have accounted for output tax. The council appealed, contending that it should have been permitted to delay accounting for output tax until it received reimbursement from the finance company (which in some cases was a year after it had reclaimed input tax on its payments to the subcontractors). The tribunal rejected this contention and dismissed the appeal, and the QB upheld this decision. Potts J held that the tax points for the input tax and output tax must be the same, that the tax point was not fixed by the date of reimbursement since these were deemed supplies, and that the only sensible time when the deemed output could take place was simultaneously with the deemed input. *Metropolitan Borough of Wirral v C & E Commrs, QB [1995] STC 597*.

1.60   A trader (S) acted as a franchisee for a company (M) which provided finance for the leasing of commercial vehicles. S sold a vehicle which he had acquired in a part-exchange transaction, and paid the proceeds of the sale to M. He then reclaimed input tax on the payment. The Commissioners issued an assessment to recover the tax, considering that S had sold the vehicle as a principal, so that there was no justification for the reclaim of input tax. S appealed, contending that he had sold the vehicle as an agent of M, and was therefore entitled to reclaim the tax by virtue of what is now *VATA 1994, s 47(2A)*. The tribunal rejected this contention and dismissed the appeal, holding on the evidence that S had made the sale as a principal, rather than as an agent, and was not entitled to reclaim the VAT as input tax. *AJ Shutt, MAN/92/219 (VTD 9817)*.

1.61   In July 1997 a woman (R) began a used car business. Because she did not have sufficient capital to purchase used cars, she allowed other vendors to display cars on her premises on the basis that, when a purchaser was found, R would purchase the car from the vendor, resell it to the purchaser and recover a commission from the vendor by deducting this from the sale price. R did not register for VAT until September 1998. The Commissioners discovered that she had become liable to register from September 1997, and issued a notice of compulsory registration, backdated accordingly. R appealed, contending that the commission which she retained had been below the registration threshold. The tribunal dismissed her appeal, holding that *VATA 1994, s 47(2A)* applied. R had supplied the cars as an agent acting in her own name, so that the gross sale price of the cars should be treated as her turnover for VAT purposes. *JP Rowan, MAN/99/92 (VTD 16357)*.

1.62   A company which dealt in antiques arranged for an antique locket to be sold at auction. It was purchased by a Kuwaiti who exported it. The company did not account for output tax on the sale of the locket. The Commissioners issued an assessment and imposed a misdeclaration penalty. The company appealed, contending that the sale should be treated as a zero-rated export. The tribunal rejected this contention and dismissed the appeal, holding that the locket was sold through the auctioneers who were agents acting in their own name. Accordingly, by virtue of *VATA 1994, s 47(2A)*, there was a supply of goods by the company to the auctioneers and a supply by the auctioneers to the Kuwaiti purchaser. Although the sale by the auctioneers was an export which qualified for zero-rating, the supply by the company to the auctioneers was standard-rated. *Bashir Mohamed Ltd, LON/99/ 188 (VTD 16762)*. (*Note*. The appeal against the penalty was also dismissed—see 49.203 PENALTIES: MISDECLARATION.)

1.63   **Nursing homes ordering incontinence pads for specific residents—whether within VATA 1994, s 47(2A).**   A company supplied incontinence pads to various nursing homes, on behalf of specific named residents. The supplies were billed to the nursing homes, which obtained payment from the residents. The company treated the supplies as zero-rated under *VATA 1994, Sch 8, Group 12, Item 2(g)*. The Commissioners issued an assessment on the basis that the nursing homes were agents acting in their own names, within *VATA 1994, s 47(2A)*, so that the supplies were not made to the residents but to the nursing homes, and the company was obliged to account for output tax. The company appealed. The tribunal allowed the appeal, holding that 'if an agent signs a contract "for and on behalf of" his principal we consider that he is not acting in his own name, but in that of his principal. In the present case the declarations which were clearly contractual documents expressly stated that the nursing home was acting "on behalf of" its handicapped residents and was using their funds'. The tribunal observed that *s 47(2A)* was apparently intended to implement *Article 5(4)(c)* of the *EC Sixth Directive*, but observed that 'the English version of *Article 5(4)(c)* differs radically from the French version' and that *s 47(2A)* appeared to be 'a very poor rendition'. Since the UK legislation failed 'to implement the *Directive* properly', the Commissioners could not 'rely on the direct effect of *Article 5(4)(c)*'. The tribunal concluded that 'the words "acts in his own name" in *section 47(2A)* do not cover an agent who is expressly acting on behalf of named principals. The wording of *section 47(2A)* cannot be reconciled with *Article 5(4)(c)* in the English version. The English version is wholly different from the French version. *Section 47(2A)* treats goods in the same way as services, whereas they are covered by different articles of the *Directive* with totally different wording. *Section 47(2A)* did not apply to the supplies.' *Express Medicare Ltd, LON/96/1382 (VTD 16969)*. (*Note*. The relevant supplies took place in 1996. With regard to the rating of the supplies, see now *VATA 1994, Sch 8, Group 12, Note 5B*, introduced by *VAT (Drugs, Medicines and Aids for the Handicapped) Order 1997 (SI 1997 No 2744)*, with effect from 1 January 1998. This provision is designed to ensure that supplies to individuals who are patients in, or attending at the premises of, a relevant institution are excluded from zero-rating, and that it is not possible to arrange for third parties to make zero-rated supplies. For the Commissioners' interpretation of this provision, see Business Brief 29/97, issued on 16 December 1997.)

1.64   See also *Mölnlycke Ltd*, 19.9 DRUGS, MEDICINES, AIDS FOR THE HANDICAPPED, ETC.

DISBURSEMENTS

1.65   **Disbursements by solicitors—whether a supply.**   See *Rowe & Maw*, 58.42 SUPPLY.

1.66   **Reimbursement of director's expenses—whether made as agent for associated company.**   Two companies (C and F) formed a third company (E) as a joint venture. C had a 25% shareholding in E, and F had a 75% shareholding. One of C's directors was appointed as a director of E. His travelling expenses were reimbursed by C. The Commissioners issued an assessment to C on the basis that the reimbursement of his expenses constituted consideration for a supply, on which output tax was chargeable. C appealed, contending that it had been acting as an agent of E when it made the reimbursements, so that no VAT was chargeable. The tribunal accepted this contention and allowed the appeal. *Rowe & Maw*, 58.42 SUPPLY, distinguished. *Alpha International Coal Ltd, LON/92/79Y3 (VTD 9795)*. (*Note*. For a subsequent application for costs, see 2.310 APPEALS.)

1.67   **Director's expenses charged to customer—whether a supply.**   See *Glassiron Ltd*, 58.50 SUPPLY, and *Medical Services & Equipment (ME) Ltd*, 58.51 SUPPLY.

1.68   **Fee for handling insurance claim—whether a disbursement.**   A company failed to account for fees which it received for handling insurance claims. The Commissioners issued an assessment charging output tax on the fees, and the company appealed, contending that the fees were disbursements and that output tax was not chargeable. The tribunal rejected this contention and dismissed the appeal, and the QB upheld this decision. *National Transit Insurance Co Ltd v C & E Commrs, QB 1974, [1975] STC 35; [1975] 1 WLR 552; [1975] 1 All ER 303.*

ESTATE AGENTS

1.69   **Estate agents—expenses charged to clients.**   See *Lea*, 58.46 SUPPLY.

1.70   **Estate agents—time of supply.**   See *Cooke*, 58.303 SUPPLY, and the cases noted at 58.304 and 58.305 SUPPLY.

NURSING AGENCIES

1.71   **Nursing agency—whether supplies made by agency as principal or as agent for nurses.**   See *Allied Medicare Nursing Services Ltd*, 31.4 HEALTH AND WELFARE; *British Nursing Co-Operation Ltd*, 31.5 HEALTH AND WELFARE; *Reed Personnel Services Ltd*, 31.6 HEALTH AND WELFARE; *Sheffield & Rotherham Nursing Agency*, 31.7 HEALTH AND WELFARE; *Parkinson*, 31.9 HEALTH AND WELFARE; *Fairburn*, 31.10 HEALTH AND WELFARE; *BUPA Nursing Services Ltd*, 58.227 SUPPLY, and *South Hams Nursing Agency*, 58.228 SUPPLY.

1.72   **Nursing services partly provided by unqualified staff—whether exempt.**   See *Elder Home Care Ltd*, 31.11 HEALTH AND WELFARE.

'PARTY PLAN' AND DIRECT SELLING

1.73   **'Party plan' sales—whether hostess acting as agent or principal.**   A company (D) established a 'party plan' system for the sale of tupperware to the public. Under the system, D appointed a number of distributors. The distributors purchased the tupperware from D, which fixed a recommended retail price for it. Each distributor then appointed a number of 'sub-distributors', who persuaded friends or acquaintances to act as 'hostesses', arranging parties at their homes, at which the 'sub-distributor' displayed tupperware and obtained orders from the guests. The sub-distributors passed these orders to the distributors, who delivered the goods to the sub-distributors for onward supply to the customers. The sub-distributor paid the distributor 70% of the recommended retail price of the goods, retaining the remaining 30% as commission. The Commissioners assessed the distributors on the full amount paid by the customers, considering that the sub-distributors were acting as agents of the distributor. A married couple acting as distributors appealed, contending that they had sold the goods to the sub-distributors, who in turn had acted as a principal rather than as an agent in selling them to the customers, so that the distributors were only liable to account for tax on the price paid to them by the sub-distributor. The CA accepted this contention and allowed the appeal. *P & R Potter v C & E Commrs, CA 1984, [1985] STC 45.* (*Note.* For subsequent proceedings in this case, see 2.350 APPEALS.)

1.74   A company (C) sold wickerwork goods, etc., using the 'party plan' system. Through its agents, it found individuals, usually housewives, to act as hostesses at parties held in private houses at which the company's goods were displayed and orders taken. In return for her services, the hostess was given a 'reward' dependent on the value of the goods ordered. This 'reward' could be taken either in cash or goods. The Commissioners issued an assessment on the basis that the company was liable to account for tax on the full value of all the goods ordered at the party. The company appealed, contending that the amount of the reward paid to the hostess should be deducted in computing the consideration. The tribunal rejected this contention and dismissed the appeal, holding that the hostess was acting as an agent rather than as an independent principal. *Churchway Crafts Ltd (No 1), LON/78/143 (VTD 782).*

1.75   A similar decision was reached in *AL Younger, LON/81/278 (VTD 1173).*

1.76   A similar decision was reached in a case concerning the sale of embroidery kits under a 'party plan'. The tribunal held that the distributors were liable to account for tax on the full amount paid by the ultimate customer, with no deduction for the commission retained by the hostess. *Potter,* 1.73 AGENTS, distinguished. *Simply Cross-stitch, [1985] VATTR 241 (VTD 1968).*

1.77   **Goods sold under 'party plan' system—value of consideration for goods supplied to hostess.** See *Pippa-Dee Parties Ltd,* 63.26 VALUATION, and *Churchway Crafts Ltd (No 2),* 63.28 VALUATION.

1.78   **Goods sold by 'direct selling'—whether salesmen agents or independent contractors.**   A company manufactured household goods, which it sold through catalogues distributed by self-employed part-time salesmen. The salesmen obtained orders from customers and passed these orders to the company, paying the company 80% of the catalogue price for the products. The Commissioners issued an assessment on the basis that the company should account for VAT on the full amount paid to the salesman by the customer, rather than on the amount paid to the company by the salesman. The tribunal allowed the company's appeal, holding that the salesmen were acting as independent contractors. *Potter,* 1.73 above, applied. *Betterware Products Ltd, LON/83/384 (VTD 1951).*

1.79   *Betterware Products Ltd,* 1.78 above, was applied in the similar subsequent case of *D & D Kelly, LON/87/173 (VTD 2452).*

1.80   **Mail order goods supplied to agents for promotional purposes.**   See *GUS Merchandise Corporation Ltd,* 54.1 RETAILERS' SPECIAL SCHEMES.

1.81   **Mail order goods sold to agents—application of Retail Scheme.**   See *GUS Merchandise Corporation Ltd (No 2),* 54.49 RETAILERS' SPECIAL SCHEMES.

1.82   **Commission received by agents.**   Appeals against assessments charging tax on commission received by agents were dismissed in *I & L Ball, MAN/91/985 (VTD 9251)* and *Merlin HC Ltd, MAN/92/743 (VTD 9251).*

1.83   A couple sold second-hand children's clothing as agents. They did not account for output tax on their commission. The Commissioners issued an assessment and the tribunal dismissed the couple's appeal, holding that tax remained due on the commission even though the sales of clothing were zero-rated. *RJ & JM Farrimond, MAN/92/278 (VTD 10831).*

2   Appeals

Cross-reference.

For appeals by partnerships see 44.1 PARTNERSHIP *et seq.*

The cases in this chapter are arranged under the following headings.

THE MAKING OF THE APPEAL

The tribunal's jurisdiction (VATA 1994, s 82(2), 83)

Note. For appeals against decisions on matters within the discretion of the Commissioners, including those involving *VATA 1994, s 84(10)*, see 2.50 *et seq.* below.

2.1   **Whether tribunal has jurisdiction in relation to future supplies.**   In a case where the substantive issue is no longer relevant, a company appealed to the QB against a tribunal decision. The tribunal hearing had related to supplies under contracts which had already been made but not yet executed. The QB struck out the appeal, holding that the tribunal had no jurisdiction in relation to future supplies. *Allied Windows (South Wales) Ltd v C & E Commrs, QB April 1973 unreported.*

2.2 Tribunals struck out appeals, applying the QB decision in *Allied Windows (South Wales) Ltd*, 2.1 above, in *DC Morgan (for Emmanuel Church, Northwood PCC), [1973] VATTR 76 (VTD 21)* and *V McCulloch, LON/90/1512Y (VTD 5949).*

2.3 *Allied Windows (South Wales) Ltd*, 2.1 above, was applied by the QB in another case where an appeal was struck out on the grounds that it related to a supply that had not taken place at the time of the appeal. *Odhams Leisure Group Ltd v C & E Commrs, QB [1992] STC 332. (Note.* For another issue in this case, see 5.57 BOOKS, ETC.)

2.4 The QB decision in *Odhams Leisure Group Ltd*, 2.3 above, was applied in a subsequent case in which an appeal was adjourned indefinitely on the grounds that it related to future supplies. *Church of Christ the King, LON/93/2029A (VTD 12783).*

2.5 Similar decisions, also applying *Odhams Leisure Group Ltd*, 2.3 above, were reached in *Anglia Energy Conservation Ltd, LON/95/2862 (VTD 14216)* and *A Stott, LON/98/352 (VTD 15622).*

2.6 **Appeal against assessment to recover input tax—application by Commissioners to strike out appeal—whether appeal within VATA 1994, s 83(b).** A university owned all the shares in a property company (G). G constructed certain buildings for the university, and granted the university an underlease of these buildings. The university gave G a certificate that it would use the buildings for relevant residential purposes (see 15.36 *et seq* CONSTRUCTION OF BUILDINGS, ETC). On 6 July 1999 the Commissioners issued a ruling that the certificate should not have been issued. On 14 July they issued an assessment to recover the input tax which the university had reclaimed. The university appealed. The Commissioners applied for the appeal to be struck out, contending that the question of whether the certificate should have been issued depended on the application of an extra-statutory concession, over which the tribunal had no jurisdiction. The tribunal rejected the application, holding that it had no jurisdiction to review the application of the concession, but, by virtue of *VATA 1994, s 83(b)*, it did have jurisdiction to consider the appeal, which was '*prima facie* valid'. (The tribunal also held that *VATA 1994, s 84(10)* did not apply, on the basis that the ruling issued on 6 July was not a 'prior decision', applying the QB decision in *Arnold*, 2.57 below.) *Greenwich Property Ltd, [2000] VATDR 166 (VTD 16746). (Notes.* (1) There has as yet been no public hearing of the substantive appeal. (2) The tribunal chairman (Mr. Oliver) specifically held that the appeal was within *s 83(b)*, although appeals against assessments are normally considered to fall within *s 83(p)*.)

2.7 **Claim for repayment of input tax following submission of return covering 23-year period—whether tribunal has jurisdiction under VATA 1994, s 83(c).** See *Royal College of Obstetricians and Gynaecologists*, 45.1 PAYMENT OF TAX.

2.8 **Appeal against assessment—application by Commissioners to strike out appeal.** A similar decision was reached in a case where a company had failed to account for output tax on supplies of silver to Bangladesh. In the export documentation, the silver was described as lead solder. The Commissioners issued an assessment charging output tax on the supplies, on the basis that they did not qualify for zero-rating since the documentation did not clearly identify the goods in question, as required by what is now *Notice No 703, para 1.10.* The company appealed, and the Commissioners applied for the appeal to be struck out on the grounds that it was outside the tribunal's jurisdiction. The tribunal rejected the application, holding that although it had 'no jurisdiction to consider the validity of the conditions laid down for zero-rating ... the assessment as such is an appealable matter under (*VATA 1994, s 83(p)*)'. *G McKenzie & Co Ltd, LON/92/2015A (VTD 11992)*. (*Notes*. (1) At a subsequent hearing the company's appeal was dismissed—see 24.12 EXPORTS. (2) The decision in this case was approved by the QB in *Arnold*, 2.57 below.)

2.9   **Appeal against assessment for period for which no return made—whether tribunal has jurisdiction to hear appeal under VATA 1994, s 83(p)(i).**   A trader appealed against ten assessments. The Commissioners lodged an application for the appeals to be struck out on the grounds that the trader had not made returns for the relevant periods, so that the appeals were not authorised by *VATA 1994, s 83(p)(i)*. The tribunal accepted this contention, holding that the requirements of *VATA 1994, s 83(p)(i)* were within the scope of *Article 22* of the *Sixth Directive*. The tribunal observed that 'the system, expressed in *Article 22* of the *Sixth Directive*, requires a taxable person to disclose in his return his own view of his liability to tax and his own assessment of the correct amount due. It is a system based on self-assessment; ... far from systematically undermining the principle that a taxpayer has a right to be taxed correctly and in accordance with the law, *section 83(p)(i)* is proportionate and complementary to the system.' *PW Coleman, [1999] VATDR 133 (VTD 15906, 16178)*. (*Note*. The trader had also appealed against nine default surcharges, for which see 2.103 below.)

2.10   An accountant appealed against three assessments. The Commissioners lodged an application for the appeal to be struck out on the grounds that the accountant had not made returns for the relevant periods, so that the appeals were not authorised by *VATA 1994, s 83(p)(i)*. The tribunal accepted this contention and struck out the appeals, observing that the accountant had 'quite simply decided not to comply with the system'. *S Mashood, [1999] VATDR 133 (VTD 15896, 16178)*. (*Note*. The substantive appeal was heard with *Coleman*, 2.9 above.)

2.11   **Repayment claim covering period of several years—whether tribunal has jurisdiction under VATA 1994, s 83(t).**   Following the decision in *Next plc*, 54.26 RETAILERS' SPECIAL SCHEMES, two associated companies which sold goods by mail order lodged substantial repayment claims under *VATA 1994, s 80*. On 18 July 1996 the Paymaster-General stated in Parliament that legislation was to be included in the 1997 Finance Bill to introduce a three-year limit for retrospective repayment claims, and to amend the law on unjust enrichment, with retrospective effect from 18 July 1996. Following this announcement, the Commissioners wrote to the companies to inform them that, although the amount of the claim was agreed, 'Customs will not be making a repayment of the claim as it relates to prescribed accounting periods of more than three years before the claim was made'. The companies appealed. Two other companies, and a partnership, which had submitted similar claims under *s 80*, appealed against similar decisions. The Commissioners applied for all the appeals to be struck out, contending that the tribunal had no jurisdiction. The tribunal rejected this application, holding that there was a dispute concerning 'a claim for the repayment of an amount under *s 80*', within *VATA 1994, s 83(t)*. *Kay & Co Ltd and Others, MAN/96/859 (VTD 14557)*. (*Note*. For subsequent developments in this case, see 45.23 PAYMENT OF TAX.)

2.12   Following the decision in the case noted at 45.19 PAYMENT OF TAX, the appellant company submitted three repayment claims, covering the entire period from the introduction of VAT in 1973 during which it had wrongly treated certain supplies as standard-rated rather than zero-rated, and a period beginning in 1991 during which it had wrongly accounted for output tax on the face value of gift vouchers, rather than on the 'subjective value' as determined by the CJEC in *Argos Distributors Ltd*, 21.131 EUROPEAN COMMUNITY LAW. The Commissioners only agreed to repay the sums which had been paid within three years of the relevant repayment claim, in accordance with the provisions of *VATA 1994, s 80(4)* as substituted by *FA 1997, s 47*. The company appealed. The Commissioners applied for the appeal to be struck out on the grounds that the tribunal had no jurisdiction. The tribunal rejected this contention, holding that there was an appealable matter within *VATA 1994, s 83(t)*. The chairman observed that it was arguable that the company had enforceable rights under European Community law which might prevail over the provisions of *s 80(4)*, and directed that the appeal should be set down for hearing. *Marks & Spencer plc, [1998] VATDR 93 (VTD 15302)*. (*Note.* For the substantive appeal, see 45.32 PAYMENT OF TAX.)

2.13   **Repayment claim—claimant failing to provide additional information requested by Commissioners—whether an appealable decision.** A company submitted a return claiming a repayment of more than £149,000. Following a control visit by a VAT officer, the Commissioners informed the company that they were 'of the opinion that the supplies amount to tax avoidance ... we need to be satisfied that the terms of the leasing agreement are consistent with the supply being at open market value. We therefore require confirmation from a duly authorised representative of the board of directors... that the purchase of computer equipment and its proposed onward leasing ... is not part of some wider tax avoidance motive which involves the leases being terminated prior to the expiry of its five-year term.' The company did not provide this confirmation, but lodged an appeal with the Tribunal Centre. Prior to the hearing of the appeal, the Commissioners sent the company four letters requesting further information, but the company refused to provide this. The Commissioners lodged an application for the appeal to be struck out on the grounds that there had 'been no appealable decision released by the Commissioner (*sic*)'. The tribunal held that 'there has to be "a decision" before the tribunal has any jurisdiction under (*VATA 1994, s 83*)' but that, on the evidence, the Commissioners had 'made a decision not to make a repayment to the appellant at least unless and until certain information is provided'. However, the company's Notice of Appeal did not comply with *VAT Tribunals Rules (SI 1986 No 590), rule 3(2)*. The tribunal directed that the company should 'provide particulars whether in an amended Notice of Appeal or otherwise, in accordance with *rule 3(2)* of the *VAT Tribunals Rules*, of the decision with respect to which the appeal is made'. *City of Sunderland College Supplies Ltd, MAN/98/252 (VTD 15701)*. (*Note.* The *Rules of the Supreme Court 1965 (SI 1965 No 1776)* refer to 'particulars'. With effect from 26 April 1999, these rules have largely been replaced by the *Civil Procedure Rules 1998 (SI 1998 No 3132)*, which refer instead to 'information'.)

2.14   A company submitted a return claiming a repayment of more than £2,000,000. The Commissioners formed the opinion that the company had wrongly treated certain supplies as zero-rated. They requested further information from the company. The company did not provide the information, but lodged an appeal with the Tribunal Centre. The Commissioners lodged an application for the appeal to be struck out on the grounds that there had been no appealable decision. The tribunal rejected the application, holding that the Commissioners had made a decision not to make a repayment until they had received further information, and that this was 'an appealable decision'. With regard to the substantive appeal, the tribunal observed that the burden of proof was on the company, and that the company 'would have been much wiser ... to have given reasonable particulars of the claims'. The tribunal directed that both parties should serve Lists of Documents, that the Commissioners should serve a Statement of Case, and the company should then serve a response to the Statement of Case. *Colaingrove Ltd (No 2), LON/00/765 (VTD 16981)*.

2.15   **Extra-statutory concessions.** See the cases noted at 2.49 to 2.59 below.

2.16   **Special Provisions Order 1995, Article 12—whether tribunal has jurisdiction to review Commissioners' direction.**   See *JH Corbitt (Numismatists) Ltd*, 56.1 SECOND-HAND GOODS, and *Christopher Gibbs Ltd*, 56.2 SECOND-HAND GOODS.

2.17   **Decision of Commissioners as to period of returns—whether appealable.**   See *Selected Growers Ltd*, 55.1 RETURNS, and *Punchwell Ltd*, 55.2 RETURNS.

2.18   **Appeal against default interest—effect of VATA 1994, s 84(6)*.**   See the cases noted at 17.1 to 17.3 DEFAULT INTEREST.

2.19   **Default surcharge—whether tribunal may hear appeal against surcharge liability notice before any surcharge has been incurred.**   A company which had been served with a surcharge liability notice lodged an appeal to the tribunal. The Commissioners applied for the appeal to be struck out, contending that it was premature and that no appeal could be lodged until a default surcharge had been imposed. The tribunal granted the Commissioners' application, holding that it had no jurisdiction to entertain an appeal against the issue of a surcharge liability notice. *Expert Systems Design Ltd, MAN/92/367 (VTD 7974)*.

2.20   Similar decisions were reached in *SR Auld, LON/93/108P (VTD 11956)* and *Castrue Ltd, LON/94/712P (VTD 12681)*.

2.21   **VATA 1994, Sch 11 para 5(2)(3)—whether tribunal has jurisdiction to hear appeal.**   In the case noted at 48.136 PENALTIES: FAILURE TO NOTIFY, a deregistered builder had issued eleven invoices purporting to charge VAT, although he was no longer registered. The Commissioners sought to recover the amount in question under *VATA 1994, Sch 11 para 5(2)(3)*. The trader appealed. The Commissioners applied for the appeal to be struck out, on the grounds that the tribunal had no jurisdiction to hear the appeal under *VATA 1994, s 83*. The tribunal granted the Commissioners' application, observing that, since the facts of the case had been fully explored in the appeal against the penalty (where the tribunal had jurisdiction under *VATA 1994, s 83(q)*), 'the lack of jurisdiction to hear an appeal against the amount due has not, in this appeal, meant that the appellant has been unable to put forward all his arguments'. *GE Alm, LON/98/961 (VTD 15863)*.

2.22   **VATA 1994, Sch 11 para 4(1)*—requirement to give security—whether appealable decision.**   The Commissioners had served a notice requiring a company to give security under what is now *VATA 1994, Sch 11 para 4(1)* in the sum of £170,801.89 in a case where approximately £80,000 of input tax had been reclaimed by the company. The company sought to appeal against this requirement. The Commissioners applied to strike out the appeal on the grounds that no such appeal lay under *VATA 1994, s 83*. The tribunal allowed the Commissioners' application, holding that it had no jurisdiction to entertain the appeal, on the grounds that no express right of appeal lay against a notice requiring security under *Sch 11 para 4(1)*. *Strangewood Ltd (No 2), [1988] VATTR 35 (VTD 2599)*. (*Note. VATA 1994, s 83(l)* only allows an appeal against a requirement to give security under *Sch 11 para 4(2)*.)

2.23   **Appeal against retrospective cancellation of registration—whether within jurisdiction of tribunal.**   A woman had registered for VAT in 1982 as a breeder of racehorses. She regularly made claims for repayment of VAT. In 1991 a VAT officer formed the opinion that she was not carrying on a business. The Commissioners issued a ruling that her registration should be cancelled with retrospective effect, and issued an assessment to recover input tax which she had reclaimed in the years 1986 to 1991 inclusive. She appealed, contending that the Commissioners' decision to backdate the cancellation of her registration was unreasonable. The Commissioners applied for a direction that the appeal should be struck out as it did not relate to an appealable matter within what is now *VATA 1994, s 83*, and thus was outside the jurisdiction of the tribunal. The tribunal dismissed the Commissioners' application, holding that the tribunal had 'a supervisory jurisdiction to review any decision to deregister'. *Anne Brookes, [1994] VATTR 35 (VTD 11752)*.

2.24   **Assessment issued to recover unpaid tax—appellant contending that assessment invalid because tax already paid—jurisdiction of tribunal.** The Commissioners issued an assessment on an individual (G), including £10,260 in respect of tax unpaid for the period ending 31 March 1985. G did not pay the tax charged by the assessment, and the Commissioners presented a bankruptcy petition. G appealed, contending that he had paid the tax by cheque in March 1985. The tribunal observed that it was doubtful whether it 'had jurisdiction to enquire into a matter which seemed to involve no issue of liability but to be concerned essentially with debt recovery', but agreed to hear the appeal on the basis 'that if the tax had originally been paid by (G) as he contended the assessment subsequently made under (*VATA 1994, s 73*) to recover it would have been bad; and that assessment was itself clearly appealable by virtue of (*VATA 1994, s 83(p)*)'. The Commissioners gave evidence that they had never received the £10,260. G produced a copy of his VAT return for the period in question, but did not produce a copy of the cheque which he claimed to have sent, or a bank statement showing that the cheque had been debited. The tribunal dismissed G's appeal, finding on the evidence that G had submitted the return and the cheque but that there was no evidence that the return had ever been received or that the cheque had been presented. G 'had not discharged the burden of proving on the balance of probabilities that the tax due for March 1985 was received by the Commissioners'. *J Goldenberg, LON/92/3294A (11591)*.

2.25   **Application to transfer appeals from Scottish tribunal to English tribunal.** A Scottish company had four English subsidiaries. The VAT affairs of all five companies were dealt with in Scotland. The English subsidiaries appealed to the Edinburgh VAT Tribunal against directions issued by the Commissioners. The companies subsequently applied for the appeals to be heard by the London Tribunal Centre, contending that since the appeals involved the application of English law to English contracts, they should be heard by an English tribunal. The Edinburgh Tribunal granted the application, holding that it had jurisdiction to hear the appeals, since 'delivery to any Tribunal Centre should be sufficient to instigate proceedings, particularly when there is one UK respondent'. However, 'in the present case where the companies are registered in England, where the contracts with which the application is concerned concern matters of English law, it is plain that the matter should be appropriately dealt with under the control of an English Tribunal Centre, from which there is an English appeal route'. *RBS Leasing & Services (No 1) Ltd (and related appeals), EDN/98/58–61 (VTD 15643)*. (*Note*. For the substantive appeal, see 63.2 VALUATION.)

Whether the recipient of a supply may appeal

Cases where the recipient was permitted to appeal

2.26   In the case noted at 58.37 SUPPLY, a company which was the recipient of a supply appealed against the Commissioners' decision that tax was payable on the supply. The Commissioners did not object to the hearing of the appeal but the tribunal considered as a preliminary matter whether the appellant had any *locus standi*. It concluded that what is now *VATA 1994, s 83* does not require the appellant to be the taxable person accountable for the tax in dispute, but that the appellant must have a sufficient legal interest in maintaining the appeal. This was clearly so in the case in question but might not apply to, for example, a member of the public buying an article from a retailer. The tribunal held that, where the appellant was the recipient of a supply, he should 'wherever possible seek the consent of the supplier to the appeal being brought by them jointly, upon such terms as to costs as they may agree'. *Processed Vegetable Growers Association Ltd, [1973] VATTR 87 (VTD 25)*.

2.27   In the case noted at 15.140 CONSTRUCTION OF DWELLINGS, ETC., where the appellant was the recipient of the relevant supply, the tribunal held that he had sufficient interest to maintain the appeal. *Payton*, 2.32 below, was distinguished, on the grounds that the appellant had deposited with the Commissioners an amount equal to the tax in dispute, on condition that it would be refunded if the appeal succeeded. *B Gilbourne, [1974] VATTR 209 (VTD 109)*.

2.28   In a case noted at 26.1 FINANCE, the tribunal held that the appellant company, which was the recipient of the relevant supplies, had sufficient interest to maintain the appeal. *Processed Vegetable Growers*, 2.26 above, applied; *Payton*, 2.32 below, not followed (and implicitly disapproved). The tribunal observed that if the appeal succeeded, and was not reversed by the courts, the Commissioners would be bound to observe it and repay or credit to the supplier the tax which he had accounted for. *Williams & Glyn's Bank Ltd, [1974] VATTR 262 (VTD 118)*.

2.29   An individual (B) had been invoiced by contractors who had carried out work on his house. The amount invoiced included VAT of £106.50. B considered that no tax was chargeable under the legislation then in force. He paid the contractor for the amount exclusive of the VAT, sent the Commissioners a cheque for £106.50 and appealed. The Commissioners refused to accept the cheque and contended at the hearing that the appellant did not have a sufficient financial interest to maintain the appeal, relying on *In re IG Farbenindustrie AG Agreement, CA [1943] 2 All ER 525*. The tribunal rejected the Commissioners' contention, distinguishing *IG Farbenindustrie* because the appellant had a statutory right of appeal. The appellant also had a sufficient financial interest in the matter as he had not paid the contractors the whole of the amount invoiced. *JR Beckley, LON/74/68 (VTD 114)*. (*Note*. Compare *Wade*, 45.3 PAYMENT OF TAX, in which the facts were broadly similar but the appellant did not query the rating of the relevant supply until after he had paid the tax to the supplier, and his appeal was dismissed by the tribunal.)

2.30   In *Kenwood Appliances Ltd*, 34.28 INPUT TAX, the tribunal accepted that a company which was not the recipient of the relevant supply, but which was required to pay the consideration under an indemnity agreement, had sufficient *locus standi* to lodge an appeal.

2.31   For examples of other cases where the tribunal entertained an appeal by the recipient of a supply, see *Barclays Bank plc*, 2.41 below; *Watters*, 6.23 BUILDINGS AND LAND; *Shearing*, 7.24 BUSINESS; *Severnside Siren Trust Ltd*, 11.9 CHARITIES; *Sussex County Association of Change Ringers*, 11.19 CHARITIES; *Leukaemic Disorders Trust*, 11.22 CHARITIES; *Thompson*, 15.30 CONSTRUCTION OF BUILDINGS, ETC.; *League of Friends of Kingston Hospital*, 15.57 CONSTRUCTION OF BUILDINGS, ETC.; *Strowbridge*, 15.84 CONSTRUCTION OF BUILDINGS, ETC.; *Midgley*, 15.86 CONSTRUCTION OF BUILDINGS, ETC.; *Shiri Guru Nanaka Sikh Temple*, 15.106 CONSTRUCTION OF BUILDINGS, ETC.; *Chipping Sodbury Town Trust*, 15.115 CONSTRUCTION OF BUILDINGS, ETC.; *Sheldon School*, 15.127 CONSTRUCTION OF BUILDINGS, ETC.; *Portland College*, 19.26 DRUGS, MEDICINES, AIDS FOR THE HANDICAPPED, ETC.; *Simmons*, 19.32 DRUGS, MEDICINES, AIDS FOR THE HANDICAPPED, ETC.; *Drummond*, 19.36 DRUGS, MEDICINES, AIDS FOR THE HANDICAPPED, ETC.; *Arthritis Care*, 19.41 DRUGS, MEDICINES, AIDS FOR THE HANDICAPPED, ETC.; *Hall*, 19.42 DRUGS, MEDICINES, AIDS FOR THE HANDICAPPED,

ETC.; *Mills*, 19.45 DRUGS, MEDICINES, AIDS FOR THE HANDICAPPED, ETC.; *Poole Shopmobility*, 19.47 DRUGS, MEDICINES, AIDS FOR THE HANDICAPPED, ETC.; *Conroy*, 19.62 DRUGS, MEDICINES, AIDS FOR THE HANDICAPPED, ETC.; *Open University*, 20.3 EDUCATION; *Joseph Rowntree Foundation*, 20.14 EDUCATION; *Nationwide Anglia Building Society*, 26.2 FINANCE; *Fairburn*, 31.10 HEALTH AND WELFARE; *Cameron*, 31.29 HEALTH AND WELFARE; *Lee*, 36.10 INSURANCE; *British Telecommunications plc*, 39.15 LAND; *Central Capital Corporation Ltd*, 39.51 LAND; *Ashworth*, 39.96 LAND; *Dowse*, 39.103 LAND; *Bondi*, 39.104 LAND; *Clarke*, 39.104 LAND; *Wilson*, 39.105 LAND; *Fisher*, 39.113 LAND; *Roberts*, 39.116 LAND; *St Anne's Catholic Church*, 52.46 PROTECTED BUILDINGS; *The Royal Academy of Music*, 52.7 PROTECTED BUILDINGS; *Walsingham College (Yorkshire Properties) Ltd*, 52.58 PROTECTED BUILDINGS; *Heart of Variety*, 58.18 SUPPLY; *Calabar Developments Ltd*, 58.19 SUPPLY; *Life Education Centre (Nottinghamshire) Ltd*, 58.32 SUPPLY; *Commonwealth Telecommunications Bureau*, 58.38 SUPPLY; *Hutchvision Hong Kong Ltd*, 58.371 SUPPLY; *John Village Automotive Ltd*, 58.391 SUPPLY, and *Everett*, 62.3 TRANSPORT. The list is not exhaustive.

Cases where the appeal was struck out

2.32   A woman had been supplied with a surgical belt for an amount which included VAT of 96p. She paid the amount 'under protest' and lodged an appeal. The tribunal held that she did not have sufficient interest to maintain the appeal. Although she had paid 'under protest', she had paid the tax voluntarily without compulsion or threats and accordingly had no right to recover the tax should her appeal succeed. *Twyford v Manchester Corporation, Ch D [1945] Ch 236; [1946] 1 All ER 621*, applied. The tribunal observed that the appeal would have succeeded (see 31.30 HEALTH AND WELFARE). *M Payton, [1974] VATTR 140 (VTD 89).* (*Note.* The decision was distinguished in *Gilbourne*, 2.27 above, and not followed in *Williams & Glyn's Bank Ltd*, 2.28 above.)

2.33   An individual (W) booked a holiday with a large company which was registered for VAT and accounted for tax under a Retail Scheme. W considered that the VAT included in the cost of the holiday was excessive, and appealed to a tribunal. The tribunal directed that the appeal be struck out, holding that the appeal was outside the scope of what is now *VATA 1994, s 83*, since W was the recipient of the supply and was not a taxable person. Previous decisions in which appeals by recipients of supplies had been entertained were distinguished, as in those cases the rating of the supply had been in issue, whereas in the present case it was accepted by all parties that the supply of the holiday was standard-rated. *C Wayment, LON/89/1854Y (VTD 4846).*

2.34   An individual (W), who was not registered for VAT, received tuition in flying in order to qualify as a commercial pilot. The cost of the courses included VAT. W appealed to the tribunal, contending that VAT should not have been charged. The tribunal dismissed his appeal, holding that W was not entitled to credit for any input tax since he was not a taxable person. (The tribunal also observed that the VAT was correctly chargeable, since the tuition was neither exempt nor zero-rated.) *FP Whitehouse, LON/92/404A (VTD 11114).*

2.35   The Commissioners issued a ruling that a property management company was supplying its services to the owners of the relevant premises, rather than to the subtenants who occupied the premises. The owners were property investors who were not registered for VAT and were therefore unable to reclaim input tax on the management services. One of them sought to lodge an appeal against the Commissioners' ruling, on the basis that if the services were deemed to be supplied to the occupiers, they would be able to recover input tax, so that the owners could charge a higher rent without making the premises more difficult to let. The tribunal struck out the appeal, holding that he did not have sufficient legal interest in the disputed decision. *Williams & Glyn's Bank*, 2.28 above, distinguished. *B Kingsley-Smith, LON/95/1563A (VTD 13787)*.

Miscellaneous

2.36 **Whether appellant may require production of Commissioners' working papers before hearing.** A trader had appealed against some estimated assessments on her and made an application for further and better particulars of the Commissioners' case under what is now *VAT Tribunals Rules (SI 1986 No 590), rule 9*. It became apparent during the hearing of the application that she wanted to see the Commissioners' working papers leading to the amount of the assessments. The tribunal rejected the application. *K Taylor (t/a Jeans), [1975] VATTR 147 (VTD 163A)*. (*Note*. The *Rules of the Supreme Court 1965 (SI 1965 No 1776)* refer to 'particulars'. With effect from 26 April 1999, these rules have largely been replaced by the *Civil Procedure Rules 1998 (SI 1998 No 3132)*, which refer instead to 'information'.)

2.37 **Whether notebooks of investigating VAT officer privileged.** A trader, whose VAT affairs were under investigation, applied to a tribunal for notes of interviews made by a VAT officer to be made available to his solicitors. The tribunal rejected the application, holding that the notes were privileged. *EYS Wat (t/a Kam Tong Restaurant), LON/76/82 (VTD 494)*.

2.38 The proprietors of a restaurant applied for records made by VAT officers carrying out observations at the restaurant to be made available to them. The tribunal granted the application, applying *dicta* in *Moti Mahal Indian Restaurant*, 47.93 PENALTIES: EVASION OF TAX, and observing that there was 'no basis upon which contemporaneous records of the kind with which this case is concerned and which are central to the assessment in question should be protected from disclosure in the ordinary way'. *F Karim, M Ali & A Majid (t/a Dhaka Tandoori Restaurant), MAN/92/1642 (VTD 10987)*.

2.39 **Solicitor withdrawing appeal on behalf of clients—clients submitting subsequent further Notice of Appeal.** A married couple had lodged an appeal against an assessment, and in October 1992 their solicitor met VAT officers to discuss the appeal. Three weeks later the solicitor wrote to the VAT office withdrawing the appeal. Subsequently the couple submitted a further Notice of Appeal relating to the same assessment. The Commissioners applied for the appeal to be struck out. The tribunal granted the Commissioners' application, finding that the couple had authorised the solicitor to act on their behalf, and holding that, by virtue of what is now *VATA 1994, s 85*, the assessment was now *res judicata*. *Dicta* in *Waugh v HB Clifford & Sons Ltd, CA [1982] 1 All ER 1095*, applied. *BD & Mrs MA Taylor, MAN/93/78 (VTD 10980)*.

2.40 **Whether former shareholders of company can be enjoined in appeal made by company.** Following the sale of a company, the new shareholders discovered, and informed the Commissioners, that some cash receipts and other transactions had not previously been reported. The Commissioners issued an estimated assessment and the company appealed. The vendors, who were liable to indemnify the company for any tax liabilities relating to the time before the sale, deposited the tax demanded but did not provide the new owners of the company with information to enable them to pursue the appeal, and lodged an application to be enjoined in the appeal. The tribunal rejected the application and the QB dismissed the vendors' appeal against this decision, holding that there would be no injustice if they were excluded because they could in the future dispute any liability under the indemnity. If the necessary information was provided to the company, the tribunal could allow the applicants to join in the appeal at a later date under *VAT Tribunals Rules (SI 1986 No 590), rules 13, 14* and *19. Schwarcz & Others v Aeresta Ltd & C & E Commrs, QB 1988, [1989] STC 230.*

2.41   **Whether third party can be joined in appeal.**   A company (V) issued credit cards and made related supplies to banks. Its supplies had been treated as exempt, but it considered that they should be standard-rated. In November 1990 the Commissioners accepted V's contention, and issued a ruling accordingly. A bank (B), to which V supplied services, objected to the ruling, since it was partly exempt and would be unable to recover much of the input tax which it would have to pay in respect of the supplies it received from V. In June 1991 B lodged a formal appeal against the ruling. V applied for a direction under *VAT Tribunals Rules (SI 1986 No 590), rule 19(3)* that it should be joined as a party to the appeal. The Commissioners supported the application, but B objected to it. The tribunal granted the application, holding that it had power to grant the application, applying *dicta* in *Schwarcz & Others v Aeresta Ltd*, 2.40 above, and that 'it would be much better equipped to do justice to the matter if (V) were joined as a party'. It was 'both necessary and expedient to have (V) as a party to the appeal'. *Barclays Bank plc v C & E Commrs and Visa International Service Association, [1992] VATTR 229 (VTD 7911).* (*Note.* For a direction as to costs, see 2.337 below.)

2.42   **Whether appeals by associated partnerships should be heard together.**   The Commissioners issued estimated assessments on two partnerships which operated restaurants. Three of the four members of each partnership were the same. Both partnerships appealed. The Commissioners applied for a direction that the appeals should be heard together. The tribunal made a direction accordingly, under *VAT Tribunals Rules (SI 1986 No 590), rule 19(3)*, applying the CA decision in *Johnson v Walden, CA 1995, [1996] STC 382 (TTC 2001, 4.16)*. One of the partnerships appealed to the QB, contending that the appeals should not be heard together. Turner J rejected this contention and dismissed the appeal, holding on the evidence that the tribunal had been entitled to make the direction in question. The tribunal's decision was 'entirely rational', and it would 'have been a mischievous result if there had been two separate hearings and witnesses whose evidence was believed in one case in relation to the same evidential matters were not believed in the other, or the other way about'. *Maharani Restaurant v C & E Commrs, QB [1999] STC 295.* (*Note.* At a subsequent hearing, the appeals were dismissed and penalties under *VATA 1994, s 60* were upheld—see 47.54 PENALTIES: EVASION OF TAX.)

2.43   **Whether appeals by related companies should be heard together.**   The decision in *Maharani Restaurant*, 2.42 above, was applied in an insurance premium tax case where the tribunal held that appeals by six related companies should be heard together. *Cresta Holidays Ltd (and related appeals), LON/00/9000–4 (VTD 16857).*

2.44   **The Notice of Appeal.**   In the case noted at 15.76 CONSTRUCTION OF BUILDINGS, ETC., the Commissioners issued an assessment on a company after discovering that it had reclaimed input tax which the Commissioners considered was attributable to an exempt supply. The company lodged an appeal against the assessment, describing its reason for appealing as being that the assessment was out of time. Subsequently the company applied to amend its Notice of Appeal to include an alternative contention that the input tax was attributable to a zero-rated supply, rather than to an exempt supply. The tribunal allowed the company's application, holding that it 'would be reluctant in the extreme to prevent a taxpayer from raising a *bona fide* defence'. *Marchday Holdings Ltd, [1992] VATTR 484 (VTD 8964).*

2.45   In 1994 a company submitted a claim for a substantial VAT repayment, contending that *Input Tax Order, Article 7* was invalid. The Commissioners rejected the claim and the company appealed. The appeal was stood over pending the CJEC decision in *Royscot Leasing Ltd*, 21.207 EUROPEAN COMMUNITY LAW. In 1998, following the CA decision in *British Telecommunications plc*, 9.83 CARS, the company applied to amend its Notice of Appeal to include an alternative contention that part of the tax in question related to delivery charges which were outside the scope of *Input Tax Order, Article 7*. The tribunal granted the application, applying *Marchday Holdings Ltd*, 2.44 above, and holding that 'the tribunal should be reluctant to prevent a taxpayer from raising a *bona fide* defence'. *Quicks plc, [1998] VATDR 491 (VTD 15836).*

2.46   A company appealed against an assessment and a misdeclaration penalty, contending in its Notice of Appeal that it had been misdirected by a VAT officer. The Commissioners made a preliminary application for the appeal to be struck out or for the company to give further particulars of the ground of appeal. The tribunal rejected the Commissioners' application, observing that while the doctrine of personal bar could not prevent the Customs from recovering any tax due, an alleged misdirection could constitute a reasonable excuse for a misdeclaration and justify the discharging of a penalty. *Albany Building Services Ltd, EDN/92/335 (VTD 10531).* (*Notes.* (1) For cases concerning the doctrine of personal bar, see 2.83 *et seq.* below. (2) The appeal was subsequently dismissed—see 49.361 PENALTIES: MISDECLARATION. The tribunal found that the VAT officer had not misdirected the company. (3) The *Rules of the Supreme Court 1965 (SI 1965 No 1776)* refer to 'particulars'. With effect from 26 April 1999, these rules have largely been replaced by the *Civil Procedure Rules 1998 (SI 1998 No 3132)*, which refer instead to 'information'.)

2.47   See also *City of Sunderland College Supplies Ltd*, 2.13 above.

2.48   **Appeal procedure where assessment reduced by Commissioners.** A partnership which operated a restaurant appealed against an estimated assessment, but did not pay the tax of £35,000 charged by the assessment. The partnership lodged a hardship application under *VAT Tribunals Rules (SI 1986 No 590)*, rule 11. The application was heard in April 1991, and the partnership was given three months to pay the tax charged. Meanwhile, in May 1991 the Commissioners reduced the assessment to £25,000. In July 1991 the partnership submitted a further notice of appeal. The Tribunal Centre allocated a new reference number to this notice of appeal, and the Commissioners applied for the appeals to be consolidated. In September 1991 the tribunal consolidated the appeals, finding that the grant of a second reference number had been an administrative error, and dismissed the appeals on the grounds that the tax charged had not been paid. The partnership appealed to the QB, contending that the appeals should not have been consolidated and that the time for paying the tax charged by the amended assessment should therefore have been extended. The QB dismissed the appeal, holding that where an assessment, against which an appeal had been lodged, was reduced, there was no need for any further appeal, nor was there any statutory provision for such an appeal. The grant of a separate reference number was of no significance and did not mean that the appeal should be treated as two separate appeals. Since the partnership had not paid the sum charged by the assessment, the tribunal had been entitled to dismiss the appeal. *Sitar Tandoori Restaurant v C & E Commrs, QB [1993] STC 591.*

MATTERS WITHIN THE DISCRETION OF THE COMMISSIONERS

2.49   **Whether a concession can be the subject of an appeal.** A company (D) applied to the Commissioners for a concession that services which it supplied under long-term contracts made before January 1973 should not be chargeable to VAT. The Commissioners rejected the claim, notifying D by letter. D and two associated companies, E and C, appealed. The tribunal struck out the appeals, holding that E and C had no *locus standi* as the decision was not communicated to them. With regard to D, the question of whether a concession should be made was not a subject of appeal within what is now *VATA 1994, s 83. Davis Advertising Service Ltd, [1973] VATTR 16 (VTD 5).*

2.50 **Special Provisions Order 1995, Article 12—whether tribunal has jurisdiction to review Commissioners' direction.** In the case noted at 56.1 SECOND-HAND GOODS, the HL held that a tribunal's jurisdiction was restricted to considering whether a trader's records complied with the statutory requirements, and that where the records did not meet those requirements, the tribunal could not consider whether the Commissioners should have used their discretion to permit the use of the scheme. *C & E Commrs v JH Corbitt (Numismatists) Ltd, HL [1980] STC 231; [1981] AC 22; [1980] 2 All ER 72.* (*Note.* This case was decided before the introduction of what is now *VATA 1994, s 84(10)* by *FA 1981.* The decision should be read in the light of *s 84(10)* — see *Christopher Gibbs Ltd,* 56.2 SECOND-HAND GOODS — but is still frequently cited as an authority.)

2.51 In the case noted at 56.2 SECOND-HAND GOODS, the tribunal considered that it had jurisdiction to overrule a Commissioners' decision that a company was not entitled to use the margin scheme for sales of antiques, since its records did not comply with the scheme requirements. The tribunal declined to follow *J H Corbitt (Numismatists) Ltd,* 56.1 SECOND-HAND GOODS, since that case had been decided before the enactment of what is now *VATA 1994, s 84(10). Christopher Gibbs Ltd, [1992] VATTR 376 (VTD 8981).*

2.52 **Commissioners' refusal to operate 'Sheldon statement'—whether within VATA 1994, s 84(10).** See *Animal Virus Research Institute,* 2.81 below.

2.53 **Commissioners refusing to backdate extra-statutory concession—whether an appealable matter within VATA 1994, s 84(10).** Before 1 April 1983, the VAT liability on the sale of a security depended on the 'place of belonging' of the purchaser. The Commissioners agreed with the Investment and Unit Trust Associations that, with effect from 1 April 1983, members of the Associations should have the option of treating the country in which the sale took place as the 'place of belonging' of the purchaser, in any case where the identity (and thus the place of belonging) of the purchaser was unknown, and also in any case where it was not known where the sale took place. An investment trust submitted a claim that the concession should be backdated to 1 April 1978. The Commissioners rejected this claim and the investment trust lodged an appeal. The tribunal struck out the appeal, holding that it had no jurisdiction and that there had been no decision within what is now *VATA 1994, s 84(10). Scottish Investment Trust plc, EDN/92/77 (VTD 9368).*

2.54 **Application of extra-statutory concession—whether within VATA 1994, s 84(10).** In the case noted at 24.29 EXPORTS, the tribunal held that it could consider the application of an extra-statutory concession, since 'the effect of (what is now *VATA 1994, s 84(10)*) is to allow the tribunal to review whether, as a matter of fact, the taxpayer has acted in accordance with guidelines prescribed by the Commissioners in the exercise of a discretion conferred on them, but not to review the laying down of the guidelines or requirements themselves'. *RW Shepherd, [1994] VATTR 47 (VTD 11753).*

2.55 A similar decision was reached in *G McKenzie & Co Ltd,* 2.8 above.

2.56 An individual who had converted an old church into a dwelling appealed against the Commissioners' refusal to apply an extra-statutory concession which would have entitled him to reclaim input tax. (The concession took effect from 21 April 1994, and the Commissioners refused to apply it to the appellant since the work in question had been completed before that date.) The tribunal dismissed the appeal, holding that it had 'no jurisdiction in regard to the operation of extra-statutory concessions'. *Dicta* of Lord Grantchester in *Farm Facilities (Fork Lift) Ltd*, 61.18 TRANSFERS OF GOING CONCERNS, applied. *Dr BN Purdue, EDN/94/511 (VTD 13430)*. (*Notes*. (1) The decision here was approved by the QB in *Arnold*, 2.57 below. (2) An alternative contention by the appellant, that the work had not been completed until after 21 April 1994, was also rejected by the tribunal — see 15.66 CONSTRUCTION OF BUILDINGS.)

2.57   In a subsequent case in which the application of the same concession was in dispute, the QB held that the tribunal had no jurisdiction in relation to the concession, which was a matter for the Commissioners. Hidden J held that the provisions of *VATA 1994, s 84(10)* only applied to a case where there were two separate decisions (as had been the case in *JH Corbitt (Numismatists) Ltd*, 56.1 SECOND-HAND GOODS) and did not apply in the present case where there had only been one decision. *G McKenzie & Co*, 2.8 above, and *Purdue*, 2.56 above, approved; *obiter dicta* of the tribunal chairman in *British Teleflower Service Ltd*, 38.49 INVOICES, disapproved. *C & E Commrs v SH Arnold, QB [1996] STC 1271.*

2.58   The decision in *Arnold*, 2.57 above, was applied in *Greenwich Property Ltd*, 2.6 above.

2.59   **Concessions, etc.—other cases.**   For the jurisdiction of the tribunal in relation to a published non-statutory arrangement, see also *McLean Homes Midland Ltd*, 34.7 INPUT TAX. There have been a large number of cases in which a tribunal has dismissed an appeal because it had no jurisdiction in non-statutory matters or because the appellant has failed to disclose a ground of appeal, but which raise no point of general interest. In the interests of space, such cases are not summarised individually in this book.

2.60   **Commissioners deciding to cancel registration under VATA 1994, Sch 1 para 13*—nature of tribunal's jurisdiction.**   See *The Source Enterprise Ltd*, 42.1 OVERSEAS TRADERS.

2.61   **Penalty under VATA 1994, s 63*—whether Commissioners acting unreasonably in imposing penalty.**   See *Food Engineering Ltd*, 49.413 PENALTIES: MISDECLARATION.

2.62   **Retrospective group registration—nature of tribunal's jurisdiction.**   In the case noted at 30.2 GROUPS OF COMPANIES, the QB held that the Commissioners have power under what is now *VATA 1994, s 43(7)* to admit group registration retrospectively. However the discretion to admit retrospective treatment was that of the Commissioners and could not be exercised by the tribunal. *C & E Commrs v Save and Prosper Group Ltd, QB 1978, [1979] STC 205.*

2.63   **VATA 1994, Sch 11 para 4*—power to require security—nature of tribunal's jurisdiction.**   See *Mr Wishmore Ltd*, 14.46 COLLECTION AND ENFORCEMENT.

2.64   **Cash accounting scheme—nature of tribunal's jurisdiction.**   See *Mainline Fabrications*, 10.4 CASH ACCOUNTING SCHEME.

2.65   **Application of VATA 1994, Sch 1 para 1(3)—nature of tribunal's jurisdiction.**   See *Hare*, 53.32 REGISTRATION, and *Timur & Timur*, 53.34 REGISTRATION.

2.66   **Direction under VATA 1994, Sch 1 para 2*—nature of tribunal's jurisdiction.**   See *Chamberlain*, 53.95 REGISTRATION, and *Gregorio & Sons*, 53.115 REGISTRATION.

2.67 Appeals

2.67 **Application for registration under VATA 1994, Sch 1 para 9*—nature of tribunal's jurisdiction.** See *Golden Pyramid Ltd*, 53.51 REGISTRATION.

2.68 **Input tax claims—VAT Regulations 1995, reg 29*—nature of tribunal's jurisdiction.** See *Vaughan*, 38.55 INVOICES AND CREDIT NOTES.

2.69 **Definition of 'tax year' for partial exemption calculations—VAT Regulations 1995, reg 99*.** See *Yorkhurst Ltd*, 43.112 PARTIAL EXEMPTION.

2.70 **Claim to pre-registration input tax—Commissioners refusing to authorise claim under VAT Regulations 1995, reg 111*—whether within jurisdiction of tribunal.** The proprietors of a rest home claimed input tax on supplies made to them before registration. The Commissioners rejected the claim and the proprietors appealed. The Commissioners applied for the appeal to be struck out on the grounds that the decision on whether to allow pre-registration input tax under what is now *VAT Regulations 1995 (SI 1995 No 2518), reg 111* was within the Commissioners' discretion and outside the jurisdiction of the tribunal. The tribunal dismissed the Commissioners' application, holding that it had jurisdiction to review the decision. The tribunal held that 'the appeal relates to input tax even though the Commissioners have decided not to authorise the appellants to treat the amounts as if they were input tax'. Accordingly, the appeal related to an appealable matter within what is now *VATA 1994, s 83(c)*. Applying *Brookes*, 2.23 above, the tribunal had jurisdiction to review the Commissioners' exercise of their discretion. *S & Mrs S Barar (t/a Turret House Rest Home), LON/93/2021A & 2224A (VTD 12707)*. (*Note.* There was no public hearing of the substantive appeal.)

2.71 **Late repayment claim by 'third country trader'—VAT Regulations 1995, regs 185–197—whether within jurisdiction of tribunal.** In the case noted at 42.5 OVERSEAS TRADERS, the tribunal held that it had no 'jurisdiction to review the exercise by Customs & Excise of any discretion it may have in its management of the collection and refund of VAT'. *Jersey Telecoms, LON/95/1965 (VTD 13940)*.

ESTOPPEL AND ALLIED MATTERS

2.72 **Commissioners' practice where taxpayer misled by VAT officer.** In a Parliamentary question and answer on 21 July 1978, the then Financial Secretary to the Treasury, Mr Robert Sheldon stated: 'When it is established that an officer of Customs and Excise, with the full facts before him, has given a clear and unequivocal ruling on VAT in writing; or it is established that an officer knowing the full facts has misled a trader to his detriment, the Commissioners of Customs and Excise would only raise an assessment based on the correct ruling from the date the error was brought to the attention of the registered person concerned.' (*Hansard Vol. 161, col. 426; C & E Notice No 48, Extra-Statutory Concession 3.5.*)

2.73 In December 1973 a company which manufactured and installed built-in wardrobes for new houses was informed by the Commissioners that its supply of such wardrobes was zero-rated under the legislation then in force. In May 1975 the Commissioners informed the company that they had changed their view, and now considered that such supplies were standard-rated. The company accepted this ruling but appealed against an assessment charging tax on supplies made before May 1975. The tribunal dismissed the company's appeal, holding that there was no question of estoppel against the Commissioners. *Cupboard Love Ltd, LON/76/40 (VTD 267)*.

2.74 A similar decision was reached in *HV Ribbans, LON/76/200 (VTD 346)*.

2.75   In a similar case, the tribunal held that 'on the existing state of the authorities we are bound to hold that no estoppel can arise against the mandatory provisions of a taxing statute'. *POH Medlam, LON/77/304 (VTD 545).*

2.76   In the case noted at 54.1 RETAILERS' SPECIAL SCHEMES, the tribunal held that an inspection of a trader's records, and a general assurance that they were in order, was insufficient to form the basis of an estoppel. *GUS Merchandise Corporation Ltd, [1978] VATTR 28 (VTD 553).*

2.77   In the case noted at 61.18 TRANSFERS OF GOING CONCERNS, Lord Grantchester held that 'there can be no estoppel against the Crown in the person of the Commissioners of Customs & Excise which prevents them from recovering tax which is lawfully due under the provisions of an Act of Parliament and Regulations made thereunder'. *Farm Facilities (Fork Lift) Ltd, [1987] VATTR 80 (VTD 2366).*

2.78   A builder had carried out work on a protected building which did not qualify as an 'approved alteration' and was therefore not eligible for zero-rating. However he did not charge VAT on the work and appealed against a subsequent assessment, contending that he had been told by a VAT officer that tax would not be chargeable. The tribunal dismissed his appeal. Applying *dicta* of Finlay J in *Williams v Grundy's Trustees KB 1933, 18 TC 271 (TTC 2001, 5.28),* 'nothing is better settled than the principle that there is no estoppel as against the Crown'. *PT Wood, MAN/91/513 (VTD 6992).*

2.79   There are a large number of other cases in which tribunals have held, applying one or more of the preceding decisions, that the Commissioners cannot be estopped from collecting VAT. Such cases appear to raise no point of general importance, and in the interests of space, are not reported individually in this book. For a list of such cases decided up to and including 31 December 1993, see Tolley's VAT Cases 1994. For a case in which costs were awarded to the appellant, see *Ness,* 2.343 below.

2.80   A company which carried on a property development business reclaimed input tax relating to exempt supplies. The Commissioners rejected the claim and the company appealed, contending that it had been misled by a VAT officer on a control visit and that the circumstances fell within what is now Extra-Statutory Concession 3.5 (see 2.72 above). The tribunal had reservations as to whether it had jurisdiction to hear the appeal, but did so in an 'arbitral capacity', and found that the company had been misled to such an extent that the statement of practice was operative. *C & G Developments Ltd, LON/86/682 (VTD 2384).*

2.81   The Commissioners made an application for an appeal to be struck out on the grounds that it pertained to what is now Extra-Statutory Concession 3.5 (see 2.72 above) and that estoppel was not one of the grounds of appeal under what is now *VATA 1994, s 83.* The tribunal dismissed the application, holding that the grounds of the appeal made it clear that the appeal was brought under what is now *VATA 1994, s 84(10)* and that, in the alternative, the appeal was against a decision of the Commissioners relating to the assessment, such appeal being under *s 83(p).* While an appeal was unlikely to succeed under either *subsection,* that was insufficient to justify a conclusion that no appeal lay to the tribunal. *Animal Virus Research Institute, [1988] VATTR 56 (VTD 2692).*

2.82   **Agreement to accept correction to return—whether Commissioners estopped from treating original return as valid.**   See *AB Gee of Ripley Ltd,* 49.28 PENALTIES: MISDECLARATION.

2.83   **Scottish appeals—whether Commissioners personally barred.**   In a Scottish case, a partnership contended that it had been misled by VAT officers and that the Commissioners were personally barred (the Scottish equivalent of estoppel) from demanding the assessed tax. The tribunal accepted that the partners had been wrongly advised, but dismissed the appeal, holding that in Scotland the plea of personal bar does not operate against the Crown in taxation matters, applying *Lord Advocate v Meiklam 1860, 22 D 1427* and other authorities. *Milne & Mackintosh (t/a Jack and Jill)*, *[1981] VATTR 61 (VTD 1063)*.

2.84 *Milne & Mackintosh*, 2.83 above, was applied in the similar subsequent cases of *Lincars Radio Taxis, EDN/81/17 (VTD 1118); J & E McClymont, EDN/82/15 (VTD 1253); G Brown, EDN/92/76 (VTD 7718)* and *St. Andrew's Motor Homes Ltd*, 19.17 DRUGS, MEDICINES, AIDS FOR THE HANDICAPPED, ETC.

2.85 **Issue estoppel per rem judicatum—direction under Rule 19(3) of Tribunals Rules.** A trader (F) had been convicted at a Crown Court under *Criminal Law Act 1977, s 1(1)*, for conspiracy to cheat the public revenue by failing to account for VAT on takings from gaming machines. The Commissioners issued assessments on him, charging tax on the takings from the machines. He appealed, contending that, notwithstanding the conviction in the Crown Court, he had not been the operator of the machines in question. The Commissioners applied for a direction under *rule 19(3)* of the *VAT Tribunals Rules* that the appellant should not be permitted to reopen issues which had been determined against him in the Crown Court. The tribunal granted the application sought by the Commissioners. The tribunal held that it had inherent jurisdiction to prevent abuse of process. The present case fell within the doctrine of 'issue estoppel per rem judicatum'. Applying *dicta* of Lord Halsbury LC in *Reichel Magrath, HL 1889, 14 AC 665*, 'it would be a scandal to the administration of justice if, the same question having been disposed of by one case, the litigant were to be permitted by changing the form of the proceedings to set up the same case again'. The tribunal chairman (Mr. Potter) held that the issue had been 'effectively covered by the criminal proceedings'. Furthermore, the fact that 'neither the learned judge nor either counsel appears to have considered those parts of the law relating to VAT' and that the judge had appeared 'sometimes to take it for granted that VAT should have been charged' was not sufficient to alter this conclusion, since 'it was open to the defence, if it saw fit, to raise all relevant matters of law; and the defence did not do so'. The criminal proceedings had found as a fact that the appellant had made the supplies in question, and the tribunal had no discretion to reach a different conclusion. *MJ Feehan, [1993] VATTR 266 (VTD 10154)*. (*Note*. For the substantive appeal, see 23.15 EXEMPTIONS: MISCELLANEOUS.)

2.86 **'Res judicata'.** In the case noted at 34.517 INPUT TAX, the Commissioners were investigating an alleged fraud concerning a company which exported beer and wine to France. The QB dismissed an application by the company for judicial review, and the Commissioners were subsequently granted summary judgment against the company in respect of unpaid excise duty of more than £8,300,000. The QB dismissed the company's appeal against the judgment, holding that the existence of the debt was *res judicata*. Applying *dicta* of Wigram VC in *Henderson v Henderson, 1843, 3 Hare 100*, 'where a given matter becomes the subject of litigation in, and of adjudication by, a court of competent jurisdiction, the court requires the parties to that litigation to bring forward their whole case, and will not (except under special circumstances) permit the same parties to open the same subject of litigation in respect of matter which might have been brought forward as part of the subject in contest, but which was not brought forward, only because they have by negligence, inadvertence, or even accident, omitted part of their case. The plea of *res judicata* applies, except in special cases, not only to points upon which the court was actually required by the parties to form an opinion and pronounce a judgment, but to every point which properly belonged to the subject of litigation, and which the parties, exercising reasonable diligence, might have brought forward at the time.' Lightman J observed that 'it would be grossly unjust that (the company) should be entitled to have an entirely fresh run after the lengthy and expensive judicial review proceedings, and the delay thereby occasioned, to any recovery of the £9,000,000 (*sic*) by the CCE. The CCE has, as it seems to me, already been kept out of its money far too long.' *C & E Commrs v Lacara Ltd, QB 11 October 1999 unreported.*

2.87   See also *Taylor*, 2.39 above.

2.88   **Assessment found to be defective—whether Commissioners estopped from issuing replacement assessment by 'res judicata' principle.**   Following the decision in the case noted at 3.17 ASSESSMENT, the Commissioners issued a replacement assessment. The trader applied for the assessment to be struck out, contending that the principle of '*res judicata*' estopped the Commissioners from issuing a replacement assessment. The tribunal rejected this contention and dismissed the trader's application. The tribunal observed that another issue in the case had been considered by the High Court (for which see 53.38 REGISTRATION) and had been remitted to a new tribunal for reconsideration. The tribunal reviewed the evidence and held that 'the interests of justice require that this appeal should be determined on its merits bearing in mind the views of the High Court ... although the newly constituted tribunal cannot now consider the original assessment and the supplementary assessment (as they have been withdrawn) the interests of justice would best be served by referring all the outstanding issues (including the new assessment) to a newly constituted tribunal for a decision on the merits'. *A Bennett (No 2), LON/98/416 (VTD 16590).*

THE REQUIREMENTS OF VATA 1994, s 84(2)

2.89   **Whether requirements of VATA 1994, s 84(2) may be waived.**   In a case where an appellant company had not made a return it was required to make, and hence had not complied with what is now *VATA 1994, s 84(2)*, the tribunal noted that the Commissioners had no objection to the hearing of the appeal and proceeded with the hearing, holding that the Commissioners could waive the requirements of the subsection. *Stilwell Darby & Co Ltd, [1973] VATTR 145 (VTD 35).*

2.90   *Stilwell Darby & Co Ltd*, 2.89 above, was applied in the similar subsequent case of *EG Gittins (t/a Robinsons Ironmongery), [1974] VATTR 109 (VTD 87).*

2.91   **Appeal against assessment covering more than one prescribed period— requirements of VATA 1994, s 84(2)*.**   A company appealed against an assessment covering nine prescribed periods, for five of which returns had not been made. The tribunal struck out the appeals against the five periods for which returns had not been made, holding that it had no jurisdiction to hear them. (The appeals against the remaining four were dismissed.) *Shaft Sports Ltd, [1983] VATTR 180 (VTD 1451).*

2.92   **Whether tax payable where returns made subject to a reservation.**   A company had submitted returns showing net tax payable of £43,073, qualified by a statement that they were 'subject to reserved claims for input tax on expenses'. The Commissioners rejected the claims and the company appealed. The Commissioners applied for the appeals to be struck out as the company had not paid the £43,073. The tribunal accepted this contention and struck out the appeals, holding that a return must be an unqualified one, any underpayments or overpayments being rectified in later returns. *DK Wright & Associates Ltd, [1975] VATTR 168 (VTD 203).*

2.93   **VATA 1994, s 84(2)—interaction with s 84(3)(b).**   A driving school proprietor initially accounted for VAT on the full amount of the school's receipts, but later formed the view that the instructors working for him were self-employed and that he need not account for VAT on the amounts which they retained. From April 1977 to

June 1978 he showed the tax due on the amounts in question on his returns, but withheld payment. The Commissioners issued an assessment to recover the tax, and he appealed. The tribunal refused to entertain the appeal, as what is now *VATA 1994, s 84(2)* had not been complied with. He applied for judicial review and an order of *certiorari* to quash the decision, contending that *VATA 1994, s 84(3)(b)* applied, and that payment of the tax would cause him hardship. Stephen Brown J accepted this contention and granted his application. *R v VAT Tribunal (ex p. Happer), QB [1982] STC 700; [1982] 1 WLR 1261.* (*Notes.* (1) *Dicta* of Stephen Brown J were subsequently disapproved by Webster J in *Minster Associates*, 2.94 below, and Rose J in *Theodorou*, 2.95 below. (2) For whether supplies of driving tuition should be regarded as made by the school proprietor or by the instructors, see the cases at 58.180 to 58.187 SUPPLY.)

2.94   The Commissioners issued an assessment on a partnership. The tribunal refused to hear the partnership's appeal, since it had not paid sums shown as due on its returns, so that what is now *VATA 1994, s 84(2)* had not been satisfied. The partnership applied for judicial review but the QB dismissed the application, holding that the tribunal had no power to hear an appeal. Webster J disapproved *dicta* of Stephen Brown J in *ex p. Happer*, 2.93 above. *R v VAT Tribunal (ex p. Minster Associates), QB [1988] STC 386.*

2.95   An individual (T) failed to pay output tax due on unpaid fees. The Commissioners issued an assessment to recover the tax and T appealed, claiming bad debt relief. The tribunal refused to hear the appeal, as T had not paid the amounts shown on his returns. T applied for judicial review but the QB rejected the application. *Dicta* of Stephen Brown J in *Happer*, 2.93 above, and *obiter dicta* of Webster J in *Minster Associates*, 2.94 above, were disapproved. Rose J held that there was no ambiguity between *s 84(2)* and *(3)*, which imposed different requirements, and that *s 84(2)* applied not only to undisputed tax shown in returns but also to disputed tax shown in returns. *R v London VAT Tribunal and C & E Commrs (ex p. Theodorou), QB 1988, [1989] STC 292.*

2.96   A trader submitted a return claiming a repayment of £75,000. The Commissioners ascertained that £77,000 of this related to an alleged payment to a company of which the trader was the controlling director, and that the relevant invoice did not comply with the statutory requirements. They therefore rejected the repayment claim, and issued an assessment charging output tax of £2,000. The trader appealed, and the Commissioners applied for the appeal to be struck out on the grounds that the trader had not paid output tax of £37,000 shown in subsequent returns. The tribunal ordered the trader to pay the amounts shown in his returns within six weeks. *RS Carter, LON/93/2827A (VTD 11838).*

2.97   A company director applied for judicial review of a decision that an appeal could not be entertained until the tax due had been paid or deposited. The QB dismissed the application and the CA upheld this decision. *R v C & E Commrs and London VAT Tribunal (ex p. Menzies), CA [1990] STC 263.*

2.98   **Tax unpaid in respect of previous business—whether VATA 1994, s 84(2) complied with.**   A married couple had carried on a hotel in partnership and were registered for VAT from 1973 until 1976, when they transferred the business to a company. The couple re-registered in 1980 and appealed against the disallowance of a claim to input tax. The tribunal struck out the appeal, finding that the couple still owed tax in respect of their previous business. *J & CL McAllister, [1981] VATTR 55 (VTD 1077).*

2.99   **Payments made in respect of assessments and surcharges—late appeals subsequently lodged—whether such tax may be reallocated against other**

assessments for purposes of VATA 1994, s 84(2). A trader made a late appeal against assessments covering the period from August 1982 to August 1987, against default surcharges for periods between December 1987 and December 1990, and against the rejection of a repayment claim of tax declared to be due for the period from 1987 to 1992. The total amount declared on his returns for the ten years in question was £106,000; his total liabilities to the Commissioners for those years (including tax assessed which had not been declared on his returns, and the default surcharges) was £182,000. He had paid a total of £109,346, some of which had been paid in respect of the assessments and surcharges. The Commissioners applied for his appeal to be dismissed, since he had not paid the tax shown as due under his most recent returns as required by what is now *VATA 1994, s 84(2)*. He objected to the application, contending that, since he had lodged late appeals against assessments and surcharges after paying part of the amounts in question, the tax paid in respect of these assessments and surcharges should be reallocated and set against the unpaid returns. The tribunal rejected this contention, granted the Commissioners' application, and struck out the appeal, holding that the condition that the tax shown as due on an appellant's returns must have been paid before an appeal could be heard was absolute and could not be interpreted as a condition that the appellant must have paid amounts equal to the amounts shown on the returns, after taking into account sums paid in respect of assessments and surcharges which were under appeal. *RJ Walker (t/a Smart Cars), LON/92/2389 (VTD 9973)*.

2.100   **Other cases.** There are a large number of other cases, which appear to raise no point of general interest, in which appeals have been dismissed because the requirements of what is now *VATA 1994, s 84(2)* have not been complied with. In the interests of space, such cases are not reported in this book. For a list of such cases decided up to and including 30 September 1989, see Tolley's VAT Cases 1990.

2.101   **Returns submitted between lodging of appeals and date of hearing.** In a case where an appellant had not submitted returns at the time of lodging appeals but submitted nil returns before the hearing, the Commissioners applied for the appeals to be struck out but the tribunal rejected this contention and allowed the appeals on the evidence. *DI Cadman, [1994] VATTR 128 (VTD 12288)*.

2.102   **Default surcharges—whether s 84(2) applicable.** In November 1996 a group of companies appealed against default surcharges. In May 1997 the Commissioners made an application under *VAT Tribunals Rules (SI 1986 No 590), rule 6* that the appeal could not be entertained as the group had not paid its VAT liability for the period ending 31 January 1997. The tribunal dismissed the application. On the evidence, at the date on which the Notice of Appeal was received, all the tax shown in the group's returns had been paid. The fact that the company had not paid default surcharges, or submitted a hardship application in respect of the surcharges, was not conclusive. Applying *dicta* in *Hubbard Foundation Scotland*, 2.107 below, the tribunal had begun to entertain the appeal on 9 December 1996, when it despatched the initial hearing notice. Applying *dicta* of Rose J in *R v London VAT Tribunal (ex p. Theodorou)*, 2.95 above, it was 'not appropriate to construe widely words which restrict rights of appeal or to hold that such words are absolute where there is an alternative construction'. The chairman held that 'the provisions of *s 84(2) and (3)* should be construed not as a jurisdictional bar but as giving the Commissioners power to apply under *rule 6* or not as they think appropriate, a power which can be waived'. Accordingly, 'the Commissioners must be taken to have waived a default by an appellant if they fail to make a *rule 6* application before the commencement of a substantive appeal hearing'. *Widnell Group, [1997] VATDR 145 (VTD 15170)*.

2.103   A trader appealed against nine default surcharges. The Commissioners lodged an application under *VATA 1994, s 84(2)* for the appeals to be struck out, on the grounds that the trader had not made returns for the relevant periods. The tribunal rejected the application, holding that the conditions of *VATA 1994, s 84(2)* were contrary to the EC principle of proportionality. The tribunal observed that *s 84(2)* was 'not concerned with the tax in dispute' and held that 'it is not easy to explain what part it plays in the compliance system without conceding that its real purpose is to impose the ultimate penalty of denial of access to tribunal justice on the non-compliant taxpayer'. The requirements of *s 84(2)* were 'susceptible of undermining the fundamental principle of correct taxation and correct application of the compliance rules'. *Dicta* of the CJEC in *Garage Molenheide BVBA & Others v Belgian State*, 21.209 EUROPEAN COMMUNITY LAW, applied. *PW Coleman, [1999] VATDR 133 (VTD 15906, 16178)*. (*Notes*. (1) For the Commissioners' practice following this decision, see Business Brief 23/99, issued on 17 November 1999. (2) The trader also appealed against ten assessments, in respect of which the appeals were struck out— see 2.9 above.)

2.104   **Appeal against notice requiring security—whether VATA 1994, s 84(2) compatible with Community law.** A company appealed against a notice requiring security. The Commissioners lodged an application under *VATA 1994, s 84(2)* for the appeal to be struck out on the grounds that the company had failed to render a return. The tribunal adjourned the hearing of the application. The chairman (Mr. Oliver) observed that it was arguable that the conditions imposed by *s 84(2)* were 'beyond the scope of the obligations that might be deemed necessary under *Article 22(8)*' (of the *EC Sixth Directive*). Firstly, in contrast to *s 84(3)*, there was no provision in *s 84(2)* for payment of outstanding tax to be waived on grounds of hardship. Secondly, it was arguable that 'the requirement in *s 84(2)* imposes an impediment to the potential appellant's right to a fair hearing'. *Formix (London) Ltd, LON/97/882 (VTD 15241)*. (*Note*. There was no further hearing of the appeal, as the company subsequently went into liquidation and the liquidator declined to continue with the appeal. See, however, *Coleman*, 2.103 above, and *Miah*, 2.105 below.)

2.105   **Appeal against penalties—whether VATA 1994, s 84(2) compatible with Community law.** A partnership appealed against ten penalties under *VATA 1994, s 60*. The Commissioners lodged an application under *VATA 1994, s 84(2)* for the appeal to be struck out on the grounds that the partnership had not made returns for the relevant periods. The tribunal rejected the application, observing that to grant the application would mean that the partners 'have no way of rebutting the allegations of dishonesty unless they put in returns for those periods and pay the tax. If they do put in the returns that are consistent with their defence they expose themselves, at the least, to misdeclaration penalties.' *M & R Miah (t/a Tandoori Nights), [1999] VATDR 133 (VTD 15925, 16178)*. (*Notes*. (1) For the Commissioners' practice following this decision, see Business Brief 23/99, issued on 17 November 1999. (2) The substantive appeal was heard with *Coleman*, 2.9 above.)

2.106   **Compulsory registration—appeal under VATA, s 83(a)—whether s 84(2) applicable.** A VAT officer formed the opinion that a partnership, which had not registered for VAT, was required to register on the grounds that its turnover had exceeded the registration threshold. The partnership subsequently submitted a return showing VAT of £17,793 as payable. The Commissioners issued an assessment charging VAT of £33,245. The partnership appealed. The Commissioners lodged an application under *VATA 1994, s 84(2)* for the appeal to be struck out on the grounds that the partnership had not made returns for the relevant periods. The tribunal rejected this contention and dismissed the Commissioners' application, holding that it was not 'precluded from entertaining an appeal against the decision of the Commissioners to register a person where that person had not made all the returns and paid the amounts shown in those returns as payable for the period(s) covering his registration'. Where an appellant was 'contending, in substance, that as a matter of law he was not required to be registered', he was 'not required to submit returns and to pay the tax' as a precondition to his appeal being heard. *M & D Khan, [1999] VATDR 133 (VTD 15907, 16178)*. (*Notes.* (1) For the Commissioners' practice following this decision, see Business Brief 23/99, issued on 17 November 1999. (2) The substantive appeal was heard with *Coleman*, 2.9 above.)

THE REQUIREMENTS OF VATA 1994, s 84(3)

Payment of assessed tax (VATA 1994, s 84(3)(a))

2.107 **Date from which appeal 'entertained'.** A Foundation was established with the main object of furthering the instruction and study of Scientology. It appealed against ten assessments without paying the tax charged. The Commissioners applied to the tribunal for the appeals to be dismissed under what is now *VATA 1994, s 84(3)(a)*. The tribunal initially rejected the application, considering that an appeal was not entertained until it was heard on the merits, but the CS overruled this decision and remitted the case to the tribunal with a direction to it to order the Foundation to pay the tax within 14 days. The CS held that there was a distinction between an appeal being 'entertained' and an appeal being 'heard'. An appeal begins to be entertained when the tribunal sets in motion the requisite procedure for its determination. *C & E Commrs v Hubbard Foundation Scotland, CS [1981] STC 593*. (*Note.* For subsequent proceedings in this case, see 2.217 below.)

2.108 **Assessment to recover input tax—application of VATA 1994, s 84(3).** A company appealed against an assessment to recover input tax which it had deducted in its returns. The Commissioners applied for a direction that the appeal should be struck out, since the company had not paid the tax charged by the assessment. The company applied for an extension of the time in which to apply for a direction excusing it from paying or depositing the tax on account of hardship. The tribunal allowed the company's application. *Boltgate Ltd, [1982] VATTR 120 (VTD 1246)*. (*Note.* The decision in this case was distinguished in *Safegold Fashions Ltd*, 2.111 below.)

2.109 *Boltgate Ltd*, 2.108 above, was applied in a subsequent case where the tax assessed had not been paid. The tribunal held that it could entertain the appeal since the question at issue was an amount of input tax. *Brian Gubby Ltd, [1985] VATTR 59 (VTD 1961)*. (*Notes.* (1) The decision in this case was distinguished in *Safegold Fashions Ltd*, 2.111 below. (2) For the substantive appeal, see 7.60 BUSINESS.)

2.110 A company which was partly exempt appealed against an assessment issued by the Commissioners to recover input tax which it had claimed. The Commissioners applied for a direction that the appeal should be struck out as the company had not paid the tax assessed. The tribunal allowed the company's application, observing that the appeal concerned a dispute over input tax within what is now *VATA 1994, s 83(c)* or *(e)*. Applying *dicta* of Lord Grantchester in *Boltgate Ltd*, 2.108 above, Parliament had intended disputes as to registration and input tax to be entertained by tribunals without payment or deposit of the disputed tax. *Trust Securities Holdings Ltd, [1990] VATTR 1 (VTD 4550)*. (*Note.* The decision in this case was disapproved by a subsequent tribunal in *Safegold Fashions Ltd*, 2.111 below.)

2.111 The Commissioners formed the opinion that a company had reclaimed input tax on the basis of false invoices. They therefore issued an assessment to recover the tax in question. The company appealed against the assessment but did not pay the tax assessed. The Commissioners applied for a direction that the appeal should be dismissed since the company had not complied with what is now *VATA 1994*, *s 84(3)*. The tribunal accepted the Commissioners' application and dismissed the appeal. Because the appeal was against an assessment, it was made under what is now *VATA 1994, s 83(p)* as well as under *s 83(c)*, and thus could not be entertained unless the tax was deposited. *Boltgate Ltd*, 2.108 above, was distinguished since it had been decided before the enactment of what is now *VATA 1994, s 73(2)*; *Brian Gubby Ltd*, 2.109 above, was distinguished since it had been decided before the amendment of that provision by *FA 1988*. *Trust Securities Holdings Ltd*, 2.110 above, was disapproved. Applying *R v C & E Commrs (ex p. Strangewood Ltd)*, 34.515 INPUT TAX, the Commissioners were not required to allow credit for all input tax claimed in a return. Where more input tax was credited or repaid than was allowable, the excess was properly assessable under *s 73(2)*. *Safegold Fashions Ltd, [1992] VATTR 105 (VTD 7343)*.

2.112   The Commissioners formed the opinion that a company had reclaimed input tax which was attributable to an exempt supply, and issued an assessment to recover the tax. The company appealed against the assessment but did not pay the tax assessed. The Commissioners applied for a direction that the appeal should be struck out as the company had not complied with what is now *VATA 1994, s 84(3)*. The tribunal accepted the application and struck out the appeal. The assessment had been properly made under what is now *VATA 1994, s 73*, and *VATA 1994, s 83(p)* therefore provided that the appeal could not be heard unless the tax was deposited. *Safegold Fashions Ltd*, 2.111 above, applied. *Boltgate Ltd*, 2.108 above, was distinguished since it had been decided before the enactment of *VATA 1994, s 73(2)*; *Brian Gubby Ltd*, 2.109 above, was distinguished because it had been decided before the amendment of that provision by *FA 1988*. *Richard Haynes Associates, LON/92/2597 (VTD 10068)*.

Applications under Tribunals Rules, rule 11 (VATA 1994, s 84(3)(b))

2.113   Assessments charging tax of over £27,000 were made on a car dealer, following his conviction for having submitted fraudulent returns. He applied under *Tribunals Rules, rule 11* for the appeal to be entertained without payment or deposit of the tax. After one adjournment the application was set down for hearing in September 1975. The dealer was represented at the hearing by counsel but did not attend. He was believed to be in Spain and the reason for his non-attendance was not known. The tribunal refused a further adjournment and dismissed the *rule 11* application. The QB upheld the tribunal decision. *PA Baird (t/a Baird Motors) v C & E Commrs, QB April 1976 unreported.*

2.114   A trader had appealed against two assessments and applied under *Tribunals Rules, rule 11* for the appeals to be entertained notwithstanding that he had not paid or deposited the tax. The notices of appeal had indicated that the trader's accountant would deal with the appeal, but neither the trader nor the accountant attended at the time fixed for the hearing of the application. The trader then applied under *rule 26(2)* for the decision to be set aside, appearing in person and contending that, because of his accountant's negligence, he had not been notified of the time fixed for hearing the *rule 11* application. The tribunal set aside its initial decision on the *rule 11* application, which it then proceeded to hear in private. *B Hallam (t/a APX Car Sales), [1977] VATTR 105 (VTD 394)*. (*Note.* The appeals were subsequently dismissed.)

2.115   A company appealed against an assessment and at the same time applied under *Tribunals Rules, rule 11* for the appeal to be entertained notwithstanding that the tax had not been paid or deposited. The company was not represented at the hearing of the application but six days previously its accountants had written to the tribunal, sending a copy of a letter from the company's bank manager refusing it an overdraft. The tribunal dismissed the application, considering that the evidence before it did not establish that payment of the tax would result in hardship. The company then applied under *rule 26(2)* for the decision to be set aside. Its accountant attended the hearing and stated that he had assumed that the letter which he had submitted would be sufficient to support the *rule 11* application, being more familiar with the informal procedures of General Commissioners with regard to income tax, etc. The tribunal decided in the circumstances to set aside its decision on the *rule 11* application which it then proceeded to rehear in private. *Cumbershourne Ltd (t/a Hockley Enterprises), [1977] VATTR 110 (VTD 369).*

2.116   A company applied for an appeal to be entertained by the tribunal without the tax in dispute being paid or deposited. The company had been prosecuted under what is now *VATA 1994, s 72*, and the proceedings had been compounded by the payment of a penalty. The company had recently purchased a freehold restaurant for more than £900,000. It had a bank overdraft of slightly under £80,000. The tax assessed was almost £115,000. The tribunal held that, in view of the company's existing overdraft, the payment of the tax would cause hardship, and therefore allowed the application. *Bentley Restaurant Ltd, LON/88/620 (VTD 4327).*

2.117   A partnership failed to pay any VAT, or make any VAT returns, for 25 successive prescribed accounting periods between 1 June 1981 and 31 August 1987. The Commissioners issued an estimated assessment covering the whole of the period, charging tax of more than £56,000. The partnership appealed and applied for the appeal to be heard without payment of the tax assessed, on the grounds that payment would cause it hardship. The tribunal was satisfied that payment of the full amount would cause hardship, but held that, as the assessment was a composite one covering several accounting periods, each period should be considered separately. On the evidence, the tribunal held that the partnership had not established that payment of the tax assessed for the last five accounting periods of the assessment (totalling slightly more than £10,000) would cause hardship, and ordered that the partnership should pay this amount. The partnership appealed to the QB, which held that the assessment had to be considered as a whole and that the appeal against the assessment should be heard without any tax being paid. The CA upheld this decision. *Don Pasquale v C & E Commrs, CA [1990] STC 556.* (*Note.* The decision in this case was unanimously disapproved by the CA in the subsequent case of *Le Rififi Ltd*, 3.70 ASSESSMENT. Millett LJ observed that 'the case has no *ratio decidendi* (and) Dillon LJ appears to have treated the question as one of first impression'. The effect of the decision in *Le Rififi Ltd* is that the notice of assessment would be deemed to comprise 25 separate assessments.)

2.118   The Commissioners issued an assessment charging tax of more than £56,000 on a married couple who operated a restaurant, and also instigated criminal proceedings against the couple for fraudulent evasion of tax. The couple appealed against the assessment and applied for the appeal to be heard without payment of the tax. The Commissioners opposed this application and in turn applied for a direction that the appeal and all proceedings other than the hardship application should be stood over pending the result of the criminal proceedings. The couple admitted fraudulent evasion of tax but disputed the quantum, admitting that they had underpaid £17,000, of which £10,000 had already been deposited with the Commissioners. The tribunal held that it would be unfair to the appellants to require them to proceed with their *rule 11* application under the threat of possible or actual criminal proceedings, and adjourned all the proceedings, including the *rule 11* application, until the completion of the criminal proceedings. *P & J Rosignoli, [1983] VATTR 266 (VTD 1502).*

2.119   There have been a number of cases, which appear to raise no point of general interest, in which hardship applications have been dismissed. In the interests of space, such cases have not been included in this book.

STATEMENTS OF CASE, ETC. (Tribunals Rules, rr 7–9)

2.120 **Application for extension of time to serve Statement of Case.** In the case noted at 58.332 SUPPLY, the tribunal had directed that the Commissioners should serve their Statement of Case by 30 November 1985. In fact the Commissioners failed to do so until 20 January 1986, when they also lodged a late application for an extension of time to serve the statement. The tribunal allowed the application, but directed that if the Commissioners were successful and the appeal was dismissed, the 50–day period from 30 November 1985 to 20 January 1986 should be excluded from the computation of any interest payable by the company. *Dormers Builders (London) Ltd, [1986] VATTR 69 (VTD 2044)*.

2.121 In the case noted at 53.37 REGISTRATION, the Commissioners imposed a penalty on a company on 22 July 1986. The company appealed and, after a local review, the Commissioners confirmed their decision on 17 October 1986. On 4 November 1986 the company lodged a notice of appeal to the tribunal. On 4 December the tribunal received an application from the Commissioners for an extension of time, until 4 February 1987, for them to serve their Statement of Case. The tribunal rejected the application, holding that there was no justification for such a delay, and ordering that the Commissioners should be confined to relying on the grounds set out in their decision dated 17 October 1986. *Optimum Personnel Evaluation (Operations) Ltd, LON/86/620 (VTD 2334)*.

2.122 On 8 October 1991 a restaurant proprietor lodged an appeal against a penalty under what is now *VATA 1994, s 60*. The hearing was arranged for 26 February 1992. The Commissioners failed to serve a Statement of Case until 20 February 1992, when they served a statement which was incomplete and without supporting documentation. At the start of the appeal hearing, the Commissioners applied for an extension of time in which to serve their completed Statement of Case and list of documents. The tribunal allowed the application, granting the Commissioners a further 21 days to serve the documents in question. *J Chan, EDN/91/206 (VTD 7289)*.

2.123 **Commissioners' failure to submit Statement of Case.** In a case where the Commissioners had rejected a claim for a refund of tax under what is now *VATA 1994, s 35*, the claimant lodged an appeal on 26 March 1992. The appeal was listed for hearing on 29 May 1992, but the Commissioners applied for an extension of time to serve their Statement of Case. The tribunal directed that the Commissioners should serve their Statement of Case by 26 June 1992. However, they did not do so until 8 July. At the hearing of the appeal, the claimant's accountant made a preliminary application that the appeal should be allowed under *rule 19(4)* of the *Tribunals Rules*, since the Commissioners had not complied with the tribunal's direction. The tribunal accepted this application and formally allowed the appeal, observing that 'if a tribunal does give a direction it expects it to be complied with and would require to be persuaded by compelling reasons and circumstances to excuse compliance'. The Commissioners had been allowed three months to serve their Statement of Case, but on the evidence it had not been completed until 26 June, and had then been sent to the London Tribunal Centre instead of to the Edinburgh Tribunal Centre. Furthermore, the statement was straightforward and added nothing to a letter which the Commissioners had sent to the claimant in March. Accordingly, there were 'no unusual circumstances and no reasonable excuses in this case'. The CS upheld the tribunal decision, holding that it could only overturn the tribunal decision if the tribunal had acted unreasonably. In the absence of any mitigating circumstances, the tribunal had been entitled to exercise its discretion under *rule 19(4)* of the *Tribunals Rules* and allow the appeal. *C & E Commrs v C Young, CS [1993] STC 394*.

2.124 The CS decision in *Young*, 2.123 above, was applied in a subsequent case in which the Edinburgh Tribunal allowed an appeal on the grounds that the Commissioners had failed to serve their Statement of Case within the time allowed. *Sonat Offshore (UK) Inc, EDN/95/189 (VTD 14021)*.

2.125   A similar decision, also applying *Young*, 2.124 above, was reached by the Manchester Tribunal in *G Costello, MAN/99/890 (VTD 16680)*.

2.126   A company appealed against an assessment and a misdeclaration penalty. On 10 June 1992 the Commissioners applied for an extension of time to serve their Statement of Case. The tribunal directed that the Commissioners should serve their Statement of Case by 8 August. The Commissioners did not comply with this direction, and were granted a further extension of time until 8 October. Again the Commissioners failed to comply, and on 9 October they applied for a further extension to 8 December. On 19 October the company lodged an application for the appeal to be allowed, since the Commissioners had not complied with the tribunal's direction to serve their Statement of Case. The tribunal heard the company's application on 17 November, by which time the Commissioners had (on 2 November) served their Statement of Case. The tribunal held that it had jurisdiction under *rule 19(4)* of the *Tribunals Rules* to allow the appeal on the grounds of the Commissioners' late service of their Statement of Case, applying *Young*, 2.123 above. However, the tribunal declined to exercise its jurisdiction in such a way, observing that 'the approach of the Scottish courts to delays and failure to comply with directions is not necessarily the same as in England and Wales'. The Commissioners were ordered to pay the costs of the application, and the tribunal observed that the Commissioners could have rendered themselves liable to a penalty under what is now *VATA 1994, Sch 12 para 10*, applying *Freight Transport Leasing Ltd*, 2.270 below. *Faccenda Chicken Ltd, [1992] VATTR 395 (VTD 9570)*.

2.127   A similar decision was reached in *Charles F Hunter Ltd, MAN/93/231 (VTD 11619)*.

2.128   In a similar case, an appeal was lodged in February 1993, and the Commissioners applied for an extension of time until 16 May to serve their Statement of Case. The tribunal allowed the application, which was not opposed by the appellant company. However, the Commissioners failed to submit their Statement of Case, and in August they applied for a further extension of time until 16 September. The tribunal again allowed the application, and the case was set down for hearing on 23 November. At the date of the hearing, the Commissioners had still not submitted their Statement of Case. The tribunal observed that there were 'no mitigating circumstances' for the long delays, and that it had 'become standard practice to apply for extensions of time for the Statement of Case and too often the Commissioners fail to observe extended time limits'. The tribunal awarded a penalty of £200 against the Commissioners under what is now *VATA 1994, Sch 12 para 10*, and directed that the Commissioners should serve their Statement of Case within twelve days. *Wine Warehouses Europe Ltd, [1993] VATTR 307 (VTD 11525)*.

2.129   See also *Vaz*, 2.271 below.

2.130   **Whether Commissioners may amend their Statement of Case.**   At the start of an appeal hearing the Commissioners applied to amend their Statement of Case. The amendment raised a new alternative ground for the assessment, and required the admission in evidence of two further documents. The appellant company objected, contending that it had been taken by surprise. The tribunal rejected the Commissioners' application, finding that the material facts and documents had been known to the Commissioners at the date on which the assessment was issued, and holding that the application was unfair to the appellant company. *Vorngrove Ltd, MAN/84/55 (VTD 1733)*.

2.131 Appeals

2.131   However, in the case noted at 58.219 SUPPLY, the Commissioners were allowed to amend a Statement of Case by introducing an alternative contention. The tribunal held that the appellant company was not prejudiced by this, since there was no rule prohibiting a party to an action from raising alternative contentions. Lord Grantchester observed that 'an assessment for a net amount of tax payable will normally involve a consideration both of output tax and input tax'. *The Football Association Ltd, LON/83/484 (VTD 1845).*

2.132   **Contents of Statement of Case.**   In the case noted at 14.7 COLLECTION AND ENFORCEMENT, where an appeal against a requirement to give security was successful, the tribunal chairman strongly criticised the Commissioners for 'inaccuracies' in their Statement of Case, observing that the Statement of Case 'must set out accurately and fully all the grounds on which the decision was taken'. *VSP Marketing Ltd, LON/94/794A (VTD 12636).*

2.133   In a case in which an appeal against a requirement for security was dismissed, the Commissioners' representative made allegations about the company which had not been included in the Commissioners' Statement of Case. The tribunal chairman observed that the drafting of the Case was 'hardly satisfactory' and that any relevant factors 'should be included in the Statement of Case, and not either left unsaid or left to be deduced by the inclusion of certain documents in their List of Documents'. *M & S Services Ltd, [1995] VATDR 512 (VTD 13610).*

2.134   **Application by appellant to strike out Commissioners' Statement of Case.**   See *Ridgeons Bulk Ltd*, 3.116 ASSESSMENT.

2.135   **Application for 'further and better particulars'—Tribunals Rules, rule 9.**   The Commissioners imposed a penalty on a partnership which operated a restaurant. The partnership appealed, stating in its Notice of Appeal that its grounds of appeal were 'basis of assessment unsafe'. The Commissioners submitted an application under *Tribunals Rules, rule 9* for the partnership to serve 'further and better particulars of the grounds of appeal', requesting 'the precise grounds of appeal and the basis on which the Commissioners' decision is disputed'. The tribunal dismissed the Commissioners' application, observing that 'given that the matters and facts relied on must be pleaded in the defence, it is difficult to see what is to be gained from asking for precise grounds at this stage. The main effect of the request is to delay the procedure and to involve paperwork which will be duplicated in the defence.' The chairman (Mr. Wallace) held that 'it is only in exceptional evasion cases that it will be appropriate to direct particulars in advance of the pleadings ... In most appeals against best judgment assessments, however, a request for particulars serves no purpose unless the appellant has been provided with a detailed knowledge of the Commissioners' case.' *Kashmir Tandoori, [1998] VATDR 104 (VTD 15363).* (*Note.* The *Rules of the Supreme Court 1965 (SI 1965 No 1776)* refer to 'particulars' and 'pleadings'. With effect from 26 April 1999, these rules have largely been replaced by the *Civil Procedure Rules 1998 (SI 1998 No 3132)*, which refer instead to 'information' and to a 'statement of case'.)

2.136   See also *Albany Building Services Ltd*, 2.46 above.

APPLICATIONS FOR THE ADMISSION OF LATE APPEALS, ETC.

2.137   **Application for late appeal granted by Court of Appeal.**   In the case noted at 63.47 VALUATION, the tribunal referred the case to the CJEC for a ruling. The appellant company applied for judicial review of the terms of reference, but this application was rejected by the QB and the CA (see 2.229 below). Following the QB decision dismissing this application, the company applied for an extension of time to appeal against the tribunal decision under *Tribunals and Inquiries Act 1992, s 11*. The CA granted the application. Sir Thomas Bingham MR observed that 'it seems to me quite clear that (the company) intended to do all it could to challenge the tribunal's decision on this point. It has not been in any sense playing the system or behaving in a mischievous manner. It has merely adopted an understandable (though in my view incorrect) means of seeking to mount the challenge.' Schiemann LJ observed that 'it is, as has been recognised by the Law Commission in its paper on judicial review, one of the defects of our law at the moment that there can be situations in which there is some doubt as to which procedural route should be adopted'. *Conoco Ltd v C & E Commrs, CA 19 July 1995 unreported. (Note.* For subsequent developments in this case, see 2.210 below.)

2.138   **Application for late appeal granted by High Court.**   The Commissioners applied to the High Court for an extension of time to appeal against the decision noted at 30.5 GROUPS OF COMPANIES. Lightman J granted the application, holding that, under the *Civil Procedure Rules 1998 (SI 1998 No 3132)*, it was no longer sufficient to apply a rigid formula in deciding whether an extension was to be granted, and that each application had to be viewed by reference to the criterion of justice. In the case in question, an extension of time should be granted since the delay had been short, there had been no prejudice to the company, the subject matter of the appeal was important, and there were strong arguments in support of the Commissioners' case. *C & E Commrs v Eastwood Care Homes (Ilkeston) Ltd and Others, QB 18 January 2000, Times 7.3.2000.*

2.139   **Application for late appeal—general principles.**   An appeal was submitted two months out of time, and the appellant applied under *Tribunals Rules, rule 19* for an extension of time. The tribunal allowed the application provided that the applicant paid the Commissioners £25 on account of their costs within ten days. The chairman observed that admitting the application would not prejudice the Commissioners and that it would be a breach of natural justice not to let the applicant pursue his appeal. *WJ Price, [1978] VATTR 115 (VTD 559). (Note.* The decision in this case was not followed by a subsequent tribunal in *Wan & Wan*, 2.144 below, on the grounds that the tribunal's reasoning was inconsistent with the subsequent CA decisions in *Norwich & Peterborough Building Society v Steed, CA [1991] 1 WLR 449; [1991] 2 All ER 880; Costello v Somerset County Council, CA [1993] 1 WLR 256* and *Ward-Lee v Lineham, CA [1993] 1 WLR 754; [1993] 2 All ER 1006.*)

2.140   A trader applied for an extension of the period in which to appeal, contending that he had been under the impression that his accountants were dealing with the matter. The tribunal allowed the application on condition that the trader paid £40 towards the Commissioners' costs. *WR Hallam, MAN/78/187 (VTD 683).*

2.141   The Commissioners had begun proceedings to recover unpaid tax from a partnership. They sought to recover some of the tax from an individual (T) who had been registered as one of the partners. T disputed liability, and in 1976 the Commissioners issued a ruling that T had been a partner in the business. In 1978 T applied for leave to lodge a late appeal against this decision. The tribunal granted the application, holding that it would not prejudice the Commissioners. *D Trippett, [1978] VATTR 260 (VTD 686). (Note.* See now, however, the subsequent decision in *Wan & Wan*, 2.144 below.)

2.142   An application for a late appeal by an appellant who appeared in person was dismissed in a case where the tribunal applied *dicta* of Lord Guest in *Ratnam v Cumarasany, PC 1964, [1965] 1 WLR 8; [1964] 3 All ER 933. N Cave, LON/95/582P (VTD 13346).*

2.143   A similar decision was reached in a case in which a company applied in February 1996 for leave to appeal against assessments which had been issued in January 1993. The tribunal held that the company had failed to give a satisfactory explanation for its failure to act within the time limit. *Costello v Somerset County Council, CA [1993] 1 WLR 256* and *Ward-Lee v Lineham, CA [1993] 1 WLR 754; [1993] 2 All ER 1006*, applied. *J Walter Thompson UK Holdings Ltd, [1996] VATDR 145 (VTD 14058).*

2.144   The decision in *J Walter Thompson UK Holdings Ltd*, 2.143 above, was applied in a subsequent case in which a partnership applied in January 1997 for leave to appeal against assessments which had been issued in May 1993. The tribunal declined to follow the decision in *Price*, 2.139 above, on the grounds that the tribunal's reasoning in that case was inconsistent with the subsequent CA decisions in *Norwich & Peterborough Building Society v Steed, CA [1991] 1 WLR 449; [1991] 2 All ER 880; Costello v Somerset County Council, CA [1993] 1 WLR 256* and *Ward-Lee v Lineham, CA [1993] 1 WLR 754; [1993] 2 All ER 1006*. The tribunal observed that the decision in *Price* 'concentrated on one issue, namely where the balance of prejudice lay, whereas the more recent decisions emphasise the importance of carrying out a discretionary balancing exercise where the balance of prejudice is only one factor to be taken into account'. *WY & YS Wan (t/a Wan's Chinese Takeaway), LON/97/160 (VTD 14829).*

2.145   A similar decision, also applying *Costello v Somerset County Council, CA [1993] 1 WLR 256*, was reached in *S Haque, [1999] VATDR 219 (VTD 16047).*

2.146   In 1992 the Commissioners issued an assessment, charging tax of more than £1,300,000, on a university. In March 1997 the university applied for leave to appeal against the assessment. The tribunal dismissed the application, applying *J Walter Thompson UK Holdings Ltd*, 2.143 above, and *Norwich & Peterborough Building Society v Steed, CA [1991] 1 WLR 449; [1991] 2 All ER 880. University of Reading, LON/x (VTD 15387).* (*Note.* Costs were awarded to the Commissioners—see 2.243 below.)

2.147   **Late appeal following tribunal decision in similar case.** A trader had reclaimed input tax relating to the training of a racehorse. In July 1977 the Commissioners issued an assessment to recover the tax, on the basis that the expenditure had not been incurred for the purposes of the trader's business. The trader paid the tax charged by the assessment. In March 1978, following the tribunal decision in *British Car Auctions Ltd*, 34.274 INPUT TAX, the trader applied to the tribunal for an extension of time in which to appeal against the assessment. The tribunal rejected the application, holding that its admission would enable the applicant to endeavour to recover tax paid voluntarily under a mistaken view of the law, although there was no general right of recovery of money so paid. *R Kyffin, [1978] VATTR 175 (VTD 617).* (*Note.* The principle that money paid under a mistaken view of the law is not recoverable was laid down by Lord Ellenborough CJ in the case of *Bilbie v Lumley, KB 1802, [1775–1802] All ER 425*, which held that 'money paid with full knowledge of all the facts cannot be recovered back by reason of its having been paid in ignorance of the law'. This principle has recently been disapproved and overruled by the HL in *Kleinwort Benson Ltd v Lincoln City Council, HL [1998] 3 WLR 1095; [1998] 4 All ER 513.*)

2.148   **Partnership appeal delayed by illness of one partner.** A husband and wife carried on a hotel in partnership. They failed to appeal against an estimated assessment until, five months after it was issued, the Commissioners threatened distraint proceedings. They then paid the tax and applied for an extension of the time in which to make an appeal. The tribunal granted the application, holding that the Commissioners would not be prejudiced as the tax had already been paid. *WW & JH Hornby, MAN/74/28A (VTD 155).*

2.149   **Late appeals during collection, etc. proceedings.**   A trader failed to make returns and the Commissioners issued assessments charging tax of £2,106 under what is now *VATA 1994, s 73(1)*. She did not appeal and the Commissioners applied for summary judgment. She sought leave to defend, contending that the tax was not due. The QB held that it was not open to the trader to raise this defence in the High Court and that the Commissioners were entitled to summary judgment. *C & E Commrs v J Holvey*, QB 1977, *[1978] STC 187; [1978] QB 310; [1978] 1 All ER 1249*. (*Note.* Under the law now in force, the trader is only entitled to appeal if a return has been made—see *VATA 1994, s 83(p)(i)* which originates from *FA 1980*.)

2.150   A similar decision was reached in a case where an accountant had failed to pay a VAT assessment, and the Revenue had issued a statutory demand. The CA held that there were no grounds for setting aside the statutory demand. *JA Cozens v C & E Commrs, CA 29 October 1999 unreported*. (*Note.* At a subsequent hearing, the tribunal dismissed a late appeal and ordered the accountant to pay costs to the Commissioners—see *LON/99/94 (VTD 16545)*.)

2.151   See also *Nawaz*, 2.218 below.

2.152   The Commissioners obtained a final judgment with costs, for the tax charged by an assessment against which no appeal had been made. The defendant then applied under *Tribunals Rules, rule 19* for an extension of the period in which he could appeal against the assessment. The tribunal dismissed this application. The defendant subsequently applied under *rule 26* for the *rule 19* application to be reinstated. The tribunal dismissed this application, holding that, in view of the High Court judgment, it had no jurisdiction to entertain the appeal. *TS Digwa, [1978] VATTR 119 (VTD 612)*.

2.153   *Digwa*, 2.152 above, was applied in *G & I Hall, MAN/78/55 (VTD 623); Glen & Padden (t/a Shieldfield Processors & Refiners), MAN/79/140 (VTD 917); N Hewitt, MAN/81/93 (VTD 1149); LR Back, MAN/82/154 (VTD 1306); M Sharif, MAN/84/188 (VTD 1701, 1886); JE & K Spiby (t/a Spymore Wall Coverings), MAN/83/72 (VTD 1812)* and *M Saeed & P Arabian, MAN/85/143 (VTD 1859)*.

2.154   In a Scottish case, the Lord Advocate took proceedings, on behalf of the Commissioners, in the Sheriff Court in respect of three assessments against which no appeal had been made to a tribunal. The defendant contended that one of the assessments had been made outside the time limit of what is now *VATA 1994, s 73*. The Sheriff Court allowed the defendant's appeal in respect of the disputed assessment, holding that although the amount of the assessment was (applying *Holvey*, 2.149 above), exclusively a matter for the tribunal, the question of whether the assessment had been made out of time was a matter of law which could be raised in collection proceedings. The CS upheld this decision, holding that, since the assessment had been made out of time, it was a nullity and did not fall within what is now *VATA 1994, s 83(p)*. The defence that the assessment was a nullity could be taken before the court even though the point had not been taken before a tribunal. *Lord Advocate v J Shanks (t/a Shanks & Co), CS [1992] STC 928*. (*Note*. The decision here appears to conflict with the established case law relating to direct tax, where it has consistently been held that the validity of assessments cannot be disputed in collection proceedings. See *CIR v Pearlberg, CA [1953] 1 All ER 388; CIR v Soul, CA 1976, 51 TC 86* and *CIR v Aken, CA [1990] STC 497*, which are summarised in Tolley's Tax Cases 2001. None of these three cases were cited in *Shanks*. In the subsequent case of *Bennett*, 53.22 REGISTRATION, the tribunal chairman expressed the view that the principle laid down in *Shanks* should be confined to cases where the issue was whether the assessment had been issued within the statutory time limit, and did not extend to cases where the point at issue was whether the assessment had been made to the best of the Commissioners' judgment.)

2.155   **Late appeal during distraint proceedings.**   On 3 November 1978 the Commissioners issued assessments charging tax of £2,153. The trader paid £153 and the Commissioners agreed to accept payment of the balance in two instalments. The trader did not keep the agreement and in January 1979 the Commissioners levied distraint on 9 January 1979, entering into a form of 'Walking Possession Agreement'. The trader then applied to lodge a late appeal. The tribunal dismissed the application and awarded costs of £100 to the Commissioners. *PJ Davies, [1979] VATTR 162 (VTD 791)*.

2.156   **Other cases.**   There are a very large number of cases in which tribunals have dismissed applications for late appeals, and where the decision appears to raise no point of general interest. In the interests of space, such cases are not reported in this book. For a list of such cases decided up to and including 30 September 1989, see Tolley's VAT Cases 1990.

2.157   **Application by Commissioners to make late appeal against tribunal decision.**   In the case noted at 62.30 TRANSPORT, the tribunal decision was released on 18 September 1991. On 13 March 1992 the successful appellant company went into voluntary liquidation. On 18 March the Commissioners made an application to lodge a late appeal to the High Court against the tribunal decision. The QB rejected the application, observing that tribunal decisions were not binding precedents, and that since the company had gone into liquidation, the Commissioners were unlikely to receive any money even if a late appeal was successful. *C & E Commrs v Facthaven Incentive Marketing Ltd, QB [1992] STC 839.*

2.158   **Application for reinstatement of appeal.**   See the cases noted at 2.211 *et seq.* below.

SETTLEMENT OF APPEALS BY AGREEMENT (VATA 1994, s 85)

2.159   A company (L) carried out construction work for a manufacturing company (P). P withheld payment of some of the invoices issued by L, considering that the work in question should have been zero-rated, and L did not account for output tax on the disputed invoices. Subsequently L issued a credit note to P in respect of the invoices which remained unpaid. L later went into receivership. The receiver formed the opinion that all the work done for P should have been zero-rated, and issued a credit note in respect of the invoices which P had paid. The receiver submitted a VAT return on behalf of L claiming a repayment of more than £1.5 million, being the amount of VAT which L had charged to P and had accounted for to the Commissioners. The Commissioners refused to repay the VAT in question, considering that the credit note should be disallowed since it had been issued for an improper purpose and that repayment would result in the 'unjust enrichment' of L. (Since L was by now in liquidation, the amount in question would have been divided between all its creditors rather than being returned to P, which had actually suffered the tax.) The Commissioners offered to repay the money directly to P, rather than to the liquidator of L. The liquidator rejected this proposal and lodged an appeal against the refusal to make the repayment. A VAT officer wrote to the liquidator on 3 January 1991 to inform him that 'the Commissioners have reconsidered their decision on the validity of the credit note issued by L ... it is now agreed that L are entitled to a refund of the VAT overpaid in error'. A few days later another officer reviewed the case. He considered that his colleague had acted incorrectly, and that the money in question should be paid to P, as the Commissioners had originally intended, rather than to L, as his colleague had subsequently promised. He wrote to the liquidator on 14 January, informing him that his colleague's letter was 'hereby withdrawn' and that the money should be repaid to P rather than to L. The liquidator refused to agree to this and his appeal against the original refusal was heard by the tribunal. The tribunal held that the letter dated 3 January 1991 constituted the settlement of the appeal by agreement, within what is now *VATA 1994, s 85(1)*. Under what is now *VATA 1994, s 85(2)*, an appellant could resile from such an agreement within 30 days, but there was no such provision whereby the Commissioners could resile from such an agreement. The letter dated 14 January, whereby the Commissioners purported to withdraw from the agreement, was therefore ineffective. *Lamdec Ltd (in receivership and liquidation), [1991] VATTR 296 (VTD 6078)*. (*Note*. The tribunal chairman also considered that, since L was in liquidation, the repayment of the tax would not result in 'unjust enrichment'. However, the chairman's *obiter dicta* with regard to 'unjust enrichment' were not followed, and were implicitly disapproved, in the subsequent case of *Creative Facility Ltd*, 45.11 PAYMENT OF TAX.)

2.160   The Commissioners issued assessments charging output tax on two companies which they considered had underdeclared tax. In December 1992 the Commissioners wrote to the companies offering them compounded settlements under *CEMA 1979, s 152*, as an alternative to criminal prosecution. On 13 January 1993 solicitors acting on behalf of the companies wrote to the Commissioners purporting to accept the offers to compound. However, in the letter the solicitors stated that the companies and their directors 'expressly deny any dishonesty or deliberate misdeclaration and reserve all their rights to challenge on appeal the quantum and the legal and/or factual basis of all or any of the assessments to which this agreement relates. It is intended to take these appeals before the tribunal'. On the same date, the solicitors lodged notices of appeal against the assessments. On 22 January the Commissioners wrote to the solicitors rejecting the proposals set out in their letter of 13 January. On 28 January the solicitors replied to the Commissioners, informing them that the companies 'do not now insist on the reservation of their rights of appeal'. On 4 February the Commissioners replied to the solicitors, accepting their proposals for settlement subject to the companies completing an undertaking to inform the tribunal that the appeals had been settled by agreement. The companies' signatories completed this undertaking on 12 February. However, they did not inform the tribunal that the appeals had been settled, and the Commissioners subsequently lodged applications for the appeals to be struck out. The tribunal accepted the Commissioners' applications, holding that the parties had entered into agreements within what is now *VATA 1994, s 85(1)* and that the appellants had not resiled from the agreements within the time limits laid down by what is now *VATA 1994, s 85(2)*. The compounding agreement was authorised by *CEMA 1979, s 152. Aspley Caterers Ltd, MAN/93/65; TBC Catering Ltd, MAN/93/67 (VTD 12235)*.

2.161   An engineering company reclaimed substantial amounts of input tax. The Commissioners rejected the claim, considering that the relevant supplies had not been made to the claimant company, but to one of its associated companies. The company appealed, and the case was set down for hearing by the tribunal in January 1994. After its counsel had made a long opening statement the case was adjourned for lunch, and during the adjournment the company's counsel and Customs' solicitor came to a provisional agreement, as a result of which they jointly asked the tribunal to adjourn the case indefinitely. The company's counsel formed the opinion that Customs' solicitor had agreed that £53,000 could be repaid to the company. In February 1994 the company's solicitors wrote to the Commissioners formally requesting the repayment. The Commissioners responded in May, rejecting the claim and stating that while the solicitor had agreed in principle that the company might be entitled to bad debt relief, this would only be possible if output tax had previously been accounted for on the transactions in question. The company's counsel replied disputing the terms of this letter, and in June the solicitor with whom he had originally discussed the case replied stating *inter alia* that 'I am happy to confirm that we agreed that (the company) would be allowed the credit for input tax calculated at £53,000 odd ... That appears to me to dispose of the appeal. The question of (the company's) entitlement to bad debt relief is a separate matter'. In the interval between these two letters, the Customs' officer responsible for the original assessment had formed the opinion that, if the company had genuinely received the supplies in question and thus been entitled to reclaim input tax, it had also made an onward supply on which it was required to account for output tax. He therefore arranged for the issue of an assessment charging output tax of £53,000. The company applied to the tribunal for a direction that the original appeal be recorded as having been settled by agreement under what is now *VATA 1994, s 85*. The case was relisted for hearing in January 1995. The tribunal dismissed the company's application, finding that the provisions of what is now *s 85(3)(a)* had not been complied with, since the agreement had not been confirmed in writing. (The tribunal observed that the assessment to output tax which had been issued in June 1994 was apparently not under appeal, but expressed the opinion on the available evidence that it had been made outside the one-year time limit of what is now *VATA 1994, s 73(6)(b)*.) *TF Mechanical Engineering Ltd, MAN/93/718 (VTD 12975)*.

2.162   In July and October 1992 a company (M) submitted returns claiming credit for substantial amounts which it had previously accounted for as output tax. It had originally treated the relevant supplies as standard-rated and had issued invoices to the recipients of the supplies, which had reclaimed the amounts in question as input tax. One of M's directors subsequently formed the opinion that, notwithstanding the invoices which M had issued, the supplies in question should have been treated as zero-rated under the law then in force. However, M failed to issue credit notes to the recipients. In November 1992 the Commissioners issued an assessment to recover £829,726 from M (this being the amount reclaimed in the return submitted in July 1992). M appealed. The appeal was settled by agreement under *VATA 1994, s 85* in May 1995. Under the agreement, M was required to issue a credit note in respect of the tax of £829,726 to the recipients of the supplies. However, although M issued a document, described as a credit note, to one of the recipients (C), it failed to refund the tax which it had charged C in respect of the supplies in question. (It had previously threatened to take legal proceedings against C in relation to another dispute concerning the contract in question.) In October 1995, having discovered that M had not made a refund to C, the Commissioners issued a further assessment to collect the tax of £829,726 from M. M appealed, contending firstly that the note it had issued to C was not a credit note and that it was under no obligation to make a refund to C, and secondly that the assessment was invalid. The tribunal rejected these contentions, upheld the October 1995 assessment, and dismissed M's appeal. The effect of the *s 85* agreement had been to uphold the November 1992 assessment. Under the agreement, M had been required to adjust its VAT account under what is now *reg 38* of the *VAT Regulations 1995*. That adjustment 'required the issue of a *bona fide* credit note, and the giving of value to (C)'. For a credit note 'to give value to the customer, it must represent a genuine entitlement by the recipient either to a refund or to some type of offset'. Such a refund or offset was 'a mandatory requirement of a person issuing a credit note'. On the evidence, the tribunal was 'quite satisfied that (M) intended neither to refund to (C) the sum for which the note was issued nor to offset such sum'. Consequently, 'the credit note issued to (C) was not valid for VAT purposes'. Furthermore, the October assessment was a valid assessment under *VATA 1994, s 73(2)*. (The tribunal also held that M had been required to give credit to C in its accounting period ending 31 May 1995, and the assessment was issued within two years of that accounting period.) *McNulty Offshore Services Ltd, MAN/96/119 (VTD 14824)*.

2.163   See also *Tourick*, 53.79 REGISTRATION.

2.164   **Compounding agreement—whether an agreement of appeal within VATA 1994, s 85.**   The Commissioners investigated the proprietor of a taxi business, whom they considered had been evading VAT. In June 1994 they issued an assessment on him, charging VAT of more than £350,000. The proprietor appealed. In January 1995 the proprietor signed an agreement with the Commissioners, under *CEMA 1979, s 152*. Under the agreement, the proprietor undertook to pay £500,000 by instalments, to include 'all arrears, interest and penalties'. The Commissioners undertook not to institute criminal proceedings against the proprietor provided that he paid the £500,000 by July 1997. When the appeal was first listed for hearing, the Commissioners applied for it to be struck out on the grounds that it had been settled by the compounding agreement. The tribunal chairman (Dr. Brice) dismissed this application and directed that the appeal should be heard in the usual way. The appeal was subsequently heard by a different chairman (Mr. Palmer), who dismissed the appeal, holding that the effect of the compounding agreement was that the appeal had been settled by agreement, within *VATA 1994, s 85*. The chairman observed that the agreement was 'clearly intended to be an agreement affecting the assessment and finally resolving any dispute between the parties relating to it'. The purpose of *s 85* was 'to encourage settlement by agreement of disputes between Customs & Excise and taxpayers. Those agreements are intended to be given finality ... the assessment is therefore effectively treated as discharged by the agreement'. *C Cummings, LON/94/1128 (VTD 14870)*.

2.165   **Appeals following criminal proceedings—whether any agreement under VATA 1994, s 85.**   In December 1997 two individuals pleaded guilty at a Crown Court to charges of fraudulent evasion of VAT. The Crown Court adjourned sentencing, thus giving the defendants the opportunity to pay the evaded tax. Following negotiations, the Commissioners formed the opinion that they had reached agreement with the defendants' accountants, and issued a notice purporting to be a confirmation of the agreement under *VATA 1994, s 85(3)*. The defendants' solicitors issued a notice under *VATA 1994, s 85(2)* resiling from the agreement (and contending alternatively that the Commissioners' notice was void as there had never been a formal agreement of the appeals). The appeals in question were then set down for hearing by the tribunal, and the Commissioners applied for the appeals to be struck out on the grounds that they had already been settled by agreement under *s 85*. The tribunal observed that the defendants' position appeared to be 'particularly unmeritorious', but held on the evidence that the appeals had not been settled by agreement and directed that the Commissioners' application be struck out. The tribunal also directed that the appeals would be dismissed unless the appellants registered for VAT and rendered returns to the Commissioners in respect of the periods covered by the assessments under appeal. *Saffron v Australian Federal Commissioners of Tax (No 2), FC(A) [1991] FCR 578* applied. *GM & CW Citrone, MAN/97/1187 & MAN/98/215 (VTD 15702)*. (*Notes*. (1) *Saffron v Australian Federal Commissioners of Tax* was a case in which it was held by a majority that a taxpayer, who had been convicted of conspiracy to defraud the Commonwealth of Australia in his income tax returns, could adduce evidence in his subsequent appeals against tax assessments which contradicted matters which had been necessarily decided against him by his conviction. (2) The assessments were subsequently reduced—*(16662)*.)

2.166   **Appeal settled by agreement—subsequent application for costs.**   See *McGinty*, 2.301 below.

2.167 Appeals

2.167 **Solicitor agreeing to withdraw appeal on behalf of clients—effect of VATA 1994, s 85.** See *Taylor*, 2.39 above.

APPLICATIONS FOR ADJOURNMENTS

2.168 **Appeal against tribunal decision—appellant applying for adjournment of High Court hearing.** The tribunal dismissed a company's appeal against an estimated assessment and the company appealed to the High Court against the tribunal decision. The case was listed for a High Court hearing in March 1992, but the hearing was adjourned because the controlling director of the company was in prison. The case was relisted for hearing in July 1992. The company's solicitors applied for a further adjournment, contending that the company needed time to obtain sufficient funds to proceed with the appeal. The QB rejected the application, holding that lack of funds was not a proper basis for an adjournment. Counsel for the company was unable to proceed with the appeal, which was dismissed with costs. *Rimland Ltd v C & E Commrs, QB 10 July 1992 unreported.*

2.169 **Adjournment refused by tribunal—whether courts should interfere.** The Commissioners issued an assessment on a partnership which operated a restaurant, covering the period from April 1973 to January 1975. When the appeal was set down for hearing, the partnership requested an adjournment. The tribunal rejected this request and held that it could not entertain the appeal as the tax had not been paid or deposited, and a return for one of the periods covered by the assessment had not been made. The partnership appealed to the QB, which upheld the tribunal's decision. Neill J held that a court should interfere with a tribunal's refusal to grant an adjournment only if the refusal would cause an injustice. *Abedin & Abedin v C & E Commrs, QB 1978, [1979] STC 426.*

2.170 In April 1989 the Commissioners issued a 'global' assessment on a builder (W), covering the period from June 1985 to 1988. In October 1989 W was convicted of two charges of fraudulent evasion of VAT, and received a sentence of imprisonment. In April 1991 W lodged a late appeal against the assessment. The hearing of the appeal was eventually fixed for December 1993, but, at W's request, was delayed until April 1994. W did not attend the hearing but was represented by an accountant who requested a further adjournment until September 1994, stating that W was outside the UK. The tribunal rejected this application and confirmed the assessment. W appealed to the QB, contending that the tribunal had been wrong to refuse a further adjournment. The QB rejected this contention and dismissed the appeal, observing that in view of the history of the case, the tribunal had been 'perfectly entitled to say that enough is enough' and to exercise its discretion to refuse a further adjournment. *GM Whatton v C & E Commrs, QB [1996] STC 519.*

2.171 See also *R v VAT Tribunal (ex p. Cohen & Others)*, 2.221 below.

2.172 **Application by the Commissioners for proceedings to be stood over pending criminal prosecution.** A company appealed against an assessment covering six years and charging tax of more than £1,000,000. The Commissioners applied for the hearing of the appeal to be stood over for six months on the grounds that they were considering criminal proceedings against the company. The tribunal chairman (Mr. Oliver, sitting alone) rejected the application, observing that the company wished the appeal to be heard and stating 'I fully recognise that there is a public interest in bringing perceived criminals to trial. I am not, however, persuaded that the hearing of a civil VAT appeal, before criminal proceedings based on a similar subject-matter take place, can frustrate that public interest.' Mr. Oliver held that the Commissioners had not 'shown that there would be any real risk of serious prejudice leading to injustice — either to the Commissioners or to (the company) — as the result of holding the VAT tribunal appeal before any criminal proceedings are concluded'. *Dicta* of Megaw LJ in *Jefferson Ltd v Bhetcha, CA [1979] 1 WLR 898; [1979] 2 All ER 1108* applied. *McNicholas Construction Co Ltd, [1997] VATDR 73 (VTD 14975).* (*Notes.* (1) For subsequent developments in this case, see 2.189 below, 3.77 ASSESSMENT, and 14.78 COLLECTION AND ENFORCEMENT. (2) Despite Mr. Oliver's decision that the hearing of the appeal would not jeopardise the criminal proceedings, the Harrow Crown Court subsequently determined that 'the evidence disclosed in public at the VAT tribunal and later published was an abuse of process, and the various defendants could not receive a fair trial'. See Taxation, 22 April 1999, p 103.)

2.173 The decision in *McNicholas Construction Co Ltd*, 2.172 above, was not followed, and was implicitly disapproved, in a subsequent case in which the tribunal held that the hearing of the appeal should await the outcome of the related criminal prosecution. *JH Smith, LON/x, 23 June 1999 unreported.*

2.174 See also *Rosignoli*, 2.118 above.

2.175 **Application by Commissioners for adjournment to enable them to consider grant of immunity to witness.** In the case noted at 38.11 INVOICES AND CREDIT NOTES, the Commissioners produced as a witness a trader (C) who had been convicted of registering in a false name. The Commissioners' case rested on the assumption that there had been collusion between C and the appellant company, and the company's solicitor submitted that C should be cautioned that he need not answer incriminating questions. C then asked for an opportunity to consult a solicitor, and the Commissioners requested an adjournment to consider whether they should grant C immunity from prosecution. The tribunal refused the Commissioners' request, holding that the Commissioners should have foreseen the course of events and that the adjournment requested would be unfair to the company. *Stewart Ward (Coins) Ltd, [1986] VATTR 129 (VTD 2108).*

2.176 **Application for adjournment for medical reasons.** A trader did not attend the hearing of an appeal. Prior to the hearing, he had sent in an unsatisfactory doctor's statement which the tribunal decided to treat as an application for an adjournment. The Commissioners opposed this, having regard to the previous history of the case, and the tribunal dismissed the application and the appeal. *P Donaldson, LON/80/ 345 (VTD 1082).*

2.177 A chartered accountant (S) who also owned an estate agency failed to account for VAT on fees and commission he had received. The Commissioners issued assessments in September 1988 charging tax on this income. S appealed, and the hearing of the appeal was delayed from November 1990 to March 1991 at his request because of his ill-health. It was then postponed again, for the same reason, and relisted for August 1991. Two weeks before the hearing was due, S requested a further postponement, enclosing a doctor's letter to confirm that he was suffering from Parkinson's disease. The Commissioners objected to the application, which was heard by the tribunal in S's absence. The Commissioners gave evidence that S had been regularly seen at business premises, including several sightings in August 1991. The tribunal rejected the application for postponement of the hearing, and proceeded to hear the appeal, which it dismissed. The tribunal observed that S was a Fellow of the Institute of Chartered Accountants, and expressed surprise at his 'conduct with regard to avoiding attendance at this hearing'. Costs of £200 were awarded to the Commissioners. *GT Swaine, MAN/90/543 (VTD 6451).*

2.178 A partnership which operated a restaurant appealed against an estimated assessment. The appeal was listed for hearing in October 1992, but was adjourned since the principal partner was suffering from angina. The case was relisted for hearing in June 1993. The partnership's accountant requested a further adjournment, since the partner was still suffering from angina and unable to attend the hearing. The tribunal rejected the application, observing that the accountant was unlikely to give any indication as to when the partner might be able to attend a hearing, and that the partnership had failed to submit information in support of its appeal. (The tribunal also dismissed the appeal.) *The Curry Garden Tandoori Restaurant, LON/91/12 (VTD 10766).*

2.179   A company appealed against three default surcharge assessments. The hearing was originally arranged for February 1994, but was postponed on five occasions on account of the prolonged illness of one of the company's two directors. In October 1995 the company requested a further postponement for the same reasons. The tribunal rejected the application, observing that the company had continued to trade despite the illness of the director in question and holding that 'the ends of justice would be better served by the hearing proceeding as called'. *A & T Barr (Electrical) Ltd, EDN/93/200 (VTD 13848). (Note.* The tribunal also dismissed the company's appeals against the surcharges.)

2.180   See also *Baird v C & E Commrs,* 2.113 above.

2.181   **Accountant not ready to present appeal.**   On the morning of the day fixed for hearing an adjourned appeal, the appellant telephoned to say that he had recently appointed an accountant who had not had time to prepare the appeal and accordingly he would not attend or be represented. The tribunal treated the telephone call as an application for a further adjournment, and in view of the circumstances, it dismissed both the application and the appeal. *J Butterfield, [1977] VATTR 152 (VTD 404).*

2.182   In the case noted at 49.206 PENALTIES: MISDECLARATION, the partnership's accountant applied for an adjournment on the grounds that he had only been instructed two days before the hearing and had not had time to prepare his case. The tribunal rejected the application, observing that the hearing had previously been adjourned because one of the partners had been ill, and stating that 'it is clearly unreasonable to instruct a new adviser two days before the second hearing date which had been fixed and expect the tribunal to grant an adjournment because the appellants did nothing earlier'. *Hounslow Sweet Centre, LON/92/271X (VTD 10026).*

2.183   **Application by former partners.**   In an appeal by a firm of solicitors which was in receivership, the tribunal allowed an application for an adjournment made on behalf of former partners in the firm so that they could serve concurrent notice of appeal. *Blyth Elfords, [1985] VATTR 204 (VTD 1939).*

2.184   **Other cases.**   There have been a large number of other cases involving applications for adjournments, in which the decision appears to raise no point of general interest. In the interests of space, such cases are not summarised individually in this book.

THE HEARING OF THE APPEAL BEFORE THE TRIBUNAL

Onus of proof

2.185   In the case noted at 3.50 ASSESSMENT, the QB and CA held that, in the hearing of an appeal against an assessment to VAT, the burden of proof was on the appellant to show, on the balance of probabilities, that the assessment was wrong, rather than on the Commissioners to show that it was correct. Macpherson J held that 'at no time do the Commissioners have any burden to prove anything before the tribunal ... it is throughout ... up to the taxpayer company, if it can, to attack the assessment in whole or in part'. *Grunwick Processing Laboratories v C & E Commrs, CA [1987] STC 357.*

2.186   *Grunwick Processing Laboratories Ltd*, 2.185 above, was applied in a subsequent case in which the proprietor of a pizza restaurant appealed against an estimated assessment. The tribunal held that the burden of proof remained on the appellant notwithstanding the fact that the assessment under appeal had been computed on the assumption that the appellant had deliberately underdeclared takings. While an allegation of fraud or dishonesty should be included in the Statement of Case and should be supported by evidence, the Commissioners were not required to prove that the appellant had acted dishonestly. *Dicta* of the tribunal in *Stewart Ward (Coins) Ltd*, 38.11 INVOICES AND CREDIT NOTES, disapproved. *E Halil, [1992] VATTR 432 (VTD 9590)*.

2.187   *Grunwick Processing Laboratories Ltd*, 2.185 above, has been applied in a very large number of subsequent cases in which tribunals have held that the burden of proof is on the appellant. In the interests of space, such cases are not reported individually in this book.

Whether appeal to be heard in private

2.188   **Application dismissed.**   In a case where the substantive issue has been overtaken by subsequent changes in the legislation, the tribunal rejected a company's application that its appeal should be heard in private, holding that 'whenever possible, decisions of these tribunals should be given in public so that they could be published for general guidance'. The tribunal observed that an appeal should be heard in private 'when a hearing in public would defeat the ends of justice, or would be likely to harm the appellant in the course of his business'. *Guy Butler (International) Ltd (No 1), [1974] VATTR 199 (VTD 106A)*.

2.189   A company applied for the hearing of an appeal to be heard in private, contending that, since the Commissioners had alleged that it had been involved in fraudulent conduct, a public hearing would be damaging to its business. The tribunal dismissed the application, observing that 'the assessments and the allegations on which they are based must be assumed to be made seriously and in good faith by the Commissioners through their own professional lawyers'. Furthermore, 'dishonesty has to be alleged in all civil penalty cases ... and in all extended time limit cases ... harm to reputation is a risk that inevitably follows from all assessments based on alleged dishonesty on the part of an appellant'. *McNicholas Construction Co Ltd (No 2), [1998] VATDR 220 (VTD 15575)*. *(Notes.* (1) For preliminary issues in this case, see 2.172 above and 14.78 COLLECTION AND ENFORCEMENT. For the substantive appeal, see 3.77 ASSESSMENT. (2) Despite the tribunal's decision that the hearing of the appeal in public would not jeopardise criminal proceedings against some of the company's employees, the Harrow Crown Court subsequently determined that 'the evidence disclosed in public at the VAT tribunal and later published was an abuse of process, and the various defendants could not receive a fair trial'. See *Taxation*, 22 April 1999, p 103.)

2.190   **Application granted.**   Two companies applied for their appeals to be heard in private. The Commissioners had no objection to the applications. The tribunal granted the applications, but observed that 'appeals should if possible be heard in public, and ... a direction to the contrary should be made only in exceptional circumstances. In our judgment exceptional circumstances would arise where the disclosure of confidential information would harm an appellant in his business, or where the evidence to be given would involve the disclosure of a process, where such disclosure would prejudice his competitive position.' *Consortium International Ltd; Consortium Communications International Club, LON/79/93, 94 (VTD 824)*.

2.191   Similar decisions were reached in *Synopsys Ltd, LON/91/2309Z (VTD 7207)* and *Lonsdale Travel Ltd, MAN/90/535 unreported.*

2.192   **Hearing in private—whether expert witness may be excluded from hearing.**   A company which had reclaimed input tax on the purchase of a yacht applied for its appeal to be heard in private, on the grounds that it was carrying out work of a 'highly sensitive' nature. The tribunal granted the application, and the Commissioners sought leave to produce an expert witness. The tribunal directed that the Commissioners' expert witness should not be present when the company's evidence was given, and the Commissioners applied by way of judicial review for an order to quash this direction. Forbes J granted the Commissioners' application. If the Commissioners satisfied the tribunal that their expert witness was a properly qualified expert in the particular field, he should be entitled to attend the tribunal throughout the hearing of the company's expert witness. It would be contrary to natural justice to prevent an expert witness listening to sensitive evidence given by the other side, even at a hearing in private, if the tribunal were satisfied that the expert witness was qualified as an expert on the matter to which the sensitive evidence related. *R v Manchester VAT Tribunal (ex p. C & E Commrs), QB February 1982 unreported.*

2.193   **Application to strike out appeal—hearing in private—whether decision to be made public.**   In the case noted at 17.5 DEFAULT INTEREST, the Commissioners had applied for an appeal to be struck out on the grounds that it was outside the tribunal's jurisdiction. The tribunal chairman rejected this contention and advised the parties that, although the hearing had been in private, she proposed to publish her decision. The Commissioners objected to this proposal, stating that 'the decision is based on an inaccurate appreciation of the facts and is wrong in law ... the decision would not be useful to the public as a helpful precedent'. The tribunal rejected the application, applying *Guy Butler (International) Ltd (No 1)*, 2.188 above, and *dicta* of Lord Halsbury in *Scott v Scott, HL [1913] AC 417*, and noting that the publication of the decision would not prejudice the appellant partnership, and that the partnership had no objection to publication. *RMSG, [1994] VATTR 167 (VTD 11921).*

Miscellaneous

2.194   **Unauthorised use of tape recorder by appellant during hearing—Contempt of Court Act 1981.**   In the case noted at 21.129 EUROPEAN COMMUNITY LAW, a shorthand writer engaged by the appellant company recorded part of the proceedings without the permission of the tribunal. The tribunal imposed restrictions on the use of the recorder, and warned that its unauthorised use had been a breach of *Contempt of Court Act 1981, ss 9, 19*, and that such contempts could be punished. *Empire Stores Ltd, [1992] VATTR 271 (VTD 8859).*

2.195   **Admissibility of hearsay evidence.**   In a case where no witness statements had been served under *Tribunals Rules, rule 8*, the QB held that it was permissible for a tribunal to admit hearsay evidence provided that there was no objection to the admission of such evidence and that the tribunal did not decide of its own volition that such evidence should be excluded. *Wayne Farley Ltd & Another v C & E Commrs, QB [1986] STC 487.* (*Note.* With regard to the use of hearsay evidence, see now *Civil Procedure Rules 1998 (SI 1998 No 3132), rule 33.*)

2.196   Hearsay evidence concerning the alleged dishonesty of an employee of the appellant company was ruled inadmissible in *Deeds Ltd*, 38.14 INVOICES AND CREDIT NOTES.

2.197   **Record book found by VAT officers at appellant's premises—whether admissible as evidence.**   In an appeal against an estimated assessment on a clothing manufacturer, the Commissioners introduced as evidence a record book which had been found by VAT officers at the manufacturer's premises. The manufacturer's solicitor objected to the production of the book, contending that it was hearsay evidence and should not be admitted. The tribunal ruled that the book was admissible as evidence. The tribunal was not satisfied that the book was hearsay evidence, and observed that 'if any part of the evidence offered to link the book and the appellant is hearsay, we can deal with that evidence as it is tendered'. *M Hanif, MAN/89/747 (VTD 6430)*. (*Notes.* (1) The appeal was subsequently dismissed. The tribunal held that it was 'not satisfied on the balance of probabilities that the book does not relate to the appellant's business'. For the award of costs to the Commissioners, see 2.241 below. (2) With regard to the use of hearsay evidence, see now the note following *Wayne Farley Ltd*, 2.195 above.)

2.198   **Notice of objection to Witness Statements.**   A gold coin dealer accounted for VAT under the margin scheme in respect of a large proportion of his takings. The Commissioners formed the impression that he had acted fraudulently, in that he had falsely attributed takings to purported second-hand transactions which had not in fact taken place, so that the conditions for the margin scheme were not satisfied and output tax was chargeable on the full amount of the takings. The dealer provided the Commissioners with the names of two people—one a Canadian and the other a resident of the USA—to whom he claimed he had made substantial supplies of gold coins under the margin scheme. The two people in question gave the Commissioners written statements denying that they had received such supplies. The Commissioners included these statements as Witness Statements with their Statement of Case. The dealer objected to the Statements being put in evidence and served a notice of objection, applying for directions, under *rule 21(4)* of the *VAT Tribunals Rules*. The tribunal rejected the dealer's application, holding that 'whether ... the statements should be given any weight as evidence is ... entirely a matter for the tribunal that hears the appeal'. *MD Bord, LON/91/2595Y (VTD 7946)*. (*Note.* For the substantive appeal, see 56.3 SECOND-HAND GOODS.)

2.199   **Exclusion of evidence—public interest immunity.**   The Commissioners issued estimated assessments on a partnership, and imposed a penalty under *VATA 1994, s 60(1)*. The partnership appealed. During the hearing of the appeal, the Commissioners applied for a direction that witnesses should not be required to answer questions in cross-examination which might serve to identify an informant, claiming public interest immunity. The tribunal granted the application, observing that 'in the case of public prosecutions, it has been settled since the eighteenth century that witnesses cannot be asked questions tending to disclose the identity of an informant. In civil cases, the rule has been applied to a range of situations where the effective functioning of an organisation established under Act of Parliament might be adversely affected by allowing the identity of informants to be disclosed.' Applying *dicta* of Lord Cross in *Alfred Crompton Amusement Machines Ltd v C & E Commrs (No 2), HL 1972, [1974] AC 405; [1972] 2 All ER 353* (a purchase tax case), 'in a case where the considerations for and against disclosure appear to be fairly evenly balanced, the courts should ... uphold a claim to privilege on the ground of public interest and trust to the head of the department concerned to do whatever he can to mitigate the ill-effects of non-disclosure'. On the evidence, the partnership had not shown that 'the withheld evidence is at all likely to be relevant to its determination of the issues in the appeals in this case'. The tribunal was obliged to observe 'the legitimate public interest of protecting the identity of informers and the contents of information obtained from them'. *Bendenoun v France, ECHR 1994, 18 EHRR 54 (TTC 2001, 25.72)*, applied. *CT, C & P Ellinas (t/a Hunts Cross Supper Bar), MAN/96/692 (VTD 15346)*. (*Note.* For subsequent developments in this case, see 47.85 PENALTIES: EVASION OF TAX.)

2.200   Appeals

2.200   **Whether tribunal entitled to refuse to admit evidence submitted very late.**   In the case noted at 54.49 RETAILERS' SPECIAL SCHEMES, the tribunal refused to admit as evidence certain correspondence which the Commissioners had sought to introduce on the third day of the hearing. The Commissioners appealed to the QB, contending as a preliminary point that the tribunal should have considered the correspondence. The QB accepted this contention and remitted the case to the tribunal. The tribunal had acted unreasonably and had been wrong in law in refusing to consider the correspondence as evidence. *C & E Commrs v GUS Merchandise Ltd, QB [1992] STC 776.*

2.201   **Tribunals Rules, rule 18(2)—appeal dismissed 'for want of prosecution'.**   In 1998 a publican appealed against a ruling that he had acquired his business as a going concern. Subsequently he left the premises, and the Commissioners were unable to trace him. They applied, under *VAT Tribunals Rules (SI 1986 No 590), rule 18(2)*, for his appeal to be dismissed 'for want of prosecution'. The tribunal dismissed the appeal, holding on the evidence that the appellant had 'wilfully refused to correspond with the tribunal' and had 'deliberately made it impossible for the tribunal to communicate with him'. *JW Power, [2000] VATDR 175 (VTD 16748).*

2.202   **Tribunals Rules, rule 21(4)—whether compatible with European Convention on Human Rights.**   See *Murrell*, 32.3 HUMAN RIGHTS.

2.203   **Tribunals Rules, rule 22—summons to third party.**   A company issued a summons, under *VAT Tribunals Rules (SI 1986 No 590), rule 22*, to a firm of accountants, seeking to inspect certain documents. The firm applied to have the summons set aside, contending that the summons was defective as it was directed to the firm and not to any named individual. The tribunal accepted this contention, granted the application and set the summons aside, holding that the summons was invalid since the *Tribunals Rules* 'did not provide for the service of a summons on a partnership as such'. The tribunal observed that a partnership was not a legal entity, and held that the effect of *rule 22(4)* was that 'the third party to whom the summons was issued must be either an individual or a body corporate'. *British Shoe Corporation Ltd v C & E Commrs (ex p. Coopers & Lybrand), [1998] VATDR 348 (C86).*

2.204   **Attendance of interpreter.**   In an appeal by a partnership which operated a Chinese restaurant, the appellants presented as an interpreter an accountant who was a partner in the firm dealing with the restaurant's affairs. The Commissioners objected to the use of the accountant as an interpreter on the basis that he 'could not be seen to be independent'. The tribunal accepted this contention and ruled that the hearing should be adjourned 'so that the name of an independent linguistic interpreter can be submitted'. *CY & TY Shek (t/a The Golden Bowl Café), EDN/99/89 & 113 (VTD 16509).*

2.205   A similar decision was reached in *TS Cheung (t/a May Wah Takeaway), EDN/99/123 (VTD 16670).*

2.206   **Tribunals Rules, rule 26.**   There have been a very large number of cases where an appellant has failed to attend the hearing of an appeal, and the tribunal has dismissed the appeal under *VAT Tribunals Rules (SI 1986 No 590), rule 26*. In the interests of space, such cases are not listed individually in this book.

2.207   **VATA 1994, Sch 12 para 5(2)—difference of opinion between tribunal members.**   A restaurant proprietor appealed against estimated assessments. His appeal was heard by a tribunal consisting of a chairman and one other member. The chairman concluded that the assessments had been made to the best of the Commissioners' judgment, and should be upheld. However, the lay member formed the opinion that the assessments had not been made to the best of the Commissioners' judgment, as required by *VATA 1994, s 73(1)*, and should be discharged. The tribunal held that, by virtue of *VATA 1994, Sch 12 para 5(2)*, which provides for the chairman to have a casting vote, 'the chairman's conclusion determines the outcome of this appeal', and dismissed the appeal. The proprietor appealed to the QB, which directed that the case should be remitted to a new tribunal for re-hearing. Carnwath J held that a tribunal should not treat an assessment as invalid merely because it disagreed as to how the Commissioners' judgment should have been exercised. An assessment should only be held to fail the 'best judgment' test of *s 73(1)* where it had been made 'dishonestly or vindictively or capriciously', or was a 'spurious estimate or guess in which all elements of judgment are missing', or was 'wholly unreasonable'. Short of such a finding, there was no justification for setting aside an assessment. Carnwath J observed that 'it is only in a very exceptional case that an assessment will be upset because of a failure by the Commissioners to exercise best judgment. In the normal case the important issue will be the amount of the assessment.' On the evidence, the approach of the lay member had been wrong, and the tribunal chairman had been entitled to conclude that the assessment had been issued to the best of the Commissioners' judgment. His reasoning on this point was 'clearly set out' and 'impeccable'. However, having concluded by virtue of *Sch 12 para 5(2)* that the assessment had been made to the best of the Commissioners' judgment, both the chairman and the lay member should then have given further consideration, acting jointly, to the amount of the assessment. It appeared that the lay member had 'taken no part in the decision on the amount of the assessment', having 'regarded his function as discharged when he had expressed his view on the best judgment issue'. There was 'at least a possibility that, if he had taken part, the decision would have been more favourable to the appellant'. *MH Rahman (t/a Khayam Restaurant) v C & E Commrs, QB [1998] STC 826.*

2.208   **Tribunal delaying release of decision.**   See *R v C & E Commrs (ex p. Dangol)*, 2.222 below.

2.209   **Failure by Commissioners to comply with direction of tribunal.**   See *Young*, 2.123 above; *Vaz*, 2.271 below, and *AR Waller & Associates*, 17.11 DEFAULT INTEREST.

2.210   **Appeal against tribunal refusal to refer question to CJEC.**   In the case noted at 63.47 VALUATION, the tribunal referred the case to the CJEC for a ruling, but rejected a request by the appellant company to refer an additional question to the CJEC seeking a ruling on whether the company was entitled to reclaim input tax. The company obtained leave from the CA to lodge a late appeal against this refusal (see 2.137 above) and, at a subsequent hearing, the QB held that the input tax question was not '*acte claire*' and that the tribunal should have referred the input tax question to the CJEC. Applying *dicta* of the CJEC in *Srl CILFIT and Lanificio di Gavardo SpA v Ministro della Sanita*, 21.3 EUROPEAN COMMUNITY LAW (the leading authority on the legal principle of '*acte claire*'), the point in dispute was not 'so obvious as to leave no scope for any reasonable doubt as to the manner in which the question raised is to be resolved'. The QB remitted the case to the tribunal to make the reference in question. *Conoco Ltd v C & E Commrs, QB [1995] STC 1022.*

APPLICATIONS FOR REINSTATEMENT OF APPEALS

Cases where the application was successful

2.211   An appellant, who had failed to attend a hearing at which his appeal was dismissed, subsequently applied for the appeal to be reinstated, contending that he had been under the impression that his solicitors were dealing with the appeal. The tribunal directed that the appeal should be reinstated on condition that the appellant paid costs of £300 to the Commissioners. *JDG Wilkinson, MAN/77/303 (VTD 583, 649)*.

2.212   In a case where a company's managing director had suffered from illness, the tribunal allowed an application for the reinstatement of an appeal on condition that the company paid £5,000 on account of the tax and £75 on account of the Commissioners' costs. *Renwalk Ltd, MAN/80/119 (VTD 1255)*.

2.213   The unsuccessful appellant in the case noted at 52.59 PROTECTED BUILDINGS subsequently applied under *rule 26(2)* of the *Tribunals Rules* to have the decision set aside, on the grounds that he had been let down by accountants who had not attended the hearing. The tribunal stated that it was 'reluctant to deny anyone a chance to argue his rights especially when problems have existed about representation', and reinstated the appeal on condition that the appellant should pay costs of £300 to the Commissioners. *P Robinson, MAN/89/131 (VTD 4530)*.

2.214   The Commissioners issued an assessment on the proprietor of a kebab shop, covering a period of four years. The proprietor appealed but did not pay the tax charged by the assessment. On 25 November 1993 the Commissioners made an application for the appeal to be struck out, and the application was set down for hearing on 13 January 1994. On receiving notification of the hearing, the proprietor applied under *rule 11* of the *Tribunals Rules* for the appeal to be heard without payment of the tax assessed, on the grounds that payment would cause him hardship. On 31 December 1993 the Commissioners served a notice opposing the hardship application. The appellant did not attend the hearing on 13 January, and in his absence the tribunal chairman gave a direction that the appeal be dismissed in accordance with *rule 19(4)*. This direction was notified to the appellant, who served a notice of application for the appeal to be reinstated under *rule 26(1)* of the *Tribunals Rules*, contending that on 11 January a member of the tribunal staff had told him by telephone that the hearing scheduled for 13 January had been adjourned and that he need not attend. The tribunal chairman accepted the appellant's evidence, set aside the previous direction, and reinstated the appeal. The chairman awarded costs against the Commissioners, observing that the notice which the Commissioners had served on 31 December had been accompanied by a letter stating that the hardship application would not be listed for 30 days, and commenting that 'it is the duty of the advocate of HM Customs and Excise ... to ensure that any direction dismissing an appeal by virtue of (*VATA 1994, s 82**) is validly given and that the tribunal is aware of any potential problem'. *C Akar (t/a Akar Kebabs), [1994] VATTR 176 (VTD 11873)*.

2.215   An application for reinstatement of an appeal was allowed in a case in which the tribunal applied *dicta* of Roskill LJ in *Samuels v Linzi Dresses, CA [1980] 2 WLR 836; [1980] 1 All ER 803* and observed that the Commissioners had not 'suffered any substantial prejudice through the delay'. *Empress of India Restaurant, [1997] VATDR 242 (VTD 15087)*. (*Note.* Costs of £300 were awarded to the Commissioners.)

2.216   Applications for the reinstatement of an appeal were also allowed in *A & IA Smith, LON/87/588X (VTD 4995)* and *Maharani Restaurant, LON/x (VTD 15088)*.

Cases where the application was unsuccessful

2.217   An appeal by an unincorporated association was dismissed on the grounds that the association had failed to pay the tax in dispute. (It had sent a cheque for the amount in question, but the cheque had been dishonoured.) Subsequently the association paid the tax and applied under *Tribunals Rules, r 19(4)* for the appeal to be reinstated.

The tribunal rejected the application, observing that the association had a history of dilatory tactics and that a letter it had sent indicated that it desired to change its grounds of appeal. *Hubbard Foundation Scotland, EDN/81/23 (VTD 1194)*. (*Note.* For other proceedings involving this association, see 2.107 above.)

2.218 In a case where the tribunal had dismissed appeals by an accountancy partnership against assessments, the partners failed to pay the tax charged and the Commissioners issued writs against the partners. One of the partners obtained a stay of proceedings by order of a Master of the Queen's Bench, conditional upon his entering a fresh appeal. He did so but the tribunal dismissed his appeal, holding that there were no grounds for reinstatement. The accountant appealed to the QB, which upheld the tribunal decision, holding that there was no matter of principle involved and observing that the accountant's only real purpose in seeking to reinstate the appeal appeared to be to delay the enforcement proceedings. *T Nawaz v C & E Commrs, QB [1986] STC 484.*

2.219 In a case where an appeal had been settled by agreement under what is now *VATA 1994, s 85*, the tribunal dismissed a subsequent application for reinstatement, holding that it had no jurisdiction to reinstate the appeal. *Abbey Life Japan Trust, LON/91/1889 (VTD 11205)*.

2.220 Applications for the reinstatement of appeals were dismissed in *A Moss, MAN/79/91 (VTD 919, 953); Rushfern Ltd, MAN/83/35 (VTD 1509); TE Formstone, MAN/88/559 (VTD 3693); Shazia Fashions Fabrics, LON/91/627 (VTD 7184); Terry Shaw Holdings, MAN/92/671 (VTD 11613); Highacre (Cambridge) Ltd, LON/93/819A (VTD 12060); Express Pipework Co, EDN/93/261 (VTD 12108); TL Dunning, LON/93/2027 & LON/94/784 (VTD 12739); IT Anderson, LON/94/1006P (VTD 13226); M Razaq, M Mushtaq & M Azam (t/a Liberty Cars), MAN/94/877 (VTD 14949)* and *MW Morgan, LON/95/2893 (VTD 16968)*.

APPLICATIONS FOR JUDICIAL REVIEW

2.221 **Application for judicial review of tribunal decision.** The Commissioners issued estimated assessments on two companies which had not submitted VAT returns, and which were the subject of an investigation by VAT officers. The Commissioners had begun criminal proceedings against the companies' directors, alleging conspiracy to defraud. The companies appealed against the assessments and applied for the appeals to be adjourned until the criminal proceedings had been completed. The tribunal granted an adjournment of the appeals for one month only, to enable the companies to submit the outstanding returns. The directors applied for judicial review of the tribunal decision. The QB rejected the application. McCullough J held that the company should have appealed under the *Tribunals and Inquiries Act. R v VAT Tribunal (ex p. Cohen & Others), QB 1983, [1984] STC 361.*

2.222 A restaurant proprietor appealed against estimated assessments. The tribunal began hearing the appeals for three days in September 1996. It then adjourned until April 1997, when it sat for a further three days, and did not conclude the hearing until August 1997. The tribunal then did not release its decision until May 1998. It held that the assessments had been made to the best of the Commissioners' judgment, but were excessive, and reduced them by one-third. The proprietor appealed to the QB and applied for judicial review, contending that the effect of the delay was that the tribunal would have forgotten parts of the evidence and that its decision was unsafe. The QB criticised the tribunal for the delays, but dismissed the proprietor's appeal and application for judicial review. Moses J held that the delay in releasing the decision was 'unjustified and unjustifiable'. However, 'unless an unsuccessful party can show that the delay has tainted the conclusion and the findings, it would be wrong to say that he is entitled as of right to have the case remitted to be heard again depriving the other side, who after all is equally not responsible for the delay, of the fruits of victory'. Moses J observed that where a hearing could not be heard on consecutive days, the delays between the hearings should be kept to a minimum, and the tribunal chairman should rarely take longer than three months from the final day of the hearing before releasing the tribunal decision. *R v C & E Commrs (ex p. Dangol), QB 1999, [2000] STC 107.*

2.223   The appellant company in the case noted at 59.9 TOUR OPERATORS AND TRAVEL AGENTS applied for judicial review of the tribunal decision. The QB rejected the application. Popplewell J held that the company should have appealed under the *Tribunals and Inquiries Act. R v VAT Tribunals (ex p. Jenny Braden Holdings Ltd), QB 10 March 1994 unreported.*

2.224   A similar decision was reached in *R v C & E Commrs and VAT Tribunal (ex p. Cohen), QB 3 December 1998 unreported.*

2.225   For a case where the QB granted judicial review of a tribunal decision, see *R v C & E Commrs (ex p. Sims)*, 27.22 FOOD.

2.226   **VATA 1994, s 84—application for judicial review.** See *R v VAT Tribunal (ex p. Minster Associates)*, 2.94 above; *R v VAT Tribunal and C & E Commrs (ex p. Theodorou)*, 2.95 above, and *R v C & E Commrs and London VAT Tribunal*, 2.97 above.

2.227   **Application for reference to CJEC.** In the case noted at 26.29 FINANCE, the QB rejected an application by the company for a reference to the CJEC. *R v C & E Commrs (ex p. Swallowfield plc), QB 1 March 1993, 1993 STI 342.* (*Note.* The company did not take the matter further. The case was heard in the QB with *BLP Group plc*, 21.192 EUROPEAN COMMUNITY LAW. The latter company appealed to the CA, which reversed the QB decision in that case and disapproved the decision in *Swallowfield*.)

2.228   In the case noted at 21.192 EUROPEAN COMMUNITY LAW, the QB rejected an application by the company for a reference to the CJEC. The company appealed to the CA, which reversed the QB decision and directed that the case should be referred to the CJEC. *R v C & E Commrs (ex p. BLP Group plc), CA 1993, [1994] STC 41.*

2.229   **Application for judicial review of terms of reference to CJEC.** In the case noted at 63.47 VALUATION, the tribunal referred the case to the CJEC for a ruling. The appellant company applied for judicial review of the terms of reference, contending that the tribunal should have added a further reference to the possibility of an input tax deduction. At a preliminary hearing, Hidden J granted leave to apply for judicial review, but at a subsequent hearing Popplewell J rejected the application, holding that the tribunal decision had not been perverse and that judicial review was not an appropriate remedy in the circumstances, since the matter was covered by the *Tribunals and Inquiries Act 1992, s 11.* The CA upheld Popplewell J's decision, but granted the company leave to lodge a late appeal under *Tribunals and Inquiries Act 1992, s 11* against the tribunal decision (see 2.137 above). *R v VAT Tribunal (ex p. Conoco Ltd), CA 19 July 1995 unreported.* (*Note.* For subsequent developments in this case, see 2.210 above.)

2.230   **Application for withdrawal of reference to CJEC.** The CA referred the cases noted at 21.207 EUROPEAN COMMUNITY LAW to the CJEC. Subsequently the CJEC gave judgment in the similar case of *EC Commission v French Republic*, 21.206 EUROPEAN COMMUNITY LAW, holding that *Article 17(6)* of the *EC Sixth Directive* permitted Member States to continue to apply provisions to limit the deduction of input tax. The Commissioners took the view that the effect of this judgment was that the appeals noted at 21.207 EUROPEAN COMMUNITY LAW would inevitably be unsuccessful, and applied to the CA for the reference to be withdrawn. The CA rejected this application, holding that, while it had power to withdraw a reference to the CJEC, it should only exercise such a power when 'it was manifest that the reference would not fulfil any useful purpose'. Since the cases would shortly be heard by the CJEC, and the appellant companies objected to the withdrawal of the reference, it would not be appropriate to withdraw it in this case. *Royscot Leasing Ltd v C & E Commrs (and related appeals), CA 5 November 1998, Times 23.11.98. (Note.* The appeals noted at 21.207 EUROPEAN COMMUNITY LAW were unsuccessful.)

2.231 **Application for judicial review of validity of Statutory Instruments.** In June 1994 a group of companies (E) which operated the Channel Tunnel terminals lodged an application for leave to apply for judicial review of the *VAT (Tax-Free Shops) Order 1992 (SI 1992 No 3131)* and the *VAT (Tax-Free Shops) Order 1994 (SI 1994 No 686)*, contending that the Statutory Instruments in question failed to implement *Article 28K* of the *EC Directive* (and the similar *Directive* relating to excise duty) correctly, and failed to prevent evasion or avoidance. The Commissioners did not oppose the application, and Tucker J granted leave to apply. A number of companies which operated tax-free shops at airports and seaports and on ferries, and which would have been adversely affected if the application were successful, subsequently issued notices of motion, applying for orders that the grant of leave to apply for judicial review should be set aside. At a subsequent hearing the QB upheld the objectors' contentions and revoked the grant of leave, observing that the original grant of leave had been made outside the normal time limits and had been made *ex parte*, and holding that the objectors had sufficient *locus standi*. E 'could not, by choosing to give informal notice of its intention to apply for judicial review to some only of the persons directly affected, viz. the Commissioners, thereby affect the right of other persons directly affected, viz. the objectors, to apply to set aside the leave granted'. While a grant of leave should be set aside only in exceptional circumstances, this was 'an exceptional case in its size, complexity and ramifications'. Although the form of the original application was an attack, by way of judicial review, on the validity of the Statutory Instruments, in its substance it was an attack on the validity of the *Directives* themselves. It was accepted that E did not have the necessary *locus standi* to challenge the validity of the *Directives* under *Article 173* of the *EC Treaty*. The objectors had shown that to uphold E's original application would 'cause severe prejudice to the objectors and to other persons not only in the UK but throughout the European Community'. Furthermore, 'the fact that the present case concerns the validity of Community measures provides no reason to disregard or modify the provisions of English domestic law concerning time limits'. *R v HM Customs & Excise (ex p. Eurotunnel plc & Others), QB 17 February 1995 unreported. (Notes.* (1) See also the subsequent case of *Eurotunnel SA & Others v SeaFrance*, 21.244 EUROPEAN COMMUNITY LAW. (2) The zero-rating of sales from 'tax-free shops' has subsequently been abolished, with effect from 1 July 1999, by the *VAT (Abolition of Zero-Rating for Tax-Free Shops) Order 1999 (SI 1999 No 1642)*. (3) The *Rules of the Supreme Court 1965 (SI 1965 No 1776)* refer to the use of a 'motion', and to applications being made '*ex parte*' or '*inter partes*'. With effect from 26 April 1999, these rules have largely been replaced by the *Civil Procedure Rules 1998 (SI 1998 No 3132)*, which refer instead to the use of an 'application', and to applications being made 'without notice' or 'on notice'.)

2.232 **Commissioners withdrawing ruling by local VAT officer—application for judicial review.** In the case noted at 63.54 VALUATION, a company (F) sold books of vouchers to car dealers, who then passed the books of vouchers to the purchasers of second-hand cars. F accounted for output tax on the amounts which it received from the car dealers for the vouchers, but the car dealers did not account for tax on their onward supply of the vouchers to their customers. In March 1998 a local VAT officer ruled that no tax was chargeable on these onward supplies, on the basis that they fell within *VATA 1994, Sch 6 para 5*. However, the scheme came to the attention of a regional office, and in June 1998 the Commissioners withdrew the first ruling and ruled that the sale of the vouchers was not within *Sch 6 para 5*, so that VAT was chargeable. The company applied for judicial review of the Commissioners' decision to withdraw their original ruling. Carnwath J reviewed the evidence in detail and held that there was no legal basis for any claim for compensation, but that, as this was 'a developing area of the law', the company's claim for damages for negligence should 'continue as though begun by writ'. Carnwath J observed that, applying *dicta* of Lord Browne-Wilkinson in *R v CIR (ex p. Matrix Securities Ltd), HL [1994] STC 272 (TTC 2001, 31.21)*, 'the test is one of fairness, not only to the taxpayer, but also to the Customs and to the general body of taxpayers'. Accordingly, 'the legitimate expectation is not that the clearance will be treated as binding come what may, but that, if there is a change in the understanding of the legal position, it will not be treated as retrospective'. The effect of the original ruling 'was not simply to lift a VAT burden from one group of taxpayers (the car dealers), but to impose it on another (the participating retailers)'. On the evidence, the officer who had made the ruling had had all the necessary information, and had made her ruling 'without making sure that it was in accordance with the Customs' current view of the law. Had she taken the precaution of consulting Policy Division or more senior officers, she would not have given the advice she did.' *R v C & E Commrs (ex p. F & I Services Ltd), QB [2000] STC 364.*

2.233   **Whether Commissioners treating taxpayers equally—late application for judicial review.**   In the case noted at 5.72 BOOKS, ETC., the tribunal held that a company which supplied satellite broadcasting services was not entitled to treat part of the subscriptions which it received as attributable to the zero-rated supply of magazines. The company subsequently applied for judicial review, contending that the Commissioners had acted unfairly because it had to account for tax in this way from June 1998, but the Commissioners had not issued similar rulings to other suppliers until July 1999 (after the tribunal decision). Langley J reviewed the evidence and granted the company's application, holding on the evidence that the company had a 'reasonably arguable claim' which should be considered in detail. Although *RSC Order 53 rule 4(1)* provided that applications for judicial review should be made within three months, in this case there was 'good reason for extending the period within which the application shall be made'. Applying *dicta* of Woolf LJ in *R v Commissioners for Local Administration (ex p. Croydon London Borough Council), CA [1989] 1 All ER 1033*, the relevant provisions were 'not intended to be applied in a technical manner ... the courts will not rely on those provisions to deprive a litigant who has behaved sensibly and reasonably of relief to which he is otherwise entitled'. *R v C & E Commrs (ex p. British Sky Broadcasting Group plc), QB 14 July 2000 unreported.*

2.234   **Delay in repayment of input tax pending enquiries by Commissioners—application for judicial review.**   See *R v C & E Commrs (ex p. Strangewood Ltd)*, 34.515 INPUT TAX, and *R v C & E Commrs (ex p. Lacara Ltd)*, 34.517 INPUT TAX.

2.235   **Commissioners failing to make repayments for previous accounting periods—application for judicial review.**   See *R v C & E Commrs (ex p. Kay & Co Ltd and Others)*, 45.23 PAYMENT OF TAX.

THE AWARD OF COSTS

Note. The cases under this heading are those which appear to raise points of general interest and are mainly separate applications for costs after the hearing of the appeal. In general a decision as to costs at the conclusion of the hearing is not referred to either here or in the note on the hearing, unless it raises a point of general interest in relation to costs.

Applications by the Commissioners

2.236   A partnership's appeal was listed for hearing on 13 March 1978. The partners did not attend and were not represented. A tribunal officer telephoned the partnership's accountant, and was told that a letter withdrawing the appeal had been posted on 9 March. The letter had not been received and the tribunal dismissed the appeal and awarded costs of £50 to the Commissioners. (The letter of withdrawal did in fact reach the Tribunal Centre on the following day, having been posted on 10 March by second-class post. The tribunal, in its decision, severely criticised the accountant's behaviour and regretted that it had no power to ensure that the accountant should pay the costs awarded.) *Slack & Taylor (t/a Olives), MAN/77/247 (VTD 537).*

2.237   In a case where an appellant failed to appear at the hearing of the appeal, the tribunal awarded costs of £100 to the Commissioners. The chairman observed that 'appellants who abandon appeals to these tribunals at the last moment or who do not attend to pursue their appeals or applications without reasonable explanation should be aware that an order for costs may be made against them'. *R Santi, MAN/80/38 (VTD 954).*

2.238   At the hearing of a company's appeal, the Commissioners were represented by three officers who gave evidence. The company was not represented and, during the hearing of the evidence, the tribunal received a letter from the company, stating that the appeal had been withdrawn. The tribunal awarded the Commissioners costs of £1,500. *Southern Girl Ltd, LON/84/160 (VTD 1803).*

2.239   In the case noted at 61.9 TRANSFERS OF GOING CONCERNS, where a company had purchased a business as a going concern, and had appealed against the disallowance of input tax, the tribunal held that the appeal was frivolous and an abuse of process, and awarded costs of £200 to the Commissioners. *Quadrant Stationers Ltd, LON/83/32 (VTD 1599).*

2.240   In a case where the tribunal upheld an estimated assessment charging tax of more than £1,700,000, the Commissioners applied for costs. The tribunal quoted from a statement by the then Financial Secretary to the Treasury, Mr Robert Sheldon in the House of Commons on 13 November 1978 (reproduced at *[1978] VATTR 266*), in which he stated that the Commissioners 'have concluded that, as a general rule, they should continue their policy of not seeking costs against unsuccessful appellants; however they will ask for costs in certain cases so as to provide protection for public funds and the general body of taxpayers. For instance, they will seek costs at those exceptional tribunal hearings of substantial and complex cases where large sums are involved and which are comparable with High Court cases, unless the appeal involves an important general point of law requiring clarification. The Commissioners will also consider seeking costs where the appellant has misused the tribunal procedure — for example, in frivolous or vexatious cases, or where the appellant has first produced at a hearing relevant evidence which ought properly to have been disclosed at an earlier stage and which could have saved public funds had it been produced timeously.' On the facts of the case, the Commissioners were awarded their costs, to be taxed by a Taxing Master. *Nose Cash & Carry Ltd, LON/87/311 (VTD 3763).* (*Note.* The *Rules of the Supreme Court 1965 (SI 1965 No 1776)*, and their precursors, refer to the 'taxation of costs', and to a 'Taxing Master'. With effect from 26 April

1999, these rules have largely been replaced by the *Civil Procedure Rules 1998 (SI 1998 No 3132)*, which refer instead to the 'assessment of costs', and to a 'costs judge'.)

2.241 In the case noted at 2.197 above, where an appeal against an estimated assessment was dismissed after a hearing lasting five days, the tribunal awarded costs of £5,657 to the Commissioners. *M Hanif, MAN/89/747 (VTD 7815)*.

2.242 In a case where the tribunal had upheld a penalty on a partnership under what is now *VATA 1994, s 60*, computed at the rate of 90% of the evaded tax, but had reduced the quantum of the assessment in respect of which the penalty was imposed, the Commissioners applied for costs of £6,390. The partnership contended that the costs claimed (most of which related to solicitors employed by the Commissioners) were excessive. The tribunal assessed the costs at £5,251, applying *dicta* in *Re Eastwood (decd), CA [1974] 3 All ER 603*, and directed that the partnership should pay two-thirds of this amount. *N Ahmed & K Akhtar (t/a The Albany Fish Bar), [1993] VATTR 262 (VTD 11509)*.

2.243 Following the decision in the case noted at 2.146 above, the Commissioners applied for costs. The tribunal granted the Commissioners' application, observing that the Parliamentary Statement reproduced at *[1978] VATTR 266* had indicated that the Commissioners would seek costs following 'tribunal hearings of substantial and complex cases where large sums are involved and which are comparable with High Court cases, unless the appeal involves an important general point of law'. Since the assessment in question charged tax of more than £1,300,000, this was clearly a case where 'large sums are involved' and there was nothing in the Parliamentary Statement to displace 'the general rule that costs should follow the event'. *University of Reading, [1998] VATDR 27 (VTD 15387)*.

2.244 In *CAL Ingot Manufacturers*, 49.353 PENALTIES: MISDECLARATION, the tribunal awarded costs of £600 to the Commissioners.

2.245 In *Isfa Management Ltd*, 47.17 PENALTIES: EVASION OF TAX, the tribunal awarded costs of £1,000 to the Commissioners.

2.246 Costs were also awarded to the Commissioners in *Ali*, 3.52 ASSESSMENT; *United Society of Poets Ltd*, 34.20 INPUT TAX, and *LMB Holdings Ltd*, 34.21 INPUT TAX.

2.247 There have been a number of other cases in which costs have been awarded to the Commissioners, where the tribunal has held that the appeal was 'frivolous and vexatious', and which appear to raise no point of general importance. In the interests of space, such cases are not reported individually in this book. For a list of such cases up to and including 30 September 1989, see Tolley's VAT Cases 1990.

2.248 **Expenses of Commissioners' representatives travelling from London to attend an Edinburgh appeal.** An appeal was listed for hearing in Edinburgh. The appellant did not attend and was not represented. The tribunal therefore dismissed the appeal. The Commissioners applied for costs in respect of two officers, one of whom was legally qualified, who had travelled from London to present their case. The tribunal held that the appellant should not be made 'liable for more than these services would cost locally, as both are available locally', and awarded total costs of £150. *A Whyte, EDN/79/4 (VTD 914)*.

2.249 A similar decision was reached in another Scottish case, where the appellant had telephoned on the morning of the hearing to state that he would not be attending. The Commissioners, who were represented by a member of their Solicitor's Office, were awarded costs of £320, but the expenses of travelling from London were not awarded, since the Commissioners could have obtained local legal representation. *WM Dempster, EDN/82/7 (VTD 1316).*

2.250   **Commissioners' expenses where representative engaged in other cases on the same day.**   In a Manchester case at which the appellant did not attend, the Commissioners were represented by a member of their Solicitor's Office, who had also been engaged in two other cases on the same day. The Commissioners applied for costs of £126. The tribunal took the view that the officer's expenses should be apportioned equally between the three cases in which he had been engaged, and awarded costs of £42. *The Eye Gee Co Ltd, MAN/81/154 (VTD 1269).*

2.251   **Tribunal awarding costs to Commissioners although no application for costs made by Commissioners.**   See the cases noted at 2.338 to 2.341 below.

Costs where the appellant was successful

2.252   Following a successful appeal against an estimated assessment, the appellant partnership made an application for costs. The tribunal found that the aggressive tone of a letter sent to the Commissioners by the partnership's accountants had led to a degree of animosity which was not conducive to a settlement between the parties and made a deduction for this in computing the award of costs. The partnership appealed to the QB which reversed the tribunal's decision on this point and awarded the partnership its costs in full, finding that a settlement had been inhibited by the contentions of the Commissioners rather than by those of the partnership. *L & E Zoungrou (t/a Highlands Steak House) v C & E Commrs, QB 1988, [1989] STC 313.*

2.253   In the case noted at 36.18 INSURANCE, the tribunal allowed a company's appeals against two assessments, holding on the evidence that the officer responsible for the assessments had not acted to the best of his judgment. However, the tribunal refused to award costs to the company, on the grounds that the company had given evidence which was untruthful. The QB dismissed the company's appeal against this decision. Lightman J held that it was clear, as a matter of principle and authority, that where a party had given false evidence on an issue relevant to the court's decision, the court could take that into account when deciding the question of costs. On the evidence, the tribunal was entitled to refuse to award the company the costs of its appeal. *Dicta of Parker LJ in Baylis Baxter Ltd v Sabath, CA [1958] 1 WLR 529; [1958] 2 All ER 209* applied. *North East Garages Ltd v C & E Commrs, QB [1999] STC 1057.*

2.254   A couple who owned a snack bar, and had successfully appealed against an estimated assessment, applied for costs. The tribunal refused the application, holding that an award of costs would be inappropriate in view of the appellants' uncooperative attitude to the Commissioners' officers. *Mr & Mrs AJ Williams (t/a Bridge St Snack Bar), CAR/77/191 (VTD 593).*

2.255   In a case where an assessment was reduced to £56, the tribunal awarded the appellant costs of £300. The appellant had also claimed tribunal costs of £916 in respect of his own time in relation to the appeal. The tribunal rejected this claim, holding that 'an appellant in a fiscal matter is not entitled to charge at profit costs for his attempts, even though successful, to avoid the effect of an assessment'. *GJ Hollingworth, MAN/77/278 (VTD 672).*

2.256   Following a successful appeal by a partnership which operated a restaurant, the tribunal awarded the appellants only half of their costs, holding that they were the architects of their own misfortune because of the unsatisfactory nature of their accounts and the late stage at which they had supplied essential information. *Yang Sing Chinese Restaurant, MAN/83/1 (VTD 1757).*

2.257   A similar decision was reached in a successful appeal against a misdeclaration penalty. *J & B Properties (Yorkshire) Ltd, MAN/92/988 (VTD 9912)*.

2.258   In the case noted at 7.40 BUSINESS, the tribunal rejected an application for costs by the successful appellant company, finding that the company had not made sufficient evidence available to the Commissioners before the hearing. *DS Supplies Ltd, MAN/95/884 (VTD 13559)*.

2.259   In the case noted at 63.103 VALUATION, the appellant applied for costs after the initial hearing. The Commissioners opposed the claim as the decision in the appellant's favour had been a decision in principle only, against which they had lodged an appeal to the QB, and they considered that the application was premature. The tribunal accepted the Commissioners' contention that it would be premature to award costs. *BH Bright, LON/88/1393X (VTD 4339)*. (*Note*. For a further subsequent application by the appellant, see 2.277 below.)

2.260   The successful appellant in the case noted at 48.81 PENALTIES: FAILURE TO NOTIFY applied for costs of more than £4,300, including more than £3,600 in respect of his accountant's services. The tribunal held that the accountant's claim to have written 41 letters and spent 63 hours on the case was excessive, and awarded costs of £2,300, representing £2,000 in respect of the accountant and £300 in respect of the appellant. *IW Dale, LON/87/562Z (VTD 4353)*.

2.261   In the case noted at 26.27 FINANCE, where the tax in dispute was £166,000, the tribunal awarded costs on the standard basis. The company claimed costs of more than £42,000, which the Commissioners objected to as excessive. The company had been represented by a leading firm of accountants, which had charged hourly rates of £186.30 for a tax partner, £117.35 for a tax senior manager and £91.10 for a tax manager. The tribunal held that these rates were reasonable, but held that the firm had spent excessive time both on the case itself and in preparing its analysis of, and claim for, costs. The tribunal awarded total costs of £30,941 (including £20,000 in respect of the accountants' charges and £8,500 in respect of counsel's fees). *Freight Transport Leasing Ltd, MAN/89/862 (VTD 7500)*. (*Note*. For another issue in this case, see 2.270 below.)

2.262   A company which had successfully appealed against a misdeclaration penalty applied for costs of £2,510, including £1,500 in respect of its accountants' fees (calculated on the basis of 12½ hours at £120 per hour). The Commissioners objected to the claim, contending that since the appeal had not involved any complex points of law, the amount of time claimed for was excessive. The tribunal rejected this contention, observing that the penalty imposed had been more than £57,000, and that the bill had only covered preparatory advice, since the accountants had not attended the hearing, at which the company had been represented by two of its officers. The tribunal upheld the claim of £1,500 in respect of the accountants, but reduced the claim in respect of the company's officers by £90, making a total award of £2,420. *Telstar Leisure Ltd, LON/91/2071X (VTD 9126)*.

2.263   A successful appellant company applied for costs of more than £7,500, including £3,375 in respect of its accountants; £3,028 in respect of a firm of VAT consultants whom the accountants had engaged to conduct the appeal; and £1,123 in respect of its own employees. The tribunal observed that the fee charged by the VAT consultants should not have exceeded £1,000, and awarded total costs of £3,500. *Small & Co Ltd, LON/91/255Y (VTD 9642)*.

2.264   A company, which had successfully appealed against a misdeclaration penalty, applied for costs of more than £5,000. £2,137 of the claim related to its solicitors; £2,000 to its accountants, and £1,002 to the company's own expenses, including 14 hours of the chairman's time. The tribunal accepted that the claim in respect of the solicitors was reasonable, but held that the claim in respect of the accountants should be reduced to £750, and that the claim for the company's own expenses was not allowable (except with regard to travelling expenses). The tribunal held that 'there was no logical distinction between a company and a litigant in person', so that the company was not entitled to claim costs in respect of the time expended by its chairman. *Rupert Page Developments Ltd, [1993] VATTR 152 (VTD 9823)*. (*Notes*. (1) This decision was not followed, and was implicitly disapproved, in the subsequent case of *Alpha International Coal Ltd*, 2.310 below. (2) Compare *GA Boyd Building Services Ltd*, 2.328 below, in which a tribunal awarded costs in respect of time spent by a company's director in preparing for an appeal, holding that the company was not affected by the provisions of the *Litigants in Person (Costs and Expenses) Act 1975*. See also the subsequent CA decision in *Jonathan Alexander Ltd v Proctor, CA 1995, [1996] 1 WLR 518; [1996] 2 All ER 334*, where the CA held that the term 'litigant in person' did not apply to a company represented by one of its directors.)

2.265   The successful appellant in the case noted at 1.4 AGENTS applied for costs, and the tribunal directed that the award be assessed by a Taxing Master. The appellant submitted claims for £67,827 in respect of loss of income from his business (which he had temporarily closed pending the hearing of the appeal) and for £17,172 in respect of loss of profit for the time he had spent on the case, together with interest. The Taxing Master rejected these claims and the CA upheld the Master's decision. The *Litigants in Person (Costs and Expenses) Act 1975* did not apply to VAT tribunals. Accordingly, an award of costs to a successful litigant in person could not exceed those costs recoverable at common law. The appellant could only recover out-of-pocket expenses and was not entitled to remuneration for the time he had spent in conducting the appeal. Since the costs were (by virtue of *Tribunals Rules, rule 29(5)*) a civil debt rather than a judgment debt, the appellant was also not entitled to interest on costs. *R Nader (t/a Try Us) v C & E Commrs, CA [1993] STC 806*. (*Note*. The *Rules of the Supreme Court 1965 (SI 1965 No 1776)*, and their precursors, refer to the 'taxation of costs', and to a 'Taxing Master'. With effect from 26 April 1999, these rules have largely been replaced by the *Civil Procedure Rules 1998 (SI 1998 No 3132)*, which refer instead to the 'assessment of costs', and to a 'costs judge'.)

2.266   A successful appellant company applied for costs of more than £18,000 (including £6,400 attributable to its solicitors, £3,600 attributable to its accountants, £5,000 attributable to one of its directors, and £3,500 attributable to counsel). The Commissioners agreed to pay costs attributable to counsel's fees, but refused to agree the remainder of the claim, considering that it was excessive. The tribunal reviewed the claim in detail and awarded £2,500 in respect of the solicitors' fees and £1,000 in respect of its accountants' fees, observing that the remainder of the amounts claimed related to work done before the appeal had been lodged. The tribunal rejected the company's claim for £5,000 attributable to work done by its director, observing that although the director was a qualified valuer, the bill in question did not relate to work 'done by him as a professional adviser'. *Broadway Video (Wholesale) Ltd, [1994] VATTR 271 (VTD 11935, 12446)*. (*Note*. The tribunal also held that the company was not entitled to interest on the costs—see 2.355 below.)

2.267   **Award of costs where appellant not legally represented.**   See the cases noted at 2.308 *et seq.* below.

2.268   **Award of costs where company appellant represented by director.**   See the cases noted at 2.319 *et seq.* below.

2.269   **Application for costs on indemnity basis.**   See the cases noted at 2.330 *et seq.* below.

2.270 **Failure by Commissioners to comply with award of costs.** In the case noted at 26.6 FINANCE, the tribunal made an interim award of costs of £10,000 to the appellant company pending the hearing of the application noted at 2.261 above. The Commissioners were ordered to pay this amount within one month. However, the Commissioners did not pay the sum in question until ten weeks after the date of the award. The tribunal met again to consider the award of a penalty against the Commissioners under what is now *VATA 1994, Sch 12 para 10*. The £10,000 had been paid by the time of this hearing, and the tribunal chose not to award any penalty. However, the tribunal rejected the Commissioners' contention that the provisions of *Sch 12 para 10* did not apply to the Commissioners, and commented that 'we strongly disapprove of the lack of efficiency which has led to the appellant's being deprived for over a month of a substantial sum of money to which it was entitled'. *Freight Transport Leasing Ltd, [1992] VATTR 120 (VTD 7000, 7515).*

2.271 **Award of costs where appellant represented by VAT consultant working on contingency basis.** In a case where an appeal had been allowed on the grounds that the Commissioners had failed to serve their Statement of Case within the prescribed time limits, the appellant applied for an award of the costs incurred by a VAT consultant who had represented him. The Commissioners objected to the claim on the grounds that the consultant had been working for the appellant on a contingency basis, and that if no award of costs were made, the appellant would have no liability to pay the consultant. The QB upheld the Commissioners' contentions and held that the amount claimed was not allowable. Macpherson J held that 'where a successful party has no liability to pay those acting for him, he has incurred no expense in respect of which an order for costs can be made in his favour'. *Gundry v Sainsbury [1910] 1 KB 645* applied. In the absence of an award of costs, the appellant had no liability to pay the consultant for his services. Accordingly, no award could be made. *C & E Commrs v VR Vaz, QB 1994, [1995] STC 14.* (*Note.* The tribunal had not issued a public report of its decision to allow the substantive appeal. Compare, however, *Young*, 2.123 above, and *Faccenda Chicken Ltd*, 2.126 above.)

Costs where the appellant was partly successful

2.272 In a case where an assessment had been reduced from £991 to £290, the appellant applied for costs of £756, the bulk of which were those of his accountants who represented him at the appeal. The tribunal awarded 70% of the admissible costs, based on the proportion by which the tax was reduced. In arriving at the admissible costs, it deducted £300 in respect of work which ought to have been done in relation to the rendering of the applicant's returns. (The tribunal also held that VAT should not be added to costs awarded to a taxable person and costs should be on a party to party basis.) *SK Ahmad, [1976] VATTR 128 (VTD 266).*

2.273 The Commissioners issued an estimated assessment on a partnership, charging tax of £2,769. On appeal, the assessment was reduced to £1,175. There had been an abortive first hearing of the appeal, and in the interval between the first and the second hearing the Commissioners had offered to reduce the assessment to £1,568, to which the partners did not respond. The partners applied for an award of costs. The tribunal observed that the need for an estimated assessment had arisen because the partners' records were defective, and the Commissioners could not be called on to bear the partners' costs because the estimate turned out to be excessive. *Ahmad*, 2.272 above, was distinguished because in that case there were errors of principle in the estimated assessment. (The partners were, however, awarded costs in respect of the first hearing because the adjournment had been caused by the Commissioners' failure to comply with *Tribunals Rules, rule 20*.) *J & J Brown (t/a Shaw's Bar), [1977] VATTR 253 (VTD 393).*

2.274   In a case where two assessments on a family partnership had been reduced to an agreed amount before the hearing, the partnership applied for costs. The senior partner, who was blind, had had to memorise details of the case, and the partnership applied for £670 in respect of his time, as well as for lesser amounts in respect of other staff. The QB held that a litigant in person was not entitled to an order for costs in respect of time expended in preparing a case to be heard by a VAT tribunal. The *Litigants in Person (Costs and Expenses) Act 1975* did not apply to VAT tribunals, and accordingly the tribunal's power under *rule 29* of the *Tribunals Rules* was confined to costs recoverable at common law. *Wendy Fair Market Club*, 2.314 below, approved. *C & E Commrs v DW Ross & Others, QB [1990] STC 353; [1990] 2 All ER 65.* (*Note.* The decision in this case was approved by the CA in *Nader*, 2.265 above.)

2.275   The appellant in the case noted at 34.401 INPUT TAX and 58.151 SUPPLY applied for costs. He had succeeded in one of the two issues in the appeal, but had been unsuccessful in the other. The Commissioners contended that in the circumstances there should be no award of costs. The tribunal rejected this contention and awarded the appellant one half of the costs of his appeal and the whole of the costs of the application. *EA Kilburn, MAN/87/277 (VTD 4866).*

2.276   The appellant company in the case noted at 20.16 EDUCATION subsequently applied for costs. The tribunal awarded costs of £340, including £250 in respect of the services of an accountant (representing five hours at £50 per hour). *North West Leicestershire Youth Training Scheme Ltd, MAN/88/548 (VTD 4929).*

2.277   The appellant in the case noted at 63.103 VALUATION applied for costs. The tribunal dismissed her application, holding that as her appeal had only succeeded with regard to 33.5% of her supplies, there should be no order as to costs. *BH Bright, LON/88/393 (VTD 5022).*

2.278   In a case where an estimated assessment had been reduced from £5,051 to £2,469, the appellant applied for costs. The tribunal held that the appellant was partly responsible for the assessment being raised as she had been dilatory in supplying information to the Commissioners, but awarded costs of £300 in respect of her accountant's services. The tribunal rejected a claim for costs in respect of the appellant's own time, applying the QB decision in *Ross*, 2.274 above, and holding that the *Litigants in Person (Costs and Expenses) Act 1975* had no application to VAT tribunals. *VD George, LON/89/1014Z (VTD 5072).*

2.279   In a case where an estimated assessment had been reduced from £46,000 to £28,060, the company applied for costs of more than £16,000. The Commissioners opposed the application, considering that the case had been prolonged by the behaviour of the company's accountant. The tribunal criticised the accountant for his lack of co-operation, but awarded the company one-half of the costs incurred after the date on which it lodged its appeal. (The company's application had included costs incurred before that date, which the tribunal held to be irrecoverable.) *Salina Ltd, LON/89/1823Y (VTD 6287).*

2.280   Following the decision in the case noted at 34.7 INPUT TAX, the appellant company applied for costs. The tribunal had dismissed the appeal in question, but the Commissioners had subsequently reduced the assessment under appeal by agreement, to take account of the view which the tribunal had expressed on an alternative issue. The tribunal rejected the application. It had dismissed the company's appeal after specifically finding that the supplies in dispute had not been made to the company. The views it had expressed on the alternative issue were *obiter dicta*. The Commissioners had been under no obligation to reduce the assessment, which they had done 'entirely within their discretion' and 'independently of the appeal'. In the circumstances, each party should pay its own costs with regard to the substantive appeal. The company was ordered to pay costs to the Commissioners in respect of the hearing of the application. *McLean Homes Midland Ltd (No 3), MAN/89/363 (VTD 6447)*.

2.281 In a case where an estimated assessment had been reduced from £4,082 to £20, the tribunal refused the appellant's application for an award of costs. The reduction in the assessment had been the result of the production by the appellant, at a late stage, of records which had not been available at the time of the control visits which resulted in the assessment. In the circumstances an award of costs was not appropriate. *Nathoo (t/a Kamona Enterprises), LON/91/1692 (VTD 6551)*.

2.282 In the case noted at 47.64 PENALTIES: EVASION OF TAX, the tribunal awarded costs to the appellant partnership, but declined to sanction an award requested by the partnership in regard to a barrister and solicitor who had both represented it, holding that the case could have been conducted by a solicitor alone. *Café Da Vinci & Da Vinci Too, EDN/90/132 (VTD 7634)*.

2.283 In the case noted at 34.415 and 34.458 INPUT TAX, where the appellant company had been partly successful, the tribunal strongly criticised the company's controlling director for having failed to co-operate with the Commissioners through not providing any information in support of the claims to input tax. On the evidence, the appeal had 'taken place mainly because of (the director's) refusal to give any reasons, until the hearing, as to why the two items might have been purchased for business purposes'. In the circumstances, the company was ordered to pay 75% of the Commissioners' total costs. *Remlock Design Ltd, LON/92/1124Y (VTD 9146)*.

2.284 A company appealed against a default surcharge, contending firstly that the amount of the surcharge was excessive since it had paid part of the tax before the due date, and secondly that it had a reasonable excuse for non-payment of the balance. Shortly before the hearing of the appeal the Commissioners accepted the company's first contention, admitting that the amount of the surcharge was excessive. At the hearing of the appeal, the tribunal rejected the company's second contention and upheld the reduced surcharge. However, the tribunal awarded costs to the company in respect of the time spent by its accountant in disputing the amount of the surcharge. *Retainco (51) Ltd (t/a The Royal Hotel), MAN/93/589 (VTD 11265)*.

2.285 Following the case noted at 47.74 PENALTIES: EVASION OF TAX, the appellant applied for costs. The tribunal rejected his application, observing that the validity of the assessment and penalty had been upheld and that the appellant had been found to have acted dishonestly, and holding that, despite the mitigation of the penalty, an award of costs was not appropriate. *Bright*, 2.277 above, applied; *Ahmad*, 2.272 above, distinguished. *JO Kyriacou, LON/92/2098A (VTD 12003)*.

2.286 In the case noted at 63.47 VALUATION, the appellant company applied for costs. The Commissioners opposed the application, contending firstly that there should be no award of costs since the appeal should have been stood over pending the CJEC decision in *Elida Gibbs Ltd*, 21.130 EUROPEAN COMMUNITY LAW, and alternatively that the award of costs should be restricted since, although the company had been successful on the issue relating to its output tax, it had been unsuccessful on an alternative contention relating to input tax (which had been the subject of the Court decisions noted at 2.137 above and 2.210 above). The tribunal rejected the Commissioners' first contention, observing that the facts in *Elida Gibbs Ltd* were distinguishable and might not have been determinative of the case. However, the tribunal accepted the Commissioners' second contention and awarded only 75% of the company's costs. The tribunal held that the input tax issue had been 'a separate issue' on which the appellant company had failed, and that the company should therefore 'be deprived of that part of its costs which related to the time spent in arguing (that) issue'. *Dicta* of Nourse LJ in *Re Elgindata (No 2), CA [1992] 1 WLR 1207; [1993] 1 All ER 232* applied. *Conoco Ltd, [1997] VATDR 47 (VTD 14814).*

2.287   **Appeal against assessment and penalty—appeal against assessment dismissed but appeal against penalty allowed—award of costs.**   In the case noted at 49.188 PENALTIES: MISDECLARATION, a trader had appealed against an assessment charging output tax and a misdeclaration penalty. The tribunal dismissed his appeal against the assessment in principle, but reduced the amount of the assessment, and allowed his appeal against the penalty on the grounds that he had a 'reasonable excuse' for the misdeclaration. The trader applied for costs of £3,700. The Commissioners opposed the application, firstly on the grounds that the appeal had only succeeded in part, and alternatively on the grounds that the trader's accountants had agreed that, if the appeal was unsuccessful, they would only charge him a total fee of £1,000. The tribunal rejected the Commissioners' contentions and allowed the trader's application in full, holding that it was 'irrelevant that only a short amount of time was spent arguing the issue of a serious misdeclaration penalty'. The fact that the accountants had agreed to reduce their fee if the appeal was unsuccessful was not relevant, since the appeal had been partly successful and they had therefore charged a fee of £3,700. *PJ Guntert (t/a Abingdon Scaffolding Co), LON/92/2183A (VTD 12127)*. (*Note.* Compare, however, the subsequent QB decision in *Vaz*, 2.271 above.)

2.288   **Appeal against assessment and penalty— assessment reduced but penalty upheld—award of costs.**   In the case noted at 47.6 PENALTIES: EVASION OF TAX, a partnership which operated a restaurant appealed against an assessment and a penalty under *VATA 1994, s 60*. The tribunal directed that the assessment should be reduced, but upheld the penalty. The Commissioners applied for costs. The tribunal observed that much of the evidence given by Customs' officers 'was of little or no use to us in coming to our decision', and directed that the appellants should only pay 85% of the Commissioners' costs. *Standard Tandoori Nepalese Restaurant, [2000] VATDR 105 (VTD 16597).*

Costs where Commissioners' decision or assessment is withdrawn

2.289   In order to arrive at its employees' emoluments for income tax, a hotel company entered in its pay sheets the value of any meals or accommodation it provided its employees without charge. The Commissioners assessed it on the basis that the amounts entered were the consideration for taxable supplies to the employees. The company appealed and the Commissioners subsequently withdrew the assessment. The tribunal awarded the company costs of £50. *Roxburghe Hotel Ltd, EDN/77/18 (VTD 456).*

2.290   In a case where a partnership had applied for costs of £4,090, the tribunal awarded costs of £626. *Nara Manufacturers, MAN/76/146 (VTD 603, 894).*

2.291   In a case where the Commissioners had withdrawn a default surcharge before the hearing, the appellant partnership sought costs in respect of bank interest which it had paid, contending that it would not have incurred the interest had it not had to pay the surcharge. The tribunal refused the partnership's claim, as the partnership had been at fault by not lodging an appeal against the surcharge at the appropriate time, but had lodged a late appeal after receiving a demand for payment. *Aladdin Window Co, MAN/88/12 (VTD 3026)*. (*Note.* The case was heard with *Newcastle Double Glazing Ltd*, 2.326 below.)

2.292   In a similar case, a trader applied for costs of £840. The tribunal awarded costs of £50 only, and awarded £30 to the Commissioners in respect of a summons the appellant had issued to a VAT officer, whose 'testimony could have no relevance to the issues'. *A Adley (t/a Jean Wenham), LON/89/1039 (VTD 4798).*

2.293   The Commissioners had attempted to deregister a trader as they had considered that he was not carrying on a business. The trader consulted a chartered accountant who made representations on his behalf, and the Commissioners subsequently accepted that his registration was valid. The trader applied for costs of £767, comprising £392 for the services of the accountant and £375 for the services of another adviser who had recommended the accountant. The tribunal allowed the £392 in respect of the accountant but only awarded £100 in respect of the adviser. The tribunal also awarded £75 in respect of the hearing of the application, making a total award of £567. *AJ Money, LON/90/669X (VTD 5655).*

2.294   The Commissioners issued an assessment on a partnership on 13 November 1990. On receipt of the assessment, the partnership telephoned its local VAT office to arrange a meeting to discuss the matter. The meeting was arranged for 23 November. On 20 November the partnership submitted a formal appeal against the assessment. At the meeting the partnership satisfied the VAT officers that the assessment was incorrect, and it was withdrawn. The partnership applied for costs in respect of its accountant's time in preparing for and attending the meeting. The Commissioners opposed any award, but the tribunal awarded costs of £309.70. The appeal had not been premature and costs incurred prior to proceedings were clearly allowable, applying *SA Pecheries Ostendaises v Merchants Marine Insurance Co, CA [1928] 1 KB 757* and *Frankenberg v Famous Lasky Film Service, [1931] 1 Ch 428. RM & DJ Jarrett, [1991] VATTR 435 (VTD 6670).*

2.295   *Jarrett*, 2.294 above, was applied in a case where the Commissioners had sought to register a college on the basis that it was conducted on a profit-making basis and was therefore ineligible for exemption under the legislation then in force, but had subsequently accepted that the college's supplies were exempt from VAT. The Commissioners contended that an award of costs was inappropriate since draft accounts which they had inspected indicated that the college was making substantial profits, and that the college had not initially indicated that the profits would be reinvested rather than distributed to its shareholders. The tribunal rejected this contention, holding that the college had not acted unreasonably and was entitled to an award of costs. Since the college had not submitted a quantified claim, the amount of the award was left to be determined by a Taxing Master of the Supreme Court. *Surrey College Ltd, [1992] VATTR 181 (VTD 9087).* (*Notes.* (1) The relevant supplies would now qualify for exemption under *VATA 1994, Sch 9, Group 6.* (2) The *Rules of the Supreme Court 1965 (SI 1965 No 1776)*, and their precursors, refer to the 'taxation of costs', and to a 'Taxing Master'. With effect from 26 April 1999, these rules have largely been replaced by the *Civil Procedure Rules 1998 (SI 1998 No 3132)*, which refer instead to the 'assessment of costs', and to a 'costs judge'.)

2.296   In a case where three assessments had been withdrawn, the appellants claimed costs totalling £6,300. £1,500 of this was attributable to the appellants' usual accountants, and £4,800 was attributable to a major firm of accountants who had been requested to assist with the case. The Commissioners contended that the claim was excessive, and that there had been a duplication of costs because of the use of two different firms of accountants. The tribunal awarded total costs of £4,500. *P Maxwell & B Hodges, LON/91/920, LON/91/1402 & LON/91/1436 (VTD 8887).*

2.297   In a case where a default surcharge had been withdrawn, the tribunal rejected an application by the appellant company for costs, observing that the company had been dilatory in providing evidence in support of its contentions. *SKN Electronics Ltd, MAN/92/1667 (VTD 10210).*

2.298   A similar decision was reached in a case where the tribunal found that a company had been dilatory in providing evidence in support of its claim to bad debt relief. *City Fine Wine plc, LON/93/1600A (VTD 12947)*.

2.299   In a case where the Commissioners had withdrawn a requirement for a company to provide security under what is now *VATA 1994, Sch 11 para 4*, the company applied for costs, and the tribunal awarded it costs of £750. *London Express Ltd, LON/93/1213A (VTD 12375)*.

2.300   In a case where costs were awarded to a sole trader following the withdrawal of an assessment, the tribunal chairman observed that the accountant's charges of £120 per hour were not 'unreasonable for an experienced practitioner in this highly specialised and contentious field'. *JC Dilley, LON/92/761 (VTD 12617)*.

2.301   The Commissioners issued an assessment on a trader who operated a removals business. He appealed, and the assessment was subsequently withdrawn by the Commissioners. The trader applied for costs. The Commissioners refused to pay his costs and the trader appealed to the tribunal. The tribunal dismissed his application, holding that the appeal had been settled by an agreement within what is now *VATA 1994, s 85*, and observing that 'if agreements are reached before any appeal is heard, then costs, if appropriate, would normally form part of any concluded agreement'. The tribunal chairman (Miss Plumptre, sitting alone) observed that she could 'find nothing in (*VATA 1994, s 83**) which would give this tribunal jurisdiction to hear this appeal'. *JJJ McGinty (t/a Alton Transport), LON/94/912A (VTD 12671)*. (*Note*. No cases were cited in the decision. Compare *Jarrett*, 2.294 above, and *Surrey College Ltd*, 2.295 above.)

2.302   In a subsequent appeal by the same trader, the tribunal again refused to make an award of costs. The tribunal held that, although it had jurisdiction under *Tribunals Rules, rule 29* to make an order for costs when an appeal had been determined under *VATA 1994, s 85*, any agreement to conclude an appeal should have the effect of disposing of the dispute between the parties. Accordingly, any application for costs should either have been incorporated in the agreement, or brought to the attention of the tribunal at the time the agreement was recorded, or dealt with within the 30–day 'cooling-off' period provided by *s 85(2)*. *JJJ McGinty (t/a Alton Transport), [1995] VATDR 193 (VTD 13463)*. (*Note*. The decision here discusses the decision in *Taylor*, 2.39 above, but does not refer to *Jarrett*, 2.294 above, or *Surrey College Ltd*, 2.295 above.)

2.303   A medical partnership appealed against a ruling by the Commissioners. After correspondence, the Commissioners withdrew the ruling. The partnership's accountant claimed costs of £7,500 plus VAT. The Commissioners considered that the claim was excessive, and offered to pay £2,864 plus VAT. The tribunal awarded costs of £4,250 plus VAT. The accountant also claimed further costs of £5,235 plus VAT in respect of the hearing. The tribunal held that this was 'excessive', and awarded £1,500 plus VAT. *Dr GP Ridsdill-Smith & Partners, LON/99/1250 (VTD 16992)*.

2.304   **Assessment issued because of misleading information given to VAT officer.**   In a case where the Commissioners withdrew an assessment under appeal, the tribunal refused the appellant's application for costs, finding that the need for an assessment had arisen because the appellant had given inaccurate information to VAT officers. *D Lawton, MAN/77/237 (VTD 576)*.

2.305   A similar decision was reached in *KJ Gagliardi, CAR/78/29 (VTD 667)*.

2.306   **Further proceedings stayed, subject to the award of costs.**   In May 1979 the Commissioners issued a ruling that certain supplies by the British Institute of

Management (BIM) were exempt. Because of BIM's input tax position, it was in its interest for the supplies to be treated as standard-rated. BIM therefore appealed and the appeal was fixed for hearing on 30 October 1979. Shortly before that date, the Commissioners informed BIM that they were withdrawing their decision and agreed that the supplies were still standard-rated. The tribunal awarded BIM costs of £1,720 (but rejected BIM's application for costs incurred prior to receipt of the Commissioners' ruling in May 1979). *British Institute of Management (No 2), [1980] VATTR 42 (VTD 900).*

2.307 **Costs claimed on indemnity basis.** The Commissioners issued an assessment charging tax of more than £650,000 on a company which supplied and fitted hearing aids. The Commissioners subsequently accepted the company's contention that the fitting of hearing aids was an exempt supply at the relevant time, and withdrew the assessment. The company applied for costs on the indemnity basis. The tribunal rejected this contention, applying *Bowen-Jones v Bowen-Jones, [1986] 3 All ER 163,* and holding that 'an award of costs on the indemnity basis will only be made in exceptional circumstances'. The tribunal approved an award of costs on the standard basis, to be taxed by a district registrar under *VAT Tribunals Rules 1986, rule 29(1)(b). Ultratone Ltd, MAN/90/299 (VTD 5536).* (*Notes.* (1) The supply of hearing aids is no longer exempt following changes to what is now *VATA 1994, Sch 9, Group 7* by *FA 1988.* Compare *Coleman,* 31.31 HEALTH AND WELFARE. (2) For cases where costs were awarded on the indemnity basis, see 2.330 *et seq.* below.)

Costs where the appellant was not legally represented

2.308 **Company appellant represented by director.** See the cases noted at 2.319 *et seq.* below.

2.309 **Appellant represented by chartered accountant.** A trader who had successfully appealed against an estimated assessment applied for costs of £2,201, comprising the costs of the services of the chartered accountant who had conducted the matter on her behalf, plus the costs of the application itself. The Commissioners opposed the application, contending that 'costs' in *Tribunals Rules, rule 29* should be confined to 'legal costs', i.e. costs recoverable in the High Court and amounts charged by solicitors. The tribunal rejected this. Under *Tribunals Rules, rule 25* 'any person' may represent an appellant and it would be 'contrary to natural justice and to the construction of *rules 25* and *29* to hold that a party is entitled to recover the taxed costs of his solicitor for conducting an appeal on his behalf whereas he is precluded from recovering the taxed costs of his accountant for performing precisely the same task, and possibly with more expertise so far as figures are concerned.' Accordingly the tribunal awarded the amount claimed (except for the costs relating to the unsuccessful interlocutory application noted at 2.36 above). *K Taylor (t/a Jeans), MAN/75/5 (VTD 163B).*

2.310 The successful appellant company in the case noted at 1.66 AGENTS applied for costs of £944. The company had been represented at the hearing by its company secretary, a certified accountant who was not a shareholder in the company. The Commissioners opposed the application, contending that since the accountant held the post of company secretary, the company should be treated as a litigant in person, so that, applying *Rupert Page Developments Ltd,* 2.264 above, costs should only be awarded in respect of out-of-pocket expenses. The tribunal rejected this contention, holding that the accountant was acting as an 'independent adviser', so that the company was not subject to the restrictions imposed upon a litigant in person. The tribunal awarded the company costs of £944 in accordance with its claim, together with a further £318 in respect of the hearing of the application. *Alpha International Coal Ltd, LON/92/79 (VTD 11441).*

2.311 **Housing Association represented by one of its officers.** A Housing Association, which was a registered charity, provided rented accommodation for people on low incomes. The Commissioners issued a ruling that tax was chargeable on certain work done on houses owned by the Association. The Association appealed, contending that the work was zero-rated under the legislation then in force. The Association was represented by its Deputy Surveyor (K), who was an Associate of the Royal Institute of Chartered Surveyors but otherwise had no professional qualifications. The appeal was successful and the Association applied for costs, made up mainly of amounts for the time spent by K in preparing and presenting the appeal. The hours and hourly rates were not disputed, but the Commissioners contended that K's costs were not allowable as he was not a qualified solicitor. The tribunal rejected this contention and allowed the claim in full. *Re Eastwood (decd), CA [1974] 3 All ER 603*, and *K Taylor*, 2.309 above, applied. *The Sutton Housing Trust (No 1), LON/81/160 (VTD 1198)*.

2.312 The applicant in the case noted at 2.311 above later made a similar application (for costs of £829) following its success in a subsequent appeal. The Commissioners again contended that K's time in preparing (as distinct from presenting) the appeal was not allowable. The tribunal again rejected this and awarded costs of £763, applying *British Institute of Management (No 2)*, 2.306 above. *The Sutton Housing Trust (No 2), LON/82/149 (VTD 1296)*.

2.313 A similar decision was reached in *Orbit Housing Association, LON/84/73 (VTD 1783)*.

2.314 **Club represented by committee member.** In the case noted at 39.4 LAND, a club had successfully appealed against the disallowance of input tax. The club's appeal had been conducted by one of its committee members (H). The club applied for costs of £1,643, of which £1,600 represented H's 'remuneration' for preparing and attending the appeal at £10 per hour. The tribunal rejected this claim, holding that in the circumstances of the case H should be treated as a litigant in person and could only recover his out-of-pocket expenses. The tribunal noted that the *Litigants in Person (Costs and Expenses) Act 1975* did not apply to appeals to a VAT tribunal. *Wendy Fair Market Club (No 1), LON/77/400 (VTD 679, 833)*. (*Note*. The decision here was approved by the QB in *C & E Commrs v DW Ross & Others*, 2.274 above.)

2.315 **Partnership appellant represented by partner.** In the case noted at 58.354 SUPPLY, the appellant partnership was unsuccessful at the tribunal but was successful in the Court of Appeal. The partnership, which had been represented by the senior partner (R), applied for costs. The tribunal directed that the determination of the partnership's costs should be referred to the Taxing Master. The chairman observed that 'normally this tribunal would treat a partner as a litigant in person and award him his out-of-pocket expenses. This is because the *Litigants in Person (Costs and Expenses) Act 1975, s 1(1)*, which might otherwise authorise an award of a sum in respect of work done and expenses or losses incurred, does not apply to tribunal proceedings'. The chairman noted that R now claimed that he had not conducted the appeal in his capacity as a partner, but in the capacity of an employee of one of the other partners, although R had produced no written evidence to support his claim. The chairman observed that 'a thorough investigation was needed ... into the basis of and *bona fides* of (R's) assertions. The hearing before the Taxing Master might be an appropriate occasion to conduct the enquiry.' *BJ Rice & Associates, LON/91/1370 (VTD 14659)*. (*Note*. The *Rules of the Supreme Court 1965 (SI 1965 No 1776)*, and their precursors, refer to the 'taxation of costs', and to a 'Taxing Master'. With effect from 26 April 1999, these rules have largely been replaced by the *Civil Procedure Rules 1998 (SI 1998 No 3132)*, which refer instead to the 'assessment of costs', and to a 'costs judge'.)

2.316 Appeals

2.316   See also *DW Ross & Others*, 2.274 above.

2.317   **Appellant represented by person with no professional qualifications.** A successful appellant (H) was represented by K, who was a law graduate and practised as a consultant, but had no professional or accountancy qualifications. H claimed costs of £2,594 represented mainly by the time of K, his clerk and his typist, which were charged at £30, £20 and £9 per hour for each respectively, plus a 35% uplift for K. The tribunal considered the hourly rates charged excessive and substituted £15 (with no uplift), £10 and £6 for K, his clerk and his typist respectively. After examining the itemised bill in detail, it awarded total costs of £582. Items wholly disallowed included those incurred because of H's neglect or because of a postponement of the appeal made to suit his convenience. *GA Harrison, [1982] VATTR 7 (VTD 1182)*.

2.318   **Application for costs by unrepresented sole appellant.** The tribunal allowed an appeal against a misdeclaration penalty after finding that the penalty assessments had been computed incorrectly. The successful appellant applied for costs. The tribunal held that, applying the QB decision in *Ross*, 2.274 above, no award could be made in respect of the time of a litigant in person, and awarded £50 to cover the appellant's expenses. *A Sprake (t/a Sprake & Tyrell), LON/92/1300P (VTD 10391)*.

Costs where company appellant represented by director

2.319   In the case noted at 9.1 CARS, the company claimed costs of £116.60 including £60 for the time spent by its director in preparing for and conducting the appeal and £15 for his travelling expenses, in addition to those already awarded, because he had travelled by Rolls Royce. The tribunal disallowed the £60 because it was not an expense incurred by the company and the £15 because the Commissioners cannot be expected to bear the extra cost of travelling by Rolls Royce. The remaining items claimed were disallowed as not being expenses of the appeal. *Chartcliff Ltd, LON/76/73 (VTD 302)*.

2.320   A company had appealed against an assessment of £1,864 made in March 1976. In September 1976 the Commissioners notified it that the assessment would be withdrawn. The company then applied to the tribunal for an award of costs, including £3 per hour for the time of one of its directors. The tribunal disallowed this, applying *Chartcliff Ltd*, 2.319 above, but awarded costs in respect of the remaining items on a party to party basis. *Rupert Page Developments Ltd, LON/76/64 (VTD 379)*. (*Note.* For a subsequent appeal by the same company, see 2.264 above.)

2.321   In the case noted at 56.5 SECOND-HAND GOODS, the appellant company had been represented by its managing director and claimed costs including £100 for its estimated loss of earnings because of the director's absence from its business for the day of appeal. The tribunal held that, as the director had been present as advocate as well as witness, the company was entitled to the cost of his services. As his average daily remuneration was £34, it considered £50 a day as reasonable for his services and allowed £100 to cover the day of the hearing plus half a day in preparing for the appeal and half a day for the hearing of the application for costs. *Re Nossen's Patent, Ch D [1969] 1 All ER 775* and *Re Eastwood (decd), CA [1974] 3 All ER 603*, applied. *Jocelyn Feilding Fine Arts Ltd, LON/78/81 (VTD 749)*.

2.322   The Commissioners had issued a ruling that a company was required to register for VAT, and the company appealed, contending that its supplies were exempt. Following the decision against them in *Tameside Metropolitan Borough Council, 39.5 LAND*, the Commissioners withdrew their ruling and the company applied for an award of £1,234 for costs incurred in preparing for the appeal. This included £400 for the work done by one of its directors (at £10 an hour) in preparing the appeal and an amount representing the director's expenses in attending (apparently as an onlooker) the *Tameside* appeal. The tribunal awarded total costs of £400, comprising £300 for legal expenses and £100 for the work done by the company director. The tribunal held that the costs incurred in attending the *Tameside* appeal were not allowable. *Meshberry Ltd, LON/78/384 (VTD 835).*

2.323   The successful appellant company in the case noted at 38.52 INVOICES AND CREDIT NOTES was represented by one of its directors. It applied for an award of costs including £360 (£60 a day) for the work done by the director and £132 for the services of two other employees who assisted him in preparing the appeal. The Commissioners opposed the claim, contending that it was excessive. The director's salary was £15,000 per annum. The tribunal held that the amounts were reasonable and, applying *Jocelyn Feilding Fine Arts Ltd*, 2.321 above, were allowable except in so far as they related to the period prior to the Notice of Appeal. The tribunal awarded costs of £390 (£300 for the director and £90 for the other employees). *Kleen Technologies International Ltd, LON/80/66 (VTD 1005).*

2.324   A private company had appealed against an assessment relating to certain transactions in silver bars, contending that it had acted as an agent in the transactions and not as an independent principal. In the event, the Commissioners accepted the company's view and agreed to limit the assessment to tax on the company's commission. The company claimed costs of £420 for the time spent by the directors in preparing for the appeal (representing 42 hours at £10 per hour). The tribunal rejected this claim, applying *Rupert Page Developments Ltd*, 2.320 above, but awarded £50 in respect of the costs incurred by the director and his wife at the hearing. *Investment Chartwork Ltd, [1981] VATTR 114 (VTD 1093).* (*Note.* The reasoning here was disapproved in *GW Martin & Co Ltd*, 2.325 below. The costs of preparing for an appeal were allowed in the subsequent cases of *Nulmay Ltd*, 2.327 below, and *GA Boyd Building Services Ltd*, 2.328 below.)

2.325   In the appeal noted at 34.252 INPUT TAX, the successful appellant company was represented by its managing director (GW). It subsequently applied for costs of £2,845. This included £1,120 for the time spent by GW in preparing for and attending the appeal, a similar amount of £540 for another director (R), £961 for the work carried out by a third director (GP) who was a practising chartered accountant, and disbursements of £224. The tribunal reviewed the evidence in detail and awarded costs of £1,024 (comprising £280 in respect of GW, £520 in respect of GP, nothing in respect of R, and the disbursements of £224). The awards in respect of GW and GP were calculated on the basis of an hourly rate of £20. The claim in respect of R was disallowed on the grounds that he had attended the appeal as a witness and his preparation time was mostly spent in preparing the proof of his evidence. *Jocelyn Feilding Fine Arts Ltd*, 2.321 above, and *Re Eastwood (decd), CA [1974] 3 All ER 603*, applied. *Investment Chartwork Ltd*, 2.324 above, was not followed, on the grounds that it was inconsistent with the decision in *Re Eastwood*. *GW Martin & Co Ltd, LON/83/263 (VTD 1448).*

2.326   Following a successful appeal in one of the cases noted at 18.104 DEFAULT SURCHARGE, the company applied for costs in respect of wages or salaries for its employees when attending the hearing. The tribunal refused the application, holding that the amounts sought were not properly recoverable. The company was, however, awarded costs of £275 in respect of its accountant's services. *Newcastle Double Glazing Ltd, MAN/88/13 (VTD 3026).* (*Note.* The case was heard with *Aladdin Window Co*, 2.291 above.)

2.327   Following a successful appeal in one of the cases noted at 18.97 DEFAULT SURCHARGE, the company applied for costs totalling £633.50. The Commissioners offered to pay £255, but the company rejected this offer and appealed to the tribunal. The tribunal held that the company should be awarded costs at the rate of £35 per hour for a period of nine hours (four hours for preparing the appeal and five hours for attending the hearing), together with travelling expenses of £31.50, making a total award of £346.50 in respect of the appeal against the surcharge. In addition, the company was awarded a further £271.50 in respect of the hearing of the application. *Nulmay Ltd, MAN/90/52 (VTD 6627)*.

2.328   Following a successful appeal in one of the cases noted at 49.50 PENALTIES: MISDECLARATION, the appellant company, which had been represented by its director, applied for costs of £426.40, including £280 in respect of time spent by its director in preparing for the appeal (computed on the basis of 6 hours at £35 per hour). The Commissioners opposed the application, contending that it was not appropriate to make any award in respect of the time spent by the director in preparing for the hearing. The tribunal granted the application in full, observing that the company was not affected by the provisions of the *Litigants in Person (Costs and Expenses) Act 1975*, and holding that the amount claimed was reasonable. *Jocelyn Feilding Fine Arts Ltd*, 2.321 above, and *Nulmay Ltd*, 2.327 above, applied. (The tribunal awarded a further £146.40 in respect of the hearing of the application.) *GA Boyd Building Services Ltd, [1993] VATTR 26 (VTD 9788)*.

2.329   See also *Broadway Video (Wholesale) Ltd*, 2.266 above.

Application for costs on indemnity basis

2.330   A company which carried on a retail clothing business successfully appealed against an estimated assessment. The tribunal awarded costs to the company on the indemnity basis. The VAT officer responsible for the assessment had suggested that there had been large-scale defalcations, but the tribunal considered that this allegation was 'without foundation and not reasonably capable of belief'. The company's records were good, and the assessment had not been made to the best of the Commissioners' judgment. There had been 'a level of competence in the investigation and assessment below that which the taxpaying public has a right to expect'. *KTS Fashions Ltd, LON/90/505 (VTD 6782)*.

2.331   In March 1988 the Commissioners issued an assessment, charging VAT of more than £104,000, on a partnership which had operated five garages. The assessment was based on allegations made by a former member of the partnership, who had not taken any active part in the running of the business, and had taken High Court proceedings against his former colleagues. The partnership appealed against the assessment, contending that it was excessive and had not been made to the best of the Commissioners' judgment. In March 1992, after prolonged correspondence and several meetings, the Commissioners reduced the assessment to £3,152. The partnership accepted this liability and withdrew the appeal. However, the partnership applied to the tribunal for an award of costs on the indemnity basis, contending that the Commissioners' conduct 'had throughout been so unreasonable and exceptional that an order for costs on an indemnity basis was appropriate'. The tribunal reviewed the evidence and held that the assessment had not been made to the best of the Commissioners' judgment, applying *dicta* of Woolf J in *Van Boeckel*, 3.1 ASSESSMENT. The officer responsible for the assessment 'had not fairly considered' information supplied by the partnership's accountants. On the evidence, 'if he had fairly considered the material put before him he would have realised that the assessment was for an amount in excess of any that could possibly be due'. Medd J held, applying *dicta* of Glidewell LJ in *Burgess v Stafford Hotel Ltd, CA [1990] 3 All ER 222*, that costs should only be awarded on an indemnity basis if the Commissioners had 'acted disgracefully to such an extent as to make this a wholly exceptional case'. In this case, the officer responsible for the assessment had not fairly considered information supplied by the partnership, either before the issue of the assessment or on a number of subsequent occasions 'both in writing and at meetings'. It appeared 'that he had convinced himself that a massive fraud had taken place and that any argument put forward which suggested to the contrary (*sic*) could not be sound and therefore need not be considered with care'. The officer who succeeded him was not trained in investigation work, and had 'adopted the same approach'. As a result, the partnership had incurred costs which were 'enormous' and 'very much larger than they need have been'. The conduct of the two VAT officers had been 'so exceptional that an order for costs on an indemnity basis was appropriate'. *H & B Motors (Dorchester), LON/88/821 (VTD 11209).*

2.332   In the case noted at 14.7 COLLECTION AND ENFORCEMENT, where the tribunal had allowed an appeal against a notice requiring security, the tribunal awarded costs to the appellant company on the indemnity basis. The tribunal chairman held, on the evidence, that the Commissioners 'did not take reasonable steps to ascertain the full and correct facts before issuing the notice'. The Commissioners' Statement of Case had contained factual inaccuracies, and had not 'set out accurately and fully all the grounds on which the decision was taken'. On the evidence, it appeared that the notice had been issued 'for an unauthorised purpose', namely to recover money owed by a company in a different ownership, the trade of which had been taken over by the appellant company. The tribunal observed that 'if Customs and Excise have used the power for an unauthorised purpose, they must bear all the financial costs borne by the taxpayer in getting the decision set aside'. *VSP Marketing Ltd, LON/94/794A (VTD 12636).*

2.333   Following the decision noted at 2.332 above, the Commissioners paid the appellant company costs of £30,000 relating to work done by its accountants. The company applied for further costs relating to work done by its solicitors. The Commissioners opposed the application on the grounds that the company had been represented by its accountants and that the costs sought in respect to the solicitors related to periods before the issue of the notice which was the subject of the appeal. The company applied to the tribunal for a ruling that the Commissioners should pay the costs sought in respect of its solicitors. The tribunal dismissed the application, holding that, if the parties were unable to agree on the amount of costs to be awarded, the matter should be the subject of a further hearing before the tribunal chairman who had determined the original appeal, and that it would not be proper to make any such preliminary ruling as the company had sought. *VSP Marketing Ltd (No 2), LON/94/794A (VTD 13167).*

2.334   Following the decision noted at 2.333 above, the appellant company applied for costs of more than £26,000 relating to work done by its solicitors and more than £38,900 in relation to work done by its accountants. The solicitors' costs were based on 58 hours at £450 per hour. The accountants' costs were based on £200 per hour for work done by an employed barrister, £250 per hour for an employed solicitor, and £469 per hour for a partner. Some of the costs which the company claimed related to work done before the date on which the disputed notice requiring security was issued. The Commissioners objected to the claim, contending that it was unreasonable to have incurred the costs of three lawyers and that the hourly charging rates of the solicitors' firm, and the partner in the accountancy firm, were unreasonable. They also contended that no costs should be awarded in respect of work done before the notice requiring security was issued. The tribunal upheld this contention, holding that its 'only jurisdiction is to award a sum of costs of and incidental to and consequent on the appeal'. Until the Commissioners had made a decision against which an appeal could be lodged, there was no appealable matter so that costs incurred before then could not be costs of the appeal. *Dicta* of Lord Grantchester in *British Institute of Management*

(*No 2*), 2.306 above, applied. The tribunal also held on the evidence that this was not 'a case which at any stage warranted the services of lawyers from two different firms', and observed that 'by the time the security notice was issued the accountancy firm were so firmly in charge of the proceedings that the services of the law firm partner were not reasonably warranted save and so far as specific research was required in order to assist the accountancy firm in the presentation of the case'. With regard to the charging rates, the tribunal held that the rate charged for the partner in the accountancy firm should not have exceeded £320 per hour (i.e. a basic rate of £200 per hour with a 60% mark-up), and that the rate charged by the solicitors' firm should not have exceeded £300 per hour. The result was the tribunal awarded costs of £26,834 in respect of the work done by the accountancy firm and £3,600 in respect of the work done by the solicitors' firm. *VSP Marketing Ltd (No 3), [1995] VATDR 328 (VTD 13587).*

2.335   An application for costs to be awarded on the indemnity basis was rejected in *Ultratone Ltd*, 2.307 above, where an assessment had been withdrawn before the hearing and the tribunal observed that 'an award of costs on the indemnity basis will only be made in exceptional circumstances'.

Miscellaneous

2.336   **Costs when parties compromise.**   After the hearing of a company's appeals had begun, there was an adjournment, during which the company and the Commissioners came to a compromise agreement. On the resumption of the hearing, the company's solicitor applied for an award of costs. The tribunal rejected the application, holding that if a party to an appeal wholly concedes his case, the tribunal can consider an award of costs, but where the parties reach a compromise agreement, the tribunal cannot continue the hearing purely in relation to costs. If one side is to be recompensed for costs, the compromise agreement must provide for this. *The Cadogan Club Ltd, LON/76/202, LON/77/194 (VTD 548).*

2.337   **Costs where third party joined in appeal.**   In the case noted at 2.41 above, the tribunal granted an application that a third party should be joined in an appeal. (The appeal was by the recipient of the services in dispute, and the third party was the supplier of those services.) The appellant company (B) applied for a direction that the third party (V) should not seek costs. The tribunal granted the application, holding that to put an appellant 'at risk for the costs of one or more other parties who subsequently establish their right to be joined could be a serious disincentive to his freedom to exercise the right of appeal'. *Barclays Bank plc v C & E Commrs and Visa International Service Association, LON/91/1159Y (VTD 9059).*

2.338   **Tribunal awarding costs to Commissioners although no application for costs made by Commissioners.**   In a case where an appeal by a firm of solicitors was dismissed, the Commissioners did not apply for costs but the tribunal nevertheless made an award of costs to the Commissioners, as a mark of 'concern at the ignorance of law and the function and procedures of the tribunal which the appellants have displayed, which is aggravated by the fact that they are a firm of practising solicitors and should know better'. *Houston Stewart, EDN/91/236 (VTD 9526).*

2.339   A VAT officer on a control visit discovered that a two-partner firm of solicitors had failed to account for VAT on receipts of more than £16,000. The solicitors were unable to provide a satisfactory explanation of this, and the Commissioners issued an assessment. The firm appealed, but neither of the solicitors attended the hearing. Six minutes before the hearing was due to start, the tribunal clerk received a faxed letter from the firm requesting an adjournment. The tribunal refused the application, dismissed the appeal, and awarded costs of £400 to the Commissioners, observing that this was 'a case where the two solicitors have no excuse for their lack of co-operation both with Customs and with this tribunal'. *Musgrave & Larkin (Solicitors), LON/92/2119A (VTD 10885).*

2.340 In the cases noted at 10.6 CASH ACCOUNTING SCHEME and 38.41 INVOICES AND CREDIT NOTES, where an invoice issued between associated companies was held to be a sham, the tribunal held that the companies had pursued their appeals 'on a vexatious and frivolous basis', and awarded costs of £1,000 to the Commissioners. *FPV Ltd, MAN/97/828; Marketing Middle East Ltd, MAN/97/1110 (VTD 15666).*

2.341 In the case noted at 34.17 INPUT TAX, where the tribunal found that a company had reclaimed input tax in respect of false invoices, the tribunal awarded costs of £2,000 to the Commissioners. *Realm Defence Industries Ltd, LON/98/799 (VTD 16831).*

2.342 **Appeal by Commissioners against High Court decision—whether Court of Appeal should impose restrictions as to costs.** In the case noted at 3.70 ASSESSMENT, the QB found in favour of the appellant company, and the Commissioners appealed to the CA. The company applied to the CA for a ruling that the QB award of costs to the company should not be disturbed, and that the Commissioners should bear the costs of both parties in the CA. The CA rejected the application, holding that the costs of the appeal to the QB should follow the result of the appeal to the CA, in accordance with normal principles. Sir Thomas Bingham MR observed that the CA 'would not wish to countenance a general rule that tax-collecting bodies can only collect small sums of revenue at their own expense'. However, in the circumstances of the case the CA imposed a condition that the Commissioners should not seek to disturb the award of costs to the company in respect of the tribunal hearing, and that, if the Commissioners' appeal to the CA was successful, each side should pay its own costs in respect of that appeal. *C & E Commrs v Le Rififi Ltd, CA [1994] STC 383.* (*Note.* The CA subsequently allowed the Commissioners' appeal on the substantive issue.)

2.343 **Appeal dismissed but costs awarded to appellant.** In a case where an appeal was dismissed, the tribunal found that the appellant had been misdirected by a VAT officer and directed that he should be awarded his costs. *JR Ness, EDN/93/116 (VTD 11559).*

2.344 In a case where an appeal against the disallowance of input tax was dismissed after a hearing lasting for five days (with an interval of six months between the second and third days), the tribunal found that the appeal had been prolonged by the conduct of the Commissioners' Solicitors' Office, and directed that the appellant should be awarded 40% of his costs. The tribunal found that the Solicitors' Office had been dilatory in disclosing documents to the appellant's agent, and that this had caused the agent additional work. On the evidence, the agent had been 'dealt with in a most unhelpful manner by the Solicitors' Office when he quite properly attempted to have rectified, for the reconvened hearing, matters which should have been before the tribunal at the outset ... had everything been conducted as it should have been by the Commissioners, the case would not have lasted five days.' *YY & MV Patel (t/a Rumi Clothing), MAN/96/489 (VTD 15268).*

2.345 **Commissioners failing to comply with directions by tribunal—award of costs.** The Commissioners had issued a ruling that certain building work undertaken by a charity failed to qualify for zero-rating. The charity appealed, and the appeal was stood over pending a CA decision (see *Jubilee Hall Recreation Centre Ltd,* 52.8 PROTECTED BUILDINGS). In September 1999 the tribunal issued a direction requiring the Commissioners to serve a Statement of Case by 8 October. The

Commissioners served the Statement of Case on 25 October. On 26 October the tribunal made several directions, which the charity complied with but the Commissioners did not. On 25 November the tribunal sent a form T19 to both parties. The charity responded but, despite a subsequent reminder, the Commissioners failed to do so. In January 2000 the case was listed for hearing by the tribunal chairman (Mr. Oliver), who awarded costs against the Commissioners, observing that 'the tribunal is concerned with the repeated failures of the Solicitors' Office (of the Commissioners) to respond to T19 letters. The matter has been taken up with the office on several occasions in the past. Moreover, in this case the Solicitors' Office had been out of time in providing the Statement of Case and had only done so in the teeth of a coercive direction from the tribunal. The Statement of Case, when it arrived, had been exiguous in the extreme and has been the subject of an application by the appellant for further and better particulars which I have allowed. The excuse offered by the solicitor for the Commissioners was that the T19 letter had been misfiled. That would have been unfortunate if it had happened only once. As it is two T19 letters went unanswered and I do not accept that both were misfiled. Taxpayers must not be prejudiced by official delays. The problems of a charity seeking to reclaim input tax are more acute than most and a proper standard of efficiency is demanded from the Commissioners in dealing with these.' *London Federation of Clubs for Young People, LON/97/283 (VTD 16477)*.

2.346   See also *Faccenda Chicken Ltd*, 2.126 above.

THE AWARD OF INTEREST (VATA 1994, s 84(8))

2.347   A company had supplied certain goods to an individual (M) in connection with work on his house. The Commissioners considered that the supply was standard-rated. The company accepted this, accounting for the relevant tax of £65 and charging it to the customer. M did not accept the Commissioners' view and, after paying the amount to the company 'without prejudice', appealed on the ground that the supply was zero-rated under the legislation then in force. The tribunal allowed the appeal and M applied for interest on the amount repayable to him. The Commissioners opposed the application, contending that the amount repayable had not been paid or deposited with them, within the meaning of what is now *VATA 1994, s 84(8)*. The tribunal rejected this contention and allowed interest at 10% per annum (the rate which M had applied for). *WJM Mahoney, [1976] VATTR 241 (VTD 258)*.

2.348   In a case where the substantive issue has been overtaken by subsequent changes in the legislation, the QB allowed an appeal by a parish church council. The tax in dispute was refunded to the council, which then applied for interest under what is now *VATA 1994, s 84(8)*. The council had paid the tax in paying the contractors' bills for the relevant work, and the Commissioners accepted that, applying *Mahoney*, 2.347 above, the council was entitled to interest. However, the parties were unable to agree the calculation of the interest, and the appeal was referred to the tribunal, which held that the rate should be that allowed from time to time on the courts' short-term investment account. *Dicta* in *Bartlett v Barclays Bank Trust Ltd, Ch D [1980] 2 All ER 92*, applied. *St Luke Great Crosby PCC, MAN/78/59 (VTD 1463)*.

2.349   **Whether interest may be compounded.**   A successful appellant company applied for interest to be awarded at 2.5% over the base rate of the Bank of Scotland, compounded quarterly. The Commissioners accepted the rate as reasonable, but objected to the compounding of the interest. The tribunal allowed the company's application, observing that 'where the taxpayer can show the specific amount which it has cost him in interest due to the non-payment of input tax by (the Commissioners) he is entitled to an award at least approximating to that loss'. The compounding of the interest was reasonable and appropriate. *Margrie Holdings Ltd,*

EDN/85/69, February 1992 unreported. (Note. The decision in this case was distinguished (and implicitly disapproved) in the subsequent case of *Peoples Bathgate & Livingston Ltd,* 2.352 below.)

2.350   **Whether interest claimable on tax overdeclared.**   In the case noted at 1.73 AGENTS, a couple trading as Tupperware distributors successfully appealed against a decision by the Commissioners that they were liable to account for tax on amounts which their agents retained as commission. Following the CA decision that the tax paid was not due, the distributors applied for a direction that it be repaid with interest under what is now *VATA 1994, s 84(8).* The tribunal dismissed the application, holding that its jurisdiction was restricted to matters specified in what is now *VATA 1994, s 83,* and that the omission of any reference to a claim for an overdeclaration or overpayment of tax suggested that the tribunals were not intended to hear and determine such matters. Remarks of Stephen Brown J in *R v VAT Tribunal (ex p. Happer),* 2.93 above, were *incuriam* and were not binding on the tribunal. Since the tribunal did not have jurisdiction the applicants' remedy lay in an action in the High Court. *R & P A Potter, [1985] VATTR 255 (VTD 1982). (Note.* The Commissioners eventually made repayments to the distributors following the HL decision in *Fine Art Developments plc,* 55.14 RETURNS.)

2.351   **Whether interest claimable where assessment withdrawn.**   A company appealed against an assessment and paid the tax charged. Subsequently the Commissioners withdrew the assessment and repaid the tax. The company lodged a claim for interest, which the Commissioners refused to pay. The tribunal rejected the company's claim. The tribunal chairman observed that the potential right to interest could not 'be defeated simply by a withdrawal of an assessment before hearing'. However, the withdrawal of the assessment in question had been concessionary. Accordingly the application was outside the scope of what is now *VATA 1994, s 84* and the tribunal had no jurisdiction to make an award of interest in such circumstances. *Trevor Toys Ltd, LON/91/1294X (VTD 9352).*

2.352   **Repayment claims—payment delayed by Commissioners—whether interest payable under VATA 1994, s 78 or VATA 1994, s 84.**   Until 1993, the Commissioners required car dealers, in accounting for VAT, to reduce the purchase price of cars which they had purchased by the amount of any refund of the relevant road fund licence. They subsequently accepted that this requirement had been incorrect, and made repayments to four dealers with interest under *VATA 1994, s 78.* The dealers appealed to the Edinburgh tribunal, contending that they should have been entitled to compound interest under *VATA 1994, s 84(8)* rather than to simple interest under *VATA 1994, s 78.* The tribunal rejected this contention and dismissed the appeals, holding that *VATA 1994, s 84(8)* was inapplicable. The tribunal observed that 'the purpose of *s 84(8)* was to empower the tribunal, on proof of the exceptional circumstances in *s 84(8)(b)* or if consequently upon a determination that a payment or deposit had to be made before the appeal could be entertained and the taxpayer had to either borrow money or incur costs or lose the benefit of funds which he should not have lost, that the tribunal had a very wide discretion in the interests of justice to make such an award by way of interest as was appropriate in the circumstances'. Furthermore, the tribunal observed that 'compounding interest unless specifically sanctioned by Statute would be a most unusual course to follow'. *Margrie Holdings Ltd,* 2.349 above, distinguished (and implicitly disapproved). The fact that the appellants had incurred overdraft interest was not conclusive. *Peoples Bathgate & Livingston Ltd, EDN/93/260; John Martin Holdings Ltd, EDN/93/262; Goulds of Glasgow, EDN/94/22; Peoples Liverpool Ltd, EDN/96/20 (VTD 14264).*

2.353   The decision in *Peoples Bathgate & Livingston Ltd,* 2.352 above, was applied in the similar subsequent case of *Seaton Sands Ltd & Others, LON/95/2609 (VTD 15381).*

2.354   The decision in *Peoples Bathgate & Livingston Ltd*, 2.352 above, was not followed in a subsequent case in which a company had submitted a repayment claim in December 1996 and the Commissioners had not made the repayment until July 1997. The Commissioners subsequently made a payment of repayment supplement under *VATA 1994, s 79*. The company claimed a further payment of interest under *VATA 1994, s 84(8)*. The Commissioners rejected this claim on the basis that the effect of *VATA 1994, s 78(2)* was that no further payment of interest was due. The tribunal allowed the company's appeal, holding that 'the words of *s 78* make it clear that it is subordinated to claims for interest under other sections' and that 'interest claimed under *s 84* prevails over an interest claim under *s 78*'. The tribunal observed that repayment supplement was 'not a payment in lieu of interest' but was 'a penalty on Customs for refusing to pay that which was due'. The tribunal directed that the company should be paid simple interest at 8% for the period from January to March 1997 and at 6% from April to July 1997 (the rates applied for). *Bank Austria Trade Services Gesellschaft mbH, EDN/97/39 (VTD 16918)*.

2.355   **Whether interest to be included in award of costs.**   In the case noted at 2.266 above, the tribunal held that it had no jurisdiction, in awarding costs, to take interest into account. (The tribunal chairman commented that 'although the lack of any jurisdiction in the tribunal to reflect the liability to interest, or to offer compensation for the loss of the use of money, can unquestionably produce an unjust result ... the present state of the law is such that it is not competent to the tribunal to provide any remedy'.) *Broadway Video (Wholesale) Ltd, [1994] VATTR 271 (VTD 12446)*.

3   Assessment

Cross-reference. For partnership assessments see 44.1 PARTNERSHIP *et seq.*

The cases in this chapter are arranged under the following headings.

WHETHER ASSESSMENT MADE TO BEST OF COMMISSIONERS' JUDGMENT (VATA 1994, s 73(1))

Cases where the assessment was upheld

3.1   The Commissioners issued an estimated assessment, covering a three-year period, on a publican. The publican appealed, contending that the assessment had not been made to the best of the Commissioners' judgment, because it was based on a sample period of only five weeks. The tribunal rejected this contention and upheld the assessment in principle, but reduced the amount of the assessment to allow for pilferage of stock. The QB upheld the tribunal decision, holding that, although the Commissioners had to exercise their judgment as to the amount of the assessment in a reasonable manner, they were under no obligation to do the work of the taxpayer by carrying out exhaustive investigations. Woolf J held that the Commissioners should 'fairly consider all material placed before them and, on that material, come to a decision which is one which is reasonable and not arbitrary as to the amount of tax which is due. As long as there is some material on which the Commissioners can reasonably act, then they are not required to carry out investigations which may or may not result in further material being placed before them . . . it is perfectly proper for the Commissioners, if they choose to do so, to make a test over a limited period such as five weeks and take the results which are thrown up by that test period of five weeks into account in performing their task of making an assessment'. Applying *dicta* of Lord Donovan in *Argosy Co Ltd v Guyana Commissioner of Inland Revenue, PC*

3.2 Assessment

[1971] 1 WLR 514, 'once a reasonable opinion that liability exists is formed, there must necessarily be guess-work at times as to the quantum of liability'. Furthermore, the fact that the original assessment had not made any allowance for pilferage did not render it invalid or unreasonable. *CPM Van Boeckel v C & E Commrs, QB 1980, [1981] STC 290; [1981] 2 All ER 505.*

3.2   The QB decision in *Van Boeckel*, 3.1 above, has been applied in a very large number of subsequent decisions. In the interests of space, such cases are not summarised individually in this book.

3.3   The Commissioners issued an estimated assessment on the proprietor of two Chinese restaurants. The assessment had been computed by assuming that the average mark-up on sales of drinks was 130%, and that takings from sales of drinks were 12% of total takings. The proprietor appealed, contending that the assessment had not been made to the best of the Commissioners' judgment. The tribunal rejected this contention and dismissed the appeal, and the CS upheld the tribunal decision. *S Y Seto v C & E Commrs, CS 1980, [1981] STC 698.*

3.4   The Commissioners issued an estimated assessment on two publicans, computed on the basis of an average mark-up of 67% on drink and 100% on sales of food. The publicans' accountant had informed a VAT officer that the publicans had made supplies of accommodation, and an estimated figure of receipts from accommodation was also included in the assessment. The publicans appealed, contending that the mark-up used in the assessment was excessive and that they had ceased to make supplies of accommodation before the start of the period covered by the assessment. The tribunal allowed their appeal in part, accepting the mark-up of 100% on sales of food but directing that the assessment be recomputed on the basis that the average mark-up on sales of drink was 62%, and that the estimate for supplies of accommodation should be reduced to nil. The result was that the tax charged by the assessment was reduced from £25,372 to £19,345. The QB upheld the tribunal decision, holding that the assessment had been made to the best of the Commissioners' judgment. *Van Boeckel*, 3.1 above, applied. *C & GP Holder v C & E Commrs, QB [1989] STC 327.*

3.5   The Commissioners issued an estimated assessment on the proprietors of an Italian restaurant, covering a five-year period. The assessment was based on a review of the restaurant's records for a period of three months, and computed by applying a weighted mark-up (of 163.07%) to sales of drinks and treating sales of drinks as 30.95% of total sales. The tribunal dismissed the proprietors' appeal and the CS upheld this decision, holding that the assessment had been made to the best of the Commissioners' judgment. *Van Boeckel*, 3.1 above, applied. *A & B Farnocchia v C & E Commrs, CS [1994] STC 881.*

3.6   The Commissioners issued an estimated assessment on a couple who operated a fish and chip shop. The couple appealed, admitting that they had suppressed some of their takings but contending that the assessment was excessive and had not been made to the best of the Commissioners' judgment. The tribunal reviewed the evidence in detail and upheld the validity of the assessment but directed that the amount of the assessment should be reduced. The CA upheld this decision, holding that the tribunal had been entitled to find that the assessment had been made to the best of the Commissioners' judgment, notwithstanding that the amount of the assessment had been reduced. The tribunal had not misdirected itself and its decision was a finding of fact with which the court could not interfere. *Van Boeckel*, 3.1 above, and *Edwards v Bairstow & Harrison, HL 1955, 36 TC 207 (TTC 2001, 4.148)* applied. *M & A Georgiou (t/a Mario's Chippery) v C & E Commrs, CA [1996] STC 463.*

(*Note.* An appeal against a penalty was also dismissed—see 47.68 PENALTIES: EVASION OF TAX and 32.1 HUMAN RIGHTS.)

3.7   The Commissioners issued a 'global' assessment on a company director who had bought and sold a number of cars. The assessment covered the period from July 1988 to April 1993, but the officer responsible for computing the assessment mistakenly included some outputs relating to previous periods. The director appealed, contending as a preliminary point that the assessment was invalid as it had not been made to the best of the Commissioners' judgment. The tribunal chairman (Mr. de Voil) rejected this contention, holding that although the officer responsible for the assessment had undoubtedly made an error, the error was not one of 'judgment', since 'judgment connotes a deliberate choice between... possible alternatives'. The fact that, in computing the assessment, the officer had 'showed a want of care' was not sufficient to render the assessment invalid. Mr. de Voil observed that 'the purpose of the "best judgment" provision is to prevent an unfair onus from being placed on an appellant—to prevent the perpetuation of an injustice which cannot be properly remedied on appeal. There is no unfair onus here; there is no irremediable injustice; there is a simple error.' *MV Gauntlett, [1996] VATDR 138 (VTD 13921).* (*Note.* The appeal was adjourned for further argument on whether the director had been acting as a car dealer. However, there was no further public hearing of the appeal.)

3.8   The Commissioners issued estimated assessments on the proprietor of a fish and chip shop, covering accounting periods from December 1993 to August 1995. In computing the last of these assessments, the officer responsible for the assessment inadvertently included purchase invoices from the period from 1 September 1995 to 11 September 1995. The proprietor appealed, contending *inter alia* that this error meant that the assessment had not been made to the best of the Commissioners' judgment. The tribunal rejected this contention and upheld the validity of the assessment while reducing it in amount, applying *Van Boeckel*, 3.1 above, and *Georgiou*, 3.6 above. The proprietor appealed to the QB, which upheld the tribunal decision. Burton J observed that 'the only legitimate grievance that the appellant could have had was that 11 days' worth of purchases were included which should not have been, and that grievance was removed by the tribunal'. *G Ahmed (t/a Lister Fisheries) v C & E Commrs, QB [1999] STC 468.* (*Note.* The appellant also contended that the tribunal chairman had been biased. The QB rejected this contention, holding that there was not 'any evidence of bias'.)

3.9   The proprietors of a fish and chip shop appealed against an estimated assessment. The tribunal reviewed the evidence in detail and found that, owing to an arithmetical error by the officer responsible for the assessment, the assessment had in fact understated the amount of underdeclared tax. The tribunal observed that 'it would offend against the obvious mischief at which *s 73* is aimed, and would be offensive to common sense, if a trader should be able to escape the consequences of his misdeclarations by reason of an arithmetical mistake on the Commissioners' part resulting in an underdeclaration of the tax properly due from him ... an arithmetical error which does not lead to an absurd or incredible result does not, by itself, lead to the result that the Commissioners have failed to exercise their best judgment in raising the assessment ... the purpose of the legislation is to ensure that traders pay the amount of tax properly due from them'. The tribunal directed that the assessment be increased in accordance with *VATA 1994, s 84(5)*. *R & YL Ho (t/a Robert's Golden Cod Fish Bar), [1996] VATDR 423 (VTD 14252).* (*Note.* An appeal against a penalty under *VATA 1994, s 60* was also dismissed.)

3.10   In the case noted at 2.207 APPEALS, Carnwath J held that a tribunal should not treat an assessment as invalid merely because it disagreed as to how the Commissioners' judgment should have been exercised. An assessment should only be held to fail the

3.11   Assessment

'best judgment' test of *s 73(1)* where it had been made 'dishonestly or vindictively or capriciously', or was a 'spurious estimate or guess in which all elements of judgment are missing', or was 'wholly unreasonable'. Short of such a finding, there was no justification for setting aside an assessment. Carnwath J observed that 'it is only in a very exceptional case that an assessment will be upset because of a failure by the Commissioners to exercise best judgment. In the normal case the important issue will be the amount of the assessment.' *MH Rahman (t/a Khayam Restaurant) v C & E Commrs, QB [1998] STC 826. (Note.* For a subsequent case in which a Scottish tribunal chairman questioned whether the *dicta* of Carnwath J in this case were applicable in Scotland, see *Cameron*, 3.19 below.)

3.11   The Commissioners issued an estimated assessment on a couple who operated a fish and chip shop. They appealed, contending that the assessment had not been made to the best of the Commissioners' judgment. The tribunal rejected this contention and dismissed their appeal, applying *Rahman*, 3.10 above. The Ch D upheld this decision (and held that the Commissioners had been entitled to register the couple from 1 October 1991). *MA & JS Henderson (t/a Tony's Fish and Chip Shop) v C & E Commrs, Ch D 30 June 2000, 2000 STI 951.*

3.12   The QB decision in *Rahman*, 3.10 above, was applied in the following subsequent cases in which appeals against estimated assessments were dismissed: *F Ghalleb & I Majid (t/a Casanovas), MAN/98/556 (VTD 16060); RW Evitts (t/a The Royal Oak Public House), MAN/96/1090 (VTD 16067); MW Morgan, LON/95/2893 (VTD 16421); A McGrath (t/a The Village Fryers), MAN/97/927 (VTD 16428); Edinburgh Petroleum Services Ltd, EDN/99/96 (VTD 16463); WY Tsang (t/a The Winson), MAN/97/463 (VTD 16497); Shabna Tandoori Takeaway, MAN/94/121 & 167 (VTD 16510); J Rahman (t/a Thurland Balti House), MAN/98/622 (VTD 16511); K Gillett, MAN/99/94 (VTD 16578); KW & HA Chan (t/a The Great Wall), LON/99/1037 (VTD 16584); Saagar Tandoori Restaurant, MAN/94/466 (VTD 16599); A Ali & H Rahman (t/a Taste of India), MAN/97/32 (VTD 16600); F Rahman (t/a The Taste of India Tandoori Restaurant & Takeaway), MAN/97/ 1220 (VTD 16603, 16950); R Gargaro (t/a Spex Opticians), EDN/98/187 (VTD 16605); Flannagan Days Ltd, MAN/99/802 (VTD 16624); M Shamsaee, MAN/ 99/59 (VTD 16635); M & O Behic, MAN/97/1001 (VTD 16658); A Subhan & A Hoque (t/a Indian Ocean Tandoori Restaurant), LON/99/1199 (VTD 16686); Beijing Licensed Restaurant Ltd, MAN/98/763 (VTD 16737); Z & M Hussain, MAN/98/193 & 194 (VTD 16755); M Razaq, M Mushtaq & M Azam (t/a Liberty Cars), MAN/94/877 (VTD 16793); Gavco 132 Ltd, MAN/99/632 (VTD 16794); JP Cunningham, MAN/98/44 (VTD 16824); SA Tompkins (t/a Rene's Patisserie), LON/99/1194 (VTD 16828); B McKinney & AE Deluca (t/a BA McKinney Building & Decorating Contractors), LON/99/253 (VTD 16865); Z Akdag, LON/ 98/038 (VTD 16924)* and *P Kalley (t/a FKI), LON/94/361 (VTD 16979).*

3.13   A clothing manufacturer appealed against an estimated assessment, contending that it had not been made to the best of the Commissioners' judgment. The tribunal rejected this contention and upheld the validity of the assessment while reducing it in amount. The tribunal observed that the officer responsible for the assessment had erred in failing to analyse a sample of goods obtained from the manufacturer. However, applying *dicta* of Carnwath J in *Rahman*, 3.10 above, 'the tribunal should not treat an assessment as invalid merely because it disagrees as to how the judgment should have been exercised. A much stronger finding is required.' Accordingly, the fact that the Commissioners had not fully considered all the material put before them did not invalidate the assessment. The tribunal observed that 'it cannot be right that a trader can escape his liabilities because an officer did not take into account something that may well not have influenced his decision in any event'. *M Desai (t/a Regency Garments), MAN/97/455 (VTD 16036).*

3.14   The Commissioners issued an assessment on a partnership which operated a fish and chip shop. The assessment was computed on the basis that 40% of takings had been suppressed. The tribunal upheld the assessment, holding that it had been made to the best of the Commissioners' judgment and had been made within the statutory one-year time limit of *VATA 1994, s 73(6)(b)*. The partners appealed to the QB, contending that the tribunal should have also considered the amount of the assessment. The QB dismissed the appeal. As a matter of principle, a tribunal should consider the amount of an assessment as well as deciding that it had been made to the best of the Commissioners' judgment. However, in the case in question, the partners had denied that there had been any suppression of takings whatsoever. As the partners had not challenged the amount of the assessment before the tribunal, there was nothing which would have enabled the tribunal to reach a different conclusion with regard to the percentage of takings that had been suppressed. Accordingly, there would be no purpose in remitting the case to the tribunal to consider the amount of the assessment. *Majid & Partners v C & E Commrs, QB 1998, [1999] STC 585.*

3.15   See also *Whatton*, 2.170 APPEALS.

3.16   **Other cases.**   There have been a very large number of other cases in which the tribunal has held that an assessment has been made to the best of the Commissioners' judgment, and has dismissed the appeal. In the interests of space, such cases are not summarised individually in this book.

Cases where the appellant was partly successful

3.17   **Estimated initial assessment followed by further assessment.**   The proprietor of a dry-cleaning business was registered for VAT in March 1996 after the Commissioners had formed the opinion that his turnover exceeded the registration threshold. In July 1996 an estimated assessment was issued by the VAT Central Unit at Southend, covering the period to May 1996. The officer who was investigating the trader's liability considered that the assessment was inadequate, and arranged for the issue of a further assessment two months later. The tribunal held that the initial assessment had not been made to the best of the Commissioners' judgment. The chairman (Mr. Wallace) observed that 'it should have been quite simple for someone to have attended from Southend who could have given first-hand evidence as to how the computer was programmed and the assessment produced ... It is not clear to us that the Commissioners are empowered to exercise their best judgment under *s 73(1)* through the agency of a computer or to authorise a computer programmer coupled with persons feeding information into a computer to assess to best judgment on their behalf.' The assessment was 'wholly inconsistent' with the details which the Commissioners had already obtained. The fact that the assessment was too low rather than too high was 'irrelevant', and the Commissioners should have withdrawn the initial assessment and substituted a new assessment for the correct figure. However, the further assessment had been made to the best of the Commissioners' judgment and was valid, since it 'was independent and did not depend on the validity of the (initial) assessment'. The proprietor appealed to the QB, which upheld the validity of the supplementary assessment. Carnwath J observed that there was 'no reason in principle or common sense why the Commissioners' conclusion on the Central Assessment, assuming it to have been correct, should deprive the Customs of the right to pursue the supplementary assessment'. *A Bennett v C & E Commrs, QB [1999] STC 248. (Notes.* (1) The Commissioners apparently did not cross-appeal against the tribunal's decision that the initial assessment was not made to the best of their judgment. They subsequently issued a replacement assessment, for which see 2.88 APPEALS. (2) For another issue in this case, see 53.38 REGISTRATION.)

3.18   Assessment

3.18   *Bennett*, 3.17 above, was applied in the similar subsequent case of *EK Rustem (t/a The Dry Cleaners), LON/96/821 (VTD 15206)*.

3.19   **Scottish tribunals—whether 'Rahman' principles applicable in Scotland.** In a Scottish excise duty case, the tribunal chairman (Mr. Coutts, sitting alone) specifically questioned the application in Scotland of the principles laid down by Carnwath J in *Rahman*, 3.10 above. Mr. Coutts expressed the view that the *dicta* of Carnwath J were not 'necessarily binding' in Scotland, and stated that 'the entire discussion of *Van Boeckel* (see 3.1 above) in *Rahman* was *obiter* and it should not be assumed that the observations therein would necessarily be followed in Scotland'. Mr. Coutts directed that the assessment under appeal should be substantially reduced. *R Cameron (t/a RC Bookmakers), EDN/98/8001 (E96)*. (*Notes*. (1) Although this was an excise duty case, Mr. Coutts' observations are clearly also relevant to VAT. (2) *Rahman* has been approved and applied in a large number of subsequent English cases: see 3.11 above to 3.13 above. With regard to the inter-relationship between English and Scottish courts in tax cases, see the judgment of Lord Reid in *Abbott v Philbin, HL 1960, 39 TC 82; [1961] AC 352; [1960] 2 All ER 763 (TTC 2001, 4.150)*. Mr. Coutts' decision in *Cameron* fails to refer to the guidelines laid down by Lord Reid.)

Cases where the appellant was successful

3.20   An appeal against an estimated assessment was allowed in a case where the officer responsible for the assessment agreed that he had wrongly used tax-inclusive figures for purchases and tax-exclusive figures for takings. The tribunal held that the assessment had not been made to the best of the Commissioners' judgment. *P Friel, [1977] VATTR 147 (VTD 396)*.

3.21   A VAT officer conducting a control visit discovered that, through a clerical error, a company had overclaimed input tax by £119. She issued an estimated assessment charging tax of more than £22,000, computed on the assumption that there had been a large number of similar errors. The company appealed, contending that the error of £119 was the only large error of its type and that the total of overclaimed input tax for the relevant period was £153. The tribunal accepted the company's evidence and reduced the assessment to this amount. The officer had not made the assessment to the best of her judgment, as it was not reasonable to suppose that the error of £119 which she had discovered was typical of other errors. There was 'no element whatsoever of evasion'. *Van Boeckel*, 3.1 above, distinguished. *WM Low & Co plc, EDN/91/78 (VTD 7162)*.

3.22   An appeal was allowed in a case where the tribunal found that the officer responsible for an assessment had failed to apply the rules relating to tax points correctly, and had charged tax twice in respect of continuous supplies of services (firstly when invoices were raised and again when payments were made in respect of those invoices). The tribunal held that the assessment must be viewed as a whole, and that the result of these errors was that the whole assessment was invalid as it had not been made to the best of the Commissioners' judgment. *Fresh Pasta Products, [1993] VATTR 238 (VTD 9781)*. (*Note*. Dicta of the tribunal were disapproved by the QB in the subsequent case of *Dollar Land (Feltham) Ltd*, 18.568 DEFAULT SURCHARGE.)

3.23   A builder made supplies to a brewery company, and issued three invoices in respect of these services. He accounted for output tax in his return for December 1990. Subsequently the brewery company questioned the invoices, and requested the builder to cancel the three original invoices and issue six replacement invoices, with more details of the work which he had carried out. He issued the replacement invoices in January 1991. In June 1992 a VAT officer discovered that the builder had issued two sets of invoices and had not issued a credit note to cancel the original set. The officer formed the opinion that the builder should have accounted for output tax on the January 1991 invoices, and should issue a credit note to recover the output tax on the original invoices, which he had accounted for in December 1990. He issued an assessment, including a charge to default interest for the period from January 1991 to June 1992. The tribunal allowed the builder's appeal, holding that the assessment had not been issued to the best of the Commissioners' judgment. *Dicta* in *Van Boeckel*, 3.1 above, applied. Furthermore, in raising the interest charge, the Commissioners had not acted 'reasonably', applying *Associated Provincial Picture Houses v Wednesbury Corporation, CA 1947, [1948] 1 KB 223; [1947] 2 All ER 680*. The tribunal chairman commented that 'the tax liability arising on the replacement invoices, and the lack of any credit note in respect of the original invoices, did not alter the fact that the amount of tax due was already in the hands of the Commissioners'. *C Callaway, LON/92/2978A (VTD 12039)*.

3.24   The Commissioners issued an estimated assessment on the proprietors of a kebab and pizza shop. The assessment was computed on the basis of an average rate of suppression of takings. The tribunal upheld the assessment and the proprietors appealed to the QB. Latham J held that the tribunal had erred in its reasoning by failing to appreciate that the proprietors had not sold pizzas for the whole of the period assessed, and by taking purchases of pizza boxes into account without making allowances for the closing stock of such boxes. On the evidence, the tribunal had 'misdirected itself or misunderstood the true nature of the issue'. Its reasoning was fundamentally flawed and the case should be remitted to a new tribunal for rehearing. *V & S Koca v C & E Commrs, QB 1995, [1996] STC 58.*

3.25   An appeal was allowed in a case involving an upholstery business, where the tribunal found that the VAT officer responsible for the assessment had failed to take account of wastage. The chairman observed that 'it is not enough to go through the motions of a mark-up exercise, however faultless one's arithmetic, merely on the basis of what one is told; one should apply some common-sense to the analysis of the situation. To assess an upholsterer ... without taking wastage into account does not constitute the exercise of best judgment'. *DJ Milliner & RF Burt, [1995] VATDR 255 (VTD 13438)*.

3.26   A partnership operated a sandwich bar which provided hot and cold food for consumption on and off the premises, so that some of its supplies were standard-rated whereas others were zero-rated. From July 1989 to September 1994 the partnership treated 60% of its sales as zero-rated. Following a control visit in September 1994, the partners agreed that this figure should be reduced to 50%. The Commissioners issued an assessment on the basis that the figure of 50% should be backdated to October 1989. The tribunal allowed the partnership's appeal, holding that the assessment was based on 'wholly inadequate material' and was not to the best judgment of the Commissioners. *Dicta* in *Van Boeckel*, 3.1 above, applied. *G & M Ramsey (t/a George's Kitchen), [1995] VATDR 484 (VTD 13582)*.

3.27   The Commissioners issued an estimated assessment on a retail shopkeeper selling newspapers, confectionery and tobacco. The shopkeeper had been using a Retail Scheme (Scheme B2, which has subsequently been withdrawn) but the assessment had not been based on a Retail Scheme calculation. The tribunal allowed the shopkeeper's appeal, holding that the assessment had not been made to the best of the Commissioners' judgment, since the Commissioners had entered into a legally binding agreement to permit the shopkeeper to use a Retail Scheme. Applying *dicta* in *Tesco plc*, 54.55 RETAILERS' SPECIAL SCHEMES, 'a scheme which has been agreed cannot be altered retrospectively'. The effect of the agreement was that any estimated assessment must be based on the agreed Retail Scheme calculation. *I Briggs, [1995] VATDR 386 (VTD 13603)*.

3.28 See also *Moti Mahal Indian Restaurant*, 47.93 PENALTIES: EVASION OF TAX, and *Li (t/a Summer Palace Restaurant)*, 47.94 PENALTIES: EVASION OF TAX.

3.29 **Assessment partly duplicating previous assessment—whether made to best of Commissioners' judgment.** Following a control visit in 1988, the Commissioners issued a 'global' assessment covering the twelve months ending 29 February 1988. In 1990 another VAT officer made a control visit to the same trader, and arranged for the issue of another 'global' assessment covering three years, and including the tax which had already been assessed in 1988. The trader appealed, contending that the assessment was invalid since it had not been made to the best of the Commissioners' judgment. The Commissioners accepted that the assessment should be reduced to take account of the duplication of the previous assessment, but contended that the assessment should still be treated as valid with regard to the periods beginning on 1 March 1988, which had not been included in the previous assessment. The tribunal allowed the trader's appeal. The officer responsible for issuing the second assessment should have considered whether she was duplicating the previous assessment. Her failure to do this meant that the assessment had not been made to the best of the Commissioners' judgment. Since the assessment had not been made to the best of the Commissioners' judgment, it was invalid and void, and could not be corrected by any subsequent amendment to it. Applying *dicta* in *International Language Centres Ltd*, 3.32 below, an assessment had to be considered as a whole and treated as either wholly valid or wholly void; if part of the assessment was invalid it followed that the whole assessment was a nullity. *Bill Hennessy Associates Ltd*, 3.102 below, distinguished. *JH Barber, [1992] VATTR 144 (VTD 7727)*.

3.30 **Other cases.** There have been a number of other cases in which the tribunal has held, on the particular facts, that an assessment has not been made to the best of the Commissioners' judgment, and has allowed the appeal. In the interests of space, such cases are not summarised individually in this book. Where the cases in question were decided before the QB decision in *Rahman*, 3.10 above, they should be read in the light of Carnwath J's judgment in that case.

TIME LIMIT FOR ASSESSMENT (VATA 1994, s 73(6))

Whether assessment made within two years of end of accounting period (VATA 1994, s 73(6)(a))

3.31 In the case noted at 27.33 FOOD, the tribunal held that an assessment covering a period of 3½ years was invalid to the extent that it covered accounting periods ending more than two years before the date on which it was issued. *Macklin Services (Vending) West Ltd, [1979] VATTR 31 (VTD 688)*.

3.32 A company which supplied educational courses to students visiting the UK formed the opinion that it had wrongly treated some of its supplies as standard-rated when it should have treated them as zero-rated under *FA 1972*, and had thereby overpaid tax of £40,560. It deducted this amount, in two stages, in computing its tax liability for the periods ending February 1979 and November 1979. In January 1982 the Commissioners issued an assessment to recover the £40,560, together with an unrelated underdeclaration of £1,436. The company appealed, contending that the assessment was out of time. The QB accepted this contention and allowed the appeal, holding that the assessment was a 'global' assessment and could not be separated into its two component parts. *International Language Centres Ltd v C & E Commrs, QB [1983] STC 394*. (*Notes.* (1) The disputed supplies were subsequently held to be standard-rated, and would be standard-rated under the law as now in force. (2) For subsequent developments in this case, see 14.60 COLLECTION AND ENFORCEMENT. (3) *Obiter dicta* of Woolf J were disapproved by the CA in the subsequent case of *House*, 3.93 below.)

3.33   *International Language Centres Ltd*, 3.32 above, was applied in a subsequent case where the Commissioners issued an assessment, covering the period from January 1988 to March 1990, in January 1991. The tribunal held that the assessment was out of time. *Greenhalgh's Craft Bakery Ltd, MAN/91/626 (VTD 10955)*. (*Note.* For another issue in this case, see 27.48 FOOD.)

3.34   A company (C) made a payment of £2,000,000 to another company (H) in February 1991. C considered that this payment should be treated as inclusive of VAT. However, H considered that the payment was outside the scope of VAT, and did not issue a VAT invoice. C reclaimed input tax in respect of the payment in its return for the period ending June 1991. The Commissioners initially accepted C's claim, and issued an assessment on H charging output tax on the payment, but H's appeal was allowed by a tribunal (see 58.116 SUPPLY). In June 1993 the Commissioners issued an assessment on C to recover the input tax which C had claimed. C appealed, contending that the assessment was outside the time limit of what is now *VATA 1994, s 73(6)(a)*, on the basis that the 'prescribed accounting period' referred to in *s 73(6)(a)* should be treated as the period in which the payment was made (i.e. the period ending March 1991), rather than the period in which the input tax was claimed. The CA rejected this contention and upheld the assessment. The 'prescribed accounting period' was the period in which the input tax had been claimed. Accordingly the assessment had been made within the statutory time limit. Thorpe LJ held that 'as a matter of practicality and good sense any limitation period to run against the Commissioners would not naturally be expected to run earlier than the date upon which they first receive notice by way of account' and observed that there could not 'be any injustice to taxpayers in holding that ... certainty is deferred until 24 months after the end of the prescribed accounting period covered by the return within which the transaction was included'. *C & E Commrs v The Croydon Hotel & Leisure Co Ltd, CA [1996] STC 1105*. (*Note.* For the hearing of the substantive appeal, see 34.510 INPUT TAX.)

Whether assessment made within one year of 'evidence of facts' (VATA 1994, s 73(6)(b))

Cases where the assessment was upheld

3.35   A company which was partly exempt reclaimed the whole of its input tax. The Commissioners issued an assessment, covering a period of 20 months, to recover the overclaimed tax. The company appealed, contending that the assessment should only cover a period of 12 months. The tribunal rejected this contention and dismissed the appeal. *FC Milnes (Bradford) Ltd, MAN/77/62 (VTD 478)*.

3.36   In May 1977 the Commissioners issued an assessment covering the period from 1 April 1973 to 30 April 1976. The trader appealed, contending that the assessment was invalid as it had been made outside the statutory time limit. The tribunal rejected this contention and dismissed the appeal, holding on the evidence that the Commissioners had not received the information necessary to issue the assessment until June 1976. *HE McCafferty, LON/77/224 (VTD 483)*.

3.37   Following a control visit, the Commissioners issued an assessment covering a period of 28 months. The officer responsible for the assessment also discovered that the trader had treated the sale of an excavator as a zero-rated export, although he was unable to produce the necessary proof of export. The trader assured the officer that the excavator had been exported, and undertook to submit evidence of this. Accordingly the liability was not included in the assessment. However, the trader subsequently failed to submit the evidence in question, and thus the Commissioners issued a further assessment charging tax of £70 on the sale of the excavator. The tribunal dismissed the trader's appeal, holding that the assessment had been made within the one-year time limit of what is now *VATA 1994, s 73(6)(b)*. *Jeudwine*, 3.83 below, distinguished. *C Judd (t/a CJ Plant Hire)*, *LON/79/9 (VTD 813)*.

3.38   In July 1976 the Commissioners issued an estimated assessment on a company trading as jewellers, covering the 21 months ending 31 December 1974. The company appealed, contending as a preliminary point that the assessment was invalid as it covered more than one accounting period. The tribunal rejected this contention and the company appealed to the CA, which upheld the tribunal decision and remitted the case to the tribunal to hear the substantive appeal. The tribunal upheld the assessment, finding that the Commissioners had been unable to quantify the assessment until December 1975, when they received details of the company's turnover. Accordingly the assessment had been made within the one-year time limit of what is now *VATA 1994, s 73(6)(b)*. *SJ Grange Ltd*, *CAR/77/120 (VTD 884)*.

3.39   *SJ Grange Ltd*, 3.38 above, was applied in the similar case of *Gatherchoice Holdings Ltd*, *LON/90/1339Y (VTD 5804)*.

3.40   A company failed to account for output tax on certain supplies which it made, treating them as exempt from VAT under the legislation then in force. In 1981 the Commissioners discovered that the supplies had taken place and appeared to be taxable. In February 1982 the Commissioners asked the company to provide details of the amounts of the supplies in question. The company did not provide these details until February 1984, and the Commissioners issued an assessment in April 1984. The company appealed, contending that the assessment was outside the statutory time limit. The tribunal rejected this contention and dismissed the appeal, and the QB upheld this decision. On the evidence, the Commissioners had not had sufficient information to raise an assessment until February 1984, so that the assessment was within the one-year time limit of what is now *VATA 1994, s 73(6)(b)*. Taylor J observed that the officer responsible for an assessment was not 'required to possess and employ the deductive powers of Sherlock Holmes and the clairvoyance of Madame Vacani'. *Schlumberger Inland Services Inc v C & E Commrs*, *QB 1986, [1987] STC 228*.

3.41   A farmer (C) registered for VAT in 1973, and also obtained a second registration in respect of a restaurant of which he was the proprietor. This separate registration was cancelled in 1976, on the basis that an individual was only entitled to one registration for all his business activities (see the cases at 53.1 *et seq.* REGISTRATION). Following this, C failed to account for output tax on his takings from the restaurant. On 22 August 1983 a VAT officer made a routine control visit to the farm. He was told of the existence of the restaurant, and was told that it was run by a limited company. In May 1984 he made a further visit, and was told that the restaurant was run by C as sole proprietor. The Commissioners issued estimated assessments in respect of the restaurant on 21 June and 3 August 1984. C appealed, contending that the assessments were out of time and invalid. The tribunal dismissed the appeal, holding that the necessary evidence of facts did not come to the Commissioners' knowledge until 22 August 1983. The fact that the Commissioners knew that C had operated a restaurant from 1973 to 1976 did not justify an inference that they were aware of the subsequent underdeclarations. The Commissioners were entitled to assume either that the restaurant had closed, or that the tax due in respect of it was being correctly accounted for under C's existing registration number. The QB upheld the tribunal decision, holding that there was no basis for inferring that the Commissioners knew of any underpayment of tax before 22 August 1983, and it followed that the assessments were not out of time. *OAS Cutts v C & E Commrs, QB 1988, [1989] STC 201.*

3.42   A trader carried on a clandestine business of manufacturing and selling counterfeit recording tapes. He did not register for VAT and kept no accounting records. The Commissioners issued assessments, against which he appealed, contending that they were out of time and invalid. The tribunal dismissed his appeals and the QB upheld this decision. Simon Brown J held that 'the reference ... to evidence of facts coming to the Commissioners' "knowledge", in my judgment, means what it says; the word does not encompass constructive knowledge'. *M Spillane v C & E Commrs, QB 1989, [1990] STC 212.*

3.43   Similar decisions were reached in *Mervyn Conn Organisation Ltd, LON/89/67Z (VTD 5205); Chatfield Applied Research Laboratories Ltd, LON/92/3393A (VTD 11117); Castlegate Holdings Ltd, MAN/92/1120 (VTD 11579); RJ & JW Furniss (t/a Newspoint), LON/96/486 (VTD 14758)* and *KN & DJ Robotham (t/a North Walsham Insurance Services), LON/97/879 (VTD 15325).*

3.44   In April 1992 a VAT officer discovered errors in the way in which the Post Office had accounted for output tax on self-supplies of stationery. In September 1992 and March 1993 the Commissioners issued assessments to the Post Office, charging output tax on self-supplies of stationery made in the periods from September 1986 to March 1992. The Post Office appealed, contending that the assessments were outside the one-year time limit of what is now *VATA 1994, s 73(6)(b)*, since the Commissioners had had all the information necessary to issue the assessments more than a year before they were actually issued. The tribunal accepted this contention but the QB remitted the case to the tribunal for rehearing, holding that the tribunal chairman had erred in law, and had wrongly treated *VATA 1994, s 73(6)(b)* as encompassing constructive knowledge. Potts J held that the words 'evidence of facts' should be construed as 'evidence of facts giving rise to a particular assessment. This is not the same as the date on which the Customs should have been aware that there was an under declaration of tax, i.e. the date on which the Customs could be said to be fixed with constructive knowledge of an error in the taxpayer's returns'. Applying *dicta* of Simon Brown J in *Spillane*, 3.42 above, 'evidence of facts ... means what it says; the word does not encompass constructive knowledge'. The QB also directed that the tribunal should reconsider its conclusion that the assessments were global assessments in the light of the CA decision in *Le Rififi Ltd*, 3.70 below. Potts J observed that 'given the contents of the assessment and the schedules and summaries attached thereto, and adopting the test and approach enunciated by the Court of Appeal in *Le Rififi*, I would have expected the tribunal to conclude that the March 1993 notice was not a global assessment, but one containing separate assessments for different accounting periods'. *C & E Commrs v The Post Office, QB [1995] STC 749.*

3.45   *Dicta* of Potts J in *The Post Office*, 3.44 above, were applied in a subsequent case in which the tribunal held that an assessment had been made within the one-year time limit of *VATA 1994, s 73(6)(b)*. *British Teleflower Service Ltd, [1995] VATDR 356 (VTD 13756).* (*Note.* For another issue in this case, see 38.49 INVOICES AND CREDIT NOTES.)

3.46   The Commissioners began criminal proceedings against the controlling director of a company which sold exotic birds. The trial was adjourned so that the amount of evaded VAT could be ascertained. On 30 April 1996 an accountant, employed by the Commissioners, calculated an appropriate mark-up of 159% for sales to the public and 104% for sales to other retailers. On 30 September 1996 an accountant representing the company put forward a lower mark-up of 80%. A meeting took place on 30 January 1997, at which a retail mark-up of 150% was agreed, and on 16 April 1997 the Commissioners issued ten quarterly assessments charging VAT. The company appealed, contending as a preliminary point that the assessments had been issued outside the one-year time limit of *VATA 1994, s 73(6)(b)*. The tribunal rejected this contention and upheld the assessments in principle, and the QB and CA upheld this decision. Aldous LJ observed that the purpose of *s 73(6)* 'is to protect the taxpayer from tardy assessment, not to penalise the Commissioners for failing to spot some fact which, for example, may have become available to them in a document obtained during a raid'. On the evidence, the Commissioners had needed to establish the appropriate mark-up figure, which had occurred at the meeting on 30 January 1997. The one-year time limit therefore ran from that date, and the assessments had been made within the statutory time limit. *Pegasus Birds Ltd v C & E Commrs, CA [2000] STC 91.* (*Note*. At a separate hearing, the director was convicted of evasion of VAT and sentenced to 12 months' imprisonment.)

3.47   The QB decision in *Pegasus Birds Ltd*, 3.46 above, was applied in *Eyesave Ltd, MAN/99/971 (VTD 16756)* and in *Fforestfach Medical Centre*, 6.16 BUILDINGS AND LAND.

3.48   See also *Majid & Partners*, 3.14 above; *McNicholas Construction Co Ltd*, 3.77 below, and *Elvington Ltd*, 59.18 TOUR OPERATORS AND TRAVEL AGENTS.

3.49   There are a large number of other cases in which tribunals have upheld the validity of assessments and have rejected appellants' contentions that the Commissioners had the necessary 'evidence of facts' more than a year before the issue of the assessment in question. In the interests of space, such cases are not reported individually in this book. For a list of such cases decided up to and including 31 December 1993, see Tolley's VAT Cases 1994.

3.50   **Assessment dated within time limit but not properly notified until after expiry of time limit.** A company carried on the business of film processing. Quantities of salvage silver produced in this photographic process were sold by some of its directors to metal dealers. Such sales were not disclosed in the company's accounts and VAT was not paid on them. When the Commissioners began investigations, large sums of money were found in the company's safe together with a number of Krugerrands, and one ton of silver was discovered on the company's premises. The Commissioners issued an assessment which was dated within the one-year time limit but was not notified to the company until after the expiry of the time limit. The company appealed, contending that the assessment was invalid. The tribunal dismissed the appeal, holding that an assessment which had not been properly notified was unenforceable until it had been notified, but was not rendered invalid by a delay in notification. The CA upheld the tribunal decision. *Grunwick Processing Laboratories Ltd v C & E Commrs, CA [1987] STC 357.* (*Note*. For another issue in this case, see 2.185 APPEALS.)

3.51   *Grunwick Processing Laboratories Ltd*, 3.50 above, was applied in a subsequent case where an assessment had been completed and signed within the one-year time limit but was not notified to the person assessed until after the expiry of the time limit. The tribunal held that 'the date on which the assessment was made is the date on which the decision to assess is recorded together with the amount of the assessment and on which this record is countersigned and dated'. *HR Babber (t/a Ram Parkash Sunderdass & Sons), [1992] VATTR 268 (VTD 5958).* (*Note*. The decision in this case was approved by the QB in *The Post Office*, 3.44 above. For another issue in this case, see 63.59 VALUATION.)

3.52   The decision in *Grunwick Processing Laboratories Ltd*, 3.50 above, was applied in the subsequent cases of *A Garavand (t/a Caspian Kebab & Pizza)*, *LON/93/217A (VTD 11847)*; *S Ali (t/a The Bengal Brasserie)*, *MAN/98/644 (VTD 16952)* and *Yuen Tung Restaurant Ltd*, 3.85 below.

3.53   A similar decision was reached in a case where the Commissioners had withdrawn an assessment following the QB decision in *Ridgeons Bulk Ltd*, 3.116 below, and had subsequently issued a replacement assessment which was not notified to the company until more than a year after the Commissioners had received the necessary 'evidence of facts'. The company appealed, contending that the assessment was out of time and invalid. The tribunal rejected this contention and dismissed the appeal, holding that 'the assessment of the amount of tax considered to be due and the notification to the taxpayer were separate operations'. *Dicta* of Balcombe LJ in *Le Rififi Ltd*, 3.70 below, applied. Accordingly the assessment under appeal had been 'made' when the form VAT 641 was countersigned by the appropriate officer, which was within the relevant one-year time limit, and was valid even though the notice of assessment (form VAT 655) had not been sent to the company until after the expiry of the one-year limit. *Classicmoor Ltd, [1995] VATDR 1 (VTD 13336)*.

3.54   In the case noted at 49.346 PENALTIES: MISDECLARATION, the assessment imposing the penalty was posted on 20 March 1991. The rate of such penalties was reduced from that date by *FA 1991*, but the penalty in question was imposed at the old rate. The Commissioners submitted evidence showing that the penalty had been computed, and the assessment prepared, on 15 March, before the reduction of the rate. The tribunal held that 'an assessment is made when the Commissioners reach a decision to make the assessment and calculate the amount due', and that 'the act of assessing and the act of notifying are two different acts that can occur on different dates'. Accordingly, the assessment here had been made on 15 March. *Din*, 3.99 below, and *Burford v Durkin, CA 1990, [1991] STC 7 (TTC 2001, 5.82)*, applied. *JL Dart, LON/91/2033 (VTD 9066)*.

3.55   A similar decision, applying *Babber*, 3.51 above, was reached in *CE Kinsella Traction, LON/92/1461 (VTD 10130)*.

Cases where the appellant was partly successful

3.56   **Assessment to rectify errors in past returns.**   The supplies made by a trader included exempt supplies, necessitating an apportionment of his input tax. He used a method approved by the Commissioners for his accounting periods up to 28 February 1974, but thereafter switched to an alternative method without obtaining the Commissioners' approval as required by the regulations then in force, although the change was apparent from his returns. The alternative method was inappropriate for his circumstances and gave him a greater credit for input tax than the method which he had originally used. In June 1976 the Commissioners issued an assessment covering the period from 1 April 1973 to 31 March 1975. The tribunal held that as the returns were in the possession of the Commissioners, the assessment was out of date with regard to the periods up to 28 February 1974, having been made outside the two years of what is now *VATA 1994, s 73(6)(a)* and no evidence of new facts having reached the Commissioners to bring the case within *VATA 1994, s 73(6)(b)*. *V Lord (t/a Lords Electrical and Fancy Goods), MAN/76/113 (VTD 320)*.

3.57   In the case noted at 58.23 SUPPLY, the Commissioners issued an assessment in March 1980, covering the accounting periods from April 1974 to December 1979 inclusive. The company appealed, contending that the assessment had been issued outside the one-year time limit of what is now *VATA 1994, s 73(6)(b)*. The tribunal allowed the appeal in part, holding that the assessment was out of time with regard to the accounting periods ending in 1974 and 1975, since the Commissioners had received full information for these years before the end of 1976, but that the assessment was valid with regard to the periods from 1976 to 1979 inclusive, since the Commissioners did not have sufficient information to quantify the assessment until 1980. The company appealed to the QB, which upheld the tribunal decision as one of fact. Sir Douglas Frank QC observed that 'the tribunal cannot substitute its own view of what facts justify the making of an assessment but can only decide when the last of those facts was communicated or came to the knowledge of the officer'. *Cumbrae Properties (1963) Ltd v C & E Commrs, QB [1981] STC 799.*

3.58   A trader (H) had been registered for VAT when carrying on a business of retailing and wholesaling poultry. In about 1975 he and his wife decided that she should start up a business of dealing in second-hand furniture. This business was duly started but, because of illness, H's wife was unable to take any part in it and it was carried on by the appellant. H did not disclose the existence of this business in his returns, and in December 1980 the Commissioners issued an assessment covering the period from 25 April 1977 to 27 September 1980, on the basis that H was liable to account for the tax on the takings of the furniture-dealing business. The tribunal found that a VAT officer was informed of the existence of the business on 28 June 1979, and held that in view of this, the assessment was out of date as regards periods ending more than two years before it was made. *M Head, MAN/80/242 (VTD 1119).* (*Note.* Compare the subsequent QB decision in *Cutts,* 3.41 above.)

Cases where the appellant was successful

3.59   Two relatives, B and N, carried on business as goldsmiths from 1975 to March 1976, when N left the business leaving B as the sole proprietor. They did not apply for registration for VAT, but were registered by the Commissioners in February 1979. In May 1979 the Commissioners issued assessments, against which they appealed. They subsequently submitted returns showing no tax due. The Commissioners were not satisfied by the returns, and in December 1981 they withdrew the original assessments and issued new assessments for the same periods. B and N appealed against the replacement assessments, contending that they were out of time. The QB accepted this contention and allowed the appeals. Woolf J held that the submission of returns showing no tax due did not constitute 'evidence of facts' within *s 73(6)(b),* so that the assessments had been made outside the time limits of *s 73(6).* Woolf J observed that 'the Commissioners were not obliged to withdraw the previous assessments which were made prior to the making of the returns, and they should have continued to rely on them'. Woolf J also observed that 'where ... the two–year period has not elapsed ... the language of the section does not appear to prevent an assessment being withdrawn and replaced by another assessment'. *B & N Parekh v C & E Commrs, QB [1984] STC 284.*

3.60   The proprietor of a fish and chip shop was deregistered in June 1985 on the basis that his turnover had declined. However, the Commissioners received information that his turnover continued to exceed the registration threshold, and made control visits in June and July 1987. In July 1988 the proprietor was informed that he was being re-registered for VAT with retrospective effect. In August 1988 the Commissioners sent the proprietor a schedule of estimated sales and tax due. In January 1990 the Commissioners issued an estimated assessment, based on the figures in this schedule, covering the period from June 1985 to January 1990. The proprietor appealed, contending that the assessment was out of time, as the Commissioners had had all the information necessary for the issue of the assessment in August 1988 but had not issued the assessment until after the expiry of the one-year time limit laid down by *s 73(6)(b).* The tribunal accepted this contention and allowed the appeal. *M Woodger, MAN/90/127 (VTD 5402).*

3.61   In December 1989 a company (W) purchased a property from another company (M), which had made an election to waive exemption. W paid a deposit of £36,000, and M issued a completion statement requesting payment of £378,000, and a VAT invoice stating the sale price as £414,000 (i.e. £360,000 plus VAT of £54,000). However, in January 1990 M issued a revised completion statement (for reasons that are not fully set out in the decision) showing a sale price of £326,400 plus VAT of £48,960. In its return for the period ending 31 January 1990, W reclaimed input tax of £48,960. At a control visit in May 1990 a VAT officer saw the earlier completion statement and the VAT invoice, and pointed out that W appeared to have underclaimed input tax by £5,040. He arranged for this amount to be repaid to W in June 1990. In May 1992 a different VAT officer saw the subsequent completion statement and formed the opinion that the £5,040 should not have been repaid to W, and in June 1992 the Commissioners issued an assessment to recover this amount. The company appealed, contending that the assessment was out of time. The tribunal allowed the appeal, finding that the VAT officer who had made the May 1990 control visit had been presented with all the relevant information concerning the transaction, so that no further facts had come to the Commissioners' knowledge after that control visit and the assessment issued in June 1992 was outside the statutory time limit. *Winturn Ltd, MAN/92/1128 (VTD 10699)*. (*Notes*. (1) An appeal against a subsequent assessment was dismissed. (2) *Dicta* of the tribunal chairman were disapproved by a subsequent tribunal in *Strollmoor Ltd*, 58.370 SUPPLY.)

3.62   A trader (M) borrowed money from a partnership. He entered into an arrangement whereby, instead of repaying the loan, he would meet leasing payments on equipment which the partnership had leased. He reclaimed input tax on these payments. A VAT officer made a control visit to M in April 1991 and formed the opinion that M had entered into a sale and leaseback arrangement with the effect that M was entitled to credit for the input tax but was required to account for output tax on the purported sale. M wrote to the VAT office explaining the true nature of the transaction, but the officer did not accept M's explanation and arranged for the issue of an assessment in October 1991. M appealed, but the appeal was not set down for hearing. A subsequent control visit took place in April 1993, and on this occasion the officer realised the true nature of the transaction. He withdrew the original assessment charging output tax, and arranged for the issue of an assessment to recover the input tax on the basis that the relevant supplies of leasing equipment had not been made to M. The assessment was dated May 1993, and covered periods from 1990 to October 1992 inclusive. The tribunal allowed M's appeal, holding that the assessment was a global assessment, and was out of time since the necessary evidence of facts had been in the Commissioners' possession for more than a year before the assessment was issued. *AD Mills, MAN/93/1263 (VTD 12312)*. (*Note*. For whether an assessment is a 'global' assessment, see now the CA decision in *Le Rififi Ltd*, 3.70 below.)

3.63   In August 1992 a VAT officer formed the opinion that a company which was partially exempt, and operated a special method of calculating its deductible input tax, had overclaimed input tax by treating too much tax as attributable to taxable supplies. Following correspondence, an assessment covering the period from January 1991 to March 1992 was issued in May 1994. The company appealed, contending that all the relevant information had been in the hands of the Commissioners since September 1992, so that the assessment was outside the twelve-month time limit of what is now *VATA 1994, s 73(6)(b)*. The tribunal accepted this contention and allowed the appeal. *Mills*, 3.62 above, applied. *Lazard Brothers & Co Ltd, LON/94/943 (VTD 13476)*.

3.64   An appeal was allowed in a case where assessments were issued in January 1995 and the tribunal found that the Commissioners had held all the necessary information since a control visit in June 1992. The tribunal held that the Commissioners' failure to issue the assessment earlier was 'perverse'. *Dicta* in *Cumbrae Properties (1963) Ltd*, 3.57 above, applied. *WA Collins, LON/95/594A (VTD 13579)*.

3.65   Similar decisions were reached in *GM & EA Flowers (t/a Soar Valley Construction)*, *MAN/95/1805 (VTD 13889)* and *Mentford Ltd, LON/99/535 (VTD 16724)*.

3.66   **Assessment dated within time limit but not properly notified until after expiry of time limit.** At a control visit in June 1990, a VAT officer discovered that a clothing manufacturer had apparently been treating clothing suitable for adult women as zero-rated rather than standard-rated. He issued an assessment in July 1990 charging tax on the supplies in question. However, the notice of assessment did not specify the accounting periods to which it related, and the Commissioners formed the opinion that the assessment could therefore have been considered invalid. Accordingly, on 21 May 1991 the Commissioners formally withdrew the defective assessment. A second assessment was issued, dated 30 May to replace the original assessment. The manufacturer appealed, contending that the second assessment was out of time and invalid as he had not received it until July 1991, which was outside the one-year time limit of *s 73(6)(b)*. The tribunal chairman (Mr. Hilton, sitting alone) accepted this contention and allowed the appeal, rejecting the Commissioners' evidence that the date of issue of the assessment had been 30 May 1991, and holding that the assessment was invalid since 'the date of notification was more than one year after the Commissioners had knowledge of the evidence of the facts which justified the assessment'. *D Mohammed (t/a Aglow Fashions), MAN/91/1044 (VTD 10246)*. (*Note.* Compare *Babber*, 3.51 above; *Garavand*, 3.52 above; *Classicmoor Ltd*, 3.53 above; *Dart*, 3.54 above, and *Kinsella Traction*, 3.55 above, in all of which it was held that an assessment had been 'made' on a date prior to that on which it was notified to the appellant. None of these cases is referred to in Mr. Hilton's decision in *Mohammed*.)

3.67   In a Scottish case, the Commissioners issued an assessment on a bank. The notification was dated 5 January 1999. The bank appealed, contending that the assessment was outside the statutory time limit, because the Commissioners had all the information necessary to raise the assessment not later than December 1997. The Commissioners produced an internal form VAT 641, dated 14 December 1998. The tribunal accepted the company's contention and allowed the appeal, holding that 'in the light of the evidence before us that an assessment whether by way of administrative action or on the merits could be stopped or altered at any time prior to the notice going out ... there is in this tribunal's view insufficient evidence to establish that an assessment was made prior to 5 January 1999'. The tribunal observed that 'it would be manifestly unsatisfactory if, say, eleven months after an officer made some calculation, which he then dignifies with the title "assessment", it was then issued to the taxpayer'. The tribunal declined to follow the English decisions in *Babber*, 3.51 above, or *Classicmoor Ltd*, 3.53 above. *Royal Bank of Scotland Group plc (No 2)*, *EDN/99/22 (VTD 16418)*. (*Notes.* (1) The decision refers to *dicta* of Potts J in *The Post Office*, 3.44 above, and to *dicta* of Millett LJ in *Le Rififi Ltd*, 3.66 below, but fails to refer to the CA decision in *Grunwick Processing Ltd*, 3.50 above. (2) A subsequent tribunal specifically declined to follow this decision in *Ali*, 3.52 above, on the grounds that it was inconsistent with the CA decision in *Grunwick Processing Ltd*, 3.50 above.)

3.68   The Commissioners issued a notice of assessment on a trader, covering the periods from January 1991 to January 1995. The trader appealed, contending that the Commissioners had had all the necessary facts in July 1995, but had not made the assessments until September 1996, so that 15 of them had been made outside the statutory time limit. The Commissioners gave evidence that the assessments had actually been made in March 1996, although they had not been notified until September. The tribunal accepted this evidence but the Ch D allowed the trader's appeal. Lawrence Collins J observed that 'assessment of VAT is an important step, and it is unsatisfactory that the process is not transparent, and not defined by legislation or even by clear administrative practice'. On the evidence in this case, although a form VAT 641 had been prepared in March 1996, it had not been signed by a 'check officer'. A further form VAT 641 had been prepared in September 1996. The relevant notification (form VAT 655) was based on the form VAT 641 which had not been completed until September 1996, rather than on the one which had been completed in March. Accordingly the assessments were outside the one-year time limit of *s 73(6)(b)*, so that only those assessments which had been issued within the normal two-year time limit were valid. *G Cheeseman (t/a Well In Tune) v C & E Commrs, Ch D [2000] STC 1119.*

Whether assessment issued within three-year time limit (VATA 1994, s 77)

Note. *VATA 1994, s 77*, as amended by *FA 1997, s 47*, provides that the normal time limit for assessment is three years after the end of the relevant accounting period. Before the enactment of *FA 1997*, the time limit was six years. (The extended time limit under *s 77(4)* remains at twenty years.) The cases in this section should be read in the light of this change.

3.69   In March 1987 the Commissioners issued an assessment on a company covering the period from 1 January 1980 to 31 December 1986. The company appealed, contending that the assessment was invalid because it was made more than six years after the start of the period assessed. The tribunal accepted this contention and allowed the company's appeal, holding that the assessment was a nullity. *Barratt Construction Ltd, [1989] VATTR 204 (VTD 4230).*

3.70   In August 1989 the Commissioners issued three forms VAT 191 to a company, assessing the periods from 1 May 1983 to 30 April 1989 inclusive. The tax due for each quarterly period was separately stated. The company appealed, contending as a preliminary point that the assessment was a single global assessment and was wholly invalid because it was made more than six years after the start of the period assessed. The tribunal accepted this contention but the CA reversed this decision, holding that the notice comprised 24 separate quarterly assessments and that only the earliest period was out of time. The decision in *Don Pasquale*, 2.117 APPEALS, was unanimously disapproved. Millett LJ observed that 'the case has no *ratio decidendi* (and) Dillon LJ appears to have treated the question as one of first impression'. Balcombe LJ observed that 'the assessment of the amount of tax considered to be due, and the notification to the taxpayer, are two separate operations'. *C & E Commrs v Le Rififi Ltd, CA 1994, [1995] STC 103. (Note.* For a preliminary issue in this case, see 2.342 APPEALS.)

3.71   The CA decision in *Le Rififi Ltd*, 3.70 above, was applied in the subsequent cases of *Baltex Clothing Manufacturers, MAN/92/108 (VTD 13777)* and *Copeland*, 47.92 PENALTIES: EVASION OF TAX.

3.72   In July 1992 the Commissioners issued a notice of assessment on a partnership which carried on business as architects. The notice of assessment covered the period from May 1985 to May 1990. Accompanying schedules indicated that the assessment comprised three distinct elements of underdeclaration. One schedule covered the period from May 1985 to April 1988. A second schedule covered the period from June 1987 to February 1990, and fifteen further schedules covered the quarterly accounting periods from May 1988 to January 1992. The partnership appealed, contending that the assessment was a global assessment and had been issued outside the statutory time limit. The Commissioners agreed to withdraw the schedule covering the period from May 1985 to April 1988, as the start of this period was clearly outside the six-year time limit, but refused to withdraw the remainder of the assessment, considering that the original assessment was a composite assessment rather than a single 'global' assessment, and that the assessments for the periods from June 1987 to January 1992 had been issued within the statutory time limit. The tribunal dismissed the partnership's appeal, holding that the original notice of appeal represented seventeen separate assessments rather than a single global assessment. Only the assessment covering the period from May 1985 to April 1988, which the Commissioners had already withdrawn, had been issued outside the statutory time limit. *International Language Centres Ltd*, 3.32 above, and *Don Pasquale*, 2.117 APPEALS, distinguished. *Georgalakis Partnership, LON/92/1692 (VTD 10083)*.

3.73   The Commissioners issued a 'global' assessment, dated 13 January 1992 and covering the period from 1 October 1985 to 31 March 1990, to a builder. The builder appealed, contending that the assessment was out of time and invalid. The Commissioners submitted that the assessment had actually been made on 13 December 1991, when the officer responsible for the assessment had completed a form VAT 641. The tribunal rejected this contention and allowed the appeal, observing that the form 641 had not been countersigned in accordance with the Commissioners' usual practice, and holding that the date on which the assessment was made was 8 January 1992, when the form was processed by a computer operator. The chairman observed that 'the assessment has not been made until it is at the stage when it simply requires clerical processing. That must be after supervisory consideration. Until then the Commissioners have not made a decision and the assessed amount has not been finally determined.' *Babber*, 3.51 above, applied. *EVW Harris, MAN/93/346 (VTD 11925)*.

3.74   **Whether assessment authorised by VAT Regulations, reg 25(1).** See *Eastgate Christian Bookshop Ltd*, 55.10 RETURNS.

3.75   **Whether assessment authorised by VAT Regulations, reg 25(5).** See *Inchcape Management Services Ltd*, 55.12 RETURNS.

Whether twenty-year time limit applicable (VATA 1994, s 77(4))

Cases held to be within s 77(4)

3.76   In December 1991 the Commissioners issued a 'global' assessment on a company covering the period from 1 August 1985 to 31 January 1990, together with assessments for the five subsequent three-month periods, charging tax of more than £90,000. The company appealed, contending that the global assessment was invalid since the start of the period was outside the six-year time limit of what is now *VATA 1994, s 77*. The Commissioners defended the assessment on the basis that the company's conduct fell within *VATA 1994, s 60(1)*, so that the extended 20–year time limit of *VATA 1994, s 77(4)* applied. (The Commissioners had not in fact imposed a penalty under what is now *VATA 1994, s 60*, and explained this in correspondence as 'an oversight on the part of the case officer'. The hearing of the appeal against the assessment was delayed pending criminal proceedings against some of the company's suppliers.) The tribunal chairman observed that 'the parties should ... ensure that all matters in dispute are formally placed before the tribunal before the hearing of the appeal as they would be in an ordinary (*VATA 1994, s 60**) appeal ... the time limit for making a (*VATA 1994, s 60**) penalty assessment has not expired, and the possibility exists, unlikely as it may be, that the appeal will extend to dealing with such an assessment'. The chairman observed that, since there was nothing in *VATA 1994, s 77(4)* 'which requires the Commissioners to have made a penalty assessment ... to bring the 20–year limitation period into operation, it follows that there need be no such penalty assessment to extend the limitation period'. The chairman also observed that the Customs officer dealing with the case seemed to have been under the misapprehension that the time limit for imposing a penalty had expired, and commented that the officer 'appeared to have little or no knowledge of the limitation period applicable to penalty assessments'. Accordingly, the tribunal held that the Commissioners were 'entitled to rely on the 20–year time limit for the making of assessments ... subject to their proving fraud or dishonesty to a high degree of probability on the part of (the company) at the substantive hearing'. (The tribunal also rejected a contention by the company that the assessments were invalid since the period assessed was not stated on a notice of amendment—see 3.97 below.) *Sirpal Trading Co Ltd, MAN/92/37 (VTD 13288)*.

3.77   In March 1997 the Commissioners issued 24 assessments, covering the period from April 1990 to March 1996, on a company (M) in the construction industry. The assessments were issued to recover input tax which M had claimed on the basis of invoices issued in the names of 12 VAT-registered nominal subcontractors, for services which the purported subcontractors had not in fact supplied, and on the basis that the circumstances fell within *VATA 1994, s 77(4)*, since certain senior employees of M had acted fraudulently and that fraudulent conduct could be attributed to M. M appealed, contending firstly that the assessments had not been made to the best of the Commissioners' judgment, and additionally that the conditions of *s 73(6)(b)* and *s 77(4)* were not satisfied and that the pre-1995 assessments had been made outside the statutory time limit. The tribunal reviewed the evidence in detail and upheld the assessments with regard to nine of the twelve subcontractors in question, finding that M had wrongly obtained credit for input tax, under *VATA 1994, s 26(1)*, for the purpose of evading VAT. (The tribunal accepted that the invoices issued by one of the subcontractors represented genuine supplies, and found that there was insufficient evidence that M's conduct with regard to the other two subcontractors fell within *VATA 1994, s 60(1)*, as required by *VATA 1994, s 77(4)(a)*.) It followed from the fact that the alleged subcontractors did not make genuine supplies to M that M 'had no right to deduct, as its input VAT, the amounts purporting to be VAT in the VAT invoices'. M had 'through its employees provided its self-employed workforce with the facility of payment without proper deduction of income tax . . . the means by which the facility was fraudulent and dishonest, and (M's) acts of claiming relief for input tax for the amounts shown as VAT on the VAT-only invoices issued in the names of the bogus subcontractors in respect of non-existent supplies were equally fraudulent and dishonest.' Although M had not actually benefited from the fraud in terms of cash, 'it achieved the commercial advantage of satisfied gangmasters and a contented workforce who regarded themselves as entitled to expect that lump fraud facilities would be available to them'. The company appealed to the QB, which upheld the tribunal decision (except that the amount of the assessments for 1992 and 1993 was slightly reduced to take account of the tribunal's finding that there was insufficient proof of dishonest conduct with regard to one of the subcontractors, deleting sums relating to that subcontractor from the assessments). Dyson J held that the tribunal had been entitled to find that there was dishonest conduct on the part of two site managers and of a contract manager who reported directly to M's chief executive, that the organisers of the fraud were not acting as agents of the nominal subcontractors, and the nominal subcontractors had not in fact supplied any labour to M. The transactions were 'shams'. Furthermore, the tribunal was correct to hold that the relevant statutory provisions required 'the attribution to (M) of the knowledge, acts and omissions of site managers and site agents', and that the conditions of *s 77(4)(a)* were satisfied. The fact that some of M's directors may have been unaware of the fraud was not conclusive. Dyson J observed that failing to attribute the site agents' knowledge to M 'would encourage those prepared to engage in fraud or turn a blind eye to fraud to set up separate VAT accounts departments for that purpose' and 'would discriminate against small companies that do not have separate accounts departments insulated from what happens on site or in contracts departments'. Additionally, the assessments had been made to the best of the Commissioners' judgment, as required by *s 73(1)*, and the Commissioners had not had sufficient 'evidence of facts' to justify an assessment until March 1996, less than twelve months before the actual issue of the assessments, so that the conditions of *s 73(6)(b)* were also satisfied. *McNicholas Construction Co Ltd v C & E Commrs, QB [2000] STC 553.* (*Note.* For preliminary issues in this case, see 2.172 and 2.179 APPEALS and 14.78 COLLECTION AND ENFORCEMENT.)

3.78   In November 1997 the Commissioners issued an assessment on a company for the period ending 31 May 1991, charging tax on a sale of property which had not been declared in the company's return. The company appealed, contending that the assessment was invalid since the start of the period was outside the three-year time limit of what is now *VATA 1994, s 77*. The Commissioners defended the assessment on the basis that the company's conduct fell within *VATA 1994, s 60(1)*, so that the extended 20–year time limit of *VATA 1994, s 77(4)* applied. The tribunal accepted the Commissioners' contentions and dismissed the company's appeal, finding that the company's return for the relevant period had wrongly stated that it had no VAT liability, that the company's accountants had acted 'irresponsibly', and that the company's controlling director had signed the return 'without checking its contents and ensuring that they were complete and correct'. Applying *Howroyd*, 47.7 PENALTIES: EVASION OF TAX, it was dishonest if a company officer signed 'a return containing a mis-statement and he has no honest belief in the truth of the statement he has made, and in particular if he makes the statement recklessly, not caring whether it is true or false'. *Adam Geoffrey & Co (Management) Ltd, MAN/98/324 (VTD 16074).* (*Note.* The tribunal also upheld a penalty imposed on the director under *VATA 1994, s 61*—see 47.8 PENALTIES: EVASION OF TAX.)

Cases held not to be within s 77(4)

3.79   In July 1995 the Commissioners issued an assessment on a married couple who operated a launderette. The assessment covered the period from 21 July 1985 to 28 February 1995. The couple appealed, contending that the extended time limit imposed by *VATA 1994, s 77(4)* was inapplicable. The tribunal accepted this contention and allowed the appeal. The assessment in question was a single 'global' assessment. The couple did not fall within *VATA 1994, s 77(4)(a)* as they had not been guilty of dishonest conduct within *VATA 1994, s 60(1)*. The assessment could not be validated under *VATA 1994, s 77(4)(b)* because the assessment had been backdated to 21 July 1985, whereas *VATA 1994, s 67* derived from provisions in *FA 1985* which had not come into force until 25 July 1985. For the purposes of *VATA 1994, s 77(1)*, the prescribed accounting period was a three-month period beginning in July 1985, rather than the whole of the extended period covered by the assessment. The Commissioners had not issued a direction under *VAT Regulations 1995, reg 25(1)(c)*, and in any event it would not 'be a proper exercise of the power to give such a direction to use it to get round the time limit in *s 77(1)*'. The officer responsible for the assessment had misunderstood the law and had not given 'proper consideration' to her power to backdate the assessment. Furthermore, applying *dicta* in *Van Boeckel*, 3.1 above, the assessment had not been issued to the best of the Commissioners' judgment. *DJ & MA Wright, MAN/95/135 (VTD 14570).*

3.80   The Commissioners were investigating the proprietor of a road haulage business. In January 1996 they issued an assessment covering more than six years. The trader appealed, contending that the assessment was invalid because the conditions of *VATA 1994, s 77(4)* were not satisfied. The tribunal allowed the appeal in part. With regard to *VATA 1994, s 77(4)(a)*, the tribunal held on the evidence that there was 'no question of a *s 60* civil penalty' because the trader's affairs had been handled by his wife, who was not herself a taxable person. (The wife had stated at interview that she 'did everything but drive the lorries'. The Commissioners had begun criminal proceedings against the trader's wife for furnishing false documents, but had not taken proceedings against the trader himself.) Furthermore, at the time the assessment was raised, the trader's wife had not been convicted of fraud. The fact that a fraud trial may be 'in prospect' did not meet the requirements of *s 77(4)(a)*, which referred to a person who 'has been convicted of fraud'. It followed that the assessment was invalid in so far as it related to accounting periods ending before January 1990. (The appeal was dismissed with regard to the six years for which the assessment was within the normal time limit of *s 77(1)* as then in force.) *RD Brooker, LON/x (VTD 15164)*.

Supplementary assessments (VATA 1994, s 77(6))

3.81   On 4 September 1996 the Commissioners issued an assessment on a building contractor, covering the periods from May 1994 to July 1996. On 10 October 1996 they issued a further assessment covering the period from 1 May 1994 to 31 July 1994. It was accepted that the Commissioners had obtained no further evidence since the issue of the September assessment, and the assessment was issued on the basis that items had been omitted from the September assessment. The contractor appealed, contending that the October 1996 assessment was invalid on the grounds that it was not authorised by *VATA 1994, s 73(6)(b)*, since the Commissioners had obtained no further evidence since the issue of the September assessment, and that the effect of *VATA 1994, s 77(6)* was that the assessment could only be issued within the two-year time limit of *VATA 1994, s 73(6)(a)*. The tribunal chairman (Mr. Heim) accepted this contention and allowed the appeal, holding that the September 1996 assessment was valid and that the result of its issue was that the Commissioners could not issue an additional assessment under *VATA 1994, s 73(6)* unless further evidence came to their knowledge after it had been made. As the Commissioners had obtained no 'further such evidence', the assessment could only be treated as a supplementary assessment under *VATA 1994, s 77(6)* and could only be made 'within the period of two years after the end of the prescribed accounting period specified in *s 73(6)(a)*'. *L Roberts, LON/98/31 (VTD 15759)*.

ASSESSMENT WHERE PURCHASES CANNOT BE RECONCILED WITH SALES (VATA 1994, s 73(7))

3.82   A trader (G) based in England carried on a business of dealing in second-hand agricultural machinery. He made his purchases in the UK but sent most of the machinery to premises he owned in Eire, and sold the machinery in Eire. The Commissioners issued an assessment under what is now *VATA 1994, s 73(7)* in relation to some 300 of his purchases over the three years to 31 March 1979. G appealed, contending that the 'missing' 300 items had been resold in Eire and that the Commissioners were estopped from assessing because his records had been inspected at a control visit in 1975. The tribunal rejected this contention and dismissed the appeal (except for one item of machinery), finding that G had not produced an adequate record of the actual machinery alleged to have been sold in Eire. *P Gutherie, [1980] VATTR 152 (VTD 986)*.

THE VALIDITY OF THE ASSESSMENT

3.83   **Assessment to rectify error in previous assessment—whether valid.**   A trader (J) failed to account for tax on sales of 168 prints at auction sales in 1974–1976, treating them as zero-rated. A VAT officer, on examining his records in September

3.84 Assessment

1976, considered that there was no proof of export. J then obtained and forwarded to the VAT officer a letter from the auctioneers, identifying certain prints which had been sold to foreign buyers, and another letter from a New York gallery stating that certain prints, which its director had purchased at one of the auctions, were for export to New York. An assessment was thereupon issued on 24 November 1976 charging tax of £187, covering the only three items sold which were not referred to in the two letters. However, the Commissioners subsequently considered that the letters were not adequate proof of export, and a further assessment was issued on 9 December 1976 in respect of all the items sold, charging tax of £1,605 with a set-off for the £187 assessed in the first assessment. J appealed against the second assessment, contending that it was invalid as no further evidence to justify it had come to light since the first assessment. The tribunal accepted this contention and allowed the appeal, holding that a further assessment could only be raised where new evidence had come to the knowledge of the Commissioners since the previous one. *WRH Jeudwine, [1977] VATTR 115 (VTD 376)*. (*Notes.* (1) *Dicta* of the tribunal chairman were implicitly disapproved by the QB in the subsequent case of *Parekh*, 3.59 above. Woolf J observed that 'the language of the section does not appear to prevent an assessment being withdrawn and replaced by another assessment'. (2) In *Foster & Foster*, 3.87 below, the tribunal declined to follow the decision in *Jeudwine* on the grounds that it had been decided before the enactment of what is now *VATA 1994, s 77* by *FA 1985*.)

3.84   *Jeudwine*, 3.83 above, was applied in the similar cases of *R Scott, MAN/76/181 (VTD 517); A Christofi, LON/77/258 (VTD 550); V Scarfe & J Cowley, LON/77/28 (VTD 703)* and *Heyfordian Travel Ltd, [1979] VATTR 139 (VTD 774)*.

3.85   In April 1991 the Commissioners issued four estimated assessments to a company which operated a restaurant. The first assessment covered the period from 1 December 1987 to 31 March 1990, and the other three assessments covered the three succeeding quarters. Through a clerical error, the period covered by the first assessment was not stated on the Notice of Assessment. The company appealed, and following the appeal the case was reviewed by a VAT officer who formed the opinion that the omission of the dates covered by the first assessment rendered it invalid. The Commissioners wrote to the company stating that the first assessment was being withdrawn, and issued a replacement assessment dated 31 May 1991. The company appealed against the replacement assessment, contending as a preliminary point that it was invalid since no new facts had come to the Commissioners' knowledge since the issue of the first assessment. The tribunal rejected this contention, holding that the effect of the withdrawal of an assessment was 'that the Commissioners are entitled to proceed as if the assessment had not been made' and that they were 'entitled, until the expiration of the time limit which applied to the withdrawn assessment, to make another assessment on the same basis'. *Jeudwine*, 3.83 above, was distinguished on the basis that, in that case, the first assessment had not been withdrawn at the time when the second assessment was issued. *Yuen Tung Restaurant Ltd (t/a The Far East Restaurant), [1993] VATTR 226 (VTD 11008)*. (*Note.* It was agreed by the appellant company and the Commissioners that the first assessment could have been considered valid since the period assessed was stated on accompanying schedules. Compare *House*, 3.93 below.)

3.86   *Yuen Tung Restaurant Ltd*, 3.85 above, was applied in the similar case of *IC Sinclair (t/a Ian Sinclair & Son), EDN/94/55 (VTD 12842)*.

3.87   A VAT officer visited a hotel in August 1993, and formed the opinion that the hotel records were incomplete and incorrect. Following his visit the Commissioners issued an assessment to the hotel proprietors in January 1994. In February 1994 the officer responsible for the assessment wrote to the proprietors to inform them that the assessment contained an error and would be withdrawn and replaced by a corrected assessment. A replacement assessment was issued in March 1994. The proprietors appealed, contending that the assessment was invalid. The tribunal rejected this contention and dismissed the appeal, applying *dicta* in *Parekh*, 3.59 above, and *Yuen Tung Restaurant Ltd*, 3.85 above, and holding that 'the result of the withdrawal of an assessment is that it has no further effect. It does not therefore limit the Commissioners' powers or their duties under *CEMA 1979, s 6* to continue to exercise those powers and to carry out those duties.' The tribunal specifically declined to follow *Jeudwine*, 3.83 above, on the grounds that that case had been decided before the enactment of what is now *VATA 1994, s 77* by *FA 1985. RA & Mrs JC Foster (t/a The Watersplash Hotel), LON/94/582A (VTD 12723).*

3.88   Similar decisions were reached in *PC Eccles, LON/93/2503A (VTD 13372)* and *Classicmoor Ltd*, 3.53 above.

3.89   **Assessment to rectify omission from previous assessment.**   See *Judd*, 3.37 above.

3.90   **Assessment showing end of period covered but not start of period—whether valid.**   The Commissioners issued an estimated assessment which was intended to cover a period of 33 months ending on 30 April 1978. However, the Notice of Assessment (form VAT 191) described the period assessed as 'period 61 ended 30 April 1978'. The tribunal held that the assessment was only valid for the three months ending on that date, found that there had been no underdeclaration for those three months, and allowed the appeal. *RE Bell, [1979] VATTR 115 (VTD 761)*. (*Notes.* (1) Form VAT 191 has subsequently been superseded by form VAT 655. (2) *Obiter dicta* of the tribunal chairman (Mr. Shirley) were disapproved by the CA in the subsequent case of *House*, 3.93 below. Sir John Balcombe observed that Mr. Shirley's decision gave to the form VAT 191 'an importance which it cannot properly bear'.)

3.91   **Error in notice of assessment—end of period correctly stated but start of period incorrectly stated.**   The Commissioners issued an assessment which was intended to cover the period from 1 March 1986 to 30 November 1990. However, the notice of assessment was incorrectly typed, and stated that the assessment was for the period from 1 March 1985 to 30 November 1990. The tribunal allowed the trader's appeal, holding that the effect of the typing error was that the assessment was invalid. *SAS Fashions Ltd*, 3.95 below, applied. *M Younis (t/a Heaton Private Hire), MAN/92/739 (VTD 11908)*. (*Note.* The decision in this case was disapproved in the subsequent case of *Solomon's Kebab House*, 3.92 below, on the grounds that it had been decided without reference to the High Court decision in *Grunwick Processing Laboratories Ltd*, 3.50 above, and was inconsistent with the subsequent CA decision in *Le Rififi Ltd*, 3.70 above.)

3.92   A partnership which operated a restaurant became liable to register in October 1989 but failed to do so. One of the partners left the partnership in December 1990. The remaining partners continued to operate the restaurant and belatedly registered for VAT in January 1992. Subsequently the Commissioners issued an assessment which covered the period from 8 December 1990 (the date of the partnership change) to 31 March 1992. Because of an error in programming the VAT Central Unit computer at Southend, the form VAT 655 described the assessment as covering the period from 9 October 1989 (the date when the original partnership had become liable to register) to 31 March 1992. The partnership appealed, contending as a preliminary issue that the effect of the error on the form VAT 655 was that the assessment was invalid. The tribunal rejected this contention and held that the assessment was valid. The result of the error was that the assessment had not been validly notified. However, applying *Grunwick Processing Laboratories Ltd*, 3.50 above,

3.93   Assessment

a delay in notification did not render the assessment invalid, but merely rendered it unenforceable until it was notified properly. Applying *dicta* of Balcombe LJ in *Le Rififi Ltd*, 3.70 above, 'the assessment of the amount of tax considered to be due, and the notification to the taxpayer, are separate operations'. The tribunal decisions in *Younis*, 3.91 above, and *SAS Fashions Ltd*, 3.95 below, were not followed, and were specifically disapproved on the grounds that they had been decided without reference to the High Court decision in *Grunwick Processing Laboratories Ltd*, 3.50 above, and were inconsistent with the subsequent CA decision in *Le Rififi Ltd*, 3.70 above. *Solomon's Kebab House, MAN/94/2107 (VTD 13560)*.

3.93   **Period assessed not stated on notice of assessment but stated on accompanying schedules.**   The Commissioners issued an assessment on a car dealer, covering the period from 1 November 1984 to 31 January 1990. On the formal notice of assessment (form VAT 655), the dates covered by the assessment were left blank, but the period assessed was indicated by accompanying schedules. The trader appealed, contending that the assessment was invalid since the period assessed was not stated on the form VAT 655. The tribunal rejected this contention and dismissed the appeal, distinguishing *Bell*, 3.90 above, because in that case the notice of assessment and the schedules were inconsistent with each other, whereas in the present case there was no inconsistency. The CA upheld this decision. Applying *SJ Grange Ltd*, 3.38 above, and *Le Rififi Ltd*, 3.70 above, the fact that the assessment was a 'global' assessment did not render it invalid. *International Language Centres Ltd*, 3.32 above, distinguished (and *obiter dicta* of Woolf J disapproved). Furthermore, a notification could be contained in more than one document provided that it was clear which document or documents were intended to contain the notification and that document or documents contained the necessary details. In the present case, the schedules contained with the assessment showed with complete clarity how the assessment had been computed. The notification in question was valid and gave rise to an enforceable obligation to pay the agreed amount of tax. *PJ House (t/a P & J Autos) v C & E Commrs, CA 1995, [1996] STC 154*.

3.94   The tribunal decision in *House*, 3.93 above, was applied in a similar subsequent case in which *SAS Fashions Ltd*, 3.95 below, was distinguished. *DJ Freeland, LON/92/2349 (VTD 11358)*.

3.95   **Assessment not stating period assessed—whether valid.**   The Commissioners issued a 'global' assessment to a company. Through a clerical error, the period intended to be covered by the assessment was not specified. The company appealed, contending that the assessment was invalid. The tribunal accepted this contention and allowed the appeal. The tribunal decision in *House*, 3.93 above, was distinguished because in that case the period covered by the assessment had been indicated in accompanying schedules, whereas that was not so in the instant case. *Dicta* in *Bell*, 3.90 above, applied; *Grunwick Processing Laboratories Ltd*, 3.50 above, distinguished. *SAS Fashions Ltd, MAN/90/1024 (VTD 9426)*. (*Note*. The decision in this case was made after the tribunal decision in *House*, 3.93 above, but before the CA decision, and was subsequently specifically disapproved by the CA. Sir John Balcombe observed that the case had been decided without reference to the High Court decision in *Grunwick Processing Laboratories Ltd*, 3.50 above, and was inconsistent with the subsequent CA decision in *Le Rififi Ltd*, 3.70 above.)

3.96   **Amendment of assessment by Commissioners—period assessed stated on original assessment but not stated on notice of amendment—whether valid.**   In July 1991 the Commissioners issued an assessment, covering more than one return period, on a partnership, charging output tax of £15,344. In July 1993 they issued a notice of amendment of assessment, indicating that the assessments had been reduced to £8,586. This notice did not specifically state the period covered by the assessments. The partnership appealed, contending as a preliminary issue that the amended assessment was invalid, and applying for a direction that the appeal should be allowed on this basis. The tribunal rejected this contention and dismissed the application, applying *House*, 3.93 above, and holding that the assessment contained the necessary minimum requirements 'in unambiguous and reasonably clear terms'. *Bell*, 3.90 above, and *SAS Fashions Ltd*, 3.95 above, distinguished. *SP & A Fairbairn (t/a Ruffles), MAN/92/1475 (VTD 12825)*.

3.97 A similar decision, also applying *House*, 3.93 above, was reached in *Sirpal Trading Co Ltd*, 3.76 above.

3.98 **Amendment of assessment—whether properly notified.** In October 1998 the Commissioners issued an assessment of a penalty to a couple who traded as shopkeepers. The couple appealed. In December 1998 the Commissioners sent a letter advising the couple's accountant that the assessment had been reduced, and stating that 'the revised Notice of Assessment will be issued to your client direct as soon as possible'. When the appeal was set down for hearing, the tribunal found that the amount of the revised assessment had not been validly notified. Applying *dicta* of Woolf J in *International Language Centres Ltd*, 3.32 above, 'the taxpayer is entitled to be informed in reasonably clear terms of the effect of the assessment'. On the evidence, the letter dated December 1998 did not inform the couple's accountants 'in reasonably clear terms of the amount of the amended assessment. It clearly leaves some further computation to be carried out.' Additionally, it appeared that the letter had not been 'intended ... to be a notice of assessment, because it contemplates that a revised notice of assessment is to be issued in the near future'. *Mr & Mrs HK Randhawa (t/a Mill Hill Food Store), MAN/97/944 (VTD 16692)*.

3.99 **Undated assessment—whether valid.** A partnership appealed against an assessment which had been delivered by hand by a VAT officer, contending that the assessment was invalid since it had not been dated. The tribunal dismissed the appeal, holding that although it was advisable for an assessment to be dated, there was no statutory requirement for this. *AK & AR Din (t/a Indus Restaurant), [1984] VATTR 228 (VTD 1746)*.

3.100 **Assessment not complying with certificate of registration—whether valid.** The proprietors of a fish-and-chip shop registered for VAT from 1 November 1998. The Commissioners formed the opinion that they should have registered for VAT from 1 November 1996. On 8 June 1999 they issued a certificate of registration requiring the proprietors to make a return covering the period from 1 November 1996 to 31 August 1999. On the following day a VAT officer issued a letter requiring them to make a return for the period from 1 November 1996 to 31 October 1998. In July 1999 the Commissioners issued an assessment covering this latter period. The proprietors appealed, contending as a preliminary point that the assessment was invalid, since the effect of *VATA 1994, s 73(1)* was that 'the only valid period for which the Commissioners could assess the appellants to tax was that from 1 November 1996 to 31 August 1999'. The tribunal accepted this contention and allowed the appeal. *DJ, J & S Plummer, MAN/99/589 (VTD 16976)*. (*Note.* For another issue in this case, see 53.161 REGISTRATION.)

THE AMOUNT OF THE ASSESSMENT

Note. For cases concerning the question of whether an assessment was made to the best of the Commissioners' judgment, as required by *VATA 1994, s 73(1)*, see 3.1 *et seq.* above.

3.101 **Estimated assessments—general.** There have been a very large number of appeals against estimated assessments, in which the decision turns entirely on the facts of the particular case. In the interests of space, such decisions are not summarised in this book. For summaries of such cases decided up to and including 31 December 1993, see Tolley's VAT Cases 1994.

3.102 **Whether amount charged by assessment may be altered after issue.** In the case noted at 18.19 DEFAULT SURCHARGE, the appellant company contended that the amount charged by an assessment could not be amended after the assessment had been issued. The tribunal rejected this contention, holding that what is now *VATA 1994, s 73* enabled the Commissioners to withdraw or reduce an assessment if they discovered that the amount of the assessment was incorrect. *Bill Hennessy Associates Ltd, LON/87/640 & 709 (VTD 2656).*

3.103 *Bill Hennessy Associates Ltd*, 3.102 above, was applied in the subsequent case of *Yuen Tung Restaurant Ltd*, 3.85 above.

3.104 **Assessment remitted to tribunal by High Court to consider amount of assessment.** The Commissioners issued estimated assessments on an accountant who had failed to submit VAT returns. The tribunal dismissed the accountant's appeals, holding that the assessments had been made to the best of the Commissioners' judgment. The accountant appealed to the QB, which directed that the case should be remitted to a new tribunal to consider the amount of the assessment. Collins J observed that it was important to distinguish between the issue of whether an assessment had been made to the best of the Commissioners' judgment (as required by *VATA 1994, s 73(1)*) and the amount of the assessment. In deciding whether an assessment had been made to the best of the Commissioners' judgment, the tribunal had a supervisory role, but once a tribunal had accepted that the Commissioners were entitled to make that assessment, the amount of the assessment was for the tribunal to decide. On the evidence, the tribunal had correctly held that the assessment had been made to the best of the Commissioners' judgment. However, the language used in the decision made it clear that the tribunal had then misdirected itself, since it had failed to consider the amount of the assessment. The tribunal 'should have considered the material put before it by the appellant and decided for itself whether the assessments should be changed'. *MYH Murat v C & E Commrs, QB [1998] STC 923. (Notes. (1)* For another issue in this case, not taken to the QB, see 48.156 PENALTIES: FAILURE TO NOTIFY. (2) Compare the subsequent decision — also by Collins J — in *Majid & Partners*, 3.14 above, where he declined to remit a case to the tribunal, since the appellant had failed to challenge the amount of the assessment at the initial hearing.)

3.105 See also *Rahman*, 2.207 APPEALS.

3.106 **VATA 1994, s 84(5)—assessment increased by tribunal.** In February 1996 the Commissioners issued estimated assessments, covering the periods from July 1993 to September 1994, on a partnership which traded as racehorse dealers. The partnership appealed. The Commissioners subsequently reduced the assessments in the light of further information, but the partnership proceeded with its appeal, which was heard by a tribunal in June 1997. The tribunal allowed the appeals with regard to the periods up to and including January 1994, holding on the evidence that these assessments had not been made to the best of the Commissioners' judgment. However, the tribunal increased the assessments for the periods from February to September 1994, finding that the assessments were inadequate and holding that it had power to increase the assessments under *VATA 1994, s 84(5)*. The partnership appealed to the QB, contending that the tribunal had acted unreasonably in increasing the assessments. The QB accepted this contention and allowed the appeal. Carnwath J held that the tribunal could exercise its power to increase assessments in order to correct arithmetical errors, or where the Commissioners had argued at the hearing that the assessments should be increased. However, the tribunal did not have 'a free-standing power to increase the assessment entirely of its own initiative'. Furthermore, if a tribunal was contemplating increasing an assessment, the appellant should be given 'a fair opportunity (by adjournment, if necessary)' to consider the position. On the evidence, the tribunal here had not given the partnership adequate notice of its intention to increase the assessments. *Elias Gale Racing v C & E Commrs, QB 1998, [1999] STC 66.*

3.107   For a case in which the tribunal increased an assessment under *VATA 1994, s 84(5)*, see *Ho*, 3.9 above.

MISCELLANEOUS

3.108   **Business taken over as going concern—assessment on transferee for liability arising before date of transfer.**   See *Ponsonby*, 61.90 TRANSFERS OF GOING CONCERNS, and *Choudhury*, 61.93 TRANSFERS OF GOING CONCERNS.

3.109   **Whether assessment issued for wrong period.**   The Commissioners issued an assessment for the period from 27 October 1983 to 31 May 1985. However, the tribunal found that the supplies to which the assessment related had taken place between 1 June and 31 August 1985. The tribunal allowed the trader's appeal, holding that the assessment was invalid since it had been made for the wrong period. *HK Sneller, LON/87/124 (VTD 2556).*

3.110   A similar decision was reached in *McGowan-Kemp (Printing Machines) Ltd, MAN/98/745 (VTD 16553).*

3.111   The Commissioners issued an assessment which purported to cover the period from 1 May 1984 to 30 April 1989. However, it also included supplies made in the period from 1 February 1984 to 30 April 1984. The company appealed, contending that the assessment was invalid for this reason. The tribunal accepted this contention and allowed the appeal, applying *dicta* of Lord Grantchester in *Sneller*, 3.109 above. *International Institute for Strategic Studies, [1992] VATTR 245 (VTD 6673).*

3.112   See also *Garnham*, 58.111 SUPPLY.

3.113   The Commissioners discovered that a company had failed to account for tax on deposits at the time of receipt. They instructed the company to include any such amounts on which tax had not been accounted for in its return for the period ending January 1991. The company failed to comply with this and the Commissioners issued an assessment for that period charging tax on the receipts in question. The company appealed, contending that the assessment was invalid because most of the deposits in question had been received before the start of the relevant return period, so that the assessment had been issued for the wrong period. The tribunal dismissed the appeal, holding that what is now *VATA 1994, Sch 11 para 2(1)* empowered the Commissioners to direct that the receipts in question should be accounted for in the return for the period ending January 1991. *Sneller*, 3.109 above, distinguished. *Cantors plc, [1993] VATTR 367 (VTD 10834).*

3.114   **Whether assessment issued to charge output tax may be treated as assessment to recover input tax.**   The Commissioners issued an assessment on a manufacturer of steel shelving, after discovering that his records indicated an unusually low gross profit rate. The assessment was originally issued to recover output tax, on the basis that the manufacturer had failed to record some sales. Subsequently, the Commissioners discovered that the discrepancy was attributable to the fact that the manufacturer had reclaimed input tax on the basis of false invoices, issued in the name of a company which had ceased trading 13 years previously. They recomputed the assessment accordingly, changing the basis of the assessment from undeclared output tax to overclaimed input tax. The manufacturer appealed, contending that an assessment issued to charge output tax could not be treated as an assessment to recover input tax. The tribunal rejected this contention and dismissed the appeal, applying *dicta* of Lord Grantchester in *The Football Association Ltd*, 58.219 SUPPLY. *MP Buxton, MAN/90/993 (VTD 10108). (Note.* Compare the subsequent QB decision in *Ridgeons Bulk Ltd*, 3.116 below.)

3.115   See also *Sooner Foods Ltd*, 58.269 SUPPLY.

3.116   **Whether assessment originally issued to recover overclaimed input tax may be treated as assessment to recover underdeclared output tax.**   A company (R) obtained a tenancy from an associated company (S), under a lease whereby no rent would be charged for the first three years in return for R agreeing to carry out certain repairs to the premises. R reclaimed input tax on the repairs. A VAT officer discovered that the relevant builders' invoices were made out to S, and issued an assessment to recover the input tax on the grounds that the supply had not been made to R. (See the cases at 34.64 *et seq.* INPUT TAX.) R appealed, contending that there had been a tripartite arrangement between it, S and the builders, so that the input tax was correctly reclaimable. The Commissioners formed the opinion that if there had been a tripartite arrangement whereby R was entitled to reclaim input tax, the effect was that R should also account for output tax on the onward supply. The Commissioners included this contention in their statement of case. R made an application for the statement of case to be struck out, contending that an assessment raised to recover input tax could not be treated as assessment charging output tax. The tribunal dismissed R's application and subsequently heard the substantive appeal (see 58.105 SUPPLY). R appealed to the QB which allowed the appeal, holding that the assessment had been issued to recover input tax and could not be treated as an assessment charging output tax. The Commissioners should have issued a new assessment to charge output tax under the provisions of what is now *VATA 1994, s 73(6). Football Association Ltd*, 2.131 above, and *Sooner Foods Ltd*, 58.269 SUPPLY, distinguished. *Ridgeons Bulk Ltd v C & E Commrs, QB [1994] STC 427.*

3.117   **Assessment covering period before date of registration.**   See *Adler Properties Ltd*, 53.20 REGISTRATION; *Bjelica*, 53.21 REGISTRATION, and *Short*, 53.25 REGISTRATION.

4   Bad Debts

Note. There have been substantial changes in the rules governing bad debt relief. The current provisions are contained in *VATA 1994, s 36*. Cases relating to the earlier provisions of *FA 1978* and *VATA 1983* should be read in the light of the changes in the legislation.

4.1   **Customer paying contract price exclusive of VAT.**   A company sold goods for £10,200 plus VAT of £816. The customer only paid £10,200 and the company claimed bad debt relief of £816. The tribunal held that the outstanding debt of £816 should be treated as a gross debt and that only the VAT element of ³⁄₂₃rds of the debt (i.e. £106.43) was eligible for bad debt relief. *Enderby Transport Ltd, MAN/83/304 (VTD 1607).*

4.2   *Enderby Transport Ltd*, 4.1 above, was applied in the similar cases of *R Huckridge, LON/85/141 (VTD 1969); Autocraft Motor Body Repairs, MAN/96/1362 (VTD 15077); WP Holdings plc, MAN/96/995 (VTD 15134)* and *Empire Contracts Ltd,* 34.378 INPUT TAX.

4.3   Similar decisions were reached in *Irrepressible Records Ltd, LON/87/615 (VTD 2947); Caernarfonshire Fatstock Group Ltd, MAN/89/748 (VTD 5033); K & D Williams, LON/91/285Y (VTD 7078); Independent Community Care Ltd, LON/91/1971Z (VTD 7735); B & PD Simmons, LON/91/947Y (VTD 7996); JJ Manpower Services, LON/92/729Y (VTD 9405); WS Parsons Ltd, LON/92/3427 (VTD 10693); Gale & Daws Ltd, LON/92/2613A (VTD 11126); B & H Carpentry & Joinery, LON/94/296A (VTD 12791); NM Williams, LON/94/1076A (VTD 12876); Triple Crown Securities Holdings Ltd, LON/94/433A (VTD 13154)* and *S Jennings, MAN/96/68 (VTD 14372).*

4.4   *Caernarfonshire Fatstock Group*, 4.3 above, was distinguished in a subsequent case in which a trader had been registered for VAT in January 1990 with retrospective effect from August 1989. Between August and December 1989 he had made supplies to an engineering company (G) on which he had not charged VAT. In February 1990 he issued an invoice to G charging VAT on these supplies. G did not pay the VAT, and went into receivership later in 1990. The trader claimed bad debt relief in respect of the whole of the amount charged by the February invoice, but the Commissioners only allowed relief of the VAT fraction of ³⁄₂₃. The tribunal allowed the trader's appeal, observing that he had contacted his local VAT office in July 1989 to enquire about registration, and the VAT office had been dilatory in dealing with his enquiry. The tribunal chairman observed that the February invoice had been issued in respect of 'a sum the entirety of which was value added tax which the appellant was attempting to recover for the Commissioners' benefit. The position might be different in the case of a trader who, culpably registering late, was attempting, belatedly, to recover from his customer sums which he should have charged at an earlier date but which, because of his own default, he has failed to charge.' In the circumstances of this case, 'the amount of tax chargeable by reference to the outstanding amount is the whole of the VAT-only invoice and the appellant is entitled to bad debt relief for the entirety of that sum'. *RC Palmer (t/a R & K Engineering), MAN/92/724 (VTD 11739).* (*Note.* An appeal against a misdeclaration penalty was also allowed.)

4.5   **Insurance company declining to pay VAT.**   A company repaired a vehicle for an insurance company. The contract price was £11,300 plus VAT of £904. The insurance company paid £11,250 only, contending that the VAT of £904 and the balance of £50 should be paid by its client. The company which had carried out the repair invoiced the client but failed to obtain payment, and claimed bad debt relief.

4.6 Bad Debts

The tribunal dismissed its appeal, holding that the only remedy open to it was civil proceedings. *Aldon Engineering (Yorkshire) Ltd, MAN/78/235 (VTD 743).*

4.6   A similar decision was reached in a case where an insurance company withheld the VAT element of the price paid to a trader who had replaced water-damaged carpets. *A Littlejohn (t/a Carpet Trades), EDN/83/72 (VTD 1716).*

4.7   A firm of solicitors acted for a company in an action to recover damages following a fire at its premises. The company was awarded costs of £7,127 plus VAT of £709. The defendants' insurers only paid £7,127. The solicitors then applied to their client company for payment of the VAT, but that company did not pay the bill and subsequently went into liquidation. The solicitors therefore claimed bad debt relief, but the Commissioners only allowed relief of ²⁄₂₃rds of the outstanding debt, i.e. £92. The tribunal upheld the Commissioners' decision. The £709 was a debt owed to the solicitors by the client, and relief could only be given on the VAT element of the gross debt. *AW Mawer & Co, [1986] VATTR 87 (VTD 2100).*

4.8   **Intermediary becoming insolvent.** A retail company traded within a large store under a concession. It dealt with the public in the normal way, but at the close of trading each day it handed its payments to the store for banking. At the end of each week the store repaid the company its receipts for that week after deducting 10% commission. The store went into liquidation owing a substantial amount to the company, and the company claimed bad debt relief. The Commissioners rejected the claim and the tribunal dismissed the company's appeal, holding that the company was in a similar position to a trader who was robbed of his weekly takings on the way to the bank. The company's contracts were with its customers, and the customers had paid it for the goods which it sold. The store was not a customer of the company, but was in the position of a person to whom the company had lent its takings for safe keeping. *Wayfarer Leisure Ltd, [1985] VATTR 174 (VTD 1898).*

4.9   **Shares received as consideration for debt under voluntary arrangement— whether bad debt relief claimable.** A company (U) had made supplies to another company (H), which was in financial difficulties. At a meeting of H's creditors, a voluntary arrangement was proposed whereby the creditors would receive ten redeemable preference shares for every £8 owed by H. A majority of H's creditors voted in favour of this proposal, although U's company secretary voted against it. Following the meeting, U received a share certificate from H in accordance with the voluntary arrangement. Subsequently U claimed bad debt relief in respect of the amounts it was owed by H. The Commissioners issued an assessment to recover the tax, considering that the share certificate issued by H to U constituted consideration for the debt, so that no bad debt relief was due. U appealed, contending that the share certificate was worthless and did not amount to satisfaction of the debt. The tribunal dismissed the appeal, holding that U was bound by the decision reached at the creditors' meeting, and that the share certificate represented full consideration for the debt. Consequently there was no longer any 'outstanding amount' within what is now *VATA 1994, s 36(2)*, and bad debt relief was not due. *Dicta* in *A-Z Electrical*, 10.9 CASH ACCOUNTING SCHEME, applied. *AEG (UK) Ltd, [1993] VATTR 379 (VTD 11428).*

4.10   **Bad debt relief allowed—surplus funds in liquidation.** A company went into creditors' voluntary liquidation. It owed money to its creditors for supplies of goods and the debts included VAT. The suppliers claimed bad debt relief and recovered over £38,000 from the Commissioners. The liquidation was finalised with a surplus of £61,000 in the hands of the liquidator after all the creditors were paid in full. The Commissioners sought to recover the £38,000 which they had allowed in bad debt relief, considering that, by repaying the VAT, they had discharged the company's contractual liability to pay to the creditors the VAT element of the contract price and were, therefore, entitled to be subrogated to the creditors' contractual rights to be paid the VAT element of the contract price. The QB rejected the claim, holding that the doctrine of subrogation did not apply. A VAT refund was not intended to operate so as to vest the creditors' continuing rights against the company in the Commissioners. Furthermore, the Commissioners had no quasi-contractual right against the company, because the VAT refund did not discharge the company's contractual liability to pay to their creditors the VAT element of the contractual price. The CA upheld this decision, holding that it was not possible to transfer the suppliers' rights of lodging proof to the Commissioners without a specific assignment by the suppliers. *C & E Commrs v TH Knitwear (Wholesale) Ltd, CA 1987, [1988] STC 79.* (*Note.* See now, however, *VATA 1994, s 36(4A)*, inserted by *FA 1997, s 39.* Where a supplier has made a valid claim to bad debt relief, the purchaser is no longer entitled to credit for input tax in respect of the VAT which has been refunded to the supplier.)

4.11   **Indemnity agreements.**   A company (C) traded as wholesalers of video cassettes, acquiring them from producers and distributing them to retailers. The producers indemnified C for losses incurred when retailers defaulted on debts. In such cases, C claimed bad debt relief from the Commissioners and was subsequently reimbursed by the producers to the extent of the loss. The Commissioners issued an assessment to recover part of the bad debt relief, considering that the amount of the reimbursement should be treated as tax-inclusive. The tribunal allowed C's appeal, holding that there was nothing in *VATA 1983, s 22* which entitled the Commissioners to recover a repayment of tax in these circumstances. *TH Knitwear (Wholesale) Ltd*, 4.10 above, applied. *CBS United Kingdom Ltd, [1987] VATTR 93 (VTD 2376).* (*Note. VATA 1983, s 22* was subsequently repealed by *FA 1990.* See now *VATA 1994, s 36* and *VAT Regulations 1995 (SI 1995 No 2518), reg 165.*)

4.12   **Relief claimed but debt already paid.**   A company (J) had made both standard-rated and zero-rated supplies to another company (V). J went into liquidation in July 1985, owing V £32,000. All its supplies to V between May and July 1985 had been zero-rated, and the total amount of these zero-rated supplies exceeded £32,000. However V claimed bad debt relief, contending that payments which J had made before going into liquidation should be allocated to the most recent zero-rated supplies, and that the outstanding £32,000 should be treated as including standard-rated supplies made before May 1985. The Commissioners rejected V's claim and the tribunal dismissed V's appeal. It was an established legal principle that payments should be allocated to earlier debts before later debts. It followed that the debt in respect of which V had claimed relief had already been paid by J, and the £32,000 outstanding at July 1985 related entirely to zero-rated supplies in respect of which relief was not due. *Virgo Plant Hire Ltd, [1990] VATTR 113 (VTD 5046).*

4.13   A similar decision was reached in *CB Kennedy, MAN/96/151 (VTD 16068).* (*Note.* Costs were awarded to the Commissioners.)

4.14   **Relief claimed—records inadequate.**   In its return for the period ending 31 March 1991, a company (E) claimed bad debt relief of £7,047 in respect of money allegedly owed to it by a company which had gone into liquidation in 1987. A VAT officer discovered that E did not have the documents required by what is now *VAT Regulations 1995 (SI 1995 No 2518), reg 168*, and issued an assessment to recover the tax in question. The tribunal dismissed the company's appeal against this decision, holding that its jurisdiction was supervisory rather than appellate, applying *dicta* of Farquharson J in *Mr Wishmore Ltd*, 14.46 COLLECTION AND ENFORCEMENT. *Easden Manufacturing Co Ltd, LON/92/1772A (VTD 10116).*

4.15 Bad Debts

4.15   A similar decision was reached in *NGS (Coatbridge) Ltd, EDN/98/68 (VTD 15970)*.

4.16   **Company claiming bad debt relief in respect of supplies made while it was a subsidiary member of a group—whether relief claimable by company making supplies or by representative member of group.** In 1990 a company (T) made some supplies in respect of which it was never paid. At the time T was a member of a group of companies, the representative member of which was a public company (P). In March 1991 P sold its interest in T, which continued trading. In November 1991 T wrote off the amount it was owed, and claimed bad debt relief under what is now *VATA 1994, s 36*. The Commissioners rejected the claim, on the grounds that the relief should have been claimed by P rather than by T, since it was P which had accounted for output tax on the supplies in question. The tribunal allowed T's appeal, observing that P had sold its shareholding in T at a valuation which treated the outstanding debts as good, and that, since T was no longer a member of the group of which P was the representative member, the intention of the legislation was that T should be entitled to the relief. The tribunal held that the fact that T had had a different VAT registration number since its departure from the group was 'irrelevant to the claim'. *Triad Timber Components Ltd, [1993] VATTR 384 (VTD 10694)*.

4.17   *Triad Timber Components Ltd,* 4.16 above, was applied in the similar case of *Proto Glazing Ltd, LON/95/573A (VTD 13410)*.

4.18   **Barter transactions—whether bad debt relief due under Article 11C1 of EC Sixth Directive.** See *Goldsmiths (Jewellers) Ltd*, 21.139 EUROPEAN COMMUNITY LAW.

4.19   **Debt assigned under factoring agreement.** A company assigned some of its bad debts to a factoring company. It received some of the debts in question from the factoring company, and claimed bad debt relief in respect of the remainder. The Commissioners rejected the claim and the tribunal dismissed the company's claim. Since the company had assigned the debts, it was not entitled to relief under what is now *VATA 1994, s 36. Skytech Aluminium Stockholding & Distribution Ltd, MAN/ 94/667 (VTD 14023)*.

4.20   **Cross-references.** For cases where credit notes were issued to cancel a debt, see 38.71 *et seq.* INVOICES AND CREDIT NOTES. See also *Vernitron Ltd*, 58.70 SUPPLY (goods sold conditionally and resold by purchaser without vendor's permission) and *Hurley Robinson Partnership*, 58.110 SUPPLY (goods invoiced—amount disputed by customer company which later went into liquidation).

5 Books, etc.

The cases in this chapter are arranged under the following headings.

Books and booklets (VATA 1994, Sch 8, Group 3, Item 1)
Goods held to qualify for zero-rating 5.1–5.20
Goods held not to qualify for zero-rating 5.21–5.36
Brochures, pamphlets and leaflets (VATA 1994, Sch 8, Group 3, Item 1)
Goods held to qualify for zero-rating 5.37–5.47
Goods held not to qualify for zero-rating 5.48–5.67
Newspapers, journals and periodicals (VATA 1994, Sch 8, Group 3, Item 2)
5.68–5.79
Music (VATA 1994, Sch 8, Group 3, Item 4) 5.80
Maps, charts, etc. (VATA 1994, Sch 8, Group 3, Item 5) 5.81

BOOKS AND BOOKLETS (VATA 1994, Sch 8, Group 3, Item 1)

Goods held to qualify for zero-rating

5.1   **Ring binders for workshop manuals.**   A company supplied ring binders for workshop manuals. It did not account for VAT on these supplies, treating them as zero-rated. The Commissioners issued a ruling that, since the binders were supplied separately from their intended contents, they were standard-rated. The tribunal allowed the company's appeal, holding that the supplies of the binders were zero-rated under what is now *VATA 1994, Sch 8, Group 3, Item 1. AE Walker Ltd, [1973] VATTR 8 (VTD 3)*. (*Note.* The decision in this case was regarded as doubtful, and as 'extremely limited' in application, by a subsequent tribunal in *International Master Publishers Ltd*, 5.23 below. For the Commissioners' practice following this decision, see Customs' VAT Manual, Part 7, chapter 3, section 3.3.)

5.2   **Textbooks supplied with correspondence course.**   A company which provided correspondence courses treated 80% of the fees which it charged students as being for the supply of textbooks and zero-rated. The Commissioners issued an assessment to charge VAT on the whole of the fees, considering that there was a single supply of tuition. The tribunal allowed the company's appeal, holding that the textbooks were eligible for zero-rating and that the company had acted correctly in apportioning the fees. *The Rapid Results College Ltd, [1973] VATTR 197 (VTD 48)*.

5.3   A publishing company supplied correspondence courses in journalism, including printed course notes and manuals. It treated part of its fees as attributable to the course notes and manuals and as zero-rated. The Commissioners issued an assessment on the basis that the company was making a single supply of tuition services and that the whole of the consideration should be standard-rated. The company appealed, contending firstly that it was making two separate supplies and had accounted for tax on the correct basis, and alternatively that if it were deemed to be making a single supply, it was making a single supply of goods which qualified for zero-rating. The tribunal accepted the company's second contention and allowed the appeal. On the evidence, the company could supply the manuals without the tuition, but it could not supply tuition without the manuals. The tribunal held that, in view of 'the small element of external tuition', the company was making a single supply of manuals to which the tuition was incidental. Accordingly, the whole supply was zero-rated. *International News Syndicate Ltd, LON/96/1306 (VTD 14425)*.

5.4   **'Course books' supplied to students of English.**   The proprietor of a business which provided tuition in English charged an inclusive fee, part of which he treated as being for the supply of course books and as zero-rated. The Commissioners issued an assessment on the basis that there was a single standard-rated supply of tuition. The tribunal allowed the proprietor's appeal, holding that the course books qualified for zero-rating and that the proprietor was entitled to apportion the fees. *JE Rendle (t/a Coventry International English Studies Centre), MAN/82/120 (VTD 1389).*

5.5   **Course manuals supplied to accountancy students.** A company which provided accountancy tuition treated part of its fees as being for the supply of course manuals and as zero-rated. The Commissioners issued an assessment on the basis that there was a single standard-rated supply of tuition. The tribunal allowed the company's appeal, holding that the manuals constituted a separate supply and qualified for zero-rating. *LSA (Full Time Courses) Ltd, [1983] VATTR 256 (VTD 1507).*

5.6   **Course books supplied with vocational retraining courses.** A company supplied residential training courses for army personnel who were about to return to civilian life. The courses available included computer tuition and driving instruction. It supplied course books to the students, and treated part of the consideration as being for the supply of these course books, and as zero-rated. The Commissioners issued an assessment on the basis that the company was making a single supply of tuition, so that the whole of the consideration was taxable at the standard rate. The company appealed. The tribunal allowed the appeal, holding that the company was making separate supplies of tuition and books. The course books were 'physically and economically dissociable from the main supply'. It was 'both practicable and realistic to treat the supply of the course books as a zero-rated supply separate from the standard-rated supply of tuition'. *Force One Training Ltd, LON/95/1594A (VTD 13619).*

5.7   **Directory supplied as part of discount scheme.** A company operated a discount scheme under which subscribers were provided with a 'Status Card' to enable them to obtain discounts from specified retailers, and a 'Status Directory' listing the retailers within the scheme and the discounts they would offer to Status Card holders. The Commissioners issued a ruling that the payments by subscribers were wholly standard-rated. The company appealed, contending that its supplies were zero-rated under what is now *VATA 1994, Sch 8, Group 3*. The tribunal allowed the appeal in part, holding that the major part of the consideration was paid for the right to receive discounts, which was a standard-rated supply of services, but that part of the consideration was attributable to the supply of the Directory, which was a booklet within what is now *VATA 1994, Sch 8, Group 3, Item 1* and qualified for zero-rating. *Status Cards Ltd, LON/74/102 (VTD 128).*

5.8   **Mail order catalogues.** Two associated companies sold goods by mail order, under a number of different trading names. They produced catalogues twice a year for distribution to agents or potential agents. The catalogues had different covers for each of the trading names which the companies used, but apart from these covers, the contents of the catalogues were identical. The catalogues were printed overseas. Most of them arrived in the UK in their finished condition. However, in case of a shortage of any particular version of the catalogue, they also had printed extra copies (known as 'float copies') of the body of the catalogue. These float copies had temporary protective covers, consisting of a sheet of white card, and the pages had not been trimmed. The Commissioners issued a ruling that the 'float copies' were not 'books' and not eligible for zero-rating, on the grounds that they would need further processing after they had been imported. The tribunal allowed the companies' appeals, holding that, even though further work would be carried out on them, the 'float copies' were still 'books' when they were imported, and thus qualified for zero-rating. *GUS Catalogue Order Ltd & GUS Merchandise Corporation Ltd, MAN/87/532 (VTD 2958).*

5.9 **Children's cut-out books.** A company published children's books, and also manufactured and sold plastic toys. It sold a sixteen-page cut-out book entitled 'The Twins on Holiday'. The narrative story was on the four inside pages. The remaining pages were designed to be cut out to form figures of two girls and of their clothing, intended to illustrate the story. The Commissioners issued a ruling that the product was not eligible for zero-rating, on the grounds that it was a toy rather than a book. The tribunal allowed the company's appeal against this decision, holding that the product was a book at the time of supply even though the reader might subsequently cut out the figures. *WF Graham (Northampton) Ltd, LON/79/332 (VTD 908).*

5.10 **Young children's publication containing yearplanner.** A company marketed a 66-page publication, priced at £2.99 and aimed at young children, which included a 24-page 'yearplanner' and a 4-page section for names, addresses and telephone numbers. The remaining 38 pages contained a number of quizzes and jokes as well as a section about money. The company did not account for output tax on sales of the product, treating it as a zero-rated book. The Commissioners issued an assessment charging tax on the basis that the product was akin to a diary and did not qualify for zero-rating. The tribunal allowed the company's appeal, holding that the product was 'much more than a diary and address book' and was 'designed to be read as entertainment'. *WF Graham (Northampton) Ltd*, 5.9 above, applied; *Colour Offset Ltd*, 5.33 below, distinguished. *Scholastic Publications Ltd, MAN/95/2087 (VTD 14213).* (*Note.* The tribunal also held that a 'dinosaur action set', marketed by the same company and containing cut-out models of dinosaurs, was a toy rather than a book and did not qualify for zero-rating.)

5.11 **Market research reports.** A company which carried on a market research business produced reports for sale to members of the public. It did not account for VAT on sales of these reports. The Commissioners issued an assessment charging tax on them, on the basis that the company was supplying services rather than goods. The tribunal allowed the company's appeal, holding that the company was supplying booklets which were zero-rated under what is now *VATA 1994, Sch 8, Group 3, Item 1. City Research Associates Ltd, [1984] VATTR 189 (VTD 1745).*

5.12 **Booklet containing audience viewing figures for TV programmes.** A company supplied reports, comprising details of audience viewing figures for TV programmes. It did not account for VAT on its receipts from these supplies, considering that the reports were booklets which qualified for zero-rating under what is now *VATA 1994, Sch 8, Group 3, Item 1.* The Commissioners issued assessments charging tax on the basis that the company was making standard-rated supplies of services, to which the reports were incidental. The tribunal allowed the company's appeal, holding that the company was supplying information in the form of a booklet, and that the booklet qualified for zero-rating. *City Research Associates Ltd*, 5.11 above, applied. *David Graham & Associates, LON/92/3394A (VTD 11068).*

5.13 **Memorandum and Articles of Association supplied for new companies.** A company carried on business as company formation agents. In accounting for VAT, it treated part of the consideration which it received as attributable to supplying eight copies of the companies' Memorandum and Articles of Association, and thus as zero-rated. The Commissioners issued a ruling that there was a single supply which did not qualify for zero-rating. The tribunal allowed the company's appeal, holding that the consideration was apportionable and the part which was attributable to the Memorandum and Articles was zero-rated. *JP Company Registrations Ltd, LON/86/302 (VTD 2249).*

5.14 Books, etc.

5.14 **Charity annual report.** A charity published its annual report for 1995 in a ring-bound format whereby the back of 12 of the 15 pages contained a monthly calendar with a photograph illustrating the charity's work. The back page of the report comprised stiff card and contained a flap intended to enable the calendar to be stood upright on a desk. The Commissioners issued a ruling that the charity was obliged to account for output tax on the cost of producing the report. The charity appealed, contending that the report was a booklet, so that it qualified for zero-rating under *VATA 1994, Sch 8, Group 3, Item 1*. The tribunal accepted this contention and allowed the appeal. The fact that the report included a calendar, and was designed so that it could stand on a desk, did not prevent it from qualifying as a 'booklet' or 'brochure'. *London Cyrenians Housing, LON/95/3173A (VTD 14426)*.

5.15 **Illustrated diary.** A company traded as a dealer in second-hand works of art. It produced a book (in a limited edition of 1,000) entitled 'Today And Tomorrow', which contained 17 illustrations of paintings by a well-known film director. Opposite each illustrated painting were pages headed with the 12 months of the year and lines ending with a printed number for each day of the month. The company did not account for tax on sales of the book, treating it as zero-rated. The Commissioners issued an assessment charging tax on the sales, on the basis that it was a diary for completion and was not within the definition of a 'book'. The company appealed. The tribunal allowed the appeal, holding that the book qualified for zero-rating under what is now *VATA 1994, Sch 8, Group 3, Item 1. Richard Salmon Ltd, LON/92/2893A (VTD 12126)*.

5.16 **Payments to trader advertising 'money-making scheme'—whether for supply of books.** A trader advertised a 'money-making scheme', inviting potential customers to send him an initial monthly 'subscription fee' of £49.95. On receipt of an initial payment, he sent his customers a 'start-up information pack', and on receipt of subsequent payments, he sent books on subjects such as 'grants and sources of free money', 'venture capital', 'loan finance', 'marketing', 'leasing finance', etc. He did not account for output tax on the payments which he received. The Commissioners issued a ruling that the payments were liable to VAT, and he appealed, contending that the payments were wholly attributable to the supply of books which qualified for zero-rating. The tribunal accepted this contention and allowed his appeal, observing that the scheme which the trader operated was 'bordering on the fraudulent' since it was clear that no recipient of the books would be able to resell them for more than the £49.95 which he had paid. On the evidence, all that the trader's customers actually received 'was the book or books themselves'. The chairman observed that 'it is true that each book was not worth £49.95 or anything like it, but at the end of the day that is all that was actually supplied, other than items to which no value can be attributed'. *MG Reece (t/a Mako Consultants), LON/94/3388 (VTD 13980)*.

5.17 **Publication supplied to members of unincorporated association—whether wholly zero-rated.** A company (H) produced the annual members' handbook of the Professional Association of Teachers. It treated its supplies of the handbook as zero-rated. The Commissioners formed the opinion that, since the handbook contained details of benefits available to members of the PAT, including a 'Spend and Save' scheme which H organised, part of the consideration should be treated as attributable to this scheme and as paid for a standard-rated supply of services. They issued an assessment, against which H appealed. The tribunal allowed H's appeal, holding that the whole of the consideration was attributable to the zero-rated supply of the handbooks, and that no part of the consideration was attributable to the supply of benefits to members of the PAT. *Hague Shaw (Marketing) Ltd, MAN/92/338 (VTD 11445, 11474)*.

5.18 **Publications supplied to members of clubs or associations as part of consideration for subscription.** See *Automobile Association*, 13.17 CLUBS, ASSOCIATIONS AND ORGANISATIONS; *Barton*, 13.18 CLUBS, ASSOCIATIONS AND ORGANISATIONS, and *Institute of Chartered Foresters*, 13.19 CLUBS, ASSOCIATIONS AND ORGANISATIONS.

5.19 **Books supplied to club members by mail order.** A company supplied books by post to members of a club which it organised. It charged a reduced price for the books, plus a contribution to the cost of postage and packing. The Commissioners issued a ruling that there were two separate supplies, one of the books and one of their delivery, and that the delivery charges were standard-rated. The tribunal allowed the company's appeal, holding that there was a single zero-rated supply. *The Leisure Circle Ltd, LON/82/198 (VTD 1362)*.

5.20 A similar decision was reached in *Book Club Associates, [1983] VATTR 34 (VTD 1363)*.

Goods held not to qualify for zero-rating

5.21 **Binders for encyclopaedias.** A company published an encyclopaedia, which was issued in weekly parts. It also supplied special binders for the encyclopaedia. The tribunal held that the binders were not a component part of a book, and that the supply of the binders was not zero-rated under either what is now *VATA 1994, Sch 8, Group 3, Item 1* or *Item 6*. *Fabbri & Partners Ltd, [1973] VATTR 49 (VTD 16)*.

5.22 *Fabbri & Partners Ltd*, 5.21 above, was applied in a similar case in which *AE Walker Ltd*, 5.1 above, was distinguished. *Marshall Cavendish Ltd, [1973] VATTR 65 (VTD 16)*.

5.23 **Binders for pictures of wildlife.** An appeal was dismissed in a case where a company supplied binders intended to be filled with cards providing pictures of, and information about, wildlife. The tribunal held that the binders were not eligible for zero-rating. *Fabbri & Partners Ltd*, 5.21 above, and *Marshall Cavendish Ltd*, 5.22 above, applied; *AE Walker Ltd*, 5.1 above, distinguished and regarded as doubtful and 'extremely limited' in application. *International Master Publishers Ltd, LON/91/2534Y (VTD 8807)*.

5.24 **Supply of component parts of book.** A company carried on business as printers and bookbinders. It supplied publishers with all the component parts of books for publication, including the covers, the endpapers, and the unfolded and uncut printed sheets of the pages. The Commissioners issued a ruling that these supplies were standard-rated. The tribunal dismissed the company's appeal, holding that the component parts of a book were not themselves a book and were not eligible for zero-rating. *AE Walker Ltd*, 5.1 above, distinguished. *Butler & Tanner Ltd, [1974] VATTR 72 (VTD 68)*.

5.25 **Albums of wedding photographs.** A trader supplied albums of wedding photographs. The actual photography was done by an independent specialist photographer, while the trader supplied the film and produced the photographs. The price quoted to the customer for proofs and the finished album included an amount to be paid by the customer to the photographer at the ceremony. The trader did not account for VAT on his supplies, and the Commissioners issued a ruling that they were standard-rated. The trader appealed, contending that he was supplying books which should be zero-rated. The tribunal dismissed the appeal, holding that the albums were not books. *DA Draper, MAN/80/197 (VTD 1107)*.

5.26 **Booklet containing vouchers for admission to entertainments in holiday area.** A company trading in a holiday area operated a complex scheme under which it supplied hoteliers and tourists with booklets entitled 'Passports to Entertainment'. Each of these booklets comprised twelve leaves, each of which comprised or included a detachable voucher entitling the holder to admission, either free or at a discount, to an entertainment in the area. It did not account for VAT on its supplies of these booklets. The Commissioners issued a ruling that they were not eligible for zero-rating, and the company appealed, contending that as booklets they were zero-rated under what is now *VATA 1994, Sch 8, Group 3, Item 1*. The tribunal dismissed the company's appeal, holding that in substance the company was making a standard-rated supply of services. *Graham Leisure Ltd, LON/81/329 (VTD 1304)*.

5.27 **'Leisure guides' containing vouchers.** A company published 'leisure guides', which consisted largely of vouchers enabling customers to obtain accommodation at hotels or guest houses, and meals at restaurants, for less than the normal price. The company did not account for VAT on the sales of these guides. The Commissioners issued a ruling that the guides were not eligible for zero-rating and the company appealed. The tribunal dismissed the company's appeal, observing that the real value was in the vouchers rather than in the booklets, and holding that in substance the company was making a supply of standard-rated services. *Interleisure Club Ltd, LON/91/1681X (VTD 7458)*.

5.28 **Computer manuals supplied with computer tuition.** A company provided courses of computer training, for which it charged a fee of £150. In accounting for VAT, it treated part of these fees as attributable to the supply of a manual, and as zero-rated. The Commissioners issued an assessment on the basis that there was a single standard-rated supply. The tribunal dismissed the company's appeal, distinguishing *The Rapid Results College*, 5.2 above, and *LSA (Full Time Courses) Ltd*, 5.5 above. On the evidence, the manuals were not sold independently and formed part of a single supply of tuition. *EW (Computer Training) Ltd, LON/90/484X (VTD 5453)*.

5.29 **Instruction manuals supplied with franchising advice.** A company provided advisory services to clients with regard to franchising. It provided its clients with a prospectus, an instruction manual and other printed materials. The text of the instruction manual was also supplied on a computer disk. The Commissioners issued a ruling that the company's supplies were entirely standard-rated. The company appealed, contending that part of the consideration which it received should be attributed to the prospectuses, instruction manuals and other printed materials, and qualified for zero-rating. The tribunal rejected this contention and dismissed the appeal, observing that the invoices which the company issued did not seek to apportion the fees and holding that the company was making a single composite supply which did not qualify for zero-rating. *Force One Training Ltd*, 5.6 above, distinguished. *Franchise Development Services Ltd, LON/95/2530A (VTD 14295)*.

5.30 **Books supplied with boxed games.** A company supplied boxed sets of 'fantasy war games'. The boxes included a rulebook, and a second book giving information about the game. In accounting for tax, the company treated part of the price of the games as attributable to the books and as zero-rated. The Commissioners issued assessments on the basis that the company was supplying games and that the supplies were entirely standard-rated. The tribunal upheld the assessments and dismissed the company's appeal, holding that 'the essential feature of the transaction is the supply of a war game' and that the books did not have 'a distinct and separate identity'. *Games Workshop Ltd, MAN/98/1073 (VTD 16975)*.

5.31 **Advertisements in guidebook.** A partnership published guidebooks which included advertisements. It did not account for VAT on the consideration which it received from the advertisers. The Commissioners issued an assessment charging tax on the consideration. The partnership appealed, contending that, since the guidebooks were zero-rated, the advertisements should also be zero-rated. The tribunal rejected this contention and dismissed the appeal. *Colourfast Printers, LON/89/910Y (VTD 4557)*.

5.32 **Surname histories supplied as scroll.** A company supplied scrolls, measuring 17 ins by 11 ins, each of which gave a history of a particular surname. The information contained in the scrolls derived from a computer database, in which were stored histories, in similar formats, of 75,000 surnames. The Commissioners issued a ruling that the scrolls were standard-rated, and the company appealed. The tribunal dismissed the appeal, holding that the scrolls were neither books nor booklets, and were not eligible for zero-rating. *The Hall of Names Ltd, LON/91/1256 (VTD 8806)*.

5.33 **Diaries and address books.** A printing company did not account for VAT on sales of diaries and address books which it produced. The Commissioners issued an assessment charging tax on these supplies, and the company appealed, contending that they were zero-rated. The QB rejected this contention and upheld the assessment. May J held that a book was something to be read or looked at. A completed diary of historical or literary interest may be a book, but a blank diary was not. Similarly, a blank address book was not a book. *C & E Commrs v Colour Offset Ltd, QB 1994, [1995] STC 85*.

5.34 **Sets of cards for learner drivers—whether zero-rated.** A company sold packs of cards which were intended to be used by learner drivers. They measured 9cm by 5.7cm, resembled small playing cards in appearance, and were printed on glossy cardboard. They were sold in packs of 170. One side of each card contained a question about road signs or the Highway Code, with the answer to the question being printed on the reverse of the card. The company did not account for output tax on sales of the cards, treating them as zero-rated. In 1994 the Commissioners issued a ruling that the cards did not qualify for zero-rating. The company appealed, contending that each set of cards should be treated as a loose-leaf reference book. The tribunal dismissed the appeal, applying the QB decision in *Colour Offset Ltd*, 5.33 above. (The tribunal noted that a VAT officer who had visited the company before 1990 had apparently accepted that the cards were zero-rated, and that the Commissioners had changed their policy on zero-rating following the tribunal decision in *Panini Publishing Ltd*, 5.55 below, but had not reissued *Leaflet No 701/10/85* to reflect this change of policy. The chairman expressed the hope that the Commissioners would apply what is now Extra-Statutory Concession 3.5, for which see 2.72 APPEALS.) *Flipcards Ltd, MAN/95/2210 (VTD 13916)*.

5.35 **Payments to company in response to advertisements—whether for supply of booklets.** A company (S) advertised in certain publications (such as 'Sunday Sport') inviting readers to send it £47.50. It informed readers that, in return for such a payment, they would be entitled to give a name of their choice to a star. (The names in question were not recognised by NASA or the International Astronomical Union, and the tribunal heard that a leading astronomer described the services which S offered as 'quite valueless and unofficial, and ... a complete waste of money'.) On receipt of such a payment, S sent the customer an acknowledgement, together with a five-page booklet giving some information about stars, and two charts showing details of constellations. It did not account for VAT on its receipts. The Commissioners issued a ruling that the receipts were liable to VAT, and S appealed, contending that it was supplying booklets which were zero-rated under what is now *VATA 1994, Sch 8, Group 3*. The tribunal dismissed S's appeal, holding that, in view of the nature of the advertisements which S placed, S was making standard-rated supplies of services. Since the booklet only comprised five pages and cost very little to produce, it was 'economically indissociable' from the supply of services and there was 'no rational basis for apportionment'. *Schoemann ISR (UK) Ltd, LON/93/1792A (VTD 11713)*.

5.36   **Charity supplying 'camera-ready copy' to publishing company—whether supplies by charity zero-rated.**   A registered charity was established to promote the study of international security issues of a political, strategic, economic, social or ecological nature. It entered into an agreement with a publishing company, whereby it submitted material to the publishing company as camera-ready copy, and the publishing company arranged for the necessary printing and marketing. Under the agreement, the charity granted the publishing company 'the sole and exclusive right to publish and sell' the publications in question. The charity did not account for output tax on the amounts which it received from the company. The Commissioners issued an assessment charging tax on such supplies, and the charity appealed, contending that it had entered into a joint venture and was making zero-rated supplies of books and journals. The tribunal dismissed the appeal, holding on the evidence that the production and publication of the books and journals was the sole responsibility of the publishing company, and that there was 'no common property in the publications'. The publishing company was acting as an independent principal, rather than as an agent of the charity. The charity was supplying services to the publishing company and its supplies were standard-rated. *International Institute for Strategic Studies, LON/95/1533A (VTD 13551)*.

BROCHURES, PAMPHLETS AND LEAFLETS (VATA 1994, Sch 8, Group 3, Item 1)

Goods held to qualify for zero-rating

5.37   **Stapled pamphlets supplied with geological kits.**   A trader supplied a product called 'British Geology', which was primarily a collection of geological specimens, but which included four printed sheets, stapled together, containing relevant information. The stapled sheets could be supplied separately for 10p (wholesale). The Commissioners issued a ruling that his supplies were wholly standard-rated, and he appealed, contending that part of the consideration was attributable to the printed sheets which were a pamphlet and should be zero-rated. The tribunal accepted this contention and allowed his appeal to this extent. (However, printed pieces of card containing instructions for polishing specimens were held to be standard-rated.) *D J Emery, MAN/75/2 (VTD 187)*.

5.38   **Dress designing kits—whether 'brochures'.**   A company supplied courses in dress designing and pattern construction. The course consisted of a folder containing an instruction booklet and instruction sheets, a teaching strip of fabric, some miniature patterns and a fabric requirement planner (a sheet of paper marked in such a way as to achieve the best use of material when cutting out). The Commissioners issued a ruling that the supply of the teaching strip, miniature patterns and fabric planner were standard-rated, and that 54% of the purchase price was attributable to these items. The company appealed, contending that the whole supply was zero-rated. The tribunal accepted this contention and allowed the appeal, holding that there was a single composite supply which, although it had some unusual features, was of a brochure and was zero-rated under what is now *VATA 1994, Sch 8, Group 3, Item 1. Betty Foster (Fashion Sewing) Ltd, [1976] VATTR 229 (VTD 299)*. (*Note.* The Commissioners regard this as 'an exceptional decision' and instruct VAT offices 'to resist its application to any other such other cases'—see Customs' VAT Manual, Part 7, chapter 3, sections 2.18(d) and 3.8.)

5.39   **Advertising materials—whether 'leaflets'.** A company which carried on a printing business produced advertising material, most of which was slightly larger than standard A4 size, and was intended to be delivered by door-to-door canvassers. The Commissioners issued a ruling that output tax was chargeable on the supplies in question. The company appealed, contending that the materials were 'leaflets' and should be zero-rated. The tribunal allowed the company's appeal in part, holding that 38 of the 40 items in question were suitably sized to be described as leaflets and were therefore zero-rated, but that the remaining two items (which measured 20 ins by 15 ins) were too large to be described as leaflets, and were therefore standard-rated. *Cronsvale Ltd, [1983] VATTR 313 (VTD 1552).*

5.40   A company produced printed sheets advertising products for people who were hard of hearing. The sheets were on thick paper, weighing about 150g per square metre, and included a tear-off slip at the bottom of each sheet. They were distributed with newspapers and magazines. The company did not account for output tax on its supplies of these sheets, treating them as zero-rated. The Commissioners issued an assessment charging tax on the supplies, and the company appealed, contending that the printed sheets were within the definition of 'leaflets'. The tribunal accepted this contention and allowed the appeal. The chairman (Mr. Lightman, sitting alone) disapproved *dicta* of Lord Grantchester in *Marylebone Cricket Club*, 5.54 below, and held that 'there is no need for a leaflet to be flimsy'. *Multiform Printing Ltd, [1996] VATDR 580 (VTD 13931).*

5.41   **A4 publication supplied at children's museum—whether 'leaflets'.** A company operated a children's museum. It accounted for output tax on its admission charges. Subsequently its accountants submitted a repayment claim on the basis that part of the admission charges should be attributed to the supply of two publications which were given to visiting children, and these information sheets were leaflets which qualified for zero-rating. The Commissioners accepted that one of the publications was a leaflet, but issued a ruling that the second publication—a folded A4 sheet entitled 'Me and My Body' —was not a leaflet. This publication contained some information about the museum, and a number of questions with spaces for the children to insert the appropriate answer, and the Commissioners considered that it was a worksheet or activity sheet, rather than a leaflet. The tribunal allowed the company's appeal, holding that the publication was within the definition of a 'leaflet'. It was flimsy, designed to be held in the hand, and the area for completion was less than 25% of the total area. *Marylebone Cricket Club*, 5.54 below, distinguished. *Eureka! The Children's Museum, MAN/97/1143 (VTD 15710).*

5.42   **Telecommunications instruction manuals—whether 'brochures'.** A company sold telecommunications equipment, including instruction manuals which it supplied to potential distributors of its equipment. It did not account for VAT on the supply of the instruction manuals, considering that they were zero-rated. The Commissioners issued an assessment on the basis that the manuals were part of a standard-rated supply of items of equipment. The tribunal allowed the company's appeal, holding that the manuals were brochures and were zero-rated. *John Harrison (Gatesby) Ltd, MAN/89/510 & MAN/89/911 (VTD 5581).*

5.43   **Folders containing postage stamps—whether 'brochures'.** A stamp dealer did not account for tax on sales of certain collector's items, originally sold by the Post Office, which consisted of documents made of stout paper or card, measuring about 17 ins by 4 ins, and folded twice so as to produce folders measuring about 7 ins by 4 ins. The folders illustrated particular themes, and included mounted postage stamps relating to that theme. The Commissioners issued a ruling that these supplies did not qualify for zero-rating, and the dealer appealed. The tribunal allowed the appeal, holding that the items were within the definition of 'brochures', so that their sale was zero-rated under what is now *VATA 1994, Sch 8, Group 3, Item 1*. *Betty Foster (Fashion Sewing) Ltd*, 5.38 above, applied. (However, the tribunal also held that old books of stamps, sold by the dealer to collectors, did not qualify for zero-rating, so that tax was chargeable on the excess of the sale price over the face value—the face value being outside the scope of VAT by virtue of what is now *VATA 1994, Sch 6 para 5*.) *SP Schusman, [1994] VATTR 120 (VTD 11835)*.

5.44 **Graphic designer—whether supplying brochures.** A graphic designer (C) agreed to produce a brochure for a building firm. He did not account for output tax on this supply, treating it as zero-rated. The Commissioners issued an assessment on the basis that C was only supplying design services, which did not qualify for zero-rating, and that the actual brochures were supplied by the printer whom C had employed. C appealed, contending that, under the relevant contract, he was wholly responsible for the production of the brochure. The tribunal accepted this contention and allowed C's appeal, holding that he was supplying brochures which qualified for zero-rating. The fact that the printer rendered a separate invoice to the customer 'did not of itself create a separate contract between the printer and the customer'. *AP Carpenter, LON/96/430 (VTD 15253)*.

5.45 **Partnership preparing marketing mailshots for insurance company— whether supplying brochures.** A partnership traded as a marketing agency. It agreed to prepare mailshot packages for an insurance company. The Commissioners issued a ruling that the partnership was making standard-rated supplies of advertising services. The partnership appealed, contending that it was supplying brochures which qualified for zero-rating. The tribunal accepted this contention and allowed the appeal, holding that the partnership was supplying brochures. The supply of the brochures was separate from any previous supply of design services. *Direct Marketing Bureau, MAN/99/581 (VTD 16696)*.

5.46 **Leaflets supplied with promotional services.** A partnership supplied promotional services, including advertising leaflets, to an insurance company. The Commissioners issued a ruling that it was required to account for output tax on the whole of its receipts. The partnership appealed, contending that part of the consideration should be attributed to the supplies of leaflets, which qualified for zero-rating. The Ch D accepted this contention and allowed the appeal. On the evidence, the insurance company ordered the leaflets when they were needed. The partnership had invoiced and itemised the leaflets separately from its promotional services. Accordingly, as a matter of commercial reality, the partnership had made separate supplies and its supplies of leaflets qualified for zero-rating. *Appleby Bowers v C & E Commrs, Ch D 21 November 2000, 2000 STI 1652*.

5.47 **Supplies of study packs to students.** A company advertised GCSE and A level courses in collaboration with colleges of further education. Under the scheme, the company advertised for students, who enrolled with one of the colleges and worked from home with materials supplied by the company, under the supervision of a tutor provided by the company. The company provided the students with 'study packs'. The Commissioners issued an assessment on the basis that the study packs were part of a supply of educational services (which did not qualify for exemption—see 20.19 EDUCATION). The company appealed, contending that the study packs were a separate supply of printed materials which qualified for zero-rating under *VATA 1994, Sch 8, Group 3, Item 1*. The tribunal accepted this contention and allowed the appeal, observing that 'the company does not supply the student with instruction, tuition or schooling. The most it does is to counsel the prospective student and to facilitate his enrolment application at the relevant college.' On the evidence, 'the students' fees relates (*sic*) to what the company provides to the students, that is the course packs coupled with the service of facilitating access to the college'. *Oxford Open Learning (Systems) Ltd (No 2), LON/99/1041 (VTD 16890).*

Goods held not to qualify for zero-rating

5.48   **Car stickers—whether 'leaflets'.** A company supplied car stickers for advertising forthcoming events, and did not account for VAT on these supplies. The Commissioners issued a ruling that the car stickers were liable to VAT, and the company appealed, contending that they were 'leaflets' and should be zero-rated. The tribunal dismissed the company's appeal, holding that a leaflet was something produced and designed to be read by one person at a time. The car stickers were not leaflets, since they were posters or notices designed to be read by the public at large. *Arbroath Herald Ltd, EDN/75/9 (VTD 182).*

5.49   **Adhesive labels in foreign languages—whether 'leaflets'.** A company published sheets of adhesive labels, bearing the names of household objects in a foreign language. They were designed as an aid to the learning of languages. The Commissioners issued a ruling that the company was required to account for output tax on its supplies. The company appealed, contending that the labels should be treated as leaflets and should be zero-rated. The tribunal rejected this contention and dismissed the appeal, holding that the labels were not within the definition of 'leaflets'. *Panini Publishing Ltd,* 5.55 below, applied. *HP Lansdown (Linguistickers) Ltd, LON/96/518 (VTD 14714).*

5.50   **Boards for displaying hairdressing charges—whether 'leaflets'.** A trader supplied black plastic boards, measuring 23 ins by 11 ins, to hairdressers, together with a book of peelable stickers to be placed on the board, to be used for displaying charges to customers. He did not account for VAT on these supplies, and the Commissioners issued an assessment charging tax on them. He appealed, contending that he was supplying leaflets which should be zero-rated. The tribunal dismissed his appeal, holding that the articles were not leaflets. *JD Mortimer, MAN/76/184 (VTD 381).*

5.51   **Advertising materials—whether 'pamphlets'.** A company carried on an advertising consultancy business. It supplied a client with quantities of window banners, door stickers and posters, together with folded 'pamphlets' comprising a single sheet of paper measuring 40 ins by 14 ins and printed on one side. These 'pamphlets' were intended to be used by the client's representatives for showing to retailers who might be interested in the client's products. The tribunal held that these 'pamphlets' qualified for zero-rating, but that the window banners, door stickers and posters were neither pamphlets nor leaflets and were standard-rated. *Arbroath Herald Ltd,* 5.48 above, applied. *Pace Group (Communications) Ltd, MAN/77/210 (VTD 510).*

5.52   **Programmes sold at stamp fairs.** A stamp dealer organised stamp fairs. He prepared for each fair a programme, with details of the exhibitors, which was sold to those attending the fair. There was no admission charge as such. He did not account for VAT on his receipts from programme sales. The Commissioners issued an assessment on the basis that only 25% of the consideration was zero-rated, the remaining 75% being standard-rated as being for admission to the fair. The dealer appealed, contending that the whole of the consideration should be zero-rated. The tribunal upheld the assessment in principle and held on the evidence that two-thirds of the consideration was standard-rated. *MH Jarmain, [1979] VATTR 41 (VTD 723).*

5.53   **Programmes included with admission charge to greyhound stadium.** *Jarmain,* 5.52 above, was applied in a similar case where admission to a greyhound stadium included the provision of a programme. The tribunal held that 15% of the admission fee was zero-rated as being attributable to the supply of the programme, the remaining 85% being standard-rated (see 63.102 VALUATION). *IC Thomas, [1985] VATTR 67 (VTD 1862).*

5.54   **Scorecards at cricket matches—whether 'leaflets'.**   A cricket club sold scorecards at its home matches. These scorecards consisted of a single sheet of card or stiff paper on which were printed the teams and certain other information relating to the match, together with a list of forthcoming fixtures and an advertisement. In 1980 the Commissioners issued a ruling that the scorecards were not eligible for zero-rating. The club appealed, contending that the scorecards were leaflets. The tribunal dismissed the appeal, holding that a leaflet 'a flimsy piece of paper containing propaganda, advertisement or similar information in writing which is distributed gratuitously or for a nominal consideration', and that the scorecards were not within the definition of 'leaflets'. *Marylebone Cricket Club, LON/81/88 (VTD 1074).* (*Note. Dicta* of Lord Grantchester were disapproved by a subsequent tribunal in *Multiform Printing Ltd,* 5.40 above.)

5.55   **Adhesive-backed photographs for insertion into albums—whether leaflets.**   Two companies in the same group distributed adhesive-backed reproductions of photographs. A description of the subject of each photograph was printed on the protective cover for the adhesive back. Each photograph formed part of a series designed to be collected and inserted into an album. The photographs were retailed by newsagents. The companies did not account for VAT on its supplies of the photographs, and the Commissioners issued a ruling that they were standard-rated. The companies appealed, contending that the photographs were leaflets and should be zero-rated. The tribunal dismissed the companies' appeals, holding that 'a leaflet must be limp, and generally if not inevitably on unlaminated paper'. The photographs were not leaflets and were therefore standard-rated. *Panini Publishing Ltd, LON/88/166Y; Mirror Group Newspapers Ltd, LON/88/887X (VTD 3876).*

5.56   **Pictures of sports personalities.**   A partnership sold pictures of sports personalities. It failed to account for output tax on its sales. The Commissioners issued an assessment charging tax on them, and the partnership appealed, contending that they should be treated as zero-rated. The tribunal rejected this contention and dismissed the appeal. *D & J Foster (t/a David Foster Associates), MAN/95/2552 (VTD 14820).*

5.57   **Illustrated children's story sheets—whether 'leaflets'.**   A company sold packs designed for pre-school children. The packs included play mats and jigsaw puzzles, which were accepted as standard-rated, and leaflets for parents, which were accepted as zero-rated. They also contained illustrated story sheets and dictionary cards. The story sheets were printed on one side of the paper, and some words were printed in red so as to correspond with the words in the dictionary cards. There were eight dictionary cards in each pack, which were held together by an elastic band. The Commissioners issued a ruling that neither of these items qualified for zero-rating. The company appealed, contending that the items were leaflets. The tribunal rejected this contention and dismissed the appeal, and the QB upheld this decision. *Betty Foster (Fashion Sewing) Ltd,* 5.38 above, applied. *Odhams Leisure Group Ltd v C & E Commrs, QB [1992] STC 332.* (*Note.* For another issue in this case, see 2.3 APPEALS.)

5.58   **Information sheets—whether 'brochures' or 'leaflets'.**   A partnership produced and distributed information sheets providing information about company law, tax and insolvency. The sheets were made of stiff plastic and measured about 9 ins by 12 ins. The Commissioners issued a ruling that the sheets were standard-rated and the partnership appealed, contending that the sheets were brochures or pamphlets, and should be zero-rated. The tribunal rejected this contention and dismissed the appeal, holding that the sheets could not be described either as brochures or as pamphlets. *Panini Publishing Ltd*, 5.55 above, applied; *Betty Foster (Fashion Sewing) Ltd*, 5.38 below, distinguished. *Infocard, LON/90/1314Z (VTD 5732).*

5.59   **Tax cards—whether 'brochures' or 'leaflets'.**   A company published glossy cards, which it described as 'tax cards', containing various items of information relating to tax. The cards measured 21½ centimetres by 10¼ centimetres, and were scored in such a way that they could be folded into three, enabling them to be kept in a jacket pocket. The company did not account for VAT on the supply of these cards. The Commissioners issued a ruling that the cards were standard-rated, and the company appealed, contending that the cards were brochures or leaflets. The tribunal rejected this contention and dismissed the appeal, holding that the cards were not brochures since they consisted of a single sheet, and were not leaflets since they were printed on stiff card whereas a leaflet must be limp. *Panini Publishing Ltd*, 5.55 above, and *Christian Art Ltd*, 5.60 below, applied. *Tax Briefs Ltd, LON/91/2541Z (VTD 9258).*

5.60   **Cards containing religious verse—whether 'leaflets'.**   A company carried on business as wholesale suppliers of religious articles. It sold laminated cards, measuring 9.5cm by 6cm, containing a prayer or religious verses. It did not account for VAT on sales of these cards. The Commissioners issued an assessment charging tax on them, and the company appealed, contending that they were 'leaflets' and should be zero-rated. The tribunal rejected this contention and dismissed the company's appeal, holding that the cards did not qualify as 'leaflets' and were not eligible for zero-rating. *Marylebone Cricket Club*, 5.54 above, and *Panini Publishing Ltd*, 5.55 above, applied. *Christian Art Ltd, LON/90/414Z (VTD 5940).*

5.61   **Laminated recipe cards—whether 'leaflets'.**   A company produced laminated cards, on which were printed recipes. The Commissioners issued a ruling that the cards were not eligible for zero-rating, and the company appealed, contending that they were leaflets and should be zero-rated. The tribunal rejected this contention and dismissed the appeal, holding that the cards did not qualify as leaflets. *Odhams Leisure Group Ltd*, 5.57 above, and *Panini Publishing Ltd*, 5.55 above, applied. *International Master Publishers Ltd, LON/91/2534Y (VTD 8807).* (*Note.* For another issue in this case, see 5.23 above.)

5.62   **Illustrated A4 cards—whether 'leaflets'.**   A company produced packs of A4 cards. The front of each card contained a copy of a painting or drawing, and the back of the card contained information about the painting or drawing in question. The Commissioners issued a ruling that output tax was chargeable on the supplies, and the company appealed, contending that the cards should be treated as leaflets and as zero-rated. The tribunal rejected this contention and dismissed the appeal. *Odhams Leisure Group Ltd*, 5.57 above, and *Panini Publishing Ltd*, 5.55 above, applied. *Philip Green Education Ltd, MAN/97/1202 (VTD 15669).*

5.63   **Inserts for telephone directories—whether leaflets.**   A printing company supplied inserts for 'Yellow Pages' telephone directories. The inserts were printed on shiny paper which was substantially heavier than the rest of the directory, so that the volume would naturally fall open at the insert and provide publicity to the advertiser. The company did not account for VAT on the inserts, and the Commissioners issued an assessment charging tax on the consideration. The company appealed, contending that the inserts were leaflets and should be zero-rated. The tribunal rejected this contention and dismissed the appeal, holding that, in view of the weight of the paper in question, the inserts did not qualify as leaflets and were not eligible for zero-rating. *Odhams Leisure Group Ltd*, 5.57 above, and *Panini Publishing Ltd*, 5.55 above, applied. *Adland Group Co Ltd, LON/92/1871A (VTD 10397).*

5.64   **Broadsheet containing information about greyhound racing—whether a 'pamphlet'.**   See *Evans & Marland Ltd*, 5.69 below.

5.65   **'Discount cards'—whether brochures.**   Two companies issued documents incorporating 'discount cards', with a face value of £14.99, entitling the holder to obtain a free course on up to twelve occasions at a stated restaurant. The Commissioners issued a ruling that output tax was payable on the supplies of the cards, and the companies appealed, contending that the cards should be treated as brochures and as zero-rated under *Sch 8, Group 3, Item 1.* The tribunal rejected this contention and dismissed the appeal. The tribunal declined to follow *obiter dicta* of Waite LJ in *Granton Ltd*, 63.53 VALUATION, on the grounds that that case had been concerned with whether the cards were within what is now *VATA 1994, Sch 6 para 5.* Although Waite LJ had stated that the cards were 'incorporated in a three-page brochure', the question of whether the cards were brochures was not an issue which the CA had been asked to determine, so that 'the use of that word by Waite LJ can therefore not have been a part of the *ratio decidendi* of that judgment'. Furthermore, Waite LJ had only stated that the card was incorporated in a 'brochure', rather than that it was a brochure. The document was perforated so that the part which entitled the bearer to a discount could be torn off. The tribunal held that this was 'the essential part of the whole A4 document' and that it was not within the definition of a 'brochure'. The discount cards were sold because they gave rise to an 'expectation of benefit', and it followed that their sale was a supply of services, rather than of goods, and was standard-rated. *Interleisure Club Ltd*, 5.27 above, applied. *Full Force Marketing Ltd; Framesouth Ltd, LON/93/783 (VTD 15270).*

5.66   **Business registration certificates.**   A company provided a service of registering business names, in accordance with the *Business Names Act 1985.* It treated part of its fees as attributable to the issue of certificates, and as zero-rated. The Commissioners issued an assessment to recover the tax, and the tribunal dismissed the company's appeal. Firstly, the company was making a single composite supply of registration services, which were standard-rated, and the supply of a certificate was incidental. *Schoemann ISR (UK) Ltd*, 5.35 above, applied. Secondly, the supply of a certificate did not qualify for zero-rating under *VATA 1994, Sch 8, Group 3, Item 1*, since a certificate was not within the definition of a 'leaflet' or 'pamphlet'. *BNR Company Services Ltd, MAN/94/1618 (VTD 13783).*

5.67   **Postal games—whether part of consideration attributable to supply of printed matter.**   See *Cropper*, 58.420 SUPPLY, and *M & E Sports Ltd*, 58.421 SUPPLY.

NEWSPAPERS, JOURNALS AND PERIODICALS (VATA 1994, Sch 8, Group 3, Item 2)

5.68   **Property guides.**   A firm of chartered surveyors and estate agents published a monthly property guide, consisting almost entirely of advertisements for houses. It was sold to other estate agents, rather than to members of the public. The firm did not account for VAT on supplies of this guide, and the Commissioners issued an assessment charging tax on them. The firm appealed, contending that the guide should be zero-rated as a 'newspaper, journal or periodical'. The tribunal rejected this contention and dismissed the appeal, and the QB upheld this decision. The guide contained nothing which could be regarded as news and thus was not a newspaper or journal. Since it was not sold to the public, it was not within the ordinary meaning of 'periodical'. *Snushall Dalby & Robinson v C & E Commrs, QB [1982] STC 537.*

5.69   **Broadsheet containing information about greyhound racing.**   A company produced a publication which gave information concerning greyhound races. It was printed on one side of the paper only, and was designed to be displayed in betting shops. 95% of its subscribers were proprietors of betting shops. It was produced on most weekdays throughout the year. The Commissioners issued a ruling that the publication did not qualify for zero-rating, and the company appealed, contending firstly that it was a 'newspaper or journal', and alternatively that it was a pamphlet. The tribunal rejected these contentions and dismissed the appeal, holding that it was not a newspaper or journal, since its predominant function was to act as a guide to betting rather than to publish new information about recent or imminent events, and its format disqualified it from being a pamphlet. *Evans & Marland Ltd (t/a Greyform Publications), [1988] VATTR 115 (VTD 3158).*

5.70   **Quarterly pictorial magazine—whether a 'periodical'.**   A publishing company produced a quarterly 32–page magazine called 'Just Seventeen Posters'. It consisted almost entirely of large poster-sized photographs. It treated its sales of the magazine as zero-rated under *VATA 1994, Sch 8, Group 3, Item 2.* The Commissioners issued a ruling that the publication did not qualify for zero-rating, and the company appealed, contending that the publication was a 'periodical'. The tribunal allowed the appeal, holding that the publication was within the ordinary meaning of the word 'periodical' notwithstanding the fact that it had very little text, and that some readers would probably unstaple it to extract some of the posters. *EMAP Consumer Magazines Ltd, LON/94/1710 (VTD 13322).*

5.71   **Bi-monthly publication with poster-sized photographs of musicians.**   In August and October 1993 a company published two issues of a bi-monthly publication devoted to a group of musicians. In 1994 it published a third issue of the publication in a somewhat different format. It did not account for output tax on its sales of the publication, treating it as a zero-rated periodical. The Commissioners issued a ruling that the publication did not qualify for zero-rating, and the company appealed. The tribunal allowed the appeal. Applying *EMAP Consumer Magazines Ltd*, 5.70 above, the fact that much of the publication consisted of poster-sized photographs did not prevent it from qualifying as a 'periodical'. The tribunal was satisfied on the evidence that it had been the company's intention 'at the relevant time to continue with regular publication, although it later decided to cease or suspend further publication'. *European Publishing Consultants Ltd, LON/94/698A (VTD 13841).*

5.72   **Broadcasting services—whether part of consideration attributable to magazine.**   A company supplied satellite broadcasting services to subscribers. It provided the subscribers with a magazine providing details of the programmes which it broadcast. The Commissioners ruled that the whole of the subscriptions were for standard-rated supplies of broadcasting services. The company appealed, contending that part of the subscription should be attributed to zero-rated supplies of the magazines. The tribunal rejected this contention and dismissed the appeal, holding that the 'true nature of the contract' between the company and the subscribers was that the company was making single supplies of broadcasting services. *Dicta* of the CJEC in *Card Protection Plan Ltd*, 21.162 EUROPEAN COMMUNITY LAW, applied; *Automobile Association*, 13.17 CLUBS, ASSOCIATIONS AND ORGANISATIONS, distinguished. *British Sky Broadcasting Group plc, [1999] VATDR 283 (VTD 16220).* (*Note.* For subsequent developments in this case, see 2.233 APPEALS.)

5.73 Books, etc.

5.73 **Quarterly magazine supplied to members of Institute—whether part of subscription attributable to magazine.** See *Institute of Chartered Foresters*, 13.19 CLUBS, ASSOCIATIONS AND ORGANISATIONS.

5.74 **Magazine distribution company—whether supplies of magazines within Group 3, Item 2.** See *Odhams Distribution Pergamon Holdings Ltd*, 1.39 AGENTS.

5.75 **Free gifts supplied with magazines—whether supplies entirely zero-rated.** A company (K) published magazines for children. It supplied free gifts with the magazines. The magazines were distributed by another company (C), which paid K 55% of the cover price of the magazines. The Commissioners issued an assessment on the basis that the free gifts were a separate supply which did not qualify for zero-rating. K appealed, contending that the free gifts cost less than 20% of the cover price of the magazines, and therefore qualified as a linked supply under what is now Extra-Statutory Concession 3.7. The tribunal rejected this contention and dismissed K's appeal, finding that the 'total cost' for the purposes of Extra-Statutory Concession 3.7 was the 55% which K received from C. C was an independent principal rather than an agent of K. Accordingly, the cost of the free gifts exceeded 20% of the total cost of the magazines, and they were a separate supply which could not be treated as zero-rated. *Keesing (UK) Ltd, LON/98/898 (VTD 16840)*.

5.76 **Company placing orders for magazines with publishers—magazines sent by publishers to subscribers—whether company making supplies of magazines within Sch 8, Group 3.** See *Nordic Subscription Service UK Ltd*, 1.41 AGENTS.

5.77 **In-house magazines distributed to employees—whether a zero-rated supply within Sch 8, Group 3.** See *The Post Office*, 58.94 SUPPLY.

5.78 **News digest supplied by fax, E-mail or internet.** A company (F) supplied a regular digest of financial news to customers by fax, E-mail or internet. The Commissioners issued a ruling that F's supplies failed to qualify for zero-rating, since the paper which produced the printed matter was provided by F's customers, rather than by F. The tribunal dismissed F's appeal, holding that 'exemptions and zero-ratings must be strictly construed' and observing that *Group 3* 'clearly refers to goods, or in the language of *Article 5* of the *Sixth Directive*, to tangible property'. F was supplying information 'in the form of electrical impulses' and it 'would be stretching the language of the statute beyond reasonable limits' to hold that F's supplies qualified for zero-rating. The tribunal observed that 'it may be that the European Court of Justice will eventually have to tackle the whole problem of electronic commerce, but we do not think that this case would be a proper one to refer on our own initiative'. *Forexia (UK) Ltd, LON/98/879 (VTD 16041)*.

5.79 **Delivery charges by newsagents—whether part of consideration for newspaper.** See *Coe*, 54.2 RETAILERS' SPECIAL SCHEMES, and the cases noted at 54.3 RETAILERS' SPECIAL SCHEMES.

MUSIC (VATA 1994, Sch 8, Group 3, Item 4)

5.80 **Flipcards containing information about music.** A company sold packs of cards which measured 9cm by 5.7cm, resembled small playing cards in appearance, and were printed on glossy cardboard. They were sold in packs of about 100. One side of each card contained a question about music, with the answer to the question being printed on the reverse of the card. The company did not account for output tax on sales of the cards, treating them as zero-rated. The Commissioners issued a ruling that the cards did not qualify for zero-rating. The company appealed, contending that each set of cards should be treated as zero-rated under *VATA 1994, Sch 8, Group*

3, Item 4. The tribunal rejected this contention and dismissed the appeal, holding that 'music' should be defined as 'the written or printed score or set of parts of a musical composition' and that the cards in question were outside this definition. *Flip Cards (Marine) Ltd, MAN/96/248 (VTD 14483).*

MAPS, CHARTS, ETC. (VATA 1994, Sch 8, Group 3, Item 5)

5.81   **Histographs.**   A company sold sets of 'histographs', which set out the family trees of the Kings and Queens of England in tabular form as historical charts. It did not account for VAT on these supplies. The Commissioners issued a ruling that they were standard-rated, and the company appealed, contending that they were zero-rated under what is now *VATA 1994, Sch 8, Group 3, Item 5.* The tribunal rejected this contention and dismissed the appeal, holding that, under the '*eiusdem generis*' principle, the reference to 'charts' in *Item 5* had to be construed in the context of the entire *Item*, and referred to geographical charts only and not to historical charts. Accordingly, the supply of historical charts was standard-rated. *Brooks Histograph Ltd, [1984] VATTR 46 (VTD 1570).*

6 Buildings and Land

Cross-references. For cases concerning the zero-rating provisions of *VATA 1994, Sch 8, Group 5*, see 15 CONSTRUCTION OF BUILDINGS, ETC. For cases concerning the zero-rating provisions of *VATA 1994, Sch 8, Group 6*, see 52 PROTECTED BUILDINGS. For cases concerning exemption under *VATA 1994, Sch 9, Group 1*, see 39 LAND.

The cases in this chapter are arranged under the following headings.

> **Developers of non-residential buildings (VATA 1994, Sch 10, paras 5–7)** 6.1–6.5
>
> **Elections to waive exemption (VATA 1994, Sch 10, paras 2, 3)**
> The date from which the election is effective 6.6–6.21
> Miscellaneous 6.22–6.35
> **Supplies between landlord and tenant** 6.36–6.44

DEVELOPERS OF NON-RESIDENTIAL BUILDINGS (VATA 1994, Sch 10, paras 5–7)

Note. *VATA 1994, Sch 10, paras 5–7* contain provisions, originally introduced by *FA 1989*, imposing a self-supply charge on developers of non-residential buildings put to exempt use within a ten-year period. The charge was phased out over the period to 1 March 1997 and was abolished for all new developments beginning after 28 February 1995.

6.1   The governors of an independent school obtained planning permission to develop new playing fields on what had previously been farmland. They incorporated a subsidiary company to administer the new facilities. The school granted the company a lease of the facilities for a period of twelve years, for a premium of £187,500 and an annual rent, and the company gave the school a non-exclusive licence to use the facilities in return for an annual licence fee. The school elected to waive exemption in respect of the lease, and reclaimed the input tax charged by the contractors who had completed the development. The Commissioners formed the opinion that the school had developed a non-residential building for the purposes of its business and was liable to account for output tax on the full cost of construction and the value of the land under what is now *VATA 1994, Sch 10, paras 5, 6*. The school appealed, contending that these provisions were not applicable since it was using the building as a licensee rather than as a developer. The tribunal accepted this contention and allowed the school's appeal, and the HL upheld this decision. *Articles 5(7)* and *6(3)* of the *EC Sixth Directive* permitted a self-supply to be treated as a taxable transaction in a case in which input tax would not have been wholly deductible if the goods or services in question had been acquired from a third person. However, the self-supply provisions did not apply where the relevant goods or services were in fact acquired from a third person, and the question of whether such input tax was deductible had to be determined in the ordinary way, i.e. according to whether it could be attributed to a taxable supply. In this case, the school was using the sports ground under the terms of the licence granted by the subsidiary company, so that the charge to tax was not in accordance with the *Sixth Directive*. Lord Hoffmann held that the fact that the school had originally developed the land and leased it to the company was irrelevant, since it was 'not permissible to take a global view of the series of transactions in the chain of supply'. Furthermore, the whole of the expenditure on the development was attributable to the taxable supply which the school made to the subsidiary company, so that the input tax was deductible in full. *Robert Gordon's College v C & E Commrs, HL [1995] STC 1093; [1996] 1 WLR 201.*

6.2   A doctor purchased the site of the surgery from which he practised. He had the old surgery demolished and a new surgery built on the same site. The Commissioners issued an assessment charging tax on the value of the land and the cost of the construction work, in accordance with what is now *VATA 1994, Sch 10 paras 5, 6*. The doctor appealed, contending firstly that the £45,000 which he had paid for the land should be disregarded, and secondly that he should not be treated as a 'developer' within *Sch 10 para 5(5)*, since he was using the surgery for the purposes of the National Health Service. The tribunal rejected these contentions and dismissed his appeal, holding firstly that the amount which the doctor had paid for the land had to be included in the computation, and secondly that the doctor occupied the surgery as a principal for his own practice. *Dr BHV Bray, LON/92/2116A (VTD 10274)*.

6.3   A medical partnership purchased a site adjacent to its surgery, at a cost of £128,000, demolished the house which had occupied the site, and built an extension to the surgery. The extension did not occupy the whole of the site in question; part of the site was used as a car park, and the remainder was landscaped. In accounting for VAT on the deemed self-supply of the surgery extension under what is now *VATA 1994, Sch 10 para 6*, the partnership did not account for tax on the whole of the £128,000 which it had paid for the site, but only on the proportion of that amount which equated to the proportion of the site which the extension occupied. The Commissioners issued a ruling that the partnership should have accounted for VAT on the whole of the £128,000, and the partnership appealed. The tribunal dismissed the appeal, holding that the whole of the value of the site had to be brought into account. *Drs Shutes Robinson & Ling, [1993] VATTR 459 (VTD 11552)*.

6.4   In 1992 a doctor purchased 9045 square feet of land, including a two-storey building with a gross external floor area of 1640 square feet, of which 878 square feet were used as a surgery. She paid £220,939, of which £160,683 was attributed to the building and £60,256 to the land. In 1994 she built an extension, with a gross external floor area of 1271 square feet, on the land. The Commissioners issued a ruling that output tax was chargeable on the deemed self-supply under *VATA 1994, Sch 10 para 5*, that the appropriate fraction under *Sch 10 para 6(2)(a)* was 1271/2911, and that this fraction was applied to the £60,256 paid for the land, so that the value of the self-supply for VAT purposes was £26,308.97. The doctor appealed, accepting that there had been a self-supply and that the 'appropriate fraction' was 1271/2911, but contending that the 'land on which the existing building stands' for the purposes of *Sch 10 para 6(2)(a)* should be treated as being restricted to the 878 square feet which were used as a surgery (i.e. 9.07% of the total land area), so that the fraction of 1271/2911 should only be applied to 9.07% of the £60,256 paid for the land, so that the value of the self-supply for VAT purposes was only £2,553.81. The tribunal rejected these contentions and dismissed the doctor's appeal, holding that 'the natural construction of the phrase "the land on which the existing building stands" includes the curtilage of the existing building'. *Dr A Garcav, LON/96/253 (VTD 14640)*. *(Note*. The doctor, who did not attend the hearing and was not represented, was given leave to apply for a further hearing to consider the application of *Articles 5(7)* and *6(3)* of the *EC Sixth Directive*. However, there was no further hearing of the appeal.)

6.5   See also *Fforestfach Medical Centre*, 6.16 below.

ELECTIONS TO WAIVE EXEMPTION (VATA 1994, Sch 10, paras 2, 3)

The date from which the election is effective

6.6   **Whether election may be retrospective.**   A unit trust owned the freehold of a building which was leased to the Law Society until August 1988. From September

6.7   Buildings and Land

1988 to March 1990 the building was unoccupied while refurbishments took place. In March 1990 it was let to a firm of solicitors. In September the trustees of the unit trust notified the Commissioners that they wished to elect to waive exemption with effect from 1 August 1989. Subsequently they reclaimed input tax which they had incurred between August 1988 and August 1989. The Commissioners refused to repay the tax incurred prior to 1 August 1989. The trustees appealed, contending that the provisions of what is now *VATA 1994, Sch 10* were inconsistent with *Article 13C* of the *EC Sixth Directive*. The tribunal rejected this contention and dismissed the trustees' appeal, holding that *Article 13C* of the *Directive* gave member states the right to restrict the scope of the option to tax such supplies. *Newcourt Property Fund, LON/90/1029X (VTD 5825)*.

6.7   *Newcourt Property Fund*, 6.6 above, was applied in the similar cases of *Bradshaw & Others (as Trustees for Taylor Dyne Ltd Pension Fund), [1992] VATTR 315 (VTD 6964)* and *Acre Friendly Society, [1992] VATTR 308 (VTD 7649)*.

6.8   A similar decision was reached in *Pinchdean Ltd, LON/91/1678Z (VTD 9796)*.

6.9   A company built an extension to its premises, which it let to an associated company. It reclaimed input tax in respect of the extension in its returns for August and November 1989. The Commissioners issued an assessment to recover the tax, considering that the input tax was not reclaimable since it related to an exempt supply. The company appealed, contending that it had intended to waive exemption in respect of the building in question. A written election was sent to the local VAT office on 14 September 1990. The tribunal dismissed the company's appeal, holding that, by virtue of what is now *VATA 1994, Sch 10 para 3(1)(a)*, the election was only effective from 14 September 1990 and could not be backdated. Under *Sch 10 para 2(4)*, input tax could not be reclaimed in respect of a supply which had taken place before the effective date of the election. *Hi-Wire Ltd, MAN/90/990 (VTD 6204)*.

6.10   Similar decisions were reached in *V Dennis (t/a Lynden Property Co), LON/92/ 641Y (VTD 11299); Hellesdon Developments Ltd*, 43.48 PARTIAL EXEMPTION, and *22A Property Investments Ltd*, 58.162 SUPPLY.

6.11   In December 1991 the trustees of a pension fund (L) purchased a leasehold property which comprised office accommodation with a residential flat. The vendor had elected to waive exemption in respect of the property, and issued an invoice including VAT. L reclaimed the VAT as input tax in its return for the period ending 31 December 1991. However, the Commissioners did not repay the tax, as L had not notified them whether it would elect to waive exemption on the property in question. In February 1992 L submitted an election to waive exemption in respect of its ownership of the property. The election was backdated to the date of purchase. The Commissioners took the view that the input tax on the purchase of the property should be treated as deductible on the date of the election, when it became clear that it had been incurred for the purpose of making a taxable supply, so that it was only repayable following receipt of the company's return for the period ending 31 March 1992. L submitted a claim for repayment supplement on the basis that the input tax should have been treated as deductible in December 1991 and repaid accordingly, and appealed against the Commissioners' refusal of the claim. The tribunal dismissed L's appeal, holding that, until L had made an election to waive exemption, there were no grounds for treating the input tax as attributable to an intended taxable supply. *Lawson Mardon Group Pension Scheme, LON/92/492 (VTD 10231)*.

6.12   **Whether letter constituted an election—whether election irrevocable.**   In November 1989 a company wrote to its local VAT office stating that 'as from our rental quarter commencing 25 December 1989 we wish to charge VAT on our rental invoices'. The VAT office treated this as an election under what is now *VATA 1994,*

Sch 10. At a control visit in July 1990, a VAT officer discovered that, despite the letter, the company had not accounted for VAT. The Commissioners issued an assessment charging tax on the rents received after 25 December. The tribunal dismissed the company's appeal, holding that the letter constituted an election and that an election was irrevocable. *Devoirs Properties Ltd, MAN/90/1061 (VTD 6646)*.

6.13   In July 1989 a property development company wrote to its local VAT office concerning a building which it had purchased, and stating 'it is our intention, as owners of the above building, to elect that as from now the building is to be treated as taxable under the commercial property regulations'. The VAT office replied, stating 'we acknowledge that you will exercise your option to tax at the standard rate supplies in respect of the above building'. In 1994 the company went into receivership, and the receivers sold the building in question. The Commissioners issued a ruling that, in view of the election to waive exemption, output tax was payable on the sale. The company appealed, contending that its letter of July 1989 'was a letter expressing intention ... at no time did we write to make the formal election'. The tribunal rejected this contention and dismissed the appeal, holding that the company had made an irrevocable election to waive exemption. *Devoirs Properties Ltd*, 6.12 above, applied. *Resource Maintenance Ltd, LON/95/137A (VTD 13204)*.

6.14   An election to waive exemption was also held to be irrevocable in *Coach House Property Management Ltd, LON/91/1709Z (VTD 7564)*.

6.15   *Coach House Property Management Ltd*, 6.14 above, was applied in the similar case of *Brollies Ltd, MAN/93/556 (VTD 11966)*.

6.16   **Letter held not to constitute election.**   A medical partnership entered into a contract to develop some land as a new medical centre. The partnership registered for VAT in 1993, and the centre was let to tenants in October 1995. In April 1996 the partnership's accountants wrote to the Commissioners, asking them to treat the letter as a 'retrospective election' to waive exemption. The Commissioners informed the accountants that, if the partnership had 'previously made exempt supplies (since 1989) on the above property, this option (*sic*) cannot take effect until you have written to Customs & Excise with full details'. Subsequently the partnership reclaimed input tax on the development. In February 1998, after further correspondence, the Commissioners issued an assessment under the self-supply provisions of *VATA 1994, Sch 10 paras 5, 6* (see 6.1 *et seq*. above), on the basis that they were not satisfied that the partnership had accounted for output tax on rents received from tenants. The partnership appealed. The tribunal dismissed the partnership's appeal, holding that the letter of April 1996 'was not, and was not capable of being, a valid notification of an election to tax with effect from any date'. *Fforestfach Medical Centre, LON/98/746 (VTD 16587)*. (*Note*. The tribunal also held that the assessment had been made within the one-year time limit of *VATA 1994, s 73(6)(b)*—see 3.47 appeals.)

6.17   **Whether election made although not notified to Commissioners.**   A company (F) let a property on an industrial estate to another company (G). On the advice of its accountants, F charged VAT on the rent. Subsequently F sold the property to G for £200,000. On the advice of its solicitor, F did not charge VAT on the sale. The Commissioners considered that, by charging VAT on the rent, F had elected to waive exemption on the property, and should therefore have charged VAT on the sale. F appealed, contending that it had not made a formal election to waive exemption, and that the sale was therefore exempt from VAT. The tribunal rejected this contention and dismissed the appeal (with liberty to apply for a further hearing as to whether the £200,000 should be held to be inclusive or exclusive of tax). The act of election and the act of notification were two distinct processes. Since F had no right to charge VAT on the rent except by making an election under what is now *VATA 1994, Sch 10 para 2*, its demands for VAT on the rent were an election that its supplies in relation to the property were no longer to be exempt from VAT. *Fencing Supplies Ltd, [1993] VATTR 302 (VTD 10451)*. (*Note*. See now *VATA 1994, Sch 10 para 3(6)* as substituted by *SI 1995 No 279* with effect from 1 March 1995.)

6.18   A similar decision was reached in *Resource Maintenance Ltd*, 6.13 above.

6.19   The decision in *Fencing Supplies Ltd*, 6.17 above, was applied in a subsequent case in which the tribunal upheld a company's claim that it had made an election to waive exemption on 31 July 1999, although it had not notified the election to Customs until 10 November 1999. *Classic Furniture (Newport) Ltd, MAN/00/34 (VTD 16977)*.

6.20   An election which had not been notified was held to be ineffective in *McMaster Stores (Scotland) Ltd*, 45.16 PAYMENT OF TAX.

6.21   A similar decision was reached in *Euro Properties (Scotland) Ltd, EDN/95/306 (15291)*.

Miscellaneous

6.22   **Amount of consideration where election to waive exemption not made.**   A development company (J) agreed to buy some agricultural land from another company (E). In its letter of offer, J described the agreed price as 'deemed to be inclusive of VAT'. The sale of the land was exempt from VAT under what is now *VATA 1994, Sch 9, Group 1*, although E could have made an election to waive exemption under *VATA 1994, Sch 10*. E did not make any such election. J took legal proceedings against E, contending that, since E could have waived exemption, and J could then have reclaimed input tax, E should repay to J the proportion of the price that would have represented VAT if an election had been made. The CS rejected this contention and dismissed the proceedings. The contract had specified a single price, and the words 'deemed to be inclusive of VAT' merely meant that the price would be deemed to include VAT if any were payable. Since no VAT was payable, the contingency implied in the clause did not take effect, and J was not entitled to any repayment. *Jaymarke Developments Ltd v Elinacre Ltd (in liquidation) & Others, CS [1992] STC 575*.

6.23   **Sale of public house—whether within Sch 10 para 2(2)(a).**   A brewery sold a disused public house, in respect of which it had elected to waive exemption. It charged output tax on the sale. The purchaser lodged an appeal, contending that the effect of what is now *Sch 10 para 2(2)(a)* was that output tax should not have been charged, since he intended to use the building as a dwelling. The tribunal accepted this contention and allowed his appeal, holding on the evidence that he had always intended to use the building as a dwelling and that he had communicated this intention to the brewery, so that the effect of *Sch 10 para 2(2)(a)* was that the sale was exempt from VAT. *J Watters, LON/94/2980A (VTD 13337)*.

6.24   A company (P) sold a disused public house to an unrelated company in the construction industry (S). P had elected to waive exemption in relation to the property. On the same day S sold the property to two purchasers, and contracted with the purchasers to build residential units on the site. P accounted for output tax on its sale to S. S appealed to the tribunal, contending that despite P's election to waive exemption, the sale should have been treated as exempt by virtue of *VATA 1994, Sch 10 para 2(2)(a)*. The tribunal rejected this contention and dismissed the appeal, holding that *Sch 10 para 2(2)(a)* only applied where the purchaser intended to use the building as a dwelling, which was not the case here. The tribunal observed that 'normally the rate of value added tax applicable to any transaction is determinable by the application of objective criteria. However, in this appeal the rate depends, unusually, on the intention of someone other than the supplier.' Accordingly 'the legislation which refers to such intention should be narrowly construed', since 'any move away from the contractual link between the vendor and the purchaser would create many difficulties'. The tribunal also held that it was necessary for the vendor to be aware of the purchaser's intention at the time of the sale and, on the evidence, S had not shown that P was aware of the intended use of the property at the time of the sale. *SEH Holdings Ltd, LON/98/1362 (VTD 16771)*.

6.25   In the case noted at 61.75 TRANSFERS OF GOING CONCERNS, the tribunal held that an election to waive exemption extended to the whole of a public house. On the evidence, none of the building was 'intended for use as a dwelling', since no part of it consisted of 'self-contained living accommodation', within *VATA 1994, Sch 8, Group 5, Note 2(a)*. Accordingly *VATA 1994, Sch 10 para 2(2)(a)* did not apply and the whole of the building was covered by the election under *VATA 1994, Sch 10 para 2(1)*. *AJ White, LON/96/1964 (VTD 15388)*.

6.26   **Building leased to charity—application of Sch 10 para 2(2)(b).**   A company reclaimed input tax on the refurbishment of a building (consisting of a shop and three flats), in respect of which it had elected to waive exemption. The Commissioners issued an assessment to recover the tax, on the basis that the ground floor of the building (the shop) was leased to a charity, so that the effect of *Sch 10 para 2(2)(b)* was that the election was ineffective. The tribunal upheld the assessment and dismissed the company's appeal. *Headway Commercial Ltd, EDN/97/179 (VTD 15535)*.

6.27   **VATA 1994, Sch 10 para 2(3AA)—election ineffective and supply remaining exempt.**   A company (P), which was the trustee of a number of personal pension schemes and was a member of a VAT group, purchased a property in respect of which the vendor had elected to waive exemption. P granted a lease of the property to three pension scheme members, who occupied the property for an exempt insurance business, and whose contributions had been used to fund the acquisition of the property. In an attempt to recover input tax on the purchase of the property, P elected to waive exemption. The Commissioners issued a ruling that the effect of *VATA 1994, Sch 10 para 2(3AA)* was that P's election was ineffective and that the lease to the pension scheme members remained exempt. The representative member of P's VAT group appealed, contending that the purpose of *Sch 10 para 2(3AA)* was to counter tax avoidance, whereas the transaction here was a legitimate commercial transaction. The tribunal dismissed the appeal and upheld the Commissioners' ruling. The pension scheme members had provided finance for the acquisition of the land, within *Sch 10 para 3A(3)(a)*. Accordingly, the conditions of *Sch 10 para 2(3AA)* were satisfied and the election was ineffective. The facts that the transactions 'were not for the avoidance of taxation', and that 'the terms of the lease were fully commercial', were not conclusive. There was no ambiguity in the legislation, so that the decision in *Pepper v Hart, HL [1992] STC 898 (TTC 2001, 65.94)* did not apply. The provisions of *Sch 10 para 2(3AA)* were authorised by *Article 13C* of the *EC Sixth Directive*. (The tribunal observed that, unlike *Articles 13A* and *13B*, *Article 13C* made no reference to the prevention of 'possible evasion, avoidance or abuse', but simply provided that 'Member States may restrict the scope of this right of option and shall fix the details of its use'.) *Winterthur Life UK Ltd (No 2), LON/98/127 (VTD 15785)*.

6.28   A company (E) and a NHS trust entered into a development agreement whereby E agreed to construct a building for the trust, the trust agreed to grant E a 99–year lease of the building, E agreed to grant an underlease of the building back to the trust (for 99 years less 3 days), and the trust agreed to grant E a sub–underlease of about 70% of the building. E made an election to waive exemption in respect of the underlease, with the intention of recovering the input tax on the construction of the building. The Commissioners issued a ruling that the effect of *VATA 1994, Sch 10 para 2(3AA)* was that P's election was ineffective and that the underlease to the trust remained exempt. The tribunal upheld the Commissioners' ruling and dismissed E's appeal, holding that E was a 'developer of the land' within *Sch 10 para 2(3AA)(a)* and *3A(2)*. The land was a capital item within *VAT Regulations 1995 (SI 1995 No 2518), regs 112(2), 113(e)*. The grant of a lease of an uncompleted building was within the definition of 'use' for the purposes of *reg 113(e)* and *114(4)(e)*. The fact that the building was incomplete did not prevent it from constituting a 'building' for the purposes of *reg 113(e)*. The grant had been made within the period laid down by *Sch 10 para 3A(2)(b)*. *East Kent Medical Services Ltd, LON/98/935 (VTD 16095)*.

6.29   **VATA 1994, Sch 10 para 3(2)—land covered by election.**   An accountancy partnership owned property in Droitwich, Worcester and Barnstaple. The partners occupied parts of the Worcester and Barnstaple properties as their offices, the remainder of those properties being let. The whole of the Droitwich property was let to tenants. In July 1989 the partnership wrote to its local VAT office, stating that it intended to elect to waive exemption in respect of all three properties. Subsequently the partners formed the opinion that it would be to their advantage to elect in respect of the Droitwich property only (as renovation work was to be carried out on that property) but not in respect of the other two properties. In October the partnership submitted a formal election to waive exemption in respect of the Droitwich property only. The Commissioners treated the July letter as an election relating to all three properties and, following a control visit, issued assessments charging tax on the rental income from the Worcester and Barnstaple properties. The partnership appealed, contending that that income was not covered by the election and was therefore exempt from VAT. The tribunal accepted this contention and allowed the appeal, finding 'on the balance of probabilities that the partners elected in relation to the Droitwich property alone'. *Devoirs Properties Ltd*, 6.12 above, and *Resource Maintenance Ltd*, 6.13 above, distinguished. *Harrison Priddey & Co, MAN/95/2291 (VTD 14089)*.

6.30   Two companies, which were members of separate groups, formed a limited partnership by a deed dated 25 September 1997. The partnership acquired 16 properties which had previously been owned by a different partnership comprising a company from each of the two groups. Of the 16 properties, four were subject of elections to waive exemption, while the remaining 12 were not. Solicitors acting for the partnership sent the local VAT office a notification that it had elected to waive exemption in respect of all 16 properties. However, this notification was dated 22 September 1997, three days before the formation of the partnership, was only signed by a representative of the general partner, and was not authorised by the partnership deed. Subsequently the Commissioners issued an assessment on the basis that the partnership had elected to waive exemption in respect of all 16 properties. The partnership appealed, contending that the notification was inaccurate and did not bind the partnership. The tribunal accepted this contention and allowed the appeal. The tribunal observed that 'an election has a separate existence from the notification and must be made on a particular date, take effect on a specified date, if different, and relate to specified land'. On the evidence, the actual election was made in respect of four properties only. To the extent that the notification purported to relate to the other 12 properties, it had no effect. Furthermore, the signature of the representative of the general partner was binding on that partner only. The signatory had no authority to bind the limited partner, because the partnership was not in existence at the time of the notification. *Blythe Limited Partnership, [1999] VATDR 112 (VTD 16011)*. (*Note*. For the Commissioners' practice following this decision, see Business

Brief 16/99, issued on 20 July 1999, and Business Brief 17/99, issued on 6 August 1999. The Commissioners state that they 'fully agree with the Tribunal's approach and will not be appealing' against the decision.)

6.31   The decision in *Blythe Limited Partnership*, 6.30 above, was applied in a subsequent case in which the tribunal found on the evidence that a family partnership had only elected to waive exemption in respect of one of three properties which it owned, and that a letter purporting to waive exemption in respect of the other two properties had been sent by a member of the family who was not in fact a partner, and was not binding on the partnership. *DS Talafair & Sons, MAN/98/956 (VTD 16144)*.

6.32   **VATA 1994, Sch 10 para 3(3)—election intended to apply only to part of building.**   A consultant (L), who was registered for VAT, owned the freehold of a three-storey building. The ground floor was occupied by two shops. The first and second floors were also divided into two independent units. One of these was used by L as his business premises. The other unit (67A) had been used as a flat, but was in need of refurbishment. In March 1990 L wrote to his local VAT office stating that he wished to elect to waive exemption in respect of 67A. The VAT office replied, informing L that the election covered all his 'transactions for the land and buildings concerned' and was irrevocable. L converted 67A into office premises, and reclaimed input tax on the work. However, he was unable to find a suitable tenant, and subsequently reconverted it into a flat which he occupied himself. At a control visit in 1994, a VAT officer discovered that, although L had reclaimed input tax relating to 67A, he had not accounted for output tax on his income from the two shops. She arranged for the issue of an assessment, against which L appealed, contending that the election should be treated as only covering 67A and not as covering the whole building. The tribunal rejected this contention and dismissed the appeal. The effect of what is now *VATA 1994, Sch 10 para 3(3)* was that the election had effect in relation to the whole of the building. Furthermore, the election was irrevocable. The fact that L had not been able to let 67A, and had subsequently reconverted it into a flat, did not alter the effect of the election. *MH Lounds (t/a Lounds Associates), MAN/95/1794 (VTD 13999)*.

6.33   **VATA 1994, Sch 10 para 3(9)—'fair and reasonable' attribution of input tax.**   The trustees of a pension fund, which was registered for VAT, constructed a commercial building and reclaimed input tax. In August 1993 they granted a 15–year lease of the building. The Commissioners issued an assessment on the deemed self-supply in accordance with *VATA 1994, Sch 10 para 6(1)*. In December 1994 the trustees elected to waive exemption and claimed 99.1% of the input tax on the self-supply, on the basis that the exempt lease had lasted for 16 months whereas the expected life of the building was 150 years. The Commissioners rejected the claim on the basis that they could not allow any revised initial attribution of input tax, since the building was within the capital goods scheme and, if the building continued to be used for taxable purposes, 86.67% of the relevant input tax would be recovered within ten years. The trustees appealed, contending that the application of the capital goods scheme did not amount to a 'fair and reasonable' attribution of the input tax, as required by *VATA 1994, Sch 10 para 3(9)*, since it would have to wait for several years to recover most of the input tax. The QB rejected this contention and upheld the Commissioners' ruling, holding that if a taxpayer elected to waive exemption, he was bound by the provisions of the capital goods scheme. What is now *VAT Regulations 1995 (SI 1995 No 2518), regs 112–116* prevented the Commissioners from agreeing a revised initial attribution. The provisions of *reg 116(2)* only permitted a revised attribution in subsequent periods, rather than in the initial period. Buxton J observed that, if a taxpayer sought to elect to waive exemption, he must be taken to have made that decision on an informed basis regarding the capital goods scheme. *C & E Commrs v Trustees for R & R Pension Fund, QB [1996] STC*

6.34　Buildings and Land

889. (*Note*. For the Commissioners' practice following this decision, see Business Brief 17/96, issued on 16 August 1996.)

6.34　See also *The Island Trading Co*, 43.114 PARTIAL EXEMPTION.

6.35　**Effect of election to waive exemption—attribution of input tax.** See *Cliff College*, 43.47 PARTIAL EXEMPTION; *R Walia Opticians Ltd*, 43.49 PARTIAL EXEMPTION, and *Royal Sun Alliance Insurance Group plc*, 43.129 PARTIAL EXEMPTION.

SUPPLIES BETWEEN LANDLORD AND TENANT

6.36　**Reverse premium by landlord to tenant—whether consideration for taxable supply of services.** See *Gleneagles Hotel plc*, 58.100 SUPPLY; *Neville Russell*, 58.101 SUPPLY, and *Hutchinson Locke & Monk*, 58.102 SUPPLY.

6.37　**Improvements to hotel paid for by tenant—whether a supply by tenant to landlord.** See *Port Erin Hotels Ltd*, 58.104 SUPPLY.

6.38　**Repairs to premises paid for by tenant in return for rent-free occupation— whether a supply by tenant to landlord.** See *Ridgeons Bulk Ltd*, 58.105 SUPPLY.

6.39　**Payment by landlord for surrender of lease by tenant—whether exempt.** See *Lubbock Fine & Co*, 21.165 EUROPEAN COMMUNITY LAW.

6.40　**Payment by tenant to landlord for surrender of onerous lease—whether exempt.** See *Central Capital Corporation Ltd*, 39.51 LAND, and *AA Insurance Services Ltd*, 39.52 LAND.

6.41　**Compensation payment by tenant for termination or surrender of taxable lease.** See *Lloyds Bank plc*, 58.117 SUPPLY.

6.42　**Rent paid while premises unoccupied—treatment of input tax.** See *Harper Collins Publishers Ltd*, 43.41 PARTIAL EXEMPTION.

6.43　**Payments under agreement capping mortgage interest—whether consideration for a supply.** See *Iliffe & Holloway*, 58.107 SUPPLY.

6.44　**Repairs to bomb-damaged building—whether supplies made to landlord or tenant.** See *Commercial Union Assurance Co plc*, 34.49 INPUT TAX.

7 Business

Note. Cases in this chapter involve the general meaning of 'business' as defined in what is now *VATA 1994, s 94(1)*. For activities deemed to be businesses by virtue of *s 94(2)(a)*, see 13 CLUBS, ASSOCIATIONS AND ORGANISATIONS. For cases where the existence of a business is not disputed, and the issue is whether there has been a supply for the purposes of the business or in the course or furtherance of the business, see 34 INPUT TAX and 58 SUPPLY. For cases where the existence of a business is not disputed, and the issue is by whom the business is carried on, see 53.133 *et seq.* REGISTRATION. Although the UK legislation refers to 'business', the relevant EC legislation (*Article 4* of the *EC Sixth Directive*) refers to an 'economic activity'. For cases concerning the definition of an 'economic activity', see 21.59 to 21.68 EUROPEAN COMMUNITY LAW. The Commissioners take the view that 'the meaning of "economic activity" is not materially different from the meaning of "business" in the UK legislation'—see Customs' VAT Manual, Part 6, section 1.3.

The cases are arranged under the following headings.

Court decisions 7.1–7.14
Tribunal decisions
  Letting of property (including lock-up garages) 7.15–7.26
  Hiring of chattels 7.27–7.46
  Conversion, etc. of buildings 7.47–7.52
  Ownership of horses 7.53–7.73
  Promotion of tourism 7.74
  Miscellaneous activities
    Cases held to constitute a business 7.75–7.91
    Cases held not to constitute a business 7.92–7.114

COURT DECISIONS

7.1   **Charity providing accommodation for schoolchildren.**   A company, limited by guarantee and accepted by the Inland Revenue as charitable, carried on the activity of providing boarding houses for the pupils of a school. The boarding fees were charged to the parents separately from the school fees and the company was conducted so as to achieve neither profits nor losses. The Commissioners issued a ruling that output tax was chargeable on the fees, and the company appealed, contending that it was not carrying on a 'business' for VAT purposes. The CS rejected this contention, holding that the company was carrying on a business within the scope of what is now *VATA 1994, s 94(1)*. The CS observed that the activities were predominantly concerned with making taxable supplies to consumers for a consideration. The supplies were of a kind which, subject to differences of detail, were made commercially by those who sought to profit from them, and were continued over an appreciable period of time and with such frequency as to amount to a recognisable and identifiable activity. Lord Emslie held that 'the natural meaning of the word "business" does not require that what is done must be done commercially ... or with the object of making profits'. *C & E Commrs v Morrison's Academy Boarding Houses Association, CS 1977, [1978] STC 1*.

7.2   **Statutory body—whether carrying on a business.**   The *Water Act 1973* set up ten water authorities in England and Wales and established the National Water Council with a wide variety of functions. The Commissioners issued a ruling that, except with regard to certain ancillary activities, the Council was not carrying on a business (so that it was not entitled to reclaim input tax). The QB allowed the Council's appeal in part, applying *Morrison's Academy Boarding Houses Association*, 7.1 above, and holding that 'business' was not restricted to activities carried on commercially with a view to profit. The fact that services were supplied in the performance of a statutory duty did not automatically prevent them from constituting supplies in the course of business. However, certain advisory and administrative services, which the Council supplied exclusively to public bodies, were outside the definition of 'business'. *National Water Council v C & E Commrs, QB 1978, [1979] STC 157.*

7.3   **Organisation distributing religious propaganda.** The Church of Scientology, an organisation established in California, acquired premises in Sussex, at which it provided training courses and sold books and other goods. It did not account for output tax on its supplies. The Commissioners issued an assessment on the basis that the Church was carrying on a business. The Church appealed, contending that an organisation which propagated a religious philosophy should not be treated as carrying on a 'business'. The tribunal rejected this contention and dismissed the appeal, and the CA upheld this decision. *Church of Scientology of California v C & E Commrs, CA 1980, [1981] STC 65; [1980] 3 CMLR 114; [1981] 1 All ER 1035.*

7.4   **Charitable trust to raise funds for construction of theatre.**   A charitable trust was set up in 1972 with the primary object of constructing a theatre in a disused hall and raising funds from the public for this. The Trust reclaimed input tax on the goods and services supplied to it for the purposes of the project. The Commissioners rejected the claim, considering that the Trust was not carrying on a business. The QB upheld this decision. Neill J held that the Trust's activities 'lacked any commercial element at all and ... cannot properly be regarded as business activities'. *Morrison's Academy Boarding Houses Association*, 7.1 above, distinguished. *C & E Commrs v Royal Exchange Theatre Trust, QB [1979] STC 728; [1979] 3 All ER 797.*

7.5   **Pheasant shoots—contributions by participants towards cost.**   A landowner (F), who was registered for VAT, organised the shooting of pheasants on his family estate. Originally, friends and relatives had been invited to shoot on the estate as family guests. F asked those he invited to make specified contributions towards the cost. He did not advertise for guests and only invited family friends and relatives. The contributions usually met about half the cost of the shooting. The Commissioners issued an assessment on the basis that F was making supplies for consideration. F appealed, contending that the running of the shoots did not amount to the carrying on of a business. The tribunal accepted this contention and allowed F's appeal, and the QB upheld this decision. *Morrison's Academy Boarding Houses Association*, 7.1 above, distinguished. *C & E Commrs v Lord Fisher, QB [1981] STC 238; [1981] 2 All ER 147.* (*Note.* For a subsequent case in which this decision was distinguished, see *Williams*, 58.122 SUPPLY.)

7.6   **Hire of aircraft by partnership to company—whether partnership carrying on a business.**   Three people, who had registered as a partnership for VAT, owned an aircraft, which they hired out to a company which carried on the business of hiring aircraft to qualified pilots. Under the charter agreement, the partnership received a fee from the company based on the number of hours for which the aircraft was hired. The Commissioners issued a ruling that the partnership was not carrying on a business, and should therefore be deregistered. The tribunal dismissed the partnership's appeal and the QB upheld this decision, holding that the charter of a single asset to a single customer did not constitute a business. *Three H Aircraft Hire v C & E Commrs, [1982] STC 653.* (*Note.* Compare, however, the subsequent CJEC decision in *Staatssecretaris van Financien v Heerma*, 21.62 EUROPEAN COMMUNITY LAW.)

7.7   Hire of shed to partnership—whether an 'economic activity'. See *Staatssecretaris van Financien v Heerma*, 21.62 EUROPEAN COMMUNITY LAW.

7.8   Apple and Pear Development Council—whether carrying on any business. See *Apple and Pear Development Council*, 21.47 EUROPEAN COMMUNITY LAW.

7.9   Institute of Chartered Accountants—whether licensing activities a business or economic activity. See *The Institute of Chartered Accountants in England and Wales v C & E Commrs*, 58.129 SUPPLY.

7.10   Holding company—whether carrying on any business. See *Polysar Investments Netherlands BV v Inspecteur der Invoerrechten en Accijnzen*, 21.61 EUROPEAN COMMUNITY LAW, and *Cumbrae Properties (1963) Ltd*, 58.23 SUPPLY.

7.11   Investment trust. See *The Wellcome Trust Ltd*, 21.66 EUROPEAN COMMUNITY LAW.

7.12   Limited partnership holding investments—whether carrying on an 'economic activity'. See *Harnas & Helm CV v Staatssecretaris van Financien*, 21.67 EUROPEAN COMMUNITY LAW.

7.13   Grant of building rights—whether an 'economic activity'. See *van Tiem v Staatssecretaris van Financien*, 21.63 EUROPEAN COMMUNITY LAW.

7.14   Prostitution—whether an 'economic activity'. See *Adoui v Kingdom of Belgium & City of Liège*, 21.64 EUROPEAN COMMUNITY LAW.

TRIBUNAL DECISIONS

Letting of property (including lock-up garages)

7.15   **Furnished letting—whether carrying on a business.** An accountant (W) owned three houses in Bradford which were let furnished under arrangements which were agreed to amount to licences to occupy land. The Commissioners issued a ruling that the letting amounted to the carrying on of a business (with the result that W was partly exempt). The tribunal dismissed W's appeal, holding that the letting amounted to a business within the ordinary meaning of the word and that W's registration as an accountant covered the business of furnished letting. The fact that the income from the letting was accepted as investment income for income tax purposes was not conclusive. *DA Walker, [1976] VATTR 10 (VTD 240)*.

7.16   **Letting of houses held as investments.** A builder (P) owned about twelve houses, the letting of which was in the hands of estate agents. The rents were treated as investment income for income tax purposes. P reclaimed the whole of his input tax. The Commissioners issued an assessment to recover some of the tax, on the basis that the rental income was a business activity with the result that P was partly exempt. The tribunal upheld the assessment and dismissed P's appeal. *Walker*, 7.15 above, applied. *J Prescott, MAN/77/239 (VTD 529)*.

7.17   **Letting of business premises.** An estate agent (S) and his wife purchased a dilapidated building and carried on the estate agency business from its basement. The ground floor was let as a hairdressing salon, and the first floor as a residential flat. Although the property was owned jointly, the rents were paid to S and were placed in a bank account in his sole name. He reclaimed the whole of his input tax and the Commissioners issued an assessment to recover the tax, on the basis that the letting was a business activity and that S was therefore partly exempt. The tribunal upheld the assessment and dismissed S's appeal. *Walker*, 7.15 above, applied. *DE Sherwin, MAN/86/171 (VTD 3299)*.

7.18   A company, 90% of the shares in which were owned by a solicitor, applied for registration, describing its business activity as 'property owning and management'. It also reclaimed input tax incurred on the refurbishment of office premises, which it had transferred under licence to an associated company, in which the solicitor also owned 90% of the shares. There was no formal agreement concerning this transfer. The Commissioners rejected the application for registration, on the basis that the company was not carrying on any business. The tribunal dismissed the company's appeal against this decision. The onus was on the company to show that its activities constituted a business which was to include the making of taxable supplies. The owning and holding of a property was not in itself a business. *Godlin Ltd, LON/99/912Y (VTD 4416)*.

7.19   A charity, which owned two buildings which it let to another charity at a rent of £1 p.a., applied for registration for VAT. The Commissioners rejected the application on the grounds that the charity was not carrying on any business, and the tribunal dismissed the charity's appeal. *Whitehall Chase Foundation Trust, LON/89/1378 (VTD 5134)*.

7.20   **Letting of lock-up garages.**   An architect (W) owned 24 lock-up garages, managed for him by estate agents who accounted to him quarterly for the net receipts. He took no direct part in the management of the garages and the Inland Revenue accepted that the rents were investment income for income tax purposes. The Commissioners issued an assessment charging output tax on the basis that the rents were from taxable supplies. (It was common ground that the rents were not exempt, being within what is now *VATA 1994, Sch 9 Group 1, Item 1(h)*.) The tribunal dismissed W's appeal, holding that the letting amounted to carrying on a business even though the day-to-day management of the garages was left to agents. *Walker*, 7.15 above, applied; *Coleman*, 7.27 below, distinguished. *JW Wilcox, [1978] VATTR 79 (VTD 546)*.

7.21   A two-person partnership carried on a retail business. The partners also jointly owned some 60 lock-up garages in the area, which they let. The Commissioners issued an assessment charging output tax on the basis that the rents were taxable. (It was common ground that they were within what is now *VATA 1994, Sch 9 Group 1, Item 1(h)* and not exempt.) The partners appealed, contending that the letting should be treated as an investment and not as a business activity. The tribunal rejected this contention and dismissed the appeal, finding that the letting was conducted on business principles and involved the provision of services for consideration. Accordingly, the letting was within the definition of a 'business'. Applying *Glassborow*, 53.1 REGISTRATION, the partnership registration covered the letting of the garages as well as the retail business. *RW & AAW Williamson, [1978] VATTR 90 (VTD 555)*.

7.22   *Williamson*, 7.21 above, was applied in the similar case of *BL & N Merrifield, LON/92/2676A (VTD 10563)*.

7.23   A married couple purchased a number of garages and let them to tenants. They did not register for VAT, and the Commissioners issued a ruling that they were liable to be registered. The couple appealed, contending that the garages had been purchased as an investment and did not constitute a business. The tribunal dismissed the couple's appeal, holding that the letting of the garages was a business activity. *Williamson*, 7.21 above, and *Morrison's Academy*, 7.1 above, applied; *Coleman*, 7.27 below, distinguished. *GW & Mrs JA Green, LON/91/2594Y (VTD 9016)*.

7.24 **Letting of beach chalet.** A retired accountant hired a 'beach chalet' from a District Council. The Council charged VAT on the hire. The accountant appealed to the tribunal, contending that VAT was not due because the Council should not be regarded as carrying on a business. The tribunal rejected this contention and dismissed his appeal, holding that the Council's letting of beach chalets were 'activities that might be carried out by any other landlord'. *HT Shearing, LON/99/885 (VTD 16723).*

7.25 **Letting of cottages purchased with business premises.** See *Johnson*, 34.177 INPUT TAX.

7.26 **Whether property let by individual to associated partnership.** A married couple owned and operated a nursing home in partnership. They built an extension to the home, and entered into an agreement whereby the wife purported to grant the partnership authority to use the extension. The wife registered for VAT and reclaimed input tax of £49,000 on the extension. The Commissioners rejected the claim and cancelled the registration, considering that the wife was not making any taxable supplies. The tribunal dismissed the wife's appeal, holding that she was not making any taxable supplies and was not entitled to be registered. The effect of *Law of Property Act 1925* was that the couple owned the whole of the nursing home as joint tenants, and the wife did 'not use or occupy the extension to the nursing home in her own right'. Accordingly, the purported agreement between the wife and the partnership was 'null and void'. *Mrs G Blandy, MAN/94/303 (VTD 13123).*

Hiring of chattels

7.27 **Letting of pleasure boat—whether a business.** An individual (C) acquired a pleasure boat and let it to a company carrying on the business of holiday boat hire. The charterers were to use the vessel in their business, taking reasonable steps to maximise the revenue from hiring it out, and paying C 45% of the hiring fees received. He applied for registration for VAT. The Commissioners rejected his application, considering that the hiring out of the vessel did not amount to the carrying on of a business. The tribunal dismissed C's appeal. The hiring out of the vessel for holiday use was a trade but he did not participate in this. His intention was to make an investment and his receipt of a share of the hire fees, and the activities on his behalf as a consequence of the charter, did not make the investment a business. *KG Coleman, [1976] VATTR 24 (VTD 242). (Note.* The decision was approved by the QB in *Three H Aircraft Hire*, 7.6 above.)

7.28 A partnership purchased a boat from a company under an agreement whereby the company was to retain possession of the boat for use in its boat hire business and to maintain and insure it and provide fuel and stores for it. Bookings could be by either the company or the partnership. The partnership received 45% of the net hire charges, as defined, where the booking was made by the company, and 50% where the partnership made the booking. The partnership advertised for bookings and applied for registration for VAT. The Commissioners rejected the application on the basis that the partnership was not carrying on any business. The tribunal allowed the partnership's appeal, holding that, in view of the efforts which the partnership made to attract customers, it was carrying on business. *Dicta* in *Morrison's Academy Boarding Houses Association*, 7.1 above, applied. *Longbow, MAN/77/253 (VTD 551).*

7.29 See also *Purdue*, 34.393 INPUT TAX.

7.30 **Motor cruiser acquired for chartering.** The purchase of a motor cruiser for chartering was held to be an investment, rather than a business activity, in *K & C Rossiter, LON/83/104 (VTD 1452).*

7.31 Business

7.31 **Chartering of sailing yacht.** A couple who owned a sailing yacht registered for VAT in 1977. In 1978 they chartered the yacht to a company, which became responsible for maintaining and insuring it and retained 50% of all hiring fees received. In 1980 the Commissioners cancelled the couple's registration on the ground that the charter of the yacht to a company did not constitute the carrying on of a business. The tribunal dismissed the couple's appeal against this decision. *G & J Tibbs (t/a Joanne Yacht Services), MAN/80/241 (VTD 1098).*

7.32 A company which carried on a pig-farming business reclaimed input tax on the purchase of a yacht, which was used by directors of the company and their families, and was also let on hire. The Commissioners issued an assessment to recover the tax and the company appealed, contending that it was carrying on a separate business of chartering. The tribunal rejected this contention and dismissed the appeal, holding that in view of the small number of lettings, the limited nature of advertising, and the company's selectivity in accepting hirers, the hiring of the yacht did not constitute a business. The chairman observed that 'evidence of performance is to be preferred to the evidence of intent where the latter is unaccompanied by performance'. *Rainheath Ltd, MAN/81/70 (VTD 1249).*

7.33 A small private company, which carried on a business of mobile crane hire, reclaimed input tax on the purchase of a yacht. The Commissioners issued an assessment to recover the tax, considering that the yacht had been acquired for the personal purpose of the company directors, rather than for business purposes. The company appealed, contending that the yacht had been purchased to set up a new business of chartering. The tribunal allowed the appeal in part, holding on the evidence that the yacht chartering constituted a business but that the yacht had partly been purchased for personal enjoyment, and that 25% of the input tax was allowable. *RF Henfrey (Midlands) Ltd, MAN/82/174 (VTD 1409).*

7.34 An accountant who had retired from full-time practice purchased a yacht and reclaimed the input tax thereon. The Commissioners issued an assessment to recover the tax and he appealed, contending that he had purchased the yacht to establish a new business of chartering. The tribunal accepted his evidence and allowed his appeal. *AG Evans, LON/83/62 (VTD 1453).*

7.35 A married couple who owned a hotel reclaimed input tax on the purchase of a yacht. The Commissioners issued an assessment to recover the tax and they appealed, contending that they had purchased the yacht for the purpose of establishing a chartering business. The tribunal accepted their evidence and allowed the appeal. *The Westbourne Hotel, EDN/84/5 (VTD 1652).*

7.36 A plant hire company reclaimed input tax on the purchase of a yacht. The Commissioners issued an assessment to recover the tax, considering that it had been acquired for the personal enjoyment of the company directors. The company appealed, contending that it had been acquired for the purpose of chartering. The tribunal dismissed the appeal, finding that there was no evidence of any steps having been taken to charter the yacht, and holding that the tax was not deductible. *Trexagrove Ltd, [1984] VATTR 222 (VTD 1758).*

7.37 A company which carried on a leasing business reclaimed input tax on the purchase of a yacht. The yacht was entered in races and was then twice let on charter before being sold. The Commissioners issued an assessment to recover the tax, considering that the yacht had not been acquired for business purposes but for the personal pleasure of the company chairman. The company appealed, contending that the yacht had been acquired for chartering. The tribunal accepted the company's evidence and allowed the appeal. *Petros Leasing Ltd, MAN/88/366 (VTD 4056).*

7.38   A similar decision was reached in a case where a holding company reclaimed input tax on two yachts. The Commissioners rejected the claim but the tribunal allowed the company's appeal, holding on the evidence that the yachts had been purchased for the purpose of a separate business of chartering. *CR King & Partners (Holdings) Ltd, LON/90/1646Z (VTD 6695)*.

7.39   A company which had carried on a property development business chartered a yacht, which was owned by its controlling director, for a five-year period. It reclaimed input tax on repairs to the yacht. The Commissioners rejected the claim, considering that the expenditure had not been incurred for business purposes. The company appealed, contending that it had acquired the yacht for the purpose of hiring it to customers. Two customers had agreed to hire the yacht, but in one case the customer withdrew from the agreement, and in the other case the company was unable to fulfil the agreement because the yacht had broken down. The tribunal allowed the company's appeal, holding on the evidence that 'it was at all times the appellant company's intention to engage in the business of boat chartering, and ... any expenditure which it may have incurred on the repair and maintenance of the boat was expenditure on goods or services to be used for the purpose of its business'. *Silicon Valley Estates Ltd, LON/92/211X (VTD 11017)*.

7.40   A company which had carried on a business of open-cast coal mining purchased a yacht at a cost of £336,000, and reclaimed input tax on the purchase. The Commissioners issued an assessment to recover the tax, considering that the yacht had been purchased for the personal pleasure of the company's principal director. The company appealed, contending that the yacht had been purchased with a view to chartering it to customers. The tribunal accepted the company's evidence and allowed the appeal. *Dicta* in *Ian Flockton Developments Ltd*, 34.248 INPUT TAX, applied. *DS Supplies Ltd, MAN/95/884 (VTD 13559)*. (*Note.* The tribunal rejected the company's application for costs, finding that the company had not made sufficient evidence available to the Commissioners before the hearing.)

7.41   The chartering of a yacht was also held to constitute a business in *Premier Motor Yacht Charters Ltd, MAN/97/223 (VTD 15506)*.

7.42   **Property company—whether yacht purchased for future chartering business.** See *Warwest Holdings Ltd*, 34.471 INPUT TAX.

7.43   **New company temporarily dormant—whether yacht purchased for future chartering business.** See *Furness Vale Yacht Hire Ltd*, 34.450 INPUT TAX.

7.44   **Financial consultant—whether yacht purchased for future chartering business.** See *Milner*, 34.470 INPUT TAX.

7.45   **Hiring out of aircraft by partnership—hire mainly to partners.** Six people interested in flying, five of whom travelled by air in their respective businesses, acquired a four seater aircraft and obtained permission to fly it from a hitherto disused airfield, with the intention of using it themselves and hiring it out as a commercial venture. They formed themselves into a partnership, registered the business name and were registered for VAT from September 1974. However, following an inspection of the partnership records, the Commissioners cancelled the registration, and the partnership appealed against this cancellation. The evidence was that, during the year to 31 August 1975, the aircraft was used mainly by the partners. When it was so used, the partner was debited with the cost. When the aircraft was hired out to the public, the partner who had introduced the customer collected the hiring charge and was debited with the amount. The total debited to the partners for their own and public use of the aircraft was £3,035. The firm made other supplies of £200 and in addition it sold the aircraft for £6,560 in the year (and replaced it). The tribunal allowed the partnership's appeal. Applying *Carlton Lodge Ltd*, 13.28 CLUBS, ASSOCIATIONS AND ORGANISATIONS, the supply of the use of the aircraft to a partner was a supply in the course of that business. *Border Flying Co, [1976] VATTR 132 (VTD 300)*.

7.46   **Hire of aircraft to flying club.**   A company which owned a light aircraft hired it to a flying club. The company was responsible for the maintenance, cleaning and insurance of the aircraft. The Commissioners issued a ruling that the company was not carrying on any business and was not entitled to be registered. The tribunal allowed the company's appeal. *Walker*, 7.15 above, applied; *Three H Aircraft Hire*, 7.6 above, and *Coleman*, 7.27 above, distinguished. *Cavendish Aviation Ltd, MAN/81/80 (VTD 1471)*.

Conversion, etc. of buildings

7.47   **Conversion of building into dwelling-house.**   A consultant, who was registered for VAT, bought 1½ acres of land with an old barn on it and with planning permission to convert the barn into a dwelling-house. The conversion of the barn was completed in October 1973 and he moved into it with his family, having sold his previous house in September. He reclaimed input tax on the conversion and the Commissioners issued an assessment to recover the tax. He appealed, contending that he should be treated as carrying on a business as a builder. The tribunal rejected this contention and dismissed his appeal, holding on the evidence that he had converted the barn for his personal occupation. *G Nixon, CAR H/75/184 (VTD 233)*. (*Note*. Relief would now be available under *VATA 1994, s 35* as amended by *FA 1996, s 30*.)

7.48   A civil servant and his wife purchased an old stable, coachhouse, etc. for conversion into a dwelling-house. He decided to do the work of conversion himself. He applied for and obtained registration as a builder and reclaimed input tax on the conversion. The Commissioners rejected his claim and the tribunal dismissed his appeal, holding that he and his wife had not acquired the buildings as partners, that he was not carrying on a business, and that the fact that he had been registered did not prevent the Commissioners from reviewing the registration. *GWH Kelly, EDN/77/43 (VTD 598)*. (*Notes*. (1) This case was distinguished in the 1995 case of *Dewhirst*, 53.55 REGISTRATION. (2) Relief would now be available under *VATA 1994, s 35* as amended by *FA 1996, s 30*.)

7.49   **Charity—conversion of building for use as centre for handicapped.**   A registered charity which ran a centre for the handicapped acquired two vacant shops and converted them into a new centre at the cost of some £37,000. Most of the labour was done by workmen, the charity being reimbursed their wages by the Manpower Services Commission. The charity reclaimed input tax on the work. The Commissioners rejected the claim, considering that the Fellowship was not carrying on a business. The tribunal dismissed the charity's appeal. *Widnes Spastic Fellowship, MAN/77/132 (VTD 455)*.

7.50   **Committee set up to enlarge church hall.**   A church established a committee to enlarge the church hall. The committee appealed against the Commissioners' refusal to register it, contending that it was carrying on a business. The tribunal rejected this contention and dismissed the appeal, holding that there was not sufficient continuity in the project to bring it within the meaning of 'business'. *Trinity Methodist Church Royton (Building Committee), MAN/78/159 (VTD 807)*.

7.51   **Intermittent property development—whether company still carrying on any business.**   A small property development company registered for VAT in 1977 and completed a contract in 1979. In January 1981 it purchased a large house which it renovated and sold at a profit in August. (The renovation was accepted as being zero-rated under legislation which has subsequently been superseded.) In 1982 the Commissioners issued a ruling that the company was not carrying on a business and was not entitled to be registered. The company appealed. The tribunal accepted the company's evidence and allowed the appeal, observing that an activity such as property development could still constitute a business even though supplies were only made infrequently. *David Wickens Properties Ltd, [1982] VATTR 143 (VTD 1284)*.

7.52   **Statutory repair work carried on by City Council—whether Council carrying on any business.**   See *Glasgow City Council*, 40.10 LOCAL AUTHORITIES AND STATUTORY BODIES.

Ownership of horses

Note. In the 1993 Budget Statement, the then Chancellor of the Exchequer announced that arrangements would be introduced to help racehorse owners to meet 'the normal business test for VAT registration'. See Customs & Excise News Release No 43/93, issued on 16 March 1993. For detailed coverage of the arrangements in question, see Tolley's VAT Business by Business Guide 2000/2001. Most of the cases below refer to periods before the introduction of the current arrangements, and should be read in that light. For cases where appellants have reclaimed input tax on the basis that the purpose of owning racehorses has been to advertise an existing business activity, see 34.248 *et seq.* INPUT TAX.

7.53   An individual (P) had owned racehorses for many years, and in 1967 decided to begin breeding them. He kept his horses at stud farms (not owned by him) in England and France. He registered for VAT in 1973, and reclaimed substantial amounts of input tax. His accounts showed small amounts of income, but consistent net losses. In 1975 the Commissioners decided to cancel his registration, considering that his activities constituted a hobby rather than business. The tribunal allowed P's appeal, holding that the breeding of horses was necessarily a long-term activity and that his activities amounted to the carrying on of a business. *DD Prenn, LON/78/406 (VTD 793)*.

7.54   The proprietor of a stud farm raced four horses, three of which had been bred at her stud, and reclaimed the input tax thereon. The Commissioners issued an assessment to recover the tax, considering that the racing of horses was not a business activity. She appealed, contending that the horses had been raced to demonstrate their value for breeding purposes. The tribunal accepted her evidence and allowed her appeal. *DB Ismay, [1980] VATTR 19 (VTD 877)*.

7.55   A similar decision was reached in *GB Turnbull Ltd, [1986] VATTR 247 (VTD 1769)*.

7.56   A company was incorporated with the object of breeding horses. It reclaimed input tax in respect of the purchase of a share in a colt. The Commissioners refused to repay the tax, considering that the company's activities did not constitute a business for VAT purposes. The tribunal allowed the company's appeal against this decision, holding that the breeding of horses could constitute a business despite the fact that supplies may be intermittent. On the evidence, the company was carrying on a business and the input tax in question was deductible. *Guest Leasing & Bloodstock Co Ltd, LON/81/133 (VTD 1227)*.

7.57   A company which operated a public house and restaurant incorporated a subsidiary company (G). G purchased a number of racehorses and applied to be registered for VAT. The Commissioners rejected the application, considering that G was not carrying on a business. The tribunal dismissed G's appeal against this decision, holding that horse racing could not constitute a business since it did not involve the making of any taxable supplies. *Guinea Grill Stakes Ltd, LON/82/129 (VTD 1291).* (*Note.* See now, however, the note preceding 7.53 above.)

7.58   A company which bought and sold horses raced some of the horses which it owned, and reclaimed input tax on their upkeep. The Commissioners issued an assessment to recover the tax, considering that the racing of horses did not constitute a business activity, and that the horses had been raced for the personal pleasure of the company's principal director. The company appealed, contending that the horses had been raced in order to advertise their value. The tribunal accepted this contention and allowed the appeal. *Andy Smith Bloodstock Ltd, LON/83/187 (VTD 1663).*

7.59   A company which carried on a welding business reclaimed input tax on the purchase of racehorses. The Commissioners issued an assessment to recover the tax and the company appealed, contending that its horse-racing activities constituted a separate business. The tribunal rejected this contention and dismissed the appeal. *Times of Wigan Ltd, MAN/83/33 (VTD 1917).* (*Note.* See now, however, the note preceding 7.53 above.)

7.60   A company which sold cars reclaimed input tax on the upkeep of several racehorses. The Commissioners issued an assessment to recover the tax, considering that the horses had been purchased for the enjoyment of the principal director, rather than for business purposes. The company appealed, contending that its horse-racing activities constituted a business in their own right. The tribunal rejected this contention and dismissed the appeal. *Brian Gubby Ltd, [1985] VATTR 59 (VTD 1961).* (*Notes.* (1) See now, however, the note preceding 7.53 above. (2) For a preliminary application in this case, see 2.109 APPEALS.)

7.61   A publican purchased some horses and reclaimed the input tax thereon. The Commissioners issued an assessment to recover the tax, considering that the horses had not been purchased for business purposes. The publican appealed, contending that he had bought the horses to begin a new business of breeding them, and that this would be a full-time business activity, since he had had to close the public house which he had operated. The tribunal accepted his evidence and allowed his appeal. *RG Creber, LON/86/450 (VTD 2623).*

7.62   A chemist, who was registered for VAT, also bought and sold horses. He had purchased two mares for breeding, but failed to make a profit on this. Subsequently he bought foals with the intention of selling them as yearlings. From 1984 to 1987 he sold five such foals at a profit. The Inland Revenue accepted that he was carrying on a trade for income tax purposes. However, the Commissioners considered that his purchase and sale of foals did not amount to a business for VAT purposes, and informed him that he could neither claim input tax on the purchase of foals, nor charge output tax on their sale as yearlings. The tribunal dismissed his appeal against this decision, holding that there was 'not sufficient frequency' in his dealing activities for them to constitute a business. *EM Thornton (t/a Forum Stud Farm), LON/88/945Z (VTD 4711).*

7.63   A company registered for VAT, describing its business as the breeding and selling of racehorses. It reclaimed input tax, and the Commissioners issued an assessment to recover the tax, considering that the company's activities were primarily recreational and that the company was not carrying on a business. The tribunal dismissed the company's appeal against the assessment. On the evidence, the company's predominant activity had been racing horses rather than breeding them, and the racing activities had been 'carried on primarily for the interest and enjoyment of the three directors'. *Prenn*, 7.53 above, distinguished. *Triangle Thoroughbreds Ltd, MAN/90/470 (VTD 5404)*. (*Note*. See now, however, the note preceding 7.53 above.)

7.64   *Triangle Thoroughbreds Ltd*, 7.63 above, was applied in a subsequent case where a company which carried on a property consultancy business had also bought and sold horses. In 1985 and 1986 the company received gross income of £7,000 and £4,700 respectively from horse-trading, but there had been no such income in 1987 and only one sale of £500 in 1989. The tribunal reviewed the evidence in detail and held that for 1985 and 1986 the company's horse-trading activities had constituted a business, but that from 1987 to 1990 they had been so sporadic that they did not amount to a business and no input tax was reclaimable. *Bailiwick Ltd, LON/91/451X (VTD 7802)*.

7.65   A company which had carried on a business of property development reclaimed input tax on the purchase of some land and a brood mare. The Commissioners refused to repay the tax, considering that the expenditure had not been incurred for the purpose of any business. The company appealed, contending that it had decided to begin a new business of breeding and selling racehorses. The tribunal accepted the company's evidence and allowed the appeal. *Mowbray Properties Ltd, MAN/90/650 (VTD 6033)*.

7.66   An individual, employed by a printing company, registered for VAT in August 1988 as a breeder of racehorses. On his registration form VAT1 he estimated his taxable supplies for the following twelve months as £23,000. In fact he only made one taxable supply in that period, selling a gelding (which he had purchased in 1986) for £2,100, and made no sales in the following year. However, he bought seven other horses and reclaimed input tax on their upkeep. In 1990 the Commissioners cancelled his registration on the grounds that he was not carrying on a business. The tribunal dismissed his appeal against this decision, holding that his activities were not 'predominantly concerned with the making of taxable supplies to consumers for a consideration'. *P Higson, LON/90/1472X (VTD 6826)*.

7.67   An appeal was dismissed in a case in which the tribunal found that a company's primary purpose was to race horses, and held that 'racing horses, as such, cannot be a business since no taxable supplies are made'. *Rykneld Thoroughbred Co Ltd, MAN/90/668 (VTD 6894)*. (*Note*. See now, however, the note preceding 7.53 above.)

7.68   A company was incorporated to breed and race horses. It applied to be registered for VAT, but the Commissioners rejected its application on the grounds that it was not carrying on a business. The tribunal dismissed the company's appeal against this decision, applying *Brian Gubby Ltd*, 7.60 above, and *Triangle Thoroughbreds Ltd*, 7.63 above. *Michael Jackson Bloodstock Ltd, LON/90/1650X (VTD 7863)*.

7.69   See also *K & K Thorogood Ltd*, 34.459 INPUT TAX.

7.70   A property developer, who was registered for VAT, reclaimed input tax on the purchase of two racehorses and two yearlings. The Commissioners issued an assessment to recover the tax and he appealed, contending that he intended to deal in horses, and that his dealing in horses constituted a business activity. Of the two racehorses in question, one had raced five times (winning once) before being sold at a loss; the other had raced 21 times (winning once) and had been offered for sale but no buyer had been found. The two yearlings had been bought for a total of £4,500 and had been sold for a total of £11,000 five months later. He had subsequently bought and sold a number of other horses, and over a four-year period had spent £134,000 on purchases and received £102,000 from sales. The Inland Revenue had accepted that he was carrying on a trade of dealing in horses. The tribunal allowed his appeal, holding that his activities constituted a business. *Andy Smith Bloodstock Ltd*, 7.58 above, applied. *RB Payne, LON/90/1476X (VTD 9211)*. (*Note*. For another issue in this case, see 34.464 INPUT TAX.)

7.71   An individual (J) was registered for VAT as a breeder of horses, some of which he raced. In 1990 the Commissioners issued a ruling that he was not entitled to be registered, considering that his horse-breeding activities were not in the course or furtherance of a business. He appealed, contending that he was carrying on a business of breeding horses to be sold as potential steeplechasers, although at the time of the appeal hearing he had not yet sold any horses. The tribunal allowed the appeal, holding that J's breeding of horses was 'a serious undertaking honestly pursued ... with reasonable or recognisable continuity'. *Triangle Thoroughbreds Ltd*, 7.63 above, and *Michael Jackson Bloodstock Ltd*, 7.68 above, distinguished. *RJ Jenks, LON/91/ 810 (VTD 10196)*.

7.72   **Racehorse breeder—appeal against retrospective cancellation of registration—whether within jurisdiction of tribunal.** See *Brookes*, 2.23 APPEALS.

7.73   **Trust Fund publishing lists of stallions and receiving registration fees from owners.** In 1983 the Thoroughbred Breeders' Association established a Trust to encourage the owners of thoroughbred stallions and mares to support British horse racing. Owners of stallions were required to pay a registration fee of £100 to the Trust for each of their stallions, and were requested to make additional contributions to the Trust Fund. The Trust undertook to help promote at least 200 races, to be held at the 34 British flat-racing courses, and to be restricted to the progeny of registered stallions. The Trust published lists of the registered stallions for this purpose. The Commissioners issued a ruling that the Trust was carrying on a business activity for VAT purposes, and was required to register for VAT and to account for tax on the registration fees and contributions which it received. The Trust appealed, contending that it was not carrying on a business and was not making any taxable supplies. The tribunal accepted these contentions and allowed the appeal, holding that in publishing the lists of registered stallions the Trustees were merely carrying out their duties under the Trust Deed, rather than supplying services to the owners of the stallions. *British European Breeders' Fund Trustees, [1985] VATTR 12 (VTD 1808)*.

Promotion of tourism

7.74   The promotion of tourism was held to constitute a business in *Netherlands Board of Tourism*, 34.396 INPUT TAX, and in *Austrian National Tourist Office*, 34.397 INPUT TAX, but was held not to constitute a business in *Turespaña*, 34.398 INPUT TAX.

Miscellaneous activities

Cases held to constitute a business

7.75   **Committee formed to organise testimonial football match.** A committee was formed to organise a testimonial football match, to raise money for the dependants of a former player. The Commissioners issued a ruling that the committee was required to register for VAT. The committee appealed, contending that it was not carrying on a business. The tribunal dismissed the appeal, holding that the committee was deemed to be carrying on a business by virtue of what is now *VATA 1994, s 94(2)(b)*. *The Eric Taylor Testimonial Match Committee, [1975] VATTR 8 (VTD 139)*.

7.76 **Dealing in second-hand cars—whether a business.** A jeweller also dealt in second-hand cars, but did not account for output tax on his sales of such cars. The Commissioners issued an assessment charging tax on these sales, and he appealed, contending that he dealt in cars as a hobby and not as a business. The tribunal dismissed his appeal, holding that his dealing in cars constituted a business. *RW Adams, BIR/75/8A (VTD 175).*

7.77 **Motorboat purchased for resale—whether a business.** See *Cavner,* 34.449 INPUT TAX.

7.78 **Catering at public house—whether a separate business.** The Commissioners issued an assessment on a publican which included tax on sales of food. The tribunal accepted the publican's contention that the catering was a separate business carried on by his wife, and reduced the assessment accordingly. *J Oldham, MAN/80/240 (VTD 1113).* (*Note.* The Commissioners might now have recourse to a direction under *VATA 1994, Sch 1 para 2.* For cases concerning this provision, see 53.95 *et seq.* REGISTRATION. See also *Smith & Smith,* 44.14 PARTNERSHIP, and the cases noted at 53.136 to 53.138 REGISTRATION.)

7.79 Similar decisions were reached in *TR Clark, LON/82/338 (VTD 1370); WD Cummins, LON/85/45 (VTD 1985); GE Moss (t/a The Red House), MAN/96/541 (VTD 14633)* and *L Young, MAN/96/387 (VTD 14987).* (*Note.* See the note following *Oldham,* 7.78 above.)

7.80 In *Gent,* 48.142 PENALTIES: FAILURE TO NOTIFY, the Commissioners accepted that catering by the wife of a publican constituted a separate business.

7.81 **Catering by educational charity.** See *Summer Institute of Linguistics Ltd,* 15.58 CONSTRUCTION OF BUILDINGS, ETC.

7.82 **Administration of Jewish ecclesiastical court.** A committee of eight people comprised a Jewish ecclesiastical court, and also issued licences to catering firms, certifying that food had been prepared in accordance with Jewish ecclesiastical law. The Commissioners issued a ruling that the committee was carrying on a business, and was required to be registered for VAT. The tribunal upheld the ruling and dismissed the committee's appeal, applying *Morrison's Academy Boarding Houses Association,* 7.1 above. *Leeds Kashrut Commission & Beth Din Administration Committee, MAN/77/137 (VTD 465).*

7.83 **Religious association.** An association which published religious books and magazines, and organised religious seminars, failed to account for output tax on its takings from such seminars. The Commissioners issued an assessment and the association appealed, contending that it was not carrying on a business. The tribunal rejected this contention and dismissed the appeal. *Holy Spirit Association for the Unification of World Christianity, LON/84/179 (VTD 1777).*

7.84 **Musical entertainment at public house—whether a separate business.** A publican arranged for an individual (B) to promote music at the public house. He paid B a nightly fee to cover B's expenses and also allowed B to charge for admission and retain such takings. The Commissioners formed the opinion that B was acting as an employee or agent of the publican, and assessed the publican on the admission takings. He appealed, contending that he had entered into the arrangement with B in order to increase his bar takings, and that B was carrying on a separate business of promoting music. The tribunal accepted the publican's evidence and allowed his appeal. *JA Conlon, LON/85/610 (VTD 2343).*

7.85 **Gaming machines and poolroom at premises used for selling cars— whether a separate business.** The Commissioners discovered that a car dealer was not accounting for output tax on takings from gaming machines and a poolroom located at his premises. They issued an assessment charging tax on such takings. The dealer appealed, contending that the machines and poolroom were operated by his wife and constituted a separate business. The tribunal accepted his evidence and allowed the appeal. *BH Hamilton, BEL/87/3 (VTD 2460).* (*Note.* The Commissioners might now have recourse to a direction under *VATA 1994, Sch 1 para 2.* For cases concerning this provision, see 53.95 *et seq.* REGISTRATION.)

7.86   **Royal Society for Prevention of Cruelty to Animals.** In 1990 the Commissioners formed the opinion that the RSPCA, which had been registered for VAT for many years, was not carrying on a business and thus should not be registered. They therefore issued an assessment to recover input tax which the RSPCA had reclaimed from 1988 to 1990. The RSPCA appealed, contending that its activities constituted a business and that the input tax had been correctly reclaimed. The tribunal allowed the RSPCA's appeal. The provision of veterinary services was a business activity, notwithstanding that the charges which the RSPCA levied for such services were treated as voluntary rather than obligatory, and that about 20% of the owners of animals treated by the RSPCA did not pay for such treatment. On the evidence, the RSPCA received consideration in respect of the majority of animals it treated. Applying *Morrison's Academy Boarding Houses Association,* 7.1 above, the fact that the RSPCA was a charity, and that its activities were not carried on for profit, did not prevent its activities from constituting a business. *Royal Society for Prevention of Cruelty to Animals, [1991] VATTR 407 (VTD 6218).*

7.87   **Breeding of sheep—whether a business.** A married couple had registered for VAT as breeders of Wiltshire Longhorn sheep, from 24 acres of land near Chippenham. For the period from 1989 to 1992 they received income of less than £800 and incurred expenditure of more than £28,000. The Commissioners formed the opinion that their breeding of sheep was a hobby rather than a business, and sought to deregister them under what is now *VATA 1994, Sch 1 para 13(3).* The couple appealed, contending that their breeding of sheep constituted a business from which they hoped to make profits in the future. The tribunal allowed their appeal, finding that their breeding of sheep constituted a business rather than a hobby. *Prenn,* 7.53 above, and *Creber,* 7.61 above, applied; *Triangle Thoroughbreds Ltd,* 7.63 above, and *Brian Gubby Ltd,* 7.60 above, distinguished. *Mr & Mrs JC Strachan, LON/91/ 2621Y (VTD 9568).*

7.88   **Company formed to promote career of racing driver—whether carrying on a business.** A company was incorporated with the aim of attracting sponsorship for a young motor racing driver. It registered for VAT. A VAT officer formed the opinion that the company's activities did not constitute a business, and the Commissioners cancelled the company's registration under what is now *VATA 1994, Sch 1 para 13.* The tribunal allowed the company's appeal, holding on the evidence that the company's activities 'were predominantly concerned with the making of taxable supplies to sponsors for a consideration'. Accordingly the company was carrying on a business and was entitled to be registered. *Bird Racing (Management) Ltd, LON/93/1889A (VTD 11630).*

7.89   **Charitable school charging fees to pupils.** See *Leighton Park School,* 15.48 CONSTRUCTION OF BUILDINGS, ETC.

7.90   **Royal Academy of Music.** See *The Royal Academy of Music,* 52.7 PROTECTED BUILDINGS.

7.91   **Bowling club.** See *Hunmanby Bowling Club,* 15.55 CONSTRUCTION OF BUILDINGS, ETC.

7.92 **Company providing services to schools.** A number of independent schools established a company to supervise the finances of the schools. The schools reimbursed the company's expenses. The Commissioners issued a ruling that output tax was payable on the amounts reimbursed. The company appealed, contending that it was not carrying on any business. The tribunal accepted this contention and allowed the appeal, applying *Processed Vegetable Growers Association Ltd*, 58.37 SUPPLY. *Allied Schools Agency Ltd, [1973] VATTR 155 (VTD 36)*.

7.93 **Provision of volunteer blood donors—whether a business activity.** An association was established to enable hospitals to contact suitable volunteer blood donors. In order to defray administrative expenses it charged a 'capitation fee', or 'transfusion fee' to hospitals which required the services of such volunteers. In 1972 the Commissioners ruled that the association's activities were outside the scope of VAT. In 1983 the association, thinking that it might be advantageous if it could register voluntarily, approached the Commissioners, who thereupon sought to register it and to make it account for VAT from March 1983. The association was then advised that it would not be in its interests to register for VAT, and it appealed against the Commissioners' decision. The tribunal allowed the association's appeal, finding that the fees were designed to be a contribution towards the administrative costs of the service in finding suitable volunteer donors and holding that this did not amount to the carrying on of a business. *Greater London Red Cross Blood Transfusion Service, [1983] VATTR 241 (VTD 1495)*.

7.94 **Subpostmaster—whether carrying on a business.** The Commissioners issued a ruling that a subpostmaster, with no other occupation, was carrying on a business and was required to register for VAT. The subpostmaster appealed. The tribunal allowed his appeal, observing that he was treated as an employee for income tax and national insurance purposes and holding that his contract with the Post Office was a contract of service and that he was an employee. *Re Appeal of Roberts, KB [1939] 4 All ER 433* (a national insurance case), applied. *R Rickarby, [1973] VATTR 186 (VTD 44)*.

7.95 Two brothers carried on a retail newsagency and catering business from various premises in Wiltshire. One of the brothers (P) applied to run a sub-post office from premises in Swindon. He was required to pay Post Office Counters Ltd (POCL) £88,560, including VAT of £13,189. The partnership reclaimed input tax on this payment. The Commissioners rejected the claim on the basis that P was an employee of the Post Office and that running a sub-post office did not constitute a business for VAT purposes. The partnership appealed, contending that P had applied to run the sub-post office for the purpose of expanding the partnership retail business. The contract between P and POCL stated that it was a contract for services and that P was an agent rather than an employee. The tribunal dismissed the appeal, holding that, despite the express statement to the contrary in the contract, the contract was a contract of service rather than a contract for services, and that P was an employee of Post Office Counters Ltd rather than an independent contractor. The chairman held that 'the most significant feature ... (is) the ability reserved by the contract to POCL to control the subpostmaster in all aspects of his running of the sub-post office' and concluded that 'after reviewing all the contractual materials including the method of appointment and having drawn the picture and stood back from it ... what emerges is not one of a person carrying on a business on his own account in running his sub-post office but that of a servant'. *Hitchcock v Post Office, EAT [1980] ICR 100* and *Tanna v Post Office, EAT [1981] ICR 374* (both unfair dismissal cases) distinguished. *H & V Patel (No 1), LON/94/2821 (VTD 14956)*. (*Note.* At a subsequent hearing, the tribunal also held that, although P had applied to run the sub-post office in order to expand the partnership retail business, the expenditure could not be apportioned and none of the input tax was deductible — see 34.441 INPUT TAX.)

7.96 **Catering at public house—whether a separate business.** See *Smith & Smith*, 44.14 PARTNERSHIP, and *Fraser*, 44.15 PARTNERSHIP.

7.97 **Sale of pictures by trust owning historic house.** The Earl of Haddington owned a large estate in Berwickshire. He decided to set up a charitable trust to preserve the house and gardens and to allow the public to have access to them. He gave the trust the house and gardens, except for a portion which he retained as his private residence. He also gave the trust seventeen pictures to be sold at auction to raise money. The pictures were sold in July and September 1987, and the trustees took over the management of the estate in October 1987. The trustees requested, and obtained, registration for VAT from 1 October 1987 on the grounds that their management of the estate constituted the carrying on of a business. Subsequently the Commissioners sought to register the trustees with effect from July, and thus to charge VAT on the sale of the pictures. The trustees appealed, contending that the sale of the pictures was an isolated transaction in the nature of the realisation of an investment, and that they were not carrying on any business until they took over the management of the estate in October. The tribunal allowed the trustees' appeal, holding that the pictures were held as capital assets, and that the trustees were not carrying on a business at the time when they sold the pictures. Although the pictures had been sold in the furtherance of a future business, the trustees were not required to be registered at the time of the sale and consequently were under no obligation to account for VAT on the proceeds. *The Trustees of the Mellerstain Trust, [1989] VATTR 223 (VTD 4256).*

7.98 **Solicitors' Discipline Tribunal.** The Scottish Solicitors' Discipline Tribunal (SSDT) was established in 1933. It applied for registration for VAT and the Commissioners refused to register it on the grounds that it was not carrying on a business. The tribunal upheld the Commissioners' decision. The activities of the SSDT had no element of commerciality or of economic activity. *The Scottish Solicitors' Discipline Tribunal, [1989] VATTR 138 (VTD 3539).*

7.99 **Radio Authority.** The Radio Authority was established by the *Broadcasting Act 1990* to take over the regulation and licensing of independent radio. It reclaimed input tax which it had incurred. The Commissioners issued a ruling that the Authority was not carrying on a business within the meaning of what is now *VATA 1994, s 4(1)*. The Authority appealed, contending that it was carrying on an economic activity within *Article 4(1)* of the *EC Sixth Directive*. The tribunal dismissed the appeal, holding that the Authority was a regulatory body which was not carrying on a business for VAT purposes. It was a body governed by public law, and accordingly *Article 4(5)* of the *Sixth Directive* directed that it was not to be considered as a taxable person. *Ufficio Distrettuale v Comune di Carpaneto*, 21.76 EUROPEAN COMMUNITY LAW, applied; *Apple & Pear Development Council*, 21.47 EUROPEAN COMMUNITY LAW, distinguished. *The Radio Authority, [1992] VATTR 155 (VTD 7826).*

7.100 **Activities of clubs, associations, etc.** In some of the cases noted in 13 CLUBS, ASSOCIATIONS AND ORGANISATIONS it was explicitly held that the club, etc. was not carrying on a business within the meaning of what is now *VATA 1994, s 94(1)*. These include *New Ash Green Village Association Ltd*, 13.1 (association providing amenities for village inhabitants); *Notts Fire Service Messing Club*, 13.5 (fire station canteen); *British Olympic Association*, 13.7 (UK National Olympic Committee).

7.101   **Arts Council.**   The Arts Council was incorporated by Royal Charter in 1946. Its main activity was the distribution of an annual Parliamentary grant. It registered for VAT in 1973. Until 1989 it provided its services free of charge, but from 1989 it began to charge fees, on a sliding scale, to the recipients of grants. In 1990 the Commissioners issued a ruling that the Council's grant-making activities did not constitute a business (so that it was not entitled to reclaim input tax attributable to these activities). The Council appealed, contending that its grant-making activities were economic activities which involved the making of taxable supplies. The tribunal dismissed the appeal, holding that the Council was not making taxable supplies, either to the Department of National Heritage or to the recipients of grants. The Council was not supplying services for consideration, and was not carrying out an economic activity within *Article 4(2)* of the *EC Sixth Directive. Staatssecretaris van Financien v Cooperatieve Vereniging 'Cooperatieve Aardappelenbewaarplaats GA',* 21.45 EUROPEAN COMMUNITY LAW, applied. Furthermore, the Council was a body governed by public law, and was acting as a public authority within *Article 4(5)* of the *Directive.* Since there was no rival authority, treating the Council as a non-taxable person did not lead to any distortion of competition. *Comune di Carpaneto Piacentino & Others v Ufficio Provinciale Imposta sul Valore Aggiunto di Piacenza,* 21.77 EUROPEAN COMMUNITY LAW, distinguished. *The Arts Council of Great Britain, [1994] VATTR 313 (VTD 11991).*

7.102   **Company receiving grant under Housing & Planning Act 1986.**   In 1995 a company was incorporated to help regenerate an urban area. It received a grant from the Secretary of State for the Environment under the *Housing & Planning Act 1986.* In 1998 it made a late claim for input tax in respect of various purchases including a computer. The Commissioners rejected the claim on the grounds that the company was not carrying on a business. The company appealed, contending that it was supplying services to its local Metropolitan Borough Council. The tribunal rejected this contention and dismissed the company's appeal, holding that it was not supplying any services and that the grant which it had received did not represent consideration for any supply. *West Central Halifax Partnership Ltd, MAN/98/262 (VTD 16570).*

7.103   **Charitable housing association.**   See *Cardiff Community Housing Association Ltd,* 15.46 CONSTRUCTION OF BUILDINGS, ETC.

7.104   **Fishing rights—whether occasional lettings constituting a business.**   A company which operated a stud farm acquired fishing rights over part of the River Spey for two weeks in May each year. It reclaimed input tax in respect of this purchase. The Commissioners issued an assessment to recover the tax, considering that the rights had not been purchased for the purpose of any business activity, but for the personal pleasure of the company's controlling director, who was a keen fisherman. The company appealed, contending that it had acquired the rights with the intention of letting them at market rents, and subsequently reselling them at a profit. The rights had been let to friends and relatives of the controlling director, and in one case to a business acquaintance of his. The tribunal dismissed the company's appeal, finding that the company had purchased the fishing rights as an investment and that any letting had been merely incidental to the hope of capital appreciation, and holding that this was neither a business nor an 'economic activity', so that the input tax was not deductible. *Coleman,* 7.27 above, applied; *Rompelman,* 21.59 EUROPEAN COMMUNITY LAW, distinguished. *Adstock Ltd, LON/91/1866A (VTD 10034).*

7.105   **Care of retired police horse.**   A former police officer (C), who owned a stable and land, agreed to care for a retired police horse. He applied for VAT registration so that he could reclaim input tax. The Commissioners rejected the claim on the grounds that he was not making any taxable supplies. The tribunal dismissed C's appeal (while observing that, if he wished to register, he 'might consider' setting up a business of selling the horse's manure). *J Casson, LON/99/330 (VTD 16535)*.

7.106   **Holding company—whether carrying on any business.**   A holding company registered for VAT with effect from November 1987. Subsequently the Commissioners formed the opinion that the company was not carrying on any business, and cancelled its registration. The company appealed, contending that it was carrying on an 'economic activity' of providing management services, within *Article 4* of the *EC Sixth Directive*. The tribunal dismissed the appeal, applying *Polysar Investments*, 21.61 EUROPEAN COMMUNITY LAW. On the evidence, the only functions carried out by the company's directors were attributable to their duties as directors of the subsidiary company to which the management services were allegedly supplied, and the services 'lacked the element of regularity necessary to constitute economic activities'. *Newmir plc, [1993] VATTR 55 (VTD 10102)*.

7.107   **Charitable trust.**   In the case noted at 21.66 EUROPEAN COMMUNITY LAW, the CJEC ruled that a company which acted as the sole trustee of a charitable trust was not carrying on a business, since an activity consisting in the purchase and sale of shares and other securities was not within the definition of an 'economic activity' for the purposes of the *EC Sixth Directive*. The case was remitted to the tribunal for the formal determination of the company's appeal. The company sought to adduce further evidence and argument. The tribunal rejected the company's application and formally dismissed the appeal. *Wellcome Trust Ltd, [1997] VATDR 1 (VTD 14813)*.

7.108   **Company organising 'jobs fairs' for educational institutes.**   A company was incorporated to organise education and jobs fairs for universities, polytechnics and colleges of higher education. It received subscriptions from such institutions, and allowed its subscribers to occupy stands at its fairs free of charge. It reclaimed substantial amounts of input tax. The Commissioners issued assessments to recover the tax, on the basis that the provision of free stand space was not a business activity, so that the company was not entitled to reclaim input tax relating to it. The tribunal upheld the assessments and dismissed the company's appeal. The effect of *VATA 1994, s 5(2)(a)* was that the provision of free stand space was not to be treated as a supply for VAT purposes. Furthermore, applying *dicta* in *BLP Group plc*, 21.192 EUROPEAN COMMUNITY LAW, 'input tax can be deducted only to the extent that the goods or services on which it has been paid are "cost components" of a taxable transaction'. *Education & Jobs Fairs Ltd, MAN/96/1063 (VTD 15231)*.

7.109   **Company carrying out refurbishment work for associated company.**   A company (P) registered for VAT in 1997. It agreed to carry out some refurbishment work at a property owned by an associated company (L), which was a member of a group of companies which operated a number of casinos. (Although P and L were associated, P was not a member of L's VAT group.) P reclaimed substantial amounts of input tax relating to the refurbishment. In 1999 the Commissioners issued a ruling that P was not entitled to be registered, as it was not making any taxable supplies. (They also issued assessments to recover input tax which P had reclaimed.) The tribunal dismissed P's appeal against this decision, holding on the evidence that it was not satisfied that P 'has made, or is to make, any taxable supplies'. *Ladbroke (Palace Gate) Property Services Ltd, LON/99/643 (VTD 16666)*.

7.110   **Dealing in shares.**   For a case where the tribunal held that dealing in shares did not constitute a business, see *National Society for the Prevention of Cruelty to Children*, 11.33 CHARITIES.

7.111   **Partnership—investment of surplus funds.**   See *Kuchick Trading*, 34.140 INPUT TAX.

7.112 **Playgroup—whether a business.** See *Newtonbutler Playgroup Ltd*, 15.45
CONSTRUCTION OF BUILDINGS, ETC.

7.113 **Construction of yacht.** In January 1995 an individual (H) applied to be registered for VAT, stating on form VAT1 that he had begun a business of constructing yachts. The Commissioners duly registered him and he reclaimed input tax. A VAT officer visited him in August 1996, ascertained that he had only constructed one yacht, and formed the opinion that his activities did not constitute a business. The Commissioners therefore issued an assessment to recover the input tax which H had claimed. The tribunal upheld the assessment and dismissed H's appeal, holding on the evidence that his construction of a single yacht was 'an isolated transaction, and one which did not amount to a recognisable and identifiable activity'. Furthermore, H 'did not conduct his activities in a regular manner on sound and recognised business principles: he did not maintain proper books and records, engaged casual labour, and seemingly made no effort to advertise or otherwise publicise his services as a boatbuilder'. *D Hetherington, LON/96/1909 (VTD 15647)*.

7.114 **VATA 1994, s 94(4)—whether office accepted in the course of any business.** See *Gardner*, 58.54 SUPPLY.

8   Business Entertainment

Note. The effect of *Input Tax Order 1992 (SI 1992 No 3222), Article 5*, is that tax is not deductible on goods or services used for the purposes of 'business entertainment'.

The cases in this chapter are arranged under the following headings.

> Cases held to constitute 'business entertainment' 8.1–8.28
> Cases where the input tax was apportioned 8.29–8.33
> Cases held not to constitute 'business entertainment' 8.34–8.44

CASES HELD TO CONSTITUTE 'BUSINESS ENTERTAINMENT'

8.1   **Expenditure in restaurants.**   A surveyor reclaimed input tax in respect of expenditure on lunches in restaurants for himself and clients. The Commissioners issued an assessment to recover the tax and the tribunal dismissed his appeal. *WB Wyatt, CAR/76/65 (VTD 263)*.

8.2   A similar decision was reached in *Mrs S Woolf (t/a Sally Woolf Interiors), LON/92/2713A (VTD 10415)*.

8.3   A similar decision was reached in a case where an architect had reclaimed input tax on the cost of meals with clients. *W Richards, MAN/92/324 (VTD 11674)*. (*Note*. For another issue in this case, see 34.108 INPUT TAX.)

8.4   **Provision of food and accommodation for trainee agents.**   Two corporations sold goods through a pyramid of distributors, who were agents rather than employees. They held regular courses for the distributors, and provided food and accommodation. They reclaimed input tax on this expenditure. The Commissioners issued an assessment to recover the tax on the basis that the expenditure constituted 'business entertainment'. The QB upheld the decision and the CA dismissed the corporations' appeals, holding that the provision of free food and accommodation was within the definition of 'entertainment', so that the input tax was not deductible. *C & E Commrs v Shaklee International and Another, CA [1981] STC 776*.

8.5   *Shaklee International*, 8.4 above, was applied in the similar cases *of Sealine International Ltd, MAN/91/1257 (VTD 10061); Able Foods Ltd, LON/92/2950A (VTD 11317)* and *Siberian Trading Co Ltd, EDN/96/4 (VTD 14229)*.

8.6   A similar decision, also applying *Shaklee International*, 8.4 above, was reached in a subsequent case where the tribunal specifically held that the recipients of the entertainment were agents rather than employees, applying *dicta* of Cooke J in *Market Investigations Ltd v Minister of Social Security, QB [1968] 3 All ER 732 (TTC 2001, 65.21)*. *Network International Group Ltd, MAN/98/782 (VTD 16554)*.

8.7   **Food provided at business discussion meetings.**   A company carried on the business of market research for manufacturers of medical goods and equipment. It arranged discussion meetings, held at hotels and attended by about ten people. It provided these people with food and drink, and reclaimed the input tax on this expenditure. The Commissioners issued an assessment to recover the tax and the tribunal dismissed the company's appeal, applying *Shaklee International*, 8.4 above. *Medicare Research Ltd, LON/80/385 (VTD 1045)*.

8.8   **Provision of meals by cricket club for visiting teams.**   A county cricket club provided lunch and tea for visiting teams and officials, including umpires and scorers, as required by the County Cricket Club Board. Unlike most county clubs, it engaged an outside caterer for this purpose, and reclaimed input tax on the amounts it paid to the caterer. The Commissioners issued an assessment to recover the tax, and the club appealed. The tribunal dismissed the appeal, holding that the expenditure was within the definition of 'business entertainment'. *Shaklee International*, 8.4 above, applied. *Lancashire County Cricket Club, MAN/81/27 (VTD 1244)*.

8.9   **Subscription for theatre tickets.**   A club, with a limited membership, was formed to assist in financing the reconstruction of a theatre. In return for their subscriptions, members were guaranteed specified seats for an evening of their choice for each weekly performance for four years. A company which purchased a subscription to the club reclaimed input tax on this expenditure. The Commissioners issued an assessment to recover the tax, considering that the expenditure constituted 'business entertainment'. The tribunal upheld the assessment and dismissed the company's appeal. *Shaklee International*, 8.4 above, applied. *William Matthew Mechanical Services Ltd, [1982] VATTR 63 (VTD 1210)*.

8.10   A similar decision was reached in *Wolf Management Services Ltd, MAN/82/7 (VTD 1270)*.

8.11   **Launching party for new premises.**   A company arranged a lunch at a local hotel to mark the opening of new premises. The lunch was attended by 25 senior employees and about 130 actual or potential customers or suppliers. The company reclaimed input tax on the cost of the lunch. The Commissioners issued an assessment to recover the tax and the tribunal dismissed the company's appeal, holding that the expenditure was on 'business entertainment', applying *Shaklee International*, 8.4 above. The proportion of the expenditure which was attributable to the company's employees was not deductible, because its provision was 'incidental to its provision for others', within what is now *Input Tax Order, Article 5(3)*. *Wilsons Transport Ltd, MAN/83/68 (VTD 1468)*.

8.12   The Fraserburgh Harbour Commissioners (a statutory body) opened a new inner harbour, which was significantly deeper than the previous inner harbour, and held a party to publicise its opening. The party was attended by the Prince of Wales, local dignitaries, and potential users of the harbour. Free food and drink was provided. The tribunal held that the input tax relating to this was not deductible, since it was within the definition of 'business entertainment'. *BMW (GB) Ltd*, 8.32 below, applied. *Fraserburgh Harbour Commissioners, EDN/98/9 (VTD 15797)*.

8.13   **Elizabethan banquets.**   A partnership carried on the business of providing Elizabethan banquets. Each banquet was attended by about 240 people. If a particular banquet failed to attract the expected number of customers, the partnership invited its employees to attend free of charge, to maintain the expected atmosphere. Most of the customers were driven to the banquet in coaches. At the banquets the customers were entertained by actors in Elizabethan costume. The partnership reclaimed input tax on the banquets. The Commissioners issued an assessment to recover the tax attributable to the food provided to the coach drivers, to the partnership's employees who attended free of charge, and to the actors. The tribunal held that the tax attributable to the food provided to the coach drivers and the employees was 'business entertainment' and was not deductible. (However, the food and drink consumed by the actors while performing was not 'business entertainment', so that the tax attributable to this was deductible.) *Elizabethan Banquets, LON/84/455 (VTD 1795)*.

8.14   **Motor racing by company—whether any provision of business entertainment.**   A company carried on the business of manufacturing and selling sunbeds. Its principal director, who had been a professional racing driver, raced cars bearing the name of the company's product. Potential customers were invited to the pits and provided with entertainment. The company reclaimed input tax on this expenditure and the Commissioners issued an assessment to recover the tax. The tribunal dismissed the company's appeal, holding that the tax was not deductible since the expenditure constituted 'business entertainment'. *Paine Leisure Products Ltd, LON/84/380 (VTD 1836)*.

8.15   **Powerboat racing—whether any provision of business entertainment.**   See *Denby*, 34.312 INPUT TAX.

8.16   **Horse racing by company—whether any provision of business entertainment.**   See *British Car Auctions Ltd*, 34.274 INPUT TAX.

8.17   **Horse racing by accountant as business entertainment.**   See *Dyer*, 34.286 INPUT TAX.

8.18   **Hospitality at golf championship.**   A partnership entertained prospective clients at the British Open Golf Championship, and reclaimed input tax on the expenditure in question. The Commissioners issued an assessment to recover the tax, considering that the hospitality was within the definition of 'business entertainment'. The tribunal upheld the assessment and dismissed the company's appeal. *PR Promotions, MAN/86/15 (VTD 2122)*.

8.19   A similar decision was reached in *Cheshire Securities Ltd, MAN/87/57 (VTD 3240)*.

8.20   **Hospitality suite at sports ground.**   A company carried on the business of selling and servicing industrial plant. It occupied a 'hospitality suite' overlooking Cardiff Arms Park, under a licence agreement with Cardiff Rugby Club. It used the suite as an office for two days each week, but also invited customers to the suite to watch rugby matches in a 'convivial atmosphere'. Under the terms of the licence, the club also provided the company with eight season tickets for the grandstand. The company reclaimed the input tax charged on its occupation of the suite. The Commissioners issued an assessment to recover two-thirds of the tax, considering that the suite was primarily occupied for the purpose of business entertainment. The QB upheld the assessment. Laws J held that what is now *Input Tax Order, Article 5* disallowed input tax on any supply which was used to a measurable extent for business entertainment. The entertainment here could not be disregarded on *de minimis* grounds. Although the Commissioners had agreed to allow one-third of the input tax, the effect of *Input Tax Order, Article 5* was that none of the tax was deductible. *C & E Commrs v Plant & Repair Services (South Wales) Ltd, QB [1994] STC 232.* (*Note.* The decision in this case was disapproved by the CA in the subsequent case of *Thorn EMI plc*, 8.30 below.)

8.21   A company leased a 'hospitality box' at a rugby league ground and reclaimed input tax on this expenditure. The Commissioners issued an assessment to recover half of the tax. The tribunal dismissed the company's appeal. (The tribunal chairman commented that, since half the input tax had been allowed, 'the assessments are unduly favourable to the appellant'.) *RW Cockroft & Co (Travel) Ltd, MAN/93/850 (VTD 11800)*.

8.22   A professional football club operated a scheme limited to 40 subscribers, whereby the subscribers were allocated particular seats at the ground and were provided with lunch in a special suite. A company which operated a property management business purchased two of the 40 subscriptions and reclaimed input tax on their cost. The Commissioners issued an assessment to recover the tax, on the grounds that it related to a supply of business entertainment. The company appealed, contending that it had not incurred the expenditure in order to entertain existing or potential customers, but partly in order to reward its staff and its financial advisor, and partly with the hope of making additional contacts. (The company had two directors, one other part-time employee, and some temporary staff.) The tribunal dismissed the company's appeal, noting that the company's business activities took place at a significant distance from the football ground, and concluding that 'if there was an element of advertising, as a business use, it must be considered to have been essentially fortuitous, and not significant enough to be measurable'. Furthermore, since one of the subscriptions had been used to entertain the company's financial advisor, who was not an employee of the company, the entertainment could not be treated as being outside the definition of 'business entertainment' in *Input Tax Order, Article 5(3)*. The chairman observed that 'given the nature and very small number of staff in (this) case, and the prominent role of (the financial advisor), it is impossible to say that the paramount purpose was provision for the employees and/or directors'. *KPMG Peat Marwick McLintock*, 8.40 below, distinguished. *Sundeck plc, LON/95/ 1297A (VTD 14051)*.

8.23   **Cabaret evenings organised by brewery.**   A brewery company organised cabaret evenings at its headquarters, and gave free admission to its customers. The company reclaimed input tax on the cost of the cabaret evenings, and the Commissioners issued an assessment to recover the tax, considering that they constituted 'business entertainment'. The tribunal dismissed the company's appeal, holding that the expenditure was within what is now *Input Tax Order 1992, Article 5*. *Northern Clubs Federation Brewery Ltd, MAN/91/1017 (VTD 8881)*.

8.24   **Free drinks provided to restaurant customers.**   A VAT officer discovered that the gross profit rate of a restaurant was unusually low. The restaurant proprietors explained that they provided free drinks to some customers. The Commissioners issued an assessment to recover input tax attributable to such drinks, on the basis that their provision constituted 'business entertainment'. The tribunal upheld the assessment and dismissed the proprietors' appeal. *Shaklee International*, 8.4 above, applied. *Polash Tandoori Restaurant, LON/92/1998A (VTD 10903)*.

8.25   **Estate agents reclaiming input tax on wine.**   A firm which carried on business as estate agents stayed open late on some evenings in December, and provided wine to people who visited its offices. It also held an anniversary celebration, to which it invited local dignitaries, and provided wine to those attending. The firm reclaimed input tax on the cost of the wine, and the Commissioners issued an assessment to recover the tax. The tribunal dismissed the firm's appeal, holding that the provision of the wine constituted 'business entertainment', and that, by virtue of what is now *Article 5(1)* of the *Input Tax Order*, the tax was not deductible. *Shaklee International Ltd*, 8.4 above, applied. *White & Sons, LON/93/1770 (VTD 11680)*.

8.26   **Cabaret at conference for members of accountancy partnership.**   A large accountancy partnership organised a conference which was attended by around 400 partners. The conference included a cabaret. The partnership reclaimed input tax on the whole cost of the conference, including the cabaret. The Commissioners issued an assessment to recover the tax relating to the cabaret. The partnership appealed, contending that the cabaret should be treated as an integral part of the conference. The tribunal rejected this contention and dismissed the appeal, holding on the evidence that the cabaret was 'pure entertainment' and that the expenditure on the cabaret had not been incurred for the purpose of the partnership's business. *Ernst & Young, [1997] VATDR 183 (VTD 15100)*. *(Notes.* (1) For another issue in this case, see 8.41 below. (2) For the Commissioners' practice following this decision, see Business Brief 25/97, issued on 10 November 1997.)

8.27   **Food and drink provided at exhibitions.**   A company organised a number of exhibitions. In conjunction with some of the exhibitions it staged receptions, at which food and drinks were provided. It reclaimed input tax on this expenditure. The

Commissioners issued an assessment to recover the tax, on the basis that the expenditure constituted 'business entertainment'. The tribunal upheld the assessment and dismissed the company's appeal. *Shaklee International*, 8.4 above, applied; *The City of Chicago Board of Trade*, 8.39 below, distinguished. *Miller Freeman Worldwide plc, LON/94/3345 (VTD 15439)*.

8.28   **Party for premiere of film.**   A company agreed to promote a film in the UK, in exchange for a share in the film's profits. It hosted a party for the UK premiere of the film, and reclaimed input tax on the party. The Commissioners rejected the claim on the basis that the expenditure was 'business entertainment'. The tribunal dismissed the company's appeal against this decision. *Shaklee International*, 8.4 above, applied; *Kilroy Television Company Ltd*, 8.43 below, distinguished. *The Entertainment Group of Companies Ltd, LON/8/994 (VTD 16639)*.

CASES WHERE THE INPUT TAX WAS APPORTIONED

8.29   **Premises partly used for business entertainment.**   A company which produced and marketed Scotch whisky reclaimed input tax relating to premises which were primarily used for business administration but were partly used as a venue for business entertainment. The Commissioners issued an assessment to recover the tax, contending that, since the premises were partly used for business entertainment, the effect of *Input Tax Order, Article 5(1)* was that the tax could not be apportioned and that none of the tax was deductible. The tribunal rejected this contention and allowed the company's appeal, holding on the evidence that 70% of the tax was deductible. *MacDonald & Muir Ltd, EDN/92/208 (VTD 10947)*.

8.30   **Hospitality chalets at air shows.**   A company manufactured complex electronic systems, which it displayed and sold at air shows. At these shows it had exhibition stands and 'hospitality chalets'. It reclaimed input tax in respect of the hospitality chalets, and the Commissioners issued an assessment to recover this tax, considering that the expenditure in question was for the purpose of business entertainment. The company appealed, contending that the chalets were essential as a place in which to hold confidential discussions with potential purchasers. The CA held that the tax should be apportioned. Millett LJ held that what is now *Article 5* of the *Input Tax Order* should be construed as permitting apportionment in the case of supplies used partly for business entertainment and partly for other business purposes. The exclusion of all credit for input tax in such a case would be a contravention of *Article 17* of the *EC Sixth Directive*. *Thorn EMI plc v C & E Commrs, CA [1995] STC 674*.

8.31   **Provision   of   beer   by   concert   promoter—whether   'business entertainment'.**   The promoter of a 'rock music' concert tour, comprising five concerts, advertised tickets at £10 each with the incentive of free beer for those attending. The tour was not a success, and only 370 tickets in total were sold for the five concerts. The promoter reclaimed input tax on the purchase of 9,600 cans of beer and lager. The Commissioners issued an assessment to recover the tax, considering that the provision of free beer and lager at concerts was within the definition of 'business entertainment', and that it was in any event unlikely that 370 customers would have drunk 9,600 cans between them. The promoter appealed, contending that the beer and lager had been provided to customers, and to his 16 employees, for the purpose of the business, and that the input tax should be treated as deductible. The tribunal allowed the appeal in part, finding that the price paid by each customer 'entitled the customer to listen to three rock bands in concert, and to drink beer and lager without paying extra for such drink'. Since the customers had paid for their tickets, the beer and lager was not within the definition of 'business entertainment', so that the input tax was deductible in principle, applying *The City of Chicago Board of Trade*, 8.39 below. However, the tribunal also found that not all of the beer purchased could have been drunk by customers. The chairman observed that 'not all the customers who attended the rock concerts would have been male ... a female attending a rock concert would not be likely to consume the same amount of drink of beer and lager as a male... it would not be credible to envisage that a female would drink some 13 cans of beer or lager'. The tribunal found on the balance of probabilities that the customers had consumed an average of eight cans each, making a total of 2,960 cans. With regard to the 16 employees, the tribunal held that the input tax was deductible in principle, but found that each employee would have consumed an average of eight cans per concert for each of the five concerts, making a total of 640 cans. Accordingly the tribunal held that the input tax on 3,600 cans was deductible but that the tax on the remaining 6,000 cans was not deductible. *D Lumby*, *MAN/94/593 (VTD 12972)*.

8.32   **Motor distributor.**   A company (BMW) carried on business as an importer and distributor of motorcars and motorcycles. It sold such vehicles to independent dealers, who in turn sold them to members of the public. In the course of its promotional activities it arranged 'track days', at which dealers and potential customers could test-drive its cars. Dealers were required to make payments ranging from £25 to £85 per person attending. (For 1994, the amount reimbursed by the dealers represented 29% of BMW's total costs in arranging the 'track days'.) BMW also arranged golfing days and curling days, and reclaimed input tax on the total costs of these activities. The Commissioners issued assessments on the basis that BMW could only recover the proportion of the input tax which equated to the proportion of the costs which was reimbursed by the dealers (i.e. 29% of the input tax on the 'track days', and 17% of the input tax on the 'curling days'), but that the remainder of the input tax was not recoverable, since it was attributable to supplies of business entertainment. BMW appealed, contending that it was not making any supply of hospitality, since it was making supplies to the dealers and it was those dealers who were supplying hospitality to their customers. The tribunal rejected this contention and upheld the assessments in principle (subject to adjustment of the figures). The tribunal observed that there were 'two quite distinct elements in the track days'. Expenditure on demonstrating BMW's products, such as test drives and brake demonstrations, was not within the definition of 'business entertainment'. However, BMW had also incurred substantial expenditure on 'hospitality'. This hospitality was supplied by BMW rather than by the dealers and only the percentage of the relevant input tax which was attributable to the supplies to the dealers was recoverable. The percentage which was attributable to the supplies to the potential customers was 'business entertainment' and was not recoverable. The QB upheld the tribunal decision. On the evidence, the supply of facilities to the customers was distinguishable from the transaction between BMW and the dealers. There was a gratuitous provision of services by BMW to the customers, which was within the definition of 'business entertainment'. *BMW (GB) Ltd v C & E Commrs, QB [1997] STC 824.*

8.33   **Dinner dance for employees of accountancy partnership.**   An accountancy partnership reclaimed input tax in respect of dinner dances which it organised for its employees. Each employee was entitled to bring one guest. The Commissioners issued an assessment to recover 45% of the tax, considering that the proportion of the expenditure which was attributable to the employees' guests constituted 'business entertainment'. The tribunal upheld the assessment and dismissed the partnership's appeal. The decision in *KPMG Peat Marwick McLintock*, 8.40 below, was disapproved and not followed, on the basis that in that case both parties had accepted in argument that the tax could not be apportioned, so that it was either wholly allowable or wholly disallowable, whereas in the subsequent case of *Thorn EMI plc*, 8.30 above, the CA had held that *Article 5* of the *Input Tax Order* should be construed as permitting apportionment in the case of supplies used partly for business entertainment and partly for other purposes. The tribunal chairman held that the tribunal hearing the previous case noted at 8.40 below had erred in drawing a distinction between the use of goods and services for business reasons and for social reasons, and had erred in applying a test of 'predominance or paramount purpose'. The chairman observed that there was nothing in the *Input Tax Order* 'which stated or implied that the provision of entertainment for non-employees was to be treated as not being business entertainment where its provision was incidental to the provision of entertainment for employees, in contrast to the specific provision made in the converse case'. Accordingly, the partnership was only entitled to credit for the tax attributable to the entertainment of its employees as distinct from its employees' guests. *KPMG (No 2), [1997] VATDR 192 (VTD 14962)*. (*Notes.* (1) For the Commissioners' practice following this decision, see Business Brief 25/97, issued on 10 November 1997. (2) The decision here was distinguished in *Ernst & Young*, 8.41 below, where employees were required to pay £15 towards the cost of their guests' attendance at a Christmas party, whereas the employees here had not been required to make any payment towards the cost.)

CASES HELD NOT TO CONSTITUTE 'BUSINESS ENTERTAINMENT'

8.34   **Hotel expenses of visiting football club met by host club.**   A Scottish football club (Celtic) took part in the European Cup organised by the Union of European Football Associations, and played teams from Romania and Hungary in successive rounds. Two games were played in each round on a 'home' and 'away' basis, and the rules provided that the home club was to pay the hotel expenses of the visiting club. Celtic reclaimed input tax in respect of the hotel accommodation which it provided in Glasgow for the Romanian and Hungarian teams. The Commissioners issued an assessment to recover the tax, considering that the expenditure constituted 'business entertainment'. Celtic appealed. The CS allowed Celtic's appeal, holding that 'entertainment' should be construed as meaning hospitality free to the recipient. Because of the reciprocal obligations under the competition rules, what the visiting teams enjoyed at Celtic's expenses was not free to them, since they were required to meet Celtic's hotel expenses for the other matches in the round. There was, therefore, no provision of 'business entertainment' within what is now *Input Tax Order, Article 5. Shaklee International*, 8.4 above, distinguished. *Celtic Football & Athletic Club Ltd v C & E Commrs, CS [1983] STC 470.*

8.35   *Celtic Football & Athletic Club Ltd*, 8.34 above, was applied in a subsequent case where the Football Association arranged and paid for hotel accommodation for visiting teams and reclaimed the input tax thereon. The tribunal allowed the Association's appeal against an assessment to recover the tax, holding that the provision of the accommodation did not constitute business entertainment. The hospitality provided by the Association was enforced and contractual, and there was a reciprocal element because the Association's teams had in previous years received such accommodation when playing abroad. *Football Association Ltd, [1985] VATTR 106 (VTD 1860)*. (*Note.* For another issue in this case, see 58.219 SUPPLY.)

8.36   **Hotel expenses of tennis players.**   See *Northern Lawn Tennis Club*, 34.14 INPUT TAX.

8.37   **Refreshments at conferences.**   A company (W) organised conferences on financial issues. The cost of some of these conferences was met by sponsors (such as banks or other financial institutions), who were entitled to nominate up to 120 delegates (usually customers or potential customers) who could attend the conferences free of charge. Meals and refreshments were provided at the conferences, which were held at hotels. W reclaimed input tax on the cost of the meals and refreshments. The Commissioners issued an assessment to recover the proportion of the tax which related to the delegates of the sponsors, considering that the provision of meals and refreshments to these delegates was within the definition of 'business entertainment'. The tribunal allowed W's appeal, holding on the evidence that the relevant entertainment was supplied to the delegates by the sponsors, rather than by W. Since W was not the person providing business entertainment, it was entitled to reclaim input tax on the supplies which it received from the hotels, although the sponsors would not be entitled to reclaim input tax on the supplies of meals and refreshments which they received from W. *Webster Communications International Ltd, [1997] VATDR 173 (VTD 14753)*.

8.38   **Theatre tickets supplied to potential customers by company incorporated to market playwright's works.**   A company was incorporated to market the works of a well-known playwright. It supplied theatre tickets to people who might wish to see plays written by the playwright, with a view to negotiating performance rights. It reclaimed input tax on the cost of these tickets. The Commissioners issued an assessment to recover the tax, considering that the supply of the tickets constituted the provision of 'business entertainment'. The tribunal allowed the company's appeal. Generally, the provision of theatre tickets would fall within the definition of 'business entertaining'. However, in the case under appeal, the tickets were supplied in the hope that the customers to whom they were supplied would be interested in producing a film or television version of the playwright's work. They were akin to 'an industrial product buyer visiting another user of the product at the instigation of the manufacturer', and no element of hospitality or entertainment was involved. *Shaklee International*, 8.4 above, and *PR Promotions*, 8.18 above, distinguished. *WR Ltd, MAN/91/116 (VTD 6968)*.

8.39   **Conference receptions.**   An association (CBOT) was established under USA law by members of the Chicago futures and options market, with the object of promoting the market. It was a member of the Futures Industry Association (FIA), which was based in the USA and which organised annual conferences in London. CBOT registered for VAT in the UK in accordance with the provisions of what is now *VATA 1994, Sch 1 para 10*. It sponsored a cocktail party and a champagne reception at the 1989 and 1990 London conferences of the FIA, and reclaimed input tax on this expenditure. The Commissioners issued an assessment to recover the tax, considering that—with the exception of the part attributable to the CBOT's own staff—it was not deductible by virtue of what is now *Input Tax Order 1992, Article 5*. The CBOT appealed, contending that the expenditure was not within the definition of 'business entertainment' since the delegates had paid to attend the conference. The tribunal accepted this contention and allowed the appeal, holding that payment was 'incompatible with the concept of entertainment or hospitality'. Since the delegates had paid to attend the conference, it followed that what they received was not 'entertainment or hospitality'. *Celtic Football & Athletic Club Ltd*, 8.34 above, applied; *Shaklee International*, 8.4 above, distinguished. *The City of Chicago Board of Trade, LON/92/766Y (VTD 9114)*.

8.40   **Dinner dance for employees of accountancy partnership.**   An accountancy partnership reclaimed input tax in respect of a dinner dance which it organised for its employees. Each employee was entitled to bring one guest. The Commissioners issued an assessment to recover the tax, considering that the function constituted 'business entertainment' and that its provision for the employees was 'incidental to its provision for others'. The tribunal allowed the partnership's appeal, finding that the attendance of the employees' guests was incidental and ancillary to the attendance of the employees themselves, and holding that this was not within the definition of 'business entertainment'. *KPMG Peat Marwick McLintock, [1993] VATTR 118 (VTD 10135)*. (*Notes.* (1) For the Commissioners' practice following this decision,

8.41 Business Entertainment

see Business Brief 21/95, issued on 8 October 1995. (2) The decision here was disapproved by a subsequent tribunal in another case involving the same partnership—see 8.33 above—on the basis that both parties had accepted in argument that the tax could not be apportioned, so that it was either wholly allowable or wholly disallowable, whereas in the subsequent case of *Thorn EMI plc*, 8.30 above, the CA had held that *Article 5* of the *Input Tax Order* should be construed as permitting apportionment in the case of supplies used partly for business entertainment and partly for other purposes. The chairman in the case noted at 8.33 above observed that there was nothing in the *Input Tax Order* 'which stated or implied that the provision of entertainment for non-employees was to be treated as not being business entertainment where its provision was incidental to the provision of entertainment for employees, in contrast to the specific provision made in the converse case', and held that the tribunal hearing the case noted here had erred in drawing a distinction between the use of goods and services for business reasons and for social reasons, and had erred in applying a test of 'predominance or paramount purpose'.)

8.41 An accountancy partnership reclaimed input tax in respect of a Christmas party and a dinner dance which it organised for its employees. For the Christmas party, each employee was required to pay £10 towards the cost, and was entitled to bring one guest to the Christmas party but was required to pay a further £15. (No guests attended the dinner dance, which took place after a conference attended by partners and employees.) With regard to the Christmas party, the Commissioners issued an assessment to recover the tax on the amount by which the cost of the party exceeded the payments made by the employees. With regard to the dinner dance, the Commissioners issued an assessment to recover the whole of the tax attributable to the cost of the disco and to the cost of alcoholic drinks which were served before and after the meal, and 50% of the tax attributable to the cost of the dinner. The partnership appealed, contending that its purpose in incurring the expenditure was to reward its staff, so that the expenditure had been incurred for the purpose of its business. The tribunal accepted this contention and allowed the appeal. The tribunal specifically disapproved the Commissioners' practice, laid down in *Leaflet 700/55/93*, of allowing only 50% of input tax attributable to entertainment of employees. With regard to the guests of the employees, the tribunal distinguished *KPMG (No 2)*, 8.33 above, on the grounds that in that case no charge had been made. Applying *dicta* of Keene J in *BMW (GB) Ltd*, 8.32 above, 'the crucial characteristic of "entertainment" within the phrase "business entertainment" is that it is provided to a person or persons who enjoy it free of charge'. Although the charge of £15 was considerably less than the cost of the party, 'it was not so small that one can say that the meal was effectively supplied free of charge'. The tribunal held that the expenditure was not within *VATA 1994, s 84(4)*, since that provision had to be read in the light of *Article 17(6)* of the *EC Sixth Directive*. Alternatively, the tribunal considered that even if the expenditure were deemed to be within *s 84(4)*, the appeal would still be successful on the grounds that 'the Commissioners were unreasonable in disallowing the expenditure because no reasonable body of Commissioners understanding the law as we have found it to be could consider that the expenditure was non-business'. *Ernst & Young, [1997] VATDR 183 (VTD 15100)*. (*Notes.* (1) For another issue in this case, see 8.26 above. (2) For the Commissioners' practice following this decision, see Business Brief 25/97, issued on 10 November 1997.)

8.42 **Debentures providing seats at tennis tournament.** A company which manufactured sports equipment purchased ten debentures issued by the All England Lawn Tennis Club, entitling it to a total of 130 seats at the annual Wimbledon tennis tournament. It reclaimed input tax on the purchase. The Commissioners issued an assessment to recover the tax, considering that the expenditure had been incurred for the purpose of business entertainment. The company appealed, contending that the expenditure had been incurred for the purpose of promoting its products, and that the business entertainment was incidental and subsidiary. The tribunal allowed the appeal in part, holding on the evidence that 50 of the seats had been purchased for entertainment, so that the input tax relating to them was not deductible, but that 80 of the seats had been purchased for employees and their relatives, so that the input tax relating to those seats was deductible. *BTR Industries Ltd, MAN/90/913 (VTD 11828)*.

8.43   **Buffet meal for participants in television programme.**   A company which produced television programmes provided modest buffet meals, costing less than £10 per head, for people who participated in the programmes. It reclaimed input tax on the cost of the meals. The Commissioners issued assessments to recover the tax, considering that the expenditure was within the definition of 'business entertainment', and the company appealed. The tribunal allowed the company's appeal, finding that the company had placed itself under a legal obligation to provide the meals. The QB upheld this decision as one of fact. The case was 'on the borderline', but on the evidence, the tribunal had been entitled to find that the meals did not constitute 'business entertainment'. *Dicta* in *Celtic Football & Athletic Club Ltd*, 8.34 above, applied; *Shaklee International*, 8.4 above, distinguished. *C & E Commrs v The Kilroy Television Company Ltd, QB [1997] STC 901*.

8.44   **Market research company—product trials for alcoholic beverages.**   A market research company organised 'product trials' for brewery companies. At the trials, members of the public were asked to consume a number of alcoholic beverages and to complete questionnaires on them. They were also provided with sandwiches or bread and cheese, and with a taxi journey home. The company reclaimed input tax on the cost of the 'product trials'. The Commissioners issued an assessment to recover the tax relating to the food, considering that this expenditure was within the definition of 'business entertainment'. The tribunal allowed the company's appeal. The Commissioners had accepted that the provision of the alcoholic beverages was not 'business entertainment'. On the evidence, the tribunal held that 'the provision of the simple food was a necessary part of the provision of the drinks, bearing in mind that the drinks were alcoholic, that the participants would not have eaten for some time before the product trial took place, and also bearing in mind the very simple quality of the food provided. Accordingly, the provision of the food was ... a necessary part of the provision of the drinks'. *Celtic Football & Athletic Club Ltd*, 8.34 above, and *The Kilroy Television Co Ltd*, 8.43 above, applied. *DPA (Market Research) Ltd, LON/95/2837 (VTD 14751)*.

9 Cars

Note. In this chapter a reference to the *Cars Order* is to the *VAT (Cars) Order 1992 (SI 1992 No 3122)*. A reference to the *Input Tax Order* is to the *VAT (Input Tax) Order 1992 (SI 1992 No 3222)*.

The cases in this chapter are arranged under the following headings.

THE DEFINITION OF 'MOTOR CAR' (Cars Order, Article 2)

Note. 'Motor car' is defined in the *Cars Order (SI 1992 No 3122), Article 2* and in the *Input Tax Order (SI 1992 No 3222), Article 2*. The definitions are relevant in relation to, *inter alia*, both the margin scheme for second-hand motor cars (*Cars Order, Article 8*) and the disallowance of input tax (*Input Tax Order, Article 7*). The definitions were amended with effect from 1 December 1999 by the *VAT (Cars) (Amendment) Order 1999 (SI 1999 No 2832)* and the *VAT (Input Tax) (Amendment) Order 1999 (SI 1999 No 2930)*. One of the effects of the amendments was to remove vehicles constructed to carry a payload of one tonne or more from the definition of a 'motor car'. The cases in this subsection (most of which are input tax cases) should be read in the light of these changes.

Vehicles held to be motor cars

9.1 **Land Rover specially adapted.** A company sold a Land Rover which its previous owner had fitted with a hard top body with side windows and upholstered seats, to enable it to be used to transport his daughters to gymkhanas. The Commissioners issued an assessment charging output tax, on the basis that the vehicle was not a 'motor car' within *Cars Order, Article 2*. The tribunal allowed the company's appeal, holding that the Land Rover had been converted into a 'motor car'. *Chartcliff Ltd, [1976] VATTR 165 (VTD 262)*. (*Note.* For another issue in this case, see 9.35 below. For an application for costs, see 2.319 APPEALS.)

9.2 A landscape gardener reclaimed input tax on the purchase of a Land Rover, which had been modified by the addition of a metal canopy with two side windows, and was registered as a heavy goods vehicle. The Commissioners issued an assessment on the basis that this modification had converted the vehicle into a motor car, so that the input tax was not deductible. The tribunal upheld the assessment and dismissed the gardener's appeal. Applying *Jeynes*, 9.17 below, the fact that the vehicle was registered as a heavy goods vehicle was not conclusive. *MCF Wigley, MAN/91/776 (VTD 7300)*.

9.3   **Whether vehicle normally used on public roads.**   A company which imported cars from Europe claimed credit for input tax incurred on the purchase of a Continental version of a Ford Escort. The Commissioners refused to allow credit for the tax, as the car was 'a motor vehicle of a kind normally used on public roads', within *Article 2*. The company appealed, contending that the Continental version of the car differed from the UK version and was not within the definition in question. The tribunal rejected this contention and upheld the Commissioners' decision, and the QB dismissed the company's appeal. The definition 'motor vehicle of a kind normally used on public roads' should be construed in its ordinary sense as referring to a broad class of motor vehicles, and should not be restricted to any particular model. *Withers of Winsford Ltd v C & E Commrs, QB [1988] STC 431*.

9.4   **Tipping truck with accommodation for carriage of employees.**   A firm which traded as roofing contractors purchased a Volkswagen 'LT 35' tipping truck which had, as well as a tipping body over the rear wheels and the usual driver's cab with room for one passenger, a second roofed cab behind the driver's cab with room for three more passengers, with side doors with windows and a window at the back. The Commissioners issued a ruling that the vehicle was a motor car as defined in the *Cars Order, Article 2*. The tribunal upheld the ruling and dismissed the company's appeal. *Weatherproof Flat Roofing (Plymouth) Ltd, LON/81/351 (VTD 1240)*.

9.5   **Estate car.**   The tribunal held that a Ford Granada estate car, used by a builder mainly for the purposes of his business, was within the definition of a 'motor car'. *MC Gardner, LON/78/23 (VTD 588)*.

9.6   The proprietor of a garage and grocery store reclaimed input tax in respect of an estate car used in his business and licensed as a goods vehicle. The Commissioners rejected his claim and the tribunal dismissed the proprietor's appeal. *R Howarth, CAR/77/451 (VTD 632)*.

9.7   Similar decisions were reached in *FW Chattin, LON/82/38 (VTD 1226); JT Thomson, EDN/82/13 (VTD 1300); LS Scargill, MAN/82/122 (VTD 1420); GA Security Systems Ltd, MAN/83/212 (VTD 1527)* and *Direct Link Couriers (Bristol) Ltd, LON/85/481 (VTD 2105)*.

9.8   A company purchased three estate cars and removed the rear seats. It reclaimed input tax on the three cars. The Commissioners issued an assessment to recover the tax, and the company appealed, contending that by removing the rear seats, it had taken the vehicles outside the definition of 'motor car' in *Cars Order, Article 2*, so that the input tax was deductible. The tribunal dismissed the appeal, holding that, despite the removal of the rear seats, the vehicles remained within the definition of 'motor cars'. *County Telecommunications Systems Ltd, LON/92/1357A (VTD 10224)*.

9.9   **Chevrolet K10.**   A contractor reclaimed input tax on a Chevrolet K10 Blazer (a vehicle of which the part of the bodywork with the rear and side windows and the rear roof is removable comparatively easily). The Commissioners rejected the claim on the basis that the vehicle was within the definition of a 'motor car'. The tribunal dismissed the contractor's appeal. *D Yarlett, LON/83/194 (VTD 1490)*.

9.10   **Volkswagen pick-up truck.**   A company reclaimed input tax on a Volkswagen long-wheelbase pick-up truck which had, to the rear of the driver's seat, roofed accommodation which was fitted with side windows. The Commissioners rejected the claim on the basis that the vehicle was within the definition of a 'motor car'. The

9.11 Cars

tribunal dismissed the company's appeal. *Readings & Headley Ltd, LON/83/193 (VTD 1535)*.

9.11 **Toyota Hiace van.**   A trader reclaimed input tax in respect of a Toyota Hiace van, fitted with side windows, which was taxed and insured as a commercial vehicle. The Commissioners rejected the claim, considering that the vehicle was within the definition of a 'motor car' by virtue of *Cars Order, Article 2(b)*. The trader appealed, contending that the vehicle was not constructed for the carrying of passengers. The tribunal dismissed his appeal, holding that the vehicle was within the statutory definition of a 'motor car'. *TW Knapp, LON/79/55 (VTD 778)*.

9.12 **Toyota Previa.**   A partnership which sold pine furniture purchased a Toyota Previa, registered as a commercial vehicle. The partners removed the middle and rear rows of seats and used it for delivering furniture. They reclaimed input tax on the purchase. The Commissioners issued an assessment to recover the tax, considering that, despite the removal of the seats, the vehicle was still within the definition of a 'motor car'. The tribunal upheld the assessment and dismissed the partnership's appeal, observing that the seats could easily be replaced. *Gorringe Pine, LON/95/2239A (VTD 14036)*.

9.13 A similar decision was reached in *RC Kenney & BJ Stiles (t/a AD Fine Art), LON/94/726 (VTD 14969)*.

9.14 **Toyota Spacecruiser.**   A partnership which manufactured women's clothing reclaimed input tax on the purchase of a Toyota Spacecruiser. The Commissioners issued an assessment to recover the tax, on the basis that the vehicle was a 'motor car'. The partners appealed, contending that because they had removed the rear seats of the vehicle and inserted a hanging rail which was used for transporting clothes, the vehicle was no longer a 'motor car'. The tribunal rejected this contention and dismissed the appeal, holding that 'the removal of the rear seats and the insertion of the hanging rail were temporary modifications' and the vehicle remained a 'motor car'. *Mr & Mrs M Gohil (t/a Gohil Fashions), LON/97/1124 (VTD 15435)*.

9.15 **Modified Datsun pick-up.**   A company had acquired a Datsun 120Y pick-up, modified by the addition of a detachable hard top superstructure with two side windows and a hatchback, fitted to the rear of the driver's seat, and having a headroom of between three and four feet and no seats or seating accommodation. The Commissioners issued a ruling that the vehicle was within the definition of a 'motor car', since the roofed accommodation brought it within *Cars Order, Article 2(b)*. The company appealed, contending that 'roofed accommodation' should be construed as referring solely to accommodation for passengers, as distinct from freight. The tribunal rejected this contention and dismissed the company's appeal. *HKS Coachworks Ltd, MAN/81/64 (VTD 1124)*. (*Note*. The decision here was disapproved by the CA in *R v C & E Commrs (ex p. Nissan UK Ltd)*, 9.39 below.)

9.16 **Range Rover.**   The tribunal held that a Range Rover, which had been modified by the anchoring of the back seat, was within the definition of a 'motor car'. *HJ Berry & Sons Ltd, MAN/82/113 (VTD 1324)*.

9.17 A trader who carried on a mobile catering business purchased two Range Rovers. He registered them as heavy goods vehicles and reclaimed input tax on their purchase. The Commissioners rejected the claim and he appealed. The QB upheld the Commissioners' decision, holding that although the vehicles had been registered as heavy goods vehicles, they remained motor cars for VAT purposes. *C & E Commrs v Jeynes (t/a Midland International (Hire) Caterers), QB 1983, [1984] STC 30*.

9.18 A Range Rover was also held to be a 'motor car' in *John Slough of London, LON/82/289 (VTD 1427)*.

9.19   **Modified jeep.**   The tribunal held that a jeep pick-up, with accommodation behind the driver with plastic windows at the sides and back and a canvas roof fitted over a roll bar, was within the definition of a motor car. *PT Jones, LON/82/360 (VTD 1401)*.

9.20   A trader reclaimed input tax on the purchase of a Suzuki jeep, which had been modified by the fitting of a rear seat, although it had no rear window. The Commissioners issued an assessment to recover the tax, considering that the jeep had been 'adapted solely or mainly for the carriage of passengers', and thus qualified as a motor car for the purposes of the *Cars Order*. The tribunal upheld this decision. *S Compton (t/a Stan Compton Electrical Engineers & Contractors), LON/92/1762A (VTD 10259)*.

9.21   **Commercial vehicle—modified by restoration of rear bench seat—whether reconverted into motor car.**   A trader (B) had purchased a vehicle which had been converted for commercial purposes by replacing the rear side windows with metal sheets and by removing the rear bench seat. B decided to sell the vehicle and, before doing so, restored the rear seat by rebolting it back into its original position. The Commissioners raised an assessment on the basis that, by doing this, he had reconverted the vehicle back into a motor car. The tribunal dismissed B's appeal, holding that by securely fixing the rear seat, he had adapted the vehicle so that it could be used solely or mainly for the carriage of passengers. *K Barbour, EDN/87/39 (VTD 2651)*.

9.22   **Converted Citroen van.**   A partnership which operated a bookshop purchased a Citroen van and reclaimed input tax. Subsequently the partnership modified the van by fitting windows behind the driver's seat. The Commissioners issued an assessment on the basis that this amounted to a conversion of the vehicle into a motor car, which was a self-supply, so that the input tax reclaimed on the purchase of the van had to be refunded by the company. The tribunal upheld the assessment and dismissed the company's appeal. *Browsers Bookshop, LON/88/47 (VTD 2837)*.

9.23   **Ford Escort.**   The tribunal held that a Ford Escort, the rear seats of which could be folded away, was within the definition of a 'motor car'. *RC Lucia, LON/90/1536 (VTD 5776)*.

9.24   **Mercedes van.**   A furniture manufacturer reclaimed input tax on the purchase of a Mercedes van, which had two passenger seats behind the driver, and had windows on either side of the van behind the driver's seat. The Commissioners issued an assessment to recover the tax, considering that the vehicle qualified as a car for VAT purposes, so that the input tax was not deductible. The tribunal dismissed the trader's appeal, holding that the vehicle was within *Article 2* of the *Cars Order*. *T Stead, EDN/91/145 (VTD 6650)*.

9.25   **Daihatsu Fourtrak Estate.**   A company purchased a Daihatsu Fourtrak Estate, and reclaimed the input tax. The Commissioners issued an assessment to recover the tax, considering that the Daihatsu was a motor car as defined in the *Cars Order*. The company appealed, contending that the input tax should be allowed because it had purchased the Daihatsu for the purpose of towing a trailer which it used to carry expensive cars such as Ferraris. The tribunal dismissed the appeal, holding that the Daihatsu was a 'motor car' and that the input tax was not deductible. *Specialised Cars Ltd, MAN/93/370 (VTD 11123)*.

9.26   A similar decision was reached in *DR Metson & Partners, LON/92/3193 (VTD 11218)*.

9.27   **Suzuki Vitara Sport.**   A grocer reclaimed input tax on the purchase of a Suzuki Vitara Sport. The Commissioners issued an assessment to recover the tax, on the basis that the vehicle was a 'motor car' within the *Cars Order*. The grocer appealed, contending that the Suzuki was a commercial vehicle. The tribunal dismissed his appeal, holding that the Suzuki was within *Cars Order, Article 2(b)*. *W McAdam, EDN/94/382 (VTD 13286)*.

9.28   A Suzuki Vitara was also held to be within the definition of a 'motor car' in *MA Lock (t/a MAL Carpenters & Joiners), LON/95/2942A (VTD 14427)*.

9.29   **Isuzu pick-up.**   A registered trader reclaimed input tax on the purchase of a Isuzu two-axle rigid body pick-up motor vehicle. The Commissioners issued an assessment to recover the tax, considering that the Isuzu was a 'motor car', so that the tax was not deductible. The trader appealed, contending that the Isuzu was not within the definition of a 'motor car', since it could carry twelve people (five, including the driver, in the cab, and seven in the rear). The tribunal rejected this contention and dismissed the appeal, holding on the evidence that the Isuzu was not 'suitable' for carrying more than six people, and was within the definition of a 'motor car'. *BC Kunz (t/a Wharfedale Finance Co), MAN/94/2546 (VTD 13514)*.

9.30   An Isuzu pick-up was also held to be a 'motor car' in *Hague Farms Ltd, LON/95/1930 (VTD 13722); CP & EA O'Dell (t/a CP Motors), MAN/94/242 (VTD 13802); DJF & PE Lamb (t/a D & R Services), MAN/94/1108 (VTD 13802); DJ & Mrs SA Banwell, LON/95/2352A (VTD 13944)* and *PAJ Eccleston, MAN/98/539 (VTD 16037)*.

9.31   **Mitsubishi pick-up.**   A Mitsubishi double-cab L200 pick-up was held to be a 'motor car' in *FWK Howells (t/a Buckingham Commercial Motor Co), LON/97/809 (VTD 16488)*.

9.32   **Volkswagen Caravelle.**   A partnership reclaimed input tax on a Volkswagen Caravelle, the rear seats of which were easily removable so that it could be used to carry goods. The Commissioners rejected the claim and the tribunal dismissed the partnership's appeal. *Intercraft UK Romania, LON/95/1947A (VTD 13707)*.

9.33   **Rally car.**   An engineer built a rally car and reclaimed input tax on the materials. The Commissioners rejected the claim, ruling that the car was a 'motor car' within *Cars Order, Article 2*. The tribunal upheld the Commissioners' ruling and dismissed the engineer's appeal. *Jeynes*, 9.17 above, applied; *Barnard*, 9.48 below, distinguished. *D Appleby, LON/95/2936 (VTD 14580)*.

9.34   **Vauxhall Monterey.**   A four-wheel drive Vauxhall Monterey was held to be a 'motor car' in *Anglia Building & Decorating Contractors*, 49.324 PENALTIES: MISDECLARATION.

Vehicles held not to be motor cars

9.35   **Van fitted with benches.**   The company in the case noted at 9.1 above sold a standard 15 cwt Ford van purchased from a builder, who had fitted it with wooden benches. It had no side windows. The company did not account for output tax on the sale, and the Commissioners issued an assessment charging output tax. The company appealed, contending that the vehicle was a 'motor car' within *Cars Order, Article 2*. The tribunal rejected this contention, holding that the van was not a 'motor car'. As it was not clear whether the company could deduct input tax in respect of the van, the appeal was adjourned to enable the parties to agree as to the amount to which the assessment should be reduced. *Chartcliff Ltd, [1976] VATTR 165 (VTD 262)*. (*Note.* For subsequent proceedings in this appeal as to costs, see 2.319 APPEALS. It was stated during those proceedings that it had been agreed that input tax was allowable and the assessment was reduced to nil.)

9.36 **Hearses—whether 'constructed for a special purpose'—Cars Order, Article 2(v).** A second-hand car dealer sold eight second-hand funeral hearses. The Commissioners issued a ruling that the hearses were 'constructed for a special purpose' within *Cars Order, Article 2(v)*, and thus could not be dealt with under the margin scheme for second-hand cars. The tribunal dismissed the trader's appeal against this decision. *KP Davies, CAR/79/65 (VTD 831)*.

9.37 **Pick-up truck with attached canopy—whether converted into a 'motor car'.** The proprietor of an engineering business purchased a pick-up truck. To protect goods from the weather and from thieves, he bought a fibreglass canopy which covered the whole of the load-carrying part of the truck and extended over the roof of the driver's cab. It was attached to the truck with clips, hooked onto hooks riveted to the side of the truck. The canopy could be removed quickly and easily, and the trader frequently used the truck without the canopy. The Commissioners issued an assessment on the basis that, by attaching the canopy to the truck, the trader had converted the truck into a motor car within the *Cars Order* and thus incurred liability to VAT. The tribunal allowed the trader's appeal, holding that, to amount to a conversion, some degree of permanence was required which was absent in this case. *KM Batty, MAN/86/122 (VTD 2199)*.

9.38 **Toyota Land Cruisers converted into recovery vehicles.** A trader purchased two Toyota Land Cruisers and converted them for use as recovery vehicles by welding onto them a trailer with the necessary equipment for vehicle recovery. He reclaimed input tax on their purchase. The Commissioners rejected the claim, considering that the vehicles were within the definition of 'motor cars'. The tribunal allowed the trader's appeal, holding that the converted vehicles did not fall within the definition of a 'motor car' by virtue of *Cars Order, Article 2(v)*, as they were 'vehicles constructed for a special purpose other than the carriage of persons'. *H Lovejoy (t/a HRS Recoveries), LON/86/743 (VTD 2488)*.

9.39 **Nissan pick-up truck—roofed accommodation not suitable for passengers.** In a case concerning provisions in the *Car Tax Act 1983* similar to *VAT (Cars) Order, Article 2(b)*, the CA held that 'accommodation' should be construed as referring only to accommodation for human passengers, rather than for freight. *HKS Coachworks Ltd*, 9.15 above, disapproved. *R v C & E Commrs (ex p. Nissan UK Ltd), CA 1987, [1988] BTC 8003*. (*Note.* The decision in this case was applied in *John Beharrell Ltd*, 9.46 below.)

9.40 **Converted Transit van.** A company which operated a detective agency purchased a Transit van and adapted it for the purpose of undertaking static surveillance work. The items that were fitted to the van included a long seat which could also be used as a bed, a frame to take a portable cooker, a sink, a wardrobe, a table which could be used as a desk, a radio aerial, an access ladder for the roof and reinforcement of the roof, and thermal and acoustic insulation. Dark glass was fitted to the windows and there were several other additional small alterations. The company disposed of the vehicle in 1984, and did not account for VAT on the disposal of the vehicle. The Commissioners issued an assessment charging output tax, and the company appealed, contending that the vehicle was a motor car, so that, as the selling price was less than the deemed acquisition price, no tax was chargeable. The tribunal rejected this contention and dismissed the appeal, holding that the vehicle had been converted from a van into a caravan and had never been a motor car. *Burgess Detective Agency Ltd, MAN/87/333 (VTD 2685)*.

9.41 A company purchased two Ford Transit vans, which it adapted by inserting rear seats large enough for two or three people. The seats were made of heavy duty plastic and were not upholstered, and the vans had no rear windows, handrails or seat belts. The company reclaimed input tax on the vans, and the Commissioners issued an assessment to recover the tax, considering that the insertion of the rear seats meant that the vans had been converted into cars for the purpose of the *Cars Order*. The company appealed, contending that the vans were mainly used for the transport of goods, which were usually placed on the rear seat. The tribunal allowed the company's appeal, holding that despite the installation of the seats, the vehicles were still not 'motor cars' within *Cars Order, Article 2. Bolinge Hill Farm*, 9.42 below, and *AL Yeoman Ltd*, 9.43 below, applied. *Chichester Plant Contractors Ltd, LON/90/372Y (VTD 6575)*.

9.42 **Land Rover fitted with two folding seats.** A farming partnership purchased a Land Rover with two folding seats in the rear. The Commissioners considered that the addition of these seats meant that the vehicle had been 'adapted solely or mainly for the carriage of passengers' within *Cars Order, Article 2*, so that the input tax was not allowable. The partnership appealed, contending that the rear seats were seldom used and were very uncomfortable in view of the hard rear suspension and the absence of armrests. The tribunal accepted this contention and allowed the appeal. *Chartcliff Ltd*, 9.1 above, distinguished. The changes made to the vehicle were relatively minor and the additional seating was 'anything but luxurious' and had been 'designed to have the least effect possible on the load carrying capacity'. The main use of the vehicle was clearly not the carriage of passengers. *Bolinge Hill Farm, LON/89/1071Z (VTD 4217)*.

9.43 **Daihatsu Fourtrak vehicles.** A company purchased two Daihatsu Fourtrak Commercial Hard Tops. Each vehicle had been equipped with two folding rear seats, described by the tribunal as 'of an insubstantial nature'. The company claimed a deduction for the input tax incurred on their purchase. The Commissioners issued an assessment to recover the tax, considering that the vehicles were 'motor cars' within the meaning of *Cars Order, Article 2*. The company appealed, contending that the vehicles in question were not motor cars, since they were not constructed 'solely or mainly for the carriage of passengers'. The tribunal allowed the appeal, holding that the vehicles were not motor cars since the seating was of a 'very rudimentary nature' and 'most uncomfortable for passengers on anything but the shortest of journeys'. *Bolinge Hill Farm*, 9.42 above, applied. *AL Yeoman Ltd, EDN/89/104 (VTD 4470)*. (*Note*. For a subsequent case in which a Daihatsu Fourtrak was held to be a 'motor car', see *Specialised Cars Ltd*, 9.25 above.)

9.44 **Land Rover with rear seats removed.** A sole trader in the construction industry had purchased a 12–seat Land Rover from which he had removed the two rear bench seats. He reclaimed the input tax on the purchase, and the Commissioners issued an assessment to recover the tax, considering that the removal of the rear seats had converted the Land Rover from a commercial vehicle into a 'motor car'. The tribunal allowed the trader's appeal against the assessment. Despite the removal of the rear bench seats, the vehicle remained suitable for carrying twelve people and had not been converted into a 'motor car'. *P Oddonetto, LON/89/1566X (VTD 5208)*.

9.45 **Land Rover with small window inserted.** A writer, who was registered for VAT, purchased a Land Rover and modified it by inserting a half-size window in the nearside rear panel. The Commissioners issued an assessment on the basis that, by doing so, he had converted the Land Rover into a motor car, so that there was a deemed self-supply on which output tax was chargeable. The tribunal allowed the writer's appeal, holding that the vehicle was not adapted 'solely or mainly for the carriage of passengers'. Applying *R v C & E Commrs (ex p. Nissan UK Ltd)*, 9.39 above, the roofed space to the rear of the driver's seat did not amount to 'accommodation' within the meaning of *Cars Order, Article 2(b)*. On the evidence, the vehicle was intended solely for the appellant's use in making expeditions to remote parts of Africa, and was within *Article 2(v)*. *TH Sheppard, LON/95/2269A (VTD 13815)*.

9.46   **Peugeot vans—whether converted into cars.**   A company which carried on business as an installer of air-conditioning equipment purchased a number of Peugeot 205 and 305 vans. It modified the vehicles by adding a window on each side, behind the driver's seat. The modifications were carried out for safety reasons, to improve visibility. The Commissioners considered that the modification amounted to the conversion of the vehicles into cars, so that there was a deemed self-supply of the vehicles, and issued an assessment to recover the input tax which the company had reclaimed on their purchase. The tribunal allowed the company's appeal, holding that the 'accommodation available behind the driver's seat in the vehicles as modified could not realistically be described as reasonably suitable for the carriage of passengers'. Applying *R v C & E Commrs (ex p. Nissan UK Ltd)*, 9.39 above, it did not constitute 'accommodation' for the purpose of the *Cars Order*, and the vehicles continued to be vans rather than cars. *John Beharrell Ltd, [1991] VATTR 497 (VTD 6530)*.

9.47   **Toyota Hilux Double Cab—whether suitable for carrying twelve or more persons—Cars Order, Article 2(i).**   A partnership which carried on a farming business reclaimed input tax on the purchase of a converted Toyota Hilux Double Cab pick-up truck. The Commissioners issued an assessment to recover the tax, considering that the vehicle was within the definition of a 'motor car'. The partnership appealed, contending that the vehicle was suitable for carrying twelve persons and thus was excluded from the definition of a motor car by *Cars Order, Article 2(i)*. The tribunal examined the vehicle and allowed the company's appeal, observing that it could carry twelve people for short journeys if most of the passengers were young, and holding that the input tax was allowable. The tribunal observed that the fact that the vehicle was not suitable for transporting elderly people or handicapped people, or for long journeys, was not conclusive. *Dicta* in *Jeynes*, 9.17 above, applied. *W Hamilton & Son, LON/96/1434 (VTD 14812)*.

9.48   **Pick-up truck—whether within Cars Order, Article 2(v).**   The proprietor of a plant hire business purchased a Ford 250 pick-up truck and undertook certain conversion work to make it more suitable for his business. He reclaimed input tax on the vehicle. The Commissioners issued an assessment to recover the tax, considering that the vehicle was within the statutory definition of a 'motor car'. The tribunal allowed the trader's appeal, holding on the evidence that the vehicle was within the exclusion in *Cars Order, Article 2(v)*, being 'constructed for a special purpose other than the carriage of persons and having no other accommodation for carrying persons than such as is incidental to that purpose'. *KV Barnard, LON/95/2629 (VTD 13865)*.

SELF-SUPPLIES (Cars Order, Article 5)

9.49   **Whether a self-supply.**   A car dealer built a car for himself, out of new and second-hand components, at a cost of £1,300. After running it for 3,000 miles, he sold it for £1,995. The Commissioners issued an assessment on the basis that there had been a self-supply of the car within *Cars Order, Article 5*. The tribunal upheld the assessment and dismissed the trader's appeal. *EG Nicol, MAN/77/322 (VTD 571)*.

9.50   The standard rate of VAT was increased from 8% to 15% with effect from 18 June 1979. A company which dealt in cars ordered a number of new V-registration cars (which could not be used on the roads before 1 August 1979). It accounted for tax on the basis that it had made a deemed self-supply of these cars before 18 June 1979. The Commissioners issued an assessment on the basis that there had been no supply of the cars until after 31 July, so that tax was chargeable at 15% on the supply of the cars. The tribunal upheld the assessment and dismissed the company's appeal. *A & B Motors (Newton-le-Willows) Ltd, [1981] VATTR 29 (VTD 1024).*

9.51   A car-dealing company held a large number of cars on a sale or return basis, under which they remained the property of the manufacturer until it decided to purchase them. On 11 June 1979 the Chancellor of the Exchequer announced that the standard rate of VAT would be increased from 8% to 15% with effect from 18 June. During the intervening week, the company earmarked 33 of the cars which it held as demonstration cars, making the necessary entries in its stock records and authorising the manufacturer to debit it with the price of the cars. The Commissioners issued an assessment on the basis that there had been no supply of the cars until after 18 June. The tribunal allowed the company's appeal, holding that there had been a self-supply before that date. *Arnold Clark Automobiles Ltd (and associated appeals), EDN/80/52–55 (VTD 1058).*

9.52   In another case where a car-dealing company held cars on a sale or return basis, and elected to purchase some of them shortly before 18 June 1979, the tribunal upheld the Commissioners' ruling that there had been no self-supply of the cars. On the evidence, the cars were not used as demonstration vehicles but were sold to customers after 18 June. *Hall Park Garage Ltd, LON/81/194 (VTD 1185).*

9.53   **Whether car used for research or development—Cars Order, Article 5(3).** A company which manufactured cars built a prototype, which it exhibited and also lent to the publishers of a specialist magazine so that they could write an article about it. The Commissioners issued an assessment on the basis that there had been a self-supply of the car. The company appealed, contending that the car was 'used solely for the purpose of research and development' so that, by virtue of *Cars Order, Article 5(3)*, there had been no self-supply. The tribunal accepted the company's evidence and allowed the appeal. *Lea-Francis Cars Ltd, MAN/81/113 (VTD 1166).*

RELIEF FOR SECOND-HAND MOTOR CARS (Cars Order, Article 8)

Whether conditions of Notice No 718 complied with (Article 8(1))

9.54   A car dealer failed to produce records to comply with the requirements specified in what is now *Notice No 718* for the 'margin scheme' for second-hand car dealers. The Commissioners issued an assessment in which the output tax was taken to be that on the full amount of the dealer's sales. The dealer appealed, contending that the assessment had not been made to the best of the Commissioners' judgment as it had not taken into account his purchases of used cars. The tribunal rejected this contention and dismissed the appeal, holding that, as the dealer had not complied with the statutory requirements so as to bring himself within the protection of the margin scheme, the Commissioners had no alternative but to charge tax on the full amount. *DA Pody, LON/75/124 (VTD 217).*

9.55   A second-hand car dealer was liable to be registered from 1 April 1973, but did not apply for registration until July 1975, whereupon he was registered with effect from 1 April 1973. He made a return for the period from 1 April 1973 to 31 December 1975 declaring tax due of £721, calculated under the margin scheme. The Commissioners considered that throughout the period his records did not comply with the requirements of what is now *Notice No 718* and issued an assessment charging tax on the full amount of his supplies. The tribunal upheld the assessment and dismissed the dealer's appeal. *DE Chappell, [1977] VATTR 94 (VTD 352).*

9.56 A second-hand car dealer accounted for tax under the 'margin scheme' but had not maintained the records specified by what is now *Notice No 718* and had not issued sales invoices. The Commissioners issued an assessment charging tax on the full amount of his supplies. The tribunal upheld the assessment and dismissed the dealer's appeal. *JH Corbitt (Numismatists) Ltd*, 56.1 SECOND-HAND GOODS, applied. *H Nixon, [1980] VATTR 66 (VTD 973)*.

9.57 Similar decisions were reached in *I Jones, CAR/75/186 (VTD 232); Charles Oliver Enterprises Ltd, MAN/76/67 (VTD 268); C Parker, MAN/76/54 (VTD 292); H Kitchen, LON/77/66 (VTD 397); Hughes Bros, CAR/77/155 (VTD 450); EJ Parish, LON/77/283 (VTD 474); TL Penfold, CAR/77/174 (VTD 524); J Smith (t/a Morecambe Used Car Centre), MAN/77/243 (VTD 554); LW & PE Kirkwood, MAN/77/135 & 136 (VTD 564); JJ Woodward, LON/77/247 (VTD 569); PS Gabrielson, CAR/77/22 (VTD 606); RA Watson, LON/78/115 (VTD 758); RS & DE Swanson, MAN/80/29 (VTD 959); McNally & Waite (t/a Macray Motor Bodies), MAN/80/169 & 170 (VTD 1109); AD Motors (Woodford), LON/83/31 (VTD 1449); Nelsons of Newark Ltd, MAN/84/91 (VTD 1751); MK Sadiq, LON/85/565 (VTD 2160); CL Howarth, LON/86/75 (VTD 2363); J Roberts, MAN/87/161 (VTD 2555); Bordergem Ltd, MAN/88/38 (VTD 2887)* and *K Tork (t/a KT Motors), LON/90/744 (VTD 7013)*.

9.58 A partnership dealing in second-hand cars failed to keep the records required by what is now *Notice No 718*. The Commissioners issued an assessment charging tax of more than £30,000, and the partnership appealed, contending that the amount demanded was inequitable. The tribunal dismissed the appeal, finding that the records kept were inadequate and holding that the Commissioners had not acted unreasonably. *GP, D & A Bardsley (t/a Bardsley Car Sales), [1984] VATTR 171 (VTD 1718)*.

9.59 *Bardsley*, 9.58 above, was applied in the similar cases of *JW Donaldson, EDN/88/179 (VTD 3668); WG McCalden, LON/88/1332 (VTD 4216); RM Lane, MAN/88/28 (VTD 5038)* and *Sellhire Autos Ltd, MAN/92/1098 (VTD 10568)*.

Whether car is a 'used motor car' (Article 8(1))

9.60 **Sale of car already registered by dealer—whether a sale of a used car.** A company which traded as a car dealer appealed against an assessment charging tax on the full sale price of some cars which it had sold, contending that the cars should be treated as used cars and dealt with under the margin scheme. The tribunal dismissed the appeal, applying *Morris Motors Ltd v Lilley, Ch D [1959] All ER 737* and holding that the cars were new cars rather than used cars, so that the margin scheme was inapplicable. *Lincoln Street Motors (Birmingham) Ltd, [1981] VATTR 120 (VTD 1100)*.

9.61 *Lincoln Street Motors (Birmingham) Ltd*, 9.60 above, was applied in the similar cases of *Queensborough Motors, EDN/81/39 (VTD 1139); Ashmall & Parkinson Ltd, MAN/82/245 (VTD 1387)* and *Finglands Travel Agency Ltd, MAN/82/232 (VTD 1447)*.

Whether acquisition within Article 8(2)

9.62 **Cars purchased from finance company—whether subsequent sale within margin scheme.** A company (P) manufactured and imported motor cars. By an agreement with a finance company (M), it sold certain cars to M to be leased to handicapped persons for a period of at least three years. When the leases expired, M repossessed the cars and sold them back to P. Both the lease by M and the sale back to P qualified for zero-rating under *VATA 1994, Sch 8 Group 12*. P subsequently resold the cars on the open market and accounted for tax under the margin scheme. The

Commissioners issued a ruling that the sales of the cars could not be dealt with under the margin scheme, on the basis that a zero-rated supply was not 'a supply in respect of which no VAT was chargeable', within *Article 8(2)* of the *Cars Order*. P appealed, contending that its acquisition of the cars, being zero-rated, was within *Article 8(2)* of the *Order*, so that it was entitled to use the margin scheme. The tribunal accepted this contention and allowed P's appeal, observing that, although *Article 26a* of the *EC Sixth Directive* indicated 'circumstances in which a taxable dealer may tax his profit margin rather than the full value of the supply', the Commissioners could not 'rely on the *Sixth Directive* to require a narrower interpretation of *Article 8(2)(a)* than it would otherwise be given, so that they cannot claim that it should be interpreted to exclude matters other than those referred to in *Article 26a(B)* ... it is quite plain from *article 8* that it is intended to apply in circumstances other than those for which *Article 26a(B)* makes provision'. *Peugeot Motor Co plc, [1998] VATDR 1 (VTD 15314)*. (*Note.* For the effect of *Article 26a* of the *EC Sixth Directive*, see also *Stafford Land Rover, 9.127* below.)

9.63 **Whether cars purchased from private individual in Republic of Ireland.** A company (R) sold cars which had been imported from the Republic of Ireland. It accounted for tax under the margin scheme. The Commissioners issued an assessment on the basis that R had obtained the cars in Ireland from an Irish dealer, and should have accounted for tax on the full sale price of the cars. R appealed, contending that it had obtained the cars from a private individual (in order to comply with regulations issued by the DETR). The tribunal rejected this contention and dismissed the appeal. On the evidence, R had obtained the cars in the Republic of Ireland from a dealer. This was not a supply in the UK, and was therefore not within *Article 8(2)* of the *Cars Order*. The purported transactions whereby R claimed to have obtained the cars from a private individual were 'documented but unreal'. They 'were shams and so "nothings" for all tax purposes'. The tribunal also held that, for the purpose of *Article 28b* of the *EC Sixth Directive*, the place of acquisition of the cars by R 'must be the United Kingdom because that is where the transportation to (R) ended'. (The tribunal also observed that the assessments had been issued on the basis that R was entitled to deduct the 'acquisition VAT properly chargeable'.) *Richmond Cars Ltd, LON/99/1207 (VTD 16942)*.

Computation of profit margin (Article 8(5))

Price at which car obtained (Article 8(5)(a))

9.64 **Whether expenses of sale deductible.** A second-hand car dealer, who bought and sold his vehicles at auctions, operated the margin scheme. He claimed that, in arriving at the consideration received for car sales, the commission, entry fee and indemnity fee paid to the auctioneer should be deducted. The Commissioners rejected this claim and the tribunal dismissed his appeal. *CG Todd, LEE/74/31 (VTD 130)*.

9.65 **Whether costs of restoration deductible.** A contention that expenditure incurred in restoring second-hand cars should be taken into account for the purposes of the margin scheme was rejected in *J Robertson, EDN/84/106 (VTD 1797)*.

9.66 Similar decisions were reached in *Peter Oates Ltd, LON/87/543 (VTD 2576)*; *PPG Publishing Ltd, LON/88/92 (VTD 3047)*; *E Barnett (t/a Barnett Motor Services), MAN/90/948 (VTD 6868)* and *JPS Doyle, LON/94/2550A (VTD 13742)*.

9.67 **Sales of repossessed cars by hire-purchase finance company.** A company (D) financed hire-purchase agreements for cars sold by dealers. Sometimes it repossessed cars from defaulting purchasers, which were then sold in the open market as second-hand vehicles. The Commissioners issued an assessment charging tax on the full amount received on the sale of certain repossessed cars. D appealed, contending that the sales should be treated under the margin scheme, and that for the purposes of the *Cars Order*, its acquisition cost was the original purchase price paid to the dealer. The tribunal rejected this contention and dismissed the appeal. On payment of the purchase price to the dealer, D acquired the ownership of the car, followed immediately by a transfer of possession to the hirer which, by virtue of what is now *VATA 1994, Sch 4 para 1(2)(b)*, was an onward supply of the car to the hirer as goods. The amount paid to the dealer was wholly exhausted as consideration for the onward supply to the hirer, and could not be used as a base for establishing the consideration for the acquisition of the car on repossession. Accordingly, whether or not the sale of the car fell to be dealt with under the margin scheme, the consideration on repossession was nil and tax was chargeable on the full amount realised on its sale. *Darlington Finance Ltd, [1982] VATTR 233 (VTD 1337).*

9.68   **Cars purchased from company which owed amounts to finance company— whether subsequent payment to finance company part of consideration.**   A company (D) purchased 23 vehicles from another company (E). E had acquired the vehicles under conditional sale agreements from a finance company (F), whereby legal title to the cars remained with F. In February 1990 E went into liquidation, having failed to pay F the full amounts which it owed in respect of the vehicles. F demanded payment of the outstanding balance from D, which paid F £32,000 in settlement of its claim. In the meantime D had sold the vehicles to customers, paying VAT of £3,050 under the margin scheme. Following its payment of £32,000 to F, D reclaimed the VAT of £3,050 from the Commissioners, on the basis that it had sold the cars at a loss and should not have accounted for any VAT in respect of the sales. The Commissioners rejected the claim, and D appealed. The tribunal allowed D's appeal, holding that the £32,000 formed part of the consideration paid by D for the vehicles. Accordingly, D had sold the cars for less than their cost of acquisition, and the effect of what is now *Article 8* of the *Cars Order* was that the sales gave rise to no VAT liability. *Daron Motors Ltd, LON/92/3165 (VTD 11695).*

9.69   **Owner of vintage car registering for VAT as restorer and supplier of vintage cars.**   An individual (D), who had purchased a vintage Bentley car for £500 in 1966, was made redundant from his employment in 1985. He decided to go into business as a restorer and supplier of vintage cars, and registered for VAT accordingly. He issued himself with a VAT invoice purporting to show that he had sold the Bentley to his business for £35,000, and reclaimed input tax accordingly. The Commissioners issued an assessment on the basis that the car had been acquired for £500 rather than for £35,000. The tribunal upheld the assessment and dismissed D's appeal. *GK Dodds, [1989] VATTR 98 (VTD 3383).*

Price at which car sold (Article 8(5)(b))

9.70   **Amount of consideration for car sold with allowance for car traded in.**   Two companies offered for sale second-hand cars at fixed prices, stating that the customer would be given a minimum of £1,500 for any car he 'traded in', with no reservations as to the true value of that car. The offer prices for the cars to be sold were inflated by sums which, it was hoped, would prevent losses on the deals. On a sale, the customer was given an invoice showing the sale price and also a credit note for the traded-in car. Subsequently the companies adjusted the credit notes to allocate the amount to show what they considered to be the true value of the traded-in car, and treated the difference between this and the amount actually credited to the customer as a 'special trade-in offer'. The traded-in car was taken into stock at its true value and the 'special trade-in offer' was deducted from the sale price of the car sold to the customer, in accounting for tax under the margin scheme. The Commissioners issued assessments on the basis that the sale price was the price agreed with, and invoiced to, the customer. The tribunal upheld the assessments and dismissed the companies' appeals. *James A Laidlaw (Edinburgh) Ltd; James A Laidlaw (Dunfermline) Ltd, EDN/82/41 & 42 (VTD 1376).*

9.71 Similar decisions were reached in *Stuart & Co (Motors) Ltd, [1984] VATTR 207 (VTD 1753); RF Taylor, MAN/87/279 (VTD 2841); W Milligan & Sons, MAN/87/342 (VTD 4297)* and *PV Coventry (t/a Vincent James of Bath), LON/91/1450X (VTD 9617).*

9.72 A company (L) accepted second-hand cars in part-exchange on the basis that the relevant transaction could be cancelled by the customer within 30 days. However, if the car taken in part-exchange had been sold, the customer was not entitled to a refund of the nominal part-exchange price stated on the order form, but to a lower 'trade value'. Initially L accounted for VAT on the basis of the sale prices shown on the order forms. However, it subsequently submitted a repayment claim on the basis that the sale price should be adjusted to reflect the 'trade value', rather than the sale price agreed with the customer. The Commissioners rejected the claim and the tribunal dismissed L's appeal, holding on the evidence that 'the price attributed to the part-exchange cars on sales of (L's) cars to customers was the price shown on the order forms and the invoices'. The Ch D upheld this decision, holding that it was an established principle that non-monetary consideration had to be valued subjectively, according to the price actually agreed by the parties to the transaction. The subjective value of the consideration was the price agreed with the customer. *Empire Stores Ltd*, 21.129 EUROPEAN COMMUNITY LAW, applied. *Lex Services plc v C & E Commrs, Ch D [2000] STC 697. (Note.* For a similar case involving new cars, see *North Anderson Cars Ltd*, 63.73 VALUATION.)

9.73 **Disposal of taxicab licences—whether a separate supply from disposal of taxi.** Until 31 March 1983, the Commissioners treated the sale of taxicab licences as outside the scope of VAT. After that date the Commissioners treated them as part of the sale of the taxicabs. The change in treatment was notified to the National Federation of Taxicab Associations and subsequently published in *Notice 700/25/ 84.* A company which disposed of one taxicab in 1986 and another in 1987 did not account for VAT on the sale of the licences. The Commissioners issued an assessment to recover the tax and the tribunal dismissed the company's appeal. *Associated Cab Co Ltd, MAN/88/97 (VTD 3394).*

9.74 A partnership sold two cars, to which it had transferred hackney carriage licences permitting them to be used as taxis in Cambridge. It contended that in computing the margin, there should be deducted not only the original cost of the cars but also an amount in respect of the licences. The tribunal rejected this contention and dismissed the appeal, holding that there was a single supply and the fact that the company had improved the value of the vehicles by attaching the licences to them was not relevant for the purposes of the margin scheme. *GT Collins & Son, LON/88/ 3134 (VTD 3738).*

9.75 *Associated Cab Co*, 9.73 above, and *GT Collins & Son*, 9.74 above, were followed in a similar subsequent case in which an appeal against an assessment charging tax on the sale of a taxicab was dismissed. *SS Natt, MAN/91/9 (VTD 6999).*

9.76 **Road fund licences sold with second-hand cars.** A company sold second-hand cars. Where a car did not have a valid road fund licence at the time of sale, the company undertook to obtain a licence on behalf of the customer. The Commissioners issued an assessment on the basis that the sale of the cars included the sale of the licences, and that VAT should be charged on the whole supply. The tribunal allowed the company's appeal, holding that the payments for road fund licences were not part of the consideration for the company's supplies. *DE Siviter (Motors) Ltd, MAN/88/458 (VTD 3556)*. (*Note*. See *Notice No 718, para 7.3*, which states 'if you offer a vehicle for sale with a valid road fund licence, or a licence is offered with the vehicle as part of the agreed sales price, you are making a single supply and the selling price entered in your stock book must include the value of the licence. But where, after negotiating the sale of a car, you agree to obtain the licence on behalf of the customer, you may treat the licence as a separate supply provided you can meet the conditions for a disbursement as explained in *Notice 700: The VAT Guide*. If you cannot meet the conditions for a disbursement, the car and licence are treated as a single supply ...')

9.77   Similar decisions were reached in *Cromford Hill Motor Sales, MAN/97/1095 (VTD 16152)* and *John Wilson Cars Ltd, MAN/99/514 (VTD 16655)*.

9.78   The decision in *Cromford Hill Sales*, 9.77 above, was distinguished in a subsequent case in which the tribunal held on the evidence that the appellant company was making a single supply of a car with a road fund licence, and was required to account for tax on the full amounts paid by its customers, in accordance with *Notice No 718, para 7.3. C Hesketh & Sons Ltd, MAN/99/823 (VTD 16963)*.

9.79   **MOT certificates supplied with second-hand cars.**   A company which sold second-hand cars obtained one-year MOT certificates for the cars which it supplied. It attributed part of the consideration which it received to its supply of the MOT certificates, and did not account for output tax on this. The Commissioners issued an assessment on the basis that the company was making a single supply of a car with a MOT (as laid down in *Notice No 718*), and was required to include the amount attributed to the MOT certificates as part of the consideration for the purposes of the second-hand margin scheme. The tribunal upheld the assessment and dismissed the company's appeal. On the evidence, the company was 'selling the MOT-tested car to the customer for a single price which covers both the gross price of the car plus the charge for the test'. *Family Car Centre Ltd, LON/98/1237 (VTD 16141)*.

9.80   *Family Car Centre Ltd*, 9.79 above, was applied in the similar subsequent case of *Depot Corner Car Sales, MAN/99/945 (VTD 16907)*.

DISALLOWANCE OF INPUT TAX (Input Tax Order, Article 7)

Note. *Input Tax Order, Article 7* was amended by *VAT (Input Tax) (Amendment) (No 3) Order 1995 (SI 1995 No 1666)* with effect from 1 August 1995.

General principles

9.81   **Whether Input Tax Order, Article 7 in accordance with EC law.**   See *Royscot Leasing Ltd*, 21.207 EUROPEAN COMMUNITY LAW.

9.82   **Delivery charges.**   A car was supplied to a company at an agreed price plus a delivery charge of £47.50. The company appealed against the Commissioners' decision that the tax on the delivery charge was not allowable as input tax. The tribunal dismissed the appeal, holding that the delivery charge was in substance and reality part of the consideration for the supply of the car and not a separate charge for the service of delivery. *Wimpey Construction UK Ltd, [1979] VATTR 174 (VTD 808)*.

9.83   A company purchased substantial numbers of cars directly from the manufacturers. The manufacturers arranged for the cars to be delivered by a transport company, which made a separate charge for this service. The company reclaimed input tax on the delivery charges. The Commissioners rejected the claim and the company appealed, contending that the delivery charge was consideration for a separate supply, on which it was entitled to reclaim input tax. The HL rejected this contention and upheld the Commissioners' ruling. Lord Slynn observed that 'if the transaction is looked at as a matter of commercial reality there was one contract for a delivered car: it is artificial to split the various parts of the transaction into different supplies for VAT purposes. What (the company) wanted was a delivered car; the delivery was incidental or ancillary to the supply of the car and it was only on or after delivery that property in the car passed.' *C & E Commrs v British Telecommunications plc*, HL *[1999] STC 758; [1999] 1 WLR 1376; [1999] 3 All ER 961*. (*Note*. For the Commissioners' practice following this decision, see Business Brief 17/99, issued on 6 August 1999.)

9.84   **Towbar fitted as optional extra.**   A salesman used a caravan, towed by his car, for exhibiting and selling the Encyclopaedia Britannica. He purchased a new car and had a tow bar fitted as an optional extra. he reclaimed input tax on the towbar. The Commissioners issued an assessment to recover the tax and the tribunal dismissed the salesman's appeal. Applying the principles established by *British Railways Board v C & E Commrs*, 62.5 TRANSPORT, there had been a single supply of a motor car fitted with a tow bar. *AC Turmeau, LON/81/164 (VTD 1135)*.

9.85   **'Car kit' supplied with car.**   A company which had ordered a new car also ordered a 'car kit', comprising side skirts and a boot lid spoiler, to be added to the car. The kit was invoiced separately from the car, and the company reclaimed input tax on the kit. The Commissioners issued an assessment to recover the tax, considering that the kit formed part of the car when it was delivered, so that the tax was not deductible by virtue of what is now *Article 7* of the *Input Tax Order*. The tribunal dismissed the company's appeal, holding that the company had been supplied with a motor car, and that the fact that the kit was invoiced separately did not alter the fact that the input tax was not deductible. *A Thompson & Sons Ltd, MAN/91/982 (VTD 7833)*.

9.86   **Police Authority—claim for refund of VAT on purchase of motor cars— effect of VATA 1994, s 33(6).**   See *R v C & E Commrs (ex p. Greater Manchester Police Authority)*, 40.3 LOCAL AUTHORITIES.

9.87   **Disallowance of input tax—other cases.**   There are a number of cases in which claims to input tax on the purchase of motor cars have been dismissed. In the interests of space, such cases are not summarised individually in this book. For the imposition of penalties in such cases, see 49.320 to 49.323 PENALTIES: MISDECLARATION.

9.88   **Input Tax Order, Article 7(2C)—whether cars supplied on letting on hire before 1 August 1995.**   *Article 7* of the *VAT (Input Tax) Order 1992 (SI 1992 No 3222)* was substantially amended by *SI 1995 No 1666* with effect from 1 August 1995. Following the changes, a leasing company (B) reclaimed input tax on six cars. The Commissioners formed the opinion that the tax was not recoverable, on the basis that B's customer had entered into a prepayment agreement with an associated company, the effect of which was that the cars had been supplied on a letting on hire prior to 1 August 1995, so that, by virtue of *Article 7(2C)*, they were not 'qualifying motor cars' within *Article 7(2A)* and the tax was not deductible. B appealed, contending that none of the cars had been supplied before 1 August 1995. The tribunal accepted this contention and allowed the appeal, and the CA upheld this decision. Pill LJ observed that none of the cars had been identified before 1 August 1995 and that B had neither made nor received payments, nor issued invoices, before that date. He held that the fact that B's customer had, before 1 August, entered into a prepayment agreement with an associated company to make an onward supply of the cars in question was not conclusive, since B was not associated with the customer and was not a party to the customer's transaction. Pill LJ expressed the view that the purpose of *Article 7(2C)* was 'to prevent *the same* taxable person, by letting before 1 August and purchasing on or after that date, from obtaining the benefit of both regimes'. *BRS Automotive Ltd v C & E Commrs, CA [1998] STC 1210. (Note.* See, however, the *VAT (Input Tax) (Amendment) Order 1998 (SI 1998 No 2767)*, which reverses the effect of this decision. The purpose of the amendment is to ensure 'that the 50% restriction on input tax recovery will apply as Parliament intended to all leased business cars also used for private motoring'. See Customs News Release 28/98, issued on 12 November 1998, and Business Brief 25/98, issued on 16 December 1998. The Financial Secretary to the Treasury described the scheme adopted by B's customer as a 'blatant avoidance scheme marketed by some of the leading accountants'.)

Whether car intended for use 'exclusively for the purposes of a business' (Article 7(2E)(2G))

Cases where the appellant was unsuccessful

9.89   A farmer reclaimed input tax on the purchase of a Daihatsu 4–track vehicle. The Commissioners rejected the claim, and the farmer appealed, contending that he intended to use the vehicle exclusively for business purposes, within *Input Tax Order, Article 7(2E)*. The tribunal dismissed the appeal, accepting that the farmer's subjective intention was to use the vehicle exclusively for business purposes, but holding on the evidence that the vehicle was available for private use within *Input Tax Order, Article 7(2G)*, so that the farmer was not entitled to reclaim the input tax. The tribunal chairman (Mr. Lightman) observed that 'it is verging on the impossible that someone who acquires a motor vehicle which is freely usable on the roads for private use would not, at that time, have it at the back of his mind that it might be so usable, and that he could therefore so make it available to himself or others. In other words, he must, in such circumstances, be treated as intending that it be available, at least to himself, for private use.' *GDG Jones (t/a Jones & Son), LON/96/357 (VTD 14535). (Note.* The decision here has been followed in a large number of subsequent cases. However, *obiter dicta* of the tribunal chairman were disapproved by a subsequent tribunal in the case of *Martinez*, 9.97 below, where Mr. Wallace expressed the view that Mr. Lightman's use of the word 'must' was inappropriate, and that the presumption was rebuttable, albeit with difficulty.)

9.90   The decision in *GDG Jones*, 9.89 above, was applied in a similar subsequent case in which a partnership's appeal against the disallowance of input tax was dismissed. The tribunal chairman (Mr. Demack) observed, applying *dicta* of the Advocate-General in *Enkler v Finanzamt Homburg*, 21.68 EUROPEAN COMMUNITY LAW, that 'the important point is that the consumer always has the opportunity to use the asset whenever he finds it necessary or desirable to do so'. *PC & AM Wood, MAN/96/413 (VTD 14804).*

9.91   *GDG Jones*, 9.89 above, was applied in a similar subsequent case in which the tribunal specifically declined to follow the decision in *Grace*, 9.104 below. *S Shepherd, EDN/98/64 (VTD 15799).*

9.92   A similar decision was reached in a subsequent case in which the tribunal specifically declined to follow the decisions in *Lowe*, 9.102 below, and *Grace*, 9.104 below. *LP & CG Brown, MAN/97/337 (VTD 16109).*

9.93   A similar decision, again applying *GDG Jones*, 9.89 above, and specifically declining to follow the decisions in *Lowe*, 9.102 below, and *Grace*, 9.104 below, was reached in *JA Heath (t/a Heath Private & Commercial Vehicles), MAN/99/63 (VTD 16212).*

9.94 Cars

9.94   *GDG Jones*, 9.89 above, and *Wood*, 9.90 above, were applied in the similar subsequent cases of *JG Jamieson, EDN/96/93 (VTD 14879); MPM Oliver, LON/96/1273 (VTD 14914); Applied Electronic Engineering Ltd, MAN/96/950 (VTD 14942); GO Cawser, MAN/96/1019 (VTD 15067); RE Desborough & MJ Delaney (t/a M & R Machinery Sales), LON/97/326 (VTD 15078); BD Williams, LON/96/1734 (VTD 15163); Highland Vessel Seafoods Ltd, EDN/97/209 (VTD 15600); AJ & JD Evans, MAN/98/16 (VTD 15860); Netherwater Environmental Ltd, MAN/98/93 (VTD 15909); S Toogood (t/a Hydro-Actif), LON/98/1314 (VTD 16005); P Rossall, EDN/98/162 (VTD 16054); C Porter (t/a Clark's Autos), EDN/99/102 (VTD 16229); Agricultural Tyres & Wheels, MAN/99/146 (VTD 16293); Electrocom Ltd, MAN/99/360 (VTD 16557)* and *JSG Commercials, MAN/99/620 (VTD 16940)*.

9.95   *GDG Jones*, 9.89 above, and *Wood*, 9.90 above, were applied in a similar case in which the tribunal chairman (Mr. de Voil) observed that 'a person is deemed to intend the natural consequences of his actions. By buying a chattel, I am thereby automatically making it available for any use I might conceivably wish to make of it: that is what buying a chattel involves. If I bought it deliberately ... I must be assumed to have bought it with the intention of making it so available.' *Thompson*, 9.101 below, was distinguished, as the cars in that case had been insured for business use only, so that any private use would have been illegal. *Webb Plant Hire Ltd, LON/97/452 (VTD 15162).* (*Note*. The decision here has been applied in a number of subsequent cases. For a case heard by the same chairman in which it was distinguished, see *Upton*, 9.108 below.)

9.96   *Webb Plant Hire Ltd*, 9.95 above, was applied in the similar subsequent cases of *RJ Everett, LON/96/1611 (VTD 15469); J Anderson (t/a R Boa Ironmonger), EDN/98/33 (VTD 15717); JVC Trim (t/a Riverside Motor Company), LON/98/419 (VTD 15853)* and *RG Unwin (t/a Unwins), LON/98/831 (VTD 15965)*.

9.97   A car dealer reclaimed input tax on the purchase of a four-wheel drive Nissan Terano. The Commissioners issued an assessment to recover the tax and the dealer appealed, contending that he had bought the Terano for the purpose of towing vehicles. The tribunal dismissed his appeal, accepting that this was the dealer's main purpose, but holding on the evidence that he had not shown 'that he did not intend to make it available for private use even in an emergency'. The tribunal chairman (Mr. Wallace) observed that 'the fact that a vehicle is insured for private use, and is kept at the trader's home, is likely to cause a tribunal to approach evidence and submissions that it is intended to be used only for business with circumspection'. *L Martinez, [1999] VATDR 267 (VTD 16320).*

9.98   Similar decisions were reached in *Mrs S Kothari, LON/98/986 (VTD 16046); D & S Patel (t/a Lidgett Lane Foodstore), MAN/99/28 (VTD 16191); NE Levett-Scrivener, LON/99/130 (VTD 16380); A Moss, LON/99/856 (VTD 16596); Nuchem Ltd, LON/99/886 (VTD 16638); Accelerated Business Growth (UK) Ltd, MAN/99/1094 (VTD 16727); A Collis (t/a AC Video Games), LON/99/687 (VTD 16734); DW & AD Bevan (t/a DW Bevan & Son), LON/99/1324 (VTD 16830); MJ Towler, MAN/99/860 (VTD 16964)* and *Standridge Farm Ltd*, 49.321 PENALTIES: MISDECLARATION.

9.99   **Leasing of car to company director—whether at undervalue—whether Input Tax Order, Article 7(2G) applicable.** A company which operated an employment agency reclaimed input tax on the purchase of a Mercedes. The Commissioners issued an assessment to recover the tax, and the company appealed, contending that it should be entitled to reclaim the tax since it was hiring the Mercedes to its managing director. The tribunal rejected this contention and dismissed the appeal, holding on the evidence that it was not satisfied that the letting of the Mercedes had been under a legally binding agreement, and furthermore that it was not satisfied that the hiring 'was intended to be on commercial terms'. Accordingly, the effect of *Article 7(2G)* of the *Input Tax Order* was that the tax was not deductible. *Orin Engineering (UK) Ltd, LON/97/163 (VTD 15254)*.

9.100   **Leasing of cars to associated company—application of Input Tax Order, Article 7(2G).** See *West Midlands Motors Ltd*, 49.409 PENALTIES: MISDECLARATION.

Cases where the appellant was successful

9.101   An accountant, who owned three cars, purchased a further four cars and reclaimed input tax on their purchase. The Commissioners issued an assessment to recover the tax, considering that they were available for private use and that the effect of *Input Tax Order, Article 7(2G)* was that the input tax was not deductible. The accountant appealed, contending that the cars were intended exclusively for business use because he already owned three cars which he could use privately, and he had insured the four cars in dispute for business use only. The tribunal accepted the accountant's evidence and allowed his appeal, observing that 'the facts of this case are extremely unusual' and holding on the evidence that the accountant had 'made the decision that these four cars would not be made available for private use, whether for himself or his staff'. *Jones*, 9.89 above, distinguished. *HAS Thompson, LON/96/357 (VTD 14777)*. (*Note.* The Commissioners consider that this was 'an exceptional case which has been very much overtaken by later decisions and therefore provides little useful precedent'—see Customs' VAT Manual, Part 13, chapter 2A, section 11.34(a).)

9.102   A trader carried on business as a breeder and supplier of game birds (pheasants). He reclaimed input tax on the purchase of a Nissan Patrol. The Commissioners rejected the claim, on the basis that the vehicle was available for private use, so that the effect of *Input Tax Order, Article 7(2E)* was that the input tax was not deductible. The trader appealed, contending that the Nissan was intended exclusively for business use, and that he had purchased it because he needed a large four-wheel drive vehicle which could be used for towing a trailer. He already owned two other vehicles, one of which was a saloon which he used for private journeys. The tribunal accepted the trader's evidence and allowed the appeal. The tribunal chairman (Mr. Lawson, sitting alone) distinguished *Jones*, 9.89 above, and *Wood*, 9.90 above, holding that those cases relied on 'inference', whereas in the present case it was clear from the trader's evidence 'that he intended from the outset to use the vehicle exclusively for business purposes' and 'never intended or needed to use the vehicle for private purposes'. *SF Lowe, LON/97/225 (VTD 15124)*. (*Note.* The decision here was not followed, and was implicitly disapproved, in the subsequent cases of *Brown*, 9.92 above, and *Heath*, 9.93 above.)

9.103   A partnership of three people carried on business as licensed artificial inseminators. The partnership reclaimed input tax on the purchase of three Citroen cars. The Commissioners rejected the claim, considering that the cars were 'available for private use', within *Input Tax Order, Article 7(2G)*. The partnership appealed, contending that the effect of the licences issued by the Ministry of Agriculture, Fisheries and Food, under which the business operated, was that the cars could not be used privately. Under the licences, the cars were treated as part of the store where the company kept its stocks of semen. The boots of the cars contained canisters of liquid nitrogen, at a temperature of -150°C, in which flasks containing semen were kept while the partners were visiting farmers whose cattle were on heat and ready for insemination. The partners owned their own cars which they used for all their private motoring including travel to and from the partnership premises. The tribunal accepted the partnership's evidence and allowed the appeal. *Southern UK Breeders, LON/97/598 (VTD 15303)*.

9.104 A trader (G), who lived at Crawley, operated catering facilities at go–kart tracks at Crawley and Eastleigh. He reclaimed input tax on the purchase of an estate car. The Commissioners issued an assessment to recover the tax. G appealed, contending that he had purchased and used the estate car solely for the purposes of his business, as he owned another car which he used for private motoring. The tribunal chairman (Miss Gort, sitting alone) accepted G's evidence and allowed the appeal. Miss Gort declined to follow the decisions in *GDG Jones*, 9.89 above, and *Webb Plant Hire Ltd*, 9.95 above, observing that *Input Tax Order, Article 7(2G)* stated only that 'a taxable person shall not be taken to intend to use a motor car exclusively for the purposes of a business carried on by him if he intends to ... make it available ... for private use'. Miss Gort observed that the fact that the car was insured for private use as well as for business use 'does not of itself show that it was (G's) intention to make it available for private use', since he had been informed by the RAC that they did not issue insurance policies for business use only. *I Grace, [1998] VATDR 86 (VTD 15323)*. (*Note.* The decision here was not followed, and was implicitly disapproved, in the subsequent cases of *Shepherd*, 9.91 above, *Brown*, 9.92 above, and *Heath*, 9.93 above.)

9.105 *Grace*, 9.104 above, was applied in a similar subsequent case in which a caterer had reclaimed input tax on the purchase of a jeep, which he used for delivering food to various sites. The tribunal chairman (Mr. Heim) noted that the trader had specifically requested that the vehicle should be insured for business purposes only, and that he had other vehicles which he could use for private motoring. *JC Aldam (t/a John Charles Associates), [1998] VATDR 425 (VTD 15851)*.

9.106 A similar decision, also applying *Grace*, 9.104 above, was reached in a case where a couple who carried on business as foresters and farmers had reclaimed input tax on a Toyota four-wheel drive dual-cab pick-up. *R & HM Swailes, EDN/98/169 (VTD 16069)*.

9.107 An appeal was allowed in another Scottish case where the tribunal chairman (Mrs. Pritchard) accepted the trader's evidence that he had purchased a Ford Mondeo for business purposes only, as he had the use of another vehicle for private motoring. *Martinez*, 9.97 above, distinguished. *J Berry (t/a Automotive Management Services), EDN/00/1 (VTD 16664)*.

9.108 A trader, who lived in Central London, carried on the business of supplying and servicing vending machines in public houses. He reclaimed input tax on the purchase of a Lamborghini. The Commissioners rejected the claim on the basis that the Lamborghini was available for private use. The tribunal allowed the trader's appeal, noting that the facts were unusual because the trader lived in Central London. On the evidence, all the shops which the trader visited were within walking distance of his home, and he always used taxis to attend social engagements, since 'when he does find a little time for socialising, he cannot imagine doing so without alcohol'. *Webb Plant Hire Ltd*, 9.95 above, and *Martinez*, 9.97 above, distinguished. *CM Upton (t/a Fagomatic), LON/99/746 (VTD 16772)*.

9.109 **Leasing of cars—whether at undervalue—whether Input Tax Order, Article 7(2G) applicable.** A company (T) purchased three cars for leasing and reclaimed input tax on the purchase. One of the cars was leased to an associated company (H) and the other two were leased to a company (R) which operated a golf centre. The Commissioners issued an assessment to recover the tax on the basis that T had intended to lease the cars for less than a commercial value, so that the effect of *Input Tax Order, Article 7(2G)* was that the cars should not be held to have been purchased for business purposes. T appealed, contending that the transactions met the test of commerciality and that *Article 7(2G)* did not apply to them. The tribunal accepted this contention and allowed the appeal. With regard to the cars which had been leased to R, the tribunal noted that R was not associated with T but that the leases in question had been entered into as a result of a 'personal friendship' between one of T's directors and a 'person connected with' R. However, although the rental payments under the leases were less than would be expected in an arm's length transaction, T had also received interest-free loans from the lessees, and the effect of this was that T would receive 'a reasonable commercial rate of return for its participation in the transaction'. Accordingly it was entitled to reclaim input tax on its purchase of the cars. *Tamburello Ltd, [1996] VATDR 268 (VTD 14305)*. (*Note*. An alternative contention by T, that *Article 7(2G)* should be disregarded as being incompatible with *Article 17* of the *EC Sixth Directive*, was rejected by the tribunal.)

FUEL FOR PRIVATE USE (VATA 1994, ss 56, 57)

9.110 **Sole trader.** An estate agent failed to account for tax on petrol used for private motoring, although he had reclaimed input tax on the petrol in question. The Commissioners issued an assessment to charge tax on the basis of the scale charges laid down by what is now *VATA 1994, s 57*. The tribunal upheld the assessment and dismissed the estate agent's appeal. *GM Child (t/a Child & Co), LON/90/1239X (VTD 6827)*. (*Note*. For another issue in this case, see 34.149 INPUT TAX.)

9.111 Similar decisions were reached in *BA Hicks, LON/92/1799P & 2075P (VTD 11215); RNM Anderson, EDN/93/32 (VTD 11776); R Desouza, LON/93/400A (VTD 11819); JA Bowles (t/a Oakey Bros Butchers), LON/93/2202 (VTD 12422); AF Sanders, MAN/94/2289 (VTD 13423); RM Bevan, MAN/95/2491 (VTD 14016); WS Thayer, LON/95/2533 (VTD 14382); MI Gross (t/a AME Engineering Services), MAN/96/19 (VTD 14454); DV Birch (t/a Robert Gibbons & Son), MAN/98/210 (VTD 15762)* and *Conway*, 15.111 CONSTRUCTION OF BUILDINGS, ETC.

9.112 A trader (P) owned three cars, two of which were used solely for business. The third car, a Mercedes, was used for business and private mileage, but P failed to account for output tax on the basis of *VATA 1994, s 57*. The Commissioners issued an assessment charging tax on the scale charge and P appealed, contending that 95% of the mileage was business mileage and that when he had used the car for private purposes he had judged the length of the journey, topped the vehicle up with fuel to cover the private use and paid for that fuel privately. The tribunal dismissed P's appeal, observing that there was no evidence to substantiate the amount of private use. There was no way of showing that fuel for private use had not been paid for out of business funds. The chairman cast doubt on the claimed 5% private use as the mileage it represented was very low, and observed that 'that doubt could only be displaced by contemporary log entries'. *G Phillips, LON/93/2934A (VTD 12184)*.

9.113 A similar decision was reached in a case where the tribunal held that the provisions of what is now *VATA 1994, s 56(1)* were within the powers granted by the relevant derogation issued by the Council of the European Communities (*86/356/EEC*). *M Kimber, LON/92/944Y (VTD 10469)*.

9.114 *Kimber*, 9.113 above, was applied in the similar subsequent case of *SJ Prosser, MAN/97/1050 (VTD 15461)*.

9.115 **Partnership—fuel supplied to partners.** A partnership which operated a hotel paid for petrol which the partners used for private motoring, but did not account for output tax in respect of the petrol, although it had previously reclaimed input tax on the purchase of the petrol. The Commissioners issued an assessment charging output tax on the basis of the scale charges laid down by what is now *VATA 1994, s 57*. The tribunal dismissed the partnership's appeal, holding that, in the absence of a detailed record of private and business mileage, the adoption of the scale charges was mandatory. *Playden Oasts Hotel, LON/90/1648Z (VTD 6468)*.

9.116   Similar decisions were reached in *Harry Friar Partnership, LON/92/1059X (VTD 9395); Brown & Rochester, MAN/92/633 (VTD 9751); RD & EC Spicer (t/a Sands Executive), LON/94/1370A (VTD 13858)* and *Seddon Investments, MAN/97/1086 (VTD 15679)*.

9.117   **Fuel supplied to employees.**   A company failed to account for VAT on petrol supplied to its employees, and the Commissioners issued an assessment computed in accordance with the scale charges laid down by what is now *VATA 1994, s 57*. The tribunal upheld the assessment and dismissed the company's appeal. On the evidence, the company paid for the petrol used by some of its employees in travelling between their homes and the company's office. This was private mileage rather than business mileage, and the company was, therefore, obliged to account for VAT thereon. *Magor Products Engineering Ltd, MAN/90/612 (VTD 6532)*.

9.118   See also the cases noted at 49.276 PENALTIES: MISDECLARATION.

9.119   An appeal was allowed in a case where the tribunal accepted the evidence of the appellant company that it only reimbursed business mileage and did not reimburse any private mileage. The tribunal chairman observed that the requirement (in what is now *Notice No 700/64/96, para 3(d)*) 'that there be detailed records was not a statutory requirement'. *Timewade Ltd, LON/94/316 (VTD 12786)*. (*Note*. The tribunal noted that the company had been dilatory in replying to the Commissioners' enquiries, and only awarded the company 50% of its costs.)

9.120   The Commissioners assessed a company which operated a garage, charging output tax under *VATA 1994, ss 56, 57* in respect of two cars which the company owned. The tribunal allowed the company's appeal in part, finding that one of the cars was not used for private purposes, but that output tax was chargeable in respect of one of the cars which was driven by the company's managing director. The chairman observed that it was 'improbable that (the director's) purchases of petrol were so accurate that he could be sure that he paid for all private use of this car'. *Deans Ltd, LON/94/1792A (VTD 13935)*.

MISCELLANEOUS

9.121   **Buying and selling cars—whether a hobby or a business.**   See *Adams*, 7.76 BUSINESS.

9.122   **Treatment of car expenses of employees or agents in relation to input tax.**   See the cases noted at 34.1 to 34.11 INPUT TAX.

9.123   **Personalised vehicle numberplates—whether input tax deductible.**   See the cases noted at 34.369 *et seq.* INPUT TAX.

9.124   **Company cars.**   For whether the provision of a company car may constitute a taxable supply, see the cases noted at 58.1 to 58.7 SUPPLY.

9.125   **Fees for arranging Ministry of Transport vehicle test—whether chargeable to VAT.**   A garage proprietor (W) was not authorised by the Department of Transport to carry out Ministry of Transport vehicle tests. He therefore arranged for such tests to be carried out at approved garages, charging his customers the test fee plus an additional amount for arranging the test. He did not account for output tax on these charges. The Commissioners issued assessments charging output tax, on the basis that only test fees charged to customers separately as disbursements were outside the scope of VAT, as stipulated in Business Brief 21/96. The tribunal dismissed W's appeal, holding that as a matter of law he was required to charge output tax on the fees. However, the chairman commented that the assessment of the fees was 'a particularly harsh decision by the Commissioners' and that 'it was incumbent upon the Commissioners to inform taxpayers such as (W) in the plainest and simplest of terms precisely what the changes they made on 1 November 1996 meant to them. I appreciate that the Commissioners cannot spell out in detail every change in practice but, where a change affects a particularly vulnerable group of people, something more should be done to help them than simply to issue Notes with VAT returns and say that a Business Brief is available further to explain changes made.' *MA Ward (t/a Acorn Garage), MAN/98/507 (VTD 15875)*.

9.126   An appeal was dismissed in another case where a company failed to account for output tax on charges for arranging MOT tests. The tribunal chairman held that 'it is not for us to enquire whether the eight conditions set out in paragraph 10.8 of the VAT Guide (all of which have, according to that paragraph, to be satisfied) are or are not reasonable as a whole. That would be a matter for the Divisional Court on an application for judicial review.' *Chandlers Garage Holdings Ltd, LON/99/271 (VTD 16610)*.

9.127   **Sale of second-hand cars—effect of Article 26a(B) of EC Sixth Directive.**   A married couple who traded in partnership as car dealers had accounted for tax under the margin scheme. Subsequently they submitted a repayment claim on the basis that their supplies should have been treated as exempt from VAT. The Commissioners rejected the claim and the tribunal dismissed the couple's appeal, holding that the margin scheme was authorised by *Article 26a(B)* of the *EC Sixth Directive*. When the couple received second-hand cars from customers in part-exchange deals, the supplies by the customers were exempt from VAT under *Article 13B(c)*, applying *EC Commission v Italian Republic*, 21.172 EUROPEAN COMMUNITY LAW. However, when the couple supplied cars to customers, the exemption in *Article 13B(c)* did not apply and they were required to account for tax on their profit margin. *Stafford Land Rover, [1999] VATDR 471 (VTD 16388)*.

10 Cash Accounting Scheme

The cases in this chapter are arranged under the following headings.

Termination of authorisation
Cases where the appellant was successful 10.1
Cases where the appellant was unsuccessful 10.2–10.6
Other matters 10.7–10.9

TERMINATION OF AUTHORISATION

Cases where the appellant was successful

10.1   In the case noted at 18.298 DEFAULT SURCHARGE, a trader had incurred a default surcharge and, as a result, the Commissioners withdrew his authority to use the Cash Accounting Scheme. The tribunal held that the trader had a reasonable excuse for the default giving rise to the surcharge and, therefore, also allowed his appeal against the withdrawal of his authorisation to use the Scheme. *SP Whitehouse, LON/91/1726 (VTD 6763).*

Cases where the appellant was unsuccessful

10.2   A company began to use the Cash Accounting Scheme in October 1987. Subsequently it incurred several default surcharges. In November 1989 the Commissioners withdrew the company's authorisation to use the scheme. The tribunal dismissed the company's appeal against this decision. *Vitech Engineering Ltd, LON/90/102X (VTD 5154).*

10.3   *Vitech Engineering Ltd*, 10.2 above, was applied in the similar cases of *AA Whyte, MAN/90/686 (VTD 5829); R Smith (t/a Ray Smith Associates), LON/91/287Y (VTD 6624)* and *DE Smith, MAN/91/453 (VTD 6668).*

10.4   An appeal was dismissed in a case where the tribunal held that its jurisdiction was supervisory rather than appellate, applying *JH Corbitt (Numismatists) Ltd*, 56.1 SECOND-HAND GOODS, and *Mr Wishmore Ltd*, 14.39 COLLECTION AND ENFORCEMENT. *Mainline Fabrications, MAN/91/435 (VTD 7010).*

10.5   Similar decisions, also applying *JH Corbitt (Numismatists) Ltd*, 56.1 SECOND-HAND GOODS, and *Mr Wishmore Ltd*, 14.39 COLLECTION AND ENFORCEMENT, were reached in *J Brown, MAN/91/709 (VTD 7747); F Fowle, LON/92/962X (VTD 9174); Industry Northwest Publications (1983) Ltd, MAN/91/1507 (VTD 9425); Mrs SM Wood (t/a Moulton Auto Hire), LON/92/600X (VTD 9565); MD Design Group Ltd, LON/92/2502A (VTD 10070); Howards Way Cleaning, MAN/92/1073 (VTD 10458)* and *Geomatrix Ltd, MAN/92/640 (VTD 10701).*

10.6   A company (M) operated the Cash Accounting Scheme. It issued an invoice to an associated company (F) in respect of future marketing services of more than £410,000. F, which did not operate the Cash Accounting Scheme, reclaimed input tax in respect of the amount charged on the invoice. The Commissioners issued a ruling withdrawing M's entitlement to operate the cash accounting scheme, and the tribunal dismissed M's appeal. By virtue of *VAT Regulations 1995 (SI 1995 No 2518), reg 64(1)(e)*, a taxable person was not entitled to operate the scheme where the Commissioners considered this necessary for the protection of the revenue. On the evidence, there was 'a clear threat to the revenue that, in allowing the claim for (F) ... no subsequent transactions will take place and the revenue will not recover that payment. The revenue clearly needs protecting against the misappropriation of funds due to the timing arising from the cash accounting system.' The chairman observed that there was 'no obvious or sustainable commercial justification for the business practice adopted other than the gaining of a tax advantage. The scheme for cash accounting was designed to give small businesses the option of accounting for VAT when they received payments rather than when they issued a tax invoice. This automatically gave bad debt relief. It is not designed to enable a business to structure its arrangements so that it issues an invoice before any supplies are made (or any costs incurred in relation thereto) where payment by design, in whole or in part, only occurs after a considerable period.' There was 'very serious doubt that there was any possibility' of F ever being able to pay the amount charged by the invoice. Applying *dicta* of Diplock LJ in *Snook v London & West Riding Investments Ltd, CA [1967] 2 QB 786; [1967] 1 All ER 518*, the tribunal was satisfied that the 'arrangements between (M) and (F) were no more than a sham'. *Marketing Middle East Ltd, MAN/97/1110 (VTD 15666)*. (*Notes.* (1) The tribunal also rejected F's claim to input tax—see 38.41 INVOICES AND CREDIT NOTES. (2) The tribunal awarded costs of £1,000 to the Commissioners, finding that M had pursued the appeal 'on a vexatious and frivolous basis'. (3) See now *VAT Regulations 1995, reg 58(2)(f)*. With effect from 3 July 1997, the cash accounting scheme cannot be used for supplies of goods or services in respect of which a VAT invoice is issued in advance of the delivery of goods or performance of services.)

10.7   There are a large number of other cases, which appear to raise no point of general importance, in which tribunals have dismissed appeals against the termination of authorisation to use the Cash Accounting Scheme. In the interests of space, such cases are not reported individually in this book. For a list of such cases decided up to and including 31 December 1992, see Tolley's VAT Cases 1993.

OTHER MATTERS

10.8   **Application of Scheme where grant received from third party.**   A company carrying on a management consultancy business operated the Cash Accounting Scheme. It took advantage of a scheme run by the Scottish Development Agency whereby the Agency paid a grant of 55% of the cost of the company's services to certain qualifying clients. The Agency stipulated that VAT should be paid by the clients on the total cost of the service, including the amount covered by the grant. The company submitted invoices to its clients charging gross fees plus VAT, and deducting the amount of any grant. The company submitted invoices to the Agency on which no VAT was charged. Thus, where the clients paid the invoices in full, the VAT was recovered from them and paid to the Commissioners. However, where the invoices were not paid by the clients, but the grants relating to the invoices were paid to the company by the Agency, the company did not account for VAT on the amount thus received. The Commissioners issued an assessment charging VAT on such amounts and the company appealed, contending that if nothing was paid for the services except the grant, no VAT should be due. The tribunal dismissed the company's appeal. The amounts paid by the Agency were clearly consideration for services which the company supplied. The fact that the consideration was paid by a third party was immaterial, applying *Lord Advocate v Largs Golf Club*, 13.5 CLUBS, ASSOCIATIONS AND ORGANISATIONS. Under the Cash Accounting Scheme, VAT had to be accounted for in the accounting period in which payment for the supply was received. *Martin Gibson Ltd, EDN/90/54 (VTD 5473)*.

10.9   **Application of Scheme where debt discharged by payment in kind.**   A partnership, which accounted for tax under the Cash Accounting Scheme, had supplied goods to a company which was in financial difficulty. The company owed the partnership £29,600. The company came to an arrangement with its creditors by which it increased its share capital and the creditors received shares as payment of the money owed to them. The partnership received shares in the company, but did not account for VAT on the £29,600. The Commissioners issued an assessment charging tax on this amount, and the partnership appealed, contending that the shares were effectively worthless and that it had never received payment. The tribunal dismissed the partnership's appeal. Applying the principles laid down in *Spargo [1873] Ch 407*, the correct analysis of the transaction was that each shareholder should be taken to have received cash in satisfaction of the debt owed to him, and to have paid the same amount of cash for his shares. Although the two deemed payments were self-cancelling, the deemed payment in respect of the supplies which the partnership had previously made was liable to VAT. *A–Z Electrical, LON/93/95A (VTD 10718)*.

11   Charities

The cases in this chapter are arranged under the following headings.

SUPPLIES TO CHARITIES—WHETHER ZERO-RATED (VATA 1994, Sch 8, Group 15)

Supplies of goods donated for sale (VATA 1994, Sch 8, Group 15, Item 1)

11.1   **Whether goods 'donated for sale'.**   A college (N), which was an educational charity, arranged for the incorporation of a wholly-owned subsidiary company which had covenanted to give all its profits to its parent charity. A neighbouring college (C), which was also a charity, wished to purchase various goods (such as photocopiers and computer equipment). In an attempt to avoid output tax from being charged on the supplies, the goods in question were treated as being supplied to N, as being donated by N to its subsidiary company and as being sold to C by the subsidiary. The subsidiary charged a small commission to C. The supplies of the goods were treated as zero-rated under *VATA 1994, Sch 8, Group 15, Item 1.* The Commissioners issued a ruling that the goods had not been 'donated for sale', and thus failed to qualify for zero-rating. N and its subsidiary company appealed. The tribunal dismissed the appeals, observing that 'as a matter of commercial reality, the transactions represented a tripartite agreement' and involved 'no requirement or justification for a "donation" of the relevant equipment to (the company)'. On the evidence, the goods were never delivered to the company, and it was clear that C 'was intended to have the beneficial use and enjoyment of the goods from the moment of delivery'. Neither N nor the company ever acquired title to the goods, and the supplies failed to qualify for zero-rating. *University of Wales College Newport; Allt-Yr-Yn & Caerleon Enterprises & Services Ltd, [1997] VATDR 417 (VTD 15280).* (*Note.* See also *Group 15, Note 1* as substituted by *FA 1997, s 33.* The substituted *Note 1* was intended to block avoidance schemes of this nature.)

Supplies of 'relevant goods' (VATA 1994, Sch 8, Group 15, Items 4, 5, Note 3)

11.2   **Equipment used by homeopathic institute—whether 'medical or scientific equipment'.**   A charity provided seminars in homeopathic and other alternative forms of medicine. Its founder and manager also ran a private practice in the field of alternative medicine, although he had no medical or scientific qualifications. The charity provided training in a technique used by its founder in his private practice, involving the use of a metal box with an electrical current flowing through it, in contact with the patient. Ampoules of various liquids, imported from Germany, were placed in the metal box, and the readings thus obtained were used for diagnosis. The Commissioners issued a ruling that the ampoules were standard-rated. The charity appealed, contending that they were zero-rated on the basis that they were 'medical or scientific equipment' and were therefore zero-rated under what is now *VATA 1994, Sch 8, Group 15, Item 5, Note 3*. The tribunal dismissed the appeal, holding on the evidence that the metal box was not 'medical or scientific equipment', and that the ampoules were used by the charity's founder in his private practice, rather than being used by the charity. *The Institute of EAV & Bio-Energetic Medicine, LON/83/303 (VTD 1667)*.

11.3   **Dental simulation equipment—whether 'relevant goods' within Group 15, Note 3(a).** A company supplied dental simulation equipment, designed for training dental students, to two universities. The Commissioners issued an assessment charging tax on the supplies. The company appealed, contending that the equipment was medical equipment, within *VATA 1994, Sch 8, Group 15, Item 5, Note 3(a)*, and therefore qualified for zero-rating. The tribunal accepted this contention and allowed the appeal. *The Anglodent Company, LON/00/271 (VTD 16891)*.

11.4   **Washing machines for cleaning surgical equipment.** The tribunal held that the supply of washing machines for the cleaning of surgical and laboratory equipment was standard-rated. Although the supply was to eligible bodies within the scope of what is now *VATA 1994, Sch 8, Group 15*, the washing machines could not properly be described as scientific equipment within *Group 15, Note 3. Lancer UK Ltd, [1986] VATTR 112 (VTD 2070)*.

11.5   **Forms used to describe injuries of accident victims.** The tribunal held that a supply of forms, used to describe the injuries of accident victims, did not qualify for zero-rating under what is now *VATA 1994, Sch 8, Group 15*, since the forms were not within the definition of 'medical equipment' and thus were not 'relevant goods' within *Group 15, Note 3. Dr CJ Eaton, LON/86/321 (VTD 2315)*.

11.6   **Observation window at centre for treating epilepsy.** A registered charity, which provided residential assessment, treatment and care for sufferers from epilepsy, incurred expenditure on refurbishing and improving its facilities, installing an observation window and a special 'soft games room' with heavily padded walls, floor and ceiling. The Commissioners issued a ruling that the work was standard-rated, and the charity appealed, contending that the work should be treated as zero-rated under what is now *VATA 1994, Sch 8, Group 15, Item 5*. The QB rejected this contention, holding that the goods were not 'medical goods' within *Group 15, Note 3*, and thus the supplies failed to qualify for zero-rating. *C & E Commrs v The David Lewis Centre, QB [1995] STC 485. (Note.* For another issue in this case, not taken to the QB, see 19.27 DRUGS, MEDICINES, AIDS FOR THE HANDICAPPED, ETC.)

11.7   **Supplies of chemicals and photographic paper to charity for use in X-ray work.** A company supplied chemicals and photographic paper to a charity for use in X-ray work. It did not account for output tax on the supplies, considering that they should be zero-rated under what is now *VATA 1994, Sch 8, Group 15*. The Commissioners issued a ruling that the supplies were not eligible for zero-rating, since the chemicals and paper were not 'relevant goods' within what is now *Group 15, Note 3*. The company appealed, contending that the chemicals and paper should be regarded as 'parts or accessories' within *Note 3(c)*. The tribunal rejected this contention and dismissed the appeal, holding that the chemicals and paper were not within the definition of 'parts or accessories'. *Norwich Camera Centre Ltd, LON/93/1610 (VTD 11629)*.

11.8   **Supply of photocopier—whether 'relevant goods' within Group 15, Note 3.**   A charity acquired a photocopier. The Commissioners issued a ruling that output tax was chargeable on the supply. The charity appealed, contending that the supply should be treated as zero-rated under *VATA 1994, Sch 8, Group 15, Item 5*. The tribunal rejected this contention and dismissed the appeal, holding that the supply did not qualify for zero-rating on the basis that the photocopier was not within the definition of 'relevant goods' in *Group 15, Note 3. Crown Treatment Centre, LON/97/1573 (VTD 15564)*.

11.9   **Warning sirens—whether 'relevant goods' within Group 15, Note 3(g).**   After two major fires at large industrial plants in the Avonmouth area, a charitable trust was established to provide and maintain an 'early warning system' in the area. It purchased a number of early-warning sirens. The Commissioners issued a ruling that the supply of the sirens was standard-rated. The trust appealed, contending that the sirens were aural equipment and were intended to be used for rescue services, and were therefore zero-rated 'relevant goods' within *VATA 1994, Sch 8, Group 15, Note 3(g)*. The tribunal accepted this contention and allowed the appeal. *Severnside Siren Trust Ltd, LON/99/88 (VTD 16640)*.

Supplies to an 'eligible body' (VATA 1994, Sch 8, Group 15, Items 4–6, Note 4)

11.10   **Registered charity providing medical facilities—whether an 'eligible body' within Group 15, Note 4.**   A registered charity provided medical and dental facilities, primarily for French-speakers in the London area. The Commissioners issued a ruling that it was not an 'eligible body' within *VATA 1994, Sch 8, Group 15, Item 5, Note 4*. The company appealed, contending that its premises were a 'hospital', within *Note 4(d)*, or 'a charitable institution providing care or medical or surgical treatment for handicapped persons', within *Note 4(f)*. The tribunal rejected this contention and dismissed the appeal, holding that the premises were 'a medical care centre with surgical facilities', rather than a hospital. The company did not deal with serious accidents, carry out operations 'other than those of a minor nature', or employ nurses or porters. Furthermore, the company's premises were not 'an institution for the treatment of the chronically sick or disabled'. The fact that some of the company's patients were within the definition of 'handicapped persons' was not conclusive, since there was no evidence that 'that class of patients amounts to a significant part of (the company's) clientele'. *Medicare Français, LON/95/2314A (VTD 13929)*.

11.11   A company arranged to provide helicopters, fully fitted out for use as air ambulances, to two charitable trusts. The Commissioners issued a ruling that output tax was chargeable on the supply of the helicopters. The company appealed, contending that its supplies should be treated as zero-rated under *VATA 1994, Sch 8, Group 15, Item 5*. The tribunal held that, as a matter of principle, the company was making separate supplies of the helicopter and of the services of the pilot, and that the supply of the pilot's services failed to qualify for zero-rating, but that the hire of the helicopter was, in principle, within *Group 15, Note 9*. The tribunal directed that the case should be relisted for further argument as to whether the charitable trusts were 'eligible bodies' within *Group 15, Note 4. Medical Aviation Services Ltd, LON/97/16 (VTD 15308)*. (*Note*. There was no further public hearing of the appeal. See now *VATA 1994, Sch 8, Group 15, Notes 4A, 4B*, introduced by *FA 1997, s 34* with effect from 26 November 1996.)

11.12   **Minibuses supplied to charities for elderly.**   A registered charity provided a variety of services to elderly people. It purchased a number of minibuses, arranged for them to be converted to carry wheelchairs, and supplied them to other charities for the benefit of elderly people. It treated its supplies as zero-rated under *VATA 1994, Sch 8, Group 15*. The Commissioners issued assessments on the basis that the charities to which the minibuses were supplied were not 'eligible bodies' within *Group 15, Note 4*, so that the supplies did not qualify for zero-rating. The tribunal allowed the appeal, holding that the recipient charities were within the definition of an 'eligible body' in *Group 15, Note 4(f)*. The QB upheld this decision. *C & E Commrs v Help The Aged, QB [1997] STC 406*. (*Note*. See now, however, *VATA 1994, Sch 8, Group 15, Notes 4A, 4B*, introduced by *FA 1997, s 34* with effect from 26 November 1996. The new provisions were intended to restrict the scope of the zero-rating provisions to 'charities providing personal care or treatment predominantly for the handicapped ... in an institutional or a domiciliary setting'.)

11.13 Registered charity providing scooters and wheelchairs for the disabled— whether an 'eligible body' within Group 15, Item 5. A registered charity provided scooters and wheelchairs for disabled people. The Commissioners issued a ruling that the scooters and wheelchairs failed to qualify for zero-rating under *VATA 1994, Sch 8, Group 15, Item 5*, as the charity was not an 'eligible body' as defined by *Note 4A*. The tribunal upheld this decision and dismissed the charity's appeal. *Poole Shopmobility, LON/98/1486 (VTD 16290)*. (*Note*. For another issue in this case, see 19.47 DRUGS, MEDICINES, AIDS FOR THE HANDICAPPED, ETC.)

11.14 Charitable trust providing 'early-warning' system in the case of emergency—whether an 'eligible body' within Group 15, Note 4(h). In the case noted at 11.9 above, the tribunal held that a charitable trust, established to provide an 'early-warning' system in the case of an emergency, was providing rescue services within *VATA 1994, Sch 8, Group 15, Note 4(h)* and was therefore within the definition of an 'eligible body'. *Severnside Siren Trust Ltd, LON/99/88 (VTD 16640)*.

Provision of care for 'handicapped persons' (VATA 1994, Sch 8, Group 15, Item 5, Note 5)

11.15 Purchase of microcomputer—whether 'the provision of care for a handicapped person'. A registered charity purchased a microcomputer and arranged for it to be delivered to an individual who was severely handicapped with muscular dystrophy. The Commissioners issued an assessment on the basis that the sale of the microcomputer was standard-rated. The charity appealed, contending that the provision of the microcomputer constituted the 'provision of care for a handicapped person', and was therefore zero-rated under what is now *VATA 1994, Sch 8, Group 15, Item 5*. The tribunal rejected this contention and dismissed the charity's appeal, holding that the 'provision of care' required that 'the provider himself provides, or assumes the responsibility of providing, something in the nature of protection or a continuing state of care for the handicapped person'. The 'absence of any continuing personal supervisory role' by the charity meant that the provision of the microcomputer did not constitute the provision of 'care', and did not qualify for zero-rating. *Medical Care Foundation, [1991] VATTR 28 (VTD 5411)*.

11.16 Spellcheckers purchased by Dyslexia Institute. The Dyslexia Institute purchased a number of 'spellcheckers' from a firm of electronic publishers. In accordance with advice from the Commissioners, the vendors charged VAT. The Institute appealed, contending that the goods should have been treated as zero-rated under what is now *VATA 1994, Sch 8, Group 15*. The tribunal dismissed the appeal, holding that dyslexics were not 'handicapped persons' as defined in *Note 5*, and that the Institute was not providing 'medical treatment' within *Item 5*. The chairman also observed that she was 'not satisfied that these "spellmasters" are computer equipment within the ordinary and natural meaning of those words'. *The Dyslexia Institute Ltd, LON/94/293A (VTD 12654)*.

11.17   *The Dyslexia Institute*, 11.16 above, was applied in the similar case of *Mrs J Smith (for Dundee & Angus Dyslexic Association), EDN/94/122 (VTD 12909).*

Supplies of advertising facilities (VATA 1994, Sch 8, Group 15, Item 8)

Note. *VATA 1994, Sch 8, Group 15, Item 8* was substituted by the *VAT (Charities and Aids for the Handicapped) Order 2000 (SI 2000 No 805)* with effect from 1 April 2000. The cases in this section should be read in the light of this change.

11.18   **Advertising posters—whether zero-rated under Group 15, Item 8.**   The Royal Society for the Encouragement of Arts, Manufacture and Commerce is a registered charity and the representative member of a VAT group. Posters, advertising a special awards scheme, were designed and prepared outside the group but printed within the group. The charity treated the self-supply of the posters as zero-rated. The Commissioners issued an assessment on the basis that the supply did not qualify for zero-rating. The QB upheld the assessment. Scott-Baker J held that the purpose of *VATA 1994, Sch 8, Group 15, Item 8* was to help charities obtain supplies of advertising services from third party suppliers, and that the legislation was not intended to promote 'in-house' advertising, which did not need such assistance. *C & E Commrs v The Royal Society for the Encouragement of Arts, Manufacture & Commerce, QB 1996, [1997] STC 437.*

11.19   **Advertisements in periodical—whether zero-rated under Group 15, Item 8.**   An association of bell-ringers, which was a registered charity, arranged for the inclusion of two advertisements in a periodical dealing with bell-ringing. The Commissioners issued a ruling that output tax was chargeable on the advertisements. The association appealed, contending that they should be zero-rated under *VATA 1994, Sch 8, Group 15, Item 8*. The tribunal allowed the appeal in part, holding that a small classified advertisement, advertising a quarterly meeting, was standard-rated but that a large display advertisement, advertising a bell-ringing festival, was zero-rated. The tribunal observed that an advertisement could be zero-rated under *Item 8* if it was either for the purpose of raising funds for the charity, or for the purpose of making known the objects of the charity. On the evidence, neither of the advertisements had been for the purpose of making known the objects of the charity. However, the second advertisement had been for the purpose of raising funds, and therefore qualified for zero-rating. *Sussex County Association of Change Ringers, LON/95/2266A (VTD 14116).* (*Note.* The association was not registered for VAT, but the Commissioners accepted that it had sufficient *locus standi* to lodge an appeal—see 2.31 APPEALS.)

11.20   **Recruitment advertising services supplied to registered charity—whether zero-rated under Group 15, Item 8.**   A registered charity arranged for an associated company (which was not a member of the same VAT group) to supply services in connection with advertising for new staff for the charity. The company and the charity treated the supplies as zero-rated under *VATA 1994, Sch 8, Group 15, Item 8.* The Commissioners issued a ruling that the supplies did not qualify for zero-rating, on the basis that the primary purpose of the advertisements was to recruit new staff, rather than 'making known the objects or reasons' of the charity, as required by *Item 8*. The company appealed, contending that the advertisements should be treated as zero-rated, on the grounds that 'making known the objects of the charity and the raising of money for it' was a substantial purpose of the recruitment advertisements. The tribunal dismissed the appeal, holding that the primary purpose of the advertisements was the recruitment of staff, which was not a qualifying purpose within *Item 8*. The tribunal observed that 'if Parliament had intended that all charitable advertisement should be zero-rated, the preamble to (*Item 8*) would have been unnecessary', and to 'allow a test less stringent than "predominance"' would mean that 'all advertisements in any way concerned with charities would pass the test for zero-rating'. *RNIB Properties Ltd, LON/97/982 (VTD 15748)*.

11.21   **Printing company supplying collection envelopes to charities—whether within Group 15, Item 8.**   A printing company supplied quantities of collection envelopes to charities. It did not account for output tax on these supplies. The Commissioners issued a ruling that the supplies were standard-rated, and the company appealed, contending that the envelopes should be treated as advertisements and as qualifying for zero-rating under *VATA 1994, Sch 8, Group 15, Item 8*. The tribunal rejected this contention and dismissed the appeal, holding that, although some of the envelopes could fairly be described as 'advertisements', the company was only making a supply of printing services, and the advertisements were actually published by the charity. *TE Penny & Co Ltd, LON/97/291 (VTD 15329)*.

11.22   **Steel badges requesting support for a charity—whether an 'advertisement' within Item 8.**   A registered charity (LDT) purchased a number of steel badges from a company. The badges bore the slogan 'please support LDT'. LDT gave these badges to donors. The Commissioners issued a ruling that the company's sales of the badges to LDT were standard-rated supplies. LDT appealed, contending that the sales should be treated as zero-rated under *VATA 1994, Sch 8, Group 15, Item 8*. The tribunal rejected this contention and dismissed the appeal, holding that the badges were not an 'advertisement' and did not qualify for zero-rating under the legislation then in force. *Leukaemic Disorders Trust, EDN/99/157 (VTD 16783)*. (*Note.* See now *Item 8* as substituted by *VAT (Charities and Aids for the Handicapped) Order 2000 (SI 2000 No 805)* with effect from 1 April 2000. It appears that the badges would now qualify for zero-rating as a 'medium of communication with the public'.)

FUND-RAISING EVENTS—WHETHER EXEMPT (VATA 1994, Sch 9, Group 12)

Note. VATA 1994, Sch 9, Group 12 was substituted by the *VAT (Fund-Raising Events by Charities and Other Qualifying Bodies) Order 2000 (SI 2000 No 802)* with effect from 1 April 2000. The cases in this section should be read in the light of this change.

11.23   **Series of fund-raising events—whether exempt.**   A registered charity arranged seven performances of a play, and a pre-release screening of a film. The Commissioners issued a ruling that the charges made for admission to these performances were chargeable to VAT at the standard rate. The charity appealed, contending firstly that the performances constituted a 'fund-raising event' and were exempt under what is now *VATA 1994, Sch 9, Group 12*. The tribunal dismissed the charity's appeal, holding that the performances constituted a 'series' and were thus excluded from exemption under the legislation then in force. The restriction of the scope of the exemption was in accordance with the provisions of *Article 13A1(o)* of the *Sixth Directive. Northern Ireland Council for Voluntary Action, [1991] VATTR 32 (VTD 5451)*. (*Note.* See now, however, *Sch 9, Group 12, Notes 4* and *5*, introduced by *SI 2000 No 802*. It appears that, as the series consisted of fewer than 15 events, they would now qualify for exemption.)

11.24   A registered charity organised a festival dinner, a race day and a carol concert. It reclaimed input tax on the expenditure related to these events. The Commissioners rejected the claim and issued a ruling that the supplies were exempt by virtue of *VATA 1994, Sch 9, Group 12*. The charity appealed, contending that the events were 'part of a series or regular run of like or similar events' and thus were excluded from exemption under the legislation then in force. The tribunal rejected this contention and dismissed the charity's appeal, holding that the events were not 'part of a series or regular run of like or similar events' on the grounds that the events were 'intrinsically dissimilar and there is no quality inherent in the nature of the events which is common to all'. *Newsvendors Benevolent Institution, LON/96/567 (VTD 14343)*.

11.25 **Real ale and jazz festival.** A sports club organised a real ale and jazz festival, lasting for three consecutive evenings. The Commissioners issued a ruling that the festival did not qualify for exemption under *VATA 1994, Sch 9, Group 12*, on the grounds that it comprised a 'series or regular run of like or similar events', and thus was excluded from exemption under the legislation then in force. The club appealed. The tribunal allowed the appeal, noting that different jazz bands played on each of the three days, and holding that the festival should be viewed as 'a single organic whole', rather than as a series of three separate events. *Northern Ireland Council for Voluntary Action*, 11.23 above, distinguished. *Reading Cricket & Hockey Club, LON/95/1093A (VTD 13656)*.

11.26 **Rugby club social events.** A rugby union club staged a number of social functions such as 'stag nights'. It did not account for output tax on its receipts from such events, treating them as exempt from VAT under *VATA 1994, Sch 9, Group 12*. The Commissioners issued an assessment on the basis that the events comprised a 'series or regular run of similar or like events', and were thus excluded from exemption under the legislation then in force. The tribunal upheld the assessment and dismissed the club's appeal. (The tribunal chairman also considered that some of the functions did not qualify as 'fund-raising events', on the grounds that the club had not shown that the main purpose of staging such events was to raise funds.) *Blaydon Rugby Football Club, [1996] VATDR 1 (VTD 13901)*.

11.27 **Student union balls—whether 'fund-raising events'.** A student union, which was a charity under *Charities Act 1993, Sch 2(w)*, and was registered for VAT, organised balls for students. It treated these balls as exempt from VAT. The Commissioners issued a ruling that the balls did not qualify for exemption, on the grounds that they were primarily social events rather than fund-raising events. The union appealed, contending that the balls were 'fund-raising events' within *VATA 1994, Sch 9, Group 12*. The tribunal accepted this contention and allowed the appeal, holding on the evidence that the raising of funds was 'a main purpose' of staging the events and 'not merely (an) incidental purpose'. *Cheltenham & Gloucester College of Higher Education Students Union, LON/97/1198 (VTD 15727)*. (*Note*. See now, however, *Group 12, Item 1* as substituted by *SI 2000 No 802*. To qualify for exemption, the 'primary purpose' of an event now has to be the raising of money.)

11.28 **Whether event staged by a 'qualifying body'.** An unincorporated committee was established to organise a testimonial football match to raise money for a fund. Most of the fund was to be paid to a former footballer, and the remainder was to be used to buy hospital equipment in a ward for patients suffering from cancer. The Commissioners issued a ruling that the supplies made by the committee did not qualify for exemption under what is now *VATA 1994, Sch 9, Group 12*, as the committee was not a 'qualifying body' within *Note 3*. The secretary of the committee appealed. The tribunal dismissed the appeal, holding that the committee was not within what is now *VATA 1994, Sch 9, Group 12, Item 1*, since most of the fund's proceeds were to be paid to the former footballer, rather than to the hospital. *P Bailes, LON/93/1430 (VTD 12459)*.

APPORTIONMENT OF INPUT TAX

11.29 A registered charity operated an art gallery. It did not charge visitors for admission to the gallery, but it received income from selling souvenirs, from organised tours and lectures, from the occasional hire of the gallery, and from charging admission fees to occasional exhibitions. The charity reclaimed the whole of its input tax, and the

Commissioners issued an assessment to recover some of the tax, considering that the charity's entitlement to input tax should be restricted to the proportion which its taxable supplies bore to its total supplies, including grants and donations. The tribunal allowed the charity's appeal in part, holding that, since only some of the charity's activities constituted a business, the Commissioners were correct to seek an apportionment of the charity's input tax, but that they were not justified in including grants and donations in the computation. The charity appealed to the QB which upheld the tribunal decision. Applying *Apple & Pear Development Council*, 21.47 EUROPEAN COMMUNITY LAW, only input tax relating to the charity's taxable supplies could be deducted. *Whitechapel Art Gallery v C & E Commrs, QB [1986] STC 156; [1986] 1 CMLR 79.*

11.30 A charity provided legal aid and assistance free of charge to poor people in the Borough of Hillingdon. It reclaimed the whole of the input tax which it incurred. The Commissioners issued an assessment on the basis that the input tax relating to the services which the charity provided free of charge was not recoverable, and that the charity's total input tax should be apportioned accordingly. The charity appealed, contending that the whole of its input tax should be recoverable. The tribunal dismissed the charity's appeal, holding that as some of the charity's services were made for no consideration, the input tax relating to those services could not be recovered. *Hillingdon Legal Resources Centre Ltd, [1991] VATTR 39 (VTD 5210).*

11.31 *Hillingdon Legal Resources Centre Ltd*, 11.30 above, was applied in the similar subsequent case of *Wolverhampton Citizens Advice Bureau, MAN/96/1145 (VTD 16411).*

11.32 A charity agreed to provide services to four councils. The Commissioners issued rulings that the agreements did not provide for any taxable supplies (so that the charity would not be able to reclaim any related input tax). The charity appealed. The tribunal reviewed the evidence submitted by the charity but concluded that it was 'not clear ... whether, and to what extent, each agreement related to matters which the authority is obliged to provide for, or which it may simply decide are desirable in the general interest; or whether the local authorities in question intended that what they were doing should be the making of a grant in such a way that its use was tightly controlled, or whether they intended to contract out the performance of statutory obligations which they could not perform themselves'. Since the charity had not furnished 'adequate factual evidence of the legal status of the service level agreements', the tribunal directed that the appeal should be adjourned. *The Pre-School Learning Alliance, LON/99/1048 & LON/00/53 (VTD 16928).*

11.33 A charity, governed by Royal Charter, had a substantial fund of investments, which produced income of more than £1,000,000 per year. Its general charitable activities were accepted as not constituting a business, but it also made a number of taxable supplies, and had regularly reclaimed about 5% of its total input tax. It submitted a claim for its investment activities to be treated as a business, with the result that a substantially greater proportion of its input tax would be treated as deductible. The Commissioners issued a ruling that the investment activities did not amount to a business, and should therefore be left out of account in determining how much of the charity's input tax should be apportioned to its business activities. The charity appealed, contending that its investment activities should be treated as a business in accordance with *Notice No 701/1/92*, which stated (on p 12) that 'if a charity becomes actively involved in buying and selling shares on a regular basis, or receives commission for brokerage services, that will be regarded as a business activity'. The tribunal dismissed the appeal, holding that the charity's investment activities could not be regarded as constituting a business in law, applying *dicta* in *Polysar Investments Netherlands BV*, 21.61 EUROPEAN COMMUNITY LAW. The tribunal strongly criticised the Commissioners for 'seeking to resile from the straightforward interpretation' of *Notice No 701/1/92*, and expressed 'the hope that the leaflet will now be withdrawn and replaced by a leaflet which Customs & Excise will support'. *National Society for the Prevention of Cruelty to Children, [1992] VATTR 417 (VTD 9325)*. (*Note. Notice No 701/1/92* has subsequently been superseded by *Notice No 701/1/95*. Customs' VAT Manual, Part 9, chapter 2, section 2.22 states that 'current policy ... is that the acquisition or disposal of shares or of any other form of security by a charity is a non-business activity'.)

11.34 In a case where the facts are not fully set out in the tribunal decision, the tribunal directed that the input tax incurred by a registered charity which engaged in both business and non-business activities should be apportioned. *British & Foreign Bible Society, EDN/92/262 (VTD 10149)*.

11.35 **Retrospective claim by museum trustees.** The Board of Trustees of the Victoria and Albert Museum was established under the *National Heritage Act*. They apportioned the Museum's input tax between business and non-business activities, operating the income-based method described in what is now *VAT Notice No 700, Appendix F*. However, they subsequently formed the opinion that this method led to too small an amount of input tax being apportioned to business activities. From April 1993 they adopted a revised method of apportionment which determined the residual input tax by using the ratio which the Museum's input tax directly attributable to its wholly taxable activities bore to the VAT incurred by the Museum on all the supplies made to it which could be directly attributed to either its taxable activities or its non-business activities. The Commissioners agreed to the use of this method for the period beginning on 1 April 1993. In September 1993 the Trustees submitted a retrospective claim to input tax for the period from 1 April 1990 to March 1993, based on using the method which they had adopted since April 1993 rather than the income-based method which they had actually operated during the three years in question. The Commissioners rejected the claim and the Trustees appealed. The tribunal dismissed the appeal and the QB upheld this decision. Turner J held that the *Appendix F* method which the Trustees had adopted was 'an acceptable method of apportionment', and was not inconsistent with *Article 17(5)* of the *EC Sixth Directive*. Although the Trustees could have chosen another acceptable method of apportionment, they had not made an 'error', and the case did not fall within what is now *VAT Regulations 1995 (SI 1995 No 2518), reg 34*. *Victoria & Albert Museum Trustees v C & E Commrs, QB [1996] STC 1016.*

11.36 **Extension to premises owned by charity and used by subsidiaries under non-exclusive licences—reclaimable proportion of input tax.** A company (M), which was a registered charity, owned a hospice. It had two wholly-owned subsidiary companies which were also charities. One of these subsidiaries operated a number of charity shops which made taxable supplies, and was registered for VAT, while the other subsidiary was not registered, since its sole activity was the provision of care for the terminally ill, which was exempt from VAT. M was registered for VAT on the basis that it was making taxable supplies to its two subsidiaries. M arranged for an extension to the hospice and reclaimed input tax of £80,000 (representing 89% of the total input tax) on the relevant construction work. The Commissioners rejected the claim on the basis that the expenditure was primarily attributable to non-business activities, so that only a much smaller proportion of the tax was reclaimable. The tribunal chairman (Mr. Heim, sitting alone) allowed M's appeal, holding that, while M had granted its two subsidiaries licences to occupy its premises, the licences did not grant an exclusive right of occupation and were therefore not exempt supplies within *VATA 1994, Sch 9, Group 1*, but were taxable supplies. Additionally, M was making taxable supplies of management services. Accordingly, M was primarily using the premises for the purpose of making taxable supplies to its subsidiaries, and the principal purpose of the construction work in question had been the making of taxable supplies. With regard to the apportionment of the tax, the tribunal held that M had adopted 'a proper approach' by initially treating 'the totality of the input tax as being referable to ... business purposes' and then deducting a proportion of the tax as relating to M's own use of the premises, which was admittedly outside the scope of VAT. *Mount Edgcumbe Hospice Ltd, LON/94/519 (VTD 14807)*. (*Notes*. (1) On the issue of whether a non-exclusive licence to occupy land is exempt from VAT, compare *Altman Blane & Co*, 39.9 LAND, which was not referred to in this decision. See also the subsequent case of *Abbotsley Golf & Squash Club Ltd*, 39.123 LAND, where the same tribunal chairman (Mr. Heim) held that a licence to occupy land did not have to be exclusive to qualify for exemption, on the grounds that exclusivity of occupation was a necessary condition for the creation of a tenancy, but was not a necessary condition for the creation of a licence. Mr. Heim's conclusion in *Abbotsley Golf & Squash Club Ltd* appears to contradict his reasoning in *Mount Edgcumbe Hospice Ltd* on the question of the taxability of the licences. The decision on this point is therefore of doubtful value as a precedent: for a fuller analysis, see the memorandum by the VAT Practitioners' Group published in the Tax Journal, 8 March 1999. (2) For the Commissioners' practice following these decisions, see Business Brief 25/97, issued on 10 November 1997, and Business Brief 22/98, issued on 3 November 1998.)

11.37   **Charity reclaiming input tax on overhead expenditure relating to transactions outside UK.** A charity, which was registered for UK VAT, purchased various goods outside the UK. It stored the goods in a warehouse in the Netherlands, and gave them away for no consideration to recipients outside the EU. Although the goods never entered the UK, their distribution was arranged by the charity's London office. The charity reclaimed input tax relating to these transactions. The Commissioners issued an assessment to recover the tax, and the tribunal dismissed the charity's appeal. Because the goods had never entered the UK, they did not qualify as exports within *VATA 1994, s 30(5)*, since '"export" involves removal from the United Kingdom'. Accordingly, there was no entitlement to input tax under *s 26(2)(a)*. There was also no entitlement to input tax credit under *s 26(2)(b)*, since the goods had been distributed for no consideration, and therefore, by virtue of *s 5(2)(a)*, did not qualify as supplies. (The tribunal also held that, even if the goods were treated as supplies, they were not made in the course or furtherance of the charity's business.) *International Planned Parenthood Federation, LON/99/993 (VTD 16922).*

11.38   **Input tax apportioned to take account of non-business use—effect of Lennartz decision.** See *North East Media Development Trust Ltd*, 45.64 PAYMENT OF TAX.

11.39   **Purchase of premises by partly exempt charity—apportionment of input tax.** See *Bristol Churches Housing Association*, 43.38 PARTIAL EXEMPTION.

MISCELLANEOUS

11.40   **Whether charity carrying on a business.** See *Morrison's Academy Boarding Houses Association*, 7.1 BUSINESS; *Royal Exchange Theatre Trust*, 7.4 BUSINESS; *Widnes Spastic Fellowship*, 7.49 BUSINESS, and *The Wellcome Trust Ltd*, 21.66 EUROPEAN COMMUNITY LAW.

11.41   **Supplies of welfare services by charity—whether exempt under Article 13A1(g) of EC Sixth Directive.** See *Yoga for Health Foundation*, 21.148 EUROPEAN COMMUNITY LAW; *International Bible Students Association*, 21.149 EUROPEAN COMMUNITY LAW; *Central YMCA*, 21.150 EUROPEAN COMMUNITY LAW;

Peterborough Diocesan Conference & Retreat House, 31.44 HEALTH AND WELFARE, and *Trustees for the Macmillan Cancer Trust*, 31.45 HEALTH AND WELFARE.

11.42   **Construction of buildings—whether for relevant charitable purpose.**   See *Meadows*, 15.41 CONSTRUCTION OF BUILDINGS, ETC.; *Shinewater Association Football Club*, 15.42 CONSTRUCTION OF BUILDINGS, ETC; *Bennachie Leisure Centre Association*, 15.43 CONSTRUCTION OF BUILDINGS, ETC.; *St Dunstan's Roman Catholic Church Southborough*, 15.47 CONSTRUCTION OF BUILDINGS, ETC.; *Leighton Park School*, 15.48 CONSTRUCTION OF BUILDINGS, ETC.; *St Dunstan's Educational Foundation*, 15.52 CONSTRUCTION OF BUILDINGS, ETC., and *League of Friends of Kingston Hospital*, 15.57 CONSTRUCTION OF BUILDINGS, ETC.

11.43   **Royal Academy of Music—whether concert hall to be used for 'relevant charitable purpose'.**   See *The Royal Academy of Music*, 52.7 PROTECTED BUILDINGS.

11.44   **Fitness centre operated by charity—whether building used for 'relevant charitable purpose'.**   See *Jubilee Hall Recreation Centre Ltd*, 52.8 PROTECTED BUILDINGS.

11.45   **Bowling club—whether a charity.**   See *Hunmanby Bowling Club*, 15.55 CONSTRUCTION OF BUILDINGS, ETC.

11.46   **Fund-raising event organised by charity—amount of consideration.**   See *Glasgow's Miles Better Mid-Summer 5th Anniversary Ball*, 63.114 VALUATION.

11.47   **Sponsorship received by charity in return for benefits—whether full amount of sponsorship constitutes 'consideration'.**   See *Tron Theatre Ltd*, 63.87 VALUATION.

11.48   **Local authority providing grants to charity—whether such grants constitute consideration for supplies.**   See *Trustees of the Bowthorpe Community Trust*, 40.9 LOCAL AUTHORITIES AND STATUTORY BODIES.

12 Clothing and Footwear

The cases in this chapter are arranged under the following headings.

WHETHER A SUPPLY OF ARTICLES 'DESIGNED AS CLOTHING'

12.1   **Article for use in push-chairs.** A company supplied an article designed for protecting a child when placed in a push-chair. In appearance the article resembled a romper-suit, but a child could not readily walk in it. The company did not account for output tax on its supplies of these articles, treating them as zero-rated. The Commissioners issued a ruling that the articles were not eligible for zero-rating, on the grounds that they were not within the definition of 'clothing'. The tribunal upheld this decision and dismissed the company's appeal. *Mothercare Ltd, LON/76/177 (VTD 323).*

12.2   **Article to support young child when carried.** A company manufactured an article, under the brand name of 'Easy Rider', which was designed to help a baby to be carried by its mother by providing warmth and support. It did not account for output tax on its supplies of these articles. The Commissioners issued a ruling that the articles were not eligible for zero-rating, on the grounds that they were not within the definition of 'clothing'. The tribunal upheld this decision and dismissed the company's appeal. *Little Rock Ltd, LON/77/121 (VTD 424).*

12.3   **'Buoyancy vest'.** A company supplied articles described as 'buoyancy vests', designed to support young children while they were learning to swim. The Commissioners issued a ruling that supplies of the buoyancy vests did not qualify for zero-rating, on the grounds that they were not within the definition of 'clothing'. The tribunal upheld this decision and dismissed the company's appeal. *British Vita Co Ltd, MAN/76/135 (VTD 332).*

12.4   **Pleating of textile material for girls' skirts.** A company carried on the business of pleating textiles for other companies which made girls' and women's clothing. It did not account for output tax on work done on material for skirts for young girls, treating such supplies as zero-rated. The Commissioners issued an assessment on the basis that the work was liable to VAT at the standard rate. The tribunal allowed the company's appeal, holding that the company was to be treated as supplying the pleated pieces of material and not merely the services of pleating. The pleated material in question was designed to be used as parts of skirts for young children and was not suitable for adult women. The pleated pieces fell within the description 'articles designed as clothing' in what is now *VATA 1994, Sch 8, Group 16, Item 1.* The QB upheld the tribunal decision. The pleated material was processed in such a way that it was only suitable to be used as clothing for young children, and the fact that further work would subsequently have to be carried out did not prevent the material from qualifying for zero-rating under *Sch 8, Group 16, Item 1. C & E Commrs v Ali Baba Tex Ltd, QB [1992] STC 590.* (*Note.* The Commissioners now accept that 'where an article has been processed to the extent that it cannot make anything other than children's clothing, new goods have been supplied'; see Customs' VAT Manual, Part 3, section 3.1.)

12.5   **Girls' elasticated headbands.** A trader manufactured elasticated headbands, intended to be worn by girls under 14 years of age. She did not account for output tax on sales of these headbands, treating them as zero-rated. The Commissioners formed the opinion that the headbands were not within the definition of 'clothing', and issued an assessment, against which the trader appealed. The tribunal dismissed her appeal, holding that the headbands did not qualify as 'other headgear' within what is now *VATA 1994, Sch 8, Group 16, Note 1*, and were therefore not eligible for zero-rating. The tribunal considered that 'headgear must be similar or analogous to hats and must give some covering or protection to the head'. *Mrs V Cassidy (t/a Balou), MAN/90/884 (VTD 5760)*.

12.6   **Badge sashes and woggles for Girl Guides and Brownies.**   Two companies manufactured and sold items designed as uniforms for Girl Guides (aged 10 to 13 inclusive) and Brownies (aged 7 to 9 inclusive). They did not account for output tax on such supplies, treating them as zero-rated. The Commissioners issued rulings that badge sashes and woggles did not qualify for zero-rating under what is now *VATA 1994, Sch 8, Group 16*, on the grounds that they were not within the definition of 'clothing'. The tribunal upheld the Commissioners' rulings and dismissed the companies' appeals. *Dauntgate Ltd, MAN/93/144Y; BG Supplies (Birmingham) Ltd, MAN/93/373W (VTD 11663)*. (*Note*. For another issue in this case, see 12.17 below.)

12.7   **Washing of children's jeans prior to sale—whether a zero-rated supply of clothing.**   A partnership carried on the business of washing denim jeans prior to sale, with the object of lightening the colour of the cloth and softening the material. It did not account for output tax on the consideration it received for washing jeans designed for children, treating such supplies as zero-rated. The Commissioners issued a ruling that the partnership was making supplies of services which did not qualify for zero-rating. The partnership appealed, contending that the washing had the effect of making the jeans more fashionable and was a 'treatment or process' within what is now *VATA 1994, Sch 4 para 2*, and thus a supply of zero-rated clothing. The tribunal dismissed the appeal, holding that, although the washing could be described as a 'treatment or process', it did not produce any goods, since 'what went into the process was a pair of jeans and that is what was there at the end of the process'. Accordingly, the partnership was making standard-rated supplies of services rather than zero-rated supplies of goods. *Ali Baba Tex Ltd*, 12.4 above, distinguished. *Warley Denim Services, MAN/92/1668 (VTD 10396)*.

12.8   **Sale of discount cards to be used for purchases of zero-rated clothing.**   See *Mothercare (UK) Ltd*, 54.8 RETAILERS' SPECIAL SCHEMES.

WHETHER ARTICLES 'NOT SUITABLE FOR OLDER PERSONS'

12.9   **Fashion knitwear.**   A company did not account for output tax on sales of eleven types of 'one-size fashion knitwear'. All, with one exception, were of approximately the same size and possessed the quality of 'stretchability'. The tribunal held that, except for one item which was significantly smaller than the others, their supply did not qualify for zero-rating. Although they were intended for the use of young children, they were also 'suitable for older persons' and were thus excluded from zero-rating. *Jeffrey Green & Co Ltd, [1974] VATTR 94 (VTD 69)*.

12.10   **Leather overcoats.**   A company did not account for output tax on a type of overcoat, bearing no size label but advertised as a 'girl's leather coat'. The coats were 35 inches in length and measured 35 inches across the bust. The Commissioners issued a ruling that, because the coats had a three-inch bust dart, they were 'suitable for wear by older persons' and did not qualify for zero-rating. The company appealed, contending that the waist and hip measurements of the coats were such that they were not 'suitable for wear by older persons'. The tribunal rejected this contention and dismissed the appeal, observing that the length of the overcoats appeared to be 'suitable on older persons' and holding that, in view of the three-inch bust dart, the overcoats in question did not qualify for zero-rating. *Walter Stewart Ltd, [1974] VATTR 131 (VTD 83)*.

12.11   Nursing shawls.   A partnership manufactured nursing shawls. It did not account for output tax on its supplies of these shawls, treating them as zero-rated. The Commissioners issued a ruling that the shawls were not eligible for zero-rating, on the grounds that they were 'suitable for older persons'. The tribunal accepted this contention and dismissed the firm's appeal. *WG Jones & Son, BIR/74/12 (VTD 117)*.

12.12   Moccasins.   A company manufactured a type of moccasin. In accounting for tax, it treated sizes up to and including 5½ as zero-rated. The Commissioners issued a ruling that the moccasins in size 3 to size 5½ inclusive did not qualify for zero-rating on the grounds that they were also suitable for some older women. The company which manufactured them appealed, contending that they were designed for young girls and should therefore be zero-rated. The tribunal dismissed the appeal, observing that 'the fact that some older persons may ... be able to wear them by reason of size ... should not in our view be relevant', but holding on the evidence that the moccasins in question were 'suitable for wear by older persons', and were therefore excluded from zero-rating. *Jeffrey Green & Co Ltd*, 12.9 above, applied. *Brays of Glastonbury Ltd, CAR/78/95 (VTD 650)*. (*Note*. The Commissioners appear to disapprove of the part of the decision which is quoted above, and state in Customs' VAT Manual, Part 7, chapter 14, section 2.19 that 'certain commercial publications seek to misuse the decision'.)

12.13   Slippers—whether unisex—effect of Notice No 714.   A company did not account for VAT on sales of slippers which it manufactured in sizes 4 and 5. The Commissioners issued an assessment charging tax on the slippers, considering that they were designed for girls and that, by virtue of *Notice No 714*, only girls' slippers up to and including size 3 could be zero-rated. The company appealed, contending that the slippers were unisex, and that *Notice No 714* indicated (at *p 21* of the 1986 edition) that unisex slippers could be zero-rated up to and including size 5½. The tribunal criticised the wording of *Notice No 714* as being inconsistent with the legislation, since 'sizes 4 or 5 in general fit girls of ages greater than 14 and some adult women'. Accordingly, any unisex slippers in those sizes were suitable for wear by 'older persons', and not eligible for zero-rating. The tribunal remitted the case to the parties to consider the different fabric colours, patterns and designs individually, on the principle that designs suitable for both sexes, and designs only suitable for girls, were not eligible for zero-rating; but designs which were only suitable for boys were eligible for zero-rating. *R Spencer (Cosy Comfort Slippers) Ltd, MAN/91/1636 (VTD 7945)*. (*Note. Notice No 714* has subsequently been revised and reissued.)

12.14   Jeans.   Boys' jeans were held, on the evidence, to be designed as clothing for young children, and not to be suitable for older persons, in *VF Corporation (UK) Ltd, BEL/79/7 (VTD 898)*.

12.15   A similar decision was reached in *R Kaur Singh, MAN/86/6 (VTD 2433)*.

12.16   Sports shorts.   A company did not account for output tax on supplies of elasticated white shorts designed to be worn by children under the age of 14 when playing games such as football or tennis, treating them as zero-rated. The Commissioners formed the opinion that some of the shorts, with advertised waist sizes of 28 ins, 30 ins and 32 ins, were suitable for people over the age of 14, and thus did not qualify for zero-rating. They issued an assessment charging tax on the supplies of these shorts, and the company appealed. The tribunal allowed the company's appeal, finding that because the waist–crotch–waist measurement of the shorts in question did not exceed

26 ins, they were too small to be suitable for people over the age of 14. (The tribunal noted that the waist measurements of the shorts 'at rest' were up to four inches smaller than the advertised waist measurements, which were measured at 'a position of comfortable stretch in wear', and also observed that 'we are not concerned with what an abnormally small person, but rather an average person of age groups, could wear'.) *Falcon Sportswear Ltd, MAN/85/374 (VTD 2019)*.

12.17   **Culottes and sweatpants for Girl Guides and Brownies.**   Two companies manufactured and sold items designed as uniforms for Girl Guides (aged 10 to 13 inclusive) and Brownies (aged 7 to 9 inclusive). They did not account for output tax on such supplies, treating them as zero-rated. The Commissioners issued rulings that neckerchiefs, culottes in sizes 30″ and 32″ waist, and Guides' sweatpants in size 32″ waist did not qualify for zero-rating on the grounds that they were 'suitable for older persons'. The companies appealed. The tribunal allowed the appeals in part, holding that the culottes did not qualify for zero-rating because their waist size rendered them suitable for 60% of all women and, although they were intended as uniform for Guides, their dark blue colour was 'perfectly standard and acceptable ... for older persons'. However, the sweatpants qualified for zero-rating because, although their waist measurement of 32″ was in principle 'suitable for older persons', the garments had a waist–crotch–waist measurement of only 23″. It followed that, unlike the culottes, they were 'not sufficiently full at lower points' to be 'suitable for older persons'. The neckerchiefs also qualified for zero-rating on the grounds that they would not be worn by 'any persons other than girl guides and boy scouts'. *Dauntgate Ltd, MAN/93/144Y; BG Supplies (Birmingham) Ltd, MAN/93/373W (VTD 11663)*. (*Note.* For another issue in this case, see 12.6 above.)

12.18   **Riding hats.**   A company manufactured riding hats. The Commissioners accepted that the hats were zero-rated up to and including size 6½, but issued a ruling that the hats were not eligible for zero-rating above 6½, on the grounds that they were suitable for older persons as well as for young children. The tribunal allowed the appeal, finding that, since cartoon characters were portrayed on the hats, which bore the words 'Kids Own', any adult who wore one would risk being exposed to 'ridicule or contempt'. Accordingly the hats were not 'suitable' for anyone over the age of 14, and qualified for zero-rating. *Charles Owen & Co (Bow) Ltd, [1993] VATTR 514 (VTD 11267)*.

12.19   **Acrylic hats with football logos.**   A company imported a quantity of knitted acrylic hats, with logos referring to well-known football teams. The Commissioners issued a ruling that the sale of the hats was standard-rated. The company appealed, contending that the hats should be zero-rated as they were designed for young children and were not suitable for older persons. The tribunal accepted this contention and allowed the appeal. On the evidence, although the hats could be stretched so that it was physically possible for an adult to wear them, they were 'too close-fitting for comfortable wear over an extended period'. Furthermore, they were intended as a 'cheap imitation' of official football club hats, to be worn by young children who could not afford the official hats. The tribunal considered that the hats 'would be unlikely to be worn by any persons other than football supporters, and supporters over 14 would want the official hats'. The hats 'would not in general be acceptable headwear for adults or children over 14'. *Benrose Ltd (t/a Multi-Stock Co), LON/98/7048 (VTD 15783)*.

13 Clubs, Associations and Organisations

Note. This chapter includes cases concerning *VATA 1994, s 94(2)(a)*, under which the provision of 'facilities or advantages' by a club, association or organisation to its members is deemed to be the carrying on of a business. *VATA 1994, s 94(3)*, which previously provided that certain bodies in the public interest were not to be treated as carrying on a business, was repealed by *FA 1999, s 20, Sch 20*, with effect from 1 December 1999. The subscriptions which, in accordance with *s 94(3)*, were previously disregarded for VAT purposes, are exempted with effect from the same date by *VATA 1994, Sch 9, Group 9, Item 1(e)*, introduced by the *VAT (Subscriptions to Trade Unions, Professional and Other Public Interest Bodies) Order 1999 (SI 1999 No 2834)*. For details, see VAT Information Sheet 11/99, dated December 1999. For cases concerning *VATA 1994, Sch 9, Group 9* (Trade unions, professional and public interest bodies) see 60 TRADE UNIONS, PROFESSIONAL AND PUBLIC INTEREST BODIES.

The cases in this chapter are arranged under the following headings.

Whether VATA 1994, s 94(2)(a) applicable 13.1–13.16
The taxation of the receipts of a club, etc.
    Annual subscriptions 13.17–13.27
    Receipts other than annual subscriptions 13.28–13.41
Other matters 13.42–13.47

WHETHER VATA 1994, s 94(2)(a) APPLICABLE

13.1   **Village development association.** An association was incorporated, as a company limited by guarantee, under a scheme for developing a large village with some 2,000 houses. The association comprised 16 'consultant members' and 18 'representative members', appointed by societies established for each of the 'neighbourhood areas' into which the village was divided. Its principal activities were the upkeep of amenity land in the village, providing and maintaining street lighting, running a village sports ground and running a village hall. Its principal income consisted of payments from all houseowners in the area under covenants which formed part of the Deeds of Transfer under which they acquired their houses. The Commissioners issued a ruling that the company was an association providing facilities to its members and was carrying on a business by virtue of what is now *VATA 1994, s 94(2)(a)*. The tribunal allowed the company's appeal against this decision, holding that the houseowners to whom its services were supplied were not its members. 'Member' could not be extended to mean any person who had entered into a contractual relationship with the association. *New Ash Green Village Association Ltd, [1976] VATTR 63 (VTD 245)*. (*Note.* See *Manor Forstal Residents Society Ltd*, 13.2 below, for an appeal by one of the neighbourhood area societies.)

13.2   **Association of local residents.** A new village was divided into a number of 'neighbourhood areas' and a society was established as a residents' association for each of the areas. Each society was registered under the *Industrial and Provident Societies Act 1965*, its members being the owners of houses in its area. It was financed by members' subscriptions and its main activities were the upkeep of the amenity land in its area and the periodical external redecoration of members' houses. The tribunal upheld the Commissioners' contention that it was an association providing facilities available to its members and hence carrying on a business by virtue of what is now *VATA 1994, s 94(2)(a)*. *Manor Forstal Residents Society Ltd, [1976] VATTR 63 (VTD 245)*. (*Note.* The case was heard with *New Ash Green Village Association Ltd*, 13.1 above.)

13.3   **Members' club operating 'timeshare' accommodation.** A members' club operated a holiday complex, comprising 26 self-contained units. It had about 1,300 members, each of which were entitled to one week's holiday at the complex each year. The members were required to pay an annual contribution to a central fund which was used to cover the cost of wages, laundry and general maintenance and management. The club registered for VAT from 1991, but applied for deregistration in 1993. The Commissioners rejected the application, on the basis that the effect of what is now *VATA 1994, s 94(2)(a)* was that the club was deemed to be carrying on a business. The tribunal dismissed the club's appeal against this decision, holding that the club was within *s 94(2)(a)*, and was making supplies for consideration. Furthermore, these supplies did not qualify for exemption under *Article 13A1(f)* of the *EC Sixth Directive. Stichting Uitvoering Financiële Acties (SUFA) v Staatssecretaris van Financiën*, 21.146 EUROPEAN COMMUNITY LAW, applied. *The Regency Villas Owners Club, LON/95/305 (VTD 16525)*.

13.4   **Company operating 'timeshare' accommodation.** The owners of a 'timeshare' holiday complex formed a limited company to maintain the accommodation at the complex. Each owner held one share in the company. The Commissioners issued a ruling that the company was carrying on a business and was required to account for VAT. The company appealed, contending that its activities were not carried on on a commercial basis. The tribunal dismissed the appeal, holding that the supplies were within *VATA 1994, s 94(2)(a)*. *Dicta* of Lord Emslie in *Morrison's Academy Boarding Houses Association*, 7.1 BUSINESS, applied. *Scandinavian Village Ltd, EDN/99/216 (VTD 16961)*.

13.5   **Canteen at fire station.** Canteen facilities were provided at a fire station. The fire service provided the canteen, cooking equipment and the cooks, and paid £1 per week to an operational fireman to act as 'mess manager'. As such he signed the accounts of the canteen which, although described as a club, was in fact very loosely organised with no constitution, rules, committee or officers. Anyone at the fire station could use the canteen and prices were fixed to cover the cost of the food supplied. The Commissioners issued a ruling that the club was required to register for VAT. The tribunal allowed the club's appeal, holding on the evidence that the canteen was not run by a club or organisation within what is now *VATA 1994, s 94(2)(a)*. The canteen was run by the mess manager, who performed his duties as an employee or agent of the fire authority. *Nottingham Fire Service Messing Club, [1977] VATTR 1 (VTD 348)*.

13.6   **Working Men's Club.** An incorporated Industrial and Provident Society provided the usual facilities of a Workmen's Club and Institute, including the provision of alcoholic drinks and recreational facilities. The facilities were available to members who were required to hold one 50p share in the Club and pay an annual subscription. The Commissioners issued a ruling that VAT was chargeable on members' subscriptions (including the payments for the shares). The tribunal dismissed the club's appeal, holding that the subscriptions were consideration for the club's provision of facilities or advantages available to members. *Southchurch Workingmen's Club & Institute Ltd, MAN/78/40 (VTD 613)*. (*Note*. The tribunal also held that the club was not within what is now *VATA 1994, Sch 9, Group 9, Item 1(e)*.)

13.7   **Association to raise funds for Olympics.** The British Olympic Association reclaimed input tax on the cost of supplying clothing for British competitors in the 1976 Olympics, and on fees charged by advertising agents who had helped it in fund-raising appeals. The Commissioners rejected the claim and the tribunal dismissed the Association's appeal. The British competitors at the Games were not, as such, members of the Association and accordingly the provision of clothing for them was not for the purpose of any deemed business of providing facilities available to the Association's members. Furthermore, applying *Morrison's Academy Boarding Houses Association*, 7.1 BUSINESS, the Association was not carrying on a business in the general sense of the term. *British Olympic Association, [1979] VATTR 122 (VTD 779).*

13.8 **English-Speaking Union.** The English-Speaking Union (ESU) was established by Royal Charter and registered as a charity, with the principal object of promoting the 'mutual advancement of the education of the English-speaking peoples of the world'. In return for their subscription, members were entitled to take part in ESU's activities. With two exceptions, non-members had an equal right to participate in, or take advantage of, these activities. The two exceptions were that the ESU journal, published every few months, was issued free to members but non-members had to pay for it, and that members could obtain contacts and introduction to other members, when travelling away from home. The Commissioners issued a decision that ESU was deemed to be carrying on a business by virtue of what is now *VATA 1994, s 94(2)(a)*, and the tribunal dismissed ESU's appeal. *The English-Speaking Union of the Commonwealth, [1980] VATTR 184 (VTD 1023).* (Note. The ESU would now probably qualify for exemption under *VATA 1994, Sch 9, Group 9, Item 1(e).*)

13.9 **Golf club—trust established to purchase course.** A golf club, which had previously held the leasehold of its course, established a trust to purchase the freehold. The trust divided the ownership into 750 units, 200 of which were allocated to the club and 550 of which were reserved for allocation to individual members, no member being entitled to more than one unit. No member was entitled to play golf on the course unless he was the holder of a unit. The Commissioners assessed the club on the basis that it was carrying on a business by providing the facilities of the golf course for consideration. The club appealed, contending that the facilities were provided by the trust which was a separate legal entity, and that it received no consideration for the supply of the units by the trust to the members. The CS rejected this contention and upheld the assessment, holding that it was the club which provided the facilities, the consideration for which was the members' subscriptions and the payments which the members made for units in the trust. *Lord Advocate v Largs Golf Club, CS [1985] STC 226.*

13.10 **Fund-raising association for Ironbridge Museum.** In 1968 the Ironbridge Museum Trust was established to preserve the history of the Ironbridge area. It was incorporated as a limited company and registered as a charity. A fund-raising association was also established, and was called the Friends of the Ironbridge Gorge Museum. In 1990 the Commissioners sought to register the Friends for VAT. The Friends appealed, contending that in law they were acting as agents of the Trust, that subscriptions from members included donations which were passed to the Trust and were not liable to VAT, and that any benefits received by members (such as free admission to sites and the receipt of a quarterly newsletter) were conferred by the Trust rather than by the Friends. The tribunal allowed the Friends' appeal, holding that the Friends were not 'quite on the same basis as a private members club'. In the case of a private members club, the subscriptions paid by members were consideration for facilities provided by the club. However, people joined the Friends not in order to receive facilities, but in order to make financial contributions to the Museum. Donations were not consideration for benefits or facilities, and were therefore outside the scope of VAT. Since any benefits received by members were supplied by the Trust rather than by the Friends, what is now *VATA 1994, s 94(2)(a)* did not apply and the Friends were not liable to be registered. *Friends of the Ironbridge Gorge Museum, [1991] VATTR 97 (VTD 5639).* (Note. For the Commissioners' practice following this decision, see Customs' VAT Manual, Part 6, chapter 3, section 6 annex, paragraph 12. The Commissioners take the view that parts of the decision are 'open to challenge' and are seeking 'a suitable test-case'.)

13.11   **Golf club—free membership given to honorary members—whether VATA 1994, s 94(2)(a) applicable.**   A limited company was established under the Business Expansion Scheme to operate a golf club. It gave honorary membership of the club to 64 of its shareholders. The Commissioners issued an assessment on the basis that the grant of honorary membership was a taxable supply by virtue of what is now *VATA 1994, s 94(2)(a)*, and that the value of the supply was the normal subscription paid by members who were not shareholders. The club appealed, contending that the only supply was the issue of shares, which was exempt from VAT. The tribunal allowed the club's appeal, holding on the evidence that the shareholders' 'paramount purpose in buying the shares was to invest in the company with a view to profit', and that the club had offered honorary membership to such shareholders as an 'incentive to invest'. *Oldbus Ltd*, 26.26 FINANCE, applied; *Exeter Golf & Country Club*, 13.31 below, distinguished. *Hinckley Golf Club Ltd*, *[1992] VATTR 259 (VTD 9527)*.

13.12   **County football association—income from fines—application of VATA 1994, s 94(2)(a).**   The Northamptonshire Football Association was registered for VAT, and reclaimed the whole of its input tax. A significant proportion of its income came from fines imposed on players who had been cautioned or dismissed from the field of play. The Commissioners issued a ruling that part of the Association's input tax should be apportioned to the receipt of fines, which related to a disciplinary activity which should be treated as outside the scope of VAT, and was not deductible. The Association appealed, contending that it was carrying on a business within what is now *VATA 1994, s 94(2)(a)* and that all its input tax related to its business activities. The tribunal accepted this contention and allowed the appeal, holding that the enforcement of the rules of the game was 'an essential element of the administration of the playing of the game'. The enforcement of the rules was 'an advantage of membership' and 'an obligation of the Association undertaken in favour of each of the members in return for ... the payment of their membership fees and subscriptions'. It was thus deemed to be part of the carrying on of a business, within what is now *VATA 1994, s 94(2)(a)*. *Scottish Solicitors' Discipline Tribunal*, 7.98 BUSINESS, distinguished. *Northamptonshire Football Association, LON/94/727 (VTD 12936)*.

13.13   **Rugby club.**   A rugby club was established as a non-profit-making body, although it charged spectators 25p for admission to first-team matches, and sold match programmes. It arranged for the construction of a new changing-room block (including separate toilets for spectators), and reclaimed input tax on this. The Commissioners issued assessments to recover the tax, on the basis that the club was not carrying on any business. The tribunal allowed the club's appeal, holding that it was carrying on a business within *VATA 1994, s 94(2)(a)*, and was making taxable supplies which were 'directly referable to the construction of the building'. The fact that the club was a non-profit-making body was not conclusive, since 'it was carrying on business (*sic*) and the construction of the changing-room block was in furtherance of that deemed business'. *Clwb Rygbi Nant Conwy, MAN/97/864 (VTD 16376)*. (*Note*. The tribunal also held that the club's supplies were excluded from exemption by *Sch 9, Group 1, Item 1(l)* and *(m)*.)

13.14   **Association of taxi drivers.**   In *Eastbourne Town Radio Cars Association*, 58.31 SUPPLY, the CA held that an association of taxi drivers was within *VATA 1994, s 94(2)(a)*.

13.15 Clubs, Associations and Organisations

13.15 Company campaigning for welfare of farm animals. Two companies had been established to campaign for the welfare of farm animals. They were registered as a group for VAT purposes. One of the companies (S) was limited by guarantee and received subscriptions from supporters of the companies' aims, but the actual campaigning was undertaken by the other company (C), which was the representative member of the group for VAT. S owned 50% of the shares in C, the other 50% being owned by an individual. Members of the public who paid subscriptions to S received a quarterly magazine, published by C. C reclaimed input tax in respect of campaigning expenditure. The Commissioners issued an assessment to recover the tax on the basis that the companies' campaigning activities did not constitute a business. C appealed, contending that they should be treated as a business for VAT purposes by virtue of *VATA 1994, s 94(2)(a)*. The tribunal rejected this contention, holding on the evidence that members of the public who subscribed to S were not 'members' of S, as required by *s 94(2)(a)*, and that the subscriptions which they paid did not give them any contractual rights. *New Ash Green Village Association Ltd*, 13.1 above, applied. *Compassion in World Farming Ltd, [1997] VATDR 281 (VTD 15204)*. (*Note.* The tribunal directed that some of the assessments under appeal should be discharged as they had been incorrectly computed and had not been made to the best of the Commissioners' judgment.)

13.16 Society for defence of hunting. An association was formed in 1930 to defend deer-hunting, stag-hunting, and similar 'blood sports', which some Members of Parliament had sought to outlaw. Between 1991 and 1995 it was active in opposing proposed legislation on this subject. It was registered for VAT and reclaimed input tax on its expenditure. It accounted for output tax on a proportion of members' subscriptions, the balance of the subscriptions being treated as attributable to exempt supplies of insurance or zero-rated supplies of printed matter. In 1993 the Commissioners issued assessments to recover some of the association's input tax, on the basis that much of the expenditure related to general propaganda which did not provide any 'facility or advantage' to the association's members and was not to be treated as a business activity. The association appealed, contending that, by campaigning against proposed legislation which would outlaw its members' leisure activities, it was providing its members with 'facilities or advantages', which constituted the carrying on of a business by virtue of *VATA 1994, s 94(2)(a)*. The tribunal accepted this contention and allowed the appeal, and the CA upheld this decision. The fact that the expenditure benefited people who participated in blood sports without being members of the association was not conclusive. On the evidence, the tribunal had been entitled to conclude that the association's propaganda provided its members with 'facilities or advantages', so that the association was entitled to reclaim input tax on its expenditure. The term 'facilities and advantages' should be construed widely. There was a direct link between the members' subscriptions and the association's campaigning activities. *C & E Commrs v British Field Sports Society, CA [1998] STC 315; [1998] 1 WLR 962; [1998] 2 All ER 1003*.

THE TAXATION OF THE RECEIPTS OF A CLUB, ETC.

Annual subscriptions

13.17 Whether subscription covers more than one supply. The Automobile Association provided members with an annual handbook and a magazine. The Commissioners issued a ruling that the whole of members' subscriptions was chargeable at the standard rate. The Association appealed, contending that part of the subscriptions were attributable to the supply of the handbook and magazine, which were zero-rated under what is now *VATA 1994, Sch 8, Group 3*. The tribunal accepted this contention and allowed the appeal, and the QB upheld this decision as one of fact. *C & E Commrs v The Automobile Association, QB [1974] STC 192; [1974] 1 WLR 1447; [1974] 1 All ER 1257.* (*Note. Obiter dicta* of Lord Widgery CJ, with regard to the distinction between questions of law and questions of fact, were disapproved by Lord Denning MR in the subsequent case of *British Railways Board*, 62.5 TRANSPORT.)

13.18   A similar decision was reached in a case concerning a society which had been formed to further the knowledge of alpine plants. Its principal activity was the supply to members of an annual handbook and a quarterly bulletin. The QB held that part of the subscriptions was attributable to these publications, and was zero-rated under what is now *VATA 1994, Sch 8, Group 3. Barton v C & E Commrs, QB [1974] STC 200; [1974] 1 WLR 1447; [1974] 3 All ER 337.*

13.19   The Institute of Chartered Foresters was established as a non-profit-making body to provide training in, and information about, forestry. In accounting for tax, it treated part of its members' subscriptions as attributable to the zero-rated supplies of a quarterly magazine (so that it could reclaim the relevant input tax). The Commissioners issued a ruling that the magazine was part of a single supply of services to the Institute's members, which failed to qualify for zero-rating but was exempt from VAT. The tribunal upheld the Commissioners' ruling and dismissed the Institute's appeal. *British Sky Broadcasting plc*, 5.72 BOOKS, ETC. applied; *The Automobile Association*, 13.17 above, distinguished. *Institute of Chartered Foresters, EDN/00/51 (VTD 16884).*

13.20   **Yacht club—whether subscriptions entirely exempt from VAT.**   See *Royal Thames Yacht Club*, 23.26 EXEMPTIONS: MISCELLANEOUS.

13.21   **Golf club subscription—whether exempt under Sch 9, Group 1.**   See *Banstead Downs Golf Club*, 39.29 LAND.

13.22   **Golf club—entrance subscriptions.**   A golf club did not account for tax on the 'entrance subscriptions' which it charged new members. The Commissioners issued an assessment charging tax on them, and the tribunal dismissed the club's appeal, holding that the subscriptions were part of the consideration for the facilities which the club supplied to its members. *Downes Crediton Golf Club, CAR/79/203 (VTD 868).*

13.23   **Golf club charging reduced subscriptions to members making loans to club—value of supply for VAT purposes.**   A golf club had raised finance through loans from members. In return for these loans, it charged a reduced level of annual subscription to such members. The Commissioners considered that, in such cases, the club should account for VAT on the full subscription rate charged to members who had not made loans to the club. The club appealed, contending that the value of the supply should be the reduced subscription actually charged, plus an amount equal to the annual interest that would be paid in the open market on loans such as those made to the club. The tribunal accepted this contention and allowed the club's appeal. *Exeter Golf Club*, 13.31 below, applied. *West Essex Golf Club, [1992] VATTR 35 (VTD 7321).*

13.24   **Sports and social club owning premises including playing fields—whether subscriptions liable to VAT.**   A limited company, describing itself as an 'athletic association' but described by the tribunal as a sports and social club, owned premises including playing fields and pitches. It established a fund, described as a sports fund, to which its members paid subscriptions. The Commissioners issued an assessment on the basis that by providing its facilities the club was carrying on a business and that the fund subscriptions were liable to VAT. The company appealed, contending that there was no direct link between the payment of subscriptions and the provision of facilities, and that the subscriptions were in the nature of donations. The tribunal dismissed the appeal, holding that on the evidence, the link between the payment of subscriptions and the provision of facilities was clearly discernible. *Belvedere & Calder Vale Sports Club*, 13.39 below, applied. *Royal Ulster Constabulary Athletic Association Ltd, [1989] VATTR 17 (VTD 3529).*

13.25   **Country club—whether subscriptions for licence to occupy land.**   See *Trewby*, 39.30 LAND.

13.26   **Holiday club—increase in subscriptions to meet special expenditure.**   See *Little Spain Club*, 39.31 LAND.

13.27   **Annual subscriptions—time at which VAT chargeable.**   See *East Kilbride Golf Club*, 58.323 SUPPLY.

Receipts other than annual subscriptions

13.28   **Club bar sales—whether supplies.**   An unincorporated members' club sold alcoholic drinks to its members. It applied for its VAT registration to be cancelled. The Commissioners rejected the application as the club's supplies exceeded the registration threshold. The club appealed, contending that, since the members were already part-owners of its stock of drinks, it was not supplying them to its members. The tribunal rejected this contention and dismissed the appeal, and the QB upheld this decision, holding on the evidence that the club was supplying its drinks to its members, notwithstanding that the members were already part-owners of the club's stock. *Carlton Lodge Club v C & E Commrs, QB [1974] STC 507; [1975] 1 WLR 66; [1974] 3 All ER 798.*

13.29   **Levy on members to meet capital expenditure.**   A club which was heavily in debt foresaw capital expenditure of up to £50,000 on its premises, partly to comply with fire precaution regulations. Its rules were altered to permit levies on members to meet its special needs, to obviate an increase in the annual subscriptions. Following this it made a levy of £7.50 per member for its financial year ending 31 January 1975. The Commissioners issued an assessment on the basis that the levies were chargeable at the standard rate. The club appealed. The tribunal dismissed the appeal, holding that the levies were to meet expenditure to provide the facilities available to the members and were therefore taxable by virtue of what is now *VATA 1994, s 94(2)(a). The Royal Scottish Automobile Club, EDN/76/7A (VTD 257).*

13.30   **Bonds issued as a condition of membership.**   A company ran a members' golf and country club, with various classes of membership. Full members and social members were required, in addition to paying the usual annual subscriptions, to subscribe for a bond in the company within 28 days of becoming members. The bond was unsecured, carried no interest, and, with regard to these classes of Members, not transferable; if for any reason the holder ceased to be a member, the Bond was cancelled after five years. The bond had a face value of £350 but the committee required members to pay more than this. The Commissioners issued a ruling that output tax was payable on the amounts which the members paid for the bonds, and the club appealed. The tribunal held that the bond was a 'security for money' within the meaning of what is now *VATA 1994, Sch 9, Group 5, Item 1* and that the real character of the transaction was a composite supply to the member comprising the bond (which was exempt) and the grant of the right to remain a member (which was standard-rated). The appeal was therefore stood over to enable the parties to arrive at a suitable apportionment under what is now *VATA 1994, s 24(5). Dyrham Park Country Club Ltd, [1978] VATTR 244 (VTD 700).* (*Note.* There was no further public hearing of the appeal.)

13.31   **Interest-free loans by club members.**   A limited company operated a golf club. It required its members, in addition to paying subscriptions, to make interest-free loans to the club to help finance its development. The loans were repayable should the member die, cease to be a full member, or reach the age of 65. The Commissioners issued an assessment on the basis that the club was required to account for output tax on the consideration which it received from members, and that this consideration included not only the amounts of the loans but also interest at the minimum lending rate. The tribunal upheld the assessment, and the CA dismissed the club's appeal against this decision. Cumming-Bruce LJ observed that 'in connection with the market value the Commissioners have been modest in their assessment of tax on their calculation because it might be thought that the hypothetical lender would not lend his money at less than the minimum lending rate plus 2%'. *Exeter Golf & Country Club Ltd v C & E Commrs, CA [1981] STC 211. (Note.* With regard to the valuation of the consideration, see the subsequent case of *Harleyford Golf Club plc*, 63.121 VALUATION, in which the tribunal held that the consideration should be taken to be interest at the minimum lending rate, declining to follow the *obiter dicta* of Cumming-Bruce LJ on the grounds that they were inconsistent with the subsequent CJEC decisions in *Naturally Yours Cosmetics Ltd (No 2)*, 21.128 EUROPEAN COMMUNITY LAW, and *Empire Stores Ltd*, 21.129 EUROPEAN COMMUNITY LAW.)

13.32   Members of a golf club were called on to make a levy or interest-free loan to meet the cost of extensive work on the clubhouse. The contribution was repayable should the member die or resign before 1 October 1980 but otherwise would then be 'deemed to be a gift to the club'. The tribunal held that the contribution was an interest-free loan and was chargeable to VAT. *Exeter Golf & Country Club*, 13.31 above, applied. *Pollok Golf Club, EDN/80/4 (VTD 1044).*

13.33   Members of a golf club were required to make interest-free loans as a condition of membership. The loans were primarily to enable the club to purchase the golf course of which it had hitherto held a tenancy. The Commissioners issued an assessment charging tax on the market value of the loans. The tribunal upheld the assessment and dismissed the club's appeal, holding that, since making the loan was a condition of membership, it was part of the consideration for the supplies made by the club. Although the member was given a letter of acknowledgement of his loan, this was not a 'security for money' or a 'security' such as a debenture. The function of the document was 'purely evidential and its commercial value were it to be assigned would be negligible'. *Hamilton Golf Club, EDN/80/65 (VTD 1150). (Note.* For a subsequent case in which the purchase of debentures in a golf club was held to be taxable consideration for supplies of services, see *Harleyford Golf Club plc*, 63.121 VALUATION.)

13.34   A similar decision was reached in a case where all playing members of a golf club were required as a condition of membership to make a compulsory loan to the club. The tribunal held that the loan was part of the consideration for the facilities which the club supplied. *Blackmoor Golf Club, LON/83/251 (VTD 2027).*

13.35   An unincorporated members' club provided facilities for its members, including a golf course and club building. Having previously held the course as lessee, the club acquired the freehold in 1976. A scheme was devised to raise the necessary finance by means of interest-free loans from members, or the payment of a subscription surcharge as a condition of membership if no loan was made. The club accounted for VAT on the subscription surcharges but not on the loans. The Commissioners issued an assessment charging output tax on the open market value of all loans, whether compulsory or voluntary. The tribunal upheld the assessment and dismissed the club's appeal, holding that the consideration for the loans was the continued supply of the club's facilities, and that the club's motive in raising the loans was irrelevant. *Rothley Park Golf Club, MAN/85/231 (VTD 2074).*

13.36   **Golf club—sale of debentures to members.**   See *Harleyford Golf Club plc*, 26.31 FINANCE and 63.121 VALUATION.

13.37   **Football club—supplies of season tickets to bondholders.**   See *The Arsenal Football Club plc*, 63.120 VALUATION.

13.38   **Rugby club—disposal of right to apply for international match tickets.**   A rugby club purchased from the Welsh Rugby Union interest-free debentures, each giving the club, *inter alia*, the right to one seat at international matches at Cardiff Arms Park (on payment for the ticket). The club then informed its members that in return for a 'donation' of £250 a member could have the right to apply for a ticket for the internationals for 25 years, to be paid for at their face value in the normal way. The member also had certain rights to extend the option after the 25 years. The option was not transferable should the member die. The Commissioners issued a ruling that the £250 was consideration for the supply of the right to apply for tickets and was standard-rated. The tribunal dismissed the club's appeal. *Abercynon Rugby Football Club, [1982] VATTR 166 (VTD 1286).*

13.39   **Sports club—match fees.**   A sports club provided its members with facilities for playing cricket, rugby union and association football. Its rules provided for the payment of annual subscriptions, but in addition each of the three main sports sections fixed 'match fees' for members actually playing in a match. These fees, which were not referred to in the club rules, were intended to cover match expenses such as travel, hire of pitches and referees' fees and expenses. The team captain, or other sports section representative who collected them, defrayed petty cash expenses out of them and paid the balance to the club treasurer. The Commissioners issued an assessment charging tax on these match fees, and the club appealed, contending that they were donations. The tribunal rejected this contention and dismissed the appeal. Applying the reasoning in *British Railways Board*, 62.5 TRANSPORT, both the annual subscriptions and the match fees together constituted the consideration for the provision by the Club of the facilities available to its members. *Belvedere & Calder Vale Sports Club, MAN/79/129 (VTD 931).*

13.40   **Rugby club match fees—whether donations.**   A rugby club levied match fees of £2, which were collected by the team captain and were used to pay the referee's expenses and to buy refreshments (principally beer) for the visiting team. Any surplus was paid to the club treasurer. The club did not account for VAT on the amounts collected, and the Commissioners issued an assessment charging tax on them. The club appealed, contending that the fees should be regarded as voluntary donations and as outside the scope of VAT. The tribunal accepted this contention and allowed the appeal, holding that the fees did not 'represent consideration for goods or services'. *Belvedere & Calder Vale Sports Club*, 13.39 above, was distinguished, on the grounds that the match fees in that case were required and formally fixed by the relevant section of the club. The chairman also doubted the correctness of the decision in *Belvedere*, and expressed the view that *British Railways Board*, 62.5 TRANSPORT, which had been regarded as an important precedent in *Belvedere*, was not 'applicable in the case of match fees or players' donations'. The chairman observed that 'there is no nexus between a voluntary kitty to pay the referee his travelling expenses and buy refreshments for the players of both teams, and the general club charges or subscription to enable the member to enjoy the privilege thereof'. *Sleaford Rugby Football Club, MAN/92/213 (VTD 9844).*

13.41   **Rugby club—bar stock acquired from cricket club using same premises.**   A rugby club operated a bar from September to April each year. During the intervening months the same bar was operated by a cricket club. A loan account was operated between the clubs. The rugby club was registered for VAT but the cricket club was not. The rugby club's treasurer deducted input tax in respect of bar stock which it acquired from the cricket club. The Commissioners issued an assessment to recover the input tax and the tribunal dismissed the club's appeal. Since the cricket club was not registered for VAT, the rugby club was not entitled to claim input tax on supplies from it. *Baildon Rugby Union Football Club, MAN/88/ 359 (VTD 3239).*

OTHER MATTERS

13.42   **Whether sports clubs separate entities.**   The Commissioners sought to register two bowling clubs, which had the same secretary and operated from the same premises, on the basis that they formed two branches of a single entity. The secretary lodged appeals, contending that the clubs were separate entities, with separate memberships and separate records and accounts, and that their supplies were below the registration threshold. The tribunal accepted the clubs' evidence and allowed their appeals. *AG Hayhoe (for Watchet Bowling Club & Watchet Indoor Bowling Club), LON/80/341 (VTD 1026).*

13.43   A sports club (C) comprised a number of 'section clubs' covering separate sports such as rugby and hockey. These section clubs used C's premises and facilities but had their own rules, annual general meetings, officers and accounts. The tribunal held that the 'section clubs' were separate entities. Accordingly, the payments they received from their own members were not liable to VAT, but the sums which C received from the 'section clubs' were liable to VAT. *Cambuslang Athletic Club, EDN/82/39 (VTD 1592).*

13.44   An 'old boys' association' of former pupils at a high school had three affiliated sports clubs; a football club, a cricket club, and a tennis club. The Commissioners issued a ruling that the association was liable to account for tax on supplies made by the clubs, on the basis that the association and the clubs were a single legal person. The association appealed, contending that the three sports clubs were separate legal entities. The tribunal reviewed the club rules and allowed the association's appeal, holding that the three sports clubs were separate legal entities. *Watchet Bowling Club*, 13.42 above, and *Cambuslang Athletic Club*, 13.43 above, applied; *Belvedere & Calder Vale Sports Club*, 13.39 above, distinguished. *Old Parkinsonians Association, LON/ 92/2573 (VTD 10908).*

13.45   **Whether limited company and unincorporated association to be treated as same legal entity.**   A limited company had been incorporated in 1930 to hold the assets of a golf club, which had previously been an unincorporated association. The club continued to function from the same premises, which were owned by the limited company. The same people comprised the club's management committee and the company's board of directors. In 1975, when income from gaming machines became liable to VAT, there were two such machines on the premises. One of these was owned by the club and the other was owned by the limited company. The Commissioners issued an assessment on the company, charging it to tax on the takings from both machines. The company appealed, contending that it was not liable to tax on the takings from the machine which was owned by the unincorporated association. The tribunal accepted this contention and allowed the appeal, holding that the company and the association were separate legal entities. *Dartford Golf Club Ltd, LON/83/37 (VTD 1576).* (*Note.* The Commissioners might now have recourse to a direction under *VATA 1994, Sch 1 para 2*. For cases concerning this provision, see 53.95 *et seq.* REGISTRATION.)

13.46 Clubs, Associations and Organisations

13.46 **Institute of Chartered Accountants—whether licensing activities a business or economic activity.** See *The Institute of Chartered Accountants in England and Wales*, 58.129 SUPPLY.

13.47 **Overpaid VAT refunded to members' club—whether club obliged to pay proportion of refund to former member.** Under the *VAT (Sport, Physical Education and Fund-Raising Events) Order 1994 (SI 1994 No 687)*, the scope of what is now *VATA 1994, Sch 9, Group 10* was extended with effect from 1 April 1994, to exempt services supplied by non-profit-making sports clubs to their members. (Such services had previously been standard-rated under UK law.) Clubs were allowed to backdate their exemption to January 1990, and were permitted to reclaim VAT which they had overpaid from January 1990 to April 1994. In a case where a members' golf club had received a substantial refund, a former member of the club took County Court proceedings against the club demanding repayment of the VAT which had been charged on his annual subscriptions from 1990 to 1993. The County Court rejected his claim. The club was a separate entity from its individual members. If a members' club were to fail to pay VAT to the Commissioners, the individual members would not be liable to pay the tax due. Under *VATA 1994, s 19(2)*, the consideration for membership of the club was the amount of the subscription inclusive of any VAT charged. A members' club was at liberty to vote to return overpaid VAT to those members from whom it was originally collected, but was under no obligation to do so. *Winfield v Stowmarket Golf Club Ltd, Ipswich County Court 22 May 1995 unreported.*

14   Collection and Enforcement

Cross-reference.

See also 46 PENALTIES: CRIMINAL OFFENCES.

The cases in this chapter are arranged under the following headings.

POWER TO REQUIRE SECURITY (VATA 1994, Sch 11 para 4)

Cases where the appellant was successful

Change in active directors

14.1   The Commissioners issued a notice requiring security of £12,900 from a company. The company's controlling director had not been involved with any other companies, but his parents had been directors of three companies which had become insolvent with substantial VAT liabilities. The tribunal allowed the company's appeal against the notice, observing that neither of the director's parents were directors or shareholders of the appellant company. *Mayor Fashions Ltd, LON/89/440Z (VTD 4429).*

14.2   The Commissioners issued a notice requiring security of £6,500 from an electronics company. The company's managing director had been involved with two previous companies which had become insolvent. The company appealed, contending that the notice was unreasonable because its VAT payments were up to date, and the director had ceased his involvement with one of the previous companies well before it became insolvent. The tribunal accepted the company's evidence and allowed the appeal. *Exact Electronics Ltd, LON/92/2754A (VTD 11391).*

14.3   The Commissioners issued a notice requiring security of £139,500 from a company (C) which carried on business as a dealer in imported carpets. The officer responsible for the notice acted on the basis that one of C's two directors (J) had previously been a director of another company (T) which had ceased to trade while owing unpaid VAT of £295,000. C appealed, contending that J had never been a director of T, although his father had been T's managing director. The tribunal allowed C's appeal, holding that the Commissioners' decision to require security was flawed because it was based on incorrect assumptions. *UK Carpets Ltd, LON/93/768A (VTD 11526).*

14.4   The Commissioners issued a notice requiring security from a company which operated a restaurant. The reason of the notice was that one of the company's employees (N) had previously been a partner in a firm which had owned the same restaurant, and that the partnership owed VAT of more than £200,000. The company appealed, contending that the requirement was unreasonable since it employed N as a chef and he was no longer involved in the management of the restaurant. The tribunal accepted the company's evidence and allowed the appeal, holding that the decision to require security was unreasonable. *Auldbrook Ltd, EDN/93/164 (VTD 11717).*

14.5   A similar decision was reached in *Tidesave Ltd (t/a Yu Chinese Restaurant), EDN/97/89 (VTD 15418).*

14.6   The Commissioners issued a notice requiring security of £19,600 from a company, on the grounds that its business was managed by an individual (P) who had been adjudged bankrupt owing more than £100,000 in unpaid VAT and surcharges. The company appealed, contending that the notice was unreasonable since, although P had previously been a director, he was in poor health and had resigned his directorship before the company had registered for VAT. The tribunal accepted the company's evidence and allowed the appeal. *BP Stone & Brickwork Contractors Ltd, MAN/93/1215 (VTD 11722).*

14.7   In May 1994 the Commissioners issued a notice requiring security of more than £800,000 from a company (V), which had been incorporated as a joint venture by a Swedish company (O) and a Dutch company (P) to trade as a distributor of petroleum products. The reason given for the notice was that two of V's directors had previously been directors of another company (N) carrying on a similar business which had been deregistered in November 1993 while owing more than £1,000,000 in unpaid VAT. V appealed, contending that the notice was unreasonable, since the controlling shareholder of N was not involved in V, O had not had any connection with N, and P had merely been a supplier of N. The two directors referred to in the notice were the controlling directors of P, but had only been appointed directors of N in December 1992, at a time when N was already in serious financial difficulties. The tribunal reviewed the evidence in detail and allowed V's appeal, noting that the ownership of N had 'nothing in common' with that of V, and that V had provided guarantees from a Dutch bank, so that 'the possibility of V being a likely risk to the revenue' was 'very remote'. *VSP Marketing Ltd, LON/94/794A (VTD 12636). (Note.* Costs were awarded to the appellant on the indemnity basis—see 2.332 APPEALS.)

14.8   The Commissioners issued a notice requiring security of £50,000 from a company (S) which operated a cellular telephone business, after discovering that a previous company (E) with two of the same directors had become insolvent owing more than £140,000 in unpaid VAT. S appealed, contending that the requirement was unreasonable, as its controlling director had not been involved with E. The tribunal allowed the appeal, holding that, since the officer responsible for the notice had ignored the fact that S's controlling director had not been involved with E, the requirement was unreasonable. *Smartone Connect Ltd, LON/94/703A (VTD 12789).*

14.9   The Commissioners issued a notice requiring security of £12,500 from a company (G) which carried on a road haulage business. The company's controlling director (B) had previously been a director of another company with a similar name operating a similar business. B and his wife had had a 50% shareholding in that company. However, he had fallen out with the other directors, and that company had ceased trading and gone into voluntary liquidation. G appealed against the notice, contending that it was unreasonable, since B had not been responsible for the administrative and financial affairs of the previous company. The tribunal accepted this contention and allowed the appeal. *Greyhound Transport (UK) Ltd, LON/94/1365A (VTD 13216).*

14.10   A similar decision was reached in *Roundstar Ltd, LON/x (VTD 15471)*.

14.11   The Commissioners issued a notice requiring security of £79,000 from a building company on the basis that two of its senior employees had been directors of previous companies which had become insolvent while owing substantial amounts of unpaid VAT. The company appealed, contending that the requirement was unreasonable because neither of the employees concerned were 'employed by it in such a role as to affect its financial viability', and its controlling director had not been involved in any of the companies in question. The tribunal accepted the company's evidence and allowed the appeal. *John Dee Ltd*, 14.28 below, and *Elliott*, 14.36 below, applied. *CSL Building Services Ltd, LON/95/3123 (VTD 14193)*.

14.12   The Commissioners issued notices requiring security from two associated companies which operated licensed premises, on the grounds that the two directors of the companies (who were sisters) had previously been directors of other businesses which had become deregistered or insolvent with substantial VAT arrears. The companies appealed, contending that although the sisters had been directors of the previous companies, they had played no part in the management of those companies, which had effectively been controlled by their parents, and that their parents were not involved in the management of the appellant companies. The tribunal accepted the companies' evidence and allowed the appeals. *Millennium Catering & Pub Co Ltd, EDN/95/353; Jointexit Ltd, EDN/96/15 (VTD 14275)*.

14.13   The Commissioners issued a notice requiring security of £16,400 from a company (S) operating a shopfitting business, on the grounds that the principal director of S had previously been the sales director of a company operating a similar business which had gone into liquidation owing more than £60,000 in unpaid VAT. S appealed, contending that the notice was unreasonable because the failure of the previous company was attributable to one of the other directors, who was not a director of S. The tribunal accepted this evidence and allowed the appeal. *Soundmethods Ltd, MAN/96/353 (VTD 14523)*.

14.14   The Commissioners issued a notice requiring security from a company supplying catering equipment, on the grounds that its principal director (R) had previously been involved in a company which had ceased trading while owing VAT. The company appealed, contending that the requirement was unreasonable because the failure of the previous company had been attributable to the behaviour of R's husband, who had also been a director of that company, and who had become 'very vindictive' towards R following the breakdown of their marriage. The tribunal accepted the company's evidence and allowed the appeal. *Central Catering Equipment Ltd, MAN/96/536 (VTD 14605)*.

14.15   The Commissioners issued a notice requiring security from a company carrying on business as a cleaning contractor, after discovering that one of its employees (J) had previously been a director of two companies which had traded from the same premises and had ceased to trade while owing unpaid VAT. The company appealed, contending that the notice was unreasonable because its controlling director had not been involved in either of the previous companies, and that J was merely an employee and was not involved in the management of the company. The tribunal accepted the company's evidence and allowed the appeal. The chairman observed that 'there may be occasions when the Commissioners have to react with great speed to the tell-tale signs of imminent insolvency' but that 'it is only the most extreme of circumstances that could justify the taking of the decision without giving the taxpayer the opportunity to explain his side of the picture'. *Restorex Ltd, [1997] VATDR 402 (VTD 15014)*.

14.16 Collection and Enforcement

14.16 *Restorex Ltd*, 14.15 above, was applied in a subsequent case where the Commissioners issued a notice requiring security from a company of which the controlling director was a married woman, whose husband was in business as a sole trader with substantial arrears. The tribunal found that the Commissioners had failed to make enquiries before issuing the notice, and observed that 'however likely a requirement may have been, it has not been shown to our satisfaction that the decision would inevitably have been the same'. *LEBS Services Ltd, LON/97/1650 (VTD 15550)*.

Other cases

14.17 **Previous liquidation of company in similar ownership attributed to fire at premises.** The Commissioners issued a notice requiring security from a company in the clothing trade, on the grounds that the company secretary had previously been secretary of two companies in the same business which had gone into liquidation owing unpaid VAT. The company appealed, contending that the requirement was unreasonable since the company was trading profitably and one of the previous liquidations had been the result of a fire at the company's premises. The tribunal allowed the company's appeal, holding that the requirement was unreasonable. *Deltaview Ltd, LON/84/540 (VTD 1832, 1876)*.

14.18 **Previous liquidation of company in similar ownership attributed to non-payment by major customer.** The Commissioners issued a notice requiring security from a company on the basis that one of its directors had previously been a director of two other companies which had become insolvent owing VAT. The company appealed, contending that the insolvency of the two previous companies had been a result of late payment by a Borough Council, and that because of the experience of the two previous companies, it was not accepting contracts with local authorities. The tribunal allowed the appeal, finding that the company had a good compliance record and that it was unreasonable for the Commissioners to have required security. *Firepower Builders Ltd, LON/88/301Y (VTD 3358)*.

14.19 Two associated companies appealed against requirements for security, contending that the requirement was unreasonable because only one of the two companies was in arrears with its VAT, and those arrears were the result of delay in receiving payment from its major customer. The tribunal accepted the companies' evidence and allowed the appeals. *Century Supplies Ltd; Euro Catering Equipment Ltd, MAN/95/483, 2566 & 2574 (VTD 14375)*.

14.20 A company (C), which provided temporary staff to distribution businesses, suffered a large number of bad debts and became insolvent, owing VAT to the Commissioners. An associated company (S) provided temporary staff to specialised transport businesses. Following C's insolvency, the Commissioners issued a notice requiring security from S. S appealed, contending that the notice was unreasonable because its client base was completely different from that of C, its clients were 'large and creditworthy', and that it had an efficient financial management structure. The tribunal accepted S's evidence and allowed the appeal. *IP Chemical & Petroleum Services Ltd, LON/x (VTD 15530)*.

14.21 **Sole trader previously employee of liquidated company.** The Commissioners issued a notice requiring security of £4,500 from a sole trader, who had previously been employed by a company owned by his parents. This company had gone into liquidation with arrears of VAT. The trader appealed against the notice, contending that it was unreasonable to require security from him as he had not been responsible for the finances of his parents' company. The tribunal allowed the appeal, holding on the evidence that the Commissioners' decision to require security was unreasonable, applying *Associated Provincial Picture Houses v Wednesbury*

Corporation, CA 1947, [1948] 1 KB 223; [1947] 2 All ER 680. D Jandu, MAN/89/232 (VTD 4475).

14.22   **Sole trader—low turnover.**   The Commissioners issued a notice requiring security of £3,750 from a sole trader who had previously been a director of two companies which had gone into liquidation owing VAT totalling almost £29,000. The trader appealed, contending that the requirement was unreasonable as his turnover was less than £10,000 a year. The tribunal allowed the appeal, holding on the evidence that the Commissioners had acted unreasonably in requiring any security. *RB Cornforth, LON/89/842 (VTD 4532).*

14.23   **Sole trader—failure to make returns but no previous history of unpaid VAT.**   An accountant (C), who had retired from a partnership and had begun a small sole practice, failed to make VAT returns but paid the tax charged by estimated assessments. The Commissioners issued a notice requiring security, and C appealed. The tribunal allowed C's appeal. The chairman (Mr. Coutts, sitting alone) observed that 'the only matter which could be relied upon to suggest that the revenue required to be protected ... was the extraordinarily cavalier attitude adopted by (C) to making actual returns' and expressed the view that ' a requirement for security for tax to be collected is a measure which should be used sparingly. It is not ... an appropriate method for ensuring that returns are made ... While it may be that, in an appropriate case, non-furnishing of returns may make it requisite to demand security for the protection of the revenue, this is not such a case. The amounts which were involved were small, and an obvious preliminary step of making a substantial assessment and seeing if it were paid was not taken by the Commissioners.' *CJ Cameron, EDN/97/222 (VTD 15779). (Note.* Mr. Coutts' *dicta* with regard to the Commissioners 'making a substantial assessment' should be read in the light of other cases such as the subsequent decision of Dyson J in *Pegasus Birds Ltd,* 3.46 ASSESSMENT, where he held that the Commissioners 'could not simply pluck figures out of the air'.)

14.24   **Sole trader—VAT office failing to take account of zero-rated supplies.**   An interior designer did a significant amount of work on listed buildings, so that some of his turnover was standard-rated and some zero-rated. He found difficulty in dividing payments for work in progress between these categories, and was advised by his local VAT office that he should submit returns on the basis that all his supplies were standard-rated and should subsequently reclaim the tax which related to zero-rated supplies. He followed this advice, but continued to submit his returns after the due date. The Commissioners issued a notice requiring security. The tribunal allowed the trader's appeal, observing that the notice had been issued from Customs' Coventry Business Centre and finding that the officer responsible for the issue of the notice had not requested information from the local VAT office, and was not aware of the specific difficulties of the trader's business. Accordingly, the notice was unreasonable. The tribunal also observed that the officer responsible for the notice 'has not distinguished in his mind the position of a sole trader from that of a limited company, where at the cessation of trading Customs & Excise have no means of recovering any outstanding VAT. This is not the case where a sole trader is concerned, such a person remaining personally liable.' *J McPhee, LON/97/1564 (VTD 15606). (Note.* For a subsequent appeal by the same appellant, see 14.35 below.)

14.25   **Current VAT liability up to date—notice requiring security held to be unreasonable.**   The Commissioners issued a notice requiring security from a partnership which traded as locksmiths. The principal partner had previously been a director of a company which had ceased trading, owing £5,900 in unpaid VAT. The tribunal allowed the partnership's appeal, holding that, since the partnership had submitted four returns and paid all the VAT shown thereon, it was unreasonable for the Commissioners to continue to require security. *C Hickson & Others (t/a Flury's), LON/93/1723A (VTD 11455).*

14.26   Similar decisions were reached in *Computer Cave Ltd, MAN/97/370 (VTD 15212); The Natural Stone Co, LON/97/717 (VTD 15272); Steel Direct Ltd, LON/97/733 (VTD 15272)* and *Janwear Ltd, MAN/97/1013 (VTD 15460).*

14.27   The Commissioners issued a notice requiring security of £2,800 from a company which carried on business in the construction industry. The controlling director of the company had previously been a director of two other companies which had gone into receivership, owing VAT to the Commissioners. The company appealed, contending that the requirement was unreasonable because the company was financially sound and 80% of its supplies were zero-rated, so that it normally owed no VAT to the Commissioners. The tribunal allowed the appeal, holding that the Commissioners had acted unreasonably and had ignored the fact that most of the company's supplies were zero-rated. *Dicta* in *Associated Picture Houses v Wednesbury Corporation, CA 1947, [1948] 1 KB 223; [1947] 2 All ER 680* applied. *Wold Construction Co Ltd, MAN/93/432 (VTD 11704).*

14.28   In January 1992 the Commissioners issued a notice requiring security of more than £350,000 from a company which had been incorporated to carry on a road haulage business. The business had previously been carried on by six associated companies in similar ownership, which had gone into receivership in January 1991, owing a total of more than £1,000,000 in unpaid VAT. The company appealed, contending that the Commissioners had acted unreasonably and should have requested further information concerning its finances, since some of its directors had not been involved with the previous companies, and it had made pre-tax profits of more than £400,000 in its first six months of trading. The tribunal upheld the notice, finding that the Commissioners had failed to take account of the company's financial status, but holding on the evidence that even if they had held additional information concerning its finances, it would still have been reasonable for them to require security. The QB allowed the company's appeal and the CA upheld this decision, holding that the tribunal's jurisdiction was appellate rather than merely supervisory. The tribunal had to consider whether the Commissioners had acted reasonably and had taken account of all relevant material, but had no power to substitute its own decision for one reached on an incorrect basis (except that it could dismiss an appeal where it was shown that, even if additional material had been taken into account, the decision would *inevitably* have been the same). Neill LJ observed that the tribunal should 'consider whether Customs had acted in a way in which no reasonable panel of Commissioners could have acted or whether they had taken into account some irrelevant matter or had disregarded something to which they should have given weight'. *Dicta* of Lord Lane in *JH Corbitt (Numismatists) Ltd*, 56.1 SECOND-HAND GOODS, applied. However, the tribunal could not exercise a fresh discretion, since 'the protection of the revenue is not a responsibility of the tribunal or of a court'. In the present case the tribunal had found that the Commissioners had failed to enquire into the company's financial status, and it was not inevitable that, if this material had been considered, the result would have been the same. *C & E Commrs v John Dee Ltd, CA [1995] STC 941.*

14.29   An established construction company (D), which had had a turnover of more than £5,000,000 in 1990, suffered financial difficulties and went into receivership, owing about £74,000 in unpaid VAT. Its principal director became a director of a new company (E), which operated a joinery business. E did not pay its VAT for the periods from July 1993 to January 1995, and in May 1995 the Commissioners issued a notice requiring security of £46,500. E appealed, contending that the notice was unreasonable because it was in a sound financial position (and had subsequently paid its VAT arrears), and D's insolvency should be disregarded as having been caused by a major recession in the building industry. The tribunal accepted E's evidence and allowed its appeal. *Extrastable Services Ltd, MAN/95/2059 (VTD 13911)*.

14.30   **Notice issued following late submission of two returns—whether notice unreasonable.**   On 15 July 1996 the Commissioners issued a notice requiring security of £10,600 from a company which had failed to submit its returns for the periods ending January 1996 and April 1996. The Commissioners received the returns in question two days later, and issued a revised notice requiring security of £4,100. The company appealed, contending that the notice was unreasonable. The tribunal accepted this contention and allowed the appeal, observing that the company had been registered for VAT since August 1994 and that its returns and payments were up-to-date at the time the revised notice was issued. *Topzone Ltd, MAN/96/855 (VTD 14782)*.

14.31   A similar decision was reached in *Dunholme Decorators Ltd, MAN/99/752 (VTD 16484)*.

14.32   **Amount of demand excessive.**   The Commissioners issued a notice requiring security of £21,800 from a retail company, on the grounds that the company's principal director had been a director of four other companies which had failed to pay VAT. The tribunal allowed the company's appeal, holding that the decision to require security was reasonable in principle, but that the amount required was unreasonable, since it had been based solely on a consideration of the company's projected annual turnover of £250,000 and had failed to take account of the fact that the company was a retailer and was entitled to credit for significant amounts of input tax. *Superstore Discount Tile Warehouse Ltd, LON/95/1077A (VTD 13393)*.

14.33   A similar decision was reached in *Ram Computercare (Sales) Ltd, LON/97/24 (VTD 16102)*.

14.34   In January 1995 the Commissioners issued a notice requiring security of £75,500 from a company which had been registered for VAT since 1979. This sum represented the current arrears of almost £36,600 together with unpaid surcharges totalling some £7,500 and an estimated six months' future liability of £31,400. The company appealed, contending that the requirement was unreasonable. The tribunal allowed the appeal, holding that, while it had been reasonable for the Commissioners to require security, the amount of the unpaid default surcharges should not have been included in the requirement, and the requirement was therefore 'flawed' and incorrect. *Qcom Maintenance Ltd, MAN/95/1399 (VTD 13933)*.

14.35   An appeal against a notice requiring security was allowed in a case where the tribunal found that the relevant VAT officer 'could not have acted reasonably in deciding on what security should be paid as he is unable to identify to us not only the amounts outstanding in relation to this appeal, but to identify how any of the figures of the various other businesses and the arrears, tie in with the figures he apparently relied on'. *J McPhee (t/a K2 Interiors), MAN/99/69 (VTD 16158)*.

14.36   **Business transferred from wife to husband—whether notice unreasonable.**   The Commissioners issued a notice requiring security of £1,750 from a trader (E) who operated a catering business including a café. E's wife had previously operated the café but had been declared bankrupt owing more than £12,000 in unpaid VAT. Following her bankruptcy the café had been transferred to E. He appealed against the notice, contending that he had not been responsible for the business when it was operated by his wife, that she had been defrauded by a dishonest manager who had stolen more than £10,000, and that the notice was unreasonable. The tribunal allowed the appeal, holding on the evidence that the officer responsible for issuing the notice had failed to consider all the relevant information. *Dicta* of Turner J in *John Dee Ltd*, 14.28 above, applied. *S Elliott, LON/95/1278A (VTD 13432)*.

14.37   **Company acquired from company formation agent.**   A company (R) acted as a company formation agent. When R formed a new company, it became the registered company secretary until the purchasers appointed a new secretary. The Commissioners issued a notice requiring security from a company (C), of which R was the registered company secretary, on the basis that 16 other companies with R as secretary had poor compliance records. C appealed, contending that it had no connection with the other 16 companies. The tribunal accepted this contention and allowed the appeal, holding that 'the function of a company secretary ... has nothing to do with the management of the business of the company in question, unless he is specifically engaged to carry out wider functions (which was not the case here)'. On the evidence, 'there was no suggestion that (R) was in some way instrumental in causing the tax debts or poor compliance' of the other 16 companies, and the Commissioners' decision to require security was unreasonable. *Control Ltd, LON/00/632 (VTD 16973)*.

Cases where the appellant was partly successful

14.38   The Commissioners issued a notice requiring security of £5,000 from a company (G) which operated an employment agency. The principal director of the company had previously been a director of five other companies which had ceased trading, owing a total of more than £50,000 in unpaid VAT. The company appealed, contending that the notice was unreasonable because the previous five companies had all carried on businesses in the motor trade. The tribunal allowed the appeal in part, holding that the decision to require security was reasonable but that the amount required was unreasonable because the turnover of the previous companies had been taken into consideration, although G was operating in a completely different line of business and had a significantly lower turnover. The tribunal directed that the amount of security should be fixed at £4,000. *Giddian Ltd, [1984] VATTR 161 (VTD 1706)*.

14.39   The Commissioners issued a notice requiring security of £40,000 from a car hire company, on the basis that two of the company's four directors, and the company secretary, had previously been involved with other companies which had gone into liquidation owing VAT. The company appealed, contending that the requirement was unreasonable since the secretary and one of the two directors in question had resigned, and it had brought its payments up to date. The tribunal allowed the appeal in part, ordering the company to provide security of £10,000 and submit monthly returns. *Dreestone Ltd, LON/85/119 (VTD 1900)*.

14.40   The Commissioners issued a notice requiring security of £10,000 from a sole trader who had previously been a director of a company which had become insolvent owing substantial VAT. The trader appealed, contending that the amount required was unreasonable. He submitted further details of his turnover, following which the Commissioners agreed to reduce the amount required to £2,900. The tribunal reviewed the evidence in detail, applying *dicta* in *Giddian Ltd*, 14.38 above, and indicating that the requirement should not exceed 30% of the trader's projected net liability for the next 12 months. It found that in this case the projected net liability was £8,800, and reduced the requirement to £2,500. *DA French (t/a Adept Architectural Aluminium), LON/91/1156Y (VTD 9706)*.

14.41   Requirements to give security were reduced in *Kaymac Fashions Ltd, LON/85/267 (VTD 1945); Fiesta Fashions Ltd, LON/85/436 (VTD 1975); Chaseside Shopfitters Ltd, LON/85/497 (VTD 2023); Highfire Ltd, LON/87/128 (VTD 2399); Pearl*

Top Services Ltd, MAN/88/168 (VTD 2888); Guttenberg & Sons, MAN/88/432 (VTD 3392); GF Port, MAN/89/25 (VTD 3772); FA Taylor, LON/88/1465Y (VTD 3882); Samrosa Ltd, LON/88/1442X (VTD 3984); Jointstock Ltd, LON/ 89/606 (VTD 4236); Tiffin Developments Ltd, MAN/89/729 (VTD 4462); Kings Norton Carpet Centre Ltd, MAN/89/762 (VTD 4749); SRJ McGleish, MAN/90/ 261 (VTD 5318); Croydon Architectural Ltd, LON/91/2711Y (VTD 7823); Integrated Allied Industries Ltd, LON/91/2700Z (VTD 7947); Casey Flooring (Contracts) Ltd, MAN/92/1698 (VTD 10205); Craig Security Services Ltd, LON/ 93/853A (VTD 11484); Denimode Ltd, LON/93/1493A (VTD 11952); Pegasus Holdings (Malvern) Ltd, MAN/94/287 (VTD 12539); Hosepower Ltd, LON/94/ 513 (VTD 12594); Astral Print Ltd, LON/94/1171 (VTD 12837) and *Moon Fashions Ltd, LON/95/218 (VTD 14324).*

Cases where the appellant was unsuccessful

14.42   The Commissioners issued a notice requiring security of £15,000. The company appealed, contending that the amount required was excessive. The tribunal dismissed the appeal. Lord Grantchester held that it was reasonable for the Commissioners to require 'security to be in an amount slightly in excess of the estimated tax liability of the trader concerned over a recent six-month period'. *Labelwise Ltd, LON/83/192 (VTD 1499).*

14.43   A company appealed against the Commissioners' requirement for security of £11,600. One of its directors had been a director of seven companies engaged in a similar business, all of which had gone into liquidation owing considerable sums of VAT to the Commissioners. The tribunal dismissed the appeal, holding that the Commissioners had not acted unreasonably. *Power Rod (UK) Ltd, [1983] VATTR 334 (VTD 1550).*

14.44   A company appealed against a notice requiring security, contending that the requirement was unreasonable since it would force it to cease trading and make its 14 employees redundant. The tribunal dismissed the appeal. Lord Grantchester held that 'such considerations do not ... require or persuade us to allow this appeal. The power conferred by Parliament on the Commissioners is expressed to be exercisable by them "for the protection of the revenue", with the result that the Commissioners must act thereunder with that purpose in mind. I can only allow an appeal against a decision of the Commissioners to act thereunder if it is one that no reasonable body of Commissioners could reach'. *Rosebronze Ltd, LON/84/154 (VTD 1668).*

14.45   The decision in *Rosebronze Ltd*, 14.44 above, has been applied in a large number of subsequent cases in which appeals against requirements for security have been dismissed. In the interests of space, such cases are not summarised individually in this book. For a list of such cases decided up to December 1995, see Tolley's VAT Cases 1996.

14.46   A company carried on business as suppliers and installers of double-glazing. Its managing director had previously been involved in two other double-glazing companies which had become insolvent with heavy liabilities, including a debt of £85,000 for VAT to the Commissioners. The company was in arrears with its VAT returns and payments, and the Commissioners issued a notice of requirement of security. The tribunal dismissed the company's appeal and the QB upheld this decision. Farquharson J held that the Commissioners were justified in requiring security in view of the conduct of the earlier companies controlled by the same director, and of the late returns of the appellant company. *Mr Wishmore Ltd v C & E Commissioners, QB [1988] STC 723.* (*Note. Obiter dicta* of Farquharson J were disapproved by the CA in the subsequent case of *John Dee Ltd*, 14.28 above.)

14.47   Collection and Enforcement

14.47   The Commissioners issued a notice requiring security of £16,500 from an electronic engineering company. The directors of this company had previously been directors of two other companies which had ceased trading with substantial arrears of VAT. The company appealed against the notice, contending that the Commissioners had not given adequate consideration to the financial history of the three companies. The tribunal dismissed the company's appeal, applying *Mr Wishmore Ltd*, 14.46 above. The Commissioners had a duty to consider all the relevant facts before them, but they were not obliged to make detailed enquiries. On the evidence, there was a long history of default by companies under the control of the same two directors for which no explanation had been given, and the Commissioners were entitled to assume that there had been financial mismanagement. *Hitron Ltd, [1989] VATTR 148 (VTD 3755).*

14.48   The Commissioners issued a notice requiring security of £253,000 from a company which had fallen into arrears with its VAT liability. One of the company's directors had previously been involved with three previous companies which had ceased trading with arrears of VAT. The company appealed, contending that the notice had been unreasonable and that the Commissioners had been unduly influenced by the director's involvement with the three previous companies. The tribunal rejected this contention and dismissed the appeal. Applying *Mr Wishmore Ltd*, 14.46 above, the tribunal's jurisdiction was supervisory rather than appellate. The tribunal could only intervene if the Commissioners had acted unreasonably, applying the standards laid down by Lord Greene MR in *Associated Provincial Picture Houses v Wednesbury Corporation, CA 1947, [1948] 1 KB 223; [1947] 2 All ER 680*. The Commissioners' decision here was not unreasonable on the evidence. *Dialrace Ltd, [1991] VATTR 505 (VTD 6328).*

14.49   The Commissioners issued a notice requiring security of £23,000 from a company (C) trading as jewellers. C's controlling director had previously been the controlling director of another company which had become insolvent, owing £300,000 in unpaid VAT. The tribunal dismissed C's appeal, holding that the decision to require security was reasonable on the evidence, applying *Mr Wishmore Ltd*, 14.46 above, and *dicta* of Lord Greene in *Associated Provincial Picture Houses v Wednesbury Corporation, CA 1947, [1948] 1 KB 223; [1947] 2 All ER 680. Colette Ltd, [1992] VATTR 240 (VTD 6975).*

14.50   *Colette Ltd*, 14.49 above, was applied in the similar case of *Felicitations Ltd, LON/93/2375 (VTD 12409).*

14.51   A company appealed against a notice requiring security of £10,425, contending that the notice was unreasonable. The tribunal rejected this contention and dismissed the appeal, applying the QB decision in *Mr Wishmore Ltd*, 14.46 above, and distinguishing *Dreestone Ltd*, 14.39 above. *Winslade Electrical Ltd, LON/93/658 (VTD 10943).*

14.52   A company appealed against a notice requiring security, contending that the notice was unreasonable and was not 'necessary for the protection of the revenue'. The tribunal rejected this contention and dismissed the appeal, applying *Rosebronze Ltd*, 14.44 above. The tribunal declined to follow *dicta* in *Club Centre of Leeds Ltd, [1980] VATTR 135 (VTD 985)* (a case concerning provisions in *FA 1972* which had subsequently been amended by *FA 1981*, but which the company had cited as an authority), observing that that case dealt with a different area of VAT law, and was 'not of direct relevance to the present case'. *IPS Currall (t/a Ian Currall & Partners), MAN/92/1567 (VTD 11652).*

14.53   The Commissioners issued a notice requiring security of £7,350 from a company controlled by a married couple, on the grounds that the wife had previously been a director of two other companies which had become insolvent owing substantial amounts of VAT. The company appealed, contending that the decision was unreasonable because the two previous companies had been controlled by the wife's parents, and that, although she had been a director, she had had no control over the management of those companies and had not been authorised to sign cheques. Her parents had subsequently returned to Italy, so that she was no longer under the influence of her father. The tribunal allowed the appeal but the QB reversed this decision, holding that the Commissioners' decision to require security had not been unreasonable. Dyson J observed that 'in exercising its supervisory jurisdiction the tribunal must limit itself to considering facts and matters which existed at the time the challenged decision was taken'. *C & E Commrs v Peachtree Enterprises Ltd, QB [1994] STC 747.* (*Note. Obiter dicta* of Dyson J were disapproved by the CA in the subsequent case of *John Dee Ltd*, 14.28 above.)

14.54   *Dicta* of Dyson J in *Peachtree Enterprises Ltd*, 14.53 above, were applied in a subsequent case in which a family company had taken over a restaurant which had previously been operated by members of the same family trading in partnership. The Commissioners issued a notice requiring security from the company and the tribunal dismissed the company's appeal. The tribunal chairman observed that, since 'the tribunal must limit itself to considering facts and matters which existed at the time the challenged decision was taken', subsequent events were 'irrelevant'. *Obiter dicta* of the tribunal chairman in the Scottish case of *Lomond Services Ltd, EDN/98/3 (VTD 15451)* (which the company had cited as an authority) were specifically disapproved. *Kushoom Koly Ltd, [1998] VATDR 363 (VTD 15591).*

14.55   The QB decision in *Peachtree Enterprises Ltd*, 14.53 above, was also applied in the similar subsequent cases of *B Harris & Son (Monumental Masons) Ltd, LON/94/661A (VTD 12626); Beefy's, MAN/94/457 (VTD 12711); Grunwick Property Ltd, MAN/94/624 (VTD 12775); Northern Contract Services Group Ltd, [1994] VATTR 419 (VTD 12807); Orton Building Services Ltd, MAN/94/78 (VTD 12822); Blue Banana Ltd, MAN/94/912 (VTD 12865); D Patey (t/a Patey & Son), LON/94/1206A (VTD 12927); Elmana Ltd, LON/93/2847A (VTD 13055); Eastwave Engineering Ltd, LON/94/900A (VTD 13107); Lees Services Ltd, MAN/94/2469 (VTD 13334); Meyvale Building Services Ltd, LON/94/2318A (VTD 13400); Typsecure Ltd (t/a CJ May Doncaster), MAN/94/2505 (VTD 13453); JB Precision Engineering Ltd, MAN/95/2029 (VTD 13655); Compass Crane & Plant Hire Ltd, MAN/94/2647 (VTD 13860); Shieldclever Services Ltd, MAN/95/2215 (VTD 13961); Limefield Laundries Ltd, MAN/96/370 (VTD 14357); Classic Interiors (UK) Ltd, MAN/96/437 (VTD 14526); Soundscape Ltd, LON/97/38 (VTD 14853); Arctic Gulf Ltd, EDN/96/196 (VTD 14897); JD Pearson (t/a J Douglas Pearson & Co), EDN/97/104 (VTD 15330); Applied Food Technology Ltd, LON/97/1273 (VTD 15371); Compact Distribution Centre Ltd, MAN/98/70 (VTD 15611); Decorum Decorators Ltd, EDN/98/62 (VTD 15621); Feldon Packaging Co Ltd, LON/98/298 (VTD 15752); Wordbarr Ltd, EDN/98/130 (VTD 15823); Heronloch Ltd, EDN/98/124 (VTD 15824); JD Shaw, LON/98/635 (VTD 15936); Logicmega Ltd, MAN/98/765 (VTD 16032); N Zezza (t/a San Remo), MAN/98/665 (VTD 16326); WM Agencies Ltd, MAN/99/537 (VTD 16461); Heyville Ltd, LON/99/880 (VTD 16540); Flinco (UK) Ltd, LON/99/669 (VTD 16548); D Cohen (t/a Splash), LON/99/1118 (VTD 16573); Regent Street Estates Investment Ltd, MAN/99/1095 (VTD 16694); Concrete Crushing Co Ltd, MAN/99/180 (VTD 16741)* and *Summerhose Ltd, MAN/00/584 (VTD 16967).*

14.56   The Commissioners issued a notice requiring security of £7,300 from a certified accountant who had consistently paid his VAT liability after the due date. The accountant appealed, contending that the requirement was unnecessary since, 'as he was a member of the association of certified accountants and would be deprived of membership thereof were he to be made bankrupt, the rules of that professional association would in themselves ensure that he paid all VAT due'. The tribunal rejected this contention and dismissed his appeal, holding that it was not 'in any way unreasonable' for the Commissioners to require security. *JL Morrell (t/a Morrell Middleton), MAN/95/1543 (VTD 13970)*.

14.57   The Commissioners issued a notice requiring security from a company which operated a restaurant. The restaurant had previously been operated by another company which had suffered financial difficulties and had gone into liquidation. The same individual had been secretary of both companies. The tribunal upheld the notice and dismissed the company's appeal, holding that the Commissioners had not acted unreasonably. *Smartone Connect Ltd*, 14.8 above, and *Greyhound Transport (UK) Ltd*, 14.9 above, distinguished. The tribunal chairman observed that 'the tribunal's jurisdiction in a security appeal is appellate not supervisory, and the tribunal must examine whether the Commissioners had rightly exercised their power to require security. The tribunal must consider whether the Commissioners have acted in a way in which no reasonable panel of Commissioners could have acted, whether they have taken into account some irrelevant matter or have disregarded something to which they should have given weight. It is not for the tribunal to exercise a fresh discretion, as the protection of the revenue is not the responsibility of any court or tribunal.' *Restaurant Portfolio Ltd (t/a L'Escargot), LON/96/1979 (VTD 15245)*.

14.58   Appeals against requirements to give security have been dismissed in a very large number of other cases, in which the decisions appear to raise no point of general interest. In the interests of space, such cases are not reported individually in this book. For a list of such cases decided up to and including 31 October 1990, see Tolley's VAT Cases 1991.

14.59   **Input tax repayment—requirement to give security—whether appealable decision.** See *Strangewood Ltd (No 2)*, 2.22 APPEALS.

RECOVERY OF VAT (VATA 1994, Sch 11 para 5(1)-(3))

14.60   **VATA 1994, Sch 11 para 5—tax declared in returns but neither paid nor assessed within time limits—whether Commissioners may take collection proceedings.** In the case noted at 3.32 ASSESSMENT, a company had correctly accounted for tax of £40,560 in its returns for the periods ending May 1976. However, it subsequently formed the view that it should have treated the supplies as zero-rated, and recovered the £40,560 by unilaterally deducting it from its liability for subsequent accounting periods. The tribunal subsequently held that the disputed supplies did not qualify for zero-rating, but the Commissioners failed to issue an assessment to recover the tax within the statutory time limits. They instead sought to recover the tax by issuing a writ against the company, on the grounds that it had declared the tax in its returns for the periods to May 1976, but had failed to pay the tax to the Commissioners. The QB upheld the writ, holding that the tax had been accounted for in the company's returns and had been borne by the company's customers. The fact that it had been declared in the company's returns meant that the Commissioners were entitled to recover it as a debt due to the Crown. *C & E Commrs v International Language Centres Ltd, QB [1986] STC 279*.

14.61   **Recovery of tax under VATA 1994, Sch 11 para 5(2).** A partner in a firm of solicitors had held the office of Clerk of the Horserace Betting Levy Board Appeal Tribunal. The firm issued three invoices in respect of services which he supplied in his capacity as Clerk, but did not account to the Commissioners for the VAT thereon. The Commissioners issued a ruling that the firm was liable to account for the VAT by virtue of what is now *VATA 1994, Sch 11 para 5(2)*. The tribunal dismissed the firm's appeal against this decision. *Hempsons, [1977] VATTR 73 (VTD 361)*. (*Note.* The appeal also concerned the application of provisions in *FA 1972, s 45* which have subsequently been superseded.)

14.62   An individual (W) acted as a management consultant. In October 1973 he incorporated a company (S) to sell his services. He had issued eight tax invoices before the incorporation of the company, and issued two further invoices after the incorporation, but did not account for VAT on any of the ten invoices. All ten invoices were issued in the name of a company which did not exist. The Commissioners brought an action against W for payment of the amount of tax shown on the invoices. The QB held that the first eight invoices had been issued by W and that he was accountable for the tax, applying *European Communities Act 1972, s 9(2)*. However, on the evidence the QB held that the last two invoices had been issued by S (which had subsequently gone into liquidation). The amounts of VAT were recoverable from W and from the liquidator of S respectively, by virtue of what is now *VATA 1994, Sch 11 para 5(2)*. *C & E Commrs v MF Wells, QB [1981] STC 588; [1982] 1 All ER 920*.

14.63   A company (L) supplied goods to a customer, and issued a tax invoice for the sale price inclusive of VAT, but did not account for the VAT shown on the invoice. The Commissioners issued an assessment to recover the tax and the tribunal dismissed L's appeal, applying what is now *VATA 1994, Sch 11 para 5(2)*. *Lancaster Fabrications Ltd, MAN/82/109 (VTD 1317)*.

14.64   In the case noted at 2.21 APPEALS, the tribunal held that it had no jurisdiction to hear an appeal under *VATA 1994, Sch 11 para 5(2)(3)*. *GE Alm, LON/98/961 (VTD 15863)*.

14.65   **Invoice issued but no actual supply—effect of VATA 1994, Sch 11 para 5(2).**   On examining a trader's records, a VAT officer discovered an invoice in the trader's name for a supply of cloth, charging VAT of £3,675. The trader had not accounted for output tax on this invoice, although the company to which the invoice was addressed had reclaimed input tax on it. The Commissioners issued an assessment charging tax and the trader appealed, contending that the invoice was a 'pro-forma' and had been cancelled, and that the supply had never taken place. The tribunal accepted the trader's evidence and allowed the appeal, holding that there had been no supply and that the assessment was not authorised by *VATA 1994, s 73*. The tribunal held that the effect of *Sch 11 para 5(2)* was that 'the Commissioners are entitled to recover from the appellant the sum of £3,675, being the amount shown as VAT on the invoice, but this is recoverable as a debt to the Crown and not by way of an assessment'. *G Kaur (t/a GK Trading), MAN/97/688 (VTD 15366)*.

DISTRAINT (VATA 1994, Sch 11 para 5(4))

Note. See now the *Distress for Customs & Excise Duties and Other Indirect Taxes Regulations 1997 (SI 1997 No 1431)*, which took effect from 1 July 1997, and which extended the Commissioners' powers of distraint.

14.66   **Perishable items.**   It was held that perishable items (such as food), which could not be restored in the same condition as when they were distrained upon, were exempt from distraint. *Morley v Pincombe, Ex D 1848, 2 Ex D 101*.

14.67   **Tools of trade.**   In a case where a Collector of Taxes had levied distraint on a piano which the debtor's wife used to give music lessons, the KB held that the tools of a debtor's trade were only exempt from distraint for rent, and were not exempt from distraint for tax. *MacGregor v Clamp & Son, KB [1914] 1 KB 288*.

14.68   **Entry to premises.**   The QB held that a bailiff was entitled to enter premises through an open window, and may also further open a window which was already partly open. *Nixon v Freeman, QB 1860, 5 H & N 647.*

14.69   The QB held that a bailiff was not entitled to open a window catch in order to enter premises without a warrant authorising him to 'break open' the premises. *Hancock v Austin, QB 1863, 14 CBNS 634.*

14.70   The QB held that a bailiff was entitled to enter premises through a partially opened skylight. *Miller v Tebb, QB 1893, 9 TLR 515.*

14.71   The QB held that a bailiff had no right to break into premises without a warrant, but was entitled to climb over a wall or fence from adjoining premises. *Long v Clark, QB [1894] 1 QB 119.*

14.72   **'Walking possession' agreement.**   The QB held that entering into a 'walking possession' agreement did not constitute the abandonment of a distraint. *Lumsden v Burnett, QB [1898] 2 QB 177.*

14.73   **Distraint levied on company—liquidation of company before sale of goods levied on.**   In October 1982 the Commissioners levied distraint on a company which owed more than £30,000 in unpaid VAT. A 'walking possession' agreement was signed on behalf of the company. In February 1983 the company went into liquidation. In May 1983 the company's plant and machinery were sold by agreement between the Commissioners and the liquidator. The Commissioners claimed the net proceeds of the sale (£27,080). The liquidator objected to the claim, and the Commissioners applied to the Ch D for a declaration that they were entitled to the proceeds. The Ch D held, applying *Herbert Berry Associates Ltd v CIR, HL 1977, 52 TC 113 (TTC 2001, 43.32),* that the court had a discretion to allow the Commissioners to retain the proceeds of the distraint, and that since there had been 'no unconscionable conduct or delay' in this case, the Commissioners were entitled to the proceeds of the distraint. *Re Memco Engineering Ltd, Ch D [1985] 3 All ER 267.*

14.74   **Late appeal after levy of distraint.**   See *Davies,* 2.155 APPEALS.

FURNISHING OF INFORMATION (VATA 1994, Sch 11 para 7)

14.75   **Customs' power to require information.**   In a purchase tax case, the HL considered the extent of Customs' power to require information. Lord Reid held that 'if a demand for information is made in the proper manner, the trader is bound to answer the demand within the time and in the form required, whether or not the answers may tend to incriminate him, and if he fails to comply with the demands, he may be prosecuted... The trader is only bound to furnish information within such time and in such form as the Commissioners require ... If the information required is simple and easily provided, the time required may be short. I do not think, however, that this entitles the Commissioners to send a representative to confront the trader, put questions to him orally and demand oral answers on the spot; and I am certainly of the opinion that it does not entitle them to send their representative to subject the trader to a prolonged interrogation in the nature of a cross-examination ...'. *C & E Commrs v Harz & Power, HL [1967] 1 All ER 177.*

14.76   **Extent of Commissioners' power to inspect and copy documents.**   Search orders (*'Anton Piller'* orders) were made against defendants in a civil action concerning the manufacture of illegally copied videocassettes. Documents belonging to two of the defendants (H and R) had been entrusted to the custody of the plaintiffs' solicitors. The Commissioners were investigating the failure of H and R to account for VAT on the sale of the illegal cassettes, and sought to inspect and copy the documents. H had authorised this but R had not. In accordance with the undertaking given by them to the Court, the solicitors declined to allow the Commissioners to inspect the documents without a specific Court order. The Commissioners made an application to the High Court which granted the order sought. Farquharson J held that, in view of the terms under which the documents were held, the solicitors were correct in refusing to allow the Commissioners access to them except by order of the Court. However, on the facts of the case it was proper to make such an order. *C & E Commrs v AE Hamlin & Co, Ch D [1983] STC 780; [1983] 3 All ER 654. (Note.* For *'Anton Piller'* orders, see *Anton Piller KG v Manufacturing Processes Ltd, CA [1976] 1 All ER 779.* The validity of such orders was upheld by the ECHR in *Chappell v United Kingdom, ECHR 1989, 12 EHRR 1.* Under the *Civil Procedure Rules 1998 (SI 1998 No 3132),* which largely took effect from 26 April 1999, such orders are now referred as search orders.)

14.77   *'Anton Piller'* orders were made against defendants in a civil action concerning the manufacture of illegally copied audiocassettes. The orders authorised the plaintiff company to remove into the custody of their solicitors counterfeit records and documents, relating to the action, which were the property of the defendants. The action was settled and the solicitors returned the goods but retained the documents. The Commissioners were investigating the defendants' failure to account for VAT on the sale of the illegal cassettes, and asked the solicitors for access to the documents. The solicitors refused to allow such access without the defendants' consent, which the defendants refused. The Commissioners thereupon issued a notice to the solicitors under what is now *VATA 1994, Sch 11 para 7* requiring the production of the documents. The solicitors applied to the High Court for directions. Sir Nicholas Browne-Wilkinson VC held that, in ordinary cases, the Commissioners could not require solicitors holding documents which had been seized under *'Anton Piller'* orders to produce those documents, and that the solicitors in such cases could not disclose the documents in question to the Commissioners except by order of the Court. However, in the circumstances of this case, the Court would authorise the documents to be disclosed. *EMI Records Ltd v Spillane & Others, Ch D [1986] STC 374. (Notes.* (1) For subsequent proceedings in this case, see 3.42 ASSESSMENT. (2) See the note following *AE Hamlin & Co,* 14.76 above, with regard to *'Anton Piller'* orders. The *Civil Procedure Rules 1998* also now refer to a 'claimant' rather than to a 'plaintiff'.)

ENTRY AND SEARCH OF PREMISES (VATA 1994, Sch 11 para 10)

14.78   The Commissioners were investigating a construction company and obtained search warrants authorising them to enter the company's premises and the homes of the company's two directors. The company and the directors applied for judicial review, contending firstly that *VATA 1994, Sch 11 para 10* should be held to be invalid under EC law, and alternatively that the warrants were unnecessary, since the company had offered to co-operate with the Commissioners. The QB rejected these contentions and dismissed the applications. *Article 22(8)* of the *EC Sixth Directive* authorised Member States to impose 'obligations which they deem necessary for the correct collection of tax and for the prevention of evasion'. On the evidence, the Commissioners' determination that search warrants were needed, and the magistrates' decision to grant the warrants, were entirely rational. The company had made a partial offer of co-operation, but it was an offer 'hedged around by conditions'. The Commissioners had merely been given the opportunity to inspect files and records of the company at the premises of the company's solicitors. This was completely unsatisfactory. McCowan LJ observed that 'Customs require to be able themselves to search all parts of the premises in question and all cupboards, cabinets, etc. Often the evidence is found on odd sheets of paper found in the backs of cupboards, desks, etc., rather than in formal files and records.' *R v C & E Commrs (ex p. X Ltd) (aka R v C & E Commrs ex p. McNicholas Construction Co Ltd & Others), QB [1997] STC 1197.* (*Note.* For a preliminary issue in this case, see 2.172 APPEALS. For subsequent developments, see 2.189 APPEALS and 3.77 ASSESSMENT.)

14.79   The Commissioners obtained warrants under *Sch 11 para 10(3)*, authorising them to search, and remove materials from, the premises of a trader and his solicitor, who had been involved in a complex avoidance scheme involving the use of several companies resident outside the UK. The trader and solicitor applied for judicial review, contending that some of the items which the Commissioners had seized from the solicitor were subject to legal privilege. The QB rejected the applications, with the exception of three small classes of documents which the Commissioners were ordered to return. Applying *dicta* of Jowitt in *R v Chief Constable of Warwickshire Constabulary and Another (ex p. Fitzpatrick & Others), QB [1998] 1 All ER 65,* 'circumstances ... may very well require decisions to be made at speed and without time for reflection or that opportunity to assess the significance of material which only becomes possible when it can be considered in the context of other material'. Furthermore, 'judicial review is not a fact-finding exercise and it is an extremely unsatisfactory tool by which to determine, in any but the clearest of cases, whether there has been a seizure of material not permitted by the search warrant'. Accordingly, 'a person who complains of excessive seizure ... should not, save in such cases, seek his remedy by way of judicial review but should rely on his private law remedy when he will have a tribunal which will be able to hear evidence and make findings of fact unfettered by *Wednesbury* principles'. Applying *dicta* of Waller LJ in *Reynolds v Commissioner of the Metropolitan Police, CA [1984] 3 All ER 649,* 'to do a detailed examination in a house would no doubt have required several police officers to be there for some days, causing disturbance to the householder, and might require comparisons to be made with other documents already in the hands of the police'. Smedley J observed that 'in judicial review cases, the court's essential function is not to act as an appellate court but to look at the material available to the decision-makers, in this case the officers of Customs & Excise, and ask whether they have acted unfairly... If, however, in the course of a legitimate search of a solicitor's office, particularly where the solicitor himself is alleged to be complicit in the offence being investigated, the officers seize material which includes items subject to legal privilege inadvertently, it cannot be that the seizure of those items renders the execution of the warrant unlawful.' The Commissioners had adopted a system of applying to the Attorney-General to nominate a barrister to sift through seized documents before deciding which of them should be retained. This procedure protected the interests of both the solicitor and of the Commissioners. *R v C & E Commrs (ex p. Popely); R v C & E Commrs (ex p. Harris), QB [1999] STC 1016.*

ORDER FOR ACCESS TO RECORDED INFORMATION (VATA 1994, Sch 11 para 11)

14.80   **Conditions for issue of a search warrant.**   A solicitor had been summoned to appear before magistrates to answer charges that he had knowingly been concerned in the fraudulent evasion of VAT by a company of which he was a director. He was remanded on bail, and a Customs officer made an *ex parte* ('without notice') application to a magistrate under what is now *VATA 1994, Sch 11 para 11(1)* for a search warrant requiring the Midland Bank to give him access to records of six accounts held in the name of the solicitor's firm, and to take copies. The magistrate granted the warrant, but the solicitor made an immediate application to the QB for an order of *certiorari* to quash it. The QB granted the order, holding that *VATA 1994, Sch 11 para 11(1)(b)* required the magistrate who granted the application to have 'reasonable grounds' for believing that an offence had been committed and that the information required was relevant. The granting of a search warrant was not a mere formality. In this case, the QB held that there was insufficient information before the magistrate which could have satisfied him that there were reasonable grounds for believing that the Midland Bank was in possession of information which might be required as evidence in respect of an offence. In certain circumstances, *ex parte* applications under *VATA 1994, Sch 11 para 11(1)* would be justified, but it was desirable that such applications should have been made on notice. In the circumstances here, the application should have been made under the *Bankers Book Evidence Act 1879* rather than under the *VATA*. *R v Epsom Justices (ex p. Bell & Another), QB 1988, [1989] STC 169*. (*Note*. The *Rules of the Supreme Court 1965 (SI 1965 No 1776)* refer to applications being made 'ex parte' or 'inter partes'. With effect from 26 April 1999, these rules have largely been replaced by the *Civil Procedure Rules 1998 (SI 1998 No 3132)*, which refer instead to applications being made 'on notice' or 'without notice'.)

14.81   The Commissioners obtained orders from a magistrates' court under *VATA 1994, Sch 11 para 11*, requiring three banks to give them access to certain certified documents relating to a company. The company's controlling directors applied for judicial review. The QB granted the applications and quashed the orders. Kennedy LJ observed that, although *VATA 1994, Sch 11 para 11* enabled the Commissioners to seek orders *ex parte* ('without notice'), it was preferable for them to proceed *inter partes* ('on notice'), unless there was 'real reason to believe that something of value to the investigation may be lost' if that course was adopted. *Dicta* of Parker LJ in *R v Epsom Justices (ex p. Bell & Another)*, 14.80 above, applied. *R v City of London Magistrates (ex p. Asif & Others), QB [1996] STC 611*. (*Notes*. (1) Compare the subsequent decision in *R v City of London Magistrates Court & Another (ex p. Peters)*, 14.82 below, where the QB held that the Commissioners had been justified in proceeding *ex parte*, rather than *inter partes*, because there was reason to believe that the director might have transferred funds abroad if the application had been made *inter partes*. (2) See the note following *R v Epsom Justices (ex p. Bell)*, 14.80 above, with regard to the *Civil Procedure Rules 1998 (SI 1998 No 3132)*.)

14.82   The Commissioners obtained an order from a magistrates' court under *VATA 1994, Sch 11 para 11*, requiring a bank to give them access to documents relating to a company which carried on a jewellery business. The company's controlling director applied for judicial review, contending firstly that the order was defective because it referred to 'reasonable grounds for suspecting' that an offence had been committed, whereas the statutory test was that there should be 'reasonable grounds for believing' that an offence had been committed, and secondly that there had been procedural irregularities. The QB dismissed the application, holding on the evidence that the officer who had applied for the order had believed that an offence had been committed, that the magistrate had believed what he was required to believe, and that the order was not defective. The officer had presented his information to the magistrates in a balanced way, and there had been no procedural irregularity. Furthermore, the Commissioners had been justified in proceeding *ex parte* ('without notice'), rather than *inter partes* ('on notice'), because there was reason to believe that the director might have transferred funds abroad if the application had been made *inter partes*. *R v City of London Magistrates (ex p. Asif & Others)*, 14.81 above, distinguished. *R v City of London Magistrates Court & Another (ex p. B & J Peters), QB 1996, [1997] STC 141*.

14.83   **Applications for access orders under Sch 11 para 11—whether criminal or civil proceedings.**   The Commissioners applied for four access orders under *VATA 1994, Sch 11 para 11*. Half a day of court time was set aside for the hearing. Two days before the date set for the hearing, the respondents' solicitors applied for an adjournment, contending that the hearing would require a complete day. The

Commissioners refused to agree to the application, but on the date fixed for the hearing, the magistrates found that insufficient time was available, and adjourned the case to be heard for a full day. At the adjourned hearing 17 days later, the magistrate granted the access orders but the respondents applied for costs, contending that the proceedings were criminal proceedings and that the Commissioners had acted unreasonably in refusing to agree to set aside a whole day for the hearing. The QB held that the proceedings were civil rather than criminal, and the magistrate had no jurisdiction to award costs. Lord Bingham CJ observed that 'although the respondents were suspected of criminal offences, no formal accusation had been made against any of them on behalf of the state or any private prosecutor and there were no proceedings in being which could have led to the conviction of the respondents of any breach of the criminal law or to their condemnation'. *C & E Commrs v City of London Magistrates' Court and Others, QB [2000] STC 447; [2000] 1 WLR 2020; [2000] 4 All ER 763.*

MISCELLANEOUS

14.84   **Company in receivership—whether receiver obliged to pay VAT to Commissioners.**   In 1972 a company issued a debenture in favour of a bank, creating a floating charge over the whole of its undertaking. In 1974, under the terms of the debenture, the bank appointed a receiver. The company continued to trade, and charged VAT on the supplies which it made. The receiver issued an originating summons for a declaration as to whether he was obliged to pay the VAT which he had collected to the Commissioners, or whether he was entitled instead to pay it to the bank under the terms of the debenture. Brightman J held that the receiver was obliged to pay the VAT to the Commissioners. He would be committing a criminal offence if he failed to do so, and had no right to pay the money to the bank instead. *Re John Willment (Ashford) Ltd, Ch D 1978, [1979] STC 286.* (*Note.* The *Rules of the Supreme Court 1965 (SI 1965 No 1776)* refer to the use of an 'originating summons'. With effect from 26 April 1999, these rules have largely been replaced by the *Civil Procedure Rules 1998 (SI 1998 No 3132)*, which refer instead to 'alternative procedure'.)

14.85   *Re John Willment (Ashford) Ltd*, 14.84 above, was approved by the CA in a similar subsequent case where there were fixed charges over specific assets, rather than a floating charge over the whole of the company's undertaking. The company's receiver collected rent from properties in respect of which the company had elected to waive exemption. The CA held that the receiver was obliged to pay the VAT on the rents to the Commissioners under *Law of Property Act 1925, s 109(8)*. Nourse LJ observed that the receiver owed duties to the company as to the bank, and was obliged to protect the company against the potentially serious consequences of failing to account to the Commissioners for the tax in question. *Sargent v C & E Commrs, CA [1995] STC 399; [1995] 1 WLR 821.*

14.86   **Liability of provisional liquidator appointed under Insolvency Act 1986, s 135.**   See *Re Grey Marlin Ltd*, 35.1 INSOLVENCY.

14.87   **Set-off of Crown debts.**   In February 1975 an order was made for the compulsory winding-up of a company. At the date of winding-up, the company owed £4,726 to the Inland Revenue and £951 to the DHSS. It was also owed £4,055 by Customs in respect of reclaimable input tax. The Commissioners repaid £3,651 of this before becoming aware of the other Crown debts. They then requested the liquidator to set the amount repaid against the other Crown debts in accordance with the *Bankruptcy Act 1914, s 31*. The liquidator refused to comply with this request and the Commissioners began proceedings for the recovery of the £3,651. The Ch D dismissed the liquidator's appeal, holding that *s 31* applied to debts due to and from the Crown immediately before the commencement of the winding-up. *Re DH Curtis (Builders) Ltd, Ch D [1978] 2 All ER 183*, applied. The £3,651 had been paid by mistake and was recoverable in law. *Re Cushla Ltd, Ch D [1979] STC 615; [1979] 3 All ER 415.* (*Note. Bankruptcy Act 1914, s 31* was repealed by *Insolvency Act 1985.* See now *Insolvency Act 1986, s 323.*)

14.88   **Commissioners obtaining 'Mareva injunction'.** The Commissioners received information that a company, which they considered owed about £264,000,000 in customs duty, intended transferring its business to a newly-formed company, without paying the outstanding duty. They therefore applied for an injunction (a '*Mareva* injunction') to restrain the company from selling or disposing of its assets. The Ch D granted the injunction. Neuberger J observed that 'the proposed sale of the business is not an arm's length transaction or in the ordinary course of trade' and held on the evidence that 'there is a real prospect of irreversible and very substantial damage to Customs' if the injunction were not granted. *C & E Commrs v Anchor Foods Ltd, Ch D [1999] 1 WLR 1139; [1999] 3 All ER 268.* (*Notes.* (1) Although the case concerned customs duty, the principles are also relevant to VAT. (2) Under the *Civil Procedure Rules 1998 (SI 1998 No 3132)*, which largely took effect from 26 April 1999, '*Mareva*' injunctions are now referred as 'freezing injunctions'. (3) The injunction was subsequently discharged. For further developments in this case, see the CA decision reported at *[2000] All ER(D) 1113.*)

14.89   **Company in receivership—input tax previously reclaimed on goods subsequently repossessed—whether a preferential debt.** See *Re Liverpool Commercial Vehicles Ltd*, 34.527 INPUT TAX.

14.90   **Group registration—liability of members other than representative member.** See *Re Nadler Enterprises Ltd*, 30.9 GROUPS OF COMPANIES.

14.91   **Group registration—representative member seeking to disclaim liability.** See *Sunfine Developments Ltd*, 30.10 GROUPS OF COMPANIES.

14.92   **Court proceedings for recovery of assessed tax—whether notification of assessment must be averred in pleadings.** In a Scottish case, the Lord Advocate took proceedings for the recovery of tax assessed by the Commissioners. The defendant appealed, contending that the sum sought had not previously been claimed from him. The Crown's pleadings contained no reference to the manner in which the assessment had been notified. Counsel for the Crown accepted that he would have to prove that such notification had been given, but contended that it was not necessary specifically to aver this in the pleadings, and did not give details of the date on which the notification was made or the address to which it was made. The CS allowed the defendant's appeal, holding that the fact that the amount assessed has been notified to the person assessed in accordance with what is now *VATA 1994, s 73(1)* must be averred in the Crown's pleadings. *Lord Advocate v Johnson, CS [1985] STC 527.*

14.93   **CEMA 1979, s 147(3)—criminal proceedings—Customs' right to appeal against lenient sentence.** A defendant was convicted for fraudulent evasion of excise duty. The magistrates fined him £500. The Commissioners considered that the sentence was unduly lenient, and appealed to the Crown Court under *CEMA 1979, s 147(3)*. The Crown Court judge held that he had no jurisdiction to entertain the appeal. The Commissioners appealed to the QB, which reversed the Crown Court decision and remitted the case to the Crown Court to hear the Commissioners' appeal. The QB held that, in proceedings under *CEMA 1979*, the prosecution had a right of appeal against any decision by a magistrates' court. This included the sentence imposed by the magistrates. *C & E Commrs v WJ Brunt, QB 10 November 1998, Times 25.11.1998.* (*Note.* Although the case concerned excise duty, the decision is also relevant to VAT. With regard to the appropriate sentence, see *R v Dosanjh, CA [1998] 3 All ER 618*, where it was suggested that the minimum appropriate sentence should be six months' imprisonment.)

14.94 **Agreement for compounding criminal proceedings and payment of liability by instalments.** The managing director of a company was arrested on 12 March 1986. Subsequently the Commissioners issued assessments on the company, charging VAT of more than £160,000. In November an agreement was made whereby the Commissioners agreed to compound criminal proceedings for alleged offences committed between 1 November 1983 and 12 March 1986, and the company agreed to pay £140,000 by instalments ending on 31 October 1987. Subsequently the company submitted its return for the quarter ending 30 April 1986, amended in manuscript to indicate that it covered the period from 12 March to 30 April only, rather than the whole of the quarter. The Commissioners issued an assessment charging VAT on sales between 1 February and 12 March 1986, and the company appealed, contending that this liability was already covered by the agreement made in November 1986. The tribunal allowed the company's appeal, holding that the compounding agreement should be construed as including all arrears for the period from 1 November 1983 to 12 March 1986. *Empress Car Company (Abertillery) Ltd, LON/88/987 (VTD 4832)*.

14.95 **Compounding agreement under CEMA 1979, s 152—whether an agreement of appeal within VATA 1994, s 85.** See *Cummings*, 2.164 APPEALS.

14.96 **Assessment not under appeal challenged in collection proceedings.** See the cases noted at 2.149 *et seq.* APPEALS.

14.97 **Assessment issued to recover unpaid tax—appellant contending that assessment invalid because tax already paid—jurisdiction of tribunal.** See *Goldenberg*, 2.24 APPEALS.

14.98 **Partnership debt—validity of bankruptcy order against one member of partnership.** See *Schooler*, 44.39 PARTNERSHIP.

14.99 **Statutory demand—Insolvency Act 1986, s 375(1).** See *Cozens*, 2.150 APPEALS, and *Re A Debtor (No 8 of 1997)*, 35.2 INSOLVENCY.

15   Construction of Buildings, etc.

Note. This chapter contains mainly cases turning on the zero-rating provisions of *VATA 1994, Sch 8, Group 5*, but also includes cases involving the application of what is now *VATA 1994, s 35* (which provides for refunds of VAT to 'persons constructing certain buildings') and *Input Tax Order, Article 6* (which disallows an input tax credit on standard-rated goods supplied to persons constructing dwellings by way of business). There have been substantial changes to the legislation in recent years. *VATA 1994, Sch 8, Group 5* was substituted by the *VAT (Construction of Buildings) Order 1995 (SI 1995 No 280)* with effect from 1 March 1995. The cases in this chapter should be read in the light of the changes in the legislation. The cases are arranged under the following headings.

DEFINITION OF 'PERSON CONSTRUCTING A BUILDING' (VATA 1994, Sch 8, Group 5, Item 1(a); VATA 1994, s 35(1)(1A))

Cases held to qualify for zero-rating or refund

15.1   **Interval between construction and sale—whether sale within Group 5, Item 1.** A housing association had built houses and let them on short tenancies. The houses were subsequently sold to the tenants. The association did not account for output tax on the sales but reclaimed input tax on the costs associated with the disposal, considering that the sales were zero-rated by virtue of what is now *VATA 1994, Sch 8, Group 5, Item 1*. The Commissioners refused to repay the tax in question, considering that because of the lettings which had taken place between the construction and sale of the buildings, the association did not qualify as a 'person constructing a building'. The tribunal allowed the association's appeal and the CS upheld this decision. The phrase 'a person constructing a building' simply meant that only the person who had constructed a building was entitled to treat its sale as zero-rated. Zero-rating was not restricted to cases where the sale took place while the building was in the course of construction. *C & E Commrs v Link Housing Association Ltd, CS [1992] STC 718*. (*Note*. For the Commissioners' practice following this decision, see Business Brief 15/92, issued on 5 October 1992.)

15.2 **Completion of partly-built house.** An individual (M) purchased a partly completed house from a developer for £25,000, the builder having gone bankrupt. The building was structurally complete and M completed the house himself, including the joinery work, installation of sanitary ware, central heating and electrical fittings, and internal and external decoration. He claimed a refund, under what is now *VATA 1994, s 35*, of tax on materials. The Commissioners rejected the claim, considering that the house had been completed when M acquired it. The tribunal allowed M's appeal, holding that the construction of a dwelling involved its completion to a habitable state, and observing that the use in the legislation of the indefinite article in 'a person constructing' indicated that the claimant need not be the only person constructing a dwelling. On the evidence, the work done by M could not be disregarded on *de minimis* grounds, and accordingly he was a person constructing the dwelling for the purposes of *s 35**. *VW McElroy, LON/77/289 (VTD 490)*.

15.3 **House added to existing house to form a pair of semi-detached dwellings.** A claimant (H) had built a house for himself in 1968, known as No 10 Rest Bay Close. Ten years later he built another house on the same plot, which became No 10A. The two dwellings formed a pair of semi-detached houses, each with its own access and services and separately owned and rated. H moved into No 10A and claimed a refund of tax under what is now *VATA 1994, s 35*. The Commissioners rejected the claim on the ground that No 10A was an enlargement of No 10. The tribunal allowed H's appeal, holding on the evidence that No 10A was clearly not an enlargement of No 10. *TJ Hill, [1982] VATTR 134 (VTD 1225)*. (*Note*. The decision was approved by the QB in *Perry*, 15.22 below.)

15.4 **Construction of flat adjacent to house.** An individual (H) constructed a garage and a flat adjacent to his house. The east wall of the garage was about four feet away from the west wall of the house. The flat was a single-storey building and was attached to the south wall of the garage but was not attached to the house. The only external access to the flat was by means of a passageway between the garage and the house, leading onto the drive. The passageway was covered, with a lockable door at each end. H claimed a refund of tax under what is now *VATA 1994, s 35*. The Commissioners rejected the claim, considering that the work constituted the enlargement of an existing building. The tribunal allowed H's appeal, holding that the interpolation of the passageway did not provide a sufficiently direct access to link the occupation of the flat and the house. *Perry*, 15.22 below, distinguished. (The tribunal also held that a refund of tax was not due in respect of the garage, as on the evidence the garage was part of the existing house rather than part of the flat.) *AA Heslop, EDN/89/43 (VTD 3862)*.

15.5 **Construction of house adjacent to offices.** A husband and wife partnership built a house adjacent to their business premises. The two buildings shared a common wall and were connected by a communicating door. The partnership reclaimed tax under what is now *VATA 1994, s 35*, but the Commissioners disallowed the claim as there was internal access between the two buildings. The partnership appealed and the tribunal allowed the appeal. *Perry*, 15.22 below, was distinguished because in that case both buildings were dwelling-houses so that the new dwelling had become an enlargement of the existing dwelling. In the instant case the existing building comprised offices whereas the new building was a house. The house could not be said to be an enlargement of the existing offices. *Waterways Services, [1990] VATTR 37 (VTD 4643).*

15.6   **Replacement of old farmhouse by new farmhouse.**   A farmer owned an old stone-built farmhouse which had been built in the late 19th century, had no foundations, and was in poor condition. He obtained planning permission for 'improvements and extension' to the building. However, in view of the absence of foundations, the whole of the old building was demolished and a completely new house was erected on the site. He claimed relief under what is now *VATA 1994, s 35*. The Commissioners rejected the claim, considering that in view of the nature of the planning permission, the work had in law constituted the reconstruction of an existing building, rather than the construction of a new one. The tribunal allowed the farmer's appeal, finding that since no part of the original farmhouse remained standing, the work was the construction of a new building and was eligible for relief. Applying *dicta* in *Waterways Services Ltd*, 15.5 above, the fact that the proposed work was described in the planning permission as an 'extension' did not render it unlawful or prevent it from qualifying as the construction of a building. *ED Bruce, [1991] VATTR 280 (VTD 6326).*

15.7   **Replacement of semi-detached cottages by detached house.**   A married couple purchased two 18th century semi-detached cottages. They obtained planning permission to convert the cottages into a single building, and reclaimed input tax under what is now *VATA 1994, s 35*. The Commissioners rejected the claim on the grounds that the work amounted to the conversion of an existing building. The couple appealed, contending that, despite the terms of the planning permission, the cottages had been in such poor condition that they had had to demolish them and construct a new building. The tribunal accepted the couple's evidence and allowed the appeal. *JS & L Bell, MAN/94/438 (VTD 13448).*

Cases held not to qualify for zero-rating or refund

15.8   **Construction of flat on top of existing building.**   A three-storey house was divided into three flats. An additional flat was built on top of the existing house. The tribunal held that the work did not qualify for relief under what is now *VATA 1994, s 35*. The flat did not have a separate entrance, had no independent foundation, and was clearly an enlargement of an existing building. *S Hardy, LON/76/46 (VTD 289).*

15.9   **Construction of flat as extension to bungalow.**   A flat was built as an extension to a bungalow. The bungalow already had a flat-roofed extension and the flat was partly at ground level, sharing a common wall with the existing extension, and partly over the existing extension. It had separate access and services and was separately rated. The tribunal held that the flat was an enlargement of the bungalow and that its construction did not qualify for relief under what is now *VATA 1994, s 35*. *DW Taylor, MAN/77/94 (VTD 454).*

15.10   **Construction of flat adjacent to house.**   A self-contained flat was constructed adjacent to an existing house. The roof of the house was extended to cover the flat. The tribunal held that the flat was an enlargement of an existing building for the purposes of what is now *VATA 1994, s 35. Taylor*, 15.9 above, applied; *Hill*, 15.3 above, distinguished. *HN Kirsopp, MAN/81/203 (VTD 1236)*.

15.11   Reconstruction of derelict cottage.   An individual bought a 17th century cottage which was derelict and uninhabitable. He carried out extensive work to make it suitable as a dwelling-house for himself but, to comply with the terms of his planning permission, he used the old foundation and some of the old building. He reclaimed tax under what is now *VATA 1994, s 35*. The Commissioners rejected the claim and the tribunal dismissed his appeal, holding that the work was the reconstruction of an existing building. *HC Morton, CAR/77/137 (VTD 438)*.

15.12   Similar decisions were reached in *T Owen, LON/78/345 (VTD 741)* and *JW Shields, EDN/96/246 (VTD 15154)*.

15.13   Sales of land on which houses built by associated company.   A company (D) was a member of a group engaged in building, for which there was no group registration. D's principal function was to acquire building land and necessary planning permission, plan the layout of the estates and see to the landscaping and the building of roads and sewers. Another group company (Y) built the houses in accordance with D's plans and specifications. D then sold the plots of land with the houses built on them. In a typical sale, D was described as the vendor and Y as the builder, and the completion statement showed separate figures for the house and the land, the former being the amount invoiced by Y to D for erecting the house. The Commissioners issued a ruling that D's sales of land were exempt. D appealed, contending that they were zero-rated and that it could therefore reclaim part of its input tax. The tribunal rejected this contention and dismissed the appeal. The functions performed by D were not those of 'a person constructing a building' for the purpose of what is now *VATA 1994, Sch 8, Group 5, Item 1. Monsell Youell Developments Ltd, [1978] VATTR 1 (VTD 538)*.

15.14   Work carried out by lessee.   In 1965 a redevelopment scheme was begun under which land owned by an educational foundation was let for 125 years to a company (C) which was to finance the redevelopment, and sublet by C to another company (M) for a similar term. The redevelopment was completed in 1971, and the foundation reclaimed the input tax incurred. The Commissioners disallowed the claim, considering that the foundation was not the 'person constructing a building' and thus not within what is now *VATA 1994, Sch 8, Group 5, Item 1*. The tribunal dismissed the foundation's appeal. The words 'person constructing a building' must be given their natural meaning. The 'construction must be physically done by the person concerned or by his servants or agents, or the person must himself directly enter into a contract or arrangement for another to do the physical construction works'. The construction work here was done under contracts to which the foundation was not a party. *Hulme Educational Foundation, [1978] VATTR 179 (VTD 625)*.

15.15   Sale by housing association of former council houses.   In March 1993 a housing association purchased a number of council houses from the district council which had built them. In 1994 the association sold four of the houses to sitting tenants, in accordance with the provisions introduced by the *Housing Act 1980*. The Commissioners issued a ruling that the sales did not qualify for zero-rating, since the association was not the 'person constructing' the dwellings. The association appealed, contending that the effect of *Article 5(8)* of the *EC Sixth Directive* was that it should be treated as the 'person constructing' the dwellings. The tribunal dismissed the appeal, holding that *Article 5(8)* was 'wholly permissive' and 'does not create a directly effective entitlement that United Kingdom taxpayers can rely on'. Furthermore, the purchase of the houses from the council by the association did not constitute the transfer of a business as a going concern. *Peddars Way Housing Association Ltd, LON/93/2619A (VTD 12663)*.

15.16   **Materials added to house after completion of contract.**   A married couple purchased a newly-built house in May 1993. They also purchased a conservatory (in kit form), additional light fittings, curtain rails, a fitted wardrobe, and additional shelving and miscellaneous hardware. All these items were attached to the house after completion of the contract. The couple reclaimed input tax under what is now *VATA 1994, s 35*. The Commissioners rejected the claim, on the grounds that the couple were not 'a person constructing a building'. The couple appealed, contending that the house had not been completed at the time they purchased it. The tribunal rejected this contention and dismissed their appeal, holding on the evidence that 'on the completion of the contract the vendor handed over a completed building'. The addition of a conservatory 'amounted to the enlargement of an existing building' and none of the other items in question 'could fairly be described as constructing a building or as completing the construction of a building'. *AG & W Simister, MAN/93/1376 (VTD 12715)*.

15.17   An appeal was dismissed in a case where a claimant had purchased a fireplace for a new house before taking occupation but after the completion certificate had been issued by the local authority. *Simister*, 15.16 above, applied. The tribunal held that 'the completion of a building is a matter of fact and evidence of completion is the local authority certificate'. *I Taylor, EDN/97/170 (VTD 15566)*.

15.18   **Sale of renovated houses.**   A company sold houses which it had renovated, and did not account for output tax on the sales. The Commissioners issued an assessment charging tax on the sales, and the company appealed, contending that the sales were zero-rated under what is now *VATA 1994, Sch 8, Group 5, Item 1*. The tribunal dismissed the company's appeal, holding that the work of renovation did not amount to 'construction' and accordingly the company was not a 'person constructing a building'. *T & D Services (Timber Preservation & Damp Proofing Contractors) Ltd, LON/80/435 (VTD 1157)*.

15.19   A similar decision was reached in *BS Horn, MAN/82/18 (VTD 1250)*.

15.20   **Extension to existing house.**   An individual (C) converted a house comprising 156 square metres into two semi-detached houses with a total area of 244 square metres. He reclaimed tax under what is now *VATA 1994, s 35*. The Commissioners rejected the claim and the tribunal dismissed C's appeal, holding that the work constituted the enlargement of an existing building. *D Childs, LON/82/330 (VTD 1373)*.

15.21   See also *Granger Builders*, 15.100 below, and the note at 15.101 below.

15.22   **Dwelling added to existing house with communicating door.**   The owner of a house built a two-storey extension to be used by members of his family. The extension had a separate entrance. However, a condition of the planning permission was that the extension was to be used 'only in conjunction with the existing building'. A communicating door was built in the party wall between the existing house and the extension. The Commissioners rejected the owner's claim for a refund of tax, considering that the work did not constitute the construction of a new building. The QB upheld the Commissioners' decision. On the evidence, the extension was an enlargement of the existing dwelling, so that relief was not due. The terms of the planning permission and the existence of the communicating door dictated the conclusion that the extension was not a separate building. *C & E Commrs v RC Perry, QB [1983] STC 383*.

15.23 Construction of Buildings, etc.

15.23   *Perry*, 15.22 above, was applied in the similar subsequent case of *W Macaulay, EDN/95/291 (VTD 14429)*.

15.24   **Reconstruction of bungalow.**   An appellant (W) purchased a bungalow which was structurally unsound. He obtained planning permission to convert it into a 'dwelling and granny flat'. The existing walls were replaced but the roof structure and windows were retained. There was little change in the external appearance of the bungalow. W claimed a refund of VAT under what is now *VATA 1994, s 35*. The Commissioners rejected the claim, considering that the work was the alteration of an existing building and that no refund was therefore due. The tribunal dismissed W's appeal, holding that the work constituted the reconstruction of an existing building rather than the construction of a new one. *D White, EDN/89/93 (VTD 4254)*.

15.25   A claimant (B) obtained planning permission for extensions to a bungalow. After beginning work on the extensions, he became aware that the existing walls had been badly affected by damp. He replaced the external walls, replaced the roof, and then demolished the internal walls. The Commissioners rejected his claim for a refund of tax, on the basis that the work constituted the reconstruction of an existing building and the bungalow had never been 'demolished completely to ground level', as required by *VATA 1994, Sch 8, Group 5, Note 18*. The tribunal upheld this decision and dismissed B's appeal. *Bruce*, 15.6 above, distinguished. *AA Bugg, LON/97/224 (VTD 15123)*.

15.26   **Reconstruction or alteration of existing building.**   There have been a large number of cases in which tribunals have found that work has constituted the reconstruction or alteration of an existing building, rather than the construction of a new building, and which appear to raise no point of general interest. In the interests of space, such cases are not summarised individually in this book. For summaries of such cases decided up to 31 December 1995, see Tolley's VAT Cases 1996.

DEFINITION OF 'BUILDING DESIGNED AS A DWELLING' (VATA 1994, Sch 8, Group 5, Items 1(a), 2(a); VATA 1994, s 35(1A)(a))

Cases held to qualify for zero-rating

15.27   **Prefabricated bungalows—whether 'buildings designed as a dwelling'.**   A married couple purchased a caravan site which was 'almost derelict', renovated the site, and built a number of luxury prefabricated bungalows for sale. The bungalows were erected on a brick foundation with a brick skirting. The couple considered that the sale of the bungalows qualified for zero-rating under what is now *VATA 1994, Sch 8, Group 5, Item 1*. Accordingly, they reclaimed input tax and did not account for output tax. The Commissioners issued an assessment to recover the input tax on the basis that the sale of the bungalows did not qualify for zero-rating, but was the grant of an interest over land which was exempt from VAT. The tribunal allowed the couple's appeal, holding that the bungalows were clearly 'buildings', rather than caravans. They were rated and insured as bungalows, and although they were described as 'mobile homes' in agreements between the purchasers and the site manager, it was unlikely that they would in fact be moved. The cost of removal would be prohibitive, and the homes were occupied and used as permanent dwellings. When they were erected on the site, they 'lost the physical characteristics which had made them mobile and they acquired new characteristics (such as the brickwork base) which made them buildings'. *Mr & Mrs N Smith, MAN/89/708 (VTD 5579)*.

15.28   **Conversion of mill into residential units—whether Sch 8, Group 5, Note 2(c) applicable.**   Two individuals obtained permission to convert a mill into two residential units. They each acquired one of the units, and retained joint ownership of a workshop which stood in the grounds of the mill. They signed an agreement under *Town and Country Planning Act 1990, s 10*, respectively covenanting not to sever the legal ownership of any part of either of the residential units or the workshop. They reclaimed tax on the conversion work under *VATA 1994, s 35*. The Commissioners rejected the claim on the grounds that the effect of the covenant was to prohibit the separate use or disposal of either of the residential units, so that the effect of *VATA 1994, Sch 8, Group 5, Note 2(c)* was that neither of the units qualified as a building 'designed as a dwelling'. The tribunal allowed the claimants' appeal, holding that since the covenants related 'to each of the three properties respectively', their effect was to prevent any further subdivision of either of the two residential units, but that they did not prohibit the separate disposal of either of the units 'in the sense contemplated by *Note 2(c)*'. *JS Sherwin & RK Green, LON/98/708 (VTD 16396)*.

Cases held not to qualify for zero-rating

15.29   **Independent building in grounds of recently-built house—whether a 'building designed as a dwelling'.** An individual purchased a house and obtained planning permission to build a new house on the same site. The structure of the new house was completed in August 1990, and the internal fitting was completed in May 1991. In October 1991 the owner applied for permission to demolish a garage block and replace it by an annexe consisting of a triple garage with office space and residential accommodation for domestic staff, and to build an indoor swimming pool. The annexe was not physically attached to the new house. Planning consent for this was granted in March 1992, and the construction of the annexe began in August 1992. The Commissioners issued a ruling that the construction of the annexe and swimming pool did not qualify for zero-rating under what is now *VATA 1994, Sch 8, Group 5, Item 2*, and the owner appealed. The tribunal dismissed the appeal, holding that the annexe did not qualify for zero-rating. The annexe was not part of a single dwelling erected in stages, but was a separate building from the house. The garage was not constructed at the same time as the house and thus did not fall within what is now *VATA 1994, Sch 8, Group 5, Note 3*. Although the annexe contained residential accommodation, it was not within the definition of 'a building designed as a dwelling'. *SA Whiteley, [1993] VATTR 248 (VTD 11292)*.

15.30   A married couple arranged for the construction of a new two-storey building, in the grounds of their existing house, and including two bedrooms, a kitchen, a bathroom and a shower. The Commissioners issued a ruling that the work did not qualify for zero-rating. The husband appealed, contending firstly that the new building was designed as a dwelling and alternatively that it was intended for use for a residential purpose. The tribunal rejected these contentions and dismissed the appeal. The effect of *VATA 1994, Sch 8, Group 5, Note 2(c)* was that the building did not qualify as a 'building designed as a dwelling', since its separate use was prohibited by the terms of the relevant planning permission. Furthermore, the fact that the couple's eldest child occupied the new building did not mean that it qualified as 'residential accommodation for students', since the child was 'occupying the new building as being a child of the appellant and part of the appellant's household rather than as a student or school pupil'. *P Thompson, [1998] VATDR 524 (VTD 15834)*.

15.31   See also *Moore*, 15.65 below.

15.32   **Conversion of stable block into 'annexe'—whether a 'building designed as a dwelling'.** An individual (H) claimed a refund of VAT under *VATA 1994, s 35* in respect of the conversion of a stable block into an 'annexe for living accommodation'. The Commissioners rejected the claim on the basis that, in view of the relevant planning permission, the converted stable block did not qualify as a 'building designed as a dwelling'. The tribunal dismissed H's appeal against this decision. *LR Hamilton, MAN/97/975 (VTD 16020)*.

15.33   **Conversion of barn into living accommodation—whether a 'building designed as a dwelling'.**   See *Ford*, 52.3 PROTECTED BUILDINGS, and *Clamp*, 52.4 PROTECTED BUILDINGS.

15.34   **University buildings used for vacation lettings.**   A university owned a number of buildings, which had been designed and used as student accommodation but which were also partly used for vacation lettings for non-educational purposes. It arranged for the refurbishment of the buildings and leased them to an associated company. It reclaimed the relevant input tax. The Commissioners rejected the claim on the grounds that the grants of the leases were exempt supplies. The university appealed, contending that, since it had originally constructed the buildings and was granting major interests in them, the grants qualified for zero-rating under *VATA 1994, Sch 8, Group 5, Item 1*. The tribunal rejected this contention and dismissed the appeal, holding that, in view of the nature of the accommodation, the buildings were not 'designed as a dwelling or number of dwellings' and were not 'intended for use solely for a relevant residential or a relevant charitable purpose'. *University of Bath, LON/95/2791A (VTD 14235)*.

15.35   *University of Bath*, 15.34 above, was applied in a subsequent case where the facts were similar. The tribunal observed that the rooms occupied by the students were not within the definition of a 'dwelling', since they contained no cooking or toilet facilities. *University Court of the University of St Andrews, EDN/96/182 (VTD 15243)*.

DEFINITION OF 'RELEVANT RESIDENTIAL PURPOSE' (VATA 1994, Sch 8, Group 5, Items 1, 2(a); VATA 1994, s 35(1A)(b))

Cases held to qualify for zero-rating

15.36   **Whether building intended as 'residential accommodation for students'.**   An educational establishment (G) provided courses in Welsh. It arranged for the construction of two buildings, to be used as accommodation for students on residential courses lasting for up to a week. It treated the work as zero-rated, on the basis that the buildings were intended to be used solely for a 'relevant residential purpose', namely as 'residential accommodation for students', within *VATA 1994, Sch 8, Group 5, Item 2(a)* and *Note 4(d)*. The Commissioners issued a ruling that VAT was chargeable on the work in question, considering that the accommodation did not qualify as 'residential accommodation', since no student occupied it for more than a week. The tribunal allowed G's appeal, holding that, although 'residence' (when used as a noun) 'clearly implies a building with a significant degree of permanence of occupation ... the word loses that clear meaning when used as an adjective. In ordinary English "residential accommodation" merely signifies lodging, sleeping or overnight accommodation. It does not suggest the need for such accommodation to be for any fixed or minimum period.' *Urdd Gobaith Cymru, [1997] VATDR 273 (VTD 14881)*.

15.37   A college arranged for the construction of four accommodation blocks intended for use by short-stay students attending courses which lasted between three and six days. The accommodation did not include catering or kitchen facilities. The Commissioners issued a ruling that output tax was chargeable on the work. The college appealed, contending that the accommodation was intended for use 'solely for a relevant residential purpose'. The tribunal accepted this contention and allowed the appeal. Applying *Urdd Gobaith Cymru*, 15.36 above, the phrase 'residential accommodation' merely signified 'lodging, sleeping or overnight accommodation'. Accordingly, the fact that there were no kitchen or catering facilities within the blocks did not prevent them from qualifying as 'residential accommodation for students'. *Denman College, [1998] VATDR 399 (VTD 15513)*.

Cases held not to qualify for zero-rating

15.38   **Construction of building in garden of private house.**   A building constructed in the garden of a private house, and comprising a garage, games room and lavatory, was held not to be suitable for residential occupation, and therefore not to qualify for zero-rating, in *AD Smith, MAN/86/26 (VTD 2164)*.

15.39   **Classroom block constructed by fee-paying school.**   The Commissioners issued a ruling that supplies in the course of construction of two classroom buildings at a fee-paying boarding school did not qualify for zero-rating. The company which operated the school appealed, contending that the buildings should be treated as being used for a relevant residential purpose. (It was accepted that the school was not a charity.) The tribunal dismissed the company's appeal, holding that the buildings did not qualify for zero-rating since they were 'intended for use solely as classrooms and for purposes associated with that use; they are thus intended to be used merely as part of a home or other institution and not as the home or institution itself'. *Riverside School (Whassett) Ltd, [1995] VATDR 186 (VTD 13170)*.

15.40   **Whether building intended as 'residential accommodation for students'.**   See *Thompson*, 15.30 above, and *University of Bath*, 15.34 above.

DEFINITION OF 'RELEVANT CHARITABLE PURPOSE' (VATA 1994, Sch 8, Group 5, Items 1, 2(a); VATA 1994, s 35(1A)(b))

Cases held to qualify for zero-rating or refund

15.41   **Changing rooms constructed for under-16s' football club.**   A builder constructed a block of changing rooms for a junior football club (whose players were all under 16 years of age), and did not account for VAT on the work. The Commissioners issued an assessment, against which he appealed, contending that the work should be zero-rated on the grounds that it was for a 'charitable purpose'. The tribunal adjourned the appeal for further evidence, finding that the club was not a registered charity but holding that it might still qualify as a charity on the basis that it was established for 'purposes beneficial to the community' (applying *Special Commissioners v Pemsel, HL 1891, 3 TC 53; TTC 2001, 9.1*) or that it fell within *Recreational Charities Act 1958, s 1. R Meadows, LON/93/213A (VTD 11817) (Note.* There was no further public hearing of the appeal. It is understood that, following the tribunal decision, the Commissioners accepted that the club was within *Recreational Charities Act 1958, s 1*.)

15.42   **Football club.**   A football club built a pavilion, with the aid of a loan from the National Playing Fields Association (NPFA). The pavilion was owned by the NPFA, which granted the club a licence to use it. The club was the principal user of the pavilion, but it was used by other organisations with the permission of a local committee of the NPFA. The club reclaimed input tax on the building of the pavilion. The Commissioners rejected the claim on the grounds that the club was not a charity and that the club was carrying on a business. The club appealed, contending that the pavilion was used by the NPFA, which was a charity, and was used 'in providing social or recreational facilities for a local community', within what is now *VATA 1994, Sch 8, Group 5, Note 6(b)*. The tribunal allowed the appeal, holding on the evidence that the construction of the pavilion was 'gratuitous work done for the

15.43 Construction of Buildings, etc.

prime benefit of the NPFA' and was 'primarily and substantially in furtherance of the activities and ownership rights of NPFA'. The pavilion was used 'for the charitable purposes of NPFA ... to the local community'. Accordingly the conditions of *Note 6(b)* were satisfied and the club was entitled to a refund of the input tax. *Hunmanby Bowling Club*, 15.55 below, distinguished. *Shinewater Association Football Club*, *LON/94/732A (VTD 12938)*.

15.43 **Leisure centre constructed by charity—whether within VATA 1994, Sch 8, Group 5, Note 6(b).** An association which was a registered charity arranged for the construction of a leisure centre. Membership of the association was automatically granted to the inhabitants of ten adjoining parishes. The Commissioners issued a ruling that the construction of the centre failed to qualify for zero-rating on the basis that the centre was operated as a business. The association appealed, contending that the construction qualified for zero-rating under what is now *VATA 1994, Sch 8, Group 5, Note 6(b)* as the centre was used similarly to a village hall, 'in providing social or recreational facilities for a local community'. The tribunal accepted this contention and allowed the appeal. The fact that the building was 'reasonably substantial' in size did not prevent it from being treated as similar to a village hall. *Ormiston Charitable Trust*, 15.50 below, distinguished. *Bennachie Leisure Centre Association, EDN/96/60 (VTD 14276)*. (*Notes.* (1) The Commissioners state, in Customs' VAT Manual, Part 9, chapter 2, section 12.13 that they 'were not happy with the finding in this particular case' and consider that 'the decision should be restricted to this case and not given general application'. However, the decision was applied by a subsequent tribunal in *Ledbury Amateur Dramatic Society*, 15.44 below. (2) The decision here was distinguished in the subsequent case of *Princess Royal Sports Club*, 15.51 below, partly on the grounds that the association's constitution here specifically provided 'that the local community are *ipso facto* members'.)

15.44 **Theatre constructed for charity—whether within VATA 1994, Sch 8, Group 5, Note 6(b).** An amateur dramatic society, based in a small town with a population of 8,000 people, was a registered charity. It arranged for the construction of a theatre. The Commissioners issued a ruling that tax was chargeable on the work. The society appealed, contending that the construction qualified for zero-rating under *VATA 1994, Sch 8, Group 5, Note 6(b)* as the theatre was used similarly to a village hall, 'in providing social or recreational facilities for a local community'. The tribunal accepted this contention and allowed the appeal. On the evidence, 90% of the society's members lived in the town where the theatre was built, so that the facilities were provided for a 'local community'. The theatre employed no full-time staff, and was used similarly to a village hall. *Bennachie Leisure Centre Association*, 15.43 above, applied; *South Molton Swimming Pool Trustees*, 15.53 below, and *Jubilee Hall Recreation Centre Ltd*, 52.8 PROTECTED BUILDINGS, distinguished. *Ledbury Amateur Dramatic Society, LON/99/634 (VTD 16845)*.

15.45 **Playgroup—whether a business.** A company, which operated a playgroup and was accepted as being a charity, reclaimed VAT under what is now *VATA 1994, s 35* on the construction of a new building. The company's turnover was less than £4,000 p.a. and, although the majority of parents made contributions to the cost of running the playgroup, such contributions were not compulsory. The Commissioners rejected the claim on the basis that the building was used in the course or furtherance of a business of providing playgroup facilities, and was therefore not used solely for a relevant charitable purpose. The tribunal allowed the company's appeal, holding that in view of the low turnover and the voluntary nature of the contributions, the playgroup was not a 'business'. *Newtownbutler Playgroup Ltd, LON/94/1457A (VTD 13741)*.

15.46   **Office block constructed for housing association—whether used 'in the course or furtherance of a business'.**   A charitable housing association, registered under the *Industrial & Provident Societies Act 1965*, arranged for the construction of an office block. The Commissioners issued a ruling that the work was standard-rated. The association appealed, contending that the offices were used for a 'relevant charitable purpose' within *VATA 1994, Sch 8, Group 5, Item 2(a)*. The tribunal accepted this contention and allowed the appeal, holding that the association had 'taken on what was formerly the duty of the State to provide housing for those people who are unable to obtain accommodation in the open market through a variety of reasons'. It had 'no autonomy in the way it functions and is obliged to function in some ways which are completely contrary to normal business practice and the usual way of carrying out economic activities'. Accordingly, it was not carrying on a business, and its offices were used 'otherwise than in the course or furtherance of a business', within *Group 5, Note 6(a)*. *Cardiff Community Housing Association Ltd, LON/99/343 (VTD 16841)*.

15.47   **Garage constructed at church.**   A Catholic Church arranged for the construction of a garage, within the curtilage of the church building, for parking cars which were provided by the parish and driven by priests resident at the presbytery. The Commissioners issued a ruling that output tax was chargeable on the work. The church appealed, contending that the garage was intended for use 'solely for a relevant charitable purpose', and therefore qualified for zero-rating under *VATA 1994, Sch 8,, Group 5, Item 2(a)*. The tribunal accepted this contention and allowed the appeal, observing that the cars were provided for pastoral use and holding that any private use was *de minimis* and could be disregarded. The tribunal held that 'the fact that a priest may from time to time use a car, which is provided for his use, for his personal shopping is irrelevant to the question whether the garage ... is used for a relevant charitable purpose'. *St Dunstan's Roman Catholic Church Southborough, [1998] VATDR 264 (VTD 15472)*.

Cases held not to qualify for zero-rating or refund

15.48   **Classroom block constructed by fee-paying school—whether within VATA 1994, Sch 8, Group 5, Note 6(a).**   A school, which was operated by a charitable company limited by guarantee, constructed a new classroom block. It applied for a certificate of zero-rating under what is now *VATA 1994, Sch 8, Group 5, Note 12(b)*. The Commissioners rejected the application, considering that the classroom block was not to be used for a relevant charitable purpose, since it was intended for use in the course of a business of providing education for a consideration. The school appealed, contending that since some of the pupils who were to be educated in the classroom block were in receipt of scholarships and bursaries, the block was partly for charitable purposes and an apportionment should be made under *Sch 8, Group 5, Note 10*. The tribunal rejected the school's contention and dismissed the appeal. None of the pupils were admitted free, so that the school was making supplies for consideration in respect of all its pupils. Applying *Morrison's Academy Boarding Houses Association*, 7.1 BUSINESS, such supplies constituted the carrying on of a business. The whole of the classroom block was to be used in the course or furtherance of that business, so that the conditions of *VATA 1994, Sch 8, Group 5, Note 6(a)* were not satisfied. Furthermore, even if many of the pupils had been educated free of charge, so that their education would not constitute a business activity, no part of the block would be used for non-business purposes unless no fee-paying pupils were educated there. *Leighton Park School, LON/91/1673Z (VTD 9392)*.

15.49   **University buildings used for vacation lettings—whether intended for use solely for relevant charitable purpose.**   See *University of Bath*, 15.34 above.

15.50 Construction of Buildings, etc.

15.50 **Sports pavilion constructed by charity—whether within VATA 1994, Sch 8, Group 5, Note 6(b).** A registered charity arranged for the construction of a building, on land at the rear of a school, to be used as a sports pavilion. The Commissioners issued a ruling that the supplies made in the course of construction did not qualify for zero-rating, on the basis that the building was not intended to be used solely for a relevant charitable purpose. The charity appealed, contending that the building was intended to be used 'in providing social or recreational facilities for a local community', within what is now *VATA 1994, Sch 8, Group 5, Note 6(b)*. The tribunal dismissed the appeal, holding that the building was not within *Note 6(b)*, on the grounds that it was not used 'similarly' to a village hall. The people to whom it provided facilities were 'a particular section of the community, not a local community', and the building was not 'operated in the way in which a village hall is carried on'. *Ormiston Charitable Trust, [1995] VATDR 180 (VTD 13187)*.

15.51 A similar decision was reached in a subsequent case in which the tribunal applied the CA decision in *Jubilee Hall Recreation Centre Ltd*, 52.8 PROTECTED BUILDINGS, and distinguished *Bennachie Leisure Centre Association*, 15.43 above, on the basis that the charity's constitution here did 'not provide that the local community are *ipso facto* members nor does it provide for any defined area of membership'. *Princess Royal Sports Club, EDN/99/43 (VTD 16227)*.

15.52 **Sports hall constructed by charity—whether within VATA 1994, Sch 8, Group 5, Note 6(b).** A registered educational charity arranged for the construction of a sports hall, which was intended to be used by an independent fee-paying school, and to be made available for community use at specified times. The Commissioners issued a ruling that the supplies made in the course of construction did not qualify for zero-rating, on the basis that the school was charging for the use of the facilities, so that the building was not intended to be used solely for a relevant charitable purpose. The charity appealed, contending that the school was also a charity and that its use of the sports hall was within *VATA 1994, Sch 8, Group 5, Note 6*. The CA rejected this contention, holding that the building was used for the purposes of a business, and was not intended for use 'in providing ... recreational facilities for a local community', since the community use was secondary to the use by the school. Sir John Vinelott observed that 'insofar as pupils at the school benefited from that facility, they did so not as members of the local community, but as pupils on whose behalf fees were paid to the school'. *C & E Commrs v St Dunstan's Educational Foundation, CA 1998, [1999] STC 381*. (*Note*. The case was heard by the CA together with *Jubilee Hall Recreation Centre Ltd*, 52.8 PROTECTED BUILDINGS.)

15.53 **Swimming pool constructed by charity—whether within VATA 1994, Sch 8, Group 5, Note 6(b).** A charity was established for the purpose of building and operating a swimming pool in a rural area of North Devon. (The area had previously been served by a pool operated by the local district council, but that pool had closed in 1991.) The Commissioners issued a ruling that output tax was chargeable on the construction of the pool. The charity appealed, contending that the pool qualified for zero-rating under *VATA 1994, Sch 8, Group 5, Note 6(b)*. The tribunal rejected this contention and dismissed the appeal, finding that the pool was 'a well-organised commercial operation' and holding that it was not solely used 'as a village hall or similarly in providing social or recreational facilities'. The tribunal also held that the pool facilities were not provided solely for a local community, since it was used by people from up to 23 miles away, whereas for the purposes of *Note 6(b)* 'the local community being referred to is on the scale of a village'. *Jubilee Hall Recreation Centre Ltd*, 52.8 PROTECTED BUILDINGS, applied. *South Molton Swimming Pool Trustees, LON/98/372 (VTD 16495)*.

15.54   **Building used by charity as sports and fitness centre—whether within VATA 1994, Sch 8, Group 5, Note 6(b).**   See *Jubilee Hall Recreation Centre Ltd*, 52.8 PROTECTED BUILDINGS.

15.55   **Bowling club—whether within VATA 1994, Sch 8, Group 5, Note 6(a).**   A bowling club reclaimed input tax on materials used for the construction of a pavilion. The Commissioners rejected the claim on the grounds that the club was not a charity and that the club was carrying on a business. The tribunal dismissed the club's appeal, holding that the club was a charity within the *Recreational Charities Act 1958*, but that it was also carrying on a business within what is now *VATA 1994, s 94*, so that the conditions of what is now *VATA 1994, Sch 8, Group 5, Note 6(a)* were not satisfied and no refund was due. *Hunmanby Bowling Club, MAN/93/862 (VTD 12136)*. (*Note*. Despite the tribunal's decision that the club was a charity, the Commissioners consider that 'sports clubs are not usually charities ... because the promotion of sport is not a charitable object in itself and such clubs usually exist to provide facilities for their members'. See Customs' VAT Manual, Part 9, chapter 2, section 3.5.)

15.56   **Royal Academy of Music—whether concert hall to be used for 'relevant charitable purpose'.**   See *The Royal Academy of Music*, 52.7 PROTECTED BUILDINGS.

15.57   **Building constructed to house scanner unit for hospital.**   A registered charity arranged for the construction of a building to house a scanner unit for a hospital. The Commissioners issued a ruling that the services supplied to the charity in the course of construction of the building did not qualify for zero-rating. The charity appealed. The tribunal dismissed the appeal, holding that since the hospital itself was not a charity, the building was not being used for a relevant charitable purpose. *League of Friends of Kingston Hospital, LON/93/1870A (VTD 12764)*.

15.58   **Building used by charity for catering supplies—whether used 'in the course or furtherance of a business'.**   A registered charity constructed a building which comprised a kitchen, two dining rooms and a coffee lounge. It claimed a refund of tax under *VATA 1994, s 35*. The Commissioners rejected the claim on the ground that the charity was using the building to make supplies of catering services 'in the course or furtherance of a business', so that the conditions of *VATA 1994, Sch 8, Group 5, Note 6(a)* were not satisfied. The tribunal dismissed the charity's appeal. Applying *Morrison's Academy Boarding Houses Association*, 7.1 above, 'the provision of catering for consideration does not cease to be a business by reason of the fact that it is not designed to make a profit'. *Summer Institute of Linguistics Ltd, LON/98/1400 (VTD 16159)*.

15.59   **Community centre—whether within VATA 1994, Sch 8, Group 5, Note 6(a).**   A community association had been formed with the objects of promoting 'the benefit of the inhabitants of Southwick and its immediate neighbourhood'. It was a registered charity, and had 60 affiliated organisations. It arranged for the construction of a new community centre. The Commissioners issued a ruling that output tax was chargeable on the work, and the association appealed, contending that it should be treated as zero-rated. The tribunal rejected this contention and dismissed the appeal. The building was available to affiliated organisations on payment of a fee, so that the conditions of *VATA 1994, Sch 8, Group 5, Note 6(a)* were not satisfied. On the evidence, the association's membership included individuals who were not resident in Southwick or 'its immediate neighbourhood', and its affiliated organisations were also not subject to such a restriction. Accordingly, the tribunal held that the building was not used 'in providing social or recreational facilities for a local community'. *Dicta* of Sir John Vinelott in *Jubilee Hall*

Recreation Centre Ltd, 52.8 PROTECTED BUILDINGS, applied. *Southwick Community Association, LON/97/1703 (VTD 16441)*.

RESIDENTIAL CONVERSIONS (VATA 1994, Sch 8, Group 5, Item 1(b); VATA 1994, s 35(1A)(c),(1D))

15.60   **Conversion of building formerly used as public house—whether a residential conversion.**   A married couple purchased a run-down building which had been used as a public house until the 1970s, but which had been unoccupied for some time and had been deemed 'unfit for human habitation' by the local council. They converted the building into a dwelling-house, and claimed a refund of tax under *VATA 1994, s 35*. The Commissioners rejected the claim on the basis that the building had been used as a dwelling after 1 April 1973, so that it was not a 'non-residential building' as defined by *VATA 1994, Sch 8, Group 5, Note 7*, and the work was therefore not a residential conversion as defined by *VATA 1994, s 35(1D)*. The tribunal dismissed the couple's appeal against this decision. *R & A Tilley, LON/96/1199 (VTD 15097)*.

15.61   An individual (T) purchased a public house, which had included residential accommodation on the upper floor, and converted it into a private dwelling-house. He claimed a refund of tax under *VATA 1994, s 35*. The Commissioners rejected the claim on the basis that the building had previously been used as a dwelling, so that it was not a 'non-residential building' as defined by *VATA 1994, Sch 8, Group 5, Note 7*, and the work was therefore not a residential conversion as defined by *VATA 1994, s 35(1D)*. The tribunal dismissed T's appeal, holding that the upper floor of the building was not 'non-residential' before the conversion. Since the building had already contained a residential part, and the conversion did not create an additional dwelling, the work was not within the definition of a 'residential conversion'. The tribunal specifically declined to follow the decision in *Temple House Developments Ltd*, 15.62 below, on the grounds that the tribunal there had erred in law by reading *Note 7* in conjunction with *Note 2*. The chairman (Mr. Lightman) held that *Note 2* was 'only intended to be relevant to the question of whether there is "a building designed as a dwelling" after the conversion', whereas the purpose of *Note 7* was to determine 'whether the building or part of the building was non-residential *before* the conversion'. *G Tobell, LON/98/1349 (VTD 16646)*.

15.62   **Public house converted into two semi-detached houses—whether within Item 1(b).**   A company purchased a public house and obtained planning permission for its conversion into two semi-detached houses. The company elected to waive exemption on the property and reclaimed input tax on the purchase and conversion. The Commissioners issued assessments to recover the tax on the basis that they were attributable to exempt supplies. The company appealed, contending that the public house had been a 'non-residential building', within *VATA 1994, Sch 8, Group 5, Item 1(b)*, so that the subsequent sales would be zero-rated supplies and the input tax was recoverable. The tribunal accepted this contention and allowed the appeal, holding on the evidence that no part of the public house 'was designed as a dwelling before the ... planning consent'. The effect of *Group 5, Notes 2, 7* was that 'there was no part of the (public house) which was not non-residential'. *Tilley*, 15.60 above, distinguished. *Temple House Developments Ltd, LON/97/787 (VTD 15583)*. (*Note.* The decision here was disapproved by a subsequent tribunal in *Tobell*, 15.61 above, on the grounds that the tribunal here had erred in law by reading *Note 2* in conjunction with *Note 7*. It was also not followed, and implicitly disapproved, by a subsequent tribunal in *Calam Vale Ltd*, 15.63 below.)

15.63   A company converted a public house into two semi-detached dwellings. The Commissioners issued a ruling that the sale of the dwellings was exempt from VAT, so that the company could not reclaim the related input tax. The company appealed, contending that the public house had been a 'non-residential building', within *VATA 1994, Sch 8, Group 5, Item 1(b)*, so that the subsequent sale was zero-rated and the input tax was recoverable. The tribunal rejected this contention and dismissed the appeal, holding that the public house was not a 'non-residential building' as defined by *VATA 1994, Sch 8, Group 5, Note 7*, and the work was therefore not a 'residential conversion'. The tribunal observed that *Sch 8, Group 5, Note 2* was 'meant to refer to a building after construction or conversion, whereas *Note 7* is meant to refer to it before its *Item 1(b)* conversion'. The tribunal also held that *Note 9* did not apply to the conversion, observing that *Note 9* was 'apparently intended not to extend *Item 1(b)* but to cut it down: conversion of a non-residential part of a building is not after all to qualify if the building contained a residential part'. The work here did not fall within *Item 1(b)*, since 'it is not the simple conversion of a non-residential part of a building but the conversion of that part plus a residential part'. *Calam Vale Ltd, LON/99/977 (VTD 16869)*.

15.64   **Conversion of building formerly used as nursing home—whether a residential conversion.**   A married couple reclaimed input tax on the conversion of a derelict building into a dwelling-house. The Commissioners rejected the claim, on the basis that the building had been used as a nursing home between 1968 and 1992, so that the effect of *VATA 1994, Sch 8, Group 5, Note 7* was that it was not a 'non-residential' building. The tribunal dismissed the couple's appeal against this decision. *Mr & Mrs GD King, LON/98/555 (VTD 15961)*.

15.65   **Conversion of barns into recreational buildings—whether within VATA 1994, s 35(1D).**   An individual (M) owned a farm which included a number of barns. He converted one of these into a dwelling-house and converted two other barns into a swimming pool and a recreation complex. He claimed a refund of VAT in respect of the conversion of all three barns. The Commissioners accepted the claim in relation to the barn which had been converted into a dwelling-house, but rejected the claim with regard to the other two barns. M appealed. The tribunal dismissed his appeal, observing that *VATA 1994, s 35(1D)* specifically referred to 'a building designed as a dwelling' and holding that the word 'building' could not 'be interpreted in the plural'. Accordingly, the construction of the swimming pool and recreation complex was not within *VATA 1994, s 35(1D)* and relief was not due. *Whiteley*, 15.29 above, applied. *JA Moore, MAN/x (VTD 15972)*.

15.66   **Time at which conversion completed.**   In the case noted at 2.56 APPEALS, an individual who had converted an old church into a dwelling reclaimed input tax on the conversion. The Commissioners rejected the claim on the grounds that the work had been completed before 21 April 1994, before the relevant provisions came into effect. (The provisions now contained in *s 35(1D)* were applied from 21 April 1994 by extra-statutory concession. The relevant certificate of completion was dated 10 March 1994.) The tribunal dismissed the claimant's appeal, holding that the conversion was complete when the building was habitable, safe and hygienic, as evidenced by the certificate of completion. The fact that some decoration and electrical work remained to be done had no bearing on the completion of the conversion. *Dr BN Purdue, EDN/94/511 (VTD 13430)*.

DEFINITION OF 'MAJOR INTEREST IN BUILDING, DWELLING OR SITE' (VATA 1994, Sch 8, Group 5, Item 1)

Cases held to qualify for zero-rating

15.67   **Lease originally granted for 21–year period—whether Deed of Rectification effective.**   A married couple arranged for the construction of a building comprising two residential flats. They registered for VAT and reclaimed input tax on the construction. Subsequently they granted a lease of one of the flats for a period of 21 years. When the Commissioners discovered this, they issued an assessment to recover the tax, since the lease did not exceed 21 years and was therefore not a 'major interest' as defined by *VATA 1994, s 96*. The couple appealed against the assessment. On legal advice, they and the lessees entered into a Deed of Rectification to extend the term of the lease to 22 years. The tribunal allowed the couple's appeal, holding that 'the mere fact that the sole purpose of the rectification is a tax advantage is not a bar to rectification'. *Taylor v Taylor & Another (re Colebrook's Conveyances), Ch D 1972, [1973] 1 All ER 132* applied. *CS & JM Isaac, MAN/96/254 (VTD 14656)*.

15.68 **Properties described as 'holiday dwelling-houses'—whether Note 13 applicable.** A company developed a site in Ayrshire, constructing a number of detached dwelling-houses. Under the relevant agreement with the local authority, it was a condition of the development that 'all houses on the development shall be used as holiday dwelling-houses only and for no other purpose'. The company treated its sales of the houses as zero-rated. The Commissioners issued an assessment on the basis that the effect of *VATA 1994, Sch 8, Group 5, Note 13* was that the sales failed to qualify for zero-rating. The tribunal allowed the company's appeal, holding on the evidence that the relevant agreement 'did not prevent the use of the holiday dwelling-houses ... as a principal private residence'. The tribunal held that 'the two states of use, namely as a holiday dwelling house or as a ... principal private residence' were not mutually exclusive, since the houses could be purchased by people whose working life involved living in tied accommodation, or by retired people 'whose time may be available on a year-round basis for 365 days as "days on which work is suspended" and "days of recreation and amusement"' (the dictionary definitions of a 'holiday'). *Livingstone Homes UK Ltd, EDN/99/98 (VTD 16649)*.

Cases held not to qualify for zero-rating

15.69 **'Time-sharing' leases—whether a grant of a major interest.** A company had constructed cottages on a holiday site in Cornwall and let them on a time-sharing basis, under which it granted customers an 80–year lease of a cottage for a specified 'holiday period' (usually one week) in each of the 80 years. It did not account for tax on the payments it received from customers, and the Commissioners issued an assessment charging tax on the payments. The company appealed, contending that, since the tenancy lasted for more than 21 years, the supply was zero-rated under what is now *VATA 1994, Sch 8, Group 5, Item 1*. The tribunal rejected this contention and dismissed the appeal, and the QB upheld this decision. Although the lease extended for more than 21 years, the grant did not constitute the grant of a major interest because the interest was not continuous. *Cottage Holiday Associates Ltd v C & E Commrs, QB 1982, [1983] STC 278*. (*Note.* See now *VATA 1994, Sch 8, Group 5, Note 13*.)

15.70 **Definition of 'site'.** A building company sold some development land, on which it had undertaken some civil engineering work including pile-driving for the foundations of buildings. The Commissioners issued an assessment to recover the input tax which the company had previously reclaimed, considering that the sale of the site was an exempt supply. The company appealed, contending that it had granted a major interest in a site, which should be treated as zero-rated under what is now *VATA 1994, Sch 8, Group 5, Item 1*. The tribunal rejected this contention and dismissed the appeal, holding that the land was not the 'site' of a specific building so that its sale did not qualify for zero-rating. *Stapenhill Developments Ltd, [1984] VATTR 1 (VTD 1593)*.

15.71 A similar decision was reached in *Permacross Ltd, MAN/94/878 (VTD 13251)*.

15.72   **Licence to occupy 'park home' erected on caravan site—whether grant of a major interest.**   A company which owned a caravan site arranged for structures, described as 'park homes', to be erected on the site, and reclaimed the relevant input tax. The Commissioners issued an assessment to recover the tax, considering that it related to exempt supplies. The company appealed, contending that the 'park homes' were buildings, and that the pitch agreements under which they were occupied constituted the grant of a major interest in land, so that the supply was zero-rated under what is now *VATA 1994, Sch 8, Group 5, Item 1*. The tribunal held that the 'park homes' were buildings, applying *Smith*, 15.27 above, but that the pitch agreements constituted an indefinite licence to occupy land, which did not amount to the grant of a major interest in land, and did not grant any interest in the 'park homes' themselves. Accordingly the pitch fees were exempt from VAT and the supplies of the 'park homes' were not within what is now *VATA 1994, Sch 8, Group 5, Item 1*. *Stonecliff Caravan Park, [1993] VATTR 464 (VTD 11097)*. (*Note.* For another issue in this case, see 65.4 ZERO-RATING.)

WHETHER SERVICES SUPPLIED 'IN THE COURSE OF CONSTRUCTION' (VATA 1994, Sch 8, Group 5, Item 2)

Cases where the appellant was successful

Note. See *VATA 1994, Sch 8, Group 5, Note 18*, introduced by *VAT (Construction of Buildings) Order 1995 (SI 1995 No 280)*. A number of appeals which had been successful before the introduction of *Note 18* would now fall within that provision and be excluded from zero-rating. Such cases have not normally been summarised in this book, except where they illustrate a point which continues to be of importance. The cases in this section should be read in the light of the changes in the legislation.

15.73   **Hall for Sunday School built alongside church.**   A church obtained planning permission for the building of a room, to be used as a Sunday School, on the site of an old vestry. The planning permission described the work as an 'extension' to the church. The work described in the planning permission was completed in December 1991, at which time there was direct access from the church to the new Sunday School room, through double doors which had formerly led to the vestry. In February 1992 the doorway between the church and the Sunday School room was blocked up with plasterboard and sealant. The Commissioners issued a ruling that the work did not qualify for zero-rating, and the company which had carried out the work appealed, contending that the Sunday School room was a new building and that its construction had not been completed until February 1992 when the old doorway was blocked. The tribunal allowed the company's appeal, holding that the work constituted an extension to the church, rather than an enlargement of the church. The fact that the architect had issued a certificate of completion in December 1991 was not conclusive. In this case, 'the work of blocking the internal access was within the course of construction of the Sunday School room', and the work qualified for zero-rating. *Carrophil Ltd, LON/92/1005 (VTD 10190)*.

15.74   **Construction of annexe to church—whether conditions of Note 17 satisfied.**   A church arranged for the construction of a new annexe to replace its existing chapel house. The Commissioners issued a ruling that the effect of *VATA 1994, Sch 8, Group 5, Note 16* was that the construction was standard-rated. The church appealed, contending that the work was within *Group 5, Note 17* and qualified for zero-rating. The tribunal accepted this contention and allowed the appeal, holding that the church had constructed an annexe within *Note 17*, rather than an extension within *Note 16*. *Macnamara*, 15.107 below, distinguished. *Grace Baptist Church, MAN/98/798 (VTD 16093)*.

15.75 **Redevelopment of group of buildings—whether within Group 5, Note 16(a).** A company owned a site which it wished to redevelop. Some of the buildings were demolished and a new building was constructed on the site. The Commissioners issued a ruling that the relevant supplies were undertaken in the course of reconstructing an existing building, and thus were excluded from zero-rating by what is now *VATA 1994, Sch 8, Group 5, Note 16(a)*. The company appealed, contending that the supplies were zero-rated. The QB accepted this contention and allowed the company's appeal, holding on the evidence that the work constituted the construction of a new building rather than the reconstruction of an existing building. The CA upheld the QB decision, holding that the work was not within the definition of 'reconstruction' because it was 'not a replication or construction anew of what was there before'. *Wimpey Group Services Ltd v C & E Commrs, CA [1988] STC 625.* (*Note.* The services in question would not now qualify for zero-rating because the building was not used for a 'relevant residential or charitable purpose'—see *Item 2(a)*, originating from *FA 1989*. However, the case remains relevant with regard to the definition of 'reconstruction'.)

15.76 **Construction of office block using walls of industrial building.** *Wimpey Group Services Ltd*, 15.75 above, was applied in a subsequent case in which most of an industrial building was demolished, with only the concrete frame and some brick party walls being retained, and an office block was constructed using parts of these walls. The tribunal held that the work should be treated as a new building and as qualifying for zero-rating under the legislation then in force. The CA upheld this decision (by a 2–1 majority, Ward LJ dissenting). Stuart-Smith LJ observed that the question at issue was 'a jury question' and a matter of 'fact, degree and impression', rather than a question of law. *C & E Commrs v Marchday Holdings Ltd, CA 1996, [1997] STC 272.* (*Notes.* (1) The work in question was carried out before the changes enacted by *FA 1989*, so that it would not qualify for zero-rating under the current legislation. With regard to when a building ceases to be an 'existing building', see now *VATA 1994, Sch 8, Group 5, Note 18*, introduced by *SI 1995 No 280* with effect from 1 March 1995. (2) For the Commissioners' practice following this decision, see Business Brief 20/97, issued on 24 September 1997. (3) For a preliminary issue in this case, see 2.44 APPEALS.)

15.77 **Block of flats constructed underneath existing building.** A company constructed a block of flats, part of which was sited underneath an existing building. The foundations of the existing building were reinforced, but the access and services to the new block were entirely independent. The Commissioners issued a ruling that the work did not qualify for zero-rating, but the tribunal allowed the company's appeal, holding that the work constituted the construction of a new building rather than the enlargement of an existing building. *John Compass Ltd, EDN/87/35 (VTD 3163).*

15.78 **Construction of flats behind existing house.** A large house was divided into two flats. The upper flat had a separate outside staircase. A building containing four more flats was built behind the house, and a new external entrance was built which also gave access to the existing upper flat. The new building was modern in appearance and was clearly distinct from the old building. The Commissioners issued a ruling that the work did not qualify for zero-rating, and the builders appealed, contending that the work was zero-rated. The tribunal allowed the appeal, holding that the new building was not an enlargement of the existing building and that the services in question qualified for zero-rating. *R & P Wellman, LON/89/1251Z (VTD 4383).*

15.79 A contractor built a flat at the back of an existing property. The ground floor of the existing property was occupied by a bank, and the two upper floors were used as workshops. The flat was built at first-floor level, supported by piers with parking space underneath. There was no internal access between the flat and the existing building, and all services to the flat were independent of those to the existing property. The Commissioners issued a ruling that the work did not qualify for zero-rating as it constituted the conversion of an existing building. The tribunal allowed the contractor's appeal, finding that the flat was visually very different from the existing building, and was used for a different purpose. Consequently, the work constituted the construction of a new building, rather than the conversion of an existing building. *J Samuel (t/a Joseph Samuel Developments), LON/90/1516 (VTD 7177)*. (*Note*. For another issue in this case, see 15.97 below.)

15.80 **Construction of flats above car park.** A company which owned a two-storey car park obtained planning permission to build 24 flats on top of the car park. The Commissioners issued a ruling that the work was standard-rated. The company appealed, contending that it was zero-rated. The tribunal allowed the company's appeal, holding that it was 'wholly inappropriate' to regard the block of flats as an enlargement of the car park. Accordingly, the building of the flats constituted the construction of a new building, rather than the conversion of an existing one. *Trident Housing Association Ltd, MAN/92/387 (VTD 10642)*.

15.81 **Construction of flats adjacent to nursing home.** A company which owned a nursing home obtained permission for the construction of a block of 15 flats, designed for elderly people in need of care, adjacent to the nursing home. The nursing home was a three-storey building, constructed in red brick, and the block of flats also comprised three storeys, but the ceilings were lower than those in the nursing home, so that the nursing home was five feet higher than the block of flats. The nursing home and the flats had a common party wall, with internal access which was used by nurses to visit the residents of the flats. The Commissioners issued a ruling that, because of the internal access, the construction of the flats was standard-rated. The company appealed, contending that the construction was zero-rated. The tribunal allowed the company's appeal, holding that the flats were not an 'extension or annexation' to the nursing home. Notwithstanding the internal access, the block of flats was a separate building rather than an enlargement of the nursing home, and the construction of the flats qualified for zero-rating. *Elliott*, 15.102 below, and *Perry*, 15.22 above, distinguished. *Associated Nursing Services plc, LON/93/1173A (VTD 11203)*.

15.82 **Construction of residential unit in grounds of nursing home—whether Note 16 applicable.** A couple operated a nursing home. The home comprised two separate units, one of which provided for medical patients and one provided for mentally infirm patients. In 1997 and 1998 the couple arranged for building work which involved the extension of the unit which housed the mentally infirm patients. As a result of the work, that unit was joined onto the unit comprising the medical patients. However, there was no internal access, and the two units were designed to operate entirely separately, in accordance with local licensing requirements. The Commissioners issued a ruling that the effect of *VATA 1994, Sch 8, Group 5, Note 16* was that the work failed to qualify for zero-rating. The tribunal upheld this ruling but the couple appealed to the QB, which remitted the case to a new tribunal for rehearing. Lightman J held that 'regard must be had only to the physical character of the buildings in course of construction at the date of the relevant supply ... the subjective intentions on the part of the appellants as to their future use, their subsequent use and the terms of the planning permission regulating their future use are irrelevant, save only in so far as they throw light upon the potential use and functioning of the buildings'. *Cantrell (t/a Foxearth Lodge Nursing Home), QB [2000] STC 100.*

15.83   **Residential building constructed in grounds of study centre—subsequently linked to main building—whether an extension to existing building.**   A charity operated a field centre. It arranged for the construction of a residential building in the grounds of the centre, to provide accommodation for students visiting the centre. There was a gap of one metre between the existing building and the residential building but, 28 days after the completion of the residential building, the contractor constructed a link between the two buildings. The Commissioners issued a ruling that the work constituted the alteration of an existing building and was standard-rated. The contractor appealed, contending that the work constituted the construction of a new building and qualified for zero-rating. The tribunal accepted this contention and allowed the appeal, observing that the construction of the link 'involved new roof works and new walls' and that 'the works involved were substantial, going far beyond ... opening a doorway in a party wall ... The link required some extensive work and some considerable expense.' *Symonds*, 15.98 below, and *Graden Builders*, 15.99 below, distinguished. *DS Menzies, EDN/97/114 (VTD 15733).*

15.84   **Residential building adjoining nursing home—subsequently linked to main building—whether an extension to existing building.**   The proprietor of a nursing home arranged for the construction of a new residential building adjoining the home, to be used for the same purposes. When the new building was completed, there was no internal access to the original building and the two homes were operated separately. However, three weeks after the new building had been completed, he arranged for an interconnecting door to be fitted so that the two homes could be operated as one unit. The Commissioners issued an assessment on the basis that the work did not qualify for zero-rating. The proprietor appealed, contending that he had genuinely intended to operate two separate nursing homes but had been forced to merge them because five of his patients had died, which had significantly reduced his income. The tribunal accepted the proprietor's evidence and allowed his appeal. *JMB Strowbridge, MAN/95/2449 (VTD 16521).*

15.85   **Replacement of barn by four-bedroomed house.**   The owner of a derelict barn obtained planning permission for its conversion into a four-bedroomed house. The barn was totally demolished, but some of the internal timber work was used in the new house. The timber in question was retained for decorative purposes only, and had no load-bearing capacity. The Commissioners issued a ruling that the work was not eligible for zero-rating as it was the conversion of an existing building. The tribunal allowed the owner's appeal, holding that the work constituted the construction of 'an entirely new building'. *MS Gill, LON/89/1359X (VTD 4904).*

15.86   **Retention of facade—whether a 'condition or requirement of statutory planning consent'—Note 18(b).**   A married couple arranged for the construction of an extension of a dilapidated farmhouse. The extension required planning permission, which they obtained. During the work, it was discovered that all except one of the existing walls were unstable and had to be demolished to ground level. The couple obtained retrospective planning permission for the 'construction of a replacement dwelling incorporating part of an existing wall'. The Commissioners issued a ruling that output tax was chargeable on the work, and the couple appealed, contending that the effect of *VATA 1994, Sch 8, Group 5, Note 18(b)* was that the building had ceased to be 'an existing building', since all that was left of the original building was one wall and the retention of that wall was 'a condition or requirement of statutory planning consent'. The tribunal accepted this contention and allowed the appeal. *R & SL Midgley, MAN/96/640 (VTD 15379).*

15.87   **Sewage treatment plant installed in course of construction of house at boarding school—whether within Group 5, Item 2.**   A company which operated a boarding school built a new boarding house. A new sewage treatment plant was installed to serve the house, in accordance with the relevant building regulations. The Commissioners accepted that the construction of the house was zero-rated, but considered that the expenditure on the sewage treatment plant did not qualify for zero-rating. The company appealed, contending that the plant was within the definition of 'any services' in what is now *VATA 1994, Sch 8, Group 5, Item 2*, and should be zero-rated since it had been supplied in the course of construction of the house. The tribunal accepted this contention and allowed the appeal. The CS upheld this decision, holding that the sewage plant qualified for zero-rating since it was contemporaneous with the construction of the new boarding house and would not have been needed but for the new boarding house. *C & E Commrs v Rannoch School, CS [1993] STC 389.*

15.88   **Access roads constructed in preparation for housing development.**   A company entered into a contract to construct access roads for a new housing development comprising seven houses, two of which were to be new buildings and the other five of which were to be conversions of existing buildings. The company initially issued an invoice charging VAT on the work. However, the customer persuaded the company that the work should be zero-rated, and the company then issued a credit note in respect of the original invoice, and treated the whole of the work as zero-rated. The Commissioners issued an assessment on the basis that, since only two of the houses were new buildings, and only one of the houses had been sold at the relevant time, only one-seventh of the work was eligible for zero-rating. The company appealed. The tribunal allowed the company's appeal in part, holding that it was not 'necessary for the construction of the individual houses to take place contemporaneously with the road works', and the fact that one of the houses had not been sold did not prevent the work attributable to that house from qualifying for zero-rating. The input tax should be apportioned between the new houses and the converted houses, so that two-sevenths of the total tax was deductible. *Lamberts Construction Ltd, MAN/91/486 (VTD 8882).*

15.89   **Construction of riverside house incorporating dock —whether construction of dock 'related to the construction' of house.**   A company constructed a house on the River Thames. The house was built on stilts, underneath which was a dock, constructed by sheet piling to hold back the riverbank, for a boat. The lower level of the house was higher than the minimum level necessary under the relevant building regulations, so that the owner could drive a boat from the river into the dock and then enter the house by a staircase. The company did not account for tax on the sheet piling work, treating it as part of the construction of the house and as zero-rated. The Commissioners issued an assessment charging tax on the work, but the tribunal allowed the company's appeal, holding on the evidence that the work was 'related to the construction' of the house and qualified for zero-rating under *VATA 1994, Sch 8, Group 5, Item 2. Rannoch School,* 15.87 above, applied. *Turner Stroud & Burley Construction Ltd, LON/97/1440 (VTD 15454).*

Cases where the appellant was unsuccessful

15.90   **Definition of 'in the course of construction'.**   In an unsuccessful appeal, where the substantive issue has subsequently been clarified by what is now *VATA 1994, Sch 8, Group 5, Note 22,* the tribunal held that 'a building remains in the course of construction until the main structure is completed, the windows glazed and all essential services and fittings, such as plumbing and electricity, have been installed therein. Thereafter the building ceases to be in the course of construction ... and the phase of fitting out and furnishing is ready to begin'. *University of Hull, LEE/75/31 (VTD 180).*

15.91 The decision in *University of Hull*, 15.90 above, was applied in the subsequent case of *Birmingham Council for Old People*, 15.127 below.

15.92 **School playgrounds—whether built 'in the course of construction' of school.** In 1979 work began on the building of a new secondary school. The school opened to pupils in 1981, although some of its original buildings were not completed until 1983. Under the original plans, the school was to have been equipped with two playgrounds. However, the playgrounds were not completed until 1994. The Commissioners issued a ruling that the construction of the playgrounds were standard-rated. The school appealed, contending that the work should be zero-rated on the grounds that it was an integral part of the school, and that the construction of the school was not complete until the construction of the playgrounds. The QB rejected this contention, holding that the work failed to qualify for zero-rating. Jowitt J held that, although zero-rating under *VATA 1994, Sch 8, Group 5, Item 2* was not restricted to the services of constructing the relevant building itself, related services could only qualify for zero-rating if there was 'a temporal connection between the construction of the building and the provision of the other services'. On the evidence, the interval between the completion of the building work on the school and the construction of the playgrounds was far too long to establish the necessary temporal link. Accordingly, the building of the playgrounds failed to qualify for zero-rating. *C & E Commrs v St Mary's Roman Catholic High School, QB [1996] STC 1091.*

15.93 **Penthouse maisonettes built on top of existing building.** A company constructed two penthouse maisonettes on the top of a six-floor building, and reclaimed input tax on the work. The Commissioners rejected the claim and the tribunal dismissed the company's appeal, holding that the work constituted the reconstruction of an existing building rather than the construction of a new building. *Northland Securities Development Ltd, LON/78/225 (VTD 785).*

15.94 **Conversion of derelict hall into house.** A company purchased a derelict nineteenth-century hall, and undertook substantial building work, raising the height of the roof and constructing new walls, floors and windows. The company sold the building and did not account for output tax on the sale, although it had previously reclaimed input tax on the work. The Commissioners issued an assessment to recover the input tax on the basis that the sale was exempt and that the work did not amount to the construction of a building. The tribunal dismissed the company's appeal, holding that the work constituted the conversion of an existing building, rather than the construction of a new building, and did not qualify for zero-rating. *St Andrews Building Co Ltd, EDN/86/12 (VTD 2127).*

15.95 **Conversion of existing building.** There have been a large number of cases in which tribunals have found that work has constituted the conversion of an existing building, rather than the construction of a new building, and which appear to raise no point of general interest. In the interests of space, such cases are not summarised individually in this book. For summaries of such cases decided up to 31 December 1995, see Tolley's VAT Cases 1996.

15.96 **Single-storey house adjoining existing house in same occupation.** The owner of a large house decided to build a separate self-contained house within its grounds. The local planning authority granted planning permission only on condition that the new house adjoined the old house and appeared to form a single dwelling with it, and that the new house must remain in the same ownership as the existing house and must not be separately let or occupied. Accordingly a single-storey extension was built, connected to two walls of the existing house, and appearing from outside to be an integral part of the existing house, but having no internal access. The company which built the extension failed to account for tax. The

Commissioners issued an assessment and the tribunal dismissed the company's appeal, holding that, having regard to the terms of the planning permission, and the common occupation of the two houses, the new building was an extension or enlargement of the old building despite its internal independence. The QB upheld this decision. Lord McCluskey held that '... in a case of this kind the decision of the tribunal is essentially a decision on the matter of fact with which this court cannot interfere'. *Charles Gray (Builders) Ltd v C & E Commrs, CS [1990] STC 650.*

15.97   **Block of flats constructed at rear of existing building—whether an extension or enlargement of existing building.**   A trader converted a Victorian house into seven flats and constructed a new block of four flats at the rear of the house. The new flats were structurally independent of the existing building except for the party wall, part of which was the original rear wall of the house. The only entrance to the new flats was through the existing building. The tribunal held that the new flats were an extension or enlargement of the existing building, so that the work was not eligible for zero-rating. *J Samuel (t/a Joseph Samuel Developments), LON/90/1516 (VTD 7177).* (*Note.* For another issue in this case, see 15.79 above.)

15.98   **Extension constructed in two stages.**   The owner of a small three-bedroomed detached house obtained planning permission for the building of a two-storey extension to it. He engaged a contractor to construct the extension as a self-contained building without internal access from the existing house. He then engaged a second contractor to cut through the party wall which divided the original house from the extension, so as to provide access at both ground-floor and first-floor level. The contractor who had constructed the initial extension did not account for VAT on the work, and the Commissioners issued an assessment on the basis that the work was not eligible for zero-rating. The tribunal dismissed the contractor's appeal. The fact that the work was carried out in two stages was not conclusive, since 'notwithstanding the form of the planning proposals the whole of the building work was in truth and in fact a single operation with a rest or pause at a convenient stage'. The fact that the work had deliberately been entrusted to two contractors, rather than one, did not change its nature. The work carried out by the first contractor 'was the first stage, and a substantial stage, of an intended and declared enlargement of an existing dwelling'. *R Symonds, LON/90/1836X (VTD 9050).*

15.99   A similar decision was reached in *Graden Builders Ltd, MAN/93/1545 (VTD 12637).*

15.100   **Enlargement of existing building.**   A building partnership demolished one wing of a farmhouse and replaced it by a new wing which had no internal access to the main farmhouse. The Commissioners issued a ruling that the new wing was an enlargement of an existing building. The partnership appealed, contending that it should be treated as zero-rated. The tribunal rejected this contention and dismissed the appeal. On the evidence, the end wall of the new wing was tied in to the wall of the main house. Since it had been built onto the main house, it was an annexation to the main house and did not qualify for zero-rating. *Granger Builders, [1996] VATDR 438 (VTD 14126).*

15.101   There have been a large number of cases in which tribunals have found that work has constituted the enlargement of an existing building, rather than the construction of a new building, and which appear to raise no point of general interest. In the interests of space, such cases are not summarised individually in this book. For summaries of such cases decided up to 31 December 1995, see Tolley's VAT Cases 1996.

15.102   **Extension to nursing home.**   A married couple owned a small nursing home, which had originally been a farmhouse. They obtained planning permission for an extension to the home. The new building was substantially larger than the old building. The two buildings were linked by an internal passageway. The Commissioners considered that the new building was an enlargement or extension of the existing building, and was therefore not eligible for zero-rating. The couple appealed, contending that, notwithstanding the terms of the planning permission, the new building was a separate entity. The QB rejected this contention, holding that the work did not qualify for zero-rating. On the evidence, the terms of the planning permission required the construction of a connecting door and passageway. It followed that the new structure was not itself a separate nursing home, but could only function in connection with the existing building. *C & E Commrs v Mr & Mrs Elliott, QB [1993] STC 369.*

15.103   The QB decision in *Elliott*, 15.102 above, was applied in the subsequent case of *Nidderdale Building Ltd, MAN/94/604 (VTD 13158).*

15.104   Similar decisions were reached in *S & H Shroufi (t/a Morris Grange Nursing Home), MAN/95/2769 (VTD 14852)* and *MJ Keeley, LON/98/679 (VTD 16219).*

15.105   **Conversion of buildings into nursing home.**   A partnership purchased a site containing four buildings, standing in a U-shaped formation and comprising a total of 15,000 square feet. It obtained planning permission to redevelop the site as a nursing home. During the redevelopment, two-thirds of the old buildings were demolished and the four buildings were joined together by intercommunicating doors. After the work, the nursing home comprised 25,000 square feet. The partnership claimed that the work carried out should be treated as zero-rated. The Commissioners rejected the claim and the tribunal dismissed the partnership's appeal, holding that the work constituted the conversion of existing buildings. *Victoria Gardens Nursing Home, MAN/91/1197 (VTD 10547).*

15.106   **Construction of extension or annexe used for relevant charitable purpose— whether Sch 8, Group 5, Note 17 applicable.**   A Sikh Temple, which was a recognised charity, arranged for the construction of an extension or annexe to its place of worship. The Commissioners issued a ruling that the work was the extension of an existing building and that the contractor was required to account for output tax on the construction. The charity appealed, contending that the work was the construction of an annexe which was intended for use solely for a relevant charitable purpose and should be treated as zero-rated. The tribunal dismissed the appeal, observing that it was not necessary to decide whether the work was within the definition of an 'annexe', since the main access to it was via the existing building, so that, although it was accepted that it was intended for use solely for a relevant charitable purpose, the effect of *VATA 1994, Sch 8, Group 5, Note 17(b)* was that it failed to qualify for zero-rating. *Shiri Guru Nanaka Sikh Temple, MAN/96/1159 (VTD 14972).*

15.107   An appeal was dismissed in a case where the tribunal held that an extension to a school building was not within the definition of an 'annexe', and did not qualify for zero-rating. The tribunal observed that, even if the extension had been treated as an 'annexe', it would still not have qualified for zero-rating, since it was not 'capable of functioning independently from the existing building', as required by *VATA 1994, Sch 8, Group 5, Note 17(a). BT Macnamara, [1999] VATDR 171 (VTD 16039).*

15.108   *Macnamara*, 15.107 above, was applied in the similar subsequent case of *Colchester Sixth Form College, LON/98/1341 (VTD 16252).*

15.109   **Reconstruction or alteration of existing building.**   There have been a large number of cases in which tribunals have found that work has constituted the reconstruction or alteration of an existing building, rather than the construction of a new building, and which appear to raise no point of general interest. In the interests of space, such cases are not summarised individually in this book. For summaries of such cases decided up to 31 December 1995, see Tolley's VAT Cases 1996.

15.110   **Reconstruction of end-of-terrace house.**   The owner of an end-of-terrace house, built from precast concrete, undertook substantial work on the house including the removal of the external concrete walls and their replacement by brickwork. The roof and the internal walls were retained, the roof being temporarily supported by telescopic posts during the work. The owner reclaimed input tax on the work, but the Commissioners rejected the claim, considering that it constituted the reconstruction of an existing building rather than the construction of a new building. The tribunal dismissed the owner's appeal against this decision. On the evidence, the building 'was never demolished to such an extent that the erection of a building as a whole could properly be said to have followed'. *DS Bird, LON/91/1922X (VTD 9292).*

15.111   **Supplies of groundwork by subcontractor.**   A subcontractor agreed to supply the groundwork (laying concrete slabs as foundations for new buildings) at a site, which he was told related to new dwellings. He therefore zero-rated his supply. However, the buildings constructed on the site were garages and workshops. The Commissioners issued an assessment charging output tax on the work, and the tribunal dismissed the subcontractor's appeal. *ME Conway, LON/93/612A (VTD 11725).* (*Note.* For another issue in this case, see 9.111 CARS.)

15.112   **Supplies by subcontractor to contractor.**   A contractor was supplying services in the course of constructing a building which was accepted as being for a 'relevant charitable purpose'. It arranged for a subcontractor to carry out the electrical installation, and told the subcontractor that the work was zero-rated, so that he need not charge VAT. The Commissioners issued an assessment on the subcontractor, charging output tax on the basis that his supplies had been made to the contractor rather than to the customer, so that the effect of what is now *VATA 1994, Sch 8, Group 5, Note 12,* was that it did not qualify for zero-rating. The tribunal upheld the assessment and dismissed the subcontractor's appeal. *ME Smith (Electrical Engineers) Ltd, MAN/94/2101 (VTD 13594).*

15.113   See also *Ian Fraser & Partners Ltd,* 49.174 PENALTIES: MISDECLARATION; *Taylor & Fraser Ltd,* 49.175 PENALTIES: MISDECLARATION, and *McRandal,* 49.176 PENALTIES: MISDECLARATION.

SUPPLIES TO RELEVANT HOUSING ASSOCIATIONS (VATA 1994, Sch 8, Group 5, Item 3)

15.114   **Conversion of 'bedsits' into self-contained flats.**   A housing association arranged for the conversion of 24 'bedsits' into self-contained flats. The Commissioners issued a ruling that output tax was chargeable on the work. The association appealed, contending that the bedsits had been 'non-residential', so that the work qualified for zero-rating under *VATA 1994, Sch 8, Group 5, Item 3.* The tribunal accepted this contention and allowed the appeal, holding that, because the bedsits had had shared bathroom and kitchen facilities, they had been neither 'designed nor adapted for use as a dwelling or number of dwellings nor for a relevant residential purpose', within *Group 5, Note 7.* The tribunal held that 'to be a dwelling in the ordinary sense each of the bedsits would have to have contained within it "all the major activities of life, particularly sleeping, cooking and feeding plus toilet facilities"'. *Dicta* in *University of Bath,* 15.34 above, applied. Furthermore, the bedsits could not be treated as one single dwelling, since they 'were more than lodgings in a shared household' and 'a building so occupied does not have the characteristics of a dwelling'. *Look Ahead Housing Association, LON/99/860 (VTD 16816).*

15.115   **Conversion of bedrooms in youth hostel.**   A YMCA, which was a registered housing association, owned a youth hostel containing 44 hostel-type bedrooms and 9 self-catering flatlets, all of which shared bath and shower facilities. It arranged for the conversion of 15 of the hostel-type bedrooms into 10 self-catering flatlets. The Commissioners issued a ruling that VAT was chargeable on the work, and the YMCA appealed, contending that it should be treated as zero-rated under *VATA 1994, Sch 8, Group 5, Item 3.* The tribunal rejected this contention and dismissed the appeal, holding that, although the new flatlets were used as a 'sole or main residence', they were not used for a relevant residential purpose within *Note 4(g)*, as they did not constitute a 'self-sufficient institution'. *Derby YMCA, MAN/00/473 (VTD 16914).* (*Note.* The tribunal allowed an appeal against a misdeclaration penalty, holding that the complexity of the law constituted a reasonable excuse.)

CONSTRUCTION OF GARAGES (VATA 1994, Sch 8, Group 5, Note 3)

15.116   **Whether dwelling and garage constructed 'at the same time'.**   A trust arranged for the construction of two semi-detached dwelling-houses. A certificate of completion was issued in December 1997. In January 1998 the trust applied for planning permission to add two garages to the dwellings. This was granted the following month. The construction of the garages began in March 1998 and was completed within two months. The Commissioners issued a ruling that VAT was chargeable on the construction of the garages, since the dwellings and garages had not been constructed 'at the same time', as required by *VATA 1994, Sch 8, Group 5, Note 3.* The trust appealed, contending that, despite the issue of the certificate of completion, the houses should not be treated as having been completed until the construction of the garages. The tribunal rejected this contention and dismissed the appeal, finding that 'the evidence ... establishes that the construction of the dwellings was in fact complete at the date of the certificate of practical completion'. *Chipping Sodbury Town Trust, LON/99/743 (VTD 16641).*

15.117   **Construction of garage in grounds of recently-built house.**   See *Whiteley*, 15.29 above.

BUILDING MATERIALS (VATA 1994, Sch 8, Group 5, Item 4; VATA 1994, s 35(1B))

Note. Whether there has been a supply of 'building materials', or articles ordinarily incorporated by builders, may arise under three VAT provisions, affecting respectively the zero-rating of the supply (*VATA 1994, Sch 8, Group 5, Item 4*), the input tax credit of the recipient of the supply (*Input Tax Order, Article 6*) and the amount of the 'do-it-yourself' housebuilders relief (*VATA 1994, s 35*). Where the appeal relates to *Sch 8, Group 5*, summaries should be read in the light of subsequent changes in the legislation. The zero-rating of most alterations to buildings was removed by *FA 1984* with respect to supplies made after 31 May 1984. The provisions now in *Note 22*, excluding certain materials etc. from *Item 4*, were introduced at the same time so as to exclude prefabricated furniture, except where designed for kitchens, and electrical or gas appliances, except for appliances falling within one of the specific exceptions. See also *VAT Information Sheet 5/00—Construction and 'Building Materials'* for Customs' interpretation of when building materials are 'ordinarily incorporated' into a building.

Finished or prefabricated furniture (Note 22(a))

15.118   **Built-in dressing table units.**   In a purchase tax case, the Ch D held that built-in dressing table units were not 'ordinarily installed by builders', since they were not 'articles which one would expect a builder to install as fixtures in the ordinary way without any special instruction'. *F Austin (Leyton) Ltd v C & E Commrs, Ch D [1968] Ch 529; [1968] 2 All ER 13.* (*Note.* The purchase tax legislation provided that furniture was chargeable to purchase tax, but excluded 'builders' hardware ... and other articles of kinds ordinarily installed by builders as fixtures'. The current VAT legislation (*Sch 8, Group 5, Note 22*) refers to 'goods of a description ordinarily incorporated by builders'.)

15.119   **Built-in wardrobes.**   The Commissioners issued a ruling that built-in wardrobes failed to qualify for zero-rating. The company which supplied the wardrobes appealed. The tribunal allowed the appeal but the QB held that the tribunal had erred in law, and remitted the case to the tribunal for rehearing. Glidewell J held that, in order to meet the conditions of being 'ordinarily installed by builders', it was not sufficient that an article fell within a general class of items which could be regarded as 'ordinarily installed', but the tribunal should also consider whether the specific type of article in question fell within the definition of 'ordinarily installed'. *C & E Commrs v Smitmit Design Centre Ltd, QB [1982] STC 525.* (*Notes.* (1) There was no further public hearing of the appeal, which apparently was dismissed by consent following Glidewell J's rulings. (2) The legislation has subsequently been amended and the phrase 'ordinarily installed' has been replaced by the phrase 'ordinarily incorporated'.)

15.120   In the case noted at 45.3 PAYMENT OF TAX, the tribunal held that wardrobes which were fitted in a new bungalow were furniture and were excluded from zero-rating. *McLean Homes Midland*, 15.123 below, distinguished. *SH Wade, MAN/94/642 (VTD 13164).* (*Note.* For the Commissioners' practice following this decision, see Business Brief 12/97, issued on 5 June 1997.)

15.121   A trader who supplied bedroom furniture and fittings failed to account for output tax on his supplies. The Commissioners issued an assessment and he appealed, contending that his supplies should be treated as zero-rated. The tribunal dismissed his appeal, distinguishing *McLean Homes Midland Ltd*, 15.123 below. The tribunal observed that the trader's supplies 'would be tailor-made to the room for which they were intended, being assembled on site and carefully fitted to the room, to produce a carefully-joined and extremely smart result'. He 'produced a design on the basis that he was fitting to an ordinarily rectangular room, with featureless walls, and by fitting his units to the size of room, provided the customer with a bespoke version of storage space which the customer would otherwise have had to provide by obtaining furniture from a furniture dealer'. The fact that he commonly used two walls as part of the wardrobe did not prevent his supplies from being within what is now *Note 22(a)(b)*. *S Leon (t/a Custom Bedrooms), MAN/94/989 (VTD 13200).*

15.122   **Shelves and rails provided for use in recesses used as wardrobes—whether 'finished or prefabricated furniture'.**   A building company purchased prefabricated houses in kit form. The plans for the houses provided for recesses which could be used as wardrobes. The kits included shelving and lengths of railing which could be used in the recessed wardrobes. The company reclaimed input tax on the shelves and rails. The Commissioners issued an assessment to recover the tax, considering that they were 'finished or prefabricated furniture' or, alternatively, that they were 'materials for the construction of fitted furniture' within what is now *Input Tax Order, Article 6*. The tribunal allowed the company's appeal, holding that the walls, floor and ceiling of the recess could not be considered as furniture, and that the materials could not therefore be considered as used for the construction of fitted furniture. *Harrington Construction Ltd, EDN/88/110 (VTD 3470).*

15.123   A company reclaimed input tax on items such as doors and shelves intended for installation in built-in wardrobes in houses which it had constructed. The walls of the rooms were used as the sides and backs of the wardrobes. The Commissioners issued an assessment to recover the tax, considering that it was not deductible by virtue of what is now *Input Tax Order, Article 6*. The tribunal allowed the company's appeal, applying *Harrington Construction Ltd*, 15.122 above, and holding that the materials in question were of a type ordinarily installed as fixtures, and were not materials for the construction of fitted furniture. Consequently the input tax was deductible. The QB upheld this decision as one of fact. Brooke J held that 'whether something was an item of furniture or not was very much a matter of impression. It was quite impossible to characterise an annex or closet or a cupboard either as being furniture or not being furniture'. *C & E Commrs v McLean Homes Midland Ltd, QB [1993] STC 335.* (*Notes.* (1) This case was distinguished in *Wade*, 15.120 above, and *Leon*, 15.121 above. (2) For the Commissioners' interpretation of the distinction between *Wade* and this decision, and for their interpretation of what constitutes 'furniture', see Business Brief 12/97, issued on 5 June 1997.)

15.124   *Harrington Construction Ltd*, 15.122 above, and *McLean Homes Midland Ltd (No 2)*, 15.123 above, were applied in a subsequent case in which the Commissioners had issued an assessment to recover input tax claimed on wardrobe doors designed to convert recesses into built-in wardrobes. The tribunal allowed the company's appeal on this point, holding that the doors were not fitted furniture, nor were they materials for the construction of fitted furniture. *McCarthy & Stone plc, LON/91/382 (VTD 7014).* (*Note.* For another issue in this case, see 15.148 below.)

15.125   *McLean Homes Midland Ltd*, 15.123 above, was applied in a similar subsequent case in which *Wade*, 15.120 above, and *Leon*, 15.121 above, were distinguished. The tribunal held that shelves and doors qualified for zero-rating, on the basis that they were 'the very simplest of internal fittings plus a set of doors separating a natural recess from the rest of the room'. The recesses in question were 'an integral part of the room and form part of the fabric of the building'. (However, wardrobes with a melamine end panel, and wardrobes with a raised wooden floor, were held to be within the definition of 'furniture', and thus failed to qualify for zero-rating.) *Moores Furniture Group Ltd, MAN/97/142 (VTD 15044).*

15.126   **Washbasin units.**   A company, which built houses for sale, installed in some of these houses washbasins which were supported by basin units rather than pedestals. It reclaimed input tax on the purchase of the basin units. The Commissioners issued an assessment to recover the tax, considering that the units were 'finished or prefabricated furniture', so that, by virtue of what is now *Article 6 of the Input Tax Order 1992*, the tax was not deductible. The company appealed, contending that the units were not within the definition of 'furniture'. The tribunal accepted this contention and allowed the appeal, holding on the evidence that the purpose of the units was simply to support the basins and to hide the piping, and that they were not intended to be used as cupboards or worktops. Accordingly they were not within the definition of 'furniture'. *Dicta* of Brooke J in *McLean Homes Midland Ltd*, 15.123 above, applied. *Edmond Homes Ltd, MAN/92/1502 (VTD 11567).* (*Note.* For the Commissioners' practice following this decision, see Business Brief 3/94, issued on 15 February 1994.)

15.127   **Staff lockers in nursing home—whether 'furniture'.**   A charity arranged for the construction of a nursing home. A number of lockers, for the use of staff, were included in the building. The Commissioners issued a ruling that the construction of these lockers was standard-rated, considering firstly that the lockers were not supplied until after the construction had been completed, and secondly that they were 'finished or prefabricated furniture' and thus excluded from zero-rating in any event by *Note 22(a)*. The charity appealed, contending that the lockers were not within the definition of 'furniture', but were zero-rated building materials which had been supplied in the course of construction. The tribunal rejected this contention and dismissed the appeal. Applying *University of Hull*, 15.90 above, the construction had been completed before the lockers were supplied. Additionally, the lockers were within the definition of 'furniture'. *Birmingham Council for Old People, MAN/96/1062 (VTD 15437)*.

15.128 **Bollards installed in school science laboratories.** A school arranged for the fitting-out of a science block containing seven laboratories. The Commissioners issued a ruling that output tax was chargeable on the installation of 42 bollards in the laboratories. The school appealed, contending that the bollards were 'building materials' within *VATA 1994, Sch 8, Group 5, Item 4*, and qualified for zero-rating. The tribunal rejected this contention and dismissed the appeal, holding that the bollards were 'finished or prefabricated furniture', within *Note 22. Edmond Homes Ltd*, 15.126 above, distinguished. *Sheldon School, LON/97/817 (VTD 15300)*.

Electrical or gas appliances (Note 22(c))

15.129 **Gas and electric fires.** The tribunal held that gas and electric fires, installed to supplement central heating, were not 'articles of a kind ordinarily installed by builders' in *Rialto Builders Ltd (No 2), [1974] VATTR 14 (VTD 53)*.

15.130 **Electric fire.** An individual (S) claimed a refund of tax on the installation of an electric fire in a stone fireplace. The Commissioners rejected the claim on the basis that the fire did not constitute 'building materials'. The tribunal dismissed S's appeal. *JH Shephard, CAR/76/24–25 (VTD 254)*.

15.131 **Gas fires fitted as standard in new houses.** A builder installed a radiant convector gas fire as standard in the lounge of each of a number of houses he built in Yorkshire. He reclaimed input tax on the basis that the fires were 'articles of a kind ordinarily installed by builders as fixtures'. The Commissioners rejected his claim but the tribunal allowed his appeal. Heating of one kind or another was normally installed in new houses and, on the evidence, a convector gas fire was one of the forms of heating normally installed by builders as fixtures. *F Austin (Leyton) Ltd*, 15.118 above, applied; *Rialto Builders Ltd (No 2)*, 15.129 above, distinguished. *F Booker Builders & Contractors Ltd, [1977] VATTR 203 (VTD 446)*.

15.132 **Gas fires and electric fittings.** An appellant contended that gas fires and electric fittings, supplied to him for the house extension he was building, were goods ordinarily installed by builders as fixtures. The tribunal accepted this contention and allowed the appeal to this extent. *SC Blake, LON/83/13 (VTD 1419)*. (*Note*. The zero-rating of alterations to buildings was removed by *FA 1984* with respect to supplies made after 31 May 1984.)

15.133 **Storage heaters.** Two partners owned a five-storey house let out as offices to various tenants (including a firm of which they were partners). They arranged for the installation of 32 electric storage heaters. The radiators were free-standing, connected by cables to wall sockets, but because of their weight were not easily movable. The tribunal held that the radiators in question were not 'of a kind ordinarily installed by builders'. *Gibb & Innes, EDN/75/1 (VTD 154)*. (*Note*. See also the note following *Blake*, 15.132 above.)

15.134 A company had installed all-electric heating systems in a number of bungalows. The systems included night storage heaters, weighing almost 300 lbs each. The tribunal held that the heaters were articles of a kind ordinarily installed by builders as fixtures for the purposes of what is now *Input Tax Order, Article 6. F Booker Builders and Contractors Ltd*, 15.131 above, and *dicta* of Lord Goddard CJ in *Billing v Pill, CA [1953] 2 All ER 1061*, applied. *Robert Dale & Co (Builders) Ltd, [1983] VATTR 61*

(VTD 1347). (Note. For the Commissioners' practice following this decision, see their Press Release of 17 June 1983, reproduced at *1983 STI 255.*)

15.135 **Cooker hoods.** A property development company reclaimed input tax in respect of cooker hoods, which it had purchased for incorporation in a block of 14 flats which it was developing. The Commissioners issued an assessment to recover the tax, considering that it was not deductible by virtue of what is now *VATA 1994, Sch 8, Group 5, Note 22(c).* The tribunal dismissed the company's appeal, holding that the cooker hoods were electrical appliances. *BGM Ltd, LON/93/851A (VTD 11793).*

15.136 **Electric security gates.** A partnership constructed expensive houses, some of which included electrically operated security gates. It did not account for tax on the supplies of the gates. The Commissioners issued an assessment on the basis that the gates failed to qualify for zero-rating under *VATA 1994, Sch 8, Group 5, Note 22* since they were not 'ordinarily incorporated by builders', and also that the gates were electrical appliances and thus excluded from zero-rating by *Note 22(c).* The tribunal upheld both the Commissioners' contentions and dismissed the partnership's appeal. *M & G McCarthy (t/a Croft Homes), LON/99/1253 (VTD 16789).*

Other items

15.137 **Mechanical ventilator units.** The tribunal held that mechanical ventilator units, which were installed for sound-proofing purposes in houses near to an airport, were articles 'of a kind ordinarily installed by builders'. *British Airports Authority (No 5), LON/77/144 (VTD 447).*

15.138 **Ventilating system.** An individual (W) claimed a refund of tax on the installation of a ventilating system in a bungalow which he had built. The Commissioners rejected his claim, considering that a ventilation system was not 'ordinarily incorporated' in a bungalow. The tribunal allowed W's appeal. Most houses did not have ventilating systems installed, but where there was no natural ventilation, a ventilation system was generally required by building regulations. On the evidence, a ventilation system was necessary for this particular bungalow. The system was an article of a type ordinarily incorporated in a building, when such installation was considered necessary. *CH Wigmore, [1991] VATTR 290 (VTD 6040).*

15.139 A company manufactured mechanical ventilation systems with heat recovery, for installation in domestic buildings. The Commissioners issued a ruling that its supplies of these systems were standard-rated, and the company appealed, contending that the systems were 'articles of a kind ordinarily installed by builders', and qualified for zero-rating under what is now *VATA 1994, Sch 8, Group 5, Item 4.* The tribunal accepted this contention and allowed the appeal. *Wigmore,* 15.138 above, applied. *2S Airchangers Ltd, BEL/93/1A (VTD 12495).*

15.140 **Scaffolding.** In the course of the construction of a house a specialist firm supplied scaffolding on hire, which it designed and erected and, on the conclusion of the hire, dismantled. The tribunal held that the services of designing, erecting and dismantling were within what is now *VATA 1994, Sch 8, Group 5, Item 2* and zero-rated, but that the scaffolding was not 'materials' within *Item 4* and was standard-rated. The consideration for the hire was therefore to be apportioned between the two, the appeal being adjourned for this to be agreed. *B Gilbourne, [1974] VATTR 209 (VTD 109).* (*Note.* The appeal was by the recipient of the supply—see 2.27 APPEALS.)

15.141 **Waste disposal units.** A company reclaimed input tax in respect of waste disposal units which it had purchased for installation in fitted kitchens. The Commissioners issued an assessment to recover the tax, considering that waste disposal units were not 'ordinarily' installed in fitted kitchens, so that the claim for input tax was prohibited by what is now *Article 6* of the *Input Tax Order*. The company appealed, contending that the flats were luxury flats and that waste disposal units were ordinarily installed in luxury flats. The tribunal dismissed the appeal, holding that 'ordinarily' implies installation in all sections of the market, not just in luxury homes. *Creighton Griffiths (Investments) Ltd, [1983] VATTR 175 (VTD 1442).*

15.142   **Telephone exchange.**   A university installed a new telephone exchange system. The Commissioners issued a ruling that the supply of the new telephone exchange was standard-rated. The university appealed, contending that the telephone exchange system was within what is now *VATA 1994, Sch 8, Group 5, Item 4* and was therefore zero-rated. The tribunal allowed the university's appeal, holding that the exchange was a fixture rather than a chattel, applying *dicta* of Scarman LJ in *Berkley v Poulett, CA 1976, 241 EG 911. University of Reading, LON/89/235 (VTD 4209).*

15.143   **Venetian blinds.**   A construction company built two houses designed for low energy consumption. They had south-facing windows, which incorporated venetian blinds which opened and closed automatically so as to admit or retain heat. The company reclaimed input tax on the blinds. The Commissioners issued an assessment to recover the tax, considering that it was not deductible by virtue of what is now *Input Tax Order, Article 6*. The company appealed, contending that the blinds were items ordinarily installed by builders, and that the tax was deductible. The tribunal rejected this contention and dismissed the appeal, holding that the blinds were not items ordinarily installed by builders, so that *Article 6* applied and the tax was not deductible. *Frank Haslam Milan & Co Ltd, MAN/87/89 (VTD 3857).*

15.144   **Timber used for shelving.**   Timber used for shelving was held to qualify as 'materials' in *John Turner & Smith Ltd, MAN/74/23 (VTD 124).*

15.145   **Conservatories, roof timbers and fire doors—whether supplied with services.**   A joinery partnership supplied two conservatories, some new roof windows and some fire doors to the owners of protected buildings, and did not account for output tax on the supplies, treating them as zero-rated. The Commissioners issued an assessment charging tax, on the basis that the supplies did not qualify for zero-rating under what is now *VATA 1994, Sch 8, Group 5, Item 4*, since the materials had not been supplied with any related zero-rated services. The partnership appealed, contending that it had supplied services as well as the materials, so that the materials qualified for zero-rating under what is now *VATA 1994, Sch 8, Group 5, Item 4*. The QB rejected this contention and upheld the assessment. Ognall J held that the partnership was doing no more than was necessary to supply goods. As a matter of law, the services found to have been provided were nothing more than the normal obligations imposed by law on a person selling any articles. The partnership had made a single supply of goods which did not qualify for zero-rating. *C & E Commrs v MD & RW Jeffs (t/a J & J Joinery), QB [1995] STC 759.*

15.146   **Kitchen units.**   The QB decision in *Jeffs*, 15.145 above, was applied in a subsequent case in which the tribunal held that supplies of kitchen units were supplies of goods and there were no related supplies of services. Accordingly the supplies did not qualify for zero-rating. *D & Mrs C Hodson (t/a Bordercraft Workshops), MAN/95/1769 (VTD 13897).*

15.147   **Snooker table.**   A partnership claimed a deduction for input tax in respect of the installation of a snooker table. The Commissioners issued an assessment to recover the tax and the partnership appealed. The tribunal dismissed the appeal, holding that snooker tables were not 'articles ordinarily installed by builders'. *Haden & Son, LON/85/615 (VTD 2209).*

15.148   **Material for soundproofing concrete floors.**   A company reclaimed input tax on the supply of a material for soundproofing concrete floors. The Commissioners issued an assessment to recover the tax, considering that the tax was not recoverable by virtue of what is now *Article 6* of the *Input Tax Order*. The tribunal dismissed the company's appeal. *McCarthy & Stone plc, LON/91/382 (VTD 7014)*. (*Note.* For another issue in this case, see 15.124 above.)

15.149   **Planting of trees and shrubs.**   A landscape gardener reclaimed input tax in respect of trees and shrubs which he had planted in the grounds of a new estate. The Commissioners issued an assessment to recover the tax, considering that the trees and shrubs were not within the definition of 'materials ... of a kind ordinarily installed by builders'. The tribunal dismissed the gardener's appeal against this decision. (The tribunal also observed that the planting of the trees was not 'in the course of construction' of the buildings.) *JW Tilbury, LON/80/407 (VTD 1102)*.

15.150   The decision in *Tilbury*, 15.149 above, was not followed in a subsequent case involving a housing development, where the tribunal held on the evidence that 'it is now normal practice for planning authorities in the case of new housing developments to require a scheme of hard and soft landscaping to be submitted and approved before the commencement of the development'. Accordingly, the tribunal held that the trees and shrubs were 'goods ordinarily at the present time incorporated in the site of buildings of the description that are involved here'. *Rialto Homes plc, [1999] VATDR 477 (VTD 16340)*. (*Note.* For the Commissioners' practice following this decision, see Business Brief 7/00, issued on 18 May 2000.)

15.151   An individual (M) claimed a refund of tax on hedging shrubs and weedkiller. The Commissioners rejected the claim on the basis that they could not be regarded as 'building materials', and the tribunal dismissed M's appeal. *A McAlister, BEL/87/14 (VTD 3148)*.

15.152   A company reclaimed input tax in respect of trees and shrubs which it had planted in the grounds of a housing development. The Commissioners issued an assessment to recover the tax, considering that it was not deductible by virtue of what is now *Article 6* of the *Input Tax Order*. The company appealed, contending that the trees and shrubs were 'articles of a kind ordinarily installed as fixtures'. The tribunal dismissed the company's appeal. The trees and shrubs were 'not articles which one would expect a builder to install as fixtures in the ordinary way'. *McLean Homes East Anglia Ltd, [1992] VATTR 460 (VTD 7748)*.

15.153   **Safe.**   An individual (J) claimed a refund of tax on the installation of a safe. The Commissioners rejected the claim on the basis that a safe was not 'ordinarily incorporated' in a dwelling-house. The tribunal dismissed J's appeal against this decision. *GE Joel, LON/88/403 (VTD 3295)*.

MISCELLANEOUS

15.154   **Interaction of VATA 1994, Sch 8, Group 5 and VATA 1994, Sch 9, Group 1.**   An individual (C) purchased a house in 1.8 acres of land. He carried out substantial demolition work, constructed a larger house on the site, and reclaimed input tax on the materials which he had used. The Commissioners rejected the claim, considering firstly that, because he had retained a small proportion of the walls of the existing house, the work did not qualify as the construction of a building, and contending alternatively that the input tax was not recoverable because C intended to sell the house after building it, so that the input tax had been incurred for the purpose of making an exempt supply under what is now *VATA 1994, Sch 9, Group 1, Item 1*. The tribunal allowed C's appeal. With regard to the first issue, the tribunal held that the work qualified as the 'construction of a building' under the legislation then in force. With regard to the Commissioners' second contention, the tribunal observed that this would 'have the effect that even if the fee simple of the land is sold by a person constructing a building designed as a dwelling, the grant of any interest in land is exempt. Being a taxing statute, these provisions must be construed strictly, and should be construed in favour of the taxpayer. Further, it is well settled that a statute should be construed so that it should have a sensible meaning.' The Commissioners' contentions 'would have, or be capable of having, the effect of nullifying the zero-rating of the grant of a major interest in land by a person constructing a building. It appears to me that that cannot have been the intention of Parliament ... it would appear that the intention was that (*Sch 9**) should apply subject to (*Sch 8**). But whether that be right or not, if (*Sch 9**) is to apply to all grants of an interest in land, then it renders (*Sch 8, Group 5, Item 1**) meaningless'. Accordingly, the input tax should be deemed not to have been incurred for the purpose of an exempt supply. *AR Carter, LON/95/1390 (VTD 13828)*. (*Note*. With regard to the definition of 'construction of a building', see now *VATA 1994, Sch 8, Group 5, Note 18*, introduced by *VAT (Construction of Buildings) Order 1995 (SI 1995 No 280)*. The work in question would not now qualify for zero-rating, but the case remains a useful authority with regard to the interaction of *VATA 1994, Sch 8, Group 5* and *VATA 1994, Sch 9, Group 1*.)

15.155   **Construction work undertaken for purpose of exempt supplies—change in law to make such supplies zero-rated from March 1995—whether input tax recoverable.**   See *Martins Properties (Chelsea) Ltd*, 43.131 PARTIAL EXEMPTION.

15.156   **VATA 1994, s 35(1)(b)—whether construction work 'lawful'.**   An appellant claimed a refund of input tax incurred in building a flat adjacent to an existing house. There was no communication between the flat and the house. The flat was separately rated and was self-contained in respect of all services. However, the relevant planning permission stated that the flat was to 'remain solely for the enjoyment of the dwelling house'. The Commissioners therefore rejected the claim, considering that the work was not within what is now *VATA 1994, s 35(1)(b)*, because it was not 'lawful'. The tribunal upheld this contention and dismissed the appeal. *RAS Alexander, EDN/89/140 (VTD 4560)*.

15.157   **VATA 1994, s 35(1)(b)—whether construction work 'otherwise than the course or furtherance of any business'.**   An individual (F) obtained planning permission for the erection of a 'dwelling house incorporating bed and breakfast facilities'. He claimed a refund of tax under *VATA 1994, s 35*. The Commissioners rejected the claim and the tribunal dismissed his appeal. *VATA 1994, s 35(1)(b)* provided that a refund was only due where the works were 'otherwise than in the course of any business'. On the evidence, F had undertaken the work with 'the intention to further the business of running a bed and breakfast establishment in the building'. *HW Flynn, LON/99/1161 (VTD 16930)*.

15.158   **Tax wrongly charged by contractor—claim for refund under VATA 1994, s 35.**   An individual (V) engaged a builder to construct a house for him. The contract excluded work on all external doors and windows. V arranged for this work to be carried out for him by a separate company. That company issued an invoice charging VAT on its services, which V paid. V applied for the tax to be refunded under what is now *VATA 1994, s 35*. The Commissioners rejected the claim on the grounds that the work was in the course of construction of the building and should have been zero-rated, so that V should have requested a refund from the company. The tribunal dismissed V's appeal against this decision, holding that *VATA 1994, s 35* only provided for refunds of tax in cases where tax was 'chargeable on the supply of goods', as in cases where articles were purchased from a builders' merchant. In the case under appeal, although the tax had been charged, it had not been properly chargeable, so that *VATA 1994, s 35* did not apply and V's remedy was against the company, rather than against the Commissioners. *RJ Vincett, LON/93/233A (VTD 10932)*.

15.159   *Vincett*, 15.158 above, was applied in the similar cases of *E Banks, LON/93/2845 (VTD 12004)* and *DM Aries, LON/93/2611A (VTD 12172)*.

15.160   A similar decision was reached in *DC Fisher, LON/93/2723A (VTD 12356)*.

15.161   **VATA 1994, s 35(1)(c)—definition of 'goods used ... for the purposes of the works'.**   A married couple claimed relief under what is now *VATA 1994, s 35* in respect of a fence and a garden wall, built for them by contractors. The Commissioners rejected the claim and the tribunal dismissed the couple's appeal, holding that the invoices in question related to supplies of services and that the goods which were included in the supply were an 'integral and incidental part of the overall single supply of a service'. Accordingly the supplies were not within what is now *VATA 1994, s 35(1)(c)* and relief was not due. *AJ & A Elliott, LON/89/1782X (VTD 4926)*.

16   Death

The cases in this chapter are arranged under the following headings.

> **Burial and cremation (VATA 1994, Sch 9, Group 8)** 16.1–16.4
> **Miscellaneous** 16.5–16.14

BURIAL AND CREMATION (VATA 1994, Sch 9, Group 8)

16.1   **Clearing of old burial ground.**   A property developer had planning permission to build a shopping complex on an area partly owned by a Borough Council. The Council arranged for a company to clear a burial ground which formed part of the area. The company reclaimed input tax on the basis that the work was zero-rated civil engineering work within *VATA 1983, Sch 5* as then in force. The Commissioners rejected the claim, considering that it was exempt under what is now *VATA 1994, Sch 9, Group 8, Item 1*. The tribunal rejected the company's contentions, holding that the work was not civil engineering work. It also held that the work was not the 'disposal of the remains of the dead' within *VATA 1994, Sch 9, Group 8, Item 1*. The normal meaning of these words confined the exemption to services supplied by undertakers as such and to cremation services. The tribunal therefore held that the work was neither zero-rated nor exempt, but standard-rated. *UFD Ltd, [1981] VATTR 199 (VTD 1172)*.

16.2   **Funeral directors—storage of cadavers and use of chapel of rest.**   A partnership which carried on business as funeral directors stored cadavers for other firms, and allowed such firms to use its chapel of rest. The Commissioners issued a ruling that these supplies were exempt from VAT under *VATA 1994, Sch 9, Group 8, Item 2*, so that the partnership could not reclaim the related input tax. The tribunal dismissed the partnership's appeal, observing that the services were 'directly involved in and concerned with the burial of the dead'. The tribunal distinguished *Network Insurance Brokers Ltd*, 16.3 below, and *Co-Operative Wholesale Society Ltd*, 16.4 below, noting that those cases 'were concerned with financial arrangements rather than physical arrangements'. *CJ Williams' Funeral Service of Telford, [1999] VATDR 318 (VTD 16261)*.

16.3   **Insurance broker—services relating to hospital fund—whether exempt under Group 8, Item 2.**   A company (N), which carried on business as a registered insurance broker, supplied services to a hospital fund which provided a funeral benefit for its members. It received commission from the fund, but did not account for output tax on the commission. The Commissioners issued an assessment charging tax on the commission and N appealed, contending that the commission should be treated as exempt under *VATA 1994, Sch 9, Group 8, Item 2*. The tribunal rejected this contention and dismissed the appeal, and the QB upheld this decision. The words 'arrangements for or in connection with the disposal of the remains of the dead' in *Item 2* should be construed in accordance with *Annex F* of the *EC Sixth Directive*, i.e. as relating to cremation services or services of the kind supplied by undertakers. Accordingly, the supplies made by N failed to qualify for exemption. *Network Insurance Brokers Ltd v C & E Commrs, QB [1998] STC 742*.

16.4   **Payment to funeral directors in relation to funeral benefit scheme—whether exempt under Group 8, Item 2.**   A major company (C) had agreed to provide funeral services to members of an insurance fund, charging a fee of £6 per member. Subsequently the company (L) which operated the fund decided that it wished to extend the choice of funeral directors providing such services for its members. The agreement was revised and, under the revised agreement, L paid C annual compensation of £1.25 for each of its members. C did not account for output tax on these payments, treating them as exempt under *VATA 1994, Sch 9, Group 8, Item 2*. The Commissioners issued an assessment on the basis that the payments failed to qualify for exemption. C appealed, contending that it was making a single supply of services and that the whole of the consideration which it received should be treated as exempt. The tribunal rejected this contention and dismissed the appeal, holding that the compensation payments were not made 'for or in connection with the disposal of the remains of the dead', as required by *Item 2*. The QB and CA upheld this decision. Simon Brown LJ held that, whereas the consideration of £6 per member paid under the original agreement was accepted as relating to exempt supplies, the additional consideration of £1.25 per member related to separate supplies which did not qualify for exemption. Where C itself provided funeral services, its supplies were accepted as exempt, but where funeral services were supplied by other funeral directors, C's services were not exempt. *Co-Operative Wholesale Society Ltd v C & E Commrs (No 3), CA [2000] STC 727*.

MISCELLANEOUS

16.5   **Death of accountant—whether excuse for late return.**   See the cases noted at 18.194 to 18.196 DEFAULT SURCHARGE.

16.6   **Death of bookkeeper—whether excuse for late return.**   See *Ernest Platt (Bury) Ltd*, 18.182 DEFAULT SURCHARGE.

16.7   **Death of bookkeeper—whether excuse for misdeclaration.**   See the cases noted at 49.40 and 49.41 PENALTIES: MISDECLARATION.

16.8   **Death of director—whether excuse for late return.**   See the cases noted at 18.161 to 18.164 DEFAULT SURCHARGE.

16.9   **Death of employee—whether excuse for late return.**   See *Semec (Engineering) Ltd*, 18.188 DEFAULT SURCHARGE, and *Group Topek Holdings Ltd*, 18.189 DEFAULT SURCHARGE.

16.10   **Death of father—whether excuse for late return.**   See *Watts*, 18.92 DEFAULT SURCHARGE, and *Chelms*, 18.93 DEFAULT SURCHARGE.

16.11   **Death of mother—whether excuse for late return.**   See the cases noted at 18.90 to 18.91 DEFAULT SURCHARGE.

16.12   **Death of partner—whether excuse for late registration.**   See *Ford*, 48.16 PENALTIES: FAILURE TO NOTIFY.

16.13   **Death of son-in-law—whether excuse for late return.**   See *Hardwick*, 18.141 DEFAULT SURCHARGE.

16.14   **Death of wife—whether excuse for late return.**   See *Stephens*, 18.88 DEFAULT SURCHARGE.

17   Default Interest

17.1   **Appeal against interest charge—effect of VATA 1994, s 84(6).**   On 20 December 1990 the Commissioners issued an assessment charging VAT of £44,158. The trader did not pay the tax until 14 February 1991, and an interest charge was imposed. The trader appealed, contending that the interest charge should be waived because he had queried the assessment with the Commissioners, and had written to the Commissioners stating that he would not pay the tax assessed until he had received further clarification. The Commissioners applied for the appeal to be struck out. The tribunal allowed the application and struck out the appeal. The interest was lawfully payable and what is now *VATA 1994, s 84(6)* provided that the tribunal had no power to vary the amount assessed. *DA Kelly, LON/91/1887Z (VTD 7941)*.

17.2   *Kelly*, 17.1 above, was applied in the following cases in which appeals against interest charged under what is now *VATA 1994, s 74* were dismissed: *Paro Ltd, LON/92/1921P (VTD 9414); Farm Services (Gillingham) Ltd, LON/92/219X (VTD 9514); Elesa Ltd, LON/92/1669A (VTD 10308); T Probyn, MAN/92/637 (VTD 10679); Inspection Equipment Ltd*, 49.109 PENALTIES: MISDECLARATION and *Stratford*, 49.178 PENALTIES: MISDECLARATION.

17.3   Similar decisions were reached in *Gateway Leisure (Caravan Sales), EDN/92/304 (VTD 9689); W Cowx, LON/92/1920 (VTD 10037); DTA Ross & Son, EDN/93/106 (VTD 10755); AWTS Transportation International Ltd, LON/93/560A (VTD 11089); WM Whitefield & Sons (Builders) Ltd, EDN/93/40 (VTD 11286); Hodge Servicing Ltd, MAN/93/264 (VTD 11561); PS Bahd (t/a Kingsbury Liquor Mart), LON/92/1954A (VTD 11688); JH Winstone, LON/93/1527 (VTD 11948); Jamie plc, LON/93/1971A (VTD 11962); Ottoman Textiles Ltd, MAN/93/1566 (VTD 12795); Kenmyn Management Services Ltd, LON/94/1561A (VTD 13765)* and *VP Bassi (t/a Imperial Wines), LON/1321 (VTD 16449)*.

17.4   A company appealed against a charge to interest under what is now *VATA 1994, s 74* (originally *FA 1985, s 18*). The Commissioners applied to strike out the appeal on the grounds that there was no appealable matter within what is now *VATA 1994, s 83*. The tribunal chairman (Miss Plumptre, sitting alone) rejected the application, holding that despite the wording of what is now *VATA 1994, s 84(6)*, an appellant 'may wish to take the opportunity to argue that the decision to assess to default interest is incompatible with the principles of European Community law'. *Audiostore Ltd (t/a Stagestruck), LON/93/2220A (VTD 11827)*. (*Notes*. (1) Miss Plumptre's decision discusses *obiter dicta* of the tribunal chairman in *London Borough of Camden*, 17.6 below, but does not refer to any of the cases noted at 17.1 to 17.3 above. (2) For the compatibility of the measures enacted in *FA 1985* with Community law, see the QB decision in *P & O Ferries*, 49.23 PENALTIES: MISDECLARATION, and the tribunal decisions in *The Central YMCA*, 18.566 DEFAULT SURCHARGE, *Impetus Engineering Co (International) Ltd*, 18.567 DEFAULT SURCHARGE, and *W Emmett & Son Ltd*, 49.411 PENALTIES: MISDECLARATION. Miss Plumptre's decision in *Audiostore Ltd* does not refer to any of these four decisions.)

17.5   A similar decision was reached (again by Miss Plumptre) in a case where a partnership had paid interest under what is now *VATA 1994, s 74* in respect of an assessment which was under appeal, and had subsequently sought repayment of the interest which it had paid. *Dicta* of Lord Goff in *Woolwich Equitable Building Society v CIR, HL [1992] STC 657 (TTC 2001, 32.2)* applied. *RSMG, [1994] VATTR 167 (VTD 11920)*. (*Note*. For another issue in this case, see 2.193 APPEALS.)

17.6 Default Interest

17.6 **Calculation of interest—whether set-off permissible.** A London Borough Council, which had admitted underdeclarations of tax, appealed against a default interest assessment, contending firstly that the Commissioners had acted unreasonably in raising it, and secondly that the assessment was wrongly computed because it failed to make allowance for unclaimed input tax which should have been set against the output tax on which the interest was charged, and which it had notified to the Commissioners on a form VAT 657. The tribunal rejected the Council's first contention, holding that what is now *VATA 1994, s 83* did not give it jurisdiction to review the Commissioners' decision to impose an interest charge. *Food Engineering Ltd*, 49.413 PENALTIES: MISDECLARATION, distinguished. However, the tribunal upheld the Council's second contention, holding that since the Council had previously notified its unclaimed input tax on a form VAT 657, the input tax unclaimed for a particular accounting period should be set against the output tax assessed for that period in computing the interest charge. (The tribunal also held that only amounts relating to the same prescribed accounting periods could be aggregated, and that any surplus of input tax for a particular period could not be carried forward.) *London Borough of Camden, [1993] VATTR 73 (VTD 10476).*

17.7 A partnership reclaimed input tax of £16,250 which was attributable to exempt supplies, and the Commissioners issued an assessment to recover the tax. They also imposed an interest charge covering the period from August 1991 to March 1992. In July 1992 the partnership lodged an election to waive exemption in respect of the property to which the input tax related. The Commissioners accepted that, following this election, the partnership was entitled to reclaim input tax of £15,200. The partnership appealed against the charge to default interest, contending that, in computing the charge, the £15,200 which was repayable should be set against the £16,250 which had been assessed, and that interest should only be charged on the balance. The tribunal dismissed the appeal, holding that the interest charge had been correctly calculated and that the subsequent repayment could not be set against the amount of the assessment. *Maybourne & Russell, LON/93/618A (VTD 11289).*

17.8 The Commissioners discovered that a trader had underdeclared output tax, and issued an assessment, covering the period from 1 April 1989 to 30 April 1991, charging output tax of £5,901, with default interest from 1 April 1990. The trader appealed against the interest charge, contending that he had underclaimed input tax of £3,657, and that this should be set against the output tax in computing the interest charge. He had notified this underclaimed input tax in March 1992, after the issue of the assessment, and the Commissioners had accepted the claim in May 1992. The tribunal dismissed the appeal, distinguishing *London Borough of Camden*, 17.6 above, on the grounds that, in that case, the input tax had previously been notified by a voluntary disclosure on form VAT 657, so that there had been 'an earlier assessment' within what is now *VATA 1994, s 74(1)(a)(ii)*. In the present case, however, there had been no such disclosure at the time when the output tax assessment was issued, so that the effect of what is now *s 74(1)(a)(i)* was that the interest charge applied to the whole of the output tax charged by that assessment, and the input tax of £3,657 could only be set against that output tax from the date in May 1992 when the Commissioners acknowledged their acceptance of the claim to input tax. The tribunal chairman observed that 'there is no provision in the legislation whereby the amount of (an) assessment can be recalculated to take account of a subsequent claim to further credit for input tax in the same accounting periods', and that 'it is unfortunate for the taxpayer that interest is charged by (*VATA 1994, s 74**) not on the amount by which his true liability for the periods in question exceeds the tax declared on his returns but on the whole amount assessed by an assessment made under (*VATA 1994, s 73**)'. *D MacKenzie, LON/92/904X (VTD 11597).*

17.9   *MacKenzie*, 17.8 above, was distinguished in a subsequent case in which a company had notified an underclaim of input tax before the Commissioners issued an assessment to recover underdeclared output tax. The tribunal held that the input tax should be set against the output tax in computing the interest charge. *London Borough of Camden*, 17.6 above, applied. *SGS Holding UK Ltd, LON/93/2016A (VTD 13018)*.

17.10   In January 1992 a company discovered that, for the period ending August 1990, it had underclaimed input tax of £7,235. It submitted a repayment claim, which the Commissioners accepted, and the sum in question was repaid to the company in February. In June 1992 a VAT officer discovered that the company had underdeclared output tax of £15,209 for the period ending August 1990. The Commissioners raised a default interest charge on this amount. The company appealed, contending that the input tax of £7,235 should be set against the output tax of £15,209 in calculating the interest charge. The tribunal accepted this contention and allowed the appeal, applying *London Borough of Camden*, 17.6 above, and observing that a Customs' Press Release of 7 September 1994 had stated that 'in general Customs will not in future seek to assess interest where it does not represent commercial restitution'. Furthermore, to charge default interest on the gross amount of output tax without taking account of the underclaimed input tax would be contrary to the principles enunciated by Lord Goff in *Woolwich Equitable Building Society v CIR, HL [1992] STC 657 (TTC 2001, 32.2)*. *R & N Miller Ltd, LON/92/2297 (VTD 13236)*.

17.11   **Calculation of interest disputed—Commissioners failing to provide clarification.**   In an appeal against default interest, the tribunal chairman held that the Commissioners had not provided sufficient details of how the interest was calculated, and adjourned the hearing with a direction that the Commissioners should, within 28 days, provide 'full details in a form readily understood of the calculation of default interest'. The Commissioners failed to comply with the direction, and at the resumed hearing the tribunal formally allowed the appeal. *AR Waller & Associates, [1993] VATTR 402 (VTD 10712)*.

17.12   **Date on which interest ceases to run.**   In 1991 a builder reclaimed input tax in respect of materials purchased for a house which he intended building for himself. Following a control visit in January 1992, the Commissioners issued an assessment to recover the tax. In April 1992 the builder submitted a claim for the tax to be treated as repayable under what is now *VATA 1994, s 35*. Meanwhile the Commissioners took proceedings to enforce payment of the tax charged by the assessment, and the builder paid the tax assessed in May 1992. His claim for the tax to be refunded under *s 35** was accepted, and the tax was repaid to him in June. The Commissioners demanded default interest on the tax charged by the assessment, and the builder appealed, contending that the charge was unfair since the officer who made the control visit in January 1992 had not told him that he would have to claim the tax under *s 35**, and that if the officer had told him this, he could have reclaimed the tax earlier. The tribunal allowed his appeal in part, holding that he had been 'misinformed as to the correct procedure for reclaiming input tax on the building of his own house, and that as a result, the repayment of that input tax was unreasonably delayed', and that had it not been for this, the tax could have been repaid in April. The tribunal held that, in the circumstances, the default interest should cease to run after 31 March 1992. *NC Stanley, MAN/92/1319 (VTD 10857)*.

17.13   **Company reclaiming input tax attributable to associated partnership— validity of interest charge.**   A company reclaimed input tax of £11,000 in its return for the period ending November 1991 which was in fact attributable to an associated partnership. The company's accountant discovered this in March 1992, and the company notified the Commissioners accordingly on 20 March. In the meantime, the company had claimed and received a repayment of £7,500, when it should have paid output tax of £3,500 to the Commissioners. The Commissioners issued an assessment charging default interest on the company from January 1992 to 21 April 1992. The company appealed, contending that the interest charge was unjust as there had been no net loss of tax. The tribunal dismissed the appeal, observing that the company and the partnership were separate entities and that the interest had been computed in accordance with what is now *VATA 1994, s 74*. *Terracopia Ltd, MAN/92/1283 (VTD 11341)*.

17.14   **Partnership failing to account for tax on payments from associated companies—validity of interest charge.** In an Isle of Man case, an accountancy partnership failed to account for tax on payments from associated companies. The Isle of Man Treasury imposed an interest charge. The partnership appealed, contending that the charge should be waived because the companies could have reclaimed the amounts in question as input tax, so that there had been no net loss of tax. The tribunal dismissed the appeal, holding that the interest was lawfully due and that neither the Treasury nor the tribunal had discretion to waive it. *Holdsworth & Co v Isle of Man Treasury, MAN/93/275 (VTD 12480)*. (*Note.* See now the Commissioners' News Release 34/94, dated 7 September 1994, indicating that Customs will no longer charge interest in such circumstances.)

17.15   **Incorrect reclaim of input tax following misdirection by VAT officer.** A company which traded as car dealers reclaimed input tax on certain transactions without holding VAT invoices. It was accepted that this was largely due to incorrect advice given by a VAT officer in 1989. In the circumstances the Commissioners did not impose a penalty under what is now *VATA 1994, s 63*. However, they did issue an assessment to recover the net amount underdeclared. They also imposed an interest charge under what is now *VATA 1994, s 74*. The company appealed against the interest charge. The tribunal dismissed the appeal, holding that there had been a temporary loss of tax to the Crown, that the default interest was lawfully due, and that the Commissioners could not be estopped from collecting it. *GUS Merchandise Corporation Ltd*, 2.76 APPEALS, and *Farm Facilities (Fork Lift) Ltd*, 2.77 APPEALS, applied. *RC & R Harding (t/a Tolcarne Motors), LON/92/986X (VTD 11809)*.

17.16   **Assessment to interest covering several different accounting periods.** In March 1996 the Commissioners issued an assessment on a trader, covering the period from August 1988 to May 1994. They subsequently issued an assessment charging interest. The trader appealed, contending firstly that the assessment to interest was invalid because it was 'global' and did not identify the separate accounting periods to which the interest related, and alternatively *VATA 1994, s 74(3)* should be interpreted as meaning that interest should be restricted to the assessments made in respect of the last three years, rather than being the interest on the whole sum outstanding calculated for the last three years. The tribunal rejected these contentions and dismissed the appeal. Applying the CA decision in *Bassimeh*, 47.2 PENALTIES: EVASION OF TAX, 'to subdivide this total figure into 18 quarterly figures and then aggregate them so as to reproduce the same figure would be ... entirely otiose and unnecessary'. With regard to the trader's alternative contention, the effect of *VATA 1994, s 74(3)* was that the interest was chargeable on the whole debt but limited to the amount in respect of the last three years. *MS Shokar (t/a Manor Fish Bar), [1998] VATDR 301 (VTD 15674)*.

17.17   **Duplicate invoices—whether assessment raised to best of Commissioners' judgment—whether Commissioners acting unreasonably in raising interest charge.** See *Callaway*, 3.23 ASSESSMENT.

17.18   **Other cases.**   There have been a number of other cases, which appear to raise no point of general interest, in which appeals against assessments to default interest have been dismissed. In the interests of space, such cases are not reported individually in this book.

18   Default Surcharge

General Note. There have been a very large number of appeals against default surcharges. All appeals to the Courts are summarised individually. However, unsuccessful appeals to tribunals are only summarised where the case appears to raise a point of general importance. The cases in this chapter are arranged under the following headings.

Payment by credit transfer
    Cases where the appellant was successful 18.497–18.499
    Cases where the appellant was unsuccessful 18.500–18.503
Other cases
    Cases where the appellant was successful 18.504–18.529
    Cases where the appellant was unsuccessful 18.530–18.565
Validity of the surcharge 18.566–18.569

THE SURCHARGE LIABILITY NOTICE (VATA 1994, s 59(2,3))

18.1   **Receipt of surcharge liability notice disputed.**   A company appealed against a default surcharge, contending that it had not received the relevant surcharge liability notice. The tribunal allowed the company's appeal, holding that the surcharge liability notice had not been served and thus the default surcharge was invalid. The QB upheld this decision, holding that the whole scheme of default surcharges was dependent upon service of the surcharge liability notice. *C & E Commrs v Medway Draughting & Technical Services Ltd, QB [1989] STC 346.*

18.2   A similar decision was reached in a case heard in the QB with the preceding case. *C & E Commrs v Adplates Offset Ltd, QB [1989] STC 346.*

18.3   There have been a large number of cases in which appellants have claimed that they have not received the relevant surcharge liability notice. Such decisions turn entirely on whether the tribunal accepts or rejects the appellant's evidence on the balance of probabilities. In the interests of space, such cases are not reported individually in this book.

18.4   **Whether surcharge liability notice withdrawn.**   In July 1987 a company received a surcharge liability notice indicating that its return for the period ending 30 April 1987 had not been received. It telephoned its local VAT office, to state that the return must have been received because the cheque which had accompanied it had been banked. (In fact the return had been received after the due date, so that the company had incurred a potential surcharge liability although the wording of the notice was inaccurate and misleading.) A VAT officer advised the company that there had been an industrial dispute at the VAT Central Unit which had resulted in a backlog of work, and advised the company to destroy the notice as it had been issued in error. In fact the company filed the notice. It submitted its next return late, and a surcharge was subsequently imposed. The company appealed, contending that the surcharge liability notice had been withdrawn, so that the surcharge was invalid. The tribunal accepted this contention and allowed the company's appeal. It was implicit in what is now *VATA 1994, s 76(9)* that a surcharge could be withdrawn, and it followed that a surcharge liability notice could also be withdrawn. The effect of the company's conversation with the VAT officer had been to withdraw the surcharge liability notice. *Montreux Fabrics Ltd, [1988] VATTR 71 (VTD 2673).*

18.5   A company submitted its return for the period ending 31 August 1987 in early October. On 21 October the Commissioners issued an estimated default surcharge. The company, knowing that the return and payment were in the post, took no action. In April 1988 the Commissioners issued a revised surcharge notice based on the figures in the company's return. The company's director telephoned the local VAT office to state that he had paid the tax in October, and was told by a VAT officer that he should ignore the notice and throw it away, which he did. Subsequently the Commissioners continued to seek payment of the surcharge and the company lodged a formal appeal. The tribunal allowed the appeal, holding on the evidence that the surcharge had been withdrawn by the officer who had discussed it with the company in April 1988. *Graham Fredericks Ltd, LON/88/201 (VTD 3304).*

18.6 Default Surcharge

18.6   A similar decision, applying *dicta* in *Montreux Fabrics Ltd*, 18.4 above, was reached in *GB White (t/a Chiffon Couture), LON/89/894Z (VTD 4785)*.

18.7   **Validity of surcharge liability notice disputed.** A company's return for the period ending 31 March 1987 was submitted on 12 May 1987 and received by the VAT Central Unit on 18 May 1987. At the time the return was received there was an industrial dispute at the VAT Central Unit. On 10 July 1987 a surcharge liability notice was issued to the company. The notice stated that the return for the period ending 31 March 1987 had not been received. Subsequently the company submitted another return late and a default surcharge was imposed. The company appealed, contending that the surcharge liability notice was invalid since it had incorrectly stated that the return for the period ending 31 March 1987 had not been received, instead of stating that the return had been received late. The tribunal accepted this contention and allowed the appeal, holding that the effect of the inaccurate wording of the notice was that it could not be considered as a valid surcharge liability notice. *Coleman Machines Ltd, MAN/88/437 (VTD 3196)*.

18.8   See also *Nixdorf*, 18.443 below, and *Columbia Veneering Co Ltd*, 18.444 below.

18.9   A tribunal had held that two companies had a reasonable excuse for a first default because their bookkeeper had been ill, but held that there was no reasonable excuse for subsequent defaults. The companies appealed against the surcharges imposed in respect of these defaults, contending that, by virtue of what is now *VATA 1994, s 59(7)*, the effect of allowing the appeal against the first default was that the remaining surcharges should be held to be ineffective. The tribunal rejected this contention and upheld the surcharges, holding that 'the consequence of the deemed non-service is no more than that one of the three requirements specified in (*s 59(2)**) for the applicability of (*s 59(4)**) ... has not been satisfied, and (it was) not therefore required to treat the surcharge period specified in (the notice) as not having been notified to (the appellant)'. *RW Joinery (Stockport) Ltd, MAN/88/830; RW Construction (Stockport) Ltd, MAN/88/831 (VTD 3761)*.

18.10   A similar decision was reached in a subsequent case where the tribunal held that the fact that a reasonable excuse had been established for the first default did not render the subsequent form VAT 164 ineffective. *Dow Engineering*, 18.13 below, and *Eidographics Ltd*, 18.14 below, distinguished. The wording of the form VAT 164 was adequate to take effect either as a surcharge liability notice within *VATA 1994, s 59(2)(b)* or as an extension notice within *VATA 1994, s 59(3)*. *Goldfinch Transport Ltd, [1996] VATDR 484 (VTD 14145)*.

18.11   A company changed its name without notifying the Commissioners. It received a surcharge liability notice addressed in its former name, and appealed against a subsequent default surcharge, contending that the notice had been invalid as it had been issued in the company's former name. The tribunal dismissed the company's appeal, finding that the company's directors had not been misled and holding that the company was at fault in not having notified the Commissioners of its change of name. *Philbor Motors Ltd, LON/90/454X (VTD 5388)*.

18.12   A similar decision was reached in *Street Magazine Ltd, MAN/93/142 (VTD 10991)*.

18.13   In a case where a surcharge liability notice had not been received, but surcharge extension notices, issued subsequently, had been received, the tribunal held that the extension notices were invalid. Applying *dicta* in *RW Joinery (Stockport) Ltd*, 18.9 above, a surcharge extension notice remained valid if the original notice had been received, even if there were subsequently held to have been a reasonable excuse for the initial default. However, since a surcharge extension notice only indicated the end of a surcharge liability period, and did not state the beginning of that period, it was not valid in a case where an appellant had not actually received the initial notice, and thus had not been notified of the date on which the period in question began. *Dow Engineering, MAN/90/657 (VTD 5771)*.

18.14   Similar decisions were reached in *Eidographics Ltd, [1991] VATTR 449 (VTD 6788); Acer Engineering Ltd, MAN/91/1063 (VTD 7536); BB Keane, LON/92/786X (VTD 9131)* and *Sig Video Gems Ltd, LON/94/236P (VTD 12486)*.

18.15   A trader had submitted four successive returns late, but had satisfied the tribunal that he had a reasonable excuse for the first default, since he had never received the appropriate blank return form (see 18.456 below). He contended that, because of this, the effect of what is now *VATA 1994, s 59(7)* was that the first surcharge liability notice was deemed not to have been served, that the extension notices issued in respect of the next default were therefore invalid, and that all the surcharges should be discharged. The Commissioners considered that the effect of *s 59(7)** was that the second default fell to be treated as the first default, the third default as the second, and the fourth default as the third, so that the trader remained liable to a 5% surcharge. The tribunal allowed the trader's appeal, holding that the effect of *s 59(7)** was to deem the notice in question never to have been received. *Dicta* of the tribunal in *RW Joinery (Stockport) Ltd*, 18.9 above, disapproved. *S Robinson, [1991] VATTR 440 (VTD 6267)*. (*Notes.* (1) Compare *Dow Engineering*, 18.13 above, in which *RW Joinery (Stockport) Ltd*, 18.9 above, was approved and applied. (2) The Commissioners have subsequently amended the wording of the surcharge liability notice to include the words 'if no surcharge period has been notified to you previously, the period beginning on the date of this notice and ending on ... is hereby specified as a surcharge period'. (3) The decision here was not followed in the subsequent case of *Goldfinch Transport Ltd*, 18.10 above, where the tribunal held that the wording of the form VAT 164 was adequate to have effect either as a surcharge liability notice within *VATA 1994, s 59(2)(b)* or as an extension notice within *VATA 1994, s 59(3)*.)

18.16   *Robinson*, 18.15 above, was applied in *Pennington Lee*, 18.505 below, in which there was held to be a reasonable excuse for the first default. (*Note.* The decision does not discuss the conflict between the decision reached in *Robinson*, 18.15 above, and those reached in *RW Joinery (Stockport) Ltd*, 18.9 above, and *Dow Engineering*, 18.13 above. See now the note following *Robinson*, 18.15 above.)

18.17   An appeal was allowed in a case where a surcharge liability notice issued in July 1991 indicated that the surcharge liability period ended in May 1991 (this being a typing error for May 1992). The tribunal held that the notice was invalid. *In Style Pleaters, LON/92/585 (VTD 7700)*.

18.18   **Whether tribunal may hear appeal against surcharge liability notice before any surcharge has been incurred.**   See *Expert Systems Design Ltd*, 2.19 APPEALS; *Auld*, 2.20 APPEALS, and *Castrue Ltd*, 2.20 APPEALS.

COMPUTATION OF THE SURCHARGE (VATA 1994, s 59(4,5))

18.19   **Surcharge originally computed on basis of estimated assessments—returns subsequently submitted showing additional liability—whether surcharges to be recomputed.**   A company failed to submit several VAT returns. The Commissioners issued estimated assessments and imposed surcharges computed on the basis of the tax charged by the assessments. Subsequently the company submitted the returns, showing a higher liability than the Commissioners had assessed. The Commissioners therefore withdrew the original surcharges and replaced them with increased surcharges computed on the basis of the tax shown in the returns. The company appealed, contending that the revised surcharges were invalid. The tribunal rejected this contention and dismissed the appeal, holding that the issue of the revised surcharges was authorised by what is now *VATA 1994, s 59(4)*. *Bill Hennessey Associates Ltd, LON/87/640 & 709 (VTD 2656)*.

18.20 **Surcharge cancelled on receipt of return showing repayment due—whether cancellation equivalent to annulment.** A company which had received a surcharge liability notice in July 1987 did not submit its return for the period ending 30 September 1987. In November 1987 the Commissioners issued an estimated assessment for the period, together with a surcharge computed at the rate of 5% of the tax charged by the estimated assessment. In December 1987 the company submitted the return, showing that a repayment was due to it for that period. Accordingly the Commissioners cancelled the surcharge. The company submitted its return for the period ending 31 December 1987 seven weeks late, and the Commissioners imposed a surcharge computed at the rate of 10% of the tax shown on the return. The company appealed, contending that, since the previous surcharge had been cancelled, the surcharge should have been computed at the rate of 5% rather than 10%. The tribunal rejected this contention and dismissed the appeal. The words 'may assess' in what is now *VATA 1994, s 76* gave the Commissioners a discretion. The fact that a surcharge of the statutory minimum had not been imposed did not mean that the default should be left out of account for the purposes of what is now *VATA 1994, s 59(5)*. *GB Techniques Ltd, [1988] VATTR 95 (VTD 3121)*.

18.21 *GB Techniques Ltd*, 18.20 above, was applied in the similar case of *Freewheeler Co Ltd, MAN/89/668 (VTD 4544)*.

18.22 A similar decision was reached in *Conference Staging Ltd, LON/93/1141P (VTD 11434)*.

18.23 **VAT office allocating payments to previous surcharges rather than to current liability.** A company which had incurred two default surcharges made lump sum payments totalling £9,000 in December 1987 in respect of its VAT liabilities. The local VAT office allocated the payments to the surcharge arrears, and did not allocate any of the payments to the company's liability for the period ending 30 November 1987. A further surcharge was consequently imposed in respect of that period. The company appealed, contending that its payments should have been used to clear its current liability first, with only the excess of the payments over the current liability being set against the surcharges. The tribunal accepted this contention and allowed the appeal. *Clifford Construction Ltd, LON/89/141X (VTD 3929)*. (*Notes*. (1) For another issue in this case, see 18.434 below. (2) Compare the subsequent decisions in *Berry*, 18.25 below; *Playford & Pope*, 18.26 below, and *APUK Ltd*, 18.27 below.)

18.24 Similar decisions were reached in *Kam (Stationery) Ltd, LON/90/1289 (VTD 5897)* and *Crusader Line Ltd (t/a Spaghetti Western), LON/93/2871A (VTD 12439, 12568)*.

18.25 A contrasting decision was reached in a case where a trader had incurred arrears totalling £1,771. He paid this amount on 14 August 1990, but then failed to pay his liability for the period ending 31 July 1990 by the due date. The Commissioners imposed a further surcharge, and the trader appealed, contending that the payment which he had made on 14 August should be set firstly against his liability for the period ending 31 July, and that only the balance should be set against the previous arrears. The tribunal rejected this contention and dismissed his appeal, holding on the evidence that the payment made on 14 August should be set against the previous arrears, rather than against the liability for the period ending 31 July. *DC Berry, LON/94/1163 (VTD 13380)*.

18.26   An appeal was dismissed in a case where a firm of solicitors, which had incurred eight successive defaults, contended that payments which it had made should be reallocated to clear its current tax liabilities, rather than being set against the surcharges. The tribunal chairman observed that 'the appellants were a firm of solicitors and were in a position to advise themselves either to appeal against the penalties or to pay the outstanding tax first before the penalties'. On the evidence, the Commissioners had not insisted 'upon the payment of the penalties before the tax; they accepted cheques sent to them by the appellants and applied them in ... a reasonable way in the circumstances of this case'. *Playford & Pope, LON/95/1151P (VTD 13989)*.

18.27   A company appealed against five default surcharges, contending that the Commissioners had acted unfairly in allocating payments which it had made to its oldest arrears, rather than to its current liability. The tribunal rejected this contention and dismissed the appeal, holding on the evidence that 'the Commissioners were entitled to allocate the payments towards the oldest debts'. *APUK Ltd, MAN/98/345 (VTD 15796)*. (*Note*. For another issue in this case, see 18.230 below.)

18.28   **Submission of cheque with words and figures differing.** A company sent a cheque for its quarterly VAT payment on which the amount in words was correctly stated but the amount in figures was incorrect. The bank returned the cheque unpaid, endorsed 'words and figures differ'. The Commissioners imposed a default surcharge but the tribunal allowed the company's appeal, holding that the bank was wrong not to honour the cheque for the amount stated in words. Under the *Bills of Exchange Act 1882, s 9(2)*, a cheque on which the words and figures differ is valid for the amount stated in words. *Covercraft Ltd, MAN/88/791 (VTD 3558)*.

18.29   A trader had a quarterly VAT liability of £5,545.98. He submitted a cheque made out for this amount in figures, but for only £5,545.00 in words. The cheque was dishonoured by his bank and the Commissioners imposed a default surcharge of £831.89, calculated at the appropriate rate of 15%. The trader appealed, contending that he had a reasonable excuse. The tribunal rejected this contention, holding that 'mere carelessness' could not constitute a reasonable excuse. However, the tribunal held that, under the *Bills of Exchange Act 1882, ss 9(2), 72*, where there is a discrepancy between the words and figures on a cheque, the amount in words is the amount payable. Consequently the cheque in question was a valid payment of £5,545.00, and should have been honoured by the bank accordingly. It followed that the trader was in default only to the extent of 98 pence. The tribunal could not ignore this on *de minimis* grounds, but the effect of this was that the surcharge should be reduced to the statutory minimum of £30. *TG Mather (t/a Economy Appliances), LON/88/581Y (VTD 3829)*.

18.30   **Submission of cheque with amount in words missing.** A partnership submitted a cheque on which the amount in figures was correctly stated, but the amount in words was missing. The Commissioners returned the cheque to the partnership for amendment without presenting it, and imposed a default surcharge. The tribunal allowed the partnership's appeal, holding that the cheque was a valid cheque within the *Bills of Exchange Act 1882, s 3(1)*, notwithstanding that the amount of the cheque was only stated in figures and not in words. *Heeney v Addy, [1910] 2 IR 688*, applied. *Exchange Car Hire, [1992] VATTR 430 (VTD 9343)*.

18.31   **Surcharge imposed but no tax due.** A company submitted a late return, showing tax payable to the Commissioners, and a default surcharge was imposed. Subsequently the company's accountant discovered that he had made a mistake in the return and that a repayment was due. The Commissioners accepted that the original return was incorrect but refused to discharge the surcharge. The tribunal allowed the company's appeal, holding that 'it cannot be appropriate to levy a surcharge on a figure which does not in truth amount to a figure for outstanding tax'. *Nationwide Hygiene Supplies Ltd, EDN/90/128 (VTD 5389).*

18.32   A trader persistently submitted returns late. The Commissioners issued estimated assessments and imposed surcharges. Subsequently the trader submitted returns showing that his liability was less than the amounts assessed, and that, viewed as a whole, his account with the Commissioners was in credit. The tribunal allowed his appeal against the surcharges, holding that there was no 'outstanding VAT' for the purposes of *VATA 1994, s 59(4)(b)*. *M Bruce, MAN/99/253 (VTD 16660).*

18.33   **Change of company name.**   A company changed its name in 1988. Prior to its change of name, it had submitted a return after the due date. Its next two returns were also submitted late, and a default surcharge was imposed. The company appealed, contending that, because of its change of name, the first default should not be taken into account. The tribunal rejected this contention and dismissed the appeal. The company continued to be the same entity despite its change of name. *Speciality Restaurants plc, LON/92/12Y (VTD 10310).*

18.34   **Surcharge imposed for return period ending on last day of surcharge period.**   A company's return for the period ending 30 April 1992 was submitted late and the Commissioners issued a surcharge liability notice, with the surcharge period extending until 30 April 1993. Its return for the period ending on that date was submitted late and a surcharge was accordingly imposed. The company appealed, contending that the surcharge was invalid because the two defaults were more than 52 weeks apart. The tribunal rejected this contention and dismissed the appeal, holding that the accounting period ending 30 April 1993 ended within the surcharge period so that the surcharge had been correctly imposed. *Mountfield Software Ltd, LON/94/865P (VTD 12816).*

18.35   See also *Sageworth Ltd*, 18.455 below, and *Shute*, 18.453 below.

18.36   **VAT Central Unit computer incorrectly programmed—surcharge imposed at excessive rate.**   A surcharge was reduced in a case where the tribunal found that the Commissioners had levied it at 15% rather than 10%, as a result of an error in programming the computer at the VAT Central Unit at Southend. *Darci Shoes Ltd, LON/94/2732 (VTD 13228). (Note.* See VAT Information Sheet 7/95, issued on 10 April 1995.)

18.37   A similar decision was reached in *P Sullivan, [1995] VATDR 85 (VTD 13245).*

18.38   **VATA 1994, s 59(5)—effect of invalidity of previous surcharge assessment.**   The Commissioners issued a surcharge assessment for October 1994 to a company which made monthly returns and had paid its liability after the due date. The surcharge was computed at the rate of 2%, but the assessment wrongly stated that it covered the three-month period from 1 August 1994 to 31 October 1994. The company also paid its November liability after the due date, and the Commissioners issued a surcharge assessment imposing a 5% surcharge. The company appealed against the surcharges, contending that it had a reasonable excuse. In October 1995 the Commissioners, having discovered that the October 1994 assessment was expressed to be for a three-month period instead of a one-month period, wrote to the company withdrawing it and purporting to reduce the November 1995 assessment from 5% to 2%. The tribunal allowed the company's appeal against the November 1994 assessment, holding that, because the October 1994 assessment was accepted by the Commissioners as invalid, 'it followed that the Commissioners could not "determine" the November 1994 surcharge assessment as

5% and that assessment was accordingly void'. The assessment 'could not be reduced either in pursuance of *VATA 1994, s 76(9)* or ... in exercise of the Commissioners' inherent power to reduce assessments'. The tribunal held that 'each liability occasioned by each default is separate' and that 'only properly notified defaults for a prescribed accounting period count (and they drop out of account if a reasonable excuse defence is sustained)'. Furthermore, 'while the Commissioners and the tribunal have power to reduce an assessment, this power exists where the assessment is excessive because, for example, it is based on an overstatement of the outstanding VAT; but the power does not exist where the assessment is ineffective because the liability is of the wrong type, for example it assesses a third default liability where it ought to have assessed a second default liability'. The power to reduce an assessment could not 'be exercised where the assessment is ineffective and so void *ab initio*'. (The tribunal observed that 'this is different from the position that obtains where a taxable person establishes the defence of reasonable excuse under *VATA 1994, s 59(7)*; the *subsection* itself appears to contemplate that the specified percentages for subsequent defaults will be adjusted accordingly'.) *Dow Chemical Company Ltd, [1996] VATDR 52 (VTD 13954)*.

18.39   A company appealed against a default surcharge, contending that the surcharge was invalid because a previous surcharge had been withdrawn. The tribunal rejected this contention, applying *dicta* in *Dow Chemical Company Ltd*, 18.38 above, and holding that 'where a taxable person establishes the defence of reasonable excuse under *VATA 1994, s 59(7)*, the *subsection* itself appears to contemplate that the specified percentages for subsequent defaults will be adjusted accordingly'. *SSR Group Services Ltd, LON/98/1506 (VTD 16033)*. (*Note*. For another issue in this case, see 18.46 below.)

DESPATCH OF RETURN AND PAYMENT TO THE COMMISSIONERS (VATA 1994, s 59(7)(a))

18.40   **Return posted one day before due date.**   In a case where a return was posted on the day prior to the due date, but was not received until the following week, the tribunal dismissed the company's appeal, holding that it was not reasonable to expect the return to be received within the time limit. *R Walia Opticians (London) Ltd, LON/90/670Y (VTD 5085)*. (*Note*. Customs & Excise have subsequently stated in correspondence that they will accept that a return has been posted in time if it was posted at least one working day prior to the due date—see *1991 STI 389*. However, despite this apparent assurance, the tribunals have continued to uphold surcharges in such circumstances in appeals where the Commissioners' representative has not drawn this statement to the attention of the tribunal. See, for example, *Nicholls*, 18.41 below; *Kingdom Amusements*, 18.41 below; *Michelotti*, 18.41 below, and *La Reine (Limoges Porcelain) Ltd*, 18.43 below.)

18.41   Similar decisions were reached in *JF Stockham, LON/89/220Z (VTD 5178); AGH Edgecox, MAN/90/450 (VTD 5334); Sonnat Ltd, MAN/90/327 (VTD 5436); Crimpers Ltd, LON/89/592Z (VTD 5466); Artinville Ltd, LON/90/729X (VTD 5515); Flame Cheater Ltd, LON/90/1420Y (VTD 5685); DT Nicholls, LON/92/616 (VTD 7960); Kingdom Amusements, EDN/92/40 (VTD 8872)* and *SL Michelotti, LON/93/1284 (VTD 11551)*.

18.42   A similar decision was reached in a case where the return was posted two days before the due date (which was a Sunday). *Silverdale Transport Ltd, LON/90/752 (VTD 5192)*. (*Note*. The decision here was not followed, and was implicitly disapproved, in the subsequent case of *Halstead Motor Company*, 18.45 below. The decision here was

18.43 Default Surcharge

made before the Commissioners' published statement reported at *1991 STI 389*, for which see the note following *R Walia (Opticians) Ltd*, 18.40 above.)

18.43   An appeal was dismissed in a case where the due date was Sunday 31 May 1992 and the tribunal found that the return had been posted at Bournemouth Post Office before 7 p.m. on Friday 29 May. The tribunal chairman held that the return had not been 'posted early enough that it was reasonable to expect that it would be received by Customs on or before Sunday 31 May'. *La Reine (Limoges Porcelain) Ltd, LON/92/2842P (VTD 10468)*. (*Note*. The decision here was not followed, and was implicitly disapproved, in the subsequent case of *Halstead Motor Company*, 18.45 below. The decision here fails to refer to the Commissioners' published statement reported at *1991 STI 389*, for which see the note following *R Walia (Opticians) Ltd*, 18.40 above.)

18.44   A similar decision was reached in *JG Brolly & Bros. Ltd, EDN/94/83 (VTD 13762)*. (*Note*. Compare *Halstead Motor Company Ltd*, 18.45 below, which was not referred to in this decision.)

18.45   An appeal was allowed in a case where the tribunal found that a return for the period ending 30 June 1994 was posted in the early afternoon of Friday 29 July. At the hearing, and despite Customs' statement reproduced at *1991 STI 389* (see the note following *R Walia Opticians (London) Ltd*, 18.40 above), the representative of Customs' Solicitor's Office contended that because the due date was Saturday 30 July, the company had not sent it 'at such a time and in such a manner that it was reasonable to expect it to be received by the Commissioners within the appropriate time limit'. The tribunal rejected this contention, declining to follow the decisions in *Silverdale Transport Ltd*, 18.42 above, and *La Reine (Limoges Porcelain) Ltd*, 18.43 above, and observing that the Commissioners were not complying with their previous statement reproduced at *1991 STI 389*. The tribunal held that, by posting the return before the last collection on Friday 29 July, the company had 'despatched the return at such a time and in such a manner that it was reasonable to expect that it would be delivered at Southend on Saturday 30 July and be received by the Commissioners within the appropriate time limit'. *Halstead Motor Company, [1995] VATDR 201 (VTD 13373)*.

18.46   The decision in *Halstead Motor Company*, 18.45 above, was applied in the similar subsequent case of *SSR Group Services Ltd, LON/98/1506 (VTD 16033)*. (*Note*. For another issue in this case, see 18.39 above.)

18.47   A similar decision was reached in a case where the tribunal found that a cheque for the period ending 30 September 1999 had been posted by first class post on Friday 29 October 1999. *A & R Robertson & Black, EDN/00/138 (VTD 16999)*.

18.48   **Return not submitted until due date.** An appeal against a default surcharge was dismissed in a case where a firm of chartered surveyors had not posted their VAT return until the due date. The tribunal held that it was not reasonable to post a return less than three days before the due date. The use of the services of the Post Office was not a derogation from the statutory limits, and posting must be effected in such a way as to satisfy the limits. *Aikman v White*, 55.6 RETURNS, was authority for the proposition that, as the Commissioners had adopted the Post Office as their agent, posting a return exonerates a taxpayer from delay or default by the Post Office. However, there was nothing in that case to support any contention that the conditions as to time limits thereby became irrelevant. *Gould & Co, LON/89/1594X (VTD 4773)*.

18.49   *Gould & Co*, 18.48 above, was applied in a subsequent case where the tribunal distinguished *Aikman v White*, 55.6 RETURNS, and *Hayman v Griffiths*, 55.7

RETURNS, on the grounds that those cases were decided on legislation prior to *FA 1985* (which introduced what is now *VATA 1994, s 59*), and that what is now *s 59* required a return to be received by the due date, rather than to be furnished by the due date. Accordingly a taxpayer was in default unless his return was received by the due date. *R Jones, LON/90/1502X (VTD 5753)*.

18.50   *Gould & Co*, 18.48 above, was also applied in *E Wigful Tools (Sheffield) Ltd, MAN/90/847 (VTD 6243)* and *Paragon Business Products Ltd*, 18.454 below.

18.51   There have been a large number of other cases in which tribunals have dismissed appeals against default surcharges after finding that the relevant return had not been posted until the due date, and holding that this failed to meet the requirements of what is now *VATA 1994, s 59(7)(a)*. In the interests of space, such cases are not reported individually in this book.

18.52   **Date of posting disputed.**   There have been a very large number of cases in which appellants have claimed that the relevant return was posted before the due date, although postmarked and received after the due date. Such decisions turn entirely on the particular facts of the case, and on whether the tribunal accepts or rejects the appellant's evidence on the balance of probabilities. In the interests of space, such decisions are not reported individually in this book.

18.53   **Receipt of return denied by Commissioners.**   An appeal was allowed in a case where a company's managing director gave evidence that he had personally delivered the return in question to the Woking VAT office before the due date. *AP Heather Ltd, LON/89/1134Z (VTD 4376)*.

18.54   A similar decision was reached in a case where a trader gave evidence that he had delivered the return to the Doncaster VAT office on the due date. *J Sheard, MAN/90/783 (VTD 6318)*.

18.55   A similar decision was reached in a case where a company's accountant gave evidence that he had personally delivered the return to the Maidenhead VAT office on the due date. *Harleyford Estate Ltd, LON/91/2487Z (VTD 7741)*.

18.56   **Return tendered to local VAT office by hand on last working day before due date—VAT office refusing to accept return.**   See *Light Wire Ltd*, 18.521 below, and *Hatfield*, 18.522 below.

18.57   **Return delivered by hand—accountant claiming to have posted it before due date.**   A surcharge was imposed on a partnership which had submitted two returns after the due date. The partnership's accountant appealed and stated in evidence that one of the returns had been posted before the due date but had been delayed by a fire at the local sorting office. The Commissioners produced evidence that both returns had been delivered by hand, rather than by post, and also submitted a letter from the Post Office confirming that there had been no fire at the sorting office in question at the relevant time. The tribunal dismissed the appeal and awarded costs to the Commissioners. *Albert Guest House, LON/90/239 (VTD 5524)*.

18.58   **Accountant claiming to have delivered return by hand before due date.**   A company's return for the period ending 31 December 1989 was received by post on 17 January 1990, postmarked 16 January. The company appealed and its accountant gave evidence that he had delivered the return by hand on 22 December. In cross-examination, his description of the size of the building and of the layout of its entrance appeared not to correspond with the actual geography of the VAT office in question. The accountant also stated that there had been a postal strike, whereas the Commissioners produced a letter from the GPO stating that there had been no strike or industrial action at the relevant period. The tribunal found, after hearing the accountant's evidence, that the return had in fact been delivered by post, and that, in view of the inaccuracy of the accountant's description of the VAT office which he claimed to have visited, he had not shown 'on the balance of probabilities' that he had actually visited the VAT office. The tribunal therefore dismissed the company's appeal. *Gundy Harris & Co Ltd, LON/90/638 (VTD 5172)*.

18.59   **Partner claiming to have delivered return by hand on due date.**   A similar decision was reached in a case where a partner gave evidence that he had delivered two returns by hand on the due date, but the Commissioners produced evidence to show that the returns had been received by post and had been postmarked after the due date. The tribunal dismissed the partnership's appeal, finding that the partner had been 'mistaken as to the circumstances in which the two returns were made'. *MF Printers, LON/90/1526Z (VTD 5770)*.

18.60   **Appellant claiming to have delivered return by hand on due date.**   An appeal was dismissed in a case where a trader contended that his return for the period ending 31 July 1990 had been delivered by hand on 31 August, although the records kept at the local VAT office indicated that it had been delivered by hand on 19 September. The tribunal stated that it was 'unable to accept the appellant's allegation that the envelope (had) been lying around the office for 19 days before being opened and dealt with'. *FJ Amsbury, LON/90/1933Y (VTD 5999)*.

18.61   **Director claiming to have delivered return by hand on due date.**   An appeal was dismissed in a case where a company's managing director stated in evidence that he had delivered the company's return to the local VAT office by hand on the due date. The tribunal commented that the director and his secretary 'may have been mistaken in their recollection'. *DW Robey & Sons Ltd, LON/91/1732Z (VTD 6967)*.

18.62   **Receipt of cheque denied by Commissioners.**   An appeal against a default surcharge was allowed in a case where the Commissioners accepted that a return had been received on time but contended that it had not contained the appropriate cheque. The tribunal found, on the balance of probabilities, that the cheque and the return were posted together, but that the cheque had been lost at the VAT Central Unit. *Romill Engineering, LON/88/132 (VTD 3109)*.

18.63   Similar decisions were reached in *SW Haulage Ltd, MAN/89/370 (VTD 4108); AK Price, LON/90/885Y (VTD 5927); J Farley, LON/90/1678 (VTD 6558)* and *Talking Point (Europe) Ltd, LON/91/2725Z (VTD 7698)*.

18.64   **Payment by credit transfer.**   A company submitted its return for the period ending 30 September 1989 before the due date (31 October). However, it paid the tax by credit transfer, and did not initiate the payment until 7 November. The payment was received by the Commissioners on 9 November, and a default surcharge was imposed. The company appealed, contending that the payment had been made within the extra seven days allowed for payments by credit transfer. The tribunal dismissed the appeal, holding that payments by credit transfer had to be received by the Commissioners by the seventh day. An explanatory leaflet sent to the company with the credit transfer warned that at least two working days must be allowed for the bank to clear the transaction, so that the money was in the Commissioners' account by the seventh day. As the company had not initiated the payment until the seventh day, there was no chance of the Commissioners receiving it within the extra seven days allowed. *Matilot Ltd (t/a Hardlife Ladder Co), MAN/89/998 & MAN/90/97 (VTD 4847)*.

18.65   Similar decisions were reached in *Leslie Wise Ltd, LON/94/3452A (VTD 13354); Consolidated Holdings Ltd, MAN/95/107 (VTD 13483); JND Ltd, LON/95/2471P (VTD 13719); FPS (UK) Ltd, MAN/98/537 (VTD 15716); Paragon Business Products Ltd*, 18.454 below; *Slough Motor Co*, 18.500 below, and *Wingate Electrical plc*, 18.501 below.

18.66   A company paid its VAT by credit transfer. For the period ending 30 June 1995, it initiated its payment on Friday 4 August 1995. The Commissioners did not receive the payment until Tuesday 8 August, and imposed a default surcharge. The company appealed, contending that payment had been made within the seven-day extended time limit. The tribunal rejected this contention and dismissed the appeal, declining to follow the decision in *Marshall*, 18.68 below, and applying *Wingate Electrical plc*, 18.501 below. *Whitport plc, LON/95/2782 (VTD 14337)*. (*Note*. The tribunal also held that the circumstances did not constitute a reasonable excuse.)

18.67   *Whitport plc*, 18.66 above, was applied in the similar subsequent cases of *Headlam (Floorcovering Distributor) Ltd (t/a Florco), LON/99/416 (VTD 16478)* and *AL Currie & Brown*, 18.542 below.

18.68   In 1987 a trader received a letter inviting him to adopt the credit transfer scheme. He did not respond to the letter, but in January 1992, having incurred several default surcharges, he decided to take advantage of the scheme. His payment for the period ending 29 February 1992 was received on 6 March. The Commissioners imposed a further surcharge but the tribunal allowed the trader's appeal, holding that in view of the letter which the Commissioners had sent him in 1987, he had been entitled to pay his VAT liability by credit transfer. *GL Marshall, LON/92/1344 (VTD 9321)*. (*Note*. The decision here was not followed, and was implicitly disapproved, in the subsequent case of *Whitport plc*, 18.66 above.)

18.69   **Payment by credit transfer—application of extended time limit to Scotland.**   See *Rowan Timber Supplies (Scotland) Ltd*, 18.497 below.

WHETHER A 'REASONABLE EXCUSE' (VATA 1994, s 59(7)(b))

Computer problems

Cases where the appellant was successful

18.70   **Installation of computer.**   A company which had installed a new computer found that it would be unable to complete its first return after the installation by the due date. It telephoned its local VAT office to ask whether some self-billing invoices could be entered on the following return instead. Following its conversation with the VAT office, the company took the view that it was more important for the return to be accurate than for it to be punctual. It therefore delayed the submission of the return, and a default surcharge was imposed. The tribunal allowed the company's appeal, holding that the VAT office should have advised the company that an estimated return would be acceptable, and that the circumstances therefore constituted a reasonable excuse. *Evans Transport, LON/87/637 (VTD 2974)*.

18.71   Delay resulting from the installation of a computer was held to constitute a reasonable excuse in *Exchange Club Ltd, MAN/88/144 (VTD 3031); Alexander Designs Ltd, LON/88/816 (VTD 3325); Bryant Glass Ltd, MAN/88/864 (VTD 3431); H Webb, MAN/89/235 (VTD 3788); Accountancy Executive Appointments, EDN/91/8 (VTD 5891); Starwest Investment Holdings Ltd, LON/91/541X (VTD 6547); Price Legand Offset International Ltd, LON/90/942Y (VTD 7066); JJ Cumpstey Ltd, LON/92/2542 (VTD 9883); Televideo, MAN/92/910 (VTD*

18.72 Default Surcharge

10052); Alert Security Supplies Ltd, MAN/94/425 (VTD 12677) and Hatton Garden Agency Ltd, LON/94/2525 (VTD 13285).

18.72 **Computer malfunction.** There have been a large number of cases in which tribunals have found that the malfunction of a computer has constituted a reasonable excuse for a late return. In the interests of space, such cases are not listed individually in this book. For a list of such cases decided up to 31 December 1994, see Tolley's VAT Cases 1995.

18.73 In a case where a computer had broken down, with loss of data, following the insertion of an unauthorised program by a former employee, the tribunal held that this constituted a reasonable excuse. *Television Information Network Ltd, LON/88/720 (VTD 3403).*

18.74 A company's computer was damaged by one of its staff in May 1987. The company found it difficult to obtain spare parts for the computer, and acquired a replacement in June. The tribunal held that this constituted a reasonable excuse for the late submission of the company's return for the period ending 30 April 1987. (There was, however, held to be no reasonable excuse for subsequent defaults.) *RK Transport Ltd, LON/91/858Y (VTD 6358).*

18.75 Damage to a computer was also held to be a reasonable excuse in *GM Supplies, LON/94/854 (VTD 12983).*

18.76 **Theft of computer.** The computer used by a firm of solicitors was stolen in October 1988. A replacement was not installed until February 1989, and the correct disk converter was not supplied until May 1989. After the disk converter had been installed, it was discovered that the back-up disks containing the firm's records for July 1988 to October 1988 had been corrupted, so that the relevant data had to be re-entered. The firm did not complete this until January 1990. In the meantime, its returns for the periods ending from 31 October 1988 to 31 October 1989 were submitted late, and default surcharges were imposed. The tribunal allowed the firm's appeal in part, holding that the disruption arising from the theft constituted a reasonable excuse for the late submission of the returns for the periods ending October 1988 and January 1989, but not for the period ending April 1989. (The tribunal also held that the firm's discovery in May 1989 that it would need to re-enter some of its old data constituted a reasonable excuse for the late submission of its returns for the periods ending July and October 1989.) *Stocken & Lambert, LON/92/2818 (VTD 10527). (Note.* For another issue in this case, see 18.310 below.)

18.77 The theft of a company's computer, together with the disks containing copies of the information needed to compile its VAT returns, was also held to constitute a reasonable excuse in *Licensed Establishments Management Services Ltd, LON/93/1908 (VTD 11777).*

Cases where the appellant was unsuccessful

18.78 **Installation of computer.** Pressure of work arising from the installation of a computer was held not to constitute a reasonable excuse in *J Martorana (t/a Mr Unique Tyre & Exhaust Centre), LON/87/591 (VTD 2557); McGeoghan Plant Hire & Excavations Ltd, LON/88/221 (VTD 3246); Gemini Fashion Accessories Ltd, MAN/88/294 (VTD 3262); Bloxwich Engineering Ltd, MAN/88/673 (VTD 3396); Freeman Box & Co, LON/88/918 (VTD 3524); Dresswell (Newtownards) Ltd, BEL/88/15 (VTD 3568); Lledo (London) Ltd, LON/89/28X (VTD 3590); Delton Electric Ltd, MAN/89/196 (VTD 3904); Delton Central Services Ltd, MAN/89/197 (VTD 3904); Charles Bell (BD) Ltd, MAN/90/172 (VTD 4887); Word (UK) Ltd,*

LON/90/619 (VTD 5224); WE Hannan & Associates Ltd, MAN/90/441 (VTD 5343); AE Technical Services, EDN/91/42 (VTD 5931); Span Computer Contracts Ltd, LON/91/327Z (VTD 6323, 6461); Finishfavour Ltd, LON/91/1652X (VTD 7053); Taylor & Taylor, LON/91/2176Y (VTD 7187); James Watts Transport Southwark Ltd, LON/93/770P (VTD 11067); Magstack Ltd (t/a Brixton Academy), LON/93/2574P (VTD 12009); J & G Associates, EDN/95/27 (VTD 13471) and Internet for Business Ltd, EDN/99/103 (VTD 16266).

18.79   The treasurer of a social club transferred its accounts onto a computer without maintaining a manual back-up system. Six months later he resigned from the treasurership and passed his successor a number of computer disks, which his successor had no means of processing. Consequently the club was unable to submit its next return in time and incurred a default surcharge. The tribunal found that the surcharge clearly arose from the actions of the former treasurer, but held that, as the club was responsible for its treasurer's actions, this did not constitute a reasonable excuse. *Rotherham Borough Council Employees Sports & Social Club, MAN/88/797 (VTD 3543).*

18.80   **Failure to keep back-up data.**   A firm appealed against a default surcharge, contending that it had a reasonable excuse because its computer had broken down. The tribunal dismissed the appeal, holding that the firm had been at fault in not keeping a back-up copy of the data fed into the computer. *JN Electrical Units, LON/88/583 (VTD 3346).*

18.81   Similar decisions were reached *in Peachman Building Services (Croydon) Ltd, LON/90/260 (VTD 5041)* and *Stella Products Ltd, MAN/90/234 (VTD 5494).*

18.82   **Computer malfunction.**   The malfunction of a computer was held not to be a reasonable excuse in *Durham City Car Co Ltd, MAN/88/723 (VTD 3604); Survey & Marketing Services, MAN/89/724 (VTD 4455); City Rentals Ltd, LON/90/81 (VTD 4806); AF Tann Ltd, LON/90/435Y (VTD 5012); Active Handling (UK) Ltd, LON/90/377 (VTD 5273); Ward Meadows (Plant) Ltd, MAN/90/1058 (VTD 5752); 100 Per Cent, LON/91/690Z (VTD 6238); JF Turkington (Engineers) Ltd, MAN/91/380 (VTD 6484); Halcove Ltd, EDN/91/227 (VTD 6935); SL Bindman, MAN/91/1248 (VTD 7340); Armstrongs Transport (Wigan) Ltd, MAN/91/1253 (VTD 7464); High Range Developments Ltd, LON/92/355Z (VTD 8989); Brakel Ltd, MAN/91/1280 (VTD 9685); A Reid, EDN/92/353 (VTD 10406); Angus Modelmakers Ltd, EDN/92/316 (VTD 10655); DC Edwick, MAN/93/187 (VTD 10962); GS & DS Bhalla (t/a Pinehurst Hotel), LON/93/1005 (VTD 11284); F & A Ponting Ltd, MAN/94/529 (VTD 12595); C & G Cheshire (t/a Jeeves of Hampshire), LON/98/174 (VTD 15624); Shan Trading Ltd, LON/98/710 (VTD 15726); Ciro Citterio Menswear plc, MAN/99/95 (VTD 16336) and R Gunn & MJ Davies, LON/99/858 (VTD 16927).*

18.83   Two companies appealed against default surcharges, contending that they had a reasonable excuse for the late submission of returns in that they had installed computer programs which had failed to work. The firm which had supplied the computer programs had subsequently gone into liquidation. The tribunal dismissed the companies' appeals, holding that they had placed reliance on the firm of computer programmers to produce an accounting system, and that what is now *VATA 1994, s 71(1)(b)* precluded this from being a reasonable excuse. *Heating & Management Services Ltd, LON/89/1191Z; Utilicom Ltd, LON/89/1206Z (VTD 4200).*

18.84   Similar decisions were reached in *The Music Shop (Romford) Ltd, LON/89/980Z (VTD 4696)* and *Sollac SA, LON/95/1842P (VTD 13688).*

18.85   Default Surcharge

18.85   **Change in VAT rate—difficulty in reprogramming computer.**   A trader appealed against a default surcharge, contending that he had a reasonable excuse because he had experienced difficulty in reprogramming his computer following the increase in the VAT rate from 15% to 17.5%. The tribunal dismissed his appeal, observing that he should have calculated his VAT manually, and holding that the circumstances did not constitute a reasonable excuse. *G Robinson (t/a Swallow Motor Co), LON/93/398P (VTD 11120).*

Illness or bereavement

Cases where the appellant was successful

18.86   **Illness or injury of appellant.**   There have been a large number of cases in which tribunals have held that illness or injury suffered by an appellant has constituted a reasonable excuse for a late return. Such cases turn entirely on the particular facts and, in the interests of space, are not summarised individually in this book. For a list of such cases decided up to 31 December 1995, see Tolley's VAT Cases 1996.

18.87   **Illness of trader's wife.**   Illness suffered by a trader's wife was held to constitute a reasonable excuse for a late return in *MHD Mortimer, LON/89/435Y (VTD 4235); J Hunter, EDN/89/191 (VTD 4566); AP Taylor, LON/91/1505X (VTD 7893); DJ Harmer, LON/92/1728P (VTD 9581); MRK Hill (t/a Marcus Builders), LON/94/2031P (VTD 13235)* and *MA Nimmock, LON/95/2821P (VTD 13857).*

18.88   **Death of trader's wife.**   In a case where a trader's wife died from cancer on 30 November 1987, the tribunal held that this constituted a reasonable excuse for the late submission of returns for the periods ending 31 October 1987 and 31 January 1988. *MD Stephens, LON/88/746Z (VTD 3963).*

18.89   **Illness of trader's husband.**   A married woman submitted two returns late and default surcharges were imposed. She appealed, contending that she had a reasonable excuse because her husband, who assisted her in the business, had suffered from prolonged illness and had been unable to work properly. The tribunal allowed her appeal. *Mrs MW Stewart (t/a Sodisk), LON/90/1832X (VTD 6013).*

18.90   **Death of trader's mother.**   A trader's mother became very ill with cancer in October 1987, and died in March 1988. The tribunal held that this constituted a reasonable excuse for the late submission of the return for the period ending 31 January 1988. *IM Barnard, LON/89/252Y (VTD 3741).*

18.91   Similar decisions were reached in *ER Hill, LON/90/234 (VTD 5001)* and *CF Dale Ltd, LON/91/2198X (VTD 7385).*

18.92   **Death of trader's father.**   The father of a sole trader was diagnosed as having cancer in April 1987. He was admitted to hospital in May and died in August. The tribunal held that this constituted a reasonable excuse for the late submission of the return for the period ending 31 May. (There was held to be no reasonable excuse for subsequent defaults.) *AP Watts, LON/89/1204X (VTD 4535).*

18.93   Similar decisions were reached in *S Chelms (t/a Central Consultancy & Training Services), LON/93/16P (VTD 10489)* and *R Badman (t/a Gardener & Badman), LON/98/342 (VTD 15938).*

18.94   **Illness or injury of partner.**   There have been a large number of cases in which tribunals have held that illness or injury suffered by one of the members of a small partnership has constituted a reasonable excuse for a late return. Such cases turn entirely on the particular facts and, in the interests of space, are not summarised individually in this book. For a list of such cases decided up to 31 December 1995, see Tolley's VAT Cases 1996.

18.95   **Illness of partner's mother.**   A husband and wife traded in partnership. The wife's mother, who lived in the Netherlands, fell ill with cancer and the wife travelled to the Netherlands to be with her. The tribunal held that this constituted a reasonable excuse for the late submission of two VAT returns. *A & A Everett, LON/88/942Y (VTD 3669).*

18.96   **Death of partner's mother.**   A husband and wife operated a hotel in partnership. The husband had to fly to Guyana at short notice when his mother, who was resident there, became ill and died. The tribunal held that this constituted a reasonable excuse for a late return. *Warren Park Hotel, LON/88/473Y (VTD 3508).*

18.97   **Illness or injury of director.**   There have been a large number of cases in which tribunals have held that illness or injury suffered by a company director has constituted a reasonable excuse for a late return. Such cases turn entirely on the particular facts and, in the interests of space, are not summarised individually in this book. For a list of such cases decided up to 31 December 1995, see Tolley's VAT Cases 1996.

18.98   **Illness of director's wife.**   A company appealed against three default surcharges, contending that it had a reasonable excuse because the wife of its principal director had been seriously ill throughout the period in question (and had subsequently died). The tribunal allowed the appeal, holding that the circumstances constituted a reasonable excuse. *Potterburn Ltd, EDN/98/195 (VTD 15912).*

18.99   **Emotional strain following trial of murderer of director's father.**   The father of a company's principal director was murdered in September 1985. A man was convicted of the murder in July 1986, but appealed to the Court of Appeal, which upheld the conviction in July 1987. The tribunal held that, in view of the emotional strain on the director, the circumstances constituted a reasonable excuse for the late submission of the company's return for the period ending 31 July 1987. (There was, however, held to be no reasonable excuse for a subsequent default.) *Calpeel Ltd, LON/88/1339Y (VTD 4194).*

18.100   **Illness of director's father.**   A company appealed against a default surcharge, contending that it had a reasonable excuse because a director who was required to sign the relevant cheque had been called away at short notice to visit his father who was ill. The tribunal allowed the appeal, holding that the circumstances constituted a reasonable excuse. (There was, however, held to be no reasonable excuse for a subsequent default.) *Gillaroo Ltd, LON/92/777 (VTD 8889).*

18.101   **Death of director's brother.**   A small family company appealed against a default surcharge, contending that it had a reasonable excuse for a late return because all its administration was carried out by one of its directors, and her brother had died suddenly shortly before the return was due. The tribunal accepted this contention and allowed the appeal. *J & T Blacksmith Ltd, EDN/00/59 (VTD 16710).*

18.102   **Illness of secretary.**   The illness of an appellant's secretary was held to constitute a reasonable excuse for a first default in *M Bowen, [1987] VATTR 255 (VTD 2535).* (*Note.* There was, however, held to be no reasonable excuse for three subsequent defaults.)

18.103   Illness of a secretary was also held to be a reasonable excuse in *J Carrick, LON/91/2442Y (VTD 7664); Lynton Group Ltd, LON/93/1008P (VTD 11049)* and *First de Parys (Dry Cleaners) Ltd, LON/93/2151P (VTD 12178).*

18.104 Default Surcharge

18.104 Illness or injury of bookkeeper. There have been a large number of cases in which tribunals have held that illness suffered by a bookkeeper has constituted a reasonable excuse for a late return. Such cases turn entirely on the particular facts and, in the interests of space, are not summarised individually in this book. For a list of such cases decided up to 31 December 1994, see Tolley's VAT Cases 1995.

18.105 Injury to bookkeeper's husband. On 27 December 1990 a company's bookkeeper received a telephone call advising her that her husband had been injured in a road accident in Scotland. The bookkeeper travelled to Scotland to be with her husband, and did not return to work until January 1991. In her absence, the company's return for the period ending 30 November was not submitted until 4 January 1991 and a default surcharge was imposed. The tribunal allowed the company's appeal, holding that the circumstances constituted a reasonable excuse. *Graphic Eye Ltd, LON/91/543X (VTD 6249)*. (*Note.* The location of the company's office is not stated in the decision, but the case was heard in London, so presumably the company's office was somewhere in Southern England. The case appears to have been decided on the basis that the husband's accident occurred a long way away from the company's office.)

18.106 Illness of bookkeeper's father. The father of a small company's bookkeeper suffered a heart attack on 24 February 1989. The bookkeeper left the office to visit him and to help look after her mother. She did not return to work until 6 March. The tribunal held that this constituted a reasonable excuse for the late submission of the return for the period ending 31 January 1989. *L & B Scaffolding Ltd, LON/89/677 & 678Z (VTD 4543)*.

18.107 Illness of bookkeeper's mother. A company appealed against a default surcharge for the period ending 31 March 1994, contending that it had a reasonable excuse because its bookkeeper, who had been entrusted with the posting of the relevant return, had been told on 28 April that her mother had been taken ill, and had travelled from Hampshire to London to visit her. The tribunal held that the circumstances constituted a reasonable excuse. *L & B Scaffolding Ltd*, 18.106 above, applied. *Southern Ski Enterprises Ltd, LON/95/2574 (VTD 13797)*.

18.108 Illness of computer operator. In a case where the only employee who could operate the computer used by two associated companies fell seriously ill, thus delaying the submission of six returns, the tribunal held that this constituted a reasonable excuse. *Servewell Site Services Ltd, LON/88/759; Plantasia Ltd, LON/88/760 (VTD 3291)*.

18.109 A similar decision was reached in *Kirkton Investment Ltd, EDN/97/36 (VTD 15096)*.

18.110 Illness of cashier. In a case where a trader's cashier was off work through illness for three weeks, the tribunal held that the circumstances constituted a reasonable excuse for a late return. *TW George, LON/89/656Y (VTD 3974)*.

18.111 The illness of a company's cashier was held to constitute a reasonable excuse for late payment in *Elcomatic Ltd, EDN/96/96 (VTD 14456)*.

18.112 Illness of wages clerk. The illness of the wages clerk employed by three associated companies was held to constitute a reasonable excuse in *All Saints Garage Ltd, MAN/90/843; All Saints Commercial Ltd, MAN/90/941; Warren Garage Ltd, MAN/90/942 (VTD 5798)*.

18.113 Illness of shop manager. A company owned a newsagency. During July 1990 its shop manager, who was responsible for maintaining its accounting records, suffered severe toothache and had two teeth extracted. He was unable to keep the company's records up to date, and the VAT return for the period ending 30 June 1990 was not submitted until 10 August. The Commissioners imposed a default surcharge but the tribunal allowed the company's appeal, holding that the circumstances constituted a reasonable excuse. *Chestergage Ltd, MAN/91/134 (VTD 6179)*.

18.114   **Illness of office manager.**   A company appealed against a default surcharge, contending that it had a reasonable excuse because its office manager, who had been responsible for its returns for 18 years, had unexpectedly been absent from work at the relevant time, suffering from menopausal depression. The tribunal allowed the appeal, holding that the circumstances constituted a reasonable excuse. *XL Refrigerators Ltd, MAN/91/1485 (VTD 9763)*.

18.115   Illness of a company's office manager was also held to constitute a reasonable excuse in *Samzou Ltd, MAN/92/1443 & MAN/93/351 (VTD 11483)* and *Voland Asphalt Co Ltd, LON/95/2649 (VTD 14553)*.

18.116   **Illness of employee.**   In a case where the only full-time employee of a fish and chip shop suffered from severe influenza in late March 1991, and was off work for two weeks, the tribunal held that the consequent disruption constituted a reasonable excuse for the late submission of the return for the period ending 28 February 1991. *R Wright (t/a Gotterson's Fish Bar), LON/91/1082X (VTD 6732)*.

18.117   Illness suffered by an employee was also held to constitute a reasonable excuse in *Alan Franks Group, MAN/94/1352 (VTD 13731); Flame Cheater International Ltd, LON/96/459 (VTD 14288); E Collins, LON/96/1759 (VTD 14888)* and *Calscot Stocktaking, EDN/98/56 (VTD 15573)*.

18.118   **Illness or injury of accountant.**   There have been a number of cases in which tribunals have held that illness or injury suffered by an accountant has constituted a reasonable excuse for a late return. Such cases turn entirely on the particular facts and, in the interests of space, are not summarised individually in this book. For a list of such cases decided up to 31 December 1994, see Tolley's VAT Cases 1995.

Cases where the appellant was unsuccessful

18.119   **Illness.**   Illness suffered by the appellant was held not to constitute a reasonable excuse in *MN Sargeson, MAN/89/686 (VTD 4480); P Turner (t/a Turner Hire & Sales), MAN/89/933 (VTD 4610); JJ Murphy, LON/90/1066Y (VTD 5475); AB Bremner, EDN/91/45 (VTD 6112); MSI Shomdul, LON/91/787X (VTD 6348); MT Khan, MAN/91/663 (VTD 6860); M Loucaides, LON/91/2553X (VTD 7707); R Bailey, MAN/92/748 (VTD 9677); G Mistry, LON/93/1931P (VTD 11624); D Slater, MAN/93/1424 (VTD 12020); D Robinson, EDN/94/60 (VTD 12667)* and *G Asker, LON/00/362 (VTD 16753)*.

18.120   **Depression.**   A sole trader appealed against a default surcharge, contending that he had a reasonable excuse in that he had been suffering from depression since his relationship with a woman had ended. The tribunal dismissed his appeal, observing that he had been able to work despite his depression and 'he should have engaged someone to take on the task of keeping his records'. *GG Wright, LON/90/1380X (VTD 5691)*.

18.121   A similar decision was reached in *M Loucaides, LON/92/2553X (VTD 9307)*.

18.122   **Single parent suffering from stress.**   A divorced electrician appealed against six default surcharges, contending that he had a reasonable excuse because he had been suffering from stress, and was having to bring up two teenage children single-handed. The tribunal dismissed his appeals, holding that the circumstances did not constitute a reasonable excuse. *BC Poland (t/a Cameron Electrical Contractors), LON/92/2154P (VTD 10536).*

18.123   **Illness of partner.**   In a case where one member of a partnership had suffered a prolonged illness, the tribunal held that this did not constitute a reasonable excuse for five separate defaults. *L & N Tiles, LON/90/442Z (VTD 5120).*

18.124   Illness suffered by a partner was also held not to be a reasonable excuse in *Mr & Mrs G Eland, MAN/90/862 (VTD 5716); Parkers Motorist Discount, MAN/91/1889 (VTD 9545); La Cucaracha, LON/92/2827P (VTD 9988); FC Foreman & Partners, LON/93/2387P (VTD 11894); The Unique Film Company, LON/94/126P (VTD 12214)* and *Ballygrant Inn, EDN/98/107 (VTD 15683).*

18.125   A partnership appealed against a default surcharge, contending that it had a reasonable excuse because one of the partners had suffered from severe depression after his wife had left him, and had had to see a psychiatrist. The tribunal dismissed the appeal, holding that this was not a reasonable excuse. *NE & RWH Murden, MAN/92/228 (VTD 9192).* (*Note.* For another issue in this case, see 18.251 below.)

18.126   **Injury to partner.**   A partnership contended that it had a reasonable excuse for several late returns extending over more than two years, as one of the partners had suffered serious head injuries in a road accident and was unable to work regularly. The tribunal dismissed the appeals, observing that one of the other partners should have arranged for the completion of the returns. *Nader & Associated Manufacturing Co, MAN/90/87 (VTD 4746).*

18.127   In a case where a husband and wife ran a restaurant, the tribunal held that chronic back pain suffered by the husband, which at times rendered him unable to work, did not constitute a reasonable excuse. *Il Pozzo Restaurant, LON/90/279Z (VTD 5195).*

18.128   A similar decision was reached in *Hillfoots Drystone Dyking, EDN/92/148 (VTD 8966).*

18.129   **Illness of partner's wife.**   Illness suffered by the wife of a partner was held not to constitute a reasonable excuse in *Haydn Welch Jewellers, LON/96/640 (VTD 14428).*

18.130   **Illness of director.**   There have been a large number of cases in which tribunals have held that illness suffered by a director has not constituted a reasonable excuse for a late return. Such cases turn entirely on the particular facts and, in the interests of space, are not summarised individually in this book. For a list of such cases decided up to 31 December 1995, see Tolley's VAT Cases 1996.

18.131   **Illness of secretary.**   In a case where a company's secretary had been admitted to hospital for surgery, the tribunal dismissed the company's appeal against a default surcharge, observing that the directors should have made alternative arrangements for submitting the relevant return. *Central Roadways Ltd, MAN/88/827 (VTD 3576).*

18.132   Illness suffered by a secretary was also held not to constitute a reasonable excuse in *Dr TSR Hardy, LON/90/809Z (VTD 5521)* and *Hiross Ltd, LON/93/229P (VTD 10630).*

18.133   **Illness of club treasurer.**   The tribunal held that the prolonged illness of a club treasurer, who was suffering from a tumour, did not constitute a reasonable excuse for seven successive defaults, as alternative arrangements should have been made. *Middlesbrough & District Motor Club Ltd, MAN/90/71 (VTD 4728).*

18.134   A similar decision was reached in *Warriors Social Club, EDN/93/78 (VTD 11146)*.

18.135   **Illness of bookkeeper.**   There have been a large number of cases in which tribunals have held that illness suffered by a bookkeeper has not constituted a reasonable excuse for a late return. Such cases turn entirely on the particular facts and, in the interests of space, are not summarised individually in this book. For a list of such cases decided up to 31 December 1994, see Tolley's VAT Cases 1995.

18.136   **Illness of accountant.**   A company appealed against a default surcharge, contending that it had a reasonable excuse because its accountant had only recently returned to work after four months' absence following a heart operation, and could only work for sixteen hours a week. The tribunal dismissed the appeal, observing that the company should have made alternative arrangements for completion of the returns. *York Avenue Garage, MAN/88/310 (VTD 3252)*.

18.137   Similar decisions were reached in *Smart County Personnel Ltd, LON/88/704 (VTD 3751); Novelminster Ltd, LON/91/2301Z & LON/91/2489Z (VTD 10314); Veda Products Ltd, LON/95/2402P (VTD 13685); Mrs J McGready (t/a Abbey Flowers), EDN/95/365 (VTD 13993)* and *Satchwell Grant Ltd, LON/96/970 (VTD 14577)*.

18.138   The tribunal held that the prolonged illness of an accountant was not a reasonable excuse for the late submission of five successive late returns, as the trader should have engaged another accountant. *C Reid, MAN/89/552 (VTD 4103)*.

18.139   In a case where a company's accountant had a history of angina and subsequently suffered two heart attacks, the tribunal held that this did not constitute a reasonable excuse for five successive defaults, as the company directors had 'let the situation continue when it was unlikely to improve'. *Lees Heginbotham & Sons Ltd, MAN/89/754 (VTD 4533)*.

18.140   **Death of trader's mother.**   A trader appealed against a default surcharge for the period ending 31 December 1988, contending that he had a reasonable excuse because he had been upset by the death of his mother in August 1988. The tribunal dismissed his appeal, finding that his turnover in the relevant quarter had not been adversely affected by his bereavement, and that he had failed to give sufficient priority to fulfilling his basic statutory obligations. *BA Smyth, LON/90/439Y (VTD 5039)*.

18.141   **Death of son-in-law.**   A trader appealed against a default surcharge, contending that he had a reasonable excuse because his son-in-law had died four months before the due date of the return in question, and he had therefore needed to spend more time with his daughter. The tribunal dismissed his appeal, holding that the circumstances did not constitute a reasonable excuse. *RL Hardwick, MAN/91/7 (VTD 5961)*.

Pregnancy and childbirth

Cases where the appellant was successful

18.142   **Secretary suffering miscarriage.**   In a case where a company's secretary had suffered a miscarriage, the tribunal held that this constituted a reasonable excuse for a late return. *Perryman Motor Factors (Greenford) Ltd, LON/87/841 (VTD 2793)*. (*Notes*. (1) There was held to be no reasonable excuse for subsequent defaults. (2) For a subsequent appeal by the same company, see 18.153 below.)

18.143   **Bookkeeper suffering miscarriage.**   An electrician's bookkeeper became pregnant. She continued to keep his books but developed complications and had to go to hospital on several occasions. She eventually suffered a miscarriage. The tribunal held that the circumstances constituted a reasonable excuse for the late submission of two returns. *N Brooks, LON/89/1269Y (VTD 4784)*.

18.144   **Director's wife developing complications during pregnancy.**   The wife of the principal director of a small company became pregnant early in 1987. She had a history of gynaecological problems. During her pregnancy she developed placenta previa, and had to be admitted to hospital. She remained in hospital until after the birth of the child in October. During her time in hospital, her husband visited her each day. The tribunal held that this constituted a reasonable excuse for the late submission of a VAT return. *Lam Cash & Carry Ltd, LON/88/991 (VTD 3400)*.

18.145   A similar decision was reached in *Interchem (Chemists Wholesale) Ltd, MAN/95/2486 (VTD 13952)*. (*Note*. There was held to be no reasonable excuse for other defaults.)

18.146   **Partner suffering complications in pregnancy.**   A married couple appealed against two default surcharges, contending that they had a reasonable excuse because the wife had suffered difficulties in pregnancy. The tribunal accepted their evidence and allowed the appeal. *RJ & Mrs GD Barker, LON/92/327Z (VTD 7952)*.

18.147   **Partner giving birth.**   A married couple who traded in partnership submitted their return for the period ending 31 May 1991 after the due date, and a default surcharge was imposed. They appealed, contending that they had a reasonable excuse because the wife had given birth to a child in April 1991. The tribunal allowed their appeal, holding that the circumstances constituted a reasonable excuse. *Mr & Mrs FJ Bamford (t/a FJ Hardy Tilers), LON/93/1286 (VTD 11584)*. (*Note*. Compare *Pinnock & Lambden*, 18.158 below, where similar circumstances were held not to constitute a reasonable excuse.)

18.148   **Director giving birth.**   A company submitted its return for the period ending 31 August 1995 after the due date and a default surcharge was imposed. The company appealed, contending that it had a reasonable excuse because one of its two directors had given birth in early September 1995 and it had been unable to transfer money from a deposit account to its current account until both directors could visit its bank. The tribunal accepted the company's evidence and allowed the appeal. *Ashvail Services Ltd, MAN/96/457 (VTD 14440)*.

18.149   **Company secretary on maternity leave—clerical error by employee temporarily carrying out her duties.**   The company secretary of a building company gave birth on 14 November 1990. The company's return for the period ending 31 October 1990 was submitted by another employee, who accidentally postdated the accompanying cheque. The Commissioners imposed a default surcharge but the tribunal allowed the company's appeal. Applying *Reddish Electronics Ltd* and *Dabchicks Sailing Club*, 18.414 below, the accidental postdating of a cheque was not a reasonable excuse. However, the absence on maternity leave of the company secretary, who had arranged for another employee to carry out her duties, did constitute a reasonable excuse. *AJW Stagg (General Builders) Ltd, LON/91/280X (VTD 6283)*. (*Note*. Compare the cases noted at 18.418 to 18.420 below, in which errors by employees or bookkeepers were held not to constitute a reasonable excuse.)

18.150   **Pregnancy of secretary.**   A company appealed against a default surcharge, contending that it had a reasonable excuse because its secretary had been pregnant and had been absent from work with morning sickness, and that the secretary had not told the principal director that she was pregnant, so that he had not realised that it might be necessary to make other arrangements for submitting the return. The tribunal accepted the company's evidence and allowed the appeal, observing that 'it is common for young ladies to keep secret their condition in the early weeks of pregnancy'. *Inter Trading Sports Associates Ltd, MAN/93/1527 (VTD 12344)*.

18.151   An appeal was allowed in a case where a company's secretary had gone into labour prematurely. *Dunkirk Panel Services Ltd, LON/94/1182P (VTD 12834)*.

Cases where the appellant was unsuccessful

18.152   **Pregnancy of bookkeeper.** A firm of estate agents did not submit its return for the period ending 30 June 1988 until 12 August. A default surcharge was imposed and the firm appealed, contending that it had a reasonable excuse because its bookkeeper had been pregnant and had given birth to a son on 17 August. The tribunal dismissed the appeal, observing that 'the appellants must have known for a considerable period of time that their only bookkeeper was going to have a baby'. *Adrian Laflin Estate Agents, LON/89/71 (VTD 3811)*.

18.153   Similar decisions were reached in *Chapman Roofing Co, LON/88/1052 (VTD 4186); Perryman Motor Factors (Greenford) Ltd, LON/90/1290, LON/91/1493 (VTD 7173); Bruce Weir & Co, LON/91/962Z (VTD 7620); Bing Transport & Trading, EDN/92/285 (VTD 9688)* and *Bedworth Car Centre Ltd, MAN/91/952 (VTD 10706)*.

18.154   A trader appealed against a default surcharge, contending that he had a reasonable excuse because his bookkeeper had been four months pregnant, and had been off work suffering from morning sickness. The tribunal dismissed the appeal, observing that the trader should have realised that the bookkeeper's pregnancy might impair her ability to work, and should have made alternative arrangements for submitting the return. *M Campbell, MAN/91/424 (VTD 6269)*.

18.155   **Wife giving birth.** A trader appealed against a default surcharge, contending that he had a reasonable excuse for the late submission of a return because his wife had given birth to a daughter less than four weeks before the return was due. The tribunal dismissed his appeal, observing that the daughter's birth 'was an event which must have been anticipated for a considerable period'. *PE Marks, LON/88/106Z (VTD 4515)*.

18.156   A similar decision was reached in *JK Birkinshaw (t/a JB Plant), MAN/93/94 (VTD 10648)*.

18.157   **Pregnancy of wife.** A trader appealed against a default surcharge, contending that he had a reasonable excuse because his wife had been heavily pregnant at the relevant time and had been 'having problems with bleeding'. The tribunal dismissed the appeal, holding that this did not constitute a reasonable excuse. *JT Lindsay (t/a Galloway Design & Inspection Services), EDN/92/32 (VTD 9151)*.

18.158   **Partner giving birth.** A two-person partnership submitted their returns for the periods ending 31 October 1991 and 31 January 1992 after the due date, and a default surcharges were imposed. The partners appealed, contending that they had a reasonable excuse because one of the partners had been pregnant and had given birth on 7 February 1992. The tribunal dismissed the appeal, holding that this was not a reasonable excuse for submitting the return late. *KS Pinnock & KJ Lambden (t/a TNT Printed Leisurewear), LON/93/45P (VTD 11263)*.

18.159   **Cashier on maternity leave.** A firm of solicitors appealed against a default surcharge, contending that it had a reasonable excuse because its cashier had been on maternity leave. The tribunal dismissed the appeal, holding that this was not a reasonable excuse. *Davidsons, LON/93/2852 (VTD 12120)*.

18.160   Default Surcharge

Loss or unavailability of key personnel

Cases where the appellant was successful

18.160 **Partner abroad on business.**   A partnership had arranged a meeting with a VAT officer, because the senior partner was not sure how to account for VAT on car fuel and did not have a copy of *Notice No 700* dealing with the car fuel scale charges. The partner delayed completing the return for the period ending 31 March 1989, intending to complete it after the meeting, which took place on 28 April. He had to travel to France on business on 29 April, and did not submit the return until after his return at the beginning of May. The Commissioners imposed a default surcharge but the tribunal allowed the partnership's appeal, distinguishing *Martorana*, 18.78 above, and observing that, while a trader should arrange his affairs so as to give priority to the performance of statutory duties such as the rendering of VAT returns, this obligation did not 'take priority even at the risk of causing damage to the business'. *Derrick A Knightley & Associates, MAN/89/897 (VTD 4972).*

18.161 **Death of director.**   A company was run by two directors, one of whom controlled the administration and was the sole signatory. The tribunal held that the death of the administrative director constituted a reasonable excuse for the late submission of a return. *Crane & Manpower Ltd, MAN/88/82 (VTD 2807).*

18.162 The sudden death, from a heart attack, of a company's managing director was held to constitute a reasonable excuse in *North West Freighters Ltd, MAN/88/584 (VTD 3341).*

18.163 The death of a company's managing director was also held to be a reasonable excuse in *R Burgin Ltd, LON/90/1779X (VTD 5916)* and *Circare Ltd, LON/91/1770Z (VTD 6903).*

18.164 **Cash-flow problems following death of director.**   See *WBL Ltd*, 18.335 below.

18.165 **Resignation of managing director.**   The wife of a company's managing director kept the company's books. Her husband resigned from the company and left almost immediately, and she ceased to act as the company's bookkeeper with effect from her husband's departure. The tribunal held that this constituted a reasonable excuse for the late submission of a return. *Manchester Scaffolding Ltd, MAN/88/96 (VTD 2855).*

18.166 The resignation of a company's managing director, who had been personally responsible for the company's VAT returns, was also held to constitute a reasonable excuse for a late return in *Jefferby Ltd, MAN/92/1425 (VTD 11057).*

18.167 **Loss of director.**   The sudden resignation of a company's finance director was held to constitute a reasonable excuse in *Gwent Technical Mouldings Ltd, LON/92/302X (VTD 7939).*

18.168 The resignation of a company's director was also held to constitute a reasonable excuse for a late return in *The Wigmore Hall Trust, LON/95/2225P (VTD 13773).* (*Note.* There was held to be no reasonable excuse for a subsequent default.)

18.169 The disappearance of one of a company's two directors was held to constitute a reasonable excuse for two late returns in *Cresthaven Contractors Ltd, LON/94/1308 (VTD 13010).* (*Note.* There was held to be no reasonable excuse for subsequent defaults.)

18.170 **Dismissal of director.**   In a case where a company had dismissed its finance director for incompetence, the tribunal held that this constituted a reasonable excuse for the late submission of a return. *Airline Computer Services Ltd, MAN/89/520 (VTD 4311).*

18.171   **Imprisonment of director.**   A company appealed against a default surcharge, contending that it had a reasonable excuse because one of its two directors had been imprisoned shortly before the start of the accounting period in question, leaving his co-director in sole charge of the company. The tribunal accepted the company's evidence and allowed the appeal. *Kewpost Ltd, LON/96/1300 (VTD 14664)*. (*Note.* Compare *Brough Bros (Kitchens & Bathrooms) Ltd*, 18.210 below, where the imprisonment of a company's controlling director was held not to constitute a reasonable excuse.)

18.172   **Director called away to deal with family problems.**   The principal director of a small company received an urgent telephone call from his sister in October 1988, asking him to stay with her in Scotland to ease relations between her and her husband, which had become strained. He left for Scotland two days later and stayed for two weeks. As a result he failed to submit the company's VAT return for the period ending 30 September 1988 in time. The Commissioners imposed a default surcharge but the tribunal allowed the company's appeal, holding that the circumstances constituted a reasonable excuse. *Balma Time Ltd, MAN/89/71 (VTD 3585).*

18.173   **Director abroad on business.**   A company (J) had entered into an agreement with a US company whereby the US company would take over J's business. The deal was due to be completed on 1 August 1989. On 13 July J's managing director was told that the US company was withdrawing from the deal. He flew to the USA on 23 July in an attempt to persuade the US company to proceed with the transaction. He did not return until 31 July. As he was the sole signatory of J's cheques, J did not pay its VAT for the quarter ending 30 June until after the due date, and the Commissioners imposed a default surcharge. The tribunal allowed J's appeal, holding that the circumstances constituted a reasonable excuse. *Jet Rod (Franchising) Ltd, MAN/89/846 (VTD 4502).*

18.174   An appeal was allowed in a case where the controlling director had had to visit Los Angeles on business shortly before the due date of a return. *Loadstone Ltd, LON/91/1774 (VTD 7878).*

18.175   **Director called away on business.**   An appeal was allowed in a case where the controlling director of a company based in Finchley, with no other employees, had to travel to Yorkshire on urgent business three days before a return was due, and did not return to Finchley in time to post the return before the due date. *Dankroy Ltd, LON/91/2738 (VTD 7743).*

18.176   A similar decision was reached in *Neruby Computing Services Ltd, LON/98/1221 (VTD 15874).*

18.177   A company's return for the period ending 31 January 1992 was not submitted until 2 March, and a default surcharge was imposed. The company appealed, contending that it had a reasonable excuse because both its directors, who were the only full-time employees, were away from the office on business at the time the return was due. The company had only one office employee, a young woman who worked part-time on two days a week (Mondays and Wednesdays). She had been instructed to complete and post the form before leaving the office on Wednesday 25 February, but had accidentally left the completed form in her desk instead of posting it. The tribunal allowed the appeal, holding that the circumstances constituted a reasonable excuse. *BS Electrical Ltd, EDN/92/145 (VTD 9199).*

18.178 Default Surcharge

18.178 **Loss of company secretary.** In a case where a company secretary had left the company at short notice following serious disputes which had become the subject of a High Court action, the tribunal held that this constituted a reasonable excuse for the late submission of a return. *Chemical Corporation (UK) Ltd, LON/87/842 (VTD 2750).*

18.179 A company secretary left his employment at short notice in May 1989, without completing the VAT return for the period ending 30 April. The tribunal held that the circumstances constituted a reasonable excuse for the late submission of the return. *EH Smith Parkinson (Motors) Ltd, MAN/89/648 (VTD 4289).*

18.180 The wife of the managing director of a small engineering company acted as the company secretary. She began a liaison with the company's only other engineer. They eloped together, and she subsequently sought and obtained a divorce. Because of the loss of his company secretary and of his only qualified colleague, the managing director was unable to complete the company's principal contract. The tribunal held that the circumstances constituted a reasonable excuse for the late submission of two VAT returns. (There was, however, held to be no excuse for four subsequent defaults.) *Briana Electronics Ltd, LON/89/1429Y (VTD 4629).*

18.181 The loss of a company secretary was also held to constitute a reasonable excuse in *Hodgson Martin Ltd, EDN/92/100 (VTD 9108).*

18.182 **Death of bookkeeper.** The death of a company's bookkeeper was held to constitute a reasonable excuse for a late return in *Ernest Platt (Bury) Ltd, MAN/94/1779 (VTD 13208).*

18.183 **Loss of bookkeeper.** The resignation of a bookkeeper at short notice was held to constitute a reasonable excuse for a late return in *Starplex Ltd, LON/87/632 (VTD 2552); CPA Environmental Control Associates Ltd, LON/88/417 (VTD 2953); Milhench Brothers, BEL/88/13 (VTD 3375); Open Rule Ltd, LON/88/311 & 312X (VTD 4130); AJ Parfitt (t/a Parfitt & Craig Hall), LON/90/1268X (VTD 5623); CG Sharpe, MAN/91/1376 (VTD 7679); G Blackburn, MAN/92/355 (VTD 8845)* and *CHS Publications Ltd, LON/97/440 (VTD 15191).*

18.184 **Temporary absence of bookkeeper.** A partnership's return for the period ending 31 August 1990 was submitted late, and a default surcharge was imposed. The partnership appealed, contending that it had a reasonable excuse because its bookkeeper had been on jury service from 17 to 26 September. She had only been notified of the jury service in August and had only expected it to last for a week. The tribunal allowed the appeal, holding that this constituted a reasonable excuse. *Groves Garage, LON/91/55X (VTD 5895).*

18.185 A similar decision was reached in *Weldwork Ltd, LON/94/1057P (VTD 12953).*

18.186 A trader, based in Maidenhead, submitted his return for the period ending 29 February 2000 late. The Commissioners imposed a surcharge, and the trader appealed, contending that he had a reasonable excuse because his bookkeeper had had to travel to Cornwall on 16 March because her father was seriously ill. She had expected to return within a week, but had stayed in Cornwall for the rest of the month. The tribunal allowed the appeal, holding that the circumstances constituted a reasonable excuse. *S Yate (t/a Yummies), LON/00/750 (VTD 16943).*

18.187 **Resignation of computer operator.** In a case where a company's computer clerk, who was responsible for the preparation of the VAT return, left at short notice sixteen days before the due date of the return, the tribunal held that this constituted a reasonable excuse. *Barnett Lawson (Trimmings) Ltd, LON/89/1316Z (VTD 4400).*

18.188   **Death of employee.**   The death of a company's office manager, sixteen days before the due date of a return, was held to be a reasonable excuse in *Semec (Engineering) Ltd, LON/91/182X (VTD 5963)*.

18.189   The death of an employee was also held to constitute a reasonable excuse for a late return in *Group Topek Holdings Ltd, EDN/94/137 (VTD 13146)*.

18.190   **Resignation of manager.**   The manager of a restaurant resigned at short notice in June 1990, following the unexpected death of his stepmother. The tribunal held that this constituted a reasonable excuse for the late submission of the return for the period ending 31 May 1990. *Futures Restaurants Ltd, LON/90/1440X (VTD 5717)*.

18.191   The resignation of a company's manager, a month before the due date of a return, was held to constitute a reasonable excuse in *Landseer Film & Television Productions Ltd, LON/93/622 (VTD 10812)*.

18.192   **Manager away on business.**   An appeal was allowed in a case where a company's general manager, who was required to sign the company's cheque in payment of its VAT, was unexpectedly called away on business shortly before the due date of a return. *Parcare International Ltd, LON/92/2196P (VTD 9773)*.

18.193   **Dismissal of accounts clerk.**   In a case where a firm of solicitors had been obliged to dismiss their accounts clerk, the tribunal held that this constituted a reasonable excuse for the late submission of the first return following the dismissal. *JV McPherson & N Weather, LON/89/1442X (VTD 4800)*.

18.194   **Death of accountant.**   The sudden death of a company's accountant was held to constitute a reasonable excuse for a first default in *Fred's Newsagents Ltd, LON/88/191 (VTD 2815)*.

18.195   The death from a heart attack of an accountant employed by a sole trader was held to constitute a reasonable excuse for a late return in *BA England, LON/90/731Y (VTD 5292)*.

18.196   A similar decision was reached in *Mrs LD McLean, LON/91/865 (VTD 6920)*.

18.197   **Dismissal of accountant.**   In a case where a company had been obliged to dismiss a newly-appointed accountant for unsatisfactory work, the tribunal held that this constituted a reasonable excuse for the late submission of the first return following the dismissal. *Formtax Plastics Ltd, LON/93/1767P (VTD 11605)*.

18.198   **Loss of accountant.**   The resignation of a company's accountant was held to constitute a reasonable excuse in *Linguarama Ltd, LON/89/312Z (VTD 4011); Bergen Transport Ltd, MAN/89/842 (VTD 4481); Goliath International (Tools) Ltd, MAN/89/1048 (VTD 4737); EBA Systems Ltd, LON/89/1381 (VTD 4770); Granmore Ltd, MAN/90/448 (VTD 5253); Button Eventures Ltd, LON/90/1948 (VTD 5995); TJ Tiling (Contractors) Ltd, MAN/90/851 (VTD 5664, 6194)* and *Wizard Accounting Solutions Ltd, LON/94/163P (VTD 12304)*.

18.199   **Staff turnover.**   Exceptional staff turnover was held to constitute a reasonable excuse in *Brearly Townsend Painters Ltd, MAN/84/419 (VTD 3126); Dexter Brent & Patterson Ltd, LON/88/489 (VTD 3136); Pizza Express Ltd, LON/88/868 (VTD 3340); Complete Maintenance Ltd, LON/89/989X (VTD 4669)* and *Lyham Property Services, LON/90/1936Y (VTD 6874)*. (*Note.* Compare the cases noted at 18.232 below, in which staff shortages were held not to constitute a reasonable excuse.)

18.200　Default Surcharge

Cases where the appellant was unsuccessful

18.200　**Partners away from office on business.**　In a case where the three members of a partnership were all working away from their office at the time when a return was due, and had not delegated the completion of the return to any of their employees, the tribunal held that this did not constitute a reasonable excuse. *Pip Systems, MAN/88/ 551 (VTD 3413).*

18.201　Similar decisions were reached in *M Haque & Co, LON/89/1622X (VTD 4517); EL & HN Miliam, LON/90/296Z (VTD 4876)* and *The Nightingale Partnership, LON/92/3028P (VTD 10219).*

18.202　**Partners abroad on business.**　A partnership of musicians appealed against a surcharge, contending that the partners and their manager had been on business in the USA when the return was due. The tribunal held that the circumstances did not constitute a reasonable excuse. *UBU Projex, LON/89/1835X (VTD 4820).*

18.203　A similar decision was reached in *P Halloran & M Hollingsworth, LON/96/465 (VTD 14412).*

18.204　**Partner on holiday.**　The absence on holiday of a partner was held not to be a reasonable excuse in *Eastbridge Joiners & Shopfitters, EDN/89/130 (VTD 4229); KR & EM Phelps, LON/89/486Y (VTD 4486); P Hagyard & A Gardiner, MAN/90/374 (VTD 5240); W & B Mahon, MAN/90/546 (VTD 5335); Andrew S Campbell Associates, LON/91/2326Y (VTD 7262); Allclean Cleaning Services, LON/92/2642 (VTD 9885); KJ & Mrs BM McGarry, LON/93/184P (VTD 10385); GE, PI & DL Greenwood (t/a Blinkers of South Cave), MAN/93/1620 (VTD 12534)* and *A Stanton-Precious & MZ Hunt (t/a Hogs Back Brewery), LON/96/1867 (VTD 14791).*

18.205　**Partner on honeymoon.**　A partnership appealed against a default surcharge, contending that it had a reasonable excuse because one of the two partners had married during the week before the due date of the return and had then gone on a honeymoon. The tribunal dismissed the appeal, observing that the wedding was 'not unforeseen' and that alternative arrangements should have been made for the submission of the return. *Ceiling Services, EDN/91/77 (VTD 6289).*

18.206　A similar decision was reached in *SM Eaton & SL Grove, LON/x (VTD 16575).*

18.207　**Resignation of director.**　A company's finance director gave notice of leaving on 14 August and left on 4 September. His replacement did not take up duty until 3 October. During the intervening period the company did not submit its return for the period ending 31 August. The tribunal held that the circumstances did not constitute a reasonable excuse, as the managing director should have made alternative arrangements for the completion of the return. *Reflexions Market Research Ltd, LON/90/208X (VTD 4850).*

18.208　A similar decision was reached in *Maranello Concessionaires Ltd, LON/96/297 & 298 (VTD 14211).* (*Note.* For another issue in this case, see 18.543 below.)

18.209　**Director in Court.**　A company did not submit its return for the period ending 31 August 1989 until November, and the Commissioners imposed a surcharge. The company appealed, contending that its director had been on trial for a criminal offence from early September until 5 October. At the end of the trial the director was sentenced to a term of imprisonment. The tribunal dismissed the company's appeal, holding that the company had not established a reasonable excuse. *Henley Glass Centre Ltd, LON/90/445Z (VTD 5236, 5921).*

18.210   **Director in prison.**   A company's return for the period ending 31 July 1991 was submitted after the due date, and a default surcharge was imposed. The company appealed, contending that it had a reasonable excuse because its controlling director had been committed to prison in May 1991, and his wife had had to take over the management of the company during his imprisonment. The tribunal dismissed the appeal, holding that the circumstances did not constitute a reasonable excuse. *Brough Bros (Kitchens & Bathrooms) Ltd, LON/92/82Z (VTD 7915)*.

18.211   **Director away from office on business.**   In a case where the principal director of a small company had to work away from the company's office for two weeks, and consequently did not submit a VAT return until after the due date, the tribunal held that the circumstances did not constitute a reasonable excuse. *Control Computers & Telecommunications Ltd, LON/88/1438Z (VTD 3461)*.

18.212   Similar decisions were reached in *James Pringle Ltd, EDN/89/85 (VTD 3945); Skingrade Ltd, EDN/89/138 (VTD 4377); Hills Diecasting Co Ltd, LON/89/1406Z (VTD 4399); Link Industrial Services Ltd, MAN/90/850 (VTD 5663); Beaver Oil Services Ltd, LON/90/1445X (VTD 5786); Leisure West Clothing Ltd, LON/91/ 42Y (VTD 5930); Senes Sportswear Ltd, LON/91/43Y (VTD 5930); Gravity Productions Ltd, LON/91/1987X (VTD 7068); Remlock Design Ltd, LON/92/ 1180Y (VTD 9145)* and *WJ Hatt Ltd, LON/93/662P (VTD 10762)*.

18.213   **Director abroad on business.**   A company appealed against a surcharge, contending that its principal director had been abroad for three weeks on business at the time the return was due. The tribunal dismissed the appeal, holding that the director should have delegated the return. *Ultracolour Ltd, LON/88/1241 (VTD 3278)*.

18.214   Similar decisions were reached in *Tradeplan Ltd, LON/89/719Z (VTD 4033); Michael Nightingale & Co Ltd, LON/89/1722Y (VTD 4873); Emmabee Fashions Ltd, LON/88/1074 (VTD 5077); Thamesdown Engineering Systems Ltd, LON/90/ 1008Y (VTD 5341); CB Group Ltd, LON/91/65 (VTD 5841); Balton Ltd, LON/90/359Z (VTD 5980); BMS Medical Manufacturer & Supplies Ltd, MAN/ 91/767 (VTD 7836); Management Consult Ltd, MAN/92/420 (VTD 9228); Interflex Data Systems Ltd, LON/92/1983P (VTD 9578)* and *UK Inspection Ltd, MAN/93/803 (VTD 11467)*.

18.215   **Director contesting Parliamentary election.**   A company submitted a return late, and the Commissioners imposed a surcharge. The company appealed, contending that its controlling director had been standing for election to the European Parliament, and had been too busy to complete the return. The tribunal dismissed the appeal, holding that this was not a reasonable excuse, since 'the date of these elections is known far in advance so that a taxpayer has every possibility of arranging his affairs in advance to comply with his statutory obligations'. *Medcross Ltd, LON/94/1515P (VTD 13080)*.

18.216   **Director on holiday.**   There have been a very large number of cases in which companies have contended that they have had a reasonable excuse because a company director has been on holiday at the relevant time, and where the tribunal has dismissed the appeal, holding that this does not constitute a reasonable excuse. In the interests of space, such cases are not reported individually in this book. For a list of such cases decided up to 31 December 1993, see Tolley's VAT Cases 1994.

18.217   **Resignation of employee.**   There have been a large number of cases in which tribunals have held that the resignation of the employee who had been responsible for VAT returns has not constituted a reasonable excuse for a late return. Such cases turn entirely on the particular facts and, in the interests of space, are not summarised

18.218 Default Surcharge

individually in this book. For a list of such cases decided up to 31 December 1995, see Tolley's VAT Cases 1996.

18.218 **Company secretary on holiday.** The absence on holiday of a company secretary was held not to be a reasonable excuse in *J McArdle (Haulage) Ltd, LON/90/1891X (VTD 5779)* and *Olympia Testing (East Anglia) Ltd, LON/92/1710P (VTD 9260)*.

18.219 **Club treasurer on holiday.** A golf club appealed against a default surcharge, contending that it had a reasonable excuse because its treasurer had been on holiday at the relevant time. The tribunal dismissed the appeal, holding that this was not a reasonable excuse. *Prestonfield Golf Club Ltd, EDN/96/244 (VTD 14841)*.

18.220 **Financial controller on holiday.** The absence on holiday of a company's financial controller was held not to be a reasonable excuse in *Picken & Son Ltd, MAN/92/1587 (VTD 10952)*.

18.221 **Redundancy of bookkeeper.** A firm of solicitors made its bookkeeper redundant in December 1989. Its VAT return for the period ending 31 March 1990 was submitted late and a default surcharge was imposed. The firm appealed, contending that it had a reasonable excuse in view of the departure of the bookkeeper. The tribunal dismissed the appeal, observing that the loss of a bookkeeper could constitute a reasonable excuse in certain circumstances, but not where the firm itself had made the decision to discharge the bookkeeper. *Greenhouse Stirton & Co, LON/90/1336Y (VTD 5481)*. (*Note*. For another issue in this case, see 18.558 below.)

18.222 A similar decision was reached in *Food-Wrap Ltd, LON/93/961P (VTD 10817)*.

18.223 **Loss of bookkeeper.** A sole trader contended that he had a reasonable excuse for the late submission of several returns because his fiancée, who acted as his bookkeeper, had left him. The tribunal dismissed his appeal, holding that this did not constitute a reasonable excuse. *RA Jones, MAN/89/776 (VTD 4664)*.

18.224 The loss of a bookkeeper was also held not to constitute a reasonable excuse in *P Ward, MAN/93/874 (VTD 11406); LC & P Allen, LON/94/802P (VTD 12547)* and *Nationwide Leisure Ltd, MAN/99/913 (VTD 16482)*.

18.225 **Bookkeeper on holiday.** The absence on holiday of the bookkeeper responsible for preparing the relevant return was held not to be a reasonable excuse in *QA (Weld Tech) Ltd, MAN/88/603 (VTD 3259); MD & J Burrows, MAN/89/213 (VTD 3844); Timverton Trading Ltd, LON/90/1543Y (VTD 5621); Kabe Engineering Ltd, LON/90/1693Y (VTD 5684); Panzer Delicatessen Ltd, LON/91/74 (VTD 6462); Griffiths & Goddard Restorations Ltd, LON/91/857Y (VTD 6704); Southgate Tubular Products Ltd, LON/90/187X (VTD 6780); Andrews Sherlock & Partners, LON/91/1625X (VTD 6949); Northwest Drawing Supplies, MAN/91/1287 (VTD 7463); Federation of Fresh Meat & Wholesalers, LON/91/2253 (VTD 7552); Ellamastic Asphalt Division Ltd, LON/91/2589X (VTD 7999); AL Rae, EDN/92/325 (VTD 10238); Diversport Ltd, MAN/93/160 (VTD 10572); MET Packaging (Services) Ltd, LON/92/2967P (VTD 10731); Brush & Palette Sign Co, LON/95/1160P (VTD 13413); Vitaldrive Ltd, MAN/94/2467 (VTD 13422); R Paterson, EDN/96/36 (VTD 14168)* and *MC Rigden, LON/96/585 (VTD 14527)*.

18.226 **Computer operator on holiday.** The absence on holiday of a company's computer operator was held not to be a reasonable excuse in *Stave-Con Ltd, MAN/90/915 (VTD 5808)*.

18.227 **Dismissal of manager.** A firm of solicitors dismissed its office manager after discovering financial irregularities. The manager had submitted two VAT returns late, and the next return was also submitted late. The Commissioners imposed a surcharge and the firm appealed, contending that the manager's dishonesty constituted a reasonable excuse. The tribunal dismissed the firm's appeal. The returns in question had all been signed by one of the partners in the firm. The partner should have been aware that the returns were being submitted late and the circumstances did not constitute a reasonable excuse. *Messrs Rowlands, MAN/88/15 (VTD 2752).*

18.228 **Office manager on holiday.** The absence on holiday of a company's office manager was held not to constitute a reasonable excuse in *Griffiths & Goddard Restorations Ltd, LON/91/1857Y (VTD 6523).*

18.229 **Loss of accountant.** In a case where a trader's accountant had emigrated unexpectedly and without warning, the tribunal held that this was not a reasonable excuse. *TTM Chau, LON/91/2323 (VTD 7244).*

18.230 A company appealed against five default surcharges, contending that it had a reasonable excuse because its accountant and his assistant had resigned within two months of each other. The tribunal dismissed the appeal, holding on the evidence that the company 'did not give sufficient priority to appointing a qualified replacement' for the accountant. The tribunal observed that it was the company's responsibility 'to obtain trained staff and, if there was difficulty in doing so, to employ professional accountants'. *APUK Ltd, MAN/98/345 (VTD 15796).* (*Note.* For another issue in this case, see 18.27 above.)

18.231 **Accountant on holiday.** The absence on holiday of the accountant responsible for submitting the relevant return was held not to be a reasonable excuse in *Curry Mahal Restaurant Manchester Ltd, MAN/89/323 (VTD 4244); M Crolla, EDN/90/17 (VTD 4701); Mrs S Helsby, MAN/91/50 (VTD 6066); London Building Co plc, LON/92/2767 (VTD 9971); Stephens Catering Equipment Co Ltd, BEL/92/72 (VTD 10150); WR McMaster (t/a Delta Bar), EDN/93/233 (VTD 12109)* and *Tetra International Ltd, LON/98/847 (VTD 15820).*

18.232 **Staff shortages.** Staff shortages were held not to be a reasonable excuse in *Wyndley Nurseries Ltd, MAN/88/826 (VTD 3637); Hexham Steeplechase Course Ltd, MAN/89/100 (VTD 3830); Vorwerk (UK) Ltd, LON/89/380Y (VTD 3969); Tudor Furnishings (Chalfont) Ltd, LON/88/1488 (VTD 4087); PGK Photo Developments Ltd, MAN/89/543 (VTD 4268); Sterling Westminster Investments Ltd, LON/90/105Y (VTD 4915); R Falconer, LON/90/1558Z (VTD 5635); Torwood Services Ltd, EDN/91/161 (VTD 6587); JM Cunningham, EDN/91/62 (VTD 6588); Project & Design Ltd, MAN/92/574 (VTD 9681); TR Blencowe (t/a Blencowe Associates), LON/93/241P (VTD 10629)* and *Whaley Engineering Ltd, MAN/97/205 (VTD 15062).*

18.233 **Staff holidays.** Staff holidays were held not to constitute a reasonable excuse in *Roy Conway Industrial Services Ltd, MAN/92/94 (VTD 9439); Crowther Print Ltd, EDN/92/319 (VTD 10241); Pipeline Protection Ltd, MAN/92/1559 (VTD 10336); BAPP Industrial Supplies Ltd, MAN/92/1787 (VTD 10632); Warwick Students Union Services Ltd, MAN/93/1618 (VTD 12166); PNDC Willan, MAN/93/1575 (VTD 12563); Lockerbie Meat Packers Ltd, EDN/95/296 (VTD 13826B)* and *Holdproud Ltd, LON/98/383 (VTD 15589).*

18.234 **Industrial action.** Industrial action by staff was held not to be a reasonable excuse in *Yorkshire & Humberside Tourist Board, MAN/89/1007 (VTD 4744).*

18.235 **Christmas holidays.** There have been a large number of cases in which tribunals have held that Christmas holidays have not constituted a reasonable excuse for a late return. In the interests of space, such cases are not summarised individually in this book. For a list of such cases decided up to 31 December 1995, see Tolley's VAT Cases 1996.

18.236   **Easter holiday.**   The closure of a business for an Easter holiday was held not to be a reasonable excuse in *P & H Pipework Ltd, LON/89/816Y (VTD 4092)* and *Norpak Engineering Ltd, MAN/91/1175 (VTD 7462)*.

Loss, unavailability or inadequacy of records

Cases where the appellant was successful

18.237   **Dismissal of bookkeeper—records missing.**   A company dismissed its bookkeeper in June 1987 for fraud and embezzlement. After the bookkeeper's departure, it was discovered that sales invoices were missing, and that both the purchases ledger and the cash book were incomplete. The tribunal held that this constituted a reasonable excuse for the late submission of the return for the period ending 31 July 1987. (There was, however, held to be no reasonable excuse for subsequent defaults.) *Auto Bodies (Hemel) Ltd, LON/89/110Y (VTD 4184)*.

18.238   **Records temporarily unavailable.**   A company's return for the period ending 30 September 1987 was submitted late, and a default surcharge was imposed. The company appealed, contending that it had a reasonable excuse because a Canadian company had offered to take over its business and, as 30 September was the end of its financial year, its books and records had been sent to a firm of accountants, who were not responsible for the firm's VAT return. The accountants had retained the books for longer than had been anticipated. The tribunal allowed the appeal, holding that the circumstances constituted a reasonable excuse. *Drillfact Ltd, MAN/88/181 (VTD 3009)*. (*Note.* Compare *Heffernan*, 18.271 below, where similar circumstances were held not to constitute a reasonable excuse.)

18.239   A trader had lent his books to his accountant to prepare accounts for income tax. On 22 December 1988 he visited his accountant to retrieve the books so that he could complete his VAT return for the period ending 30 November 1988. The accountant was not in his office and his secretary refused to hand over the books. The trader did not succeed in obtaining the books until 5 January, so that his return was submitted late. The tribunal allowed his appeal, holding that the circumstances constituted a reasonable excuse. *DP Hollick, LON/89/499X (VTD 3956)*.

18.240   A similar decision was reached in a case where a rugby club dispensed with the services of a firm of accountants whose work had been 'inadequate', but was unable to recover its records from the firm for three weeks. *Llandaff Athletic Rugby Club, LON/89/945Z (VTD 4143)*.

18.241   A company took over the business of an associated company as a going concern, and wrongly reclaimed input tax on the stock taken over. The Commissioners discovered this at a control visit in October 1987, and a further visit was made on 1 December 1987, at which the company's VAT records were taken away by two VAT officers for detailed inspection. The Commissioners supplied photocopies of some of the documents which had been taken, but some of the copies were of poor quality, and they did not supply copies of the invoices. In July 1988 the documents were released to the company's accountants, who were to hold them to the order of the Commissioners rather than to the order of the company. The company had been unable to submit any returns while its records were unavailable, and its records for the period to February 1988 were not completed until November 1988. In January 1989 the company's accountant contacted the VAT office to arrange a meeting, but the officer dealing with the case was not available and it was agreed that the VAT office would contact the accountant to arrange a convenient time. The officer concerned did not contact the accountant until June 1989, and the outstanding returns were submitted in July 1989. In the meantime the company had incurred six default surcharges. The tribunal allowed the company's appeal in part, holding that the retention of the company's records by the Commissioners constituted a reasonable excuse for the late submission of the returns due from February 1988 to November 1988 inclusive. (There was, however, held to be no excuse for the late submission of the returns due in February and May 1989.) *Windows Direct Ltd, MAN/90/16 (VTD 4762)*.

18.242   In a case where a penalty under what is now *VATA 1994, s 60* had been imposed on a partnership, the tribunal allowed the partnership's appeal against two default surcharges, finding that the relevant returns could not have been submitted on time because the records were being examined by VAT officers and the partnership had not been provided with copies. (The Commissioners' contention that the partnership should have requested copies was rejected.) *New Bengal Tandoori Restaurant, LON/89/171Y, 174Y & 177Y (VTD 5211)*.

18.243   Similar decisions were reached in *Falcon Plastics Ltd, MAN/93/1582 (VTD 13050); Peking Inn (Cookham) Ltd, LON/95/3106 (VTD 14079)* and *KH Ching, HB Yi & HC Yong (t/a Chef Peking-on-Thames), LON/95/3068P (VTD 14079)*.

18.244   A company's return for the period ending 31 December 1990 was not submitted until 7 January and a default surcharge was imposed. The company appealed, contending that it had a reasonable excuse because its books had been in the hands of its accountants from late November until 6 January. The company had been suffering cash-flow problems and had an overdraft of more than £70,000. On 26 November its bank had insisted that audited accounts should be submitted if the overdraft facility was to be continued. The tribunal allowed the appeal, holding that the circumstances constituted a reasonable excuse. *McKenzie Bain Ltd, LON/91/360 (VTD 5994)*.

18.245   A similar decision was reached in *McFarlane Roofing Ltd, MAN/92/1586 (VTD 10845)*.

18.246   An appeal was allowed in a case where the proprietor of a restaurant had posted the relevant records to her accountant for him to complete the VAT return, and the records had been delayed for ten days in the post. *C Boniface, LON/92/1184Y (VTD 9954)*.

18.247   A trader appealed against several default surcharges, contending that he had a reasonable excuse because the Inland Revenue had taken possession of his records in October 1989, and had retained them for 21 months. The tribunal allowed his appeal in part, holding that this was a reasonable excuse for the late submission of the return for the period ending September 1991, but that there was no reasonable excuse for subsequent defaults. *JE Hewitt (t/a James E Hewitt Associates), MAN/93/543 (VTD 11177)*.

18.248   In a Northern Ireland case, a social club appealed against a surcharge, contending that it had a reasonable excuse because its records had been held by the Royal Ulster Constabulary. The tribunal accepted this evidence and allowed the appeal. *Shamrock Sports & Social Club, LON/94/307P (VTD 12767)*.

18.249   **Details of input tax not available.**   An appeal was allowed in a case where a company had submitted returns late because of delays in receiving invoices in respect of imported goods. *Appleyard Lees & Co, MAN/88/145 (VTD 2928)*.

18.250   An agricultural contractor had not received all his invoices from his suppliers for the period ending 31 October 1987. He telephoned his local VAT office to ask whether he could submit a return on the basis of the figures actually available, but was told that he could not submit an incomplete return. He therefore delayed the submission of the return, and a default surcharge was imposed. The tribunal allowed his appeal, holding that he should have been advised that he could estimate part of his input tax in accordance with what is now *VAT Regulations 1995 (SI 1995 No 2518), reg 29(3)*, and that the circumstances constituted a reasonable excuse. *KVJ Joyce, LON/88/ 394 (VTD 3224)*.

18.251   *Appleyard Lees & Co*, 18.249 above, and *Joyce*, 18.250 above, were applied in the similar case of *NE & RWH Murden, MAN/92/228 (VTD 9192)*. (*Note*. For another issue in this case, see 18.125 above.)

18.252   A similar decision was reached in *Weru (UK) Ltd, LON/94/862 (VTD 12738)*.

18.253   **Industrial action by Post Office staff—consequent delay in receiving invoices.**   In a case where industrial action by Post Office staff led to a company receiving many invoices much later than usual, the tribunal held that this constituted a reasonable excuse for the late submission of a return. *Social Surveys (Gallup Poll) Ltd, LON/89/321Z (VTD 3775)*.

18.254   A similar decision was reached in *Mercuri Urval Ltd, LON/89/821Y (VTD 4438)*.

18.255   **Details of income not available.**   A company which published music obtained royalties from record sales and from the performance of songs on radio and television. In respect of the latter, a payment was made by the Performing Rights Society Ltd and, for the purposes of calculating its income, the company relied on a quarterly statement from the society. For the period ending 30 June 1987 the figures were seriously understated in the statement, and so the company contacted its local VAT office to explain that it could not furnish a correct return until the true figures were available. The Commissioners imposed a default surcharge but the tribunal allowed the company's appeal, holding that the VAT office should have advised the company to submit an estimated return, and that the circumstances therefore constituted a reasonable excuse. *Minder Music Ltd, LON/87/838 (VTD 2678)*.

18.256   A company which operated a knitting business sent fabric to dyers according to customers' requirements. The dyers despatched the dyed fabric directly to the customers. However the dying process involved a loss in weight through evaporation and shrinkage. Thus the weight and length of cloth delivered to customers was about 5% less than its weight and length when it left the factory. The company made out blank invoices when the fabric left the factory, and completed the invoices when the customers notified it of the weight of the cloth they had received. This procedure led to delay in completing quarterly returns, and the company later abandoned it, but not before it had incurred a default surcharge. The tribunal allowed the company's appeal, holding that the unusual circumstances constituted a reasonable excuse. *Knittex Ltd, MAN/89/42 (VTD 3541)*.

18.257   An appeal was allowed in a case where invoices were issued in Italy on behalf of a UK company which supplied English-language tuition to Italian students. The tribunal found that a VAT officer had given the company's director the impression that he should delay the company's returns until he had received confirmation of the issue of such invoices, even if this meant that the return would have to be delayed until after the due date, and held that this misunderstanding constituted a reasonable excuse. *David Leslie (Hairfashions) Ltd*, 18.280 below, distinguished. *Butler School of Languages, LON/91/700 (VTD 7067)*. (*Note*. There was held to be no reasonable excuse for other defaults.)

18.258   **Return delayed while records verified.**   A trader appealed against a default surcharge, contending that he had a reasonable excuse because his accountant had discovered errors in previous returns, and had advised him to delay submitting the return until a control visit by a VAT officer. The tribunal allowed the appeal, holding that the circumstances constituted a reasonable excuse. *T Harrison, MAN/88/307 (VTD 3078)*.

18.259 Similar decisions were reached in *Capricorn Business Services Ltd, LON/89/1815X (VTD 4802); The Garage Door Co, EDN/93/87 (VTD 11144); Belgian Trading Co, LON/94/817P (VTD 12644)* and *QEN Spearing, LON/98/370 (VTD 16314)*.

18.260 An appeal was allowed in a case where a company's directors discovered errors in the company's records, and delayed submitting a return until they had verified the figures. *Dust Extraction (International) Ltd (VTD 3175)*.

18.261 Similar decisions were reached in *Intersport Manchester Ltd, MAN/89/16 (VTD 3625); Provident Direct Sales (Holdings) Ltd, MAN/89/233 (VTD 3952); A Needham, MAN/90/257 (VTD 5150); AL Watkins (t/a Fence-Tech), MAN/94/818 (VTD 12819)* and *PJ Moody (t/a PMS Telecom), LON/94/3128P (VTD 13234)*.

18.262 In October 1989 a company's accountant discovered that the company's bookkeeper had failed to pay cash takings into the company's bank account, and had apparently pocketed the cash in question. The accountant spent the whole of the next week examining the company's records, with the result that the company's return for the period ending 30 September was submitted late and a default surcharge was imposed. The tribunal allowed the company's appeal, holding that the circumstances constituted a reasonable excuse. *Square Moves Ltd, LON/90/395 (VTD 5050)*.

18.263 A similar decision was reached in *Maddermarket Theatre Trust Ltd, LON/92/3332 (VTD 10393)*.

18.264 In a case where some of a hotelier's invoices were accidentally damaged by water, requiring an additional ten hours' work in summarising them for the quarterly return, the tribunal held that the circumstances constituted a reasonable excuse. *TN Thorne, MAN/91/82 (VTD 6231)*.

18.265 An appeal was allowed in a case where a company's bookkeeper gave evidence that he had been surprised by the unusually high amount of input tax shown on the return, and had therefore delayed submission of the return for four days while she checked the relevant figures. *Peter Boizot (Franchises) Ltd, LON/93/456P (VTD 10773)*.

18.266 A paper merchant, who imported quantities of paper and paid for this by direct debit, habitually awaited receipt of his monthly bank statement before completing his VAT return. Normally he received his bank statement before the end of the month and was therefore able to submit his return before the due date. However, his September bank statement had not arrived by 30 October. He therefore telephoned his bank to obtain details of the payments he had made, but was told that the statement was in the post and that the figures were not available. He received the statement on 5 November, and submitted the return on 6 November. The Commissioners imposed a default surcharge but the tribunal allowed his appeal, holding that the circumstances constituted a reasonable excuse. *J Purcell (t/a John Purcell Paper), LON/93/752P (VTD 10925)*.

18.267 **Imported goods—delay in receiving C79 certificate from Customs.** A trader imported flowers from outside the UK, using the services of an import agent. In preparing his VAT returns, he relied on the monthly issue of forms C79 from Customs to ascertain how much tax he could reclaim in respect of the goods which he had imported. On two occasions in 1992, Customs did not send him the C79 in time for him to complete his VAT return. The trader delayed submitting the returns until he had received the C79, and the Commissioners imposed a default surcharge. The tribunal allowed the trader's appeal, holding that the delays by Customs in sending the forms C79 constituted a reasonable excuse. *A Fitzpatrick, MAN/92/1180 (VTD 10282)*.

18.268   See also *Chandler Forest Products Ltd*, 18.517 below.

Cases where the appellant was unsuccessful

18.269   **Omission in records.**   A company's accountants found that the bookkeeper had failed to enter an invoice in the company's books, and delayed the VAT return. The tribunal dismissed the appeal, holding that this was not a reasonable excuse. *RSM Industries Ltd, MAN/88/55 (VTD 2810)*.

18.270   Similar decisions were reached in *BR Camp, MAN/88/927 (VTD 3605)* and *CDA Fasteners Ltd, MAN/91/511 (VTD 6389)*.

18.271   **Records temporarily unavailable.**   A sole trader appealed against a default surcharge, contending that he had a reasonable excuse because his accountants had kept his records so that they could prepare his annual accounts, and had delayed returning them to him. The tribunal dismissed his appeal, observing that what is now *VATA 1994, s 71(1)(b)* precluded delay by the accountants from constituting a reasonable excuse. *DRM Heffernan, LON/93/454 (VTD 10735)*.

18.272   A similar decision was reached in *RS Coombe, LON/93/323P (VTD 11154)*.

18.273   A trader appealed against four default surcharges, contending that he had a reasonable excuse because his records had been held by his solicitors. The tribunal dismissed his appeal, observing that the trader should have demanded the return of his records from his solicitors, and that what is now *VATA 1994, s 71(1)(b)* precluded reliance on a third party from constituting a reasonable excuse. *Jenkinson*, 48.80 PENALTIES: FAILURE TO NOTIFY, distinguished. *NG Hughes (t/a Lightning Couriers), MAN/92/519 (VTD 11685)*.

18.274   **Details of input tax not available.**   A company which imported raw materials required certificates from Customs detailing the amount of input tax paid at the port when the goods were imported. Its certificate relating to the period ending 30 November 1987 was not available until 8 December. The company did not submit its return until 10 January 1988, and a default surcharge was imposed. The company appealed, contending that it was unfair for the Commissioners to require it to submit a return within only 22 days of receiving the certificate. The tribunal dismissed the appeal, holding that the circumstances did not constitute a reasonable excuse. *RAAR Associates Ltd, LON/88/437Y (VTD 3365)*.

18.275   The late arrival of import certificates from import agents was held not to be a reasonable excuse, on the grounds that the company should have submitted estimated returns. *Clinkscale Radio & Musical Ltd, EDN/89/76 (VTD 4279)*.

18.276   Similar decisions were reached in *West Heat (Eltra) Ltd, LON/89/1430Z (VTD 4772); A dos Santos Tavares, LON/90/270 (VTD 4956)* and *J Drennan Partnership, LON/97/117 (VTD 15190)*.

18.277   A company appealed against a default surcharge, contending that it had a reasonable excuse because there had been a delay in receiving invoices, in respect of which it wished to claim input tax, from suppliers. The tribunal dismissed the appeal, holding that this was not a reasonable excuse. *The Deva Trading Co Ltd, MAN/88/714 (VTD 3421)*.

18.278   Similar decisions were reached in *Harrier Shoes Ltd, LON/89/310X (VTD 3814); Lyezeal Ltd, LON/89/127 (VTD 3823); Middlesbrough Football & Athletic Co*

(1986) Ltd, MAN/89/14 (VTD 3836); AV Turner & Sons Ltd, LON/88/1463Z (VTD 3877); CP Evans, MAN/89/955 (VTD 4717); DJ Watkinson, MAN/91/40 (VTD 5794) and *A Pereira, LON/90/1856Z (VTD 5835).*

18.279   A barrister did not submit his return for the period ending 28 February 1988 until April, and the Commissioners imposed a default surcharge. The barrister appealed, contending that he had a reasonable excuse because he had been unable to find certain receipts for expenses on which he wished to reclaim input tax. He had eventually found the receipts in a box in the playroom used by his two-year-old daughter. The tribunal dismissed his appeal, observing that it was the barrister's responsibility to keep the papers necessary for completion of the return in a safe place. *DM Moore, LON/88/1095 (VTD 5244).*

18.280   **Details of income not available.**   Delays in obtaining details of income from departmental branches of a business were held not to be a reasonable excuse in *David Leslie (Hairfashions) Ltd, LON/88/1091 (VTD 3446).*

18.281   Similar decisions were reached in *Lloyd Scotter Electrical Ltd, MAN/89/803 (VTD 4482); Hindi Picture Ltd, LON/89/1495Z (VTD 4490); Zetland Garage (Southport) Ltd, MAN/89/936 (VTD 4676)* and *PJ Sansom, MAN/91/937 (VTD 7121).*

18.282   **Cessation of business—firm wishing to check final VAT return with final accounts.**   A firm which had ceased to trade delayed submitting its final VAT return so that it could reconcile the figures with its final accounts. The tribunal held that this did not constitute a reasonable excuse. *Photographics, LON/88/1246X (VTD 3407).*

18.283   **Return delayed while figures verified.**   In a case where a company's accountant delayed the submission of a VAT return so that he could reconcile the figures with the accounts, the tribunal held that this was not a reasonable excuse. *Glossop Sectional Buildings Ltd, MAN/89/466 (VTD 4100).*

18.284   Similar decisions were reached in *George & George, LON/89/1402Z (VTD 4562); Southern Fabrics Ltd, LON/88/791Z (VTD 4781); Acorn Origination Ltd, LON/90/1257 (VTD 5517); Digital Intelligence Systems Ltd, MAN/90/696 (VTD 6500); Trowbridge Trades & Labour Club & Institute Ltd, LON/91/1313 (VTD 6640); Frank Coleman (Luton) Ltd, LON/91/1598X (VTD 6653); CA Mandelberg (t/a Andrew Mandelberg & Co), MAN/91/701 (VTD 7114); Femco Engineering Co Ltd, LON/91/2101X (VTD 7454); DT Engineering Ltd, LON/92/598Y (VTD 7912); DI Wright, MAN/92/464 (VTD 9254); Kitchens For You Ltd, LON/93/828P (VTD 10802); BCC (Building Services) Ltd, LON/X (VTD 13211); Bercor Ribbon Co Ltd, MAN/95/2198 (VTD 14025)* and *Alan Davison (Construction) Ltd, MAN/96/426 (VTD 14531).*

18.285   **Integration of company's records with those of parent company.**   The shares of a company (F) were purchased by another company in January 1989. The new parent company decided to integrate F's records with its own. However, the companies remained separate entities and F's return for the quarter ending 31 December 1989 was submitted late. The tribunal dismissed F's appeal, holding that the extra work required by the integration of the companies' records did not amount to a reasonable excuse. *Forth Skips Ltd, EDN/90/55 (VTD 5016).*

18.286   **Records under investigation with Commissioners.**   In June 1987 two VAT officers made a control visit to a company. They formed the opinion that some purchase invoices, in respect of which the company had reclaimed input tax, were fictitious. In July they interviewed the company's directors and removed a large number of documents. They informed the directors that they would provide photocopies of the documents on request, but the company did not request copies. In the meantime the company did not submit its returns for the periods ending 30 June and 30 September 1987, and a default surcharge was imposed. The company appealed, contending that the circumstances constituted a reasonable excuse. The tribunal dismissed the appeal, holding that the company should have requested copies and that it was not reasonable for the directors to have decided to withhold the company's returns. 'A person in the appellant's position, who knows that improper conduct of some sort is alleged against him, is not entitled to sit back and postpone his returns'. *G & J Spencer Ltd, MAN/89/50 (VTD 5428)*.

18.287   A similar decision was reached in *JF Laughlin, EDN/92/338 (VTD 10499)*.

18.288   **Company's records in Chinese.** A company appealed against a default surcharge, contending that it had a reasonable excuse because its accounts clerk for the relevant period had kept its records in Chinese. He had subsequently left the company and his successor could not read Chinese. The tribunal dismissed the appeal, holding that the circumstances did not constitute a reasonable excuse. *P Jennings & Sons Ltd, LON/91/1533 (VTD 6696)*.

18.289   **Change of address.** See *Fishwick*, 18.536 below.

Change of accounting dates

Cases where the appellant was successful

18.290   A company appealed against a default surcharge, contending that it had a reasonable excuse for the late submission of a return because, at a control visit, it had requested that its accounting periods for VAT (which ended in February, May, August and November) should be changed to end on 31 March, 30 June, 30 September and 31 December, so that they would coincide with its annual accounting date for corporation tax. It had followed this with a request in writing, to which the Commissioners had not replied. Subsequently the Commissioners issued an estimated assessment, and imposed a surcharge, for a period of one month ending on 30 June. However, as the company's previous period had ended on 31 May, its accountant wrote to the Commissioners stating that he had assumed that the next return should be for a period ending on either 31 August (if the existing dates were continued) or 30 September. The tribunal allowed the company's appeal, holding that, in view of the Commissioners' failure to reply to correspondence, there was a reasonable excuse for the company's failure to make a return for June. *IPMC Ltd, LON/88/5 (VTD 2797)*.

18.291   A similar decision was reached in *Discount Window Systems Ltd, BEL/92/58 (VTD 10159)*.

18.292   A company, whose accounting periods had ended in January, April, July and October, applied to change its quarterly periods so that they ended in February, May, August and November. The Commissioners approved this change, and the company anticipated that its next return would cover the four-month period from 1 November 1987 to 29 February 1988. In mid-January 1988 the company received a return form expressed to be for the period from 1 November 1987 to 31 January 1988. In mid-February 1988 it received a further return form covering the period from 1 February to 29 February. The company submitted both returns together in late March, and a default surcharge was imposed in respect of the first return. The tribunal allowed the company's appeal, holding that the circumstances constituted a reasonable excuse. *United Cutlers Ltd, MAN/88/324 (VTD 3116)*.

18.293   Similar decisions were reached in *Egerton Transport Ltd, MAN/91/227 (VTD 6505); Nova Group (London) Ltd, LON/92/2923P (VTD 10252, 10409); Nova*

Roofing Co Ltd, LON/92/2924P (VTD 10252, 10409); Rawlings & Lucas (Builders) Ltd, LON/92/2925P (VTD 10252, 10409) and *Express Vending Ltd, LON/95/323P (VTD 13252).*

18.294   On 6 April 1987 a company, which had previously submitted returns for the quarterly periods ending in March, June, September and December, applied to change its quarterly periods so that they would end in January, April, July and October. This request was accepted, but on 14 May the company applied for a further change so that its periods would end in February, May, August and November. The Commissioners replied on 27 May, accepting this request but asking for a return for the one-month period ending 30 April to be submitted by 31 May. The company did not comply and a surcharge was subsequently imposed. The tribunal allowed the company's appeal, holding that it was unreasonable for the Commissioners to expect a one-month return at such short notice. *Snow & Rock Sports Ltd, LON/88/596 (VTD 3223).*

18.295   A company whose accounting periods had ended in December, March, June and September applied to change its accounting dates so that its future accounting periods would end in February, May, August and November. In February 1988 the Commissioners issued an amended certificate of registration stating 'returns to be made in respect of period ending 31 May 1988 and three-monthly thereafter' and including the words 'recipients of amended certificates are required to furnish by the due dates previously notified any returns outstanding in respect of periods ending prior to that shown above'. The company took the view that it could submit a return covering the five months to 31 May 1988, and need not submit a separate return for the period ending 31 March. The Commissioners imposed a surcharge for the late payment of the tax due for those three months and the company appealed, contending that the amended certificate had been ambiguous and had not made it clear that the Commissioners would still require a separate return for the period ending 31 March. The tribunal allowed the company's appeal, holding that the wording of the certificate was 'extremely ambiguous' and that the circumstances constituted a reasonable excuse. *Industrial Fabrication Systems Ltd, LON/89/881Y (VTD 4219).*

18.296   *Industrial Fabrication Systems Ltd*, 18.295 above, was applied in a subsequent case where a company applied to change its accounting periods and submitted its first subsequent return after the due date. *Anti-Static Technology Ltd, LON/90/327Z (VTD 5065).*

18.297   In a case where a small company applied to change its accounting dates in March 1989, but was not allowed to implement the change until the following quarter, the tribunal held that the circumstances constituted a reasonable excuse for the late submission of the return for the period ending 30 April 1989, because the company had not been given adequate warning that it would still need to submit a return for that period. *Northwood Garage (Whitstable) Ltd, LON/89/1364Y (VTD 4352).*

18.298   A similar decision was reached in *SP Whitehouse, LON/91/1726 (VTD 6763)*. (*Note*. For another issue in this case, see 10.1 CASH ACCOUNTING SCHEME.)

18.299   A sole trader's accounting periods had ended in February, May, August and November. She decided to transfer the business to a limited company with effect from 1 January 1997. Her accountant visited the local VAT office in November 1996 to make the necessary arrangements. Following this conversation, he assumed that his client would be permitted to submit a final return for the four methods ending 31 December 1996 instead of the normal quarterly return for the three months ending 30 November 1996. On 22 January 1997 he submitted a return covering the final four months of trading. The Commissioners imposed a default surcharge for the late submission of the return for the three months ending 30 November, but the tribunal allowed the trader's appeal, holding that the circumstances constituted a reasonable excuse. *DF Macris (t/a Helena's Unisex Beauty Centre), LON/97/550 (VTD 15073).*

18.300   A married couple carried on a home improvement business and were registered for VAT with accounting periods ending in March, June, September and December. Subsequently they began a second business with a separate trading name and obtained a separate registration with accounting periods ending in February, May, August and November. In August 1990 they also purchased a public house, and applied for a third registration number. The Commissioners informed the couple that they could only have one registration, in accordance with the QB decision in *Glassborow*, 53.1 REGISTRATION, and that the input tax and output tax relating to all three businesses should be aggregated and included on the same return form. The couple included the figures for all three businesses in a single return for the period ending 30 September 1990 as requested, but because of the extra work, the return was submitted late. The Commissioners imposed a default surcharge, against which the couple appealed. The tribunal allowed the couple's appeal, holding that the extra work caused by having to alter the accounting period of one of the businesses, and include all three businesses on the same return for the first time, constituted a reasonable excuse. *G & BM Beaumont (t/a Beaumont Home Improvements), MAN/91/112 (VTD 6063).*

Cases where the appellant was partly successful

18.301   A partnership's quarterly return periods had ended in February, May, August and November. It applied for these to be changed so that they ended in March, June, September and December. The Commissioners issued a return covering the single month of March 1999 and a return covering the three months ending June 1999. The partnership submitted both returns after the due date, and the Commissioners imposed a default surcharge. The partnership appealed, contending that the change of accounting dates constituted a reasonable excuse. The tribunal allowed the appeal in part, holding that the circumstances constituted a reasonable excuse for the late submission of the return for March 1999 but that there was no reasonable excuse for the return for the period ending June 1999. *P & J Cook (t/a Blacksmiths Arms), MAN/00/54 (VTD 16770).*

Cases where the appellant was unsuccessful

18.302   In a case where a partnership had applied to change its accounting periods, and had then overlooked the effect of the change, the tribunal held that this did not constitute a reasonable excuse. *N & Mrs M Tulip, MAN/88/402 (VTD 3243).*

18.303   Similar decisions were reached in *Worldstill Ltd, MAN/89/142 (VTD 3796); VJ Wall, LON/89/1027Y (VTD 4795); Sewards (Electrical) Ltd, LON/92/2356P (VTD 9709); Watco Design Ltd, EDN/95/351 (VTD 14136)* and *Packwell Cartons Ltd, LON/96/478 (VTD 14314).*

18.304   Extra work caused by a change of accounting date was held not to constitute a reasonable excuse in *CEM Computers, BEL/88/42 (VTD 3647)* and *Clive White Chartered Surveyors, LON/88/963Z (VTD 3989).*

18.305   A company's financial year ended on 31 August, but its quarterly return periods ended on 31 January, 30 April, 31 July and 31 October. It did not submit its return for the period ending 31 July 1994 by the due date, but on 1 September 1994 it submitted a request for its return periods to be changed so that they ended on 28 February, 31 May, 31 August and 30 November. The Commissioners accepted this request, but refused to apply it retrospectively, and imposed a default surcharge for the three-month period ending on 31 July 1994. The company appealed, contending that the circumstances constituted a reasonable excuse. The tribunal dismissed the appeal, observing that the company was already in default at the time it submitted its request to change its accounting periods, and holding that the circumstances did not constitute a reasonable excuse. *Basicflex Ltd (t/a Proline Engineering), LON/94/ 3125 (VTD 13370).*

18.306   A company's financial year ended on 31 December, but its quarterly return periods had ended in February, May, August and November. In July 1998 it applied to change its accounting dates so as to coincide with its financial year. The Commissioners issued a one-month return covering September 1998, followed by a three-month return ending on 31 December 1998. The company submitted both of these returns late. The Commissioners accepted that the change constituted a reasonable excuse for the late delivery of the September return, but imposed a default surcharge for the quarterly period ending in December. The tribunal dismissed the company's appeal, holding that there was no reasonable excuse for the late submission of this return. *Tameplace Ltd, LON/00/360 (VTD 16736).*

Insufficiency of funds (VATA 1994, s 71(1)(a))

Cases where the appellant was successful

18.307   **Dishonesty of former company secretary.**   The whole of the shares of a private company were sold in 1984. The vendors did not tell the purchaser that the company owed £24,000 in unpaid tax. The former company secretary had drawn cheques for various sums to the Inland Revenue and Customs, but had not posted them. He had recorded the amounts in question in the company's books as having been paid. When the purchaser discovered the tax liabilities, he made arrangements to pay them by instalments, and they were paid in full by 1987. However, in the meantime the company had suffered cash-flow problems and its current VAT had fallen into arrears. The Commissioners imposed a surcharge, and the company appealed. The tribunal allowed the appeal, holding that although an insufficiency of funds was not of itself a reasonable excuse, the dishonesty of the former company secretary did constitute a reasonable excuse. The QB upheld the tribunal decision. The company's explanation for non-payment was not simply a temporary cash shortage, but was that the dishonesty of its former secretary had deprived it of the means to pay. The restriction in what is now *VATA 1994, s 71(1)(a)* therefore did not automatically apply, and the tribunal was entitled to find that the circumstances constituted a reasonable excuse. *C & E Commrs v Salevon Ltd, QB [1989] STC 907.*

18.308   **Dishonesty of former managing director.**   *Salevon Ltd*, 18.307 above, was applied in a similar subsequent case where the tribunal held that the dishonesty of a company's former managing director constituted a reasonable excuse. *Dove Services (Manchester) Ltd, MAN/90/695 (VTD 5510).*

18.309   Similar decisions, also applying *Salevon Ltd*, 18.307 above, were reached in *Primboon Ltd, LON/91/2053Y (VTD 7757)* and *Reflex Synthesisers Controllers Ltd, LON/92/ 1044 (VTD 8815).*

18.310   **Dishonesty of former partner.**   A firm of solicitors submitted five returns late and the Commissioners imposed surcharges. The firm appealed, contending that it its auditors had discovered that one of its partners had apparently misappropriated £40,000. He had subsequently been expelled from the partnership and suspended from practice by the Law Society. The tribunal allowed the firm's appeal, applying *Salevon Ltd*, 18.307 above, and holding that the circumstances constituted a reasonable excuse. *Stocken & Lambert, LON/92/2818 (VTD 10527)*. (*Note*. For another issue in this case, see 18.76 above.)

18.311   **Dishonesty of bookkeeper.**   In a case where a trader had dismissed his bookkeeper for stealing from him, the tribunal held that this constituted a reasonable excuse for non-payment. *AG Hurlstone, LON/90/1746 (VTD 6167)*.

18.312   A similar decision was reached in *MM Carew & Son Marble Co Ltd, LON/93/1888P (VTD 11681)*.

18.313   **Dishonesty of employee.**   In a case where an employee of a partnership had stolen £25,000 from the partnership while the partners were on holiday, the tribunal held that this constituted a reasonable excuse for non-payment. *Swift Catering Services, LON/91/1400Y (VTD 6740)*.

18.314   The theft of funds by employees was also held to constitute a reasonable excuse in *Mid-Rhondda Central Workmen's Institute Ltd, LON/91/1206X (VTD 6770)* and *WL Finch, LON/98/1066 (VTD 15826)*.

18.315   **Account frozen by bank.**   A sole trader sold a large quantity of goods for £55,000. His bank initially cleared the purchaser's cheque for this amount, but subsequently informed him that the cheque was a forgery, and froze his account. Consequently he was unable to send a quarterly VAT payment, and the Commissioners imposed a surcharge. The tribunal allowed his appeal, observing that he had sufficient funds to pay the VAT, but had been denied access to them by the bank's action in freezing his account. *RG Richardson (t/a Castle Mouldings), LON/89/525Y (VTD 3898)*.

18.316   In December 1990 a company issued a cheque for £2,220.50. However, when the cheque was presented, the company's bank wrongly debited its account with £22,205.50. This substantially increased the company's overdraft, and the bank froze its account. The bank did not admit its error until the following month, so that the company was unable to pay its quarterly VAT liability. The tribunal held that the bank's error constituted a reasonable excuse. *Premier Roofing Systems Ltd, MAN/91/246 (VTD 6338)*.

18.317   **Overdraft limit unexpectedly reduced by bank.**   In a case where a company's bank unexpectedly reduced its overdraft limit from £470,000 to £220,000, the tribunal held that this constituted a reasonable excuse for the company's inability to pay its VAT liability by the due date. *Kingston Craftsmen (1981) Ltd, MAN/90/603 (VTD 5409)*.

18.318   Similar decisions have been reached in a considerable number of subsequent cases. In the interests of space, such cases are not summarised individually in this book. For a list of such cases decided up to 31 December 1995, see Tolley's VAT Cases 1996.

18.319   **Delay in receiving loan from bank.**   A company appealed against a default surcharge, contending that it had a reasonable excuse for late payment because it had anticipated a loan or overdraft extension from its bank, but the negotiations 'turned out to be more protracted than it would have been reasonable to expect'. The tribunal allowed the appeal, holding that the bank's procrastination constituted a reasonable excuse. *VP Rollers Ltd, LON/93/2623 (VTD 12065)*.

18.320   A similar decision was reached in *Messenger & Co, LON/93/1072P (VTD 12413)*.

18.321   **Repayment awaited from Customs.**   A partnership could not pay its liability for the period ending 30 April 1988, because it had not received a repayment due from Customs in respect of an earlier period. The tribunal held that this constituted a reasonable excuse. *GT Shaw & MA Whilock, MAN/88/616 (VTD 3530)*.

18.322 A similar decision was reached in *Samzou Ltd, MAN/93/351 (VTD 11013)*.

18.323 **VAT repayment due from other EC State.** A company appealed against a default surcharge, contending that it had a reasonable excuse because it was owed almost £9,000 in VAT by the Luxembourg Government. The tribunal accepted this contention and allowed the appeal. *DPC European Transport, LON/98/850 (VTD 16177)*.

18.324 **Excessive balancing payment falling due under Annual Accounting Scheme—whether a reasonable excuse for late payment.** A company had been allowed to adopt the Annual Accounting Scheme from August 1988, and was required to pay £956 per month. In May 1989 its payments were reduced to £10 per month, but in October 1990 they were increased to £1,200 per month. For the year ending July 1991 it was required to make a balancing payment of £15,200. It was unable to pay this amount within the statutory period, and a surcharge was imposed. The company appealed, contending that it had a reasonable excuse because of the dramatic fluctuations in the amount of the payment required from it by the Commissioners. The tribunal allowed the appeal, observing that 'the whole purpose of the Annual Accounting Scheme is to reduce the possibility of a cash-flow crisis for the taxpayer by enabling him to make regular payments of a reasonably consistent amount throughout the year towards his tax liability' and holding that the Commissioners 'had a duty of care to respond effectively to notified changes in circumstances by setting revised realistic monthly payments'. The Commissioners' failure to do so constituted a reasonable excuse. *Lineplan Ltd, EDN/92/173 (VTD 9369)*.

18.325 **Liquidation of customers.** There have been a large number of cases in which tribunals have held that the liquidation of the appellant's customers has constituted a reasonable excuse for non-payment, applying the principles in *Salevon Ltd*, 18.307 above. Such cases turn entirely on the particular facts and, in the interests of space, are not summarised individually in this book. For a list of such cases decided up to 31 December 1993, see Tolley's VAT Cases 1994.

18.326 **Late payment from Council.** A contractor worked almost exclusively for a London borough council, which persistently paid him late, so that he incurred two surcharges. The tribunal allowed his appeal and the CA upheld this decision (by a 2–1 majority). Notwithstanding the provisions of what is now *VATA 1994, s 71(1)(a)*, an insufficiency of funds could constitute a reasonable excuse 'if the exercise of reasonable foresight and of due diligence and a proper regard for the fact that the tax would become due on a particular date would not have avoided the insufficiency'. On the evidence here, if the trader had brought further pressure to bear on the council, 'he would probably have received no further orders and the bulk of his livelihood would have disappeared'. (Nolan LJ commented that 'as a general rule a small trader dealing with larger organisations and having difficulty in securing the prompt payment of his bills should elect to account for his Value Added Tax on the cash basis and would have no reasonable excuse for failing to do so'.) *C & E Commrs v JB Steptoe, CA [1992] STC 757*.

18.327 **Late payment by major client.** *Steptoe*, 18.326 above, has been applied in a large number of subsequent cases in which late payment, or non-payment, by a major client has been held to constitute a reasonable excuse for non-payment of VAT. In the interests of space, such cases are not reported individually in this book. For a list of such cases decided up to 31 December 1992, see Tolley's VAT Cases 1993.

18.328 **Delay in receiving compensation following compulsory purchase order.** In a case where a company's premises had been the subject of a compulsory purchase order, and the payment of compensation to the company had been delayed, the tribunal held that this constituted a reasonable excuse for non-payment. *Bridge Metal Services (Thurrock) Ltd, LON/92/325Z (VTD 7921).*

18.329   A similar decision was reached in *Sandwell Scaffold Co Ltd, MAN/94/713 (VTD 12823).*

18.330   **Persistent late payment by majority of trader's customers.** A trader appealed against two surcharges, contending that she had a reasonable excuse because more than 85% of her customers delayed paying her for periods of 80 days or more. The tribunal allowed her appeal, applying the principle in *Steptoe*, 18.326 above. *SA Jones, LON/92/1837P (VTD 9616).*

18.331   Similar decisions, also applying the principle in *Steptoe*, 18.326 above, have been reached in a large number of subsequent cases. In the interests of space, such cases are not reported individually in this book. For a list of such cases decided up to 31 December 1993, see Tolley's VAT Cases 1994.

18.332   **Cash-flow problems following industrial action by Post Office staff.** As a result of industrial action by Post Office staff, a company failed to receive payment from some of its customers and could not only pay about £12,000 of a VAT liability of about £17,000. The Commissioners imposed a surcharge but the tribunal allowed the company's appeal, holding that the circumstances constituted a reasonable excuse, applying *Salevon Ltd*, 18.307 above. *A Lockett & Co Ltd, MAN/89/28 (VTD 3546).*

18.333   *A Lockett & Co Ltd*, 18.332 above, was applied in the similar case of *David Taylor Tool Hire Ltd, MAN/89/355 (VTD 4969).*

18.334   A similar decision was reached in *Intertrade (GB) Ltd, LON/92/1491P (VTD 9610).*

18.335   **Cash-flow problems following death of director.** One of the three directors of a building company was killed in a car accident in October 1990. This led to a sharp drop in the company's income, and the company was unable to pay its VAT liability for the period ending January 1992. The Commissioners imposed a surcharge but the tribunal allowed the company's appeal, holding that the circumstances constituted a reasonable excuse. *WBL Ltd, LON/91/985Z (VTD 6606).*

18.336   **Cash-flow problems following death of employee.** The proprietors of a hotel appealed against a default surcharge, contending that they had a reasonable excuse because they had scheduled an annual dance for 14 November 1992, but had been forced to cancel it at short notice following the death of one of their employees in a road accident on 12 November. The loss of the expected income from this dance had prevented them from paying their VAT liability. The tribunal allowed the appeal, holding that the circumstances constituted a reasonable excuse. *Corriegour Lodge Hotel, EDN/93/92 (VTD 11536).*

18.337   **Cash-flow problems following fire.** A company suffered a fire at its factory in October 1989, which stopped production for three weeks. This caused cash-flow problems, and it was unable to pay the full amount of VAT due for the period ending 30 November 1989. The Commissioners imposed a surcharge but the tribunal allowed the company's appeal, applying *Salevon Ltd*, 18.307 above. *Baronshire Engineering Ltd, EDN/90/56 (VTD 5027).*

18.338   A similar decision was reached in *Forgeville Ltd, LON/96/433 (VTD 14298).*

18.339   **Theft of cash.** Theft of cash was held to constitute a reasonable excuse for non-payment of VAT in *Top Quality Seconds Prescot Ltd, MAN/90/207 (VTD 5096); Fat Sam's American Food & Beverage Co Ltd, LON/90/1408Z (VTD 5785);*

HA Lindsay, MAN/91/946 & MAN/92/1130 (VTD 9530); DA Parfitt, LON/92/3172 (VTD 10184); RE Tidy, LON/93/660P (VTD 11957); Electritec Ltd, LON/94/392A (VTD 12423) and *DS Rosenberg (t/a Crusade), LON/95/3166 (VTD 14049).*

18.340   **Cash-flow problems following computer malfunction.** Following a computer malfunction, a company was unable to send out its invoices promptly and suffered cash-flow problems. The tribunal held that this constituted a reasonable excuse. *Belco Manufacturing Co Ltd, LON/90/1126Y (VTD 5918).* (*Note.* For other cases concerning computer malfunction, see 18.70 to 18.85 above.)

18.341   **Cash-flow problems attributed to increase in loan repayments.** A company had obtained a loan from Barclays Bank, which it was repaying by monthly payments of £530. A new branch manager insisted that the payments should be increased to £1,488 per month. This caused the company financial problems, and it incurred a surcharge. The tribunal allowed the company's appeal, holding that the 'unexpected' conduct of the bank constituted a reasonable excuse. *Project Research & Evaluation Ltd, LON/94/2097P (VTD 13183).*

18.342   **Other cases.** There have been a small number of other cases in which tribunals have held that, notwithstanding the provisions of *VATA 1994, s 71(1)(a)*, an insufficiency of funds has been attributable to exceptional and unavoidable circumstances which have amounted to a reasonable excuse, but where the nature of the case is such that it is of little if any value as a precedent. In the interests of space, such cases are not summarised individually in this book. For such cases reported up to 31 December 1993, see Tolley's VAT Cases 1994.

Cases where the appellant was partly successful

18.343   A company failed to pay its VAT liabilities for five accounting periods by the due dates, and the Commissioners imposed default surcharges. The company appealed, contending that its failure to pay was attributable to non-payment by some of its customers. The tribunal reviewed the evidence in detail and found, applying the principles laid down in *Steptoe*, 18.326 above, that there was no reasonable excuse for the first three defaults in question, but that there was a reasonable excuse for the last two defaults. The company appealed to the QB, which upheld the tribunal decision as one of fact. On the evidence, the tribunal had been entitled to draw a distinction between the first three defaults and the last two defaults. *TE Davey Photo-Service Ltd v C & E Commrs, QB 1995, [1997] STC 889.*

Cases where the appellant was unsuccessful

18.344   **Repayment claimed to be due to associated company.** A company appealed against 13 surcharges, contending that it had a reasonable excuse for some of the defaults because the Commissioners had taken eight months to make a repayment of VAT to an associated company. The tribunal dismissed the appeals, holding that the default was attributable to cash-flow problems which could not constitute a reasonable excuse. The company appealed to the CS, which upheld the tribunal decision. The tribunal was entitled to conclude that the only reason for the company's non-payment was insufficiency of funds. Furthermore, the company had taken no steps to register itself or any associated company as a group, and could not claim that non-payment to a separate legal entity was a reason for its own non-payment. *Artful Dodger (Kilmarnock) Ltd v C & E Commrs, CS [1993] STC 330.*

18.345   Similar decisions were reached in *Tape Recorder Hi-Fi Centre, LON/88/387 (VTD 3221); Computer Aided Systems (UK) Ltd, LON/88/657X (VTD 3729); Errey's*

Furnishing Ltd, MAN/89/630X (VTD 4110); Bondcloak Ltd, MAN/90/201 (VTD 4858); Amesbury Motor Co, LON/92/1448 (VTD 9644); AT & T Rentals Ltd, BEL/92/16P (VTD 10790) and Hazel Grove Timber & Building Supplies Ltd, MAN/95/1409 (VTD 13801).

18.346 **Repayment claimed to be due to associated partnership.** A sole trader appealed against a default surcharge, contending that she had a reasonable excuse because the Commissioners had delayed making a repayment to a family partnership of which she was a member. The tribunal dismissed her appeal, holding that this was not a reasonable excuse. *E Fitzpatrick, BEL/90/7 (VTD 5427).*

18.347 A similar decision was reached in *M Davidson, EDN/99/79 (VTD 16207).*

18.348 A company appealed against a default surcharge, contending that it had a reasonable excuse for non-payment because the Commissioners owed money to an associated partnership. The tribunal dismissed the appeal, holding that this was not a reasonable excuse. *Quad (Civil Engineering) Ltd, MAN/91/119 (VTD 6093).*

18.349 A similar decision was reached in *Philip Maddison Haulage Ltd, MAN/90/931 (VTD 6428).*

18.350 **Cash-flow problems following withdrawal from Cash Accounting Scheme.** A company which had adopted the Cash Accounting Scheme found that its turnover had almost reached the statutory maximum, and therefore applied to revert to the normal rules for VAT accounting. Its first return under the normal rules showed an increased VAT liability, and was submitted late. The Commissioners imposed a surcharge and the company appealed, contending that the cash-flow problems resulting from its withdrawal from the Cash Accounting Scheme constituted a reasonable excuse. The tribunal dismissed the appeal, holding that the insufficiency of funds was foreseeable and did not constitute a reasonable excuse. *Broadgate Software Ltd, MAN/90/778 (VTD 5662).*

18.351 A similar decision was reached in *Aquability Partnership, MAN/92/1105 (VTD 10635).*

18.352 **Overdraft limit reduced by bank.** The reduction of a company's overdraft limit was held not to constitute a reasonable excuse in *Philipson Studios Ltd, MAN/92/1629 (VTD 10488); WGM Decorating, LON/95/445P (VTD 13344); Executive Security (Wentworth) Ltd, LON/97/469 (VTD 15052)* and *Industcool Engineering Ltd, LON/97/850 (VTD 15196).* (*Note.* Compare, however, *Kingston Craftsmen (1981) Ltd,* 18.317 above, and the note at 18.318 above.)

18.353 **Cheque from customer delayed in post.** A company which was suffering cash-flow problems had to pay VAT of about £21,000 for its period ending February 1988. It was expecting a cheque of about £20,000 from a customer. This cheque was posted on or about 24 March but was delayed in the post by an industrial dispute. On 5 April, as the cheque had still not arrived, the company's managing director visited the customer and obtained a duplicate cheque which he banked on the same day. He then drew a cheque for the VAT due and delivered it personally to the VAT Central Unit on 6 April. The Commissioners imposed a surcharge and the company appealed. The tribunal dismissed the appeal, holding that the case was therefore governed by what is now *VATA 1994, s 71(1)(a)* and the circumstances did not constitute a reasonable excuse. *Lennick Precision Engineering Ltd, LON/88/1085 (VTD 3342).*

18.354 Similar decisions were reached in *Glendower Cutting Tools Ltd, MAN/88/917 (VTD 3564)* and *PF Baines & J McDonough (t/a Still Visual), LON/89/1551X (VTD 4921).*

18.355   **Cash-flow problems following late payment by principal customer.**   A trader was unable to pay his VAT liability for the period ending February 1991, and a surcharge was imposed. The trader appealed, contending that he had a reasonable excuse because 80% of his work was carried out for one customer, who owed him more than £200,000. The tribunal dismissed his appeal, holding that the problems were 'relatively short-term', and the business was not solely dependent on the defaulting customer, so that what is now *VATA 1994, s 71(1)(a)* prevented the circumstances from constituting a reasonable excuse. *Steptoe*, 18.326 above, was distinguished because the trader there 'was totally dependent on one customer for the continued existence of his business and because of the identity of the customer was unable to exert normal business pressures to induce payment'. *J McCaig, EDN/91/142 (VTD 6362).*

18.356   *Steptoe*, 18.326 above, has also been distinguished in several subsequent cases where defaulting customers accounted for less than 75% of the appellant's turnover. In the interests of space, such cases are not reported individually in this book.

18.357   **Cash-flow problems following personal bankruptcy of financial director.**   A company had an overdraft facility of £60,000, supported by a personal guarantee given by one of its directors. In 1991 the director became bankrupt, and the bank withdrew the overdraft facility. The company was unable to pay its next VAT liability, and a surcharge was imposed. The tribunal dismissed the company's appeal, holding that the circumstances did not constitute a reasonable excuse. *Relay Couriers Ltd, LON/91/2098Z (VTD 7990).*

18.358   **Cash-flow problems following receivership of major shareholder.**   A company (S) failed to pay its VAT liability for the period ending July 1991 by the due date, and a surcharge was imposed. S appealed, contending that 33% of its share capital was owned by another company (R), which had gone into receivership in June 1991. The tribunal dismissed the appeal, holding that the circumstances did not constitute a reasonable excuse. *Sea-Change Ltd, MAN/93/1268 (VTD 11759).*

18.359   **Cash-flow problems attributed to economic recession.**   A company which had been unable to pay its VAT liability appealed against a default surcharge, contending that its cash-flow problems were caused by the 'severe effects of the recession', rather than by any culpable default. The tribunal dismissed the appeal, holding that 'the general state of the economy cannot in itself be a satisfactory excuse for late payment' and that the case was governed by what is now *VATA 1994, s 71(1)(a). The Gardens Entertainments Ltd, LON/92/136Z (VTD 8972).*

18.360   Similar decisions were reached in *Faxlink Communications, LON/91/2747Y (VTD 7766); Northern Software Consultants Ltd, MAN/91/1021 (VTD 9027); Flan-Form Ltd, LON/92/1444P (VTD 9415); Melroad Ltd (t/a UK Pipework Fabrications), MAN/92/102 (VTD 9438); Gableglade Ltd, LON/92/2006 (VTD 9597); Merseyside Trailer Hire, MAN/92/801 (VTD 10136); Alucast (Diecastings) Ltd, MAN/92/912 (VTD 10291); Tipton Non-Ferrous Foundry Ltd, MAN/92/913 (VTD 10328) and E Steventon & Co Ltd, LON/93/1449P (VTD 11250).*

18.361   **Cash-flow problems attributed to labour costs.**   A company appealed against a default surcharge, contending that it had needed to make some of its employees redundant in order to reduce its labour costs, but that the statutory redundancy payments had increased its short-term cash-flow problems. The tribunal dismissed the appeal, holding that the circumstances did not constitute a reasonable excuse. *ADM (North East) Ltd, MAN/93/1473 (VTD 12640).*

18.362   **Cash-flow problems attributed to change of premises.**   A company appealed against a default surcharge, contending that it had a reasonable excuse because of the cost of changing premises. The tribunal dismissed the appeal, holding that the circumstances did not constitute a reasonable excuse. *Performance Print Ltd, MAN/98/572 (VTD 15810).*

18.363 **Payment by instalments.** A partnership was unable to pay the whole of its quarterly VAT liability by the due date. It submitted a valid cheque for part of the amount due, and a postdated cheque for the remainder. The Commissioners imposed a surcharge and the tribunal dismissed the partnership's appeal. *London Bridge Cycles, LON/87/593 (VTD 2550).*

18.364 A company was unable to pay its quarterly liability due on 31 October 1989. It posted a letter to the Commissioners on 26 October 1989, offering payment by instalments. The director concluded the letter with the words 'I hope that this arrangement is acceptable to you, if it is not please contact me by return post'. The Commissioners did not reply to the letter but imposed a surcharge. The tribunal dismissed the company's appeal, holding that an offer to pay tax by instalments without the Commissioners' approval or consent could not be a reasonable excuse for not making such payments at the time and in the manner laid down by Parliament. The fact that the Commissioners had not sent an immediate reply to the company's letter could not be taken as implying either approval or consent. *Alexis Modes Ltd, LON/90/27Z (VTD 4780).*

18.365 Similar decisions were reached in *Orka Trading Co Ltd, LON/89/1841X (VTD 4936); Union Clothing Ltd, LON/92/1727 (VTD 10564); LJ Harvey & Associates (Bournemouth) Ltd, LON/92/2580P (VTD 10739); Insider Publications Ltd, EDN/93/120 (VTD 11162); Bridge Motors (Dudley) 1990 Ltd, MAN/93/670 (VTD 11329); Connect Transport Ltd, EDN/94/27 (VTD 12552); Geoffrey Davis (Menswear) Ltd, LON/94/521P (VTD 12576); Total Storage & Distribution Ltd, LON/95/1470 (VTD 13506); Mark Feldmann & Co, LON/95/1849P (VTD 13658); Gara Rock Hotel Ltd, LON/95/444P (VTD 13691); PG Davies, LON/96/1350 (VTD 14713)* and *S Bateman (t/a Super Bike Sales), LON/97/1148 (VTD 15281).*

18.366 **Payment by postdated cheque.** Three associated partnerships paid their VAT liability for the period ending 30 April 1987 with cheques postdated to 1 June. The Commissioners imposed default surcharges and the tribunal dismissed the partnerships' appeals, observing that the obligation to effect payment by the due date was not satisfied by the delivery of a cheque dated after the due date had expired, and holding that there was no reasonable excuse for the defaults. *John Oliver Haircutters (Colchester); Hair by John Oliver; John Oliver Haircutters, [1987] VATTR 239 (VTD 2532).*

18.367 *John Oliver Haircutters (Colchester),* 18.366 above, was applied in the similar cases of *Double D Freight Services Ltd, MAN/89/333 (VTD 3987); Eurowear Fashions Ltd, LON/88/654 (VTD 3600, 4012); North Birmingham & Aldridge Motor Co Ltd, MAN/89/108 (VTD 4014); Valewood Furniture Ltd, LON/93/1203 (VTD 12447)* and *Southern Ski Enterprises Ltd,* 18.107 above.

18.368 There have been a very large number of other cases in which tribunals have held that the submission of postdated cheques has not constituted a reasonable excuse for the late payment of the VAT due. In the interests of space, such cases are not summarised individually in this book. For a list of such cases decided up to 31 December 1995, see Tolley's VAT Cases 1996.

18.369 For cases where a cheque was accidentally postdated, see 18.414 below.

18.370 **Postdated cheques previously accepted by Commissioners.** A partnership which had submitted a postdated cheque in payment of its liability appealed against a default surcharge, contending that the Commissioners had always accepted postdated cheques in the past. The tribunal dismissed the appeal, holding that this did not constitute a reasonable excuse. *JP Sim & Co, EDN/87/78 (VTD 2543)*.

18.371   Similar decisions were reached in *DVK Executive Hotels, LON/90/68X (VTD 4786)* and *AD High & Sons Ltd, LON/95/1306 (VTD 13399)*.

18.372   **Temporary insufficiency of funds.**   See *Palco Industry Co Ltd*, 18.408 below.

18.373   **Cash-flow problems attributed to absence of financial controller on holiday.**   See *Picken & Son Ltd*, 18.220 above.

18.374   **Cash-flow problems following loss of credit controller.**   A company's credit controller gave one month's notice on 6 June 1991, and left her employment on 6 July 1991. Following her departure, the company's cash-flow deteriorated, and the company was unable to pay its liability for the periods ending 31 July and 31 October by the due date. The Commissioners accepted that there was a reasonable excuse for the non-payment of the tax for the period ending 31 July, but imposed a surcharge in respect of the following period. The tribunal dismissed the company's appeal, holding that the circumstances did not constitute a reasonable excuse. *Q-Com Maintenance Ltd, MAN/92/1834 (VTD 12918)*.

18.375   **Cash-flow problems attributed to divorce.**   An accountant appealed against two default surcharges, contending that he had a reasonable excuse for non-payment since his wife had left him and he had suffered cash-flow problems as a result of the divorce settlement. The tribunal dismissed his appeal, holding that this did not constitute a reasonable excuse. *MS Ramsey, LON/95/2783 (VTD 14280)*.

18.376   **Other cases.**   There have been a very large number of other cases in which appellants have contended that they could not pay the tax due because of cash-flow problems, and in which the appeals have been dismissed. In the interests of space, such cases are not reported individually in this book.

Cheque dishonoured or incorrectly made out

Cases where the appellant was successful

18.377   **Cheque wrongly dishonoured by bank.**   A company paid its quarterly liability by a cheque drawn on the Royal Bank of Scotland. The bank failed to honour the cheque. The company protested to the bank, which apologised and confirmed that the cheque should have been met, but had been dishonoured through a 'clerical error'. The company subsequently paid the VAT with a banker's draft, but this was not sent until after the due date and the Commissioners imposed a default surcharge. The tribunal allowed the company's appeal, holding that the bank's error constituted a reasonable excuse for the late payment. *Hydrabell Ltd, LON/88/1256 (VTD 3519)*.

18.378   Similar decisions have been reached in a considerable number of subsequent cases. in the interests of space, such cases are not summarised individually in this book. For a list of such cases reported up to 31 December 1996, see Tolley's VAT Cases 1997.

18.379   An appeal was allowed in a case where a bank had failed to honour an agreement that it would telephone a company before dishonouring a cheque in payment of VAT. *Speedy Products Ltd, MAN/91/406 (VTD 6754)*.

18.380   Similar decisions were reached in *KCS Management Systems, LON/91/2703 (VTD 9013)* and *A Boon (t/a Allan Boon Haulage), LON/92/2257P (VTD 9952)*.

18.381 Default Surcharge

18.381 A similar decision was reached in a case where a bank dishonoured a cheque although the company in question had adequate funds in another account, and the bank had previously checked the state of the other account before dishonouring a cheque. (There was, however, held to be no reasonable excuse for other defaults.) *Around the Clock Ltd, LON/91/1304Y (VTD 7157)*.

18.382 Similar decisions were reached in *Bowden Associates Ltd, MAN/91/133 (VTD 7449)*; *JMG Gregory, LON/92/738Y (VTD 7979)*; *Mikelyjos Process Automation Ltd, LON/93/894 (VTD 11305)*; *WGM Decorating, LON/93/2850P (VTD 12401)*; *Computer Technology Solutions Ltd, LON/94/1007 (VTD 12721)* and *Purite Ltd, LON/99/84 (VTD 16161)*.

18.383 An appeal was allowed in a case where a bank had returned a cheque to the Commissioners endorsed 'signature differs', and the company's managing director gave evidence that he had signed the cheque and was an authorised signatory. *Kirkcroft Skips Ltd, MAN/91/1226 (VTD 7560)*.

18.384 An appeal was allowed in a case where the appellant had paid sufficient funds into his account two days before the Commissioners presented his cheque, but the bank had dishonoured the cheque and returned it endorsed 'effects uncleared'. *AL Evans, MAN/91/1498 (VTD 7639)*.

18.385 Similar decisions were reached in *Awnhail Ltd, MAN/93/911 (VTD 11465)*; *MD McDonald, MAN/93/655 (VTD 12153)* and *AJ Buthwick, LON/94/1300P (VTD 12782)*.

18.386 An appeal was allowed in a case where a bank cashier had failed to process a cheque which had been submitted for payment by bank giro. The tribunal held that the cashier's error constituted a reasonable excuse and that the restriction in *VATA 1994, s 71(1)(b)* did not apply. *Isis Specialist Office Supplies Ltd, LON/95/987 (VTD 13389)*.

18.387 **Bank returning cheque unpaid endorsed 'refer to drawer please represent'.** A partnership's cheque was dishonoured by its bank, being returned endorsed 'refer to drawer please represent'. The Commissioners imposed a default surcharge and the partnership appealed, contending that the cheque would have been honoured if it had been represented, and producing a letter from the bank to confirm this. The tribunal allowed the appeal, finding on the evidence that the bank would have honoured the cheque if it had known that the Commissioners adopted a policy of not representing cheques, and holding that the circumstances constituted a reasonable excuse. *M Simpson & G Scoffin, MAN/91/1130 (VTD 7390)*. (*Notes.* (1) For the Commissioners' policy in not representing cheques which have been dishonoured, see *VAT Notes No. 2 (1991)*. (2) No other cases were referred to in the decision. Compare *Palco Industry Co Ltd*, 18.408 below, *Walsh*, 18.411 below, and the cases noted at 18.412 and 18.413 below.)

18.388 **Commissioners delaying presentation of cheque—company wrongly assuming cheque had gone astray and cancelling original cheque—whether a reasonable excuse.** A company delivered its return and cheque for the period ending 31 March 1991 to its local VAT office by hand on 30 April. In mid-May the company received an estimated assessment for the relevant period, with a covering letter stating that its return and payment had not been received. The company's director assumed that the cheque had been lost in transit. He therefore cancelled the original cheque and issued a replacement. In the meantime, the Commissioners belatedly presented the original cheque, which was returned unpaid by the company's bank. The Commissioners imposed a default surcharge but the tribunal allowed the company's appeal. In assuming that the original cheque had been lost in transit, and consequently cancelling it, the company had not acted unreasonably and there was no justification for a penalty being imposed. *Shearer Holdings Ltd, EDN/91/214 (VTD 7088)*.

18.389 **Cheque delayed in post and dishonoured when belatedly presented.** A company sent its quarterly VAT payment on 27 April 1988. It was delayed in the post and the cheque was dishonoured when it was belatedly presented. The tribunal accepted evidence that the cheque would have been honoured if it had been presented before 1 May, and held that the delay in presentation constituted a reasonable excuse. *Elmcrown Hotels Ltd, LON/88/278 (VTD 3595)*. (*Note*. Compare the QB decision in *Palco Industry Co Ltd*, 18.408 below.)

18.390 A company submitted a return shortly before moving its bank account from Barclays to National Westminster. The return was delayed in the post and the cheque which accompanied it was not presented until after the closure of the Barclays account. In the meantime Barclays had already returned a number of cheques, unpaid, to the company instead of forwarding them to National Westminster in accordance with normal banking practice. When the director realised that the return had been delayed, he personally gave a cheque drawn on the National Westminster account to a VAT officer. The tribunal held that the circumstances constituted a reasonable excuse. *Artic Shield Ltd, MAN/89/248 (VTD 3789)*.

18.391 A similar decision was reached in another unrelated case where a company's accountant had submitted a return while in the process of transferring the relevant bank account from Barclays to National Westminster. Although there were adequate funds in the account for the cheque to be cleared, Barclays dishonoured the cheque instead of forwarding it to National Westminster in accordance with normal banking practice. The tribunal allowed the company's appeal, holding that the circumstances constituted a reasonable excuse. *Donnison & Smith Engineering Ltd, MAN/90/770 (VTD 5651)*.

18.392 A similar decision was reached in *Jardin Trim Ltd, LON/92/288 (VTD 7695)*.

18.393 **Cheques previously represented by Commissioners.** A company's cheque for the period ending 31 March 1991 was returned unpaid by its bank, endorsed 'refer to drawer—please represent'. However, the Commissioners did not represent the cheque, and imposed a default surcharge. The company appealed, contending that the cheque would have been honoured on representation, and that its cheque for the period ending 30 September 1990 had been similarly dishonoured when first presented but had subsequently been represented and honoured without a surcharge being imposed. The company's accountant referred the tribunal to a statement by Customs Press Office, reproduced in *Tolley's Practical Tax 1986* at p 120, which stated that 'provided that a cheque, which is subsequently honoured, is received by the Commissioners on or before the due date, a default will not be recorded'. The tribunal allowed the appeal. The company was clearly in default and its insufficiency of funds could not constitute a reasonable excuse. However, the fact that the Commissioners had previously represented dishonoured cheques, and had publicly stated that they would do so without imposing surcharges, and had not advised the company of their change of policy, meant that the company had a reasonable excuse for its late payment. *Professional Testing Services Ltd, EDN/91/166 (VTD 6689)*. (*Notes*. (1) Compare *Palco Industry Ltd*, 18.408 below; *Walsh*, 18.411 below, and the cases noted at 18.413 below. (2) For the Commissioners' policy in no longer representing cheques which have previously been dishonoured, see *VAT Notes No. 2 (1991)*, issued in July 1991.)

18.394 *Professional Testing Services Ltd*, 18.393 above, was applied in the similar case of *Cleshar Contract Services Ltd, LON/91/1066 (VTD 7621)*.

18.395 Default Surcharge

18.395   **Cheque accidentally postdated.**   In a case where a cheque was inadvertently dated 31 November 1988 rather than 31 October 1988, the tribunal held that this error was a reasonable excuse, applying *Corton Bashforth Screenprint Ltd*, 18.397 below, and distinguishing *Dabchicks Sailing Club*, 18.414 below. *Holland Studio Craft Ltd, MAN/89/34 (VTD 3771)*.

18.396   The accidental postdating of a cheque was also held to constitute a reasonable excuse in *Jackson & Padgett Ltd, MAN/88/795 (VTD 3435); Robinson Cooke, LON/88/806Y (VTD 4040); SP Caswell, LON/89/1172X (VTD 4176); JCB Electronics Ltd, LON/89/1360Y (VTD 5004); SA Gee, MAN/90/832 (VTD 5656); AK Masson, LON/91/1298Z (VTD 6542); B Short, MAN/91/769 (VTD 6694); DL Powell, LON/92/447Z (VTD 7933); LV Turner, MAN/94/777 (VTD 12839)* and *GH Poole (t/a Glenwood Polishing & Manufacturing 1992), MAN/99/573 (VTD 16339)*.

18.397   **Cheque out of date.**   An appeal was allowed in a case where a company had inadvertently dated a cheque 1986 instead of 1988. *Corton Bashforth Screenprint Ltd, MAN/88/491 (VTD 3232)*.

18.398   Similar decisions were reached in *Alsuna Ltd, MAN/89/278 (VTD 3845); RA & E Hodgson, MAN/90/92 (VTD 5052); Singh & Choudry, LON/92/201 (VTD 7654); J Austin, LON/91/1442X (VTD 7668)* and *Guy Engraving & Engineering Co, LON/92/2003P (VTD 9337)*.

18.399   **Cheque not signed in accordance with bank mandate.**   An appeal was allowed in a case where a company had submitted a cheque signed by two signatories who were not directors, but had overlooked the fact that, as the cheque was for more than £2,000, it should have been signed by a director in accordance with the bank mandate. *Swanlion Ltd, MAN/88/341 (VTD 3399)*. (*Note*. Compare the cases noted at 18.418 to 18.420 below, where similar circumstances were held not to constitute a reasonable excuse.)

18.400   An appeal was allowed in a case where a company had submitted a cheque signed by only one director, when its bank mandate required the signature of two directors, and gave evidence that the omission was accidental. *Green Cook Ltd, LON/90/1749X (VTD 5781)*.

18.401   A similar decision was reached in *Megatron Ltd, LON/92/1369 (VTD 9207)*.

18.402   **Alteration to cheque not initialled.**   A trader submitted a VAT return with a cheque on which the date had been altered in manuscript, but the alteration had not been initialled. (The alteration in question amended the date by one calendar month, and the cheque had not been postdated.) The bank did not honour the cheque but returned it unpaid, endorsed 'alteration required drawer's signature'. The Commissioners imposed a default surcharge, and the trader appealed. The tribunal allowed the appeal, holding, following a dictum in *Halsbury's Laws of England vol. 3(1) para 180*, that it was unreasonable for the bank not have honoured the cheque, since the cheque was neither postdated nor out of date, regardless of whether the original date or the altered date was taken as the date of issue. *C Rees, LON/89/734 (VTD 4440)*.

18.403   A similar decision was reached in a case where the date on a cheque had been altered from 1931 to 1991, and the alteration had not been initialled. The tribunal commented that the bank were 'not justified' in failing to honour the cheque. *Party Paragon The Shop Ltd, LON/91/1886 (VTD 7242)*.

18.404 An appeal was allowed in a case where the appellant had failed to initial an alteration to a cheque, and the Commissioners had returned the cheque to him for amendment without presenting it. *R Smallman, LON/93/1990 (VTD 11538)*.

18.405 A similar decision was reached in *Dellastreet Systems Ltd, MAN/92/330 (VTD 11965)*.

18.406 **Cheque submitted for incorrect amount.** The tribunal allowed an appeal against a default surcharge in a case where a firm had sent a cheque in the sum of £6,322.22 in respect of a payment due, as shown on the return, of £6,332.22. *Shirlaw Allan & Co, EDN/87/111 (VTD 2596)*.

18.407 Similar decisions were reached in *RS Wainwright, BEL/88/14 (VTD 3150); AG Hill, MAN/89/276 (VTD 3809); Dixons, LON/89/802Z (VTD 4053); Deepblue Ltd, LON/89/448Y (VTD 4126); Nightingale Music Ltd, LON/90/630X (VTD 5060)* and *Lysander Systems Ltd, LON/95/222P (VTD 13672)*.

Cases where the appellant was unsuccessful

18.408 **Cheque delayed in post.** A company (P), which had an overdraft facility of £1 million, posted its return for the period ending 31 October 1988 by recorded delivery on 28 November. A cheque for the tax due was sent with the return. The return was not delivered until 7 December. However, because the cheque was for more than £10,000, it was presented by the Commissioners on the day of receipt. The cheque was dishonoured and a default surcharge was imposed. The company appealed, contending that the cheque would have been cleared if it had been delivered promptly by the Post Office. The QB upheld the surcharge, holding that it was the responsibility of the drawer of a cheque to ensure that there were adequate funds available to meet that cheque. A cheque was only valid as payment if it was honoured on due presentation, which did not require immediate presentation or presentation on some precisely calculated day. A payer could not dictate when a cheque was to be paid. What is now *VATA 1994, s 71(1)(a)* specifically excluded an 'insufficiency of funds' as a reasonable excuse for the failure to pay any tax due. The despatch of a worthless cheque could not amount to the despatch of tax. *C & E Commrs v Palco Industry Co Ltd, QB [1990] STC 594*.

18.409 *Palco Industry Co Ltd, 18.408 above*, was applied in the similar cases of *SJ Sloan, MAN/90/802 (VTD 5641); Apollo Security Services plc, LON/90/1636Y (VTD 5830); A Harris, LON/91/409Y (VTD 6065); Realmead Ltd, LON/90/1205 (VTD 6168); Pollards Motorway Services Ltd, MAN/91/190 (VTD 6392); N Vyas, MAN/90/720 (VTD 6424); FAS Young, MAN/91/538 (VTD 6425); Bob Sparshott Engineering Ltd, LON/91/1280Y (VTD 6585); Adam Removals Ltd, LON/91/1276Y (VTD 6586); KW Dove, LON/91/2722Z (VTD 7510); Floral Tubs Ltd, MAN/91/1110 (VTD 7540); Pneumatic Punchers Ltd, LON/91/2609Z (VTD 7812); DJ Wortley (t/a Mass Mitec), LON/91/2475Y (VTD 7851); DA Cunningham, LON/92/129X (VTD 7874); Target Design & Marketing Ltd, LON/92/185X (VTD 7910); RC Construction Ltd, LON/91/682 (VTD 7998); Associated Collection Services Ltd, LON/92/225 (VTD 8888); Trench Packaging Ltd, LON/92/1131 (VTD 9152); R Young (t/a Ray Young Associates), LON/92/1608P (VTD 9202); Mr & Mrs Robbins, LON/91/2705X (VTD 9364); Fereligh Ltd, LON/92/1890P (VTD 9398); PC Scholes, MAN/92/1508 (VTD 9762); Peter V Moore Dutton Ltd, MAN/92/962 (VTD 9924); Mr & Mrs GM McManus (t/a La Campagnola), MAN/92/919 (VTD 9933); TA Ratcliffe, MAN/92/956 (VTD 10016); DJ Wortley (t/a Mass Mitec), LON/92/950 (VTD 10377); Hire It (Southern) Ltd, LON/92/2964P (VTD 10461); Abba Consultants (Automation) Ltd, LON/93/397 (VTD 10666); Magright Ltd, LON/93/620P (VTD 10816); N*

Wilson (t/a Stamford Poste Hotel), LON/92/1411 (VTD 10902); Music Marketing Services Ltd, LON/93/1180P (VTD 11204); Southwest Telecoms Ltd, LON/93/1645 (VTD 11628); Cohort Specialist Security Services Ltd, MAN/93/1420 (VTD 12200); GRE & DJ Gregory, LON/92/2770A (VTD 12453); ASD Engineering Ltd, MAN/94/613 (VTD 12697); Concrete Restorations Ltd, LON/94/1304 (VTD 13035); A Murray (t/a Eccles Glass Co), MAN/95/1035 (VTD 13593) and *Enigma Industries Ltd, LON/96/495 (VTD 14477).*

18.410 Similar decisions were reached in *Air Link Transformers (Tordidal) Co Ltd, LON/88/1367 (VTD 3417); JG Hennigan, LON/89/823Y (VTD 4078); Banham Motor Co, LON/91/2382Y (VTD 7931); DW Jones, LON/91/1062 (VTD 9664); Aire Autos Ltd, MAN/93/226 (VTD 10571); Country Dairy Products Ltd, MAN/93/151 (VTD 10578)* and *B & AS Greenfield (t/a B & A Greenfield), LON/94/647 (VTD 12529).*

18.411 **Cheque not represented by Commissioners.** A trader's contention that a dishonoured cheque should have been represented by the Commissioners, since it might have been honoured if represented, was rejected by the tribunal in *JS Walsh, MAN/89/81 (VTD 3706).*

18.412 The decision in *Walsh*, 18.411 above, was applied in *Wiltshire & Gloucestershire Draining Co Ltd, LON/91/1102 (VTD 6559); Aztec Computer Products Ltd, LON/91/1753Y (VTD 7127); Lady Jane (London) Ltd, LON/91/2263Y (VTD 7143); Sophia Ltd, LON/91/1243Y (VTD 7261)* and *Valley Industrial Services Ltd, LON/91/2231Y (VTD 9302).*

18.413 Similar decisions were reached in *Marketing Tactics Ltd, MAN/89/405 (VTD 4190); Wilkinson Embroidery Ltd, MAN/89/579 (VTD 4606); WJ Higginson, BEL/89/24 (VTD 4938); Mills Dyers Ltd, MAN/91/837 (VTD 6714); Ellis & Perry (Ellesmere Port) Ltd, MAN/91/881 (VTD 6837); One Way Circuits Ltd, LON/91/1279Y (VTD 6879); LT Sargeant (t/a Barbara Collins Design Associates), LON/91/2268 (VTD 7243); Plaster Design Ltd, EDN/91/290 (VTD 7271); Ashley Management Conferences plc, LON/91/1736 (VTD 7349); ABC Graphics Ltd, LON/91/2576Z (VTD 7472); I Bruce, EDN/91/289 (VTD 7636); Mrs Westell, LON/92/18Y (VTD 8931); Hinkrose Ltd, MAN/91/1528 (VTD 8963); KD Anderson, MAN/92/29 (VTD 9196); HA Tipton (t/a Craven Construction Co), MAN/92/980 (VTD 9943); MW Coverson, MAN/92/747 (VTD 10025); Coote & Hall (Engineers) Ltd, MAN/93/122 (VTD 10447); AM Widdowson & Son Ltd, MAN/92/1486 (VTD 10450); Pertemps Ltd, MAN/93/33 (VTD 10538); M Ffransis, LON/92/247 (VTD 10716); The Soft Brick Co Ltd, MAN/92/1716 (VTD 10835); Ro-Rand Industries Ltd, MAN/92/548 (VTD 10976); Burke Edwards, MAN/93/645 (VTD 11036); G & G Ponton Ltd, EDN/93/101 (VTD 11231); Barford Hire Ltd, LON/93/1763P (VTD 11839); Durston Plant Contractors Ltd, LON/93/2230P (VTD 12402)* and *Kinghorn Mee, EDN/94/83 (VTD 13297).*

18.414 **Cheque accidentally postdated.** The submission of an accidentally postdated cheque was held not to constitute a reasonable excuse in *Reddish Electronics Ltd, MAN/88/452 (VTD 3210); Sanam, MAN/88/570 (VTD 3215); Dabchicks Sailing Club, LON/88/954 (VTD 3309); GJ, G & C Schofield, MAN/88/775 (VTD 3521); Spool Ltd, MAN/89/283 (VTD 3787); Overland Contracts (Holdings) Ltd, MAN/89/194 (VTD 3794); Overland Transport Services Ltd, MAN/89/254 (VTD 4004); SBM Warehouses Ltd, LON/89/548X (VTD 4006); JH Smith, LON/89/743Y (VTD 4038); Goldbeat Ltd, MAN/89/521 (VTD 4265); Heavy Goods Vehicle Enterprises Ltd, MAN/89/519 (VTD 4332); William M Smith (Decorators) Ltd, MAN/89/742 (VTD 4396, 4639); PG Hawkins & Sons Ltd, LON/89/1301Y (VTD 4571); CW Winter, LON/89/1252Z (VTD 4602); Padgbury Lane Service*

Station Ltd, MAN/89/969 (VTD 4633); PG Shorrock, MAN/89/413 (VTD 4729); Shutter Door Fixers Ltd, LON/89/1628X (VTD 4775); KR Lodge, LON/90/73Y (VTD 4792); Gentlesound Ltd, LON/89/1822Y (VTD 4797); Tottenham Liberal & Radical Club, LON/89/1857Z (VTD 4827); Evertex Ltd, MAN/90/118 (VTD 4891); JR Rafferty, LON/89/500X (VTD 4982); Power Precision Ltd, EDN/90/93 (VTD 5127); After Hours Cleaning Co Ltd, MAN/89/760 (VTD 5237); R Wilson, MAN/90/491 (VTD 5263); C & H Binding, LON/90/1195Z (VTD 5470); Reldan Ltd, LON/90/1230X (VTD 5516); Manor Packaging, MAN/90/779 (VTD 5681); P Bayley (t/a Applied Cutting Technology), LON/90/1331 (VTD 5832); Nimrod Services (Electronics) Ltd, LON/90/416Z (VTD 5848); Lion Structural Engineers Ltd, EDN/91/21 (VTD 5859); Elletson Properties Ltd, MAN/90/404 (VTD 5878); Matchpoint Photo Litho Ltd, MAN/91/72 (VTD 6088); Colchester Lister Associates Ltd, LON/91/1179 (VTD 6371); Multi-Site Services, LON/91/866 (VTD 6472); B Moore, LON/91/769Y (VTD 6584); Smith Earl Associates Ltd, LON/91/1345 (VTD 6700); Albion (Norfolk) Ltd, LON/91/1603 (VTD 7005); Peter Martyn Property Group Ltd, LON/91/122 (VTD 7125); Staycare Ltd, LON/91/1334Y (VTD 7386); TR Noakes & AS Peplow (t/a Teepee Art & Design), LON/92/541X (VTD 7613); Centre 365 Ltd, LON/92/251Y (VTD 7868); AC Causton Ltd, LON/91/2097Z (VTD 7869); PM Jones-Davies, MAN/92/469 (VTD 9002); J Trechman (t/a Kenrick Translation Services), LON/92/2068P (VTD 9825); RS Bright (t/a R Bright Transport), MAN/92/542 (VTD 9946); GWC Tanner, LON/92/2640P (VTD 10042); Thomas M Devon & Co Ltd, EDN/93/8 (VTD 10407); Sigma Engraving, LON/93/2735P (VTD 12084); Ipswich Gardening Services Ltd, LON/93/2277P (VTD 12192); RJ Howard, LON/94/1316P (VTD 12847); Lotmod Ltd (t/a Natterjacks), LON/95/2059P (VTD 13689) and *L Thompson, MAN/96/862 (VTD 14795).*

18.415   **Cheque out of date.** A company submitted a cheque dated 1989 instead of 1990. The cheque was not honoured by its bank and a default surcharge was imposed. The tribunal dismissed the company's appeal, holding that the circumstances did not constitute a reasonable excuse. *CBR System Ltd, LON/90/1905Y (VTD 5871).*

18.416   Similar decisions were reached in *Lois Engineering Ltd, MAN/91/783 (VTD 7327); Selmar Burglar Alarms Co Ltd, LON/92/347Y (VTD 7740); Eglington DIY Ltd, BEL/92/56 (VTD 9858); Pedersen Caterers, LON/93/193P & 523P (VTD 10818); JE Hill, MAN/93/83 (VTD 10967); Cambridge Connectivity Ltd, LON/94/1694P (VTD 13046)* and *Fourth Road Consultants Ltd, EDN/95/22 (VTD 13626).*

18.417   **Unsigned cheque.** There have been a very large number of cases in which the tribunal has held that the accidental failure to sign the cheque tendered in payment of the VAT due does not constitute a reasonable excuse for non-payment. In the interests of space, such cases are not reported individually in this book. For a list of such cases decided up to 31 December 1994, see Tolley's VAT Cases 1995.

18.418   **Cheque not signed in accordance with bank mandate.** A company submitted a cheque for its quarterly VAT payment with only one signature, although its bank mandate required two signatures. The bank did not honour the cheque and the tribunal held that the oversight did not constitute a reasonable excuse. *Hamperbay Ltd, LON/88/547 (VTD 3048).*

18.419   *Hamperbay Ltd,* 18.418 above, was applied in *Readon Holdings Ltd, MAN/89/183 (VTD 3705).*

18.420   Similar decisions were reached in *Fairview Windows Ltd, MAN/88/788 (VTD 3619); Sign Specialists Ltd, MAN/89/681 (VTD 4477); Wardhire Ltd, LON/90/136Y (VTD 5622); Freeway Marketing Ltd, LON/90/1751Y (VTD 5905); The Cloth Development Co Ltd, LON/90/1854Z (VTD 5985); J & S Glass Mirror Centre,*

18.421   Default Surcharge

LON/91/64Y (VTD 6117); Graphicad Ltd, MAN/91/228 (VTD 6503); Bardon Environmental Services Ltd, MAN/91/651 (VTD 6504); Portswood Haulage Contractors, LON/91/965X (VTD 6556); A Sinclair (t/a The Magpie Bar), EDN/91/98 (VTD 6589); P Hodgkiss, EDN/91/144 (VTD 6825); Quality Embryo Transfer Co Ltd, MAN/91/324 (VTD 7538); LWM Alexander Oliver Bennett Partnership, EDN/92/151 (VTD 9153); Thousand Yard Store, LON/93/1676P (VTD 12006); Brainstormers Web Factory Ltd, LON/98/730 (VTD 15761); Merriman White, LON/97/516 & LON/98/1449 (VTD 16045) and *Excel Shopfitting Ltd, LON/98/1265 (VTD 16270).*

18.421   **Alterations to cheque not initialled.**   A company's cheque was dishonoured by its bank because the date on the cheque had been altered but the alteration had not been initialled. The tribunal held that the failure to initial the alteration was not a reasonable excuse. *KBC Tent & Marquee Hire Ltd, MAN/90/26 (VTD 4765).*

18.422   Similar decisions were reached in *Applied Cutting Technology, LON/91/1138Z (VTD 6489)* and *R & R Herman (t/a Retell), LON/99/241 (VTD 16591).*

18.423   **Words and figures on cheque differing.**   An appeal was dismissed in a case where a trader had submitted a cheque on which the amount shown in words differed from that shown in figures, and the VAT Central Unit returned the cheque to the trader for amendment without presenting it. *PA Delaney, LON/91/438Y (VTD 6105). (Note.* For the validity of such a cheque, see *Covercraft Ltd,* 18.28 above, and *Mather,* 18.29 above. Neither of these cases were referred to in the decision.)

18.424   Similar decisions were reached in *Magpie Court Ltd, LON/91/473Z (VTD 6166); MM Chea, LON/91/1127Y (VTD 6357); RG Crabb, LON/91/1546Y (VTD 9091); DP Stephenson (t/a Sutton Chauffeuring), MAN/92/527 (VTD 9914); CW Aberdeen (t/a Smithfield Electronics), MAN/91/801 & MAN/92/1437 (VTD 9944)* and *Rebel Fashions, MAN/97/112 (VTD 15057).*

18.425   **Cheque made out for incorrect amount.**   An appeal was dismissed in a case where the company had submitted a cheque for a lesser amount than the liability shown on its return, and contended that the error was accidental. *A Williams & Son, LON/89/801Z (VTD 4191).*

18.426   Similar decisions were reached in *Nature's Larder, EDN/90/44 (VTD 4856); WA Lawson, LON/90/506X (VTD 5823); Anglian Farming Contracts Ltd, LON/92/635X (VTD 7928)* and *NB McMahon, LON/94/1306P (VTD 12904).*

Misleading advice from Customs

Cases where the appellant was successful

18.427   **Telephone conversation with VAT office.**   A company had obtained permission from the Commissioners to submit returns covering twelve-week periods rather than quarterly periods. It was sent a return covering a period from 15 August 1987 to 7 November 1987. The due date for this return was stated on the return form to be 7 December 1987. However, one of the company's directors telephoned the Halifax VAT office and was informed by that office that the due date was 31 December 1987. The return was actually sent on 29 December and received on 31 December. The Commissioners imposed a default surcharge, but the tribunal allowed the company's appeal. The date by which the return was legally due remained 7 December 1987, as stated on the return form. However, the Halifax VAT office had incorrectly informed the company that the due date was 31 December, and the company therefore had a reasonable excuse for believing that that was the due date. *ASJ Manufacturing Ltd, MAN/88/156 (VTD 2832).*

18.428   Similar decisions were reached in *Wallace King plc, LON/91/566Z (VTD 6498); Lycett Industries Ltd, MAN/91/1563 (VTD 11672)* and *Martin Groundland & Co Ltd, EDN/98/82 (VTD 15696)*.

18.429   A company did not have sufficient funds to pay its VAT liability for the period ending 30 April 1988. Its managing director telephoned the local VAT office in mid-May and asked whether it would be acceptable to pay by three postdated cheques, the last cheque to be dated 21 June. The conversation that followed was disputed, but the tribunal found that the VAT officer who took the call had led the director to believe that the submission of such cheques would be acceptable. Accordingly the circumstances constituted a reasonable excuse. *Harley Engineering Ltd, LON/88/768 (VTD 3271)*.

18.430   Similar decisions were reached in *Archway (Shoes) Ltd, LON/89/1147Y (VTD 4250); Slee Blackwell Solicitors, LON/91/1312Z (VTD 7263); A Better Choice Ltd, LON/92/1501P (VTD 9048); EJ Scarlett (t/a Spectrum Building Services), LON/92/2173P (VTD 9618); Mo's Music Machine Ltd, LON/92/2843 (VTD 10032); Wentworth Sawmills Ltd, MAN/92/640 (VTD 10105); A Erskine Electrical Co Ltd, MAN/92/1536 (VTD 10139); Unique Sealed Units Ltd, LON/92/2904 (VTD 10235); Vitalia Ltd, LON/93/1900P (VTD 11682); EAP Ltd, LON/93/2193P (VTD 12089)* and *Dawson Strange Photography Ltd, LON/98/1411 (VTD 15967)*.

18.431   A company which was suffering cash-flow problems did not send its payment for the period ending 31 March 1999 until 30 April. The Commissioners imposed a surcharge but the tribunal allowed the company's appeal, finding that a VAT officer had agreed to allow the late payment in a telephone conversation with the company's accountants. *Gray Dunn & Co Ltd, EDN/00/71 (VTD 16839)*.

18.432   A video producer had arranged to be abroad on business from 15 January 1991 to 2 March 1991. In December 1990 she telephoned her local VAT office to ask whether she could delay her return for the period ending 31 January 1991 until after she returned to the UK. The officer to whom she spoke asked her to write to the office with details. She wrote to the office on 3 January, stating that she would submit the return as soon as possible after 2 March. She received no reply, and a default surcharge was imposed, against which she appealed. The tribunal allowed her appeal, holding that, when she telephoned her local VAT office, she should have been advised to submit an estimated return. She had been given misleading advice by the VAT office and, in view of this, her absence abroad constituted a reasonable excuse. *SG Flinders, LON/91/1022X (VTD 6349)*.

18.433   **Misleading advice by VAT officer.**   A company appealed against a default surcharge, contending that its managing director had been informed by a VAT officer that so long as the return was submitted by the due date, the company would not be surcharged even if the tax was paid late. The officer in question, an executive officer at the local VAT office, stated in evidence that he 'did not use the words "default surcharge" because they were things I was not certain about. I did not know for certain how the surcharge system worked so I did not mention it specifically'. The tribunal chairman commented that it seemed 'strange that a VAT inspector, visiting a trader to discuss a late return, however inexperienced, should be uncertain of the default surcharge system'. On the evidence, the company had clearly been misled by the VAT officer and had therefore established a reasonable excuse for its non-payment of the tax. *Trendadd Ltd, LON/88/479 (VTD 3222)*.

18.434   Misleading advice by a VAT officer was also held to constitute a reasonable excuse in *RA Dentith v The Treasury of the Isle of Man Government (VTD 4272); Business Post Holdings Ltd, LON/89/879 & LON/90/69Y (VTD 5002); TJD Garrard, LON/90/1061Y (VTD 5447); PDS (Gold Plating) Co Ltd, LON/90/328Z (VTD 5468);*

18.435   Default Surcharge

PJ Woods, MAN/91/202 (VTD 6134); ASI Glass Processing Ltd, MAN/94/441 (VTD 12631); TM Technology Ltd, MAN/96/480 (VTD 14509); Hannah Auto Electronics Ltd, EDN/97/231 (VTD 15429) and *Clifford Construction Ltd*, 18.23 above.

18.435   An appeal was allowed in a case where a VAT officer had agreed to accept payment of a partnership's quarterly liability by instalments, and had not informed the partnership that this agreement would not prevent a default surcharge from being imposed. The tribunal held that the circumstances constituted a reasonable excuse for the late payment. *Andrews Kent & Stone, LON/92/309X (VTD 7753)*.

18.436   Similar decisions were reached in *T Cooper-Cocks, LON/92/1380 (VTD 9062); Qubit UK Ltd, LON/92/1685 & 1847 (VTD 9073); K Coombes, LON/92/1068Y (VTD 9417); Key Personnel (Midlands) Ltd, MAN/92/668 (VTD 9833)* and *CDN Property Services Ltd, LON/94/301 (VTD 12275)*.

18.437   In the March 1991 Budget, the Chancellor of the Exchequer announced that the standard rate of VAT would be increased from 15% to 17½% with effect from 1 April 1991. A partnership which supplied windows had already taken a large number of provisional orders, in respect of which it had quoted prices on the basis that the rate of VAT would be 15%. It consulted the Balham VAT office as to the effect of the change, and was told that it must charge VAT at 17½% unless the tax point was before 1 April. In order to create a tax point before the increase in the rate, it issued invoices in respect of these provisional orders dated March 1991. Because of the increased work which this caused, its return for the period ending 31 March was not submitted until after the due date, and a default surcharge was imposed. The partnership appealed, contending that the increased workload constituted a reasonable excuse. The tribunal accepted this contention and allowed the appeal, observing that the Balham VAT office should have informed the partnership of the effect of what is now *VATA 1994, s 89*, under which VAT could have been charged at 15% in respect of contracts made before 1 April, even if the tax point was not until 1 April. *Brytahomes Window Company, LON/91/1599X (VTD 9379)*.

18.438   **Misunderstanding between appellant and VAT officer.**   An appeal was allowed in a case where the appellant contended that he had been given permission by a VAT officer to delay payment until the following period. The tribunal accepted his evidence in respect of the conversation that had taken place between him and the officer. The Commissioners could 'otherwise allow or direct', within what is now *VAT Regulations 1995 (SI 1995 No 2518), reg 40(3)*, for payment of tax and submission of returns at a time different from that laid down by *SI 1995 No 2518, reg 25*. It appeared that the officer was not authorised to make such a concession, but the conversation had given the appellant the impression that additional time had been granted, and the circumstances therefore constituted a reasonable excuse. *D Caro, MAN/88/34 (VTD 3284)*.

18.439   Similar decisions were reached in *Q & B Motor Accessories Ltd, LON/91/83Z (VTD 6037); AT Healan, LON/92/1565P (VTD 9351); Birchall Blackburn, MAN/91/1444 (VTD 9547); Green Business Co Ltd, LON/93/196P & 197P (VTD 10523); Ollerton Hotel (Kirkcaldy) Ltd, EDN/92/269 (VTD 10530)* and *MJ Shanahan (t/a MJS Haulage), LON/94/279 (VTD 12634)*.

18.440   In a case where the facts were similar, the tribunal held that a VAT officer, who had agreed to accept payment of a company's VAT liability by 25 April rather than 31 March, had effectively allowed an extension of the due date under *VAT Regulations 1995 (SI 1995 No 2518), reg 40(3)*. *Starlite (Chandeliers) Ltd, [1999] VATDR 313 (VTD 16188)*.

18.441   A company had failed to submit returns for the three quarters ending 31 March 1986, although it had submitted subsequent returns. A VAT officer made a control visit in July 1988 and agreed to collect the outstanding returns a month later. Following the visit, the company did not submit its return for the quarter ending 30 June 1988, but gave it to the VAT officer on 23 August with the earlier returns. A surcharge was subsequently imposed and the company appealed, contending that it had a reasonable excuse because its director had believed that the agreement for collection of the earlier returns also applied to the current return. The tribunal found that there had been a genuine misunderstanding and allowed the company's appeal. *Interior Design & Construction Ltd, LON/89/192Y (VTD 3484)*.

18.442   A similar decision was reached in *Secure Areas Ltd, MAN/91/1006 (VTD 7969)*.

18.443   **Surcharge liability notice—whether misleading.**   A trader had submitted three repayment returns late. An estimated default surcharge had been issued, but had been cancelled following receipt of the returns. Subsequently the trader submitted a further return, showing a tax liability, after the due date. A surcharge was imposed at the rate of 15%. The trader appealed, contending that the cancellation of the previous surcharges was equivalent to their annulment and that the surcharge should be at the rate of 5% applicable to a first default. The tribunal held that the 15% was correct and in accordance with the terms of what is now *VATA 1994, s 59*. However, the tribunal also held that the wording of the surcharge liability notice issued by the Commissioners was ambiguous, since it could lead a reader to believe that a surcharge liability period expired on the final date indicated, whereas in law the period included the return for the period ending on the date in question. In view of the wording of the notice, the appellant had a reasonable excuse for considering that the notice did not cover the period for which he eventually defaulted. Accordingly, the tribunal allowed the appeal. *DN Nixdorf, MAN/89/517 (VTD 4276)*.

18.444   A similar decision was reached in *Columbia Veneering Co Ltd, LON/90/1843Y (VTD 5907)*.

18.445   See also *Montreux Fabrics Ltd*, 18.4 above, and *Coleman Machines Ltd*, 18.7 above, where misleading surcharge liability notices were held to be invalid.

18.446   **Notice No 700—whether misleading.**   An appeal was allowed in a case where the tribunal held that a passage in *Notice No 700* was misleading and could lead a trader to believe that repayment returns would not be taken into account for default surcharge purposes. The passage in question afforded a reasonable excuse. *Dicta* in *HTV v Price Commission, CA [1976] ICR 170* and *R v CIR (ex p. Preston), HL [1985] STC 282 (TTC 2001, 31.14)*, applied. *B Giddy, LON/90/37 (4710)*. (*Note*. The passage in question has now been omitted. This decision was distinguished in *Karl Joh (UK) Ltd*, 18.452 below.)

18.447   **Misleading letter from local VAT office.**   A partnership elected to pay its VAT liabilities by credit transfer. It had received a letter signed by a senior VAT officer, stating that 'if you do elect to pay via a credit transfer system the Commissioners will allow you a further 7 days in which to pay the tax due and furnish the VAT return'. It paid its liability for the quarter ending 31 January 1989 by a bank giro credit dated 6 March, and its liability for the quarter ending 31 July by a bank giro credit dated 7 August. The Commissioners imposed a default surcharge and the partnership appealed, contending that the payments had been made within the time limit as extended by the letter from the VAT officer. The tribunal found that the partners had misunderstood the terms of the officer's letter. The VAT return explicitly stated that taxpayers must ensure that returns and payments were received by the due date, and this advice was repeated in the *VAT Guide*. It was not sufficient to submit a return or a payment on the due date; returns and payments must be submitted in time to arrive on or before the due date. However, as the officer's letter was not clear on this matter, and as the Commissioners had not informed the partnership that its practice was incorrect until October 1989, seven months after the first default, the partners had a reasonable excuse for their incorrect belief that their system of making payments on the final or penultimate day satisfied the Commissioners. *Barney & Freeman, [1990] VATTR 119 (VTD 4849)*. (*Note.* The decision here has not been followed in subsequent cases, and therefore appears to be of doubtful value as a precedent. A subsequent tribunal specifically declined to follow it in *Wingate Electrical plc*, 18.501 below. In *Slough Motor Co*, 18.500 below, the tribunal held that a 'reasonable competent businessman using the bank giro credit system and seeking to effect payment within a shorter period than two days should make sure that this is possible under the particular banking procedures used by him'. See also *Paragon Business Products Ltd*, 18.454 below, and the cases noted at 18.503 below.)

18.448   A similar decision was reached in *WG Beynon & Sons Ltd, LON/92/2368P (VTD 10043)*.

18.449   An appeal was allowed in a subsequent case where the tribunal held that a letter from a VAT office had been misleading, and had given the recipient company the incorrect impression that its VAT liability could be paid by direct debit. *Stream International Ltd, EDN/97/164 (VTD 15602)*.

18.450   A trader had fallen into arrears with his VAT liability. He visited the Coventry VAT office to ascertain how much he owed, and was told that he owed £1,222, which he paid. Two weeks later he received a letter from the VAT office, not referring to his visit, and informing him that he owed £817. He formed the opinion that his payment of £1,222 had not been taken into account, and that he had overpaid £405. He therefore withheld this amount from his next payment, and the Commissioners imposed a default surcharge. The tribunal allowed his appeal, finding that the letter sent to him by the VAT office had been incorrect and had misled the trader into believing that he had overpaid, and holding that this constituted a reasonable excuse. *RM Kelly, MAN/93/553 (VTD 11347)*.

Cases where the appellant was unsuccessful

18.451   **Notice of security—whether misleading.**   A company was served with a notice of requirement to give security of £7,500, but was unable to pay this amount. It continued to trade, but did not issue further VAT invoices or submit its next VAT return. It appealed against a default surcharge, contending that it had been misled by the wording of the notice of requirement to give security, which neither its accountant nor its solicitor could understand. The tribunal dismissed the appeal, stating that it might be understandable for a layman not to understand the notice, 'but it is astonishing that neither a chartered accountant nor a solicitor of the Supreme Court could understand it. It is equally astonishing that neither of them was able to or did seek advice on the matter.' *Actel Group Ltd, LON/88/591 (VTD 3301)*.

18.452   **VAT Guide—whether misleading.**   A company appealed against a default surcharge, contending that it had been misled by the Commissioners' *VAT Guide* into believing that the late submission of two returns showing repayments due would not count as defaults. The tribunal dismissed the appeal. *Giddy*, 18.446 above, was distinguished because the appellant there had been an individual who consistently made repayment claims, whereas the company here usually had an excess of output tax over input tax, its only two repayment returns having been for 'trivial amounts', and was in a position 'to act through servants or advisors'. *Karl Joh (UK) Ltd, EDN/90/156 (VTD 5537)*.

18.453   **Surcharge liability notice—whether misleading.** A company had been served with a surcharge liability notice covering the period to 31 December 1992. However, it submitted its return for the period ending 31 December 1992 after the due date, and a default surcharge was imposed. The company appealed, contending that it had a reasonable excuse because the due date for the return in question was 31 January 1993, and it had assumed that no surcharge would be imposed because the surcharge liability period had ended before the due date. The tribunal dismissed the appeal, holding that the surcharge had been in accordance with what is now *VATA 1994, s 59(4)*, and that the circumstances did not constitute a reasonable excuse. *JW & YE Shute, LON/93/559 (VTD 11303)*.

18.454   **Form VAT 597—whether misleading.** A company paid its VAT liability by credit transfer. It appealed against a default surcharge, contending that it had a reasonable excuse because the wording of the form VAT 597 which it had received when it joined the scheme in 1991 was misleading in that it implied that a trader only had to initiate a payment within the seven-day extension and did not make it clear that the payment had to be received by the Commissioners within the extra seven days. The tribunal dismissed the appeal, accepting that the form had been potentially misleading and had subsequently been revised in 1992, but holding that the circumstances did not amount to a reasonable excuse since a 'reasonably conscientious businessman' would have 'been aware that payment had to be effected at least two banking days before the due date, given that this warning appears on the bank giro credit book'. (The tribunal also observed that the bank through which the payments were made was acting as the agent of the company rather than as the agent of the Commissioners.) *Paragon Business Products Ltd, LON/95/2570P (VTD 14263)*. (*Note.* Since 1992 the form VAT 597 has contained the words 'you must allow at least two banking days for the bank to complete the transaction. The amount due must be in the department's account on the seventh day; if the seventh day falls on the weekend, the amount due must be received by the Friday.')

18.455   **Whether appellant misled by VAT officer.** A company appealed against a default surcharge, contending that it had a reasonable excuse because the defaults in question occurred exactly twelve months apart, and its director had been told by a VAT officer that no surcharge would be imposed unless the company defaulted more than once in a twelve-month period. The tribunal dismissed the appeal, observing that the imposition of the surcharge was in accordance with what is now *VATA 1994, s 59(2)*, finding that the trader had not specifically questioned a VAT officer about the position since receiving a surcharge liability notice, and holding that the circumstances did not constitute a reasonable excuse. *Sageworth Ltd (t/a Anton Hammes), LON/93/1030P (VTD 11151)*.

Return form not available

Cases where the appellant was successful

18.456   **Non-receipt of blank VAT return form.** A trader appealed against a default surcharge, contending that he had a reasonable excuse because he had not received a blank return form despite having telephoned his local VAT office to request one. The tribunal allowed his appeal, holding that the failure to receive a blank return form could only be accepted as a reasonable excuse if the trader took steps to obtain a duplicate form, but also holding that one telephone call was sufficient for this purpose. *S Robinson, [1991] VATTR 440 (VTD 6267)*. (*Note.* For another issue in this case, see 18.15 above.)

18.457 Default Surcharge

18.457 Similar decisions have been reached in a considerable number of subsequent cases. In the interests of space, such cases are not summarised individually in this book. For a list of such cases decided up to 31 December 1995, see Tolley's VAT Cases 1996.

18.458 **VAT return form mislaid.** A trader appealed against a default surcharge, contending that he had a reasonable excuse because he had mislaid the blank VAT return form, but had requested a replacement form as he had realised that he had lost the original, and submitted the return as soon as he received the replacement form. The tribunal allowed the appeal, holding that the circumstances constituted a reasonable excuse. *PE Burns, BEL/88/10 (VTD 3151)*.

18.459 A similar decision was reached in *Brown's Boathouse Ltd, MAN/89/1047 (VTD 4726)*.

18.460 An appeal was allowed in a case where a company, which had mislaid its return form, submitted its quarterly details in manuscript instead, and enclosed a cheque for the VAT due. On receiving the manuscript details, the Commissioners sent the company a duplicate return, but this was not completed and returned until after the due date. The tribunal held that, since the company had not realised that it could be issued with a duplicate return form, the circumstances constituted a reasonable excuse. *J & C Pendleton Ltd, MAN/91/122 (VTD 6092)*.

Cases where the appellant was unsuccessful

18.461 **Non-receipt of blank VAT return form.** A company did not receive a blank VAT return form for the period ending 31 October 1987. It did not request a duplicate form until January 1988. The Commissioners imposed a default surcharge and the tribunal dismissed the company's appeal, holding that the delay in requesting a duplicate form was unreasonable and that the circumstances did not constitute a reasonable excuse. *Goddard & Phillips Ltd, LON/88/566 (VTD 3218)*.

18.462 There have been a very large number of other cases in which the tribunal has found that the appellant did not receive the appropriate blank VAT return form, but did not request a form until after the due date, and has held that the delay in requesting a duplicate form did not constitute a reasonable excuse. In the interests of space, such cases are not reported individually in this book. For a list of such cases decided up to 31 December 1993, see Tolley's VAT Cases 1994.

18.463 **VAT return form mislaid.** In a case where a trader lost her VAT return form, and did not request another form until after the due date, the tribunal held that this did not constitute a reasonable excuse. *N Matthews (t/a Tradewinds Restaurant), LON/90/237Z (VTD 5189)*.

18.464 Similar decisions were reached in *R Bernstein QC, LON/88/1056X (VTD 4816); Mainstream Productions Ltd, LON/90/696 (VTD 5301); M Sarwar, MAN/91/1039 (VTD 7120); D Childs, MAN/91/1172 (VTD 7328); JB Lynch, LON/91/2670Z (VTD 7392); Nelson Stokes Ltd, LON/92/241X (VTD 7690); MacGregor Nash & Co, LON/91/2540 (VTD 7873); JW Meyer, LON/93/778P (VTD 10899)* and *Woodstock Timber Products, LON/93/1460 (VTD 11693)*.

18.465 **Receipt of return form disputed.** A partnership appealed against a default surcharge, contending that it had a reasonable excuse for the late submission of two returns as it had not received return forms and had had to request duplicates. The Commissioners produced the completed return forms in evidence, showing that these were the original forms and were not duplicates, and gave evidence that no request for duplicates had been received and no duplicates had been sent. The tribunal dismissed the appeal, finding that it was satisfied that the partnership's evidence was untruthful. *DJ Electrical Contractors, LON/89/100X (VTD 3916)*.

18.466   Similar decisions were reached in *RW Dodds (Marlow) Ltd, LON/89/155Z (VTD 4016); KAG Gingell, LON/88/922Z (VTD 5168)* and *Sprintman Ltd, MAN/90/607 (VTD 5810).*

Sole trader—absence from usual address

Cases where the appellant was successful

18.467   **Appellant in prison.**   A trader was imprisoned on 13 March 1988, after a criminal trial lasting two months. The tribunal held that this constituted a reasonable excuse for the late submission of the return for the period ending 31 March 1988. (There was, however, held to be no excuse for a subsequent default, the tribunal holding that the trader should have delegated subsequent returns to his wife or son who carried on his business during his imprisonment.) *T Creasey, LON/90/308X (VTD 5116).* (*Note.* Compare *Squire,* 18.470 below.)

18.468   **Appellant abroad on business.**   In a case where the appellant was abroad on business at the time a return was due, the tribunal held that this constituted a reasonable excuse. *RT Burridge, MAN/89/151 (VTD 3723).*

18.469   See also *Flinders,* 18.432 above.

Cases where the appellant was unsuccessful

18.470   **Appellant in prison.**   In December 1987 an accountant and tax adviser was imprisoned for six weeks after being convicted of defrauding the Inland Revenue. He appealed against six successive default surcharges covering the periods ending 28 February 1987 to 31 May 1988, contending that he had a reasonable excuse because of the worry of preparing for the trial and the trauma of being sent to prison. The tribunal dismissed his appeal, holding that the circumstances did not constitute a reasonable excuse. On the evidence, the accountant's business had continued to operate 'with a substantial turnover', and his wife had previously submitted most of his VAT returns. *A Squire, MAN/90/715 (VTD 5821).*

18.471   In a case where a sole trader had been in prison for three months beginning on 14 April 1989, the tribunal held that this did not constitute a reasonable excuse for the late submission of her returns for the periods ending 28 February 1989 and 31 May 1989. *R Molino, LON/91/1997Y (VTD 9056).*

18.472   **Appellant abroad on business.**   An appellant's claim that he had a reasonable excuse for the late submission of a return, because he had been abroad on business when the return was due, was rejected in *JR Harpur, LON/88/41 (VTD 2930).*

18.473   Similar decisions were reached in *SH Nuttall, MAN/90/789 (VTD 5892); C Curwood, LON/90/935X (VTD 5915); N Horrox, MAN/91/313 (VTD 6270); TCT Wellesley-Miller, LON/91/2564Y (VTD 7691); J Barry, MAN/91/536 (VTD 11281); DH Kinnon (t/a Henderson Associates), EDN/96/80 (VTD 14461); DC Campbell, EDN/96/183 (VTD 14723)* and *FJ Lee (t/a Gladrags), LON/98/1570 (VTD 16028).*

18.474   **Frequent business travel.**   A dancer appealed against a default surcharge, contending that her work involved frequent travel and that this constituted a reasonable excuse for late submission of VAT returns. The tribunal dismissed her appeal, holding that the circumstances did not constitute a reasonable excuse. *PJ Atkins, MAN/89/460 (VTD 4142).*

18.475   Business travel was also held not to be a reasonable excuse in *RM Doveton, LON/89/967 (VTD 4164); JC Byrne, LON/88/1145Z (VTD 4202); SP Newton,*

LON/90/633X (VTD 5367); C Dunstan, MAN/90/791 (VTD 5705); PA Garraway, LON/91/1242Y (VTD 6479); AG Hood, LON/92/418Z (VTD 7994); D Chancellor, LON/92/1015Z (VTD 9051); SP Wilcock (t/a The Hi-Fi People), LON/92/2062P (VTD 9737); KJ Sherriff, LON/93/915P (VTD 10820); TA Ratcliffe, MAN/93/1502 (VTD 12396); T Wood (t/a Thomas Wood Associates), MAN/97/69 (VTD 15028); JC Wythe, LON/97/528 (VTD 15054) and MJ Smithers, LON/98/512 (VTD 16100).

18.476   **Appellant on holiday.**   A trader contended that he had a reasonable excuse for the late submission of a return because he had been abroad on holiday. The tribunal dismissed his appeal, holding that this was not a reasonable excuse. *DE Murray, EDN/89/37 (VTD 3692)*.

18.477   There have been a very large number of other cases in which tribunals have held that the absence on holiday of the appellant has not constituted a reasonable excuse for the late payment of the VAT due. In the interests of space, such cases are not summarised individually in this book. For a list of such cases decided up to 31 December 1995, see Tolley's VAT Cases 1996.

18.478   **Appellant on honeymoon.**   A hairdresser was married on 23 September 1989 and went to Jamaica for a fortnight's honeymoon immediately after the wedding. She did not submit her return for the quarter ending 31 August until after the honeymoon. The tribunal held that, as the honeymoon had been arranged four months in advance, this was not a reasonable excuse. *S Bannon, LON/90/203Z (VTD 4877)*.

Matrimonial and domestic problems

Cases where the appellant was successful

18.479   **Divorce.**   A trader was divorced in July 1989 after nineteen years of marriage. The tribunal held that this constituted a reasonable excuse for the late submission of the return for the period ending 31 July 1989. *GD Williams, MAN/90/17 (VTD 4810)*.

18.480   A company appealed against a default surcharge, contending that it had a reasonable excuse for the late submission of two successive returns because its principal director had been in the process of divorcing his wife. The tribunal accepted the company's evidence and allowed the appeal. *Thomas Moriarty Associates Ltd, LON/92/1841 (VTD 10668)*.

18.481   **Matrimonial difficulties.**   Matrimonial difficulties were held to constitute a reasonable excuse for the late submission of two successive returns in *MJC Sims, LON/90/1599X (VTD 5928)* and *JL Thurley, LON/92/1095Y (VTD 9509)*.

18.482   **Domestic problems.**   A trader appealed against a default surcharge, contending that he had a reasonable excuse because his daughter had been served with a notice to quit the accommodation where she was living, and he had had to help her find new accommodation. The tribunal accepted this contention and allowed his appeal. *H McAulay, LON/89/682Y (VTD 4372)*. (*Note*. There was, however, held to be no reasonable excuse for subsequent defaults.)

18.483   See also *PM Power & DG Clark*, 18.513 below.

Cases where the appellant was unsuccessful

18.484   **Marriage breakdown.**   A trader appealed against a series of default surcharges, contending that he had a reasonable excuse because he had been badly affected by the breakdown of his marriage in October 1987. The Commissioners accepted that this was a reasonable excuse for the late submission of the return for the period ending 30

November 1987, but considered that it did not constitute a reasonable excuse for the late submission of subsequent returns. The tribunal dismissed the trader's appeal. *AW Lock, LON/90/1141 (VTD 6768)*.

18.485   **Divorce.**   A trader appealed against four successive default surcharges, contending that he had a reasonable excuse because he had been 'going through a somewhat traumatic divorce'. The tribunal dismissed his appeal, holding that this was not a reasonable excuse. *BJ Davies, MAN/92/1297 (VTD 10676)*.

18.486   **Cash-flow problems following divorce.**   See *Ramsey*, 18.375 above.

18.487   **Matrimonial difficulties.**   A husband and wife traded in partnership as retailers. In 1986 the wife began having an affair with one of their employees. This led to matrimonial difficulties, and they subsequently separated. In the meantime the partnership submitted three returns late. The tribunal dismissed the appeal, holding that the circumstances did not constitute a reasonable excuse. *Jumpers, LON/88/708Z (VTD 4052)*.

Difficulty in computing liability

Cases where the appellant was successful

18.488   **VAT officer directing change in accounting methods.**   An appeal was allowed in a case where a VAT officer on a control visit had instructed a company to change its system of claiming input tax. The tribunal held that, in view of the officer's instructions, the company had a reasonable excuse for having mistakenly believed that accuracy was more important than promptness in submitting its returns. *Rok Crete Units Co Ltd, LON/87/690 (VTD 2660)*.

18.489   Similar decisions were reached in *Goldfinch Blinds Ltd, LON/87/821 (VTD 2671); Auto-Factors Ltd, LON/88/38 (VTD 3055); Carmichael Jennifer May Ltd, LON/88/409 (VTD 3159); MSK (Insulation Services) Ltd, LON/89/723Z (VTD 4198); K Eyre, LON/89/996Y (VTD 5200); McGrath Brothers (Engineering) Ltd, BEL/90/23X (VTD 5551)* and *Harbury Estates Ltd, MAN/90/1111 (VTD 8851)*.

Cases where the appellant was unsuccessful

18.490   **Appellant expecting control visit by VAT officer.**   A trader appealed against a default surcharge, contending that he had delayed submitting his return because he was expecting a control visit by a VAT officer and wished to check that the return was correct. The tribunal dismissed his appeal, holding that this did not constitute a reasonable excuse. *T Norman, MAN/88/543 (VTD 3257)*.

18.491   Similar decisions were reached in *Cloudmead Ltd, LON/88/943 (VTD 3290); S Hampson, LON/88/447Z (VTD 3402); Gilberts Motors Ltd, LON/88/916Z (VTD 3424); The Commercials Trading Co Ltd, LON/89/924Z (VTD 3962); Soft Solutions Ltd, LON/89/1113X (VTD 4793); HJ Michaels, LON/89/313 (VTD 4958); South Wales Industrial Valve Services Ltd, LON/90/10X (VTD 5222); Rentexit Ltd (t/a Leadair Technical & Refrigeration), MAN/92/1731 (VTD 10335); JA Rainford, MAN/93/437 (VTD 11011); Derby Plating Services Ltd, MAN/93/545 (VTD 11352, 12018); Hi-Life Promotions Ltd, LON/94/1622P (VTD 13033); JK Hunter, EDN/94/88 (VTD 13099); Bulgin Powersource plc, MAN/95/2414 (VTD 13915); Vinhispania Ltd, LON/97/288 (VTD 14939)* and *Darvill*, 49.356 PENALTIES: MISDECLARATION.

18.492   **Doubt as to liability of supplies.**   A roofing contractor contended that he had a reasonable excuse for the late submission of several returns, because it was not always clear whether his work was standard-rated or zero-rated. The tribunal dismissed his appeal, holding that this was not a reasonable excuse. *EP Basnett (t/a EB Roofing Services), MAN/89/205 (VTD 3795)*.

18.493   Similar decisions were reached in *Faststar Ltd, LON/89/1645 (VTD 4707); Chasekey Personnel Ltd, EDN/92/4 (VTD 9101)* and *Diamond Investigations Ltd, EDN/97/91 (VTD 15176)*.

18.494   A trader appealed against several default surcharges, contending that he had a reasonable excuse because he had been unsure as to how to account for tax on disbursements. The tribunal dismissed his appeal, observing that 'the law is clearly stated in the case of *Rowe & Maw* (see 58.42 SUPPLY), of which the appellant was made aware', and holding that the circumstances did not constitute a reasonable excuse. *DJ Wilson, LON/98/180 (VTD 15919)*.

18.495   **Company wishing to claim bad debt relief and delaying return until it had contacted accountant.** A company appealed against a default surcharge, contending that it had delayed submitting the relevant return because it had wished to claim bad debt relief and had been unable to contact its accountant. The tribunal dismissed the appeal, holding that the circumstances did not constitute a reasonable excuse. *Smith & Choyce Ltd, LON/92/174Z (VTD 7817)*.

18.496   A similar decision was reached in *Transam Ltd, LON/95/2483 (VTD 13987)*.

Payment by credit transfer

Cases where the appellant was successful

18.497   **Payment by credit transfer—application of extended time limit.** In a Scottish case, a company submitted its return for the period ending 28 February 1999 before the due date of 31 March. It paid the tax by credit transfer from its account with the Bank of Scotland, and initiated the payment on 1 April. However, the payment was not received by the Commissioners until 8 April, and a default surcharge was imposed. The company appealed, contending that the payment had been initiated within the seven-day extended time limit. The company also queried the position with the Bank of Scotland, which stated in reply that 'the nature of the transaction requires the transfer of funds from Scotland to England. The clearing cycles in either countries is (*sic*) two working days but cross-border transactions require an extra day making it three working days.' The tribunal accepted the company's evidence and allowed the appeal, describing the letter from the Bank of Scotland as 'quite extraordinary' and holding that, since the payment had been initiated within the extended time limit, the circumstances constituted a reasonable excuse. *Rowan Timber Supplies (Scotland) Ltd, EDN/99/118 (VTD 16305)*.

18.498   In another Scottish case, a company initiated a credit transfer payment on 5 November 1997, but the Commissioners did not receive the payment from the company's bank until 10 November. The Commissioners imposed a default surcharge but the tribunal allowed the company's appeal, holding that the circumstances constituted a reasonable excuse. *Hydril UK Ltd, EDN/99/166 (VTD 16508)*.

18.499   A company which paid its VAT by credit transfer had consistently initiated payment on the last day of the seven-day extended period, so that the Commissioners did not receive payment until after the time limit had expired. Nevertheless, the Commissioners did not impose surcharges until June 2000, when they imposed a surcharge for the period ending 30 April 2000. The company appealed, contending that the Commissioners' failure to impose surcharges for previous periods had led it to assume that its practice of initiating the payment within the seven-day period was acceptable. The tribunal allowed the appeal, holding that the circumstances constituted a reasonable excuse, since it was reasonable for the company 'to have relied on the consistent practice of the Commissioners'. The tribunal noted that the failure to impose surcharges previously had been attributable to a fault in the Commissioners' computer, and observed that the Commissioners 'should have warned the taxpayer that their computer problems had been cured so that, for the future, the full rigour of the penalty regime would be imposed'. *Renlon Ltd, LON/00/809 (VTD 16987)*.

Cases where the appellant was unsuccessful

18.500   **Payment by credit transfer—misunderstanding of extended time limit.**   A company paid its VAT liability by credit transfer. Its payment for the quarter ending 30 June 1993 was not received by Customs until 8 July 1993, and a default surcharge was imposed. The company appealed, contending that it had a reasonable excuse because it had given the bank transfer slip to its bank (which was not one of the four main 'clearing' banks) on 6 July, and had believed that this constituted payment within the extended seven-day time limit allowed by the Commissioners. The tribunal dismissed the appeal, holding that the circumstances did not constitute a reasonable excuse, since a 'reasonable competent businessman using the bank giro credit system and seeking to effect payment within a shorter period than two days should make sure that this is possible under the particular banking procedures used by him'. *Slough Motor Co, LON/93/2450P (VTD 11818)*.

18.501   *Slough Motor Co*, 18.501 above, was applied in a similar subsequent case in which the extended due date was Monday 7 August 1995, and the company had initiated payment on Friday 4 August 1995. The tribunal specifically declined to follow the decision in *Barney & Freeman*, 18.447 above. *Wingate Electrical plc, LON/95/3067P (VTD 14078)*.

18.502   *Slough Motor Co*, 18.501 above, and *Whitport plc*, 18.66 above, were applied in the similar subsequent case of *AL Currie & Brown, LON/96/1359 (VTD 14678)*.

18.503   Similar decisions were reached in *Pan Graphics Industrial Ltd, LON/94/2529 (VTD 13126); Consolidated Holdings Ltd, MAN/95/107 & MAN/96/220 (VTD 13875, 14352); Cell Ltd, LON/95/3005 (VTD 13942); Hydewood Ltd, LON/96/1944 (VTD 14828); Jayhard Ltd, LON/97/720 (VTD 15306); J & S Joiners & Builders (Paisley) Ltd, EDN/00/109 (VTD 16892); Headlam (Floorcovering Distributor) Ltd*, 18.67 above; *Maranello Concessionaires Ltd*, 18.208 above, and *Paragon Business Products Ltd*, 18.454 above.

Other cases

Cases where the appellant was successful

18.504   **Burglary.**   In a case where the appellant's business premises had been burgled and set on fire, the tribunal held that this constituted a reasonable excuse for a late return. *R Collyer, MAN/87/314 (VTD 2628)*.

18.505   A burglary at a company's premises was held to constitute a reasonable excuse for a late return in *Parkgate Quarries Ltd, BEL/88/40 (VTD 3712); Cirrus Reynolds & Co Ltd, MAN/89/929 (VTD 4951); Ricocrest Ltd, LON/88/379Z (VTD 5179); Knight Guard Security Ltd, LON/90/1565X (VTD 5788); C & C Engineering (WGC) Ltd, LON/91/1207X (VTD 6605); Pennington Lee Ltd, MAN/91/518 (VTD 6625)* and *MM Skip Hire Ltd, LON/94/121 (VTD 12528)*.

18.506 Default Surcharge

18.506 **Fire at premises.** A company suffered a serious fire in April 1988, damaging its records and causing considerable disruption. It had to move to temporary premises, and was unable to submit its returns for the periods ending 31 March and 30 June 1988 until August. The Commissioners imposed a default surcharge but the tribunal allowed the company's appeal, holding that the circumstances constituted a reasonable excuse. *Philip Law Ltd, LON/88/1177Y (VTD 3466).*

18.507 Similar decisions were reached in *Mobile Radio Ltd, LON/89/425X (VTD 3994); Ernest William (Drums) Ltd, LON/88/827Y (VTD 4278); WE Cary Ltd, MAN/90/197 (VTD 5056); PC Clarke, LON/95/904 (VTD 13728)* and *Himalaya Carpets Ltd, LON/97/140 (VTD 14892).*

18.508 **Cash-flow difficulties resulting from fire.** See *Baronshire Engineering Ltd,* 18.337 above.

18.509 **Flooding at premises.** In a case where a firm's premises had been flooded, the tribunal held that this constituted a reasonable excuse for the late submission of a return. *Motorways Auto Spares, LON/89/780X (VTD 4045).*

18.510 **Premises damaged by gales.** A trader submitted a VAT return six days late and a default surcharge was imposed. He appealed, contending that he had a reasonable excuse because his premises had been damaged by gales and he had had to spend considerable time repairing the roof of the premises. The tribunal allowed the appeal, holding that this constituted a reasonable excuse. *J Stickland, LON/90/1596X (VTD 5971).*

18.511 **Premises damaged by bombs.** In a case where a company's premises had been damaged by bomb attacks, the tribunal held that this constituted a reasonable excuse for two late returns. *CSC Electrix Ltd, LON/98/902 (VTD 15956).*

18.512 **Change of business premises.** A change of business premises was held to constitute a reasonable excuse in *Computer Presentations Ltd, MAN/88/190 (VTD 3039); Kingston Craftsmen (1981) Ltd, MAN/89/229 (VTD 3838); Wagstaffe Ellis & Associates, MAN/90/315 (VTD 5115); GL Owen (t/a New Product Research & Development), LON/90/1131 (VTD 5363); City Industries Ltd, LON/91/270Z (VTD 6097); KCP Computer Services Ltd, LON/92/1187Y (VTD 8877); C & S Cladding Ltd, LON/93/862 (VTD 11102); William O'Hanlon & Co Ltd, MAN/93/1346 (VTD 12309); Gamefishing Publications Ltd, EDN/94/39 (VTD 12553); Anozinc Ltd, MAN/94/564 (VTD 12695); Cresthaven Contractors Ltd, LON/94/1308 (VTD 12845)* and *Pavigres-Wich Ltd, LON/94/2925P (VTD 13414).*

18.513 **Sudden termination of partnership.** P and C operated a garage in partnership. On 22 August 1990 C informed P that, because of 'domestic difficulties' with his wife, his assets had been frozen and he therefore had to withdraw from the partnership. P wished to continue the business, and therefore had to raise sufficient cash to purchase C's share in it. The tribunal held that the circumstances constituted a reasonable excuse for the late submission of the partnership return for the period ending 31 July 1990. *PM Power & DG Clark, LON/90/1812Y (VTD 6120).*

18.514 **Dispute between directors.** In a case where the facts are not fully set out in the decision, the tribunal held that 'a bitter and long-standing conflict' between a company's only two directors constituted a reasonable excuse for a late return. *Croydon Power & Light Ltd, LON/95/587P (VTD 13296).*

18.515 **Litigation with major client.** A sole trader became involved in litigation with his major client. The tribunal held that the disruption and stress resulting from this constituted a reasonable excuse for the late submission of a return. *TM O'Callaghan, LON/90/1068Y (VTD 5981).*

18.516   **Exceptional workload.**   Exceptional pressure of work was held to constitute a reasonable excuse in *Blackburn & District Group Training Association Ltd, MAN/87/ 493 (VTD 2735); WJ Mullen, BEL/88/6 (VTD 3374); Foster Cars (Rotherham) Ltd, MAN/89/45 (VTD 3586); Calderprint, MAN/89/807 (VTD 4541); Composite Technics Ltd, LON/89/1760 (VTD 4683); PC Adams, LON/90/1602Y (VTD 5665); NSR Gee, LON/90/1192Z (VTD 5687); Southern Groundworks, LON/90/ 1731Z (VTD 5970); See Europe Ltd, LON/91/1614Z (VTD 6926); D Molyneux, LON/92/1499P (VTD 9265); Churchill Express (London) Ltd, LON/92/1720 (VTD 9726); Briggs 'Palm Shoes' Ltd, MAN/92/541 (VTD 9840); TK Colgate (t/a Shrewsbury English School), MAN/92/1671 (VTD 10329); PJ McMahon, LON/ 92/3114 (VTD 11308); Sandmar Technologies Ltd, LON/93/1559P (VTD 11326); F Duval (t/a L'Ecluse Restaurant), LON/93/2622P (VTD 12082)* and *HS & HK Sagar (t/a AMR Pipeline Products Co), MAN/94/423 (VTD 12692).*

18.517   **Industrial action by Customs staff.**   A company which imported timber operated a deferred payment system, the import formalities for which were handled by different import agents. The company found that the import agents' documents were often inaccurate, and considered it advisable to check these against a computer statement produced monthly by the VAT Central Unit. The tribunal held that delays in issuing this statement, arising from industrial action by Customs staff, constituted a reasonable excuse for a late return. *Chandler Forest Products Ltd, LON/87/620 (VTD 2612).*

18.518   **VAT officer demanding immediate payment of assessed tax from money earmarked for current liability.**   A company's managing director went abroad on 14 February 1991 for two weeks' holiday. He entrusted the company's sales clerk with the task of completing the company's return for the period ending 31 January, and left her a signed cheque made payable to the Commissioners but with the amount left blank. On 15 February the company received a letter from its local VAT office, giving details of errors discovered following a control visit in the previous week, and an assessment charging tax in respect of these errors. A week later, a VAT officer called with bailiffs demanding payment of the tax charged by the assessment. The sales clerk gave the VAT officer the cheque which the director had intended to accompany the January return. Consequently, the tax shown in that return could not be paid until the first week in March, after the director had returned from holiday. The Commissioners imposed a default surcharge but the tribunal allowed the company's appeal, criticising the VAT office for its conduct in threatening to levy distraint within a few days of the issue of the assessment, and holding that the circumstances constituted a reasonable excuse for the company's inability to pay the liability shown in its January return by the due date. *Direct Valeting Ltd, MAN/91/ 1149 (VTD 7118).*

18.519   **Concessionary   practice   previously   agreed   by   Commissioners.**   A partnership traded as printers and stationers. In December 1972 the Commissioners had agreed in writing that it could adopt a concessionary practice whereby, in cases where a tax invoice was issued not later than six weeks after the end of the month in which goods were delivered, the date on which the invoice was issued could be treated as the tax point. The partnership consistently submitted its returns two weeks late. It incurred a default surcharge and appealed, contending that the terms of the concessionary practice had led the partners to believe that late returns were acceptable. The tribunal accepted this contention and allowed the appeal. *Bernard & Smith, LON/87/683 (VTD 2607).*

18.520   A company consistently submitted returns six weeks after the end of its accounting period. It appealed against a default surcharge, contending that in 1974 a VAT officer had authorised it to submit its returns in this way. The tribunal accepted this evidence and allowed the appeal, holding that the circumstances constituted a reasonable excuse. *T & H Collard Ltd, LON/87/692 (VTD 2654)*.

18.521   **Return tendered to local VAT office by hand on last working day before due date—VAT office refusing to accept return.**   A company appealed against a surcharge for the period ending 30 September 1991, contending that one of its directors had visited the Chesterfield VAT office in the late afternoon of 30 October to deliver the return by hand, but had been instructed to post the return to the VAT Central Unit in Southend. The tribunal accepted the company's evidence and allowed the appeal. *Light Wire Ltd, MAN/92/115 (VTD 7967)*.

18.522   A similar decision was reached in *R & MR Hatfield, LON/92/1891P (VTD 11677)*.

18.523   **Industrial action by Post Office staff.**   Because of industrial action by Post Office staff, letterboxes in the Wythenshawe area were sealed for most of September 1988, and a company operating in that area was unable to post its VAT return. The tribunal allowed its appeal against a default surcharge, holding that the closure of the letterboxes constituted a reasonable excuse. *Ernest Lee (Electrical Services) Ltd, MAN/89/67 (VTD 3584)*.

18.524   A similar decision was reached in *Geoffrey Davis (Menswear) Ltd, LON/94/521P (VTD 12576)*. (*Note.* An appeal against a subsequent surcharge was dismissed—see 18.365 above.)

18.525   **Industrial action by Post Office staff—consequent delay in receiving invoices.**   See *Social Surveys (Gallup Poll) Ltd*, 18.253 above, and *Mercuri Urval Ltd*, 18.254 above.

18.526   **Cash-flow problems following industrial action by Post Office staff.**   See *A Lockett & Co Ltd*, 18.332 above, and *David Taylor Tool Hire Ltd*, 18.333 above.

18.527   **Postage of return delayed by gale.**   A married couple carried on a farming and haulage business in a remote and heavily wooded part of Devon, two miles from the nearest post box. On 30 January 1990 some trees in the area were blown down by a gale, blocking several roads. Because of this, the couple were unable to post their return for the period ending 31 December 1989 at their usual post box. They arranged for a young woman who worked for them to post the return at a different post box, near to her home. The return was eventually posted in the early evening, after the last collection from the box in question. The tribunal held that the circumstances constituted a reasonable excuse for the late delivery of the return. *PR & NA Hoskin (t/a Parsons & Son), LON/90/715Z (VTD 5306)*.

18.528   **Hotel proprietor—application for deregistration.**   The owner of a hotel suffered from ill-health and handed over the running of the hotel to his son in June 1990. Neither he nor his son submitted any VAT returns thereafter. The Commissioners imposed default surcharges and the owner appealed, contending that he had applied for deregistration in June 1990 when he had handed over the running of the hotel to his son. The Commissioners gave evidence that they had never received the application for deregistration. The tribunal accepted the hotelier's evidence and allowed his appeal, finding that he had applied for deregistration and holding that, since his turnover was below the appropriate threshold and he had genuinely believed that he was no longer registered, he had a reasonable excuse for not having submitted the returns in question. *A F Lasrado, LON/93/296P (VTD 10656)*.

18.529   **Other cases.**   There have been a small number of other cases turning on very unusual facts in which tribunals have found that the particular circumstances have constituted a reasonable excuse, but where the nature of the case is such that it is of little if any value as a precedent. In the interests of space, such cases have been omitted from this book. For such cases reported up to 31 December 1993, see Tolley's VAT Cases 1994.

Cases where the appellant was unsuccessful

18.530 Appellant facing criminal charges. An accountant appealed against several default surcharges, contending that he had a reasonable excuse because during the period in question he had been involved in a prolonged criminal investigation and had been indicted for theft by the Crown Prosecution Service. The tribunal dismissed the accountant's appeal, holding that this did not constitute a reasonable excuse. *GAW Sprosson, LON/93/2578P (VTD 12073)*.

18.531 Effects of fire. A company suffered from a serious fire on 16 August 1987. It submitted its return for the period ending 30 September 1987 after the due date, and a default surcharge was imposed. The company appealed, contending that the effects of the fire constituted a reasonable excuse. The tribunal dismissed the appeal, holding that the period between the fire and the due date of the return was long enough for the company to have attended to its VAT affairs. *John Pargeter & Sons Ltd, MAN/88/435 (VTD 3318)*.

18.532 A similar decision was reached in *R Booth (t/a Discovery Trading Co), MAN/94/755 (VTD 12778)*.

18.533 Effects of robbery. There was a robbery at a partnership's premises in November 1986. The Commissioners accepted that the disruption caused by this constituted a reasonable excuse for the late submission of the return for the period ending 31 December 1986. One of the partners refused to work at the premises again after the robbery. The tribunal held that her refusal to work at the premises did not constitute a reasonable excuse for six further defaults. *G Ross & S Metcalfe, MAN/89/1062 (VTD 4835)*.

18.534 Dyslexia. A builder, who was dyslexic, submitted four VAT returns late. The tribunal rejected his contention that his dyslexia constituted a reasonable excuse. *JCNT Taylor, MAN/88/839 (VTD 3408)*.

18.535 Dyslexia was also held not to constitute a reasonable excuse in *NJ Fisher, MAN/92/1397 (VTD 11238)*.

18.536 Change of address. In a case where a trader was preparing to move house, and had packed his records away in boxes in anticipation of the move, the tribunal held that this did not constitute a reasonable excuse. *AG Fishwick, MAN/88/874 (VTD 3642)*.

18.537 A trader's change of address was held not to constitute a reasonable excuse in *MK McMullan, LON/89/1754Y (VTD 4917); MD Rowley, LON/89/1779 (VTD 5089); Dr MEC Randle, MAN/92/379 (VTD 9000); A Gibb (t/a Business Post Fife), EDN/93/104 (VTD 11166); K Elliott (t/a Harbourne Engineering), LON/98/988 (VTD 16010) and JM Sheldrake, LON/99/6 (VTD 16119)*.

18.538 Change of business premises. The change of a company's premises was held not to constitute a reasonable excuse in *Hall Garage, LON/88/1018Z (VTD 3749); Aviss Holdings Ltd, LON/89/751Z (VTD 3982); Birchwatt Productions Ltd, LON/89/1011 (VTD 4182); Network Data Ltd, LON/89/676Y (VTD 4393); CBA Enterprises Ltd, MAN/89/883 (VTD 4741); Interhouse Ltd, LON/90/32X (VTD 4782); Makebrite Ltd, MAN/90/222 (VTD 5490); Young Street Management Services Ltd, EDN/90/194 (VTD 5711); CW Aberdeen, MAN/91/801 (VTD 7027); Magill Business Associates Ltd, MAN/91/516 (VTD 7855); JFD Cartons Ltd,*

18.539 Default Surcharge

MAN/92/1692 (VTD 10293); Soundvision Ltd, LON/94/2098P (VTD 12977) and *Taylor Construction, LON/94/3126P (VTD 13269).*

18.539 **Cash-flow problems following change of premises.** See *Performance Print Ltd*, 18.362 above.

18.540 **Reliance on director.** Reliance on a company director was held not to constitute a reasonable excuse in *True Engineers Ltd, LON/89/591Z (VTD 4032); Alpha Numeric Ltd, LON/89/1448 (VTD 5519); SC Campbell (Plastics) Ltd, MAN/90/1081 (VTD 6086); P & A Fencing & Sheds Ltd, MAN/91/19 (VTD 6089); Maltby Motors Ltd, MAN/91/968 (VTD 7026); LJ Harvey & Associates (Bournemouth) Ltd, LON/92/3263P (VTD 10389); Normaco Ltd, LON/93/2137 (VTD 11821); SC Driver (Opticians) Ltd, LON/94/278P (VTD 12410); Beatwood Ltd (t/a Royals of London), LON/95/83P (VTD 13229)* and *Letchworth Polishing & Plating Co Ltd, LON/95/902P (VTD 13675).*

18.541 **Reliance on accountant.** A company appealed against a number of default surcharges, contending that it had a reasonable excuse because its accountant (who was an employee of the company) had submitted the returns in question after the due date and had concealed the surcharges from the directors. The tribunal dismissed the appeal, holding that the circumstances did not constitute a reasonable excuse, and the QB upheld this decision. The tribunal had been entitled to find that the reason for the late payment was the dilatoriness of the accountant. The fact that the accountant was an employee of the company did not take him outside the definition of 'any other person' for the purposes of *VATA 1994, s 71(1)(b)*, and the effect of *s 71(1)(b)* was that the circumstances could not constitute a reasonable excuse. Macpherson J observed that, when the 1985 Finance Bill (which introduced what is now *VATA 1994, s 71*) was being debated, the Minister responsible had stated that 'if all one had to do to have a reasonable excuse was to find an accountant who would delay everything, there would be easy pickings to be made'. *Profile Security Services Ltd v C & E Commrs, QB [1996] STC 808.*

18.542 *Profile Security Services Ltd*, 18.541 above, was applied in the similar subsequent cases of *Young Construction (London) Ltd, LON/96/1027 (VTD 14565); Olympiad Signs Ltd, LON/96/1029 (VTD 14566)* and *Corps of Commissionaires Management Ltd, LON/96/872 (VTD 14593).*

18.543 A company appealed against a default surcharge, contending that it had a reasonable excuse because it had relied on its accountant, who had been dilatory. The tribunal dismissed the appeal, applying *Harris*, 48.85 PENALTIES: FAILURE TO NOTIFY. *Jenkinson*, 48.80 PENALTIES: FAILURE TO NOTIFY, was distinguished because in that case the accountant had deliberately given the appellant false information, whereas in the case under appeal the accountant had not been guilty of any misrepresentation. *Global Security Services Ltd, EDN/89/91 (VTD 4035).*

18.544 Reliance on accountants has been held not to constitute a reasonable excuse in very many other cases. In the interests of space, such cases are not reported individually in this book. For a list of such cases reported up to 31 October 1990, see Tolley's VAT Cases 1991.

18.545 **Reliance on secretary.** A company appealed against a default surcharge, contending that it had a reasonable excuse because its managing director had delegated the company's VAT affairs to the company secretary, who had transpired to be inefficient and had subsequently been dismissed. The tribunal dismissed the appeal, holding that the inefficiency of the company secretary did not constitute a reasonable excuse. *Polarstar Ltd, LON/96/623 (VTD 14445).*

18.546   There have been a large number of cases in which reliance on a secretary has been held not to be a reasonable excuse. In the interests of space, such cases are not summarised individually in this book. For a list of such cases reported up to and including 31 December 1995, see Tolley's VAT Cases 1996.

18.547   **Reliance on treasurer.**   Reliance on the treasurer of a golf club was held not to be a reasonable excuse in *Poulton Park Club Ltd, MAN/89/1005 (VTD 4653)*.

18.548   Reliance on the treasurer of a rugby club was held not to constitute a reasonable excuse in *Crowborough Rugby Football Club Ltd, LON/90/1676Z (VTD 6023)*.

18.549   **Reliance on employee.**   There have been a very large number of cases in which reliance on an employee has been held not to be a reasonable excuse. In the interests of space, such cases are not summarised individually in this book. For a list of such cases decided up to 31 December 1995, see Tolley's VAT Cases 1996.

18.550   **Reliance on bookkeeper.**   Reliance on a bookkeeper has been held not to constitute a reasonable excuse in a very large number of cases, which appear to raise no point of general importance. In the interests of space, such cases are not reported individually in this book. For a list of such cases decided up to 31 December 1993, see Tolley's VAT Cases 1994.

18.551   **Reliance on wife.**   In a case where the wife of a partner had forgotten to submit a return, the tribunal held that this did not constitute a reasonable excuse. *Nealeplan, LON/88/1215Z (VTD 3457)*.

18.552   Reliance on the wife of a sole trader was held not to constitute a reasonable excuse in *R Swain, MAN/90/351 (VTD 5286); AJ Howe-Davies (t/a D & B Contracts), LON/90/1240 (VTD 5609); M Shalloe, MAN/90/1036 (VTD 6234); D Hickford, EDN/91/126 (VTD 6290); CV Weedon, LON/92/2908P (VTD 10181); PG Davies, LON/93/1886P (VTD 11456)* and *Wynd Consulting, LON/96/1756 (VTD 14773)*.

18.553   **Club treasurer unaware of issue of surcharge liability notice.**   A golf club had submitted two returns after the due dates and had been issued with a surcharge liability notice. A new treasurer took office in late 1987 and was unaware of the issue of the notice. He submitted the return for the period ending 31 March 1988 after the due date and the Commissioners imposed a default surcharge. The tribunal dismissed the club's appeal, holding that it was the club's responsibility to ensure that the new treasurer was aware of the issue of the notice. *Stourbridge Golf Club Ltd, MAN/88/658 (VTD 3359)*.

18.554   See also *Rotherham Borough Council Employees Sports & Social Club*, 18.79 above, in which the fact that a new club treasurer was not told that his predecessor had received a surcharge liability notice was held not to constitute a reasonable excuse.

18.555   **Company accountant not aware of surcharge liability notice.**   A company appointed a new accountant in September 1988. It had previously received a surcharge liability notice, but the managing director did not tell the accountant this. When a subsequent return was submitted after the due date, the Commissioners imposed a default surcharge. The tribunal dismissed the company's appeal, holding that, since the company had received and been aware of the issue of the notice, it was the company's responsibility to inform its accountant. *John Hilditch Plant Hire, LON/89/732X (VTD 4151)*.

18.556   **Company director unaware of surcharge liability notice.**   A company appealed against a default surcharge, contending that its previous bookkeeper had not told the managing director (who was her father) that the company had received a surcharge liability notice. The tribunal dismissed the appeal, holding that the circumstances did not constitute a reasonable excuse. *Surecliff Ltd, LON/92/188X (VTD 8922)*.

18.557 **Cheque accidentally not submitted with return.** In a case where the person whose responsibility it was to submit a VAT return accidentally omitted to enclose the necessary cheque, the tribunal held that this was not a reasonable excuse. *Brecon Brewery Ltd, LON/87/862 (VTD 3053)*.

18.558 Similar decisions were reached in *JBW Cunningham, MAN/89/223 (VTD 3828); Cuffley Motor Co Ltd, LON/89/500 (VTD 3998); P Thorrold, LON/89/1484Y (VTD 4523); Britton & Black, MAN/89/970 (VTD 4677); PR Allen, LON/89/1626X (VTD 4935); Press Graphics Ltd, LON/90/726X (VTD 5100); BM Forward, LON/90/759X (VTD 5145); DV & AEN Lewis, LON/90/45Y (VTD 5215); Esson Ltd, LON/90/828Y (VTD 5227); DL Flitton, LON/90/338 (VTD 5272); IC Waland, EDN/90/138 (VTD 5406); Ravi Bhushan Bhardwaj Specsavers (Wokingham Road) Ltd, LON/90/1353X (VTD 5463); HM & AJ Jones (t/a Contract Services), MAN/91/433 (VTD 6299); EL Ritson, LON/90/1839X (VTD 6969); JR Potts, LON/91/2597Y (VTD 7360); Hom Construction (London) Ltd, LON/91/2525X (VTD 7861); B Shaer, LON/92/2103 (VTD 9600); RM Kago (t/a The Bingham Hotel), LON/94/84P (VTD 12217); J Henderson (t/a AH Sales), EDN/94/81 (VTD 12968); Meteorites Productions Ltd, LON/94/1858P (VTD 13000); T Levy, LON/94/2736P (VTD 13110); ED Duncan, EDN/94/324 (VTD 13520)* and *Greenhouse Stirton & Co*, 18.221 above.

18.559 In a case where a company contended that it had submitted a cheque with the return, but a VAT officer gave evidence that there was no cheque enclosed in the envelope containing the return, the tribunal found that the cheque had not been sent and held that the company did not have a reasonable excuse. *Camden (Hardchrome) Ltd, MAN/89/123 (VTD 3724)*.

18.560 Similar decisions were reached in *GA Mackay, EDN/90/174 (VTD 5547); Brockholes Electrics Co Ltd, LON/91/1171 (VTD 6519); RK Midda, LON/92/254Y (VTD 8951)* and *TL Smart (t/a On Tour Catering), LON/92/2476P (VTD 10303)*.

18.561 **Chequebook not available.** A trader appealed against a default surcharge, contending that he could not have paid his VAT on time because he had run out of blank cheques and his bank had not supplied him with a new chequebook. The tribunal dismissed his appeal, holding that this was not a reasonable excuse. *C Beckett, MAN/90/30 (VTD 4766)*.

18.562 Similar decisions were reached in *Barking Vehicle Rentals Ltd, LON/90/169Y (VTD 4934); JA Armstrong, MAN/90/350 (VTD 5262); Lynben Ltd, EDN/91/299 (VTD 7291)* and *City Shredding Services Ltd, LON/92/1447P (VTD 9329)*.

18.563 **Difficulty in posting return.** A company appealed against a default surcharge, contending that it had a reasonable excuse for having posted the return late, because its directors did not have a car and the nearest post-box was three miles away. The tribunal dismissed the appeal, holding that this did not constitute a reasonable excuse. *Webbro Ltd, MAN/92/380 (VTD 8999)*.

18.564 A company appealed against a default surcharge, contending that it had a reasonable excuse for having posted the return late, because one of its employees had intended to deliver the return to its local VAT office on the due date, but had been delayed by traffic congestion and had eventually posted the return instead. The tribunal dismissed the appeal, holding that this did not constitute a reasonable excuse. *New Concept Ltd, EDN/97/71 (VTD 15174)*.

18.565   **Other cases.**   There have been a large number of unsuccessful appeals which appear to raise no point of general importance but where appellants have contended that the surcharge has been unjust. In the interests of space, such cases are not reported individually in this book.

VALIDITY OF THE SURCHARGE

18.566   A YMCA appealed against a default surcharge, contending that the imposition of the surcharge was contrary to the legal principle of 'proportionality'. The tribunal rejected this contention and dismissed the appeal, applying *W Emmett & Son Ltd*, 49.411 PENALTIES: MISDECLARATION, and observing that 'a national revenue department may well feel that default must be legislated against with even more vigour than mistakes'. *The Central Young Men's Christian Association, LON/92/1179X (VTD 9318)*. (*Note.* For the principle of 'proportionality', see *Internationale Handelsgesellschaft GmbH v Einfuhr- und Vorratstelle für Getriede und Futtermittel, CJEC [1970] ECR 1145; [1972] CMLR 255*.)

18.567   Similar decisions, applying *W Emmett & Son Ltd*, 49.411 PENALTIES: MISDECLARATION, and *dicta* of Simon Brown J in *P & O Ferries*, 49.412 PENALTIES: MISDECLARATION, were reached in *Impetus Engineering Co (International) Ltd, MAN/92/669 (VTD 10596); JF Bower (t/a Bean Bower & Co), [1995] VATDR 294 (VTD 13224); Finaplan Ltd, MAN/93/478 & 796 (VTD 13224); Advanced Security Installations Ltd, LON/96/447 (VTD 14297)* and *Universal Display Fittings Co Ltd, LON/98/463 (VTD 15838)*.

18.568   Three associated companies appealed against eighteen default surcharges, contending that they were invalid because the Commissioners had imposed them automatically without considering the exercise of their discretion under what is now *VATA 1994, s 76*. The tribunal dismissed the appeals, holding that the surcharge assessments were valid, since in the circumstances of the case in question there was 'no possibility that their discretion would have been exercised otherwise than to impose the surcharges'. The QB upheld this decision. Judge J specifically disapproved *obiter dicta* of the tribunal chairman in *Food Engineering Ltd*, 49.413 PENALTIES: MISDECLARATION, and the decision reached by Miss Gort in *Tamdown Ltd*, 49.415 PENALTIES: MISDECLARATION. Judge J held that the right of appeal to a VAT tribunal provided for by what is now *VATA 1994, s 83* was confined to an appeal against the liability to surcharge or against the amount of the surcharge. There was no right to appeal against the Commissioners' discretionary power whether or not to make a surcharge assessment. The remedy against any improper exercise of the Commissioners' discretionary power to impose a surcharge would be an application for judicial review. On the facts of this case, the decision to impose the surcharges was inevitable. *Dollar Land (Feltham) Ltd v C & E Commrs (and associated appeals), QB [1995] STC 414*.

18.569   The QB decision in *Dollar Land (Feltham) Ltd*, 18.568 above, was applied in the subsequent similar cases of *Mrs AM Rogers (t/a Quality Records), LON/95/2970 (VTD 13991)* and *Stafford & Worcester Property Co Ltd, MAN/98/880 (VTD 16302)*.

19   Drugs, Medicines, Aids for the Handicapped, etc.

Note. The scope of *VATA 1994, Sch 8, Group 12* has been significantly restricted by the amendments made by the *VAT (Drugs, Medicines and Aids for the Handicapped) Order 1997 (SI 1997 No 2744)*, which came into force on 1 January 1998. The cases in this chapter should be read in the light of these provisions. The cases are arranged under the following headings.

Supplies of goods by registered practitioner (VATA 1994, Sch 8, Group 12, Items 1, 1A) 19.1–19.5

Supplies to handicapped people (VATA 1994, Sch 8, Group 12, Items 2, 3)
  Medical or surgical appliances (*VATA 1994, Sch 8, Group 12, Item 2(a)*) 19.6–19.11
  Adjustable beds designed for invalids (*VATA 1994, Sch 8, Group 12, Item 2(b)*) 19.12–19.14
  Motor vehicles (*VATA 1994, Sch 8, Group 12, Item 2(f)*) 19.15–19.17
  Whether 'equipment and appliances ... designed solely for use by a handicapped person' (*VATA 1994, Sch 8, Group 12, Item 2(g)*) 19.18–19.43
  Parts and accessories (*VATA 1994, Sch 8, Group 12, Item 2(h)*) 19.44–19.47
  Services of adapting goods for a handicapped person (*VATA 1994, Sch 8, Group 12, Item 3*) 19.48–19.49

Supplies of widening doorways, etc. (VATA 1994, Sch 8, Group 12, Items 8, 9) 19.50–19.56

Supplies of bathrooms, washrooms, etc. (VATA 1994, Sch 8, Group 12, Items 10, 11) 19.57–19.62

Supplies of lifts (VATA 1994, Sch 8, Group 12, Items 16–18) 19.63–19.66

SUPPLIES OF GOODS BY REGISTERED PRACTITIONER (VATA 1994, Sch 8, Group 12, Items 1, 1A)

19.1   **Supply on prescription of lotion to patients at clinics.**   A company, the controlling director of which was a registered pharmacist, manufactured a pharmaceutical product, minoxidil, which was made into a lotion for the treatment of alopecia and was only available on prescription. It supplied this lotion to three clinics which specialised in such treatment, and did not account for VAT on these supplies. The Commissioners issued assessments charging tax on them, considering that the company was making supplies of goods to the clinics, and that these supplies did not qualify for zero-rating. The company appealed, contending that it was making its supplies to the patients and that the supplies should be zero-rated under what is now *VATA 1994, Sch 8, Group 12, Item 1*. The tribunal accepted this contention and allowed the appeal, holding on the evidence that the lotion remained the company's property until it was dispensed to the patients, that the company was supplying the lotion to the patients rather than to the clinic, and that the payments from the clinic qualified for zero-rating. *Parsons Green Ltd, [1990] VATTR 194 (VTD 5044)*. (*Note. See now, however, VATA 1994, Sch 8, Group 12, Note 5A, introduced by VAT (Drugs, Medicines and Aids for the Handicapped) Order 1997 (SI 1997 No 2744), with effect from 1 January 1998.*)

19.2   **Provision of drugs from hospital dispensary—whether within VATA 1994, Sch 8, Group 12, Item 1.**   A company operated a private hospital. It supplied patients with drugs in the course of their treatment. It did not account for VAT in respect of these drugs, considering that the supply was zero-rated under what is now *VATA 1994, Sch 8, Group 12, Item 1*. The Commissioners issued a ruling that the supplies of drugs were not eligible for zero-rating, but were exempt supplies by virtue of what is now *VATA 1994, Sch 9, Group 7, Item 4*. The tribunal allowed the company's appeal, holding on the evidence that the drugs were prescribed by an 'appropriate medical practitioner' within *Medicines Act 1968, s 67(2)(a)*, and were a separate zero–rated supply, rather than merely a part of a composite exempt supply of care in a hospital. The CA upheld this decision (by a 2–1 majority, Kennedy LJ dissenting). Millett LJ held that, for VAT purposes, the Commissioners could treat as separate transactions what the contracting parties had treated as a single supply, but the Commissioners could not join together what the contracting parties had treated as separate. The supply of drugs was a separate supply of goods which qualified for zero–rating. *Wellington Private Hospital Ltd v C & E Commrs, CA [1997] STC 445. (Notes.* (1) See now, however, *VATA 1994, Sch 8, Group 12, Note 5A*, introduced by *VAT (Drugs, Medicines and Aids for the Handicapped) Order 1997 (SI 1997 No 2744)*, with effect from 1 January 1998. (2) For another issue in the tribunal appeal in this case, not taken to the QB, see 43.82 PARTIAL EXEMPTION. (3) The *dicta* of Millett LJ in this case should now be read in the light of the subsequent CJEC decision in *Card Protection Plan Ltd*, 21.162 EUROPEAN COMMUNITY LAW, where the CJEC held that 'a supply which comprises a single service from an economic point of view should not be artificially split'.)

19.3   Similar decisions were reached in two cases which were heard in the QB and CA with *Wellington Private Hospital Ltd*, 19.2 above. *C & E Commrs v British United Provident Association Ltd (No 1); C & E Commrs v St Martins Hospital Ltd, CA [1997] STC 445. (Note.* For another issue in the *British United Provident Association Ltd* case, see 19.8 below.)

19.4   **Supply on prescription of primrose oil products.**   A company supplied primrose oil products. The Commissioners issued a ruling that the supply of these products, when dispensed by a registered pharmacist on the prescription of a doctor, failed to qualify for zero–rating under what is now *VATA 1994, Sch 8, Group 12, Item 1* on the grounds that the products had 'no demonstrable medicinal properties'. (The products were not available under the National Health Service, but were sometimes prescribed by private medical practitioners.) The company appealed, contending that the products were useful for patients suffering from multiple sclerosis, arthritis and pre-menstrual tension, and qualified for zero–rating under *Group 12, Item 1* when prescribed by a doctor and dispensed by a pharmacist. The tribunal allowed the appeal, holding that 'goods' for the purposes of *Group 12, Item 1* included 'pharmaceutical products normally used for health care, prevention of diseases, and treatment for medical purposes properly prescribed by a doctor (or other person mentioned in *Item 1*), and dispensed by a registered pharmacist'. The products in dispute were pharmaceutical products, so that their supply qualified for zero–rating. *Bio Oil Research Ltd, MAN/92/1320 (VTD 12252).*

19.5   **Drugs personally administered by NHS doctor—whether zero-rated under VATA 1994, Sch 8, Group 12, Item 1A.**   In 1997 the Commissioners issued a ruling that drugs and other medical items personally administered by a general practitioner working in the NHS formed part of a single exempt supply of medical care, so that the related input tax was not recoverable. A partnership of doctors appealed, contending that the supplies of drugs which were personally administered by a NHS doctor were supplies of goods which qualified for zero–rating under *VATA 1994, Sch 8, Group 12, Item 1A*. The tribunal accepted this contention and allowed the appeal. When treating a patient under the *National Health Service (Pharmaceutical Services) Regulations 1992*, a doctor was 'making two separate supplies, one of goods and one of services'. In construing *Group 12, Item 1A*, it would be 'artificial to distinguish between those drugs administered to a patient under *regulation 20* which were not personally administered by a doctor, and those which are administered by him in a situation of an emergency, which would come from the same stock'. Where a doctor administered drugs to such a patient, he was 'providing not just his own services, but also a supply of goods which is economically dissociable from his services'. *Drs Woodings, Rees, Crossthwaite & Jones, [1999] VATDR 294 (VTD 16175). (Note.* For the Commissioners' practice following this decision, see Business Brief 22/99, issued on 13 October 1999. The Commissioners 'consider that the tribunal's finding in this case is entirely dependent upon its interpretation of the facts of the case itself. In view of this, they consider that the effects of the decision are limited to the appellants alone and will not seek to apply it to other NHS GPs.')

SUPPLIES TO HANDICAPPED PEOPLE (VATA 1994, Sch 8, Group 12, Items 2, 3)

Medical or surgical appliances (VATA 1994, Sch 8, Group 12, Item 2(a))

19.6   **'Airbaths' supplied to hospitals.**   A company designed 'airbaths', which were intended to relieve pains in the neck and upper back by directing underwater currents of hot air at the appropriate parts of the body. It supplied these to hospitals, and did not account for VAT on these supplies. The Commissioners issued a ruling that they were liable to VAT, and the company appealed, contending that they should be zero-rated under what is now *VATA 1994, Sch 8, Group 12, Item 2(a)*. The tribunal dismissed the company's appeal, holding that the airbaths were neither 'medical or surgical appliances' within *Item 2(a)* nor 'designed solely for use by a handicapped person within *Item 2(g)'*. *The Princess Louise Scottish Hospital*, 19.29 below, applied. *Aquakraft Ltd, MAN/85/350 (VTD 2215).*

19.7   **Transcutaneous electrical nerve stimulators—whether within Sch 8, Group 12, Item 2(a).**   A company supplied transcutaneous electrical nerve stimulators, which were intended to relieve pain by applying electrical currents to the skin through surface electrodes. It did not account for VAT on its supplies, treating them as zero-rated. The Commissioners issued a ruling that the supplies of the stimulators did not qualify for zero-rating, and the company appealed. The tribunal allowed the appeal, holding on the evidence that the stimulators had been 'designed solely for use by chronic pain sufferers' and 'solely for the relief of a severe abnormality or a severe injury', and were thus within what is now *VATA 1994, Sch 8, Group 12, Item 2(a)*. (The tribunal observed that any sales to individuals who were not within the definition of 'a handicapped person' would not qualify for zero-rating.) *Neen Design Ltd, LON/93/1586A (VTD 11782). (Note.* For the Commissioners' practice following this decision, see Business Brief 4/94, issued on 21 February 1994.)

19.8   **Supplies of prostheses—whether within Sch 8, Group 12, Item 2(a).**   A company which operated a number of hospitals did not account for tax on supplies of prostheses (manufactured parts designed to replace or supplement natural components of the human body, such as hip joints and heart valves), but reclaimed the input tax relating to such supplies. The Commissioners issued a ruling that the supply of prostheses was an integral part of a composite supply of medical care, which was exempt from VAT, so that the related input tax was not recoverable. The company appealed, contending that the supplies of prostheses were separate supplies which qualified for zero-rating under what is now *VATA 1994, Sch 8, Group 12, Item 2(a)*, and that the services relating to the supplies of hip replacements qualified for zero-rating under what is now *VATA 1994, Sch 8, Group 12, Item 7*. The tribunal allowed the company's appeal in part, holding that the replacement hip joints fell within *Group 12, Item 2(a)* and that the services involved in the supply of replacement hip joints qualified for zero-rating under *Group 12, Item 7*, but that apparatus used for splint lumbro-sacral fusion, and plates used for osteotomy, were not designed 'solely for the relief of a severe abnormality or severe injury', and thus failed to qualify for zero-rating. The CA upheld this decision (by a 2–1 majority, Kennedy LJ dissenting). Millett LJ held that, for VAT purposes, the Commissioners could treat as separate transactions what the contracting parties had treated as a single supply, but the Commissioners could not join together what the contracting parties had treated as separate. The supply of prostheses was a separate supply of goods which qualified for zero-rating under *Item 2(a)*, and the services involved in implanting them qualified for zero-rating under *Item 7*. *British United Provident Association Ltd v C & E Commrs (and cross-appeal), CA [1997] STC 445.* (*Notes.* (1) See now, however, *VATA 1994, Sch 8, Group 12, Note 5B*, introduced by *VAT (Drugs, Medicines and Aids for the Handicapped) Order 1997 (SI 1997 No 2744)*, with effect from 1 January 1998. (2) For another issue in this case, see 19.3 above.)

19.9   **Incontinence pads—whether supplies made to handicapped people.**   A company manufactured and imported incontinence pads. It entered into contracts with three NHS trusts and a nursing home for the sale of these products for use by patients. The contracts provided for the ownership of the incontinence pads to pass directly from the company to the patients. The company did not account for output tax on the supplies, treating them as zero-rated. The Commissioners issued a ruling that the supplies failed to qualify for zero-rating, accepting that the patients were within the definition of a 'handicapped person' and that the incontinence pads were within *VATA 1994, Sch 8, Group 12, Item 2(a)*, but considering that the supplies were made to the trusts and the nursing home, rather than to the patients. The tribunal reviewed the evidence and allowed the appeal in part, holding that in cases where the patients were living in their own homes, the supplies were made to the patients and that the fact that the consideration was paid by a third party was not material. However, where the patients were living in a nursing home (whether an independent nursing home or a home run by an NHS trust), the tribunal held that the supplies were not made to the patients. The chairman observed that 'although the evidence was that the pads are stored in the room occupied by the patient, it seems ... that an arrangement which precludes the trust from using pads allocated to one patient for another if stock runs short is unreal. Because of his mental condition, the patient cannot consent to part of the stock in his room being switched.' *Mölnlycke Ltd, LON/96/55 (VTD 14641).* (*Notes.* (1) The tribunal rejected an alternative contention by Customs that *VATA 1994, s 47(2A)* applied, holding that '*s 47(2A)* cannot have been intended to affect the application of the zero-rating provisions'. (2) See now *VATA 1994, Sch 8, Group 12, Note 5B*, introduced by *VAT (Drugs, Medicines and Aids for the Handicapped) Order 1997 (SI 1997 No 2744)*, with effect from 1 January 1998. This provision is designed to ensure that supplies to individuals who are patients in, or attending at the premises of, a relevant institution are excluded from zero-rating, and that it is not possible to arrange for third parties to make zero-rated supplies. For the Commissioners' interpretation of this provision, see Business Brief 29/97, issued on 16 December 1997.)

19.10   *Mölnlycke Ltd,* 19.9 above, was applied in the similar subsequent case of *PM & RI Morgan (t/a J Bishop & Co), MAN/96/758 (VTD 15218).*

19.11   See also *Express Medicare Ltd,* 1.63 AGENTS (where the tribunal held that incontinence pads fell within *Item 2(g)* rather than *Item 2(a)*).

Adjustable beds designed for invalids (VATA 1994, Sch 8, Group 12, Item 2(b))

19.12   **Electromagnetic mattress, pillow and Kenkobio machine.**   See *Back In Health Ltd,* 19.34 below.

19.13   **Adjustable beds—whether within Sch 8, Group 12, Item 2(b).**   A company manufactured physiotherapy products, including adjustable beds. The beds were of unusually strong construction, adjustable in height, and included two cycloidal vibrator massage units which were embedded in the mattress. The Commissioners issued a ruling that the beds did not qualify for zero-rating under what is now *VATA 1994, Sch 8, Group 12, Item 2(b)*, on the grounds that they were not 'designed for invalids'. The company appealed, contending that the beds were designed for invalids, and the fact that they could also be used by people who were not invalids was not conclusive. The tribunal allowed the appeal, holding on the evidence that the beds were not 'designed for normal sleep and rest' but were 'designed for a special purpose' and were 'designed for invalids'. Accordingly they qualified for zero-rating. *Niagara Holdings Ltd, [1993] VATTR 503 (VTD 11400)*.

19.14   A company imported adjustable beds from Germany. The Commissioners issued a ruling that the supplies of the beds did not qualify for zero-rating under *VATA 1994, Sch 8, Group 12, Item 2(b)*, on the grounds that they were suitable for able-bodied people and were not designed specifically for disabled customers. The company appealed, contending that the beds were designed for invalids, and the fact that they could also be used by people who were not invalids was not conclusive. The tribunal accepted this contention and allowed the appeal, holding on the evidence that 'the bed was specifically designed for people who are less than able'. The chairman observed that 'whilst the promotional literature is not specific in stating that the bed is designed for invalids, it is clear from all the features incorporated in the design that it is so suitable' and found that 'it was the intention of the manufacturers ... to produce a bed which was suitable for people who were temporarily in a state of invalidity, or suffering from permanent minor disabilities'. *Niagara Holdings Ltd, 19.13 above, applied. Hulsta Furniture (UK) Ltd, LON/98/936 (VTD 16289)*.

Motor vehicles (VATA 1994, Sch 8, Group 12, Item 2(f))

19.15   **Motor vehicle supplied to paraplegic.** A paraplegic reclaimed input tax on the purchase of a motor car with an automatic gearbox and a special grab handle fitted to the driver's door. The Commissioners rejected the claim, and the paraplegic appealed. The tribunal dismissed his appeal, finding on the evidence that the car in question was not 'designed or substantially adapted for the carriage of a person in a wheelchair', and holding that it was therefore outside what is now *VATA 1994, Sch 8, Group 12, Item 2(f)* and did not qualify for zero-rating. *JG Oliver, MAN/92/1065 (VTD 10579)*.

19.16   **Motor caravan.** A company which designed and built motor caravans supplied a motor caravan with a door 30 inches wide, designed to accommodate a wheelchair, and a ramp to enable the wheelchair to be loaded. The Commissioners issued a ruling that the caravan did not qualify for zero-rating, on the basis that it was capable of carrying more than five persons other than the wheelchair passenger, and thus was not within what is now *VATA 1994, Sch 8, Group 12, Item 2(f)*. The company appealed. The tribunal allowed the appeal, finding on the evidence that the vehicle was 'not designed or adapted to carry more than five persons apart from the person in the wheelchair'. *Emperor Enterprises Ltd, LON/93/803 (VTD 11038)*.

19.17   A company did not account for tax on the sale of a motor caravan to a handicapped person. The Commissioners issued an assessment charging tax on the sale, and the company appealed, contending that it should be treated as zero-rated under what is now *VATA 1994, Sch 8, Group 12, Item 2(f)*. The tribunal rejected this contention and dismissed the appeal, holding on the evidence that, although the caravan had been purchased by a handicapped person, it had not been 'designed or substantially and permanently adapted for the carriage of a person in a wheelchair or on a stretcher', so that the conditions of *Item 2(f)* were not satisfied. *St Andrew's Motor Homes Ltd, EDN/96/5 (VTD 14100). (Note.* The tribunal also rejected a contention by the company that the Commissioners were personally barred from raising the assessment—see 2.84 APPEALS.)

Whether 'equipment and appliances ... designed solely for use by a handicapped person' (VATA 1994, Sch 8, Group 12, Item 2(g))

19.18 **Alterations to kitchen at home of handicapped persons.** A householder, whose wife and son were both registered as disabled, had work carried out on his kitchen to make it easier for them to use. The work included altering two doors, supplying new cupboards and fitting electric points. He claimed that the work should be treated as zero-rated. The Commissioners rejected his claim and the tribunal dismissed his appeal, holding that none of the equipment was 'designed solely for use by a handicapped person'. *The Princess Louise Scottish Hospital*, 19.29 below, applied. *D Bell, LON/83/147 (VTD 1480)*.

19.19 Two handicapped persons purchased a bungalow and arranged for certain work to be done to the kitchen. The Commissioners issued a ruling that the work did not qualify for zero-rating, and the purchasers appealed. The tribunal upheld the Commissioners' ruling and dismissed the appeal. *AC Bruce & ML Hull, LON/86/315 (VTD 2248)*.

19.20 The tribunal held that a specially-designed 'rise and fall' sink was designed solely for use by a handicapped person and was thus zero-rated under what is now *VATA 1994, Sch 8, Group 12, Item 2(g)*. *WN Heaton & Son Ltd, MAN/86/336 (VTD 2397)*.

19.21 **Fitted kitchen for handicapped person—whether supply zero-rated.** A company supplied fitted kitchens. It provided a range of such kitchens which were specially designed to be suitable for disabled people. The Commissioners issued a ruling that the kitchens did not qualify for zero-rating, on the grounds that they were suitable for use by people who were not handicapped. The company appealed, accepting that some of the kitchen units (such as an oven, a hob and an extractor fan) failed to qualify for zero-rating, but contending that certain units were specifically designed for people in wheelchairs, and thus were within *Group 12, Item 2(g)*. The tribunal accepted this contention and allowed the appeal. On the evidence, several of the kitchen units stood on a high and deeply-recessed plinth, which was designed 'solely for use by a handicapped person'. The sink facing, a special knee-face hob unit, and wall cupboards with internal pull-out drop-down fittings, also qualified for zero-rating. *Bruce & Hull*, 19.19 above, distinguished. *Softley Ltd (t/a Softley Kitchens), LON/96/1810 (VTD 15034)*. (*Note*. For the Commissioners' practice following this decision, see Customs' VAT Manual, Part 7, chapter 12, annex C, paragraph 8. The Commissioners state that they 'continue to maintain that suppliers of mass production kitchen equipment cannot benefit from zero-rating, even if that equipment might be of more use to disabled people than others'.)

19.22 **Extension to house occupied by handicapped person.** Extensions to a house occupied by a handicapped person were held not to qualify for zero-rating in *JA Gow (t/a Falkirk Building Co), EDN/88/2 (VTD 2983); Cheverton Construction Ltd, LON/88/164 (VTD 3254)* and *KWS & BK Panesar (t/a KSP Builders and Panesar Building & Plumbers' Merchants), MAN/98/420 (VTD 16143)*.

19.23 **Extension containing renal dialysis unit.** A married couple arranged for an extension to their house to contain a renal dialysis unit, since the husband was suffering from a condition which required renal haemodialysis treatment two or three times each week. The Commissioners accepted that the provision of the renal dialysis unit, and the provision of a lavatory in the extension, qualified for zero-rating under what is now *VATA 1994, Sch 8, Group 12, Items 2(g)* and *10* respectively. However, they issued a ruling that the goods and services supplied in the building of the extension did not qualify for zero-rating. The wife appealed, contending that the proportion of the cost which was attributable to the room containing the dialysis unit

(79/235 of the total cost) should be treated as zero-rated. The tribunal rejected this contention and dismissed her appeal. *Mrs LJ Brailsford, MAN/95/562 (VTD 13472).*

19.24 **Architect's services in designing conversion of house for handicapped person.** An architect was employed to design the conversion of a house for the use of a handicapped person. The tribunal held that the architect's services did not qualify for zero-rating. *Dr AN Strachan, MAN/86/155 (VTD 2165).*

19.25 **Surveyors' services.** *Strachan,* 19.24 above, was applied in a similar case where a firm of surveyors had failed to account for VAT on services relating to work carried out for a County Council in relation to accommodation for the handicapped. The tribunal held that the surveyors' services did not qualify for zero-rating. *Hewitt Overall Associates, LON/92/536Z (VTD 9374).*

19.26 **Covered walkways erected at college for disabled.** A registered charity operated a college providing training and education for the disabled. It engaged a contractor to construct covered walkways at the college. The Commissioners issued a ruling that the work was standard-rated, and the college appealed, contending that it was zero-rated under what is now *VATA 1994, Sch 8, Group 12.* The tribunal dismissed the appeal, holding that the walkways did not qualify for zero-rating under *Group 12, Item 2(g)* since they were not 'designed solely for use by a handicapped person'. *The Princess Louise Scottish Hospital,* 19.29 below, applied. *Portland College, MAN/92/226 (VTD 9815).* (*Note.* The tribunal also held that the walkways failed to qualify for zero-rating under *Group 12, Item 8*—see 19.51 below.)

19.27 **Conversion and refurbishing of buildings at centre for treating epilepsy.** A registered charity provided residential assessment, treatment and care for sufferers from epilepsy. It occupied a 170–acre site, and incurred expenditure on refurbishing and improving its facilities. The Commissioners issued a ruling that the expenditure was not eligible for zero-rating, and the charity appealed, contending that much of the expenditure should be treated as zero-rated. The tribunal allowed the appeal in part, holding that the installation of a specially-designed heating system, enabling water to be circulated at lower temperatures than normal in order to reduce the risk of burning if a patient were to fall against them, qualified for zero-rating under what is now *VATA 1994, Sch 8, Group 12, Item 2(g).* However, expenditure on woollen carpets, purchased to protect patients from scorching when falling as a result of an epileptic seizure, did not qualify for zero-rating since the carpets were not specifically designed for the use of the handicapped. Similarly, changing facilities at a sports hall did not qualify for zero-rating, since they were 'no different to what may be found in a sports hall elsewhere', and a physiotherapy unit and gymnasium also failed to qualify for zero-rating. *The David Lewis Centre, MAN/92/69 (VTD 10860).* (*Notes.* (1) For other issues in this case, taken to the QB, see 11.6 CHARITIES. (2) The Commissioners did not appeal against the tribunal decision that the heating system qualified for zero-rating, but have subsequently stated that they do not accept that the ruling 'creates a precedent'—see Customs' VAT Manual, Part 7, chapter 12, annex C, paragraph 7.)

19.28 **Hydrotherapy pool at school for disabled.** A registered charity arranged for the installation of a hydrotherapy pool at a school which it ran for disabled children. The Commissioners issued a ruling that output tax was chargeable on the relevant supplies. The charity appealed, contending that the supplies qualified for zero-rating under what is now *VATA 1994, Sch 8, Group 12.* The tribunal allowed the appeal in part, holding on the evidence that the pool itself, and the 'environmental control system', were designed solely for use by the handicapped and qualified for zero-rating, but that the supply of the building housing the pool did not qualify for zero-rating. *The David Lewis Centre*, 19.27 above, applied. *Boys' and Girls' Welfare Society, MAN/96/1041 (VTD 15274)*. (*Note*. For another issue in this case, see 19.60 below.)

19.29 **Overbed tables—whether within Group 12, Item 2(g).**   A hospital purchased a number of specially-designed overbed tables which could be adjusted by one hand or foot. The Commissioners issued a ruling that VAT was chargeable on the tables, and the hospital appealed, contending that they were zero-rated under what is now *VATA 1994, Sch 8, Group 12, Item 2(g) or (h)*. The tribunal dismissed the appeal, holding that the tables were not zero-rated since they were not 'designed solely for use by a handicapped person'. The tribunal observed that the tables were 'eminently practical and convenient for all sorts of hospital patients and (were) not designed with a particular class in mind'. *The Princess Louise Scottish Hospital, [1983] VATTR 191 (VTD 1412)*.

19.30 **'Airbaths' supplied to hospitals.**   See *Aquakraft Ltd*, 19.6 above.

19.31 **Bath equipment for handicapped children.**   A company designed and supplied bath equipment intended for handicapped children. The Commissioners issued a ruling that the equipment was not eligible for zero-rating, since it could also be used by children who were not handicapped. The tribunal allowed the company's appeal, holding on the evidence that the equipment was 'designed solely for use by a handicapped person', and qualified for zero-rating under what is now *VATA 1994, Sch 8, Group 12, Item 2(g)*. *Kirton Designs Ltd, LON/86/641 (VTD 2374)*.

19.32 **Air conditioning units.**   A woman who suffered from multiple sclerosis purchased two air conditioning units and reclaimed input tax. The Commissioners rejected her claim and she appealed, contending that the units should be zero-rated since she was a handicapped person. The tribunal dismissed her appeal, holding that the units were not eligible for zero-rating since they were not 'designed solely for use by a handicapped person'. *The Princess Louise Scottish Hospital*, 19.29 above, applied. *E Simmons, LON/90/1557Z (VTD 6622)*.

19.33 **Sloping writing board—whether 'designed solely for use by a handicapped person'.**   A company manufactured a magnetic sloping writing board, called the 'Posturite Board', which was designed to reduce neck and back pain when writing and reading. It did not account for VAT on supplies of the board. The Commissioners issued a ruling that the supplies were standard-rated, and the company appealed, contending that the supplies should be zero-rated since the board was particularly helpful to people in wheelchairs. The tribunal dismissed the company's appeal, holding that the board was not designed solely for use by handicapped people and thus did not qualify for zero-rating. *Posturite (UK) Ltd, LON/91/2723Z (VTD 7848)*.

19.34 **Electromagnetic mattress, pillow and Kenkobio machine.**   A company imported and distributed electromagnetic mattresses, pillows, and 'Kenkobio' machines (which were designed to reduce pain by introducing an electromagnetic field to the affected part of the body). It did not account for VAT on the sales of these items, considering that they should be zero-rated under what is now *VATA 1994, Sch 8, Group 12*. The Commissioners issued a ruling that the supplies did not qualify for zero-rating, and the company appealed. The tribunal dismissed the appeal, holding on the evidence that the items in question were not designed solely for use by handicapped people. *Dicta* in *The Princess Louise Scottish Hospital*, 19.29 above, applied. *Back In Health Ltd, MAN/91/1139 (VTD 10003)*.

19.35 **High-density foam mattress and pillow—whether 'designed solely for use by a handicapped person'.**   A company manufactured high-density foam mattresses and pillows. The Commissioners issued a ruling that the supplies of these items did not qualify for zero-rating, on the basis that they were not 'designed solely for use by a handicapped person'. The company appealed, contending that the items were designed solely for use by people who were chronically sick and were therefore within the definition of 'handicapped person' in *VATA 1994, Sch 8, Group 12, Note 3*. The tribunal allowed the company's appeal. Applying *dicta* of Lord Grantchester in *Kirton Designs Ltd*, 19.31 above, the tribunal should 'apply a subjective test and consider what was in the mind of the designer'. On the evidence, the foam and the mattress had been designed 'solely for the use of those suffering long-term pain'. The foam had a strong odour, which made it 'most unlikely that it would be purchased by anyone who does not suffer from long-term pain or pressure sores'. The fact that the mattress could, in principle, be used by a normal person was not conclusive. Furthermore, 'long-term pain and pressure sores' were 'within the meaning of "chronically sick" because the conditions last a long time, and are not soon over, and those suffering from the conditions are ill, or unhealthy, or suffering from an ailment'. *Tempur Pedic (UK) Ltd, LON/95/458A (VTD 13744)*.

19.36   **Central heating system.**   An appellant had a three-year-old daughter who suffered from cystic fibrosis. He reclaimed input tax on the purchase of a central heating system. The Commissioners rejected the claim and he appealed, contending that the system was necessary for his daughter's health. The tribunal dismissed his appeal, as the system was not 'designed solely for use by a handicapped person'. *P Drummond, EDN/94/177 (VTD 13100)*.

19.37   **Supplies of pesticide sprays.**   A company manufactured aerosol pesticide sprays, designed to kill dust mites. It supplied the sprays to pharmacists for sale to asthmatics or sufferers from eczema. The Commissioners issued a ruling that output tax was chargeable on the supply of the sprays. The company appealed, contending that supplies of the sprays to asthmatics or sufferers from eczema should be treated as zero-rated under *VATA 1994, Sch 8, Group 12, Item 2*. The tribunal dismissed the appeal, holding on the evidence that not all sufferers from asthma could be described as 'chronically sick or disabled' within *Group 12, Note 3*. Accordingly, the sprays were not 'designed solely for use by a handicapped person', and thus failed to qualify for zero-rating. *GD Searle & Co Ltd, LON/94/1290A (VTD 13439)*.

19.38   **Products designed for sufferers from house dust allergy.**   A company marketed a number of products which were designed for people who were allergic to house dust. The Commissioners accepted that a nebuliser qualified for zero-rating under *VATA 1994, Sch 8, Group 12, Item 2*. However, they ruled that the other products — bedding covers, a vacuum cleaner, a dehumidifier, a medication system, and an anti-allergen system — failed to qualify for zero-rating. The company appealed, contending that all five products were 'equipment and appliances ... designed solely for use by a handicapped person', within *Item 2(g)*. The tribunal accepted the company's evidence and allowed the appeal, finding that the products were specifically designed for people who suffered from allergy to house dust to such an extent that they were 'chronically sick', within *Group 12, Note 3*. *GD Searle & Co Ltd*, 19.37 above, distinguished. *Medivac Healthcare Ltd, LON/99/1271 (VTD 16829)*.

19.39   **Single-seat golf buggies.**   A partnership manufactured single-seat golf buggies, which it marketed for sale to elderly golfers. It did not account for output tax on the sale of the buggies, and the Commissioners issued an assessment. The partnership appealed, contending that the buggies should be treated as zero-rated. The tribunal rejected this contention, holding that the buggies 'were not, viewed as a whole, designed solely for the use of handicapped persons'. *Foxer Industries, LON/95/*

1452A (VTD 13817). (*Note.* For a subsequent appeal by the same partnership, see 19.48 below.)

19.40   *Foxer Industries*, 19.39 above, was applied in the similar subsequent case of *CF Leisure Mobility Ltd, LON/99/1063 (VTD 16790).*

19.41   **Fire escape—whether within Group 12, Item 2(g).**   A charity operated a hotel which provided accommodation for people suffering from arthritis, and for people caring for them. It arranged for the construction of a fire escape. The Commissioners issued a ruling that output tax was chargeable on the work, and the charity appealed, contending that it should be treated as zero-rated. The tribunal dismissed the appeal, holding that the fire escape did not qualify for zero-rating, since it was not 'designed solely for use by a handicapped person' as required by *VATA 1994, Sch 8, Group 12, Item 2(g). Arthritis Care, LON/95/2611A (VTD 13974).*

19.42   **Computer system supplied to handicapped student.**   A student, who was accepted as being a 'handicapped person' within *VATA 1994, Sch 8, Group 12, Note 3*, ordered a new computer system. The Commissioners issued a ruling that only certain parts of the system qualified for zero-rating, within *VATA 1994, Sch 8, Group 12, Item 2(g)*. The tribunal allowed the student's appeal, holding on the evidence that the system had to be viewed as a single supply and that it was 'designed solely for use by a handicapped person'. *WM Hall, LON/00/463 (VTD 16989).*

19.43   **Incontinence pads ordered by nursing homes—whether within Group 12, Item 2(g).**   See *Express Medicare Ltd*, 1.63 AGENTS.

Parts and accessories (VATA 1994, Sch 8, Group 12, Item 2(h))

19.44   **Overbed tables.**   See *The Princess Louise Scottish Hospital*, 19.29 above.

19.45   **Electric generator.**   A young girl suffered from severe asthma and needed to use a nebuliser several times a day. Her father purchased an electric generator to power the nebuliser. The Commissioners issued a ruling that VAT was chargeable on the supply, and he appealed, contending that the generator should be treated as zero-rated under what is now *VATA 1994, Sch 8, Group 12, Item 2(h)*. The tribunal rejected this contention and dismissed his appeal, holding on the evidence that the generator was not 'designed solely for use by a handicapped person'. *I Mills, LON/85/33 (VTD 1893).*

19.46   A similar decision was reached in *AC Wesley, LON/92/407Y (VTD 9074).*

19.47   **Batteries for use in invalid scooters and wheelchairs.**   A charity purchased a number of batteries for use in invalid scooters and wheelchairs. The Commissioners issued a ruling that VAT was chargeable on the supply of the batteries. The charity appealed, contending that the supply should be treated as zero-rated under *VATA 1994, Sch 8, Group 12, Item 2(h)*. The tribunal rejected this contention and dismissed the charity's appeal. *Poole Shopmobility, LON/98/1486 (VTD 16290).* (*Note.* For another issue in this case, see 11.13 CHARITIES.)

Services of adapting goods for a handicapped person (VATA 1994, Sch 8, Group 12, Item 3)

19.48   **Adapted golf buggies.**   A partnership manufactured single-seat golf buggies for elderly golfers. Following the decision noted at 19.39 above, in which the tribunal held that the buggies did not qualify for zero-rating under *VATA 1994, Sch 8, Group 12, Item 2(g)*, the partnership claimed that work done in adapting some of the buggies for specific customers should be treated as qualifying for zero-rating under *Item 3*. The partnership claimed that 21 supplies should be treated as within this provision. The tribunal found that only 9 of the 21 customers in question were within the definition of a 'handicapped person' in *Note 3*. In one of these cases, the modifications to the basic design were so fundamental that the entire buggy should be treated as zero-rated under *Item 2(g)*. In the other eight cases, an appropriate proportion of the price (fixed by the tribunal at 13.4% of the total) should be treated as zero-rated under *Item 3*. *Foxer Industries, LON/95/1452 (VTD 14469)*.

19.49   **Work at properties owned by housing trust.**   A company carried out work at properties which were owned by a housing trust (which was not a charity) and were occupied by handicapped people. It did not account for tax on the work. The Commissioners issued an assessment and the company appealed, contending that the services were within *VATA 1994, 8 Sch, Group 12, Item 3*. The tribunal dismissed the appeal, holding on the evidence that the relevant supplies had been made to the housing trust rather than to the tenants, so that they failed to qualify for zero-rating. *Redrow Group plc*, 34.59 INPUT TAX, distinguished. *Cross Electrical & Building Services Ltd, MAN/99/1070 (VTD 16954)*.

SUPPLIES OF WIDENING DOORWAYS, ETC. (VATA 1994, Sch 8, Group 12, Items 8, 9)

19.50   **Widening of doorways at house inherited by handicapped person but not occupied by her.**   A handicapped woman inherited a house from her mother and incurred expenditure on widening the ground-floor doorways to make the house suitable for her occupation. However, before the work could be completed, the woman decided that she wanted to sell the house. The Commissioners issued an assessment charging tax on the work. The tribunal upheld the assessment, holding that the work in question was not eligible for zero-rating under what is now *VATA 1994, Sch 8, Group 12, Item 8*, since the woman had never occupied the house as her private residence. *PA Macrae, LON/90/1734Z (VTD 7849)*.

19.51   **Covered walkways erected at college for disabled.**   In the case noted at 19.26 above, a registered charity, which operated a college providing training and education for the disabled, engaged a contractor to construct covered walkways at the college. The Commissioners issued a ruling that output tax was chargeable on the work, and the college appealed, contending *inter alia* that the work should be treated as zero-rated under what is now *VATA 1994, Sch 8, Group 12, Item 8*. The tribunal rejected this contention and dismissed the appeal. *Portland College, MAN/92/226 (VTD 9815)*.

19.52   **Installation of new patio doors and internal doors.**   A handicapped person, who was confined to a wheelchair, purchased a bungalow. Some of the internal doors were too small to accommodate his wheelchair, and he arranged for a builder to undertake substantial alterations to the bungalow. A new entrance hall, suitable for entry in a wheelchair, was built. A new shower-room and bathroom were installed, and wider internal doorways were provided. A new kitchen was installed, the lounge window was replaced by sliding patio doors, and the level of the ground outside these doors was raised to enable the wheelchair to pass through them. A new car port was built. The Commissioners accepted that the building of the new entrance hall qualified for zero-rating under what is now *VATA 1994, Sch 8, Group 12, Item 8*, and that the new shower-room qualified for zero-rating under what is now *VATA 1994, Sch 8, Group 12, Item 10*. However, they issued a ruling that the remainder of the work was standard-rated. The builder appealed. The tribunal allowed the appeal in part, holding that the installation of the new internal doorways and the raising of the ground outside the patio doors qualified for zero-rating under *Item 8*, and the new bathroom qualified for zero-rating under *Item 10*. However, the new kitchen, patio doors, and car port were not eligible for zero-rating. *DJ Avis (t/a Property Alterations), LON/92/1663 (VTD 10664)*.

19.53   **Extension to bedroom also used as access to handicapped person's bedroom.**   A handicapped person reclaimed input tax on work done at his residence. The work included the extension of a bedroom which was adjacent to the bedroom he slept in, and which he used as a means of access to his bedroom on occasions when a lift, which was his normal means of access to his bedroom, was not working. The Commissioners issued a ruling that this part of the work did not qualify for zero-rating. The tribunal allowed the claimant's appeal, holding that the bedroom in question, although it was principally used as a bedroom, also qualified as a 'passage' for the purpose of what is now *VATA 1994, Sch 8, Group 12, Item 8*. Accordingly the work qualified for zero-rating. *BH Cannings-Knight, LON/92/2256A (VTD 11291)*. (*Note*. The Commissioners consider that 'the particulars of this case were unique'. For their interpretation of this decision, see Customs' VAT Manual, Part 7, chapter 12, section 5.13(a).)

19.54   **Supply of building materials to handicapped person—whether supplied 'in connection' with services under Group 12, Item 8.**   A barrister, who suffered from multiple sclerosis and was a 'handicapped person' within what is now *VATA 1994, Sch 8, Group 12, Note 3*, arranged for two builders to carry out construction work at his home. It was accepted that the builders' services qualified for zero-rating under what is now *VATA 1994, Sch 8, Group 12, Item 8*. The barrister also purchased certain building materials. The Commissioners issued a ruling that these materials did not qualify for zero-rating, since they had not been supplied by the builders who had supplied the construction services. The barrister appealed, contending that the materials had been supplied in connection with the supplies of construction services, that the fact that they were supplied by a different supplier was not conclusive, and that they qualified for zero-rating under *Sch 8, Group 12, Item 13*. The tribunal accepted this contention and allowed the appeal. *G Flather, LON/93/1832 (VTD 11960)*. (*Note*. Where building services are zero-rated under *VATA 1994, Sch 8, Group 5, Item 2*, any materials supplied in connection with those services can be zero-rated under *Item 3* only if supplied by the same person. However, there is no similar provision in *VATA 1994, Sch 8, Group 12, Item 13*.)

19.55   **Widening of doorways, etc. at tennis club used by charity for the handicapped.**   A tennis club allowed its premises to be used by a charity for the disabled. To enable disabled people to use the premises, various doorways were widened, access ramps were built, and special WCs and showers were installed in the changing rooms. The club paid for the work and was subsequently reimbursed by the charity. The Commissioners issued a ruling that the work in question was standard-rated, as the relevant supplies had been made to the club rather than to the charity. The trustee of the charity (who was also the secretary of the club) appealed, contending that the work should be treated as qualifying for zero-rating under what is now *VATA 1994, Sch 8, Group 12*. The tribunal rejected this contention and dismissed the appeal. Since the relevant supplies had not been made to the charity, they failed to qualify for zero-rating. *DM Brand (as Trustee of Racket Sports for Children with Special Needs), LON/95/2751 (VTD 14080)*.

19.56   **Supply of conservatory at home of handicapped person.**   A married couple arranged for the construction of a conservatory at the rear of their house. The husband suffered from severe arthritis and was confined to a wheelchair. The couple reclaimed VAT on the construction of the conservatory. The Commissioners agreed to refund VAT on the widening of the existing doorway from the house to the conservatory, and on the construction of two ramps, but refused to refund the remainder on the basis that it failed to qualify for zero-rating. The wife appealed, contending that the supply of the conservatory should be treated as zero-rated. The tribunal rejected this contention and held that only the construction of the ramps and the widening of the doorway qualified for zero-rating. *GV Johnson, MAN/99/864 (VTD 16672).*

SUPPLIES OF BATHROOMS, WASHROOMS, ETC. (VATA 1994, Sch 8, Group 12, Items 10, 11)

Note. *VATA 1994, Sch 8, Group 12, Item 11* was substituted by the *VAT (Charities and Aids for the Handicapped) Order 2000 (SI 2000 No 805)* with effect from 1 April 2000. The cases in this section should be read in the light of this change.

19.57   **Bathroom and lavatory at annexe to house for handicapped person.** A company extended a building by adding an annexe designed for the use of a handicapped person. The annexe included a specially-designed bathroom and lavatory. The company did not account for VAT on the work. The Commissioners accepted that 30% of the work in question was zero-rated, as being attributable to the supply of the bathroom and lavatory, but issued an assessment charging tax on the remaining 70%. The tribunal upheld the assessment and dismissed the company's appeal. *Heathill Developments Ltd, LON/87/30 (VTD 2412).*

19.58   See also *Brailsford*, 19.23 above, and *Avis*, 19.52 above.

19.59   **Hot water system of residential home.** A home for the disabled provided accommodation for 25 residents. It updated the hot water system by installing thermostatic control valves. The Commissioners accepted that such work was zero-rated in so far as it related to bathrooms and lavatories, but issued a ruling that it was standard-rated in so far as it related to washbasins and showers in the residents' bedrooms. The home appealed, contending that the bedrooms should be regarded as washrooms for the purpose of what is now *VATA 1994, Sch 8, Group 12, Item 11*, since the residents used them for washing as well as for sleeping in. The tribunal rejected this contention and dismissed the appeal, holding that a washroom was a room which primarily provided washing facilities, whereas the rooms in question primarily provided sleeping facilities. *Mid-Derbyshire Cheshire Home, MAN/89/546 (VTD 4512).* (*Note.* See also *Sch 8, Group 12, Note 5K,* introduced by the *VAT (Charities and Aids for the Handicapped) Order 2000 (SI 2000 No 805)* with effect from 1 April 2000. *Note 5K* defines a 'washroom' as 'a room that contains a lavatory or washbasin (or both) but does not contain a bath or a shower or cooking, sleeping or laundry facilities'.)

19.60   **Special radiators in residential unit for disabled children.** A registered charity operated a residential unit for disabled children. It arranged for the installation of new radiators with a low surface temperature. The Commissioners issued a ruling that output tax was chargeable on the supply of the radiators, and the charity appealed, contending that they should be treated as zero-rated under what is now *VATA 1994, Sch 8, Group 12.* The tribunal allowed the appeal in part, holding that the radiators did not qualify for zero-rating under *Item 2(g)*, since such radiators were not 'designed solely for use by a handicapped person', but that they qualified for zero-rating under what is now *Item 11* where they were installed in bathrooms, washrooms or lavatories. *Boys' and Girls' Welfare Society, MAN/96/1041 (VTD 15274).* (*Note.* For another issue in this case, see 19.28 above.)

19.61   **Renovation of shower-room used by handicapped woman.** A woman, who was accepted as being a 'handicapped person' within what is now *VATA 1994, Sch 8, Group 12,* occupied a house with a shower-room on the first floor. She had the roof and window of the shower-room replaced, and had a new central heating system fitted. She appealed against the Commissioners' decision that this work did not qualify for zero-rating. The tribunal dismissed her appeal. The conversion of a bathroom into a shower-room was within the scope of *Group 12, Item 10*, but the additional work at issue in this case was not. It was necessary because the house was not in a good state of repair, rather than because the appellant was a handicapped person. *J Drury, LON/90/1398Y (VTD 6030)*.

19.62   **Installation of WCs and shower at tennis club used by charity for the disabled.**   See *Brand*, 19.55 above.

SUPPLIES OF LIFTS (VATA 1994, Sch 8, Group 12, Items 16–18)

19.63   **Supplies of lifts to unregistered nursing home.**   The proprietor of an unregistered nursing home arranged for the installation of a lift. The Commissioners issued a ruling that output tax was chargeable on the supply, and she appealed, contending that the supply should be zero-rated because all the residents of the nursing home were chronically sick or disabled. The tribunal dismissed her appeal, holding that the supply failed to qualify for zero-rating because the supply had been made to the proprietor, who was 'neither a handicapped person or a charity'. *KA Conroy, LON/85/115 (VTD 1916)*. (*Notes*. (1) The case was decided on the provisions of *VATA 1983* as originally enacted, prior to the introduction of what is now *VATA 1994, Sch 8, Group 12, Items 16–18*, which date from 1986. However, *Items 16–18* only provide for the zero-rating of lifts where the supply is made to a handicapped person or a charity, so that the decision remains relevant to *Items 16–18*. (2) The tribunal also held that the supply failed to qualify for zero-rating under *VATA 1983* on the grounds that the lift had not been 'designed solely for use by a handicapped person'. The decision on this point has been overtaken by the introduction of *Items 16–18*.)

19.64   A similar decision was reached in *Brian Perkins & Co Ltd, LON/88/952Y (VTD 3885)*.

19.65   **Installation of lift at building occupied by Student Union.**   A Student Union occupied premises on four floors of the university campus. An external lift was installed to enable disabled students to have access to the top two floors. The Commissioners issued a ruling that the installation of the lift was standard-rated. The Union appealed, contending that it should be treated as zero-rated under *VATA 1994, Sch 8, Group 12, Item 17*. The tribunal dismissed the appeal, holding that, since the Student Union premises existed 'to provide facilities for students generally both to the able-bodied and the handicapped', it could not be 'properly described as a "day-centre" within the ordinary use of the term' and thus failed to qualify for zero-rating. *Union of Students of the University of Warwick, [1995] VATDR 219 (VTD 13821)*.

19.66   **Installation of lift at art gallery.**   A charity installed a lift at an art gallery which it operated. The Commissioners issued a ruling that output tax was chargeable on the installation. The charity appealed, contending that the lift should be treated as zero-rated under *VATA 1994, Sch 8, Group 12, Item 17*. The tribunal dismissed the appeal, holding that the gallery was not within the definition of a 'day-centre', so that the lift failed to qualify for zero-rating. *Union of Students of the University of Warwick*, 19.65 above, applied. The tribunal observed that 'had Parliament intended to zero-rate lifts provided for the handicapped, this could have been done without restricting the provision to day-centres provided by a charity'. *Aspex Visual Arts Trust, LON/97/683 (VTD 16419)*. (*Note*. The tribunal also held that the lift was not a 'chair lift' within *Item 2(d)*.)

20   Education

Note. *VATA 1994, Sch 9, Group 6* derives from *VATA 1983, Sch 6, Group 6,* which was substituted by the *VAT (Education) Order 1994 (SI 1994 No 1188)*, with effect from 1 August 1994. Most of the cases in this chapter were heard under the previous wording of *VATA 1983, Sch 6, Group 6,* and should be read in the light of this change. The cases are arranged under the following headings.

> Provision of education by an 'eligible body' (VATA 1994, Sch 9, Group 6, Item 1(a)) 20.1–20.13
> The provision of research (VATA 1994, Sch 9, Group 6, Item 1(b)) 20.14
> Vocational training (VATA 1994, Sch 9, Group 6, Items 1(c), 5) 20.15–20.19
> Private tuition (VATA 1994, Sch 9, Group 6, Item 2) 20.20–20.24
> Incidental goods and services (VATA 1994, Sch 9, Group 6, Item 4) 20.25–20.29
> Youth club facilities (VATA 1994, Sch 9, Group 6, Item 6) 20.30–20.34

PROVISION OF EDUCATION BY AN 'ELIGIBLE BODY' (VATA 1994, Sch 9, Group 6, Item 1(a))

Note. Before 1 August 1994, *Item 1* referred to the provision of education by a 'school, eligible institution or university'. The cases in this section should be read in the light of this change.

20.1   **Tuition by barrister at university.**   A barrister gave tuition to law students at Cambridge University. He did not account for VAT on the fees he received from the colleges. The Commissioners issued a ruling that VAT was chargeable on the fees, but the tribunal allowed the barrister's appeal, holding that he was acting as an employee of the colleges, so that the fees were exempt under what is now *VATA 1994, Sch 9, Group 6, Item 1. CI Cant, [1976] VATTR 237 (VTD 317).*

20.2   **Lectures and seminars provided by musicians at universities.**   A partnership of four musicians gave lectures, seminars and tutorials at Cambridge and Glasgow Universities. The musicians did not account for VAT on their fees for these services, and the Commissioners issued an assessment on the partnership. The partnership appealed, contending that the services were exempt from VAT by virtue of what is now *VATA 1994, Sch 9, Group 6.* The tribunal allowed the appeal, holding that the relevant services were supplied to the students by the two universities, and that the universities had procured the partnership to provide the tuition as agents of the universities. Accordingly the services were exempt under what is now *VATA 1994, Sch 9, Group 6, Item 1. Alberni String Quartet, [1990] VATTR 166 (VTD 5024). (Notes.* (1) The assessment appealed against also covered certain other supplies, with regard to which the tribunal held that there was insufficient evidence for it to reach a final conclusion, and gave guidelines for the parties to reach agreement, with liberty to apply for a further hearing. There was no further public hearing of the appeal. (2) An alternative contention by the partnership's accountant, that the partners had made the supplies as individuals, rather than as a partnership, was rejected.)

20.3   **Open University courses—whether BBC supplying education.**   The BBC invoiced the Open University in respect of expenditure which it incurred in broadcasting television and radio programmes relating to Open University courses. The Commissioners issued a ruling that VAT was chargeable on the amounts invoiced. The Open University lodged an appeal, contending that the amounts should be treated as exempt from VAT. The tribunal dismissed the appeal, holding that the services of the BBC did not qualify for exemption, since the BBC was not itself providing education. *The Open University, [1982] VATTR 29 (VTD 1196).*

20.4   **Unregistered school.**   A former schoolteacher opened a nursery school in the basement of her home. She also began teaching English to foreign children living in London. However, the Department of Education and Science refused to register her school. She did not account for VAT on the fees which she received, and the Commissioners issued an assessment on them. The tribunal dismissed her appeal, holding that the fees did not qualify for exemption. *JG Barker, [1984] VATTR 147 (VTD 1671).*

20.5   **School visits to cavern.**   A company owned a cavern, to which the public were admitted on payment. School groups were admitted at reduced rates. The company did not account for VAT on the amounts it received from school parties and the Commissioners issued an assessment on them. The company appealed, holding that the relevant supplies should be treated as exempt under what is now *VATA 1994, Sch 9, Group 6.* The tribunal dismissed the appeal, holding that, although the school visits were instructional, they did not qualify as 'education ... of a kind provided by a school or university', since each visit lasted for only one hour, and was equivalent to a single lesson rather than to a course of instruction. *Buxton & District Civic Association Ltd, MAN/87/385 (VTD 3380).*

20.6   **Ballroom dancing.**   A company, limited by guarantee, was formed to encourage dancing. It organised tests for ballroom dancers under the age of 16. It did not account for VAT on these, and the Commissioners issued a ruling that they were liable to VAT at the standard rate. The company appealed, contending that they were exempt from VAT under what is now *VATA 1994, Sch 9, Group 6.* The tribunal allowed the appeal, applying the tribunal decision in *Phillips,* 20.7 below, and holding that the teaching of ballroom dancing was within the definition of 'education of a kind provided by a school'. The fact that dancing had a 'recreational element' did not mean that the tests in question were excluded from exemption. *Allied Dancing Association Ltd, [1993] VATTR 405 (VTD 10777).* (*Note.* For another issue in this case, see 60.1 TRADE UNIONS, PROFESSIONAL AND PUBLIC INTEREST BODIES.)

20.7   **Motorcycle instruction.**   An individual (P) provided courses in motorcycle instruction. He did not account for output tax on his fees. The Commissioners issued assessments, against which he appealed, contending that his supplies should be treated as exempt under what is now *VATA 1994, Sch 9, Group 6.* The tribunal allowed his appeal, holding that education was not confined to 'formal instruction in the classroom'. *Dicta* of Lord Hailsham in *CIR v McMullen, HL 1980, 54 TC 413 (TTC 2001, 9.44)* applied. *TK Phillips (t/a Bristol Motorcycle Training Centre), [1992] VATTR 77 (VTD 7444).*

20.8   **Zoological society.**   A zoological society, which operated a large zoo near Chester, accounted for output tax on its admission charges, but subsequently submitted a repayment claim, contending that it should have treated these charges as consideration for exempt supplies of education. The Commissioners rejected the claim and the tribunal dismissed the society's appeal. The fact that, in a 1959 rating case (*North of England Zoological Society v Chester Rural District Council, CA [1959] 1 WLR 773; [1959] 3 All ER 116*), the CA had held that the society had the advancement of education as an object, and conducted the zoo as an 'educational undertaking', was not conclusive. The tribunal observed that 'education is capable of being advanced without that factor which results in the advancement itself qualifying as education', and that 'a person determined on spending a relaxing day at the zoo simply viewing its exhibits is hardly likely to regard the visit as one of education'. Although the society's supplies had an 'educational content', they were essentially recreational. The QB upheld this decision. Carnwath J held that, in the context of the *EC Sixth Directive*, 'the VAT legislation is referring to education in the sense of a course or class or lesson of instruction, rather than the broader sense in which that expression was used by the Court of Appeal in the 1959 case'. *North of England Zoological Society v C & E Commrs, QB [1999] STC 1027.*

20.9   **VATA 1994, Sch 9, Group 6, Note 1(e)—definition of 'eligible body'.**   A charity provided educational courses for foreign students. Its income exceeded its expenditure by a substantial margin, the surplus being retained with a view to subsequent expansion. The Commissioners registered the trust for VAT, considering that it was not eligible for exemption under the legislation then in force because it was making profits (compare now the definition of an 'eligible body' in *Group 6, Note 1(e)*). The trust appealed, contending that the courses were provided 'otherwise than for profit' and thus were exempt from VAT, so that it was not required to be registered. The tribunal allowed the trust's appeal, holding that there was no profit motive as the surplus created had to be applied for charitable purposes. The CA upheld this decision. Sir Nicholas Browne-Wilkinson VC held that the words 'otherwise than for profit' 'refer to the objects for which an organisation is established and not to the budgeting policy being pursued for the time being by the organisation in question'. *C & E Commrs v Bell Concord Educational Trust Ltd, CA [1989] STC 264; [1989] 2 All ER 217; [1989] 1 CMLR 845.*

20.10   *Bell Concord Educational Trust Ltd,* 20.9 above, was applied in a similar case where the tribunal held that, in considering whether payments received for supplies exceeded the costs of making those supplies, indirect costs could be taken into account and it should consider the position over a period of time rather than on a year-to-year basis. *The University of Edinburgh, EDN/92/196 (VTD 10936).*

20.11   *Bell Concord Educational Trust Ltd,* 20.9 above, was distinguished in a subsequent case where a company which operated an accountancy college appealed against registration, contending that all its supplies were exempt. The tribunal rejected this contention and dismissed the appeal, finding that the company had paid remuneration to its directors and holding that this amounted to a distribution of profit for the purposes of *Group 6, Note 1(e)*. (The chairman commented that 'we cannot see that it makes any difference in principle that it was taken as remuneration and not as dividend'.) *North London College of Accountancy Ltd, LON/95/417A (VTD 14054).*

20.12   **Students Union—whether part of an 'eligible body'.**   A Students Union operated a shop from which it made various supplies to students. It lodged a repayment claim, contending that it had wrongly accounted for output tax on certain supplies which qualified for exemption. The Commissioners rejected the claim on the basis that the Union was not an 'eligible body' within *VATA 1994, Sch 9, Group 6, Note 1(e)*. The tribunal considered this point at a preliminary hearing and held that the Union was 'an integral part of the University', and was therefore part of an 'eligible body'. The Union was therefore 'party to the principal supply of education' within *Group 6, Item 4*. The tribunal directed that the substantive appeal of the repayment claim should be listed for hearing. *University of Leicester Students Union, MAN/99/543 (VTD 16792).* (*Note.* There has as yet been no further hearing of the appeal.)

20.13   **Residential courses in English as a foreign language—whether VATA 1994, Sch 9, Group 6, Note 2 applicable.**   A company, which was accepted as falling within *VATA 1994, Sch 9, Group 6, Note 1(f)*, organised a number of courses for overseas students in the teaching of English as a foreign language. Most of the courses were residential, although in some cases students stayed with English families. The company treated its supplies as exempt. The Commissioners issued an assessment charging tax on the basis that the effect of *Group 6, Note 2* was that some of the company's supplies did not qualify for exemption. The company appealed, contending that its supplies should be treated as an integral part of the provision of education by an eligible body, and as exempt. The CA accepted this contention and allowed the appeal. Schiemann LJ held that *Group 6* should be construed in accordance with *Article 13A1* of the *EC Sixth Directive*. Accordingly, *Note 2* should not be construed in such a way as to exclude supplies which were 'closely related' to the teaching of English as a foreign language. The company's supplies of catering and accommodation, and of various types of excursions, were 'closely related to the supply of the teaching of English as a foreign language' and were exempt from VAT. *C & E Commrs v Pilgrims Language Courses Ltd (and cross-appeal), CA [1999] STC 874*. (*Note*. For the Commissioners' practice following this decision, see Business Brief 18/99, issued on 18 August 1999.)

THE PROVISION OF RESEARCH (VATA 1994, Sch 9, Group 6, Item 1(b))

20.14   A charitable institution, based in York, operated a fund to help families who were caring for severely handicapped children. The fund's data was kept on a computer operated by the University of York. The University invoiced the charity for a proportion of the salaries of the staff who updated the database, but did not charge VAT on the invoices. The Commissioners issued an assessment charging output tax. The charity appealed, contending that the supplies should be treated as exempt under what is now *VATA 1994, Sch 9, Group 6, Item 1(b)*, as the provision of research by an eligible body. The tribunal accepted this contention and allowed the appeal, holding on the evidence that the database was 'a valuable research resource' of statistical data for use in the sphere of social studies. The Commissioners appealed to the QB, which remitted the case for further findings of fact. The tribunal heard further evidence and found that there were a series of contracts between the charity and the university and that it was an obligation of each of the contracts that the University would maintain and update the database, and would produce 'applied information'. The tribunal expressed the opinion that 'the characteristics of such supplies were such that ... they constituted the provision of education or research (and) did not constitute the provision of welfare or social security services'. *Joseph Rowntree Foundation, MAN/92/537 (VTD 14534)*. (*Note*. There was no further hearing of the appeal by the QB. It is understood that the Commissioners accepted the tribunal's findings and agreed to withdraw the assessment.)

VOCATIONAL TRAINING (VATA 1994, Sch 9, Group 6, Items 1(c), 5)

20.15   **Director of company providing lectures for Manpower Services Commission.**   A company provided courses of lectures for the Manpower Services Commission. It was accepted that the supplies by the company were exempt under VAT under what is now *VATA 1994, Sch 9, Group 6*. The company paid its principal director for providing the lectures. The director issued invoices to the company for his services, on the basis that in giving the lectures he was acting on his own account and not as an official or employee of the company. He did not charge VAT on the invoices, and the Commissioners issued an assessment on the amounts in question. The tribunal dismissed the director's appeal, holding that although the director was supplying lecturing services to the company, these supplies by themselves did not qualify as 'training'. *AD Knowles, MAN/87/471 (VTD 3393)*.

20.16   **Services of YTS trainees.**   A company, limited by guarantee, was established as a non-profit-making body to act as an agent for the Manpower Services Commission. It placed trainees with local employers. The employers contracted to make payments to the company every four weeks, as contributions towards training. The Commissioners issued an assessment on these payments. The company appealed, contending that they were exempt under what is now *VATA 1994, Sch 9, Group 6*. The tribunal dismissed the appeal, holding that the supplies which the company made to the trainees were exempt under what is now *VATA 1994, Sch 9, Group 6*, but that the supplies which the company made to the employers were a provision of the trainees' services, which did not qualify for exemption. *North-West Leicestershire Youth Training Scheme Ltd, [1989] VATTR 321 (VTD 4476)*. (*Note*. For the award of costs in this case, see 2.276 APPEALS.)

20.17   *North-West Leicestershire Youth Training Scheme*, 20.16 above, was applied in the similar subsequent case of *Lite Ltd, MAN/97/264 (VTD 15223)*.

20.18   **Supplies to new businesses under Employment and Training Act 1973— whether 'vocational training'.** A company supplied services to new businesses under agreements with a local Training and Enterprise Council, in accordance with the *Employment and Training Act 1973*. The Commissioners issued a ruling that output tax was chargeable on the supplies. The company appealed, contending that it was making supplies of vocational training, which qualified for exemption under *VATA 1994, Sch 9, Group 6, Item 1(c)*. The tribunal accepted this contention and allowed the appeal. *Harrogate Business Development Centre Ltd, [1998] VATDR 466 (VTD 15565)*.

20.19   **Supplies of GCSE and A level courses—whether vocational training.** A company, which was not an 'eligible body' within *VATA 1994, Sch 9, Group 6, Item 1*, advertised GCSE and A level courses in collaboration with three colleges of further education. Under the scheme, the company advertised for students, who enrolled with one of the three colleges and worked from home with materials supplied by the company, under the supervision of a tutor provided by the company. The colleges received funding from the Further Education Funding Council, and paid the company 79% of the funds relating to the company's students. The company did not account for output tax on the amounts which it received from the colleges. The Commissioners issued an assessment charging tax on these, and the company appealed, contending that they should be treated as exempt under *VATA 1994, Sch 9, Group 6, Item 5*. The tribunal rejected this contention and dismissed the appeal, holding that 'for a course to be vocational training it must . . . constitute training or retraining for a *specific* trade, profession or employment', and finding that GCSE and A level courses were not within the definition of 'vocational training'. *Oxford Open Learning (Systems) Ltd, LON/98/1478 (VTD 16160)*. (*Note*. For a subsequent appeal involving the same company, see 5.47 BOOKS, ETC.)

PRIVATE TUITION (VATA 1994, Sch 9, Group 6, Item 2)

20.20   **Whether 'a subject ordinarily taught in a school or university'.** An experienced English teacher became interested in a process, originating in California, whereby pupils with reading difficulties caused by sciotopic sensitivity syndrome were cured by the use of glasses with coloured lenses. She began acting as a consultant and, after publicity on local television, her turnover increased to above the registration threshold. On the advice of her accountant, she charged tax on her supplies. However, she subsequently formed the opinion that they should be exempt under what is now *VATA 1994, Sch 9, Group 6*. The Commissioners issued a ruling that they were standard-rated, and she appealed. The tribunal dismissed her appeal, holding that her supplies were not within *Group 6*, since they could not be described as 'tuition in subjects which are normally taught in the course of education provided by a school or university'. *AE Wright, LON/92/1468A (VTD 10408)*.

20.21   **Whether 'teacher acting independently of an employer'.**   A qualified teacher taught mathematics in accordance with a method devised by a private company, with which she had entered into a licence agreement and to which she paid 50% of her fees. She did not account for VAT on her fees, and the Commissioners issued an assessment charging tax on them. She appealed, contending that her services were exempt under what is now *VATA 1994, Sch 9, Group 6*. The tribunal allowed her appeal, holding that, despite her obligations to the company which had devised the method by which she taught, she was providing private tuition and 'acting independently of any employer or organisation'. 'So far as there is an element of dependence ... it is not the sort that excludes (the appellant's) supplies from the scope of ... *Group 6*'. Accordingly, her supplies qualified for exemption. *V Ellicott, LON/92/3017A (VTD 11472).*

20.22   The proprietor of a tutorial institute provided tuition in cranio-sacral therapy to healthcare practitioners, physiotherapists and massage therapists. He provided 60% of the tuition himself, but arranged for other tutors to provide the remaining 40%. The Commissioners issued a ruling that, where he was not carrying out the tuition himself, he was required to account for output tax on the supplies, on the basis that the tutors were not 'acting independently of any employer or organisation'. The tribunal upheld the Commissioners' ruling and dismissed the proprietor's appeal, holding that 'supplies given via paid lecturers in subjects which the appellant himself was not qualified to teach cannot in any reasonable way be described as a supply of private tuition by an individual teacher acting independently of an employer'. *Ellicott*, 20.21 above, distinguished. *J Page (t/a Upledger Institute), EDN/99/144 (VTD 16650). (Note.* The Commissioners accepted that cranio-sacral therapy was 'a subject ordinarily taught in a school or university'.)

20.23   A tutor offered GCSE tuition in several subjects. In some cases he undertook the tuition himself, but in some cases he employed other tutors. The Commissioners issued a ruling that, where he was not carrying out the tuition himself, he was required to account for output tax on the supplies, on the basis that the tutors were not 'acting independently of any employer or organisation'. The tribunal upheld the Commissioners' ruling and dismissed the proprietor's appeal. *Ellicott*, 20.21 above, distinguished. *B Graham (t/a Excel Tutoring Services), LON/98/213 (VTD 16814).*

20.24   **Partnerships—ballroom dancing tuition.**   Two partnerships provided tuition in ballroom dancing. The Commissioners issued assessments charging tax on them. The partnerships appealed, contending that the tuition qualified for exemption under *VATA 1994, Sch 9, Group 6, Item 2*. The tribunal accepted this contention and allowed the appeals. The fact that the teachers were members of partnerships did not alter the fact that the tuition was provided by an 'individual teacher' within *Item 2*. *C & E Clarke; A & H Clarke, LON/96/1446 (VTD 15201). (Note.* For the Commissioners' practice following this decision, see Business Brief 1/98, issued on 7 January 1998.)

INCIDENTAL GOODS AND SERVICES (VATA 1994, Sch 9, Group 6, Item 4)

20.25   **Sale of batteries.**   A trader did not account for VAT on batteries which he sold to students. The Commissioners issued an assessment and the trader appealed, contending that the supplies were exempt by virtue of what is now *VATA 1994, Sch 9, Group 6, Item 4*. The tribunal dismissed his appeal, holding that the supplies did not qualify for exemption. *WH Saint, LON/81/112 (VTD 1147).*

20.26   **Supplies of conference facilities to eligible bodies.**   A trust operated a large house, which had previously been used as a convent. It provided conference facilities and accommodation to a variety of organisations, many of which were religious or charitable bodies. The Commissioners issued a ruling that these supplies were standard-rated. The trust appealed, contending that where the supplies were made to an organisation which was an 'eligible body' within *VATA 1994, Sch 9, Group 6, Note 1*, its supplies should be treated as exempt either under *Group 6, Item 4* or under *Article 13A1(i)* of the *EC Sixth Directive*. The tribunal rejected this contention and dismissed the appeal, holding that the supplies failed to qualify for exemption under *Group 6, Item 4* because that provision only exempted supplies to an eligible body which was making a 'principal supply'. On the evidence here, the recipients of the trust's supplies did not make any onward supplies for consideration which could qualify as 'principal supplies'. The tribunal also held that the condition that there must be an onward exempt supply was in accordance with the *EC Sixth Directive*, since 'in looking at the *Sixth Directive* one must not just look at *Article 13* but must also take account of the provisions of *Article 2* and also of *Article 4 ... Article 2* provides that it is the supply of goods or services effected for consideration which is subject to value added tax, and this governs the United Kingdom requirement that there should be a supply. The fact that under *Article 4* a "taxable person" is defined as a person who independently carries out any "economic activity" does not in the tribunal's view displace the requirement in *Article 2* that the supply of goods or services shall be effected for a consideration since *Article 4* refers back to *Article 2*'. *Glenfall House Trust, LON/99/308 (VTD 16657)*. (*Note*. For the Commissioners' practice, see *Notice No 701/30, para 6.4*, which states that 'if you are under contract to provide closely related goods and services (including conference facilities) to another eligible body rather than direct to its pupils, etc., these supplies are exempt only if the body receiving them makes supplies of education in the course or furtherance of business'.)

20.27 **Supplies by Students Union—whether within Item 4.** See *University of Leicester Students Union*, 20.12 above.

20.28 **School photographs—whether supplied by school.** See *H Tempest Ltd*, 63.17 VALUATION.

20.29 **Supply of facilities at school premises to photographers—whether supply made by school or by local education authority.** See *Lancashire County Council*, 58.279 SUPPLY.

YOUTH CLUB FACILITIES (VATA 1994, Sch 9, Group 6, Item 6)

20.30 **World Association of Girl Guides.** The World Association of Girl Guides and Girl Scouts reclaimed input tax in respect of payments which it received from its affiliated organisations. The Commissioners issued a ruling that the Association's services were exempt from VAT under what is now *VATA 1994, Sch 9, Group 6, Item 6*, so that the Association was not entitled to reclaim input tax. The Association appealed. The tribunal allowed the appeal, holding that the Association was not itself an 'association of youth clubs' within what is now *VATA 1994, Sch 9, Group 6, Item 6*, although its constituent members were associations of youth clubs. Although references to an organisation within *Sch 9, Group 9* specifically included an association of organisations falling within it, there was no such provision in relation to *Sch 9, Group 6*. Accordingly the Association's supplies were not exempt and it was entitled to reclaim input tax. *World Association of Girl Guides and Girl Scouts, [1984] VATTR 28 (VTD 1611)*.

20.31 **Local YMCA.** The Commissioners formed the opinion that a YMCA which carried on religious and sporting activities was not a 'youth club' within what is now *VATA 1994, Sch 9, Group 6*, and issued an assessment on its income. The tribunal allowed the YMCA's appeal, holding that a 'youth club' was an organisation that provided recreational, educational, social or cultural activities for members who were mainly, but not necessarily exclusively, under 21 years of age, and finding that the appellant YMCA was within this definition. *Hastings & Rother YMCA, LON/86/388 (VTD 2329).*

20.32   **National Council of YMCAs—whether supplies of facilities to non-members exempt under Sch 9, Group 6.**   The National Council of YMCAs administered five 'day camps', which were made available to both members and non-members. The Commissioners issued assessments on the basis that the supply of these facilities to non-members was liable to VAT. The Council appealed, contending that such supplies were exempt under what is now *VATA 1994, Sch 9, Group 6, Item 6.* (It was common ground that the supplies to members were exempt under this provision.) The tribunal allowed the Council's appeal, holding that once it was established that the facilities in question were provided by a youth club or association of youth clubs, and were available to members, the provision of those facilities remained an exempt supply even where, as here, the facilities had also been provided to non-members. *National Council of YMCAs Inc, [1990] VATTR 68 (VTD 5160).* (*Note.* For subsequent developments in this case, see 45.68 and 45.72 PAYMENT OF TAX.)

20.33   **Gymnastic club.**   A company which operated a gymnastic club appealed against the Commissioners' decision that it was not a 'youth club' within what is now *VATA 1994, Sch 9, Group 6, Item 6.* The tribunal dismissed the company's appeal, finding that the company was not recognised as charitable and that the club provided income for its directors, rather than being organised on a non-profit-making basis. *International Gymnastic School Ltd, LON/91/186X (VTD 6550).*

20.34   **Junior section of golf club.**   A members' golf club operated a 'junior section'. The Commissioners issued a ruling that VAT was chargeable on the subscriptions from members of the 'junior section'. The club appealed, contending that the 'junior section' should be treated as a youth club within what is now *VATA 1994, Sch 9, Group 6, Item 6.* The tribunal rejected this contention and dismissed the appeal, disapproving a statement in *VAT Leaflet No 701/35/84*, and holding that the exemption in *Item 6* could not be extended to a youth or junior section of a senior club. *Haggs Castle Golf Club, EDN/95/164 (VTD 13653).* (*Note. Leaflet No 701/35/84* has since been superseded by *Leaflet No 701/35/95.*)

21   European Community Law

Note. The first significant steps towards the present-day European Union were taken in 1951, when the European Coal & Steel Community (ECSC) was established by the Treaty of Paris. This was followed by the establishment of the Council of Ministers and of the European Court of Justice. In 1957 the Treaties of Rome established the European Atomic Energy Community (EAEC) and the European Economic Community (EEC). The UK joined all three Communities with effect from 1 January 1973, following the *European Communities Act 1972*. In February 1992 the UK Government signed the Treaty on European Union (also known as the Maastricht Treaty), which made significant amendments to the EEC Treaty. These included changing the title of the Community from the 'European Economic Community' to the 'European Community', and changing the name of the Council from the 'Council of the European Communities' to the 'Council of the European Union'. However, the names of the Commission of the European Communities and the Court of Justice of the European Communities, which are the bodies principally concerned with European VAT law, remained unchanged. The EC Treaty was further amended by the Treaty of Amsterdam, which was signed in October 1997, came into effect on 1 May 1999, and has had the effect, *inter alia*, of renumbering the articles of the EC Treaty. In *Proceedings of the Court of Justice & the Court of First Instance of the EC 31/98*, the CJEC note that 'this could create some confusion in the mind of the user between the version of an article before the entry into force of the Amsterdam Treaty and that subsequent to that date . . . the Court has therefore decided, in the interests of clarity and consistency, to implement a uniform system of citation of the provisions of the four treaties (ECSC, Euratom, EC, EU) in the judgments of the Court and the Opinions of the Advocates-General. Thus, as from the entry into force of the Amsterdam Treaty, references to the provisions of the treaties are to consist of an Arabic numeral designating the article plus two designating the treaty, for example "Article 2 EC". See also the Press Release reported at *1999 STI 1618* and *[1999] AEECR 481*.

European VAT law is still referred to as 'European Community law' because it remains based on the provisions of the EC Treaty, on the Directives deriving from the Commission of the European Communities, and on the decisions of the Court of Justice of the European Communities. For cases concerning the European Convention for the Protection of Human Rights, see 32 HUMAN RIGHTS.

The cases in this chapter are arranged under the following headings.

EC TREATY

21.1   **EC Treaty, Article 234EC*—whether case should be referred to CJEC.**   In a 1974 case, concerning a dispute between French companies which produced champagne and two English companies which produced cider, the French companies requested the case to be referred to the CJEC under what is now *Article 234EC(2)* of the *EC Treaty*. The QB refused to refer the case, and the CA upheld this decision. Lord Denning observed that the effect of *Article 234EC(3)** was that the House of Lords was required to refer questions of European law to the CJEC, since there was 'no judicial remedy under national law' against decisions of the HL. However, the High Court and Court of Appeal fell under *Article 234EC(2)** rather than *Article 234EC(3)**. The effect of *Article 234EC(2)** was that a national court 'may ... request the Court of Justice to give a ruling', but it was not required to do so, since 'the cases which get to the House of Lords are substantial cases of the first importance ... whereas the points in the lower courts may not be worth troubling the European Court about'. Stephenson LJ observed that *Article 234EC(2)** 'confers a power', whereas *Article 234EC(3)** 'imposes an obligation'. *HP Bulmer Ltd & Another v J Bollinger SA & Others, CA [1974] Ch 401; [1974] 2 All ER 1226.*

21.2   In a 1980 case concerning the import of pornographic material, Lord Diplock stated that English judges should 'not ... be too ready to hold that, because the meaning of the English text (which is one of six of equal authority) seems plain to them, no question of interpretation can be involved'. *R v Henn & Darby, HL 1980, [1981] AC 850; [1980] 2 All ER 166.* (*Note.* This was the first case which the HL referred to the CJEC for a preliminary ruling.)

21.3   In an Italian case, the CJEC held that a case should be referred under *Article 234EC(3)** unless the national court considered that the question was 'acte claire', i.e. that the correct application of Community law was 'so obvious as to leave no scope for any reasonable doubt as to the manner in which the question raised is to be resolved'. *Srl CILFIT and Lanificio di Gavardo SpA v Ministro della Sanita, CJEC Case 283/81; [1982] ECR 3415; [1983] 1 CMLR 472.*

21.4   *Srl CILFIT and Lanificio di Gavardo SpA v Ministro della Sanita*, 21.3 above, was applied by the QB in *Conoco Ltd*, 2.210 APPEALS.

21.5   However, in a subsequent German case, Advocate-General Jacobs held that it was not 'appropriate, or indeed possible, for the Court to continue to respond fully to all references which, through the creativity of lawyers and judges, are couched in terms of interpretation, even though the reference might in a particular case be better characterised as concerning the application of the law rather than its interpretation'. *Wiener SI GmbH v Hauptzollamt Emmerich, CJEC Case C-338/95; [1998] 1 CMLR 1110.*

21.6   *Wiener SI GmbH v Hauptzollamt Emmerich,* 21.5 above, was applied in a subsequent customs duty case where the QB upheld the tribunal decision in favour of the appellant company, and rejected the Commissioners' contention that the case should be referred to the CJEC. Dyson J observed that 'there is no indication in the *CILFIT* judgment that the doctrine of "acte claire" has any application other than to references by a court of last instance under (*Article 234EC(3)**)', and stated that 'it is preferable for a court falling outside (*Article 234EC(3)**) not to use this phrase'. *Dicta* of Lord Denning in *HP Bulmer Ltd & Another v J Bollinger SA & Others,* 21.1 above, applied. *C & E Commrs v Anchor Foods Ltd, QB 1998, [1999] VATDR 425.*

21.7   **Application for withdrawal of reference to CJEC.**   See *Royscot Leasing Ltd,* 2.230 APPEALS.

21.8   **EC Treaty, Article 87EC*—State aid.**   The CA held that differential rates of insurance premium tax, introduced by *FA 1997,* constituted a 'state aid' within the meaning of what is now *Article 87EC* of the *EC Treaty,* and should therefore have been notified to the EC Commission in accordance with what is now *Article 88EC. R v C & E Commrs (ex p. Lunn Poly Ltd and Another), CA [1999] STC 350.*

21.9   The decision in *R v C & E Commrs (ex p. Lunn Poly Ltd and Another),* 21.46 above, was distinguished in the VAT case of *University of Sussex,* 45.30 PAYMENT OF TAX.

EC DIRECTIVES—GENERAL PRINCIPLES

21.10   **EC Directives—whether directly applicable.**   In the case noted at 21.174 below, the CJEC held that 'wherever the provisions of a Directive appear, as far as their subject matter is concerned, to be unconditional and sufficiently precise, their provisions may ... be relied upon as against any national provision which is incompatible with the Directive or in so far as the provisions define rights which individuals are able to assert against the state'. *U Becker v Finanzamt Münster-Innenstadt, CJEC Case 8/81; [1982] ECR 53; [1982] 1 CMLR 499.*

21.11   In a case concerning unequal treatment of men and women by a health authority, the CJEC held that a directive could be relied on against a state authority acting as an employer. *Marshall v Southampton & South-West Hampshire Health Authority, CJEC Case 152/84; [1986] ECR 723; [1986] 1 CMLR 688; [1986] 2 All ER 584.*

21.12   In a case concerning unequal treatment of men and women by a statutory corporation, the CJEC held that a directive was directly applicable 'against a body, whatever its legal form, which had been made responsible, pursuant to a measure adopted by the State, for providing a public service under the control of the State and has for that purpose special powers beyond those which result from the normal rules applicable in relations between individuals'. *Foster & Others v British Gas plc, CJEC Case C-188/89; [1990] ECR 3313; [1990] 3 All ER 897.*

21.13   In a German case, where a directive had been transposed into German law in 1995, the CJEC held that from the date on which the directive was transposed, individuals could no longer rely on the provisions of the directive 'unless the national implementing measures are incorrect or inadequate in the light of the directive'. *Kampelmann & Others v Landschaftsverband Westfalen-Lippe & Others, CJEC Cases C-253/96 & C-258/96; [1997] 1 ECR 2771.*

21.14   See also *Defrenne v Sabena*, 21.31 below; *Lord Mayor & Citizens of the City of Westminster*, 21.75 below; *Yoga for Health Foundation*, 21.148 below; *International Bible Students Association*, 21.149 below, and the cases noted at 21.175 below.

21.15   In an Italian case, the CJEC held that a Member State which had failed to implement the provisions of a directive could not rely on the terms of the directive against individuals. *Pubblico Ministero v Ratti, CJEC Case 148/78; [1979] ECR 1629; [1980] 1 CMLR 96.*

21.16   In an Italian case concerning a consumer protection directive which not had been implemented in Italian law, the CJEC held that, since directives did not have direct effect against private entities, consumers could not derive rights against traders from the directive. *F Dori v Recreb Srl, CJEC Case C-91/92; [1994] 1 ECR 3325; [1994] 1 CMLR 665; [1995] AEECR 1.*

21.17   **Primacy of EC Directives over national legislation.** In a 1964 case, the CJEC held that Community law takes precedence over national law. *Costa v ENEL, CJEC Case 6/64; [1964] ECR 585; [1964] CMLR 425.*

21.18   In a 1978 case, the CJEC held that 'a national court which is called upon, within the limits of its jurisdiction, to apply provisions of Community law, is under a duty to give full effect to those provisions, if necessary refusing of its own motion to apply any conflicting provision of national legislation, even if adopted subsequently, and it is not necessary for the court to request or await the prior setting aside of such provisions by legislative or other constitutional means'. *Amministrazione delle Finanze dello Stato v Simmenthal SpA, CJEC Case 106/77; [1978] ECR 629; [1978] 3 CMLR 263.*

21.19   *Amministrazione delle Finanze dello Stato v Simmenthal SpA*, 21.18 above, was applied by the VAT tribunal in *Merseyside Cablevision Ltd*, 34.444 INPUT TAX, where the tribunal held that 'the law of the European Economic Community ... prevails over any contrary provision in national law'.

21.20   However, in the subsequent case noted at 58.363 SUPPLY, the tribunal held, applying *dicta* of Lord Templeman in *Duke v GEC Reliance Ltd, HL [1988] 1 AC 718; [1988] 1 All ER 626*, that the *European Communities Act 1972* does not 'enable or constrain a British court to distort the meaning of a British statute in order to enforce against an individual a Community directive which has no direct effect between individuals'. Further, 'there is no rule of law compelling, or enabling, any court to construe a pre-existing statute of the United Kingdom in order to comply with a Directive subsequent in time, where the legislature or executive of the United Kingdom has not implemented that Directive'. *George Kuikka Ltd, [1990] VATTR 185 (VTD 5037).*

21.21   Similarly, in the case noted at 27.125 FOOD, the tribunal chairman held that 'the principles of European law ... do not, in my view, inhibit or constrain a court here into adopting an unnecessarily narrow interpretation of the statutory provisions in order to limit the scope of relief'. *McCormick (UK) plc, LON/97/1193 (VTD 15202).*

21.22   In a 1990 UK case, concerning regulations issued under the *Merchant Shipping Act 1988*, the CJEC held that a national court was required to set aside a rule of national law which it considered was the sole obstacle preventing it from granting interim relief in a case concerning Community law. *Amministrazione delle Finanze dello Stato v Simmenthal SpA*, 21.18 above, applied. *Factortame Ltd & Others v Secretary of State for Transport (No 2), CJEC Case C-213/89; [1990] 1 ECR 2433; [1990] 3 CMLR 375; [1991] 1 All ER 70.*

21.23   In a 1993 case, the CA held that 'the fact that a national court, in considering a case on the basis of national legislation implementing a directive but where the directive itself is not directly pleaded, did not refer to the relevant case law of the European Court on the directive, is a factor which contributes to a finding that the judgment is unreliable and should be quashed'. *Wren v Eastbourne Borough Council, CA [1993] 3 CMLR 166.*

21.24   **State liability to pay damages for failure to implement Directive.**   In an Italian case, the CJEC held that the Italian government was liable to pay compensation to employees of an insolvent company, who had suffered financial loss through Italy's failure to implement a directive guaranteeing such employees their arrears of wages. *Francovich v Italian State, CJEC Case C-6/90; [1991] 1 ECR 5357; [1993] 2 CMLR 66.* (*Note.* For the procedure to be adopted in the UK in seeking to apply the principles laid down in this case, see *R v Secretary of State for Employment (ex p. Equal Opportunities Commission)*, 21.30 below.)

21.25   The principles laid down in *Francovich v Italian State*, 21.24 above, were applied in two subsequent cases in which national legislation was held to be contrary to EC law. The CJEC ruled that 'the principle that Member States are obliged to make good damage caused to individuals by breaches of Community law attributable to the state is applicable where the national legislature was responsible for the breach in question'. *Brasserie du Pêcheur SA v Federal Republic of Germany; R v Secretary of State for Transport (ex p. Factortame Ltd & Others) (No 3), CJEC Cases C-46/93, C-48/93; [1996] 1 ECR 1029; [1996] 1 CMLR 889; [1996] 2 WLR 506; [1996] AEECR 301.*

21.26   The decisions in *Brasserie du Pêcheur SA v Federal Republic of Germany; R v Secretary of State for Transport (ex p. Factortame Ltd & Others) (No 3)*, 21.25 above, were applied in the subsequent case of *R v Ministry of Agriculture, Fisheries & Food (ex p. Hedley Lomas (Ireland) Ltd, CJEC Case C-5/94; [1996] 1 ECR 2553; [1996] 2 CMLR 391; [1996] AEECR 493.*

21.27   In a case concerning claims for compensation by German residents following the insolvency of two German tour operators, the CJEC held that 'failure to take any measure to transpose a directive in order to achieve the result it prescribes within the period laid down for that purpose constitutes *per se* a serious breach of Community law and consequently gives rise to a right of reparation for individuals suffering injury if the right prescribed by the directive entails the grant to individuals of rights whose content is identifiable, and a causal link exists between the breach of the state's obligation and the loss and damage suffered'. *Dillenkofer & Others v Federal Republic of Germany, CJEC Case C-178/94, C-179/94; [1996] 1 ECR 4845; [1996] 3 CMLR 469; [1996] AEECR 917.*

21.28   The decisions in *Brasserie du Pêcheur SA v Federal Republic of Germany; R v Secretary of State for Transport (ex p. Factortame Ltd & Others) (No 3)*, 21.25 above, were distinguished in a case in which the CJEC held that a breach of *Directive 90/435/EC* was not sufficiently serious to give rise to a claim to compensation. *R v HM Treasury (ex p. British Telecommunications plc), CJEC Case C-392/93; [1996] 1 ECR 1631; [1996] 2 CMLR 217; [1996] 3 WLR 303; [1996] AEECR 401.*

21.29   A similar decision was reached in *Denkavit International BV & Others v Bundesamt für Finanzen, CJEC Case C-283/94; [1996] STC 1445; [1996] 1 ECR 5063 (TTC 2001, 25.38).*

21.30   **Claims to compensation under Francovich principle—procedure to be adopted.**   In a case in which the HL held that certain provisions of the *Employment Protection (Consolidation) Act 1978* were incompatible with what is now *Article 141EC* of the *EC Treaty*, Lord Keith of Kinkel observed that 'if there is any individual who believes that he or she has a good claim to compensation under the

Francovich principle, it is the Attorney-General who would be defendant in any proceedings directed to enforcing it'. *R v Secretary of State for Employment (ex p. Equal Opportunities Commission), HL [1994] 1 All ER 910.*

STATUS OF CJEC DECISIONS

21.31   **Application of CJEC decisions—whether retrospective.**   In a Belgian case concerning what is now *Article 141EC* of the *EC Treaty* (which lays down the principle 'that men and women should receive equal pay for equal work'), the CJEC held that, although *Article 141EC** had direct effect, its decision could not have retrospective effect for periods prior to the date of the judgment, except with regard to those who had 'already brought legal proceedings or made an equivalent claim'. The CJEC observed that 'important considerations of legal certainty affecting all the interests involved, both public and private, make it impossible in principle to reopen the question as regards the past'. *Defrenne v SA Belge de Navigation Aerienne Sabena, CJEC Case 43/75; [1976] ECR 455; [1976] 2 CMLR 98; [1981] 1 All ER 122.*

21.32   *Defrenne v Sabena,* 21.31 above, was applied in a subsequent case concerning occupational pension schemes. The CJEC held that 'overriding considerations of legal certainty preclude legal situations which have exhausted all their effects in the past from being called into question where this might upset retroactively the financial balance of many contracted-out pension schemes'. Accordingly, *Article 141EC** of the *Treaty* 'may not be relied on in order to claim entitlement to a pension, with effect from a date prior to that of this judgment, except in the case of workers or those claiming under them who have before that date initiated legal proceedings or raised an equivalent claim under the applicable national law'. *Barber v Guardian Royal Exchange Assurance Group, CJEC Case 262/88; [1990] 1 ECR 1889; [1990] 2 CMLR 513; [1990] 2 All ER 660.*

21.33   *Defrenne v Sabena,* 21.31 above, and *Barber v Guardian Royal Exchange Assurance Group,* 21.32 above, were distinguished in the case noted at 21.246 below. The CJEC held that, since the EC Commission had warned the Danish government that the levy in question appeared to be a breach of Community law, it was inappropriate to limit the temporal scope of the judgment. *Dansk Denkavit ApS & Others v Skatteministeriet, CJEC Case C-200/90; [1992] 1 ECR 2217; [1994] 2 CMLR 377; [1994] STC 482.*

21.34   The decision in *Dansk Denkavit ApS & Others v Skatteministeriet,* 21.33 above, was applied in a subsequent case in which the CJEC held that 'the financial consequences which might ensue for a government owing to the unlawfulness of a tax have never justified in themselves limiting the effects of a judgment of the Court ... to limit the effects of a judgment solely on the basis of such considerations would considerably diminish the judicial protection of the rights which taxpayers have under Community fiscal legislation'. *Roders BV & Others v Inspecteur der Invoerrechten en Accijnzen, CJEC Case C-367/93; [1995] 1 ECR 2229.*

TIME LIMITS

21.35   **Time limit imposed by national law—whether valid under Community law.**   In a German case, the CJEC held that 'the right conferred by Community law must be exercised before the national court in accordance with the conditions laid down by national rules ... The laying down of such time limits with regard to actions of a fiscal procedure is an application of the fundamental principle of legal certainty protecting both the taxpayer and the administration concerned'. *Rewe-Zentralfinanz* *eG & Rewe-Zentral AG v Landwirtschaftskammer für das Saarland, CJEC Case 33/76; [1976] ECR 1989; [1977] 1 CMLR 533.*

21.36   In a French case, the CJEC held that 'a national legislature may not, subsequent to a judgment of the Court from which it follows that certain legislation is incompatible with the *EC Treaty*, adopt a procedural rule which specifically reduces the possibilities of bringing proceedings for recovery of taxes which were wrongly levied under that legislation'. *Deville v Administration des Impôts, CJEC Case 240/87; [1988] ECR 3513; [1989] 3 CMLR 611.*

21.37   In an Irish case, a national time limit for claiming a social security benefit was held to be invalid, since the time limit in question 'had the result of depriving the applicant of any opportunity whatever to rely on her right to equal treatment under the directive'. *Emmott v Minister for Social Welfare & Another, CJEC Case C-208/90; [1991] 1 ECR 4269; [1991] 3 CMLR 894.*

21.38   The decision in *Emmott v Minister for Social Welfare & Another*, 21.37 above, was distinguished in a subsequent Netherlands case in which a national law, under which payment of arrears of benefits was restricted to a maximum period of twelve months, was held to be valid. *Steenhorst-Neerings v Bestuur van de Bedrijfsvereniging voor Detailhandel, Ambachten en Huisvrouwen, CJEC Case C-338/91; [1993] 1 ECR 5475; [1995] 3 CMLR 323.*

21.39   The decision in *Steenhorst-Neerings v Bestuur van de Bedrijfsvereniging voor Detailhandel, Ambachten en Huisvrouwen*, 21.38 above, was applied in the similar subsequent case of *Johnson v Chief Adjudication Officer (No 2), CJEC Case C-410/92; [1994] 1 ECR 5483; [1994] 1 CMLR 725; [1995] AEECR 258.*

21.40   In a Belgian case, a partnership had appealed against a charge to tax. During the proceedings, it sought to raise an alternative contention based on what is now *Article 43EC* of the *EC Treaty*. The Belgian Court of Appeal held that, under Belgian law, this contention could not be considered on the grounds that it had been raised outside the 60–day time limit laid down by the Belgian Tax Code, and referred the case to the CJEC to consider whether the relevant provision was compatible with Community law. The CJEC held that the time limit was invalid under Community law, and directed that the substantive question of whether the charge to tax was compatible with the *EC Treaty* should be considered by the Belgian court. *SCS Peterbroeck Van Campenhout & Cie v Belgium, CJEC Case C-312/93; [1995] 1 ECR 4599; [1996] 1 CMLR 793; [1996] AEECR 242.*

21.41   In a Danish case in which a five-year limitation period was held to be reasonable, the CJEC observed that 'the setting of reasonable limitation periods for bringing proceedings is compatible with Community law. Such periods cannot be regarded as rendering virtually impossible or excessively difficult the exercise of rights conferred by Community law, even if the expiry of those periods necessarily entails the dismissal, in whole or in part, of the action brought'. *Fantask A/S & Others v Industriministeriet, CJEC Case C-188/95; [1998] 1 CMLR 473; [1998] AEECR 1.*

21.42   In an Italian case, the CJEC held that 'the fact that the Court has given a preliminary ruling interpreting a provision of Community law without limiting the temporal effects of its judgment does not affect the right of a Member State to impose a time-limit under national law within which, on penalty of being barred, proceedings for repayment of charges levied in breach of that provision must be commenced. Community law does not prohibit a Member State from resisting actions for repayment of charges levied in breach of Community law by relying on a time-limit under national law of three years.' *Edilizia Industriale Siderurgica Srl v Ministero delle Finanze, CJEC Case C-231/96, [1998] 1 ECR 4951.*

21.43   Similar decisions were reached in *Aprile Srl v Amministrazione delle Finanze dello Stato, CJEC Case C-228/96, 17 November 1998 unreported* and *Roquette Frères SA v Direction des Services Fiscaux du Pas-de-Calais, CJEC Case C-88/99, [2000] All ER(D) 2008.*

21.44   In a Belgian case, the CJEC held that 'in the absence of Community rules governing a matter, it is for the domestic legal system of each Member State to lay down the detailed procedural rules governing actions for safeguarding rights which individuals derive from the effect of Community law'. Furthermore, 'the position of the VAT authorities cannot be compared with that of a taxable person. The authorities do not have the information necessary to determine the amount of the tax chargeable and the deductions to be made until, at the earliest, the day when the return referred to in *Article 22(4)* of the *Sixth Directive* is made ... In the case of an inaccurate return, or where it turns out to be incomplete, it is therefore only from that time that the authorities can start to recover the unpaid tax. Thus, the fact that the five-year limitation period begins to run as against the tax authorities on the date on which the return should in principle be made, whereas an individual may exercise his right to deduction only within a period of five years as from the date on which that right arose, is not such as to infringe the principle of equality.' *Société Financière d'Investissements SPRL (SFI) v Belgian State, CJEC Case C-85/97, [2000] STC 164.*

EC SIXTH DIRECTIVE

Scope of the Directive (Article 2)

21.45   **Article 2(1) of EC Sixth Directive—definition of 'supply of goods or services effected for consideration'.**   A Dutch co-operative operated a cold store for the benefit of its members, who paid a storage charge, fixed annually. In 1975 and 1976 the co-operative levied no charges on its members. The Dutch authorities raised a VAT assessment on the basis that the members had received a benefit as a consequence of the failure to make a charge. The co-operative appealed and the case was referred to the CJEC, which held that there was no consideration for the supply of the storage services. Consideration for a supply for VAT purposes must have a direct link with the services supplied and must be capable of being expressed in money. It followed that a provision of services for which no definite subjective consideration was received did not constitute a provision of services 'against payment'. *Staatssecretaris van Financien v Cooperatieve Vereniging 'Cooperatieve Aardappelenbewaarplaats GA', CJEC Case 154/80; [1981] ECR 445; [1981] 3 CMLR 337.* (*Note*. The case was argued on the provisions of the *EC Second Directive*, the relevant provisions of which were very similar to those now in *Article 2* of the *EC Sixth Directive*, except that, in the English version of the *Directive*, the words 'against payment' have been replaced by the words 'for consideration'. The wording of the French, German, Italian and Dutch versions remained unchanged.)

21.46   The Hong Kong Trade Development Council was a trade organisation founded to promote trade between Hong Kong and other countries by providing information and advice about the country free of charge (and for no other form of consideration). The cost of this activity was financed partly by a grant from the Hong Kong government and partly from a levy on products imported into and exported from Hong Kong. The services were provided free of charge and the CJEC was asked to rule on whether the Council could be regarded as a taxable person. The CJEC held that the provision of services for no consideration could not be subject to VAT and, where no other activity was involved, the provider of the services could not be regarded as a taxable person, and could not therefore register for VAT. *Article 2(1)* of the *Sixth Directive* effectively excludes from the scope of the tax any person who habitually provides services free of charge, since 'services provided free of charge are different in character from taxable transactions which, within the framework of the value added tax system, presuppose the stipulation of a price or consideration'. *Staatssecretaris van Financiën v Hong Kong Trade Development Council, CJEC Case 89/81; [1982] ECR 1277; [1983] 1 CMLR 73.*

21.47   The Apple & Pear Development Council was established in 1966 by a statutory instrument, with the principal object of promoting the sale of apples and pears in England and Wales. The Council comprised 14 members, appointed by the Minister for Agriculture, the majority of whom were growers nominated by the National Farmers Union. All commercial growers with two hectares or more, and 50 or more trees, had to register with it and pay a compulsory annual charge, based on the area of their land, to meet its expenses. Initially the Commissioners accepted that its activities were business activities, on which it was entitled to reclaim input tax, and that its compulsory charges to growers were outside the scope of VAT. However, in 1981 the Commissioners issued a ruling that its activities did not constitute a business and that it was not entitled to reclaim input tax. The Council appealed to the HL, which held that an activity could only constitute a 'business' if it involved the making of taxable supplies for consideration, and referred the case to the CJEC. The CJEC held that, for a supply of services to be for consideration within *Article 2(1)* of the *EC Sixth Directive*, there must be a direct link between the service provided and the consideration received. On the evidence, there was no relationship between the level of the benefits which individual growers obtained from the Council's services and the amount of the mandatory charges which they were obliged to pay. Accordingly, the compulsory annual charges did not constitute 'consideration' and the Council was not making supplies of services for consideration. *Apple & Pear Development Council v C & E Commrs, CJEC Case 102/86; [1988] STC 221; [1988] ECR 1443; [1988] 2 CMLR 394; [1988] 2 All ER 922.*

21.48   In two Netherlands cases, the CJEC held that the illegal sale of drugs such as amphetamines or hashish was not an 'economic activity' and thus not a supply for VAT purposes. While the principle of fiscal neutrality precluded 'a generalised differentiation between lawful and unlawful transactions', supplies of narcotic drugs were outside the scope of this principle, since 'because of their very nature, they are subject to a total prohibition on their being put into circulation in all the Member States, with the exception of strictly controlled economic channels for use for medical and scientific purposes'. *Mol v Inspecteur der Invoerrechten en Accijnzen, CJEC Case 269/86; [1988] ECR 3627; [1989] BVC 205; [1989] 3 CMLR 729; Vereniging Happy Family Rustenburgerstrat v Inspecteur der Omzetbelasting, CJEC Case 289/86; [1988] ECR 3655; [1989] BVC 216; [1989] 3 CMLR 743.* (*Note.* These decisions were distinguished in the subsequent cases of *R v Goodwin & Unstead*, 21.49 below; *Staatssecretaris van Financiën v Coffeeshop 'Siberië' vof*, 21.50 below, and *Lange v Finanzamt Fürstenfeldbruck*, 21.187 below.)

21.49   Two individuals were convicted for selling counterfeit perfume, contrary to *VATA 1994, s 72*. They appealed to the CA, contending that VAT was not chargeable on counterfeit goods. The CA directed that the case should be referred to the CJEC for a ruling as to whether counterfeit goods were within the scope of *Article 2* of the *EC Sixth Directive*. The CJEC held that the supply of counterfeit perfumes was within *Article 2*, and VAT was chargeable accordingly. The principle of fiscal neutrality 'precludes a generalised differentiation between lawful and unlawful transactions, except where, because of the special characteristics of certain products, all competition between a lawful economic sector and an unlawful sector is precluded'. *Mol v Inspecteur der Invoerrechten en Accijnzen* and *Vereniging Happy Family Rustenburgerstrat v Inspecteur der Omzetbelasting*, 21.48 above, were distinguished, on the grounds that they concerned goods 'which, because of their special characteristics, may not be placed on the market or incorporated into economic channels'. The prohibition on counterfeit products such as perfumes, however, stemmed from the fact that they infringed intellectual property rights and was 'conditional, not absolute as in the case of narcotics or counterfeit currency'. Furthermore, there was scope for competition between counterfeit perfumes and perfumes which were traded lawfully, so that counterfeit perfumes could not 'be regarded as *extra commercium*'. *R v Goodwin & Unstead, CJEC Case C-3/97; [1998] STC 699; [1998] 3 WLR 565; [1998] AEECR 500.*

21.50   In a Netherlands case, the proprietor of a coffee shop hired a table to a dealer in cannabis. The proprietor did not account for output tax on the rent received from the dealer. The Netherlands authorities demanded payment, and the proprietor appealed, contending that since the sale of cannabis was illegal under Netherlands law, the rent should be treated as outside the scope of VAT. The case was referred to the CJEC, which rejected the proprietor's contentions and held that renting out a space for the sale of narcotic drugs was within the scope of the *EC Sixth Directive*. *Vereniging Happy Family Rustenburgerstrat v Inspecteur der Omzetbelasting*, 21.48 above, was distinguished, on the grounds that 'the activity to be taxed in this case is not the sale of narcotic drugs, but a supply of services consisting in making available a place where the sale of those products is effected'. The CJEC observed that 'renting out a place intended for commercial activities is, in principle, an economic activity and therefore falls within the scope of the *Sixth Directive*. The fact that the activities pursued there constitute a criminal offence, which may make the renting unlawful, does not alter the economic character of the renting and does not prevent competition in the sector, including that between lawful and unlawful activities. Not to charge VAT thereon would undermine the fiscal neutrality of the VAT scheme.' *Staatssecretaris van Financiën v Coffeeshop 'Siberië' vof, CJEC Case C-158/98, [1999] STC 742; [1999] AEECR 560.*

21.51   In a Netherlands case, an individual who played a barrel organ on the public highway, and invited passers-by to leave donations in a tin, was assessed to output tax on his takings. He appealed, contending that his takings were outside the scope of VAT. The case was referred to the CJEC, which held that the playing of music on the public highway for which no payment was stipulated did not constitute a 'supply of ... services effected for consideration', and VAT was not chargeable. There was no agreement between the parties, and there was also 'no necessary link between the musical service and the payments to which it gives rise'. *Tolsma v Inspecteur der Omzetbelasting Leeuwarden, CJEC Case C-16/93; [1994] STC 509; [1994] 1 ECR 743; [1994] 2 CMLR 908.*

21.52   See also *Stirling*, 58.62 SUPPLY.

21.53   **Foreign exchange credit transactions—whether supplies of services within Article 2(1).**   A bank reclaimed input tax in respect of foreign exchange credit transactions. (The transactions concerned credits opened in foreign currency, and did not involve the physical exchange of banknotes.) The Commissioners rejected the claim, on the basis that the transactions did not constitute supplies for the purposes of VAT. The bank appealed. The tribunal allowed the appeal but the QB referred the case to the CJEC for a ruling as to whether such transactions constituted supplies within *Article 2(1)* of the *EC Sixth Directive*. The CJEC upheld the tribunal decision that the transactions were supplies of services for consideration, observing that 'to hold that currency transactions are taxable only when effected in return for payment of a commission or specific fees ... would ... allow a trader to avoid taxation if he sought to be remunerated for his services by providing for a spread between the proposed transaction rates rather than by charging such sums'. (The CJEC also held that, where no fees or commission were calculated with regard to certain specific transactions, the taxable amount was 'the net result of the transactions of the supplier of the services over a given period of time'.) *C & E Commrs v First National Bank of Chicago, CJEC Case C-172/96; [1998] STC 850; [1998] AEECR 744; [1999] 2 WLR 230*. (*Note*. For the Commissioners' practice following this decision, see Business Brief 16/98, issued on 28 July 1998, and Business Brief 24/98, issued on 2 December 1998.)

21.54   **Sale of property partly used for business purposes and partly used for private purposes—application of Article 2(1) of Sixth Directive.** In a German case, a hotelier sold a guesthouse, part of which he had used for private purposes rather than for business purposes. He was assessed on the whole of the proceeds, and appealed, contending that he should only be required to account for tax on the proportion of the proceeds which was attributable to the part of the guesthouse which he had used for business purposes. The case was referred to the CJEC, which ruled that where a taxable person sold property, part of which he had chosen to reserve for private use, the sale of that part was outside the scope of *Article 2(1)* of the *EC Sixth Directive. Finanzamt Ülzen v Armbrecht, CJEC Case C-291/92; [1995] STC 997; [1995] 1 ECR 2775; [1995] AEECR 882.*

21.55   **Article 2(2) of EC Sixth Directive—imports of goods from outside European Community.** A German woman had imported and sold quantities of morphine, although this was illegal under German law. The German authorities charged VAT on the import and sale of the morphine. She appealed, contending that there was no VAT liability on the illegal import of narcotic drugs. The CJEC upheld this contention and allowed her appeal. *Einberger v Hauptzollamt Freiburg (No 2), CJEC Case 294/82; [1984] ECR 1177; [1985] 1 CMLR 765.*

21.56   In a Finnish case, the CJEC held that VAT was chargeable on sales of ethyl alcohol which had been smuggled into the EU. *Einberger v Hauptzollamt Freiburg (No 2)*, 21.55 above, was distinguished on the grounds that it dealt with 'products which may not be introduced into economic channels because of their intrinsic character of illegal goods. Ethyl alcohol, however, does not have that character ... an intrinsically lawful product such as ethyl alcohol may not be equated with a narcotic drug'. *Tullihallitus v Salumets & Others, CJEC Case C-455/98, [2000] All ER(D) 891.*

21.57   In a German case, the CJEC ruled that the importation of counterfeit money was outside the scope of VAT. *Einberger v Hauptzollamt Freiburg (No 2)*, 21.55 above, applied. Advocate-General Jacobs observed that 'a line must be drawn between, on the one hand, transactions that lie so clearly outside the sphere of legitimate economic activity that, instead of being taxed, they can only be the subject of criminal prosecution, and, on the other hand, transactions which though unlawful must nonetheless be taxed, if only for ensuring in the name of fiscal neutrality, that the criminal is not treated more favourably than the legitimate trader'. *Witzemann v Hauptzollamt München-Mitte, CJEC Case C-343/89; [1993] STC 108; [1991] 1 ECR 4477.*

21.58   The Spanish government exempted the import of armaments, ammunition and equipment for military use. The European Commission brought an action under what is now *Article 226EC* of the *EC Treaty*, seeking a declaration that Spain had failed to fulfil its obligations under the *Treaty*. The CJEC accepted this contention and granted the declaration. *EC Commission v Kingdom of Spain, CJEC Case C-414/97, 16 September 1999 unreported.*

Taxable persons (Article 4)

General (Article 4(1))

21.59   In a Dutch case, a couple acquired a future title to two units which were intended to be used as showrooms and which were under construction. They gave notice that the showrooms would be let to traders and that they would opt for the supply to be taxable under the provisions of Dutch law. They applied for a refund of input tax incurred before the premises had been let. The Dutch authorities rejected the claim on the grounds that the couple had not, at that time, made any taxable supplies. The couple appealed, and the case was referred to the CJEC, which ruled that a person undertaking acts preparatory to the carrying on of an economic activity qualified as a 'taxable person' within *Article 4(1)* of the *EC Sixth Directive*, and that input tax was recoverable in such circumstances. The purpose of the system whereby input tax could be deducted was to relieve a trader entirely of the burden of VAT suffered in the course of his economic activities, which included preparatory acts such as the purchase of immovable property. *DA Rompelman & EA Rompelman-van-Deelen v Minister van Financien, CJEC Case 268/83; [1985] ECR 655; [1985] 3 CMLR 202.*

21.60   See also *Clarina Live-In Care Service*, 1.37 AGENTS, and *Merseyside Cablevision Ltd*, 34.444 INPUT TAX.

21.61   **Holding company—whether a 'taxable person'.** In a Dutch case, a company (P) which acted as a holding company, and did not carry on any commercial or management activity, reclaimed input tax. The Dutch authorities issued an assessment to recover the tax, considering that since the company did not carry on any commercial activity, it was not a taxable person and could not reclaim any input tax. P appealed and the case was referred to the CJEC, which held that a holding company whose sole purpose was to hold shares in other undertakings, without any direct or indirect involvement in the management of those undertakings, was not a taxable person and had no right to deduct or reclaim input tax. *Polysar Investments Netherlands BV v Inspecteur der Invoerrechten en Accijnzen, CJEC Case C-60/90; [1991] 1 ECR 3111; [1993] STC 222.* (*Note.* For the Commissioners' practice following this decision, see their News Release 59/93, issued on 10 September 1993.)

21.62   **Article 4(1) of EC Sixth Directive—whether economic activity carried on 'independently'.** A married couple operated a farming business in partnership. The husband owned a shed and let it to the partnership for an annual rent. The tax authority ruled that the letting was not to be regarded as an independent economic activity, so that the husband was not a taxable person within *Article 4(1)*. The case was referred to the CJEC, which held that the fact that the husband's economic activity was confined to letting an item of tangible property to the partnership of which he was a member was immaterial to the question of whether he was acting independently. Applying *Enkler v Finanzamt Homburg*, 21.68 below, the hiring out of intangible property with a view to obtaining income therefrom on a continuing basis was an 'economic activity' within *Article 4(2)*. Accordingly, where a person's sole economic activity consisted in the letting of an item of intangible property to a company or partnership of which he was a member, the letting was to be regarded as an independent activity within the meaning of *Article 4(1)* of the *Sixth Directive*. *Staatssecretaris van Financien v Heerma, CJEC Case C-23/98, 27 January 2000, 2000 STI 102.*

Economic activities (Article 4(2))

21.63   In a Dutch case, an appellant had granted a company building rights over land in return for an annual payment. He then reclaimed input tax which he had suffered on the acquisition of the property. The Dutch court referred the case to the CJEC for a ruling on whether the grant of a right of user over property was within the definition of an 'economic activity' in *Article 4(2)* of the *EC Sixth Directive*. The CJEC held that the grant of building rights over immovable property, in the form of a grant of a right of user over the property for a specified period and in return for payment, was to be regarded as an economic activity. Accordingly the input tax was reclaimable by the appellant. *WM van Tiem v Staatssecretaris van Financien, CJEC Case C-186/89; [1990] 1 ECR 4363; [1993] STC 91.*

21.64   In a Belgian case, the CJEC held that prostitution was an 'economic activity' (with the result that the Belgian government was not entitled to deport a French prostitute working in Liège, since it had not taken action to prevent Belgian women from working as prostitutes in the same city). *Adoui v Kingdom of Belgium & City of Liège, CJEC Case 115/81; [1982] ECR 1665; [1982] 3 CMLR 631.*

21.65   In a Belgian case, a company was established with the object of developing processes for turning sea and brackish water into drinking water. It reclaimed input tax on the costs of a profitability study, but went into liquidation without beginning to trade. The Belgian tax authority issued an assessment to recover the tax which the company had reclaimed. The liquidators of the company appealed, and the case was referred to the CJEC. The CJEC held that initial investment expenditure incurred for the purposes of a business could in principle be regarded as an economic activity within *Article 4(2)* of the *EC Sixth Directive*. However, *Article 4* did not preclude a tax authority from requiring objective evidence in support of a declared intention to commence economic activities which would give rise to taxable transactions. A taxable person only acquired that status definitively if he made such a declaration in good faith. In cases of fraud or abuse, a tax authority could claim repayment retrospectively on the ground that the deductions had been made on the basis of false declarations. Accordingly, the CJEC ruled that when a tax authority had accepted that a company which had declared an intention to begin an economic activity had the status of a taxable person, the commissioning of a profitability study could be regarded as an economic activity and the company's status as a taxable person could only be withdrawn 'in cases of fraud or abuse'. *Intercommunale voor Zeewaterontzilting (in liquidation) v Belgian State, CJEC Case C-110/94; [1996] STC 569; [1996] 1 ECR 857.*

21.66   A company, which was registered for VAT, acted as the sole trustee of a charitable trust. In 1992 it sold a large number of shares in a public company, The shares in question had been obtained by the trust in 1986, in exchange for shares which had been bequeathed to the trust in 1936. The company reclaimed input tax in respect of expenses incurred in relation to the sale of such shares to people resident outside the EC. The Commissioners rejected the claim, on the grounds that the company's investment activities did not constitute a business. The company appealed, contending that its investment activities were carried out on such a large scale that they constituted an 'economic activity' within *Article 4(2)* of the *EC Sixth Directive*. The tribunal referred the case to the CJEC, which held that the exercise of the right of ownership could not by itself be regarded as an economic activity. Neither the scale of a sale of shares, nor the employment of consultancy undertakings in connection with it, could constitute criteria for distinguishing between the activities of a private investor, which were outside the scope of VAT, and those of a larger investor. The question of whether or not the sale of shares and securities was the predominant concern of the activity in the course of which the sales took place could not affect the classification of investment activity. Accordingly, the concept of economic activities, within *Article 4(2)* of the *EC Sixth Directive*, did not include an activity consisting in the purchase and sale of shares and other securities by a trustee in the course of the management of a charitable trust. *The Wellcome Trust Ltd v C & E Commrs, CJEC Case C-155/94; [1996] STC 945; [1996] 1 ECR 3013; [1996] 2 CMLR 909; [1996] AEECR 589.*

21.67   In a Netherlands case, a limited partnership held shares and bonds. It reclaimed input tax which it had incurred in connection with loan transactions. The Netherlands authority rejected the claim on the basis that the partnership was not carrying on any economic activity. The partnership appealed, and the case was referred to the CJEC, which ruled that the mere acquisition and holding of bonds and the receipt of income therefrom were not to be regarded as economic activities within *Article 4(2)* of the *EC Sixth Directive*. *Polysar Investments Netherlands BV v Inspecteur der Invoerrechten en Accijnzen*, 21.61 above, applied. *Harnas & Helm CV v Staatssecretaris van Financien, CJEC Case C-80/95; [1997] STC 364; [1997] 1 ECR 745; [1997] 1 CMLR 649; [1997] AEECR 267.*

21.68   In a German case, a married woman (E) was employed by her husband who carried on business as a tax consultant. In 1984 she notified the tax authority that she was beginning a business of hiring out motor caravans. She purchased a caravan, reclaimed input tax and accounted for output tax, most of which represented payments from her husband. In 1986 she notified the tax authority that she intended to use the caravan for private purposes only. Subsequently the tax authority issued an assessment on the basis that E had never been acting as a trader. E appealed and the case was referred to the CJEC for rulings on the interpretation of *Article 4(2)* and *Article 11A1(c)* of the *EC Sixth Directive*. The CJEC held that the hiring out of tangible property was an 'economic activity' within *Article 4(2)* of the *Sixth Directive* if it was 'done for the purpose of obtaining income therefrom on a continuing basis'. The question of 'whether the hiring out of tangible property such as a motor caravan is carried on with a view to obtaining income on a continuing basis' was 'for the national court to evaluate in all the circumstances of the particular case'. With regard to the calculation of the taxable amount, *Article 11A1(c)* should be interpreted as meaning that the taxable amount in respect of transactions treated as supplies of services within *Article 6(2)(a)* of the *EC Sixth Directive* must include expenses which were incurred during a period in which the goods were at the disposal of the taxable person in such a way that he could use them at any time for non-business purposes, and the proportion of the total expenses to be included must be proportionate to the ratio between the total duration of actual use of the goods and the duration of actual use for non-business purposes. *Enkler v Finanzamt Homburg, CJEC Case C-230/94; [1996] STC 1316; [1996] 1 ECR 4517; [1997] 1 CMLR 881.*

21.69   See also *The Arts Council of Great Britain*, 7.101 BUSINESS; *Newmir plc*, 7.106 BUSINESS; *EC Commission v Netherlands*, 21.74 below; *Park Commercial Developments plc*, 26.25 FINANCE; *Merseyside Cablevision*, 34.444 INPUT TAX, and *Norwich City Council*, 40.5 LOCAL AUTHORITIES AND STATUTORY BODIES.

Occasional transactions (Article 4(3))

21.70   In a German case, the CJEC held that a transaction which consisted of a contract for the sale of land which had not been built on, and contracts for the supply of work and services in connection with the construction and supply of a building on that land, did not constitute a 'supply of buildings ... and land on which they stand' within the meaning of *Article 4(3)(a)* of the *EC Sixth Directive*. The supply had to be regarded as a supply of building land within *Article 4(3)(b)*. The German government was, therefore, entitled to impose VAT on the transaction. *Kerrutt & Another v Finanzamt Mönchengladbach-Mitte, CJEC Case 73/85; [1986] ECR 2219; [1987] BTC 5015; [1987] 2 CMLR 221.*

21.71   In a German case, a woman (B) registered as a car dealer and began building work with the aim of constructing a repair workshop. However, she was unable to complete the work for financial reasons, and subsequently sold the partly completed building and the land on which it stood. She purported to waive exemption on the building but not the land, with the intention of reclaiming input tax on the building work without having to account for output tax on the sale of the land. The German tax authority ruled that an election to waive exemption could not be limited to buildings alone, and had to include the land on which the buildings stood. B appealed and the case was referred to the CJEC, which held that 'for the purposes of VAT, buildings or parts of buildings and the land on which they stand cannot be dissociated from each other'. *Article 4(3)(a)* of the *EC Sixth Directive* had to be interpreted as meaning that the option for taxation 'must relate inseparably to the buildings or parts of buildings and the land on which they stand'. *Finanzamt Goslar v Breitsohl, CJEC Case C-400/98, 8 June 2000, 2000 STI 1513.*

21.72   In a Netherlands case, a local authority appealed against an assessment charging tax on a supply of land, contending that the land was not 'building land' within *Article 4(3)(b)* of the *EC Sixth Directive*, and that the supply was therefore exempt under *Article 13B(h)*. The case was referred to the CJEC for a ruling on the definition of 'building land'. The CJEC held that it was for the Member States to define the concept of 'building land' within the meaning of *Article 4(3)(b)* and *Article 13B(h)*. It was not for the court to specify what degree of improvement had to be exhibited by land which had not actually been built on in order to be categorised as within the definition of 'building land'. *Gemeente Emmen v Belastingdienst Grote Ondernemingen, CJEC Case C-468/93; [1996] STC 496; [1996] 1 ECR 1721; [1996] AEECR 372.*

Associated persons (Article 4(4))

21.73   See *Barclays Bank plc*, 30.15 GROUPS OF COMPANIES; *Osman*, 53.99 REGISTRATION, and *Shamrock Leasing Ltd*, 58.376 SUPPLY.

Public authorities (Article 4(5))

21.74   In a case concerning the treatment for VAT purposes of notaries and bailiffs in the Netherlands (where they were not public employees but independent officers performing their duties on behalf of their clients), the CJEC held that they were taxable persons within *Article 4* of the *Sixth Directive*, since they independently carried out economic activities, and were not bodies governed by public law within *Article 4(5)*. Where public officers, who were not employees of the public authorities, provided services to individuals in return for payment by their clients, they carried out an economic activity. The fact that their activities consisted in the performance of duties which were conferred and regulated by law in the public interest did not alter the situation. The CJEC held that 'bodies governed by public law are not automatically exempted in respect of all the activities in which they engage, but only in respect of those which form part of their specific duties as public authorities'. *EC Commission v Netherlands, CJEC Case 235/85; [1987] ECR 1471; [1988] 2 CMLR 921.*

21.75   Westminster City Council managed a hostel providing accommodation to homeless men. The Commissioners issued an assessment, charging VAT on the basis that the Council was making supplies of accommodation and catering. The Council appealed, contending that the supplies should be treated as exempt. The tribunal held that, although the Council operated the building for social reasons in pursuance of its welfare obligations, the operation of the building was nevertheless a business for VAT purposes, following *Morrison's Academy*, 7.1 BUSINESS, and *Lord Fisher*, 7.5 BUSINESS. The operation of the building was also not exempt under what is now *VATA 1994, Sch 9, Group 1, Item 1*, because although the building would not normally be regarded as a hotel, inn or boarding house, it was a 'similar establishment' to a hotel, inn or boarding house, and therefore fell within what is now *Item 1(d)*. However, the tribunal held that the operation of the building was exempt under *Article 4(5)* of the *EC Sixth Directive*, which provided that 'local government authorities and other bodies governed by public law shall not be considered taxable persons in respect of the activities or transactions in which they engage as public authorities ...'. The accommodation provided by the Council was of such a type that the Council was clearly not supplying services in competition with proprietors of commercial hotels, inns or boarding houses. The tribunal also held that the operation of the building fell within the provisions of *Article 13A1(g)*, as the supplies were closely linked to welfare and social security work and were made by a body governed by public law. *The Lord Mayor and Citizens of the City of Westminster, [1989] VATTR 71 (VTD 3367)*.

21.76   In two Italian cases, local authorities appealed against assessments charging VAT on receipts from various transactions, contending that as local authorities they were not taxable persons and therefore not required to charge VAT on the transactions in question. The Italian courts referred the cases to the CJEC for guidance on the interpretation of *Article 4(5)* of the *EC Sixth Directive*. The CJEC held that activities pursued 'as public authorities' were those engaged in by bodies governed by public law under the special legal regime applicable to them, but did not include activities pursued by them under the same legal conditions as those applying to private traders. Bodies subject to public law should be treated as taxable persons in respect of activities which could also be engaged in by private individuals in competition against them. *Ufficio Distrettuale delle Imposte Dirette di Fiorenzuola d'Arda v Comune di Carpaneto Piacentino; Ufficio Provinciale Imposta sul Valore Aggiunto di Piacenza v Comune di Rivergaro and Others, CJEC Case 231/87; [1989] ECR 3233; [1991] STC 205*. (*Notes*. (1) For subsequent proceedings, see 21.77 below. (2) For the Commissioners' practice following this decision, see Business Brief 10/93, issued on 26 March 1993.)

21.77   Following the decision in the cases noted at 21.76 above, a similar case involving the same local authorities was also submitted to the CJEC. The CJEC held that bodies subject to public law should be treated as taxable persons 'in respect of activities in which they engage as public authorities where those activities may also be engaged in, in competition with them, by private individuals, in cases in which their treatment as non-taxable persons could lead to significant distortion of competition'. *Comune di Carpaneto Piacentino & Others v Ufficio Provinciale Imposta sul Valore Aggiunto di Piacenza, CJEC Case C-4/89; [1990] 1 ECR 1869; [1990] 3 CMLR 153*.

21.78   In a Spanish case, the CJEC held that *Article 4(5)* was not applicable where a local authority entrusted the collection of taxes to independent third parties, who were treated as self-employed and remunerated on a percentage basis. Accordingly, the payments made by the local authority to the tax collectors were subject to VAT. *Ayuntamiento de Sevilla v Recaudadores de las Zonas Primera y Segunda, CJEC Case C-202/90; [1991] 1 ECR 4247; [1993] STC 659; [1994] 1 CMLR 424*.

21.79   In a German case, a municipality reclaimed input tax on the costs of constructing a building. The tax authority rejected the claim on the basis that the municipality was exempt from VAT and was not a taxable person. The municipality appealed, and the case was referred to the CJEC for a ruling on the interpretation of *Article 4(5)* of the *EC Sixth Directive*. The CJEC held that *Article 4(5)* permitted Member States to treat public bodies as non-taxable persons even where they had acted in a similar manner to private traders. *Finanzamt Augsburg-Stadt v Marktgemeinde Welden, CJEC Case C-247/95; [1997] STC 531; [1997] 1 ECR 779; [1997] AEECR 665*.

21.80   The European Commission brought an action against the United Kingdom, seeking a declaration that, by failing to subject tolls to VAT, the UK had failed to fulfil its obligations under the *Sixth Directive*. The UK defended the action, contending that such tolls were exempt under *Article 4(5)*. The CJEC rejected this contention, holding that the exemption only applied where the tolls were operated directly by bodies governed by public law, and finding that 'in the United Kingdom, the activity of providing access to roads on payment of a toll is carried out in certain cases not by a body governed by public law but by traders governed by private law'. Accordingly, the CJEC held that the UK should subject tolls to VAT, and should account to the Commission for the tax which should have been levied, with interest from 1994. *Commission of the European Communities v United Kingdom, CJEC Case C-359/97, [2000] STC 777.* (*Note*. For the Commissioners' practice following this decision, see their News Release 36/00, issued on 12 September 2000, and Business Brief 15/00, issued on 21 November 2000.)

21.81   Similar decisions were reached in *Commission of the European Communities v France, CJEC Case C-276/97, 12 September 2000 unreported* and *Commission of the European Communities v Ireland, CJEC Case C-358/97, 12 September 2000 unreported.*

21.82   However, contrasting decisions were reached in two cases involving the Netherlands and Greece, where the CJEC found that the tolls in question were operated exclusively by bodies governed by public law, within *Article 4(5)* of the *Sixth Directive*. *Commission of the European Communities v Netherlands, CJEC Case C-408/97, 12 September 2000 unreported* and *Commission of the European Communities v Hellenic Republic, CJEC Case C-260/98, 12 September 2000 unreported.*

21.83   In a Portuguese case, a city council appealed against a demand for VAT on its receipts form parking meters and car parks. The case was referred to the CJEC, which held that the council was acting a public authority, within *Article 4(5)* of the *EC Sixth Directive*. However, the council could be treated as a taxable person, since the Finance Minister of a Member State could be authorised by a national law to define 'significant distortions of competition', provided that such decisions could be reviewed by the national courts. *Fazenda Pública v Câmara Municipal do Porto, CJEC Case C-446/98; [2000] All ER(D) 2281.*

21.84   See also *The Radio Authority*, 7.99 BUSINESS; *The Arts Council of Great Britain*, 7.101 BUSINESS; *Norwich City Council*, 40.5 LOCAL AUTHORITIES AND STATUTORY BODIES; *Metropolitan Borough of Wirral*, 40.6 LOCAL AUTHORITIES AND STATUTORY BODIES; *Rhondda Cynon Taff County Borough Council*, 40.7 LOCAL AUTHORITIES AND STATUTORY BODIES, and *The Royal Academy of Music*, 52.7 PROTECTED BUILDINGS.

Taxable transactions (Articles 5–7)

21.85   **Article 5 of EC Sixth Directive—definition of supplies of goods.**   In a Dutch case, the taxpayer carried out repairs, some of which were extensive, on school books. He contended that he was supplying goods, which under Dutch law were chargeable to VAT at 4%. The Dutch authorities considered that he was supplying services, which were chargeable at 18%. The CJEC held that the production of goods from materials supplied by customers only took place where the contractor produced a new article, i.e. one the function of which was different from that of the materials provided. Repairs, however extensive, did not amount to the supply of goods. *Van Dijk's Boekhuis BV v Staatssecretaris van Financien, CJEC Case 139/84; [1985] ECR 1405; [1986] 2 CMLR 575.*

21.86   In another Dutch case, the CJEC held that a supply of goods could take place even without the transfer of legal ownership, although the supplier should have the right to dispose of the property in question as owner. It was the function of the national court concerned to determine, on the facts of the case, whether the transferee had obtained the right to dispose of the property in question as owner. *Staatssecretaris van Financien v Shipping & Forwarding Enterprise (SAFE) BV, CJEC Case 320/88; [1990] 1 ECR 285; [1991] STC 627; [1993] 3 CMLR 547.*

21.87 A Danish company provided meals on board ferries travelling between Denmark and Germany. The German authorities issued assessments on the basis that the company was making supplies of goods within *Article 5(1)* of the *EC Sixth Directive*, so that, by virtue of *Article 8(1)*, some of the supplies would be deemed to take place in Germany. The company appealed, contending that the supplies were supplies of services within *Article 6(1)*, so that, by virtue of *Article 9(1)*, the supplies were deemed to take place in Denmark, where its business was established. The case was referred to the CJEC, which upheld the company's contentions. Restaurant transactions were to be regarded as supplies of services within *Article 6(1)*, so that, by virtue of *Article 9(1)*, they were deemed to be carried out at the place where the supplier had established his business. The CJEC observed that, applying *Berkholz v Finanzamt Hamburg-Mitte-Altstadt*, 21.108 below, the place where the supplier had established his business was the 'primary point of reference', and that regard was only to be had to another establishment from which the services were supplied if the reference to the place where the supplier had established his business did not 'lead to a rational result for tax purposes' or if it created 'a conflict with another Member State'. *Faaborg-Gelting Linien A/S v Finanzamt Flensburg, CJEC Case C-231/94; [1996] STC 774; [1996] 1 ECR 2395; [1996] 3 CMLR 535; [1996] AEECR 656.* (*Note*. Despite this decision, the Commissioners still treat such supplies as supplies of goods which are outside the scope of UK VAT when supplied on board international or intra-EC passenger transport: see Customs' VAT Manual, Part 4, chapter 2B, para 10.8.)

21.88 **Article 5(4)(c) of EC Sixth Directive.** See *Express Medicare Ltd*, 1.63 AGENTS.

21.89 **Article 5(6) of EC Sixth Directive—private use of business assets.** An oil company distributed vouchers to customers who purchased 12 litres of petrol. When customers had collected a certain number of such vouchers, they could be exchanged for goods. The Commissioners issued a ruling that the company was liable to account for output tax on the cost of the goods it supplied in this way. The company appealed, and the case was referred to the CJEC for a ruling on the interpretation of *Article 5(6)* and *Article 11A3(b)* of the *EC Sixth Directive*. The CJEC held that the application by an oil company of goods in exchange for vouchers must be treated as a supply for consideration, within *Article 5(6)*. Advocate-General Fennelly observed that, under the company's sales promotion scheme, the goods were described as gifts, and that the amounts paid by the customers were entirely attributable to their purchases of fuel and could not be treated as consideration for the goods. The exchange of goods for the vouchers was a 'disposal free of charge', and was taxable accordingly. *Kuwait Petroleum (GB) Ltd v C & E Commrs, CJEC Case C-48/97, [1999] STC 488; [1999] AEECR 450.* (*Notes.* (1) The CJEC also held that there was no 'price discount' allowed to the customer, so that *Article 11A3(b)* did not apply. (2) For the Commissioners' practice following this decision, see Business Brief 17/99, issued on 6 August 1999. (3) The company subsequently made an unsuccessful appeal to the Ch D—see 21.90 below.)

21.90 The CJEC decision in *Kuwait Petroleum (GB) Ltd*, 21.89 above, was applied in a subsequent appeal by the same company. The tribunal dismissed the company's appeal and the Ch D upheld this decision. Laddie J held that, in the light of the ruling by the CJEC, the tribunal was entitled to find that the redemption goods 'were supplied to customers "otherwise than for consideration" and were therefore within *Article 5(6)*'. *Kuwait Petroleum (GB) Ltd v C & E Commrs, Ch D [2000] All ER(D) 2378.* (*Note.* The Ch D also rejected an alternative contention by the company, holding that *Article 11C* of the *Sixth Directive* did not apply.)

21.91 See also *Gallaher Ltd*, 63.48 VALUATION.

21.92   **Article 5(6) of EC Sixth Directive—private use of business assets—whether land included in business assets.** In a Dutch case, a building contractor purchased a plot of land with an existing building. He obtained planning permission to build two houses on the land. He kept one of the houses for his private use, and sold the other house. As he had reclaimed input tax on the goods and services used in the construction of the houses, he accounted for an identical amount of output tax. The Netherlands tax authority, however, took the view that there had been a single supply consisting of the land as well as the buildings, and issued an assessment charging output tax on the value of the land. The contractor appealed, contending that he had acquired the land in a private capacity, and it had never formed part of his business assets. The case was referred to the CJEC for a preliminary ruling concerning the interpretation of *Article 5(6)* of the *EC Sixth Directive*. The CJEC held that, where a taxable person acquired land solely for private use but built a dwelling on that land in the course of his business, only the house (and not the land) was to be regarded as having been a business asset applied for private use for the purposes of *Article 5(6)*. The CJEC observed that 'the purpose of *Article 5(6)* ... is to ensure equal treatment as between a taxable person who applies goods forming part of the assets of his business for private use and an ordinary consumer who buys goods of the same type. In pursuit of that objective, that provision prevents a taxable person who has been able to deduct VAT on the purchase of goods used for his business from escaping the payment of VAT when he transfers ... those goods from his business for purely private purposes and from thereby enjoying advantages to which he is not entitled by comparison with an ordinary consumer who buys goods and pays VAT on them'. *P de Jong v Staatssecretaris van Financien, CJEC Case C-20/91; [1992] 1 ECR 2847; [1992] 3 CMLR 260; [1995] STC 727.*

21.93   **Article 5(7)(a) of EC Sixth Directive—self-supplies of goods.** See *Robert Gordon's College*, 6.1 BUILDINGS AND LAND.

21.94   **Article 5(8) of EC Sixth Directive—transfer of 'totality of assets'.** In a Dutch case, the CJEC held that there could be a transfer of a business even if there had been a cessation of trading before the date on which the transfer took place 'if the wherewithal to carry on the business, such as plant, building and employees, are available and are transferred'. The fact that there was no transfer of goodwill or existing contracts was not conclusive. *JMA Spijkers v Gevroeders Benedik Abattoir CV, CJEC Case 24/85; [1986] ECR 1119; [1986] 2 CMLR 296.*

21.95   See also *Peddars Way Housing Association Ltd*, 15.15 CONSTRUCTION OF BUILDINGS, ETC.

21.96   **Article 6(1) of EC Sixth Directive—definition of supply of services.** In a German case, a dairy farmer undertook to discontinue milk production and was granted a compensation payment under an EC regulation. The German tax authority issued an assessment on the basis that the compensation payment was subject to VAT. The farmer appealed, and the case was referred for a preliminary ruling on the definition of a 'supply of services' in *Article 6(1)* of the *EC Sixth Directive*. The CJEC held that the undertaking given by the farmer did not constitute a supply of services, so that the compensation was outside the scope of VAT. In compensating farmers who undertook to cease milk production, the Community did not acquire goods or services for its own use but acted in the common interest of promoting the proper functioning of the Community milk market. The farmer's undertaking did not entail any benefit, either for the Community or for the national authority, which would enable them to be considered as consumers of a service. *Mohr v Finanzamt Bad Segeberg, CJEC Case C-215/94; [1996] STC 328; [1996] 1 ECR 959; [1996] AEECR 450.*

21.97   A similar decision was reached in a subsequent case in which a German farming company had received compensation for an undertaking not to harvest at least 20% of its potato crop. The CJEC held that the undertaking did not constitute a supply of services, so that the compensation was not taxable. *Landboden-Agrardienste GmbH & Co KG v Finanzamt Calau, CJEC Case C-384/95; [1998] STC 171.*

21.98   See also *Faaborg-Gelting Linien A/S v Finanzamt Flensburg*, 21.87 above, and *Mirror Group Newspapers Ltd*, 26.30 FINANCE.

21.99   **Article 6(2) of EC Sixth Directive—treatment of private use of goods as supply of services.**   In a German case, the taxpayer had purchased a second-hand car from a non-taxable person. The car was purchased with the intention of being used for both private and business purposes. The German tax authority charged VAT on the private use, based on the depreciation of the car and the proportion to which it was used privately. The taxpayer appealed, contending that *Article 6(2)* of the *EC Sixth Directive* precluded a charge to tax where no tax had been deducted on the acquisition of the asset from a non-taxable person. The CJEC held that *Article 6(2)* was unconditional and could be relied upon by a taxpayer against any national provision which was incompatible with it. The power of Member States to derogate from the obligation to charge tax on private use of business assets did not allow them to impose tax where VAT was not wholly or partly deductible. Accordingly VAT was not chargeable in the circumstances of the case. *Kühne v Finanzamt München III, CJEC Case 50/88; [1989] ECR 1925; [1990] STC 749; [1990] 3 CMLR 287.*

21.100   See also *Lennartz v Finanzamt München III*, 21.216 below.

21.101   In a German case, an assessment was made charging VAT on the private use of a car which had been treated as a business asset. The assessment included a proportion of certain expenses relating to the use of the car, on which the owner had not reclaimed input tax. The owner appealed and the case was referred to the CJEC, which held that ancillary services relating to the private use of goods did not fall within *Article 6(2)(a)* of the *EC Sixth Directive* and, where the owner of the goods had not been able to deduct input tax in respect of such services, taxation of such private use was precluded. *Finanzamt München III v Mohsche, CJEC Case C-193/91; [1993] 1 ECR 2615; [1997] STC 195.*

21.102   **Employer providing transport for employees—whether within Article 6(2) of Sixth Directive.**   In a German case, a building company provided transport to enable some of its employees to travel from their homes to the sites where they were working. The case was referred to the CJEC for a ruling on whether this should be treated as a supply of services for consideration, within *Article 6(2)* of the *EC Sixth Directive*. The CJEC held that, in principle, the provision of free transport by an employer was within *Article 6(2)*, since it served the employees' private purposes and thus purposes other than those of the business. However, *Article 6(2)* did not apply when, having regard to special circumstances such as changes in the place of work and difficulty in finding other means of transport, the requirements of the business made it necessary for the employer to provide transport for employees, in which case the supply of those services was not effected for purposes other than those of the business. It was for the national court to determine whether particular circumstances made it necessary for an employer to provide such transport. *Julius Fillibeck Söhne GmbH & Co KG v Finanzamt Neustadt, CJEC Case C-258/95; [1998] STC 513; [1998] 1 WLR 697; [1998] AEECR 466.*

21.103   **Article 6(3) of EC Sixth Directive—self-supplies of services.**   See *Robert Gordon's College*, 6.1 BUILDINGS AND LAND.

21.104   **Article 7 of EC Sixth Directive—imports.**   In a Dutch case, the CJEC held that the entry into the Netherlands of goods coming from the Netherlands Antilles had to be regarded as entry into the EC for the purposes of applying *Article 7(1) of the EC Sixth Directive. Van der Kooy v Staatssecretaris van Financiën, CJEC Case C-181/97; 28 January 1999 unreported.*

Place of taxable transactions (Articles 8, 9)

21.105   **Article 8 of EC Sixth Directive—place of supply of goods.**   A German company, not resident in the UK, had entered into a contract with a UK company to supply and install a bulk material handling system. It also appointed another UK company to act as its sales representative and to supply technical services. It claimed a refund of input tax from the UK under the *EC Eighth Directive*, contending that, under *Article 8* of the *EC Sixth Directive*, the goods should be deemed to have been supplied in Germany. The Commissioners rejected the claim and the tribunal dismissed the company's appeal. The place of supply was the site where the components of the systems were installed and commissioned. As this site was in the UK, the supply of goods was deemed to have taken place in the UK. *Azo-Maschinenfabrik Adolf Zimmerman GmbH (No 2), [1987] VATTR 25 (2296). (Note.* See now *VATA 1994, s 7(3),* deriving from *F(No 2)A 1992.)*

21.106   Compare *George Kuikka Ltd,* 58.363 SUPPLY, in which machine tools were treated as supplied outside the UK.

21.107   See also *Faaborg-Gelting Linien A/S v Finanzamt Flensburg,* 21.87 above; *Centrax Ltd,* 22.15 EUROPEAN COMMUNITY: SINGLE MARKET, and *Peninsular & Oriental Steam Navigation Co,* 58.366 SUPPLY.

21.108   **Article 9(1) of EC Sixth Directive—place of supply of services—definition of 'fixed establishment'.**   A German trader installed gaming machines on two ferry boats operating between Germany and Denmark, and contended that the services provided from such machines were provided from a fixed establishment located on the ship. The CJEC ruled that such services could be regarded as being provided from a fixed establishment only if there was a permanent presence on board the ship of both human and technical resources necessary to provide the services in question. *G Berkholz v Finanzamt Hamburg-Mitte-Altstadt, CJEC Case 168/84; [1985] ECR 2251; [1985] 3 CMLR 667. (Notes.* (1) For another issue in this case, see 21.189 below. (2) Despite this decision, the Commissioners still treat such supplies as outside the scope of UK VAT when supplied on board international or intra-EC passenger transport: see Customs' VAT Manual, Part 4, chapter 2B, para 10.8.)

21.109   A leasing company, established in the Netherlands, supplied a number of cars to customers in Belgium and stored a number of cars with Belgian dealers. It paid VAT to the Netherlands tax authority in respect of such transactions, and submitted a repayment claim on the basis that the place of supply was in Belgium. The Netherlands tax authority rejected the claim on the basis that the company had no fixed establishment in Belgium, so that the place of supply was in the Netherlands. The company appealed and the case was referred to the CJEC for a ruling on the interpretation of *Article 9(1)* of the *EC Sixth Directive.* The CJEC held that services could not be deemed to be supplied at an establishment other than the main place of business unless that establishment had a minimum degree of stability derived from the permanent presence of both the human and technical resources necessary for the provision of the services. *Berkholz v Finanzamt Hamburg-Mitte-Altstadt,* 21.108 above, applied. Accordingly, a leasing company did not supply cars from a fixed establishment in another Member State if it did not have an office or any premises on which to store the cars there. *ARO Lease BV v Inspecteur der Belastingdienst Grote Ondernemingen Amsterdam, CJEC Case C-190/95; [1997] STC 1272; [1997] 1 ECR 4383.*

21.110   A similar decision was reached in *Lease Plan Luxembourg SA v Belgium, CJEC Case C-390/96; [1998] STC 628.* (*Note.* For another issue in this case, see 21.254 below.)

21.111   **Veterinary services.**   A Netherlands veterinary partnership supplied services to Belgian cattle farmers. The Netherlands authority required the partnership to account for output tax on such supplies on the basis that the services were supplied in the Netherlands. The partnership appealed, contending that the services should be treated as falling within *Article 9(2)* of the *EC Sixth Directive* and as being supplied in Belgium. The case was referred to the CJEC, which rejected the partnership's contention, holding that the services fell within *Article 9(1)* rather than *Article 9(2)*, and should be treated as being supplied in the place where the partnership had established its business. *Dudda v Finanzamt Bergisch Gladbach*, 21.117 below, applied. *Maatschap MJM Linthorst & Others v Inspecteur der Belastingdienst/ Ondernemingen Roermond, CJEC Case C-167/95; [1997] STC 1287.* (*Note.* For the Commissioners' practice following this decision, see Business Brief 12/98, issued on 21 May 1998.)

21.112   **Transport services—Article 9(2)(b) of EC Sixth Directive.**   A company provided a maritime passenger and freight service between the Italian mainland and Sardinia, and appealed against the imposition of VAT in respect of that part of the journey which took place in international waters. The CJEC held that *Article 9(2)(b)* of the *Sixth Directive* did not preclude a Member State from applying its VAT legislation to a transport operation between two points within its national territory even where a part of the journey was completed outside its national territory, provided that it did not encroach on the tax jurisdiction of other states. *Trans Tirreno Express SpA v Ufficio Provinciale IVA, CJEC Case 283/84; [1986] ECR 231; [1986] 2 CMLR 100.*

21.113   The French government exempted from VAT transport between mainland France and Corsica. The EC Commission applied for a declaration that the exemption of such transport was in breach of the *EC Sixth Directive*, contending that the place of supply was entirely within France. The CJEC dismissed the application, holding that transport between mainland France and Corsica which took place in or above international waters was not supplied in France, and that the French government was not required to impose VAT thereon. *EC Commission v French Republic, CJEC Case C-30/89; [1990] 1 ECR 691.*

21.114   The Greek government exempted sea voyages in territorial waters from VAT. The EC Commission applied to the CJEC for a declaration that this was in breach of the *EC Sixth Directive*, contending that the place of supply was entirely within Greece. The CJEC upheld this contention and granted the declaration sought, holding that the Greek government had failed to fulfil its obligations under the *Directive*. *EC Commission v Hellenic Republic, CJEC Case C-331/94; [1996] STC 1168; [1996] 1 ECR 2675.*

21.115   In a German case, a company organised cross-frontier coach tours. The German tax authority charged VAT on the basis that the consideration which the company received should be apportioned between the countries concerned on the basis of the distances covered. The company appealed, contending that the time spent in the countries concerned could also be taken into account. The CJEC rejected this contention, holding that, in a case where cross-frontier transport was supplied on an all-inclusive basis, the total consideration must be allocated on a pro rata basis, having regard to the distances covered in each state. *Reisebüro Binder GmbH v Finanzamt Stuttgart-Körperschaften, CJEC Case C-116/96; [1998] STC 604.*

21.116   See also *Faaborg-Gelting Linien A/S v Finanzamt Flensburg*, 21.87 above; *British Sky Broadcasting Ltd*, 58.372 SUPPLY; *The Chinese Channel Ltd (HK)*, 58.373 SUPPLY, and *WH Payne & Co*, 58.397 SUPPLY.

21.117   **Sound engineering services—whether within Article 9(2)(c) of EC Sixth Directive.**   In a German case, a trader supplied sound engineering services for concerts and similar events. The German tax authority assessed him for VAT on the whole of his turnover, even where the concerts took place outside Germany. He appealed, contending that his services were 'services relating to ... entertainment or similar activities', within *Article 9(2)(c)* of the *Sixth Directive*, so that the place of supply was where the services were physically carried out. The case was referred to the CJEC which upheld the trader's contention, holding that, where such sound engineering services were 'a prerequisite for the performance of the principal artistic or entertainment service supplied', they were within *Article 9(2)(c)*. *Dudda v Finanzamt Bergisch Gladbach, CJEC Case C-327/94; [1996] STC 1290; [1996] 1 ECR 4595; [1996] 3 CMLR 1063.*

21.118   **Article 9(2)(e) of EC Sixth Directive—definition of 'advertising services'.**   The European Commission applied for a ruling that the French government was in breach of its obligations under Community law, in that it had applied restrictions to the definition of 'advertising services', thus failing properly to implement the provisions of *Article 9(2)(e)* of the *EC Sixth Directive*. The CJEC granted the rulings sought by the Commission, holding that a promotional activity was within the definition of an 'advertising service' if it involved 'the dissemination of a message intended to inform the public of the existence and the qualities of the product or service which is the subject matter of the activity, with a view to increasing the sales of that product or service'. *EC Commission v French Republic, CJEC Case C-68/92; [1993] 1 ECR 5881; [1997] STC 684; [1995] 2 CMLR 1.*

21.119   Similar decisions were reached in *EC Commission v Kingdom of Spain, CJEC Case C-73/92; [1993] 1 ECR 5997; [1997] STC 700; [1995] 2 CMLR 1* and *EC Commission v Grand Duchy of Luxembourg, CJEC Case C-69/92; [1993] 1 ECR 5907; [1997] STC 712; [1995] 2 CMLR 1.*

21.120   See also *Diversified Agency Services Ltd (aka Omnicom UK plc)*, 58.377 SUPPLY; *Austrian National Tourist Office*, 58.378 SUPPLY; *Miller Freeman Worldwide plc*, 58.387 SUPPLY, and *International Trade & Exhibitions J/V Ltd*, 58.390 SUPPLY.

21.121   **Services of arbitrator—whether within Article 9(2)(e).**   A German professor of law acted as an arbitrator for the International Chamber of Commerce, based in France. The German tax authority charged turnover tax on the fees which the professor received. He appealed, contending that the services were within *Article 9(2)(e)* of the *EC Sixth Directive*, so that the place of supply was in France. The case was referred to the CJEC, which rejected the professor's contentions, holding that the services of an arbitrator were not within *Article 9(2)(e)*. *Von Hoffmann v Finanzamt Trier, CJEC Case C-145/96; [1997] STC 1321; [1997] AEECR 852.*

21.122   **Article 9(2)(e) of EC Sixth Directive—definition of 'forms of transport'.**   A German company purchased goods in Hong Kong which were packed in a container and sent by sea to Hamburg and then overland to Frankfurt. The CJEC was asked for a ruling as to whether transport by container could be considered as a form of transport within *Article 9(2)(e)* of the *EC Sixth Directive* (as substituted by *Article 1* of the *EC Tenth Directive*). The CJEC held that transport by a container could not be considered as a form of transport for this purpose. *Hauptzollamt Frankfurt am*

Main-Ost v Deutsche Olivetti GmbH, CJEC Case C-17/89; [1990] 1 ECR 2301;
[1992] 2 CMLR 859.

21.123   The proprietor of a yacht charter business, operating from Kiel in Germany,
appealed against the imposition of VAT on the charter of the yachts, contending that
the place of supply was where the yachts were used, which was mainly outside
German territorial waters. The case was referred to the CJEC for a ruling on whether
the yachts were 'movable tangible property' within *Article 9(2)(e)* of the *Sixth
Directive*, or 'forms of transport' which were excluded from *Article 9(2)(e)* and fell
under the general rule in *Article 9(1)*. The CJEC held that yachts hired for pleasure
were 'forms of transport', with the result that, under *Article 9(1)*, the place of supply
was in Germany where the business was established. *Hamann v Finanzamt
Hamburg-Eimsbuttel, CJEC Case 51/88; [1989] ECR 767; [1991] STC 193; [1990]
2 CMLR 377.*

21.124   See also *BPH Equipment Ltd*, 58.402 SUPPLY.

Chargeable event (Article 10)

21.125   **Article 10(2) of EC Sixth Directive—derogation for transactions to become
chargeable on payment.**   In an Italian case, a company had commissioned a
contractor to construct a building. The contractor issued a 'proforma' invoice in 1980
but did not issue a VAT invoice until 1982. The Italian VAT office penalised the
company for breaching an Italian law requiring the recipient of a 'proforma' invoice
to account for the VAT due thereon. The company appealed, contending that the
effect of the derogation in *Article 10(2)* of the *EC Sixth Directive* was that the VAT
was not chargeable until it had paid the contractor for the building. The case was
referred to the CJEC, which ruled that Member States which availed themselves of
the derogation in question were not required to lay down detailed rules providing for
situations where a service had been supplied but the relevant invoice had not been
issued and payment had not been made. (The Advocate-General expressly
considered that the relevant Italian legislation was not inconsistent with the *Directive*,
but the CJEC did not issue an explicit ruling on this point.) *Ufficio IVA di Trapani v
Italittica SpA, CJEC Case C-144/94; [1995] STC 1059; [1995] 1 ECR 3653.*

21.126   **Article 10(3)—chargeable event on importation.**   In an Italian case, a company
temporarily imported a quantity of wheat from Canada in 1982 in order to process it
into semolina. It re-exported the semolina but retained the by-products of the
processing, which it released for consumption in 1985. The Italian authorities
required payment of an agricultural levy, VAT and interest in respect of the
importation of the by-products. Subsequently the company began proceedings to
seek repayment of the interest, contending that the effect of *Article 10(3)* of the *Sixth
Directive* was that the chargeable event had not occurred until 1985 when it released
the by-products for consumption. The case was referred to the CJEC, which upheld
the company's contention with regard to the interest charged on the VAT, ruling that
Article 10(3) precluded a Member State from requiring interest on VAT for the
period between temporary importation and definitive importation in respect of goods
which were subject to inward processing arrangements. (However, the CJEC upheld
the validity of the charge to interest on the agricultural levy.) *Pezzullo Molini Pastifici
Mangimifici SpA v Ministero delle Finanze, CJEC Case C-166/94; [1996] STC 1236;
[1996] 1 ECR 331.*

Taxable amount (Article 11)

21.127   **Article 11A1(a) of EC Sixth Directive—definition of 'consideration'.**   In a
German case, the CJEC held that interest awarded by a court, in respect of the late

payment of taxable consideration, was not itself part of the consideration for the services in question. *BAZ Bausystem AG v Finanzamt München für Körperschaften, CJEC Case 222/81; [1982] ECR 2527; [1982] 3 CMLR 688.*

21.128 A company which sold cosmetics supplied some of its goods to agents at greatly reduced prices. The Commissioners issued an assessment charging output tax on the normal wholesale price of such goods. The company appealed, contending that, by virtue of *Article 11A1* of the *EC Sixth Directive*, the consideration should be treated as the amount actually paid by the agents. The tribunal referred the case to the CJEC for guidance on the meaning of 'consideration' in Community law. The CJEC held that, for the purposes of *Article 11A1(a)* of the *Directive*, the taxable amount included not only the monetary consideration actually paid for the product but also the value of the services provided by the agents to the company in obtaining and rewarding hostesses. The value of this service was the difference between the normal wholesale price and the amount actually paid by the agents, so that VAT was chargeable on the whole of the normal wholesale price. *Naturally Yours Cosmetics Ltd v C & E Commrs (No 2), CJEC Case 230/87; [1988] STC 879; [1988] ECR 6365; [1989] 1 CMLR 797.*

21.129 A company sold goods by mail order. It offered new customers, and existing customers who introduced new customers, certain goods (such as a kettle, a toaster or an iron) free of charge as inducements. Such goods were supplied after new customers had made their first order. The value of such goods did not exceed £10. The company accounted for VAT on the cost of the goods, and the Commissioners issued assessments charging tax on 150% of the cost price, being their estimate of the market value of the supply. The tribunal directed that the case should be referred to the CJEC for a ruling whether, for the purposes of *Article 11A1* of the *EC Sixth Directive*, the supply of goods not in the company's current catalogue was made for a consideration separate from the sum of money payable to the supplier for goods ordered from the catalogue; and, if there was any such separate consideration, how it was to be determined. The CJEC ruled that the goods in question were supplied to the customers in consideration for a service, namely the introduction of a potential customer, and not in return for the purchase by the new customer of goods from the catalogue. Applying *Naturally Yours Cosmetics Ltd (No 2)*, 21.128 above, the value of the goods was to be determined subjectively. The value in question was that attributed by the recipient of the services (i.e. the company). Accordingly the taxable amount for VAT purposes was the cost of the articles to the company. *Empire Stores Ltd v C & E Commrs, CJEC Case C-33/93; [1994] STC 623; [1994] 1 ECR 2329; [1994] 1 CMLR 751; [1994] 2 All ER 90.* (*Notes.* (1) For the Commissioners' practice following this decision, see Business Brief 15/94, issued on 19 July 1994. (2) For a preliminary issue in this case, see 2.194 APPEALS. (3) Following the CJEC decision, the tribunal discharged the assessments—*[1994] VATTR 145.*)

21.130 A company which manufactured toiletries issued vouchers entitling customers to discounts on the purchase of its products. It also operated a sales promotion scheme, entitling customers who purchased and returned three of its toothpaste cartons to a £1 refund. It claimed a repayment of output tax which it had previously accounted for, contending that the reimbursement of this money constituted a retrospective discount which reduced the consideration for its supplies. The Commissioners rejected the claim on the basis that there was no direct link between the sale of the toothpaste by the retailer and the reimbursement of the money by the manufacturer. The company appealed. The tribunal referred the case to the CJEC for rulings on whether the taxable amount was the amount originally charged by the manufacturer to the wholesaler or retailer, or whether the discounts allowed by the manufacturer were deductible from that amount. The CJEC held that the 'taxable amount' within *Article 11A1(a)* of the *EC Sixth Directive* could not exceed the amount actually paid by the final consumer. Accordingly, the amounts refunded by the manufacturer had to be deducted from the original selling price in computing the taxable amount. *Elida Gibbs Ltd v C & E Commrs, CJEC Case C-317/94; [1996] STC 1387; [1996] 1 ECR 5339; [1997] 2 WLR 477; [1997] AEECR 53. (Notes.* (1) The case was heard in the CJEC with *Argos Distributors Ltd*, 21.131 below. (2) For the Commissioners' practice following this decision, see Business Brief 25/96, issued on 6 December 1996.)

21.131   A company (D) operated a retail business. It operated a voucher scheme, under which it sold vouchers at a discount to other traders for distribution to members of the public. It had consistently accounted for output tax on the face value of the vouchers, as instructed by the Commissioners. In 1993 it formed the opinion that that it should only have been required to account for tax on the discounted amounts at which it sold the vouchers to other traders. It claimed repayment of more than £1,000,000 in tax which it considered that it had overpaid in the previous ten years. The Commissioners rejected the claim and D appealed. The tribunal referred the case to the CJEC for a ruling on whether *Article 11A1(a)* of the *EC Sixth Directive* was to be interpreted so that the part of the consideration represented by the voucher was the face value of the voucher or the sum actually obtained by the supplier of the goods from the sale of the voucher. The CJEC held that the consideration for the purposes of *Article 11A1(a)* was the subjective value actually received, and that the part of the consideration represented by the voucher was the sum actually obtained by the supplier from the sale of the voucher. *Argos Distributors Ltd v C & E Commrs, CJEC Case C-288/94; [1996] STC 1359; [1996] 1 ECR 5311; [1996] 3 CMLR 569; [1997] 2 WLR 477. (Notes.* (1) The case was heard in the CJEC with *Elida Gibbs Ltd*, 21.130 above. (2) For the Commissioners' practice following this decision, see Business Brief 25/96, issued on 6 December 1996.)

21.132   In a Belgian case, a company appealed against assessments charging output tax, contending that, where customers made payment by credit card, the amount which the credit card company retained as commission should be excluded in computing the consideration on which VAT was chargeable. The CJEC rejected this contention, holding that in a credit card transaction, the commission retained by the credit card company must be included in the consideration which was chargeable to VAT. The fact that the purchaser did not pay the agreed price directly to the supplier, but paid it to an intermediary who retained some of the payment as commission, could not change the taxable amount. *Chaussures Bally SA v Belgian Ministry of Finance, CJEC Case C-18/92; [1993] 1 ECR 2871; [1997] STC 209.*

21.133   In a German case, a company which operated gaming machines was required to pay out as winnings 60% of all coins inserted. It only accounted for VAT on the 40% of the takings which it retained. The German tax authority issued an assessment on the basis that the company was required to account for output tax on the full amount of the takings, including the amounts which were paid out as winnings. The company appealed, and the case was referred to the CJEC, which ruled that the effect of *Article 11A1* of the *EC Sixth Directive* was that, in the case of gaming machines offering the possibility of winning, the taxable amount did not include the statutorily prescribed proportion of the total coins inserted which corresponded to the winnings paid out to players. *HJ Glawe Spiel und Unterhaltungsgeräte Aufstellungsgesellschaft mbH & Co KG v Finanzamt Hamburg-Barmbek-Uhlenhorst, CJEC Case C-38/93; [1994] STC 543; [1994] 1 ECR 1679; [1995] 1 CMLR 70.*

21.134   See also *First National Bank of Chicago*, 21.53 above; *Peugeot Motor Co plc*, 45.8 PAYMENT OF TAX; *Medical Centre Developments Ltd*, 58.109 SUPPLY, and E*mily Patrick*, 63.66 VALUATION.

21.135   **Article 11A1(c) of EC Sixth Directive.**   See *Enkler v Finanzamt Homburg*, 21.68 above.

21.136   **Article 11A3(b) of EC Sixth Directive.**   A major retail company operated sales promotion schemes whereby vouchers were given on the purchase of particular goods. The vouchers could be redeemed against the purchase of other goods. The company accounted for VAT on cash received but did not account for VAT on the face value of the vouchers. The Commissioners issued an assessment charging tax on the face value of the vouchers and the company appealed, contending that the amount of the vouchers constituted a discount which could be excluded from the consideration under *Article 11A* of the *EC Sixth Directive*. The case was referred to the CJEC, which upheld the company's contention that the amount of the vouchers constituted a 'price discount or rebate allowed to the customer and accounted for at the time of supply'. Accordingly, the amount of the vouchers fell within *Article 11A3(b)* of the *EC Sixth Directive* and did not form part of the taxable consideration. *Boots Co plc v C & E Commrs, CJEC Case 126/88; [1990] STC 387; [1990] 1 ECR 1235; [1990] 2 CMLR 731.*

21.137   See also *Kuwait Petroleum Ltd*, 21.89 above, and *Co-Operative Retail Services Ltd*, 63.61 VALUATION.

21.138   **Article 11A3(c) of EC Sixth Directive.**   See *Plantiflor Ltd*, 23.2 EXEMPTIONS: MISCELLANEOUS.

21.139   **Article 11C1 of EC Sixth Directive—reduction of taxable amount.**   A company (G) which traded as jewellers made a supply of goods, valued at more than £200,000, to another company (R) which promised to provide advertising services to G as consideration. However, R went into liquidation without providing the full amount of the services agreed. G claimed bad debt relief in respect of the £135,000 for which services had not been provided. The Commissioners rejected the claim, on the basis that relief was only available where supplies were made for monetary consideration. G appealed, contending that it should be entitled to relief under the provisions of *Article 11C1* of the *EC Sixth Directive*. The tribunal held that the matter should be referred to the CJEC for a ruling on the interpretation of the second sentence of *Article 11C1*. The CJEC held that the derogation in *Article 11C1* did not authorise a Member State, which had enacted provisions for the refund of VAT in cases of non-payment of the consideration, to refuse such a refund for consideration in kind when it permitted such a refund for consideration in money. *Goldsmiths (Jewellers) Ltd v C & E Commrs, CJEC Case C-330/95; [1997] STC 1073; [1997] 1 ECR 3801; [1997] 3 CMLR 520.* (*Note.* Following the CJEC decision, the tribunal allowed the company's appeal—see *[1997] VATDR 325*. For the Commissioners' practice following the decision, see Business Brief 21/97, issued on 3 October 1997. *VATA 1994, s 36* has now been amended by *FA 1998, s 23.*)

21.140   See also *Kuwait Petroleum (GB) Ltd*, 21.90 above; *British Telecommunications plc*, 38.92 INVOICES AND CREDIT NOTES, and *AEG (UK) Ltd*, 63.109 VALUATION.

Exemptions (Articles 13–16)

Activities in the public interest (Article 13A)

21.141   **Article 13 of EC Sixth Directive—exemptions.**   The Italian government had exempted the services of veterinary surgeons from VAT. The EC Commission brought a case against the Italian government on the grounds that such an exemption did not comply with the provisions of the *EC Sixth Directive*. The CJEC held that the exemption in question was outside the terms of *Article 13* and the Italian government was in breach of its obligations under the *Directive*. *EC Commission v Italian Republic, CJEC Case 122/87; [1988] ECR 2919; [1989] 3 CMLR 844.*

21.142   The EC Commission applied to the CJEC for a ruling that the UK had failed to fulfil its obligations under *Article 13A* of the *Sixth Directive*, in that it had exempted the supply of medicines and corrective spectacles from VAT. The CJEC granted the application, ruling that such supplies were not eligible for exemption. *EC Commission v United Kingdom, CJEC Case 353/85; [1988] STC 251; [1988] ECR 817.* (*Note.* The UK complied with this ruling by introducing *FA 1988, s 13.* See now *VATA 1994, Sch 9 Group 7.* The supply of medicines and corrective spectacles is generally now standard-rated. However, the supply of medicines in a hospital or similar approved institution remains exempt under *VATA 1994, Sch 9 Group 7, Item 4*, and the supply of prescribed medicines by registered pharmacists is zero-rated under *VATA 1994, Sch 9 Group 12, Item 1.* The supply of opticians' services in connection with the supply of spectacles may be treated as an exempt supply of services—see *Leightons Ltd*, 31.12 HEALTH AND WELFARE.)

21.143   **Article 13A1(b) of EC Sixth Directive—hospital and medical care.**   Under French law, VAT was chargeable on fixed allowances for the taking of samples for medical analysis. The Commission of the EC applied to the CJEC for a declaration that France had failed to fulfil its obligations under *Article 13A(1)(b)* of the *Sixth Directive.* The CJEC granted the declaration. *EC Commission v French Republic, CJEC Case C-76/99, 11 January 2001 unreported.*

21.144   See also *Gregg*, 21.153 below, and *Kaul (t/a Alpha Care Services)*, 31.35 HEALTH AND WELFARE.

21.145   **Article 13A1(c) of EC Sixth Directive—provision of medical care.**   In an Austrian case, a doctor was appointed by a court to establish, on the basis of a genetic test, whether a claimant was a child of a defendant. She included VAT on the invoice which she issued to the Austrian Federal Treasury in respect of her services. The Treasury appealed, contending that the relevant services should be treated as exempt under *Article 13A1(c)* of the *EC Sixth Directive.* The case was referred to the CJEC which held that the relevant services did not qualify for exemption, on the grounds that *Article 13A1(c)* did 'not apply to services consisting, not in providing care to persons by diagnosing and treating a disease or any other health disorder, but in establishing the genetic affinity of individuals through biological tests'. *Dotter v Willimaier (aka D v W), CJEC Case C-384/98, [2000] All ER(D) 1195.*

21.146   **Article 13A1(f) of EC Sixth Directive—'services supplied by independent groups of persons'.**   In a Dutch case, a charity (S) organised lotteries for another charity (A) on behalf of social and cultural organisations affiliated to A. A reimbursed the costs incurred by S. S did not account for VAT on the amounts it received from A. The Dutch authorities charged VAT on the supplies, and S appealed, contending that they should be treated as exempt under *Article 13A1(f)* of the *EC Sixth Directive.* The CJEC ruled that the exemption only applied to independent groups of persons rendering services for their own members. Services supplied by one foundation for another foundation, where the second foundation was not a member of the first, did not qualify for the exemption. Advocate-General Mischo observed that 'any exemptions, as exceptions to the general rule that VAT is levied on all economic activity, are to be interpreted strictly and must not exceed what is expressly and clearly provided for'. *Stichting Uitvoering Financiële Acties (SUFA) v Staatssecretaris van Financiën, CJEC Case 348/87; [1989] ECR 1737; [1991] 2 CMLR 429.*

21.147   The decision in *Stichting Uitvoering Financiële Acties (SUFA) v Staatssecretaris van Financiën*, 21.146 above, was applied in *The Regency Villas Owners Club*, 13.3 CLUBS, ASSOCIATIONS AND ORGANISATIONS, and *Peterborough Diocesan Conference & Retreat House*, 31.44 HEALTH AND WELFARE.

21.148   **Article 13A1(g) of EC Sixth Directive—services and goods 'closely linked to welfare and social security work'.** A registered charity, which had been established to promote the practice of yoga, owned a residential centre. It did not account for output tax on its supplies of accommodation at the centre. The Commissioners issued an assessment charging tax on the supplies, and the charity appealed, contending firstly that it was not carrying on any business and alternatively that its supplies should be treated as exempt from VAT. The QB accepted the charity's alternative contention and allowed the appeal. Applying *dicta* of Romer LJ in *Berry v St Marylebone Borough Council, CA 1957, [1958] Ch 406; [1957] 3 All ER 677*, 'the expression "social welfare" means the well-being (whether in the physical, mental or material sense) of individuals as members of society ... the provision of benefits which tends directly to improve the health or conditions of life of individuals comes prima facie within the expression "social welfare"'. Accordingly, the charity's aims were within the definition of 'welfare' for the purposes of *Article 13A1(g)* of the *EC Sixth Directive*, which provided that 'the supply of services ... closely linked to welfare' should be exempt from VAT, and which should be treated as having direct effect in the UK. *Yoga for Health Foundation v C & E Commrs, QB [1984] STC 630; [1985] 1 CMLR 340. (Note.* See now *VATA 1994, Sch 9 Group 7, Items 9 & 10* and *Notes 5–7.)*

21.149   The International Bible Students' Association organised conventions to promote the teachings of the Jehovah's Witnesses. Admission to the conventions was free, but the association made profits from catering at the conventions. The Commissioners issued an assessment charging VAT on the receipts from catering. The QB allowed the association's appeal, holding that the association had been established to promote 'spiritual welfare' and that its activities were therefore exempt from VAT under *Article 13A1(g)* of the *EC Sixth Directive. International Bible Students' Association v C & E Commrs, QB 1987, [1988] STC 412; [1988] 1 CMLR 491. (Note.* See now *VATA 1994, Sch 9 Group 7, Items 9 & 10* and *Notes 5–7.)*

21.150   A YMCA operated a club in London, which offered leisure and sporting facilities. The Commissioners issued a ruling that VAT was due on the club subscriptions, and the YMCA appealed, contending that they should be treated as exempt under *Article 13A1(g)* of the *EC Sixth Directive.* (It was accepted that the supplies did not qualify for exemption under what is now *VATA 1994, Sch 9 Group 6.)* The tribunal dismissed the appeal, holding that the club facilities were not within the definition of 'services closely linked to welfare and social security work'. On the evidence, 60% of the club's members were over 30 years of age, and paid annual subscriptions of more than £300, which was 'beyond the means of people in financial need'. Fewer than 5% of the club's members were aged 20 or less, and the club was not therefore 'designed to supplement the needs of the young'. (The tribunal also observed that sporting facilities were the subject of *Article 13A1(m)* of the *Directive*, and commented that 'a supply which is essentially a supply of sporting or physical education facilities covered by *paragraph 1(m)* will in principle be outside the scope of *paragraph 1(g)'.) Yoga For Health Foundation,* 21.148 above, distinguished. *Central YMCA, [1994] VATTR 146 (VTD 12425).*

21.151   See also *Peterborough Diocesan Conference & Retreat House,* 31.44 HEALTH AND WELFARE, and *Trustees for the Macmillan Cancer Trust,* 31.45 HEALTH AND WELFARE.

21.152   In a Dutch case, a woman operated a day nursery as a sole proprietor. She made a profit from the nursery, and used the profit to meet her living expenses. The Dutch authority issued a ruling that her supplies were taxable, and she appealed. The case was referred to the CJEC, which held that the exemption in *Article 13A1(g)* was only available to 'bodies governed by public law or other organisations', and did not apply to sole proprietors. Consequently the nursery in question did not qualify for exemption. *Bulthuis-Griffioen v Inspector der Omzetbelasting, CJEC Case C-453/93; [1995] STC 954; [1995] 1 ECR 2341.* (*Note.* This decision was not followed in the subsequent case of *Gregg*, 21.153 below.)

21.153   **Article 13A1(g)—whether exemption applicable to partnership.**   A married couple operated a nursing home in partnership, with a number of employees. The Commissioners issued a ruling that they were not entitled to register for VAT, on the grounds that all their supplies were exempt from VAT under *VATA 1994, Sch 9 Group 7, Item 4.* The couple appealed, contending that they should not be treated as exempt since the exemption should be construed in accordance with *Article 13A1(b)* and *(g)* of the *EC Sixth Directive*, which confined such exemption to 'bodies governed by public law'. The tribunal referred the case to the CJEC, which held that *Article 13A1* should be 'interpreted as meaning that the terms "other duly recognised establishments of a similar nature" and "other organisations recognised as charitable by the Member State concerned" ... do not exclude from that exemption natural persons running a business'. Accordingly the Commissioners were justified in treating the couple's supplies as exempt and declining to register them. The CJEC distinguished *Bulthuis-Griffioen v Inspector der Omzetbelasting*, 21.152 above, holding that 'the terms "establishment" and "organisation" are in principle sufficiently broad to include natural persons as well. It may be added that none of the language versions of *Article 13A* of the *Sixth Directive* include the term "legal person", which would have been clear and unambiguous, instead of the abovementioned terms. It may be inferred that, in employing those terms, the Community legislature did not intend to confine the exemptions referred to in that provision to the activities carried on by legal persons, but meant to extend the scope of those exemptions to activities carried on by individuals. It is true that the terms "establishment" and "organisation" suggest the existence of an individualised entity performing a particular function. Those conditions are, however, satisfied not only by legal persons but also by one or more natural persons running a business. That interpretation, to the effect that the terms "establishment" and "organisation" do not refer only to legal persons, is, in particular, consistent with the principle of fiscal neutrality inherent in the common system of VAT ... the principle of fiscal neutrality precludes, *inter alia*, economic operators carrying on the same activities from being treated differently as far as the levying of VAT is concerned. It follows that that principle would be frustrated if the possibility of relying on the benefit of the exemption provided for activities carried on by the establishments or organisations referred to in *Article 13A(1)(b)* and *(g)* was dependent on the legal form in which the taxable person carried on his activity.' *J & M Gregg v C & E Commrs, CJEC Case C-216/97, [1999] STC 935; [1999] AEECR 775.*

21.154   **Article 13A1(h)—services and goods 'closely linked to the protection of children and young persons'.**   See *Prospects Care Services Ltd*, 31.39 HEALTH AND WELFARE.

21.155   **Article 13A1(i)—children's or young people's education.**   See *Glenfall House Trust*, 20.26 EDUCATION.

21.156   **Article 13A1(l) of EC Sixth Directive—whether organisation's aims of 'a trade union nature'.**   The Institute of the Motor Industry was established in 1920. In 1996 it applied for a ruling that its supplies should be treated as exempt from VAT under *VATA 1994, Sch 9 Group 9*. The Commissioners ruled that the Institute did not qualify for exemption, and the Institute appealed. The tribunal referred the case to the CJEC for a ruling as to whether the Institute qualified for exemption under *Article 13A1(l)* of the *EC Sixth Directive*, observing that the English-language text of this provision, referring to 'an organisation with aims of a trade-union nature', did not appear to be as wide as the French or German text. The CJEC held that 'an organisation with aims of a trade-union nature', within *Article 13A1(l)*, was 'an organisation whose main aim is to defend the collective interests of its members— whether they are workers, employers, independent professionals or traders carrying on a particular economic activity—and to represent them vis-à–vis the appropriate third parties, including the public authorities'. However, a non-profit-making organisation which aimed to promote the interests of its members could not be regarded as having objects of a trade union nature 'where that object is not put into practice by defending and representing the collective interests of its members vis-à–vis the relevant decision-makers'. It was for the national tribunal to decide whether the Institute was within the definition and qualified for exemption. With regard to the apparent differences between the different texts of *Article 13A1(l)*, the CJEC observed that 'the wording used in one language version of a Community provision cannot serve as the sole basis for the interpretation of that provision, or be made to override the other language versions in that regard ... In the event of divergence between the language versions, the provision in question must be interpreted by reference to the purpose and general scheme of the rules of which it forms a part'. *Institute of the Motor Industry v C & E Commrs, CJEC Case C-149/97, [1998] STC 1219.* (*Note.* Following the CJEC decision, the tribunal dismissed the Institute's appeal, finding that its main aim was not 'supplying defence and representational services' and holding that its supplies failed to qualify for exemption—see 60.22 TRADE UNIONS, PROFESSIONAL AND PUBLIC INTEREST BODIES.)

21.157   **Article 13A1(l) of EC Sixth Directive—whether organisation's aims of 'a philanthropic or civic nature'.**   See *Institute of Leisure and Amenity Management*, 60.12 TRADE UNIONS, PROFESSIONAL AND PUBLIC INTEREST BODIES; *British Tenpin Bowling Association*, 60.14 TRADE UNIONS, PROFESSIONAL AND PUBLIC INTEREST BODIES, and *Committee of Directors of Polytechnics*, 60.15 TRADE UNIONS, PROFESSIONAL AND PUBLIC INTEREST BODIES.

21.158   **Article 13A1(m) of EC Sixth Directive—services closely linked to sport or physical education.**   The Spanish government exempted private sports bodies from VAT on condition that their entry fees did not exceed certain specified amounts. The European Commission brought an action against the Spanish government, seeking a declaration that this condition was not authorised by *Article 13A1(m)* of the *EC Sixth Directive*. The CJEC granted a declaration accordingly, holding that the criterion of the amount of membership fees was contrary to *Article 13A1(m)*, since it could result in a non-profit-making body being excluded from exemption, or in a profit-making body being able to benefit from it. Accordingly, the Spanish government had failed to fulfil its obligations under the *Directive*. *EC Commission v Spain, CJEC Case C-124/96; [1998] STC 1237.*

21.159   See also *Keswick Golf Club*, 23.21 EXEMPTIONS: MISCELLANEOUS; *Chard Bowling Club*, 23.24 EXEMPTIONS: MISCELLANEOUS and *Royal Pigeon Racing Association*, 23.27 EXEMPTIONS: MISCELLANEOUS.

21.160   **Article 13A1(o) of EC Sixth Directive—exemption for fund-raising events by charities, etc.**   See *Northern Ireland Council for Voluntary Action*, 11.23 CHARITIES.

21.161   **Article 13A2 of EC Sixth Directive—restrictions on exemptions.**   See *Keswick Golf Club*, 23.21 EXEMPTIONS: MISCELLANEOUS, and *The Zoological Society of London*, 23.30 EXEMPTIONS: MISCELLANEOUS.

Other internal exemptions (Article 13B)

21.162   **Article 13B(a) of EC Sixth Directive—exemption for insurance transactions.**   A company (C) operated a service whereby, in return for a payment of £16, a customer whose credit cards were lost or stolen would be indemnified up to £750 against any claim made against him in respect of loss caused by fraudulent use of the cards. C engaged an insurance broker to arrange for an appropriate insurance policy. C failed to account for VAT on the payments received from customers for this service. The Commissioners issued a ruling that the payments were taxable and C appealed, contending that they should be treated as exempt under the provisions of *VATA 1983* (see the note preceding 36.14 INSURANCE), or alternatively that it should be treated as making multiple supplies so that part of the payments qualified for exemption. The HL referred the case to the CJEC for rulings as to what was the proper test to be applied in deciding whether a transaction consisted of a single composite supply or of two or more independent supplies; whether supplies of the kind made by C constituted or included 'insurance' within *Article 13B(a)* of the *EC Sixth Directive*, and whether the restriction of the exemption for insurance transactions to supplies made by authorised insurers was compatible with *Article 13B(a)* of the *EC Sixth Directive*. The CJEC held that Member States could not restrict the scope of the exemption for insurance transactions exclusively to supplies by insurers who were authorised by national law. It was for the national court to determine whether the particular transactions in this case were to be regarded as comprising two independent supplies, namely an exempt insurance supply and a taxable card registration service. The CJEC observed that 'having regard to the diversity of commercial operations, it is not possible to give exhaustive guidance on how to approach the problem correctly in all cases.' However, 'a supply which comprises a single service from an economic point of view should not be artificially split'. There was 'a single supply in particular in cases where one or more elements are to be regarded as constituting the principal service, whilst one or more elements are to be regarded, by contrast, as ancillary services which share the tax treatment of the principal service. A service must be regarded as ancillary to a principal service if it does not constitute for customers an aim in itself, but a means of better enjoying the principal service supplied'. *Card Protection Plan Ltd v C & E Commrs, CJEC Case C-349/96; [1999] STC 270; [1999] 3 WLR 203; [1999] AEECR 339.*

21.163   See also *Century Life plc*, 36.11 INSURANCE.

21.164   **Article 13B(b) of EC Sixth Directive—exemptions for leasing or letting of immovable property.**   In a Danish case, two blocks of twelve garages were constructed in conjunction with a building development comprising 37 linked houses. Some of the garages were let to residents of the development and some were let to non-residents. The case was referred to the CJEC for a ruling on whether the letting of the garages was exempt from VAT under *Article 13B(b)* of the *Sixth Directive*, as the 'letting of immovable property', or was excluded from that exemption by *Article 13B(b)(2)*, as the 'letting of premises and sites for the parking of vehicles'. The CJEC held that where the letting of parking places was 'closely linked to lettings of immovable property' which were themselves exempt from VAT under *Article 13B(b)*, such lettings could not be excluded from exemption. *Skatteministeriet v Henriksen, CJEC Case 173/88; [1989] ECR 2763; [1990] STC 768; [1990] 3 CMLR 558.*

21.165   An accountancy partnership surrendered the lease of offices which it had occupied, and received a payment of £850,000 from the landlords for the surrender. The partnership did not account for VAT on the £850,000, and the Commissioners issued an assessment charging tax on it. The partnership appealed, contending that, by virtue of *Article 13B* of the *EC Sixth Directive*, the payment should be treated as exempt from VAT. The tribunal referred the case to the CJEC, which held that a transaction whereby a tenant surrendered his lease and returned the immovable property to his immediate landlord was within *Article 13B(b)*, and was therefore exempt from VAT. Where the rent paid under such a lease was exempt from VAT,

Article 13B did not authorise a Member State to tax the consideration paid in respect of such a surrender. *Lubbock Fine & Co v C & E Commrs, CJEC Case C-63/92; [1993] 1 ECR 6665; [1994] STC 101; [1994] 3 WLR 261; [1994] 3 All ER 705.* (*Note.* The relevant legislation was amended by *VAT (Land) Order 1995 (SI 1995 No 282)* with effect from 1 March 1995.)

21.166   An unlimited company which carried on a stockbroking business took an assignment of an underlease. It received £1,500,000 from the assignor as consideration. The Commissioners issued an assessment on the basis that this consideration was taxable. The company appealed, contending that it was exempt under *Article 13B(b)* of the *EC Sixth Directive*. The QB directed that the case should be referred to the CJEC. Moses J observed that the limitations of the principle laid down in *Lubbock Fine & Co*, 21.165 above, were 'both important and uncertain', and that 'the proper identification of those limitations is vital in order to achieve a system of indirect taxation which is simple and uniform'. *C & E Commrs v Cantor Fitzgerald International, QB [1998] STC 948.* (*Notes.* (1) The CJEC has registered the case as *Case C-108/99*. The Advocate-General has not yet delivered an Opinion. (2) For the Commissioners' policy pending the hearing of the appeal, see Business Brief 28/97, issued on 12 December 1997.)

21.167   In 1993 a publishing company (M) agreed to lease five floors of a multi-storey building, with an option to lease a further four floors. The lessor paid an inducement of £12,000,000 into an escrow account, to be paid to M in instalments. The lessor also paid VAT of £2,100,000, which M accounted for as output tax. In 1994 and 1995 M exercised its option with regard to three further floors, and £1,400,000 was repaid to the lessor in 1995 in respect of M's unexercised option for the remaining floor. Subsequently M claimed repayment of the £2,100,000 from the Commissioners, contending firstly that it had accounted for this in error as it did not relate to any supply, and alternatively that the relevant supply was exempt under *Article 13B(b)* of the *EC Sixth Directive*. The tribunal rejected M's first contention, holding that the inducement of £12,000,000 was consideration for a supply of services made by M in the course of relocating its business. However, the tribunal held that part of the payment qualified for exemption. Applying *Lubbock Fine*, 21.165 above, a supply could qualify for exemption under *Article 13B(b)* even where it was made by the tenant rather than by the landlord. The tribunal held that, in view of the terms of the agreement in question, the inducement had to be apportioned. On the evidence, £5,500,000 of the inducement related solely to the option for M to lease a further four floors. Since 'the act of entering into the lease was not the real *quid pro quo* for (M's) entitlement to the whole or part of the £5,500,000', none of the £5,500,000 could be treated as exempt. The balance of £6,500,000, however, did qualify for exemption, since 'the arrangements can properly be described as the leasing or letting of immovable property by (M) for a consideration consisting of the £6,500,000'. *Mirror Group plc, [1998] VATDR 206 (15443).* (*Note.* The Commissioners appealed to the QB, which has referred the case to the CJEC. The CJEC has registered the case as *Case C-409/98*. For the Commissioners' practice pending the hearing of the appeal, see Business Brief 17/98, issued on 7 August 1998.)

21.168   The French Government exempted the letting of caravans, tents and mobile homes from VAT. The European Commission applied for a declaration that this exemption went beyond the scope of *Article 13B(b)* of the *EC Sixth Directive*. The CJEC granted the declaration, holding that France had failed to fulfil its obligations under *Article 2* of the *Directive*. *EC Commission v French Republic, CJEC Case C-60/96; [1997] 1 ECR 3827; [1999] STC 480.*

21.169   Under German law, the leasing and letting of immovable property was exempt from VAT (in accordance with *Article 13B(b)* of the *EC Sixth Directive*), but lettings for 'short-term accommodation of guests' were excluded from exemption. A woman who let property to refugee families was assessed to output tax on her income from these lettings. The letting agreements were always for periods of less than six months, but many of the refugees stayed in the accommodation for more than a year. She appealed, and the case was referred to the CJEC for a ruling on whether the provision of short-term accommodation for guests should be excluded from exemption under *Article 13B(b)(1)*, and as to the period of accommodation which could properly be regarded as short-term. The CJEC held that *Article 13B(b)(1)* provided Member States with a margin of discretion, could be construed as meaning that the provision of short-term accommodation for guests was taxable, and did not preclude taxation in respect of agreements concluded for a period of less than six months. It was for the national court to determine whether the duration stated in the letting agreement reflected the true intention of the parties. Where the letting agreement did not reflect the true intention of the parties, the actual duration of the accommodation, rather than that specified in the letting agreement, would have to be taken into consideration. *Blasi v Finanzamt München I, CJEC Case C-346/95; [1998] STC 336; [1998] AEECR 211.*

21.170   Under Spanish law, the letting of business premises was subject to VAT. A tenant appealed to the Spanish courts, contending that this infringed *Article 13B(b)* of the *EC Sixth Directive*. The case was referred to the CJEC, which held that *Article 13B(b)* allowed Member States 'to subject to VAT lettings of immovable property and, by way of exception, to exempt only lettings of immovable property to be used for dwelling purposes'. *J Amengual Far v M Amengual Far, CJEC Case C-12/98, 3 February 2000; [2000] All ER(D) 117.*

21.171   See also *Central Capital Corporation Ltd*, 39.51 LAND; *Ashworth*, 39.96 LAND; *Colaingrove Ltd*, 39.101 LAND, and *Aquarium Entertainments Ltd*, 58.418 SUPPLY.

21.172   **Article 13B(c) of EC Sixth Directive.**   The EC Commission took proceedings against the Italian Republic for failing to implement *Article 13B(c)* of the *EC Sixth Directive*, which exempts the supplies of goods used wholly for an exempt activity, when these goods have not given rise to a right of deduction of input tax. The Italian VAT system effectively treated such supplies as being outside the scope of VAT. This did not necessarily have the same effect as exempting the supplies, for in cases where a partial exemption calculation applied, the Italian provisions resulted in a reduction in the denominator of the fraction. The CJEC held that, by enacting legislation which did not exempt from VAT supplies of goods used wholly for an exempted activity, the Italian Republic had failed to fulfil its obligations under *Article 13B(c)*. *EC Commission v Italian Republic, CJEC Case C-45/95; [1997] STC 1062; [1997] 1 ECR 3605.* (*Note.* For the Commissioners' interpretation of the effects of this decision, see Business Brief 24/99, issued on 25 November 1999.)

21.173   See also *Stafford Land Rover*, 9.127 CARS.

21.174   **Article 13B(d) of EC Sixth Directive—exemption for granting of credit.**   In a German case, a credit negotiator claimed exemption under *Article 13B(d)* of the *EC Sixth Directive*. The CJEC held that *Article 13B(d)* had direct effect despite the fact that it had not been implemented in German law at the relevant time. *U Becker v Finanzamt Münster-Innenstadt, CJEC Case 8/81; [1982] ECR 53; [1982] 1 CMLR 499.*

21.175   *Becker v Finanzamt Münster-Innenstadt*, 21.174 above, was applied in *RA Grendel GmbH v Finanzamt für Körperschaften Hamburg, CJEC Case 255/81; [1982] ECR 2301; [1983] 1 CMLR 379; G Kloppenburg v Finanzamt Leer, CJEC Case 70/83; [1984] ECR 1075; [1985] 1 CMLR 205* and *G Weissgerber v Finanzamt Neustadt an der Weinstraße, CJEC Case 207/87; [1988] ECR 4433; [1991] STC 589.*

21.176   In a Dutch case, the CJEC held that a supplier who allowed a customer to defer payment in return for interest was in principle granting credit which was exempt from VAT under *Article 13B(d)* of the *EC Sixth Directive*. However, where payment was only deferred until delivery of the goods or services (as in the case which was the subject of the appeal), interest was not in fact consideration for a separate supply of credit but was part of the taxable consideration for the supply, within *Article 11A1(a)*. *Muys en De Winter's Bouw-en Aannemingsbedrijf BV v Staatssecretaris van Financiën, CJEC Case C-281/91; [1993] 1 ECR 5405; [1997] STC 665; [1995] 1 CMLR 126.*

21.177   In a Danish case, an association of savings banks provided services comprising the execution of transfers, the provision of advice on and trade in securities, and the management of deposits, purchase contracts and loans. The association claimed repayment of VAT which it had accounted for on such transactions, contending that it should have treated them as exempt. The case was referred to the CJEC for rulings on the interpretation of *Article 13B(d)* of the *EC Sixth Directive*. The CJEC held that the exemption was not restricted to transactions effected by a particular type of institution, by a particular type of legal person, or wholly or partly by electronic means or manually. It was not necessary for the service to be provided by an institution which had a legal relationship with the final customer, and the fact that a transaction covered by the provisions was actually effected by a third party, rather than by the customer's bank, did not preclude exemption. Transactions concerning transfers and payments, and services consisting of the management of deposits, purchase contracts and loans, included operations carried out by a data-handling centre if those operations were distinct in character and were specific to, and essential for, the exempt transactions. However, services which merely consisted of making information available to banks and other users did not qualify for exemption. The CJEC also held that, provided that a supply of services fulfilled the criteria for exemption and was specified in an invoice which only concerned that service, the fact that, for organisational reasons, the service was invoiced by a third party did not prevent the transaction to which it related from qualifying for exemption. *Sparekassernes Datacenter v Skatteministeriet, CJEC Case C-2/95; [1997] STC 932; [1997] 1 ECR 3017; [1997] 3 CMLR 999; [1997] AEECR 610.*

21.178   See also *FDR Ltd*, 26.3 FINANCE; *Civil Service Motoring Association*, 26.13 FINANCE; *Continuum (Europe) Ltd*, 26.33 FINANCE; *Nightfreight plc*, 26.34 FINANCE; *Republic National Bank of New York*, 58.158 SUPPLY, and *F & I Services Ltd*, 63.54 VALUATION.

21.179   **Article 13B(f) of EC Sixth Directive—exemptions for betting, etc.**   In a German case, a trader operated a form of roulette without official authorisation. He was assessed to turnover tax and appealed. The case was referred to the CJEC, which held that the unlawful operation of games of chance was within the scope of the *Sixth Directive*. Applying *Lange v Finanzamt Fürstenfeldbruck*, 21.187 below, 'the principle of tax neutrality precludes a generalised distinction from being drawn ... between lawful and unlawful transactions'. *Mol v Inspecteur der Invoerrechten en Accijnzen* and *Vereniging Happy Family Rustenburgerstrat v Inspecteur der Omzetbelasting*, 21.48 above, were distinguished, on the grounds that they concerned goods 'which, because of their special characteristics, may not be placed on the market or incorporated into economic channels'. However, the CJEC also held that the exemption under *Article 13B(f)* of the *Directive* could not be restricted 'solely to lawful games of chance', and that VAT could not be imposed on unlawful games of chance where the corresponding activity was exempt when 'carried on by a licensed public casino'. *Fischer v Finanzamt Donaueschingen, CJEC Case C-283/95; [1998] STC 708; [1998] AEECR 567.*

21.180   See also *Feehan*, 23.15 EXEMPTIONS, and *Ryan*, 46.17 PENALTIES: CRIMINAL OFFENCES.

21.181   **Article 13B(h) of EC Sixth Directive.**   See *Gemeente Emmen v Belastingdienst Grote Ondernemingen*, 21.72 above, and *Norbury Developments Ltd*, 21.238 below.

Option for taxation (Article 13C)

21.182   **Article 13C of EC Sixth Directive—option to tax letting and leasing of immovable property.**   A Belgian law, enacted in 1992, allowed taxpayers to opt to tax the letting and leasing of immovable property. However, the law in question was repealed in 1994. A company which had opted to tax certain property, and had reclaimed input tax in respect of it, appealed against the rejection of its claim, contending that it had been granted an option to tax under *Article 13C* of the *Sixth Directive*, that the abolition of that option was contrary to Community law, and that the principle of legal certainty precluded the retrospective repeal of the national law in question. The case was referred to the CJEC, which held that a Member State which had granted its taxpayers the right to opt for taxation of certain lettings of immovable property, in accordance with *Article 13C*, was not precluded from subsequently abolishing that right of option and returning to 'the basic rule that leasing and letting of immovable property are exempt from tax'. It was for the national court to determine whether the retrospective repeal of the law in question was a breach of the principle of protection of legitimate expectation or of the principle of legal certainty. *Belgocodex SA v Belgium, CJEC Case C-381/97; [2000] STC 351.*

21.183   See also *Newcourt Property Fund*, 6.6 BUILDINGS AND LAND; *Winterthur Life UK Ltd (No 2)*, 6.27 BUILDINGS AND LAND, and *R Walia Opticians Ltd*, 43.49 PARTIAL EXEMPTION.

Exemptions on importation (Article 14)

21.184   **Article 14 of EC Sixth Directive—exemptions on importation.**   A Luxembourg national entered Belgium as a student at Liege University in 1976. In 1978 he married a French national who worked in Liege. While staying in Belgium, he used successively two cars bought and registered in Luxembourg, where VAT was paid. In 1980 the Belgian tax authorities informed him that, as he had been normally resident in Liege since his marriage, he must pay VAT on the importation of the two cars. On appeal, the CJEC ruled that the *Sixth Directive* precluded the levying of VAT by a Member State on the importation of a motor vehicle purchased in another Member State where VAT had been paid and the vehicle registered, when the vehicle was used by a national of the second Member State. A student from another Member State remains a temporary visitor for VAT purposes, regardless of any marriage, unless the couple settle in the host State in such a way as to show their intention of not returning to the Member State of origin when the studies are completed. *Ministère Public & Ministry of Finance v V Profant, CJEC Case 249/84; [1985] ECR 3237; [1986] 2 CMLR 378.*

21.185   A Belgian resident was employed in France and was provided by his employer with a car registered in France. He used the car for business and private purposes. The Belgian authorities sought to charge VAT on the importation of the car into Belgium. The CJEC held that VAT could not be charged in such circumstances. The private use of the car in Belgium constituted temporary importation, which was exempt from VAT under *Article 14* of the *EC Sixth Directive*. *Profant*, 21.184 above, applied. *Ministère Public & Ministre des Finances du Royaume de Belgique v Ledoux, CJEC Case 127/86; [1988] ECR 3741; [1991] STC 553.*

21.186   The Italian government imposed VAT on the importation of free commercial samples of low value, although supplies of such samples within Italy were exempt from VAT. On an application by the EC Commission, the CJEC ruled that, by taxing such importations, the Italian government had failed to fulfil its Treaty obligations. Accordingly the imposition of VAT in such circumstances was illegal. *EC Commission v Italian Republic, CJEC Case 257/86; [1988] ECR 3249; [1990] 3 CMLR 718; [1991] BTC 5104.*

Exemption of exports (Article 15)

21.187   **Article 15 of EC Sixth Directive—whether exemption extends to goods exported unlawfully.**   In a German case, a trader exported information systems to countries in respect of which the Community had imposed a ban on such exports. The German authorities sought to impose VAT, and the trader appealed, contending that the exports were exempt under *Article 15* of the *EC Sixth Directive* notwithstanding the illegality of the exports. The case was referred to the CJEC which upheld the trader's contention, holding that the principle of tax neutrality precluded a generalised distinction between lawful and unlawful transactions. *Mol v Inspecteur der Invoerrechten en Accijnzen* and *Vereniging Happy Family Rustenburgerstrat v Inspecteur der Omzetbelasting*, 21.48 above, were distinguished, on the grounds that they concerned goods 'which, because of their special characteristics, may not be placed on the market or incorporated into economic channels'. *Lange v Finanzamt Fürstenfeldbruck, CJEC Case C-111/92; [1993] 1 ECR 4677; [1994] 1 CMLR 573; [1997] STC 564.*

21.188   **Article 15(4) of EC Sixth Directive—exemption for fuelling and provisioning vessels used at sea.**   In a Dutch case, a company (V) sold to another company (F) two consignments of bunker oil which were delivered to tanks rented by F and were subsequently loaded onto seagoing vessels. V did not account for VAT on the oil supplied to F, and the Dutch authorities issued an assessment charging tax on the supplies. V appealed, contending that the supplies should be treated as exempt from VAT. The Dutch court referred the case to the CJEC for a ruling on whether the exemption under *Article 15(4)* of the *EC Sixth Directive* applied only to supplies of fuel made directly to seagoing vessels, or whether it also extended to supplies made at prior stages in the marketing chain where the goods were ultimately to be used for the fuelling and provisioning of such vessels. The CJEC held that the exemption applied only to supplies of goods made to the operator of a vessel in order to be used by him for fuelling and provisioning, and could not be extended to supplies of those goods made at an earlier marketing stage. However, the supply of the goods did not have to coincide with the fuelling and provisioning, and the fact that the goods were stored after delivery and before fuelling and provisioning did not cause the benefit of the exemption to be lost. The supplies in this case, therefore, qualified for exemption. *Staatsecretaris van Financien v Velker International Oil Co Ltd NV, CJEC Case C-185/89; [1990] 1 ECR 2561; [1991] STC 640.*

21.189   **Article 15(8) of EC Sixth Directive.**   In the case noted at 21.108 above, the CJEC held that the operation of gaming machines on board ships did not qualify for exemption under *Article 15(8)* of the *EC Sixth Directive*. The CJEC held that 'the only services exempted under *Article 15(8)* are those which are directly connected with the needs of sea-going vessels or their cargoes, that is to say services necessary for the operation of such vessels'. *G Berkholz v Finanzamt Hamburg-Mitte-Altstadt, CJEC Case 168/84; [1985] ECR 2251; [1985] 3 CMLR 667.*

21.190   **Article 15(10) of EC Sixth Directive.**   See *MEP Research Services Ltd*, 58.379 SUPPLY.

Deductions (Articles 17–20)

Right to deduct (Article 17)

21.191   French legislation restricted the input tax deductible in respect of the construction or purchase of a leased building, where the annual rental income was less than one-fifteenth of the value of the building. The CJEC held that, where there are no provisions in Community law which permit Member States to limit a taxable person's right to deduct input tax, the full amount of the input tax could be deducted immediately. Taxable persons who had exercised their right to treat the supply of leases as taxable were entitled to deduct the relevant input tax at the time when it was incurred. *EC Commission v French Republic, CJEC Case 50/87; [1988] ECR 4797; [1989] 1 CMLR 505.*

21.192   A holding company provided management services to a group of subsidiary trading companies. In 1991 it disposed of 95% of the shares in a German subsidiary company. It was accepted that this disposal was an exempt supply within what is now *VATA 1994, Sch 9 Group 5.* However, the company reclaimed input tax in respect of professional services supplied in relation to this disposal by a merchant bank, a firm of solicitors and a firm of accountants. The Commissioners issued an assessment to recover the tax, with the exception of a small proportion which they accepted as forming part of the company's general overhead expenses and as not being directly used for the disposal in question. The tribunal dismissed the company's appeal, holding that the tax was not deductible since it related entirely to the making of an exempt supply. The CJEC upheld the tribunal decision, holding that input tax was only deductible under *Article 17* of the *EEC Sixth Directive* if the goods or services in question had a direct and immediate link with taxable transactions. The fact that the ultimate aim of the taxable person was the carrying out of a taxable transaction was irrelevant. *BLP Group plc v C & E Commrs, CJEC Case C-4/94; [1995] STC 424; [1995] 1 ECR 983; [1996] 1 WLR 174; [1995] AEECR 401.*

21.193   A bank, which was partly exempt, incurred legal costs in defending a claim alleging negligent misrepresentation in relation to the sale of a company. The bank's client was a US corporation, and its supplies to the client were accepted as zero-rated under the legislation then in force. The bank reclaimed the whole of the input tax relating to the claim. The Commissioners issued assessments on the basis that the tax should be apportioned between taxable supplies and exempt supplies. The bank appealed, contending that the tax was wholly attributable to the zero-rated taxable supplies which it had made to its US client. The QB referred the case to the CJEC, which held that input tax was only deductible if there was a direct and immediate link between a particular input transaction and a particular output transaction. It was for the national court to apply the 'direct and immediate link' test to the facts of each particular case. A taxable person could not deduct the full amount of input tax incurred on services which had been utilised, 'not for the purpose of carrying out a deductible transaction, but in the context of activities which are no more than the consequence of making such a transaction, unless that person can show by means of objective evidence that the expenditure involved in the acquisition of such services is part of the various cost components of the output transaction'. *C & E Commrs v Midland Bank plc, CJEC Case C-98/98, [2000] STC 501; [2000] 1 WLR 2080; [2000] AEECR 673.*

21.194   In a German case, a company acquired development rights in respect of building land. It subsequently elected to waive exemption in respect of the land. It began construction work in January 1994 and reclaimed input tax. The tax authority issued assessments to recover the tax, on the basis that the possibility of waiving exemption in such cases had been withdrawn by an amendment to German law which came into force on 1 January 1994 and had retrospective effect. The company appealed, contending that the retrospective restriction of its right to opt for taxation was a breach of the Community law principle of legitimate expectation. The case was referred to the CJEC, which held that the effect of *Article 17* of the *EC Sixth Directive* was that input tax incurred on intended taxable supplies was deductible despite the subsequent change in the law. The CJEC observed that, under *Article 17(1)*, the right to deduct arose at the time when the deductible tax became chargeable. The CJEC held that 'in the absence of fraud or abuse and subject to any adjustments to be made' under the conditions laid down in *Article 20*, the right of deduction was 'retained even if the taxable person has been unable to use the goods or services which gave rise to a deduction in the context of taxable transactions by reason of circumstances beyond his control'. In such circumstances, 'the taxable person is entitled immediately to deduct the VAT due or paid on the goods or services supplied with a view to the performance of the economic activities which it envisages carrying out'. The principles of the protection of legitimate expectations and of legal certainty 'preclude its being deprived retroactively of that right by a legislative amendment postdating the supply of those goods or services'. *Grundstückgemeinschaft Schloßstraße GbR v Finanzamt Paderborn, CJEC Case C-396/98, 8 June 2000 unreported.*

21.195   See also *Thorn EMI plc*, 8.30 BUSINESS ENTERTAINMENT; *Apple & Pear Development Council*, 21.47 above; *Lennartz v Finanzamt München III*, 21.216 below; *Fishguard Bay Developments Ltd*, 43.12 PARTIAL EXEMPTION; *Cooper & Chapman (Builders) Ltd*, 43.118 PARTIAL EXEMPTION, and *North East Media Development Trust*, 45.64 PAYMENT OF TAX.

21.196   **Article 17 of EC Sixth Directive—whether a right to deduct input tax where no output tax is to be charged.**   See *Hurd*, 34.186 INPUT TAX, and *F & M Mounty & Sons*, 34.219 INPUT TAX.

21.197   **Article 17(2)(a) of EC Sixth Directive.**   In a Dutch case, petrol was supplied to a company's employees, used exclusively for the purposes of the company's business, and invoiced to the company. The company reclaimed input tax on the petrol and appealed against the Dutch authorities' refusal to allow the deduction. The Netherlands Supreme Court referred the case to the CJEC for a ruling on whether the fact that the petrol was supplied directly to the employees precluded the deduction by the employer of the VAT paid on the petrol. The CJEC ruled that, although *Article 17(2)(a)* of the *EC Sixth Directive* restricted a taxable person's right to deduct tax to amounts due or paid 'in respect of goods ... supplied to him', the purpose of that provision could not be to prevent such a person deducting VAT paid on goods which were sold to him for use in his business, albeit that the goods were actually physically delivered to his employees. Accordingly, VAT could be reclaimed by an employer in such circumstances. *Leesportfeuille 'Intiem' CV v Staatssecretaris van Financien, CJEC Case 165/86; [1988] ECR 1471; [1989] 2 CMLR 856.*

21.198   In the case noted at 21.54 above, a hotelier sold a guesthouse, part of which he had used for private purposes rather than for business purposes. The case was referred to the CJEC, which ruled that where a taxable person sold property, part of which he had chosen at the time of acquisition not to assign to his business, only the part assigned to the business was to be taken into account for the application of *Article 17(2)(a)* of the *EC Sixth Directive*. *Finanzamt Ülzen v Armbrecht, CJEC Case C-291/92; [1995] STC 997; [1995] 1 ECR 2775.*

21.199   In a Belgian case, a company had purchased some land in 1980. It had work carried out on the land, and reclaimed input tax on these supplies. In 1983 it was required by Ghent Council to dispose of the land, without having ever used it for any taxable transactions. The Belgian government sought to recover the tax which the company had reclaimed, and the company appealed. The case was referred to the CJEC for a ruling on the interpretation of *Article 17(2)* of the *EC Sixth Directive*. The CJEC held that the right of deduction was exercisable and remained acquired where, by reason of circumstances beyond his control, the taxable person had never actually used the goods and services in question for the purposes of taxable transactions (while observing that such a supply might give rise to a subsequent adjustment under *Article 20*). *Belgium v Ghent Coal Terminal NV, CJEC Case C-37/95; [1998] STC 260; [1998] AEECR 223.*

21.200   See also *Glasse Brothers*, 34.30 INPUT TAX.

21.201   **Article 17(2)(a) of EC Sixth Directive—tax invoiced but not properly chargeable—whether deductible.**   In a Dutch case, a company reclaimed input tax which had been invoiced to it by two subcontractors but was not properly due. The Dutch authorities issued an assessment to recover the tax, and the company appealed. The Dutch court referred the case to the CJEC for a preliminary ruling as to whether the right to deduct input tax under *Article 17(2)(a)* of the *EC Sixth Directive* extended to tax which was due solely because it was charged on the invoice. The CJEC answered the question in the negative, holding that the right to deduct could only be exercised in respect of tax which was actually due under a transaction which was subject to VAT. The right to deduct input tax did not extend to tax which was not lawfully due but was wrongly charged on an invoice. *Genius Holding BV v Staatssecretaris van Financien, CJEC Case 342/87; [1989] ECR 4227; [1991] STC 239.*

21.202   *Genius Holding BV v Staatssecretaris van Financien*, 21.201 above, was applied in two subsequent German cases where traders had issued bogus invoices in respect of supplies which they had not actually made. The CJEC held that it was for Member States 'to lay down the procedures to apply as regards the adjustment of improperly invoiced VAT'. Adjustments could be made conditional on the issuer of the invoice having 'in sufficient time wholly eliminated the risk of any loss in tax revenues'. Advocate-General Fennelly observed that where VAT was 'mentioned erroneously or fictitiously on invoices ... the issuer of the invoice in question must be able to establish, to the satisfaction of the relevant national tax authorities, that no loss of VAT revenue will occur'. *Schmeink & Cofreth AG & Co KG v Finanzamt Borken; Strobel v Finanzamt Esslingen, CJEC Case C-454/98, [2000] STC 810.*

21.203   See also *Podium Investments Ltd*, 34.518 INPUT TAX.

21.204   **Article 17(3)(a) of EC Sixth Directive.**   See *The Liverpool Institute of Performing Arts*, 43.103 PARTIAL EXEMPTION.

21.205   **Article 17(5) of EC Sixth Directive.**   See *The Trustees of the Victoria & Albert Museum*, 11.35 CHARITIES, and *Pearl Assurance plc*, 43.68 PARTIAL EXEMPTION.

21.206   **Article 17(6) of EC Sixth Directive—expenditure not eligible for deduction of input tax.**   Under a law dating from 1967, the French Republic did not permit input tax to be deducted in respect of vehicles designed for the transport of persons (including motor cars, motorcycles, bicycles, boats, aeroplanes and helicopters). The EC Commission applied to the CJEC for a declaration that, by denying the right to deduct VAT incurred on means of transport, the French Republic had failed to fulfil its obligations under *Article 17* of the *EC Sixth Directive*. The CJEC rejected this contention and dismissed the application, holding that the effect of *Article 17(6)* of the *Directive* was that the French Republic was entitled to retain the exclusions in question. *EC Commission v French Republic, CJEC Case C-43/96; [1998] STC 805; [1998] AEECR 951.*

21.207   Two associated companies reclaimed input tax on motor cars purchased for leasing businesses. The Commissioners issued assessments to recover the tax, on the basis that the deduction of the input tax was prohibited by *Input Tax Order, Article 7*. The companies appealed, contending that *Input Tax Order, Article 7* was incompatible with the right of deduction of input tax in *Article 17* of the *EC Sixth Directive*. The tribunal dismissed the appeals, holding that the restriction was permitted under *Article 17(6)* of the *Directive*. Until the European Council had decided what expenditure should not be eligible for an input tax deduction, Member States could retain all the exclusions provided for under their national laws. The exclusion of any deduction of input tax on motor cars did not contravene the principle of proportionality. The QB upheld this decision but the CA directed that the case should be referred to the CJEC for a ruling on whether *Input Tax Order, Article 7* was valid under European law. The CJEC held that *Article 17(6)* authorised Member States 'to retain general exclusions from the right to deduct the value added tax payable on the purchase of motor cars used by a taxable person for the purposes of his taxable transactions, even though those cars were essential tools in the business of the taxable person concerned, or those cars could not, in a specific case, be used for private purposes by the taxable person concerned'. *Royscot Leasing Ltd v C & E Commrs (and related appeals), CJEC Case C-305/97, [1999] STC 998; [2000] 1 WLR 1151; [1999] AEECR 908.*

21.208   **Article 17(7) of EC Sixth Directive—definition of 'capital goods'.** In a Dutch case, the CJEC defined 'capital goods' as 'goods used for the purposes of some business activity and distinguishable by their durable nature and their value and such that the acquisition costs are not normally treated as current expenditure but written off over several years'. *Verbond van Nederlandse Ondernemingen v Inspecteur der Invoerrechten en Accijnzen, CJEC Case 51/76; [1977] ECR 113; [1977] 1 CMLR 413.* (*Note.* The case was argued on the provisions of the *EEC Second Directive*, but the decision is clearly relevant to the *Sixth Directive*.)

Rules governing right to deduct (Article 18)

21.209   The Belgian tax authorities refused to refund an amount of input tax reclaimed by a company, because they suspected that the company had 'engaged in fictitious circular sales which artificially created an apparent credit'. The company appealed, and the case was referred to the CJEC (together with three other appeals where the facts were similar). The CJEC ruled that the withholding of the amounts claimed was in accordance with *Article 18(4)* of the *EC Sixth Directive*. In such cases, it was for the national court to examine whether or not the measures in question, and the way in which they were applied, were proportionate. *Garage Molenheide BVBA & Others v Belgian State, CJEC Case C-286/94; [1998] STC 126; [1998] 1 CMLR 1186; [1998] AEECR 61.*

21.210   See also *Douros*, 43.133 PARTIAL EXEMPTION, and *Byrd*, 43.135 PARTIAL EXEMPTION, and *University of Sussex*, 45.30 PAYMENT OF TAX.

The deductible proportion (Article 19)

21.211   In a French case, a company which had substantial income from dividends reclaimed the whole of its input tax. The French authorities issued an assessment computed on the basis that the company was only entitled to reclaim a proportion of its input tax, since the dividend income should be included in the denominator of the fraction laid down by *Article 19(1)* of the *EC Sixth Directive* as turnover in respect of which input tax was not deductible. The company appealed, contending that dividends should not be taken into account in the denominator, and the Conseil d'Etat referred the case to the CJEC. The CJEC upheld the company's contention, holding that the receipt of dividends was not within the scope of VAT, since it did not amount to consideration for any economic activity. Consequently dividends on shares were to be excluded from the denominator of the fraction laid down by *Article 19(1)* for the purposes of calculating the deductible proportion of input tax. *Sofitam SA (aka Satam SA) v Ministre du Budget, CJEC Case C-333/91; [1993] 1 ECR 3513; [1997] STC 226.*

21.212   In a French case, a company which carried on a property management business invested sums which it received as advances from co-owners and lessees, and retained the interest which it received. This interest amounted to about 14% of the company's income. It reclaimed the whole of its input tax, including the input tax relating to such investments. The tax authority took the view that, because the interest was exempt from VAT under *Article 13B* of the *EC Sixth Directive*, the effect of *Article 19(2)* of the *Directive* was that only a proportion of the input tax was deductible, and that the amount of interest received should be included in the denominator of the fraction used to calculate the deductible proportion of input tax. The company appealed, contending that the transactions were 'incidental financial transactions' for the purposes of *Article 19(2)*. The case was referred to the CJEC, which ruled that the transactions were not 'incidental financial transactions' for the purposes of *Article 19(2)*, since the receipt of such interest was a 'direct, permanent and necessary extension of the taxable activity of property management companies'. Accordingly, the amount of interest received should be included in the denominator of the fraction used to calculate the deductible proportion of input tax. *Sofitam SA v Ministre du Budget*, 21.211 above, distinguished. *Régie Dauphinoise-Cabinet A Forest Sarl v Ministre du Budget, CJEC Case C-306/94; [1996] STC 1176; [1996] 1 ECR 3695; [1996] 3 CMLR 193.*

21.213   In a Belgian case, two holding companies received dividends and interest from trading subsidiary companies. The holding companies reclaimed the whole of their input tax. The Belgian authorities sought to recover some of the tax on the basis that it was partly attributable to the receipt of income which was exempt from VAT. The companies appealed and the case was referred to the CJEC for guidance on the interpretation of *Article 19* of the *Sixth Directive*. The CJEC held that dividends paid by a subsidiary company to a holding company were outside the scope of VAT and had to be excluded from the denominator of the fraction used to calculate the deductible proportion of input tax. Interest paid on loans to subsidiaries should be similarly excluded where the relevant loans did not constitute 'an economic activity of the holding company', within *Article 4(2)*. Whether the relevant loans were within the charge to VAT was a question to be decided by the national court, applying the principles laid down in *Régie Dauphinoise-Cabinet A Forest Sarl v Ministre du Budget*, 21.212 above. *Floridienne SA v Belgian State; Berginvest SA v Belgian State, CJEC Case C-142/99; [2000] STC 1044.*

21.214   See also *Dean & Chapter of the Cathedral Church of St Peter*, 43.77 PARTIAL EXEMPTION.

Adjustments of deductions (Article 20)

21.215   See *Tremerton Ltd*, 43.50 PARTIAL EXEMPTION; *Briararch Ltd*, 43.125 PARTIAL EXEMPTION; *Curtis Henderson Ltd*, 43.126 PARTIAL EXEMPTION, and *University of Wales College Cardiff*, 43.128 PARTIAL EXEMPTION.

21.216   **Article 20(2) of EC Sixth Directive—adjustments of input tax on capital goods.** In a German case, a tax consultant purchased a car. Initially he used the car mainly for private purposes, and did not reclaim any input tax on the purchase. In the following year his business use of the car increased, and he reclaimed a proportion of the input tax incurred on the purchase of the car. The German tax authority refused to repay the tax, considering that the consultant should be treated as having initially bought the car wholly for private use, and that he was not entitled to reclaim any input tax on the subsequent business use of the car. The consultant appealed and the German court referred the case to the CJEC for a ruling on whether input tax could be reclaimed under *Article 20(2)* on a capital item which was not initially used for business purposes, but was used for business purposes within five years from its acquisition. The CJEC held that the question of whether input tax was deductible was to be determined solely by reference to the capacity in which the purchaser of goods was acting at the time of the purchase. *Article 20(2)* did not itself contain any provisions as to the origin of the right to deduct, but merely established the procedure for calculating adjustments to the initial deduction. Therefore, if a person purchased goods for private purposes but subsequently used them for business purposes, no input tax would be deductible. However, the immediate use of the goods for either taxable or exempt supplies was not of itself 'a condition for the application of *Article 20(2)*'. The question of whether goods had been purchased for the purposes of an 'economic activity' was a question of fact which had to be determined in the light of all the relevant circumstances. Where goods were purchased partly for the purposes of taxable business transactions and partly for private purposes, the taxable person could reclaim the whole of the input tax but would then have to account for output tax on the private use. *Lennartz v Finanzamt München III, CJEC Case C-97/90; [1991] 1 ECR 3795; [1993] 3 CMLR 689; [1995] STC 514.* (*Note.* For the Commissioners' practice following this decision, see Business Brief 4/92, issued on 10 February 1992, and Customs' VAT Manual, Part 13, chapter 2, sections 5.11,5.12.)

Persons liable for payment of tax (Article 21)

21.217   **Article 21(1) of Sixth Directive—recipient of 'credit note'.**   In a German case, a farmer who was liable to account for VAT at 7% supplied pigs to livestock dealers. He subsequently received documents described as credit notes (but akin to self-billing invoices) from some of the dealers, which included VAT at 13% rather than at 7%. The farmer originally accepted the VAT liability of 13%, but subsequently sought to reduce his liability. The German tax authority resisted the claim and the case was referred to the CJEC, which held that the credit notes qualified as a 'document serving as an invoice', and that the effect of *Article 21(1)* of the *EC Sixth Directive* was that a trader who had received a credit note serving as an invoice which included an amount of VAT, and had not contested the amount included, was liable to pay the amount in question even if it was greater than the amount actually owed. *Finanzamt Osnabrück-Land v Langhorst, CJEC Case C-141/96; [1997] STC 1357; [1997] 1 ECR 5073; [1998] 1 WLR 52; [1998] AEECR 178.*

Obligations of persons liable for payment (Articles 22, 23)

21.218   **Article 22(3) of EC Sixth Directive—invoices.**   In a Belgian case, a trader reclaimed input tax in respect of invoices which did not state the registration number of the supplier, the date of the supply, or the full name of the person to whom the supply was made. The CJEC held that, by virtue of *Article 22(3)(c)* of the *EC Sixth Directive*, Member States could specify the criteria with which invoices had to comply, for the correct levying of tax and the prevention of fraud. The relevant criteria should, however, be necessary for the collection of tax and its control by the tax authorities, and should not make the exercise of the right of deduction 'practically impossible or excessively difficult'. *L Jorion (née Jeunehomme) & Société Anonyme d'Etude et de Gestion Immobilière 'EGI' v Belgian State, CJEC Case 123/87; [1988] ECR 4517.*

21.219 In a German case, an appellant failed to produce original invoices in support of a claim to input tax. The tax authority rejected his claim, and he appealed. The case was referred to the CJEC, which ruled that *Article 22(3)* of the *EC Sixth Directive* conferred on Member States the power to require production of an original invoice in order to establish the right to deduct input tax. *Reisdorf v Finanzamt Köln-West, CJEC Case C-85/95; [1996] 1 ECR 6257; [1997] STC 180; [1997] 1 CMLR 536.*

21.220 **Article 22(5) of EC Sixth Directive—interim payments.** In an Italian case, the CJEC held that *Article 22(5)* of the *EC Sixth Directive* authorised Member States to derogate from the rule that payment had to be made on submission of the return, and to demand interim payments. However, payment could only be demanded for transactions which had actually been carried out. An Italian provision, which required traders to pay an amount of VAT equal to 65% of the estimated total amount payable for a period which had not yet elapsed, was contrary to *Article 22(5)* of the *EC Sixth Directive*, which could be invoked by any traders required to make such payments. *M Balocchi v Ministero delle Finanze dello Stato, CJEC Case C-10/92; [1993] 1 ECR 5105; [1997] STC 640; [1995] 1 CMLR 486.*

21.221 **Article 22(8) of EC Sixth Directive—obligations imposed by Member States.** See *Formix (London) Ltd*, 2.104 APPEALS; the cases noted at 2.105 APPEALS, and *Bjelica*, 53.21 REGISTRATION.

Special schemes (Articles 24–26a)

21.222 **Article 24 of EC Sixth Directive—small undertakings.** See *Byrd*, 43.135 PARTIAL EXEMPTION.

21.223 **Article 24(6) of EC Sixth Directive.** See *Eastwood Care Homes (Ilkeston) Ltd*, 30.5 GROUPS OF COMPANIES.

21.224 **Article 25 of EC Sixth Directive—flat-rate schemes.** In 1981 the Italian government introduced a flat-rate scheme for VAT refunds to be paid to producers of beef, pork and unconcentrated and unsweetened milk. On an application by the EC Commission, the CJEC held that the scheme contravened the provisions of the *Sixth Directive*. *EC Commission v Italian Republic, CJEC Case 3/86; [1988] ECR 3369; [1989] 3 CMLR 748.*

21.225 **Article 26 of EC Sixth Directive—travel agents and tour operators.** In a Dutch case, the CJEC ruled that *Article 26* of the *EC Sixth Directive* applied to cases where a travel agent only provided accommodation, and was not restricted to cases where transport was also provided. *Beheersmaatschappij Van Ginkel Waddinxveen BV & Others v Inspecteur der Omzetbelasting Utrecht, CJEC Case C-163/91; [1992] 1 ECR 5723; [1996] STC 825.*

21.226 The European Commission applied for a ruling that the German Federal Republic had failed to comply with its obligations under the *EC Sixth Directive*, in that it had exempted tour operators' margins for supplies within the Community, whereas *Article 26* of the *Directive* only provided for exemption in respect of supplies outside the Community. The CJEC granted the application, ruling that Germany had failed to comply with its obligations. *EC Commission v Federal Republic of Germany, CJEC Case C-74/91; [1992] 1 ECR 5437; [1996] STC 843.* (*Note.* For the Commissioners' practice following this decision, see their News Release 43/94, issued on 25 October 1994. The Tour Operators' Margin Scheme was amended with effect from 1 January 1996. See *Notice No 709/5/96*.)

21.227 The proprietors of a hotel in Devon provided coach transport to and from the hotel for customers from Northern England. On Saturdays the coach collected customers from Leeds and certain pick-up points en route, returning to Leeds each Friday. In addition, each Tuesday the coach was used to provide customers with a sight-seeing trip around Devon. About 90% of the hotel's customers used the coach. The Commissioners issued a ruling that the hotel proprietors were acting as tour operators, within *VATA 1994, s 53(3)*, and were required to operate the Tour Operators' Margin Scheme. The proprietors appealed, contending firstly that they were not within the definition of 'tour operators', and alternatively that the basis of apportionment laid down in *Leaflet 709/5/88* was contrary to *Article 26* of the *EC Sixth Directive*. The QB referred the case to the CJEC, which ruled that the proprietors were acting as 'travel agents' within *Article 26* of the *EC Sixth Directive*. To make the application of the margin scheme depend on whether a trader was formally classified as a travel agent or tour operator would create distortion of competition. Ancillary travel services which constituted 'a small proportion of the package price compared to the accommodation' would not lead to a hotelier falling within *Article 26*, but where a hotelier, in return for a package price, habitually offered his customers travel to the hotel 'from distant pick-up points' in addition to accommodation, such services could not be treated as purely ancillary. However, the CJEC upheld the proprietors' alternative contention, holding that the margin scheme under *Article 26* applied solely to the services supplied by third parties. A method based on actual costs (such as the scheme imposed by *Leaflet 709/5/88*) required a series of complex sub-apportionment exercises and meant substantial additional work for the trader. A trader could not be required to calculate the part of the package corresponding to the in-house services by such a method, where it was possible to identify that part of the package on the basis of the market value of the relevant services (which, in the instant case, were the prices charged by the hotel to 'non-package' customers). *TP Madgett & RM Baldwin (t/a Howden Court Hotel) v C & E Commrs, CJEC Cases C-308/96 & C-94/97, [1998] STC 1189*. (*Note*. For the Commissioners' practice following this decision, see Business Brief 10/99, issued on 22 April 1999.)

21.228   See also *Aer Lingus plc*, 59.2 TOUR OPERATORS AND TRAVEL AGENTS, and *Independent Coach Travel (Wholesaling) Ltd*, 59.3 TOUR OPERATORS AND TRAVEL AGENTS.

21.229   **Article 26(2) of EC Sixth Directive—definition of 'fixed establishment'.**   A Danish company (D), which carried on a travel business, established a UK subsidiary company (L) to act as an agent. Under the agency agreement, L received a commission of 19% on all package tours which it sold on behalf of D. L accounted for VAT on this commission, but D did not account for VAT on its profit on such sales. The Commissioners issued a ruling that D was required to register for UK VAT, and that where L sold package tours on behalf of D, D was required to account for UK VAT on its margin. D appealed, contending that it was not liable to UK VAT since it did not have a fixed establishment in the UK. The QB referred the case to the CJEC for a ruling on the interpretation of the term 'fixed establishment' in *Article 26(2)* of the *EC Sixth Directive*. The CJEC ruled that, in such a case, it was necessary to ascertain whether the subsidiary company was independent of the tour operator and to verify whether its establishment was of a requisite minimum size in terms of human and technical resources. On the facts found by the tribunal, particularly with regard to the number of D's employees established in the UK, it was clear that D did 'display the features of a fixed establishment' in the UK. *C & E Commrs v DFDS A/S, CJEC Case C-260/95; [1997] STC 384; [1997] 1 ECR 1005; [1997] 1 WLR 1037; [1997] AEECR 342*. (*Note*. For the Commissioners' practice following this decision, see Business Brief 12/98, issued on 21 May 1998.)

21.230   **Article 26a of EC Sixth Directive—special arrangements applicable to second-hand goods.**   See *Peugeot Motor Co plc*, 9.62 CARS, and *Stafford Land Rover*, 9.127 CARS.

Simplification procedures (Article 27)

21.231   **Article 27 of EC Sixth Directive—special measures for derogation.** In December 1977 the UK Government notified the European Commission of various special measures which it wished to retain under *Article 27* of the *EC Sixth Directive*. These included *FA 1972, Sch 3 para 2* (the precursor of what is now *VATA 1994, Sch 6 para 2*). However, in 1981 the provision in question was amended by *FA 1981, s 14*. The UK Government did not notify this amendment to the Commission. Subsequently a company, to which the Commissioners had issued a direction under *FA 1972, Sch 3* requiring it to account for tax on the open market value of goods supplied to agents, appealed against the direction, contending that it was invalid. The CJEC held that the amended provision was invalid, so that the UK was not authorised to depart from the provision in *Article 11* of the *Directive* that the taxable amount in respect of a supply should be the consideration received by the supplier. Furthermore, the CJEC held that *Article 11* had direct effect and could be invoked by the appellant company to claim rights not enacted in UK legislation. *Direct Cosmetics Ltd v C & E Commrs, CJEC Case 5/84; [1985] STC 479; [1985] ECR 617; [1985] 2 CMLR 145*. (*Note.* The UK Government subsequently obtained a derogation from the Council of the European Communities authorising *VATA 1983, Sch 4 para 3* (which is now *VATA 1994, Sch 6 para 2*). For a subsequent case in which the validity of the derogation was upheld, see 21.232 below.)

21.232   Acting under the derogation issued by the Council of the European Communities following the case noted at 21.231 above, the Commissioners issued directions under what is now *VATA 1994, Sch 6 para 2* to the company involved in that case and to a company which sold school photographs through the agency of the school's head teachers. The companies appealed, contending that the direction was ultra vires and outside the scope of the *EC Sixth Directive*, since *Article 27* only permitted derogation for the purpose of preventing tax evasion or avoidance. The tribunal referred the cases to the CJEC for a ruling on the validity of the direction. The CJEC ruled that the derogation issued by the Council of the European Communities and the direction issued by the Commissioners were valid. *Article 27(1)* of the *Sixth Directive* was not confined to situations where there was a deliberate intention to avoid tax, but included business arrangements undertaken for genuine commercial reasons, if the effect of such arrangements was that tax was avoided. *Direct Cosmetics Ltd v C & E Commrs (No 2); Laughtons Photographs Ltd v C & E Commrs, CJEC Case 138/86; [1988] STC 540; [1988] ECR 3937*.

21.233   The Belgian government provided for the use of catalogue prices as a minimum taxable amount for charging VAT on the supply and importation of new cars, and notified these provisions to the EC Commission as a special measure under *Article 27(5)* of the *EC Sixth Directive*. On an application by the EC Commission, the CJEC held that the use of catalogue prices did not constitute a valid derogation from the provisions of *Article 11*, as they were too general in nature and were disproportionate to the need to prevent tax evasion or avoidance. *EC Commission v Kingdom of Belgium, CJEC Case 324/82; [1984] ECR 1861; [1985] 1 CMLR 364*.

21.234   German law provided that, for certain supplies between associated persons, the cost of the supply was to be the 'taxable amount'. A landlord, who let a number of properties to a company owned by his wife and son, appealed against an assessment issued on this basis, and the case was referred to the CJEC for a ruling on whether the relevant provision was authorised by *Article 27* of the *EC Sixth Directive*. The CJEC held that the provision was not covered by *Article 27*, since it was not confined to what was 'strictly necessary to deal with the risk of tax evasion or avoidance'. *EC Commission v Kingdom of Belgium*, 21.233 above, applied. (The CJEC observed that rents were often set at a low level for social or political reasons, whereas building costs were generally high, and that there was nothing to prevent a provision formulated in general or abstract terms from excluding cases in which the agreed rent was lower than the amount normally necessary to amortise building costs but was in accordance with normal market rent.) *Finanzamt Bergisch Gladbach v Skripalle, CJEC Case C-63/96; [1997] STC 1035; [1997] 1 ECR 2847.*

21.235   In 1989 the EC Council issued a Decision under *Article 27(1)* of the *EC Sixth Directive*, authorising the French Republic to apply a measure derogating from *Article 17(6)* of the *Directive*, and excluding the deduction of input tax on accommodation, food, hospitality and entertainment. In subsequent proceedings, two French companies contended that the Council Decision was invalid. The case was referred to the CJEC, which held that the Council Decision was invalid because it was 'not compatible with the principle of proportionality' which was 'part of the general principles of Community law'. The Decision authorised the French Republic 'to deny traders the right to deduct the VAT charged on expenditure which they are able to show to be strictly of a business nature'. National legislation 'which excludes from the right to deduct VAT expenditure in respect of accommodation, hospitality, food and entertainment without making any provision for the taxable person to demonstrate the absence of tax evasion or avoidance in order to take advantage of the right of deduction is not a means proportionate to the objective of combating tax evasion and avoidance'. *Ampafrance SA v Directeur des Services Fiscaux de Maine-et-Loire, CJEC Case C-177/99; Sanofi Synthelabo v Directeur des Services Fiscaux du Val-de-Marne, CJEC Case C-181/99, 19 September 2000 unreported.*

21.236   See also *Kimber*, 9.113 CARS; *Next plc*, 54.26 RETAILERS' SPECIAL SCHEMES; *Grattan plc*, 54.27 RETAILERS' SPECIAL SCHEMES; *Primback Ltd*, 54.39 RETAILERS' SPECIAL SCHEMES, and *RBS Leasing & Services (No 1) Ltd*, 63.2 VALUATION.

Transitional provisions (Articles 28–28o)

21.237   **Article 28 of EC Sixth Directive.**   The Commission of the European Communities applied to the CJEC for a ruling that the UK had failed to fulfil its obligations under *Article 28* of the *EC Sixth Directive* in that it had applied a zero rate of tax to several types of supplies which were not eligible for zero-rating under the *Directive*. The CJEC allowed the application in part. It ruled that the supply of sewerage services and water to industry; the supply of news services to undertakings such as banks and insurance companies; the supply of fuel and power; the construction of buildings—other than local authority housing—and of civil engineering; and the supply of protective boots and helmets were not eligible for zero-rating and should be charged to a positive rate of tax. However, it ruled that the zero-rating of animal feeding stuffs, seeds or other means of propagation of plants used for human and animal foodstuffs, and live animals which yielded food for human consumption was within the terms of the *Directive*. *EC Commission v United Kingdom (No 2), CJEC Case 416/85; [1988] STC 456; [1988] ECR 3127.* (Note. The UK introduced the required changes in *FA 1989*, which restricted the scope of *VATA 1983, Sch 5*. See *VATA 1994, Sch 8* for the current zero-rating provisions.)

21.238   **Article 28(3) of EC Sixth Directive.**   A company contracted to purchase some land. It obtained planning permission to build on the land, and sold the land at a profit. It reclaimed input tax on the purchase of the land. The Commissioners issued an assessment to recover the tax, since the land was exempt from VAT under what is now *VATA 1994, Sch 9 Group 1, Item 1*. The company appealed, contending that the relevant provisions of *VATA* were inconsistent with *Article 13B(h)* of the *EC Sixth Directive*, since the land in question was 'building land' and *Article 13B(h)* provided for the exemption of 'land ... other than building land'. The tribunal found that the land was 'building land', and referred the CJEC for a ruling on whether the relevant provisions of *VATA*, which exempted the supply of 'building land', were authorised by the transitional provisions of *Article 28(3)(b)* of the *Directive*. The CJEC held that a Member State was entitled to exempt the supply of building land under *Article 28(3)(b)* of the *EC Sixth Directive*, even though there had been some changes to the relevant exemption provisions since the adoption of the *Directive*. *EC Commission v Federal Republic of Germany*, 21.226 above, distinguished. The CJEC observed that whilst *Article 28(3)(b)* 'precludes the introduction of new exemptions or the extension of the scope of existing exemptions following the entry of the *Sixth Directive*, it does not prevent a reduction of those exemptions, since their abolition constitutes the objective pursued by *Article 28(4)* of the *Sixth Directive*'. *Norbury Developments Ltd v C & E Commrs, CJEC Case C-136/97, [1999] STC 511; [1999] AEECR 436*.

21.239   In a Belgian case, a company supplied international coach transport, which was taxed at 6%. It appealed to the CJEC, contending that it was inequitable for Belgium to treat international air transport as exempt from VAT but to charge VAT on international coach transport. The CJEC rejected this contention, holding that the effect of *Article 28(3)(b)* of the *EC Sixth Directive* was that Member States were entitled to exempt international air transport. The CJEC observed that 'it is for the Community legislature to establish the definitive Community system of exemptions from VAT and thereby to bring about the progressive harmonisation of national VAT laws'. The Community principle of equal treatment did not preclude national legislation 'which on the one hand, in accordance with *Article 28(3)(b)* of the *Sixth Directive*, continues to exempt international passenger transport by air, and on the other hand taxes international passenger transport by coach'. *Idéal Tourisme SA v Belgium, CJEC Case C-36/99, [2000] All ER(D) 971*.

21.240   **Article 28a(1)(b) of EC Sixth Directive—transitional arrangements for taxation of new means of transport.** See *Patterson*, 22.12 EUROPEAN COMMUNITY: SINGLE MARKET.

21.241   **Article 28a(5)(b) of EC Sixth Directive—transfer of own goods between Member States.** See *Centrax Ltd*, 22.15 EUROPEAN COMMUNITY: SINGLE MARKET.

21.242   **Article 28b of EC Sixth Directive—place of transactions.** See *Richmond Cars Ltd*, 9.63 CARS.

21.243   **Article 28c of EC Sixth Directive—transitional arrangements for exemptions.** See *FEA Briggs Ltd*, 22.1 EUROPEAN COMMUNITY: SINGLE MARKET, and *Centrax Ltd*, 22.15 EUROPEAN COMMUNITY: SINGLE MARKET.

21.244   **Article 28k of EC Sixth Directive.** A group of companies (E) which operated the Channel Tunnel terminals brought proceedings before the French courts challenging the validity of *Article 28k* of the *EC Directive* (and the similar *Directive* relating to excise duty). The CJEC held that the validity of provisions in Directives could be challenged before a national court, even though the person mounting the challenge had not brought an action for annulment of the relevant provisions under what is now *Article 230EC* of the *EC Treaty*, but held that the applicant had not shown that the provisions of *Article 28k* were invalid. *Eurotunnel SA & Others v SeaFrance, CJEC Case C-408/95; [1998] BTC 5200*.

Taxes other than turnover taxes (Article 33)

21.245   **Tax on gaming machines—whether permissible under Article 33 of EC Sixth Directive.** In a French case, a trader appealed against an assessment to a tax imposed on the operation of automatic gaming machines, contending that the tax was a tax on turnover and was not permissible under *Article 33* of the *EC Sixth Directive*. The CJEC rejected this contention, holding that, since the tax was assessed solely on the basis of the machine being placed 'at the disposal of the public, without in fact taking account of the revenue which could be generated thereby', it could not be regarded as a turnover tax. The tax was also not incompatible with what is now *Article 90EC* of the *EC Treaty*. *Bergandi v Directeur Général des Impôts, CJEC Case 252/86; [1988] ECR 1343; [1991] STC 529; [1989] 2 CMLR 933.*

21.246   **Danish employment levy—whether permissible under Article 33 of EC Sixth Directive.**   In a Danish case, the CJEC held that an 'employment levy', which had been introduced with effect from 1988, was a turnover tax and was not permissible under *Article 33* of the *EC Sixth Directive*. *Dansk Denkavit ApS & Others v Skatteministeriet, CJEC Case C-200/90; [1992] 1 ECR 2217; [1994] STC 482; [1994] 2 CMLR 377.* (*Note*. For another issue in this case, see 21.33 above.)

21.247   **Austrian tax on tourism—whether permissible under Article 33 of EC Sixth Directive.**   Three Austrian states imposed charges on all traders in their territory which had an economic interest in tourism. Several traders appealed, contending that the charges were not permissible under *Article 33* of the *EC Sixth Directive*. The CJEC rejected this contention, holding that the charges were not precluded by the *Directive*. The charges were 'not passed on to the final consumer in a manner characteristic of VAT' and were 'not levied on commercial transactions in a manner comparable to VAT'. *Dansk Denkavit ApS & Others v Skatteministeriet,* 21.246 above, distinguished. *Pelzl & Others v Steiermärkische Landesregierung & Others, CJEC Cases C-338/97, C-344/97 & C-390/97; 8 June 1999 unreported.*

21.248   **Article 33—other cases.**   There have been a number of other cases concerning *Article 33* of the *EC Sixth Directive*, which turn on the particular facts of the tax in question. In the interests of space, such cases are not summarised individually in this book.

EC EIGHTH DIRECTIVE

21.249   **Article 2 of Eighth Directive.**   An Italian bank, which was partly exempt, made a repayment claim under the *Eighth Directive* for input tax incurred in France. The French authorities rejected the claim and the case was referred to the CJEC, which held that *Article 2* of the *Eighth Directive* must be interpreted as granting taxable persons which were partly exempt a right to 'partial refund'. By virtue of *Article 5*, the refundable amount should be calculated 'first, by determining which transactions give rise to a right to deduction in the Member State of establishment and, second, by taking account solely of the transactions which would also give rise a right of deduction in the Member State of refund if they were carried out there and of the expenses giving rise to a right to deduction in the latter State'. *Ministre du Budget v Société Monte Dei Paschi Di Siena, CJEC Case C-136/99, 13 July 2000, 2000 STI 1515.*

21.250   **Article 3 of Eighth Directive.**   A lawyer established in Belgium hired a car, to be used for the purposes of his profession, from a Netherlands company. Lawyers' services were exempt from VAT in Belgium under the transitional provisions of *Article 28* of the *Sixth Directive*. The lawyer applied to the Netherlands tax authority for a refund of the VAT charged to him on the hire of the car. The Netherlands authority rejected the claim, as the lawyer did not have a certificate of the type required by *Article 3* of the *Eighth Directive*. (Since the lawyer's services were exempt in Belgium, the Belgian authorities had not issued him with such a certificate.) The lawyer appealed and the case was referred to the CJEC, which ruled that the lawyer was not entitled to a refund. Since the lawyer benefited from an exemption granted by the Belgian authorities, he was not entitled to a certificate of the type required by *Article 3* of the *Eighth Directive*. He was therefore not entitled to a refund of VAT charged on services supplied to him in another Member State in which he was not established. *Debouche v Inspecteur der Invoerrechten en Accijnzen Rijswijk, CJEC Case C-302/93; [1996] STC 1406; [1996] 1 ECR 4495; [1997] 2 CMLR 511.*

21.251 In a German case, the CJEC held that applications for a refund under *Article 3(a)* of the *Eighth Directive* 'must, in principle, be accompanied by the original invoices or import documents establishing the amount of VAT in respect of which is a refund is sought'. However, Member States could provide for a duplicate invoice or import document to be used as proof of entitlement to a refund, 'provided that the transaction which led to the refund occurred and there is no risk of further applications for a refund'. *Société Générale des Grandes Sources d'Eaux Minérales Françaises v Bundesamt für Finanzen, CJEC Case C-361/96; [1998] STC 981.*

21.252 **Article 5 of Eighth Directive.**   See *Ministre du Budget v Société Monte Dei Paschi Di Siena*, 21.249 above.

21.253 **Article 7(1) of Eighth Directive.**   See also *Nova Stamps AB*, 22.14 EUROPEAN COMMUNITY: SINGLE MARKET.

21.254 **Article 7(4) of Eighth Directive.**   In the case noted at 21.110 above, the CJEC held that it was contrary to what is now *Article 49EC* of the *EC Treaty* for national rules to provide that taxable persons not established in a Member State, who applied for a refund of VAT but were not reimbursed within the six-month period laid down by *Article 7(4)* of the *Eighth Directive*, were entitled to interest only from such time as notice to pay was served on that Member State, and at a lower rate than that applied to the interest paid to taxable persons established in the territory of that State. *Lease Plan Luxembourg SA v Belgium, CJEC Case C-390/96; [1998] STC 628.*

EC THIRTEENTH DIRECTIVE

21.255 See *Jack Camp Productions*, 24.6 EXPORTS, and *CR Investments SRO*, 42.4 OVERSEAS TRADERS.

MISCELLANEOUS

21.256 **The principle of 'legal certainty'.**   In a French case, the CJEC held that 'rules imposing charges on the taxpayer must be clear and precise so that he may know without ambiguity what are his rights and obligations and may take steps accordingly'. *Administration des Douanes v Société Anonyme Gondrand Freres, CJEC Case 169/80; [1981] ECR 1931.*

21.257 See also *Barber v Guardian Royal Exchange Assurance Group*, 21.32 above.

21.258 **Recovery of charges levied in breach of Community law.**   In an Italian case, the CJEC held that the Italian government was not entitled to withhold repayment of charges which had been levied contrary to Community law. *Amministrazione delle Finanze dello Stato v San Giorgio SpA, CJEC Case C-199/82; [1983] ECR 3513; [1985] 2 CMLR 658.*

21.259 *Amministrazione delle Finanze dello Stato v San Giorgio SpA*, 21.258 above, was applied in a subsequent Italian case in which the CJEC held that Community law precluded a Member State from making repayment of taxes, which had been levied contrary to Community law, 'subject to a condition, such as the requirement that such duties or taxes have not been passed on to third parties, which the plaintiff must show he has satisfied'. *Dilexport Srl v Amministrazione delle Finanze dello Stato, CJEC Case C-343/96; [2000] AEECR 600.*

21.260   **Claim to repayment of VAT levied in breach of Community law—whether repayment should be retrospective.**   In a case where the CJEC held that a Greek law restricting the reclaim of input tax was incompatible with the *EC Sixth Directive*, the appellant company claimed that it should be refunded the tax which it had incurred since 1987 (when the relevant law came into force). The CJEC accepted the company's claim, holding that 'a taxable person may claim, with retroactive effect from the date on which the arrangements at issue came into force, a refund of VAT paid without being due'. *Barra & Others v Belgian State and City of Liège, CJEC Case 309/85; [1989] 1 CMLR 337; [1988] ECR 355* applied. *BP Supergas Anonimos Etairia Geniki Emporiki-Viomichaniki kai Antiprossopeion v Greece, CJEC Case C-62/93; [1995] STC 805; [1995] 1 ECR 1883; [1995] AEECR 684.*

21.261   **Recovery of charges levied in breach of Community law—whether repayment may be refused on grounds of 'unjust enrichment'.**   In 1992 the CJEC issued a ruling that certain dock dues which had been imposed in the French overseas departments had been in breach of Community law. The relevant importers claimed repayment of the charges in question, but the French authorities rejected the claim on the grounds that, since the charges had been passed on to the purchasers of the goods sold, repayment to the importers would lead to 'unjust enrichment'. The case was referred to the CJEC, which ruled that a Member State could resist repayment to traders of charges levied in breach of Community law only where it was established that the charge had been borne in its entirety by another person and that reimbursement of the trader would constitute unjust enrichment. It was for the national courts to determine, in the light of the facts in each case, whether those conditions had been satisfied. Furthermore, where an illegally levied charge had been passed on to the purchaser, it was for the national courts to determine whether its illegal levying had caused damage to the trader to the extent that enrichment would not be 'unjust'. *Société Comateb & Others v Directeur Général des Douanes et droits indirects, CJEC Case C-192/95; [1997] STC 1006; [1997] 1 ECR 165; [1997] 2 CMLR 649.*

22   European Community: Single Market

22.1   **Sale of goods to customer claiming to be taxable person in another Member State—application of conditions imposed by Notice No 703.** A company sold two tables to a customer who claimed to be registered for VAT in the Netherlands. The company did not account for output tax on the sale. The Commissioners issued an assessment charging tax and the company appealed, contending that the sale should be treated as zero-rated. The tribunal dismissed the appeal, holding that the transaction did not qualify for zero-rating because the company had not complied with the conditions of *Notice No 703*, which were authorised by what is now *VATA 1994, s 30(8)* and *VAT Regulations 1995 (SI 1995 No 2518), reg 134*. The tribunal also observed that the conditions thus imposed were authorised by *Article 28c* of the *EC Sixth Directive*. *FEA Briggs Ltd, LON/94/1156A (VTD 12804)*.

22.2   A similar decision was reached in *Red Giant Promotions Ltd, MAN/97/647 (VTD 15667)*.

22.3   **Whether goods removed from UK—application of Notice No 703.** A trader (K) did not account for output tax on the sale of a quantity of clothing. The Commissioners issued an assessment charging tax on the sale, and K appealed, contending that the goods had been sold to a German trader and should be treated as zero-rated under *VATA 1994, s 30*. The tribunal dismissed the appeal, holding that K had failed to comply with the conditions laid down by *Notice No 703*, and that there was no clear evidence that the goods in question had been removed from the UK. *G Kaur, MAN/94/1407 (VTD 13537)*.

22.4   A similar decision was reached in *AR Vig (t/a One by One Fashions), MAN/96/137 (VTD 14504)*. (*Note.* A subsequent appeal against a misdeclaration penalty was also dismissed—see 49.199 PENALTIES: MISDECLARATION.)

22.5   Similar decisions, applying *dicta* of Lord Denning in *Henry Moss of London Ltd*, 24.1 EXPORTS, were reached in *Ornamental Design plc, MAN/97/360 (VTD 15364)* and *SR Talbot (t/a SRT Labels), MAN/98/279 (VTD 15774)*.

22.6   A similar decision was reached in *R Kumar, MAN/99/233 (VTD 16893)*.

22.7   A VAT officer formed the opinion that a company had not obtained sufficient evidence, as required by *Notice No 703*, to justify treating a number of supplies as zero-rated. The officer examined a sample of 234 supplies, and ascertained that 80 of these — i.e. 34% of the sample — did not have a certificate of shipment. He therefore issued an assessment charging tax of more than £500,000, on the assumption that 34% of the supplies which the company had treated as zero-rated did not qualify for zero-rating. The company appealed, contending that there was sufficient evidence to show that the goods had been removed from the UK. The tribunal accepted this contention and allowed the company's appeal, holding on the evidence that 'the package of documents provided in each stockist's file, when it contains evidence of payment for identified goods dispatched to a named stockist in the EU, together with the customer's order, any relevant correspondence, the invoice, the "picking list", and the packing list ... does constitute sufficient evidence of removal of the goods in question from the UK for the purposes of *paragraph 8.7* of *Notice 703*'. The tribunal held that it was not essential for the company to have produced certificates of shipment since, 'by virtue of *paragraph 8.7* of *Notice 703* ... the production of certificates of shipment are (*sic*) not the sole requirement for demonstrating removal of goods from the UK to an EU customer'. *Harriet's House Ltd, LON/99/35 (VTD 16315)*.

22.8 **Sale of van to unregistered customer in Republic of Ireland.** In January 1993 a company sold a van to a resident of the Republic of Ireland, and did not account for VAT. The purchaser was not registered for VAT, and the Commissioners issued a ruling that the company was required to account for output tax. The tribunal dismissed the company's appeal. *Somerset Car Sales Ltd, LON/93/ 1581 (VTD 11986).*

22.9 *Somerset Car Sales Ltd*, 22.8 above, was applied in a similar subsequent case in which a company sold three lorries to a resident of the Republic of Ireland, who was not registered for VAT. *T Naughton Ltd, MAN/99/815 (VTD 16702).*

22.10 **Acquisition of car from Germany—application of VATA 1994, s 10.** A British army officer, who was stationed in Germany, purchased a car in Germany on 6 June 1994, having paid a deposit on 6 May. In September 1994 he was posted to the UK, and he arranged for the car to be transported to the UK on 4 September. The Commissioners charged VAT on the transfer of the car, on the basis that it was a 'new means of transport', so that VAT was chargeable under *VATA 1994, s 10*. The tribunal dismissed the officer's appeal, holding that the car was a 'new means of transport', within the definition in *VATA 1994, s 95(3)*, because less than three months had elapsed since its first entry into service. The fact that the officer had paid a deposit more than three months before the car was transported to the UK was not relevant. *PJI Lane, LON/95/2071A (VTD 13583). (Note. VATA 1994, s 95(3)* has subsequently been amended, increasing the relevant period from three months to six months.)

22.11 In November 1994 a British officer, serving in Germany, purchased a car for the use of his wife. In July 1995, while he was still in Germany, he purchased a Saab car for his own use. In September 1995 he and his wife returned to the UK. The Commissioners issued a ruling that VAT was chargeable on the transfer of the Saab to the UK. The officer appealed, contending that he should be given the benefit of an extra-statutory concession (TR/60/205/1) so that tax should not be charged. The tribunal rejected this contention and dismissed the appeal. The relevant concession contained a clause providing that 'no more than one motor vehicle, vessel or aircraft per entitled person may be relieved of tax under the concession in any period of twelve months'. Since the Saab was the second car which the officer had purchased within twelve months, he had been unable to register it with British Forces Germany and the concession did not apply. *RB Howard-Williams, LON/96/238 (VTD 14474).*

22.12 A British citizen (P) worked in Germany from June 1991 to December 1993. Shortly before his return to the UK, he purchased a car in Germany, having paid VAT at the German rate of 15%. On his return to the UK, the Commissioners informed him that he would have to pay VAT on the car at the UK rate of 17.5%. He appealed. The tribunal dismissed his appeal, holding that the car was a 'new means of transport', within what is now *VATA 1994, s 95(3)*, when P brought it into the UK. Furthermore, the provisions of *s 95(3)* were in accordance with *Article 28a(1)(b)* of the *EC Sixth Directive. RM Patterson, LON/94/611A (VTD 13669).*

22.13 **Acquisition of cars from Republic of Ireland.** See *Richmond Cars Ltd*, 9.63 CARS.

22.14 **Time limit for repayment claim—VAT Regulations, reg 179.** In May 1997 a Swedish company submitted a claim, under the *EC Eighth Directive*, for the repayment of VAT which had been charged in 1995. The Commissioners rejected the claim on the basis that it had been made outside the six-month time limit of *VAT Regulations 1995 (SI 1995 No 2518), reg 179(1)*. The company appealed. The tribunal dismissed the appeal, holding that the time limit was mandatory and was in accordance with *Article 7(1)* of the *EC Eighth Directive*. *Jack Camp Productions*, 24.27 EXPORTS, and *Jersey Telecoms*, 42.5 OVERSEAS TRADERS, applied. *Nova Stamps AB, LON/97/964 (VTD 15304)*.

22.15   **Removal of goods from UK—Commissioners issuing assessments charging output tax—whether assessments compatible with Sixth Directive.**   A UK company carried on the business of manufacturing, repairing and maintaining gas turbine generators. It sold its turbines to customers throughout the EU, and maintained turbines which it had installed. It transported a quantity of goods (parts to be used for maintenance) from the UK to Italy. The Commissioners issued assessments on the basis that the removal of goods from the UK gave rise to a deemed supply under *Sch 4 para 6(1)*, on which the company was required to account for output tax. The company appealed, contending that the effect of *Article 28a(5)(b)* of the *EC Sixth Directive* was that the transport of the goods should not be treated as a supply for consideration, since it had been undertaken for the purpose of a supply under the conditions laid down by *Article 8(1)(a)*. The tribunal accepted this contention and allowed the appeal, On the evidence, 'the parts were transported to Italy for the purposes of their subsequent installation and assembly by or on behalf of the appellant within the first indent of *Article 28a(5)(b)*, so that there is no deemed supply under the *Directive*'. The tribunal observed that what is now *VATA 1994, s 7(3)(b)* 'must be interpreted in accordance with the *Directive*, or, if this is impossible, it must be disapplied. Either way, the appellant succeeds.' Furthermore, even if there had been a deemed supply, the condition laid down by *Notice No 725, para 2.4*, that a trader removing his own goods from the UK must be registered for VAT in the country of destination or account for UK VAT on the transfer, was unreasonable, and was not authorised by *Article 28c(A)* of the *EC Sixth Directive*. *Article 28c* authorised Member States to lay down conditions 'for the purpose of ensuring the correct and straightforward application of the exemptions provided for ... and preventing any evasion, avoidance or abuse'. However, the conditions could not 'be used as a method of ensuring the registration requirements in the other Member State', could not 'be used merely to ensure the integrity of the Single Market', and could not 'be imposed to counteract the fact that registration may not be obligatory in another Member State. The integrity of the Single Market is the responsibility of the (EC) Commission.' *Centrax Ltd, [1998] VATDR 369 (VTD 15743)*. (*Note*. For the Commissioners' practice following this decision, see Business Brief 22/99, issued on 13 October 1999. The Commissioners state that 'because of the uncertain position regarding retrospective VAT registration in Italy, Customs have agreed that Centrax can exceptionally zero-rate transfers of their own goods from the UK to Italy using their VAT registration number in Italy, even though they were not registered in Italy at the time the transfers took place.')

22.16   **Failure to submit EC sales statement—penalty under VATA 1994, s 66.**   See *Sloan Electronics Ltd*, 50.5 PENALTIES: REGULATORY PROVISIONS.

23 Exemptions: Miscellaneous

Cross-references.

For cases falling within *VATA 1994, Sch 9, Group 1* (Land), see 39 LAND. For cases falling within *VATA 1994, Sch 9, Group 2* (Insurance*)*, see 36 INSURANCE. For cases falling within *VATA 1994, Sch 9, Group 5* (Finance), see 26 FINANCE. For cases falling within *VATA 1994, Sch 9, Group 6* (Education), see 20 EDUCATION. For cases falling within *VATA 1994, Sch 9, Group 7* (Health and welfare), see 31 HEALTH AND WELFARE. For cases falling within *VATA 1994, Sch 9, Group 8* (Burial and cremation), see 16.1 *et seq.* DEATH. For cases falling within *VATA 1994, Sch 9, Group 9* (Trade unions, professional and public interest bodies) see 60 TRADE UNIONS, PROFESSIONAL AND PUBLIC INTEREST BODIES. For cases falling within *VATA 1994, Sch 9, Group 12* (Fund-raising events by charities and other qualifying bodies), see 11 CHARITIES. For exemptions under the *EC Sixth Directive*, see 21.141 *et seq.* EUROPEAN COMMUNITY LAW.

The cases in this chapter are arranged under the following headings.

Group 3—Postal services 23.1–23.5
Group 4—Betting, gaming and lotteries 23.6–23.17
Group 10—Sport, sports competitions and physical education 23.18–23.27
Group 13—Cultural services 23.28–23.31

GROUP 3—POSTAL SERVICES

23.1 **Additional charge for postage and packing—whether taxable.** A married couple supplied mounted wedding photographs. Where the photographs were to be posted to the customer, an additional charge was made varying with the number of photographs. In accounting for tax, the couple deducted 10% in arriving at their gross takings to cover the postal charge which they considered should be exempt. The Commissioners issued an assessment charging tax on the amount deducted. The tribunal dismissed the couple's appeal, holding that the additional charge did not qualify for exemption under what is now *VATA 1994, Sch 9, Group 3. Mr & Mrs WHG Swinger, LON/77/127 (VTD 414).*

23.2 **Delivery of plants by parcel post—whether exempt.** A company (P) supplied plants by mail order. It arranged for the plants to be delivered by the Post Office, by parcel post. It charged its customers £2.50 for this, and paid £1.63 to the Post Office, retaining the balance. It did not account for output tax on the amounts paid to the Post Office, treating them as consideration for an exempt supply by the Post Office (and dealing with such payments through a separate 'suspense account' for book-keeping purposes). The Commissioners issued a ruling that P was required to account for output tax on the full amount paid by the customers. P appealed, contending that the delivery of the plants was a separate supply which qualified for exemption. The CA accepted this contention and allowed P's appeal, holding that in arranging for delivery, P was acting as an agent for its customers, and was not liable to account for output tax on the payments of £1.63 to the Post Office. *Plantiflor Ltd v C & E Commrs, CA [2000] STC 137. (Note.* The Commissioners have appealed to the House of Lords against this decision. For their practice pending the hearing of the appeal, see Business Brief 7/00, issued on 18 May 2000.)

23.3 **Goods sent by post—postage paid by customer.** A company sold goods by post. It invoiced customers for the net price plus the cost of the postage, and the goods were not despatched until the invoiced amount had been received. The company accounted for tax only on the price of the goods, treating the amount received for postage as exempt under what is now *VATA 1994, Sch 9, Group 3, Item*

1. The Commissioners issued an assessment on the basis that the company was liable to account for tax on the amount received for postage. The tribunal dismissed the company's appeal, holding that the amounts in question failed to qualify for exemption. Applying *Rowe & Maw*, 58.42 SUPPLY, the company supplied the service of procuring the Post Office to deliver the goods in consideration of the payment from the customer of an amount equal to the charge made by the Post Office. *BSN (Import & Export) Ltd, [1980] VATTR 177 (VTD 998).*

23.4   *BSN (Import & Export) Ltd,* 23.3 above, was applied in the similar case of *Basebuy Ltd, LON/93/1080A (VTD 12088).*

23.5   **Supply of books by mail order to 'club members'.**   See *The Leisure Circle Ltd,* 5.19 BOOKS, ETC., and *Book Club Associates,* 5.20 BOOKS, ETC.

GROUP 4—BETTING, GAMING AND LOTTERIES

23.6   **Provision of bingo facilities by club.**   A members' club organised bingo sessions. Participants paid separate amounts in respect of, or for, entrance fees, jackpot participation fees, bingo boards and jackpot cards. The club did not register for VAT. The Commissioners issued a ruling that the club was required to register, accepting that the supply of the boards and cards was exempt under what is now *VATA 1994, Sch 9, Group 4, Item 1,* but treating the entrance fees and jackpot participation fees as within *Note 1(a)(b)* and standard-rated, so that the club's taxable turnover exceeded the registration threshold. The club appealed, contending that, in arriving at the taxable takings, the percentage of its takings which was set aside for jackpot prizes should be deducted. The tribunal rejected this contention and dismissed the appeal. *Fakenham Conservative Association Bingo Club, LON S/73/164 (VTD 76). (Note.* Compare the subsequent decision in *WMT Entertainments Ltd,* 23.8 below.)

23.7   A members' club provided various forms of live entertainment and regular bingo sessions. On the evenings on which both live entertainment and bingo were provided, members wishing to play bingo were charged amounts varying from 10p to 65p. The club appealed against an assessment on these receipts, contending that they were consideration for the provision of bingo within the exemption of what is now *VATA 1994, Sch 9, Group 4, Item 1.* The QB held that the payments by members were partly for the bingo facilities (exempt) and partly for the live entertainment (taxable) and should be apportioned accordingly, and remitted the case to the tribunal to consider the apportionment. *Tynewydd Labour Working Men's Club & Institute Ltd v C & E Commrs, [1979] STC 570. (Note.* The tribunal directed an apportionment of 15% to bingo and 85% to the live entertainment—see 63.99 VALUATION.)

23.8   A company operated a number of bingo clubs. It sold books of bingo cards to customers at 6p per book. It retained some of these fees, the remainder being distributed as prize money. (Customers were also required to pay stake money of £1.80, one-sixth of which was distributed as prize money.) The company only accounted for VAT on the amounts which it retained, and the Commissioners issued an assessment on the basis that it should also have accounted for VAT on the amounts distributed as prizes. The company appealed, contending that these amounts were exempt under what is now *VATA 1994, Sch 9, Group 4.* The tribunal accepted this contention and allowed the appeal. The amounts which the company retained were excluded from exemption by *Sch 9, Group 4, Note 1(b),* but the amounts which it distributed as prize money were not within *Note 1(b)* and therefore qualified for exemption under *Sch 9, Group 4, Item 1. WMT Entertainments Ltd, MAN/91/282 (VTD 9385). (Note.* Compare *Fakenham Conservative Association Bingo Club,* 23.6 above, which was not referred to in this decision.)

23.9 Exemptions: Miscellaneous

23.9 **Payments to take part in card games returnable to players as winnings.** A company operated a casino and organised card games. It did not account for tax on its takings from the card games. The Commissioners issued an assessment charging tax on them, and the club appealed, contending that the takings were not taxable because all the payments were returned to the players in the form of winnings, and that it regarded the games as 'loss leaders' in relation to its other activities. The tribunal upheld the assessment and dismissed the company's appeal, holding that the payments from the members were to enable them to participate in the game, and were therefore excluded from exemption by *Sch 9, Group 4, Note 1(b)*. *Rum Runner Casino Ltd, MAN/80/33 (VTD 1036)*.

23.10 **Payments for use of card room.** A partnership operated a proprietary social club, which included a card room. It charged club members £1.80 per hour for the use of this room. It did not account for output tax on these charges, treating them as exempt. The Commissioners issued a ruling that output tax was chargeable on the payments, and the partnership appealed. The tribunal allowed the appeal, holding on the evidence that the payments were for the right to use the club's facilities, rather than for the right to play a particular game. The card games were organised by the members themselves, rather than by the partnership. Accordingly, the payments were exempt under *VATA 1994, Sch 9, Group 4, Item 1* and were not excluded from exemption by *Note 1(b)*. *Rum Runner Casino Ltd*, 23.9 above, distinguished. *WG Lee & N Sarrafan (t/a The Regal Sporting Club), LON/97/940 (VTD 15563)*.

23.11 **Shooting gallery—whether a provision of a game of chance.** A partnership ran shooting galleries at Blackpool. In return for 35p a customer was allowed four or five shots (the number dependent on the range) with a.22 inch calibre rifle at a cardboard target, and was given a prize if he completely obliterated the white bull's-eye. The bull's-eye was.312 inch in diameter. The Commissioners issued an assessment charging tax on the partnership's receipts. The partnership appealed, contending that the gallery was a 'game of chance' within *VATA 1994, Sch 9, Group 4, Item 1*. Evidence was given of two experts, of whom one had obliterated the bull's-eye in only two out of 25 attempts, while the other had no successful attempts. On average, there was about one success in 600 by members of the public. The tribunal accepted the partners' evidence and allowed the appeal, holding on the evidence that, while simply placing four shots in the bull's-eye required skill, it would require superlative skill to eliminate the element of chance in completely obliterating the bull's-eye. (The tribunal stressed that the decision was based on the particular facts and was not to be taken as applying to all forms of small-bore rifle shooting.) *W & D Grantham, MAN/79/102 (VTD 853)*. (*Note. Gaming Act 1968, s 52*—see *Group 4, Note 2*—provides, *inter alia*, that 'game of chance' includes a game of chance and skill combined and that 'in determining ... whether a game which is played otherwise than against one or more other players is a game of chance and skill combined, the possibility of superlative skill eliminating the element of chance shall be disregarded'.)

23.12 **Provision of casino accommodation on cruise ship.** A company (S) carried on business as a casino operator. It entered into an agreement with a company operating cruise ships (P & O) whereby P & O granted to it the exclusive right to operate gaming on its cruise ships in return for 50% of the gross profits from such gaming. The Commissioners issued a ruling that the rights which P & O granted to S amounted to the granting of a licence or concession to operate certain games of chance, which was a supply of services taxable at the standard rate. S appealed, contending that what P & O supplied to it under the agreement were facilities for the playing of games of chance, and that these facilities were exempt under what is now *VATA 1994, Sch 9, Group 4, Item 1*. The tribunal allowed S's appeal, holding that the right granted by P & O to S constituted the provision of a facility for playing a game of chance and was therefore exempt. *J Seven Ltd, [1986] VATTR 42 (VTD 2024)*.

23.13   **Takings from gaming machines.**   A trader failed to account for tax on takings from gaming machines located in pubs and clubs. The Commissioners issued an assessment charging tax on them, and the trader appealed, contending that they should be treated as exempt under *Group 4, Item 2* as the granting of a right to take part in a lottery. The tribunal rejected this contention and dismissed his appeal, holding that the machines were not 'lotteries' and the takings were excluded from exemption by *Group 4, Note 1(d)*. *G McCann (t/a Ulster Video Amusements), [1987] VATTR 101 (VTD 2401)*.

23.14   See also *Ryan*, 46.17 PENALTIES: CRIMINAL OFFENCES.

23.15   **Video poker machines.**   The Commissioners issued assessments charging output tax on the owner of a number of 'video poker' machines. The owner appealed, contending that the takings should be treated as exempt from VAT under what is now *VATA 1994, Sch 9, Group 4*. The tribunal dismissed his appeal, holding that the takings were excluded from exemption by *Group 4, Note 1(d)*, and that this exclusion was not inconsistent with *Article 13B(f)* of the *EC Sixth Directive*, since the relevant exemption was 'subject to conditions and limitations laid down by each Member State'. The QB upheld the tribunal decision, applying *Ryan*, 46.17 PENALTIES: CRIMINAL OFFENCES, and *HJ Glawe Spiel*, 21.133 EUROPEAN COMMUNITY LAW. *MJ Feehan v C & E Commrs, QB 1994, [1995] STC 75*. (*Note*. For another issue in this case, not taken to the QB, see 2.85 APPEALS.)

23.16   **Hire of machines for sorting roulette chips—whether within Sch 9, Group 4, Item 1.**   A company which operated casinos owned a number of machines designed for sorting roulette chips, and let these on hire. It did not account for VAT on its takings from the hire of these machines, considering that they were exempt from VAT under what is now *VATA 1994, Sch 9, Group 4, Item 1*. The Commissioners issued an assessment charging tax on the takings in question, on the basis that the machines were not used as an intrinsic or essential part of the playing of the game of roulette. The QB upheld the assessment, holding that the payments did not qualify for exemption. Schiemann J held that *Item 1* merely excluded gambling itself from the scope of VAT, and did not have the effect of requiring the exemption of supplies of equipment such as roulette wheels or sorting machines which were to be used for subsequent gambling. *C & E Commrs v Annabel's Casino Ltd, QB 1994, [1995] STC 225*. (*Note*. For another issue in this case, not taken to the QB, see 43.55 PARTIAL EXEMPTION.)

23.17   **Horse-racing betting game.**   A company operated a betting game whereby customers could bet, on a premium-rate telephone line, on one racehorse each day for a period of 24 days. Customers had to register by telephone before competing, each registration lasting about six minutes. Each telephone call was treated as a £1 bet, and any customer who accumulated £100 or more in winnings in a 24–day period won a special bonus. The company reclaimed input tax on its costs, and the Commissioners issued an assessment to recover the tax, considering that the company's supplies were exempt from VAT under *VATA 1994, Sch 9, Group 4*. The company appealed, contending that the telephone registration services should be treated as separate taxable supplies. The tribunal rejected this contention and dismissed the company's appeal, holding that the company was making a single supply of providing facilities for betting. The registration of the customers was 'an integral part of the game and hence the provision of betting facilities'. *Logic Ltd, LON/95/2634 (VTD 13934)*.

23.18 Exemptions: Miscellaneous

GROUP 10—SPORT, SPORTS COMPETITIONS AND PHYSICAL EDUCATION

Note. *VATA 1994, Sch 9, Group 10* has been substantially amended by the *VAT (Sport, Sports Competitions and Physical Education) Order 1999 (SI 1999 No 1994)*, with effect from 1 January 2000. The *Order* replaces references to 'an eligible body' for the previous references to 'a non-profit-making body', so that 'supplies which would otherwise fall to be exempt . . . will only do so if they are made by an eligible body'. The cases in this section should be read in the light of the changes to the legislation.

23.18　**Rugby club match fees—whether exempt.**　A rugby union club charged its players a match fee of £2.50. These fees were used to defray the purchase of shirts and rugby balls, and to pay referees' fees. The club failed to account for output tax on the match fees, and the Commissioners issued an assessment charging tax on them. The club appealed, contending that the fees should be treated as exempt under what is now *VATA 1994, Sch 9, Group 10*. The tribunal rejected this contention and dismissed the appeal, holding that the match fees did not qualify for exemption, regardless of whether they related to league matches or to friendly matches. The club's friendly matches were not within the definition of 'competitions', and with regard to the league matches, the match fees were not consideration for any 'grant' by the club to its players within the scope of *Group 10. Wimborne Rugby Football Club, LON/89/755Y (VTD 4547).*

23.19　**Admission to sports centre—whether exempt under Group 10, Item 3.**　A charitable trust operated a sports centre. It sold 'privilege cards', which granted the holders free admission to the centre, and the use of certain facilities (such as a swimming pool) at a reduced rate. Adults were required to pay £29.95 for such cards, and there were reduced rates for students and pensioners. It charged for admission to individuals who did not hold privilege cards. It did not account for output tax on such payments, treating them as exempt under *VATA 1994, Sch 9, Group 10, Item 3.* The Commissioners issued a ruling that the trust was required to account for output tax on payments from individuals who did not hold privilege cards, on the grounds that the privilege cards were a membership scheme and that the effect of *Item 3* was that payments from non-members did not qualify for exemption. The trust appealed, contending firstly that the privilege cards did not amount to a membership scheme, and alternatively that the provision in *Item 3* excluding payments by non-members from exemption was not in accordance with *Article 13A2(b)* of the *EC Sixth Directive*. The tribunal accepted the first contention and allowed the appeal, holding that the privilege cards did not amount to a membership scheme, since the concept of a 'membership scheme' involved 'an element of participation or belonging which is absent in the present case'. *Basingstoke & District Sports Trust Ltd, [1995] VATDR 405 (VTD 13347).* (*Note.* For the Commissioners' practice following this decision, see Business Brief 3/96, issued on 16 February 1996.)

23.20　**Golf club—whether a 'non-profit-making body'.**　The Commissioners issued a ruling that a limited company which operated a golf club was not within the definition of a 'non-profit-making body', so that its supplies did not qualify for exemption under *VATA 1994, Group 10, Item 3.* The club appealed, contending that, although it had been founded as a proprietary club, the holding company which had originally owned it had sold it and it was now managed as a members' club. The tribunal reviewed the evidence in detail and allowed the appeal. The facts that the club paid significant sums in rent to the company which owned its course, and paid management fees to a management company, did not necessarily take it outside the definition of a 'non-profit-making body', since 'income is not profit'. On the evidence, the tribunal was satisfied that any surplus which remained after paying the club's overheads (which included rent and management fees) would be 'used in the improvement of the club's facilities'. Accordingly, the club was within the definition of a 'non-profit-making body', and its supplies to its members qualified for exemption under *Group 10, Item 3*. *Chobham Golf Club, [1997] VATDR 36 (VTD 14867)*. *(Notes*. (1) The Commissioners appealed to the High Court against this decision (see Business Brief 18/97, issued on 22 August 1997) but subsequently withdrew their appeal—see Business Brief 18/98, issued on 11 September 1998. (2) See the note at the head of this section with regard to the *VAT (Sport, Sports Competitions & Physical Education) Order 1999 (SI 1999 No 1994).*)

23.21   **Golf club—supplies to non-members—effect of Group 10, Item 3.**   A members' golf club allowed non-members to play on its course in return for payment of a 'green fee'. The Commissioners issued a ruling that the club was required to account for tax on the green fees, and the club appealed, contending that they should be treated as exempt. The tribunal rejected this contention and dismissed the club's appeal. The fees did not qualify for exemption under *VATA 1994, Sch 9, Group 10, Item 3*, and the exclusion of supplies to non-members from the scope of this exemption was not inconsistent with *Article 13A1(m)* of the *EC Sixth Directive*, since such restrictions were permitted by *Article 13A2* of the *Directive*. *Keswick Golf Club (and related appeals), [1998] VATDR 267 (VTD 15493).*

23.22   **Golf club—non-refundable fee for place on membership waiting list.**   A members' golf club had a waiting list of more than 18 months for membership. It required prospective members to pay a non-refundable fee of £20 for a place on this list. This fee was deducted from the first subscription if membership was subsequently taken up. The club did not account for VAT on these fees, treating them as exempt. The Commissioners issued a ruling that the fees failed to qualify for exemption under *VATA 1994, Sch 9, Group 10*, and were therefore standard-rated. The tribunal dismissed the club's appeal. On the evidence, the payment was 'consideration for the right to be on the waiting list, and as such standard-rated'. *Milnathort Golf Club Ltd, EDN/98/139 (VTD 15816).*

23.23   **Golf club—transfer of business to non-profit-making body.**   See *Tall Pines Golf & Leisure Co Ltd*, 39.10 LAND.

23.24   **Bowling club—payments from members for casual play.**   A bowling club registered for VAT from September 1994. In its first VAT return, it treated fees charged to its members for competitions as exempt under *VATA 1994, Sch 9, Group 10* but treated all fees received for casual play (whether received from members or non-members) as standard-rated. This resulted in the club's exempt input tax being less than the *de minimis* limits, and to the club reclaiming more than £6,800 in input tax. A VAT officer visited the club and formed the opinion that the return was incorrect because fees received from members for casual play should have been treated as exempt, with the result that the exempt input tax exceeded the *de minimis* limits and the repayment actually due to the club was only £1,036. The Commissioners issued a ruling accordingly, and the club appealed, contending that casual play was not 'closely linked and essential to sport'. The tribunal dismissed the appeal, holding that the services which the club provided to enable casual play were 'closely linked with and essential to sport', and were therefore exempt from VAT under *VATA 1994, Sch 9, Group 10, Item 3*. The tribunal also held that the terms of *Item 3* were not inconsistent with *Article 13A1(m)* of the *EC Sixth Directive*. *Chard Bowling Club, LON/95/1121 (VTD 13575).*

23.25   **Yacht club—whether berthing fees exempt from VAT.**   A yacht club did not account for VAT on berthing fees which it received from its members. The Commissioners issued an assessment charging tax on such fees, and the club appealed, contending that they qualified for exemption under *VATA 1994, Sch 9, Group 10, Item 3*. The tribunal allowed the appeal, holding that the yacht club's members were people 'taking part in sport' and that the berthing fees were paid for services which were 'closely linked with and essential to sport'. *Swansea Yacht & Sub Aqua Club, [1996] VATDR 89 (VTD 13938)*.

23.26   **Yacht club—whether subscriptions entirely exempt from VAT.**   A yacht club offered two classes of membership. Ordinary members paid a subscription of £430 p.a. but approximately 7% of members paid a reduced rate of £178 plus VAT, which enabled them to use the clubhouse but not to compete in yachting events. The club did not account for VAT on the subscriptions paid by ordinary members, treating them as exempt under *VATA 1994, Sch 9, Group 10, Item 3*. The Commissioners issued a ruling that part of the subscriptions should be attributed to a taxable supply of clubhouse facilities which did not qualify for exemption. The club appealed, contending that it was making a single supply of services closely linked to sport. The tribunal rejected this contention and dismissed the appeal, holding on the evidence that the club was making separate supplies of sporting facilities and clubhouse facilities. The clubhouse facilities were not incidental to the sporting facilities, since they could be 'characterised as supplies of all the facilities of a substantial free-standing London club capable of being enjoyed to the exclusion of the sporting facilities', as was shown by the 7% of members who paid a reduced subscription which did not entitle them to use the sporting facilities. *Royal Thames Yacht Club, LON/94/1469 & 2081 (VTD 14046)*.

23.27   **Pigeon racing—whether a sport.**   The Commissioners issued a ruling that pigeon racing did not qualify for exemption under *VATA 1994, Sch 9, Group 10, Item 3*. The Royal Pigeon Racing Association appealed against the ruling. The tribunal dismissed the appeal, holding that to qualify for exemption under *Group 10, Item 3* 'the individual must be taking part in the sport, which we interpret to the main sporting activity and not some ancillary activity'. Pigeon racing did not qualify for exemption because the only relevant physical activities were undertaken by the pigeons, rather than by their owners. Applying *dicta* of the CJEC in *Stichting Uitvoering Financiele Acties (SUFA) v Staatssecretaris van Financien, 21.146* EUROPEAN COMMUNITY LAW, the scope of any exemption contained in the *EC Sixth Directive* had to be 'interpreted strictly'. *Royal Pigeon Racing Association, LON/94/2910A (VTD 14006)*.

GROUP 13—CULTURAL SERVICES

23.28   **Restored Victorian garden—whether a 'museum'—Group 13, Item 2(a).**   In the 1840s a large garden was established in a steep ravine by the River Helford in Cornwall. It included many plants from different parts of the world. After the Second World War the garden was substantially neglected. In 1981 the property was purchased by a couple who set about restoring the garden. In 1990 they transferred the property and garden to a trust and charged visitors for admission to the garden. They did not account for output tax on the admission charges. The Commissioners issued a ruling that they were taxable and the trust appealed, contending that the charges qualified for exemption from VAT under *VATA 1994, Sch 9, Group 13*. The tribunal rejected this contention and dismissed the appeal, holding that, 'even allowing for the great age of many of the trees', the garden could not be described as a 'museum', within *Group 13, Item 2(a)*. *Trebah Garden Trust, LON/98/1372 (VTD 16598)*.

23.29   **Museum—whether 'managed and administered on a voluntary basis by persons who have no direct or indirect financial interest in its activities'—Group 13, Note 2(c).**   The trustees of Glastonbury Abbey did not account for output tax on admission charges to the Abbey museum, treating them as exempt. The Commissioners issued an assessment charging tax, considering that the Abbey did not qualify for exemption as the trustees had two paid employees, so that the Abbey was not 'managed and administered on a voluntary basis by persons who have no direct or indirect financial interest in its activities', as required by *Group 13, Note 2(c)*. The trustees appealed. The tribunal allowed the appeal, finding that the admission fees totalled about £125,000 p.a. and the employees' salaries totalled £19,800 p.a. Accordingly, the payments to the two employees did not mean that the Abbey was not 'managed and administered on a voluntary basis', and thus did not prevent the trustees from qualifying for exemption within *Note 2(c)*. *Glastonbury Abbey, [1996] VATDR 307 (VTD 14579)*.

23.30   **Zoological society—whether 'managed and administered on a voluntary basis by persons who have no direct or indirect financial interest in its activities'—Group 13, Note 2(c).** The Zoological Society of London, a registered charity, accounted for output tax on admission charges, but subsequently submitted a claim for repayment of the tax, contending that it should have treated its supplies as exempt under *VATA 1994, Sch 9, Group 13*. The Commissioners rejected the claim on the grounds that the management and administration of the society was in the hands of paid employees, so that the society was not 'managed and administered on a voluntary basis by persons who have no direct or indirect financial interest in its activities', as required by *Group 13, Note 2(c)*. The society appealed, contending that the responsibilities for management and administration were in the hands of the members of its Council, who were in the position of trustees, and that the fact that it paid employees who performed some functions of management and administration did not prevent it from qualifying for exemption. The tribunal accepted this contention in principle, but the QB directed that the case should be referred to the CJEC for guidance on the interpretation of the words 'managed and administered on an essentially voluntary basis' in *Article 13A2(a)* of the *EC Sixth Directive*. Lightman J observed that 'the question raised is what tier of paid management and administration operates to disqualify an otherwise eligible body from exemption'. This issue was 'clearly of great importance in the field of VAT and there is a need for uniformity of construction throughout the Community'. To make an immediate reference would avoid 'the delay and expense of appellate proceedings which may lead only to a reference at a later stage'. *C & E Commrs v The Zoological Society of London, QB [1999] BTC 5284*. (*Note*. The CJEC has registered the case as *Case C-267/00*. The Advocate-General has not yet delivered his Opinion.)

23.31   **Chapel—whether 'managed and administered on a voluntary basis by persons who have no direct or indirect financial interest in its activities'—Group 13, Note 2(c).** The Commissioners issued a ruling that the trustees of a chapel, which included a historic library, were required to account for output tax on admission charges for entry to the chapel. They appealed, contending that the charges should be treated as exempt from VAT under *VATA 1994, Sch 9, Group 13*. The tribunal rejected this contention and dismissed the appeal. The tribunal held that, in view of the chapel's collections of historic books and other items of historic or artistic interest, the chapel could be described as a 'museum', within *Group 13, Item 2(a)*. However, the trustees were not an 'eligible body' within *Item 2*, since the stipends of the dean and canons who acted as the trustees were 'at least in material part, paid for the management duties and roles they perform, and have always had to perform'. Accordingly, they were 'remunerated to a material extent for their management activities', and it followed that the chapel was not 'managed and administered on a voluntary basis by persons who have no direct or indirect financial interest in its activities', as required by *Group 13, Note 2(c)*. (The tribunal also observed that the trustees had not shown that it applied any profits from the admission charges to the 'continuance or improvement of the facilities made available by means of the supplies', as required by *Note 2(b)*.) *Dean & Canons of Windsor, LON/97/552 (VTD 15703)*.

24 Exports

Note. This chapter covers cases concerning exports of goods outside the European Community. For cases concerning transactions within the Community, see 22 EUROPEAN COMMUNITY: SINGLE MARKET.

The cases in this chapter are arranged under the following headings.

Notice No 703 24.1–24.12
Retail export schemes (Notice No 704) 24.13–24.23
Miscellaneous 24.24–24.31

NOTICE No 703

24.1   **Whether requirements of Notice No 703 unreasonable.** Two companies traded as clothing wholesalers, with substantial export sales. They failed to provide the evidence of export called for by *Notice No 703* in respect of a number of cases where they had treated goods as exported. The Commissioners issued assessments on the basis that the companies were required to account for output tax on such sales. The companies appealed, contending that the relevant sales were made 'over-the-counter', the customers had claimed that the goods were for export, and they had handed the customers a form C273 as required by *Notice No 703* but had not received the forms back from the customers duly stamped with confirmation of export. The tribunal dismissed the companies' appeals and the CA upheld this decision. Lord Denning observed that 'the Commissioners were entitled to impose very strict conditions for being satisfied. Unless there were strict conditions, value added tax could be evaded very easily.' Accordingly, 'it was necessary for the Commissioners to devise machinery to prevent people from getting out of paying value added tax ... the machinery is just about as good as could be devised to stop evasion'. Templeman LJ observed that the trader 'could bring pressure to bear on the customer by requiring payment by the customer of the whole or part of the appropriate VAT as a deposit until the certificate (C273) is produced'. *Henry Moss of London Ltd v C & E Commrs; The London Mob (Great Portland Street) Ltd v C & E Commrs, CA 1980, [1981] STC 139; [1981] 2 All ER 86.*

24.2   A trader reclaimed input tax in respect of 155 water filters, claiming that they had been exported to Nigeria. The Commissioners rejected the claim, as the trader had not produced the evidence of export required by *Notice No 703*. The tribunal dismissed the appeal, holding that there was 'nothing unreasonable in the conditions required to prove export as set out in *Notice No 703*'. *JA Fashanu, LON/94/2897 (VTD 13137). (Note.* For another issue in this case, see 38.36 INVOICES AND CREDIT NOTES.)

24.3   A company (M) supplied goods to an export house in June 1994. The goods were exported to Libya eight weeks later. The Commissioners issued an assessment charging tax on the supply, on the grounds that the goods had not been exported within one month of the supply as required by *Notice No 703*. M appealed, accepting that it had not complied with this requirement but contending that the requirement in question was unreasonable. The tribunal dismissed the appeal, holding that it had no jurisdiction to consider whether the requirements were unreasonable, and that their validity could only be challenged by judicial review. *Henry Moss of London Ltd*, 24.1 above, applied. *Megalith Ltd, LON/96/1505 (VTD 15207).*

24.4   *Henry Moss of London Ltd*, 24.1 above, has been applied in a large number of similar cases. In the interests of space, such cases are not reported individually in this book. For a list of such cases decided up to 31 December 1993, see Tolley's VAT Cases 1994.

24.5   **Whether requirements of Notice No 703 complied with.**   A trader sold some contact lenses and accessories to a doctor who was resident in Bombay. As the trader's husband was shortly travelling to Bombay by air, she arranged for him to take the goods with him for delivery to the Bombay customer. Some three weeks before her husband travelled, the trader wrote to the local VAT office for information as to the evidence required for zero-rating exported goods, but was not told of the requirements until after the goods had been exported. As a result she was not able to produce a form C273 to verify the exportation. The Commissioners issued a ruling that the supply of the goods did not qualify for zero-rating, and the trader appealed. The tribunal dismissed the appeal, finding that it was satisfied from the evidence that the goods had been exported, but holding that since the requirements of *Notice No 703*, issued in accordance with what is now *VAT Regulations 1995 (SI 1995 No 2518), reg 129*, had not been complied with (in that form C273 had not been produced), the supply could not be zero-rated. *AA Sadri (t/a Hutosh Commercial), LON/78/265 (VTD 694).*

24.6   A company sold lengths of cloth used for Nigerian national costume. The sales were mostly to Nigerians who came to the company's London premises to select and pay for the goods. Usually the company arranged the transport of the goods to Nigeria but sometimes the customer made his own arrangements. At the relevant period, Nigeria had banned the import of textiles. Accordingly, at the instigation of the customers, the goods were misdescribed on the packages containing them, and the company arranged that they were also misdescribed in the relevant carriage and export documentation. There was no misdescription in the company's own books and invoices. On discovering the discrepancies between the invoices and the documentation, the Commissioners considered that there was no satisfactory evidence that the goods had been exported and issued assessments charging tax on them. There were 133 disputed supplies. The tribunal held on the evidence that 128 of the supplies were zero-rated and reduced the assessment from £165,958 to £3,291. *Middlesex Textiles Ltd, [1979] VATTR 239 (VTD 866).*

24.7   A company (S) supplied goods to another company (V) for export to Libya, and treated the goods as zero-rated. The Commissioners requested evidence that the goods had been exported. S produced a bill of lading and eight airway bills, but the descriptions in these bills could not be related to any of the goods invoiced. The Commissioners were not satisfied that the goods had been exported and issued an assessment charging tax on them. The tribunal upheld the assessment and dismissed S's appeal, holding that S had not produced sufficient documentary evidence to satisfy the Commissioners, acting reasonably, that the goods which it had supplied to V had been exported. *Stockton Plant & Equipment Ltd, [1986] VATTR 94 (VTD 2093).*

24.8   A company failed to account for VAT on items of thermal clothing, considering that they should be zero-rated as they had been supplied to members of the Forces serving overseas. The Commissioners issued assessments on the basis that the supplies in question did not qualify for zero-rating as there was insufficient proof of export. The company appealed against the assessments and the tribunal allowed the appeal in part, finding that it was satisfied that four of the invoices in question related to goods in respect of which proof of export had been provided, but that the company had not proved that goods specified in other invoices had been exported. *Dicta* of Lord Denning in *Henry Moss of London*, 24.1 above, applied. *Kingdom Sports Ltd, [1991] VATTR 55 (VTD 5442).*

24.9   Appeals have been dismissed in a large number of cases in which tribunals have held that the requirements of *Notice No 703* have not been complied with. In the interests of space, such cases are not reported individually in this book. For a list of such cases decided up to 31 December 1993, see Tolley's VAT Cases 1994.

24.10   See also the cases noted at 49.197 to 49.203 PENALTIES: MISDECLARATION.

24.11   **Goods sold at auction.**   An antique dealer failed to account for output tax on goods sold at auction. The Commissioners issued an assessment charging tax on the sales, and the dealer appealed, producing a letter from the auctioneers stating that the goods had been sold to overseas buyers. The tribunal dismissed his appeal, holding on the evidence that the sales did not qualify for zero-rating since the dealer had not produced the evidence of export required by *Notice No 703*, issued in accordance with what is now *VAT Regulations 1995 (SI 1995 No 2518), reg 129. Dicta* of Lord Denning in *Henry Moss of London Ltd*, 24.1 above, applied. The chairman observed that 'if the auction houses are unable or unwilling to produce the necessary material for the sales to be zero-rated, that is a matter between them and the seller'. *JV Cambridge, LON/90/151 (VTD 5104).*

24.12   **Misdescription of goods allegedly exported.**   A company failed to account for output tax on supplies of silver to Bangladesh. In the export documentation, the silver was described as lead solder. The Commissioners issued an assessment charging output tax on the supplies, on the basis that they did not qualify for zero-rating since the documentation did not clearly identify the goods in question, as required by *Notice No 703*. The company appealed, contending that the goods had been wrongly described to reduce the risk of theft in transit. The tribunal dismissed the appeal, holding that the requirement in *Notice No 703* that the appellant should hold proof of export which clearly identifies the goods was clearly authorised by *Article 15* of the *EC Sixth Directive*. The appellant company did not hold such proof and thus the supplies did not qualify for zero-rating. *G McKenzie & Co Ltd, LON/92/2015 (VTD 12949).* (*Note.* For a preliminary issue in this case, see 2.8 APPEALS.)

RETAIL EXPORT SCHEMES (NOTICE No 704)

24.13   A company sold some fur skins to a customer who paid for them by a draft on an external US dollar account. An employee of the company travelled with the skins and the customer to Heathrow Airport, where the customer had booked a flight to America. They were delayed en route to the airport and the customer took the skins with him as luggage, without producing them to a Customs officer as required by what is now *VAT Regulations 1995 (SI 1995 No 2518), reg 131(1)*. The Commissioners issued a ruling that the company was required to account for output tax on the sale. The tribunal dismissed the company's appeal, holding that the Commissioners had to be satisfied that the statutory conditions had been met. If the conditions were not complied with, the Commissioners had no jurisdiction to waive the tax. *Randall Bros. (Furs) Ltd, LON/75/163 (VTD 210).*

24.14   A UK resident (J) visited an Edinburgh jeweller's shop with his fiancée, a US citizen, and purchased a ring for her. Shortly afterwards she flew to the USA, taking the ring with her. J claimed a refund of the VAT charged on the sale of the ring. The Commissioners rejected the claim and the tribunal dismissed J's appeal. The ring had been supplied to J, who was a UK citizen, and not to his fiancée. Furthermore, even if the supply had been to his fiancée, she had not complied with the conditions laid down by *Notice No 704*, not having produced the ring to a Customs officer on exportation. *P Johnstone, EDN/75/16 (VTD 211).*

24.15   An individual (G) emigrated from the UK to New Zealand in March 1977, travelling by air. Shortly before he left, he bought a new motorcycle from a retailer. It was delivered to his home untaxed and without registration plates, and was later shipped to New Zealand with his household and personal effects. The Commissioners refused to refund the VAT on the motorcycle, and G appealed. The tribunal dismissed his appeal, holding that it had not been exported by the retailer and it was not within the personal retail export schemes, as it had been supplied to G at his home in the UK and not directly to the ship in which it was exported. Further, a motorcycle did not qualify as 'goods' within the schemes, as under what is now *VAT Regulations 1995 (SI 1995 No 2518), reg 117(4)*, the term does not include motor vehicles. *GJ Alden, LON/77/255 (VTD 461)*.

24.16   A company sold 18 fur coats and stoles to a Japanese customer, who wished to travel to Japan by air next day with the furs. The company therefore attempted to deal with the sale under the 'over-the-counter' retail export scheme. The customer was given possession of the furs with a form VAT 414 completed on behalf of the company as prescribed in *Notice No 704* (as then in force). However, the customer did not obtain the necessary certification. The company treated the sale as covered by the zero-rating of exports. The Commissioners issued an assessment on the basis that the sale was not zero-rated, and the tribunal dismissed the company's appeal. Although the furs had been exported, they were not capable of being dealt with under the retail export schemes. They should have been dealt with in accordance with the relevant provisions of *Notice No 703*, which had not been complied with. *Helgor Furs Ltd, LON/78/339 (VTD 728)*. (*Note*. Form VAT 414 has subsequently been replaced by form VAT 407.)

24.17   An appeal was dismissed in a case where a company failed to obtain the evidence of exportation required by *Notice No 704*. *Miss Worth Ltd, LON/83/328 (VTD 1623)*.

24.18   Similar decisions were reached in *P Gandesha, LON/89/588Z (VTD 5111)* and *M Vojtisek (t/a TV & Hi-Fi Studio), LON/94/311A (VTD 12905)*.

24.19   A company treated various sales as zero-rated under the Retail Export Scheme. The Commissioners issued an assessment on the basis that the goods did not qualify for treatment under the Retail Export Scheme, since the purchaser had acquired them for business purposes. The tribunal upheld the assessment and dismissed the company's appeal, observing that the company's director 'had not read *Notices 704* or *703*' and that 'the burden is on the appellant of convincing us, on a balance of probabilities, that the Commissioners' assessment is wrong'. *GK Electrical UK Ltd, MAN/87/198 (VTD 2861)*. (*Note*. Goods exported for business purposes may only be dealt with under the Retail Export Scheme if their value does not exceed £600—see *Notice No 704*.)

24.20   An appeal was dismissed in a case where the tribunal found that forms VAT 407 submitted by a company had not been stamped or signed by a Customs officer as required by what is now *VAT Regulations 1995 (SI 1995 No 2518), reg 131(1)*. *East London Fancy Goods Ltd, LON/89/1203X (VTD 5542)*.

24.21   A similar decision was reached in *HJF Enterprises Ltd, LON/94/70A (VTD 13788)*.

24.22   An individual (C) purchased a computer from an Eire company, which was registered as an overseas trader in the UK. He reclaimed the VAT charged on the purchase. The Commissioners rejected the claim and C appealed, contending that he intended to export the computer to Botswana. The tribunal dismissed his appeal, holding that the conditions laid down by *Notice No 704* had not been fulfilled, since C had taken delivery of the computer in the UK. *A Coxshall, EDN/96/32 (VTD 14317)*.

24.23   See also *Richmond Design Interiors Ltd*, 47.55 PENALTIES: EVASION OF TAX.

24.24   **VATA 1994, s 30(6)—company by which goods exported.** A large group of companies had a significant export trade. It formed a subsidiary export company (E), to which all goods produced by the group and intended for export could be sold, so that E would effect the sales to the overseas buyers. E could, therefore, submit monthly returns rather than quarterly returns, with consequent cash-flow advantages. E was duly registered for VAT in 1980 and rendered monthly returns. In January 1989 the Commissioners wrote to E stating that they had reviewed its operations and considered that the goods which the group exported were not genuinely supplied to E by the other group companies, but were supplied directly to the overseas buyers, so that E was not entitled to reclaim input tax. The QB allowed E's appeal against this decision. Roch J observed that the legislation showed 'a clear intention on the part of Parliament that a wide interpretation should be given to the provisions of the *Act* so that any transaction for a consideration will be either the supply of goods or a supply of services if the supplier is registered for VAT'. *Philips Exports Ltd v C & E Commrs, QB [1990] STC 508.*

24.25   A company (G) carried on business as an importer and distributor of pharmaceutical and other products. It received orders from Poland for a large quantity of body sprays. The orders in question were passed to G by another company (L) which acted as a broker. G ordered these items from independent manufacturers, and arranged for the manufacturers to send them directly to a seaport. G did not account for VAT on the supply of the goods, treating them as zero-rated exports. The Commissioners issued assessments on the basis that G had supplied the goods to L, that only L was entitled to treat its services in relation to the supply of the goods as zero-rated, and that G should have treated its supplies as standard-rated. G appealed, contending that it had exported the goods in question, and that L was acting as its agent. The tribunal accepted G's evidence and allowed the appeal, holding that L was acting as G's agent and that G had exported the goods for the purpose of what is now *VATA 1994, s 30(6). Geistlich Sons Ltd, MAN/93/383 (VTD 11468).*

24.26   **VATA 1994, Sch 8, Group 13, Item 3—definition of 'patterns'.** A company supplied overseas customers with internegatives, to be used for the production of motion picture bulk release prints. The Commissioners issued an assessment charging output tax on the supplies. The company appealed, contending that the internegatives were within the definition of 'patterns' for the purposes of *VATA 1994, Sch 8, Group 13, Item 3*, so that the supplies qualified for zero-rating. The tribunal rejected this contention and dismissed the appeal, holding that the internegatives were not within the definition of 'patterns'. *Technicolor Ltd, LON/96/898 (VTD 14871).*

24.27   **Claim for refund of tax lodged outside time limit.** A company resident and carrying on business in the Cayman Islands, and not carrying on business in the UK, claimed a repayment of VAT in respect of goods exported to it. The Commissioners refused the claim, as it had been made outside the six-month time limit laid down by what is now *VAT Regulations 1995 (SI 1995 No 2518), reg 192*. The tribunal dismissed the company's appeal, observing that the time limit was in accordance with the provisions of the *EC Thirteenth Directive. Jack Camp Productions, LON/90/1539X (VTD 6261).*

24.28   **Export of telephone cards to collectors.** A trader sold British Telecom phonecards to collectors of such cards who were resident abroad. He did not account for VAT on such exports, treating the supplies as zero-rated. The Commissioners issued a ruling that the export of the cards had to be treated as a supply of services rather than of goods, and thus, where the cards still contained any credits which could be used to make telephone calls, were not eligible for zero–rating. The tribunal upheld the Commissioners' ruling. *R Farrow, LON/91/1665Y (VTD 10612)*.

24.29   **Export of boat—application of Extra-Statutory Concession 4.1.** A boatbuilder failed to account for VAT on the sale of a boat. The Commissioners issued an assessment charging tax on the sale. The builder appealed, contending that the sale should have been treated as zero–rated under what is now *Extra-Statutory Concession 4.1*, since he had originally arranged to sell the boat to a customer who had intended to sail it outside the UK, but the customer was unable to complete the purchase for financial reasons, and he had subsequently exported the boat to a Norwegian. The tribunal allowed the appeal, finding that the evidence was 'sufficient to establish on the balance of probabilities' that the boat would have been exported within the seven-day time limit if the customer had not fallen into financial difficulties. *Extra-Statutory Concession 4.1** did not require that the boat should actually be exported within seven days of its delivery, but to the customer *intending* that it should be exported. The tribunal held that it could consider the application of the concession, since 'the effect of what is now (*VATA 1994, s 84(10)**) is to allow the tribunal to review whether, as a matter of fact, the taxpayer has acted in accordance with guidelines prescribed by the Commissioners in the exercise of a discretion conferred on them, but not to review the laying down of the guidelines or requirements themselves'. *RW Shepherd, [1994] VATTR 47 (VTD 11753)*.

24.30   **Goods supplied from vending machines at airports.** A company supplied goods such as condoms and sanitary towels from vending machines in airport buildings which were used by passengers awaiting departure. The Commissioners issued a ruling that it was liable to account for output tax on such supplies. The company appealed, contending that some of the supplies in question should be treated as zero–rated exports. The tribunal dismissed the appeal, observing that some of the goods might be purchased by airport staff rather than by passengers, and holding that the supplies did not qualify for zero–rating. *Mates Vending Ltd, [1995] VATDR 266 (VTD 13429)*.

24.31   **Charity reclaiming input tax on overhead expenditure relating to transactions outside UK.** See *International Planned Parenthood Federation*, 11.37 CHARITIES.

25 Farming

25.1   **Flat-rate scheme for farmers—appeal against cancellation of certificate.**   A married couple farmed land in the Isles of Scilly, as tenants of the Duchy of Cornwall. They grew and sold bulbs and flowers, and let holiday accommodation. They also bought and resold flowers from other growers. They had registered for VAT from 1987. In 1995 they applied for a flat-rate farming certificate, which was granted. In 1997 the Commissioners cancelled the certificate, considering that the couple were not eligible for the scheme because at least 20% of the flowers which they sold were bought from other growers, rather than grown on their own farm, and their total income from resale of such flowers and supplies of holiday accommodation exceeded the registration threshold. The couple appealed. The tribunal allowed the appeal, finding that the couple had 'made full disclosure of their activities ... (including) matters like packaging, plant food and postage, and the holiday lets'. The tribunal held that the buying and selling of cut flowers were not separate parts of the couple's business, and held that 'as the bought-in flowers are mixed in with the flowers actually grown by the appellant on his (*sic*) own ground, there is no way in which the bought-in flowers can be described as a separate business, isolated from the appellant's own production, and excised from it in such a way as to treat that as a separate business of a florist or a dealer in flowers'. The couple carried on a business which qualified as 'growing of fruit and vegetables, flowers and ornamental plants' within *VAT (Flat-Rate Scheme for Farmers) (Designated Activities) Order 1992 (SI 1992 No 3220)*. Applying *TP Madgett & RM Baldwin (t/a Howden Court Hotel) v C & E Commrs*, 21.227 EUROPEAN COMMUNITY LAW, 'a farmer who buys in a certain amount of produce with the intention of incorporating it with his own produce either for reasons of quality or to make it easier to sell his produce, to render it attractive or to present it to customers in the most propitious way, is carrying out activities ancillary to those of a farmer and ... those ancillary activities cannot, unless they reach a significant proportion, be considered separately, treated in isolation, or taken to characterise the main supply.' *A & H Julian, LON/97/1241 (VTD 16532)*.

25.2   **Renovation of farmhouse—whether input tax deductible.**   For cases where input tax was apportioned, see 31.190 to 31.199 INPUT TAX. For unsuccessful appeals against the disallowance of input tax, see 31.211 to 31.214 INPUT TAX. For appeals concerning the application of *VATA 1994, s 24(3)* to farming businesses, see *RS & EM Wright Ltd*, 31.237 INPUT TAX, and *FJ Meaden Ltd*, 34.243 INPUT TAX.

26   Finance

Note. See the *VAT (Finance) Order 1999 (SI 1999 No 594)*, introduced with effect from 10 March 1999 'to clarify the scope of the *Group* following recent litigation, redefining the exemptions for payment and credit transfer services and for intermediary services, and making it explicit that third party credit management is not exempt'. The cases in this chapter should be read in the light of the changes in the legislation.

The cases in this chapter are arranged under the following headings.

Dealings with money (VATA 1994, Sch 9, Group 5, Item 1) 26.1–26.5
The provision of instalment credit finance (VATA 1994, Sch 9, Group 5, Items 3, 4) 26.6–26.8
Intermediary services (VATA 1994, Sch 9, Group 5, Item 5) 26.9–26.24
Dealings with securities (VATA 1994, Sch 9, Group 5, Item 6) 26.25–26.32
Arrangements for dealings with securities (VATA 1994, Sch 9, Group 5, Item 7) 26.33–26.34
Miscellaneous 26.35–26.37

DEALINGS WITH MONEY (VATA 1994, Sch 9, Group 5, Item 1)

26.1   **Transport of cash.** The Commissioners issued a ruling that the services provided by Securicor, in transporting cash between bank branches, were chargeable to output tax at the standard rate. A bank which used Securicor's services appealed, contending that the services should be treated as exempt under what is now *VATA 1994, Sch 9, Group 5, Item 1*. The tribunal dismissed the appeal, holding that 'dealing with money' connoted financial transactions or operations, and not simply the handling of money. *Williams & Glyn's Bank Ltd, [1974] VATTR 262 (VTD 118)*. (*Note.* For the status of the bank as appellant, see 2.28 APPEALS.)

26.2   **Building society—restocking of automated cash machines.** A building society operated about 750 automated cash machines at various sites. It arranged for Securicor to restock the machines with cash on a daily basis, collecting the required cash from the building society's bank. Securicor accounted for VAT on the charges which it made to the building society for this service. The society appealed, contending that the supply should be treated as exempt under what is now *VATA 1994, Sch 9, Group 5*. The tribunal dismissed the appeal, holding that the services did not qualify for exemption because the money remained the property of the building society throughout the operation, so that 'in no part of this cycle is there any dealing with money as money', and Securicor's services 'could just as well relate to any other goods which might be counted, packed, delivered, collected and reconciled'. *Williams & Glyn's Bank Ltd*, 26.1 above, applied; *Barclays Bank plc*, 26.15 below, distinguished. *Nationwide Anglia Building Society, [1994] VATTR 30 (VTD 11826)*.

26.3   **Credit card services—whether exempt transfers of money.** A company (F) provided credit card services for a number of banks. The Commissioners issued a ruling that F was required to account for output tax on its supplies. F appealed, contending that its supplies should be treated as transfers of money which were exempt from VAT under *VATA 1994, Sch 9, Group 5, Item 1*. The tribunal accepted this contention and allowed the appeal in principle (subject to a further hearing with regard 'to whether other supplies are properly to be regarded as part of the principal supply or as ancillary thereto or are independent'). The CA upheld the tribunal decision, holding that the tribunal was entitled to conclude that there was 'a single or core supply'. These supplies were within *Article 13B(d)(3)* of the *EC Sixth Directive* and therefore qualified for exemption. *Sparekassernes Datacenter v Skatteministeriet*,

21.177 EUROPEAN COMMUNITY LAW, applied. *C & E Commrs v FDR Ltd, CA [2000] STC 672.* (*Note.* The case was decided on the wording of *VATA 1994, Sch 9 Group 5* before the introduction of *Notes 2A, 2B*, which were introduced by *VAT (Finance) Order 1999 (SI 1999 No 594)* with effect from 10 March 1999. The change to the legislation was intended 'to clarify ... that third party credit management is not exempt'. However, the judgment of Laws LJ suggests that, notwithstanding this change to the UK legislation, the company's supplies would still be held to be exempt from VAT by virtue of *Article 13B(d)(3)* of the *EC Sixth Directive*. Compare *Becker v Finanzamt Münster-Innenstadt*, 21.174 EUROPEAN COMMUNITY LAW. For Customs' response to the decision, see Business Brief 10/2000, issued on 8 August 2000. Customs have applied to the House of Lords for leave to appeal against the CA decision, on the grounds that it 'challenges the UK's interpretation of European law'. The Business Brief also states that 'until the status of these types of services is finally settled, businesses operating identical arrangements to those of FDR will not have to account for VAT in respect of these services. It remains Customs' view that these services are properly subject to VAT at the standard rate and that the UK legislation correctly implements *Article 13B(d)(3)*. Where VAT is not accounted for on these services, our officers will issue assessments for the tax we contend is due. No action will be taken to enforce payment of such assessments until the final outcome of the FDR appeal. If the final decision is in Customs' favour, we will require payment of the tax and interest.')

26.4   **Unsecured bonds issued by incorporated members' club.**   In the case noted at 13.30 CLUBS, ASSOCIATIONS AND ORGANISATIONS, the tribunal defined a 'security for money' as 'a document under seal or under hand at a consideration containing a covenant, promise or undertaking to pay a sum of money'. The tribunal held that 'a document to be such a "security for money" does not have to be either "marketable" or "transferable" or "negotiable"'. *Dyrham Park Country Club Ltd, [1978] VATTR 244 (VTD 700).*

26.5   **Voucher—whether a 'security for money'.**   In the case noted at 63.44 VALUATION, a company (P) issued vouchers which could be exchanged for goods of a retail value equal to the face value of the voucher. The Ch D held that each voucher was a 'security for money' within *VATA 1994, Sch 9, Group 5, Item 1*, and that the supplies which P made to K were therefore exempt from VAT. *Kingfisher plc v C & E Commrs, Ch D [2000] STC 992.*

THE PROVISION OF INSTALMENT CREDIT FINANCE (VATA 1994, Sch 9, Group 5, Items 3, 4)

26.6   **Provision of finance for lease purchase agreements.**   A finance company provided finance for the purchase of vehicles under lease-purchase agreements. It did not separately identify the finance charge, but quoted customers the purchase price and the number and amount of instalments. It did not account for VAT on the amount which represented the finance charge, treating this as exempt under what is now *VATA 1994, Sch 9, Group 5*. The Commissioners considered that, since the amount of the finance charge was not separately quoted, the full amount paid was liable to VAT at the standard rate, and issued an assessment accordingly. The tribunal allowed the company's appeal. The amount of the finance charge could be ascertained by a simple calculation. Since the company's customers were all businesses, a specific statement of the separate charge was not as important as it would be in a consumer credit transaction. The charges were within *Group 5, Item 3* and qualified for exemption. *Freight Transport Leasing Ltd, [1991] VATTR 142 (VTD 5578).* (*Note.* For subsequent developments in this case, see 2.261 and 2.270 APPEALS.)

26.7   **Sale of motor vehicles by hire-purchase—whether 'option fee' exempt.** A company sold motor vehicles by hire-purchase. It charged customers 'option fees', and accounted for output tax on these fees. In 1996 it submitted a repayment claim on the basis that the 'option fees' should have been treated as exempt from VAT under *VATA 1994, Sch 9, Group 5*. The Commissioners rejected the claim, considering that the 'option fees' were taxable consideration paid by the customers for the option to purchase the vehicles. The company appealed. The tribunal dismissed the appeal, holding that 'it is plain on the face of (the) agreements that the payment is for the option . . . what is being supplied is the right to secure, if the necessary conditions are fulfilled, ownership of the car which throughout is the ultimate objective of the agreement'. *General Motors Acceptance Corporation (UK) plc, [1999] VATDR 456 (VTD 16137)*.

26.8   **Sale of motor vehicles by hire-purchase—whether 'administration fee' exempt.** A company provided finance for customers who wished to buy motor vehicles by hire-purchase. It charged customers 'administration fees', and accounted for output tax on these fees. In 1998 it submitted a repayment claim on the basis that the 'administration fees' should have been treated as exempt from VAT under *VATA 1994, Sch 9, Group 5*. The Commissioners rejected the claim, considering that the 'administration fees' related to the supply of the vehicles as well as to the supply of credit, and therefore failed to qualify for exemption. The company appealed. The tribunal allowed the appeal, holding that the company had provided the customers with 'the facility of instalment credit finance' within *Group 5, Item 3*, for a separate charge which was disclosed to the customer. On the evidence, the tribunal held that the company 'distances itself from the actual sale of the car' and the administration fees were 'in no way related to transfer of title'. *General Motors Acceptance Corporation (UK) plc*, 26.7 above, distinguished. *Wagon Finance Ltd, LON/98/215 (VTD 16288)*. (*Note.* For the Commissioners' practice following this decision, see Business Brief 27/99, issued on 21 December 1999.)

INTERMEDIARY SERVICES (VATA 1994, Sch 9, Group 5, Item 5)

Note. *Group 5, Item 5* was substituted by the *VAT (Finance) Order 1999 (SI 1999 No 594)*, with effect from 10 March 1999. The cases in this section should be read in the light of the changes in the legislation.

26.9   **Trade association acting as clearing house for members.** A federation of retailers acted as a clearing house for its members. The members sent the federation monthly statements received from their suppliers, with cheques for the total amounts payable thereunder. The federation paid the suppliers the amounts due from members. It made a small charge to the members for each statement dealt with, and did not account for output tax on these charges. The Commissioners issued a ruling that the charges were taxable at the standard rate, and the federation appealed, contending that they should be treated as exempt under what is now *VATA 1994, Sch 9, Group 5, Item 5*. The tribunal accepted this contention and allowed the appeal. *British Hardware Federation, [1975] VATTR 172 (VTD 216)*.

26.10   **Interest received by solicitors—whether consideration for exempt supplies of financial services.** A firm of solicitors kept two clients' general bank deposit accounts, and also kept a building society account in the names of the partners, into which the undistributed profits of the firm were deposited and out of which were paid the partners' income tax liabilities. The Commissioners issued an assessment to recover part of the input tax which the firm had reclaimed, considering that the interest which it received was consideration for exempt supplies of financial services, to which part of the firm's input tax should be attributed. The tribunal allowed the firm's appeal in part, holding that the deposits in the building society account were allocations of profit already earned, so that the interest on that account was not consideration for any supply by the firm, but that the interest received on the clients' accounts was consideration for exempt supplies, since the making of deposits in these accounts was an integral part of the manner in which the firm carried on its business. *Hedges & Mercer, [1976] VATTR 146 (VTD 271)*.

26.11   **Money retained as commission by companies issuing charge cards.**   Two companies issued charge cards, which could be used by customers for making payments to retailers. When the companies made the necessary payments to the retailers, they retained certain sums as commission. The Commissioners formed the opinion that this commission constituted consideration for supplies of financial services, which were exempt from VAT under what is now *VATA 1994, Sch 9, Group 5, Note 4*, with the result that the companies were subject to the partial exemption provisions and their deductible input tax had to be restricted accordingly. They issued assessments on this basis, against which the companies appealed. The CA upheld the assessments, holding that the companies were making exempt supplies within *Sch 9, Group 5* and that the commission which they retained constituted consideration for these supplies. *C & E Commrs v Diners Club Ltd; C & E Commrs v Cardholders Services Ltd, [1989] STC 407; [1989] 2 All ER 385*.

26.12   *Diners Club Ltd*, 26.11 above, was applied in a subsequent case where a retail company (T) had deducted amounts charged to it by the issuers of credit cards in accounting for VAT on sales by credit card. The Commissioners issued an assessment to charge tax on the full amount of the sales, and the tribunal dismissed the company's appeal. T was making taxable supplies of goods to its customers. The exempt supplies of credit were made by the companies which issued the credit cards, rather than by T. *Thayers Ltd, LON/91/1081 (VTD 7541)*.

26.13   **Commission received by company for encouraging use of credit cards.**   A company limited by guarantee operated a credit card scheme, whereby it encouraged its members to use a credit card issued by a bank, and received commission from the bank. It did not account for output tax on the commission which it received. The Commissioners issued an assessment charging tax on the commission, and the company appealed, contending that the commission should be treated as exempt from VAT under *VATA 1994, Sch 9, Group 5, Item 5*. The tribunal accepted this contention and allowed the company's appeal, holding that the fact that the company was not the person actually granting credit to the cardholders was not conclusive. The CA upheld the tribunal decision. On the facts found by the tribunal, the arrangement between the company and the bank was an arrangement for the granting of credit to the company's members. The commission had been received as consideration for 'the making of arrangements for ... the granting of any credit', and therefore qualified for exemption. *C & E Commrs v Civil Service Motoring Association, CA 1997, [1998] STC 111. (Note.* See now, however, the note at the head of this section with regard to the substitution of *Item 5* by *SI 1999 No 594*.)

26.14   **Company operating fuel card schemes—whether making exempt supplies of financial services.**   A company (H) operated five fuel card schemes. The Commissioners issued a ruling that the card fees and service charges paid by cardholders, and the amounts which the company received from retailers, were consideration for exempt supplies of financial services (with the result that it was not entitled to reclaim the relevant input tax). H appealed, contending that the fuel cards were agency cards rather than charge cards or credit cards and that its supplies were taxable rather than exempt. The tribunal reviewed the evidence in detail and allowed H's appeal in part, holding that in the case of three of the schemes (principally concerning supplies of fuel for heavy goods vehicles, but also including a scheme under which the cardholder had to present his card to the retailer before receiving the fuel), H purchased the fuel from the retailers and made taxable supplies of the fuel to the cardholders. However, in the case of the two standard schemes, the retailers were supplying fuel directly to the cardholders, so that H was making exempt supplies of financial services. *Diners Club Ltd*, 26.11 above, applied. *The Harpur Group Ltd, [1994] VATTR 180 (VTD 12001).* (*Note.* For the Commissioners' practice following this decision, see Business Brief 25/94, issued on 16 December 1994.)

26.15   **Banking services.**   Securicor provided a credit checking service and a money-changing service for customers of a bank. It collected and opened sealed cash containers from the customers, and advised the bank of the amounts contained. The Commissioners issued a ruling that these services were chargeable to output tax at the standard rate. The bank which received the services appealed, contending that they should be treated as exempt under what is now *VATA 1994, Sch 9, Group 5, Item 5*. The tribunal allowed the bank's appeal, holding that the services in question were 'services which were normally performed by the bank as an integral part of its banking activities', and qualified for exemption. *Williams & Glyn's Bank Ltd*, 26.1 above, distinguished. *Barclays Bank plc, [1988] VATTR 23 (VTD 2622).* (*Note.* See now, however, the note at the head of this section with regard to the substitution of *Item 5* by *SI 1999 No 594*.)

26.16   **Partnership acting as financial investigator for bank.**   A partnership acted as a financial investigator for a bank, checking and verifying the credentials of proposed assignees of the bank and ensuring that notice of assignment was given to debtors. It did not account for output tax on the fees which it received for these services. The Commissioners issued an assessment charging tax on them, and the partnership appealed, contending that they should be treated as exempt under what is now *VATA 1994, Sch 9, Group 5*. The tribunal rejected this contention and dismissed the appeal [*LON/85/326Z (VTD 4580)*]. The partnership appealed to the QB, which upheld the tribunal decision. *Minster Associates v C & E Commrs, QB 2 April 1992 unreported.*

26.17   **Company providing services relating to hire-purchase arrangements for sale of cars.**   A company (V), which was a member of a major group of companies in the motor industry, provided hire-purchase facilities in connection with the sale of cars manufactured by its group. It arranged for another company (L), which was a member of a major banking group, to provide various services relating to the 'necessary support functions', including making recommendations as to whether hire-purchase applications should be accepted or rejected. The Commissioners issued a ruling that the services which L supplied to V were taxable. L appealed, contending that its services qualified for exemption under *VATA 1994, Sch 9, Group 5, Item 5*. The tribunal accepted this contention and allowed L's appeal, and the QB upheld this decision. On the evidence, L was making a single composite supply of services which qualified as 'the making of arrangements' for 'the granting of any credit' within *Sch 9, Group 5. C & E Commrs v Lloyds TSB Group Ltd; C & E Commrs v Volkswagen Financial Services (UK) Ltd, QB [1998] STC 528.* (*Note.* See now, however, the note at the head of this section with regard to the substitution of *Item 5* by *SI 1999 No 594*.)

26.18   **Estate agents arranging for provision of financial advice to clients.**   A firm of estate agents entered into arrangements with a financial company and a firm of solicitors to provide financial advice to clients. The estate agents provided an office for the use of the advisor. The advisors received commission from institutions to whom they introduced clients, and paid a proportion of this commission to the estate agents. The estate agents did not account for tax on this commission. The Commissioners issued assessments charging tax on this, and the estate agents appealed, contending that the commission should be treated as exempt under what is now *VATA 1994, Sch 9, Group 5, Item 5* or alternatively (where insurance policies were concluded) under *VATA 1983, Sch 6, Group 2, Item 3* (which has since been superseded). The tribunal dismissed the appeal, holding that the facilities which the estate agents provided did not amount to 'the making of arrangements'. *Ford*, 36.14 INSURANCE, and *Barclays Bank plc*, 36.25 INSURANCE, distinguished. *Wright Manley Ltd, MAN/92/466; Wright & Partners, MAN/92/467 (VTD 10295)*.

26.19   The decision in *Wright Manley Ltd*, 26.18 above, was applied in a similar subsequent case in which the tribunal observed that 'simple introduction on a generic basis is not sufficient to gain exemption'. *Ford*, 36.14 INSURANCE, distinguished. *Cheshire Trafford Estates Ltd, MAN/97/839 (VTD 15495)*.

26.20   **Submission of financial reports to lending institutions.**   A financier registered for VAT in 1988. A VAT officer formed the opinion that he was not entitled to registration, since all his supplies were exempt, and rejected a claim for repayment of input tax. The trader appealed, contending that, although most of his supplies were exempt from VAT, he also supplied financial reports to lending institutions on behalf of clients, and these supplies were taxable. The tribunal dismissed the appeal, holding that, since the financial reports were prepared for the purpose of obtaining loans for the trader's clients, they were exempt under what is now *VATA 1994, Sch 9, Group 5, Item 5. DP Devoti (t/a Belmont Associates), MAN/92/374 (VTD 11868)*.

26.21   A company carried on a business of providing financial advice. It assisted a merchant bank to launch a new investment trust, and did not account for output tax on the fee paid to it by the merchant bank. The Commissioners issued an assessment charging tax on the payment, and the company appealed, contending that the payment should be treated as exempt under what is now *VATA 1994, Sch 9, Group 5*. The tribunal dismissed the appeal, finding that the company's activities were 'of a promotional and marketing nature' and 'were not sufficiently part of, nor sufficiently closely connected with, the share issue transactions themselves, to make them exempt'. *Hargreaves Lansdown Asset Management Ltd, LON/93/547A (VTD 12030)*. (*Note*. The company was given leave to apply for a further hearing to pursue a contention, not argued in detail at the hearing, that part of its fee should be apportioned to work done for its own clients which might fall within the scope of the exemption. However, there was no further hearing of the appeal.)

26.22   **Contract for procurement of business finance—whether initial fee exempt under VATA 1994, Sch 9, Group 5.**   A company was incorporated with the object of helping businesses to raise finance. It charged clients an application fee of 0.1% of the amount of finance required, and a funding fee of 1% of the amount of finance obtained. It accepted that the 1% funding fees related to exempt supplies, but reclaimed input tax on the basis that the initial application fee related to a taxable supply of financial consultancy. The Commissioners formed the opinion that both fees related to exempt supplies, and issued an assessment to recover the input tax which the company had reclaimed. The tribunal dismissed the company's appeal, holding on the evidence that there was 'one contract for a service of making arrangements for an advance', and that the entire service was exempt from VAT under what is now *VATA 1994, Sch 9, Group 5. Lindum Resources Ltd, MAN/93/784 (VTD 12445)*.

26.23   **Goods sold on interest-free credit by retailer—whether retailer making supply within VATA 1994, Sch 9, Group 5, Item 5.**   See *Primback Ltd*, 54.39 RETAILERS' SPECIAL SCHEMES.

26.24   **Sales of discount vouchers by car dealers—whether within VATA 1994, Sch 9, Group 5, Item 5.**   In the case noted at 63.54 VALUATION, the QB held that the sale of books of discount vouchers by car dealers did not qualify for exemption under *VATA 1994, Sch 9, Group 5, Item 5. F & I Services Ltd v C & E Commrs, QB [2000] STC 364.*

DEALINGS WITH SECURITIES (VATA 1994, Sch 9, Group 5, Item 6)

26.25   **Development company—input tax relating to raising of share capital.**   A company was incorporated in 1984. Its directors intended that it should purchase land for development, erect office buildings thereon, and dispose of the freeholds of the new office premises. It raised capital under the Business Expansion Scheme, and reclaimed input tax on services made to it by a licensed share dealer which helped it to raise this capital. The Commissioners raised an assessment to recover the input tax, on the basis that the dealer's services had been supplied in connection with the issue of the company's shares, which was an exempt supply. The company appealed, contending that the input tax should be treated as deductible because it had been incurred for the purpose of future trading activities. The tribunal dismissed the appeal, distinguishing *Rompelman*, 21.59 EUROPEAN COMMUNITY LAW, and *Merseyside Cablevision*, 34.444 INPUT TAX. The expenditure in this case was laid out 'in order to obtain the services of professional men in connection with issuing shares in the company for the purpose of raising capital'. It could 'not be regarded as expenditure preparatory to the carrying on of an economic activity of the sort mentioned in *Article 4(2)*' of the *EC Sixth Directive. Park Commercial Developments plc, [1990] VATTR 99 (VTD 4892).*

26.26   **Reorganisation of share capital.**   A company which was incorporated in 1980, and which operated a flying club, reorganised its share capital in 1984 and 1986. In 1984 it redeemed loan stock and replaced it, pound for pound, with ordinary shares; and in 1986 it made a rights issue under which each existing shareholder was given the right to subscribe £1 for a further ordinary £1 share. The Commissioners issued an assessment on the basis that the subscription monies provided by the shareholders were paid for the supply of services and were liable to VAT at the standard rate. The company appealed, contending that the supplies should be treated as exempt under what is now *VATA 1994, Sch 9, Group 5, Item 6.* The tribunal allowed the company's appeal, holding on the evidence that the additional subscriptions did not confer additional benefits or facilities. Both transactions were simply issues of shares and were therefore exempt supplies. *Southchurch Workingmen's Club & Institute Ltd,* 13.6 CLUBS, ASSOCIATIONS AND ORGANISATIONS, and *Trewby,* 39.30 LAND, distinguished. *Oldbus Ltd, LON/89/1657 (VTD 5119). (Note.* The Commissioners consider that this decision should be treated 'as applying only to cases with identical facts'—see Customs' VAT Manual, Part 6, chapter 3, section 6, para 3.5(a).)

26.27   A company reclaimed input tax in respect of fees paid to an investment bank in respect of a rights issue of shares. The Commissioners issued an assessment to recover the tax, considering that it related to an exempt supply. The tribunal upheld the assessment and dismissed the company's appeal. *Banner Management Ltd,* 43.30 PARTIAL EXEMPTION, distinguished. *MBS plc, LON/88/1396X (VTD 7542).*

26.28   A similar decision, also distinguishing *Banner Management Ltd,* 43.30 PARTIAL EXEMPTION, was reached in *Celtic plc, EDN/96/47; Celtic Football & Athletic Co Ltd, EDN/96/48 (VTD 14898).*

26.29   A public company, which was the representative member of a trading group, financed the acquisition of another company by a substantial share issue. It reclaimed input tax in respect of expenditure relating to the share issue. The Commissioners rejected the claim, on the grounds that the issue of the shares was an exempt supply. The company appealed, contending that the input tax should be treated as deductible since the share issue was not itself a supply and that the purpose of the share issue was to facilitate its trading activities, in the course of which it made taxable supplies. The tribunal dismissed the appeal, holding that the share issue was an exempt supply and that the expenditure in question was directly attributable to this exempt supply. *Swallowfield plc, [1992] VATTR 212 (VTD 8865)*. (*Note.* An application by the company for the case to be referred to the CJEC was rejected by the QB—see 2.228 APPEALS. For a ruling by the CJEC in a similar case, see *BLP Group plc*, 21.192 EUROPEAN COMMUNITY LAW.)

26.30   A company reclaimed input tax on professional fees relating to an issue of additional shares, to raise finance for its business. The Commissioners issued an assessment to recover the tax relating to the share issue where the shares were sold to people resident in the EU. (It was accepted that the company was entitled to reclaim input tax relating to sales of shares to people resident outside the EU.) The company appealed, contending that the input tax should be treated as deductible since the issue of a company's own shares was not itself a supply and the purpose of the share issue was to facilitate its trading activities, in the course of which it made taxable supplies. The tribunal dismissed the appeal and the QB upheld this decision. The issue of a company's shares was a supply within *Article 6(1)* of the *EC Sixth Directive*. The supply was exempt from VAT and the expenditure in question was directly attributable to this exempt supply, so that the input tax in question was not deductible. The fact that the supply did not involve any depletion of the company's resources was not conclusive. *BLP Group plc*, 21.192 EUROPEAN COMMUNITY LAW, applied. *Mirror Group Newspapers Ltd v C & E Commrs, QB [2000] STC 156*.

26.31   **Golf club—sale of debentures to members.** A limited company was incorporated to operate a golf club. It required most members (other than junior members or social members) to purchase debentures in it. The Commissioners issued a ruling that the sale of the debentures constituted a taxable supply of services. The company appealed, contending that the sales should be treated as exempt from VAT under *VATA 1994, Sch 9, Group 5, Item 6*. The tribunal rejected this contention and dismissed the appeal, holding that the act of purchasing a debenture represented 'non-monetary consideration for the supply of services, namely the grant of membership rights'. *Harleyford Golf Club plc, LON/95/3076 (VTD 14466)*. (*Note.* For the valuation of the supplies, see 63.121 VALUATION.)

26.32   **Initial charge for managed personal equity plan.** A company managed personal equity plans. It levied initial charges to new clients. In cases where the shares contained in the plan were selected by the client, the Commissioners accepted that the charges were exempt from VAT under *VATA 1994, Sch 9, Group 5, Item 6*. However, in the majority of cases where the shares contained in the plan were selected by the company, the Commissioners ruled that the charges failed to qualify for exemption. The CS allowed the company's appeal (reversing the tribunal decision). On the evidence, the initial charge was applicable to both the self-selected plans and to the managed plans. Since the charges were identical, and it was accepted that the initial charges for the self-selected plans qualified for exemption, the initial charges for the managed plan were also for the purchase of securities, and qualified for exemption. *Ivory & Sime Trustlink Ltd v C & E Commrs, CS [1998] STC 597*. (*Note.* For the Commissioners' practice following this decision, see Business Brief 7/99, issued on 23 March 1999.)

ARRANGEMENTS FOR DEALINGS WITH SECURITIES (VATA 1994, Sch 9, Group 5, Item 7)

Note. *Group 5, Item 7* was revoked by the *VAT (Finance) Order 1999 (SI 1999 No 594)*, with effect from 10 March 1999. See now *Item 5*, as substituted by *SI 1999 No 594*, which refers to the 'provision of intermediary services in relation to', rather than to 'the making of arrangements for' any transactions within *Item 6*, and restricts the exemption to services provided 'by a person acting in an intermediary capacity', as defined by *Item 5A*. The cases in this section are now, therefore, primarily of historical interest, but may still be of some relevance to the provisions now contained in *Item 5*.

26.33   **Services relating to personal equity plans.**   A company (C) supplied services to a group of companies (S) which issued personal equity plans. C dealt with telephone enquiries and with replies to advertisements which S had placed, sent application forms to potential customers and checked completed application forms. The Commissioners issued a ruling that C was required to account for output tax on its supplies. C appealed, contending that its supplies should be treated as exempt under *VATA 1994, Sch 9, Group 5, Item 7*. The tribunal accepted this contention and allowed C's appeal, but the Commissioners appealed to the QB, which directed that the case should be referred to the CJEC for a ruling on the application of *Article 13B(d)* of the *EC Sixth Directive*. *C & E Commrs v Continuum (Europe) Ltd (aka CSC Financial Services Ltd), QB 20 May 1999, Times 21.5.1999. (Notes.* (1) See the note at the head of this section with regard to the repeal of *Item 7* by *SI 1999 No 594*. (2) The CJEC has registered the case as *C-235/00*. The Advocate-General has not yet delivered his Opinion. (3) For the Commissioners' response to the QB decision, see News Release 19/99, issued on 20 May 1999.)

26.34   **Accountants' services relating to flotation of shares.**   A company which traded as a haulage contractor wished to increase its capital by flotation on the London Stock Exchange. It arranged a firm of accountants to prepare some reports in relation to the flotation. The accountants charged output tax on its supplies of these services, and the company reclaimed input tax on the supplies. The Commissioners rejected the claim, on the basis that the services had not been supplied for the purposes of the company's business. The company and the accountants then claimed that the services should have been treated as exempt under *VATA 1994, Sch 9, Group 5, Item 7*, so that no VAT was due on the supplies. The Commissioners rejected this claim and issued a ruling that the accountants' services were standard-rated. The company appealed. The tribunal upheld the Commissioners' ruling and dismissed the company's appeal, holding that the accountants' services constituted the provision of financial information and failed to qualify for exemption, either under *Group 5, Item 7* or under *Article 13B(d)(5)* of the *EC Sixth Directive*. *Continuum (Europe) Ltd*, 26.33 above, distinguished. *Nightfreight plc, MAN/97/747 (VTD 15479).*

MISCELLANEOUS

26.35   **Bank dealing in foreign currency bank notes—whether a supply.**   See *Republic National Bank of New York*, 58.158 SUPPLY.

26.36   **Foreign exchange transactions not involving physical supplies of banknotes—whether a supply.**   See *The First National Bank of Chicago*, 21.53 EUROPEAN COMMUNITY LAW.

26.37   **Bank—application of special partial exemption method.**   See *The Governor and Company of the Bank of Scotland*, 43.98 PARTIAL EXEMPTION.

27 Food

The cases in this chapter are arranged under the following headings.

SUPPLIES IN THE COURSE OF CATERING (VATA 1994, Sch 8, Group 1(a))

Definition of 'catering'

27.1 **Sale of food from mobile vans.** A trader sold food from mobile vans and did not account for VAT on the sales. The Commissioners issued an assessment on the basis that the supplies were in the course of catering and were standard-rated. The tribunal allowed the trader's appeal, holding that the food was not supplied in the course of catering. *BR James, [1977] VATTR 155 (VTD 388)*. (*Notes*. (1) Compare the subsequent QB decision in *Cope*, 27.36 below. (2) Supplies of hot food from mobile vans would now be standard-rated by virtue of *VATA 1994, Sch 8, Group 1, Note 3(b)*, originating from *FA 1984*. For cases concerning this provision, see 27.46 *et seq.* below.)

27.2 *James*, 27.1 above, was applied in the similar case of *B Spragge, [1977] VATTR 162 (VTD 408)*.

27.3 For sales of cold food from mobile vans, where the issue was whether the food was sold for consumption on defined 'premises' within what is now *VATA 1994, Sch 8, Group 1, Note 3(a)*, see *Cooper*, 27.23 below, and *Skilton & Gregory*, 27.38 below.

27.4 **Meals provided at client's premises.** A trader supplied cooked meals at clients' premises. He did not account for VAT on these supplies. The Commissioners issued an assessment charging tax on them and the tribunal dismissed the trader's appeal, holding that the supplies were in the course of catering. *RH Noorman, LON/79/174 (VTD 887)*.

27.5 **Set meals supplied by butcher.** A butcher supplied food to customers to order, on the basis of eleven menus with set meals and fixed prices. He did not account for VAT on these supplies. The Commissioners issued an assessment charging tax on them, on the basis that they were 'in the course of catering' and thus did not qualify for zero-rating. He appealed, contending that his supplies were not in the course of catering, since any catering was undertaken by the customers to whom he supplied the meals. The tribunal rejected this contention and dismissed his appeal, observing that the food which he supplied was ready for immediate consumption in individual portions, and that the supplies were linked to functions organised by the recipient. Accordingly, the supplies were in the course of catering. *RV Vodden, MAN/84/74 (VTD 1842)*.

27.6   **Delicatessen orders delivered to customers.**   A company trading as retail grocers supplied and delivered delicatessen orders to customers. The company advertised this service as 'home party catering'. However, many of the items supplied required some further preparation before they could be served. Loaves of bread were not sent out cut, gateaux were often sent out frozen, chicken joints and cocktail sausages needed to be cooked or warmed, and coffee was supplied in the form of coffee beans. The Commissioners issued a ruling that the supplies were in the course of catering and were standard-rated. The company appealed, contending that the supplies were zero-rated. The tribunal allowed the company's appeal in part, holding that because of the additional preparation required, the actual catering for the parties was done by the customer and thus the supplies were zero-rated. However, buffet boxes supplied by the company and containing complete meals were held to be supplies in the course of catering, and standard-rated. *C Chasney Ltd, [1989] VATTR 152 (VTD 4136)*.

27.7   **Delicatessen orders collected by customers.**   See *Wendy's Kitchen*, 27.13 below.

27.8   **'Party trays' sold from delicatessen counters.**   A major retail company sold a range of 'party trays' of food from its delicatessen counters. Such trays had to be ordered in advance and collected from the counter. The company did not account for output tax on its supplies of the trays, treating them as a zero-rated supply of food. The Commissioners issued an assessment charging tax on the basis that the trays were a standard-rated supply of catering, and the company appealed. The tribunal allowed the appeal, holding that the company was making supplies of food, and that the arrangement of the food on trays did not amount to 'catering'. The QB upheld this decision. There had been no delivery to, or service at, the location where the food was to be consumed. There had been no waiter service and no provision of cutlery, etc. The company would normally have no knowledge as to whether the food was for a specific event or occasion. The tribunal had been entitled to find that the supplies were not in the course of catering. *Vodden*, 27.5 above, and *C Chasney Ltd*, 27.6 above, distinguished. *C & E Commrs v Safeway Stores plc, QB 1996, [1997] STC 163*.

27.9   **Sandwiches supplied on platters.**   A partnership operated a sandwich shop. It supplied platters of sandwiches to customers (mostly to nearby offices), and did not account for tax on such supplies, treating them as zero-rated. The Commissioners issued assessments charging tax on the supplies, on the basis that they did not qualify for zero-rating since they were within the definition of 'catering'. The partnership appealed. The tribunal allowed the appeal, holding that the arrangement of sandwiches on platters did not amount to 'catering'. *C Chasney Ltd*, 27.6 above, and *Cope*, 27.36 below, distinguished. *Out To Lunch, MAN/93/1182 (VTD 13031)*.

27.10   A similar decision was reached in a subsequent case where the tribunal held that 'there is very little difference between sandwiches sold in a bag and sandwiches sold on a platter' and that 'the delivery of the platters was a very minor part' of the business. *R & A Bardetti (t/a Obertelli Quality Sandwiches), LON/99/561 (VTD 16758)*. (*Note*. For another issue in this case, see 54.33 RETAILERS' SPECIAL SCHEMES.)

27.11 Food

'Finger buffets' delivered to customers. A married couple traded in partnership as food retailers. As part of their business, they supplied 'finger buffets' to local offices, such as accountancy firms. The cheapest type of finger buffet which they offered comprised sandwiches and fruit tarts; more expensive buffets also included pies, sausage rolls, crisps, salad, cakes, etc. Initially the couple accounted for VAT on these buffets. Subsequently, on the advice of their accountants, they submitted a repayment claim, on the basis that the supplies should have been zero-rated. The Commissioners rejected the claim, considering that the supplies were in the course of catering, and thus were excluded from zero-rating. The couple appealed. The tribunal dismissed the appeal, observing that the couple described themselves in their leaflets and brochures as 'quality outside caterers', and finding that each of the finger buffets was a supply in the course of catering. *Safeway Stores plc*, 27.8 above, and *Out To Lunch*, 27.9 above, distinguished. *PJ & LJ Lawson (t/a Country Fayre), MAN/96/5 (VTD 14903).*

27.12 *Lawson*, 27.11 above, was applied in a subsequent case where the facts were similar. The tribunal distinguished *Safeway Stores plc*, 27.8 above, on the grounds that the supplies in that case were not delivered to customers; and distinguished *Out To Lunch*, 27.9 above, on the grounds that that case only concerned supplies of sandwiches, whereas in the present case the appellants' menu 'included a large variety of items other than sandwiches; in particular cakes, cheeseboard and fruit, which permitted a meal rather than a snack to be provided'. *C & E Taylor (t/a Sandwich Heaven), MAN/98/757 (VTD 16211).*

27.13 **'Finger buffets' collected by customers.** A partnership operated a catering and delicatessen business from a shop. It advertised two types of menus for finger buffets. The food provided with the finger buffets included sandwiches, rolls, sausage rolls, pies, chicken drumsticks, crisps, nuts, etc. It accounted for VAT on these finger buffets where it delivered them to its customers. However, where customers collected the buffets from the shop, the partnership did not account for tax on the supplies, treating them as zero-rated. The Commissioners issued an assessment charging tax on the basis that the finger buffets were supplied in the course of catering even when they were collected by the customers, and were excluded from zero-rating. The partnership appealed. The tribunal dismissed the appeal, holding on the evidence, including the partnership's advertising material, that the supplies were within the definition of catering. *Safeway Stores plc*, 27.8 above, and *Out To Lunch*, 27.9 above, distinguished. *Wendy's Kitchen, MAN/95/1073 (VTD 15531).*

27.14 A similar decision, also distinguishing *Safeway Stores plc*, 27.8 above, was reached in *AC & Mrs Y Hodge (t/a Priory Kitchen), MAN/97/326 (VTD 16185).*

27.15 **Supply of sandwiches ordered by electronic mail—whether within definition of 'catering'.** A company began a service whereby office employees could order sandwiches, confectionery and drinks by electronic mail. The items which had been ordered were delivered in refrigerated vans to the office where the employees worked. The Commissioners issued a ruling that the supply of the sandwiches was made in the course of catering, and was therefore standard-rated. The company appealed. The tribunal allowed the appeal, holding that the fact that the company's promotional literature described its services as 'catering' was not conclusive. *Bergonzi*, 27.44 below, was distinguished on the grounds that in that case 'the person supplying the food was physically present on the premises of the employer'. The tribunal observed that the company's supplies were equivalent to a sandwich delivery service, and were not within the ordinary definition of 'catering'. *Emphasis Ltd, [1995] VATDR 419 (VTD 13759).*

27.16 **Supplies from aircraft stand at airport.** A company sold take-away food from a large vehicle situated at an aircraft stand at an airport terminal. It accounted for output tax on its supplies of hot food, but treated its supplies of cold food as zero-rated. The Commissioners issued an assessment charging output tax on the basis that all the company's supplies were in the course of catering. The tribunal allowed the company's appeal, holding that 'the ordinary person would not regard the supplies by the appellant as being done in the course of catering'. *E & G Catering Services Ltd, LON/97/1571 (VTD 15552)*.

27.17   **Meals provided on aircraft.**   See *British Airways plc*, 62.6 TRANSPORT.

Whether food supplied 'for consumption on the premises' (VATA 1994, Sch 8, Group 1, Note 3(a))

Cases held to qualify for zero-rating

27.18   **Sale of doughnuts at Ideal Home Exhibition.**   A company manufactured bakery equipment, including machinery designed for the manufacture of doughnuts. It displayed this machinery at the Ideal Home Exhibition, and gave sample doughnuts to traders who visited its stand and expressed interest in renting or buying its machines. It also sold some doughnuts to members of the public, mainly in batches of six. It did not account for VAT on these sales. The Commissioners issued an assessment charging tax on the basis that they were supplies in the course of catering and thus not eligible for zero-rating. The tribunal allowed the company's appeal, holding on the evidence that the doughnuts were not sold for consumption on the premises, since they were mostly sold in batches of six and it was unlikely that the purchasers intended to consume all six doughnuts immediately. *DCA Industries Ltd, [1983] VATTR 317 (VTD 1544)*.

27.19   **Sale of doughnuts from mobile vans.**   In *Skilton & Gregory*, 27.38 below, the tribunal held that sales of doughnuts from mobile vans in Battersea Park were zero-rated, since 'there was no delineated area capable of constituting the premises where the consumption took place'.

27.20   **Food sold from kiosks in shopping centre.**   A trader operated one of six food kiosks within a shopping centre. She did not account for VAT on her supplies. The Commissioners issued an assessment charging tax on 60% of her supplies, on the basis that 60% of the food which she sold was consumed within the shopping centre, and that the shopping centre constituted the premises on which the food was supplied. The tribunal allowed the trader's appeal, holding that there was no delineated area capable of constituting 'premises' where the actual consumption of food supplied by the trader took place. The shopping centre was akin to a public thoroughfare and did not constitute 'premises'. Accordingly the supplies were not within the definition of 'catering', and were zero-rated. *M Armstrong, [1984] VATTR 53 (VTD 1609)*.

27.21   A company sold food from a kiosk in the hall of a shopping centre. It did not account for tax on its sales of cold take-away food. The Commissioners issued an assessment charging tax on such supplies. The company appealed, contending that the supplies qualified for zero-rating. The tribunal allowed the company's appeal. Although much of the food which the company sold was consumed within the shopping centre, the shopping centre was akin to a 'public thoroughfare'. The food was not supplied for consumption 'on the premises', and thus was not excluded from zero-rating. *Armstrong*, 27.20 above, applied; *Crownlion (Seafood) Ltd*, 27.39 below, distinguished. *Peek Catering Ltd, EDN/92/162 (VTD 10628)*.

27.22   **Snack bar in office block.**   A trader operated a snack bar from a room on the first floor of an office block. Most of her supplies were of sandwiches. She did not account for VAT on her supplies, and the Commissioners issued an assessment charging tax on them. She appealed, contending that, since none of the food which she supplied was consumed in the room in which the snack bar was located, the supplies were zero-rated. The tribunal allowed her appeal in part, finding that 70% of her supplies were to customers who worked in the same office block as the snack bar and that 30% were to customers from other buildings, and holding that the 70% of the supplies which were consumed within the office block were standard-rated. The trader applied for judicial review of this decision. The QB granted a declaration that the supplies were entirely zero-rated. The tribunal had erred in law in regarding the whole building as the 'premises'. The word 'premises' in what is now *VATA 1994, Sch 8, Group 1, Note 3(a)* should be construed as including only the room which the trader occupied. *R v C & E Commrs (ex p. Sims (t/a Supersonic Snacks)), QB 1987, [1988] STC 210.* (*Note.* The decision in this case was distinguished in the subsequent case of *Bergonzi,* 27.44 below, on the grounds that it related to a multi-tenanted office block to which members of the public had access.)

27.23   **Sandwiches sold from tray taken around offices.**   A trader sold sandwiches from a mobile van and from a tray taken around offices in an office block. The Commissioners issued an assessment on the basis that his supplies were 'in the course of catering' and were standard-rated. The tribunal allowed the trader's appeal, holding that the food was not supplied in the course of catering. Sales from a van were not intended for consumption 'on the premises', since the public thoroughfare did not amount to 'premises'; and the sales of sandwiches were not for consumption 'on the premises', since the trader did not necessarily intend the sandwiches to be consumed within the office block and the customers could, for example, have taken them to a nearby park. *M Cooper, MAN/87/269 (VTD 2665).*

27.24   A company sold sandwiches and fruit salads at offices in the City of London. The sandwiches and salads were placed in large baskets, and each basket was given to an employee to visit a number of office blocks. Most sales took place in the reception areas of the offices. The company had accounted for VAT on more than 75% of the sandwiches which it sold, but had not accounted for VAT on any of the sales of fruit salad. The Commissioners issued an assessment charging VAT on more than 75% of the sales of fruit salad. On receiving the assessment, the company director consulted an accountant, who considered that none of the supplies should have been standard-rated. He wrote to the Commissioners accordingly, and lodged an appeal. The tribunal allowed the appeal, holding that none of the food was supplied for consumption 'on the premises', applying the QB decision in *Sims,* 27.22 above. Where the food was consumed was of no consequence to the company. Food was only supplied 'for consumption on the premises on which it is supplied' where the supplier had some right or duty to supply the food on those premises. *Zeldaline Ltd, [1989] VATTR 191 (VTD 4388).*

27.25   **Sandwiches sold by company trading within hospital site—whether supplied for consumption on the premises.**   A company trading from a room within a hospital site sold sandwiches, etc., and accounted for tax on the basis that these sales were zero-rated. The Commissioners issued an assessment on the basis that 80% of the sales were for consumption within the 'hospital site' and were therefore deemed to be supplied in the course of catering. The tribunal allowed the company's appeal, holding that the 'premises' in which the food was supplied was the room in which the company operated, rather than the whole of the 'hospital site'. Applying the QB decision in *Sims,* 27.22 above, any food consumed outside that particular room was not supplied 'for consumption on the premises'. *Ashby Catering Ltd, MAN/89/144 & MAN/89/426 (VTD 4220).*

27.26   **Seafood sold from kiosk in public park.**   A company sold seafood from a kiosk in a public park at Barry Island. The park was about 700 yards in circumference, and contained at least 20 shops or kiosks. The company did not account for VAT on these sales, considering that they were zero-rated. The Commissioners issued an assessment charging tax on the sales, considering that the park constituted 'premises' so that the sales were in the course of catering. The tribunal allowed the company's appeal, holding that the park did not constitute premises and that the supplies were zero-rated. *Armstrong*, 27.20 above, and *Sims*, 27.22 above, applied; *Cope*, 27.36 below, and *Crownlion (Seafood) Ltd*, 27.39 below, distinguished. *Fresh Sea Foods (Barry) Ltd*, *[1991] VATTR 388 (VTD 6658)*.

27.27   **Supplies of cold food from school tuck shop.**   The governors of a school formed a limited company to operate the school 'tuck shop', which sold hot and cold food. The tuck shop was located within the main school building, in two rooms which had previously formed a cloakroom. The company failed to account for output tax on its sales of food. The Commissioners issued an assessment charging tax on the sales, and the company appealed, accepting that output tax was due on supplies of hot food, but contending that the supplies of cold food qualified for zero-rating, on the basis that the food was not supplied for consumption on the tuck shop premises. The tribunal accepted this contention and allowed the appeal, holding that the supplies were not within the general definition of 'catering', and also that they were not excluded from zero-rating by what is now *VATA 1994, Sch 8, Group 1, Note 3(a)*, since the 'premises' should be construed as meaning the two rooms occupied by the tuck shop itself, rather than the whole of the school building. *Armstrong*, 27.20 above, applied; *Cope*, 27.36 below, distinguished. *St Benedict Trading Ltd, MAN/93/1375 (VTD 12915)*.

27.28   **Supplies of cold food from kiosks at railway stations.**   A company sold cold take-away food from kiosks at railway stations. The Commissioners issued a ruling that the company's sales were standard-rated, on the basis that the food was supplied for consumption on the premises at which it was supplied. The company appealed, contending that the 'premises' should be interpreted as its kiosks, rather than the whole of the railway stations in question, so that the sale of food consumed outside its kiosks should be treated as zero-rated. The tribunal allowed the appeal, holding that the fact that the kiosks were situated at railway stations was not sufficient to bring them within the general definition of 'catering', and that, from the company's point of view, it was immaterial whether the food which it supplied was to be consumed on the station at which it was sold. The 'premises' on which the food was supplied were the company's kiosks, rather than the whole of the railway stations. *Sims*, 27.22 above, and *Zeldaline Ltd*, 27.24 above, applied; *Cope*, 27.36 below, distinguished. *Travellers Fare Ltd, MAN/94/1190 (VTD 13482)*.

Cases held not to qualify for zero-rating

27.29   **Supply of food from buffets at football ground.**   A football supporters' club sold food from a number of kiosks at a football ground. It did not account for VAT on these supplies. The Commissioners issued a ruling that the supplies were standard-rated on the basis that they were for consumption on the premises on which they were supplied. The club appealed, contending that its premises were the kiosks from which the food was sold, rather than the whole football ground. The tribunal rejected this contention and dismissed the appeal against this decision, holding that the whole of the football ground constituted the 'premises'. *Bristol City Football Supporters Club*, *[1975] VATTR 93 (VTD 164)*. (*Note*. The decision was approved by the QB in *Cope*, 27.36 below.)

27.30   A similar decision was reached in *Parker (t/a The Roker Park Suite), MAN/80/58 (VTD 956)*.

27.31 Food

27.31 **Sale of food at working men's club.** A company which operated a restaurant obtained the right to sell food at a nearby working men's club. It did not account for VAT on these sales. The Commissioners issued an assessment charging tax on these sales and the company appealed, contending that its premises should be treated as the kitchen which it occupied, rather than the whole club. The tribunal rejected this contention and dismissed the appeal, holding that the whole of the club, including the car park, constituted the 'premises'. Accordingly the supplies were standard-rated. *Bristol City Football Supporters Club*, 27.29 above, applied. *Ivy Café Ltd, MAN/76/73 (VTD 288).*

27.32 **Drinks supplied from vending machines.** An employees' social club operated two vending machines, dispensing hot and cold drinks, on its employers' premises. It did not account for VAT on its receipts from these machines. The Commissioners issued an assessment charging tax on the supplies. The tribunal dismissed the club's appeal, holding that the drinks were supplied 'for consumption on the premises'. *Burnham Radio Recreational & Welfare Club, CAR/77/157 (VTD 518).*

27.33 A company operated a number of vending machines, dispensing hot and cold drinks, which were installed at various premises such as factories and garages. It did not account for VAT on its receipts from these machines. The Commissioners issued an assessment charging tax on the supplies. The tribunal dismissed the company's appeal, holding that the nature of the supplies was such that they were intended for early consumption. Accordingly they were intended 'for consumption on the premises on which they were supplied'. *Macklin Services (Vending) West Ltd, [1979] VATTR 31 (VTD 688).* (*Note.* For another issue in this case, see 3.31 ASSESSMENT.)

27.34 An accountancy partnership operated a coin-operated vending machine which dispensed hot drinks. Each week the partners were supplied with 5p coins to obtain drinks from the machine. The partners' drawings accounts were debited accordingly. The partnership did not account for VAT on the takings from the machines. The Commissioners issued an assessment charging tax on them. The tribunal dismissed the partnership's appeal, holding that the partnership was supplying the drinks to the partners and that the supplies were in the course of catering and therefore standard-rated. *Atkins Macreadie & Co, MAN/86/333 (VTD 2381).*

27.35 Drinks supplied from vending machines were also held to be standard-rated in *Streamline Taxis (Southampton) Ltd, LON/85/499 (VTD 2016); Triangle Press Ltd, LON/92/1122Y (VTD 9648)* and *Bourne*, 49.207 PENALTIES: MISDECLARATION.

27.36 **Supplies of food from mobile stall at race meetings.** A trader sold seafood for immediate consumption from a mobile stall at race meetings. The Commissioners issued an assessment on the basis that his supplies were within the definition of 'catering' and were therefore standard-rated. He appealed, contending that they were zero-rated. The QB upheld the assessment, observing that the food was supplied for consumption at the racecourses, which were within the definition of 'premises' for the purposes of *Note 3*. Furthermore, the word 'includes' in *Note 3* was not intended to be restrictive, and 'catering' included the provision of food incidental to some other activity, such as football matches, race meetings, wedding receptions, etc. Accordingly the trader's supplies were in the course of catering. *C & E Commrs v BH Cope, QB [1981] STC 532.*

27.37 *Cope*, 27.36 above, was followed in a case where a company supplied food and drink at a 'point-to-point' course for racehorses. The tribunal held that the company's supplies were in the course of catering and thus were standard-rated. *Q Inns Ltd, LON/92/295Z (VTD 8929).*

27.38   **Sale of doughnuts from mobile vans.**   A partnership sold doughnuts from mobile vans. Most of the sales took place at horse-race meetings or agricultural shows, but some took place in Battersea Park. The partnership did not account for VAT on the sales, treating them as zero-rated. The Commissioners issued an assessment charging VAT on the basis that the sales were supplies in the course of catering, and thus excluded from zero-rating. The tribunal allowed the partnership's appeal in part, holding that the sales at horse-race meetings and agricultural shows were for consumption on the premises on which they were supplied, and were therefore deemed to be supplies in the course of catering and excluded from zero-rating. However, the sales in Battersea Park were zero-rated, since 'there was no delineated area capable of constituting the premises where the consumption took place'. *Cope*, 27.36 above, and *Cooper*, 27.23 above, applied. *Skilton & Gregory, LON/92/662X (VTD 11723)*. (*Note*. An appeal against a misdeclaration penalty was allowed.)

27.39   **Food sold from kiosks in shopping centre.**   A company sold seafood from a kiosk in a shopping centre. The kiosk was one of a number of kiosks, all of which sold food of various types, surrounding a courtyard which had tables and chairs for almost 400 people. The company did not account for VAT on its supplies, and the Commissioners issued an assessment charging tax on them. The tribunal dismissed the company's appeal, holding that the courtyard and the kiosks together constituted 'premises', so that the supplies were of food 'for consumption on the premises on which it is supplied' and were not eligible for zero-rating. *Armstrong*, 27.20 above, distinguished. *Crownlion (Seafood) Ltd, [1985] VATTR 188 (VTD 1924)*.

27.40   A partnership sold food from a snack bar on the first floor of a shopping centre. The snack bar was adjacent to two similar kiosks. About twelve feet from the kiosks was a raised seating area containing 20 tables, each of which could seat four people. The partnership did not account for VAT on its sales of food. The Commissioners issued an assessment charging tax on the supplies, considering that the kiosks and the seating area constituted 'premises', so that the food was supplied in the course of catering and was not eligible for zero-rating. The tribunal upheld the assessment and dismissed the partnership's appeal, applying *Crownlion (Seafood) Ltd*, 27.39 above, and distinguishing *Armstrong*, 27.20 above. *Breezes Patisserie, EDN/92/295 (VTD 10081)*.

27.41   **Seafood sold in public houses and clubs.**   A trader sold seafood in public houses and clubs. The Commissioners issued an assessment on the basis that the seafood was supplied in the course of catering and was therefore standard-rated. He appealed, contending that his supplies were zero-rated. The tribunal reduced the assessment to take account of a small number of sales made in the street, which were zero-rated, but held that the sales in public houses and clubs were within the definition of 'catering' and thus were standard-rated. *K Mowbray, [1986] VATTR 266 (VTD 2239)*.

27.42   **Food sold at public house.**   Food sold at a public house was held to be standard-rated in *MJ Hellaby, LON/89/715Z (VTD 4790)*.

27.43   **Food supplied from shed in country park.**   A company supplied food from a shed in a 360–acre country park. The park was private property, and members of the public had to pay for admission to the park. Where appropriate, the food was supplied in containers, but no plates were provided. There were no tables or seats near to the shed, and no food was consumed inside the shed. The company did not account for VAT on its supplies. The Commissioners issued an assessment, charging tax on the basis that the food was supplied 'in the course of catering'. The tribunal dismissed the company's appeal, holding that the country park constituted 'premises' so that the supplies were standard-rated. *Mylos of Reading (Catering & Ices) Ltd, LON/86/575 (VTD 2538).*

27.44   **Snack bar in office block.**   A trader operated a snack bar from two rooms on the seventh floor of an office block. The whole of the office block was occupied by a single group of companies. The trader accounted for output tax on supplies of hot food, but did not account for tax on supplies of cold food. The Commissioners issued an assessment charging tax on the supplies of cold food, on the basis that they were supplies in the course of catering and thus excluded from zero-rating. The trader appealed, contending that the supplies should be treated as zero-rated, applying the decision in *Sims*, 27.22 above. The tribunal dismissed the appeal, distinguishing *Sims* because in that case 'the licence was intended to allow the grantee to deal with the general public', whereas in the present case 'the licence was granted exclusively for the benefit of the employees of the group of companies'. Applying the principle in *Cope*, 27.36 above, the supplies of food were incidental to the business activities of the group of companies, and were thus within the definition of 'catering'. Furthermore, the whole of the seventh floor of the office block constituted the premises on which the food was supplied, so that the food was supplied for consumption on the premises, and the supplies were excluded from zero-rating by what is now *VATA 1994, Sch 8, Group 1, Note 3. GME Bergonzi (t/a Beppi's Buffet Service), LON/93/ 1756A (VTD 12122).*

27.45   **Snack bar at auction site.**   A partnership operated a snack bar at a site used for car auctions, under a licence agreement with the auctioneers. The partnership did not account for VAT on food sold at the snack bar, and the Commissioners issued an assessment charging tax on the supplies. The partnership appealed, contending that the supplies should be treated as zero-rated. The tribunal dismissed the appeal, observing that the snack bar existed for the purpose of enabling food to be consumed at the auctioneers' premises. *Cope*, 27.36 above, applied; *Sims*, 27.22 above, and *Ashby Catering Ltd*, 27.25 above, distinguished. *Bramley Caterers, MAN/90/1072 (VTD 6385).*

Whether food supplied 'hot' (VATA 1994, Sch 8, Group 1, Note 3(b))

27.46   **Hot pies sold from baker's shop.**   A company trading as bakers sold freshly-baked pies from retail shops. The final baking of such pies was carried out in the shop oven, so that they were hot at the time of sale. Some customers purchased pies to consume immediately, whereas others purchased them to take away and eat later. The Commissioners issued an assessment charging tax on some of the sales, on the basis that the pies which were eaten while hot were excluded from zero-rating. The company appealed, contending that it did not heat the pies for the purpose of enabling them to be consumed at a temperature above the ambient air temperature, but in order to produce a smell which was designed to attract customers. The QB allowed the company's appeal, holding that, on the evidence accepted by the tribunal, the pies were not within the definition of 'hot food' in what is now *VATA 1994, Sch 8, Group 1, Note 3(b)(i)*. The CA upheld this decision. *John Pimblett & Sons Ltd v C & E Commrs, CA 1987, [1988] STC 358.*

27.47   *John Pimblett & Sons Ltd*, 27.46 above, was followed in a similar case where a shop sold freshly-baked Cornish pasties. It was accepted that a substantial proportion of the pasties were sold at a temperature above the ambient air temperature. However, the tribunal accepted that the company's purpose was solely to sell freshly-baked pasties, and that no pasties were reheated or deliberately kept warm after baking. Accordingly, the pasties were not supplied in the course of catering, and their sale was zero-rated. *Lutron Ltd, LON/88/1148Z (VTD 3686).*

27.48   *John Pimblett & Sons Ltd*, 27.46 above, and *Lutron Ltd*, 27.47 above, were applied in
a subsequent case where a company sold freshly-baked pies, pasties and sausage rolls.
The tribunal held that the sales were zero-rated, since the company's purpose in
heating the food was that the items should be seen to be freshly-baked, rather than to
enable them to be consumed at a temperature above the ambient air temperature.
The fact that some of the items may have been consumed above the ambient air
temperature was incidental. *Redhead*, 27.52 below, distinguished. *Greenhalgh's Craft
Bakery Ltd, MAN/91/626 (VTD 10955)*. (*Note.* For another issue in this case, see
3.33 ASSESSMENT.)

27.49   A similar decision, also applying *John Pimblett & Sons Ltd*, 27.46 above, was reached
in *Three Cooks Ltd, LON/94/2558A (VTD 13352)*.

27.50   **Chip butties—whether roll containing chips may be zero-rated.**   A trader
operated a fish and chip shop, from which he sold 'chip butties' (consisting of hot
chipped potatoes inside a cold bread roll). He treated part of the price of the chip
butties as attributable to the roll, and as zero-rated. The Commissioners issued an
assessment on the basis that he was supplying hot food which did not qualify for
zero-rating. The tribunal dismissed the trader's appeal, holding that he was making a
single supply of hot food which was entirely standard-rated. *PA Marshall (t/a Harry
Ramsbottom's), MAN/95/692 (VTD 13766)*.

27.51   **Baked potatoes with cold fillings—whether wholly standard-rated.**   A
trader sold baked jacket potatoes with a variety of fillings, some of which were cold.
The Commissioners issued an assessment on the basis that his sales of potatoes,
including the fillings, was standard-rated. The trader appealed, contending that he
should be treated as making separate supplies of the potatoes and the fillings, and that
the cold fillings should be treated as zero-rated. The tribunal rejected this contention
and dismissed the appeal, holding that he was making a single supply of hot food
which was entirely standard-rated. *M Rourke (t/a The Market Pantry), MAN/99/
446 (VTD 16671)*.

27.52   **Sale of heated waffles.**   A trader carried on business selling hot and cold snacks,
including waffles. She treated the sale of waffles as zero-rated. The Commissioners
issued an assessment charging tax on the sale of waffles, on the basis that they were
within the definition of 'hot food'. The trader appealed, contending that her purpose
in heating the waffles was merely to ensure that they were crisp, rather than to enable
them to be consumed at a temperature above the ambient air temperature. The
tribunal allowed her appeal in part, finding that only some of the waffles were still hot
when they were sold, and holding that although all the waffles had been heated for
consumption 'at a temperature above the ambient air temperature', only those waffles
which were still above the ambient temperature when sold were excluded from
zero-rating. The waffles which were no longer above the ambient air temperature at
the time of sale were zero-rated. *WD Redhead, MAN/87/167 (VTD 3201)*.

27.53   **Sale of heated croissants.**   A company sold heated filled croissants. The
Commissioners issued a ruling that the croissants were within the definition of 'hot
food' so that the company was required to account for output tax on these supplies.
The company appealed, contending that the purpose of heating the croissants was to
keep them fresh and to prevent them from hardening, rather than to enable them to
be consumed at a temperature above the ambient air temperature. The tribunal
dismissed the appeal, finding that the 'application and retention of heat' was
necessary 'to create attractive and palatable food'. The tribunal observed that there
would be 'a degree of artificiality in separating the appellant's intention to produce
food for sale which is attractive and palatable because it is "hot" and its intention to
sell that food while it is attractive and palatable, but not because it is "hot". On the

evidence, the company's 'predominant purpose in cooking the savoury croissants and presenting them for sale hot was "for the purposes of enabling (them) to be consumed at a temperature above the ambient air temperature"'. *Pret A Manger (Europe) Ltd, LON/C/1423 (VTD 16246).*

27.54　**Sale of roast chickens in department stores.**　A company owned three large department stores. It sold many types of food, including roast chickens. It did not account for VAT on the sales of chickens, treating them as zero-rated. The Commissioners issued an assessment on the basis that the chickens were within the definition of 'hot food' in what is now *VATA 1994, Sch 8, Group 1, Note 3(b)*, and were accordingly deemed to be supplied in the course of catering and standard-rated. The tribunal allowed the company's appeal, holding on the evidence that the company's predominant purpose in keeping the chickens hot until sale was to comply with hygiene requirements. Although the chickens were still hot when sold, this was not for the purpose of enabling them to be consumed above the ambient air temperature. They were not marketed in such a way as to be eaten shortly after purchase. The tribunal commented that to eat a roast chicken 'as one would eat a pie or pasty would be an unpleasantly messy process'. *The Lewis's Group Ltd, MAN/89/389 (VTD 4931).*

27.55　**Sale of cooked chicken pieces in supermarkets.**　A company which operated a number of supermarkets did not account for output tax on the sale of cooked chicken pieces, treating them as zero-rated. The Commissioners issued an assessment charging tax on such supplies, on the basis that they did not qualify for zero-rating since they were hot when they were sold. The company appealed, contending that the food was not heated 'for the purposes of enabling it to be consumed at a temperature above the ambient air temperature', but in order to comply with food hygiene regulations. The tribunal accepted this contention and allowed the appeal. *John Pimblett & Sons Ltd*, 27.46 above, and *The Lewis's Group Ltd*, 27.54 above, applied. *Stewarts Supermarkets Ltd, BEL/93/60A (VTD 13338).*

27.56　**Sale of cooked chickens and chicken pieces from take-away shop.**　A trader operated two take-away food shops from which she sold chickens and chicken portions, as well as other types of foodstuffs. Where she sold chickens and chicken portions with chipped potatoes, she treated the sales as standard-rated. However, where she sold chickens or chicken portions on their own, she treated the sales as zero-rated. The Commissioners issued an estimated assessment charging tax on such sales. The trader appealed, contending that the purpose of heating the chickens was to comply with food hygiene regulations. The tribunal accepted this contention and allowed the appeal in respect of these sales, applying *Stewarts Supermarkets Ltd*, 27.55 above. *NM Holmes (t/a The Chicken Shop), MAN/98/355 (VTD 16264).*

27.57　**School meals.**　A catering firm supplied cooked lunches to a school. The lunches were cooked at the firm's premises and delivered to the school by minibus. The lunches were usually delivered in aluminium trays, and were kept warm at the school on electrically-heated metal trolleys. The Commissioners issued an assessment charging VAT on the lunches, on the basis that they were a supply in the course of catering. The firm appealed, contending that the supplies should be treated as zero-rated. The tribunal dismissed the appeal. On the evidence, the lunches were hot when they left the firm's premises, having been cooked in order that they could be consumed 'at a temperature above the ambient air temperature'. *John Pimblett & Sons Ltd*, 27.46 above; *Lutron Ltd*, 27.47 above, and *The Lewis's Group Ltd*, 27.54 above, distinguished. *P & S Catering, LON/90/1222Z (VTD 6382).*

27.58　**Hot meal delivery service.**　A trader provided a meals delivery service for the elderly and disabled. He did not account for VAT on his supplies. The

Commissioners issued an assessment charging tax on them, and the tribunal dismissed the trader's appeal, finding that the supplies covered by the assessment were of hot food and were therefore excluded from zero-rating. (The tribunal chairman expressed the opinion, however, that such supplies would not be excluded from zero-rating if the purpose of heating the food was solely to comply with food hygiene regulations, rather than to enable the food to be consumed at a temperature above the ambient air temperature.) *PJ Bridgewater, LON/91/1486Y (VTD 10491)*. (*Note*. The *obiter dicta* of the chairman with regard to the food hygiene regulations were not followed, and were implicitly doubted, in the subsequent case of *Malik*, 27.59 below.)

27.59   A trader operated a meals delivery service. Until 1994 she treated her supplies as standard-rated. Subsequently she began to treat her supplies as zero-rated, and submitted a claim for repayment of output tax which she had accounted for in 1994. The Commissioners rejected the claim on the basis that her supplies were of hot food which was excluded from zero-rating. She appealed, contending that she had only heated the food for the purpose of complying with the relevant food hygiene regulations, so that, following *obiter dicta* of the tribunal chairman in *Bridgewater*, 27.58 above, her supplies should be treated as zero-rated. The tribunal rejected this contention and dismissed her appeal, and the QB upheld this decision. On the evidence, the trader had heated the food with a dual purpose, and the tribunal had been entitled to conclude that her main purpose was to enable customers to eat the food hot if they so wished. *John Pimblett & Sons Ltd*, 27.46 above, distinguished. *MA Malik v C & E Commrs, QB [1998] STC 537*.

WHETHER 'FOOD OF A KIND USED FOR HUMAN CONSUMPTION' (VATA 1994, Sch 8, Group 1, General Item 1)

27.60   **Ritual slaughter of animals in accordance with Jewish law.** An unincorporated association provided the services of employees to carry out the ritual slaughter of animals for human consumption in accordance with Jewish dietary law. The Commissioners issued a ruling that the association's services were liable to VAT at the standard rate. The association appealed, contending that its services should be zero-rated under what is now *VATA 1994, Sch 8, Group 1*. The tribunal accepted this contention and allowed the appeal, holding that the employees were applying a process to the animals within what is now *VATA 1994, Sch 4 para 2*, and that the supply of their services was therefore a deemed supply of the meat, within *Sch 8, Group 1, General Item 1*. *The London Board for Shechita, [1974] VATTR 24 (VTD 52)*.

27.61   **Abattoir services.** A borough council provided a public slaughterhouse, the running of which it shared with a company representing the principal users. The company was responsible for the killing of the animals and the processing of the carcasses, while the Council was responsible for the lairage (penning of the animals awaiting slaughter), for a cooling hall in which the carcass meat was hung before collection by the owner, and for the inspection and stamping of the meat. The Council and the company made separate charges in respect of animals brought to the abattoir. The Commissioners assessed the Council on the basis that its charges were standard-rated except in so far as they were for lairage, meat inspection and a Meat Livestock Commission levy. The Council appealed, contending that since the abattoir was used to produce food for human consumption, its supplies should be treated as zero-rated. The tribunal dismissed the appeal, holding that the Council merely provided facilities for the slaughtering and carcass processing by the company which, on the evidence, was an independent principal and not an agent or employee of the Council. *Darlington Borough Council, [1980] VATTR 120 (VTD 961)*.

27.62   **Cod liver oil products.**   A company supplied cod liver oil and related products. The Commissioners issued a ruling that the supplies were liable to VAT at the standard rate, and the company appealed, contending that they were zero–rated under what is now *VATA 1994, Sch 8, Group 1*. The tribunal dismissed the company's appeal, holding that the supplies were not within the definition of 'food'. *Marfleet Refining Co Ltd, [1974] VATTR 289 (VTD 129)*.

27.63   **Royal Jelly capsules.**   The Commissioners issued an assessment on a company which distributed 'Royal Jelly' capsules. The company appealed, contending that the capsules were 'food' and should be zero–rated. The tribunal dismissed the appeal, holding that the capsules were not food. They were meant to be swallowed undissolved, with water, and had an unpleasant taste if retained in the mouth. *Marfleet Refining Co Ltd*, 27.62 above, applied. *Grosvenor Commodities Ltd, LON/ 90/1805X (VTD 7221)*. (*Note*. The tribunal also rejected a contention by the company that the Commissioners were estopped from raising the assessment. For cases concerning estoppel, see 2.72 *et seq.* APPEALS.)

27.64   **Chlorella pyrenoidosa tablets.**   A company sold tablets of chlorella pyrenoidosa (an edible green micro–algae which contained protein, vitamins and minerals). It did not account for output tax on its sales of these tablets, treating them as zero–rated. The Commissioners issued a ruling that the sales did not qualify for zero–rating, on the grounds that the chlorella tablets were not 'food of a kind used for human consumption'. The company appealed. The tribunal dismissed the appeal, holding that although the tablets were 'palatable', they were not within the definition of 'food'. *Nature's Balance Ltd, LON/93/2953A (VTD 12295)*.

27.65   **Algae tablets.**   A company sold algae tablets and powdered algae. The Commissioners issued a ruling that its supplies did not qualify for zero–rating, on the grounds that algae were not 'food of a kind used for human consumption'. The tribunal dismissed the company's appeal. *Nature's Balance Ltd*, 27.64 above, applied. *Hunter Ridgeley Ltd, LON/94/2028 (VTD 13662)*.

27.66   **Fruit and vegetable tablets.**   A company manufactured two types of tablets, called 'Juice Plus Fruit Blend Tablets' and 'Juice Plus Vegetable Blend Tablets'. They were made from juices and powders derived from various fruits and vegetables, and were approximately 1.5cm in diameter. The Commissioners issued a ruling that the supplies of the tablets were standard–rated. The company appealed, contending that the tablets were within the definition of 'food of a kind used for human consumption' and were therefore zero–rated. The tribunal rejected this contention and dismissed the appeal, observing that 'taking the word "food" in its normally understood sense, tablets do not look like food or taste like food' and holding that 'these tablets are not food in the normal present-day meaning of the word'. *National Safety Associates of America (UK) Ltd, LON/95/3185A (VTD 14241)*.

27.67   **Dietary supplement containing powdered gelatine.**   A company sold a powder which was marketed as a dietary supplement and was intended to be mixed with water and drunk. 85% of the powder consisted of edible gelatine (also known as collagen hydrolysate); the remaining 15% consisted of vitamins, minerals, colouring and flavouring. The Commissioners issued a ruling that sales of the powder were standard–rated. The company appealed, contending that the powder was within the definition of food, and qualified for zero–rating. The tribunal accepted this contention and allowed the appeal, observing that the case was 'very finely balanced' but that the powder had a very high protein value and holding that, in view of its high 'nutritional value', it qualified as a food. *Arthro Vite Ltd, MAN/96/1190 (VTD 14836)*.

27.68   **Powder for making sports drinks.**   A company supplied products consisting
primarily of carbohydrate or creatine, in powder form, which were designed to be
mixed with water and drunk by people competing in, or training for, sporting events.
Initially the Commissioners accepted that these products qualified for zero-rating.
However, they reviewed their policy with effect from December 1997 and issued a
ruling that the products should be treated as standard-rated from that date. The
company appealed, contending that, as the products consisted primarily of
carbohydrate or protein, they were within the definition of 'food'. The tribunal
accepted this contention and allowed the appeal. On the evidence, the products were
consumed for nutritional purposes. *VATA 1994, Sch 8, Group 1, Note 1* provided
that '"food" includes drink', so that a 'drinkable substance' could be within the
definition of 'food'. The tribunal observed that 'food frequently contains large
amounts of water: indeed, if it did not, it might be difficult or impossible to consume'.
On the evidence, the products in question were 'for the preparation of food
supplements (technically, "dietary integrators")'. The 'benefit to the consumer' was
'the carbohydrate and protein, alternatively pure protein, present in the product,
which the consumer takes for nourishment'. *SIS (Science in Sport) Ltd, [2000]
VATDR 194 (VTD 16555).*

27.69   **Aloe vera gel products.**   A company supplied a number of products based on aloe
vera gel. They were marketed in litre bottles, but customers were advised not to
consume more than 110ml twice daily, as larger doses would have a laxative effect.
The Commissioners issued a ruling that the products were standard-rated, and the
company appealed, contending that they should be zero-rated as 'food of a kind used
for human consumption'. The tribunal rejected this contention and dismissed the
appeal, holding on the evidence that none of the products had 'any nutritional value
whatsoever'. *Arthro Vite Ltd*, 27.67 above, distinguished. *Forever Living Products Ltd,
MAN/97/907 (VTD 16263).*

27.70   **Paan.**   A retailer sold a preparation called 'paan', which consisted of a mixture of
betel nut, coconut, rose petals, sugar and honey, wrapped in betel leaves. It was
intended to be chewed on the completion of a meal until the flavour had been released
and swallowed, the remaining fibrous constituents being spat out. The
Commissioners issued a ruling that sales of paan were standard-rated, on the basis
that betel nut (the main ingredient) was a stimulant rather than a food. The retailer
appealed, contending that paan should be zero-rated as food for human
consumption. The tribunal allowed his appeal, finding that paan had a measurable
nutritive value and holding that it was within the definition of 'food'. *GR Soni,
[1980] VATTR 9 (VTD 897).*

27.71   **Herbal fruit concentrate.**   A company imported and sold a herbal fruit
concentrate, marketed in plastic containers and described by the tribunal as a 'dark,
stiff, sticky fruit paste'. Cane sugar comprised 70% of its ingredients, but the tribunal
found that its taste was somewhat less sweet than most jams. It was marketed to be
eaten by the spoonful, rather than by being spread on bread. The Commissioners
issued a ruling that the concentrate did not constitute 'food', and thus did not qualify
for zero-rating. The tribunal allowed the company's appeal, holding that the
concentrate was within the definition of 'food'. (Herbal tablets sold by the same
company were held not to be food, and thus to be standard-rated.) *Ayurveda Ltd,
LON/88/1372X (VTD 3860).*

27.72   **Laxative fruit cubes.**   A company manufactured laxative fruit cubes, which
contained a mixture of dried fruits such as figs and senna pods. It did not account for
VAT on the sale of the cubes, considering that they were zero-rated under what is
now *VATA 1994, Sch 8, Group 1*. The Commissioners issued a ruling that the cubes
did not constitute food and thus were not eligible for zero-rating. The tribunal

dismissed the company's appeal, finding that the cubes 'were neither sold nor bought as a form of nourishment, nor were they consumed for pleasure'. The cubes were designed 'to remedy or to prevent constipation'. They were a remedial preparation, and did not constitute 'food'. *Brewhurst Health Food Supplies, LON/91/2488Z (VTD 8928)*.

27.73   **Chinese herbal tea prescribed by doctor.**   A doctor, who was registered for VAT, operated a Chinese herbal and homeopathic clinic. She prescribed and dispensed preparations of Chinese herbal tea for some of her patients. The exact ingredients of the herbal tea varied from patient to patient. The Commissioners issued a ruling that, since the prescriptions were individually prepared for medical reasons, they were not 'food of a kind used for human consumption' and thus did not qualify for zero-rating. The doctor appealed, contending that the herbal tea preparations were within the definition of 'food' and qualified for zero-rating under *VATA 1994, Sch 8, Group 1, Overriding Item No 4*. The tribunal allowed the appeal. On the evidence, the herbal tea had 'some nutritive value' and 'people drink herbal teas as part of their normal daily diet, in many cases as a substitute for what they would otherwise drink'. The ingredients of the preparations 'were substantially the same as the ingredients of sachets of herbal teas sold commercially'. The fact that the herbal teas were prescribed by a doctor did not prevent them from constituting food. *C & E Commrs v Beecham Foods Ltd, HL [1972] 1 WLR 241; [1972] 1 All ER 498* (a purchase tax case) applied. *Dr X Hua, LON/95/2069A (VTD 13811)*.

27.74   **JS4 soft roll concentrate.**   A company manufactured a product known as 'JS4 soft roll concentrate', which was not itself edible but was used as an aid for the baking of soft rolls. The concentrate consisted mainly of sugar, dextrose, salt, and edible oil. Flour, water and yeast had to be added to it before baking could take place. After baking, the flour, yeast and water constituted about 95% of the soft rolls; the concentrate comprised the remaining 5%. The company did not account for VAT on sales of the concentrate, considering that it should be zero-rated. The Commissioners considered that it was not eligible for zero-rating and issued an assessment charging tax on the sales, against which the company appealed. The tribunal allowed the company's appeal and the CS upheld this decision. Zero-rating was not restricted to food which was virtually ready for human consumption in the state in which it was supplied. The words 'food of a kind used for human consumption' in what is now *VATA 1994, Sch 8, Group 1, Item 1* reflected the fact that many foods for human consumption were retailed in a form in which they were not fit to be consumed without some further preparation. The fact that part of the preparation was carried out at a stage before the food was sold to the ultimate consumer did not prevent the ingredients from qualifying for zero-rating. *C & E Commrs v MacPhie & Co (Glenbervie) Ltd, CS [1992] STC 886*.

27.75   **Sausage casings.**   A company manufactured sausage casings, which were made from reconstituted collagen (a structural animal protein), with the addition of a permitted additive E460 which was designed to modify the texture and which also had the effect of aiding digestion by helping in the functioning of the bowel. The Commissioners issued a ruling that the casings were not 'food of a kind used for human consumption' and were not eligible for zero-rating. The tribunal allowed the company's appeal. The sausage casings were clearly edible and were designed to be eaten. The fact that the casings had to be incorporated into a sausage after being manufactured and being consumed did not prevent them from qualifying as 'food'. *Devro Ltd, EDN/91/259 (VTD 7570)*.

27.76   **Haddock and mackerel sold to fishermen.**   See *North Isles Shellfish Ltd, 27.90* below.

27.77   **Biscuits packed in tin—whether wholly zero-rated.** A company which manufactured biscuits sold tins containing four varieties of biscuits. It treated its supplies of these tins as zero-rated. The cost of the tins comprised 55% of the total cost. The Commissioners issued a ruling that the tins should be treated as a mixed supply and partly standard-rated, since the tins cost more to produce than the biscuits they contained. The tribunal allowed the company's appeal, holding that the entire supply was zero-rated. On the evidence, the packaging of the biscuits in a tin was 'both normal and necessary'. The company sought to make a profit on the biscuits, rather than on the tins, and the tins were 'designed to look as attractive as possible to sell the product with the minimum expenditure necessary for a quality product'. The fact that the tins could be used after the biscuits had been consumed was not material. The CS upheld the tribunal decision. Applying the reasoning in *British Airways plc*, 62.6 TRANSPORT, 'the tin was incidental to the biscuits, rather than the biscuits being incidental to the tin'. *C & E Commrs v United Biscuits (UK) Ltd (t/a Simmers), CS [1992] STC 325.*

27.78   **Biscuits packed in ceramic jar—whether wholly zero-rated.** *United Biscuits (UK) Ltd*, 27.77 above, was applied in a similar subsequent case in which small quantities of luxury biscuits were sold in ceramic self-sealing jars. The cost of the jars comprised 70% of the total cost. The Commissioners issued a ruling that part of the consideration was attributable to the supply of the jar and was standard-rated, but the tribunal allowed the company's appeal, holding that the whole of the consideration was attributable to the supply of biscuits and qualified for zero-rating. *Paterson Arran Ltd, EDN/96/249 (VTD 15041).*

ANIMAL FEEDING STUFFS (VATA 1994, Sch 8, Group 1, General Item 2)

27.79   **Polymer additive for cattle feed.** A company, which sold animal feeding stuffs, sold an additive for cattle feed. The additive was in the form of a powder. It was a polymer, with no significant nutritive value, and was biologically inert, but was advertised as being able to increase the nutritive value of silage by enabling the cattle to digest more of the silage. The company accounted for VAT on the basis that the additive was zero-rated, and the Commissioners issued an assessment charging VAT on the sales of the additive. The tribunal dismissed the company's appeal, holding on the evidence that the additive was not itself a nutrient and thus was not within the definition of 'animal feeding stuffs'. *Chapman & Frearson Ltd, MAN/88/618 (VTD 4428).* (*Note.* Costs were awarded to the Commissioners in connection with the appearance of an expert witness.)

27.80   **Worms and maggots supplied with ornamental fish.** A married couple trading in partnership sold ornamental fish. With the fish they also supplied worms and maggots, which were used to feed the fish when in transit. They accepted that the ornamental fish were standard-rated, since they were not intended to be eaten, but in accounting for VAT they treated part of the consideration received as zero-rated, on the basis that it was attributable to the supply of the worms and maggots. The Commissioners issued an assessment charging tax on the whole of the amounts paid, and the tribunal dismissed the couple's appeal. The subject of each sale was the fish, rather than the worms and the maggots, and since the worms and maggots were not intended for resale, they did not qualify for zero-rating. *Pier Aquatics, MAN/90/1019 (VTD 7063).*

27.81   **Maggots sold from vending machines.** A company sold tins of maggots from vending machines. The maggots were intended to be used by fishermen as bait. The company treated its sales of the maggots as zero-rated, and the Commissioners issued an assessment charging tax on them. The company appealed, contending that the maggots were 'animal feeding stuffs' which were zero-rated under *VATA 1994,*

Sch 8, Group 1, General Item 2, since they were sold and used by fishermen to feed fish with a view to attracting them to an area where they could be caught. The tribunal rejected this contention and dismissed the appeal, holding that it was 'not the intrinsic nature of the item supplied which is relevant, but the purpose for which it is sold . . . in order to determine the nature of the supply, the purpose of the seller has to be looked at.' The company's purpose in selling the maggots was to enable its customers to catch the fish, rather than to feed the fish. *North Isles Shellfish Ltd*, 27.90 below, was distinguished, on the basis that the bait used in that case 'was not only intended for use in catching the lobsters but was also intended to be eaten by them once captured, to sustain them prior to sale'. The QB upheld this decision. Laddie J held that the fact that the maggots were edible did not mean that they fell within the definition of 'animal feeding stuffs'. In view of the way in which the maggots were supplied, they did not qualify for zero-rating. *Fluff Ltd (t/a Mag-It) v C & E Commrs, QB 11 May 2000, 2000 STI 752.*

27.82   **Whether animal food excluded from zero-rating by Excepted Item No 6.**   See the cases at 27.130 *et seq.* below.

27.83   **Charges made by stud farm—whether any part of consideration apportionable to zero-rated supplies of animal feeding stuffs.**   A farmer kept two stallions at stud. Mares served were usually kept at grass on the farm until it was considered that there had been a pregnancy. In such cases there was a single contract under which the owner of the mare paid a fixed 'service charge' of £100 plus a weekly amount for the time the mare was kept at the farm. He accounted for output tax on the service charges, but did not account for tax on the weekly charges. The Commissioners considered that the whole of the consideration was standard-rated, and assessed him accordingly. He appealed, contending that the weekly charge was for the keep of the mare and should be zero-rated as 'animal feeding stuffs'. The QB rejected this contention and upheld the assessment. Applying the test used in *British Railways Board*, 62.5 TRANSPORT, the farmer was supplying the single service of keeping the mare with everything that was involved in maintaining her 'in reasonable condition and safety'. *C & E Commrs v DD Scott, QB 1977, [1978] STC 191.*

27.84   *Scott*, 27.83 above, was applied in the similar case of *C & E Commrs v DW & MJ Bushby, QB 1978, [1979] STC 9.*

27.85   *Scott*, 27.83 above, and *Bushby*, 27.84 above, were applied in the similar case of *LE Barr, LON/96/780 (VTD 14529)*, and in *Banstead Manor Stud Ltd*, 37.1 INTERNATIONAL SERVICES.

27.86   **Casual grazing licences—whether any part of consideration apportionable to zero-rated supplies of animal feeding stuffs.**   See *JA King*, 39.35 LAND.

27.87   **Supply of grass feed for horses kept at livery.**   A partnership carried on a livery business. They advertised for customers to send them horses to be kept at livery. They invoiced their customers for supplies of grass to the animals, and did not account for output tax on these supplies, treating them as zero-rated. The Commissioners issued an assessment charging tax on the supplies, on the basis that the partnership was making a single standard-rated supply of the keep of animals. The tribunal allowed the partnership's appeal, distinguishing *Scott*, 27.83 above, and *Smith*, 27.89 below. The partnership did not operate a stud and, on the evidence, any additional services were undertaken as agents for the owners and thus did not affect the zero-rating of the supplies of grass. *RW & JR Fidler (t/a Holt Manor Farm Partners), LON/94/798A (VTD 12892).*

27.88   A similar decision, also distinguishing *Scott*, 27.83 above, and *Smith*, 27.89 below, was reached in *S & J Marczak (t/a Suzanne's Riding School), LON/94/1682A (VTD 13141).*

27.89 **Rearing and keeping of cattle—whether feeding of cattle constitutes separate supply.** A trader whose main activity was the rearing and keeping of other persons' heifers accounted for tax on the basis that part of the charges which he made were for a separate zero-rated supply of animal feeding stuffs. The Commissioners issued an assessment on the basis that the whole of his supplies were standard-rated. The tribunal upheld the assessment and dismissed the trader's appeal. *Scott*, 27.83 above, and *Bushby*, 27.84 above, applied. *ARM Smith, MAN/ 87/321 (VTD 2954).*

27.90 **Fish sold as lobster bait.** A company sold haddock and mackerel as lobster bait. It did not account for output tax on such sales, treating them as zero-rated animal feeding stuffs. The Commissioners issued an assessment charging output tax on the basis that the sales did not qualify for zero-rating. The company appealed. The tribunal allowed the appeal, holding on the evidence that the fish qualified for zero-rating under what is now *VATA 1994, Sch 8, Group 1, General Item 2*. The tribunal observed that 'in addition to enticing the lobster it was intended that the lobster should eat the fish as a start to and a part of the fattening process which continued whilst the lobster was in captivity. This is not a case of a poisoned bait but of supplying the animal with feeding stuff which had also assisted to entrap it'. (The tribunal also considered that the haddock and mackerel qualified for zero-rating under *General Item 1* as 'food of a kind used for human consumption', on the basis that the fish was edible and that 'the motive of the purchaser in obtaining the fish is irrelevant'.) *North Isles Shellfish Ltd, [1995] VATDR 415 (VTD 13083).* (*Note.* The tribunal's opinion that that 'the motive of the purchaser in obtaining the fish is irrelevant' was disapproved in the subsequent case of *Fluff Ltd (t/a Mag-It)*, 27.81 above, where the tribunal held that it was 'not the intrinsic nature of the item supplied which is relevant, but the purpose for which it is sold . . . in order to determine the nature of the supply, the purpose of the seller has to be looked at.')

MEANS OF PROPAGATION OF PLANTS (VATA 1994, Sch 8, Group 1, General Item 3)

27.91 **Kits for growing mushrooms.** A farming partnership supplied kits for growing mushrooms. Each kit comprised a bucket, a label and instruction leaflet, a growing medium infused with spawn, and peat, etc. It did not account for VAT on its supplies, treating them as zero-rated under what is now *VATA 1994, Sch 8, Group 1, General Item 3*. The tribunal held that the supplies had to be apportioned and that 40% of the consideration was standard-rated as referable to the bucket and label. The remaining 60% was attributable to the growing medium and the peat, and was zero-rated. *Cheshire Mushroom Farm, [1974] VATTR 87 (VTD 71).*

LIVE ANIMALS (VATA 1994, Sch 8, Group 1, General Item 4)

27.92 **Koi carp.** A fish farmer sold Koi carp (an ornamental type of fish originating in Japan). He did not account for VAT on these sales. The Commissioners issued an assessment charging tax on them, and the farmer appealed, contending that sales of fish were zero-rated. The tribunal dismissed the farmer's appeal, finding that the fish in question were sold for ornamental purposes, rather than to be eaten. There was no evidence that anyone had ever eaten a Koi carp, and that the fact that, in theory, they were edible was not conclusive. They were not marketed as food, and were not within the definition of 'food of a kind used for human consumption'. *JR Chalmers, LON/82/99 (VTD 1433).*

27.93 **Dinkelsbuhl carp.** A fish farmer did not account for VAT on sales of Dinkelsbuhl carp. The Commissioners issued an assessment charging tax on his sales, on the basis that the carp were sold for ornamental purposes rather than as food. The tribunal allowed the farmer's appeal, finding that eating carp was 'uncommon' but was not eccentric. The Commissioners appealed to the QB which quashed the decision and remitted the case to a new tribunal to be reheard, holding that the tribunal had misdirected itself in its reasoning. *C & E Commrs v RT Lawson-Tancred, QB [1988] STC 326.* (*Note.* There was no further public hearing of the appeal. Compare the subsequent case of *Fluff Ltd (t/a Mag-It)*, 27.81 above, where the tribunal held that it was 'not the intrinsic nature of the item supplied which is relevant, but the purpose for which it is sold . . . in order to determine the nature of the supply, the purpose of the seller has to be looked at.')

27.94   **Trout fishery supplying right to catch edible trout—whether part of consideration zero-rated.** A partnership which operated a trout fishery sold tickets which allowed customers to catch trout. It only accounted for output tax on part of the consideration. The Commissioners issued an assessment charging tax on the full amount of the ticket price, and the partnership appealed, contending that there were two separate supplies, namely a standard-rated supply of the right to fish and a zero-rated supply of the trout as food. The tribunal rejected this contention and dismissed the appeal, holding that as a matter of substance and reality all that the partnership supplied was the right to catch fish, which was a standard-rated supply. *Chalk Springs Fisheries, LON/86/706 (VTD 2518).*

27.95   The proprietor of a trout fishery charged anglers a total cost of £9.50 for a whole day, computed as £6.50 for the privilege of fishing and £3 for the cost of fish taken. The £3 cost of fish was, however, payable whether or not the angler caught any fish. The proprietor did not account for output tax on this £3, treating it as zero-rated, and the Commissioners issued an assessment on the basis that the whole of the £9.50 was subject to tax at the standard rate. The tribunal upheld the assessment and dismissed the proprietor's appeal, applying *Chalk Springs Fisheries*, 27.94 above. *RC Haynes, LON/87/624 (VTD 2948).*

ICE CREAM, ETC. (VATA 1994, Sch 8, Group 1, Excepted Item 1)

27.96   **Frozen desserts.** A company launched a range of frozen desserts. The Commissioners issued a ruling that the desserts did not qualify for zero-rating, since they were 'similar frozen products', within *VATA 1994, Sch 8, Group 1, Excepted Item 1*. The company appealed, contending that the term 'similar frozen products' should be construed as meaning similar to 'water ices' (the immediately preceding item in *Excepted Item 1*). The tribunal rejected this contention and dismissed the appeal, holding that the term 'similar frozen products' should be construed as referring to all the items in the list preceding it, including ice cream, ice lollies and frozen yoghurt as well as water ices. The tribunal observed that, as a matter of principle, and applying a statement of Sir Ernest Gowers in '*The Complete Plain Words*', 'commas are always put after each item in (a) series (of nouns or phrases) up to the last but one, but practice varies about putting a comma between the last one and the *and* introducing the last. Neither practice is wrong.' Accordingly, the tribunal concluded that 'no help is available in answering the question from a purely grammatical angle'. However, it appeared that 'the intention of *Excepted Item 1* is to deny zero-rating to certain iced products, be they cream-based or water-based. To achieve that result it is necessary to read *Excepted Item 1* as if it includes a comma after the phrase "water ices"'. *Ross Young Holdings Ltd, [1996] VATDR 230 (VTD 13972).*

27.97   **Frozen yoghurt.** A retail company sold a product described as 'soft frozen yoghurt'. When sold, it took the form of a liquid of high viscosity, with a temperature of between -1°C and -5°C. The Commissioners issued a ruling that sales of the product were standard-rated, since the product was 'frozen yoghurt', within *VATA 1994, Sch 8, Group 1, Excepted Item 1*. The company appealed, contending that at the time of sale the product was 'a liquid of high viscosity' which could not be described as 'frozen', and therefore qualified for zero-rating. The Ch D rejected this contention and dismissed the company's appeal, holding that the product was 'frozen yoghurt' and was therefore standard-rated. Hart J held that 'frozen yoghurt' should be construed as 'yoghurt reduced to a temperature below the freezing point of water'. *Meschia's Frozen Foods v C & E Commrs, Ch D 2000, [2001] STC 1.*

27.98   A company made wholesale supplies of frozen yoghurt to retailers. The yoghurt was supplied at a temperature of -18°C but was intended for consumption at -5°C. The Commissioners issued a ruling that sales of the product were standard-rated, since the product was 'frozen yoghurt', within *VATA 1994, Sch 8, Group 1, Excepted Item 1*. The company appealed, contending that the product was 'yoghurt unsuitable for immediate consumption when frozen', within *Sch 8, Group 1, Overriding Item 1*, and therefore qualified for zero-rating. The tribunal rejected this contention and dismissed the company's appeal, holding that the product was 'frozen yoghurt' and was therefore standard-rated. The tribunal observed that 'there is a distinction between food which is consumed for the purpose of nourishment and food which is consumed as ... an "amusement or entertainment"'. Ordinary yoghurt falls into the former category, frozen yoghurt into the latter.' At the time the yoghurt in question was supplied to retailers, it had 'passed the point of no return: the added stabilisers and emulsifiers have rendered the yoghurt unsuitable for use as "nutritional" yoghurt and stamped it indelibly with the characteristic of "amusement or entertainment" yoghurt, which can only be eaten frozen.' Furthermore, 'a yoghurt which is designed and intended to be eaten frozen, which will be eaten frozen, and which is not suitable to be eaten unfrozen, cannot be described as "unsuitable for immediate consumption when frozen" simply because it has at one point been frozen down to a temperature at which it happens to be inedible, for the purpose of supply to a customer who will not in any case be consuming it'. *Tennessee Secret (UK) Ltd, LON/99/1328 (VTD 16945).*

CONFECTIONERY, ETC. (VATA 1994, Sch 8, Group 1, Excepted Item 2)

27.99   **Sweetened popcorn.**   In a purchase tax case, the QB held that sweetened popcorn was within the definition of 'confectionery'. *C & E Commrs v Clark's Cereal Products Ltd, QB 1965, [1968] 3 All ER 778.*

27.100   A similar decision was reached in *C & E Commrs v Popcorn House Ltd, QB 1965, [1968] 3 All ER 782.*

27.101   **Toffee apples.**   In a purchase tax case, the Ch D held that toffee apples were not within the definition of 'confectionery'. Cross J observed that 'despite the toffee coating, the apple is still there as a live fruit which has not been tampered with in the same way as a dried or roasted almond or raisin that has been coated in sugar or chocolate and which is not a live fruit'. Furthermore, the fact that 'drained, glacé or crystallised fruits' were specifically included in the statutory definition of confectionery indicated that toffee apples were not to be treated as confectionery. *Candy Maid Confections Ltd & Others v C & E Commrs, Ch D [1968] 3 All ER 773.* (*Note.* The Commissioners accept that, following this decision, toffee apples are zero-rated for VAT—see Customs' VAT Manual, Part 7, chapter 1, part A, section 4.11(e).)

27.102   **Biscuits for use in ice-cream trade.**   A company manufactured biscuits for the ice-cream trade, suitable for eating only in conjunction with ice-cream. Most of its sales were of wafers and cones, which were agreed to be zero-rated. However, it also manufactured 'nougat wafers', which comprised two wafer biscuits with a sandwich filling of albumen, glucose and sugar, and were lightly coated with a powder comprising sugar and skimmed milk powder. The Commissioners issued a ruling that the 'nougat wafers' were confectionery and thus were standard-rated. The tribunal allowed the company's appeal, holding that, since the products were baked, they were not within the definition of confectionery. *Boni Faccenda Ltd, [1975] VATTR 155 (VTD 196)*.

27.103   **'Chocolate Dundees'.**   A company manufactured a product known as 'Chocolate Dundees', which were circular and the base of which comprised 55.5% flour, 17% fat and 19.7% sugar. They were baked, partly covered with chocolate, and individually wrapped. The Commissioners issued a ruling that the 'Chocolate Dundees' were confectionery and thus did not qualify for zero-rating. The tribunal dismissed the company's appeal, finding that the 'Chocolate Dundees' were 'biscuits wholly or partly covered with chocolate', and were therefore confectionery and standard-rated. *Adams Foods Ltd, [1983] VATTR 280 (VTD 1514)*.

27.104   **'Chocolate Marzipan Walnuts'.**   A company manufactured a product known as 'Chocolate Marzipan Walnuts', which had a meringue base to which was added marzipan, walnuts, buttercream and a chocolate coating. The Commissioners issued a ruling that the products were confectionery and therefore excluded from zero-rating. The company appealed, contending that the products were cakes and were therefore zero-rated. The tribunal accepted the company's contention and allowed the appeal. *Goodfellow & Steven Ltd, EDN/87/10 (VTD 2453)*.

27.105   **'Zebra Shortcake Rings and Fingers'.**   A company manufactured biscuits, sold in transparent packets of five or six and known as 'Zebra Shortcake Rings' and 'Zebra Shortcake Fingers'. The top of the biscuits included thin stripes of chocolate. The chocolate comprised about 1% of the total content of the biscuits. The Commissioners issued a ruling that the products were standard-rated through being 'biscuits ... partly covered with chocolate'. The company appealed, contending that the chocolate was merely for decorative purposes and should not be regarded as providing a covering. The tribunal dismissed the company's appeal, holding that the fact that there was some chocolate on the biscuits meant that they were excluded from zero-rating. *North Cheshire Foods Ltd, MAN/86/216 (VTD 2709)*.

27.106   **'Caramel Shortcake'.**   A partnership manufactured a product known as 'Caramel Shortcake', which consisted of biscuit crumbs mixed with margarine, condensed milk, syrup and chocolate. The Commissioners issued a ruling that the product was confectionery, on the basis that it was a biscuit 'wholly or partly covered with chocolate'. The partnership appealed, contending that the product was a cake and was therefore zero-rated. The tribunal dismissed the appeal, holding that the product was not a cake and was within the definition of 'confectionery'. *In Good Taste, EDN/88/30 (VTD 2956)*. (*Note.* See, however, the subsequent decision in *Marks & Spencer plc*, 27.107 below. Following that decision, the Commissioners now accept that caramel shortcake is zero-rated—see Customs' VAT Manual, Part 7, chapter 1, part A, section 4.7(a).)

27.107   **'Caramel Shortcake Slices'.**   A company retailed a product named 'Caramel Shortcake Slices'. The shortcake base of this product contained 50% flour, 33% butter, and 12.5% sugar. This base constituted 52% of the product, the remaining 48% comprising caramel and chocolate. The product was baked, and had a maximum life of 25 days. The Commissioners issued a ruling that the product constituted confectionery, and was therefore not eligible for zero-rating. The company appealed, contending that the product was a cake and was therefore zero-rated. The tribunal allowed the company's appeal, holding on the evidence that the product was a cake. *Marks & Spencer plc, LON/88/1316Y (VTD 4510).*

27.108   **'Jaffa Cakes'.**   A company manufactured a product known as 'Jaffa Cakes'. The product consisted of a small round piece of sponge cake, on which was a small amount of sweet orange jam, and which was entirely covered by a thin layer of chocolate. The Commissioners issued a ruling that the 'Jaffa Cakes' were biscuits covered with chocolate, falling within what is now *VATA 1994, Sch 8, Group 1, Excepted Item 2,* and were therefore standard-rated. The company appealed, contending that the 'Jaffa Cakes' were cakes rather than biscuits, and were therefore zero-rated. The tribunal accepted this contention and allowed the appeal, observing that the ingredients of the sponge part of the 'Jaffa Cake' were 'virtually the same' as the ingredients of a traditional sponge cake. The 'Jaffa Cakes' were moist and had the texture of a sponge cake, and the sponge was a substantial part of the product in bulk and texture, rather than simply a base for the jam and chocolate. *United Biscuits (UK) Ltd, LON/91/160 (VTD 6344).*

27.109   **Carob-coated wafer biscuits.**   A company manufactured a product consisting of thin wafer biscuits with a sweet creamy filling and a carob coating. The Commissioners issued a ruling that the product was confectionery and was not eligible for zero-rating. The tribunal dismissed the company's appeal, holding that the product was within the definition of 'confectionery'. *E Round & Son Ltd, MAN/85/165 (VTD 2069).*

27.110   *E Round & Son Ltd,* 27.109 above, was applied in the similar case of *WH Cotterell, MAN/89/560 (VTD 4573).*

27.111   **'Swedish Snowballs'.**   A company manufactured a product known as 'Swedish Snowballs'. They were sweet, produced by cooking, and described as similar to marshmallow. The Commissioners issued a ruling that they were confectionery, and the tribunal upheld this decision. *Swedish Snowball Production Ltd, MAN/86/305 (VTD 2311).*

27.112   **Fruit and nut mixtures.**   A company manufactured packets of 'Big D Tropical Fruits and Nuts', containing a mixture of raisins, peanuts, coconut chips, banana chips and pineapple pieces. The banana chips and pineapple pieces contained added sugar. The added sugar comprised about 10% of the finished product by weight. The Commissioners issued a ruling that the product was confectionery and was standard-rated. The tribunal allowed the company's appeal in part, holding that the raisins, peanuts and coconut chips qualified for zero-rating, and that the consideration should be apportioned. *Smiths Foods Ltd, [1983] VATTR 21 (VTD 1346).* (*Note.* The Commissioners now accept that fruit and nut mixtures may be wholly zero-rated if the weight of standard-rated items (e.g. sweetened fruits, pieces of chocolate or roasted nuts) does not exceed 25% of their total net weight. See *Notice No 701/14/97, para 4.2.*)

27.113   **Diet bars.**   A company imported and supplied 'diet bars', which included peanuts, bran and other ingredients, and were marketed as a slimming aid to replace meals. The Commissioners issued a ruling that the diet bars were confectionery and therefore standard-rated. The tribunal allowed the company's appeal, finding that, although the bars were edible, they were not palatable. The high cost and the taste would preclude them being eaten for pleasure. Only a negligible amount of sweetener was included. Accordingly the bars were not confectionery, and were zero-rated. *Texas Touch Dallas Diet Ltd, [1984] VATTR 115 (VTD 1664).*

27.114   **Cereal bars.**   The Commissioners issued a ruling that two varieties of cereal bar were confectionery, and were therefore excluded from zero-rating. The tribunal dismissed the manufacturers' appeal, finding that the bars contained a substantial quantity of honey. Accordingly they were items of 'sweetened prepared food ... normally eaten with the fingers' within the definition of confectionery in what is now *VATA 1994, Sch 8, Group 1, Note 5. W Jordans (Cereals) Ltd, LON/88/514Z (VTD 3275)*.

27.115   **Energy bars.**   A trader imported 'energy bars' from the USA. The bars contained fructose, glucose, oat bran, brown rice, syrup, peanut butter and honey. They were marketed for sale to people competing in endurance sports such as marathons and triathlons. They were priced at £1.50 per bar. The Commissioners issued a ruling that the bars constituted confectionery, and were therefore excluded from zero-rating. The tribunal dismissed the trader's appeal, finding that the bars were 'an item of sweetened prepared food which is normally eaten with the fingers', and were thus within the definition of confectionery. *EJ Huczek, MAN/92/507 (VTD 8850)*.

27.116   **'Horlicks' and 'Lucozade' tablets.**   A company manufactured 'Horlicks' and 'Lucozade' tablets. It did not account for VAT on sales of these, treating them as zero-rated. In 1991 the Commissioners issued a ruling that the tablets were not eligible for zero-rating, since they were 'sweetened prepared food which is normally eaten with the fingers' and thus within the definition of confectionery in what is now *VATA 1994, Sch 8, Group 1, Note 5*. The company appealed, contending that the tablets should not be treated as confectionery, since they were not deliberately 'sweetened'. The tribunal allowed the appeal, holding that the 'Horlicks' tablets were not 'sweetened' on the basis that, although they contained some sugar, they did not taste sweet; and that the 'Lucozade' tablets were not sweetened on the basis that they consisted primarily of maltodextrin and dextrose, which were themselves sweet food products which were not the subject of any further sweetening, whereas the reference to 'sweetened prepared food' in *Note 5* should be construed as referring to items which had been deliberately made sweeter. *Smith Kline Beecham plc, [1993] VATTR 219 (VTD 10222)*.

27.117   **Marshmallow cones.**   A company sold cones (of the type commonly used to contain ice-cream) which were filled with marshmallow and which had a sugar topping. The Commissioners issued a ruling that the cones were standard-rated 'confectionery'. The tribunal dismissed the company's appeal, holding that the cones were confectionery rather than biscuits, and were therefore standard-rated. *Kathy's Kones Ltd (No 1), MAN/93/994 (VTD 11705)*. (*Note.* For a subsequent appeal by the same company, see 27.118 below. Following the subsequent decision, the Commissioners now accept that the product in question is zero-rated—see Customs' VAT Manual, Part 7, chapter 1, part A, section 4.8(b).)

27.118   The company in the case noted at 27.117 above appealed against a subsequent ruling with regard to the same product. Its appeal was heard by a differently-constituted tribunal which declined to follow the previous decision, observing that the 1975 decision in *Boni Faccenda Ltd*, 27.102 above, where nougat wafers were held to be zero-rated biscuits, had not been cited in that case. The tribunal found that the cones were 'eaten by children as if they were biscuits' and concluded that 'the man in the street would ... regard the cones as biscuits ... notwithstanding the earlier tribunal decision to the contrary'. Accordingly the tribunal allowed the company's appeal. *Kathy's Kones Ltd (No 2), LON/96/1726 (VTD 14880)*. (*Note.* Following this decision, the Commissioners now accept that the product in question is zero-rated—see Customs' VAT Manual, Part 7, chapter 1, part A, section 4.8(b). Compare, however, the subsequent decision in *Marcantonio Foods Ltd*, 27.119 below, where similar cones were held not to be 'biscuits'.)

27.119   **Waffle cones lined with chocolate.**   A company manufactured waffle cones, similar to ice-cream cones, but lined with chocolate. The Commissioners issued a ruling that the cones were standard-rated, on the basis that they were 'biscuits wholly or partly covered with chocolate', within *Excepted Item 2*. The company appealed, contending that the cones were sold as incomplete products, to be used as edible containers for desserts or ice-cream, and were not 'biscuits'. The tribunal accepted this contention and allowed the appeal. *Kathy's Kones Ltd (No 2)*, 27.118 above, was distinguished on the basis that the product in that case 'was not made for use in combination with any other food products, but was made for consumption on its own'. The tribunal held that 'one of the salient characteristics of a biscuit is that it is eaten in the hand, and in the case of a sweet biscuit, it is eaten on its own'. *Marcantonio Foods Ltd, LON/97/602 (VTD 15486)*.

27.120   **Spherical wafers with hazelnut filling and coating.**   A company manufactured two types of small spherical wafers. The wafers were filled with a soft hazelnut filling; both types were covered with chopped hazelnuts and one of the types was also covered in light meringue. Hazelnuts comprised 28% of the product, while 27% consisted of sugar, 15% was vegetable fat and 10% was vegetable oil. The products were individually wrapped, and had to be consumed within about eight months of manufacture. If they were exposed to the air, the wafers would absorb the filling and become too soft. The Commissioners issued a ruling that the products were confectionery. The company appealed, contending that the products were 'biscuits' and qualified for zero-rating. The tribunal accepted the company's contentions and allowed the company's appeal (by a 2–1 majority, with the chairman dissenting). The CA upheld the majority tribunal decision as one of fact. The tribunal had correctly determined that the question of law was whether the products were biscuits, and had correctly ruled that the word 'biscuit' should be given its ordinary meaning. Accordingly, the tribunal decision was a finding of fact which could not be overturned on appeal. Hutchison LJ observed that 'there is no ideal concept, conformity with every aspect of which is necessary before an aspiring manufacturer can call his product a biscuit. It is a question of fact in each case whether the article in question can properly and sensibly be said to be a biscuit.' *C & E Commrs v Ferrero UK Ltd, CA [1997] STC 881*.

BEVERAGES (VATA 1994, Sch 8, Group 1, Excepted Item 4)

Note. The scope of what is now *Excepted Item No 4* was extended by the *VAT (Beverages) Order 1993 (SI 1993 No 2498)*, which took effect from 1 December 1993. Before that date, *Excepted Item No 4* had referred to 'manufactured beverages', rather than simply to 'beverages'.

27.121   **'Kosher' meals including fruit juice—whether entirely zero-rated.**   A company supplied prepacked meals, which it certified as 'Kosher' (prepared in accordance with Jewish ecclesiastical law). It treated its supplies of these meals as entirely zero-rated. In 1987 the Commissioners issued a ruling that, as the meals contained fruit juice, which was excluded from zero-rating by what is now *VATA 1994, Sch 8, Group 1, Excepted Item 4*, the supplies were deemed to be mixed supplies and part of the consideration had to be treated as standard-rated. The tribunal dismissed the company's appeal against this decision. *Hermolis & Co Ltd, [1989] VATTR 199 (VTD 4137)*.

27.122   **'Bio-Light'.**   A company manufactured a product named 'Bio-Light', which was an opaque brown fluid sold by chemists and health food shops. The product was packaged in small bottles, and was intended to be diluted with water before consumption. It was described in the company's advertising as 'a natural detoxifying and slimming food supplement'. The company did not account for tax on sales of the product. The Commissioners issued a ruling that the product was standard-rated, on the basis that it was a 'manufactured beverage' and was excluded from zero-rating by what is now *VATA 1994, Sch 8, Group 1, Excepted Item 4*. The company appealed, contending that the product was a food supplement which should not be treated as a 'beverage', since it was designed to be sipped slowly at intervals, and would act as a violent laxative if drunk by the glassful. The tribunal allowed the appeal, observing that the product had an unpleasant taste and would not 'be consumed for pleasure', and holding that it was not within the definition of 'beverage'. The tribunal chairman observed that a beverage was a liquid that was 'characteristically taken to increase bodily liquid levels, to slake the thirst, to fortify or to give pleasure'. *Bioconcepts Ltd, LON/92/2852 (VTD 11287)*.

27.123   **Drink containing water, fibre and fruit juice.**   A company manufactured and distributed a drink containing water, fibrous extracts and fruit juice. The fibrous extracts comprised 20% of the total product. The drink was more expensive than standard fruit juice drinks, being priced at 69p for 250 ml. The Commissioners issued a ruling that the product was a 'beverage' and thus excluded from zero-rating. The company appealed, contending that the inclusion of significant quantities of fibre meant that the product was outside the definition of 'beverage', so that the supplies should be zero-rated. The tribunal rejected this contention and dismissed the appeal. On the evidence, 'the consistency was not that of syrup but of a slightly thickened fruit juice'. The product was packaged and marketed as a drink, and was within the definition of a 'beverage'. *Bioconcepts Ltd*, 27.122 above, distinguished. *Smith Kline Beecham plc, LON/95/1704A (VTD 13674)*.

27.124   **Powder for making sports drinks.**   See *SIS (Science in Sport) Ltd*, 27.68 above.

27.125   **Spices for making mulled wine—whether within Excepted Item No 4.**   A company sold packs of spices, designed to be used for making mulled wine. The Commissioners issued a ruling that the packs were within *VATA 1994, Sch 8, Group 1, Excepted Item No 4*, as 'products for the preparation of beverages', and were therefore standard-rated. The company appealed, contending that the packs were not within *Excepted Item No 4*, and qualified for zero-rating. The tribunal accepted this contention and allowed the appeal, holding that the words 'products for the preparation of beverages' had 'to be construed "*eiusdem generis*" with the preceding words "syrups, concentrates, essences, powders, crystals" and do not comprehend every kind of product for the preparation of beverages but only those which perform the same function as syrups, concentrates, essences, etc. ... what is meant by those words is something from which a beverage is made by reconstitution, dilution or infusion and not just any ingredient of the finished drink. The spices which go into mulled wine, whilst a most important ingredient, do not ... fulfil anything like that kind of function.' (The chairman also observed that 'the principles of European law ... do not, in my view, inhibit or constrain a court here into adopting an unnecessarily narrow interpretation of the statutory provisions in order to limit the scope of relief'.) *McCormick (UK) plc, LON/97/1193 (VTD 15202)*.

27.126   **Fruit-flavoured 'iced tea'—whether within Sch 8, Group 1, Overriding Item No 4.**   A company manufactured four varieties of fruit-flavoured 'iced tea'. Tea powder comprised less than 2% of the products, the main ingredients of which were water, glucose syrup and citric acid. The Commissioners issued a ruling that supplies of the products were standard-rated, being excluded from zero-rating by *VATA 1994, Sch 8, Group 1, Excepted Item No 4*. The company appealed, contending that the products were within the definition of 'tea' and so were zero-rated under *VATA 1994, Sch 8, Group 1, Overriding Item No 4*. The tribunal rejected this contention and dismissed the appeal, holding that the products were not 'tea pure and simple in the ordinary use of the term ... in terms of taste and smell the fruit flavouring predominates over the tea'. The fact that the products were marketed as 'tea' was not conclusive. *Snapple Beverage Corporation, LON/94/1991A (VTD 13690)*.

27.127 **'Norfolk Punch'—whether within Sch 8, Group 1, Overriding Item No 4.** A company manufactured a beverage called 'Norfolk Punch', which contained a variety of herbs as well as substantial quantities of sugar and honey. The Commissioners issued a ruling that sales of the product were standard-rated by virtue of *VATA 1994, Sch 8, Group 1, Excepted Item No 4.* The company appealed, contending that the beverage was a 'similar product' to herbal tea, and was therefore zero-rated by virtue of *VATA 1994, Sch 8, Group 1, Overriding Item No 4.* The tribunal rejected this contention and dismissed the appeal, holding on the evidence that, although it contained a variety of herbs, the beverage was not a 'similar product' to herbal tea. The tribunal observed that the common characteristic of tea, maté and herbal teas was 'that they are drinks obtained by a straightforward process of infusing leaves, without more' and were 'not the products of a manufacturing process'. The product at issue, however, was 'the result of a fairly complicated manufacturing process involving several stages and with quite a large variety of ingredients'. *Orchid Drinks Co Ltd, MAN/95/2419 (VTD 14222)*.

27.128 **'Rivella'—whether within Sch 8, Group 1, Overriding Item No 6.** A company manufactured a beverage called 'Rivella', which was made from lactoserum but contained no milk protein, and could therefore be drunk by people who were allergic to cows' milk. Lactoserum comprised 35% of the beverage, while water comprised more than 50% of it. The Commissioners issued a ruling that sales of the product were standard-rated by virtue of *VATA 1994, Sch 8, Group 1, Excepted Item No 4.* The company appealed, contending that the beverage was made from extracts of milk, and was therefore zero-rated by virtue of *VATA 1994, Sch 8, Group 1, Overriding Item No 6.* The tribunal accepted this contention and allowed the appeal. *Rivella (UK) Ltd, LON/99/562 (VTD 16382)*.

PET FOOD, ETC. (VATA 1994, Sch 8, Group 1, Excepted Item 6)

27.129 **Liver brawn sold for cats and dogs.** A couple who operated a petrol station also sold rolls of liver brawn, weighing about 2lbs each and marketed as 'dog and cat food'. The couple did not account for output tax on these supplies. The Commissioners issued an assessment on the basis that the food was pet food which was excluded from zero-rating. The couple appealed, contending that the brawn should be zero-rated because it was suitable for pigs and poultry as well as for pet dogs and cats. The tribunal dismissed the appeal, holding on the evidence that the brawn was 'obviously stocked for sale to passing motorists who would have an interest in purchasing the same for their dogs or cats' and observing that 'the nature of the packaging was appropriate for small purchases by owners of one or two pets, rather than by farmers who could be expected to purchase in bulk'. *E & J Crooks, EDN/83/65 (VTD 1602)*.

27.130 **1lb packs of meat—whether 'packaged pet food'.** A company sold meat, advertised as pet food, in 1lb packs. The Commissioners issued a ruling that the sales were of 'packaged pet food' and were therefore excluded from zero-rating by what is now *VATA 1994, Sch 8, Group 1, Excepted Item No 6.* The tribunal upheld this decision. *Freezerman (UK) Ltd, LON/85/454 (VTD 2061)*.

27.131 **Raw meat sold in plastic bags—whether 'pet food'.** A company which operated a licensed slaughterhouse sold raw meat in plastic bags. It advertised the meat as pet food, but its customers included zoos, greyhound trainers, animal experimental establishments, security organisations (for guard dogs), dog breeders, farmers (for sheep dogs), and pet shop owners as well as private individuals. The

Commissioners issued an assessment charging VAT on the sales, on the basis that it was advertised as pet food and thus was excluded from zero-rating by what is now *VATA 1994, Sch 8, Group 1, Excepted Item No 6*. The tribunal allowed the company's appeal in part, observing that a pet was an animal 'which is kept primarily as an object of affection', and holding on the evidence that most of the company's supplies were not 'primarily intended for pets', but were 'produced and offered for sale ... as foods for animals generally' and thus were not excluded from zero-rating. *Freezerman (UK) Ltd*, 27.130 above, was not followed, and was implicitly disapproved. The appeal was adjourned for the parties to agree figures. *Popes Lane Pet Food Supplies Ltd, [1986] VATTR 221 (VTD 2186)*. (*Notes.* (1) There was no further public hearing of the appeal. (2) For the Commissioners' practice following this decision, see Customs' VAT Manual, Part 7, chapter 1, part D, section 3.2.)

27.132   **Minced chicken—whether 'pet food'.**   A company sold minced chicken, as food for animals, in 1lb and 5lb packs. It did not account for VAT, considering that the sales were zero-rated under what is now *VATA 1994, Sch 8, Group 1, General Item No 2*. The Commissioners issued an assessment on the basis that the sales were of pet food and thus excluded from zero-rating by what is now *VATA 1994, Sch 8, Group 1, Excepted Item No 6*. The company appealed, contending that most of the minced chicken was sold to owners of working dogs, including the local police force and greyhound trainers. The tribunal allowed the appeal, holding that the minced chicken was not sold as pet food, and was therefore zero-rated. *Popes Lane Pet Food Supplies Ltd*, 27.131 above, applied. *Norman Riding Poultry Farm Ltd, [1989] VATTR 124 (VTD 3726)*.

27.133   **Meat sold as dog food—whether 'pet food'.**   A partnership sold meat as dog food from a market stall and from a nearby shop. The meat was not fit for human consumption. The partnership treated the sales of the meat as zero-rated, but the Commissioners issued an assessment on the basis that the meat was sold as pet food and was therefore standard-rated. The partnership appealed, contending that most of the meat was sold to owners of 'working dogs' such as guard dogs and greyhounds. The tribunal allowed the appeal in part, holding that all the sales from the market stall were zero-rated but that the sales from the shop should be apportioned between zero-rated sales to owners of pets and standard-rated sales to owners of working dogs. The appeal was adjourned in the hope that the parties could agree an apportionment. *LJ & H Norgate (t/a Dog's Dinner), LON/89/1221Z (VTD 5241)*. (*Note.* There was no further public hearing of the appeal.)

27.134   A partnership sold frozen meat, intended as dog food, from a shop. Above the freezer from which the meat was sold was a handwritten notice stating 'frozen pet food'. The partnership did not account for output tax on such sales, treating them as zero-rated. The Commissioners issued a ruling that the sales should have been treated as standard-rated, on the basis that they were supplies of pet food and thus were excluded from zero-rating by what is now *VATA 1994, Sch 8, Group 1, Excepted Item 6*. The partnership appealed, contending that some of the sales were to owners of working dogs rather than to owners of pets. The tribunal held that all sales to the general public were standard-rated, since the effect of the notice by the freezer was that the food was being advertised for sale as pet food. However, some of the sales were in response to orders placed by regular customers, and in such cases the effect of the notice was 'insignificant'. The tribunal adjourned the appeal in the hope that the parties could agree an apportionment. *P Peters & K P Riddles (t/a Mill Lane Farm Shop), LON/94/1221 (VTD 12937)*. (*Note.* There was no further public hearing of the appeal.)

27.135   **Rabbit food—whether 'packaged pet food'.**   The proprietor of a pet shop did not account for VAT on sales of rabbit food. Some of this food was sold in 4lb bags, while some was kept in a large container, and was only weighed and placed into a bag when requested by a customer. The Commissioners issued an assessment charging tax on these supplies, and the proprietor appealed, contending that the supplies were zero-rated. The tribunal allowed the appeal in part. On the evidence, it was accepted that the food was sold for consumption by rabbits which were kept as pets. It followed that it was excluded from zero-rating by what is now *VATA 1994, Sch 8, Group 1, Excepted Item No 6* if it was 'packaged', but was not so excluded if it was not packaged. Applying the wording in *Notice No 705/21/86*, the food could only be regarded as packaged where it had been placed into a 4lb bag prior to being sold. Putting loose food into a container at the point of sale did not constitute the packaging of that food. *B Beresford, MAN/92/99 (VTD 9673)*. (*Note*. The Commissioners now accept that, since 85% of rabbits kept in the UK are reared for food, rather than kept as pets, 'rabbit food sold in any quantity is only standard-rated if it is supplied, packaged, specifically for pet rabbits'—see Customs' VAT Manual, Part 7, chapter 1, part D, section 3.3(d).)

27.136   **Nuts sold as bird food.**   A firm operated a leisure garden which contained several caged birds. It sold nuts which visitors could use to feed the birds. It did not account for output tax on its sales of these nuts. The Commissioners issued an assessment charging tax on the sales, and the firm appealed, contending that the sales should be treated as zero-rated. The tribunal dismissed the appeal, holding that the nuts were 'packaged foods (not being pet foods) for birds other than poultry or game' and were therefore excluded from zero-rating by what is now *VATA 1994, Sch 8, Group 1, Excepted Item No 6. Merley Bird Gardens, LON/92/2221 (VTD 12426)*. (*Note*. See now *Notice 701/15/95, para 16*, and compare the subsequent decision in *Hardman*, 45.18 PAYMENT OF TAX.)

28   Fuel and Power

Note. Until 31 March 1993, supplies of fuel and power were zero-rated subject to the detailed conditions laid down in *VATA 1983, Sch 5, Group 7*. This provision had been substituted by *FA 1989, s 21* in relation to supplies made on or after 1 July 1990, to restrict zero-rating to supplies for domestic use or use by a charity otherwise than in the course or furtherance of a business. Cases relating to supplies before that date should be read in the light of this change. Supplies of fuel and power for domestic and charitable use were charged at 8% from 1 April 1994 to 31 August 1997 and at 5% from 1 September 1997.

28.1	**Supply of cylinders for butane gas.** A company supplied butane gas through authorised dealers. The customer entered into a standard 'Cylinder Refill Authority Agreement', on completion of which, and on payment of £5, he was supplied with a cylinder. When empty, the cylinder could be exchanged for a filled one on payment of £1 (or the price for gas current at the time). The cylinders remained the property of the company. The company did not account for output tax on its receipts, treating them as zero-rated. The Commissioners issued an assessment on the basis that only £1 of the £5 was eligible for zero-rating, the remaining £4 being for the supply of services relating to the cylinder and being standard-rated. The tribunal dismissed the company's appeal, holding that the £4 related to a standard-rated supply of services. *Calor Gas Ltd, [1973] VATTR 205 (VTD 47).*
28.2	**Coin-operated washing machines in launderette.** See *Mander Laundries Ltd*, 65.1 ZERO-RATING: MISCELLANEOUS.
28.3	**Coin-operated special lighting in club billiards room.** A members' club had a billiards room with three tables for billiards or snooker. Those using it obtained lighting over the tables by inserting coins in a meter in the room. It did not account for output tax on the takings, treating them as zero-rated. The Commissioners issued an assessment charging tax on them and the tribunal dismissed the club's appeal, holding that the supplies were standard-rated because the cost of the electricity used was only a small proportion of the money inserted, which was paid for the supply of facilities for playing billiards or snooker. *Washwood Heath & Ward End Conservative and Unionist Club Ltd, BIR/73/12 (VTD 50).*
28.4	A club, incorporated as a company limited by guarantee, provided its members with facilities for playing squash and lawn tennis. The squash courts and some of the lawn tennis courts were equipped with artificial lighting, operated by prepayment meters. Members using these courts paid a booking fee and a fee for using the meters, as well as inserting coins in the meters. The Commissioners issued an assessment made on the basis that the coins inserted in the meters were consideration for using the courts and chargeable at the standard rate. The tribunal dismissed the company's appeal, holding that, applying the test used in *British Railways Board*, 62.5 TRANSPORT, the meter payment was for the supply of the facility to enjoy the game, rather than simply for the supply of electricity. *St Anne's-on-Sea Lawn Tennis Club Ltd, [1977] VATTR 229 (VTD 434).*
28.5	**Electricity provided in holiday accommodation.** A husband and wife who supplied self-catering holiday accommodation took over the running of a hotel. They charged their visitors for food and accommodation and, in accounting for VAT, sought to attribute part of their takings to the supply of electricity, which was zero-rated. The Commissioners raised an assessment on the basis that the supplies actually made were of food and accommodation, and were entirely standard-rated. The tribunal upheld the assessment and dismissed the couple's appeal. *Lt Col TJ & Mrs ST Pine-Coffin, LON/83/367 (VTD 1620).*

28.6   A company provided holiday accommodation in chalets and static caravans. It charged £10 per week in respect of gas and electricity, neither of which were metered. The Commissioners assessed the company on the basis that the charge was standard-rated. The company's appeal was dismissed. The supply of the gas and electricity was provided as part of a composite supply and the charge made for it bore no relation to the amounts actually used. *Hazelwood Caravans & Chalets Ltd, [1985] VATTR 179 (VTD 1923).*

28.7   *Hazelwood Caravans & Chalets Ltd*, 28.6 above, was followed in the similar case of *CMC (Preston) Ltd, MAN/88/78 (VTD 3858).*

28.8   **Electricity provided at site for touring caravans.** *Hazelwood Caravans & Chalets Ltd*, 28.6 above, and *CMC (Preston) Ltd*, 28.7 above, were distinguished in a subsequent case where the owners of a caravan site offered the use of electricity for a standard charge of £1.50 per day. Customers had to use their own caravans, none being provided by the owners of the site, whereas in *Hazelwood* the accommodation was in caravans owned by the company. Most customers occupied the site for a week or less, whereas in *Hazelwood* and *CMC (Preston)* many customers stayed for long periods. The tribunal held that the electricity supplied to the caravan owners was a separate supply, rather than a notional allocation of part of an inclusive rent, and that the payments for the electricity were therefore zero-rated. *J Adams, AC Woskett & Partners, LON/91/2182Z (VTD 9647).*

28.9   **Electricity provided in sheltered housing.** A housing association provided sheltered accommodation to tenants. It made a separate charge in respect of electricity used for heating. The Commissioners issued a ruling that the supplies of electricity were part of a single supply of accommodation which was exempt from VAT. The association appealed, contending that the electricity was the subject of a separate supply which was chargeable to VAT at the reduced rate of 8%. The tribunal accepted this contention and allowed the appeal, observing that there was 'a long-standing practice of separate charge and indeed separate payment', rather than a single inclusive rent. *Adams Woskett & Partners*, 28.8 above, applied. *Suffolk Heritage Housing Association Ltd, LON/94/2563 (VTD 13713).*

28.10   **Supplies of charcoal.** A married couple supplied charcoal to retailers. They failed to account for output tax on these supplies. The Commissioners issued an assessment charging tax on the supplies, and the couple appealed, contending that the supplies should be treated as zero-rated. The tribunal dismissed the appeal, holding that the supplies did not qualify for zero-rating since they were intended for resale by the recipients. Accordingly they were excluded from zero-rating by what is now *VATA 1994, Sch A1 para 2(b). Mr & Mrs J Wyld (t/a Wyldwood Coppice), LON/93/3007A (VTD 12420).*

29 Gold

29.1 A gold dealer (S) had agreed to supply a company (C) with quantities of 9–carat gold, and had issued invoices accordingly, but had in some cases delivered fine gold instead of 9–carat gold. In such cases C had arranged for the gold to be converted into 9–carat gold, but S had unilaterally sent C a set of substitute invoices and credit notes, describing the supplies as being of fine gold. C had refused to accept the substitute invoices and credit notes, but S had adjusted his returns on the basis that he was not required to account for output tax on the disputed transactions. The Commissioners issued three assessments cancelling the adjustments (and also charging tax on a number of other transactions where S had failed to account for tax). S appealed, contending that the effect of what is now *VATA 1994, s 55* was that he was not required to account for tax on his supplies of fine gold to C, and that the assessments were not made to the best of the Commissioners' judgment. The tribunal rejected these contentions and upheld the assessments in principle (while reducing one of them by a small amount). The tribunal held that, as S had agreed to supply C with 9–carat gold, he was required to account for output tax on the transactions in question. The effect of the agreement between C and S was that what is now *VATA 1994, s 55* 'never had application in relation to the supplies in issue. VAT was correctly charged and paid in respect of all the supplies to (C) described as relating to 9–carat gold.' C had been entitled to refuse to accept the substitute invoices and credit notes, as 'the accounting obligation for VAT was that of (S), not that of (C) ... the liability to account for tax remained that of the appellant supplier'. *P Sheldon (t/a Nova Gold), MAN/94/282 & 621 (VTD 16551).*

30   Groups of Companies

Note. See *FA 1999, s 16, Sch 2*, which made substantial changes to the legislation concerning the VAT treatment of groups of companies, including the repeal of *VATA 1994, s 43(3)-(8)* and their replacement by *VATA 1994, ss 43A-43C*. The revised provisions took effect from 27 July 1999. For details of the changes, see Tolley's Value Added Tax.

The cases in this chapter are arranged under the following headings.

Group registration 30.1–30.15
Miscellaneous 30.16–30.29

GROUP REGISTRATION

30.1   **Whether Commissioners have discretion to accept group registration where statutory requirements not met.**   A company applied for group registration for itself and two associated companies. None of the companies controlled either of the others but all three were controlled by the same individuals (not in partnership). The Commissioners rejected the application and the tribunal dismissed the company's appeal, holding that, while group registration would have been administratively convenient, the Commissioners had no discretion to permit it where the statutory requirements for it were not met. *E Du Vergier & Co Ltd, [1973] VATTR 11 (VTD 4)*.

30.2   **Whether group registration may be retrospective.**   A group registration took effect from April 1973. In October 1973 the business of a subsidiary company, covered by the group registration, was transferred to a hitherto dormant company in the group. The holding company (which was the representative member of the group) did not notice at the time that the group registration did not cover this company. The holding company discovered the omission in 1977 and asked the Commissioners to permit the group registration to operate retrospectively with regard to the omitted subsidiary. The Commissioners refused, on the ground that they had no power to admit group treatment retrospectively. The QB upheld the Commissioners' ruling. Neill J held that the discretion to admit retrospective treatment was that of the Commissioners and could not be exercised by a tribunal. *C & E Commrs v Save & Prosper Group Ltd, QB 1978, [1979] STC 205*.

30.3   In 1982 a company applied to include a subsidiary company in its group registration with retrospective effect from 1979. The Commissioners agreed to include the subsidiary in the group registration from the date of the application, but refused to apply the application retrospectively. The tribunal dismissed the company's appeal. Applying *dicta* of Viscount Simon LC in *Charles Osenton & Co v Johnston, HL [1941] 2 All ER 245*, 'the appellate tribunal is not at liberty merely to substitute its own exercise of discretion for the discretion already exercised by the judge. In other words, appellate authorities ought not to reverse the order merely because they would themselves have exercised the original discretion, had it attached to them, in a different way.' On the evidence, the Commissioners' decision had clearly not been unreasonable. *Blue Boar Property & Investment Co Ltd, [1984] VATTR 12 (VTD 1579)*.

30.4   Similar decisions were reached in *MJ Foster Ltd, LON/74/7 (VTD 75)* and *Homecraft Manufacturing Ltd, LON/92/986Z (VTD 9300)*.

30.5   **Companies registered as group from August 1995—requesting backdated separate registrations from 1992 to July 1995—whether Commissioners entitled to cancel separate registrations.**   A holding company and seven subsidiaries, which were partly exempt, registered for VAT as a group with effect from 1 August 1995. In July 1996, following the introduction of new *de minimis* partial exemption provisions, the group's accountants submitted applications for five of the subsidiaries to be separately registered with effect from 1992 to July 1995. On 2 August 1996 the Commissioners accepted the applications. However, on 15 August the Commissioners cancelled the separate registrations. The companies appealed. The tribunal allowed the appeals, holding that under *Article 24(6)* of the *EC Sixth Directive*, 'a person who is eligible for exemption can opt to be subject to VAT and he will then be entitled to deduct input tax in accordance with the rules for deduction as they apply in his country'. On the evidence, 'if the group treatment had not existed, the appellants' applications for retrospective registration would have been accepted without demur'. The subsequent group treatment could not deprive the companies of their rights under the *EC Sixth Directive*, or bar them from exercising those rights. The tribunal held that 'in so far as (*VATA 1994, Sch 1*) purported not to grant those rights, or to bar them, or to confer on the Commissioners a discretion to refuse them, it is contrary to and cannot stand with the express provisions of the *Sixth Directive*'. Accordingly, the cancellation of the separate registrations was 'unlawful and invalid'. *Merseyside Cablevision Ltd*, 34.444 INPUT TAX, applied. *Eastwood Care Homes (Ilkeston) Ltd (and related appeals), [1999] VATDR 369 (VTD 16231)*. (*Note*. The Commissioners have appealed to the High Court against this decision — see 2.138 APPEALS.)

30.6   **Requirements of VATA 1994, s 43A*.**   The British Airways Board (BAB) applied for a trust company, which administered its pension fund, to be included in BAB's group registration. The Commissioners rejected the application, on the grounds that the trust company was not controlled by BAB for the purpose of provisions in *FA 1972* which became *VATA 1994, s 43(3)*. The Trust company had no issued share capital and the Board was not a member of it, so that the Board was not its holding company within the meaning of the *Companies Act*. It had twelve management trustees of whom the Board nominated six, including the chairman who had a casting vote. The tribunal dismissed BAB's appeal, holding that the provisions in *FA 1972* which became *VATA 1994, s 43(8)* were an exhaustive definition of 'control'. Accordingly, as the Board was not the company's holding company, it could be said to control it only if it was empowered by statute to control its activities, which it was not. *British Airways Board; British Airways Pension Fund Trustees Ltd (VTD 846)*. (*Note. VATA 1994, s 43(3)(8)* have now been replaced by *VATA 1994, s 43A(1)-(3)*—see *FA 1999, Sch 2*.)

30.7   **Whether application for a company to cease to be part of a group must be in writing.**   A subsidiary company within a group sold one of its assets after it had ceased to trade. An assessment was raised on the parent company of the group for the VAT due on the asset. The parent company appealed, contending that when the subsidiary had ceased to trade, a Customs officer had been informed on a control visit that it was no longer a member of the group, and that the statement to the officer was an application to exclude the subsidiary from the group registration. The tribunal dismissed the appeal, holding that there was no requirement to make an application in writing, but that the statement to the officer did not amount to an application to exclude the subsidiary. *Marine & General Print Holdings Ltd, MAN/85/416 (VTD 2120)*.

30.8   **Group registration—right of appeal.**   In *Davis Advertising Service Ltd*, 2.49 APPEALS, the tribunal held that, in the case of a group registration, only the representative member had a right of appeal.

30.9   **Group registration—liability of members other than representative member.**   P, the parent company of a group, and S, one of its subsidiaries, went into creditors' voluntary liquidation at the same time. A group registration covering both companies was in force and the Commissioners claimed tax due from P, in its capacity as representative member of the group, as a preferential debt in the winding-up of S. The liquidator of S rejected the claim and referred the matter to the High Court by way of originating summons. The Ch D upheld the Commissioners' claim, holding that, by virtue of what is now *VATA 1994, s 43*, the tax could be claimed from the other members of the group, who were jointly and severally liable for the amounts unpaid. Accordingly, any VAT not paid by P could be claimed preferentially in the winding-up of S. *Re Nadler Enterprises Ltd, Ch D [1980] STC 457; [1981] 1 WLR 23; [1980] 3 All ER 350.* (*Note.* The *Rules of the Supreme Court 1965 (SI 1965 No 1776)* refer to the use of an 'originating summons'. With effect from 26 April 1999, these rules have largely been replaced by the *Civil Procedure Rules 1998 (SI 1998 No 3132)*, which refer instead to 'alternative procedure'.)

30.10   **Group registration—representative member seeking to disclaim liability.**   A company (S) had been registered for VAT as the representative member of a group comprising two companies, itself and a wholly-owned subsidiary. The subsidiary went into liquidation, owing more than £33,000 in VAT, and the Commissioners issued assessments to recover this amount from S. S appealed, contending that it should not be held liable for the debt incurred by its subsidiary. The tribunal upheld the assessments and dismissed S's appeal. *Sunfine Developments Ltd, MAN/89/931 (VTD 6124).*

30.11   **Whether overseas company may be included in UK VAT group.**   A registered group of companies applied for a company which was resident in Eire, and was controlled by the same Netherlands holding company as the members of the group, to be included in the group for VAT purposes. The Eire company traded as a factoring company, purchasing trade debts from the UK group and appointing a UK company in the group as its agent in collecting the factored debts. The Commissioners rejected the application, considering that a company which was not resident in the UK could not be included in a UK group. The representative member of the group appealed, contending that the Eire company should be treated as having 'an established place of business in the UK'. The tribunal dismissed the appeal, finding that the Eire company did not have an office in the UK and that all its employees were based in Eire. The fact that the managing director of the Eire company regularly visited the UK company's office did not make that office an 'established place of business' of the Eire company. *Newey & Eyre Group Ltd, [1995] VATDR 244 (VTD 13311).* (*Note.* See also the subsequent case of *Shamrock Leasing Ltd*, 58.376 SUPPLY, where the tribunal held that an overseas company could not be included in a UK group, and *VATA 1994, s 43A(1)*, introduced by *FA 1999, Sch 2*, under which a body corporate now has to be 'established' in the UK, or have a 'fixed establishment' in the UK, to be eligible for membership of a UK group.)

30.12   The representative member of a group of banking companies applied for an Eire company (U) to be included in its VAT group. The Commissioners rejected the application, on the basis that the refusal of the claim was 'necessary for the protection of the revenue', within *VATA 1994, s 43(5A)*, since the application appeared to have been made for the purpose of avoiding a 'reverse charge' under *VATA 1994, s 8* on services which U supplied to the group. The company appealed, contending that the application had been made for administrative reasons, and that the Commissioners' refusal of the application was unreasonable. The tribunal reviewed the evidence in detail and noted that the company's application had failed to give the statutory 90 days' notice required by *VATA 1994, s 43(7)*, with the result that 'a fresh application will be necessary which will fall to be determined on the basis of the facts and the law at the time when it is made and considered'. The tribunal held that the words 'necessary for the protection of the revenue' could include 'any loss of revenue which is not *de minimis*, whether or not it follows from the normal operation of grouping. It certainly covers an artificial avoidance scheme but it also covers a straightforward case which could not be characterised as avoidance or abusive.' The tribunal declined to follow *dicta* in *Club Centre of Leeds Ltd, [1980] VATTR 135 (VTD 985)* (a case concerning provisions in *FA 1972* which had subsequently been amended by *FA 1981*, but which the company had cited as an authority), observing that that case dealt with a different area of VAT law, and had been cited out of context. The tribunal held that 'the phrase "necessary for the protection of the revenue" must be considered as a totality and involves a balancing exercise in which the Commissioners must weigh the effect on the appellant of refusal of grouping against the loss of revenue likely to result from grouping'. On the evidence in this case, the Commissioners should have requested further information before refusing the application. *Dicta* in *John Dee Ltd*, 14.28 COLLECTION AND ENFORCEMENT, applied. *National Westminster Bank plc, [1999] VATDR 201 (VTD 15514)*. (*Notes.* (1) See the subsequent tribunal decision in *Shamrock Leasing Ltd*, 58.376 SUPPLY, where the tribunal held that an overseas company could not be included in a UK group. See also *VATA 1994, s 43A(1)*, introduced by *FA 1999, Sch 2*, under which a body corporate now has to be 'established' in the UK, or have a 'fixed establishment' in the UK, to be eligible for membership of a UK group. (2) For the Commissioners' interpretation of the decision, see Business Brief 15/99, issued on 12 July 1999.)

30.13   In the case noted at 58.376 SUPPLY, the tribunal held that the Commissioners were 'not in law entitled' to treat an overseas company as a member of a UK VAT group. *Shamrock Leasing Ltd, LON/98/184 (VTD 15719)*.

30.14   **Application for group registration—definition of prescribed accounting period.**   See *Atlas Interlates Ltd*, 49.1 PENALTIES: MISDECLARATION.

30.15   **Date on which company ceases to be treated as part of group of companies.**   On 27 February 1995 a banking company (B) gave the share capital of one of its subsidiaries to a charitable trust. The Commissioners informed B that the subsidiary would be removed from B's group with effect from 1 July 1995. B appealed, contending that as a matter of law the subsidiary had ceased to be a member of its group at the time of the transfer of the share capital. The tribunal accepted this contention and allowed B's appeal, and the Ch D upheld this decision. Ferris J held that under *Article 4(4)* of the *EC Sixth Directive*, Member States could only treat two or more legally independent entities as a single taxable person if they were 'closely bound to one another by financial, economic and organisational links'. It would not be correct to interpret *VATA 1994, s 43* as 'conferring group treatment on an entity which was formerly entitled to that treatment but has ceased to be eligible for it'. *Barclays Bank plc v C & E Commrs, Ch D [2000] STC 665*. (*Note*. The decision discusses *VATA 1994, s 43(6)*, which was repealed with effect from 27 July 1999 by *FA 1999, Sch 2*. Similar provisions are, however, contained in the new *VATA 1994, s 43C(3)(4)*.)

MISCELLANEOUS

30.16   **Interpretation of VATA 1994, s 43.**   In *Thorn EMI plc*, 36.20 INSURANCE, the tribunal held that what is now *VATA 1994, s 43* 'has the effect of excluding supplies within the group from the charged tax, (but) it cannot have the effect of altering the character of a supply made to a person outside the group'. A similar decision was reached in *Canary Wharf Ltd*, 41.10 MANAGEMENT SERVICES. In *Thorn Materials Supply Ltd*, 30.27 below, Lord Nolan held that the purpose of what is now *s 43(1)* 'was to enable a group to be treated as if it were a single taxable entity'.

30.17   **Services provided by member of group to holding company for benefit of pension trust —whether VATA 1994, s 43(1) applicable.**   A bank was under a continuing obligation to provide investment advisory services free of charge to a pension trust, which was not a member of the bank's group for VAT purposes. The bank paid a subsidiary company, which was a member of its VAT group, for the services to be supplied to the pension trust. The bank did not account for VAT on the services in question, considering that they had been supplied by the subsidiary to the bank, and therefore fell to be disregarded for VAT purposes by virtue of what is now *VATA 1994, s 43(1)*. The Commissioners issued an assessment on the supply, considering that the services had in effect been supplied by the subsidiary directly to the pension trust, so that the bank, as the group representative member, was required to account for VAT on the supply. The tribunal allowed the bank's appeal. On the evidence, the subsidiary company had supplied its services to the bank, and the supply therefore fell to be disregarded for VAT purposes by virtue of *s 43(1)*. The fact that the services were supplied for the ultimate benefit of the pension trust did not alter the fact that the supply by the subsidiary had been to the bank. *Kingfisher plc*, 30.23 below, applied. *Midland Bank plc, [1991] VATTR 525 (VTD 6129)*.

30.18   **Change of representative member—validity of assessment.**   Until March 1996 a company (TE) had been the representative member of a group of companies (the T group). In March 1996 a new company (TP) was incorporated and became the representative member of the group. In September the Commissioners issued an assessment to TP, charging tax on supplies made by a member of the group (TU) between October 1994 and March 1995. TP appealed, contending as a preliminary point that the assessment was invalid because it had not been the representative member of the group at the time the supplies were made. The tribunal rejected this contention and held that the assessment had been validly made. The tribunal observed that 'the Commissioners could not in law have assessed (TE) in September 1996; it no longer had any of the statutory functions or obligations of representative member of the VAT group that included (TU)'. Furthermore, 'substitution of one representative member for another within the same group registration cannot ... remove the Commissioners' power of assessment of VAT due on account of the former representative member's failure to make a complete and correct return.' Applying *dicta* of Viscount Dunedin in *Whitney v CIR, HL 1925, 10 TC 88 (TTC 2001, 5.64)*, when it had been determined that there was a tax liability, 'it is antecedently highly improbable that the statute should not go on to make that liability effective. A statute is designed to be workable, and the interpretation thereof by a court should be to secure that object'. *Thorn plc, [1998] VATDR 80 (VTD 15283)*. (*Note.* For the substantive appeal, see 63.11 VALUATION.)

30.19   **Management services within group of companies.**   See *Tilling Management Services Ltd*, 41.1 MANAGEMENT SERVICES.

30.20   **Management services supplied to company not registered for VAT— recipient company subsequently joining same VAT group as supplier of services.**   See *Svenska International plc*, 41.16 MANAGEMENT SERVICES.

30.21   **Management services—time of supply.**   See *Legal & Contractual Services Ltd*, 41.4 MANAGEMENT SERVICES; *Pentex Oil Ltd*, 41.5 MANAGEMENT SERVICES; *Missionfine Ltd*, 41.6 MANAGEMENT SERVICES, and *Waverley Housing Management Ltd*, 41.7 MANAGEMENT SERVICES.

30.22   **Payments between associated companies—whether loans or consideration for management services.**   See *London Regeneration Project Services Ltd*, 41.2 MANAGEMENT SERVICES.

30.23 **Retail sales paid for by credit card issued by member of same group of companies as retailer—time of supplies.** A group of companies traded as retailers. One of the companies in the group (T) provided a consumer credit service for use in shops owned by members of the group, and issued credit cards to customers for this purpose. The holding company (K) did not account for tax on sales paid for by the credit cards issued by T until the users of the cards had paid the amounts in question to T. The Commissioners issued assessments on the basis that K should account for tax on the basis that the time of supply was when the sale took place, as with any other credit card. K appealed, contending that sales by means of T's credit cards should be distinguished from sales by other credit cards, as the credit had been provided by one of K's subsidiary companies, rather than by an independent operator. The tribunal allowed K's appeals and the QB upheld this decision. Popplewell J held that, under what is now *VATA 1994, s 43*, K was deemed to carry on the retail businesses of its retail subsidiaries, and also T's credit business. Accordingly, K's deemed retail sales were financed by its deemed credit business, and the sales in question were 'self-financed credit sales'. As indicated in *Notice No 727 (1987 edition), para 9*, tax need not be accounted for in respect of self-financed credit sales until payment was received. *C & E Commrs v Kingfisher plc, QB 1993, [1994] STC 63. (Note. Notice No 727 (1987 edition)* was subsequently replaced by *Notice No 727 (1997 edition).* The 'standard' method of accounting (under which tax on self-financed credit sales was not due until payment was received) was withdrawn with effect from 1 March 1997.)

30.24 **Deduction of input tax by holding companies.** See *Polysar Investments Netherlands BV v Inspecteur der Invoerrechten en Accijnzen,* 21.61 EUROPEAN COMMUNITY LAW, and *Sofitam SA v Ministre du Budget,* 21.211 EUROPEAN COMMUNITY LAW.

30.25 **Group of companies—application of partial exemption.** A group of three companies, with a single VAT registration, made both taxable and exempt supplies. In 1990 the group applied for permission to use a special method of computing its deductible input tax. The Commissioners approved the use of a special method, under which the deductible portion of residual input tax was to be computed using output values. At a control visit in 1991, a VAT officer discovered that the group was calculating the deductible input tax for each of the three companies individually, and then aggregating the totals to arrive at the group liability. He considered that the group should have aggregated the companies' input tax and applied the special method to the aggregate totals, and that the effect of the group's computations was that it had overclaimed input tax of more than £26,000. The Commissioners issued an assessment to recover this tax, and the group appealed. The tribunal allowed the group's appeal, holding that nothing in what is now *VATA 1994, s 43* required the companies' input tax to be aggregated, and observing that *para 3* of *Notice No 706* directed that the businesses carried on by the members of a group were to be treated separately, with the effect that 'each company in the group individually should begin its calculation of its deductible input tax after having excluded the items listed in (*para 16*)'. *Joseph Nelson Investment Planning Ltd, MAN/92/845 (VTD 10964).*

30.26 A group of companies carried on business as retailers and fitters of parts for motor cars. It incorporated a company to supply insurance services to their customers. The group adopted the standard method of apportioning input tax between taxable and exempt supplies. The Commissioners formed the opinion that the standard method led to the group being able to reclaim too much input tax, and issued a direction requiring the use of a special method whereby any input tax which was not directly attributable to taxable or exempt supplies should be apportioned between companies 'on the same basis that both direct and indirect costs are allocated to members by means of the group's accounting system', and that the deductible proportion of input tax should then be ascertained separately for each company. The group appealed, contending that the method directed by the Commissioners was unreasonable. The CS accepted this contention and allowed the appeal, holding that the wording of the direction was ambiguous, and it was therefore 'invalid and of no legal effect'. *Kwik-Fit (GB) Ltd v C & E Commrs, CS 1997, [1998] STC 159.*

30.27   **Avoidance scheme operated by group of companies—vendor companies becoming separately registered before delivery of goods—time of supply for VAT purposes.**   A group of companies adopted a scheme with the object of reducing the group's VAT liability. Two companies in the group agreed with a third company in the group to sell motor cars and other goods to that third company. 90% of the purchase price was paid in advance by the purchasing company to the two vendor companies, and was then lent back to the purchasing company by the vendor companies. At the date of the agreement, and at the time of the advance payment, all three companies were covered by a single group registration. However, the two vendor companies became separately registered for VAT before the delivery of the goods (when the remaining 10% of the price became payable). The Commissioners issued a ruling that the vendor companies should account for output tax on the whole of the purchase price. The companies appealed, contending that output tax was only payable on the amount which was paid on delivery, and that tax was not chargeable on the advance payment of 90% because, under what is now *VATA 1994, s 6(4)*, the time of supply was when the payment was made, at which time the companies were covered by the same group registration. The CA rejected this contention and upheld the Commissioners' rulings, and the HL dismissed the companies' appeals (by a 4–1 majority, Lord Hoffmann dissenting). Lord Nolan observed that there was nothing in *VATA* which warranted excluding the payment of 90% from the charge to VAT. Neither *Article 4(4)* of the *EC Sixth Directive*, nor what is now *VATA 1994, s 43(1)*, was 'designed to confer exemption or relief from tax. They are designed to simplify and facilitate the collection of tax by treating the representative member as if it were carrying on all the businesses of the other members as well as its own, and dealing on behalf of them all with non-members.' What is now *s 43(1)* 'may have the effect of deferring the charge to tax upon the added value of goods until they are the subject of a supply outside the group, but it does not prevent that charge'. Therefore, the liability for output tax on the full amount of the consideration, including the 90% which had been paid in advance, arose on the delivery date. *Thorn Materials Supply Ltd v C & E Commrs; Thorn Resources Ltd v C & E Commrs, HL [1998] STC 725; [1998] 1 WLR 1106; [1998] 3 All ER 384.*

30.28   **Avoidance scheme operated by group of companies—company incurring expenditure on property for subletting to company within group— company ceasing to be member of group—whether entitled to credit for input tax.**   A company (J) leased an office block, which needed substantial fitting-out work, from another company (N). Under the agreement, which was dated 14 October 1994, J agreed to undertake the fitting-out work, and N paid J £1,146,660 plus VAT as a contribution to the cost. On 25 October 1994 J sublet the office block to an associated company (M), which was the representative member of the same VAT group, for a premium of £36,500,000 and a small annual rent. M paid the premium on the same day. No tax invoice was issued, as the payment was for a supply within M's VAT group. On 26 October J applied to leave M's VAT group and set up a new VAT group. On 27 October J entered into an agreement with another associated company (P), whereby P agreed to carry out the fitting-out work on the office block. P subsequently invoiced J for £12,000,000 plus VAT in respect of this work. J paid this amount and reclaimed input tax on the payment. The Commissioners issued an assessment to recover the tax on the basis that it was not attributable to any taxable supply. J appealed, contending firstly that it was attributable to the supply which it had made to N on 14 October, and alternatively that it was attributable to the annual rent which it would receive from M. The tribunal upheld the assessment in principle, but directed that it should be reduced (from £2,069,894 to £1,898,492) to take account of the supply which J had made to N. With regard to the remainder of the tax, the tribunal held that it was attributable to the premium which M had paid J while the two companies were within the same VAT group, rather than to the future payments of rent. On the evidence, it was 'clear that (J) sought to obtain repayment of the input tax without incurring substantial related output tax'. Under *VAT Regulations 1995 (SI 1995 No 2518), reg 101(2)*, input tax was only directly attributable to taxable supplies if it related to goods or services which were 'used or to be used ... exclusively in making taxable supplies'. Under *Article 17(2)* of the *EC Sixth Directive*, input tax was deductible 'in so far as the goods or services are used for the purposes of ... taxable transactions'. Accordingly, 'the fact that (J) used the services supplied to a substantial extent for the purposes of an intra-group transaction, which under *VATA 1994, s 43(1)(a)* is disregarded as an output, does not have the effect that those services are to be regarded as exclusively used in making further supplies to the same company arising from the same contract, which were and are taxable because they no longer fall to be disregarded'. *JP Morgan Trading & Finance, [1998] VATDR 161 (VTD 15373)*.

30.29 **Insolvency Act 1986, Sch 6—application of Crown preference to group of companies.** Two companies (V and S) were members of the same group. In March 1991 the group incurred a substantial VAT liability in respect of a sale of land. In April 1991 V went into receivership. In June 1992 S paid the Commissioners more than £400,000 in respect of the VAT liability. Subsequently S went into liquidation. In proceedings between V and S, S sought relief in respect of V's share of the VAT, contending that it was entitled to the preference which the Commissioners would have had under *Insolvency Act 1986, Sch 6*, on the basis that any co-obligant in a joint and several obligation, who discharged the liability of any of the other co-obligants, was entitled to the benefit of all the rights which were available to the principal creditor, including the right of preference, without the need for an assignation. Lord Penrose accepted this contention, holding that an appropriate part of the total VAT liability would have fallen to be paid out of V's resources. That should be paid as if the Commissioners had demanded payment from V's receivers, as a preferential debt, in priority to V's secured creditors. Lord Penrose observed that any other result would unjustly benefit V's creditors at the expense of S's creditors. *Villaswan Ltd v Sheraton (Blythswood) Ltd, CS 9 November 1998, Times 27.1.1999.*

31   Health and Welfare

The cases in this chapter are arranged under the following headings.

SUPPLIES OF SERVICES BY REGISTERED PRACTITIONERS, ETC. (VATA 1994, Sch 9, Group 7, Item 1)

31.1   **Acupuncture supplied by registered nurse.**   A state registered nurse (E) carried on an acupuncture practice from his clinic. The Commissioners issued a ruling that he was required to register for VAT, and he appealed, contending that his supplies were exempt under what is now *VATA 1994, Sch 9, Group 7, Item 1(d)*. The tribunal dismissed his appeal, holding that although he was registered as a qualified nurse, acupuncture treatment was not within the scope of a registered nurse. The exemption of *Sch 9, Group 7, Item 1* must be construed as being limited to services supplied by persons in the specified categories in the course of their professions or vocations. The services supplied by E were not supplied in his capacity as a registered nurse. *Dr AR Evans, [1976] VATTR 175 (VTD 285)*.

31.2   **Company hiring radiological scanner to health authorities.**   A company purchased a radiological scanner with the intention of hiring it to health authorities. It reclaimed input tax on the purchase of the scanner, but the Commissioners rejected the claim on the grounds that the company's supplies were exempt under what is now *VATA 1994, Sch 9, Group 7, Item 1*. The tribunal allowed the company's appeal against this decision, holding that the company's supplies were excluded from exemption by *Sch 9, Group 7, Note 1*, since they consisted of the letting of goods on hire. The services supplied by the radiographer who accompanied the scanner were subsidiary to the letting on hire of the scanner. *Aslan Imaging Ltd, [1989] VATTR 54 (VTD 3286)*.

31.3   **Mobile chest X-ray service.**   The Commissioners refused an application for registration by the proprietors of a mobile chest X-ray service, considering that the supplies in question were exempt from VAT. The proprietors appealed, contending that their supplies were excluded from exemption by what is now *VATA 1994, Sch 9, Group 7, Note 1*. The tribunal rejected this contention and dismissed their appeal, holding that they were supplying services rather than goods, and that their services were exempt under *Sch 9, Group 7, Item 1(c)*. *Aslan Imaging Ltd, 31.2 above*, distinguished. *Cleary & Cleary (t/a Mobile X-Rays), LON/91/2295Y (VTD 7305)*.

31.4   **Nursing agency.**   A company which carried on business as a nursing agency registered for VAT. In 1989 the Commissioners directed that the company should be deregistered on the grounds that its supplies of nursing services were exempt under what is now *VATA 1994, Sch 9, Group 7, Item 1(d)*. The company appealed, contending that it was not making exempt supplies of nursing services, but was acting as an agent of the nurses whom it represented, and that its income arose from the placement of nursing staff, which did not qualify for exemption. The tribunal dismissed the company's appeal, holding that it was acting as a principal rather than as an agent of the nurses. On the evidence, the nurses were employed by the company under a contract of service, and the company's supplies were exempt. *Allied Medicare Nursing Services Ltd, MAN/89/484 (VTD 5485)*.

31.5   *Allied Medicare Nursing Services Ltd*, 31.4 above, was distinguished in a subsequent case in which a major nursing agency successfully appealed against a ruling by the Commissioners that it was making exempt supplies as well as taxable supplies (and therefore should have applied the partial exemption provisions). The tribunal observed that, in *Allied Medicare*, 'although the decision does not say so in terms, the inference must be that the tribunal did not accept that the documentation in that case reflected the true position'. In the case under appeal, however, there was no reason to doubt the accuracy of the documents which treated the nurses as self-employed. On the evidence, the relationship between the agency and the nurses was 'not that of master and servant', and 'such elements of control as there may be' were 'no more than are necessary for the agent/principal relationship specified in the Conditions'. The arrangements were 'wholly lacking in many of the normal features of a contract of service'; there was no guarantee of work, no minimum hours, no holiday or sick pay, no potential redundancy payment and no continuity of work. On the evidence, the nurses were self-employed, and they themselves entered into contracts with clients of the agency. The agency was not the employer of the nurses and did not make any exempt supplies. *British Nursing Co-Operation Ltd, LON/91/1696Y (VTD 8816)*.

31.6   *British Nursing Co-Operation Ltd*, 31.5 above, was applied in a subsequent case where the facts were broadly similar, although the relevant contracts did not specifically state that the agency (R) was acting as an agent for the nurses. The Commissioners issued a ruling that R was making exempt supplies (and thus was not entitled to recover the whole of its input tax). The tribunal allowed R's appeal, holding that R was not making any exempt supplies since it supplied nurses rather than nursing services. On the evidence, and despite the ambiguity of the relevant contracts, R was merely acting as an agent for the nurses, who were supplying their services to the hospitals as independent principals. The QB upheld the tribunal decision as one of fact. Laws J observed that 'although the contracts fully distribute parties' private law duties and rights, they do not put beyond question the nature of the supplies made by (R), nor was it their function to do so. What those supplies was (*sic*) was accordingly a matter of fact for the tribunal. That being the case, there is no proper basis on which this court should interfere with the tribunal's conclusions.' *C & E Commrs v Reed Personnel Services Ltd, QB [1995] STC 588*.

31.7   A similar decision was reached in a subsequent case in which the Commissioners issued an assessment on the basis that a partnership which operated a nursing agency was itself supplying nursing services to clients, and that since these supplies were exempt, the partnership was not entitled to reclaim input tax. The partnership appealed, contending that it was not acting as a principal, and that its only supplies were of introduction services for which it charged commission which was standard-rated, so that it had reclaimed input tax on the correct basis. The tribunal accepted the partnership's evidence and allowed the appeal, holding that the partnership was acting as an agent of the nurses rather than as a principal. *Allied Medicare Nursing Services Ltd*, 31.4 above, distinguished. *Sheffield & Rotherham Nursing Agency, MAN/92/414 (VTD 11279)*.

31.8   See also *BUPA Nursing Services Ltd*, 58.227 SUPPLY, and *South Hams Nursing Agency*, 58.228 SUPPLY.

31.9   The Commissioners sought to register a woman who operated a nursing agency. She appealed, contending that she was not required to register since all her supplies were exempt. The tribunal allowed her appeal, holding that although her business was described as an agency, she carried on business as a principal, rather than simply as an agent of the nurses registered with her. The services which she supplied were nursing services and were within what is now *VATA 1994, Sch 9, Group 7, Item 1(d)*. *MG Parkinson, LON/90/1083Y (VTD 6017)*.

31.10   **Commission for supply of nurses.** A company which operated a nursing agency supplied two nurses to a nursing home. The company charged VAT on its commission. The proprietor of the nursing home lodged an appeal, contending that the commission should be treated as exempt under *VATA 1994, Sch 9, Group 7, Item 1(d)*. The tribunal rejected this contention and dismissed the appeal, holding on the evidence that the company was acting as an agent and 'did not purport to provide nursing services but nurses'. It 'acted as an intermediary only and correctly charged VAT on its commission'. *Dr RA Fairburn, LON/96/1613 (VTD 15904)*.

31.11   **Nursing services partly provided by unqualified staff.** A company provided nursing services to patients in their own homes. Some of the company's employees were registered nurses but others were unqualified. The company did not account for tax on these supplies, considering that they were exempt. The Commissioners issued an assessment charging tax on the basis that the supplies did not qualify for exemption, since some of the supplies were not provided by registered nurses. The tribunal allowed the company's appeal, finding that the company exercised 'a very high standard of supervision' and holding that there was 'no necessity for the supervisor and the employee to be in the same premises if ready communication is available'. On the evidence, the services were 'directly supervised' within the meaning of what is now *VATA 1994, Sch 9, Group 7, Note 2* and qualified for exemption under what is now *VATA 1994, Sch 9, Group 7, Item 1(d)*. *Parkinson*, 31.9 above, applied. *Elder Home Care Ltd, EDN/93/23 (VTD 11185)*. (*Note*. For the Commissioners' revised interpretation of what constitutes 'direct supervision', see Customs & Excise News Release 23/96, issued on 11 April 1996.)

31.12   **Dispensing of corrective spectacles.** A company carried on business as opticians. It employed eight doctors and an ophthalmic optician to provide eye tests, and also employed several dispensing opticians to dispense spectacles. The Commissioners issued a ruling that its supplies of corrective spectacles were supplies of goods which did not qualify for exemption and were standard-rated. The company appealed, contending that, in addition to providing the spectacles, it made supplies of services which were exempt under what is now *VATA 1994, Sch 9, Group 7, Item 1*. The tribunal allowed the company's appeal, holding that the primary purpose of the dispensing opticians was to advise patients, rather than merely to sell spectacles, so that the payments received by the company should be apportioned. The QB upheld the tribunal decision, holding that in substance and reality there were two distinct supplies. *C & E Commrs v Leightons Ltd, QB [1995] STC 458*. (*Notes*. (1) For the Commissioners' practice following this decision, see Business Brief 2/99, issued on 13 January 1999, and VAT Information Sheet 8/99, issued on 22 June 1999. (2) For cases concerning repayment claims following this decision, see *Green*, 45.5 PAYMENT OF TAX, *Hayward Gill & Associates Ltd*, 45.6 PAYMENT OF TAX, and *CL Dyer & Co*, 45.7 PAYMENT OF TAX.)

31.13   A similar decision was reached in *C & E Commrs v Eye-Tech Opticians, QB [1995] STC 458*. (*Note*. The case was heard in the QB with *C & E Commrs v Leightons Ltd*, 31.12 above.)

31.14 **Services provided by doctor.** A doctor had gained considerable experience in acting as an expert medical witness before various courts and tribunals, and had become an Associate of the Chartered Institute of Arbitrators. The Commissioners issued a ruling that services provided by the doctor in conducting medical examinations, paternity testing, issuing medical certificates, assessing insurance claims, and preparing medical reports for personal injury and medical negligence cases were exempt under *VATA 1994, Sch 9, Group 7, Item 1* (so that the doctor was unable to reclaim input tax relating to these services). The doctor appealed, contending that these services should be treated as taxable. The tribunal rejected this contention, holding that all these services qualified for exemption under UK law. The chairman observed that all the disputed services 'bear the hallmarks of something done which is of a medical nature which meets the particular needs of a particular person'. However, the tribunal directed that the case should be referred to the CJEC to consider whether the exemption under *Group 7, Item 1* was inconsistent with the provisions of *Article 13A1(c)* of the *EC Sixth Directive*. *PL d'Ambrumenil; Dispute Resolution Services Ltd, LON/x (VTD 15977). (Note.* For the Commissioners' views on the liability of 'medico-legal' services supplied by doctors, see Business Brief 26/96, issued on 19 December 1996.)

31.15 **Unregistered optician—whether supplies 'directly supervised' by registered optician—9 Sch, Group 7, Note 2.** The Commissioners issued a ruling that supplies by an unregistered optician failed to qualify for exemption under *VATA 1994, Sch 9, Group 7, Item 1.* The optician appealed, contending that his supplies were directly supervised by a registered optician, and thus qualified for exemption by virtue of *Group 7, Note 2.* The tribunal accepted this contention and allowed the appeal, holding on the evidence that the supplies were supervised by a registered optician even though there was no explicit contract requiring the supervisor to undertake this task. The tribunal observed that 'a contract may be valuable evidence of responsibility' but that its absence did 'not prove that there is no responsibility'. On the evidence, 'supervision was an implicit term of the relationship'. *AJ Land (t/a Crown Optical Centre), LON/97/162 (VTD 15547).*

31.16 *Land,* 31.15 above, was distinguished in a subsequent case in which the tribunal held on the evidence that an unregistered optician was not directly supervised by a registered optician, so that his supplies failed to qualify for exemption. *A & S Services, LON/97/812 (VTD 16025).*

31.17 **Supplies by unregistered practitioner—whether 'directly supervised' by referring practitioners.** The Commissioners issued a ruling that supplies by a chiropractor, who was not a registered practitioner within *VATA 1994, Sch 9, Group 7, Item 1,* did not qualify for exemption. She appealed, contending that her supplies should be treated as 'directly supervised' by the registered practitioners who referred patients to her, and thus as exempt by virtue of *Group 7, Note 2.* The tribunal dismissed her appeal, holding on the evidence that the chiropractor's services were not 'directly supervised'. *Elder Home Care Ltd,* 31.11 above, distinguished. *C Pittam, LON/94/1975A (VTD 13268). (Note.* See now *VATA 1994, Sch 9, Group 7, Item 1(ca),* introduced by the *VAT (Chiropractors) Order 1999 (SI 1999 No 1575)* with effect from 29 June 1999. The effect of this is that supplies by a chiropractor who is registered under the *Chiropractors Act 1994* now qualify for exemption.)

31.18 **Anti-smoking therapy—whether supplies 'directly supervised' by registered medical practitioner.** A company supplied group therapy and training manuals to clients who wished to stop smoking tobacco. It did not account for output tax on its supplies, treating them as exempt. The Commissioners issued a ruling that the supplies failed to qualify for exemption under *VATA 1994, Group 7, Item 1* and that the company was required to account for output tax. The company appealed, contending that its supplies should be treated as 'directly supervised' by a registered medical practitioner, and therefore as exempt from VAT. The tribunal rejected this contention and dismissed the appeal. On the evidence, a registered medical practitioner visited the company's directors three times a year, and his services were 'of an informal advisory nature'. Accordingly, the company's supplies were not 'directly supervised' by a registered medical practitioner, as required by *Group 7, Note 2. Elder Home Care Ltd*, 31.11 above, distinguished. *Easyway Productions Ltd, LON/95/2613 (VTD 14938)*.

DENTAL SERVICES (VATA 1994, Sch 9, Group 7, Item 2)

31.19   **Sales by dentist to other dentists.** A dentist sold X-ray equipment to other dentists, and did not account for VAT. The Commissioners issued an assessment on the supplies, and the dentist appealed, contending that they were exempt under what is now *VATA 1994, Sch 9, Group 7, Item 2*. The tribunal dismissed his appeal, holding that the supplies did not qualify for exemption. *AW Roberts, LON/76/175 (VTD 353)*.

31.20   **Definition of 'dental technician'.** An individual, who was licensed by the British Institute of Surgical Technologists, manufactured crowns and bridges for dentists. He reclaimed input tax, but the Commissioners rejected his claim, considering that his supplies were exempt under what is now *VATA 1994, Sch 9, Group 7, Item 2(c)*. The tribunal dismissed his appeal, holding that he was within the definition of a 'dental technician'. *JA Bennett, LON/79/231 (VTD 865)*.

31.21   **Supply of 'study models' by dental technician.** A dental technician was registered for VAT. The Commissioners sought to cancel his registration on the grounds that all his supplies were exempt under *VATA 1994, Sch 9, Group 7, Item 2*. He appealed, contending that he was making supplies of 'study models', which were supplies of goods rather than supplies of services, and were therefore taxable supplies. The tribunal rejected this contention and dismissed the appeal, observing that 'the model of an individual's mouth does not instantly suggest as a matter of common sense that it is a supply of goods'. The appellant 'was applying his professional expertise to supply a service to dentists and not an item of property to dentists'. Furthermore, even if the study models were to be regarded as goods, their supply would be ancillary to the supply of services, since 'it would be wholly unrealistic to regard the study model as having any independent use, value or utility'. *F Steven (t/a City Ceramic Dental Laboratory), EDN/98/137 (VTD 16083)*.

31.22   **Supplies of mouthguards—whether part of consideration attributable to supply of dental services.** A company supplied mouthguards, which were intended to be used by schoolchildren participating in contact sports, and were individually customised by a dental technician. The mouthguards cost between £21.95 and £35.95. The Commissioners issued a ruling that the company was making supplies of goods which were entirely standard-rated. The company appealed, contending that part of the consideration was attributable to the services of the dental technician, which were exempt from VAT. The tribunal accepted this contention and allowed the appeal, observing that 'if a parent is prepared to pay between 11 and 18 times as much for the appellant's bespoke mouthguard as for an off-the-peg "boil and bite", it is those professional services for which he is paying the extra'. *O-Pro Ltd, LON/99/971 (VTD 16780)*.

PROVISION OF CARE, ETC. IN HOSPITAL OR SIMILAR INSTITUTION (VATA 1994, Sch 9, Group 7, Item 4)

31.23   **Company providing ancillary services at hospitals.** A company supplied services to about 45 hospitals. The services included cleaning, duties relating to patients which could be entrusted to non-nursing personnel, duties for hospital staff, and the services of telephonists and receptionists. The company did not account for VAT and the Commissioners issued a ruling that the services did not qualify for exemption under what is now *VATA 1994, Sch 9, Group 7*. The tribunal allowed the company's appeal in part, holding that services which involved personal contact with patients were exempt under *Sch 9, Group 7, Item 4*, but (by a 2–1 majority) that services which did not involve contact with patients were standard-rated. *Crothall & Co Ltd, [1973] VATTR 20 (VTD 6).* (*Note.* The Commissioners now state that 'we no longer accept that the specific services considered by the *Crothall* decision are exempt, as the case predates the *EC Sixth Directive*, which refers to "medical care", and we cannot accept that the services in the *Crothall* decision are medical care'. See Customs' VAT Manual, Part 7, chapter 22, section 3.4(b).)

31.24 **Hospitals providing accommodation for mothers of very young children.**   A charity ran 32 private hospitals. When young children were taken into one of the hospitals, it provided accommodation for the children's mothers as well as for the children. It made separate charges for the mothers' accommodation. The Commissioners raised an assessment on the basis that the supplies of accommodation to the mothers were standard-rated to the extent that they related to food consumed by the mothers. The charity appealed, contending that its supplies were exempt under what is now *VATA 1994, Sch 9, Group 7, Item 4*. The tribunal allowed the appeal, holding that the provision of food and accommodation for the mother of a child patient was an exempt supply, because it was a necessary ingredient of the supply of care by the hospital for the child. *Nuffield Nursing Home Trust, [1989] VATTR 62 (VTD 3327).*

31.25 **Provision of telephones in hospital.**   An organisation arranged for the provision of 33 coin-operated telephones in a large hospital. Until 1988 it did not make any profit from this, but from 1989 the amounts which it received from users of the telephones began to exceed the amounts which it paid to British Telecom. The Commissioners issued a ruling that the organisation was required to account for VAT on its surplus takings. The organisation appealed, contending that the supply of the telephones constituted the 'provision of care' which was an exempt supply under what is now *VATA 1994, Sch 9, Group 7, Item 4*. The tribunal dismissed the appeal, holding that the provision of telephones was not within the definition of 'care'. *Dicta* in *Crothall & Co Ltd*, 31.23 above, applied. *Poole General Hospital League of Friends, LON/92/2204 (VTD 10621).*

31.26 **Drugs supplied from hospital dispensary.**   See *Wellington Private Hospital*, 19.2 DRUGS, MEDICINES, AIDS FOR THE HANDICAPPED, ETC.

31.27 **Provision of treatment at acupuncture clinic.**   The proprietor of an acupuncture clinic appealed against registration, contending that he was providing medical treatment which should be treated as exempt from VAT. The tribunal dismissed his appeal, finding that the clinic was not a registered institution within what is now *VATA 1994, Sch 9, Group 7, Item 4*. *Dr J D'Ambrosio, BIR/73/1 (VTD 15).*

31.28 See also *Evans*, 31.1 above.

31.29 **Supply of meals to doctor in hospital dining room.**   A resident doctor at Bradford Royal Infirmary regularly ate meals in the hospital dining room. As required by a ruling under what is now *VATA 1994, s 41(2)*, the hospital accounted for VAT on its income from catering. The doctor lodged an appeal, contending that the catering should be treated as exempt from VAT under what is now *VATA 1994, Sch 9, Group 7, Item 4*, on the basis that it was supplied in connection with the provision of medical treatment. The tribunal dismissed her appeal, holding that the catering did not qualify for exemption. *Dr AJ Cameron, [1973] VATTR 177 (VTD 41)*.

31.30 **Surgical belt supplied to wearer by manufacturer but fitted at hospital.**   In the case noted at 2.32 APPEALS, an individual had, on the recommendation of her doctor, purchased a surgical belt from a manufacturer. The doctor fitted the belt for her at a hospital. The tribunal held that the supply qualified for exemption under what is now *VATA 1994, 9 Sch, Group 7, Item 4. M Payton, [1974] VATTR 140 (VTD 89)*.

31.31 **Supply and fitting of hearing aids on hospital premises.**   An individual (C) supplied audiology services and hearing aids. The Commissioners accepted that his audiology services were exempt under what is now *VATA 1994, Sch 9, Group 7, Item 1(e)*. However, the Commissioners considered that since this exemption was confined to services rather than goods, the supply of hearing aids (which had been exempt from VAT before the changes made by *FA 1988*) did not qualify for exemption, but was standard-rated. C appealed, contending that, although the supply of hearing aids was not itself exempt, the fitting of hearing aids should be treated as exempt under *Item 4* where it was carried out on hospital premises. The tribunal dismissed the appeal, holding that the fitting of hearing aids did not qualify as 'the provision of care or medical or surgical treatment', and accordingly was not within *Sch 9, Group 7, Item 4. MJ Coleman, LON/92/1274A (VTD 10512)*.

31.32 **Unregistered hair transplant clinic.**   A company opened a hair transplant clinic in 1977. However, the clinic was not registered under the *Nursing Homes Act 1975* until 31 October 1978. The Commissioners accepted that the supplies at the clinic after that date were exempt under what is now *VATA 1994, Sch 9, Group 7, Item 4*, but issued a ruling that the supplies before that date did not qualify for exemption. The tribunal dismissed the company's appeal against this decision. *Huntley Hair Transplants Ltd, LON/77/414 (VTD 823)*.

31.33 **Nursing home.**   The proprietor of a nursing home reclaimed input tax in respect of work carried out at the home. The Commissioners issued an assessment to recover some of the tax, considering that the supplies made by the home were exempt under what is now *VATA 1994, Sch 9, Group 7, Item 4*. The tribunal upheld the assessment and dismissed the proprietor's appeal. *Dr A Hill, MAN/88/888 (VTD 5658)*.

31.34 A similar decision was reached in *FA Saleem, EDN/94/169 (VTD 12995)*.

31.35 The proprietor of a nursing home was registered for VAT. The Commissioners issued a ruling that he was not entitled to be registered, on the grounds that all his supplies were exempt from VAT under what is now *VATA 1994, Sch 9, Group 7, Item 4*. The proprietor appealed, contending that he should not be treated as exempt since the exemption should be construed in accordance with *Article 13A1(b)* of the *EC Sixth Directive*, which confined such exemption to 'bodies governed by public law'. The tribunal accepted this contention and allowed the appeal. *Dicta* of the CJEC in *Bulthuis-Griffioen v Inspector der Omzetbelasting*, 21.152 EUROPEAN COMMUNITY LAW, applied. The chairman observed that the exemptions in *Article 13A* had to be construed strictly, and it was 'not unnatural, particularly in a European context, that exemptions which are clearly directed towards activities which are socially beneficial should, in certain cases, apply to such activities only if they are carried on by organisations rather than by individuals'. *P Kaul (t/a Alpha Care Services), [1996] VATDR 360 (VTD 14028)*. (*Note*. For the Commissioners' practice following this decision, see Business Brief 1/97, issued on 24 January 1997.)

31.36 See also *Gregg*, 21.153 EUROPEAN COMMUNITY LAW.

31.37   **Unregistered retirement home.** The proprietors of a retirement home reclaimed input tax on work carried out at the home. The Commissioners issued an assessment to recover some of the tax in question, considering that the supplies made at the home were exempt under what is now *VATA 1994, Sch 9, Group 7, Item 4*. The tribunal allowed the proprietors' appeal, finding that at the relevant time the home was not registered as a Nursing Home, and holding that none of the supplies made by the proprietors were exempt from VAT. *Hill*, 31.33 above, distinguished. *B & E Latimer, EDN/90/175 (VTD 6486)*.

31.38   **Construction of premises for use as retirement home—apportionment of input tax.** A couple constructed a building with residential accommodation for six people. They reclaimed input tax on the basis that they intended to use the building as a retirement home. However, they were unable to fill the home, and offered three of the places to the local authority's Social Services Department under an Adult Placement Scheme. The other three places remained unfilled. The Commissioners issued an assessment to recover the tax which the couple had claimed, since the accommodation under the Adult Placement Scheme was within the provision of the *Registered Homes Act 1984*, and thus was exempt from VAT. The couple appealed, contending that they had sought to let the accommodation to tenants who did not require any degree of personal care, and any supplies to such tenants would have been taxable. The tribunal allowed the appeal in part, directing that the tax should be apportioned on the basis that the part attributable to the units of accommodation which had been taken up under the Adult Placement Scheme was attributable to exempt supplies, but that the part attributable to the other three units was attributable to intended taxable supplies. *PJ & AL Haines, MAN/95/1275 (VTD 13834)*.

31.39   **Accommodation for children in need of care.** A company provided accommodation for children in need of care, in accordance with the *Children Act 1989, s 23*. It received payment from local authorities who placed children in its care. Its turnover exceeded the registration threshold, but it failed to register for VAT. The Commissioners issued a ruling that the company was required to register. The company appealed, contending that its supplies should be treated as exempt under *VATA 1994, Sch 9, Group 7* or under *Article 13A1(h)* of the *EC Sixth Directive*. The tribunal rejected these contentions and dismissed the appeal. The tribunal held that the supplies failed for exemption under *Group 7, Item 4*, since, construing the legislation in accordance with the *eiusdem generis* principle, '*Item 4* is ... concerned with a provision of a care in a medical connotation'. The supplies also failed to qualify for exemption under *Group 7, Item 9*, since the company was not a 'charity or public body', and failed to qualify under *Article 13A1(h)* of the *EC Sixth Directive*, since the company was not 'a body governed by public law'. *Prospects Care Services Ltd, [1997] VATDR 209 (VTD 14810)*.

HUMAN BLOOD, ORGANS AND TISSUE (VATA 1994, Sch 9, Group 7, Items 6–8)

31.40   **Recombinant Factor VIII.** A company supplied a product known as Recombinant Factor VIII to the National Health Service. The Commissioners issued a ruling that the company was required to account for output tax on these supplies. The company appealed, contending firstly that the product was 'derived from human blood' within *VATA 1994, Sch 9, Group 7, Item 7* and alternatively that it was 'human ... tissue' within *VATA 1994, Sch 9, Group 7, Item 8*. The tribunal rejected these contentions and dismissed the appeal. Types of factor VIII which were derived from human plasma were exempt from VAT under *VATA 1994, Sch 9, Group 7, Item 7*. However, the product in question was not derived from human plasma and did not qualify for exemption. The tribunal observed that it was an established principle that exemptions should be strictly construed, and held that it appeared to be the intention of the legislation 'only to exempt naturally occurring parts of the human body and not to exempt substances produced as a matter of manufacture or production'. *Baxter Healthcare Ltd, LON/96/177 (VTD 14670).*

SUPPLIES OF WELFARE SERVICES (VATA 1994, Sch 9, Group 7, Item 9)

31.41   Equipment supplied with nursery services.   A company supplied nursery management services to businesses, primarily to enable employees of such businesses to have young children cared for at or near their place of work. It was accepted that these services were exempt from VAT under what is now *VATA 1994, Sch 9, Group 7*. However, the company treated supplies of various items of equipment, installed when a new nursery unit was established, as separate standard-rated supplies. It therefore accounted for output tax on the installation of such equipment, reclaimed input tax on the purchase of the equipment, and carried out partial exemption computations in which the supplies of the equipment were treated as standard-rated. The Commissioners issued an assessment to recover the input tax, on the basis that the equipment was supplied as an integral part of an exempt supply. The company appealed, contending that the equipment was a separate standard-rated supply and that it had accounted for tax on the correct basis. The tribunal dismissed the appeal, holding that the supplies of equipment were 'an integral part of the contract to supply child care services' and thus were exempt from VAT. *Kids of Wilmslow Ltd, MAN/93/945 (VTD 12341).*

31.42   Supplies of catering to elderly people in sheltered housing accommodation.   A housing association, which was a registered charity, provided sheltered housing accommodation for the elderly. Some of the accommodation included kitchen facilities, but some did not. Where the accommodation did not include kitchen facilities, the association supplied catering services to the residents (most of whom were aged 80 or over, and were considered incapable of looking after themselves). It did not account for output tax on the supplies, treating them as exempt under *VATA 1994, Sch 9, Group 7, Item 9.* The Commissioners issued a ruling that the supplies were excluded from exemption by *Note 7,* and thus were standard-rated. The association appealed, contending that the supplies should be treated as ancillary to the provision of care to the residents, so that the restriction in *Note 7* was inapplicable. The tribunal allowed the appeal, holding on the evidence that the association was providing care because its staff helped the residents with tasks such as dressing, undressing and bathing. The supply of catering was therefore ancillary to the provision of care and qualified for exemption. *Viewpoint Housing Association Ltd, EDN/94/104 (VTD 13148).*

31.43   Home help for elderly people.   A housing association, which was accepted as being a charity, supplied 'home help' services to 90 elderly clients under a contract with the local District Council. Each client received an average of two hours' help each week. The Commissioners issued a ruling that it was required to account for output tax on these supplies. The association appealed, contending that the supplies should be treated as exempt under *VATA 1994, Sch 9, Group 7, Item 9.* The tribunal accepted this contention and allowed the appeal, holding on the evidence that the clients had 'major difficulty in safely carrying out some key daily living tasks' and relied on help from social services to continue to live in their own homes. Accordingly, the supplies were within the definition of 'welfare services'. *Watford & District Old People's Housing Association Ltd (t/a Watford Help In The Home Service), [1998] VATDR 477 (VTD 15660).* (*Note.* For the Commissioners' practice following this decision, see Business Brief 24/98, issued on 2 December 1998, and Business Brief 4/99, issued on 16 February 1999.)

31.44   **Supplies by Retreat House—whether exempt.**   A charity operated a Retreat House from premises in the Diocese of Peterborough. It was registered for VAT and accounted for output tax, but subsequently formed the opinion that some of its supplies of services should be treated as exempt, and lodged a retrospective claim for repayment of tax. The Commissioners rejected the claim, with the exception that they accepted that certain supplies of training qualified for exemption under what is now *VATA 1994, Sch 9, Group 6*, and that some 'retreats' which the charity organised qualified as exempt supplies of spiritual welfare under what is now *VATA 1994, Sch 9, Group 7, Item 9*. The charity appealed. The tribunal reviewed the evidence in detail and allowed the appeal in part, holding that supplies relating to a 'workshop' conducted by a psychotherapist were supplies of spiritual welfare which qualified for exemption but that the remaining supplies (including supplies of accommodation and catering) did not qualify for exemption, either under the UK legislation or under *Article 13A1* of the *EC Sixth Directive*. *Stichting Uitvoering Financiële Acties (SUFA) v Staatssecretaris van Financiën*, 21.146 EUROPEAN COMMUNITY LAW, applied. (The tribunal also held that, even if the supplies had been held to be exempt, the tax in question would not be repayable as the tax had been passed on to the customers and repayment would have led to 'unjust enrichment'.) *Peterborough Diocesan Conference & Retreat House, LON/94/2078 (VTD 14081)*.

31.45   **Charity providing hotel accommodation for cancer patients—whether Group 7, Note 7 applicable.**   A registered charity purchased a hotel and used it to provide accommodation for cancer patients and their families. The Commissioners issued a ruling that output tax was payable on the supplies of accommodation. The charity appealed, contending that it was supplying welfare services which were exempt under *VATA 1994, Sch 9, Group 7, Item 9*. The tribunal accepted this contention and allowed the appeal. The building in which the accommodation was provided was 'not a hotel in the normal sense of the word', since it was 'open only to those suffering from cancer or associated with them, only upon professional recommendations (and) only for a specific length of time', but was 'an institution providing welfare'. The tribunal held that 'the provision of accommodation and catering are ancillary to the provision of welfare', so that the supplies were not excluded from exemption by *Group 7, Note 7*. The tribunal also expressed the view that the restriction laid down by *Group 7, Note 7* was incompatible with the provisions of *Article 13A1(g)* of the *EC Sixth Directive*, which had direct effect. The tribunal observed that 'the fact that old people's homes are included in *Article 13A1(g)* and that this inclusion is, from the context, an example of what is to be included, shows that services incorporating accommodation can be exempt, without conditions that the supply of accommodation shall be ancillary to the supply of welfare services'. *Trustees for the Macmillan Cancer Trust, [1998] VATDR 289 (VTD 15603)*.

SUPPLIES OF TRANSPORT SERVICES (VATA 1994, Sch 9, Group 7, Item 11)

31.46   **Transport of human organs, etc. for transplant operations.**   A trader carried on business supplying transport services for human organs and blood for use in transplant operations, and for teams of people involved in such operations. The Commissioners issued a ruling that he was required to account for output tax on his supplies. He appealed, contending that they should be treated as exempt under *VATA 1994, Sch 9, Group 7, Item 11*. The tribunal rejected this contention and dismissed his appeal. *M Peverley (t/a Lifeline Medical Transport Service), MAN/97/472 (VTD 15353)*.

32   Human Rights

Note. The European Convention for the Protection of Human Rights was adopted in 1950, as a treaty of the Council of Europe. (This body predates, and is entirely separate from, the European Community which originates from the 1957 Treaty of Rome.) Article 1 of the First Protocol of the European Convention provides that 'every natural or legal person is entitled to the peaceful enjoyment of his possessions' but goes on to add that 'the preceding provisions shall not ... in any way impair the right of a State to enforce such laws as it deems necessary to control the use of property in accordance with the general interest or to secure the payment of tax or other contributions and penalties'. The Convention is recognised as part of European Community law by article 6 of the 1997 Treaty of Amsterdam. For recent discussions of the Convention and its impact on UK tax law, see the article by Christopher Wallworth in 'Taxation', 15 June 2000, pp 284–287, and the detailed article by Philip Baker in 'British Tax Review', 2000, pp 211–377.

32.1   **Determination of penalty under VATA 1994, s 60—whether any breach of European Convention on Human Rights.**   In the case noted at 47.68 PENALTIES: EVASION OF TAX, the Commissioners had imposed a penalty under *VATA 1994, s 60* on a partnership. The penalty was originally imposed at the rate of 95% of the evaded tax. The tribunal upheld the penalty in principle, but reduced it to 75% of the evaded tax. The CA upheld the tribunal decision. The partners subsequently applied to the ECHR, contending that the imposition of the penalty was a breach of the *European Convention on Human Rights.* The ECHR rejected this contention, holding that it was 'manifestly ill-founded within the meaning of *Article 35*' of the Convention, and unanimously declared the application inadmissible. The ECHR held, *inter alia*, that 'the interests of justice did not require leading counsel to be instructed on the applicants' behalf'. Furthermore, 'in the light of the circumstances of the present case seen as a whole', there was 'no appearance of unfairness within the meaning of *Article 6* of the *Convention*'. The length of the proceedings was 'justified by complexity of the case (*sic*) and conduct of the applicants'. *Article 1 of the First Protocol* of the *Convention* provided that a State could 'enforce such laws as it deems necessary to control the use of property in accordance with the general interest or to secure the payment of taxes or other contributions or penalties'. Applying *Gasus Dossier GmbH v Netherlands, ECHR 23 February 1995 unreported*, 'the Court will respect the legislature's assessment in such matters unless it is devoid of reasonable foundation'. *M & A Georgiou v United Kingdom, ECHR Case 40042/98, 16 May 2000 unreported.*

32.2   **Penalties under VATA 1994, s 60—whether a 'criminal charge' within Article 6 of European Convention on Human Rights.**   In three appeals involving penalties under *VATA 1994, s 60*, the tribunal considered, as a preliminary issue, whether the imposition of a penalty under *VATA 1994, s 60* gave rise to a 'criminal charge' within *Article 6* of the *European Convention on Human Rights*. The tribunal observed that the nature of the offence, involving a charge of dishonesty, pointed 'towards the penalties ranking as criminal charges despite their place in the civil penalty code'. Furthermore, applying the guidelines in *Engel v Netherlands, ECHR 1980, 1 EHRR 647*, the penalties were 'sufficiently burdensome to fall on the criminal side of the line'. Accordingly, the tribunal held that the penalties in question were 'criminal charges' within *Article 6(1)*. The chairman observed that 'the implications of their being so will depend on the circumstances of the particular case'. *Han & Yau; Martins & Martins; Morris, LON/x (VTD 16990).*

32.3   **Penalty apportioned to director under VATA 1994, s 61—effect of Human Rights Act 1998.**   A penalty was imposed on a company director under *VATA 1994, s 61*. The director appealed and applied for a postponement of the hearing as he was in Australia. His solicitors wrote to the tribunal claiming that it would be a breach of the *Human Rights Act 1998* to hear the appeal in the director's absence. The tribunal rejected this contention, observing that the director 'was fully aware of the hearing date and no evidence that he could not afford to be present had been given'. Furthermore, the right to a fair trial 'does not prevent a hearing in absentia if the appellant has been given notice of the hearing'. The tribunal also held that the scale of the penalty meant that the case should be treated as a criminal one for the purposes of *Article 6* of the *European Convention on Human Rights*. Accordingly, the right to a fair trial under *Article 6* meant that the tribunal was entitled to read a witness statement submitted by the director, despite the prohibition on witness statements where notice of objection is given under *VAT Tribunals Rules 1986 (SI 1986 No 590), rule 21(4)*. The tribunal reviewed the evidence and held that the director's conduct had constituted 'evasion', applying *R v Dealy*, 46.10 PENALTIES: CRIMINAL OFFENCES, and that (with the exception of two small invoices) it was clear that 'the appellant knew that what he was doing or omitting would be regarded as dishonest according to the ordinary standards of reasonable and honest people'. *Dicta* of Lord Lane CJ in *R v Ghosh, CA [1982] 3 WLR 110; [1982] 2 All ER 689* applied. The tribunal therefore dismissed the appeal with the exception of two invoices where it held that dishonesty had not been proved, reducing the penalty from £59,170 to £55,354. *JL Murrell, LON/99/121 (VTD 16878)*.

32.4   See also *Edwards*, 47.11 PENALTIES: EVASION OF TAX.

33   Imports

General Note. This chapter deals with the provisions applying to importations of goods into the UK from outside the Member States of the European Union.

33.1   **Import from outside European Community.**   An individual (M) imported a Porsche from the USA into the UK. The Commissioners issued a ruling that VAT was chargeable on the import. The tribunal upheld the Commissioners' ruling and dismissed M's appeal. *N Murray, LON/97/677 (VTD 15149).*

33.2   A similar decision was reached in a case where a civil servant had imported a car from Cyprus. The tribunal observed that Cyprus was not part of the European Union and that 'the British Sovereign base area in Cyprus forms no part of the territory of the European Union for the purpose of value added tax'. *M Dullaghan, [2000] VATDR 188 (VTD 16407).*

33.3   **Import VAT certificates—duplicated claim for input tax.**   See the cases noted at 49.148 PENALTIES: MISDECLARATION to 49.150 PENALTIES: MISDECLARATION, and those noted at 49.164 PENALTIES: MISDECLARATION to 49.166 PENALTIES: MISDECLARATION.

33.4   **Import certificates—delay in issuing GSP exemption certificate.**   See *John Lanham Watts (Carpets) Ltd*, 49.151 PENALTIES: MISDECLARATION.

33.5   **Import certificates wrongly made out to associated company.**   See *Rosedew Ltd*, 49.152 PENALTIES: MISDECLARATION, and the cases noted at 49.153 PENALTIES: MISDECLARATION.

33.6   **Input tax assessed on importation—premature reclaim.**   See *Ericsons Fashions Ltd*, 49.158 PENALTIES: MISDECLARATION.

33.7   **Input tax reclaimed on imported goods before receipt of import certificate.**   See *Quay Marine Ltd*, 49.159 PENALTIES: MISDECLARATION, and *Analog & Numeric Devices Ltd*, 49.160 PENALTIES: MISDECLARATION.

33.8   **Imported goods—tax repaid in error to agent by Commissioners.**   A company (M) imported a machine valued at about £370,000. It provided a banker's draft for the VAT of £55,000, which was made payable to the Commissioners and was handed to the Commissioners' office in Portsmouth, where it was credited to the account of the company (E) which M had nominated to act as its import agent for this transaction. When the machine arrived at Portsmouth, the VAT officer dealing with the import wrongly charged VAT of only £14,000. The remaining £41,000 of the £55,000 paid by M, which the Commissioners had credited to an account in E's name, was later reclaimed by, and repaid to, E without reference to M. Subsequently M claimed credit for the whole of the £55,000 as input tax, but the Commissioners only allowed credit for the £14,000 which had been charged at the time of the import. Meanwhile E had gone into liquidation without accounting for the balance of £41,000. The tribunal allowed M's appeal. The chairman observed that 'the problem which has arisen here stems entirely from the oversight of the officer of Customs' and considered that 'as a matter of justice, the loss caused by the default of E should in this case be borne by the Commissioners rather than by the appellant'. The full amount of the VAT properly due had been paid by M to the Commissioners by a banker's draft. It was not M's fault that the Commissioners had, under a private arrangement with the agent, credited the money to the agent's account and subsequently allowed the agent to withdraw the money, when it should have been clear that the money did not belong to the agent, but was money provided by M as principal for the purpose of paying VAT. *Mills Marketing Services Ltd, LON/89/1180Y (VTD 4861)*.

33.9 **Input tax reclaimed on imported goods—tax not paid to Commissioners by import agent.** A company traded as importers of steel wool. It used the services of an import agent. The agent sent the company invoices for six shipments of imported goods, and the company paid the invoiced amounts to the agent. However, the agent went into liquidation without accounting for the tax to the Commissioners. The company reclaimed input tax in respect of the transactions, and the Commissioners issued an assessment to recover the tax. The tribunal dismissed the company's appeal. The agent had been an agent of the company, rather than an agent of the Commissioners. The fact that the company had paid the money to the agent did not amount to payment to the Commissioners, and the fact that the agent had been approved did not amount to an authority to receive moneys on behalf of the Commissioners. The company did not hold a C79 certificate in respect of the transactions in question, and the Commissioners had not authorised the company to reclaim input tax thereon. *The Metallic Wool Co Ltd, LON/94/1062A (VTD 13495)*.

33.10 *The Metallic Wool Co Ltd*, 33.9 above, was applied in the similar subsequent case of *Leather Fashions Ltd, LON/93/2319 (VTD 15016)*. (*Note.* An appeal against a misdeclaration penalty was, however, allowed.)

33.11 See also *James*, 49.156 PENALTIES: MISDECLARATION.

33.12 **Import of goods—time at which input tax reclaimable.** A company (C) imported computer parts. It paid the VAT due on these imports each month by direct debit, and reclaimed the amounts in question as input tax. In April 1991 the standard rate of VAT was increased from 15% to 17.5%. However, as a result of a programming error in its accounts computer, C continued to account for VAT at the old rate of 15%. It discovered the error at the beginning of June, notified the Commissioners, and submitted a form C305 indicating the underpayments for April and May 1991 together with a cheque for the amount in question. The Commissioners acknowledged receipt of the C305 on 21 June. On 27 June C submitted its monthly return for May, in which it reclaimed the amounts shown on the C305 as input tax. The Commissioners formed the opinion that, since the C305 had only been submitted in June, the tax shown thereon should have been reclaimed in C's June return, rather than in the May return. They therefore issued an assessment, including a charge to default interest for one month. C appealed, contending that, since the tax related to goods which had been imported in April and May, and had been paid before submission of the May return, it had been entitled to reclaim the input tax in its May return. The tribunal accepted this contention and allowed the appeal, holding that, since the C305 had been acknowledged by the Commissioners, C had been entitled to reclaim the amounts as input tax by virtue of what is now *VAT Regulations 1995 (SI 1995 No 2158), reg 29(2)*. *Compaq Computer Manufacturing Ltd, EDN/92/126 (VTD 10354)*.

33.13 **Input tax reclaimed on imported goods—no certificate held.** See *Vin-Dotco (UK) Ltd*, 49.167 PENALTIES: MISDECLARATION.

33.14 **Imported goods—input tax reclaimed by import agent.** A company (C) carried on business as freight forwarders and shipping agents. It paid VAT due on certain imports of goods by its clients, in order to obtain an Entry Acceptance device enabling the goods to be cleared without lodging manual documents. After Customs had issued forms C79, C reclaimed the tax as input tax. The Commissioners issued an assessment to recover the tax, considering that it was not deductible since the goods had not been imported for the purpose of C's business, as required by what is now

VATA 1994, s 24(1)(b). The tribunal upheld the assessment and dismissed C's appeal. *Cavenco Ltd, LON/93/540A (VTD 11700)*.

33.15   In a case where the facts were unusual and in dispute, a VAT officer discovered that a Portuguese company had exported some goods to a UK company (M), but had mistakenly issued the relevant form C79 to a trader (S) who had previously acted as M's import agent, but was no longer acting as such. S had reclaimed the relevant input tax, and the Commissioners issued an assessment to recover the tax from S, and allowed M to reclaim the tax even though it did not hold the C79. The tribunal upheld the assessment and dismissed S's appeal, finding that S had 'not been wholly candid with the Commissioners or, for that matter, with this tribunal'. *B Shokrollahi (t/a BS Mondial), MAN/94/526 (VTD 13781)*.

33.16   **Whether goods imported as agent or as principal.**   A company resident outside the EU, which carried on a clothing business, appointed a woman resident in the UK (W) as a representative. She took orders for the company's clothing from UK retailers, and faxed these to the company. In many cases, the retailers were treated as the importers of the clothing. However, in some cases the retailers refused to be treated as the importers, and W was treated as the importer. She was registered for VAT and accounted for the tax due on importation. She reclaimed this as input tax. The amount was initially repaid to her, but the Commissioners subsequently formed the opinion that W was acting as an agent and that the repayment had been made in error, and issued an assessment to recover the tax. W appealed, contending that she had been acting as an independent principal and was entitled to credit for the input tax. The tribunal dismissed her appeal, holding on the evidence that she had been acting as an agent and was not entitled to credit for the input tax. *Angela Walker, LON/92/1339A (VTD 12421)*.

33.17   **VATA 1994, s 21—value of imported goods.**   An individual (M) purchased a quantity of gemstones from a Canadian company for £52,318. He paid VAT of £8,879 in accordance with *VATA 1994, s 1*. Subsequently he discovered that the gemstones were only worth about £11,000. He submitted a claim for part of the VAT which he had paid on their importation to be refunded to him. The Commissioners rejected the claim and he appealed. The tribunal dismissed his appeal, holding that the original valuation had been in accordance with *VATA 1994, s 21*, which required the gemstones to be valued for VAT purposes at the amount which M had actually paid to the vendors. *AJ Maden, [1996] VATDR 449 (VTD 14603)*.

34   Input Tax

Note. For cases concerning the disallowance of input tax under *Input Tax Order 1992, Article 5*, see 8 BUSINESS ENTERTAINMENT. For cases concerning *Input Tax Order 1992, Article 6*, see 15 CONSTRUCTION OF BUILDINGS, ETC. For cases concerning *Input Tax Order 1992, Article 7*, see 9 CARS. For cases concerning the evidence required to support a claim to input tax, see 38 INVOICES AND CREDIT NOTES.

WHETHER SUPPLIES MADE TO THE APPELLANT

Motoring expenses

34.1   **Whether petrol supplied to company or to agents.**   A company which sold clothing appointed a number of self-employed agents on a commission basis. The agents had to undertake extensive travelling, for which they used their own cars. They were allowed to deduct the amounts spent on petrol from the amounts they collected for the company, on condition that they provided the company with invoices from the garages, made out in the company's name. The company reclaimed input tax on the amounts in question, and the Commissioners issued an assessment to recover the tax. The tribunal dismissed the company's appeal. On the evidence, the agents were independent contractors rather than employees. Accordingly, the petrol had been supplied to the agents rather than to the company, and the company was not entitled to reclaim the input tax. *Berbrooke Fashions, [1977] VATTR 168 (VTD 426).*

34.2   *Berbrooke Fashions*, 34.1 above, was applied in the similar cases of *S & U Stores Ltd, BIR/76/89 (VTD 726)* and *Holywell International (Engineering) Ltd, MAN/83/90 (VTD 1470).*

34.3   Similar decisions were reached in *James Trevor Ltd, LON/83/5 (VTD 1425)* and *Fairway Lubricants Ltd, LON/83/161 (VTD 1577).*

34.4   **Whether petrol supplied to contractor or to subcontractors.**   A partnership which operated a dairy business sold milk to the public by means of regular deliveries from vans to householders. It engaged van drivers as self-employed subcontractors with contractual responsibilities to deliver regular orders to customers, collect the sums owing and pay them to the partnership. The partnership gave the van drivers money to pay for their petrol, which was to be purchased from one of a selected number of garages. The partnership reclaimed input tax in respect of the fuel purchased by the van drivers, and the Commissioners issued an assessment to recover the tax. The tribunal dismissed the partnership's appeal, holding that the petrol was supplied to the van drivers rather than to the partnership, so that the partnership was not entitled to credit for the input tax. *R Wiseman & Sons, [1984] VATTR 168 (VTD 1691).*

34.5   A similar decision, applying *Berbrooke Fashions Ltd*, 34.1 above, was reached in *BC Allum, LON/93/1452A (VTD 12646).*

34.6   **Mileage allowances to employees.** A company which retailed clothing employed 175 salesmen. It agreed with their trade union that each of them should receive a weekly allowance to cover the cost of six gallons of petrol. No record was kept of the employees' actual mileage. The company reclaimed input tax in respect of these payments and the Commissioners issued an assessment to recover the tax. The tribunal dismissed the company's appeal, accepting evidence that the allowance covered only part of the actual expenditure, but holding that the petrol had been supplied to the employees as individuals rather than to the company, so that the company could not reclaim input tax. *Stirlings (Glasgow) Ltd, [1982] VATTR 116 (VTD 1232). (Note.* See now the *VAT (Input Tax) (Person Supplied) Order 1991 (SI 1991 No 2306).)*

34.7   A company provided senior employees with cars. The employees were allowed to use the cars privately, and were responsible for buying petrol. They were paid a mileage allowance calculated according to a fixed formula per mile travelled from the managers' homes to sites and back, with a reduction of twelve miles per day to represent private mileage. The company reclaimed input tax on the mileage allowances. The Commissioners issued an assessment to recover the tax claimed in respect of the journeys between the employees' homes and the sites at which they worked. The tribunal dismissed the company's appeal, holding that the supplies of petrol were made to the employees and not to the company. (However, the tribunal observed that if the petrol were to be treated as being supplied to the company, input tax would be reclaimable in respect of the whole of the mileage allowances paid, since they were paid for the purpose of the company's business. Because the managers had no normal workplace, the journeys from their homes to the sites were for business purposes. It also followed that, if the petrol were to be treated as being supplied to the company, it could not be expected to account for output tax in respect of either the petrol itself or the mileage allowances, since there would be neither any transfer of the petrol nor any private use of it.) *McLean Homes Midland Ltd, MAN/89/363 (VTD 5010). (Notes.* (1) Following this decision, the assessment under appeal was reduced from £20,819 to £7,566 by agreement. For a subsequent application for costs, see 2.280 APPEALS. (2) See also the note following *Stirlings (Glasgow) Ltd*, 34.6 above.)

34.8   *McLean Homes Midland Ltd*, 34.7 above, was applied in a subsequent case where the tribunal held that petrol had been supplied to the employees of a company rather than to the company itself, and that the company was therefore not entitled to reclaim any input tax in respect of the petrol in question. *Klockner Ferromatik Desma Ltd, MAN/90/144 (VTD 7061). (Note.* See the note following *Stirlings (Glasgow) Ltd*, 34.6 above.)

34.9   **Input tax reclaimed on car leased on behalf of associated company.** A company (W) leased a car for the benefit of an associated company (J). W paid the first five instalments and was reimbursed by J, which paid the next nine instalments. The lease was then reassigned to J, which reclaimed input tax in respect of the fourteen instalments which had been paid while the car was leased to W. The Commissioners disallowed the claim since the supply had been made to W rather than to J. The tribunal upheld the Commissioners' decision and dismissed J's appeal. *Johanson Ltd, MAN/84/200 (VTD 1730).*

34.10   **Input tax reclaimed on termination of lease of car.**   A company (T) leased a car from a finance company (M). Under the leasing agreement, which was to last for three years, the car remained the property of M. T subsequently decided to end the lease after only one year, and in accordance with the terms of the agreement, M required payment of £10,726 plus VAT of £1,609, totalling £12,335. T ascertained from a car dealer (S) that the car was only worth £10,000, and arranged that S should purchase the car from M for a nominal price of £12,335, of which £2,335 would be reimbursed to S by T. T then reclaimed the VAT of £1,609 as input tax and appealed against the Commissioners' rejection of the claim. The tribunal dismissed T's appeal. The car had been sold to S rather than to T, and since the car had not been supplied to T, T was not entitled to reclaim the input tax. *Telequick Ltd, MAN/90/318 (VTD 5319).*

34.11   **Land Rover purchased by an employee—whether input tax reclaimable by employer.**   A foreman employed by a construction company purchased a Land Rover. The company reclaimed input tax on the purchase and the Commissioners issued an assessment to recover the tax. The tribunal dismissed the company's appeal, holding that as the supply was made to the employee rather than to the company, the company was not entitled to reclaim input tax. *Binof Construction Ltd, MAN/90/105 (VTD 5113).*

Accommodation

34.12   **Board and accommodation supplied to employees of company installing machinery—input tax reclaimed by purchaser.**   A company (B) contracted with a Dutch company to purchase a brickmaking machine. It was agreed that the machine would be installed by engineers employed by the Dutch company, and that B would arrange and pay for the engineers' board and accommodation. B reclaimed the input tax on the supplies of accommodation, and the Commissioners issued an assessment to recover the tax, considering that the accommodation had been supplied to the engineers rather than to B. The tribunal dismissed B's appeal, holding that the accommodation had been supplied to B by the hotel and by B to the engineers, so that although B was entitled to credit for input tax on the accommodation supplied by the hotel, it was liable to account for a corresponding amount of output tax on the supply by it to the engineers. *Ibstock Building Products Ltd, [1987] VATTR 1 (VTD 2304).* (*Note.* For a case in which this decision was distinguished with regard to output tax, see *Stormseal (UPVC) Window Co Ltd*, 58.221 SUPPLY.)

34.13   **Accommodation supplied for lecturers at conferences.**   An institute which organised conferences provided overnight accommodation, in the hotels where the conferences were held, for any lecturer who required it. The institute reclaimed input tax on the accommodation and the Commissioners issued an assessment to recover the tax, against which the institute appealed. The tribunal dismissed the appeal, holding that the accommodation was supplied by the hotel directly to the lecturers rather than to the institute. (Input tax was also disallowed on refreshments supplied to the lecturers on the grounds that they were business entertainment.) *Institute of Purchasing & Supply, [1987] VATTR 207 (VTD 2533).*

34.14   **Accommodation provided for tennis players by club organising tournament—whether accommodation supplied to club.**   A tennis club organised an annual tournament and provided bed and breakfast accommodation at a hotel for the top eight seeded players in the men's and ladies' singles. The accommodation was booked by the club, but the hotel made the bills out to the players, who paid the bills and presented them to the club for reimbursement. The club reclaimed input tax on the basis that the hotel had supplied the accommodation to it. The Commissioners issued an assessment to recover the tax, contending that the hotels made the supplies directly to the players rather than to the club. The club appealed. The tribunal held that the hotel supplied the accommodation to the club rather than to the players, applying *Ibstock Building Products Ltd*, 34.12 above, and distinguishing *Institute of Purchasing & Supply*, 34.13 above. The fact that the bills were made out to the players, rather than to the club, was a matter of administrative convenience only, and did not affect the legal nature of the supplies. An alternative contention by the Commissioners, that the rooms were provided for the purpose of business entertainment, was also rejected by the tribunal. The essence of entertainment was that it was provided free to the recipient, applying *Celtic Football & Athletic Club*, 8.34 BUSINESS ENTERTAINMENT. However, the tribunal upheld a third contention for the Commissioners, that having received supplies from the hotel the club had made those supplies to the players, and thus, although the club could reclaim the input tax on the supplies by the hotel, it had to account for a corresponding amount of output tax on the supplies deemed to have been made by it to the players. *Northern Lawn Tennis Club, [1989] VATTR 1 (VTD 3528)*.

34.15   **Accommodation reserved and paid for by employees—employees subsequently reimbursed by employer—whether employer entitled to reclaim input tax.** An insurance company (which was partly exempt) required some of its employees to travel on business. The employees sometimes had to reserve and pay for overnight hotel accommodation. The company reimbursed them for this, and reclaimed input tax. The Commissioners rejected the claim and the tribunal dismissed the company's appeal. The tribunal held that, where the accommodation in question was reserved by the company, it was supplied to the company and the input tax formed part of the company's residual input tax, to be apportioned between taxable and exempt supplies. However, where the accommodation was reserved by the employees, it was supplied by the hotels to the employees and the company was not entitled to reclaim input tax. Furthermore, the company was not itself making any supplies of accommodation to the employees. *Leesportfeuille 'Intiem' CV v Staatssecretaris van Financiën*, 21.197 EUROPEAN COMMUNITY LAW, applied; *Ibstock Building Products Ltd*, 34.12 above, and *Northern Lawn Tennis Club Ltd*, 34.14 above, distinguished. *Co-Operative Insurance Society Ltd, [1997] VATDR 65 (VTD 14862)*. (*Note.* For the Commissioners' practice following this decision, see Business Brief 16/97, issued on 21 July 1997.)

Associated companies

34.16   **Partnership reclaiming input tax in respect of receivership of associated company.** A married couple traded in partnership as producers of slides and computer graphics. The husband (L) was also one of two directors of a company which traded from the same premises. The partnership had invested approximately £60,000 in the company. However, a serious dispute arose between L and his co-director, as a result of which L instructed solicitors to apply for an order appointing a receiver for the company. An accountant agreed to act as receiver on condition that L indemnified him for any costs incurred as receiver which the company was unable to meet. L accepted this condition, and the accountant was duly appointed as receiver of the company. He discovered that L's co-director had been acting fraudulently and had used the company's funds for his personal purposes. The receiver invoiced the company for his professional fees, which the partnership paid in accordance with the indemnity agreement which L had previously entered into. The partnership reclaimed input tax in respect of the amounts paid. The Commissioners issued an assessment to recover the tax, considering that the relevant services had been supplied to the company rather than to the partnership. The tribunal dismissed the partnership's appeal, holding that the receiver's services had not been supplied to the partnership, so that the partnership was not entitled to reclaim the relevant input tax. *M & RJ Lister, LON/92/1336 (VTD 9972)*.

34.17   **Input tax reclaimed on supplies to associated company.**   A company (S) purchased some tooling equipment, on which it reclaimed input tax. It subsequently suffered financial difficulties, transferred its business as a going concern to an associated company (R) and went into liquidation. R's controlling director persuaded the companies which had supplied S with the tooling equipment to issue credit notes to S and to issue fresh invoices to R. R then reclaimed input tax. When the Commissioners discovered what had happened, they issued an assessment to recover the tax. The tribunal dismissed R's appeal, holding that the relevant supplies had been made to S rather than to R, that the credit notes were ineffective and that the replacement invoices were false. *Realm Defence Industries Ltd, LON/98/799 (VTD 16831)*. (*Note.* The tribunal awarded costs of £2,000 to the Commissioners.)

34.18   See also *Collins*, 38.18 INVOICES AND CREDIT NOTES; *Tortoise Factory Units Ltd*, 38.19 INVOICES AND CREDIT NOTES, and *Gavacan*, 38.20 INVOICES AND CREDIT NOTES.

34.19   **Purported supply between associated companies—whether input tax reclaimable.**   A company (C) was in financial difficulties. Its controlling director had incorporated a further company (M). He arranged for C to issue M with an invoice charging £298,500 plus VAT in respect of his services. M reclaimed input tax (of more than £52,000) in respect of this invoice. C did not account for the output tax, and was subsequently dissolved. The Commissioners rejected M's claim for repayment of the input tax, and the tribunal dismissed M's appeal, observing that the director had not shown that the invoice 'related to any supply of services from C to M for a consideration of £298,500 or any other agreed consideration', and that the director's evidence as to the reasons for the invoice showed a 'lack of credibility'. *Morston Properties Ltd (No 2), LON/97/1107 (VTD 15444)*.

34.20   The appellant company (M) in the case noted at 34.19 above issued seven invoices to another company (U) incorporated by its controlling director, purporting to charge VAT of more than £69,000. Most of this related to the director's services, while some related to the sale of assets. U reclaimed this amount as input tax, while M ceased trading, owing more than £54,000 in unpaid VAT. The Commissioners rejected U's repayment claim, and the tribunal dismissed U's appeal. With regard to the purported transfers of assets, the tribunal found that, in the case of the majority of the items, there was no evidence of any actual supply. In the case of the three remaining items (a printer, some printer toner and some bookmarks) the purported transfer was at a price at least 50% more than M had been charged for them. The tribunal observed that 'since each of those three items was an everyday item whose second-hand value must have been less than its original value, we are unable to accept that the supplies were genuine taxable supplies to (U)'. With regard to the invoice in respect of the director's purported services, the tribunal was 'unable to accept that the single invoice raised by (M) represented genuine supplies of services' and found that M 'did not make a genuine taxable supply of services to (U)'. *United Society of Poets Ltd, LON/98/182 (VTD 15772)*. (*Note.* The tribunal awarded costs of £500 to the Commissioners, finding that the appeal was 'frivolous in nature'.)

34.21   **Purported transfer of goods from company to associated partnership—whether input tax reclaimable.**   A company (K) was in financial difficulties, and the Commissioners began distraint proceedings against it. Bailiffs visited K's premises in May 1995, and sought to distrain on five motor vehicles and five items of plant and machinery. K's directors produced an invoice purporting to show that the assets in question had been sold two months earlier to an associated partnership comprising K's controlling shareholders. The Commissioners did not accept the validity of the sale, but did not execute the distraint. Although the invoice produced by K's directors indicated that it had charged VAT of £13,000 on the sale of the goods in question to the partnership, K did not pay this to the Commissioners as output tax. Subsequently an associated company (L) reclaimed the amount in question as input tax in its return for the period ending October 1996. The Commissioners rejected the claim and L appealed, contending that it had purchased the goods in question from the partnership on 25 October 1996, for the same price as the partnership had paid to K. (K had ceased trading in November 1996 and went into voluntary liquidation.) The tribunal dismissed L's appeal, holding on the evidence that it was not satisfied that 'any sale of the assets ever took place ... There is no dispute that no cash or cheque for the purchase price and VAT was ever paid by (L) to the partnership on 25 October 1996 and it is clear that no such payment has ever been made subsequently. The VAT returns of the partnership for the period ending 31 May 1996 to 28 February 1997 show that the partnership was not trading during these periods and no input or output tax nor supplies are recorded.' On the evidence, 'there was never any intention that (L) should pay any money to the partnership for the assets and no payment has been made. The entries in (L's) books are ... paper entries and do not evidence or record a genuine sale of the assets.' *LMB Holdings Ltd, MAN/97/382 (VTD 15739)*. (*Note*. Costs were awarded to the Commissioners.)

Leasing

Cases where the appellant was successful

34.22 **Whether lease supplied to solicitors' partnership or to company.** A firm of solicitors, with a view to future expansion, leased premises which were larger than they required, and sublet part of the premises. They incorporated a company for the purpose of holding the lease and assigning the subleases. They reclaimed input tax in respect of their expenditure on the lease. The Commissioners issued an assessment to recover the tax, on the basis that the relevant supply had been made to the company rather than to the partnership. The tribunal allowed the partnership's appeal, holding that in substance the supply had been made to the partnership for the purpose of the partnership's business. *Bird Semple & Crawford Herron, [1986] VATTR 218 (VTD 2171)*.

Cases where the appellant was unsuccessful

34.23 **Whether supplies made to landlord or to leaseholder.** A company agreed to purchase the premises which it occupied, but was unable to proceed with the purchase for financial reasons. The landlords agreed to release the company from the contract on condition that the company paid the landlords' costs. The landlords were not registered for VAT, and the company reclaimed the input tax on the costs. The Commissioners rejected the claim and the tribunal dismissed the company's appeal, holding that the legal services had been supplied to the landlords and not to the company. *WJ Brown Toys Ltd, MAN/83/333 (VTD 1684)*.

34.24 A photographer reclaimed input tax in respect of repairs and improvements to premises which he occupied. The Commissioners issued an assessment to recover the tax, considering that the supplies in question had been made to the landlord of the premises rather than to the photographer. The tribunal upheld the assessment and dismissed the photographer's appeal. *LA Barnett, LON/88/753 (VTD 3245)*.

34.25   A company which held a tenancy of part of a building also acted as the managing agent of that building. It reclaimed input tax on expenditure relating to the management of the building. The Commissioners issued an assessment to recover the tax, on the basis that the relevant supplies had been made to the landlord, rather than to the company. The tribunal upheld the assessment and dismissed the company's appeal. *WS Atkins (Services) Ltd, LON/92/1872 (VTD 10131)*.

34.26   **Payments made by guarantor of leases following default by tenant— whether supply made to guarantor.** In 1986 a company (V) acquired a subsidiary (G). G acquired a number of leasehold properties. The landlords required V to guarantee that G would meet its obligations with regard to the leases. In 1988 V sold its shareholding in G to an unrelated company (C), but V continued to be bound by its guarantees. In 1991 C went into receivership. The landlords claimed substantial sums from V under the guarantees. In cases where the landlords had waived exemption under the leases, the claims included VAT. V reclaimed input tax in respect of its payments to the landlords. The Commissioners rejected the claim, on the grounds that the payments were not consideration for any supplies made to V. The tribunal dismissed V's appeal, holding that the landlords had made supplies to G rather than to V. Although V had paid consideration in respect of these supplies, it was not the recipient of the supplies and was therefore not entitled to reclaim input tax. *Vivat Holdings plc, [1995] VATDR 348 (VTD 13568)*.

34.27   A similar decision was reached in a case where an accountant had been a shareholder in a company which occupied rented premises, and had issued a guarantee to the landlord in respect of the rent. The company failed to pay the rent, and the accountant was called upon to pay the unpaid rent in accordance with the guarantee. The tribunal held that the accountant was not entitled to reclaim input tax on the payment. *F Cable, EDN/94/269 (VTD 13845)*.

34.28   A similar decision was reached in a case where a company (K) had accepted the assignment of a lease under conditions whereby it indemnified the assignor against default. Nine months later K assigned the lease to an unrelated company (F) which subsequently defaulted and went into liquidation. The lessor demanded and obtained payment of arrears of rent from the company (T) which had acted as surety under the original underlease, and T in turn demanded payment from K. K appealed to the tribunal, contending that the original lessee was entitled to credit for input tax on the payment which T had made to the lessor (so that its liability under the indemnity agreement would be reduced accordingly). The tribunal dismissed the appeal, holding that the relevant supplies were made to F, rather than to the original lessee, which was not entitled to input tax thereon. The chairman observed that it was a 'basic principle that it is the recipient of the supply who obtains the credit regardless of whether it is he who provides the consideration'. *Kenwood Appliances Ltd, [1996] VATDR 127 (VTD 13876)*. (*Note.* The Commissioners accepted that K had sufficient *locus standi* to lodge an appeal. Compare the cases at 2.26 to 2.31 APPEALS.)

34.29   **Whether sunbeds supplied by vendor to leasing company or to lessee.** A company (T) sold sunbeds. In cases where customers wished to acquire sunbeds under a leasing agreement, rather than by outright purchase, it delivered the sunbed to the customer but transferred the ownership of the sunbed to a leasing company. In such cases it paid the initial amount of rent due by the customer to the leasing company under the leasing agreement, and reclaimed input tax in respect of such payments. The Commissioners issued an assessment to recover this tax, considering that the effect of the agreement was that T sold the sunbed to the leasing company rather than to the ultimate customer, but that in paying the initial rent it was paying a liability of the customer, and that since it had made no supply to the customer, it was not entitled to reclaim input tax in respect of its payment of the customer's initial rental liability. The tribunal upheld the assessment and dismissed T's appeal. *Tantol Ltd, MAN/91/430 (VTD 10013)*.

Legal costs

Cases where the appellant was successful

34.30   Legal services supplied to farming partnership. Two brothers who were in partnership as farmers held the tenancy of their farm jointly with their father. The father took no part in the partnership's farming activities. The partners and their father purchased the freehold of the farm. They subsequently sold this farm and purchased another farm. The partners reclaimed input tax in respect of services supplied to them by two firms of land agents and a firm of solicitors in connection with these transactions. The Commissioners issued an assessment to recover the tax, considering that as the partners had owned the farms jointly with their father who was not a partner, the services were not strictly attributable to the partnership. The tribunal allowed the brother's appeal, finding that the VAT officer who had raised the assessment had acted under a misapprehension, and holding that each of the supplies was a supply to the taxable persons, the two brothers, even though the supplies were also made to their father. *Article 17(2)(a)* of the *EC Sixth Directive* made it clear that the important requirement was that the supply in question was used for the purposes of the taxable transactions of the taxable person. *Glasse Brothers, [1989] VATTR 143 (VTD 3716)*.

34.31   Parent company requiring solicitors to investigate affairs of subsidiary company—whether services supplied to parent or to subsidiary. A company (C), which was registered for VAT, had a subsidiary company (L), which was not registered. C's directors became concerned about the way in which one of L's directors was acting, and engaged a firm of solicitors to undertake a confidential investigation of L's affairs. C reclaimed the input tax in respect of the solicitors' services, although the relevant invoice had been made out to L rather than to C. The Commissioners issued an assessment to recover the tax, considering that the services in question had actually been supplied to L, and that since L was not registered for VAT, the tax was not reclaimable. The tribunal allowed C's appeal against the assessment, finding that the invoice had been made out in L's name in error and holding that the services had actually been supplied to C and had been supplied for the protection of C's business. *Crompton Enterprises Ltd, [1992] VATTR 321 (VTD 7866)*.

Cases where the appellant was partly successful

34.32   Legal costs of sale of hotel equipment. A farmer (J) also operated a hotel, which he leased from a company. He had a 25% shareholding in the company, and was one of the three directors. The hotel was sold in 1988. J reclaimed input tax on legal costs incurred in connection with the sale of the hotel. The Commissioners issued an assessment to recover the tax, considering that, since the hotel was owned by the company rather than by J, the legal costs had not been incurred in connection with J's business. J appealed, contending that he should be entitled to reclaim input tax since he had been treated as carrying on the business of the hotel and had accounted for tax accordingly, and that the hotel equipment and a staff bungalow in the hotel grounds were owned by him personally rather than by the company. The tribunal allowed J's appeal in part, holding that the legal costs incurred in connection with the sale of the hotel freehold were incurred by the company but that the legal costs incurred in connection with the sale of the hotel equipment and the staff bungalow were incurred by J himself for the purpose of a business which he had operated. The tribunal apportioned the total input tax shown on the relevant invoices and directed that ⁵/₁₈ of the total input tax should be treated as allowable. *RJ Jones, LON/89/1302Y (VTD 5701)*.

Cases where the appellant was unsuccessful

34.33 **Legal costs relating to breach of covenant.**   A husband and wife carried on business in partnership. They acquired the lease of a commercial building. In 1982 the freeholders of the property took them to Court for breach of their repairing covenants under the lease. The couple lost the action and were ordered to pay costs to the freeholders. They reclaimed input tax on the costs and the Commissioners issued an assessment to recover the tax. The tribunal dismissed the couple's appeal, finding that the costs were in respect of supplies of legal services made to the freeholders, and holding that the lessees were not entitled to reclaim the input tax thereon. *JG & MV Potton, LON/87/592 (VTD 2882)*.

34.34 **Unsuccessful legal action—whether losing party may claim input tax on costs.**   A trader (T) who carried on business as a market gardener had previously been director of a company which was in liquidation. He began legal actions against the liquidator of the company and against a firm of solicitors. His actions were dismissed by the High Court which ordered him to pay the defendants' costs. He reclaimed the VAT on the costs as input tax and the Commissioners issued an assessment to recover the tax. The tribunal dismissed his appeal, holding that the relevant supplies had been made to the defendants, rather than to T, so that the input tax was not deductible. The QB upheld this decision. *NO Turner (t/a Turner Agricultural) v C & E Commrs, QB [1992] STC 621*. (*Note.* For another issue in this case, see 34.423 below.)

34.35 *Turner*, 34.34 above, was applied in the similar subsequent cases of *KC & HM Barnes (t/a Sidlesham Common Carriage Company), LON/95/2983A (VTD 14090); M Olivant, MAN/97/344 (VTD 15422)* and *Dow-Nell Construction Co Ltd, LON/99/1336 (VTD 16871)*.

34.36 A firm of architects took legal action against a client. The client won the case and the firm was ordered to pay his costs, totalling more than £60,000. The firm reclaimed input tax on these costs. The Commissioners rejected the claim, as the legal services in question had been supplied to the successful client rather than to the firm. The tribunal dismissed the firm's appeal against this decision, applying *Francis Jackson Homes Ltd*, 34.41 below. *Nye Saunders & Partners, LON/93/1318A (VTD 11384)*.

34.37 *Nye Saunders & Partners*, 34.36 above, was applied in the similar subsequent case of *R Carr, MAN/97/327 (VTD 15411)*.

34.38 Similar decisions were reached in *EG Davey (t/a EG Davey & Co), LON/95/527A (VTD 13538)* and *K Tulsidas & MK Bhatt (t/a Amazon International), MAN/98/770 (VTD 16335)*.

34.39 A trader failed to pay a bill of £1,300 from her solicitors. The solicitors took legal action against her, and she was ordered to pay the fees and the legal costs. She appealed, but subsequently withdrew her appeal and agreed to pay the solicitors £23,000 in full settlement. She reclaimed input tax on this payment. The Commissioners rejected the claim and she appealed. The tribunal dismissed her appeal, applying *Turner*, 34.34 above. *AC Slot, LON/94/1089 (VTD 15076)*. (*Note.* For another issue in this case, see 39.111 LAND.)

34.40   **Legal fees relating to transfer of share capital.** A company (B) wished to acquire the share capital of another company (G). G's owners insisted that B should pay all legal fees relating to the transaction. B reclaimed input tax on the vendors' legal fees and the Commissioners issued an assessment to recover the tax. The tribunal dismissed B's appeal, holding that the solicitors had supplied their services to the vendors of G's shares, rather than to G or B. *Brucegate Ltd, MAN/89/ 761(VTD 4903).*

34.41   **Solicitors' fees on sale of land—whether services supplied to vendors or purchaser.** A company purchased some land for development, and agreed to pay the solicitors' fees incurred by the vendors. It reclaimed the input tax on these fees, and the Commissioners issued an assessment to recover the tax, since the solicitors had supplied their services to the vendors rather than to the company. The tribunal upheld the assessment and dismissed the company's appeal. *Francis Jackson Homes Ltd, LON/90/1228Z (VTD 6352).*

34.42   **Legal costs relating to abortive purchase of premises—whether supplied to vendor or purchaser.** See *WJ Brown Toys Ltd*, 34.23 above.

34.43   **Legal costs—whether supplied to partnership or to individual partner.** A partnership was dissolved in 1986 and one of the partners continued in business as a sole trader. He incurred legal and accountancy fees in the course of a dispute with his former partner, and reclaimed the VAT on the fees as input tax. The Commissioners issued an assessment to recover the tax and he appealed, contending that the expenditure had been incurred to protect his business reputation. The tribunal dismissed his appeal, holding that the expenditure was incurred in the course of the partnership business and that the partnership was a separate entity from the appellant's own business. *GG Ingram (t/a Ingram & Co), MAN/89/30 (VTD 4605).*

34.44   A partnership which provided services to publishers traded from a room in a house owned by the principal partner. The partner decided to sell the freehold of the house to raise finance, and the partnership reclaimed input tax on the legal costs incurred. The Commissioners issued an assessment to recover the tax, considering that the supply had not been made to the partnership and that the costs had not been directly incurred for the purposes of the partnership's business. The tribunal dismissed the partnership's appeal, applying *Rushgreen Builders Ltd*, 34.74 below. The partnership had not had any interest in the property, and had not incurred the expenditure in question. The supplies had been made to the individual partner rather than to the partnership. *Rock Lambert, LON/90/1544Y (VTD 6637).*

34.45   Two relatives traded in partnership. In 1986 one of the partners (T) was injured in a road traffic accident. He took legal proceedings, which were not settled until 1995 (by which time the partnership had ceased to be registered). He reclaimed input tax on his solicitors' costs. The Commissioners rejected the claim on the basis that the solicitors' services had been supplied to T as an individual, rather than to the partnership. The tribunal dismissed T's appeal, applying *Rock Lambert*, 34.44 above. *KW Taylor, MAN/96/21 (VTD 14244).*

34.46   A two-person partnership ceased trading and deregistered in January 1990. Subsequently one of the partners (S) formed the opinion that the other partner had been defrauding him. He engaged a solicitor to undertake enquiries, and reclaimed input tax on the solicitor's fees. The Commissioners rejected his claim and he appealed. The tribunal dismissed his appeal, holding that the tax was not deductible since the services in question had been supplied to S as an individual, rather than to the partnership. *B Stone, LON/94/37 (VTD 12442).*

34.47   Transfer of employer's pension funds—legal advice provided for employees affected—whether services supplied to employer. See *The Plessey Co Ltd*, 51.7 PENSION FUNDS.

Expenditure on premises

Cases where the appellant was successful

34.48   **Whether supplies made to managing agent or freeholders.**   An estate agent (S) acted as manager of a block of flats. He was informed by the local authority that urgent work should be carried out on the flats, and arranged for contractors to undertake the required work. However, the freeholders and leaseholders of the flats refused to accept liability for the work, contending that there had been a contravention of *Landlord and Tenant Act, s 20*. S therefore paid the contractors himself, and reclaimed the relevant input tax. The Commissioners issued an assessment to recover the tax, considering that the supply had been made to the freeholders of the flats, rather than to S, and that S was acting as an agent rather than as a principal. The tribunal allowed the appeal, holding that the supply had been made to S, who had 'accepted the obligations of principal to the contract'. The payment had been made to protect the reputation of S's business and the input tax was deductible. *GHJA Scott (t/a Chancellor & Sons), LON/90/1637Y (VTD 6922).*

34.49   **Repairs to bomb-damaged building—whether supplies made to landlord or tenant.**   A major insurance company carried on business from premises in London, which it leased. The premises were badly damaged by IRA bombs, and the insurance company arranged for repairs and improvements to be carried out. The repairs were estimated to cost almost £18,000,000, and the proposed improvements were estimated to cost more than £12,000,000. The insurance company reclaimed input tax on the repairs. The Commissioners rejected the claim on the basis that the relevant supplies should be treated as having been made to the landlord, rather than to the insurance company which had effectively been acting as the landlord's agent. The insurance company appealed, contending that, in arranging for the repair work, it had acted as an independent principal. The tribunal accepted this contention and allowed the appeal. *Commercial Union Assurance Co plc, LON/95/2756 (VTD 14195)*. (*Note*. The tribunal also held that a payment of £5,250,000 by the landlord to the insurance company, made as a contribution to the cost of the improvement works, represented consideration for a taxable supply of services by the insurance company to the landlord.)

34.50   **Construction of farm building—whether supply made to landlord or tenant.**   A tenant farmer reclaimed input tax on the construction of a grain store at the farm. The grain store cost £57,894 plus VAT. The landlord paid £57,000 and the tenant paid the balance. The Commissioners discovered that most of the cost had been met by the landlord of the farm, and issued an assessment to recover the tax. The tenant appealed. The tribunal allowed the appeal. On the evidence, the landlord had been 'under no legal or contractual obligation' to pay the £57,000. The tenant had been responsible for the erection of the building, and would be entitled to remove it under the *Agricultural Holdings Act 1986*. Accordingly, he was entitled to credit for the input tax. *JA Nichols, MAN/96/33 (VTD 14521).*

34.51   **Input tax reclaimed on supplies for property development—whether company acting as principal or agent.**   See *Drexlodge Ltd*, 1.38 AGENTS.

34.52   Input Tax

Cases where the appellant was unsuccessful

34.52   **Whether supplies made to surveyor or to clients.**   A surveyor supervised the work of an extension to clients' premises. When the work was nearly complete, a defect was discovered. The clients required that this be put right, but the builders who were constructing the extension went into liquidation. The clients had the work carried out by another company at a cost of £7,423, including VAT of £550. They claimed damages from the surveyor, who paid them the amount in full and also paid the clients' legal costs of £1,188 including VAT of £88. The surveyor reclaimed the £638 as input tax and the Commissioners issued an assessment to recover this amount. The tribunal dismissed the surveyor's appeal, holding that the relevant supplies were clearly made to the clients rather than to the surveyor. *ME Coster, LON/80/394 (VTD 1057).*

34.53   **Remedial work on house—input tax reclaimed by original builder.**   A couple, who had purchased a house from the company which had built it, discovered several structural defects and arranged for another firm of builders to remedy these. They claimed the costs of this work from the company which had built the house. The matter was referred to arbitration and the company was ordered to pay the couple more than £20,000 as compensation. The company reclaimed input tax in respect of some of the remedial work for which the purchasers had paid. The Commissioners rejected the claim on the grounds that the relevant supplies had been made to the couple who had purchased the house, rather than to the company. The tribunal upheld the Commissioners' decision and dismissed the company's appeal. *D & K Builders & Sons (Ampthill) Ltd, LON/88/1046Z (VTD 4287).*

34.54   **Surveyors' fees—whether supplied to lender or to borrower.**   A company (H) carried on the business of restoring old buildings and reconstructing them for residential use. It borrowed money from a finance company. The finance company arranged for surveyors to inspect the work which H had done before making stage payments, and deducted the amount of the surveyors' fees from the amounts it paid to H. H reclaimed input tax in respect of the surveyors' fees, and the Commissioners issued an assessment to recover the tax, considering that the relevant supplies had been made to the finance company, rather than to H. The tribunal upheld the assessment and dismissed H's appeal. *Heritage Venture Enterprises Ltd, MAN/92/559 (VTD 10741).*

34.55   **Whether services of surveyors and solicitors supplied to bank or to construction company.**   A building company (P) obtained a bank loan in order to convert a property into residential units. The bank instructed a firm of surveyors to monitor the progress of the work. The bank paid the surveyors' fees and charged these, plus certain solicitors' fees, to P. P reclaimed input tax on these amounts. When the Commissioners discovered this, they issued an assessment to recover the tax. The tribunal dismissed P's appeal, holding that the relevant services had been supplied to the bank, rather than to P. *Dalesid Ltd, 38.17* INVOICES AND CREDIT NOTES, and *Eagle Trust plc, 34.85* below, applied; *Redrow Group plc, 34.59* below, distinguished. *Poladon Ltd, MAN/99/1022 (VTD 16825).*

34.56   **Work carried out to comply with Clean Air Act 1956—whether supplies made to Borough Council or to individual householders.**   See *Doncaster Borough Council, 40.2* LOCAL AUTHORITIES AND STATUTORY BODIES.

Miscellaneous

Cases where the appellant was successful

34.57   **Whether central heating boiler supplied to claimant.**   An individual (M) was building a house for his own use. He arranged for the plumbing to be done by L, who was not registered for VAT, and who was area representative for a company (W) from which he could obtain central heating equipment at a special discount. It was agreed that L should obtain the central heating boiler and associated equipment for the house from W, but that L should keep his special discount. L therefore charged M the full price of the boiler and equipment plus the VAT of £14.87 he had paid W on the discounted price. M reclaimed the £14.87 under what is now *VATA 1994, s 35*, but the Commissioners rejected the claim on the basis that the supply had been made to L rather than to M. The tribunal allowed M's appeal, holding on the evidence that L had bought the boiler and equipment as an agent for M, who was therefore entitled to the refund. *MB Murden, LON/75/173 (VTD 207).*

34.58   **Chamber of Commerce operating training scheme for Manpower Services Commission—whether supplies made to Chamber or to trainees.**   A Chamber of Commerce operated a training scheme for employees under a contract with the Manpower Services Commission. It reclaimed input tax in respect of expenditure which it incurred in connection with the training. The Commissioners refused to allow the claim, considering that the supplies in question were made to the individual trainees, the Commission or the employers. The tribunal allowed the Chamber's appeal, holding that the supplies were made to the Chamber, which was under a contractual obligation both to the Commission and to the employers. *Aberdeen Chamber of Commerce, EDN/88/115 (VTD 3622).*

34.59   **Housebuilding company arranging for sale of houses already owned by prospective purchasers—whether estate agents' services supplied to company.**   A group of housebuilding companies instituted a scheme for prospective purchasers of its houses, whereby it nominated an estate agent to sell the houses already owned by such purchasers, and paid the agents' fees. The scheme was instituted because most prospective purchasers could not proceed with a purchase until they had found a buyer for their existing homes. The group reclaimed input tax on the fees which it paid to the estate agents. The Commissioners issued an assessment to recover the tax, considering that the supplies were made to the owners of the houses, rather than to the company. The representative member of the group appealed, contending that it was acting as a joint principal and was a joint recipient of the supply, so that it was entitled to reclaim the input tax. The tribunal accepted this contention and allowed the appeal, holding on the evidence that the agents' services were provided both to the company and to the potential purchaser. The CA reversed this decision but the HL unanimously allowed the company's appeal and restored the decision of the tribunal. Applying *Belgium v Ghent Coal Terminal NV*, 21.199 EUROPEAN COMMUNITY LAW, the supplies had been 'received in connection with the business activities of the taxable person, for the purpose of being incorporated within its economic activities'. Lord Hope observed that 'the fact that someone else—in this case, the prospective purchaser—also received a service as part of the same transaction does not deprive the person who instructed the service and who has had to pay for it of the benefit of the deduction'. *C & E Commrs v Redrow Group plc, HL [1999] STC 161; [1999] 1 WLR 408; [1999] 2 All ER 1.* (*Note.* For the Commissioners' practice following this decision, see Business Brief 27/99, issued on 21 December 1999. The Commissioners take the view that 'the decision only applies ... where there is a claim to input tax credit by a taxable person who has commissioned the goods or services and contracted with the supplier for them'. They consider that the decision 'has no relevance to circumstances where a third party is simply meeting the costs of another'. See, however, the subsequent tribunal decision in *British Airways plc (No 3)*, 34.60 below.)

34.60   **Meals provided for delayed airline passengers—whether supplied to airline or directly to passengers.**   A company which operated an airline made arrangements whereby passengers whose flights were delayed for more than two hours were given meal vouchers which could be exchanged for food up to a specified value at a number of restaurants at the airport. It paid the restaurant the amount shown on the vouchers, and reclaimed input tax on the amounts which it paid. The Commissioners issued a ruling that the company was not entitled to credit for the input tax, on the grounds that the restaurants were supplying the food directly to the passengers rather than to the company. The company appealed, contending that the restaurants should be treated as supplying the food to the company, and that the company was making onward supplies of the food to the passengers which would be zero-rated as part of the overall supply of transport. The tribunal allowed the company's appeal, applying *dicta* of Lord Hope in *Redrow Group plc*, 34.59 above, and declining to follow the previous tribunal decision in *British Airways plc (No 2)*, 34.79 below, on the grounds that it was inconsistent with the HL decision in *Redrow*. *British Airways plc (No 3)*, *[2000] VATDR 74 (VTD 16446)*.

34.61   **Repairs to repossessed motor coach—whether supply made to vendor.**   A company traded as motor distributors. In 1987 it sold a coach under a hire-purchase agreement. In 1990 the purchaser failed to make the required payments, and the company sought to repossess the coach. The company had some difficulty in tracing the coach, but eventually discovered that it had been damaged in an accident. It reclaimed input tax on repairs to the coach. The Commissioners issued an assessment to recover the tax, on the basis that the repairs had been supplied to the purchaser of the coach, rather than to the company. The tribunal allowed the company's appeal, holding on the evidence that the company 'had at no time parted with the ownership of the vehicle', and that it was entitled to reclaim the input tax. *Blythswood Motors Ltd, EDN/95/325 (VTD 14203)*.

34.62   **Purchase of vehicle—conditional sale agreement in name of trader's son.**   A trader (B) carried on a vehicle hire business. He wished to purchase an 8–seat motor vehicle, and applied to a finance company for credit. However, the company rejected his application. His son then applied to the same company for credit and was accepted. The vehicle was registered in B's name and B made the monthly repayments to the finance company. B reclaimed input tax on the purchase, but the Commissioners rejected the claim on the grounds that the conditional sale agreement was in the name of B's son, rather than in the name of B himself. The tribunal allowed B's appeal, observing that in the particular circumstances it was required 'to look at all the facts and not just at the formal agreement between (the finance company) and (B's son)'. Applying *dicta* of Laws J in *Reed Personnel Services Ltd*, 31.6 HEALTH AND WELFARE, 'contractual documents determining the private law obligations of the parties involved do not necessarily conclude the issue for VAT'. The fact that the relevant documents were addressed to B's son was not conclusive. *Collins*, 38.18 INVOICES AND CREDIT NOTES, and *Newland Technical Services Ltd*, 38.68 INVOICES AND CREDIT NOTES, distinguished. *JR Beagley, LON/96/1001 (VTD 15107)*. (*Note*. For another issue in this case, see 61.28 TRANSFERS OF GOING CONCERNS.)

34.63   **Retailer reimbursing independent concessionaires for discounts offered to customers using 'storecard'—whether supply of services by concessionaire to retailer.**   A company (B) operated a number of retail department stores. It allowed independent concessionaires to operate within its premises, in return for a licence fee based on turnover. It operated a 'storecard' (in-house credit card) scheme, under which discounts were allowed to customers. The discounts applied to purchases from B's concessionaires as well as to purchases from B itself. B reimbursed the concessionaires and reclaimed input tax on these reimbursements. The Commissioners issued a ruling that B was not entitled to make adjustments in respect of purchases from B's concessionaires, on the basis that the payments were consideration for the original supply of goods to the customer. B appealed. The tribunal allowed the appeal, holding that the payments which B made to the concessionaires were consideration for supplies of services by the concessionaires to B, being the concessionaires' agreement to accept the 'storecard' and give the relevant discount. Accordingly, VAT was chargeable on the supply, the valuation of which was the amount of the discount, and B was entitled to treat that VAT as its input tax. *JE Beale plc, LON/97/1096 (VTD 15920)*.

Cases where the appellant was partly successful

34.64   **Whether supplies made to company or to controlling shareholder.**   An individual (R) purchased a 44–ton vessel in 1961 which he and his wife used for pleasure cruising. Following his retirement, he purchased a larger vessel in 1972 and, early in 1973, lent both vessels to a company (S) which he had incorporated to carry on the business of chartering them. The company, which was wholly owned by R and his wife, paid nothing for the loan but undertook to keep the vessels in good and seaworthy condition. The second vessel was overhauled in 1974 at a cost of £12,579 including VAT of £932. The invoice was addressed to 'R Esq, S Ltd', and R paid the bill himself. R then repossessed the ship and sold it through agents who charged a commission of £1,250 including VAT of £250. The company reclaimed both the £932 and the £250 as input tax and appealed against an assessment to recover these amounts. The tribunal dismissed the appeal with regard to the £250, finding that the sale had been by R and not by the company, but allowed the appeal with regard to the £932, finding that the repairs had been carried out on behalf of the company. *Setar Lines Ltd, LON/76/155 (VTD 316)*.

Cases where the appellant was unsuccessful

34.65   **Whether supplies made to partnership or individual partner.**   A firm of chartered accountants reclaimed input tax in respect of a caravan which had been purchased by one of the partners. The Commissioners issued an assessment to recover the tax and the firm appealed, contending that the caravan was used for the purpose of the firm's business. The tribunal dismissed the appeal, holding that the 'taxable person' was the partnership, and that, as the caravan had been supplied to one of the individual partners rather than to the partnership itself, the partnership was not entitled to reclaim the input tax. *Smith Wheeler & Hay, LON/81/331 (VTD 1208)*.

34.66   A partnership traded from premises which were leased by one of the partners. The partnership reclaimed input tax on the rent payable to the landlord under the lease. The Commissioners issued an assessment to recover the tax, on the grounds that the relevant supplies were made to the partner rather than to the partnership. The tribunal upheld the assessment and dismissed the partnership's appeal. *Bird Semple & Crawford Herron*, 34.22 above, and *Glasse Brothers*, 34.30 above, distinguished. *Fantasia (Knutsford), MAN/93/15 (VTD 12515)*.

34.67   An appeal was dismissed in a case where a joiner had reclaimed input tax relating to an unregistered partnership of which he was a member. *MJ White, LON/93/2368 (VTD 12360)*.

34.68   A similar decision was reached in *S Grange, MAN/96/456 (VTD 15706)*.

34.69   See also *Ingram*, 34.43 above; *Stone*, 34.46 above, and *Mills*, 34.123 below.

34.70   **Whether supply made to company or to director.**   A company reclaimed input tax in respect of a franchise fee which its managing director had paid before the company was incorporated. The Commissioners rejected the claim and the tribunal dismissed the company's appeal, holding that the supply was made to the director as an individual rather than to the company. *Foxmead Services (Northern) Ltd, MAN/83/296 (VTD 1625).*

34.71   Similar decisions were reached in *Bleyer Hair Clinic Ltd, MAN/84/279 (VTD 1947); Goodpass Ltd, LON/95/1749 (VTD 14088); Mowco Ltd, EDN/98/29 (VTD 15657)* and *Associated Concrete Repairs Ltd, LON/98/827 (VTD 15963).*

34.72   An appeal was dismissed in a case where a sole trader reclaimed input tax on a supply made to a company of which he had been a director. *PM Herbert, LON/86/425 (VTD 2350).*

34.73   See also *Collins*, 38.18 INVOICES AND CREDIT NOTES, and *Gavacan*, 38.20 INVOICES AND CREDIT NOTES.

34.74   **Sale of house owned by company director—whether input tax on estate agent's services reclaimable by company.**   The principal director of a building company sold his house to raise finance for the company, which reclaimed input tax on the commission paid by the director to the estate agent. The Commissioners issued an assessment to recover the tax and the tribunal dismissed the company's appeal, holding that the services had been supplied to the director rather than to the company. *Rushgreen Builders Ltd, LON/87/116 (VTD 2470).*

34.75   The principal director of a property company, which had a large overdraft, obtained a second mortgage on his private residence as security against the overdraft. Subsequently the bank decided to call in the overdraft and required the director to sell the house. The company reclaimed input tax on the solicitors' fees and agents' fees relating to the sale. The Commissioners issued an assessment to recover the tax, on the basis that the relevant supplies were made to the director rather than to the company. The company appealed, contending that the input tax should be treated as deductible since the proceeds of the sale had been applied for the purposes of the business. The tribunal dismissed the company's appeal, observing that 'the critical question is whether the services were rendered to the business'. The services here had been rendered to the director rather than to the company. *Dean*, 34.420 below, and *Rushgreen Builders Ltd*, 34.74 above, applied. *WH Blatch Investments Ltd, LON/95/918A (VTD 13727).*

34.76   **Input tax reclaimed in respect of goods supplied to winners of bingo prizes.**   A company (J) carried on the business of an amusement arcade. It issued vouchers with a face value of £1 each to winners at bingo. The winners could use the vouchers for the purchase of goods from J or from a nearby firm (C), or could exchange them for vouchers issued by another company (A). J reimbursed C for the vouchers which C accepted at face value, and reclaimed input tax in respect of the goods which the winners of the vouchers had purchased from C. The Commissioners issued an assessment to recover the tax, considering that the goods were supplied by C to the winners of the vouchers rather than to J. The tribunal upheld the assessment and dismissed J's appeal. *Jomast Trading & Development Ltd, [1984] VATTR 219 (VTD 1735).*

34.77   See also *Sooner Foods Ltd*, 58.269 SUPPLY.

34.78   **Lunches provided for students at language school—whether supplied to students or to school.**   A company operated a language school. It paid students a lunch allowance of £17, with which the students bought lunch at a nearby restaurant for themselves and for their tutor. The students gave receipted bills to the school, which reclaimed input tax thereon. The Commissioners issued an assessment to recover the tax, considering that the lunches were supplied to the students, rather than to the school. The tribunal accepted this contention and dismissed the company's appeal. *Butler Question Method School of Languages Ltd, LON/90/223Y*

(VTD 5677). *(Note.* An appeal against an estimated assessment on undeclared takings was also dismissed.)

34.79 **Meals provided for delayed airline passengers—whether supplied to airline or directly to passengers.** A company which operated an airline made arrangements whereby passengers whose flights were delayed for more than two hours were given meal vouchers which could be exchanged for food up to a specified value at a number of restaurants at the airport. It paid the restaurant the amount shown on the vouchers, and reclaimed input tax on the amounts which it paid. The Commissioners issued a ruling that the company was not entitled to credit for the input tax, on the grounds that the restaurants were supplying the food directly to the passengers rather than to the company. The company appealed, contending that the restaurants should be treated as supplying the food to the company, and that the company was making onward supplies of the food to the passengers which would be zero-rated as part of the overall supply of transport. The tribunal dismissed the appeal, holding that the food was supplied directly by the restaurants to the passengers. *P & O European Ferries*, 34.143 below, was distinguished on the grounds that it related to supplies of services, whereas the supplies made by the restaurants were supplies of goods. The QB upheld the tribunal decision as one of fact. *British Airways plc v C & E Commrs (No 2)*, QB [1996] STC 1127. *(Note.* See now, however, the subsequent decision in *British Airways plc (No 3)*, 34.60 above.)

34.80 **Input tax reclaimed by company managing pop group—whether acting as principal or agent.** See *World Chief Ltd*, 1.13 AGENTS.

34.81 **Input tax claimed on purchase of paper—whether goods purchased as principal or as agent.** See *LS & A International Ltd*, 1.14 AGENTS.

34.82 **Goods purchased by partnership—whether input tax reclaimable by single partner as sole trader.** A sole trader reclaimed input tax in respect of goods which he had purchased while carrying on a previous business in partnership with his wife. The Commissioners issued an assessment to recover the tax, considering that the two businesses were unconnected. The tribunal dismissed the trader's appeal. Although registration related to persons rather than businesses, two or more persons carrying on business together were regarded as being separate from one of those persons carrying on business on his or her own account. *Dicta* of May J in *Glassborow*, 53.1 REGISTRATION, applied. *JR Michaelis, LON/90/925Z (VTD 5734)*.

34.83 **Trust employing accountants to provide services to investment trust—to which trust services supplied.** In a case where the facts were complex and unusual, a trust established by will, and registered for VAT, supplied management and investment services to related trusts. From 1987 it managed an investment trust, which was not registered for VAT, and employed accountants to provide services to that trust. It reclaimed input tax in respect of the accountants' fees. The Commissioners issued an assessment to recover the tax, considering that the accountants' services had been supplied to the investment trust and not to the management trust. The tribunal upheld the assessment and dismissed the trust's appeal. *Apple & Pear Development Council*, 21.47 EUROPEAN COMMUNITY LAW, applied. *Sir Alexander MacRobert Memorial Trust, [1990] VATTR 56 (VTD 5125)*.

34.84 **Pension funds defrayed by employer—whether input tax reclaimable.** See *Linotype & Machinery Ltd*, 51.2 PENSION FUNDS; *Talbot Motor Co Ltd*, 51.3 PENSION FUNDS, and *Ultimate Advisory Services Ltd*, 51.4 PENSION FUNDS.

34.85 **Whether supplies made to appellant or to appellant's bank.** A company requested a substantial increase in its overdraft facility from its bank. The bank requested a detailed report from the company's accountants. The accountants submitted their report to the bank but sent invoices to the company rather than to the bank. The company reclaimed input tax in respect of these invoices. The Commissioners rejected the claim and the tribunal dismissed the company's appeal, holding on the evidence that the accountants had supplied their services to the bank rather than to the company. *Dalesid Ltd*, 38.17 INVOICES AND CREDIT NOTES, applied. *Eagle Trust plc, MAN/93/1125 (VTD 12871)*.

34.86   See also *Poladon Ltd*, 31.49 above, and *Dalesid Ltd*, 38.17 INVOICES AND CREDIT NOTES.

34.87   **Public house transferred as going concern—Court order for payment to supplier of goods.**   The business of a public house was transferred as a going concern from one company (H) to another company (S) in March 1991. H went into liquidation in April 1991. A wholesaler who had supplied drinks to the public house began proceedings against two individuals in respect of money allegedly owed to it for drinks supplied before the transfer of the business. The court gave judgment in favour of the wholesaler, and ordered the named individuals to pay the wholesaler £65,000. The liquidator of H reclaimed input tax in respect of the payment, and S also reclaimed input tax in respect of the same payment. The Commissioners accepted the liquidator's claim and rejected the claim by S. The tribunal dismissed the appeal, holding that S was not entitled to credit for the input tax since it had not carried on the business at the material time (and also noting that it did not hold an invoice in support of its claim). *A Hughes & Sons Ltd (t/a The Derby House), LON/94/2419 (VTD 13504)*. (*Note*. The relationship between the individuals and the companies is not made clear in the decision, but it is assumed that the individuals had been directors of both the companies concerned.)

34.88   **Other cases.**   There have been a number of other cases, which appear to raise no point of general interest, in which appeals against the disallowance of input tax have been dismissed on the grounds that the relevant supply had not been made to the appellant. In the interests of space, such cases are not summarised individually in this book.

WHETHER SUPPLIES USED FOR THE PURPOSES OF THE BUSINESS

Note. In the cases below the issue is whether the supplies were for use in the existing business. Where the issue is whether the supplies were for the purposes of a future business or business activity, see 34.444 below *et seq.* See also, for accounting periods beginning after 27 July 1993, *VATA 1994, s 84(4)*, deriving from *FA 1993, s 46*. This provides that a tribunal can only allow an appeal against the disallowance of input tax on a 'luxury, amusement or entertainment' where the tribunal considers that the Commissioners 'could not reasonably have made' the determination which is the subject of the appeal. Cases relating to periods before the enactment of *FA 1993* should be read in the light of this change.

Luxuries, amusements and entertainments (VATA 1994, s 84(4))

34.89   **Tennis club subscription for controlling director.**   A company which supplied lecturing services reclaimed input tax on a subscription to a tennis club for its controlling director. The Commissioners rejected the claim on the ground that the expenditure had not been incurred for the purpose of the company's business. The tribunal dismissed the company's appeal, holding that 'the expenditure was not directly referable to the purpose of the business' and that it was not satisfied that the benefit of the company was 'the real purpose in the mind of (the director)' when he incurred the expenditure. Furthermore, the subscription was a 'luxury, amusement or entertainment' within what is now *VATA 1994, s 84(4)*. *John Price Business Courses Ltd, [1995] VATDR 106 (VTD 13135)*.

34.90 **Personalised vehicle numberplates—whether a 'luxury'.** In *College Street Market Gardens*, 34.384 below, the tribunal held that personalised vehicle numberplates were a 'luxury' within *VATA 1994, s 84(4)*.

34.91 **Family partnership—purchase of racing car.** A family partnership carried on business as monumental masons. In January 1994 they purchased a racing car at a cost of £19,000 and reclaimed the input tax thereon. The Commissioners issued an assessment to recover the tax, considering that the car had not been purchased for the purposes of the business, but for the personal pleasure of one of the partners (M), and that the car was a 'luxury, amusement or entertainment', within what is now *VATA 1994, s 84(4)*. The partnership appealed, contending that the car had been purchased for advertising purposes. In 1994 M had driven the car in a competition, sponsored by Dunlop Rover, which comprised twelve races, and this had attracted publicity for the partnership in local newspapers and on local radio. The car had been sold in early 1995. The tribunal accepted the partnership's evidence and allowed the appeal. Applying *dicta* in *Ian Flockton Developments Ltd*, 34.248 below, the tribunal was satisfied that the car had been purchased for advertising purposes. Furthermore, the tribunal held that the car was not a 'luxury, amusement or entertainment', so that *s 84(4)* did not apply. The tribunal chairman also observed that, even if the car were deemed to fall within *s 84(4)*, the assessment would have been unreasonable on the grounds that the VAT officer responsible for it had not attempted to interview any of the partners. *Myatt & Leason, [1995] VATDR 440 (VTD 13780)*.

34.92 **Christmas party for employees—whether within VATA 1994, s 84(4).** In *Ernst & Young*, 8.41 BUSINESS ENTERTAINMENT, the tribunal held that expenditure on a Christmas party for employees (who were required to make a contribution towards the cost) did not fall within *VATA 1994, s 84(4)*.

Motoring expenses

34.93 **Motoring expenses—whether petrol supplied to appellant.** See *Berbrooke Fashions*, 34.1 above, and the cases noted at 34.2 above to 34.8 above.

34.94 **Use of car for transport of employees.** The proprietors of a hairdressing salon reclaimed input tax on petrol and the Commissioners issued an assessment to recover the tax. The partners appealed, giving evidence that their employees were sometimes required to work in the evenings and, when this happened, the cars were used to drive the employees home. The tribunal held that the tax in respect of these journeys was deductible, and reduced the assessment accordingly. *E & S Blyth-Palk (t/a John Baxter Hair Fashions), LON/78/295 (VTD 718)*.

34.95 **Rental payments for car no longer used in business—whether input tax deductible.** Two individuals (S and H) had operated a restaurant in partnership. The partnership had leased a car, which was used by S partly for partnership purposes and partly for private purposes. S left the partnership and agreed with H that he would retain possession of the car, and that H would pay the rental payments on the car for the remaining 13 months of the lease. H reclaimed input tax on these payments. The Commissioners issued an assessment to recover the tax and the tribunal dismissed H's appeal. The tax was not deductible since the car was no longer used for the purposes of the business. H's motive for making the rental payments was to obtain S's share of the ownership of the restaurant. *Mrs Hague, LON/81/262 (VTD 1159)*.

34.96 **Accountancy partnership—accessories fitted to partner's car.** An accountancy partnership reclaimed input tax on accessories which had been fitted to a car owned by one of the partners, and used partly for partnership purposes and partly for private purposes. The Commissioners issued an assessment to recover the tax, and the partnership appealed. The tribunal directed that the tax should be apportioned. *Broadhead Peel & Co, [1984] VATTR 195 (VTD 1737)*.

34.97 **Repairs to car used by hotelier.** A hotelier reclaimed input tax on repairs to a car. The Commissioners issued an assessment to recover part of the tax, considering that the car was partly used for private purposes and that the cost should be apportioned accordingly. The tribunal allowed the appeal in part, finding that the private use of the car was very slight and holding that 95% of the tax was allowable. *WG Tregenza, LON/85/130 (VTD 1907)*.

34.98 **Repairs to vintage car used for advertising purposes.** A company dealt in 'classic' cars. It used a Lagonda car (a racing car built before World War II) for promotional purposes, although the car was actually owned by its managing director rather than the company. The car was driven in a long-distance race in Italy, and subsequently required repairs. The company reclaimed input tax on the cost of the repairs. The Commissioners issued an assessment to recover the tax but the tribunal allowed the company's appeal, holding on the evidence that the expenditure had been incurred in order to promote the company's business. *Terry Cohn Ltd, LON/97/311 (VTD 15962)*.

34.99 **Management consultancy partnership—upgrading of Aston Martin.** A partnership carried on a management consultancy business. It reclaimed input tax on the upgrading of an engine of an Aston Martin motor car. The car was approximately ten months old, had originally cost £145,000 and had covered 6,054 miles. The upgrading of the engine cost £50,000, and enabled the car to travel at 175 miles per hour. The Commissioners rejected the claim on the basis that the work seemed 'to have been commissioned to enhance performance rather than to effect repair and maintenance'. The partnership appealed, contending that the tax should be treated as deductible since the car was driven for business purposes. The tribunal dismissed the appeal, holding that 'there is no obvious and clear association between the business of a management consultancy and the expenditure on upgrading, as opposed to repairing an engine, simply to achieve driving speeds grossly in excess of permitted speed limits'. Accordingly, the tribunal held that the expenditure was not for the purposes of the partnership's business. *Dicta* in *Rosner,* 34.145 below, applied. *Trade Development Associates, LON/94/347A & 419A (VTD 12699)*.

34.100 **Transporter partly used privately.** The tribunal directed that input tax should be apportioned in a case where a trader purchased a transporter partly for business purposes and partly for private purposes. *LVJ Brooks, LON/84/29 (VTD 1722)*.

34.101 **Motoring offences—legal costs.** See *Scott,* 34.148 below, and *Child,* 34.149 below.

34.102 **Renovation of old vans.** A company reclaimed input tax on the renovation of two old vans, which were painted in pre-war livery and taken to local rallies. The vans did not bear the company's name, but a notice was displayed at the rallies indicating that they were sponsored by the company. The Commissioners issued an assessment to recover the tax and the company appealed, contending that the expenditure had been incurred for the purpose of advertising its business. The tribunal dismissed the company's appeal, finding that the expenditure had been incurred to enable the controlling director 'to enjoy his hobby of restoring old vans'. *Ron Miller Ltd, LON/90/1191Z (VTD 5827)*. (*Note.* For another issue in this appeal, see 58.157 SUPPLY.)

Clothing

34.103 **Formal clothing purchased by barrister—whether input tax deductible.** A new barrister reclaimed input tax on the purchase of two dark three-piece suits, three white tunic shirts, twelve detachable collars, two pairs of black shoes, several pairs of black socks and a suitcase. The Commissioners issued an assessment to recover the tax, considering that the clothing had not been purchased exclusively for professional purposes, since it could also be worn privately. The barrister appealed, contending that he had purchased the items in question for appearing in court, since the Bar Council required such clothing to be worn in court, and that before becoming a barrister he had habitually worn two-piece suits, coloured socks and brown shoes, which were not acceptable for court wear. The tribunal allowed his appeal in part, holding that the three tunic shirts and detachable collars, and one of the two three-piece suits, could be regarded as having been purchased for professional purposes. However, the tax on the second suit and on the shoes, socks and suitcase was not allowable. *EM Alexander, [1976] VATTR 107 (VTD 251)*.

34.104   Fur coat purchased by authoress.   An authoress and scriptwriter decided to travel to New York in 1979 to attempt to gain a lucrative literary contract. Shortly before her departure she bought a mink coat for £4,950. She reclaimed the VAT on this as input tax. The Commissioners issued an assessment to recover the tax, considering that the coat had been purchased for private purposes rather than for professional purposes. She appealed, contending that her main purpose in buying the coat had been to impress the people that she would be meeting in New York and thus to improve her chances of gaining the literary contract. The tribunal held that the coat had been partly purchased for professional purposes and partly for private purposes, so that the cost should be apportioned. The appeal was adjourned in the hope that the parties could agree an apportionment. *RA Sisson, LON/80/310 (VTD 1056)*. (*Note*. There was no further public hearing of the appeal. See now *VATA 1994, s 84(4)*, deriving from *FA 1993, s 46*.)

34.105   Art consultant—whether clothing purchased for business purposes.   An art consultant reclaimed input tax on the purchase of items of clothing costing more than £8,500. The Commissioners issued an assessment to recover the tax, considering that the clothing had not been purchased for the purposes of her business. She appealed, contending that she had purchased the clothing in question 'to cultivate a professional image drawing prospective clients' attention to herself'. The tribunal dismissed her appeal, holding that she had 'failed to establish that the expenditure ... was expenditure incurred for the purposes of her business, within (*VATA 1994, s 24(1)*)'. *PJ Stone Ltd*, 34.110 below, applied. *Alexander*, 34.103 above, was distinguished since the clothing there had been purchased to comply with the rules of the Bar Council. *Sisson*, 34.104 above, was distinguished since the fur coat there had been found to have been purchased for the purpose of attempting to obtain one specific contract. *BJ Brown, LON/91/1681 (VTD 6552)*.

34.106   Retailers—input tax reclaimed on suits worn while working.   In the case noted at 1.6 AGENTS, two retailers had reclaimed input tax on the cost of suits which they wore while working. The tribunal held that 'to dress well in order to conform with the standards of a particular lifestyle' was not a business expense, and that the tax was not deductible. *JK Hill & SJ Mansell (t/a JK Hill & Co), LON/86/472 (VTD 2379)*.

34.107   Electrician—input tax reclaimed on suits worn while working.   An electrician reclaimed input tax on suits which he wore at work. The Commissioners issued an assessment to recover the tax and he appealed, contending that he often had to work in dirty conditions and therefore did not wear the clothing in question when not at work. The tribunal held that 75% of the tax in question was allowable. *PR Younghusband, LON/91/913Y (VTD 7443)*.

34.108   **Architect—input tax reclaimed on suits worn while working.**   An architect reclaimed input tax on the cost of suits which he wore while working. The Commissioners issued an assessment to recover the tax and the tribunal dismissed the architect's appeal, applying *Hill & Mansell*, 34.106 above. *W Richards, MAN/92/ 324 (VTD 11674).* (*Note.* For another issue in this case, see 8.3 BUSINESS ENTERTAINMENT.)

34.109   **Actor—whether clothing purchased for business purposes.**   An actor, who worked mainly as an 'extra' in television and films, reclaimed input tax on items of clothing such as dress suits. The Commissioners issued an assessment to recover 50% of the tax in cases where the clothing was also suitable for private wear. The actor appealed, contending that he had purchased the clothing for the purpose of his work as an actor and had not worn it privately, so that the whole of the tax should be deducted. The tribunal allowed his appeal, applying *Ian Flockton Developments Ltd*, 34.248 below, and *Lennartz*, 21.216 EUROPEAN COMMUNITY LAW. On the evidence, the actor's sole intention in buying the clothing was to wear it while acting. The Commissioners had not shown that the clothing had actually been worn privately, and the fact that it could be worn privately did not prevent the tax from being deductible. *J Pearce, LON/91/1638Y (VTD 7860).* (*Note.* For another issue in this case, see 34.437 below.)

34.110   **Clothing purchased by company for wear by principal director—whether for purpose of company's business.**   A company carried on a management consultancy business from the home of its principal director. It purchased a number of items of clothing and jewellery to be worn by the director. These items included a pair of black leather boots and a sapphire mink jacket. The company reclaimed input tax on these items and the Commissioners issued an assessment to recover the tax, considering that the expenditure had not been incurred for the purpose of the company's business. The company appealed, contending that the clothing served the purpose of the company's business since, when its director attended meetings, she should be 'dressed in such a way that people would have confidence in her judgment'. The tribunal dismissed the appeal, holding that the company had not established that the clothing and jewellery in question had been purchased for business purposes. *PJ Stone Ltd, LON/86/396 (VTD 2241).*

34.111   **Wig purchased by professional musician—whether for professional purposes.**   A professional jazz musician reclaimed input tax on the purchase of a wig. The Commissioners issued an assessment to recover the tax, considering that he had purchased the wig for private purposes rather than for professional purposes. He appealed, contending that he had always worn his hair long and had gained an 'image' as having a thick head of hair, but that his hair had recently begun to fall out and that he needed to wear a wig to maintain his image. The tribunal allowed his appeal. Applying *Ian Flockton Developments Ltd*, 34.248 below, the tribunal was satisfied that 'on the balance of probability the object in the taxpayer's mind at the time the expenditure was incurred was that the goods and services in question were to be used for the purpose of the business'. *JM Collie, LON/90/1328X (VTD 6144).* (*Note.* See now, however, *VATA 1994, s 84(4)*, deriving from *FA 1993, s 46*.)

Legal costs—civil cases

Cases where the appellant was successful

34.112   **Legal services supplied to farming partnership.**   See *Glasse Brothers*, 34.30 above.

34.113   **Legal costs incurred by parent company in investigating affairs of subsidiary company.**   See *Crompton Enterprises Ltd*, 34.31 above.

34.114   **Equine chiropractor.**   An equine chiropractor (W) practised from premises which were subject to an 'agricultural condition', whereby they had to be occupied by a person 'wholly or principally employed in agriculture'. The local council issued a ruling that W's work did not comply with this condition, and took enforcement proceedings. W incurred legal costs in instructing solicitors to defend the proceedings and to seek the removal of the 'agricultural condition'. He was unsuccessful, and subsequently sold the premises in question. He reclaimed the input tax on the costs. The Commissioners issued an assessment to recover some of the tax, on the basis that the expenditure had been partly incurred for private purposes. The tribunal allowed W's appeal, holding that 'there was a clear nexus between the incurring of the expenditure on the relevant services and the purposes of the appellant's business as a chiropractor'. Accordingly, the whole of the input tax was deductible. *M Windsor, MAN/95/2208 (VTD 14185)*.

34.115   **Bank—whether legal costs partly attributable to exempt supplies.**   See *Midland Bank plc*, 21.193 EUROPEAN COMMUNITY LAW.

Cases where the appellant was partly successful

34.116   **Surveyor—legal action against former partners.**   A dispute arose between the members of a partnership of quantity surveyors. One of them (M) took legal proceedings against the other partners, who responded by expelling him from the partnership. The action was subsequently settled. M began a sole practice and reclaimed the input tax on the legal costs he had incurred in his action against his former partners. The Commissioners rejected the claim, and he appealed. The tribunal allowed his appeal in part, holding that the tax relating to expenditure incurred after he had begun his sole practice was reclaimable, since it had been incurred to protect his professional reputation, but that the tax relating to the recovery of his capital from the partnership was not reclaimable. *BP McCallum, [1980] VATTR 79 (VTD 945)*.

34.117   **Consultant—costs of libel action and of obtaining discharge from bankruptcy.**   A consultant reclaimed input tax in respect of legal costs incurred in obtaining his discharge from bankruptcy, in conducting a libel action, and in being represented before a Parliamentary Commission of Enquiry. The Commissioners rejected his claim and he appealed. The tribunal allowed his appeal in part, holding that tax was not reclaimable in respect of his discharge from bankruptcy or of the Parliamentary Commission of Enquiry, but that tax was deductible in respect of his successful conduct of the libel action, since this had affected his integrity in a business capacity. *WG Stern, LON/84/416 (VTD 1970)*.

34.118   **Company—costs of libel action.**   The directors of a company which operated a health spa began libel actions against a magazine. The company was awarded damages of £7,500 and the directors were awarded damages totalling £90,000 as individuals. The company reclaimed the input tax incurred in respect of the directors' legal costs as well as that incurred in respect of its own costs. (It appears that the bill of costs did not distinguish between those referable to the company's action and those referable to the directors' actions.) The tribunal held that the directors' main purpose in incurring the expenditure had been to clear their own reputations, and that only 25% of the tax in question was allowable. *Ormac (No 49) Ltd, EDN/90/185 (VTD 6537)*.

34.119   **Sole trader—former cohabitee claiming to be a partner—legal costs.**   An electrician (C) registered for VAT, as a sole trader, in 1984. In 1985 he began cohabiting with a woman (P). Their relationship deteriorated, and in 1991 C left their house. P took possession of his van, and C took legal proceedings against her to recover it. During the proceedings, P claimed that she should be treated as a 50% partner in the business. The proceedings were eventually settled in 1996, and P was ordered to return the van to C. C reclaimed input tax on his legal costs. The Commissioners rejected the claim, on the basis that the expenditure primarily related to a domestic dispute. C appealed. The tribunal allowed his appeal in part, holding on the evidence that one-third of the tax was deductible. *Dicta* of Latham J in *Rosner*, 34.145 below, applied. *D Clark (t/a Clark Electrical Services), MAN/98/679 (VTD 15927)*.

Cases where the appellant was unsuccessful

34.120   **Legal costs relating to breach of covenant.**   See *Potton*, 34.33 above.

34.121   **Legal costs of application for judicial review.**   An import and export dealer (J), who was registered for VAT, had a brother who was an undischarged bankrupt. J employed his brother to export engines to Egypt, paying his remuneration from an overseas source into an overseas bank account, with a view to keeping it out of the reach of IS's trustee in bankruptcy. Subsequently the brother was arrested and charged with five offences under *CEMA 1979, s 68(2)*. He was committed for trial and was granted bail, subject to a surety of £100,000 which J provided. While on bail, the brother went to the USA and did not return to the UK. The Court made an estreatment order for the surety of £100,000, and J applied for judicial review. His application was dismissed, and he paid the £100,000. He had to pay costs to his solicitors, and reclaimed the VAT thereon as input tax. The Commissioners issued an assessment to recover the tax, considering that the expenditure had been incurred for personal reasons rather than for business reasons. The tribunal upheld the Commissioners' contentions and dismissed J's appeal. *JH Smalley, MAN/88/657 (VTD 3894)*.

34.122   **Legal costs of civil action concerning land purchase.**   A firm of scrap dealers purchased the freehold of a site. They had previously occupied part of the site as tenants. Seven other tenants issued a writ against the firm, claiming that it had previously arranged to share part of the land with them, and seeking a share of the profits from the land. The firm reclaimed input tax on legal costs incurred in resisting this action. The Commissioners rejected the claim and the tribunal dismissed the firm's appeal, holding that expenditure arising from a dispute about the ownership of land did not qualify as expenditure for the purpose of the firm's business. *Shaw Lane Estates, MAN/88/680 (VTD 4420)*.

34.123   **Legal fees relating to partnership dispute.**   A trader (M) had previously been in a partnership trading as garage proprietors. The partnership included his ex-wife. She withdrew from the partnership in 1974 and they were divorced the following year. Under the divorce agreement M was required to pay his ex-wife an amount in respect of her share in the partnership. There were delays in valuing the amount due, but in 1987 the couple agreed that M should pay her £5,000 in full and final settlement of her claims. M's solicitors charged him £2,500 for work done in respect of the partnership dispute. Meanwhile, in 1983 the partnership had been dissolved and M had registered for VAT as a sole trader, selling wine. He reclaimed input tax on the solicitors' fees and the Commissioners issued an assessment to recover the tax. The tribunal dismissed M's appeal, holding that the solicitors' services had not been rendered to M for the purpose of his business as a wine retailer. *C Mills, LON/89/1423Y (VTD 4864)*.

34.124 A registered trader had been in partnership with his wife until the marriage broke down, from when he continued his business as a sole trader. The couple were divorced, and the ex-wife made an application under the *Married Women's Property Act 1882, s 17*. The trader was ordered to pay costs of more than £55,000 to his ex-wife. He reclaimed input tax on the costs and the Commissioners issued an assessment to recover the tax. The tribunal dismissed the trader's appeal, holding that the relevant supplies had not been made for the purpose of the trader's business. *Turner*, 34.34 above, applied. *K Lister, MAN/93/1079 (VTD 13044)*. (*Note*. An appeal against a misdeclaration penalty was, however, allowed.)

34.125 **Legal fees relating to transfer of share capital.** A company (F) carried on the business of manufacturing refractory fibre products. Its controlling shareholders entered into negotiations for the sale of their shares to another company, but were unable to agree satisfactory terms. During the course of the negotiations, the shareholders consulted accountants and solicitors, who charged F for their work. F reclaimed input tax on this expenditure, and the Commissioners issued an assessment to recover the tax. The tribunal dismissed F's appeal, holding that the expenditure had not been incurred for the purpose of F's business. *Ash Fibre Processors Ltd, MAN/93/568 (VTD 12201)*.

34.126 See also *Brucegate Ltd*, 34.40 above.

34.127 **Legal costs incurred by director of insolvent company.** An individual (H), who carried on business as a self-employed consultant, was appointed as managing director of a company. He resigned his directorship in May 1988, and the company went into liquidation later in that year. In 1991 the Department of Trade and Industry applied for an order under *Company Directors Disqualification Act 1986, s 6* barring H from acting as a company director. He successfully opposed the application, and reclaimed input tax on his legal costs. The Commissioners rejected the claim, on the basis that the expenditure did not relate to H's consultancy business. The tribunal dismissed H's appeal, applying *Rosner*, 34.145 below. *AJ Handyside (t/a Stratagem International), LON/94/1226A (VTD 13182)*.

34.128 *Handyside*, 34.127 above, was applied in the similar subsequent cases of *ML Keam, LON/99/897 (VTD 16685)* and *R Redgrove, LON/99/911 (VTD 16817)*.

34.129 **Solicitor's fees on transfer of deeds of house.** A builder who had been divorced from his wife arranged for a solicitor to transfer the title deeds of his home from joint names to his sole name. He reclaimed input tax on the solicitor's fees and appealed against an assessment to recover the tax, contending that the house was a business asset as he had used it as security for a bank loan. The tribunal dismissed his appeal against the assessment, applying *Dean*, 34.420 below, and finding that the house was predominantly a private residence rather than a business asset. *SD Jordan, LON/90/1692Y (VTD 5071)*.

34.130 **Legal costs on sale of property owned by partner and partly used by partnership—whether input tax deductible.** See *Rock Lambert*, 34.44 above.

34.131 **Solicitor's fees on transfer of land.** See *Francis Jackson Homes Ltd*, 34.41 above.

34.132 **Legal costs of defending action for repossession of house.** A trader borrowed money from a bank to purchase a house. She defaulted on the loans and the bank began proceedings to repossess the house. The trader reclaimed input tax on the costs which she incurred in defending the proceedings. The Commissioners issued an assessment to recover the tax, considering that the expenditure had been incurred for personal reasons rather than for business purposes. The trader appealed, contending that the tax should be treated as deductible since she ran her business from the house. The tribunal dismissed her appeal, holding that the expenditure had been incurred for personal purposes and that the tax was not deductible. *Rosner*, 34.145 below, applied. *S McLeod (t/a Sally McLeod Associates), LON/94/1080A (VTD 12886).*

34.133   **Legal costs incurred by company in relation to director's previous business.**   A company reclaimed input tax in respect of legal costs which its principal director had incurred in the course of a dispute with his previous company, having been dismissed from his directorship with that company. The Commissioners issued an assessment to recover the tax and the tribunal dismissed the company's appeal, holding that the legal costs had clearly not been incurred for the purpose of the appellant company's business. *Ingram*, 34.43 above, applied. *Morgan Automation Ltd, LON/90/396X (VTD 5539).*

34.134   A company (R) sold leisurewear. Its principal director (L) had previously been director of another company (B) which had gone into liquidation. L considered that the reason for B's liquidation was that its finance director had withdrawn funds without authorisation, and that B's bank had been negligent in that it had cleared cheques which only bore the signature of the finance director, although the bank mandate required a second signature. The Official Receiver declined to take legal action against the bank, so L arranged for R to pay £1 to the Receiver in return for the Receiver assigning B's right of action against the bank and the finance director. Following this assignment, R and B issued a writ against the bank claiming substantial damages. Subsequently the bank agreed to pay R £168,000, plus costs, in settlement of the claims. R reclaimed input tax on its costs, but the Commissioners rejected the claim on the basis that the expenditure had not been incurred for the purpose of R's business. The tribunal dismissed R's appeal, holding that 'it is not possible to identify the services which were the subject of the legal fees charged to (R) as the cost component of any taxable transaction of that company'. *BLP Group plc*, 21.192 EUROPEAN COMMUNITY LAW, and *Neuvale Ltd*, 43.14 PARTIAL EXEMPTION, applied. *Rushcombe Ltd, LON/96/847 (VTD 14727).*

34.135   **Legal fees in respect of work done before registration.**   See *Charles-Greed*, 34.481 below, and *Sherman & Perilly*, 34.482 below.

34.136   **Legal costs of defending action against former employer.**   An individual (M) had been managing director of a company dealing in men's clothing. In 1989 he left that company and registered for VAT as a self-employed marketing consultant. He was paid £36,000 by his former employer, and also retained a BMW car valued at £12,000. The company demanded the return of the car. M refused to return the car and his former employer obtained judgment against him in the Westminster County Court. M reclaimed input tax in respect of his solicitor's fees in defending the action. The Commissioners issued an assessment to recover the tax and the tribunal dismissed M's appeal, holding that the expenditure had not been incurred for the purposes of his business. *Wallman Foods Ltd*, 34.151 below, and *Mills*, 34.123 above, applied. *HD Marks, LON/92/2951A (VTD 11381).*

34.137   **Legal costs of taking action against former employer.**   An individual (O) was dismissed from his employment after borrowing £40 from his employer's petty cash. He was unable to find another job, and began self-employment as a management consultant. He registered for VAT. He took legal action against his former employer in an industrial tribunal, and reclaimed input tax on his legal costs. The Commissioners rejected his claim, on the basis that the expenditure had not been incurred for the purpose of his business. The tribunal dismissed his appeal, holding that the expenditure had been incurred for personal purposes rather than for the purposes of O's management consultancy business. *P Oldfield, MAN/93/955 (VTD 12233).*

34.138   **Legal costs of civil action following car accident.**   A builder (D) was injured in a car accident. He took a civil action against the other driver, and was awarded damages. However, as the damages awarded were less than the amount which the other driver had offered before the hearing, D had to pay a substantial proportion of his legal costs. He reclaimed input tax on these. The Commissioners issued an assessment to recover the tax, considering that the expenditure had not been incurred for the purposes of D's business. The tribunal dismissed D's appeal. Applying the QB decision in *Rosner*, 34.145 below, the tribunal held that input tax could only be deducted if the expenditure was 'directly referable to what the business is in fact doing'. The expenditure here was of benefit to D's business, but was not 'directly referable to the business of building'. Accordingly the tax was not deductible. *CB Dureau, LON/96/987 (VTD 14643)*.

34.139   **Legal costs of unsuccessful civil action.**   See *Nye Saunders & Partners*, 34.36 above, and *Davey*, 34.38 above.

34.140   **Legal costs of realising investments.**   A partnership carried on business as wholesalers and retailers of clothing, textiles and household goods. The partnership purchased a 10% interest in a residential property, as an investment. Subsequently the ownership of this property was transferred to a non-resident company, and the partnership took legal action against the couple who had held the 90% interest in the property. Meanwhile, in 1989 the partnership sold its wholesale business, and in 1990 it closed its retail shop. The partnership's action concerning the investment property was settled out of court, and the partnership reclaimed input tax on its solicitors' charges. The Commissioners issued an assessment to recover the tax, considering that the expenditure had not been incurred for the purpose of the partnership's business. The partnership appealed, contending firstly that it was carrying on a business of investing its surplus funds, and alternatively that the expenditure was incurred for the purpose of recovering money which was to be used for the purposes of its clothing business. The tribunal dismissed the appeal, holding on the evidence that the partners 'did not conduct their investment activities in such a manner that they amounted to a business' and that the funds which were recovered were not used, or intended to be used, for the purposes of the clothing business. *Kuchick Trading, MAN/91/1190 (VTD 12131)*.

34.141   A retailer purchased a 50% shareholding in a nursing home. A dispute arose between him and the other shareholders, and he consulted a solicitor. He reclaimed input tax on the solicitor's fees. The Commissioners issued an assessment to recover the tax, considering that the expenditure had not been incurred for the purpose of the retailer's business. The tribunal dismissed the retailer's appeal, holding that the shareholding was 'a personal investment rather than a business activity', and that there was no 'real connection or nexus between the legal services and the purposes of the business'. *R Anwar, MAN/93/1524 (VTD 12748)*.

34.142   **Transfer of employer's pension funds—legal advice provided for employees affected.**   See *The Plessey Co Ltd*, 51.7 PENSION FUNDS.

Legal costs—criminal cases

Cases where the appellant was successful

34.143   **Legal costs of company employees charged with manslaughter.**   A company operated a number of ferries across the English Channel. One of its ferries sailed from Zeebrugge with its doors open and capsized with heavy loss of life. The company and seven of its employees were charged with manslaughter. The company spent about £3,500,000 on the defence of the employees, and reclaimed the input tax incurred on this. The Commissioners issued an assessment to recover the tax, considering that the expenditure had not been incurred for the purpose of the company's business. The tribunal allowed the company's appeal, holding that the conviction of any of the employees 'would have caused severe damage to the public perception of the company's business'. The expenditure had clearly been incurred for the purposes of the company's business, notwithstanding that it had also had the effect of benefiting the individual employees. *Wallman Foods Ltd*, 34.151 below, and *Britwood Toys Ltd*, 34.152 below, distinguished. *P & O European Ferries (Dover) Ltd, [1992] VATTR 221 (VTD 7846)*. (*Note.* The Commissioners consider that this decision 'was based on the very particular and unusual facts ... and most apparently similar cases can be distinguished on the facts'. See Customs' VAT Manual, Part 13, chapter 2, section 3.3.)

34.144   **Legal costs incurred by gold dealer in defending criminal charges.**   A gold dealer was arrested and charged with offences under *CEMA 1979, s 170(1)(a)* concerning the evasion of Customs duties on gold which he had purchased from another registered dealer. He was acquitted and reclaimed input tax on his legal costs. The Commissioners rejected the claim on the basis that the expenditure had been incurred for a 'personal reason rather than for a business reason'. The tribunal allowed the dealer's appeal, observing that 'the activities described in the indictment were all steps taken in the normal course of (the dealer's) carrying on of his gold dealing business', and distinguishing *Rosner*, 34.145 below. It was not alleged that the dealer 'had in any way been involved in smuggling in the sense of knowingly importing gold with intent to defraud Her Majesty of duty ... had (he) been charged with a smuggling offence under *s 170(1)(b)* his legal expenses might not have been deductible'. *SR Brooks, LON/94/412A (VTD 12754)*.

Cases where the appellant was unsuccessful

34.145   **Legal costs of sole trader charged with criminal offence.**   The proprietor of a private educational establishment was convicted of conspiracy to defraud, in relation to the provision of false information under the *Immigration Act 1971* and in assisting overseas visitors to the UK in making false representations about whether they were genuine students. He was fined and ordered to pay the costs of the prosecution. He also paid the costs of an appeal by one of his students, and incurred legal costs in negotiating with Customs for a compounded penalty to avoid criminal proceedings regarding evasion of VAT. He reclaimed input tax in respect of the legal costs incurred, and the Commissioners issued an assessment to recover the tax, considering that the expenditure had not been incurred for the purposes of the business. The proprietor appealed, contending that the expenditure had been incurred for the purpose of his business, since he had been liable to imprisonment and if he had been imprisoned for any length of time his business may have been forced to close. The QB upheld the assessment, holding that the fact that the business had benefited from the expenditure was not conclusive, since 'there must be a real connection, a nexus between the expenditure and the business'. On the evidence, there was no clear nexus between the expenditure in question and the business. Accordingly, the expenditure in question had not been incurred for the purpose of the business and none of the tax was deductible. *C & E Commrs v FW Rosner, QB 1993, [1994] STC 228*.

34.146   In *Spillane*, 3.42 ASSESSMENT, the QB held that VAT on legal fees, incurred by a sole trader in defending proceedings for committal to prison for contempt of court, was not deductible as input tax.

34.147   A similar decision was reached in *RN Scott, MAN/92/1244 (VTD 11574)*.

34.148   **Legal costs of farmer charged with motoring offence.** A farmer was prosecuted for reckless driving. He reclaimed input tax in respect of his solicitors' and counsel's fees. The Commissioners rejected his claim and the tribunal dismissed his appeal, holding that the expenditure had not been incurred for the purpose of his business. *RN Scott, MAN/86/96 (VTD 2302)*. (*Note*. For a subsequent appeal by the same appellant, see 34.147 above.)

34.149   **Legal costs of estate agent charged with motoring offence.** An estate agent was charged with driving when under the influence of alcohol, and refusing to take a breathalyser test. He reclaimed input tax in respect of legal costs incurred in defending himself. The Commissioners issued an assessment to recover the tax, considering that the expenditure had been incurred for personal reasons rather than for business reasons. The tribunal dismissed the estate agent's appeal, applying *Scott*, 34.148 above. 'The criminal offence of failing to take a breath test to ascertain the content of alcohol in the appellant's blood had no connection to a supply of goods or services used for the purpose of the appellant's business'. *GM Child (t/a Child & Co), LON/90/1239X (VTD 6827)*. (*Note*. For another issue in this case, see 9.110 CARS.)

34.150   **Legal costs of surveyor charged with motoring offence.** A surveyor was convicted of driving with excessive alcohol and was disqualified from driving for three years. He reclaimed input tax on his legal costs. The Commissioners rejected the claim and the tribunal dismissed the surveyor's appeal, applying *dicta* in *Rosner*, 34.145 above. *VW Evans, LON/96/1271 (VTD 14662)*.

34.151   **Legal costs of company director charged with criminal offence.** A company carried on a grocery business, including a supermarket. In the course of its business it acquired and sold a quantity of confectionery, in relation to which W, its managing director and principal shareholder, was later charged with handling stolen property. He was convicted and served six months in prison. At his request, the solicitors who had handled his defence invoiced the company for the legal costs incurred. The company paid these and reclaimed the VAT thereon as input tax. The Commissioners issued an assessment to recover the tax and the tribunal dismissed the company's appeal. The legal services had been rendered to W personally and not to the company. The expenditure might have had the effect of benefiting the business, but it was not incurred for the purpose of the business. *Wallman Foods Ltd, MAN/83/41 (VTD 1411)*.

34.152   The managing director of a company was charged with corruption in relation to the acquisition of stock by the company. He was acquitted and the company reclaimed input tax in respect of the costs of his defence. The Commissioners rejected the claim and the tribunal dismissed the company's appeal. The charges were brought against the director personally. The expenditure had benefited the company's business but had not been incurred for the purpose of the company's business and accordingly the input tax was not deductible. *Wallman Foods Ltd*, 34.151 above, applied. *Britwood Toys Ltd, LON/86/280 (VTD 2263)*.

34.153   A company carried on business as a building contractor and property developer. In 1985 the company and its principal director were charged with obtaining money from the National Coal Board by deception, by falsely representing that the company had completed work for the Board when this was not the case. The Board also began civil proceedings against the director. The company reclaimed input tax in respect of the costs of defending the actions. The Commissioners agreed to allow the tax in respect of the civil action, but only agreed to allow 50% of the tax in respect of the criminal proceedings. The tribunal dismissed the company's appeal against this decision, holding that the company had not shown that more than 50% of the costs could be regarded as having been incurred for business purposes. (The tribunal also held that, as the company was partly exempt, the tax in question should be apportioned between taxable and exempt supplies.) *Dennis Rye Ltd, MAN/88/764 (VTD 4545)*. (*Note.* For a subsequent appeal by the same company, see 43.62 PARTIAL EXEMPTION.)

34.154 The director of a computer software company was charged with assaulting a British Rail employee, and was convicted. The company reclaimed input tax on the costs of his defence. The Commissioners issued an assessment to recover the tax, and the tribunal dismissed the company's appeal. *Wallman Foods Ltd*, 34.151 above, and *Britwood Toys Ltd*, 34.152 above, applied. *LHA Ltd, LON/93/924A (VTD 11911)*. (*Note.* For another issue in this case, see 34.451 below.)

34.155 An individual (M) had been the principal director of a company (T) which had gone into liquidation. The company's affairs were investigated by the Serious Fraud Office, and M was charged with fraudulent trading, contrary to *Companies Act 1985, s 458*. M was also chairman of another company (K) which had been incorporated to develop a power station. K paid substantial legal fees in defending M against the charges of fraudulent trading, and reclaimed input tax on these fees. The Commissioners rejected the claim, considering that the expenditure had not been incurred for the purpose of K's business. The tribunal dismissed K's appeal, applying the QB decision in *Rosner*, 34.145 above. The fact that the expenditure had benefited K was not conclusive. On the evidence, the legal services could not 'properly be said to have been used for the purposes of the business of the company'. *P & O European Ferries*, 34.143 above, distinguished. *Kingsnorth Developments Ltd, LON/93/1616 (VTD 12544)*.

Renovation and acquisition of premises—sole traders

Cases where the appellant was successful

34.156 **Shopkeeper.** A shopkeeper lived above the shop from which he traded. He reclaimed input tax incurred on renovating the premises, and the Commissioners issued an assessment to recover the tax. The tribunal allowed his appeal, finding that the expenditure related to the retail shop and holding that the whole of the tax was allowable. *JPR Hampton, MAN/86/93 (VTD 2196)*.

34.157 **Grocer—renovation of kitchen used for take-away food business.** A grocer traded from two adjoining cottages, using the upper floor of one of them as living accommodation. He began to offer sandwiches and hot take-away food for sale, and renovated the kitchen of one of the cottages. He reclaimed the input tax on the relevant expenditure, but the Commissioners issued an assessment to recover the tax, considering that the use of the equipment was domestic rather than commercial. The tribunal allowed the grocer's appeal, holding on the evidence that the element of private use was insignificant and that the expenditure had been incurred for business purposes. *PA Farley, MAN/87/208 (VTD 2567)*.

34.158 **Farmer—erection of conservatory for use as office.** A farmer reclaimed input tax on the erection of a conservatory at her house. The Commissioners issued an assessment to recover the tax, and the farmer appealed, contending that the conservatory had been erected to be used as an office, so that the input tax should be treated as deductible in full. The tribunal accepted the farmer's evidence and allowed her appeal. *MA Murray, EDN/95/172 (VTD 13907)*.

Cases where the appellant was partly successful

34.159   **Fish farmer.**   A fish farmer owned five ponds, covering 3 acres, in land of 48 acres. The only accommodation at the farm was a prefabricated bungalow, which was nearing the end of its life. He built a new bungalow to replace the existing one, and reclaimed input tax on the expenditure. The Commissioners issued an assessment to recover the tax but the tribunal allowed his appeal in part, holding that in view of his need to live near the fish ponds, 50% of the tax was deductible. *D Mears, [1981] VATTR 99 (VTD 1095)*. (*Note*. The tribunal rejected an alternative contention by the appellant, that the work was within what is now *VATA 1994, s 35*. For cases concerning *s 35*, see 15 CONSTRUCTION OF BUILDINGS, ETC.)

34.160   **Farmer.**   A farmer owned an estate of 2,000 acres, and lived in a mansion on the estate. Part of the estate was used as a caravan site. The administration of the estate, including the farming and the caravan site, was carried on from the mansion. The farmer reclaimed input tax in respect of extensive repairs to the mansion. The tribunal held that the expenditure had been incurred partly for business purposes and partly for private purposes, and held that 60% of the tax in question was deductible. *Sir Ian MacDonald of Sleat, [1981] VATTR 223 (VTD 1179)*. (*Note*. See now Business Brief 18/96, issued on 27 August 1996, for guidelines which have been agreed with the National Farmers' Union regarding input tax claims for repairs and renovations to farmhouses.)

34.161   A farmer renovated a bungalow, which had previously been vacant, to use as a home for his family and as a base from which he could run his farming business. He reclaimed the input tax incurred on the renovation. The Commissioners considered that the work had primarily been incurred for private purposes rather than business purposes, and issued an assessment to recover 80% of the tax in question. The farmer appealed. The tribunal reviewed the evidence in detail and found that half the total expenditure had been incurred for private purposes and half had been incurred for dual purposes. Of the half that had been incurred for dual purposes, 60% should be apportioned to the business, with the result that 30% of the total input tax should be treated as allowable. The assessment was reduced accordingly. *RJ Blomfield, MAN/90/592 (VTD 5759)*. (*Note*. See also the note following *Sir Ian MacDonald of Sleat*, 34.160 above.)

34.162   A sheep farmer reclaimed input tax on the restoration of a farm house. The Commissioners issued an assessment to recover the tax, on the basis that the expenditure had been incurred for private purposes rather than for the purposes of the farmer's business. The farmer appealed. The tribunal allowed the appeal in part, finding that the expenditure had been incurred for a dual purpose and holding that 40% of the tax was allowable. *MS Riches, [1994] VATTR 401 (VTD 12210)*. (*Notes*. (1) An alternative contention by the appellant, that the work qualified for zero-rating under what is now *VATA 1994, Sch 8 Group 5*, was rejected by the tribunal. Compare the cases noted at 15.90 to 15.113 CONSTRUCTION OF BUILDINGS, ETC. (2) An appeal against a misdeclaration penalty was allowed. (3) See also the note following *Sir Ian MacDonald of Sleat*, 34.160 above.)

34.163   **Car dealer.**   A car dealer purchased and renovated a run-down property. He used it as his family home and ran his business from one room. He reclaimed the input tax on the renovation work, and the Commissioners issued an assessment to recover the tax. The tribunal allowed his appeal in part, holding that one-eighth of the tax was attributable to the business and was deductible. *RJ Ferguson, MAN/83/198 (VTD 1578)*.

34.164   **Solicitor.**   A solicitor reclaimed input tax on the purchase of some materials for the construction of a house, one room of which he intended to use as an office. The

Commissioners rejected the claim, and the solicitor appealed. The tribunal held that the expenditure had primarily been incurred for personal purposes, and that only 5% of the tax was deductible. *PF Bilton, MAN/86/162 (VTD 2324).*

34.165   **Stud proprietor—refurbishment of house partly used for business purposes.** The proprietor of a stud in Oxfordshire had to visit Newmarket frequently to take his mares to be covered by stallions there, to meet clients, and to buy and sell horses at auction. He leased a small house in Newmarket to stay in overnight, and reclaimed input tax on the expenditure incurred in refurbishing it. The Commissioners issued an assessment to recover the tax, considering that the expenditure had been incurred for personal reasons rather than for business reasons. The tribunal allowed the proprietor's appeal in part, holding that his primary purpose was 'to provide himself with a place where he could do business with his customers on the many occasions when, in connection with that business, he needed to go to Newmarket'. *Farrington,* 34.181 below, distinguished. However, since the house was partly used for business entertainment, the tribunal held that only 50% of the tax in question was deductible. *TD Rootes (t/a The Shutford Stud), LON/91/ 339X (VTD 6808).*

34.166   **Subpostmaster and general retailer.** A subpostmaster and general retailer refurbished his premises. The work included the creation of an office downstairs and a bedroom and bathroom upstairs. He reclaimed input tax on the refurbishment. The Commissioners rejected his claim, considering that the expenditure had not been incurred for the purpose of his retail business. The tribunal allowed his appeal in part, finding that the work had partly been incurred in order to provide better storage facilities for the business, but had also partly been incurred for the purpose of his office as a subpostmaster and partly with the intention of letting or selling the upper floor of the premises. The tribunal directed that the input tax should be apportioned. *JJ Gartland, MAN/90/877 (VTD 7331).*

34.167   **Forester.** The owner of a forest in Ulster, who was registered for VAT, reclaimed input tax on the construction of storage buildings on his estate, and on the construction of a driveway leading to his house and to the storage buildings. (Previously, access to the house had been by means of a road which crossed land owned by the National Trust.) The Commissioners issued an assessment to recover the tax, considering that the expenditure had been incurred for private purposes, rather than for the purpose of administering the forest which he owned. He appealed, contending that the buildings had been constructed for the purpose of storing business assets, and that the driveway had been constructed to avoid the need to cross National Trust land. The tribunal allowed his appeal in part, holding that 50% of the expenditure on the storage buildings and on a part of the driveway leading to those buildings, and 25% of the expenditure on the remainder of the driveway, had been incurred for business purposes. *Earl of Belmore, BEL/92/13X (VTD 9775).*

34.168   **Haulage contractor.** A haulage contractor reclaimed input tax on the building of a two-storey extension at the rear of his home. The Commissioners issued an assessment to recover the tax and he appealed, contending that he had built the extension to provide himself with an office. Initially he had used the lower part of the extension as his office, but subsequently he had rearranged the ground floor so that a room at the front of his house (which had previously been a lounge) became his office and the new room became a dining-room. The tribunal allowed his appeal in part, accepting that the lower floor of the extension had been built with the intention of being used as an office, finding that two-thirds of the expenditure was attributable to the lower floor, and holding that two-thirds of the disputed tax was allowable. *J Bryant, LON/90/1588A (VTD 11212).*

34.169   **Ceramic designer.**   A ceramic designer, who worked from home, reclaimed input tax on the construction of an extension to her home. The Commissioners issued an assessment to recover 45% of the tax, on the basis that the expenditure had been incurred for private purposes as well as for business purposes. The tribunal allowed the designer's appeal in part, finding that the business purpose was the primary purpose but that the desire to improve the value of her home was a subsidiary purpose, and holding that 80% of the tax was deductible. *J Willingale, LON/93/2325A (VTD 12029)*.

34.170   **Plant hire contractor.**   The proprietor of a plant hire business reclaimed input tax on the renovation of a farmhouse. The Commissioners issued an assessment to recover the tax, considering that the expenditure had been incurred for domestic purposes rather than for business purposes. The proprietor appealed, contending that the expenditure had been incurred for the purpose of providing accommodation for his daughter and son-in-law, and that since his son-in-law was employed by him in the business, the tax was deductible. The tribunal held that the expenditure had been incurred for a dual purpose but that the domestic purpose was the primary purpose, and held that 10% of the tax was deductible. *LG Cook (t/a Ellon Plant Hire), EDN/93/216 (VTD 12302)*.

Cases where the appellant was unsuccessful

34.171   **Doctor.**   A doctor built a house on land which he owned and reclaimed input tax on the materials used. The Commissioners issued an assessment to recover the tax and the tribunal dismissed the doctor's appeal, holding that the supply of the materials was not for the purposes of his business. *Dr M Davies, CAR/75/162 (VTD 219)*. (*Note*. The relevant supplies were before the introduction of what is now *VATA 1994, s 35*. See 15 CONSTRUCTION OF BUILDINGS, ETC. for cases concerning this provision.)

34.172   **Fisherman.**   A fisherman reclaimed input tax on expenditure incurred in renovating the barn where he and his family lived. The Commissioners issued an assessment to recover the tax on this expenditure and the tribunal dismissed his appeal. *DC Bean, CAR/76/163 (VTD 339)*.

34.173   **Builder.**   A builder purchased an old blacksmith's forge to convert into a house for his own occupation, and reclaimed input tax on building materials relating to this work. The Commissioners issued an assessment to recover the tax, and the tribunal dismissed his appeal, holding that the materials had not been supplied for the purposes of his business. *TDO Jones (t/a Evan Jones & Son), CAR/76/75 (VTD 365)*.

34.174   A builder, who had previously lived in a caravan, converted a barn for him and his family to live in. He reclaimed input tax on the materials used, and the Commissioners issued an assessment to recover the tax. The tribunal dismissed his appeal against the assessment, holding that the barn had not been converted for the purposes of his business. *W Ball, MAN/88/821 (VTD 3865)*.

34.175   An appeal was dismissed in a subsequent case where a builder had reclaimed input tax in respect of materials used to renovate two houses which he and his wife used as private residences. *RD Elton, LON/92/2058A (VTD 11590)*.

34.176   **Publican.**   A publican reclaimed input tax on redecorating and carpeting the living accommodation on the upper floor of the public house. The Commissioners issued an assessment to recover the tax and the tribunal dismissed his appeal, holding that the expenditure had not been incurred for business purposes. *RTG Britton, MAN/77/39 (VTD 445)*.

34.177   **Coal merchant.**   A coal merchant purchased a disused quarry and five Victorian cottages nearby. He used the quarry as his business premises. He renovated five of the cottages and reclaimed input tax in respect of the materials used for the renovation. The Commissioners issued an assessment to recover the tax, against which he appealed. The tribunal dismissed his appeal, holding that the cottages were not assets of his business and had not been renovated for the purpose of his business. *SJ Johnson, MAN/82/185 (VTD 1367)*.

34.178   **Architect.**   An architect reclaimed input tax on expenditure incurred in renovating an office building of which he was the joint owner. The Commissioners issued an assessment to recover the tax, considering that he had purchased an interest in the building as an investment, so that the expenditure had not been incurred for the purpose of his profession. The tribunal upheld the assessment and dismissed the architect's appeal. *DT Morgan-Jones, LON/83/173 (VTD 1340)*.

34.179   An architect reclaimed input tax on materials used in renovating his house. The Commissioners issued an assessment to recover the tax and the tribunal dismissed the architect's appeal. *CR Butterworth, LON/82/240 (VTD 1395)*.

34.180   **Accountant.**   An accountant reclaimed input tax on alterations carried out at the house which he and his wife occupied. The Commissioners issued an assessment to recover the tax and the tribunal dismissed the accountant's appeal. *CR Groom, MAN/83/244 (VTD 1630)*.

34.181   **Actor.**   An actor lived in London but frequently worked in Manchester. He purchased and renovated a house in Manchester so that he could stay there when necessary in preference to a hotel. The Commissioners issued an assessment to recover the tax and the tribunal dismissed the actor's appeal, holding that the expenditure had been incurred for personal reasons rather than for the purposes of his profession. *K Farrington, LON/86/230 (VTD 2177)*.

34.182   **Furniture dealer.**   A furniture dealer reclaimed input tax on the renovation of a flat which he occupied, including the purchase of kitchen and bathroom fittings. The Commissioners issued an assessment to recover the tax and the tribunal dismissed his appeal, holding that there was no connection between his occupation of the flat and his furniture business. *DB Bray, LON/90/326 (VTD 5538)*.

34.183   **Bookseller.**   A bookseller lived at Westcliff-on-Sea, where he had a shop, and also owned a warehouse at Burton-on-Trent. He purchased two houses, one in London and one in Burton-on-Trent, and reclaimed input tax on renovation work at the houses. The Commissioners issued an assessment to recover the tax and the tribunal dismissed the bookseller's appeal, holding that the houses had been purchased for personal reasons, rather than for the purposes of the business. *JR Hodgkins (t/a Clifton Books), LON/90/1514Y (VTD 6496)*.

34.184   **Surveyor.**   A chartered surveyor, who was a paraplegic, converted two barns into a cottage. He reclaimed the input tax incurred on the work, and the Commissioners issued an assessment to recover the tax. He appealed, contending that the expenditure had been incurred for business purposes as he needed the active assistance of someone living nearby. He gave evidence that he had intended the cottage to be used as accommodation for his son, who was aged 19 and living at home. However, at the relevant time the cottage was let on short-term tenancies. The tribunal dismissed the surveyor's appeal, holding on the evidence that the renovation of the cottage had not been carried out for the purposes of his business. *ACH Bond, LON/89/1246Y (VTD 4722)*.

34.185   **Conversion of houseboat intended to be used for bed and breakfast accommodation—whether input tax wholly deductible.**   The owner of a large houseboat undertook conversion work on it so that it could be used to provide bed and breakfast accommodation. He reclaimed the whole of the input tax incurred on the work. The Commissioners issued an assessment to recover 50% of the tax, since the owner was living in the houseboat and it appeared that he would continue to use half of the houseboat for his own occupation. The tribunal upheld the assessment and dismissed the owner's appeal. *C Pollock, LON/91/195 (VTD 6638)*. (*Note*. The appellant also contended that the work was within what is now *VATA 1994, s 35*, but the tribunal rejected this contention since the houseboat was not a building and he was converting it rather than constructing it. For cases concerning *s 35*, see 15 CONSTRUCTION OF BUILDINGS, ETC.)

34.186   **Farmer—repair to farmhouse roof.**   A farmer incurred expenditure on repairs to the roof of his farmhouse, and reclaimed the whole of the input tax. The Commissioners issued an assessment to recover 30% of the tax, considering that the expenditure had been partly incurred for private purposes, so that only a proportion of the tax was deductible. The farmer appealed, contending that the effect of *Article 17* of the *EC Sixth Directive*, as interpreted in *Lennartz v Finanzamt München*, 21.216 EUROPEAN COMMUNITY LAW, was that the whole of the input tax should be treated as deductible. The tribunal dismissed his appeal, holding that the principle in *Lennartz* only applied to supplies of goods and that the subsequent private use of such goods was treated as a supply of services on which output tax was chargeable. However, the farmhouse was immovable property rather than goods, and the use of the farmhouse for private purposes could not be treated as a taxable supply of services. Since the input tax was not paid wholly for the purposes of actual or deemed taxable transactions, it followed that the decision in *Lennartz* was distinguishable and only a proportion of the input tax was deductible. *WD Hurd, [1995] VATDR 128 (VTD 12985)*. (*Note*. The case was heard by the tribunal with *F & M Mounty & Sons*, 34.219 below.)

34.187   **Caterer.**   A married woman carried on a small catering business from her home. She reclaimed the whole of the input tax on the refurbishment of the kitchen. The Commissioners issued an assessment to recover 80% of the tax, considering that the kitchen was primarily used to prepare meals for the trader's family. She appealed, contending that the whole of the tax should be treated as allowable because the kitchen had to meet the standards set by the Health and Safety Inspectorate. The tribunal dismissed her appeal, finding that she had 'not discharged the burden of proof' that the purpose of the work was to comply with these standards. *E Gent (t/a Elizabeth Corke Catering), MAN/96/54 (VTD 14438)*.

34.188   **Haulage contractor.**   A haulage contractor reclaimed input tax relating to the building of an extension at the bungalow where he lived. The Commissioners issued an assessment to recover the tax, considering that it had not been incurred for the purposes of his business. The tribunal upheld the assessment and dismissed the contractor's appeal. *BCW Bushell, LON/96/411 (VTD 15094)*.

Renovation and acquisition of premises—partnerships

Cases where the appellant was successful

34.189   **Family farming partnership—conversion of cowshed into cottage.**   A married couple who carried on a farming business in partnership renovated an old cowshed, converting it into a cottage for the husband's mother to live in. The couple reclaimed input tax on the materials used in the renovation and the Commissioners issued an assessment to recover the tax. The couple appealed, contending that the tax should be treated as deductible since the mother did some agricultural work for them. The tribunal allowed the couple's appeal, holding on the evidence that their principal purpose had been to enable the husband's mother to continue to work for them on the farm. *CSJ & DJ Whitfield, LON/88/452 (VTD 3506)*.

34.190 **Family farming partnership—renovation of farmhouse.** A family farming partnership farmed a substantial area of land including three farms, each of which had a farmhouse. One of the farmhouses was occupied by the senior partner (D), the second was occupied by an employee, and the third, which was owned by D rather than by the partnership, was in very poor condition. D decided to renovate it. The work was paid for by the partnership, which reclaimed the input tax. The Commissioners issued an assessment to recover the tax, considering that the work had been carried out for D's private purposes rather than for the purposes of the partnership. The tribunal allowed the partnership's appeal, holding on the evidence that the farmhouse had been renovated to be used as a business asset of the partnership. *D Dyball & Son, LON/89/1449X (VTD 4863)*.

34.191 **Retailers—whether premises purchased for expansion of business or for letting.** A married couple traded in partnership, selling bicycles and perambulators from a retail shop. In 1979 they acquired the adjacent premises, which were in poor condition. They renovated the premises and converted the first floor into offices, some of which they used for storage. They reclaimed input tax on the materials used. The Commissioners issued an assessment to recover the tax, considering that the work had not been carried out for the purposes of the couple's retail business and that the renovated premises were probably intended for letting. The tribunal allowed the couple's appeal, finding that the original premises were crowded and congested, and that expansion was an 'attractive proposition'. *JF & SD Pank, MAN/89/805 (VTD 4930)*.

34.192 **Hotel owned and managed by married couple—enlargement of hotel.** A married couple owned and managed a hotel which contained 19 bedrooms. They occupied one of the bedrooms and their daughter occupied another bedroom, the remaining 17 being let to guests. They arranged for the building of an extension, and the bedrooms which they had previously occupied were subsequently let to guests. They reclaimed the input tax incurred in building the extension. The Commissioners issued an assessment to recover the tax, considering that the work had been undertaken to provide the couple with better living accommodation, rather than for the purposes of the business. The tribunal allowed the couple's appeal, holding on the evidence that the extension had been built for the purpose of the hotel business although it had also had the effect of improving the proprietors' living accommodation. *JA & GL Perez, LON/90/988Z (VTD 6758)*.

34.193 **Partnership carrying on property development business.** A married couple carried on a property development business in partnership. They reclaimed input tax on the building of a two-storey extension at their house. The extension comprised one room which was used as an office, together with a kitchen, a bathroom, and two upstairs rooms which could be used as bedrooms or for office purposes. The Commissioners issued an assessment to recover 50% of the tax, on the basis that the expenditure was partly for private purposes. The couple appealed, contending that the whole of the expenditure had been incurred for business purposes, and that both the upstairs rooms had been used as offices. The tribunal accepted the couple's evidence and allowed the appeal. *DLR & Mrs LM Chiplen, LON/93/1458A (VTD 12280)*. (*Note*. The assessment under appeal also covered a duplicated claim to input tax, in respect of which the appeal was dismissed.)

34.194 **Building partnership.** A married couple traded in partnership as builders. In 1990 they purchased a mill which had planning permission for conversion into a private house. They reclaimed input tax on the purchase and subsequent conversion work. In 1992 they moved into the mill. In 1994 the Commissioners issued an assessment to recover the tax, on the basis that the mill had been purchased to be used as their private residence. The couple appealed, contending that they had intended to sell the mill at a profit and were still hoping to do so, having instructed three different estate agents. The tribunal accepted the couple's evidence and allowed their appeal. *GM & JA Storrie, MAN/95/1929 (VTD 14543)*.

Cases where the appellant was partly successful

34.195   **Family farming partnership—conversion of oasthouse into farmhouse.**   A family farming partnership converted an oasthouse for use as a farmhouse, and reclaimed the input tax on the work. The Commissioners issued an assessment to recover the tax, and the partnership appealed. The tribunal allowed the appeal in part, directing that the tax in question should be apportioned. *K & D Chapman, LON/81/213 (VTD 1209)*.

34.196   **Family farming partnership—conversion of mill into dwelling-house for partners.**   A family farming partnership, consisting of a married couple and their son and his wife, converted a mill into a dwelling-house for the two senior partners. The partnership reclaimed the input tax on this work and the Commissioners issued an assessment to recover the tax, considering that it had been undertaken for private purposes rather than for business purposes. The tribunal allowed the partnership's appeal in part, holding that 50% of the tax was allowable. *Herrod-Taylor & Co, LON/83/143 (VTD 1475)*.

34.197   **Family farming partnership—conversion of barn into dwelling-house for partner.**   A family farming partnership reclaimed input tax in respect of the conversion of a barn into a dwelling-house for one of the partners and his wife. The Commissioners issued an assessment to recover the tax, considering that the expenditure had been incurred for domestic purposes rather than private purposes. The partnership appealed, contending that the purpose of the work had been to enable the relevant partner, who had suffered a stroke and was unable to walk long distances, to live in close proximity to the farm. The tribunal allowed the appeal in part, finding that the work had a dual purpose, of which the business purpose was the dominant purpose, and holding that 70% of the tax in question was allowable. *W Cupit & Sons, MAN/89/891 (VTD 5403)*.

34.198   **Family farming partnership—conversion of granary into dwelling-house for partner.**   A family farming partnership comprised a married couple and their son. The partnership converted an old granary into a dwelling-house for the son and his fiancée, and reclaimed the input tax thereon. The Commissioners issued an assessment to recover the tax, considering that the work had been undertaken for domestic reasons rather than for the purposes of the business. The partnership appealed, contending that the work had been undertaken for business purposes since it was essential that the son should live on the farm. The tribunal held that the work had been undertaken with a dual purpose and adjourned the hearing in the hope that the parties could agree on an apportionment of the tax. *J & B Stanwix & Son, MAN/90/772 (VTD 6347)*. (*Note*. There was no further public hearing of the appeal.)

34.199   **Family farming partnership—renovation of farmhouse and cottage.**   A family farming partnership owned a large farmhouse and a number of cottages. The active partners lived in the farmhouse. The partnership incurred expenditure on renovating the farmhouse and one of the cottages, and reclaimed the input tax on this expenditure. The Commissioners issued an assessment to recover 70% of the tax on the farmhouse and the whole of the tax on the cottage. The tribunal allowed the partnership's appeal in part, holding that the tax in respect of the cottage was wholly allowable, since it was intended that it should be occupied by employees, but upheld the Commissioners' decision to allow only 30% of the tax in respect of the farmhouse. *J Korner & Others, EDN/85/73 (VTD 2008)*. (*Note*. See now Business Brief 18/96, issued on 27 August 1996, for guidelines which have been agreed with the National Farmers' Union regarding input tax claims for repairs and renovations to farmhouses.)

34.200   A family farming partnership incurred expenditure in renovating and extending their farmhouse. The extension comprised 2,063 square feet, of which 1,290 were accepted as relating entirely to living accommodation. The partnership reclaimed 773/2,063 of the total input tax, and the Commissioners issued an assessment to recover most of this, considering that only 10% of the total tax was deductible. The tribunal reviewed the evidence in detail and allowed the appeal in part, holding that 20% of the total tax was deductible. *PM & JB Paice, LON/92/1007Y (VTD 9649)*. (*Notes*. (1) An appeal against a misdeclaration penalty was allowed. (2) See also the note following *Korner & Others*, 34.199 above.)

34.201   A married couple carried on a livestock farming business from a hill farm not suitable for arable crops. The husband was also a partner in a nearby firm of surveyors. They incurred expenditure on renovating the farmhouse, which was described as 'an imposing period house with landscaped gardens' resembling 'a country mansion'. They reclaimed one-third of the input tax on this expenditure. The Commissioners considered that only 10% of the tax in question should be allowed, and issued an assessment to recover the balance. The tribunal allowed the couple's appeal in part, holding on the evidence that 20% of the input tax was deductible. (An appeal against the disallowance of input tax incurred on resurfacing the driveway was dismissed.) *ATB & Mrs SDL Jones, LON/92/1763A (VTD 11410)*. (*Notes*. (1) For another issue in this case, see 34.299 below. (2) See also the note following *Korner & Others*, 34.199 above.)

34.202   **Family farming partnership—installation of security system in farmhouse.**   A family farming partnership reclaimed input tax in respect of the installation of a security system in the farmhouse. The Commissioners issued an assessment to recover the tax but the tribunal allowed the partnership's appeal in part, holding that 40% of the tax in question was allowable. *The Grange Farm, LON/86/680 (VTD 2344)*. (*Note*. See now the note following *Korner & Others*, 34.199 above.)

34.203   **Family farming partnership—renovation of cottage.**   A family farming partnership restored an old cottage adjoining the farmhouse. Immediately after the restoration the cottage was occupied by one of the partners, but it was subsequently occupied by an employee. The partnership reclaimed the input tax on the work. The Commissioners issued an assessment to recover the tax but the tribunal allowed the partnership's appeal in part, holding that 70% of the tax in question was allowable. *ACS Eccles & Co, EDN/85/71 (VTD 2057)*. (*Note*. See now the note following *Korner & Others*, 34.199 above.)

34.204   A similar decision was arrived at in a subsequent case where the tribunal allowed 70% of the input tax on the cost of renovating and extending a cottage close to the main farmhouse. *WJL Greig & Son, EDN/88/56 (VTD 2918)*. (*Note*. See now the note following *Korner & Others*, 34.199 above.)

34.205   **Grocery partnership.**   A grocery partnership reclaimed input tax in respect of building materials which were partly used for business purposes and partly for private purposes. The Commissioners issued an assessment to recover the tax. The tribunal allowed the partnership's appeal in part, holding that 50% of the tax in question was allowable. *AS Purewal & Others, MAN/85/119 (VTD 2055)*.

34.206   **Lighthouse open to viewing by public and used as partners' private residence.**   A retired naval commander and his wife had carried on a business of buying and selling pictures. In 1984 the husband bought a derelict lighthouse, and spent three years restoring it. In 1986 they closed their business of buying and selling pictures, and in 1987 they opened the lighthouse for viewing by the public in return for admission fees. They also used the lighthouse as their private residence. They reclaimed input tax on the materials used in renovating the lighthouse, and the Commissioners issued an assessment to recover the tax. The tribunal held that the expenditure had been incurred for a dual purpose and that 40% of the tax was allowable, applying *Ian Flockton Developments Ltd*, 34.248 below. *Waterford Galleries, LON/88/896X (VTD 3448)*.

34.207   **Hotel owned and managed by married couple—conversion of outbuildings into accommodation for relatives working at hotel.**   A married couple purchased a hotel in 1987. They incurred expenditure in converting outbuildings into residential accommodation, and reclaimed input tax on this. The Commissioners discovered that the accommodation in question was occupied by the couple's widowed mothers, who had contributed to the cost of the work, and issued an assessment to recover the tax. The couple appealed, contending that, since their mothers worked for them at the hotel, the expenditure had been incurred for business reasons and the tax was deductible. The tribunal allowed the appeal in part, holding that the expenditure had been incurred for a dual purpose and that one-third of the tax was deductible, applying *Ian Flockton Developments Ltd*, 34.248 below. *BG & PL Menheneott, MAN/92/90 (VTD 10542)*.

34.208   **Renovation of bungalow adjacent to hotel—whether expenditure incurred for purpose of business.**   A married couple had purchased a hotel in Godalming in 1983. In 1986 they also purchased a bungalow in grounds adjoining the hotel. They used the bungalow as their private residence. In April 1988 they installed a new kitchen in the bungalow. However, in May 1988 they purchased another hotel some distance away, and on 1 September they left the Godalming hotel to live in the new hotel. Between August 1988 and February 1989 they arranged for the construction of a two-storey extension to the bungalow at the Godalming hotel. This bungalow was initially occupied by hotel employees, but in December 1989 they sold it. The couple reclaimed input tax on the kitchen and the extension, and the Commissioners issued an assessment to recover the tax, considering that the expenditure had not been incurred for business purposes. The tribunal allowed the couple's appeal in part, holding that the tax on the kitchen was deductible since at that time the partners were living in the bungalow and were doing so for the purpose of running the business. However, the tax on the extension was not deductible, because at the time the expenditure was incurred the couple had left the Godalming hotel, and since the subsequent sale of the bungalow was an exempt supply, the extension had never been used for the making of taxable supplies. *Mr & Mrs M Cummings (t/a Inn On The Lake), LON/91/1170 (VTD 8891)*.

34.209   **Design consultants reclaiming input tax on conservatory.**   An unmarried couple carried on business as design consultants from the cottage where they lived. They reclaimed input tax on the supply of a conservatory at the cottage, and the Commissioners issued an assessment to recover the tax, considering that the expenditure had not been incurred for business purposes. The couple appealed, contending that the conservatory was used as a showroom and for meetings with clients. The tribunal allowed the appeal in part, holding on the evidence that 60% of the tax on the conservatory was deductible. *B Muir & G Edwards (t/a Muir-McGill Associates), LON/91/1684X (VTD 7469).*

34.210   **Solicitors' partnership—swimming pool constructed in grounds.**   See *Willcox & Co*, 34.413 below.

Cases where the appellant was unsuccessful

34.211   **Building partnership—materials for house built for partner.**   A partnership which carried on a construction business reclaimed input tax in respect of materials used in building a house for one of the partners. Most of the work was done by the partner concerned. The Commissioners issued an assessment to recover the tax and the tribunal dismissed the partnership's appeal. *RGB Contractors, LON/74/70 (VTD 133).*

34.212   **Family retail partnership—purchase of property.**   A family partnership, which carried on a retail business, reclaimed input tax on the purchase of a property. The Commissioners rejected the claim and the tribunal dismissed the partnership's appeal, finding that 'it is not established that the property was purchased as a business asset' and that, even if it was, 'it was purchased by way of an investment and not for the purpose of obtaining income therefrom'. *Morrison's Academy Boarding Houses Association*, 7.1 BUSINESS, and *Adstock Ltd*, 7.104 BUSINESS, applied. *T, EC, PT & A Worthington (t/a Conochies), EDN/98/128 (VTD 16228).*

34.213   **Garage built at partners' residence.**   A married couple trading in partnership reclaimed input tax on a garage built at their residence. The Commissioners issued an assessment to recover the tax and the tribunal dismissed the couple's appeal, holding on the evidence that the garage was not used for business purposes. *DF & A Everett, MAN/83/252 (VTD 1606).*

34.214   A similar decision was reached in *Mr & Mrs G Vitzthum (t/a Leeds Wine Services), MAN/92/1505 (VTD 11076).*

34.215   **Family farming partnership—renovation of castle.**   A married couple who owned a livestock farm lived in a seventeenth-century castle, from which they administered the farm. They reclaimed input tax on renovation of part of the castle. The Commissioners issued an assessment to recover 90% of the tax, considering that the work had primarily been undertaken for domestic reasons. The tribunal upheld the assessment and dismissed the couple's appeal. *CMM & ISMM Crichton, EDN/87/105 (VTD 2748). (Note. See now the note following Korner & Others*, 34.199 above.)

34.216   **Family farming partnership—renovation of farmhouse.**   A married couple purchased 1,500 acres of farmland, including an old nine-bedroomed house which was a protected building. The house was in disrepair, and they had it renovated at a cost of more than £1,000,000. They reclaimed 30% of the input tax relating to this expenditure. The Commissioners issued an assessment to recover two-thirds of the amount reclaimed, considering that only 10% of the expenditure could be regarded as having been for the purposes of their business activities (which included occasional lettings for shooting weekends as well as the administration of the farm). The tribunal upheld the assessment and dismissed the couple's appeal. *RF & RJ Macaire, LON/92/1139Z (VTD 10741). (Note. See now the note following Korner & Others*, 34.199 above.)

34.217   A family partnership reclaimed input tax on a payment made to a firm of quantity surveyors in connection with the renovation of the farmhouse. The Commissioners issued an assessment to recover 50% of the tax, on the basis that the expenditure had been partly incurred for private purposes. The tribunal dismissed the partnership's appeal. The chairman observed that Customs had been 'very generous indeed' in agreeing an apportionment of 50%. *CJ, JD & EN Aplin, LON/95/1943 (VTD 14660)*. (*Note*. See now the note following *Korner & Others*, 34.199 above.)

34.218   **Family farming partnership—conversion of coach-house into residence for partner.**   A family farming partnership arranged for the conversion of a coach-house into a dwelling-house for one of the partners. The partnership reclaimed 40% of the input tax relating to this work. The Commissioners only agreed to repay 10% of the tax in question. The tribunal upheld the Commissioners' decision and dismissed the partnership's appeal. *Riches*, 34.162 above, distinguished. *DM Walthall & LD Crisp, LON/98/519 (VTD 15979)*.

34.219   **Farming partnership—repair to farmhouse roof.**   A family farming partnership incurred expenditure on repairs to the roof of a house which was occupied by one of the partners, and reclaimed the whole of the input tax. The Commissioners only agreed to repay 18% of the tax, considering that the expenditure had been primarily incurred for private purposes, so that only a proportion of the tax was deductible. The partnership appealed, contending that the effect of *Article 17* of the *EC Sixth Directive* as interpreted in *Lennartz v Finanzamt München*, 21.216 EUROPEAN COMMUNITY LAW was that the whole of the input tax should be treated as deductible. The tribunal dismissed the appeal, holding that the principle in *Lennartz* only applied to supplies of goods and that the subsequent private use of such goods was treated as a supply of services on which output tax was chargeable. However, the farmhouse was immovable property rather than goods, and the use of the farmhouse for private purposes could not be treated as a taxable supply of services. Since the input tax was not paid wholly for the purposes of actual or deemed taxable transactions, it followed that the decision in *Lennartz* was distinguishable and only a proportion of the input tax was deductible. *F & M Mounty & Sons, [1995] VATDR 128 (VTD 12985)*. (*Notes.* (1) The case was heard by the tribunal with *Hurd*, 34.186 above. (2) See also the note following *Korner & Others*, 34.199 above.)

34.220   **Partnership providing consultancy services—acquisition of property.**   See *RMSG*, 49.336 PENALTIES: MISDECLARATION.

Expenses by or on behalf of employees or agents

Cross-reference. For the liability to output tax in respect of supplies to employees (including company cars), see 58.1 *et seq.* SUPPLY.

34.221   **Expenditure incurred on employees' pension funds—whether for purpose of company's business.**   See the cases noted at 51.1 to 51.6 PENSION FUNDS.

34.222   **Hotel bills of employees on subsistence allowances.**   A BBC employee was absent from home for four nights in the course of his duties. He received a flat-rate subsistence allowance from the BBC. His actual outlay included hotel expenses of £8.80, including VAT of 80p, for which he obtained a tax invoice. The BBC reclaimed the 80p as input tax. The Commissioners rejected the claim and the tribunal dismissed the BBC's appeal. Although the hotel accommodation had been supplied to the employee for the purposes of the BBC's business, it had not been supplied to the BBC within the meaning of what is now *VATA 1994, s 24(1)*. *British Broadcasting Corporation, [1974] VATTR 100 (VTD 73)*.

34.223   **Fixed allowances to employees to cover subsistence and petrol.**   *British Broadcasting Corporation*, 34.222 above, was applied in another case in which a company paid its travellers fixed amounts for their expenditure on subsistence and petrol and reclaimed one-eleventh of the amounts so paid as input tax (the standard rate was then 10%). The Commissioners issued an assessment to recover the tax and the tribunal dismissed the company's appeal. *Ledamaster Ltd, BIR/76/121 (VTD 344).*

34.224 **Company reimbursing petrol expenditure of self-employed representative.** See *Berbrooke Fashions*, 34.1 above, and the cases noted at 34.2 and 34.3 above.

34.225 **Mileage allowances to employees.** See *Stirlings (Glasgow) Ltd*, 34.6 above; *McLean Homes Midland Ltd*, 34.7 above, and *Klockner Ferromatik Desma Ltd*, 34.8 above.

34.226 **Use of car for transport of employees.** See *Blyth-Palk*, 34.94 above.

34.227 **Personalised numberplates for managing director's car.** See *Ava Knit Ltd*, 34.376 below; *B J Kershaw Transport Ltd*, 34.377 below; *Empire Contracts Ltd*, 34.378 below; *Quality Care Homes Ltd*, 34.379 below; *Industrial Doors (Scotland) Ltd*, 34.379 below; *The Redington Design Co Ltd*, 34.379 below, and *NEP Group Ltd*, 49.331 PENALTIES: MISDECLARATION.

34.228 **Land Rover purchased by an employee—whether input tax reclaimable by employer.** See *Binof Construction Ltd*, 34.11 above.

34.229 **Clothing purchased by company for wear by principal director—whether for purpose of company's business.** See *PJ Stone Ltd*, 34.110 above.

34.230 **Refurbishment of houses provided for Cathedral vergers.** The Dean and Chapter of Hereford Cathedral were registered for VAT since they operated a restaurant and shop at the Cathedral, and also staged exhibitions for which visitors were charged admission. They incurred expenditure in refurbishing two houses which were situated in the Cathedral cloisters, built in 1472, and were used as residences for the Cathedral's two vergers. They reclaimed input tax on the refurbishment. The Commissioners rejected the claim, considering that the tax was not reclaimable since the Cathedral's religious and spiritual activities were not business activities, the provision of domestic accommodation for clergy and other officers was 'essentially a non-business use', and the expenditure had not been incurred for the purpose of the Cathedral's business activities. The Cathedral appealed, contending that the whole of the input tax should be treated as deductible. The tribunal allowed the appeal in part, finding that 'in the modern Cathedral the business activities constitute a significant part of the overall purpose for which a Cathedral exists ... the cost of maintaining a Cathedral which has existed for hundreds of years for the advancement of religion cannot be met without the finance guaranteed by secular or business activities'. The tribunal held, on the evidence, that the 'relative importance' of the business activities and the religious activities was equal, so that 50% of the tax in question was deductible. *The Dean & Chapter of Hereford Cathedral, [1994] VATTR 159 (VTD 11737).* (*Note.* For a case concerning similar expenditure on houses occupied by the Dean and Canons of a Cathedral, see *Dean & Chapter of Bristol Cathedral*, 34.440 below.)

34.231 **Bed and breakfast supplied to employees.** A company carried on the business of leasing amplification and lighting equipment for the popular music business. It had four full-time employees who maintained its equipment. When the equipment was on hire, they travelled with it to set it up, operate it, and dismantle it. The company paid for the employees' bed and breakfast when on tour, and reclaimed the input tax. The Commissioners issued an assessment to recover the tax and the company appealed. The tribunal allowed the company's appeal, holding that the supplies were made to the company and were for the purpose of the company's business. *Power Leasing Ltd, [1984] VATTR 104 (VTD 1661).*

34.232   **Removal expenses.**   A company had carried on business as a supplier of industrial electronic instruments from premises in Lincolnshire. It became insolvent and went into liquidation. The liquidator sold the shares to an individual (F) who had previously worked in London. F became the company's controlling director and moved the company's base from Lincolnshire to Peterborough. He moved his private address from London to Uppingham to be nearer the company's premises. The company reclaimed input tax on the removal expenses. The Commissioners issued an assessment to recover input tax relating to F's change of address. The tribunal allowed the company's appeal, holding on the evidence that the expenditure had been incurred for the purposes of the company's business, rather than for F's personal purposes. *SSL Ltd, LON/87/254 (VTD 2478). (Note.* The case was decided prior to the enactment of what is now *VATA 1994, s 24(3),* but remains an authority on the allowability of removal expenses, particularly in view of the subsequent decision in *Michael Sellers & Co Ltd,* 34.247 below, where the tribunal held that *s 24(3)* did not apply to removal expenses.)

34.233   A similar decision was reached in *Riftmain Ltd, LON/87/828 (VTD 2819).*

34.234   **Legal costs of director charged with criminal offence.**   See *Wallman Foods Ltd,* 34.151 above.

34.235   **Legal costs of employees charged with manslaughter.**   See *P & O European Ferries (Dover) Ltd,* 34.143 above.

34.236   **Swimming pool constructed for use of employees of firm of solicitors.**   See *Willcox & Co,* 34.413 below.

Domestic accommodation for directors (VATA 1994, s 24(3))

Note. *VATA 1994, s 24(3),* deriving from *FA 1990,* provides that input tax is not deductible in respect of goods or services supplied to or imported by a company and used, or to be used, in connection with the provision of accommodation by the company where the accommodation is used, or to be used, by a director of the company or by a person connected with a director of the company. Cases relating to periods before the enactment of *FA 1990* have been omitted.

34.237   **Carpets.**   A farming company reclaimed input tax on the purchase of carpets for use in the farmhouse, where its directors lived. The Commissioners issued an assessment to recover the tax, considering that the expenditure had not been incurred for the purposes of the company's business. The tribunal dismissed the company's appeal. *GI Hadfield & Son Ltd, MAN/90/1075 (VTD 6421).*

34.238   **Furniture.**   An appeal was dismissed in a case where a company had reclaimed input tax in respect of furniture purchased for its directors' private residence. *Setlode Ltd, LON/91/2223 (VTD 7765).*

34.239   **Double glazing.**   A company reclaimed input tax on the cost of installing double glazing at the residence of its controlling directors, one room of which was used as an office. The Commissioners issued an assessment to recover five-sixths of the tax, considering that the expenditure fell within what is now *VATA 1994, s 24(3).* The tribunal upheld the assessment and dismissed the company's appeal. *Newland Technical Services Ltd, LON/92/1255A (VTD 9294). (Note.* For other issues in this case, see 38.68 INVOICES AND CREDIT NOTES, and 49.93 and 49.309 PENALTIES: MISDECLARATION.)

34.240   **Conversion of premises—lease to director at low rent.**   A family company which traded as builders' merchants reclaimed input tax on the conversion of part of its premises to provide residential accommodation for one of its directors. The Commissioners issued an assessment to recover the tax, and the company appealed, contending that it was leasing the accommodation to the director and should be allowed to reclaim the input tax. The tribunal rejected this contention and dismissed the appeal, observing that the lease was at a low rent and holding that the effect of *VATA 1994, s 24(3)* was that the tax was not deductible. *FD Todd & Sons Ltd, MAN/96/724 (VTD 14731).*

34.241 **Short-term accommodation in Scotland.** A company, the registered office of which was in Surrey, carried on an oil consultancy business. It purchased two weeks' time-share accommodation in Scotland, about 40 miles from Aberdeen, and reclaimed input tax on the purchase. The Commissioners issued an assessment to recover the tax, considering that the accommodation had been purchased as holiday accommodation for the company's directors. The company appealed, contending that it had been purchased for business reasons, to be used for meetings with clients. The tribunal held that the accommodation had been purchased for a dual purpose, and that 25% of the tax in question was deductible, applying *Ian Flockton Developments Ltd*, 34.248 below. *Suregrove Ltd, LON/92/571X (VTD 10740).*

34.242 **Farming company—expenditure on farmhouse.** A company which operated a farming business incurred expenditure on converting two derelict cottages into a farmhouse. It reclaimed input tax on the work. The Commissioners rejected the claim, considering that the effect of what is now *VATA 1994, s 24(3)* was that the tax was not deductible. The tribunal allowed the company's appeal in part, finding that the farmhouse was primarily used as domestic accommodation for the company's directors but that a small part of the expenditure related to the conversion of a pigsty into an office, and holding that 10% of the tax was deductible. *RS & EM Wright Ltd, MAN/94/220 (VTD 12984).*

34.243 **Family farming company—renovation of bungalow for occupation by employee—employee related to company directors.** A family farming company was controlled by a married couple. The company owned a bungalow, which had been occupied by an employee but had subsequently become vacant. The couple's son, who was an employee of the company, married in 1990. The company renovated the bungalow to enable him to occupy it. The company reclaimed input tax on this expenditure. The Commissioners issued an assessment to recover the tax, on the basis that the effect of what is now *VATA 1994, s 24(3)* was that the tax was not deductible, since the son was 'a person connected with a director of the company'. The company appealed. The tribunal allowed the appeal in part, holding that the expenditure had been incurred for a dual purpose and that 50% of the tax should be treated as deductible. *FJ Meaden Ltd, LON/94/1766A (VTD 13215).* (*Note.* The Commissioners did not appeal against this decision, but state in Customs' VAT Manual, Part 13, chapter 2A, section 14.7 that they 'do not agree with the apportionment method adopted' and instruct their officers that they 'should allow apportionment only using the objective method taken by the tribunal in *RS & EM Wright Ltd*' (see 34.242 above).)

34.244 **Property development company—repairs to house occupied by directors.** A company which carried on a property development business reclaimed input tax on repairs to a house occupied by its directors and their family. The Commissioners issued an assessment to recover the tax and the company appealed, contending that a proportion of the tax should be treated as deductible since two of the rooms in the house were used entirely for the company's business. The tribunal allowed the appeal in part, finding that one of the rooms was used wholly for business purposes and that a second room was used partly for business purposes, and holding that 5% of the input tax in question should be treated as deductible. *Wellright Ltd, MAN/96/303 (VTD 14646).*

34.245   **Company in bloodstock industry—renovation of house used for meetings and for domestic use of company chairman.**   A company, which was a member of a group, carried on the business of breeding and training thoroughbred racehorses. It owned a large house, which was used by the company chairman as a residence and for business meetings. It incurred expenditure on refurbishing the house, and reclaimed input tax on the work. The Commissioners issued an assessment on the basis that none of the tax relating to the upper floor was deductible, and that only 20% of the tax relating to the ground floor was deductible. (This was computed on the basis that, in 1995/96, the house was used for business purposes on 64 days.) The representative member of the group appealed, accepting that the tax relating to the upper floor was not deductible, but contending that 61.5% of the tax relating to the ground floor should be allowed as a deduction (on the basis that the house had been used for business purposes on 64 days and for non-business purposes on 40 days, ignoring days when the house was not used at all). The tribunal rejected this contention and dismissed the appeal, observing that, while there was 'a legitimate business element in this case', whenever the chairman stayed overnight 'he was using the accommodation including the group floor for domestic purposes', and that 'it would be unrealistic to treat every waking hour which he spent at (the house) as devoted to business'. The Commissioners' allowance of 20% of the expenditure 'was adopted in an effort to be fair and reasonable, avoiding troublesome calculations'. *Sangster Group Ltd, LON/97/394 (VTD 15544).*

34.246   **Garage provided for director.**   A company which supplied engineering services received planning permission for the construction of a double garage in the grounds of the house which its controlling director owned and occupied. The ownership of the plot on which the garage was built was transferred by the director to the company. The garage was used to house a car which the company owned, and which the director drove mainly but not exclusively for business purposes. The company reclaimed input tax on the construction of the garage. The Commissioners issued an assessment to recover the tax, on the basis that the effect of what is now *VATA 1994, s 24(3)* was that the tax was not deductible. The tribunal allowed the company's appeal in part, holding that the provision of the garage fell within *s 24(3)* and that the tax should be apportioned. (The tribunal rejected the Commissioners' contention that the use of the garage for business purposes was a breach of the relevant planning permission and that the tax was therefore not deductible.) On the evidence, the tribunal held that 85% of the use of the garage was for business purposes, so that 85% of the input tax was deductible. *Giffenbond Ltd, MAN/94/1238 (VTD 13481).*

34.247   **Removal expenses—whether within VATA 1994, s 24(3)*.**   A company carried on a financial consultancy business from the home of its controlling director. The director and the company moved from Yorkshire to Peterborough and reclaimed input tax on the removal expenses. The Commissioners issued an assessment to recover 90% of the tax, on the basis that 90% of the use of the property was for domestic purposes and that what is now *VATA 1994, s 24(3)* applied. The company appealed, contending that the move had been for business reasons rather than for domestic reasons. The tribunal accepted the company's evidence and allowed the appeal, holding that *VATA 1994, s 24(3)** did not apply. *Michael Sellers & Co Ltd, LON/92/574X unreported. (Note.* This decision appears not to have been publicly released by the Tribunal Centre, but is cited in Customs' VAT Manual, Part 13, chapter 2A, section 14.6.)

Horse racing

Note. The cases listed below are those where input tax has been reclaimed on the basis that the purpose of owning racehorses has been to advertise an existing business activity. For cases where it has been contended that the ownership of horses constitutes a business activity in its own right, see 7.53 *et seq.* BUSINESS. See also *VATA 1994, s 84(4)*, deriving from *FA 1993*. This provides that a tribunal can only allow an appeal against the disallowance of input tax relating to a 'luxury, amusement or entertainment' where the tribunal considers that the Commissioners 'could not reasonably have made' the determination which is the subject of the appeal. Cases relating to periods before the enactment of *FA 1993* should be read in the light of this change.

Cases where the appellant was successful

34.248   **Company manufacturing plastic storage tanks.** A company which manufactured plastic storage tanks reclaimed input tax on the training and upkeep of a racehorse. The Commissioners issued an assessment to recover the tax and the company appealed, contending that it had purchased the horse for promotional purposes. The principal director gave evidence that this was the sole object which he had in mind when he decided to buy the horse. The tribunal upheld the assessment, accepting the director's evidence but holding that it should apply an objective test and that the company 'ought not to have had any commercial belief that the purchase and running of the racehorse could have been for the purpose of its business'. The QB allowed the company's appeal against this decision, holding that the tribunal had been wrong to substitute an objective test for the test of what was actually in the mind of the witness at the time of the expenditure. On the facts found by the tribunal, the company's sole object in buying the horse was to promote its business. Stuart-Smith J observed that this finding was 'a surprising one', but held that it was a finding of fact with which the court could not interfere. *Ian Flockton Developments Ltd v C & E Commrs, QB [1987] STC 394. (Note.* The decision here conflicts with the established case law relating to direct tax, where the HL has held that the conscious motive of the taxpayer at the time of the expenditure is not conclusive; see the judgment of Lord Brightman in *Mallalieu v Drummond, HL [1983] STC 665 (TTC 2001, 60.192).* However, Customs did not take the case further, and the decision here has been followed by tribunals in many subsequent cases. For the Commissioners' interpretation of the decision, see Customs' VAT Manual, Part 13, chapter 2, section 4.5. See also the note at the head of this section with regard to the effect of *VATA 1994, s 84(4)*.)

34.249   **Shirt manufacturing company.** A company which carried on business as designers and manufacturers of shirts purchased seven racehorses and reclaimed input tax on their purchase. The horses were given names which were identifiable with the company's shirts. The Commissioners issued an assessment to recover the tax and the company appealed, contending that the horses had been purchased for the purpose of advertising its business. The tribunal accepted this contention and allowed the appeal. *Hillingdon Shirt Co Ltd, MAN/78/26 (VTD 678).*

34.250   **Farming partnership.** A farming partnership reclaimed input tax on the upkeep of racehorses, some of which it had bred. The Commissioners issued an assessment to recover the tax and the partnership appealed, contending that the expenditure had been incurred for the purpose of advertising a caravan site which the partners owned. The tribunal accepted the partners' evidence and allowed the appeal. *AE House & Son, LON/85/373 (VTD 2620). (Note.* For an appeal by an associated company, heard with this case, see 39.98 LAND.)

34.251   **Engineering company.** A company which carried on an engineering business reclaimed input tax on the upkeep of three racehorses. The Commissioners issued an assessment to recover the tax, considering that the expenditure had not been incurred for the purposes of the company's business, but for the pleasure of the company's managing director (who owned a stud farm). The tribunal allowed the company's appeal, holding on the evidence that the expenditure had been incurred for promotional purposes. *Bridge Book Co Ltd*, 34.280 below, was distinguished because in that case horse racing was the main recreational activity of the director concerned. *Skeltools Ltd, LON/80/63 (VTD 968)*.

34.252   A similar decision was reached in a subsequent case also involving an engineering company. *GW Martin & Co Ltd, LON/82/263 (VTD 1390)*. (*Note*. For the award of costs in this case, see 2.325 APPEALS.)

34.253   In another case where an engineering company had reclaimed input tax on expenditure incurred in keeping racehorses, the tribunal allowed the company's appeal against an assessment issued to recover the tax in question, applying *Ian Flockton Developments Ltd*, 34.248 above. On the evidence, the tribunal was satisfied that the managing director's purpose in purchasing and running the racehorses was to promote the company's business. *J Martin Engineers (Wishaw) Ltd, EDN/90/206 (VTD 6667)*.

34.254   **Heating engineering company.**   A company which carried on a heating engineering business reclaimed input tax on the upkeep of a racehorse. The Commissioners issued an assessment to recover the tax but the tribunal allowed the company's appeal. On the evidence, none of the directors had had any previous material interest in horse racing, and the tribunal was satisfied that the horse had been run for the purpose of advertising the company's business. *A & E Mechanical Services Ltd, MAN/80/47 (VTD 1069)*.

34.255   **Company owning public house.**   A company acquired a public house in Glasgow in 1977, changing its name to 'The Captain's Rest'. The company acquired three racehorses, the first of which it named 'Captain's Rest', and the third of which it named 'Restless Captain'. The company reclaimed input tax on the upkeep of the racehorses and the Commissioners issued an assessment to recover the tax. The company appealed, submitting evidence that the horses had attracted interest and enthusiasm among customers. The annual turnover of the pub had increased from £55,000 in 1977 to £260,000 in 1980. The tribunal allowed the company's appeal, holding on the evidence that the horses had been acquired for the purpose of promoting the company's business. *Demor Investments Ltd, [1981] VATTR 66 (VTD 1091)*.

34.256   **Housebuilding company.**   A company which carried on business as housebuilders reclaimed input tax on the purchase of three racehorses, which it named Mr Sinclair, Major Sinclair and Miss Sinclair. The Commissioners issued an assessment to recover the tax and the company appealed, contending that it had acquired the horses for the purpose of promoting its business. The tribunal allowed the company's appeal, holding that the fact that the names given to the horses were closely connected to the company's name indicated that they had been purchased for advertising purposes. *Sinclair Developments Ltd, MAN/82/127 (VTD 1466)*.

34.257   An appeal was allowed in a case where a small building company based in Wantage had purchased a 50% share in a racehorse, and reclaimed input tax on the upkeep of the horse. The tribunal held that, since there were several stables in the Wantage area, the acquisition of a horse could reasonably be considered to have been for the purpose of promoting the company's business. *C & P Building & Welding (Wantage) Ltd, LON/85/466 (VTD 2062)*.

34.258   **Builders' merchants.**   A company trading as builders' merchants reclaimed input tax on the upkeep of a racehorse. The Commissioners issued an assessment to recover the tax, considering that the horse had been purchased for the recreational interest of one of the directors, who had previously owned a racehorse of her own. The company appealed, contending that the purpose of the expenditure had been to promote its business. The tribunal accepted the company's evidence and allowed the appeal. *Ian Flockton Developments Ltd*, 34.248 above, applied; *Queghan Construction Co Ltd*, 34.276 below, and *Sheet & Roll Convertors Ltd*, 34.289 below, distinguished. *Wenlock Building Centre Ltd, MAN/90/1136 (VTD 10893)*.

34.259 **Company selling cleaning materials.** A company which sold cleaning materials, principally to restaurants and licensed premises, reclaimed input tax on the upkeep of several racehorses. The Commissioners issued an assessment to recover the tax but the tribunal allowed the company's appeal, holding on the evidence that the expenditure had been incurred for the purpose of promoting the company's business. *EL Davis & Co Ltd, LON/83/76 (VTD 1477)*.

34.260 **Company selling glassware.** An appeal was allowed in a case where a company which sold glassware to restaurants and licensed premises had reclaimed input tax on the upkeep of racehorses. *Dickins Ltd, LON/83/77 (VTD 1477)*. (*Note.* The case was heard with *EL Davis & Co Ltd*, 34.259 above.)

34.261 **Company manufacturing packaging.** A company which carried on business as a manufacturer of packaging materials reclaimed input tax on the purchase of some racehorses. The Commissioners issued an assessment to recover the tax and the company appealed, contending that the horses had been purchased for promotional purposes and that by attending meetings where the horses raced, it had obtained additional customers. The tribunal accepted the company's evidence and allowed the appeal. *AJ Bingley Ltd, LON/83/333 (VTD 1597)*.

34.262 **Shopfitting company.** A company which carried on business as shopfitters reclaimed input tax on the purchase of racehorses. The Commissioners issued an assessment to recover the tax and the company appealed, contending that it had purchased the horses in the hope of obtaining additional customers in the brewing industry. The tribunal accepted the company's evidence and allowed the appeal. *William Cowan & Son Ltd, EDN/84/74 (VTD 1792)*.

34.263 **Retail furniture company.** A company which sold furniture by retail reclaimed input tax on the purchase and upkeep of several racehorses. Some of the horses had names which reflected the company's name, and the horseblankets were used to advertise the company's business. In addition, the company sent 70,000 customers a racing calendar with a covering letter encouraging them to follow its horses and make further purchases from the company, and stating that if a customer bet 50p on one of the company's horses, that sum would be deducted from any bill paid by the customer in one of its shops. The Commissioners issued an assessment to recover the tax but the tribunal allowed the company's appeal, holding that the horses had been raced for the purpose of promoting the company's business. *J Boardmans Ltd, MAN/84/293 (VTD 2025)*.

34.264 **Haulage contractors.** A company which carried on business as haulage contractors reclaimed input tax on the upkeep of racehorses. The Commissioners issued an assessment to recover the tax but the tribunal allowed the company's appeal, holding on the evidence that the expenditure had been incurred for the purpose of promoting the company's business. *Brian Yeardley Continental Ltd, MAN/85/225 (VTD 2035)*.

34.265 **Printing company.** A company which carried on a printing business purchased a 50% share in a racehorse and reclaimed input tax on the upkeep of the horse. The horse's blanket was used to advertise the company's name at races, and advertisements were placed in local papers to emphasise the link between the company and the horse. The Commissioners issued an assessment to recover the tax but the tribunal allowed the company's appeal, holding on the evidence that the expenditure had been incurred for the purpose of promoting the company's business. *Hickling & Squires Ltd, MAN/86/80 (VTD 2287)*.

34.266 A similar decision was reached in a subsequent case where a printing company had reclaimed input tax on the purchase and upkeep of racehorses. *Alito Colour Ltd, LON/91/1268X (VTD 7504)*.

34.267 **Sports equipment retailers.** A company which carried on business as a retailer of sports equipment purchased a racehorse, and reclaimed input tax on the upkeep of the horse. Photographs and newspaper cuttings of the horse were used for publicity on the shop premises. The Commissioners issued an assessment to recover the tax but the tribunal allowed the company's appeal, holding on the evidence that the horse had been purchased for the purpose of advertising the company's business. *Solihull Sports Services Ltd, MAN/86/408 (VTD 2713)*.

34.268 **Nightclub owner.** The owner of a nightclub reclaimed input tax in respect of expenditure incurred on a racehorse. The Commissioners issued an assessment to recover the tax and he appealed, contending that the horse was used to advertise the business. The nightclub was called the 'King of Clubs', and the horse was named 'KC's Dancer'. The tribunal allowed his appeal, applying *Ian Flockton Developments Ltd*, 34.248 above, and holding that the expenditure had been incurred for the purpose of promoting the nightclub. *P Holder, LON/91/509Z (VTD 6446)*.

34.269 **Interior decorating company.** A company which carried on an interior decorating business reclaimed input tax on the purchase and upkeep of a racehorse. The horse had competed in several races, but had never finished higher than eighth. The Commissioners issued an assessment to recover the tax, considering that the racehorse had not been acquired for the purpose of the company's business. The tribunal allowed the company's appeal. On the evidence, one of the company's directors also owned racehorses privately, and, partly because of her contacts, more than half of the company's trade came from within racing circles. The tribunal was satisfied that the company's intention in purchasing the horse was to promote its business. *Ian Flockton Developments Ltd*, 34.248 above, applied. *Beckett & Graham Ltd, LON/90/1162Z (VTD 6878)*.

34.270 **Quarrying company.** A company which operated five chalk and limestone quarries reclaimed input tax on the training and upkeep of a racehorse. The Commissioners issued an assessment to recover the tax, considering that the expenditure had not been incurred for the purpose of the company's business. The company appealed, contending that one of its quarries was located in an area of North Yorkshire which was well-known for the training of racehorses, and there were nine racing stables within two miles of the quarry. It wished to exploit land adjoining the existing quarry, for which it would need planning permission, and was concerned at the possibility of the racehorse trainers objecting to an application for such permission. Accordingly, the company had purchased the horse for the purpose of promoting its goodwill among the racing fraternity. The tribunal allowed the appeal, applying *Ian Flockton Developments Ltd*, 34.248 above, and observing that, since the quarry had an annual turnover of £1 million, expenditure of £5,000 on a racehorse was 'well within any tolerance limits' of promoting the goodwill of the company. *Fenstone (Quarries) Ltd, MAN/91/423 (VTD 7236)*.

Cases where the appellant was partly successful

34.271 **Company promoting work of sportswriter.** A company was incorporated to promote the work of its controlling director, who was a professional sportswriter who had written two books about horse racing. It purchased a part-share in a racehorse, and reclaimed input tax on its purchase and upkeep. It also reclaimed input tax on the upkeep of racehorses which were part-owned by its controlling director. The Commissioners issued an assessment to recover the tax, and the company appealed, contending that the expenditure had been incurred for the purpose of promoting its director's reputation among people interested in horse racing. The tribunal reviewed the evidence in detail and allowed the appeal in part, holding that the input tax attributable to the racehorse which was part-owned by the company was allowable, but the input tax attributable to the horses which were part-owned by the director as an individual was not allowable. *Ian Flockton Developments Ltd*, 34.248 above, applied. *Sportswords Ltd, MAN/90/278 (VTD 11178)*.

34.272   **Company operating holiday centre.** A family company which owned and operated a 'holiday centre' in Devon purchased ten racehorses between 1989 and 1991, and reclaimed input tax on their purchase and upkeep. In October 1991 the horses were sold to an associated company which operated a stud farm. Following a control visit in 1993, the Commissioners issued assessments to recover some of the tax, considering that the expenditure had not been wholly incurred for the purposes of the company's business, but had been partly incurred for the personal pleasure of the company's directors. The company appealed, contending that the expenditure had been incurred for advertising purposes and that the incidental personal enjoyment of the directors was irrelevant. The tribunal reviewed the evidence in detail and allowed the appeal in full with regard to the period up to October 1990 (during which time four horses had been purchased). *Dicta* of Stuart-Smith J in *Ian Flockton Developments Ltd*, 34.248 above, applied. With regard to the period from November 1990 to October 1991, the tribunal found that by October 1990 it was apparent that the use of the racehorses for advertising had not been profitable, and that the directors had decided to operate a stud farm. The tribunal granted the company liberty to apply for a further hearing to consider whether any of the expenditure between November 1990 and October 1991 inclusive had been incurred for business purposes. *Kingsley Holidays Ltd, LON/94/2241 (VTD 13487)*. (*Note.* There was no further public hearing of the appeal.)

Cases where the appellant was unsuccessful

34.273   **Music publishing company.** A music publishing company purchased six racehorses and reclaimed input tax on their purchase. The Commissioners issued an assessment to recover the tax, considering that the horses had been purchased for the purposes of the company's managing director, who was a bloodstock dealer. The company appealed, contending that the horses had been purchased for the purposes of its business. The tribunal dismissed the appeal and the QB upheld the decision. *Ashtree Holdings Ltd v C & E Commrs, QB [1979] STC 818*.

34.274   **Car auctioneering company.** A company which carried on a car auctioneering business purchased two racehorses and reclaimed input tax on their purchase and upkeep. The Commissioners issued an assessment to recover the tax and the company appealed, contending that the horses had been acquired for advertising purposes. The tribunal dismissed the appeal, holding on the evidence that the horses had been purchased to facilitate the entertainment of customers at race meetings. Accordingly, the expenditure constituted business entertainment and the tax was not deductible by virtue of what is now *Input Tax Order, Article 5. British Car Auctions Ltd, [1978] VATTR 56 (VTD 522)*.

34.275   **Housebuilding company.** A company which carried on a housebuilding business purchased three racehorses and reclaimed input tax on their upkeep. The Commissioners issued an assessment to recover the tax and the company appealed, contending that the horses had been purchased for the purpose of advertising its business. The tribunal dismissed the appeal, holding that there was insufficient connection between the company's business and the racing activities to justify the deduction of the tax. There was no evidence to suggest that any purchasers of houses built by the company had been influenced by its horse racing activities. *Tallishire Ltd, [1979] VATTR 180 (VTD 834)*.

34.276   A company based in Oldham, which carried on a housebuilding business, reclaimed input tax on the purchase and upkeep of a horse which it named 'Miss Oldham'. The Commissioners issued an assessment to recover the tax and the tribunal dismissed the company's appeal, holding on the evidence that the horse had not been used to promote the company, since its name did not reflect the company's name and there was no evidence of any connection between the company's customers and the horse racing. *Queghan Construction Co Ltd, MAN/83/171 (VTD 1538)*.

34.277   Similar decisions were reached in *Robertson Robertson Construction Co, EDN/85/124 (VTD 2071)* and *RV Young Ltd*, 49.335 PENALTIES: MISDECLARATION.

34.278   **Builder.**   A builder reclaimed input tax on the purchase and upkeep of two racehorses. The Commissioners issued an assessment to recover the tax and the tribunal dismissed his appeal, holding that the expenditure had not been incurred for business purposes. *J Dayani, LON/88/489Y (VTD 3491)*.

34.279   **Metal-dealing company.**   A company which carried on a metal-dealing business reclaimed input tax on the upkeep of a racehorse (which had died after running in five races). The Commissioners issued an assessment to recover the tax and the tribunal dismissed the company's appeal, holding that the company had not proved that the expenditure had been for the purposes of its business. *MSS (North West) Ltd, [1980] VATTR 29 (VTD 882)*.

34.280   **Bookselling company.**   An appeal was dismissed in a case where a company which carried on the business of buying and selling 'remaindered' paperback books had reclaimed input tax on the purchase and upkeep of racehorses. *The Bridge Book Co Ltd, LON/80/18 (VTD 935)*.

34.281   **Professional singer.**   A professional singer became interested in horse racing and purchased several racehorses. She reclaimed input tax on the upkeep of the horses and the Commissioners issued an assessment to recover the tax. The tribunal dismissed her appeal, holding that she had not acquired the horses for the purpose of her profession as a singer. *D Squires, LON/82/165 (VTD 1436)*.

34.282   **Tool-manufacturing company.**   A company which carried on a business of tool manufacturing leased a number of racehorses from its chairman, who had bred horses for several years. The company reclaimed input tax on the upkeep of the horses and the Commissioners issued an assessment to recover the tax. The tribunal dismissed the company's appeal, holding that the horse racing had been undertaken for the purposes of conferring a benefit on the chairman. *Metal Woods Ltd, LON/83/15 (VTD 1473)*.

34.283   **Contract cleaner.**   The proprietor of a contract cleaning business reclaimed input tax on the purchase and upkeep of two racehorses, named 'Glynfield Portion' and 'Glynfield Cleaner'. The Commissioners issued an assessment to recover the tax and the tribunal dismissed the proprietor's appeal, holding that he had not satisfied it that the horses had been acquired for the purpose of promoting his business. *C Reid (t/a Glynfield Cleaning Contractors), MAN/83/141 (VTD 1543)*.

34.284   **Farmer.**   A farmer reclaimed input tax on the purchase and upkeep of several racehorses. The Commissioners issued an assessment to recover the tax and the tribunal dismissed the farmer's appeal, holding that the racehorses had not been purchased for the purposes of his business. *TN Bailey, LON/83/79 (VTD 1587)*.

34.285   **Company manufacturing footwear.**   A company which manufactured slippers purchased several racehorses and reclaimed input tax on their purchase and upkeep. The Commissioners issued an assessment to recover the tax and the tribunal dismissed the company's appeal, holding on the evidence that the horses had not been purchased to promote the company's business, to which they bore no relation, but had been purchased because of the principal director's interest in horse racing. *H Lister (Slippers) Ltd, MAN/83/237 (VTD 1747)*.

34.286   **Accountant.**   An accountant reclaimed input tax on the upkeep of several racehorses. The Commissioners issued an assessment to recover the tax, considering that the expenditure had not been incurred for the purposes of his practice. He appealed, contending that the expenditure had been incurred for promotional purposes. The tribunal dismissed his appeal, finding that there was no evidence that the horses had been used for advertising purposes, and holding that they had been used as an adjunct to business entertainment, so that the input tax was not deductible. *British Car Auctions Ltd*, 34.274 above, applied. *T Dyer, EDN/90/89 (VTD 5356)*.

34.287   **Engineering company.**   An engineering company purchased a one-eighth share in each of four racehorses, and reclaimed input tax thereon. The Commissioners issued an assessment to recover the tax, considering that the expenditure had not been incurred for business purposes. The company appealed, contending that the expenditure had been incurred for the purpose of advertising its business. One of the four horses was registered with the Jockey Club in the name of the company's secretary; the other three were registered in the names of people unconnected with the company. The tribunal dismissed the company's appeal, finding that the company derived 'no advertising benefits whatsoever' from its ownership of the shares in the horses. *EW Ambrose Ltd, MAN/90/548 (VTD 5766)*.

34.288   A company carrying on the business of construction and civil engineering reclaimed input tax on the purchase and upkeep of two racehorses. The Commissioners issued an assessment to recover the tax, considering that the horses had not been purchased for the purpose of the company's business. The company appealed, contending that the horses had been purchased for advertising purposes. The tribunal dismissed the company's appeal, observing that the horses' names did not reflect the company's name and holding that 'no ordinary businessman would have incurred this expenditure on racehorses and their upkeep as part of his business expenditure'. On the evidence, 'the expenditure was not the result of a considered commercial decision'. *Dicta* in *Ian Flockton Developments Ltd*, 34.248 above, applied. *Heyrod Construction Ltd, MAN/91/1256 (VTD 7882)*.

34.289   **Company manufacturing plastics.**   A company which manufactured plastic products reclaimed input tax on the upkeep of racehorses. The Commissioners issued an assessment to recover the tax and the company appealed, contending that the horses had been purchased for the purpose of advertising its business. The tribunal dismissed the company's appeal, holding on the evidence that the horses had been purchased as a 'private recreational interest' of the controlling director. *Sheet & Roll Convertors Ltd, LON/92/119 (VTD 7991B)*.

34.290   **Printing company.**   A printing company named Mayspark reclaimed input tax on the purchase and upkeep of a racehorse, which it named 'Mayspark Lad'. The Commissioners issued an assessment to recover the tax, considering that the expenditure had not been incurred for the purposes of the company's business. The company appealed, contending that the horse had been purchased for advertising purposes. The tribunal dismissed the appeal, holding that, despite its name, the horse was not in fact used to advertise the company's business. The tribunal observed that 'the use of the name Mayspark Lad is the only feature of any real value' to the company's case, but found that 'even here nothing was done in the way of advertising to associate Mayspark Lad in the minds of racegoers with (the company's) printing business'. *Mayspark Ltd, LON/94/1339 (VTD 13152)*.

34.291   **Company owning and racing horses—whether carrying on a business.**   See *Guinea Grill Stakes Ltd*, 7.57 BUSINESS.

Show jumping and other equine activities

34.292   **Manufacturing company—whether horse and horsebox purchased for advertising purposes.**   A company carried on business as a dealer in horse carcasses and manufacturer of meat products, bone meals, tallows and animal oils. Its principal product was named 'Sterilox'. It purchased a luxury horse box, costing £50,000, on which the name 'Sterilox' was prominently displayed, and subsequently purchased a horse, which it named 'Sterilox Bay Grange', and which it entered in show-jumping events. It reclaimed input tax on the horse and the horsebox, and the Commissioners issued an assessment to recover the tax, considering that the expenditure had been incurred for the pleasure of the company's directors, rather than for the purpose of the company's business. The tribunal allowed the company's appeal, holding on the evidence that the horse and the horsebox had been acquired for the purpose of advertising the company's business. *A Hughes & Son (Skellingthorpe) Ltd, MAN/81/206 (VTD 1301)*.

34.293   **Accountant.**   An accountant reclaimed input tax on the purchase and upkeep of a pony which he had entered in show-jumping events. The Commissioners issued an assessment to recover the tax, and the accountant appealed, contending that he had purchased it to advertise his business. The tribunal dismissed his appeal, holding on the evidence that the pony had been purchased for the benefit of his daughters. *M Lake, LON/82/393 (VTD 1388)*.

34.294   **Tomato-dealing company.**   A tomato-dealing company reclaimed input tax on the upkeep of horses for show-jumping and three-day events. The Commissioners issued an assessment to recover the tax but the tribunal allowed the company's appeal, holding on the evidence that the horses had been acquired to publicise the company's business. *Van Heyningen Brothers Ltd, LON/83/201 (VTD 1675)*.

34.295   **Management company.**   A company managed a number of housing associations and marketed the houses to young couples. It reclaimed input tax on the purchase and upkeep of show-jumping horses. The Commissioners issued an assessment to recover the tax but the tribunal allowed the company's appeal, holding on the evidence that the company's show-jumping activities had been undertaken for advertising purposes. *Management Services Ltd, LON/86/631 (VTD 2503)*.

34.296   **Company manufacturing marine equipment.**   A company carried on business as a manufacturer of marine equipment such as chains and mooring systems. It reclaimed input tax on the purchase and upkeep of six show-jumping horses. The Commissioners issued an assessment to recover the tax, considering that the expenditure had not been incurred for the purposes of the company's business. The tribunal allowed the appeal, holding on the evidence that the director had intended the horses to be used to advertise the company. *Ian Flockton Developments Ltd*, 34.248 above, applied. *Griffin-Woodhouse Ltd, MAN/91/977 (VTD 8942)*. (*Note*. An appeal against a misdeclaration penalty was also allowed.)

34.297   **Partnership selling wall coverings.**   A married couple traded in partnership, selling wall coverings. Their daughter competed in dressage events, and the partners reclaimed input tax in respect of expenditure on the horses which she rode in these events. The Commissioners issued an assessment to recover the tax, considering that the expenditure had been incurred for family reasons rather than for the purposes of the business. The tribunal upheld the assessment and dismissed the couple's appeal. *Mr & Mrs BJ Hooton (t/a BJH Supplies & Services), LON/92/1645 (VTD 10118).*

34.298 **Company trading as air conditioning engineers.** A company which carried on business as air conditioning engineers reclaimed input tax on the purchase of a trailer for transporting horses. The trailer was used for transporting two horses to dressage events, where they were ridden by the daughter of the company's controlling director. The Commissioners issued an assessment to recover the tax, considering that the expenditure had been incurred for the personal pleasure of the company's principal director. The company appealed, contending that the trailer had been purchased for the purpose of advertising its business. The tribunal accepted the company's evidence and allowed the appeal. *Delta House Installations Ltd, LON/93/2521 (VTD 12151).*

34.299 **Equestrian centre at farm—whether expenditure incurred for business purposes or as benefit for farmers' daughter.** A married couple owned a large farm. They incurred expenditure on establishing equestrian facilities at the farm, including stables and fences for jumping tuition, and reclaimed input tax on this expenditure. The Commissioners issued an assessment to recover the tax, considering that the expenditure had been incurred for the purpose of benefiting the couple's daughter, who was a keen rider. The couple appealed, contending that the equestrian centre was 'a legitimate diversification enterprise' designed to increase their income from the farm. The tribunal allowed the appeal in part, finding that the expenditure had been incurred for a dual purpose and that the desire to assist the couple's daughter was 'the main element in the decision', and holding that 30% of the input tax was allowable. *ATB & SDL Jones, LON/92/1763A (VTD 11410).* (*Note.* For another issue in this case, see 34.201 above.)

34.300 **Farm horses also used for hunting.** A family farming company reclaimed input tax on the upkeep of three horses which were used for hunting by the company's principal director and his daughter. The Commissioners issued an assessment to recover the tax, and the company appealed. The tribunal concluded that the horses were used partly for business purposes and partly for private purposes, and directed that the assessment should be recomputed on the basis that input tax should be allowed for the maintenance and feeding of one horse. *JC & NC Ward Ltd, LON/83/8 (VTD 1416).*

34.301 **Company trading as dealers in second-hand vehicles—input tax reclaimed on horses used by director for hunting.** A company carried on business as a dealer in second-hand vehicles, primarily Land Rovers and Range Rovers. It reclaimed input tax on the purchase and upkeep of horses which its director used for hunting. The Commissioners issued an assessment to recover the tax, considering that the horses had not been used for the purposes of the company's business. The company appealed, contending that it had bought the horses for the purpose of enabling it 'to make and maintain contact with current and potential customers'. The tribunal dismissed the appeal. The director had been involved in hunting from an early age, and it was his principal recreation. On the evidence, less than 2% of the company's turnover was attributable to hunting contacts. The fact that the expenditure may have resulted in an incidental benefit for the business did not mean that it had been incurred for the purpose of the business. *Ian Flockton Developments Ltd*, 34.248 above, distinguished. *Walter E Sturgess & Sons Ltd, MAN/90/615 (VTD 9009).*

34.302 **Horses purchased by engineering company.** See *K & K Thorogood Ltd*, 34.459 below.

34.303   **Company incorporated to breed horses—whether colt purchased for purposes of business.** See *Guest Leasing & Bloodstock Co Ltd*, 7.56 BUSINESS.

34.304   **Horse boxes used by trader's family.** A trader reclaimed input tax on the purchase of three horse boxes. The Commissioners issued an assessment to recover the tax and the trader appealed, contending that they had been purchased for advertising purposes. The tribunal dismissed his appeal, finding that they had been purchased for the private purposes of the trader and his family, who rode horses and ponies as a hobby. The QB upheld this decision. *MA Lenihan v C & E Commrs, QB [1992] STC 478.* (*Note.* For another issue in this case, see 58.60 SUPPLY.)

34.305   **Horse box used by trader's son.** A publican reclaimed input tax on the purchase of a horse box, which was used by his son who competed in show-jumping events. The Commissioners issued an assessment to recover the tax and the publican appealed, contending that he had purchased the horse box for the purpose of advertising his business. The tribunal dismissed the appeal, holding on the evidence that the publican had not shown 'on a balance of probability' that the expenditure had been incurred for the purposes of his business. *P McCourt (t/a The Millstone Inn), MAN/96/136 (VTD 14452).*

34.306   **Horse box used by director's daughter.** A company reclaimed input tax on the purchase of a horse box. The Commissioners rejected the claim and the tribunal dismissed the company's appeal, finding that the horse box had been purchased in order to transport horses owned by the managing director's daughter to show-jumping events. *Harveys & Co (Clothing) Ltd, MAN/87/381 (VTD 3166).*

34.307   **Horse box used by director's son.** A company trading as wholesale suppliers of fruit and vegetables reclaimed input tax on the lease of a horse box. The Commissioners issued an assessment to recover the tax, considering that the horse box had not been acquired for the purpose of the company's business, but to provide transport for the managing director's son, who was an English international show-jumper. The company appealed, contending that the horse box had been acquired for advertising purposes. The tribunal held that the horse box had been acquired with a dual purpose and the tax should be apportioned by virtue of what is now *VATA 1994, s 24(5).* The tribunal held, on the evidence, that 20% of the tax in question was deductible. *Freshgro (Bicester) Ltd, LON/91/321Y (VTD 7250, 7832).*

34.308   **Whether horse breeding activities of individual a business.** See *Prenn*, 7.53 BUSINESS, *Creber*, 7.61 BUSINESS, and *Thornton*, 7.62 BUSINESS.

34.309   **Whether company carrying on a business of horsebreeding.** See *Guest Leasing & Bloodstock Co Ltd*, 7.56 BUSINESS, and the cases noted at 7.63 to 7.65 BUSINESS.

Powerboat racing

34.310   A company, which carried on a business of cleaning industrial premises, reclaimed input tax on powerboat racing. The Commissioners issued an assessment to recover the tax but the tribunal allowed the company's appeal, holding on the evidence that the expenditure had been incurred for advertising purposes. *20th Century Cleaning & Maintenance Co Ltd, LON/78/89 (VTD 838).* (*Note.* See now, however, *VATA 1994, s 84(4)*, deriving from *FA 1993, s 46.*)

34.311   A firm of estate agents claimed a deduction for input tax incurred on powerboat racing, contending that the expenditure was incurred for the purpose of advertising their business. The Commissioners issued an assessment to disallow the deduction, considering that the powerboat racing was a hobby of one of the partners. The tribunal held on the evidence that the boat was used to promote the firm's business and allowed the firm's appeal, applying *Ian Flockton Developments Ltd*, 34.248 above. *Hamptons, LON/88/861Y (VTD 3883)*. (*Note*. See now, however, *VATA 1994, s 84(4)*, deriving from *FA 1993, s 46*. The Paymaster-General singled out this case in the Finance Bill Committee on 8 June 1993, observing that the firm's appeal 'would not succeed under the law as it shall be rewritten. It is right to rewrite the law so as not to permit such a case to take place and succeed before a tribunal.')

34.312   A self-employed gas engineer reclaimed input tax in respect of the purchase of a powerboat, which he used for racing. The Commissioners issued an assessment to recover the tax, considering that the boat had been purchased partly for private purposes and partly to be used for business entertainment. The engineer appealed, contending that he had purchased the boat for advertising purposes. The tribunal dismissed the appeal, holding on the evidence that the boat had been purchased to be used for business entertainment, so that the tax was not deductible. *C Denby, MAN/92/238 (VTD 9668)*.

34.313   **Motorboat purchased by bakery partnership.** A partnership which owned a bakery business purchased a motorboat and reclaimed the input tax. The Commissioners issued an assessment to recover the tax and the partnership appealed, contending that the boat had been purchased for advertising purposes. The tribunal dismissed the appeal, holding on the evidence that the boat had been purchased for private use. *Motcombe Bakeries, LON/86/54 (VTD 2216)*.

34.314   **Boat acquired by engineering company—whether input tax deductible.** See *Diesel Generating (Tetbury) Ltd*, 34.426 below.

34.315   **Motorboat purchased by married couple for restoration and resale—whether input tax deductible.** See *Cavner*, 34.449 below.

34.316   **Motorboat—whether purchased for future chartering business.** See *Castle*, 34.469 below.

Motor racing and rallying

Note. The cases in this section should be read in the light of *VATA 1994, s 84(4)*, originating from *FA 1993, s 46*. This section, which took effect for accounting periods beginning after 27 July 1993, provides that a tribunal can only allow an appeal against the disallowance relating to a 'luxury, amusement or entertainment' where the tribunal considers that the Commissioners 'could not reasonably have made' the determination which is the subject of the appeal. Cases relating to accounting periods beginning before 28 July 1993 should be read in the light of this change.

Cases where the appellant was successful

34.317   **Motor racing—metal dealers.** A partnership carried on the business of dealing in metals. One of the partners (S) was a New Zealander who had been a successful amateur motor racing driver. He competed in several televised races, and actively sought sponsorship for his motor racing. The partnership advertised on the car which S raced, and paid for some of the expenditure incurred in running the car. It reclaimed input tax on this expenditure. The Commissioners issued an assessment to recover the tax, considering that it had not been incurred for business purposes, but the tribunal allowed the partnership's appeal. *Atlas Marketing, LON/85/27 (VTD 1905)*.

34.318   **Motor racing—company supplying amusement machines.** A company supplied electronic amusement machines. Its market consisted of people who distributed amusement machines or who controlled premises where amusement machines were commonly to be found. It purchased a Formula Ford racing car and reclaimed the input tax thereon. The Commissioners issued an assessment to recover the tax and the company appealed, contending that the expenditure had been incurred for advertising purposes. The tribunal accepted the company's evidence and allowed the appeal. *Terropol Ltd, MAN/86/237 (VTD 3021)*.

34.319   **Motor racing—company manufacturing downhole tools for oil industry.**   A company carried on the business of manufacturing specialist downhole tools for the oil industry. It reclaimed input tax on expenditure incurred in running a Ferrari 308 racing car, which was driven by its controlling director. The Commissioners issued an assessment to recover the tax, considering that the expenditure had not been incurred for the purposes of the company's business. The company appealed, contending that the expenditure had been incurred for advertising purposes. The tribunal accepted the company's evidence and allowed the appeal, applying *Ian Flockton Developments Ltd*, 34.248 above. *Petroline Wireline Services Ltd, EDN/92/29 (VTD 9200)*.

34.320   **Motor racing—company providing TV production consultancy services.**   A company was incorporated to provide consultancy services with regard to the production of television programmes and videos. Its controlling director was an amateur motor racing driver. The company purchased a 1964 Lotus racing car and spent £100,000 on restoring it. It reclaimed the relevant input tax. The Commissioners issued an assessment to recover the tax, considering that the expenditure had been incurred for the personal pleasure of the director, rather than for the purposes of the company's business. The company appealed, contending that the expenditure had been incurred for advertising purposes. The tribunal accepted the company's evidence and allowed the appeal. *Richard Drewitt Productions Ltd, LON/93/2A (VTD 11999)*.

34.321   **Motor racing—company hiring drape curtains.**   A company carried on the business of hiring out drape curtains to the organisers of large exhibitions, trade shows and concerts. It reclaimed input tax on the purchase and maintenance of a racing car. At first the car was driven by the company's principal director, but he was not very successful and a more experienced driver was subsequently engaged. The Commissioners rejected the claim, considering that the expenditure had been incurred for the personal pleasure of the company's principal director. The company appealed, contending that the expenditure had been incurred for advertising purposes. The tribunal accepted the company's evidence and allowed the appeal, applying *Ian Flockton (Developments) Ltd*, 34.248 above, and distinguishing *Fenwick Builders Ltd*, 34.331 below. *Acrejean Ltd, LON/93/1774A (VTD 12262)*.

34.322   **Motor racing—monumental masons.**   See *Myatt & Leason*, 34.91 above.

34.323   **Motor rallying—plant hire company.**   The managing director of a plant hire company was also a successful rally driver, who had won a national championship. The company reclaimed input tax on the purchase of a rally car which the director drove in races and which displayed the company's name. The Commissioners issued an assessment to recover the tax and the company appealed, contending that the car had been purchased for the purpose of advertising its business. The tribunal allowed the company's appeal, applying *Ian Flockton Developments Ltd*, 34.248 above. *Steve Hill (Plant Hire) Ltd, LON/90/725X (VTD 5507)*.

34.324   **Kart racing.**   A company reclaimed input tax relating to the purchase and maintenance of a kart. The kart was raced by the company's managing director, and the company's name was painted on the kart. The Commissioners issued an assessment to recover the tax and the company appealed. The tribunal allowed the appeal, holding on the evidence that the kart had been purchased and raced for the purpose of promoting the company's business. *Ian Flockton Developments Ltd*, 34.248 above, applied. *NCS Northern Communications Systems Ltd, MAN/87/310 (VTD 4242)*.

34.325   **Motorcycle racing—transport firm.**   A married couple operated a transport business in partnership. They reclaimed input tax relating to motorcycle racing. The Commissioners issued an assessment to recover the tax and they appealed, contending that the expenditure had been incurred for advertising purposes. The tribunal accepted their evidence and allowed their appeal. *JA & IA Miller (t/a Miller Transport), BEL/85/14 (VTD 2041)*.

Cases where the appellant was partly successful

34.326   **Motor racing—braid manufacturing company.**   The principal director of a company which manufactured braid was a former motor racing driver. In 1984 he resumed motor racing after several years in retirement. The company reclaimed input tax on its director's motor racing activities and the Commissioners issued an assessment to recover the tax. The company appealed, contending that its director had resumed motor racing with the object of promoting the company. The tribunal found that the motor racing had a dual purpose and held that 45% of the disputed tax was deductible. *TD Reid (Braids) Ltd, BEL/89/30 (VTD 4638)*.

34.327   **Motor racing—sand extraction company.**   A company carried on the business of sand extraction. Its managing director was a motor racing driver, and the company reclaimed input tax on his motor racing activities. The Commissioners issued an assessment to recover the tax, considering that the expenditure had been incurred for the personal pleasure of the director, rather than for the purposes of the company's business. The tribunal held that the expenditure had been incurred for a dual purpose, observing that it was doubtful whether 'an ordinary businessman with a business in a defined location would have spent 41% of his advertising budget on motor racing, most of which took place outside the area'. *Fenwick Builders Ltd*, 34.331 below, applied; *Steve Hill (Plant Hire) Ltd*, 34.323 above, distinguished. The tribunal directed that the input tax should be apportioned, and adjourned the appeal in the hope that the parties could reach agreement on an apportionment. *Chambers (Homefield Sandpit) Ltd, LON/92/276X (VTD 9012)*. (*Notes.* (1) There was no further public hearing of the appeal. (2) An appeal against a misdeclaration penalty was dismissed—see **49.340** PENALTIES: MISDECLARATION.)

34.328   **Motor rallying—grocery company.**   A grocery company reclaimed input tax on expenditure incurred in motor rallying. The Commissioners issued an assessment to recover the tax and the company appealed, contending that the expenditure had been incurred for the purpose of advertising its business. The tribunal allowed the appeal in part, holding that one-third of the expenditure in question was allowable. *Lurgan Cash & Carry, BEL/84/4 (VTD 1738)*.

34.329   **Hot-rod racing—car repair business.**   The proprietor of a car repair business took part in hot-rod racing and reclaimed input tax relating to this. The Commissioners issued an assessment to recover the tax and he appealed, contending that the expenditure was for advertising purposes. The tribunal allowed his appeal in part, holding that the expenditure had a dual purpose and that 70% of the tax was deductible. *Ian Flockton Developments Ltd*, 34.248 above, applied. *L Dallas, BEL/87/16 (VTD 3620)*.

Cases where the appellant was unsuccessful

34.330   **Motor   racing—building   company—whether   for   promotional purposes.**   The appellant company carried on business as a building contractor. Its employees included B, the son-in-law of H, its managing director. B was an enthusiastic motor racing driver and, through him, H became very interested in motor racing. The directors decided to acquire a car to be raced by B in the company's name and deducted the tax on its expenses of racing the car in its returns. The appeal was against an assessment withdrawing the deduction. The tribunal dismissed the appeal, holding that the company had acquired the car firstly to take part in motor racing activities as to which B and H had become enthusiastic, and secondly to enhance their personal prestige and, incidentally, that of the company. In the circumstances of the case it was unrealistic to say that the car had been raced for the purposes of the company's business. *Hubbard & Houghton Ltd, LON/80/314 (VTD 1028)*.

34.331   A building company reclaimed input tax on expenditure incurred in racing two motor cars which were driven by its managing director. The Commissioners issued an assessment to recover the tax, considering that the expenditure had not been incurred for business purposes. The company appealed, contending that the motor racing had had the effect of advertising its business. The tribunal dismissed the appeal, finding that the motor racing had been a hobby 'with a "spin-off" in the form of business contacts' and holding that the input tax was not deductible. *Fenwick Builders Ltd, LON/90/928Z (VTD 5801)*.

34.332   **Motor racing—aviation company.**   A company which carried on an air taxi business claimed to deduct input tax on motor racing activities. Its appeal against an assessment withdrawing the deduction was dismissed. The tribunal held that, although the motor racing activity was begun with the object of promoting the name of the company and attracting additional business, there was never a reasonable chance of it being successful in this objective. *Renco Aviation Ltd, LON/83/203 (VTD 1646)*.

34.333   **Motor racing—sunbed manufacturers.**   See *Paine Leisure Products Ltd*, 8.14 BUSINESS ENTERTAINMENT.

34.334   **Renovation of March racing car by member of group of companies dealing in cars—whether for business purposes.**   A company, which was a member of a group of companies which dealt in expensive cars such as BMWs, Mercedes and Porsches, purchased a March racing car which was in need of extensive renovation, and reclaimed input tax on this expenditure. The Commissioners issued an assessment to recover the tax, considering that the company had purchased the car so that it could be raced by the controlling director of the group for his own pleasure, and had not been purchased for business purposes. The company appealed, contending that the car had been purchased for advertising and promotional purposes. The tribunal dismissed the appeal, finding that the racing of the car 'was unattended by any form of promotion of the group and its business' and that the group had previously engaged in motor racing but that this 'had produced very little in the way of sales'. On the evidence, the company had not shown that the car had been purchased for promotional purposes. *PLR Ltd, LON/91/1379 (VTD 9501)*.

34.335   **Motor rallying—whether for purposes of wife's motor-dealing business.**   A married woman (T) was a dealer in motor cars and equipment. However, although the business was in her name the running of it was largely left to her husband, an undischarged bankrupt, who was a well-known motor rally driver. She claimed input tax on some of her husband's rally expenses. The expenses, some of which were invoiced to her in her business name, were mainly the cost of tyres when not donated by sponsors of her husband's rally driving. He had received over £15,000 from sponsors and also some amounts from the sale of used tyres, but none of this had gone into the appellant's business account. He had circulated potential sponsors but the circulars had not mentioned his wife's business. On this and other evidence the tribunal held that the disputed tax related to supplies for the personal activities of the husband and was not incurred for the purposes of the wife's business. The appeal was dismissed and costs were awarded to the Commissioners. *A Thompson (t/a AY Cars), MAN/80/115 (VTD 1043).*

34.336 **Motor rallying—building company.** The appellant company carried on business as building contractors. It sought to claim input tax on the purchase of and cost of maintenance of two rally cars. The Commissioners disallowed the claim on the basis that the cars were not rallied for the purpose of the business, and issued an assessment to recover the tax. The company's appeal was dismissed. *John McMillan & Son Ltd, BEL/83/11 (VTD 1610).*

34.337 **Motor rallying—coal merchants.** A married couple and their son traded in partnership as coal merchants. The son was also a keen rally driver. The partnership name was displayed on the front and sides of his rally car, and the partnership paid for all repairs and spare parts for the car. The partnership reclaimed the input tax on this expenditure, and the Commissioners issued an assessment to recover the tax, considering that the expenditure had not been incurred for the purpose of the partnership's business. The tribunal upheld the assessment and dismissed the partnership's appeal. *RH Pearson & Sons, EDN/91/154 (VTD 7287).*

34.338 **Motor rallying—jeweller.** An appeal was dismissed in a case where a jeweller, who was also a keen motor rally driver, had reclaimed input tax which was attributable to his rally driving. *JR Joannides, MAN/91/1338 (VTD 11373).* (*Note.* For another issue in this case, see 58.365 SUPPLY.)

34.339 **Drag-car racing—whether part of business activities.** A company carried on business as a builder and developer. It incurred input tax on the import of components for a drag-racing car, which was raced by the son of the managing director, who won various championships. The company logo appeared on the car. The Commissioners disallowed the input tax and the company appealed, contending that the input tax was incurred for the purpose of its business. The tribunal dismissed the appeal, holding that, whilst the company was carrying on two separate activities of building and drag-racing, on the facts the drag-racing activity did not form part of the business activities of the company. *W & J Barrs Ltd, LON/87/409 (VTD 2564).*

34.340 **Motorcycle racing.** A company which traded in a wide variety of goods reclaimed input tax on expenditure incurred in motorcycle racing. The Commissioners issued an assessment to recover the tax and the tribunal dismissed the company's appeal. *Fundmain Ltd, MAN/82/135 (VTD 1493).*

34.341 **Motorcycles purchased by electrical dealers.** A married couple who sold electrical accessories reclaimed input tax on the purchase of motorcycles. The Commissioners issued an assessment to recover the tax and the tribunal dismissed the couple's appeal. *Mr & Mrs CA Eadon (t/a Motaelectrics), MAN/84/29 (VTD 1692).*

34.342 **Motorcycle purchased by design company.** A design company reclaimed input tax on the purchase of a motorcycle and spare parts. The Commissioners issued an assessment to recover the tax and the tribunal dismissed the company's appeal. *R & M Baker Ltd (t/a Castle Designs), MAN/83/339 (VTD 1695).*

34.343 **Motorcycle purchased by clothing shop.** A clothing shop reclaimed input tax on the purchase of a motorcycle used for competing in moto-cross events. The Commissioners issued an assessment to recover the tax and the tribunal dismissed the company's appeal. *C & W Clothiers Ltd, MAN/84/163 (VTD 1756).*

34.344 **Motorcycle racing—manufacturing company.** A small manufacturing company reclaimed input tax relating to motorcycle racing. The motorcycle in question was ridden by a nephew of the company secretary. The Commissioners issued an assessment to recover the tax and the tribunal dismissed the company's appeal. *TLV (Manufacturing) Ltd, MAN/85/298 (VTD 2058).*

34.345 **Motorcycle—numberplate dealers.** The proprietor of a business which sold motorcar and motorcycle numberplates reclaimed input tax on the purchase of a racing motorcycle by her son. The Commissioners issued an assessment to recover the tax and the tribunal dismissed her appeal. *PD Wood, LON/89/1112X (VTD 4644).*

Yachting

34.346 **Manufacturing company.** A company which manufactured industrial doors reclaimed input tax on the purchase of a yacht. The Commissioners issued an assessment to recover the tax, considering that the yacht had been purchased for the personal pleasure of the company's managing director. The company appealed, contending that the yacht had been purchased for advertising purposes. The tribunal held that the yacht had been purchased for a dual purpose but that the principal purpose was for the pleasure of the director, and that only a proportion of the input tax was deductible. The tribunal adjourned the appeal for the parties to consider the apportionment. *Freelance Door Services Ltd, MAN/82/183 (VTD 1384). (Notes.* (1) There was no further public hearing of the appeal. (2) See now *VATA 1994, s 84(4),* originating from *FA 1993, s 46.*)

34.347 **Car sales company.** A company which dealt in cars reclaimed input tax on the purchase of a yacht. The Commissioners issued an assessment to recover the tax and the tribunal dismissed the company's appeal, holding that the yacht had not been purchased for business purposes. *Omega Cars Ltd, MAN/82/48 (VTD 1528).*

34.348 A similar decision was reached in *Hill & Son (Manor Park) Ltd, LON/83/416 (VTD 1629).*

34.349 **Dairy produce company.** A company which sold dairy produce reclaimed input tax on a 51ft racing yacht which cost more than £140,000. The company's managing director skippered the yacht in races. The company reclaimed input tax on the yacht and the Commissioners issued an assessment to recover the tax. The tribunal dismissed the company's appeal, holding on the evidence that the yacht had not been acquired for business purposes. *Ernest George Ltd, LON/83/354 (VTD 1760).*

34.350 **Machine tool company.** A company dealing in machine tools reclaimed input tax on the purchase of a yacht. The Commissioners refused to repay the tax, considering that the yacht had not been acquired for business purposes. The company appealed, contending that the yacht had been acquired to provide an 'upmarket setting' for meetings with potential customers, and had regularly been used for that purpose. The tribunal allowed the appeal in part, holding on the evidence that the yacht was used partly for business purposes and partly for private recreational purposes, and that 50% of the tax in question was deductible. *Tower Steel (Holdings) Ltd, LON/89/1839X (VTD 5029). (Note.* See now, however, *VATA 1994, s 84(4),* deriving from *FA 1993, s 46.*)

34.351 **Company repairing car engines.** A company which carried on a business of repairing car engines purchased a yacht from its managing director, and then purchased a second yacht, using the first yacht as part-exchange. The company reclaimed input tax on the purchase of the second yacht. The Commissioners issued an assessment to recover the tax and the company appealed, contending that it had acquired the yacht for research purposes and that it hoped to diversify its business into repairing yacht engines. The tribunal dismissed the appeal, holding on the evidence that this research was remote from the company's existing business and that the yacht had primarily been acquired for recreational purposes. *GL Motor Services Ltd, LON/87/245 (VTD 2413)*.

34.352   **Farming company—whether yacht purchased for chartering.**   See *Rainheath Ltd*, 7.32 BUSINESS.

34.353   **Mobile crane hire company—whether yacht purchased for chartering.**   See *RF Henfrey (Midlands) Ltd*, 7.33 BUSINESS.

34.354   **Accountant—whether yacht purchased for chartering.**   See *Evans*, 7.34 BUSINESS.

34.355   **Hotel proprietors—whether yacht purchased for chartering.**   See *Westbourne Hotel*, 7.35 BUSINESS.

34.356   **Plant hire company—whether yacht purchased for chartering.**   See *Trexagrove Ltd*, 7.36 BUSINESS.

34.357   **Leasing company—whether yacht purchased for chartering.**   See *Petros Leasing Ltd*, 7.37 BUSINESS, and *CR King & Partners (Holdings) Ltd*, 7.38 BUSINESS.

34.358   **Property development company—whether yacht purchased for chartering.**   See *Silicon Valley Estates Ltd*, 7.39 BUSINESS.

34.359   **Property company—whether yacht purchased for future chartering business.**   See *Warwest Holdings Ltd*, 34.471 below.

34.360   **Mining company—whether yacht purchased for chartering.**   See *DS Supplies Ltd*, 7.40 BUSINESS.

34.361   **New company temporarily dormant—whether yacht purchased for future chartering business.**   See *Furness Vale Yacht Hire Ltd*, 34.450 below.

34.362   **Financial consultant—whether yacht purchased for future chartering business.**   See *Milner*, 34.470 below.

34.363   **Building contractors—whether yacht purchased for future shipbuilding business.**   See *Penjen Ltd*, 34.463 below.

Aircraft

34.364   **Kitchen equipment company.**   A company which supplied kitchen equipment reclaimed input tax on the purchase and restoration of an aircraft. The Commissioners issued an assessment to recover the tax, considering that the expenditure had not been incurred for the purpose of the company's business. The company appealed, contending that the aircraft had been acquired for advertising purposes. The tribunal rejected this contention and dismissed the appeal. *Spoils Kitchen Reject Shops Ltd, LON/86/157 (VTD 2200)*.

34.365   **Heating engineers.**   A partnership which carried on business as heating engineers reclaimed input tax on the purchase of an aircraft. The partnership name was painted on the wings in letters 50cm high. The Commissioners issued an assessment to recover the tax and the partners appealed, contending that they had purchased the aircraft for business purposes. The tribunal dismissed the appeal. On the evidence, the aircraft was not used in the business, and the 'visual impact' of the partnership name on the wings when the aircraft was flying at 1000 feet was negligible. *IM & PA Munster (t/a M & M Heating Services), MAN/91/867 (VTD 7961)*.

34.366   **Computer consultancy company.**   A company which carried on a computer consultancy business reclaimed input tax on the purchase of a microlight aircraft. The Commissioners rejected the claim, considering that the aircraft had not been purchased for business purposes, and the company appealed, contending that the aircraft had been purchased for advertising purposes. The tribunal dismissed the company's appeal, finding that the aircraft had been purchased for the pleasure of the company's managing director, and holding that the input tax was not deductible. *Eddystone Computers Ltd, LON/92/3036A (VTD 11018).*

34.367   **Property company.**   A property company reclaimed input tax on the purchase of an aircraft and a helicopter. The Commissioners issued an assessment to recover the tax, considering that the expenditure had not been incurred for business purposes. The tribunal allowed the company's appeal in part, finding on the evidence that the aircraft had been purchased for the purpose of flying between the sites of its properties and for viewing potential properties, but that the helicopter had been purchased for private purposes. *Key Properties Ltd, LON/92/2266A (VTD 11778).* (*Note.* For other issues in this case, see 39.92 LAND and 49.267 PENALTIES: MISDECLARATION.)

34.368   **Company operating garage.**   A company which owned a garage reclaimed input tax on the maintenance and running costs of an aircraft. The Commissioners issued an assessment to recover the tax, considering that the expenditure had been incurred for the personal pleasure of the company's controlling director. The company appealed, contending that the aircraft had been purchased for advertising purposes. The tribunal upheld the assessment and dismissed the company's appeal. *Willpower Garage Ltd, MAN/91/1269 (VTD 12114).*

Personalised vehicle numberplates

Cases where the appellant was successful

34.369   **Sole trader.**   A haulage contractor, whose initials were MWA, reclaimed input tax on the purchase of a personalised numberplate bearing the registration 'MWA 2'. He affixed the numberplate to a car, which he used 75% for business purposes and 25% privately. The Commissioners issued an assessment to recover the tax, but the tribunal allowed the contractor's appeal, applying *Ian Flockton Developments Ltd*, 34.248 above, and holding that it was satisfied that he had purchased the numberplate for the purpose of advertising his business. *Jones*, 34.386 below, and *Ava Knit Ltd*, 34.376 below, distinguished. *MW Alexander, LON/91/1191Z (VTD 7208).* (*Note.* See now, however, *VATA 1994, s 84(4)*, originating from *FA 1993, s 46*.)

34.370   A management consultant (S) purchased a vehicle numberplate '100 S' for £4,400. He fixed the numberplate to a Range Rover which he drove for business purposes, and reclaimed input tax on the purchase. The Commissioners rejected the claim, and S appealed, contending that he had purchased the numberplate as an investment and to disguise the age of the Range Rover. The tribunal chairman (Miss Gort, sitting alone) accepted his evidence and allowed his appeal, applying *dicta* in *Ian Flockton Developments Ltd*, 34.248 above, and holding that the numberplate was not a 'luxury', so that the provisions of *VATA 1994, s 84(4)* did not apply. *MJ Shaw (t/a Shaw Associates), LON/97/277 (VTD 15099).* (*Notes.* (1) The decision in this case was not followed, and was implicitly disapproved, by a subsequent tribunal in *Marinello*, 34.388 below, on the grounds that Miss Gort had not referred to the decision in *Rosner*, 34.145 above, where the QB had held that there must be 'a nexus between the expenditure and the business'. (2) Compare the decision in *College Street Market Gardens*, 34.384 below, in which the tribunal held that personalised vehicle numberplates were within the definition of a 'luxury' for the purposes of *VATA 1994, s 84(4)*.)

34.371   **Partnership.**   A partnership operated a supermarket under the name 'Sunner & Son'. It purchased a personalised numberplate '7 SUN' at a cost of £6,300. The numberplate was affixed to a Sierra 2.9 litre car which was owned by one of the partners, and which was normally parked outside the supermarket. The partnership reclaimed input tax on the purchase. The Commissioners issued an assessment to recover the tax, and the partnership appealed, contending that the numberplate had been purchased for advertising purposes. The tribunal accepted the partnership's evidence and allowed the appeal. *Jones*, 34.386 below, and *Philips*, 34.387 below, distinguished. *Sunner & Sons, MAN/91/1205 (VTD 8857)*. (*Note.* See now, however, *VATA 1994, s 84(4)*, originating from *FA 1993, s 46*.)

34.372   **Limited company.**   A company carried on a business of selling, renting and repairing televisions and video recorders. In 1992 it purchased a numberplate '3 TV' and fixed it to a Lexus car which was driven by its controlling director. Later in the year it purchased a numberplate '9 TV' and fixed it to a Rover car which was driven by the director's wife, who worked for the company on a part-time basis. It reclaimed the input tax on these numberplates. The Commissioners issued an assessment to recover the tax, on the basis that the expenditure had not been incurred for the purposes of the business. The company appealed, contending that the expenditure had been incurred for advertising purposes. The tribunal allowed the appeal, observing that the initials 'TV' referred to the company's trade rather than to the initials of the director, and that if the director had wished to purchase such numberplates for his own prestige or vanity, he would have purchased numberplates bearing his own initials. *Ava Knit Ltd*, 34.376 below, and *BJ Kershaw Transport Ltd*, 34.377 below, distinguished. *Hamlet's (Radio & TV) Ltd, MAN/93/1285 (VTD 12716)*.

34.373   A group of companies carried on a business of providing financial and advisory services. It purchased a numberplate '1 FAS', which it affixed to a BMW which was driven by the group's managing director, and reclaimed input tax on the purchase. The Commissioners issued an assessment to recover the tax, considering that the expenditure had not been incurred for the purpose of the group's business. The holding company appealed, contending that the numberplate had been purchased for advertising purposes and that '1 FAS' was intended to stand for 'Independent Financial Advisory Services'. The tribunal accepted the company's evidence and allowed the appeal, observing that 'the initials are not associated with the name of the managing director himself'. *Hamlet's (Radio & TV) Ltd*, 34.372 above, applied. *New Mansion Pension Managers Ltd, MAN/94/1866 (VTD 13527)*.

Cases where the appellant was partly successful

34.374   A car dealer bought a personalised car numberplate, 'LEW 1S', for £36,000 plus VAT, and reclaimed the relevant input tax. The Commissioners issued an assessment to recover the tax, on the basis that he had not purchased the numberplate for the purposes of his business. The dealer appealed, contending that he had purchased the numberplate as an investment, to resell it at a profit in the future, and also for advertising purposes. The tribunal allowed the appeal in part, finding that the numberplate had been partly purchased for advertising purposes, partly for resale, and partly for personal enjoyment, and held that 75% of the tax was deductible. *RA Lewis, MAN/91/1348 (VTD 9845)*. (*Note.* See now, however, *VATA 1994, s 84(4)*, originating from *FA 1993, s 46*.)

34.375   A chartered surveyor, whose initials were 'MJD', reclaimed input tax on the purchase of a personalised numberplate 'MJD2'. The Commissioners rejected the claim and the surveyor appealed. The tribunal held that, since the initials reflected the surveyor's trading name, 25% of the tax was deductible. *Dicta* in *Rosner*, 34.145 above, applied; *Marinello*, 34.388 below, distinguished. *MJ Dant, LON/94/318 (VTD 16043)*.

Cases where the appellant was unsuccessful

34.376   **Limited company.** A company which manufactured women's clothing reclaimed input tax on the purchase of a personalised numberplate '714 ROD' for its managing director's car. The initials did not reflect the company's name, but were chosen because the director's Christian name was Rodney. The Commissioners issued an assessment to recover the tax and the tribunal dismissed the company's appeal, holding that the numberplate was not acquired for the purposes of the company's business, but for the personal pleasure of the director. *Ava Knit Ltd, MAN/82/219 (VTD 1461)*.

34.377   A company which carried on a transport business reclaimed input tax on the purchase of a personalised numberplate 'BK 4'. The company was named after its controlling director, and the initials reflected those of the director. The Commissioners issued an assessment to recover the tax and the tribunal dismissed the company's appeal, finding that the relationship between the numberplate and the company was so tenuous that the plate could not reasonably be expected to serve the object of promoting the company. *BJ Kershaw Transport Ltd, MAN/84/229 (VTD 1785)*.

34.378   An appeal was dismissed in another case where a company reclaimed input tax on a personalised numberplate bearing the initials of the company's managing director. The initials (GJW) were not reflected in the company's name. The tribunal held that the numberplate had not been purchased for the purpose of promoting the company's business. *Empire Contracts Ltd, MAN/90/937 (VTD 7200)*.

34.379   Similar decisions were reached in *Quality Care Homes Ltd, MAN/91/302 (VTD 7391); Industrial Doors (Scotland) Ltd, EDN/94/26 (VTD 12656)*, and *The Redington Design Co Ltd, LON/98/1432 (VTD 12656)*.

34.380   A company which operated amusement arcades reclaimed input tax in respect of two personalised numberplates. The numberplates bore the letters 'LC', which were the initials of the son and daughter-in-law of the managing director, and were attached to cars driven by the son and daughter-in-law. The Commissioners issued an assessment to recover the tax and the tribunal dismissed the company's appeal, observing that the numberplates did not reflect the company's name and finding that the company's 'predominant motive' was to give the director's son and daughter-in-law 'the pleasure of driving cars with their initials displayed on the numberplates'. *Alexander*, 34.369 above, distinguished. *Stardust Leisure Ltd, LON/92/1248A (VTD 9740)*.

34.381   A company reclaimed input tax on the purchase of a personalised numberplate '3 MB' bearing the initials of the company's managing director, which were not reflected in the company's name. The numberplate was fixed to a Bentley car, costing more than £100,000, which was driven by the managing director. The Commissioners rejected the claim and the tribunal dismissed the company's appeal, holding that it was 'difficult to accept that (the director) really believed that the numberplate would genuinely benefit the business'. *Sunner & Sons*, 34.371 above, distinguished. *Welbeck Video plc, LON/93/162A (VTD 11383)*.

34.382 A company which dealt in electrical goods purchased a personalised numberplate 'FEL 1X' at a cost of more than £50,000. The company was named after its managing director, and the initials reflected the director's name. The company fixed the numberplate to a Mercedes which the director drove, and reclaimed input tax on the purchase. The Commissioners issued an assessment to recover the tax, and the company appealed. The tribunal dismissed the appeal, holding that there was 'no clear nexus between the expenditure on the numberplate and the business itself'. *Rosner*, 34.145 above, applied. *Felix Quinn Enterprises Ltd, EDN/93/171 (VTD 12411).*

34.383 See also *NEP Group Ltd*, 49.331 PENALTIES: MISDECLARATION.

34.384 **Partnership.** A family partnership which operated a market gardening business reclaimed input tax on the purchase of four personalised numberplates. The numberplates reflected the initials of the individual partners, but did not reflect the trading name of the partnership. The Commissioners issued an assessment to recover the tax, and the tribunal dismissed the partnership's appeal, finding that the numberplates had been 'purchased out of a natural pride in the partners' own evident individual success and that the use of these numbers would enhance their own individual images'. *College Street Market Gardens, LON/95/2712 (VTD 14118).* (*Note.* The tribunal also held that the numberplates were within the definition of a 'luxury', so that, by virtue of *VATA 1994, s 84(4)*, it would only have allowed the appeal if the Commissioners' decision had been unreasonable.)

34.385 A similar decision was reached in *Engineering Quality Consultants, EDN/99/190 (VTD 16634).*

34.386 **Accountant.** A chartered accountant, whose initials were ENJ, reclaimed input tax on the purchase of a numberplate bearing the registration 'ENJ 8'. The Commissioners rejected the claim and the tribunal dismissed his appeal. The test of whether expenditure was incurred for business purposes was a subjective test, applying *Ian Flockton Developments Ltd*, 34.248 above. However, the tribunal did 'not believe that his motive in buying the number was as a business purpose ... we think his subjective motive more likely to have been to possess a personalised number personally which could do the practice no harm'. *EN Jones, MAN/90/15 (VTD 5023).*

34.387 **Printer.** A printer, whose Christian name was David, purchased a personalised numberplate 'DAV 10' at a cost of £38,775. He fixed the numberplate to a BMW, and reclaimed input tax on the purchase. The Commissioners issued an assessment to recover the tax, and the tribunal dismissed the printer's appeal, holding that 'the standards and thinking of the ordinary businessman in the position of the appellant ... makes it improbable that the acquisition of the numberplate was for the purposes of the business'. *Dicta* in *Ian Flockton Developments Ltd*, 34.248 above, applied. *D Philips, EDN/92/3 (VTD 7883).* (*Note.* For another issue in this case, see 49.305 PENALTIES: MISDECLARATION.)

34.388 **Publican.** A publican, who also had a number of other business interests, reclaimed input tax on the purchase of a personalised numberplate 'PEM 1'. (The publican's initials were 'PEM'.) The Commissioners issued an assessment to recover the tax, on the basis that he had purchased the numberplate for personal reasons rather than for business reasons. The tribunal dismissed the publican's appeal. Applying *dicta* of the QB in *Rosner*, 34.145 above, there had to be 'a nexus between the expenditure and the business'. On the evidence, 'there was no real nexus between the number on the numberplates and any of (the publican's) businesses'. The tribunal specifically declined to follow the decision in *Shaw*, 34.370 above, on the basis that the chairman in that case had failed to refer to the QB decision in *Rosner. PE Marinello, EDN/98/119 (VTD 15915)*.

34.389   **Haulage contractor.**   See *Windsor*, 49.332 PENALTIES: MISDECLARATION.

Associated companies

34.390   **Whether expenditure incurred for business of subsidiary company or of parent company.**   A leasing company (F) was a subsidiary of a banking company (C), which was itself the subsidiary of a US banking company. A large proportion of C's supplies were exempt from VAT, so that it could reclaim less than half of its input tax, whereas F could reclaim the whole of its input tax. F purchased some computer equipment which it leased to C for a period of eight years, and reclaimed the input tax incurred on the purchase. The Commissioners issued an assessment to recover the tax, considering that the equipment had not been purchased for the purposes of F's business. The tribunal allowed F's appeal, holding that the transactions were not a sham and that the input tax was deductible. *Friary Leasing Ltd, LON/88/1026Z (VTD 3893)*. (*Note. VATA 1994, s 44* now provides that there is a deemed self-supply where a going concern is transferred to a partly exempt group.)

34.391   **Enterprise Zone Trust established by property development company.**   A company (V) which carried on the business of property development established an Enterprise Zone Trust to promote the sale of units in a shopping precinct which it was developing in an Enterprise Zone in the West Midlands. V reclaimed input tax on the expenditure incurred in establishing the Trust. The Commissioners issued an assessment to recover the tax, considering that, since the Trust was a separate legal entity, the expenditure was not directly for the purpose of V's business, although it would have the effect of benefiting V's business. The tribunal allowed V's appeal. Applying *Ian Flockton Developments Ltd*, 34.248 above, 'the sole purpose of incurring the expenditure was for the more advantageous and efficient way of carrying on (V's) business'. *Wallman Foods Ltd*, 34.151 above, distinguished. *V & P Midlands Ltd, MAN/90/520 (VTD 7589)*.

34.392   A similar decision was reached in *Property Enterprise Managers Ltd, LON/91/234Z (VTD 7711)*.

34.393   **Repairs to boats hired to associated company—whether for business purposes.**   A married couple carried on a computer consultancy business in partnership, and were registered for VAT. They purchased three boats, and hired them to a company which they controlled. The company advertised the boats as holiday accommodation, but attracted very few customers, and traded at a loss. In 1988 the partnership had invoiced the company for the use of the boats, but, because of the company's financial difficulties, it did not issue any more invoices to the company until 1991. In the meantime the partnership undertook repairs to the boats, and reclaimed input tax. The Commissioners issued an assessment to recover the tax, considering that, because the partnership was not invoicing the company for the hire of the boats, the hire of the boats to the company did not amount to a business activity. The tribunal allowed the partners' appeal, holding that the hire of the boats was a business despite the temporary cessation of payment by the company, so that the partnership was entitled to credit for the relevant input tax. *JR & S Purdue, [1994] VATTR 387 (VTD 11779)*.

34.394   **Antique furniture purchased by registered company and leased to tenant of unregistered associated company.**   A company (J), which was not registered for VAT, owned business premises which it leased to an unrelated company (V). V owed J rent of £5,250. The principal director of J also controlled another company (R), which operated a public house and was registered for VAT. The director arranged for

R to purchase some antique furniture from V for £5,250, and lease the furniture back to V. The £5,250 was lent by J to R, paid by R to V for the furniture, and finally paid by V to J as arrears of rent, so that effectively it travelled in a circle. R reclaimed input tax on the furniture, and the Commissioners issued an assessment to recover the tax, considering that R had not purchased the furniture for the purpose of its business. The tribunal dismissed R's appeal, finding that it was satisfied that R's intention 'at the time when the expenditure was incurred on the furniture was not that the furniture should be used for the purposes of its business'. (The tribunal also observed that, although it was not necessary to apply the principle laid down in *Furniss v Dawson, HL [1984] STC 153 (TTC 2001, 71.191)* to the facts here, it was 'clear ... that the *Furniss v Dawson* principle could apply to cases relating to the recovery of input tax'.) *Raceshine Ltd, MAN/91/1135 (VTD 7688).* (*Note.* An appeal against a misdeclaration penalty was also dismissed.)

34.395   **Company refurbishing accommodation for associated charity.**   A trading company covenanted all its profits to a charity for the homeless. It incurred expenditure in refurbishing a property for the homeless, and reclaimed the input tax on this work. The Commissioners issued an assessment to recover the tax, considering that the expenditure had been incurred for the purposes of the charity, rather than for the purpose of the company's business. The tribunal dismissed the company's appeal, holding on the evidence that 'the refurbishing of the accommodation was ... for the purpose of carrying out the objectives of the charity'. *Emmaus Ltd, LON/93/699A (VTD 11679).*

Promotion of tourism

34.396   **Tourist board.**   The Netherlands Tourist Bureau, which had been established by the Netherlands Government as a non-profit-making organisation to encourage people to visit the Netherlands, operated a branch in London. The branch was registered for VAT in 1989 under the name of the Netherlands Board of Tourism, and reclaimed the whole of its input tax. In March 1994 the Commissioners issued a ruling that only part of the input tax incurred by the Board was attributable to supplies made for business purposes, and that the remainder of the tax related to supplies made to the Netherlands Government and was not deductible. The Board appealed, contending firstly that all its supplies were made to commercial sponsors, and alternatively that those supplies which were not made to commercial sponsors were made to its parent Bureau in the course of its business. The tribunal allowed the appeal, accepting the Board's alternative contention and holding that those supplies which were not made to commercial sponsors were made through the Bureau to the Netherlands Government and were made in the course of the Board's business. *Imperial War Museum,* 43.2 PARTIAL EXEMPTION, applied; *Apple & Pear Development Council,* 21.47 EUROPEAN COMMUNITY LAW, distinguished. *Netherlands Board of Tourism, LON/94/607A (VTD 12935).*

34.397   The London branch of the Austrian National Tourist Office (ANTO) reclaimed the whole of its input tax. The Commissioners issued a ruling that only part of the input tax was deductible, and that part of the tax related to supplies made to the Austrian Federal Government (and the Federal States) which were essentially 'the activities of a government agency', and was not deductible. The tribunal allowed ANTO's appeal, holding that ANTO was carrying on a business for VAT purposes and that the whole of its input tax was deductible. *Netherlands Board of Tourism,* 34.396 above, applied; *Turespaña,* 34.398 below, was distinguished on the grounds that the Spanish government had a degree of control over Turespaña, whereas ANTO could not 'be regarded as part of the Austrian Government even in the widest sense'. *Austrian National Tourist Office, LON/96/674 (VTD 15561).* (*Note.* For another issue in this case, see 58.378 SUPPLY.)

34.398   Turespaña (T) was established as a statutory body to encourage tourists to visit Spain. It claimed credit for input tax on supplies of advertising services. (For the obligation on the supplier of these services to account for output tax, see *Diversified Agency Services Ltd*, 58.377 SUPPLY.) The Commissioners rejected the claim, considering that, although T was carrying on a business for VAT purposes in that it made supplies of exhibition facilities to third parties, the promotion of tourism by a statutory body was not an economic activity or a business for the purposes of VAT law. T appealed, contending that the grants which it received from the Spanish Government represented consideration for the supplies which it made to that Government. The tribunal dismissed the appeal, holding on the evidence that 'in carrying out its activities (T) was discharging its statutory duties'. Its activities were controlled by the Spanish Government, and were 'far removed from the usual concept of supplies'. *Staatssecretaris van Financiën v Hong Kong Trade Development Council*, 21.46 EUROPEAN COMMUNITY LAW, applied. *Netherlands Board of Tourism*, 34.396 above, was distinguished on the grounds that 75% of the income of the appellant in that case was commercially generated. *Turespaña, LON/96/002 (VTD 14568)*. (*Note.* The decision here was distinguished in the subsequent case of *Austrian National Tourist Office*, 34.397 above, on the grounds that the Spanish government had a degree of control over Turespaña, whereas the Austrian National Tourist Office could not 'be regarded as part of the Austrian Government even in the widest sense'.)

Miscellaneous

Cases where the appellant was successful

34.399   **Provision of Christmas street lighting by Chamber of Commerce.** A Chamber of Commerce organised a festival of street lighting each Christmas. It reclaimed input tax on the relevant expenditure. The Commissioners rejected the claim but the tribunal allowed the Chamber's appeal, holding that the expenditure had been incurred for the purpose of promoting the trade of the members of the Chamber. *Sittingbourne Milton & District Chamber of Commerce, LON/76/178 (VTD 341)*.

34.400   **Radios purchased by broadcaster.** A broadcaster and writer (H) reclaimed input tax on the purchase of a transistor radio and a car radio. The Commissioners issued an assessment to recover the tax, considering that the radios had been purchased for private purposes rather than professional purposes. H appealed, contending that he had purchased the radios to listen to rival broadcasters. The tribunal accepted his evidence and allowed his appeal. *R Hough, LON/77/106 (VTD 488)*.

34.401   **Computer—whether purchased for business purposes.** A trader who had carried on business as a general builders' merchant, and also supplied management services, purchased a computer for £13,000 and reclaimed input tax on the purchase. The Commissioners issued an assessment to recover the tax but the tribunal allowed the trader's appeal, holding on the evidence that the computer had been purchased for business purposes rather than for private purposes. *EA Kilburn, MAN/87/277 (VTD 3937)*. (*Note.* For another issue in this case, see 58.151 SUPPLY. For a subsequent application for costs, see 2.275 APPEALS.)

34.402   **Actor joining health club.** An actor joined a health club, and reclaimed input tax on his entrance fee and subscriptions. The Commissioners issued an assessment to recover the tax, considering that the expenditure had been incurred for private purposes since membership of such a club was not 'essential to the acting profession'. The actor appealed, contending that he had joined the club for the purpose of undertaking a specific role in a television series, which required him to portray a character with a high level of physical fitness. In the series he was filmed swimming underwater, running, and weight training. The tribunal allowed his appeal, applying *Ian Flockton Developments Ltd*, 34.248 above, and holding on the evidence that he had joined the club to serve the purposes of his profession. *A Anholt, [1989] VATTR 297 (VTD 4215)*. (*Note*. See now, however, *VATA 1994, s 84(4)*, originating from *FA 1993, s 46*.)

34.403   **Purchase of typesetting machines by company formerly engaged in typesetting but now engaged in finance—whether for business purposes.** A company had for many years been engaged in manufacturing typesetting machines and related software, but sold this business in 1984. It continued to receive investment income, while an associated company provided financial services, mainly to companies engaged in typesetting. In the following year the company incurred expenditure in refurbishing three old typesetting machines of historic interest, and reclaimed the input tax on this expenditure. The Commissioners issued an assessment to recover the tax, considering that the machines had been refurbished as a personal hobby of the principal director, rather than for the purpose of the company's business. The tribunal allowed the company's appeal, holding on the evidence that the purchase and refurbishment of the old machines had been undertaken for the purpose of publicising the group's business of providing finance for the purchase of typesetting machines. *M & H Whittaker & Son Ltd, MAN/88/174 (VTD 3554)*.

34.404   **Renovation of property owned by transport company.** A company carried on the business of road transport and haulage, and had also bought and sold property. In 1986 it purchased land close to a garage which it owned. The land contained a bungalow, which the company's managing director occupied, and a row of pigsties. The company converted the pigsties into stables and reclaimed the input tax on this work. The Commissioners issued an assessment to recover the tax, considering that the expenditure had not been incurred for the purpose of the company's business. The company appealed, contending that the expenditure had been incurred to make the land more attractive to a developer. The tribunal allowed the appeal, holding that the company's business should be regarded as including property development as well as road transport and haulage. *Philip Drakard Trading Ltd, LON/89/1473X (VTD 5030)*. (*Note*. For another issue in this case, taken to the QB, see 58.89 SUPPLY.)

34.405   **Landscaping work at company's premises—whether input tax deductible.** A company carried on the business of providing architectural services. In 1987 it acquired new premises, which included a courtyard which was 'no more than a mud patch'. It incurred expenditure on landscaping the courtyard, erecting banking and installing steps and brickwork, and reclaimed input tax on this work. The Commissioners issued an assessment to recover the tax, considering that the work had been undertaken with a view to improving the property's resale value, rather than for the purpose of the company's business. The company appealed, contending that the work was needed because staff had to cross the courtyard, and because they had wanted to make the courtyard 'an attractive feature of the property which would impress clients'. The tribunal allowed the company's appeal, holding that the expenditure had been incurred for business purposes. *Thorpe Architecture Ltd, LON/91/391 (VTD 6955)*.

34.406   **Golf club—improvements to clubhouse—whether carried out for purpose of club's business or to benefit landlord.** A golf club leased its clubhouse from a limited company, most of the shares in which were held by members of the club. The club undertook extensive improvements to the clubhouse and reclaimed the input tax thereon. The Commissioners issued an assessment to recover the tax, considering that the work had been carried out to benefit the company which owned the premises, rather than for the purposes of the club's business. The tribunal allowed the club's appeal, finding that the club's 'sole intention in carrying out the improvements was to improve the facilities for members and the appellants' business'. *Scott*, 34.429 below, distinguished. *Burntisland Golf Club, EDN/91/10 (VTD 6340)*.

34.407   **Expenditure on demolition of company's previous premises.**   A small engineering company, controlled by a married couple, moved to new premises. Its directors decided that they would have to sell the company's previous premises (the freehold of which was owned by the directors rather than by the company) to raise funds. They considered that the sheds and outbuildings at its previous site reduced the resale value of the site, and the company incurred expenditure in demolishing them. It reclaimed input tax on this expenditure. The Commissioners issued an assessment to recover the tax, considering that the expenditure had not been incurred for the purposes of the company's business, but for the financial benefit of the directors. The tribunal allowed the company's appeal, finding that the company had paid for the expenditure in order to enable more money to be injected into the company, and holding that although the directors' loan account with the company would be increased by the amount injected, the expenditure had still been incurred for the purpose of the company's business. *AW Mills Engineering Ltd, LON/94/ 2757A (VTD 13196)*.

34.408   **Dogs—whether used for business purposes as guard dogs.**   A company carried on a computer graphics and printing business from the home of its controlling shareholder. It purchased two dogs, one of which subsequently gave birth to a litter of five puppies, three of which the director gave away and two of which he kept. The company reclaimed input tax on the upkeep of the dogs. The Commissioners issued an assessment to recover the tax, considering that the dogs were primarily kept as pets and that it would not have been necessary to keep more than one dog as a guard dog. The company appealed, contending that the dogs had been kept as guard dogs. The tribunal accepted the company's evidence and allowed the appeal, applying *Ian Flockton Developments Ltd*, 34.248 above. *Music View Ltd, LON/91/2191 (VTD 9122)*.

34.409   **Marketing consultant—expenditure on maintaining licence as helicopter pilot.**   A marketing consultant (K), who was a qualified helicopter pilot, had owned a helicopter which he had used for business travel. However, because of a decline in his turnover, he decided that he could not afford the cost of running the helicopter, and sold it in 1990. He retained his licence as a pilot, and reclaimed input tax on his licence fees in 1991 and 1992. The Commissioners issued an assessment to recover the tax, considering that since K no longer owned a helicopter, the cost of maintaining his licence had not been incurred for the purpose of his consultancy business. K appealed, contending that he hoped that his turnover would increase and that he would again be able to afford a helicopter for business travel. If he had not maintained his licence, he would have had to incur substantial retraining costs before he could be granted a new one. The tribunal accepted K's evidence and allowed his appeal, holding that it was satisfied that at the time the expenditure was incurred, K had decided to retain his licence in the belief that he would require it for the purpose of his business. *CJ Kent (t/a Market Integration), LON/94/2886A (VTD 13214)*.

Cases where the appellant was partly successful

34.410   **Burglar alarm.**   An appeal was allowed in part in a case where the appellant, who carried on business from his home, had reclaimed input tax on the installation of a burglar alarm after he had been burgled on two occasions. The tribunal held that 50% of the tax in question was allowable. *A Kitson, MAN/85/239 (VTD 2030).* (*Note.* The nature of the appellant's business is not stated in the decision.)

34.411   **Heating equipment.**   A business consultant, who worked from home, reclaimed input tax on the purchase of Aga heating equipment. The Commissioners considered that only 22% of the tax was deductible, since the house comprised nine rooms and only two of these were used for business purposes. The tribunal allowed the appeal in part, finding that the heater was kept on for 24 hours per day and that the appellant worked for up to 55 hours per week, and holding that 30% of the tax should be treated as deductible. The tribunal observed that 'to base the apportionment entirely upon the number of rooms in use for business purposes, without regard to the actual use of the heating system, is unrealistic'. *MF Phipps, [1996] VATDR 241 (VTD 13839).*

34.412   **Club subscriptions.**   Two solicitors in partnership in Belfast reclaimed input tax on subscriptions to the Ulster Reform Club. The Commissioners issued an assessment to recover the tax, considering that the expenditure had been incurred for private purposes rather than for professional purposes. The solicitors appealed. The tribunal allowed the appeal in part, holding that the tax should be apportioned. *KEG Morrow & AE Wells, BEL/86/4 (VTD 2424).*

34.413   **Swimming pool constructed in grounds of solicitors' practice.**   The principal partner in a firm of solicitors owned a large house in Norfolk, eight miles outside Norwich, in 6.5 acres of grounds. A building in the grounds, which had originally been a coach house, was used as the firm's offices. The firm paid no rent to the partner for its occupation of the building. The firm reclaimed input tax on the construction of a swimming pool in the grounds of the partner's house. The Commissioners issued a ruling that the tax was not reclaimable, considering that the expenditure had been incurred for the personal pleasure of the partner and his family. The firm appealed, contending that the pool had been built for the benefit of its staff, since it had experienced difficulty in recruiting staff and had decided that 'in an attempt to make the work conditions more congenial, some recreation facilities should be provided to compensate for the isolation and lack of amenities in the immediate surrounding area'. The pool was used by employees with 'very little restriction', and changing rooms had been provided for their use. The tribunal allowed the appeal in part, holding that the partner's main purpose in deciding to build the pool was to provide a valuable benefit for the firm's employees, but that since the pool was also used by the partner and his family, and was built on land owned by them, the tax should be apportioned. The tribunal ruled that 35% of the tax in question was allowable. *Willcox & Co, [1992] VATTR 472 (VTD 8813).* (*Note.* See now, however, *VATA 1994, s 84(4),* originating from *FA 1993, s 46.*)

34.414   **Swimming pool constructed by farmer.**   See *Nielsen,* 34.455 below.

34.415   **Video cassette recorder.**   A company carried on a design consultancy business from the home of its principal director. It reclaimed input tax on the purchase of a video cassette recorder. The Commissioners issued an assessment to recover the tax, and the company appealed. Prior to the hearing, the company had failed to give the Commissioners any details of the way in which the recorder was used for business purposes, but at the tribunal hearing the director gave evidence that it was used to record technical programmes while he was away from home, and that it was not normally used privately, since he already owned a VCR which was attached to a different set which he and his family used for private viewing. The tribunal held on the evidence that 50% of the tax was deductible. *Remlock Design Ltd, LON/92/1124Y (VTD 9146).* (*Notes.* (1) For another issue in this case, see 34.458 below. (2) For the award of costs, see 2.283 APPEALS. (3) Compare *Cobb's Croft Service Station*

Ltd, 34.456 below, and *Smith*, 34.457 below, in which input tax on video cassette recorders was held not to be deductible.)

34.416   **Motor cruiser principally used for chartering but with element of private use—whether input tax to be apportioned.**   A trader purchased a motor cruiser which he let on charter during the summer. He reclaimed the whole of the input tax on the purchase. The Commissioners issued an assessment to recover 5% of the tax, on the basis that the trader sometimes used the cruiser privately. The tribunal upheld the assessment, finding that one of the reasons why the trader had purchased the cruiser 'was so that he could get some personal enjoyment and use of it', and holding that 5% could not 'be regarded as an excessive disallowance'. *HA Lovejoy (t/a HRS Recoveries), LON/93/2754 (VTD 12835)*. (*Note*. For another issue in this case, see 39.17 LAND.)

34.417   **Rolex watches.**   Two brothers carried on business in partnership as plumbing and heating engineers. They purchased two Rolex watches at a cost of £1,350 each, and reclaimed input tax on the purchase. The Commissioners issued an assessment to recover the tax, and the partners appealed, contending that the watches had been purchased for their reliability, durability and ability to withstand heat, vibration and humidity. The tribunal allowed the appeal in part, holding that some of the input tax should be allowed since the partners needed watches to measure gas flows, but that the partners had not shown that 'these extravagant watches were to be solely used for the purposes of the business' and it appeared that they had largely been purchased 'for their investment purposes and/or as status symbols'. The tribunal held that only 25% of the input tax was deductible. *Trigg's Plumbing & Heating, LON/95/2614 (VTD 14142)*.

34.418   **Input tax reclaimed by charities—apportionment of input tax.**   See the cases noted at 11.29 *et seq.* CHARITIES.

Cases where the appellant was unsuccessful

34.419   **Family farming partnership—tuition of partner as pilot.**   A farming partnership comprised a married couple and their two sons. The partnership paid for one of the sons to have flying lessons, and reclaimed input tax on the fees, although they did not own an aircraft. The Commissioners issued an assessment to recover the tax and the partnership appealed, contending that they had incurred the expenditure because they considered that at some time in the future they might need an aircraft for crop-spraying and for business travel. The tribunal dismissed the appeal, holding that the expenditure had not been incurred for the purposes of the farming business. *GWM Warner & Others, LON/82/324 (VTD 1402)*.

34.420   **Estate agent's charges on sale of property.**   A married couple took over the tenancy of a public house. To finance improvements, they sold their existing house and bought a smaller one. They reclaimed input tax in respect of the estate agent's charges. The Commissioners issued an assessment to recover the tax, and the couple appealed. The tribunal dismissed the appeal, holding that the agent's services had been supplied to the couple as owners of their house, rather than as publicans. *Mr & Mrs AF Dean, LON/83/137 (VTD 1455)*.

34.421   *Dean*, 34.420 above, was applied in the similar case of *DL Jones, LON/93/585A (VTD 11430)*. (*Note*. For another issue in this case, see 49.195 PENALTIES: MISDECLARATION.)

34.422   See also *Rushgreen Builders Ltd*, 34.74 above.

34.423   **Surveyor's fees.**   A local council proposed to make a compulsory purchase order in respect of a house owned by a market gardener. He considered that the council were undervaluing his house, and consulted a surveyor. He reclaimed input tax in respect of the surveyor's fees. The Commissioners issued an assessment to recover the tax, and the tribunal dismissed the appeal, holding that the expenditure had not been incurred for the purpose of the gardener's business. The QB upheld the tribunal decision. *NO Turner (t/a Turner Agricultural) v C & E Commrs, QB [1992] STC 621. (Note.* For another issue in this case, see 34.34 above.)

34.424 **Music recording company—whether supplies made for purposes of company's business.** A company carried on the business of manufacturing and selling records of popular music. It reclaimed input tax on the hire of two recording studios for the use of a specific group which was under contract to it. The Commissioners rejected the claim on the grounds that the studios in question had been hired for the purposes of the group's business, rather than for the company's business, and the company's role had been the provision of finance. The tribunal upheld the assessment and dismissed the company's appeal. *The Bacon Empire (Publishing) Ltd, LON/83/464 (VTD 1688).*

34.425 **Lunch.** A sole trader reclaimed input tax on the cost of lunch while he was working. The Commissioners issued an assessment to recover the tax and the tribunal dismissed the trader's appeal. *Dicta* of Lord Davey in *Strong & Co of Romsey Ltd v Woodifield, HL 1906, 5 TC 215 (TTC 2001, 61.80)* applied. *DG Mutch, MAN/87/109 (VTD 2559).*

34.426 **Engineering company—whether boat acquired for business purposes.** The managing director of an engineering company purchased a boat which had been damaged by fire and had it refurbished by the company. The company reclaimed input tax on this expenditure, and the Commissioners issued an assessment to recover the tax. The tribunal dismissed the company's appeal, holding that the company had not shown any connection between the expenditure in question and its business. *Diesel Generating (Tetbury) Ltd, LON/87/165 (VTD 2702).*

34.427 **Computer consultancy company—whether boat used for business purposes.** A company which carried on a computer consultancy business reclaimed input tax on the repair and maintenance of a boat. The Commissioners issued an assessment to recover the tax and the company appealed, contending that the boat was used as an office and as a venue for business meetings. The tribunal dismissed the appeal, finding that the boat was primarily used for private purposes and holding that the company had failed to produce sufficient evidence to justify the allowance of any of the input tax. *Parker Bond Ltd, MAN/94/504 (VTD 13160).*

34.428 **Farmer—purchase of shotguns.** A farmer purchased two Purdy shotguns at a cost of £34,000, and reclaimed input tax on their purchase. The Commissioners rejected the claim and the tribunal dismissed the farmer's appeal, holding on the evidence that the farmer had failed to prove that the guns had been acquired for the purposes of his business. *JD Leavesly, MAN/88/95 (VTD 2987).*

34.429 **Kitchen equipment—whether acquired for publican's business or for wife's catering business.** A publican reclaimed input tax in respect of the purchase of kitchen equipment. The catering at the public house was carried on by his wife, and was treated as a separate business for tax and VAT purposes. The turnover of the wife's catering business was below the VAT registration threshold. The Commissioners issued an assessment to recover the tax, considering that the kitchen equipment had been purchased for the wife's catering business rather than for the publican's own business, and that since the wife did not account for output tax on her sales of food, input tax could not be reclaimed on the equipment purchased for her use. The tribunal upheld the assessment and dismissed the publican's appeal. *MJ Scott, LON/88/1447Z (VTD 4257).*

34.430   **Cigarettes purchased by accountant—whether for business purposes.**   An accountant reclaimed input tax on the purchase of quantities of cigarettes. The Commissioners issued an assessment to recover the tax and he appealed, contending that he had purchased the cigarettes in order to give them to his employees and customers, for the purposes of maintaining the goodwill of his practice. The tribunal dismissed his appeal, holding on the evidence that the cigarettes had not been supplied for the purposes of his business. *AG Fine, MAN/89/304 (VTD 4977)*.

34.431   **Music centre.**   A company reclaimed input tax on the purchase of a music centre, which was installed in a house which the company owned and where its principal director lived. The Commissioners issued an assessment to recover the tax and the tribunal dismissed the company's appeal, holding that the music centre had not been purchased for the purpose of the company's business. *The Gourmet Sandwich Ltd, MAN/90/428 (VTD 5505)*.

34.432   **Building materials—whether purchased for purposes of company or director.**   A company was incorporated by a retired builder (R) to provide management services for an associated design company, and for any other associated companies with which he might subsequently become involved. R arranged for two builders to erect an extension at a client's residence. The management company purchased the materials to be used for the extension, and reclaimed the input tax thereon. R was paid an agency fee for arranging the transaction. The Commissioners rejected the company's claim, considering that the building materials had not been purchased for the purpose of the management company's business. The tribunal upheld this decision and dismissed the company's appeal. *S Robertson (Management) Ltd, LON/90/251Y (VTD 5597)*.

34.433   **Oil painting.**   A company carried on business as a retailer of confectionery and cigarettes. It reclaimed input tax on the purchase of an oil painting, which had cost £4,950 and which was kept at the home of its managing director. The Commissioners issued an assessment to recover the tax, considering that the expenditure had not been incurred for the purposes of the company's business. The company appealed, contending that it intended to display the painting in a new boardroom, which had not been completed at the time of the hearing, and that it had been purchased to impress visitors to the boardroom. The tribunal dismissed the appeal, finding that the painting had not been purchased for the purpose of the company's business. *Cough & Candy Ltd, MAN/90/724 (VTD 5952)*.

34.434   **Antique train sets.**   A company which carried on the business of supplying lighting equipment purchased four antique train sets, at a total cost of more than £16,000, and reclaimed input tax on the purchase. The Commissioners issued an assessment to recover the tax and the tribunal dismissed the company's appeal, finding that the train sets had not been purchased for the purpose of the company's business. *Leadstar Ltd, LON/91/1596 (VTD 7153)*.

34.435   **Furniture sold by tenant to landlord—whether landlord entitled to reclaim input tax.**   A married couple were registered for VAT as proprietors of a property management business. They owned the freehold of a hotel, which was let to a company of which they were shareholders and directors. The company suffered financial difficulties and the local authority threatened distraint proceedings for non-payment of rates. In September 1991 the company sold the couple the furniture of the hotel for £35,000 (expressed as being inclusive of VAT). The couple paid the company a cheque for £35,000, and the company then paid the couple a cheque for £29,900 in respect of arrears of rent. The couple reclaimed input tax in respect of the payment of £35,000. The Commissioners issued an assessment to recover the tax, on the basis that the transaction had not been carried out for the purpose of the couple's business. The tribunal dismissed the couple's appeal, noting that the company had not accounted for output tax on the purported sale and holding on the evidence that there had been no actual supply of the furniture. Furthermore, even if there had been a supply, the supply would not have been for the purpose of the couple's business, since 'the business of the appellants was the management of property and the leasing of services and it was not suggested to us how that purpose could be served by the acquisition of furniture in a hotel belonging to their tenants ... the purpose of the transaction was to safeguard the hotel business and sell it on as a going concern'. *Dr & Mrs P Frost, EDN/94/151 (VTD 13045).*

34.436 **Military vehicle—whether purchased for advertising purposes.** A company, which traded in surplus nuts and bolts, reclaimed input tax on the purchase of a military vehicle (a Vickers-Armstrong self-propelled gun). The Commissioners rejected the claim on the basis that the vehicle had not been purchased for the purposes of the company's business. The company appealed, contending that the vehicle had been purchased for advertising purposes. The tribunal reviewed the evidence and dismissed the appeal, observing that the company's controlling director had conducted a high-profile publicity campaign against his local council, and finding that he used the vehicle 'for the purposes of private campaigns' and had not purchased it with the aim of promoting the company's business. *Dicta* of Stuart-Smith J in *Ian Flockton Developments Ltd*, 34.248 above, applied. *Worldwide Surplus Supplies Ltd, LON/98/833 (VTD 16198).*

34.437 **Jacuzzi purchased by actor.** An actor reclaimed input tax on the purchase of a jacuzzi. The Commissioners issued an assessment to recover the tax, considering that it had not been purchased for the purposes of his profession. He appealed, contending that he had suffered from back trouble and had purchased the jacuzzi in the hope that it would help him to return to work more quickly. The tribunal dismissed the appeal, holding that 'in seeking to return to health and fitness his object must ... have been that of any normal person. The measures he took to return to health and fitness were no different to those which other private individuals take'. *Anholt*, 34.402 above, distinguished. *J Pearce, LON/91/1638Y (VTD 7860).* (*Note.* For another issue in this case, see 34.109 above.)

34.438 **Computer equipment purchased by accountant.** An accountant was also a shareholder and director of a company which sold computer systems. In 1990 the accountant purchased some items of computer equipment for the company, and reclaimed input tax on these items. The company went into liquidation in February 1991. When the Commissioners discovered what had happened, they issued an assessment to recover the input tax. The tribunal dismissed the accountant's appeal, holding that he had not purchased the equipment for the purpose of his accountancy practice. *L Ramm (t/a Ramm Louis & Co), LON/92/2465A (VTD 11242).*

34.439 **Religious cassettes.** A company which operated a travel agency reclaimed input tax on the purchase of some audiocassettes, which propagated the 'Sai Madhura' religious teachings of Sai-Christ of Canada, Incorporated. The Commissioners issued an assessment to recover the tax. The tribunal dismissed the company's appeal, holding that the cassettes had not been purchased for the purpose of the company's business. *Jet Across Ltd, MAN/94/18 (VTD 12541, 13526).*

34.440 **Refurbishment of houses occupied by Cathedral Dean and Canons.** The Dean and Chapter of Bristol Cathedral were registered for VAT since they operated a shop and refectory at the Cathedral. They reclaimed input tax on the refurbishment of the houses occupied by the Dean and the three Canons. The Commissioners only agreed to allow 25% of the tax in question. The tribunal upheld the Commissioners' ruling and dismissed the Dean's appeal. *Dean & Chapter of Bristol Cathedral,*

LON/96/126 (VTD 14591). (*Note*. For a case concerning similar expenditure on houses occupied by Cathedral vergers, see *Dean & Chapter of Hereford Cathedral*, 34.230 above.)

34.441   **Retail partnership—payment to secure appointment of partner as sub-postmaster—whether for purpose of retail business.**   In the case noted at 7.95 BUSINESS, a member of a retail partnership applied to run a sub-post office. He was required to pay Post Office Counters Ltd £88,560, including VAT of £13,189. The partnership reclaimed input tax on this payment. The Commissioners rejected the claim and the tribunal dismissed the partnership's appeal, holding that, although the partner had applied to run the sub-post office in order to expand the partnership retail business, the expenditure could not be apportioned and none of the input tax was deductible. *H & V Patel (No 2), LON/94/2821 (VTD 15328)*.

34.442   The decision in *Patel*, 34.441 above, was applied in the similar subsequent case of *JH & H Pugh, LON/95/654 (VTD 16034)*.

34.443   **Input tax reclaimed by import agent—whether goods imported for purpose of agent's business.**   See *Cavenco Ltd*, 33.14 IMPORTS.

WHETHER SUPPLIES INTENDED FOR USE IN FUTURE BUSINESS

Cases where the appellant was successful

34.444   **Cable television company—pre-trading expenditure.**   In 1982 a company (M) was incorporated to carry on the business of supplying cable television in the Merseyside area. It incurred considerable preliminary expenditure, and applied to be registered for VAT to enable it to reclaim input tax on this. Initially the Commissioners refused to register the company on the grounds that it was not trading. Subsequently M supplied consultancy services to another associated company, and renewed its application for registration. It was registered in December 1983, the registration being backdated to May 1982 at its request. In January 1984 it submitted its first VAT return, covering the period from May 1982 to 31 December 1983, and reclaiming more than £33,000 as input tax. In August 1985 the Commissioners formally rejected the claim, ruling that M was not entitled to be registered under the legislation then in force (*VATA 1983, Sch 1*) and that the registration should be treated as void since M was not making taxable supplies. The tribunal allowed M's appeal against this decision. Applying *Amministrazione delle Finanze dello Stato v Simmenthal SpA*, 21.18 EUROPEAN COMMUNITY LAW, 'the law of the European Economic Community ... prevails over any contrary provision in national law'. Under *Article 4* of the *EC Sixth Directive*, any person carrying on an economic activity was a 'taxable person'. If goods or services were supplied to him by another taxable person, and he used those goods or services for the purposes of his taxable transactions, he was entitled to deduct the tax he had suffered on the supplies made to him from the tax for which he was accountable on the supplies made by him. Applying *Rompelman & Another v Minister van Financien*, 21.59 EUROPEAN COMMUNITY LAW, a person who carried on activities which were preparatory to the carrying on of an economic activity was to be treated as a person carrying on that economic activity. M had had a fixed and continuing intention to operate a cable television service, which qualified it as a 'taxable person' within *Article 4(1)* of the *EC Sixth Directive*. The fact that, under the UK legislation then in force, M was not entitled to be registered for VAT, did not alter the fact that, under Community law, it was a taxable person and was entitled to credit for the input tax it had suffered. *Merseyside Cablevision Ltd, [1987] VATTR 134 (VTD 2419)*. (*Notes*. (1) The relevant provisions of *VATA 1983, Sch 1* were subsequently amended by *FA 1988*.

(2) For a case in which this decision was distinguished, see *Park Commercial Developments plc*, 26.25 FINANCE.)

34.445   **Property development.** A partnership was formed to develop an estate. It acquired the freehold of the land, obtained planning permission, widened roads, and installed drainage, gas and electricity. It reclaimed input tax on the professional expenses incurred. Subsequently it sold 75% of the land on the estate to a company carrying on the business of property development. The Commissioners issued an assessment to recover the input tax which the company had previously reclaimed, considering that, in view of the sale of the land, the expenditure could not be attributed to any taxable supplies. The company appealed, contending that the input tax was correctly reclaimable since its activities had been undertaken with the intention of making taxable supplies, and that the sale of the land constituted the transfer of a part of the business as a going concern. The tribunal accepted the partnership's evidence and allowed the appeal. The fact that, at the time of the sale, the partnership had not made any supplies in respect of the land was not conclusive. *The Golden Oak Partnership, LON/90/958Z (VTD 7212)*. (*Note*. For a subsequent case in which this decision was distinguished, see *Gulf Trading & Management Ltd*, 43.121 PARTIAL EXEMPTION.)

34.446   **Landowner.**   In 1988 a landowner (H) applied for registration as an 'intending trader', and informed the Commissioners that he intended to begin selling timber in 1990. The Commissioners accepted the application, and allowed him to make provisional claims for repayment of input tax. However, such repayment claims were expressed to be 'subject to the condition, provided for by (*VATA 1994, s 25(6)**), that the Commissioners may require you, on request, to refund all or any of the input tax claimed, if you do not make taxable supplies by way of business, or if in respect of input tax claimed prior to a period in which taxable supplies in the course of business are made, that input tax is not commensurate with the related output tax'. H reclaimed input tax of £2,290. However, in March 1990 he sold the land, and in September 1990 the Commissioners issued an assessment to recover the input tax which H had reclaimed. H appealed, contending that the conditions attached to his original registration were invalid. The tribunal allowed the appeal, holding that the conditions were 'discriminatory and unenforceable'. Applying *Rompelman & Another v Minister van Financien*, 21.59 EUROPEAN COMMUNITY LAW, acts which were preparatory to commercial exploitation were 'to be considered as an economic activity'. The expenditure incurred by H had been incurred for the purpose of an economic activity notwithstanding that H had never made any taxable supplies. The sale of the land had constituted the transfer of a business as a going concern, so that the purchaser of the land would have to account for output tax in due course. *ACS Hordern, [1992] VATTR 382 (VTD 8941)*. (*Note*. Compare the subsequent decision in *Wilson*, 34.466 below, in which the tribunal held that conditions imposed under *VATA 1994, s 25(6)** were valid. For a case in which the sale of land was held not to constitute the transfer of a going concern, see *Gulf Trading & Management Ltd*, 43.121 PARTIAL EXEMPTION.)

34.447   See also *Belgium v Ghent Coal Terminal NV*, 21.199 EUROPEAN COMMUNITY LAW.

34.448   **Restoration of patrol boats for exhibition and hire.**   A consultant reclaimed input tax on the costs of restoring several old naval patrol boats, which he had purchased with a view to exhibiting and hiring them out. The Commissioners rejected the claim but the tribunal allowed his appeal, holding on the evidence that he had purchased the craft for the purpose of a future business and that the input tax was deductible. *Rompelman & Another v Minister van Financien*, 21.59 EUROPEAN COMMUNITY LAW, applied. *WG Haydon-Baillie, [1986] VATTR 79 (VTD 2072)*.

34.449 **Motorboat purchased by married couple for restoration and resale—whether input tax deductible.**   A married couple traded in partnership as dealers in cars and mobile homes. In 1990 they purchased an expensive motorboat and reclaimed the input tax on the purchase. The Commissioners issued an assessment to recover the tax, considering that the motorboat had been purchased for private pleasure, rather than for business purposes. The couple appealed, contending that they had intended to restore the motorboat and sell it at a profit. They had advertised it for sale in yachting magazines, but had not received an acceptable offer. The tribunal allowed the appeal, holding on the evidence that the couple had purchased the boat for the purpose of an intended business of dealing in boats. *SB & JM Cavner, LON/91/1212 (VTD 7714)*. (*Note*. See now, however, *VATA 1994, s 84(4)*, deriving from *FA 1993, s 46*.)

34.450 **Yacht—whether purchased for future chartering business.**   A company registered for VAT with effect from 1 August 1990. In its first return it reclaimed input tax on the purchase of a yacht. In October 1993 the Commissioners issued an assessment to recover the tax, on the basis that the yacht was not being used for business purposes. The company appealed, contending that it had purchased the yacht for the purpose of chartering it to an associated engineering company, for the purpose of entertaining customers. However, the engineering company had subsequently been hit by financial difficulties, and had not made use of the yacht until May 1994. The tribunal accepted the company's evidence and allowed the appeal, finding that it was satisfied that it remained the company's purpose to use the yacht for future chartering. The chairman observed that 'although to a suspicious mind the dates of the invoice and the charter were ominously close to the date of the hearing, I am satisfied that the purpose of the charter, both from the appellant's and the engineering company's points of view, were genuine'. *Furness Vale Yacht Hire Ltd, MAN/94/16 (VTD 12628)*. (*Note*. Compare the subsequent decision in *Warwest Holdings Ltd*, 34.471 below, in which this case was distinguished.)

34.451 **Vintage cars—whether purchased for future business.**   A computer software company reclaimed input tax on the restoration of four vintage cars. The Commissioners issued an assessment to recover the tax, considering that the cars had not been purchased for business purposes, and the company appealed. The tribunal allowed the appeal, holding that the cars had been purchased as an investment, for the purpose of being sold at a profit, so that the input tax was deductible. *LHA Ltd, LON/93/924A (VTD 11911)*. (*Note*. For another issue in this case, see 34.154 above.)

34.452 A similar decision was reached in a subsequent case where a company had purchased three vintage cars and had reclaimed the input tax thereon. The tribunal accepted the company's evidence and held that the input tax was deductible. *Rompelman & Another v Minister van Financien*, 21.59 EUROPEAN COMMUNITY LAW, and *LHA Ltd*, 34.451 above, applied. *Tarrakarn Ltd, [1996] VATDR 516 (VTD 14279)*.

34.453 **Restoration of vintage car—whether for purposes of future tourism business.**   An individual (H) registered for VAT as an 'intending trader' in 1989. In 1990 and 1991 he reclaimed input tax on the restoration of a vintage Jaguar car. Following a control visit in 1995 the Commissioners became aware that H had never accounted for output tax and appeared never to have made any taxable supplies. They therefore issued an assessment to recover the input tax which H had reclaimed on the repairs to the car. H appealed, contending that he had arranged for the repairs with the intention of using the car for chauffeuring foreign tourists on conducted tours of historic sites in Devon and Cornwall, but that he had not yet completed the necessary accommodation although he hoped to do so in 1997. The tribunal accepted H's evidence and allowed his appeal. On the evidence, the tribunal was satisfied that, at the time the expenditure was incurred, H intended to use the car for business purposes. *Dicta* of Stuart-Smith J in *Ian Flockton Developments Ltd*, 34.248 above, applied. The tribunal held that 'the time at which the relevant intention of the taxpayer is to be ascertained was the time at which the relevant expenditure was incurred'. *JH Halsey, [1996] VATDR 508 (VTD 14313)*.

34.454   **Surveyor—arbitration proceedings to resolve dispute with former partners—whether expenditure incurred for subsequent consultancy business.**   Disputes arose between the partners in a firm of surveyors. One of the partners (H) issued a writ seeking the dissolution of the partnership. The other partners responded by issuing a notice expelling him from the partnership. The matter was referred to arbitration. The arbitrator upheld the expulsion notice, but H was allowed to retain certain clients (which, under the partnership deed, he would not have been permitted to do). H subsequently registered for VAT as a consultant. In his first return he reclaimed input tax relating to the arbitration proceedings. The Commissioners issued an assessment to recover the tax but the tribunal allowed H's appeal, holding on the evidence that there was a clear nexus between the arbitration proceedings and H's subsequent consultancy business. The chairman observed that, as a direct result of pursuing the arbitration proceedings, H had been able to continue working with clients whom he might otherwise have lost. *McCallum*, 34.116 above, distinguished. *P Hartridge (t/a Hartridge Consultancy), MAN/97/1158 (VTD 15553)*.

Cases where the appellant was partly successful

34.455   **Swimming pool constructed by farmer.**   In 1989 a farmer built a swimming pool in the grounds of his house. He reclaimed the input tax on this work. The Commissioners issued an assessment to recover the tax, considering that it had been incurred for private purposes, and as an investment to improve the value of his property, rather than for business purposes. The farmer appealed, contending that the swimming pool had been built for the purpose of a future business activity, and that in 1992 he had begun to open it to paying guests on six days each week, having been unable to do so earlier because of difficulties with planning permission and with dehumidification. The tribunal allowed the appeal in part, finding on the evidence that the work had been undertaken for a dual purpose but that the predominant purpose was for the purpose of a future business activity, and holding that 75% of the tax was deductible. *J Nielsen, LON/92/2874A (VTD 11852)*.

Cases where the appellant was unsuccessful

34.456   **Video recorder—whether purchased for future business.**   A company which operated a service station reclaimed input tax on a video recorder. The Commissioners issued an assessment to recover the tax and the company appealed, contending that the video recorder had been purchased for use in future business activities. The tribunal dismissed the appeal, holding on the evidence that the company had not shown that the recorder was to be used for business purposes. *Cobb's Croft Service Station Ltd, [1976] VATTR 170 (VTD 269)*.

34.457   A similar decision was reached in a case where an electrical engineer purchased a video recorder and reclaimed the input tax, contending that he was considering setting up a new business as a wedding photographer. *DA Smith, MAN/84/40 (VTD 1830)*.

34.458   **Yamaha keyboard—whether purchased for future business.**   A company which carried on a design consultancy business from the home of its principal director reclaimed input tax on the purchase of a Yamaha keyboard. The

Commissioners issued an assessment to recover the tax and the company appealed, contending that the keyboard had been purchased so that the controlling director's son could 'write musical software for a computer ... with a view to developing this as a business proposition'. The tribunal dismissed the appeal, holding on the evidence that the keyboard had not been purchased for the purposes of any future business activity. *Remlock Design Ltd, LON/92/1124Y (VTD 9146)*. (*Notes*. (1) For another issue in this case, see 34.415 above. (2) For the award of costs, see 2.283 APPEALS.)

34.459   **Horses purchased by engineering company—whether for future business of riding instruction.**   A company was incorporated in 1976 to carry on an engineering business. In 1977 and 1978 it purchased two horses. From 1979 the company's income from engineering declined substantially. In 1980 the company's Memorandum of Association was amended to include references to horse breeding, training and riding instruction. In 1981 the company rented some land on which it built stables, and in December 1982 the daughter of the couple who controlled the company qualified as an intermediate riding instructor. The company reclaimed income tax on its equine activities. The Commissioners issued an assessment to recover the tax in question (covering the period from December 1976 to August 1981), considering that the expenditure had not been incurred for business purposes, but for the personal enjoyment of the directors and their daughter. The company appealed, contending that it had purchased the horses with the intention of beginning a business of horse breeding and riding instruction. The tribunal dismissed the appeal, holding on the evidence that the company had not carried on any such business until December 1982. During the period covered by the assessment, the company's equine activities had not involved the making of taxable supplies. The tribunal held that 'in commencing a new business, there may be a period of gestation prior to the making of taxable supplies' but 'it must be contemplated that taxable supplies be made (*sic*) in the reasonably foreseeable future, in the course of or furtherance of the business'. Accordingly the input tax was not deductible. *Evans*, 7.34 BUSINESS, distinguished. *K & K Thorogood Ltd, LON/82/318 (VTD 1595)*.

34.460   **Refurbishment of stables—whether for purpose of future livery business.**   An individual, who had been registered as a shopkeeper but had subsequently sold his shop, reclaimed input tax on the refurbishment of some stables which he had purchased. The Commissioners issued an assessment to recover the tax, considering that he was not carrying on a business. He appealed, contending that he had purchased the stables with a view to setting up a livery stable to be run as a business. The tribunal dismissed his appeal, holding that he had not purchased the stables for the purposes of any future business, but to further his own interest in horses. *R McLintock, EDN/85/94 (VTD 2102)*.

34.461   **Construction company—expenditure on farm.**   A construction company reclaimed input tax on expenditure on a farm which its managing director had purchased. The Commissioners issued an assessment to recover the tax and the company appealed, contending that the farm had been purchased with a view to diversification of its business. The tribunal dismissed the appeal. *F Jones & Sons (Cheltenham) Ltd, LON/88/1078Y (VTD 4511)*.

34.462   **Farming company—renovation of house—whether intended for future business.**   A company which carried on a farming business incurred substantial expenditure on renovating a large house on its land, which it had not previously used for business purposes, and reclaimed input tax on the work. It subsequently sold the house, and the Commissioners issued an assessment to recover the input tax, on the basis that the sale of the renovated house was exempt from VAT. The company appealed, contending that it had incurred the expenditure with the intention of using the house for a future business of making supplies of accommodation to people interested in shooting or fishing, but, because of financial difficulties attributed to economic recession and an increase in interest rates, it had subsequently changed its intention and had sold the house instead. The tribunal dismissed the appeal, holding on the evidence that the company had failed to establish that it had incurred the expenditure in question for the purpose of making taxable supplies. *Stockton Park (Leisure) Ltd, LON/95/1658A (VTD 14548)*. (*Note.* The tribunal also rejected an alternative contention by the company that the work on the farmhouse should be treated as zero-rated construction. The tribunal held that the work amounted to the reconstruction of an existing building rather than the construction of a new building.)

34.463 **Building contractors—whether yacht purchased for future shipbuilding business.** A company which had carried on business as a building contractor reclaimed input tax on the refitting of a 21–foot yacht, which was owned by one of its directors. The Commissioners issued an assessment to recover the tax, considering that the expenditure had not been incurred for business purposes. The company appealed, contending that it intended to carry on the business of shipbuilding and repairing. The tribunal dismissed the appeal, finding that the yacht had been refitted for the benefit and private purposes of the controlling director, and that there was no evidence that the company intended to carry on a business of shipbuilding. *Penjen Ltd, LON/89/1167X (VTD 5882)*.

34.464 **Purchase of helicopter—whether for future business.** A property developer, who was registered for VAT, reclaimed input tax on the purchase of a helicopter. The Commissioners issued an assessment to recover the tax and he appealed, contending that he had intended to use the helicopter for a prospective business of setting up a helicopter flying school, and that when this proved impractical he had begun leasing the helicopter. The tribunal dismissed his appeal, holding that no ordinary businessman would have purchased a helicopter in such circumstances. *Three H Aircraft Hire*, 7.6 BUSINESS, applied; *Rompelman*, 21.59 EUROPEAN COMMUNITY LAW, distinguished. *RB Payne, LON/90/1576X (VTD 9211)*. (*Note.* For another issue in this case, see 7.70 BUSINESS.)

34.465 **Tuition as helicopter pilot—whether for future business.** The proprietor of a road haulage business reclaimed input tax on the cost of lessons in flying a helicopter. The Commissioners issued an assessment to recover the tax, and the proprietor appealed, contending that he had incurred the expenditure in the hope of starting a new business of helicopter transport. The tribunal reviewed the evidence and dismissed the appeal, holding that it was satisfied that the proprietor wished to become a commercial helicopter pilot, but observing that 'he will find it difficult to put in the necessary hours' and that 'even if he does put in the hours and he does get qualified, it is not immediately clear what business he is likely to run'. *J English, MAN/98/7 (VTD 15879)*.

34.466 **Input tax reclaimed by 'intending trader'—no taxable supplies made.** In October 1989 an individual (W) applied to be registered for VAT as a freelance pilot. The Commissioners accepted his application 'subject to the condition, provided for by (*VATA 1994, s 25(6)**), that the Commissioners may require you, on request, to refund all or any of the input tax claimed, if you do not make taxable supplies by way of business'. In fact W never made any taxable supplies, and in November 1990 he applied to be deregistered. The Commissioners issued an assessment to recover the input tax which he had reclaimed while he had been registered. The tribunal dismissed W's appeal, holding that the Commissioners were entitled 'to require in their discretion a refund of all or any of the input tax claimed, on the ground that the appellant had not made taxable supplies by way of business'. *K Wilson, EDN/92/341 (VTD 12042)*.

34.467   **Development company—input tax relating to raising of share capital.**   See *Park Commercial Developments plc*, 26.25 FINANCE.

34.468   **Development company—expenditure on property let on short-term leases.**   See the cases at 43.10 to 43.13 PARTIAL EXEMPTION.

34.469   **Motorboat—whether purchased for future chartering business.**   A builder reclaimed input tax on the purchase of a motorboat. The Commissioners issued an assessment to recover the tax and he appealed, contending that he had purchased the boat with the intention of setting up a future chartering business. The tribunal dismissed the appeal, finding that the builder had failed to produce sufficient evidence in support of his claim. *LD Castle (t/a Langford Building Supplies)*, *LON/94/604A (VTD 12813)*.

34.470   **Financial consultant—whether yacht purchased for future chartering business.**   In 1990 a financial consultant (M), who was employed as the chief executive of a large company, ordered a luxury yacht at a cost of £200,000. The yacht was delivered in 1991. In February 1992 M left the company which had employed him and became self-employed as a financial consultant. He registered for VAT from September 1992. In 1993 he reclaimed input tax in respect of the running costs of the yacht. The Commissioners rejected the claim on the grounds that the yacht had been purchased for private purposes rather than for business purposes. He appealed, contending that since the delivery of the yacht, he had intended to use it for chartering. He had received income from chartering totalling £1,800 up to the end of 1994, and of £5,000 in 1995. (The running costs of the yacht amounted to some £1,500 per year.) He also submitted a belated claim for input tax on the purchase of the yacht, contending that it should be treated as deductible by virtue of the principles laid down in *Lennartz v Finanzamt München III*, 21.216 EUROPEAN COMMUNITY LAW. The tribunal rejected this contention and dismissed M's appeal. On the evidence, at the time when M had decided to purchase the yacht, he had done so with the intention of using it for his own enjoyment. His subsequent decision that he would have to charter the yacht 'was not part of the purpose of the expenditure; it was an exercise in damage limitation'. The tribunal chairman also observed that, although M had received income of £6,800 from chartering by the time of the hearing, 'no business yet exists'. *KJ Milner, LON/95/1949 (VTD 13648)*.

34.471   **Property company—whether yacht purchased for future chartering business.**   In 1992 a property company purchased a yacht from an associated company at a cost of £117,500, and reclaimed input tax on the purchase. The Commissioners issued an assessment to recover the tax, on the basis that the yacht had not been purchased for business purposes. The company appealed, contending that the yacht had been purchased with the intention of being used for chartering, although this had not materialised and the yacht had eventually been sold at a loss in 1995. The tribunal reviewed the evidence in detail and dismissed the appeal, observing that there was 'no obvious and clear association between the taxpayer company's business and the expenditure concerned' and holding that the company had failed to prove that the expenditure had been incurred for business purposes. *Dicta* in *Rosner*, 34.145 above, applied; *Furness Vale Yacht Hire Ltd*, 34.450 above, distinguished. *Warmest Holdings Ltd, LON/93/2972 (VTD 14114)*.

PRE-REGISTRATION INPUT TAX

34.472   **Input tax reclaimed on purchases of stock.**   An ice-cream salesman, who had traded for some time before registering for VAT, reclaimed input tax on supplies made to him before registration. The Commissioners rejected his claim and the tribunal dismissed his appeal. There was no evidence that the supplies in question were still in his possession when he registered, and it was reasonable to assume that most of the stock would have been sold to customers. He had not been asked to account for output tax on supplies before registration and he could not reclaim input tax on purchases before registration. *M Allard, [1984] VATTR 157 (VTD 1566)*.

34.473   **Shopfitting—whether supplies of goods or services.**   A company which owned a number of retail opticians' shops registered for VAT from 1 September 1988. This followed the enactment of *FA 1988, s 13*, as a result of which the company's supplies, which had previously been exempt, became standard-rated. The company reclaimed input tax on expenditure which it had incurred before registering for VAT on refurbishing and fitting out several shops. The Commissioners issued an assessment to recover the tax relating to expenditure incurred more than six months before the date of registration, considering that the supplies were supplies of services and that the tax thereon was not recoverable as the company had only made exempt supplies at the relevant time. The company appealed, contending that the supplies were compound supplies, consisting of the supply of goods and the supply of services for fitting those goods, and that the input tax attributable to the goods themselves was deductible in accordance with the practice laid down in *VAT Notes No 2 1989/90* (see the *Note* at the end of this summary). The QB accepted this contention, holding that the services of fitting out the shops were multiple supplies rather than single supplies, so that part of the input tax related to supplies of goods and was deductible. *Bophutatswana National Commercial Corporation*, 37.2 INTERNATIONAL SERVICES, and the CA decision in *Card Protection Plan Ltd*, 21.162 EUROPEAN COMMUNITY LAW, applied. *Rayner & Keeler Ltd v C & E Commrs, QB [1994] STC 724*. (*Note*. The supplies in question took place before 1 March 1988, at a time when all supplies by opticians were exempt. The supply of goods by opticians became taxable after 31 August 1988 following the amendment of *VATA 1983, Sch 6, Group 7* by *FA 1988, s 13*. The Commissioners had agreed to allow opticians to reclaim input tax on goods held at 1 September 1988. However, the Commissioners only agreed to allow input tax to be deducted in respect of supplies of services where the services were supplied within the six months prior to 1 September 1988, this being the date on which the opticians were required to register for VAT.)

34.474   *Rayner & Keeler Ltd*, 34.473 above, was distinguished in a subsequent case in which the proprietors of a small shop which sold greeting cards reclaimed input tax in respect of shop fittings carried out more than six months before they registered for VAT. The Commissioners rejected the claim on the basis that the relevant supplies were supplies of services, so that the effect of what is now *VAT Regulations 1995, reg 111(2)* was that the input tax was not deductible. The tribunal dismissed the proprietors' appeal, holding that the supplies amounted to 'an elaborate decoration of a room' and had to be treated as supplies of services. *MEJ Burgess & AP Holmes (t/a Cards'N Cuddles), LON/96/292 (VTD 14475)*.

34.475   **Covering of mares—whether supplies of goods or services.**   A horse-breeding company registered for VAT in 1992. In its first return, it reclaimed input tax on fees which it had paid to the owners of stallions which had covered its mares between 1987 and 1991. The Commissioners rejected the claim, on the grounds that the tax related to pre-registration supplies of services. The company appealed, contending that it related to supplies of semen which should be treated as supplies of goods. The tribunal rejected this contention and dismissed the company's appeal. *Bristol Bloodstock Ltd, LON/93/436A (VTD 11955)*.

34.476   **Research and development study—whether supplies of goods or services.**   A company registered for VAT in July 1991. It reclaimed input tax in respect of supplies which it had received more than six months before its date of registration. The supplies in question related to a research and development study concerning the development of two pieces of electronic equipment. The Commissioners rejected the claim, on the basis that the supplies were supplies of services so that the tax was not deductible by virtue of what is now *VAT Regulations 1995, reg 111(2)(c)*. The company appealed, contending that the supplies were directed to the production of prototypes, and should be classified as supplies of goods rather than as supplies of services. The tribunal dismissed the appeal, holding on the evidence that what the company 'obtained and paid for was a research and development study into each of the two inventions concerned' and that it was not 'possible, as a matter of common-sense, to divorce the production of the working models from the rest of the study and the reports based upon it'. The company had received a single supply of services and was not entitled to credit for the disputed input tax. *Aegis Technology Ltd, LON/94/2916A (VTD 13588)*.

34.477   **Payment to patent agents—whether for supplies of goods or services.**   A partnership registered for VAT from April 1998. It reclaimed input tax in respect of supplies from patent agents. The relevant invoices were dated from June 1996 to June 1997. The Commissioners issued an assessment to recover the tax, on the basis that the invoices related to supplies of services, so that the tax was not recoverable. The partnership appealed, contending that the payments related to patent and trademark registrations which should be treated as goods. The tribunal rejected this contention, holding that the supplies were of services so that the input tax was not reclaimable. *H Parker & M Hornsby (t/a Water Two), MAN/98/746 (VTD 16225)*.

34.478   **Deregistered trader re-registering for VAT and claiming input tax on goods held.**   A furniture maker had deregistered, and had accounted for output tax of £893 on the machinery and equipment which he held at the date of deregistration, in accordance with *VATA 1994, Sch 4 para 8*. He subsequently re-registered and claimed the £893 as input tax. The Commissioners rejected the claim and he appealed, contending that he should be entitled to credit for the £893 as he still held the machinery and equipment in question. The tribunal dismissed the appeal, observing that 'once it is appreciated that a purchase of the equipment by the appellant from an unregistered trader, who in fact passed on all or part of the tax he himself suffered on purchase, would not entitle the appellant to input tax credit, it is less surprising if he receives no credit in the circumstances in the present case'. *D Haugh, LON/97/171 (VTD 15055)*.

34.479   **Input tax on leased vans.**   A trader registered for VAT in January 1991. Since 1988 he had leased two vans, and he reclaimed the total input tax incurred under the lease agreements. The Commissioners agreed to allow the total input tax incurred in the six months immediately before his registration, but refused to allow the input tax incurred before that time. The tribunal dismissed the trader's appeal against this decision. *RL Windeatt, LON/91/750Z (VTD 6571)*.

34.480   **Computer services.**   An appeal was dismissed in a case where a builder reclaimed input tax on supplies of computer services dating from more than six months before he registered for VAT. *B Woodcock, LON/91/1711X (VTD 7459)*.

34.481   **Solicitors' fees.**   An appeal was dismissed in a case where an architect registered for VAT in 1990 and reclaimed input tax in respect of solicitors' fees relating to work which he had completed in 1983. *Dicta* of Fox LJ in *Apple & Pear Development Council*, 21.47 EUROPEAN COMMUNITY LAW, applied. *P Charles-Greed, LON/91/1958 (VTD 7790)*.

34.482   Two individuals, S and P, registered for VAT as a partnership from 1 January 1998. In November 1997, before they had registered, they had provided consultancy services to an accountancy partnership (G). They issued individual invoices for these services. G did not pay for the services, and S and P incurred solicitors' costs. They reclaimed input tax on these costs on their partnership VAT returns. The Commissioners issued an assessment to recover the tax, and S appealed. The tribunal dismissed the appeal, finding that the claim related to outputs which were not subject to tax, and holding that they were 'not therefore "cost components" of a taxable transaction'. *Dicta* of Potts J in *Schemepanel Trading Ltd*, 34.486 below, applied. The Ch D upheld this decision. Jacob J observed that, on the facts found by the tribunal, S and P were suing on individual contracts, rather than as a partnership. *J Sherman & S Perilly v C & E Commrs, Ch D 18 January 2001 unreported.*

34.483   **Building services.**   An appeal was dismissed in a case in which a partnership which operated an inn and restaurant had reclaimed input tax on supplies relating to the refurbishment of the restaurant, made more* than six months before its registration. *Portnacraig Inn & Restaurant, EDN/93/44 (VTD 11528).*

34.484   **Reclaim of input tax relating to outputs made before registration.**   A company was incorporated in 1993 to organise a three-day conference which was to run from 29 April 1994 until 1 May 1994. It received most of the fees for the conference by 31 March 1994. It registered for VAT on 14 April 1994. In its first return it reclaimed input tax relating to customers who had paid their fees before 14 April, although it did not account for output tax on such fees. The Commissioners issued an assessment to recover the tax which related to customers who had paid before 14 April. The tribunal dismissed the company's appeal. The company was not a 'taxable person' before 14 April 1994, since it was neither registered, nor required to be registered, for VAT. Accordingly, it was not entitled to credit for the relevant input tax. Applying *dicta* of Mustill LJ in *Neuvale Ltd*, 43.14 PARTIAL EXEMPTION, 'tax on inputs should be set off against tax on the outputs to which the inputs related, and against nothing else'. *Perth Junior Chamber Conferences 1994 Ltd, EDN/94/323 (VTD 13450).*

34.485   A builder reclaimed input tax on materials which he had purchased more than six months before registration, and which had been the subject of onward supplies made before his registration. The Commissioners rejected his claim and the tribunal dismissed his appeal. *HE Morgan (t/a Hayden Trading Co), LON/97/471 (VTD 15177).*

34.486   **Building services—payments made after registration relating to work done before registration.**   A building company registered for VAT from 1 October 1994. At that time it was supplying building services to a nursing home. It had received payments on account totalling £54,000 between July and September 1994, and received a further £25,000 in November 1994. It had arranged for some of the work to be done by a subcontractor, to whom it paid £11,750 in September 1994 (including VAT of £1,750) and £57,000 (also including VAT) between October and December 1994. In its first return, for the two months ending 30 November 1994, it accounted for output tax on the £25,000 which it had received in that month, and reclaimed input tax of £8,000 on payments which it had made to the subcontractor, thereby claiming a repayment. The Commissioners only agreed to allow input tax of £3,234, rejecting the balance of the claim on the grounds that it related to supplies made before the company had registered. The company appealed, accepting that it was not entitled to reclaim input tax on the payment which it had made in September, since it was not then a 'taxable person' within the definition in *VATA 1994, s 24*, but contending that it should be entitled to input tax on all the payments which it had made in October and November, since it was a taxable person at the time of making the payments. The tribunal rejected this contention and dismissed the appeal, holding that *VATA 1994, s 24* should be interpreted as restricting the definition of 'input tax' to tax on supplies made to a taxable person who was also a taxable person when he used those supplies. The disputed supplies received by the company 'were the cost components of supplies made by the appellant which were not chargeable to tax'. They were 'effectively outside the VAT system' and did not 'confer a right to deduct input tax'. The QB upheld the tribunal decision. The relevant inputs related to supplies that were made before the company became a taxable person and which were not subject to output tax. *Dicta* of Mustill LJ in *Neuvale Ltd*, 43.14 PARTIAL EXEMPTION, and Advocate-General Lenz in *BLP Group plc*, 21.192 EUROPEAN COMMUNITY LAW, applied. *Schemepanel Trading Ltd v C & E Commrs, QB [1996] STC 871.*

34.487   **Input tax reclaimed on pre-registration supplies—whether deductible under VAT Regulations 1995, regulation 111*.**   See *Douros*, 43.133 PARTIAL EXEMPTION; *Byrd*, 43.135 PARTIAL EXEMPTION, and *Jolly Tots Ltd*, 43.136 PARTIAL EXEMPTION.

34.488   **Expenditure incurred when business exempt from VAT and unregistered— business becoming liable to VAT and registered accordingly—whether input tax reclaimable.**   See *Reading & Crabtree*, 43.137 PARTIAL EXEMPTION.

34.489   **Input tax reclaimed on pre-registration supplies of services—appeal dismissed.**   An appeal was dismissed in a case where a trader had reclaimed input tax on supplies of services received more than six months before registering for VAT. *IF Dunham, MAN/94/468 (VTD 13359).*

ADVANCE PAYMENTS

34.490   **Advance payment—goods not supplied.**   A company which sold pine beds made an advance payment of £12,000 to one of its suppliers. It treated this amount as tax-inclusive and reclaimed the 'VAT fraction' as input tax. However, it did not receive any goods from the supplier to whom it had made the payment. When the Commissioners discovered what had happened, they issued an assessment to recover the tax. The tribunal upheld the assessment and dismissed the company's appeal. *Weldons (West One) Ltd, LON/80/196 (VTD 984).*

34.491   Similar decisions were reached in *P Hansen, LON/80/439 (VTD 1154); T Smith, LON/80/440 (VTD 1155); JA McCall, BEL/83/7 (VTD 1588); F McSorley, BEL/85/7 (VTD 1938); Ronton Haulage Ltd, LON/86/420 (VTD 2234); IMO Precision Controls Ltd, LON/91/1360X (VTD 7948)* and *Rodeo Catering Ltd, LON/91/2218Z (VTD 11870).*

34.492   A company (T) ordered nine yachts and paid deposits which included VAT. Shortly afterwards, the supplier went into liquidation and the yachts were never delivered. T reclaimed input tax on the deposits. The Commissioners issued an assessment to recover the tax and the tribunal dismissed T's appeal, holding that input tax could not be reclaimed as no supply had taken place. *Howard*, 34.500 below, applied. *Theotrue Holdings Ltd, [1983] VATTR 88 (VTD 1358).*

34.493   *Theotrue Holdings Ltd*, 34.492 above, was applied in the similar cases of *JL Laycock, MAN/85/133 (VTD 1887); Monks & Sons, LON/92/2630A (VTD 10401)* and *W Puddifer (Junior) Ltd, [1996] VATDR 237 (VTD 13898).*

34.494   A company paid for a supply of fertiliser. Only part of the fertiliser was delivered, as the supplier went into liquidation before completing the supply. The company reclaimed input tax in respect of the whole payment, and the Commissioners issued an assessment to recover the tax relating to the fertiliser which had not been delivered. The tribunal dismissed the company's appeal, holding that the company was not entitled to reclaim tax on a supply that had not taken place. *Northern Counties Co-Operative Enterprises Ltd, [1986] VATTR 250 (VTD 2238).*

34.495   A jewellery manufacturer paid for a quantity of bullion, but never received the supply. He reclaimed input tax on the payment and appealed against the Commissioners' rejection of the claim. The tribunal allowed his appeal, observing that the value of the bullion was such that the supplier was clearly liable to be registered, and holding that as the manufacturer had undoubtedly made the payment in question, he was entitled to credit for the input tax. *DN Greenall, MAN/85/114 (VTD 2362).* (*Note.* Compare the subsequent QB decision in *Pennystar Ltd,* 34.497 below.)

34.496   A similar decision was reached in a case where a company which operated a wholesale business ordered and paid for a substantial quantity of goods, but never received them. The Commissioners issued an assessment to recover the tax but the tribunal allowed the company's appeal. *Tom Wilson (Tobacco) Ltd, MAN/98/466 (VTD 16437).* (*Note.* The decision fails to refer to the QB decision in *Pennystar Ltd,* 34.497 below, or to any of the tribunal decisions noted at 34.490 to 34.494 above, and must therefore be regarded as of doubtful authority.)

34.497   A company reclaimed input tax of £11,910 on a payment for some computers which were not in fact delivered. The Commissioners rejected the claim and the company appealed. The QB upheld the Commissioners' ruling, holding that the property in the computers had never passed and there had been no supply. Accordingly the company was not entitled to input tax. *C & E Commrs v Pennystar Ltd, QB 1995, [1996] STC 163.*

34.498   *Theotrue Holdings Ltd,* 34.492 above, and *Pennystar Ltd,* 34.497 above, were applied in the similar subsequent cases of *Birchview Ltd, MAN/96/1326; Birchview, MAN/96/1327 (VTD 15275).*

34.499   *Pennystar Ltd,* 34.497 above, was also applied in the similar subsequent case of *Icon Construction Services Ltd, LON/99/59 (VTD 16416).*

34.500   **Payment to fraudulent trader for purchase of non-existent goods.**   A trader paid amounts, including VAT, to purchase some containers. He was given what purported to be VAT invoices, and reclaimed the VAT as input tax. However, the supplier, which was the subject of police investigation, did not deliver the containers and did not pay the VAT to the Commissioners. The Commissioners issued an assessment to recover the tax and the tribunal dismissed the trader's appeal, finding on the evidence that the containers had never existed. Applying *Oliver,* 58.132 SUPPLY, there could be no taxable supply of non-existent goods, and it followed that there could be no deduction of input tax in respect of a non-existent supply. *P Howard, LON/80/457 (VTD 1106).*

34.501   M, the proprietor of a business leasing heavy goods vehicles, agreed to purchase two lorries and six refrigerated trailers from a partnership comprising a father (JA) and son (A), and lease them back to the partnership. M paid for the vehicles in February and May 1986, and leased them back to the partnership as agreed. In December 1986 the partnership offered to repurchase the vehicles and this was also agreed, the leasing agreements being terminated. However, the partnership did not pay for the vehicles, and, on the same day that the vehicles were sold to the partnership, one of the partners (JA) was murdered. Five months later, the surviving partner (A) was arrested on a charge of incitement to murder his father. It transpired that he had been involved in several fraudulent transactions, and that the eight vehicles, which the partnership had purported to sell to, and repurchase from, M, had never existed. M began proceedings against the partnership, but these proved difficult since one partner was dead and the other was awaiting trial for incitement to murder him. The surviving partner (A) was the sole executor of the deceased partner's will, but could not obtain probate and was believed to have dissipated much of the estate without bothering with the formalities of probate. When the Commissioners discovered what had happened, they issued assessments on M, disallowing the input tax claimed in respect of the purchases of the eight vehicles, on the grounds that the vehicles had never existed and there could not be a supply of a non-existent vehicle. M appealed to the tribunal which upheld the assessment, applying *Howard*, 34.500 above, and *Theotrue Holdings Ltd*, 34.492 above. *MS Munn, [1989] VATTR 11 (VTD 3296)*.

34.502   A similar decision was reached in a subsequent case where an insurance company (N) had entered into an agreement with two other companies (C and W) to purchase eight electric generators from, and lease them back to, those companies. N reclaimed input tax on the generators. C and W subsequently went into liquidation and the Commissioners discovered that the generators had never existed. The tribunal dismissed N's appeal against an assessment issued to recover the input tax. *Norwich Union Life Insurance Society, LON/90/1809 (VTD 7205)*.

34.503   A similar decision was reached in a case where a company had reclaimed input tax in respect of the purported purchase of video equipment from a company whose controlling director had subsequently been convicted of conspiracy to defraud. The equipment had never been delivered to the appellant company, and the tribunal found that there was no evidence that it had ever existed. The tribunal held that the appellant company was not entitled to credit for input tax in respect of non-existent supplies. *Howard*, 34.500 above, and *Theotrue Holdings Ltd*, 34.492 above, applied. *Alvabond Ltd, LON/90/429A (VTD 10598)*.

34.504   **Amount paid to fraudulent trader for purchase of goods not owned by trader.**   A finance company (N) entered into six agreements with another company (H) under which N was to provide funds to enable H to purchase items of equipment for use in its business. Under the agreements, ownership of the equipment was to be transferred from a supplier (M) to N and N was to lease the equipment back to H. N reclaimed input tax on the payments which it made under the agreement (and accounted for output tax on the leasing payments which it received from H). In fact M did not own or supply any equipment, and H did not purchase any new equipment with the funds which N had paid, although the equipment described in the invoices produced in M's name corresponded with equipment which H was already using under previous lease-purchase agreements with other finance companies. H subsequently went into receivership and N discovered that the equipment which H was using in its business was owned by finance companies, so that N was unable to establish title to any of the equipment. When the Commissioners discovered what had happened, they issued an assessment to recover the input tax in question. The tribunal upheld the assessment and dismissed N's appeal, holding on the evidence that the equipment in question had never been supplied to N. At the time of the purported supplies, all the equipment which H was using was owned by other finance companies. The company from which H had claimed to have purchased the equipment was 'a business sham of no substance' and the relevant invoices 'were wholly fictitious' and had been 'prepared to enable the directors of (H) to obtain finance based on fictitious purchases of equipment'. The tribunal observed that 'it is beside the point that equipment might have existed at the premises of (H) which, with the application of false serial numbers, conformed to the descriptions in the documents produced as invoices'. *Norfolk & Suffolk Finance Ltd, LON/97/894 (VTD 15288)*.

34.505   **Deposit paid for purchase of land—contracts exchanged but never completed—whether input tax deductible.**   A property company (B) entered into a contract for the purchase of some land at a price of £13.5 million (excluding VAT). It paid a deposit of £1,350,000 to the vendors' solicitors, who provided a postdated invoice showing the total VAT to be charged and the amount due on completion. The contract was never completed, partly because B did not have sufficient funds to proceed. Accordingly, B forfeited its deposit. However, B reclaimed input tax on the proposed purchase. The Commissioners rejected the claim, and B appealed. The tribunal dismissed the appeal, holding that the postdated invoice did not entitle B to reclaim the input tax, and that there had been no supply of the land. *Genius Holding BV*, 21.201 EUROPEAN COMMUNITY LAW, applied. *Broadwell Land plc, [1993] VATTR 346 (VTD 10521) (Note.* The decision here was approved by the CA in *BJ Rice & Associates*, 58.354 SUPPLY.).

COMPENSATION AND DAMAGES PAYMENTS

34.506 **Payment of damages to customer—whether tax reclaimable.** A company which dealt in scrap metal repeatedly made short deliveries to one of its customers. When the customer discovered this, it threatened to take legal action, and the company paid £223,500 as damages in an out-of-court settlement. The company reclaimed tax on this payment. The Commissioners rejected the claim, considering that the payment was outside the scope of VAT. The tribunal dismissed the company's appeal. *Whites Metal Co, LON/86/686 (VTD 2400).*

34.507 A company (H) which operated a wholesale business was sued by one of its suppliers. The case went to the County Court, which gave judgment for the supplier and ordered H to pay the supplier £12,300. H reclaimed input tax on this payment. The Commissioners rejected the claim, considering that the payment constituted damages or compensation and was outside the scope of VAT. The tribunal dismissed H's appeal, holding that the payment did not relate to any taxable supply and that the Court Order was 'by way of compensation or damages (which) is outside the scope of VAT'. *Reich*, 58.113 SUPPLY, and *Holiday Inns (UK) Ltd*, 58.116 SUPPLY, applied. *Hometex Trading Ltd, MAN/94/741 (VTD 13012).*

34.508 **Input tax reclaimed on settlement payment to solicitors.** See *Slot*, 34.39 above.

34.509 **Input tax reclaimed on compensation payment to lessor.** In April 1990 a company (F) entered into a 'finance lease' of an expensive printing machine. In December 1990 F went into receivership, and the lease was terminated. The lessors claimed substantial compensation, and their claim was upheld by the Court of Session. F reclaimed input tax on the compensation payment. The Commissioners rejected the claim, and F appealed. The tribunal dismissed the appeal, holding that the termination of the lease was not a supply of services. Since the lessor had not supplied any services in return for the compensation payment, the payment was outside the scope of VAT. *Holiday Inns (UK) Ltd*, 58.116 SUPPLY, applied; *Bass plc*, 58.76 SUPPLY, distinguished. *Financial & General Print Ltd, LON/95/1281A (VTD 13795).*

34.510 A company (C) made a payment of £2,000,000 to another company (H) in February 1991. C considered that this payment should be treated as inclusive of VAT. However, H considered that the payment was outside the scope of VAT, and did not issue a VAT invoice. C reclaimed input tax in respect of the payment in its return for the period ending June 1991. The Commissioners initially accepted C's claim, and issued an assessment on H charging output tax on the payment, but H's appeal was allowed by a tribunal (see *Holiday Inns (UK) Ltd*, 58.116 SUPPLY). In 1993 the Commissioners issued an assessment on C to recover the input tax which C had claimed. The tribunal allowed C's appeal, disapproving and declining to follow the previous decision in *Holiday Inns (UK) Ltd*, on the grounds that it was inconsistent with the subsequent CJEC decision in *Lubbock Fine & Co*, 21.165 EUROPEAN COMMUNITY LAW. The tribunal held that the payment was consideration for a supply of services, and that C was entitled to reclaim the input tax even though H had not issued a VAT invoice, and despite the fact that the previous tribunal had held that H was not required to account for output tax on the payment. The tribunal held that 'the right to deduct is not limited to the case where output tax has been paid but also extends to the case where it is payable ... the recipient of a supply can claim input tax even though the supplier fails to account for the output tax in his return or becomes insolvent before the output tax is paid'. *Croydon Hotel & Leisure Co Ltd, [1997] VATDR 245 (VTD 14920)*. (*Notes.* (1) For a preliminary issue in this case, see 3.34 ASSESSMENT. (2) Compare *Financial & General Print Ltd*, 34.509 above, which was not referred to in this decision. (3) For the corporation tax treatment of the payment, see *Croydon Hotel & Leisure Co Ltd v Bowen, Sp C [1996] SSCD 466 (TTC 2001, 61.72)*.)

POST-CESSATION INPUT TAX

34.511   A retail shopkeeper had entered into a long-term contract for the hire to him of various shop fittings including a counter and shelving. He closed the business in March 1973 but had to continue paying the hire charges until September 1973. He reclaimed input tax in respect of the hire charges paid from April to September. The Commissioners rejected his claim on the grounds that he was not carrying on any business at that time. The tribunal dismissed his appeal against this decision. *PT Miles, LON/73/87 (VTD 33)*.

34.512   A company which owned a factory ceased to trade. Subsequently it decided to let the factory, and had work carried out on it to make it suitable for letting. It reclaimed input tax in respect of this work and the Commissioners issued an assessment to recover the tax. The tribunal dismissed the company's appeal, holding that the company had not incurred the expenditure for the purpose of any business. *GA Hurley Ltd, MAN/88/538 (VTD 3510)*.

34.513   A married couple who had operated a hotel closed it in October 1990. They then renovated the building with the intention of reopening it as a registered residential home (which would be exempt from VAT). They reclaimed input tax incurred in the renovation on a return relating to the hotel business. On discovering what had happened, the Commissioners issued an assessment to recover the tax. The tribunal dismissed the couple's appeal, holding that since the hotel business had ceased before the renovation, the input tax was not reclaimable. *G & C Brown, EDN/91/266 (VTD 7430)*.

34.514   A married couple had operated a carpet business in partnership, but the wife withdrew from the partnership in February 1993 and the husband continued to operate the business as a sole proprietor, continuing to use the partnership registration number. Subsequently he reclaimed input tax on the renovation of some flats which were jointly owned by him and his wife. The Commissioners issued an assessment to recover the tax, and the tribunal dismissed his appeal, holding that he could not reclaim the tax since it related to a partnership activity but the partnership had ceased to trade and was no longer registered for VAT. (The chairman also noted that it appeared that the expenditure had been incurred for the purpose of making supplies of accommodation which would be exempt from VAT.) *AT Sinnett, MAN/95/2671 (VTD 14201)*.

MISCELLANEOUS MATTERS

34.515   **Repayment of input tax—accuracy of claim in doubt.**   A company made a claim for repayment of a substantial amount of input tax. The Commissioners withheld repayment, since the company and its principal director were under investigation for purporting to make exports of goods which had allegedly never taken place. The company applied for judicial review, contending that the Commissioners were obliged to repay the amount claimed prior to any further investigations. The QB dismissed the application, holding that the Commissioners were not obliged to repay excess input tax claimed where they had grounds for suspecting the accuracy of the claim. The Commissioners were entitled to a reasonable opportunity to investigate such a claim, and the delay in this case had not reached unreasonable proportions. *R v C & E Commrs (ex p. Strangewood Ltd)*, QB *[1987] STC 502*.

34.516   The decision in *R v C & E Commrs (ex p. Strangewood Ltd)*, 34.515 above, was applied in *Pennine Carpets Ltd*, 61.45 TRANSFERS OF GOING CONCERNS.

34.517   The QB reached a similar decision in a subsequent case where the Commissioners were investigating an alleged fraud concerning a company which exported beer and wine to France. The company had claimed repayment of more than £200,000, while the Commissioners had issued assessments charging tax of more than £1,400,000, on the basis that the company had overclaimed input tax. Keene J observed that the company had been used 'as an apparently unnecessary middleman' and that there seemed 'little commercial sense' in its involvement 'unless . . . there was a fraudulent intent to achieve a sufficiently complex structure of companies as to enable drawback to be improperly claimed. No credible explanation has been provided to this court for this trading structure on a legitimate basis'. The Commissioners had 'evidence of prolonged wholesale fraud' and there was 'nothing unnecessary about the (Commissioners') requirements for greater verification of claims in the circumstances which have arisen'. It would clearly be premature for the court to make a declaration in favour of the company, when its appeals against the assessments had not yet been heard by the tribunal. *R v C & E Commrs (ex p. Lacara Ltd)*, QB 30 *March 1998, 1998 STI 576*. (*Note*. In 1999 the Commissioners were granted summary judgment against the company in respect of unpaid excise duty of more than £8,000,000. The QB dismissed the company's appeal against the judgment— see 2.86 APPEALS.)

34.518   **Tax properly chargeable differing from tax charged by contractor.** A company arranged with a firm of contractors for the conversion of two houses into flats. The bill submitted by the contractors included £2,250 in respect of input tax. However some of the work was zero-rated, so that the tax properly chargeable was only £1,023. Shortly after the conversion was completed, the contractors went into liquidation. The company claimed a deduction for the input tax charged of £2,250, and the Commissioners would only allow a deduction of £1,023. The tribunal accepted the Commissioners' contention and dismissed the company's appeal, holding that the 'tax' of what is now *VATA 1994, s 24(1)* is the tax properly chargeable, if different from that charged. *Podium Investments Ltd, [1977] VATTR 121 (VTD 314)*.

34.519   See also *Genius Holding BV v Staatssecretaris van Financien*, 21.201 EUROPEAN COMMUNITY LAW.

34.520   **Input tax reclaimed in respect of stolen goods.** A demolition contractor reclaimed input tax in respect of the purchase of an item of equipment which had been stolen. The item was later repossessed by the police and returned to its rightful owner. The Commissioners issued an assessment to recover the tax and the tribunal dismissed the contractor's appeal, holding that there was no right to reclaim input tax in respect of stolen goods. *CR Hudson (t/a 21st Century Demolition & Plant Hire)*, *MAN/91/1016 (VTD 9666)*.

34.521   **Goods supplied in France but paid for in the UK.**   A company (B), which carried on international haulage work, had an arrangement with an international fuel company (S) under which S supplied diesel fuel to B's vehicles while they were travelling in France. S provided B with monthly invoices showing the gross costs of those supplies in French currency, including French VAT (TVA). B reclaimed input tax, at the UK rate of 15%, on the sterling equivalent of the amounts in question. The Commissioners issued an assessment to recover the tax, and the tribunal dismissed B's appeal, holding that credit for input tax was limited to UK VAT charged on a supply made in the UK. *British Iberian International Transport Ltd, LON/85/654 (VTD 2101)*. (*Note.* The appellant had used the *EC Eighth Directive* to recover TVA paid in France for a period subsequent to that covered by the assessment, but the French authorities had refused a late claim under that provision for the period of the assessment as being out of time.)

34.522   A claim to deduct TVA as input tax was also rejected in *Normal Films Ltd, LON/97/1031 (VTD 15558)*.

34.523   An appeal was dismissed in another case where a UK company (D) had reclaimed input tax on supplies of goods which had taken place in France, although the supplier had also been a UK company. The supplier had initially issued a VAT invoice, but had subsequently realised its mistake and had issued a credit note. The tribunal held that, since the place of supply was in France, D was not entitled to reclaim UK input tax on the supplies in question. *Duffy & Carr Group plc, LON/93/1525A (VTD 11728)*.

34.524   **Yacht moored in Greece—input tax reclaimed by UK purchaser.**   A UK company purchased a yacht from an associated company. At the time of the purchase the yacht was moored in Greece. However, the purchaser reclaimed input tax on the yacht. The Commissioners issued an assessment to recover the tax and the tribunal dismissed the company's appeal. Since the yacht was moored in Greece, the supply had taken place outside the UK and was not subject to UK VAT. *Da Conti International Ltd, LON/90/444Z (VTD 6215)*.

34.525   **Self-billing.**   See the cases noted at 38.44 to 38.49 INVOICES AND CREDIT NOTES.

34.526   **Credit note received for tax already deducted as input tax.**   See *Silvermere Golf and Equestrian Centre Ltd*, 38.86 INVOICES AND CREDIT NOTES.

34.527   **Repossession of goods under conditional sale—input tax previously reclaimed by purchaser.**   A company (L) arranged to purchase a number of commercial vehicles from another company (V). The vehicles were supplied under contracts of conditional sale which provided that V would retain their ownership until L had paid for them in full. V accounted for VAT on the delivery of the vehicles, and L reclaimed the VAT as input tax. Subsequently, before the vehicles had been fully paid for, L went into receivership. V repossessed the vehicles and gave the receivers a credit note for an amount which included the VAT paid. The receivers applied to the Ch D for directions as to whether the VAT in question constituted a preferential debt. The Commissioners contended that, since the original sale had been conditional, L had only had a conditional entitlement to reclaim the input tax, so that the tax should rank as a preferential debt. The Ch D rejected this contention. The delivery of the goods by V was admitted to have been a supply. There were no grounds 'on which a delivery of goods pursuant to a contract which contains a title retention clause, and which constitutes a supply in respect of which VAT has become due within the clear terms of the legislation, can later be said not to constitute a supply because the goods are repossessed by the vendor'. (Accordingly, since the input tax related to a transaction which had taken place more than twelve months before the date of the receivership, the VAT was not a preferential debt.) *Re Liverpool*

Commercial Vehicles Ltd, Ch D [1984] BCLC 587. (*Note.* For the Commissioners' practice following this decision, see their Press Notice No 931 dated 3 August 1984.)

34.528   **Whether excess input tax post-receivership can be set off against pre-receivership tax liabilities.**   The joint receivers and managers of a company sought judicial review of the Commissioners' decision not to repay the excess of input tax over output tax generated by the company since the receivership, but to set the excess input tax against pre-receivership output tax liabilities. The QB dismissed the application, holding that the Commissioners were entitled to make the set-off. *R v C & E Commrs (ex p. Richmond & another), QB 1988, [1989] STC 429.*

34.529   **Estimated assessment to correct alleged overclaim of input tax.**   See *WM Low & Co plc,* 3.21 ASSESSMENT.

34.530   **Failure to claim input tax in correct period—whether tax may be recovered in a later period.**   A company had consistently failed to reclaim input tax on certain supplies which it had received. In 1990 it submitted a return in which it reclaimed the tax in question for a period of ten years up to 31 March 1988, totalling more than £161,000. The Commissioners issued an assessment to recover the tax, considering that the claim should have been made on the returns for the accounting periods in which the expenditure had been incurred. The company appealed, contending that the late claim was in accordance with *Notice No 700 (1987 edition).* The tribunal allowed the appeal, applying *dicta* of Lord Keith in *Fine Art Developments plc,* 55.14 RETURNS. On the evidence, the failure to claim the input tax in the prescribed periods had been the result of inadvertence, and *Notice No 700 (1987 edition)* permitted such an error to be adjusted in a subsequent return. *Aer Lingus plc, [1992] VATTR 438 (VTD 8893).* (*Notes.* (1) The input tax in question would no longer be deductible in view of the introduction of the margin scheme for tour operators by the *VAT (Tour Operators) Order 1987.* See 59.2 TOUR OPERATORS AND TRAVEL AGENTS for an appeal by the same company on this issue. (2) *Notice No 700* has subsequently been amended and the passage in question has been deleted.)

34.531   **Goods paid for in US dollars—correct exchange rate for input tax claim.**   A UK company purchased goods from a US company with a place of business in the UK. The invoices stated the value of the goods and the VAT thereon, both in UK currency and in US dollars. The company was required to pay for the goods in dollars, and did so. By the time that payment was made, the value of the pound had declined against the dollar. The company claimed as its input tax the tax fraction of the amounts it actually paid to purchase the dollars. The Commissioners considered that the input tax actually due was the amount stated in sterling on the invoice, and issued an assessment to recover the balance. The tribunal dismissed the company's appeal. The tax stated in sterling on the invoices was the tax for which the company was entitled to credit. *Advansys plc, MAN/88/870 (VTD 4427).*

34.532   **Arrangement between retail company and finance company—whether input tax reclaimable.**   A company (E) carried on business as a retailer of domestic electrical appliances. Many of its sales were on a hire-purchase basis, in co-operation with a finance company which was granted an option over the appliances until the customer had paid for them in full. E agreed with the finance company concerned that, if customers defaulted, it would pay any amount outstanding under the agreement in return for reclaiming the option. E then took steps to repossess the goods from the customers. E reclaimed input tax on the appliances concerned. The Commissioners issued an assessment to recover the tax, considering that, in the absence of a formal assignation of the finance company's rights, E was not entitled to reclaim input tax. The tribunal allowed E's appeal, holding that the terms of the agreement were sufficient to constitute a supply even in cases where E had not established either physical possession or legal ownership of the goods. *Excell Consumer Industries Ltd, [1985] VATTR 94 (VTD 1865)*.

34.533 **Claim to assign repayment of input tax.** An accountant submitted a client's return showing a repayment due of £389. With the return he submitted a written request that £258 of the repayment should be repaid to him, rather than to the client. However, the Commissioners sent the £389 to the client. Subsequently the accountant withheld the sum of £258 from his own return. The Commissioners levied distraint to recover this amount from him, and he then lodged an appeal to the tribunal, contending that the input tax had been assigned to him. The tribunal dismissed his appeal, holding that the written request submitted by the accountant did not constitute a formal assignment of the repayment. *NS Daws, MAN/91/957 (VTD 7643)*.

34.534 **Input tax reclaimed by unregistered claimant.** See *Wayment*, 2.33 APPEALS, and *Whitehouse*, 2.34 APPEALS.

35 Insolvency

35.1 **Provisional liquidator—Insolvency Act 1986, s 135.** An individual was appointed provisional liquidator of a company, under *Insolvency Act 1986, s 135*, in September 1997, on an application by the Commissioners. The liquidation was completed in March 1998 by the sale of the business as a going concern. The company had continued to trade, under the liquidator's supervision, in the interim period, and made sales in respect of which it was liable to pay VAT. The liquidator applied to the Ch D for directions with regard to his liability to account for the VAT, and to whether he could deduct his expenses. The Ch D held that the liquidator was under a duty to ensure that tax was accounted for, in its entirety, to the revenue authorities. This duty took priority to the liquidator's claim for expenses which he had incurred under *Insolvency Rules 1986 (SI 1986 No 1925), rule 4.218. Re Grey Marlin Ltd, Ch D [1999] 3 All ER 429.*

35.2 **Statutory demand—Insolvency Act 1986, s 375(1).** A father and son who traded in partnership failed to pay a VAT assessment. The Commissioners made a statutory demand against the son. He applied to have the statutory demand set aside. His application was rejected, and he applied to another district judge under *Insolvency Act 1986, s 375(1)*. The district judge dismissed the application, and he appealed to the Ch D. The Ch D dismissed the appeal, holding on the evidence that the district judge had properly exercised his discretion. *Re A Debtor (No 8 of 1997), The Debtor v C & E Commrs, Ch D 30 November 1998 unreported.*

35.3 See also *Cozens*, 2.150 APPEALS.

35.4 **Partnership debt—validity of bankruptcy order against one member of partnership.** See *Schooler*, 44.39 PARTNERSHIP.

35.5 **Appeal by undischarged bankrupt.** An individual who had been made bankrupt lodged a late appeal against an assessment issued before the date of bankruptcy. The tribunal adjourned the appeal, holding that the bankrupt had no *locus standi*, and that it was for his trustee in bankruptcy to decide whether an appeal should be lodged. *DT Hunt, [1992] VATTR 255 (VTD 10147).*

35.6 **Supplies by undischarged bankrupt.** A consulting engineer (S) was made bankrupt in 1981 but continued to carry on business. He appealed against an assessment, contending that he could not be held to be trading while he was an undischarged bankrupt. The tribunal rejected this contention and dismissed his appeal. The fact that S was trading in breach of the law of bankruptcy did not alter the fact that he was trading. He had remained a legal person and continued to offer and supply his services as an independent principal. *JE Scally, [1989] VATTR 245 (VTD 4592).*

35.7 **Business transferred as going concern following bankruptcy—deposits taken before bankruptcy but supplies made following transfer.** A furniture retailer became bankrupt in April 1994. The business was transferred, as a going concern, to a limited company seven days later. Following the transfer, the company failed to account for output tax on supplies of furniture for which deposits had been received before the bankruptcy of the previous proprietor and the transfer of the business. The Commissioners issued an assessment charging output tax, and the company appealed, contending that the liability should be treated as that of the transferor's trustee in bankruptcy. The tribunal rejected this contention and dismissed the appeal, holding that there were two separate tax points. The tax point in respect of the deposit was the time when the deposit was taken. However, the tax point in respect of the balance of the price was the time when the furniture was delivered or the time when payment was made. *JD Fox Ltd*, 58.340 SUPPLY, applied. *Camford Ltd (t/a The Cotswold Collection), LON/95/221A (VTD 13339)*.

35.8   **Bankruptcy—whether excuse for non-registration.**   See *Ambrose*, 48.132 PENALTIES: FAILURE TO NOTIFY.

35.9   **Legal costs of discharge from bankruptcy—input tax not reclaimable.**   See *Stern*, 34.117 INPUT TAX.

35.10   **Bankruptcy of company director—whether excuse for non-payment of VAT.**   See *Relay Couriers Ltd*, 18.357 DEFAULT SURCHARGE.

35.11   **Company in receivership—obligation of receiver to pay VAT to Commissioners.**   See *Re John Willment (Ashford) Ltd*, 14.84 COLLECTION AND ENFORCEMENT.

35.12   **Set-off of Crown debts.**   See *Re Cushla Ltd*, 14.87 COLLECTION AND ENFORCEMENT.

35.13   **Company in receivership—input tax previously reclaimed on goods subsequently repossessed—whether a preferential debt.**   See *Re Liverpool Commercial Vehicles Ltd*, 34.527 INPUT TAX.

35.14   **Continuous supplies of services—payments received after liquidation.**   A company which had made continuous supplies of construction services, within *regulation 90* of the *VAT Regulations 1995 (SI 1995 No 2518)*, went into liquidation. The liquidator failed to account for payments which he received on behalf of the company, and the Commissioners issued an assessment charging tax on them. The tribunal dismissed the liquidator's appeal, holding that since the company had never issued VAT invoices in respect of the services in question, output tax was chargeable when payment was received. *Glenshane Construction Services Ltd (in liquidation), LON/95/2061 (VTD 14160)*.

35.15   **Group registration—liability of members other than representative member.**   See *Re Nadler Enterprises Ltd*, 30.9 GROUPS OF COMPANIES.

35.16   **Insolvency Act 1986, Sch 6—application of Crown preference to group of companies.**   See *Villaswan Ltd v Sheraton (Blythswood) Ltd*, 30.29 GROUPS OF COMPANIES.

35.17   **Insolvency of customers—whether excuse for non-payment of VAT.**   See *BD (Refrigeration Services) Ltd*, 18.325 DEFAULT SURCHARGE.

35.18   **Insolvency of customers—whether a supply.**   See the cases noted at 58.151 to 58.153 SUPPLY.

36 Insurance

Note. *VATA 1994, Sch 9, Group 2* was substituted by *FA 1997, s 38* with effect from 19 March 1997. The substituted legislation is intended to make it 'more difficult to avoid VAT when insurance is supplied with other goods and services'. The cases in this chapter should be read in the light of the changes in the legislation. The cases are arranged under the following headings.

> The provision of insurance and reinsurance (VATA 1994, Sch 9, Group 2, Item 1) 36.1–36.10
>
> Services of an insurance intermediary (VATA 1994, Sch 9, Group 2, Item 4) 36.11–36.13
>
> Superseded legislation 36.14–36.31

THE PROVISION OF INSURANCE AND REINSURANCE (VATA 1994, Sch 9, Group 2, Item 1)

36.1   **Provision of hired cars—whether part of consideration attributable to supply of insurance.**   A company carried on a car hire business and had arranged insurance for its cars with a recognised insurer. In accounting for output tax, it treated part of the consideration which it received from its customers as attributable to an exempt supply of insurance. The Commissioners issued an assessment charging output tax on the whole of the consideration, and the tribunal dismissed the company's appeal, holding that the company was making a single supply of the hire of the car. The only supply of insurance was made by the insurance company to the car hire company, rather than by the car hire company to the customer. *CJ Kiff Ltd, [1981] VATTR 88 (VTD 1084).*

36.2   Similar decisions were reached in *AJ Turner, MAN/85/105 (VTD 1965); Kings Lynn Motor Co Ltd, LON/90/50Y (VTD 5312); CA Vine (t/a Cornish Car Hire), LON/91/1104Z (VTD 7467); R Stratton (t/a SRG Hire), LON/97/1510 (VTD 16879)* and *Motor & Legal Group Ltd,* 58.361 SUPPLY.

36.3   **Provision of motor insurance.**   A company which supplied motor insurance reclaimed the whole of its input tax. The Commissioners issued an assessment to recover the tax, on the basis that it related to exempt supplies of insurance. The tribunal upheld the assessment and dismissed the company's appeal. *International Warranty Co (UK) Ltd, EDN/85/28 (VTD 1934).*

36.4   A company which owned a garage allowed some of its employees to drive its cars privately. It extended its insurance cover accordingly and made deductions from its employees' wages. The Commissioners issued an assessment on the basis that the company had made its employees a standard-rated supply of the right to use its cars. The company appealed, contending that the deductions from its employees' salaries were for insurance and should therefore be treated as exempt under what is now *VATA 1994, Sch 9, Group 2.* The tribunal dismissed the appeal, holding that the insurance was supplied to the company and not to the employees, and that the money recovered from the employees did not qualify for exemption. On the evidence, what was supplied to the employees 'was not the insurance cover nor the making of arrangements by the appellant company for extended insurance cover, but the right to use the cars for private and pleasure purposes for the consideration which was measured by the cost of the extended insurance cover'. *T & B Garage (Wimbledon), LON/89/803Z (VTD 4613).*

36.5   **Valuation of car for insurance purposes.**   A company carried on business as an insurance broker and arranged for the provision of motor insurance. It valued cars which were to be the subject of such insurance, and charged clients a fee of £8 for determining the agreed value. The Commissioners issued a ruling that these valuation fees were chargeable to VAT at the standard rate, and the company appealed, contending that they formed part of the consideration for a supply of insurance, and should be treated as exempt from VAT under what is now *VATA 1994, Sch 9, Group 2*. The tribunal allowed the company's appeal, applying *British Railways Board*, 62.5 TRANSPORT, and *British Airways plc*, 62.6 TRANSPORT, and distinguishing *Dogbreeders Associates*, 36.21 below. 'The determination of the agreed value was an integral part of the provision of the particular insurance policies.' *Lancaster Insurance Services Ltd, LON/90/607X (VTD 5455)*.

36.6   **Goods sold by 'party plan' system—insurance provided to distributors.**   A company sold pottery and ceramics on a 'party plan' system, through distributors whom it provided with kits of goods. It required its distributors to pay two-thirds of the retail value of any goods which were broken or stolen. In 1982 it began a scheme whereby the distributors could insure themselves against such thefts and breakages, in return for payments of 50p per week. It did not account for VAT on these payments, and the Commissioners issued a ruling that they were standard-rated. The company appealed, contending that the payments should be treated as exempt from VAT under what is now *VATA 1994, Sch 9, Group 2, Item 1*. The tribunal dismissed the appeal, holding that the services supplied by the company did not qualify for exemption. *John E Buck & Co Ltd, LON/83/208 (VTD 1525)*.

36.7   **Insurance of television sets.**   Two groups of companies let television sets on hire. With each of the groups, the sets were let on hire by one subsidiary company, and another subsidiary provided insurance. 70% of the total consideration was allocated to the rental subsidiary, the other 30% being allocated to the insurance subsidiary. The groups did not account for output tax on the amounts allocated to the insurance subsidiaries, treating them as exempt from VAT. The Commissioners issued assessments charging output tax on the full amounts of the payments, on the basis that there was a single composite supply which did not qualify for exemption. The groups appealed. The tribunal allowed the appeals, holding that there were two separate supplies in each case. The rental subsidiaries supplied the service of letting the goods on hire, and the insurance subsidiaries supplied insurance. The payments for insurance qualified for exemption under what is now *VATA 1994, Sch 9, Group 2, Item 1*. *Thorn EMI plc; Granada plc, [1993] VATTR 94 (VTD 9782)*. (*Note*. For the Commissioners' practice following this decision, see Customs' VAT Manual, Part 7, chapter 17, section 5.8. Customs state that 'traders who argue that the insurance element of their supplies qualifies for exemption as a result of (these) cases will have to demonstrate that they have created an insurance company which is a permitted insurer'.)

36.8   **Video hire business.**   A couple operated a video hire business in partnership. They made an annual charge of £2 to each of their customers in order to cover damage to videocassettes. They did not account for output tax on this charge. The Commissioners issued an assessment charging tax on it, and the couple appealed, contending that it was for a supply of insurance which should be treated as exempt. The tribunal rejected this contention and dismissed the appeal. The couple were not authorised to carry on insurance business and the charges did not qualify for exemption under *VATA 1994, Sch 9, Group 2. K & V Peters, LON/95/2904 (VTD 14328)*.

36.9   **Personal pension schemes.**   A group of companies operated two personal pension schemes. The Commissioners issued a ruling that VAT should be charged at the standard rate on the services which the group supplied in connection with the schemes. The representative member of the group appealed, contending that the supplies qualified for exemption under *VATA 1994, Sch 9, Group 2, Item 1*. The tribunal accepted this contention and allowed the appeal. On the evidence, the services in question were not simply trust administration services. The schemes embodied insurance contracts, and 'were part and parcel of the provision of insurance'. *Federated Pensions Services Ltd*, 36.26 below, distinguished. *Winterthur Life UK Ltd, LON/96/1787 (VTD 14935)*.

36.10 **Storage insurance.** An individual (L) arranged with a removal and storage contractor for his personal possessions to be placed in storage. He requested insurance cover, for which the contractor charged £97.50 plus VAT. L wrote to the Commissioners querying why VAT should be charged on the insurance. The Commissioners issued a ruling that VAT was chargeable since the contractor was not an authorised insurer, as required by *VATA 1994, Sch 9, Group 2, Item 1*. L appealed. The tribunal allowed his appeal, holding on the evidence that L was insured with an authorised insurer under the storage contractor's policy, and that the contractor should be treated as L's agent for this purpose. The tribunal held that it was 'not strictly necessary that there should be any correlation between the amount paid by customer to contractor on the one hand and the amount paid by contractor to insurer on the other ... The correct analysis of the arrangements embodied in the master policy as between the insurer and (the contractor) is ... that the insurer, in consideration of the annual premium, undertakes to keep open and unrevoked an offer to grant insurance cover to any customer of (the contractor) up to the stated limit of the insurer's liability.' *AA Lee, LON/97/446 (VTD 15205)*.

SERVICES OF AN INSURANCE INTERMEDIARY (VATA 1994, Sch 9, Group 2, Item 4)

36.11 **Insurance agent reviewing pension policies for mis-selling on behalf of insurance company.** A company (L) had sold a number of personal pension policies between 1988 and 1994. The Securities Investment Board and Personal Investment Authority required all such policies to be reviewed to determine whether there had been any mis-selling. L arranged for another company (C) to undertake this review. C did not account for output tax on these supplies. The Commissioners issued an assessment charging tax on them, and C appealed, contending that they should be treated as exempt under *VATA 1994, Sch 9, Group 2, Item 4*. The QB accepted this contention and allowed the appeal, and the CA upheld this decision. Jacob J held that the supplies fell within *Article 13B(a)* of the *EC Sixth Directive*. The fact that the services were not supplied by L itself, but by C acting on its behalf, did not prevent them from qualifying for exemption. The services were not merely ancillary, but were 'a vital part of the administration of the contracts'. *Century Life plc v C & E Commrs, CA 2000, [2001] STC 38*.

36.12 **Hire of motor vehicles—whether partnership acting as an 'insurance intermediary'.** A partnership hired a number of motor vehicles to customers. In accounting for VAT, they treated part of the consideration which they received as relating to the insurance of the vehicles, and as exempt. The Commissioners issued an assessment on the basis that the consideration was standard-rated, and the partnership appealed. The tribunal dismissed the appeal, holding that the partnership did not qualify as an 'insurance intermediary' within *VATA 1994, Sch 9, Group 2, Item 4, Note 1*, since the relevant insurance policy named the partnership, rather than the customer, as the insured party. The tribunal observed that 'it is the appellants who are in a contractual relationship with the insurance company, not the drivers. As such the appellants cannot broker a contract between the insurers and the insured because they themselves are the insured.' Additionally, the partnership was not making separate supplies, but was making a single standard-rated supply of an insured motor vehicle. *GM Craddock & BM Walker (t/a Warwick Garages), MAN/99/111 (VTD 16513).*

36.13 **Warranty insurance for double glazing—whether 'relevant requirements' of Notes 4 and 5 fulfilled.** A company supplied and installed double glazing and related products. It arranged warranty insurance, and treated such supplies as exempt from VAT under *VATA 1994, Sch 9, Group 2, Item 4*. The Commissioners issued an assessment charging tax on the supplies, on the basis that the 'relevant requirements' of *Sch 9, Group 2, Notes 4* and *5* were not fulfilled. The company appealed. The tribunal reviewed the evidence in detail and held that the company's supplies made between January 1997 and June 1998 failed to qualify for exemption on the grounds that the company's documentation failed to meet the requirements of *Note 5*, since the specific amount of the premium was not stated. The tribunal held that the fact that the amount could be ascertained by an arithmetical calculation was not sufficient to meet the statutory requirements, since 'the customer has to be able to identify what he is paying for the warranty insurance. A stated sum tells him; a formula does not.' The tribunal observed that 'even if the contract enabled the customer by a process of elimination to identify the amount, that would not be sufficient because that it is not setting out the amount, as the legislation requires'. *CR Smith Glaziers (Dunfermline) Ltd, EDN/98/209 (VTD 16327).* (*Notes.* (1) The tribunal allowed the company's appeal in part with regard to the period ending 31 December 1996, holding that the company's supplies qualified for exemption before the changes to *Group 2* introduced by *FA 1997*. However, the tribunal held that supplies under a transitional arrangement which the company had adopted in cases where contracts had been agreed before December 1996, but services had not yet been completed, failed to qualify for exemption on the grounds that it was the company, rather than the customer, which had absorbed the extra costs of arranging the insurance. (2) The company had altered the form of its contracts with effect from July 1998, and it was accepted that the contracts from July 1998 met the requirements of *Notes 4* and *5*.)

SUPERSEDED LEGISLATION

Note. *VATA 1983, Sch 6, Group 2* became *VATA 1994, Sch 9, Group 2*, which was substituted by *FA 1997, s 38* with effect from 19 March 1997. What had been *Group 2, Item 3*, providing for exemption for 'the making of arrangements for the provision of any insurance or reinsurance', was not re-enacted in the substituted legislation. Accordingly, the cases summarised in the following paragraphs do not necessarily qualify for exemption under the current legislation. Some of the cases may, however, remain of interest as illustrating matters of general principle with regard to the treatment of insurance for VAT purposes.

36.14 **Pensions insurance provided by financial adviser.** A chartered accountant (F) also carried on business as a financial adviser. He worked in close association with another individual (S), who had special knowledge and experience of pensions insurance. They shared commissions received from brokers for pensions insurance effected as a result of their work. The Commissioners issued assessments on the basis that F's share of these commissions was standard-rated. F appealed, contending that the transactions constituted the making of arrangements for the provision of insurance and were exempt from VAT under the legislation then in force. The tribunal accepted this contention and allowed the appeal. *D Ford (t/a Donald Ford Financial Services), [1987] VATTR 130 (VTD 2432).*

36.15 **Sale of second-hand cars—breakdown insurance arranged by vendor.** A partnership which sold second-hand cars offered its purchasers an insurance policy against mechanical breakdown for a cost of £250. In accounting for output tax, the partnership treated such payments as exempt from VAT. The Commissioners issued an assessment charging tax on them, and the company appealed. The tribunal allowed the company's appeal, holding that the payments qualified for exemption under the legislation then in force. *HB & DD Geddes, LON/88/681 (VTD 3378)*.

36.16   *Geddes*, 36.15 above, was distinguished in a subsequent case where a dealer who sold sports cars attributed a large proportion of the sale price of such cars to insurance warranties, and did not account for output tax on the amounts attributed to the warranties. In a case where an MG which had been bought for £2,650 was sold for £3,895, the dealer attributed £1,045 of this price to the warranty, and only accounted for output tax on £200 (i.e. £2,850, being the price after deducting the amount attributed to the warranty, minus the purchase price of £2,650). The maximum claim under the warranty was normally £250. The Commissioners issued assessments on the basis that, since the normal price of such a warranty was £82, only that amount could be treated as being for an exempt supply. The tribunal dismissed the dealer's appeal, observing that it was 'not impressed by (the appellant) as a witness' and finding that he fixed the figures 'so as to confer a tax advantage'. On the evidence, 'the whole process of fixing the warranty price was a sham. The figure attributed on the invoices by (the dealer) to the warranty bears no relationship whatsoever either to the amount charged by insurers or to the part played by (the dealer) in arranging the insurance'. (The tribunal also observed that, to the extent that any supplies were exempt under what is now *VATA 1994, Sch 9, Group 2*, the partial exemption rules would apply and require a restriction of input tax, although the dealer had made no such adjustment.) *G Charlesworth (t/a Centurions), LON/91/2150 (VTD 9015)*. (*Note*. See also *Notice No 711, para 19* and Business Brief 7/94, issued on 7 March 1994.)

36.17   See also *Brisbane*, 47.38 PENALTIES: EVASION OF TAX.

36.18   A company trading as car dealers arranged for insurance to be provided by an associated insurance company. It charged customers £950 for such insurance. It treated the whole of this £950 as exempt from VAT, but only passed £80 to the insurance company, retaining £870 as commission. The Commissioners issued assessments charging output tax on the basis that only the cost of £80 was attributable to insurance. The tribunal held that the company's returns were incorrect and that the Commissioners were entitled to apportion the price of £950. However, the tribunal allowed the company's appeal, holding on the evidence that the officer responsible for the assessment had not acted to the best of his judgment. *Dicta* in *Van Boeckel*, 3.1 ASSESSMENT, applied. *North East Garages Ltd, MAN/96/63 (VTD 15734)*. (*Note*. For another issue in this case, taken to the QB, see 2.253 APPEALS.)

36.19   **Letting of holiday cottages—obligatory insurance premium against cancellation.**   A company let holiday cottages. It charged customers an obligatory cancellation insurance premium, and took out relevant insurance policies with an authorised insurer. In accounting for tax, it treated the amounts which it charged its customers for insurance as exempt for VAT. The Commissioners issued a ruling that the company was making a single composite supply which did not qualify for exemption. The tribunal allowed the company's appeal, holding that there were two separate supplies and that the supply of insurance was exempt under the legislation then in force. *Rosemoor Holdings Ltd, LON/88/1275Z (VTD 4068)*.

36.20   **Insurance premiums paid with taxable rent—whether a separate exempt supply.**   A company owned a property which it let to tenants, and in respect of which it had elected to waive exemption. It insured the property, and required its tenants to pay it a specified proportion of the insurance premiums as rent. It did not account for output tax on such payments, treating them as a separate supply of exempt insurance. The Commissioners issued an assessment charging output tax on the payments, on the basis that they were payments of rent in respect of which the company had elected to waive exemption. The tribunal dismissed the company's appeal, holding that the company had 'made a single supply consisting of the grant of a legal estate in land ... the provisions of the lease relating to insurance cannot realistically be extricated from the lease and considered separately'. The tribunal also held that the premiums were not paid as disbursements for the tenants, since there was 'no element of agency'. *Globe Equities Ltd, [1995] VATDR 472 (VTD 13105)*.

36.21   **Retainer paid by insurance broker to partnership engaged in selling dogs.**   A husband and wife partnership advertised dogs for sale. They traded in a similar way to estate agents, acting as an intermediary between dogbreeders and members of the public. They received commission and annual retainers from the breeders to whom they introduced buyers. They also encouraged purchasers of dogs to take out insurance with an insurance broker, and received an annual retainer from the broker. They did not account for VAT on this retainer, and the Commissioners issued a ruling that it was standard-rated. The partners appealed, contending that the retainer should be treated as exempt from VAT under the legislation then in force. The tribunal dismissed the appeal, holding that the insurance arrangements were made by the broker rather than by the partnership, and that the retainer did not qualify for exemption. *Dogbreeders Associates, [1989] VATTR 317 (VTD 4295)*.

36.22   **Insurance provided by commercial removal service.**   The proprietor of a commercial removal service offered customers insurance against loss or damage of goods being moved. More than 90% of his customers requested this insurance cover, the usual charge for which was 8% of the value of the insured goods. The proprietor himself took out a policy with an established insurance company. The Commissioners issued an assessment charging tax on the amounts paid for the insurance, and the proprietor appealed, contending that the payments should be treated as exempt under *VATA 1983, Sch 6, Group 2, Item 3*. The tribunal dismissed the appeal, finding that the proprietor himself provided insurance to his customers, and holding that this was not a supply within the provision in question, since that only applied where an intermediary made arrangements for a third party to provide insurance, rather than where a principal provided insurance himself. (The supply also failed to qualify for exemption under what is now *VATA 1994, Sch 9, Group 2, Item 1*, since the proprietor was not a person permitted to carry on insurance business within *Insurance Companies Act 1982, s 2*.) *EJ Mooney (t/a Company Moves), [1990] VATTR 50 (VTD 4667)*.

36.23   *Mooney (t/a Company Moves)*, 36.22 above, was distinguished in three subsequent appeals, heard together, in which the tribunal found that the customers were parties to the insurance contracts and had rights against the insurance companies under the contracts. Accordingly the relevant supplies were directly related to the making of arrangements for the provision of insurance, and were exempt from VAT under the legislation then in force. *Robinsons Removals (Cleveland) Ltd, MAN/92/1644; E Pearson & Sons (Teesside) Ltd, MAN/92/1710; KW Devereux & Sons, MAN/92/1301 (VTD 11187)*.

36.24   **Insurance against loss of credit cards.**   See *Card Protection Plan Ltd*, 21.162
EUROPEAN COMMUNITY LAW.

36.25   **Direct marketing by insurance broker.**   A company which carried on business as an insurance broker undertook direct marketing to potential customers. It received commission from other companies in the same group when customers took out policies with one of the group companies. The Commissioners issued a ruling that the direct marketing services were standard-rated, and the company appealed, contending that they should be treated as exempt from VAT under the legislation then in force. The tribunal allowed the appeal, holding that the direct marketing consisted of 'services related to insurance transactions'. *Barclays Bank plc, [1991] VATTR 466 (VTD 6469)*. (*Note.* See now, however, *VATA 1994, Sch 9, Group 2, Note 7*, introduced with effect from 19 March 1997.)

36.26 **Pension fund trustees—contributions invested in insurance policies— whether trustees making arrangements for provision of insurance.** A company acted as trustee and administrator of a number of pension schemes. It invested the contributions paid by members of the schemes in insurance policies. It did not account for VAT on the fees which it received for this, and the Commissioners issued a ruling that they were standard-rated. The company appealed, contending that the fees should be treated as exempt under the legislation then in force. The tribunal dismissed the company's appeal, holding that the company was trading as a principal and was the person receiving the benefits of the insurance, rather than the provider of the insurance. It was making a single composite supply of trusteeship and administrative services, which did not qualify for exemption. *Federated Pensions Services Ltd, [1992] VATTR 358 (VTD 8932)*.

36.27 **Company formed by insurance brokers—whether supplies exempt.** A number of insurance brokers established a limited company (C) to devise new insurance products and to conduct negotiations with insurers for the underwriting of such products. C did not account for VAT on its supplies. The Commissioners issued a ruling that the supplies were standard-rated, and C appealed, contending that the supplies should be treated as exempt under the legislation then in force. The tribunal accepted this contention and allowed the appeal. *Countrywide Insurance Marketing Ltd, [1993] VATTR 277 (VTD 11443)*. (*Note.* See now, however, *VATA 1994, Sch 9, Group 2, Note 7*, introduced with effect from 19 March 1997.)

36.28 **Arrangements for provision of travel insurance.** A company (C) acted as an advertising agent for ferry operators. It also arranged travel insurance for the ferry operators with an insurance company. It received commission from the insurance company, and did not account for VAT on this, considering that it was exempt. The Commissioners issued on the basis that the commission did not qualify for exemption, since C did not itself make any arrangements with the customers of the ferry operators. The tribunal allowed C's appeal, holding that its services qualified for exemption under the legislation in force. *Curtis Edington & Say Ltd, LON/93/1651A (VTD 11699)*. (*Note.* For the Commissioners' practice following this decision, see News Release 52/94, issued on 15 December 1994. See also *VATA 1994, Sch 9, Group 2, Note 7*, introduced with effect from 19 March 1997.)

36.29 **Insurance of central heating systems.** A company (D) carried on business as heating engineers, installing and maintaining domestic central heating systems. It operated a service plan in conjunction with a leading insurance company, whereby it charged customers an annual fee of £99 and paid £54 of this to the insurance company, which then issued insurance certificates indemnifying the customers against any charges in the event of the equipment breaking down within twelve months. D treated the whole of the £99 as exempt from VAT. The Commissioners issued a ruling that only the £54 paid to the insurance company was exempt. D appealed. The tribunal allowed the appeal in part, holding that the £54 paid to the insurance company was wholly exempt, and that a proportion of the £45 which D retained should also be attributed to the making of arrangements for the supply of insurance, and thus as qualifying for exemption. The tribunal chairman expressed the opinion that, on the evidence, £67.50 should be treated as exempt and £31.50 as taxable, but gave the parties leave to apply for a further hearing within two months to adduce further evidence as to the quantum of the apportionment. *Domestic Service*

Care Ltd, MAN/93/163 (VTD 11869). (*Note*. There was no further public hearing of the appeal.)

36.30   **Exclusivity payment by insurance company.**   A company (H) received a payment from an insurance company (E) in return for granting E the exclusive right to provide insurance to its members. H did not account for output tax on the payment. The Commissioners issued an assessment, and H appealed, contending firstly that it had not made any supply to E, and alternatively that the payment was exempt from VAT under the legislation then in force. The tribunal rejected these contentions and dismissed H's appeal, holding that the payment was consideration for a supply of services and that the supply did not qualify for exemption. *Dogbreeders Associates*, 36.21 above, applied. *The British Horse Society Ltd, MAN/98/736 (VTD 16204)*.

36.31   **Estate agents arranging for provision of financial advice to clients.**   See *Wright Manley Ltd*, 26.18 FINANCE.

37 International Services

Note. With effect from 1 January 1993, revised provisions covering the place of supply of services were introduced by the *VAT (Place of Supply of Services) Order 1992 (SI 1992 No 3121)*, and *VATA 1983, Sch 5, Group 9* was substituted by the *VAT (International Services & Transport) Order 1992 (SI 1992 No 3223)*. The current zero-rating provisions are contained in *VATA 1994, Sch 8, Group 7*. Many supplies which would have been treated as zero-rated before 1 January 1993 are now treated as taking place outside the UK, and thus outside the scope of UK VAT.

The cases in this chapter are arranged under the following headings.

Zero-rating (VATA 1994, Sch 8, Group 7) 37.1–37.2
Reverse charge on services received from abroad (VATA 1994, s 8, Sch 5) 37.3–37.14

ZERO-RATING (VATA 1994, Sch 8, Group 7)

37.1 **Stud fees paid for servicing of mare—whether whole consideration zero-rated under Group 7, Item 1.** A company which owned a stud farm in the UK arranged for a mare, which was owned by a non-resident, to be serviced by a stallion at the stud. The company did not account for VAT on the consideration paid by the owner of the mare, treating it as wholly zero-rated under what is now *VATA 1994, Sch 8, Group 7, Item 1*. The Commissioners issued an assessment charging tax on part of the consideration, on the basis that it was attributable to the keep of the mare and did not qualify for zero-rating. The tribunal allowed the company's appeal, holding that there was a single supply of the servicing of the mare. The mare constituted 'goods' and the stallion's services constituted 'work carried out' within what is now *Item 1*, so that the whole of the consideration qualified for zero-rating. *Banstead Manor Stud Ltd, [1979] VATTR 154 (VTD 816)*.

37.2 **Diplomatic services—whether within Group 7, Item 2.** A company owned and maintained properties which were used as the official residences of the Bophutatswana Government in the UK. The premises were used to encourage tourism and investment in Bophutatswana by UK residents. The company did not account for tax on the consideration paid by the Bophutatswana Government, and the Commissioners issued an assessment charging output tax. The company appealed, contending that its services consisted of the making of arrangements for supplies of tourism and financial services which would take place in Bophutatswana, and were therefore zero-rated under what is now what is now *VATA 1994, Sch 8, Group 7, Item 2*. The tribunal dismissed the appeal, holding that the company was providing 'a single supply of services of the sort that would be supplied by an accredited diplomatic mission', but the QB remitted the case to the tribunal for rehearing, holding that the company was making multiple supplies which the tribunal had wrongly treated as a single supply. The CA upheld the QB decision, holding that it was essential to analyse the individual supplies of goods and services in order to determine how the money paid by the Bophutatswana Government should be apportioned between them. *Bophutatswana National Commercial Corporation Ltd v C & E Commrs, CA [1993] STC 702. (Note.* There was no further public hearing of the appeal.)

REVERSE CHARGE ON SERVICES RECEIVED FROM ABROAD (VATA 1994, s 8, Sch 5)

37.3 **VATA 1994, Sch 5 para 2—definition of 'advertising services'.** In 1991 and 1992 a trader distributed envelopes, containing information about a lottery, for a

Netherlands company. He did not account for tax on his receipts for these services. The Commissioners issued an assessment charging tax on them, and he appealed, contending that his services were within the definition of 'advertising services' (and were thus zero-rated under the legislation then in force). The tribunal dismissed his appeal, holding that he was supplying 'distribution and delivery services', rather than advertising services. *P Lawrence (t/a PLC), LON/94/1233A (VTD 13092)*.

37.4   See also *Austrian National Tourist Office*, 58.378 SUPPLY; *Miller Freeman Worldwide plc*, 58.387 SUPPLY; *International Trade & Exhibitions J/V Ltd*, 58.390 SUPPLY, and *John Village Automotive Ltd*, 58.391 SUPPLY.

37.5   **Advertising services—validity of VAT (Place of Supply of Services) Order.** See *Diversified Agency Services Ltd*, 58.377 SUPPLY.

37.6   **VATA 1994, Sch 5 para 3—services of consultants.** A French company acquired a UK subsidiary, and supplied management services relating to 'new consolidation systems' and 'group structure re-organisation'. The Commissioners issued an assessment on the basis that the services were 'services of consultants', within *VATA 1994, Sch 5 para 3*, so that the UK subsidiary was liable to account for tax under the 'reverse charge' provisions of *VATA 1994, s 8*. The company appealed, contending that the relevant supplies were not 'services of consultants' and that the place of supply was in France, so that there should be no liability to UK VAT. The tribunal rejected this contention and dismissed the appeal, holding on the evidence that the relevant services were 'of a strategic, rather than a clerical or administrative nature', and were therefore 'services of consultants', within *Sch 5 para 3*. *Vision Express Ltd, MAN/99/719 (VTD 16848)*.

37.7   See also *MEP Research Services Ltd*, 58.379 SUPPLY.

37.8   **VATA 1994, Sch 5 para 3—engineering services.** See *Hutchvision Hong Kong Ltd*, 58.371 SUPPLY.

37.9   **VATA 1994, Sch 5 para 3—services of accountants.** See *WH Payne & Co*, 58.397 SUPPLY.

37.10   **VATA 1994, Sch 5 para 3—data processing.** See *Laurentian Management Services Ltd*, 58.374 SUPPLY.

37.11   **VATA 1994, Sch 5 para 3—exclusion of services relating to land.** See *Brodrick Wright & Strong Ltd*, 58.384 SUPPLY, *Mechanical Engineering Consultants Ltd*, 58.385 SUPPLY, and *Aspen Advisory Services Ltd*, 58.386 SUPPLY.

37.12   **VATA 1994, Sch 5 para 5—definition of 'financial services'.** See *Gardner Lohman Ltd*, 58.399 SUPPLY, and *Culverpalm Ltd*, 58.400 SUPPLY.

37.13   **VATA 1994, Sch 5 para 6—definition of 'supplies of staff'.** See *American Institute of Foreign Study (UK) Ltd*, 58.401 SUPPLY.

37.14   **VATA 1994, Sch 5 para 7—definition of 'goods other than means of transport'.** See *BPH Equipment Ltd*, 58.402 SUPPLY.

38   Invoices and Credit Notes

The cases in this chapter are arranged under the following headings.

WHETHER DOCUMENTS TO BE TREATED AS VAT INVOICES (VAT Regulations 1995, reg 14)

General principles

38.1   **Incomplete invoices.** See *Jeunehomme v Belgian State*, 21.218 EUROPEAN COMMUNITY LAW.

Documents held to constitute valid invoices

38.2   **Invoices issued one day prior to receivership—whether valid.**   A company issued a set of invoices to British Telecom on 15 September 1992. It went into receivership on the following day, and subsequently went into liquidation. The Commissioners formed the opinion that, because British Telecom operated a 'self-billing' system, the invoices were not effective, and that the supplies in question had not taken place until after the company had gone into receivership, so that the tax chargeable was recoverable from the receivers. The company appealed, contending that the invoices were genuine, so that the tax was recoverable as a debt in the liquidation. The tribunal accepted this contention and allowed the appeal. The tribunal chairman (Mr. de Voil, sitting alone) stated that the self-billing procedure was 'a gross violation of the integrity of the VAT system' and 'a dangerous procedure' which 'should be strictly controlled and policed'. The fact that a customer operated a 'self-billing' system did not oblige a supplier to refrain from issuing a normal invoice. *UDL Construction plc (in administrative receivership and compulsory liquidation), [1995] VATDR 396 (VTD 13714).*

38.3   **Invoices prepared by customer on behalf of supplier.**   A company (W) carried on business as steel constructional engineers. It agreed that a newly formed company (B) should do work for it as a subcontractor. The agreement was with M who held himself out as a director of B. B was registered for VAT but had no stationery or invoices of its own and, at M's request, W had duplicate invoices printed for B. The work done by B was costed and agreed weekly. An employee of W then prepared a duplicate invoice for B showing the amount due inclusive of VAT, paid this amount to M and retained the top copy of the invoice. The Commissioners refused to accept the invoices as evidence of the tax borne for input tax purposes, and assessed W for the tax on the ground that this was a case of 'self-billing' for which the company had not obtained the Commissioners' approval as was required by what is now *VAT*

Regulations 1995 (SI 1995 No 2518), reg 13. The tribunal allowed W's appeal. Although the tribunal accepted the evidence for the Commissioners that B had not accounted for the tax and could not now be traced, it also accepted W's evidence as to what took place. This was not a case of 'self-billing' as the invoices had been printed and prepared on behalf of B. *Weldstruct Ltd, [1977] VATTR 101 (VTD 374). (Note.* Compare the cases noted at 38.44 to 38.49 below.)

38.4   A similar decision was reached in *Ocean Leisure International Ltd, MAN/94/147 (VTD 13169).*

38.5   **Invoices issued in wrong name.**   A wholesaler (B) wished to obtain a credit account with a manufacturing company (G Ltd) but was unable to do so. G's products were in great demand and B arranged with some of G's sales representatives that goods which he required should be ordered in the name of, and invoiced and delivered to, an existing customer. The representative then collected the goods with the invoice and delivered them to B who handed the representative a cheque drawn in favour of G Ltd. It was stated that a number of wholesalers, unable to open an account with G, had entered into similar arrangements. B deducted the tax on the invoices as input tax and appealed against an assessment withdrawing the deduction. The tribunal allowed the appeal, holding that the goods had been supplied to B and the invoices were valid tax invoices. *AL Booth, [1977] VATTR 133 (VTD 385).*

38.6   A sole trader reclaimed input tax in respect of invoices made out to a company of which he was a director, and which had a similar name to his trading name. The Commissioners issued an assessment to recover the tax but the tribunal allowed the trader's appeal, holding on the evidence that the invoices related to supplies made to the trader, that the incorrect insertion of the company's name on the invoices was a clerical error by the supplier, and that in the circumstances it would be unreasonable to reject the trader's claim to input tax. *JE Morgan (t/a Wishmore Morgan Investments), LON/86/165 (VTD 2150).*

38.7   See also *Crompton Enterprises Ltd*, 34.31 INPUT TAX.

38.8   **Invoices bearing false VAT number.**   A company (M) purchased two items of heavy earth-moving equipment and deducted input tax on the purchases. The invoices bore fictitious VAT numbers and the addresses stated on the invoices were false. The Commissioners therefore disallowed the input tax claimed on the purchases. The tribunal allowed M's appeal, holding that the vendors were clearly taxable persons since the value of the items in question was in excess of the registration limits. On the evidence, M was held not to be in any way party to the false invoices. *Morshan Contractors Ltd, MAN/84/202 (VTD 1861). (Note.* A subsequent tribunal specifically declined to follow this decision in *Pride & Leisure Ltd*, 38.24 below.)

38.9   The proprietor of an off-licence reclaimed input tax in respect of invoices which bore a false VAT number and did not show the name or address of the supplier. The Commissioners issued an assessment to recover the tax, and the trader appealed, contending that the invoices recorded genuine transactions. At the hearing of the appeal the trader produced copies of delivery notes relating to the transactions, together with his chequebook stubs and copies of his bank statements. He stated in evidence that he had contacted the supplier who had refused to provide signed invoices, and that he was no longer dealing with the supplier in question. The tribunal allowed the appeal, finding that the invoices recorded genuine transactions and holding that the trader was entitled to credit for the input tax. *Montalbano*, 38.57 below, distinguished. *GN Chavda (t/a Hare Wines), LON/92/97 (VTD 9895).*

38.10 Invoices and Credit Notes

38.10 A company engaged a contractor to erect a building comprising four industrial units. Payment was made in cash on a weekly basis, and at the completion of the work the contractor issued an invoice showing a total charge of £33,100 plus VAT of £4,965. The company paid the balance due, and reclaimed the £4,965 as input tax. The Commissioners discovered that the registration number on the invoice was false and that the contractor was not registered for VAT. They therefore rejected the company's input tax claim. The company appealed. The tribunal allowed the appeal, holding that since the contractor's turnover clearly exceeded the registration threshold of *Sch 1 para 1*, he was a 'taxable person' and the company was entitled to credit for the input tax. *Libdale Ltd*, 38.12 below, and *Greenall*, 34.495 INPUT TAX, applied; *Pride & Leisure Ltd*, 38.24 below, distinguished. *Ellen Garage (Oldham) Ltd, [1994] VATTR 392 (VTD 12407)*.

38.11 **Authenticity of invoices disputed.** The Commissioners issued an assessment to recover input tax reclaimed by a company (S) trading as a coin dealer. The trader who had issued the invoices had been registered in a false name, and had been convicted and fined for this. The Commissioners formed the view that S was a party to the deception, and that the invoices were not authentic. The tribunal allowed S's appeal, holding that the Commissioners had not proved that S was implicated in any deception. *Stewart Ward (Coins) Ltd, LON/85/548 (VTD 2108, 2134)*. (*Notes*. (1) For a preliminary application in this case, see 2.175 APPEALS. (2) *Dicta* of the tribunal were disapproved by a subsequent tribunal in *Halil*, 2.186 APPEALS.)

38.12 Two companies (L and C) reclaimed input tax in respect of substantial purchases of precious metals from a sole trader (F). F had previously been registered for VAT, but had changed his address without notifying the Commissioners, and his registration had been cancelled. He had issued VAT invoices in respect of the transactions, but had not accounted for the VAT, and had subsequently been convicted for cheating the public revenue and sentenced to two years' imprisonment. The Commissioners formed the opinion that the directors of L and C had been aware that F did not intend to account for VAT on the transactions, and had been involved in a conspiracy to cheat the public revenue. They were convicted and their convictions were upheld by the CA (see 46.16 PENALTIES: CRIMINAL OFFENCES). The Commissioners issued assessments to recover the input tax which L and C had reclaimed. L and C appealed, contending that the invoices recorded transactions which had actually taken place and that they were entitled to credit for the input tax even though F had not in fact paid the VAT to the Commissioners. The tribunal allowed the appeals, finding that the transactions had actually taken place and that F had been a taxable person at the time of the transactions, even though his registration had wrongly been cancelled. VAT was therefore chargeable on the transactions, and L and C were entitled to credit for the input tax. *Libdale Ltd; Clycol Precious Metals Ltd, [1993] VATTR 425 (VTD 11543)*.

38.13 See also *Tom Wilson (Tobacco) Ltd*, 34.496 INPUT TAX.

38.14 **Self-billing—subcontractor producing false registration certificate.** A company reclaimed input tax on payments made to a subcontractor under a self-billing arrangement. The subcontractor had produced a false registration certificate and did not account for the tax. The Commissioners rejected the claim but the tribunal allowed the company's appeal, holding that the tax was allowable since the subcontractor was a 'taxable person'. *Deeds Ltd, LON/82/20 (VTD 1500)*. (*Note*. For another issue in this case, see 2.196 APPEALS.)

38.15 **Invoice issued by deregistered supplier.** A trader (P) reclaimed input tax of £1,750 on the purchase of a vehicle. The supplier had previously been registered for VAT, but had subsequently deregistered. No VAT number was shown on the invoice, although P had obtained the supplier's old VAT number. The Commissioners issued an assessment to recover the tax, but the tribunal (Mr. Porter, sitting alone) allowed P's appeal, holding that the Commissioners ought to have exercised their discretion to treat the invoice as a VAT invoice. *T Postlethwaite (t/a TP Transport), MAN/96/930 (VTD 14925)*. (*Note*. No other cases were cited in the decision. With regard to supplies received from deregistered traders, compare *Direct Drilling*, 38.33 below, and the cases noted at 38.34 below. With regard to the nature of the tribunal's jurisdiction, compare the QB decision in *Kohanzad*, 38.59 below. With regard to the Commissioners' power to require production of an original invoice, see also *Reisdorf v Finanzamt Köln-West*, 21.219 EUROPEAN COMMUNITY LAW.)

Documents held not to constitute valid invoices

38.16   **Contractor reclaiming input tax in respect of invoices made out to customer.**   A kitchen fitter arranged for a retailer to supply kitchen units to his customers. The retailer sold the units directly to the customers and invoiced them accordingly. The fitter retrieved the invoices from the customers and reclaimed input tax in respect of them. The Commissioners issued an assessment to recover the tax and the tribunal dismissed the fitter's appeal, holding that the goods had been supplied to the customers rather than to the fitter, and that the fitter was not entitled to reclaim the input tax. *M Perks, MAN/82/228 (VTD 1556)*.

38.17   A construction company had agreed to carry out certain services for a bank which had granted it a loan facility. The company reclaimed input tax in respect of six invoices made out to the bank. Three of the invoices were issued by surveyors, one by a firm of valuers, and two by a firm of solicitors. The Commissioners issued an assessment to recover the tax and the company appealed, contending that it had paid for the supplies in question and that the bank was acting as its agent. The tribunal dismissed the appeal, holding that there was no evidence that the bank had agreed to act as an agent. Since the invoices were made out to the bank, the company had no right to reclaim the input tax in question. *Dalesid Ltd, LON/90/1941 (VTD 9147)*.

38.18   **Invoices made out to associated company.**   An appeal was dismissed in a case where a sole trader reclaimed input tax in respect of invoices made out to an associated company. The tribunal observed that 'although the particulars listed are onerous, there are sound reasons why claims for input tax should be supported by proper documentation. The name and address of the person to whom goods or services are supplied is of considerable importance'. *A Collins (t/a Inta Colour Brochures), LON/90/937X (VTD 6491)*. (*Note*. The *Rules of the Supreme Court 1965 (SI 1965 No 1776)* refer to 'particulars'. With effect from 26 April 1999, these rules have largely been replaced by the *Civil Procedure Rules 1998 (SI 1998 No 3132)*, which refer instead to 'information'.)

38.19   A company reclaimed input tax on supplies made before its registration, the invoices for which were made out to an associated company which had subsequently gone into liquidation. The Commissioners rejected the claim and the tribunal dismissed the company's appeal. *Tortoise Factory Units Ltd, LON/89/712 (VTD 4932)*.

38.20   An appeal was dismissed in a case where a sole trader had reclaimed input tax in respect of a number of invoices, but the tribunal found that the supplies in question had in fact been made to an associated company which had subsequently gone into liquidation. *Booth*, 38.5 above, and *Morgan*, 38.6 above, distinguished. *JW Gavacan, LON/94/2776A (VTD 13670)*.

38.21   See also *Herbert*, 34.72 INPUT TAX.

38.22 Invoices and Credit Notes

38.22 **Invoice bearing false VAT number.** A trader reclaimed input tax in respect of two invoices bearing false VAT numbers and issued in the names of unregistered traders. The Commissioners issued an assessment to recover the tax and the tribunal dismissed the trader's appeal. *FP Spain, MAN/83/147 (VTD 1555).*

38.23 A company reclaimed input tax on the basis of an invoice purportedly issued by a company which did not exist. The registration number shown on the invoice was false. The tribunal dismissed the company's appeal, holding that the company should have taken steps to verify the VAT number. *Henry Hadaway Organisation Ltd, LON/84/379 (VTD 2042).*

38.24 A similar decision was reached in a subsequent case where a company which had reclaimed VAT produced a purported invoice in the name of a non-existent company and bearing a false registration number. The tribunal declined to follow *Morshan Contractors Ltd*, 38.8 above, or *Deeds*, 38.14 above, holding that the Commissioners had exercised their discretion correctly in refusing to allow the claim. On the evidence, the appellant company had not proved that it had actually paid all the money shown on the fictitious invoice. The tribunal observed that 'a request for payments in cash in the course of a substantial contract would have put any trader on enquiry' and observed that the company's 'failure to obtain a proper tax invoice from a properly registered trader (if this was the position of the contractor) ... seems all the more remarkable'. *Pride & Leisure Ltd, MAN/91/212 (VTD 6911).*

38.25 *Pride & Leisure Ltd*, 38.17 above, was applied in the similar case of *D & D Coombes (t/a CH Chipp & Sons), LON/95/57 (VTD 13541).*

38.26 Similar decisions were reached in *Skycastle Ltd, LON/84/45 (VTD 1774)*; *Zintell Ltd, LON/90/985Z (VTD 7556)*; *Shalako of London Ltd, LON/90/1740 (VTD 7847)*; *Rimland Ltd, LON/90/170 (VTD 9962)*; *Papas Fashions, LON/91/2375X (VTD 10562)*; *J & B Construction Co Ltd, LON/92/1293A (VTD 11529)*; *Hermolis & Co Ltd, LON/93/1170 (VTD 11594)*; *MG Holloway, LON/94/2105 (VTD 13133)*; *Mrs J Newark, MAN/94/377 (VTD 13143)*; *EEB Nelken, LON/94/1029A (VTD 13176)*; *JA Taylor, MAN/94/502 (VTD 13822)*; *AR Brooks, LON/95/2716 (VTD 14256)*; *D Blount (t/a Office Equipment Consultants), MAN/95/1534 (VTD 15489)*; *Pitchworth Ltd, EDN/97/110 (VTD 15516)*; *PK Kishore & S Kumari (t/a Britannia Shoes), LON/99/90 (VTD 16886)*; *NK Kishore & S Kumari (t/a Eastern Arts & Crafts and Shambo Shoes), LON/99/91 (VTD 16886)*; *Buxton*, 3.114 ASSESSMENT; *Moda Ltd*, 47.12 PENALTIES: EVASION OF TAX and *Suitmart Ltd*, 49.349 PENALTIES: MISDECLARATION.

38.27 A similar decision was reached in a subsequent case where the tribunal held, applying *dicta* of Schiemann J in *Kohanzad*, 38.59 below, that its jurisdiction was supervisory and the Commissioners had not acted unreasonably. *Progressive Purification Systems Ltd, LON/95/2526 (VTD 13936).*

38.28 Similar decisions, also applying *dicta* of Schiemann J in *Kohanzad*, 38.59 below, were reached in *BAR Dann, LON/96/1265 (VTD 14811)*; *Joytot Ltd, LON/97/514 (VTD 15502)*; *Paramount Contractors Ltd, LON/98/168 (VTD 15642)*; *Cinetek Ltd, LON/99/161 (VTD 16572)* and *Elite Designs International Ltd, LON/99/635 (VTD 16925).*

38.29 **Business transferred as going concern—tax charged by vendor.** A trader (J) purchased a retail video business as a going concern for £18,000. The vendor's solicitors advised J that the price included VAT. J therefore reclaimed the VAT fraction of the purchase price as input tax. The Commissioners rejected the claim and J appealed, accepting that the business had been transferred as a going concern but contending that she should be allowed to reclaim the VAT which she had been charged by the vendor, and citing as authority a passage in the 'British VAT Reporter' (published by CCH). The tribunal rejected this contention and dismissed J's appeal, criticising the 'British VAT Reporter'. The chairman commented that the passage which J had cited as authority 'appears to me to contain a degree of misunderstanding ... if the vendor purports to charge VAT the sum paid is not, in fact, VAT, because the transaction is not one which attracts VAT'. Furthermore, the letter from the vendor's solicitors was not an invoice for VAT purposes. It had no registration number, did not state the vendor's name or address, and did not state the amount or rate of VAT. In any event, a VAT invoice could not exist where there was no taxable supply. *KK Jalf, MAN/90/260 (VTD 5767)*.

38.30   **Purported supply between associated companies—whether input tax reclaimable.**   See *Morston Properties Ltd (No 2)*, 34.19 INPUT TAX, and *United Society of Poets Ltd*, 34.20 INPUT TAX.

38.31   **Purported transfer of goods from company to associated partnership—whether input tax reclaimable.**   See *LMB Holdings Ltd*, 34.21 INPUT TAX.

38.32   **Purported transfer of goods from company to associated partnership—whether input tax reclaimable.**   See *Corke*, 43.141 PARTIAL EXEMPTION.

38.33   **Invoice issued by deregistered supplier.**   In May 1990 a partnership (D) reclaimed input tax of £1,200 on the basis of an invoice issued by another partnership (M), which had previously been registered for VAT, but had deregistered from September 1989. The Commissioners issued an assessment to recover the tax and the tribunal dismissed D's appeal, observing that the £1,200 was not VAT, but was in effect a premium charged by M, and that D's remedy was against M rather than against the Commissioners. *Direct Drilling, LON/93/401A (VTD 11071)*.

38.34   Similar decisions were reached in *A Hussain (t/a Villa Bombay), LON/93/1853 (VTD 11961); J McGowan, MAN/87/143 (VTD 11967); RN Gray (t/a RN Gray & Co), LON/93/1520A (VTD 12661); Kellpak Ltd, EDN/95/283 (VTD 14018); Sundial International plc, MAN/97/549 (VTD 16698)* and *Vickers Reynolds & Co (Lye) Ltd, MAN/99/1088 (VTD 16965)*.

38.35   **Invoice issued by unregistered supplier.**   A company (C) reclaimed input tax on the basis of three invoices issued by a company which was not registered for VAT. The three invoices all included the words 'VAT number applied for', but the supplier had never registered for VAT and subsequently ceased trading without accounting for the tax. The Commissioners issued an assessment to recover the tax and the tribunal dismissed C's appeal. *Active Clothing Ltd, MAN/92/1714 (VTD 11363)*.

38.36   Similar decisions were reached in *Dynamic Construction Ltd, MAN/93/730 (VTD 12079); JA Fashanu, LON/94/2897 (VTD 13137)* and *JD Ogilvie (t/a O & D Consultants), LON/96/611 (VTD 14536)*.

38.37   **Invoices bearing word 'proforma'.**   A 'proforma' invoice was held not to constitute a valid tax invoice in *Harlech Estates Ltd, MAN/90/986 (VTD 9548)*.

38.38   See also *Ufficio IVA di Trapani v Italittica SpA*, 21.125 EUROPEAN COMMUNITY LAW; *Ford Fuels Ltd*, 49.81 PENALTIES: MISDECLARATION; *South Caernarvon Creameries Ltd*, 49.121 PENALTIES: MISDECLARATION, and the cases noted at 49.122 PENALTIES: MISDECLARATION.

38.39   **Application for payment not intended to constitute tax invoice.**   See *ABB Power Ltd*, 58.318 SUPPLY, and *Finch*, 58.319 SUPPLY.

38.40 **Purchases from retailers—whether till slips evidence for input tax.** A company which operated a sauna purchased goods from local retailers. It reclaimed input tax on the evidence of till slips from such retailers. The Commissioners issued an assessment to recover the tax and the tribunal dismissed the company's appeal. *Mancumi & Sons Ltd, LON/81/365 (VTD 1213).*

38.41 **Invoices issued by associated company—whether shams.** A company (M), which operated the Cash Accounting Scheme, issued an invoice to an associated company (F) in respect of future marketing services of more than £410,000. F, which did not operate the Cash Accounting Scheme, reclaimed input tax in respect of the amount charged on the invoice. The Commissioners rejected the claim and the tribunal dismissed M's appeal, finding that there was 'very serious doubt that there was any possibility' of F ever being able to pay the amount charged by the invoice, and holding on the evidence that the 'arrangements between (M) and (F) were no more than a sham'. *Dicta* of Diplock LJ in *Snook v London & West Riding Investments Ltd, CA [1967] 2 QB 786; [1967] 1 All ER 518*, applied. *FPV Ltd, MAN/97/828 (VTD 15666).* (*Notes.* (1) The tribunal also dismissed an appeal by M against the termination of its right to use the Cash Accounting Scheme—see 10.6 CASH ACCOUNTING SCHEME. (2) The tribunal awarded costs of £1,000 to the Commissioners, finding that the companies had pursued the appeals 'on a vexatious and frivolous basis'.)

38.42 **Invoices described by issuer as fraudulent.** See *Sandell*, 58.138 SUPPLY.

38.43 **Supply of faulty goods—customer issuing supplier with 'invoice' claiming compensation—whether supplier entitled to reclaim input tax.** A company (G) supplied another company (M) with a quantity of material for the manufacture of wetsuits. M paid £20,700 plus VAT for the material. Subsequently M discovered that the material was faulty, and was not waterproof. M issued G with a purported invoice, reclaiming £21,100 and the VAT. G reclaimed the VAT shown on the purported invoice as input tax. The Commissioners issued an assessment to recover the tax, considering that the invoice did not represent any supply by M, but was intended to represent a claim to compensation. The tribunal dismissed M's appeal, holding that the purported invoice was not valid for VAT purposes as it did not relate to any taxable supply, and that the payment of compensation was outside the scope of VAT. *Holiday Inns (UK) Ltd, 58.116 SUPPLY*, applied. *Galaxy Equipment (Europe) Ltd, MAN/91/1457 (VTD 11415).*

38.44 **'Self-billing' invoices.** A company had approval from the Commissioners to operate the 'self-billing' method of issuing invoices. It issued such an invoice on behalf of a trader who had been deregistered. The Commissioners issued an assessment to recover the tax and the tribunal dismissed the company's appeal, holding that one of the conditions for the approval of the self-billing method had not been satisfied, so that the invoice was not effective. *Credit Ancillary Services Ltd, [1986] VATTR 204 (VTD 2172).*

38.45 Similar decisions were reached in *Shani Fashion Industries Ltd, LON/92/1483A (VTD 9789); MJ Gleeson plc, LON/94/1868A (VTD 13332)* and *Outis Ltd, LON/x (VTD 14864).*

38.46 An appeal was dismissed in a case where a company reclaimed input tax on the basis of 'self-billing' invoices which it had issued in the names of scaffolding contractors, although it had not been authorised to operate a self-billing system as required by what is now *Notice No 700, para 6.9(a). Midland Plant & Scaffolding Ltd, MAN/93/260 (VTD 11603).* (*Note.* An appeal against a charge to default interest was also dismissed.)

38.47   A similar decision was reached in *MP Lonergan, LON/95/639A (VTD 13305)*.

38.48   See also the cases noted at 49.262 to 49.264 PENALTIES: MISDECLARATION; *Glinski*, 49.350 PENALTIES: MISDECLARATION; *Beveridge*, 49.397 PENALTIES: MISDECLARATION, and the cases noted at 58.426 to 58.429 SUPPLY.

38.49   **'Self-billing invoices'—whether within Extra-Statutory Concession 3.9.**   A company which had operated the self-billing system incorrectly by issuing invoices on behalf of deregistered traders appealed against an assessment covering a period of almost six years, contending that the case fell within what is now Extra-Statutory Concession 3.9. The tribunal rejected this contention and dismissed the appeal, holding that a document issued on behalf of an unregistered person was not an 'invoice' and thus was not within Extra-Statutory Concession 3.9*. *British Teleflower Service Ltd, [1995] VATDR 356 (VTD 13756)*. (*Note.* The tribunal also found that the assessment had been issued within the one-year time limit of *VATA 1994, s 73(6)(b)*—see 3.45 ASSESSMENT.)

38.50   **Associated   partnerships—circular   transactions.** See   *CAL   Ingot Manufacturers*, 49.353 PENALTIES: MISDECLARATION.

INPUT TAX RECLAIMED WITHOUT INVOICES (VAT Regulations 1995, reg 29)

Cases where the appellant was successful

38.51   **Invoices destroyed accidentally.**   A trader failed to produce invoices in support of a claim to input tax. The Commissioners issued an assessment to recover the tax, and the trader appealed, contending that the invoices had been accidentally burnt. The tribunal accepted the trader's evidence and allowed the appeal. *JJ Newman, LON/79/32 (VTD 781, 903)*. (*Note.* See now, however, the subsequent case of *Reisdorf v Finanzamt Köln-West*, 21.219 EUROPEAN COMMUNITY LAW, in which the CJEC ruled that *Article 22(3)* of the *EC Sixth Directive* conferred on Member States the power to require production of an original invoice in order to establish the right to deduct input tax.)

38.52   A similar decision was reached in *Kleen Technologies International Ltd, LON/80/66 (VTD 970)*. (*Note.* For the award of costs in this case, see 2.323 APPEALS.)

38.53   **Invoices lost.**   A partnership appealed against an assessment withdrawing an input tax credit, contending that the relevant tax invoices had been lost on a change of residence by a partner of the business, and hence were not available for inspection by a VAT officer on a subsequent normal control visit. The details had been entered in the firm's VAT book and these entries had been checked in detail by the firm's accountant, to whom the receipts and invoices had been produced. The tribunal allowed the appeal, considering that the Commissioners had acted unreasonably in refusing to accept the firm's audited records, on the ground only that the original documentation was no longer available. *C Read & D Smith, [1982] VATTR 12 (VTD 1188)*. (*Note.* See now the note following *Newman*, 38.51 above.)

38.54   *Read & Smith*, 38.53 above, was applied in the similar case of *D Wright, LON/93/ 2720A (VTD 12451)*.

38.55   At a control visit in December 1994, VAT officer discovered that a farmer did not hold invoices relating to input tax which he had claimed from 1992 to July 1994, and issued an assessment to recover the tax in question. The farmer appealed, contending that he had lost the invoices when he had changed his address in August 1994. The tribunal accepted his evidence and allowed the appeal for the periods from 1992 to June 1994, finding that at the time he had claimed the input tax, the farmer had held invoices as required by *Article 18(1)* of the *EC Sixth Directive*. The fact that he had subsequently lost the invoices did not deny him the right to reclaim the tax. *Kohanzad*, 38.59 below, was distinguished on the grounds that the tribunal there had not been satisfied that the claimant had ever possessed the invoices which he had claimed to have lost. The tribunal held that 'the issue whether, at the time of claiming the deduction of input tax, the appellant held the required documents (here invoices) is a question of fact to be determined by the tribunal on the evidence, the burden of proof being on the appellant ... If the assessing officer forms the view that the requisite documents were not in fact held at the relevant time, then he must go on to consider the exercise of the discretion under (*VAT Regulations 1995, reg 29**) to allow other documentary evidence if there was such evidence. However, the fact that, on appeal against the exercise of that discretion, an appellant must show that the Commissioners did not act reasonably, does not affect the fact that on the prior issue of whether he did hold the documents the tribunal has a full appellate jurisdiction.' (The appeal was dismissed with regard to the input tax relating to July 1994, on the grounds that the farmer had already lost the invoices at the time he had submitted the relevant return.) *MS Vaughan, [1996] VATDR 95 (VTD 14050)*. (*Note.* See now the note following *Newman*, 38.51 above.)

38.56   **Unregistered supplier—no invoice issued.**   A company took delivery of a machine called a Yamazaki Machining Centre, for which it paid £122,500, plus purported VAT of £18,375, by banker's draft. The vendor failed to supply a VAT invoice, although it had previously been agreed that the price was inclusive of VAT. The company reclaimed the £18,375 as input tax. The Commissioners refused to allow the claim on the ground that no VAT invoice had been obtained and the machine had not been supplied by a taxable person. The tribunal allowed the company's appeal, holding on the evidence that the machine had been supplied by a taxable person and that the input tax was therefore allowable notwithstanding that an invoice had not been obtained. *Syston Tooling & Design Ltd, MAN/89/119 (VTD 4553)*.

Cases where the appellant was unsuccessful

38.57   **Invoices not produced by claimant.**   The Commissioners discovered that a trader had reclaimed input tax without holding supporting invoices, and issued an assessment to recover the tax. The tribunal dismissed the trader's appeal, observing that 'the Commissioners have a discretion whether or not to accept evidence other than tax invoices' but holding that, on the evidence, the Commissioners had been justified in refusing to accept the claims in question. *S Montalbano, LON/85/591 (VTD 2113)*. (*Note.* The decision in this case was approved by the QB in *Kohanzad*, 38.59 below.)

38.58   *Montalbano*, 38.57 above, was applied in the similar cases of *Floyde Brothers, LON/89/1530 (VTD 6765)* and *DH Morgan, LON/90/367X (VTD 6805)*.

38.59   The Commissioners issued estimated assessments on a jeweller after Customs officers had discovered quantities of undeclared gold and Krugerrands in his car. The jeweller appealed, contending that the assessments should be reduced to allow input tax on his purchases of the gold and Krugerrands in question. However, he failed to produce purchase invoices. The tribunal dismissed his appeal and the QB upheld this decision. Where an appellant failed to produce invoices, the Commissioners had a discretion as to whether to allow credit for input tax. Where they declined to allow such credit, the tribunal had a supervisory jurisdiction, the burden of proof being on the appellant to show that the Commissioners had acted unreasonably. On the evidence, the Commissioners had acted reasonably in rejecting the jeweller's claim. *A Kohanzad v C & E Commrs, QB [1994] STC 967*.

38.60   Similar decisions were reached in *Miss Charlie Ltd, LON/90/361 (VTD 9301);
Templegate Accounting Services Ltd, LON/96/43 (VTD 14446); PJ & AJ Nicholas
(t/a A & P Scaffolding), LON/98/894 (VTD 15898); Glinski*, 49.350 PENALTIES:
MISDECLARATION and *WFS Metals Ltd*, 49.351 PENALTIES: MISDECLARATION.

38.61   *Kohanzad*, 38.59 above, was applied in a subsequent case in which the tribunal held
that its jurisdiction in such appeals was supervisory rather than appellate. *Dicta* in
Bardsley, 9.58 CARS, applied; *John Dee Ltd*, 14.28 COLLECTION AND ENFORCEMENT,
distinguished. *Richmond Resources Ltd (in liquidation), LON/94/1496A (VTD
13435)*.

38.62   Similar decisions, also applying *Kohanzad*, 38.59 above, were reached in *Sparrow
(UK) Ltd, LON/99/1085 (VTD 16642)* and *N O'Driscoll, LON/99/1265 (VTD
16941)*.

38.63   The Commissioners discovered that a trader had reclaimed input tax without holding
supporting invoices, and issued an assessment to recover the tax. The trader
appealed, contending that he could not produce the invoices as his accountant was
holding them as security for unpaid fees. The tribunal dismissed the appeal, holding
that the trader had not produced evidence to justify the claim. *HR Jalota,
MAN/87/206 (VTD 2684)*. (*Note*. For an explanation of the circumstances in which
an accountant may retain a client's records as security for unpaid fees, see *Woodworth
v Conroy, CA [1996] 1 All ER 107*. The Ch D has held that the effect of *Companies
Act 1985, s 221* is that an accountant cannot retain a company's sales invoices—see
DTC (CTC) Ltd v Gary Sargent & Co, Ch D [1996] BCC 290.)

38.64   **Invoices allegedly stolen.**   A married couple traded in partnership as clothing
retailers. The Commissioners discovered that they had reclaimed input tax without
supporting invoices. They issued an assessment to recover this tax, and the partners
appealed, contending that the invoices had been stolen from their car. The tribunal
dismissed their appeal, observing that this was the second occasion on which the
partners had claimed that records had been stolen and finding that the officer had
reason for suspecting that the theft 'could have been invented for the purpose of
avoiding production of the VAT records'. The tribunal chairman observed that 'the
Commissioners should act in a way which will protect the revenue; they are a public
body dispensing and receiving public money and they are accountable for that. For
them to pay out money to an individual or firm when there was no evidence of
entitlement to the money would be inconsistent with the discharge by them of their
public duty'. *VK & Mrs U Dilawri (t/a East & West Textiles), MAN/91/632 (VTD
11409)*.

38.65   *Dilawri*, 38.64 above, was applied in the similar subsequent cases of *JD Maloney,
LON/96/785 (VTD 14754)* and *D Hudson, MAN/97/1200 (VTD 15618)*.

38.66   Similar decisions were reached in *WA Oloyede, LON/93/1083A (VTD 11944)* and
Elegant Clothing (Blackburn) Ltd, MAN/96/788 (VTD 14739).

38.67   **Invoices allegedly destroyed.**   The Commissioners discovered that a trader had
reclaimed input tax without holding supporting invoices, and issued an assessment to
recover the tax. The trader appealed, contending that the invoices had been
destroyed when his premises were flooded. The tribunal dismissed his appeal,
holding that the Commissioners had not acted unreasonably in refusing to accept his
claims. *Van Boeckel*, 3.1 ASSESSMENT, applied. *JC Horton, LON/90/837Z (VTD
7258)*.

38.68   **Invoices not issued by supplier—whether Commissioners should permit
claims to input tax under VAT Regulations, reg 29*.**   A company (N)
reclaimed input tax in respect of a payment which it had made to a company which

supplied registration marks, although it had received neither the registration mark in question nor a tax invoice. The Commissioners issued an assessment to recover the tax and the tribunal dismissed N's appeal, holding that although what is now *VAT Regulations 1995 (SI 1995 No 2518), reg 29* gave the Commissioners the right to accept claims for input tax without supporting invoices, the tribunal's jurisdiction in such cases was supervisory rather than appellate, and the Commissioners had not acted unreasonably in this case. *Newland Technical Services Ltd, LON/92/1255A (VTD 9294). (Note. For other issues in this case, see 34.239 INPUT TAX, and 49.93 and 49.309 PENALTIES: MISDECLARATION.)

38.69   **Other cases.**   There are a large number of other cases, which appear to raise no point of general importance, in which appeals against the disallowance of input tax have been dismissed on the grounds that the appellant has failed to provide sufficient evidence in support of the claim. In the interests of space, such cases are not included in this book.

CALCULATION OF VAT ON INVOICES

38.70   **Rounding of invoices.**   A company which operated a hotel adopted a policy of rounding down fractions of a penny in respect of individual items included in invoices. The Commissioners issued an assessment on the basis that the company was only entitled to round down the total amount of tax included on any invoice, rather than individual items included within that invoice. The tribunal upheld the assessment and dismissed the company's appeal. *Catchlord Ltd, [1985] VATTR 238 (VTD 1966).*

CREDIT NOTES

Whether credit note effective for VAT purposes

38.71   A company (B) invoiced its parent company (U) for an amount described as 'service charges' including VAT. In accounting for its tax, U treated as input tax the whole of the tax on the amounts invoiced to it. In fact, most of the supplies made by U were exempt, so that it was entitled to deduct only a proportion of the tax. On discovering this, the Commissioners issued an assessment to recover input tax overdeducted up to March 1974. Thereupon B issued credit notes to U cancelling the service charges from April 1973 to October 1975, and took credit for the tax on the charges cancelled in its subsequent returns. The Commissioners considered that the credit notes were not valid for VAT purposes, and issued an assessment to recover the tax, against which B appealed. The tribunal allowed the appeal in part, holding that, to the extent that the 'service charges' represented payments to employees, B was acting as an agent for U and not as an independent principal, and that the credit notes were effective in respect of this outlay. Insofar as the service charge was for rent, rates and overheads of the head office building, there had been a taxable supply by B and the credit notes were ineffective. The tribunal held that a credit note was only effective for VAT purposes if it had been 'issued *bona fide* in order to correct a genuine mistake or overcharge, or to give a proper credit'. (The ascertainment of the figures was left for agreement by the parties.) *British United Shoe Machinery Co Ltd, [1977] VATTR 187 (VTD 463).*

38.72   A firm of architects and surveyors invoiced a company for work carried out, and accounted for output tax of £373. However, the company subsequently went into liquidation without paying the amount invoiced. In July 1974 the firm thereupon issued a credit note for the amount invoiced and deducted the £373 in its next return. The Commissioners issued an assessment to recover the £373 and the tribunal dismissed the firm's appeal. Applying *dicta* in *British United Shoe Machinery Co Ltd*, 38.71 above, the credit note had not been issued in order to correct a genuine mistake or overcharge, and was therefore ineffective for VAT purposes. *Peter Cripwell & Associates, CAR/78/131 (VTD 660).*

38.73   In 1980 a company (M) sold a machine to another company (E) for £45,910 plus VAT of £6,886, issuing a tax invoice for this amount. Under the terms of the sale, the whole of the VAT plus 20% of the £45,910 was payable on delivery of the machine, the remaining 80% carrying interest and being payable in instalments. E paid the deposit, the VAT and the first instalment, but failed to pay subsequent instalments and M repossessed the machine. E was then in receivership, and M sent the receiver a purported credit note for the amount originally invoiced, together with a purported invoice for £27,055 (including VAT of £3,122), for E's use of the machine. M submitted a VAT return which included the £3,122 as output tax and deducted the £6,886 as input tax. The Commissioners issued an assessment to recover the difference of £3,764, and the tribunal dismissed M's appeal, holding that the 'credit note' was not effective for tax purposes. *Mannesmann Demag Hamilton Ltd, [1983] VATTR 156 (VTD 1437).*

38.74   A company (S) sold commercial vehicles to a finance company for subsequent resale to customers under hire-purchase agreements. The invoices which S issued to the finance company showed an inflated sale price (overvaluing old vehicles taken in part-exchange in order to meet the finance company's requirement for a minimum deposit). Subsequently S issued credit notes to the customers under the hire-purchase agreements, to correct the overcharge. The Commissioners issued an assessment on the basis that S was obliged to account for output tax on the full amount shown on the invoices which it had issued to the finance company. S appealed. The tribunal dismissed the appeal, holding that the supply had been to the finance company, not to the customer, and that the credit notes were not effective for VAT purposes. *Sheepcote Commercial (Vehicles) Ltd, LON/86/334 (VTD 2378).*

38.75   *Sheepcote Commercial (Vehicles) Ltd*, 38.74 above, was applied in the similar subsequent case of *Senator Marketing Ltd, LON/90/79Y (VTD 5598).*

38.76   A similar decision was reached in *Howletts (Autocare) Ltd, MAN/94/483 (VTD 14467). (Note.* Costs were awarded to the Commissioners.)

38.77   A similar decision was reached in a case in which a company (F) trading as a car dealer agreed discounts with customers who purchased cars under hire-purchase agreements whereby legal ownership of the cars passed to the finance company involved in the transaction, but issued invoices to the finance company showing the gross undiscounted price and treating the discount as a deposit. F subsequently issued credit notes to the customers, and the Commissioners issued an assessment on the basis that the credit notes were ineffective for VAT purposes. The tribunal dismissed F's appeal, holding that the credit notes were ineffective since they had been issued to the customer whereas the relevant supply had been made to the finance company. *First County Garages Ltd, LON/95/2962 (VTD 14417).*

38.78   Purported credit notes were also held to be ineffective for VAT purposes in *Temple Gothard & Co, LON/78/238 (VTD 702); Castle Wines Ltd, MAN/82/31 (VTD 1271); RSM Macro, MAN/83/100 (VTD 1533); Larullah Ltd, LON/84/172 (VTD 1779); Levis's Compressors Ltd, MAN/84/36 (VTD 1871); Bury's Transport (Oxon) Ltd, LON/85/129 (VTD 1928); Paul Verma & Co, LON/45/487 (VTD 2104); Thermalex Window Systems Ltd, MAN/86/209 (VTD 2299); Reddiglaze Ltd, MAN/86/210 (VTD 2299); Castle Associates Ltd, MAN/87/448 (VTD 3497); J Rickard, LON/88/802Z (VTD 3711); ME Braine (Boatbuilders) Ltd, MAN/88/594 (VTD 3881); SAW Freeman, LON/89/1205X (VTD 4652); AS Verdi,*

38.79 Invoices and Credit Notes

LON/89/1392Y (VTD 5228); Britel Communications Ltd, LON/90/819X (VTD 6890); WR Dyke, LON/91/1612Z (VTD 7351); AJ Freeman, LON/90/1566X (VTD 7384); TA Costello, LON/91/1865X (VTD 9163); LJ Gerrard, LON/92/ 2735A (VTD 10158); Ten Bob A Week Ltd, MAN/92/553 (VTD 10678); HT Shepherd (Ibstock) Building Contractors Ltd, MAN/92/1445 (VTD 11084); Yorkshire Pine Products (UK) Ltd, MAN/94/160 (VTD 13175); McNulty Offshore Services Ltd, 2.162 APPEALS; *Realm Defence Industries Ltd*, 34.17 INPUT TAX, *Engineering Building Services*, 49.237 PENALTIES: MISDECLARATION, and the cases noted at 49.238 PENALTIES: MISDECLARATION.

38.79   In a case where the facts were complex, a number of credit notes had been issued in respect of management charges raised between associated companies for the use of capital. The Commissioners issued an assessment on the basis that the credit notes were not effective for VAT purposes. The tribunal reviewed the evidence in detail and allowed the company's appeal in part. *Laurence Scott Ltd, [1986] VATTR 1 (VTD 2004).*

38.80   In 1979 a company issued invoices for fees including VAT of £4,960.49. The customer did not pay the fees and the company began legal proceedings. The proceedings were dismissed in 1987. The company then issued a credit note and reclaimed the VAT in its next quarterly return. The Commissioners issued an assessment to recover the tax, considering that the credit note had not been issued bona fide. The tribunal allowed the company's appeal, holding on the evidence that the money had not been due to the company in the first place. The credit note had been correctly issued to correct a genuine overcharge. *Cobojo Ltd, MAN/89/746 (VTD 4055).*

38.81   A company which installed security alarm systems, under agreements which provided for continuing hire and maintenance of the systems, issued credit notes in cases where customers had left their premises without paying for the hire or maintenance. The Commissioners issued an assessment in respect of such credit notes, considering that they had been issued to write off bad debts and were not effective for VAT purposes. The company appealed. The tribunal allowed the company's appeal, holding that in cases where customers had left the premises it seemed reasonable to suppose that the systems in question would not have been hired or maintained. Accordingly, the credit notes had been issued in good faith and were effective for VAT purposes. *British United Shoe Machinery Co Ltd*, 38.71 above, applied. *Securicor Granley Systems Ltd, [1990] VATTR 9 (VTD 4575).*

38.82   *Securicor Granley Systems Ltd*, 38.81 above, was applied in a case where a company which fitted baby seats in cars had contracted to refund the price of the seat to any customers who returned the seat and the receipt after the fourth birthday of the child for whose use it was fitted. Where these conditions were fulfilled, the company issued credit notes. The tribunal held that there was a single transaction and that the credit notes had been issued in good faith and were effective for VAT purposes. *Kwik Fit (GB) Ltd, [1992] VATTR 427 (VTD 9383).*

38.83   A company in the motor trade offered customers a comprehensive repair service whereby it undertook to repair damaged cars and provided a substitute vehicle for the customer's use while his own vehicle was being repaired. The substitute car was provided without charge to the customer, but the company instructed the customer's solicitors to include in the relevant claim the amount of hire charges which it would otherwise have required the customer to pay. When the repairs had been completed, the customer was required to return the hire car and reclaim his own. An invoice was prepared for the amount of the hire charges, including VAT, and sent to the solicitors. Where the amount recovered was less than the amount included in the invoice (e.g. where the customer had been guilty of contributory negligence) the company prepared a credit note for the amount of the difference. The credit note was not sent to the solicitors, but was taken into account in computing the company's VAT liability. The Commissioners issued an assessment to recover the tax which was the subject of the credit notes, considering that they were not effective for VAT purposes and that the company should have claimed bad debt relief instead. The tribunal allowed the company's appeal in part, holding that the credit notes were valid in cases where it was subsequently agreed that the rate of charge was excessive. However, where the amount paid was less than the amount invoiced because of the customer's contributory negligence, or where the amount invoiced was reduced because the period of hire was subsequently agreed to have been excessive, the customer remained nominally liable to the company for the invoiced amount and the company should have claimed bad debt relief instead of issuing a credit note. Similarly, where the company had issued a credit note because it could not recover the invoiced amount from the third party, the credit note was not effective and the company should have claimed bad debt relief instead. *Barras (Garages) Ltd, MAN/91/268 (VTD 6913)*.

38.84   In a case where the facts were unusual, the tribunal held that two credit notes had been correctly issued, since the companies to whom they had been issued had not reclaimed the tax in question as input tax. *The Friary Electrical Co Ltd, LON/91/2145 (VTD 7554)*. (*Note*. An appeal against a misdeclaration penalty was also allowed.)

38.85   See also *Lamdec Ltd*, 2.159 APPEALS; *Dixons Group plc*, 63.108 VALUATION, and *AEG (UK) Ltd*, 63.109 VALUATION.

38.86   **Whether recipient of supply obliged to account for tax in respect of disputed credit note issued by supplier.**   A company (G) supplied goods and services to another company (S) in 1974 and 1975, invoicing S for the supply for an amount including VAT of £7,393 which G duly accounted for and which S deducted as input tax. In 1978, following a change of practice under which the Commissioners accepted that the relevant supplies were zero-rated, G was permitted to reclaim the £7,393 and issued a credit note for the amount. However, S did not receive the credit note and was not aware of the credit until told of it by VAT officers at a meeting in January 1980. Meanwhile there had been court proceedings between G and S, as a result of which the credit note was 'commercially worthless'. The Commissioners issued an assessment on S for the £7,393 for the period to 31 January 1980. The tribunal allowed the appeal, finding that S had never received the original credit note and holding that S was entitled to credit for the £7,393 and was under no obligation to take any action in respect of the disputed credit note. *Silvermere Golf & Equestrian Centre Ltd, [1981] VATTR 106 (VTD 1122)*. (*Note. Notice No 700, para 7.1* states that 'any VAT adjustment arising from the ... receipt of a credit or debit note must be made in the VAT account for the period in which you enter the adjustment in your business accounts'.)

38.87   *Silvermere Golf & Equestrian Centre Ltd*, 38.86 above, was applied in a similar subsequent case where the Commissioners had issued an assessment to recover input tax which a company had deducted on receipt of an invoice, for which the supplier had purportedly issued a subsequent credit note. The tribunal found that the company had never received the credit note in question, and allowed its appeal against the assessment. *Highsize Ltd, LON/90/945Y (VTD 7098)*.

38.88   For a case in which a credit note issued by the receivers of a company was held to have been wrongly issued, and to be worthless, see *Wade*, 45.3 PAYMENT OF TAX.

Miscellaneous

38.89 **VAT Regulations 1995, reg 38—whether any decrease in consideration.** A company (M) had supplied goods to another company (S). S went into receivership, owing M more than £15,000. M repossessed goods to the value of this debt. In its return for the period ending December 1991, M deducted the output tax relating to the repossessed goods. The Commissioners issued an assessment to recover the tax, and M appealed, contending that the repossession amounted to a 'decrease in consideration' within what is now *VAT Regulations 1995 (SI 1995 No 2518), reg 38*. The tribunal dismissed M's appeal, holding that the repossession did not amount to a decrease in consideration. *Morley Electronic Fire Systems Ltd, MAN/92/1119 (VTD 10957)*.

38.90 A company made sales of bottled mineral water, on which it accounted for VAT. Following the introduction of the *VAT (Beverages) Order 1993 (SI 1993 No 2498)* with effect from 1 December 1993, it became aware that, although all such supplies were standard-rated after that date, some of its supplies could have been treated as zero-rated before that date, as the supplies were of natural mineral water which was not 'manufactured' and was not therefore excluded from zero-rating by the law previously in force. At first the Commissioners rejected the company's claim that any of the supplies had qualified for zero-rating, and the company had to lodge a formal appeal against a ruling that the sales had been standard-rated, but in September 1996, before the appeal had been heard by a tribunal, the Commissioners accepted the company's claim. In the meantime, the company agreed with three of its customers (all major retailers) that it would issue them with credit notes for the sums charged as VAT, together with invoices for approximately 85% of the sums as additional consideration for the original supplies. (The effect of this scheme was that the company would recover approximately 85% of the overpaid VAT and the customers would recover approximately 15%.) In its return for the period ending October 1996, the company reclaimed VAT of more than £2,000,000. The Commissioners considered that the effect of the three-year cap introduced by a Budget Resolution under *Provisional Collection of Taxes Act 1968* (and subsequently enacted by *FA 1997*) was that more than £926,000 of the amount claimed was not repayable. They therefore made a repayment of approximately £1,100,000. The company appealed, contending that its transactions with its customers constituted decreases in consideration for the original supplies, within *VAT Regulations 1995 (SI 1995 No 2518), reg 24*, so that it had been entitled to adjust its VAT account under *reg 38* and the balance of £926,000 was repayable accordingly. The tribunal rejected this contention and dismissed the appeal. Applying *dicta* of Lord Hope in *McMaster Scotland Stores Ltd*, 45.16 PAYMENT OF TAX, what is now *reg 38* 'is concerned only with the making of adjustments to the VAT account to reflect an increase or a decrease in consideration which includes an amount of tax chargeable on the supply'. The tribunal held that the consideration for the supplies in this case 'did not include an amount of VAT, with the consequence that the procedure under *regulation 38* is not available to the appellant and the appellant's claim fails'. The only way in which the company could claim repayment was under *VATA 1994, s 80*. *The Robinson Group of Companies Ltd, MAN/97/348 (VTD 16081)*.

38.91 See also *McMaster Scotland Stores Ltd*, 45.16 PAYMENT OF TAX, and *Copson*, 55.19 RETURNS.

38.92 **Decrease in consideration—whether credit note must be issued.** A company made refunds to some of its customers in some cases where the goods which it had supplied did not meet the customers' expectations. It accounted for output tax on the basis that it could reduce the amount of the supply by the amount of the refund, although it did not always issue a credit note. The Commissioners issued a ruling that the company could only reduce the amount of the supply, as shown on the invoice, where it issued a credit note in accordance with the *VAT Regulations*. The company appealed, contending that the effect of *Article 11C1* of the *EC Sixth Directive* was that it was entitled to treat the taxable amount as being reduced by the amount of the refund even where it did not issue a credit note. The tribunal rejected this contention and dismissed the company's appeal. *Article 11C1* provided that the taxable amount was to be reduced 'under conditions which shall be determined by the Member States'. The relevant conditions were laid down in *regulation 38* of the *VAT Regulations 1995*, which had to be read in conjunction with the definition of a 'decrease in consideration' in *regulation 24*. The tribunal observed that 'to suggest that increases or decreases in consideration could be effective for VAT purposes without any credit note or other similar document changing the amount of consideration in the original invoice does run counter to the scheme both of the *Sixth Directive* ... and indeed the national primary legislation which requires accounting for value added tax to be on the basis of invoices'. *British Telecommunications plc, LON/95/3145 (VTD 14669)*.

38.93   **Article 21(1)(c) of Sixth Directive—appeal by recipient of credit note.**   See *Finanzamt Osnabrück-Land v Langhorst*, 21.217 EUROPEAN COMMUNITY LAW.

38.94   **Treatment of credit note in partial exemption computation.**   See *London International Financial Futures Exchange*, 43.60 PARTIAL EXEMPTION.

38.95   **Delay in processing credit notes—effect of VAT Regulations 1995, reg 34*.**   See *Copson*, 55.19 RETURNS.

39 Land

Note. The cases in this chapter are those dealing with *VATA 1994, Sch 9, Group 1*. For cases dealing with *VATA 1994, Sch 10*, see 6 BUILDINGS AND LAND. For cases dealing with *VATA 1994, Sch 8, Group 5*, see 15 CONSTRUCTION OF BUILDINGS. For cases dealing with *VATA 1994, Sch 8, Group 6*, see 52 PROTECTED BUILDINGS.

The cases in this chapter are arranged under the following headings.

WHETHER A LICENCE TO OCCUPY LAND (VATA 1994, Sch 9, Group 1, Item 1)

General

Cases held to be exempt

39.1   **Concession to operate shops at airport.**   Under an agreement with the British Airports Authority, a company operated two shops at Heathrow Airport. It paid the BAA a percentage of its turnover. The Commissioners issued a ruling that the agreement granted a licence to occupy land, so that the BAA's input tax had to be apportioned accordingly. The tribunal dismissed the BAA's appeal, and the CA upheld this decision. Scarman LJ observed that 'the court is under an obligation to look at the substance of the agreement and to reach a conclusion as to its nature quite irrespective of its form, or the language in which the agreement is embodied ... the true nature of this agreement is that it is a licence to occupy the two shops—i.e. land'. *British Airports Authority v C & E Commrs (No 1), CA 1976, [1977] STC 36; [1977] 1 WLR 302; [1977] 1 All ER 497.*

39.2   **Licence to produce play in theatre.**   A company (T) granted another company a licence to produce a play in a theatre. The Commissioners issued a ruling that the licence was a licence to occupy land within what is now *VATA 1994, Sch 9, Group 1,* so that T's input tax had to be apportioned. The tribunal dismissed T's appeal against this decision. *Theatres Consolidated Ltd, [1975] VATTR 13 (VTD 141)*.

39.3   **Part of premises sublet—rents paid direct to head lessor.** A partnership leased certain premises, most of which it sublet to three associated companies. These companies paid their rents direct to the head lessor. The Commissioners issued an assessment on the basis that the partnership had granted the companies licences to occupy land, which were exempt from VAT, so that the partnership's input tax had to be apportioned. The tribunal upheld the assessment and dismissed the partnership's appeal. *Star Automatics, BIR/75/117 (VTD 311)*.

39.4   **Receipts linked with rental payments for market sites.** In a case in which the facts were complex, a company which operated markets and fairs experienced difficulties in trading on Sundays because of the *Shops Act 1950*. It therefore established a club to carry out Sunday trading. The club received payments from traders who occupied sites provided by the company. The tribunal held that these payments were exempt under what is now *VATA 1994, Sch 9, Group 1* as consideration for licences to occupy land. *Wendy Fair Market Club, LON/77/400 (VTD 679)*. (*Note.* For other matters in this case, see 2.314 APPEALS.)

39.5   **Letting of market stall for one day.** A Borough Council controlled various markets and fairs. It let two market stalls for periods of one day only. The market was open for trading from 9.00 a.m. to 5.30 p.m., and the stallholder could not bring his goods into the market before 8.15 a.m. nor leave them there after 6.15 p.m. The Council did not account for VAT on its receipts from these lettings, considering that they were exempt. The Commissioners formed the opinion that the short duration of the lettings prevented them from qualifying for exemption, and issued an assessment charging tax on the receipts in question. The tribunal allowed the Council's appeal, holding that the stallholders were granted licences to occupy land within what is now *VATA 1994, Sch 9, Group 1*, and that the short duration of the licences was immaterial. *Tameside Metropolitan Borough Council, [1979] VATTR 93 (VTD 733)*.

39.6   **Serviced office accommodation.** A company supplied serviced office accommodation. The services in question included cleaning and the services of a telephone switchboard. The Commissioners issued a ruling that the supplies in question were a licence to occupy land, so that the consideration was exempt from VAT under what is now *VATA 1994, Sch 9, Group 1*, and the company was not able to reclaim the related input tax. The tribunal dismissed the company's appeal, applying *British Airports Authority (No 1)*, 39.1 above. *Business Enterprises (UK) Ltd, [1988] VATTR 160 (VTD 3161)*.

39.7   A company which supplied serviced office accommodation to tenants reclaimed input tax. The Commissioners issued an assessment to recover the tax, considering that the company's supplies were exempt from VAT. The tribunal upheld this contention and dismissed the company's appeal. *Birchforest Ltd, MAN/90/1063 (VTD 6046)*.

39.8   A similar decision, applying *Business Enterprises (UK) Ltd*, 39.6 above, was reached in *WS Atkins (Services) Ltd*, 34.25 INPUT TAX.

39.9   **Licence giving non-exclusive occupation of office.** A firm of chartered accountants formed a limited company to provide investment advice. The company operated from a room in the firm's office, and paid rent to the firm. However, the company did not have exclusive occupation of the room, since it was also used at times by the firm. The firm did not account for output tax on the rental payments from the company, treating them as exempt. The Commissioners issued an assessment charging tax on the payments, on the basis that they did not qualify for exemption since the company's occupation of the room was not exclusive. The tribunal allowed the firm's appeal, holding that the supply was of a licence to occupy land and qualified for exemption even though the licence did not grant exclusive occupation. *Altman Blane & Co, LON/93/740 (VTD 12381)*. (*Notes.* (1) For Customs' current interpretation of what constitutes a licence to occupy land, see Business Brief 21/99, issued on 7 September 1999, and *Amendment 3 (October 1999)* to *Notice 742: Land and Property*. (2) For another issue in this case, see 58.25 SUPPLY.)

39.10   **Golf club—transfer of business to non-profit-making body.**   A company (T), which owned a golf club, had registered for VAT in 1989. In 1998 it undertook a transaction, devised by a tax consultancy firm, whereby it transferred part of its business to a newly-formed non-profit-making body (C). The transfer was treated as the transfer of a going concern, and was intended to take advantage of the exemption in *VATA 1994, Sch 9, Group 10, Item 3* (so that C would not be required to account for output tax although T could reclaim input tax). Following the transfer, T submitted a return claiming a repayment of input tax. The Commissioners rejected the claim and issued a ruling that T had granted C a licence to occupy land, which was exempt under *Sch 9, Group 1*. C appealed, contending that the effect of the transfer agreement was that there had been separate supplies of the use of the land and of the use of sporting equipment. The tribunal rejected this contention and dismissed the appeal, holding that there had been a single supply of 'a licence to occupy a fully equipped golf course' and that this supply was exempt under *Sch 9, Group 1*. *Tall Pines Golf & Leisure Co Ltd, LON/99/266 (VTD 16538)*.

39.11   **Licence giving non-exclusive occupation of golf course.**   See *Abbotsley Golf & Squash Club Ltd*, 39.123 below.

39.12   **Installation of amusement machines in leisure club.**   The proprietor of a business which supplied amusement machines paid £15,000 to a leisure club at a holiday resort for the right to install a number of machines in a room at the club. He reclaimed input tax in respect of this payment, and the Commissioners issued an assessment to recover the tax, considering that the payment was for a licence to occupy land and was exempt from VAT. The tribunal dismissed the proprietor's appeal, holding that the payment was for the right to occupy a specific room in the leisure club and this amounted to a licence to occupy land. *A Higgins, MAN/90/748 (VTD 6205)*.

39.13   **Installation of cigarette vending machines in public houses.**   A company operated coin-operated vending machines for cigarettes. It entered into agreements to install such machines in public houses. The Commissioners issued a ruling that the agreements constituted the grant of licences to occupy land, so that payments under the agreements were exempt from VAT and the company was unable to reclaim the related input tax. The CA dismissed the company's appeal. Ward LJ held that the only relevant supply was the licence 'to place the machine on, or annex it to, the premises'. That was a licence to occupy land. *C & E Commrs v Sinclair Collis Ltd, CA [1999] STC 701*.

39.14   The QB decision in *Sinclair Collis Ltd*, 39.13 above, was applied in the similar subsequent case of *MD Johnson (t/a Johnson Vending Services), LON/97/73 (VTD 15989)*.

39.15   **Installation of coin-operated telephones in hospitals.**   British Telecom (BT) paid commission to the owners of hospital sites for the right to install coin-operated telephones at the hospitals. BT charged itself VAT on self-billing invoices and reclaimed it as input tax. The Commissioners issued an assessment to recover the tax, on the basis that it related to licences to occupy land, which were exempt from VAT.

BT appealed, contending that the use of land was merely incidental and was not the dominant nature of the supply. The tribunal rejected this contention and dismissed the appeal, applying the CA decision in *Sinclair Collis Ltd*, 39.13 above. *British Telecommunications plc, LON/96/1135 (VTD 16244)*.

39.16   **Payment made under Tomlin order to settle dispute over land.**   A family farming partnership had occupied a 47–acre farm since 1960, under an agreement entered into by the then senior partner. In 1961 the partnership had paid rent to the company which owned the freehold of the land. It had made no further payments thereafter. The company began legal action against the senior partner and the partnership. They defended the proceedings, contending that the company's claim to ownership of the land was barred by the *Limitation Act 1939*, so that the land had become the property of the senior partner. In 1989 the dispute was settled by means of a Tomlin order, under which the partner relinquished his claim to the land, and the company agreed to pay him £450,000. The partnership did not account for VAT on this amount, and the Commissioners issued an assessment on the basis that it related to a standard-rated supply of services. The partnership appealed, contending that the payment related to a licence to occupy land and was therefore exempt from VAT under what is now *VATA 1994, Sch 9, Group 1*. The tribunal accepted this contention and allowed the appeal, holding that the supply was of an interest in land, which was exempt from VAT. *JE Greves & Son, [1993] VATTR 127 (VTD 9777)*.

39.17   **Payment for occupation of part of vehicle workshop.**   A trader operated a vehicle recovery service. He allowed an unrelated partnership, which operated a repair business, to occupy part of his workshop in return for payment. He did not account for tax on the amounts which he received from the partnership. The Commissioners issued an assessment charging tax on the payments, and the trader appealed, contending that they were for a licence to occupy land and thus were exempt. The tribunal allowed the appeal, holding on the evidence that he had granted the partnership a licence to occupy a part of the premises, rather than merely a licence to use the workshop facilities. *HA Lovejoy (t/a HRS Recoveries), LON/93/2754 (VTD 12835)*. (*Note*. For another issue in this case, see 34.416 INPUT TAX.)

39.18   **Pitch fees for 'park homes' at caravan site.**   See *Stonecliff Caravan Park*, 15.72 CONSTRUCTION OF DWELLINGS, ETC.

39.19   **Refurbishment of restaurant prior to grant of licence.**   See *Sheffield Co-Operative Society Ltd*, 43.20 PARTIAL EXEMPTION.

39.20   **Refurbishment of houses prior to sale.**   A housing association refurbished a number of houses and sold them. It reclaimed input tax on the refurbishment. The Commissioners issued an assessment to recover the tax, on the basis that the input tax related to exempt supplies. The association appealed, contending that it had made standard-rated supplies of 'refurbishment services' in consideration for a reduction below the market value of the purchase price of each house. The tribunal rejected this contention and dismissed the appeal, holding that the input tax was entirely attributable to exempt supplies. *Ridgeons Bulk Ltd*, 58.105 SUPPLY, distinguished. *Maritime Housing Association Ltd, MAN/98/402 (VTD 16232)*.

39.21   **'Reverse consideration' on sale of freehold property.**   See *Brammer plc*, 43.24 PARTIAL EXEMPTION.

Cases held to be partly exempt

39.22   **Serviced office accommodation.**   A company supplied serviced office accommodation, including the handling of mail and the provision of a telephone answering service. The tribunal held that, although part of the consideration paid by the company's tenants was for the grant of licences to occupy land, the services of mail handling and telephone answering were taxable supplies. Accordingly the consideration paid by the company's tenants had to be apportioned. *Business Enterprises (UK) Ltd*, 39.6 above, distinguished. *Sovereign Street Workplace Ltd, MAN/91/403 (VTD 9550)*.

39.23 A company leased a building, which it divided into office accommodation and let to tenants. It charged tenants a rent of £55 per square foot, treating £15 of this as attributable to an exempt supply of land, and £40 as attributable to taxable supplies of services such as cleaning, maintenance, electricity and insurance. It reclaimed input tax in respect of the furniture which it installed in the building, and on amounts paid in respect of cleaning the offices. The Commissioners issued an assessment to recover the input tax, considering that it was attributable to exempt supplies. The company appealed. The tribunal allowed the appeal in part, holding that the company was making multiple supplies and that the consideration paid by the tenants had to be apportioned. *Business Enterprises (UK) Ltd*, 39.6 above, distinguished. The tribunal held that, since the offices could have been let unfurnished, the whole of the input tax on the furniture was attributable to taxable supplies, and was reclaimable in full, but that 'the totality of the cleaning services supplied to the appellant are used in making exempt supplies of the premises, and so the input tax is not deductible'. *First Base Properties Ltd, LON/93/3122A (VTD 11598)*.

39.24 **Licence to trade from retail shops.** A group of companies owned a number of retail shops. It entered into agreements whereby licensees could trade from two of the shops. The licensees were required to pay fixed fortnightly sums to the group, and to stock products supplied by the group, and were entitled to keep all profits. The group incurred expenditure in respect of these shops, and reclaimed the relevant input tax. The Commissioners issued an assessment to recover the tax, on the basis that the expenditure related to the grant of licences to occupy land, which were exempt from VAT. The representative company appealed, contending that it had granted trading rights, and that these grants were standard-rated. The tribunal allowed the appeal in part, holding on the evidence that the licensees 'received much more than a mere licence to occupy land', and that 'as a matter of economics a substantial proportion of the consideration must have been attributable to the trading rights'. The tribunal directed that the tax should be apportioned. *Cullens Holdings plc, LON/93/1179 (VTD 12376)*.

39.25 **Alexandra Palace.** See *Haringey Borough Council*, 40.1 LOCAL AUTHORITIES AND STATUTORY BODIES.

Cases held not to be exempt

39.26 **Right to take car on harbour property.** Harbour Trustees charged motorists for access to quays or jetties. They did not account for tax on the toll receipts. The Commissioners issued an assessment and the Trustees appealed, contending that the tolls were exempt under what is now *VATA 1994, Sch 9, Group 1*. The tribunal dismissed the appeal, holding that the tolls did not qualify for exemption. *Mevagissey Harbour Trustees, BIR/74/14 (VTD 111)*.

39.27 **Grant of facilities at airport.** The British Airports Authority granted a company the right to supply goods Gatwick Airport, in return for a percentage of the company's gross takings. The Commissioners issued a ruling that the agreement gave the company a right over land, so that the company's payments to the Authority were exempt from VAT. The Authority appealed, contending that the agreement did not amount to a licence to occupy land, so that it was entitled to reclaim input tax. The tribunal allowed the Authority's appeal, holding that the right to pass through a control point at an airport did not amount to 'an interest in or right over land'. *British Airports Authority (No 2), LON/74/151 & 152 (VTD 146)*.

39.28   A similar decision was reached in a case where the British Airports Authority granted an airline company the use of certain 'transfer desks' at Heathrow Airport. The tribunal held that the grant was not of an interest over land, so that the payments were not exempt from VAT. *British Airports Authority (No 3), LON/74/153 (VTD 147)*.

39.29   **Golf club subscription.**   A golf club used a course which was on common land, in accordance with a licence granted by the local authority. The club held the freehold of the clubhouse which was on land adjoining the course. It appealed against an assessment charging tax on members' subscriptions, contending that they should be treated as exempt under what is now *VATA 1994, Sch 9, Group 1, Item 1*. The tribunal rejected this contention and dismissed the appeal. *Banstead Downs Golf Club, [1974] VATTR 219 (VTD 229)*.

39.30   **Unincorporated country club—members' subscriptions.**   An unincorporated members' club owned land including tennis courts and croquet lawns. It failed to account for output tax on its subscriptions. The Commissioners issued an assessment on the club secretary, charging tax on them. The secretary appealed, contending that they should be treated as exempt under what is now *VATA 1994, Sch 9, Group 1, Item 1*. The QB rejected this contention and dismissed the appeal. The subscriptions entitled members to the privilege of entering the grounds rather than to a share in the beneficial ownership of the club property. A 'right over land' must be interpreted as a legal or equitable interest, and it was impossible to say that members had a licence to occupy any part of the club's premises. *Trewby (Hurlingham Club) v C & E Commrs, QB [1976] STC 122; [1976] 1 WLR 932; [1976] 2 All ER 199*.

39.31   **Holiday club—increased subscriptions.**   A holiday club occupied land under a sublease. It decided to purchase the headlease of the land, and increased its subscriptions to meet this. It failed to account for tax on its increased subscriptions, and the Commissioners issued an assessment charging VAT. The club appealed, contending that the increase should be treated as exempt under what is now *VATA 1994, Sch 9, Group 1, Item 1*. The QB rejected this contention and upheld the assessment, holding that the additional payments were subscriptions rather than rent or premiums for a licence to occupy land. *C & E Commrs v Little Spain Club, QB 1978, [1979] STC 170*.

39.32   **Provision of rest room for taxi drivers.**   A partnership operated a taxi business. Its drivers used their own vehicles, and paid the partnership £20 per week for the use of radio equipment and a rest room at the business premises while awaiting calls. The partnership did not account for VAT on these payments, and appealed against an assessment on them, contending that part of the payments should be treated as rent for the use of the rest room, and thus exempt from VAT. The tribunal dismissed the appeal, holding that the use of the room was not a licence to occupy land and did not qualify for exemption. *Ferris & Budd (t/a Z Cars), BIR/76/194 (VTD 412)*.

39.33   A similar decision was reached in *Parker Radio Cars (Sutton Coldfield) Ltd, MAN/87/25 (VTD 2504)*.

39.34   **Payments by driving instructors for use of driving school offices.**   A similar decision was reached in a case where self-employed driving instructors made weekly payments to a driving school in return for the use of an office. *CW & JA Garner, LON/83/61 (VTD 1476)*.

39.35   **Casual grazing licences.**   A farmer owned two fields which were suitable for grazing. He grazed his own animals on them and, from time to time, allowed other people to place horses or ponies in the fields in return for weekly payments. He did not account for tax on these payments. The Commissioners issued an assessment charging tax on them, and the farmer appealed, contending that the payments were exempt under what is now *VATA 1994, Sch 9, Group 1*. The tribunal rejected this contention and dismissed his appeal, holding that the grazing facilities did not amount to licences to occupy land and thus did not qualify for exemption. *JA King, [1980] VATTR 60 (VTD 933)*. (*Note*. The tribunal also held that the supply could not be treated as a zero-rated supply of animal feeding stuffs.)

39.36   Promotion of concerts at halls owned by Council.   The Greater London Council owned several concert halls, and granted licences to promoters to stage public performances at the halls. In several cases, it agreed to provide stewards and to supply admission tickets. It did not account for VAT on the fees it received from the promoters, considering that they were exempt under what is now *VATA 1994, Sch 9, Group 1*. The Commissioners issued an assessment on the basis that the provision of stewards and of admission tickets was a separate supply which did not qualify for exemption, and raised an assessment accordingly. The tribunal upheld the assessment in principle, directing that the amounts which the GLC received should be apportioned between taxable and exempt supplies. (However, in a case where the GLC acted as co-promoter, the tribunal held that there was no supply by the GLC to the promoter, and the GLC was only liable to account for VAT on the supplies it made to the public.) *Greater London Council, [1982] VATTR 94 (VTD 1224)*.

39.37   Antique fair in hotel room.   A trader organised and promoted antique fairs which were held in hotels or public houses. She charged other traders for the right to use tables at the fairs, and also charged the public for admission. She did not account for VAT on her receipts from traders. The Commissioners issued an assessment charging tax on them and she appealed, contending that the receipts were exempt under what is now *VATA 1994, Sch 9, Group 1*. The tribunal dismissed her appeal, holding that the provision of tables did not amount to a licence to occupy land, so that the receipts did not qualify for exemption. *WB Enever, LON/83/220 (VTD 1537)*. (*Note*. The tribunal also held that the supplies were excluded from exemption by *FA 1972, Sch 5 Group 1, Item 1(g)*. This exclusion was repealed by *FA 1989*, but the supplies would still not qualify for exemption through not being held to be for a licence to occupy land.)

39.38   Payments from associated company for use of office facilities.   A company (U), which provided financial services, owned the office from which it operated. It had two associated companies, which operated from the same premises and which also provided financial services. One of these companies paid U £3,500 p.a. for the use of its facilities. U did not account for tax on these payments, and the Commissioners issued an assessment charging tax on them. U appealed, contending that the payments should be treated as exempt from VAT under what is now *VATA 1994, Sch 9, Group 1*. The tribunal dismissed the appeal, holding that U had not granted its associated company a licence to occupy any land, and that the payments were made under 'an informal arrangement to share facilities' which did not qualify for exemption. *Ultimate Advisory Services Ltd, MAN/91/1488 (VTD 9523)*. (*Note*. For another issue in this case, see 51.4 PENSION FUNDS.)

39.39   Installation of amusement machines in public houses.   A company which owned several public houses arranged for coin-operated amusement machines to be installed therein, in return for payments from the owners of the machines. The Commissioners formed the opinion that, by allowing the owners of the machines to install them on the premises, the company had granted the owners licences to occupy land, with the result that the company was making exempt supplies as well as taxable supplies and could only reclaim a proportion of its input tax. They therefore issued an assessment to recover some of the input tax which the company had reclaimed. The tribunal allowed the company's appeal against the assessment, holding that none of the agreements granted a licence to occupy land. *The Wolverhampton & Dudley Breweries plc, [1990] VATTR 131 (VTD 5351)*. (*Note.* The decision in this case was subsequently disapproved by the QB in *Sinclair Collis Ltd*, 39.13 above.)

39.40   **Grant of facilities for crane to pass through airspace.**   A property developer paid a surveyor for permission to swing a tower crane above the surveyor's premises. The surveyor did not account for output tax on this payment, and the Commissioners issued an assessment charging tax thereon. The surveyor appealed, contending that the payment related to a licence to occupy land, and should be treated as exempt from VAT. The tribunal dismissed the appeal, holding that the agreement gave the developer the right to pass through the surveyor's airspace, rather than to occupy the surveyor's airspace. *RH Carter (t/a Protheroe Carter & Eason Ltd), LON/93/93A (VTD 12047)*.

39.41   **Payments for use of stand at exhibition.**   The Swiss National Tourist Office (SNTO) hired a stand at an exhibition. It used part of the stand itself, and sublet the remainder of the stand to a number of Swiss organisations or businesses. It reclaimed input tax on its payment to the exhibition organisers. The Commissioners issued an assessment to recover the tax, on the basis that the supplies made by the SNTO were grants of a licence to occupy land, which was exempt from VAT. The SNTO appealed. The tribunal allowed the appeal, holding that 'the real substance of the supply was ... the right to full participation in the Switzerland stand'. The entitlement to use facilities such as a meeting and storage room, and to be included in a catalogue which was produced by the exhibition organisers, was 'just as important as the right to occupy the table and chairs and the space where they were situated'. The supplies 'went far beyond licences to occupy land'. *Swiss National Tourist Office, LON/94/223A (VTD 13192)*.

39.42   See also *International Trade & Exhibitions J/V Ltd*, 58.390 SUPPLY.

39.43   **Concession to sell goods from retail shop.**   A shoe retailer (L) allowed a watch retailer (J) to sell watches from his shop, receiving 12.5% of J's turnover as consideration. L did not account for output tax on the payments which he received from J, treating them as exempt. The Commissioners issued an assessment charging tax on the payments, and L appealed, contending that he had granted J a licence to occupy land. The tribunal rejected this contention and dismissed the appeal. On the evidence, L had not granted J 'a clearly defined area or site'. J had the right to install two display units and to display his watches in one of the shop windows, but the remainder of the shop was shared. The payments which J made were not rent, but were 'for use of facilities at the premises according to user'. *PJ Lamb (t/a Footloose), MAN/96/1232 (VTD 15136)*. (*Note.* For the Commissioners' practice following this decision, see Business Brief 25/97, issued on 10 November 1997.)

39.44   **Charity granting non-exclusive licences to wholly-owned subsidiaries.**   See *Mount Edgcumbe Hospice Ltd*, 11.36 CHARITIES.

39.45   **Commission retained by property management agents.**   A company carried on the business of managing residential property for landlords. It did not account for output tax on its commission. The Commissioners issued an assessment, and the company appealed, contending that the payments should be treated as exempt from VAT. The tribunal rejected this contention and dismissed the appeal. The company was a manager rather than a tenant, so that its commission did not qualify for exemption. *Peter Anthony Estates Ltd, MAN/94/653 (VTD 13250)*.

39.46　**Service charges.**　Under a lease, the leaseholders were obliged to keep their properties in 'good order and repair'. The landlords reserved the right to appoint a factor to ensure that this was done. The landlords subsequently appointed such a factor, and VAT was imposed on the service charges. One of the leaseholders appealed, contending that the service charges should be treated as exempt. The tribunal rejected this contention and dismissed the appeal, holding that the charges did not qualify for exemption because they were not part of the original supply of land. The tribunal also noted that the charges did not fall within the scope of what is now Extra-Statutory Concession 3.18, holding that the charges were not mandatory in the sense required by the concession, since there was 'a distinction between the obligations on the proprietors to maintain the property (which were mandatory) and the method by which the proprietors chose to implement those obligations. The proprietors were not required to appoint a factor — the Owners' Association could make some other arrangement to deal with their obligations.' *J Devine, EDN/97/97 (VTD 15312)*.

39.47　Domestic service charges, paid to trustees appointed under an agreement between a freeholder and a lessor, were held not to qualify for exemption in *Trustees of the Nell Gwynn House Maintenance Fund*, 58.34 SUPPLY. (*Note*. The relevant supplies took place before the introduction of what is now Extra-Statutory Concession 3.18. It appears that the supplies might now fall within the scope of the concession, but compare *Devine*, 39.46 above.)

Surrenders of leases

Cases held to be exempt

39.48　**Payment by landlord for surrender of lease—whether exempt under Article 13B(b) of EC Sixth Directive.**　See *Lubbock Fine & Co*, 21.165 EUROPEAN COMMUNITY LAW.

39.49　**Payment for assignment of lease—whether exempt under Article 13B(b) of EC Sixth Directive.**　See *Cantor Fitzgerald International*, 21.166 EUROPEAN COMMUNITY LAW.

39.50　**Payment by tenant to landlord for surrender of onerous lease.**　A company (M) which carried on a consultancy business, and also dealt in shares, occupied leased premises, part of which it sublet. Its landlord had elected to waive exemption on the rent which M paid. However, M had not elected to waive exemption on the rent it received from its subtenant. M decided that it wished to terminate the lease before its expiry, and paid a 'reverse premium' of £67,500 to its landlord. It treated this premium as relating to an exempt supply of land. The Commissioners issued an assessment on the basis that, since the landlord had elected to waive exemption in respect of the premises, the payment did not qualify for exemption. The tribunal allowed M's appeal, holding that by surrendering its lease, M had made an exempt supply of land to the landlord. *Marbourne Ltd, LON/93/590A (VTD 12670)*. (*Notes*. (1) For the Commissioners' practice following this decision, see Business Brief 18/95, issued on 4 September 1995. The Commissioners initially appealed to the High Court, contending that it must be the person receiving payment, the landlord, who made the supply in question. However, the Commissioners did not pursue the appeal, because the company had ceased trading and would not have been represented before the High Court, and because they considered that the correct legal principle was established in the subsequent case of *Central Capital Corporation Ltd*, 39.51 below, where the tribunal held that the relevant supply of land was made by the landlord rather than by the tenant. A similar decision was reached in *AA Insurance Services Ltd*, 39.52 below. For a more detailed analysis, see British Tax Review 1998, p 596. The writer (Hugh McKay) comments that the *Marbourne* decision was 'the right end result but the wrong reasoning'. (2) The case also concerned the operation of the partial exemption provisions prior to their substitution by *SI 1992 No 3102*. The decision here was largely in favour of the Commissioners, but does not appear to be directly relevant to the current provisions. The company had reclaimed the whole of its input tax, and an appeal against a misdeclaration penalty was dismissed—see 49.326 PENALTIES: MISDECLARATION.)

39.51   In another case concerning a 'reverse surrender', the tribunal declined to follow the decision in *Marbourne Ltd*, 39.50 above, and held that the relevant supply of land was made by the landlord rather than by the tenant. However, the tribunal held that the payment made by the tenant was exempt from VAT. The tenant was the recipient of the supply, and, applying *Williams & Glyns Bank Ltd*, 2.28 APPEALS, had a right of appeal against the Commissioners' decision that the supply was taxable. Applying the CJEC decision in *Lubbock Fine & Co*, 21.165 EUROPEAN COMMUNITY LAW, the supply by the landlord qualified for exemption under *Article 13B(b)* of the *EC Sixth Directive*. Since the original grant of the lease was not taxable, the subsequent 'reverse surrender' of that lease was also not taxable. *Central Capital Corporation Ltd, MAN/94/2393 (VTD 13319)*. (*Note*. For the Commissioners' practice following this decision, see Business Brief 18/95, issued on 4 September 1995.)

39.52   A similar decision was reached in a case where a tenant company wished to surrender its lease, and the landlord agreed to accept the surrender on condition that the tenant paid a premium of £120,000 plus VAT. The tenant reclaimed input tax on this payment. The Commissioners rejected the claim and the tribunal dismissed the tenant's appeal, holding that the relevant supply was made by the landlord and was exempt from VAT, so that the tenant was not entitled to recover input tax. *AA Insurance Services Ltd, [1999] VATDR 361 (VTD 16117)*.

Cases held to be partly exempt

39.53   **Payment made partly for surrender of old lease and partly as inducement to enter new lease.**   A cricket club had leased a site which had development potential. The trust which owned the site wished to develop it as a supermarket. The local council would only grant planning permission if the trust and the development company entered into an agreement with the club under *Town and Country Planning Act 1971, s 52*, whereby the club would be provided with a new site. The trust agreed to pay the club £70,000 for the surrender of the existing lease and the development company agreed to pay the club £110,000 in return for the club surrendering the existing lease and entering into the agreement under *Town and Country Planning Act 1971, s 52*. The Commissioners issued an assessment charging tax on the payment of £110,000. The club appealed, contending that the payment should be treated as exempt from VAT. The tribunal allowed the appeal in part, finding that 'there were two distinct requirements made of the club' and holding that half of the payment was attributable to the surrender of the existing lease and was exempt from VAT, applying *Lubbock Fine & Co*, 21.165 EUROPEAN COMMUNITY LAW, but that the other half was paid as an inducement to enter into the agreement under the *Town and Country Planning Act* and was standard-rated, applying *Neville Russell*, 58.101 SUPPLY. *Grantham Cricket Club, MAN/93/457 (VTD 12287, 12863)*. (*Note*. For subsequent developments in this case, see 45.14 PAYMENT OF TAX.)

Cases held not to be exempt

39.54   **Payment for surrender of lease.**   In December 1987 a company (C) purchased the headlease of a building which was used as office accommodation. The building was let to a tenant until June 1989, when C paid the tenant £36,000 as an inducement to surrender its sublease. C sold the headlease in July 1989. In its next return, C reclaimed input tax on the payment it had made to the tenant. The Commissioners issued an assessment to recover the tax, considering that the payment related to the transfer of an interest in land, which was exempt from VAT under what is now *VATA 1994, Sch 9, Group 1.* The tribunal upheld the assessment and dismissed C's appeal, applying *Brasplern (Group Services) Ltd*, 43.10 PARTIAL EXEMPTION, and *Rentorn Ltd*, 43.11 PARTIAL EXEMPTION. *Cedar Court Business Centre Ltd, LON/91/ 1132 (VTD 6976).* (*Note.* Compare *Lubbock Fine*, 21.165 EUROPEAN COMMUNITY LAW.)

Hairdressing salons

Cases held to be exempt

39.55   A hairdresser (Q) owned two salons, one for men and one for women, in the same town. He found that he was losing money at the men's salon. He dismissed his three employees but offered them the right to continue their profession on a self-employed basis, using the same chair, washbasin and cupboard as before, and paying him a fixed weekly payment. They accepted this offer, and made regular payments to Q as agreed. Q did not account for VAT on these payments, and the Commissioners issued an assessment charging tax on them. Q appealed, contending that the payments were exempt under what is now *VATA 1994, Sch 9, Group 1.* The tribunal allowed Q's appeal, holding that he had granted his ex-employees a licence to occupy land. *R Quaife, LON/82/305 (VTD 1394).*

39.56   A similar decision was reached in *M Bullimore, MAN/86/154 (VTD 2626).*

39.57   A couple who owned a number of hairdressing salons did not account for tax on part of the amounts which they received from the stylists who worked at the salons. The Commissioners issued assessments charging tax on the payments, and the couple appealed, contending that the payments were for licences to occupy land and should be treated as exempt under what is now *VATA 1994, Sch 9, Group 1.* The tribunal reviewed the evidence and allowed the appeal in part, holding that the agreements in force from September 1991, which restricted each of the stylists to a specific area of the salon, constituted licences to occupy land and the payments thereunder qualified for exemption. (However, the agreements in force prior to September 1991, which did not provide for any specific interest in the premises, did not qualify for exemption.) *GG & Mrs HK Daniels (t/a Group Montage), MAN/91/572 (VTD 12014).* (*Note.* The Commissioners announced that they had appealed to the High Court against this decision—see Business Brief 16/94, issued on 25 July 1994—but subsequently withdrew the appeal because, at the hearing, their representative 'had accepted that the agreements used accurately reflected what actually happened in the salon, i.e. that the stylists were genuinely restricted to a particular area of the salon'. See Customs' VAT Manual, Part 8, section 7.10(e). Customs state that 'it would be most unusual for the business to be carried on in this way. If ... the stylists, juniors under their direction, or their clients move outside the designated area ... the *Group Montage* decision is irrelevant'.)

Cases held not to be exempt

39.58   A partnership owned a hairdressing salon with eight chairs. They allowed two other hairdressers to use the premises in return for weekly payments. They did not account for VAT on these payments, and the Commissioners issued an assessment charging tax on them. The partnership appealed, contending that the payments were exempt under what is now *VATA 1994, Sch 9, Group 1.* The tribunal dismissed the appeal, holding that the arrangements did not amount to licences to occupy land. *Quaife,*

39.55 above, was distinguished because the hairdressers in that case had been allocated specific chairs, which was not the case here. *N & J Price, LON/83/47 (VTD 1443)*.

39.59   A married couple, who had operated a hairdressing salon in partnership, incorporated a number of companies. Each stylist who worked at the salon was employed by one of the companies, and the couple gave each company the right to use specified chairs and washbasins. The couple did not account for VAT on the payments they received from the companies, and the Commissioners issued an assessment charging tax on them. The tribunal dismissed the couple's appeal, holding that they had not granted the companies licences to occupy land. *PM & Mrs P Field (t/a Paul Field Hair & Beauty Salon), LON/84/569 (VTD 2047)*.

39.60   The proprietor of a hairdressing salon let two chairs in the salon to one of the hairdressers. He did not account for tax on these payments, and appealed against the Commissioners' ruling that they were taxable, contending that they were exempt under what is now *VATA 1994, Sch 9, Group 1*. The tribunal dismissed his appeal, holding that he had granted the hairdresser facilities which did not amount to a licence to occupy land and did not qualify for exemption. *M Genc, [1988] VATTR 16 (VTD 2595)*. (*Note*. For another issue in this case, see 48.8 PENALTIES: FAILURE TO NOTIFY.)

39.61   In the case noted at 58.206 SUPPLY, the Commissioners refused to accept a salon proprietor's contention that the payments he received from the stylists qualified for exemption under what is now *VATA 1994, Sch 9, Group 1*. The tribunal dismissed the proprietor's appeal, holding that the payments were for the use of the 'general facilities of the salon' and were 'certainly not a licence to occupy exclusively or in company with others any land, but a mere incident or ingredient of what is in substance a business facility'. *Genc*, 39.60 above, applied; *Bullimore*, 39.56 above, distinguished. *ME Hosmer, LON/89/1851 (VTD 7313)*.

39.62   A similar decision was reached in *Characters (Hairdressers) Ltd, MAN/96/919 (VTD 15351)*.

39.63   A company which owned a hairdressing salon allowed its directors to use one of the chairs at the salon. It did not account for output tax in respect of this use, although it accounted for tax on amounts received from other self-employed stylists. The Commissioners issued an assessment charging tax on the basis that, since the company treated the directors as self-employed and did not account for tax on their takings, it had made a deemed supply of the use of the chair and should have accounted for VAT thereon under what is now *VATA 1994, s 19(3)*. The company appealed, contending that the supply in question was a licence to occupy land which was exempt from VAT. The tribunal dismissed the appeal, applying *Genc*, 39.60 above, and holding that the terms under which the directors made use of the chair did not constitute a licence to occupy land. *Biburtry Ltd, LON/92/2243A (VTD 10615)*.

39.64   In the case noted at 58.216 SUPPLY, self-employed hairstylists working at a salon paid the proprietor 57% of their gross takings. The proprietor only accounted for tax on 10% of the gross takings, treating the other 47% as being for a licence to occupy land, and exempt. The Commissioners issued a ruling that the payments did not qualify for exemption. The tribunal dismissed the proprietor's appeal, finding that 'although the individual stylists did have their own chair, they did not necessarily use that chair and the chairs generally were interchangeable within the salon', so that there was not 'a total exclusive use of an allocated space'. Accordingly, the proprietor had not granted the stylists a licence to occupy land, and the payments did not qualify for exemption. *A Winder (t/a Anthony & Patricia), MAN/92/1653 (VTD 11784)*.

39.65   A similar decision was reached in a case in which the tribunal held that 'what the stylist obtained was the right to practise her vocation as a hairdresser, using the general facilities of the salon. The occupation, albeit exclusive, of two chairs (was) a mere incident or ingredient in what was in substance the use of business facilities.' *W Walker (t/a Ziska), EDN/92/334 (VTD 11825)*.

39.66   An appeal was dismissed in a case where the tribunal held that the supplies which a company operating a hairdressing salon made to each of its stylists were single supplies of services and that any licence to occupy land was 'ancillary or incidental'. The chairman observed that 'the licences are economically useless without the other elements, the most important of which are services of the juniors and the use of the wash basins and the dryers ... as a matter of common sense there were single supplies.' *Simon Harris Hair Design Ltd, [1996] VATDR 177 (VTD 13939)*. (*Note*. For the Commissioners' practice following this decision, see Business Brief 13/96, issued on 1 July 1996.)

39.67   The decision in *Simon Harris Hair Design Ltd*, 39.66 above, was applied in a subsequent case where the tribunal held that the salon proprietors had made 'a single composite supply of the right to carry on a business of hairdressing by providing a package of hairdressing facilities'. Applying the CJEC decision in *Card Protection Plan Ltd*, 21.162 EUROPEAN COMMUNITY LAW, 'a supply which comprises a single service from an economic point of view should not be artificially split'. Accordingly, the proprietors' supplies were wholly standard-rated. *Mr & Mrs Broadley (t/a Professional Haircare), LON/x (VTD 16643)*.

39.68   Similar decisions, also applying *Simon Harris Hair Design Ltd*, 39.66 above, and *Card Protection Plan Ltd*, 21.162 EUROPEAN COMMUNITY LAW, were reached in *Mr Francis Ltd, EDN/99/163 (VTD 16804)* and *Q & M Olivieri, LON/99/956 (VTD 16991)*.

39.69   A company operated a hairdressing salon for self-employed stylists. It received payments from stylists in respect of the use of chairs and washbasins, and did not account for tax on these payments. The Commissioners accepted that the use of separate cubicles or rooms amounted to a licence to occupy land, but issued an assessment charging tax on the payments which were made in respect of chairs and washbasins in the main hairdressing area. The company appealed, contending that these payments were also consideration for a licence to occupy land, and were exempt from VAT. The tribunal rejected this contention and dismissed the appeal, applying *Simon Harris Hair Design Ltd*, 39.66 above. The tribunal held that the supply of washbasins was 'an integral part of a hairdressing business' and did not qualify for exemption. While the provision of chairs and mirrors could amount to a licence to occupy land, the use of the chair and mirror was 'subsumed into the hairdressing business', so that 'that licence cannot be considered to be dissociable from the other services supplied in relation to the hairdressing business in the general area of the salon'. Accordingly the supplies were standard-rated. *Herbert of Liverpool (Hair Design) Ltd, MAN/97/754 (VTD 15949)*.

39.70   A similar decision, also applying *Simon Harris Hair Design Ltd*, 39.66 above, was reached in *George*, 53.46 REGISTRATION.

39.71   See also *Jamieson*, 49.385 PENALTIES: MISDECLARATION.

HOTEL ACCOMMODATION, ETC. (VATA 1994, Sch 9, Group 1, Item 1(d))

39.72   **University hall of residence.**   The Commissioners sought to register a hall of residence at Manchester University, considering that the fees paid by the resident students were excluded from exemption by what is now *VATA 1994, Sch 9, Group 1, Item 1(d)*. The tribunal allowed the hall's appeal, holding that the hall was not a 'similar establishment' to a boarding house and was thus not excluded from exemption under *Sch 9, Group 1. J McMurray (a Governor of Allen Hall), [1973] VATTR 161 (VTD 39).* (*Note.* The tribunal also considered that the supplies should be exempted under the then equivalent of *VATA 1994, Sch 9, Group 6.*)

39.73   **Accommodation for overseas students.**   A registered charity provided accommodation, in four buildings in London, for overseas students. The Commissioners issued a ruling that the charity was required to account for VAT on the fees which it received, on the basis that the buildings were a 'similar establishment' to a boarding house so that the fees were excluded from exemption by *VATA 1994, Sch 9, Group 1, Item 1(d).* The tribunal allowed the charity's appeal, holding that the buildings were not a 'similar establishment' to a boarding house and accordingly the fees were not excluded from exemption. The tribunal observed that the 'predominant characteristic' of a hotel, inn or boarding house was 'the offer of use of accommodation for gain'. The charity was offering accommodation as part of its purpose of helping overseas students and improving international relations. *International Student House, LON/95/3142 (VTD 14420).*

39.74   **Accommodation at Buddhist centre.**   A registered charity, established to propagate the teachings of a 13th century Buddhist sage, owned a substantial property set in 80 acres of land, which it used as a base for residential courses. It reclaimed input tax on expenditure relating to the property. The Commissioners rejected the claim and issued a ruling that the supplies of accommodation were exempt under *VATA 1994, Sch 9, Group 1.* The charity appealed, contending that the supplies should be treated as excluded from exemption by *Item 1(d).* The tribunal rejected this contention and dismissed the appeal, holding on the evidence that the property was used as a religious centre and was not 'an establishment with a function similar to a hotel'. *Namecourt Ltd*, 39.75 below, distinguished. *Soka Gakkai International UK, LON/95/2554 (VTD 14175).*

39.75   **Hostel for homeless and unemployed.**   A company owned a large property in London, where it provided 'bed and breakfast' accommodation for about 260 homeless and unemployed people. Most residents stayed for six months or more, and relied on financial support from the DHSS. The company did not account for VAT on the charges which it made for the accommodation. The Commissioners issued an assessment on the amounts charged, and the company appealed, contending that its supplies were exempt under what is now *VATA 1994, Sch 9, Group 1.* The tribunal dismissed the appeal, holding that the supplies were excluded from exemption by *Sch 9, Group 1, Item 1(d). Namecourt Ltd, [1984] VATTR 22 (VTD 1560).*

39.76   Compare *Lord Mayor & Citizens of the City of Westminster*, 21.75 EUROPEAN COMMUNITY LAW.

39.77   **Serviced flats.**   An individual (M) purchased a building which was divided into flats but was in need of renovation. He renovated the flats and let them on a long-stay basis. He registered for VAT and reclaimed the input tax he had incurred. The Commissioners rejected his claim, considering that his supplies were exempt under what is now *VATA 1994, Sch 9, Group 1.* He appealed, contending that he intended to convert the flats into a hotel and that the supplies were excluded from exemption by *Sch 9, Group 1, Item 1(d).* The tribunal dismissed his appeal, holding that the flats were not a 'similar establishment' to a hotel and that he was granting licences to occupy land, which were exempt from VAT. *BL Mills, LON/84/91 (VTD 1686).*

39.78   **Guest-house for permanent residents.**   The owner of a guest-house, providing 'bed and breakfast' accommodation, failed to account for VAT on her receipts. The Commissioners issued an assessment and she appealed, contending that her supplies were exempt and that the guest-house was not similar to a hotel because she regarded her customers as permanent residents. The tribunal dismissed her appeal, holding that the guest-house was a 'similar establishment' to a boarding house and that the supplies were therefore excluded from exemption by what is now *VATA 1994, Sch 9, Group 1, Item 1(d)*. *HD Paddon, LON/85/132 (VTD 1987)*.

39.79   **Long-term accommodation in boarding house.**   The proprietor of a boarding house failed to account for VAT on payments received from long-term residents. The Commissioners issued an assessment to recover the tax, against which she appealed. The tribunal dismissed her appeal, holding that the accommodation was excluded from exemption by what is now *VATA 1994, Sch 9, Group 1, Item 1(d)*. *Namecourt Ltd*, 39.75 above, applied. The QB upheld this decision. *Mrs RI McGrath v C & E Commrs, QB [1992] STC 371*.

39.80   **Board and lodging in flats above restaurant.**   The proprietor of a restaurant provided board and lodging in flats above the restaurant, but did not account for output tax on these supplies. The Commissioners issued an assessment charging tax on the receipts and the tribunal dismissed the proprietor's appeal, holding that the supplies were excluded from exemption by *VATA 1994, Sch 9, Group 1, Item 1(d)*. *AT Hussain (t/a Al Ameer), MAN/97/508 (VTD 15668)*.

39.81   **Deposits for hotel accommodation—whether excluded from exemption by Sch 9, Group 1, Item 1(d).**   A company which owned a hotel failed to account for VAT on deposits. The Commissioners issued an assessment and the company appealed, contending that the deposits were exempt under what is now *VATA 1994, Sch 9, Group 1*. The tribunal dismissed the appeal, holding that the deposits were excluded from exemption by what is now *VATA 1994, Sch 9, Group 1, Item 1(d)*. *Camilla Enterprises Ltd, EDN/92/247 (VTD 10426)*.

39.82   **Hire of rooms for wedding receptions—whether excluded from exemption by Sch 9, Group 1, Item 1(d).**   A hotelier did not account for VAT on the hire of rooms for wedding receptions. The Commissioners issued a ruling that VAT was chargeable on these supplies, on the basis that they were 'for the purpose of a supply of catering' and were therefore excluded from exemption by what is now *VATA 1994, Sch 9, Group 1, Item 1(d)*. The hotelier appealed. The tribunal chairman held that 'the fact that the bar is open in the evening to function guests' did not necessarily mean that the function room was provided for the purpose of a supply of catering. However, the burden of proof was on the appellant to show 'that the function room was not provided for the purpose of a supply of catering ... So far no clear evidence of the purpose has been produced. As matters stand I do not find the facts sufficiently clear to reach any conclusion on the assessment. It may be that on some occasions the room was used in the evening for the purpose of a supply of catering and on some occasions any catering was not the substantial purpose.' The tribunal therefore adjourned the appeal for further argument. *S Packford, LON/93/234A (VTD 11626)*. (*Note*. There was no further public hearing of the appeal. It appears from Customs' VAT Manual, Part 8, section 8.37, that Customs subsequently accepted that some of the hire charges were exempt, on the basis that 'catering was not the substantial purpose' of the hiring. Compare, however, the subsequent cases of *Willerby Manor Hotels Ltd*, 39.84 below, and *Blendhome Ltd*, 39.85 below. The decision here was not followed in *Willerby Manor Hotels*, on the grounds that it was inconsistent with the CJEC decision in *Card Protection Plan Ltd*, 21.162 EUROPEAN COMMUNITY LAW.)

39.83   The hire of rooms for wedding receptions was held to be excluded from exemption by *VATA 1994, Sch 9, Group 1, Item 1(d)* in *Seamill Hydro, 1998 (unreported)*. (*Note*. This decision has not been publicly released by the Tribunal Centre, but was cited as an authority by a subsequent tribunal in *Blendhome Ltd*, 39.85 below.)

39.84 A company did not account for VAT on the hire of rooms for evening wedding receptions. The Commissioners issued a ruling that VAT was chargeable on these supplies, on the basis that they were 'for the purpose of a supply of catering' and were therefore excluded from exemption by what is now *VATA 1994, Sch 9, Group 1, Item 1(d)*. The company appealed, contending that the hire of rooms was a separate supply which qualified for exemption, applying *Packford*, 39.82 above. The tribunal rejected this contention and dismissed the appeal, declining to follow *Packford* on the grounds that it had been decided before the CJEC decision in *Card Protection Plan Ltd*, 21.162 EUROPEAN COMMUNITY LAW. The tribunal held that 'the hire of a function room for an evening reception is a supply ancillary to those of wedding reception facilities and is integral to the reception arrangements: it is a means of better enjoying the principal service supplied'. Accordingly, the company had 'made a composite supply of a standard-rated package of wedding reception facilities, the main ingredient in which was a supply of catering'. *Willerby Manor Hotels Ltd, MAN/99/871 (VTD 16673)*.

39.85 **Wedding reception at hotel—'exclusivity fee'—whether excluded from exemption by Sch 9, Group 1, Item 1(d).** A company which operated a hotel charged customers an 'exclusivity fee' of £900 entitling the guests at wedding receptions to the exclusive use of the hotel and its grounds. The Commissioners issued a ruling that the 'exclusivity fees' were paid 'for the purpose of a supply of catering' and were therefore excluded from exemption by *VATA 1994, Sch 9, Group 1, Item 1(d)*. The company appealed, contending that the 'exclusivity fees' were paid for the right of exclusive occupation of land, which should be treated as exempt from VAT. The tribunal rejected this contention and dismissed the appeal. Applying *dicta* of the CJEC in *Card Protection Plan Ltd*, 21.162 EUROPEAN COMMUNITY LAW, the 'exclusivity fee' was a 'means of better enjoying the principal service supplied'. It followed that the fees were paid 'for the purpose of a supply of catering' and were therefore excluded from exemption. *Blendhome Ltd (t/a Stanhill Court Hotel), LON/98/866 (VTD 16048)*.

HOLIDAY ACCOMMODATION (VATA 1994, Sch 9, Group 1, Item 1(e))

39.86 **Short lettings of furnished flats advertised as holiday accommodation.** A married couple owned a house in Highgate comprising three furnished flats. One of the flats was let under a controlled tenancy. The other two were let for short periods. The couple registered with the English Tourist Board and advertised the flats as 'fully furnished holiday accommodation'. They did not account for VAT on the rent from the flats and the Commissioners issued an assessment charging tax on the rents, on the basis they were excluded from exemption by what is now *VATA 1994, Sch 9, Group 1, Item 1(e)*. The couple appealed, contending that they had only advertised the flats as holiday accommodation in order to ensure that the tenancies would not be controlled, and that at least half of their lettings were not to holidaymakers. The tribunal dismissed their appeal, holding that, as the flats were advertised as holiday accommodation, the rents were excluded from exemption. *RW & B Sheppard, [1977] VATTR 272 (VTD 481)*.

39.87 Three flats located above a grocery shop, and advertised as holiday accommodation, were held to be excluded from exemption by what is now *VATA 1994, Sch 9, Group 1, Item 1(e)* in *VWS Morgan, CAR/77/437 (VTD 633)*.

39.88 **'Time-share' holiday accommodation.** A company built a number of houses on an estate. It sold 'holiday certificates', entitling the purchaser to occupy one of the houses for up to twelve weeks each year. It did not account for VAT on these sales. The Commissioners issued an assessment charging tax on them, and the company appealed, contending that they should be treated as exempt from VAT. The tribunal dismissed the appeal, holding that the sales were excluded from exemption by what is now *VATA 1994, Sch 9, Group 1, Item 1(e)*. *American Real Estate (Scotland) Ltd, [1980] VATTR 80 (VTD 947)*.

39.89 A couple converted a barn in Cornwall into holiday accommodation. They sold nine weekly units in the accommodation, giving each purchaser the right to occupy it for a specified week for a period of 25 years. The freehold of the property was conveyed to a bank as a trustee, to be sold after 25 years. Each purchaser of a 'time-share' unit was invited to make an additional payment of £350 to purchase a 2% interest in the sale proceeds. Seven of the nine purchasers did so. The couple did not account for VAT on their receipts and the Commissioners issued an assessment. The tribunal dismissed the couple's appeal, holding that the supplies were excluded from exemption by what is now *VATA 1994, Sch 9, Group 1, Item 1(e)*. *P & V Cretney, [1983] VATTR 271 (VTD 1503)*.

39.90 A company owned a number of cottages in Devon. It gave its shareholders the right to one week's holiday each year in one of the cottages for a period of 25 years. It advertised some of its shares for sale, at a price which depended on the cottage and time of year chosen by the shareholder. The Commissioners issued a ruling that the company was carrying on a business of supplying holiday accommodation and was required to be registered for VAT. The company appealed, contending that the only supplies which it made were of shares, which were exempt from VAT. The tribunal dismissed the appeal, observing that an intending shareholder reading the company's prospectus would be bound to notice the different subscription rates charged for the shares. The tribunal held that the amount paid by shareholders should be apportioned, with £1 being attributed to the exempt supply of a share and the balance being attributed to the taxable supply of holiday accommodation. *Court Barton Property plc, [1985] VATTR 148 (VTD 1903)*.

39.91 The time-sharing of a yacht was held to be standard-rated in *Oathplan Ltd, [1982] VATTR 195 (VTD 1299)*.

39.92 A company reclaimed input tax on the purchase of a property. The Commissioners issued an assessment to recover the tax on the basis that the property had been purchased for the purpose of making exempt supplies. The company appealed, contending that it had purchased the property 'for commercial use'. The tribunal dismissed the company's appeal, finding that the company had stated that it intended refurbishing the property with the intention of letting it as timeshare accommodation, and observing that such supplies would be exempt from VAT. (Since the building was not a 'new' building as defined by what is now *Group 1, Note 4*, the effect of *Group 1, Note 12* was that the exclusion in *Item 1(e)* would not apply—although this is not explicitly stated in the decision.) The tribunal also observed that 'it is for the appellant to show that the input tax for which he claims credit relates to taxable supplies made or to be made by him in the course or furtherance of his business, and, in respect of a provisional deduction of input tax, that no part of the input tax relates to goods or services used or to be used by him in making exempt supplies'. *Key Properties Ltd, LON/92/2266A (VTD 11778)*. (*Note*. For other issues in this case, see 34.367 INPUT TAX and 49.267 PENALTIES: MISDECLARATION.)

39.93 A company which had sold timeshare licences repurchased some of the licences from a bank which had taken over the licences after the original purchasers had defaulted. The company reclaimed input tax in respect of the repurchases. The Commissioners issued an assessment to recover the tax, considering that the repurchases were exempt from VAT under what is now *VATA 1994, Sch 9, Group 1*. The tribunal dismissed the company's appeal, holding that the repurchases were exempt and that the effect of *Group 1, Note 12* was that the exclusion in *Item 1(e)* did not apply. *Interlude Houses Ltd, EDN/94/65 (VTD 12877)*.

39.94   **House converted into flats and advertised as holiday accommodation but subsequently leased—apportionment of input tax.**   See *Cooper & Chapman (Builders) Ltd*, 43.118 PARTIAL EXEMPTION.

39.95   **Beach huts.**   A borough council did not account for VAT on income received from letting beach huts. The Commissioners issued a ruling that the income was liable to VAT on the basis that it was excluded from exemption by what is now *VATA 1994, Sch 9, Group 1, Item 1(e)*. The tribunal upheld the Commissioners' ruling and dismissed the council's appeal. 'Holiday accommodation' was not restricted to residential accommodation. The huts were capable of being used for cooking, eating, shelter, changing clothes and a variety of other uses. Accordingly they were within the definition of 'holiday accommodation'. *Poole Borough Council, [1992] VATTR 88 (VTD 7180)*.

39.96   **Lease of house precluding occupation in February of each year.**   In 1988 a married couple were assigned a 98–year lease of a riverside property in Cambridgeshire. Under the lease, the lessees were not permitted to occupy the property during the month of February. Since they had no other residence, they spent each February with their daughter in Germany. Following amendments to *VATA 1983* by *SI 1990 No 2553*, the company which owned the freehold charged the couple VAT on the ground rent and service charge. The couple objected, and the Commissioners issued a formal ruling that the payments were standard-rated because of the covenant prohibiting residence throughout the year, which had the effect that the lease fell within what is now *VATA 1994, Sch 8 Group 5, Note 7* and *VATA 1994, Sch 9, Group 1, Note 11*. The wife appealed, contending that the restrictions imposed by *SI 1990 No 2053* were not in accordance with *Article 13B* of the *EC Sixth Directive*. The tribunal accepted this contention and allowed the appeal, observing that *Article 13B(b)* excluded 'the provision of accommodation in holiday camps or on sites developed for use as camping sites'. It was accepted that the property in question was not situated in a holiday camp. The terms of *SI 1990 No 2053* were outside the scope of *Article 13B*, and the introduction of what is now *VATA 1994, Sch 9, Group 1, Note 11* 'was an excessive exercise of the power given by *Article 13B(b)*'. It had led to the appellant suffering an inequality of treatment as compared with lessees who were free to occupy their homes throughout the year. Such inequality of treatment was not objectively justifiable and was therefore 'arbitrary, discriminatory and illegal'. *Dicta* of the CJEC in *Groupment des Hauts Fourneaux et Acieres Belges v High Authority of the European Coal and Steel Community, CJEC [1958] ECSC 245* applied. *BA Ashworth, [1994] VATTR 275 (VTD 12924)*.

CARAVAN FACILITIES (VATA 1994, Sch 9, Group 1, Item 1(f))

39.97   **Storage.**   Winter storage of caravans was held not to be exempt from VAT in *MP & CM Warner, MAN/86/385 (VTD 2409)*.

39.98   A similar decision was reached in *Unity Farm Holiday Centre Ltd, LON/87/145 (VTD 2620)*. (*Note.* For an appeal by an associated partnership, heard with this case, see 34.250 INPUT TAX.)

39.99   In *DH Commercials (Leasing) Ltd*, 39.110 below, the tribunal chairman held that 'for the provision of a pitch for a caravan to fall within (*Sch 9, Group 1, Item 1(f)*) it must necessarily be on a site where at some stage in the year ... the caravan must be available for human habitation'.

39.100   **Seasonal pitches for caravans.**   A caravan site was only open from 1 March to 31 October in each year, this being a condition of the relevant planning permission. The proprietors of the site did not account for output tax on receipts from licences to occupy the site for periods extending for more than one year, treating the receipts as exempt. The Commissioners issued an assessment on the basis that the receipts were excluded from exemption by what is now *VATA 1994, Sch 9, Group 1, Item 1(f)* and *Note 14*, and thus were standard-rated. The proprietors appealed. The tribunal dismissed the appeal, holding that the effect of what is now *Note 14(b)* was that the licences were for seasonal pitches and thus were excluded from exemption. *T & M Smith, MAN/94/45 (VTD 13052).*

39.101   A similar decision was reached in a subsequent case in which the tribunal held that the provisions of *VATA 1994, Sch 9, Group 1, Item 1(f)* were in accordance with *Article 13B* of the *EC Sixth Directive*. Applying *dicta* of Advocate-General Jacobs in *Blasi v Finanzamt München*, 21.169 EUROPEAN COMMUNITY LAW, 'the last sentence of *Article 13B(b)* is broadly worded so as to allow the Member States a large degree of discretion in placing limits on the scope of the exemption'. *Colaingrove Ltd, [2000] VATDR 82 (VTD 16187).*

39.102   **Caravan sites—whether input tax reclaimable.**   See *Stonecliff Caravan Park*, 65.4 ZERO–RATING: MISCELLANEOUS.

PARKING FACILITIES (VATA 1994, Sch 9, Group 1, Item 1(h))

39.103   An individual rented a garage for £4 per month plus VAT. He lodged an appeal against the charge to VAT, contending that he had been granted a right over land, which was exempt from VAT. The tribunal dismissed his appeal, holding that the supply was excluded from exemption by what is now *VATA 1994, Sch 9, Group 1, Item 1(h)*. *AJ Dowse, LON/73/102 (VTD 46).*

39.104   *Dowse*, 39.103 above, was applied in the similar cases of *F Bondi, LON/75/70 (VTD 173)* and *LO Clarke, CAR/77/29 (VTD 457).*

39.105   An individual who leased three garages appealed against the charge to VAT, contending that he had been granted rights over land, which were exempt from VAT, and that the exclusion of 'parking facilities' did not apply, since he was using the garages for storage purposes. The tribunal rejected this contention and dismissed his appeal, holding that the garages were within the definition of 'parking facilities', so that the leases were excluded from exemption by what is now *VATA 1994, Sch 9, Group 1, Item 1(h)*. *GG Wilson, [1977] VATTR 225 (VTD 428).*

39.106   A company (H) owned a cinema with an adjacent plot of land which it used as a car park for its employees and customers. On the other side of the car park was a supermarket. H granted a licence to the company which owned the supermarket, allowing that company's employees and customers to use the car park. Under the licence, H received payments from the supermarket. H did not account for VAT on these payments, and the Commissioners issued an assessment charging tax on them. The tribunal dismissed H's appeal, holding that the payments were excluded from exemption by what is now *VATA 1994, Sch 9, Group 1, Item 1(h)*. *Henley Picture House Ltd, BIR/79/107 (VTD 895).*

39.107   A company which carried on business as motor vehicle auctioneers charged customers for parking vehicles which they wished to sell. The Commissioners issued an assessment on the basis that the payments by the customers were liable to VAT, and the tribunal dismissed the company's appeal. *Inter City Motor Auctions Ltd, EDN/86/83 (VTD 2319).*

39.108   The lease of two parking spaces was held to be within *VATA 1994, Sch 9, Group 1, Item 1(h)*, and thus excluded from exemption, in *Internoms Ltd, LON/98/1112 (VTD 16527)*.

39.109   A company owned a number of lock-up garages and converted stables, which it leased. Where lessees had indicated that they wished to use the garages for storage, the company did not account for tax on the payments received under the leases, considering that they were exempt under what is now *VATA 1994, Sch 9, Group 1*. The Commissioners issued an assessment charging tax on the payments, considering that they constituted parking facilities which were excluded from exemption by *Sch 9, Group 1, Item 1(h)*. The CS upheld the assessment. Where lock-up garages were let, the plain implication was that facilities had been granted for parking a vehicle. Moreover, even if, before entering the lease, the parties had agreed that the purpose of the letting was domestic storage, the terms of the lease did not preclude the lessee from using the facilities for parking a vehicle. Accordingly, where an unqualified lease of a lock-up garage was granted, the necessary implication was that there had been a grant of facilities for parking a vehicle. *C & E Commrs v Trinity Factoring Services Ltd, CS [1994] STC 504*.

39.110   A company provided storage facilities for caravans. It did not account for output tax on its receipts. The Commissioners issued a ruling that the receipts were liable to VAT, and the company appealed, contending that they should be treated as exempt under *VATA 1994, Sch 9, Group 1*. The tribunal dismissed the appeal, holding that the company was supplying parking facilities, which were excluded from exemption by *Group 1, Item 1(h)*. *DH Commercials (Leasing) Ltd, MAN/95/2125 (VTD 14115)*. (*Note*. The tribunal also held that the supplies did not fall within *Item 1(f)*—see 39.99 above.)

39.111   *DH Commercials (Leasing) Ltd*, 39.110 above, was applied in the similar subsequent case of *AC Slot, LON/94/1089 (VTD 15076)*. (*Note*. For another issue in this case, see 34.39 INPUT TAX.)

39.112   See also *Skatteministeriet v Henriksen*, 21.164 EUROPEAN COMMUNITY LAW.

MOORING FACILITIES, ETC. (VATA 1994, Sch 9, Group 1, Item 1(k))

39.113   **Provision of berth.**   An individual held a licence to berth a boat at a wharf on the River Wey. He was charged £120 plus VAT, and lodged an appeal against the charge to VAT, contending that he had been granted a right over land, which was exempt from VAT. The tribunal dismissed his appeal, holding that the supply was excluded from exemption by what is now *VATA 1994, Sch 9, Group 1, Item 1(k)*. *JW Fisher, LON/75/47 (VTD 179)*.

39.114   A company owned land alongside the River Thames. It built a creek leading from the river, and allowed members of the public to moor boats at specified plots of land alongside the creek. It did not account for VAT on the amounts which it charged for the facilities. The Commissioners issued an assessment charging tax on them, and the company appealed, contending that it had granted rights over land, which should be treated as exempt from VAT. The tribunal dismissed the company's appeal, holding that the supplies were excluded from exemption by what is now *VATA 1994, Sch 9, Group 1, Item 1(k)*. *Strand Ship Building Co Ltd, LON/84/74 (VTD 1651)*.

39.115   A similar decision was reached in *Threshfield Motors Ltd, MAN/98/305 (VTD 16699)*.

39.116   A married couple, who lived on a yacht moored at a quay on the River Medina, appealed against the imposition of VAT on the mooring fees, contending that they should be treated as exempt from VAT. The tribunal dismissed the couple's appeal, holding that the fees were specifically excluded from exemption by what is now *VATA 1994, Sch 9, Group 1, Item 1(k)*. *DM & PJ Roberts, [1992] VATTR 30 (VTD 7516)*. (*Note*. The tribunal also held that, although it was accepted that the couple lived on the yacht, the yacht was not a 'houseboat' for the purposes of *VATA 1994, Sch 8 Group 9*—see 65.8 ZERO-RATING: MISCELLANEOUS.)

SPORTS GROUNDS, ETC. (VATA 1994, Sch 9, Group 1, Item 1(l))

39.117   **Admission to rugby league ground.**   A rugby league club did not account for VAT on amounts paid by spectators for admission to its home matches. The Commissioners issued an assessment on the payments and the club appealed, contending that they were exempt from VAT. The tribunal dismissed the club's appeal, holding that the payments did not qualify for exemption. *Rochdale Hornets Football Club Ltd, [1975] VATTR 71 (VTD 161)*. (*Note*. The case also concerned zero-rating provisions in *FA 1972, Sch 4 Group 5*, which was repealed with effect from 1 May 1985.)

39.118   **Admission to rugby union ground.**   See *Clwb Rygbi Nant Conwy*, 13.13 CLUBS, ASSOCIATIONS AND ORGANISATIONS.

39.119   **Executive boxes at football ground.**   A football club granted seasonal licences of executive boxes at its ground. In accounting for VAT, it treated 97.36% of the consideration as attributable to an exempt licence to occupy land, and 2.64% as being excluded from exemption by *VATA 1994, Sch 9, Group 1, Item 1(l)*. The Commissioners issued an assessment charging tax on the basis that 98% of the consideration was excluded from exemption by *VATA 1994, Sch 9, Group 1, Item 1(l)*. The club appealed, contending that the ground was only used for football matches for 96 hours per year, whereas its licencees could use the boxes for 3,640 hours per year (i.e. 364 days at 10 hours per day), so that on a time basis, only 2.64% of the consideration should be treated as being within *Item 1(l)*. The tribunal rejected this contention and dismissed the appeal, subject to an adjustment to the assessments so that some of the consideration could be attributed to the provision of light refreshments on match days. In principle, the exception in *Item 1(l)* should be interpreted as operating only when a box was actually available to view a football match, since the purpose of the provision was 'to tax entertainment'. However, on the evidence, although some licensees made limited use of their boxes on days other than match days, others used them only to watch matches. The value of the right to use a box for 'a given unit of time for a period whilst a match was taking place was much greater than that outside such a period'. The club's calculations were wrong in principle since they 'ignored the issue of value'. The Commissioners had acted fairly and reasonably in treating 98% of the consideration as falling within *Item 1(l)*. *Southend United Football Club, [1997] VATDR 202 (VTD 15109)*.

FACILITIES FOR PLAYING SPORT (VATA 1994, Sch 9, Group 1, Item 1(m))

39.120   **Supply of football ground for international match.**   The company which owned Hampden Park allowed the Scottish Football Association to use it for international matches. The Commissioners issued a ruling that the supplies of the use of Hampden Park constituted licences to occupy land, which were exempt from VAT, so that the company's input tax had to be apportioned. The company appealed, contending that the supply amounted to the granting of facilities for playing sport, which was excluded from exemption by what is now *VATA 1994, Sch 9, Group 1, Item 1(m)*, and thus was standard-rated. The tribunal allowed the company's appeal, holding that the presence of paying spectators did not prevent the facilities from falling within *Item 1(m)*. *Queens Park Football Club Ltd, [1988] VATTR 76 (VTD 2776)*.

39.121   **Use of rugby union ground.**   See *Clwb Rygbi Nant Conwy*, 13.13 CLUBS, ASSOCIATIONS AND ORGANISATIONS.

39.122   **Grant of licence to occupy land for teaching golf—whether excluded from exemption by Item 1(m).**   A golf club professional (J) granted assistant professionals licences to use a practice range at the club for teaching people how to swing a golf club. He did not account for tax on the money which he received from the assistant professionals, treating them as exempt from VAT. The Commissioners issued assessments charging tax on J's receipts on the basis that they were excluded from exemption by *VATA 1994, Sch 9, Group 1, Item 1(m)*. The tribunal upheld the assessments and dismissed J's appeal. Applying *Skatteministeriet v Henriksen*, 21.164 EUROPEAN COMMUNITY LAW, exemptions were to be construed narrowly and exceptions to exemptions were to be construed widely. The practice area was within the curtilage of the golf course and should be treated as a facility for playing sport, within *Item 1(m)*. *LH Johnson, LON/97/9 (VTD 14955)*.

39.123   **Grant of non-exclusive licence to occupy golf courses—whether excluded from exemption by Item 1(m).**   A company (G) which owned two golf courses granted a golf club a non-exclusive licence to occupy its courses, receiving a licence fee of £280,000. G did not account for output tax on this fee, treating it as being consideration for a licence to occupy land and thus as exempt from VAT. The Commissioners issued an assessment on the basis that the payment was taxable, considering that it was excluded from exemption by *VATA 1994, Sch 9, Group 1, Item 1(m)*, as being 'the grant of facilities for playing any sport'. The tribunal allowed G's appeal, holding that the fact that the licence was not exclusive did not prevent it from constituting a 'licence to occupy land', within *Item 1*. Applying *dicta* of Lord Templeman in *Street v Mountford, HL [1985] 1 AC 809; [1985] 2 All ER 289*, exclusivity of occupation was an essential condition of a tenancy but was not an essential condition of a licence. The chairman observed that 'what distinguishes a tenancy from a licence is that the former grants a legal right to exclusive possession of the land for a particular period'. The chairman declined to follow *dicta* in *Mount Edgcumbe Hospice Ltd*, 11.36 CHARITIES (which the Commissioners had cited as an authority), observing that 'the issue in the appeal of *Mount Edgcumbe . . .* was not similar to that in the present case'. The tribunal also held that *VATA 1994, Sch 9, Group 1, Item 1(m)* did not apply, since G had granted the club 'a licence to occupy land, not facilities for playing any sport or participating in any physical recreation'. The club had occupied the land for the purpose of granting such facilities to its members, but what G had granted the club was simply a licence to occupy land. The chairman observed that 'the licence envisaged that the club would occupy the property for use as a golf course and club, but that object of the licence is not the grant of the facilities which would be created after the grant. It would be a distortion of language to say that (G) was granting facilities for playing sport or participating in physical recreation to the club.' *Abbotsley Golf & Squash Club Ltd, [1997] VATDR 355 (VTD 15042)*. (*Notes*. (1) For the Commissioners' practice following this decision, see Business Brief 25/97, issued on 10 November 1997, and Business Brief 22/98, issued on 3 November 1998. For their current interpretation of what constitutes a licence to occupy land, see Business Brief 21/99, issued on 7 September 1999, and *Amendment 3 (October 1999)* to *Notice 742: Land and Property*. (2) The decisions in *Mount Edgcumbe Hospice Ltd* and *Abbotsley Golf & Squash Club Ltd* were reached by the same tribunal chairman (Mr. Heim), although his reasoning in the latter case appears to contradict his reasoning in the previous case on the question of the taxability of the licences. For a fuller analysis, see the memorandum by the VAT Practitioners' Group published in the Tax Journal, 8 March 1999.)

39.124　**Hire of gymnasium to gymnastic clubs—whether excluded from exemption by Item 1(m).**　A registered charity was established to build and own a gymnasium, to be used by local gymnastic clubs and other organisations. Initially it accounted for output tax on its income from letting the gymnasium to clubs, but in 1996 its treasurer wrote to the VAT office, asking for the income to be treated as exempt. The Commissioners rejected the claim and issued a ruling that the supplies were standard-rated. The tribunal dismissed the charity's appeal, holding that the supplies were excluded from exemption under *Group 1* by *Item 1(m)*. The tribunal observed that *Note 16* did not apply because none of the gymnastic clubs had exclusive use of the facilities, as required by *Note 16(b)(iv)*. (The tribunal also observed that the supplies were not exempt under *Group 10, Item 3* because they were not made to individuals.) *Colchester School of Gymnastics, LON/97/1172 (VTD 15370)*.

MISCELLANEOUS

39.125　**Whether VATA 1994, Sch 9, Group 1, Item 1 consistent with EC Sixth Directive.**　See *Norbury Developments Ltd*, 21.238 EUROPEAN COMMUNITY LAW.

40   Local Authorities and Statutory Bodies

40.1   **Rebuilding of Alexandra Palace—whether input tax reclaimable.**   In 1980 most of Alexandra Palace was destroyed by fire. Between 1985 and 1990 Haringey Borough Council, which was the trustee of the Palace, reclaimed input tax incurred in rebuilding it. The Commissioners initially accepted the repayment claims, but in December 1990 they issued an assessment to recover much of the tax, considering that a significant proportion of the expenditure was attributable to the hire of the Palace as an exhibition centre, and that such supplies were exempt from VAT under what is now *VATA 1994, Sch 9 Group 1*. The Council appealed, contending firstly that it had incurred the expenditure in the course of its statutory duties under the *Alexandra Park & Palace (Public Purposes) Act 1900*, so that the whole of the tax was reclaimable under what is now *VATA 1994, s 33(1)*, and alternatively that any input tax attributable to exempt supplies was 'an insignificant proportion' of the total tax, and should therefore be refunded under *VATA 1994, s 33(2)*. The QB rejected the Council's first contention, holding that the business purpose could not be treated as irrelevant or incidental, but accepted the Council's second contention, holding that the Council had been justified in treating the proportion of its input tax attributable to exempt supplies as insignificant. On the facts found by the tribunal, no more than 8% of the total expenditure related to exempt supplies, and this was within the definition of 'insignificant'. Furthermore, the Commissioners had made the initial repayments on a lawful basis, and there had been no misrepresentation by the Council. 'The opinions which led the Commissioners to make refunds ... between 1985 and 1990 were ones which they were entitled to form'. It was not open to the Commissioners to resile from their initial acceptance that the exempt input tax could be treated as insignificant. *Mayor & Burgesses of the London Borough of Haringey v C & E Commrs (and cross-appeal), QB [1995] STC 830*. (*Note.* For the Commissioners' practice following this decision, see Business Brief 11/95, issued on 2 June 1995, and Notice No 749, paras 4.4 and 4.5.)

40.2   **Grants made by Council for work in reducing smoke emissions—whether input tax reclaimable.**   A Borough Council declared parts of its district as 'smoke control areas' under the *Clean Air Act 1956*, and made grants to householders who arranged for contractors to carry out specified work with the aim of reducing smoke emissions. The Department of the Environment reimbursed 4/7 of the amounts which the Council paid. The Council had to bear the remaining 3/7 of the cost itself, and reclaimed the input tax included in the contractors' charges. The Commissioners rejected the claim, on the grounds that the supplies were made to the householders rather than to the Council. The Council appealed, contending that the tax should be treated as reclaimable under what is now *VATA 1994, s 33*. The tribunal dismissed the appeal, holding that the Council could not reclaim the input tax since it was 'not involved in the transactions between any of the householders who obtained grants from it and the contractors who carried out the grant-aided works'. *Doncaster Borough Council, MAN/93/1157 (VTD 12458)*.

40.3   **VATA 1994, s 33(3)(f)—definition of 'police authority'.**   The *Police Act 1997* established a Service Authority for the National Crime Squad (NCS), with responsibility for investigating and preventing major criminal activities, and a National Criminal Intelligence Service (NCIS) to provide tactical and strategic intelligence on major organised crime. NCS and NCIS claimed refunds of VAT under *VATA 1994, s 33*. The Treasury rejected the claims on the basis that neither NCS nor NCIS qualified as a 'police authority' within *VATA 1994, s 33(3)(f)*. NCS and NCIS applied for judicial review. The QB dismissed the applications, holding that NCS and NCIS were not police authorities within *Police Act 1996, s 101(1)* and therefore were also not police authorities for the purposes of *VATA 1994, s 33(3)(f)*. Furthermore, the Treasury had been entitled not to make an order treating them as specified bodies within *s 33(3)(k)*. Applying *dicta* of Sir Thomas Bingham MR in *R v Ministry of Defence (ex p. Smith), CA 1995, [1996] QB 517; [1996] 1 All ER 257*, 'the court may not interfere with the exercise of an administrative discretion on substantive grounds save where the court is satisfied that the decision is unreasonable in the sense that it is beyond the range of responses open to a reasonable decision-maker'. *R v HM Treasury & Another (ex p. Service Authority for the National Crime Squad and Others), QB [2000] STC 638.*

40.4   **Police Authority—claim for refund of VAT on purchase of motor cars—effect of VATA 1994, s 33(6).**   A police authority made a claim, under *VATA 1994, s 33(1)*, for a refund of VAT paid on the purchase of new motor cars. The Commissioners rejected the claim, on the basis that the effect of the *VAT (Input Tax) Order 1992 (SI 1992 No 3222), article 7* was that the tax was not repayable. The authority applied for judicial review. The QB rejected the application and upheld the Commissioners' ruling. Collins J held that the effect of *VATA 1994, s 33(6)* was that *article 7* of the *Input Tax Order*, which was made in accordance with *VATA 1994, s 25(7)*, applied to refund claims under *s 33(1)*. Accordingly, the authority was not entitled to a refund of the tax in question. *R v C & E Commrs (ex p. Greater Manchester Police Authority), QB [2000] STC 620.*

40.5   **Advertising facilities supplied by Council in return for sponsorship payments—whether a supply 'in the course or furtherance of a business'.**   A City Council, which was registered for VAT in accordance with what is now *VATA 1994, s 42*, granted advertising facilities to commercial sponsors of various campaigns organised by the Council, including a child safety campaign and an anti-smoking campaign. However, the Council did not account for tax on the sponsorship payments which it received. The Commissioners issued an assessment charging tax on the payments, and the Council appealed, contending that it had not made the supplies in question 'in the course or furtherance of a business', so that output tax was not chargeable. The tribunal dismissed the appeal, holding that the Council 'were carrying on business activities as the means of performing their statutory functions'. Furthermore, the supplies were 'economic activities' within *Article 4(2)* of the *EC Sixth Directive*, and were not excluded from VAT by *Article 4(5)* of the *Directive*, since the supplies to the sponsors were 'under the same legal conditions as those that apply to private traders'. *Morrison's Academy Boarding Houses Association*, 7.1 BUSINESS, and *Ufficio Distrettuale delle Imposte Dirette di Fiorenzuola d'Arda v Comune di Carpaneto Piacentino*, 21.76 EUROPEAN COMMUNITY LAW, applied. *Norwich City Council, LON/93/1950A (VTD 11822)*.

40.6   **Supplies of information by District Council—whether Article 4(5) of EC Sixth Directive applicable.**   A District Council operated an information service, collecting and distributing information relating to the county in which it was located, in accordance with the provisions of *Local Government Act 1985, s 88*. It supplied such information to an urban development corporation (which had been created under *Local Government, Planning & Land Act 1980, s 135*), and did not account for output tax on these supplies. The Commissioners issued an assessment charging tax on them, and the Council appealed, contending that the effect of *Article 4(5)* of the *EC Sixth Directive* was that it should not be considered a 'taxable person'. The tribunal rejected this contention and dismissed the appeal. *Article 4(5)* stated that local authorities should 'be considered taxable persons ... where treatment as non-taxable persons would lead to significant distortions of competition'. On the evidence, the tribunal held that the work in question could have been undertaken by a private organisation, and that to treat the Council as a non-taxable person 'would bear unfairly on private organisations which would be accountable for VAT on similar work'. The Council was making supplies to the corporation for consideration, in the course or furtherance of a business, and was therefore required to account for output tax. *Metropolitan Borough of Wirral, MAN/95/77 (VTD 14674)*.

40.7   **Provision and maintenance of cemeteries by Borough Council—whether Council acting as a 'taxable person' within Article 4(5) of EC Sixth Directive.**   A Borough Council reclaimed input tax, under *VATA 1994, s 33*, on supplies which it received for the purpose of providing and maintaining cemeteries. The Commissioners issued a ruling that the Council's provision and maintenance of cemeteries was a business activity, so that its supplies were exempt supplies and it was not entitled to reclaim input tax. The Council appealed, contending that the effect of *Article 4(5)* of the *EC Sixth Directive* was that it should not be considered a 'taxable person'. The tribunal accepted this contention and allowed the appeal. Applying *Ufficio Distrettuale delle Imposte Dirette di Fiorenzuola d'Arda v Comune di Carpaneto Piacentino*, 21.76 EUROPEAN COMMUNITY LAW, the Council provided and maintained cemeteries 'as a public authority' and thus 'was not a taxable person in respect of those activities'. Furthermore, since the great majority of cemeteries and crematoria were operated by local authorities, 'the treatment of local authorities as non-taxable persons in connection with these activities would not lead to significant distortions of competition'. *Rhondda Cynon Taff County Borough Council, [2000] VATDR 149 (VTD 16496)*. (*Note.* For the Commissioners' practice following this decision, see Business Brief 4/2000, issued on 17 March 2000.)

40.8   **Application of Article 4(5) of EC Sixth Directive.**   See also *The Lord Mayor & Citizens of the City of Westminster*, 21.75 EUROPEAN COMMUNITY LAW; *Ufficio Distrettuale delle Imposte Dirette di Fiorenzuola d'Arda v Comune di Carpaneto Piacentino*, 21.76 EUROPEAN COMMUNITY LAW; *Comune di Carpaneto Piacentino & Others v Ufficio Provinciale Imposta sul Valore Aggiunto di Piacenza*, 21.77 EUROPEAN COMMUNITY LAW; and *Ayuntamiento de Sevilla v Recaudadores de las Zonas Primera y Segunda*, 21.78 EUROPEAN COMMUNITY LAW.

40.9   **Local authority providing grants to charity—whether such grants constitute consideration for supplies.**   A County Council made grants to a registered charity which ran workshops providing work experience for the physically and mentally handicapped. The charity reclaimed input tax on the construction of a new workshop. The Commissioners rejected the claim on the grounds that the workshop was not used for making taxable supplies. The charity appealed, contending that the grants which it received from the Council represented consideration for supplies to the Council. The tribunal dismissed the appeal, holding that the charity was making its supplies to the individual disabled persons for no consideration, and that the grants from the Council were donations which were outside the scope of VAT. *Trustees of the Bowthorpe Community Trust, LON/94/1276A (VTD 12978)*.

40.10   **Statutory repair work carried on by City Council—whether any supply by Council.**   Under the *Housing (Scotland) Act 1987*, Glasgow City Council repaired a number of buildings where the owners had failed to comply with statutory repair notices. Initially it accounted for VAT on the amounts which it charged to the owners in respect of this work. In 1996 it submitted a claim for a substantial repayment, on the basis that the repair work was not supplied in the course of any business and was not liable to VAT. The Commissioners rejected the claim, and the Council appealed. The tribunal allowed the appeal, holding that, in exercising its statutory authority, the Council was not making any supply of services within the scope of *VATA 1994*. The tribunal observed that 'the whole procedure has a compulsory flavour about it which points away from the consensual element present in most circumstances where a supply occurs'. *Apple & Pear Development Council*, 21.47 EUROPEAN COMMUNITY

LAW, applied. Furthermore, the works could not 'properly be described as being carried out in the course or furtherance of a business'. *Glasgow City Council, [1998] VATDR 407 (VTD 15491)*. (*Notes.* (1) For the Commissioners' practice following this decision, see Business Brief 19/98, issued on 15 September 1998. (2) For subsequent developments in this case, see 45.29 PAYMENT OF TAX.)

41   Management Services

41.1   **Management services within a group of companies.** A company (T) provided management services for the operating companies of a large group. It took this function over from the parent company on the introduction of VAT. It charged for its services insofar as they related to property or were legal services (as to which there was no dispute) but made no charge for its other services and consequently incurred substantial losses in providing them. It therefore arranged with the parent company that it would surrender its corporation tax losses to other companies in the group as 'group relief' under what is now *Income and Corporation Taxes Act 1988, s 402* in return for payments as permitted by that legislation. This arrangement was embodied in a formal agreement between T and the parent company. T did not account for tax on the payments and the Commissioners issued an assessment charging tax on them. The QB upheld the assessment, holding that T was supplying services for consideration. *C & E Commrs v Tilling Management Services Ltd, QB 1978, [1979] STC 365.*

41.2   **Payments between associated companies—whether loans or consideration for management services.** A company (P) set up a subsidiary company (L) to provide management services. P made regular payments to L, which did not account for output tax on these. The Commissioners issued assessments charging tax on the payments, on the basis that they represented consideration for management services. L appealed, contending that the payments were loans, and had been made solely for the purpose of keeping its bank account in credit. The tribunal accepted L's evidence and allowed the appeal, finding that the payments 'were not payments on account of management charges, but were in reality made for the purpose of maintaining (L's) account in credit'. *London Regeneration Project Services Ltd, LON/92/1442A (VTD 12062).*

41.3   A similar decision was reached in *Glengate KG Properties Ltd, LON/95/2520A (VTD 14239).*

41.4   **Management services—time of supply.** A company (L) and two subsidiaries were registered as a group of companies with effect from November 1982. L did not account for tax on management charges which its subsidiaries paid after the group registration, but which related to services performed before the group registration. The Commissioners issued an assessment charging tax on the payments but the tribunal allowed L's appeal, holding that the time of supply was the date of payment. *Legal & Contractual Services Ltd, [1984] VATTR 85 (VTD 1649).*

41.5   In the case noted at 49.111 PENALTIES: MISDECLARATION, a holding company had made supplies to two subsidiary companies, the value of which was recorded by credit and debit entries in the companies' books. The tribunal held that the supplies were within what is now *VAT Regulations 1995 (SI 1995 No 2518), reg 90(1)*, and that the time of supply was when the entries were made in the companies' books, on the grounds that 'payment may be made by offsetting a debt owed against a debt due, e.g. by journal transfer between purchase and sales ledger accounts, or by making a credit entry in an inter-company current account having a debit balance' and that the time of payment was 'the date on which the appropriate entry is made in the accounting records'. *Pentex Oil Ltd, EDN/91/140 (VTD 7989, 7991).*

41.6   A company's accounts for the year ending 30 September 1990 were signed by the directors on 7 January 1991. The accounts included management charges from an associated company, but the company did not account for tax on this. The Commissioners issued an assessment and imposed a misdeclaration penalty. The company appealed, contending that the tax point should have been treated as 1 July 1991 (when the accounts were adopted by the shareholders at the company's Annual General Meeting), rather than 7 January 1991. The tribunal dismissed the company's appeals, holding that the time of supply was 7 January. *Missionfine Ltd (t/a GT Air Services), MAN/92/293 (VTD 10331)*.

41.7   A company (W) managed a number of properties for an associated company (T). Between March 1992 and October 1992 W did not issue any invoices for management charges to T, and also did not pay any of the rents it had collected to T. The Commissioners issued a ruling that, by retaining the rents instead of paying them to T, W had effectively held them as payment for its supplies of management services, so that the effect of what is now *regulation 90(1)* of the *VAT Regulations 1995* was that VAT became chargeable at that time. The tribunal allowed W's appeal, holding that the withholding of the rents did not amount to payment for the management services which W supplied to T, and that 'receipt of rent by authorised agents of a principal could not amount to payment of the agent's fee'. *Waverley Housing Management Ltd, EDN/93/105 (VTD 11765)*.

41.8   **Company issuing invoices to associated company and subsequently going into liquidation without accounting for output tax—whether associated company entitled to reclaim input tax.** In November 1993 a company (E), which was in financial difficulties and owed more than £10,000 in unpaid VAT, issued an invoice for management services to a subsidiary company (W). E issued further such invoices in February 1994 and March 1994, but failed to account for the output tax shown on the invoices. In April 1994 E went into liquidation. W reclaimed the input tax shown on the three invoices. The Commissioners rejected the claim and W appealed, contending that the assessment was unfair, since in 1987 the Commissioners had accepted that E had supplied management services to W, and had issued an assessment charging output tax on that basis. The tribunal rejected this contention and dismissed W's appeal, holding on the evidence that it was not satisfied that E had made any supplies of management services in 1993 or 1994. Furthermore, 'the Commissioners were fully entitled to reconsider the management charges in a situation where no output tax would be recoverable because of (E's) liquidation'. *The Withies Inn Ltd, LON/95/1778 (VTD 14257)*.

41.9   A company (E) issued an invoice for 'administration charges' to an associated company (D). D reclaimed input tax on the invoice, but E went into liquidation without accounting for output tax. When the Commissioners discovered this, they issued an assessment to recover the tax which D had reclaimed. The tribunal upheld the assessment and dismissed D's appeal, holding on the evidence that E had not made any supplies to D. *Warmfield Developments Ltd, MAN/99/577 (VTD 16953)*.

41.10   **Whether management services supplied to headlessee or underlessees.** A company (C) held the head lease of an industrial estate, most of the buildings in which were let to tenants on underleases. A management company was joined as a party to the underleases, and covenanted to provide various services such as repairs and maintenance. The Commissioners issued a ruling that the management company was supplying its services to C as the headlessee, that C was then making the supplies to the underlessees as part of an exempt supply of an interest in land, and that where the management company was in the same VAT group as C, the effect of the group registration was that there was a single exempt supply. C appealed, contending firstly that the management company was making its supplies directly to the underlessees, and secondly that the group registration did not have the effect of changing the character of a supply from a taxable supply of services to an exempt supply of goods. The tribunal accepted both these contentions and allowed the appeal. The effect of 'the wording and the structure of the underlease' was that the management company was making the disputed supplies of services directly to the underlessees. Some of the supplies conferred a benefit on the headlessee, but they were 'of their nature services to be used and paid for by' the underlessee. Furthermore, *VATA 1994, s 43* did not have the effect of 'transforming a standard-rated supply of services into an exempt supply of goods'. *Dicta* in *Thorn EMI plc*, 36.7 INSURANCE, applied; *Kingfisher plc*, 30.23 GROUPS OF COMPANIES, distinguished. *Canary Wharf Ltd, [1996] VATDR 323 (VTD 14513)*.

41.11   **Provision of employees' services—whether a taxable supply.**   See the cases noted at 58.18 to 58.41 SUPPLY.

41.12   **Management services—set-offs between accountancy partnership and associated service company.**   An accountancy partnership held all the shares in an unlimited company which provided certain financial services for the partnership's clients. The partnership and the company occupied the same premises and used the same staff, who were employed and paid by the company, which periodically invoiced the partnership for a proportion of the salaries with a set-off being made for overhead expenses borne by the partnership and attributable to the company, and for a management fee representing work done by the partners for the company. In November 1975 the company issued an invoice to the partnership for £66,218, computed on the basis that staff salaries paid by the company and attributable to the partnership totalled £93,858, from which were deducted overhead expenses of £22,640 borne by the partnership and attributable to the company, and a management fee of £5,000 charged by the partnership to the company. The Commissioners issued assessments on the basis that the company had made taxable supplies to the partnership of £93,858, and that the partnership had made taxable supplies to the company of £27,640. The partnership and the company appealed, contending that they should only be required to account for VAT on the net amount of £66,218. The tribunal rejected this contention and dismissed the appeals. *Smith & Williamson; Smith & Williamson Securities, [1976] VATTR 215 (VTD 281)*.

41.13   **Management services—whether credit notes effective.**   See *Laurence Scott Ltd*, 38.79 INVOICES AND CREDIT NOTES.

41.14   **Payments between associated companies—whether for single composite supply of management services.**   See *TS Harrison & Sons Ltd*, 58.417 SUPPLY.

41.15   **Payment received by publishing company—whether for taxable supply of management services or distribution of profits.**   A company published a number of magazines. It did not account for output tax on payments it received from the editor of three magazines. The Commissioners issued assessments on the basis that the payments represented consideration for taxable supplies of management services. The company appealed, contending that the payments should be treated as a distribution of profits and as outside the scope of VAT. The tribunal rejected this contention and dismissed the appeal, holding that the payments represented consideration for supplies of services. *JRL Newsletters Ltd, LON/95/2758 (VTD 14394)*.

41.16   **Management services supplied to company not registered for VAT—recipient company subsequently joining same VAT group as supplier of services.**   A Swedish bank owned a UK subsidiary company (S), which was registered for VAT. S supplied management services to the London branch of the bank, which was not registered for VAT. It was accepted that these services were 'continuous supplies of services', within what is now *VAT Regulations 1995 (SI 1995 No 2518), reg 90*. S reclaimed input tax on its related expenditure. In August 1991, before any invoice had been raised or any payment made for the services, the London branch was registered for VAT and joined the VAT group of which S was the representative member. The Commissioners issued an assessment to recover the input tax which S had reclaimed, and S appealed. The tribunal upheld the assessment, holding that the Commissioners were entitled to recover the tax under what is now *VAT Regulations 1995, reg 107*. The CA upheld this decision and the HL dismissed S's appeal (by a 4–1 majority, Lord Lloyd dissenting). Where there was a continuous supply of services, no supply was treated as having been made until there had been a payment or the issue of an invoice. The effect of the entry of the London branch into the VAT group was that S had claimed credit for intended supplies which, under VAT law, had never taken place. The CJEC decision in *Belgium v Ghent Coal Terminal NV*, 21.199 EUROPEAN COMMUNITY LAW (which S had cited as an authority) was distinguished, on the grounds that 'it related to circumstances where the taxable person could not make the intended supply because of circumstances outside its control', whereas 'in the present case the bringing of London Branch into the group was not by reason of circumstances beyond the control of (S) but was made with the concurrence of (S)'. The relevant supplies, for which S had received credit, had to be considered as having been appropriated for use in making exempt supplies to third parties. S was therefore required to account for tax accordingly. Lord Hope observed that 'the guiding principle as to relief for input tax as against output tax is that of fiscal neutrality . . . the various statutory rules which must be applied in this case have produced a result which is consistent with that principle'. *Svenska International plc v C & E Commrs, HL [1999] STC 406; [1999] 1 WLR 769; [1999] 2 All ER 906*. (*Note.* See also the anti-avoidance provisions in *VATA 1994, Sch 9A*, introduced by *FA 1996* in relation to events occurring after 28 November 1995.)

41.17   **Management services supplied to unregistered investors—whether any right to appeal.** See *Kingsley-Smith*, 2.35 APPEALS.

42   Overseas Traders

42.1   **Whether Canadian company having a business establishment in the UK—VATA 1994, Sch 1 para 10.**   A company registered in Canada, which sold dartboards in Canada, owned a property in Lancashire. Its directors visited the UK occasionally, and purchased goods for resale in Canada. However, the company made no sales in the UK. It had registered for VAT in 1976. In 1988 it made a VAT repayment claim. The Commissioners formed the opinion that the company should not have been registered for VAT in the UK, and refused to repay the amount claimed. Subsequently they cancelled the company's registration. The company appealed, contending that it had a business establishment in the UK, and was therefore entitled to be registered under what is now *VATA 1994, Sch 1 para 10*. The tribunal allowed the company's appeal. The company's directors used the Lancashire property as a base when visiting the UK to purchase goods. The fact that the property was not continuously occupied did not prevent it from constituting a 'business establishment' in the UK. (The tribunal also held that its jurisdiction in the case was appellate rather than merely supervisory.) *The Source Enterprise Ltd, MAN/91/450 (VTD 7881)*.

42.2   **Whether German company supplying goods in UK or Germany—Article 8 of EC Sixth Directive.**   See *Azo-Maschinenfabrik Adolf Zimmerman GmbH (No 2)*, 21.105 EUROPEAN COMMUNITY LAW.

42.3   **Time limit for repayment claim—VAT (Repayments to Third Country Traders) Regulations 1987.**   See *Jack Camp Productions*, 24.27 EXPORTS.

42.4   **Repayment claim by 'third country trader'—VATA 1994, s 39.**   A company established in the Czech Republic claimed repayments of VAT under *VATA 1994, s 39* and the *EC Thirteenth Directive*. The Commissioners rejected part of the claims on the grounds that they related to 'day-to-day living expenses which are not directly business-related', and that, in several cases, the claims were not supported by invoices. The tribunal dismissed the company's appeal, finding that the relevant supplies appeared to have been made directly to the company's representatives, rather than to the company itself. Furthermore, it appeared that the supplies had been made for the personal benefit of the representatives, rather than for the purposes of the company's business. *CR Investments SRO, LON/97/1201–1204 (VTD 15474)*.

42.5   **Repayment claim by 'third country trader'—time limit for claim—VAT Regulations 1995, reg 192.**   In September 1994 a Jersey company claimed a substantial repayment of VAT under what is now *VATA 1994, s 39*. The Commissioners rejected the claim on the grounds that it had been made outside the statutory six-month time limit laid down by what is now *VAT Regulations 1995 (SI 1995 No 2518), reg 192*. The tribunal dismissed the company's appeal against this decision. Applying *dicta* of Lord Lane in *JH Corbitt (Numismatists) Ltd*, 56.1 SECOND-HAND GOODS, and of Neill LJ in *John Dee Ltd*, 14.28 COLLECTION AND ENFORCEMENT, the tribunal had no 'jurisdiction to review the exercise by Customs & Excise of any discretion it may have in its management of the collection and refund of VAT'. *Jersey Telecoms, LON/95/1965 (VTD 13940)*.

43 Partial Exemption

General Note. The law concerning the deduction of tax by partly exempt persons was substantially amended from 1 April 1987, and there were further changes with effect from 1 April 1992. See now *VATA 1994, ss 14, 15* and *VAT Regulations 1995 (SI 1995 No 2518), regs 99–111.*

NON-BUSINESS INPUT TAX (VAT Regulations 1995, reg 100)

43.1 **College of further education.** A college of further education was partly exempt, making some taxable supplies and some exempt supplies of educational services. It also provided free education for a number of students aged under 19. This was treated as outside the scope of VAT. However, in its returns, the college reclaimed input tax relating to these services. The Commissioners issued an assessment to recover the tax, on the basis that the relevant goods or services were not 'used or to be used for the purposes of any business' within *VATA 1994, s 24(1)*, so that the effect of *VAT Regulations 1995 (SI 1995 No 2518), reg 100* was that the input tax was not deductible. The tribunal upheld the assessments and dismissed the college's appeal. *North East Worcestershire College, MAN/98/717 (VTD 16665).*

ATTRIBUTION OF INPUT TAX TO TAXABLE SUPPLIES (VAT Regulations 1995, reg 101)

Input tax held to be used 'exclusively in making taxable supplies' (Regulation 101(2)(b))

43.2   **Museum admitting school parties free of charge.**   In 1989 the Imperial War Museum began charging visitors admission, but continued to allow free admission to school parties, and to other visitors at restricted times. It reclaimed the whole of its input tax. In 1991 the Commissioners formed the opinion that, in allowing some visitors free admission, the Museum was making 'non-taxable supplies', and that not all of its input tax was deductible. They concluded that only 85% of the Museum's input tax was deductible, and issued an assessment to recover the remaining 15%. The Museum appealed, contending that all its input tax was deductible. The tribunal allowed the appeal. The running of the Museum amounted to a business. The general overheads incurred by the Museum were used for the purpose of making taxable supplies. The Museum did not make any exempt supplies, and the fact that some visitors were admitted free of charge did not alter the fact that all the Museum's supplies were taxable. Thus the whole of the input tax was incurred for the purpose of making taxable supplies, even though it was not exclusively used for this purpose. *Whitechapel Art Gallery*, 11.29 CHARITIES, was distinguished since in that case the free art displays had been separate from the gallery's business activities. On the facts here, there was a single business activity of running the exhibition area of the Museum. Applying what is now *VAT Regulations 1995 (SI 1995 No 2518), reg 101*, all of the input tax fell to be attributed to this activity, and therefore all the input tax was deductible. *Imperial War Museum, [1992] VATTR 346 (VTD 9097)*.

43.3   **Property let for one week as holiday accommodation and subsequently sold.**   In 1987, a company acquired a lease of a flat in London, with the intention of letting it as holiday accommodation. It incurred expenditure on refurbishing the flat, and advertised it as holiday accommodation for overseas visitors. However, it only attracted one customer, who occupied the flat for a week in 1988, paying £500 plus VAT. Subsequently the company sold the flat to one of its directors for £190,000. Since this sale was an exempt supply, the Commissioners considered that most of the input tax which the company had reclaimed should be attributed to this exempt supply, and issued assessments to recover $^{1900}/_{1905}$ of the tax. The company appealed, contending that since it had incurred the expenditure with the intention of making taxable supplies, and the whole of the flat had been the subject of a taxable supply, it was entitled to credit for the whole of the input tax. The tribunal accepted this contention and allowed the appeal. *Briararch Ltd*, 43.125 below, and *Cooper & Chapman (Builders) Ltd*, 43.118 below, distinguished. *Pembridge Estates Ltd, LON/90/1803X (VTD 9606)*. (*Note*. The decision here was not followed in the subsequent case of *Key*, 43.19 below.)

43.4   **Input tax on legal fees—whether to be apportioned or attributed to taxable supply.**   An insurance company, which was partly exempt, resisted a claim under a policy which it had entered into, claiming that the other party had been guilty of misrepresentation. It incurred legal fees in resisting the claim, which was eventually settled by a compromise agreement. The company reclaimed the full amount of the input tax relating to the fees in question. The Commissioners issued an assessment to recover part of the tax, considering that the expenditure was a general overhead of the business and should be treated as residual input tax, to be apportioned. The company appealed, contending that the input tax was entirely recoverable since it related to the supply of a zero-rated policy. The tribunal allowed the company's appeal, holding that the legal services had been used in the making of the taxable supply, rather than merely as a consequence of having made the supply, and accordingly the whole of the input tax was deductible. The QB upheld this decision. Auld J held that the legal services were causally connected with the making of the payment of the claim if and when it was made, and were therefore used 'exclusively in making taxable supplies'. *C & E Commrs v Deutsche Ruck UK Reinsurance Co Ltd, QB [1995] STC 495*. (*Note*. For the Commissioners' practice following this decision, see Business Brief 6/95, issued on 28 March 1995.)

43.5 **Bank—whether legal costs wholly attributable to taxable supplies.** See *C & E Commrs v Midland Bank plc*, 21.193 EUROPEAN COMMUNITY LAW.

43.6 **Bank—acquisition of leasing companies.** A bank, which was partly exempt, had operated an equipment leasing business for several years. In 1987 this business had suffered losses. In 1990 and 1991 the bank acquired the share capital of three existing leasing companies. It took over the leasing businesses formerly operated by these companies, which became dormant subsidiaries. The bank reclaimed input tax on fees which it paid to solicitors and brokers relating to the acquisition of the companies. The Commissioners issued an assessment to recover some 28% of the tax, considering that it was partly attributable to exempt supplies. The bank appealed, contending that all the input tax should be treated as reclaimable, since it had acquired the companies for the purpose of making taxable supplies. The tribunal accepted this contention and allowed the bank's appeal, holding that there was 'no need to distinguish between the share purchases and the subsequent purchases of the businesses'. The CA upheld this decision. On the evidence, the tribunal had been entitled to find that there was a direct link between the acquisitions and the making of taxable supplies. *BLP Group plc*, 21.192 EUROPEAN COMMUNITY LAW, distinguished. *C & E Commrs v UBAF Bank Ltd, CA [1996] STC 372*. (*Note*. For the Commissioners' practice following this decision, see Business Brief 7/96, issued on 3 May 1996.)

43.7 **Tourist board—installation of improved internet site.** A tourist board was partly exempt. It arranged for the installation of an improved internet site. Initially it treated the relevant input tax as residual input tax, but subsequently it submitted a repayment claim on the basis that it should have been attributed to taxable supplies. The Commissioners rejected the claim and the board appealed. The tribunal allowed the appeal in principle (subject to agreement as to figures), holding on the evidence that the expenditure had been incurred 'for the primary purpose of making taxable supplies, i.e. the booking service for which a charge is made'. *Scottish Tourist Board, EDN/00/46 (VTD 16883)*.

43.8 **Nursing agency—whether subject to partial exemption provisions.** See *British Nursing Co-Operation Ltd*, 31.5 HEALTH AND WELFARE.

43.9 **College supplying free prospectuses.** See *West Herts College*, 58.95 SUPPLY.

Input tax held to be used 'exclusively in making exempt supplies' (Regulation 101(2)(c))

43.10 **Short-term lease of building pending sale.** A company was unable to sell a building which it had constructed, and therefore let it on a short-term lease. The Commissioners issued an assessment to recover the input tax which the company had claimed, considering that it should be attributed to an exempt supply. The company appealed, contending that the input tax should be allowed since it intended to sell the building, and any sale would be a taxable (zero-rated) supply. The tribunal dismissed the appeal, holding that the company had made an exempt supply and the input tax had to be attributed to that supply. *Brasplern (Group Services) Ltd, MAN/83/223 (VTD 1558)*.

43.11 A building company was unable to sell four houses which it had built, and in respect of which it had reclaimed input tax. It therefore leased them on two-month renewable leases. The Commissioners issued an assessment to recover the tax, on the basis that it had to be attributed to the leases which were exempt supplies. The tribunal upheld the assessment and dismissed the company's appeal, applying *Brasplern (Group Services) Ltd*, 43.10 above. *Rentorn Ltd, EDN/88/105 (VTD 3334)*. (*Note*. This case was distinguished in *Curtis Henderson Ltd*, 43.126 below. Compare also *Briararch Ltd*, 43.125 below.)

43.12 **Conversion of property let on short-term leases—whether expenditure to be attributed to future taxable supply.** A company was registered as an intending trader with effect from August 1980. It converted a large house, which its managing director had purchased, into two self-contained units, and reclaimed the input tax incurred. It also reclaimed input tax incurred in building four houses. However, it did not make any taxable supplies, but let the properties on short-term leases. Accordingly, as the only supplies made were exempt from VAT, the Commissioners issued assessments to recover the tax. The company appealed, contending that it was entitled to reclaim the tax under *Article 17* of the *EC Sixth Directive*. The tribunal dismissed the appeal, holding that the Commissioners were entitled to reject claims for input tax where no taxable supply was made within a reasonable period. What is now *VAT Regulations 1995 (SI 1995 No 2518), reg 101* conformed to the provisions of the *EC Sixth Directive*. Furthermore, the company had accepted the conditions as to registration and the reclaim of input tax originally imposed by the Commissioners. *Fishguard Bay Developments Ltd, LON/87/625X (VTD 3225, 4549)*.

43.13 A property development company purchased a building and converted it into a number of self-contained flats or apartments. It reclaimed input tax on the work, although it let the apartments on short-term leases. The Commissioners issued an assessment to recover the tax on the basis that the expenditure should be attributed to the leases which were exempt supplies. The company appealed, contending that the short-term leases were only intended to be temporary, and that it intended to use the building as a hotel, so that the building would be used for taxable supplies. The tribunal dismissed the appeal, finding that the building had not been used for taxable supplies and holding that the company had not proved that it had any intention of using the building for taxable supplies. *Celahurst Ltd, LON/92/257 (VTD 13502)*. (*Note*. An appeal against a misdeclaration penalty was also dismissed.)

43.14 **Refurbishment costs incurred against future exempt supplies.** Two companies reclaimed input tax on expenditure incurred in refurbishing a property to be used as offices and warehouses. The Commissioners issued assessments to recover the tax, as the expenditure related to future exempt supplies. The tribunal dismissed the companies' appeals and the CA upheld this decision. Mustill LJ observed that 'tax on inputs should be set off against tax on the outputs to which the inputs related, and against nothing else'. The leasing of the property would be an exempt supply, and the tax incurred for the purpose of making exempt supplies could not be deducted as input tax. *Neuvale Ltd & Frambeck Ltd v C & E Commrs, CA [1989] STC 395*. (*Note*. The claims related to periods before 1 April 1987. *VATA 1983, s 15* was amended by *FA 1987, s 12*, to specifically limit credit for input tax to input tax attributable to taxable supplies made, or to be made, by the taxable person. See now *VATA 1994, s 26*.)

43.15 *Neuvale Ltd*, 43.14 above, was applied in a subsequent case where a company had reclaimed input tax which the tribunal found to have been wholly attributable to the making of exempt supplies. *Montague Burton Developments Ltd, LON/90/1551Z (VTD 10090)*.

43.16   **Premises leased after refurbishment.** A company purchased business premises and reclaimed input tax on their refurbishment. Subsequently it granted a lease of part of the premises to an associated partnership. The Commissioners issued an assessment to recover the input tax, on the basis that it should be attributed to the supply of the lease which was exempt from VAT under what is now *VATA 1994, Sch 9 Group 1*. The tribunal upheld the assessment and dismissed the company's appeal. *North West Business Centres Ltd, MAN/89/768 (VTD 4594)*.

43.17   A similar decision was reached in *Wigan Metropolitan Development Co (Investment) Ltd, MAN/89/591 (VTD 4993)*.

43.18   In 1988 a holding company acquired the freehold of an office building in London. It began refurbishing the building later that year, with the intention of using it as an office. In 1989 it realised that the building would be inadequate for its intended purposes, and it sold the freehold. The sale was an exempt supply, but the company reclaimed the input tax incurred on the refurbishment. The Commissioners issued an assessment to recover the tax. The company appealed, contending that the tax should be treated as deductible since it had purchased the building for the purpose of its business. The tribunal dismissed the appeal. Applying *Sheffield Co-Operative Society Ltd*, 43.20 below, where input tax related specifically to an exempt supply, a general commercial intention was not relevant. *The Really Useful Group plc, LON/91/136Y (VTD 6578)*.

43.19   **Refurbishment work undertaken for purpose of exempt supply—short-term taxable supply made before exempt supply.** A property developer (K) converted a barn into a house, with the intention of selling it. It was accepted that the sale would be exempt for VAT under the legislation then in force. However, before selling the converted house, K used it to make four short-term supplies of bed and breakfast accommodation. He accounted for output tax on these supplies, and reclaimed input tax on the refurbishment. The Commissioners issued an assessment to recover the tax, and K appealed, contending that the input tax should be attributed to the taxable supplies which he had actually made. The tribunal rejected this contention and dismissed his appeal, finding on the evidence that it was satisfied that he had incurred the expenditure for the purpose of making an exempt supply, and holding that he was not entitled to recover the tax in question. Applying the principles laid down in *Briararch Ltd*, 43.125 below, and *Curtis Henderson Ltd*, 43.126 below, where input tax was incurred with the intention of making 'a supply of a particular nature', the tax should be attributed on the basis of that intended supply, 'notwithstanding that for a short time he made a supply of a different nature before making the intended supply'. *WEH Key, MAN/97/480 (VTD 15354, 15794)*. (*Note.* The conversion of a barn into a house would normally now qualify for zero-rating. See Tolley's Value Added Tax.)

43.20   **Costs of refurbishing department store restaurant—whether attributable to taxable supplies.** A company, which was partly exempt, operated a department store which contained a restaurant. It decided to refurbish the restaurant and grant a licence to an independent operator, in order to attract more customers to the store. The restaurant was extensively refurbished and a licence was subsequently granted. The company reclaimed the whole of the input tax incurred on the cost of the refurbishment. The Commissioners issued assessments to recover the tax, considering that it was directly related to the grant of the licence, which was an exempt supply under what is now *VATA 1994, Sch 9 Group 1*. The company appealed, contending that the input tax should be attributed to taxable supplies because its intention in incurring the expenditure had been to attract more customers to the department store. The tribunal dismissed the company's appeal, holding that the company's motive of improving its trade was not to be confused with the objective purpose of the expenditure, which had to be treated as directly attributable to the exempt supply. *Sheffield Co-Operative Society Ltd, [1987] VATTR 216 (VTD 2549).*

43.21   **Costs of refurbishing Masonic temple.**   A company owned a building which was used as a Masonic temple. It let the building to several Masonic Lodges, these lettings being exempt from VAT. The building also contained a bar, where drinks were sold, these sales being standard-rated supplies for VAT purposes. The company incurred expenditure on refurbishing the building and reclaimed the relevant input tax. The Commissioners issued an assessment to recover the tax, on the basis that the expenditure was directly attributable to the lettings which were exempt supplies. The company appealed, contending that the expenditure was partly attributable to its standard-rated supplies of drinks, so that the expenditure should be apportioned. The tribunal dismissed the appeal, holding that the expenditure was directly attributable to the exempt supplies. *Richard Haynes Associates*, 43.43 below, and *Sovereign Street Workplace Ltd*, 39.22 LAND, distinguished. *Ashwell House (St Albans) Ltd, LON/93/2757A (VTD 12483).*

43.22   **Company operating parks for 'mobile homes'.**   A company operated six residential parks for 'mobile homes'. Its business comprised the sale of some such homes, the letting or licensing of the pitches on which the mobile homes were situated, and the performance of work for the occupiers of such homes. The 'pitch fees' were accepted as being exempt from VAT (compare *Stonecliff Caravan Park*, 15.72 CONSTRUCTION OF BUILDINGS, ETC.) and the company was therefore partly exempt. In accounting for tax, it treated input tax relating to the maintenance and improvement of its parks as relating to both taxable and exempt supplies, and as apportionable. It also reclaimed input tax on its purchase of building materials relating to the siting of new park homes (such as concrete bases and pipework for the connection of services). The Commissioners issued an assessment on the basis that both these categories of input tax were solely attributable to the grant of exempt licences to occupy land, and thus the tax was not recoverable. The company appealed. The QB upheld the assessment, holding that all the expenditure in question should be attributed to the land on which the mobile homes stood, rather than to the mobile homes themselves. The pitch fees which the company received under the agreements were wholly exempt from VAT, and thus all the relevant input tax was attributable to exempt supplies. *Dicta* of the CJEC in *BLP Group plc*, 21.192 EUROPEAN COMMUNITY LAW, applied. *C & E Commrs v Harpcombe Ltd, QB [1996] STC 726.*

43.23   *Harpcombe Ltd*, 43.22 above, was applied in the similar subsequent case of *Tingdene Developments Ltd, LON/99/274 (VTD 16546).*

43.24   **'Reverse consideration' on sale of freehold property.**   A company (B) owned the freehold of a large building. It granted another company (L) a 51–year lease on the property. Subsequently it received an offer for the freehold of the property from another company (A). A also wished to take over the lease. L only agreed to relinquish the lease in return for consideration of £2,460,500. A considered that this price was excessive, and only agreed to proceed with the transaction after receiving a 'reverse consideration' of £370,500 from B. B reclaimed input tax on this payment. The Commissioners rejected the claim, considering that the payment had been made in order to facilitate the sale of the freehold, which was an exempt supply. The tribunal dismissed B's appeal, holding that the 'reverse consideration' should be attributed to the exempt supply, since 'the entire series of transactions were concerned with the ownership of interests in land and the transfer thereof'. *Brammer plc, MAN/90/123 (VTD 6420).*

43.25   **Legal costs of aborted purchase of property.**   A property investment company (L) entered into negotiations to purchase a building which had previously been used by a bank. The vendors subsequently sold the building to a brewery. L reclaimed input tax on its legal costs. The Commissioners rejected the claim and the tribunal dismissed L's appeal, holding that the effect of *VATA 1994, s 26* was that the input tax was not reclaimable, because it related to an abortive exempt supply and could not be related to any taxable supply. *London & Exmoor Estates Ltd, LON/x (VTD 16707).*

43.26   **Lease of commercial property—zero-rated when lease entered into but exempt at time of subsequent expenditure—effect of change in rating of supply.**   In 1987 a building company (H) granted a lease of a commercial property which it had constructed to a bank. The lease was zero-rated under the legislation then in force. From 1 April 1989, such leases became exempt from VAT, except where an election was made to waive exemption. Subsequently H faced claims (the details of which are not fully set out in the decision) in relation to its construction of the property, and incurred legal costs in defending these claims. It reclaimed input tax in respect of these claims. The Commissioners rejected the claim, since the lease was exempt from VAT at the time the expenditure was incurred, and H had not elected to waive exemption. H appealed, contending that since the lease had been zero-rated when it was entered into, the input tax should be treated as relating to a taxable supply rather than to an exempt supply. The tribunal rejected this contention and dismissed the appeal, holding that 'the supplies of services representing the input tax in issue in this appeal (were) not so closely identifiable with the original supply as to remain unaffected by the legislation reclassifying the entire class of transaction from zero-rated to exempt supplies'. *HDG Harbour Development Group Ltd, LON/90/1482Y (VTD 9386).*

43.27   **Professional fees in connection with disposal of shares.**   See *BLP Group plc*, 21.192 EUROPEAN COMMUNITY LAW.

43.28   **Professional fees in connection with reorganisation of share capital.**   See *MBS plc*, 26.27 FINANCE; *Celtic plc*, 26.28 FINANCE; *Swallowfield plc*, 26.29 FINANCE, and *Mirror Group Newspapers Ltd*, 26.30 FINANCE.

43.29   **Construction work undertaken for purpose of exempt supplies—change in law to make such supplies zero-rated from March 1995—whether input tax recoverable.**   See *Martins Properties (Chelsea) Ltd*, 43.131 below.

Input tax held to be used 'in making both taxable and exempt supplies' (Regulation 101(2)(d))

Professional fees

43.30   **Professional services incurred in connection with share issue and bank loan—apportionment of input tax.**   A building company raised additional capital by making a share issue and by obtaining a bank loan. It received professional advice from accountants and solicitors in connection with this, and reclaimed input tax on the fees. The Commissioners issued an assessment to recover the tax, considering that it related to exempt supplies and was not therefore deductible. The company appealed, contending that the need for the services was partly attributable to the taxable supplies made by the company, and that the input tax should therefore be apportioned between taxable and exempt supplies. The tribunal allowed the appeal in part, holding that the accountants' services were partly used in connection with the making of exempt supplies (the issue of shares) and partly with the making of taxable supplies, but that the solicitors' services were wholly used in connection with exempt supplies. *Banner Management Ltd, [1991] VATTR 254 (VTD 5678)*.

43.31   **Professional fees incurred in connection with management buy-out— apportionment of input tax.**   A company incurred lawyers' and accountants' fees in connection with a management buy-out, including arranging a loan and an overdraft facility. It reclaimed the whole of the input tax on these fees. The Commissioners issued a ruling that the input tax was not deductible, since it related to exempt supplies of shares and loan stock. The company appealed, contending that the whole of the input tax was deductible since the professional fees had been incurred in connection with the company's general business intentions of making taxable supplies, rather than exclusively in the making of exempt supplies. The tribunal allowed the appeal, holding that the issue of shares and loan stock was 'purely incidental' to the company's trading objectives and that the professional fees partly related to the loan and overdraft facility. Accordingly, the supplies of professional services were 'for mixed use' and fell within what is now *VAT Regulations 1995 (SI 1995 No 2518), reg 101(2)(d)*. (Since the overwhelming majority of the company's supplies were taxable, it followed that the whole of the input tax was deductible.) *Edgemond Group Ltd, MAN/93/35 (VTD 11620)*. (*Notes*. (1) The Commissioners initially appealed to the High Court against this decision, but subsequently withdrew their appeal. Despite failing to pursue their appeal, they take the view that this decision is inconsistent with the CJEC decision in *BLP Group plc*, 21.192 EUROPEAN COMMUNITY LAW. See Customs' VAT Manual, Part 15, chapter 3, sections 1.3, 1.4. (2) The decision here was distinguished in the subsequent case of *RAP Group plc*, 43.32 below.)

43.32   **Professional fees incurred in connection with share issue and management services—apportionment of input tax.**   A company (R) acquired the share capital of another company (W). Each of W's shareholders was issued one new ordinary share in R, plus a warrant, in exchange for each 130 ordinary shares in W. R reclaimed input tax on professional fees paid to stockbrokers, accountants and solicitors relating to this transaction. The Commissioners issued a ruling that the input tax was used 'exclusively in making exempt supplies' within *VAT Regulations, reg 101(2)(c)*. R appealed, contending that the fees related to its supplies of management services to W, so that the tax should be apportioned under *reg 101(2)(d)*. The Ch D allowed the appeal in part, holding on the evidence that the services supplied by the stockbrokers and the accountants related entirely to the share issue, which was an exempt supply. However, the solicitors' services were not 'limited to the issue of shares' but had been partly used for the purposes of making taxable supplies, so that the tax shown on the invoice from the solicitors should be apportioned. *RAP Group plc v C & E Commrs, Ch D [2000] STC 980*.

43.33   **Solicitors' fees incurred in transfer of part of business—whether input tax reclaimable.**   A company, which was a subsidiary member of a banking group, carried on an assurance business and held a number of properties as investments. It sold a property which it had let under a lease, and in respect of which it had elected to waive exemption. The sale of the property was treated as the transfer of part of a business as a going concern. The company which was the representative member of the group reclaimed input tax on its solicitors' fees in relation to the transfer. The Commissioners issued an assessment on the basis that, since the transfer of a going concern was not a supply for VAT purposes, the input tax in question could not be directly attributed to taxable supplies and had to be treated as residual input tax within *VAT Regulations 1995 (SI 1995 No 2518), reg 101(2)(d)*. The tribunal upheld the assessment and dismissed the company's appeal. The tribunal observed that the letting of the property had not been 'a separate identifiable business activity'. The transfer costs 'were incurred in the ordinary course of making and managing investments in its property investment portfolio so as to provide the real underlying business, the assurance business, with funds to meet the claims of insured persons and annuitants'. *Abbey National plc, [1997] VATDR 224 (VTD 14951)*. (*Note*. The company appealed to the QB, which referred the case to the CJEC. The CJEC has registered the case as Case C-408/98. Advocate-General Jacobs delivered his Opinion on 13 April 2000. He held that, where the assets transferred were those of a business which made both taxable and exempt supplies, the tax should be apportioned in accordance with *Articles 17(5)* and *19* of the *EC Sixth Directive*—i.e. treated as residual input tax. However, where the assets were those of a business making only taxable supplies, the tax should be treated as wholly deductible. The CJEC has not yet issued judgment.)

Expenditure on premises

43.34 **Company owning tourist village including cottages let to tenants— apportionment of input tax.** A company owned a village which it sought to preserve in an unspoilt condition, as an attraction to tourists. Cars were banned, and tourists were charged £1 for admission. The company accounted for VAT on the admission charges. The village included about 80 cottages, which were let to tenants on condition that they were occupied for at least eight months in the year. The company reclaimed input tax on the repair, redecoration and refurbishment of the cottages, and the Commissioners issued an assessment to recover the tax, considering that the expenditure in question was wholly attributable to the letting of the cottages, which were exempt supplies. The tribunal allowed the company's appeal in part, holding that the work of repair and redecoration was carried out in accordance with the terms of the leases of the cottages and was attributable solely to exempt supplies. However, on the evidence, some of the refurbishment which had been carried out was not required by the leases, and had partly been undertaken to make the village more attractive to tourists, i.e. for the purpose of taxable supplies. *Clovelly Estate Co Ltd, [1991] VATTR 351 (VTD 6353)*.

43.35 **Workshops let to tenants—apportionment of input tax.** A married couple purchased an old pottery. They occupied part of the premises for an antiques business, and let several workshops at the pottery on short-term tenancies. They reclaimed input tax in respect of building work carried out at the premises. The Commissioners issued an assessment to recover 80% of the tax, on the basis that that percentage of the input tax was attributable to exempt supplies. The couple appealed, contending that their ultimate intention was to use the whole site for their own business, and that they had only let the workshops on a short-term basis while their business grew. The tribunal reviewed the evidence in detail and held that 60% of the input tax in question should be treated as attributable to exempt supplies and 40% to taxable supplies. *Mr & Mrs Buckley (t/a Wheelcraft Centre & Original Homes), LON/90/943Y (VTD 7150)*.

43.36 **Remedial work to building partly used as office accommodation and partly to be used as residential accommodation—apportionment of input tax.** A company (C) owned a building, part of which it used as business office accommodation, and part of which was surplus to its requirements. It obtained planning permission to reconvert the latter part into residential flats, with the intention to lease or sell them. Before the conversion was completed, the building was damaged by council workmen who were replacing the main sewer. C incurred expenditure on rectifying this, and reclaimed the whole of the relevant input tax. The Commissioners formed the opinion that the expenditure had been incurred for the purpose of making exempt supplies (the sale or lease of flats) as well as of taxable supplies (the company's office accommodation) and should be apportioned accordingly. They issued an assessment to recover 55% of the tax in question. C appealed, contending that since the conversion had not been completed until after the expenditure had been incurred, the whole of the expenditure should be attributed to taxable supplies. The tribunal rejected this contention and dismissed C's appeal. *Sheffield Co-Operative Society Ltd*, 43.20 above, applied. *Circa Ltd, LON/92/113Z (VTD 9908)*.

43.37   **Redevelopment of property partly used as café and partly leased to finance company—apportionment of input tax.**   A married woman purchased a café in 1987, and registered for VAT in February 1990. During 1989 and early 1990 she redeveloped the café, and reclaimed the whole of the input tax incurred. The Commissioners discovered that the upper floor of the property was let, under an informal lease, to a finance company of which the proprietor's husband was managing director. They issued an assessment to recover one-third of the input tax, on the basis that it was attributable to an exempt supply. The tribunal upheld the assessment and dismissed the proprietor's appeal. *S McElroy (t/a Boundary Café), MAN/92/564 (VTD 10540)*.

43.38   **Purchase of premises by partly exempt charity—apportionment of input tax.**   A housing association, which was a registered charity, required larger premises, and in January 1991 it began negotiations for the purchase of such premises. It registered for VAT in May 1991, and elected to waive exemption on the sale of its existing leasehold premises. In June 1991 it purchased the leasehold interest in new premises from a development company for £803,250 plus VAT, and assigned its interest in its previous premises to the same company for £389,400 plus VAT. In its return for the period ending 30 June 1991, the association accounted for output tax on the disposal of its premises, and reclaimed input tax in respect of its new premises, claiming a substantial net repayment. It subsequently applied to be deregistered with effect from July 1991. The Commissioners issued a ruling that the association was not entitled to credit for the input tax in question, and the association appealed. The tribunal allowed the appeal in part, holding that a proportion of the input tax could be apportioned to the association's management activities, which were taxable supplies, and was therefore deductible. *Bristol Churches Housing Association, LON/91/2008Z (VTD 10515)*.

43.39   **Refurbishment of premises.**   A company which carried on business as a stockbroker and financial adviser acquired new premises, and reclaimed the whole of the input tax on their refurbishment. The Commissioners rejected the claim, considering that the tax had to be apportioned. The company appealed, contending that the whole of the tax should be treated as deductible. The tribunal dismissed the appeal, holding that the expenditure in question was 'part of the management of the company's business', so that the tax had to be apportioned. *Fox-Pitt Kelton Ltd, LON/93/1296A (VTD 11556)*.

43.40   The *Housing (Scotland) Act 1988* established a statutory body (S) for the purpose of providing housing and promoting the provision of housing. It took over a stock of about 75,000 houses. During the next ten years it sold about 25,000 of these and transferred about 40,000 to housing associations. In 1999 it submitted a retrospective reclaim of input tax relating to the refurbishment of some of the properties which it let to tenants. The Commissioners rejected the claim, on the basis that the input tax was wholly attributable to exempt supplies. S appealed, contending that it was entitled to apportion the tax in accordance with *VAT Regulations 1995 (SI 1995 No 2518), reg 101(2)(d)*, because although it was currently letting the houses in question, it hoped to sell some of them in due course. The tribunal accepted this contention and allowed the appeal in principle (subject to agreement as to figures). *Scottish Homes (No 2), EDN/99/126 (VTD 16644)*.

43.41 **Office premises no longer needed for business purposes—temporarily left vacant and subsequently let—whether input tax recoverable.** A publishing company leased a five-storey building, with the intention of using it for business purposes. In 1990 the company formed the opinion that it no longer needed the whole of the premises for its business, and vacated two of the floors. One of the floors remained unoccupied until October 1992, when it was let to a tenant, while the other floor remained unoccupied until January 1993, when it too was let. In May 1993 the company elected to waive exemption in respect of the rents. It continued to reclaim the input tax incurred in respect of the whole of the premises. The Commissioners issued an assessment to recover the input tax from September 1991 to February 1993, on the basis that it was attributable to exempt supplies. The company appealed, contending that the input tax attributable to the vacant periods should be treated as residual input tax and as recoverable. The tribunal accepted the company's evidence and allowed the appeal, finding that the company had retained the two floors 'exclusively for the purpose of making taxable supplies and not carrying out any other activity. The original purpose of taking the leases was never departed from and could have been carried out at short notice whenever the opportunity presented itself ... the vacant periods should be treated as residual, the rents being unattributable overheads of the business during these periods, not being attributable either to taxable or exempt supplies'. *Harper Collins Publishers Ltd, EDN/92/219 (VTD 12040)*.

43.42 **Conversion of hotel into residential home—attribution of input tax.** A married couple owned a hotel. In 1988 they purchased the adjoining premises, which was a large house let as bed-sitting rooms, with the intention of converting the two buildings into one and using them as a registered residential home. They obtained the necessary registration under the *Registered Homes Act 1984* in September 1989. They reclaimed input tax in respect of the conversion work. The Commissioners issued an assessment to recover the tax, on the basis that since the provision of care in the residential home was exempt from VAT under what is now *VATA 1994, Sch 9 Group 7*, the tax should be attributed to exempt supplies. The couple appealed, contending that the tax should be apportioned since they had continued to accept guests at the hotel during the conversion. The tribunal accepted this contention and adjourned the appeal to enable the parties to consider the apportionment. *JJ & BM Gallagher, MAN/91/118 (VTD 12140)*. (*Note*. There was no further hearing of the appeal.)

43.43 **Expenditure on property intended to be used for taxable supplies but initially used for exempt supplies—attribution of input tax.** A partnership which carried on a management consultancy business reclaimed input tax on the construction of a self-contained flat. The Commissioners discovered that the flat was let on an assured shorthold tenancy, and issued an assessment to recover the tax, on the basis that the expenditure related to exempt supplies. The partnership appealed, contending that the tax should be apportioned since, at the time the expenditure was incurred, it had intended to use the flat to make serviced supplies of accommodation which would be excluded from exemption. The tribunal accepted the partnership's evidence and allowed the appeal, holding that the tax should be apportioned. *Briararch Ltd*, 43.125 below, and *Curtis Henderson Ltd*, 43.126 below, applied. *Richard Haynes Associates, LON/92/2597 (VTD 12300)*.

43.44 **Exempt supplies preceding taxable supplies—attribution of input tax.** See *C & E Commrs v University of Wales College Cardiff*, 43.128 below, and *Royal & Sun Alliance Insurance Group plc*, 43.129 below.

43.45 **Property company—attribution of input tax.** The Commissioners issued assessments on a property company which was partly exempt but had failed to operate the partial exemption provisions correctly. The company appealed, contending that the assessments were unfair because some of the input tax which the

Commissioners had apportioned should have been directly attributed to taxable supplies under the standard method of attribution then in force. The tribunal upheld the assessments and the QB dismissed the company's appeal. Laws J observed that it was frequently impossible to discover the exact or literal extent to which 'mixed use' supplies were used in the making of taxable supplies. The assessments in question had been based on information supplied by the company, and had been made to the best of the Commissioners' judgment. Applying *dicta* of Woolf J in *Van Boeckel*, 3.1 ASSESSMENT, 'the use of the words "the best of their judgment" does not envisage the burden being placed on the Commissioners of carrying out exhaustive investigations'. The company had failed to produce 'facts or figures to demonstrate the extent to which mixed use supplies had been deployed for the making of taxable supplies'. *Dwyer Property Ltd v C & E Commrs, QB [1995] STC 1035.*

43.46 **Nursing home.** A company which operated a nursing home arranged for the construction of an extension, and reclaimed the whole of its input tax. The Commissioners issued an assessment to recover part of the tax. The tribunal upheld the assessment and dismissed the company's appeal, holding that the company was partly exempt and should have operated the partial exemption provisions. *The Laurels Nursing Home Ltd, MAN/96/1065 (VTD 15259).* (*Note.* An appeal against a misdeclaration penalty was subsequently allowed—see 49.291 PENALTIES: MISDECLARATION.)

43.47 **Effect of election to waive exemption—attribution of input tax.** A college which provided religious education arranged for the construction of two buildings to be used for conferences. It formed a subsidiary company to conduct the conference activities, and in September 1989 elected to waive exemption in respect of the rent paid by the subsidiary company. It reclaimed input tax relating to the construction of the buildings, and, in calculating its deductible input tax for the purpose of applying the partial exemption provisions, treated this input tax as attributable to taxable supplies. The Commissioners formed the opinion that the input tax relating to the buildings should be excluded from the partial exemption calculation, and issued an assessment to recover some of the input tax which the college had reclaimed. The tribunal allowed the appeal in part, holding that the expenditure was used for the purpose of making taxable supplies following the election to waive exemption which took effect from September 1989. The tribunal upheld the assessment with regard to the periods preceding the election, but discharged the assessment with regard to the periods subsequent to the election. *Cliff College, MAN/92/695 (VTD 12000).*

43.48 A property company registered for VAT in 1994. It was accepted as partly exempt, and adopted the standard method of attributing input tax. In May 1997 it elected to waive exemption in respect of its stock of properties. The company reclaimed input tax on the basis that the election should be treated as retrospective, so that its exempt input tax for the period ending April 1997 was *de minimis*. The Commissioners issued an assessment on the basis that the election could not have retrospective effect and that the relevant input tax had to be apportioned. The tribunal upheld the assessment and dismissed the company's appeal. *Hellesdon Developments Ltd, LON/99/354 (VTD 16833).* (*Note.* The tribunal also held that certain correspondence between the company and the Commissioners did not amount to the agreement of a special method.)

43.49 **Rent paid on properties subject to election to waive exemption—attribution of input tax.** A company trading as opticians from leased premises made both taxable and exempt supplies. The landlords of three of the properties from which the company traded had elected to waive exemption in respect of the properties. The company reclaimed the whole of the input tax on the rent. The Commissioners rejected the claim, on the basis that the tax had to be attributed between the company's taxable and exempt supplies. The company appealed, contending that a landlord should not be permitted to exercise an election to waive exemption where a tenant made exempt supplies and was therefore unable to reclaim the whole of the input tax. The tribunal rejected this contention and dismissed the appeal, holding that there was 'nothing in the fundamental principles of Community law ... that in any material respect cuts down the discretion given to the Member State to enact its own "option to tax" provisions in such a way that the landlord should be precluded from exercising his option where his tenant is a partially exempt trader'. *R Walia Opticians Ltd, [1997] VATDR 368 (VTD 15050)*.

43.50   **Bowling club constructing clubhouse—attribution of residual input tax on costs of construction.**   A bowling club, which was partly exempt, arranged for the construction of a clubhouse. For the year ending 31 March 1996, it had adopted the standard method of attribution and had treated 25% of the relevant input tax as attributable to taxable supplies. In June 1996 it wrote to its VAT office, estimating that, following the opening of a bar in the clubhouse, 56% of its supplies would be taxable, and requesting 56% of its residual input tax to be treated as attributable to taxable supplies. The Commissioners rejected the claim, on the grounds that there was nothing in *VAT Regulations 1995 (SI 1995 No 2518), reg 101* which permitted estimation of expected future supplies. The club appealed. The tribunal dismissed the appeal, applying *University of Wales College Cardiff*, 43.128 below. The chairman observed that the wording of *reg 101* allowed 'no room for any interpretation that would replace sales made in the period by estimated sales to be made at some later date'. *Chard Bowling Club, [1997] VATDR 375 (VTD 15114)*. (*Note*. An appeal against the Commissioners' refusal to allow the retrospective application of a special method was also dismissed—see 43.89 below.)

Miscellaneous

43.51   **Building society reclaiming input tax in respect of deemed self-supply— method of apportionment.**   A building society, most of whose supplies were exempt, made a small number of taxable supplies such as the provision of services to its staff. The total value of its taxable supplies in 1990 was approximately 0.25% of the total value of all its supplies. The society also produced a large amount of printed material, mostly for internal use. This printed material was a deemed self-supply for VAT purposes, and the society accounted for output tax accordingly. The company reclaimed input tax on the whole value of this self-supplied stationery. The Commissioners rejected the claim, since not all the stationery was used in connection with taxable supplies, so that the deductible input tax was only that proportion of the relevant total input tax which corresponded with the proportion of taxable supplies to total supplies. The tribunal dismissed the society's appeal. The society had suffered VAT on a large proportion of the value of the printed matter which it had produced, but this was clearly in accordance with the intention of the legislation, since if VAT was not paid on such self-supplies, businesses producing printed matter for their own commercial use might gain a commercial advantage. *The National & Provincial Building Society, MAN/90/694 (VTD 6293)*. (*Note*. See also *VAT Regulations 1995 (SI 1995 No 2518), reg 104*, which provides that 'where ... a person makes a supply to himself the input tax on that supply shall not be allowable as attributable to that supply'.)

43.52   **Company trading as mortgage broker and estate agent—apportionment of input tax.**   A company traded as a mortgage broker and estate agent. It reclaimed input tax on alterations to its premises. The Commissioners issued an assessment to recover most of the tax, considering that it was partly attributable to the exempt supplies which the company made as a mortgage broker. The tribunal upheld the assessment in principle but reduced it in amount, finding on the evidence that 29% of the company's time was taken up by its estate agency business, and holding that 29% of the tax in question was deductible. *Ace Estates Ltd, LON/90/255Y (VTD 6216)*.

43.53   **Company incorporated to organise annual motor rally—whether input tax apportionable.**   A company was incorporated to organise an annual motor rally. Most of its income came from sponsorship, which was standard-rated, but it also received significant income from entry fees, such income being exempt from VAT. The company reclaimed input tax on the expenditure it incurred in organising the rally. The Isle of Man Treasury issued an assessment to recover the tax, considering that the costs of organising the rally should be set against the entry fees received, and that, as the entry fees were exempt from VAT, the whole of the expenditure related to exempt supplies and was not recoverable. The company appealed, contending that, since its sole purpose was to organise the rally, the input tax should be treated as relating to the whole of its income and should therefore be apportioned. The tribunal allowed the company's appeal. The sponsorship was received for the specific purpose of organising the rally. The rally was the subject of a supply to the sponsors as well as to the competitors, and the appropriate proportion of the input tax was, therefore, deductible. *Manx International Rally Ltd v The Isle of Man Treasury, MAN/91/196 (VTD 6711)*.

43.54   **Partnership operating caravan site—apportionment of input tax.**   A partnership operated a caravan site. The letting of caravans on the site was exempt from VAT, but the partnership also made some sales, which were taxable supplies, and let six seasonal pitches, the income from which was also taxable. The partnership incurred substantial expenditure on a new water main, and reclaimed the relevant input tax. The Commissioners issued an assessment on the basis that 80% of the expenditure should be treated as attributable to exempt supplies, so that only 20% of the input tax was deductible. The partnership appealed, contending that 50% of the tax should be treated as deductible. The tribunal reviewed the evidence in detail and allowed the appeal in part, holding that 30% of the tax was deductible. *RBF & NJ Morris (t/a Roundstone Caravan Depot), LON/92/2346A (VTD 11092)*.

43.55   **Purchase of helicopter by group of companies making taxable and exempt supplies—apportionment of input tax.**   A group of companies operated casinos in four cities in the UK. The group's income from gambling in the casinos was exempt from VAT, but the group also received taxable income from gaming machines, vending machines and bar sales. It was therefore partly exempt, and was permitted to treat 16% of its general input tax as being attributable to exempt supplies. The group purchased a helicopter, which was used for transporting company directors and officers from one city to another to supervise each of the casinos. The group reclaimed the whole of the input tax attributable to the helicopter (and accounted for output tax on its sale two years later). At a subsequent control visit, a VAT officer formed the opinion that the company should only have reclaimed 16% of the input tax, since the helicopter had been purchased for the purpose of supervising the whole of the group's business activities, which included exempt supplies as well as taxable supplies. The Commissioners therefore issued an assessment to recover 84% of the input tax in question. The tribunal upheld the assessment and dismissed the group's appeal. *Annabel's Casino Ltd, MAN/92/1037 (VTD 10859)*. (*Note*. For another issue in this case, see 23.16 EXEMPTIONS: MISCELLANEOUS.)

43.56   **Building society—costs of television advertisements—attribution of input tax.**   A building society incurred expenditure in making television advertisements. It accounted for input tax on the basis that the relevant input tax was residual input tax which should be apportioned between its taxable and exempt supplies (under the terms of its special method). The Commissioners issued a ruling that the relevant input tax should be treated as wholly attributable to exempt supplies. The society appealed. The tribunal allowed the appeal, holding on the evidence that the advertisements were not directly attributable to the making of exempt supplies. They were not advertising individual financial products but were intended to inform viewers that the society provided a variety of services, so that the input tax was residual and fell to be apportioned. *Britannia Building Society, MAN/96/174 (VTD 14886).*

43.57   **Partly exempt charity—input tax on machinery and packaging materials.** A registered charity had been incorporated to provide work for psychiatric patients. It made taxable supplies of packaging to commercial customers and exempt supplies of training to its clients. It reclaimed input tax on purchases of machinery and packaging materials. The Commissioners issued a ruling that this input tax was used in making both taxable and exempt supplies, within *VAT Regulations 1995, reg 101(2)(d)*, so that only a proportion of the input tax was reclaimable. The charity appealed, contending that the input tax in question should be wholly attributed to its taxable supplies of commercial packaging. The tribunal rejected this contention and dismissed the appeal. *Reading Industrial Therapy Organisation Ltd, LON/96/1545 (VTD 15132).*

43.58   **Supplies made before, but paid for after, a change in partial exemption rules—whether old or new method of attribution applicable.** A butcher purchased a property in June 1986. Between July 1986 and April 1987 he redeveloped it in order to be able to let it. The relevant materials and services were all supplied before 1 April 1987 (when the rules regarding attribution of input tax between taxable supplies and exempt supplies were amended) but some of them were not paid for until after that date. The butcher reclaimed input tax on the basis that the old rules for attributing input tax between taxable and exempt supplies applied, as the time of supply was in all cases before 1 April 1987. However, the Commissioners issued an assessment to recover some of the tax, considering that, as the input tax had not been reclaimed until after 1 April 1987, the new method of attribution applied with the result that the input tax in respect of the supplies which were not paid for until after that date was attributable to an exempt supply and was not reclaimable. The tribunal allowed the butcher's appeal, holding that as the time of supply was before 1 April 1987 the old rules for attributing input tax applied. *V Perna, [1990] VATTR 106 (VTD 5017).*

43.59   **Bank reclaiming input tax on assignments of debts.** A bank, which was partly exempt, had loaned large sums of money to a number of South American countries. The debtors were unable to keep up the interest payments on the loans. The bank assigned a number of the debts either for cash or for other debts. In 1988 it adjusted its calculations of input tax in respect of some of the debts which had been assigned from 1985 to 1988. The Commissioners issued an assessment to recover the tax in question. The bank appealed, contending that the assignments were not exempt supplies and that accordingly they should be taken into account in determining the percentage of its costs which related to taxable service charge income. The tribunal allowed the bank's appeal, holding that the bank was entitled to include the assignments in its input tax calculation. *Barclays Bank plc, [1991] VATTR 115 (VTD 5616).*

43.60   **Partial exemption—treatment of credit note.** The London International Financial Futures Exchange (LIFFE) became partly exempt with effect from January 1990, following the enactment of what is now *VATA 1994, Sch 9, Group 5, Item 7*. It agreed a special 'direct attribution' method of calculating its deductible input tax. The Commissioners issued an assessment charging tax of more than £3,700,000, on the basis that LIFFE had calculated its deductible input tax incorrectly in two ways. Firstly, it had treated a credit note, which it had received in respect of computer systems and equipment which it had ordered before it became partly exempt, as reducing the amount of input tax wholly attributable to exempt supplies, and secondly, it had reclaimed the full amount of input tax on construction services supplied to it by an associated company. LIFFE appealed, contending that its calculation of deductible input tax had been correct. The tribunal allowed the appeal in part. The credit note should not have been treated as reducing the amount of input tax wholly attributable to exempt supplies, since it related to supplies made before the start of the period for which the calculation of deductible input tax had to be made. However, on the evidence, the construction services supplied by LIFFE's associated company were wholly used in making taxable supplies, and the input tax in respect of them was deductible in full. *London International Financial Futures Exchange (Administration & Management), [1993] VATTR 474 (VTD 11611).*

43.61   **Insurance broker.** A company which traded as an insurance broker, but also made some taxable supplies, registered for VAT from June 1992. It reclaimed the whole of its input tax, without operating the partial exemption provisions. The Commissioners formed the opinion that the tax should have been apportioned and that most of it should have been attributed to exempt supplies. They therefore issued an assessment to recover most of the tax. The company appealed, contending that the amounts of its input tax solely attributable to exempt supplies were less than £7,200 p.a., and thus within the *de minimis* limits as then in force, whereas the Commissioners had treated £7,310 as attributable to exempt supplies. The tribunal upheld the assessment and dismissed the company's appeal, holding that the company's calculations were incorrect because they depended on wrongly attributing input tax of £150 to taxable supplies. *Credit Risk Management Ltd, MAN/94/416 (VTD 12971).*

43.62   **Property development company—purchase of sites for future development.** A company which carried on business as a builder and property developer, and was partly exempt, purchased two sites for future development. It included the input tax on these purchases in calculating its deductible input tax under the (pre–1992) standard method as then in force. The Commissioners formed the opinion that the inclusion of these purchases had distorted the input tax calculation and produced an unfair result. They recalculated the apportionment without reference to the acquisition of the two sites and issued an assessment, against which the company appealed. The QB upheld the assessment. The standard method in force at the relevant time did not prescribe the manner of ascertaining the relative extent to which supplies were to be used. However, the manner of ascertainment had to be one which achieved a fair and reasonable attribution of the tax paid on the inputs which the company used to make both taxable and non-taxable supplies. The attribution arising from the company's calculation was distortive, and the distortion made the attribution unfair and unreasonable. What was required was a fair and reasonable attribution of the use to which the residual inputs were to be put. The method which the company had adopted was not effective to ascertain the extent to which the residual inputs in the relevant quarters were used in making taxable supplies, and thus did not do what the *VAT Regulations* required. *C & E Commrs v Dennis Rye Ltd, QB 1995, [1996] STC 27.*

43.63   **Computation of residual input tax—exclusion of capital expenditure.** A building society, which was partly exempt, submitted a repayment claim in which, in computing the fraction of residual input tax to be treated as repayable, it excluded capital expenditure from the denominator but not from the numerator. The Commissioners rejected the claim on the grounds that capital expenditure should be excluded from both the numerator and the denominator. The tribunal dismissed the society's appeal. The chairman observed that 'the object of excluding capital goods from the fraction is to exclude the value of inputs whose inclusion would distort the results of the calculation'. *Derbyshire Building Society, MAN/95/2311 (VTD 14026)*.

Input tax in respect of 'capital goods' (Regulation 101(3)(a))

43.64   Trustees who administered an estate sold some land which was needed for the construction of a by-pass. They reclaimed input tax relating to the sale. The Commissioners issued an assessment to recover the tax, on the basis that it was attributable to a 'supply of capital goods', within *VAT Regulations 1995 (SI 1995 No 2518), reg 101(3)(a)*. The tribunal upheld the assessment and dismissed the trustees' appeal, holding that it was clear that 'the land constituted a capital asset of the business'. *Trustees of the Whitbread Harrowden Settlement (and related appeals), LON/99/1091 (VTD 16781)*. (*Note*. A misdeclaration penalty was upheld in principle but mitigated by 25%—see 49.395 PENALTIES: MISDECLARATION.)

Input tax held to be used for 'incidental supplies' (Regulation 101(3)(b))

43.65   **Partly exempt holding company—input tax on share disposals.**   A company (H) was the holding company of a group of companies in the construction industry, and was partly exempt. In 1985 it reclaimed input tax incurred in respect of share disposals and of a rights issue of its shares. In calculating the deductible proportion of its input tax, it ignored money it had received for the sale of a minority holding of shares in another public company (B). The Commissioners considered that H had reclaimed an excessive proportion of its input tax, and issued an assessment to recover part of the tax. The tribunal allowed H's appeal in part, holding on the evidence that H was an active industrial holding company and was not a passive investment company. Accordingly, the sale of its minority shareholding in B was incidental to its business, so that what is now *VAT Regulations 1995 (SI 1995 No 2518), reg 101(3)(b)* applied, and the proceeds of the sale fell to be excluded from the partial exemption calculation. The tribunal chairman observed that 'the ordinary everyday meaning of "incidental" is "occurring or liable to occur in fortuitous or subordinate conjunction with"'. The QB upheld this decision. H was not carrying on a business similar to an investment company, and the sale of its holding of shares in B was incidental to its business. *C & E Commrs v CH Beazer (Holdings) plc, QB [1989] STC 549*.

43.66   For a case concerning the definition of 'incidental financial transactions', see *Régie Dauphinoise-Cabinet A Forest Sarl v Ministre du Budget*, 21.212 EUROPEAN COMMUNITY LAW.

SPECIAL METHODS (VAT Regulations 1995, reg 102)

Approval or direction of special method (Regulation 102(1))

43.67   **Whether special method agreed by Commissioners.**   A group of companies made both taxable and exempt supplies, but had reclaimed input tax on all supplies received. The Commissioners threatened criminal proceedings to recover the tax which had been wrongly reclaimed. In December 1978 the companies sent the Commissioners a cheque for £13,456, which was the VAT due based on a calculation using a special method (the 'Stanlor' method) approved under the *VAT (General) Regulations* as then in force. The Commissioners cashed the cheque and the group continued to use the method in question without having formally agreed this with the Commissioners. In May 1980 the Commissioners wrote to the representative company (S) instructing it not to use the Stanlor method. S did not comply with this instruction, and the Commissioners issued an assessment to recover the input tax which S had reclaimed. The tribunal allowed S's appeal with regard to the period up to May 1980, holding that the Commissioners had implicitly approved the group's use of the Stanlor method in December 1978, but dismissed S's appeal with regard to the period after May 1980, holding that S should not have continued to use the Stanlor method after it had been instructed not to do so. The QB upheld this decision, holding that the Commissioners' letter of May 1980 was a valid notice under what is now *VAT Regulations 1995 (SI 1995 No 2518), reg 102(3)*. *S & U Stores plc v C & E Commrs, QB [1985] STC 506.*

43.68   A life assurance company, which was partly exempt, submitted a substantial repayment claim covering a period of almost six years. The Commissioners rejected the claim on the basis that the company's returns had been made in accordance with its agreed special partial exemption method. (The method in question excluded the values of taxable supplies of properties and securities, on the basis that the inclusion of such figures would distort the calculation.) The company appealed, contending firstly that the method which it had initially adopted had never been 'approved or directed' by the Commissioners, within *VAT Regulations 1995 (SI 1995 No 2518), reg 102(1)*, and alternatively that, if the method had been 'approved or directed', that approval or direction was invalid under *Article 17(5)* of the *EC Sixth Directive*. The tribunal rejected these contentions and dismissed the appeal. On the evidence, the company was 'at all relevant times . . . calculating its residual input tax by a method which excluded from the numerator and the denominator of the partial exemption fraction the values of both all supplies of securities and all supplies of property'. This method had been approved by the local VAT office. *The Wellington Private Hospital Ltd*, 43.82 below, applied. Furthermore, the use of the method in question was authorised by *Article 17(5)(c)* of the *Sixth Directive. Pearl Assurance plc, LON/98/ 428 (VTD 15960)*.

43.69   In the case noted at 43.48 above, the tribunal held that certain correspondence between the company and the Commissioners did not amount to the agreement of a special method. *Hellesdon Developments Ltd, LON/99/354 (VTD 16833)*.

43.70   **Arrangement between trustees and Commissioners—whether an agreed special method.**   A charitable trust operated a school. Most of the trustees' supplies were therefore exempt from VAT, but they also made a number of taxable supplies. The trustees registered for VAT with effect from April 1973. Between then and May 1974 they entered into correspondence with the Commissioners concerning their right to reclaim input tax. Following this correspondence, the trustees only reclaimed input tax which was specifically attributable to taxable supplies. Subsequently the trustees consulted an accountancy firm, which considered that the trustees should also have been permitted to reclaim a proportion of residual input tax, and submitted a claim for repayment of more than £140,000. The Commissioners rejected the claim, on the basis that the correspondence in May 1974 amounted to the formal agreement of a special method for attributing input tax, and that this special method could not be altered retrospectively. The trustees appealed, contending that they had never specifically applied to use a special method and that the correspondence did not constitute a formal agreement to adopt a special method. The tribunal accepted this contention and allowed the trustees' appeal in principle, holding on the evidence that 'the arrangement which was made was ... simply an arrangement whereby the appellants reclaimed input tax on taxable supplies and what has happened is that the appellants did not actually seek to make any apportionment at all of input tax which arose in respect of both taxable and exempt supplies'. The question of apportioning input tax between taxable and non-taxable or exempt supplies 'was simply not addressed'. Accordingly, the arrangement could not 'purport to restrict the right of the appellants to seek to use the UK equivalent of the pro rata rule and seek to apportion input tax between the taxable and non-taxable supplies'. *The University of Edinburgh*, 43.92 below, applied; *GUS Merchandise Corporation Ltd*, 54.49 RETAILERS' SPECIAL SCHEMES, distinguished. *Ampleforth Abbey Trust, MAN/97/21 (VTD 15763)*.

43.71 **Company changing special method by agreement with Commissioners— whether entitled to revert to previous method unilaterally.** A company (J) provided financial services, of which some were standard-rated and some were exempt. In 1981 it agreed a special method with the Commissioners for calculating its deductible input tax. In early 1986 the Commissioners agreed a method of attributing the input tax of partly exempt finance companies with the Finance Houses Association. This method differed from that used by J, and at a subsequent control visit a VAT officer ascertained that, for the year ending 31 May 1986, J would be able to deduct more input tax if it used the method adopted by the Finance Houses Association than if it continued to adopt the method which it had used in 1981. J agreed to use the method adopted by the Finance Houses Association, and its VAT liability for the year ending 31 May 1986 was calculated accordingly. However, in December 1986 J changed its accountant, and the new accountant reverted to the previous special method which J had used from 1981 to the year ending 31 May 1985. The Commissioners did not discover this until the company's next control visit in early 1989. The VAT officer who carried out the visit ascertained that, for the periods from June 1987 to November 1988, J had accounted for a lesser amount of tax than would have been the case if it had continued to use the special method adopted by the Finance Houses Association. The Commissioners issued an assessment calculated on the basis that J should have continued to use the latter method. The tribunal dismissed J's appeal, finding that there had been an agreement in 1986 that J should use the method adopted by the Finance Houses Association, and holding that J was not entitled to revert to its previous method unilaterally. *Julian Hodge Bank Ltd, LON/92/232 (VTD 10197)*.

43.72 **Special method verbally agreed by VAT officer—company subsequently deciding to adopt standard method—whether Commissioners entitled to insist on use of special method.** A property company registered for VAT with effect from October 1993. It made exempt supplies to residential tenants and standard-rated supplies to commercial tenants. In its first return it reclaimed part of the input tax relating to service charges, attributing the relevant input tax by reference to floor area rather than by reference to the relative value of its taxable and exempt supplies, and also reclaimed the whole of the input tax relating to professional expenses for the acquisition of its property. A VAT officer visited the company in February 1994 and agreed that the company could apportion its input tax on the basis of floor area, rather than by reference to the relative value of its taxable and exempt supplies. He did not query the reclaim of input tax attributable to acquisition costs at his visit, but did so subsequently, in a letter dated June 1994, informing the company that this input tax should also be apportioned. In August 1994 the Commissioners issued an assessment to recover that part of the input tax which they considered should be attributed to exempt supplies. The company appealed, accepting in principle that the input tax relating to the acquisition expenses should be apportioned, but contending that it had only intended its special method of attributing input tax by reference to floor area to apply to its service charge inputs, and that it should be allowed to use the standard method of apportioning the input tax relating to the acquisition expenses. The tribunal accepted this contention and directed that the assessment should be recomputed using the standard method of apportionment. On the evidence, the correspondence could not 'be construed as constituting or evidencing approval of a special method of apportionment which included the acquisition inputs'. The Commissioners did not wish the 'floor area' method of apportionment to apply solely to the service charges input tax (which was relatively small) and the company had not agreed to such a special method applying to the whole of its input tax. Accordingly, the whole of the company's input tax should be apportioned using the standard method of attribution under what is now *VAT Regulations 1995 (SI 1995 No 2518), reg 101. Trustcorp Ltd, LON/95/1054 (VTD 13779)*.

43.73   **Commissioners directing use of special method—whether direction unreasonable.**   The Dean and Chapter of Liverpool Cathedral were registered for VAT, and received both taxable and exempt income. They had agreed a method of apportioning their input tax with the local VAT office. In 1995 the Commissioners agreed a system of apportioning residual input tax with a representative body known as the Churches Main Committee. In 1996 the Commissioners issued a direction that the Cathedral should cease using its existing method of apportionment, and should adopt the method agreed with the Churches Main Committee, under which 65% of its residual input tax would be recoverable. The Cathedral appealed, contending that the direction was unreasonable, since, unlike most cathedrals, it had elected to waive exemption in respect of the cathedral building, and should therefore be entitled to apportion more than 65% of its residual input tax to taxable supplies. The tribunal accepted this contention and allowed the Cathedral's appeal. *Dean & Chapter of the Cathedral Church of Christ, MAN/x (15068)*.

43.74   **Company applying for change to agreed special method—appeal against Commissioners' refusal.**   In 1989 a company, which provided funeral services and which was therefore partly exempt, had agreed a special method of apportioning its input tax with the Commissioners. This agreed special method was based on the company's outputs, and resulted in about 8% of the company's residual input tax being treated as recoverable. In 1996 the company applied for an amendment to the special method which would change the base of two of the calculations from outputs to inputs, and would have the result in about 22% of its residual input tax being treated as recoverable. The Commissioners rejected the claim on the basis that the changes 'would not produce a fair and reasonable attribution of residual input tax', since 'the funeral parlour operating expenses essentially relate to what is a core exempt supply' whereas there was 'relatively high value input tax in catering, flowers and obituary notices'. The tribunal reviewed the evidence and dismissed the company's appeal, holding that the company's suggested method of attribution was 'unfair and unreasonable in principle'. *Co-Operative Wholesale Society Ltd (No 2), MAN/96/1059 (VTD 15633)*.

43.75   **Whether special method void for unfairness.**   A company had agreed a special method with the Commissioners. The Commissioners discovered that the company had apparently reclaimed more input tax than it was entitled to, and issued an assessment accordingly. The company appealed, contending that the special method was unfair and should be treated as void. The tribunal rejected this contention and dismissed the appeal. *Dennis Rye Ltd, MAN/97/120 (VTD 15848)*.

Termination of special method (Regulation 102(3))

43.76   **Whether letter from Commissioners constituted valid notice under Regulation 102(3).**   See *S & U Stores plc*, 43.67 above.

43.77   **Cathedral operating special method—whether entitled to terminate use of method unilaterally.**   A cathedral owned a shop, at which a variety of goods were sold to tourists. It also ran a school which charged fees to pupils, these fees being exempt from VAT. In 1984 the Commissioners authorised a special method for attributing the cathedral's input tax. The required calculation was based on income levels, and grants and donations which the cathedral received were included in the computation of the denominator. The cathedral initially operated the special method, but subsequently formed the view that the result of including grants and donations in the computation was that too little of its input tax was being attributed to taxable supplies, and unilaterally ceased to operate the special method. The Commissioners issued an assessment on the basis that the cathedral should have continued to operate the special method. The tribunal dismissed the cathedral's appeal, holding that it had not been entitled to stop using the special method without the agreement of the Commissioners. The tribunal also observed that the inclusion of grants and donations in the computation was in accordance with *Article 19* of the *EC Sixth Directive*. *Dean & Chapter of the Cathedral Church of St Peter, LON/87/832X (VTD 3591)*.

43.78   **Whether change from special method to standard method may be retrospective.**   In 1984 a company began using a special 'direct attribution' method of apportioning its input tax between taxable and exempt supplies. Following a control visit in 1991, it realised that it would have been to its advantage to have reverted to the standard method of attribution as amended with effect from 1 April 1987. The Commissioners agreed to allow it to change to the standard method and to backdate the change to 1 April 1990, but refused to allow it to recompute its input tax in accordance with the special method for the period from April 1987 to March 1990. The tribunal dismissed the company's appeal against this decision. *PL Schofield Ltd, MAN/91/878 (VTD 7736)*.

43.79   A company carried on the businesses of building and of property management. In 1976 it received permission to adopt a special method of calculating its deductible input tax. In 1985 it received the Commissioners' agreement to a change in the method of apportioning its input tax. In 1990 its accountant formed the view that this method had led to insufficient input tax being treated as deductible, and submitted a claim for repayment of tax, computed on the basis that the standard method of apportionment should have been used with effect from 1 April 1987. The Commissioners refused to accept a retrospective claim and the company appealed. The tribunal dismissed the appeal, holding that the Commissioners had not acted unreasonably in refusing to accept a retrospective claim. *T Clark & Son Ltd, LON/91/239Z (VTD 8933)*.

43.80   A similar decision was reached in a subsequent case where the tribunal held, applying *dicta* of Neill LJ in *John Dee Ltd*, 14.28 COLLECTION AND ENFORCEMENT, and of the tribunal chairman in *BMW (GB) Ltd*, 43.85 below, that its jurisdiction was limited to deciding whether the Commissioners' decision was a reasonable one. On the evidence, the Commissioners had not acted unreasonably in refusing to accept a retrospective claim. *The Chartered Society of Physiotherapy, LON/97/185 (VTD 15108)*.

43.81   A college, which was partly exempt, had agreed a special method with the Commissioners. It subsequently formed the opinion that the method was unfair, as other colleges were not adopting a similar method of attributing their input tax. The college therefore lodged an appeal, contending that it had only agreed to the special method on the understanding that other colleges would be using a similar method, and that it should be therefore allowed to recompute its input tax for the previous seven accounting periods. The tribunal rejected this contention and dismissed the appeal. On the evidence, the college had agreed a special method and there had been no misrepresentation by Customs. Accordingly, the college could not recompute its input tax retrospectively. *Dicta* in *The Wellington Private Hospital Ltd*, 43.82 below, applied. *James Watt College, EDN/98/6 & 7 (VTD 15916)*.

43.82   **Company using special method without written permission—no objection raised by VAT officer at control visit—whether company entitled to revert to standard method retrospectively.**   A company which operated a private hospital, and made both taxable and exempt supplies, began to operate a special method for the apportionment of its input tax with effect from its accounting period ending 31 May 1987. It had not received written permission to adopt this special method, but its records were inspected by VAT officers in December 1987 and again in 1988. It continued to adopt this special method for all its returns up to and including May 1989. On the advice of its accountants, it unilaterally reverted to the standard method for subsequent returns. The Commissioners refused to accept this change for the periods up to and including 31 August 1991 (the returns for which were submitted late). The company's accountants also calculated that, as a result of having adopted the special method, the input tax which it had reclaimed for the periods from 1 March 1987 to 31 May 1989 was £157,000 less than would have been the case if it had adopted the standard method. It submitted a retrospective claim for this amount, which the Commissioners rejected. The company appealed, contending that since it had never requested nor received permission to use a special method, all its returns should have been submitted using the standard method. The tribunal allowed the appeal in part, finding that, since the company's use of the special method for the periods from 1 March 1987 to 30 November 1987 had not been approved by the Commissioners, it was entitled to use the standard method for those periods. However, when the company had been visited by VAT officers in December 1987, its use of the special method had been approved and permitted. Accordingly, after having received this permission, the company was not entitled to revert to the standard method until its accounting period ending November 1991. *The Wellington Private Hospital Ltd, [1993] VATTR 86 (VTD 10627).* (*Note.* For another issue in this case, taken to the QB, see 19.2 DRUGS, MEDICINES, AIDS FOR THE HANDICAPPED, ETC.)

43.83   *The Wellington Private Hospital,* 43.82 above, was applied in the similar case of *BMW Finance (GB) Ltd, EDN/94/71 (VTD 13131).* (*Note.* For a subsequent 'partial exemption' appeal by an associated company, see 43.85 below.)

43.84   **Commissioners directing termination of special method—whether unreasonable.**   Two associated companies which administered pension funds owned a number of properties, some of which produced taxable income and some produced exempt income. In 1991 the companies had agreed special methods for attributing their input tax. In 1995 the Commissioners issued directions terminating the special methods and requiring the companies to adopt the standard method of attribution. The companies appealed, contending that the adoption of the standard method would be unreasonable. The tribunal accepted this contention and allowed the appeals. Applying *dicta* of the CA in *John Dee Ltd,* 14.28 COLLECTION AND ENFORCEMENT, the tribunal's jurisdiction was appellate rather than merely supervisory. The enabling provision for the relevant regulations was *VATA 1994, s 26(3),* which provided that the regulations should be for the purpose of 'securing a fair and reasonable attribution of input tax'. On the evidence, the 1991 methods were 'unsatisfactory' but the adoption of the standard method would be 'even more unsatisfactory in that it was likely to lead to greater distortions'. The Commissioners could reasonably have directed the use of an alternative special method, such as one based on the rental values of the relevant properties. However, they had not done so. Since the standard method was less satisfactory than the 1991 schemes, the directions were flawed in that they did not achieve an attribution which was more fair and reasonable. *Merchant Navy Officers Pension Fund Trustees Ltd; Merchant Navy Ratings Pension Fund Trustees Ltd, LON/95/2944 (VTD 14262).*

43.85   A company (B) was the representative member of a large VAT group, which made both taxable and exempt supplies. It had used a special method of attributing its input tax, which was very similar to the standard method as it was based on the values of supplies made. However, the Commissioners had not formally approved this method (which, because it included the values of cars sold under hire-purchase agreements, had yielded a recovery rate of 93% of input tax in 1994, and 84% in 1995). In April 1996 the Commissioners issued a direction that this method should be terminated, and that a new special method, based on the method agreed with the Finance Houses Association and described in *Notice No 700/57/95*, should be adopted. B appealed, contending that the proposed method did not give a fair and reasonable attribution of input tax because it ignored the fact that taxable leasing supplies involved more overheads than exempt hire-purchase supplies. The tribunal dismissed the appeal, holding that its jurisdiction was limited to deciding whether the Commissioners' decision to issue the direction was a reasonable one. *Dicta* of Neill LJ in *John Dee Ltd*, 14.28 COLLECTION AND ENFORCEMENT, applied. On the evidence, the method which B had adopted prior to the direction had not secured a fair and reasonable attribution of input tax. Where a car was sold under a hire-purchase agreement, the costs which B incurred related to the exempt provision of finance, rather than to the taxable sale of the cars. The Commissioners had 'acted reasonably in seeking to alter the method used'. Although it was accepted that a leasing transaction was more complex than a hire-purchase transaction, B's proposals for taking this into account could not 'be objectively verified ... without unreasonable effort'. Accordingly, the Commissioners' direction had been reasonable. *BMW (GB) Ltd, LON/96/733 (VTD 14823)*.

43.86   A similar decision was reached in a case in which the Commissioners had issued a direction terminating a special method used by a bowling club and requiring the club to use the standard method. The tribunal held that the Commissioners' direction was reasonable. *Merchant Navy Officers Pension Fund Trustees*, 43.84 above, distinguished. *Glasgow Indoor Bowling Club, EDN/96/75 (VTD 14889)*.

Date from which special method effective (Regulation 102(4))

43.87   **Whether special method may be backdated.** At a meeting on 26 February 1988 between a VAT officer and a company which was partly exempt, a special method for attributing the company's input tax was agreed. However, the company failed to account for input tax in accordance with the agreement. When the Commissioners discovered this, they issued an assessment in accordance with the special method, covering the period from 1 April 1987 to 31 March 1989. The tribunal allowed the company's appeal in part, holding that the Commissioners could not insist on the use of the special method for any period prior to 26 February 1988. *North British Housing Association Ltd, MAN/91/45 (VTD 7195)*.

43.88   A bank, which was partly exempt and had agreed a special method of calculating its deductible input tax, went into liquidation in February 1991. It ceased to trade but the liquidator incurred input tax. The liquidator formed the opinion that the existing special method had been to the bank's detriment as the percentage of deductible input tax had been unreasonably low. In April 1992 the accountants acting for the liquidator wrote to the local VAT office proposing a new special method. The Commissioners agreed to the revised method being used with effect from 1 April 1992, but refused to allow the revised method to be backdated. The liquidator appealed, contending that the revised method should be used retrospectively for the period from 1 July 1991 to 31 March 1992. The tribunal dismissed the liquidator's appeal, holding that the Commissioners had not acted unreasonably in refusing to allow the revised special method to be backdated. *AJ Barrett (as provisional liquidator for Rafidain Bank), LON/92/2732A (VTD 11016)*.

43.89   A bowling club applied for permission to adopt a special method of attributing its input tax with retrospective effect, to take account of an anticipated future increase in the proportion of its taxable supplies. The Commissioners rejected the application and the tribunal dismissed the club's appeal. Applying *dicta* in *BMW (GB) Ltd*, 43.85 above, the tribunal's jurisdiction was limited to deciding whether the Commissioners' decision was a reasonable one. On the evidence, the Commissioners had not acted unreasonably in refusing to accept a retrospective claim. *Chard Bowling Club (No 2), [1997] VATDR 375 (VTD 15114)*. (*Note*. For another issue in this case, see 43.50 above.)

Miscellaneous

43.90   **Partial exemption—definition of 'significant change in business'.**   A bank, which was partly exempt, had agreed with the Commissioners a special method of calculating its deductible input tax. The agreement stipulated that any significant change in the bank's business must be notified. In 1986 the bank made zero-rated supplies of gold bullion totalling more than £395 million. The Commissioners rejected the bank's input tax claim, considering that the supplies of bullion constituted a significant change in the bank's business. The tribunal allowed the bank's appeal, holding on the evidence that the supplies in question did not amount to a significant change in the bank's business. *Union Bank of Switzerland, [1987] VATTR 221 (VTD 2551)*.

43.91   **Commissioners refusing to permit special method—nature of tribunal's jurisdiction.**   An estate agent, who was partly exempt, reclaimed the whole of his input tax. The Commissioners issued an assessment to recover part of the tax. The assessment was computed using the standard method of attributing input tax. The estate agent appealed, contending that the standard method was inequitable and that the Commissioners should have allowed him to use a special method. The tribunal dismissed his appeal, holding that the Commissioners 'had a discretion, which they chose not to exercise, to allow or direct the use of another method'. The tribunal had 'no power to interfere with such an exercise of discretion unless it is unreasonable to the extent that no reasonable body of Commissioners could have reached such a conclusion'. *JG Whitelaw, EDN/89/28 (VTD 4299)*.

43.92   **University operating special method—whether residual input tax may be reclaimed.**   The value of the exempt outputs of a university is much greater than the value of its taxable outputs. Since 1973 the Commissioners have therefore approved special arrangements for universities, whereby each activity giving rise to an output tax liability may be dealt with separately. Under these arrangements there has to be separate accounting for each taxable activity, and the input tax attributable to each such activity may be set off against the relevant output tax. In 1990 Edinburgh University, which had previously considered that it was not worth reclaiming any residual input tax not directly attributable to a taxable activity, made a claim for repayment of residual input tax attributable to its computer services department. The Commissioners refused to repay the tax, considering that the special method which had been agreed did not allow a claim for residual input tax. The tribunal allowed the University's appeal, holding that it was entitled to reclaim the residual input tax and that its failure to have done so previously was an error which it was 'now entitled to have put right'. *The University of Edinburgh, EDN/91/55 (VTD 6569)*.

43.93   A similar decision was reached in a subsequent case where a university had lodged a substantial retrospective repayment claim. The tribunal held that the agreement between the Commissioners and the university had left 'very substantial amounts of input tax untouched', and that to restrict 'the university's entitlement to what it has actually claimed would be to deprive it of rights of deduction under the pro rata rule given to it in the EU VAT directives'. On the evidence, the tribunal held that 'the content of the special method is not to be found in the narrow confines contended for by the Commissioners and does include the ability to recover residual input tax as claimed by the university'. *Ampleforth Abbey Trust*, 43.68 above, applied. *The University of Sussex, LON/98/851 (VTD 16221)*. (*Note.* At a subsequent hearing, the tribunal held that the university could only reclaim retrospectively for three years—see 45.30 PAYMENT OF TAX.)

43.94   **Holding company—whether supplies made by subsidiary to be treated as taxable under special method.** A holding company had agreed with the Commissioners a special method of attributing input tax. Under the agreement one of its subsidiaries, which supplied taxable computer services to a customer outside the group, was treated as fully taxable, so that its input tax was wholly deductible. Subsequently the subsidiary began making supplies to other members of the group. The Commissioners considered that, since these supplies were, by virtue of what is now *VATA 1994, s 43(1)(a)*, not subject to VAT, the subsidiary's input tax should be restricted accordingly. They therefore issued an assessment to recover some of the subsidiary's input tax. The holding company appealed, contending that the wording of the special method agreed with the Commissioners required that all the subsidiary's input tax should be treated as allowable, even though some of its supplies were no longer subject to VAT. The tribunal accepted this contention and allowed the company's appeal. *Fidelity International Management Holdings Ltd, LON/91/1915 (VTD 7323)*.

43.95   **Group of companies—application of special method.** See *Joseph Nelson Investment Planning Ltd*, 30.25 GROUPS OF COMPANIES, and *Kwik-Fit (GB) Ltd*, 30.26 GROUPS OF COMPANIES.

43.96   **Input tax on refurbishment of premises—whether deductible under special method.**   A company which made taxable supplies also made exempt dealings in securities and let part of its premises to tenants, so that it was partly exempt. It had agreed a special method of apportioning its input tax, by which tax relating to the 'general management and general upkeep of the structure and common areas of the premises' was to be apportioned on the basis of the percentage of the total floor space which it occupied, but any remaining input tax was to be deductible in full. It undertook substantial refurbishment of the premises, and reclaimed the whole of the input tax relating to this work. The Commissioners issued an assessment to recover part of the tax, considering that it should have been apportioned under the terms of the special method. The company appealed, contending that, in view of the scale of the refurbishment, the expenditure was not within the definition of 'general upkeep... of the premises', and therefore fell within the definition of 'remaining input tax' and was deductible in full. The tribunal accepted the company's contentions and allowed the appeal. The tribunal chairman commented that it was 'remarkable that ... the Commissioners did not use words to make it crystal clear that the tax on ... the capital costs of the refurbishment and construction works ... was to be included in the amounts to be apportioned'. *Louis Dreyfus & Co Ltd, LON/90/236Z (VTD 10795)*.

43.97   **Statutory body operating special method—whether entitled to reclaim input tax on non-business activities.** The *Housing (Scotland) Act 1988* established a statutory body (S) for the purpose of providing housing and promoting the provision of housing. Until 30 June 1990, S was entitled to reclaim input tax on non-business activities under what is now *VATA 1994, s 33*. From 1 July 1990 S lost this status and became partly exempt. Its accountants subsequently applied for permission to operate a special method of calculating its deductible input tax. The Commissioners replied approving an alternative method subject to the exclusion of 'the value of any goods or services not supplied by way of business'. In 1993 the

Commissioners discovered that S had been treating its distribution of grants to housing associations as a business activity and reclaiming a proportion of the input tax relating to this. The Commissioners took the view that the provision of grants to housing associations was not a business activity, and that none of the input tax was deductible. They therefore issued an assessment to recover some of the input tax which S had treated as deductible. The tribunal dismissed S's appeal, observing that the Commissioners had directed that 'non-business supplies must be excluded' from the partial exemption calculations, and holding that the Commissioners were entitled to treat the provision of grants as a non-business activity. *Scottish Homes, EDN/94/138 (VTD 13292)*. (*Note*. For a subsequent appeal by the same association, see 43.40 above.)

43.98   **Bank operating special method—treatment of service charge income.**   A group of companies carried on a retail banking business, and was partly exempt. It had agreed a special method for calculating its deductible input tax. Under the special method, the total percentage of input tax recoverable would be sum of the percentage of costs relating to lending income, multiplied by the product of the group's taxable lending income divided by the total of its taxable and exempt lending income, and the percentage of costs relating to service charge income, multiplied by the product of the group's taxable service charge income divided by the total of its taxable and exempt service charge income. Items which were outside the scope of VAT were to be ignored. Subsequently the Commissioners discovered that, for some periods, the costs which the group was treating as attributable to service charge income exceeded the service charge income itself. In 1994 they issued an assessment to recover more than £425,000 of input tax which the group had reclaimed. The group appealed, contending that it had operated the special method correctly, and that the reason that the service charge income was less than the associated costs was that a large number of its customers kept their accounts in credit and were provided with free banking facilities. The tribunal accepted this contention and allowed the group's appeal, holding that the free banking facilities should be treated as being supplies for consideration, so that the bank was entitled to reclaim the relevant proportion of input tax. *The Governor and Company of the Bank of Scotland, EDN/94/114 (VTD 13854)*.

43.99   **Finance company—operation of special method involving 'transaction count'.**   A finance company, which was partly exempt, operated a special method which stated, *inter alia*, that 'the taxable percentage applied to VAT directly attributable to sales and new business administration costs should be calculated by using a transaction method of taxable new deals created in the tax period over all new deals created in the tax period'. The company treated hire-purchase transactions as wholly exempt, so that they were included in the denominator of the appropriate fraction, but not in the numerator. Subsequently the company formed the opinion that a hire-purchase transaction should have been treated as both a taxable deal (the hiring of goods) and an exempt deal (credit finance), and lodged a backdated repayment claim accordingly. The Commissioners rejected the claim on the basis that, because a hire-purchase transaction was not wholly taxable, it did not qualify as a 'taxable deal'. The tribunal allowed the company's appeal, holding that it was entitled to treat a hire purchase transaction as two deals (i.e. included once in the numerator and twice in the denominator) in arriving at the appropriate fraction. *Sovereign Finance plc, MAN/97/778 (VTD 16237)*.

43.100   **Recovery of input tax on currency transactions—application to change special method.**   A company, established in the British Virgin Islands, operated a number of 'bureaux de change' in the UK. In 1993 the Commissioners wrote to the company, specifying the terms of a special partial exemption method, under *VAT Regulations, reg 102*, for calculating its recoverable input tax. Under the method, the input tax relating to overheads was to be recovered by reference to customers' domicile, on a transaction count basis. Initially the company accounted for tax on the basis that 38% of the residual input tax was recoverable, on the basis that 38% of its transactions were with customers domiciled outside the EU. Subsequently the company formed the opinion that it should be allowed to reclaim more than 38% of its residual input tax, and lodged a retrospective repayment claim, computed on the basis that 45% of the currency which it received for exchange was non-EU currency. The Commissioners rejected the claim and the company appealed. The tribunal reviewed the evidence in detail and dismissed the appeal, observing that 'the currency presented by a customer ... need not represent the country of domicile. While it is perfectly plausible that a tourist from country A visiting country B will carry the currency of country A, it is equally possible that a tourist may be carrying the currency of other countries which he has visited before arriving in country B'. Furthermore, some of the company's customers would be people domiciled in the UK who had acquired surplus foreign currency when travelling outside the EU and wished to change it into sterling. On the evidence, the tribunal held that the company had 'not established that the transaction count method was in any way wrong' and had 'not shown that the calculations based on the currency method invalidate that original method ... (or) that the conclusions which it draws from the currency method to invalidate the transaction count method stand up to scrutiny'. *Chequepoint (UK) Ltd, LON/98/1543 (VTD 16754)*.

43.101   **Investment trust operating special method—treatment of 'stock-lending' transactions.**   An investment trust agreed a special partial exemption method in 1988. In 1997 it began to carry out 'stock-lending' transactions. The Commissioners issued a ruling that the value of the exempt supplies should be treated as including the open market values of the stocks lent, as laid down by *Notice No 701/44*. The trust appealed, contending that the value of the relevant supplies was simply the amounts paid to it for the transactions in question. The tribunal accepted this contention and allowed the appeal, finding that 'the only trading benefit obtained by the appellants was their fee' and holding that it would 'be wholly artificial and unreal to attempt to attribute a consideration based upon the whole value of shares which were transferred for a temporary purpose'. *Scottish Eastern Investment Trust plc, EDN/99/211 (VTD 16882)*.

ATTRIBUTION OF INPUT TAX TO FOREIGN AND SPECIFIED SUPPLIES (VAT Regulations 1995, reg 103)

43.102   A Japanese corporation was established to promote Japanese horse racing. It established an office in the UK, and registered for UK VAT under what is now *VATA 1994, Sch 1 para 10*. It reclaimed the whole of the input tax incurred in respect of its London office, on the basis that it was attributable to supplies which would be taxable supplies if they were made in the UK. The Commissioners rejected the claim and issued a ruling that most of the tax had to be attributed to supplies of betting facilities which would have been exempt from UK VAT under what is now *VATA 1994, Sch 9, Group 4*. The tribunal allowed the corporation's appeal, finding that none of the supplies made by the UK office were attributable to betting activities, and holding that the return had been made in accordance with what is now *VAT Regulations 1995 (SI 1995 No 2518), reg 103*. *Japan Racing Association, LON/93/1830A (VTD 11489)*.

43.103   **Advertising services supplied to German company.**   An educational institute (L) did not begin accepting students (thereby making exempt supplies of educational services) until 1995, but in 1993 it had entered into a sponsorship agreement with a German company (G), whereby G made substantial payments to L in return for advertising and publicity services. It was accepted that the effect of the *VAT (Place of Supply of Services) Order 1992 (SI 1992 No 3121), article 16* was that the place of supply of these services was in Germany. The Commissioners issued a ruling that these supplies were not to be treated as taxable supplies for the purposes of the partial exemption provisions, but should be apportioned in accordance with what is now *VAT Regulations 1995 (SI 1995 No 2518), reg 103*. L appealed, contending that, even though the supplies were deemed to be made outside the UK, they should be treated as taxable supplies in the denominator of the fraction prescribed by what is now *VAT Regulations 1995 (SI 1995 No 2518), reg 101(2)(d)* (so that it was able to reclaim all its input tax in 1993 and 1994, and a substantial proportion of its input tax in 1995). The CA unanimously rejected this contention and upheld the Commissioners' ruling. Nourse LJ held that the input tax attributable to 'out of country supplies' was outside the scope of *reg 101*. It would be anomalous to include the value of such supplies in the denominator of the fraction laid down by *reg 101(2)(d)*. What is now *regulation 103* 'was intended to institute a separate regime for out of country and specified supplies'. *C & E Commrs v Liverpool Institute for Performing Arts (aka The Liverpool School of Performing Arts), CA [1999] STC 424*. (*Note.* For the Commissioners' practice following this decision, see Business Brief 8/99, issued on 31 March 1999.)

ATTRIBUTION OF INPUT TAX ON SELF-SUPPLIES (VAT Regulations 1995, reg 104)

43.104   **Building society operating special method—self-supplies of stationery.**   A building society, which was partly exempt, had operated a special method on the lines agreed by the Building Societies Association and laid down in *Notice No 700/57/95*. It sought to modify the method and proposed that inputs should be attributed to taxable supplies on the basis of the time spent by its staff in connection with the making of taxable supplies, including time spent by its printing staff in producing stationery. The Commissioners refused to accept that time spent by the printing staff ought to be included, and the society appealed. The tribunal rejected the society's claim, holding that the effect of *VAT Regulations 1995, reg 104* was that the Commissioners were 'acting properly in refusing to allow a method which treats the input tax on self-supplies of stationery, however calculated, as attributable to taxable supplies'. *Leeds & Holbeck Building Society, MAN/96/670 (VTD 15356)*. (*Note.* The appeal also concerned the validity of *VATA 1994, s 80(4)*, in respect of which the appeal was adjourned pending the hearing of the substantive appeal in *Marks & Spencer plc*, 45.32 PAYMENT OF TAX.)

TREATMENT OF INPUT TAX ATTRIBUTABLE TO EXEMPT SUPPLIES AS BEING ATTRIBUTABLE TO TAXABLE SUPPLIES (VAT Regulations 1995, reg 106)

Note. *VAT Regulations 1995, regulation 105* was omitted by the *Value Added Tax (Amendment) (No 2) Regulations 1999 (SI 1999 No 599)*, with effect from 10 March 1999.

43.105   **Interpretation of de minimis limits.**   A partnership, which was partly exempt, used a special direct attribution method. Its annual adjustment period for this purpose ended on 30 April 1987. New partial exemption regulations were introduced with effect from 1 April 1987, but the partnership contended that the old *de minimis* rules should be treated as applying to it for the whole of the period to 30 April 1987. The Commissioners issued a ruling that the old rules could only be applied in considering the period up to 31 March 1987, and that the new method laid down by *SI 1987 No 510* should be applied to the partnership's input tax for April 1987. The tribunal upheld the Commissioners' ruling and dismissed the partnership's appeal, holding that there was 'nothing in either *FA 1987* or *SI 1987 No 510* that expressly or by necessary implication extends the life of the old *de minimis* rules ... beyond 31 March 1987'. *BC & ME Risby, LON/90/1300Y (VTD 6544). (Note.* The regulations introduced by *SI 1987 No 510* were themselves subsequently substituted by *SI 1992 No 645*. The *de minimis* rules are now contained in *VAT Regulations 1995 (SI 1995 No 2518), reg 106*.)

43.106   A partnership became liable to register for VAT from October 1986, but did not actually do so until October 1988. Its first VAT return covered the 31 months from October 1986 to April 1989. Until October 1988, all its activities related to taxable supplies, but from October 1988 it began work on converting a barn, the disposal of which would be an exempt supply. The partnership reclaimed input tax of £2,030 attributable to the work on the barn, but the Commissioners refused to repay the tax, considering that it was not recoverable since it related to an exempt supply. The partnership appealed, contending that, since the tax in question was less than £3,000, it was within the *de minimis* limit of £100 per month prescribed by the *VAT (General) Regulations* as then in force. (The Commissioners considered that the tax in question could only be averaged over the twelve months ending on 30 April 1989, and therefore exceeded the *de minimis* limit.) The tribunal accepted the partnership's contention and allowed the appeal. By issuing the partnership with a return covering the period from October 1986 to April 1989, the Commissioners had established the whole of that period as the 'prescribed accounting period' for the purposes of what is now *VAT Regulations 1995 (SI 1995 No 2518), reg 99(1)(b). JR Williams & RJS Wallis, LON/91/300Z (VTD 7286). (Note.* This case was distinguished in the subsequent cases of *Eltham Park Insurance Brokers Ltd*, 43.111 below, and *Dr Dunn & Others*, 43.113 below.)

43.107   A company reclaimed input tax of £797 in its return for the period ending 31 March 1990, although the invoice was dated July 1989. The input tax related to an exempt supply, and the Commissioners issued an assessment to recover the tax, since the company's total input tax for the period ending 30 September 1989 (when the invoice was issued) exceeded the *de minimis* limits. The company appealed, contending that the input tax should be allowed since its input tax for the period ending 31 March 1990 did not exceed the *de minimis* limits. The tribunal dismissed the appeal, holding that the reference to an accounting period in what is now *VAT Regulations 1995 (SI 1995 No 2518), reg 106* was 'to the period in which the supply to which the tax relates was made, rather than to the period in which it was claimed'. *Trevor Toys Ltd, LON/91/1760Y (VTD 7805).*

43.108   The decision in *Trevor Toys Ltd*, 43.107 above, was applied in the similar subsequent case of *Dayrich Bookmakers, MAN/96/153 (VTD 15492).*

43.109   A company which operated a swimming pool made both taxable and exempt supplies. The input tax attributable to its exempt supplies was usually within the *de minimis* limits, with the result that it was able to reclaim the whole of its input tax. However, in 1991 it had to replace the sand filters at the pool. Because of this expenditure, its input tax for that year was much greater than usual, and the input tax attributable to exempt supplies exceeded the *de minimis* limits for the first time. The Commissioners restricted the deductible input tax accordingly, and the company appealed, contending that, since the sand filters were capital expenditure which had to be paid for out of reserves rather than out of current profits, the input tax relating to them should be spread over a five-year period. The tribunal rejected this contention and dismissed the appeal, holding that there was nothing in the *VAT Regulations* which permitted input tax to be spread in this way. *Chester Swimming Association, MAN/91/900 (VTD 10969).*

43.110   A company reclaimed the whole of its input tax for a three-month period, although its exempt input tax for that period was more than the *de minimis* limit laid down by what is now *VAT Regulations 1995 (SI 1995 No 2518), reg 106*. The Commissioners issued an assessment to recover the tax and the company appealed, contending that its input tax for the quarterly period in question should be aggregated with the previous quarter, since the effect of aggregating the two quarters was to bring the exempt input tax below the *de minimis* limit. The tribunal dismissed the appeal, holding that the exempt input tax could not be averaged in this way, and that the reference in *regulation 106(1)** to 'any longer period' was to a period ending on 31 March, as laid down by *regulation 99**. *Polo Farm Sports Club, LON/93/909A & LON/93/1225P (VTD 11386)*. (*Note.* An appeal against a misdeclaration penalty was, however, allowed.)

43.111   A similar decision was reached in a subsequent case in which the tribunal found that a partly exempt company which had registered retrospectively had wrongly informed the Newry VAT office that its exempt input tax was more than 50% of its total input tax, although this was not in fact the case. The tribunal held that the company was not entitled to adopt a non-standard tax year (for the purpose of manipulating the transitional *de minimis* limits) without the approval of the Commissioners. *Williams & Wallis*, 43.106 above, distinguished. *Eltham Park Insurance Brokers Ltd, LON/96/108 (VTD 14306)*.

43.112   A company, which made both exempt and taxable supplies, registered for VAT with effect from 1992. For the period ending 31 May 1993, its exempt input tax was within the *de minimis* limits, so that it was able to reclaim all its input tax. However, for the two years ending 31 May 1995 its exempt input tax exceeded the *de minimis* limits. Nevertheless, it reclaimed the whole of its input tax for those years, and the Commissioners issued an assessment to recover the tax attributable to exempt supplies. The company appealed, contending that, for the purposes of what is now *VAT Regulations 1995, reg 99(1)(d)*, the 34 months from 1 August 1992 to 31 May 1995 should be treated as the company's 'tax year' (thus bringing the exempt input tax within the *de minimis* limit). The tribunal rejected this contention and dismissed the appeal, holding that the effect of *VAT Regulations 1995, reg 99(1)(d)* was that the Commissioners had a discretion whether or not to extend the period to be treated as the 'tax year', and that their refusal to exercise this discretion in this case was not unreasonable. *Yorkhurst Ltd, MAN/95/2757 (VTD 14458)*.

43.113   A medical partnership registered for VAT from 1 January 1994. Its first accounting period ended on 28 February 1994, but its accounting dates were then amended, at its request, so that its second accounting period ended on 30 June 1994. Following a control visit, the Commissioners issued an assessment on the basis that the partnership had overclaimed input tax for the year ending 31 March 1995, by reclaiming input tax which was attributable to exempt supplies and failing to observe the *de minimis* limits. The partnership appealed, contending that because of its change of accounting dates, its first 'tax year' for the purposes of what is now *VAT Regulations 1995, reg 99(1)(d)* was the year beginning on 1 April 1995. The tribunal rejected this contention and dismissed the appeal. On a proper interpretation of what is now *VAT Regulations 1995, reg 99(1)(d)*, the partnership's first 'tax year' was the year beginning on 1 April 1994. Their total exempt input tax for that year exceeded the *de minimis* limits. *Williams & Wallis*, 43.106 above, distinguished. *Dr Dunn & Others, LON/96/620 (VTD 14788)*.

ADJUSTMENTS OF ATTRIBUTIONS (VAT Regulations 1995, regs 107–110)

Whether Regulation 107 applicable

43.114   **Short-term lease of premises purchased for taxable purposes—whether any adjustment of attribution of input tax required.**   A company carried on a business of providing management and marketing services. In July 1991 it purchased a freehold property, and reclaimed input tax on the purchase and refurbishment of the property. In August 1992 it granted a two-year lease of part of the premises. In January 1993 it elected to waive exemption in respect of the lease. The Commissioners formed the opinion that some of the input tax which the company had reclaimed should be attributed to the exempt supplies which it had made between August 1992 and December 1992, and issued an assessment for the period ending November 1992 to recover part of the tax (£4,120). The company appealed, contending firstly that, at the time of purchase, it had intended to use the whole of the property for the purpose of its taxable business activities, but had subsequently been obliged to lease part of the property because it had been unable to dispose of its previous premises; and also contending that the £4,120 input tax which the Commissioners had sought to recover was within the *de minimis* limits of what is now *VAT Regulations 1995, reg 106*. The tribunal accepted these contentions and allowed the appeal, holding that the initial reclaim of input tax had been in accordance with the decision in *Briararch Ltd*, 43.125 below. The effect of what is now *VAT Regulations 1995, reg 107* was that the initial attribution did not fall to be adjusted until the end of the company's tax year in May 1993, and *reg 108(2)* did not require the attribution to be adjusted in the November 1992 return. With regard to the period ending May 1993, the *de minimis* limits of what is now *VAT Regulations 1995, reg 106* applied, so that, again, no adjustment was required. (The tribunal also held that *VATA 1994, Sch 10 para 3(9)** did not empower the Commissioners to require a retrospective amendment to the November 1992 return as a condition of accepting the election to waive exemption.) *The Island Trading Co Ltd, [1996] VATDR 245 (VTD 13838).*

43.115   **Company wrongly treating subscription income as outside scope of VAT and failing to reclaim related input tax—whether entitled to adjust attribution of input tax retrospectively—effect of VAT Regulations 1995, reg 107.**   A company with political objectives derived some income from non-business activities, including donations. It was partly exempt, and operated a special method of attributing its input tax. In its returns for 1994 and 1995, it treated some of its subscription income as outside the scope of VAT, and failed to reclaim the relevant input tax. In 1998 it submitted two 'voluntary disclosures' seeking to correct its annual adjustments for 1994 and 1995 in order to reclaim the tax. The Commissioners rejected the claim on the basis that such errors could only be corrected through the special procedures laid down by *VAT Regulations 1995 (SI 1995 No 2518), regs 34* and *35*. The company appealed. The tribunal dismissed the appeal, holding that 'we cannot accept that *regulation 107* applies to the present situation. Our principal reason is that *regulation 107* is concerned exclusively with annual adjustments of attributions of input tax to taxable supplies.' The tribunal held that *reg 107* 'has no bearing on the antecedent question of whether the tax incurred by the taxable person is or is not input tax. That is covered by (*VATA 1994, s 24(5)*) and by the agreed method designed to determine what person's "tax incurred" ... is referable to his business'. Furthermore, 'neither the special method nor *regulation 107* makes any reference to error correction either through the annual adjustment or at all'. By contrast, *regs 34* and *35* provided 'a specific mechanism for correcting errors'. The tribunal held that 'the presence of such specific mandatory provisions for correcting errors ... removes any necessity for incorporation of error correction into the special method of a taxable person'. *Greenpeace Ltd, LON/99/532 (VTD 16681).*

43.116   **VAT Regulations 1995, reg 107(1)(c)—failure to make annual adjustment.**   An appeal was dismissed in a case where the tribunal found that a college, which was partly exempt, had failed to make the annual adjustment required by *VAT Regulations 1995, reg 107(1)(c)*. (The tribunal also found that the Commissioners and the college had agreed that its 'tax year', as defined in *reg 99(1)(d)*, should begin on 1 August, in order to coincide with the academic year.) *Ruskin College, LON/99/443 (VTD 16726)*.

43.117   **Management services supplied to company not registered for VAT—recipient company subsequently joining same VAT group as supplier of services—effect of VAT Regulations 1995, reg 107***.   See *Svenska International plc*, 41.16 MANAGEMENT SERVICES.

Whether Regulation 108 applicable

43.118   **House converted into flats and advertised as holiday accommodation but subsequently leased—apportionment of input tax.** A company (C) converted a large house at Richmond-on-Thames into ten self-contained furnished flats. It advertised these flats as holiday accommodation for people visiting London. Some of the flats were thus occupied between December 1988 (when the conversion was completed) and February 1989. In February 1989 C received an offer from a US company to enter into a lease of the whole building so that the flats could be used to house the US company's employees. C reclaimed the whole of the input tax incurred on the conversion. The Commissioners issued an assessment to recover part of the tax, considering that it related to the supply of a lease which was exempt from VAT. C appealed, contending that the whole of the conversion work had been undertaken for the purpose of providing holiday accommodation, which was a taxable supply. The tribunal rejected C's contentions, holding that each floor of the building had to be considered separately, and that the input tax should be apportioned between that charged on supplies used for the making of taxable supplies of holiday accommodation, and that charged on supplies used for the supply of the tenancy to the US company. The QB upheld this decision. There was 'no causative nexus between the publication of the advertisement of holiday flats and the letting of the whole building for some quite different purpose'. The company had made a supply which was not a supply of holiday accommodation and thus not excluded from exemption. *Sheppard*, 39.86 LAND, distinguished. Furthermore, the relevant provisions of the *VAT Regulations* were in accordance with *Article 17* of the *EC Sixth Directive*, which permitted the amount of input tax provisionally treated as deductible to be subject to a subsequent adjustment on the basis of actual use. *Cooper & Chapman (Builders) Ltd v C & E Commrs, QB 1992, [1993] STC 1*.

43.119   **Input tax reclaimed on purchase of land—land sold as exempt supply six months later—adjustment to input tax claim.**   A company purchased some land in January 1990. The vendor had elected to waive exemption, so that the purchase price included VAT of £105,000, which the company reclaimed as input tax. Six months later the company sold the land without electing to waive exemption. The Commissioners issued an assessment for the period ending 31 January 1990 to recover the input tax, on the basis that it was attributable to an exempt supply. The company appealed, contending that when it had purchased the land, it had intended to build a warehouse and use the land for taxable supplies, but it had subsequently decided that it could not afford the cost of construction. The Commissioners thereupon withdrew the assessment and issued an assessment for the same amount for the period ending 31 July 1990, on the basis that the effect of what is now *VAT Regulations 1995 (SI 1995 No 2518), reg 108* was that the company should have adjusted its claim to input tax when it submitted its return for the period in which the sale was made. The tribunal upheld this assessment and dismissed the company's appeal. *Franco F'Lli Ltd, LON/91/242X (VTD 13153)*.

43.120   Similar decisions were reached in the Isle of Man cases of *Old Chelsea Properties Ltd v Isle of Man Treasury, MAN/96/850; Villiers Group plc v Isle of Man Treasury, MAN/96/851 (VTD 15230)*.

43.121   A company purchased a plot of land in 1998. It reclaimed input tax on professional fees relating to plans for building houses on the land. However, it subsequently sold the land without developing it. The Commissioners issued an assessment on the basis that the input tax had to be attributed to the exempt sale of the land, in accordance with *VAT Regulations 1995 (SI 1995 No 2518), reg 108*. The company appealed, contending that its sale of the land was the transfer of a going concern, rather than an exempt supply. The tribunal rejected this contention and dismissed the appeal, observing that 'the land was not being actively developed when it was sold'. Accordingly, the sale of the land was an exempt supply, rather than the transfer of a going concern, and the company was obliged to adjust its input tax under *reg 108*. *Golden Oak Partnership*, 34.445 INPUT TAX, was distinguished, on the grounds that the partnership in that case had 'carried out substantial infrastructural works' and the land there 'was in the course of active development' when it was sold. *Gulf Trading & Management Ltd, LON/99/842 (VTD 16847)*.

43.122   A company purchased some land with the intention of developing it. The vendor had elected to waive exemption, so that the purchase price included VAT, which the company reclaimed as input tax. Subsequently it received an offer from a housing association, and agreed to sell the land to the association under a contract whereby it agreed to construct a number of flats on the land. The Commissioners issued an assessment on the basis that the whole of the input tax which the company had reclaimed should be attributed to the exempt sale of the land, in accordance with *VAT Regulations 1995 (SI 1995 No 2518), reg 108*. The company appealed, contending that, because it had agreed to make zero-rated supplies of construction services to the housing association, only part of the input tax was attributable to the exempt sale of the land, and part was attributable to the zero-rated supplies of construction services. The tribunal accepted this contention and allowed the appeal. *Wiggett Construction Ltd, MAN/99/1047 (VTD 16984)*.

43.123   **Input tax reclaimed on expenditure relating to redevelopment of property—subsequent exempt supply of property—whether regulation 108 applicable.**   In 1995 a company (T) purchased a property with the intention of redeveloping it as residential accommodation. It obtained the necessary planning permission, and reclaimed input tax on services supplied by planning consultants, engineers, surveyors, etc. relating to the proposed redevelopment. However, it was unable to raise the necessary finance to proceed with the redevelopment, and in May 1996 it made an exempt supply of the site (with the benefit of the planning permission) to a Jersey company. The Commissioners issued an assessment to recover the input tax which T had reclaimed. The tribunal dismissed T's appeal, holding that the effect of *VAT Regulations 1995 (SI 1995 No 2518), reg 108* was that the input tax had to be attributed to the exempt supply which T had actually made, rather than to the taxable supply which it had originally intended to make. The provisions of *regulation 108* were consistent with *Article 20(1)* of the *EC Sixth Directive*. The wording of *Article 20(1)* was 'wide enough ... to include a change of intention which results in a change of the VAT status of a transaction from taxable to exempt'. The QB upheld this decision. Carnwath J observed that there had been a 'change ... in the factors used to determine the amount to be deducted', within *Article 20(1)(b)*. The tribunal had been entitled to find that there had been a sufficient direct and immediate link between the supplies which T received and the supply which it made for the input tax to be reattributed from the intended taxable supply to the actual exempt supply. *Belgium v Ghent Coal Terminal NV*, 21.199 EUROPEAN COMMUNITY LAW, distinguished. *Tremerton Ltd v C & E Commrs, QB [1999] STC 1039*.

43.124   **Company registering with intention of making taxable supplies—subsequently making exempt supplies—whether Regulation 108 applicable.**   A company registered for VAT in 1996, stating that it intended to supply counselling services. It failed to attract any clients, and in 1997 it began letting rooms at its premises. The Commissioners issued an assessment to recover input tax which the company had reclaimed from 1996 to 1999. The tribunal reviewed the evidence in detail and upheld the assessment in principle (subject to agreement as to figures), holding that, from 1996 to October 1997, the company 'was entitled to be registered as an intending trader' but that from November 1997 this was no longer the case. Accordingly *VAT Regulations 1995 (SI 1995 No 2518), reg 108* applied and the company was obliged to repay the input tax. *Infinite Mind Ltd, LON/99/1349 (VTD 16980)*.

Whether Regulation 109 applicable

43.125   **Grant of short tenancy pending sale of major interest in building—adjustment of attribution of input tax.**   A company (B) restored a listed building with the intention of selling a leasehold interest in it. However, it was unable to find a lessee who would accept a long lease, and therefore granted a four-year tenancy to provide it with temporary rental income. It reclaimed the whole of the input tax incurred on the restoration. The Commissioners issued an assessment to recover the tax, considering that it should be wholly attributed to the four-year tenancy, which was an exempt supply. B appealed, contending that it remained its intention to sell a long lease, which would be a taxable supply, and that the input tax should therefore be apportioned between the exempt supply and the future taxable supply. The tribunal allowed B's appeal, holding that, since the Commissioners had accepted B's evidence that it intended to make a taxable supply of a 25–year lease in the building, it followed that $^{25}/_{29}$ of the input tax which B had incurred related to this future taxable supply and was therefore deductible. The QB upheld the tribunal decision. The regulations envisaged that input tax should be apportioned in such cases, and such an apportionment was in accordance with *Article 20* of the *EC Sixth Directive. C & E Commrs v Briararch Ltd, QB [1992] STC 732*. (*Notes.* (1) The case was heard in the QB with *Curtis Henderson Ltd*, 43.126 below. (2) For the Commissioners' practice following this decision, see Business Brief 15/92, issued on 5 October 1992.)

43.126   A development company built a house with the intention of selling it, and reclaimed the input tax incurred on its construction. The house was completed in April 1989. The company was unable to sell the house, and in August 1990 the house was let on a short lease. The tenant remained in occupation for nine months, and the house was subsequently sold in September 1990. When the Commissioners became aware of the letting of the house, they issued an assessment to recover the input tax that had been repaid to the company. The company appealed, contending that it was entitled to credit for the input tax. The tribunal allowed the appeal in part, holding that the tax should be apportioned, applying *Briararch Ltd*, 43.125 above, and distinguishing *Rentorn Ltd*, 43.11 above. The QB upheld the tribunal decision. The regulations envisaged that input tax should be apportioned in such cases, and such an apportionment was in accordance with *Article 20* of the *EC Sixth Directive. C & E Commrs v Curtis Henderson Ltd, QB [1992] STC 732*. (*Notes.* (1) The case was heard in the QB with *Briararch Ltd*, 43.125 above. (2) For the Commissioners' practice following this decision, see Business Brief 15/92, issued on 5 October 1992.)

43.127   **Expenditure relating to transfer of freehold of airport—rental income received prior to any taxable supply.**   In October 1988 a company (F) acquired the freehold of Eastleigh Airport, which had previously been owned by a Jersey company. Both before and after the acquisition, the airport was leased to the British

Airports Authority. In March 1989, F sold a 50% interest in the airport to another company (R) for £30 million. F and R applied for planning permission to develop the airport as a 'business park'. F reclaimed the input tax on fees which it had incurred in respect of its acquisition of the airport. The Commissioners issued an assessment to recover the tax, since the rental income which F received in respect of the airport was exempt from VAT. F appealed, contending that it intended to make taxable supplies in the future, and that the input tax should be apportioned to take account of this. The tribunal held that the input tax should be apportioned, applying *Briararch Ltd*, 43.125 above, and *Curtis Henderson Ltd*, 43.126 above. In making the apportionment, residual input tax which could not be directly apportioned to either exempt or taxable supplies should be apportioned on the basis that the proposed 'business park' development had a value of £35 million and that the rest of the airport had a value of £15 million. *Findhelp Ltd, [1991] VATTR 341 (VTD 6431, 7015).*

43.128   **Building initially used for exempt supplies—subsequently used for taxable supplies—adjustment of attribution.**   A university constructed two buildings. It began to use the buildings, in making exempt supplies of educational services, in October 1990. In April 1992, on the advice of its accountants, it leased the buildings to an associated company for a 20–year period, and elected to waive exemption. In its return for the period ending 31 July 1992, it reclaimed 93% of the input tax on the construction of the buildings. The Commissioners issued an assessment to recover part of the tax, considering that since 51% of the university's income for the year ending July 1990 had been standard-rated, only 51% of the input tax was allowable. The university appealed, contending that 93% of the input tax on the first building (and 97% of the tax on the second building) should be treated as deductible since, on a time-apportionment basis, the buildings had been used for exempt supplies for no more than 18 months and were to be used for taxable supplies for at least 20 years. The QB rejected this contention and upheld the assessment. Carnwath J held that the effect of the company's contentions would be that adjustments to recoverable input tax could be made without any time limit as long as a building existed. Such a result would lead to an unacceptable degree of uncertainty, and was contrary to the spirit of the *EC Sixth Directive*, which contemplated a capital goods adjustment period of not more than ten years. The provisions of the *VAT Regulations* permitted specific adjustments for a period of up to six years, and were in accordance with *Article 20* of the *EC Sixth Directive*, which permitted Member States to lay down procedures as to the input tax to be allowed. *C & E Commrs v University of Wales College Cardiff, QB [1995] STC 611.*

43.129   A group of insurance companies held the leasehold of a number of properties. The group had originally used the properties for the purposes of its insurance business, but subsequently vacated them, and decided to sublet them. In 1995 it elected to waive exemption in respect of the properties. It subsequently claimed a repayment of input tax incurred on rents and service charges relating to the properties prior to the election, while they were vacant, although it had initially attributed this input tax to exempt supplies. The Commissioners rejected the claim and the representative member of the group appealed, contending that it was entitled to make an adjustment under *VAT Regulations 1995 (SI 1995 No 2518), reg 109*. The Ch D accepted this contention and allowed the appeal. Park J held that, within the six-year period prescribed by *reg 109*, the group had 'formed an intention to use the inputs in making taxable supplies'. The rents which the group paid while the properties were vacant 'were cost components of the taxable supplies' which the group subsequently made. There was a 'direct and immediate link' between the relevant inputs and outputs. Accordingly, the group was entitled to recover the input tax. *Royal & Sun Alliance Insurance Group plc v C & E Commrs, Ch D [2000] STC 933.*

43.130   **Bank reclaiming input tax on obsolete stationery.**   A banking company, which was partly exempt, had a large quantity of stationery which became obsolete. It supplied this to a scrap paper merchant to be destroyed. It reclaimed input tax in respect of the stationery. The Commissioners issued an assessment to recover the tax. The bank appealed, contending that it should be entitled to recover the tax under *VAT Regulations 1995 (SI 1995 No 2518), reg 109*. The tribunal rejected this contention and dismissed the appeal. *Nationwide Building Society*, 57.1 SELF-SUPPLY, was distinguished, on the grounds that it related to a building society which had printed its own stationery, whereas the bank here purchased printed stationery. On the evidence, the bank could not prove 'in connection with any particular supply, what provisional attribution was made, and what was the final use of each of the items in any particular supply ... in the absence of such proof, the Commissioners could not reasonably be satisfied that (the bank) was entitled to adjust under *regulation 109*'. Furthermore, *reg 109* did not apply because each supply of stationery to the bank was a single composite supply, and the bank had 'simply used some of the goods comprised in the supply for a different taxable supply from the one originally intended'. *Halifax plc, MAN/98/282 (VTD 16697)*.

43.131   **Construction work undertaken for purpose of exempt supplies—change in law to make such supplies zero-rated from March 1995—whether attribution of input tax to exempt supplies may be adjusted.**   In 1994 a construction company incurred expenditure on the construction of penthouse apartments to be let on long leases. Such supplies were exempt under the legislation then in force, but became zero-rated from 1 March 1995, following the *VAT (Construction of Buildings) Order 1995 (SI 1995 No 280)*. In June 1995 the company submitted a claim for the input tax to be attributed to taxable supplies. The Commissioners rejected the claim and the tribunal dismissed the company's appeal, holding that 'a change of law cannot affect prior attributions of input tax'. *Perna*, 43.58 above, and *Gulland Properties*, 43.138 below, applied. *Martin's Properties (Chelsea) Ltd, LON/95/2945A (VTD 14092)*.

EXCEPTIONAL CLAIMS FOR VAT RELIEF (VAT Regulations 1995, reg 111)

Note. With regard to the Commissioners' interpretation of what is now *VAT Regulations 1995 (SI 1995 No 2518), reg 111*, see Business Brief 30/93, issued on 24 September 1993.

43.132   **Company registering for VAT on 1 April 1987 (when partial exemption rules changed) and claiming input tax incurred before registration—whether old or new method of attribution applicable.**   A company registered for VAT with effect from 1 April 1987. In its first return, it reclaimed input tax which it had incurred before registration, in accordance with what is now *VAT Regulations 1995 (SI 1995 No 2518), reg 111*. The company was partly exempt, and calculated the deductible amount of the input tax in question under the partial exemption rules in force up to 31 March 1987. The Commissioners formed the opinion that, since the company had not registered for VAT until 1 April 1987, it should have calculated its deductible input tax under the revised rules introduced from that date, and calculated the repayable amount accordingly. The tribunal dismissed the company's appeal against this decision, holding that, since there had been no entitlement to reclaim the relevant input tax until after the change in the input tax rules on 1 April 1987, it followed that the deductible input tax had to be calculated under the rules in force from that date. *Perna*, 43.58 above, distinguished. *St George's Home Co Ltd, MAN/90/876 (VTD 10213)*.

43.133   **Input tax reclaimed on pre-registration supplies—whether deductible under regulation 111*.**   A trader who provided financial services registered for VAT from April 1993. Most of his supplies were exempt from VAT but he also made a few taxable supplies. He reclaimed input tax on office equipment which he had purchased between 1988 and 1992. The Commissioners rejected his claim and he appealed, contending that the input tax should be treated as deductible under what is now *VAT Regulations 1995 (SI 1995 No 2518), reg 111*. The tribunal dismissed his appeal, holding that the office equipment had been almost exclusively used for making exempt supplies and that, since he had not reclaimed the tax at the time it became chargeable, the effect of *Article 18(3)* of the *EC Sixth Directive* was that the Commissioners had a discretion as to whether to allow the claim to input tax. The tribunal chairman observed that *regulation 111** did not specify how the pre-registration inputs of a partly exempt trader should be treated, and held that the Commissioners' policy of using a direct attribution method for all such claims was justified, since 'partial exemption involves complicated calculations which are not appropriate to unregistered traders who may not have kept the right records for the purpose'. (The chairman also commented that 'this case is what might be termed the pre-registration toothbrush trick but applied to the financial services industry'.) *T Douros (t/a Olympic Financial Services), LON/93/2523A (VTD 12454).*

43.134   *Douros*, 43.133 above, was applied in the similar subsequent case of *M Jenkins (t/a Lifetime Financial Services), LON/96/3072 (VTD 14784).*

43.135   An insurance broker also supplied photocopying and fax facilities. His turnover from his insurance brokerage, which was accepted as being exempt from VAT, exceeded £60,000 per annum. His receipts from photocopying and fax facilities were between £500 and £600 per annum. He registered for VAT with effect from April 1992. In his first return he reclaimed input tax on various items of office equipment which he had purchased since September 1987. The Commissioners rejected the claim, on the basis that what is now *VAT Regulations 1995 (SI 1995 No 2518), reg 111* only permitted the claiming of pre-registration input tax which had been incurred for the purposes of making taxable supplies. The broker appealed, contending that the combined effect of *regs 106** and *111** was that the tax should be treated as deductible. The tribunal dismissed the appeal, applying *dicta* in *Douros*, 43.133 above, and holding that *regulation 111** was 'a free-standing provision notwithstanding that it is to be found in *(Part XIV*)* of the *(VAT Regulations*)*'. The Commissioners' exercise of their discretion not to allow the input tax had not been unreasonable, and did not contravene *Article 18* of the *EC Sixth Directive*. The broker had been 'a taxable person for the purposes of the *Sixth Directive* before he became a taxable person for the purposes of *VATA*'. His right to deduct input tax in accordance with *Article 17* of the *Sixth Directive* had arisen 'when the supplies to him were used for the purposes of his taxable transactions'. At that time he had chosen to be treated as exempt from tax under *Article 24*. Accordingly, the effect of *Article 24(5)* was that he was not entitled to deduct the tax in question. The tribunal observed that 'it is consistent with the *Sixth Directive* and the observations in *Rompelman* (see 21.59 EUROPEAN COMMUNITY LAW) for the Commissioners to restrict credit to so much of the tax claimed as can be demonstrated to have been used for the purposes of his taxable transactions'. *GN Byrd (t/a GN Byrd & Co), MAN/93/1433 (VTD 12675).*

43.136   A company which operated a nursery school registered for VAT from August 1993. Most of its supplies were exempt from VAT. However, it also supplied swimming lessons, sold sweatshirts, and hired its premises for children's parties. These supplies were accepted as taxable. In its first return it reclaimed input tax on supplies which it had received before registration. The Commissioners rejected the claim, on the basis that pre-registration input tax was only reclaimable if it was directly attributable to taxable supplies. The company appealed, contending that the tax should be treated as deductible under what is now *VAT Regulations 1995 (SI 1995 No 2518), reg 111*. The tribunal dismissed the appeal, applying *Douros*, 43.133 above. *Merseyside Cablevision Ltd*, 34.444 INPUT TAX, distinguished. *Jolly Tots Ltd, MAN/93/1356 (VTD 13087)*.

43.137   **Expenditure incurred when business exempt from VAT and unregistered—business becoming liable to VAT and registered accordingly—whether input tax reclaimable.**   A nursing home opened in April 1991 but was unsuccessful. In May 1992 the proprietors ceased to use the building as a nursing home and opened it as a licensed hotel. In October 1992 they registered for VAT. They reclaimed input tax on expenditure which they had incurred while the building was used as a nursing home. The Commissioners rejected the claim and the proprietors appealed, contending that the input tax should be treated as deductible under what is now *VAT Regulations 1995 (SI 1995 No 2518), reg 111*. The tribunal dismissed the appeal, holding that the tax was not deductible since it had been used for the purpose of making exempt supplies and there had been no intention to make taxable supplies at the time the expenditure was incurred. *Neuvale Ltd*, 43.14 above, and *Byrd*, 43.135 above, applied. *R Reading & R Crabtree (t/a Mostyn Lodge Hotel), MAN/93/1353 (VTD 12756)*.

43.138   A similar decision was reached in *Gulland Properties, LON/95/370A (VTD 13955)*.

43.139   **Claim to pre-registration input tax—Commissioners refusing to authorise claim under VAT Regulations 1995, reg 111*—whether within jurisdiction of tribunal.**   See *Barar & Barar (t/a Turret House Rest Home)*, 2.70 APPEALS.

43.140   **Claim to pre-registration input tax—effect of VAT Regulations 1995, reg 111(2)*.**   See *Burgess & Holmes*, 34.474 INPUT TAX.

43.141   **Claim to pre-registration input tax—application of VAT Regulations 1995, reg 111(3)*.**   A trader registered for VAT in 1995. He reclaimed input tax under *VAT Regulations 1995 (SI 1995 No 2518), reg 111* in respect of an invoice purportedly issued by a company he controlled, which had ceased trading (and had been struck off of the Register of Companies six days before the date of the invoice). The Commissioners rejected the claim and the tribunal dismissed the trader's appeal. *Reg 111(3)* provided that a claim had to be supported by 'invoices and other evidence'. The Commissioners had to be satisfied that the company had made a supply to the trader for consideration. The trader had failed to provide 'satisfactory evidence' of the purported supply. *NR Corke, LON/98/1125 (VTD 16832)*.

43.142   **VAT Regulations 1995, reg 111(5)—claim for repayment after deregistration.**   A couple who operated a nursing home deregistered for VAT, and subsequently submitted a claim for repayment of input tax relating to professional advice. The Commissioners rejected the claim on the basis that the tax in question was attributable to the general overheads of the business, rather than to taxable supplies. The tribunal dismissed the couple's appeal against this decision. *Mr & Mrs L Jones, MAN/97/1027 (VTD 15595)*.

44 Partnership

The cases in this chapter are arranged under the following headings.

Partnership assessments 44.1–44.5
Partnership appeals 44.6
Partnership registration 44.7–44.8
Whether a partnership exists 44.9–44.38
Miscellaneous 44.39–44.45

PARTNERSHIP ASSESSMENTS

44.1   **Assessment issued in partnership name.**   A restaurant was registered for VAT as a partnership of three people. A control visit took place in November 1986 and the VAT officer was told by the partnership's accountant that one of the partners had left. The VAT office wrote to the partner in question but received no reply. Subsequently an assessment was raised on the partnership, in the partnership name, charging tax on undeclared takings. The partnership did not dispute the amount of the assessment, but lodged an appeal, contending that the assessment was invalid because it was issued in the partnership name and a partnership was not an entity in English law. The tribunal rejected this contention and dismissed the appeal. The partnership here was at fault in not having notified the Commissioners of the partnership change in writing, as required by what is now *VAT Regulations 1995 (SI 1995 No 2518), reg 4*. The issue of an assessment in the partnership name was in accordance with the requirements of what is now *VATA 1994, s 45*. *The Bengal Brasserie, [1991] VATTR 210 (VTD 5925)*.

44.2   An assessment in a partnership name was held to be valid, notwithstanding a change in the members of the partnership, in *Eleanor Cleaning Services, LON/93/652 (VTD 11353)*.

44.3   Similar decisions, applying *The Bengal Brasserie*, 44.1 above, were reached in *JE, JH & AG Jones (t/a S Jones & Son), LON/93/2663A (VTD 13308)* and *Oysters Fish Bar, MAN/96/1256 (VTD 16203)*.

44.4   **Change of partnership—old partner continuing in new partnership.**   A partnership which operated a Chinese restaurant decided to sell it as a going concern. The purchaser decided to take one of the old partners into partnership with him. The Commissioners issued an assessment on the basis that there had been no sale of the business, merely a change of partners. The tribunal allowed the new partners' appeal, holding that the new partnership was a separate entity so that what is now *VATA 1994, s 45* had no application and a new registration number should have been issued. *Hoi Shan Chinese Restaurant, LON/86/299 (VTD 2368)*.

44.5   **Assessment of penalty under VATA 1994, s 60.**   See *Akbar & Others*, 47.5 PENALTIES: EVASION OF TAX; *Standard Tandoori Nepalese Restaurant*, 47.6 PENALTIES: EVASION OF TAX, and *Santi Bag Restaurant*, 47.62 PENALTIES: EVASION OF TAX.

PARTNERSHIP APPEALS

44.6   **Appeal delayed by illness of partner.**   See *Hornby*, 2.148 APPEALS.

PARTNERSHIP REGISTRATION

44.7   Separate businesses carried on by the same individuals in partnership. See *Glassborow and Another*, 53.1 REGISTRATION, and the cases noted at 53.2 to 53.4 REGISTRATION.

44.8   Limited partnerships comprising one limited partner and one general partner—whether entitled to separate registrations. Two individuals each practised as a patent agent on his own, one in Middlesex and the other in Kent. Each was registered for VAT. In order to protect their respective practices should either die or be incapacitated, they entered into reciprocal arrangements under which each formed a partnership with the other as a limited partner. The limited partner contributed £250 as capital but drew no profits and took no part in the management of the practice. The partnership was to terminate on the death or incapacity of the general partner, but the limited partner was then required to offer his services to the business for up to six months so as to preserve the goodwill pending sale. The Commissioners issued a ruling that the two businesses should be covered by the same registration (in the name of either firm). The choice between the two firms was left to the two individuals, who appealed against the decision. The tribunal allowed their appeals, distinguishing *Glassborow*, 53.1 REGISTRATION, on the grounds that it related to general partnerships. A limited partner, taking no part in the management of the business, could not be said to have made taxable supplies in the course of that business. Furthermore, he did not carry on the business in partnership 'within the meaning and intent' of what is now *VATA 1994, s 45(1)*, so that since each of the limited partnerships was carried on by a different active partner, each was entitled to a separate registration. *H Saunders & T G Sorrell, [1980] VATTR 53 (VTD 913)*.

WHETHER A PARTNERSHIP EXISTS

44.9   Country club—whether operated as a partnership. The Commissioners issued an assessment on a country club in Cornwall which had been registered for VAT as a partnership between two individuals, L and C. C appealed, contending that she was not a partner and that L was the sole proprietor. It was accepted that the club had been run by L as the sole proprietor until 1975, when C moved to the club. Later that year L moved to the USA, although he told C that he intended to return in the near future. The club's bank account remained in L's sole name, but C had authority to sign cheques. C had told a VAT officer in 1976 that she was in partnership with L, and the club had been registered accordingly. C had also signed form VAT2 as a partner. At the hearing C produced a letter from L, who was still in the USA, stating that he had never taken her into partnership in the club. The tribunal dismissed C's appeal, finding that she had acted as a partner in her dealings with the Commissioners, and had been responsible for the operation of the club since late 1975 when L had left the country. The fact that L and C had subsequently claimed not to be in partnership was not conclusive, applying *dicta* of Cozens-Hardy MR in *Weiner v Harris, CA [1910] 1 KB 285*. On the evidence, C had been in partnership with L in running the business of the club. *B Leighton-Jones & A Craig (t/a Saddletramps), CAR/77/231 (VTD 597)*.

44.10   Health club—whether operated as a partnership. The proprietor of a health club failed to account for output tax on income from aerobics classes at the club. The Commissioners issued an assessment charging tax on them, and he appealed, contending that the aerobics was a separate business which he carried on in partnership with his father (who had lent him money to help finance the club). The tribunal rejected this contention and upheld the assessment, observing that there was no written partnership agreement and that the proprietor's father 'played no part in the conduct or management of the aerobics activities'. The QB dismissed the proprietor's appeal against this decision. On the evidence, the tribunal decision was not in any way unreasonable. *Associated Provincial Picture Houses v Wednesbury Corporation, CA 1947, [1948] 1 KB 223; [1947] 2 All ER 680*, applied. *RJ Burrell (t/a The Firm) v C & E Commrs, QB [1997] STC 1413.*

44.11   **Hairdresser—alleged partnership with sons.**   The Commissioners registered a hairdresser on the basis that he was the proprietor of two salons. He appealed, contending that he was only the sole proprietor of one of the salons, and that he was operating the second salon in partnership with his three sons, all of whom were below the age of 18. The tribunal rejected this contention and dismissed his appeal, finding that he was the sole proprietor of both salons, and observing that the existence of a partnership requires a consensus between the partners which was entirely lacking in this case. *JP Bridgeman, MAN/81/162 (VTD 1206).*

44.12   **Hairdressers—whether trading in partnership.**   Four women carried on business as hairdressers from a salon in Blackpool. The Commissioners issued a notice of compulsory registration on the basis that they were trading in partnership. They appealed, contending that they were trading as individuals and not as a partnership, and were not required to register as their individual turnover was below the registration threshold in each case. The tribunal accepted this contention and allowed their appeal. On the evidence, the business had 'very little passing or casual trade' and each hairdresser had 'her own established clientele which she has built up over the years'. Customers were 'not attracted to the salon but to the individual stylist by word of mouth and recommendation'. The hairdressers were each conducting their own business from shared premises, and the fact that they shared certain overheads did not mean that they were trading in partnership. *C Hunter, A Kiernan, M Wigglesworth & LA Wright, MAN/99/376 (VTD 16558).*

44.13   **Husband and wife trading in partnership—whether wife also carrying on separate business.**   A married couple operated a public house in partnership. They did not account for output tax on receipts from catering at the public house, and the Commissioners issued an assessment charging tax on these receipts. The couple appealed, contending that the catering was a separate business, carried on by the wife as a sole trader, and that VAT was not chargeable because these receipts were below the limits of *Sch 1 para 1*. The tribunal accepted the couple's evidence and allowed their appeal, holding that the catering was a separate business. *P & V Marner, MAN/77/140 (VTD 443). (Notes.* (1) The Commissioners might now have recourse to a direction under *VATA 1994, Sch 1 para 2*. For cases concerning this provision, see 53.95 *et seq.* REGISTRATION. (2) See also *Smith & Smith*, 44.14 below, and the cases noted at 53.136 to 53.138 REGISTRATION.)

44.14   The decision in *Marner*, 44.13 above, was not followed in a subsequent case where a married couple who operated a public house did not account for VAT on supplies of catering and accommodation, and claimed that these were a separate business carried on by the wife. The tribunal reviewed the evidence in detail and applied *dicta* of Lord Lindley (see *Lindley & Banks on Partnership, 17th edition, para 16.28*) that 'a partner ... is not allowed in transacting the partnership affairs, to carry on for his own sole benefit any separate trade or business which, were it not for his connection with the partnership, he would not have been in a position to carry on. Bound to do his best for the firm, he is not at liberty to labour for himself to their detriment; and if his connection with the firm enables him to acquire gain, he cannot appropriate that gain to himself on the pretence that it arose from a separate transaction with which the firm had nothing to do.' Accordingly, the use of the public house for catering and accommodation was a partnership activity 'unless the partners arrived at a clearly defined commercial arrangement whereunder (the wife) alone were to benefit from them'. On the evidence, 'there was no arrangement in this case operating to separate the catering and accommodation activities from the rest of the activities of the public house'. *J & Mrs SF Smith (t/a The Salmon Tail), MAN/99/213 (VTD 16190)*.

44.15   *Smith*, 44.14 above, was applied in the similar subsequent case of *AE & Mrs ME Fraser, LON/99/453 (VTD 16761)*.

44.16   A married couple were registered for VAT as proprietors of a car hire business. The Commissioners discovered that they had not accounted for VAT on contract work, and issued an assessment charging tax. The couple appealed, contending that the contract work was a separate business, carried on by the wife as a sole trader. The tribunal rejected this contention and dismissed the appeal, holding on the evidence that 'there was in reality only one business'. *W & B Brough (t/a Chaddy Cars), MAN/98/702 (VTD 16700)*.

44.17   **Husband and wife trading in partnership—whether husband also carrying on separate business.**   See *Jackson*, 44.20 below, and *Parker & Parker*, 53.162 REGISTRATION.

44.18   **Husband and wife—whether trading in partnership.**   The Commissioners issued an assessment in respect of the takings of a driving school and of a motor accessories shop. The assessment was made on the basis that both activities were a single business carried on by a married couple in partnership. The husband appealed, contending that the driving school was a separate business, carried on by him alone. The tribunal allowed the appeal, holding on the evidence that the two activities comprised a single business and that the husband was the sole proprietor of both the driving school and the shop, so that the assessment was invalid. There was no profit-sharing, and the wife had no share in the capital of the business. The tribunal observed that 'especially as between husband and wife ... there should, in order to establish a legal partnership, be some positive contractual evidence'. *PI & JY Cooper, LON/81/325 (VTD 1218)*.

44.19   A married woman was registered for VAT as the proprietor of a public house. She was subsequently declared bankrupt. The Commissioners formed the opinion that the public house had in fact been operated by the woman and her husband in partnership. They issued an amended certificate of registration and an assessment accordingly. The couple appealed, contending that the wife had run the public house as a sole trader with her husband acting as an employee. The tribunal rejected this contention and dismissed the appeal, holding on the evidence that the couple had traded in partnership. *R & Mrs J Wilson (t/a Mountain View Hotel), MAN/98/639 (VTD 16404)*.

44.20   An individual (R) was registered for VAT as the proprietor of a retail shop. In May 1981 a small amusement arcade was opened at the same premises. R did not account for output tax on takings from the machines, but reclaimed input tax on their purchase. The Commissioners discovered this and discovered that accounts had been drawn up showing that the shop was operated by a partnership of R and his wife, rather than by R as a sole trader. They therefore issued an assessment to recover the tax. R appealed, contending that, notwithstanding the accounts which had been submitted to the Inland Revenue, he remained the sole proprietor of the shop and had purchased the machines in this capacity and had hired them to a separate partnership business comprising himself and his wife, the turnover of which was below the VAT registration threshold. The tribunal reviewed the evidence and dismissed the appeal, holding that the shop was run by R and his wife in partnership but that R was the sole proprietor of the amusement arcade. The tribunal held that the purported rental of the machines was 'an afterthought' and that the partnership had not purchased the amusement machines for the purpose of the retail shop business. Accordingly the partnership was not entitled to reclaim input tax on the purchase. *RD & SL Jackson, LON/85/70 (VTD 1959)*. (*Note*. See also *VATA 1994, Sch 1 para 2*, deriving from *FA 1986*. The effect of a direction under this provision would be that output tax would now be chargeable on the takings from the amusement machines.)

44.21 A husband and wife traded as newsagents in partnership, and were registered for VAT accordingly. Subsequently the husband began a shopfitting business, which occupied him for at least 40 hours per week. His wife kept the books and records for this business, but there was no formal partnership agreement. The Commissioners considered that the husband was operating the shopfitting business as a sole trader and should be registered as such. He appealed, contending that the business was a partnership between him and his wife. The tribunal dismissed his appeal, holding that his wife was assisting him under an informal domestic arrangement which fell short of being a partnership. *VJ Britton, [1986] VATTR 209 (VTD 2173)*.

44.22 A married couple purchased a shop as a going concern in 1988. Their takings were lower than they had anticipated, and in 1991 the husband purchased a car hire business with money he had received on being made redundant from a previous employment. They submitted accounts to the Inland Revenue indicating that both the shop and the car hire business were run as a partnership (with the husband being allocated most of the profit from the car hire business, and the profits and losses of the shop being split equally). The couple did not register for VAT, and in 1998 the Commissioners issued a notice of compulsory registration. The couple appealed, contending that, notwithstanding the accounts which they had submitted to the Inland Revenue, the car hire business was actually being run by the husband as a sole trader while the shop was run by the wife as a sole trader. The tribunal rejected this contention and dismissed the appeal, observing that they had signed the accounts as partners and that 'the accounts are more likely to have shown the true position'. *Britton, 44.21 above, distinguished. CD & MD Gow, LON/99/28 (VTD 16272)*.

44.23 A married couple, who traded from a café at a seaside resort, did not register for VAT. The Commissioners issued a retrospective notice of compulsory registration. The couple appealed, contending that the husband was operating the café as a sole trader while the sale of ice creams for consumption off the premises was a separate business, carried on by the wife as a sole trader. The tribunal rejected this contention, holding on the evidence that the couple were trading in partnership. *Cooper, 44.18 above, distinguished. PC & VL Leonidas, LON/97/1594 (VTD 16588)*. (*Notes*. (1) The tribunal allowed the couple's appeal against a penalty for failure to register—see 48.31 PENALTIES: FAILURE TO NOTIFY. (2) For another issue in this case, see 55.10 RETURNS.)

44.24 A management consultant, who was registered for VAT, owned a flat which was let as holiday accommodation. He did not account for output tax on his income from this, and the Commissioners issued an assessment. He appealed, contending that the letting of the flat should be treated as a partnership between him and his wife. The tribunal dismissed his appeal, holding that the burden of proof was on the appellant and finding that he had not produced evidence to show that his wife took any part in the management of the business. The fact that he had paid some of the rental income to his wife was not conclusive. *AG Pole, LON/94/2467A (VTD 13225)*.

44.25 **Joint venture agreement—whether a partnership.** A company (S) carried on a management consultancy business and also engaged in property development. It did not account for tax on its receipts from property development and the Commissioners issued an assessment. S appealed, contending that its receipts were remuneration for joint ventures which amounted to a partnership. The tribunal dismissed S's appeal, holding that participation in joint venture agreements did not amount to a partnership. The fact that S had only received a specified percentage of the total profits was not conclusive. The essential requirements of a partnership were not fulfilled. S had agreed to supervise the work carried out and this was a taxable supply of services. *Strathearn Gordon Associates Ltd, [1985] VATTR 79 (VTD 1884)*.

44.26   A company (K) carried on the business of property development. It received commission of £125,000 from a larger company (L) with which it had made a profit-sharing agreement, but did not account for VAT on this. The Commissioners issued an assessment and K appealed, contending that it had been in partnership with L. The tribunal dismissed K's appeal, holding that although it had entered into a profit-sharing agreement with L, and had supplied services to L, this did not amount to a partnership. *Strathearn Gordon Associates*, 44.25 above, applied. *Keydon Estates Ltd, LON/88/1225X (VTD 4471)*.

44.27   A company (F) carried on the business of property development. It entered into a joint venture agreement with a larger company (C) under which it was to receive £75,000 plus 5% of the profits of the venture. It did not account for VAT on its receipts under the agreement, and the Commissioners issued an assessment. F appealed, contending that the agreement amounted to a partnership. The tribunal dismissed F's appeal, applying *Strathearn Gordon Associates*, 44.25 above, and *Keydon Estates Ltd*, 44.26 above, and holding that the agreement did not amount to a partnership. *Fivegrange Ltd, LON/89/1631Y (VTD 5338)*.

44.28   *Strathearn Gordon Associates*, 44.25 above, *Keydon Estates Ltd*, 44.26 above, and *Fivegrange Ltd*, 44.27 above, were applied in the similar subsequent case of *Forestmead Ltd, LON/98/219 (VTD 15852)*.

44.29   **Partnership operating hotel—whether catering operated by partnership or by one partner as individual.**   See *Albert*, 53.140 REGISTRATION.

44.30   **Partnership owning fish and chip shop—whether mobile van operated by partnership or by one partner as individual.**   See *Insley & Clayton*, 58.272 SUPPLY.

44.31   **Builders—whether trading in partnership.**   See *Malin & Malin*, 48.30 PENALTIES: FAILURE TO NOTIFY.

44.32   **Bookmakers—alleged partnership.**   See *SP Graham Ltd & Others*, 53.54 REGISTRATION.

44.33   **Partnership of musicians—whether supplies of tuition services made as individuals or by partnership.**   See *Alberni String Quartet*, 20.2 EDUCATION.

44.34   **Partnership operating retail shop—invoices issued for graphic design services—whether relevant supplies made by partnership or by individual partner.**   See *W & J Tang (t/a Ziploc)*, 58.248 SUPPLY.

44.35   **Partnership operating retail shop—undeclared wholesale supplies to other traders—whether relevant supplies made by partnership or by individual partner.**   See *M & N Singh*, 58.249 SUPPLY.

44.36   **Partnership operating restaurant—kitchen also used for take-away sales from adjacent premises.**   See *Yung*, 58.250 SUPPLY.

44.37   **Whether partnership temporarily discontinued.**   See *Barnett & Larsen*, 49.285 PENALTIES: MISDECLARATION.

44.38   **Other cases.**   There are a number of other cases, which appear to raise no point of general importance, in which the issue has been whether a partnership existed. Such cases turn entirely on their own facts and, in the interests of space, are not summarised individually in this book. For a list of such cases decided up to 31 October 1990, see Tolley's VAT Cases 1991.

MISCELLANEOUS

44.39 Partnership debt—validity of bankruptcy order against one member of partnership. A married couple operated a wine business in partnership. There was no formal partnership deed. The partnership failed to account for substantial amounts of VAT, and the Commissioners served statutory demands on both partners. The husband made an individual voluntary arrangement with his creditors under *Insolvency Act 1986, Part VIII*. However the wife's creditors rejected a similar proposal, and in March 1994 the wife (who was engaged in matrimonial proceedings against her husband) was declared bankrupt. The CA dismissed her appeal against the order. *Article 15(3)* of the *Insolvent Partnerships Order 1986* expressly dispensed with any need to couple the presentation of a bankruptcy petition with a petition to wind up the partnership. A creditor could rely on an admitted or indisputable debt, including one established by an unsatisfied statutory demand, as a proper basis for a bankruptcy petition. The joint debt of a partner was a debt owed by that partner for the purposes of *Insolvency Act 1986, s 267(1)*. The fact that one member of a partnership had entered into an individual voluntary arrangement did not protect other members of the partnership from enforcement by a partnership creditor against their separate estates. *VGM Schooler v C & E Commrs, CA 20 July 1995 unreported.*

44.40 Retirement of partner—subsequent VAT repayment to partnership—whether former partner entitled to share of repayment. From 1985 to 1992 two individuals (H and S) traded in partnership as opticians. In 1992 H retired. Subsequently S submitted a claim to Customs for repayment of overpaid VAT, and in January 1996 Customs made a substantial repayment. H took proceedings against S, claiming that he was entitled to a share of the part of the VAT repayment relating to the period when the business had been carried on in partnership. The QB accepted this contention and gave judgment for H, holding that the terms of the partnership deed did not bar H from his right to a share in the repayment. *Hawthorn v Smallcorn, Ch D [1998] STC 591.*

44.41 Supplies by firm to a partner—whether in course of firm's business. See *Border Flying Co*, 7.45 BUSINESS, and *RGB Contractors*, 34.211 INPUT TAX.

44.42 Partner's caravan partly used for purposes of partnership business—whether tax on costs ranks for partnership input tax. See *Smith Wheeler & Hay*, 34.65 INPUT TAX.

44.43 Retention of possession of leased car by outgoing partner—whether car used for purpose of business. See *Mrs Hague*, 34.95 INPUT TAX.

44.44 Partnership Act business—whether a business for VAT purposes. See *Three H Aircraft Hire*, 7.6 BUSINESS.

44.45 Family farming partnership—whether second dwelling-house on farm occupied by a partner used for the purposes of the business. See *Herrod-Taylor & Co*, 34.196 INPUT TAX.

45   Payment of Tax

The cases in this chapter are arranged under the following headings.

PAYMENT OF VAT CREDITS (VATA 1994, s 25)

45.1   **Application of VATA 1994, s 25.**   On the introduction of VAT, the Royal College of Obstetricians and Gynaecologists did not apply for registration, on the basis that its supplies were predominantly exempt. In 1995 its advisers became aware that it would have been to the College's advantage to register for VAT, as it had made taxable supplies and would have been able to recover significant amounts of input tax. It thereupon applied for registration in October 1995. The Commissioners accepted the application and issued a VAT return covering the period from 1 April 1973 to 31 December 1995. In January 1996 the College submitted the return, claiming a repayment of more than £640,000. On 18 July 1996 the Paymaster-General stated in Parliament that legislation was to be included in the 1997 Finance Bill to introduce a three-year limit for retrospective repayment claims with retrospective effect from 18 July 1996. Following this announcement, the Commissioners wrote to the College stating that they were only willing to repay £47,454. The College lodged an appeal against this ruling. The Commissioners applied for the appeal to be struck out, contending that the tribunal had no jurisdiction. The tribunal rejected this application holding that there was a dispute concerning 'the amount of input tax which may be credited', within *VATA 1994, s 83(c)*. The tribunal also allowed the College's appeal, observing that *VATA 1994* 'provides for no specified time within which, and no precise date by which, the Commissioners are required to make a payment found to be due from them to a taxpayer under *s 25*', but holding that the Commissioners had no 'discretion to delay or defer such a payment' and that *s 25* 'envisages that the Commissioners will diligently, expeditiously and scrupulously deal with any claim by a taxpayer'. *Royal College of Obstetricians and Gynaecologists, MAN/96/967 (VTD 14558)*. (*Note.* For a subsequent application for judicial review, see *R v C & E Commrs (ex p. Kay & Co Ltd and Others)*, 45.23 below.)

45.2   **Interaction of VATA 1994, s 25 and VATA 1994, s 80(4)—whether three-year time limit applicable to claims for repayment of input tax.**   See *BICC plc*, 45.26 below, and *Royal Bank of Scotland Group plc*, 45.28 below.

45.3 Payment of Tax

REPAYMENT OF TAX (VATA 1994, s 80)

Note. *VATA 1994, s 80*, which lays down the conditions under which a taxable person may claim recovery of overpaid VAT, was amended by *FA 1997, ss 46, 47*. *VATA 1994, s 80(3A)-(3C)*, which are intended to provide that a taxable person may not claim repayment if he does not intend to pass the repayment to his customers, were introduced by *FA 1997, s 46* with effect from 19 March 1997. *VATA 1994, s 80(4)* was amended by *FA 1997, s 47* to introduce a three-year time limit for retrospective repayment claims with effect from 18 July 1996. Cases relating to periods before 19 March 1997 should be read in the light of the changes in the legislation.

Recovery of overpaid VAT (VATA 1994, s 80(1))

45.3 **Goods supplied to building firm and resold to purchaser of bungalow—purchaser subsequently lodging repayment claim.** In 1988 an individual (W), who was not registered for VAT, purchased a new bungalow from a building firm. He also ordered a number of wardrobes, which were supplied to the building firm by a company (S) and installed in the bungalow. S went into receivership in April 1993. The accountancy firm which was appointed as receivers considered that the wardrobes could have been treated as zero-rated, and issued a purported credit note to the builders, observing in a covering letter that the credit note had no commercial value since there were no funds to pay unsecured creditors. In December 1993 W wrote to the Commissioners applying for a refund of the tax charged on the supply of the wardrobes under what is now *VATA 1994, s 80*. The Commissioners rejected the claim and he appealed to a tribunal. The tribunal dismissed his appeal, holding that he was not entitled to a repayment of tax since S had supplied the wardrobes to the building firm, rather than to W. W was not a person who had 'paid an amount to the Commissioners' within *s 80(1)*, and thus he had no right to claim repayment. *Williams & Glyns Bank Ltd*, 2.28 APPEALS, distinguished. (The tribunal also held that the wardrobes in question had been correctly treated as standard-rated, distinguishing *McLean Homes Midland Ltd*, 15.123 CONSTRUCTION OF BUILDINGS, ETC., and observed that the receivers had misunderstood the relevant law and had been wrong to issue the purported credit note.) *SH Wade, MAN/94/642 (VTD 13164)*.

45.4 **Output tax wrongly charged on surrender of lease—claim for repayment from Commissioners.** In February 1991 a company (E) paid another company (G) £17,250, including VAT of £2,250, in relation to the surrender of a lease. G subsequently went into receivership. Following the CJEC decision in *Lubbock Fine & Co*, 21.165 EUROPEAN COMMUNITY LAW, E formed the opinion that the surrender should have been treated as exempt. It claimed repayment of the £2,250 from the Commissioners. The Commissioners rejected the claim on the grounds that the tax had been accounted for by G rather than E, and that they had no power to refund the tax to anyone other than G. The tribunal dismissed E's appeal, holding that the claim was outside the scope of *VATA 1994, s 80*. *Aberdeen Estates Ltd, EDN/94/235 (VTD 13622)*.

45.5 **Repayment claim by optician—whether returns submitted on provisional basis—whether method of apportionment acceptable.** Prior to May 1995, the Commissioners treated the sale of spectacles by opticians as a single standard-rated supply. In August 1993, a tribunal held that, while the sale of spectacles was taxable, the services supplied by the optician who dispensed the spectacles was a separate supply which qualified for exemption. The Commissioners appealed against this decision, but it was upheld by the QB in March 1995 (see *Leightons Ltd*, 31.12 HEALTH AND WELFARE). In May 1995 the Commissioners announced that they had accepted the QB decision and would accept repayment claims on certain conditions (see Business Brief 8/95). Meanwhile, in January 1994, an optician who had apportioned his takings between exempt and taxable supplies until February 1993, but had accounted for tax on the whole of his takings from March 1993 to November 1993 in accordance with the Commissioners' instructions, submitted a repayment claim, backdated to August 1988. In the claim, he apportioned his takings on the basis that he had sold spectacles at a 33% mark-up, and that the remainder of his output tax (approximately 30%) related to his exempt supplies of dispensing services. The Commissioners rejected the claim, considering firstly that the repayment should be restricted to the nine-month period from March to November 1993, and secondly that the method of apportionment used in the claim was unacceptable. The optician appealed. The tribunal allowed the appeal in part, finding that the optician's returns for the periods from March 1993 had been submitted on a provisional basis, and holding firstly that the method of valuation used in the claim was acceptable and secondly that the optician was entitled to repayment of the amount claimed for the period from March 1993 to May 1995. (However, the tribunal rejected the claim for the period from August 1988 to February 1993, finding that the returns for those periods had not been provisional and that the method of apportionment used in those returns had also been acceptable.) *MWJ Green, LON/96/321 (VTD 14844)*. (*Note*. For the Commissioners' current practice with regard to the apportionment of opticians' income, see Business Brief 2/99, issued on 13 January 1999.)

45.6 **Repayment claim by optician—initial claim computed on provisional basis—subsequent claim based on different method of computation.** In July 1994, following the tribunal decision in *Leightons Ltd*, 31.12 HEALTH AND WELFARE, a company trading as opticians submitted a repayment claim. In March 1995, following the QB decision in that case, the Commissioners accepted the claim, and in June 1995 they repaid the company £258,000 plus interest. The company then wrote to the Commissioners, stating that its initial claim had been 'based on information produced by the industry prior to Business Brief 31A/93 ... (and) did not include contact lens dispensing fees'. In April 1996 the company submitted a second repayment claim, based on the 'full cost apportionment method' set out in Business Brief 8/95. The Commissioners rejected this claim on the basis that 'in order for a further claim to be entertained, there must have been an indication, at the time the first claim was submitted, that this was a provisional or interim claim' but there had been 'no mention ... that the records were unsatisfactory or likely to produce an inaccurate reflection of the dispensing element. The actual wording ... implies a pricing policy which makes an apportionment formula unnecessary'. The company appealed, contending that the initial claim had been submitted in order 'not to be prejudiced by any time limit which might be applicable to a claim for a refund' and that, at the relevant time, 'there was no authoritative information as to how any overpayment should be calculated'. The tribunal accepted this contention and allowed the company's appeal, observing that 'there is nothing on the face of *s 80* which in terms provides that only one claim may be made. If the claimant can show that tax has been overpaid, *prima facie* there is a liability on the Commissioners to repay it.' The initial claim did not give rise to *res judicata*, since 'there has been no adjudication on the claim by an independent authority'. There had been no specific agreement to calculate the amount of the overpaid tax by use of the method put forward in the initial claim, since 'what took place in fact took place pursuant to the provisions of a statute and it is inappropriate to seek to regard what occurred as amounting to a contract or binding agreement between the parties'. The company was not estopped from recalculating the amount of the overpayment, since it was 'impossible to see what detriment the Commissioners have suffered'. The initial repayment had not been 'made in reliance on any representation but in pursuance of the statutory obligation under *s 80(1)*'. *Hayward Gill & Associates Ltd, [1998] VATDR 352 (VTD 15635)*. (*Notes*. (1) For the Commissioners' current practice with regard to the apportionment of opticians' income, see Business Brief 2/99, issued on 13 January 1999. (2) The decision in this case was distinguished in the subsequent case of *CL Dyer & Co*, 45.7 below.)

45.7   *Hayward Gill & Associates*, 45.6 above, was distinguished in a subsequent case in which a partnership trading as opticians made an initial repayment claim in December 1993 and a subsequent claim, computed on a different basis, in September 1996. The tribunal held on the evidence that 'in no way can the method used to formulate the second claim be described as an "accurate" claim'. Customs had 'allowed themselves to be persuaded by the professional bodies representing opticians that they could in defined circumstances accept an apportionment based upon the cost-plus method in order to dispose of the past'. However, it was 'inherently impossible (except by accident) that a method relying on the mark-up on sundries (mostly contact lens solutions with sell-by dates and subject to wastage ...) will correctly identify the element in the price paid for spectacles that is attributable to the "hardware"'. The tribunal was 'not persuaded that the original claim did not produce a fair and reasonable attribution' and was satisfied that 'the second claim certainly did not produce one that was more fair and reasonable'. *CL Dyer & Co*, *LON/97/1013 (VTD 16053)*.

45.8   **Companies trading as car dealers—claim for repayment of tax attributable to free insurance.**   Two associated companies, which carried on business as car dealers, submitted claims for substantial repayments of output tax. The Commissioners repaid a small percentage of the amount claimed by one of the companies, but rejected the bulk of the claims, most of which related to supplies of 'free insurance' (i.e. insurance supplied to purchasers of cars for no extra charge). The companies appealed. The tribunal reviewed the evidence in detail and allowed the appeals in part. Where the companies sold cars directly to consumers, the effect of *Article 11A1(a)* of the *EC Sixth Directive* was that the companies were only required to account for output tax on the payments which they actually received, rather than on the invoice price, applying *dicta* of Hutchinson LJ in *Primback Ltd*, 54.39 RETAILERS' SPECIAL SCHEMES. The tribunal chairman (Mr. Wallace) held that 'it cannot be material that (the companies) paid the insurers, whereas in *Primback* the finance company deducted the cost of the credit when paying *Primback*'. However, this principle could not be extended to sales through independent dealers which were 'intermediaries in the supply chain'. The sales by the companies to such dealers 'were of goods only and did not include supplies of insurance by the insurers'. The fact that the companies had agreed to pay the relevant insurance was not conclusive, since 'it is difficult to see how the consideration for the supplies of cars to dealers could be affected by the separate supplies of insurance by the insurers to customers, neither of whom were party to the supplies in question'. *Elida Gibbs Ltd*, 21.130 EUROPEAN COMMUNITY LAW, was distinguished, since the decision in that case 'was based on a single chain of supply' and could not be extended 'so as to cover supplies by a third party where intermediaries are involved'. Additionally, the principle laid down by Hutchinson LJ 'cannot be applied to sales where the direct nexus between the supplier and customer receiving the third party supply is broken by the insertion of a finance company'. Furthermore the companies could not be treated as if they themselves were supplying insurers. On the evidence, the customers 'received the supplies direct from the insurers'. *Peugeot Motor Co plc; Citroen UK Ltd, LON/98/388 (VTD 16104)*. (*Note*. The Commissioners have appealed to the HL against the majority CA decision in *Primback Ltd*, and the HL has referred the case to the CJEC.)

Unjust enrichment (VATA 1994, s 80(3))

45.9   **VATA 1994, s 80(3)—whether repayment would lead to 'unjust enrichment'.**   A company carried on business as a dealer in car registration numberplates. In many such transactions, it acted on an agency basis, keeping registers of clients who wished to sell particular plates and of clients who wished to buy particular plates, and introducing the clients to each other in return for commission. The company accounted for VAT on the commission which it received. In May 1990 the Commissioners issued a ruling that the company was acting as a principal, rather than as an agent, in respect of such transactions, and should therefore account for VAT on the full sale price, rather than only on its commission. The company appealed, and in December 1991 the Commissioners belatedly accepted that the company was acting as an agent, and withdrew the disputed ruling. During the period for which the ruling was in force, however, the company had accounted for output tax on the full sale price in accordance with the ruling. Following the withdrawal of the ruling, the company submitted a claim for repayment of the amount which it had paid in accordance with the Commissioners' ruling, and which it would not have had to pay if the Commissioners had accepted that it was only liable to account for VAT on its commission. The Commissioners rejected the claim, considering that it would lead to the 'unjust enrichment' of the company, within what is now *VATA 1994, s 80(3)*. The tribunal allowed the company's appeal, finding that the company had lost potential customers through being forced to account for VAT on the full sale price, and holding that 'far from being enriched by repayment from the respondents, the appellants are no more than compensated for the loss of commission which they suffered'. *Tayside Numbers Ltd, [1992] VATTR 406 (VTD 8874)*. (*Note*. See now, however, *VATA 1994, s 80(3A)-(3C)*, introduced by *FA 1997, s 46* with effect from 19 March 1997.)

45.10   A partnership carried on business as a dealer in vehicle numberplates. In most of its transactions it acted as an agent, but in some cases it acted as an independent principal. For the year to 31 July 1990, it had accounted for output tax as if it had been acting as a principal in all its transactions. In 1995 it submitted a claim for repayment of the amount overpaid. The Commissioners rejected the claim on the basis that it would lead to 'unjust enrichment', and the partnership appealed. The tribunal allowed the appeal in principle, holding on the evidence that the partnership had suffered a loss of business as a result of having set its selling prices at VAT-inclusive amounts. *Tayside Numbers Ltd*, 45.9 above, applied. However, the tribunal also found that the claim submitted was excessive, holding that 'the VAT which the partnership should have accounted for in respect of a transaction should be calculated on the basis that the VAT-inclusive commission was equal to the difference between the amount paid by the partnership to the seller and the total amount paid by the purchaser inclusive of VAT but net of the DVLA fee'. *SJ & CA Frampton (t/a Framptons), LON/95/2438 (VTD 14065)*. (*Note*. See the note following *Tayside Numbers Ltd*, 45.9 above.)

45.11   Two companies went into voluntary liquidation and were deregistered. Subsequently the companies' liquidator discovered that the companies had accounted for VAT on some supplies which had qualified for zero-rating. In May 1992 he submitted repayment claims in respect of these supplies. The Commissioners rejected the claims, considering that the repayment would result in unjust enrichment, as the liquidator did not intend to pass the benefit of the repayment back to the customers. The liquidator appealed, contending that there would be no unjust enrichment since the funds would be distributed to the company's creditors. The tribunal dismissed the appeals, holding that, under the principles of natural justice, if the Commissioners were to repay the money to the liquidator, the liquidator should repay the money to the customers who had actually paid the VAT to the company. Since the liquidator was not proposing to refund the money to the original customers, but to distribute it in accordance with insolvency law, any repayment would result in 'unjust enrichment'. *Dicta* of the tribunal in *Lamdec Ltd*, 2.159 APPEALS, were regarded as *obiter*, and were not followed. *Creative Facility Ltd, MAN/92/1157; Oblique Press Ltd, MAN/92/1158 (VTD 10891)*.

45.12   A married couple were registered for VAT as the proprietors of a hotel and some holiday chalets. In April 1990 they signed a deed of partnership whereby one of their sons was accepted as a partner in the hotel business, but not in the chalet business. They did not notify the Commissioners of this change, and continued to account for VAT in respect of both businesses under the same registration number. In December 1992 they submitted a claim for repayment of the output tax for which they had accounted in respect of the chalet business, on the basis that the turnover of that business, if treated separately, was below the registration threshold. The Commissioners rejected the claim, considering that the effect of what is now *VATA 1994, s 80* was that no repayment was due. The tribunal dismissed the couple's appeal, holding that, since the couple did not intend to repay the VAT to the customers to whom they had originally charged it, any repayment to the couple would result in 'unjust enrichment'. *P & E Daynes, EDN/93/16 (VTD 10988)*.

45.13   A similar decision was reached in *Peterborough Diocesan Conference & Retreat House*, 31.44 HEALTH AND WELFARE.

45.14   A trust had paid a cricket club £70,000 as consideration for surrendering a lease. The club accounted for VAT (of £10,500) on this. However, following the decisions in *Lubbock Fine & Co*, 21.165 EUROPEAN COMMUNITY LAW, and *Grantham Cricket Club*, 39.53 LAND, the club formed the opinion that the payment should have been treated as exempt, and claimed repayment of the £10,500 from the Commissioners. The Commissioners rejected the claim under *VATA 1994, s 80(3)*, on the basis that repayment would unjustly enrich the club. The club appealed. The tribunal dismissed the appeal, holding on the evidence that the repayment would be unjust, since the VAT had been borne by the landlord and repayment would mean that the club 'would be in receipt of funds it would not have had in the first place and which it never expected to retain'. *Tayside Numbers Ltd*, 45.9 above, distinguished. *Grantham Cricket Club (No 2), MAN/97/465 (VTD 15527)*.

45.15   A golf club registered for VAT from 1973. For all its accounting periods until 1 April 1994, it accounted for output tax on its membership subscriptions as taxable supplies, and was allowed credit for input tax. On 1 April 1994 its membership subscriptions became exempt following the introduction of what is now *VATA 1994, Sch 9, Group 10* by *SI 1994 No 687*. This was intended to give effect to *Article 13A1(m)* of the *EC Sixth Directive*, which the UK should have implemented by 1 January 1990. Accordingly, under EC law, the requirement for the club to account for output tax was unlawful with effect from 1 January 1990. The club submitted a repayment claim, as invited by the Commissioners' News Release dated 10 March 1994. The Commissioners made a net repayment of the amount of wrongly-paid output tax reduced by the amount of input tax for which credit had been allowed. Subsequently the club submitted a further claim for the amount of the input tax. The Commissioners rejected the claim and the club appealed. The tribunal dismissed the appeal, holding that the club 'would be unjustly enriched if repaid an amount which has already been credited to or received by them as input tax'. Applying *Becker v Finanzamt Münster-Innenstadt*, 21.174 EUROPEAN COMMUNITY LAW, 'an individual who relies on the *(Sixth) Directive* as the source of his Community law right to exemption for his supplies must accept that this carries with it the corresponding disqualification of relief for input tax on goods and services used in making those supplies'. The club could not 'invoke *Article 13A1(m)* and claim exemption in isolation; it must accept as a concomitant "disadvantage", in asserting its Community law right to exemption, that deduction for input tax is not available'. The tribunal observed that 'where there is a net liability to output tax, it will never be appropriate for a taxable person to be "repaid" input tax by the Commissioners, since full credit for that input tax will already have been given. The most that they could ever be required to repay will be what has actually been paid over to them, namely the "gross" amount of output tax less the input tax properly recoverable against that tax by way of credit or deduction'. *Sunningdale Golf Club, [1997] VATDR 79 (VTD 14899)*.

45.16   A company owned seven department stores, parts of which it rented to tenants. In 1990 it informed the tenants that it had elected to waive exemption on the rents paid by such tenants, and following the election it accounted for output tax on the rents. In December 1992 the company went into receivership. The receivers discovered that the company had failed to notify the Commissioners of the election to waive exemption, and formed the opinion that the election was invalid under what is now *VATA 1994, Sch 10 para 3(6)*. They issued credit notes to the tenants, and reclaimed the output tax from the Commissioners. The Commissioners rejected the claim, considering that the credit notes did not comply with what is now *VAT Regulations 1995 (SI 1995 No 2518), reg 38*, and that, since the company was in liquidation, the tax should not be repaid on the grounds that to do so would result in 'unjust enrichment' within what is now *VATA 1994, s 80(3)*. The receivers appealed. The tribunal allowed the appeal, holding that the repayment would not result in unjust enrichment. The CS upheld this decision, holding that, although that the credit notes did not comply with what is now *reg 38**, the tax was correctly repayable under what is now *VATA 1994, s 80*. Lord Hope held that, although the repayment would result in the company's enrichment, the question of whether that enrichment was 'unjust' was 'a question of fact and degree which ought to be left to the decision of the tribunal, subject to review only where it can be shown that that decision was erroneous in point of law or on the facts was wholly unsustainable'. In the present case, the tribunal had been entitled to conclude that the company's enrichment would not be 'unjust'. *C & E Commrs v McMaster Scotland Stores Ltd (in receivership), CS [1995] STC 846. (Note.* See now *VATA 1994, s 80(3A)-(3C)*, introduced by *FA 1997, s 46* with effect from 19 March 1997.)

45.17   Until 1990 a building society accounted for VAT on fees which it received from its customers for producing title deeds. In 1990 the Commissioners issued a ruling that VAT was not chargeable on such fees. The society submitted a claim for repayment of the VAT for which it had accounted on such fees between 1979 and 1989. The Commissioners rejected the claim on the grounds that the repayment would 'unjustly enrich' the society, contrary to *VATA 1994, s 80(3)*, since the fees would not be returned to the society's customers. The tribunal allowed the society's appeal, holding that the repayment would not lead to unjust enrichment under the legislation then in force, on the grounds that the society had not reduced the fees after the ruling that VAT was not chargeable, but had retained the same fees and had increased its profit margins. *Daynes*, 45.12 above, distinguished. *National & Provincial Building Society, [1996] VATDR 153 (VTD 14017). (Note.* See now, however, *VATA 1994, s 80(3A)-(3C)*, introduced by *FA 1997, s 46* with effect from 19 March 1997.)

45.18   A trader (H) sold nuts, intended as bird food for wild birds, from a market stall. On the instructions of her local VAT office, she accounted for output tax on her sales. In 1995 the Commissioners issued a revised statement (see *Notice 701/15/95, para 16*) following which they accepted that H's sales qualified for zero-rating, since they were neither 'pet food' nor 'packaged'. H then submitted a claim for repayment of the tax for which she had accounted since 1974. The Commissioners rejected the claim on the basis that it would 'unjustly enrich' H, contrary to *VATA 1994, s 80(3)*. H appealed. The tribunal allowed her appeal in principle (subject to agreement on figures), holding on the evidence that the repayment would not 'unjustly enrich' H, since she had not fixed her prices by reference to the rate of VAT, and had not increased her prices when the VAT rate had increased in 1979 and 1991. *National & Provincial Building Society*, 45.17 above, applied. *DA Hardman, MAN/92/1424 (VTD 14045)*. *(Note*. See now, however, *VATA 1994, s 80(3A)-(3C)*, introduced by *FA 1997, s 46* with effect from 19 March 1997.)

45.19   A major retail company submitted two claims for repayment of substantial amounts of VAT. One of the claims related to sales of boys' socks for shoe sizes 4 to 7, which the company had treated as standard-rated until May 1995, although the Commissioners had accepted that they qualified for zero-rating from April 1994. The tribunal allowed the company's appeal with regard to this claim, observing that the company had not reduced its prices when it began to treat the socks as zero-rated, and holding on the evidence that the VAT had been absorbed by the company. The other claim related to sales of chocolate-covered teacakes, which the company had treated as standard-rated from 1973 until 1994, when the Commissioners accepted that they qualified for zero-rating. The Commissioners agreed to repay 10% of the amount claimed, but rejected the balance of the claim on the grounds that repayment would 'unjustly enrich' the company, contrary to *VATA 1994, s 80(3)*. The tribunal dismissed the company's appeal with regard to this claim, observing that the company had reduced its prices when it began to treat the teacakes as zero-rated, and holding on the evidence that the balance of the VAT had been passed on to the purchasers of the teacakes. The company appealed to the CA, which upheld the tribunal decision. The tribunal had been entitled to find on the evidence that the burden of VAT had been passed on to the company's customers, and that its imposition had caused no loss of profit. *Marks & Spencer plc v C & E Commrs, CA 1999, [2000] STC 16*. *(Notes*. (1) See the note following *Hardman*, 45.18 above. (2) For another issue in this case, see 45.32 below.)

45.20   A company sold standard forms of contract documents, principally relating to building contracts. In 1994 the Commissioners issued a ruling that sales of such documents did not qualify for zero-rating. Subsequently the Commissioners accepted that most of the documents qualified for zero-rating under *VATA 1994, Sch 8, Group 3, Item 1*. The company submitted a claim for repayment of tax on such supplies. The Commissioners agreed to pay a small percentage of the claim (slightly under 10%), but refused to repay the balance, on the grounds that the VAT had been borne by the company's customers and that repaying it to the company would lead to 'unjust enrichment'. The company appealed, contending that, since it had covenanted to pay its profits to the Royal Institute of British Architects, which was a registered charity, it would not be unjustly enriched by the repayment. The tribunal rejected this contention and dismissed the company's appeal, observing that 'this structure, whereby a charity puts its taxable trading activities into a separate trading company, which undertakes to make an annual payment back to the charity of profits, is a common one. . . . That the repayment will not be retained by (the company) is the voluntary decision' of the company, and was 'a very different' type of obligation to that under the law of receivership or liquidation'. *McMaster Scotland Stores Ltd*, 45.16 above, and *Lamdec Ltd*, 2.159 APPEALS, distinguished. *RIBA Publications, [1999] VATDR 230 (VTD 15983)*.

45.21   For another case in which it was held that repayment would not lead to 'unjust enrichment', see *Norman Allen Group Travel*, 59.4 TOUR OPERATORS AND TRAVEL AGENTS.

45.22   **Repayment claim by company in liquidation—whether any 'unjust enrichment'.** See *Lamdec Ltd*, 2.159 APPEALS.

Three-year time limit (VATA 1994, s 80(4))

45.23   **Repayment claim lodged before amendment to VATA 1994, s 80(4) by FA 1997—effect of Parliamentary announcement by Paymaster-General.**

Following the decision in *Next plc*, 54.26 RETAILERS' SPECIAL SCHEMES, two associated companies which sold goods by mail order lodged substantial repayment claims under *VATA 1994, s 80*. On 18 July 1996 the Paymaster-General stated in Parliament that legislation was to be included in the 1997 Finance Bill to introduce a three-year limit for retrospective repayment claims, and to amend the law on unjust enrichment, with retrospective effect from 18 July 1996. Following this announcement, the Commissioners wrote to the companies to inform them that, although the amount of the claim was agreed, 'Customs will not be making a repayment of the claim as it relates to prescribed accounting periods of more than three years before the claim was made'. The companies appealed. Two other companies, and a partnership, which had submitted similar claims under *s 80*, appealed against similar decisions. The tribunal allowed the appeals, holding that it was implicit from *s 79* that the Commissioners were 'expected to make payment in most cases within a period of 30 days'. The *Tribunal Rules* did not confer power on the tribunal to direct the Commissioners to make payments, but if the Commissioners were dilatory in making repayments, the proper remedy would be judicial review. The companies then applied to the QB for judicial review of the Commissioners' refusal to make the repayments. The QB granted the applications, holding that the Commissioners had no power to defer payment of a claim once it had been established as well-founded. Keene J observed that the Commissioners' policy document 'simply proceeded on the basis that the legislation would be passed. It was not ... simply suggesting that claims should be deferred until Parliament had expressed its will one way or the other. In so doing, it was to that extent an unlawful and *ultra vires* policy.' The Commissioners were entitled to check the validity of any claim. However, they did 'not have a discretion to defer payment of sums due from them to the taxpayer, once a claim by the latter has been established as well-founded'. In the cases in question, the amount of the claims had been agreed, and the applicants were entitled to payment of the outstanding sums without further delay. *R v C & E Commrs (ex p. Kay & Co Ltd and Others), [1996] STC 1500. (Notes.* (1) See now *VATA 1994, s 80(4)* as amended by *FA 1997, s 47.* (2) For a preliminary issue in this case, see 2.11 APPEALS.)

45.24   The company which employed the Building Societies Ombudsman registered for VAT with effect from 1987, and accounted for output tax on subscriptions which it received from participating building societies. In 1995 accountants acting for the company wrote to the Commissioners, expressing the view that it was not in fact making any taxable supplies. The Commissioners delayed a reply, but following the QB decision in *Institute of Chartered Accountants in England and Wales*, 58.129 SUPPLY, they accepted the accountants' contention. The company's accountants submitted a formal repayment claim in August 1996. However, the Commissioners did not immediately repay the amount claimed, as in July 1996 the Paymaster-General had stated in Parliament that legislation was to be included in the 1997 Finance Bill to introduce a three-year limit for backdated repayment claims, with retrospective effect. On 2 December 1996, following the QB decision in *R v C & E Commrs (ex p. Kay & Co Ltd and Others)*, 45.23 above, the tribunal directed the Commissioners to make the repayment claimed. The Commissioners made the repayment in January 1997. Meanwhile, on 4 December 1996, the House of Commons had passed a Budget Resolution under *Provisional Collection of Taxes Act 1968*, imposing a three-year time limit on repayment claims by means of an amendment to *VATA 1994, s 80(4)*. In May 1997, following the confirmation of the retrospective three-year time limit by *FA 1997, s 47*, the Commissioners issued an assessment to recover the part of the refund which was outside the three-year time limit. The company applied for judicial review. The CA granted the application. Rix LJ held that the introduction of the retrospective three-year time limit did not 'permit the Commissioners to use their new clawback powers so as to override a judicial decision which pre-dates 4 December 1996'. *R v C & E Commrs (ex p. Building Societies Ombudsman Co Ltd)*, *CA [2000] STC 892.*

45.25 **Repayment claim lodged before amendment to VATA 1994, s 80(4) by FA 1997—effect of Budget Resolution passed by House of Commons.** Following the CA decision in *Potter*, 1.73 AGENTS, the Commissioners had made a repayment of £48,000 to a Tupperware distributor in 1990. In March 1996, following the 1994 CJEC decision in *Empire Stores Ltd*, 21.129 EUROPEAN COMMUNITY LAW, the distributor submitted a further repayment claim for £2,193, contending that she should have accounted for tax only on the cost price of certain goods supplied to her sub-distributors, rather than on their normal retail price. The Commissioners rejected the claim on the basis that the distributor's documentary evidence was insufficient. The distributor appealed. The appeal was not heard until December 1996, shortly after the House of Commons had passed a Budget Resolution under *Provisional Collection of Taxes Act 1968* imposing a three-year time limit on repayment claims by means of an amendment to *VATA 1994, s 80(4)*. The tribunal deferred its decision until January 1997, by which time the amendment in question had been published as *clause 47* of the annual Finance Bill. The tribunal found on the evidence that the distributor had overpaid tax but that the overpayment claimed had been excessive, and found that the actual overpayment was £948. The tribunal observed that the Budget Resolution passed by the House of Commons had temporary statutory effect, but that it was not yet 'possible to say that all the conditions imposed by the *Provisional Collection of Taxes Act* would be satisfied. For example, *clause 47* of the Finance Bill may be amended in its passage through Parliament'. The tribunal therefore deferred a final decision 'so that the appellant may make an application for a further hearing if the conditions in the *Provisional Collection of Taxes Act* are not met or if *clause 47* of the Finance Bill is amended prior to its enactment'. *A Isaacs, LON/96/1238 (VTD 14676)*. (*Note. Clause 47* was subsequently enacted without amendment as *FA 1997, s 47*.)

45.26 **Application of VATA 1994, s 80(4) as substituted by FA 1997.** In April 1997 a company, which was partly exempt, submitted a claim for repayment of VAT which it had paid during 1992, considering that it had wrongly attributed some of its input tax to exempt supplies. The Commissioners rejected the claim on the basis that it had been made outside the three-year time limit laid down by *VATA 1994, s 80(4)* (as substituted by *FA 1997*). The company appealed, contending firstly that as the overpayment related to underclaimed input tax, it was outside the scope of *VATA 1994, s 80(4)*, and alternatively that *VATA 1994, s 80(4)* should be held to be invalid under European law. The tribunal rejected the company's first contention, holding that *VATA 1994, s 80(4)* applied to the claim, so that the tax was not repayable under UK law. The tribunal observed that 'as a matter of principle, the entitlement to deduct input tax is, both under the *Sixth Directive* and in *VATA 1994*, an integral part of the determination of the liability of a taxable person to account for and pay tax to the Commissioners on that person's taxable supplies'. *BICC plc, [1998] VATDR 224 (VTD 15324)*. (*Note.* The tribunal directed that the appeal should be stood over pending a further hearing on the question of whether *s 80(4)* violated European law. There has been no further hearing of the appeal. See, however, the subsequent decision in *Marks & Spencer plc*, 45.32 below.)

45.27 *BICC plc*, 45.26 above, was applied in a similar subsequent case in which the tribunal held that 'so far as domestic legislation is concerned, the . . . appeal must fail'. The tribunal observed that the tribunal decision in *Marks & Spencer plc*, 45.32 below, was the subject of an appeal to the High Court, and gave the appellants 'the right to pursue the matter further before the tribunal on the wider European issue should they so wish'. *JB & PA Haigh, MAN/97/1214 (VTD 15835)*.

45.28 In a subsequent Scottish case where a company claimed a repayment of input tax, the tribunal chairman (Mr. Coutts) declined to follow the decision in *BICC plc*, 45.26 above, with regard to the interaction of *VATA 1994, s 25* and *VATA 1994, s 80(4)*. Mr. Coutts accepted the company's contention that the provisions of *s 80(4)* were 'inapplicable to a claim for input tax underclaimed in error'. Applying the CS decision in *Morgan Guaranty Trust Co of New York v Lothian RC, CS [1995] SLT 299*, 'by the common law of Scotland sums paid in error, whether of fact or law, are recoverable unless the defender establishes factors which would make retention of the money equitable'. The tribunal held that, for the purposes of *VATA 1994, s 80*, references to 'VAT' should be construed as references to output tax. The tribunal distinguished the QB decision in *Marks & Spencer plc*, 45.32 below, on the grounds that it related to output tax rather than input tax. *The Royal Bank of Scotland Group plc, [1999] VATDR 122 (VTD 16035)*. (*Notes*. (1) Customs have appealed to the Court of Session against this decision. For their practice pending the hearing of the appeal, see Business Brief 12/99, issued on 27 May 1999. (2) The decision here was not followed, and was specifically disapproved, in the subsequent case of *University of Sussex*, 45.30 below, where the tribunal observed that 'had the draftsman meant to confine *s 80(1)* simply to overpayments of output tax it would have been easy enough for him to have done so, as he has in (*s 78*) in providing for the Commissioners to pay interest in certain cases of official error'. (3) See now *VAT Regulations (SI 1995 No 2518) regs 29(1A)* and *34(1A)(1B)*, introduced with effect from 1 May 1997 by *SI 1997 No 1086*.)

45.29 Following the decision noted at 40.10 LOCAL AUTHORITIES, the Commissioners repaid more than £22,000,000, plus interest of more than £12,000,000, to Glasgow City Council. The Council claimed further repayments covering periods from May 1988 to January 1992. The Commissioners rejected the claim on the basis that they were outside the three-year time limit laid down by *VATA 1994, s 80(4)*. The tribunal reviewed the evidence in detail and allowed the appeal in part, holding that the 'capping' provisions, as in force at the relevant time, applied to 'payment traders only (i.e.) to taxable persons who have paid more sums by way of VAT than they have deducted from VAT otherwise due by virtue of input tax or refunds'. On the evidence, for the first four periods in dispute, the Council was a 'payment trader', so that the payments were caught by the 'capping provisions' of *s 80*. However, the fifth return contained a number of errors and, if these errors had been corrected, 'the result would have been that a repayment would have been made to the Council'. The tribunal also held that, applying the CA decision in *Marks & Spencer plc*, 45.32 below, the Council's right to reclaim the repayments 'was not an enforceable Community right but a right under national legislation'. *Glasgow City Council, EDN/97/33 (VTD 16613)*. (*Note*. See now *VAT Regulations (SI 1995 No 2518) regs 29(1A)* and *34(1A)(1B)*, introduced with effect from 1 May 1997 by *SI 1997 No 1086*, under which 'repayment traders' are also now subject to the 'three-year cap'.)

45.30 Following the decision noted at 43.93 PARTIAL EXEMPTION, the university claimed a repayment of tax dating back to 1973. The Commissioners only agreed to repay tax within the three-year time limit laid down by *VATA 1994, s 80(4)*. The tribunal dismissed the university's appeal against this decision, applying the decision in *BICC plc*, 45.26 above, and declining to follow the decision in *The Royal Bank of Scotland Group plc*, 45.28 above. The tribunal held that 'an amount of VAT due from any person ... is a net amount. In other words that is the amount of the taxpayer's bill. The right to deduct, properly viewed, is part of the mechanism to arrive at the amount of the bill. It is not part of the means of paying it.' The tribunal also held that the conditions in *Becker v Finanzamt Münster-Innenstadt*, 21.10 EUROPEAN COMMUNITY LAW, were not satisfied, so that the university was 'unable to assert any directly effective Community law right arising under *Article 18(3)* of the (*EC Sixth*) *Directive* to the payment it is claiming'. Furthermore, the fact that the legislation in force between July 1996 and May 1997 discriminated in favour of 'repayment traders' and against 'payment traders' did not amount to a 'state aid' within *R v C & E Commrs (ex p. Lunn Poly Ltd and Another)*, 21.46 EUROPEAN COMMUNITY LAW. *University of Sussex, LON/x (VTD 16656)*.

45.31   In 1993 a university, which had not previously claimed residual input tax, submitted a repayment claim, backdated to 1973. The Commissioners accepted the claim and made the repayment. In October 1996 the university made a further claim including the same period. The Commissioners rejected the claim with regard to the period prior to August 1993, on the ground that it was outside the three-year time limit laid down by *VATA 1994, s 80(4)*. The tribunal dismissed the university's appeal against this decision, observing that the claim made in October 1996 could not be treated as an amendment to the claim made in 1993. *University of Liverpool, MAN/96/728 (VTD 16769)*.

45.32   **Validity of VATA 1994, s 80(4) as substituted by FA 1997.**   Following the decision in the case noted at 45.19 above, the appellant company submitted three repayment claims, covering the entire period from the introduction of VAT in 1973 during which it had wrongly treated certain supplies of teacakes as standard-rated rather than zero-rated, and covering a period beginning in 1991 during which it had wrongly accounted for output tax on the face value of gift vouchers, rather than on the 'subjective value' as determined by the CJEC in *Argos Distributors Ltd*, 21.131 EUROPEAN COMMUNITY LAW. The Commissioners only agreed to repay the sums which had been paid within three years of the relevant repayment claim, in accordance with the provisions of *VATA 1994, s 80(4)* as substituted by *FA 1997, s 47*. The company appealed, contending that *VATA 1994, s 80(4)* (as substituted by *FA 1997*) should be held to be invalid under European law, as it had rights under European law which overrode the provisions of *FA 1997, s 47*. The tribunal rejected this contention and dismissed the appeal, but the CA directed that the case should be referred to the CJEC. With regard to the supplies of teacakes, the CA upheld the tribunal decision that any right to recover overpayments arose because of a breach of domestic law, rather than because of a breach of Community law. Accordingly, there had been no infringement of the general principles of Community law. With regard to the supplies of vouchers, the CA upheld the tribunal decision that, until 31 July 1992, *VATA 1983, s 10* could not be construed in a way which was compatible with *Article 11A1* of the *EC Sixth Directive*, so that, for that period, the company's rights derived from Community law rather than from the domestic legislation. The CA also upheld the tribunal decision that the changes made by *F (No 2) A 1992* meant that, from 1 August 1992, the domestic legislation was compatible with the *Directive*, even though the Commissioners had 'misconstrued the *Directive*'. Schiemann LJ held that the effect of the CJEC decision in *Becker v Finanzamt Münster-Innenstadt*, 21.10 EUROPEAN COMMUNITY LAW, was that 'an individual may assert an enforceable Community law right on the basis of a Directive *only* where ... the Member State has failed to transpose or has failed properly to transpose the Directive into domestic legislation'. Applying the CJEC decision in *Kampelmann & Others v Landschaftsverband Westfalen-Lippe & Others*, 21.13 EUROPEAN COMMUNITY LAW, from 1 August 1992 onwards, the company could not rely on Community law, and the misconstructions which had led to the company 'paying VAT in circumstances where they should not have paid it' did not deprive the company of any rights, since the company 'could have asserted their rights in the national court but failed to do so. The proper remedy for a misconstruction of this kind by administrators is an application to the national courts.' With regard to the period up to 31 July 1992, where the CA held that Community law principles were relevant, Schiemann LJ observed that the company 'had, throughout the early 1990s, an effective opportunity to assert their directly enforceable right but chose not to take it — presumably either because they did not know that they had such a right or were not prepared to incur the potential liability in time and costs of asserting it'. However, Community law was unclear 'on the question whether it is permissible to amend with immediate effect a limitation period so as to deprive those, possessed under domestic law of a right to reclaim payments which should not have been made, of that right'. Accordingly, the case should be referred to the CJEC for a ruling 'on whether it is compatible with Community law to enforce legislation which removes with retrospective effect a right under national law to reclaim VAT, which right has existed unexercised for more than three years'. *Marks & Spencer plc v C & E Commrs, CA 1999, [2000] STC 16.* (*Notes.* (1) The CJEC has registered the case as *Case C-62/00.* The Advocate-General has not yet delivered his Opinion. (2) For a preliminary issue in this case, see 2.12 APPEALS.)

Calculation of claim (VATA 1994, s 80(6))

45.33   **Gaming machine takings.**   A company operated gaming machines. Small prizes were paid out in cash but larger prizes were paid in tokens, which customers could exchange for gift vouchers. The company did not keep any record of the tokens which it placed in the machines, but the directors subsequently realised that this resulted in an overdeclaration of VAT, since the tokens which were replaced in the machines represented amounts won by the customers which, applying the principles in *HJ Glawe Spiel und Unterhaltungsgeräte Aufstellungsgesellschaft mbH & Co KG v Finanzamt Hamburg-Barmbek-Uhlenhorst,* 21.133 EUROPEAN COMMUNITY LAW, did not form part of the company's turnover. The company therefore submitted a repayment claim on the basis that the amounts of tokens exchanged for vouchers should have been excluded from its turnover. The Commissioners rejected the claim on the basis that some of the tokens which were exchanged for vouchers did not represent prizes paid out by the machines, but were refunds of amounts which customers had previously paid for tokens. The tribunal reviewed the evidence and held that 'the only just solution would be to allow a proportion of the amount claimed', and directed that 50% of the amount claimed should be repaid. *Morris Amusements Ltd, EDN/97/197 (VTD 15829).*

REPAYMENT SUPPLEMENT (VATA 1994, s 79)

45.34   **Whether repayment instruction 'issued' by Commissioners—VATA 1994, s 79(2)(b).**   A return claiming a repayment of VAT was received by the VAT Central Unit on 10 November 1989. According to the records kept at the Central Unit, a payable order was authorised for issue to the claimant on the same day. However, the order was not received by the claimant, nor was it cashed by any other person. On 5 January 1990 the claimant telephoned his local VAT office to complain that he had not received the repayment. The original payable order was cancelled, and a replacement order was sent on 24 January. No repayment supplement was included. The Commissioners refused to pay any repayment supplement, and informed the claimant that supplement was not due since the repayment had been made within 30 days of receiving his telephone call on 5 January. The claimant appealed, contending that repayment supplement was due since the repayment had not been issued within 30 days of the receipt of his return on 10 November. He also gave evidence that he had telephoned the local VAT office in November and December, to state that the repayment had not been received. The tribunal accepted the claimant's evidence and allowed the appeal. The Commissioners had not proved, on the balance of probabilities, that the payable order authorised on 10 November had actually been sent to the claimant. The instruction that a repayment should be made had not therefore been 'issued' as required by what is now *VATA 1994, s 79(2)(b)*. *AA Aston, [1991] VATTR 170 (VTD 5955)*.

45.35   **Excessive repayment claim—effect of VATA 1994, s 79(2)(c).**   A company submitted a return claiming a repayment of £3,095. The Commissioners ascertained that £1,176 of this amount was not supported by an invoice, and only repaid £1,919. They refused to pay any repayment supplement on the grounds that the repayment claimed had exceeded the repayment due by more than the limits laid down in what is now *VATA 1994, s 79(2)(c)*. The tribunal dismissed the company's appeal against this decision. *Trent Manor Farms, LON/93/1523A (VTD 11216)*.

45.36   **Periods to be left of account—VATA 1994, s 79(3)(a).**   A company's return for the period ending 30 September 1988 showed a repayment due. On 15 November 1988 the Commissioners queried the figures in the return. Initially the company refused to co-operate with the Commissioners, but on 23 December the company telephoned its local VAT office and made an appointment for an officer to visit its premises on 3 January 1989. The company satisfied the Commissioners that the return was correct, and on 5 January the Commissioners authorised a repayment. The company claimed a repayment supplement, as the Commissioners had failed to repay the VAT within 30 days of the receipt of the return. The Commissioners issued a ruling that no repayment supplement was due by virtue of what is now *VATA 1994, s 79(3)(a)*, which provides that, in calculating the thirty days, no account should be taken of the period for the raising and answering of any reasonable enquiry relating to the return. The company appealed, contending that the enquiry was not 'reasonable'. The tribunal dismissed the appeal, holding that there was nothing unreasonable in the Commissioners' decision to make an enquiry. *Kitsfern Ltd, [1989] VATTR 312 (VTD 4472)*.

45.37   A company (O) had traded for several years and, because most of its supplies were zero-rated, had regularly received repayments of VAT. In June 1989 it applied for group registration for itself and for its new parent company. It was allocated a new registration number, and the Commissioners instructed it that its next return should cover the period from 1 May 1989 to 30 September 1989. The completed return was received by the Commissioners on 18 October, and showed a repayment due of more than £20,000. The repayment was not received until 29 November and the company claimed a repayment supplement. The Commissioners refused the claim, considering that what is now *VATA 1994, s 79(3)* applied, as they had had to make enquiries before authorising the repayment, and accordingly a VAT officer had visited the company on 14 November. The company appealed, contending that the Commissioners' enquiries had not been reasonable. The tribunal dismissed the company's appeal, holding that the enquiries had been reasonable. *Olive Tree Press Ltd, LON/90/186X (VTD 5349)*.

45.38   A company's return for April 1990, claiming a repayment of tax, was received by the Chester VAT office on 4 June. It was forwarded by the Chester office to the VAT Central Unit, which processed it on 14 June. The Central Unit computer indicated that the repayment which had been claimed required investigation. The case was referred back to the Chester office, and a control visit was arranged for 4 July. At the visit, the VAT officer was satisfied that the repayment was due. The company claimed a repayment supplement, which the Commissioners refused, considering that what is now *VATA 1994, s 79(3)(a)* applied. The tribunal allowed the company's appeal, holding that the Commissioners' enquiries had been reasonable but that, on the evidence, the Commissioners had not actually informed the company of the nature of their enquiries until the visit on 4 July. The only time which could properly be left out of account for the purposes of what is now *VATA 1994, s 79(3)* was two days; i.e. the day on which the queries were made and answered, plus one day for the officer to make her report. It followed that repayment supplement was due. The Commissioners appealed to the QB, which upheld the tribunal decision. *C & E Commrs v L Rowland & Co (Retail) Ltd, QB [1992] STC 647.* (*Note.* See now, however, *VATA 1994, s 79(4)*, deriving from *F(No 2)A 1992, s 15.*)

45.39   A company submitted a return for November 1989 claiming a repayment of more than £210,000. This was primarily due to reclaiming input tax on development work at its premises. The return was received by the Commissioners on 5 January 1990, and on 26 January the local VAT office telephoned the company to request an appointment to verify the return. The director responsible for the return was not available, and a VAT officer visited the company without an appointment three days later. The director was unable to see him, and the officer sent the company a letter requesting further information. The company stated in evidence that it never received that letter. Following a reminder, a visit was arranged for 20 March and repayment was authorised on that date. The Commissioners refused to pay repayment supplement, considering that what is now *VATA 1994, s 79(3)* applied, and that in computing the 30–day period laid down in *VATA 1994, s 79(2)*, the period from 26 January to 20 March should be left out of account. The tribunal dismissed the company's appeal against this decision. The Commissioners' enquiries were reasonable. On the evidence, the tribunal was not satisfied that the company had not received the Commissioners' letter of 29 January. *Olive Tree Press Ltd*, 45.37 above, applied. *The Wren Group Ltd, LON/90/1553Z (VTD 5998).*

45.40   A company submitted a return for June 1990 claiming a repayment of more than £470,000. The return was received by the VAT Central Unit on 9 July. On 18 July the case was referred to the Westminster VAT office to verify the repayment. The relevant notification was not received by the Westminster office until 23 July. The company was telephoned on 26 July, and a visit was arranged for 31 July. After considering the case further, the Westminster office authorised the repayment on 10 August. The repayment was issued on 14 August, and the company received it on 17 August. The company claimed a repayment supplement. The Commissioners rejected the claim, considering that no supplement was due, by virtue of what is now *VATA 1994, s 79(3)*. The company appealed, contending that the Commissioners' enquiries had not been raised with them until 31 July, and had been answered by them on that date, so that one day was the only time which, by virtue of *VATA 1994, s 79(3)*, should be left out of account in computing the 30–day period of *VATA 1994, s 79(2)(b)*. The tribunal allowed the appeal, holding that the Commissioners' enquiries had effectively begun on 26 July, when the company had been telephoned (rather than on 9 July, as contended by the Commissioners, or on 31 July, as contended by the company). The enquiries had been fully answered at the meeting on 31 July. Therefore, the only time that fell to be left out of account, by virtue of *VATA 1994, s 79(3)*, in computing the 30–day period of *VATA 1994, s 79(2)(b)*, was the six days from 26 July to 31 July inclusive. *L Rowland & Co (Retail) Ltd*, 45.38 above, applied. *Kitsfern Ltd*, 45.36 above, distinguished, as in that case the company had failed to co-operate with the Commissioners, whereas the company here had co-operated with the Commissioners' enquiries. *Five Oaks Properties Ltd, LON/90/1674 (VTD 6085).* (*Note.* See now, however, *VATA 1994, s 79(4)*, deriving from *F(No 2)A 1992, s 15.*)

45.41   In October 1998 a partnership submitted a return claiming a repayment of more than £1,000,000. On 9 November the Chester VAT office issued a letter rejecting the bulk of the claim. Subsequently the Commissioners agreed that the claim was correct, and made a repayment of interest under *VATA 1994, s 78*, covering the period from 13 November 1998 to 1 February 1999. The interest paid was £16,580. The partnership claimed that it was entitled to a repayment supplement of £66,980 under *VATA 1994, s 79*. The Commissioners rejected the claim and the partnership appealed. The tribunal allowed the appeal, holding that the conditions of *VATA 1994, s 79(2)* were satisfied. The Commissioners' enquiries had been raised on 26 October and had been answered by 9 November. The Commissioners had failed to issue a written instruction within the relevant period. With regard to the repayment already made under *VATA 1994, s 78*, the tribunal held that 'the intention of the legislation would not permit a *s 79* payment without deducting any lesser relevant *s 78* payment already made, and ... the mechanics of this is achieved through the operation of *s 78A*'. Accordingly, the partnership was 'entitled to the repayment supplement which it is claiming, but pursuant to *s 78A* it is obliged to repay the interest payment already made pursuant to *s 78*'. *THI Leisure Two Partnership, LON/99/373 (VTD 16876).*

45.42   **Delayed repayment—application of VATA 1994, s 79(4).**   On 16 February 1995 a company submitted a return claiming a repayment of £221,000 (which was attributable to the purchase of a new site). This was received by the VAT Central Unit at Southend on 17 February. The Central Unit referred the claim to a specialist office at Liverpool. On 13 March the Liverpool office referred the claim to the company's local VAT office at Uxbridge. That office telephoned the company on 16 March and confirmed that the repayment claim was correct. The Liverpool office received the report from the Uxbridge office on 20 March. It approved the repayment claim on 21 March, and the repayment was credited to the company's bank account on 24 March. The company subsequently claimed a repayment supplement on the grounds that the repayment had not been made within 30 days of the receipt of the return. The Commissioners rejected the claim, considering that the effect of *VATA 1994, s 79(4)* was that the period from 16 March to 20 March should be left out of account, and that the payment had been authorised on 21 March, which was within the 30–day period as extended by *s 79(3)*. The company appealed, contending that the Commissioners' inquiry had been answered on 16 March, the date on which it was raised, so that only one day should be left out of account in computing the 30–day period. The tribunal rejected this contention and dismissed the company's appeal. By virtue of *VATA 1994, s 79(4)*, the period to be left out of account ended with the date on which the Commissioners satisfied themselves that they had received a complete answer to their inquiry. The tribunal held that this date was 20 March (the date on which the Liverpool office was satisfied) rather than 16 March (the date on which the Uxbridge office was satisfied). Accordingly, the repayment had been made within the extended 30–day period and no supplement was due. (The tribunal declined to follow the decision in *Five Oaks Properties Ltd*, 45.40 above, on the grounds that that case had been decided before the enactment of *VATA 1994, s 79(4)*.) *Watford Timber Co Ltd, LON/96/1223 (VTD 14756).*

45.43   An appeal against the refusal of repayment supplement was dismissed in a case where the tribunal found that the Commissioners had raised an enquiry at a control visit in June 1990 and that the company had not answered the enquiry until a subsequent visit in July 1991. *Tary Cash & Carry Ltd, LON/92/1419P (VTD 11850).*

45.44   **Company claiming repayment in return containing errors—whether Commissioners obliged to make repayment pending investigation of errors.**   A company submitted a return claiming a repayment of VAT of more than £18 million. The Commissioners discovered that there were errors in the return, and raised detailed enquiries with the company. The company formally claimed a repayment supplement on the basis of the figures in the return, notwithstanding the errors which the Commissioners had discovered. The Commissioners refused to make a provisional repayment and the company appealed, contending that the Commissioners were obliged to make a repayment on the basis of the figures in the return subject to any errors which were discovered within 30 days. The tribunal dismissed the appeal, holding that what is now *VATA 1994, s 79* did not confer an automatic right to repayment supplement in such circumstances. Where the amount

EDN/93/191 (VTD 12853). (Note. An appeal against a default surcharge was also dismissed.)

45.55 Similar decisions were reached in *Thomas M Devon & Co, EDN/94/142 (VTD 13098)* and *MB Champion, LON/95/56A (VTD 13307)*.

45.56 A company accounted for tax, under the 'reverse charge' provisions, on management charges levied by its parent company, which was resident outside the UK. Following a change of accountants, it subsequently reclaimed the tax, on the basis that the services in question were not 'relevant services' within *VATA 1994, Sch 5*, so that the 'reverse charge' provisions did not apply. The Commissioners accepted the repayment claim and the company submitted a claim to be repaid interest under *VATA 1994, s 78*. The Commissioners rejected the claim to interest on the grounds that the overpayment was not attributable to any 'official error'. The tribunal dismissed the company's appeal, holding that the overpayment was not 'due to' an error on the part of the Commissioners and was therefore not within the scope of *s 78(1)*. *Rogers Torbay Ltd*, 45.50 above, and *Wheeler*, 45.57 below, applied; *CGI Pension Trust Ltd*, 45.65 below, and *Wydale Hall*, 45.67 below, distinguished. *Avco Trust plc, LON/x (VTD 16251)*.

45.57 **Estimated assessment—whether any 'official error'.** In August 1988 the Commissioners issued an estimated assessment charging tax of more than £34,000 on a motor dealer for the periods ending March 1987. The dealer submitted returns claiming repayments for the periods ending June 1988 and September 1988. The Commissioners set the repayments against the tax assessed for the previous periods. In November 1990 the dealer closed his business, and the Commissioners were unable to enforce payment of the unpaid tax. In August 1991 the accountants acting for the dealer requested clarification of how the assessment had been computed. The Commissioners replied in February 1992. The accountants did not respond to this letter until 1993, and in April 1993 the Commissioners withdrew the assessment. However, the Commissioners asked to review the dealer's records from 1988 to the date of cessation. In January 1994 the accountants replied that this was not possible, as the records had been destroyed in 1991. In February 1994 the Commissioners repaid the tax for the periods ending June and September 1988. The dealer submitted a claim to interest under what is now *VATA 1994, s 78*. The Commissioners rejected the claim and the tribunal dismissed the dealer's appeal. On the evidence, there had been reasonable grounds for the Commissioners' having issued the estimated assessment in August 1988. Applying *Rogers Torbay Ltd*, 45.50 above, it would be 'repugnant to commonsense and to the intention of the legislation' to conclude that the failure to repay the tax for the periods ending September 1988 was due to any error on the part of the Commissioners. The true cause of the delay in repaying the tax was 'the failure by (the dealer) or of those acting for him to provide that information which, had it been provided timeously, would have obviated the need for an assessment or led to its early withdrawal'. *AD Wheeler (t/a Wheeler Motor Co), LON/95/1780A (VTD 13617)*.

45.58 *Wheeler*, 45.57 above, was applied in the similar subsequent case of *Alan Glaves International Ltd, MAN/99/29 (VTD 16151)*.

45.59 **Use of inappropriate Retail Scheme.** A company registered for VAT in 1973 and operated a Retail Scheme. In 1991 a VAT officer visited the company and discovered that it was making wholesale supplies as well as retail supplies, and informed the company that it should not use a Retail Scheme for wholesale supplies. Subsequently the company's directors formed the opinion that the result of having operated Scheme G was that it had paid more tax than was necessary, and submitted a claim for repayment of more than £100,000, together with interest. The

Commissioners rejected the claim and the tribunal dismissed the company's appeal, observing that the company 'had the benefit of professional advice from the commencement of VAT' and holding that 'any claim for interest under (*VATA 1994, s 78*) is barred by the provisions of (*s 78(11)*)'. *RJN Creighton Ltd, BEL/93/57 (VTD 12395)*.

45.60   Use of inappropriate Retail Scheme—retrospective recalculation permitted by Commissioners—whether any 'official error'.   A married couple who owned a village shop accounted for tax under Retail Scheme D from 1989 to 1995. Since part of their business consisted of the sale of home-made cakes, they were not in fact eligible to use Scheme D. In 1995 they applied to make a retrospective change to Scheme F. The Commissioners accepted the application and subsequently made a repayment to the couple. The couple then applied for interest on the repayment. The Commissioners rejected the claim and the couple appealed, contending that a VAT officer who had visited them in 1990 should have advised them that Scheme D was inappropriate, and that they should therefore be entitled to interest under *VATA 1994, s 78*. The tribunal rejected this contention and dismissed the appeal, finding on the evidence that there had been 'no error on the part of the Commissioners'. *JL & PA Peart (t/a The Border Reiver), MAN/96/433 (VTD 14672)*. (*Note*. Retrospective changes of retail scheme are only allowed in exceptional cases, and the maximum period of recalculation is now three years.)

45.61   Assessment issued to recover input tax—Commissioners subsequently accepting that assessment incorrect—whether an 'official error'.   In 1985 a trader (G) reclaimed input tax relating to the renovation and extension of a cottage. A VAT officer formed the opinion that this work had not been carried out for the purpose of G's business, and the Commissioners issued an assessment to recover the tax. G appealed, but, on the advice of his solicitor, subsequently withdrew the appeal and paid the tax. In 1995 another VAT officer visited G and discovered that, from 1990, he had been letting the cottage as holiday accommodation, but had not been accounting for tax on this income. He arranged for the issue of an assessment charging output tax on this income. G complained that it was unfair that he should have to pay output tax on this income when his previous claim for input tax had been disallowed. The Commissioners accepted that, since the cottage was being used for business purposes, the input tax should be repaid. However, they refused to pay interest. G appealed, contending that the VAT officer who had visited him in 1985 had made an 'error', within *VATA 1994, s 78(1)*. The tribunal rejected this contention and dismissed his appeal, finding that it was not 'conceivable that (the officer) would have acted in the way he did if (G) had said that the intended use of the cottage was for holiday lets'. Applying *dicta* in *Rogers Torbay Ltd*, 45.50 above, it would be 'repugnant to commonsense and to the intention of the legislation' to conclude that the incorrect assessment was due to an error on the part of the Commissioners. *RJ Gynn, LON/97/595 (VTD 15360)*.

45.62   Attribution of input tax to exempt income—part of income capable of attribution to zero-rated income—whether any 'official error'.   In March 1978 the Institute of Bankers agreed with the Commissioners that its subscription income should be treated as exempt from VAT under what is now *VATA 1994, Sch 9 Group 9*. Subsequently one of the Institute's employees wrote to the Commissioners, requesting permission to treat a large proportion of the subscription income as attributable to the supply of a zero-rated journal to its members, and to apportion its input tax accordingly. However, in 1980 the Institute's principal finance officer informed the Commissioners that, as it did 'not in any way wish to imperil the exempt status of members' subscriptions', it 'would prefer to leave the present arrangements undisturbed rather than court any such risk'. In 1992 the Institute engaged a new accountant, who formed the opinion that part of the subscription income should be treated as attributable to its zero-rated supplies. In May 1993 he wrote to the Commissioners submitting repayment claims for the period from 1984 to 1993. The Commissioners accepted the claims and made the requested repayment. In May 1995 he submitted a further claim covering the period from 1973 to 1984. The Commissioners again made the requested repayment. In 1997 the Institute submitted a claim for interest under *VATA 1994, s 78*. The Commissioners rejected the claim on the basis that there had been no 'official error'. The tribunal dismissed the Institute's appeal against this decision, holding on the evidence that there had been no misdirection by the Commissioners. On the evidence, the Institute's principal finance officer had decided in 1980 that it would not be in its interests to attribute part of its income to zero-rated supplies. Since the Institute had 'decided its position', there had not been 'a relevant error on the part of the Commissioners'. (The tribunal also observed that, with regard to the period from 1984 to 1993, where the repayment claim had been made in May 1993, the claim to interest was outside the statutory time limit.) *The Chartered Institute of Bankers, LON/97/1598 (VTD 15648)*.

Cases where the appellant was partly successful

45.63   **Input tax wholly attributed to exempt supplies—whether any 'official error'.**   Fifteen associated housebuilding companies (not comprising a VAT group) operated a scheme for prospective purchasers of their houses whereby they agreed to acquire the purchaser's existing house in part-exchange. From 1981 to 1996 they treated the input tax attributable to such acquisitions as wholly attributable to exempt supplies. In 1996 they formed the opinion that part of the tax could have been attributed to their zero-rated supplies of new houses, and submitted repayment claims accordingly, which the Commissioners accepted. The companies then claimed interest under *VATA 1994, s 78*. The Commissioners rejected the claim to interest on the basis that there had been no 'official error' within *s 78*. The companies appealed. The tribunal reviewed the evidence in detail and dismissed fourteen of the appeals, while allowing the appeal by one company on the basis of a specific letter which it had received from the Nottingham VAT office in 1985. (The letter was only produced on the morning of the hearing, and the Commissioners accepted that it gave erroneous advice, falling within the scope of *s 78*.) The tribunal observed that each of the companies 'was a separate entity for VAT purposes and ... each should have dealt with its own VAT affairs'. *Barratt Homes Ltd (and associated appeals), MAN/99/250 (VTD 16533)*.

Cases where the appellant was successful

45.64   **Input tax apportioned to take account of non-business use—effect of Lennartz decision.**   In May 1987 a charity submitted a return claiming a repayment of input tax of more than £25,000. The Commissioners formed the opinion that some of the input tax was not directly related to business activities and should therefore be apportioned in accordance with what is now *VATA 1994, s 24(5)* (see 11.29 *et seq.* CHARITIES). In 1991 the CJEC gave judgment in the case of *Lennartz v Finanzamt München*, 21.216 EUROPEAN COMMUNITY LAW. The charity's accountants formed the opinion that, in the light of this decision, the charity should have been permitted to reclaim the whole of the input tax in question. The Commissioners accepted this and repaid the input tax, and the charity made a claim for interest under what is now *VATA 1994, s 78*. The Commissioners rejected the claim to interest, and the charity appealed. The tribunal allowed the appeal, holding that what is now *VATA 1994, s 24(5)* was inconsistent with *Article 17* of the *EC Sixth Directive* as interpreted in *Lennartz*. The Commissioners' correspondence to the company in 1987 had been based on an erroneous interpretation of the law, and this error had led to the company failing to claim credit for input tax to which it had in fact been entitled. *North East Media Development Trust Ltd, MAN/94/448 (VTD 13104)*. (*Note.* For subsequent developments, see 45.70 and 45.71 below.)

45.65 **Failure to claim input tax on disposals of shares outside EC —whether any 'official error'.** A company which managed a pension fund disposed of various shares on markets outside the EC. In 1987 a VAT officer informed the company that such disposals were exempt supplies, so that the input tax on associated expenses was not deductible, and the company was no longer entitled to be registered. The company followed the officer's advice, and duly deregistered. In 1995 the company engaged a firm of accountants to review its VAT affairs. The accountants realised that the company was making disposals which qualified for zero-rating until the end of 1992, and thereafter were outside the scope of VAT but with the right of recovery of input tax. As a result of this, the company re-registered and reclaimed input tax relating to the supplies in question, backdated to 1987. The Commissioners repaid the tax in question, but refused to pay any interest. The company appealed, contending that it was entitled to interest under *VATA 1994, s 78*. The tribunal accepted this contention and allowed the appeal. On the evidence, the tribunal found that the officer had been 'supplied with complete and correct information and documents by (the company), so that he was provided with everything necessary to enable him properly to consider whether any of the company's transactions in securities qualified for zero-rating'. The officer 'should have known, or should have realised, that typically a pension fund, and particularly one of an international company with its main base outside the UK as in this case, would have made share sales to persons overseas, and that the input VAT on expenses relating thereto qualified for zero-rating'. The tribunal observed that it was 'essential that, before Customs' officers give definitive advice . . ., they be sure they understand the reality of the situation with which they are dealing, and give rulings according with that reality'. The company's failure to claim its input tax at the appropriate time was attributable to the incorrect information given by the VAT officer who had visited the company. *CGI Pension Trust Ltd, MAN/98/85 (VTD 15926)*.

45.66 **Retail Scheme—overdeclaration of tax—whether any official error.** A retailer, who had overdeclared tax in respect of newspaper delivery charges, claimed a repayment. The Commissioners repaid tax of £13,900, but refused to repay any interest. The trader appealed, contending that she had been misled by a VAT officer and was entitled to interest under *VATA 1994, s 78*. The CS accepted this contention and allowed her appeal (reversing the tribunal decision). Lord Macfadyen held that, on the evidence, it was accepted that the scheme proposed and adopted by the trader was an adaptation of what is now Direct Calculation Scheme 1. However, the officer whom the trader had consulted had been under the impression that the trader was adopting an apportionment scheme. The advice given by the officer had been incomplete and misleading, and the only reasonable conclusion on the evidence was that the trader was entitled to interest under *VATA 1994, s 78*. Dicta in *Edwards v Bairstow & Harrison, HL 1955, 36 TC 207 (TTC 2001, 4.148)* applied. *Mrs ID Mathieson v C & E Commrs, CS [1999] STC 835*.

45.67 **Output tax accounted for on exempt supplies—whether any 'official error'.** A religious organisation ran educational courses from its premises. Until early 1994 it accounted for output tax on these supplies. In 1994 it engaged a tax consultant who ascertained that these courses should have been treated as exempt and claimed repayment of the overdeclared tax together with interest under what is now *VATA 1994, s 78**. The Commissioners accepted the claim for repayment of output tax but rejected the claim to payment of interest on the grounds that there had not been any 'official error'. The organisation appealed, contending that the Commissioners' *Leaflet 701/30/87* was misleading as it had not reflected the changes enacted by the *VAT (Education) Order 1987 (SI 1987 No 1259)*, and that it had been misled at a control visit by a VAT officer who had given it the impression that it should account for output tax on the supplies in question. The tribunal accepted this contention and allowed the appeal. *Wydale Hall, MAN/94/687 (VTD 14273)*. (*Note. Leaflet 701/30/87* has subsequently been superseded by *Leaflet 701/30/97*.)

Computation of interest

45.68   The successful appellant association in the case noted at 20.32 EDUCATION applied for an award of interest under what is now *VATA 1994, s 78*. The Commissioners made a payment of interest of £75,655, computed in accordance with the rates laid down by *SI 1991 No 1754*. The association appealed to the tribunal, contending that the interest should have been compounded. The tribunal rejected this contention and dismissed the appeal, holding that there was no statutory provision for compounding the award of interest under *VATA 1994, s 78*. *National Council of YMCAs Inc, [1993] VATTR 299 (VTD 10537)*. (*Note*. For a subsequent unsuccessful application by the association, see 45.72 below.)

45.69   The proprietors of a hotel submitted a return for the period ending 30 September 1990, claiming a repayment of £1,924. On 15 November a VAT officer made a control visit to the hotel. He formed the opinion that only £691 should be repaid, and that the proprietors were liable to a misdeclaration penalty of £369. The Commissioners repaid the balance of £322 to the proprietors on 29 November 1990. Following representations by the proprietors, the penalty was withdrawn and the sum of £369 was repaid to them on 4 April 1991. Following a further control visit on 27 September 1991, the Commissioners accepted that the original repayment claim had been correct and that the VAT officer had been wrong to refuse it. The balance of £1,233, together with interest of £119, was repaid to the proprietors in October 1991. The proprietors complained that the interest paid to them was inadequate, and in February 1992 the Commissioners made a payment of interest of £151 under what is now *VATA 1994, s 78*. The proprietors appealed to the tribunal, contending that they were entitled to a more substantial payment. The tribunal allowed their appeal in part, holding that the rates of interest were fixed by statutory instrument (*SI 1991 No 1754*) and could not be altered, but finding that the Commissioners' computation of interest had only begun on 29 December 1990, whereas the commencement date should have been 29 November 1990. The tribunal chairman noted that 'the appellants are out of pocket to the extent that the Commissioners' error cost them interest on their bank account which exceeded the interest payable by the Commissioners', and recommended 'that the Commissioners consider making an ex gratia payment to the appellants'. *S & DE Jarman, MAN/92/632 (VTD 11637)*.

45.70   Following the decision in the case noted at 45.64 above, the company claimed interest on the whole of the input tax which the Commissioners had wrongly refused to repay. The Commissioners considered that interest should only be payable on the excess of the input tax over the output tax which the company would have had to pay if the principles in *Lennartz v Finanzamt München*, 21.216 EUROPEAN COMMUNITY LAW, had been adopted. They applied to the tribunal for clarification of the amount of interest payable. The tribunal upheld the Commissioners' contention, holding that 'interest should be computed upon an amount equal to the input tax net of the output tax underpaid'. Interest should be computed on this amount from the date determined under what is now *VATA 1994, s 78(5)* to the date on which the Commissioners authorised the relevant repayment. *North East Media Development Trust Ltd, [1995] VATDR 240 (VTD 13425)*. (*Note*. For subsequent developments in this case, see 45.71 below.)

45.71 Payment of Tax

45.71 Following the decision in the case noted at 45.70 above, the Commissioners repaid interest of £19,000 to the company. The Commissioners calculated the interest on the basis that interest ceased to run in December 1993, when they repaid the disputed input tax. However, the Commissioners did not repay the interest until 1995. The company applied to the tribunal for a ruling that it was entitled to interest on the £19,000 from December 1993 until the date on which it was actually paid. The tribunal accepted this contention and directed that a further payment of interest should be made to the company. The chairman observed that, applying *Hunt v RM Douglas (Roofing) Ltd, HL [1990] 1 AC 398*, 'a person to whom money is due is not to be deprived of his interest simply because the paying party is unable to calculate the amount to which he is entitled'. There was 'nothing offensive in the notion that the Commissioners should pay interest upon interest'. The Commissioners should have repaid the £19,000 in December 1993 but had not done so, with the result that the company had been deprived of the use of its money. *North East Media Development Trust Ltd (No 3), [1996] VATDR 396 (VTD 14416)*. (*Note.* See now, however, *VATA 1994, s 78(1A)*, introduced by *FA 1997, s 44* with retrospective effect.)

45.72 **Computation of interest—application of VATA 1994, s 78(1A).** The Commissioners repaid interest of £75,655 to the successful appellant association in the case noted at 20.32 EDUCATION. The association subsequently applied for a further payment of interest on the lines of the payment made in *North East Media Development Trust Ltd (No 3)*, 45.71 above. The tribunal dismissed the application, declining to follow the decision in *North East Media Development Trust Ltd (No 3)* because of the subsequent enactment, with retrospective effect, of *VATA 1994, s 78(1A)*. The effect of *s 78(1A)(b)* was that interest under *s 78* was not payable on interest. *National Council of YMCAs, LON/97/797 (VTD 15247)*.

45.73 **Repayment claims—payment delayed by Commissioners—whether interest payable under VATA 1994, s 78 or VATA 1994, s 84.** See *Peoples Bathgate & Livingston Ltd*, 2.352 APPEALS; *Seaton Sands Ltd & Others*, 2.353 APPEALS, and *Bank Austria Trade Services Gesellschaft mbH*, 2.354 APPEALS.

MISCELLANEOUS

45.74 **Whether overpaid tax may be set against current tax due.** See *Fine Art Developments plc*, 55.14 RETURNS.

45.75 **Payment by credit transfer.** See *Matilot Ltd*, 18.64 DEFAULT SURCHARGE.

45.76 **Commissioners' right of set-off.** See *R v C & E Commrs (ex p. Richmond)*, 34.528 INPUT TAX.

45.77 **VATA 1994, Sch 11 para 5—tax declared in returns but neither paid nor assessed within time limits—whether Commissioners may take collection proceedings.** See *International Language Centres Ltd*, 3.32 ASSESSMENT.

45.78 **Assessment issued to recover unpaid tax—appellant contending that assessment invalid because tax already paid—jurisdiction of tribunal.** See *Goldenberg*, 2.24 APPEALS.

45.79 **VAT Regulations 1995, reg 40—Commissioners' power to 'allow or direct' extension of normal time limit.** See *Caro*, 18.438 DEFAULT SURCHARGE, and *Starlite (Chandeliers) Ltd*, 18.440 DEFAULT SURCHARGE.

46 Penalties: Criminal Offences

The cases in this chapter are arranged under the following headings.

Offences under VATA 1994, s 72 46.1–46.13
Common law offences 46.14–46.18

OFFENCES UNDER VATA 1994, s 72

46.1 **Failure to register—whether taking steps to evade tax.** A trader who had failed to register for VAT was convicted for 'being knowingly concerned in, or in the taking of steps with a view to the fraudulent evasion of tax', contrary to what is now *VATA 1994, s 72(1)*. He appealed, contending that inaction did not amount to 'the taking of steps'. The CA rejected this contention and dismissed his appeal. *R v McCarthy, CA Criminal Division [1981] STC 298.*

46.2 A similar decision was reached in *R v Fairclough, CA Criminal Division 25 October 1982 unreported.*

46.3 **Indictment under VATA 1994, s 72—whether void for duplicity.** A defendant was convicted of conduct involving the commission of offences under what is now *VATA 1994, s 72(1)* and *(3)*, contrary to *s 72(8)*. He appealed, contending that the indictment was void for duplicity. The CA rejected this contention and dismissed his appeal, holding that *VATA 1994, s 72(8)* could embrace the commission of numerous offences, which, if the details were known, could have been charged individually under *s 72(1)* and *(3)*. *R v Asif, CA Criminal Division 1985, 82 Cr AR 123; [1985] CLR 679.*

46.4 *R v Asif*, 46.3 above, was applied in a similar case in which the CA upheld the convictions of two partners in a restaurant business. The CA observed that, while it was preferable for an indictment to charge a defendant with a particular offence under what is now *VATA 1994, s 72(1)* or *(3)*, the provisions of *s 72(8)* covered a case where a 'deficiency was so striking that it was possible to say that a fraud had been perpetrated but impossible to say how it was done'. *R v Choudhury; R v Uddin, CA Criminal Division [1996] STC 1163.*

46.5 **Indictment under VATA 1994, s 72—whether defective.** A woman was convicted of conduct involving the commission of offences under *VATA 1994, s 72*, in that she had made claims for refunds of VAT to which she was not entitled, and had furnished or made use of forms VAT 407 on which false Customs stamps had been applied. She appealed, contending that the indictment was defective in that it failed to make any specific reference to fraudulent intent or intent to deceive. The CA rejected this contention and dismissed her appeal, holding that the jury had been correctly directed and that there had been no miscarriage of justice. *R v Ike, CA Criminal Division 1995, [1996] STC 391.*

46.6 **Amendment of indictment under VATA 1994, s 72—whether unfair to appellant.** An individual (S) was charged with offences under *VATA 1994, s 72*, comprising the understatement of output tax and the submission of false claims to input tax. He indicated that he was prepared to plead guilty to the charge relating to input tax, but not to the charge relating to output tax. The Crown therefore applied to amend the indictment so as to split the single count into two separate counts, one relating to input tax and one relating to output tax. The trial judge accepted the application, and S appealed to the CA, contending that the amendment was unfair. The CA rejected this contention and dismissed his appeal, holding that there were good reasons for the amendment and that the amended indictment was not defective. *R v Stanley, CA Criminal Division 17 September 1998, Times 8.12.1998.*

46.7   **Conviction for fraudulent evasion of VAT—whether Customs' officers' notebooks admissible in evidence.** VAT officers formed the opinion that the proprietors of a fish and chip shop had been underdeclaring VAT. Two officers observed the shop, recording the numbers of people entering it. The proprietors were convicted of fraudulent evasion of VAT. They appealed to the CA, contending that there had been an irregularity in the course of the trial and that the notebooks kept by the VAT officers who had conducted the observations should not have been admitted in evidence. The CA allowed the appeals, holding that the notebooks were inadmissible, and that the VAT officers should not have been allowed to refer to the notebooks to refresh their memories of what had happened. *R v Kelsey 1981, 74 Cr App R 213*, was distinguished since in that case the police officer's notebook which was admitted as evidence had been checked by an observer at the time the relevant entry was made, whereas in the present case there had been no check on the accuracy of what each of the VAT officers had written down. The prosecution had admitted that there were some errors and omissions in the notebooks. Nolan LJ described the prosecution evidence as 'fundamentally flawed'. *R v Eleftheriou & Another, CA Criminal Division [1993] BTC 257.*

46.8   **Offences under VATA 1994, s 72(1)—whether to be tried summarily or on indictment.** A trader was charged under what is now *VATA 1994, s 72* with being knowingly concerned in the fraudulent evasion of VAT, in that he had been controlling director of a company which had used an obsolete VAT registration number and charged customers output tax of £193,000 but had not paid this to the Commissioners. The local magistrates decided to deal with the case by way of summary proceedings. The Commissioners sought judicial review of the magistrates' decision, contending that, since the maximum penalty by way of summary proceedings was six months' imprisonment, the magistrates' decision was perverse and the case should be tried on indictment. The QB held that the magistrates' decision was unreasonable, since in the absence of mitigating factors or unusual circumstances, a sentence of more than six months' imprisonment might be expected where an amount of almost £200,000 was involved. The case should therefore be tried on indictment. *R v Northampton Magistrates' Court (ex p. C & E Commrs), QB [1994] BVC 111.*

46.9   An accountant was charged with fraudulent conduct after submitting a claim for repayment of VAT by a company for which he acted, although the company did not hold an invoice in support of the claim. The local magistrates ruled that the case should be dealt with by summary proceedings and the Commissioners sought judicial review of their decision. The QB granted the Commissioners' application and remitted the case to a different panel of magistrates for them to reconsider the case, applying *dicta* of Schiemann J in *R v Northampton Magistrates' Court (ex p. C & E Commrs)*, 46.8 above. *R v Flax Bourton Magistrates' Court (ex p. C & E Commrs), QB 29 January 1996, Times 6.2.1996.*

46.10   **Fraudulent evasion of tax—definition of 'evasion'.** A company director was convicted of four counts of being knowingly concerned in the fraudulent evasion of VAT. He appealed, contending that his conduct did not amount to 'evasion' since he had not intended to permanently deprive Customs of the VAT due, but had refrained from submitting VAT returns while the company was trading at a loss. The CA dismissed his appeal, holding that deliberate non-payment of tax was within the definition of 'evasion', and that the prosecution did not have to prove that the defendant intended to permanently deprive Customs of the VAT in question. *Dicta* in *R v Fairclough*, 46.2 above, applied. *R v JC Dealy, CA Criminal Division 1994, [1995] STC 217: [1995] 1 WLR 658.*

46.11   **Fraudulent evasion of tax—conviction upheld.** A partner in a scrap metal business was convicted of fraudulent evasion of VAT after Customs officers had discovered that purchase invoices from unregistered suppliers, which did not include any VAT, had been destroyed, and that input tax had been reclaimed on the basis of false invoices. The CA dismissed the partner's appeal against his conviction. *R v Collier, CA Criminal Division 26 March 1997, 1997 STI 474.*

46.12   **Fraudulent evasion of tax—conviction for unlawful supply of steroids.**   Two defendants were convicted for fraudulent evasion of VAT, in that they had failed to account for output tax on supplies of anabolic steroids. They appealed to the CA, contending that since their supplies had been unlawful under *Medicines Act 1968*, no VAT was due on them, and that this question should have been referred to the CJEC. The CA rejected this contention and dismissed their appeal. Under the principle of fiscal neutrality, unlawful supplies were subject to VAT except where, because of the special characteristics of certain goods, all competition between a lawful and an unlawful economic sector was precluded. *R v Goodwin & Unstead,* 21.49 EUROPEAN COMMUNITY LAW, applied. *R v C & J Citrone, CA Criminal Division 1998, [1999] STC 29.*

46.13   **Conviction for supply of counterfeit goods.**   See *R v Goodwin & Unstead,* 21.49 EUROPEAN COMMUNITY LAW.

COMMON LAW OFFENCES

46.14   **Common law offence of cheating public revenue.**   The director of a company was convicted of cheating the public revenue by failing to account for VAT on sales of gold. The CA dismissed his appeal against conviction, holding that *Theft Act 1968, s 32(1)* retains the common law offence of cheating the public revenue even though other statutory offences (e.g. under what is now *VATA 1994, s 72*) might be in point. Drake J held that 'the common law offence of cheating does not necessarily require a false representation, either by words or conduct. Cheating can include any form of fraudulent conduct which results in diverting money from the revenue and in depriving the revenue of money to which it is entitled.' *R v Mavji, CA Criminal Division [1986] STC 508.*

46.15   The proprietor of a business dealing in motor vehicles was convicted of cheating the public revenue by charging VAT to customers while not being registered, and not accounting to the Commissioners for the tax charged. The CA dismissed his appeal against conviction, holding that *Theft Act 1968, s 32(1)* retained the common law offence of cheating the public revenue notwithstanding that other statutory offences might be relevant. The CA also held that the common law offence of cheating the Revenue was satisfied by omission, and a positive act of deception was not required. *R v Redford, CA Criminal Division [1988] STC 845.*

46.16   Convictions for cheating the public revenue were also upheld in *R v Fisher, R v Hooper; CA Criminal Division 21 March 1989, 1989 STI 269.*

46.17   Three individuals, who had failed to account for VAT on takings from gaming machines, were convicted of cheating the public revenue. They appealed, contending that the takings should be treated as exempt under *Article 13B(f)* of the *EC Sixth Directive.* The CA rejected this contention and dismissed their appeals, holding that *Article 13B(f)* did not require all forms of gambling to be exempt from VAT, since Member States were authorised to limit the scope of the exemption. Accordingly, the restriction laid down by what is now *VATA 1994, Sch 9 Group 4, Note 1(d)* was not incompatible with the *Sixth Directive. R v E Ryan (and related appeals), CA Criminal Division [1994] STC 446.*

46.18   See also *Feehan,* 2.85 APPEALS.

47   Penalties: Evasion of Tax

Note. The cases in this chapter are arranged under the following headings.

COMPUTATION OF THE PENALTY

47.1   **Whether penalty may be imposed under VATA 1994, s 60 where trader has never registered.**   A company traded without being registered for VAT. The Commissioners imposed a penalty of £46,000 under what is now *VATA 1994, s 60*, attributed to the controlling director under *VATA 1994, s 61*. Both the company and the director appealed, contending that they were not liable to any penalty under *VATA 1994, s 60* since, in the absence of returns, there had not been any false claims or understatements. The CA rejected this contention and dismissed the appeals. It had clearly been the intention of Parliament that *VATA 1994, s 60** should be capable of applying to cases of non-registration. *VATA 1994, s 60(3)** provided 'a formula for the calculation of the statutory maximum in those cases where the method of tax evasion is a fraudulent understatement of output tax or overstatement of input tax ... (but) was not intended to provide a formula where the method of evasion was not to register or make declarations at all'. Peter Gibson LJ observed that 'the dishonest omission by a person to register for VAT or, having registered, to make a return, ... would plainly fall within (*VATA 1994, s 60(1)**)'. The provisions of *VATA 1994, s 60(3)* had 'no application to a case of non-registration or an omission by a registered person to make a return. In such a case ... the amount of the penalty is equal to the amount of tax evaded by that person's conduct.' *CS Stevenson v C & E Commrs (and related appeal), CA [1996] STC 1096.*

THE ASSESSMENT OF THE PENALTY (VATA 1994, s 76)

47.2   **Whether notice must apportion penalty to specific accounting periods.**   The Commissioners imposed a penalty of £65,000 on a company under what is now *VATA 1994, s 60*, covering 18 prescribed accounting periods. The company had had three directors during the period in question, but the Commissioners attributed the whole of the penalty to one director (B) under *VATA 1994, s 61*, and notified B of the liability without specifically apportioning the penalty to the particular accounting periods. The CA dismissed B's appeal, holding that both the assessment and its notification were valid. The legislation did not require the Commissioners to carry out, or notify, any unnecessary calculations, and it was not necessary to refer to individual quarterly figures within the overall period to which the penalty related. *Le Rififi Ltd*, 3.70 ASSESSMENT, and *House*, 3.93 ASSESSMENT, applied. *N Bassimeh v C & E Commrs, CA 1996, [1997] STC 33. (Note. The CA also* held that, where directors had collaborated in a company's dishonest conduct, each director was *prima facie* responsible for the whole penalty.)

47.3 **Whether penalty properly notified to company directors.** The Commissioners imposed a penalty under what is now *VATA 1994, s 60* on a company which manufactured women's clothing, on the grounds that it had reclaimed input tax in respect of false invoices. They sought to recover half of the penalty from the company's controlling directors under what is now *VATA 1994, s 61*. The directors appealed, contending that the penalty had not been properly notified. The tribunal chairman (Mr. Miller, sitting alone) accepted this contention and allowed the appeals. It was 'an antecedent step to the portion of the basic penalty being recoverable from the named officer as his liability that there is service of a notice under (*s 61**), which must mean a valid notice'. There was no prescribed form of notice, but it was essential that the notice should show the amount of the basic penalty and that it should state that the Commissioners 'propose to recover from the officer to whom ... the notice is addressed the portion of the penalty which is specified in the notice'. The fact that the notices did not set out separate amounts in respect of each relevant accounting period did not render them defective. However, the notices did not inform the appellants what portion of the penalty it was proposed to recover from each of them and, because they failed to do this, the notices were defective. The chairman observed that 'it would have been the easiest of things for the Commissioners to have stated the portion which they proposed to recover from the appellants', and held that 'each appellant had to be told in the notice addressed to him the precise portion of the penalty which the Commissioners proposed to recover from him'. The chairman commented that 'this may seem a very technical point, but imposition of tax and penalties depend upon the requirements prescribed by Parliament being satisfied'. *MK & ME Nazif, LON/92/70P (VTD 13616)*.

47.4 The Commissioners imposed a penalty under *VATA 1994, s 60* on a company which had failed to account for VAT on certain supplies, and apportioned the whole of the penalty to the company's controlling director under *VATA 1994, s 61*. They issued a notice, addressed to the company for the attention of the director, and subsequently issued a further notice, similarly addressed, reducing the amount of the penalty. The company and the director appealed, contending as a preliminary point that the notices were defectively worded and should be held to be invalid, since each of the notices had been addressed to both the company and the director. The tribunal rejected this contention, holding that each of the notices had been validly served and observing that 'although each of the ... notices could have been more satisfactorily worded, each of them sufficiently stated the matters specified in *s 61(2)*'. The tribunal held that, for the purposes of *s 61(1)*, 'one notice will suffice, provided that both parties (i.e. the company and the director) receive it'. The QB upheld this decision. Keene J held that a *s 61* notice did not have to be in any particular form, or use any particular wording. *Bassimeh*, 47.2 above, and *House*, 3.93 ASSESSMENT, applied. The notice had sufficiently identified the director, and had been properly served both on the company and on the director. *Nidderdale Building Ltd v C & E Commrs; J Lofthouse v C & E Commrs, QB [1997] STC 800*.

47.5 **Penalty assessed on partnership—validity of assessment.** The Commissioners imposed a penalty under *VATA 1994, s 60* on a partnership. The partners appealed, contending as a preliminary point that separate assessments should have been raised on each of the partners individually, and that a penalty assessment on the partnership was invalid. The tribunal rejected this contention and upheld the validity of the penalty, holding that a penalty assessment under *s 60* 'can be validly made against several persons together, whether the dishonest conduct alleged is alleged to have been that of all of them together or is alleged to have been that of one or more of them in circumstances where the liability for the penalty is imposed on all of them'. *The Bengal Brasserie*, 44.1 PARTNERSHIP, and *Santi Bag Restaurant*, 47.62 below, applied. The tribunal declined to follow *obiter dicta* of Glidewell J in *Evans & Others*, *QB 1981, [1982] STC 342* (which the appellants had cited as an authority), observing that the relevant legislation had been amended by *FA 1982* to reverse the effect of that decision. *GK, RK, GK, M, FB & KG Akbar (t/a Mumtaz Paan House), [1998] VATDR 52 (VTD 15386)*. (*Note.* The substantive appeal was subsequently dismissed—see 47.49 below.)

47.6   The decision in *Akbar (t/a Mumtaz Paan House)*, 47.5 above, was applied in the similar subsequent case of *Standard Tandoori Nepalese Restaurant, LON/97/535 (VTD 16458)*. (*Note.* For the award of costs in this case, see 2.288 APPEALS.)

LIABILITY OF DIRECTORS (VATA 1994, s 61)

Cases where the appellant was unsuccessful

47.7   The Commissioners imposed a penalty, reduced by 50% to take account of co-operation, on a company which had carried on business as a building contractor, and which had made returns in which its output tax was understated and its input tax was overstated. The penalty was attributed to the company's controlling director under *VATA 1994, s 61*. The tribunal dismissed the director's appeal, holding that 'if a return contains a misstatement, and the person who makes the return has no honest belief in the truth of the statement (and in particular, if he makes the statement recklessly, not caring whether it is true or false), that is dishonesty according to the ordinary standards of reasonable and honest people'. *Dicta* of Lord Herschell in *Derry v Peek, HL 1889, 14 AC 337 (TTC 2001, 6.20)* applied. *PG Howroyd, MAN/88/841 (VTD 5582)*.

47.8   *Howroyd*, 47.7 above, was applied in the similar subsequent case of *DG Cohen, MAN/98/325 (VTD 16074)*. (*Note.* The tribunal also upheld the validity of the underlying assessment on the company—see 3.78 ASSESSMENT.)

47.9   The Commissioners imposed a penalty, mitigated by 50%, on a civil engineering company which had failed to account for output tax and had subsequently ceased trading. They sought to recover the whole of the penalty from the controlling director under what is now *VATA 1994, s 61*, on the grounds that the penalty was wholly attributable to his dishonesty. The tribunal dismissed the director's appeal, holding on the evidence that the director had acted dishonestly and that the fact that he had not withdrawn the evaded tax from the company was not a ground for waiving the penalty. *I Turnbull, LON/92/1257A (VTD 9903)*.

47.10   A similar decision was reached in *B Reeve, LON/93/2422P (VTD 12430)*.

47.11   A company went into liquidation without accounting for output tax on the sale of a boat. The Commissioners imposed a penalty on the company, under *VATA 1994, s 60*, in September 1992. In May 1993 they issued a notice under *VATA 1994, s 61*, attributing the penalty to the company's controlling director. The director appealed, contending that the delay of eight months was a breach of *Article 6(3)(a)* of the European Convention on Human Rights. The tribunal rejected this contention and dismissed the appeal. *CW Edwards, LON/93/2423 (VTD 16245)*.

47.12   Following an investigation into the garment trade, the Commissioners formed the opinion that a company (M) had reclaimed input tax in respect of false invoices, issued in the names of five non-existent traders. A handwriting expert gave evidence that the invoices were written by two individuals in the garment trade who had been convicted of offences under what is now *VATA 1994, s 72*. The Commissioners issued assessments to recover the tax, imposed penalties under what is now *VATA*

1994, s 60, and issued notices under *VATA 1994, s 61* that the penalties should be recovered from M's controlling director. M and the director appealed, and the director claimed in evidence that the invoices represented genuine supplies. The tribunal dismissed the appeals, holding on the evidence that the Commissioners had proved 'to a high degree of probability' that the director had acted dishonestly, and that the 'limited co-operation' given by the director did not justify any mitigation. *Moda Ltd, LON/91/205 & 1925; D Costa, LON/91/1926 (VTD 10761)*.

47.13   An appeal against a penalty under what is now *VATA 1994, s 60* and a direction under *VATA 1994, s 61* was dismissed in another case where a company in the rag trade had reclaimed input tax in respect of false invoices and had subsequently ceased trading. *A Kocaman, LON/92/3382A (VTD 11730)*.

47.14   Similar decisions were reached in *H Kirbas, LON/91/2528X (VTD 12329)* and *BS Bhambra, LON/96/1732 (VTD 15503)*.

47.15   An appeal was dismissed in a case where the tribunal found that the manager of a company had deliberately created false 'self-billing' invoices and reclaimed input tax accordingly. *S Hillas, MAN/92/1603 (VTD 12630)*.

47.16   The Commissioners imposed a penalty under what is now *VATA 1994, s 60* (at the rate of 50% of the evaded tax) on a company which had reclaimed input tax on the basis of false invoices. They issued notices under what is now *VATA 1994, s 61* to recover the penalty from the company's two directors, 50% of the penalty being apportioned to each director. One of the directors appealed, contending that the dishonesty had been perpetrated by his fellow-director. The tribunal dismissed his appeal, observing that he had signed the return in question and finding that 'he was well aware at the time he signed the return that it overstated (the company's) entitlement to a refund of input tax and that he had knowingly closed his eyes to its falsity'. *P Robinson, MAN/93/745 (VTD 12325)*.

47.17   The Commissioners discovered that the controlling director of a company in the construction industry had altered VAT-exclusive invoices issued by suppliers in respect of work which was zero-rated, and had reclaimed input tax on the supplies. They imposed a penalty under what is now *VATA 1994, s 60* and issued a notice under what is now *VATA 1994, s 61*, attributing the penalty to the director. (The penalty was mitigated by 35% to take account of co-operation.) The company and the director appealed. The tribunal upheld the penalty and dismissed the appeals. *Isfa Management Ltd; AQ Mohammed, MAN/94/987 (VTD 14999)*. (*Note*. Costs of £1,000 were awarded to the Commissioners.)

47.18   An appeal against a notice under what is now *VATA 1994, s 61* was dismissed in a case where the director of a company, which had operated a restaurant and had subsequently gone into liquidation, had admitted suppressing takings. *M Khan (Jesmond Tandoori Takeaway Ltd), MAN/91/210 (VTD 12336)*.

47.19   A similar decision was reached in a case where a company had failed to account for tax on sales of second-hand cars. *Bugmile Ltd, MAN/93/485 (VTD 12574)*.

47.20   A similar decision was reached in a case where a company which operated a nightclub had underdeclared its takings, and the Commissioners had attributed the whole of the penalty to the controlling director. *Hamore Ltd; JA Stott, MAN/96/374 (VTD 15061)*.

47.21   In the case noted at 47.46 below, the Commissioners imposed a penalty on a company which operated a restaurant. They issued a notice under *VATA 1994, s 61* directing that the penalty should be attributed to the company's principal director. The tribunal upheld the notice, holding that the standard of proof was the normal civil standard of the balance of probabilities. The director appealed to the CS, contending that the tribunal should have held that the standard of proof was the criminal standard of 'beyond reasonable doubt'. The CS rejected this contention and dismissed the appeal, holding that it was clear that Parliament had intended the standard of proof for penalties under *ss 60* and *61* to be the normal civil standard of the balance of probabilities. *SA Chowdhury v C & E Commrs, CS 1997, [1998] STC 293.*

47.22   The Commissioners imposed a penalty, reduced by 75% to take account of co-operation, on a company in the 'rag trade' which had failed to register for VAT and had subsequently ceased trading. They sought to recover the whole of the penalty from the company's controlling director, under *VATA 1994, s 61*. The tribunal upheld the penalty and dismissed the director's appeal. Applying *dicta* of Lord Lane CJ in *R v Ghosh, CA [1982] 3 WLR 110; [1982] 2 All ER 689*, 'it is dishonest for a defendant to act in a way which he knows ordinary people consider to be dishonest even if he asserts or genuinely believes that he is morally justified in acting as he did'. *K Georghiou, LON/96/1193 (VTD 14970).*

47.23   The Commissioners imposed a penalty, mitigated by 50%, on a company in the construction industry which had failed to account for output tax on a substantial invoice, and had subsequently ceased trading. They sought to recover 50% of the penalty from the company's sole director and 50% from the company secretary. The director appealed, contending that he had not been dishonest and that the VAT returns were the responsibility of the company secretary. The tribunal rejected this contention and dismissed his appeal, holding on the evidence that the company's conduct 'was in part attributable to the dishonesty of the appellant', that he had 'an equal responsibility' and that 50% of the penalty should be recovered from him. *JJ Kelly, LON/97/1609 (VTD 15637).* (*Note.* Costs were awarded to the Commissioners.)

47.24   Three companies which manufactured clothing failed to account for VAT and went into liquidation. All three companies were run by the same family, with the mother and daughter acting as directors and the father (N) acting as an employee. The Commissioners imposed penalties, mitigated by 10%. 50% of the penalties were attributed to N and the remaining 50% were attributed to the directors. They appealed, contending, *inter alia*, that the dishonesty was largely attributable to N, who was the head of the family, and that the directors were merely carrying out N's instructions. The tribunal dismissed the appeals, holding on the evidence that, 'although (the directors) may not have known every detail of the companies' businesses, they knew the purpose ... of withholding the returns and payments of VAT'. Accordingly, the directors 'ought to bear an equal responsibility'. *A & T Neocli; F Darker, MAN/95/2377 (VTD 15771).*

47.25   The Commissioners imposed a penalty, reduced by 75% to take account of co-operation, on a company which had failed to submit VAT returns and had failed to appeal against estimated assessments which were inadequate. They sought to recover the whole of the penalty from the company's controlling director, under *VATA 1994, s 61*. The tribunal upheld the penalty and dismissed the director's appeal, applying *dicta* of Lord Lane CJ in *R v Ghosh, CA [1982] 3 WLR 110; [1982] 2 All ER 689* (see 47.22 above). *NCS Associates Ltd; JC Gymer, LON/98/952 (VTD 16007).*

47.26   See also *Bassimeh*, 47.2 above.

Cases where the penalty was increased by the tribunal

47.27   The Commissioners imposed a penalty on a company which had failed to account for output tax. The penalty was attributed to the company's controlling director, and was mitigated by 75% to take account of co-operation. The director appealed, contending that the underdeclaration was attributable to an employee who had subsequently been dismissed. (The employee had sued the company for unfair dismissal, but the Industrial Tribunal had rejected the claim, finding that the contract of employment was 'tainted with illegality' since the director and employee had 'connived in paying (the employee) a net salary of £1,000 per month in such a way that involved a loss of tax to the Revenue'.) The tribunal rejected the director's contentions and dismissed his appeal. The tribunal also directed that the level of mitigation of the penalty should be reduced from 75% to 65% of the tax since, in the course of his appeal, the director had 'contradicted in large measure what he had already said to HM Customs & Excise, on the basis of which co-operation he had been accorded a 75% mitigation'. The tribunal held that it should exercise its discretion under *VATA 1994, s 70(2)* to cancel or reduce the mitigation of a penalty 'where the time of the tribunal is taken up contradicting material, on the basis of which a generous mitigation was accorded to the appellant'. *WA Tanner (Redland Auto Service Centre Ltd), LON/96/1701 (VTD 15691)*. (*Note*. Costs were awarded to the Commissioners.)

Cases where the penalty was reduced by the tribunal

47.28   The Commissioners imposed a penalty on a company, with three directors, which had evaded tax. The investigating officers accepted a statement by one of the directors that he was not involved in the evasion, and apportioned the penalty among the other two directors under what is now *VATA 1994, s 61*. One of these directors appealed, contending that he should only be liable for one-third of the total penalty, as all three directors were involved in the evasion. The tribunal accepted this contention on the evidence and reduced the director's share of the penalty accordingly. *JC Lock, LON/92/273 (VTD 9720)*.

47.29   The Commissioners formed the opinion that a company which operated an Indian restaurant had failed to account for tax on more than one-third of its takings. They imposed a penalty under what is now *VATA 1994, s 60* and sought to recover the penalty from two of the three directors under what is now *VATA 1994, s 61*. The tribunal reviewed the evidence in detail and upheld the penalty on one of the directors, finding that he was 'personally involved in the suppression of takings', but discharged the penalty on the second director, finding that there was no evidence that he was also involved, and considering it possible that he might have been defrauded by his co-director. (The tribunal also found that there was no evidence that the first director had been guilty of dishonest conduct in return periods prior to 1989, when VAT officers had begun investigating the restaurant.) *JU Ahmed & JA Wahab, LON/90/1889 (VTD 10120)*.

47.30   The Commissioners imposed a penalty under what is now *VATA 1994, s 60* on a company in the garment trade, which had reclaimed input tax on the basis of invoices issued in the name of a company which had been deregistered three years previously. The Commissioners sought to apportion the penalty to the company secretary and his son under the provisions of what is now *VATA 1994, s 61*. The tribunal reviewed the evidence in detail and upheld the penalty on the company secretary, finding that his evidence was 'untrue and that he acted dishonestly in claiming input relief'. However, the tribunal allowed the appeal by the secretary's son, holding that the Commissioners had failed to establish that the dishonest conduct was partly attributable to him. *M & F Bolukbasi, LON/91/2689 (VTD 11293)*.

47.31   The Commissioners imposed a penalty under what is now *VATA 1994, s 60* on a company in the rag trade, which had reclaimed input tax in respect of false invoices issued in the names of three dormant companies, and had subsequently gone into liquidation. (The supplier of the invoices had been convicted in criminal proceedings, and had been sentenced to 18 months' imprisonment.) They sought to recover the penalty from the company's controlling director under what is now *VATA 1994, s 61*. The tribunal reviewed the evidence in detail and upheld the penalty in respect of the majority of the invoices, but held that it had not been proved that the invoices issued in the name of the third company were not genuine. The assessment and penalty were reduced accordingly. The tribunal also held that there were no grounds for mitigating the penalty. *C Celikyay, LON/91/2695Z (VTD 11491)*.

47.32   A VAT officer discovered that a company which operated a confectionery business had underdeclared tax. The company's controlling director admitted that he had understated the company's output tax liability, and stated that he had done so because of the company's cash-flow problems. The Commissioners imposed a penalty under what is now *VATA 1994, s 60*, computed at the rate of 50% of the tax allegedly evaded, and issued a notice under what is now *VATA 1994, s 61* to recover the penalty from the director. (The company had subsequently gone into liquidation.) The tribunal upheld the penalty and the notice in principle, holding that a 'general intention to pay at some uncertain date' did not constitute a defence, applying *Corbyn v Saunders, QB [1978] 1 WLR 400; [1978] 2 All ER 697*. However, the tribunal reduced the amount charged in respect of one return period. *K Gold, LON/92/318Y (VTD 11939)*.

47.33   The Commissioners imposed a penalty under *VATA 1994, s 60* on a company which sold electrical goods, and issued a notice under *VATA 1994, s 61* apportioning the penalty to the company's managing director. The penalty was computed at the rate of 80% of the tax allegedly evaded. The tribunal upheld the penalty in principle, but found that the assessments on which the penalty was based were excessive, and reduced them to 80% of the amount originally charged. The tribunal held that the reduction of 20% in the penalty was 'adequate in all the circumstances', and upheld the notice apportioning the penalty to the director, holding on the evidence that the evasion of tax was attributable to the dishonesty of the director. (The tribunal also held that, applying the CS decision in *First Indian Cavalry Club Ltd*, 47.46 below, the standard of proof was the normal civil standard of 'the balance of probabilities'.) *Best Electrical Factors Ltd; IJ Davis, MAN/96/1021, 1173 & 1174 (VTD 15508)*.

47.34   The Commissioners imposed a penalty under what is now *VATA 1994, s 60*, mitigated by 50%, on a development company which had reclaimed input tax on the basis of invoices which had been altered by the company's controlling director to treat the invoiced sums as inclusive of VAT. They sought to recover the whole of the penalty from the controlling director under what is now *VATA 1994, s 61*. The director appealed, contending that he should be liable for half of the total penalty, since his co-director had been equally involved in the evasion. The tribunal upheld the penalty in principle, holding that the company had acted dishonestly, but accepted that both directors had been involved in the evasion and directed that only half the penalty should be apportioned to the controlling director. *AJF Tottey, LON/93/1014P (VTD 12149)*. (*Note.* Compare, however, the subsequent CA decision in *Bassimeh*, 47.2 above, where it was held that, where directors had collaborated in a company's dishonest conduct, each director was *prima facie* responsible for the whole penalty.)

47.35   **Penalty imposed in respect of more than one return—whether each return culpable—mitigation of penalty.**   The Commissioners imposed a penalty under what is now *VATA 1994, s 60* on a company which had reclaimed input tax in respect of false invoices and had subsequently ceased trading. They also imposed a penalty in respect of an earlier return in which the company had reclaimed input tax in respect of what the Commissioners considered to be expenditure not relating to any business activity. The whole of the penalty was apportioned to the controlling director, and the Commissioners made no reduction for mitigation. The tribunal upheld the penalty in respect of the false invoices, finding that the controlling director was responsible for the return in question, but allowed the appeal in respect of the earlier return, finding that the Commissioners had not proved 'that the return was despatched without any genuine belief that the claim to credit for input tax which it contained was or would in due course be justifiable'. The tribunal also directed that the penalty in respect of the false invoices should be mitigated by 25% to take account of co-operation. (The tribunal observed that the mitigation was limited because the director's 'professed ignorance of what had been done made it more difficult for the Commissioners to ascertain the facts'.) *Checkstatus Ltd; PJ Fitzpatrick, [1996] VATDR 81 (VTD 13168, 13893).*

47.36   **Mitigation of penalty attributed to company director under VATA 1994, s 61.**   The Commissioners imposed a penalty under *VATA 1994, s 60* on a company in the construction industry which had failed to account for output tax and had subsequently ceased trading. The penalty was imposed at the rate of 90% of the evaded tax, and was attributed to the company's controlling director under *VATA 1994, s 61*. The tribunal upheld the penalty in principle, applying *dicta* of Lord Lane CJ in *R v Ghosh, CA [1982] 3 WLR 110; [1982] 2 All ER 689* (see 47.22 above). However, the tribunal reduced the amount of the penalty from 90% to 65% of the evaded tax to take account of co-operation. *Brentwood Construction & Development Ltd; A Cowley, MAN/97/1175 & MAN/98/182 (VTD 16073).*

47.37   A similar decision, also applying *dicta* of Lord Lane CJ in *R v Ghosh, CA [1982] 3 WLR 110; [1982] 2 All ER 689* (see 47.22 above), was reached in a case where a company had failed to appeal against inadequate estimated assessments. The tribunal upheld the penalty in principle, finding that the company and its controlling director had acted dishonestly. However, the tribunal reduced the amount of the penalty from 45% to 35% of the evaded tax to take account of co-operation. The tribunal also observed that the company had been assessed to default surcharges in respect of the same accounting periods, and directed that the penalty should be reduced by the amount of the surcharges. *F Thornber, MAN/98/65 (VTD 16235).*

47.38   The Commissioners discovered that a company which traded as a car dealer had treated part of its takings as attributable to the sale of warranties which were exempt from VAT. They formed the opinion that the transactions in question did not qualify for exemption. They issued an assessment covering the period from June 1993 to February 1996, and imposed a penalty under *VATA 1994, s 60*, at the rate of 55% of the evaded tax. The penalty was attributed to the company's controlling director under *VATA 1994, s 61*. The director appealed, contending *inter alia* that 'the manipulation of the selling price' had not begun until March 1994. The tribunal accepted this contention and allowed the appeal to that extent. With regard to the period from March 1994 to February 1996, the tribunal upheld the penalty in principle, but reduced it from 55% to 50% of the evaded tax. *GT Brisbane, MAN/97/281 (VTD 16691).*

47.39   **Penalty apportioned to director under VATA 1994, s 61—effect of Human Rights Act 1998.**   See *Murrell*, 32.3 HUMAN RIGHTS.

Cases where the appellant was successful

47.40   The Commissioners imposed a penalty under what is now *VATA 1994, s 60* on a company in the construction industry which had failed to issue invoices or account for VAT on various contracts carried out for associated companies, and which had subsequently ceased to trade. The penalty was assessed on the company's controlling director under what is now *VATA 1994, s 61*. The director appealed, contending that he had not acted dishonestly and that invoices had not been issued because the companies in question were all suffering financial difficulties. The tribunal allowed the appeal, observing that the director's 'conduct in this matter left a great deal to be desired', but holding that 'the crucial question which we have to decide is whether the Commissioners have satisfied us that that conduct was for the purpose of dishonestly evading tax'. Applying *Khawaja v Secretary of State for the Home Department, HL [1983] 1 All ER 765*, the tribunal 'should not be satisfied with anything less than probability of a high degree' and 'we do not find the case put against (the appellant) proved to that standard'. *A Canton, LON/92/2482 (VTD 11485)*.

47.41   A company (L) was incorporated on 6 March 1992 and began to trade as a scrap metal merchant. It registered for VAT and, in its first return (for the period ending 30 April 1992), claimed a repayment of slightly more than £2,000. It did not submit any subsequent returns. When L was incorporated, it had one director (C), but on 20 July 1992 he was replaced by his father (M), who had been released from prison on 19 March. On 30 September 1992 Customs officers searched L's premises and formed the opinion that it had been involved in a VAT fraud. The Commissioners subsequently imposed a penalty under *VATA 1994, s 60*, mitigated by 50%. They attributed the penalty to M. (C had been convicted on a charge of fraud, unrelated to L, and had been sentenced to five years' imprisonment.) M appealed, contending that he had not been involved in the underdeclaration. The tribunal reviewed the evidence in detail and allowed M's appeal. The tribunal was satisfied that the company had reclaimed input tax in respect of false invoices, but found that 'there were no false invoices after he (M) formally became a director'. M's release from prison had been unexpected. It appeared that L had been set up by C 'as a vehicle for an input tax fraud'. However, the Customs officer responsible for attributing the penalty to M had apparently assumed that C had set the company up for M to run when he came out of prison. The tribunal found that this supposition was 'very unlikely', and held that the question of whether M 'knew about the mechanics of false invoicing remains unproven'. There was insufficient evidence to justify an inference that M 'was wholly or partly responsible for being deliberately involved with the false invoices'. *CR Matthews, LON/95/1039 (VTD 15935)*.

47.42   A company (M) was incorporated in 1994 and began trading in August 1995. It did not register for VAT until January 1996. During the intervening period, it used the VAT number of an associated company (B), which had been registered for VAT for several years. One of M's directors (C) was also a director of B, but the other director (W) was not. However, it failed to account for the tax charged. The Commissioners discovered this in July 1996, and imposed a penalty under *VATA 1994, s 60*, mitigated by 75%. The mitigated penalty was apportioned equally between C and W. W appealed, contending that he had not acted dishonestly, as he had repeatedly asked his co-director to sort out the VAT position, and had believed that the two companies would be covered by some form of group registration. The tribunal accepted W's evidence and allowed his appeal, holding that the Commissioners had not proved that W had acted dishonestly, since 'he had been taking steps from August 1995 through to July 1996 to regularise the position', including 'regularly attempting to persuade (C) to regularise the situation'. The tribunal accepted that W 'genuinely believed' that M could use B's VAT number, and while such ignorance would not amount to a 'reasonable excuse', W was not guilty of 'intentional or reckless dishonesty'. *WJ Ward, LON/97/1350 (VTD 15713)*. (*Note*. The tribunal chairman (Miss Gort) also expressed the view that *VATA 1994, s 60* did not cover amounts 'attributable to VAT', within *VATA 1994, s 67(1)(c)*, and observed that the Commissioners could have taken steps to recover the tax under *Sch 11 para 5*. However, Miss Gort's suggestion that *VATA 1994, s 60* should not include amounts within *VATA 1994, s 67* appears to be *incuriam*, as her decision here fails to refer to the CA decision in *Stevenson*, 47.1 above, where the CA held that *VATA 1994, s 60* was capable of applying to offences under *VATA 1994, s 67*.)

OTHER CASES

Cases where the appellant was unsuccessful

47.43   A husband and wife, who carried on business as hairdressers, instructed contractors to carry out reconstruction works to a castle which they owned. The castle was a protected building and the works were zero-rated. The contractors sent ten invoices to the appellants, four of which made no reference to VAT and the other six of which stated that no VAT was due. The husband altered each of the invoices by adding VAT in his own handwriting, but did not pay any VAT to the contractors. The appellants submitted a VAT return claiming repayment of the amounts which the husband had inserted on the invoices, and received payment accordingly from the Commissioners. After a routine visit by a Customs officer eight months later, the Commissioners issued a civil penalty which was upheld by the tribunal. On the facts, the Commissioners had proved that the appellants had acted dishonestly in deliberately acquiring payments to which they knew they were not entitled. It was dishonest to alter the invoices without informing the contractors or the Commissioners, to claim, receive and retain a substantial sum of money to which the appellants knew they were not entitled, and to use the money for the appellants' own business purposes. Costs were awarded to the Commissioners. *DC & LM Leslie, EDN/88/121 (VTD 3294)*.

47.44   In a case where the tribunal upheld two assessments on a restaurant which had suppressed purchases and substantially underdeclared takings, the Commissioners issued a civil penalty assessment. The tribunal held that the Commissioners had established that the proprietors of the restaurant had consistently and dishonestly submitted incorrect returns with the intention of evading tax. Applying *dicta* of Lord Bridge in *Khawaja v Secretary of State for the Home Department, HL [1983] 1 All ER 765*, 'the civil standard of proof by a preponderance of probability will suffice, always provided that, in view of the gravity of the charge of fraud which has to be made out and of the consequences which will follow if it is, the court should not be satisfied with anything less than probability of a high degree'. The proprietors had also failed to co-operate with the Commissioners, so that there were no grounds for any mitigation of the penalty. The appeal against the penalty was dismissed. *Gandhi Tandoori Restaurant, [1989] VATTR 39 (VTD 3303)*.

47.45   *Gandhi Tandoori Restaurant*, 47.44 above, has been applied in a large number of subsequent appeals in which appeals against penalties under what is now *VATA 1994, s 60* have been dismissed. In the interests of space, such cases are not listed individually in this book.

47.46   The Commissioners formed the opinion that a company which operated a restaurant was underdeclaring its takings, and imposed a penalty. The tribunal upheld the penalty (in a slightly reduced amount), holding that the standard of proof was the normal civil standard of the balance of probabilities. The company appealed to the CS, contending that the tribunal should have held that the standard of proof was the criminal standard of 'beyond reasonable doubt'. The CS rejected this contention and dismissed the appeal, holding that it was clear that Parliament had intended the standard of proof for penalties under *VATA 1994, s 60* to be the normal civil standard of the balance of probabilities. *First Indian Cavalry Club Ltd v C & E Commrs, CS 1997, [1998] STC 293.* (*Note.* The penalty was attributed to the controlling director under *VATA 1994, s 61*—see 47.21 above.)

47.47   An appeal was dismissed in a similar subsequent case in which the tribunal applied the CS decision in *First Indian Cavalry Club Ltd,* 47.46 above, and *dicta* of Lord Nicholls in *Re H, HL 1995, [1996] 1 All ER 1. C Antoniou (t/a Cosmos Patisserie), LON/96/958 (VTD 15781).*

47.48   The decision in *First Indian Cavalry Club Ltd,* 47.46 above, was also applied in the similar subsequent cases of *S Ahmed & SA Haque (t/a Taj Tandoori Restaurant), LON/96/1714 (16262)* and *ME Ismail, LON/99/69 (VTD 16423).*

47.49   The decisions in *First Indian Cavalry Club Ltd,* 47.46 above, and *Antoniou,* 47.47 above, were applied in a subsequent case in which an appeal against a penalty under *VATA 1994, s 60*—which the Commissioners had mitigated by 5%—was dismissed. The tribunal found that there were no grounds for any further reduction in the penalty, since 'the evidence points to the appellants having done everything in their power to frustrate the Commissioners in so determining that liability'. The tribunal also specifically disapproved *dicta* of the tribunal chairman in *Nandera,* 47.104 below, on the grounds that they were inconsistent with the established principles laid down by Lord Lane CJ in *R v Ghosh, CA [1982] 3 WLR 110; [1982] 2 All ER 689* (see 47.22 above). The partners appealed to the QB, which upheld the tribunal decision. Dyson J held that, in considering whether to mitigate a penalty to take account of co-operation, the Commissioners were entitled to take into account all relevant matters up to the date on which the penalty was assessed, including the conduct of the appeal against any relevant assessment. *GK, RK, GK, M, FB & KG Akbar (t/a Mumtaz Paan House), QB [2000] STC 237.* (*Note.* For a preliminary issue in this case, see 47.5 above.)

47.50   The QB decision in *Akbar,* 47.49 above, was applied in the similar subsequent case of *PA Ellinas, MAN/94/1980 (VTD 16576).*

47.51   The Commissioners imposed a penalty under what is now *VATA 1994, s 60* on a company which sold clothing, after discovering that it had claimed input tax in respect of purported invoices totalling £88,000, issued in the name of a non-existent company and bearing a false registration number. The tribunal dismissed the company's appeal, applying *Gandhi Tandoori Restaurant,* 47.44 above. On the evidence, it was clear that the company had not paid £88,000 in cash, and the obvious explanation was that the purported invoices had been created 'in order to reclaim the input tax shown on them'. The input tax claim had been made 'for the purpose of evading tax, and this conduct involved dishonesty'. There were no grounds for reducing the amount of the penalty. *D & J Singh (t/a Sandhu Brothers), MAN/91/1019 (VTD 9387).*

47.52   The Commissioners imposed a penalty under what is now *VATA 1994, s 60* on a family farming partnership which had failed to account for VAT on sales of milk quotas. The tribunal dismissed the partnership's appeal, applying *dicta* of the CS in *Mullan v Anderson, CS [1993] SLT 835,* to the effect that the standard of proof in civil cases was 'a balance of probabilities', rather than 'a high degree of probability'. The evidence here was 'sufficient to establish the (Commissioners') case on a balance of probabilities'. *Norman Wood & Sons, EDN/92/15 (VTD 10558).*

47.53   The Commissioners imposed a penalty under what is now *VATA 1994, s 60* on a farmer who had failed to account for VAT on sales of milk quota, but had submitted returns declaring no output tax liability but claiming repayments of input tax. The farmer appealed, contending that he had not acted dishonestly, but had delayed declaring the tax due because of financial difficulties. The tribunal dismissed his appeal and upheld the penalty, applying *dicta* of Lord Lane CJ in *R v Ghosh, CA [1982] 3 WLR 110; [1982] 2 All ER 689* (see 47.22 above), that 'it is dishonest for a defendant to act in a way which he knows ordinary people consider to be dishonest even if he asserts or genuinely believes that he is morally justified in acting as he did'. *MH Wright, LON/91/1605 (VTD 10760)*.

47.54   The principles laid down in *R v Ghosh, CA [1982] 3 WLR 110; [1982] 2 All ER 689* (see 47.22 above) were also applied in the subsequent cases of *Metrogold Ltd, MAN/91/30 (12002); RW & J Hodgson, MAN/96/1350 (VTD 15165); Bourne Vehicle Hire Ltd, LON/97/711 (VTD 15267); Maharani Restaurant, LON/96/830 & 858 (VTD 16537)* and *C & H Prebble (t/a Monks Kitchen), LON/98/1327 (VTD 16631)*.

47.55   A company carried on the business of providing interior design services. It issued six invoices relating to the furnishing of a flat in Kensington. The customer submitted forms VAT 407, stamped by the Ministry of Works in Bahrain, certifying that the goods which the company had supplied would be exported. The company treated the supplies as zero-rated exports. A VAT officer on a control visit discovered that the supplies in question appeared to consist of furniture and soft furnishings which had been delivered to the flat, and which did not appear appropriate for personal export. Following this visit, the Commissioners issued an assessment to charge output tax on the invoiced amounts, and also imposed penalties under *VATA 1994, s 60*. (The penalties were imposed at the rate of 25% of the tax assessed.) The company appealed, contending firstly that the supplies should be zero-rated and secondly that it had not acted dishonestly. The tribunal dismissed the appeals. The company had not complied with the requirements of *VATA 1994, s 30(8)*, and accordingly the supplies did not qualify for zero-rating. On the evidence, the tribunal found that the company's director was not 'a truthful or credible witness'. The tribunal was 'satisfied to a high degree of probability' that the director 'knew that the goods had not been exported and that they were still in the flat ... she knew that ordinary people would regard it as dishonest to refund the value added tax to a customer who had not exported the goods ... she therefore acted dishonestly'. *Gandhi Tandoori Restaurant*, 47.44 above, applied. Furthermore, since the penalties had only been imposed at the rate of 25% of the assessed tax, no further reduction was appropriate. *Richmond Design Interiors Ltd, LON/95/99P (VTD 13549)*.

47.56   In 1993 a company disclosed to the Commissioners that it had underdeclared VAT by more than £100,000 over a period of ten years. The company co-operated with the Commissioners in ascertaining the amount of the underdeclaration, and the Commissioners imposed a penalty under *VATA 1994, s 60* at the rate of 25% of the assessed tax. The company appealed, contending that the penalty should be mitigated still further. The tribunal rejected this contention and dismissed the appeal. The chairman observed that 'the statutory provisions ... make it clear that the tribunals have the power both to reduce and to increase the amount of mitigation allowed by the Commissioners ... this is not a case in which the power of the tribunal is limited to quashing the decision if it is satisfied that it was made incorrectly ... the appeal is one in which the tribunal can exercise a fresh discretion'. *John Dee Ltd*, 14.28 COLLECTION AND ENFORCEMENT, distinguished. On the evidence, the chairman also observed that 'I doubt whether I would have thought it appropriate to mitigate this penalty by as much as 75%' and held that 'it is not appropriate to mitigate the penalty any more than the Commissioners have already done'. However, the amount of the penalty would not be increased, since 'that power should be exercised cautiously, and only in the clearest cases when the tribunal is satisfied that the level of mitigation allowed by the Commissioners is manifestly too generous ... the sanction upon the frivolous or vexatious appellant should be effected by means of an order for costs, and not by means of an increase in the penalty'. *James Ashworth Waterfoot (Successors) Ltd, [1996] VATDR 66 (VTD 13851).*

47.57　The decision in *James Ashworth Waterfoot (Successors) Ltd*, 47.56 above, was applied in the similar subsequent case of *RA Tabner, MAN/98/141 (VTD 16155).*

47.58　There have been a large number of other cases, which appear to raise no point of general importance, in which appeals against penalties under what is now *VATA 1994, s 60* have been dismissed. In the interests of space, such cases are not reported individually in this book. For summaries of such cases decided up to 31 December 1991, see Tolley's VAT Cases 1992.

Cases where the penalty was increased by the tribunal

47.59　The Commissioners imposed a penalty under *VATA 1994, s 60*, at the rate of 25% of the evaded tax, on a trader who carried on business as a tyre dealer. The trader appealed, contending that he had not acted dishonestly. The tribunal rejected this contention and directed that the penalty should be increased to 50% of the evaded tax, observing that neither the trader nor his accountant had co-operated with the Commissioners, and holding that 'in reducing the penalty to the 25% level, the Commissioners acted with a generosity that was totally unjustified'. *K Lee (t/a Euro Impex), MAN/95/1391 & 1459 (VTD 15427).*

Cases where the penalty was reduced by the tribunal

47.60　**Penalty reduced to 95%.**　The Commissioners imposed a penalty under what is now *VATA 1994, s 60* on a publican who had failed to account for VAT on a substantial proportion of his takings. The penalty was imposed at the rate of 100% of the evaded tax. The tribunal upheld the penalty in principle but reduced it to 95% of the evaded tax to take account of a degree of co-operation by the publican. *JT Egan, MAN/91/11 (VTD 7528).* (*Note.* An appeal against an estimated assessment was dismissed.)

47.61　**Penalty reduced to 90%.**　The Commissioners imposed a penalty under what is now *VATA 1994, s 60* on a clothing manufacturer after discovering that he had failed to account for VAT on a large number of adults' sweatshirts and T-shirts, incorrectly treating them as zero-rated children's clothing. The tribunal upheld the penalty in principle, applying *Gandhi Tandoori Restaurant*, 47.44 above, but reduced the rate of the penalty from 100% to 90% to take account of co-operation. *AU Khan, MAN/89/823 (VTD 6450).* (*Note.* An appeal against an estimated assessment was also dismissed.)

47.62　**Penalty reduced to 85%.**　A penalty was reduced to 85% of the evaded tax in a case where the tribunal found that one of two partners in a restaurant was guilty of dishonest conduct and that the other partner was innocent. (The tribunal also observed that the effect of *Partnership Act 1890, s 10* was that both partners were jointly and severally liable for the penalty, even though only one of them had acted dishonestly.) *Santi Bag Restaurant, MAN/93/1177 (VTD 13114).*

47.63　**Penalty reduced to 80%.**　The Commissioners issued an estimated assessment on a partnership which operated two cafés. The partners admitted suppressing takings of £200 per week, and after hearing evidence the tribunal directed that the assessment be recomputed on the basis of an underdeclaration of takings of £250 per week. The Commissioners also imposed a penalty under what is now *VATA 1994, s 60* at the rate of 100% of the evaded tax. The tribunal directed that the penalty should be reduced to 80% to take account of the partners' co-operation. *Café Da*

Vinci & Da Vinci Too, EDN/90/132 (VTD 7298). (*Note.* For a subsequent application for costs, see 2.282 APPEALS.)

47.64   The Commissioners imposed a penalty under what is now *VATA 1994, s 60* on the proprietor of a kebab shop who had not registered for VAT, although his turnover had exceeded the statutory threshold. The penalty was computed at the rate of 90% of the evaded tax, covering the period from 1 July 1986 to 31 July 1989. The tribunal reviewed the evidence in detail and found that, while the trader's turnover had exceeded the threshold throughout the period in question, his failure to register could not be proved to be dishonest with regard for the period from July 1986 to 31 March 1988. For the period beginning on 1 April 1988, however, his turnover had exceeded the threshold by such an amount that the 'inescapable conclusion' was that his conduct had been dishonest. Accordingly the penalties were correctly imposed for the period from 1 April 1988 to 31 July 1989. With regard to the computation of the penalty, the tribunal held that the appropriate rate was 80% of the evaded tax, to take account for a degree of co-operation. *K Sedat (t/a Sherry's Kebab & Burger Bar), LON/90/1780Y (VTD 9566).* (*Note.* Appeals against estimated assessments were dismissed.)

47.65   **Penalty reduced to 75%.**   The Commissioners imposed a penalty under what is now *VATA 1994, s 60* on the proprietors of a fish and chip shop, after VAT officers had discovered documents which appeared to be takings records and which indicated that the proprietors had failed to account for tax on about 10% of their takings. The tribunal upheld the penalty in principle but reduced it to 75% of the evaded tax to take account of co-operation. *AR & A Smith (t/a Ginger's Fish & Chip Shop), EDN/90/32 (VTD 5694).*

47.66   The Commissioners imposed a penalty under what is now *VATA 1994, s 60* on a partnership operating a restaurant, which had only declared about 50% of its takings. The penalty was calculated at the rate of 90% of the evaded tax. The tribunal upheld the penalty in principle, but reduced it to 75% of the tax to take account of a 'degree of co-operation' by the principal partner. *The Nawab Tandoori Restaurant, LON/89/1829Z (VTD 6636).*

47.67   A similar decision was reached in *SS Alam & SU Ahmed (t/a Anarkali Tandoori Restaurant), MAN/95/572 (VTD 14584).*

47.68   The Commissioners imposed a penalty under what is now *VATA 1994, s 60* on a couple who operated a fish and chip shop. The penalty was imposed at the rate of 95% of the evaded tax. The tribunal upheld the penalty in principle, but reduced it to 75% of the evaded tax. The CA dismissed the couple's appeal against this decision, holding that the penalty had been validly imposed and that the reduction of 25% was sufficient. *M & A Georgiou (t/a Mario's Chippery) v C & E Commrs, CA [1996] STC 463.* (*Note.* For another issue in this case, see 3.6 ASSESSMENT. For a subsequent unsuccessful application to the ECHR, see 32.1 HUMAN RIGHTS.)

47.69   **Penalty reduced to 70%.**   The Commissioners imposed a penalty under what is now *VATA 1994, s 60* on the proprietors of a Chinese restaurant. The penalty was computed at the rate of 85% of the tax allegedly evaded. The tribunal found on the evidence that the assessment, which was computed on the basis that 20% of takings were suppressed, was excessive, partly because the restaurant was located in a 'run-down' area which the Customs officers considered unsafe. The tribunal reduced the assessment to amounts which the proprietors had admitted to have been underdeclared, and also held that the reduction in the penalty to take account of co-operation should be 30% rather than 15%. *WC & LT Wan, MAN/91/1502 (VTD 10107).*

47.70   **Penalty reduced to 65%.** The Commissioners imposed a penalty on the proprietor of a Chinese takeaway who had underdeclared takings. The penalty was imposed at the rate of 90% of the evaded tax. The tribunal upheld the penalty in principle but reduced it to 65% of the evaded tax. *Mrs M Tai (t/a North Bersted Chinese Takeaway), LON/99/448 (VTD 16451).*

47.71   **Penalty reduced to 60%.** A retired police officer and his wife operated a café in partnership. The Commissioners discovered that the couple had wrongly treated a number of supplies as zero-rated, and imposed a penalty under *VATA 1994, s 60*, at the rate of 90% of the evaded tax. The tribunal upheld the penalty in principle but reduced it to 60% of the evaded tax. The partnership appealed to the QB, which upheld the tribunal decision. Carnwath J held that 'in most cases it is a straightforward jury question whether there has been dishonesty'. On the evidence, the tribunal had been entitled to conclude that the husband had pursued a dishonest system of calculating the partnership's zero-rated sales. *B & D Stuttard (t/a De Wynns Coffee House) v C & E Commrs, QB [2000] STC 342.*

47.72   The Commissioners imposed a penalty on a couple who operated a fish and chip shop, and had underdeclared takings and had wrongly treated a number of supplies as zero-rated. The penalty was imposed at the rate of 65% of the evaded tax. The tribunal upheld the penalty in principle but reduced it to 60% of the evaded tax relating to the overstatement of zero-rated sales (while maintaining it at 65% in respect of underdeclared takings). *SS & MK Mann (t/a Chaucer Fish Bar), LON/98/1318 (VTD 16442).*

47.73   **Penalty reduced to 55%.** The Commissioners imposed a penalty under what is now *VATA 1994, s 60* on the proprietor of a restaurant who had admitted understating his takings. The penalty was imposed at the rate of 80% of the evaded tax. The proprietor appealed, contending that the penalty should be reduced as he had co-operated fully with the investigating officer. The tribunal found that the proprietor 'gave marginally less than full co-operation' but that the Commissioners had 'acted unreasonably in pitching the penalty at such a high percentage'. The penalty was reduced to 55% of the evaded tax. *P Pang (t/a Lafite's), EDN/91/20 (VTD 7065).*

47.74   **Penalty reduced to 50%.** The Commissioners imposed a penalty under what is now *VATA 1994, s 60* on the proprietor of a Greek restaurant. The penalty was computed at the rate of 75% of the tax allegedly evaded. The proprietor appealed, contending that the assessment was excessive and that, since he had co-operated with the Commissioners, the penalty should be reduced to 50% of the culpable tax. The tribunal accepted these contentions, holding that the assessment was justified on the evidence but that the allowance for wastage should be increased and that 5% of the sales should be treated as of cold take-away food, and that the penalty should be reduced to 50% to take account of the appellant's co-operation. *JO Kyriacou (t/a Niki Taverna), LON/92/2098A (VTD 11537).* (*Note.* A subsequent application by the appellant for costs was rejected—see 2.285 APPEALS.)

47.75   The Commissioners issued an estimated assessment on the proprietor of a Chinese restaurant, charging tax of more than £16,000, after a VAT officer had formed the opinion that more than 50% of the restaurant takings had not been declared. The Commissioners also imposed a penalty under what is now *VATA 1994, s 60*, computed at the rate of 90% of the tax allegedly underdeclared. The proprietor appealed, admitting that he had failed to declare some takings, but contending that both the assessment and the penalty were excessive. The tribunal allowed the appeals in part, finding that the VAT officer had overestimated the takings and that the tax actually evaded was only £2,764, and holding that since the proprietor had co-operated by admitting not having declared all his takings, the penalty should be reduced by 50%. *JHK Fu, MAN/90/579 & MAN/91/331 (VTD 11718)*.

47.76   A similar decision, also reducing a penalty from 90% to 50% of the evaded tax, was reached in *Stevie's Restaurant Ltd, EDN/93/123 & 160 (VTD 12349)*.

47.77   A penalty was reduced from 80% to 50% of the evaded tax in *J Allen-Fletcher, MAN/92/807 (VTD 12898)*.

47.78   **Penalty reduced to 40%.**   A penalty was reduced from 65% to 40% of the evaded tax in *J Marquez (t/a Kwick Chick Barbecue), MAN/95/1844 (VTD 15767)*.

47.79   A penalty was reduced from 60% to 40% of the evaded tax in *Oriental Kitchen, MAN/94/481 (VTD 13736)*.

47.80   **Penalty reduced to 35%.**   A penalty was reduced from 65% to 35% of the evaded tax in *MS Amiji, MAN/96/754 (VTD 16552)*.

47.81   **Penalty reduced to 30%.**   A penalty was reduced from 35% to 30% of the evaded tax in *MA & DJ Collinson (t/a Megazone), LON/98/21 (VTD 15942)*.

47.82   **Penalty reduced to 25%.**   A penalty was reduced from 30% to 25% of the evaded tax in *Evans Brothers (Glass & Glazing) Ltd, LON/95/3190 (VTD 14333)*.

47.83   **Penalty reduced to 20%.**   A penalty was reduced from 30% to 20% of the evaded tax in a case where a company had failed to account for output tax on the sale of seven coaches under a leaseback agreement. *Staffordian Travel Ltd, MAN/96/1044 (VTD 15135)*.

47.84   A trader failed to submit six successive VAT returns. The Commissioners issued estimated assessments which were inadequate. When the Commissioners discovered that the tax due was substantially greater than the tax charged by the estimated assessments, they imposed a penalty under *VATA 1994, s 60* (mitigated to 25% of the evaded tax to take account of co-operation). The tribunal upheld the penalty in principle, finding that the trader's 'conduct was dishonest by the standards of the reasonable and honest person, and he knew this'. However, the tribunal reduced the penalty to 20% of the evaded tax. *RK Johnson, LON/98/231 (VTD 15868)*.

47.85   The Commissioners imposed a penalty under *VATA 1994, s 60* on a partnership which sold take-away food, and which had underdeclared its output tax. The penalty was computed at the rate of 40% of the evaded tax. The tribunal upheld the penalty in principle but reduced it to 20% of the evaded tax to take account of co-operation. *CT, C & P Ellinas (t/a Hunts Cross Supper Bar), MAN/97/193 (VTD 16105)*. (*Notes.* (1) For a preliminary issue in this case, see 2.199 APPEALS. (2) The tribunal also considered appeals against estimated assessments, in respect of which the tribunal dismissed the appeal with regard to the last four accounting periods but allowed it with regard to earlier accounting periods.)

47.86   **Penalty reduced to 15%.**   A sole trader submitted nil returns for the two years ending October 1992. He was questioned about this at a control visit in April 1994, and told the VAT officer that he had not worked during that period because of injuries sustained in a fall. In July 1994, at an interview which had been arranged at his request, he admitted that he had done some work during this period and provided the Commissioners with full information about the underdeclarations. The evaded tax totalled £7,741, and the Commissioners imposed a penalty under *VATA 1994, s 60*. The penalty was mitigated by 80% to take account of co-operation. The trader appealed, contending that the penalty should be mitigated still further. The tribunal accepted this contention, holding that, since the disclosure was 'full and unprompted', the penalty should be reduced by 85%. *AR Carter, LON/95/2763P (VTD 14217).*

Cases where the appellant was successful

47.87   Undeclared output tax—standard of proof. A farmer (P) sold milk quotas for more than £150,000, but failed to account for VAT on these sales. He submitted a VAT return claiming a repayment. The Commissioners imposed a penalty under what is now *VATA 1994, s 60(1)* for dishonest evasion of tax. P appealed, contending that he had not acted dishonestly. His former bookkeeper gave evidence that P had told her to omit the invoices in question from the VAT returns. P denied this. The tribunal stated that it did not find the former bookkeeper to be a reliable witness. On the evidence, it considered that it was possible that the bookkeeper had made a mistake in omitting the milk quotas from the VAT returns, 'and was endeavouring to blame the appellant for the instructions which she said he had given'. The Commissioners had to prove deliberate dishonesty 'to a high degree of probability'. On the evidence, P was clearly guilty of great negligence, but the tribunal was 'unable to make a finding of deliberate tax evasion'. The appeal was, therefore, allowed. *IW Parker, [1989] VATTR 258 (VTD 4473).* (*Note.* Compare, with regard to the standard of proof, the subsequent case of *Norman Wood & Sons,* 47.52 above, where the tribunal held, applying *dicta* of the CS in *Mullan v Anderson, CS [1993] SLT 835,* that the standard of proof in civil cases was 'a balance of probabilities', rather than 'a high degree of probability'.)

47.88   The Commissioners imposed a penalty under what is now *VATA 1994, s 60* on the proprietors of a shop which sold hot and cold food for consumption on and off the premises. The proprietors had only accounted for VAT on 9% of their total sales, and the Commissioners considered that the proprietors had deliberately and wrongly treated substantial sales of hot food as zero-rated. Under questioning by a VAT officer, one of the proprietors estimated that about 40% of their take-away sales related to cold food. The tribunal found that the proprietors' returns were incorrect, and upheld an estimated assessment issued by the Commissioners. However, with regard to the penalty, the tribunal held that the onus was on the Commissioners 'to establish on a high degree of probability that (the proprietors) deliberately and dishonestly evaded the tax due'. The tribunal did not regard it as 'highly probable that (the active partner) was deliberately dishonest'. The appeal against the penalty was, therefore, allowed. *MAG & G Morga, EDN/89/31 (VTD 4905).*

47.89   An engineer (M), who was not registered for VAT, issued invoices on which he charged VAT to his customers, although no registration number was shown. When the Commissioners discovered this, M admitted that he should have registered for VAT, and stated that he had intended to register, but had not done so because of cash-flow difficulties caused by some of his customers failing to pay him. He had kept full records, which he produced to the VAT officers who interviewed him, and denied any intention of defrauding the Commissioners. The Commissioners imposed a penalty for dishonest evasion of tax, against which he appealed. The tribunal allowed his appeal, finding that 'he was not guilty of any dishonest intention' and that 'he eventually intended to account for the tax'. There was 'no evidence of any device or attempt to conceal the transactions of which he was engaged; his records were ready for inspection and accepted as accurate; and his disclosure of the factual background was frank and consistent throughout'. *R McDivitt, EDN/89/210 (VTD 5203).* (*Note.* Compare, however, the subsequent decision in *Wright,* 47.53 above.)

47.90   The Commissioners imposed a penalty under what is now *VATA 1994, s 60* on a partner in a building firm, after discovering that receipts had been issued in his name in respect of cash sales which had not been included in the partnership records. The partner appealed, contending that he had not made any unrecorded sales and that he had not issued the receipts in question. The tribunal allowed his appeal, holding that the Commissioners had not proved that the partner had made any of the purported cash sales in respect of which the receipts had been issued. *JH Martin, LON/89/ 927X (VTD 5543)*.

47.91   In a case where the tribunal dismissed an appeal against an estimated assessment on a pizza restaurant, an appeal against a penalty under what is now *VATA 1994, s 60* was allowed. The tribunal was satisfied on the evidence that the restaurant proprietor had underdeclared his takings, but was not satisfied that this was deliberate or dishonest. On the evidence, 'the underdeclaration might very possibly have been caused innocently ... by the failure of (the appellant's) staff to see that all bills were properly recorded at the cash desk or by his slipshod methods of keeping his records'. *B Gallo, MAN/88/478 (VTD 7686)*.

47.92   Similar decisions were reached in *NM & HN Patel, MAN/92/1722 (VTD 11635); CL Copeland, MAN/91/1554 (VTD 13325); KW Lam (t/a Dragon Inn Chinese Restaurant), MAN/96/244 (VTD 14974)* and *The Mild Seven Chinese Takeaway, MAN/97/600 (VTD 16962)*.

47.93   The Commissioners imposed a penalty under what is now *VATA 1994, s 60* on a married couple who operated an Indian restaurant. The tribunal allowed the appeal, holding that the Commissioners had not discharged the burden of proof required by *VATA 1994, s 60(7)*. *Van Boeckel*, 3.1 ASSESSMENT, applied. *Moti Mahal Indian Restaurant, [1992] VATTR 188 (VTD 9375)*. (*Note. Obiter dicta* of the tribunal were disapproved by the QB in the subsequent case of *Dollar Land (Feltham) Ltd*, 18.568 DEFAULT SURCHARGE.)

47.94   Similar decisions were reached in *CS Leung (t/a Driffield Tasty House), MAN/ 94/86 (VTD 13862); SW & XM Li (t/a Summer Palace Restaurant), MAN/95/ 1321 (VTD 15133); HS & KK Ahluwalia (t/a Kings Headlines), LON/96/501 (VTD 15258); K & H Nicolaides, MAN/95/2201 (VTD 15355)* and *B & A Heaton (t/a Freshmaid Sandwiches Take Away), MAN/97/313 (VTD 16661)*.

47.95   The Commissioners formed the opinion that a firm of clothing manufacturers had wrongly treated sales of clothing as zero-rated when they did not qualify for zero-rating. They issued an estimated assessment charging tax on such supplies, and imposed a penalty under what is now *VATA 1994, s 60*. The tribunal dismissed the firm's appeal against the assessment, but allowed the appeal against the penalty, holding that the 'evidence does not irresistibly lead to an inference to dishonesty', since the errors could have been attributable to 'gross carelessness'. *Hytex Clothing, MAN/91/1214 (VTD 10700)*.

47.96   Similar decisions were reached in *BH Taylor, LON/93/774P (VTD 12061)* and *Baltex Clothing Manufacturers, MAN/92/108 (VTD 12606)*.

47.97   An appeal against a penalty was allowed in another case where the appellant company contended that an underdeclaration of tax was attributable to carelessness and overwork, rather than dishonesty. The tribunal held that the Commissioners had 'failed to discharge the burden of proof' that the company's conduct had been dishonest. *Smith & Byford Ltd, [1996] VATDR 386 (VTD 14512)*.

47.98   A similar decision was reached in *I Denizli & N Karaca, LON/96/239 (VTD 14644)*.

47.99   The Commissioners issued estimated assessments on a couple who sold Indian clothing and silk, after discovering that their records indicated that they had been trading at a gross loss for some periods. They also imposed a penalty under what is now *VATA 1994, s 60*. The couple appealed against the penalty, contending that they had not acted dishonestly. The tribunal allowed their appeal, finding that documents which the VAT officers had regarded as takings records may have related to the previous year, and holding that the Commissioners had not proved to 'a high degree of probability' that the couple had acted dishonestly. *Shazia Fashion Fabrics, LON/92/22 (VTD 11020)*.

47.100 The Commissioners imposed a penalty under what is now *VATA 1994, s 60* on a partnership which operated a fish and chip shop, after a VAT officer had discovered that the records of a company which supplied the partnership showed transactions which did not appear in the partnership's records, and had concluded that the partnership had underdeclared its takings. The partnership appealed, contending that the supplier's records were incorrect and that it had not received the supplies which the supplier claimed to have made. The tribunal accepted the partnership's evidence and allowed the appeal, finding that the disputed supplies had not been made to the appellant partnership, but had in reality been made to unregistered traders. *G, A & C Andreucci (t/a Joe's Chip Shop), EDN/92/260 & EDN/93/107 (VTD 11223)*.

47.101 A similar decision was reached in a subsequent case involving the proprietor of a fish and chip shop. The tribunal found that the Commissioners had not proved, to the necessary degree of probability, that the proprietor had been the recipient of the disputed supplies. *Dicta* in *Khawaja v Secretary of State for the Home Department, HL [1983] 1 All ER 765*, applied. *CC Mann, LON/96/462 & 1574 (VTD 15182)*.

47.102 A company trading as car dealers purchased a number of cars for the purpose of hiring them to customers, and reclaimed input tax. It subsequently sold 88 of the cars (of which 36 had actually been used as hire cars and 52 had not). It accounted for output tax under the margin scheme for second-hand cars, rather than on their full sale price. When the Commissioners discovered this, they imposed a penalty under *VATA 1994, s 60*. The company appealed, accepting that its returns had been incorrect but contending that it had made a 'genuine error'. The tribunal accepted this contention and allowed the appeal. (The tribunal also strongly criticised the Commissioners for delays in investigating the case.) *Brown & Frewer Ltd, MAN/96/1199 (VTD 15209)*.

47.103 The Commissioners imposed a penalty under what is now *VATA 1994, s 60* on a company which operated an aviation business, after discovering that it failed to account for VAT on some of its income. The company appealed against the penalty, contending that it had not acted dishonestly but that the director who had completed the return had not received the necessary information from his co-director. The tribunal allowed the appeal, finding that the company had underdeclared tax, but holding that 'mere evidence of underdeclarations is not enough to discharge the burden of proof required in respect of a penalty imposed under (*VATA 1994, s 60*) ... in this case the necessary mental element of dishonesty could not readily be inferred from the fact of underdeclarations alone'. *Airspeed Aviation Ltd, MAN/91/1358 (VTD 11544)*.

47.104 **'Self-billing' invoices—failure to account for tax.** The Commissioners imposed a penalty under what is now *VATA 1994, s 60* on a clothing manufacturer who had failed to account for VAT on 'self-billing' invoices issued by one of the retailers to whom he supplied clothing. The manufacturer appealed against the penalty, contending that he had not understood the self-billing system and had not deliberately intended to evade tax. The tribunal allowed the appeal, holding that 'the standard of proof required to establish dishonesty must be a very high degree of probability, not a mere balance of probabilities'. On the evidence, there was a 'reasonable possibility' that the manufacturer's failure to account for tax on the 'self-billing' invoices had been the result of misunderstanding and carelessness, rather than deliberate dishonesty. *KS Nandera, MAN/91/123 (VTD 7880)*. (*Note. Dicta* of the tribunal chairman were disapproved by a subsequent tribunal in *Akbar (t/a Mumtaz Paan House)*, 47.49 above. The chairman here applied a subjective definition of 'dishonesty', whereas in other cases tribunals have applied an objective test, in accordance with the principles laid down by Lord Lane CJ in *R v Ghosh, CA [1982] 3 WLR 110; [1982] 2 All ER 689* (see 47.22 above).)

47.105 **Alleged overclaim of input tax.** A publican reclaimed input tax on the refurbishment of the public house which he owned. Most of the refurbishment was carried out by two people acting in partnership, at a cost of £30,500. The partnership issued the publican with an invoice charging VAT on this work. The publican paid the invoice and reclaimed the VAT as input tax. However, the partnership was not registered for VAT and the VAT number shown on the invoice had never been allocated. The Commissioners therefore rejected the claim, and a VAT officer subsequently interviewed the publican and formed the opinion that he had known that the invoice in question was fictitious. The Commissioners therefore imposed a penalty under what is now *VATA 1994, s 60*. The publican appealed against the penalty, contending that he had paid the amount to the partnership in good faith, and had assumed that the partners must have been registered for VAT, since they had charged him VAT. The tribunal accepted his evidence and allowed the appeal. *R Dickinson, MAN/89/199 (VTD 6309)*.

47.106 The Commissioners formed the opinion that a trader had reclaimed input tax on the basis of four false invoices. They issued an assessment to recover the tax, and imposed a penalty under what is now *VATA 1994, s 60*. The trader appealed, contending that the invoices were genuine. The tribunal reviewed the evidence in detail, finding that two of the invoices represented genuine supplies, upholding the assessment in respect of the other two invoices, and allowing the trader's appeal against the penalty, on the grounds that the Commissioners had 'failed to show' that the appellant had been responsible for producing the two invoices in question. *R Crompton, MAN/92/765 (VTD 12033)*.

47.107 A married couple operated a hotel in partnership. They reclaimed input tax of more than £44,000 in respect of building work allegedly done at the hotel by a company which the husband controlled. Most of the work was carried out in 1992, but the invoice was not issued until April 1993, at which time the company was in financial difficulties. The company went into receivership shortly afterwards without accounting for the output tax shown on the invoice. The Commissioners formed the opinion that the invoice overstated the cost of the work, and that the price of the work had been artificially inflated for tax reasons. They rejected the claim to input tax, and imposed a penalty for alleged evasion of tax. The partnership appealed. The tribunal allowed the appeal against the penalty. On the evidence, it was satisfied that the invoice was issued in April 1993 'because the appointment of the receivers was imminent and (the husband) was about to lose control of the situation'. However, it was satisfied that the invoice represented supplies which the company had made to the partnership, and that the work 'was of the value claimed'. *CJ & K Snape (t/a The Homelea Hotel), LON/94/645P (VTD 13465)*.

MISCELLANEOUS

47.108 **Penalty under VATA 1994, s 60—effect of Human Rights Act 1998.** See *Han & Yau*, 32.2 HUMAN RIGHTS.

48   Penalties: Failure to Notify, etc.

The cases in this chapter are arranged under the following headings.

DEFINITION OF 'RELEVANT VAT' (VATA 1994, s 67(1))

48.1   A trader became liable to register on 1 August 1987 but did not do so until 8 December. The Commissioners imposed a penalty calculated at the rate of 30% of the tax due for the period from 1 August to 8 December, and he appealed, contending that the penalty should only be applied to the tax for the period from 1 August until 31 October, since if he had been registered, the tax for the period from 1 November to 8 December would not have been payable until 29 February 1988. The tribunal rejected this contention and dismissed his appeal. The tax for which he was 'liable' included tax on supplies made between the date on which he should have registered and the date on which he in fact did so, even though he was not required to pay the tax in question until after the date on which he notified the Commissioners. *WJ Corthine, [1988] VATTR 90 (VTD 3012)*. (*Note*. The penalty would now only be 5% of the relevant tax—see *VATA 1994, s 67(4)*.)

48.2   **Whether penalty chargeable for period in respect of which appellant could have applied for deregistration.** In the case noted at 53.73 REGISTRATION, a trader's turnover exceeded the registration threshold in 1987 but dropped below the deregistration threshold in 1990. The Commissioners imposed a penalty covering the whole period from November 1987 to 16 August 1990 (the date on which he had notified the VAT office that he had previously been liable to register). He appealed, contending that the penalty should cease to run with effect from March 1990, when he could have applied for deregistration. The tribunal rejected this contention and dismissed his appeal. *RR Bissmire, LON/90/1563X (VTD 7303)*.

48.3   **Imposition of penalty where assessment issued to collect outstanding tax.** A trader became liable to register in 1975 but did not do so until 1987. The Commissioners imposed a penalty under what is now *VATA 1994, s 67* and also issued an assessment covering the period in question. The trader appealed, contending that a penalty under what is now *VATA 1994, s 67* should not be imposed where the Commissioners had issued an assessment to collect the outstanding tax in respect of which the penalty had been imposed. The tribunal dismissed the appeal and the QB upheld this decision. Leonard J held that there was 'nothing in the legislation which supports the proposition that penalty and assessment are alternative processes' and observing that it was 'inevitable that the tax lost should be the yardstick by which both are measured'. *V Bjellica (t/a Eddy's Domestic Appliances) v C & E Commrs, QB [1993] STC 730. (Note.* For another issue in this case, taken to the CA, see 53.21 REGISTRATION.)

48.4   **Assessment not made to best judgment of Commissioners—whether any 'relevant VAT'.**   In February 1997 the Commissioners issued a ruling that the proprietor of a shop selling take-away food had been liable to register for VAT from July 1990. They issued a notice of compulsory registration and an estimated assessment covering the period from July 1990 to January 1997, charging tax of £92,000. They also imposed a penalty of £12,800 for failure to notify. The trader appealed, contending that the assessment was excessive because most of his sales were zero-rated (and that this was a reasonable excuse for his failure to register). The tribunal reviewed the evidence in detail and held that the trader had become liable to register in October 1990, and that there was no reasonable excuse for his failure to do so. However, the tribunal also held that the estimated assessment had not been made to the best of the Commissioners' judgment, and held that 'because the assessment has fallen, the civil penalty ... assessed by the Commissioners must also fall'. The tribunal held that there was 'no relevant VAT' for the purposes of *VATA 1994, s 67(1)*, and also held that it had no jurisdiction to impose the £50 penalty referred to in *s 67(1)*. *D Barrett (t/a The Carib Takeaway), LON/678 (VTD 15389).*

DATE FROM WHICH PENALTY COMMENCES (VATA 1994, s 67(3))

48.5   A trader became liable to register from 21 July 1985, but did not do so until 23 December 1985. The Commissioners imposed a penalty under *FA 1985, s 15* (now *VATA 1994, s 67*) and he appealed, contending that *FA 1985, s 15* created a single offence, which in his case had occurred before 25 July 1985 when the relevant provisions came into force. The tribunal dismissed his appeal, holding that *FA 1985, s 15* created a continuous offence rather than a single offence. Since the failure to register had continued at the time when the provisions of *FA 1985, s 15* came into force, the penalty should be calculated from that date. *JF Gale, [1986] VATTR 185 (VTD 2138).*

48.6   A similar decision was reached in *Kelvingold Ltd, LON/86/180 (VTD 2110).*

48.7   A trader became liable to register in July 1984 but did not do so until May 1986. The Commissioners imposed a penalty under what is now *VATA 1994, s 67* and he appealed, raising the same contention as the appellant in *Gale*, 48.5 above. The Ch D rejected this contention and upheld the penalty, holding that what is now *VATA 1994, s 67* recognised a continuing obligation to notify a liability to register and that there was no presumption against retrospection. *C & E Commrs v Shingleton, Ch D 1987, [1988] STC 190.*

48.8   The Ch D decision in *Shingleton*, 48.7 above, was followed in *Genc*, 39.60 LAND, and *Typeflow Ltd, LON/88/808 (VTD 3264).*

DATE ON WHICH PENALTY CEASES (VATA 1994, s 67(3))

48.9   **Claim of earlier notification.**   An actor became liable to register for VAT in August 1985. He did not notify the Commissioners of this until July 1987, and they imposed a penalty under what is now *VATA 1994, s 67*. He appealed, contending that he had submitted an application for registration in May 1986, so that the penalty should only be calculated to that time. The tribunal dismissed his appeal, finding on the evidence that the Commissioners had not been notified of his liability to register until July 1987. *PS Dean, LON/89/795Z (VTD 4314)*.

48.10   Similar decisions were reached in *S & SJ Hayes, MAN/89/352 (VTD 4693)*; *RP Lambourne, LON/89/1324 (VTD 4771)*; *A Patel (t/a Swami Stores), LON/89/1002Y (VTD 4912)*; *FJ Kwiatkowski, LON/90/1250Z (VTD 5457)*; *Ryan Evans Ltd, LON/90/637X (VTD 5682)*; *Country Manor Manufacturing Ltd, LON/91/1413X (VTD 6518)* and *Betar Aluminium Fixings Ltd, MAN/92/1151 (VTD 9432)*.

48.11   A trader became liable to register for VAT in March 1983, but did not do so. He visited his local VAT office in June 1984 to apply for registration. A VAT officer helped him to complete a form VAT 1, but he heard nothing further from the office. At first he did not pursue the matter, but eventually he visited the office again. By this time the officer to whom he had previously spoken had left. (The VAT office had no record of this second visit and the trader could not recall its date.) He was still not registered after this second visit, and visited the office for a third time in June 1986. The Commissioners then imposed a penalty under what is now *VATA 1994, s 67*. The tribunal allowed the trader's appeal, finding that the trader had notified the Commissioners of his liability to register in June 1984. *RV McLaren, MAN/89/393 (VTD 4117)*.

WHETHER A REASONABLE EXCUSE (VATA 1994, s 67(8))

Illness or bereavement

Cases where the appellant was successful

48.12   **Illness of wife.**   A trader, whose wife acted as his bookkeeper, appealed against a penalty under what is now *VATA 1994, s 67*, giving evidence that his wife had been ill, and thus had been unable to keep his books up to date. He had therefore been unaware that his turnover had exceeded the registration threshold. The tribunal allowed the appeal, holding that the circumstances constituted a reasonable excuse. *J Warnock, EDN/90/106 (VTD 5396)*.

48.13   An engineer became liable to register for VAT from April 1988, but did not do so until May 1991. The Commissioners imposed a penalty under what is now *VATA 1994, s 67* and he appealed, contending that he had a reasonable excuse because in March 1988 his wife had been diagnosed as having cervical cancer, and he had required medical and psychiatric treatment for stress. In 1991 he and his wife had divorced. The tribunal allowed his appeal, holding that the circumstances constituted a reasonable excuse for his failure to register. *N McPherson, LON/92/144Z (VTD 9580)*.

48.14   **Illness of company director.**   A company appealed against a penalty under what is now *VATA 1994, s 67*, contending that it had a reasonable excuse because at the relevant time the controlling director and his wife had both suffered from illness, the director's mother had died, and their landlord had attempted to evict them from their house. The tribunal allowed the appeal, holding that the circumstances constituted a reasonable excuse for the company's failure to register. *RHS Structural Engineering Ltd, LON/91/2036Z (VTD 7354)*.

48.15   **Illness of bookkeeper.**   A florist became liable to register for VAT in April 1986, but did not do so until April 1990, and a penalty under what is now *VATA 1994, s 67* was imposed. The florist appealed, contending that she had a reasonable excuse because her bookkeeper had sent a form VAT 1 to the local VAT office in December 1987, and had failed to follow this up because she had been ill and had spent several periods in hospital. A photocopy of the form VAT 1 was produced in evidence. The Commissioners gave evidence that the form VAT 1 had never been received. The tribunal allowed the appeal in part, upholding the penalty for the period from April 1986 to December 1987, but holding that there was a reasonable excuse for the period from December 1987 to April 1990. The chairman observed that the prolonged failure to follow up an application for registration would not normally constitute a reasonable excuse, applying *dicta* in *Hislop*, 48.101 below, and *Pacey Rogers & Co*, 48.120 below, and disapproving *obiter dicta* of the tribunal chairman in *Selwyn*, 48.100 below. However, the prolonged illness of the bookkeeper did constitute a reasonable excuse for the failure to follow up the application which had been sent in December 1987. *CD Tomkins (t/a Options), MAN/90/995 (VTD 11738)*.

48.16   **Death of partner.**   A married couple purchased a riding stable in February 1989. The vendors had not been registered for VAT, since their turnover had been below the statutory threshold. In August 1989 the husband, who had been worried about the couple's finances, committed suicide. His widow continued to run the stable as a sole proprietor. Her husband's affairs were in a 'terrible state', and it took her several months to straighten them out. She did not register for VAT until August 1990 and the Commissioners imposed a penalty under what is now *VATA 1994, s 67*. The tribunal allowed her appeal, holding that the circumstances of her husband's suicide and the ensuing difficulties constituted a reasonable excuse. *P Ford (t/a Children's Riding Stables), MAN/91/109 (VTD 6855)*.

Cases where the appellant was unsuccessful

48.17   **Injury to partner.**   A married couple ran a café in partnership. They became liable to register for VAT in July 1986 but did not do so. In September 1986 the husband fell off a bridge and seriously injured his back. He remained in hospital for several months. The partnership did not apply for registration until August 1988 and the Commissioners imposed a penalty under what is now *VATA 1994, s 67*. The couple appealed, contending that the husband's injury was a reasonable excuse. The tribunal dismissed the appeal, observing that the couple had become liable to register two months before the injury occurred. *DB & JP Blake, MAN/88/862 (VTD 3515)*.

48.18   **Solicitor suffering miscarriage.**   A female solicitor became liable to register for VAT in January 1987, but did not do so until September 1988. The Commissioners imposed a penalty under what is now *VATA 1994, s 67* and she appealed, contending that she had a reasonable excuse because she had hoped to conceive and stop working, but that although she had become pregnant, she had suffered a miscarriage in August 1987. The tribunal dismissed her appeal, observing that both her pregnancy and her miscarriage had occurred after she had become liable to register and thus could not constitute a reasonable excuse. *CDA From, LON/90/1621X (VTD 5605)*.

48.19   **Illness of bookkeeper.**   A contractor (C) became liable to register in December 1991 but did not do so until June 1994. The Commissioners imposed a penalty and C appealed, contending firstly that he had a reasonable excuse because his father, who had acted as his bookkeeper, had been ill with cancer at the relevant time, and secondly that the penalty should be mitigated. The tribunal dismissed the appeal, observing that C had been incorrectly issuing invoices with a registration number which related to a business previously carried on by his father, and holding that, in view of the length of time for which the situation had continued, there was no reasonable excuse for C's failure to register. (The tribunal also held that, in view of the serious nature of the default, the penalty should not be mitigated.) *AJP Cheek (t/a Swanley Contractors), LON/95/1302P (VTD 13456).*

Liability uncertain

Cases where the appellant was successful

48.20   **Computation of turnover uncertain.** A freelance sports journalist became liable to register for VAT from November 1987, but did not do so until 1991. The Commissioners imposed a penalty under what is now *VATA 1994, s 67*, and he appealed, contending that he had a reasonable excuse because part of his income consisted of reimbursements of expenses which he had incurred abroad, and he had not realised that this should have been included in his turnover for VAT purposes. The tribunal allowed his appeal in part, holding on the evidence that he had a reasonable excuse for failing to register between November 1987 and 1 November 1989, but not for his continuing failure thereafter. *P Nichols, LON/92/657 (VTD 9304).*

48.21   Similar decisions were reached in *A Garrett, LON/92/3089P (VTD 10798)* and *JFE Tyrrel, LON/93/166A (VTD 11984).*

48.22   A curtain manufacturer became liable to register for VAT in January 1989, after her turnover had exceeded the statutory threshold in the quarter ending December 1988. However, she did not register until June 1989, and the Commissioners imposed a penalty under what is now *VATA 1994, s 67*. She appealed, contending that she had a reasonable excuse because her turnover in the quarter ending December 1988 had included an advance payment from a major customer which she had needed to purchase materials, and she had regarded this advance payment as a loan and had not realised that it formed part of her turnover. The tribunal allowed her appeal against the penalty, holding that the circumstances constituted a reasonable excuse. *M Nield (t/a Soft Options), MAN/92/137 (10677).*

48.23   A medical partnership became liable to register for VAT in October 1990, after the building of a new surgery which was a deemed self-supply under what is now *VATA 1994, Sch 10*. They failed to register, and the Commissioners subsequently imposed a penalty under what is now *VATA 1994, s 67*. The partners appealed, contending that they had a reasonable excuse for not having realised that the effect of the construction of their new surgery was that they should have registered for VAT. The tribunal accepted their evidence and allowed their appeal. *Dr Lock & Partners, LON/93/771 (VTD 10946).*

48.24   **Death of bookkeeper—turnover uncertain.** An appeal was allowed in a case where a partnership gave evidence that its bookkeeper had died while its books were in her possession, and that the partners had been unable to recover the books for six months, and thus had not realised that their turnover had exceeded the threshold. *AM Autos, LON/89/442 (VTD 3698).*

48.25   **Illness of bookkeeper.** See *Warnock*, 48.12 above.

48.26   **Contractor using subcontract labour.** A ceiling fitter arranged for himself and three colleagues to carry out some work for a company. He did not register for VAT, and the Commissioners imposed a penalty under what is now *VATA 1994, s 67*. He appealed, contending that he had not realised that his three colleagues would be treated as his subcontractors and that the amounts he paid to them would be treated as part of his turnover for VAT purposes. The tribunal allowed his appeal, holding that the circumstances constituted a reasonable excuse. *P Bailey, LON/88/200 (VTD 2851).*

48.27   *Bailey*, 48.26 above, was applied in the similar cases of *WA Scott, LON/88/315 (VTD 2938, 4208); JG Wallace, LON/92/178Z (VTD 7487)* and *G Gillespie, EDN/93/202 (VTD 11504).*

48.28   Similar decisions were reached in *WG Hubbard, LON/88/207 (VTD 2913); SR Ling, LON/88/262 (VTD 3099); L Dugdale & Son, MAN/90/713 (VTD 5431)* and *K Kavanagh, LON/90/1113X (VTD 6409).*

48.29   **Band leader receiving payments for band of musicians.**   A musician (K) organised a band, comprising himself and three other musicians, to play at a holiday camp. K received the payments for the band, and paid the other three musicians at Musicians' Union rates. The amounts paid to K exceeded the registration threshold but the amounts retained by him after making payments to the other musicians were below the threshold. He did not register for VAT and the Commissioners imposed a penalty under what is now *VATA 1994, s 67.* K appealed against the penalty, contending that he had a reasonable excuse because he had not realised that the amounts which he paid to the other musicians formed part of his turnover for VAT purposes. The tribunal allowed his appeal, holding that the circumstances constituted a reasonable excuse. *BJ Kirkby, LON/91/375Y (VTD 6545).*

48.30   **Dispute over existence of partnership—whether a reasonable excuse.**   Two brothers traded as builders. They each had their own premises, and each had accounts drawn up as if they were trading as individuals. However, in 1987 they began advertising for work under a partnership name, and in October 1988 they took out a joint public liability insurance policy. They subsequently obtained several contracts from the local council. They registered for VAT as a partnership in December 1989. The Commissioners discovered that their joint turnover had exceeded the VAT registration threshold for several years, and imposed a penalty under what is now *VATA 1994, s 67* on the basis that they should have registered as a partnership in October 1988 (when they had taken out their joint public liability insurance policy). The brothers appealed, contending that, until December 1989, they had regarded themselves as being sole traders rather than a partnership. The tribunal held that the brothers had been members of a *de facto* partnership from October 1988, applying *Moore v Davis, Ch D 1879, 11 Ch D 261* and *dicta* of Cozens-Hardy MR in *Weiner v Harris, CA [1910] 1 KB 285.* However, the tribunal allowed their appeal against the penalty, holding that the complexity of the relevant law constituted a reasonable excuse. *J & E Malin, LON/91/2224 (VTD 10085).*

48.31   *Malin*, 48.30 above, was applied in *Leonidas*, 44.23 PARTNERSHIP, where the tribunal held that a married couple had been trading in partnership but had a reasonable excuse for regarding themselves as sole traders.

48.32   **Hairdressing salon—proprietor believing that amounts retained by stylists not forming part of turnover for VAT purposes—whether a reasonable excuse.**   The proprietor of a hairdressing salon became liable to register for VAT in 1988, but failed to do so. The Commissioners imposed a penalty under what is now *VATA 1994, s 67.* The proprietor appealed, contending firstly that the amounts retained by the stylists should not be treated as forming part of her turnover, and alternatively that she had a reasonable excuse for not treating them as part of her turnover. The tribunal held that the relevant services were supplied to customers by the salon proprietor, rather than by the employees. However, since the proprietor had acted in good faith, there was a reasonable excuse for her failure to register. *B Harrison, LON/91/880 (VTD 12351).* (*Note.* Compare *Hopkins*, 48.63 below, where similar circumstances were held not to constitute a reasonable excuse.)

48.33   **Computation of turnover—misleading advice from VAT office.**   A builder appealed against a penalty for late registration, contending that he had a reasonable excuse because he had telephoned his local VAT Advice Centre, which had told him that for the purposes of the registration threshold, each year of trading would be treated separately, and had failed to explain that his turnover needed to be monitored on a 'rolling year' basis. The tribunal accepted his evidence and allowed his appeal, holding that the misleading advice constituted a reasonable excuse. *A Edwards, LON/00/246 (VTD 16849)*.

48.34 **Belief that supplies exempt.**   An orthodontist became liable to register for VAT from March 1984 but did not do so. The Commissioners imposed a penalty under what is now *VATA 1994, s 67*, and he appealed, contending that he had a reasonable excuse because he had been advised that his supplies were exempt. The tribunal accepted his evidence and allowed his appeal. *G Davies, LON/86/174 (VTD 2126)*.

48.35 Two associated partnerships operated chiropractic clinics. They became liable to register for VAT in 1986 and 1987 respectively, but did not do so until February 1992. The Commissioners imposed penalties under what is now *VATA 1994, s 67* and the partnerships appealed, contending that they had a reasonable excuse because they had believed that their supplies were exempt from VAT, and that this had been confirmed by a telephone call to the Newcastle VAT office. The tribunal allowed the appeals in part, holding on the evidence that the partnerships had a reasonable excuse for their failure to register before May 1991, but that since the partnerships had consulted accountants in the spring of 1991, there was no excuse for the continuing failure to register after May 1991. The tribunal chairman commented that 'it was the duty of (the) accountants to make full and proper enquiries as to the position with regard to ... registration for value added tax'. *Dr KP & P Burns (t/a North Ferriby Chiropractic Clinic), MAN/92/987; Dr KP & Mrs LM Burns (t/a Sheffield Clinic of Complementary Medicine), MAN/93/401 (VTD 12046)*.

48.36 **Belief that supplies zero-rated.**   A writer of textbooks failed to register for VAT, and the Commissioners imposed a penalty under what is now *VATA 1994, s 67*. He appealed, contending that he had a reasonable excuse because he had assumed that the writing of such textbooks was outside the scope of VAT. The tribunal accepted his evidence and allowed his appeal. *Neal, 48.48 below, distinguished. JD Waugh, MAN/90/274 (VTD 5344, 6206)*.

48.37 Similar decisions were reached in *P Palliser, LON/91/1120 (VTD 6262); PJ Doyle, LON/92/17Y (VTD 8811); K Sharpe, MAN/91/924 (VTD 8914)* and *GM Neville & MR Clark (t/a Trueline Interiors), LON/92/3238P (VTD 10350)*.

48.38 **School operating 'tuck shop' and selling tickets for school play—bursar unaware that such sales within the scope of VAT.**   A school operated a 'tuck shop' under the control of the bursar, who had previously been the school secretary. Most of the sales at the tuck shop were of sweets and crisps, but the shop also sold stationery, calculators, and school uniforms. In December 1987 the school also sold tickets for a school play, with the result that its turnover exceeded the threshold for registration. The bursar did not realise that the school was liable to register, and no steps were taken to register until January 1991, when the headmaster applied for registration after the governors had sought advice on the subject. The Commissioners imposed a penalty under what is now *VATA 1994, s 67* and the school appealed, contending that it had a reasonable excuse for having failed to register previously since neither the headmaster nor the bursar had realised that it was liable to do so. The tribunal allowed the school's appeal. Although the supplies at the tuck shop were clearly made by the school, it was accepted that the supplies of education at the school (which were exempt from VAT) were, for VAT purposes, made by the local education authority, and it was at least arguable that the school play should not be deemed to be supplied by the school as principal, but as agent for the local education authority. In view of the complexity of the case, the school had a reasonable excuse for its failure to register. *St Benedict's School, MAN/91/950 (VTD 7235)*.

48.39   **Sales of timber—incorrect belief that such supplies outside the scope of VAT.**   A solicitor and his wife bought an area of woodland in 1988. In 1989 they sold a large quantity of timber. They did not register for VAT, and the Commissioners imposed a penalty under what is now *VATA 1994, s 67*. They appealed, contending that they had assumed that the sales of timber were outside the scope of VAT. The tribunal allowed the appeal against the penalty. The sale of timber was a taxable supply under VAT law, but the solicitor and his wife had genuinely believed that, in selling the timber, they were not carrying on any business. Ignorance of the primary law relating to VAT was not a reasonable excuse, but ignorance of the detailed provisions of VAT law could constitute a reasonable excuse. *MJ & KE Prior, LON/92/432Y (VTD 7978)*.

48.40   **Subcontractors claiming to be employees.**   The Commissioners imposed penalties under what is now *VATA 1994, s 67* on three painters, working for the same company, who had not registered for VAT. One of the painters was aged 26 and the other two were teenagers. The painters appealed, contending firstly that they should be treated as employees rather than as self-employed, and alternatively that the circumstances constituted a reasonable excuse for their failure to register. The tribunal rejected the appellants' first contention, finding that they were self-employed and were not employees. However, the tribunal allowed their appeals on the grounds that they had acted reasonably, in view of their age and 'social and educational circumstances', in coming to the incorrect view that they were not required to register for VAT, and therefore had a reasonable excuse. *SJ Geary, LON/86/395; G Jackson, LON/86/530; C Pook, LON/86/394 (VTD 2314)*.

48.41   *Geary & Others*, 48.40 above, was applied in the similar cases of *WJS Gillard, LON/90/141Z (5040); PG Hughes, LON/90/55X (VTD 5223)* and *M & GA Stone, LON/91/427X (VTD 7798)*.

48.42   Similar decisions were reached in *S Butler, MAN/87/119 & 185 (VTD 3067); JA Bell, BEL/91/61X (VTD 7411); MB Beardshaw, MAN/91/1316 (VTD 9245)* and *KS Brown, LON/92/2063P (VTD 9614)*.

48.43   **Salesman claiming to be employee.**   A salesman was granted a franchise to act as an agent, on a commission-only basis, for a company selling windows, doors and conservatories. He failed to register for VAT, and the Commissioners imposed a penalty under what is now *VATA 1994, s 67*. He appealed, contending that his agreement with the company indicated that the company would be responsible for paying VAT on the commission which it paid him. The tribunal allowed his appeal, holding that the wording of the agreement constituted a reasonable excuse. *JAJ Dickson, MAN/87/218 (VTD 2560)*.

48.44   A similar decision was reached in a case involving a double-glazing salesman. *BF James, LON/90/153X (VTD 5078)*.

48.45   **Actor claiming to be employee.**   A Swedish actor was offered and accepted a part in a musical in London. At the end of his contract he consulted an accountant who advised him that he had become liable to register for VAT. The Commissioners imposed a penalty under what is now *VATA 1994, s 67*. He appealed, contending that he had a reasonable excuse for not registering, as income tax had been deducted from his salary by the producers of the musical, and he had therefore believed that he was an employee and had not realised that he would be expected to register for VAT. The tribunal allowed his appeal, holding that the circumstances constituted a reasonable excuse. *BTG Korberg, LON/88/553 (VTD 2966)*.

48.46   Place of supply uncertain—whether a reasonable excuse. A Dutch subsidiary of a UK company sold goods which had been manufactured in the UK. Some of its sales were to UK customers, and it became liable to register for VAT in 1991, but did not do so until the following year. The Commissioners imposed a penalty under what is now *VATA 1994, s 67* and the company appealed, contending that it had a reasonable excuse because it had believed that its supplies took place in the Netherlands and were outside the scope of UK VAT. The tribunal allowed the appeal, holding that the circumstances constituted a reasonable excuse. *HMG Europe BV, EDN/92/251 (VTD 9814)*.

48.47   Uncertainty of time of supply of services—whether a reasonable excuse. An architect became liable to register in February 1989 but did not do so until February 1990. He appealed, contending that he had a reasonable excuse because he had believed that the tax point for his supplies was either the time he received payment or the time he issued invoices, whereas the Commissioners had treated the time of supply as being the time when the services were actually performed. The tribunal allowed his appeal, holding that the Commissioners were correct in treating the time of performance as the tax point, but observing that 'where, as here, the correct analysis of which tax point applies ... is a question of some difficulty, then the taxpayer may be forgiven for getting the answer wrong'. *AM Weldon-Hollingworth, LON/94/592A (VTD 13248)*.

Cases where the appellant was unsuccessful

48.48   Ignorance of VAT. A freelance model began self-employment in April 1985, when she was 19 years of age. She became liable to register for VAT in October 1985, but did not do so until March 1986. The Commissioners imposed a penalty under what is now *VATA 1994, s 67* and she appealed, contending that she had no knowledge of VAT and was unaware that her income exceeded the registration limits. The tribunal dismissed her appeal, holding that her ignorance of the law could not constitute a reasonable excuse. The QB upheld this decision, observing that VAT was 'now well enough established in our daily commerce that anyone, however inexperienced, ought to recognise the need to become acquainted with its basic requirements when embarking upon a career'. *Jo-Ann Neal v C & E Commrs, QB 1987, [1988] STC 131*.

**48.49   *Jo-Ann Neal*, 48.48 above, has been applied in a large number of subsequent cases in which appeals against penalties under what is now *VATA 1994, s 67* have been dismissed. Such cases appear to raise no point of general importance, and, in the interests of space, are not reported individually in this book. For a list of such cases decided up to 31 December 1993, see Tolley's VAT Cases 1994.

48.50   A barrister became liable to register for VAT in May 1987, but did not do so until November 1988. He appealed against a penalty under what is now *VATA 1994, s 67*, contending that he had assumed that fees which he had received could be spread over earlier years, and that what is now *VAT Regulations 1995 (SI 1995 No 2518), reg 92*, which provided that services supplied by barristers were to be treated as taking place on receipt of the relevant fees, was *ultra vires*. The tribunal rejected this contention and dismissed his appeal, observing that 'a barrister who was in practice throughout the period from the introduction of VAT in 1973 until 1988 should have made himself familiar with the provisions relating to the way VAT should be accounted for to the Customs & Excise by members of the Bar'. *Regulation 92 was valid and properly made. On the evidence, the barrister had previously defended a client on a charge of evading VAT, and had read the *VATA* at the time. Even if he had genuinely believed that a regulation was *ultra vires*, he should have taken such a point on appeal. An erroneous view of the law did not provide a barrister with a reasonable excuse for failing to register. *JD Seal, LON/89/1200X (VTD 4586)*.

48.51 An appeal was dismissed in a case where a self-employed sales agent, working on a commission basis for one company only, contended that she had assumed that she should not be required to register. *ME Smith, LON/90/887Y (VTD 6921)*.

48.52 **Separate businesses operated by sole trader—ignorance of 'Glassborow principle'.** A trader who operated two separate businesses failed to register for VAT. The combined turnover of the businesses exceeded the registration threshold and the Commissioners imposed a penalty under what is now *VATA 1994, s 67*. The trader appealed, contending that it was not reasonable to aggregate the turnover of the businesses and that he had a reasonable excuse for not registering. The tribunal dismissed his appeal. Applying *Glassborow*, 53.1 REGISTRATION, a registration is of a person and not of the businesses he carries on. Furthermore, the trader's failure to seek advice on the position meant that the circumstances could not constitute a reasonable excuse. *BW Dawson, LON/90/216X (VTD 5216)*.

48.53 **Turnover uncertain.** A film production manager appealed against a penalty under what is now *VATA 1994, s 67*, contending that although he was aware that his supplies had exceeded the quarterly threshold then in force, he was not certain whether they would exceed the annual threshold. The tribunal dismissed his appeal, holding that he should have registered as soon as his supplies exceeded the quarterly threshold. *WF Shephard, LON/86/318 (VTD 2232)*.

48.54 *Shephard*, 48.53 above, was applied in the similar cases of *PK Cruse, LON/90/750X (VTD 5975)* and *G Wisker, LON/91/2585A (VTD 9716)*.

48.55 Similar decisions were reached in *Spurtrade Ltd, LON/86/725Z (VTD 2290); Managerial Problem Solving Ltd, LON/88/331 (VTD 2826)* and *LR Thorne, LON/92/2982P (VTD 10051, 10175)*.

48.56 A self-employed salesman, who sold goods produced by a limited company, appealed against a penalty under what is now *VATA 1994, s 67*, contending that he had a reasonable excuse in that he had not been certain whether his turnover consisted of his total sales or of his commission only, and that the company which produced the goods which he sold had not given him adequate advice. The tribunal dismissed his appeal, holding that the circumstances did not constitute a reasonable excuse. *JG Smith, MAN/87/189 (VTD 2917)*.

48.57 A barrister appealed against a penalty under what is now *VATA 1994, s 67*, contending that he had a reasonable excuse as he was uncertain as to the amount of his turnover. The tribunal rejected this contention and dismissed his appeal. *MA Syed, LON/88/1077X (VTD 3534)*.

48.58 Similar decisions were reached in *KA Metzger, LON/89/1534X (VTD 5304); GW Baxter, EDN/92/124 (VTD 9152); N Slater, LON/92/1541A (VTD 9865); Norman Adams Artists & Potters, LON/92/1457 (VTD 9964); P Newby (t/a Peter Newby & Co), MAN/92/898 (VTD 10395); DN Mawhinney, BEL/92/86 (VTD 10475); GC Barrie, MAN/93/89 (VTD 11470); PB Abrook, LON/93/1827P (VTD 11473); NP Scott-Dickinson & AF Nunn, LON/92/3173A (VTD 11859)* and *Gent*, 48.142 below.

48.59 See also *Optimum Personnel Evaluation (Operations) Ltd*, 53.37 REGISTRATION, and *Sullivan*, 53.93 REGISTRATION.

48.60 **Illiteracy.** A trader became liable to register for VAT in January 1983, but did not do so until December 1988. The Commissioners imposed a penalty under what is now *VATA 1994, s 67* and he appealed, contending that he had a reasonable excuse because he was illiterate and had believed that his turnover was below the registration threshold. The tribunal dismissed his appeal, applying *Neal*, 48.48 above, and distinguishing *Geary*, 48.40 above. On the evidence, the appellant had been ignorant of the basic principles of VAT law, namely the requirement for liability to register. *Mason*, 48.112 below, was distinguished because the appellant here was 'capable of benefiting from oral communication'. *D Searle, LON/90/1407Z (VTD 5900)*.

48.61 **Contractor using subcontract labour.** An engineer, working as a contractor with one subcontractor, appealed against a penalty under what is now *VATA 1994, s 67*, contending that he had a reasonable excuse because he had not realised that the amounts he had paid to his subcontractor formed part of his turnover for VAT purposes. The tribunal dismissed his appeal, holding that ignorance of the law was not a reasonable excuse. *AD Morris, LON/88/852X (VTD 3456)*.

48.62 Similar decisions were reached in *SG Pinder, MAN/88/909 (VTD 3582); AS Worboys, LON/88/408Y (VTD 3866)* and *LP Marsh, LON/92/135Y (VTD 9810)*.

48.63 **Hairdressing salon—proprietors believing that amounts retained by stylists not forming part of turnover for VAT purposes—whether a reasonable excuse.** A partnership which operated a hairdressing salon became liable to register for VAT from February 1988, but failed to do so. The Commissioners imposed a penalty under what is now *VATA 1994, s 67*. The partners appealed, contending that they had a reasonable excuse for their failure to register because their accountant had led them to believe that the amounts which were retained by the hairstylists who worked for them did not form part of their turnover for VAT purposes. The tribunal dismissed the appeal, finding that the partners had attempted to rely on a 'flimsy avoidance scheme' and that the circumstances did not constitute a reasonable excuse. *GD & M Hopkins (t/a Marianne's Hair Salon), LON/93/1969 (VTD 11587)*.

48.64 **Belief that supplies exempt.** The Commissioners imposed a penalty under what is now *VATA 1994, s 67* on two partners who sold videotapes on commission. They appealed, contending that they had a reasonable excuse because they had been wrongly advised by their accountant that commission was exempt from VAT. The tribunal dismissed their appeal, holding that the error amounted to simple and basic ignorance of VAT law, which was not a reasonable excuse. *RFS Phillips & Another, LON/88/314 (VTD 2829)*.

48.65 A private hospital, which made standard-rated supplies as well as exempt supplies, appealed against a penalty under what is now *VATA 1994, s 67*, contending that uncertainty as to the liability of its supplies constituted a reasonable excuse. The tribunal rejected this contention and dismissed the appeal. *Warwickshire Private Hospital, MAN/88/863 (VTD 3531)*.

48.66 An educational college appealed against a penalty under what is now *VATA 1994, s 67*, contending that it had a reasonable excuse because it had believed that its supplies were exempt. The tribunal dismissed the appeal, finding that the college's supplies did not qualify for exemption and holding that the college had no reasonable excuse for having failed to ascertain this. *Metro College of English, LON/93/1465P (VTD 11312)*.

48.67 **Belief that supplies zero-rated.** A bricklayer failed to register for VAT and the Commissioners imposed a penalty under what is now *VATA 1994, s 67*. He appealed, contending that he had a reasonable excuse because the buildings for which he was laying bricks were zero-rated, and he had therefore assumed that his work must be zero-rated. The tribunal dismissed his appeal, holding that such ignorance was not 'reasonable'. *Geary & Others*, 48.40 above, distinguished. *D Farrow, LON/91/ 1051X (VTD 6410)*.

48.68   Similar decisions were reached in *CS Bruce, LON/93/2380A (VTD 11861)* and *KA Wales, MAN/94/24 (VTD 12561)*.

48.69   A consultant became liable to register for VAT in January 1985, but did not do so until April 1987. The Commissioners imposed a penalty under what is now *VATA 1994, s 67*. He appealed, contending that many of his supplies were zero-rated under *VATA 1983, Sch 5 Group 9*, and he had assumed that they could be ignored in considering whether he was liable to register. The tribunal dismissed his appeal, holding that he should have read *Notice No 700* with greater care and should have sought advice from his local VAT office. *DA Smith, LON/90/1212Y (VTD 6598)*.

48.70   A similar decision was reached in *T Haycock, LON/91/162Y (VTD 6850)*.

48.71   A company which carried on business as a landscaping contractor became liable to register in January 1987 but did not do so until August 1990. The Commissioners imposed a penalty under what is now *VATA 1994, s 67* and the company appealed, contending that it had a reasonable excuse because it had assumed that its supplies were zero-rated. The tribunal dismissed the company's appeal, holding that 'the default was entirely due to basic ignorance of the law' and that such ignorance could not constitute a reasonable excuse. *Neal*, 48.48 above, applied; *Bailey*, 48.26 above, and *Scott*, 48.27 above, distinguished. *Revelstar Ltd, LON/91/1036 (VTD 6734)*.

48.72   A chartered surveyor appealed against a penalty for late registration, contending that he had a reasonable excuse because he had believed that his supplies were zero-rated and that he was not required to register. The tribunal dismissed his appeal, observing that he should have sought advice. *KW Paterson, LON/91/1224Z (VTD 7423)*.

48.73   A similar decision was reached in a case where the proprietor of a shop selling take-away food contended that he had believed that he was not required to register as most of his supplies were zero-rated. *D Barrett (t/a The Carib Takeaway), LON/678 (VTD 15389)*. (*Note*. For another issue in this case, see 48.4 above.)

48.74   A building worker appealed against a penalty under what is now *VATA 1994, s 67*, contending that he had assumed that he would not be liable to register for VAT as all his work had been zero-rated until April 1989, and that although his work had become standard-rated following the enactment of *FA 1989*, he had been unaware of the changes and of the need to register. The tribunal dismissed the appeal, holding that the appellant had been ignorant of 'fairly basic VAT law' and that this did not constitute a reasonable excuse. *KJ Hopkins, LON/92/654 (VTD 8890)*.

48.75   **Belief that activities not constituting a 'business'.** An unincorporated association was established to organise a conference. It became liable to register for VAT in September 1985 but did not do so until March 1987, after the conference had taken place. The Commissioners imposed a penalty under what is now *VATA 1994, s 67*. The association appealed, contending that its officers had not appreciated that it was carrying on a 'business' for VAT purposes. The tribunal dismissed the appeal, holding that there was no real doubt that the organisation of a conference for profit constituted a business activity, so that the circumstances did not constitute a reasonable excuse. *First International Conference on Emergency Medicine, MAN/88/ 218 (VTD 2881)*.

48.76   **Consultant claiming to be an employee.** An appeal was dismissed in a case where a consultant, who had previously worked as an employee for the same company, contended that he had not realised the implications of the consultancy agreement. The tribunal held that the circumstances did not constitute a reasonable excuse. *NJR Kay, MAN/87/74 (VTD 2373)*.

48.77   **Self-employed salesman claiming to be an employee.**   An appeal was dismissed in a case where a salesman, working for a single company on a self-employed basis, contended that he had believed that he was an employee and therefore not liable to register for VAT. *T Lowrie, LON/90/763 (VTD 5965)*.

48.78   See also *Osborn*, 48.143 below, and *Sullivan*, 58.235 SUPPLY.

48.79   **Contractor claiming to be an employee.**   An appeal against a penalty was dismissed in a case where a contractor contended that he had considered that he was an employee and had not realised that he was required to register for VAT. The tribunal held that the circumstances did not constitute a reasonable excuse. *J Divers, MAN/93/185 (VTD 12525)*.

Reliance on third party (VATA 1994, s 71(1)(b))

Cases where the appellant was successful

48.80   **Misrepresentation by acquaintance.**   J, who had previously been an employee, began self-employment in May 1987. He sought advice concerning VAT from G, an acquaintance whom he had met while travelling to work by train. G had told J that he was a qualified accountant, and promised J that he would arrange his registration for VAT. In May 1987 he gave J a registration number, which J used on his invoices. In September 1987 J telephoned his local VAT office to enquire why he had not received a VAT return. It transpired that the number which G had given to J was not an official registration number, and G had not registered J for VAT. J subsequently discovered that G was not in fact a qualified accountant. The Commissioners imposed a penalty on J under what is now *VATA 1994, s 67*, and J appealed, contending that he had a reasonable excuse because he had genuinely believed that he was registered. The tribunal allowed J's appeal, applying *dicta* in *Bowen*, 18.102 DEFAULT SURCHARGE, and distinguishing *Neal*, 48.48 above. Merely delegating a task to a third party was not a reasonable excuse, but in this case J had actually been given what he believed to be a registration number, and G's misrepresentations did amount to a reasonable excuse. *KE Jenkinson, [1988] VATTR 45 (VTD 2688)*.

48.81   **Misleading advice from former partner.**   Two brothers (R and ID) had carried on business together in partnership. They dissolved the partnership in July 1985 and ID continued as a sole trader. R, who had been the senior partner, told ID and their accountant that he had notified the VAT office that ID was continuing the business, although in fact he had not done so. ID gradually became concerned that he was not receiving VAT forms, and consulted an accountant in June 1986, as a result of which he registered for VAT in July 1986. The Commissioners imposed a penalty under what is now *VATA 1994, s 67*, but the tribunal allowed ID's appeal, finding that he had genuinely believed that he remained registered despite his brother's resignation from the partnership, and holding that he therefore had a reasonable excuse. *IW Dale, LON/87/562 (VTD 3385)*. (*Note*. For the award of costs in this case, see 2.260 APPEALS.)

48.82   Two individuals (R and S) began a double-glazing business in partnership in July 1988. They completed and signed a VAT registration form, and R told S that he would send the form to the VAT office. Six months later R flew to Africa with a female companion, having withdrawn all the money from the partnership's bank account. S subsequently discovered that R had never sent the VAT registration form to the VAT office. He was unable to contact R, and carried on the double-glazing business as sole proprietor. The Commissioners imposed a penalty on him under what is now *VATA 1994, s 67*. He appealed, contending that he had a reasonable excuse in that R had told him that the registration form had been submitted. The tribunal allowed his appeal, observing that both S and the Commissioners had been defrauded by R, and holding that S had a reasonable excuse for his failure to register. *DB Smith, LON/90/1094X (VTD 5561)*.

48.83   **Misleading advice from bookkeeper.**   In a case where a sole trader had received misleading advice from a qualified bookkeeper, and had subsequently dispensed with the bookkeeper's services and appointed an accountant, the tribunal held that this constituted a reasonable excuse, applying *Jenkinson*, 48.80 above. *PAF Parker, MAN/89/120 (VTD 3810)*.

48.84   **Appellant misled by accountant.**   The Commissioners imposed a penalty under what is now *VATA 1994, s 67* on a subcontractor who had become liable to register in November 1989 but had failed to do so. The subcontractor appealed, contending that he had a reasonable excuse because he had completed a form VAT 1 and had given it to his accountant. He had subsequently asked the accountant for his registration number on several occasions, and the accountant had indicated that he was waiting for a reply from the Commissioners. In 1991 the accountant disappeared without leaving a forwarding address, and the subcontractor discovered that the Commissioners had never received the VAT 1 and that the Inland Revenue had not received his accounts. The tribunal allowed the appeal, holding that the accountant's misrepresentations constituted a reasonable excuse. *GW Chapman, [1992] VATTR 402 (VTD 7843)*. (*Note.* Compare the QB decision in *Harris*, 48.85 below, which was not referred to in this decision. The tribunal decision in *Chapman* was specifically disapproved by a subsequent tribunal in *Roebuck*, 48.89 below, on the grounds that it was inconsistent with the QB decision in *Harris*, which should have been treated as a binding precedent.)

Cases where the appellant was unsuccessful

48.85   **Reliance on accountant.**   A married couple should have registered for VAT in March 1987 but did not do so until March 1988. The Commissioners imposed a penalty under what is now *VATA 1994, s 67* and the couple appealed, contending that they had a reasonable excuse in that their accountant had told them that it was not necessary to register. The QB upheld the penalty, holding that what is now *VATA 1994, s 71(1)(b)* prevented reliance on an accountant from constituting a reasonable excuse. *C & E Commrs v D & DA Harris, QB [1989] STC 907*.

48.86   The QB decision in *Harris*, 48.85 above, was followed in *KJ Graham, MAN/89/656 (VTD 4350); B & S Tomlinson, MAN/89/93 (VTD 4351); Uncles the Original Pawnbrokers Ltd, MAN/89/811 (VTD 4437); Beaumont English Language Centre, LON/89/1834Z (VTD 4907); Trioport Ltd, LON/90/160Y (VTD 4923); PW Willert, MAN/89/525 (VTD 4970); J Powell, MAN/90/593 (VTD 5261); B Endersby, LON/90/603 (VTD 5754); FM Peach, MAN/91/884 (VTD 6499); JF Spokes, LON/92/1658P (VTD 10191)* and *C Hadley, LON/92/512 (VTD 10663)*.

48.87   In a similar case where a partnership's solicitor contended that *Jenkinson*, 48.80 above, should be applied, the tribunal distinguished *Jenkinson* because in that case the agent had given the trader a purported registration number, although the number given turned out to be false. In the case under appeal the partners had not asked their accountant what their registration number was, and their reliance on a dilatory accountant was precluded from constituting a reasonable excuse by what is now *VATA 1994, s 71(1)(b)*. *RM Joinery & Double Glazing, MAN/88/533 (VTD 3658)*.

48.88 A similar decision, applying *Harris*, 48.85 above, and distinguishing *Jenkinson*, 48.80 above, was reached in a case where a trader had been wrongly advised by his accountant that he was not liable to register. *GS Davies, LON/90/249X (VTD 5182)*.

48.89 The QB decision in *Harris*, 48.85 above, was also followed in a subsequent case in which the tribunal decision in *Chapman*, 48.84 above, was specifically disapproved as being inconsistent with the QB decision in *Harris*. *JB Roebuck, MAN/92/1189 (VTD 10171)*.

48.90 In a case where the appellant had been told by a firm of chartered accountants that VAT was only payable on net earnings (rather than on gross turnover), the tribunal held that the inaccuracy of the advice could not constitute a reasonable excuse. *Lt Col RH Stafford, LON/88/961 (VTD 3472)*.

48.91 There have been a very large number of other cases where reliance on an accountant has been held not to constitute a reasonable excuse. In the interests of space, such cases are not summarised individually in this book. For a list of such cases decided up to 31 December 1994, see Tolley's VAT Cases 1995.

48.92 **Reliance on manager.** A company appealed against a penalty under what is now *VATA 1994, s 67*, contending that it had relied on its manager to comply with the requirements for registration, but that the manager had been dismissed following the discovery of cash discrepancies, and that he had not notified the Commissioners of the company's liability to register. The tribunal dismissed the appeal, holding that what is now *VATA 1994, s 71(1)(b)* prevented this from constituting a reasonable excuse. *Vinetay Ltd, EDN/86/68 (VTD 2230)*.

48.93 **Reliance on secretary.** Reliance on a secretary was held not to be a reasonable excuse in *RJ Harrison, LON/89/1152Y (VTD 4908)*.

48.94 **Reliance on club treasurer.** An operatic society had at one time been registered for VAT, but had subsequently deregistered because its turnover was below the then statutory threshold. It became liable to re-register in 1987 but did not do so until 1990. The Commissioners imposed a penalty under what is now *VATA 1994, s 67* and the society appealed, contending that it had a reasonable excuse because its treasurer had not realised that it needed to register for VAT. The tribunal dismissed the society's appeal, holding that reliance on the society's treasurer did not constitute a reasonable excuse. *Canterbury Amateur Operatic Society, LON/90/1575Y (VTD 5709)*.

48.95 **Reliance on bookkeeper.** Reliance on a company's bookkeeper was held not to constitute a reasonable excuse in *Earlswood Environmental Systems Ltd, MAN/87/416 (VTD 2605)*.

48.96 **Reliance on wife.** A builder appealed against a penalty under what is now *VATA 1994, s 67*, contending that he had relied on his wife who acted as his bookkeeper. The tribunal dismissed his appeal, holding that this did not constitute a reasonable excuse. *GA Brannan (t/a G Brannan Builders), LON/90/1828Z (VTD 5939)*.

48.97 **Shop operated under franchise agreement—franchisee placing reliance on franchisor.** A newsagent operated a shop under a franchise agreement. He was accepted as self-employed for income tax and national insurance purposes, but did not register for VAT, and a penalty under what is now *VATA 1994, s 67* was imposed. He appealed, contending that the company which had granted him the franchise had advised him that it was not necessary for him to register. The tribunal dismissed his appeal, holding that the misleading advice given could not constitute a reasonable excuse. *Harris*, 48.85 above, applied; *Geary*, 48.40 above, and *Butler*, 48.42 above, distinguished. *FW Greer, MAN/90/914 (VTD 6070)*.

48.98   **Reliance on Inland Revenue.**   A self-employed computer programmer became liable to register for VAT not later than 1 February 1988 (on the basis of turnover for the year ended 31 December 1987), but did not do so until June 1990. The Commissioners imposed a penalty under what is now *VATA 1994, s 67* and he appealed, contending that he had a reasonable excuse because in March 1989 he had asked the Inland Revenue for advice on VAT. He had repeated this request in January 1990 but without success. The tribunal dismissed his appeal, holding that the appellant was clearly ignorant of basic VAT law, and such ignorance could not constitute a reasonable excuse. *Neal*, 48.48 above, applied; *Geary*, 48.40 above, distinguished. Furthermore, he had made no enquiry whatsoever until almost fourteen months after he had become liable to register, and had not followed up this enquiry for ten months, whereas in *Hislop*, 48.101 below, the tribunal had regarded five months as being the longest delay that could be considered excusable in following up an application. *JA Farrington, LON/90/1338Y (VTD 5456)*.

48.99   **Director in prison.**   A company became liable to register for VAT at a time when its principal director was in prison. During his imprisonment he had left the management of the company in the hands of his brother, who was not a director. The tribunal dismissed the appeal, holding that this amounted to reliance on a third party, which was specifically precluded from constituting a reasonable excuse by what is now *VATA 1994, s 71(1)(b)*. *Cosmogen Ltd, LON/88/74 (VTD 3347)*.

Miscellaneous

Cases where the appellant was successful

48.100   **Registration form posted but not received by VAT office.**   A self-employed film editor became liable to register for VAT in December 1984. His accountant submitted a registration form in April 1985. However, the Commissioners did not receive the form, and subsequently imposed a penalty under what is now *VATA 1994, s 67* for failure to register by 25 July 1985 (when the relevant provisions came into force). The editor appealed, contending firstly that the submission of the form constituted notification, and alternatively that he had a reasonable excuse for not being registered because he had completed the appropriate form. The tribunal accepted the second contention and allowed the appeal. The postage of a form VAT 1 did not of itself constitute notification of liability to register. *Aikman v White*, 55.6 RETURNS, was distinguished because it related to the furnishing of returns rather than to the notification of liability to register. In the case of notification of liability to register, the Post Office was an agent of both parties, but this agency was an agency to carry and not an agency to receive information. However, the editor had 'done everything that was reasonably required of him', and therefore had a reasonable excuse for failing to notify his liability to register. *L Selwyn, [1986] VATTR 142 (VTD 2135)*. (*Note*. *Dicta* of the tribunal chairman were disapproved by a subsequent tribunal in *Tomkins*, 48.15 above.)

48.101   Similar decisions were reached in *Celtic Trading (Midlands), MAN/86/118 (VTD 2194); B Birks, MAN/86/64 (VTD 2201); MP Hislop (t/a Dorchester Productions), LON/86/583 (VTD 2258); Z & C Savva, MAN/87/153 (VTD 2561); Timeplas Ltd, LON/87/369 (VTD 2570); Cobrabrook Ltd, LON/88/969 (VTD 3185); M Ali (t/a The Candy Bar), EDN/88/156 (VTD 3441)* and *Beverley Video, BEL/88/46 (VTD 3550)*.

48.102   Commissioners failing to provide registration form.   A trader became liable to register for VAT on 1 September 1985. His brother-in-law telephoned the local VAT office in September, November and December to request a registration form. However, the office did not send a form until December. The trader submitted the completed form later that month, but the Commissioners imposed a penalty under what is now *VATA 1994, s 67*. The tribunal allowed the trader's appeal, holding that the Commissioners' failure to provide a registration form constituted a reasonable excuse. *S Zaveri (t/a The Paper Shop), [1986] VATTR 133 (VTD 2121).*

48.103   *Zaveri*, 48.102 above, was applied in the similar case of *J Brennan, LON/92/505Z (VTD 11657).*

48.104   Similar decisions were reached in *DS Nolan, LON/86/712 (VTD 2283); GK Millar & JD Turner (t/a Britannia Wine Bar), LON/87/82 (VTD 2389); Y Lucky & Another (t/a Le Bistenoo), LON/87/858 (VTD 2701); P Alexandrou, LON/88/244 (VTD 2944); Russguild Ltd, MAN/88/610 (VTD 3321); SJ Cutting, LON/88/ 1048Y (VTD 3443); GJ & GM Flanaghan, MAN/89/999 (VTD 4648); R Kelly, MAN/90/266 (VTD 5026); Hollies Discount Furniture Centre Ltd, MAN/90/277 (VTD 5243); J Marchant, LON/93/1226P (VTD 11026) and HW Lloyd, LON/ 92/3206 (VTD 11307).*

48.105   A partnership telephoned a local VAT office in April 1988 to notify its liability to VAT. No form VAT 1 was received, and the partnership made a further telephone request in June. The VAT office had no record of the previous call, and sent a form VAT 1 which the partnership returned later that month. The Commissioners imposed a penalty under what is now *VATA 1994, s 67* but the tribunal allowed the partnership's appeal, holding that the delay of less than two months in following up the earlier call was not unreasonable. *Ventnor Towers Hotel, LON/89/386X (VTD 4537).*

48.106   Mistaken belief that registration already in force.   The shares of a newly-formed company were sold by company formation agents to an individual who became the company's principal director. On the invoice from the company formation agents was typed 'with compliments VAT No 241 1563 95'. The director assumed that this was the company's registration number, whereas it was in fact the number of the company formation agents, who had not registered the new company for VAT. The tribunal allowed the company's appeal against a penalty under what is now *VATA 1994, s 67*, finding that the director had been misled by the invoice and had genuinely believed that the company had been registered by the formation agency. *Electric Tool Repair Ltd, [1986] VATTR 257 (VTD 2208).*

48.107   The tenant of a public house walked out after a disagreement with the brewery. A married couple took over the tenancy on a temporary basis. Because they had only taken over the tenancy temporarily, the husband continued to work full-time for his previous employers. The couple did not register for VAT. The Commissioners imposed a penalty under what is now *VATA 1994, s 67* and the couple appealed, contending that they had assumed that they would simply take over the existing registration. The tribunal allowed the couple's appeal, holding that the circumstances constituted a reasonable excuse. *Mr & Mrs J Daltry, MAN/86/261 (VTD 2277).* (*Note.* Compare *James*, 48.125 below, in which similar circumstances were held not to constitute a reasonable excuse.)

48.108   The shares of a company (B) had been purchased by its directors from a company formation agency. B's directors did not realise that it had not been registered for VAT by the agency. One of them telephoned the firm of accountants they had appointed and asked for B's registration number. The partner dealing with B's affairs was on holiday, and the director spoke to a woman employed by the firm, who gave him a registration number. Unknown to the director, the number given to him by the woman was the registration number of the accountants' firm. Subsequently B's directors had letterheads printed showing the number as if it were B's own. The accountants did not discover this until the end of B's first accounting period. They then notified the Commissioners, who imposed a penalty under what is now *VATA 1994, s 67*, against which B appealed. The tribunal allowed B's appeal, finding that B's directors had acted in the genuine belief that it was registered and holding that the circumstances constituted a reasonable excuse for B's failure to register. *Beaublade Ltd, MAN/88/374 (VTD 3066)*.

48.109   A trader had been registered for VAT in 1982, but had subsequently ceased self-employment, and his registration had been cancelled. He resumed self-employment in November 1987 and visited the Dudley VAT office to ask if he could use his old VAT registration number. He was advised by a VAT officer that this would be acceptable. However, the officer in question kept no record of his visit and did not ask him to complete an application form. Subsequently the Commissioners imposed a penalty under what is now *VATA 1994, s 67*. The tribunal allowed the trader's appeal, holding that the incorrect advice given by the VAT officer had led him to believe that his old registration would remain in force. *A Hill, MAN/89/464 (VTD 4973)*.

48.110   **Director not aware of company's deregistration.**   A company was formed in 1982 and was registered for VAT. Later that year the principal director went abroad and left his accountant in charge of the company. The accountant deregistered the company. The director returned to the UK in 1985 and the company resumed making taxable supplies in September 1985. The accountant did not tell the principal director that the company had been deregistered, and the director did not become aware that this was so until the Commissioners advised him of it in January 1986. The Commissioners imposed a penalty under what is now *VATA 1994, s 67*, but the tribunal allowed the company's appeal, finding that the director was unaware that the company had been deregistered in his absence. *Standoak Ltd, LON/86/500 (VTD 2250)*.

48.111   A similar decision was reached in a case where a company had been dormant for some time before recommencing business, and the Commissioners had deregistered it, but the director gave evidence that he had not received notification of the deregistration. *Folknoll Ltd, LON/89/20Y (VTD 4022)*.

48.112   **Deafness.**   An appellant contended that he had a reasonable excuse for failure to register because he was profoundly deaf and had great difficulty in communicating. He had difficulty in reading and could only communicate with his accountant through an interpreter. The tribunal allowed his appeal, holding that, as the 'normal sources of enquiry' were not open to him, he had a reasonable excuse for late registration. *Neal*, 48.48 above, distinguished. *CW Mason, MAN/88/861 (VTD 3517)*.

48.113   **Increase in turnover following redundancy of wife.**   A subcontractor (K), whose turnover was below the VAT registration threshold, was married to a woman with a salary of about £30,000 p.a. However, she was unexpectedly made redundant in February 1991. Following her redundancy, K had to work substantially longer hours in order to meet their financial commitments. His turnover therefore increased, and he became liable to register for VAT from August 1991, but did not do so until 1992. The Commissioners imposed a penalty under what is now *VATA 1994, s 67*, but the tribunal allowed K's appeal, holding that the exceptional workload following the redundancy of K's wife constituted a reasonable excuse. *A Kear, LON/92/2605P (VTD 9896)*.

48.114   **Marriage breakdown.**   A woman became liable to register for VAT in July 1986, but did not do so until April 1990. The Commissioners imposed a penalty under what is now *VATA 1994, s 67* and she appealed, contending that she had a reasonable excuse because her husband had been an alcoholic and had been violent towards her, and she had to work very long hours which had led to her turnover exceeding the registration threshold by a small amount. The marriage had finally broken down in the autumn of 1989 when her husband left her, and she had subsequently consulted an accountant. The tribunal allowed the appeal, finding that throughout the period in question the appellant 'was grossly overworked, intimidated and suffering acute stress as a result of her business responsibilities and domestic problems'. Since her turnover had 'only marginally exceeded the statutory limits', the circumstances constituted a reasonable excuse. *J Braes (t/a Aquarius), EDN/93/155 (VTD 11951)*.

48.115   **Sole trader taking wife into partnership.**   The proprietor of a haulage business took his wife and son into partnership with him. The partnership did not apply for registration and the Commissioners imposed a penalty under what is now *VATA 1994, s 67*. The partners appealed, contending that they had a reasonable excuse because they had not realised that they had to apply for a separate registration instead of using the registration number previously allocated to the husband. The tribunal allowed the appeal, holding that the circumstances constituted a reasonable excuse. *Peter Jones & Son, MAN/88/309 (VTD 2990)*.

48.116   A similar decision was reached in *JA & J Wright (t/a Euro-Dec), MAN/89/105 (VTD 3540)*.

48.117   **Dissolution of partnership—one partner continuing as sole trader.**   A husband and wife had traded in partnership as hairdressers. The marriage broke down and the wife ceased working in the business in June 1988. Draft accounts to 30 June 1988 were prepared in October, and the husband notified the Commissioners that the partnership had ceased and that he was continuing in business as a sole trader. The Commissioners imposed a penalty under what is now *VATA 1994, s 67*, on the basis that he should have notified this in July. He appealed, contending that he had a reasonable excuse because he had hoped that his wife would change her mind, and that he had not realised that he could not continue to use the partnership's existing registration number. The tribunal allowed his appeal, holding that, in the circumstances, his uncertainty about the future of his marriage constituted a reasonable excuse. *MJ Lewis, MAN/89/526 (VTD 4150)*.

48.118   **Partners initially intending to trade through limited company.**   The two directors of a limited company, which operated a number of public houses and was registered for VAT, sought to purchase a licensed restaurant. Initially they intended that the company would acquire and operate the restaurant. However, they were only able to raise sufficient capital as individuals rather than through the company. They therefore purchased the restaurant as a partnership and traded as such. They became liable to register for VAT in November 1985 but did not do so until June 1986, and the Commissioners imposed a penalty under what is now *VATA 1994, s 67*. The tribunal allowed the partners' appeal, accepting that at the time they began to operate the restaurant, they still hoped to transfer it to their company, and holding that, although the case was 'near the borderline', their conduct in awaiting the outcome of negotiations was not unreasonable. *PHV Hutchings & JH Liggett (t/a Cashlandoo Inn), [1987] VATTR 58 (VTD 2313)*.

Cases where the appellant was unsuccessful

48.119   **Failure to follow up preliminary enquiry.**   A company, aware that it might be liable to register for VAT, wrote to its local VAT office but received no reply. It did not pursue the matter until five months after its initial enquiry. The Commissioners imposed a penalty under what is now *VATA 1994, s 67* and the tribunal dismissed the company's appeal, holding that the delay of five months in following up the enquiry meant that the circumstances did not amount to a reasonable excuse. *Barmor Engineering Ltd, LON/86/305 (VTD 2214)*.

48.120   Similar decisions were reached in *P Roberts & D Brooke, MAN/86/189 (VTD 2153); R Jones, LON/86/270 (VTD 2182); SL Martin, LON/86/494 (VTD 2224); Pacey Rogers & Co, LON/87/13 (VTD 2308); GC Molyneux, MAN/88/609 (VTD 3322); DJI Electrical Services Ltd, LON/88/1059X (VTD 3671); BS Watkins, LON/89/1136X (VTD 4668); PH Leighton & JP Henry (t/a Lacy's Wine Bar), BEL/92/20X (VTD 9793); London Brick Company King's Dyke Social Club, LON/92/2462A (VTD 10387); Soul Jazz Records, LON/93/1093P (VTD 11066); Mr & Mrs F Raywood, LON/93/2031 (VTD 11945); PA Heron, LON/95/847 (VTD 13529B)* and *R Sheikh, EDN/98/84 (VTD 15684)*.

48.121   **Pressure of work.**   A company appealed against a penalty under what is now *VATA 1994, s 67*, contending that its directors had overlooked the need for registration because of pressure of work. The tribunal dismissed the appeal, holding that this was not a reasonable excuse. *Pepper Personnel Ltd, LON/86/424 (VTD 2175)*.

48.122   There have been many other cases in which tribunals have held that pressure of work does not constitute a reasonable excuse for failure to register. In the interests of space, such cases are not listed individually in this book.

48.123   **Formation of accountancy partnership.**   A firm of chartered accountants was established on 1 October 1985. Each of the partners had been registered for VAT as a sole practitioner, but they did not register as a partnership until February 1986. The Commissioners imposed a penalty under what is now *VATA 1994, s 67*. The tribunal dismissed the firm's appeal, holding that there was no excuse for its failure to register at the appropriate time. *Beaton Snelling & Co, LON/86/459 (VTD 2206)*.

48.124   **Former partner continuing business as sole trader.**   A restaurant had previously been run by two people in partnership. One of the partners left the country and the other continued to trade as sole proprietor. The partnership had been registered for VAT but the remaining partner did not notify the Commissioners that he had continued to trade as a sole proprietor. The tribunal dismissed his appeal against a penalty under what is now *VATA 1994, s 67*, holding that there was no reasonable excuse for his failure to make the required notification. *SH Liakat (t/a Banaras Tandoori Restaurant), LON/88/940 (VTD 3300)*.

48.125   **Business acquired as going concern.**   A publican took over a public house which had previously been registered for VAT. He did not notify the Commissioners, and they imposed a penalty under what is now *VATA 1994, s 67*. He appealed, contending that he had a reasonable excuse as he had assumed that the existing registration would be transferred to him. The tribunal dismissed his appeal, holding that his grounds for appeal amounted to ignorance of the law, which was not a reasonable excuse. *GA James, LON/86/363 (VTD 2207)*.

48.126   Similar decisions were reached in *Bistro Inns Ltd, LON/97/1476 (VTD 15613)* and *R Cuthbert, EDN/99/61 (VTD 16518)*.

48.127   **Dyslexia.**   A partnership appealed against a penalty under what is now *VATA 1994, s 67*, contending that it had a reasonable excuse because one of the partners was dyslexic and misread the annual threshold for registration as £25,000 when in fact it was £20,500. The tribunal dismissed the partnership's appeal, holding that this was not a reasonable excuse. *JE & JB Fletcher, MAN/87/39 (VTD 2356)*.

48.128   Dyslexia was also held not to be a reasonable excuse in *EP McKay, LON/88/988Z (VTD 3406)*.

48.129   **Marriage breakdown.**   A plumber appealed against a penalty under what is now *VATA 1994, s 67*, contending that he had a reasonable excuse because his marriage had broken down. The tribunal dismissed his appeal, holding that this was not a reasonable excuse. *CJ Talbot, LON/89/759Y (VTD 4807)*.

48.130   A similar decision was reached in *A Veitch (t/a Pine Products), EDN/94/4 (VTD 11963)*.

48.131   **Wife giving birth.**   A taxi driver became liable to register for VAT in January 1989 but did not do so until March 1990. The Commissioners imposed a penalty under what is now *VATA 1994, s 67* and he appealed, contending that he had a reasonable excuse as his wife, who acted as his bookkeeper, had given birth to a daughter in February 1989. The tribunal dismissed his appeal, holding that this did not constitute a reasonable excuse. *M Hazell, LON/90/1018Z (VTD 5574)*.

48.132   **Bankruptcy.**   The tribunal held that the fact that a trader had been an undischarged bankrupt throughout the period of his liability to register did not constitute a reasonable excuse. *CH Ambrose, LON/86/711 (VTD 2303)*.

48.133   **Other cases.**   There have been a large number of unsuccessful appeals which appear to raise no point of general importance, but where appellants have claimed that the penalty imposed has been unjust. In the interests of space, such cases are not reported individually in this book.

UNAUTHORISED ISSUE OF INVOICES (VATA 1994, s 67(1)(c))

48.134   A company was incorporated on 11 June 1979 and registered for VAT from 9 July 1979. On 7 September 1985, the managing director wrote to the Commissioners stating that he was resident in the Netherlands and that all VAT forms should be sent to the Netherlands. The Commissioners issued notices cancelling the company's registration and exempting it from registering for VAT in the UK. In January 1987 the managing director and his wife, who was a co-director and the company secretary, returned to the UK. The company entered into a contract for services in London, and issued a VAT invoice. The Commissioners imposed a penalty under what is now *VATA 1994, s 67(1)(c)* for the unauthorised issue of a VAT invoice. The tribunal allowed the company's appeal, finding that there had been no malicious intent but that the directors had been confused as to the legal consequences of their return to the UK, and holding that this constituted a reasonable excuse. *Countgold Ltd, MAN/88/155 (VTD 2894)*.

48.135   An appeal against a penalty under what is now *VATA 1994, s 67(1)(c)* was dismissed in a case where a trader had issued unauthorised invoices before applying for registration. The tribunal accepted that the trader had intended to register and subsequently to pay the tax charged by the invoice, but held that the circumstances did not constitute a reasonable excuse. *J Scott-Martin (t/a SM Harris), LON/92/1109Z (VTD 8954)*.

48.136   A builder registered for VAT in 1982 but deregistered in 1992. In 1996 and 1997 he issued eleven invoices purporting to charge VAT, although he was no longer registered. When the Commissioners discovered this, they imposed a penalty under *VATA 1994, s 67(1)(c)*. The tribunal dismissed the builder's appeal, holding that there was no reasonable excuse and no grounds for mitigation. *GE Alm, LON/98/961 (VTD 15863)*. (*Note.* For another issue in this case, see 2.21 APPEALS.)

48.137   The proprietor of a business, who had not been registered for VAT, died and the business was taken over by his son. The son did not register for VAT, but issued invoices charging VAT, and the Commissioners imposed a penalty under what is now *VATA 1994, s 67(1)(c)*. The tribunal allowed the son's appeal, holding that since he had succeeded to the business with no knowledge of the details of the business, or of business matters generally, he had a reasonable excuse for having issued the invoices in question. *A Kulka (t/a Kulka Models), MAN/92/1246 (VTD 9753)*.

48.138   A company was incorporated in February 1996, as a non-profit-making organisation limited by guarantee. It did not register for VAT, but issued three invoices to its sole customer. The invoices purported to charge VAT. When the Commissioners discovered this, they imposed a penalty under *VATA 1994, s 67(1)(c)*. The company appealed. The tribunal upheld the penalty in principle, holding that there was no reasonable excuse, but directed that the penalty should be mitigated by 50% in view of the fact that the company was a non-profit-making organisation. *Global Trade Centre Ltd, LON/96/1559 (VTD 14866)*.

MITIGATION OF PENALTIES (VATA 1994, s 70)

Cases where the penalty was mitigated by the tribunal

48.139   The Commissioners imposed a penalty under what is now *VATA 1994, s 67* on a trader who had become liable to register for VAT from 1 January 1993 but had failed to notify his liability until 13 January 1994. The tribunal held that the trader had no reasonable excuse, but considered whether the penalty should be mitigated under what is now *VATA 1994, s 70* (introduced by *FA 1993*). The tribunal observed that, in considering mitigation, 'essentially the question is one of how far the taxpayer is to blame for the defaults. If he is wholly blameworthy, the full penalty will be the proper amount; otherwise there may be a case for a reduction'. On the evidence, the trader's turnover 'went through the registration threshold progressively. It was the result of increments to his earnings and may not have been immediately apparent ... The second feature in (the appellant's) favour is that he wasted little time in putting things right after he realised that he should probably have registered. He engaged and paid an accountant to investigate his personal liability'. The tribunal mitigated the penalty by 40%. *TR Jordan, [1994] VATTR 286 (VTD 12616)*.

48.140   A penalty under what is now *VATA 1994, s 67* was mitigated by 30% in a case where the tribunal applied *dicta* in *Jordan*, 48.139 above. The tribunal observed that it could take into account the fact that the trader had been unable to get credit for input tax, and that 'this was not a case where a trader gained a competitive advantage against others who had registered'. *MB Cohen, [1994] VATTR 290 (VTD 12732)*.

48.141   A penalty was mitigated by 40% in a case where the tribunal took into account the fact that the appellant's income was 'somewhat erratic'. *RJ Dodd (t/a Able Machines), MAN/94/511 (VTD 12856)*.

48.142   The wife of a publican provided catering at her husband's public house. The Commissioners accepted that the catering was a separate business for VAT purposes. In March 1991 a VAT officer discovered that the wife's turnover had exceeded the VAT registration threshold. It was subsequently discovered that she should have registered with effect from August 1988. The Commissioners imposed a penalty of £2,771. The tribunal held that there was no reasonable excuse for the failure to register, since the wife had relied on her accountant, but directed that, since she had young children to look after, and had not tried to mislead the Commissioners, the penalty should be reduced to £1,250. *L Gent, LON/95/82 (VTD 13227)*.

48.143 A self-employed salesman, who worked on a commission basis for a single company, became liable to register in May 1988 but did not do so until October 1990. The Commissioners imposed a penalty for late registration. He appealed, contending that he had a reasonable excuse because he had assumed that he could be treated as an employee, and had telephoned the Reading VAT office in 1988. The tribunal held that the circumstances did not constitute a reasonable excuse, because the appellant should have sought professional advice or should have written to the VAT office rather than telephoning them. However, since the appellant had made a voluntary telephone call to the VAT office, and there had been no attempt to evade registration, the tribunal directed that the penalty should be mitigated by 50%. *GA Osborn, LON/94/3450 (VTD 13254)*.

48.144 A penalty was mitigated by 50%, to take account of co-operation, in *CM Broadbent, MAN/98/244 (VTD 15809)*.

48.145 The Commissioners imposed a penalty on a sole trader who had failed to register. The tribunal upheld the penalty in principle, holding that there was no reasonable excuse for the failure to register. However, the tribunal directed that the penalty should be mitigated by 90% to take account of the fact that the trader's turnover had only exceeded the registration threshold for a period of three months and had then fallen to below the threshold. *J Barnard (t/a Baron Security), LON/96/128 (VTD 14206)*.

48.146 The Commissioners imposed a penalty on the proprietors of a dry-cleaning business who had become liable to register for VAT from 31 July 1988 but had failed to do so. The proprietors appealed, contending that they had a reasonable excuse because they had believed that their turnover was below the registration limits. The tribunal rejected this contention, finding that the proprietors should have been registered from 31 July 1988 to 20 March 1991 and holding that there was no reasonable excuse for their failure to do so. *Neal, 48.48 above*, applied. However, the tribunal directed that the penalty should be mitigated by 50% to take account of the facts that the proprietors had not previously been in business, that their turnover had been below the registration limits when they took over the business, and that they had co-operated with the Commissioners. *Jordan, 48.139 above*, and *Cohen, 48.140 above*, applied. *T & L Mehmet (t/a Leyla Dry Cleaners), LON/96/464 & 468 (VTD 14473)*.

48.147 In November 1997 a VAT officer visited an unregistered trader and formed the opinion that he had become liable to register from November 1995. In July 1998, after having consulted an accountant, the trader applied for registration. In July 1999 the Commissioners formally registered him, and in December 1999 they imposed a penalty covering the period from November 1995 to July 1998. The tribunal held that there was no reasonable excuse for the trader's failure to register, applying *Neal, 48.48 above*, but held that, since the Commissioners had 'delayed inordinately', the penalty should be mitigated to nil. *SJ Whereat, LON/99/937 (VTD 16751)*.

48.148 A penalty was mitigated by 50% in a case where the tribunal found that a trader's turnover had exceeded the annual registration threshold by only £952. *AA Abdullah (t/a Aladdin's Cave Kebab House), MAN/99/1116 (VTD 16774)*.

48.149 See also *Global Trade Centre Ltd, 48.138 above*.

Cases where the penalty was mitigated by the Commissioners

48.150 The Commissioners imposed a penalty on a woman who had failed to register. They mitigated the penalty by 50%, the grounds for mitigation being that the woman had been harassed and assaulted by her former partner. She appealed, contending that the penalty should be mitigated still further. The tribunal dismissed her appeal, holding that 'the 50% mitigation already allowed is fair and reasonable and that there would be no justification for any increase'. *K Doherty, EDN/94/459 (VTD 13075)*.

48.151 A trader became liable to register for VAT in January 1988 but did not do so until September 1993. He appealed, contending that the penalty should be mitigated because his wife who had acted as his bookkeeper had been ill, he had been unable to afford an accountant until 1993, and during the period in question he had been acting as a director of a boatbuilding company which had been in serious financial difficulties. The Commissioners mitigated the penalty by 50% and the tribunal upheld their decision, applying *dicta* in *Jordan*, 48.139 above. (The tribunal also held that the trader did not have a 'reasonable excuse' for his failure to register.) *EM Vann, LON/95/1612P (VTD 13581)*.

48.152 A similar decision, also applying *dicta* in *Jordan*, 48.139 above, was reached in a case where the tribunal found that a self-employed minibus driver was suffering from 'acute shyness and a difficulty in leaving his home'. The Commissioners mitigated the penalty by 50%, to take account of 'the age, experience and level of education of the trader, and the fact that Customs were notified promptly of (his) requirement to be registered once it was discovered'. The tribunal held that no further mitigation was appropriate. *H Haines, LON/95/2494 (VTD 13986)*.

Cases where the penalty was not mitigated

48.153 A builder became liable to register for VAT in February 1989 but did not do so until after he was visited by a VAT officer in August 1994. The Commissioners imposed a penalty and the builder appealed, contending that the penalty should be mitigated since he had co-operated in establishing his turnover for the period in question. The tribunal dismissed his appeal, observing that 'that kind of co-operation is in a different category from the concept of "full co-operation" in the context of a (*VATA 1994, s 60**) case, and carries very much less weight'. *Cohen*, 48.140 above, was distinguished on the grounds that many of the builder's customers were not registered for VAT, so that 'some advantage would have accrued to the appellant as a result of his not charging VAT to his customers, whilst the disadvantage of being unable to claim input tax may have been small'. On the evidence, the builder was 'wholly to blame for the defaults and the full penalty is the proper amount'. *FD Snow, LON/94/2178 (VTD 13283)*.

48.154 A similar decision, again distinguishing *Cohen*, 48.140 above, was reached in *JS Upson, LON/94/2742 (VTD 13350)*.

48.155 In July 1994 the Commissioners imposed a penalty on a partnership which operated a taxi business and which had become liable to register for VAT in 1990 but had failed to do so. The partners appealed, contending that the penalty should be mitigated because they had relied on an accountant and that the amount of such penalties had subsequently been reduced by *FA 1995*. The tribunal dismissed the appeal, observing that 'neither partner made any attempt to assist with the investigations; in fact they went out of their way to be obtuse'. *P Khan & M Parvez (t/a On Time Cars), MAN/96/179 (VTD 14293)*.

48.156 A chartered accountant became liable to register for VAT in 1983 but failed to do so. His turnover dropped to below the registration threshold in 1991 but he became liable to register again in 1992. He again failed to notify the Commissioners. The Commissioners discovered this in 1995, and in January 1996 they imposed penalties under *VATA 1994, s 67*. The tribunal dismissed the accountant's appeal, holding on the evidence that there was no reasonable excuse and no grounds for mitigation.

48.157 Penalties: Failure to Notify, etc.

MYH Murat, LON/96/295 (VTD 14759). (*Note*. For another issue in this case, taken to the QB, see 3.104 ASSESSMENT.)

48.157 **Illness of bookkeeper.** See *Cheek (t/a Swanley Contractors)*, 48.19 above.

49   Penalties: Misdeclaration

Note. The misdeclaration penalty was originally introduced by *FA 1985, s 14*. There have been substantial changes to the provisions during the succeeding years, with significant changes being made by *FA 1994, s 45*. The current legislation is contained in *VATA 1994, ss 63, 64*. Cases relating to accounting periods beginning before 31 May 1994 (when *FA 1994, s 45* came into force) should be read in the light of the changes in the legislation.

The cases in this chapter are arranged under the following headings.

49.1   Penalties: Misdeclaration

DEFINITION OF PRESCRIBED ACCOUNTING PERIOD (VATA 1994, s 63(1))

49.1   A company had been registered for VAT since 1984, with monthly accounting periods. On 20 March 1991 it applied to be included in a VAT group. In April 1991 it submitted a return for the period ending 31 March 1991, in which it overclaimed input tax by more than £35,000. The Commissioners imposed a misdeclaration penalty and the company appealed, contending that the penalty was not valid because the effect of its application for group registration was that the period in question was no longer a 'prescribed accounting period'. The tribunal dismissed the appeal. The Commissioners had not authorised the group registration until June 1991. Being treated as a member of a group did not absolve a company joining the group from its liability to be registered under *Sch 1*. At the time when the return in question was made, the company had been required to submit a return for the period ending 31 March, which was therefore a 'prescribed accounting period' as laid down by what is now *regulation 25* of the *VAT Regulations (SI 1995 No 2518)*. *Atlas Interlates Ltd, MAN/91/1468 (VTD 7904)*.

WHETHER A RETURN HAS BEEN 'MADE' (VATA 1994, s 63(1)(a))

49.2   **Whether return a 'nullity'.**   A county council's return for April 1991 included a negative figure for output tax. It was accepted that this resulted from an error by a clerical officer in making an incorrect subtraction from the cumulative figure of output tax indicated by the council's computer. The Commissioners imposed a misdeclaration penalty. The tribunal allowed the council's appeal, holding that 'the mistake was so fundamentally wrong that the April return was not, in the opinion of the tribunal, "made" for the purposes of (*VATA 1994, Sch 11 para 2(1)**) and (*VAT Regulations 1995, reg 25**)'. The return had to be treated as a nullity, and since no return had been made, no penalty under what is now *VATA 1994, s 63* was due. *Gwent County Council, LON/90/1389X (VTD 6153)*. (*Note.* The decision in this case was disapproved by the QB in *Nomura Properties Management Services Ltd*, 49.4 below.)

49.3   The principal director of a company also carried on a farming business in partnership with his wife. The Commissioners sent a return to the company, but the director's wife inadvertently completed the return as if it related to the partnership. This resulted in a lower VAT liability being declared than would have been the case if the return had been correctly completed. When the Commissioners discovered this, they imposed a misdeclaration penalty on the company. The tribunal allowed the company's appeal, holding that the director 'was not acting in the course of his duties, nor was he purporting to do so, when he mistakenly used the appellant's return form as the means of supplying the figures for his own partnership farming business'. The company could 'not be said to have furnished a return showing the tax payable by, and other information in respect of, it and containing the requisite declaration'. *Tannington Growers (1984) Ltd, [1992] VATTR 135 (VTD 6877)*.

49.4   A company submitted a return in which the value of outputs was included in Box 1 instead of Box 4; the value of inputs was included in Box 5 rather than Box 2; the amounts of output tax and input tax were entered in Boxes 4 and 5 instead of Boxes 1 and 2; and in Box 3 was entered the excess of inputs over outputs, rather than the excess of input tax over output tax. This resulted in the return claiming a repayment of £218,718, whereas the repayment actually due was £32,808. The Commissioners imposed a penalty under what is now *VATA 1994, s 63*. The company appealed, contending that the return should be treated as a 'nullity'. The QB rejected this contention and upheld the penalty. An inaccurate return was still a return and a penalty arose as a result. Furthermore, the penalty was not invalidated by the subsequent correction of the return. *PCC (Agriculture) Ltd*, 49.26 below, approved; *Gwent County Council*, 49.2 above, disapproved. *C & E Commrs v Nomura Properties Management Services Ltd, QB [1994] STC 461.*

INADEQUATE ESTIMATED ASSESSMENT (VATA 1994, s 63(1)(b))

Cases where the appellant was successful

49.5   The Commissioners had not received a trader's return for the period ending 31 July 1990 by the due date of 31 August. They therefore issued an estimated assessment charging tax of £2 and imposed a default surcharge of £30 (the statutory minimum). In February 1991 a VAT officer discovered that the amount of tax actually due for the period in question was £9,670. The Commissioners therefore imposed a penalty under what is now *VATA 1994, s 63(1)(b)*. The trader appealed, contending that he had delivered the return by hand to the Maidenhead VAT office in September 1990. The Commissioners denied receiving the return. The tribunal allowed the trader's appeal, finding on the balance of probabilities that the trader had delivered the return and that it had been lost at the VAT office, and holding that by delivering the return the trader had taken 'all such steps as are reasonable to draw the understatement to the attention of the Commissioners'. *PM Carr (t/a P & L Packaging), LON/91/1561X (VTD 6726)*. (*Note*. For other cases where the Commissioners have denied receiving a return but tribunals have accepted appellants' evidence that the return has been delivered by hand to a VAT office, see 18.53 and 18.55 DEFAULT SURCHARGE.)

49.6   *Carr*, 49.5 above, was applied in a subsequent case where an appellant gave evidence that his bookkeeper had posted the return in question to the local VAT office. The tribunal did not consider that 'Parliament intended that a penalty should apply in a case such as this where a return was lost in the post'. *KR Meads, LON/91/1677Z (VTD 7283)*.

49.7   In a case where the facts are not fully recorded in the decision, the tribunal accepted that a company had a reasonable excuse for not having realised that an estimated assessment was inadequate, and allowed the company's appeal against a penalty under what is now *VATA 1994, s 63(1)(b)*. *Southwest Blasting Ltd, LON/92/2210 (VTD 9657)*.

49.8   An appeal was allowed in a case where the tribunal held that the notice of assessment had been defective, in that it had not included a specific statement that the return for the relevant period had not been received. *HG Jones & Associates, LON/92/3141 (VTD 10399)*.

49.9   **Bookkeeper suffering stress following pregnancy of common-law wife.**   An appeal was allowed in a case where the tribunal found that a company's bookkeeper had not notified the directors that an estimated assessment was inadequate because he was suffering from stress following the pregnancy of his common-law wife, and held that this constituted a reasonable excuse. *Acquisitions (Fireplaces) Ltd, LON/92/2516 (VTD 10097)*.

49.10   **Prolonged illness of partner.**   A married couple operated a public house. The husband suffered prolonged illness, and their VAT affairs fell into arrears. The Commissioners issued estimated assessments which were subsequently discovered to be inadequate. Accordingly the Commissioners imposed penalties under what is now *VATA 1994, s 63(1)(b)*. The tribunal allowed the couple's appeals against the penalties, holding that the husband's illness constituted a reasonable excuse. *DN & JF Thomas, LON/92/2005 (VTD 11040)*.

49.11   Penalties: Misdeclaration

49.11   **Computer malfunction.**   A company appealed against a penalty under what is now *VATA 1994, s 63(1)(b)*, contending that it had a reasonable excuse because its computer had been erratic and unreliable, and its officers had not known what its true VAT liability was. The tribunal accepted the company's evidence and allowed the appeal. *Physical Distribution Services Ltd, LON/93/2538P (VTD 12069).*

Cases where the appellant was unsuccessful

49.12   A company failed to submit its return for the period ending 31 August 1990. The Commissioners issued an estimated assessment charging VAT of £23,000, which the company paid. In November 1990 a control visit took place and the VAT officer discovered that the assessment had been inadequate. A further assessment was issued and a penalty under what is now *VATA 1994, s 63(1)(b)* was imposed. The company appealed, contending that it had a reasonable excuse because its accountant, who had begun working for the company on 13 August, had proved to be incompetent and had been dismissed in November. The tribunal dismissed the appeal, holding on the evidence that the company's finance director had been negligent in not supervising the accountant's work and in not ensuring that the relevant return was submitted. *Granmore Ltd*, 18.198 DEFAULT SURCHARGE, distinguished. *New Western (Panels) Ltd, MAN/91/317 (VTD 6990).*

49.13   The proprietors of a hotel failed to submit a VAT return for the period ending 30 September 1990. The Commissioners issued an estimated assessment charging tax of £6,350. The proprietors did not appeal. Subsequently the Commissioners discovered that the true liability for the period was almost £25,000. They therefore imposed a penalty under what is now *VATA 1994, s 63(1)(b)*. The proprietors appealed, contending that they had not appealed since they had assumed that the estimated assessment was 'about right'. The tribunal dismissed the appeal, holding that the principal partner 'should have been aware from his knowledge of his turnover' that the assessment was a 'gross underestimate'. *Muirtown Motel, EDN/91/313 (VTD 7431).*

49.14   A similar decision was reached in *C Stevenson, EDN/91/308 (VTD 7598).*

49.15   In a case where the proprietor of a Chinese restaurant could not understand English and relied on his son to deal with official correspondence, the tribunal held that there was no reasonable excuse for the acceptance of inadequate estimated assessments. *Neal*, 48.48 PENALTIES: FAILURE TO NOTIFY, applied. *YY Wong, MAN/91/860 (VTD 7591).*

49.16   A company failed to appeal against an inadequate estimated assessment, and a penalty under what is now *VATA 1994, s 63(1)(b)* was subsequently imposed. The company appealed against the penalty, contending that it had a reasonable excuse for not having checked the estimated assessment because of pressure of work following a change of premises. The tribunal dismissed the appeal, holding that the circumstances did not constitute a reasonable excuse. *Leckwith Engineering Ltd, LON/92/88Z (VTD 7702).*

49.17   An appeal was dismissed in a case where a company with a VAT liability of £32,000 failed to appeal against an estimated assessment of £1,420, and contended that it had had difficulty in balancing its books for the period in question. *Spinnaker MDC Ltd, LON/92/266Z (VTD 7841).*

49.18   A company failed to submit four successive returns. The Commissioners issued estimated assessments, which the company paid. Subsequently the Commissioners ascertained that the estimated assessments were inadequate, and imposed penalties under what is now *VATA 1994, s 63(1)(b)*. The company appealed, contending that it had a reasonable excuse because its bookkeeper had suffered from prolonged illness. The tribunal dismissed the appeal, holding that in view of the prolonged nature of the bookkeeper's illness, the company should have taken steps to keep its affairs up to date. *Social Workline Ltd, LON/92/2746P (VTD 10351)*. (*Note.* Appeals against default surcharges were also dismissed.)

49.19 A company failed to submit a number of returns and the Commissioners imposed estimated assessments which subsequently transpired to be inadequate. They therefore imposed penalties under *VATA 1994, s 63(1)(b)*. The company appealed, contending that the penalties should be waived because the Commissioners should have exercised their discretion not to impose them. The tribunal dismissed the appeal, applying *dicta* of Judge J in *Dollar Land (Feltham) Ltd*, 18.568 DEFAULT SURCHARGE. *Dicksmith Properties Ltd, LON/94/1789P (VTD 13136)*.

49.20 The Commissioners did not receive a company's return for the period ending August 1995, and issued an estimated assessment charging tax of £958. Subsequently they discovered that the company's tax liability for that period had been more than £39,000. They imposed a penalty under *VATA 1994, s 63(1)(b)*. The company appealed, contending that it had a reasonable excuse because it had posted the return in question. The tribunal rejected this contention and dismissed the appeal, finding on the evidence that the company's postal arrangements were 'casual and inefficient' and, on the balance of probabilities, the return had never been posted. Accordingly there was no reasonable excuse. *Yorkshire Rural Investments Ltd, MAN/96/614 (VTD 15083)*.

49.21 Appeals against penalties under what is now *VATA 1994, s 63(1)(b)* were also dismissed in *TR Cawthorne, LON/91/2249Z (VTD 7877); PRG Whatling, LON/92/1435P (VTD 9322); JR Bridges (t/a Plastering Contractors Ltd), LON/91/2490P (VTD 9653); Davies & Davies Ltd, LON/92/444Z (VTD 9692); JE Hewitt, MAN/92/128 (VTD 9910); J Eftekhari, MAN/91/1448 (VTD 10271); ACP Technical Services Ltd, MAN/92/131 (VTD 10332); Apex Denim & Fabric Finishers, MAN/93/166 (VTD 10989); Systemplay Ltd, MAN/93/325 (VTD 11030); A Ansari (t/a Northside House Hotel), LON/93/735 (VTD 11093); KRG Designs Ltd, MAN/93/307 (VTD 11348); A Mohammed, EDN/97/199 (VTD 15438); K & A Uddin (t/a Sangam Balti House), MAN/99/254 (VTD 16337); Aura Trading Ltd, MAN/99/912 (VTD 16534)* and *J Saunders-Pederson (t/a Advanced Information Systems UK)*, 49.399 below.

DEFINITION OF 'TAX WHICH WOULD HAVE BEEN LOST' (VATA 1994, s 63(2))

49.22 **Whether tax 'lost'.** In the case noted at 49.32 below, a company contended that the penalty was invalid because the tax in respect of which it had been imposed had been only temporarily lost to the Commissioners, since its auditors would have discovered the error in due course. The tribunal rejected this contention, holding that 'tax lost' could include 'tax delayed'. *Knight v CIR, CA [1974] STC 156 (TTC 2001, 6.4)* and *R v Holborn Commrs (ex p. Rind Settlement Trustees), QB [1974] STC 567 (TTC 2001, 6.5)* applied. *Fritz Bender Metals (UK) Ltd, [1991] VATTR 80 (VTD 5426)*.

49.23 A partnership failed to account for output tax of £2,400, and the Commissioners imposed a misdeclaration penalty. The partnership appealed, contending that the tax in question had not been 'lost' since it would have been declared in its next return. The tribunal rejected this contention and dismissed the appeal, applying *dicta* of Lord Widgery in *R v Holborn Commrs (ex p. Rind Settlement Trustees), QB [1974] STC 567 (TTC 2001, 6.5)*. *A Oliver & Sons, EDN/90/180 (VTD 5953)*.

49.24 Penalties: Misdeclaration

49.24   Similar decisions were reached in *Pursol Ltd, EDN/90/188 (VTD 5721); ACC American Car Centre Ltd, LON/90/1847Y (VTD 5883); Livebrace Ltd, MAN/90/973 (VTD 5957); Swithland Motors plc, MAN/90/943 (VTD 6125); BES Holdings Ltd, LON/91/559Y (VTD 6405); Blue Boar Computers Ltd, LON/91/997 (VTD 6416); Poloco SA, LON/91/929 (VTD 6565)* and *Sweetmate Ltd, LON/90/1667Y (VTD 6676)*.

WHETHER RETURN CORRECTED BY SUBSEQUENT RETURN (VATA 1994, s 63(8))

49.25   **Error in original return—corrected return sent after error discovered by VAT officer.**   A company submitted a return for the period ending 30 June 1990 which included a misdeclaration attributable to a clerical error. The return was received by the VAT Central Unit on 17 July 1990, and the error was discovered almost immediately by a VAT officer on a control visit. Following the visit, the company's director sent a replacement return which corrected the original return. The Commissioners imposed a misdeclaration penalty and the company appealed, contending that the first return should be treated as having been superseded by the second return. The tribunal dismissed the appeal, holding that the initial misdeclaration could not be rendered ineffective by sending an amended return after the error had been discovered. *Masterscore Ltd, MAN/90/746 (VTD 5611)*.

49.26   Similar decisions were reached in *PCC (Agriculture) Ltd, MAN/91/585 (VTD 9034); Stalwart Environmental Services Ltd,* 49.48 below, and *Ridgeway,* 49.87 below.

49.27   A similar decision was reached in a subsequent case where a return for the period ending October 1990 contained a duplication of input tax, and a VAT officer discovered this at a control visit on 27 November. On 28 November the company submitted a corrected return by fax to the VAT Central Unit. (The company had not informed either the Central Unit or the VAT officer that it proposed to do this.) The Commissioners imposed a misdeclaration penalty, and the tribunal dismissed the company's appeal, holding that the original incorrect return 'did not cease to be a return on a further return being submitted'. *Oddbins Ltd, LON/91/648Y (VTD 9011)*.

49.28   A company submitted a return for the period ending 30 June 1990 in which it reclaimed input tax in respect of an invoice issued in March 1990, which had already been included in its previous return. The error was discovered at a control visit on 31 July 1990. The officer conducting the visit warned the company that a misdeclaration penalty would arise. The company's managing director telephoned the VAT Central Unit, stating that an error had been discovered but not stating that a control visit was in progress, and arranged to send a corrected return by fax. Nevertheless, the Commissioners imposed a penalty in respect of the original return. The company appealed, contending that the amended return should be treated as correcting the original return. The tribunal allowed the company's appeal, holding that 'in the circumstances the Commissioners are estopped from treating the original return as valid ... If the Commissioners represent to a taxable person that they will give him the opportunity of formally declaring that a return which he has made is to be treated as ineffective, and the taxable person acts on the representation, ... there is nothing in law to prevent the representation from creating a binding estoppel, notwithstanding that the Commissioners thereafter refuse to give him the opportunity which they had promised him'. It followed that the original return should be treated as ineffective and that the faxed return should be treated as the effective return. *Masterscore Ltd,* 49.25 above, was distinguished on the grounds that in that case there had been no such arrangement between the company and the VAT Central Unit as had occurred in the instant case. *AB Gee of Ripley Ltd, [1991] VATTR 217 (VTD 5948)*. (*Note.* For cases concerning estoppel, see 2.72 to 2.84 APPEALS.)

WHETHER A 'REASONABLE EXCUSE' (VATA 1994, s 63(10)(a))

Clerical errors

Cases where the appellant was successful

49.29   **Misdeclaration following malfunction of computer.** A company submitted a VAT return for April 1990 in which it claimed a repayment of more than £114,000. A VAT officer visited the company and discovered that it had included in its April return input tax of £70,653 relating to invoices for services supplied in May. The Commissioners therefore imposed a misdeclaration penalty. The company appealed, contending that it had a reasonable excuse for the error, which followed the installation of a new computer on 1 April. The company's accounts manager had been absent on study leave for two weeks in early May, and his assistant had been absent unexpectedly on sick leave for three weeks at the same time. On their return they faced a backlog of work and did not notice that, because of a fault in the programming in the computer, the printout from which they prepared the April return included a large number of invoices relating to May. The tribunal allowed the appeal, finding that the accounts manager was 'conscientious and competent', and holding that it was not unreasonable for him to have assumed that the computer would have been programmed correctly. Applying the standpoint of 'a reasonable conscientious businessman', there was a reasonable excuse for the misdeclaration. *Appropriate Technology Ltd, [1991] VATTR 226 (VTD 5696)*.

49.30   *Appropriate Technology Ltd*, 49.29 above, was applied in the similar cases of *Zonner Industries Ltd, LON/90/1722Y (VTD 6031); JJH (Building Developments) Ltd, LON/91/649Y (VTD 6651); Hare Wines Ltd, LON/91/1376Z (VTD 6721); Arco British Ltd, LON/91/1406 (VTD 7041); Holmen Paper AB, LON/91/2379X (VTD 7628); Thanet District Council, LON/92/770Z (VTD 9308)* and *Godiva Bearings (Southern) Ltd, LON/92/2172 (VTD 9778)*. (*Note.* For cases where the malfunction of a computer was held not to be a reasonable excuse, see 49.56 and 49.57 below.)

49.31   Computer malfunction was also held to constitute a reasonable excuse for a misdeclaration in *Warehouse & Interior Design Ltd, LON/90/1718X (VTD 5893); Trident Exhibitions Ltd, LON/90/1912Z (VTD 6028); J & V Printing Services Ltd, MAN/91/5 (VTD 6136); Good Marriott & Hursthouse Ltd, MAN/91/553 (VTD 6633); F Hurley & Sons Ltd, LON/91/1056X (VTD 6719); The Midland Repetition Co Ltd, MAN/91/57 (VTD 6869); Peter Turner Associates, LON/91/1438 (VTD 6896)* and *JC Merrett (Builders) Ltd, LON/92/83 (VTD 10279)*.

49.32   **Company bookkeeper receiving medication.** A company submitted an incorrect return for April 1990. The amount of output tax in Box 1 was understated by £17,175 and the amount of input tax in Box 2 was overstated by £20,000. The Commissioners discovered the error at a control visit in August 1990, and imposed a misdeclaration penalty. The company appealed, contending that the errors were clerical errors by its bookkeeper. The output tax error arose from an error in transcription, and the input tax error arose from an error in addition. At the relevant time the bookkeeper was receiving medication for high blood pressure, and the company produced medical evidence that the prescribed medication had caused side-effects of lethargy, fatigue and decreased concentration. The company had not been aware that the bookkeeper was receiving medical treatment until after the errors had been discovered. The tribunal allowed the company's appeal, applying the reasoning in *Salevon Ltd*, 18.307 DEFAULT SURCHARGE. Although reliance on a bookkeeper could not of itself constitute a reasonable excuse, the tribunal was entitled to examine the reason for the bookkeeper's errors. On the evidence, 'the mistakes from which the inaccuracy resulted were caused by the drugs as opposed to simple human error'. *Fritz Bender Metals (UK) Ltd, [1991] VATTR 80 (VTD 5426).* (*Note.* For another issue in this case, see 49.22 above.)

49.33   *Fritz Bender Metals (UK) Ltd*, 49.32 above, was applied in the similar cases of *Tecnomare (UK) Ltd, LON/91/732Y (VTD 6329); Hayter Brothers Ltd, LON/91/ 2581X (VTD 9378)* and *Timark Warehousing Ltd, MAN/92/1127 (VTD 10360).*

49.34   Similar decisions were reached in *Peter Scott (Printers) Ltd, MAN/91/552 (VTD 6356)* and *K Malin, LON/91/2015X (VTD 7623).*

49.35   **Appellant partly blind.**   An appeal was allowed in a case where a man who was visually handicapped had gone into business as a retailer, but the business had been unsuccessful and had closed after five months, and both the VAT returns which he had submitted had contained clerical errors. The tribunal held that the circumstances constituted a reasonable excuse. *S Lancaster, LON/92/1288P (VTD 9261).*

49.36   **Illness of appellant.**   An appeal was allowed in a case where a sole trader gave evidence that he was recovering from a heart bypass operation at the time when he submitted a return which underdeclared output tax, and that he would have noticed the error had it not been for his ill-health. The tribunal held that the circumstances constituted a reasonable excuse. *RL Curley (t/a Scan Print Services), LON/93/233P (VTD 10691).*

49.37   **Illness of employee.**   The illness of the employee responsible for the submission of the relevant return was held to constitute a reasonable excuse for a misdeclaration in *Kenkay Ltd, LON/91/1480X (VTD 6923); Anti-Sonics Ltd, MAN/91/218 (VTD 7196); A & M Insulations Ltd, MAN/91/839 (VTD 7498); Wright & Son (Building Contractors) Ltd, MAN/91/1652 (VTD 10055); Southcombe Brothers Ltd, LON/91/745Z (VTD 10151); JH Palmer & Sons, LON/92/2470P (VTD 10230); Guardian Building Services, MAN/91/1060 (VTD 11050); AOC International Ltd, EDN/93/31 (VTD 11139); Artistic Ironworkers Supplies Ltd, MAN/93/502 (VTD 11228); Allman Holdings Ltd, LON/93/1694 (VTD 11285)* and *Food Engineering Ltd*, 49.413 below.

49.38   **Illness of employee—clerical error by inexperienced substitute.**   A company submitted a return in which its input tax was overstated by £18,123. The Commissioners imposed a misdeclaration penalty. The company appealed, contending that it had a reasonable excuse because, at the time the return was submitted, its bookkeeper had been unable to work for two weeks through illness, and the employee who prepared the return in her place had inadvertently carried forward input tax from the previous period. The tribunal allowed the company's appeal, holding that the circumstances constituted a reasonable excuse. *Draxtech Ltd, LON/91/962X (VTD 6432).*

49.39   Similar decisions were reached in *Robeda Ltd, LON/91/1435Z (VTD 7781); Burley Estates Ltd, LON/92/30X (VTD 7937); HA & DB Kitchin Ltd, LON/92/1410P (VTD 9513)* and *Alan Franks Group, MAN/92/211 (VTD 10146).*

49.40   **Death of employee.**   A company's bookkeeper died in March 1990. A replacement was appointed, and prepared the company's returns for the periods ending 30 June 1990 and 30 September 1990. However, in the September return, the new bookkeeper inadvertently reclaimed input tax on an invoice which had already been included in the June return. The Commissioners imposed a misdeclaration penalty. The tribunal allowed the company's appeal, holding that the disruption caused by the death of the bookkeeper constituted a reasonable excuse. *Coxhill Electronics Ltd, LON/91/675 (VTD 6433)*.

49.41   Similar decisions were reached in *Charnwood Holdings Ltd, LON/91/276 (VTD 7056)* and *Communications Consultants Ltd, LON/91/2526X (VTD 8973)*.

49.42   **Change of bookkeeper.**   An appeal was allowed in a case where a company had changed its bookkeeper shortly before the due date of a return, and attributed an error in dealing with management charges to the fact that the new bookkeeper had found her predecessor's working papers 'impossible to follow'. The tribunal held that the circumstances constituted a reasonable excuse. *Stanhope Properties plc, LON/91/1539X (VTD 6971)*.

49.43   A change of bookkeeper was also held to constitute a reasonable excuse for a misdeclaration in *C Maguire (t/a TC Autos), BEL/90/47X (VTD 7056)* and *Standen Ltd, LON/93/669 (VTD 10785)*.

49.44   **Bereavement of employee.**   A company appealed against a misdeclaration penalty, contending that it had a reasonable excuse because the employee responsible for the return had suffered from a bereavement shortly before completing the return. The tribunal allowed the appeal, holding that the circumstances constituted a reasonable excuse. *Danish Firma Center plc, LON/91/442Z (VTD 6196)*.

49.45   **Terminal illness of partner's father—consequent strain on partner.**   A married couple carried on business in partnership. The wife was responsible for the completion of the partnership's VAT returns. She reclaimed an excessive amount of input tax in the return for the period ending 31 July 1990 and the Commissioners imposed a misdeclaration penalty. The partners appealed, contending that the wife had been suffering from severe strain at the time because her father was terminally ill. The tribunal allowed the appeal, holding that the circumstances constituted a reasonable excuse. *ED & M Middleton, MAN/91/33 (VTD 6208)*.

49.46   **Exceptional workload.**   A company carried on business as travel agents. It decided to change its trading name after a large agency with a similar name went into liquidation with adverse publicity. The change of the company's trading name necessitated considerable extra work. During this period the company submitted a VAT return in which it reclaimed input tax on invoices made out to an associated company. The Commissioners imposed a misdeclaration penalty, but the tribunal allowed the company's appeal, holding that the 'sudden and disconcerting pressure' of additional work constituted a reasonable excuse. *Zenith Holdings Ltd, LON/90/884Z (VTD 6032)*.

49.47   There have been a small number of other cases in which exceptional pressure of work has been held to constitute a reasonable excuse for a misdeclaration. In the interests of space, such cases have not been summarised individually in this book. For a list of such cases decided up to 31 December 1996, see Tolley's VAT Cases 1997.

49.48   **Company entering into contract with local authority—lack of co-operation by local authority staff—whether a reasonable excuse.**   In October 1990 a company which carried on a refuse collection business entered into a contract with Harrow Borough Council. Under the contract, it was to be paid by the Council each month in arrear, and the work done was to be valued and agreed before it could issue invoices to the Council. Many of the Council staff objected to the refuse collection being carried out by a private company, since this had previously been undertaken by the Council's own staff. Therefore, the procedures for valuing the work fell behind schedule, and the company's general manager advised its accountant that it was unlikely to issue any invoices for its return period ending 30 November 1990. On

6 December, the accountant submitted a return showing no output tax due. However, despite the statement made by the manager, the company did in fact issue an invoice at the end of November. It sent a copy of this to the accountant, but it did not arrive until after 6 December. A VAT officer discovered this at a control visit on 21 December and drew it to the attention of the accountant, who issued a corrected return with a cheque for the VAT payable. The Commissioners imposed a misdeclaration penalty, but the tribunal allowed the company's appeal, holding that, in view of the lack of co-operation the company had suffered from the Council's staff, the circumstances constituted a reasonable excuse. *Stalwart Environmental Services Ltd, LON/91/791Y (VTD 7179)*. (*Note*. The tribunal rejected an alternative contention by the company that the penalty should be discharged by virtue of what is now *VATA 1994, s 63(8)*—see 49.26 above.)

49.49 **Invoice sent by fax not included in return.** A contractor's wife acted as his bookkeeper. She prepared his VAT return from carbon copies of the invoices which he issued. During the period ending August 1990 her husband issued one invoice by fax. Since there was no carbon copy, she did not include it in the relevant return. The Commissioners imposed a misdeclaration penalty, but the tribunal allowed the contractor's appeal, holding that the unusual nature of the invoice constituted a reasonable excuse. *M Smith, MAN/91/1212 (VTD 7439)*.

49.50 **Isolated clerical error.** There have been a number of cases in which an isolated clerical error has been held to constitute a reasonable excuse. In the interests of space, such cases are not summarised individually in this book. For a list of such cases decided up to 31 December 1996, see Tolley's VAT Cases 1997.

49.51 **Misreading of dates on return form.** An appeal was allowed in a case where a company's first return was issued for the period ending 30 November 1990, with a due date of 31 December 1990, but the company's controlling director included its transactions for December 1990 in the return and stated in evidence that he had misread the return. *GC Parts Ltd, LON/91/2248Z (VTD 7545)*.

49.52 **Mistaken belief that underdeclaration corrected by subsequent assessment.** In July 1990 a VAT officer made a control visit to a company and discovered that certain sales had been omitted from its returns. He issued an assessment to recover the tax due for the period omitted from the return for the period ending March 1990. The company paid the tax charged. In June 1991 a second control visit took place by a different officer, who discovered that some sales had been omitted from the company's return for the period ending June 1990. The Commissioners imposed a penalty and the company appealed, contending that it had a reasonable excuse because its directors had assumed that the errors had been included in the assessment which had been issued following the previous control visit. The tribunal allowed the appeal, holding that the fact that the officer had seen the June 1990 records at the July 1990 visit made it reasonable for the company to have assumed that the errors in the June 1990 return would have been corrected by the assessment issued immediately afterwards. *People Products Ltd, MAN/91/1080 (VTD 7379)*.

49.53 **Duplicate invoices issued by contractor.** In a case where a contractor issued duplicate invoices in respect of the same transaction, and the customer reclaimed input tax in respect of both invoices, the tribunal held that the circumstances constituted a reasonable excuse. *WH Clarkson & Son, MAN/91/1564 (VTD 7479)*. (*Note*. Compare *McLaughlin*, 49.76 below, in which the receipt of duplicate invoices was held not to be a reasonable excuse.)

49.54 A similar decision was reached in *Manchester Young Men's Christian Association, MAN/91/255 (VTD 9215)*.

49.55 **Duplicate payment made to contractor.** In October 1990 a district council made two payments to one contractor in respect of the same invoice. The contractor only banked one of the cheques, and returned the duplicate cheque in early November. However, in its October VAT return the council reclaimed input tax in respect of both cheques. When the Commissioners discovered this, they imposed a misdeclaration penalty. The tribunal allowed the council's appeal, holding that since the council had actually issued two cheques there was a reasonable excuse for the misdeclaration. *Vale of White Horse District Council, LON/91/587Y (VTD 6924).*

Cases where the appellant was unsuccessful

49.56 **Reliance on computer.** The Commissioners imposed a misdeclaration penalty on a firm which had underdeclared its output tax by £4,606. The firm appealed, contending that it had a reasonable excuse because its computer had failed to account for VAT on sales at one of the firm's shops. The tribunal dismissed the firm's appeal, holding that what is now *VATA 1994, s 71(1)(b)* precluded reliance on a computer programmer from constituting a reasonable excuse. *City Cycles, EDN/90/199 (VTD 5699).*

49.57 Computer errors were also held not to constitute a reasonable excuse in *Cheyne Motors Ltd, LON/90/1799 (VTD 5854); London Borough of Camden, LON/90/1592X (VTD 6123); Bristol Street Motors (Bromley) Ltd, LON/91/153 (VTD 6381); Blyth Valley Borough Council, MAN/91/414 (VTD 6417); Hancock & Wood Ltd, MAN/91/544 (VTD 6691); PJ Hall, LON/90/1892X (VTD 6722); Spelthorne Borough Council, LON/91/1475X (VTD 6958); Kubota (UK) Ltd, LON/90/1309Y (VTD 6960); Campus Martius Ltd, MAN/91/756 (VTD 7199); Jordans Plumbing Merchants Ltd, LON/91/1817 (VTD 7822); Apple Contractors (Northern) Ltd, MAN/91/1264 (VTD 7853); JMD Group plc, LON/92/483X (VTD 9129); Bruce Miller & Co, EDN/92/158 (VTD 9402); NS Dajani (t/a Lancashire Marketing Consultants), MAN/92/1701 (VTD 10861)* and *Dunelm (Castle Homes) Ltd,* 49.387 below.

49.58 **Clerical error by bookkeeper.** The Commissioners imposed a misdeclaration penalty on a borough council which had claimed a repayment of VAT for April 1990 which exceeded the amount actually due by more than £50,000, as a result of a clerical error by a member of staff who had accidentally included on the return the input tax relating to the first two weeks in May. The tribunal dismissed the council's appeal, holding that, although the error was a 'mere accident', it did not constitute a reasonable excuse. *Taunton Deane Borough Council, LON/90/1225Z (VTD 5545).* (*Note.* For another issue in this case, see 49.363 below.)

49.59 *Taunton Deane Borough Council,* 49.58 above, was applied in the similar cases of *EA Chiverton Ltd, LON/90/1397 (VTD 6130); Whitehead & Wood Ltd, MAN/91/232 (VTD 6341); Waterlink Distribution Ltd, LON/91/2611X (VTD 7913)* and *Tong Garden Centre plc, MAN/93/1056 (VTD 12103).*

49.60 A company failed to charge VAT on an invoice of £39,060. The error was discovered on a control visit after the company had claimed a repayment of more than £10,000. The Commissioners imposed a misdeclaration penalty and the company appealed, contending that it had a reasonable excuse because its bookkeeper had accidentally forgotten to include any VAT on the invoice. The tribunal dismissed the company's appeal, holding that what is now *VATA 1994, s 71(1)* prevented this from being a reasonable excuse. *Victoria Alloys (UK) Ltd, [1991] VATTR 163 (VTD 5608).*

49.61 A similar decision was reached in *Scanland Agencies Ltd, MAN/91/37 (VTD 6648).*

49.62   Penalties: Misdeclaration

49.62   *Victoria Alloys (UK) Ltd*, 49.60 above, was applied in a subsequent case where the tribunal held that there was no reasonable excuse for a clerical error which caused a company to claim a repayment of £173,000 when the correct figure was £18,000. *Appropriate Technology Ltd*, 49.29 above, distinguished. *Cavendish Constructors plc, LON/91/5901 (VTD 6957)*.

49.63   A police authority submitted a VAT return claiming a repayment of tax. The return included a claim for input tax of £104,204 in respect of a cheque made payable to British Telecom. However, the cheque had been cancelled and a replacement issued for a slightly smaller amount. The tax of £97,257 included in the second cheque was also included on the return, which therefore overclaimed input tax by £104,204. The Commissioners discovered the error on a control visit, and imposed a misdeclaration penalty. The authority appealed, contending that the inclusion of the amount of the first cheque in the return was a clerical error by one of its staff. The tribunal dismissed the appeal. The chairman stated that he was 'amazed that the authority adopted a system which allowed such an elementary mistake to pass undetected at the time of origin'. The management 'was aware of the frailty of the system yet it allowed the verification procedure to be given a low priority'. The authority's chief accountant had 'been aware of certain problems for several months yet a simple weekly check was not performed'. The circumstances did not constitute a reasonable excuse for the error. *Merseyside Police Authority, [1991] VATTR 152 (VTD 5654)*.

49.64   In July 1989 a borough council, which submitted monthly returns, sought permission from the Commissioners to estimate part of its deductible input tax. The Commissioners agreed to this request, and allowed the council to reclaim an estimated amount of £123,000 in its next return. In December the Commissioners wrote to the Council again, requesting it to review the figure of £123,000, which it had continued to carry forward as an estimated credit, and ascertain the average amount of input tax due for the previous six months. The council's accountant computed this average as £113,000. In the return for January 1990 she claimed estimated input tax of £113,000 accordingly, but also continued to claim credit for the original estimate of £123,000. The VAT office discovered the error and explained the position. The next three returns were computed on an acceptable basis, but in the May 1990 return the council's accountant again claimed credit for a cumulative figure of two months' input tax. The Commissioners imposed a misdeclaration penalty. The council appealed, contending that the complexity of the estimation procedure, and pressure of work caused by the introduction of the community charge (or 'poll tax'), constituted a reasonable excuse. The tribunal dismissed the council's appeal. On the evidence, the system had been explained to the council's accountant after the detection of the error in the January return, and subsequent returns had been correctly completed. It should have been clear to the accountant, or to her supervisors, that the May return was incorrect. Pressure of work might, in certain circumstances, excuse 'minor clerical errors', but it could not excuse a fundamental error of the type which had occurred in this case. *Havant Borough Council, LON/90/1360Y (VTD 6080)*.

49.65   A company submitted a return in which it overstated its input tax by £37,000, so that it claimed a repayment of £30,000 instead of declaring a liability of £7,000. The Commissioners imposed a misdeclaration penalty and the company appealed, contending that it had a reasonable excuse because the return had been completed by an inexperienced member of staff who had only been employed for one month, and the company secretary had been too busy to check the return. The tribunal dismissed the appeal, holding that what is now *VATA 1994, s 71(1)(b)* 'applies equally to the maker of the original mistake, the compiler of the return, and anyone whose job it may have been to check the figures'. The QB upheld this decision. The fact that a mistake had been made by an employee need not prevent the tribunal from looking behind the fact of the mistake to the reason for the mistake, applying the principle laid down in *Salevon Ltd*, 18.307 DEFAULT SURCHARGE. However, on the evidence here, the misdeclaration arose from a simple human error which could have been discovered if the figures had been checked. The unavoidable conclusion was that there was no reasonable excuse for the misdeclaration. *Frank Galliers Ltd v C & E Commrs, QB 1992, [1993] STC 284.*

49.66   There are a very large number of other cases in which clerical errors by bookkeepers or employees have been held not to constitute a reasonable excuse. In the interests of space, such cases are not listed individually in this book. For a list of such cases decided up to 31 December 1993, see Tolley's VAT Cases 1994.

49.67   **Absence of employee through illness.**   See *South Caernarvon Creameries Ltd*, 49.121 below.

49.68   **Clerical error by accountant.**   Clerical errors by accountants were held not to constitute a reasonable excuse in *Elanders (UK) Ltd, MAN/91/63 (VTD 6137); W Mayne-Flower, MAN/91/641 (VTD 6513); Progenitive Chemicals Ltd, EDN/91/ 171 (VTD 6591); Americana Europe Ltd, EDN/91/232 (VTD 6712); Imagebase Technology Ltd, LON/91/1230Z (VTD 6720); Golden Cloud Solarium, LON/91/ 1110Z (VTD 6761); KM Muir (t/a Ken Muir Nurseries), LON/91/1611Z (VTD 6830); Shoot Super Soccer Ltd, EDN/91/90 (VTD 6882); Holman Kelly Paper Co Ltd, LON/91/951Z (VTD 6899); Broadside Colours & Chemicals Ltd, MAN/91/ 807 (VTD 6994); JE Smallman, MAN/91/58 (VTD 7228); Lam Watson & Woods, LON/91/2001 (VTD 7307); Resincrest Ltd, LON/91/2168X (VTD 7310); Bidco Impex Ltd, MAN/91/540 (VTD 7406); D Carey, LON/91/2393 (VTD 7619); R Caira (t/a The Ambassador Leisure Club), EDN/91/130 (VTD 7625); Coller Paper Co Ltd, LON/92/60X (VTD 7890); R Eggleton, LON/92/546X (VTD 7932); RG Francis, LON/92/596Z (VTD 9063); Pet-Reks Southern Ltd, LON/92/1364P (VTD 9070); Boz Ltd, LON/92/1520P (VTD 9353); Eversleigh Investments & Property Co Ltd, LON/92/1784 (VTD 9646); Gleeds Chartered Quantity Surveyors, LON/92/2219P (VTD 9770, 10069); Tex Holdings plc, LON/92/3117 (VTD 10416); MBS Rüter Fassadenbau GmbH, LON/92/3258P (VTD 10472)* and *AB Transport, MAN/94/53 (VTD 12481).*

49.69   A shopkeeper was sentenced to a term of imprisonment in January 1991. His accountant submitted his VAT return for the period ending 31 December 1990. The return overclaimed input tax, and the Commissioners imposed a misdeclaration penalty. The shopkeeper appealed, contending that he had a reasonable excuse because he would have been able to check the return had it not been for his imprisonment. The tribunal dismissed the appeal, holding that what is now *VATA 1994, s 71(1)(b)* precluded the circumstances from constituting a reasonable excuse. *AJ Whitehead, MAN/92/1468 (VTD 10696).*

49.70   **Clerical error by director.**   A company reclaimed input tax twice in respect of the same transaction, and the Commissioners imposed a misdeclaration penalty. The company appealed, contending that this was an innocent clerical error by a director. The tribunal dismissed the appeal, holding that an innocent mistake could not of itself constitute a reasonable excuse without further extenuating circumstances. *M Holt (Manchester) Ltd, MAN/91/6 (VTD 6312).*

49.71   Clerical errors by directors were also held not to constitute a reasonable excuse in *Turmeaus Ltd, MAN/90/969 (VTD 6052); Integrated Furniture System Ltd, LON/ 91/421 (VTD 6549); Landowner Liquid Fertilisers Ltd, MAN/91/615 (VTD 6692); The Art Store (British Isles) Ltd, MAN/91/1094 (VTD 6938); Duvan Estates Ltd, LON/91/804 (VTD 7040) Geoffery Clarke Grain Co Ltd, LON/91/1251Z (VTD 7142); Morgan Brothers (Mid-Wales) Ltd, MAN/91/1247 (VTD 8913); Bornfleet*

Forwarding Ltd, LON/92/1509P (VTD 9704); Fast Technology Ltd, LON/92/2114A (VTD 9974); School Book Fairs (GB) Ltd, LON/93/422P (VTD 10553); D & M Electro Plating Ltd, MAN/92/1421 (VTD 10966) and *AG Tisdall & Co Ltd, LON/93/1914P (VTD 11521).*

49.72   **Deliberate clerical error by managing director suffering from illness—whether reasonable excuse.**   The Commissioners discovered that a company failed to account for VAT of more than £30,000 in respect of the sale of property, although the amount had been paid by the customer. The amount in question had been paid into an account in the names of the managing director and his wife, rather than into the company account. The Commissioners imposed a misdeclaration penalty and the company appealed, contending that it had a reasonable excuse because the managing director had been ill at the relevant time. The tribunal dismissed the appeal, observing that 'there was a deliberate understatement of outputs' and that 'no taxpayer who had a responsible attitude to his duties as a taxpayer, and who conscientiously sought to ensure that his returns were accurate, would make a deliberate understatement of outputs'. *Markdome Ltd,* 49.130 below, applied. *Amspray Ltd (t/a Champion Tools & Supplies), MAN/93/225 (VTD 10888).*

49.73   **Clerical error by partner.**   Clerical errors by partners were held not to constitute a reasonable excuse in *Messrs WB Erskine, EDN/91/136 (VTD 6310); The Main Pine Company, MAN/91/305 (VTD 6384); RWJB & GH Pryce, BEL/91/4 (VTD 6398); Sutton Kitchens, LON/91/2147Y (VTD 7432); Good Roofing (Devon), LOM/91/2414Y (VTD 7845); Tudor Hotel & Restaurant, MAN/92/554 (VTD 9683); A & M Soni, MAN/92/938 (VTD 9919)* and *JW & MJ Whitefield & AJ & JA Osbourne, LON/93/714P (VTD 10926).*

49.74   **Clerical error by appellant.**   Clerical errors by the appellant were held not to constitute a reasonable excuse in *D Malloch, EDN/91/22 (VTD 5811); A Frost, EDN/90/216 (VTD 5813); J Doherty, LON/91/28X (VTD 6609); RJ Bird, LON/91/37X (VTD 6715); GM Harris, LON/92/851Y (VTD 9069); GF Bateman, MAN/91/1678 (VTD 9344); KA Terry (t/a Advanced Laboratory Techniques), LON/92/2541P (VTD 9803); M Bott (t/a Clothesline), EDN/92/225 (VTD 10267); A Reid, EDN/92/353 (VTD 10403)* and *K Round (t/a Circle Interiors), MAN/93/203 (VTD 10844).*

49.75   **Marriage breakdown—whether excuse for clerical error in return.**   A trader appealed against a penalty imposed in respect of a duplicated claim for input tax, contending that he had a reasonable excuse because he had been suffering from stress following the breakdown of his marriage. The tribunal dismissed his appeal, holding that this was not a reasonable excuse. *JD Pauline, MAN/93/500 (VTD 11029).*

49.76   **Duplicate invoices issued by supplier.**   In a case where an oil company issued duplicate invoices to a garage proprietor in respect of the same transaction, and the proprietor reclaimed input tax in respect of both invoices, the tribunal dismissed the proprietor's appeal, holding that the circumstances did not constitute a reasonable excuse. *R McLaughlin, BEL/91/62 (VTD 7514).*

49.77   **Supplies to associated partnership—failure to account for tax.**   An appeal was dismissed in a case where a company had failed to account for VAT on supplies to an associated partnership with a similar name, and contended that this was attributable to a clerical error. The tribunal held that the circumstances did not constitute a reasonable excuse. *Appropriate Technology Ltd,* 49.29 above, and *The Clean Car Co Ltd,* 49.83 below, distinguished. *Auto-Plas (International) Ltd, LON/91/2350X (VTD 8860).*

49.78   See also *Michael Rogers Ltd*, 49.270 below.

49.79   **Sale to associated company—failure to account for tax.**   See *Precious Metal Industries (Wales) Ltd*, 49.268 below, and the cases noted at 49.269 below.

Misunderstanding of the time of supply

Cases where the appellant was successful

49.80   **Input tax reclaimed prematurely.**   A company reclaimed input tax on two proforma invoices. The tribunal held that the company had a reasonable excuse for believing that the date shown on the 'proforma' invoices was the time of supply. *Enterprise Safety Coaches Ltd, [1991] VATTR 74 (VTD 5391)*. (*Note*. The reasoning in this case was disapproved by a subsequent tribunal in *GB Capital Ltd*, 49.325 below. There was held to be no reasonable excuse for reclaiming VAT on 'proforma' invoices in *South Caernarvon Creameries Ltd*, 49.121 below, or in the cases noted at 49.122 below.)

49.81   Similar decisions were reached in *Joe Pole Construction Co Ltd, MAN/91/392 (VTD 7101); Ford Fuels Ltd, LON/91/20Y (VTD 7213)* and *The Austin Company of UK Ltd, LON/91/1990X (VTD 7981)*.

49.82   A company arranged to purchase a coach under a leasing agreement. It reclaimed the whole of the input tax due under the agreement at the time when it made the first payment. The Commissioners imposed a misdeclaration penalty. The company appealed, contending that its bookkeeper had mistakenly treated the agreement as a hire-purchase agreement. The tribunal allowed the appeal, holding that the circumstances constituted a reasonable excuse. *Chartercoach Holidays Ltd, LON/93/1464P (VTD 11193)*.

49.83   A company reclaimed input tax on the basis of an architect's certificate dated 29 June 1990, although the contractor had not issued the relevant tax invoice until 2 July and the company had paid the amount due on 6 July. The Commissioners imposed a misdeclaration penalty but the tribunal held that the circumstances constituted a reasonable excuse. *The Clean Car Company Ltd, [1991] VATTR 234 (VTD 5695)*. (*Note*. There was held to be no reasonable excuse for the claim of input tax on the basis of an architect's certificate in *Pepis (Marina) Ltd*, 49.119 below, *Breese Brick Ltd*, 49.120 below, or *Robert S Monk Ltd*, 49.386 below.)

49.84   Similar decisions were reached in *Banbridge District Enterprises Ltd, BEL/91/20X (VTD 6406); Fielder & Sons (Enfield) Ltd, LON/91/1647Z (VTD 7017); Crosstyle plc, LON/91/257Y (VTD 7169); Sprowston Hall Hotel Ltd, LON/91/255Y (VTD 7253); Coventry Motors & Sundries Co Ltd, MAN/91/104 (VTD 7378); NCC Developments Ltd, LON/91/2137X (VTD 7388)* and *Mitchells of Hailsham Ltd, LON/91/1806X (VTD 9862)*.

49.85   A company reclaimed input tax on the basis of an application for payment dated 27 September, although the contractor did not issue a VAT invoice until 11 October. The tribunal held that the circumstances constituted a reasonable excuse. *TS International Freight Forwarders Ltd, MAN/91/399 (VTD 7080)*.

49.86   Similar decisions were reached in *Equiname Ltd, MAN/91/609 (VTD 7592)* and *Wyndley Nurseries Ltd, MAN/91/970 (VTD 10269)*.

49.87   A trader ordered, and paid for, some materials in June 1990. He reclaimed the input tax in his return for the period ending 30 June, although he had not yet received the materials or the invoice. The Commissioners imposed a misdeclaration penalty but the tribunal held that the trader had a reasonable excuse for the premature claim.

49.88 Penalties: Misdeclaration

PJ Ridgeway, MAN/90/664 (VTD 6140). (*Note*. For another issue in this case, see 49.26 above.)

49.88   Similar decisions were reached in *Wisebeck Construction Ltd, LON/91/1020Z (VTD 6612)* and *M Farrey, MAN/91/478 (VTD 6709)*.

49.89   A company received a large quantity of fuel from Texaco on 28 September 1990 and reclaimed the relevant input tax in its return for the period ending 30 September, although Texaco had not issued the invoice until 4 October. The Commissioners imposed a misdeclaration penalty but the tribunal held that the circumstances constituted a reasonable excuse. *Croft Fuels Ltd, MAN/91/630 (VTD 6644)*.

49.90   Similar decisions were reached in *Jones Executive Coaches Ltd, MAN/90/1110 (VTD 6870)* and *Z Hussain (t/a Zabar Hosiery), MAN/91/634 (VTD 6895)*.

49.91   An company trading as a car dealer entered into contracts in July 1990 for the delivery of some H-registration cars which could not legally be delivered until August. The company reclaimed the relevant input tax in the period ending 31 July. The tribunal held that it had a reasonable excuse for the premature claim. *Olympian Automotive Ltd, LON/91/1048Z (VTD 7141)*.

49.92   A trader agreed to purchase two tractors by four annual instalments. He received an invoice for the 1990 instalment in April and reclaimed the relevant input tax in his return for that period, although he did not pay the invoice until September. The tribunal held that there was a reasonable excuse for the premature claim. *MR Hampden-Smith, LON/91/790 (VTD 7468)*.

49.93   In the case noted at 38.68 INVOICES AND CREDIT NOTES, a company reclaimed input tax in respect of a payment made to a supplier which went into liquidation shortly afterwards without supplying either the goods paid for or an invoice for them. The tribunal held that there was a reasonable excuse for the misdeclaration. *Newland Technical Services Ltd, LON/92/1255A (VTD 9294)*. (*Note*. For other issues in this case, see 34.239 INPUT TAX and 49.309 below.)

49.94   A firm of solicitors paid its annual contributions to the Solicitors Indemnity Fund in two instalments, due on 1 September and 1 March. In August 1991 the Fund sent the firm an invoice for its 1991/92 contributions. The firm reclaimed input tax in respect of both instalments in its return for the period ending 31 August 1991. The Commissioners imposed a misdeclaration penalty, since, by virtue of what is now *VAT Regulations 1995 (SI 1995 No 2518), reg 90(2)*, the tax was not reclaimable until the due dates for payment. The tribunal held that there was a reasonable excuse for the premature claim. *The Simkins Partnership, LON/92/1553 (VTD 9705)*.

49.95   A trader who operated the Cash Accounting Scheme reclaimed input tax by reference to the dates on which he received invoices, rather than the dates on which he made payment. The Commissioners imposed a misdeclaration penalty but the tribunal held that the circumstances constituted a reasonable excuse. *BD Cake, MAN/91/1068 (VTD 10272)*.

49.96   **Imports—input tax reclaimed prematurely.** See the cases noted at 49.142 to 49.157 below.

49.97   **Delay in reclaiming input tax.** An appeal was allowed in a case where a company had delayed reclaiming input tax on certain invoices until the end of its accounting year, although the invoices had been issued in previous accounting periods. *Colorlam Ltd, LON/92/895Z (VTD 9412)*.

49.98   **Misleading invoices issued by finance company.** A company leased two vehicles from a finance company. The invoices issued by the finance company included the total rental, including VAT, payable in respect of twelve monthly instalments from May 1990 to April 1991. The company reclaimed this total figure of VAT as input tax in its return for the period ending June 1990. The Commissioners imposed a penalty but the tribunal held that there was a reasonable excuse for the misdeclaration. *Wrights International Leather Ltd, BEL/91/10 (VTD 6399)*.

49.99   **Input tax reclaimed on supplies before registration.**   A trader reclaimed input tax on supplies he had received before registration. The Commissioners imposed a misdeclaration penalty. The tribunal allowed the trader's appeal in part, observing that, under what is now *VAT Regulations 1995 (SI 1995 No 2518), reg 111*, the Commissioners had discretion to allow credit for input tax on supplies received before registration. *DW Wyck, LON/91/845X (VTD 6619)*. (*Note*. For another issue in this case, see 49.321 below.)

49.100   **Delay in accounting for output tax.**   A company supplied goods to an associated company. It issued a single invoice, at the end of each accounting year, for the goods supplied in that year. The Commissioners imposed a misdeclaration penalty on the basis that the company should have accounted for tax at the time the goods were removed, as required by what is now *VATA 1994, s 6(2)*. The tribunal allowed the company's appeal, holding that the circumstances constituted a reasonable excuse. *Jamestown Concrete Co Ltd, EDN/91/3 (VTD 5722)*.

49.101   A golf club professional (Q) accounted for VAT at the time when he received payment, rather than when he issued invoices. The Commissioners imposed a misdeclaration penalty but the tribunal held that Q had a reasonable excuse. *AD Quarterman, MAN/90/1056 (VTD 6200)*.

49.102   Similar decisions were reached in *Watson Norrie Ltd, MAN/91/31 (VTD 6248); Tal Ltd, BEL/90/56X (VTD 6397); The Parr Partnership, EDN/91/177 (VTD 6733); PT Garrett & Sons (Contractors) Ltd, LON/91/1028X (VTD 7073); H James Builders (Wolverhampton) Ltd, MAN/91/213 (VTD 7102); JC Lewis Partnership, LON/91/1954X (VTD 7368); Ryebank Heating Ltd, MAN/91/1371 (VTD 7405); Avonline Communications (Bristol) Ltd, LON/90/1504X (VTD 9204); V Brice, LON/92/1387P (VTD 9721)* and *P Zimmatore, LON/92/1008A (VTD 10376)*.

49.103   A partnership had a contract with a local council, which insisted upon paying the partnership in twelve monthly instalments. The partnership did not include the VAT in the invoices for the instalments, but, after receiving payment from the council, issued further invoices charging VAT on the amounts paid. The Commissioners imposed a penalty but the tribunal held that the circumstances constituted a reasonable excuse. *D & J Nuttall, MAN/91/444 (VTD 6343)*.

49.104   A contractor did not account for VAT on payments for work in progress. The Commissioners imposed a penalty but the tribunal held that there was a reasonable excuse for the misdeclaration. *RM Bridgeman (t/a Bridgeman Building & Public Works Contractors), LON/91/611 (VTD 6563)*.

49.105   Similar decisions were reached in *Hill Welsh, LON/91/1510 (VTD 6828); McKean Smith & Co Ltd, MAN/91/1151 (VTD 10334); GN Mellor, MAN/92/626 (VTD 10703)* and *PH Hardwill, LON/93/2582 (VTD 13958)*.

49.106   A company (G) which submitted monthly returns contracted to sell 15 trailers to a customer, and agreed that the customer should pay G within 30 days of delivery. It issued an invoice on 1 August. Nine of the trailers were delivered in August, but the delivery of the other six was delayed until 3 September. G issued a credit note to cancel the August invoice, and issued a replacement invoice on 1 September. G declared the output tax in its September return. The Commissioners imposed a penalty on the basis that G should have accounted for tax on the first nine trailers in its August return. G appealed, contending that there had been a single contract to supply 15 trailers, so that it had assumed that the tax point was 3 September. The tribunal held that the circumstances constituted a reasonable excuse. *GB Express Ltd, LON/91/1167Z (VTD 6822).*

49.107   An accountancy partnership (H) employed a VAT consultant, and hired his services to a number of associated partnerships. H did not issue a formal VAT invoice for the consultant's services, and did not request payment from its associated partnerships until after the end of its financial year. The Commissioners imposed a penalty, considering that H should have accounted for VAT when the consultant's services were supplied. H appealed, contending firstly that the consultant's services were continuous supplies within what is now *VAT Regulations 1995 (SI 1995 No 2518), reg 90*, and alternatively that it had a reasonable excuse for having treated the consultant's services as a continuous supply on which payment of VAT could be delayed. The tribunal allowed the appeal, holding that the services were not within *reg 90*, and that the supplies had taken place at the time when the services were performed, but that H had a reasonable excuse for the misdeclaration. *Halpern & Woolf, LON/92/40Y (VTD 10072).*

49.108   **Failure to account for VAT at time of receipt of deposits—whether a reasonable excuse.**   A company which supplied interior furnishings did not account for VAT when it received deposits. The Commissioners imposed a misdeclaration penalty but the tribunal held that the company had a reasonable excuse, observing that *Notice No 700* stated that 'some types of deposit are not consideration for a supply and their receipt does not create a tax point'. *Colson & Kay Ltd, MAN/91/59 (VTD 6148). (Note.* For whether VAT is chargeable at the time a deposit is received, see the cases noted at 58.320 to 58.357 SUPPLY.)

49.109   Similar decisions were reached in *Jelson Holdings Ltd, MAN/91/551 (VTD 6682); Mr & Mrs I Foster, MAN/91/493 (VTD 6787); Inspection Equipment Ltd, LON/92/278X (VTD 10237); Simplelink Ltd (t/a Homecare Exteriors), LON/93/801A (VTD 11593)* and *Rivers Machinery Ltd,* 58.349 SUPPLY.

49.110   **Advance payments—failure to account for tax.**   A company was established to set up an indoor bowls centre. In order to finance the building of the centre, it offered life membership in return for a payment of £500. In its first VAT return, it did not account for output tax on such payments. The Commissioners imposed a misdeclaration penalty but the tribunal held that the circumstances constituted a reasonable excuse. *Bournemouth Indoor Bowls Centre Ltd, LON/96/766 (VTD 14335B).*

49.111   **Continuous supplies of services—delay in accounting for tax.**   A holding company (P) supplied services to two subsidiary companies. The companies were not registered as a group for VAT purposes. The value of the services was recorded by regular credit and debit entries in the companies' books, but P frequently delayed issuing invoices, and did not account for tax until it had issued invoices. The Commissioners imposed a penalty, on the basis that the supplies were within what is now *VAT Regulations 1995 (SI 1995 No 2518), reg 90(1)*, and that the time of supply was when the entries were made in the companies' books. The tribunal held that the time of payment was 'the date on which the appropriate entry is made in the accounting records', but also held that there was a reasonable excuse for the misdeclaration. *Pentex Oil Ltd, EDN/91/140 (VTD 7989, 7991).*

49.112   *Pentex Oil Ltd,* 49.111 above, was applied in the similar cases of *Bishop & Knight Ltd, LON/92/256 (VTD 9315)* and *A Kane, LON/92/993X (VTD 9784).*

49.113   **Continuous supplies of services—business transferred as going concern—misunderstanding of time of supply.**   A company sold a holiday caravan park to a partnership as a going concern. The company had accounted for output tax on the site fees on a receipts basis, since it had been making continuous supplies of services. The partnership failed to account for output tax in respect of fees which had been due before the transfer but not collected until after the transfer. The Commissioners imposed a misdeclaration penalty but the tribunal held that the circumstances constituted a reasonable excuse. *Marine Caravan Park, MAN/92/231 (VTD 12342).*

49.114   **Deemed self-supply under VATA 1994, Sch 10—delay in accounting for output tax.**   See *Vaughan*, 49.254 below.

49.115   **Invoices issued prematurely and subsequently cancelled.**   A company (S) carried on the business of servicing and repairing office equipment. Towards the end of the guarantee period of equipment it had supplied, it wrote to its customers offering to extend the guarantee for 12 months for a fixed sum, and enclosing invoices which included VAT. When customers did not respond to the letter, S telephoned them, and where the customer indicated that it did not wish to extend the guarantee, S treated the invoices as cancelled and did not account for output tax. The Commissioners imposed a misdeclaration penalty but the tribunal held that the circumstances constituted a reasonable excuse. *SET (Services) Ltd, LON/91/2245Z (VTD 7420).*

49.116   **Application for payment not intended by issuing company to constitute tax invoice.**   See *ABB Power Ltd*, 58.318 SUPPLY.

Cases where the appellant was unsuccessful

49.117   **Input tax reclaimed prematurely.**   A company (B) submitted a VAT return for May 1990 claiming a repayment of tax. The return included input tax relating to hire-purchase transactions. The goods which were the subject of the transactions were collected by B in May, but the hire-purchase company did not issue the VAT invoices until June. The Commissioners imposed a misdeclaration penalty, and the tribunal dismissed B's appeal. The time of supply for VAT purposes was in June 1990 when the invoices were issued, and the circumstances did not constitute a reasonable excuse. *Enterprise Safety Coaches Ltd*, 49.80 above, distinguished. *Bulkhaul Ltd, MAN/90/792 (VTD 5725).*

49.118   A company which owned a hotel incurred expenditure on reconstruction work. The work was completed in May 1990, but the contractor did not issue a VAT invoice until 13 June 1990. However, the company reclaimed the input tax shown on the invoice in its return for May 1990. The Commissioners imposed a misdeclaration penalty and the tribunal dismissed the company's appeal, holding that the circumstances did not constitute a reasonable excuse. *Cawley Hotels & Leisure Ltd, EDN/90/213 (VTD 5812).*

49.119   A company reclaimed input tax in its return for the period ending 30 June 1990 in respect of construction work for which it held an architect's certificate dated June 1990, but the relevant VAT invoice was dated 16 July. When the Commissioners discovered this, they imposed a misdeclaration penalty. The tribunal dismissed the company's appeal. On the evidence, the company's bookkeeper had known that the sum in question could not be claimed as input tax 'unless it was supported by a tax invoice which had been issued during the relevant accounting period', but had failed to check whether the invoice had been issued at the appropriate time. *The Clean Car Co Ltd*, 49.83 above, distinguished; *dicta* in *Appropriate Technology Ltd*, 49.29 above, applied. *Pepis (Marina) Ltd, MAN/91/794 (VTD 5879).*

49.120   Similar decisions were reached in *Breese Brick Ltd, LON/90/1117X (VTD 6009)* and *Robert S Monk Ltd*, 49.386 below.

49.121   An appeal was dismissed in a case where a company had reclaimed input tax in respect of two documents described as 'proforma invoices', which were not VAT invoices. *South Caernarvon Creameries Ltd, MAN/90/727 (VTD 6230)*. (*Note*. An alternative contention by the company, that it had a reasonable excuse because of the long-term illness of an employee who might have noticed the error, was also rejected.)

49.122   Similar decisions were reached in *Kirklees Developments Ltd, MAN/91/417 (VTD 6785); Floris Merchandise Ltd, MAN/91/496 (VTD 7437)* and *Triton Properties Ltd, LON/91/1168Z (VTD 7492)*.

49.123   An appeal was dismissed in a case where a company reclaimed input tax in respect of an amount it had paid to a solicitor as a stakeholder. *Stonehills Television Ltd, MAN/91/1516 (VTD 8993)*.

49.124   There was also held to be no reasonable excuse for the premature reclaim of input tax in *Harrison Meillam Construction Ltd, MAN/90/900 (VTD 5875); ACH Transport Ltd, LON/90/1475X (VTD 6006); Farnglobe Ltd (t/a Tooto's The Club), LON/91/905X (VTD 6582); CHA Ltd, LON/91/1044Z (VTD 6618); B Mullan & Son (Contractors) Ltd, BEL/91/58 (VTD 6833); GPC Properties Ltd, LON/91/342 (VTD 7044); HJ Surgenor, BEL/91/30X (VTD 7223); Vedilux Ltd, LON/91/1497Z (VTD 7252); Springvale EPS Ltd, BEL/91/67 (VTD 7421); Walker Navigation, MAN/91/1356 (VTD 7775); Rouse Kent Ltd, LON/91/1593X (VTD 8862); Paradise Forum Ltd, MAN/91/216 (VTD 8885); Chartridge Construction Ltd, LON/92/2043P (VTD 9449); Brechin Motor Co Ltd, EDN/92/228 (VTD 9525); Pierre Leon Ltd, LON/91/1180X (VTD 9794); Tritin Ltd, LON/91/1513Y (VTD 10254)* and *Simon Macczak Transport, MAN/91/849 (VTD 10887)*.

49.125   **Company operating Cash Accounting Scheme but reclaiming input tax before paying invoices.** A company which operated the Cash Accounting Scheme reclaimed input tax in respect of invoices which it had received but had not paid. When the Commissioners discovered this, they imposed a misdeclaration penalty. The tribunal dismissed the company's appeal, holding that there was no reasonable excuse for the company's premature claim. *Training Technology International Ltd, LON/91/291Z (VTD 6727)*.

49.126   Similar decisions were reached in *SSY Research Services Ltd, LON/91/2364Z (VTD 7306); Coastal Design, MAN/92/24 (VTD 9001)* and *RLO Fyffe, EDN/92/112 (VTD 9686)*.

49.127   **Delay in accounting for output tax—whether a reasonable excuse.** An opera singer received payments from opera companies which did not include VAT, and had to issue invoices to recover the VAT due. He accounted for the VAT when he received it from the opera companies, rather than when he received the fees themselves. When the Commissioners discovered this, they imposed a misdeclaration penalty. The singer appealed, contending that his misunderstanding of the correct accounting procedure constituted a reasonable excuse. The tribunal dismissed his appeal, holding that the circumstances did not constitute a reasonable excuse. *A Shore, LON/90/1649 (VTD 5799)*.

49.128   A similar decision was reached in a case involving a company trading as a building subcontractor, where the main contractor made payments which were exclusive of VAT and the company had to issue additional invoices to recover the VAT. The tribunal held that the company should have sought advice from its local VAT office, from an accountant, or from other companies in the construction industry. *Talon Holdings Ltd, LON/91/658Z (VTD 6897)*.

49.129   *Talon Holdings Ltd*, 49.128 above, was applied in the similar case of *Nivek Holdings Ltd, LON/91/670 (VTD 7383)*.

49.130   A company registered for VAT from 1 May 1990. It was required to submit a return covering the month to 31 May 1990. During this period it issued one invoice on 29 May. However, it submitted a return showing no output tax liability. The Commissioners imposed a misdeclaration penalty and the company appealed, contending that it had submitted the incorrect return to avoid incurring a default surcharge. The tribunal dismissed the appeal, holding that this was not a reasonable excuse. *Markdome Ltd, LON/90/1761Z (VTD 6007)*.

49.131   An appeal was dismissed in a case where a building contractor had failed to account for VAT on stage payments for which he had issued invoices. *TJ Ditchfield v The Isle of Man Treasury, MAN/91/173 (VTD 6533)*.

49.132   A company which was carrying on the business of property development agreed to develop a site and sell it to an insurance company for £13,000,000. In August 1990 it issued an invoice for the sale of four office blocks at the site. The invoice charged VAT, but the company did not include the VAT in its return for the period ending 31 August. The Commissioners imposed a misdeclaration penalty and the company appealed, contending that it had not intended the invoices to be VAT invoices and that the tribunal should apply the principles in *Watson Norrie Ltd*, 49.102 above. The tribunal dismissed the appeal, observing that 'although the facts in *Watson Norrie Ltd* bear some resemblance to those in this case it is not binding on us; in any event in reasonable excuse cases the facts are crucial'. On the evidence, there was no reasonable excuse for the company's failure to account for the VAT shown on the invoice in question. *Western Road Properties Ltd, LON/91/867Z (VTD 7304)*.

49.133   Failure to account for tax on 'progress payments' was also held not to be a reasonable excuse in *Regis Commercial Property, LON/91/121 (VTD 6617); Feal & Oats, LON/91/1101 (VTD 6706); Trevalyn Estates Ltd, MAN/90/398 (VTD 6749); Cindason, MAN/90/399 (VTD 6749); Marshall Brown Aluminium Ltd, EDN/91/111 (VTD 6853); The Window Glazing Consultancy, LON/91/142 (VTD 6982); Poyser & Holmes, MAN/91/639 (VTD 7059); North Scene Video Ltd, EDN/91/255 (VTD 7136); SM & E Properties Ltd, MAN/91/616 (VTD 7140); P Burke Construction Ltd, LON/91/1670Y (VTD 7222); Carter Morris Roofing Ltd, MAN/91/1171 (VTD 7229); K Rose (t/a KJ Rose Building Services), LON/92/879X (VTD 7694); Hookcroft Ltd, LON/91/725 (VTD 8870); Acoustiolox Suspended Ceilings, LON/91/2713Y (VTD 9049); DC Burdett, LON/92/2279 (VTD 9695); Reverse Osmosis Systems Ltd, MAN/92/821 (VTD 10436); WSJ (Contractors) Ltd, MAN/93/36 (VTD 11602)* and *J Tolley (t/a WH Tolley & Son), LON/93/2056P (VTD 11627)*.

49.134   An appeal was dismissed in a case where a company received a substantial payment for sale of property on 23 October 1990, but dated the relevant VAT invoice 2 November, and did not include the VAT in question in its return for the period ending 31 October. *D & M Builders (Hamilton) Ltd, EDN/91/210 (VTD 6713)*.

49.135   An appeal was dismissed in a case where a company had failed to account for VAT in respect of invoices it had issued which remained unpaid. *Renaissance Bronzes Ltd, LON/91/341Y (VTD 6849)*.

49.136   Similar decisions were reached in *JR Kircher, LON/91/1075Z (VTD 7352); RJ Wheeler, LON/91/1995Y (VTD 7366); Hastings Borough Council, LON/92/1112X (VTD 8934); CB Dureau, LON/92/36X (VTD 9355); Meldreth Construction Ltd,*

49.137 Penalties: Misdeclaration

LON/92/1136Z (VTD 9418); Oceana Holdings plc, LON/92/2359 (VTD 9961); AR Waller & Associates, LON/92/3402P (VTD 10297); Arrowfinch, LON/92/3340 (VTD 10413); William Johnson & Sons (Contractors) Ltd, MAN/93/164 (VTD 11028) and *Tru-Form Sheet Metal Ltd*, 58.71 SUPPLY.

49.137   **Management charges—delay in accounting for output tax.**   See *Missionfine Ltd*, 41.6 MANAGEMENT SERVICES.

49.138   **Failure to account for VAT on deposits.**   An appeal was dismissed in a case where a company had failed to account for VAT on the receipt of a large deposit. The tribunal held that, since the company was used to receiving deposits, and in many cases issued invoices for deposits, there was no reasonable excuse for its failure to account for VAT. *Cleco Ltd, MAN/91/361 (VTD 7084).*

49.139   A partnership which organised jazz festivals failed to account for VAT on deposits, and the Commissioners imposed misdeclaration penalties. The partnership appealed, contending that it had a reasonable excuse because the partners had assumed that they did not have to account for VAT on deposits until the time when the festivals took place. The tribunal dismissed the appeal, finding that the principal partner was 'a competent and intelligent businessman', but had not 'made any significant efforts to get any help or advice on how to prepare his returns' and had not 'made any serious attempt to understand the *General Notice*'. *Don Aldridge Associates, LON/93/713P (VTD 11452).*

49.140   An appeal was dismissed in a case where a company which organised music concerts failed to account for output tax on advance payments. *Regular Music Ltd, EDN/98/46 (VTD 15571).*

49.141   **Failure to account for tax on advance royalties.**   A company failed to account for tax on advance royalties. The Commissioners imposed a misdeclaration penalty and the company appealed, contending firstly that the payments should be regarded as loans which did not give rise to any VAT liability, and alternatively that it had a reasonable excuse for not having regarded them as giving rise to a liability. The tribunal dismissed the company's appeal, finding that the payments were clearly described as advance royalties in the relevant contract, and holding that there was no reasonable excuse for the company's failure to account for tax on them. *Software One Ltd, LON/92/1904A (VTD 11090).*

Imported goods

Cases where the appellant was successful

49.142   **Imports—input tax reclaimed prematurely.**   A company traded as an importer of goods, using an agent to deal with the payment of duty and VAT. On 30 September 1990 it was telephoned by its agent, who requested a cheque for duty of £1,150 and VAT of £3,922. The cheque was sent on that day and the company reclaimed the VAT as input tax in its return for the period ending 30 September 1990. However, the agent did not issue an invoice until 2 October. When the Commissioners discovered this, they imposed a misdeclaration penalty. The tribunal allowed the company's appeal. Although the tax point for the transaction was 2 October, the fact that the company had sent a cheque for the VAT in question on 30 September meant that it had a reasonable excuse for having believed that that date had been the tax point. *Pennine Industrial Equipment Ltd, MAN/91/390 (VTD 6512).*

49.143   A similar decision was reached in *Sealjet UK Ltd, LON/91/1098Y (VTD 6683).*

49.144   An appeal against a misdeclaration penalty was allowed in a case where a company purchased goods from an agent of an overseas manufacturer, and the bill of lading in respect of the goods was dated 25 September 1990 but the VAT invoice was dated 8 October. *Enterprise Safety Coaches Ltd*, 49.80 above, applied. *Senit Steels Ltd, LON/91/1358X (VTD 6898)*.

49.145   An appeal was allowed in a case where a double-glazing manufacturer reclaimed input tax in respect of goods he had imported and for which he had received invoices from the supplier but had not received import certificates from Customs. *Dicta* in *Appropriate Technology Ltd*, 49.29 above, applied. *MRW Richardson, MAN/90/961 (VTD 6937)*.

49.146   Similar decisions were reached in *European Computer Centre Ltd, LON/91/2131X (VTD 7220)* and *Severnside Machinery Ltd, MAN/91/1546 (VTD 10828)*.

49.147   A company imported a production machine from the USA. The machine arrived in the UK on 30 November 1990 but did not clear Customs until 1 December. The company reclaimed input tax on the machine in its return for the period ending 30 November. The Commissioners imposed a misdeclaration penalty but the tribunal allowed the company's appeal, holding that the circumstances constituted a reasonable excuse. *DCB Mouldings, EDN/91/35 (VTD 7522)*.

49.148   **Import VAT certificates—effect of new arrangements for goods imported after 30 September 1990—duplicated claim for input tax.** The Commissioners introduced new arrangements for import VAT certificates with effect from 1 October 1990 (see *VAT Notes No 2 (1990)*). Previously, import certificates had been produced weekly and distributed via shipping agents. Under the new arrangements, the weekly certificates were replaced by a single monthly certificate to be issued direct to importers. A company which imported textiles received both a weekly certificate and a monthly certificate in respect of the same transactions, and reclaimed input tax in respect of both certificates. When the Commissioners discovered this, they imposed a misdeclaration penalty. The company appealed, contending that it had not received a copy of either *VAT Notes No 2 (1990)* or of a VAT information sheet entitled *Import VAT Certificates* which explained the change of arrangements. The tribunal held that, since the company had not been aware of the new arrangements, the duplication of import certificates constituted a reasonable excuse for the duplicated claim to input tax. (There was, however, held to be no reasonable excuse for other misdeclarations on the same return.) *Rose Household Textiles Ltd, MAN/91/973 (VTD 7105)*.

49.149   **Import VAT certificates—no deferment account operated—duplicated claim for input tax.** A company was incorporated in 1991 to import goods from the Netherlands for distribution to retailers in the UK. It did not have a deferment account, and paid VAT on its imports to a freight company on receipt of an invoice. In its VAT return for the period ending 31 May 1991, which was prepared by its accountants, it included the input tax shown on its certificate for May, although it did not pay the amount shown on that certificate until early June, after receiving an invoice from the freight company. Its next VAT return was prepared by its company secretary, who prepared the return from the invoices received in the period, and thus included the amount shown on the May certificate, although this had already been included in the previous return. The Commissioners imposed a misdeclaration penalty and the company appealed, contending that it had a reasonable excuse because the company secretary had made an innocent error, and that its local VAT office had failed to reply to a request to open a deferment account. The tribunal allowed the appeal, holding that 'the duplication of the figures on the VAT certificates and the invoices received from the freight company was ... a source of understandable confusion' which constituted a reasonable excuse. *Eltraco (UK) Ltd, LON/92/731Y (VTD 9089)*.

49.150   **Import VAT certificates—payment entered by Customs on wrong C79— whether a reasonable excuse for duplicated claim for input tax.**   A company which made substantial imports of goods paid £4,200 to Customs by bankers' draft in May 1991. The amount of the draft was entered into the company's records for that month. The payment was not included in the company's C79 certificate issued by Customs on 12 June 1991 covering payments in May 1991. However, it was included on a subsequent C79 issued by Customs on 12 July, covering payments in June 1991. Following receipt of this C79, the company entered the amount of the payment in its records for June. Since the payment had been entered in its records for two successive months, the company made a duplicated claim for input tax. The Commissioners imposed a misdeclaration penalty, and the company appealed, contending that it had a reasonable excuse because it had never previously found it necessary to reconcile its records of payments with the C79 certificates. The tribunal allowed the appeal, finding that 'the error by Customs & Excise, in entering the amount in the wrong C79, was a contributory factor to the second entry of that sum in the appellant's accounts', and holding that the circumstances therefore constituted a reasonable excuse. *Plastic Protection Ltd, LON/92/583Y (VTD 9259)*. (*Note.* For another issue in this case, see 49.228 below.)

49.151   **Import VAT certificates—new arrangements after 30 September 1990— delay in receiving certificate from Customs—input tax mistakenly reclaimed on exempt supply.** The Commissioners introduced new arrangements for import VAT certificates with effect from 1 October 1990, under which weekly certificates distributed via shipping agents were replaced by monthly certificates issued direct to importers (see *VAT Notes No 2 (1990)*). A company which imported carpets had not received its certificate for October 1990 by 23 November, and felt obliged to complete its October return on that date without the certificate. In the return it reclaimed input tax in respect of goods which had been received by its agent on 31 October, and for which it had paid import duty, but for which the agent had subsequently issued a GSP exemption certificate on 8 November. The Commissioners imposed a misdeclaration penalty, since the issue of the GSP certificate confirmed that the transaction was exempt from VAT, and the import duty which had been paid in error had subsequently been repaid. The company appealed, contending that the inclusion of the amount in the return had been a genuine error, which would not have occurred but for the delay in receiving the October certificate from the Commissioners. The tribunal allowed the company's appeal, holding that the circumstances constituted a reasonable excuse. *John Lanham Watts (Carpets) Ltd, MAN/91/763 (VTD 8846)*.

49.152   **Import VAT certificates wrongly made out to associated company.**   A company (R) imported goods from China. It used the services of an import agent. This agent also acted for E, a company associated with R. During the period ending 30 September 1990, the agent mistakenly issued certificates to E in respect of goods imported by R. R reclaimed the input tax shown on these certificates, and the Commissioners imposed a misdeclaration penalty. The tribunal allowed R's appeal, observing that there had been no loss of tax, and holding that the agent's error constituted a reasonable excuse for the misdeclaration. *Rosedew Ltd, LON/92/514X (VTD 9619)*.

49.153   Similar decisions were reached in *Arendal Smelterwork AS, LON/93/1599P (VTD 11427)* and *Downey Ltd, LON/93/361P (VTD 11862)*.

49.154   **Input tax incorrectly reclaimed by company acting as import agent.**   A Japanese company had established a UK subsidiary (T) to sell its products in the UK. T reclaimed input tax in respect of supplies which were invoiced and delivered to its principal UK customer. The Commissioners imposed a misdeclaration penalty, since the tax should have been reclaimed by the customer rather than by T. T appealed, contending that its misunderstanding of the provisions was a reasonable excuse. The tribunal allowed the appeal, holding that this was 'neither a deliberate nor a careless error but an error based on a genuine misunderstanding' and that the circumstances constituted a reasonable excuse. *Taito (Europe) Corporation Ltd, LON/91/396 (VTD 7758).*

49.155   Similar decisions were reached in *CP Textiles, MAN/92/352 (VTD 11031)* and *Cauillez (UK) Ltd, MAN/92/353 (VTD 11031).*

49.156   **Input tax reclaimed on imported goods—tax not paid to Commissioners by import agent.**   A trader imported goods, using the services of a company which acted as an import agent. He received an invoice from the company dated 27 April 1990, and paid the amount in question to the company. He reclaimed the amount he had paid as input tax in his return for the period ending 31 May 1990. However, the company was suffering financial difficulties, and had not paid the tax to the Commissioners. (The company had subsequently gone into liquidation.) When the Commissioners discovered that the trader had reclaimed the tax without holding a valid certificate C79, they imposed a misdeclaration penalty. The trader appealed, contending that since he had received an invoice from the import agent, and had paid the amount demanded to the agent, he had a reasonable excuse for his premature claim. The tribunal accepted this contention and allowed the appeal against the penalty, holding that the circumstances constituted a reasonable excuse for the incorrect claim. *Quay Marine Ltd, 49.159 below, distinguished. MP James, LON/92/1312A (VTD 10474). (Note.* An appeal against a subsequent penalty was dismissed.)

49.157   A similar decision was reached in *Leather Fashions Ltd,* 33.10 IMPORTS.

Cases where the appellant was unsuccessful

49.158   **Input tax assessed on importation and reclaimed before assessment paid.**   A company imported clothing from Asia for resale in the UK. It paid commission to a US company under an agency agreement, but did not account for VAT on such commission. When the Commissioners discovered this, they issued an assessment charging tax on these payments. With the assessment was a covering letter stating 'subject to the normal rules you may claim the amount of VAT paid in box 2 of your VAT return only when you have received from Customs the VAT copy of the post-clearance demand note (form C18) after processing by Customs'. Despite this instruction, the company reclaimed the amount as input tax before it had paid the assessment. The Commissioners imposed a misdeclaration penalty, and the tribunal dismissed the company's appeal, holding that there was no reasonable excuse for the incorrect claim. *Ericsons Fashions Ltd, LON/90/1880Z (VTD 6241).*

49.159   **Input tax reclaimed on imported goods before import VAT certificate received.**   An appeal was dismissed in a case where a company reclaimed input tax on imported goods in its return for the period ending 31 December 1990, although the goods in question had not cleared Customs until 11 January 1991. (The company had sent a cheque as payment for the goods on 23 December 1990.) The tribunal held that, as the company was aware that it should not claim input tax on imported goods without holding a certificate, there was no reasonable excuse for the premature claim. *Quay Marine Ltd, LON/91/668X (VTD 9054).*

49.160   A similar decision was reached in *Analog & Numeric Devices Ltd, MAN/91/550 (VTD 9340)*. (*Note*. For another issue in this case, see 49.414 below.)

49.161   **Customs duty reclaimed as input tax.** A company which manufactured clothing imported materials from overseas. It paid customs duty on the import of such materials, and reclaimed the duty as input tax. When the Commissioners discovered this, they imposed a misdeclaration penalty. The tribunal dismissed the company's appeal, holding that there was no reasonable excuse for the incorrect claim. *Leofabs Ltd, MAN/91/401 (VTD 6632)*.

49.162   A similar decision was reached in *NGF 90 (Gateshead) Ltd, MAN/92/666 (VTD 9816)*.

49.163   **Input tax reclaimed on supply made to import agents.** An appeal was dismissed in a case where a trader who had imported four haulage vehicles from a French company reclaimed input tax in respect of an invoice made out to his import agents. The tribunal held that the appellant was at fault through not having followed the guidelines in *para 15* of *VAT Notice No 702* (subsequently updated by *Notice No 702/94*) and that the circumstances did not constitute a reasonable excuse. *PJ Robinson, MAN/91/1107 (VTD 7145)*.

49.164   **VAT on imports—deferment limit exceeded—whether a reasonable excuse for duplicated claim for input tax.** A company which manufactured flexible hosing imported certain items and had adopted the deferment scheme. Its agreed deferment limit was £3,000, but it exceeded this limit in the accounting periods ending 31 July 1990 and 31 October 1990. Because it had exceeded its deferment limit, it was required to pay invoices which had been raised by its freight forwarders for the duty and VAT attributable to certain imports and was unable, so far as those imports were concerned, to avail itself of the deferment scheme. It made a duplicated claim for input tax in respect of the amounts shown on the freight forwarders' invoices. The Commissioners imposed a misdeclaration penalty, and the company appealed, contending that the unusual nature of the invoices concerned constituted a reasonable excuse. The tribunal rejected this contention and dismissed the appeal, holding that the director who was responsible for the company's returns had not 'acted with the standard of care which is reasonably to be expected', and that there was no reasonable excuse for the duplicated claim. *Arctrend Ltd, MAN/91/1294 (VTD 10011)*.

49.165   A similar decision was reached in *Barnett Gray Ltd, LON/93/879P (VTD 11155)*.

49.166   There was also held to be no reasonable excuse for duplicated input tax claims in respect of imports in *Strong (UK) Ltd, LON/93/772 (VTD 10799)*.

49.167   **Input tax reclaimed on imported goods—no certificate held.** An appeal was dismissed in a case where a company had reclaimed input tax on imported goods without holding a certificate as required by what is now *VATA 1994, s 24(6)(a)*. *Vin-Dotco (UK) Ltd, MAN/92/935 (VTD 11346)*.

Supplies incorrectly treated as zero-rated

Cases where the appellant was successful

49.168   **Misunderstanding of VATA 1994, Sch 8, Group 8*.** A company carried on business as a subcontractor in the ship-repairing industry. In 1990 it undertook the painting of two new ships. It did not account for VAT on this work, considering that the work was zero-rated under what is now *VATA 1994, Sch 8, Group 8*. The Commissioners imposed a misdeclaration penalty and the company appealed, contending that it had made an innocent error which constituted a reasonable excuse. The tribunal accepted this contention and allowed the appeal. *Nor-Clean Ltd, [1991] VATTR 239 (VTD 5954).*

49.169   **Misunderstanding of VATA 1994, Sch 8, Group 6*.**   A construction company was carrying out work on a listed building. The work was inspected monthly by an architect employed by the customer. After each inspection the architect issued an RIBA certificate, which was not a VAT invoice but which indicated the amount of VAT payable on the work carried out. In June 1990 the architect issued a certificate for work carried out to the value of £36,171, but stating that only £5,425 of this was subject to VAT. The company issued an invoice accordingly. However the Commissioners subsequently ascertained that the whole of the £36,171 should have been treated as standard-rated, so that the company should have charged VAT of £5,425 rather than £814. They therefore imposed a misdeclaration penalty. The tribunal allowed the company's appeal against the penalty, holding that, in view of the information on the architect's certificate, the company had a reasonable excuse for having assumed that most of the work in question was zero-rated. *Shelston (Construction) Ltd, LON/91/934X (VTD 6616).*

49.170   A builder undertook the substantial reconstruction of an old house (No. 7 Albany Villas) in a conservation area. He did not account for VAT on the work. The Commissioners ascertained that the building was not listed as a protected building (although Nos. 2–5 Albany Buildings were protected) and that VAT should have been charged on the work. They imposed a misdeclaration penalty. The builder appealed, accepting that the work should have been standard-rated but contending that he had a reasonable excuse since he had previously worked on No. 2 Albany Villas which was a protected building, and that the detailed planning restrictions which had been imposed because the building was in a conservation area had led him to believe that No. 7 was also a protected building. The tribunal allowed his appeal, holding that the circumstances constituted a reasonable excuse. *BA Lowe (t/a BA Lowe Construction), LON/91/838Z (VTD 6806).*

49.171   A trader did not account for tax on the construction of a building within the curtilage of a protected building, but separate from it. The Commissioners imposed a misdeclaration penalty and the trader appealed, contending that he had a reasonable excuse because he had believed that the work was zero-rated. The tribunal allowed his appeal, holding that the circumstances constituted a reasonable excuse. *BK Sergeant, LON/92/874X (VTD 9039).*

49.172   A company failed to account for VAT in respect of work carried out on a listed building. The Commissioners ascertained that the work did not qualify for zero-rating, and imposed a misdeclaration penalty. The company appealed against the penalty, contending that it had a reasonable excuse since the contractor for whom it had carried out the work had advised it that it was zero-rated. The tribunal allowed the appeal, holding that the circumstances constituted a reasonable excuse. *E Coules & Son Ltd, LON/92/976Y (VTD 9608).*

49.173   A similar decision was reached in *P Lewsey, LON/93/711 (VTD 10784).*

49.174   **Misunderstanding of VATA 1994, Sch 8, Group 5*.**   A company agreed to install a new heating and lighting system in a parish church. It did not charge VAT, having been advised by the main contractor that the work was zero-rated since the church was accepted as a charity. The Commissioners ruled that, since the company was undertaking the work for the main contractor, rather than making supplies directly to the charity, it should have charged and accounted for VAT, and imposed a misdeclaration penalty. The tribunal allowed the company's appeal, holding that the circumstances constituted a reasonable excuse. *Ian Fraser & Partners Ltd, EDN/91/115 (VTD 6931).*

49.175   *Ian Fraser & Partners Ltd*, 49.174 above, was applied in the similar case of *Taylor & Fraser Ltd, EDN/92/163 (VTD 8977).*

49.176   A similar decision was reached in *T McRandal, LON/92/2102 (VTD 9860).*

49.177   A bricklayer failed to account for VAT in respect of work carried out in building extensions to a church and to a nursing home. The Commissioners imposed a misdeclaration penalty and the bricklayer appealed, contending that he had a reasonable excuse as he had assumed that the work was zero-rated. The tribunal allowed his appeal, holding that the circumstances constituted a reasonable excuse. *M Inger, MAN/91/1524 (VTD 9522).*

49.178   A builder failed to account for VAT in respect of scaffolding work at an old people's home, and of the installation of ramps for disabled students at a school. The Commissioners imposed a misdeclaration penalty and the builder appealed, contending that he had a reasonable excuse as he had assumed that the work was zero-rated. The tribunal allowed his appeal, holding that the circumstances constituted a reasonable excuse. *DM Stratford, LON/91/2681Y (VTD 9621).* (*Note.* For another issue in this case, see 17.2 DEFAULT INTEREST.)

49.179   An appeal against a misdeclaration penalty was allowed in a case where a builder, who had only recently registered for VAT, failed to account for VAT on the construction of a clubhouse at a golf course, and on extensions to houses. The tribunal held that the circumstances constituted a reasonable excuse. *PJ Bowen, LON/92/3399A (VTD 11167).*

49.180   A building company failed to account for VAT on work carried out in extending a church. The Commissioners imposed misdeclaration penalties and the company appealed, contending that it had a reasonable excuse because its director had been told by a surveyor that the work was zero-rated. The tribunal allowed the company's appeal, holding that the misleading advice from the surveyor constituted a reasonable excuse for the misdeclaration. *Lacy Simmons Ltd, LON/93/1000P (VTD 11211).*

49.181   *Lacy Simmons Ltd*, 49.180 above, was applied in the similar subsequent case of *Partridge Homes Ltd, LON/97/1279 (VTD 15289).*

49.182   An appeal against a penalty was allowed in a case where a partnership failed to charge VAT on the installation of a built-in kitchen, and contended that it had a reasonable excuse since the partners had assumed that the work was zero-rated. *DA Phillips & Sons, LON/91/523Y (VTD 7006).*

49.183   A similar decision was reached in *David Morris Homes Ltd, MAN/91/330 (VTD 7081).*

49.184   A company undertook excavation work for the London Borough of Islington. The Borough Council advised the company that some of the work in question was zero-rated. A VAT officer on a control visit formed the opinion that the work should have been standard-rated, and asked the company for evidence that the work qualified for zero-rating in view of the changes implemented by *FA 1989*. Neither the company nor the Council produced such evidence, and the Commissioners imposed a misdeclaration penalty. The tribunal allowed the company's appeal, holding that in view of the information provided by the Council, the company had a reasonable excuse for having incorrectly treated the work as zero-rated. *Walsh Brothers (Tunnelling) Ltd, LON/91/1451 (VTD 7186).*

49.185   A similar decision was reached in *Bomanite (Southeast), LON/95/2478 (VTD 13745)*.

49.186   A company undertook to construct a workshop for a registered charity. It did not charge VAT on the work, considering that it was zero-rated. However, the Commissioners ascertained that the new workshop was linked to an existing building by a covered walkway, so that the work was not eligible for zero-rating. They imposed a misdeclaration penalty. The tribunal allowed the company's appeal against the penalty, holding that the circumstances constituted a reasonable excuse. *DJ Trimming Ltd, LON/91/1327 (VTD 7733)*.

49.187   A local authority arranged for a company to construct an overflow chamber to alleviate flooding on a housing estate. The local authority advised the company that the work would be zero-rated, and the company did not account for VAT. The Commissioners ascertained that the work was not eligible for zero-rating, and imposed a misdeclaration penalty. The company appealed, contending that in view of the advice given by the local authority, it had a reasonable excuse for not having accounted for VAT. The tribunal allowed the appeal, holding that the circumstances constituted a reasonable excuse. *Barhale Construction plc, [1992] VATTR 409 (VTD 9137)*.

49.188   A scaffolder erected and dismantled scaffolding for the use of building contractors. He did not account for tax on the consideration which he received. The Commissioners issued an assessment charging tax on the consideration, on the basis that, by leaving the scaffolding on the site, he was supplying a standard-rated service to the contractors. They also imposed a misdeclaration penalty. The scaffolder appealed. The tribunal held that the scaffolder was supplying standard-rated services, but allowed his appeal against the penalty, holding that the complexity of the law constituted a reasonable excuse. *PJ Guntert (t/a Abingdon Scaffolding Co), LON/92/2183 (VTD 10604)*. (*Note*. For the award of costs in this case, see 2.287 APPEALS.)

49.189   A builder failed to account for VAT on progress payments received for the construction of a sports pavilion. The Commissioners imposed a misdeclaration penalty, and the builder appealed, contending that he had a reasonable excuse as he had been misled by his former accountant and had believed that the work was zero-rated. The tribunal accepted the builder's evidence and allowed the appeal. *Colin Maynard Builders, LON/93/295P (VTD 10895)*.

49.190   A builder failed to account for output tax on the construction of a swimming pool complex in the grounds of an existing house. The Commissioners imposed a misdeclaration penalty and the builder appealed, contending that he had a reasonable excuse because he had believed that the work qualified for zero-rating. The tribunal allowed the appeal, holding that he had a reasonable excuse for the misdeclaration. *C Hall, LON/92/1194 (VTD 14131)*.

49.191   See also *Derby YMCA*, 15.115 CONSTRUCTION OF BUILDINGS, ETC.

49.192   **Goods treated as zero-rated exports—Commissioners not satisfied that necessary conditions complied with—VATA 1994, s 30(6).**   An appeal was allowed in a case where a company had treated certain supplies of goods to India as zero-rated, but had been unable to produce copy bills of lading which the Commissioners had required as proof of export. The tribunal was satisfied that the goods had been exported, and held that the company had a reasonable excuse for having zero-rated them despite not having the necessary evidence of export. *TC Plastics (Manchester) Ltd, MAN/91/1426 (VTD 7684)*.

49.193   A similar decision was reached in *Roopers Export Sales Ltd, LON/92/2896P (VTD 10801)*.

49.194   A company sold some machinery to a Pakistani and did not account for VAT on the sale, treating it as zero-rated. The Commissioners discovered that the purchaser also had an address in Rochdale, and imposed a misdeclaration penalty. The company appealed. The tribunal held that the transaction did not qualify for zero-rating since the purchaser had a business address in the UK, but allowed the appeal against the penalty, holding that the company had a reasonable excuse for having mistakenly treated the sale as zero-rated. *Print On Time (Pontefract) Ltd, MAN/93/417 (VTD 11458)*.

49.195   **Misunderstanding of VATA 1994, Sch 8, Group 3*.**   A graphic designer (J) failed to account for VAT on the provision of artwork for the production of a booklet, and the Commissioners imposed a misdeclaration penalty. J appealed, contending that he had a reasonable excuse because he had assumed that the artwork would be zero-rated. The tribunal allowed his appeal, holding that the circumstances constituted a reasonable excuse. *DL Jones, LON/93/585A (VTD 11430)*. (*Note*. For another issue in this case, see 34.421 INPUT TAX.)

49.196   **Misunderstanding of VATA 1994, Sch 8, Group 1*.**   See *Skilton & Gregory*, 27.38 FOOD.

Cases where the appellant was unsuccessful

49.197   **Goods wrongly treated as zero-rated exports—conditions of VATA 1994, s 30(6) not satisfied.**   An appeal was dismissed in a case where a company had failed to charge VAT on goods invoiced to an overseas company but delivered to an address in London, and contended that it had assumed that the goods would be zero-rated. The tribunal held that the company was at fault in not having referred to the *VAT Guide*. *Dynic (UK) Ltd, LON/91/2043X (VTD 7412)*.

49.198   A similar decision was reached in a subsequent case where the tribunal held that the company's evidence failed to show that identifiable goods had been removed from the UK, or that the documentation related to any of the invoices in respect of which the penalties had been imposed. *Dallas Knitwear (Manchester) Ltd, MAN/96/407 & 660 (VTD 14653)*.

49.199   *Dallas Knitwear (Manchester) Ltd*, 49.198 above, was applied in a similar subsequent case in which an appeal against a misdeclaration penalty was dismissed. The tribunal observed that the appellant had an annual turnover of some £6,000,000, and held that there was no reasonable excuse. (The tribunal also held that there were no grounds for mitigating the penalty.) *AR Vig (t/a One by One Fashions), MAN/96/137 (VTD 14837)*.

49.200   A similar decision was reached in a case where a company had failed to account for VAT on the sale of three helicopters, and contended that they had been exported. *MW Helicopters Ltd, LON/00/49 (VTD 16888)*.

49.201   A company based in England failed to account for VAT on goods which it supplied to a Welsh branch of an American company. The Commissioners imposed a misdeclaration penalty, and the company appealed, contending that it had a reasonable excuse because it had believed that the goods could be described as exports and were therefore zero-rated. The tribunal dismissed the appeal, holding that there was no reasonable excuse for having treated the transactions as exports. *JW Froelich (UK) Ltd, LON/91/1667Y (VTD 10193)*.

49.202   A company sold a machine which was intended to be exported to Australia. It issued an invoice to an export house on 13 April 1992. The machine was actually exported on 30 May 1992. The company did not account for output tax on the invoice which it issued, treating the sale as zero-rated. The Commissioners issued an assessment charging tax on the sale, since the conditions laid down under what is now *VATA 1994, s 30(6)* and *VAT Regulations 1995 (SI 1995 No 2518)* had not been satisfied. They also imposed a misdeclaration penalty. The company appealed. The tribunal dismissed the appeals, holding that the sale did not qualify for zero-rating and that there was no reasonable excuse for the company's failure to account for output tax on the sale. *Butler Newall Ltd, MAN/93/1004 (VTD 12292).*

49.203   In the case noted at 1.62 AGENTS, the tribunal held that there was no reasonable excuse for a company's failure to account for tax on a supply within *VATA 1994, s 47(2A)*. The tribunal held that 'an experienced trader taking part in a normal transaction of sale by auction has an obligation to be aware of the law regarding value added tax on such sale and the existence of the deeming provision. Its complications, and its possible inconveniences, do not afford a reasonable excuse for the misdeclaration.' *Bashir Mohamed Ltd, LON/99/188 (VTD 16762).*

49.204   **Misunderstanding of VATA 1994, Sch 8, Group 1*.**   A trader sold hot food from a transit van. He did not account for VAT on such sales and the Commissioners imposed a misdeclaration penalty. He appealed, contending that his accountants had not told him that his sales were liable to VAT. The tribunal dismissed his appeal, holding that the circumstances did not constitute a reasonable excuse. *S Lamming, LON/91/1045Z (VTD 6635).*

49.205   An appeal was dismissed in a case where a restaurant proprietor had failed to account for VAT on sales of hot take-away food. *M Siddique, MAN/91/918 (VTD 9244).*

49.206   An appeal was dismissed in a case where the tribunal found that a partnership, which operated a restaurant selling take-away food as well as food for consumption on the premises, had treated an excessively high percentage of its sales as zero-rated. *Hounslow Sweet Centre, LON/92/271X (VTD 10026). (Note.* For a preliminary application in this case, see 2.182 APPEALS.)

49.207   A trader (B) failed to account for output tax on supplies of beverages from vending machines. The Commissioners imposed a misdeclaration penalty, and B appealed, contending firstly that he was making zero-rated supplies to the company on whose premises the machines were sited, and that that company was making onward supplies to the consumers, and alternatively that he had a reasonable excuse because he had assumed that his supplies qualified for zero-rating. The tribunal rejected these contentions and dismissed B's appeal, holding that he was making standard-rated supplies to the consumers and that there was no reasonable excuse for his failure to account for tax. (The tribunal also held that there were no grounds for mitigating the penalty.) *SA Bourne, LON/96/1973 (VTD 16023).*

49.208   **Misunderstanding of VATA 1994, Sch 8, Group 5*.**   An appeal was dismissed in a case where, in the period ending September 1990, a partnership trading as building contractors had failed to charge VAT on extensions to houses. The work in question would have been zero-rated before 1984 under *VATA 1983, Sch 5 Group 8* (the predecessor of *VATA 1994, Sch 8, Group 5*), and the principal partner gave evidence that he was unaware of the change in the law. The tribunal held that this was not a reasonable excuse. *Alan Wright & Partners, MAN/91/54 (VTD 6114).*

49.209   Similar decisions were reached in *GJ Bennett & Co (Builders) Ltd, MAN/90/1003 (VTD 6457); Bolton Consultants Ltd, LON/91/1147X (VTD 6611); H Turner & Sons (Construction) Ltd, LON/91/1589Z (VTD 6657); Matrec Ltd, MAN/91/667*

(*VTD 6693*); *Premier Aluminium & Glass Ltd, LON/91/758X (VTD 6831); Ashe Construction Southern Ltd, LON/91/723X (VTD 7075); MG Lineham (t/a MG Lineham Homes & Improvements), LON/91/1671Z (VTD 7410); T & GA Russell, MAN/91/1434 (VTD 7534); Swaffer Truscott Ltd, LON/91/1948 (VTD 7780); Italpaving Ltd, LON/92/398 (VTD 7807); Fida Interiors Ltd, EDN/92/138 (VTD 8907); Nationwide Roofing Co, LON/92/566Z (VTD 9861); R & F Building Services, MAN/92/1143 (VTD 11083)* and *BE Roose, LON/92/3166 (VTD 12350).*

49.210 **Misunderstanding of VATA 1994, Sch 8, Group 6*.** An appeal was dismissed in a case where a company had failed to account for output tax in respect of work carried out on a listed building, although the work did not qualify for zero-rating under what is now *VATA 1994, Sch 8, Group 6* since the building was used as an office and not as a residence. *DJ Trimming Ltd, LON/91/1327 (VTD 7733)*. (*Note.* For another issue in this case, see 49.186 above.)

49.211 **Misunderstanding of VATA 1994, Sch 8, Group 10*.** See *Premiair Charter Ltd*, 49.383 below.

Supplies incorrectly treated as exempt

Cases where the appellant was successful

49.212 **Misunderstanding of VATA 1994, Sch 9, Group 1—failure to account for output tax.** A company purchased some land, this purchase being exempt from VAT under what is now *VATA 1994, Sch 9, Group 1*. It constructed two industrial buildings on the land. It sold one of the buildings, with the land on which it stood, to an associated company. It did not account for tax on the sale, and the Commissioners imposed a misdeclaration penalty. The company appealed, contending that it had a reasonable excuse for not having accounted for tax since it had assumed that, because its purchase of the land had been exempt from VAT, its sale of the land would also be exempt. The tribunal allowed the appeal, observing that this was a 'borderline case' but holding that, since the transaction 'involved both an understanding of the law of real property and of the way in which land and buildings are to be dealt with in VAT law', the circumstances constituted a reasonable excuse for the failure to account for tax. *Prior Diesel Ltd, LON/93/2820 (VTD 10306)*.

49.213 **Election to waive exemption—failure to account for output tax.** In March 1990 a company elected to waive exemption in respect of a property it owned and occupied. In December 1991 it sold the property without accounting for output tax. The Commissioners imposed a misdeclaration penalty. The company appealed, contending that it had a reasonable excuse because it had undergone a change of ownership and its finance director, who had suffered from illness, had forgotten the election. The tribunal allowed the appeal, describing the election as 'an insignificant event' and holding that the circumstances constituted a reasonable excuse. *Lynton Tool & Die Ltd, LON/93/1206 (VTD 11288)*. (*Note.* Compare *Satnam Investments Ltd*, 49.214 below, *Black Eagle Ltd*, 49.215 below, *Embleton Ltd*, 49.215 below, and *Fairhome Ltd*, 49.216 below, in all of which there was held to be no reasonable excuse for a failure to account for output tax following an election to waive exemption.)

Cases where the appellant was unsuccessful

49.214 **Election to waive exemption—failure to account for tax.** A company made an election to waive exemption in respect of property which it owned. However, it failed to account for VAT on the rents it received in respect of the property. The Commissioners imposed a misdeclaration penalty and the tribunal dismissed the company's appeal, holding that there was no reasonable excuse for the failure. *Satnam Investments Ltd, LON/91/1039 (VTD 6746)*.

49.215   Similar decisions were reached in *Black Eagle Ltd, MAN/91/1325 (VTD 7682)* and *Embleton Ltd, LON/93/3034P (VTD 12897)*.

49.216   A company sold a property in respect of which it had lodged an election to waive exemption, but failed to account for output tax on the sale. The Commissioners imposed a misdeclaration penalty and the tribunal dismissed the company's appeal, holding that there was no reasonable excuse for the company's failure to account for tax. *Fairhome Ltd, LON/93/500P (VTD 11314)*.

49.217   **Misunderstanding of VATA 1994, Sch 9, Group 1.**   An appeal was dismissed in a case where a company had failed to account for VAT on the sale of a property which it had built, and contended that it had assumed that the sale would be exempt under what is now *VATA 1994, Sch 9, Group 1*. The tribunal held that since the company was carrying on business as a developer of commercial property, it should have sought professional advice. The company appeared to have been ignorant of the basic liability of the supplies which it made. Applying *Neal*, 48.48 PENALTIES: FAILURE TO NOTIFY, this ignorance could not constitute a reasonable excuse. *Cotel Developments Ltd, LON/92/243X (VTD 9149)*.

49.218   See also *Jamieson*, 49.385 below.

49.219   **Misunderstanding of VATA 1994, Sch 9, Group 6.**   An appeal against a misdeclaration penalty was dismissed in a case where a college failed to account for output tax on fees which it received from students for educational services, although the relevant supplies failed to qualify for exemption under *VATA 1983, Sch 6, Group 6* (the predecessor of *VATA 1994, Sch 9, Group 6*). The tribunal found that the college's proprietor and accountant had 'behaved irresponsibly having recklessly given themselves the benefit of the doubt', and held that there was no reasonable excuse for the college's failure to account for output tax on the fees in question. *London International College, LON/92/907 (VTD 10886)*.

Incorrect claims for bad debt relief

Cases where the appellant was successful

49.220   In November 1990 a company claimed bad debt relief in respect of eight debts where the customer had ceased trading. However, one of the companies was not formally in liquidation, so that under the law then in force no relief was due. When the Commissioners discovered this, they imposed a misdeclaration penalty. The tribunal allowed the company's appeal against the penalty. Ignorance of general VAT law was not a reasonable excuse, but the detailed rules concerning bad debt relief were complex, and the claim would have been allowed if the supply had been made after 31 March 1991, when the law was changed by the *VAT (Refunds for Bad Debts) Regulations (SI 1991 No 371)*. The tribunal chairman observed that she did 'not consider that Parliament, when legislating for serious misdeclaration penalties, intended that these penalties would be applied in circumstances such as these'. *Vision Computer Products Ltd, LON/91/1511Y (VTD 7072)*. (*Note.* The decision in this case was disapproved by a subsequent tribunal in *Ramm Contract Furnishing (Northern) Ltd*, 49.227 below, where the tribunal observed that 'we cannot accept that the application of the basic provisions for bad debt relief was so complex as to afford (the appellant) a reasonable excuse for making a premature claim for bad debt relief'.)

49.221   Penalties: Misdeclaration

49.221   In April 1991 a company claimed bad debt relief in respect of debts which had been incurred in 1987. The Commissioners disallowed the claim, as the company had been unable to submit the evidence of insolvency required by *VATA 1983, s 22* and the supplies had taken place before the revised provisions of *FA 1990, s 11* came into force. They also imposed a misdeclaration penalty. The company appealed against the penalty, contending that it had a reasonable excuse for having made the incorrect claim, since its director had wrongly assumed that the provisions of *FA 1990, s 11* were retrospective. The tribunal allowed the appeal, holding that the circumstances constituted a reasonable excuse. (There was, however, held to be no reasonable excuse for other misdeclarations on the return in question.) *James Yorke (Holdings) Ltd, LON/92/1121Y (VTD 9583).*

49.222   A company (D) carried on business as paper merchants. In November 1991 one of its customers went into liquidation, owing it £62,000. D claimed bad debt relief in respect of this in its return for the period ending March 1992. The Commissioners imposed a misdeclaration penalty, since the claim had been made before the expiry of the one-year time limit laid down by *FA 1990, s 11* (as amended by *FA 1991, s 15*). D appealed, contending that it had a reasonable excuse because it had been unaware of the changes to the rules for bad debt relief made by *FA 1990*, and that, since the customer was formally in liquidation, the claim would have been allowable under the previous provisions of *VATA 1983, s 22*. The tribunal allowed the appeal, observing that in cases of insolvencies, the 1990 changes had made the law 'much harsher' and that the rules had been changed in 'an unexpected and irrational way', and holding that D's ignorance of the relevant changes in the legislation constituted a reasonable excuse. *David John (Papers) Ltd, LON/92/2762 (VTD 10084).*

49.223   A similar decision was reached in *Leberl Advertising Ltd, LON/92/3234P (VTD 10599).*

49.224   A company (T) which carried on business as shipping and freight forwarding agents paid tax on behalf of a customer. The customer failed to reimburse T for the payment, and subsequently went into liquidation. T claimed bad debt relief, but the Commissioners rejected the claim, since T had not made any supply. The Commissioners also imposed a misdeclaration penalty, but the tribunal allowed T's appeal against the penalty, holding that the circumstances constituted a reasonable excuse. *Toga Freight Services (UK) Ltd, LON/91/2170X (VTD 9906).*

Cases where the appellant was unsuccessful

49.225   A trader supplied satellite dishes to a company in which he had a 50% shareholding. The company then sold the dishes to members of the public. Subsequently, the company went into voluntary liquidation. The trader reclaimed bad debt relief of more than £12,000 in respect of supplies which he claimed to have made to the company, although he had no VAT invoices in support of this claim. When the Commissioners discovered this, they imposed a misdeclaration penalty. The tribunal dismissed the trader's appeal, holding that the circumstances did not constitute a reasonable excuse for reclaiming bad debt relief without supporting invoices. *JD Spellar (t/a Allied Satellite Systems), LON/91/813X (VTD 6829).*

49.226   A company (M) operating the 'self-billing' system did a substantial amount of work for a company (J). J went into liquidation owing M £86,000. M had accounted for tax on a VAT invoice issued by J, showing a VAT liability of £1,765. No other outstanding VAT invoices had been issued by J, and M had not accounted for any other unpaid VAT. Although M had only paid VAT of £1,765 to Customs, it claimed bad debt relief of £12,980. When the Commissioners discovered this, they imposed a misdeclaration penalty in respect of the false claim. The tribunal dismissed M's appeal. There was no reasonable excuse for reclaiming amounts as bad debt relief where no VAT had ever been accounted for on such amounts in the first place. *Magright Ltd, LON/91/275X (VTD 6925).*

49.227   An appeal was dismissed in a case where a company had claimed bad debt relief without holding a liquidator's certificate as required by the legislation then in force. The tribunal declined to follow the decision in *Vision Computer Products Ltd*, 49.220 above, observing that 'we cannot accept that the application of the basic provisions for bad debt relief was so complex as to afford (the appellant) a reasonable excuse for making a premature claim for bad debt relief'. *Ramm Contract Furnishing (Northern) Ltd, MAN/91/1127 (VTD 9098).* (*Note.* The law relating to bad debt relief was subsequently amended by *FA 1991.* See now *VATA 1994, s 36.*)

49.228   An appeal was dismissed in a case where a company had claimed bad debt relief before the expiry of the one-year period laid down by *FA 1991, s 15. Plastic Protection Ltd, LON/92/583Y (VTD 9259).* (*Notes.* (1) For another issue in this case, see 49.150 above. (2) The one-year period has subsequently been reduced to six months—see *VATA 1994, s 36(1)(c).*)

49.229   Similar decisions were reached in *Highview Ltd, LON/92/1680 (VTD 9564); Post Form Products Ltd, LON/92/757X (VTD 9767); Trade Direct Ltd, MAN/92/1391 (VTD 10142)* and *Kernot Cases & Cartons Ltd, MAN/93/1082 (VTD 11564).*

Credit notes—incorrect treatment

Cases where the appellant was successful

49.230   **Return wrongly amended to take account of subsequent credit note.**   A company issued an invoice on 30 June 1990 including VAT of £1,508. On 21 July 1990 a credit note was issued cancelling the invoice. The company's VAT return for the period ending 30 June 1990 was prepared by its accountant and included the tax on the invoice in question. When the company's managing director received the completed return from the accountant, he amended the return to exclude the £1,508. The Commissioners imposed a misdeclaration penalty, and the company appealed, contending that it had a reasonable excuse for the error, because its director had genuinely believed that there was no need to account for VAT on the invoice since it had subsequently been cancelled. The tribunal allowed the appeal. The return should have included the tax of £1,508 and the credit note should have been taken into account in the following return. However, the director's belief that the return should be amended, to take account of the subsequent credit note, was not unreasonable. *NCJ Electrical Ltd, MAN/91/224 (VTD 6383).*

49.231   **Delay in receiving credit note from finance company.**   A building company leased an excavator from a finance company. In April 1990 the agreement was cancelled, and a similar agreement was entered into in respect of another similar machine. The finance company issued a credit note for rebate of rentals due under the first agreement, stating that the tax point was April 1990, and that the building company should account for the VAT shown on the credit note. However, the building company did not receive the credit note until August 1990, and did not account for the VAT in question until its return for the period ending August 1990. When the Commissioners discovered this, they imposed a misdeclaration penalty, as the tax should have been accounted for in the company's return for the period ending May 1990. The tribunal allowed the company's appeal, holding that the delay in receiving the credit note from the finance company constituted a reasonable excuse. *GJ Bennett & Co (Builders) Ltd, MAN/90/1003 (VTD 6457).* (*Note.* For other issues in this case, see 49.209 above and 49.364 below.)

49.232   **Credit note prepared to cancel invoice but not issued to customer—whether a reasonable excuse.**   A small company (M) agreed to supply three lifeboats to a large company (H) which was constructing an oil platform. 10% of the agreed price was paid as a deposit. It was agreed that a further 80% should be paid after H had taken delivery of the boats and confirmed their acceptability, and that the final 10% should be paid after M had provided a warranty bond. The boats were completed in October 1990, and M issued an invoice for 80% of the price, although H had not yet confirmed their acceptability. On 3 November H advised M that it did not consider the boats to be of an acceptable standard, and would not pay the invoice. M then prepared a credit note, which it backdated to 31 October. The credit note was mistakenly not issued, although it was entered in M's records. On 12 November H advised M that it had decided that the boats were acceptable after all, and would pay the invoice. M prepared a second invoice to reverse the effect of the credit note in its records, but, since it had discovered that it had not issued the credit note to H, it did not issue the second invoice to H. In preparing its VAT return for the period ending 31 October, M did not include the output tax charged on the first invoice, treating it as having been cancelled by the credit note dated 31 October. When the Commissioners discovered that the output tax had not been included in the return, they imposed a misdeclaration penalty. The company appealed, contending that it had believed that the first invoice should not be treated as effective since at the time it was issued H had not accepted the lifeboats and the amount charged was not due under the terms of the contract. The tribunal allowed the appeal. On the evidence, the tax should have been accounted for in the October return, since the invoice had been issued in that period but the credit note had not. However, applying dicta in *The Clean Car Co Ltd*, 49.83 above, the company 'ought not to be blamed for taking the view that' the tax point was November rather than October. *Offshore Marine Engineering Ltd, MAN/91/712 (VTD 6840)*.

49.233   **Validity of credit notes disputed by Commissioners.**   A company (P) was carrying out building work for a customer. The customer ran into financial difficulties and could not continue to pay for the work. P issued the customer with credit notes for £202,800 plus VAT. The Commissioners took the view that the credit notes were not effective for VAT purposes (see the cases noted at 38.71 *et seq.* INVOICES AND CREDIT NOTES), and imposed a misdeclaration penalty. The tribunal allowed the company's appeal against the penalty, observing that 'the validity of the credit notes in these circumstances is a difficult item over which an ordinary conscientious businessman might well make a mistake'. *Portal Contracting Ltd, LON/92/1458A (VTD 10234)*.

49.234   See also *The Friary Electrical Co Ltd*, 38.84 INVOICES AND CREDIT NOTES.

Cases where the appellant was unsuccessful

49.235   **Failure to account for tax shown on credit note.**   An appeal against a misdeclaration penalty was dismissed in a case where a company had failed to account for tax shown on a credit note. *V Tech Electronics Ltd, LON/91/139Y (VTD 6677)*.

49.236   Similar decisions were reached in *Scomark Engineering Ltd, MAN/91/826 (VTD 9104)* and *Meadow Contracts Group plc, LON/92/98X (VTD 9431)*.

49.237   **Credit note not effective for VAT—failure to account for tax.**   A company (E) was carrying out work on an office development for a client. It issued an invoice for £357,000 plus VAT. The client disputed the amount of the invoice, and E issued a credit note for the amount. Subsequently E began litigation against the client. In the meantime E did not account for tax on the invoice. The Commissioners formed the opinion that the purpose of the credit note had not been to correct a mistake or error, but to avoid liability to VAT, so that the credit note was not effective for VAT purposes. They imposed a misdeclaration penalty. The tribunal dismissed E's appeal, holding that there was no reasonable excuse for E's failure to account for tax on the invoice in question. *Engineering Building Services Ltd, LON/92/2552A (VTD 10875). (Note.* For whether a credit note is effective for VAT purposes, see the cases at 38.71 to 38.82 INVOICES AND CREDIT NOTES.)

49.238 Similar decisions were reached in *Vaughans of Dudley's Ltd, MAN/92/1292 (VTD 11374)* and *Bartram Planned Preventative Maintenance Ltd, MAN/93/473 (VTD 12418).*

Failure to account for output tax—other cases

Cases where the appellant was successful

49.239 **Payment received following lodgement of insurance claim for damaged goods—whether a reasonable excuse for not treating payment as taxable.** A company which manufactured paper took delivery of two consignments of pulp which were subsequently found to have been contaminated. The company lodged a claim with its insurers. Subsequently it received payment from a salvage association acting on behalf of the insurance company. It did not account for VAT on this payment. Following a control visit by a VAT officer, the company accepted that the payment was taxable since it related to the sale of the damaged pulp by the salvage association. The Commissioners imposed a misdeclaration penalty and the company appealed, contending that until the control visit, it had believed that the payment was not liable to VAT. The tribunal allowed the company's appeal, holding that the circumstances constituted a reasonable excuse. *Caledonian Paper plc, EDN/91/74 (VTD 6139).*

49.240 **Incorrect operation of self-billing system—whether a reasonable excuse for underdeclaration of output tax.** A company (R) worked on a building project as a subcontractor for another company (W), which operated a self-billing system. W issued to R a 'self-billing' invoice for £73,720 in respect of work done by R. No VAT was included on the invoice, although the work was standard-rated and VAT should have been charged. The Commissioners imposed a misdeclaration penalty but the tribunal allowed R's appeal, holding that the inaccuracy of the invoice issued by W was a reasonable excuse for R's failure to account for the VAT in question. *RC Frame Erectors Ltd, LON/91/1535X (VTD 7042). (Note.* Compare the cases noted at 49.262 to 49.264 below, in which similar circumstances were held not to constitute a reasonable excuse.)

49.241 A similar decision was reached in *AE Pipework Services Ltd, MAN/92/1257 (VTD 10724).*

49.242 **Failure to account for tax on management charges.** A partnership issued invoices to an associated company in respect of management charges, but did not account for VAT in respect of these. The Commissioners imposed a misdeclaration penalty and the partnership appealed, contending that it had a reasonable excuse because it had not realised that the management charges were liable to VAT, and there had been no loss of revenue as the company had not reclaimed any input tax. The tribunal held that the circumstances constituted a reasonable excuse. *Ardmore Direct, BEL/90/50X (VTD 7055). (Note.* Compare *Mr Builder (1987) Ltd,* 49.266 below, and the cases noted at 49.267 below.)

49.243 Similar decisions were reached in *Rawlings Bros (GS) Ltd, MAN/91/1183 (VTD 7533); AM Proos & Sons Ltd, MAN/90/932 (VTD 7717, 7734); Scorpio Marine Enterprises Ltd, LON/92/1178X (VTD 9121); Diacutt Concrete Drilling Services Ltd,*

LON/92/934X (VTD 9728); Cargo Express (UK) Ltd, LON/92/1798 (VTD 9779); Robert Matthews Ltd, LON/92/2561 (VTD 9801); Adcon Holdings Ltd, MAN/92/1407 (VTD 10324) and *Plantation Wharf Management Ltd, LON/93/1484P (VTD 12755).*

49.244   **Failure to account for output tax on amounts invoiced for supplies of staff.** A company operated a retail newsagency. Some of its shops also housed sub-post offices. In such shops, it appointed one of its directors as the nominal subpostmaster and provided employees to carry out the running of the sub-post offices. The nominal subpostmaster was paid a salary by the Post Office, which was accepted as being outside the scope of VAT (see *Rickarby*, 7.94 BUSINESS). He paid this to the company, which paid his salary and the salaries of its employees who actually worked in the sub-post offices. The company did not account for output tax on the amounts which it paid to such staff. The Commissioners issued an assessment charging output tax on the deemed supplies of staff, and imposed a misdeclaration penalty. The company accepted the assessment, but appealed against the penalty, contending that the complexity of the arrangements constituted a reasonable excuse. The tribunal accepted this contention and allowed the appeal. *United News Shops (Holdings) Ltd, MAN/92/1394 (VTD 12321).*

49.245   **Borough council acting as agent for water authority—effect of Water Act 1989 (privatisation)—whether a reasonable excuse for failure to charge output tax.** A borough council acted as agent for its local water authority. It submitted claims for reimbursement to the authority. Prior to the *Water Act 1989*, the council had not been required to charge VAT on the supply of its services to the water authority. However, after the passing of the *Water Act*, the water authority became a limited company (instead of a statutory body), so that the council was required to charge VAT on such supplies. The council did not appreciate the significance of this, and failed to charge VAT on its supplies in the two months following the privatisation of the water authority. The Commissioners imposed a misdeclaration penalty, but the tribunal allowed the council's appeal, holding that the circumstances constituted a reasonable excuse. *Chesterfield Borough Council, MAN/91/808 (VTD 7104).*

49.246   *Chesterfield Borough Council*, 49.245 above, was applied in the similar case of *Wyre Borough Council, MAN/91/1391 (VTD 8880).*

49.247   A similar decision was reached in *Eden District Council, MAN/92/1061 (VTD 10245).*

49.248   **Misunderstanding of place of supply—supplies of services treated as outside scope of VAT.** A consulting engineer supplied services to a Belgian company in relation to the supply of furnaces used for water treatment. He did not charge or account for VAT. The Commissioners ruled that his services were excluded from zero-rating, since they were 'services relating to land' within what is now *VATA 1994, Sch 5 para 3*, and imposed a misdeclaration penalty. The engineer appealed, contending that he had a reasonable excuse for believing that the supplies were zero-rated. The tribunal allowed the appeal, holding that the circumstances constituted a reasonable excuse. *DC Day, LON/91/2492 (VTD 7764).*

49.249   **Reverse premium—failure to account for tax.** The Commissioners imposed a misdeclaration penalty on a company which had failed to account for tax on a reverse premium. The company appealed, contending that it had a reasonable excuse because its financial controller had not realised that the payment was liable to VAT. The tribunal allowed the appeal, holding that the circumstances constituted a reasonable excuse. *Anacomp Ltd, LON/92/322Z (VTD 7824).*

49.250   A similar decision was reached in *Silver Knight Exhibitions Ltd, MAN/92/1826 (VTD 10569)*.

49.251   **Payments for supplies at hairdressing salon—whether a reasonable excuse for regarding supplies as being made by individual stylist rather than by salon proprietor.**   In the case noted at 58.208 SUPPLY, the proprietor of a hairdressing salon had only accounted for VAT in respect of the 60% of the gross takings which he retained, and did not account for VAT on the 40% of the takings which he paid to the stylists. The Commissioners imposed a misdeclaration penalty, but the tribunal allowed the proprietor's appeal against the penalty. On the evidence, the supplies to customers were made by the salon proprietor, and he should have accounted for VAT on the full amount of the takings. However, his belief that he only needed to account for VAT on the takings which he retained was not unreasonable, and thus there was a reasonable excuse for his failure to account for VAT. *DL Freer, LON/91/1069Y (VTD 7648)*. (*Note.* Compare the subsequent case of *S Taylor (Machine Tools) Ltd*, 49.280 below, where similar circumstances were held not to constitute a reasonable excuse.)

49.252   **Separate businesses operated by sole trader—turnover of one business below registration threshold—failure to account for tax on supplies of that business.**   A self-employed hairdresser had not been registered for VAT, as his turnover had consistently been below the registration threshold. In 1989 he began a separate business of selling water purifiers. He hoped that his turnover in this business would exceed the threshold, and therefore registered for VAT. However, he did not account for VAT on his income from hairdressing, and the Commissioners imposed a misdeclaration penalty. He appealed, contending that he had a reasonable excuse because he had only intended to register in respect of his business of selling water purifiers, and had not realised that the effect of this was that he would also have to account for VAT on his hairdressing income. The tribunal allowed his appeal against the penalty, holding that although he should have accounted for VAT on his hairdressing supplies, his ignorance of the need to do so constituted a reasonable excuse. *AD Laurie (t/a Betterwater Systems), LON/91/1899X (VTD 7889)*. (*Note.* Compare *Bobacre Ltd (t/a Geary Drive Hire)*, 49.282 below. For cases in which it was held that a registration covers more than one business, see 53.1 *et seq.* REGISTRATION. For a case in which it was held that ignorance of this principle was not a reasonable excuse for failure to register, see *Dawson*, 48.52 PENALTIES: FAILURE TO NOTIFY.)

49.253   A similar decision was reached in *R Gallo (t/a The Fun Pub), EDN/93/36 (VTD 11502)*.

49.254   **Deemed self-supply under VATA 1994, Sch 10—failure to account for tax.**   A medical partnership had arranged for the construction of a new surgery. They registered for VAT, and reclaimed the input tax incurred on the building costs. They began using the new surgery in May 1991, before the work had been completed, but did not account for VAT on the deemed self-supply in that accounting period, as required by what is now *VATA 1994, Sch 10*. The Commissioners imposed a misdeclaration penalty, and the partnership appealed, contending that they had a reasonable excuse because they had been under the impression that they did not need to account for VAT until after the final invoice had been received from the contractors. The tribunal allowed the appeal, holding that the circumstances constituted a reasonable excuse for the failure to account for tax. *Dr Vaughan & Others, MAN/92/1325 (VTD 10172)*. (*Note.* The self-supply charge under *VATA 1994, Sch 10* was abolished for all new developments beginning after 28 February 1995—see the note preceding 6.1 BUILDINGS AND LAND. For further details, see Tolley's Value Added Tax.)

49.255   Failure to account for VAT on rents collected by assignee—whether a reasonable excuse.   A company (C) leased computer equipment to customers. It purchased such equipment from suppliers, and, after leasing the equipment, it sold it to a finance company (F) and agreed to repurchase the equipment from F on a hire-purchase basis. It executed deeds of assignment whereby it assigned to F the rents receivable under the leases. Following the execution of these deeds, C did not account for VAT on the payments which its customers made to F as its assignee. The Commissioners ruled that, despite the assignments, C remained legally responsible for invoicing and for accounting for VAT, and imposed a misdeclaration penalty. C appealed, contending that it had a reasonable excuse since it had assumed that F was responsible for the VAT. The tribunal allowed the appeal against the penalty, holding that the circumstances constituted a reasonable excuse. *Capital Computers Ltd, LON/92/561Z (VTD 9095).*

49.256   Failure to account for tax on disposal of part of business—vendor considering that disposal constituted transfer of business as going concern.   A company (J) which manufactured and sold household consumer products disposed of a blow moulding business. It did not account for VAT on the disposal, and the Commissioners imposed a misdeclaration penalty. J appealed, contending that it had regarded the disposal as the transfer of a business as a going concern, on which output tax was not chargeable. The tribunal allowed the appeal, holding that it had not been unreasonable for J to have treated the disposal as the transfer of a going concern. *Jeyes Ltd, LON/92/1277P (VTD 10513).*

49.257   In May 1991 a trader purchased 15 public houses, all of which were let to tenants, from a brewery. The purchase was treated as the transfer of a going concern, so that no tax was charged. The trader elected to waive exemption in respect of the properties, so that the rents were chargeable to tax. Later in 1991 he sold one of the houses to the tenant, and did not account for output tax on the transfer. The Commissioners imposed a misdeclaration penalty, and the trader appealed, contending that he had assumed that the sale could be treated as the transfer of a going concern, on which no tax was due. The tribunal allowed the appeal, holding that the circumstances constituted a reasonable excuse. *EQ Melville, EDN/92/253 (VTD 10548).*

49.258   A building company owned three properties, in respect of which it had elected to waive exemption. It sold two of these properties to tenants in September 1991, and sold the other property in December 1991. It did not account for output tax on these sales. The Commissioners imposed misdeclaration penalties and the partnership appealed, contending that it had a reasonable excuse because the partners had assumed that the sale of the properties constituted the transfer of a business as a going concern. The tribunal allowed the appeals, holding that the circumstances constituted a reasonable excuse. *Spencer & Harrison, MAN/93/138 (VTD 10697).*

49.259   Stolen takings—failure to account for tax.   A VAT officer on a control visit formed the opinion that a trader who sold garden furniture had underdeclared his takings. Following the officer's visit, the Commissioners issued an estimated assessment and imposed a misdeclaration penalty. The trader appealed, contending that the discrepancy was attributable to takings which had been stolen. The tribunal dismissed the trader's appeal against the assessment, applying the principle in *Benton*, 58.289 SUPPLY. However, the tribunal allowed the appeal against the penalty, holding that the circumstances constituted a reasonable excuse. *DF Venton, LON/92/1859A (VTD 10526).*

49.260   Customer in liquidation after work carried out but before invoice sent— whether a reasonable excuse for failure to account for output tax.   A trader carried out work for a company which went into liquidation before he had submitted an invoice for the work done. The trader did not account for tax on the work in question, and the Commissioners imposed a misdeclaration penalty. The tribunal allowed the trader's appeal against the penalty, holding that the circumstances constituted a reasonable excuse. *C Dillon, MAN/92/1565 (VTD 10681)*.

49.261   **Sale of capital assets to finance company—whether a reasonable excuse for failure to account for output tax.**   A coach operator had had to arrange an overdraft in order to finance the building of some new coaches. She sold the completed coaches to a finance company but failed to account for output tax on the sale. The Commissioners imposed a misdeclaration penalty but the tribunal allowed the trader's appeal, holding that since this was the first time she had entered into transactions of this nature, the circumstances constituted a reasonable excuse. *A Jones (t/a Jones Motors of Ynysybwl), LON/98/235 (VTD 15861)*.

Cases where the appellant was unsuccessful

49.262   **Incorrect operation of self-billing system—whether a reasonable excuse for underdeclaration of output tax.**   An engineering company (A) acted as subcontractor for another company (R), which operated a 'self-billing' system. R provided A with remittance advices intended to show the net amount due to A and the amount of VAT due in respect of that amount. However, the advices received by A did not show any VAT details, and A did not account for VAT on the payments from R. When the Commissioners discovered this, they imposed a misdeclaration penalty. A appealed, contending that it had a reasonable excuse because the misdeclaration resulted from R's failure to operate the 'self-billing' system correctly. The tribunal dismissed A's appeal. The operation of the 'self-billing' system 'did not shift the responsibility for accounting for the VAT' from A to R, and reliance on R was in any event precluded from constituting a reasonable excuse by *VATA 1994, s 71(1)(b)*. *Alpha Engineering Services Ltd, LON/90/1978Y (VTD 5775)*.

49.263   *Alpha Engineering Systems Ltd*, 49.262 above, was applied in the similar case of *Clover Asphalte (IOM) Ltd v The Isle of Man Treasury, MAN/91/342 (VTD 6645)*.

49.264   Similar decisions were reached in *C & S Glaziers (North Wales) Ltd, MAN/91/40 (VTD 6247); Red Barn Contracting Ltd, MAN/90/1094 (VTD 6294); Yazaki (UK) Ltd, LON/91/776Z (VTD 7128); Specialist Rainwater Services Ltd, LON/91/2548Z (VTD 7732); General Metals (Glasgow) Ltd, EDN/92/224 (VTD 9399); Overburn Properties Ltd, EDN/92/323 (VTD 9966)* and *Throston Ltd, MAN/93/991 (VTD 11770)*.

49.265   See also *Beveridge*, 49.397 below.

49.266   **Failure to account for tax on management charges.**   An appeal against a misdeclaration penalty was dismissed in a case where a company had failed to account for tax on management charges. *Mr Builder (1987) Ltd, MAN/91/319 (VTD 6265)*.

49.267   Similar decisions were reached in *Euroweb Ltd, LON/91/1672Z (VTD 6843); Gardith Construction Ltd, LON/91/1348Z (VTD 6959); M & N Dwek & Co Ltd, MAN/91/989 (VTD 7082); Trina Ltd, LON/91/1928 (VTD 7713); Cleshar Contract Services Ltd, LON/91/1641Z (VTD 8803); WM Ayrton & Co (Holdings) Ltd, MAN/92/188 (VTD 9195); Pet-Reks (Southern) Ltd, LON/92/1364P (VTD 9347); PR Mitchell Ltd, LON/92/1708P (VTD 9394); Minstead House Care Management Ltd, LON/91/2315X (VTD 9506); Michael Cooney & Co Ltd, MAN/92/433 (VTD 9627); Blake Paper Ltd, LON/92/2155 (VTD 9829); Temple Avenue Finance Ltd, LON/92/2669P (VTD 9965); Omega Design & Marketing Ltd, MAN/92/848 (VTD 10004); West London Air Conditioning Ltd, LON/93/705P*

(VTD 10797); Churchill Radio Cars Ltd, LON/92/2899A (VTD 11658); Slouand Ltd, MAN/93/438 (VTD 11701); Key Properties Ltd, LON/92/2266A (VTD 11778); NEP Group Ltd, 49.331 below and *Missionfine Ltd*, 41.6 MANAGEMENT SERVICES.

49.268   **Supply to associated company—failure to account for tax.**   An appeal against a misdeclaration penalty was dismissed in a case where a company had failed to account for VAT on a sale to an associated company. *Precious Metal Industries (Wales) Ltd, LON/91/2712 (VTD 7750).*

49.269   Similar decisions were reached in *Mart Play Ltd, LON/91/2080X (VTD 9046); RC & CH Hunt, LON/92/619Y (VTD 9135); Deeside Welding Co, MAN/91/910 (VTD 9238); William Youngs & Son (Farms) Ltd, LON/92/1510P (VTD 9660); Arrowin Ltd, MAN/91/1341 (VTD 10575); Irish Roofing Felts Ltd, BEL/93/27 (VTD 11425); LEP Luma Ltd, LON/93/1167P (VTD 11490); Euromer Stevedores Ltd, MAN/91/1111 (VTD 11755); I Loftus & Son Ltd, LON/93/1346 (VTD 12678); Antrobus Farm Ltd, MAN/98/258 (VTD 16029); London & Newcastle Holdings plc, LON/99/850 (VTD 16402)* and *I & N Martin*, 49.378 below.

49.270   **Supplies to associated partnership—failure to account for tax.**   A company failed to account for VAT on supplies to an associated partnership. The Commissioners imposed a misdeclaration penalty and the company appealed, contending that it had not realised that the supplies were liable to VAT. The tribunal dismissed the appeal, holding that there was no reasonable excuse for the company's failure to account for tax, and that the fact that the partnership could have reclaimed the appropriate input tax was irrelevant. *Mr Builder (1987) Ltd*, 49.266 above, applied; *Ardmore Direct*, 49.242 above, and *AM Proos & Sons Ltd*, 49.243 above, distinguished. *Michael Rogers Ltd, LON/91/2454Z (VTD 9157).*

49.271   Similar decisions were reached in *R Baker, MAN/93/915 (VTD 11634)* and *TRS Cabinet Co Ltd, MAN/91/1640 (VTD 11750).*

49.272   See also *Auto-Plas (International) Ltd*, 49.77 above.

49.273   **Supply by partnership to retiring partner—failure to account for tax.**   A partnership transferred a vehicle valued at £18,000 to a retiring partner, and failed to account for output tax. The Commissioners imposed a misdeclaration penalty and the tribunal dismissed the partnership's appeal, holding that there was no reasonable excuse for the failure to account for tax. *Coombes Transport, MAN/92/1462 (VTD 11275).*

49.274   **Failure to account for output tax on sale of property.**   See *Porters End Estates Ltd*, 49.381 below, and *Nightingale Holdings*, 49.382 below.

49.275   **Failure to account for tax on lease premium.**   An appeal against a misdeclaration penalty was dismissed in a case where a solicitor had failed to account for output tax on the receipt of a premium for the grant of a lease. *WT Stockler, LON/96/288 (VTD 15350).*

49.276   **Private use of fuel.**   Failure to account for tax on petrol used privately was held not to constitute a reasonable excuse in *Claremont Construction (London) Ltd, LON/91/1301Y (VTD 7016)* and *Property & Investment Centre Ltd, LON/93/2037P (VTD 11686).*

49.277   **Failure to account for tax on profit on sale of car.**   In 1988 a company purchased a rare Ferrari car for £315,000. In April 1990 it sold the car for £700,000. It failed to account for VAT on its profit. The Commissioners imposed a misdeclaration penalty and the tribunal dismissed the company's appeal, holding that there was no reasonable excuse for the company's failure to seek advice on the tax consequences of the sale. *T Baden Hardstaff Ltd, MAN/90/808 (VTD 7230).*

49.278   **Sales made as agent—failure to account for tax on commission.**   A farmer acted as an agent for a landowner, selling grain on behalf of the landowner and retaining 25% of the sale price as his commission. He failed to account for VAT on the sums which he retained, and the Commissioners imposed a misdeclaration penalty. The tribunal dismissed the farmer's appeal, holding that there was no reasonable excuse for the failure to account for tax. *P Forster, LON/92/1047Z (VTD 9367).*

49.279   **Commission.**   Failure to account for tax on commission was held not to constitute a reasonable excuse in *ND Lieder, LON/92/2308A (VTD 10400); Alcatel Business Systems Ltd, LON/92/2398 (VTD 11411)* and *Merlin HC Ltd,* 1.82 AGENTS.

49.280   **Payments for supplies at hairdressing salon—whether a reasonable excuse for regarding supplies as being made by individual stylists rather than by salon proprietor.**   A company which operated hairdressing salons only accounted for output tax on the amounts which it retained, and did not account for tax on the amounts which were retained by the stylists. The Commissioners imposed a misdeclaration penalty. The company appealed, contending firstly that it should only be required to account for tax on the amounts which it retained, and alternatively that it had a reasonable excuse for having believed that it was only required to account for tax on these amounts. The tribunal dismissed the appeal, holding on the evidence that the supplies were made by the company, rather than by the individual stylists, and that there was no reasonable excuse for the misdeclaration since the company 'chose to depart from the normal straightforward method of conducting its business and to enter into confused and imprecise arrangements. The complexity was of the appellant's own making.' *S Taylor (Machine Tools) Ltd, LON/92/860A (VTD 11171).*

49.281   **Payments for supplies of chauffeur-driven car hire—whether a reasonable excuse for regarding supplies as being made by drivers rather than by partnership.**   A partnership provided a chauffeur-driven car hire business. It only accounted for VAT on the amounts which it retained, and did not account for VAT on the amounts which were paid to the drivers who worked for it. The Commissioners issued an assessment charging output tax on the full amounts paid by the customers, and imposed a misdeclaration penalty. The tribunal dismissed the partnership's appeal against both the assessment and the penalty, holding that the supplies were made by the partnership and that there was no reasonable excuse for the partnership's failure to account for tax on the correct basis. *Japan Executive Chauffeur, LON/92/3128A (VTD 11836).*

49.282   **Company acquiring assets of separate business—whether a reasonable excuse for failure to account for tax.**   A company (B), which was registered for VAT, took over the assets of a separate business and continued to trade both under its existing trading name and under the trading name of the new business. It did not account for output tax on its income under the trading name of the second business. The Commissioners imposed a misdeclaration penalty and the tribunal dismissed the company's appeal, holding that there was no reasonable excuse for the failure to account for tax. *Bobacre Ltd (t/a Geary Drive Hire), MAN/94/761 (VTD 12829).*

49.283   **Incorrect operation of Retail Scheme.**   An appeal against a misdeclaration penalty was dismissed in a case where a married couple who operated a newsagency had operated their Retail Scheme incorrectly and had failed to account for tax on several items of income. *BK & U Sood (t/a Good News), LON/92/2435 (VTD 9950).*

49.284   Similar decisions were reached in *DK Popat, MAN/91/684 (VTD 10452)* and *AP &
P Renshall (t/a Kingsway Convenience Store), MAN/98/1092 (VTD 16273)*.

49.285   **Failure to comply with direction under VATA 1994, Sch 1 para 2.**   The
proprietors of a public house failed to account for output tax on receipts from
catering, treating it as a separate business carried on by one of the partners (B) as an
individual. In October 1988 the Commissioners issued a direction under what is now
VATA 1994, Sch 1 para 2, against which the partners did not appeal. However, the
partners continued not to account for tax on the catering receipts. When the
Commissioners discovered this, they imposed a misdeclaration penalty. The partners
appealed, contending that they had terminated the partnership on 18 March 1990 but
had recommenced it on 8 April, and that they had considered that the result of the
temporary termination of the partnership was that the direction under *VATA 1994,
Sch 1 para 2* was no longer valid. The tribunal dismissed the partners' appeal, finding
that the partnership had continued throughout the period and holding that there was
no reasonable excuse for the partners' failure to account for tax. *PG Barnett & TG
Larsen, MAN/92/1585 (VTD 11056)*.

49.286   **Underdeclaration of takings—estimated assessment upheld by tribunal—
whether any excuse for misdeclaration.**   A VAT officer formed the opinion
that a publican had underdeclared takings, and issued an estimated assessment using
a mark-up calculation. Following further information from the publican's
accountant, the mark-up was reduced to 55.9%, and the revised assessment was
confirmed by the tribunal, applying *Van Boeckel*, 3.1 ASSESSMENT. The
Commissioners also imposed a misdeclaration penalty. The tribunal dismissed the
publican's appeal against the penalty, holding on the evidence that there was no
reasonable excuse for the failure to keep an accurate record of takings. *MA Rimmer,
LON/92/2410A (VTD 11397)*.

49.287   Similar decisions were reached in *M Mahoney, LON/93/2542A (VTD 12063); CA
McCourtie, LON/92/191 (VTD 12239); RD Stavrinou, LON/93/1670A (VTD
12546); Digbeth Cash & Carry Ltd, MAN/94/342 (VTD 13180); H Jin-Xu (t/a
Wong Kok Fish & Chips), MAN/98/984 (VTD 16520)* and *Sessions*, 49.376 below.

49.288   An appeal against a misdeclaration penalty was dismissed in a case where the tribunal
found that a trader had failed to account for VAT in respect of several invoices which
he had issued. *C Jacobson, MAN/92/289 (VTD 11741)*.

49.289   Similar decisions were reached in *Caroline General Services Ltd, LON/93/4911A
(VTD 12048)* and *HS Savin, MAN/93/662 (VTD 12104, 12873)*.

Incorrect input tax claims—other cases

Cases where the appellant was successful

49.290   **Failure to apply partial exemption provisions.**   A company was incorporated
to sell houses and plots of land. In its first return it reclaimed the whole of its input
tax. The Commissioners imposed a misdeclaration penalty, since some of the
supplies related to the sale of plots of land, so that the company should have restricted
its input tax claims by applying the partial exemption provisions. The tribunal
allowed the company's appeal, holding that the circumstances constituted a
reasonable excuse. *Scotia Homes Ltd, EDN/90/211 (VTD 6044)*.

49.291   There was also held to be a reasonable excuse for failure to apply the partial
exemption provisions in *Murrayfield Indoor Sports Club, EDN/91/147 (VTD 6613);
M & P McNaughton, MAN/91/346 (VTD 7438); F Wright, LON/91/1840 (VTD
7465); Humatt Holdings Ltd, LON/92/2292Z (VTD 10236); PJ Robinson, MAN/*

92/322 (VTD 13102); The Laurels Nursing Home Ltd, MAN/96/1065 (VTD 16092); Five Steps Community Nursery, LON/99/701 (VTD 16684) and *Polo Farm Sports Club*, 43.110 PARTIAL EXEMPTION.

49.292   **Input tax relating to exempt supply.**   A hairdresser purchased a boarding house and had work carried out on it to convert it into a retirement home. His accountant advised him that he could reclaim the input tax on the conversion, and he did so. However, on a subsequent control visit, a VAT officer informed him that the supplies made by the retirement home would be exempt under what is now *VATA 1994, Sch 9, Group 7, Item 4*, and that the input tax was therefore not reclaimable. The Commissioners imposed a misdeclaration penalty, but the tribunal allowed the proprietor's appeal. Although it was not necessary to decide the point, the tribunal considered it possible that the supplies might be excluded from exemption under what is now *VATA 1994, Sch 9, Group 1, Item 1(d)*, applying *Namecourt Ltd*, 39.75 LAND. In view of the uncertainty over the status of the supplies, the proprietor had a reasonable excuse for having reclaimed the relevant input tax. *J Bowe, MAN/91/303 (VTD 6748)*.

49.293   An appeal against a misdeclaration penalty was allowed in a case where a company had reclaimed input tax in respect of repairs to premises which it let to a tenant. The tribunal held that the complexity of the relevant law was a reasonable excuse for the misdeclaration. *Du Beau Ltd, LON/91/2521X (VTD 7667)*.

49.294   Similar decisions were reached in *The Communications & Leisure Group of Companies, LON/91/1149X (VTD 7788); ST Rafferty, LON/92/638 (VTD 8911); GAG Cooper, LON/92/1633P (VTD 9719); Abbasford Ltd (t/a Watford Electronics), LON/92/3200P (VTD 10229)* and *Terard Ltd, LON/99/126 (VTD 16949)*.

49.295   A company had reclaimed input tax in respect of work carried out on land which it owned, and on which it had intended to build a house. However in 1991, before construction of the house had started, the company sold the site. The sale was an exempt supply, but the company failed to repay the input tax it had previously reclaimed, as required by what is now *VAT Regulations, reg 108*. The Commissioners imposed a misdeclaration penalty, and the company appealed, contending that it had a reasonable excuse since it had not been aware of the relevant regulation. The tribunal allowed the appeal, holding that the circumstances constituted a reasonable excuse. *Time (Ancient & Modern) Ltd, LON/92/810 (VTD 8814)*.

49.296   A married couple sold a farm for £1,800,000. Their solicitor charged them £300,000, plus VAT of £45,000, for his advice with regard to the sale. The couple reclaimed the £45,000 as input tax. The Commissioners imposed a misdeclaration penalty, since the sale of the farm had been an exempt supply, so that the input tax was not deductible. The couple appealed, contending that they had a reasonable excuse for having believed that they were entitled to reclaim the tax. The tribunal allowed the appeal, holding that the circumstances constituted a reasonable excuse. *FFJ & FK Forrest, MAN/91/1355 (VTD 10576)*.

49.297   A company purchased a public house. The vendor had elected to waive exemption, and accordingly charged output tax on the sale. The purchaser reclaimed input tax without making any election to waive exemption. The Commissioners therefore issued an assessment to recover the tax, and also imposed a misdeclaration penalty. The tribunal upheld the assessment but allowed the company's appeal against the penalty, holding that the circumstances constituted a reasonable excuse. *Maplefine Ltd, MAN/97/1103 (VTD 15499)*.

49.298   See also *John Lanham Watts (Carpets) Ltd*, 49.151 above.

49.299   **Input tax reclaimed on zero-rated supply.** A company (V) purchased a portable office building. The invoice which it received for this supply did not show any VAT, because the supplier had treated the building as zero-rated. However, V's accountant treated the invoice as being inclusive of VAT, and reclaimed input tax on 3/23 of the total sum invoiced (this being the 'VAT fraction' at the relevant time). The Commissioners imposed a misdeclaration penalty but the tribunal allowed V's appeal, holding that the circumstances constituted a reasonable excuse. *Vimech Ltd, LON/91/800 (VTD 6723).*

49.300   A farmer arranged for builders to carry out work on his farmhouse, which was a listed building. The work should have been zero-rated under what is now *VATA 1994, Sch 8, Group 6,* but the builders included VAT on their invoices. The farmer paid the VAT to the builders, and reclaimed it as input tax. The Commissioners imposed a misdeclaration penalty but the tribunal allowed the farmer's appeal, holding that he had a reasonable excuse for having reclaimed the input tax. *AS Macgregor, LON/91/1841Y (VTD 7840).*

49.301   **Input tax reclaimed on motor car.** A company which carried on the business of leasing motor vehicles reclaimed input tax on cars which it had purchased. The Commissioners rejected the claim and imposed a misdeclaration penalty. The company appealed against the penalty, contending that it had a reasonable excuse for reclaiming this input tax, since what is now *Notice No 700/64/96, para 35* indicated that 'if you are a car dealer—a person whose business is the selling of cars—you can reclaim VAT you are charged on unused cars imported for sale'. The company contended that its directors were justified in believing that it qualified as a 'car dealer'. The tribunal allowed the appeal. For the purposes of the case it was not necessary to decide whether the company actually qualified as a car dealer, but it was not unreasonable for the company's directors to have considered that it would qualify as a car dealer. *EP Mooney Ltd, MAN/91/360 (VTD 6418).*

49.302   An appeal was allowed in a case where a partnership reclaimed input tax on the import of a Chevrolet car which was 'cannibalised' for spare parts. The tribunal held that the circumstances constituted a reasonable excuse. *DR Auto Repair Tech, LON/92/220Y (VTD 7489).*

49.303   An appeal was allowed in a case where a company had reclaimed input tax on a car purchased for demonstration purposes. The tribunal held that, since the car was not purchased for resale, the company had a reasonable excuse for having reclaimed the input tax. *Top Grade Cars Ltd, LON/91/337Z (VTD 7602).*

49.304   **Input tax reclaimed by tour operator.** A company trading as a tour operator in South Wales failed to operate the appropriate margin scheme and submitted a return reclaiming input tax. The Commissioners imposed a misdeclaration penalty. The tribunal allowed the company's appeal, finding that a VAT officer had failed to make it clear to the directors that they should have operated the margin scheme, and holding that this constituted a reasonable excuse. *City Centre Ticketline Ltd, LON/91/1937Y (VTD 7553).*

49.305   **Input tax reclaimed on supply not used for business purposes.** In the case noted at 34.387 INPUT TAX, the tribunal had held that a printer was not entitled to reclaim input tax on the purchase of a personalised car numberplate. However, the tribunal allowed the printer's appeal against a misdeclaration penalty, holding that since he had been advised by his accountant that he could reclaim the tax in question, he had a reasonable excuse for having done so. *D Philips, EDN/92/3 (VTD 7883).* (*Note.* Compare *NEP Group Ltd,* 49.331 below, in which an appeal against a penalty imposed in similar circumstances was dismissed, partly on the grounds that the appellant company in that case had not sought professional advice.)

49.306 A similar decision was reached in *Lister*, 34.124 INPUT TAX.

49.307 **Input tax reclaimed on supply not wholly for business purposes.** A married couple carried on in partnership the business of providing television facilities and production services to television companies. They installed a swimming pool at their premises for clients to use, and reclaimed the whole of the input tax attributable to the pool. A VAT officer formed the view that the pool, which the partners used themselves, had been primarily installed for private purposes, the business purpose being subsidiary. He issued an assessment on the basis that only one-third of the input tax was allowable. The Commissioners also imposed a misdeclaration penalty. The partners accepted that only one-third of the tax was deductible and did not appeal against the assessment, but did appeal against the penalty, contending that they had reclaimed the input tax in good faith since the pool had been used for business purposes and that they had not realised that the input tax should be apportioned. The tribunal allowed their appeal against the penalty, holding that the circumstances constituted a reasonable excuse. *Mr & Mrs Memmott (t/a Free Range Video), LON/91/707Y (VTD 6783)*.

49.308 A newsagent, who lived above the shop from which he traded, incurred expenditure on refurbishing the premises. He reclaimed input tax on the whole of the expenditure. The Commissioners ruled that only part of the tax was reclaimable, and imposed a misdeclaration penalty. The tribunal allowed the newsagent's appeal against the penalty. The Commissioners were correct in requiring the expenditure to be apportioned. However, the primary purpose of the expenditure had been to improve the business premises, so that more than half of the input tax was deductible. The newsagent had not acted unreasonably in reclaiming the whole of the tax. *B Singh, MAN/91/987 (VTD 7584)*.

49.309 In the case noted at 34.239 INPUT TAX, where a company had reclaimed input tax in respect of double glazing installed at its directors' house, the tribunal held that only one-sixth of the tax claimed was deductible, but allowed the company's appeal against a misdeclaration penalty, holding that the circumstances constituted a reasonable excuse for the claim. *Newland Technical Services Ltd, LON/92/1255A (VTD 9294)*. (*Note.* For other issues in this case, see 38.68 INVOICES AND CREDIT NOTES and 49.93 above.)

49.310 **Input tax reclaimed on transfer of going concern.** An ice-cream salesman reclaimed input tax on the purchase of the van and stock of another salesman. The Commissioners issued an assessment to recover the tax, considering that the transaction constituted the transfer of a business as a going concern,. They also imposed a misdeclaration penalty. The tribunal dismissed the salesman's appeal against the assessment, holding that the transaction did constitute the transfer of a going concern, but allowed his appeal against the penalty, holding that the circumstances constituted a reasonable excuse. *A Black, EDN/92/58 (VTD 7919)*.

49.311 See also *Mawji*, 61.46 TRANSFERS OF GOING CONCERNS.

49.312 **Input tax reclaimed by associated company—whether a reasonable excuse.** A company (O) operated a restaurant. Its directors wished to transfer the business to a new company (C), which they incorporated for this purpose. The companies' accountant asked a VAT officer whether it would be possible to transfer O's registration to C, and was told that this would be acceptable. However, before this had been done, C incurred expenditure on refurbishing the restaurant. Since C was not yet registered for VAT, O reclaimed the relevant input tax. The Commissioners imposed a misdeclaration penalty, but the tribunal allowed O's appeal, holding that the circumstances constituted a reasonable excuse. *Orbvent Ltd, LON/91/967 (VTD 6602)*.

49.313   Penalties: Misdeclaration

49.313   An appeal was allowed in a case where a partnership had reclaimed input tax in respect of invoices made out to an associated company. The tribunal held that the circumstances constituted a reasonable excuse. *Gateway Leisure (Caravan Sales), EDN/92/85 (VTD 7943)*. (*Note.* Compare *Stockwell Carpets Ltd*, 49.344 below, where similar circumstances were held not to constitute a reasonable excuse.)

49.314   Similar decisions were reached in *Long's Supermarket Ltd, BEL/91/21X (VTD 9309)* and *Leaders (North East) Ltd, MAN/92/110 (VTD 9004)*.

49.315   **Input tax incorrectly reclaimed by agent.**   In 1990 a caravan site was flooded and 25 of the caravans were damaged. The owner of the site (N), who was registered for VAT, arranged for the necessary repairs and insurance claims. (The caravans themselves were owned by private individuals, rather than by N.) The contractors who carried out the repairs submitted invoices which included VAT, but the insurance company failed to pay the VAT shown on the invoices. N therefore paid the VAT himself, and reclaimed it as input tax. The Commissioners issued an assessment to recover the tax, since the supply had been to the insurance company rather than to N, who had in effect been acting as an agent. They also imposed a misdeclaration penalty. N appealed against the penalty, contending that he had a reasonable excuse for the incorrect claim since the insurance company had advised him that he was entitled to reclaim the VAT. The tribunal allowed his appeal against the penalty, holding that the circumstances constituted a reasonable excuse for the incorrect claim. *PC Nock, MAN/92/157 (VTD 10169)*. (*Note.* For the consequences of an insurance company failing to pay a VAT liability, see also the cases noted at 4.5 to 4.7 BAD DEBTS.)

49.316   **Input tax reclaimed on supply not made to claimant—whether a reasonable excuse.**   A company (C) arranged a loan from another company (S), and agreed to pay S's solicitors' fees. C reclaimed input tax on the fees in question, and the Commissioners imposed a misdeclaration penalty, since the solicitors had supplied their services to S rather than to C, so that C was not entitled to reclaim the input tax. The tribunal allowed C's appeal against the penalty, holding that the circumstances constituted a reasonable excuse. *Crux Engineering Ltd, LON/92/179 (VTD 7706)*.

49.317   **Previous underclaim of input tax—whether a reasonable excuse for duplication of correction of error.**   A company had underclaimed its input tax and overdeclared output tax by a total of £33,000 in its return for the period ending June 1990. Its accountant reclaimed this amount by including it as input tax in its return for August 1990. However, on 28 September 1990, while the accountant was on holiday, his assistant completed a voluntary disclosure form in respect of the error, without disclosing the fact that the accountant had already effectively corrected the error by adjusting the figures in the August return. When the Commissioners discovered this, they imposed a misdeclaration penalty. The tribunal allowed the company's appeal against the penalty, finding that the duplication was accidental and holding that the circumstances constituted a reasonable excuse. *Verson Wilkins Ltd, MAN/91/1616 (VTD 9628)*.

Cases where the appellant was unsuccessful

49.318   **Input tax reclaimed on supply outside UK.**   A company (J) was a UK subsidiary of a US company, and normally acted as agent for the US company in arranging for goods to be exported from the USA to the UK, and thereafter re-exported to foreign customers. In the period ending May 1990 J also undertook a transaction in which the goods were exported directly from the USA to the Netherlands, so that any VAT due would be payable to, and reclaimable from, the Dutch authorities. However, J reclaimed VAT on this transaction from the UK

Customs & Excise instead. The Commissioners imposed a misdeclaration penalty and the tribunal dismissed J's appeal, holding that the circumstances did not constitute a reasonable excuse. *JLG Industries (UK) Ltd, EDN/91/13 (VTD 5814)*.

49.319   See also *The Edinburgh Piano Company Ltd*, 49.390 below.

49.320   **Input tax reclaimed on motor car.**   An appeal against a misdeclaration penalty was dismissed in a case where a trader had reclaimed input tax on the purchase of a car. *PM Birkin, EDN/91/81 (VTD 6113)*.

49.321   Similar decisions were reached in *DW Wyck, LON/91/845X (VTD 6619); Hardys of Telford, MAN/91/353 (VTD 6791); Nightingales Motors (Exmouth) Ltd, LON/ 91/1032Y (VTD 6842); KJ Hodgson, MAN/91/326 (VTD 7138, 7159); Page Motors (Ferndown) Ltd, LON/91/1174 (VTD 7517); S Travers, EDN/92/109 (VTD 7942); RAF Aldergrove Service Institute Fund, BEL/91/12X (VTD 8812); CT Finance Ltd, MAN/91/978 (VTD 9286); Transtrek Ltd (t/a Thropton Motor Co), MAN/91/785 (VTD 9749); Nigel Sullivan Fibres Ltd, MAN/92/169 (VTD 9842); Maple Network Consultancy Ltd, LON/93/6A (VTD 11488); RG Barnes, EDN/96/106 (VTD 14463); BD Williams, LON/96/1734 (VTD 15163)* and *Standridge Farm Ltd, MAN/00/18 (VTD 16850)*.

49.322   See also *West Midlands Motors Ltd*, 49.409 below.

49.323   In a similar case where a trader had reclaimed input tax on the purchase of a Land Rover, the tribunal held that there was no reasonable excuse for the trader's failure to realise that the Land Rover was a 'car' for the purposes of the VAT legislation. *RJ Holloway, LON/91/2578Z (VTD 7493)*.

49.324   A similar decision was reached in a case where a partnership reclaimed input tax on two four-wheel drive Vauxhall Montereys. The tribunal held that the vehicles were 'cars' and there was no reasonable excuse for reclaiming input tax on them. *Anglia Building & Decorating Contractors, MAN/00/306 (VTD 16852)*.

49.325   **Failure to apply partial exemption provisions.**   An appeal against a misdeclaration penalty was dismissed in a case where a company which was partly exempt had reclaimed the whole of its input tax. The tribunal held that the fact that the company had relied on its accountant could not be a reasonable excuse, applying the QB decision in *Harris*, 48.85 PENALTIES: FAILURE TO NOTIFY. *Dicta* of the tribunal in *Enterprise Safety Coaches Ltd*, 49.80 above, were disapproved. *GB Capital Ltd, EDN/91/31 (VTD 6138)*.

49.326   There was also held to be no reasonable excuse for the failure to apply the partial exemption provisions in *Palatine Hotel Ltd v The Isle of Man Treasury, MAN/91/ 600 (VTD 6534); ETS (Scotland) Ltd, EDN/91/219 (VTD 6987); M Ramzan, MAN/91/1071 (VTD 7725); Sefton I-Tec Ltd, MAN/92/284 (VTD 7813); Discovery Housing Association Ltd, EDN/92/119 (VTD 8847); Pack & Moore Builders Co Ltd, LON/92/1202 (VTD 9130); Ashbolt Ltd, LON/91/2081Y (VTD 11019); Regent Investment Fund Ltd, EDN/92/203 (VTD 12152); Liam Findlay Architects, EDN/98/8 (VTD 15568); Marbourne Ltd*, 39.50 LAND, and *Trustees of the Whitbread Harrowden Settlement*, 49.395 below.

49.327   **Incorrect operation of partial exemption provisions.**   An appeal against a misdeclaration penalty was dismissed in a case where a company had operated the partial exemption provisions incorrectly, and thus had reclaimed more input tax than it was entitled to. *Landene Investments Ltd, LON/92/106Y (VTD 9510)*.

49.328 Similar decisions were reached in *Hexham Steeplechase Co Ltd, MAN/92/538 (VTD 10481); Dayrich Bookmakers, MAN/96/153 (VTD 14638)* and *Hexham Golf Club*, 49.392 below.

49.329 **Input tax relating to exempt supply.** An appeal against a misdeclaration penalty was dismissed in a case where a company had reclaimed input tax relating to an exempt supply. *Bristow & Darlington Ltd, LON/91/1126Y (VTD 6961)*.

49.330 Similar decisions were reached in *Tregarn Developments Ltd, LON/91/1815Y (VTD 7358); South Tyne Chalets Ltd, MAN/91/350 (VTD 7377); Binof Construction Ltd, MAN/91/559 (VTD 7404); Eagle Capital Corporation Ltd, MAN/91/1108 (VTD 7447); Unwin Estates Ltd, LON/91/2078X (VTD 7955); Charles Church Spitfires Ltd, LON/91/850X (VTD 9512); Northumbria & Cumbria Estates Ltd, MAN/92/1270 (VTD 10366); Woodward & Stalder Ltd, LON/91/1893X (VTD 10378); Masstype Properties Ltd, LON/92/450X (VTD 11124); DC Smith, LON/93/812A (VTD 11382); Woods Place Management Ltd, LON/93/1920A (VTD 12812); Dinglis Property Services Ltd, LON/97/801 (VTD 15159); Crestbond Ltd*, 49.392 below, and *Celahurst Ltd*, 43.13 PARTIAL EXEMPTION.

49.331 **Input tax reclaimed on supply not used for business purposes.** A company reclaimed input tax on the purchase of a personalised car numberplate. The Commissioners considered that the tax was not deductible, applying *Ava Knit Ltd*, 34.376 INPUT TAX, and *BJ Kershaw Transport Ltd*, 34.377 INPUT TAX. They imposed a misdeclaration penalty. The tribunal dismissed the company's appeal, holding that the company should have sought professional advice on whether the tax was deductible, and there was no reasonable excuse for its failure to do so. *NEP Group Ltd, MAN/91/418 (VTD 6751)*. (*Note.* For another issue in this case, see 49.267 above.)

49.332 A similar decision was reached in *AT Windsor (t/a ATW Transport), LON/92/520 (VTD 11241)*.

49.333 A married couple registered for VAT as landlords of a commercial building, on which they made an election to waive exemption. They reclaimed input tax on the construction of a tennis court at their home. The Commissioners imposed a misdeclaration penalty, and the tribunal dismissed the couple's appeal. *GS & H Randhawa, LON/91/2445Y (VTD 7704)*.

49.334 A married couple who owned a retail shop reclaimed input tax on school fees for their two children and golf club membership for the husband. The Commissioners imposed a misdeclaration penalty, and the tribunal dismissed the couple's appeal. *DL & LE Cheesman (t/a Kraft E), LON/92/917 (VTD 10347)*.

49.335 A building company, which had constructed a number of purpose-built residential flats for the elderly, reclaimed input tax on the upkeep of two racehorses. The Commissioners issued an assessment to recover the tax, on the basis that the expenditure had not been incurred for the purpose of the company's business. They also imposed a misdeclaration penalty. The company appealed against both the assessment and the penalty. The tribunal dismissed both appeals, finding that the horses were not maintained for the purposes of the company's business, since 'there was no link between horse racing and the company's business'. On the evidence, the Commissioners 'had every justification for seeking to impose a serious misdeclaration penalty'. The company had been reckless, and had 'not satisfied the burden of proving that it had a reasonable excuse for overclaiming the input tax'. *RV Young Ltd, LON/93/925A (VTD 12123)*.

49.336 A married couple traded in partnership providing business consultancy services. The partnership reclaimed input tax in respect of invoices relating to a property which was divided into three flats, one of which was owned by the husband and two of which had been purchased by a trust which the husband controlled. The Commissioners imposed a misdeclaration penalty and the tribunal dismissed the couple's appeal. *RMSG, LON/93/723A (VTD 12520)*.

49.337   An appeal against a misdeclaration penalty was dismissed in another case where the tribunal found that a partnership had reclaimed input tax in respect of items of private expenditure. *Golden Echo Productions, MAN/93/674 (VTD 11747)*.

49.338   See also *Raceshine Ltd*, 34.394 INPUT TAX.

49.339   **Input tax reclaimed on supply not wholly for business purposes.**   A farming company reclaimed all the input tax incurred in respect of a farmhouse which it owned and which was occupied by its managing director. The Commissioners considered that only one-third of the tax in question was allowable, the remaining two-thirds having been incurred for the personal purposes of the director. They imposed a misdeclaration penalty. The tribunal dismissed the company's appeal, holding that there was no reasonable excuse for the misdeclaration. *Hazel Street Ltd, LON/91/120X (VTD 6229)*.

49.340   In the case noted at 34.327 INPUT TAX, where the tribunal had held that expenditure on motor racing was primarily incurred for private pleasure rather than for business purposes, the tribunal dismissed an appeal against a misdeclaration penalty, holding that no reasonable businessman would have claimed the whole of the input tax in question. *Chambers (Homefield Sandpit) Ltd, LON/92/276X (VTD 9012)*.

49.341   An appeal against a misdeclaration penalty was dismissed in another case where an appellant had reclaimed the full amount of input tax in respect of supplies which were partly for private purposes. *L Dewar, EDN/92/60 (VTD 7899)*.

49.342   **Input tax reclaimed on supply made to agent.**   An incorporated foundation reclaimed input tax in respect of invoices which were not made out to it, but to a company which acted as its agent. The Commissioners imposed a misdeclaration penalty and the tribunal dismissed the foundation's appeal, holding that the tax should have been reclaimed by the company and that there was no excuse for the foundation having incorrectly reclaimed it. *Dolmetsch Foundation Inc, LON/90/1801X (VTD 5876)*.

49.343   **Company acting as agent for overseas suppliers—reclaiming input tax on supplies made to overseas principals.**   A company, which acted as an agent for overseas suppliers, reclaimed input tax in respect of supplies which had been imported on behalf of its overseas principals, although it did not recharge the necessary output tax to the overseas principals. When the Commissioners discovered this, they imposed a misdeclaration penalty. The tribunal dismissed the company's appeal, holding that the circumstances did not constitute a reasonable excuse. *MB Appleton Yarns & Co, MAN/91/916 (VTD 7083)*.

49.344   **Input tax reclaimed on supply to associated company.**   There was held to be no reasonable excuse for the reclaiming of input tax on invoices made out to an associated company in *Stockwell Carpets Ltd, LON/92/77Y (VTD 7782)*.

49.345   A similar decision was reached in a case where a sole trader reclaimed input tax in respect of invoices made out to a company of which he was the principal director. *J Johnson (t/a London Angling Supplies), LON/92/660A (VTD 9898)*.

49.346   **Input tax reclaimed on electrical appliances for installation in new flats.**   A builder constructed a block of flats and reclaimed input tax on electrical appliances (such as washing machines and refrigerators) which he had purchased for installation in the flats. The Commissioners rejected his claim, since the input tax was not deductible by virtue of what is now *Article 6* of the *Input Tax Order 1992*. They also imposed a misdeclaration penalty. The builder appealed against the penalty, contending that he had a reasonable excuse since he had been unaware that the input tax was not deductible. The tribunal dismissed his appeal, holding that the circumstances did not constitute a reasonable excuse. The regulations which prevented the deduction of the tax dated from 1984, and concerned the appellant's 'main area of trade'. Furthermore, a previous claim by the appellant for input tax on a cooker had been disallowed, and this should have drawn the appellant's attention to the need to seek advice on whether the tax was deductible. *JL Dart, LON/91/2033 (VTD 9066)*. (*Note.* For another issue in this case, see 3.54 ASSESSMENT.)

49.347 **Input tax reclaimed on transfer of business as going concern.**   A company reclaimed input tax on the transfer of a business as a going concern. The Commissioners imposed a misdeclaration penalty and the tribunal dismissed the company's appeal, holding that there was no reasonable excuse for the incorrect reclaim of input tax. *Windowmaker UPVC Ltd, MAN/91/1206 (VTD 9939)*.

49.348 Similar decisions were reached in *Magnum Craft Ltd, LON/92/2953 (VTD 11316)* and *RN Banbury (t/a Creative Impressions), LON/96/1720 (VTD 15047)*.

49.349 **Input tax reclaimed on basis of documents not constituting tax invoices.**   A company reclaimed input tax of £11,600 on the basis of documents purporting to be invoices issued by an associated company. The associated company had gone into liquidation without accounting for the tax in question, and the invoices did not comply with the requirements of the *VAT Regulations*. The Commissioners issued an assessment to recover the tax in question, and imposed a misdeclaration penalty. The company appealed, contending that the invoices had been issued in respect of management charges. The tribunal dismissed the appeal, holding that the invoices did not constitute tax invoices, and that there was no reasonable excuse for the company having used them to reclaim the input tax, since 'the most favourable construction (of the company's) action in claiming input tax relief of the four invoices is that they were recklessly giving themselves the benefit of the doubt'. *Suitmart (UK) Ltd, LON/92/1659A (VTD 10392)*.

49.350 An appeal against a misdeclaration penalty was dismissed in a case where a gold dealer had reclaimed input tax without supporting invoices. The tribunal rejected the trader's contention that he should have been allowed to use the 'self-billing' method of issuing invoices. *C Glinski (t/a Redcliffe Precious Metals), LON/92/2752A & LON/93/169 (VTD 11300)*.

49.351 A similar decision was reached in *WFS Metals Ltd, MAN/93/914 (VTD 12293)*.

49.352 There have been a number of other cases in which misdeclaration penalties have been imposed on traders who have reclaimed input tax on the basis of documents not constituting tax invoices. In the interests of space, such cases are not reported individually in this book.

49.353 **Associated partnerships—circular transactions.**   A partnership reclaimed input tax in respect of certain invoices relating to alleged purchases from an associated partnership with different return periods. A VAT officer formed the opinion that the transactions were fictitious and that the invoices had been created for the purpose of obtaining repayments of VAT which would give the partnerships a cash-flow advantage. The Commissioners issued an assessment to recover the tax, and also imposed a misdeclaration penalty. The tribunal dismissed the partnership's appeals, holding that the assessments had been made to the best of the Commissioners' judgment, that there were reasonable grounds for regarding the invoices as fictitious, that the partnerships had not submitted evidence to prove that the transactions had actually taken place, and that there was no reasonable excuse for the partnership's incorrect claims. *CAL Ingot Manufacturers, LON/93/816 (VTD 12298, 13069)*.

Miscellaneous

Cases where the appellant was successful

49.354   **Error corrected before due date—whether a reasonable excuse.**   Two partners took over a business of selling and hiring videotapes. They mistakenly believed that the letting on hire of videotapes was not subject to VAT, and therefore accounted for VAT only on sales, rather than on receipts from hire and sales. Their return, for the period ending 30 June 1990, was submitted on 6 July and the figures were queried by VAT Central Unit. A VAT officer visited the partners and informed them that the hiring out of videotapes was standard-rated. The partners submitted an amended return and a cheque for the tax due. The amended return and cheque were both received before the due date. However, the Commissioners imposed a misdeclaration penalty. The partners appealed, contending that they had a reasonable excuse as they had genuinely misunderstood the rating of their supplies and had shown their good faith by correcting the error before the due date. The tribunal accepted this contention and allowed their appeal. Applying *Jenkinson*, 48.80 PENALTIES: FAILURE TO NOTIFY, 'there is no overriding rule of law in relation to the words "reasonable excuse" that ignorance or mistake of law can never be an excuse'. The mistake had been put right before the due date and this was 'not an appropriate case to impose the penalty'. *T & D Kennedy, [1991] VATTR 157 (VTD 5880)*.

49.355   **Dishonesty of former director.**   A company required one of its directors to resign after discovering that he had misappropriated company funds. Subsequently a VAT officer discovered that management charges, for which the director in question was responsible, had not been accounted for in the relevant VAT return. The Commissioners imposed a misdeclaration penalty but the tribunal allowed the company's appeal, holding that there was no reason for the continuing directors to have suspected the error, and that the circumstances constituted a reasonable excuse. *Foster Penny Ltd, EDN/92/46 (VTD 7716)*.

49.356   **Incorrect Retail Scheme operated.**   An appeal was allowed in a case where a trader had continued to operate a Retail Scheme for which his business was no longer eligible. *JT Darvill, LON/92/560Z (VTD 9299)*. (*Note.* For another issue in this case, see 18.491 DEFAULT SURCHARGE.)

49.357   **Incorrect operation of Tour Operators' Margin Scheme.**   A company which carried on business as a tour operator, and operated the Tour Operators' Margin Scheme, submitted a return for November 1991 in which it failed to make the annual adjustment required by the Scheme for the year ending 31 October 1991, and consequently underdeclared tax by more than £1,000,000. The Commissioners imposed a misdeclaration penalty, and the company appealed, contending that it had a reasonable excuse for its inability to make the adjustment in time. The tribunal allowed the appeal, observing that the Tour Operators' Scheme was 'a highly complicated scheme which clearly puts an additional burden on traders in that field beyond the normal requirements of the VAT system'. The company had only a short period of time to make the necessary calculations, and had submitted the necessary details to the Commissioners in February 1992, which was not unreasonable in view of the complexity of the case. Accordingly, the circumstances constituted a reasonable excuse for the misdeclaration. (The tribunal observed that 'the company would be ill-advised to suppose that the same result would necessarily be achieved in respect of a future period when the circumstances might be different'.) *Owners Abroad Group plc, LON/92/859Y (VTD 9354).*

49.358   Other cases.   There have been a small number of other cases turning on very unusual facts in which tribunals have found that the particular circumstances have constituted a reasonable excuse, but where the nature of the case is such that it is of little if any value as a precedent. In the interests of space, such cases have not been summarised individually in this book. For such cases reported up to 31 December 1995, see Tolley's VAT Cases 1996.

Cases where the appellant was unsuccessful

49.359   Return amended to deduct output tax previously accounted for in respect of unpaid invoice.   A trader carried out work for a customer and accounted for the relevant VAT in his return for the period ending 31 July 1990. However, the customer was in financial difficulty and did not pay for the work. The trader therefore deducted the output tax in question in his return for the period ending 31 October 1990. When the Commissioners discovered this, they imposed a misdeclaration penalty. The tribunal dismissed the trader's appeal, holding that there was no reasonable excuse for the deduction. *R Clark (t/a Norblast), EDN/91/ 181 (VTD 7043).*

49.360   Wages deducted in computing tax liability.   A sole trader, who operated a business of hiring sunbeds, deducted the wages which he paid to his employees in computing his VAT liability. The Commissioners imposed a misdeclaration penalty, and the tribunal dismissed the trader's appeal, holding that there was no reasonable excuse for the misdeclaration. *W Graham (t/a Sunlover Sunbeds), EDN/92/303 (VTD 10148).*

49.361   Company claiming to have been misdirected by VAT officer.   A company appealed against a misdeclaration penalty, contending that it had a reasonable excuse because it had been misdirected by a VAT officer. The tribunal dismissed the appeal, finding that the officer had not misdirected the company. *Albany Building Services Ltd, EDN/92/335 (VTD 11294).*

49.362   Other cases.   There have been many other cases, which appear to raise no point of general importance, in which appeals against misdeclaration penalties have been dismissed. In the interests of space, such cases are not reported individually in this book.

WHETHER ERROR VOLUNTARILY DISCLOSED (VATA 1994, s 63(10)(b))

49.363   In the case noted at 49.58 above, the error in the return was noticed by the council's principal accountant while he was collecting papers for a VAT officer who was conducting a control visit. The council contended that the penalty should be discharged because its own accountant had brought the error to the attention of the VAT officer. The tribunal rejected this contention, finding that the error had been discovered at a time when the Commissioners were making enquiries into the council's tax affairs, so that the conditions of what is now *VATA 1994, s 63(10)(b)* were not satisfied. The tribunal held that the purpose of *s 63(10)(b)* was 'to provide a defence to a taxpayer who makes a truly voluntary disclosure; and a disclosure made under the shadow of an official review is not a voluntary disclosure as envisaged'. *Taunton Deane Borough Council, LON/90/1225Z (VTD 5545).*

49.364   Similar decisions were reached in *Tyre Team Ltd, LON/91/34X (VTD 6407); Shipquay Enterprises Ltd, BEL/91/38 (VTD 6741); Venture Capital Ltd, MAN/90/ 899 (VTD 6794); Rhymney Valley District Council, LON/91/722 (VTD 6939);*

S Atkinson, MAN/90/1053 (VTD 6989); Jones & Attwood Ltd, MAN/91/729 (VTD 7046); Redland Timber Co Ltd, LON/91/2217Z (VTD 7558); Elmec (Blackburn) Ltd, MAN/92/445 (VTD 9222); WB Crewlyn (Electrical Contractors) Ltd, LON/92/2608 (VTD 10027); Holden Plant Hire Ltd, LON/92/300X (VTD 10685); Orchard Associates Ltd, MAN/93/734 (11576); Wall Colmonoy Ltd, LON/92/1385P (13210); Whitehead & Wood Ltd, 49.59 above; *Tong Garden Centre plc,* 49.59 above; *Springvale EPS Ltd,* 49.124 above; *GJ Bennett & Co (Builders) Ltd,* 49.209 above, and *Thornsett Structures Ltd,* 49.380 below.

49.365   A company appointed a new financial director in June 1990. After his appointment, he discovered that there were several errors in the company's records. When a control visit was arranged, he informed the VAT office that he had discovered two errors in previous VAT returns, and would welcome the visit, which took place in October 1990. During the visit, the VAT officer discovered further errors, in respect of which a misdeclaration penalty was imposed. The company appealed, contending that it had made a full disclosure and that the penalty should be waived under what is now *VATA 1994, s 63(10)(b)*. The tribunal dismissed the appeal, applying *dicta* in *Taunton Deane Borough Council,* 49.363 above. The fact that there were errors in the company's returns had not been disclosed until after the Commissioners had sought to arrange a control visit. Accordingly, the disclosure had not been made at a time when the company 'had no reason to believe that enquiries were being made', as required by what is now *VATA 1994, s 63(10)(b)*. Further, although the company had disclosed that there were errors in its returns, it had not supplied 'full information with respect to the inaccuracy concerned'. *Vernon Packaging Ltd, LON/91/233Z (VTD 6360)*.

49.366   *Taunton Deane Borough Council,* 49.363 above, and *Vernon Packaging Ltd,* 49.365 above, were applied in the similar case of *Britannia Steel Ltd, LON/92/892 (VTD 11675)*.

49.367   A borough council submitted a return for May 1990 which included cumulative figures for both April and May instead of the monthly figures for May. For June 1990 it submitted a return which included the cumulative figures for April, May and June. The Commissioners queried the June return and the council's senior accountant discovered the errors. She notified the VAT office of the errors by telephone. The Commissioners imposed a misdeclaration penalty, and the council appealed, contending that it had voluntarily furnished the Commissioners with full information regarding the inaccuracies concerned, so that what is now *VATA 1994, s 63(10)(b)* applied. The tribunal accepted this contention and allowed the appeal. The fact that the voluntary disclosure had not occurred until after the Commissioners had queried the June return did not alter the fact that the council had supplied full information concerning the errors. Accordingly, this was not 'a suitable case for a penalty to be imposed'. *Tewkesbury Borough Council, MAN/90/765 (VTD 5773)*.

49.368   An appeal was allowed in a case where a company which had discovered a misdeclaration sent the Commissioners a cheque for the tax due, without providing a written explanation of the circumstances. The Commissioners, instead of asking the company for details of the payment, repaid it. A VAT officer discovered the misdeclaration at a control visit, and a penalty was imposed. The tribunal held that the penalty was not due, since the company had effectively advised the Commissioners of the misdeclaration when it had sent a cheque for the tax due, and the Commissioners should have requested further information instead of repaying the amount to the company. *Maston (Property Holding) Ltd, LON/91/974 (VTD 6564)*.

49.369   A company reclaimed input tax in respect of work carried out on developing a hotel and restaurant. Some of the invoices in question were made out to the directors, rather than in the name of the company. The directors advised the company's VAT office of this in October 1990, before a control visit took place. However, the Commissioners imposed a misdeclaration penalty. The tribunal allowed the company's appeal, holding that the company had made a voluntary disclosure within what is now *VATA 1994, s 63(10)(b)*. *Gean House Hotel Ltd, EDN/91/164 (VTD 6687)*.

49.370   On 30 September 1990 a company submitted an invoice to an associated partnership for work done. The input tax shown on the invoice was included in the partnership's return for the relevant period, but the output tax was not included in the company's return. In November a VAT officer made a control visit to the partnership and examined the invoice in question. The senior partner told the VAT officer that the output tax had not been included in the company's September return, because the company could not afford to pay the tax charged, but would be included in the following return. The Commissioners imposed a misdeclaration penalty on the company. The company appealed, contending that it had made a voluntary disclosure within what is now *VATA 1994, s 63(10)(b)*. The tribunal accepted this contention and allowed the appeal. At the time of the disclosure, the Commissioners were making enquiries into the partnership's affairs, but they were not making any enquiries into the company's affairs. *Moor Lodge Developments Ltd, LON/91/2192X (VTD 7285)*. (*Note*. Compare the subsequent case of *FR Jenks (Overseas) Ltd*, 49.374 below, in which a tribunal held that the fact that a control visit had not been arranged to inspect the affairs of an appellant company, but to inspect the affairs of an associated company, did not provide a defence against the penalty, since 'the wording of (*VATA 1994, s 63(10)(b)**) does not limit its scope to formal enquiries, or those of which advance warning has been given, but include impromptu enquiries of the kind which occurred here'.)

49.371   An appeal was allowed in a case where the tribunal accepted a company's evidence that its managing director had told a VAT officer that invoices relating to a contract with Cambridgeshire County Council had not been included in its returns, but that it had accounted for tax on the contract in question on a cash basis, since there were long delays in receiving payment from the Council. The tribunal found that 'the disclosure was made at a time when the appellant company had no reason to believe that enquiries were being made by the Commissioners into its affairs', and held that it was sufficient for the director 'to have volunteered the nature of the error and the periods in which it had occurred'. *Bekelect Ltd, LON/92/126X (VTD 7779)*.

49.372   *Bekelect Ltd*, 49.371 above, was applied in a subsequent case where the tribunal found that a company's director had made a voluntary disclosure by telephone to the local VAT office. *Knockhatch Leisure Ltd, LON/93/14P (VTD 10518)*.

49.373   A company, which was a member of a group, received a control visit by a VAT officer in November 1991. Following the visit, the officer wrote to the company in December 1991 querying five transactions with a company which was not a member of the group for VAT purposes, and a recent share issue. The company did not reply to the letter, but in January 1992 the company's accountant met the company's auditors to review its VAT affairs. The auditors ascertained that the company had failed to account for VAT on four management charges within the group of companies. In March 1992 the company wrote to its local VAT office disclosing this, and the Commissioners imposed a misdeclaration penalty. The company appealed, contending that it had made a voluntary disclosure within what is now *VATA 1994, s 63(10)*. The tribunal accepted this contention and allowed the appeal, holding that, since the question of intra-group management charges had not been discussed at the

November 1991 control visit, or referred to in the VAT officer's letter of December 1991, 'the voluntary disclosure was not therefore the response of the taxpayers to (the officer's) letter'. At the time the voluntary disclosure was made, the company had no 'reason to believe that enquiries were being made into the matter of management charges within the company grouping'. *Hunter Saphir plc, LON/92/1941 (VTD 10770)*.

49.374   A company reclaimed input tax in respect of a management charge which it had paid to its holding company. A VAT officer made a control visit to the company. During the visit she also asked to see the holding company's books. While she was looking at these, one of the directors of the two companies admitted that, although the subsidiary company had reclaimed input tax in respect of the management charge, the holding company had not accounted for the relevant output tax. The Commissioners imposed a misdeclaration penalty on the holding company. The holding company appealed, contending that it had made a voluntary disclosure. The tribunal dismissed the appeal. The fact that the control visit had been arranged to inspect the records of the subsidiary company, rather than those of the holding company, was not material. Applying *dicta* in *Taunton Deane Borough Council*, 49.363 above, 'the wording of (*VATA 1994, s 63(10)(b)*) does not limit its scope to formal enquiries, or those of which advance warning has been given, but includes impromptu enquiries of the kind which occurred here'. *FR Jenks (Overseas) Ltd, MAN/91/1142 (VTD 8858)*.

49.375   There have been a number of other cases in which the appellant has contended that an error has been voluntarily disclosed, but the tribunal has found that the conditions of what is now *VATA 1994, s 63(10)(b)* have not been satisfied, and has dismissed the appeal. In the interests of space, such cases are not included in this book.

MITIGATION OF PENALTIES (VATA 1994, s 70)

Cases where the penalty was mitigated by the tribunal

49.376   **Underdeclaration of takings—misdeclaration penalty imposed—mitigation of penalty.**   The Commissioners discovered that a married couple who operated a public house had not declared the whole of their takings. They therefore issued an estimated assessment and imposed a misdeclaration penalty of £2,391. The tribunal upheld both the assessment and the penalty in principle, finding that the assessment had been made to the best of the Commissioners' judgment. However, the tribunal also held that the penalty should be reduced by £378. *DG & C Sessions, MAN/92/490 (VTD 13162)*.

49.377   A partnership understated its takings by £100,000 in the period ending February 1996. (The partnership declared its net sales as £60,000 rather than £160,000.) The Commissioners imposed a misdeclaration penalty, mitigated by 25%. The tribunal upheld the penalty in principle, but directed that it should be mitigated by 50%. The chairman considered that 'a 75% penalty would be appropriate for a business which had behaved reprehensibly over a period of time (but) was not appropriate for a business which, until this incident, had had an exemplary record'. *DR Evans & GL Rees (t/a L & R Building Contractors), MAN/97/841 (VTD 15738)*.

49.378   **Failure to account for output tax on transfers to associated company.**   A partnership transferred some of its fixed assets to an associated company, but failed to account for output tax on the transfers. The Commissioners imposed a misdeclaration penalty, and the partnership appealed, contending firstly that there was a reasonable excuse for the misdeclaration, and alternatively that the penalty should be mitigated. The tribunal rejected the first contention, holding that the circumstances did not amount to a 'reasonable excuse'. However, the tribunal held that, in view of the unusual nature of the transactions, and 'the generally good record of the partnership in its VAT affairs', the penalty should be mitigated by 50%. *Dicta* in *Jordan*, 48.139 PENALTIES: FAILURE TO NOTIFY, and *Cohen*, 48.140 PENALTIES: FAILURE TO NOTIFY, applied. *I & N Martin (t/a Beechwood Studios), LON/95/24P (VTD 13805)*.

49.379   In another case where a company had failed to account for output tax on supplies to subsidiary companies, the tribunal upheld the penalty in principle but mitigated it by 50% to take account 'of the complexity and of the fact of the paper nature of the transaction'. *Clycan Management Ltd, EDN/99/218 (VTD 16651)*.

49.380   In a case where three associated companies had failed to account for output tax on certain supplies to another associated company, the Commissioners imposed a penalty at the rate of 15% of the evaded tax. The tribunal upheld the penalty in principle but reduced it to 10% of the evaded tax to take account of co-operation. *Thornsett Structures Ltd (and related appeals), LON/x (VTD 15934)*. (*Note*. The tribunal also held that the penalty had not been voluntarily disclosed—see 49.364 above.)

49.381   **Failure to account for output tax on sale of property.**   A company owned eleven garages, from which it derived rental income. It sold the garages to its controlling director and failed to account for output tax on the sale. The Commissioners imposed a misdeclaration penalty, mitigated by 25%. The company appealed, contending firstly that there was a reasonable excuse for the misdeclaration, and alternatively that the penalty should be mitigated. The tribunal rejected the first contention, holding that the circumstances did not amount to a 'reasonable excuse'. However, the tribunal held that the penalty should be mitigated by 75% since this was an unusual transaction and the director's accountant had not warned him about the VAT liability. The chairman commented that 'it might have been expected that a chartered accountant experienced in tax matters, and whose advice he sought about the disposal of the property, would have adverted to the question without prompting by a lay client . . . the tribunal considers that (the director) did not receive the advice he was entitled to expect'. *Porters End Estates Ltd, LON/98/700 (VTD 15872)*.

49.382   A company sold a property, in respect of which it had elected to waive exemption. It failed to account for output tax on the sale and the Commissioners imposed a misdeclaration penalty. The tribunal upheld the penalty in principle but mitigated it by 75%. *Nightingale Holdings, LON/132/00 (VTD 16721)*.

49.383   **Supplies incorrectly treated as zero-rated—mitigation of penalty.**   In 1995 and 1996 a company transported a quantity of goods from the UK to France and failed to account for output tax on these supplies. The Commissioners imposed a misdeclaration penalty and the company appealed, contending firstly that it had a reasonable excuse because the services had been zero-rated before 1993 and its directors had been unaware of the change in the law, and alternatively that the penalty should be mitigated. The tribunal held that, applying 'the standpoint of the reasonable businessman', the company did not have a reasonable excuse. However, the tribunal directed that the penalty should be mitigated by 75%, observing that the director in question had acted in accordance with her understanding of the law and that a passage in the current issue of *Notice No 744* was misleading and could have led her to believe that the supplies still qualified for zero-rating. *Premiair Charter Ltd, LON/97/252 (VTD 15129)*.

49.384   In a case where a builder had incorrectly treated supplies as zero-rated, the tribunal held that there was no reasonable excuse for the misdeclaration, but directed that the penalty should be mitigated by 50%. *AB Mearns, EDN/00/76 (VTD 16947)*.

49.385   **Supplies incorrectly treated as exempt—mitigation of penalty.** The proprietor of a hairdressing salon failed to account for output tax on income from letting chairs at the salon to other stylists. The Commissioners imposed a misdeclaration penalty and the stylist appealed, contending that he had believed that the payments qualified for exemption. The tribunal upheld the penalty in principle, holding that there was no reasonable excuse for the misdeclaration, but mitigated the penalty by 75% to take account of the fact that the appellant had been badly advised by an accountant. The tribunal observed that the 'reduction is in recognition of the fact that there was a serious misdeclaration but also that the actings (*sic*) of an agent have got to be accepted and paid for by the principal however incorrect'. *H Jamieson, EDN/98/157, 99/65 & 99/97 (VTD 16476)*.

49.386   **Duplicated claim to input tax—mitigation of penalty.** A property development company claimed input tax in respect of an architect's certificate in December 1994, although it did not receive the relevant invoice or make the relevant payment until January 1995. The Commissioners imposed a misdeclaration penalty. The tribunal held that there was no reasonable excuse for the misdeclaration (distinguishing *Clean Car Co Ltd*, 49.83 above), but held that the penalty should be mitigated by 50%. *Robert S Monk Ltd, MAN/95/2679 (VTD 14346)*.

49.387   The Commissioners imposed a misdeclaration penalty on a company which had duplicated a claim to input tax. The company appealed, contending that the misdeclaration was attributable to a clerical error by its computer operator. The tribunal held that there was no reasonable excuse for the misdeclaration, but directed that the penalty be reduced from £4,871 to £3,000 to take account of mitigation. *Dunelm (Castle Homes) Ltd, MAN/98/824 (VTD 16052)*.

49.388   **Overclaim of input tax—mitigation of penalty.** A company which carried on a contracting business overclaimed input tax by more than £23,000 as a result of a mistake by its office manager. The Commissioners imposed a misdeclaration penalty and the company appealed. The tribunal allowed the appeal in part, holding that there was no reasonable excuse for the error, but observing that the company had previously had 'an unblemished VAT record' and that the office manager had been working for 12 hours each day. The tribunal directed that the penalty should be mitigated by 70%. *Robert S Monk Ltd*, 49.386 above, applied; *Derbyshire*, 49.407 below, distinguished. *R Moulding (Contractors Plant) Ltd, MAN/x (VTD 15102)*.

49.389   A penalty was mitigated by 80% in a case where the tribunal found that an overclaim of input tax was attributable to an isolated clerical error by a 'competent and diligent bookkeeper'. *Marine Electronic Services Ltd, LON/96/1983 (VTD 15172)*.

49.390   A company reclaimed input tax in respect of two purchases from Germany. The Commissioners imposed a misdeclaration penalty. The tribunal held that the company should have sought advice, so that there was no reasonable excuse for the misdeclaration, but mitigated the penalty by 20% because the wording of form VAT 100 was 'confusing'. *The Edinburgh Piano Company Ltd, EDN/99/42 (VTD 16132)*.

49.391   A penalty was mitigated by 40% in a case where a couple who operated a public house had reclaimed input tax without invoices. *N & T Foster (t/a Foster Leisure), MAN/97/1060 (VTD 16617)*.

49.392   **Input tax reclaimed on exempt supplies.** A company reclaimed input tax relating to exempt supplies, although the value of such supplies exceeded the *de minimis* limits. The Commissioners imposed a penalty, mitigated by 20%. The tribunal upheld the penalty in principle, holding that there was no reasonable excuse for the misdeclaration, but directed that the penalty should be mitigated by one-third. *Crestbond Ltd, LON/96/1582 (VTD 15728)*.

49.393   **Incorrect partial exemption computation—overclaim of input tax.** A golf club, which was partly exempt, overclaimed input tax as a result of an error in computing its annual adjustment for the year ended 31 March 1995. The tribunal upheld the penalty in principle, holding that there was no reasonable excuse for the misdeclaration, but directed that the penalty should be mitigated by 75% to take account of the club's 'unblemished record in VAT matters' and the fact that its treasurer had been misled by a misleading article in a golfing magazine. *Hexham Golf Club, MAN/97/454 (VTD 15286).*

49.394   In a case where a company which was partly exempt had reclaimed too much input tax, the Commissioners imposed a penalty which they mitigated by 50%, but the tribunal increased the mitigation to 75%. *Adam Smith Ltd, EDN/99/87 (VTD 16282).*

49.395   In the case noted at 43.64 PARTIAL EXEMPTION, the tribunal upheld a penalty in principle, holding that the complexity of the partial exemption provisions was not a reasonable excuse, but mitigated the penalty by 25% since the law was 'complicated and constantly changing and ... the Commissioners' published guidance on the point is not always of the clearest'. *Trustees of the Whitbread Harrowden Settlement (and related appeals), LON/99/1091 (VTD 16781).*

49.396   **Input tax wrongly reclaimed by agent—unclear advice by local VAT office—mitigation of penalty.** A trader reclaimed input tax in respect of two transactions for which he had acted as an agent. The Commissioners imposed a penalty and the trader appealed, contending firstly that he had a reasonable excuse because of the nature of the transactions and alternatively that the penalty should be mitigated. The tribunal rejected the first contention, observing that this was not 'a complex liability matter' and that 'the reasonable and conscientious businessman has an obligation to consider his VAT position', so that there was no reasonable excuse for the misdeclarations. However, the tribunal found that the trader had visited his local VAT office between the two transactions, and that, while the VAT officer to whom he spoke had 'tried to explain the procedures to him in a measure of detail, . . . the position may not have been explained very clearly'. Accordingly, the tribunal directed that the penalty in respect of the second transaction should be mitigated by 50%. *MJ Evans (t/a ATC), MAN/96/452 (VTD 14665).*

49.397   **'Self-billing' invoices—underdeclaration of output tax—mitigation of penalty.** In a case where a contractor had accepted 'self-billing' invoices which did not charge VAT, the tribunal held that there was no reasonable excuse for the misdeclaration, but mitigated the penalty by 90% to take account of co-operation. *W Beveridge, EDN/99/54 (VTD 16205).*

49.398   **Output tax accounted for on cash basis—input tax reclaimed on receipt of invoices—mitigation of penalty.** A trader accounted for output tax on the basis of payments received, but reclaimed input tax when he received invoices, rather than when he paid for the items in question. When the Commissioners discovered this, they imposed a misdeclaration penalty, computed on the basis that the retailer had underdeclared output tax, and mitigated by 50%. The trader appealed. The tribunal held that there was no reasonable excuse for the misdeclaration, but that the penalty should be mitigated in full. The tribunal observed that the retailer had been eligible to operate the cash accounting scheme, and had apparently been attempting to do so. The penalty would have been 'substantially less' if it had been computed on the basis that the retailer had been claiming input tax prematurely, rather than on the basis that he had been dilatory in accounting for output tax. The trader had co-operated fully, had not attempted to conceal any part of the transactions, and had made a 'genuine mistake'. *PG Morrison, EDN/97/49 (VTD 15244).*

49.399   **Inadequate estimated assessments—incompetence of accountant—mitigation of penalty.**   A trader failed to appeal against a number of inadequate estimated assessments, and the Commissioners imposed a penalty under *VATA 1994, s 63(1)(b)*. The tribunal held that there was no reasonable excuse for the trader's conduct, but directed that the penalty should be mitigated by 30%. The chairman held that the fact that the trader 'was ill-informed as to the requirements of VAT law and his ... statutory obligations is not a mitigating factor; those who engage in business have some duty to inform themselves of what is required of them and of their fiscal obligations ... However, if one does employ an accountant one is entitled to expect that he will carry out his instructions competently.' The trader's accountant appeared 'to have done nothing, although it must have been clear to him that the appellant was relying upon him to do his accounts and to deal with the VAT returns'. *J Saunders-Pederson (t/a Advanced Information Systems UK), LON/98/222 (VTD 15675)*.

49.400   **Misleading advice from accountants—mitigation of penalty.**   A penalty was mitigated by 50% in a case where the tribunal held that a misdeclaration was 'entirely due to wrong advice' by the company's accountants. *M & J Investment Co Ltd, MAN/00/669 (VTD 16996)*.

49.401   **Mitigation allowed—other cases.**   In a case where a Swedish company had failed to account for output tax on supplies in the UK, the tribunal directed that the penalty should be mitigated by 75%. *Wartsila NSD Sweden AB, EDN/00/78 (VTD 16921)*.

49.402   In a case where the facts were not fully set out in the decision, the tribunal directed that the amount by which a penalty was to be mitigated should be increased from 50% to 75%. *PK Graphics, LON/96/41 (VTD 14117)*.

49.403   A similar decision was reached in *BL & GJ Alford, LON/97/1027 (VTD 15310)*.

Cases where the penalty was mitigated by the Commissioners

49.404   **Penalty mitigated by Commissioners—no further mitigation appropriate.**   In a case where a partnership had reclaimed input tax prematurely, the Commissioners imposed a misdeclaration penalty which they mitigated by 50%. The tribunal dismissed the partnership's appeal, holding that there was no reasonable excuse and no grounds for any further mitigation. *WHD, PM & AD Hobson, MAN/96/591 (VTD 14671)*.

49.405   In a case where a restaurant proprietor had underdeclared output tax, the Commissioners imposed a misdeclaration penalty which they mitigated by 55% to take account of co-operation. The tribunal dismissed the proprietor's appeal, holding on the evidence that the mitigation allowed by the Commissioners was 'positively generous' and 'should have amply satisfied both the appellant and his advisers'. *SM Choudhury (t/a Eastcheap Tandoori), LON/96/1754 (VTD 15003)*.

49.406   In a case where a trader had underdeclared her tax liability as a result of a clerical error, the Commissioners imposed a misdeclaration penalty which they mitigated by 10%. The trader appealed, contending that the penalty should be mitigated further. The tribunal rejected this contention and dismissed the appeal, observing that the trader had failed to make a voluntary disclosure when her accountant had drawn the matter to her attention, and that she was 'fortunate in having received 10% mitigation'. *E Williams (t/a Memories on Video), LON/96/60 (VTD 14960)*.

Cases where the penalty was not mitigated

49.407   **Whether returns incorrect through incompetence or recklessness—whether any grounds for mitigation of penalty.**   A sole trader appealed against three misdeclaration penalties. His accountant contended that the penalties should be mitigated on the grounds that the errors 'were the result of incompetence rather than recklessness'. The tribunal dismissed the appeal, holding that there was no reasonable excuse and finding that there were also no grounds for mitigation, since the trader's wife, who completed the returns in question, had admitted that she guessed at some of the figures which she had included. *Dicta* in *Jordan*, 48.139 PENALTIES: FAILURE TO NOTIFY, applied. *CB Derbyshire, MAN/94/505 (VTD 12963)*.

49.408   **Underdeclaration of takings—whether any grounds for mitigation of penalty.**   The Commissioners imposed misdeclaration penalties on the proprietor of a Chinese restaurant, after discovering that he had underdeclared takings. The proprietor appealed, contending that the penalties should be mitigated. The tribunal dismissed the appeal, holding on the evidence that there were no grounds for mitigation of the penalties. The chairman observed that 'a penalty should be mitigated only where the trader, by co-operation or remorse, or for some other similar reason, has demonstrated that it is deserved. That is plainly not the case here.' *PDJ Lee (t/a Jumbo Express), MAN/95/1126 & 1312 (VTD 14127)*.

49.409   **Input tax reclaimed on purchase of cars—whether any grounds for mitigation of penalty.**   A company reclaimed input tax on the purchase of a Mercedes and a Range Rover. The Commissioners issued an assessment to recover the tax, and imposed a misdeclaration penalty. The company appealed, contending that it should be entitled to reclaim the input tax because it had purchased the vehicles in order to lease them to an associated company. The tribunal dismissed the appeal, holding that the effect of *Input Tax Order, Article 7(2G)(a)* was that the tax was not deductible. Furthermore, there was no reasonable excuse for the misdeclaration and there were no grounds for mitigation, since, although the tribunal accepted 'on the balance of probabilities' that the company had acted in good faith, the effect of *VATA 1994, s 70(4)(c)* was that 'acting in good faith is specifically excluded when a tribunal considers mitigation'. *West Midlands Motors Ltd, MAN/98/990 (VTD 16512)*.

49.410   **Application for mitigation rejected.**   Applications for penalties to be mitigated were rejected in *Hunters Hereditaments Ltd, MAN/96/637 (VTD 14748); K Kaur & N Singh (t/a Andy's Fish Bar), MAN/96/772 (VTD 14857); European Lift Services Ltd, LON/98/261 (VTD 15551); J Ali & F Rahman (t/a Dilraj Indian Tandoori Takeaway), LON/x/294 (VTD 16277); A & A Ali (t/a Dos Tandoori & Balti House Restaurant), LON/99/1220 (VTD 16803); AR Vig (t/a One by One Fashions)*, 49.199 above; *Bourne*, 49.207 above, and *Dinglis Property Services Ltd*, 49.330 above.

VALIDITY OF THE PENALTY

49.411   **Whether misdeclaration penalty contrary to principle of 'proportionality'.**   The Commissioners imposed a misdeclaration penalty on a company which had failed to include output tax of more than £36,000 on a monthly return. The company appealed, contending that the penalty should be regarded as void since it was contrary to the legal principle of 'proportionality'. The tribunal rejected this contention and dismissed the appeal. Applying *R v Secretary of State for the Home Department (ex p. Brind), HL [1991] 2 WLR 588; [1991] 1 All ER 720*, 'the doctrine of proportionality is not a part of the law of the United Kingdom'. It followed that 'the penalties imposed by Parliament can only be struck down if they infringe a clear principle of European law which is binding on the Government of this country'. Applying *Amsterdam Bulb v Produktsckap voor Sietegewassen, CJEC [1977] ECR 137*, the Treaty of Rome 'allows the various Member States to choose the measures which they consider appropriate' to ensure the fulfilment of the Treaty obligations. *FA 1985, s 14* had been enacted following a detailed report after considering a great deal of evidence, and it was 'clear that the UK Government considered the penalties appropriate for the purpose of enforcing the provisions of the *EC Sixth Directive* which related to the rendering and accuracy of returns'. It would be an abuse of the jurisdiction of the tribunal for it to interfere with the decision of Parliament. *W Emmett & Son Ltd, [1991] VATTR 456 (VTD 5459, 6516)*.

49.412   The tribunal decision in *W Emmett & Son Ltd*, 49.411 above, was approved by the QB in a case in which Simon Brown J observed that 'member States must inevitably have the very widest margin of appreciation for determining just what penalties are appropriate to underpin the efficient functioning of the value added tax system'; and that, while *FA 1985, s 14* was 'a blunt and heavy instrument', this was 'a feature of penalties imposed to encourage the initiation and maintenance of better procedures rather than necessarily an indication of disproportionality'. *C & E Commrs v The Peninsular & Oriental Steam Navigation Co plc (t/a P & O Ferries), QB [1992] STC 809.* (Note. Another issue in this case, concerning the interpretation of *FA 1985, s 14(4)*, was taken to the CA. However, the relevant legislation was subsequently amended by *FA 1994, s 45* to reverse the effect of the CA decision, which is no longer relevant to the current legislation.)

49.413   **Whether Commissioners' discretionary power in imposing penalties exercised unreasonably.**   In one of the cases noted at 49.37 above, the company contended that the Commissioners had exercised their discretion unreasonably in imposing the penalty. The tribunal rejected this contention, holding that the tribunal's power of supervision in such a case was supervisory rather than appellate, and that the onus was for the appellant to establish that the Commissioners had acted unreasonably, applying the principles in *Associated Provincial Picture Houses Ltd v Wednesbury Corporation, CA 1947, [1948] 1 KB 223; [1947] 2 All ER 680*. On the evidence, it had not been unreasonable for the Commissioners to have imposed a penalty in this case, notwithstanding that the tribunal had held that the circumstances constituted a reasonable excuse for the misdeclaration in question. *Food Engineering Ltd, [1992] VATTR 327 (VTD 7787)*. (Note. Obiter dicta of the tribunal chairman were subsequently disapproved by the QB in *Dollar Land (Feltham) Ltd*, 18.568 DEFAULT SURCHARGE.)

49.414   Similar decisions, also applying *Associated Provincial Picture Houses Ltd v Wednesbury Corporation, CA 1947, [1948] 1 KB 223; [1947] 2 All ER 680*, were reached in *Pilling House Properties Ltd, MAN/93/812 (VTD 12965)* and *Analog & Numeric Devices Ltd*, 49.160 above.

49.415   *Food Engineering Ltd*, 49.413 above, was distinguished in a subsequent case where the Commissioners had written a letter to a company stating that 'the imposition of the penalty is not at the discretion of the individual officer. A penalty is imposed automatically when a detected error fails the objective tests set out in *FA 1985, s 14*'. The VAT officer responsible for imposing the penalty stated in evidence that he had followed the Commissioners' instructions and had acted on the basis that 'if a return fails the objective tests set out in *FA 1985, s 14* then a serious misdeclaration penalty is imposed automatically unless it has been corrected in the next return'. The tribunal allowed the company's appeal, holding that the effect of what is now *VATA 1994, s 76(1)* was that the Commissioners had a discretionary power, rather than a mandatory duty, to impose a penalty, and that they were at fault in not having considered whether they should have exercised their discretion not to impose the penalty. The tribunal chairman (Miss Gort, sitting alone) made 'no finding as to whether or not there was in fact a reasonable excuse' but held that 'the fact that the Commissioners reviewed the decision to impose a penalty subsequently is of no avail to them: there is a statutory requirement that they exercise their discretion, and this must be done before imposing the penalty, not afterwards'. *Tamdown Ltd, LON/92/ 2921P (VTD 10180)*. (*Notes*. (1) The decision in this case was specifically disapproved by the QB in the subsequent case of *Dollar Land (Feltham) Ltd*, 18.568 DEFAULT SURCHARGE. Judge J held that the right of appeal to a VAT tribunal provided for by what is now *VATA 1994, s 83* did not include a right to appeal against the Commissioners' discretionary power whether or not to make a penalty assessment. The remedy against any improper exercise of the Commissioners' discretionary power to impose a penalty would be an application for judicial review. (2) Compare the direct tax case of *Baylis v Roberts & Roberts, Ch D [1989] STC 693 (TTC 2001, 53.7)*, in which the Ch D held that the use of the word 'may' in tax legislation did not confer a general discretion as to whether an assessment should be raised, and that an inspector had acted correctly in considering that it was his mandatory duty to issue an assessment. Miss Gort's decision in *Tamdown* makes no reference to the Ch D decision in *Baylis v Roberts*.)

49.416 A similar decision was reached (again by Miss Gort sitting alone) in *J Abassi, LON/92/1053 (VTD 10411)*. (*Note*. See the notes following *Tamdown Ltd*, 49.415 above.)

50   Penalties: Regulatory Provisions

50.1   **Penalty under VATA 1994, s 69.**   A company carried on the business of selling women's clothing from market stalls. Its registered office was the premises of its accountants, but on its form VAT 1 it cited its principal director's house as its business address. The Commissioners wished to carry out a control visit to inspect the company's records in accordance with what is now *VATA 1994, Sch 11 para 7*, and asked the company to make its records available at its business address. The company failed to comply with repeated requests, and the Commissioners imposed a penalty under what is now *VATA 1994, s 69*. The tribunal dismissed the company's appeal against the penalty, holding that it was not unreasonable for the Commissioners to have required to inspect the records at the business address and that there was no reasonable excuse for the company's failure to comply with the notice. *Fabco Ltd, LON/92/1009Y (VTD 9739)*.

50.2   In January 1993 a VAT officer telephoned a construction company to arrange a control visit. The company subsequently telephoned the VAT office to cancel the appointment, and also cancelled several subsequent appointments. In July the Commissioners issued a formal notice calling for the production of specified documents in accordance with what is now *VATA 1994, Sch 11 para 7(2)*. The company did not produce the documents, and in February 1994 the Commissioners issued a penalty assessment under what is now *VATA 1994, s 69*, charging a penalty of £5 per day. The company appealed, contending that it had a reasonable excuse because the documents in question were held by its accountants. The tribunal dismissed the appeal, holding that the circumstances did not constitute a reasonable excuse. The company was obliged to produce the documents at its principal place of business 'and it should have been possible to arrange for the records to be returned for one day, or longer if necessary, to enable them to be inspected'. *HEM Construction Ltd, LON/94/489A (VTD 12449)*.

50.3   The company in the case noted at 50.2 above appealed against a subsequent penalty of £500. The tribunal dismissed the appeal, holding that there was no reasonable excuse for the company's failure to produce the required documents, and awarded costs of £300 to the Commissioners. *HEM Construction Ltd (No 2), LON/94/1964P (VTD 13203)*.

50.4   Appeals against penalties under *VATA 1994, s 69* were also dismissed *in M Safdar, MAN/95/1612 (VTD 13646); H, H & M Suleyman (t/a Red Rose Dry Cleaners), LON/95/2619 (VTD 13753)* and *T Dyer, EDN/97/178 & 230 (VTD 16359)*.

50.5   **Failure to submit EC sales statement—penalty under VATA 1994, s 66.**   The Commissioners imposed two penalties on a company under *VATA 1994, s 66* for failure to submit EC sales statements. The tribunal upheld the penalties and dismissed the company's appeal, finding that the notices had been validly served, that the company's system 'for preparing and despatching their *(sic)* EC sales statements was deficient' and that there was no reasonable excuse. *Sloan Electronics Ltd, MAN/98/596 (VTD 16062)*.

50.6   The Commissioners imposed a penalty of £500, under *VATA 1994, s 66*, on a trader who had failed to submit an EC sales statement. The trader appealed, contending that the penalty was unfair and disproportionate because his supplies in the relevant quarter had only totalled £178. The tribunal dismissed his appeal, finding that the notice had been validly served and observing that there were no powers of mitigation in the case of penalties under *s 66*. *M Radford (t/a Atlantis Trading Co), MAN/99/88 (VTD 16243)*.

50.7 Penalties: Regulatory Provisions

50.7   A partnership submitted an EC sales statement six weeks late and the Commissioners imposed a penalty of £215 under *VATA 1994, s 66*. The partnership appealed, contending that the penalty was unfair. The tribunal rejected this contention and dismissed the appeal. *Fitch (MW) & Slade (B) (t/a Michael W Fitch Antiques), LON/99/1292 (VTD 16880).*

50.8   The Commissioners imposed penalties under *VATA 1994, s 66* on an antique dealer who had failed to submit an EC sales statement. The dealer appealed, contending that he had a reasonable excuse because he had not received the relevant form VAT 101. The tribunal dismissed his appeal, holding that he should have requested a copy of the form, and that 'the simple failure to obtain the form when it was easily within his power to do so does not provide the appellant with a reasonable excuse. It is the taxpayer's responsibility to complete and submit the EC sales list by the due date, just as it is his responsibility to complete and submit his VAT return.' *J Proops (t/a JP Antiques), LON/99/744 (VTD 16409).*

50.9   A similar decision was reached in *Beaches Ltd, LON/97/569 (VTD 16448).*

50.10   The Commissioners imposed penalties on a company which had submitted two EC sales statements after the due date. The company appealed, contending that it had a reasonable excuse because its computer had broken down. The tribunal dismissed the appeal, holding on the evidence that the circumstances did not constitute a reasonable excuse. *CJW Manufacturing Ltd, LON/99/727 (VTD 16417).*

50.11   The Commissioners imposed penalties on a company which had submitted EC sales statements after the due date. The company appealed, contending that it had a reasonable excuse because it had had difficulties in obtaining correct registration numbers from customers in the Irish Republic (some of whom had cited nine-digit numbers although Irish VAT numbers contain only eight digits). Furthermore, its director had written to its VAT office in October and November 1997 asking for advice, but had not received a reply until October 1998. The tribunal allowed the appeal, holding that it was unreasonable for the Commissioners 'to have ignored (the director's) pleas for some 11 months while further penalties were imposed'. *The Decal Co Ltd, EDN/98/194 (VTD 16274).*

50.12   A company appealed against a penalty under *VATA 1994, s 66*, contending that it had posted its sales list before the due date. The tribunal accepted the company's evidence and allowed the appeal. *Eurospray Midlands Ltd, MAN/00/205 (VTD 16775).*

51   Pension Funds

51.1   **Professional services supplied to employer as trustee of pension fund—whether input tax reclaimable.** The British Railways Board received professional advice from merchant bankers and others concerning its employees' pension funds, of which it was the trustee. It reclaimed the input tax charged to it on such services. The Commissioners rejected the claim but the tribunal allowed the Board's appeal and the CA upheld this decision. The management of the pension funds was one of the Board's functions as an employer and there was no justification for the Commissioners' refusal to allow the claim. *C & E Commrs v British Railways Board, CA [1976] STC 359; [1976] 1 WLR 1036; [1976] 3 All ER 100.*

51.2   **Pension fund trustees' expenses defrayed by employer (not a trustee)—whether input tax reclaimable.** A company defrayed the expenses incurred by the trustees of a pension fund established for its employees and for employees of subsidiary companies. However the company was not itself a trustee of the fund. The company reclaimed the input tax incurred by the trustees. The Commissioners issued an assessment to recover the tax. The tribunal upheld the assessment and dismissed the company's appeal. *British Railways Board,* 51.1 above, was distinguished because in that case the employer had been a trustee of the fund. The relevant services here had been supplied to the trustees and not to the company. *Linotype & Machinery Ltd, [1978] VATTR 123 (VTD 594).*

51.3   Similar decisions were reached in *Talbot Motor Co Ltd, MAN/82/242 (VTD 1728)* and *Rambla Properties, LON/94/298A (VTD 13030).*

51.4   A similar decision, applying *Linotype & Machinery Ltd,* 51.2 above, and *Talbot Motor Co Ltd,* 51.3 above, was reached in *Ultimate Advisory Services Ltd, MAN/91/1488 (VTD 9523).* (*Note.* For another issue in this case, see 39.38 LAND.)

51.5   **Pension funds of company established by statute—whether input tax reclaimable.** A company was established by statute to administer a canal. It had established three pension schemes, which were administered by committees on its behalf, and appointed and paid actuaries for each of the three schemes. It reclaimed input tax on the expenses of the schemes. The Commissioners rejected the claim but the QB allowed the company's appeal. Applying *British Railways Board,* 51.1 above, the provision of pension funds was within the functions of an employer and the actuaries' advice as to the solvency of the funds had been incurred for the purpose of the company's business. *Linotype & Machinery Co Ltd,* 51.2 above, distinguished. *Manchester Ship Canal Co v C & E Commrs, QB [1982] STC 351.*

51.6   **Company acting as trustee of pension funds for employees of associated companies—whether input tax reclaimable.** A company was established to act as trustee of two pension funds for employees of associated companies. The companies were registered as a group for VAT, and the parent company reclaimed the input tax incurred by the company established to act as trustee of the pension funds. The Commissioners rejected the claim but the tribunal allowed the company's appeal. The services in question were deemed to have been supplied to the parent company by virtue of what is now *VATA 1994, s 43(1)(b),* and the investment of the pension funds was within the scope of the company's business. *BOC International Ltd, [1982] VATTR 84 (VTD 1248).*

51.7   **Transfer of employer's pension funds—legal advice provided for employees affected—whether services supplied to employer.** A company was taken over by a larger company and its pension funds were transferred to other pension schemes. Legal advice was provided for representatives of the employees affected by the change. The company reclaimed input tax on these legal costs. The Commissioners rejected the claim on the basis that the relevant supplies had not been made to the company. The tribunal dismissed the company's appeal. It was accepted that, if the solicitors' services had been made to the trustees of the pension funds, these would be treated as supplies to the company for VAT purposes. However, the supplies in this case had been made to independent representatives of the beneficiaries. The beneficiaries 'were clients being separately advised ... the advice was given to the representative beneficiaries and not to the trustees'. *P & O European Ferries (Dover) Ltd*, 34.143 INPUT TAX, distinguished. *The Plessey Co Ltd, LON/94/254A (VTD 12814)*.

51.8   **Services supplied by employer to trustees of pension fund—whether output tax chargeable.**   The National Coal Board operated a contributory pension scheme for its employees. The Board was not itself a trustee of the fund, but it was responsible for the routine administration and management of the scheme. The Commissioners sought to charge tax on the services supplied by the Board for the trustees. The QB allowed the Board's appeal, holding that although the Board had provided services for the trustees, the services had not been provided for a consideration, and, by virtue of what is now *VATA 1994, s 5(2)(a)*, did not constitute a supply for VAT purposes. *National Coal Board v C & E Commrs, QB [1982] STC 863*.

51.9   **Pension fund—failure to claim input tax on disposals of shares outside EC.**   See *CGI Pension Trust Ltd*, 45.65 PAYMENT OF TAX.

52   Protected Buildings

Note. *VATA 1994, Sch 8, Group 6* was substituted by the *VAT (Protected Buildings) Order 1995 (SI 1995 No 283)*, with effect from 1 March 1995. The cases in this chapter should be read in the light of the changes in the legislation.

The cases in this chapter are arranged under the following headings.

Definition of 'protected building' (VATA 1994, Sch 8, Group 6, Note 1) 52.1–52.9

Whether a 'substantial reconstruction' (VATA 1994, Sch 8, Group 6, Item 1, Note 4) 52.10–52.14

Whether an 'approved alteration' (VATA 1994, Sch 8, Group 6, Item 2, Note 6)
Cases held to constitute an approved alteration 52.15–52.24
Cases where the tax was apportioned 52.25–52.33
Cases held not to constitute an approved alteration 52.34–52.58

Whether a supply of services (VATA 1994, Sch 8, Group 6, Item 2) 52.59–52.62

Miscellaneous 52.63–52.64

DEFINITION OF 'PROTECTED BUILDING' (VATA 1994, Sch 8, Group 6, Note 1)

52.1   **Listed building—change of use from nursing home to country club.**   In 1986 planning permission was obtained for the conversion of a protected building into a nursing home. In 1988 a further application was made for conversion of the same building into a country club. Planning permission for this was granted in 1989. The contractor did not account for VAT on the conversion, and the Commissioners issued an assessment charging output tax. The contractor appealed, contending that the work should be treated as zero-rated under what is now *VATA 1994, Sch 8, Group 6*. The tribunal dismissed the appeal, holding that since the building was intended to be used as a country club, it was not 'designed to remain as or become a dwelling or ... intended for use solely for a relevant residential purpose or a relevant charitable purpose'. Accordingly the building did not qualify as a protected building under *Sch 8, Group 6, Note 1*, and the contractor's supplies did not qualify for zero-rating. The tribunal observed that the contractor had not taken 'proper steps to verify that the supplies he was making ... were of a description entitling him to treat them as zero-rated'. *P Butland (t/a Harrogate Site Services), MAN/91/193 (VTD 6531).*

52.2   **Conversion of barn into music room.**   The owner of a 17th century barn, which stood in the grounds of the owner's house and was a listed building under the *Planning (Listed Buildings and Conservation Areas) Act 1990*, engaged a building partnership to convert the barn into a music room. The terms of the listed building consent required the barn not to be occupied as a 'separate unit of residential accommodation', but only to be occupied as an adjunct to the house in the grounds of which it stood. The partnership did not account for VAT on the work. The Commissioners issued an assessment charging output tax, and the partnership appealed, contending that the work should be zero-rated under what is now *VATA 1994, Sch 8, Group 6*. The tribunal dismissed the appeal, holding on the evidence that the barn was not 'designed to remain as or become a dwelling', and therefore did not qualify as a protected building within *Sch 8, Group 6, Note 1*. *MKM Builders, LON/92/2421A (VTD 10511).*

52.3   **Conversion of barn into living accommodation—effect of Group 6, Note 2(c).**   An individual (F) owned a house, which had been built in around 1780 and was a protected building. About 8 feet from the house stood a barn, which had been built in around 1730 and was a listed building. F obtained listed building consent to convert the barn into dwelling accommodation. The relevant planning permission provided that 'the barn conversion ... shall be occupied solely for purposes incidental to the occupation and enjoyment of (the house) as a dwelling and shall not be used as a separate unit of accommodation'. The Commissioners issued a ruling that, because of this, the conditions of *VATA 1994, Sch 8, Group 6, Note 2(c)* were not satisfied and the barn did not qualify as a 'protected building' within *Group 6, Note 1*. The tribunal upheld this decision and dismissed F's appeal. *DS Ford, LON/x (VTD 16271)*.

52.4   A couple converted a barn, which stood in the grounds of a protected building, into living accommodation. The Commissioners issued a ruling that output tax was chargeable on the conversion. The couple appealed, contending that it should be treated as zero-rated under *VATA 1994, Sch 8, Group 6*. The tribunal rejected this contention and dismissed the appeal, holding that the conditions of *Group 6, Note 2(c)* were not satisfied, since the relevant planning permission prohibited the separate use or disposal of the barn. *Morfee*, 52.22 below, was distinguished, since 'in that case the outbuilding which was a part of the listed building had been used as part of the domestic accommodation, with the main building' whereas the barn here had not previously been domestic accommodation. The tribunal observed that the fact that the main building 'is a domestic building and is a protected building does not mean that all the buildings within its curtilage, even if covered by the listing, are domestic buildings'. *D & L Clamp, [1999] VATDR 520 (VTD 16422)*.

52.5   **Conversion of outbuilding within grounds of protected building.**   The owner of a listed building arranged for the conversion of a barn into living accommodation. The Commissioners issued a ruling that output tax was chargeable on the work. The owner appealed, contending that the work qualified for zero-rating on the basis that the barn was 'designed to remain as or become a dwelling', within *VATA 1994, Sch 8, Group 6, Note 2*. The tribunal accepted this contention and allowed the appeal, observing that the restriction in *Note 2(c)* did not apply, because the relevant planning permission did not prohibit the separate disposal of the dwelling. *N Hopewell-Smith, LON/99/947 (VTD 16725)*.

52.6   See also *Forman Hardy*, 52.21 below; *Morfee*, 52.22 below; *Zielinski Baker & Partners*, 52.22 below; *CM Lee*, 52.52 below, and *Kernahan*, 52.53 below.

52.7   **Whether building to be used 'for relevant charitable purpose'.**   The Royal Academy of Music arranged for a contractor to carry out reconstruction work on a listed building which it used as a concert hall. It applied for a certificate that the work qualified for zero-rating. The Commissioners rejected the claim on the basis that the building was not 'intended for use solely for a relevant residential purpose or a relevant charitable purpose', as required by *VATA 1994, Sch 8, Group 6, Note 1*, but was intended to be used for business purposes. The Academy appealed, contending that it was not carrying on a business, and that the effect of *Article 4(5)* of the *EC Sixth Directive* was that it should not be treated as a 'taxable person'. The tribunal dismissed the appeal, holding that the Academy was carrying on a business activity. The fact that its objects were charitable or philanthropic was not conclusive. Furthermore, the Academy was not a 'public authority', and was not 'governed by public law', so that *Article 4(5)* was not applicable. *Morrison's Academy Boarding Houses Association*, 7.1 BUSINESS, and *Ufficio Distrettuale delle Imposte Dirette di Fiorenzuola d'Arda v Comune di Carpaneto Piacentino*, 21.76 EUROPEAN COMMUNITY LAW, applied. *Royal Academy of Music, [1994] VATTR 105 (VTD 11871)*.

52.8   A charity used premises on the first floor of a listed building to run a sports and fitness centre. It arranged for substantial refurbishment of the premises. The

Commissioners issued a ruling that VAT was chargeable on the work. The charity appealed, contending that the work should be zero-rated under *VATA 1994, v6*, on the basis that the building was intended for use solely for a 'relevant charitable purpose'. The tribunal rejected this contention and dismissed the appeal, and the CA upheld this decision. On the evidence, the use of the building was not 'similar to the use of a village hall in providing social or recreational facilities for a local community'. Sir John Vinelott held that the conditions of what is now *VATA 1994, 8 Sch, Group 5, Note 6(b)* were only satisfied 'where a local community is the final consumer in respect of the supply of the services . . . in the sense that the local community is the user of the services (through a body of trustees or a management committee acting on its behalf) and in which the only economic activity is one in which they participate directly'. *EC Commission v United Kingdom (No 2)*, 21.237 EUROPEAN COMMUNITY LAW, applied. *C & E Commrs v Jubilee Hall Recreation Centre Ltd, CA 1998, [1999] STC 381*.

52.9 **Insufficient evidence.** An appeal was dismissed in a case where the appellant company failed to submit evidence that the building in question was a 'protected building' within the definition laid down by *VATA 1994, 8 Sch, Group 6, Note 1. DM Builders (Chichester) Ltd, LON/91/778 (VTD 7618)*.

WHETHER A 'SUBSTANTIAL RECONSTRUCTION' (VATA 1994, Sch 8, Group 6, Item 1, Note 4)

52.10 **Renovation.** A property developer bought two protected buildings, which he renovated and sold. He did not account for tax on the sale, but reclaimed input tax on the work. The Commissioners rejected the claim, considering that the sale of the properties was exempt from VAT. He appealed, contending that the work was zero-rated under what is now *VATA 1994, Sch 8, Group 6*. The tribunal dismissed his appeal, holding on the evidence that the work was 'a minor enlargement of the building and a modernisation of its interior'. This did not amount to 'substantial reconstruction'. *D Barraclough, LON/86/699 (VTD 2529)*.

52.11 A building contractor obtained permission for the 'renovation of the roof, repositioning of the back door, provision of first floor bathroom and reflooring on ground floor' of a protected building. He carried out the work in question and sold the building. The Commissioners issued a ruling that the sale was exempt and he appealed, contending that it should be zero-rated under what is now *VATA 1994, Sch 8, Group 6*. The tribunal dismissed his appeal, holding that the work did not amount to 'substantial reconstruction'. *TR Bates, LON/87/623 (VTD 2925)*.

52.12 The owner of a Grade II listed building had it restored at a cost of £900,000. He reclaimed the input tax incurred, and then sold the building. The Commissioners issued an assessment to recover the tax, on the basis that the sale was an exempt supply. The vendor appealed, contending that the sale should be treated as zero-rated under what is now *VATA 1994, Sch 8, Group 6*. The tribunal dismissed the appeal, holding that the work in question did not amount to 'substantial reconstruction', so that the sale did not qualify for zero-rating. *ADJ Lee, LON/90/93X (VTD 5887)*.

52.13 A company which owned a protected building obtained permission for alterations to the building including underpinning, rewiring, repointing and overhauling of the roof. It reclaimed input tax on the work. The Commissioners issued an assessment to recover the tax, and the company appealed, contending that the work should be zero-rated under what is now *VATA 1994, Sch 8, Group 6*. The tribunal dismissed the appeal, holding that the work did not amount to 'substantial reconstruction', since there had been 'no material reconstruction of the building looked at as a whole'. *Barraclough*, 52.10 above, applied. *Vivodean Ltd, EDN/90/134 (VTD 6538)*.

52.14   The addition of a two-storey extension to a dilapidated farmhouse, which was a Grade II listed building, was held not to constitute 'substantial reconstruction' in *NB Church (t/a Milton Antique Restoration), LON/92/2751 (VTD 12427)*.

WHETHER AN 'APPROVED ALTERATION' (VATA 1994, Sch 8, Group 6, Item 2, Note 6)

Cases held to constitute an approved alteration

52.15   **Replacement of roof.**   The owner of a protected building obtained consent for replacement of the roof, which was of slate. The Commissioners issued a ruling that the work did not qualify for zero-rating, on the basis that it was 'repair or maintenance' and was excluded from zero-rating by what is now *VATA 1994, Sch 8, Group 6, Note 6*. The tribunal allowed the owner's appeal, holding that the works were 'works of alteration', rather than 'repair or maintenance', and qualified for zero-rating. Applying *dicta* of Lord Diplock in *C & E Commrs v Viva Gas Appliances, HL [1983] STC 819; [1983] 1 WLR 1445* (a case concerning provisions in *FA 1972* which have since been superseded) applied, 'alteration' should be construed as including 'any work upon the fabric of the building except that which is so slight or trivial as to attract the application of the *de minimis* rule'. *CN Evans, MAN/88/587 (VTD 4415)*. (*Note.* Compare the subsequent decisions in *The Vicar and Parochial Church Council of St Petroc Minor*, 52.36 below; *Meanwell Construction Co Ltd*, 52.39 below, and *Windflower Housing Association*, 52.40 below. In *The Vicar and Parochial Church Council of St Petroc Minor* the tribunal specifically declined to apply *dicta* of Lord Diplock in *Viva Gas*, observing that in that case the word 'alteration' was used 'in a context which no longer appears in (*VATA 1994*). That contextual interpretation is therefore of no help now.')

52.16   A company rethatched the roofs of two listed buildings, and did not account for output tax on the work. The Commissioners issued an assessment charging tax, and the company appealed, contending that the work constituted 'approved alterations' which qualified for zero-rating. The tribunal accepted this contention and allowed the appeal. In each case, the roof had previously been thatched with straw, whereas the company had used reeds, which altered the appearance of the roofs. Furthermore, neither of the roofs had been in specific need of repair, and the work went beyond 'repair or maintenance'. *Windflower Housing Association*, 52.40 below, and *Kain*, 52.41 below, distinguished. *Dodson Bros. (Thatchers) Ltd, [1995] VATDR 514 (VTD 13734)*.

52.17   A parish church council arranged for the replacement of the existing church roof with a new roof made of lead. The Commissioners issued a ruling that the work constituted 'repair or maintenance', so that output tax was chargeable. The church council appealed, contending that the work was an 'approved alteration' and qualified for zero-rating. The tribunal accepted this contention and allowed the appeal. *Windflower Housing Association*, 52.40 below, distinguished. *Parochial Church Council of St Andrew's Church Eakring, MAN/97/368 (VTD 15320)*.

52.18   **Replacement of guttering.**   The guttering of a church was replaced in order to improve drainage from the church roof. The new guttering was laid onto new soles, sloping in a different direction to the old soles and leading to new exit chutes. The Commissioners issued a ruling that the work did not qualify for zero-rating under what is now *VATA 1994, Sch 8, Group 6*, on the basis that it constituted 'repair or maintenance'. The church council appealed. The tribunal reviewed the evidence in detail and allowed the appeal in principle, holding that the replacement of the gutter was an alteration, rather than repair or maintenance. (The appeal was adjourned to consider the apportionment of the time spent by the contractors between this work and other work which did not qualify for zero-rating.) *All Saints Church (Tilsworth) Parochial Church Council, [1993] VATTR 315 (VTD 10490)*. (*Note*. There was no further public hearing of the appeal.)

52.19   **Insertion of additional floor timbers.**   A protected building was converted from a nursing home into a residential home. Additional floor timbers were inserted in the course of the work. The Commissioners issued an assessment charging output tax on the company which had carried out the work. The company appealed, contending that the work should be zero-rated under what is now *VATA 1994, Sch 8, Group 6*. The tribunal allowed the company's appeal, holding that, since the timbers were 'part of the fabric', the work was an alteration, and was not merely 'repair or maintenance'. *Davenport Brickwork Ltd, LON/92/1688 (VTD 10692)*.

52.20   **Installation of lighting in church.**   A vicar arranged for the installation of a new lighting system in his church, which was a protected building. The Commissioners issued a ruling that VAT was chargeable on the work. The vicar appealed, contending that the work constituted an 'approved alteration'. The tribunal accepted this contention and allowed the appeal. Applying *Holy Trinity Church (Heath Town Wolverhampton) Parochial Church Council*, 52.29 below, the installation of new lighting was within the definition of an 'alteration'. On the evidence, the work here was 'a one-off in the sense of exceptional expenditure ... and cannot be categorised as repair or maintenance'. *All Saints with St Nicholas Church Icklesham, LON/x (VTD 16321)*. (*Note*. For the Commissioners' revised policy on mains wiring, following this case, see Business Brief 7/2000, issued on 18 May 2000.)

52.21   **Alterations to outbuilding within grounds of protected building.**   The owner of a listed building obtained listed building consent for alterations to a secondary building which was within the curtilage of the listed building but was separated from it by a driveway which was 18 foot wide. The Commissioners issued a ruling that the work did not qualify for zero-rating, on the basis that the secondary building did not form part of the protected building. The owner appealed, contending that the outbuilding should be treated as part of the listed building since it was used as a games room and effectively formed part of his private residence. The tribunal allowed the appeal, distinguishing *Lee*, 52.52 below, on the grounds that the outbuilding in that case was not used a part of the owner's private residence, whereas in this case the outbuilding formed part of the entity of the owner's dwelling-house. The tribunal chairman also observed that the legislation in question derived from *FA 1989*, and statements made by Government ministers during the relevant Finance Bill debates indicated that it had been intended to retain zero-rating for protected buildings which were used as private residences. *N Forman Hardy, [1994] VATTR 302 (VTD 12776)*.

52.22   *Forman Hardy*, 52.21 above, was applied in the similar subsequent cases of *RG Morfee, LON/94/725A (VTD 13816)* and *Zielinski Baker & Partners, LON/98/950 (VTD 16722)*.

52.23   A trader purchased a farmhouse, which was a protected building, with the aim of converting it into a nursing home. He obtained listed building consent to convert the farmhouse into a nursing home, and to convert some redundant agricultural buildings, which stood in the grounds of the home, into flats and an office to be used in conjunction with the home. The partnership which carried out the work treated it as zero-rated. The Commissioners issued an assessment on the basis that the work relating to the office did not qualify for zero-rating. The partnership appealed. The tribunal allowed the appeal, holding that, although the office did not contain any sleeping accommodation, 'residential accommodation clearly includes a number of ancillary matters without which the building or institution could not properly function. In the present case it was expedient to house the administration side in a separate building, rather than to have some of the old people sleeping in one building and some in another'. *Forman Hardy*, 52.21 above, applied. *Hill Ash Developments, LON/99/537 (VTD 16747)*.

52.24   **Indoor swimming pool connected to protected building by covered walkway.**   The owner of a farmhouse, which was a listed building, arranged for the construction of an indoor swimming pool, connected to the farmhouse by a covered walkway. The Commissioners issued a ruling that the restriction in what is now *VATA 1994, Sch 8, Group 6, Note 10* applied, so that the work was standard-rated. The owner appealed, contending that the work was an approved alteration to the farmhouse, which was a protected building, so that the work should be treated as zero-rated under *Sch 8, Group 6*. The tribunal allowed the appeal, holding that the swimming pool was part of the protected building, so that the restriction in *Sch 8, Group 6, Note 10* did not apply and the work was an alteration of the protected building which qualified for zero-rating. The QB upheld the tribunal decision as one of fact. *C & E Commrs v M Arbib, QB [1995] STC 490*.

Cases where the tax was apportioned

52.25   **Replacement of roof.**   The owner of a protected building obtained permission for the replacement of the roof, which was made of stone slates and comprised 14 pitches. The builder who carried out the work treated it as zero-rated. The Commissioners issued an assessment charging tax on the work, on the basis that it was 'repair or maintenance' which did not qualify for zero-rating. The builder appealed, contending that the work was an 'alteration' because it had been necessary to raise some of the valleys and alter the pitches, and to demolish an unsafe chimney and roof over three skylights. The tribunal allowed the appeal in part, holding that 'the work of replacing or renewing a tile comes within the definition of repair and maintenance' but that 'the work of changing the height of the ridges and the pitches of the roof slopes as well as increasing the height of the valleys does not come within the term "repair and maintenance"'. Furthermore, the removal of the chimney did not qualify for zero-rating, since it was not covered by the listed building consent. The tribunal directed that the expenditure should be apportioned. *CN Foley, LON/94/2772A (VTD 13496)*.

52.26   The owner of a protected building obtained listed building consent to cover the roof with stone tiles. The contractor responsible for the work did not account for output tax on it, treating it as zero-rated. The Commissioners issued an assessment charging tax on the basis that the work was 'repair or maintenance' which did not qualify for zero-rating, and the contractor appealed. The tribunal reviewed the evidence in detail and allowed the appeal in part. On the evidence, approximately 65% of the roof area had been in need of repair, and the re-roofing of this section was 'repair or maintenance' which did not qualify for zero-rating. However, the remaining 35% of the roof had been in good condition, and the re-roofing of this section was not within the definition of 'repair or maintenance' and therefore qualified for zero-rating. *NF Rhodes, MAN/96/9 (VTD 14533)*.

52.27   **Rebuilding of external walls—replacement of roof.**   A building company obtained listed building consent for the 'refurbishment' of a dilapidated 16th century farmhouse. The work included the rebuilding of the external walls and the replacement of the roof. The company did not account for output tax on the work, treating it as zero-rated. The Commissioners issued an assessment charging tax on the basis that the work constituted 'repair and maintenance' and failed to qualify for zero-rating. The tribunal allowed the company's appeal in part, holding on the evidence that the rebuilding of the external walls and the insertion of a new window constituted an 'approved alteration'. However, applying the QB decision in *Windflower Housing Association*, 52.40 below, the replacement of the roof was 'repair and maintenance' which failed to qualify for zero-rating. The fitting of new gutters and of new external gates, the construction of a new garage, the laying of new pavings and the landscaping of the grounds also failed to qualify for zero-rating. *Logmoor Ltd, MAN/95/2750 (VTD 14733).*

52.28   **Internal alterations including installation of septic tank and installation of damp-proofing.**   A married couple purchased a listed building, which was in a run-down condition, and obtained listed building consent for various internal alterations, including the lowering of some windows, the replacement of a door with a window, the construction of various partitions, and the installation of a septic tank. The work which was eventually carried out was more extensive than the work for which listed building consent had been obtained. The Commissioners accepted that the lowering of windows and the replacement of a door with a window were approved alterations which qualified for zero-rating, but ruled that the remainder of the work did not qualify. The couple appealed, contending that 25 further items of work (including the installation of the septic tank, the installation of damp-proofing, the replacement of a staircase, the relocation of a fireplace and the lowering of a ceiling) should be treated as qualifying for zero-rating. The tribunal reviewed the evidence in detail and allowed the appeal in part, holding that seven of the 25 items (including the installation of the septic tank, and the removal and erection of various partitions) qualified for zero-rating, but that the remaining 18 items did not. Of the items which failed to qualify, some (including the installation of damp-proofing and the replacement of a staircase) were within the definition of 'repair and maintenance', while others (including the relocation of a fireplace and the lowering of a ceiling) were not covered by the grant of listed building consent and thus did not meet the requirements of *Sch 8, Group 6, Note 6(c)*. *Mr & Mrs MP Wells, MAN/96/11 (VTD 15169).*

52.29   **Installation of lighting in church.**   A parochial church council arranged for the installation of a new lighting system in the church, which was a protected building. The Commissioners issued a ruling that VAT was chargeable on the work. The church council appealed, contending that the work constituted an 'approved alteration'. The tribunal reviewed the evidence in detail and allowed the appeal in part, holding that the installation of new lighting was within the definition of an 'alteration' but that much of the work was within the definition of 'repair and maintenance' and thus failed to qualify for zero-rating. *Dicta* of Medd J in *All Saints Church (Tilsworth) PCC*, 52.18 above, applied. *Holy Trinity Church (Heath Town Wolverhampton) Parochial Church Council, MAN/94/1910 (VTD 13652).*

52.30   **New drainage system.**   A company owned a 21-acre estate which included a Grade II listed building. The sewage treatment plant at the estate was found to be inadequate. It obtained planning permission and listed building consent for a new sewage treatment plant. The Commissioners issued a ruling that output tax was chargeable on the cost of the plant, since it constituted 'repair or maintenance' rather than an 'approved alteration' within what is now *VATA 1994, Sch 8, Group 6*. The company appealed, contending that the work qualified for zero-rating. The tribunal allowed the appeal in part, holding that the work 'went far beyond mere repair or maintenance' but finding that part of the work related to three cottages on the estate which were not a part of the listed building. The tribunal directed that the tax should be apportioned accordingly. *Walsingham College (Yorkshire Properties) Ltd, [1995] VATDR 141 (VTD 13223).*

52.31 Protected Buildings

52.31 **Erection of railings around church.** A contractor erected railings around a churchyard. On the northern part of the site, the railings were fixed to the top of the churchyard wall, but on the southern part of the site they were free-standing with a small gap where they reached the church. The church was a protected building, and listed building consent had been obtained for the work. The contractor did not account for output tax on the work, treating it as zero-rated. The Commissioners issued an assessment charging tax on the work, and he appealed, contending that it was an 'approved alteration'. The tribunal allowed the appeal in part. The churchyard wall formed part of the protected building, and the erection of railings on top of this wall was within the definition of an 'approved alteration'. However, an approved alteration 'must touch the fabric of the building', so that the erection of free-standing railings around the southern part of the site did not qualify for zero-rating. *RG Powell (t/a Anwick Agricultural Engineers), MAN/96/284 (VTD 14520).*

52.32 **Construction of boundary wall.** The owner of a 16th century cottage, which was a protected building, obtained listed building consent for the replacement of a boundary fence by a wall. He reclaimed input tax on the cost of the wall. The Commissioners rejected the claim on the basis that the construction of the wall did not qualify as an approved alteration to a building. He appealed. The tribunal allowed the appeal in part, holding on the evidence that a short section of the wall, which was linked to the cottage by a 'timber-boxing' arrangement, qualified for zero-rating on the basis that it should 'be considered as part of the cottage'. However, the effect of *VATA 1994, Sch 8, Group 6, Note 10* was that the remainder of the wall did not qualify for zero-rating. *C Mason, MAN/99/109 (VTD 16250).*

52.33 **Construction of greenhouse, stables and swimming pool in grounds of protected building.** The owner of a protected building, which dated from the 15th century, obtained listed building consent for various alterations to the building. The Commissioners accepted that the work which was carried out on the building itself qualified for zero-rating. However, they issued a ruling that the construction of a greenhouse attached to the protected building, and of stables and a swimming pool enclosure in the grounds of the building did not qualify for zero-rating. The owner appealed. The tribunal allowed the appeal in part, holding that the construction of the greenhouse was an 'approved alteration' and thus qualified for zero-rating, but that the construction of the stables and the swimming pool enclosure did not qualify. On the evidence, the greenhouse was not a separate building, since it was 'attached to and integrated with the two pre-existing walls' of the protected building. However, the swimming pool enclosure was not sufficiently attached to the protected building to amount to an alteration to that building, and the stables were also a separate building, the construction of which was excluded from zero-rating by what is now *VATA 1994, 8 Sch, Group 6, Note 10. CW Mann, LON/95/2066 (VTD 14004).*

Cases held not to constitute an approved alteration

52.34 **Rebuilding of wall.** The owner of a Grade II listed building demolished and rebuilt part of the boundary wall. The tribunal held that the work did not qualify as an 'approved alteration', since the owner had not obtained the formal consent required by what is now *VATA 1994, Sch 8, Group 6, Note 6(c). J Hollier, LON/87/456 (VTD 3758).*

52.35 **Partial rebuilding of walls.** The owner of a protected building obtained listed building consent for the partial rebuilding of the front main wall. The tribunal held that the work was 'repair or maintenance', which was excluded from zero-rating by what is now *VATA 1994, Sch 8, Group 6, Note 6.* The tribunal observed that 'it is difficult for repair and maintenance not to involve some element of alteration, but it was not alteration for the sake of alteration or for any other reason apart from the more effective repair and maintenance of the building. If the most effective way to repair or maintain a building is by employing modern methods which involve the use of different building materials, the alteration ... so involved does not prevent the work from being essentially a work of repair and maintenance and therefore not eligible for zero-rating.' *Cheeseman*, 52.37 below, applied; *All Saints Church (Tilsworth)*, 52.18 above, distinguished. *Dr NDF Browne, LON/93/480A (VTD 11388)*.

52.36   A similar decision was reached in a subsequent case in which the tribunal specifically declined to apply *dicta* of Lord Diplock in *C & E Commrs v Viva Gas Appliances, HL [1983] STC 819; [1983] 1 WLR 1445* (a case concerning provisions in *FA 1972* which have since been superseded, and which the appellant had cited an authority), observing that the word 'alteration' was used 'in a context which no longer appears in (*VATA 1994*). That contextual interpretation is therefore of no help now.' On the evidence, the tribunal held that 'to the extent that there may be an element of alteration it is incidental, resulting from the carrying out of the maintenance work'. *The Vicar and Parochial Church Council of St Petroc Minor, LON/98/1381 (VTD 16450)*.

52.37   **Strengthening of walls.**   The owner of two protected buildings arranged for the rear walls of the buildings, which were unstable, to be strengthened by the injection of certain chemicals. The tribunal held that the work amounted to 'repair or maintenance' and was therefore excluded from zero-rating by what is now *VATA 1994, Sch 8, Group 6, Note 6. B Cheeseman, LON/89/1344Z (VTD 5133)*.

52.38   **Replacement of roof.**   The owner of a protected building obtained permission to reconvert it from three flats to a single dwelling. He also reslated the roof with natural slate, replacing the existing mixture of slate and asbestos. He reclaimed the input tax relating to the reslating of the roof. The Commissioners rejected the claim, since this work was not referred to in the application for listed building consent, so that it did not constitute an 'approved alteration'. The tribunal dismissed the owner's appeal, holding that 'an "approved alteration" for the purposes of zero-rating requires written consent of the appropriate authority and oral consent, even if proved, would not be sufficient'. *N Brice, LON/91/708Y (VTD 6376)*.

52.39   A construction company obtained listed building consent to replace the roof of a protected building. The tribunal held that the work constituted 'repair or maintenance' and was excluded from zero-rating by what is now *VATA 1994, Sch 8, Group 6, Note 6. Meanwell Construction Co Ltd, MAN/91/1225 (VTD 10726)*.

52.40   A housing association, which owned a Grade II listed building, obtained listed building consent for the improvement of the roof structure. The existing cast lead was removed and wooden divisions were erected to support a new rolled lead covering. The length of the parapet gutters was reduced, and the roof plane was raised. The Commissioners issued a ruling that the work was standard-rated, on the basis that it constituted 'repair or maintenance'. The association appealed, contending that the work was an 'approved alteration' and should be treated as zero-rated. The QB rejected this contention and upheld the Commissioners' ruling. Ognall J held that the work was within the definition of 'repair or maintenance', and thus did not qualify for zero-rating. The raising of the roof plane was an alteration, but since it was an integral part of wider works of repair or maintenance, it fell to be treated likewise. *C & E Commrs v Windflower Housing Association, QB [1995] STC 860*.

52.41   The owners of a protected building, which had had a thatched straw roof, obtained listed building consent to rethatch the roof with reeds. The tribunal held that the work was 'repair or maintenance' which did not qualify for zero-rating. *SH & VS Kain, LON/93/2588A (VTD 12331)*.

52.42   A listed building was badly damaged by fire. The roof had to be replaced and part of the exterior walls had to be rebuilt. The builder who carried out this work treated it as zero-rated. The Commissioners issued an assessment on the basis that it did not qualify for zero-rating, and the builder appealed, contending that the whole of the work should be treated as approved alterations and as zero-rated under what is now *VATA 1994, Sch 8, Group 6*. The QB rejected this contention, holding that the work did not qualify for zero-rating under *Group 6* (but remitted the case to a new tribunal to consider whether they qualified for zero-rating under *Group 5*). Moses J observed that what is now *VATA 1994, Sch 8, Group 6* excluded works of reconstruction, except where they could be described as an alteration which was not repair or maintenance. *C & E Commrs v CR Morrish, QB [1998] STC 954*.

52.43   **Improvement of windows.**   A company patented and supplied a perimeter sealing system for sliding sash windows. The system was installed in a number of listed buildings. The tribunal held that the installation of the system constituted 'repair or maintenance', which did not qualify for zero-rating. *Ventrolla Ltd, MAN/92/1825 (VTD 12045)*.

52.44   **Removal of asbestos.**   The owner of a protected building engaged a contractor to carry out substantial work on the building, including the removal of asbestos. The tribunal held that, since the work did not affect the character of the building, it constituted 'repair or maintenance' which was excluded from zero-rating by *Sch 8, Group 6, Note 6. RW Gibbs, LON/89/1681X (VTD 5596)*.

52.45   **Painting of exterior of listed building.**   A company applied two coats of masonry paint to the exterior of a listed building, and did not account for output tax on this work. The tribunal held that the work was 'repair or maintenance', which was excluded from zero-rating by *VATA 1994, Sch 8, Group 6, Note 6. Wrencon Ltd, LON/95/264 (VTD 13968)*.

52.46   **Redecoration of church—whether an 'alteration'.**   The priest of a Catholic church arranged for the church to be redecorated in its original Victorian style. The tribunal held that the services of the contractors who had carried out the redecoration were standard-rated, since the work did not amount to an 'alteration'. Applying *dicta* of Lord Roskill in *ACT Construction Ltd v C & E Commrs, HL 1981, [1982] STC 25; [1981] 1 WLR 1542; [1982] 1 All ER 84* (a case concerning provisions in *FA 1972* which have since been superseded), an 'alteration' must be construed as a 'structural alteration'. *St Anne's Catholic Church, [1994] VATTR 102 (VTD 11783)*. (*Note.* The Commissioners regard the decision in *ACT Construction Ltd* as establishing the principle that an alteration must 'be structural to qualify for relief'—see Customs' VAT Manual, Part 8A, chapter 2, section 5.13.)

52.47   **Internal alterations.**   The owner of a listed building had obtained consent for the construction of three dormer windows and 'minor alterations'. The work was carried out by a contractor, but the owner also arranged for a friend (R) to supply kitchen and bathroom fittings, tiles, wallpaper and curtains. The tribunal held that R's supplies did not qualify for zero-rating. *R Irving (t/a Rosemary Irving Contracts), LON/96/912 (VTD 15188)*.

52.48   **Construction of garage within curtilage of protected building.**   The owner of a protected building obtained planning permission to erect a double garage within its curtilage. The garage was physically separate from the rest of the building. The tribunal held that the work did not qualify for zero-rating, since the garage was a separate building and the work constituted the construction of a new building rather than an alteration to the existing building. *JH Bradfield, [1991] VATTR 22 (VTD 5339).*

52.49   Similar decisions were reached in *CA Orme, LON/92/1885 (VTD 9975)* and *DL Wilson, LON/97/1651 (VTD 15803).*

52.50   *Orme,* 52.49 above, was applied in the similar case of *PVR Nicholls, LON/93/1041A (VTD 11115).*

52.51   **Construction of shed within grounds of protected building.**   An old rectory, standing in 16 acres of land with a walled garden and outbuildings, was a protected building. Its owner obtained listed building consent for the construction within its grounds, and attached to an existing garden wall, of a building to comprise a garage, a workshop, and changing rooms for a swimming pool. The tribunal held that the work constituted the construction of a new building, rather than the alteration of the existing rectory. *K & G Levell, LON/89/896X (VTD 6202).*

52.52   **Conversion of outbuilding within grounds of protected building.**   The owner of a protected building obtained planning permission for the conversion of an outbuilding, which was within the curtilage of the protected building and about 20 feet away from it, into a study. The tribunal held that the outbuilding was 'not an integral part of the main house', so that the work was not an alteration to the protected building. (The tribunal also observed that the outbuilding was not itself a 'protected building', since it was not a dwelling either before or after the work in question.) *CM Lee, LON/92/980 (VTD 10662).*

52.53   *Lee,* 52.52 above, was applied in a similar subsequent case in which *Forman Hardy,* 52.21 above, was distinguished. The tribunal observed that 'the provision of study/office accommodation and secure garaging was not enough to make (the outbuilding) an integral part of the main house'. *AJ & L Kernahan, LON/97/307 (VTD 15203).*

52.54   See also *Ford,* 52.3 above, and *Clamp,* 52.4 above.

52.55   **Construction of swimming pool in grounds of protected building.**   The owner of a protected building arranged for the construction of a swimming pool complex within the curtilage of the existing building. The tribunal held that the work did not qualify for zero-rating, since the swimming pool complex was not 'integral to the house'. *Dr A Heijn, LON/96/1338 (VTD 15562).*

52.56   **Construction of car park in grounds of listed building.**   A builder constructed a car park in the grounds of a listed building. The tribunal held that the work did not qualify for zero-rating. *MD Plumb, LON/94/2040A (VTD 13621).*

52.57   **Listed building consent obtained retrospectively.**   A building company carried out alterations to a protected building. The work was completed in 1995, but the relevant listed building consent was not granted until January 1996. The Commissioners issued a ruling that the work failed to qualify for zero-rating. The tribunal dismissed the company's appeal, holding that there were 'no grounds for reading the words of *Note 6* as incorporating retrospective approvals'. *Alan Roper & Sons Ltd, MAN/96/1169 (VTD 15260).*

52.58   **Listed building consent not obtained.**   See *Hollier,* 52.34 above, and *Brice,* 52.38 above. There have been a number of other cases in which appeals have been dismissed on the grounds that the appellant has not obtained the formal listed building consent required by what is now *VATA 1994, Sch 8, Group 6, Note 6(c).* In the interests of space, such cases are not reported individually in this book.

52.59 Protected Buildings

52.59 Materials purchased by owner of protected building. A builder owned a Grade II listed building, which he used as his business address. He reclaimed input tax relating to materials which he had used in altering the building. The Commissioners rejected the claim and the tribunal dismissed his appeal, holding that there had been no supply of services as required by what is now *VATA 1994, Sch 8, Group 6, Item 2*. The tribunal observed that there was no provision in *Group 6* for zero-rating supplies of goods, and such goods could be zero-rated under *Group 5, Item 4* only if there were a supply of services within *Group 6*. *P Robinson, MAN/89/131 (VTD 4063)*. (*Note*. For subsequent developments in this case, see 2.213 APPEALS.)

52.60 A couple who owned a protected building obtained planning permission and listed building consent for alterations to it. They purchased the necessary materials and arranged for four workmen to carry out the work. They reclaimed input tax on the cost of the materials which they had purchased. The Commissioners rejected the claim, and the couple appealed, contending that the materials should be treated as zero-rated. The tribunal rejected this contention and dismissed the appeal, holding that materials were only zero-rated under what is now *VATA 1994, Sch 8, Group 5, Item 4* if they were supplied by a supplier of services within *Sch 8, Group 6, Item 2*, which was not the case here. *A & A Goddard, LON/93/1655A (VTD 11983)*.

52.61 Conservatories, roof timbers and fire doors—whether supplied with services. See *Jeffs*, 15.145 CONSTRUCTION OF BUILDINGS, ETC.

52.62 Installation of kitchen in protected building—whether supplier of goods also supplying services. The owner of a protected building obtained permission for approved alterations including the installation of a modern kitchen. He purchased kitchen units from a supplier (M), which arranged for the necessary measurement and design work. The actual fitting of the units was undertaken by a carpenter who was engaged by the owner of the building, rather than by M. The Commissioners issued a ruling that the supply of the kitchen units was a standard-rated supply of goods. The owner appealed, contending that M had also supplied services within what is now *VATA 1994, Sch 8, Group 6, Item 2*, so that the goods qualified for zero-rating under what is now *VATA 1994, Sch 8, Group 5, Item 4*. The tribunal allowed the appeal, holding on the evidence that M had supplied the services of visiting and measuring the site, designing the kitchen, and manufacturing non-standard parts. The tribunal chairman observed that '"services" in (*Sch 8**) is not limited to the service of fitting the goods on site'. *PW Cook, LON/93/1952A (VTD 12571)*.

MISCELLANEOUS

52.63 Contractor originally treating work as standard-rated—whether work may be zero-rated retrospectively. A contractor carried out work on a protected building. His accountant issued invoices on his behalf charging VAT on the work. The customer disputed the amount charged, and a surveyor was consulted. The surveyor pointed out that the work qualified for zero-rating, and, at his suggestion, the contractor issued revised invoices which did not charge VAT. The Commissioners issued an assessment charging tax on the work, and the contractor appealed. At the hearing the Commissioners accepted that the work qualified for zero-rating, but contended that it could not be zero-rated retrospectively. The tribunal allowed the contractor's appeal, holding that the effect of what is now *VATA 1994, s 30* was that no tax was chargeable on the supplies in question. *A Kleanthous (t/a AK Building Services), LON/92/389Z (VTD 9504)*.

52.64   **Apportionment of input tax where protected building used as private residence before grant of major interest.**   An individual (M) reclaimed input tax on the renovation of a protected building. The Commissioners rejected the claim on the grounds that M had lived in the house for 3½ years while the work was being carried out. M appealed, contending that he had only occupied the house on a temporary basis, and had not intended to occupy it as a permanent residence. The tribunal accepted M's evidence and allowed the appeal in part, holding that the tax should be apportioned on a time basis, the denominator being 20 years and the input tax relating to the proportion of those 20 years in which M had occupied the house not being recoverable. Accordingly $^{33}/_{40}$ of the input tax was deductible. *I Mason, MAN/92/1308 (VTD 12406).*

53   Registration

Note. The provisions concerning registration are contained in *VATA, Sch 1*. There have been substantial changes in recent years. Significant changes were effected by *FA 1990, s 9*, which provided, *inter alia*, that the previous quarterly threshold limit was abolished after 20 March 1990, as was the need to anticipate future annual turnover after that date. A person is now liable to be registered at the end of any month, if the value of his taxable supplies in the period of one year then ending has exceeded the threshold limit (£52,000 after 31 March 2000); such a person must notify the Commissioners within 30 days of the end of the month in which he becomes liable to be registered. A person is also liable to be registered if at any time there are reasonable grounds for believing that the value of his taxable supplies in the next 30 days will exceed the threshold limit; such a person must notify the Commissioners before the end of the period by reference to which the liability arises. Cases relating to periods before 21 March 1990 should be read in the light of subsequent changes in the law. For penalties imposed for failure to register, see 48 PENALTIES: FAILURE TO NOTIFY. For cases concerning the registration of groups of companies, see 30 GROUPS OF COMPANIES. For cases concerning partnership registration, see 44.7 PARTNERSHIP *et seq*. For cases concerning the provisions of *Sch 1 para 1(2)*, where the question at issue is whether a business has been transferred as a going concern, see 61.77 to 58.82 TRANSFERS OF GOING CONCERNS.

The cases in this chapter are arranged under the following headings.

LIABILITY TO BE REGISTERED (VATA 1994, Sch 1 para 1)

Whether registration covers more than one business

53.1   **Partnership operating separate businesses.**   A married couple carried on two separate businesses in partnership, with different trading names, one as estate agents and the other as land developers. The Commissioners issued a ruling that the couple were entitled to only one registration. The couple appealed, contending that they were entitled to a separate registration for each trading name. The QB rejected this contention and upheld the Commissioners' ruling, holding that a registration is of a taxable person, rather than of the business(es) he carries on. *C & E Commrs v Glassborow and Another, QB [1974] STC 142; [1975] QB 465; [1974] 1 All ER 1041.*

53.2   Four persons carried on a business in partnership and were registered in the firm's name from 6 August 1973. The business did not flourish and two of the partners left in November 1973. The remaining partners notified the VAT office of the change and continued to carry on the business, although with a low turnover. They had throughout carried on in partnership an entirely separate business, the takings of which were well below the *Sch 1 para 1* limit and in respect of which they had not applied for registration. They appealed against an assessment for the year to 30 November 1974 covering both businesses. The tribunal dismissed the appeal, holding that the retirement of the two partners in November 1973 meant that, applying *Glassborow*, 53.1 above, the August 1973 registration thereafter covered both businesses. *J & E Harris, CAR/76/220 (VTD 373).*

53.3   A married couple, who carried on a dealing business in partnership and were registered for VAT, also operated a guest-house. They did not account for output tax on the takings from the guest-house, and the Commissioners issued an assessment charging tax on them. They appealed, contending that the guest-house should be treated as a separate entity and that the turnover of the guest-house was below the registration threshold. The tribunal dismissed the appeal, holding that the partnership registration covered the guest-house as well as the dealing business. *CAM & P Humphreys (t/a Wilmington Trading Co), LON/93/1871A (VTD 13007).*

53.4   A partnership operated a motor repair business, the turnover of which was below the registration threshold. In July 1991 they registered for VAT in respect of a second business of the supply of toner cartridges for photocopiers and printers. They duly accounted for VAT in respect of their takings from this business, but did not account for VAT on their takings from their motor repair business. The Commissioners issued an assessment charging tax on the takings from that business, and the tribunal dismissed the partnership's appeal. *Glassborow*, 53.1 above, applied. *K & G Taylor, LON/95/657A (VTD 13475).*

53.5   A partnership, which was registered for VAT, carried on a joinery business. The partners also provided building services under a different trading name, and using a separate bank account. They did not account for tax on these takings. The Commissioners issued an assessment charging tax on them, and the tribunal dismissed the partnership's appeal. *Clarke Street Joinery (t/a Clarke Street Building Services), MAN/99/816 (VTD 16805).*

53.6   **Sole trader operating more than one business.**   A married woman was registered from 1 April 1973 in respect of a taxi business. The Commissioners discovered that she was also carrying on a separate business as ladies' hairdresser which had not been disclosed in her returns, and assessed her for the 2¾ years to 31 December 1975 for the tax on the takings from the hairdressing business which, unless aggregated with those of the taxi business, would have been below the then registration threshold limits. The tribunal upheld the assessment and dismissed her appeal. Applying *Glassborow*, 53.1 above, her registration covered both businesses. *M Padmore, MAN/76/163 (VTD 345).*

53.7   Similar decisions, also applying *Glassborow*, 53.1 above, were reached in *Scanes, LON/76/209 (VTD 347); N & M Basran, MAN/82/151 (VTD 1312); MD Podbury (t/a Moordown Graphics), LON/85/43 (VTD 1906); R Glendinning, LON/89/107Y (VTD 5245); LF Callaghan, LON/90/1627X (VTD 6445); D Richardson, MAN/91/1219 (VTD 8849); AM Steele, LON/92/400 (VTD 9017);*

53.8 Registration

WD Allen, LON/92/1592A (VTD 11000); B Stratton, MAN/94/1175 (VTD 13185); JD & J Harley (t/a The Treasure Chest), LON/95/499 (VTD 13533); M & TEJ Hollosi, LON/95/1348A (VTD 13757); R Knight, LON/95/2136A (VTD 13769); K Fitton, MAN/95/1040 (VTD 13844); JD Lovejoy (t/a Crumbs), MAN/95/2723 (VTD 14370) and JJ Duffy, LON/x (VTD 15343).

53.8 **Partnership with turnover below threshold—partners also acting as directors of limited companies carrying on similar businesses.** Two individuals operated a dry-cleaning business in partnership. They were also directors of three limited companies, each of which operated a dry-cleaning business at different premises. Neither the partnership, nor any of the companies, were registered for VAT. The Commissioners issued a notice of compulsory registration to the partnership, backdated to January 1996. The partnership appealed, contending that its turnover was below the registration threshold, so that it was not required to register for VAT. The Commissioners defended the notice on the basis that the four businesses 'constituted supplies made by a single taxable person for the purposes of (*VATA 1994, ss 3, 4*)'. The officer responsible for the notice gave evidence that 'she had not considered issuing a direction under *paragraph 2* of *VATA 1994, Schedule 1* related to the artificial separating of business activities, as she considered that there had only ever been one business'. The tribunal allowed the partnership's appeal. The tribunal observed that 'the majority of cases involving separation of business activities have been in connection with directions made by (the) Commissioners under (*Sch 1 para 2*). Those cases have involved ... a consideration of whether activities are closely bound to one another by financial, economic and organisational links. The issues of those cases ... involve different considerations to the issues in the present appeal which relate to *paragraph 1* of *Schedule 1*.' On the evidence, the tribunal held that there were four separate businesses, and the Commissioners had 'acted unreasonably in treating the activities as one business carried on by one taxable person'. *Burrell*, 44.10 PARTNERSHIP, distinguished. *S Garton & J Davies (t/a The Dolly Tub)*, MAN/98/927 (VTD 16260).

53.9 **Business changed—whether old registration continues.** A trader had been registered as a dairy roundsman from 1 April 1973. In June 1973 he began a new business as a ladies' hairdresser, giving up his dairy roundsman's business a few days later. He informed the VAT office of his change of business, but did not state that his takings as a hairdresser would be substantially below the threshold limit of *Sch 1 para 1* (then £5,000). He failed to account for output tax on the takings of his hairdressing business. The Commissioners issued an assessment charging tax on them, and the tribunal dismissed the trader's appeal. Applying *Glassborow*, 53.1 above, the original registration covered the hairdressing business. *C Wiper*, LEE/74/57A (VTD 152).

53.10 A similar decision was reached in a case where a wholesaler began trading as a taxi driver. *H Zemmel*, LON/77/298 (VTD 498).

53.11 A married woman had carried on a guest-house until her death in October 1974. The takings from the guest-house were below the threshold of *Sch 1 para 1*, and she had not been registered for VAT. Following her death, her husband, who was registered as a coal merchant, took over the guest-house. He transferred his previous business to his daughter in March 1975 but did not inform the Commissioners of the change and he did not make any returns in respect of the guest-house business. On discovering the position, the Commissioners issued an assessment charging tax on the takings of the guest-house. He appealed. The tribunal upheld the assessment and dismissed his appeal, holding that his registration covered the guest-house business as well as the business he had originally carried on. *WA Renton*, EDN/79/12 (VTD 870).

53.12 **Cross-references.** The reasoning in *Glassborow* was applied in relation to what is now *VATA 1994, s 84(2)* in *McAllister*, 2.98 APPEALS. For other cases in which it was held that one registration covered more than one business, see *Walker*, 7.15 BUSINESS, *Williamson*, 7.21 BUSINESS, *Dawson*, 48.52 PENALTIES: FAILURE TO NOTIFY, *Laurie*, 49.252 PENALTIES: MISDECLARATION, and *Wood*, 53.133 below.

The date from which registration is effective (VATA 1994, Sch 1 para 1(5))

Note. For cases concerning the provisions of *Sch 1 para 1(2)*, where the question at issue is whether a business has been transferred as a going concern, see 61.77 to 61.89 TRANSFERS OF GOING CONCERNS.

53.13   A married couple began a hairdressing business in February 1973 and became liable to register in August 1973. They failed to register and a VAT officer issued a notice of compulsory registration. The couple appealed, contending that their accountant had advised them that they did not have to consider registration until the end of their first year of trading. The tribunal rejected this contention and dismissed their appeal. *EF & Mrs K Norton, LON/75/5 (VTD 151)*.

53.14   A similar decision was reached in *G & E Aspinall (t/a Aspinall Consulting), MAN/93/1231 (VTD 12676)*.

53.15   A trader became liable to register for VAT from October 1974 but did not notify the Commissioners until December 1974. Her registration was backdated and she appealed, contending that she should not have been registered retrospectively. The tribunal dismissed her appeal, holding that the Commissioners were obliged to backdate her registration and had no discretion to waive the statutory provisions. *SJ Whitehead, [1975] VATTR 152 (VTD 202)*.

53.16   *Whitehead*, 53.15 above, was applied in the similar cases of *JR Atkinson, CAR/76/ 142 (VTD 309); P & G Dyer, LON/77/50 (VTD 390); GJ Jelley, MAN/90/321 (VTD 6790); P & F Arnaoutis (t/a Trafford Chip Shop), MAN/95/403 (VTD 13829); D Kirk, MAN/95/379 (VTD 14042)* and *Lindley*, 58.133 SUPPLY.

53.17   A sole trader, who was registered for VAT, transferred his business to a company with effect from August 1975. The company was not informed of its registration number until April 1976 and did not charge its customers VAT on its supplies in the intervening period. The Commissioners issued an assessment charging tax on the supplies in question, and the tribunal dismissed the company's appeal. *JJ Foggon Ltd, MAN/78/164 (VTD 789)*.

53.18   *JJ Foggon Ltd*, 53.17 above, was followed in a case where a trader had applied for registration on 1 October 1987 but was not informed of his registration number until 13 November, and did not charge VAT on supplies made in the intervening period. *JC Tobin, [1991] VATTR 165 (VTD 5740)*.

53.19   A similar decision was reached in *M Lucas & G Jones (t/a Mayfair Building & Roofing Services), LON/92/96 (VTD 10715)*.

53.20   A company applied for registration from 1 October 1987. On a subsequent control visit the Commissioners discovered that the company should have been registered from 1 August rather than 1 October, and issued an assessment charging tax on the supplies made in August and September. The company's appeal against this assessment was dismissed by the tribunal. Although the company was not registered in August and September 1987, it was required to be registered, and its supplies in that period were taxable accordingly. *Adler Properties Ltd, LON/89/688X (VTD 4088)*.

53.21   A trader applied for registration from 1 November 1987. At a control visit in 1989, a VAT officer discovered that he should have registered from April 1975. In January

1990 the Commissioners issued a return to the trader covering the period from April 1975 to October 1987. The trader failed to complete the return, and in May 1990 the Commissioners issued an assessment covering the period in question. The trader appealed, contending that the date of registration could not be altered retrospectively. The tribunal rejected this contention and dismissed the appeal, and the CA upheld this decision. The trader had been required to be registered throughout the period covered by the return and the assessment. The Commissioners had been entitled to issue the return in question, and the assessment had been made to the best of their judgment. The validity of the assessment was not altered by the fact that the trader had subsequently transferred the business to a family partnership which used the same trading name. The obligations imposed by the Commissioners were in accordance with *Article 22* of the *EC Sixth Directive*. Neill LJ observed that *'Article 22(4)* was not intended to prevent or inhibit the collection of tax from those who ... had continued to trade without paying tax'. *V Bjellica (t/a Eddy's Domestic Appliances) v C & E Commrs, CA [1995] STC 329*. (*Note*. An appeal against a penalty under what is now *VATA 1994, s 67* was also dismissed—see 48.3 PENALTIES: FAILURE TO NOTIFY.)

53.22   The CA decision in *Bjellica*, 53.21 above, was applied in the similar subsequent cases of *M Yasin & M Hussain, MAN/94/959 (VTD 15804)* and *A Goni & A Ali (t/a Curry Centre Tandoori Restaurant), LON/98/67 (VTD 15840)*.

53.23   See also *Henderson*, 3.11 ASSESSMENT.

53.24   **Certificate of registration issued with wrong date.**   A sailing club became liable to register for VAT with effect from July 1975 but did not do so until April 1977. The certificate of registration issued by the Commissioners incorrectly stated the date of registration as 20 April 1977, and subsequently the Commissioners issued a return to the club for the period from 20 April 1977 to 30 June 1977. The club submitted the return, claiming a repayment of £57. The Commissioners then discovered the error in the registration date and issued an estimated assessment for the period from 21 July 1975, together with an amended certificate of registration. The club appealed, contending that the Commissioners were bound by their first certificate of registration and that, as the club had not been called on to make a return for the period from 21 July 1975, the assessment was not authorised by what is now *VATA 1994, s 73(1)*. The tribunal rejected this contention and dismissed the appeal, holding that the Commissioners were under no obligation to issue a certificate of registration. Furthermore, the liability to make returns was laid down by what is now *VAT Regulations 1995 (SI 1995 No 2518), reg 25* and was absolute, notwithstanding that the requisite form on which to make the return had not been provided. *DG Oliver (for Maidstone Sailing Club), LON/77/359 (VTD 511)*.

53.25   **Trader re-registered by Commissioners following application for deregistration—date from which re-registration effective.**   A hairdresser, who was registered for VAT, dismissed one of his employees in May 1981. He estimated that, following this, his turnover would decline to below the deregistration threshold of what is now *Sch 1 para 4*. He therefore applied for deregistration with effect from 1 June 1981. The Commissioners accepted his application. However, his turnover did not decline to the extent that he had anticipated, and in the following year he applied to be re-registered with effect from 1 April 1982. At a control visit in October 1982, a VAT officer ascertained that the value of the hairdresser's supplies in the year ended 30 June 1981 had exceeded the threshold in *Sch 1 para 1(1)*, so that he had been liable to re-register with effect from 30 July 1981. The Commissioners issued an assessment charging tax on the hairdresser's supplies from that date, and the tribunal dismissed the hairdresser's appeal. *HR Short, [1983] VATTR 94 (VTD 1408)*.

53.26   **Form VAT 1 incorrectly completed—whether date of commencement can be amended.**   See *Bruce*, 53.48 below, and *Rowe*, 53.49 below.

53.27   **Application to backdate voluntary registration.**   See *Attwater*, 53.57 below, and the cases noted at 53.58 below.

53.28   **Deliberate mis-statement on form VAT1—effect of VAT Regulations, reg 5(2).**   See *The Gables Nursing Home*, 53.61 below.

Subsequent decline in turnover (VATA 1994, Sch 1 para 1(3))

53.29   **Sch 1 para 1(3)—whether Commissioners should have been satisfied that future supplies would not exceed threshold.**   In the case noted at 48.53 PENALTIES: FAIURE TO NOTIFY, Lord Grantchester held that the exception in what is now *Sch 1 para 1(3)* 'can only be sought to be relied upon by a trader, where he has not applied to the Commissioners at the right time to consider all the relevant circumstances, if the value of his taxable supplies in the year did not exceed the relevant amount and he establishes that no reasonable body of Commissioners at the relevant time could have come to any conclusion other than that his taxable supplies in the year would not exceed the relevant amount'. *WF Shephard, LON/86/318 (VTD 2232).*

53.30   A similar decision was reached in *DE Cannon, LON/84/350 (VTD 2486)*.

53.31   A subcontractor became liable to register from June 1990, but did not do so. The Commissioners did not discover this until February 1991, by which time he had ceased working, as the contractor for which he worked had ceased trading and subsequently went into liquidation. His turnover for the period from 1 June 1990 to 10 February 1991 was below the threshold laid down by *Sch 1 para 1(3)*. The tribunal chairman (Miss Plumptre, sitting alone) held that he could not be required to register retrospectively. *R Fawson, LON/92/1350A (VTD 9724)*. (*Note*. No other cases were cited in this decision, which was subsequently disapproved by the Ch D in *Gray*, 53.36 below.)

53.32   An individual (G), who was registered for VAT, ran a dry-cleaning business, which consisted of a small retail unit and a number of agency contracts with hotels and similar businesses. In July 1993 G sold the retail unit and some of the agency contracts to another individual (H). At the time of the transfer, H was operating an existing dry-cleaning agency business in partnership with his wife. The Commissioners issued a ruling that H should be registered for VAT by virtue of *Sch 1 para 1(2)* with effect from the date of transfer. H appealed. The tribunal allowed his appeal, accepting that the business had been acquired as a going concern, within *Sch 1 para 1(2)*, but holding on the evidence that the Commissioners should have accepted H's contention that his turnover in the 12 months following the transfer would not exceed the then threshold in *Sch 1 para 1(3)*. The tribunal held that, notwithstanding the wording of *Sch 1 para 1(3)*, it had an appellate jurisdiction in considering an appeal against registration. Applying *dicta* in *JH Corbitt (Numismatists) Ltd*, 56.1 SECOND-HAND GOODS, the officer responsible for the relevant decisions (and who did not give evidence to the tribunal) had acted unreasonably in taking the partnership turnover into account when concluding that H should be required to register. *A Hare (t/a Imperial Dry Cleaners), MAN/95/ 2347 (VTD 14202)*. (*Note*. Compare the subsequent decision in *Timur & Timur*, 53.34 below, in which the tribunal held that its jurisdiction under *Sch 1 para 1(3)* was only supervisory.)

53.33   Registration

53.33   The owner of a minicab business, who was registered for VAT, transferred it, as a going concern, to a partnership comprising his wife and son. His accountant advised the Commissioners that the owner had ceased trading, but did not advise them that the business had been transferred. Accordingly the business was deregistered with the effect from the date of the transfer. Subsequently the Commissioners discovered that the business had continued to trade, and issued an assessment on the basis that *Sch 1 para 1(2)* applied. The partners appealed, contending that following the transfer, their turnover had declined to below the registration threshold and that the effect of *Sch 1 para 1(3)* was that they should not be required to account for tax. The tribunal rejected this contention and dismissed the appeal. It was accepted that the partners' turnover had in fact declined to below the registration threshold, but there were no grounds on which the Commissioners could be expected, at the date of the transfer, to have believed that this would be the case. Applying *dicta* of Lord Grantchester in *WF Shephard*, 53.29 above, the exception in what is now *Sch 1 para 1(3)* 'can only be sought to be relied upon by a trader, where he has not applied to the Commissioners at the right time to consider all the relevant circumstances, if ... he establishes that no reasonable body of Commissioners *at the relevant time* could have come to any conclusion other than that his taxable supplies in the year would not exceed the relevant amount'. The decision in *Fawson*, 53.31 above, was specifically disapproved, on the grounds that the chairman in that case had not referred to the previous decisions in *Shephard*, 53.29 above, or *Cannon*, 53.30 above. *RJ & J Nash, MAN/96/1132 (VTD 14944)*. (*Note.* The decision here was approved by the Ch D in *Gray*, 53.36 below.)

53.34   *Nash & Nash*, 53.33 above, was applied in a similar subsequent case in which the tribunal held that it had a supervisory jurisdiction and could not substitute its own discretion or decision for that of the Commissioners, provided that the Commissioners' decision was reasonable. *Dicta* in *JH Corbitt (Numismatists) Ltd*, 56.1 SECOND-HAND SCHEMES, applied. On the evidence, the Commissioners had acted reasonably in not being satisfied that the appellants' turnover would not fall below the threshold of *Sch 1 para 1(3)*. *B & J Timur (t/a Istanbul Kebab House), LON/97/319 (VTD 15305)*. (*Note.* An appeal against a penalty for failure to notify was also dismissed.)

53.35   Similar decisions, also applying *Nash & Nash*, 53.33 above, were reached in *D Harry (t/a Principal Financial Associates), LON/97/1322 (VTD 15747)* and *M & EJ Burr (t/a Penny's Place), LON/x (VTD 16866)*.

53.36   In February 1997 a VAT officer discovered that a building contractor (G) had become liable to register from September 1996. The Commissioners issued a notice of registration and imposed a penalty. G appealed, contending that his turnover would not exceed the threshold in future periods, because he had arranged for some work to be carried on by a registered company which he controlled. The tribunal dismissed his appeal, holding on the evidence that the Commissioners had acted reasonably in not being satisfied that G's turnover would fall below the threshold. The Ch D upheld this decision. Ferris J held that the effect of *Sch 1 para 1(3)* was that 'a VAT tribunal, or this court itself, can only interfere with the decision if it is shown that the decision is one which no reasonable body of Commissioners could reach'. Where a trader registered late, 'the Commissioners must give effect to *para 1(3)* by considering the case as at the date from which registration would otherwise take effect and, by looking forward, asking themselves whether they are or are not satisfied that turnover will not exceed the threshold amount'. *JG Gray (t/a William Gray & Son) v C & E Commrs, Ch D [2000] STC 880.*

Registration on basis of future turnover (VATA 1994, Sch 1 para 1(1)(b))

Note. The 'future turnover' test under what is now *VATA 1994, Sch 1 para 1(1)(b)* was significantly amended with effect from 21 March 1990. A trader is now only required to register under *1 Sch 1(1)(b)* if there are reasonable grounds for believing that his turnover will exceed the registration threshold (currently £51,000) in the next 30 days, rather than (as previously) in the next twelve months. The practical effect of this is, as stated in Customs' Press Notice dated 20 March 1990, that the 'future turnover' test no longer applies to most new or expanding businesses. The cases noted at 53.37 to 53.39 below relate to periods before 21 March 1990.

53.37   A company which operated a recruitment agency applied for registration in January 1986. The Commissioners formed the opinion that it should have been registered from September 1985, when it had taken over a number of clients from another company, under what is now *Sch 1 para 1(1)(b)*. They imposed a penalty, against which the company appealed. The tribunal dismissed the company's appeal. Lord Grantchester observed that the test under *Sch 1 para 1(1)(b)* was an 'objective test' and 'involves a consideration of the question whether, on balance, taking all the relevant factors into consideration, it was more reasonable to believe that the value of the taxable supplies would exceed the stipulated amount rather than fall short thereof'. *Optimum Personnel Evaluation (Operations) Ltd, LON/86/620 (VTD 2334)*. (*Note.* For a preliminary issue in this case, see 2.121 APPEALS.)

53.38   The proprietor of a dry-cleaning business was registered for VAT in March 1996 after the Commissioners had formed the opinion that his turnover exceeded the registration threshold under what is now *VATA 1994, Sch 1 para 1(1)(a)*. The registration was backdated to 11 March 1990. The proprietor appealed, contending that he had not been liable to register. The tribunal reviewed the evidence and concluded that the proprietor had been liable to register under the 'future turnover' test of what is now *VATA 1994, Sch 1 para 1(1)(b)*. (The tribunal observed that 'it seems likely' that the proprietor had also been liable to register under the 'historic turnover' test of *Sch 1 para 1(1)(a)*, as the Commissioners had contended, but did not state this as a firm conclusion.) The proprietor appealed to the QB, which remitted the case to a new tribunal for rehearing, holding that the previous tribunal had erred in law in its interpretation of *Sch 1 para 1(1)(b)*. Carnwath J held that the test applied by Lord Grantchester in *Optimum Personnel Evaluation (Operations) Ltd*, 53.37 above, was 'understandable and capable of application to a particular point in time, at which there is some identifiable change in the nature or scale of the business' but was 'practically unworkable if it is applied not to a specific date defined by external circumstances, but on a rolling basis from day to day'. Applying the CJEC decision in *Administration des Douanes v Société Anonyme Gondrand Freres*, 21.47 EUROPEAN COMMUNITY LAW, 'rules imposing charges on the taxpayer must be clear and precise so that he may know without ambiguity what are his rights and obligations and may take steps accordingly'. Accordingly, 'the principle of legal certainty . . . requires the implication of some objectively definable criterion for bringing *subparagraph (b)* into play'. The tribunal had failed to make a firm finding that the proprietor was liable to register under *Sch 1 para 1(1)(a)*. Its statement that 'it seems likely' that he had done so was 'an incidental observation, rather than an alternative basis for the decision'. Accordingly the case should be remitted to a new tribunal for a rehearing. *A Bennett v C & E Commrs, QB [1999] STC 248*. (*Note.* For other issues in this case, see 2.88 APPEALS and 3.17 ASSESSMENT.)

53.39   The Commissioners issued a ruling that the proprietor of a taxi business was required to register for VAT from 6 July 1988 under the provisions of what is now *Sch 1 para 1(1)(b)*. The proprietor appealed. The tribunal reviewed the evidence in detail and allowed the appeal, finding that 'given the condition and nature of the business which the appellant took over, and his evidence, which we accept, about its development, we do not believe that, looked at objectively, there were reasonable ground (*sic*) for believing that the appellant's rental income would reach the stipulated threshold within his first year of trading beginning on 6 July 1988'. *M Nawaz (t/a Elvis Private Hire), MAN/94/224 (VTD 16017)*.

Capital assets (VATA 1994, Sch 1 para 1(7))

53.40   **Sale of motor cars—whether capital assets.** A company (H) acquired a number of motor cars from its parent company and leased them to a customer for period averaging less than six months. When the leases had expired, it sold the cars back to the original dealers. It failed to register for VAT. The Commissioners discovered that its turnover had exceeded the statutory threshold, and issued a notice of compulsory registration. H appealed, contending that the cars which it had sold to the original dealers were capital assets, so that these sales should be disregarded in computing its turnover, by virtue of *VATA 1994, Sch 1 para 1(7)*. The tribunal rejected this contention and dismissed the appeal, holding on the evidence that 'the motor cars were not intended to be of a durable nature within the context of the business of the appellant'. Furthermore, 'the sales of the cars were frequent and usual and did not make drastic changes in turnover for one year'. Accordingly, the cars were not 'capital assets'. *Harbig Leasing Two Ltd, LON/99/1216 (VTD 16843)*.

CESSATION OF LIABILITY TO REGISTER (VATA 1994, Sch 1 para 4)

53.41   A married couple, who had recently acquired a small restaurant, registered for VAT from 1 April 1973. In June 1974 they applied for deregistration on the basis that their takings for the following year would probably be below the threshold of what is now *VATA 1994, Sch 1 para 4* (which was then £4,000). The Commissioners were not satisfied that their takings would be less than the threshold, and formally rejected the application on 10 July 1974. The tribunal dismissed the couple's appeal, noting that their takings for the year ended 31 July 1974 were £4,178 and holding that it was not clear that the takings for the year from 10 July 1974, the date of the Commissioners' decision, would be £4,000 or less. *Mr & Mrs K Savva (t/a Venus Restaurant), LON/74/94 (VTD 127)*.

53.42   *Savva*, 53.41 above, was applied in a case where the Commissioners agreed to deregister a partnership from 31 December 1985, and the partners unsuccessfully contended that they should be deregistered from 1 January 1985. *RE & EM Harvey, MAN/88/938 (VTD 4899)*.

53.43   A trader (D) who carried on two small businesses registered for VAT from 1 April 1973 and applied for deregistration on 30 July 1973. The Commissioners rejected this application but subsequently agreed to deregister him from 16 February 1974, the date on which he discontinued one of the businesses. D appealed, contending that he should have been allowed to deregister from July 1973. The tribunal rejected this contention and dismissed his appeal. *JF Delves (No 2), LEE/75/3 (VTD 157)*.

53.44   **Application for deregistration accepted—whether subsequent application for deregistration from earlier date precluded.** A hairdresser closed her business on 31 January 1977 and was deregistered from 1 February. The Commissioners subsequently discovered that she had underpaid £90 VAT and sought to recover this amount. She appealed, contending that, for some time before she ceased trading, her annual turnover had been below £5,000 (the then limit of *Sch 1 para 1*) and that she could have applied for deregistration earlier. The tribunal dismissed her appeal, holding that, as she had applied for deregistration from 1

February 1977, she could not subsequently claim to be deregistered from an earlier date. *B Jackson (t/a Suite Sixe), MAN/77/20 (VTD 469).*

53.45 **Delay in application for deregistration—retrospection not permitted.** A married couple operated a fish and chip shop and were registered for VAT. Their turnover was less than the registration threshold and they did not account for any output tax. The Commissioners issued an assessment to charge output tax on the supplies they had made. They appealed, contending that they had assumed that, although they were registered, they did not have to charge VAT since their turnover was below the threshold, and that in the circumstances they should be allowed to deregister retrospectively. The tribunal dismissed their appeal, holding that deregistration could not be retrospective. *B & C Parker, MAN/87/59 (VTD 2454).*

NOTIFICATION OF LIABILITY AND REGISTRATION (VATA 1994, Sch 1 para 5)

53.46 **Sch 1 para 5(2)—date from which registration is effective.** A hairdresser had been registered for VAT from 1975 to 1988, when he deregistered. In December 1997 the Commissioners discovered that his turnover had exceeded the threshold again in the year ending 31 March 1996, and registered him from 1 May 1996. He appealed, contending that he should not be required to re-register retrospectively. The tribunal dismissed his appeal, observing that *VATA 1994, Sch 1 para 5(2)* 'contains no provision for discretion' and holding that the Commissioners were obliged to backdate his registration. *G George (t/a Top Six Hairdressing), LON/99/ 927 (VTD 16971).*

53.47 See also the cases noted at 53.13 to 53.25 above.

53.48 **Form VAT 1 incorrectly completed—whether date of commencement can be amended.** A trader began to carry on business on 11 April 1990. On 29 October he applied to register for VAT, and began to account for tax from 1 November. Because he had stated on the form VAT1 that he had begun to trade on 11 April, the Commissioners registered him from that date, and subsequently issued an assessment charging tax on his supplies from that date. The tribunal dismissed his appeal, finding that the Commissioners had not acted unreasonably. *PS Bruce, LON/93/2930 (VTD 12484).*

53.49 A partnership which operated a restaurant kept a daily record of takings, and passed the registration threshold of *Sch 1 para 1* (which was £45,000 at the relevant time) on 7 June 1994. The partners submitted a form VAT 1 notifying the Commissioners that they were required to be registered from 7 June. Subsequently their accountants advised them that, by virtue of what is now *VATA 1994, Sch 1 para 5*, their registration need not have taken effect until 1 August 1994. They applied to the Commissioners requesting that the effective date of registration be amended accordingly. The Commissioners rejected this request but the tribunal allowed the partnership's appeal, holding that the effect of what is now *VATA 1994, Sch 1 para 5(2)* was that the partnership was not required to be registered until 1 August unless it agreed to an earlier date, and the incorrect completion of the form VAT 1 did not amount to such an agreement. *AJ & AE Rowe (t/a Arthur's), LON/95/423A (VTD 13650).*

53.50 **Appeals against retrospective registration.** There have been a large number of cases, which appear to raise no point of general importance, in which appeals against retrospective registration have been dismissed. In the interests of space, such cases are not listed individually in this book. For summaries of such cases decided up to 31 December 1992, see Tolley's VAT Cases 1993.

53.51   Registration

53.51   A company was incorporated in April 1991 and applied to be registered for VAT as an 'intending trader' under the provisions of what is now *VATA 1994, Sch 1 para 9(1)*. The Commissioners rejected the application on the grounds that the company had not supplied satisfactory evidence of its intention to trade. It appeared to have done nothing other than to purchase a fax machine, and the address given on the company's application form was that of its professional advisers, rather than a business address. The company appealed, contending that it was unreasonable for the Commissioners to have rejected its assertions that it hoped to begin trading. The tribunal rejected this contention and dismissed the appeal, holding that its jurisdiction was supervisory rather than appellate, applying *JH Corbitt (Numismatists) Ltd*, 56.1 SECOND-HAND GOODS. The company had not submitted objective evidence of an intention to trade and the Commissioners had not acted unreasonably in rejecting the application. *Golden Pyramid Ltd, LON/91/1306Y (VTD 9133)*.

53.52   In 1988 a Swiss property developer purchased a site in Newcastle-upon-Tyne. In 1990 he applied for registration as an 'intending trader'. The Commissioners rejected his application. In 1992 the site which he had purchased was taken over by the Tyne & Wear Development Corporation under a compulsory purchase order, the question of compensation being referred to a tribunal. In 1993 he made a further application for registration, which the Commissioners again rejected. He appealed, contending that he wished to waive exemption in respect of the site so that he could reclaim input tax which he had incurred. The tribunal dismissed his appeal, holding that since he was no longer the owner of the site, he was no longer an 'intending trader' and was no longer entitled to registration. *L Landau, LON/95/1944 (VTD 13644)*.

53.53   In 1995 a charity, which was not registered for VAT, purchased a former hotel, which was subsequently converted and used as a residential home for the elderly (i.e. a 'relevant residential building' within *VATA 1994, Sch 8 Group 5*). In 1997 the charity applied for retrospective registration, backdated to 1995. The Commissioners refused to backdate the registration, on the basis that in 1995 the charity had neither made any taxable supplies, nor intended to do so. The charity appealed, contending that at the time when the building was being converted, it had intended to transfer a major interest (i.e. a lease of at least 21 years) in the building, and was therefore entitled to registration under *Sch 1 para 9*. The tribunal reviewed the evidence in detail and dismissed the appeal. The chairman found that he was 'not satisfied that the appellants formed an intention to grant a major interest in the property at the relevant period, July to October 1995. I am satisfied that that intention only existed and arose some time between October 1996 and April 1997. An intention is different from a hope or a discussion or a consideration. An intention implies that the mind has been directed upon or fixed upon a purpose.' *Birmingham Royal Institution for the Blind, MAN/97/912 (VTD 16386)*.

53.54   A company operated a chain of 23 bookmaking shops. It had not registered for VAT, since its supplies were exempt under what is now *VATA 1994, Sch 9, Group 4, Item 1*. In May 1995 the company's accountants submitted 23 retrospective applications for registration, backdated to April 1993, on the basis that the company had transferred each of its shops to a partnership in which it held a 95% interest, and that the partnerships had been making taxable supplies of tea and coffee to employees at the shops. The Commissioners rejected the applications, considering firstly that the alleged partnerships did not in fact exist, and alternatively that if the partnerships were deemed to exist, they were not making any taxable supplies. The company and its alleged partners appealed, contending that they were entitled to register under *VATA 1994, Sch 1 para 9*. The tribunal rejected this contention and dismissed the appeal. Under *Sch 1 para 9*, an applicant had to satisfy the Commissioners that he was making, or intending to make, taxable supplies. On the evidence presented, the Commissioners were not satisfied that the alleged partnerships were making taxable supplies, and their conclusion was 'reasonable' and 'correct in law'. There were no separate bank accounts for each partnerships, no partnership accounts, and no partners' meetings. None of the alleged partnerships owned any business assets or held bookmakers' licences. Applying *dicta* of Lord Clyde in *CIR v Williamson, CS 1928, 14 TC 335 (TTC 2001, 40.10)*, 'you do not constitute or create or prove a partnership by saying that there is one'. *SP Graham Ltd & Others, LON/96/1121 (VTD 14789)*.

53.55   In June 1994 an individual (D) applied for registration as an 'intending trader'. The Commissioners rejected his application, and he appealed, contending that he intended to undertake building work for a VAT-registered partnership of which he was a member, and to continue in business as a commercial building contractor. The tribunal accepted his evidence and allowed the appeal, holding that D had satisfied 'the conditions specified in the legislation' and that the Commissioners were 'required to register him'. On the evidence, the VAT officers responsible for rejecting his application had failed to 'consider the case put to them' and had 'closed their minds to the possibility that he could be carrying on business'. *Golden Pyramid Ltd*, 53.51 above, and *Kelly*, 7.48 BUSINESS, distinguished. *JP Dewhirst, LON/94/2414A (VTD 13793)*.

53.56   See also *22A Property Investments Ltd*, 58.162 SUPPLY.

53.57   **Date from which voluntary registration effective.**   In March 1997 a dentist applied to be registered for VAT with retrospective effect, to enable him to reclaim input tax for previous years. The Commissioners agreed to register him with effect from 1 April 1994, but rejected his application to backdate his registration to 1 April 1992. He appealed. The tribunal dismissed his appeal, holding that the effect of *Sch 1 para 9* was that a voluntary registration took effect 'from the day on which the request is made or from such earlier date as may be agreed'. Applying *dicta* in *John Dee Ltd*, 14.28 COLLECTION AND ENFORCEMENT, the tribunal's jurisdiction was limited to considering whether the Commissioners had acted unreasonably. On the evidence, the Commissioners' decision had not been unreasonable. *A Attwater, MAN/97/903 (VTD 15496)*.

53.58   Similar decisions, also applying *dicta* in *John Dee Ltd*, 14.28 COLLECTION AND ENFORCEMENT, were reached in *PJ & ML Edwards, MAN/97/1084 (VTD 15533)* and *R & M Davis (t/a El Shaddai Private Nursing Home) (and related appeals), LON/98/260 (VTD 16275)*.

53.59   A similar decision was reached in a case where the appellant contended that he had submitted a previous form VAT1, but had sent it to an office which had closed almost two years previously. The tribunal held, applying *dicta* in *Selwyn*, 48.100 PENALTIES: FAILURE TO NOTIFY, that 'the postage of a form VAT1 does not of itself constitute notification to the Commissioners of liability to register'. *Dr J Hill, LON/97/1526 (VTD 15543)*.

53.60   **Registration as 'intending trader'—conditional registration requiring repayment of input tax in certain circumstances—whether conditions valid.**   See *Hordern*, 34.446 INPUT TAX, and *Wilson*, 34.466 INPUT TAX.

53.61   **Incorrect statement on form VAT1—effect of VAT Regulations, reg 5(2).**   On 1 May 1995 a nursing home was transferred from a company to a partnership. The partnership submitted a form VAT1, applying to be registered with effect from April 1992. The Commissioners initially accepted the application, and sent the partnership a VAT return covering the period from April 1992. The partnership completed the return and submitted it to the Commissioners, claiming a substantial repayment of VAT. A VAT officer visited the nursing home to verify the claim and discovered that the partnership had only begun to carry on the business on 1 May 1995. The Commissioners issued a ruling under *VAT Regulations 1995 (SI 1995 No 2518), reg 5*, that the registration should be amended so that it ran from 1 May 1995 rather than from 1992, with the result that no tax was repayable. The tribunal upheld the Commissioners' ruling and dismissed the partnership's appeal, holding on the evidence that the Commissioners had been 'misled by the untrue statement in the application for registration and ... having discovered the truth, they were entitled to put the matter right'. The effect of *reg 5(2)* was that the Commissioners were entitled to alter the date of registration. *The Gables Nursing Home, MAN/97/51 (VTD 15456)*.

CANCELLATION OF REGISTRATION (VATA 1994, Sch 1 para 13)

53.62   **Cancellation of one of two registrations—whether appealable.**   A trader carried on two separate businesses and obtained separate registration numbers for each. When the Commissioners discovered this, they cancelled one of the registrations. The tribunal struck out the trader's appeal against this, holding that there was no appealable matter within what is now *VATA 1994, s 83(a)*, since the remaining registration number covered both businesses. *KN Weakley, LON/73/142 (VTD 56)*.

53.63   **Appeal against retrospective cancellation of registration—whether within jurisdiction of tribunal.**   See *Brookes*, 2.23 APPEALS.

53.64   **Group registration—appeal against cancellation of separate registration covering earlier periods.**   See *Eastwood Care Homes (Ilkeston) Ltd*, 30.5 GROUPS OF COMPANIES.

53.65   **Registration but no business carried on.**   A civil service canteen had applied to be registered from 1 April 1973. The Commissioners had accepted this application. However it was subsequently agreed that the carrying on of the canteen was not a business for VAT purposes, and that the application for registration had been mistaken. On 27 September 1973 the canteen applied for the registration to be cancelled. The Commissioners agreed to cancel the registration from 27 September, but refused to make the cancellation retrospective. The tribunal dismissed the canteen's appeal against this decision. *CH Goodyear, BIR/73/43 (VTD 230)*.

53.66   In 1995 a company purchased some land and registered for VAT under *VATA 1994, Sch 1 para 9*. It reclaimed input tax on the land. It did not make any taxable supplies and did not respond to correspondence from the Commissioners. In 1999 the Commissioners cancelled the company's registration. The company appealed, contending that it still intended to develop the land. The tribunal reviewed the evidence, rejected this contention and dismissed the appeal. Applying *Associated Provincial Picture Houses v Wednesbury Corporation, CA 1947, [1948] 1 KB 223; [1947] 2 All ER 680*, the tribunal's jurisdiction was supervisory. The Commissioners' decision had been 'entirely reasonable'. *DCM Leisure Ltd, MAN/00/323 (VTD 16966)*. (*Note*. The tribunal also upheld an assessment under *Sch 4 para 8*—see 63.16 VALUATION.)

53.67   See also *Three H Aircraft Hire*, 7.6 BUSINESS; *Blandy*, 7.26 BUSINESS; *Tibbs*, 7.31 BUSINESS; *Kelly*, 7.48 BUSINESS; *Trinity Methodist Church*, 7.50 BUSINESS; *Higson*, 7.66 BUSINESS; *Newmir plc*, 7.106 BUSINESS; *Ladbroke (Palace Gate) Property*

Services Ltd, 7.109 BUSINESS, and *Apple & Pear Development Council*, 21.47 EUROPEAN COMMUNITY LAW.

53.68   **Cancellation of registration—whether appellant carrying on a business.** For successful appeals against the cancellation of registration, in cases where the issue was whether the appellant was carrying on a business, see *Border Flying Co*, 7.45 BUSINESS; *Prenn*, 7.53 BUSINESS; *Jenks*, 7.71 BUSINESS; *Bird Racing (Management) Ltd*, 7.88 BUSINESS, and *Merseyside Cablevision Ltd*, 34.444 INPUT TAX.

53.69   **Registration but all supplies exempt from VAT—appeal against subsequent cancellation of registration.** The proprietors of a residential home for the elderly registered for VAT in January 1986, although all their supplies were exempt under what is now *VATA 1994, Sch 9 Group 7, Item 4*. When the Commissioners discovered this, they cancelled the registration. The tribunal dismissed the proprietors' appeal against this decision, holding that they had never been entitled to be registered. *DR Bramley & MA Bradley, [1987] VATTR 72 (VTD 2349)*.

53.70   A similar decision was reached in *MV Wright, LON/94/196A (VTD 12701)*.

53.71   See also *Steven*, 31.21 HEALTH AND WELFARE, and *Llanfyllin Group Practice*, 53.94 below.

53.72   **Application for retrospective cancellation of registration.** A hairdresser ceased to be required to be registered with effect from 15 March 1989, when the deregistration threshold of what is now *VATA 1994, Sch 1 para 4* was increased. She applied for her registration to be cancelled with effect from June 1988. The Commissioners agreed to cancel her registration from 31 March 1989, but refused to backdate the cancellation. The tribunal dismissed her appeal against this decision. *S Gilmour, EDN/90/57 (VTD 5305)*.

53.73   A trader's turnover exceeded the threshold of *Sch 1 para 1* in 1987 but dropped below the threshold of what is now *VATA 1994, Sch 1 para 4* in 1990, so that although he remained entitled to be registered under what is now *VATA 1994, Sch 1 para 9*, he was no longer required to be registered under *Sch 1 para 1*. The tribunal rejected the trader's contention that his registration should be cancelled retrospectively, holding that 'a tribunal cannot decide a question of deregistration with the benefit of hindsight'. *Dicta* in *Harvey*, 53.42 above, applied. *RR Bissmire, LON/90/1563X (VTD 7303)*. (*Note*. For another issue in this case, see 48.2 PENALTIES: FAILURE TO NOTIFY.)

53.74   Similar decisions, also applying *Harvey*, 53.42 above, were reached in *RG Henderson (t/a La Coupe), EDN/95/67 (VTD 13469)* and *P Constantine (t/a The Red Lion Inn), MAN/98/308 (VTD 15792)*.

53.75   Similar decisions were reached in *Professor RM Young, LON/91/2710X (VTD 7922); AD Davidson, LON/91/2056Z (VTD 9537); M Jones, LON/95/997 (VTD 13302); J Dunhill, MAN/93/964 (VTD 13313); TR O'Driscoll (t/a Kitchenfit), MAN/95/2266 (VTD 14350); S Moloney, LON/96/1723 (VTD 14873); C Bond Ltd, EDN/97/75 (VTD 15515); N & A Grogan (t/a Valet Plus), EDN/98/201 (VTD 16084)* and *Royal British Legion Drumnadrochit Branch, EDN/00/58 (VTD 16957)*.

53.76   **Registered business acquired as going concern—application for retrospective cancellation of registration.** A trader took over a business as a going concern in April 1992, and registered for VAT from that date. However, his turnover never exceeded the threshold of *Sch 1 para 1*, and in September 1992 he applied for his registration to be cancelled. The Commissioners agreed to cancel his registration with effect from 1 October 1992, but refused to backdate the cancellation, and issued an assessment charging output tax on the supplies which he had made between 1 April and 30 September. The tribunal dismissed the trader's appeal, holding that the effect of what is now *VATA 1994, Sch 1 para 13* was that a valid registration could only be cancelled from the date on which an application for cancellation was made, or from an agreed later date, and that registration could not be cancelled retrospectively. *JD Rana, LON/92/3295A (VTD 11842)*.

53.77 A similar decision was reached in *SM Alexander, LON/94/570A (VTD 12810)*.

53.78 **Registration cancelled following sale of business—whether Commissioners entitled to require repayment of input tax.** In 1985 an individual (R) purchased some land, which he intended to develop as a timber estate. He registered for VAT as an 'intending trader', although he had not begun to make taxable supplies and was not likely to do so for some time. During the next four years he reclaimed substantial amounts of input tax. He faced financial problems, and in 1989 he sold the land to trustees. The Commissioners cancelled his registration, and issued an assessment to recover the input tax which he had reclaimed. The tribunal allowed R's appeal against the assessment. On the evidence, R had sold a quantity of stone from the land in 1987, and this was a taxable supply. Furthermore, although the sale of the land was an exempt supply, R had also sold a quantity of fertiliser to the trustees, and this too constituted a taxable supply. Since R had made two taxable supplies, the Commissioners were not entitled to require repayment of the input tax which he had previously incurred. *D Rye, MAN/90/158 (VTD 7578)*.

53.79 **Registration cancelled following cessation of business—whether Commissioners entitled to require repayment of input tax.** An insurance broker (T) had been registered for VAT as a partly exempt trader since 1973. At a control visit in July 1990, a VAT officer formed the impression that T had not made any taxable supplies since December 1988. T disagreed with this, contending that he had made a taxable supply in the period ending 30 June 1990. Nevertheless, the Commissioners issued an assessment to recover the input tax which T had reclaimed for the periods between 1 January 1989 and 30 June 1990. The Commissioners also cancelled T's registration with effect from 1 July 1990. In January 1991 the case was reviewed by a senior VAT officer, who decided that the disputed assessment would have to be withdrawn since T had only been deregistered with effect from July 1990. T was therefore notified that the assessment was being withdrawn. In August 1991 the Commissioners wrote to T again, requesting him to refund the input tax which had previously been assessed; and in September 1991 the Commissioners issued a further notice retrospectively cancelling T's registration for the period from 1 January 1989 to 30 June 1990. T appealed against the retrospective deregistration and the demand for tax, contending firstly that the Commissioners had acted unreasonably in renewing their demand for the tax after having withdrawn the original assessments, and additionally that he had made a taxable supply in June 1990, so that he was entitled to remain registered until 30 June 1990. The tribunal adjourned the hearing for further argument, but severely criticised the Commissioners for their handling of the case, observing that the original assessment appeared to have been withdrawn by agreement under what is now *VATA 1994, s 85*, and that the Commissioners were in effect attempting 'having lost the match, (to) move the goalposts and demand a replay'. *M Tourick (t/a RM Tourick & Co), LON/91/1938Y (VTD 7712)*. (*Note.* There was no further public hearing of the appeal.)

53.80 **Voluntary registration before turnover reaching statutory threshold— subsequent application for cancellation of registration not permitted.** A partnership began to trade in April 1992. On the advice of their accountant, they registered for VAT from May 1992. However, their turnover had not reached the statutory threshold (and did not do so until December 1992). The accountant realised that the partnership need not have made its application for registration, and in June the partnership applied for cancellation of its registration. The Commissioners rejected the application, considering that deregistration was not appropriate as the partnership's turnover made it likely that the registration threshold would be exceeded within the next twelve months. The tribunal dismissed the partnership's appeal against this decision, holding that what is now *VATA 1994, Sch 1 para 13* did not enable the Commissioners 'to reverse a decision retroactively'. *M & P Stosic (t/a Dave & Sidas Fish Bar), MAN/92/1727 (VTD 10728).*

53.81   *Stosic*, 53.80 above, was applied in a case in which a couple purchased a Chinese restaurant in June 1992. The restaurant had previously been closed for some time, so that it was accepted that the transfer did not constitute the transfer of a going concern. However, the couple applied for registration with effect from the date on which they took over the restaurant. In August 1992 their accountant realised that they did not need to have registered from that date, and applied for the registration to be cancelled retrospectively. The Commissioners agreed to cancel the registration from the date on which they received this application, but refused to backdate the cancellation to June. The tribunal dismissed the couple's appeal against this decision, observing that the couple had been entitled to register under what is now *VATA 1994, Sch 1 para 9*, so that the application for registration was valid and effective until the subsequent application for cancellation. *Mr & Mrs Y Luong (t/a Golden Lion), [1994] VATTR 349 (VTD 12234).*

53.82   Similar decisions were reached in *G McMenemy, EDN/95/184 (VTD 13878); Faimana Properties Ltd, LON/96/375 (VTD 14600)* and *ST Oshitola, LON/96/489 (VTD 15487).*

53.83   *Luong*, 53.81 above, was applied in a subsequent case in which a retrospective application to amend the date of a voluntary registration was rejected. *FL Lewis-Cox (t/a The Hair Emporium), MAN/96/120 (VTD 14349).*

53.84   A similar decision, also applying *Luong*, 53.81 above, was reached in *KW Weale, MAN/96/212 (VTD 14654).*

53.85   **Anticipated future decline in turnover—application for cancellation of registration.**   An application for cancellation of registration was dismissed in a case where a trader had contended that her turnover would decline to below the registration threshold, although at the time of making the application it was still above the threshold. The tribunal held that its jurisdiction was supervisory and that the Commissioners' decision to refuse the application was not unreasonable. *N Smith (t/a The Chippy), MAN/93/822 (VTD 11806).*

53.86   Similar decisions were reached in *TE Darker (t/a Fig Tree Coffee Shop), MAN/99/413 (VTD 16620)* and *S Wilkes (t/a Dipton Chippy), MAN/99/189 (VTD 16652).*

53.87   See also the cases noted at 53.41 to 53.45 above (which deal with applications for deregistration under what is now *VATA 1994, Sch 1 para 4*, for periods before the introduction of what is now *VATA 1994, Sch 1 para 13* by *FA 1988*).

53.88   **Anticipated future change in rating of supplies—application for cancellation of registration.**   In January 1998 an osteopathy partnership applied for cancellation of its registration, on the basis that the partners had arranged to be registered under the *Osteopaths Act 1993*, and that their supplies would subsequently become exempt under *VATA 1994, Sch 9 Group 7*. The Commissioners rejected the application, on the basis that the partnership's services were still standard-rated at the relevant time. The tribunal dismissed the partnership's appeal, holding that the Commissioners had not acted unreasonably. *Associated Provincial Picture Houses v Wednesbury Corporation, CA 1947, [1948] 1 KB 223; [1947] 2 All ER 680*, applied. *RN & BA Lloyd, MAN/98/307 (VTD 15786). (Note. VATA 1994, Sch 9 Group 7* was amended by the *VAT (Osteopaths) Order 1998* to provide for the exemption of supplies by registered osteopaths with effect from 12 June 1998. The Commissioners agreed to backdate exemption to 9 May 1998 by extra-statutory concession.)

53.89   A similar decision was reached in *MG Duffree, MAN/98/231 (VTD 15793)*.

53.90   *Lloyd*, 53.88 above, and *Duffree*, 53.89 above, were applied in the similar subsequent case of *RG Wadsworth, MAN/98/762 (VTD 16128)*.

53.91   **Canadian company appealing against cancellation of registration— interpretation of VATA 1994, Sch 1 para 10.** See *The Source Enterprise Ltd*, 42.1 OVERSEAS TRADERS.

EXEMPTION FROM REGISTRATION (VATA 1994, Sch 1 para 14)

53.92   The proprietor of a restaurant and 'take-away' food shop had applied to be registered for VAT, but discovered that most of her supplies were zero-rated under the legislation then in force, so that she was usually entitled to a repayment of input tax. She applied for exemption from registration under what is now *VATA 1994, Sch 1 para 14*. The Commissioners rejected her application but the tribunal allowed her appeal against this decision, holding that it had jurisdiction to consider how the Commissioners' powers under *Sch 1 para 14* should be exercised, and that the refusal of the application would be unreasonable. *TK Fong, [1978] VATTR 75 (VTD 590)*.

53.93   A builder had registered for VAT in 1988. Following a decline in his turnover, he deregistered in September 1991. However, in February and March 1992 his turnover increased significantly as a result of a short-term contract, and he again became liable to register. However, he failed to do so. The contract in question finished at the end of March, and his monthly turnover dropped to around £3,000. In September 1992, on the advice of his accountants, he made a retrospective application for exemption from registration under what is now *VATA 1994, Sch 1 para 14*. The Commissioners rejected the application and the tribunal dismissed his appeal against this decision. In view of his turnover in February and March, the builder had become liable to register from 1 May 1992. The tribunal's jurisdiction on applications under *Sch 1 para 14* was supervisory, rather than appellate. Since the builder's turnover from April to August 1992 had continued to average £3,000 per month (at a time when the registration threshold was an annual turnover of £36,600), the Commissioners had not acted unreasonably in deciding that he should not be exempted from registration. *PT Sullivan (t/a Property Trade Services), LON/92/3331P (VTD 10349). (Note.* An appeal against a penalty under what is now *VATA 1994, s 67* was also dismissed.)

53.94   A medical partnership, which had not been registered from VAT, applied in 1995 for exemption from registration under *VATA 1994, Sch 1 para 14*. The Commissioners accepted the application. Subsequently, in January 1997, the partnership applied to be registered retrospectively from April 1992, and submitted a claim for repayment of input tax. The Commissioners agreed to register the partnership from January 1997, but, in view of the partnership's previous application for exemption, refused to backdate the registration to 1992, and refused to repay input tax which the partnership had incurred from April 1992 to January 1997. The tribunal dismissed the partnership's appeal, applying the decision in *Bramley & Bradley*, 53.69 above. *Llanfyllin Group Practice, MAN/98/703 (VTD 16156)*.

REGISTRATION OF ASSOCIATED PERSONS AS A SINGLE TAXABLE PERSON (VATA 1994, Sch 1 para 2)

Cases where the direction was upheld

53.95   **Associated companies operating launderettes.**   A trader purchased a number of launderettes which he transferred to separate companies. The Commissioners made directions under what is now *VATA 1994, Sch 1 para 2* that the trader, the various companies, and two partnerships with which he was involved, should be treated as a single taxable person. The tribunal upheld the directions, finding that the businesses were conducted in such a way with the specific aim of avoiding VAT. The QB upheld this decision. *Chamberlain v C & E Commrs, QB [1989] STC 505.*

53.96   Similar decisions were reached in *I Lyons, [1987] VATTR 187 (VTD 2451); South West Launderettes Ltd, LON/87/35 (VTD 2608); B Bills, Mrs SA Bills, and Matcroft Ltd (VTD 14715)* and *Halls Dry Cleaning Co Ltd, MAN/96/1269 (VTD 15069).*

53.97   **Dry-cleaning and ironing from same premises.**   A couple registered for VAT as proprietors of a dry-cleaning business, which also provided ironing services. In 1998 the couple's accountant informed the Commissioners that he intended to treat the ironing as a separate business, operated by the husband as a sole proprietor. The Commissioners issued a direction under *VATA 1994, Sch 1 para 2* requiring the couple and the husband to be treated as a single taxable person. The tribunal upheld the direction and dismissed the couple's appeal. *I & H Jackson, MAN/x (VTD 16001).*

53.98   A similar decision, applying *Chamberlain*, 53.95 above, and *Osman*, 53.99 below, was reached in the subsequent case of *S & C Ahmed, LON/99/852 (VTD 16998).*

53.99   **Tax consultancy and accountancy services.**   A tax consultant, also providing financial and accounting services, acted as a sole practitioner. His wife provided similar services, also as a sole practitioner, from the same office. Additionally he and his wife provided similar services in partnership, again from the same office, and a company controlled by him and his wife also provided similar services from the same office. The Commissioners issued a direction that all four businesses should be treated as one business under what is now *VATA 1994, Sch 1 para 2.* The tribunal upheld the direction and the QB dismissed the consultant's appeal, holding that *Sch 1 para 2* was authorised by *Article 4(4)* of the *EC Sixth Directive*, which allowed persons to be brought together for VAT purposes if they were 'closely bound to one another by financial, economic and organisational links'. *Osman v C & E Commrs, QB [1989] STC 596.*

53.100   Similar decisions were reached in the subsequent cases of *HD Mitchell (t/a Mitchell & Co), LON/99/613 (VTD 16547)* and *DB Jones, MAN/99/1009 (VTD 16796).*

53.101   **Married couple operating café and bread shop from the same premises.**   A trader operated a café and a bread shop from the same premises.. In 1985 he transferred the café to his wife. The Commissioners issued a notice directing that the couple should be treated as a single taxable person. The tribunal dismissed the couple's appeal. *TSD & ME Williams, LON/87/132 (VTD 2445).*

53.102   **Fish and chip shop.**   A married couple, registered as a partnership, ran a take-away fish and chip shop. In 1984 they applied to be deregistered, claiming that they had decided to divide the business between them, each operating the shop at different times. The Commissioners issued a direction that they should be treated as a single taxable person. The tribunal dismissed the couple's appeal. *I & AJ Lee, MAN/87/252 (VTD 2640).*

53.103   **Hairdressers.**   A hairdresser, who owned two salons, failed to account for VAT on supplies made at the salons by his wife and three other female hairdressers. The Commissioners issued a direction treating them as a single taxable person. The tribunal upheld the direction. *AS Lewis, MAN/88/260 (VTD 3329).*

53.104   **Gymnasium.**   A trader (S) operated a gymnasium. The premises also contained sunbeds. In 1988 S applied for deregistration, claiming that he was now only operating the gymnasium on three days a week for female customers, while his son was operating it on three days a week for male customers, and his wife was responsible for the sunbeds. The Commissioners issued a direction that S and his wife and son should be treated as a single taxable person. The tribunal upheld the direction. *M, J & P Summers, MAN/88/513 (VTD 3498).*

53.105   A similar decision was reached in *S Gibson (t/a Miss Toner), EDN/94/224 (VTD 13293).*

53.106   **Fitness club and beauty salon at same premises.**   A company operated a fitness club and was registered for VAT. One of the company's directors and his wife operated a beauty salon in partnership at the same premises. The partnership was not registered for VAT. The Commissioners issued a direction that the company and the partnership should be treated as a single taxable person. The tribunal upheld the direction. *West End Health & Fitness Club, EDN/89/70 (VTD 4070).*

53.107   **Catering at public house.**   The wife of a publican provided catering at the public house of which her husband was the tenant. The husband was registered for VAT, but did not account for VAT on the catering. The Commissioners issued a direction that the couple should be treated as a single taxable person. The tribunal upheld the direction. *P & R J Jervis, MAN/88/596 (VTD 3920).*

53.108   *Jervis,* 53.107 above, was applied in the similar subsequent case of *DJ & PA Coe, LON/92/2371A (VTD 10911).*

53.109   An unmarried couple operated a public house and were registered for VAT as a partnership. The partnership did not account for VAT on receipts from catering at the public house, treating it as a separate business operated by the female partner (T) as an individual. The Commissioners issued a direction under what is now *VATA 1994, Sch 1 para 2* that T and the partnership should be treated as a single taxable person. T appealed, contending that the catering had been treated as a separate business for the purpose of providing her with an independent source of income in case of any rift in her relationship with her partner, and not for the purpose of avoiding VAT. The tribunal dismissed her appeal and upheld the direction. *TJ Ilott, LON/92/3384 (VTD 10942).*

53.110   **Catering and accommodation at public house.**   A publican did not account for VAT on income from catering and accommodation at the public house, claiming that these were a separate business carried on by his wife. The Commissioners issued a direction that the couple should be treated as a single taxable person, and the tribunal dismissed the couple's appeal. *WP & DKM Spence, EDN/90/142 (VTD 5698).*

53.111   **Service station and video club at same premises.**   A company operated a service station. The son of one of its directors opened a video club at the same premises. The Commissioners issued a direction that the company and the club proprietor should be treated as a single taxable person. The tribunal upheld the direction. *Old Farm Service Station Ltd & L Williams, MAN/89/56 (VTD 4261).*

53.112   **Manufacture and sale of model aircraft kits.**   A former Customs officer (H) began a business of manufacturing and selling model aircraft kits. Some of these were exported to Germany. In June 1989 he formed a partnership with his wife. The partnership took over the existing UK business, but H continued the export business in his own name. The Commissioners issued a direction under what is now *VATA 1994, Sch 1 para 2*. The tribunal upheld the direction and dismissed H's appeal. *AD Head, LON/90/109Y (VTD 4828)*.

53.113 **Taxi and wedding car hire.** The proprietor of a taxi business did not account for VAT on the hire of cars for weddings, claiming that this was a separate business which he operated in partnership with his wife. The Commissioners issued a direction that the couple should be treated as a single taxable person. The tribunal upheld the direction. *A & J Harris (t/a Gribbens Taxis & Wedding Cars), EDN/89/211 (VTD 4882)*.

53.114 **Holiday cottages and restaurant.** A married woman provided self-catering holiday accommodation from five cottages. In 1987 her husband, who had been unemployed for more than a year, opened a restaurant in a room of their own house, about 100 yards from the cottages. From 1987 to 1990 their accountant drew up combined accounts covering both the restaurant and the holiday cottages. However, for 1991 and 1992 separate accounts were prepared. In 1992 the Commissioners issued a direction that the couple should be treated as a single taxable person. The tribunal upheld the direction. *S & L Taylor, EDN/92/115 (VTD 9125)*.

53.115 **Ice-cream vendors.** An ice-cream vendor (G) had six ice-cream vans, one of which he drove himself, and three of which were driven by his sons, who were aged between 20 and 21. In 1991 he sold a van to each of his three sons, and applied for deregistration, claiming that his turnover would fall below the deregistration threshold. The Commissioners issued a direction that G and his sons should be treated as a single taxable person. The tribunal upheld the direction. *D Gregorio & Sons, MAN/91/1262 (VTD 9105)*.

53.116 **Restaurant and gift shop.** The proprietor of a restaurant and gift shop had registered for VAT with effect from April 1980. In 1983 he transferred the gift shop to his wife, and deregistered. In 1991 the Commissioners issued a direction that the couple should be treated as a single taxable person. The tribunal upheld the direction. *J Roy, EDN/92/50 (VTD 9384)*.

53.117 **Car sales and car washing at same premises.** A partnership which sold cars did not account for VAT on receipts from an automatic car wash at its premises, and treated these as accruing to the wife of one of the partners (E), although she was in full-time employment elsewhere and only visited the premises at weekends. The Commissioners issued a direction that the partnership and E should be treated as a single taxable person. The tribunal upheld the direction. *Allerton Motors, MAN/91/903 (VTD 9427)*.

53.118 **Fairground amusement operators.** A married couple and their son were registered for VAT as proprietors of fairground amusements. At a control visit, VAT officers discovered that they had not accounted for VAT on some of their income, but had treated it as accruing to one of the partners as an individual, to the married couple as a partnership excluding the son, or to the father and son as a partnership excluding the mother. The Commissioners issued a direction that all three partners should be treated as a single taxable person. The tribunal upheld the direction. *EM, PG & CP Evans, LON/92/1247 (VTD 10532)*.

53.119 **Computer supplies.** A married couple carried on business in partnership, providing services of computer programming, system analysis and related training. They were not registered for VAT. They subsequently incorporated a limited company which supplied computer hardware. The company registered for VAT.

The Commissioners issued a direction that the partnership and the company should be treated as a single taxable person. The tribunal upheld the direction. *A & S Essex (t/a Essex Associates), LON/97/175 (VTD 15072)*.

53.120 **Market traders—relevance of cohabitation.** A man and woman, who were not married but lived together, both sold leather goods from separate market stalls in the same market. The Commissioners issued a direction under *VATA 1994, Sch 1 para 2*. The woman appealed, contending that she was carrying on a separate business and wanted to keep her finances separate from those of the man with whom she was living. There were four independent stalls between her stall and that of her cohabitee. The tribunal reviewed the evidence and dismissed her appeal, holding that the fact that both traders had previously had broken marriages, and wished to keep their finances separate, was not conclusive. On the evidence, the two stalls 'were closely bound to one another by financial, economic and organisational links' and the Commissioners' direction had not been unreasonable. *DY Sharples, MAN/99/164 (VTD 16234)*. *(Note.* For another case involving cohabitees, see *Ilott*, 53.109 above.)

53.121 **Failure to comply with direction under VATA 1994, Sch 1 para 2.** See *Barnett & Larsen*, 49.285 PENALTIES: MISDECLARATION.

Cases where the appellant was successful

Note. See now *VATA 1994, Sch 1 para 1A*, introduced by *FA 1997, s 31*, and the amendments to *VATA 1994, Sch 1 para 2* enacted by *FA 1997, s 31*. The amended legislation now provides that a direction is valid if the avoidance of VAT is an effect of the separation of the business. The previous requirement for the Commissioners to be satisfied that the avoidance of VAT liability was a 'main reason' for the way in which the business is organised has been abolished with effect from 19 March 1997. The cases in this section should be read in the light of the changes in the legislation.

53.122 **Tea room at furniture shop.** A husband and wife owned a shop which sold furniture. The wife's parents, who were both retired, sold tea and coffee from a room at the same premises. The Commissioners issued a direction that both couples should be treated as a single taxable person. The tribunal allowed the traders' appeal against this direction, finding that the two businesses were quite separate and holding that the tea room was not operated with a view to tax avoidance. *JT & SM Myers, MAN/89/157 (VTD 3951)*. *(Note.* See now the note at the head of this section.)

53.123 **Catering at public house.** The wife of a publican provided catering at the public house of which her husband was the tenant. The husband was registered for VAT, but he did not account for VAT on the catering. The Commissioners issued a direction that the husband and wife should be treated as a single taxable person, although the VAT officer responsible for the direction had not interviewed the wife. The tribunal allowed the couple's appeal against the direction, holding that there was no evidence to justify the officer's conclusion that the avoidance of VAT was the reason for the catering being operated as a separate business. *G & Mrs W Grisdale, [1989] VATTR 162 (VTD 4069)*. *(Note.* This case was distinguished in *Coe*, 53.108 above. See also the note at the head of this section.)

53.124 **Fencing contractors operating from same premises.** Two brothers and a brother-in-law operated as fencing contractors from the same premises. The Commissioners issued a direction that all three should be treated as a single taxable person, and they appealed. The tribunal allowed their appeal, finding that, although there was a close connection between the trades of the two brothers, the business of the brother-in-law was entirely independent. The VAT officer dealing with the case had not interviewed the younger brother or the brother-in-law. He had made assumptions which were unreasonable and the notice was therefore invalid. *Thompson, Thompson & Giblin, MAN/88/819 (VTD 4196)*.

53.125 **Hairdressers working from same premises.** The Commissioners issued a direction that two hairdressers carrying on business at the same premises should be treated as a single taxable person. The hairdressers had previously worked for several years on a self-employed basis. In 1989 they leased new premises, the lease being in their joint names. They kept separate tills, ledgers and appointment books. The tribunal allowed the hairdressers' appeal against the direction, holding on the evidence that the VAT officer responsible for the direction had acted unreasonably in considering that the avoidance of VAT had been one of the main reasons for the hairdressers trading as individuals rather than as partners. *RJ Knights & WC Wendon, LON/90/147 (VTD 5165)*.

53.126 Two hairdressers, who had previously been employees, took a joint lease of premises which they used as a hairdressing salon. They opened a joint bank account, for payment of common liabilities, and also operated individual bank accounts. The Commissioners issued a direction under what is now *VATA 1994, Sch 1 para 2*, against which they appealed. The tribunal allowed their appeal, holding on the evidence that the avoidance of VAT was not the main reason for the hairdressers deciding to trade as individuals, rather than as partners. *W Cringan & T Watson, EDN/91/330 (VTD 7519)*.

53.127 **Farming and pony trekking.** A farmer's first wife had begun a pony trekking business in 1981. This was treated as a separate business from the husband's farming. In 1984 the couple divorced and the husband took over the pony trekking business, which he ran alongside his farming business. He accounted for VAT on both businesses. In 1985 the farmer remarried and handed over the running of the pony trekking business to his second wife. In 1988 he formally transferred the pony trekking business to her. As the turnover of the pony trekking business was below the registration threshold, she stopped charging and accounting for VAT. The Commissioners issued a direction under what is now *VATA 1994, Sch 1 para 2* that the farmer and his wife should be treated as a single taxable person. The tribunal allowed the couple's appeal against this direction, finding that the two businesses were genuinely independent and holding that the conditions of *Sch 1 para 2* were not satisfied. *D & LM Horsman, [1990] VATTR 151 (VTD 5401)*. (*Note.* See now the note preceding 53.122 above.)

53.128 **Farming and bed and breakfast facilities.** A farmer had been registered for VAT since 1973. His wife provided bed and breakfast facilities from the farmhouse and from a converted building adjacent to it. The Commissioners issued a direction under what is now *VATA 1994, Sch 1 para 2* that the couple should be treated as a single taxable person. The couple appealed, contending that the two businesses were not 'closely bound by financial, economic and organisational links', and that the wife had wanted an independent source of income. The tribunal allowed the couple's appeal, finding that the officer responsible for the direction had acted unreasonably and that tax avoidance was not the reason for the operation of two separate businesses. *HD & DM Hundsdoerfer, [1990] VATTR 158 (VTD 5450)*.

53.129 **Bookselling and launderettes.** A trader (P) was registered for VAT from 1973 as the proprietor of a mail order bookselling business and of three launderettes. In April 1991 he notified the Commissioners that he had taken his wife (whom he had married in 1988) into partnership in the bookselling business. He also notified the Commissioners that he would only continue to operate one of the launderettes, since he had transferred one of the launderettes to his wife, and had taken his son (by a previous marriage) into partnership in the third launderette. Following this notification, the couple continued to account for output tax in respect of the bookselling business, since its turnover remained above the registration threshold, but the couple did not account for output tax in respect of the launderettes, since the turnover of each of the launderettes, treated independently, was below the threshold. The Commissioners issued a direction under what is now *VATA 1994, Sch 1 para 2* that P, his wife and the two partnerships should be treated as a single taxable person for VAT purposes. P and his wife and son appealed, contending that the main reason for the division of the business was not the avoidance of VAT, but was the desire to avoid inheritance tax and to provide P's wife with an independent source of income. The tribunal allowed the appeal, holding that on the evidence that P's decision to take his wife into partnership was not to avoid liability to be registered, since the wife had been acting as a *de facto* partner since their marriage. Furthermore, since P was considerably older than his wife, it was understandable that P should have wished to transfer one of the launderettes to her, while the taking of P's son into partnership in one of the other launderettes 'clearly achieved potential inheritance tax savings'. Accordingly, the Commissioners 'could not reasonably have been satisfied' that the avoidance of VAT was the reason for P's reorganisation of his business activities. *P, C & J Allen, LON/93/2586A (VTD 12209)*. (*Note.* See now the note preceding 53.122 above.)

53.130 **Dry-cleaning businesses.** An individual (IR) operated a dry-cleaning business from a shop in Leigh-on-Sea. His mother (AR) operated a similar business from a shop in Westcliff-on-Sea, and his common law wife (C) operated a similar business from a shop in Shoeburyness. All three shops used the same trading name, but had separate sets of records and separate bank accounts. The Commissioners issued a direction that all three shops should be treated as a single taxable person. The proprietors appealed, contending that, although IR and C lived together and had three children together, they operated the shops as individuals because they wanted to maintain their independence, both having previously been divorced. The shop in Westcliff had originally been purchased by IR's father (AR's husband), who had subsequently died. The tribunal accepted the proprietors' evidence and allowed the appeals, holding that the officer responsible for the direction had not made adequate enquiries but had relied on outdated information obtained at a time when AR was recovering from a hip operation. The tribunal observed that 'the fact that there was substantial mutual assistance between three traders who were related to one another does not necessarily mean that the businesses should properly be regarded as one'. *I Reayner, J Colegate & A Reayner, LON/97/431 (VTD 15396)*.

53.131 **Jewellers carrying on business from same premises.** From 1981 to 1990 two individuals (H and S) carried on business from the same premises. H sold jewellery, while S specialised in the retail sale of second-hand jewellery and antiques. In 1990 they went into partnership and registered for VAT, but in March 1993 they decided to terminate the partnership, applied for deregistration, and reverted to trading separately (while continuing to operate from the same premises). In November 1994 the Commissioners issued a direction that, despite the termination of the partnership, they should be treated as a single taxable person. They appealed against the direction, contending that they had terminated the partnership because of disagreements about trading policy, particularly with regard to the purchase of second-hand jewellery for resale, and that they were searching for separate premises. They had separate bank accounts as well as a joint account which was used for meeting joint expenses. They kept separate records. The tribunal accepted their evidence and allowed their appeals, holding that the VAT officers responsible for the direction had not given sufficient weight to the reasons for terminating the partnership, and had given too much weight to the existence of a joint bank account. On the evidence, 'the officers were unreasonable in inferring and concluding that the avoidance of VAT liability was the main reason, or one of the reasons, for the appellants carrying on the activities in the manner in which they did'. *J Humphrey & AG Smith (t/a Abacus Jewellery & Antiques), MAN/95/1133 (VTD 13561)*.

53.132   **Whether direction under VATA 1994, Sch 1 para 2 may be retrospective.**   On 5 June 1997 the Commissioners issued a direction under *VATA 1994, Sch 1 para 2* on a married couple. The direction stated that it took effect from 1 June 1997. The couple appealed, contending that a direction under *Sch 1 para 2* could not be retrospective. The tribunal accepted this contention and allowed the appeals, holding that 'it is plain from the terms of (*Sch 1 para 2*) that the date on which registration takes effect must be the date of the direction or some later date specified in the direction, but not an earlier date'. The error could not be regarded as immaterial, and the direction was, therefore, invalid and ineffective. *RD & SM Elder, EDN/97/126 & 127 (VTD 15881, 15882)*.

THE PERSON BY WHOM THE BUSINESS IS CARRIED ON

Note. For cases concerning whether a business is operated in partnership, see 44.9 *et seq.* PARTNERSHIP.

Cases where the appellant was unsuccessful

53.133   **Undischarged bankrupt.**   The wife of an undischarged bankrupt carried on a small business of making car number plates. She employed her husband and son in this business. Her husband had previously been self-employed as a car dealer, and after his bankruptcy he continued to arrange for the buying and selling of cars. The wife paid for the purchase of cars for resale, and also paid for advertisements, but left the actual purchases and sales entirely to her husband. She did not account for VAT on the cars sold and appealed against an assessment issued by the Commissioners, contending that the car dealing was a separate business carried on by her husband. The tribunal dismissed her appeal, holding that the car dealing could not be treated as her husband's business because, as an undischarged bankrupt, the husband was precluded from carrying on any business. *PO Wood, LON/80/317 (VTD 1037)*. (*Note.* Compare, however, *Scally*, 35.6 INSOLVENCY.)

53.134   **Hotel—by whom operated.**   The Commissioners sought to register the proprietor of a small hotel. He appealed, contending that the management of the hotel was delegated to three companies, one of which supplied the accommodation, one of which supplied the food, and one of which ran the bar, and that the turnover of each of the three companies was below the registration limit. The tribunal rejected his contentions and dismissed his appeal. *APG McGuire, LON/82/22 (VTD 1305)*. (*Note.* See also now *VATA 1994, Sch 1 para 2*, and the cases noted at 53.95 *et seq.* above.)

53.135   **Public house—by whom operated.**   A company which operated a public house failed to register for VAT. The Commissioners issued a notice of compulsory registration, and the company appealed, contending that it was merely acting as an agent for a number of Panamanian companies which operated the public house successively. The tribunal rejected the company's evidence and dismissed the appeal. *Blusins Ltd, EDN/96/195 (VTD 15119)*.

53.136   **Catering at public house—whether supplied by publican.**   A publican did not account for VAT on receipts from catering, and the Commissioners issued an assessment charging tax on them. The publican appealed, contending that the catering was a separate business carried on by his wife. The Inland Revenue had accepted that the catering should be treated as a separate business. The tribunal dismissed the appeal, observing that the publican's accountant had prepared a single balance sheet and that the publican had reclaimed input tax on items which were used for catering. On the evidence, the couple 'may well have intended to run the two sides of the business separately, but ... their intention was not carried into effect'. *ME Brown, LON/92/2804A (VTD 11429)*.

53.137   Similar decisions were reached in the subsequent cases of *B Davies, MAN/93/416 (VTD 12023)* and *A Odell & M Ogden, MAN/95/1436 (VTD 13512)*.

53.138   A similar decision was reached in a subsequent case in which the public house was run by a partnership of four people, and the Inland Revenue had accepted accounts showing the catering as a separate business of one of the partners. The tribunal held that there was a single business for VAT purposes, observing that 'we do not know what information was supplied to the Inland Revenue or what if any inquiries were made. We however have heard evidence over a period of 2 days and are satisfied that there was not in fact a separate business in respect of the catering activities. In the circumstances the income tax treatment does not assist or cause us to alter the conclusion to which we have come.' *Burrell*, 44.10 PARTNERSHIP, applied. *SH, HA, BP & D Allen (t/a The Shovel), MAN/98/808 (16906)*.

53.139   See also *Smith & Smith*, 44.14 PARTNERSHIP.

53.140   **Catering at hotel—whether separate business.** A partnership operated a hotel. It did not account for VAT on catering receipts. The Commissioners issued an assessment charging tax on such receipts, and the partnership appealed, contending that the catering was a separate business carried on by one of the partners as an individual. The tribunal dismissed the appeal, holding on the evidence that the catering was a part of the partnership business. *JG & SJ Albert (t/a The Groves Hotel), MAN/92/1601 (VTD 11651)*.

53.141   The proprietor of a hotel failed to account for VAT on receipts from catering. The Commissioners issued an assessment charging output tax and the proprietor appealed, contending that the catering was supplied by a friend of hers. The tribunal rejected this contention and dismissed her appeal. *CA Cherry, MAN/93/150 (VTD 13861)*.

53.142   **Manager acting for non-resident.** The owner of a property conveyancing business was resident outside the UK and showed little or no interest in the business, which was run by a manager. The Commissioners sought to register the manager and he appealed, contending that he could not be registered since he was not the legal owner of the business. The tribunal dismissed his appeal, holding that the manager was making supplies and was therefore liable to account for tax on those supplies. *RJ Culverhouse, LON/86/125 (VTD 2130)*.

53.143   **Restaurant—by whom operated.** A company which owned a hotel and restaurant applied to be deregistered on the basis that it no longer operated the restaurant. The application was accepted, but during the course of a control visit a Customs officer discovered that the restaurant business had not in fact ceased to function and therefore reregistered the company. The company appealed, contending that the wife of the principal director had taken over the restaurant as a separate business and that there was insufficient turnover for her to register for VAT. The tribunal dismissed the appeal, finding on the evidence that the wife was not the proprietor of the business but that the restaurant had at all times been run by the company. *Waterwynch House Ltd, LON/87/505 (VTD 2734)*.

53.144   A similar decision was reached in a case where the tribunal upheld the Commissioners' contentions that a fish and chip shop and an Indian restaurant operating from adjacent premises were both run by the same individual (U), and rejected U's contention that the Indian restaurant was a separate business operated by his common law wife. *Brown*, 53.136 above, and *Davies*, 53.137 above, applied. *DS Uppal (t/a Mr Chips), MAN/94/512 (VTD 14074)*.

53.145   **Launderette—by whom operated.**   The Commissioners issued an assessment on a trader (S), charging tax on the takings of a launderette and a fish-and-chip shop. He appealed, accepting that he was the proprietor of the fish-and-chip shop, but contending that the launderette was operated by his wife. The tribunal rejected this contention and dismissed his appeal, finding on the evidence that S was the proprietor of both businesses. *RS Sahota, MAN/96/379 (VTD 14986)*.

53.146   **Computer consultant—whether self-employed or employee.**   A computer engineer provided software consultancy services for a company (F), for which he charged £500 per week. In 1983 he began working for another company (T) but still continued to supply some services to F until September 1984. He was treated as self-employed for income tax purposes. In September 1987 the Commissioners issued a ruling that he was liable to register for VAT with effect from April 1982. He appealed, contending that he was not liable to register because he was an employee of T. The tribunal rejected this contention and dismissed his appeal, holding on the evidence that he was self-employed and was not an employee of T. *AJ Scott, LON/87/713 (VTD 2926)*. (*Note.* An appeal against a penalty for failure to register was also dismissed.)

53.147   **Franchise agreement.**   A buffet at a railway station was operated under a franchise agreement. The franchisee contended that he only sold food and that the sale of liquid refreshments at the buffet was a separate business carried out by another trader. The tribunal dismissed the franchisee's appeal, holding on the evidence that the franchise agreement made it clear that the franchisee was responsible for the sale of both food and drink. *D Duwel, LON/88/703Y (VTD 3483)*.

53.148   The Commissioners registered an individual (E) on the basis that he was the franchisee of a warehouse, and was therefore a 'taxable person'. E appealed, contending that he was an employee rather than a franchisee. The tribunal dismissed his appeal, holding on the evidence that he was acting as a franchisee, notwithstanding that he had not signed the formal franchise agreement, and that he was therefore liable to be registered for VAT. *DR Evans, LON/94/409A (VTD 13290)*.

53.149   **Fish and chip shop.**   The Commissioners issued an assessment on an individual (S), who had registered for VAT as the proprietor of a fish and chip shop. S appealed, contending that he had registered in error and that the business was actually carried on by his wife. The tribunal dismissed the appeal, holding on the evidence that the business was carried on by S. *S Sajawal, MAN/92/428 (VTD 10971)*.

53.150   **Kebab shop.**   The Commissioners issued an assessment on a couple who had registered for VAT as the proprietors of a kebab shop. They appealed, contending that they only operated the shop on four days each week, and that for the other three days it was operated by a licencee. The tribunal rejected this contention and dismissed the couple's appeal, holding on the evidence that there was a single business which was operated by the couple. *L & A Eleftheriou (t/a Picnic Kebab House), MAN/99/13 (VTD 16659)*.

53.151   **Car hire business.**   See *Brough*, 44.15 PARTNERSHIP.

53.152   **Partnership operating retail shop—invoices issued for graphic design services—whether relevant supplies made by partnership or by individual partner.**   See *Tang & Tang (t/a Ziploc)*, 58.248 SUPPLY.

53.153 **Hairdressing salons.** A hairdresser (M) began trading in August 1992. In November 1993 he acquired a licence to trade from adjoining premises. He continued to operate as a men's hairdresser from his original premises, while the new premises were used as a ladies' hairdressing salon. The premises shared a common entrance, and were divided by a counter and a cabinet, rather than by a wall. M did not account for VAT on the income from the ladies' salon. The Commissioners issued an assessment charging tax on them, and M appealed, contending that the ladies' salon was a separate business operated by his wife. The tribunal rejected this contention and upheld the assessment in principle, holding on the evidence that there was a single business. The fact that there were separate tills was not conclusive. On the evidence, M's wife was not a hairdresser, and M acted as the proprietor of the ladies' section as well as of the men's section. *AY Mehmet, LON/98/1394 & 1561 (VTD 16189).*

53.154 In 1996 a hairdresser (C), who had been registered for VAT since 1985, applied for his registration to be cancelled on the basis that three stylists working at his premises were working as independent contractors and were supplying their services directly to the customers. The Commissioners rejected the application and issued assessments charging tax on the full amount of the takings, on the basis that the services at the salon were still being supplied by C, and the fact that the stylists were self-employed was not conclusive. The tribunal upheld the Commissioners' contentions and dismissed C's appeal. *K Colby, MAN/98/314 (VTD 16387).*

53.155 See also *Jane Montgomery (Hair Stylists) Ltd*, 58.203 SUPPLY, and the cases noted at 58.204 to 58.209 SUPPLY.

53.156 **Retail shops—by whom operated.** A married couple was registered for VAT as the proprietors of four retail shops. The Commissioners discovered that there had been underdeclarations of takings at the shops and issued an assessment. The couple appealed, contending that the registration had been made in error because three of the shops were run by their sons. The tribunal dismissed the appeal, finding that 'no written evidence was produced to justify the assertion that the businesses were separate and independent'. *MA Shad (Newsagents), EDN/94/133 (VTD 13145).*

53.157 **Garages purchased by plumber with money lent by wife—whether letting of garages carried out by plumber or wife.** See *King*, 58.243 SUPPLY.

Cases where the appellant was successful

53.158 **Institute of Management establishing charitable trust—whether separate registrations required.** The British Institute of Management was formed in 1947 as a company limited by guarantee. In 1977 it established a charitable trust (the Foundation), with the Institute as its sole trustee. The Commissioners considered that the Institute's existing registration for VAT could not cover the activities of the Foundation, and that a separate registration was required. The tribunal allowed the Institute's appeal against this decision, holding that the activities of the Foundation were part of the activities of the Institute. Part of the Institute's services were supplied through the Foundation, and, as sole trustee, it carried on the Foundation's business in the course of its own business. *British Institute of Management (No 1), [1978] VATTR 101 (VTD 565).*

53.159 **Restaurant operated under franchise agreement.** See *Nasim*, 58.271 SUPPLY.

53.160 **Take-away restaurant—by whom operated.** A partnership, which was registered for VAT, had operated a take-away burger restaurant and a take-away Indian restaurant from adjacent premises. It sold the lease of the premises to an individual (G). Following the sale, G's son took over the burger restaurant and was registered for VAT. G's wife took over the Indian restaurant and applied for deregistration on the basis that her turnover was below the registration threshold. A VAT officer visited the premises and formed the opinion that both businesses were being run by G's son. He issued an assessment to G's son, charging output tax on the sales made from the Indian restaurant. The tribunal allowed the son's appeal, finding on the evidence that he was only operating the burger restaurant, and that the Indian restaurant was being run as a separate business by G's wife. *B Ghafoor, LON/94/462A (VTD 13329).*

53.161   **Adjacent   take-away   restaurants—whether   operated   by   same partnership.**   In the case noted at 3.100 ASSESSMENT, a married couple had owned two adjacent shops, both of which were used as take-away restaurants. They registered for VAT from November 1998. One of the restaurants mainly sold fish and chips, while the other mainly sold chicken and kebabs. The Commissioners issued a notice of registration on the basis that the two restaurants had constituted a single business for VAT purposes since 1996, carried on by the couple and their son. They appealed, contending that from 1996 to October 1998 the son had only been a partner in the fish and chip shop and had not been a partner in the shop selling chicken and kebabs. They gave evidence that they had intended to involve their daughter in this business, but she had emigrated to Spain in 1998 and they had merged the shops following her emigration. The tribunal accepted their evidence and allowed the appeal. *DJ, J & S Plummer, MAN/99/589 (VTD 16976).*

53.162   **Fish and chip shop—whether operated by couple or by husband as an individual.**   A married couple opened a café in 1995, but did not register for VAT as their turnover was below the registration threshold. In 1996 the husband purchased a second-hand fryer and began to sell fish and chips. Subsequently the Commissioners registered the couple on the basis that their turnover had exceeded the threshold. They appealed, contending that the sales of fish and chips were a separate business carried on by the husband as an individual. The tribunal accepted this contention and allowed the appeal, observing that there were separate menus and separate financial arrangements. *Burrell*, 44.10 PARTNERSHIP, distinguished. *BR & JG Parker (t/a Sea Breeze Café), LON/98/1284 (VTD 16350).*

53.163   **Associated partnerships operating hotel and holiday flats in same road— whether a single business.**   In 1987 a married couple purchased a hotel. In 1994 their son and son-in-law purchased a house, divided into holiday flats, on the opposite side of the same road. The turnover of each partnership was below the registration threshold. In 1999 the Commissioners issued a ruling that the two couples formed a single partnership which was carrying on a single business for VAT purposes and should be registered accordingly. The couples appealed. The tribunal allowed their appeal, holding that there were two separate businesses. *EL, CM, KC & E Hodges, MAN/99/941 (VTD 16983).*

53.164   **Father and son operating cleaning businesses from same premises— whether trading in partnership.**   A father and son had traded in partnership, operating a dry-cleaning business, from 1989 to 1992. By the end of 1992 their turnover had fallen to below the VAT deregistration threshold and they deregistered. They then decided to run separate businesses at the same premises. The father (AJ) carried on specialist cleaning work, while the son (GJ) carried on general dry-cleaning work. Subsequently the Commissioners issued a notice of compulsory registration on the basis that AJ and GJ were still carrying on a single business in partnership. They appealed. The tribunal allowed their appeal, holding on the evidence that they were carrying on separate businesses. *AC & GC James, LON/00/29 (VTD 16988).*

53.165 **Engineering business.** The Commissioners sought to register an individual (D) whom they considered was the sole proprietor of an engineering business from 1982 to 1987. D appealed, contending that the business was operated by a limited company. The company in question had previously been owned by D and a former partner of his (B), with whom he had subsequently fallen out. Originally B and D had been registered at Companies House as the directors of the company, but Companies House had subsequently been advised by an accountant, apparently acting on behalf of B, that D had resigned and that B and Mrs B were the sole directors. However accounts had been submitted to the Inland Revenue, by a different accountant, showing that the company was trading with D and Mrs D as directors. The tribunal found that D and his wife had remained shareholders and directors of the company, and allowed D's appeal, holding that he had not carried on a business as a sole trader during the years in question. *H Demack, MAN/89/190 (VTD 5534).*

53.166 **Hairdressing salons.** A married woman (F), whose husband was a chartered accountant, carried on business from an office in Edinburgh, collecting income for four companies which operated hairdressing salons, of which she was a director and in which her husband had a controlling interest. One of these companies had been temporarily struck off the register but subsequently restored with retrospective effect, and some returns lodged with the Registrar of Companies indicated that the companies were no longer trading. The Commissioners issued an assessment charging tax on the full amount of the income which she collected, on the basis that she was carrying on the business previously carried on by the companies. She appealed, contending that the companies had continued to trade, that the information supplied to the Registrar of Companies was incorrect, and that her only income was the 10% commission which she retained, which was below the VAT registration threshold. The tribunal allowed her appeal, finding (by a 2–1 majority) that the four companies had traded continuously throughout the period concerned, and holding that the income in question belonged to the individual companies rather than to F. *F Shanks, EDN/91/308 (VTD 11015).*

53.167 See also the cases noted at 58.211 to 58.218 SUPPLY.

53.168 **Counterfeit audiocassettes.** The Commissioners sought to register an individual (M) whom they considered was carrying on a business of manufacturing and selling counterfeit audiocassettes. M appealed, contending that he was an employee and was not required to be registered. The tribunal accepted his evidence and allowed his appeal. *M McGuckin, EDN/92/345 (VTD 12659).*

MISCELLANEOUS

53.169 **Business transferred to subsidiary—whether registration number can be transferred.** A company, registered for VAT, changed its name and transferred its business to a newly formed subsidiary bearing its old name. The new company applied for registration and requested that, to enable it to use the old company's unused stationery, etc., it should be allocated the registration number of the old company which should be given a new number. The Commissioners rejected this request and the tribunal dismissed the company's appeal, holding that the allocation of numbers was within the administrative discretion of the Commissioners. *L Reich & Sons Ltd, LON H/74/34 (VTD 97).*

54   Retailers' Special Schemes

General Note. The Special Schemes for retailers were substantially amended during 1997, with the 15 original retail schemes being replaced by the Point of Sale scheme, Apportionment Schemes 1 and 2 and Direction Calculation Schemes 1 and 2. The key changes were

- Schemes A and F continue in revised form as the Point of Sale Scheme;

- Scheme D continues in revised form as Apportionment Scheme 1;

- Scheme H continues in revised form as Apportionment Scheme 2;

- Schemes B and E continue in revised form as the Direct Calculation Scheme 1;

- Schemes B1 and E1 continue in revised form as the Direct Calculation Scheme 2; and

- Schemes B2, C, D1, G, J, J1 and J2 were withdrawn for supplies made after 31 March 1998.

For details of the changes, see *Notice 727, Notices 727/2* to *727/5*, and Tolley's Value Added Tax. The cases in this chapter should be read in the light of the changes. The cases are arranged under the following headings.

What supplies are within the schemes 54.1–54.10
Retrospective changes of scheme 54.11–54.22
Transitional matters 54.23–54.32
Gross takings 54.33–54.43
Expected selling prices 54.44–54.45
Point of Sale Scheme 54.46–54.48
Apportionment Schemes 54.49–54.50
Direct Calculation Schemes 54.51–54.55
Miscellaneous 54.56–54.58

WHAT SUPPLIES ARE WITHIN THE SCHEMES

54.1   **Whether schemes extend to supplies other than retail sales—goods supplied to selling agents for promotional purposes.**   A large mail order company operated through agents, most of whom were housewives. It sent new agents a 'free gift' of a teaset of a value not exceeding £10. The Commissioners issued assessments charging tax on the value of the teasets. The company appealed, contending firstly that the teasets were gifts within what is now *VATA 1994, Sch 4 para 5(2)(a)*, and secondly that, if the teasets were deemed to be supplies, they should be dealt with under the company's Retail Scheme. The tribunal rejected these contentions and dismissed the company's appeal, and the CA upheld this decision. The teasets were not gifts, since the agent had a contractual right to them. They were not within the Retail Schemes, and the company was obliged to account for VAT in the normal way. *GUS Merchandise Corporation Ltd v C & E Commrs, CA [1981] STC 569; [1981] 1 WLR 1309.* (*Note.* For other matters raised at the tribunal hearing but not pursued in the courts, see 2.76 APPEALS.)

54.2   **Newspaper delivery charges—whether to be included in Retail Scheme calculation.**   A couple operated a newsagency and charged customers 6p per week for delivery. They accounted for tax under a Scheme which has since been replaced, but was similar to the new Apportionment Scheme 1. The Commissioners issued a ruling that the delivery charges should be taken into account in arriving at the gross takings for the purposes of the Scheme. The couple appealed, contending that the charges should be treated as zero-rated and the effect of including them as takings within the Scheme was that they would be paying tax on a zero-rated supply. The tribunal dismissed the appeal, holding that, by electing to account for tax under a Retail Scheme, the couple had elected to have their zero-rated supplies determined in accordance with that Scheme instead of by any other manner. *NG & BE Coe, LON/75/35 (VTD 165)*.

54.3   Similar decisions were reached in *PD Hayhoe, LON/78/3 (VTD 568); BM Coleman (t/a D & A Newsagents), LON/80/256 (VTD 1013); L & R Harrison, MAN/95/ 1427 (VTD 13544); AD & JR Eckels, MAN/97/1024 (VTD 15593)* and *Fryer*, 54.19 below.

54.4   **Newspaper delivery charges—treatment under Scheme H (now Apportionment Scheme 2).** A married couple operated a newsagency and accounted for tax under Retail Scheme H (which, in revised form, is now Apportionment Scheme 2). In accounting for tax, they did not include the charges which they made to customers for delivering newspapers. Subsequently they formed the opinion that these charges should be treated as part of the expected selling prices of the zero-rated newspapers, and in March 1994 they submitted a claim for repayment of tax which they considered that they had overdeclared as a result of failing to treat the newspaper delivery charges as attributable to zero-rated supplies. The Commissioners agreed the claim with respect to periods beginning after 1 May 1990 but rejected the claim with regard to periods from 1 December 1987 to 1 May 1990, considering that while such adjustments were permitted by *Leaflet 727/14/90* with effect from 1 May 1990, they had not been permitted by *Leaflet 727/14/87* as previously in force. The couple appealed. The tribunal allowed the appeal, holding that the effect of what the couple had done had been to increase the total of their estimated standard-rated supplies as compared with their estimated zero-rated supplies and to increase the proportion of their total takings which were to be attributed to standard-rated supplies under Scheme H. Furthermore, the Commissioners had not been justified in limiting the repayment of tax to payments made since 1 May 1990. *PK & PM Lloyd, MAN/94/2506 (VTD 13562)*. (*Note*. See now, however, the three-year limit on repayment claims introduced by *FA 1997* with effect from 18 July 1996.)

54.5   **Newspaper delivery charges—treatment under Scheme B (now Direct Calculation Scheme 1).** In the case noted at 45.66 PAYMENT OF TAX, Lord MacFadyen observed that, while newspaper delivery charges had to be included in gross turnover, a VAT officer should have advised the trader that the charges should also be 'included in the sum deducted as the expected selling price of zero-rated supplies'. *Mrs ID Mathieson v C & E Commrs, CS [1999] STC 835*.

54.6   **Electricity stamps—whether to be included in gross takings.** A partnership traded as retailers and operated Scheme D (which, in revised form, is now Apportionment Scheme 1). It included the sale of electricity stamps, which it purchased at a 3% discount from the local Electricity Board, in its Scheme calculations. The Commissioners issued an assessment on the basis that the stamps should have been dealt with outside the Scheme, but the tribunal allowed the partnership's appeal, holding that there was nothing in the 'ordinary meaning of the words of the statute or notices' which prevented the partnership from including the relevant transactions within its calculations. *TE, M & IJ Parr, [1985] VATTR 250 (VTD 1967)*. (*Note*. The Commissioners subsequently amended *Notice No 727* to require the sale of electricity stamps to be dealt with outside the Retail Schemes.)

54.7   **Retail florist—amounts received from delivery service.** A retail florist accounted for tax using Retail Scheme E (which, in revised form, is now Direct Calculation Scheme 1). He received sums from a national flower delivery service, and dealt with these receipts under the Scheme. A VAT officer formed the opinion that these receipts were outside the scope of the Retail Scheme, and that the florist should have accounted for tax on them independently. He issued an assessment charging tax on these receipts. The florist appealed, contending that the flowers in question had been included in the stock of purchases from which he had calculated his liability under Scheme E, using a 20% mark-up. The tribunal allowed the florist's appeal, holding on the evidence that his returns were 'not incomplete or incorrect', so that there was no justification for the assessment. *NR Williams, MAN/92/1756 (VTD 11361)*.

54.8   **Subscriptions for discount cards.** A company (M) sold children's clothing and a variety of other goods. About 50% of its sales of goods were zero-rated. In 1988 it introduced a 'discount scheme' for regular customers. Customers who held a credit card issued by M could purchase a discount card for an annual subscription of £25. This card entitled them to a discount of 20% against all future credit card purchases. In 1989 the Commissioners issued a ruling that the discount card subscriptions were standard-rated. M appealed, contending that the subscriptions were 'an integral part of the consideration for the purchases subsequently made', and should be treated as part of its gross takings, to be apportioned between standard-rated goods and zero-rated goods under Retail Scheme J (which has subsequently been withdrawn). The tribunal allowed the appeal, holding that there was a direct link between the payments for the discount cards and the subsequent payments for goods. *British Railways Board*, 62.5 TRANSPORT, applied. *Mothercare (UK) Ltd, [1993] VATTR 391 (VTD 10751)*. (*Note.* See now *Notices No 727/3, 727/4* and *727/5* for the treatment of sales of discount vouchers and discount cards.)

54.9   **Supplies to registered traders—whether within Retail Schemes.** A co-operative society operated Retail Scheme B (which, in revised form, is now Direct Calculation Scheme 1). A number of its supplies were to registered traders. The Commissioners considered that these supplies could not be dealt with within a Retail Scheme, and that, as the exclusion of such supplies meant that more than 50% of the society's takings were from zero-rated supplies, it was not eligible to use Scheme B. The society appealed, contending that supplies to other registered traders could be dealt with under a Retail Scheme, and that the inclusion of its supplies to registered traders meant that less than 50% of its takings were zero-rated, so that it remained entitled to use Scheme B. The tribunal dismissed the appeal, holding that the effect of *Notice No 727* was that supplies to registered traders had to be dealt with outside the Retail Schemes. The QB upheld this decision. *Oxford Swindon & Gloucester Society Ltd v C & E Commrs, QB [1995] STC 583*.

54.10   **Hire of videos—whether within Retail Scheme.** A trader operated Retail Scheme C (which has subsequently been withdrawn). In the course of his business he hired videocassettes to customers. He treated his takings from this as being within the Scheme, with the result that he only accounted for output tax on a proportion of the takings. The Commissioners considered that the hire of videocassettes should be dealt with outside the Retail Schemes, and issued an estimated assessment to charge tax on the full amount of the receipts from video hire. The tribunal dismissed the trader's appeal, holding that the supply of videos on hire was a supply of services which was outside the scope of the Retail Schemes. *R Singh (t/a Best Buy Conventional Store), MAN/94/418 (VTD 13011)*.

54.11 Retailers' Special Schemes

RETROSPECTIVE CHANGES OF SCHEME

Note. Customs will now only allow retrospective changes of a retail scheme in exceptional cases. The maximum period for recalculation following an agreed retrospective claim is three years. See *Notice No 727, para 11*. The previous conditions, set out in *Notice No 727 (1993 edition), para 85*, under which Customs were prepared to consider recalculations for earlier years have now been withdrawn. For a case where a recalculation was accepted by the Commissioners, see *Peart & Peart*, 45.60 PAYMENT OF TAX.

54.11 **Appeal dismissed.** A couple who carried on business as newsagents, tobacconists and confectioners originally operated Scheme 2 (which subsequently became Scheme G, and has since been withdrawn) but, realising that this was not to their advantage, applied in August 1973 to change to Scheme 3 (which subsequently became Scheme J, and has also since been withdrawn) with effect from 1 April 1973. The Commissioners allowed the change from 10 October 1973 but refused a retrospective change. The tribunal dismissed the couple's appeal against this decision. *P & M Summerfield, BIR/74/24 (VTD 108).*

54.12 A retailer operated Scheme 2 (which subsequently became Scheme G, and has since been withdrawn). By November 1975 he began to suspect that he was paying too much tax, and asked a VAT officer for someone to see and advise him as quickly as possible. A VAT officer visited him in January 1976 and, without going into the matter deeply, told him that his increasing liability was probably due to the expansion in his business. The retailer then consulted a tax adviser, who wrote to the Commissioners in March 1976 asking for the liability to be recomputed under Scheme E (which, in revised form, is now Direct Calculation Scheme 1) or Scheme H (which, in revised form, is now Apportionment Scheme 2) with effect from 1 April 1975. The Commissioners agreed to allow retrospective treatment from 1 October 1975 but not from any earlier date. The retailer appealed. The tribunal dismissed his appeal, holding that he had failed to establish any special circumstances to justify his claim. *RJ Vulgar, [1976] VATTR 197 (VTD 304).*

54.13 *Vulgar*, 54.12 above, was applied in the similar cases of *J Boden, MAN/76/188 (VTD 377); Brookfields, LON/78/79 (VTD 577); EWA Charles, LON/77/388 (VTD 596)* and *Marine Confectioners & Tobacconists Ltd, LON/90/6X (VTD 5435).*

54.14 A trader began business as a retail newsagent and tobacconist in January 1979. His weekly turnover was within the limits of both Scheme B (which, in revised form, is now Direct Calculation Scheme 1) and Scheme G (which has subsequently been withdrawn). He elected to use Scheme G. However, in December 1979 he realised that he had made the wrong choice and should have elected to use Scheme B, under which he calculated that his liability up to September 1979 would have been £2,500 less. He applied to change to Scheme B retrospectively with effect from January 1979. The Commissioners agreed to allow him to change from October 1979 but refused to admit a retrospective change from January. The tribunal dismissed the trader's appeal, holding that it had no jurisdiction to order the Commissioners to operate a retrospective change. *JH Corbitt (Numismatists) Ltd,* 56.1 SECOND-HAND GOODS, applied. *JM Patel (t/a Magsons), LON/80/39 (VTD 936).*

54.15 A similar decision was reached in a case where the tribunal chairman observed that a retrospective change of scheme 'could only be justified in exceptional circumstances' and 'the fact that, in retrospect, one scheme might have proved less advantageous than another scheme did not constitute exceptional circumstances. It is of course the case that one scheme may operate differently, for better or worse, as to the amount of value added tax which results, but in other respects, a scheme may be more advantageous in providing a system of accounting which is more convenient to the particular retailer concerned. It is for the retailer to choose the scheme most suited to himself in the light of his own knowledge about his own business.' *RB & MR Patel (t/a Rama Stores), MAN/82/152 (VTD 1392)*.

54.16   *Patel & Patel (t/a Rama Stores)*, 54.15 above, was applied in the similar case of *MP & EM Dean (t/a Hartlebury Store), MAN/93/1320 (VTD 12116)*.

54.17   Two partners carried on business as grocers, confectioners, tobacconists and newsagents from two premises, one of which was also an off-licence and the other contained a sub-post office. They chose to operate Scheme 2 (which subsequently became Scheme G, and has since been withdrawn). This resulted in their paying more VAT than if they had operated alternative schemes. They had received *Notice No 727*, issued in February 1975, warning of the possible disadvantage of Scheme G. Between 1976 and 1981 four control visits were made to the partners, during which VAT officers pointed out the unsuitability of Scheme G and advised the adoption of alternatives. The partners declined to do so until 1981 when they finally applied to change to Scheme E (which, in revised form, is now Direct Calculation Scheme 1). The Commissioners agreed to the change with effect from 1 April 1981 but refused to approve a retrospective change from 1 April 1977. The tribunal dismissed the partners' appeal against this decision, holding that although the Commissioners had a discretion to allow a retrospective change, the tribunal had no jurisdiction to consider whether that discretion should be exercised in any particular case. *Patel (t/a Magsons)*, 54.14 above, applied. *RJ Withers & S Gibbs (t/a The General Stores), [1983] VATTR 323 (VTD 1553)*.

54.18   A married couple who operated a newsagency applied to change retrospectively from Scheme D to Scheme B. The Commissioners refused to allow a retrospective change and the tribunal dismissed the couple's appeal, applying *Vulgar*, 54.12 above, and *Dean*, 54.16 above. The tribunal observed that its power in such an appeal was supervisory and it could only allow an appeal if the Commissioners' decision was unreasonable, which was not the case here. The tribunal declined to follow the decision in *Wadlewski*, 54.22 below, observing that the tribunal there had 'misconstrued the purpose of the £100 requirement' (in *Notice No 727, 1993 edition, para 85*) and holding that the fact that 'a retrospective change would result in an adjustment of tax significantly in excess of £100' did not in itself amount to 'exceptional circumstances'. The tribunal held that 'the amount of tax concerned is not to be measured by reference to the figure of £100 but, rather, to the turnover or profit of the business'. *L & J Lewis, [1996] VATDR 541 (VTD 14085)*.

54.19   The decision in *Lewis*, 54.18 above, was applied in the similar subsequent cases of *L & P Fryer, MAN/95/1532 (VTD 14265)* and *Mr & Mrs MAR Killingbeck, MAN/95/2452 (VTD 14592)*.

54.20   A similar decision was reached in a case where the tribunal held that it was 'only entitled to investigate the exercise of discretion by the Commissioners with a view to seeing if they have taken into account any matters that ought not to be taken into account, or disregarded matters that ought to have been taken into account, or have acted in a manner in which no reasonable body of Commissioners could have acted. The tribunal cannot override the decision of the Commissioners save as a judicial authority concerned to see whether they have contravened the law by acting in excess of their power'. *AC & PS Gyte, [1999] VATDR 241 (VTD 16031)*.

54.21   Appeals against the Commissioners' refusal to allow a retrospective change of scheme were also dismissed in *R & A Powell, CAR/77/164 (VTD 601)*; *GA & DM Lunn, MAN/83/157 (VTD 1518)*; *LM & R Food Stores, MAN/84/222 (VTD 1936)*; *Maystore Ltd, LON/85/391 (VTD 2096)*; *Bryan Markwell & Co Ltd, LON/89/895 (VTD 4358)*; *Mr & Mrs A Pollitt, MAN/89/160 (VTD 4463)*; *JE Low, LON/90/*

54.22 Retailers' Special Schemes

848X (VTD 5586); SJ West (t/a Stallard News), LON/90/57Z (VTD 5802); JR Buckley, MAN/91/793 (VTD 7644); Garcha Group, LON/94/241A (VTD 13130); K, J & M Patel (t/a Dhruva Newsagents), LON/95/2327 (VTD 14843); O Neilson (t/a The News Shop), EDN/97/63 (VTD 15197); SS & JK Jutla, LON/97/002 (VTD 15446); I & J Hamilton, EDN/97/61 (VTD 15556); RSK Newsagents Ltd, EDN/97/168 (VTD 15750); P & E Waring, MAN/97/1059 (VTD 15864); KS Tiwana, MAN/98/350 (VTD 16202); E Wallace, EDN/99/52 (VTD 16281) and K Jamil, MAN/99/869 (VTD 16795).

54.22 **Appeal allowed.** A couple operated a grocery shop. From 1983 they accounted for tax under Retail Scheme G (which has subsequently been withdrawn). They subsequently discovered that the effect of using Retail Scheme G was that they were overpaying tax by about £8,000 per year, amounting on average to about 40% of their annual profits. They applied to change to Scheme F with retrospective effect. The Commissioners agreed that they could use Scheme F, but refused to allow a retrospective change. They issued a formal ruling to this effect in March 1994, and the couple appealed. The tribunal chairman (Mr. Heim, sitting alone) allowed the appeal, holding that the Commissioners had erred in failing to take account of the amount of the overpayments which had resulted from the couple using Scheme G, and noting that entry into Scheme G had been closed with effect from 1991 because it had been recognised that it produced overpayments of tax, although existing traders had been allowed to use it. The tribunal held that it had a supervisory jurisdiction, and that the Commissioners had exercised their discretion unreasonably by giving insufficient consideration to the 'exceptional circumstances'. *Bryan Markwell & Co*, 54.21 above, and *Buckley*, 54.21 above, distinguished. *A & C Wadlewski, LON/94/1849A (VTD 13340).* (*Note.* The decision here was not followed, and was implicitly disapproved, by subsequent tribunals in *Lewis*, 54.18 above; *Fryer*, 54.19 above; *Neilson*, 54.21 above, and *Jutla*, 54.21 above.)

TRANSITIONAL MATTERS

54.23 **Receipts after increase in rate from sales before the increase.** A trader sold flowers, garden produce, garden machinery and allied goods and services. Before 18 June 1979 his supplies were variously zero-rated, chargeable at the standard rate of 8%, or chargeable at the higher rate of 12½%. He accounted for tax under Scheme F (which, in revised form, is now the Point of Sale Scheme), using the 'standard method' for arriving at his gross takings. As from 18 June 1979, the two positive rates were replaced by a single standard rate of 15%. The trader accounted for tax under the old rates in respect of takings from 18 June under agreements, etc. entered into before that date. The Commissioners issued an assessment on the basis that tax should have been accounted for by reference to the increased rate as regards all his takings from 18 June. The tribunal upheld the assessment and dismissed the trader's appeal. *AS Gandy, LON/80/253 (VTD 1029).*

54.24 *Gandy*, 54.23 above, was applied in the similar case of *Norman Lavelle Ltd, MAN/82/8 (VTD 1330).*

54.25 A similar decision was reached in *Wesley Barrell (Witney) Ltd, LON/80/465 (VTD 1087).*

54.26 A company (N) which sold clothing by mail order operated Retail Scheme H (which, in revised form, is now Apportionment Scheme 2), using the 'standard method' of computing its gross takings. On 1 April 1991 the standard rate of VAT was increased from 15% to 17.5%, with the result that the VAT fraction changed from $3/23$ to $7/47$. Consequently, N was required to calculate its output tax beginning on 1 April 1991 by applying the VAT fraction of $7/47$. It did so, except in respect of its takings from self-financed credit sales entered into before 1 April 1991, on which it calculated output tax applying the old fraction of ³/₂₃. The Commissioners issued assessments covering the accounting periods from 1 February 1991 to 31 January 1992, charging tax on receipts after 31 March 1991 from self-financed credit sales made before 1 April 1991 at the new rate rather than at the old rate. N appealed, contending that the assessments were invalid as the requirements of *Appendix C* of *Notice No 727 (1993 edition)* did not conform with *Article 27* of the *EC Sixth Directive*. The tribunal accepted this contention and allowed N's appeal, and the QB upheld this decision. *C & E Commrs v Next plc, QB [1995] STC 651. (Notes.* (1) The decision in this case was disapproved and overruled by the CA in the subsequent case of *R v C & E Commrs (ex p. Littlewoods Home Shopping Group Ltd)*, 54.35 below. Millett LJ observed that, when the VAT rate was increased, the adoption of the 'standard method' of calculating gross takings, rather than the normal method of calculating the VAT due, would not affect the ultimate consumer, since the consumer 'is invoiced for his purchases at the time of supply for a price which is inclusive of VAT at the rate then in force. Later increases in the rate of tax before he completes payment in full do not affect the amount of the outstanding payments for which he is liable.' For the Commissioners' practice following the CA decision, see Business Brief 22/98, issued on 3 November 1998. (2) The 'standard method' of calculating gross takings was withdrawn with effect from 1 March 1997.)

54.27   A similar decision was reached in a case which was heard in the QB with *Next plc*, 54.26 above. *C & E Commrs v Grattan plc, QB [1995] STC 651.*

54.28   **Business taken over as going concern—Direct Calculation Scheme applied—treatment of opening stock.**   A trader purchased an existing business, selling both standard-rated and zero-rated goods, and accounted for tax under Scheme B (which, in revised form, is now Direct Calculation Scheme 1). *Notice No 727B, para 10* explicitly stated that, in arriving at the zero-rated goods received in the first period for which the scheme is used, goods held at the beginning must not be included. However, in arriving at the liability for the first period of her business, the trader included, in the zero-rated goods, stock which she had taken over with the business. The Commissioners issued an assessment to exclude the stock from the calculation. The tribunal upheld the assessment and dismissed the trader's appeal. *AL Housden, [1981] VATTR 217 (VTD 1178). (Note. Notice No 727B* has since been replaced. See now *Notice No 727/5.)*

54.29   In April 1992 a co-operative (CWS), which operated Retail Scheme B (which, in revised form, is now Direct Calculation Scheme 1), took over, as a going concern, the business of another co-operative which had operated Retail Scheme H (which, in revised form, is now Apportionment Scheme 2). It accounted for tax under Scheme B in respect of the sale of the stock it had taken over. The Commissioners considered that such stock should have been excluded from the Scheme B calculation, and that the result of including it was that CWS had underdeclared tax. They issued an assessment, against which CWS appealed. The tribunal allowed the appeal, holding that CWS had acted correctly in treating the stock taken over in its Scheme B calculation, and the QB upheld this decision. Carnwath J held that, although the effect of what is now *Article 5* of the *VAT (Special Provisions) Order* was that the transfer of goods to CWS was not to be treated as a supply, it did not follow that it should be ignored altogether. Scheme B was not confined to goods acquired through a taxable supply. The goods had been 'received for resale' and should therefore be included in the Scheme B calculation. The fact that the transferor had operated Scheme H was irrelevant. *Dicta* of the tribunal decision in *Kelly*, 54.54 below, were disapproved. *C & E Commrs v Co-Operative Wholesale Society Ltd, QB [1995] STC 983. (Note.* The decision here was distinguished in the subsequent case of *Iceland Foodstores Ltd*, 54.31 below.)

54.30 **Business transferred as going concern—Direct Calculation Scheme applied—treatment of stock.** A co-operative, which used Retail Scheme B (which, in revised form, is now Direct Calculation Scheme 1), transferred its food-retailing business to an associated company, as a going concern, in two stages. The business assets of two of the foodstores were transferred in January 1996, the assets of the remaining foodstores being transferred in February 1996. For its accounting period ending in January 1996, the co-operative accounted for tax on the basis that the zero-rated stock which was included in the first transfer should be excluded from its daily gross takings, but included in the computation of 'zero-rated goods received, made or grown for resale', at its expected retail price. The Commissioners issued a ruling that the stock should have been wholly excluded from the calculations. The tribunal upheld the ruling and the CA dismissed the co-operative's appeal. Jonathan Parker J held that, since a disposal of zero-rated goods on a transfer of a business as a going concern was a sale which was not a retail sale, the transferor had not received the 'expected selling price'. Accordingly, it was necessary to make an adjustment in respect of such goods, as directed in *Notice No 727*, issued in accordance with the Commissioners' powers under *VAT Regulations 1995 (SI 1995 No 2518), reg 67*. The 'only appropriate adjustment' was to exclude from the calculation the figure which had initially been included as the expected selling price. *United Norwest Co-Operatives Ltd v C & E Commrs, CA [1999] STC 686.* (*Note.* For another appeal relating to the transfer, heard with this case by the tribunal but not taken to the QB or CA, see *United Norwest Food Markets Ltd*, 54.51 below.)

54.31 A company took over a retail business as a going concern and began to use Retail Scheme B1 (which, in revised form, is now Direct Calculation Scheme 2). In its first return, it treated the stock which had been transferred to it with the business as goods received for resale in the tax period. On this basis, it declared negative output tax of more than £9,000,000 and claimed a repayment of more than £18,000,000. The Commissioners issued a ruling that the stock should be treated as stock held at the beginning of the year, with the result that the repayment due to the company was reduced from £18,600,000 to £7,300,000. The tribunal upheld the Commissioners' ruling and dismissed the company's appeal, holding that the stock in question 'was not to be included in the calculations until the end of the year'. *Co-Operative Wholesale Society Ltd*, 54.29 above, was distinguished, firstly on the basis that it dealt with Scheme B rather than Scheme B1, and Scheme B 'required no adjustment, annual or otherwise, to allow for differences between opening and closing stock', and secondly because the appellant company in that case was already carrying on business when it received the stock in question. *Iceland Foodstores Ltd, [1998] VATDR 498 (VTD 15833).*

54.32 **Business transferred as going concern—different Retail Schemes applied—treatment of stock.** A retail company (D) had a number of departments, some of which accounted for tax under Retail Scheme A (which, in revised form, is now the Point of Sale Scheme), some of which accounted for tax under Retail Scheme B (which, in revised form, is now Direct Calculation Scheme 1), and some of which accounted for tax under Retail Scheme H (which, in revised form, is now Apportionment Scheme 2). Its parent company (B), which was the representative member of the VAT group, considered that the use of Scheme H was disadvantageous, and that it would be beneficial to use Scheme B instead. A new subsidiary company (J) was incorporated and the businesses of D's departments which had used Schemes B and H were transferred to that company as a going concern. In B's next return, no adjustment was made to D's Scheme B and Scheme H calculations to take account of the stock which had been transferred to J. The Commissioners issued an assessment on the basis that, since the stock transferred to

J was not a retail supply, the relevant calculations should have been adjusted by reducing the value of the zero-rated expected selling prices by the value of that stock (and effectively increasing the value attributed to standard-rated outputs for the period). B appealed. The tribunal upheld the assessment and dismissed B's appeal, observing that the stock had not been sold by retail and that the transfer had had the effect of reducing the stock available for sale by retail. The tribunal held that 'the operation of Scheme B would be distorted if no account was taken of self-supply or gratuitous supply by traders. So also would it be distorted if no adjustment were made for transfers of a going concern as those in this case.' *The Burton Group plc, LON/96/1116 (VTD 15046)*. (*Note*. For another appeal relating to the transfer, heard with this case, see *Jubilee Fashions Ltd*, 54.52 below.)

GROSS TAKINGS

Note. The 'standard method' of calculating gross takings, which had been introduced in 1973 (and which provided that credit sales should not be included in gross takings until payments were received in respect of them), was withdrawn with effect from 1 March 1997. See *R v C & E Commrs (ex p. Littlewoods Home Shopping Group Ltd)*, 54.35 below, for a case concerning the consequences of this withdrawal.

54.33   **VAT Regulations, reg 67(2)(c)—whether value of standard-rated supplies agreed by Commissioners.**   A partnership operated a snack bar. Following a visit by a Customs officer in 1996, they accounted for tax on the basis that 13% of their supplies were standard-rated and 87% were zero-rated. In 1998 a subsequent Customs officer formed the opinion that 41% of the partnership's supplies were standard-rated. He arranged for the issue of an assessment covering the periods from September 1996 to November 1998, computed on the basis that the percentage of standard-rated supplies had increased from 13% to 41% during that time. The partnership appealed, contending that the previous officer had agreed that 13% of their supplies were standard-rated and this agreement should be treated as binding until the subsequent visit. The tribunal accepted this contention and allowed the appeal, holding that the effect of *VAT Regulations 1995, reg 67(2)(c)* was that the agreement reached in 1996 was valid and could not be changed retrospectively. *R & A Bardetti (t/a Obertelli Quality Sandwiches), LON/99/561 (VTD 16758)*. (*Note*. For another issue in this case, see 27.10 FOOD.)

54.34   **Direction under VAT Regulations, reg 68*—whether unreasonable.**   A company was incorporated to take over the trade of a retail furnishings company, which had adopted the optional method of calculating gross takings. The new company wished to adopt the 'standard method' as then in force, but the Commissioners issued a direction under what is now *VAT Regulations, reg 68*, instructing it to use the optional method of calculating gross takings. The company appealed, contending that the direction was unreasonable and that the ultimate tax liability would be the same whichever method was used, although the use of the standard method would give it a legitimate cash-flow advantage. The tribunal allowed the company's appeal, holding that the direction was unreasonable, and observing that deferment of tax under the standard method was not a tax advantage as the correct amount of tax still had to be paid. The QB upheld this decision. *C & E Commrs v J Boardmans (1980) Ltd, QB 1985, [1986] STC 10*. (*Note*. The 'standard method' of computing gross takings has subsequently been withdrawn—see the note preceding this section.)

54.35   **Withdrawal of standard method of calculating gross takings—application for judicial review.**   A company (L) sold goods by mail order. On the introduction of VAT in 1973 the Commissioners had stated that a trader who adopted the standard method of calculating gross takings (which provided that credit sales should not be included until payments were received in respect of them), and included as gross takings payments received in respect of supplies made before the introduction of VAT, would not normally be required to account for VAT on payments due to him at the end of the last period in which he used a retail scheme. L adopted the standard method and accounted for tax accordingly. In the November 1996 Budget, the Chancellor of the Exchequer announced that the standard method would be withdrawn with effect from 1 March 1997. The Commissioners also announced that retailers who financed their own credit sales would have to account for VAT at the time of supply even if payment had not been received. L applied for judicial review, contending that the Commissioners were not entitled to withdraw the assurances they had made in 1973. The QB dismissed the application but the CA allowed L's appeal. The CA held that the cases of *Next plc*, 54.26 above, and *Grattan plc*, 54.27 above, had been 'wrongly decided and should be overruled'. The decision to charge output tax on outstanding balances, on the withdrawal of the 'standard method' of calculating gross takings, would result in double taxation. This would be 'neither fair nor reasonable' and would be incompatible with *Articles 11* and *12* of the *EC Sixth Directive*. The decision had 'no statutory basis', and was unlawful. *R v C & E Commrs (ex p. Littlewoods Home Shopping Group Ltd)*, CA [1998] STC 445. (*Note*. For the Commissioners' practice following this decision, see Business Brief 11/98, issued on 1 May 1998.)

54.36   **Mail order business—inclusion of full value of credit sales in gross takings—whether compatible with EC law.**   A company which operated a mail order business had computed its gross takings in accordance with the standard method in force until 28 February 1997. On 27 February 1997 the Commissioners issued a letter withdrawing this method, and instructing the company to include in gross takings the full amount of all credit sales to agents, without deducting the 10% discounts which it credited to the agents. In its returns for the periods ending April 1997 and July 1997, the company continued to treat the discounts which it credited to its agents as a deduction in computing its gross takings. The Commissioners issued assessments charging tax on the amounts in question, and the company appealed, contending that the Commissioners' direction contravened *Article 11A* of the *EC Sixth Directive*. The tribunal directed that the case should be referred to the CJEC for a preliminary ruling on the interpretation of *Article 11A* and the definition of the taxable amount in the circumstances of the case. *Freemans plc, LON/97/1035 (VTD 15670)*. (*Note*. The CJEC has registered the case as *C-86/99*. Advocate-General Mischo delivered his Opinion on 11 January 2000, supporting the company's contention that the 10% discounts which the company credited to its agents should be allowed as a deduction in computing the 'taxable amount'. At the time of writing, the CJEC has not yet given judgment.)

54.37   **Application of Point of Sale Scheme—whether takings deemed to comprise cash in till or readings on till rolls.**   A company which operated a large number of public houses accounted for VAT under Retail Scheme A (now the Point of Sale Scheme), using the standard method of computing gross takings. It computed its takings by reference to the total cash in its tills, rather than by reference to the takings recorded on its till rolls. The Commissioners issued an assessment on the basis that the company's practice was incorrect, and had resulted in an underdeclaration of tax. (The company's declared takings over the periods assessed were £716,500,000. The Commissioners analysed a sample of the company's takings, and formed the opinion that the company's incorrect method of computing its takings led to 0.1013% of the total takings not being declared. This percentage was then applied to the whole of the period in question, resulting in an assessment being raised on an estimated underdeclaration of £725,774.) The tribunal dismissed the company's appeal, holding that the company had been at fault in failing to account for tax on some of the takings recorded on its till rolls, and the Commissioners' extrapolation of an estimated total underdeclaration from a particular sample was reasonable in the circumstances. *Courage Ltd, LON/92/319Y (VTD 8808)*.

54.38 **Stock deficiency attributed to assumed thefts of cash—whether assumed thefts to be included in daily gross takings.** A group of retail companies accounted for tax under Retail Scheme F (now the Point of Sale Scheme) and Retail Scheme J (which has now been withdrawn). The representative member of the group treated the amount recorded on the till rolls as the daily gross takings. However, the group's accounts indicated stock deficiencies of between £15,000,000 and £23,000,000 per year. This was primarily attributed to theft by customers and employees. The Commissioners formed the opinion that part of this discrepancy was attributable to theft by employees of cash which had not been recorded on the till rolls, rather than to thefts of stock. They issued assessments computed on the basis that about 27% of the stock deficiencies were attributable to thefts by employees, of which about 20% was attributable to thefts of cash, rather than to thefts of stock. The company appealed, contending as a preliminary point that the assessments had not been made to the best of the Commissioners' judgment. The tribunal rejected this contention and dismissed the appeal in principle (giving the company leave to apply for a further hearing with regard to the amount of the assessments). Applying *dicta* of Lord Donovan in *Argosy Co Ltd v Guyana Commissioner of Inland Revenue, PC [1971] 1 WLR 514*, 'once a reasonable opinion that liability exists is formed, there must necessarily be guess-work at times as to the quantum of liability'. *WH Smith Ltd, [2000] VATDR 1 (VTD 16505)*.

54.39 **Application of Point of Sale Scheme—goods sold on interest-free credit—whether discount retained by finance company may be deducted in computing gross takings.** A company (P) operated Retail Scheme A (now the Point of Sale Scheme). It arranged for customers to be provided with 'interest-free credit' by a finance company. In such cases, the finance company did not pay P the full price charged to the customer, but paid a net amount after retaining a 'discount' which was equivalent to the amount that the finance company would have charged the customer for the loan at a commercial rate. In accounting for output tax on such transactions, P only included as gross takings the amount which it actually received from the finance company. The Commissioners issued an assessment on the basis that P should have included the full amount charged to the customer in its gross takings. P appealed, contending that it had made two separate supplies, a supply of goods and a supply of arranging credit, and that it should only be required to account for tax on the amount which it actually received. The HL directed that the case should be referred to the CJEC for a ruling on the definition of the 'taxable amount' in the circumstances of the case. *Primback Ltd v C & E Commrs, HL 4 December 1997 unreported*. (*Notes*. (1) The CJEC has registered the case as *Case C-34/99*. Advocate-General Alber delivered his Opinion on 18 January 2001. He proposed that the court should hold that 'in the case where a retail trader offers goods at a single price and offers interest-free credit for payment of that price — the credit being provided by a person other than the retail trader and at no additional cost to the customer — and thus where the true costs of the credit are not separately indicated, the taxable amount for purposes of value added tax is the full amount payable by the customer'. (2) For the Commissioners' practice pending the determination of the appeal, see Business Brief 15/96, issued on 22 July 1996, and Business Brief 1/98, issued on 7 January 1998.)

54.40 **Point of Sale Scheme—payments made by retailer to company operating promotion scheme—whether deductible from gross takings.** A company (C) trading as carpet retailers used Retail Scheme A (now the Point of Sale Scheme). It operated a promotion scheme, whereby customers who spent £200 or more on its carpets could apply to a travel company for a voucher. The nominal value of the voucher was half of the cost of the carpets (up to a maximum of £750), and the voucher could be redeemed against certain holidays offered by the travel company. C paid 2% of the sale price of the carpets covered by the scheme to the company which had devised the scheme (L). Initially C accounted for tax on the full amount of its receipts, but it subsequently submitted a repayment claim on the basis that it should have deducted the amounts which it paid to L. The Commissioners rejected the claim, and C appealed. The tribunal dismissed the appeal, and the QB upheld this decision. On the evidence, although the vouchers were within the definition of 'trading stamps', C had never made any delivery of the vouchers, which were supplied to customers by the travel company and never became C's property. L and the travel company were running the scheme independently, and the travel company was not acting as an agent of C. The payments which C made were calculated by reference to the value of the carpets which it sold, rather than by reference to the number of the vouchers delivered, and were not consideration for the purchase of the vouchers. Accordingly, C was not entitled to deduct the amounts which it paid to L in computing its gross takings. *Allied Carpets Group plc v C & E Commrs, QB [1998] STC 894.*

54.41   **Newspaper delivery charges—inclusion in gross takings.**   See *Coe*, 54.2 above, and the cases noted at 54.3 above.

54.42   **Subscriptions for discount cards.**   See *Mothercare (UK) Ltd*, 54.8 above.

54.43   **Retail sales paid for by credit card issued by member of same group of companies as retailer—time of supplies.**   See *Kingfisher plc*, 30.23 GROUPS OF COMPANIES.

EXPECTED SELLING PRICES

54.44   **Newspaper delivery charges—treatment under Scheme H (now Apportionment Scheme 2).**   See *Lloyd*, 54.4 above.

54.45   **Business transferred as going concern—different Retail Schemes applied.**   See *The Burton Group plc*, 54.32 above.

POINT OF SALE SCHEME

54.46   **Application of Point of Sale Scheme—whether takings deemed to comprise cash in till or readings on till rolls.**   See *Courage Ltd*, 54.37 above.

54.47   **Application of Point of Sale Scheme—goods sold on interest-free credit— whether discount retained by finance company may be deducted in computing gross takings.**   See *Primback Ltd*, 54.39 above.

54.48   **Point of Sale Scheme—payments made by retailer to company operating promotion scheme—whether deductible from gross takings.**   See *Allied Carpets Group plc*, 54.40 above.

APPORTIONMENT SCHEMES

54.49   **Mail order goods sold to agents—application of Apportionment Scheme.**   A group of companies sold goods by mail order, sending copies of its catalogues to agents. Such agents received commission of 10% of the catalogue price on sales to third parties, and were credited with a discount or rebate of 10% on goods which they purchased personally. Where agents purchased goods personally, the companies accounted for VAT on the net amount paid by the agent, but where goods were sold to agents on behalf of third parties, the companies accounted for VAT on the whole of the catalogue price. Some of the goods sold were standard-rated and others zero-rated, and the companies had, by agreement with the Commissioners, operated a modified version of Retail Scheme H (which, in revised form, is now Apportionment Scheme 2). In October 1987 the group formed the opinion that it had treated a significant number of sales, which in fact had been made to agents, as having been made to third parties, and had therefore accounted for VAT on the catalogue price instead of on the net amounts paid by agents. In its return for the period ending 31 December 1987, the group increased the proportion of its sales which it treated as having been made for the agents' own use. In its return for the period ending 31 December 1988, it made a deduction for output tax which it considered that it had overdeducted in earlier periods by treating too many sales as having been made to third parties. The Commissioners accepted that, for periods after 1 January 1988, the companies could alter the proportion of its sales which they treated as being for agents' own use, but considered that the companies could not make a retrospective alteration. They therefore issued assessments on the basis that the companies should have continued to adopt the previous percentage in its return to 31 December 1987, and were not entitled to make a retrospective deduction of output tax in its return for the period ending 31 December 1988. The QB upheld both assessments. The correspondence in question showed that the companies had adopted a modified version of Retail Scheme H. The correspondence between the companies and the Commissioners constituted a series of offers to cover the ensuing three-year period, and when such offers were accepted (by the submission of the first return made on the offered basis) this acceptance was binding on the companies for the next three years. The companies appealed to the CA, which upheld the QB decision. The parties had entered into a binding agreement and the group was not entitled to resile from it. *GUS Merchandise Corporation Ltd (No 2) v C & E Commrs, CA 1994, [1995] STC 279.* (*Note.* For a preliminary issue in this case, see 2.200 APPEALS.)

54.50   **Newspaper delivery charges.**   See *Coe*, 54.2 above, and the cases noted at 54.3 and 54.4 above.

DIRECT CALCULATION SCHEMES

54.51   **Commissioners refusing application to use Direct Calculation Scheme—whether refusal unreasonable.**   A company took over (in two stages) the food-retailing business of a co-operative as a going concern. The co-operative had accounted for tax using Retail Scheme B (which, in revised form, is now Direct Calculation Scheme 1). The Commissioners issued a ruling that the company was not permitted to use Scheme B, on the grounds that its use would 'distort the output tax ... and not give a fair and reasonable result'. The company appealed. The tribunal allowed the appeal, holding that the Commissioners' ruling was unreasonable. *Dicta* in *JH Corbitt (Numismatists) Ltd*, 56.1 SECOND-HAND GOODS, applied. The decision to refuse Scheme B was 'flawed', since the officer responsible for the ruling had treated the transfers as a tax avoidance scheme, which was not the case. The tribunal held that, although the transfers brought fiscal advantages, they 'would have been carried out as they were carried out even if no fiscal advantages had existed'. The fiscal advantages of the arrangements were 'inherent in the proper and legitimate use of Scheme B'. *United Norwest Food Markets Ltd, MAN/96/423 (VTD 14923).* (*Note.* For an appeal by the transferor, heard with this appeal and dismissed, see *United Norwest Co-Operatives Ltd*, 54.30 above.)

54.52   A retail company had a number of departments, some of which accounted for tax under Retail Scheme A (now the Point of Sale Scheme), some of which accounted for tax under Retail Scheme B (which, in revised form, is now Direct Calculation Scheme 1), and some of which accounted for tax under Retail Scheme H (which, in revised form, is now Apportionment Scheme 2). The parent company considered that the use of Scheme H was disadvantageous, and that it would be beneficial to use Scheme B instead. A new subsidiary company (J) was incorporated and the businesses of those departments which had used Schemes B and H were transferred to J as a going concern. In its first return (submitted in March 1996 and covering the period ending February 1996), J claimed a repayment of more than £3,000,000. The Commissioners repaid the amount claimed in April 1996. However, the Commissioners made a routine control visit to the companies in May 1996, and in June they issued a ruling under *VAT Regulations 1995, reg 68*, refusing J permission to use Scheme B and instructing it to resubmit its return using another Scheme. J appealed, contending firstly that the repayment made in April amounted to acceptance that J could use Scheme B, and alternatively that the refusal was unreasonable. The Commissioners accepted the first contention and allowed J's appeal, holding that 'by making an unconditional repayment the Commissioners permitted the use of Scheme B ... having permitted use of the Scheme, the Commissioners were not entitled to resile from the permission with retrospective effect.' The tribunal also held that the officer responsible for the ruling had acted unreasonably, in that he had informed J that he had issued the ruling because J's return had included a figure of negative output tax. The tribunal observed that 'if he had relied on the size of the negative output tax, he could not have been criticised but ... reliance on the fact of negative output tax was an irrelevant matter and wrong in law'. Applying *dicta* of Lord Lane in *JH Corbitt (Numismatists) Ltd*, 56.1 SECOND-HAND GOODS, the officer had taken irrelevant matter into account. *Jubilee Fashions Ltd, LON/96/1116 (VTD 15046)*. (*Note*. For an appeal by the transferor, heard with this appeal and dismissed, see *The Burton Group plc*, 54.32 above.)

54.53   **Improper use of Direct Calculation Scheme.**   A partnership carrying on a retail business as confectioners, tobacconists and newsagents accounted for tax under Scheme B (which, in revised form, is now Direct Calculation Scheme 1), although it was not entitled to do so as its zero-rated supplies were more than half of its total supplies. The Commissioners therefore issued assessments on the basis that the partnership should have accounted for tax under Scheme D (which has subsequently been withdrawn). The tribunal dismissed the partnership's appeal. *NG & MG Patel, LON/87/48 & LON/87/189 (VTD 2463)*.

54.54   A partnership operating Retail Scheme B (which, in revised form, is now Direct Calculation Scheme 1) included the estimated selling prices of zero-rated opening stock in estimating its zero-rated outputs for its first period of trading. The Commissioners issued an assessment on the basis that the opening zero-rated stock should not have been brought into the partnership's computation of zero-rated goods received in the period. The tribunal accepted the Commissioners' contentions and dismissed the partnership's appeal. If opening zero-rated stock were brought into a computation, closing zero-rated stock would need to be deducted. Scheme B did not provide for such adjustments, but operated on the assumption that the percentage of stock which was zero-rated remained constant. *JM & MC Kelly, LON/87/576X (VTD 4139)*. (*Note. Dicta* of the tribunal chairman were subsequently disapproved by Carnwath J in *Co-Operative Wholesale Society Ltd*, 54.29 above.)

54.55   **Direct Calculation Scheme—deduction for wastage.**   In 1991 the Commissioners permitted a major retail company (T) to calculate the value of its standard-rated supplies by an adaptation of Scheme B1 (which, in revised form, is now Direct Calculation Scheme 2, and under which output tax is paid on daily gross takings minus expected zero-rated sales). In calculating the expected zero-rated sales, deductions were made for wastage. In 1993 the Commissioners formed the opinion that T had been underestimating its wastage, with the result that it had been making deductions for zero-rated sales which were too high, and thus had been underdeclaring its output tax. They issued an assessment charging tax of more than £2,500,000. T appealed, contending that it had operated the scheme in accordance with its agreement with the Commissioners, and that the assessment had not been made to the best of the Commissioners' judgment. The tribunal reviewed the evidence in detail and allowed the appeal, holding that the agreement as to how the scheme was to be operated was 'a contract binding on both sides from which one party cannot resile'. On the evidence, the Commissioners had given 'a final and unqualified assent' to T's proposals. The tribunal observed that 'once a permission has been granted, then it could be refused for the future if it was found that the scheme did not produce a fair and reasonable valuation. However, ... a scheme which has been agreed cannot be altered retrospectively just because Customs and Excise then find that it does not produce a fair and reasonable valuation'. Furthermore, T had not made any misrepresentation of fact, and had acted 'honestly and *bona fide*'. The tribunal held that 'in entering into a retail scheme agreement, there is no wider duty of disclosure than applies under the normal law of contract'. It followed that the assessment was invalid. *Tesco plc, [1994] VATTR 425 (VTD 12740)*.

MISCELLANEOUS

54.56   **Estimated assessment on trader using Retail Scheme—whether assessment must be based on Retail Scheme calculation.**   See *Briggs*, 3.27 ASSESSMENT.

54.57   **Company incorrectly adopting Retail Scheme for wholesale supplies— subsequent claim for repayment of tax allegedly overpaid.**   See *RJN Creighton Ltd*, 45.59 PAYMENT OF TAX.

54.58   **Use of inappropriate Retail Scheme—retrospective recalculation permitted by Commissioners—whether any 'official error'.**   See *Peart*, 45.60 PAYMENT OF TAX, and *Mathieson*, 45.66 PAYMENT OF TAX.

55 Returns

The cases in this chapter are arranged under the following headings.

Accounting periods 55.1–55.5
Making of returns (VAT Regulations 1995, reg 25) 55.6–55.13
Correction of errors (VAT Regulations 1995, regs 34, 35) 55.14–55.20
Miscellaneous 55.21–55.24

ACCOUNTING PERIODS

55.1 **Whether returns may be made for periods not specified in Regulations.** A company requested permission to use accounting periods of longer than the three months specified by what is now *VAT Regulations 1995 (SI 1995 No 2518), reg 25(1)*. The Commissioners rejected the request and the company appealed. The tribunal struck out the appeal, holding that there was no appealable matter within what is now *VATA 1994, s 83*. It also considered that there was no provision permitting departure from the requirements of the *Regulations. Selected Growers Ltd, LON/73/21 (VTD 10)*.

55.2 **Decision of Commissioners as to period of returns on registration— whether appealable.** A company was registered with effect from 1 May 1980 and was instructed to make a return for the period to 30 September 1980, which it did. On 18 December 1980, the Commissioners wrote to the company stating that it was now considered necessary to vary the length of its first accounting period which would now be deemed to end on 30 November 1980 and that the return already made was 'of no effect'. The company applied for an extension of the period in which to appeal against this decision and the Commissioners contended as a preliminary issue that there was no appealable matter within what is now *VATA 1994, s 83(a)*. The tribunal accepted this contention and struck out the appeal. *Punchwell Ltd, [1981] VATTR 93 (VTD 1085)*.

55.3 **Return issued by Commissioners covering twelve-year period for which trader failed to register.** See *Bjelica*, 53.21 REGISTRATION.

55.4 **Return covering 23–year period following prolonged failure to register.** See *Royal College of Obstetricians & Gynaecologists*, 45.1 PAYMENT OF TAX.

55.5 **Definition of 'prescribed accounting period' for purposes of VATA 1994, s 77.** See *Wright*, 3.79 ASSESSMENT.

MAKING OF RETURNS (VAT Regulations 1995, reg 25)

55.6 **Whether return 'made' when posted.** A taxpayer was charged with failing to furnish a VAT return as required by what is now *VAT Regulations 1995 (SI 1995 No 2518), reg 25*. He had posted the return in Edinburgh in the envelope supplied, but it had not been received. The Sheriff acquitted the taxpayer, holding that he had furnished the return when he posted it. The CS dismissed the Commissioners' appeal against this decision, holding that the return had been furnished because the form instructed the taxpayer to send the return to the Controller in the envelope provided. Lord Dunpark held that the effect of this wording was that the Commissioners 'were appointing the Post Office as their agent to receive the return on their behalf'. Therefore the return was 'furnished' when it was completed and posted. *Aikman v White, CS 1985, [1986] STC 1. (Note. The VAT (General)*

Regulations as in force at the relevant time used the words 'furnish' and 'furnished', whereas the *VAT Regulations 1995* use the words 'make' and 'made'. The Commissioners subsequently altered the wording of the form so that it reads 'You must ensure that the completed form and any VAT payable are received no later than the due date by the Controller'. In *W Timms & Son (Builders) Ltd*, 55.8 below, the QB distinguished this case as having been decided in the context of criminal liability, under the provisions of *VATA 1983, s 39(8)* which had subsequently been repealed. For the purposes of *FA 1985, ss 19, 20* (which have now become *VATA 1994, ss 59, 79*), the QB held that a return was furnished at the time it was received, rather than at the time it was posted.)

55.7   *Aikman v White*, 55.6 above, was followed in the English cases of *Hayman v Griffiths & Another* and *Walker v Hanby QB [1987] STC 649*. (*Note.* See now, however, the note following 55.6 above.)

55.8   A company's return for the period ending 31 August 1987, due to be received by the Commissioners by 30 September 1987, indicated that a repayment was due. The company claimed a supplement in respect of this repayment. The Commissioners contended that no repayment supplement was due because the return was not received by them until more than thirty days after the due date. The tribunal found, on the evidence, that the return in question was posted by the company on 15 September 1987 but was not received by the Commissioners until 31 March 1988. The QB held that, on the facts found by the tribunal, repayment supplement was not due. What is now *VATA 1994, s 79(1)* required a return to be received by the Commissioners within one month of the due date. *VATA 1994, ss 59, 79*, which were related provisions and should be construed to harmonise with each other, drew a clear distinction between the despatching and the receiving of a return. *Aikman v White*, 55.6 above, and *Hayman v Griffiths*, 55.7 above, were distinguished since they had been decided on the basis of the wording of the return forms issued at the relevant time, which had subsequently been altered, and in the wholly different context of criminal liability under *VATA 1983, s 39(8)*, which had subsequently been repealed. *C & E Commrs v W Timms & Son (Builders) Ltd, QB [1992] STC 374*.

55.9   Similar decisions were reached by tribunals in *Jones*, 18.49 DEFAULT SURCHARGE, *Gale*, 48.5 PENALTIES: FAILURE TO NOTIFY, and *Selwyn*, 48.100 PENALTIES: FAILURE TO NOTIFY. In *Selwyn* the tribunal observed that, while the Commissioners had appointed the Post Office as their agent, this was an agency to carry information, not an agency to receive information.

55.10   **Application of VAT Regulations, reg 25(1)(b).** On 1 September 1992 a company was struck off the Register of Companies, under *Companies Act 1985, s 652*. In November 1997 the company was restored to the Register, under *Companies Act 1985, s 653*, and was deemed to have continued in operation as if it had not been struck off. The Commissioners issued a return covering the period from 2 September 1992 to 30 April 1998. The company submitted this return and claimed a repayment. The Commissioners considered that the return was incorrect, and rejected the claim and issued an assessment covering the whole of the period covered by the return. The company appealed. The tribunal dismissed the appeal, holding that the effect of *VAT Regulations 1995 (SI 1995 No 2518), reg 25(1)(b)* was that the period was a single prescribed accounting period. Accordingly, as the assessment covered a single accounting period, the relevant time limits ran from the end of that single accounting period. *Eastgate Christian Bookshop Ltd, LON/00/381 (VTD 16766)*.

55.11   **Application of VAT Regulations, reg 25(1)(c).** In the case noted at 44.23 PARTNERSHIP, the Commissioners issued an assessment on a married couple in 1999, covering the period from 1 April 1991 to 31 August 1997. The couple appealed, contending that, because the Commissioners had not issued a direction under *VAT Regulations 1995 (SI 1995 No 2518), reg 25(1)(c)*, the assessment was a global assessment covering separate accounting periods and was therefore invalid through having been made outside the statutory time limit. The tribunal accepted this contention and allowed the appeal, holding that 'there was no sufficiently clear instruction to the appellants which could constitute a direction under *rule (sic) 25*'. Dicta in *Inchcape Management Services Ltd*, 55.12 below, applied. *House*, 3.93 ASSESSMENT, was distinguished, on the grounds that, in that case, 'all relevant documents were received on the same day'. *PC & VL Leonidas, LON/97/1594 (VTD 16588)*.

55.12   **Interpretation of VAT Regulations, reg 25(5).**   In 1992 a company received a substantial interim payment of compensation from the Department of Transport in return for surrendering its interest in some land under a compulsory purchase order. It did not account for output tax on the compensation, although it had previously elected to waive exemption in respect of the land in question. In 1994 it made a voluntary disclosure of the liability, advising the Commissioners that the amount of compensation had not been finally agreed. The compensation was finally agreed in 1997. Following subsequent correspondence, the Commissioners wrote to the company in March 1998, instructing it to account for tax on the compensation on its next return, in accordance with *VAT Regulations 1995 (SI 1995 No 2518), reg 35*. The company refused to do so, and in August 1998 the Commissioners issued an assessment, purporting to be for the prescribed accounting period ending in May 1998, charging tax of more than £1,600,000 on the compensation. The company appealed, contending that the assessment was invalid as it had been made outside the statutory time limit. The Commissioners defended the assessment on the basis that, by virtue of *VAT Regulations 1995 (SI 1995 No 2518), reg 25(5)*, they had exercised their power to 'allow VAT chargeable in any period to be treated as being chargeable in such later period as they may specify'. The tribunal allowed the company's appeal, observing that the Commissioners had not made an immediate reply to the company's letter of 1994, and holding that 'there is no evidence that they put their minds to the possibility of the exercise of the *regulation 25(5)* power until they came to draft their Statement of Case.' The tribunal held that 'the interests of legal certainty (a fundamental principle of Community law which applies to VAT) require that the taxable person be told that the power has been exercised and be told precisely what his new obligations are'. On the evidence, there had not been 'an effective exercise by the Commissioners of their *regulation 25(5)* power'. Since the Commissioners had not exercised their power under *reg 25(5)*, it followed that the assessment had been issued more than three years after the end of the relevant accounting period, and it was therefore out of time. *Inchcape Management Services Ltd, [1999] VATDR 397 (VTD 16256)*.

55.13   **Whether tax payable where return qualified.**   See *DK Wright & Associates Ltd*, 2.92 APPEALS.

CORRECTION OF ERRORS (VAT Regulations 1995, regs 34, 35)

55.14   **Unilateral correction of error by company.**   Following a direction made by the Commissioners under what is now *VATA 1994, Sch 6 para 2* that tax should be accounted for on the open market value of goods sold, a company paid a sum of £1,399,000 in tax to the Commissioners. It subsequently transpired that, in the light of the CJEC decision in *Direct Cosmetics Ltd*, 21.231 EUROPEAN COMMUNITY LAW, the Commissioners' direction had no legal effect and was void. The Commissioners refused to repay the tax previously paid, and the company therefore deducted the amount from the amount owing on its next return. The Commissioners issued a writ for the sum concerned and applied for summary judgment under *Rules of the Supreme Court 1965* as then in force. The HL rejected the application, holding that it did not matter whether the previous error was one of law or fact, since what is now *VATA 1994, s 25* allowed the company to correct errors in previous returns. Where a taxpayer had been required to pay VAT on a basis which was subsequently held to be contrary to the law, the taxpayer was entitled to deduct the wrongly paid tax from his next return. Furthermore, the Commissioners' publications could only be construed as giving the legal right to make a deduction for a past overdeclaration made in error. *C & E Commrs v Fine Art Developments plc, HL [1989] STC 85; [1989] 2 WLR 369; [1989] 1 All ER 502; [1989] 2 CMLR 185*. (*Notes*. (1) Under *VAT Regulations 1995 (SI 1995 No 2518), reg 34(3)*, it is only permissible to adjust errors on a subsequent return where the net value of errors discovered does not exceed £2,000. In other cases, the VAT office must be informed in writing. (2) The *Rules of the Supreme Court 1965* have now been replaced by the *Civil Procedure Rules 1998 (SI 1998 No 3132)*, of which *rule 24* deals with applications for summary judgment.)

55.15   **Error in original return—corrected return submitted by fax.**   See *AB Gee of Ripley Ltd*, 49.28 PENALTIES: MISDECLARATION.

55.16   **Unilateral 'correction' of unappealed assessment in subsequent return.**   A company failed to make a VAT return, because its records had been mislaid. The Commissioners issued an estimated assessment charging tax of £3,816, which the company paid. Subsequently the company attempted to reconstruct its records and formed the view that, for the relevant period, its input tax had exceeded its output tax by £2,649. For its next accounting period it accordingly deducted the aggregate of these two amounts (£6,465) as input tax. The Commissioners issued an assessment to recover the tax. The tribunal dismissed the company's appeal against this assessment, holding that as the company had not appealed against the original assessment, it could not be entitled to adjust its next return in this manner without the Commissioners' consent. *Greenspear Products Ltd, MAN/86/32 (VTD 2124)*. (*Note*. See also the note following *Fine Art Developments plc*, 55.14 above.)

55.17   **Unilateral correction of errors in past returns—effect of Notice No 700.**   A company which manufactured bone china offered its major customers a 5% discount for settlement within 30 days. It initially accounted for VAT on the full price shown in the invoices, but subsequently took the view that it should only account for tax on the actual price received. In its next return it therefore deducted an amount of £2,044 in respect of output tax allegedly overdeclared, and also deducted a further sum of £310 in respect of interest. The Commissioners issued an assessment to recover the tax, and the tribunal dismissed the company's appeal. Firstly, the company had failed to comply with the procedure for the correction of errors set out in *Notice No 700* (as then in force). It had not issued credit notes to correct the errors on the invoices it had issued to its customers. Secondly, there was no justification for the claim to deduct a sum in respect of interest. *Springfield China Ltd, MAN/89/180 (VTD 4546)*. (*Note*. See also the note following *Fine Art Developments plc*, 55.14 above.)

55.18   For a case in which an error was held to have been properly corrected in a subsequent return by virtue of *Notice No 700* (as then in force), see *Aer Lingus plc*, 34.530 INPUT TAX. For a case in which a company was held not to be entitled to make a unilateral correction to recover tax which it had allegedly overpaid, see *GUS Merchandising Corporation Ltd*, 54.49 RETAILERS' SPECIAL SCHEMES.

55.19   **Delay in processing credit notes—effect of VAT Regulations 1995, reg 34*.**   A trader received two credit notes in 1991. However, he failed to process the notes until 1994. In his return for the period ending June 1994 he claimed credit for the tax shown by the credit notes. The Commissioners considered that the effect of what is now *VAT Regulations 1995 (SI 1995 No 2518), reg 38* was that the trader was no longer entitled to credit for the amounts shown on the credit notes. They therefore issued an assessment to recover the tax in question, and the trader appealed, contending that the effect of *VAT Regulations, reg 34** was that he was entitled to correct the return for the period in which he had received the credit notes. The tribunal allowed the appeal, holding that the regulations did not give a trader 'the right to process credit notes as and when he chooses' but finding that 'the original failure to process the credit notes was an accounting error which the appellant was entitled to rectify on discovery'. *J Copson (t/a Compressors & Air Equipment), MAN/94/833 (VTD 13335)*.

55.20 **Commissioners instructing company to correct error under VAT Regulations, reg 35.** See *Inchcape Management Services Ltd*, 55.9 above.

MISCELLANEOUS

55.21 **Return showing negative amount of output tax—whether 'made' for purposes of VATA 1994, Sch 11 para 2(1).** See *Gwent County Council*, 49.2 PENALTIES: MISDECLARATION.

55.22 **Return relating to partnership business submitted on form relating to associated company—whether made by company.** See *Tannington Growers (1984) Ltd*, 49.3 PENALTIES: MISDECLARATION.

55.23 **Whether part of return withdrawn.** In November 1991 a company (C) submitted a VAT return for the period ending 30 September, claiming a repayment of £324,000. The Commissioners queried the claim, £310,000 of which related to a computer which had been imported from France. C's accounts manager asked if the £310,000 relating to the computer could be 'put on hold' and the remaining £14,000 repaid to the company. The Commissioners agreed to this and repaid the £14,000. In December 1991 C transferred ownership of the computer to an associated company. In its return for the period ending 31 December, it repeated its claim for input tax on the computer, and declared a corresponding amount of output tax. The return claimed a net repayment of £1,200, which was duly repaid by the Commissioners. In March C lodged a claim for repayment supplement on the basis that the £310,000 input tax relating to the computer should have been repaid following receipt of its September return. The Commissioners rejected the claim and the tribunal dismissed C's appeal. On the evidence, C had withdrawn the relevant claim from its September return when the Commissioners had queried it, and had subsequently claimed the relevant input tax in its December return. The tribunal observed that C could not 'have it both ways' and that 'the only basis on which (C) could lawfully claim input credit for December 1991 for the import VAT was that it had either accepted the disallowance or, which comes to the same, had withdrawn that part of the September 1991 return'. *Computer Equipment Investors Ltd, LON/92/1161Z (VTD 10092)*.

55.24 **VAT Regulations 1995, reg 40—Commissioners' power to 'allow or direct' extension of normal time limit.** See *Caro*, 18.438 DEFAULT SURCHARGE, and *Starlite (Chandeliers) Ltd*, 18.440 DEFAULT SURCHARGE.

56   Second-Hand Goods

Note. The 'margin scheme' of accounting was extended to all second-hand goods, works of art, antiques and collectors' items (except precious metals and gemstones) with effect from 1 January 1995. For a full explanation of the changes, see Tolley's Value Added Tax. For cases concerning the scheme for sales of second-hand cars, see 9.54 to 9.79 CARS. The cases in this chapter are arranged under the following headings.

> Records and accounts 56.1–56.4
> Works of art, etc. 56.5–56.8
> Miscellaneous 56.9

RECORDS AND ACCOUNTS

56.1   **Special Provisions Order 1995, Article 12—whether tribunal has jurisdiction to review Commissioners' decision.**   The Commissioners issued a ruling that a company which dealt in old coins and medals could not use the 'margin scheme' on the grounds that its records did not comply with the requirements laid down under what is now *Special Provisions Order 1995, Article 12*. The company appealed, contending that the Commissioners should have exercised their discretion to permit it to use the scheme. The HL rejected this contention and dismissed the appeal, holding that the tribunal could consider whether the records complied with the statutory requirements, but where the records did not meet those requirements, the tribunal could not consider whether the Commissioners should have exercised their discretion to permit the use of the scheme. *C & E Commrs v JH Corbitt (Numismatists) Ltd, HL [1980] STC 231; [1981] AC 22; [1980] 2 All ER 72. (Note.* This decision was not followed in the 1992 case of *Christopher Gibbs Ltd,* 56.2 below, on the grounds that it had been decided before the enactment of what is now *VATA 1994, s 84(10).* However, *dicta* of Lord Lane were applied by the CA in the 1995 case of *John Dee Ltd,* 14.28 COLLECTION AND ENFORCEMENT.)

56.2   The Commissioners issued an assessment charging tax on the full sale price of two antique tables, considering that the conditions for the application of the margin scheme had not been satisfied. The tribunal held that it had jurisdiction to review the Commissioners' decision, applying *dicta* in *Bardsley,* 9.58 CARS, and not following *JH Corbitt (Numismatists) Ltd,* 56.1 above, since that case had been decided before the enactment of what is now *VATA 1994, s 84(10).* The tribunal reviewed the evidence in detail and held that one of the tables should have been dealt with under the margin scheme, because all the relevant details were recorded except for the purchaser's signature. Since there was no reasonable doubt that the table had been sold to the person named, the tribunal held that the need for the purchaser to sign the invoice 'should ... have been dispensed with'. However, in the case of the second table, the details of the purchase price had not been recorded, so that the company was obliged to account for tax on the full sale price. *Christopher Gibbs Ltd, [1992] VATTR 376 (VTD 8981).*

56.3   **Purchaser giving false name and address—whether vendor entitled to apply margin scheme.**   A gold coin dealer accounted for VAT under the margin scheme for works of art, etc. where the coins were within the definition of 'collectors' pieces', or were more than 100 years old. The Commissioners discovered that his records indicated that he had sold a consignment of coins to a resident of the USA for £93,000, and another consignment to a Canadian for £181,000. The invoices recorded the name and address of the alleged purchasers, but they both denied having purchased the coins in question. The Commissioners formed the opinion that the dealer had acted fraudulently, by inventing the supposed transactions so as to avoid paying tax on supplies which did not qualify for the margin scheme. The trader appealed, contending that the transactions had been genuine, and that it appeared that the real purchasers of the antique coins had given him false names and addresses. The tribunal allowed the appeal, finding that, on the balance of probabilities, the sale to the Canadian purchaser had actually taken place despite the alleged purchaser's subsequent denial, and that the other sale had been to an unidentified American who had given a false name and address. The records complied with the requirements of the scheme, and there was no obligation on the dealer to check the identity of his customer. *MD Bord, LON/91/2595Y (VTD 9824)*. (*Note.* For a preliminary issue in this case, see 2.198 APPEALS.)

56.4   **Other cases.**   There have been a large number of cases in which tribunals have found that a trader's records have not complied with the requirements of the margin scheme or the global accounting scheme, and have dismissed appeals against assessments charging tax on the full amount of the takings. In the interests of space, such cases are not reported individually in this book. For summaries of such cases decided up to 31 December 1993, see Tolley's VAT Cases 1994.

WORKS OF ART, ETC.

56.5   **Works of art sold at auction—amount of consideration.**   A company sold works of art at auction. Under the relevant conditions of sale, the vendor received the 'hammer price' (the price at which the item was 'knocked down' to the buyer) less a 6% commission which was retained by the auctioneer. The buyer was also required to pay to the auctioneer a premium of 10% of the 'hammer price'. The Commissioners issued an assessment treating the buyer's premium as part of the consideration. The company appealed, contending that the consideration was the 'hammer price'. The tribunal accepted this contention and allowed the appeal. *Jocelyn Feilding Fine Arts Ltd, [1978] VATTR 164 (VTD 652)*. (*Notes.* (1) For the award of costs in this case, see 2.321 APPEALS. (2) There is now an optional scheme for auctioneers acting in their own name. Where this scheme is used, the purchase price is the hammer price less the VAT-inclusive commission charged to the vendor, and the selling price is the hammer price plus the buyer's premium, including VAT.)

56.6   **Definition of 'collectors' pieces'.**   In two German cases, the CJEC defined 'collectors' pieces' as 'objects which possess the requisite characteristics for inclusion in a collection, that is to say pieces which are relatively rare, are not normally used for their original intention, are the subject of special transactions outside the normal trade in similar utility pieces and are of greater value'. *E Daiber v Hauptzollamt Reutlingen, CJEC Case 200/84, [1985] ECR 3363; Collection Guns GmbH v Hauptzollamt Koblenz, CJEC [1985] ECR 3387*. (*Note.* The cases concerned Customs duty, but the decision is clearly relevant to *Special Provisions Order 1995, Article 12(2)(a)*, which deals with supplies of 'collectors' items'.)

56.7   *Daiber v Hauptzollamt Reutlingen*, 56.6 SECOND-HAND GOODS, was applied in the subsequent German case of *U Clees v Hauptzollamt Wuppertal, CJEC Case C-259/97, 3 December 1998 unreported.*

56.8   **Antique model railway train—whether a 'collector's piece'.**   An individual imported into the UK a Märklin gauge 3 model train, originally sold in 1900. The Commissioners issued a ruling that VAT was due on the importation. He appealed, contending that the train was a 'collector's piece of historical interest' so that no VAT was chargeable under the legislation then in force. The tribunal allowed his appeal, finding that the train in question was 'a special article representing a culminating period in the evolution of toy manufacture having an economic and sociological significance and representing a technological achievement in the history of that manufacture and the evolution of industry'. Accordingly it qualified as a 'collector's piece of historical interest'. *Daiber v Hauptzollamt Reutlingen* and *Collection Guns GmbH v Hauptzollamt Koblenz*, 56.6 above, applied. *D Pressland, [1995] VATDR 432 (VTD 13059).*

MISCELLANEOUS

56.9   **Cost of fitting out hull—whether part of cost of boat.**   A company carried on a business of hiring out boats. It acquired four bare hulls, which it fitted out and commissioned. It used the hulls in its business for several years before selling them. In accounting for tax under the margin scheme, it included the cost of fitting out and commissioning the hulls as part of the cost of acquiring them. The Commissioners issued an assessment on the basis that only the actual cost of the hulls could be deducted. The tribunal dismissed the company's appeal and the QB upheld this decision. For the purposes of what is now *Special Provisions Order 1995, Article 12*, the acquisition cost was restricted to the actual cost of the hulls. *Wyvern Shipping Co Ltd v C & E Commrs, QB 1978, [1979] STC 91.*

57 Self-Supply

Note. For cases concerning the self-supply provisions of *VATA 1994, Sch 10 para 5*, see 6 BUILDINGS AND LAND. For cases concerning the provisions of *VAT (Cars) Order, Article 5*, see 9.49 to 9.53 CARS.

57.1 **Printed stationery destroyed before use—whether a self-supply.** A building society printed its own stationery. It accounted for VAT at the time of printing, under the self-supply rules now contained in *Article 11* of the *VAT (Special Provisions) Order 1995 (SI 1995 No 1268)*. It destroyed a quantity of stationery on which it had already accounted for tax, and reclaimed the VAT in question. The Commissioners rejected the claim, considering that the deemed self-supply had taken place at the time the stationery was printed, so that the tax could not be refunded. The tribunal allowed the society's appeal, holding that there had never been any supply of the stationery, since the stationery had never been used by the society for the purpose of its business as required by what is now *Article 11(1)*. *Nationwide Building Society, [1993] VATTR 205 (VTD 10117)*.

57.2 **Self-supplies of stationery by building society operating partial exemption method.** See *Leeds & Holbeck Building Society*, 43.104 PARTIAL EXEMPTION.

57.3 **Chequebooks and credit slip books—whether within Special Provisions Order, Article 11(1)(a).** A major bank had accounted for VAT on the basis that it had made a 'self-supply', within *Article 11* of the *VAT (Special Provisions) Order 1995 (SI 1995 No 1268)*, of chequebooks, credit slip books, and bank statements. Subsequently it formed the opinion that it should not have accounted for tax on these items, on the basis that, when they were sent to customers, they were 'supplied to another person' within the meaning of *Article 11(1)(a)*. The bank claimed a substantial repayment. The Commissioners rejected the claim, considering that the items were not 'supplied' within the meaning of *Article 11*, since they were supplied as part of a financial service, rather than as goods. The bank appealed. The tribunal allowed the bank's appeal, holding that the items had been 'supplied to another person' and were therefore outside the scope of the self-supply provisions. *National Westminster Bank plc (No 2), LON/99/406 (VTD 17000)*.

57.4 **Self-supply of advertising posters.** See *The Royal Society for the Encouragement of Arts, Manufacture & Commerce*, 11.18 CHARITIES.

57.5 **Special Provisions Order, Article 11(2)(c)—direction issued by Commissioners—whether direction should have been withdrawn retrospectively.** In 1973 a university examination board had applied for, and had been granted, a direction that the self-supply provisions contained in what is now *VAT (Special Provisions) Order (SI 1995 No 1268), Article 11* should not apply to it, on the basis that the tax attributable to its self-supplies of printed materials was negligible. Subsequently the in-house printing activities of the examination board increased in number. In 1996 its accountants applied for the declaration to be withdrawn retrospectively, and submitted a consequential claim for repayment of about £2,500,000 in input tax. The Commissioners rejected the claim, on the grounds that they could only withdraw a direction under *Article 11(2)(c)* 'from a current or future date', and could not withdraw such a direction respectively. The examination board appealed. The tribunal dismissed the appeal, holding that, although the Commissioners had a discretionary power to withdraw such a direction respectively, it was not unreasonable for them to have refused to do so in this case. The tribunal observed that, when the original direction was issued in 1973, the examination board had undertaken to notify the Commissioners of 'any change in the general pattern or volume of self-supplied printed matter', but had failed to do so. Accordingly, the Commissioners had not acted unreasonably. *Dicta* of Lord Lane in *JH Corbitt (Numismatists) Ltd*, 56.1 SECOND-HAND GOODS, applied. *University of Cambridge Local Examination Syndicate, [1997] VATDR 245 (VTD 15015).*

57.6   **Assets used for private purposes—whether a self-supply.**   See *Broadhurst*, 58.83 SUPPLY, and *Mellor*, 58.84 SUPPLY.

57.7   **Assets retained on cessation of trade—whether a self-supply.**   See the cases noted at 58.85 to 58.88 SUPPLY.

58 Supply

The cases in this chapter are arranged under the following headings.

WHETHER THERE HAS BEEN A SUPPLY

Note. In the cases under this heading it is accepted that there is a business within what is now *VATA 1994, s 94*, and the issue is whether there has been a supply in the course or furtherance of that business. For whether a supply has been received for the purpose of a business, see 34 INPUT TAX. For cases where the existence of a business is disputed, see 7 BUSINESS.

Supplies to employees (including company cars)

Note. For the deduction of input tax in respect of the expenses (including car expenses) of employees or agents, see 34.222 INPUT TAX *et seq.*

58.1   **Payments by employee for private use of company car.**   The employee of a company was provided with a company car which he was entitled to use privately on payment of £4 per month to the company. The Commissioners issued a ruling that tax was chargeable on the supply of the car for private use, and the tribunal dismissed the company's appeal. *W & JR Watson Ltd, [1974] VATTR 83 (VTD 67). (Note.* The provisions concerning the VAT treatment of private motoring were changed with effect from 1 August 1995. See Tolley's Value Added Tax 2000/01, para 45.18. Although charges for the use of a motor car remain taxable in principle, the making available of a motor car for private use is not a taxable supply if VAT was wholly excluded from credit on the purchase of the vehicle.)

58.2   *W & JR Watson Ltd*, 58.1 above, was applied in the similar subsequent case of *William Peto & Co Ltd, MAN/78/66 (VTD 736).*

58.3   A company provided its directors with cars and allowed them to use the cars privately. The directors paid the company for this private use. The Commissioners issued assessments charging tax on the payments and the tribunal dismissed the companies' appeals. *Mitchell Haselhurst Ltd, [1979] VATTR 166 (VTD 812). (Note.* See now the note following *W & JR Watson Ltd*, 58.1 above.)

58.4   A company which carried on a brewery business supplied a large number of its employees with cars. It deducted sums from the employees' salaries to cover the private use of the cars. The Commissioners issued a ruling that VAT was chargeable on the sums in question. The company appealed, contending that, since it had not been able to deduct input tax on the purchase of the cars, no output tax should be due. The tribunal dismissed the appeal, holding that 'the input tax on the cost of the car is not sufficiently linked to the output tax on the supply as to offend the neutrality principle'. *Allied Lyons plc, [1994] VATTR 361 (VTD 11731). (Note.* See now the note following *W & JR Watson Ltd*, 58.1 above.)

58.5   **Employees provided with company car and receiving lower salary than employees not provided with cars.**   A company provided some of its employees with cars. Such employees were paid less than the scale salary for their grade, the reduction in salary being calculated by reference to the price of the car. Once an employee accepted that he would receive a lower salary in return for being provided with a car, he was not permitted to revert to the normal scale salary, even if he was banned from driving. The Commissioners took the view that the reduction in salary constituted consideration paid by the employee for the provision of the car, and was therefore chargeable to VAT. The company appealed, contending that the acceptance of a reduced salary did not constitute the giving of 'consideration' for the private use of the car. The tribunal accepted this contention and allowed the appeal, applying *Goodfellow*, 58.13 below. The provision of the car was taken into account in fixing the employee's gross salary, which remained the same whether or not he actually used the car. His gross salary was the amount specified in his contract, and there was therefore no reduction of salary which could constitute 'consideration'. *Co-Operative Insurance Society Ltd, [1992] VATTR 44 (VTD 7109).* (*Note.* See now the *VAT (Treatment of Transactions) Order 1992 (SI 1992 No 630)*, which gives statutory effect to this decision.)

58.6   **Provision of parking facility to employee.**   A university charged one of its employees for the provision of a parking space. The Commissioners issued a ruling that output tax was chargeable on the amount in question. The employee appealed. The tribunal allowed the appeal, holding that the university was not providing the parking facility in the course of its business. *RA Archer (No 2), [1975] VATTR 1 (VTD 134).*

58.7   **Whether employee's car supplied by employer.**   A company had introduced a complex 'private car scheme', designed to ensure that an employee would have an inducement to look after his car well. Under the scheme, the company paid 90% of the cost of the car and the employee paid the balance. When the car was replaced—generally after two years—the allowance for the old car was similarly shared. There were appropriate rules as to how the cost of running and maintaining the car was to be borne. The employee could not use the car privately for more than 10% of the total mileage except with the company's approval. The employee could negotiate the purchase of the car but the purchase invoice, car registration and insurance were in the company's name, and the make of car and the price range were defined by the company. The Commissioners issued assessments on the basis that, under the scheme, there was a taxable supply of the car to the employee. The tribunal allowed the company's appeal, holding that the arrangement resulted in joint ownership of the car and accordingly the company did not supply it to the employee. *TBS (South Wales) Ltd, [1981] VATTR 183 (VTD 1144).*

58.8   **Long service awards to employees.**   Two associated companies in the clothing trade customarily presented gold watches or similar articles to its employees on completing 25 years' service. The Commissioners issued a ruling that such presentations constituted a supply of goods in the course of the company's business, and that output tax was chargeable accordingly. The companies appealed, contending that the articles had not been supplied in the course of their business, since their business consisted of the supply of clothing rather than of gold watches, etc. The tribunal dismissed the appeals, holding that the articles had been supplied in the course of the companies' business. *UDS Group Ltd; UDS Tailoring Ltd, [1977] VATTR 16 (VTD 333).*

58.9   The Commissioners issued an assessment on a bakery company, charging tax on the value of long-service awards to employees. The company appealed, contending that as the value of the presentation was part of the employee's emoluments for income tax purposes, it was not a supply in the course of the business. The tribunal rejected this contention and dismissed the appeal, and the QB upheld this decision, holding that the fact that payments in kind were treated as emoluments for income tax did not prevent them from constituting supplies within the charge to VAT. *RHM Bakeries (Northern) Ltd v C & E Commrs, QB 1978, [1979] STC 72.*

58.10   Under a company's conditions of employment, its employees were entitled to the choice of a 'variety of gifts' on completing 25 years' service and a further gift on retiring. The Commissioners issued a ruling that tax was chargeable on the awards, and the tribunal dismissed the company's appeal. *Grants of St James's Ltd, MAN/77/103 (VTD 427)*.

58.11   **Receipts of canteen provided by employer.** A company provided canteen facilities for the employees at its factory. The canteen staff were paid by the company and the expenses and receipts were met out of, or paid into, the company's general funds. The company did not account for output tax on its receipts from the canteen. The Commissioners issued an assessment charging tax on them and the tribunal dismissed the company's appeal. *MB Metals Ltd, LON/77/466 (VTD 666)*.

58.12   The proprietors of a poultry farm provided a canteen for their staff. Meals were provided at cost and the canteen was run by employees of the proprietors. The proprietors appealed against an assessment charging tax on the canteen receipts, contending that they did not supply the meals. The tribunal dismissed the appeal. On the evidence, the food was purchased, prepared and cooked by one of the proprietors' employees. The proprietors were supplying the meals through the employee. *M & E Barker, MAN/89/138 (VTD 4589)*.

58.13   **Board and lodging provided to hotel employees—whether a supply.** The proprietors of a hotel provided board and lodging to their employees. They made deductions from their employees' wages in respect of the board and lodging. However the Commissioners sought to charge tax on the board and lodging provided to the employees, and the hoteliers appealed. The tribunal allowed their appeal, holding that the board and lodging was provided as part of the employees' remuneration and the effect of what is now *VATA 1994, Sch 6 para 10* was that the deductions made from the wages were not consideration for VAT purposes. *RW & MJ Goodfellow, [1986] VATTR 119 (VTD 2107)*.

58.14   **Clothing supplied to employees.** A company carried on business as a retailer of women's and children's clothing. It supplied clothing to its employees, and did not account for tax on such supplies. The Commissioners issued an assessment charging tax on the clothing in question, and the company appealed, contending that VAT should not be chargeable since the clothing was intended to be worn as a uniform. The tribunal dismissed the appeal. On the evidence, the clothing in question was suitable for everyday wear. The supply of clothing to employees was a taxable supply. The fact that the company required its employees to wear clothing from its retail stock did not mean that the supply was outside the scope of VAT. *Zoo Clothing Ltd, LON/91/572X (VTD 9161)*.

58.15   **Cable network connections provided to employees.** A company carried on the business of providing telecommunications and cable television services. It provided its employees with free connections to its cable television and telephone networks. The Commissioners issued an assessment charging tax on these supplies under *VAT (Supply of Services) Order 1993 (SI 1993 No 1507)*. The company appealed, contending that it had made the supplies for the purposes of its business, so that the provision in *article 3* of the *Order* was not satisfied. The tribunal rejected this contention and dismissed the appeal, holding that although the supplies brought some incidental benefits to the company, the company's 'relevant purpose here is the non-business purpose of providing all employees who are in a position to make use of them with the benefit of cable television and free line rental at home'. *Telecential Communications Ltd, LON/97/321 (VTD 15361)*.

58.16   **Provision of sports tickets to employees under staff incentive scheme— whether any supply.** A company (P) awarded tickets to football matches and motor races to some of its employees under a staff incentive scheme. The Commissioners issued assessments charging tax under *VAT (Supply of Services) Order 1993 (SI 1993 No 1507)*. P appealed, contending that it had made the supplies for the purposes of its business, so that the provision in *article 3* of the *Order* was not satisfied. The tribunal accepted this contention and allowed the appeal, finding that the scheme had 'proved successful in reducing absenteeism' and had 'encouraged the submission of ideas to improve efficiency'. On the evidence, P had 'acted for purely business reasons' and 'the personal benefit derived by (P's) employees was of secondary importance compared to the needs of its business'. *Peugeot Motor Co plc, MAN/99/856 (VTD 16731)*.

58.17   In-house magazines supplied to employees.   See *The Post Office*, 58.94 below.

Provision of employees' services and administrative services

Cases held to constitute a supply

58.18   A charitable organisation (H) presented cinema films in Children's Homes throughout the country. In this it received the co-operation of a leading cinema operator (EMI) of which one of its members was an executive. Seven projectionists were used of whom five were 'borrowed' from EMI and two were engaged by H. These two were placed on EMI's payroll and the wages and expenses of all seven were paid through the wages officer of EMI. H reimbursed EMI monthly for the amounts so paid but EMI made no further charge for its services. The Commissioners issued a ruling that the arrangement involved a taxable supply of services by EMI and that EMI should account for output tax. H appealed. The tribunal dismissed the appeal, observing that 'the concepts of consideration and profit are wholly different, and the fact that a trader makes no profit on a supply does not ... mean that there is no consideration for it'. *Heart of Variety, [1975] VATTR 103 (VTD 168)*.

58.19   A company (U) supplied a caretaker to an associated company (C). U continued to pay the caretaker's wages and charged them to C at cost plus 9½%. The Commissioners issued a ruling that output tax was chargeable on the supply. C, which was exempt and therefore unable to reclaim input tax, appealed. The tribunal upheld the Commissioners' ruling and dismissed the appeal, holding that there had been a taxable supply. *Calabar Developments Ltd, [1976] VATTR 1 (VTD 218)*.

58.20   A company (M) sold electrical goods and also provided accounting, bookkeeping and administrative services to two wholly owned subsidiaries and to an associated company. One of the three companies was a finance company not registered, or required to be registered, for VAT. The other two were trading companies and registered. There was no group registration. M charged the other three companies for the services it supplied but did not account for output tax. The Commissioners issued an assessment charging tax on the supplies and the tribunal dismissed M's appeal. *Heart of Variety*, 58.18 above, applied; *Processed Vegetable Growers*, 58.37 below, distinguished. *Metravision (GB) Ltd, [1977] VATTR 26 (VTD 340)*.

58.21   A company (P) was one of a group of companies operating casinos throughout the country, two of which it operated itself. Among its employees were three chartered accountants who spent a considerable part of their time visiting the casinos of the group to look after their books and security arrangements and advise them generally. It also provided management services to its own subsidiaries. In its accounts it credited substantial round sum amounts charged to some casinos as management fees and consultant fees respectively. It did not account for output tax on these charges.

The Commissioners issued an assessment charging tax on these supplies and the tribunal dismissed P's appeal. *Pleasurama Casinos Ltd, LON/76/181 & 208 (VTD 357).*

58.22   The British Airways Board (BAB) provided the services of some of its employees to a subsidiary (H), which in turn supplied the services of some of the employees to a housing society, which had been formed by employees of the British Overseas Airways Corporation (BOAC) in 1947 to help BOAC employees find living accommodation within travelling distance of Heathrow Airport. BOAC had been absorbed by BAB following the *Civil Aviation Act 1971*. H reimbursed BAB the salaries of the employees in question and made a management charge to the housing society in respect of the employees who had been 'seconded' to the Society. The tribunal held that BAB was supplying the employees' services in the course of its business, and that output tax was chargeable on the supply. *Heart of Variety*, 58.18 above, and *Metravision (GB) Ltd*, 58.20 above, applied. *British Airways Board; British Airways Housing Trust Ltd, LON/78/191A & 191B (VTD 663).*

58.23   A company (C) owned and managed commercial property in the UK and Australia. In order to join the company pension scheme, eight individuals employed by the company's controlling shareholder or by a subsidiary company gave up their existing employments to become employees of C. They were immediately seconded to their previous employers, and the salaries which C paid to them were reimbursed to it by the employers. C did not account for output tax, and the Commissioners issued an assessment charging tax on the basis that the supply of the seconded employees was a supply in the course of C's business. The tribunal dismissed C's appeal and the QB upheld this decision. The company existed exclusively for business purposes and was created specifically to administer the controlling shareholder's business affairs. All of its activities were part of an overall scheme to further those business purposes. The particular activity of providing staff was interrelated to its activities in that it was intrinsically part of a normal business activity to make pension provisions. *Cumbrae Properties (1963) Ltd v C & E Commrs, QB [1981] STC 799.* (*Note.* For another issue in this case, see 3.57 ASSESSMENT.)

58.24   A company (T) was the representative member of a group of companies registered for VAT. It had a subsidiary company (M) which traded as an insurance broker, all its supplies being exempt. T seconded some of its employees to M and paid their salaries. The Commissioners issued an assessment on the basis that T was making taxable supplies of its employees' services to M. T appealed, contending that it was acting as an agent and had not made any supply to M. The QB rejected this contention and upheld the assessment, and the CA dismissed T's appeal, holding on the evidence that T retained the right to direct its employees and was acting as a principal rather than as an agent. The supply of employees' services was a taxable supply. *C & E Commrs v Tarmac Roadstone Holdings Ltd, CA [1987] STC 610.*

58.25   The CA decision in *Tarmac Roadstone Holdings Ltd*, 58.24 above, was applied in the similar cases of *International Advisory Co Ltd, LON/93/1654 (VTD 12186); Job Creation (UK) Ltd, LON/93/1653 (VTD 12186)* and *Altman Blane & Co*, 39.9 LAND.

58.26   A group of companies operated a chain of launderettes. The Commissioners issued an assessment on the basis that cleaners who worked at the launderettes were employed by the holding company, which was making a taxable supply of their services to the subsidiary companies. The tribunal upheld the assessment and dismissed the holding company's appeal. *Launderette Investments Ltd, MAN/86/57 (VTD 2360).*

58.27 Supply

58.27   A company (P), which was a wholly-owned subsidiary of a US company, provided management services to a number of UK companies in the same group. It did not account for output tax on sums paid to it by such companies, although some of the companies were not in the same group of companies as P for VAT purposes. The Commissioners issued an assessment charging tax on payments by companies which were not in P's VAT group, on the basis that they represented consideration for taxable supplies of administrative services. P appealed, contending that it was not supplying such services in the course or furtherance of its business. The tribunal rejected this contention and dismissed P's appeal, applying the CA decision in *Tarmac Roadstone Holdings Ltd*, 58.24 above. *PHH Europe plc, LON/93/927A (VTD 12027)*.

58.28   A company made an annual charge to a subsidiary company to cover the use of its office and the services of two of its employees. It did not account for VAT on the charges and the Commissioners issued an assessment on the basis that the company had made a taxable supply of services to its subsidiary. The tribunal upheld the assessment and dismissed the company's appeal. On the evidence, the charge was for supplies made by the company, and was not merely a reimbursement of expenses. *Marvelle Bras (London) Ltd, LON/92/1196Z (VTD 9350)*.

58.29   A printer provided the services of some of his employees to a company, and failed to account for VAT on these supplies. The Commissioners issued an assessment charging tax on the supplies, and the tribunal dismissed the printer's appeal, applying the CA decision in *Tarmac Roadstone Holdings Ltd*, 58.24 above. *SCS Beresfors (t/a Elidaprint), LON/92/2246A (VTD 11555)*.

58.30   A company in the construction industry (W) arranged for some of its employees and subcontractors to work for an associated company. It charged these costs to the associated company, but did not account for output tax on the costs. The Commissioners issued an assessment charging tax on the basis that W had made a taxable supply of services. The tribunal upheld the assessment and dismissed W's appeal. *WJ Marston & Son Ltd, LON/97/388 (VTD 15208)*.

58.31   An association was established to provide premises and a communications network for cab drivers in the Eastbourne area. It employed an office manager and telephone operators. It registered for VAT in 1991. In 1994 it applied for deregistration, contending that it was simply acting as an agent of its members and was not making any supplies for VAT purposes. The Commissioners rejected the application, considering that the association was making supplies to its members. The tribunal dismissed the association's appeal and the CA upheld this decision. For VAT purposes, an unincorporated association was a legal entity, separate from its members. On the evidence, the association was supplying facilities or advantages to its members for consideration, and was required to register for VAT. *Dicta* in *Carlton Lodge Club Ltd*, 13.28 CLUBS AND ASSOCIATIONS, and *Trewby*, 39.30 LAND, applied; *Durham Aged Mineworkers' Homes Association*, 58.40 below, distinguished. *Eastbourne Town Radio Cars Association v C & E Commrs, CA [1998] STC 669*.

58.32   A Training and Enterprise Council supplied the services of one of its employees to a charity, which was not registered for VAT. The TEC charged output tax on the supply. The charity appealed to a tribunal, contending that output tax should not have been charged on the supply. The tribunal rejected this contention and dismissed the appeal, holding that VAT had been correctly charged. *Life Education Centre (Nottinghamshire) Ltd, MAN/98/846 (VTD 16499)*.

58.33   An educational charity (F) owned a number of schools, which were operated by an associated charity (C). F received £1,000,000 from C, and did not account for output tax on this. The Commissioners issued an assessment charging tax on it. F appealed, contending that the payment did not represent consideration for any supply. The Ch D rejected this contention and upheld the assessment. On the evidence, F had used the payment to improve the premises used by the schools which C operated. Neuberger J held that 'there was a sufficient degree of reciprocity or mutuality' between the making of the payment and the effecting of the improvements. Accordingly the payment was consideration for supplies of services. *The Church Schools Foundation Ltd v C & E Commrs, Ch D [2000] STC 651.*

58.34   Three solicitors acted as the trustees of a fund for the maintenance of a large building, containing 435 luxury apartments and some commercial premises. They employed 17 staff for this purpose. They did not account for output tax on maintenance contributions which they received from tenants, or on service charges which they received from the company which held the lease of the building. The Commissioners issued an assessment charging tax on these receipts. The trustees appealed, contending that they only supplied the limited services of arranging for the employees to carry out maintenance services, for which they accepted remuneration on which they accounted for output tax, but that the maintenance services were supplied by the employees directly to the tenants. The HL rejected this contention and upheld the assessments. On the evidence, the trustees made a supply to the tenants by supplying the services of staff, thereby enhancing the enjoyment and amenity of the flats and the building as a whole. The maintenance contributions paid by tenants to the fund were consideration for the provision of services by the trustees to the tenants. Lord Slynn observed that it would 'be wrong and artificial to regard the suppliers of the services as the individual employees'. Furthermore, the contributions were part of the taxable amount, within *Article 11A1* of the *EC Sixth Directive*, and were not 'repayment for expenses' within *Article 11A3(c)* of the *EC Sixth Directive. HJ Glawe Spiel und Unterhaltungsgeräte Aufstellungsgesellschaft mbH & Co KG v Finanzamt Hamburg-Barmbek-Uhlenhorst*, 21.133 EUROPEAN COMMUNITY LAW, distinguished. *C & E Commrs v Trustees of the Nell Gwynn House Maintenance Fund, HL 1998, [1999] STC 79; [1999] 1 WLR 174; [1999] 1 All ER 385.* (*Note.* The HL also held that the payments did not qualify for exemption under what is now *VATA 1994, Sch 9, Group 1*—see 39.47 LAND.)

58.35   See also *United News Shops (Holdings) Ltd*, 49.244 PENALTIES: MISDECLARATION.

58.36   **Management services within group of companies.**   See *Tilling Management Services Ltd*, 41.1 MANAGEMENT SERVICES.

Cases held not to constitute a supply

58.37   Members of the National Farmers Union set up a company to promote the interests of vegetable growers. Some of the company's employees were transferred to the NFU, to enable them to be included in the NFU pension scheme. The NFU invoiced the company for the employees' salaries. The Commissioners issued a ruling that output tax was chargeable on the amounts invoiced. The tribunal allowed the company's appeal, holding that the secondment of the employees was a 'domestic arrangement' and not a taxable supply. *Processed Vegetable Growers Association Ltd, [1973] VATTR 87 (VTD 25).* (*Note.* For a preliminary issue in this case, see 2.26 APPEALS.)

58.38   In 1972 the Post Office agreed that one of its employees (A) should be released from his Post Office duties to work for a statutory body (CTB). The Post Office continued to pay his normal Post Office salary, etc., and also paid him additional amounts as salary from CTB. CTB reimbursed the Post Office for all its payments and also paid it an administration charge. The Commissioners issued a ruling that the amounts invoiced by the Post Office to CTB for sums due to it under the agreement were taxable. CTB appealed. The tribunal allowed the appeal in part, holding on the evidence that A was an employee of CTB in the relevant period, so that the Post Office was not supplying A's services and tax was payable only on the administration charge. *Commonwealth Telecommunications Bureau, LON H/75/25 (VTD 189)*.

58.39 The general manager of a company which operated a gaming club also managed the affairs of a subsidiary company with a similar trade. The Commissioners issued an assessment on the basis that the parent company had made a taxable supply of the manager's services to the subsidiary company. The tribunal allowed the company's appeal, holding that, as the manager received salary from the subsidiary company as well as from the parent company, there was a dual employment rather than a taxable supply. *The Midland Wheel Club Ltd, LON/84/284 (VTD 1770)*.

58.40 A charity, established to provide housing for aged mineworkers, owned office accommodation which it shared with an associated company (M). The Commissioners issued an assessment charging output tax on the payments which the charity received from M. The QB allowed the charity's appeal, holding that the only reasonable conclusion on the evidence was that the charity was acting as an agent for M and was not supplying services to M. *Rowe & Maw*, 58.42 below, applied; *Tarmac Roadstone Holdings Ltd*, 58.24 above, distinguished. *Durham Aged Mineworkers' Homes Association v C & E Commrs, QB [1994] STC 553*.

58.41 **Retail partnership operating sub-post office—whether any supply of employees' services to Post Office.** A married couple operated a retail shop in partnership. The shop included a sub-post office, the husband being the subpostmaster. They had one employee, who spent approximately 25% of her time on Post Office work. The Commissioners issued an assessment on the basis that the couple were making a deemed supply of their employee's services to the Post Office. The couple appealed. The tribunal allowed the appeal, holding on the evidence that the couple did not receive any consideration from the Post Office in respect of the work performed by their employee. The subpostmaster's remuneration was based entirely on the turnover of the sub-post office, and none of the remuneration related to staff salaries. *RA & BD Hampton (t/a Tongue Electrics), EDN/96/99 (VTD 15171)*.

Reimbursements of expenses

58.42 **Disbursements by solicitors—whether a supply to client.** A firm of solicitors charged travelling expenses to clients as 'disbursements'. The firm did not account for tax on these disbursements and the Commissioners issued an assessment. The tribunal dismissed the firm's appeal and the QB upheld this decision. The travelling expenses in question were a part of the whole taxable supply of legal services by the firm to the client. *Rowe & Maw v C & E Commrs, QB [1975] STC 340; [1975] 1 WLR 1291; [1975] 2 All ER 444*.

58.43 **Telegraphic transfer fees for remittance of sums from solicitors' client account—whether a supply by solicitor.** See *Shuttleworth & Co*, 58.246 below.

58.44 **Surveyor's expenses charged to clients.** A surveyor failed to account for VAT on out-of-pocket expenses charged out to clients. The Commissioners issued an assessment charging tax on the amounts in question and the tribunal dismissed the surveyor's appeal, applying *Rowe & Maw*, 58.42 above. *BL Westbury, LON/81/291 (VTD 1168)*.

58.45 A similar decision was reached in *RK Short, LON/89/410 (VTD 4296)*.

58.46 **Estate agents' expenses charged to clients.** An estate agency charged clients a fixed commission of 1% and also charged in respect of 'marketing expenditure' such as advertisements, 'For Sale' boards, etc. The agency did not account for VAT on these items and the Commissioners issued an assessment charging tax on them. The tribunal dismissed the agency's appeal, applying *Rowe & Maw*, 58.42 above. *J & L Lea, MAN/85/261 (VTD 2018)*.

58.47   **Consultant's expenses charged out to clients.**   A financial consultant charged various expenses to clients but did not account for VAT on the amounts in question. The Commissioners issued an assessment charging tax on these amounts and the tribunal dismissed the consultant's appeal, applying *Rowe & Maw*, 58.42 above. *SD McDonald, LON/90/739Y (VTD 5313)*.

58.48   Similar decisions, also applying *Rowe & Maw*, 58.42 above, were reached in *P Barron, LON/91/345Y (VTD 6370)* and *JK Nawrot, EDN/92/250 (VTD 11775)*.

58.49   **Chauffeur-driven tours—chauffeur's expenses charged out to customer.**   A company carried on the business of organising chauffeur-driven tours for overseas visitors, and employed about 50 chauffeurs. Each chauffeur was given a cash float for the tour to cover his food and overnight accommodation (at a flat rate) and any minor incidental expenses such as parking fees. At the end of the tour he returned the balance of the float with a statement of his expenses and the relevant bills. The company charged these amounts to the customers, but did not account for VAT on them. The Commissioners issued an assessment charging tax on the amounts in respect of food and accommodation. The tribunal dismissed the company's appeal, applying *Rowe & Maw*, 58.42 above. The costs incurred by the chauffeur and billed to the customer constituted part of the consideration for the supply of services by the company. *Camelot Cars Couriers Ltd, LON/83/152 (VTD 1474)*.

58.50   **Director's expenses charged to customer.**   A company supplied the services of its managing director to a customer. It charged the customer £200 as an advance payment of its director's expenses, but did not account for VAT on this amount. The Commissioners issued an assessment charging tax on the £200 and the tribunal dismissed the company's appeal, applying the principles in *Rowe & Maw Ltd*, 58.42 above. *Glassiron Ltd, [1989] VATTR 245 (VTD 4592)*. (*Note.* An appeal against a penalty under what is now *VATA 1994, s 67* was also dismissed.)

58.51   A similar decision, also applying *Rowe & Maw*, 58.42 above, was reached in *Medical Services & Equipment (ME) Ltd, LON/94/1702A (VTD 13077)*.

58.52   **Subcontractor's expenses reimbursed by contractor.**   A subcontractor failed to account for VAT on payments received from the contractor for whom he worked, as reimbursements of expenditure on materials and petrol. The Commissioners issued an assessment charging tax on such payments and the tribunal dismissed the subcontractor's appeal, holding that the payments were chargeable to VAT. *JT Giles, MAN/90/475 (VTD 6789)*.

58.53   **Art gallery proprietor.**   The proprietor of an art gallery invoiced artists for 50% of various costs he incurred such as the production of catalogues and advertisements, postage, insurance, etc. He did not account for VAT on such amounts. The Commissioners issued a ruling that VAT was chargeable on them, and the proprietor appealed, contending that they should be treated as disbursements and as outside the scope of VAT. The tribunal rejected this contention and dismissed his appeal, holding that the amounts in question constituted consideration for taxable supplies of services. *Rowe & Maw*, 58.42 above, applied. *DS Campbell, LON/95/2323 (VTD 15051)*.

58.54   **Prince of Wales Trust—reimbursed expenses.**   The chairman-designate of the Prince of Wales Trust, who had been employed in local government, became self-employed as a business consultant and registered for VAT. At the time he began self-employment, he had not taken up his office as chairman of the Trust, although his appointment had been confirmed in writing. As chairman of the Trust he received no salary but his expenses were reimbursed. The Commissioners issued an assessment on the basis that he had accepted this office in the course of his business and, by virtue of *VATA 1994, s 94(4)*, should have accounted for VAT on the reimbursed expenses. The tribunal allowed his appeal against the assessment, holding that he had not accepted the chairmanship of the Trust in the course of his business, as his consultancy business had not begun at the time he accepted the office. *JJ Gardner, [1989] VATTR 132 (VTD 3687)*.

58.55 **Chartered secretary appointed as Complaints Administrator—reimbursed expenses.** A chartered secretary, who was registered for VAT, was appointed by the Secretary of State for Wales as the Independent Groundwater Complaints Administrator for the Cardiff Bay Barrage, under the *Cardiff Bay Barrage Act 1993*. She reclaimed input tax in respect of solicitors' bills and photocopying relating to this office. The Commissioners rejected the claim and she appealed. The tribunal dismissed her appeal, holding that it was not 'proper for her to charge value added tax in respect of her services as administrator, but not to charge value added tax in respect of the legal services and purchases for the office on the basis that she was the end user'. The items of expenditure had been 'incurred in the course of her work as administrator and as such should have been charged to the corporation'. *EM Lee, LON/99/649 (VTD 16750). (Note.* Compare *Ridgeons Bulk Ltd*, 3.116 ASSESSMENT, where the QB held that an assessment which had been issued to recover input tax could not be treated as an assessment charging output tax.)

58.56 **Reimbursement of director's expenses—whether reimbursement made as agent for associated company.** See *Alpha International Coal Ltd*, 1.66 AGENTS.

Sales of assets

58.57 **Sale of vans used in business.** A company sold some vans which it had used in its radio and television business. The Commissioners issued an assessment charging tax on the sales and the tribunal dismissed the company's appeal. *HB Mattia Ltd, [1976] VATTR 33 (VTD 243)*.

58.58 **Sale of lorry.** *HB Mattia Ltd*, 58.57 above, was applied in a subsequent case where a haulage contractor failed to account for tax on the sale of a lorry. *JE Hughes, MAN/77/262 (VTD 552)*.

58.59 A similar decision was reached in *T Naughton, MAN/91/422 (VTD 7854)*.

58.60 **Sale of horse boxes.** A registered trader sold two horse boxes and charged VAT on their sale. He subsequently appealed to the QB, contending that he should not have charged output tax since the sales had not been in the course of his business. The QB dismissed his appeal, holding that his case was without merit. *MA Lenihan v C & E Commrs, QB [1992] STC 478. (Note.* For another issue in this case, see 34.304 INPUT TAX.)

58.61 **Sale of jewellery.** A retail jeweller sold some jewellery which had been owned by his wife, and did not account for VAT on the sale. The Commissioners issued an assessment charging tax on the proceeds, and he appealed, contending that the jewellery had not been sold in the course of his business. The tribunal rejected this contention and dismissed his appeal, holding that the jewellery had been sold in the furtherance of the business, so that VAT was chargeable. *JS Mittu, MAN/82/32 (VTD 1275)*.

58.62   **Sale of private assets to raise capital for business.**   A farmer (S) had inherited a large estate from his father, but was faced with a large capital gains tax liability. He therefore decided to lease his late father's house to a rifle club. The house was let fully furnished. During the term of the lease S kept a number of valuable paintings in the house, some of these being locked away in storerooms but others being displayed in the rooms used by the club. When the lease expired S sold the house. The paintings, and a valuable stamp collection, were sold separately and the proceeds were paid into his business account as capital. The Commissioners issued an assessment charging tax on these proceeds, considering that the paintings and stamp collection had been business assets. The tribunal allowed S's appeal, observing that *Article 2* of the *EC Sixth Directive* taxes supplies 'by a taxable person acting as such', and thus implicitly excludes a supply by a taxable person in his personal capacity, and holding that the assets sold were personal assets, not connected with S's business. *RWK Stirling, [1985] VATTR 232 (VTD 1963).*

58.63   An engineer had, for many years, collected items of machinery as a hobby. In 1990 and in 1991 he was suffering financial difficulties, and sold some of these items. He did not account for VAT on the sales, and the Commissioners issued an assessment charging tax on them. He appealed, contending that they were private transactions and should not be subject to VAT. The tribunal allowed his appeal, holding that the sales had not been supplies in the course or furtherance of any business, but that he had had 'to realise private investments or personal possessions to provide moneys to tide him over'. *MR Atkinson, LON/93/31A (VTD 12763).*

58.64   **Sale of boat previously hired out.**   A registered trader failed to account for VAT on the sale of a boat which he had occasionally let on hire. The Commissioners issued an assessment charging tax on the sale of the boat, and the trader appealed, contending that no tax was due since the boat had not been a business asset. The tribunal dismissed the appeal, finding that the trader had previously described the boat as a business asset (for the purpose of reclaiming input tax) and was 'evasive in his evidence'. On the evidence, the trader had not discharged the onus of showing that the boat was not used for business purposes. *WJ Collins (t/a Triangle TVs), BEL/89/11 (VTD 6804).*

58.65   **Sale of assets after business given up.**   An individual (M) had carried on business as a yacht charterer and sailing instructor, using two yachts which he had purchased for business purposes but also used privately. He had registered for VAT from April 1973 but had to give up the business in November 1973 and sold the two yachts shortly afterwards. His registration was cancelled in November 1974. The Commissioners issued an assessment on the basis that tax was chargeable on the sale proceeds. The tribunal upheld the assessment and dismissed M's appeal. Although he ceased to be a taxable person on giving up his business, he was deemed to have then disposed of the yachts in the course of the business. *AJD Marshall, [1975] VATTR 98 (VTD 166).*

58.66   A trader (W) carried on a coach hire business, using two coaches. He was registered for VAT from 1 April 1973. He sold one of the coaches in October 1973, closed the business on 10 November 1973 and was deregistered from 31 January 1974. The Commissioners issued an assessment charging output tax on the sale of the two coaches. The tribunal upheld the assessment and dismissed W's appeal. *M Wolfe (t/a Arrow Coach Services), LEE/75/22 (VTD 171).*

58.67   **Sale of shop.**   A trader failed to account for output tax on the sale of a shop. The Commissioners issued an assessment and the tribunal dismissed the trader's appeal. *VAT (Special Provisions) Order, article 5(1)* did not apply since the shop's turnover was below the registration threshold and the purchaser was not a 'taxable person'.

However, the vendor had been a taxable person, and he was therefore required to account for output tax. *RC Blackburn, MAN/94/810 (VTD 13798)*.

58.68   **Sale of fixtures and fittings on surrender of lease.** A married couple had operated a public house which they had leased from a brewery. They surrendered the lease to the brewery, which took over fixtures and fittings which the couple had installed, paying them £10,000 in cash and releasing them from a debt of £3,958. The Commissioners issued a ruling that the couple were required to account for VAT on ⁷/₄₇ of the £13,958. The tribunal dismissed the couple's appeal, holding that, in view of the terms of the agreement in question, the £13,958 was taxable consideration for the sale of the fixtures and fittings. *Mr & Mrs D Campbell, MAN/95/1029 (VTD 14410)*.

58.69   **Publishing company—sale of paintings used as artwork.** A publishing company sold a number of paintings which it had used as artwork, and did not account for VAT on the proceeds. The Commissioners issued an assessment charging tax on the sale, and the company appealed, contending that the sale had not been made in the course of its business. The tribunal dismissed the appeal, distinguishing *Stirling*, 58.62 above. The paintings had been bought for business purposes and the fact that they had been stored for several years did not cause them to lose their character as business assets. *Blackie & Sons Ltd, EDN/91/274 (VTD 7632)*.

Conditional supplies (VATA 1994, Sch 4 para 1)

58.70   **Goods sold subject to reservation of title.** A company (V) sold goods to another company under a conditional sale agreement, whereby V retained legal ownership until the purchase price had been paid in full. The purchaser company went into receivership without paying for the goods, and had in the meantime resold some of the goods without V's approval or knowledge. The Commissioners issued an assessment on the basis that V had made a taxable supply of the goods. The tribunal upheld the assessment, holding that there had been a supply when the goods had been consigned to the purchaser and observing that 'it makes no difference that the legal title to the goods may not have passed contemporaneously with the moment of supply'. *Vernitron Ltd, [1978] VATTR 157 (VTD 615)*.

58.71   A similar decision was reached in *Tru-Form Sheet Metal Ltd, MAN/91/998 (VTD 9240)*. (*Note*. An appeal against a misdeclaration penalty was also dismissed.)

58.72   A company (T) carried on business as a supplier and installer of lighting systems. One of its customers (L) went into liquidation after paying about £56,000 for services which T had carried out under a contract to install a discotheque lighting system. By the time of the liquidation, most of the equipment had been installed, but T retained their legal ownership by virtue of a *Romalpa* clause in the contract. T had also issued another invoice, which remained unpaid, for a further £8,400. T did not account for output tax on any of the sums paid by L, and the Commissioners issued an assessment charging tax on the amounts in question. The tribunal dismissed T's appeal, holding that the system was to be treated as supplied at the time the payments were made. The QB upheld this decision. Although the contract had not been completed, the goods were in the possession of the customer, which had received the benefit of T's services. There had been a supply despite the fact that T retained the legal ownership of the system. T had issued invoices and had received payment. By virtue of what is now *VATA 1994, s 6(4)*, the time of payment was the time of supply. *Tas-Stage Ltd v C & E Commrs, QB [1988] STC 436*.

58.73   A company (E) which supplied computer equipment agreed to sell some equipment to an Eire company, subject to the condition that it would retain title to the equipment until the customer paid for them in full. The goods were invoiced to the Eire company and were collected by a freight company which was acting as agent for the Eire company. The Eire company had intended to sell the equipment to a company registered in Hong Kong which carried on business in Switzerland. However, the necessary export licence had not been obtained, and the equipment was impounded at Manchester Airport and subsequently forfeited under *CEMA 1979, s 139, Sch 3*. The Eire company never paid for the equipment, so that E retained legal ownership of the equipment, and did not account for VAT on the sale. The Commissioners issued an assessment on the basis that there had been a taxable supply, and E appealed, contending that there had been no supply, since it had retained the ownership of the equipment. The tribunal rejected this contention and dismissed the appeal, holding that the delivery of the goods to the freight company, which was acting as agent for the Eire customer, constituted a transfer of possession of the equipment which was a supply by virtue of what is now *VATA 1994, Sch 4 para 1(2). Oliver*, 58.132 below, applied. *ESS International Ltd, [1992] VATTR 336 (VTD 7771)*.

58.74   See also *Re Liverpool Commercial Vehicles Ltd*, 34.527 INPUT TAX, and *Mannesmann Demag Hamilton Ltd*, 38.73 INVOICES AND CREDIT NOTES.

58.75   **Provisional sale agreement not proceeded with—whether a supply.**   A company (C) wished to sell a number of machines. It made a provisional agreement to sell them to an associated company (M) to which it owed more than £600,000. Under this agreement, if M was unable to sell any of the machines to an external buyer, the machines would remain the property of C. Despite this condition, C recorded the sale of the machines to M in its accounts for the year ended 30 June 1987. M was only able to sell one of the machines, and in January 1989 C issued a credit note to M in respect of the remaining machines, the provisional sale agreement being treated as cancelled. C had not accounted for VAT on the sale of the machines to M, and the Commissioners issued an assessment on the basis that the sale recorded in C's accounts had taken place and was a taxable supply. C appealed, contending that, despite the entry in its accounts, it had never transferred possession or ownership of the machines to M. The tribunal allowed C's appeal, describing the agreement as 'obscure and contradictory' and finding that there had been no sale of the machines, which had remained the property of C. 'Once the legal position is identified, the state of affairs between the parties cannot be changed by the description of the transaction by one of the parties in its accounts. The accounts were wrong; but that error cannot transform a contingent liability to pay an unascertainable amount into the receipt of payment for the purposes of (*VATA 1994, s 6(4)**).' *Creditgrade Ltd, [1991] VATTR 87 (VTD 5390)*.

58.76   **Charge made for booking hotel room where booking not fulfilled— whether a supply.**   A company operated a chain of hotels. In cases where customers booked accommodation at the hotels, but failed to fulfil the booking, it levied a charge of the agreed price of the room, less the amount which would have represented VAT if the room had been occupied. (At the relevant time the VAT rate was 15%, so that the charge levied was $^{100}/_{115}$ of the price of the room.) It did not account for VAT at such charges, and the Commissioners issued an assessment to charge tax on the amounts in question. The company appealed, contending that since the rooms had not been occupied, there had been no supply and no liability to VAT. The QB rejected this contention and upheld the assessment. The company was charging the customer for the room, whether or not the customer occupied it. Making the room available was a supply for VAT purposes. *C & E Commrs v Bass plc, QB 1992, [1993] STC 42*.

58.77   **Payment in advance of order—whether a supply.**   See *Weldons (West One) Ltd*, 34.490 INPUT TAX.

58.78 Supply

Transfers of assets (VATA 1994, Sch 4 paras 5, 8)

58.78 **Mail order company—goods given to agents as incentives.** See *GUS Merchandise Corporation Ltd*, 54.1 RETAILERS' SPECIAL SCHEMES.

58.79 **Goods donated to promote business.** A company which manufactured fastenings did a considerable amount of business with local boatbuilders, and donated some of its products to assist a British yacht competing in the Americas Cup. It also purchased some playground equipment and donated this to the local council. The Commissioners issued an assessment on the basis that the donation of the goods in question was a taxable supply. The tribunal dismissed the company's appeal, holding that what is now *VATA 1994, Sch 4 para 5(1)* provided that the donations were to be treated as a taxable supply. *TR Fastenings Ltd, LON/80/290 (VTD 1016)*.

58.80 A similar decision was reached in a case where a company operating a 'time-share' business provided 'gifts' to potential purchasers. The company had reclaimed input tax on the 'gifts', but had not accounted for output tax. The tribunal dismissed the company's appeal against an assessment charging tax on the market value of the supplies. *Mitrolone Ltd, LON/88/1335X (VTD 4301)*.

58.81 **Free films supplied to customers by film processing company.** A company carried on the business of processing photographic films for members of the public. Most of the films which it processed were delivered by customers to retail shops such as pharmacies, from which they were collected by van drivers acting on behalf of the company. As part of a promotional scheme, the company provided customers with a free unexposed film when it returned their processed film. The Commissioners issued an assessment charging tax on the value of the free films, considering that they were supplied to the retailers and were within what is now *VATA 1994, Sch 4 para 5*. The company appealed, contending that the films were supplied to the customers rather than to the retailers, and were free gifts which fell outside *Sch 4 para 5*. The tribunal accepted the company's contention and allowed the appeal. The gift of the film was within *Sch 4 para 5(2)*, since it was a free gift which did not form part of a series of gifts to the same person and which cost the company less than £10. *United Photographic Laboratories Ltd, LON/92/527 (VTD 10071)*.

58.82 **Vouchers and wine given to householders by salesmen—whether a supply for consideration.** The proprietor of a business which sold carpet cleaning equipment provided salesmen working for him with wine and vouchers for hotel accommodation to give to householders when they visited their homes to demonstrate the equipment. The Commissioners issued an assessment on the cost of the wine and vouchers, considering that they were supplied as consideration for the right to enter the householder's premises. (The cost of the wine was 99p per bottle and the cost of the vouchers ranged from 50p to £1 each.) The proprietor appealed, contending that the wine and vouchers were gifts which were outside the scope of VAT by virtue of what is now *VATA 1994, Sch 4 para 5(2)(a)*. The tribunal allowed the proprietor's appeal. It was entirely at the salesman's discretion whether or not he gave a voucher or a bottle of wine. The customer did not obtain any contractual right to receive an item in return for allowing a salesman into his home, and he could not therefore have given consideration for the supply of such an item. *Mitrolone Ltd*, 58.80 above, distinguished. *QJ Cartlidge, LON/91/546 (VTD 7152)*.

58.83 **Assets used for private purposes—whether a self-supply.** A married couple who traded as central heating engineers carried out work on their own house. The work was invoiced to the husband and the necessary materials were purchased from their business bank account, but they did not account for VAT. The Commissioners issued an assessment on the basis that there had been a deemed supply of materials under what is now *VATA 1994, Sch 4 para 5(1)*, and the tribunal dismissed the couple's appeal. *Mr & Mrs Broadhurst (t/a RMS Heating), MAN/85/157 (VTD 2007)*.

58.84   A similar decision was reached in *GN Mellor, MAN/92/626 (VTD 10703)*. (*Note.* For another issue in this case, see 49.105 PENALTIES: MISDECLARATION.)

58.85   **Assets retained on cessation of trade—whether a self-supply.**   A partnership ceased to trade and the partners retained the partnership assets. Although they had previously claimed input tax on the assets in question, they failed to account for output tax and the Commissioners issued an assessment charging tax on the basis that the partners' retention of the assets was a deemed self-supply. The tribunal upheld the assessment and dismissed the partners' appeal. *J Kerr, E Lloyd & R Flatman, EDN/86/40 (VTD 2193)*.

58.86   Similar decisions were reached in *RJ McHarg, LON/90/1238Z (VTD 7254)* and *MF Lyons (t/a Trendz Jewellery), LON/93/219A (VTD 12243)*.

58.87   A similar decision was reached in a case where a couple who traded from a shop were evicted by their landlord for not paying their rent, and the landlord took over the traders' stock. The tribunal held that the traders were required to account for output tax on the value of the stock, observing that 'what occurred to the stock thereafter is not relevant'. *Mr & Mrs Rashid (t/a Handy Store), EDN/94/153 (VTD 13321)*.

58.88   See also *Mendes*, 63.12 VALUATION; *Ambu-Medics Ltd*, 63.13 VALUATION, and *McCormick*, 63.14 VALUATION.

58.89   **Transfer of vehicles previously held under hire-purchase agreement—whether a supply.**   A company (P) had held two vehicles under a hire-purchase agreement. Because of financial difficulties, it could not make the payments required by the agreement. It therefore transferred the vehicles to a sole trader (M), who promised to settle the hire-purchase agreement. P's managing director indemnified the hire-purchase company against any loss. The Commissioners issued an assessment on the basis that P had supplied the vehicles to M, the consideration being the amount outstanding under the hire-purchase agreement. The tribunal dismissed P's appeal and the QB upheld this decision. Where a person paid off the settlement figure under a hire purchase agreement to a finance company, it was reasonable to conclude that he did so on behalf of the hirer, since only the hirer had the contractual right to pay the amount in question to acquire ownership. The essence of the agreement was that P would supply the vehicles to M and that M would pay the amount outstanding to the hire-purchase company. *Philip Drakard Trading Ltd v C & E Commrs, QB [1992] STC 568*. (*Note.* For another issue in this case, not taken to the QB, see 34.404 INPUT TAX.)

58.90   A similar decision was reached in *RP Childs, LON/90/1072 (VTD 6120)*.

58.91   **Transfer of furniture to associated company.**   A registered trader failed to account for output tax on the transfer of some items of furniture to a company which he controlled, although he had previously reclaimed input tax on the purchase of the furniture. The Commissioners issued an assessment charging output tax on the supply. The tribunal dismissed the trader's appeal and the QB upheld this decision as one of fact, applying *Edwards v Bairstow & Harrison, HL 1955, 36 TC 207 (TTC 2001, 4.148)*. *BJ Sandley (t/a Bemba Sandley Management Co) v C & E Commrs, QB [1995] STC 230*.

58.92   **Social club providing free drinks for committee members.**   A social club provided free drinks to members of its committee, each committee member being entitled to three pints of beer in return for attending committee meetings. The

Commissioners issued an assessment charging output tax on the supply of these drinks. The club appealed, contending that the committee members should be treated as employees, so that there should be no output tax liability. The tribunal rejected this contention and dismissed the appeal, holding that the committee members were not employees and that the effect of what is now *VATA 1994, Sch 4 para 5* was that the club was required to account for output tax. *Glendale Social Club, [1994] VATTR 372 (VTD 12869)*.

58.93   **Caps presented to international footballers.**   See *Scottish Football Association*, 63.9 VALUATION.

58.94   **Supply of magazines to staff—whether within Sch 4 para 5(1).**   The Post Office distributed three periodical magazines to current and former employees. It reclaimed input tax on the related production costs, on the basis that it was making supplies of the magazines, within *Sch 4 para 5(1)*, which were zero-rated under *Sch 8, Group 3*. The Commissioners accepted the claim with regard to one of the magazines, but rejected the claim with regard to the other two, on the basis that the magazines were intended to 'inform employees of developments and current thinking within the Post Office business', were 'akin to the publications one finds circulating or on staff notice boards in any large organisation' and remained 'assets of the business after distribution to the employees, in the same sense as any other consumable overhead of the business such as stationery or pens'. The tribunal allowed the Post Office's appeal against this decision, holding on the evidence that the Post Office intended 'to transfer the property in each of the three magazines with which this appeal is concerned', and that there was a supply of each of the magazines on delivery. Accordingly the Post Office was entitled to reclaim the input tax in question. *The Post Office, MAN/95/1322 (VTD 14075)*.

58.95   **College supplying free prospectuses—whether a supply of goods.**   A college, which was partly exempt, issued free prospectuses to local residents. It claimed that, for the purposes of its partial exemption calculation, the issue of these prospectuses should be treated as free supplies, so that their deemed value should be included in the computation of total taxable supplies and the input tax related to their design and production should be treated as attributable to taxable supplies. The Commissioners rejected the claim and the college appealed. The tribunal allowed the appeal, holding that the issue of the prospectuses was within *VATA 1994, Sch 4 para 5(1)*. The tribunal held that, although the cost of producing each prospectus was less than the £15 limit in *Sch 4 para 5(2)*, it was not excluded from *Sch 4 para 5(1)* since, on the evidence, the prospectuses were 'as a matter of course, distributed to the same local households on a regular basis'. Accordingly, each prospectus formed 'part of a series or succession of gifts made to the person from time to time'. *The Post Office*, 58.94 above, applied. *West Herts College, LON/99/749 (VTD 16733)*.

Donations

58.96   **Donations by Freemasons to Masonic Association.**   The Commissioners issued an assessment on a Masonic association, charging tax on donations from Masons. The tribunal allowed the Association's appeal, holding that the donations were outside the scope of VAT since there was no relevant supply of goods or services. *Swindon Masonic Association Ltd, [1978] VATTR 200 (VTD 682)*.

58.97   **Donations to Masonic company for use of car park.**   A Masonic company owned a large building with a car park behind it. The building included a suite of rooms which was mainly used for Masonic purposes but was sometimes let out for other functions. No charge was made for use of the car park, but some users, including a local solicitors' firm, made voluntary annual payments. The

Commissioners issued an assessment on the basis that these payments were taxable consideration for parking facilities, but the tribunal allowed the company's appeal, holding that the payments were donations which were not liable to VAT. *Warwick Masonic Rooms Ltd, BIR/79/33 (VTD 839)*.

58.98 **Sponsorship fee received from bank—whether consideration for a supply.** A non-profit-making association organised an annual film competition. It received a sponsorship fee of £7,500 from a bank, and did not account for VAT on this. The Commissioners issued an assessment charging tax on the fee. The association appealed, contending that, as it had passed the money to the winner of the competition, VAT should not be chargeable. The tribunal dismissed the association's appeal, holding that the £7,500 was paid in respect of services in the form of advertising and publicity rights supplied to the bank, and that VAT was chargeable thereon despite the fact that the money had been earmarked for the winner of the competition. *Oxford Film Foundation, LON/89/911Y (VTD 5031)*.

58.99 **Donations received by musician performing on public highway.** See *Tolsma v Inspecteur der Omzetbelasting Leeuwarden*, 21.51 EUROPEAN COMMUNITY LAW.

Inducement payments ('reverse premiums') and rent-free periods, etc.

58.100 **Reverse premium—whether a supply.** The landlord of a hotel granted a lease to a company, and paid a 'reverse premium' of £1.4 million to help the company repair the property. The Commissioners issued an assessment on the basis that the payment was liable to VAT. The company appealed, contending that there had been no supply. The tribunal dismissed the company's appeal, holding that the £1.4 million was consideration paid by the landlord for the company's agreement to provide more valuable benefits under the lease. *Gleneagles Hotel plc, [1986] VATTR 196 (VTD 2152)*.

58.101 In a similar case, a firm of chartered accountants appealed against an assessment in respect of a payment of £940,000 made to it in connection with the renewal of a lease on premises of which it held the tenancy. The £940,000 comprised three elements: £240,000 constituted a rent rebate to take into account that two floors were not required; £400,000 was an amount paid by the freeholder to enable the firm to refurbish the property; and £300,000 was paid by the freeholder as an inducement for the acceptance of the lease. The tribunal reduced the assessment to £700,000, holding that there was no supply with regard to the payment of £240,000. However, the £400,000 paid to enable the firm to refurbish the premises was consideration for a taxable supply under the principle laid down in *Gleneagles Hotel plc*, 58.100 above. The £300,000 paid as an inducement to enter into the lease, i.e. as a reverse premium, was an amount paid for the execution of the new lease and consequently, for tax purposes, represented a supply of services. *Neville Russell, [1987] VATTR 194 (VTD 2484)*.

58.102 A firm of architects received a 'reverse premium' of £340,000 from a company which had granted it a lease of two floors of a building. It did not account for VAT on this amount, and the Commissioners issued an assessment, against which the firm appealed. The tribunal dismissed the firm's appeal, holding that, by accepting an inducement to enter into the lease, the firm had made a taxable supply of services for consideration. *Neville Russell*, 58.101 above, applied. *Hutchinson Locke & Monk, LON/88/1028 & LON/89/1763 (VTD 5212)*.

58.103 See also *Mirror Group plc*, 21.167 EUROPEAN COMMUNITY LAW.

58.104 **Improvements to hotel paid for by tenant—whether a supply by tenant to landlord.** A company (P) operated two hotels in the Isle of Man. The hotels were owned by P's parent company (C). P paid for alterations and improvements to the hotels. C did not reimburse P for this work, but agreed not to charge P any rent for the hotels. The Isle of Man Treasury issued an assessment on the basis that P had made taxable supplies to C and should account for VAT on the costs of the alterations and improvements. The tribunal dismissed P's appeal, applying the principles laid down in *Neville Russell*, 58.101 above. The waiver of rent by C constituted consideration for the work carried out by P. Since the transaction was not at arm's length and the consideration was non-monetary, the costs of the work carried out should be treated as the open market value of the supplies. *Port Erin Hotels v The Isle of Man Treasury, MAN/89/722 (VTD 5045)*.

58.105 **Repairs to premises paid for by tenant in return for rent-free occupation—whether a supply by tenant to landlord.** A company (R) obtained a tenancy of some premises from an associated company (S). The premises were in need of repair, and it was agreed that R would pay for the repairs in return for being allowed to occupy the premises rent-free for three years. R reclaimed the input tax on the repairs, and the Commissioners issued an assessment on the basis that the supply had been to S as the landlord, so that R was not entitled to reclaim the input tax. The tribunal held that R had made an onward supply to S and that the consideration for that supply was the right to occupy the premises rent-free for three years, so that, although R was entitled to reclaim input tax, it was required to account for a corresponding amount of output tax. R appealed to the QB, which upheld the tribunal's reasoning, applying *Gleneagles Hotel plc*, 58.100 above, but allowed R's appeal on the grounds that the assessment had been issued to recover input tax and was not effective to charge output tax, and that the Commissioners should have issued a new assessment in accordance with what is now *VATA 1994, s 73(6)* (see 3.116 ASSESSMENT). *Ridgeons Bulk Ltd v C & E Commrs, QB [1994] STC 427*.

58.106 **Sale of houses after refurbishment—whether any supply of 'refurbishment services' by vendor.** See *Maritime Housing Association Ltd*, 39.20 LAND.

58.107 **Payments under agreement capping mortgage interest—whether consideration for a supply.** A partnership carried on the business of letting commercial property. It entered into an agreement with a development company for the lease of an industrial unit from the company at a peppercorn rent. Under the agreement, the partnership paid a premium of £86,000 plus VAT to the development company. The partnership had to borrow part of this amount, and under a 'mortgage-capping' agreement, the development company agreed to pay the partnership any amount by which its interest payments in the first two years after completion of the lease exceeded 12.5%. The partnership elected to waive exemption in respect of the property. During the first two years of the lease, interest rates were high, and the development company paid the partnership £2,250 under the 'mortgage-capping' agreement. The partnership did not account for tax on these payments. The Commissioners issued an assessment charging output tax on them, on the basis that the payments were equivalent to reverse premiums. The partnership appealed, contending that the payments did not constitute consideration for any supply. The tribunal accepted this contention and allowed the appeal, holding that the 'mortgage-capping' agreement was not an inducement to enter the leasing agreement, but was supplemental to that agreement and 'was part and parcel of the overall transaction'. *Gleneagles Hotel plc*, 58.100 above, and *Neville Russell*, 58.101 above, distinguished. *N Iliffe & DC Holloway, [1993] VATTR 439 (VTD 10922)*.

58.108 **Inducement payment by lessor to lessee.** See *Mirror Group plc*, 21.167 EUROPEAN COMMUNITY LAW.

58.109   **Inducement payments to development company by health authority.**   A local health authority made four payments of £49,500 each to a development company (M), under a tripartite agreement whereby M agreed to purchase a hospital site from the Department of Health, to construct surgeries for two medical practices on the site, and to grant the health authority an underlease of the surgeries. M did not account for output tax on the payments, and the Commissioners issued assessments charging tax on them. M appealed, contending that the payments did not represent consideration for a supply of services, but should be treated as grants which were outside the scope of VAT. The tribunal rejected this contention and dismissed M's appeal. On the evidence, the payments were consideration for a service supplied by M in agreeing to enter into the agreement. *Mirror Group plc*, 21.167 EUROPEAN COMMUNITY LAW, applied; *Iliffe & Holloway*, 58.107 above, distinguished. Furthermore, the payments were 'subsidies directly linked to the price' of the relevant supplies, and thus formed part of the taxable amount, within *Article 11A1* of the *EC Sixth Directive. Medical Centre Developments Ltd, LON/95/2714 & 2860 (VTD 15601)*.

Compensation payments

58.110   **Compensation payment following disputed bill.** An architectural partnership (H) was commissioned by a firm of contractors (G) to design a building. H sent G an interim payment application for £10,000 plus VAT of £800 (the standard rate of VAT being 8% at the relevant time). G disputed the amount demanded, and the matter was referred to solicitors. Subsequently G went into liquidation, and H received compensation of £15,000 from the intended purchaser of the building. H failed to account for output tax on this payment, and the Commissioners issued an assessment charging tax of £800, on the basis that £10,800 of the payment represented consideration for H's services, and that only the balance of £4,200 was outside the scope of VAT. The tribunal upheld the assessment and dismissed H's appeal. *Hurley Robinson Partnership, BIR/78/231 (VTD 750)*.

58.111   **Payment by contractor to subcontractor—whether consideration for taxable supplies.** A partnership, which carried out road resurfacing work, had acted for several years as a subcontractor for a civil engineering company (B). In 1997 B stopped providing the partnership with new work, and also failed to pay for work which the partnership had previously done. The partnership issued a writ against B, claiming payment of more than £130,000. The proceedings were eventually settled by an agreement under which B paid the partnership £115,000, expressed as including 'any liability to VAT'. The partnership failed to account for output tax on this receipt. The Commissioners issued an assessment charging tax on it, and the partnership appealed, contending that it should be treated as compensation which was outside the scope of VAT. The tribunal rejected this contention and upheld the assessment in principle, holding that 'a mere payment of compensation would be outside the scope of VAT' but that the payment here was consideration for work which the partnership had carried out. B had 'in substance and reality agreed to pay the £115,000 in respect of work which (the partnership) had carried out'. (However, the tribunal observed on reviewing the evidence that 'the assessment had probably been made for the wrong accounting period'—a point that had not been raised by the appellants. The Commissioners subsequently accepted that the assessment had been made for the wrong accounting period, and agreed to withdraw the assessment. No costs were awarded to either side.) *Mr & Mrs Garnham (t/a Pro-Mac Surfacing), LON/98/571 (VTD 15918)*.

58.112   **Payment for surrender of rights to product name—whether consideration for a supply.** A company (C) had used a particular trading name and style of logo for some time. In 1983 it became aware that another company (U) was using a similar trading name and logo, and that this was damaging C's business. C began proceedings against U. In 1988 U paid C £30,000 in full and final settlement of C's claims, under an agreement by which C abandoned its rights to the disputed trading name and logo. The Commissioners issued an assessment charging VAT on the payment of £30,000. The tribunal dismissed C's appeal against the assessment. Under what is now *VATA 1994, s 5(2)*, 'anything which is not a supply of goods but is done for a consideration (including, if so done, the granting, assignment or surrender of any right) is a supply of services'. C had surrendered a right in return for the £30,000, which was, therefore, consideration for a deemed supply of services. *Neville Russell*, 58.101 above, applied. *Cooper Chasney Ltd, LON/89/1409Z (VTD 4898)*.

58.113   **Payment received as 'out-of-court' settlement—whether consideration for a supply.**   A broker began legal proceedings against a company (H) which traded as a travel agent, claiming that he had provided H with information concerning a number of shops which were for sale, but that H had failed to pay him the commission which had been agreed. The broker had claimed £45,000 from H, but agreed to accept £35,000 under a *Tomlin* order as an out-of-court settlement. The Commissioners issued an assessment charging tax on the £35,000, and the broker appealed. The tribunal allowed the broker's appeal, holding that, since he had not obtained judgment against H, it had not been proved that there had been any actual supply of services, and the payment included an element of compensation. The payment should be treated as being outside the scope of VAT, in accordance with the Commissioners' *Press Notice 82/87. L Reich, MAN/92/454 (VTD 9548)*.

58.114   Compare *Whites Metal Co*, 34.506 INPUT TAX.

58.115   **Compensation payment for loss of consultancy—whether a taxable supply.**   A consultant had provided services to a company for nine years, mainly in training its salesmen. In 1989 the company informed him that his services were no longer required, and paid him £30,000 as compensation, in return for which he agreed not to divulge information concerning the company to its competitors. He did not account for tax on this payment, and the Commissioners issued an assessment on the basis that it represented consideration for a taxable supply of services. He appealed, contending that the payment should be treated as being outside the scope of VAT. The tribunal accepted this contention and allowed his appeal. *F Penny (t/a FMS Management Services), LON/92/722 (VTD 10398)*.

58.116   **Compensation payment for loss of future fees—whether a taxable supply.**   A company (C) owned a hotel, which was managed by another company (H) under a written agreement. In 1991 C terminated the agreement, paying H £2,000,000 as compensation. The Commissioners issued an assessment charging tax on the payment. The tribunal allowed H's appeal, holding that the payment constituted liquidated damages for the loss of future income, and did not represent consideration for a taxable supply. *Cooper Chasney Ltd*, 58.112 above, distinguished. *Holiday Inns (UK) Ltd, [1993] VATTR 321 (VTD 10609). (Note.* The decision in this case was disapproved by a subsequent tribunal in *Croydon Hotel & Leisure Co Ltd*, 34.510 INPUT TAX, on the grounds that it was inconsistent with the subsequent CJEC decision in *Lubbock Fine & Co*, 21.165 EUROPEAN COMMUNITY LAW.)

58.117   **Compensation payment by tenant for termination or surrender of taxable lease.**   A bank occupied a leased property. The landlord of the property had elected to waive exemption in respect of the property. The bank decided to vacate the property, and paid the landlord £597,220 as compensation. The Commissioners issued a ruling that output tax was chargeable on this payment, on the basis that it represented consideration for a taxable supply of services. The bank appealed, contending that the payment should be treated as compensation and as outside the scope of VAT. The tribunal rejected this contention and dismissed the appeal, holding on the evidence that 'the contemporaneous granting and exercise' of the option to terminate the lease amounted to a supply of services by the landlord in return for the payment made by the bank. Applying *dicta* of the tribunal in *Central Capital Corporation*, 39.51 LAND, 'what governs the taxability or otherwise of any transaction in leasehold property is whether the grant of the original lease, underlease or licence was taxable or not. If it was taxable, then all subsequent transactions based on the original contractual relationship are taxable'. *Holiday Inns (UK) Ltd*, 58.116 above, and *Financial & General Print Ltd*, 34.509 INPUT TAX, distinguished. *Lloyds Bank plc, LON/95/2524 (VTD 14181)*.

58.118   **Compensation for surrender of handguns.**   A company (P) manufactured and sold handguns. Following a shooting at a primary school in Scotland, where a number of children were killed, Parliament enacted the *Firearms (Amendment) Act 1997*, which made the possession and sale of most handguns an offence. A compensation scheme was instituted, whereby compensation was paid for the surrender of such handguns. P surrendered a substantial number of guns, and was paid more than £500,000 as compensation. The Commissioners issued an assessment charging tax on this. P appealed, contending that it had not made any supply of the guns. The tribunal rejected this contention and dismissed the appeal, holding that the surrender of each gun was a supply of goods for consideration equal to the amount of compensation. The QB upheld the tribunal decision. Moses J held that, in order to determine whether or not there had been a supply, it was necessary to identify whether there had been a consumption. However, consumption did not depend upon the question of whether the guns were acquired for further use or were to be destroyed, but upon 'the acquisition of title to the goods'. P had transferred title to the guns to the Government, which gave rise to consumption by the Government. It followed that there had been a supply of goods. The payments of compensation to P represented consideration for that supply. *Mohr v Finanzamt Bad Segeberg*, 21.96 EUROPEAN COMMUNITY LAW, and *Landboden-Agrardienste GmbH & Co KG v Finanzamt Calau*, 21.97 EUROPEAN COMMUNITY LAW, distinguished. *Parker Hale Ltd v C & E Commrs, QB [2000] STC 388*. (*Note*. For the Commissioners' policy on compensation payments for the surrender of firearms, see Business Brief 27/97, issued on 21 November 1997.)

58.119   **Compensation payment for faulty goods.**   See *Galaxy Equipment (Europe) Ltd*, 38.43 INVOICES AND CREDIT NOTES.

58.120   **Compensation payment made by order of Court.**   See *Hometex Trading Ltd*, 34.507 INPUT TAX, and *Financial & General Print Ltd*, 34.509 INPUT TAX.

Whether supply 'in the course or furtherance of any business' (VATA 1994, s 4(1))

Note. In the cases under this heading it is accepted that there is a business within what is now *VATA 1994, s 94*, and the issue is whether there has been a supply in the course or furtherance of that business. For cases where the existence of a business is disputed, see 7 BUSINESS.

58.121   **Sale of sporting rights by farmer.**   An individual (R) purchased a farm in March 1979 and sold sporting rights over the farmland for £12,000 in July 1980. The Commissioners issued an assessment on the basis that the sale of the sporting rights was a standard-rated supply of goods or services. The tribunal upheld the assessment and dismissed R's appeal. It was not essential for an asset to have been used for the purpose of a business for its sale to be in the course or furtherance of that business. There had been the exploitation of an asset of the farming business which, applying what is now *VATA 1994, s 94(6)*, was made in the course or furtherance of the business. Alternatively, as the purpose of the sale was to reduce the business overdraft, it followed that it was 'in furtherance' of the business. *A Ridley, [1983] VATTR 81 (VTD 1406).*

58.122 **Farmer organising shooting syndicate—whether making supplies in course or furtherance of business.** A farmer, who was registered for VAT, organised a shooting syndicate on his farm. Members of the syndicate paid him subscriptions in return for the right to shoot. He did not account for output tax on these subscriptions. The Commissioners issued an assessment charging tax on them and he appealed, contending that the shooting was organised for pleasure, was not on a commercial basis, and did not constitute a business. (The Inland Revenue treated the shooting as 'hobby farming', giving rise to neither a profit nor a loss.) The tribunal dismissed the appeal, holding on the evidence that the organisation of the shooting went 'much farther ... than just being a particularly well-run pleasure activity'. The farmer was carrying on a business and was supplying the right to shoot in the course or furtherance of a business. *Lord Fisher*, 7.5 BUSINESS, distinguished. *JO Williams, LON/95/2173A (VTD 14240).*

58.123 **Chairman of Prince of Wales Trust—whether making supplies to Trust in course or furtherance of business.** See *Gardner*, 58.54 above.

58.124 **Chartered Secretary appointed as Complaints Administrator.** See *Lee*, 58.55 above.

58.125 **Paid lectures given by practising barrister.** A barrister received fees for lecturing at a course for Patent Agents, but did not account for VAT on these fees. The Commissioners issued an assessment charging tax on the fees, and the barrister appealed, contending that he had not given the lectures 'in the course or furtherance of his business'. The tribunal rejected this contention and dismissed the appeal. The barrister specialised in patent law and had been engaged to lecture at the course because of his professional expertise. Accordingly, he had undertaken the lectures in the course or furtherance of his business as a barrister, and was obliged to account for VAT on the fees. *BC Reid, LON/93/1373A (VTD 11625).*

58.126 **Professional football club providing services to associated members' club—whether in course or furtherance of business.** A professional football club, which was registered for VAT, established a 'members' club', in accordance with guidelines issued by the Football League. Part of the ground was set aside for the exclusive use of members of the 'members' club'. The Commissioners issued a ruling that the club was required to account for VAT on the sums which it received from 'members'. The club appealed, contending that the supplies were not made in the course or furtherance of its business. The tribunal dismissed the appeal, holding that the benefits provided by the club to the members were taxable supplies in the course or furtherance of the club's business, within what is now *VATA 1994, s 4(1)*. (The tribunal chairman observed that what is now *VATA 1994, s 94(3)(a)* was not relevant, since the 'members' club' was not in law a true members' club, but was in fact a proprietary club run as a business by the limited liability company which owned the football club. The tribunal also held that the whole of the sums paid by members were standard-rated, rejecting the club's contention that part of the consideration should be apportioned to zero-rated supplies of a booklet and a monthly newspaper.) *Southend United Football Club, LON/93/121A (VTD 11919).*

58.127 **Sale of private assets to raise capital for business.** See *Stirling*, 58.62 above, and *Atkinson*, 58.63 above.

58.128 **Administrative supplies to associated companies.** See *PHH Europe plc*, 58.27 above.

58.129   **Institute of Chartered Accountants—whether licensing activities 'in the course or furtherance of a business'.**   The Institute of Chartered Accountants in England and Wales is registered for VAT as an organisation providing advantages or facilities to its members, within what is now *VATA 1994, s 94(2)*. It is also a 'recognised professional body' under *Financial Services Act 1986, s 17* and *Insolvency Act 1986, s 391* and a 'recognised supervisory body' under *Companies Act 1989*, and issues certificates accordingly, authorising (or 'licensing') practitioners to carry on investment business, insolvency work and audit work. The Commissioners issued a ruling that the services supplied by the Institute in the course of its licensing activities were not supplied in the course or furtherance of a business, so that it was not required to account for output tax on them and was not entitled to reclaim input tax in respect of them. The Institute appealed, contending that its licensing functions amounted to a 'business' or an 'economic activity'. The tribunal rejected this contention and dismissed the appeal, holding that the relevant supplies were not 'of a kind which ... are commonly made by those who seek to make profit from them', nor were the relevant activities 'predominantly concerned with the making of taxable supplies for a consideration'. The predominant concern of the licensing activities was 'the implementation of the statutory policy of protecting the public interest through self-regulation of the relevant practitioners', and 'charging fees for investigative and monitoring services is not the predominant concern or characteristic of the activities'. The Ch D, CA and HL unanimously upheld this decision. Applying *Polysar Investments Netherlands BV v Inspecteur der Invoerrechten en Accijnzen*, 21.61 EUROPEAN COMMUNITY LAW, 'it is not enough merely to point to the fact that there is a supply of services in return for a money payment and some loose economic connection, but . . . the activities must be of an "economic character"'. Lord Slynn observed that the Institute was carrying out a regulatory function, on behalf of the State, to ensure that only fit and proper persons were licensed or authorised to carry out the various activities and to monitor what they did. This was not in any real sense a trading, commercial or economic activity, and the fact that fees were charged for the grant of the licences did not convert it into one. Performing a licensing function on behalf of the State was not a 'business'. *The Institute of Chartered Accountants in England and Wales v C & E Commrs, HL [1999] STC 398; [1999] 1 WLR 701; [1999] 2 All ER 449.*

58.130   **Advertising facilities supplied by Council in return for sponsorship payments—whether a supply 'in the course or furtherance of a business'.**   See *Norwich City Council*, 40.5 LOCAL AUTHORITIES AND STATUTORY BODIES.

Miscellaneous—supplies of goods

58.131   **Contract rendered void through misrepresentation by purchaser.**   A company (L) which dealt in electrical goods had regularly supplied goods to a large hotel group (T). The orders were regularly placed on behalf of T by one of its employees (G). G told L that he had ceased to work for T and had set up in business on his own account. In that capacity he ordered 150 television sets from L, stating that they were for installation in T's hotels. He collected the sets and L invoiced him for them, giving him one month's credit. He did not pay for them within the month. L was unable to trace him, and notified the police. Some months later G was arrested, and was subsequently convicted of theft of the sets, having obtained them by deception through having falsely represented that they were for installation in T's hotels. L did not account for tax on the sets, and the Commissioners issued an assessment on the basis that the sets had been supplied when L issued G with an invoice. The tribunal allowed L's appeal, holding that the contract with G had been rendered void by G's deception and L's prompt notification of the facts to the police.

On the evidence, the sets had been stolen by G and L had not supplied them. *Harry B Litherland & Co Ltd, [1978] VATTR 226 (VTD 701)*.

58.132   **Sale of stolen cars.**   A second-hand car dealer sold a number of stolen cars at auction. He did not account for VAT on the sales, and the Commissioners issued an assessment charging tax on the amounts received. He appealed, contending that there had been no supply since he did not own the cars. The QB rejected this contention and upheld the assessment. The fact that the dealer had no legal title to the cars did not alter the fact that he had supplied them. Supply was 'the passing of possession in goods pursuant to an agreement whereunder the supplier agrees to part and the recipient agrees to take possession'. *Dicta* in *Carlton Lodge Club Ltd*, 13.28 CLUBS, ASSOCIATIONS AND ORGANISATIONS, applied. *C & E Commrs v JRR Oliver, QB 1979, [1980] STC 73; [1980] 1 All ER 353. (Note.* Compare the subsequent case of *Hudson*, 34.520 INPUT TAX, in which a tribunal held that there was no right to reclaim input tax in respect of acquisitions of stolen goods.)

58.133   *Oliver*, 58.132 above, was applied in the similar case of *D Lindley, MAN/92/716 (VTD 12037)*.

58.134   **Supply of waste for extraction of silver content—value not ascertainable until subsequent processing.**   A company (R) carried on the business of recovering silver from photographic waste. It had no facilities for producing refined silver, and therefore disposed of its products, comprising silver and ash with a high silver content, to another company (M) which used them with its own products to form rough silver bars for disposal to a third company (J) which traded as silver brokers and was able to produce and dispose of refined silver bars. It was only at this stage that a monetary value could be placed on the preceding supplies by R and M. M accounted for VAT on the amounts it received from J and passed to R the net amount due on it. R did not account for VAT on its supplies of swarf and ash to M, and appealed against an assessment on them. The tribunal dismissed the appeal. Any difficulty arising from the delay in ascertaining the value of the supply could have been met by a request for a direction under what is now *VATA 1994, s 6(6)*. *United Refining Co (Precious Metals) Ltd, MAN/79/51 (VTD 1019)*.

58.135   **Refundable deposits for goods—whether a supply.**   A partnership acted as distributors for an American company. It had a large number of its own distributors, to whom it provided 'training tools', the sale of which would have been illegal under the *Fair Trading Act 1973*, in return for a refundable deposit. The deposits exceeded the cost of the tools. The Commissioners issued an assessment charging tax on the deposits and the partnership appealed, contending that the deposits did not represent consideration for a supply. The tribunal dismissed the partnership's appeal, holding that the distribution of the tools was a supply by the partnership and that the deposits were the consideration. *BJ Executive Services, LON/85/13 (VTD 2048)*.

58.136   **Commemorative coins issued under sales promotion scheme—whether a supply.**   A company distributed to purchasers of its products more than 150,000 commemorative £2 coins in presentation folders under a sales promotion scheme. The Commissioners issued an assessment on the basis that the distribution constituted a standard-rated supply. The tribunal dismissed the company's appeal, holding that, for VAT purposes, the distributions were supplies of coins which were collector's pieces and were chargeable to tax. *Milk Marketing Board, LON/87/495 (VTD 3389)*.

58.137   **Subcontract work where materials provided by contractor—whether a supply of materials to subcontractor.**   A construction company engaged independent subcontractors to carry out specific work. All materials were invoiced to the company and all accounts were settled by the company. The Commissioners issued an assessment on the basis that the arrangements constituted a supply by the contractor to the subcontractor of the materials and plant hire, at cost, and a supply back to the contractor by the subcontractor of the finished job. The company appealed, contending that the subcontractors were supplying labour only. The tribunal allowed the company's appeal, holding that the materials were the sole responsibility of the main contractor from start to finish. *J Hopkins (Contractors) Ltd, [1989] VATTR 107 (VTD 3511).*

58.138   **Invoices for supplies of gold described by issuer of 'shams'—whether any supply.**   A taxi driver issued VAT invoices showing sales of gold to an individual who was an acquaintance of his. In accounting for tax he only accounted for output tax on a small proportion of the amount shown on the invoices he had issued to the acquaintance, and reclaimed input tax in respect of purported invoices which he subsequently admitted to be false. The Commissioners issued an assessment to require payment of the full amounts of output tax shown on the invoices issued by the taxi driver, and to recover the input tax which he had fraudulently reclaimed. The taxi driver appealed, contending that all the invoices were shams and that he had not made any actual supplies of gold, but had issued the invoices at the request of the acquaintance, who was in possession of a large quantity of gold which he had acquired illegally and in respect of which he wished to reclaim input tax. (The Commissioners had taken criminal proceedings against the acquaintance, but he had been acquitted by a jury.) The tribunal accepted the taxi driver's evidence and allowed his appeal on the grounds that the assessment had not been made to the best of the Commissioners' judgment. On the evidence, the purported transactions were 'fiscal nullities' and, notwithstanding the issue of fraudulent invoices, could not form the basis of any claims for input tax or any liability to output tax. (The tribunal also observed that the Commissioners should have assessed the acquaintance to recover the input tax shown on the invoices issued to him by the taxi driver.) *Sandell, LON/91/1000X (VTD 9665).*

58.139   **Contract for supply of jewellery—goods not of required standard—whether a supply.**   A company (B) agreed to supply another company (G) with substantial quantities of gold-plated jewellery. B purchased the jewellery from a third company (S), which imported the jewellery from Korea. G ascertained that some of the jewellery was not in fact gold-plated. It returned 60,000 items to B, and B refunded the money which G had paid for these items. B returned the items in question to S, and S paid £175,000 to B. The Commissioners issued assessments charging output tax on these payments. B appealed, contending that it had retained title to the goods, notwithstanding that it had paid it £175,000 and that the goods had been physically returned to S. The tribunal accepted this contention and allowed the appeal, finding that the terms of the agreement were such that title to the goods would not pass from B to S until it was established that G would not take any further proceedings against B. *Basdring Ltd, MAN/92/1036 (VTD 13263).*

58.140   **Supply of counterfeit goods.**   See *R v Goodwin & Unstead,* 21.49 EUROPEAN COMMUNITY LAW.

58.141   **Unlawful supplies of anabolic steroids.**   See *R v C & J Citrone,* 46.12 PENALTIES: EVASION OF TAX.

58.142   **Purchase by partners from partnership—whether a supply.**   See *Atkins Macreadie & Co,* 27.34 FOOD.

58.143   **Takings stolen—whether a supply.**   See *Benton,* 58.289 below, and the cases noted at 58.290 below.

58.144 Supply

58.144 **Whether there can be a taxable supply of non-existent goods.** See *Howard*, 34.500 INPUT TAX.

58.145 **Arrangement between retailer and finance company—whether a supply.** See *Excell Consumer Industries Ltd*, 34.532 INPUT TAX.

Miscellaneous—supplies of services

Cases held to constitute a supply

58.146 **Vouchers issued under incentive scheme—whether a supply.** A company (N) issued vouchers, with a face value of £3, to purchasers of its products. These vouchers could be redeemed for vouchers of the same face value exchangeable for goods at stores owned by another company (F). The company did not account for VAT on the issue of the vouchers and the Commissioners issued an assessment on the basis that the issue of the vouchers was a taxable supply. The tribunal held that when N exchanged the vouchers for F's vouchers it made a taxable supply of services, the consideration for which was the face value of F's vouchers. *Normal Motor Factors Ltd, [1978] VATTR 20 (VTD 499)*.

58.147 See also the cases noted at 63.43 to 63.55 VALUATION.

58.148 **Payments from manufacturer under promotion scheme.** A company, limited by guarantee, had been established as a mutual concern by companies engaged in the cash and carry trade. Its principal activity was to organise promotions of selected products in co-operation with the manufacturers. The manufacturers contributed to the costs of the promotions, and made additional payments computed by reference to the sales of the products being promoted. The company distributed such payments to its members on the basis of their sales of the products in question. The company did not account for tax on the payments from the manufacturers and appealed against an assessment charging tax on them. The tribunal dismissed the appeal, holding that the payments were consideration for a supply within what is now *VATA 1994, s 5(2)(b)*. *The Landmark Cash & Carry Group Ltd, [1980] VATTR 1 (VTD 883)*.

58.149 **Money received for abandoned project.** An architect failed to account for VAT on payment he had received for carrying out work for a project which had subsequently been abandoned. The Commissioners issued an assessment charging tax on the payment and he appealed, contending that the payment represented compensation and should not be treated as liable to VAT. The tribunal dismissed his appeal, holding that the payment constituted consideration. *WG Richards, MAN/86/154 (VTD 2355)*.

58.150 **Payment described as 'interest-free loan'—whether consideration for a supply.** A firm of architects performed various services relating to a potential development scheme, for which it received interim payments on which VAT was correctly accounted for. Subsequently its client informed the firm that the project might be aborted, and it would therefore be unable to make further payments. The firm protested at this and it was agreed that, in view of the work which the firm had already undertaken, the client would pay the firm £50,000, described as an 'interest-free loan', repayable on a specified date if the project was proceeded with and further payments became due. The specified date passed without any more work being carried out and without repayment of the loan being made or requested. The Commissioners issued an assessment charging VAT on the £50,000, and the tribunal dismissed the firm's appeal, holding that the payment was consideration for the services which the firm had supplied. *Shingler Risdon Associates, LON/88/248 (VTD 2981)*.

58.151   **Customer in liquidation—payment not received.**   A trader supplied management services to a company which subsequently went into liquidation without paying for the services. Invoices were issued to the company, but the trader did not account for the VAT shown on the invoices. The Commissioners issued an assessment charging tax on the invoices, and the trader appealed, contending that the invoices had been issued in error by one of his staff without his knowledge. The tribunal dismissed his appeal, finding that either the appellant or his bookkeeper had been responsible for the issue of the invoices, which were genuine invoices for services that the trader had supplied to the company. *EA Kilburn, MAN/87/277 (VTD 3937)*. (*Note*. For another issue in this case, see 34.401 INPUT TAX.)

58.152   An appeal was dismissed in a case where a company had failed to account for tax in respect of services it had supplied to an associated company which had subsequently gone into liquidation. *Charles Forrington & Partners Ltd, LON/90/358Z (VTD 5540)*.

58.153   A similar decision was reached in *JR Nicholson, LON/91/860 (VTD 6707)*.

58.154   **Payphone in public house.**   A publican failed to account for VAT on receipts from a 'payphone' which he had installed in the public house. The Commissioners issued an assessment charging tax on the receipts and he appealed, contending that he should not have to account for VAT since he did not make a separate charge to the customers. The tribunal dismissed the appeal, holding that the service was clearly a supply by the publican for consideration. *K Hodson, MAN/89/606 (VTD 4709)*.

58.155   **Payphones in launderettes.**   A company which operated a number of launderettes installed payphones in the launderettes but did not account for output tax on the receipts from these. The Commissioners issued an assessment charging tax on them and the tribunal dismissed the company's appeal. *Hodson, 58.154 above*, applied. *Chamberlain Domestic Services Ltd, LON/93/2764A (VTD 12492)*.

58.156   **Free meals provided to coach drivers—whether a supply.**   A company which operated motorway service stations provided free meals to coach drivers in return for bringing passengers to the service stations. To claim a free meal, a driver had to be carrying at least 20 passengers, and also had to sign a book and produce his PSV licence. Drivers were also given gift stamps which could be exchanged for goods. The Commissioners issued assessments charging tax on the value of the free meals, on the basis that the company was making supplies for a consideration. The company appealed, contending that there was no taxable transaction. The tribunal dismissed the appeal, holding that the allowance of a free meal and a gift stamp constituted a supply by the company for consideration. The driver was given his free meal as consideration for bringing potential customers to the service station. *Granada Group plc, [1991] VATTR 104 (VTD 5565)*. (*Note*. For the valuation of such supplies, see *Westmorland Motorway Services Ltd*, 63.122 VALUATION.)

58.157   **Royalty agreement.**   A company carried on the business of supplying milk and other grocery products from two depots. It agreed to transfer the operation of one of the depots to a franchisee in return for a royalty of one penny per pint on all milk sold from that depot. The company did not account for tax on payments received under that agreement, and the Commissioners issued an assessment charging tax on such receipts. The company appealed, contending that the receipts should not be subject to VAT since they were, in effect, for the sale of milk, which was zero-rated. The tribunal dismissed the appeal, holding that tax was chargeable on the royalties by virtue of what is now *VAT Regulations 1995 (SI 1995 No 2518), reg 91. Ron Miller Ltd, LON/90/1191Z (VTD 5827)*. (*Note*. For another issue in this case, see 34.102 INPUT TAX.)

58.158   **Bank dealing in foreign currency bank notes—whether a supply.**   The
London branch of a United States bank dealt in bank notes in 150 currencies. It had
no retail branches, dealing entirely with other banks and with travel agents. It was
registered for VAT and had been accepted as partly exempt. However, in 1992 the
Commissioners formed the opinion that the bank's supplies of notes did not
constitute the making of supplies for consideration (with the result that the bank
would no longer be entitled to use the partial exemption special method which had
previously been agreed, and would have to restrict its input tax claims). The bank
appealed, contending that the supplies of notes were made for profit and were
therefore supplies of services for consideration. The tribunal allowed the bank's
appeal. The provision of bank notes in one currency, in return for an undertaking to
pay in another currency, was a supply for consideration. The transactions fell within
Article 13B(d)(4) of the *EC Sixth Directive. Republic National Bank of New York,
[1992] VATTR 299 (VTD 7894).*

58.159   **Foreign exchange transactions not involving physical supplies of
banknotes.**   See *C & E Commrs v First National Bank of Chicago*, 21.53 EUROPEAN
COMMUNITY LAW.

58.160   **Transfer of rights under hire-purchase agreement.**   In 1991 a trader acquired
a van under a hire-purchase agreement. In 1992 he disposed of the van to a company.
The company agreed to pay the amounts outstanding under the hire-purchase
agreement. The trader did not account for output tax on the disposal, and the
Commissioners issued an assessment, against which he appealed. The tribunal
dismissed his appeal. As indicated in *Notice 700/5/85*, the transfer of rights under a
hire-purchase agreement was a standard-rated supply of services, and the
consideration for the supply was the amount outstanding under the hire-purchase
agreement. *ME Noble, MAN/93/1294 (VTD 12346).*

58.161   **Competitions under contract expressed not to be legally binding.**   A
company organised a number of 'spot-the-ball' competitions. It accounted for VAT
on the full amount of entry fees, but subsequently submitted a repayment claim on
the basis that it should have deducted the amounts which it paid out in prizes,
applying   the   principles   in   *HJ   Glawe   Spiel   und   Unterhaltungsgeräte
Aufstellungsgesellschaft mbH & Co KG v Finanzamt Hamburg-Barmbek-Uhlenhorst,*
21.133 EUROPEAN COMMUNITY LAW. The Commissioners rejected the claim and the
company appealed. The tribunal rejected the company's primary contention (see
63.124 VALUATION), but directed that the case should be referred to the CJEC to
consider an alternative contention that, applying the CJEC decision in *Tolsma v
Inspecteur der Omzetbelasting Leeuwarden*, 21.51 EUROPEAN COMMUNITY LAW, the
competitions should be deemed not to be taxable supplies since they were not
governed by a legally binding contract (with the effect that the company would only
be required to account for tax on its supplies of prizes). Both sides appealed to the
QB, which held that both questions should be referred to the CJEC. Carnwath J
observed that the CJEC had stated in *Tolsma* that there had to be a 'legal relationship'
between the provider of a service and the recipient. The precise meaning of that
expression had not been clarified by any subsequent CJEC decision. *Town & County
Factors Ltd v C & E Commrs (and cross-appeal), QB [1998] STC 225.*

58.162   **Assignment of right to share in proceeds of litigation—whether a supply of
services.**   A property company (P) had acquired an option to purchase a piece of
land. The owners of the land decided to sell the land to a third party, and agreed to
pay P £3,100,000 for forgoing its option. However, the landowners' solicitors missed
the completion date and the deal collapsed. Because of a fall in property prices, the
land had to be sold at a lower price than had originally been agreed. P only received
£1,900,000 for its option and began legal proceedings against the landowners'

solicitors. The litigation was protracted and P entered into an agreement with an associated company (J) whereby, in return for financial support, it assigned J a right to share in the proceeds of the litigation. Subsequently P applied to register for VAT. The Commissioners rejected the application on the basis that P was not making any taxable supplies. The tribunal allowed P's appeal, holding that the assignment of a right to share in the proceeds of litigation was a taxable supply of services and the payments which P was receiving from J were consideration for that supply, so that P was entitled to register. *22A Property Investments Ltd, MAN/96/264 (VTD 14544)*. (*Note.* The tribunal also upheld the Commissioners' ruling that P was not entitled to make a late election to waive exemption in respect of its disposal of its option.)

58.163   **Charge for abortive visit—whether consideration for a supply of services.**   A telecommunications company (BT) arranged for visits by engineers to rectify faults reported by customers. The visits were arranged at times agreed with the customers. Where the engineer was unable to gain access to the premises at the agreed time, BT levied an 'abortive visit charge'. It did not account for output tax on these charges. The Commissioners issued an assessment charging tax on the basis that the charges represented consideration for taxable supplies of services. BT appealed, contending that the charges should be treated as 'liquidated damages' and as outside the scope of VAT. The tribunal rejected this contention and dismissed the appeal, holding that BT was providing a 'fault repair service ... from the time the fault is reported until it has been corrected'. *Bass plc*, 58.76 above, applied. *British Telecommunications plc, LON/94/5730 (VTD 14830)*.

58.164   **Parking charges—whether a supply of services.**   A company imposed parking charges on certain sites which it administered, including penalties for 'excess or improper parking'. The Commissioners issued an assessment charging output tax on such charges, and the tribunal dismissed the company's appeal. *Town & City Parking Ltd, EDN/96/142 (VTD 15730)*.

58.165   **Takings stolen—whether a supply.**   See *Benton*, 58.289 below, and the cases noted at 58.290 below.

58.166   **Fees for arranging Ministry of Transport vehicle test—whether chargeable to VAT.**   See *Ward*, 9.125 CARS.

58.167   **Statutory repair work carried on by City Council—whether any supply by Council.**   See *Glasgow City Council*, 40.10 LOCAL AUTHORITIES AND STATUTORY BODIES.

58.168   **Tenant of bomb-damaged building arranging for repairs—landlord making contribution to cost—whether a supply of services by tenant to landlord.**   See *Commercial Union Assurance Co plc*, 34.49 INPUT TAX.

58.169   **Payments from parent company to subsidiary company—whether consideration for supplies of services.**   See *Tilling Management Services Ltd*, 41.1 MANAGEMENT SERVICES.

58.170   **Tourist board—whether making supplies to overseas State.**   See *Netherlands Board of Tourism*, 34.396 INPUT TAX , and *Austrian National Tourist Office*, 34.397 INPUT TAX.

Cases held not to constitute a supply

58.171   **Cartage by fisherman—whether a supply.**   A fisherman owned two fishing boats operating from Harwich, manned by him and three relatives. He took one-third of the net proceeds of the catch and his relatives shared the remainder. He was registered for VAT but his relatives were not. He carried most of the catch in his own van to Lowestoft to be sold there at auction. The Lowestoft auctioneers prepared for him a document showing the gross proceeds of the catch, their commission, and an amount for 'cartage' to be retained by him before sharing the net proceeds with his relatives. The Commissioners issued an assessment charging VAT on the cartage but the tribunal allowed his appeal, holding that the cartage was not a taxable supply. *FVE Good, [1974] VATTR 256 (VTD 119).*

58.172   Examination fees received by tutor from part-time employment.   A former teacher began self-employment as a tutor and registered for VAT. While a teacher, she had held a part-time employment as an examiner. She continued this work after beginning self-employment, but did not account for VAT on her examiner's salary. The Commissioners issued an assessment charging tax on the salary, but the tribunal allowed her appeal, holding that the salary was not connected with her profession as a tutor and was outside the scope of VAT. *ME Holland, [1978] VATTR 108 (VTD 580).*

58.173   Sole trader negotiating agreements with manufacturers—whether making supply to manufacturers.   A sole trader operated a bulk purchasing organisation for electrical wholesalers, who paid him a membership fee plus quarterly subscriptions. He negotiated agreements with electrical manufacturers whereby they paid him rebates calculated by reference to the volume of sales made to his subscribers. The Commissioners issued an assessment on the basis that he was making a supply to the manufacturers and that the rebates which he received constituted consideration for this supply. He appealed, contending that he was not making any supply to the manufacturers, and that the rebates belonged to his subscribers. The tribunal accepted this contention and allowed his appeal, holding that there was 'a direct link between the rebate ... received by the member and the supplies to the member of goods by the manufacturer'. Accordingly, the rebates were 'contingent rebates in respect of the sales of goods by the manufacturers to the members'. *Landmark Cash & Carry Group Ltd,* 58.148 above, was distinguished on the basis that in that case 'any link was broken by the particular role of that company, a separate legal entity'. *M Morris (t/a Reward), LON/99/796 (VTD 16846).*

58.174   Optional service charges—whether a supply.   See *NDP Co Ltd,* 63.91 VALUATION.

58.175   Musician performing on public highway—whether supplying services for consideration.   See *Tolsma v Inspecteur der Omzetbelasting Leeuwarden,* 21.51 EUROPEAN COMMUNITY LAW.

58.176   Local authority providing grants to charity—whether such grants constitute consideration for supplies.   See *Trustees of the Bowthorpe Community Trust,* 40.9 LOCAL AUTHORITIES AND STATUTORY BODIES.

58.177   Payments from parent company to subsidiary company—whether consideration for supplies of services.   See *London Regeneration Project Services Ltd,* 41.2 MANAGEMENT SERVICES, and *Glengate KG Properties Ltd,* 41.3 MANAGEMENT SERVICES.

58.178   Invoices issued by parent company to subsidiary company—whether any supply of management services.   See *The Withies Inn Ltd,* 41.8 MANAGEMENT SERVICES.

58.179   Tourist board—whether making supplies to overseas State.   See *TurespaÒa,* 34.398 INPUT TAX.

BY WHOM THE SUPPLY WAS MADE

Driving tuition

58.180   **Driving school—whether tuition supplied by school or instructors.**   A company carried on business as a school of motoring. It had on its books a number of instructors, and provided for each of them a dual-control car for which it paid the insurance, car tax and repairs. The instructors paid for petrol, oil and cleaning. The fees for the lessons were collected by the instructors and shared between the company and the instructor, the scale of fees being fixed at meetings between the instructors and a representative of the company. Until March 1977 these arrangements were not committed to writing, but thereafter each instructor was required to sign a document headed 'Conditions of Employment' providing, *inter alia*, for 'commission' to be paid to the instructors and including the statement: 'you are self-employed therefore it is your responsibility to pay your tax and stamp your card'. The instructors were accepted as self-employed for income tax and national insurance purposes. The tribunal held on the evidence that until March 1977 the instructors provided the tuition as independent contractors, but that thereafter they were employees of the company, giving the tuition on behalf of the company which was therefore liable to account for VAT on the full amount of the tuition fees. *New Way School of Motoring Ltd, [1979] VATTR 57 (VTD 724).*

58.181   *New Way School of Motoring Ltd*, 58.180 above, was applied in a subsequent case in which the tribunal held that driving tuition was supplied by a partnership which operated a driving school, rather than by the instructors as individuals. *JW & MW Chalmers, LON/82/84 (VTD 1354).*

58.182   Similar decisions were reached in *JS Phillips Ltd, EDN/86/52 (VTD 2359); DJ Whitley, LON/87/106 (VTD 2435)* and *TDA (School) Ltd, LON/89/982 (VTD 4900).*

58.183   A trader (R) was the sole proprietor of four driving schools in different cities, and was the controlling director of a company which also owned a driving school. Instructors at the five schools were employed under franchise agreements, by which they were to pay the schools an agreed weekly fee and keep any remaining fees for themselves. However, in practice, the instructors paid the whole of their receipts to the schools, which then returned some of the receipts to the instructors. The Commissioners issued assessments on the basis that the driving tuition at the schools was provided by the schools. R and the company appealed, contending that the tuition was provided by the instructors rather than by the schools. The tribunal dismissed the appeals, holding on the evidence that pupils contracted for their tuition with the schools and not with individual instructors. The instructors were agents of the schools, and it was the schools which provided the tuition. *E Reeds, MAN/84/270 & MAN/86/105; Reeds School of Motoring (Nottingham) Ltd, MAN/86/103 (VTD 4578).*

58.184   The decisions in *Reeds* and *Reeds School of Motoring (Nottingham) Ltd*, 58.183 above, were not followed in a subsequent case involving an associated company which provided driving tuition in a different area. Payments were made to a third company in the same ownership, rather than to the individual instructors. The tribunal chairman (Mr. Simpson, sitting alone) held on the evidence that the instructors were making supplies of driving tuition as independent principals. The company's role was 'to provide a supporting organisation by which the instructors were provided with the means to give tuition'. The chairman observed that 'the tight control which the appellant maintained over the instructor ... which in earlier days might have been argued to suggest that the instructor's business was really the appellant's, is nowadays a common characteristic of franchise agreements, where the franchisor does not carry on the business in question ... but instead licenses another to do so under a name and method of operation which are, or are intended to be, distinctive and well-known'. The third company 'was a mere depositary, notwithstanding that it was controlled by (the same directors) and that it acted on the instructions of the appellant'. *Reeds School of Motoring (Sheffield) Ltd, MAN/92/85 (VTD 13404)*.

58.185   The proprietor of a driving school appealed against a decision that he should be registered for VAT, contending that the driving tuition was provided by the individual instructors and that he was not liable to account for VAT on takings retained by the instructors. The tribunal dismissed his appeal, applying *New Way School of Motoring Ltd*, 58.180 above. The proprietor owned the cars, all of which bore the name of the driving school. Although the instructors were independent contractors, they were supplying the services of tuition on behalf of the school proprietor. The QB upheld this decision. On the evidence, the tribunal had been justified in reaching the conclusion that the tuition was supplied by the proprietor. *J Cronin (t/a Cronin's Driving School) v C & E Commrs, QB [1991] STC 333*.

58.186   A married couple carried on a driving school in partnership. They granted franchises to a number of drivers, under which the drivers were treated as self-employed subcontractors. The instructors collected fees from pupils and paid the couple agreed amounts each week. The Commissioners issued an assessment on the basis that the couple should account for tax on the amounts retained by the instructors, considering that the driving tuition was supplied by the school rather than by the individual instructors. The couple appealed, contending that the tuition was supplied by the individual instructors. The tribunal allowed the appeal, holding that the drivers 'were genuinely in business on their own account and that they were making a supply of tuition services to the pupils'. *Cronin*, 58.185 above, and *Niven*, 63.81 VALUATION, distinguished. *Mr & Mrs ABC McIver (t/a Alan's School of Motoring), EDN/90/28 (VTD 5315)*. (*Note*. The decision does not refer to *New Way School of Motoring*, 58.180 above, or to any of the cases noted at 58.181 to 58.183 above.)

58.187   A partnership operated a driving school which provided facilities for driving instructors in return for weekly payments. The facilities consisted of a booking office, staffed by a receptionist; a waiting room for pupils; and advertising. The fees charged for driving tuition were fixed by the individual instructors, rather than by the school, and were paid to the instructors, rather than to the school. The Commissioners accepted that the instructors who used the school's facilities were self-employed, but issued an assessment on the school on the basis that the driving tuition provided by the instructors was supplied by the school. The partnership appealed, contending that the tuition was supplied by the instructors as principals. The tribunal allowed the appeal, distinguishing *Cronin*, 58.185 above, and applying *MacIver*, 58.186 above. On the evidence, there was 'no element of control or direction' and each instructor remained free 'to run his own business as he chose, while nevertheless making use of the communal facilities provided by the appellant'. *Fleet School of Motoring, MAN/90/1064 (VTD 7299)*.

58.188   Three driving schools, operated by members of the same family, failed to account for VAT on the full amounts charged to customers. The Commissioners issued assessments charging tax on the full amounts paid, and the schools appealed, contending that the driving instructors who worked for them were independent principals, so that they were not liable to account for tax on the amounts retained by the instructors. (The instructors were accepted as self-employed, but the cars which they used were owned or leased by the driving schools, and the driving schools arranged for the insurance of the cars.) The tribunal dismissed the appeals, observing that 'the extent of the control exercised by the appellant over its instructors was considerable, and not indicative of the instructors being able to conduct their instruction of pupils as they themselves would have done so left to their own devices'. On the evidence, the instructors were supplying their services as agents of the driving schools, so that the driving schools were required to account for tax on the full amounts which customers paid. *Cronin*, 58.185 above, applied. *ADI School of Motoring, MAN/93/7; ADI Driving School 'A', MAN/93/8; ADI Driving School, MAN/93/9 (VTD 11469).*

Taxi and minicab drivers

58.189   **'Dial-a-taxi' agency—whether supplies to accounts customers made by driver or by agency.**   A firm carried on a 'dial-a-taxi' agency for a number of mini-cab drivers. The drivers owned their vehicles and maintained them and provided the petrol for them. The firm advertised and generally organised the service which involved two-way radio communication between the firm and the drivers, the firm providing the radio installation. It received a fixed weekly amount from each driver who otherwise retained the full fares from customers. In accordance with their normal practice, the Commissioners accepted that the firm and the driver were agent and principal respectively and that, as the gross takings of the drivers were below the threshold limits of *Sch 1*, VAT was not chargeable on fares paid to the drivers in cash. However certain customers could, by arrangement with the firm, become 'accounts customers', and pay their fares monthly. The Commissioners issued an assessment charging tax on the amounts invoiced to the 'accounts customers', but the tribunal allowed the firm's appeal, holding on the evidence that the cash customers and the accounts customers were not distinguishable. *Triumph & Albany Car Service, LON/80/115 (VTD 977, 1004).*

58.190   The decision in *Triumph & Albany Car Service*, 58.189 above, was not followed in a subsequent case in which the tribunal upheld an assessment charging tax on the amounts invoiced to 'accounts customers'. The tribunal observed that the proprietor of the business set the fares for accounts work, allowed discounts to accounts customers, and insisted on drivers reporting for work by 6.00am if they wished to undertake accounts work. Accordingly, the tribunal held that 'the supply of services to an account customer is made by the appellant using the services of the self-employed drivers'. On the evidence, although the proprietor was acting as an agent of the drivers in respect of cash work, he was acting as an independent principal in respect of accounts work. *Dicta* of Woolf J in *Johnson*, 1.1 AGENTS, applied; *Carless*, 58.191 below, distinguished. *A Hussain (t/a Crossleys Private Hire Cars), MAN/ 99/20 (VTD 16194).*

58.191   A trader (C) was the proprietor of a taxi and private car hire business, and also ran a local removal and delivery service. He had two employees who acted as drivers, and also subcontracted work to a number of self-employed drivers who paid him a percentage of their takings. Some of these drivers used their own cars, while others used cars provided by C. Some customers paid in cash but others were allowed credit accounts. A VAT officer examining C's records discovered that there were a number of contra entries relating to money passing between C and the self-employed drivers, and formed the opinion that C had failed to account for VAT on some of the money credited to him from the drivers in respect of these transactions. He issued an assessment on the basis that, where credit customers were allocated to drivers who were not C's employees, C was dealing with such customers as an agent of the drivers, and was making supplies to the drivers and was liable to account for VAT on the amounts credited to him. C appealed, contending that he made all the relevant supplies to the credit customers, that his transactions with the drivers should be treated as not giving rise to any VAT liability, and that he had accounted for VAT on the correct basis. The tribunal upheld the assessment, holding that C was acting as an agent for the self-employed drivers for both cash and account customers, and finding that he 'had incorrectly dealt with the income and expenditure relating to the credit customers'. The QB upheld the tribunal decision as one of fact. *Cronin*, 58.185 above, distinguished. *FG Carless v C & E Commrs, QB [1993] STC 632.*

58.192   See also *Blanks*, 63.105 VALUATION, and *A2B Radio Cars*, 63.106 VALUATION.

58.193   **Taxi hired to driver who provides transport on behalf of owner.**   A trader (M) owned a number of taxi-cabs which he hired at fixed weekly rates to independent self-employed drivers. A term of the hire was that, if called on, the driver was to do work under long-term contracts between M and an education authority and British Rail respectively. The driver doing this work was not paid in cash but was given a signed voucher for the amount of the hire. The driver sent these vouchers to M weekly with an amount of cash which, with the amounts on the vouchers, would make up his weekly hire payment. M invoiced the authority and BR monthly for the amounts on the vouchers with an addition for VAT. Hence over a period M received from the drivers cash and vouchers, which together equalled the hire payments for the taxi. In accounting for VAT he treated his output tax as one-eleventh of the cash plus one-tenth of the amount of the vouchers (the VAT rate at the relevant time being 10%). The Commissioners issued assessments in which the output tax was taken as one-eleventh of the aggregate of the cash and the vouchers, plus one-tenth of the amount of the vouchers. M appealed, contending that he had been doubly charged on the amount of the vouchers. The tribunal dismissed the appeal, holding that there had been two separate supplies, one the hire of the taxis to the drivers and the other the supply of transport to the authority and BR. *E Mann (t/a Black & Gold Taxis), LEE/75/70 (VTD 204).*

58.194   A partnership operated taxis, which it hired to drivers on the basis that the drivers could retain 30% of their fares and had to pay 70% of the fares to the partnership. The partnership only accounted for tax on the 70% of the fares which it received from the drivers. The Commissioners issued an assessment on the basis that the partnership should have accounted for VAT on the full amount of the fares charged to customers. The partnership appealed, contending that the drivers were independent principals who were providing services to customers on their own account. The tribunal rejected this contention and dismissed the appeal, holding that the drivers were acting as agents of the partnership. *Cronin*, 58.185 above, applied; *Music & Video Exchange*, 1.7 AGENTS, distinguished. *Hamiltax, LON/91/1420X (VTD 8948).*

58.195   A similar decision was reached in a subsequent case in which *Triumph & Albany Car Service*, 58.189 above, was distinguished. *J Knowles (t/a Rainbow Taxis), MAN/95/ 948 (VTD 13913).*

58.196   *Hamiltax*, 58.194 above, and *Knowles*, 58.195 above, were applied in a similar subsequent case in which *Camberwell Cars Ltd*, 58.200 below, was distinguished. The tribunal held on the evidence that the drivers were acting as agents of the proprietor, who was 'the principal in all transactions involved in his business whether account or cash'. *R Snaith (t/a English Rose Collection), LON/00/428 (VTD 16997).*

58.197   Similar decisions were reached in *JARS, MAN/94/337 (VTD 13451)* and *Japan Executive Chauffeur*, 49.281 PENALTIES: MISDECLARATION.

58.198   **Taxi company—whether director acting as principal.**   The director of a taxi company owned a taxi which he drove himself. The Commissioners issued an assessment on the basis that the company was liable to account for tax on the hire of this taxi. The company appealed, contending that the director supplied his services as a principal and not as an agent of the company. The tribunal allowed the appeal on the grounds that the taxi in question was owned by the director and not by the company. (The company was, however, held to be liable for tax in cases where the director drove a taxi which the company owned.) *Jivelynn Ltd, LON/80/430 (VTD 1092).*

58.199   **Partnership operating taxi and car hire business—whether partner supplying services on behalf of firm or as individual.**   A couple operated a taxi and car hire business as a partnership. The partnership owned several taxis at the relevant time, and also used the services of a number of drivers who owned their own vehicles. The Commissioners discovered that the partnership had failed to account for VAT on the takings in respect of two cars which the partners owned, and issued an assessment charging tax on them. The partnership appealed, contending that the supplies in question had been made by the partners as individuals, rather than by the partnership. The tribunal allowed the appeal, holding on the evidence that the partners were making supplies to their customers as independent principals and that the partnership was not liable to account for tax on the takings in question. *Triumph & Albany Car Service*, 58.189 above, and *MacHenrys*, 58.211 below, applied; *Hamiltax*, 58.194 above, distinguished. *GA & AE Kearns (t/a Victoria Cars), MAN/93/337 (VTD 11655).*

58.200   **Minicab company with accounts customers and cash customers—whether supplies to cash customers made by company or by drivers as individuals.**   A company operated a minicab business, using the services of drivers who owned their own cars. The company had a considerable number of accounts customers, and encouraged its drivers to undertake such work. The company accounted for VAT in respect of fares from accounts customers. However, the company did not account for VAT in cases where the drivers accepted fares from casual customers who paid cash. The Commissioners issued an assessment charging tax on such supplies, and the company appealed, contending that in such cases the relevant supply was made by the driver as an individual and not by the company. The tribunal allowed the appeal, holding on the evidence that there was 'a real distinction between the conduct of the account work and the cash work', and that the company accepted telephone enquiries from casual cash-paying customers 'on behalf of the drivers and not in furtherance of its own business'. *Hamiltax*, 58.194 above, distinguished. *Camberwell Cars Ltd, LON/92/2167A (VTD 10178). (Note.* The decision here was distinguished in the subsequent case of *Snaith*, 58.196 above, where the drivers used cars belonging to the business proprietor.)

58.201   **Taxi driver—whether an employee.**   A taxi driver appealed against assessments on his takings, contending that he should be treated as an employee. The tribunal rejected this contention and dismissed his appeal, holding that he was self-employed and was making taxable supplies of his services. *RJ Newall, LON/95/2715 (VTD 14109).*

58.202   **Taxibus service—vehicles owned by drivers—whether drivers acting as agents or principals.**   A garage proprietor obtained a licence to operate a 'taxibus' service using minibuses. He purchased a number of minibuses, which he sold to the drivers who worked for him. All the minibuses were painted in a standard livery. The drivers paid him a fixed fee of £45 per week. He only accounted for output tax on the amounts paid to him by the drivers, and did not account for tax on the amounts which the drivers retained. The Commissioners issued an assessment on the basis that the drivers were acting as his agents, and he appealed, contending that the drivers were independent principals. The tribunal dismissed his appeal, holding that 'the service must be regarded as a single enterprise'. The chairman observed that 'it is possible to operate a taxi service ... as an individual. It is not, in my judgment, possible to operate a bus service of the scale of that described to me in that fashion. No one driver alone could conceivably provide the frequency of service which is offered.

The timetables make it abundantly clear that the drivers are working as a group and not as individuals'. The proprietor appealed to the QB, which upheld the tribunal decision as one of fact. *RD Clark v C & E Commrs, QB 1995, [1996] STC 263.*

Hairdressing

Supplies held to be made by salon proprietor

58.203 A company which owned a hairdressing salon entered into a franchise agreement with three hairstylists who worked at the salon, whereby the franchisees were to be entitled to retain their individual takings but were to pay the company amounts in respect of rent, reception charges, bookkeeping charges, secretarial charges and franchise fees. The takings were entered in the salon till under a code number identifying the stylist to whom they belonged, and were paid to the stylists by the company accountant after deducting the sums due to him and to the salon under the franchise agreement. The Commissioners took the view that the supplies at the salon were still being made by the company, and issued a notice of compulsory registration, against which the company appealed. The CS upheld the notice. In such cases, it was necessary to look at the substance of what had been established, rather than at matters of form. On the evidence, there was only one business being carried on at the salon. The stylists did not act 'in ways that independent contractors would be expected to act in, for example, in advertising their business or otherwise acting independently'. Whether the stylists acted under contracts of service or contracts for services was not conclusive. The services provided by the stylists were made by the company and formed part of its turnover. *C & E Commrs v Jane Montgomery (Hair Stylists) Ltd, CS 1993, [1994] STC 256.*

58.204 The Commissioners issued assessments on two hairdressing partnerships and an associated company, on the basis that tax had not been accounted for in respect of supplies made by hairstylists employed at salons which they operated. The partnerships and the company appealed against the assessments, contending that the hairstylists were independent contractors supplying their services directly to customers. The tribunal dismissed the appeal, following the principles laid down in *New Way School of Motoring Ltd*, 58.180 above, and holding that the stylists were engaged under contracts of service rather than under contracts for service. The proprietors of the salons provided the materials and equipment, and set the fees to be charged by the stylists. The stylists took no financial risks and had no responsibility for management. *Francis John, EDN/85/78; Francis John Hair Studio, EDN/85/79; Francis John (Saltcoats) Ltd, EDN/85/80 (VTD 3447).*

58.205 The proprietors of two associated hairdressing salons engaged hairstylists on the basis that the stylists could retain 40% of their takings, and that the salon proprietors would keep the other 60%. The salon proprietors did not account for VAT on the amounts which were retained by stylists working at the salons, and the Commissioners issued assessments on the basis that the supplies to customers were made by the salon proprietors, who should account for VAT on the full amount of the takings. The tribunal upheld the assessments and dismissed the proprietors' appeals. *Headline, LON/88/1392Z; Just Hair, LON/88/1291Y (VTD 4089).*

58.206 *Headline*, 58.205 above, was applied in a subsequent case in which the tribunal distinguished *Ashmore*, 58.213 below, and held that hairdressing services at a salon were supplied by the salon proprietor, regardless of whether the hairstylists were employees or self-employed. As in *Headline*, the salon proprietor received 60% of the gross takings, the stylist retaining 40%. There was a standard price list at the salon, although stylists could charge more than the amount shown in the list if this was agreed with the customer. The tribunal noted that the salon appeared 'physically to be a single business; one well-ordered room with seven chairs or places, nothing differentiating the employee chairs from the self-employed chairs'. *ME Hosmer, LON/89/1851 (VTD 7313)*. (*Note*. For another issue in this case, see 39.61 LAND.)

58.207   In another case involving hairstylists working at a salon, the tribunal held that the stylists were self-employed but that they were supplying their services to the salon proprietor rather than directly to the customers. Each stylist paid 55% of his or her gross takings to the proprietor, and the stylists did not have the right to a specific chair. Cheques and credit cards were made out to the salon, rather than to the stylist. On the evidence, customers at the salon were entering into contracts with the salon proprietor, rather than with the stylists. *Dicta* in *Cronin*, 58.185 above, applied. *LC Ong, LON/91/1395 (VTD 7460)*.

58.208   A similar decision was reached in another case involving hairstylists working at a salon, where the salon proprietor retained 60% of the gross takings. The stylists were treated as self-employed by the Inland Revenue. The tribunal held that 'the arrangements for the collection of the money paid by customers and the fixing of prices by (the salon proprietor) indicate that the customers contracted with (the proprietor) and not with the individual hairstylist'. *Dicta* in *Cronin*, 58.185 above, applied. *DL Freer, LON/91/1069Y (VTD 7648)*. (*Note*. For another issue in this case, see 49.251 PENALTIES: MISDECLARATION.)

58.209   The proprietor of a hairdressing salon failed to account for tax on the takings at the salon. The Commissioners issued assessments charging output tax and she appealed, contending that the stylists working at the salon were independent contractors who were supplying their services directly to the customers. The tribunal rejected this contention and dismissed the appeals, holding on the evidence that the stylists were not 'the prime functionaries' at the salon. The fact that the stylists were accepted as being self-employed, rather than employees, was not conclusive. *Jane Montgomery (Hair Stylists) Ltd*, 58.203 above, applied. *LJB Clarke (t/a Snips & Snips Hair & Beauty Salon), EDN/95/293 & 295 (VTD 14227)*.

58.210   Similar decisions were reached in *Harrison*, 48.32 PENALTIES: FAILURE TO NOTIFY; *Hopkins (t/a Marianne's Hair Salon)*, 48.63 PENALTIES: FAILURE TO NOTIFY; *S Taylor (Machine Tools) Ltd*, 49.280 PENALTIES: MISDECLARATION, and *Colby*, 53.154 REGISTRATION.

Supplies held to be made by hairstylists as independent contractors

58.211   A partnership and an associated company operated hairdressing salons. For some time they had treated the hairstylists working for them as employees, and had accounted for tax on the full amount of the takings at the salons. Subsequently they began to treat their senior stylists as self-employed, and ceased to account for VAT on the takings retained by the stylists. The stylists received no salary or wages from the proprietors, and were required to insure against liability to the public. They were accepted as self-employed by the Inland Revenue. The Commissioners issued assessments on the basis that the proprietors should continue to account for VAT on the full amount of the takings. The tribunal allowed the salon proprietors' appeals, applying *dicta* in *New Way School of Motoring Ltd*, 58.180 above, and holding that 'according to the weight which we give to each factor, the position is more consistent with the performance by the senior stylists of their hairdressing treatments being carried out under contracts for services rather than contracts of service'. The QB upheld this decision as one of fact. Having found that the stylists were self-employed, the tribunal was entitled to hold, on the evidence, that they supplied their services directly to the public. *C & E Commrs v MacHenrys (Hairdressers) Ltd & MacHenrys, QB 1992, [1993] STC 170*. (*Note*. It was agreed that payments by the stylists to the salon proprietors, for the use of chairs in the salon, were exempt from VAT through being for licences to occupy land, following *dicta* in *Niven*, 63.81 VALUATION. Compare the cases noted at 39.55 to 39.63 LAND.)

58.212   A similar decision was reached in another case where hairstylists working at a salon were accepted as self-employed by the Inland Revenue and the DSS. They received no holiday or sick pay, and their contracts were liable to be terminated at short notice, without compensation for unfair dismissal. The tribunal held that the relevant supplies were made by the stylists, rather than by the salon proprietors. On the evidence, the proprietors provided 'co-ordination rather than control'. *Dicta* of Lord Denning in *Massey v Crown Life Insurance Co, CA [1978] 1 WLR 676; [1978] 2 All ER 576*, applied; *Francis John*, 58.204 above, and *Headline*, 58.205 above, distinguished. *Mr & Mrs Giles, LON/90/509Z (VTD 5449)*. (*Note*. Compare the subsequent cases noted at 58.206 to 58.209 above, in all of which it was held that the fact that stylists were self-employed was not conclusive for VAT purposes, and that the salon proprietor was obliged to account for VAT in respect of services provided by self-employed stylists.)

58.213   In another case involving hairstylists working at a salon, the tribunal held that the stylists were self-employed and were supplying their services as principals, rather than as agents of the salon proprietor. The stylists, who paid 57% of their takings to the proprietor, had to obtain clients through their efforts, since clients were not introduced to them by the proprietor. The tribunal therefore allowed the proprietor's appeal against an assessment charging tax on the full amount of the stylists' takings. *P Ashmore, LON/90/252Y (VTD 6910)*. (*Note*. See the note following *Giles*, 58.212 above.)

58.214   The QB decision in *MacHenrys*, 58.211 above, was applied in a similar subsequent case in which self-employed stylists retained 40% of their gross takings, paying the remaining 60% to the salon proprietor. *Hosmer*, 58.206 above, and *Ong*, 58.207 above, were distinguished. The tribunal held that the fact that the stylists were self-employed was not conclusive, but that, on the evidence, the self-employed stylists were 'in a position to render to the customer the entire supply which that customer received'. The stylists were supplying their services to the customers, rather than to the salon proprietor. It followed that the salon proprietor was only liable to account for tax on the amounts which he received from the stylists, and was not liable to account for tax on the amounts which the stylists retained. *JA Wragg (t/a Take 5 Hair Design), MAN/91/398 (VTD 10574)*.

58.215   A similar decision, also applying *MacHenrys*, 58.211 above, was reached in a similar subsequent case in which self-employed stylists retained 35% of their gross takings, paying the remaining 65% to the salon proprietors. *D & S Hooper (t/a Masterclass), LON/99/487 (VTD 16764)*.

58.216   The proprietor of a hairdressing salon applied for deregistration. The Commissioners rejected his application, on the grounds that the turnover of the salon was above the threshold for deregistration. The proprietor appealed, contending that the supplies to customers at the salon were made by the individual stylists, so that his turnover should be restricted to the amounts which he received from the stylists, rather than the full amounts paid by the customers. (The stylists, who were accepted as self-employed, paid the proprietor 57% of their gross takings.) The tribunal allowed the appeal, holding on the evidence that the stylists were supplying their services directly to the customers. *A Winder (t/a Anthony & Patricia), MAN/92/1653 (VTD 11784)*. (*Note*. For another issue in this case, see 39.64 LAND.)

58.217   A similar decision was reached in *P Sorisi, LON/97/808 (VTD 15453)*.

58.218   In 1995 a woman (L) took over a hairdressing business which had previously been operated by her husband. The premises included a ladies' salon, where three stylists worked, and a men's salon with one stylist (S). S kept 40% of his takings and paid 60% to L. The Commissioners issued a ruling that L was required to register for VAT from December 1996, on the basis that the whole of S's takings should be treated as part of her turnover. She appealed, contending that S was an independent contractor who supplied his services directly to his customers, and that the 40% which S retained did not form part of her turnover. The tribunal accepted this contention and allowed her appeal, observing that 'a gentlemen's hairdresser operates quite differently to a ladies' hairdressers'. *C Lyons (t/a Wayne Anthony's), MAN/99/338 (VTD 16791)*.

Supplies of accommodation

58.219   **Hotel expenses of visiting teams met by Football Association—whether accommodation supplied to teams by hotels or by Association.**   The Football Association organised a competition for national youth teams in accordance with regulations laid down by the Union of European Football Associations, of which it was a member. These regulations required the Association to provide accommodation for the participating teams. The Association arranged and paid for such accommodation in suitable hotels, and reclaimed the input tax thereon. The Commissioners assessed the Association on the basis that it had supplied the accommodation to the visiting teams and should account for output tax on the accommodation. The Association appealed, contending that it had not made any supply. The tribunal allowed the appeal, holding that, although the Association had paid for the accommodation, it had not made any supply of the accommodation. The supplies had been made by the hotels. The making of payment for a supply of goods or services, under an arrangement with a third party, did not constitute an onward supply of the goods or services in question. *Football Association Ltd, [1985] VATTR 106 (VTD 1860)*. (*Note.* For a preliminary issue in this case, see 2.131 APPEALS.)

58.220   **Accommodation supplied to students attending language school—whether accommodation supplied by school.**   A language school found accommodation for many of its students. The accommodation was provided by families who lived close to the school. The school paid the families, and charged the students, for the accommodation. The amounts it charged the students exceeded the amounts it paid the families. The Commissioners issued an assessment on the basis that the school should account for VAT on the full amount of the accommodation charges which it received from the students. The school appealed, contending that it should only account for VAT on the difference between the amounts it received from the students and the amounts it paid to the families with whom the students stayed, on the grounds that the accommodation was supplied by the families and the school was merely acting as the students' agent. The Commissioners contended that the school was acting as a principal rather than an agent. The tribunal dismissed the school's appeal, holding on the evidence that the school supplied the accommodation through the agency of the families. The school was therefore liable to account for VAT on the full amounts it charged to the students. *City College of Higher Education Ltd*, 58.277 below, distinguished. *Cicero Languages International, LON/89/272Y (VTD 4286)*.

58.221   **Hotel accommodation supplied for subcontractors—whether supplied by company.**   Two associated companies successively carried on the business of manufacturing, supplying and fitting new and replacement windows and entrance doors. The doors and windows were installed by self-employed subcontractors. The companies arranged and paid for hotel accommodation for the subcontractors when necessary. The companies reclaimed the tax on the accommodation as input tax and the Commissioners issued assessments to recover the tax, considering that the accommodation had been supplied by the companies to the subcontractors and that the companies were therefore obliged to account for output tax on the supply. The tribunal allowed the companies' appeals, holding that although there had been a supply by the hotel to the company, it did not follow that there had been a supply by the company to the subcontractors. The accommodation was not used for the subcontractors' own purposes, but was used solely in the course of their work. *Football Association Ltd*, 58.219 above, applied. *Ibstock Building Products Ltd*, 34.12 INPUT TAX, was distinguished on the grounds that the engineers in that case were engaged by the vendors rather than by the appellant. *Northern Lawn Tennis Club*, 34.14 INPUT TAX, was distinguished on the grounds that the tennis players competed in the tournaments in furtherance of their own careers, rather than simply on the club's business. *Stormseal (UPVC) Window Co Ltd; Probelook Ltd, [1989] VATTR 303 (VTD 4538).*

58.222   **Supply of accommodation to tennis players by club organising tournament.**   See *Northern Lawn Tennis Club*, 34.14 INPUT TAX.

58.223   **Supply of accommodation to employees of company providing services to appellant.**   See *Ibstock Building Products Ltd*, 34.12 INPUT TAX.

58.224   **Supply of accommodation to visiting lecturers.**   See *Institute of Purchasing and Supply*, 34.13 INPUT TAX.

58.225   **Holiday accommodation—whether supplied by married couple in partnership or by wife as individual.**   A married couple purchased a farm in 1988, and registered for VAT in 1989. The farm incorporated a cottage which they let as holiday accommodation. Their VAT returns for the periods up to February 1990 included the income from letting the cottage. However, they did not include such income on subsequent returns. When the Commissioners discovered this, they issued an assessment charging tax on this income, and the couple appealed, contending that, with effect from 1 March 1990, the cottage had been operated by the wife as a sole trader, and that since the income from the cottage was below the registration threshold, she was not required to account for VAT on the income. The tribunal accepted the couple's evidence and allowed the appeal. *A & K Hurst, EDN/92/252 (VTD 9756).*

Employees—whether making supplies as individuals or on behalf of employer

58.226   **Service washes at launderette—whether supplies made by company owning launderette or by attendants at launderette.**   A company owned a launderette, at which it employed part-time attendants. These attendants provided 'service washes' whereby they would process laundry left by customers. A notice on one of the launderette walls stated that the service washes were 'a private arrangement between customers and staff'. The company did not specify a set price for the service washes, which were a matter for negotiation between the attendants, and the customers, some attendants charging different rates. The attendants kept the difference between the amounts paid by customers and the amounts which they had to feed into the machines. The company did not account for VAT on the amounts retained by the attendants, and the Commissioners issued an assessment charging tax on these receipts. The company appealed, contending that the service washes were supplied by the attendants and not by the company. The tribunal accepted this contention and allowed the appeal, holding that the attendants were acting on their own account and not as agents of the company. *Ivychain Ltd, LON/89/1601Y (VTD 5627).*

58.227   **Nursing services—whether supplied by nursing agency or by nurses as individuals.**   A nursing agency operated a register of self-employed nurses, whom it introduced to clients. Clients paid the agency for the nurses' services, and the agency paid the nurses their fees weekly in arrear. The agency required the nurses to wear uniform and to obey certain rules of conduct (such as not wearing high-heeled shoes or nail varnish while on duty, and not smoking on duty). The Commissioners issued an assessment on the basis that the nurses were supplying their services to the agency, and that the agency was supplying those services to clients, and was obliged to account for VAT on the amounts paid by the clients. The agency appealed, contending that the nurses supplied their services directly to the clients, and that it was merely acting as an agent. The tribunal accepted this contention and allowed the appeal. *British Nursing Co-Operation Ltd*, 31.5 HEALTH AND WELFARE, applied. The contracts which the agency entered into clearly indicated that it was acting as an agent rather than as a principal, and nothing in the rules of conduct which the agency laid down was inconsistent with its position as an agent. *BUPA Nursing Services Ltd, MAN/92/92 (VTD 10010).*

58.228   *BUPA Nursing Services Ltd*, 58.227 above, was applied in the similar case of *South Hams Nursing Agency, LON/94/904A (VTD 13027).*

58.229   Compare the cases noted at 31.4 to 31.9 HEALTH AND WELFARE.

58.230   **Food supplied at licensed club—whether supplied by club or by steward.**   A licensed club employed a steward, who was required to work for 51 hours per week and was provided with accommodation. The steward was permitted to supply food to customers at the club, paying the club £5 per week for the use of the kitchen, and to keep all profits from sales of food. The club did not account for VAT on the sales of food. The Commissioners issued an assessment on the club charging tax on these supplies, and the club appealed, contending that the food was supplied by the steward as an individual, rather than by the club. The tribunal accepted this contention and allowed the appeal. On the evidence, the steward was supplying food to club members on his own account, rather than on behalf of the club. *MacHenrys*, 58.211 above, applied. *Beckenham Constitutional Club Ltd, LON/92/1037 (VTD 10041).*

58.231   **Consultancy services—whether supplied as individual or as director of company.**   An individual (P) did not register for VAT or account for VAT on consultancy fees which he received. The Commissioners issued an assessment on him charging tax on these supplies. He appealed, contending that some of the supplies had not been made by him as an individual but by a company of which he and his wife were directors, but that he had been dismissed from employment with that company in May 1989 and had made supplies as an individual after that date. The tribunal dismissed his appeal. The company had never declared P as an employee on any of its P35 returns, nor had it deducted any tax from payments made to him. He had paid Class 2 National Insurance contributions, and had issued invoices to the company for consultancy fees. He had therefore supplied the consultancy services in question as an individual, rather than as a director of the company. *R Preston, LON/90/174Z (VTD 5702).*

58.232   **Sale of commercial vehicle by company director—whether sold on behalf of company.**   The director of a company dealing in commercial vehicles bought a second-hand vehicle from a private individual and sold it at a profit. The Commissioners issued an assessment to the company charging tax on the sale. The company appealed, contending that the director had bought and sold the vehicle in a private capacity and had not been acting on behalf of the company. The tribunal accepted this contention and allowed the appeal. *Bedworth Commercials Ltd, MAN/91/164 (VTD 7585).*

58.233   **Sale of second-hand electrical goods by company director—whether sold on behalf of company.** A company dealt in specialised lighting. Because of the economic recession, its managing director had to reduce his income from the company. He began attending local auctions to buy cheap second-hand electrical goods, which he sold at a profit. As his income from such sales was below the VAT registration threshold, he did not account for VAT. The Commissioners formed the opinion that the director was acting on behalf of the company, and assessed the company on the income from these sales. The company appealed, contending that the director was acting as a private individual. The tribunal accepted this contention and allowed the appeal, holding on the evidence that the director had not made the sales in the course of the company's business, and observing that the sales were 'of a different class of goods which had been bought from a different class of supplier, made at a different time to a different class of customers in a different way'. *Mittu*, 58.61 above, distinguished. (The tribunal chairman also observed that the Commissioners could have issued a direction under what is now *VATA 1994, Sch 1 para 2*.) *Southern Counties Lighting Ltd, LON/93/564A (VTD 11438)*.

58.234   **Painting and decorating services—whether supplied by company or by director.** The Commissioners issued an assessment on a company which carried on a painting and decorating business. The company appealed, contending that the supplies in question had been made by its controlling director as an individual, rather than by the company. The tribunal rejected this contention and dismissed the appeal, holding on the evidence that 'the only real segregation was between work undertaken for customers who would not be concerned about paying VAT, and work for those who would. (The director's) keeping separate accounting records and preparing separate accounts were no more than an inevitable consequence of a device designed to enable the appellant to avoid charging VAT to certain of its customers. In reality, this was not a case of there being two businesses, but of two vehicles being used to carry on a single business.' *E Stringer (Paints) Ltd, MAN/99/79 (VTD 16319)*.

58.235   **Salesman—whether acting as individual or as employee of company.** In December 1987 an individual (S) entered into an agreement with a company (K) which sold kitchen units. The agreement specifically stated that S was self-employed, and that 'nothing in this agreement shall be construed as giving rise to the relationship of employer and employee'. S also undertook to pay all VAT due. In July 1988 S and K entered into a new agreement which was described as a contract of employment, and under which S's employment with K was deemed to have begun on 1 July 1988. S failed to account for VAT on the amounts paid to him by K, and the Commissioners issued an assessment charging tax on the amounts paid before 1 July 1988. S appealed, contending that, despite the specific wording of the 1987 agreement, he had in fact been an employee of K since January 1987. The tribunal rejected this contention and dismissed the appeal, finding that before 1 July 1988 S's 'relationship with K was that of an independent contractor'. *J Sullivan, MAN/90/94 (VTD 5881)*. (*Note.* An appeal against a penalty for failure to register was also dismissed.)

58.236   **Apprentice jockeys riding in races—whether riding as individuals or as employees of racehorse trainers.** A couple, who carried on business in partnership as racehorse trainers, arranged for apprentice and conditional jockeys, employed at their stables, to ride customers' horses in races. The Commissioners issued assessments charging output tax on the basis that the trainers were supplying the services of the apprentice and conditional jockeys to the owners of the racehorses, and should have accounted for tax accordingly. The trainers appealed, contending that, when riding in races, the apprentices should be treated as self-employed and as supplying their own services directly to the owners. The tribunal accepted this contention and allowed the appeal, but the QB remitted the case to a new tribunal for rehearing. Moses J held that it appeared that the tribunal had erred in the way in which it had analysed the relevant agreements, and had failed to have regard to the fact that apprentice and conditional jockeys were answerable to the partnership. Furthermore, the tribunal had erred in attaching weight to the fact that fully-fledged jockeys were self-employed. It did not follow that, because fully-fledged jockeys were self-employed, apprentice and conditional jockeys were also self-employed. *Edwards v Bairstow & Harrison, HL 1955, 36 TC 207 (TTC 2001, 4.148)*, applied. *C & E Commrs v RJ & AS Hodges, QB [2000] STC 262.*

58.237   **Computer engineer—whether acting as individual or employee.**   See *Scott*, 53.146 REGISTRATION.

58.238   **Engineer—whether acting as individual or director of company.**   See *Demack*, 53.162 REGISTRATION.

58.239   **Supplies of counterfeit audiocassettes—whether made as individual or employee.**   See *McGuckin*, 53.166 REGISTRATION.

Deemed supplies under Sch 4 para 7

58.240   **Sale of mortgaged aircraft.**   A company mortgaged an aircraft as security for a loan. The company defaulted on the loan, and the lender sold the aircraft. The Commissioners issued an assessment on the basis that the sale constituted a deemed supply by the company under *Sch 4 para 7*. The tribunal upheld the assessment and dismissed the company's appeal. *Aiseireigh Investments Ltd, LON/97/376 (VTD 15988).*

Miscellaneous

Cases where the appellant was unsuccessful

58.241   **Stock car racing—whether provided by promoter or by stadium owner.**   A company (P) promoted stock car race meetings at a stadium owned by another company. The arrangement between the two companies was complex. The Commissioners assessed P on the basis that it was liable to account for VAT on gate receipts and car park receipts at the meetings. P appealed, contending that, since part of the receipts in question were paid to the stadium owner, it should only be liable to account for VAT on the share of the receipts which it retained. The tribunal rejected this contention and dismissed the appeal, holding that the true nature of the agreement was a licence to P to occupy the stadium for the purpose of the meetings, and that P was liable to account for VAT on the whole of the receipts for admission and car parking. *Mike Parker Productions Ltd, [1976] VATTR 115 (VTD 275).*

58.242   **Admission to hostess bar—by whom supply made.**   A company operated a 'hostess bar' in West London. It engaged a man and a woman, on a self-employed basis, to operate the front kiosk which allowed admission to the bar. No wages were paid, but the kiosk operators were allowed to retain the whole of the admission fees which they collected. The company did not account for tax on these fees. The Commissioners issued an assessment charging tax on the fees, and the company appealed. The tribunal dismissed the appeal, holding that the entrance fee was an integral part of the supplies which the company made to customers visiting the bar. The kiosk operators were not carrying on business on their own account, but were acting on behalf of the company. *Ablefame Ltd, LON/89/1283Z (VTD 5560).*

58.243   **Garages purchased by plumber with money lent by wife—whether letting of garages carried out by plumber or wife.**   A plumber, registered for VAT, purchased a number of garages with money lent to him by his wife. The garages were let to tenants. The plumber did not account for VAT on the rental income, although it was included in the accounts which his accountant submitted to the Inland Revenue. When the Commissioners discovered this, they issued an assessment charging tax on the rents. The plumber appealed, contending that the rental income should be treated as belonging to his wife, rather than to himself. The tribunal rejected this contention and dismissed his appeal. *R King, MAN/90/496 (VTD 7201)*.

58.244 **Fitting of kitchen furniture—whether supplies made by fitters as individuals or by partnership which sold furniture.** A married couple traded in partnership as suppliers of kitchen furniture. They arranged for such furniture to be fitted by self-employed fitters. They accounted for output tax on the amounts paid for the supply of the items of furniture, but did not account for output tax on the fitting charges. The Commissioners issued an assessment charging tax on these services, and the couple appealed, contending that the fitting services were supplied by the fitters as individuals, rather than on behalf of the couple. The tribunal dismissed the appeal, holding on the evidence that the couple were supplying services as well as goods. The fact that the fitters were self-employed was not conclusive. There was no written agency agreement between the couple and the fitters. Customers had the right to sue the couple for any defect in the fitting services. The fitters were supplying their services to the partnership, rather than directly to the customers. The couple were required to account for output tax on the full amounts paid by the customers. *I & PA Ramsay (t/a Kitchen Format), LON/93/949A (VTD 12393)*.

58.245 **Goods sold at auction following compulsory purchase of business premises by Council—whether goods sold by proprietors of business or by Council.** A County Council issued a compulsory purchase order to acquire premises which were used as a drapers' shop. Following the compulsory purchase, the goods held at the shop, and the fixtures and fittings, were sold at auction. The partnership which had owned the shop did not account for output tax on the sale proceeds. The Commissioners issued an assessment, and the partnership appealed, contending that the sale had been made by the Council. The tribunal dismissed the appeal, holding on the evidence that the items had been sold by the partnership. *Iqbal Jaurah & Sons, MAN/93/285 (VTD 12501)*.

58.246 **Telegraphic transfer fees for remittance of sums from solicitors' client account—whether supply made by solicitors or by bank.** A firm of solicitors arranged for money to be transferred from its client account to the client accounts of other solicitors under the Clearing Houses Automated Payments Service. Its bank charged it £25 for each such transfer, and it recharged these amounts to the appropriate clients. The firm did not account for output tax on these charges. The Commissioners issued a ruling that the firm was required to account for tax on the charges, and the firm appealed, contending that the relevant supplies were made to its clients by the bank. The tribunal dismissed the appeal, holding that the bank was supplying its services to the firm and that the firm was then making a separate supply to its clients. *Rowe & Maw, 58.42 above, applied. Shuttleworth & Co, [1994] VATTR 355 (VTD 12805)*.

58.247 **Sale of plant—whether supply made by partnership or by company.** A married couple carried on a farming business in partnership and were registered for VAT. They were also the controlling directors of a company which carried on a water bottling business, using plant which the couple leased to the company. The company suffered financial difficulties and it was agreed to sell the plant, and an adjacent field containing the source of the water, to an outside purchaser. The vendors charged the purchaser VAT of £15,750 on the sale of the plant, but did not account for this to the

Commissioners. Subsequently the company ceased trading, went into liquidation, and submitted a VAT return declaring the £15,750 output tax. The Commissioners issued an assessment on the partnership, on the basis that the supply of the plant had been made by the partnership rather than the company. The partners appealed, contending that the supply should be treated as having been made by the company. The tribunal rejected this contention and dismissed the appeal, holding on the evidence that the plant had been owned by the partnership and had been sold by the partnership. *D & DA Veale, LON/95/3182A (VTD 14637)*.

58.248 **Partnership operating retail shop—invoices issued for graphic design services—whether relevant supplies made by partnership or by individual partner.** A partnership operated a retail shop. One of the partners had previously been a graphic designer, and he issued a number of invoices in his own name in respect of such work. The income from this work was paid into the partnership bank account, but the partnership did not account for output tax on it. The Commissioners issued an assessment charging tax on it, and the partnership appealed, contending that the relevant supplies had been made by the partner as an individual. The tribunal rejected this contention and dismissed the appeal, holding on the evidence that the supplies had been made by the partnership. The chairman observed that 'the critical and decisive factor' was 'the inclusion of the proceeds in the partnership accounts as income of the partnership'. *W & J Tang (t/a Ziploc), MAN/97/1123 (VTD 15426)*.

58.249 **Partnership operating retail shop—undeclared wholesale supplies to other traders—whether relevant supplies made by partnership or by individual partner.** A married couple operated a general store and off-licence in partnership. The Commissioners discovered that they had not accounted for output tax on wholesale supplies of alcoholic drinks to other traders. They issued an assessment charging tax on these supplies. The couple appealed, contending that the wholesale supplies had been made by the husband as an individual, rather than by the partnership. The tribunal rejected this contention and dismissed the appeal, holding that 'the wholesale selling of alcohol, whether legitimate or not, is business of the same kind as the retail selling of alcohol. Whatever (the wife) did or did not know, and whatever the wholesale customers did or did not know, (the husband's) course of conduct was such that those customers would have been entitled to look to the partnership for any remedies to which they were entitled in respect of anything done by (the husband) in relation to the wholesale supplies.' The tribunal observed that 'when one enters into the relationship of partnership ... one voluntarily surrenders certain rights, including the right, if such it be, not to suffer the consequences of another person's actions. A partner who, for whatever reason, does not keep herself informed as to what her partner is doing cannot be heard to complain of the consequences.' *M & N Singh (t/a The Food Palace & Wine King), LON/98/1064 (VTD 16378)*.

58.250 **Partnership operating restaurant—kitchen also used for take-away sales from adjacent premises.** A married couple registered for VAT as proprietors of a restaurant. They also used the restaurant kitchen to prepare take-away food, which was sold from adjacent premises. They did not account for VAT on the take-away sales. The Commissioners issued an assessment, and the couple appealed, contending that the take-away business was operated by a three-person partnership which also included one of their uncles (L). The tribunal rejected this contention and dismissed the appeal, holding on the evidence that L's involvement was 'apparently limited to an injection of capital and to a right, of which he does not avail himself, to a share in the profits ... in substance and in reality, the extension of the restaurant and takeaway business to the adjacent premises, with the assistance of any capital injected by (L) was simply an expansion of the existing business run by the existing partnership'. *P & A Yung (t/a Chilli Restaurant & Hong Kong Food), LON/00/90 (VTD 16695)*.

58.251   **Admission to playground including miniature railway.**   A Town Council operated a children's playground, charging £1 for admission. Included in the playground was a miniature railway, operated by a private contractor, who was not registered for VAT. The contractor paid the Council a nominal rent and received 30% of the admission fees. The Council only accounted for VAT on the net amount which it retained. The Commissioners issued an assessment on the basis that the Council should have accounted for VAT on the full amount of the admission fees. The Council appealed, contending that, with regard to the 30% which it passed on to the contractor, it was acting as an agent of the contractor. The tribunal rejected this contention and dismissed the Council's appeal, holding on the evidence that the contractor was supplying his services to the council and the council was making a single supply of the right to use the playground. Accordingly the Council was obliged to account for VAT on the full amount of the admission fees, including the amounts which it passed to the contractor. *Hemsworth Town Council, MAN/96/1391 (VTD 14985)*.

58.252   **Fish and chip shop—proprietor out of UK for extended holiday—whether supplies made by proprietor or by temporary tenant.**   The proprietor of a fish-and-chip shop appealed against an assessment, contending that he had temporarily transferred the operation of his business to a tenant while he took an extended holiday in Italy. The tribunal dismissed his appeal, holding on the evidence that the proprietor remained 'the taxable person liable to account for VAT' and observing that a trader 'can make an interpersonal arrangement or contract for a third party to meet the liability, but he cannot absolve himself of his own direct statutory responsibility without fully discharging any liability in that respect'. *F Di Rienzo (t/a Franco's Fish Bar), EDN/98/10 (VTD 15599B)*.

58.253   **Massage parlour—whether services supplied by masseuses or by salon proprietor.**   The proprietor of a sauna and massage parlour failed to register for VAT. The Commissioners issued a notice of compulsory registration and an assessment charging tax on the total takings at the salon. He appealed, contending that the massage services were supplied by the individual masseuses who worked at the salon on a self-employed basis. Customers were charged a £20 entrance fee, which included a basic massage, but were also charged between £50 and £70 for 'personal relaxation massages'. The proprietor retained the £20 entrance fees, and gave evidence that the masseuses paid him a room rental of £20 per day but retained the amounts they received for 'relaxation massages'. The Commissioners called a former masseuse as a witness. She gave evidence that there was no room rental and she was required to pay the proprietor £10 for each 'relaxation massage'. The tribunal accepted the evidence of this witness and dismissed the proprietor's appeal, finding that there was 'one unified business' and the proprietor fixed the prices charged for 'relaxation massages'. Accordingly, the proprietor was required to account for tax on the full amounts paid by customers, including the amounts which the masseuses retained. *SP Rudd (t/a Duo's Spa & Sauna), LON/99/1176 (VTD 16844)*.

58.254   See also *Niven*, 63.81 VALUATION.

58.255   **Fortune-telling services—whether supplied by company or by individual fortune-tellers.**   A company advertised fortune-telling services. Customers paid £3 to enter the company's premises and paid a further fee of about £10 to the fortune-teller. The fortune-tellers retained 60% of this, paying 40% to the company. The Commissioners issued an assessment charging tax on the full amounts paid by the customers. The company appealed, contending that the fortune-tellers were supplying their services directly to the customers, so that it should not be required to account for tax on the amounts which the tellers retained. The tribunal rejected this contention and dismissed the appeal, holding that 'in substance what was being offered to the public was a supply by the company'. The fortune-tellers were supplying their services to the company and the company was then supplying those services to the public. *Infocall Universal Ltd (t/a The Psychic Centre), EDN/00/38 (VTD 16909)*.

58.256 **Motorcycle courier service—whether supplies to cash customers made by company operating service or by individual couriers.** See *Prontobikes Ltd*, 1.25 AGENTS.

58.257 **Goods sold at auction organised by fund-raising committee—whether committee selling as principals or as agents.** See *The Cheltenham Countryside Race Day*, 1.33 AGENTS.

58.258 **Company providing staff for clients.** See *Hays Personnel Services Ltd*, 1.36 AGENTS.

58.259 **Partnership providing live-in carers—whether acting as principal or agent.** See *Clarina Live-In Care Service*, 1.37 AGENTS.

58.260 **Embroidery kits sold under 'party plan' system—by whom supplied.** See *Simply Cross-stitch*, 1.76 AGENTS.

58.261 **Supplies by undischarged bankrupt.** See *Scally*, 35.6 INSOLVENCY.

58.262 **Business transferred as going concern following bankruptcy—deposits taken before bankruptcy but supplies made following transfer.** See *Camford Ltd*, 35.7 INSOLVENCY.

58.263 **Buffet restaurant—whether supplies made by franchisee.** See *Duwel*, 53.147 REGISTRATION.

58.264 **Retail shops—by whom supplies made.** See *Shad*, 53.156 REGISTRATION.

58.265 **Canteen for employees—by whom supplies made.** See *MB Metals*, 58.11 above, and *Barker*, 58.12 above.

Cases where the appellant was successful

58.266 **Partner in solicitors' firm also acting for Borough Council—whether services supplied by firm or by solicitor as an individual.** A partner in a firm of solicitors also held a part-time appointment as a solicitor to a Borough Council. The Commissioners issued a ruling that the firm should account for VAT on the solicitor's salary from the Council. The tribunal allowed the firm's appeal, holding that the contract was with the solicitor as an individual and not with the firm. *Lean & Rose, [1974] VATTR 7 (VTD 54)*.

58.267 **Sales of racehorses owned by syndicates—whether supply by syndicate or by individual member.** A racehorse breeder had a one-fortieth share in two syndicates which each owned a stallion at stud, one in the UK and the other in Ireland. The affairs of each syndicate were managed by a committee on behalf of its members. Each committee, after obtaining the requisite approval of a majority of the members, sold the syndicate's stallion to a Japanese breeder to whom it was exported. The Commissioners assessed the breeder on his share of the sale proceeds. The tribunal allowed the breeder's appeal, holding that in each case the committee had supplied the stallion. The supply of the stallion in Ireland, being a supply outside the

UK, was outside the scope of VAT. The stallion in the UK had been exported and its supply was accordingly zero-rated. *Sir John Astor, [1981] VATTR 174 (VTD 1030).*

58.268 **House-to-house sales of goods from vans.** A firm sold domestic household goods by 'door-to-door' selling. It had a number of vans, each of which was under the charge of a 'supervisor', two of whom were partners in the firm and five of whom were treated as self-employed. The firm determined the retail price of the goods and invoiced the supervisor for 50% of this price in respect of the goods loaded on his van. The Commissioners issued an assessment on the basis that the supervisors were selling the goods on behalf of the firm, so that tax was chargeable on the full retail price. The firm accepted that this was so in respect of the two supervisors who were partners, but appealed against the assessment in respect of sales by the other supervisors, contending that the supervisors had purchased the goods from the firm and sold them on their own account. The tribunal accepted this contention and allowed the appeal to this extent, holding that, in the case of the self-employed supervisors, the firm was only liable to account for tax on the amounts invoiced to them. *Headley Enterprises, LON/82/65 (VTD 1295).*

58.269 **Goods exchanged for coupons under promotional scheme—by whom supplied.** A company (S) manufactured foodstuffs, principally crisps, and sold them to retailers. In 1975 it introduced a promotional scheme, administered by another company, whereby each box of crisps contained coupons, which retailers could exchange for a variety of goods. The company which administered the scheme supplied the goods requested, and issued invoices to S to cover the cost of the goods in question, plus a service charge. VAT was charged on these invoices, and S reclaimed this as input tax. The Commissioners issued assessments on the basis that S had supplied the goods to the retailers, and should account for output tax on their value. S appealed, contending that the goods were not supplied by it, but by the company which administered the scheme. The tribunal accepted this contention and allowed S's appeal. The Commissioners appealed to the QB which upheld the tribunal's decision that the goods had not been supplied by S, but also held that S had not been entitled to reclaim input tax on the supplies, and directed that the assessments should be amended accordingly. *C & E Commrs v Sooner Foods Ltd, QB [1983] STC 376.*

58.270 **Feedstuffs supplied to racehorses—whether supplied by company or by controlling shareholder.** A company carried on the business of training racehorses. Its controlling shareholder (R) was a farmer, who supplied feedstuffs to the company and owned a number of racehorses which the company trained. R only invoiced the company for feedstuffs consumed by horses owned by other customers and did not charge it for feedstuffs consumed by his own horses. The Commissioners issued an assessment on the basis that the company should account for output tax on the open market value of the feedstuffs it provided for the horses owned by R. The company appealed, contending that it had not made any supply of the feedstuffs in question, which had remained the property of R until consumed by the horses. The QB accepted this contention and allowed the appeal, holding that the company had only supplied training facilities and had not made any supply of the feedstuffs. *Spigot Lodge Ltd v C & E Commrs, QB [1985] STC 255.*

58.271 **Restaurant operated under franchise agreement.** The proprietors of an Indian restaurant wished to retire from the active running of the business, while retaining the tenancy of the premises. They therefore disposed of the restaurant business to the head waiter (M) under a franchise agreement. M paid one of the tenants a percentage of the profits, and the tenant assisted M with the bookkeeping. Subsequently M died, having failed to account for VAT in respect of the restaurant's takings. The Commissioners issued an assessment to recover the tax from the tenants of the premises. The QB allowed the tenants' appeal, holding on the evidence that the effect of the franchise agreement was that, after the date of that agreement, the business was operated by the franchisee rather than by the tenants. It was the franchisee, rather than the tenants, who had made the relevant supplies. *Nasim & Another v C & E Commrs, QB [1987] STC 387.*

58.272   **Partnership owning fish and chip shop—whether mobile van operated by partnership or by one partner as individual.**   An unmarried couple operated a fish and chip shop in partnership, and were registered for VAT accordingly. The male partner also sold fish and chips from a mobile van, but did not account for VAT on such sales. The Commissioners issued an assessment on the basis that the van was part of the partnership business. The partnership appealed, contending that the van was a separate business which the partner carried on as a sole trader, and that the stocks for the shop and the van were kept separately. The tribunal accepted the partners' evidence and allowed the appeal, observing that the absence of a separate business bank account was inconclusive. *SR Insley & L Clayton (t/a S & L Caterers), MAN/95/1284 (VTD 13677).*

58.273   **Fish and chip shop—proprietors out of UK for six-week holiday—whether supplies made by proprietors or by temporary tenants.**   A married couple operated a fish and chip shop in partnership. They took a six-week holiday in Italy, and arranged for a temporary tenant to carry on the business during their absence. They did not account for output tax on the takings during this six-week period. The Commissioners issued an assessment charging tax on the takings, but the tribunal allowed the couple's appeal, holding that the relevant supplies had been made by the temporary tenant. *Di Rienzo*, 58.252 above, distinguished. *F & M Cortellesa, EDN/98/136 (VTD 16333).*

58.274   *Cortellesa*, 58.273 above, was applied in the similar subsequent cases of *G & M Treta (t/a The Golden Fry), EDN/99/119 (VTD 16690)* and *G Pacitti, EDN/98/44 (VTD 16759).*

58.275   **Delivery charge for meals—whether service of delivery supplied by restaurant proprietor.**   The proprietor of a take-away restaurant (H) arranged for a contractor (Y) to deliver meals to customers where customers required this. H paid Y £12 per night in return for Y making himself available, and Y also charged customers between 90p and £1.60 per delivery. The Commissioners issued an assessment on the basis that H was required to account for output tax on the amounts paid to Y. H appealed, contending that Y was an independent contractor and was making a separate supply of services. The tribunal accepted this contention and allowed the appeal, finding that, under the terms of the agreement between H and Y, the safe delivery of the meals was the responsibility of Y, rather than of H. The tribunal held on the evidence that the delivery of the order was a separate supply of services, and that the supply of delivery was made by Y, so that H was not required to account for output tax on the payments in question. *CK Ho (t/a New Lucky Ho), EDN/97/189 (VTD 15605).*

58.276   **Sale of imported radios.**   A company (O) carried on business as a haulage contractor and worked as a subcontractor for another company (L). The directors of the two companies decided to organise the importation and sale of radios from Korea. Initially the radios were imported on the basis that L was the importer, and L's VAT number was used. Subsequently O's principal director became personally involved in selling large numbers of the radios, and arranged substantial sales to UK wholesalers using L's invoices. The Commissioners assessed O in respect of the sales of the radios. O appealed, contending that it had made no supplies of the radios, and that the supplies had been made by L. The tribunal accepted this contention and allowed the appeal. *O'Reilly Transport (Newry) Ltd, BEL/86/1 (VTD 2434).*

58.277 **Examination fees collected by college on behalf of examining boards.** A college of higher education was an approved centre for examinations set by boards approved by the Department of Education and Science. The college collected examination fees on behalf of the examining boards, and also charged additional fees to candidates who sat examinations at its premises. It accounted for VAT on the fees which it charged, but not on the fees which it collected on behalf of the examining boards. The Commissioners assessed the college on the fees which it collected on behalf of the boards, and the college appealed. The tribunal allowed the college's appeal, holding that the examinations were supplied by the boards rather than by the college. *City College of Higher Education Ltd, LON/87/203 (VTD 2500).*

58.278 **Hostesses at night club—whether services supplied by club or by hostesses.** A company operated a 'gentlemen's night club' in London. On entering the club premises, a customer would be approached by a young woman, described as a 'hostess', who would invite him to come to the club's basement with her. Customers who accepted such an invitation were required to buy a bottle of champagne from the company, priced at not less than £60. They were also expected to pay a fee to the hostess in return for her company, either in cash or by credit card. The company did not account for VAT on these fees, and the Commissioners issued an assessment on the basis that the company should have charged VAT on fees which the customers had paid by credit card. The company appealed, contending that the hostesses had been supplying their services directly to the customers, and the fees were not consideration for any supply by the company. The tribunal accepted this contention and allowed the company's appeal. *Leapmagic Ltd, LON/91/90Z (VTD 6441).*

58.279 **Supply of facilities at school premises to photographers—whether supply made by school or by local education authority.** A company photographed schoolchildren at school premises and sold the photographs to parents. It made payments to the schools in return for the use of the school facilities. Following *dicta* of the tribunal chairman in *H Tempest Ltd (No 2)*, 63.18 VALUATION, the Commissioners took the view (set out in VAT Information Sheet 5/94) that the schools were acting as agents of the local education authorities, so that the local education authorities should account for output tax on the amounts received from the company. They issued an assessment on a County Council which had failed to account for output tax on this basis. The Council appealed, contending that the effect of the *Education Act 1993* was that the school facilities were supplied by the school governors rather than by the County Council. The tribunal accepted this contention and allowed the appeal, holding that 'while the head teacher is nominally an employee of the local education authority, in truth his authority to manage the school derives from his appointment by the governing body and ... he does so as their representative'. *Lancashire County Council, [1996] VATDR 550 (VTD 14655).* (*Note.* For the Commissioners' practice following this decision, see Business Brief 11/97, issued on 9 May 1997, and Business Brief 21/97, issued on 3 October 1997.)

58.280 **Goods sold under 'party plan' system—by whom supplied.** See *Potter*, 1.73 AGENTS.

58.281 **Goods sold by 'direct selling'—whether salesmen agents or independent contractors.** See *Betterware Products Ltd*, 1.78 AGENTS, and *Kelly*, 1.79 AGENTS.

58.282 **Optional service charge in restaurant—whether supplies made by company operating restaurant or by waiters.** See *NDP Co Ltd*, 63.91 VALUATION.

58.283   **Sales of car numberplates—by whom supplied.** See *Wood*, 53.133
REGISTRATION.

58.284   **Gaming machines in shop—whether supplies to customers made by owner
of machines or by owner of shop.** See *Bennetts of Sheffield Ltd*, 63.113
VALUATION.

58.285   **Goods exported by group of companies—company by which supply
made.** See *Philips Exports Ltd*, 24.24 EXPORTS.

58.286   **Export of goods—more than one company involved—by whom supply
made.** See *Geistlich Sons Ltd*, 24.25 EXPORTS.

58.287   **Canteen for employees—by whom supplies made.** See *Notts Fire Service
Messing Club*, 13.5 CLUBS, ASSOCIATIONS AND ORGANISATIONS.

58.288   **Company placing orders for magazines with publishers—magazines sent
by publishers to subscribers—whether supplies to subscribers made by
publishers or by company placing orders.** See *Nordic Subscription Service UK
Ltd*, 1.41 AGENTS.

THE TIME OF SUPPLY (VATA 1994, s 6)

Time of supply of goods (VATA 1994, s 6(2))

58.289   **Stolen takings.**   A hotel proprietor appealed against an estimated assessment,
contending that the underdeclared takings had been stolen by dishonest bar staff.
The tribunal held that the proprietor was still liable to account for tax on the stolen
takings, as the time of supply was when the goods were handed to the customer. *G
Benton, [1975] VATTR 138 (VTD 185)*.

58.290   *Benton*, 58.289 above, was applied in the subsequent cases of *AJ Furby, MAN/77/
316 (VTD 622); Townville (Wheldale) Miners Sports & Recreation Club & Institute,
MAN/78/212 (VTD 719); Moorthorpe Empire Working Men's Club, MAN/80/84
(VTD 1127); West Way Garage (Bournemouth) Ltd, LON/86/204 (VTD 2151); CJ
Huntley & RJ Brookes (t/a Brimar Guest House), LON/90/1237X (VTD 5847); JP
Sharp, MAN/91/520 (VTD 6795); Mr & Mrs AA Lewis, LON/92/2429A (VTD
11596)* and *Metrogold (Building Contractors) Ltd, MAN/00/202 (VTD 16911)*.

58.291   See also *Courage Ltd*, 54.37 RETAILERS' SPECIAL SCHEMES.

58.292   **Vending machines.**   The standard rate of VAT was increased from 8% to 15%
with effect from 18 June 1979. A firm which operated a number of vending machines
was unable to modify some of its machines in time to pass on this increase to its
customers. In cases where it had been unable to alter the machines, it accounted for
output tax at 8%. The Commissioners issued an assessment on a time-
apportionment basis, treating the appropriate proportion of the takings as chargeable
at 15%. The tribunal upheld the assessment and dismissed the firm's appeal.
Glasgow Vending Services, LON/79/334 (VTD 943).

58.293   **Supplies of coins.**   On 31 March 1982 it was announced that supplies of gold
coins, which had previously been exempt under *FA 1972*, were to become
standard-rated from the following day. A partnership which traded as coin dealers
had many customers on the day of the announcement, and had to order extra coins to
meet the demand. These coins were delivered on 1 April. The partnership failed to
account for output tax on coins which customers had ordered on 31 March, but
which it had been unable to supply to the customers until 1 April. The
Commissioners issued an assessment charging tax on these supplies (except that

where a deposit had been paid on 31 March, tax was not due on the amount of the deposit). The tribunal dismissed the partnership's appeal and the QB upheld this decision. By virtue of what is now *VATA 1994, s 6(2)*, the time of supply was 1 April. *Purshotam M Pattni & Sons v C & E Commrs, QB 1986, [1987] STC 1.*

58.294   **Goods sold subject to reservation of title—time of supply.**   A company (V) sold bus chassis under agreements whereby it retained title until receipt of payment. The chassis were delivered to coachbuilders nominated by the customers. V did not account for output tax until the completed coaches were delivered by the coachbuilders to the customers, and the Commissioners issued an assessment on the basis that the chassis were supplied when V delivered them to the coachbuilders. The tribunal upheld the assessment and dismissed V's appeal. *Volvo Trucks (GB) Ltd, [1988] VATTR 11 (VTD 2579).*

58.295   **Machine tools made available for demonstration purposes—whether within VATA 1994, s 6(2)(c).**   A company manufactured machine tools which were intended to be mounted on grinding machines. It delivered some of these tools to agents of grinding wheel manufacturers for demonstration purposes. The Commissioners issued an assessment on the basis that the tools were delivered to the manufacturers on a sale or return basis, within what is now *VATA 1994, s 6(2)(c)*. The company appealed, contending that the transactions were not within *s 6(2)*. The tribunal allowed the company's appeal, finding that the tools remained the company's property and that, when a tool was delivered, it was not the expectation of either party that that particular tool would be sold to a customer, but that a customer would see the way in which the tools worked and would then order one meeting his own particular requirements. On the evidence, 'property in the goods was not intended to pass unless and until the agent by a separate act signified that he wished to buy the (tool) on show and appropriated it in order to sell it on to his buyer'. *Diaform Ltd, LON/93/469A (VTD 11069).*

58.296   **Transfer of assets by trader to associated company—time of supply.**   A sole trader (J), who had for many years competed in Formula 3 and Formula 3000 motor racing, developed a Formula 1 racing car. In 1990 he and his wife purchased the whole of the shares in a limited company, which he used to seek finance and sponsorship for Formula 1 motor racing. His accountant prepared draft accounts, with a journal entry indicating that, on 27 September 1990, J had transferred assets relating to the Formula 1 car to his company. The Commissioners issued an assessment, including a charge to default interest, on the basis that there had been a supply of the assets on that date. J appealed, contending that despite the journal entry, the assets had not been transferred until 1991, when the company first began to race the Formula 1 cars. The tribunal allowed the appeal, finding that the accounts were 'erroneous' and that the journal entry did not constitute a tax point, so that for VAT purposes the time of supply was in 1991. *E Jordan (t/a Eddie Jordan Racing), LON/92/734 (VTD 11310).*

58.297   **Transfer of land—time of supply.**   The Cumbernauld Development Corporation, which had begun the development of the Cumbernauld area in 1956, transferred some of its remaining land to a local golf club in exchange for some land owned by the club. Under the agreement, there was no monetary consideration for either transfer, but the Corporation had to pay for work to be carried out on the golf club's course and for a new clubhouse. The Commissioners issued an assessment on the basis that the time of the supply was the date of the relevant disposition. The Corporation appealed, contending that the supply had taken place previously, when the land was made available to the club (with the result that the assessment was outside the statutory time limit). The tribunal rejected this contention and dismissed the appeal, holding that 'there requires to be a fixed point at which it can be said that the major interest in land has been supplied. Since the major interest in land is defined as "the estate or interest of a proprietor of a *dominium utile*" the only point at which that can be said to have been transferred is at the time of the exchange of dispositions'. *Cumbernauld Development Corporation (No 2), EDN/99/134 (VTD 16920)*. (*Note*. For the valuation of the supply, see 63.72 VALUATION.)

58.298   **Retail sales paid for by credit card issued by member of same group of companies as retailer—time of supply.**   See *Kingfisher plc*, 30.23 GROUPS OF COMPANIES.

58.299   **Retail sales by mail order—whether within VATA 1994, s 6(2)(c).**   A company supplied goods by mail order. Prior to the QB decisions in *Next plc*, 54.26 RETAILERS' SPECIAL SCHEMES and *Grattan plc*, 54.27 RETAILERS' SPECIAL SCHEMES, it had accounted for tax on the basis that the time of supply was the time of the first payment. Following those decisions, it submitted a repayment claim on the basis that the time of supply was the time the goods were despatched, so that, in the case of goods which had been despatched when the VAT rate was 15% but the first payment had not been made until after the rate had been increased to 17.5%, it should have accounted for VAT at 15% rather than 17.5%. The Commissioners made a provisional repayment of the amount claimed, but subsequently formed the opinion that the goods were supplied 'on approval or sale or return or similar terms', within what is now *VATA 1994, s 6(2)(c)*, and that the time of supply should be taken as 14 days after the delivery of the goods. They issued an assessment charging tax on this basis. The company appealed. The tribunal allowed the appeal, holding on the evidence that the supplies were within *s 6(2)(a)* rather than *s 6(2)(c)*. The tribunal held that *s 6(2)(c)* applied to transactions where there was no contract of sale 'unless and until the person concerned adopts or is deemed to have adopted the transaction', whereas *s 6(2)(a)* applied to transactions where there was a contract of sale but the buyer had the right to rescind the contract if he wished. Accordingly the time of supply was the date of despatch of the goods. *Diaform Ltd*, 58.295 above, distinguished. *Littlewoods Organisation plc, [1997] VATDR 408 (VTD 14977)*. (*Note*. The QB decisions in *Next plc*, 54.26 RETAILERS' SPECIAL SCHEMES and *Grattan plc*, 54.27 RETAILERS' SPECIAL SCHEMES, were subsequently disapproved by the CA in *R v C & E Commrs (ex p. Littlewoods Home Shopping Group Ltd)*, 54.35 RETAILERS' SPECIAL SCHEMES.)

Time of performance of services (VATA 1994, s 6(3))

58.300   **Supplies of accommodation.**   The proprietors of a guest-house registered for VAT with effect from June 1977. They had taken several bookings before registration for clients to stay at the guest-house after the date of registration. They did not account for output tax on such supplies. The Commissioners issued an assessment charging tax on them and the tribunal dismissed the proprietors' appeal. By virtue of what is now *VATA 1994, s 6(3)*, the accommodation was not supplied until the clients arrived at the guest-house. *E & B Palotai, LON/78/149 (VTD 656)*.

58.301   The standard rate of VAT was increased from 8% to 15% in June 1979. A company which carried on business as a tour operator continued to account for VAT at 8% on supplies which it made after the change of rate. The Commissioners issued an assessment charging tax at 15% and the company appealed, contending that the accommodation had been booked before the increase in rate and that tax should only be charged at 8%. The tribunal rejected this contention and dismissed the appeal. By virtue of what is now *VATA 1994, s 6(3)*, the time of the supply was the supply was the time when the accommodation was provided, except where an invoice had previously been issued or payment had previously been made. *Scottish Highland Hotel Group Ltd, [1981] VATTR 146 (VTD 1115)*.

58.302   For cases concerning the payment of deposits for holiday accommodation, see *Caine*, 58.341 below, and *Moonraker's Guest House Ltd*, 58.343 below.

58.303   **Estate agents—fees agreed before registration.** An estate agent began trading on 24 June 1982 but did not register for VAT until 1 April 1983. He did not account for VAT on fees which had been agreed before April 1983 and the Commissioners issued an assessment charging tax on such supplies where completion took place on or after 1 April 1983. The tribunal upheld the assessment and dismissed the agent's appeal, holding that the time of supply was the date of completion. *WJ Cooke, MAN/84/265 (VTD 1844).*

58.304   Similar decisions were reached in *Madisons, LON/87/276 (VTD 2516); J Calland, MAN/87/201 & 202 (VTD 2627)* and *S & J Property Centres, MAN/00/101 (VTD 16985).*

58.305   In a case where a contract for the sale of two houses was signed on 16 February 1987, but completion did not take place until 1 July, the Commissioners issued an assessment on the basis that the estate agents' services were not supplied until completion took place (with the result that changes to the partial exemption rules which took effect from 1 April 1987 applied to the input tax in question). The tribunal upheld the assessment, applying *Madisons* and *Calland*, 58.304 above, and holding that 'where the services are performed over a period of time and there is one consideration for the services as a whole, then the "time when services are performed" must ... mean the point in time when all the services to be supplied have been performed'. *Trustees for the Greater World Association Trust, [1989] VATTR 91 (VTD 3401).*

58.306   **Supplies of double glazing.** In March 1984 the Chancellor of the Exchequer announced that building alterations, which had previously been zero-rated, would be treated as standard-rated after 31 May 1984. A company which supplied double glazing did not account for output tax in cases where it had agreed contracts before June 1984 although the relevant work was not carried out until after 31 May. The Commissioners issued an assessment charging tax on the basis that the time of supply was after 31 May so that VAT was chargeable on the work. The tribunal upheld the assessment and dismissed the company's appeal. *APD Insulations [Group] Ltd, [1987] VATTR 36 (VTD 2292).*

58.307   For a case where the tribunal held that double glazing work had been paid for before 1 June 1984, see *Dolomite Double Glazing Ltd*, 58.325 below. For a case where the tribunal held that such work had not been paid for before that date, see *Double Shield Window Co Ltd*, 58.324 below. For a case where the tribunal held that the time of supply for double glazing was the date on which the relevant invoice was issued, see *Tingley*, 58.317 below.

58.308   **Building contractor—quotations issued before registration.** A building contractor registered for VAT with effect from 1 February 1989. He failed to account for VAT on a contract where he had issued a quotation in January 1989, but had not carried out the work until after 1 February. The Commissioners issued an assessment on the basis that VAT was chargeable on the contract. The tribunal dismissed the contractor's appeal. By virtue of what is now *VATA 1994, s 6(3)*, the time of supply was when the contract was carried out. *NCJ Hughes, MAN/92/208 (VTD 8916).*

58.309   A similar decision was reached in *Chiltern Windows Ltd, LON/93/2604A (VTD 12208).*

58.310   **Solicitor—instructions received before registration but services performed after registration.** A solicitor registered for VAT in September 1991. He did not account for tax on services which he supplied to two clients who had given him instructions before he had registered, although the relevant services had been supplied after the date of registration. The Commissioners issued a ruling that the solicitor was obliged to account for output tax on the services supplied after registration, and the tribunal dismissed the solicitor's appeal, applying *Cooke*, 58.303 above, and *Madisons*, 58.304 above. *WN Bagshawe (t/a Bagshawes), LON/95/ 1675A (VTD 14103)*.

58.311   **Conversion of building into flats—contract price not payable until five years after completion—time of supply.** A company agreed to convert a building into five flats at a price of £72,500 plus VAT. The price was not payable until five years after completion of the work. The work was completed by November 1987, when the first tenant moved in, and all the flats were occupied by February 1988. The Commissioners issued an assessment on the basis that the supply had taken place in the company's return period ending 29 February 1988. The company appealed, contending that it had an obligation to maintain the building until the contract price became five years after completion, and that the time of supply should be treated as being the time when payment was due. The tribunal upheld the assessment in principle, holding that, by virtue of what is now *VATA 1994, s 6(3)*, the time of supply for VAT purposes was the time when the services were performed, and the Commissioners were therefore correct to assess the company on the basis that tax became chargeable in the period ending February 1988. (However, the tribunal also held that the value of the consideration should be reduced to take account of the delay in reaching the due date for payment and the possibility of the final price being reduced to allow for any defects in the work—see 63.118 VALUATION.) *Mercantile Contracts Ltd, LON/88/786 (VTD 4357)*.

58.312   **Commission for hotel bookings—time of supply.** A company received commission from hotels in return for introducing potential clients. It initially sent the hotels 'pro forma' invoices which did not include VAT, and subsequently issued further invoices for the VAT. It did not account for output tax until it had received payment of the second invoices from the hotels. The Commissioners issued an assessment on the basis that the company should have accounted for VAT when it introduced the clients to the hotels, in accordance with what is now *VATA 1994, s 6(3)*. The tribunal upheld the assessment and dismissed the company's appeal. *Hotel Booking Service Ltd, LON/92/1856 (VTD 10606)*.

58.313   **Restaurant 'discount cards'—time of supply.** Two companies issued 'discount cards' entitling the holder to obtain a price reduction on up to twelve occasions at a stated restaurant. The Commissioners issued a ruling that, by virtue of *VATA 1994, s 6(3)*, the time of supply was when the cards were consigned to the immediate recipients (marketing companies which resold the cards to the ultimate consumers). The companies appealed, contending that the time of supply should be taken as the time of payment, when the cards were actually sold to the ultimate consumer. The tribunal rejected this contention and dismissed the appeal, holding that the time of supply was 'the time when the supply of the services is performed for the consideration fixed at the time of consignment and that the time when the services of consignment are performed is when the consignee can use the services consigned to it by making a reconsignment'. *Granton Marketing Ltd; Wentwalk Ltd, [1999] VATDR 383 (VTD 16118)*.

58.314   **Stolen takings.** See *Benton*, 58.289 above, and the cases noted at 58.290 above.

Issue of invoice (VATA 1994, s 6(4))

58.315   **Car dealer—date of issue of invoices.** The standard rate of VAT was increased from 8% to 15% with effect from 18 June 1979. A company which traded as a car dealer had received several orders for cars before 18 June 1979, but the cars were not ready for delivery until after that date. In such cases, the company prepared its normal triplicate invoices before 18 June and asked the prospective purchasers to confirm their agreement to the details on the invoices. It accounted for output tax at 8% on these invoices. The Commissioners issued an assessment on the basis that the company should have accounted for tax at 15%. The company appealed, contending that the invoices had been issued before 18 June 1979. The QB rejected this contention and upheld the assessment. The invoices had not been given to the prospective purchasers until after 18 June 1979, and consequently had not been 'issued' before that date. *C & E Commrs v Woolfold Motor Co Ltd, QB [1983] STC 715.*

58.316 **Accountancy partnership.** An accountancy partnership did not account for output tax until it received payment for its supplies. The Commissioners issued an assessment on the basis that the partnership should have accounted for tax at the time it issued invoices. The tribunal dismissed the partnership's appeal, holding that the effect of what is now *VATA 1994, s 6(4)* was that a supply should be treated as taking place at the earlier of the time of the receipt of payment or the issue of an invoice, and not at the later of the two. *P Smith & AR Ashton, MAN/88/333 (VTD 3317).*

58.317 **Invoices issued after 1 April 1991 for contracts agreed before 1 April 1991—time of supply.** The standard rate of VAT was increased from 15% to 17.5% with effect from 1 April 1991. A double glazing contractor had entered into contracts with customers before that date, but had not completed the work or issued an invoice. In such cases, he accounted for VAT at 15%. The Commissioners issued an assessment charging VAT at 17.5%, on the basis that the tax point was the date of issue of the invoices. The tribunal upheld the assessment and dismissed the contractor's appeal. *D Tingley (t/a Homecare Exteriors), LON/93/800A (VTD 11592).*

58.318 **Application for payment—whether an invoice for purposes of VATA 1994, s 6(4).** A company (P) was building a power station for an associated company (L). It issued applications for progress payments in accordance with the terms of the relevant contract. It intended that these applications should not be treated as tax invoices, so that the time of the supply would be the date of receipt of the payment. However, on 30 July 1990 it issued such an application which stated that the tax point was 30 July 1990. L treated this application as a tax invoice and reclaimed input tax accordingly, but P did not account for output tax. When the Commissioners discovered what had happened, they formed the opinion that the document constituted a tax invoice, so that L had acted correctly in reclaiming input tax and P had acted wrongly in failing to account for output tax. They issued an assessment imposing a misdeclaration penalty and interest, on the basis that the time of supply was 30 July 1990. P appealed, contending that the entry of 30 July 1990 in the space marked 'tax point' was a clerical error and the document did not constitute an invoice, so that the time of the supply was when L made the relevant payment, rather than when the document was issued. The tribunal accepted this contention and allowed P's appeal, holding that the document was not a tax invoice and did not have the effect of making 30 July 1990 the tax point. *ABB Power Ltd, [1992] VATTR 491 (VTD 9373).*

58.319 *ABB Power Ltd,* 58.318 above, was applied in a subsequent case where a builder had failed to account for VAT shown on applications for payment which he had issued to customers, and the Commissioners issued an assessment treating the applications as invoices and thus as giving rise to a tax point. The tribunal allowed the trader's appeal, holding that the documents were not invoices and thus their date of issue was not to be treated as the time of supply. *SR Finch, LON/91/1950A (VTD 10948).*

Receipt of payment (VATA 1994, s 6(4))

Advance payments

58.320   **Secretarial college—fees received in advance.**   The proprietor of a secretarial college charged its students fees in advance. The Commissioners issued an assessment on the basis that the time of supply was when the fees were received. The proprietor appealed, contending that the fees should be apportioned over the period in which the tuition was to be given. The tribunal rejected this contention and dismissed the appeal. *H Walters (t/a St George's Secretarial College), MAN/78/60 (VTD 602).*

58.321   **Club subscriptions paid in advance.**   A company which had operated a golf club went into liquidation. Members' subscriptions had been payable in advance, the members being supplied with a tax invoice. The liquidator admitted proofs of debts from members for the proportion of their subscriptions referable to the period after the beginning of the winding-up. He appealed against an assessment on the company, contending that it should be reduced by the tax relating to the subscriptions which he hoped to refund to the members. The tribunal dismissed the appeal. The letters admitting proofs of debts due to the members were not credit notes for VAT purposes, and, by virtue of what is now *VATA 1994, s 6(4)*, the supplies of services to the members were treated as having been made when the company issued tax invoices for them. *George Hamshaw (Golf Services) Ltd, [1979] VATTR 51 (VTD 722).*

58.322   A club for former pupils of an independent school invited the parents of current pupils to make termly advance payments towards future life membership of the club. It did not account for output tax on these payments. The Commissioners issued an assessment on the basis that tax was chargeable when the payments were made. The club appealed, contending that it did not supply any services until the pupil had been elected to membership. The tribunal accepted this contention and allowed the appeal. *The Old Chigwellians' Club, [1987] VATTR 66 (VTD 2332).*

58.323   A golf club instituted a scheme whereby members could pay part of their subscriptions in advance by monthly standing order. The Commissioners issued a ruling that VAT was chargeable when the payments were made. The tribunal dismissed the club's appeal, observing that what is now *VATA 1994, s 6(4)* provided that the supply should be treated as taking place at the time when payment was received. *East Kilbride Golf Club, EDN/90/101 (VTD 5503).*

58.324   **Payment made to solicitor as stakeholder—whether within VATA 1994, s 6(4).**   In March 1984 the Chancellor of the Exchequer announced that building alterations, which had previously been zero-rated, would be treated as standard-rated after 31 May 1984, but that, under transitional provisions, such work could be treated as zero-rated if it was paid for before 1 June 1984. A company which supplied double glazing instigated a scheme whereby customers who had placed orders before 1 June 1984 were encouraged to pay the agreed price for the work to its solicitors before that date. The solicitors undertook not to release the amounts to the company until the customer had confirmed in writing that he was satisfied with the work. The Commissioners issued an assessment on the basis that the payments to the solicitors did not constitute payment within what is now *VATA 1994, s 6(4)*, so that the supplies were not eligible for zero-rating. The tribunal upheld the assessment and dismissed the company's appeal. *Double Shield Window Co Ltd, MAN/84/227 (VTD 1771).*

58.325   **Cost of supply lent to customer by supplier—whether payment within VATA 1994, s 6(4).**   A double glazing company (D) had agreed to carry out work valued at £2,370 for a customer (S). S became aware that, if he paid for the work before 1 June 1984, it would be zero-rated. However, he could not afford to pay the full amount until June. He therefore asked one of D's directors if he would lend him the money for a month. The director agreed to this, and gave S a cheque for £2,370 on 29 May 1984. On 31 May S gave D a cheque for the same amount. The work was completed on 18 June. S repaid most of the loan on that date, and repaid the balance in September. The Commissioners issued an assessment on the basis that the exchange of cheques did not constitute payment, so that the time of supply was 18 June and the work was not eligible for zero-rating. The tribunal allowed D's appeal, holding that payment was made on 31 May. If S had refused to repay the loan after the work was completed, D would have had to sue him for repayment of the loan, rather than for payment for the work. *Dolomite Double Glazing Ltd, [1985] VATTR 184 (VTD 1922).*

58.326   **Circular payments—whether within VATA 1994, s 6(4).**   A company (D) had entered into a contract with an associated construction company (F) in 1983, whereby it was agreed that F would carry out alterations to a property for D. In March 1984 the Chancellor of the Exchequer announced that such work would be standard-rated after 31 May 1984, unless it was paid for before 1 June 1984. The principal director of D and F arranged with D's bank for it to advance the whole of the contract price so that it could pay F on 31 May. At the same time D and F entered into an agreement whereby F, having received the money in question, would lend it back to D at 6% p.a. interest, and the loan would be repaid by D as the work proceeded. On 31 May D and F exchanged cheques as agreed. The Commissioners issued an assessment charging VAT on the contract price on the basis that the exchange of cheques did not constitute payment within what is now *VATA 1994, s 6(4)* The tribunal allowed F's appeal and the CA upheld this decision. The payment made discharged D's liability under the building contract and left F with no right to sue for payment thereunder. The payment was in law a genuine contractual payment, and the court was not entitled to disregard its legal effect and treat it as something else. *C & E Commrs v Faith Construction Ltd, CA [1989] STC 539; [1990] 1 QB 905; [1989] 2 All ER 938.*

58.327   A similar decision was reached in a case which the CA heard with *Faith Construction Ltd*, 58.326 above. *C & E Commrs v West Yorkshire Independent Hospital (Contract Services) Ltd, CA [1989] STC 539; [1990] 1 QB 905; [1989] 2 All ER 938.*

58.328   **Payment by cheque—time of supply.**   Building alterations became standard-rated after 31 May 1984, unless payment was made before 1 June 1984. A builder who was carrying out work for a customer in May 1984 received a cheque for the full amount of the work in May but did not present the cheque to his bank until June. The Commissioners issued an assessment charging tax on the work. The tribunal dismissed the builder's appeal, holding that payment did not take place until the cheque was presented. *MH Rampling, [1986] VATTR 62 (VTD 2067).*

58.329   Similar decisions were reached in *Aldford Aluminium Products, MAN/86/38 (VTD 2190)* and *BJ Charman, LON/86/638 (VTD 2270).*

58.330   **Money placed in joint account by recipient—whether payment within VATA 1994, s 6(4).**   Building alterations became standard-rated after 31 May 1984, unless payment was made before 1 June 1984. A company instigated a scheme whereby it agreed with customers that, if they paid the full agreed price for such work before 1 June, it would place 75% of the amount paid in a building society account in the joint names of it and the customer. The Commissioners issued an assessment charging tax on the work in question and the company appealed, contending that the money placed in the joint account had been paid to it before 1 June 1984 for the purposes of what is now *VATA 1994, s 6(4)*. The tribunal accepted this contention and allowed the company's appeal, holding that although the company had voluntarily placed the money in a joint account, the payment remained the company's property. *Key Kitchens Ltd, LON/85/228 (VTD 2261)*.

58.331   *Key Kitchens Ltd*, 58.330 above, was applied in the similar case of *S Rankin (t/a RDR Construction), BEL/88/5 (VTD 3623)*.

58.332   **Money paid into builder's deposit account for release against architect's certificates.**   In May 1984 a development company borrowed £600,000 from a bank to finance the refurbishment of some flats. It paid the £600,000 into a deposit account at the same bank, in the name of the building company which was to carry out the work. The money was held in the deposit account subject to the condition that it could not be transferred into the building company's current account until the work carried out had been verified by architect's certificates. None of the money was transferred in this way until after 31 May 1984, when building alterations became liable to VAT at 15%. The Commissioners issued an assessment charging tax on the work. The QB allowed the company's appeal, holding that payment had taken place before 1 June 1984 so that the work was zero-rated. The CA upheld this decision. Although the payment was made under arrangements which restricted the recipients' use of the money received, it discharged the contractual liability of the development company to the building company, and left the building company with no right to sue for payment. *C & E Commrs v Dormers Builders (London) Ltd, CA [1989] STC 539; [1989] 2 All ER 938*. (*Note*. For a preliminary issue in this case, see 2.120 APPEALS.)

58.333   Similar decisions were reached in *C & E Commrs v Nevisbrook Ltd, CA [1989] STC 539; [1989] 2 All ER 938*, and *DL Rhodes, MAN/87/339 (VTD 2883)*.

58.334   **Advance payments for time-share accommodation.**   A company which constructed time-share lodges received advance payments from potential purchasers. These payments were refundable if the accommodation was not completed by a specified date. The company failed to account for tax on such payments and the Commissioners issued an assessment on the basis that tax was chargeable at the time the payment was made. The tribunal dismissed the company's appeal, applying *Purshotam M Pattni & Sons*, 58.293 above. *Clowance plc, LON/87/103 (VTD 2541)*.

58.335   **Advance payment received by vehicle manufacturers.**   A partnership which manufactured vehicles received an advance payment on 26 October 1990 in respect of a vehicle which it had agreed to manufacture in the following quarter. The partnership did not account for tax on the payment in its return for the period ending 31 October 1990 and the Commissioners issued an assessment charging tax on the payment in question. The tribunal dismissed the partnership's appeal, holding that the time of supply for VAT purposes was 26 October 1990, the date on which the payment was received. *Marquiss of Scotland, EDN/91/256 (VTD 7161)*. (*Note*. An appeal against a misdeclaration penalty was also dismissed.)

58.336   **Advance payments for theatre bookings.**   A company which operated a theatre did not account for tax on ticket sales until the time of the performance in question, even where payment had been made in advance of the performance. Money received for advance sales was kept in a deposit account until the time of the performance, at which time it was transferred to a current account and an agreed percentage was paid to the producer of the play. The Commissioners issued an assessment on the basis that the company should have accounted for tax at the time when it received payment. The company appealed, contending that since it might have to refund the money if the performance were to be cancelled, it should not be required to account for tax until the performance had actually taken place. The QB rejected this contention and upheld the assessment. The terms of the sale of the ticket did not give the customer any proprietary interest in the money paid and received for the theatre performance, so that output tax was due at the time of payment. Furthermore, even if the customers had had an equitable interest in the money paid, the payment would still be an advance payment in respect of a supply and would still give rise to output tax liability. *C & E Commrs v Richmond Theatre Management Ltd, QB [1995] STC 257.*

58.337 **Advance payments for football matches.** A football club required all spectators to purchase tickets in advance. It sold 'season books' which contained a total of 82 numbered vouchers. 40 of these provided for admission to specific matches, 20 were for use when applying for tickets for away matches, and the remaining 22 were for use when applying for tickets for Cup matches or friendly matches. It also sold more restricted 'season books', which only provided for admission to 16 or 18 league matches. In accounting for VAT, the club treated the vouchers as falling within *VATA 1994, Sch 6 para 5*, so that it only accounted for output tax when the vouchers were presented by the purchasers on a match-by-match basis. The Commissioners issued a ruling that VAT was chargeable on the amount paid for the 'season books' at the time of their purchase, by virtue of *VATA 1994, s 6(4)*. The tribunal upheld the Commissioners' ruling and dismissed the club's appeal. The chairman observed that 'what has happened and does happen in this case is that the supporter prepays his ticket ... the specific supply, although provided later, is paid for at an earlier stage and ... VAT is due on the payment when made. That view is in accordance with logic and common sense. What has been purchased is specific—the right to attend the match in question.' *Richmond Theatre Management Ltd*, 58.336 above, and *Granton Marketing Ltd*, 63.53 VALUATION, applied. *Celtic plc, [1997] VATDR 111 (VTD 14762).*

58.338 **Advance royalties.** See *Software One Ltd*, 49.141 PENALTIES: MISDECLARATION.

58.339 **Advance payment for construction of oil rig.** A company (T) entered into a contract to construct an oil rig for a customer. The customer made an advance payment of £800,000, and T did not account for VAT on this payment. The Commissioners issued an assessment, including a charge to default interest, on the basis that VAT was chargeable at the time when the £800,000 was paid. T appealed, contending that the £800,000 was a 'forward funding' payment, and there was no VAT liability until the work in question was carried out. The tribunal upheld the assessment and dismissed T's appeal, holding that the payment was consideration and that, in accordance with what is now *VATA 1994, s 6(4)*, the tax point occurred when the payment was received. *THC Fabricators (UK) Ltd, MAN/92/659 (VTD 11414).*

Deposits

58.340 **Sale of furniture—rate of tax increased between payment of deposit and payment of balance.** A company which manufactured furniture had received deposits for a number of items of furniture before 18 June 1979, but had not delivered the furniture in question. On 18 June 1979 the standard rate of VAT was increased from 8% to 15%. The company only accounted for VAT on 8% on furniture for which it had held deposits at 18 June, although the items were not delivered and paid for until after 18 June. The Commissioners issued an assessment on the basis that only the deposits could properly be treated as taxable at 8%, and that the balance of the payments in question were taxable at 15%. The tribunal dismissed the company's appeal, holding that, by virtue of what is now *VATA 1994, s 6(4)*, the tax point for the deposit was the time when it was paid, but the tax point for the remainder of the payment was when the furniture was delivered. The tribunal also held that there was a taxable supply when the deposit was paid, even if the customer did not complete the purchase. *JD Fox Ltd, LON/80/237 (VTD 1012).*

58.341   **Deposits for holiday accommodation.** A couple who provided accommodation in holiday flats failed to account for VAT on deposits for such accommodation. The Commissioners issued an assessment charging tax on the deposits and the tribunal dismissed the couple's appeal. The deposit was a payment in respect of a supply, within what is now *VATA 1994, s 6(4)*. *MH & ST Caine, LON/86/440 (VTD 2398)*.

58.342   A similar decision was reached in *G Thompson, MAN/87/112 (VTD 2666)*.

58.343   A company which provided holiday accommodation failed to account for VAT on deposits. The Commissioners issued an assessment charging tax on the deposits and the company appealed, contending that it regarded the deposits as fully refundable and as remaining the property of its customers. The QB rejected this contention and upheld the assessment. Whether the deposits remained the property of the payer was a question of law. On the evidence, the deposits formed part payment of the total price payable, and thus did not remain the property of the payer. *Caine*, 58.341 above, and *Bethway & Moss Ltd*, 58.344 below, approved. *C & E Commrs v Moonraker's Guest House Ltd, QB [1992] STC 544*.

58.344   **Deposits for fitted kitchen units.** A company which supplied fitted kitchen units required payment of a deposit by customers when an order was signed, but did not account for VAT on these deposits until the units were delivered. The Commissioners issued an assessment on the basis that tax should have been accounted for when the deposit was received. The tribunal dismissed the company's appeal, holding that a deposit constituted payment in respect of a supply, within what is now *VATA 1994, s 6(4)*. *Bethway & Moss Ltd, MAN/86/331 (VTD 2667)*. *(Note. The decision was approved by the QB in *Moonraker's Guest House Ltd*, 58.343 above.)*

58.345   **Deposits received by shopfitters.** A shopfitting firm generally took deposits of 50% of the agreed price, but did not account for tax on the deposits. The Commissioners issued an assessment on the basis that tax should have been accounted for when the deposit was received. The tribunal dismissed the firm's appeal, applying *Bethway & Moss Ltd*, 58.344 above. *Regalstar Enterprises, LON/88/197 (VTD 3102)*.

58.346   **Deposits received by company manufacturing sails.** A company which manufactured sails charged customers deposits, which were refundable in certain circumstances. The company did not account for VAT on the deposits, and the Commissioners issued an assessment. The tribunal dismissed the company's appeal, applying *Bethway & Moss Ltd*, 58.344 above, and *Regalstar Enterprises*, 58.345 above. *Bruce Banks Sails Ltd, [1990] VATTR 175 (VTD 4896)*.

58.347   **Deposits for bathroom furniture.** A company which sold bathroom furniture did not account for tax until sales were completed, although it frequently received deposits from customers. The Commissioners issued an assessment on the basis that the company should have accounted for tax when it received the deposits. The tribunal dismissed the company's appeal, applying *Regalstar Enterprises*, 58.345 above, *Bruce Banks Sails Ltd*, 58.346 above, and *Purshotam M Pattni & Sons*, 58.293 above. The deposit was a payment in respect of a supply, within what is now *VATA 1994, s 6(4)*. *Bristol Bathroom Co, LON/89/571Z (VTD 5340)*.

58.348   **Deposits for furniture.** A company failed to account for output tax on deposits for the supply of furniture. The Commissioners issued an assessment on the basis that the supply took place when the deposit was paid. The tribunal dismissed the company's appeal, applying *Bethway & Moss Ltd*, 58.344 above. *UNO Upholstery Superstores Ltd, MAN/93/1493 (VTD 13036)*.

58.349   **Deposits for machine tools.**   A company which supplied machine tools failed to account for VAT on deposits. The Commissioners issued an assessment charging tax on the deposits, and the tribunal dismissed the company's appeal, applying *Bethway & Moss Ltd*, 58.344 above, and *East Kilbride Golf Club*, 58.323 above. The deposits were received in respect of taxable supplies. *Rivers Machinery Ltd, LON/91/542X (VTD 7505)*. (*Note.* An appeal against a misdeclaration penalty was allowed. Compare the cases noted at 49.138 and 49.139 PENALTIES: MISDECLARATION.)

58.350   **Deposits received for entertainment functions.**   A trader promoted entertainment functions, for which he received deposits. He did not account for output tax on the deposits. The Commissioners issued an assessment, including a charge to default interest, on the basis that the trader should have accounted for output tax at the time of receipt of the deposits. The tribunal upheld the assessment and dismissed the trader's appeal, applying the QB decision in *Moonraker's Guest House Ltd*, 58.343 above. *MJ Kirtley (t/a Encore International), MAN/93/1350 (VTD 12471)*.

58.351   **Sale of sports cars—whether initial deposit within VATA 1994, s 6(4).**   A company had a franchise to sell Ferrari sports cars. There was a limited supply of such cars, and the company asked prospective customers to make an initial deposit of about £5,000. When a firm order was placed, the customer was asked to increase the deposit to 10% of the price of the car. The company did not account for VAT on the initial deposits, and the Commissioners issued an assessment charging tax on these. The company appealed, contending that the initial deposits did not relate to any definite supply, and that there was no tax point until a firm order was placed and a 10% deposit was received. The tribunal accepted this contention and allowed the appeal, holding that the initial deposit did not create any contractual relationship, but it was only 'an agreement to make an agreement'. *East Kilbride Golf Club*, 58.323 above, and *Bristol Bathroom Co*, 58.347 above, distinguished. *Nigel Mansell Sports Co Ltd, LON/90/613Y (VTD 6116)*.

Miscellaneous

58.352   **Accountant transferring money from clients' account to working account.**   An accountant transferred sums of money from his clients' account to his working account without issuing VAT invoices. The Commissioners issued an assessment on the basis that the transfer of the money constituted its receipt by the accountant and, by virtue of what is now *VATA 1994, s 6(4)*, was therefore to be treated as the time of supply. The tribunal upheld the assessment and dismissed the accountant's appeal. *MR Ghaus (t/a Ghaus & Co), LON/89/1217 (VTD 4999)*.

58.353   A similar decision was reached in a subsequent appeal by the same accountant. *MR Ghaus (t/a Ghaus & Co), LON/91/950 (VTD 10419)*.

58.354   **Tax consultants receiving payment after registration for work done before registration.**   A firm of tax consultants registered for VAT in October 1986. Earlier in that year they had invoiced a client for work done, but had not received payment and eventually wrote the amount off as a bad debt. In 1991 the client contacted the firm again to ask them to carry out further work. The firm requested payment of the previous debt and the client paid the outstanding amount. The Commissioners issued a ruling that the payment was liable to VAT by virtue of what is now *VAT Regulations 1995 (SI 1995 No 2518), reg 90*, and the firm appealed. The CA allowed the appeal (by a 2–1 majority, Sir Ralph Gibson LJ dissenting). Staughton LJ held that since the supply had taken place before the firm had registered for VAT, it was not then a 'taxable person' within what is now *VATA 1994, s 4(1)*. The question of whether there had been a chargeable transaction had to be determined at the time when the supply was actually made, and the provisions of what is now *VATA 1994, s 6* only applied if there was a charge to tax within the ordinary meaning of *s 4(1)**. Ward LJ held that 'the fictions for determining the time of supply for accounting purposes do not ... govern the ordinary meaning of the language in (*VATA 1994, s 4**) which make supply by a taxable person a prerequisite of liability'. What is now *VATA 1994, s 6** only determined when, rather than whether, a supply was chargeable to VAT. *Dicta* of the tribunal in *Broadwell Land plc*, 34.505 INPUT TAX, approved and applied. *BJ Rice & Associates v C & E Commrs, CA [1996] STC 581. (Notes.* (1) Compare, however, the subsequent HL decision in *Svenska International plc*, 41.16 MANAGEMENT SERVICES, where the HL held that there was no supply until there was an invoice or a payment. (2) For a subsequent application for costs, see 2.315 APPEALS.)

58.355 **Overpayments by telephone subscribers credited to next accounts—time of supply.** In cases where customers of British Telecom (BT) made overpayments, BT retained the amounts overpaid and credited them to the customers' next accounts, unless the customers requested repayment of the amounts involved. It accounted for VAT on the amounts it had invoiced, and thus did not account for any VAT on the overpayments until the issue of an invoice against which they could be set. The Commissioners issued an assessment, charging tax of more than £2,600,000, on the basis that the receipt of the overpayments constituted a tax point for VAT purposes, and that BT should have accounted for VAT accordingly. BT appealed, contending that the overpayments were accidental and did not constitute consideration for any supply. The tribunal allowed the appeal, holding that an accidental overpayment, which was paid 'under mistake of fact', 'lacked the consensual element required for consideration', and that BT could not 'convert a payment made under a mistake into consideration simply by crediting it to the customer's account'. The CA upheld this decision. Millett LJ held that, for a payment to represent consideration for a supply of services, there had to be a 'direct link' with the service provided. The inadvertent overpayment of a current debt was not a payment on account of a future liability. It was not paid on account of, or in respect of, future supplies. Under English law the recipient of an accidental overpayment was under an immediate obligation to repay it. A creditor could not appropriate a payment to a debt unless that debt was presently due and payable. There was no payment in respect of future supplies until the relevant invoice was issued. *C & E Commrs v British Telecommunications plc, CA [1996] STC 818; [1996] 1 WLR 1309.*

58.356 **Avoidance scheme operated by group of companies—vendor companies becoming separately registered after payment but before delivery—time of supply.** See *Thorn Materials Supply Ltd*, 30.27 GROUPS OF COMPANIES.

58.357 **Stolen takings.** See *Benton*, 58.289 above, and the cases noted at 58.290 above.

Continuous supplies of services (VAT Regulations 1995, reg 90)

58.358 **Rental payments between associated companies—time of supply.** A company (C) made regular payments of rent to an associated company (D). On 7 April 1992 the companies' directors reviewed the accounting period ending 31 December 1991, considered that the rental payments had been inadequate, and decided to charge an additional rent for that period of £6,000,000. This was entered in the companies' accounts, but the companies did not account for VAT. A VAT officer discovered this at a control visit in December 1992. Following his visit, D issued an invoice to C on 16 December for £6,000,000 plus VAT. The invoice was backdated to 30 November (to enable C to claim the VAT as input tax in its return for that period). The Commissioners issued an assessment and a misdeclaration penalty on the basis that the time of the supply had been 7 April 1992, when the companies' directors had agreed to make the payment. D appealed, contending that the time of supply was 30 November, being the date on the invoice. The tribunal held on the evidence that the payment was within what is now *VAT Regulations 1995 (SI 1995 No 2518), reg 90* as being for a continuous supply of services, and therefore that the time of supply was 16 December, the date on which the invoice was actually issued. The tribunal therefore allowed D's appeal, while criticising the directors' conduct in having backdated the invoice, and observing that an award of costs was inappropriate. *Diggor Gaylord Ltd; CP Holdings Ltd, LON/93/536A (VTD 11380).*

58.359   **Management services—time of supply.**   See *Legal & Contractual Services Ltd*, 41.4 MANAGEMENT SERVICES; *Pentex Oil Ltd*, 41.5 MANAGEMENT SERVICES; *Missionfine Ltd*, 41.6 MANAGEMENT SERVICES; *Waverley Housing Management Ltd*, 41.7 MANAGEMENT SERVICES, and *Svenska International plc*, 41.16 MANAGEMENT SERVICES.

58.360   **Accountancy services—whether a continuous supply of services within regulation 90*.**   See *Halpern & Woolf*, 49.107 PENALTIES: MISDECLARATION.

58.361   **Car hire—time of supply.**   A company (M) operated a fleet of motor cars. It agreed with another company (D) that, in return for payment from D, it would make such cars available to motorists who had lost the use of their own cars as a result of an accident. D described itself as an insurance company, but was not an authorised motor insurer, and M had a block insurance policy with an authorised insurer. The Commissioners issued a ruling that the arrangements between D and M resulted in separate supplies each time an individual vehicle was hired, with the result that there was a tax point at the end of each hire period. M appealed, contending that the effect of the arrangements was that there was a continuous supply, so that VAT was only payable when payment was received or when an invoice was issued. The tribunal allowed M's appeal, holding that there was a continuous supply and that the tax point fell to be determined under what is now *VAT Regulations 1995 (SI 1995 No 2518), reg 90. Halpern & Woolf*, 49.107 PENALTIES: MISDECLARATION, distinguished. *Motor & Legal Group Ltd, MAN/93/896 (VTD 12036). (Note.* An alternative contention by M, that part of the consideration should be treated as being for insurance and as exempt from VAT under what is now *VATA 1994, Sch 9, Group 2*, was rejected—see 36.2 INSURANCE.)

58.362   **Continuous supplies of services—payments received after liquidation—time of supply.**   See *Glenshane Construction Services Ltd (in liquidation)*, 35.14 INSOLVENCY.

THE PLACE OF THE SUPPLY (VATA 1994, s 7)

Place of supply of goods

58.363   **Machine tools manufactured overseas but assembled and installed in UK.**   A company traded as a selling agent on behalf of a number of overseas manufacturers of machine tools, and received commission based on the value of the machine tools ordered. The company did not account for tax on this commission, and the Commissioners issued an assessment charging output tax. The company appealed, contending that the goods were supplied outside the UK (and thus were zero-rated under the legislation then in force). The tribunal allowed the appeal, holding that, by virtue of what is now *VATA 1994, s 7(7)*, the machine tools were to be treated as supplied outside the UK. The tribunal distinguished *Azo-Maschinenfabrik Adolf Zimmerman*, 21.105 EUROPEAN COMMUNITY LAW, holding that 'there is no rule of law compelling, or enabling, any court to construe a pre-existing statute of the United Kingdom in order to comply with a Directive subsequent in time, where the legislature or executive of the United Kingdom has not implemented that Directive'. *George Kuikka Ltd, [1990] VATTR 185 (VTD 5037).*

58.364   **Purchase of yacht moored in Greece—place of supply.** See *Da Conti International Ltd*, 34.524 INPUT TAX.

58.365   **Whether cars sold in Germany or UK.** A jeweller sold two Peugeot cars, one to a German and one to a resident of Scotland. The Commissioners issued an assessment charging tax on the sales. The jeweller appealed, contending that the sales had taken place in Germany and were thus outside the scope of UK VAT. The tribunal accepted the jeweller's evidence and allowed the appeal. *JR Joannides, MAN/91/1338 (VTD 11373). (Note.* For another issue in this case, see 34.338 INPUT TAX.)

58.366   **Goods sold on board ships.** A company operated a ferry from Portsmouth to Spain. It sold various goods to passengers. The Commissioners issued a ruling that VAT was chargeable on the sales, on the basis that the place of supply was the UK, in accordance with the *Place of Supply of Goods Order 1992 (SI 1992 No 3283).* The company appealed, contending that the effect of *Article 8(1)(c)* of the *EC Sixth Directive* was that VAT should not be charged on sales made when the ferry was outside EC territorial waters. The tribunal rejected this contention and dismissed the appeal, and the QB upheld this decision. Lightman J held that *Article 8(1)(c)* was 'clear and unambiguous'. Its effect was that, in the absence of a stop in a third territory, 'in the case of goods supplied between the first point of passenger embarkation within the Community and the last point of disembarkation within the Community, the place of supply of goods shall be deemed to be the first point of passenger embarkation, and this general rule operates irrespective of the fact that in the course of the journey between the two points the ship travels through territorial waters or the high seas'. Accordingly, 'on intra-Community sailings supplies of goods made on the high seas outside the territory of Member States fall within the scope of VAT'. *Peninsular & Oriental Steam Navigation Company v C & E Commrs, QB [2000] STC 488.*

Place of supply of services

Place where supplier or recipient belongs (VATA 1994, ss 7(10),9)

58.367   **Accountancy services supplied to company registered in UK but operating abroad.** An accountancy firm supplied services to a company which traded in Jamaica but had its registered office in the UK. It did not account for output tax on these supplies. The Commissioners issued an assessment charging tax on them, and the firm appealed, contending that the services were supplied outside the UK and thus were zero-rated under the legislation then in force. The tribunal dismissed the appeal, holding that the company's registered office was a 'fixed establishment' for the purpose of what is now *VATA 1994, s 9(2).* Accordingly, the place of supply was in the UK. *Binder Hamlyn, [1983] VATTR 171 (VTD 1439).*

58.368   Similar decisions were reached in *Vincent Consultants Ltd, [1988] VATTR 152 (VTD 3091); Singer & Friedlander Ltd, [1989] VATTR 27 (VTD 3274); Chantrey Vellacott, [1992] VATTR 138 (VTD 7311)* and *A Marks (t/a Marks Cameron Davies & Co), LON/95/1773 (VTD 15541).*

58.369   **Supply of management services to companies resident in Monaco but registered in the UK.** A UK-resident company (S) was the parent company of thirteen investment companies resident in Monaco but incorporated in the UK and having their registered offices in the UK. The subsidiary companies owned property in the UK, from which they received rental income. S supplied the services of accounting and administrative staff to the investment companies, and did not account for tax on these supplies. The Commissioners issued an assessment charging tax on them, and S appealed, contending that the supplies were supplies of staff within what is now *VATA 1994, Sch 5 para 6*, so that the supplies took place outside the UK and were zero-rated under the legislation then in force. The tribunal rejected this contention and dismissed the appeal, holding that the services were general management services, rather than simply the supply of staff. Each of the investment companies had a fixed establishment in the UK for the purpose of what is now *VATA 1994, s 9(2)*, and the staff were used to administer and collect rent from properties in the UK. Accordingly, the place of supply was in the UK. *Strollmoor Ltd, LON/90/1506X (VTD 5454)*.

58.370   The company in the case noted at 58.369 above appealed against a subsequent assessment charging tax on supplies of management services to its Monaco subsidiaries. The tribunal dismissed the appeal. *Strollmoor Ltd, LON/94/632A (VTD 12765)*. (*Note*. An alternative contention by the company, that the assessment was out of time and invalid, was also rejected—see 3.49 ASSESSMENT.)

58.371   **Television signals transmitted from UK to overseas recipient.** A Hong Kong company contracted for British Telecom to transmit BBC World Service television to a receiving station in Hong Kong. The Commissioners issued a ruling that VAT was chargeable on these supplies. The Hong Kong company appealed, contending that the supplies should be treated as supplies of engineering services, within what is now *VATA 1994, Sch 5 para 3*, and as taking place outside the UK. The tribunal rejected this contention and dismissed the appeal, holding that the supplies were not within the definition of 'engineering services' and that the place of supply was where the supplier belonged, which was in the UK. *Hutchvision Hong Kong Ltd, LON/92/2736A (VTD 10509)*. (*Note*. With regard to the place of supply of telecommunication services, see now *VAT (Place of Supply of Services) Order 1992 (SI 1992 No 3121), articles 19 & 20*, introduced by *SI 1997 No 1524*.)

58.372   A UK company supplied satellite television broadcasts. The Commissioners issued a ruling that the company was required to account for output tax on such supplies to residents of Eire and the Channel Islands. The company appealed, contending that the services were 'entertainment services', within *Article 9(2)(c)* of the *EC Sixth Directive*, and should be deemed to be supplied where they were received. The tribunal dismissed the appeal, holding that although the services could be described as 'entertainment', they were not within *Article 9(2)(c)* of the *EC Sixth Directive*, which should be construed as 'dealing with the case of the supplier of the service moving between countries ... entertainment services which do not involve performance before a live audience are not covered'. Accordingly, the effect of *Article 9(1)* of the *EC Sixth Directive* was that the services were deemed to be supplied where the supplier was established, which was in the UK. *British Sky Broadcasting Ltd, [1994] VATTR 1 (VTD 12394)*. (*Note*. See now the note following *Hutchvision Hong Kong Ltd*, 58.371 above.)

58.373   **Satellite television company—whether carrying on business in UK.** A company (H), which was incorporated in Hong Kong, provided Chinese-language satellite television programmes to subscribers in Western Europe (including the UK). It had an associated company (C) which operated from premises in the UK, and which assisted in broadcasting the satellite signals to subscribers, providing local news items and editing some of the tapes which H provided. The Commissioners issued a ruling that H was carrying on business in the UK through C as its agent, so that, by virtue of *VATA 1994, s 9(5)*, C was liable to account for output tax on the relevant supplies of broadcasting services. H appealed, contending that it was making the supplies of broadcasting services itself, that it was not carrying on business in the UK, that C was an independent principal acting as a subcontractor rather than an agent, and that the place of supply of the services in question was in Hong Kong. The tribunal accepted H's evidence and allowed its appeal, finding that the greater part of the broadcasting business, such as the selection of programmes and the establishment of timetables, took place in Hong Kong, and holding that the relevant supplies were made from Hong Kong, where H was established. The QB upheld this decision as one of fact. Moses J observed that *Article 9* of the *EC Sixth Directive* 'requires a factual judgment as to whether the service is supplied from a fixed establishment'. *DFDS A/S*, 21.229 EUROPEAN COMMUNITY LAW, distinguished. *C & E Commrs v The Chinese Channel (Hong Kong) Ltd, QB [1998] STC 347.* (*Note.* For the Commissioners' practice following this decision, see Business Brief 12/98, issued on 21 May 1998.)

58.374   **Data processing and related services—whether supplied in UK.**   Two UK companies imported data processing and related services from a Canadian company. The Commissioners issued a ruling that the services were within *VAT (Place of Supply of Services) Order 1992 (SI 1992 No 3121), article 16,* and were supplied where they were received, i.e. in the UK. The companies appealed, accepting that approximately 60% of the relevant services fell within *article 16,* but contending that about 40% of the services were outside the scope of *article 16* and thus were supplied in Canada, where the supplier belonged. The tribunal accepted this contention and allowed the appeal, holding that 'the services appear to vary widely both in nature and in taxability'. *Bophutatswana National Commercial Corporation Ltd,* 37.2 INTERNATIONAL SERVICES, applied. *Laurentian Management Services Ltd; Lincoln Assurance Ltd, LON/96/1017 & 1018 (VTD 16447).*

58.375   **Lease of aircraft to Jersey company.**   A UK company leased a Cessna aircraft to a Jersey company. It did not account for output tax on the consideration, and the Commissioners issued an assessment charging tax thereon. The company appealed, contending that the place of supply was outside the EC so that no output tax was due. The tribunal dismissed the appeal, holding that the effect of what is now *VATA 1994, s 7(10)* was that the supply was to be treated as having taken place in the UK. *IDS Aircraft Ltd, LON/93/2684 (VTD 12452).*

58.376   **Overseas company admitted to UK group under extra-statutory concession—whether company deemed to 'belong' in UK for purposes of VATA 1994, s 9.**   A UK company (L) made supplies of leasing office and computer equipment to a US company (P). Although P had no business establishment in the UK, it had been accepted as a member of a UK VAT group. The Commissioners issued an assessment on L on the basis that, because P was a member of a UK VAT group, it was deemed to belong in the UK for the purpose of *VATA 1994, s 9,* so that the place of supply was in the UK and L was required to account for output tax. The tribunal allowed L's appeal, holding that P could only be treated as a member of the group if it was established in the UK within the meaning of *Article 4(4)* of the *EC Sixth Directive* and if *VATA 1994, s 43* was capable of being interpreted accordingly. On the evidence, P was neither established nor resident in the UK, and 'the Commissioners were not in law entitled to treat (P) as a member of a UK VAT group. The result of this is that the consequences of grouping cannot be applied when determining the place of supply which must therefore be in the USA. The grouping, which was extra-statutory, falls to be disregarded.' *Shamrock Leasing Ltd, [1998] VATDR 323 (VTD 15719).*

58.377   **Advertising services—whether supplied in UK.**   A UK company supplied advertising services to the Spanish Tourist Board. It did not account for output tax on such supplies. The Commissioners issued assessments charging tax on the company, on the basis that the Spanish Tourist Board was not receiving the supplies for the purposes of a business, so that the supplies did not meet the conditions of *Article 16(b)* of the *VAT (Place of Supply of Services) Order*, and the place of supply was therefore in the UK, where the supplier belonged. The company appealed, contending that *Article 16(b)* of the *VAT (Place of Supply of Services) Order 1992 (SI 1992 No 3121)* was incompatible with *Article 9(2)* of the *EC Sixth Directive*, and that the effect of *Article 9(2)(e)* of the *EC Sixth Directive* was that the supplies should be deemed to have taken place in Spain. The tribunal rejected this contention and upheld the assessments for accounting periods from 1 January 1993, holding that the Spanish Tourist Board had not received the advertising services for the purpose of any business, since it was a government body and its promotion of tourism was 'not an economic activity or a business in the VAT sense of those expressions'. Accordingly the conditions of *Article 16(b)* of the *VAT (Place of Supply of Services) Order* were not satisfied, and the services had to be treated as supplied in the UK. Furthermore, the *VAT (Place of Supply of Services) Order* was not incompatible with the *EC Sixth Directive*. The tribunal observed that 'the structure of *Article 9* of the *Directive* is to lay down as a presumptive rule that the member state of origin is to tax supplies of services made by its taxable persons, unless any of the exemptions in *paragraph 2* apply to transfer the right to tax to the member state of receipt'. The fact that the Spanish Tourist Board was registered for VAT in Spain was not conclusive, since it was a state authority within *Article 4(5)* of the *Directive*, rather than a taxable person. The QB upheld this decision. Owen J held that, for *Article 9(2)(e)* of the *Directive* to apply, it was not sufficient for a recipient of the services to be a 'taxable person', but 'he must also receive the service as one who is carrying on an economic activity so that the cost of the services is included in the price of the goods which will bring into operation the reverse charge mechanism'. *Diversified Agency Services Ltd (aka Omnicom UK plc) v C & E Commrs, QB 1995, [1996] STC 398.* (*Notes.* (1) The appeal to the tribunal also concerned periods before 1 January 1993, in respect of which the tribunal allowed the company's appeal, holding that the relevant supplies were zero-rated under the UK legislation then in force. (2) In a subsequent appeal, it was held that the Spanish Tourist Board could not reclaim input tax on the payments—see 34.440 INPUT TAX.)

58.378 **Promotion of tourism—whether services supplied in UK.** The London branch of the Austrian National Tourist Office (ANTO), which was registered for UK VAT, organised two workshops in London, at which it made supplies of services to Austrian businesses. It did not account for output tax in respect of these supplies, treating them as supplies of advertising services which, by virtue of *VAT (Place of Supply of Services) Order 1992 (SI 1992 No 3121), article 16*, were deemed to be supplied in Austria, where the recipients belonged. The Commissioners issued a ruling that output tax was chargeable on the supplies, on the basis that the supplies were not within the definition of 'advertising services' and that, since the supplies were made from a fixed establishment in the UK, the place of supply was in the UK. The tribunal dismissed ANTO's appeal, holding that the definition of an 'advertising service' in *EC Commission v French Republic,* 21.118 EUROPEAN COMMUNITY LAW, should be restricted to promotional activities involving the dissemination of a message 'by the person providing the service' and that ANTO's supplies were not within this definition since ANTO 'provides facilities for others to disseminate that message'. The tribunal held that it was 'apparent from the Court's judgment that what it had in contemplation was the provision, particularly by an advertising agency ... of advertising services to include promotional activities for a particular client. That is not the case here.' *Austrian National Tourist Office, LON/96/674 (VTD 15561).* (*Note.* For another issue in this case, see 34.397 INPUT TAX.)

58.379 **Consultancy services supplied to MEPs—whether received 'for the purpose of a business'.** A UK company supplied research and consultancy services to

Members of the European Parliament. It did not account for tax on these supplies. The Commissioners issued a ruling that it was required to account for output tax. The company appealed, contending that since it was supplying services within *VATA 1994, Sch 5 para 3*, the place of the supply was where the recipients belonged, which was outside the UK. The tribunal rejected this contention and dismissed the appeal. It was accepted that the company's supplies were within *Sch 5 para 3*. However, the Members of the European Parliament were not receiving the supplies 'for the purpose of a business', as required by *VAT (Place of Supply of Services) Order 1992 (SI 1992 No 3121), article 16(b)(i)*. Accordingly, the provisions of *article 16* did not apply, and the place of the supply was where the company belonged, which was in the UK. (The tribunal also held that the supplies did not qualify for exemption under *Article 15(10)* of the *EC Sixth Directive*.) *MEP Research Services Ltd, LON/96/1284 (VTD 16044)*.

58.380   **VATA 1994, s 9(3)*—definition of 'usual place of residence'.**   In a case where the substantive issue (involving the liability of certain supplies of insurance) has been overtaken by subsequent changes in the legislation, the tribunal held that US Forces personnel living in England on a three-year tour of duty had their 'usual place of residence' in the UK. During the tour of duty their houses in the USA were let, and, if they returned for training to the USA, their families remained in the UK. They could not therefore be regarded as having their usual place of residence in the USA. *USAA Ltd, LON/92/1950A (VTD 10369)*.

58.381   In August 1992 an Indian woman (H) entered the UK as an employee in domestic service. She left her employers in November 1992 and began legal proceedings against them. She remained in the UK during the proceedings, which were eventually settled in October 1996 by a consent order, under which her former employers were liable to pay her legal costs. The Commissioners issued a ruling that the place of supply was in the UK, so that VAT was chargeable on the costs. Her former employers appealed, contending that H's usual place of residence was in India so that the services were deemed to be supplied in India and UK VAT was not chargeable. The tribunal accepted this contention and allowed the appeal. The fact that H had been physically present in the UK throughout the period when the services were performed was not conclusive. *USAA Ltd*, 58.380 above, distinguished. *SA Razzak & MA Mishari, [1997] VATDR 392 (VTD 15240)*.

58.382   **VATA 1994, s 9(5)—services supplied through branch or agency.**   The Commissioners sent a notice to a Jersey company at the York office of a UK company, which the Commissioners considered was acting as a branch or agency of the Jersey company. The Jersey company appealed against that notice. The tribunal upheld the notice and dismissed the appeal, holding that the conditions of what is now *VATA 1994, s 9(5)(a)* were satisfied. Accordingly, when a UK resident used the services of the Jersey company, the services had been supplied in the UK. *Interbet Trading Ltd (No 2), [1978] VATTR 235 (VTD 696)*.

58.383   For a case where the tribunal held that the provisions of *VATA 1994, s 9(5)* were inconsistent with *Article 9* of the *EC Sixth Directive*, see *WH Payne & Co*, 58.397 below.

Services relating to land (VAT (Place of Supply of Services) Order, article 5)

58.384   **Surveyors' services—whether 'services relating to land'.**   A company surveyed damage to a jetty and lock at Hull and Immingham respectively. The work was carried out for companies registered in Hong Kong and Bermuda, and the company did not account for output tax on the supplies. The Commissioners issued a ruling that output tax was chargeable. The tribunal dismissed the company's appeal, holding that the work constituted 'services relating to land', within what is now *VAT (Place of Supply of Services) Order 1992 (SI 1992 No 3121), Article 5*, so that the place of supply was in the UK and the work did not qualify for zero-rating. *Brodrick Wright & Strong Ltd, LON/86/461 (VTD 2347)*.

58.385   **Services relating to commissioning of industrial waste incinerator—whether 'services relating to land'.**   A company supplied services to a Swiss company relating to the commissioning of an industrial waste incinerator complex in Cheshire. The Commissioners issued a ruling that the services were 'services relating to land', within *VAT (Place of Supply of Services) Order 1992 (SI 1992 No 3121), Article 5*, so that the services should be treated as supplied in Cheshire. The company appealed, contending that the effect of *Article 9* of the *EC Sixth Directive* was that the services should be treated as supplied in Switzerland, where the recipient was established. The tribunal dismissed the appeal, holding that the services were 'services relating to land', since 'it is a general rule of English law that anything affixed to land becomes part of it'. Furthermore, the waste incinerator complex was 'immovable property', so that under *Article 9(2)* of the *EC Sixth Directive* the services were also to be treated as supplied in the UK. *Mechanical Engineering Consultants Ltd, MAN/93/1074 (VTD 13287)*.

58.386   **Management services supplied by UK company to Channel Islands companies—whether 'services relating to land'.**   A UK company supplied management services to two companies registered in the Channel Islands companies, in respect of properties situated in the UK which those companies owned. The Commissioners issued an assessment charging tax on the supplies. The company appealed, accepting that 25% of the fees which it charged related to specific properties in the UK, and were therefore supplies relating to UK land and thus standard-rated, but contending that the remaining 75% of its fees should be treated as relating to accountancy and bookkeeping services, in respect of which the place of supply was the Channel Islands where the recipient companies belonged. The tribunal rejected this contention and dismissed the appeal, holding on the evidence that the whole of the services in question were services relating to land, within *VAT (Place of Supply of Services) Order 1992 (SI 1992 No 3121), Article 5*, so that the supplies were deemed to take place in the UK. *Aspen Advisory Services Ltd, LON/94/2773A (VTD 13489)*.

58.387   **Provision of display space at exhibitions—whether 'advertising services' or 'services relating to land'.**   A company organised exhibitions. Before 1996, it treated its supplies of display space to exhibitors as licences to occupy land. Since it had elected to waive exemption, it accounted for tax on these supplies. Following the tribunal decision in *International Trade & Exhibitions J/V Ltd*, 58.390 below, it applied to the Commissioners for authority to treat its supplies as advertising services falling within *Article 16* of the *VAT (Supply of Services) Order 1992 (SI 1992 No 3121)*, so that, where the recipient of the supplies belonged outside the UK, it should not be required to account for output tax. The Commissioners rejected the application and ruled that, despite the decision in *International Trade & Exhibitions J/V Ltd*, the company was granting licences to occupy land and, in view of its election to waive exemption, output tax was chargeable. The tribunal upheld the Commissioners' ruling and dismissed the company's appeal, holding on the evidence that the company was supplying 'the right to occupy space at the venue to which the exhibitor expects that the sort of customer he wants to attend will come. What he is getting, in effect, is the right to set up his stall so that his potential customers can visit him there.' The supplies were not within the definition of 'advertising services', since there was 'a legitimate distinction to be drawn between a supplier providing particular clients in the course of an advertising campaign with the means to get across a message about their products and services, and the situation here where what is provided is the opportunity in a specific location for clients to be there and do all the work of promoting themselves to those potential customers who attend the exhibition'. *Tameside Metropolitan Borough Council*, 39.5 LAND, applied; *International Trade & Exhibitions J/V Ltd*, 58.390 below, distinguished (and implicitly disapproved). *Miller Freeman Worldwide plc, [1998] VATDR 435 (VTD 15452)*.

Use of customer's registration number (VAT (Place of Supply of Services) Order, article 14)

58.388   A UK trader supplied transport services, beginning in France, to a UK company which was registered for VAT. He failed to account for tax on the supply and the Commissioners issued an assessment. The tribunal dismissed the trader's appeal, observing that *VAT (Place of Supply of Services) Order 1992 (SI 1992 No 3121), article 14* provided that where a supply of services 'consists of ancillary transport services provided in connection with the intra-Community transport of goods, and the recipient of those services makes use, for the purpose of the supply, of a registration number, then the supply shall be treated as made in the member State which issued the registration number if ... the supply would otherwise be treated as taking place in a different member State'. *J Blair, EDN/00/17 (VTD 16767)*.

Services supplied where performed (VAT (Place of Supply of Services) Order, article 15)

58.389   **Payment for services of jockey—whether for 'sporting services'.**   An Irish trainer paid a UK company £150,000 for the right to have first claim on the services of a leading UK jockey for races outside the UK. The Commissioners issued an assessment charging VAT on the payment. The company appealed, contending that the supply was a supply of sporting services, within what is now *VAT (Place of Supply of Services) Order 1992 (SI 1992 No 3121), Article 15*, so that the place of supply was outside the UK. The tribunal accepted this contention and allowed the company's appeal. *Patrick Eddery Ltd, [1986] VATTR 30 (VTD 2009)*.

Services supplied where received (VAT (Place of Supply of Services) Order, article 16)

58.390   **VATA 1994, Sch 5 para 2—definition of 'advertising services'.**   A UK company supplied an exhibition stand to a Georgian institute for an exhibition in Bahrain. It reclaimed input tax under *VATA 1994, s 26(2)(b)* on the costs of providing the stand. The Commissioners rejected the claim, considering that the supply was a 'service relating to land' which would have been an exempt supply if made in the UK, so that the company could not recover the attributable input tax. The company appealed, contending that the services were not 'relating to land' but were advertising services falling within *Article 16* of the *VAT (Supply of Services) Order 1992 (SI 1992 No 3121)*, and that it was entitled to recover this input tax. The tribunal accepted these contentions and allowed the appeal, holding that the service should not be treated as a 'service relating to land', since 'the right of occupation of the land at the exhibition centre was not ... the dominant feature of the supply'. The company was supplying 'advertising services' within *Article 9(2)(e)* of the *EC Sixth Directive*. *Tameside Metropolitan Borough Council*, 39.5 LAND, distinguished. *International Trade & Exhibitions J/V Ltd, [1996] VATDR 165 (VTD 14212)*. (*Notes*. (1) For the Commissioners' practice following this decision, see Business Brief 24/96, issued on 28 November 1996. (2) The decision in this case was not followed, and was implicitly disapproved, in the subsequent case of *Miller Freeman Worldwide plc*, 58.387 above.)

58.391   A company operated a motor racing team. Its income was derived almost entirely from sponsorship. Some of its sponsors were established outside the EC. It did not account for tax on its payments from such sponsors, treating them as consideration for supplies of advertising services which, by virtue of *VAT (Place of Supply of Services) Order 1992 (SI 1992 No 3121), article 16*, were deemed to be supplied where the recipients belonged. The Commissioners issued an assessment charging tax on the basis that the company was supplying sporting services which, by virtue of *VAT (Place of Supply of Services) Order 1992 (SI 1992 No 3121), article 15*, should be treated as being supplied in the UK. The company appealed. The tribunal allowed the appeal, holding on the evidence that 'the overwhelmingly predominant element of the services supplied by the appellant to the sponsors was advertising' and observing that 'the fact that the publicity was to be provided by means of the appellant's taking part in a sporting event did not turn what, in our judgment, would otherwise have been beyond question a supply of advertising services into a supply of sporting services'. *John Village Automotive Ltd, [1998] VATDR 340 (VTD 15540).*

58.392   See also *Lawrence*, 37.3 INTERNATIONAL SERVICES, and *Miller Freeman Worldwide plc*, 58.387 above.

58.393   **Advertising services—whether supplied to Liechtenstein recipient or UK recipient.**   In 1996 an organisation (G) was formed in Liechtenstein, primarily to criticise the policies adopted by the European Union. It arranged for a UK partnership (B) to supply advertisements in the UK, calling for a referendum on European issues. B sent G invoices in respect of these services, treating them as zero-rated on the basis that the place of supply was where G belonged, which was outside the EU. The Commissioners issued an assessment charging tax on B, on the basis that the advertisements had actually been supplied to a UK political party (R), so that the place of supply was in the UK. G appealed, contending that it was the recipient of the services in question, so that the supplies were therefore zero-rated. The tribunal accepted this contention and allowed the appeal, holding that B was supplying the relevant services to G, and that 'the fact that (R) may also have received a service or benefit as part of the same transaction does not alter the position'. *The Goldsmith Foundation for European Affairs, [2000] VATDR 97 (VTD 16544).*

58.394   **Advertising services—validity of VAT (Place of Supply of Services) Order.**   See *Diversified Agency Services Ltd*, 58.377 above.

58.395   **VATA 1994, Sch 5 para 3—services of consultants.**   See *Vision Express Ltd*, 37.6 INTERNATIONAL SERVICES, and *MEP Research Services Ltd*, 58.379 above.

58.396   **VATA 1994, Sch 5 para 3—engineering services.**   See *Hutchvision Hong Kong Ltd*, 58.371 above.

58.397   **Accountancy services supplied to overseas companies owning UK property—whether within VATA 1994, Sch 5 para 3.**   An accountancy firm supplied accountancy and taxation services to a number of overseas companies which owned properties in the UK, the properties in question being let to tenants. The firm did not account for output tax on the supplies in question. The Commissioners issued an assessment on the basis that the supplies should be treated as having taken place in the UK so that VAT was chargeable. The firm appealed, contending that the effect of *Article 9(2)(e)* of the *EC Sixth Directive* and of *VATA 1994, Sch 5 para 3* was that the services should be treated as being supplied where the recipients belonged and that the place of supply was therefore outside the UK. The tribunal allowed the appeal, holding on the evidence that the recipient companies did not have a 'fixed establishment' in the UK. *Dicta* of the Advocate-General in *Berkholz v Finanzamt Hamburg-Mitte-Altstadt*, 21.108 EUROPEAN COMMUNITY LAW, applied; *Binder Hamlyn*, 58.367 above, was distinguished on the grounds that the recipient company in that case had its registered office in the UK. The tribunal held that the fact that the companies had appointed agents to manage their UK properties was not conclusive, and that the provisions of *VATA 1994, s 9(5)*, treating a person who carries on business through a branch or agency as having a business establishment in that country, were inconsistent with *Article 9* of the *Sixth Directive* as interpreted in *Berkholz*. The supplies in question had taken place where the recipient companies were established, which was outside the UK. *WH Payne & Co, [1995] VATDR 490 (VTD 13668)*. (*Note*. The Commissioners announced that they were appealing to the High Court against this decision. For their statement of policy pending the hearing of the appeal, see Business Brief 26/96, issued on 19 December 1996, and Customs' VAT Manual, Part 4, sections 5.10, 7.4 and 16.11. However, there was no further hearing of the appeal. With regard to the definition of a 'fixed establishment', see the subsequent CJEC decision in *DFDS A/S*, 21.229 EUROPEAN COMMUNITY LAW. For the Commissioners' practice following the CJEC decision in *DFDS*, see Business Brief 12/98, issued on 21 May 1998.)

58.398   **VATA 1994, Sch 5 para 3—exclusion of services relating to land.** See *Brodrick Wright & Strong Ltd*, 58.384 above, *Mechanical Engineering Consultants Ltd*, 58.385 above, and *Aspen Advisory Services Ltd*, 58.386 above.

58.399   **VATA 1994, Sch 5 para 5—definition of 'financial services'.** A company trading as a metal broker acquired options for the purchase of a quantity of cadmium, and gave corresponding options to a client company. The company had reclaimed input tax on the amount it had paid for the options, but failed to account for tax on the amount it had received for them. The Commissioners issued an assessment charging tax on the amount received. The company appealed, contending firstly that it had made supplies of goods and that the place of supply was where the cadmium was situated, which was outside the UK, and alternatively, that if the supply was of services, that it was a supply of financial services within what is now *VATA 1994, Sch 5 para 5*, so that it was zero-rated under the legislation then in force. The tribunal rejected these contentions and dismissed the appeal, holding that the grant of an option to acquire cadmium was not a financial service within what is now *VATA 1994, Sch 5 para 5*. Lord Grantchester held that the words 'financial services' should 'be confined to services in connection with money and credit'. *Gardner Lohman Ltd, [1981] VATTR 76 (VTD 1081)*.

58.400   In a case where a company had unsuccessfully appealed against assessments on payments which a company received for property management, the tribunal held that rent collection was not a financial service within what is now *VATA 1994, Sch 5 para 5*. *Culverpalm Ltd, [1984] VATTR 199 (VTD 1727)*.

58.401   **VATA 1994, Sch 5 para 6—definition of 'supplies of staff'.** A UK company provided the services of travel couriers to two associated US companies. It did not account for tax on such supplies. The Commissioners issued an assessment charging tax of more than £150,000. The company appealed, contending that the supplies were supplies of staff, within *VATA 1994, Sch 5 para 6*, and were therefore, by virtue of *VAT (Place of Supply of Services) Order 1992 (SI 1992 No 3121), article 16*, deemed to take place where the recipient companies belonged, which was outside the EU. The tribunal accepted this contention and allowed the appeal, observing that it was 'more natural to describe the provision of couriers by the UK company as the supply of couriers than as the supply of courier services'. *American Institute of Foreign Study (UK) Ltd, LON/95/898A (VTD 13886)*.

58.402   **VATA 1994, Sch 5 para 7—definition of 'goods other than means of transport'.** A UK company hired cranes to a Netherlands company. The Commissioners issued an assessment on the basis that the supply was deemed to take place in the UK. The company appealed, contending that the effect of what is now *VATA 1994, Sch 5 para 7* and *VAT (Place of Supply of Services) Order 1992 (SI 1992 No 3121), article 16*, was that the supply was deemed to take place in the Netherlands.

The tribunal accepted this contention and allowed the appeal, rejecting the Commissioners' contention that the cranes should be treated as 'means of transport'. The fact that the cranes had an engine, caterpillar tread, gearing and brakes was not sufficient to bring them within the definition of 'means of transport', since 'transport' should be construed as involving 'movement from one place to another'. *Dicta* of Lord Widgery CJ in *Blackpool Pleasure Beach Co*, 62.22 TRANSPORT, applied. The cranes were 'not intended for travelling on roads' and their 'primary function (was) not to carry goods from A to B but to position them when on site'. *BPH Equipment Ltd, MAN/94/530 (VTD 13914)*.

MIXED AND COMPOSITE SUPPLIES

58.403 **General principles.** In the case noted at 21.162 EUROPEAN COMMUNITY LAW, the CJEC held that it was for the national court to determine whether the particular transactions in dispute were to be regarded as comprising two independent supplies, namely an exempt insurance supply and a taxable card registration service. The CJEC observed that 'having regard to the diversity of commercial operations, it is not possible to give exhaustive guidance on how to approach the problem correctly in all cases.' However, 'a supply which comprises a single service from an economic point of view should not be artificially split'. There was 'a single supply in particular in cases where one or more elements are to be regarded as constituting the principal service, whilst one or more elements are to be regarded, by contrast, as ancillary services which share the tax treatment of the principal service. A service must be regarded as ancillary to a principal service if it does not constitute for customers an aim in itself, but a means of better enjoying the principal service supplied'. *Card Protection Plan Ltd v C & E Commrs, CJEC Case C-349/96; [1999] STC 270; [1999] 3 WLR 203; [1999] AEECR 339*. (*Note*. The HL allowed the company's appeal in January 2001.)

58.404 **Subscriptions including handbooks or magazines—whether apportionable.** See *Automobile Association*, 13.17 CLUBS, ASSOCIATIONS AND ORGANISATIONS; *Barton*, 13.18 CLUBS, ASSOCIATIONS AND ORGANISATIONS, and *Institute of Chartered Foresters*, 13.19 CLUBS, ASSOCIATIONS AND ORGANISATIONS.

58.405 **Subscriptions for broadcasting services—whether apportionable.** See *British Sky Broadcasting plc*, 5.72 BOOKS, ETC.

58.406 **Correspondence course including textbooks—whether fees apportionable.** See *The Rapid Results College Ltd*, 5.2 BOOKS, ETC. and *International News Syndicate Ltd*, 5.3 BOOKS, ETC.

58.407 **English tuition including course books—whether fees apportionable.** See *Rendle*, 5.4 BOOKS, ETC.

58.408 **Accountancy tuition including course manuals—whether fees apportionable.** See *LSA (Full Time Courses) Ltd*, 5.5 BOOKS, ETC.

58.409 **Computer tuition including casework manuals—whether fees apportionable.** See *EW (Computer Training) Ltd*, 5.28 BOOKS, ETC., and *Computeach International Ltd*, 63.104 VALUATION.

58.410 **Course books supplied with vocational retraining courses—whether fees apportionable.** See *Force One Training Ltd*, 5.6 BOOKS, ETC.

58.411 **Stud farm—whether charges apportionable.** See *Scott*, 27.83 FOOD, *Bushby*, 27.84 FOOD, and *Banstead Manor Farm*, 37.1 INTERNATIONAL SERVICES.

58.412   **Rearing and keeping of cattle—whether feeding of cattle constitutes separate supply.**   See *Smith*, 27.89 FOOD.

58.413   **Trout fishery—supply of right to catch fish.**   See *Chalk Springs Fisheries*, 27.94 FOOD, and *Haynes*, 27.95 FOOD.

58.414   **Sale price of dishwasher including delivery—whether apportionable.**   A company manufactured and sold dishwashers which, at the relevant time, were chargeable to a higher rate of VAT. It treated part of the sale price as being for delivery of the dishwasher and chargeable at the standard rate rather than the higher rate. The tribunal held that the whole of the consideration was chargeable at the higher rate. *Lylybet Dishwashers (UK) Ltd, LON/79/244 (VTD 915).*

58.415   **Goods sent to customers by post—whether any supply of postal services.**   See *The Leisure Circle Ltd*, 5.19 BOOKS, ETC; *Book Club Associates*, 5.20 BOOKS, ETC; *Swinger*, 23.1 EXEMPTIONS: MISCELLANEOUS, *Plantiflor Ltd*, 23.2 EXEMPTIONS: MISCELLANEOUS, *BSN (Import & Export) Ltd*, 23.3 EXEMPTIONS: MISCELLANEOUS, and *Basebuy Ltd*, 23.4 EXEMPTIONS: MISCELLANEOUS.

58.416   **Hire of agricultural machinery including petrol.**   A company carried on the business of hiring agricultural machinery, such as tractors, to farmers. Where requested, it supplied petrol with the machinery. In accounting for VAT, it treated part of the consideration which it received as being attributable to the supply of petrol and as zero-rated. The Commissioners issued an assessment on the basis that there had been a single composite supply which was entirely standard-rated. The tribunal dismissed the company's appeal, holding that the petrol was 'in substance and reality an integral part of the contract and not a separate or severable supply'. *British Airways plc*, 62.6 TRANSPORT, applied. *Showtry Ltd, EDN/92/117 (VTD 10028).*

58.417   **Payments between associated companies—whether single supply or multiple supply.**   In a case where the facts are complex and unusual, a subsidiary company (H) which manufactured and sold engineering products had made various payments to its holding company. The holding company had charged VAT in respect of these payments, and H reclaimed the VAT as input tax. The Commissioners formed the opinion that some of the payments related to the provision of finance by the holding company, which was an exempt supply, and that some were advance payments of pension contributions, with the result that not all the payments were liable to VAT and H was not entitled to reclaim the full amounts of input tax shown on the invoices. They issued assessments to recover some of the tax, and H appealed, contending that the payments were for a single supply of management services, which was wholly standard-rated. The tribunal rejected this contention and upheld the assessments, holding that the payments were in respect of multiple supplies, some of which were exempt and some of which were standard-rated. *TS Harrison & Sons Ltd, MAN/91/1178 (VTD 11043).*

58.418   **Fire equipment supplied with exempt lease of premises—whether a separate supply.**   A company had operated an aquarium for many years. In September 1990, following a visit from a local authority fire officer, it agreed to purchase fire equipment for the premises and arranged for a contractor to carry out work recommended by the fire officer. It reclaimed input tax on the supplies. In December 1990, following adverse publicity, it leased the premises to an unrelated company, and assigned the contract for the work recommended by the fire officer to the tenant. Under the lease, the purchaser was to pay £72,500 p.a. for the premises, and £40,000 p.a. for the equipment. The Commissioners issued an assessment to recover the tax on the fire equipment, on the basis that the supply of the fire equipment was part of the supply of the premises, which was exempt from VAT. The company appealed, contending that the fire equipment was the subject of a separate supply. The tribunal allowed the appeal, holding that the effect of *Article 13B(b)(3)* of the *EC Sixth Directive* was that the letting of the equipment was to be treated as a separate taxable supply for the purposes of VAT. *Aquarium Entertainments Ltd, [1994] VATTR 61 (VTD 11845)*.

58.419 **Company purchasing building from development company and arranging for renovation to be carried out by associated building company—whether a single exempt supply of a renovated building.** A company (L), which traded as a travel agent, agreed to purchase a freehold property for £100,000 from a development company (D), and to pay a construction company (B) £145,000 plus VAT for the renovation of the property. B and D were associated companies. L reclaimed the input tax on the renovation, and the Commissioners issued an assessment to recover the tax, on the basis that there was in reality a single exempt supply of a renovated building. L appealed, contending that there were two separate supplies. The tribunal accepted this contention and allowed L's appeal. On the evidence, the transactions were genuine and were not a sham. B had supplied its services to L as an independent principal, rather than as an agent for D, and L was entitled to credit for the input tax. *Lonsdale Travel Ltd, MAN/90/535 (VTD 12113)*.

58.420 **Postal computer games—whether a single supply of services.** An individual (C) operated a number of postal computer games. Players paid a joining fee of £10, part of which was accepted as for standard-rated supplies of services and part of which was for a rulebook which was accepted as zero-rated. Subsequently players who wished to continue had to pay a 'turn fee' of £1.80 per turn and were supplied with cards, described as 'turn cards', on which they could direct a number of actions to take place. C then processed the various 'turn cards' and sent to each player a computer-generated report of the results of his turn. The Commissioners issued a ruling that the 'turn fees' represented consideration for a single supply of services, so that VAT was chargeable on the whole of the amount paid. C appealed, contending that the fees should be apportioned and attributed in part to supplies of documents which qualified for zero-rating. The tribunal rejected this contention and dismissed C's appeal, holding that the 'turn fees' were consideration for supplies of standard-rated services. *KJ Cropper (t/a KJC Games), MAN/95/180 (VTD 13679)*.

58.421 *Cropper*, 58.420 above, was applied in a similar subsequent case involving a 'fantasy football' game. The tribunal held that the whole of the consideration was attributable to the supply of a fantasy football game, and that none of it could be apportioned to zero-rated supplies of printed matter. *M & E Sports Ltd, MAN/98/461 (VTD 16051)*.

58.422 **Cross-references—single supply.** In the following cases the consideration was held to cover a single supply, not apportionable: *PBK Catering Ltd*, 1.5 AGENTS (catering services supplied to charity); *International News Syndicate Ltd*, 5.3 BOOKS, ETC. (supply of manuals and course books); *Franchise Development Services Ltd*, 5.29 BOOKS, ETC. (advisory services including instruction manual); *Games Workshop Ltd*, 5.30 BOOKS, ETC. (supplies of boxed games including books); *Betty Foster (Fashion Sewing) Ltd*, 5.38 BOOKS, ETC. (dress designing kit); *BNR Company Services Ltd*, 5.66 BOOKS, ETC. (supply of registering business names including registration certificate); *Wimpey Construction UK Ltd*, 9.82 CARS (delivery charges for cars); *British Telecommunications plc*, 9.83 CARS (delivery charges for cars); *Downes Crediton Golf Club*, 13.22 CLUBS, ASSOCIATIONS AND ORGANISATIONS (entrance fee and annual subscription to golf club); *Hall*, 19.42 DRUGS, MEDICINES, AIDS FOR THE HANDICAPPED ETC. (computer system supplied to handicapped student); *Pilgrims Language Courses Ltd*, 20.13 EDUCATION (supplies to overseas students learning English); *United Biscuits (UK) Ltd*, 27.77 FOOD (biscuits sold in tins); *Paterson Arran*

Ltd, 27.78 FOOD (biscuits packed in ceramic jars); *Pier Aquatics*, 27.80 FOOD (worms and maggots supplied with ornamental fish); *Pine-Coffin*, 28.5 FUEL AND POWER (electricity in holiday accommodation); *Hazelwood Caravans & Chalets Ltd*, 28.6 FUEL AND POWER (electricity in holiday accommodation); *CMC (Preston) Ltd*, 28.7 FUEL AND POWER (electricity in holiday accommodation); *Kids of Wilmslow Ltd*, 31.41 HEALTH AND WELFARE (equipment supplied with nursery services); *Lancaster Insurance Services Ltd*, 36.5 INSURANCE (valuation fee charged as part of motor insurance policy); *Craddock & Walker*, 36.12 INSURANCE (supply of insured motor vehicles); *Globe Equities Ltd*, 36.20 INSURANCE (insurance premiums paid as rent); *Federated Pensions Services Ltd*, 36.26 INSURANCE (company acting as pension fund trustee and administrator); *Tall Pines Golf & Leisure Co Ltd*, 39.10 LAND (licence to occupy golf course); *Banstead Downs Golf Club*, 39.29 LAND (annual subscription to golf club); *Willerby Manor Hotels Ltd*, 39.84 LAND (hire of rooms for wedding reception); *Blendhome Ltd*, 39.85 LAND (exclusivity fee in conjunction with hire of rooms for wedding reception); *Mothercare (UK) Ltd*, 54.8 RETAILERS' SPECIAL SCHEMES (discount card for use in retail clothing shop); *Southend United Football Club Ltd*, 58.126 above (club subscriptions including provision of booklet and newspapers); *Hemsworth Town Council*, 58.251 above (admission to playground including miniature railway); *Aspen Advisory Services Ltd*, 58.386 above (management services relating to UK properties); *British Railways Board*, 62.5 TRANSPORT (student railcard); *British Airways plc*, 62.6 TRANSPORT (air transport including catering); *Granada Group plc*, 62.24 TRANSPORT (admission to theme park including miniature railway); *Big Pit (Blaenafon) Trust Ltd*, 62.25 TRANSPORT (guided tour around disused coal mine); *Mander Laundries Ltd*, 65.1 ZERO-RATING (launderette charges). The list is not exhaustive.

58.423   **Cross-references—multiple supply.**   In the following cases the consideration was held to cover more than one supply and to be apportionable: *Ultratone Ltd*, 2.307 APPEALS (supplying and fitting of hearing aids); *Status Cards Ltd*, 5.7 BOOKS, ETC. (cards enabling holders to obtain discounts); *JP Company Registrations Ltd*, 5.13 BOOKS, ETC. (services of company formation agency including Memorandum and Articles of Association); *Direct Marketing Bureau*, 5.45 BOOKS, ETC. (separate supplies of design services and brochures); *Appleby Bowers*, 5.46 BOOKS, ETC. (separate supplies of promotional services and leaflets); *Jarmain*, 5.52 BOOKS, ETC. (admission to stamp fair by programme); *Thomas*, 5.53 BOOKS, ETC. (admission to greyhound stadium by programme); *Keesing (UK) Ltd*, 5.75 BOOKS, ETC. (free gifts supplied with magazines); *Medical Aviation Services Ltd*, 11.11 CHARITIES (supply of helicopter and pilot); *Dyrham Park Country Club Ltd*, 13.30 CLUBS, ASSOCIATIONS AND ORGANISATIONS (bond subscribed for as condition of club membership); *Wellington Private Hospital Ltd*, 19.2 DRUGS, MEDICINES, AIDS FOR THE HANDICAPPED, ETC. (drugs provided from hospital dispensary); *Tynewydd Working Men's Club*, 23.7 EXEMPTIONS: MISCELLANEOUS (entry payments covering both live entertainment and bingo); *Royal Thames Yacht Club*, 23.26 EXEMPTIONS: MISCELLANEOUS (yacht club subscriptions including sporting facilities and clubhouse facilities); *Thayers Ltd*, 26.12 FINANCE (retail sales paid for by credit card); *Cheshire Mushroom Farm*, 27.91 FOOD (kit for growing mushrooms); *Smiths Foods Ltd*, 27.112 FOOD (packets of fruits and nuts); *Hermolis & Co Ltd*, 27.121 FOOD (Kosher meals for airlines); *Adams Woskett & Partners*, 28.8 FUEL AND POWER (electricity at caravan site); *Suffolk Heritage Housing Association Ltd*, 28.9 FUEL AND POWER (electricity in sheltered housing); *Leightons Ltd*, 31.12 HEALTH AND WELFARE (provision of opticians' services in conjunction with supply of spectacles); *O-Pro Ltd*, 31.22 HEALTH AND WELFARE (provision of dental services in conjunction with supply of mouthguards); *Rayner & Keeler Ltd*, 34.473 INPUT TAX (refurbishment of shops including supply of furniture); *Thorn EMI plc & Granada plc*, 36.7 INSURANCE (insurance supplied with letting on hire of televisions); *Bophutatswana National*

Commercial Corporation Ltd, 37.2 INTERNATIONAL SERVICES (supplies of diplomatic services by company to government of Bophutatswana); *Greater London Council*, 39.36 LAND (consideration for use of concert hall); *Court Barton Property plc*, 39.90 LAND (shares in company owning holiday accommodation); *Primback Ltd*, 54.39 RETAILERS' SPECIAL SCHEMES (retailer arranging for supply of credit); *Ho*, 58.275 above (delivery of meals); *Laurentian Management Services Ltd*, 58.374 above (data processing and related services); *Virgin Atlantic Airways Ltd*, 62.7 TRANSPORT (chauffeur-driven car service supplied by airline company); *Virgin Atlantic Airways Ltd (No 2)*, 62.15 TRANSPORT (river transport including supplies of catering); *Sea Containers Services Ltd*, 62.16 TRANSPORT (supplies of catering on luxury train); *El Al Airlines Ltd*, 62.26 TRANSPORT (payments to airline company for preferential facilities); *British Airports Authority (No 4)*, 62.28 TRANSPORT (payments by airline for facilities at airport). The list is not exhaustive.

MISCELLANEOUS MATTERS

58.424   **VATA 1994, Sch 11 para 5(2)—recovery of tax if tax invoice issued.**   See the cases noted at 14.61 to 14.63 COLLECTION AND ENFORCEMENT.

58.425   **VATA 1994, s 41(2)—supplies by Government departments.**   See *Cameron*, 31.29 HEALTH AND WELFARE.

58.426   **'Self-billing'—responsibility of supplier for accuracy regarding VAT.**   A contractor (S) was carrying out work on renovating council houses for a local authority. Some of the electrical work was carried out by the appellant company (L) as subcontractor for S. S invoiced the local authority for all work done and, with the approval of the Commissioners, operated the 'self-billing' system, under which it periodically issued payment certificates to L for the work it did. The certificates did not include VAT and L, knowing that part of its work could be standard-rated, queried this with the Commissioners. The result was that the Commissioners assessed L for the tax on its standard-rated supplies to S. There was no dispute about the figures but L was unlikely to get reimbursement of the tax from S, which had gone into liquidation. The tribunal dismissed L's appeal. The fact that 'self-billing' had been used did not absolve L from its obligation to ensure the accuracy of the payment certificates from S. *TA Landels & Sons Ltd, MAN/78/52 (VTD 521).* (*Note. VATA 1994, s 29* allows the Commissioners the discretion to collect the tax due from the recipient of the services and not the supplier where the recipient produces the tax invoice.)

58.427   *TA Landels & Sons Ltd*, 58.426 above, was applied in the similar case of *Heath Plastering Co Ltd, MAN/92/923 (VTD 10680).*

58.428   Similar decisions were reached in *M & D Price Bros Ltd, BIR/78/143 (VTD 713)* and *EC Shearer, EDN/92/189 (VTD 10608).*

58.429   A company (S), which traded as a scrap metal dealer, sold a quantity of gold bullion to a dealer who purported to operate as an authorised purchaser under the 'gold scheme'. (This was a scheme operated by the Commissioners to combat fraud whereby, if the strict conditions of the scheme were complied with, the purchaser rather than the seller accounted for tax on the supply.) VAT shown on twelve invoices issued on a self-billing arrangement by the purchaser was never paid to the Commissioners. The required undertaking to pay VAT was stamped on the invoices but in no case was it signed. S had deducted the input tax and was assessed on the corresponding output tax. S appealed, contending that under the scheme the responsibility for paying the VAT should rest on the buyer rather than the seller. The tribunal dismissed the appeal, holding that the scheme did not absolve S from its statutory liability to account for the tax due. *K Squire Group Ltd, [1985] VATTR 97 (VTD 1841)*.

58.430   See also the cases noted at 49.262 to 49.265 PENALTIES: MISDECLARATION.

58.431   **'Self-billing' system operated by customer—whether supplier obliged to refrain from issue of invoices.**   See *UDL Construction plc*, 38.2 INVOICES AND CREDIT NOTES.

59 Tour Operators and Travel Agents

The cases in this chapter are arranged under the following headings.

Definition of 'tour operator' (VATA 1994, s 53(3)) 59.1–59.8
Tour Operators' Margin Scheme 59.9–59.18

DEFINITION OF 'TOUR OPERATOR' (VATA 1994, s 53(3))

59.1   A company which supplied holiday accommodation in Spain failed to account for VAT. The Commissioners issued an assessment in accordance with the *VAT (Tour Operators) Order 1987 (SI 1987 No 1806)*. The tribunal dismissed the company's appeal, holding that the company was a 'tour operator' within what is now *VATA 1994, s 53(3)*. *Coastrider Holidays Ltd, LON/89/1730 (VTD 5289)*.

59.2   **VATA 1994, s 53(3)—whether consistent with Article 26 of EC Sixth Directive.** A company which traded as a tour operator reclaimed input tax in respect of hotel room bookings and car hirings used for an 'executive bonus scheme', under which passengers travelling in executive class from Eire to London were provided with vouchers offering one night's free hotel accommodation or 24 hours' free car hire. The Commissioners rejected the claim, considering that the tax was not deductible by virtue of the *VAT (Tour Operators) Order 1987 (SI 1987 No 1806)*. The tribunal dismissed the company's appeal. The company was a tour operator as defined in what is now *VATA 1994, s 53(3)*. The bookings of hotel accommodation and car hire were supplies of services within *Article 3(1)(a)* of the *VAT (Tour Operators) Order*. They were not integral or incidental to the supply of air transport. Accordingly, the input tax on those supplies was not deductible by virtue of *Article 12* of the *Order*. Furthermore, *s 53(3)* was in accordance with *Article 26* of the *EC Sixth Directive*. *Aer Lingus plc, [1992] VATTR 438 (VTD 8893)*. (*Note.* For another issue in this case, see 34.530 INPUT TAX.)

59.3   A company carried on business by making block bookings of ferry crossings over the English Channel and the Irish Sea, and of hotel accommodation, and reselling these bookings to coach companies which provided Continental holidays. It did not deal directly with members of the public, and did not operate the Tour Operators' Margin Scheme. The Commissioners formed the opinion that the company should have operated the Scheme, and had underpaid tax through failing to do so, and issued an assessment accordingly. The company appealed, contending firstly that it was not within the definition of 'tour operator' in what is now *VATA 1994, s 53(3)* and that its supplies were not of a 'designated travel service' within *Article 3(1)* of the *VAT (Tour Operators) Order (SI 1987 No 1806)*, and alternatively that its supplies were not within *Article 26* of the *EC Sixth Directive*, which was inconsistent with the UK legislation and should be treated as having direct effect. The tribunal allowed the company's appeal, holding that the company was a 'tour operator' and was supplying 'designated travel services' within the terms of the UK legislation, but that it was not within *Article 26* of the *EC Sixth Directive*, since it did not deal with members of the public. The tribunal held, after comparing the text of the *Directive* with other language texts, that the reference to 'customers' in *Article 26(1)* should be construed as a reference to 'travellers', and that *Article 26* applied only to travel agents who dealt with travellers, and not to travel agents who acted as wholesalers making supplies to retailers. *Independent Coach Travel (Wholesaling) Ltd, [1993] VATTR 357 (VTD 11037)*. (*Note.* Compare the subsequent decision in *Gulliver's Travel Agency Ltd*, 59.5 below.)

59.4   *Independent Coach Travel (Wholesaling) Ltd*, 59.3 above, was applied in the similar subsequent case of *Norman Allen Group Travel Ltd, [1996] VATDR 405 (VTD 14158)*. (*Note*. For the Commissioners' practice following this decision, see Business Brief 14/97, issued on 30 June 1997.)

59.5   A Japanese company (G), with a place of business in the UK, made supplies to Japanese tour operators by arranging for the provision of hotel accommodation, restaurant meals, tour guides and theatre tickets for Japanese tourists visiting the UK. The Commissioners issued a ruling that G's supplies should be treated as taking place in the UK by virtue of *Article 2* of the *VAT (Tour Operators) Order*. G appealed, contending that its supplies took place outside the UK and that it was not within the *Order*, and that the *Order* was incompatible with the *EC Sixth Directive*. The tribunal reviewed the evidence in detail and allowed G's appeal in part, holding that the supplies of hotel accommodation and of tour guides were made by G, as an independent principal, in the UK, applying *Ibstock Building Products Ltd*, 34.12 INPUT TAX, and *Northern Lawn Tennis Club*, 34.14 INPUT TAX, and distinguishing *Institute of Purchasing and Supply*, 34.13 INPUT TAX, and *Football Association Ltd*, 8.35 BUSINESS ENTERTAINMENT. However, the tribunal held that with regard to the supplies of restaurant meals, G was merely supplying services and was not actually supplying the meals itself, observing that 'at no stage was it ever contemplated that G should become the owner of the roast beef or have any proprietorial interest in it' and holding that G's services were supplied at its head office in Japan rather than in the UK. With regard to the theatre tickets, G was acting as an agent for the tour operators and its supplies of agency services were made at its Japanese head office and were outside the scope of the *Order*. The tribunal distinguished *Independent Coach Travel (Wholesaling) Ltd*, 59.3 above, on the grounds that G was not supplying 'designated travel services' within *Article 3* of the *VAT (Tour Operators) Order*, and held that it was only *Article 3* of the *Order* which was *ultra vires* and ineffective. The expression 'for the benefit of travellers' covered 'supplies by wholesale providers of travel services to retail providers', so that G's supplies were within *Article 2* of the *Order*. *Gulliver's Travel Agency Ltd, [1994] VATTR 210 (VTD 12494)*.

59.6   A company arranged hotel accommodation overseas for UK customers, but did not arrange transport. It did not operate the Tour Operators' Margin Scheme. The Commissioners issued a ruling that the company was required to operate the Margin Scheme. The tribunal dismissed the company's appeal, holding that the company was within the definition of a 'travel agent' and thus was within *VATA 1994, s 53(3)*. *Beheersmaatschappij Van Ginkel Waddinxveen BV & Others v Inspecteur de Omzetbelasting Utrecht*, 21.225 EUROPEAN COMMUNITY LAW, applied. *Hotels Abroad Ltd, LON/93/255A (VTD 13026)*.

59.7   **Limousine services.**   In the case noted at 62.7 TRANSPORT, the Commissioners issued a ruling that an airline company, which supplied a chauffeur-driven car service to some of its passengers on international flights, was within what is now *VATA 1994, s 53*, so that the input tax in question was not deductible. The tribunal allowed the company's appeal on this point, observing that the fact that the company was supplying a bought-in transport service did not mean that it had to be treated as a 'travel agent' or 'tour operator' within what is now *VATA 1994, s 53(3)*. *Virgin Atlantic Airways Ltd, [1993] VATTR 136 (VTD 11096)*.

59.8   **Hotel proprietors providing transport.**   See *Madgett & Baldwin v C & E Commrs*, 21.227 EUROPEAN COMMUNITY LAW.

TOUR OPERATORS' MARGIN SCHEME

59.9   **Incorrect operation of Scheme—definition of 'specified method'—whether supplies within definition of 'designated travel services'.**   In June 1989 a

VAT officer wrote to a company trading as tour operators and providing holidays for language students, attempting to explain the Tour Operators' Margin Scheme, and setting out calculations of the company's VAT liability for an earlier period. However, the officer wrongly treated a large part of the company's inputs as zero-rated, when in fact they were standard-rated. The company accounted for tax on the basis set out in the officer's letter, with the result that it accounted for less tax than would have been the case if it had followed the methods laid down by *Leaflet No 709/5/88*. At a subsequent control visit in March 1990, a different VAT officer formed the opinion that the company was accounting for VAT incorrectly. However, since the company's records were in arrear, he was unable to confirm this, and asked the company to bring its records up to date so that he could clarify the position. The company cancelled subsequent visits on the grounds that its financial director was ill, and failed to submit VAT returns. A further control visit finally took place in September 1992, and in October 1992 the Commissioners issued assessments charging tax on the basis of *Leaflet No 709/5/88*. The company appealed, contending as a preliminary point that the VAT officer's letter should be treated as a specified method conforming with the Tour Operators' Order (*SI 1987 No 1806*). The tribunal rejected this contention, holding that the leaflet was an 'exhaustive supplement to the *Order*', and had the force of law. The VAT officer's letter of June 1989 did not qualify as a 'specified method'. At a subsequent hearing, the company contended that certain services which it had received from local organisers, and which the Commissioners had treated as general overheads, should be dealt with under the Scheme, thereby reducing its taxable margin. The tribunal allowed the company's appeal in part, holding on the evidence that 'all the services supplied by the local organisers are enjoyed unchanged and in kind by the travellers ... the local organiser provides the services of engaging the accommodation which is occupied by the students; she hires the halls and the local teachers and the benefit of both are enjoyed by the students'. The appeal was adjourned for further argument on the question of whether the provision of hired halls, tutors' services and educational books were definition of 'designated travel services' within *VAT (Tour Operators) Order 1987 (SI 1987 No 1806), article 3. Jenny Braden Holidays Ltd, LON/92/2699 & 3095 (VTD 10892, 12860)*. (*Notes*. (1) There was no further public hearing of the appeal. (2) An application by the company for judicial review was dismissed—see 2.223 APPEALS. (3) *Leaflet 709/5/88* has subsequently been replaced by *Notice 709/5/96*.)

59.10 **Day trips by rail—whether a 'designated travel service'.** A trader supplied weekend trips (including rail travel and hotel accommodation) and day trips by rail. For the day trips, he hired an engine and coaches from railway companies, and provided stewards and catering facilities. He accepted that the weekend trips fell within the Tour Operators' Margin Scheme, but accounted for tax on the basis that the day trips fell outside the scheme and that he was making zero-rated supplies of passenger transport. The Commissioners issued a ruling that the day trips were a 'designated travel service', within *VAT (Tour Operators) Order 1987 (SI 1987 No 1806), article 3*. The trader appealed, contending that his provision of stewards and catering constituted 'further processing', so that the effect of *article 3(b)* of the *Order* was that his supplies were outside the definition of a 'designated travel service'. The tribunal rejected this contention and dismissed his appeal, holding that the provision of stewards and catering did not amount to 'further processing', since they 'may make the journeys more pleasurable and safer but they do not alter what he has bought in'. Accordingly, he was supplying a 'designated travel service'. *N Harvey (t/a Green Express Railtours), MAN/97/594 (VTD 15608)*.

59.11 **Tour Operators' Margin Scheme—holidays sold through travel agents at discounts—treatment of discounts.** A company (F), within the Tour

Operators' Margin Scheme, sold holidays through travel agents. It paid the agents commission (usually 10%) on sales. In some cases agents arranged sales at cheaper prices than those published in F's brochures. In such cases the agents still had to pay F the full brochure price, thereby effectively reducing their commission. Initially F accounted for VAT on the basis that the sum 'paid or payable', within *article 7* of the *VAT (Tour Operators) Order 1987 (SI 1987 No 1806)* was its brochure price. Subsequently it submitted a repayment claim on the basis that the sum 'paid or payable' was the price actually paid by the customer. The Commissioners rejected the claim but the tribunal allowed F's appeal and the QB upheld this decision. Neuberger J held that 'the crucial point in the present case is that, where a travel agent agrees that a customer need only pay a reduced price, while (F) receives the published list price for the holiday ($£1,000$) it only receives the reduced price ($£950$) from the customer and the balance ($£50$) from the travel agent. The language of *Article 26(2)* (of the *Sixth Directive*) requires the margin to be assessed, not merely by reference to "the total amount to be paid" to (F), but by reference to "the total amount to be paid by the traveller" to (F).' Applying the principles in *Litster v Forth Dry Dock & Engineering Co Ltd, HL 1989, [1990] 1 AC 546; [1989] 1 All ER 1134*, it was 'appropriate to imply into *article 7* a term that, when assessing the sums paid or payable to the tour operator for a particular travel service, one only takes into account sums paid by the customer'. Accordingly, 'where a customer is charged a reduced price for a holiday, the difference between the published list price and the reduced price should not be taken into account when assessing the margin under the TOMS order'. *C & E Commrs v First Choice Holidays plc, QB [2000] STC 609.*

59.12   **Tour Operators' Margin Scheme—calculation of depreciation.** The Commissioners issued a direction to a partnership which operated a number of buses and coaches, requiring the partnership to account for tax under the Tour Operators' Margin Scheme, in accordance with *Leaflet 709/5/88*. The partnership appealed, contending that it should be allowed to adopt a calculation of depreciation based on replacement cost, and to include general overheads in the calculation of liability under the Scheme. The tribunal allowed the partnership's appeal in part, holding that the calculation of depreciation should be based on historic cost rather than on replacement cost, and that general overheads could not be included in the calculation of liability under the Scheme, but that costs which could be regarded 'as an indirect cost of the tour operations' (such as the provision of garage facilities) could be included in the calculation. *RA, DL & GA Whittle (t/a Go Whittle), [1994] VATTR 202 (VTD 12164).* (*Notes.* (1) *Leaflet 709/5/88* has subsequently been replaced by *Notice 709/5/96.* (2) This case was distinguished—and, in part, implicitly disapproved—in the subsequent case of *Cicero Languages International*, 59.14 below.)

59.13   **Tour Operators' Margin Scheme—expenses to be included in cost of in-house standard-rated supplies.**   A company operated two hotels. Most of its customers were simply supplied with hotel accommodation ('full paying' customers) but, during less busy periods, it also offered 'package holidays'. 'Package holiday' customers were not only supplied with accommodation but also with transport to and from the hotel and coach outings to nearby places of interest. In an effort to reduce costs, they were offered a more restricted menu than the 'full paying' customers. The company operated the Tour Operators' Margin Scheme in respect of these supplies. The Commissioners formed the opinion that the company had calculated its liability incorrectly, in that it had failed to include any overhead expenses in the cost of its 'in-house' standard-rated supplies of hotel accommodation. They issued an assessment on the basis that various overheads (including salaries, rates, lighting, heating and repairs) should be included as part of the cost of the in-house standard-rated supplies. The company appealed, contending firstly that overheads should not be included in the calculation of cost, and secondly that, in apportioning the cost of standard-rated in-house supplies between the 'full paying' customers and the 'package holiday' customers, an adjustment should be made to reflect 'the lower standard of supplies made to the package holiday guests'. The tribunal allowed the company's appeal in part, observing that *Leaflet 709/5/88* was 'difficult to understand' but should be construed in such a way as to achieve 'a fair allocation of the total profit on a mixed package of margin scheme supplies and in-house supplies between those two categories of supplies so that the margin scheme supplies are only taxed on the margin and so that the in-house supplies are taxed in the usual way'. The tribunal held that a proportion of the rent, rates, water, lighting, heating and depreciation of the premises used by the package holiday guests should be treated as part of the cost of the hotel accommodation. However, management and administration salaries, repairs and maintenance, gardening expenses, insurance and various other expenses should be treated as part of the general expenses of the business, not forming part of the cost of the 'in-house' supplies. With regard to the company's second contention, the tribunal held that the apportionment between the 'full paying' customers and the 'package holiday' customers should be made 'by reference to the number of nights spent by each category of guests, weighted to take account of the reduced standard of accommodation available to the package holiday guests'. *The Devonshire Hotel (Torquay) Ltd, LON/94/584A (VTD 14448).* (*Note. Leaflet 709/5/88* has subsequently been replaced by *Notice 709/5/96.*)

59.14   Tour Operators' Margin Scheme—expenses to be included in cost of bought-in supplies of designated travel services. A partnership which supplied educational services made a number of designated travel services, and operated the Tour Operators' Margin Scheme. In accounting for tax under the Scheme, it included as negative amounts incidental costs which were linked with bought-in supplies, such as the costs of supervising, and advertising for, accommodation to be supplied to students. The Commissioners issued an assessment charging tax on the basis that the inclusion of such incidental costs was incorrect, and that, in the case of supplies of accommodation, the negative amounts should be limited to the amounts which the partnership actually paid host families for accommodating its students. The partnership appealed. The tribunal dismissed the appeal. With regard to the amounts which the partnership spent on advertising for suitable accommodation, the tribunal observed that the advertising services were supplied to the partnership 'for its own benefit to enable it to build up its own stock of accommodation available for onward supply. The newspapers were not, however, supplying the advertising services for the benefit of (the partnership's) student-customers.' Similar principles applied to the cost of inspecting the accommodation provided by host families, the cost of training host families, the cost of staff time, and the amounts which the partnership spent on bank charges and postage. The chairman observed that 'it is not enough that the bought-in supplies are for the benefit of the tour operator's business of making onward supplies of accommodation, etc. The bought-in services, i.e. the supplies in return for which the sums were paid by (the partnership), must themselves have been supplied for the benefit of the traveller.' *The Devonshire Hotel (Torquay) Ltd*, 59.13 above, applied; *Whittle*, 59.12 above, distinguished (and implicitly disapproved). *Cicero Languages International, LON/97/603 (VTD 15246).*

59.15   Danish company—tours sold by UK subsidiary company—whether company having a 'fixed establishment' in UK. See *DFDS A/S*, 21.229
EUROPEAN COMMUNITY LAW.

59.16   Application of Leaflet No 709/5/88, para 23—election for separate computation of non-EC supplies. A company operated the Tour Operators' Margin Scheme. In accordance with *Leaflet No 709/5/88, para 23*, it dealt with all its supplies for 1989 to 1993 in a single computation. However, in 1994 it formed the opinion that it would have been to its advantage if it had accounted for tax on supplies outside the EC separately, and submitted a retrospective repayment claim. The Commissioners rejected the claim on the basis that an election to treat non-EC supplies separately must be made in advance, and could not be retrospective. The tribunal dismissed the company's appeal. The chairman held that 'the time by which a valid election to use the separated method must have been made is the time when the tour operator adjusts his VAT account under *paragraph 23* after the end of the financial year in question and makes his next return of VAT accordingly. If he uses the primary method ... he thereby demonstrates that he has not elected to use the separated supplies method for that year, and it is not open to him thereafter to elect to use it'. The QB upheld this decision. *Article 26(3)* of the *EC Sixth Directive* provided that certain services supplied by travel agents should be treated as exempt under *Article 15*, which in turn provided that Member States could lay down conditions 'for the purpose of ensuring the correct and straightforward application of such exemptions and of preventing any evasion, avoidance or abuse'. The scheme as implemented in the UK provided for tour operators to elect if they wished to use the 'separated supplies' method. Neither the standard method of calculation nor the 'separated supplies' method contained any inherent disadvantage for a tour operator, and the question of which method was more advantageous would depend on the particular composition of each operator's business. There was nothing unreasonable in refusing retrospective applications. *Aspro Travel Ltd v C & E Commrs, QB 1996, [1997] STC 151*. (*Note. Leaflet 709/5/88* has subsequently been replaced by *Notice 709/5/96*.)

59.17   *Aspro Travel Ltd*, 59.16 above, was applied in the similar subsequent case of *Best Travel Ltd (in liquidation), LON/96/500 (VTD 15753)*.

59.18   A company operated the Tour Operators' Margin Scheme. It agreed to treat its supplies outside the EC separately, as permitted by *Leaflet 709/5/88, para 23*. However, from 1991 to 1994 it wrongly treated supplies to the Canary Islands in its computation of zero-rated EC supplies. The Commissioners discovered the error in 1994 and issued an assessment to correct it. The company appealed, contending that the assessment was outside the statutory time limit of what is now *VATA 1994, s 73(6)*. The tribunal rejected this contention and dismissed the company's appeal. The chairman observed that it was 'unfortunate' that the terms of the agreement to treat the non-EC supplies separately was not in writing, since 'the calculations under Part I of the working method in the *Leaflet* required modification but the specific modifications were not specified'. The chairman also observed that the tribunal had 'reservations as to whether the unmodified method involving rolling together EC and non-EC supplies is compatible with *Article 26* of the *Sixth Directive*'. *Elvington Ltd, LON/96/350 (VTD 14537)*. (*Note. Leaflet 709/5/88* has subsequently been replaced by *Notice 709/5/96*.)

60   Trade Unions, Professional and Public Interest Bodies

Note. The scope of *VATA 1994, Sch 9, Group 9* has been expanded with effect from 1 December 1999 to extend exemption to subscriptions to certain bodies in the public interest, which had previously been held to be outside the scope of VAT by virtue of *VATA 1994, s 94(3)*. See *VATA 1994, Sch 9, Group 9, Item 1(e)*, introduced by the *VAT (Subscriptions to Trade Unions, Professional and Other Public Interest Bodies) Order 1999 (SI 1999 No 2834)*. The cases in this chapter should be read in the light of the changes to the legislation. The cases are arranged under the following headings.

> **Associations held to be within VATA 1994, Sch 9, Group 9**
> Professional bodies (*VATA 1994, Sch 9, Group 9, Item 1(b)*) 60.1–60.2
> Learned societies (*VATA 1994, Sch 9, Group 9, Item 1(c)*) 60.3–60.4
> Public interest bodies (*VATA 1994, Sch 9, Group 9, Item 1(e)*) 60.5
> **Associations held not to be within VATA 1994, Sch 9, Group 9** 60.6–60.23
> **Miscellaneous** 60.24

ASSOCIATIONS HELD TO BE WITHIN VATA 1994, Sch 9, Group 9

Professional bodies (VATA 1994, Sch 9 Group 9, Item 1(b))

60.1   **Association of dancing teachers.**   A company, limited by guarantee, was formed to encourage dancing. The Commissioners issued a ruling that its subscriptions from dancing teachers were standard-rated, and the company appealed, contending that they were exempt from VAT by virtue of what is now *VATA 1994, Sch 9, Group 9, Item 1(b)*. The tribunal accepted the company's contention and allowed the appeal, holding that the teaching of dancing was a profession and that the association was within the definition of a professional association. *Dicta* of Du Parcq LJ in *Carr v CIR, CA [1944] 2 All ER 163 (TTC 2001, 55.79)*, applied. *Allied Dancing Association Ltd, [1993] VATTR 405 (10777)*. (*Notes.* (1) The tribunal held that the association qualified for exemption under *Item 1(c)* as well as *Item 1(b)*. The Commissioners accepted the decision with regard to *Item 1(b)*, but state in Customs' VAT Manual, Part 7, chapter 24, section 5.4 that they 'do not accept' the tribunal's decision with regard to *Item 1(c)*. (2) For another issue in this case, see 20.6 EDUCATION.)

60.2   **Institute of Shipbrokers.**   The Commissioners issued a ruling that the Institute of Chartered Shipbrokers was obliged to account for VAT on its members' subscriptions. The Institute appealed, contending that it was a professional association, and that its supplies were exempt from VAT under *VATA 1994, Sch 9, Group 9*. The tribunal accepted this contention and allowed the appeal, observing that shipbroking involved 'considerable expertise' and that the Institute set examinations which 'have a substantial intellectual element as well as purely practical aspects'. The Institute required 'certain standards of conduct and takes sanctions against those who fall short'. Accordingly, the Institute was within the definition of a 'professional association' in *Group 9, Item 1(b)*. *Dicta* of Scott LJ and Du Parcq LJ in *Carr v CIR, CA [1944] 2 All ER 163 (TTC 2001, 55.79)* applied. *Institute of Chartered Shipbrokers, LON/96/1743 (VTD 15033)*.

Learned societies (VATA 1994, Sch 9, Group 9, Item 1(c))

60.3   **Organic farmers.**   An unincorporated association was established with the aim of promoting research into organic farming. The Commissioners issued a ruling that it was required to account for output tax on its members' subscriptions. The association appealed, contending that its supplies should be treated as exempt under what is now *VATA 1994, Sch 9, Group 9*. The tribunal accepted this contention and allowed the appeal, holding that organic farming was a science, so that the association's services came within *Group 9, Item 1(c)*, which provided exemption for associations whose primary purpose was the advancement of a particular branch of science. *British Organic Farmers, [1988] VATTR 64 (VTD 2700)*.

60.4   **British Association for Counselling.**   The British Association for Counselling was formed in 1977, as a non-profit making organisation, with funding from the DHSS and the Home Office. By 1993 it had 11,600 individual members. It published a quarterly journal and a number of directories, organised conferences, and ran an information service. The Commissioners issued a ruling that it did not qualify for exemption under what is now *VATA 1994, Sch 9, Group 9*, on the grounds that counselling was not a profession. The Association appealed, contending that it was exempt under what is now *VATA 1994, Sch 9, Group 9, Item 1(c)*. The tribunal accepted this contention and allowed the appeal, holding that counselling was not a profession, but that the primary purpose of the Association was 'the advancement of a particular branch of knowledge ... connected with the past or present professions or employments of its members'. Accordingly the services which the Association supplied to its members were exempt from VAT. *The British Association for Counselling, LON/93/1494 (VTD 11855)*.

Public interest bodies (VATA 1994, Sch 9, Group 9, Item 1(e))

60.5   **Rotary Clubs.**   Rotary International (RI), an unincorporated association of Rotary Clubs in the UK, was registered for VAT in 1973. In 1988 it applied to be deregistered. The Commissioners rejected the application and RI appealed, contending that it was a body with objects of a philanthropic nature (see now *VATA 1994, Sch 9, Group 9, Item 1(e)*), and therefore should not be required to account for output tax. The tribunal accepted this contention and allowed the appeal. *Rotary International, [1991] VATTR 177 (VTD 5946)*.

ASSOCIATIONS HELD NOT TO BE WITHIN VATA 1994, Sch 9, Group 9

60.6   **Royal Photographic Society.**   The Royal Photographic Society was a company limited by guarantee established to promote the general advancement of photographic science. It had some 6,000 members. Membership was open to any person interested in photography whether or not professionally. The Commissioners issued a ruling that the Society was required to register for VAT. The Society appealed, contending that it was a professional body within what is now *VATA 1994, Sch 9, Group 9*. The tribunal rejected this contention and dismissed the appeal, holding that the Society was not within *Item 1(b)* and, although it was an association for the advancement of a particular branch of knowledge, it was not within *Item 1(c)* by virtue of *Note 4*. *Royal Photographic Society, [1978] VATTR 191 (VTD 647)*.

60.7   **Bookmakers' association.**   A company limited by guarantee, with no share capital, had a membership of bookmakers in London and the Home Counties, each paying an annual subscription. The Commissioners issued a ruling that it was liable to account for VAT on the subscriptions it received. The company appealed, contending that it was within the exemption of what is now *VATA 1994, Sch 9, Group 9*. The tribunal rejected this contention and dismissed the appeal, holding on the evidence that the company's main activity was advising and helping its members in their day-to-day business. This was not for the advancement of a 'branch of knowledge'. The association did nothing to foster its members' expertise and, even if it did, their expertise was not professional. *The Bookmakers' Protection Association (Southern Area) Ltd, [1979] VATTR 215 (VTD 849)*.

60.8   **Association of taxi-cab owners.**   A company was incorporated as an association of taxi-cab proprietors. Its members paid a basic subscription of £2 per week and an optional 'radio subscription' of £11.89 per week. The most important facility it provided was a 24–hour radio taxi service, with the loan of a radio, for those members (nearly 90% of the total) who paid the 'radio subscription'. The Commissioners issued an assessment charging VAT on all members' subscriptions, and the company appealed, contending that they were exempt under what is now *VATA 1994, Sch 9, Group 9*. The tribunal rejected this contention and dismissed the appeal, holding that the association was not within *Item 1(a)* as its main activity was the provision of the radio service and in any event its members were not employees. It was also not a professional association within *Item 1(b)*; applying *dicta* of Du Parcq LJ in *Carr v CIR, CA [1944] 2 All ER 163 (TTC 2001, 55.79)*, 'no ordinary intelligent man today would regard the driving of a taxi cab as a profession'. *City Cabs (Edinburgh) Ltd, EDN/79/30 (VTD 928)*.

60.9   **Bee farmers.**   The Commissioners issued an assessment on an association of bee farmers, charging tax on members' subscriptions. The association's treasurer appealed, contending that its supplies were exempt under what is now *VATA 1994, Sch 9, Group 9*. The tribunal rejected this contention and dismissed the appeal, holding that beekeeping was not 'a particular branch of knowledge' and did not involve 'professional expertise'. On the evidence, the association resembled a craft guild, its primary purpose being to further the commercial interests of beekeepers. *MJ Chandler (as Treasurer of the Bee Farmers Association), LON/83/248 (VTD 1565)*.

60.10   **Cleaning contractors.**   A company was established to promote 'the science of cleaning'. The Commissioners issued a ruling that it was required to register for VAT, and the company appealed, contending that its supplies were exempt under what is now *VATA 1994, Sch 9, Group 9*. The tribunal rejected this contention and dismissed the appeal, holding that cleaning could not be regarded as a particular branch of knowledge and that those engaged in the cleaning industry were not exercising 'professional expertise'. *The British Institute of Cleaning Science Ltd, LON/85/184 (VTD 1981)*.

60.11   **National Association of Funeral Directors.**   An association had been established to organise, watch over, maintain, promote and assist the rights and interests of funeral directors. The Commissioners issued a ruling that it was required to account for output tax on its subscriptions. The Association appealed, contending that its subscriptions were exempt from tax under what is now *VATA 1994, Sch 9, Group 9, Item 1(c)*. The tribunal rejected this contention and dismissed the appeal, holding that, although the Association fostered expertise about the techniques of funeral directing and related matters, funeral directors were not members of a recognised profession and accordingly the primary aim of the Association could not be for the advancement of a particular branch of knowledge or the fostering of professional expertise. *National Association of Funeral Directors, LON/84/467 (VTD 1989)*.

60.12   **Institute of Leisure and Amenity Management.**   An institute was established in 1983 to represent people employed in the management of leisure and amenity facilities. The Commissioners issued an assessment charging tax on its subscriptions. The institute appealed, contending that it was a professional association within what is now *VATA 1994, Sch 9, Group 9*, and alternatively that its aims were of a 'civic nature' and exempt under *Article 13A1(l)* of the *EC Sixth Directive*. The tribunal rejected this contention and dismissed the appeal, and the QB upheld this decision. On the evidence, the Institute had been set up to serve the needs of a particular industry and it could not be said that the members were practising a profession.

Furthermore, the expression 'of a civic nature' did not include everyday and generally expected municipal services such as parks, leisure centres and other similar facilities. *Institute of Leisure & Amenity Management v C & E Commrs, QB [1988] STC 602; [1988] 3 CMLR 380.*

60.13   **Institute of Employment Consultants.** A company was established to represent and educate workers in the employment agency industry. The Commissioners issued a ruling that it was required to account for output tax on its subscriptions, and the company appealed, contending that its supplies were exempt under what is now *VATA 1994, Sch 9, Group 9.* The tribunal rejected this contention and dismissed the appeal, holding that the recruitment industry was not a recognised profession. *The Institute of Employment Consultants Ltd, LON/86/410 (VTD 2309).*

60.14   **Tenpin Bowling Association.** The Commissioners issued a ruling that the British Tenpin Bowling Association was required to register for VAT. The association appealed, contending that its supplies should be treated as exempt under what is now *VATA 1994, Sch 9, Group 9* or under *Article 13A1(l)* of the *EC Sixth Directive.* The tribunal rejected these contentions and dismissed the appeal. *Institute of Leisure & Amenity Management,* 60.12 above, applied. *British Tenpin Bowling Association, [1989] VATTR 101 (VTD 3213, 3552).*

60.15   **Committee of Directors of Polytechnics.** The Committee of Directors of Polytechnics was a company limited by guarantee and registered as an educational charity. The Commissioners issued a ruling that it was required to account for output tax on its subscriptions. The committee appealed, contending that its supplies should be treated as exempt under what is now *VATA 1994, Sch 9, Group 9.* The tribunal rejected this contention and dismissed the appeal, and the QB upheld this decision. The committee was not a professional association, since there was no such profession as that of being a polytechnic director. *Carr v CIR, CA [1944] 2 All ER 163 (TTC 2001, 55.79),* applied. The primary purpose of the committee was not to advance a particular branch of knowledge, nor to foster professional expertise, but was to raise the standards of teaching in polytechnics. Furthermore, the aims of the committee were not aims of a civic nature within *Article 13A1(l)* of the *EC Sixth Directive. Committee of Directors of Polytechnics v C & E Commrs, QB [1992] STC 873.*

60.16   **Association of Payroll and Superannuation Administrators.** The Commissioners issued an assessment charging tax on the subscriptions which the Association of Payroll and Superannuation Administrators received from its members. The Association appealed, contending that its subscriptions were exempt under what is now *VATA 1994, Sch 9, Group 9, Item 1(b).* The tribunal rejected this contention and dismissed the appeal. Applying *Carr v CIR, CA [1944] 2 All ER 163 (TTC 2001, 55.79),* payroll and pension administration did not constitute a 'profession'. *The Association of Payroll & Superannuation Administrators, MAN/90/1015 (VTD 7009).*

60.17   **Institute of Legal Cashiers and Administrators.** The Institute of Legal Cashiers and Administrators was founded in 1978 as a non–profit-making organisation. It provided correspondence courses and arranged examinations, and had a disciplinary committee which administered a code of ethics and heard charges of incompetence or misconduct. The Commissioners issued a ruling that it did not qualify for exemption under what is now *VATA 1994, Sch 9, Group 9.* The Institute appealed, contending that it was a professional body. The tribunal rejected this contention and dismissed the appeal, holding that 'the severely technical and very constricted nature of the skill which its members acquire is inconsistent with the character of a profession as it is normally understood'. Furthermore, the purpose of the Institute was not 'the advancement of a particular branch of knowledge' since the phrase must have an academic connotation to some degree at least, and that in turn presupposes some element of research or reflection being characteristic of the way in which the subject in question is addressed'. *The Institute of Legal Cashiers and Administrators, LON/93/2444A (VTD 12383).*

60.18   **Pensioners' organisation.**   The Civil Service Pensioners' Alliance (CSPA) was established to protect the interests of retired civil servants. The Commissioners issued a ruling that it was liable to account for output tax on its subscriptions. The CSPA appealed, contending that it qualified for exemption under what is now *VATA 1994, Sch 9, Group 9* or alternatively under *Article 13A1* of the *EC Sixth Directive.* The tribunal rejected these contentions and dismissed the appeal. The CSPA was not a trade union, because it consisted of pensioners rather than workers, and was not a professional organisation. Furthermore, it was not within *Article 13A1(1)* of the *Sixth Directive. Civil Service Pensioners' Alliance, [1995] VATDR 228 (VTD 13024).*

60.19   **Association of reflexologists.**   The Association of Reflexology was established in 1984 to promote the study of the body's reflexes as a guide to behaviour. The Commissioners issued a ruling that it was liable to account for output tax on its income from subscriptions. The Association appealed, contending that it should be treated as exempt under what is now *VATA 1994, Sch 9, Group 9.* The tribunal rejected this contention and dismissed the appeal. The tribunal found that the practice of reflexology largely consisted of 'treating particular bodily ailments and general stress carried out through massage on the soles of the feet, on the principle that specific areas of the feet relate to specific parts and organs of the body', and held that reflexology was not within the definition of a 'profession', since there was not 'sufficient general acceptance of reflexology as a subject for the practice of it to be generally regarded as a profession'. Furthermore, reflexology did not qualify as 'a particular branch of knowledge', within *Item 1(c). The Association of Reflexologists, LON/94/403A (VTD 13078).*

60.20   **Fund to raise money for former footballer.**   See *Bailes,* 11.28 CHARITIES.

60.21   **Working Men's Club.**   See *Southchurch Workingmen's Club & Institute Ltd,* 13.6 CLUBS, ASSOCIATIONS AND ORGANISATIONS.

60.22   **Association of workers in motor industry.**   Following the decision noted at 21.156 EUROPEAN COMMUNITY LAW, the Institute for the Motor Industry applied to the tribunal for a further hearing of its claim to exemption. The tribunal dismissed the Institute's appeal, finding that the main aim of the Institute was not 'supplying defence and representational services' and holding that its supplies failed to qualify for exemption. *Institute of the Motor Industry, [2000] VATDR 62 (VTD 16586).*

60.23   **Expert Witness Institute.**   The Expert Witness Institute was incorporated in 1997. It claimed that its supplies should be treated as exempt from VAT under *VATA 1994, Sch 9, Group 9, Item 1.* The Commissioners rejected the claim and the tribunal dismissed the Institute's appeal, holding that 'the ordinary man would not consider that an expert witness is carrying on a separate profession', so that the Institute was not a 'professional association'. Additionally, the primary purpose of the Institute was not 'the fostering of professional expertise', and the Institute did not have objects of a 'civic nature', since 'the word "civic" however defined has connotations with a locality or public affairs'. *The Expert Witness Institute, LON/99/ 1173 (VTD 16842).*

MISCELLANEOUS

60.24   **Quarterly magazine supplied to members of Institute—whether part of subscription attributable to magazine.**   See *Institute of Chartered Foresters,* 13.19 CLUBS, ASSOCIATIONS AND ORGANISATIONS.

61   Transfers of Going Concerns

The cases in this chapter are arranged under the following headings.

Cases held to fall within Special Provisions Order, Article 5(1)
 Reclaim of input tax by purchaser 61.1–61.30
 Output tax 61.31–61.34
Cases held not to fall within Special Provisions Order, Article 5(1)
 Assessments to recover input tax—appellant successful
  Retail businesses 61.35–61.40
  Manufacturing and wholesale businesses 61.41–61.49
  Miscellaneous 61.50–61.67
 Vendor failing to account for output tax 61.68–61.74
Land and buildings (Special Provisions Order, Article 5(2)) 61.75–61.76
Liability to register (VATA 1994, Sch 1 para 1(2)) 61.77–61.89
Liability to account for tax (VAT Regulations 1995, reg 6) 61.90–61.96

CASES HELD TO FALL WITHIN SPECIAL PROVISIONS ORDER, ARTICLE 5(1)

Reclaim of input tax by purchaser

61.1   Two partners purchased an existing business, and reclaimed input tax on the stock. The Commissioners issued an assessment to recover the tax, and the tribunal dismissed the partners' appeal, holding that the business had been transferred as a going concern, within what is now *VAT (Special Provisions) Order (SI 1995 No 1268), Article 5. E & E Phillips, LON/81/131 (VTD 1130)*.

61.2   A partnership purchased a restaurant. Following the purchase, the restaurant was closed for eight days for redecoration. The partnership reclaimed input tax on the purchase. The tribunal rejected the claim, holding that the eight-day closure did not prevent the transferred business from being within the definition of a 'going concern'. *The Old Red Lion Restaurant, LON/83/28 (VTD 1446)*.

61.3   A similar decision was reached in a case where a public house had been closed for 2½ months before reopening. *G Draper (Marlow) Ltd, LON/85/439 (VTD 2079)*.

61.4   A company (S) purchased the plant, equipment, stock, vehicles, fixtures and fittings of an associated company (D) which had ceased to trade and subsequently went into liquidation. S reclaimed input tax on the purchase. The tribunal rejected the claim, holding that the transaction constituted the transfer of a business as a going concern, and observing that D had failed to pay the purported VAT to the Commissioners. *Shire Equip Ltd, MAN/83/52 (VTD 1464)*. (*Note*. Where an amount charged as VAT has been paid to Customs, they will allow the purchaser to recover it—see Customs' VAT Manual, Part 10, chapter 2, section 3.2.)

61.5   A similar decision was reached in *Jaymix, LON/83/265 (VTD 1526)*.

61.6   See also *Jalf*, 38.29 INVOICES AND CREDIT NOTES.

61.7   A parachute club became insolvent and ceased to operate on 8 December 1982. On 12 January 1983 its assets were purchased by another club. The tribunal held that, despite the gap of five weeks, the transaction constituted the transfer of a business as a going concern. *Thruxton Parachute Club, LON/84/331 (VTD 1816)*.

61.8   A company took over a division of another company, paying VAT of £15,000 in respect of the stock taken over. It reclaimed the £15,000 as input tax. The tribunal rejected the claim, holding that the transaction constituted the transfer of a business as a going concern. *Advanced Business Technology Ltd, LON/83/195 (VTD 1488)*.

61.9 A company had reclaimed input tax on the purchase of five shops. The purchase agreement attributed only £1 to goodwill, the remainder of the price being attributed to the premises, fixtures and fittings and stock. The Commissioners issued an assessment to recover the tax, and the tribunal dismissed the company's appeal. *Quadrant Stationers Ltd, LON/83/32 (VTD 1599)*. (*Note*. Costs were awarded to the Commissioners—see 2.239 APPEALS.)

61.10 A couple reclaimed input tax on the purchase of a sweetshop. The Commissioners issued an assessment to recover the tax, considering that the shop had been transferred as a going concern. The tribunal upheld the assessment and dismissed the couple's appeal. Applying *dicta* of Widgery J in *Kenmir Ltd v Frizzell, QB [1968] 1 WLR 329; [1968] 1 All ER 414* (a case concerning the *Contracts of Employment Act 1963*), 'in deciding whether a transaction amounted to the transfer of a business, regard must be had to its substance rather than its form, and consideration must be given to the whole of the circumstances ... In the end the vital consideration is whether the effect of the transaction was to put the transferee in possession of a going concern, the activities of which he could carry on without interruption.' The tribunal indicated that the conclusive factor was the transfer of the premises, observing that 'the focal point of goodwill is the premises to which persons may be expected to gravitate'. *RP & DK Agnihotri, MAN/84/165 (VTD 1765)*.

61.11 *Dicta* of Widgery J in *Kenmir Ltd v Frizzell, QB [1968] 1 WLR 329; [1968] 1 All ER 414* (see 61.10 above) have been applied in a large number of subsequent cases in which appeals against the disallowance of input tax have been dismissed. In the interests of space, such cases are not summarised individually in this book.

61.12 A company (F) sold reproduction furniture from leased premises. It became insolvent, and another company (D) agreed to purchase the lease, fixtures, fittings and stock. D reclaimed input tax on the stock and the Commissioners issued an assessment to recover the tax, considering that the business had been transferred as a going concern. D appealed, contending that its motive had been to obtain the lease of the premises, and that its directors did not intend to continue selling reproduction furniture but intended to set up a new trade of selling fitted kitchens and bedrooms. The QB upheld the assessment. In deciding whether a business had been transferred as a going concern, the question was whether it could be carried on without interruption, not whether it would be carried on without interruption. The transactions here constituted the transfer of a business as a going concern and D's intention of changing the nature of the business in the future was irrelevant. *C & E Commrs v Dearwood Ltd, QB [1986] STC 327*. (*Note*. A Scottish tribunal specifically declined to follow this decision in *Sawadee Restaurant, 61.87 below*. See also *Hartley Engineering Ltd, 61.48 below*.)

61.13 The QB decision in *Dearwood Ltd, 61.12 above*, was applied in *PN Rakshit, LON/87/716 (VTD 3287); Andjohn Ltd, LON/90/896Z (VTD 5853); D Kellman (t/a Just Music), LON/91/612Y (VTD 6973); A Ablett (t/a Brush Strokes), LON/91/749Y (VTD 6981); MJ Cashmore & JD Talbot, LON/92/1291 (VTD 9797); Wishbone Print Ltd, MAN/92/1395 (VTD 11970); Electragate Ltd, MAN/94/2670 (VTD 13752); Anley Foundations Ltd, LON/95/1874A (VTD 13827); Wellington Engineering Co Ltd, LON/95/2523 (VTD 14187, 15383); Tayplace Ltd, EDN/97/186 (VTD 15484); HG Retail Ltd, LON/97/989 (VTD 15557); Bags More Ltd, MAN/98/839 (VTD 16124); S Potter & K Farmer (t/a S & K Builders), MAN/x (VTD 16739)* and *Banbury, 49.348* PENALTIES: MISDECLARATION.

61.14   The QB decision in *Dearwood Ltd*, 61.12 above, was also followed in a case in which the tribunal disapproved the reasoning in *Westpark Interiors Ltd*, 61.35 below, on the grounds that *Kenmir Ltd v Frizzell* (see 61.10 above) had not been cited in that case, and that *Westpark Interiors* had applied a subjective test whereas *Kenmir Ltd v Frizzell* and *Dearwood Ltd* had laid down an objective test. *Curtain Clearance, MAN/92/1215 (VTD 10683)*.

61.15   A company (A) was formed to take over a pet food shop from another company (C) which carried on business as a pet food retailer. C purported to charge A tax on the stock, fixtures and fittings which it sold to A. However C, which already had substantial VAT liabilities, did not account for the tax to the Commissioners. A reclaimed the input tax which C had purported to charge and appealed against the Commissioners' refusal to repay the amounts in question. The tribunal dismissed A's appeal, holding that what is now *Special Provisions Order, Article 5* was to be 'construed as including every transfer of a separate business as a going concern, notwithstanding that the business and assets transferred constituted only a part of the businesses of the transferor'. *Acrefirst Ltd, [1985] VATTR 133 (VTD 1857)*.

61.16   A company (C) carrying on business as ventilation engineers purchased the assets of one of the branches of another company with a similar business. C reclaimed input tax on the transfer. The Commissioners rejected the claim and the tribunal dismissed C's appeal, holding that the transaction constituted the transfer of a going concern. The tribunal observed that 'the fact that part of a business can only run if integrated into another business which has the facilities to support it does not ... necessarily mean that it is incapable of separate operation'. *Cosalt Coolair Ltd, MAN/85/38 (VTD 1908)*.

61.17   A company carried on the business of leasing cars and computer equipment. It sold its business to another company (B), which occupied adjoining premises. B reclaimed input tax on the transaction. The Commissioners issued an assessment to recover the tax and the tribunal dismissed B's appeal, holding that the business had been transferred as a going concern. *Baltic Leasing Ltd, [1986] VATTR 98 (VTD 2088)*.

61.18   A company (F) was established as a subsidiary of a company whose business included the hiring and repairing of fork lift trucks. F purchased some of the parent company's assets, including 29 fork lift trucks. The parent company purported to charge VAT on the assets in question, but did not pay this to the Commissioners, and subsequently went into receivership. However, F reclaimed the amounts concerned as input tax, and obtained repayment from the Commissioners. On discovering what had happened, the Commissioners issued an assessment to recover the tax from F. The tribunal dismissed F's appeal, holding that the transaction constituted the transfer of a business as a going concern. *Farm Facilities (Fork Lift) Ltd, [1987] VATTR 80 (VTD 2366)*. (*Note*. An alternative contention by F, that the repayment of the amounts claimed in its return meant that the Commissioners were estopped from recovering the tax, was also rejected. For cases concerning estoppel, see 2.72 APPEALS *et seq.*)

61.19   *Farm Facilities (Fork Lift) Ltd*, 61.18 above, was applied in the similar cases of *Safety Boat Services Ltd, EDN/91/40 (VTD 6487)* and *S Scotford-Smith, LON/95/1869 (VTD 14609)*.

61.20   A company purchased a DIY shop. The shop was closed for two months before re-opening. The company reclaimed input tax but the Commissioners rejected the claim and the tribunal dismissed the company's appeal, holding that there had been the transfer of a going concern despite the two-month closure. *Montrose DIY Ltd, EDN/87/98 (VTD 2652)*.

61.21 Transfers of Going Concerns

61.21 A company purchased a petrol station as a going concern. Under a separate contract, it also purchased the vendor's stock of 22 cars, and reclaimed input tax on these. The Commissioners rejected the claim and the tribunal dismissed the company's appeal, holding that the purchase of the cars was a part of the transfer of the vendor's business as a going concern. *Fondbane Motors, LON/87/229 (VTD 2813)*.

61.22 An individual purchased a nightclub. He intended to convert the premises into a restaurant. However, he kept the nightclub open for one week before closing it. He reclaimed input tax on the purchase. The Commissioners rejected his claim and the tribunal dismissed his appeal, holding that the fact that he intended to use the premises as a restaurant did not alter the fact that he had purchased the nightclub as a going concern. *BO Jones, MAN/90/136 (VTD 6141)*.

61.23 A company (P) manufactured furniture and sold it to a company (V) with 16 retail shops. P suffered financial difficulties and transferred its manufacturing business to V. V reclaimed input tax on the purchase. The Commissioners issued an assessment to recover the tax, on the basis that V had acquired P's business as a going concern. The tribunal upheld the assessment and dismissed V's appeal, holding that the business had been transferred as a going concern despite the switch from wholesale to retail sales. *Village Collection Interiors Ltd, LON/90/1882 (VTD 6146)*.

61.24 A manufacturing company (E) purchased the plant and stock of a company (D) carrying on a similar business, and reclaimed input tax on the purchase. The Commissioners rejected the claim and the tribunal dismissed E's appeal, observing that 'where, as in this case, the purchaser by a separate contract with a third party, executed contemporaneously and also having immediate effect, has put himself in the position to be able to carry on the vendor's business, there can be a transfer of that business as a going concern'. *Augusta Extrusions Ltd, LON/91/2298Y (VTD 8892)*.

61.25 A company (H) which carried on a property investment business purchased a leasehold estate. The vendor had granted the lease a year before the sale, electing to waive exemption. H also elected to waive exemption, and reclaimed input tax on the purchase of the estate. The Commissioners rejected the claim on the basis that the sale of the estate constituted the transfer of a business as a going concern. The tribunal dismissed H's appeal, holding that the letting and management of the estate was a part of the vendor's business, consisting of the receipt of rental income. *Hallborough Properties Ltd, MAN/92/877 (VTD 10849)*.

61.26 In December 1991 an individual (L) purchased the leasehold premises, goodwill and furniture and fittings of a café. He closed the business for two days and reopened it as a 'take-away' restaurant. He reclaimed input tax on the purchase. The tribunal rejected the claim, finding that L had 'purchased all that was needed to carry on the vendors' business, the premises, the fixtures and fittings and the goodwill'. Applying *Kenmir Ltd v Frizzell* (see 61.10 above), and *Dearwood Ltd*, 61.12 above, this constituted the transfer of a going concern. *L Louca (t/a Gardner's Café), LON/94/930A (VTD 13186)*.

61.27 In April and early May 1995 a company (F) purchased three quantities of stock, and two quantities of materials, from another company (L). On 19 May 1995 F purchased L's business as a going concern. F reclaimed input tax on the five invoices relating to the prior purchases of stock and materials. The Commissioners rejected the claim, considering that the transactions in question constituted part of the transfer of L's business. The tribunal dismissed F's appeal, holding that the transactions were 'consistent with a series of transactions comprising the transfer of a business' and that the relevant assets were intended 'to be used in carrying on the same kind of business'. *Fairmatch Ltd, LON/95/3171A (VTD 14194)*.

61.28   A trader (F) had operated a coach hire business. He sold his only coach to another trader (B), who already carried on a similar business. F then ceased to trade. B reclaimed input tax on the coach, but the tribunal rejected his claim, holding that the transaction constituted the sale of F's business as a going concern. *JR Beagley, LON/96/1001 (VTD 15107)*. (*Note*. For another issue in this case, see 34.62 INPUT TAX.)

61.29   See also *Black*, 49.310 PENALTIES: MISDECLARATION.

61.30   There are a large number of other cases, which appear to raise no point of general importance, in which appeals against the disallowance of input tax on the transfer of a going concern have been dismissed. In the interests of space, such cases are not reported individually in this book. For a list of such cases decided up to 31 October 1990, see Tolley's VAT Cases 1991.

Output tax

61.31   **Vendor failing to account for output tax—whether Special Provisions Order, Article 5 applicable.**   A trader operated a mobile simulator (a type of hydraulic machine which simulated the effect of various forms of travel, and which customers paid to spend short periods of time in). He sold the machine and did not account for VAT on the sale. The Commissioners issued an assessment charging output tax and the trader appealed, contending that the sale constituted the transfer of a business as a going concern. The tribunal allowed the appeal, finding that 'the business consisted solely of the simulator' and holding that it had been sold as a going concern, so that no VAT was chargeable. *A Wrenshall, MAN/92/1031 (VTD 10963)*.

61.32   A company (F) had operated a retail clothing business. It suffered financial difficulties and owed more than £90,000 to creditors. F's two managers (neither of whom were directors) offered to take over its stock and its liabilities. The stock was valued at £100,000. F did not account for VAT on this stock, and the Commissioners issued an assessment charging tax on it. F appealed, contending that its business had been transferred as a going concern, so that no VAT was chargeable. The tribunal accepted this contention and allowed the appeal. *Westpark Interiors Ltd*, 61.35 below, distinguished. *Flashshine Ltd, LON/92/202A (VTD 11433)*.

61.33   See also *The Golden Oak Partnership*, 34.445 INPUT TAX, and *Jeyes Ltd*, 49.256 PENALTIES: MISDECLARATION.

61.34   **Business transferred as going concern—liability of transferee for unpaid output tax arising before date of transfer.**   See the cases noted at 61.90 *et seq.* below.

CASES HELD NOT TO FALL WITHIN SPECIAL PROVISIONS ORDER, ARTICLE 5(1)

Assessments to recover input tax—appellant successful

Retail businesses

61.35   **Purchase of stock of furniture.**   A company carried on business as interior designers and suppliers of furniture and furnishings. It decided to close one of its branches, and sold the stock of that branch to another company (W). W reclaimed input tax, and the Commissioners rejected the claim, considering that the business had been transferred as a going concern. The tribunal allowed W's appeal, holding that the sale of the stock of one branch which had been earmarked for closure did not amount to the transfer of a business as a going concern. *Westpark Interiors Ltd, [1983] VATTR 289 (VTD 1534)*. (*Note.* The decision here was not followed, and was implicitly disapproved, in the subsequent case of *Curtain Clearance*, 61.14 above, on the grounds that the QB decision in *Kenmir Ltd v Frizzell* (see 61.10 above), which had been treated as a binding precedent in the subsequent QB case of *Dearwood Ltd*, 61.12 above, had not been cited to the tribunal, and that the tribunal had erred in applying a subjective test rather than an objective test.)

61.36   **Purchase of stock of confectionery.** A confectioner purchased stock and office furniture from a business which was closing down, and reclaimed the input tax thereon. The Commissioners rejected the claim, considering that this constituted the transfer of a business as a going concern, and he appealed. The tribunal allowed his appeal, holding that the business from which he purchased the items was not transferred as a going concern. The tribunal observed that 'for the transfer of a business as a going concern there must ... be a consensus between the vendor and the purchaser ... in cases such as the present where evidence of consensus may be lacking or suspect, the expression "transfer of a going concern" must be interpreted as meaning succession by way of continuity of the previous business, succession by itself not being conclusive'. *EJ Caunt (t/a Edward James Confectionery), MAN/83/160 (VTD 1561).*

61.37   **Purchase of stock of hi-fi equipment.** A partnership (S) traded as retailers of hi-fi equipment. It agreed to purchase from another company (H) the trading stock of a shop which H owned, which had been trading at a loss. Under the agreement, H was to retain the tenancy of the shop premises, and was to receive 25% of the shop profits. S reclaimed input tax on the stock, and the Commissioners issued an assessment to recover the tax, considering that the transaction constituted the transfer of a business as a going concern. The tribunal allowed S's appeal, holding that the transaction was not the transfer of a going concern, applying *Westpark Interiors Ltd*, 61.35 above, and *dicta* of Plowman J in *Baytrust Holdings Ltd v CIR, Ch D [1971] 3 All ER 76* (a stamp duty case). The tribunal observed that S's occupation of the premises was unlawful, and that S would have no rights against the head landlord, although the partners might have 'some equitable rights against H'. There was no assignment of the premises, and no transfer of goodwill. On the evidence, S had previously bought stock from H, and even if S had declined to purchase the stock which was involved in the transaction, H would still have agreed to let S trade from the shop in question in return for a share of the profits. The purchase of the second-hand stock was, therefore, a normal trading transaction. *Dearwood Ltd*, 61.12 above, was distinguished because in that case the sales manager employed by the transferor was re-employed by the transferee, whereas in this case the previous shop manager was not re-employed by S. *PW Lee-Kemp & PM O'Brien (t/a Sevenoaks Hi-Fi & Video), LON/91/1068 (VTD 7772)*. (*Note.* The decision in *Westpark Interiors* was not followed, and was implicitly disapproved, in the subsequent case of *Curtain Clearance*, 61.14 above, on the grounds that the QB decision in *Kenmir Ltd v Frizzell* (see 61.10 above), which had been treated as a binding precedent in the subsequent QB case of *Dearwood Ltd*, 61.12 above, had not been cited to the tribunal, and that the tribunal had erred in applying a subjective test rather than an objective test.)

61.38   **Purchase of assets of petrol station licencee.** A partnership acquired the licence of a petrol station. They purchased, from the previous licencee, two refrigerators, stocks of confectionery and groceries, and a computer. They reclaimed input tax on these items. The Commissioners issued an assessment to recover the tax, considering that the items in question had been acquired as part of the transfer of the previous licencee's business as a going concern. The tribunal allowed the partnership's appeal, finding that none of the items in question 'form any part of the property of, or come within the terms of operation which the ... licencees are required to observe'. The tribunal concluded that 'either on or before the outgoing licencee vacated the property the chattels and equipment belonging to that licence were removed', so that 'the terms of the licence having been complied with, there was an interruption in the supply of sweets, groceries, ice cream and coca-cola'. The business transferred as a going concern only consisted of the sale of the motor fuel and lubricants produced by the company which owned the petrol station and granted the relevant licences. The ancillary items on which the partnership had reclaimed input tax did not form part of that transfer of a going concern. *M Ryan & M Townsend (t/a Reliables Fuel Plus), LON/94/512A (VTD 12806)*.

61.39   **Purchase of stock of motor accessories from director's fiancée.**   A trader (N) owned two shops, one in Thurrock and one in Ilford, selling cycles and motor accessories. He decided to sell the Ilford shop, and moved his stock of cycles to the Thurrock shop. His fiancée (J), who worked at the Ilford shop, agreed to purchase that shop's stock of motor accessories for £5,000 including VAT. The stock was duly sold to a company of which J was the controlling director. The Ilford shop then closed. N did not account for output tax on the £5,000 which the company had paid him. The company opened a shop in Romford, seven miles from the Ilford shop, with the stock of motor accessories which it had purchased, and reclaimed input tax on the basis that the £5,000 which it had paid to N was inclusive of VAT. The Commissioners rejected the claim on the basis that the transaction was the transfer of a going concern. The company appealed, contending that it had merely purchased stock, and had adopted a different trading name and sold to different customers, so that the transaction was not the transfer of a business as a going concern. The tribunal allowed the appeal, observing that 'the form of the sale was very clearly not that of the sale of a business as a going concern, but simply the sale of specific goods'. No rights or obligations were transferred, and there was no transfer of goodwill. *Bonnet To Boot Ltd, LON/95/1273A (VTD 13466)*.

61.40   **Purchase of stock of photocopiers.**   In June 1994 a woman (G) registered for VAT as a photocopier dealer. In July 1994 she purchased a quantity of photocopiers from a company which had carried on a similar business. The company's directors had decided to cease trading and had advertised the photocopiers in 'Exchange and Mart'. G reclaimed input tax on the purchase. The Commissioners issued an assessment to recover the tax, considering that G had purchased the company's business as a going concern. The tribunal allowed G's appeal. On the evidence, G had not taken over the company's business premises, furniture, fixtures and fittings or any outstanding contracts. There had been no transfer of goodwill and G had not taken on any of the company's employees. Her purchase of the company's stock did not constitute the transfer of the company's business as a going concern. *AS Godfrey, LON/95/2163A (VTD 14648)*.

Manufacturing and wholesale businesses

61.41   **Purchase of plant for manufacturing furniture.**   A company (C) manufactured furniture from a site in Daventry. It had an associated company (V) which sold 'self-assembly' furniture from a site in Merseyside. In 1989 both companies began suffering financial difficulties, and in late 1989 some plant was transferred from C to V. C's turnover declined substantially after the loss of this plant, and V continued to trade at a loss, so that in October 1990 the directors decided to transfer the plant back from V to C. V issued an invoice charging tax on the transfer, and C reclaimed the tax as input tax. In December 1990 V went into receivership. The receivers were unable to sell the business as a going concern, and the Merseyside premises were purchased by the holding company in March 1991. C began to trade from these premises under an 'informal licence', until they were sold to an outside purchaser in June 1991. The Commissioners issued an assessment to recover the tax which C had reclaimed on the transfer of the plant, considering that the transactions amounted to the transfer of V's business as a going concern. The tribunal allowed C's appeal, holding on the evidence that, at the time the plant was transferred, the directors still hoped that V would continue to trade, and that since the furniture produced by C differed from that produced by V, the sale of the plant did not amount to the transfer of a going concern. *Cedac Structures Ltd*, 61.57 below, applied. *Computech Development Ltd, LON/91/2090A (VTD 9798)*.

61.42   A company (S), which manufactured furniture, suffered financial difficulties and went into liquidation. Its liquidator sold some of its assets to a newly-incorporated company (B). B reclaimed input tax on the purchase. The Commissioners issued an assessment to recover the tax, on the basis that the transaction constituted the transfer of S's business as a going concern. The tribunal allowed B's appeal, holding on the evidence that S's business had ceased to exist and had not been transferred as a going concern. *Bristol Engineering & Hydraulics Ltd, LON/97/41 (VTD 15431)*.

61.43   **Purchase of assets of company manufacturing ladders.** A company (W) which had manufactured ladders went into liquidation in June 1985. Another company (H) agreed to purchase W's assets, in order to set up a similar business. The purchase took place in August 1985, and H began to trade in October 1985. H reclaimed input tax on the purchase, but the Commissioners rejected the claim, considering that W's business had been transferred as a going concern. The tribunal allowed H's appeal, holding that, since W had already ceased to trade and gone into liquidation, the transactions amounted to a transfer of assets rather than to the transfer of a going concern. *Hardlife Ladder Co Ltd, LON/87/218 (VTD 2715)*.

61.44   **Purchase of stock of clothing.** A company (C), which carried on business as manufacturers and wholesalers of leather and fur clothing, reclaimed input tax on the purchase of stock from another company (R). R had been in financial difficulties, owing C £80,000, and had made its staff redundant. Three days after the transfer of the stock, C took possession of R's premises. C also purchased some machinery from R, and re-employed some of the staff whom R had made redundant. The Commissioners rejected the input tax claim, considering that the stock had been purchased as part of the transfer of a business as a going concern. The tribunal allowed C's appeal, holding on the evidence 'that there was no consensus between the parties ... either tacit or otherwise, that the business should be transferred as a going concern'. *C Cohen (Furriers) Ltd, EDN/89/155 (VTD 4933)*.

61.45   **Purchase of carpets.** A company (P) was incorporated in May 1986 to manufacture and sell carpets. Two of its three directors (M and his wife) were also directors of another company (F) which carried on a similar business; the third director was employed by F but was not a director of F. P and F shared the same office, which was owned by M and his wife. F was contractually obliged to sell through six regional agents, who also acted for other manufacturers. In August 1987 P purchased various items of machinery from F, and in September and October P purchased various items of stock from F. P reclaimed input tax in respect of the transactions. In November 1987 F dismissed its employees, all of whom were re-employed by P. In January 1988 F went into voluntary liquidation. The Commissioners issued an assessment to recover the tax, considering that the transactions constituted the transfer of a business as a going concern. The tribunal allowed P's appeal in part, holding that the transfer of the machinery fell within what is now *Article 5* of the *Special Provisions Order*, but that the sale of the items of stock did not. On the evidence, the stock had been manufactured by F's employees, and the price paid by P was reasonable. *Pennine Carpets Ltd, MAN/88/614 (VTD 5894)*. (*Note*. For another issue in this case, see 34.516 INPUT TAX.)

61.46   Purchase of machine for manufacturing plastic forks.   A trader (W) carried on the business of manufacturing plastic forks by injection moulding. The forks were sold to fish and chip shops and other take-away food shops. He agreed to sell the machine and ancillary equipment to three brothers. The brothers registered for VAT as a partnership and reclaimed the input tax on the machinery. The Commissioners rejected the claim, considering that the partnership had purchased W's business as a going concern. The partnership appealed, contending that the transaction did not constitute the transfer of a business, since they had not taken over any stock or raw material, or any lists of suppliers or customers. The tribunal allowed the appeal, applying *dicta* in *Kenmir Ltd v Frizzell* (see 61.10 above), and distinguishing *Dearwood Ltd*, 61.12 above. *AK, VK & HK Mawji, MAN/91/564 (VTD 7769, 10829)*. (*Note.* An appeal against a misdeclaration penalty was also allowed.)

61.47   Purchase of assets of textile company.   A company (M), which traded as textile merchants, suffered financial difficulties, and a creditor issued a winding-up petition against it. M's principal director decided to form a new company (P), which was incorporated on 7 April 1992. Two days later M sold two vehicles, some office furniture and equipment, and many items of textile products to P (these items being sold at cost, and representing 70% of M's total stock). In June 1992 a winding-up order was made against M. P reclaimed input tax on the items it had purchased from M, and the Commissioners issued an assessment to recover the tax, considering that the transactions constituted the transfer of M's business as a going concern. P appealed, contending that the transactions did not constitute the transfer of a going concern, since at the time they took place, the director still hoped that M would continue to trade, and that, whereas M's customers had been in the textile trade, he had intended P to seek customers from outside the trade, such as hotels and nursing homes. The tribunal allowed the appeal, holding on the evidence that 'there was no intention to transfer any part of a business (but) simply to sell assets in the form of certain equipment and some stock'. The QB upheld this decision. Schiemann J held that the tribunal had been entitled to take the intentions of the transferor and the transferee into account, although such intentions were not conclusive. The fact that the transferor and the transferee were controlled by the same person was also not conclusive. The tribunal decision was not inconsistent with the evidence. *C & E Commrs v Padglade Ltd, QB [1995] STC 602.*

61.48   Purchase of metal-turning machinery.   A company (P) which produced machined parts ceased to trade in December 1991, and subsequently went into liquidation. One of its shareholders incorporated a new company (H) to carry on an engineering business, and purchased P's metal-turning machinery from the liquidators. H reclaimed input tax on the machinery, and the Commissioners issued an assessment to recover the tax, considering that H had taken over part of P's business as a going concern. The tribunal allowed H's appeal, holding on the evidence that, although the businesses carried on by P and H both obtained the cutting of metal, they had nothing else in common and were 'entirely different'. The tribunal chairman (Mr. de Voil) distinguished *Dearwood Ltd*, 61.12 above, and declined to follow *Kenmir Ltd v Frizzell* (see 61.10 above), since that case had dealt with an employment law provision (*Contracts of Employment Act 1963, Sch 1 para 10(2)*), the wording of which was significantly different from the wording of *Special Provisions Order, Article 5*. The *Special Provisions Order* included the words 'where the assets are to be used by the transferee in carrying on the same kind of business'. Mr. de Voil observed that '"are to be" does not mean "could" as distinct from "would"'... "are to be" suggests an intention — presumably that of the transferee and presumably at the moment of transfer'. *Hartley Engineering Ltd, [1994] VATTR 453 (VTD 12385)*. (*Note.* The decision in this case was approved in the subsequent Scottish case of *Sawadee Restaurant*, 61.87 below.)

61.49 Transfers of Going Concerns

61.49   Purchase of assets of company manufacturing nursery products.   A company (G) manufactured electrical products, including underblankets, heating pads and baby alarms. In September 1989 it launched a range of nursery products. In October 1989 its directors acquired a newly-formed company (B) which marketed the nursery products which G manufactured. In 1991 G began to suffer financial problems, despite recruiting two new directors, one of whom lent it substantial funds. In September 1991 a creditor presented a winding-up petition. In October 1991 G agreed to sell to B the injection mould tooling for the nursery merchandise which it manufactured. In November 1991 G sold its stock of nursery products, and other items of manufacturing equipment, to B. In January 1992 G sold to B, for the nominal sum of £10, its rights and interest in the trade marks under which the nursery products were marketed. Later that month G went into liquidation. B reclaimed input tax on the various items which it had purchased from G. The Commissioners issued an assessment to recover the tax, considering that the transactions constituted the transfer of G's business as a going concern. The tribunal allowed B's appeal, holding that there was 'no evidence of any overall agreement between G and B for G to transfer its business or any part of its business to B'. *Babytec Ltd, LON/92/3219A (VTD 12391).*

Miscellaneous

61.50   Purchase of scrapyard.   A trader had purchased scrap metal from members of the public and used it himself. He sold the scrapyard to a company which began to sell the processed scrap metal to the public. The company reclaimed input tax on the purchase and the Commissioners issued an assessment to recover the tax, considering that the scrapyard had been transferred as a going concern. The tribunal allowed the company's appeal, holding that the business was not transferred as a going concern since the company sold scrap metal to the public whereas the vendor had not done so. *Eric Ladbroke (Holbeach) Ltd, LON/83/184 (VTD 1557).*

61.51   Purchase of assets of printing company.   A company (S) reclaimed input tax on the purchase of some of the stock of a printing company, which ceased to trade after the sale. The vendor had had nine employees, six of whom were subsequently re-employed by S. The Commissioners rejected the claim, considering that the purchase constituted the transfer of a business as a going concern. The tribunal allowed S's appeal, holding that since it had not taken over the whole of the vendor's stock, and had only taken on some of the employees, the purchase was a purchase of assets rather than the transfer of a going concern. *Staimer Productions Ltd, EDN/83/68 (VTD 1605).*

61.52   Purchase of vehicles.   A company (E) which carried on a haulage and removal business wished to purchase some vehicles from a company which had ceased to trade. The vendor company would only agree to sell the vehicles if E also took over its other assets, i.e. its premises, plant and stock. E paid a total price of £40,000, and reclaimed input tax accordingly. The Commissioners issued an assessment to recover the tax, considering that the transactions constituted the transfer of a business as a going concern. The tribunal allowed E's appeal, holding that the sale of the assets in question did not constitute the transfer of a going concern. *Euromove International Movers Ltd, LON/84/153 (VTD 1710).*

61.53   Purchase of assets of vehicle body repairers.   An individual (L) worked as a self-employed motor mechanic from a shed owned by a company (C) which traded as vehicle body repairers. In July C gave him notice to leave the shed, as it was closing its business. L decided to purchase C's premises. C would only agree to sell its premises if L also purchased its other assets (some workshop equipment, a truck, some office equipment and some spare parts). L reclaimed input tax. The Commissioners rejected the claim, considering that L had purchased C's business as a going concern. The tribunal allowed L's appeal, holding that since C had already ceased to trade, the transactions did not constitute the transfer of a going concern. *WPJ Lawson, LON/84/164 (VTD 1749)*.

61.54   A similar decision was reached in *SA Sutton (t/a Dunchurch Motor Co), LON/92/1229A (VTD 9987)*.

61.55   **Purchase of quarries.**   A civil engineering company wished to expand into road laying, but found it impossible to obtain materials from quarry owners at suitable prices. It therefore purchased the freehold of one quarry and the leasehold of another quarry, and reclaimed the input tax charged. The Commissioners rejected the claim, considering that the quarries had been transferred as a going concern. The tribunal allowed the company's appeal, finding that the company had only wished to acquire the raw materials and had not purchased any goodwill, debtors or work in progress from the vendors. Accordingly the purchase of the quarries did not constitute the transfer of a going concern. *ICB Ltd, BEL/84/8 (VTD 1796)*.

61.56   **Purchase of farm equipment.**   A partnership (F) ran one of three farms on an estate in Scotland. The other two farms were run by the landowner (R), who was a member of another partnership (S), which carried on a contracting business, and had become insolvent. R subsequently retired from farming, and assigned the lease of the two farms to F. F purchased various items of farm equipment from S, and reclaimed input tax on the purchase. The Commissioners rejected the claim, considering that F had acquired S's business as a going concern. The tribunal allowed F's appeal, holding that since S was already insolvent, and F did not continue the contracting business, the transactions did not amount to the purchase of a going concern. *Auchtertyre Farmers, EDN/87/109 (VTD 2822)*.

61.57   **Purchase of assets of civil engineering company.**   A civil engineering company (C) was in financial difficulties. In February and March 1987 it sold most of its assets to an associated company (S). In April 1987 C went into receivership and ceased trading. Its three outstanding contracts were transferred to S. S reclaimed input tax on the items it had purchased from C. The Commissioners rejected the claim, considering that C's business had been transferred as a going concern, and S appealed. The tribunal allowed the appeal, holding on the evidence that at the time when the assets were transferred it was still hoped that C could continue trading. The transfer of C's three contracts in April 1987 had been the transfer of a going concern, but the previous transfer of assets had not been the transfer of a going concern. *Cedac Structures Ltd, LON/88/522 (VTD 3307)*.

61.58   **Purchase of public houses.**   A brewery company (M) purchased the freehold of 98 public houses from an investment company (E), and reclaimed input tax on the purchase. The public houses in question had previously been leased by E to another brewery company (C), which owned 50% of the shares in E, and had been sublet by C to tenants as tied houses. The Commissioners rejected the claim, considering that the transaction constituted the transfer of a business as a going concern. The tribunal allowed M's appeal. If the sale had been subject to the existing leases to C, it would have constituted the transfer of a business as a going concern. However, the sale was not subject to the leases to C, and following the sale, the houses were let by M directly to the tenants. The operation of the public houses had not formed a part of E's business, since E had leased them to a single customer. Accordingly, E had not transferred part of its business as a going concern. *Dearwood Ltd, 61.12 above, distinguished. Morland & Co plc, [1992] VATTR 411 (VTD 8869)*.

61.59   A public house, which had been run by a licensee, closed at the end of 1991. The owner of the premises obtained an order for repossession of the premises and applied for the licence to be transferred to his wife. He refurbished the premises and reopened them, under a new name, in March 1992 as an 'upmarket' public house providing food as well as drinks. The Commissioners issued a ruling that the business had been transferred as a going concern. The tribunal allowed the owner's appeal against this decision, holding on the evidence that the business had been 'too moribund to deserve the description of a going concern', and that the owner had 'had to present a new business with a new name and new image'. *Dicta* in *Kenmir Ltd v Frizzell* (see 61.10 above), applied. *JG McLaughlin (t/a The Hip Flask), EDN/92/309 (VTD 10920).*

61.60   **Purchase of steel.**   A sole trader (N) had worked as a subcontractor in the sheet metal industry for many years. He had not registered for VAT as his turnover had been below the statutory threshold. From July 1990 to January 1991 he had worked for one contractor (C). However, in January 1991 C suffered financial difficulties when his main customer ceased trading. C was unable to continue paying N, and made his employees redundant. N had to look for new work. He found three companies which were willing to provide him with work, and took over premises which had, for the previous six months, been used by C. He registered for VAT in February 1991. He purchased some steel from C, and reclaimed input tax on the purchase. The Commissioners issued an assessment to recover the tax, considering that N had purchased C's business as a going concern. The tribunal allowed N's appeal, observing that C had already disposed of his equipment and premises and had made his employees redundant, and holding that the transfer of the steel from C to N did not amount to the transfer of a business. *JP Neville (t/a JP Neville Engineering), LON/92/2527A (VTD 10128).*

61.61   **Purchase of builders' skips.**   A company (R) carried on business in the building industry. It owned a large quantity of skips, some of which it hired out to builders' merchants. In April 1992 one of its directors established another company (W) with a very similar name, to carry on a waste recycling business. W used an identical logo to that used by R, and took on two employees whom R had made redundant. In May W purchased 90 skips and a lorry from R, and reclaimed input tax. In July 1992 R ceased trading. The Commissioners rejected the input tax claim, considering that the transaction constituted the transfer of part of R's business as a going concern. The tribunal allowed W's appeal, holding that the sale was simply a sale of assets, and did not amount to the transfer of R's business of skip hire. *Westpark Interiors Ltd*, 61.35 above, applied. *Richards & Goldsworthy (Wales) Ltd, LON/92/2671A (VTD 10346).* (*Note.* The decision in *Westpark Interiors* was not followed, and was implicitly disapproved, in the subsequent case of *Curtain Clearance*, 61.14 above, on the grounds that the QB decision in *Kenmir Ltd v Frizzell* (see 61.10 above), which had been treated as a binding precedent in the subsequent QB case of *Dearwood Ltd*, 61.12 above, had not been cited to the tribunal, and that the tribunal had erred in applying a subjective test rather than an objective test.)

61.62   **Purchase of workshop and office equipment.**   A company (M) carried on the business of selling and leasing commercial vehicles. In May 1991 it purchased four vehicles and some workshop and office equipment from an associated company (P) which was in financial difficulties. It leased the equipment back to P, and reclaimed the input tax on the purchase. In July 1991 P went into liquidation and M leased the equipment to the liquidator until October, when it leased it to a third company which had been formed to take over P's former business. The Commissioners issued an assessment on the basis that the sale constituted the transfer of P's business as a going concern. The tribunal allowed M's appeal, observing that M was not carrying on the same type of business as P, and holding that the sale and leaseback did not amount to the transfer of a business as a going concern. *Mohawk (Contract Hire & Leasing) Ltd, LON/92/2031 (VTD 10998).*

61.63   **Purchase of machinery used for peat extraction.**   In 1990 a company (N) purchased some items of machinery from a sole trader (W), who had carried on the business of extracting peat for sale as fuel or compost. N reclaimed input tax on the purchase. W was made bankrupt in 1991, and N took over the lease of some land from which W had previously traded. N began the business of recycling mushroom waste on the land. The Commissioners issued an assessment to recover the input tax which N had reclaimed, considering that the sale had constituted the transfer of W's business as a going concern. The tribunal allowed N's appeal, finding on the evidence that W had ceased to trade before the transfer of the machinery, and holding that since N carried on the business of recycling mushroom waste whereas W had carried on a business of peat extraction, the sale of the machinery had not amounted to the transfer of a business of a going concern. *Natural World Products Ltd, BEL/92/55 (VTD 11064)*.

61.64   **Purchase of assets of company installing and maintaining security systems.**   In May 1992 a company (D), which had carried on a business of maintaining and installing security systems, ceased to trade. Some of its assets (comprising stock, fixtures and fittings, and a car) were transferred to another company (S), which began a similar trade on the following day. However, S did not take over D's contracts. S reclaimed input tax on the assets. The Commissioners rejected the claim, considering that the transaction constituted the transfer of part of D's business as a going concern. S appealed, contending that as it had not taken over D's contracts, and acquired less than 30% of D's customers, the sale did not constitute the transfer of a going concern. The tribunal accepted this contention and allowed the appeal. *IHD Security Ltd, LON/94/138A (VTD 12359)*.

61.65   **Purchase of tanks used for transport and storage of bulk liquid.**   A company (R) carried on the business of selling and leasing tanks used for the transport and storage of bulk liquid. It purchased a quantity of such tanks from another company (C), which it granted C a 20% shareholding together with £40,000 redeemable shares and £60,000 in cash. R reclaimed input tax, and the Commissioners issued an assessment to recover the tax. R appealed, contending that it had deliberately decided not to purchase C's business as a going concern, since C had liabilities which it did not wish to take over, and that the transaction had been a sale and purchase of assets. The tribunal allowed the appeal, holding on the evidence that 'the terms of the sale agreement are far more consistent with a sale of assets than the sale of part of a business as a going concern'. *Riverward Ltd, MAN/93/1055 (VTD 13094)*.

61.66   **Purchase of assets of roofing company.**   A company (S), which carried on a business of fitting flat roofs, was looking for new premises. Its directors became aware that an unrelated company (R), which carried on a business of fitting pitched roofs, had gone into receivership. The receivers were only willing to sell the premises if S also took over R's debtors, plant and machinery, and other assets. S did so, and reclaimed input tax on the purchase. The Commissioners issued an assessment to recover the tax, considering that S had purchased R's business as a going concern. The tribunal allowed S's appeal, holding on the evidence that, at the time of the invoice, there was no longer any business carried on by R 'which could be described as a going concern'. R had no work in progress, and S only fitted flat roofs whereas R had only fitted pitched roofs. S had entered into the transaction to acquire new premises, rather than to acquire a business. *Standard Flat Roofing Co Ltd, LON/94/1461A (VTD 13151)*.

61.67   **Purchase of assets of photographic processing company.**   A company (C) operated a photographic processing laboratory. It also produced and sold rubber stamps. It ceased trading after 15 months and its premises were repossessed. Its assets (including some camera equipment and 140,000 postcards) were purchased by an associated company (M). M reclaimed input tax on the purchase. The Commissioners issued an assessment to recover the tax, considering that M had purchased C's business as a going concern. The tribunal allowed M's appeal in part, finding that C had never used most of the assets which it had sold (including the camera equipment and postcards) but had purchased them for the purpose of future trading activities, and holding that M had no intention of carrying on a business of photographic processing. Accordingly, the input tax was deductible (except for tax on 600 rolls of film and a small stock of rubber stamps, which the tribunal held constituted separate businesses which had been transferred as going concerns). *Morston Properties Ltd, LON/97/96 (VTD 15004)*. (*Note.* For a subsequent appeal involving these companies, see 34.19 INPUT TAX.)

Vendor failing to account for output tax

61.68   A company carried on the business of acquiring newsagents' shops and granting franchise agreements. In 1982 it set up a newsagency and appointed a married couple as its franchisees. In 1984 it sold the newsagency, including goodwill and fixtures and fittings, to the couple. It did not account for VAT on the sale, and the Commissioners issued an assessment. The company appealed, contending that the sale of the newsagency was the transfer of a business as a going concern, so that no output tax was due. The tribunal dismissed the appeal, holding that since the company was carrying on the business of granting franchises, the sale was a sale of business assets and did not constitute the transfer of part of its business. *Delta Newsagents Ltd, [1986] VATTR 260 (VTD 2220)*.

61.69   The proprietors of a shop sold the fixtures, fittings and goodwill of the shop for £20,000. They did not account for VAT on this amount and the Commissioners issued an assessment. They appealed, contending that the business had been sold as a going concern. The tribunal dismissed their appeal, finding that there was no evidence that the business had been sold as a going concern. *JH & M Clayton, MAN/90/988 (VTD 6207)*.

61.70   A partnership, which carried on the business of property ownership and management, sold the freehold of four industrial units to the trustees of a retirement benefit scheme, and did not account for output tax on the sale. The Commissioners issued an assessment charging tax, and the partnership appealed, contending that the sale constituted the transfer of a business as a going concern. The tribunal dismissed the appeal, holding that although the transfer was of a going concern, the transferee was not a taxable person, so that what is now *Special Provisions Order, Article 5(1)(a)(ii)* was not satisfied, and output tax should therefore have been charged. *Gould & Cullen, [1993] VATTR 209 (VTD 10156)*.

61.71   In 1992 a company (F), which had been incorporated to act as a jewellery and giftware trade association, sold the intellectual copyright in two publications, 'British Jeweller' and 'British Jeweller Year Book', to a newly-formed company, which was established as a joint venture between it and the publishing company which had been responsible for the publishing of the publications since 1989. F did not account for output tax on the sale. The Commissioners issued an assessment charging output tax, and F appealed, contending that the sale constituted the transfer of part of its business as a going concern. The tribunal dismissed the appeal, holding that the sale was not within what is now *Special Provisions Order, Article 5*, since the assets were not intended 'to be used by the transferee in carrying on the same kind of business ... as that carried on by the transferor'. It was significant that F had not itself carried on a publishing business, but had only held the intellectual property rights in the publications. Accordingly the publications were business assets, rather than part of F's business. The new company 'was not put in possession of a going concern the activities of which it could carry on without interruption ... two different business assets coming together to create a new enterprise cannot amount to the transfer of going concerns'. *British Jewellery & Giftware Federation Ltd, MAN/93/993 (VTD 12194).*

61.72 A public company (K) which carried on a retail business purchased a number of foodstores and transferred them to a wholly-owned subsidiary. It did not account for output tax on these transfers. The Commissioners issued an assessment charging tax on them, including a charge to interest. K appealed, contending that the transfers were outside the scope of VAT, since they constituted the transfers of going concerns. The tribunal dismissed the appeal, holding on the evidence that since K had never actually operated the foodstores, the transactions did not fall within *Article 5* of the *Special Provisions Order*. K had transferred the business assets to its subsidiary and was required to account for output tax on the transfers. *Kwik Save Group plc, [1994] VATTR 457 (VTD 12749). (Note.* The Commissioners accepted that the subsidiary could reclaim the VAT charged by the assessment as input tax, so that the substantive issue was K's liability to pay interest to the Commissioners which the subsidiary was unable to reclaim.)

61.73 A partnership supplied security services. It entered into a contract with a company, under which the company took over certain security contracts (valued at £180,000) from the partnership and agreed to pay £90,000 in instalments. (The company subsequently became insolvent after paying £70,000 of this amount.) The partnership did not account for output tax on the payments which it received from the company, and the Commissioners issued assessments charging tax on them. The partnership appealed, contending that it had transferred part of its business as a going concern. The tribunal rejected this contention and dismissed the appeal, observing that 'contracts such as these ... do not constitute part of a business capable of separate operation'. *Derbyshire Security Services, LON/96/384 (VTD 14809). (Note.* An appeal against a misdeclaration penalty was also dismissed.)

61.74 A car dealer sold his stock for £19,000. He did not account for output tax on this, and the Commissioners issued an assessment. The dealer appealed, contending that he had transferred his business as a going concern so that the sale should not be treated as a supply. The tribunal rejected this contention and dismissed his appeal, holding that the purchaser was not a 'taxable person', so that the conditions of *Article 5* of the *Special Provisions Order* were not satisfied and output tax was due on the supply. *J Balmain (t/a Glenrothes Motor Factors), EDN/99/146 (VTD 16678).*

LAND AND BUILDINGS (Special Provisions Order, Article 5(2))

61.75 A company sold a public house, in respect of which it had elected to waive exemption. The purchaser reclaimed input tax on the basis that the effect of *Article 5(2)* of the *Special Provisions Order* was that the transfer of the land and buildings was a taxable supply. The Commissioners issued an assessment to recover part of the tax, considering firstly that 44% of the premises was used for a non-business purpose, so that that proportion of the input tax was not recoverable in any event, and secondly that part of the purchase price was attributable to a transfer of fixtures, fittings and goodwill which was not covered by the election to waive exemption, and was not therefore within *Article 5(2)* but which had been transferred as a going concern within *Article 5(1)*. The purchaser appealed, and it was agreed that the question of whether *Article 5(2)* applied should be considered at a separate preliminary hearing. The tribunal reviewed the evidence and held that the company's election extended to the whole of the land and buildings in question, on the basis that no part of the premises was 'designed as a dwelling' or consisted of 'self-contained living accommodation'. The tribunal also held that the fixtures and fittings were not part of the land and were therefore not covered by the election to waive exemption, so that the input tax which related to the fixtures and fittings was not within *Article 5(2)* and was, in principle, not deductible by virtue of *Article 5(1)* (unless the purchaser could show, at a subsequent hearing, that the business had not in fact been transferred as a going concern). However, with regard to the goodwill, while it was established that goodwill could exist as a separate intangible asset, the goodwill of this particular business was 'an attribute of the venue' and there was 'no separate goodwill in the reputation and clientele'. Accordingly, the goodwill attached to the land and was not severable from it. *AJ White, LON/96/1964 (VTD 15388)*. (*Note*. The tribunal directed that the question of whether part of the premises had been purchased for a non-business purpose, and the quantification of the deductible input tax, should be considered at a separate hearing. There has as yet been no further public hearing of the appeal.)

61.76   A company, which was a registered charity, purchased a rented property at auction. The vendor had elected to waive exemption in respect of the property, and it was accepted that the letting of the property constituted a business. Following the exchange of contracts, the charity elected to waive exemption in respect of the property. The Commissioners issued a ruling that tax was chargeable on the transfer. (The effect of the ruling was that, by virtue of the transfer, the property became a 'capital item' within the capital goods scheme, so that if the property were to be used for exempt or non-business purposes within the following ten years, there would be a charge to tax by means of an adjustment to the initial deduction of input tax.) The charity appealed, contending that the effect of *Article 5* of the *Special Provisions Order* was that the transfer should not be treated as a supply. The tribunal rejected this contention and dismissed the appeal. The effect of *Article 5(2)* was that the transfer was to be treated as a supply, unless the transferee had elected to waive exemption 'no later than the relevant date'. The effect of *Article 5(3)* was that the relevant date was the date of the contract, rather than the date of completion. The tribunal observed that conveyancing solicitors were generally aware of the Commissioners' view that 'where it is intended that the transfer of otherwise taxable property is to be regarded as the transfer of a going concern, then the purchaser must elect prior to the tax point relating to the transfer'. The tribunal also held that the relevant legislation was not inconsistent with the *Sixth Directive*, since *Article 5(8)* of the *Directive* 'provides a specific power to Member States to take the necessary measures to prevent distortion of competition in cases where the recipient of assets is not wholly liable to tax'. The charity appealed to the QB, which upheld the tribunal decision. Moses J held that 'the relevant date is the date when the deposit was paid'. Since the charity had not made an election on or before that date, it was liable to pay output tax on the purchase. *Higher Education Statistics Agency Ltd v C & E Commrs, QB [2000] STC 332*.

LIABILITY TO REGISTER (VATA 1994, Sch 1 para 1(2))

61.77   **Business transferred as a going concern—application of Sch 1 para 1(2).**   The proprietor of a snooker club, who had been registered for VAT, ceased trading in November 1991. He sold the assets of the club to an individual (C) five weeks later. C registered for VAT, stating on the form VAT 1 that he had acquired the club as a going concern. However, C subsequently engaged an accountant who formed the opinion that C need not have registered for VAT, and applied for the registration to be cancelled. The Commissioners refused to cancel the registration, and C appealed, contending that he should not be required to register as his turnover had not exceeded the threshold laid down by *Sch 1 para 1(1)*. The tribunal dismissed C's appeal, holding on the evidence that the business had been transferred as a going concern despite the fact that the club had been closed for five weeks. Since the business had been transferred as a going concern, C was required by *Sch 1 para 1(2)* to register with effect from the date on which he purchased the business. *Montrose DIY Ltd*, 61.20 above, applied. *CA Curtis (t/a Green Baize Snooker), LON/92/2655 (VTD 11128).*

61.78   Similar decisions were reached in *L'Image Ltd and M Turner, LON/93/2282A (VTD 12028); S Grieco (t/a Globetrotters Fish Bar), EDN/94/131 (VTD 13194); JDs, EDN/95/182 (VTD 13703); A & A Poullais (t/a Nightingale Café, LON/ 96/73 (VTD 14140); C Ravanfar, LON/95/2540A (VTD 14159); J Singh & G Kaur (t/a Denim House Clothing Co), MAN/96/339 (VTD 14532); The Walnut Tree at Yalding Ltd, LON/95/19 (VTD 14551, 15082); DJ Whittaker (t/a Cheslyn Hay Fish Bar), MAN/96/182 (VTD 14585); D Ojeh, LON/97/213 (VTD 15369); PA Malik, MAN/97/1205 (VTD 15711); C Menendez (t/a La Casona), MAN/98/300 (VTD 15784); P Holland, MAN/x (VTD 15996); D Barnes (t/a The Haven), LON/98/1254 (VTD 16371); Bistro Inns Ltd*, 48.126 PENALTIES: FAILURE TO NOTIFY, and *Cuthbert*, 48.126 PENALTIES: FAILURE TO NOTIFY.

61.79   The tenancy of a public house changed hands on 30 September 1993. The previous tenant had been registered for VAT, but the new tenant did not register. The Commissioners issued a ruling that he was required to register from 1 October, on the basis that he had taken over the tenancy as a going concern. The tenant appealed, contending that the tenancy had not been transferred as a going concern, because the old tenant had closed the public house for a few days before 30 September, and he had not been able to open it until a few days thereafter. The tribunal dismissed the appeal, holding that the fact that the new tenant 'wished to place the premises in better shape and thus there was a very small gap before he opened his doors does not mean that there was not a transfer of a going concern'. *Spijkers v Gevroeders Benedik Abattoir CV*, 21.94 EUROPEAN COMMUNITY LAW, applied. The tribunal also held that the fact that the two tenants sold different brands of beer was 'not relevant'. *AT Harber, LON/94/972 (VTD 12979).*

61.80   *Harber*, 61.79 above, was applied in the similar cases of *GA & P Andrews, MAN/94/939 (VTD 13310); G Coward, MAN/95/179 (VTD 13542)* and *S Lagumina & A Bottiglieri (t/a La Piazza), LON/97/1515 (VTD 15542).*

61.81   The leasehold premises, goodwill and furnishings and equipment of an Indian restaurant were sold in October 1993. The purchaser closed the restaurant for several weeks, and reopened it as an Italian restaurant. The vendor had been registered for VAT, and the Commissioners issued a ruling that the purchaser was required to register from the date of purchase, on the basis that the restaurant had been transferred as a going concern. He appealed, contending that he had not acquired the business as a going concern, since he had changed the nature of the business. The tribunal dismissed his appeal, holding that the vendors had transferred the restaurant as a going concern. The fact that the purchaser had elected 'to close for a period of a number of weeks so that he could make all the necessary preparations to reopen in a radically different form' did not alter 'the fact that what was transferred to him was a restaurant business which enabled him to trade as such'. *Dearwood Ltd*, 61.12 above, and *Montrose DIY Ltd*, 61.20 above, applied. *H Tahmassebi (t/a Sale Pepe), MAN/94/197 (VTD 13177).*

61.82   *Tahmassebi*, 61.81 above, was applied in the similar subsequent case of *M Onemli, B Onemli, A Onemli & R Karadal (t/a West Kebab), LON/95/2989A (VTD 13983).*

61.83   Similar decisions were reached in *M Haroun (t/a Prince of Bengal Restaurant), MAN/95/2736 (VTD 14232)* and *Mr & Mrs Dulay (t/a Star Fisheries), MAN/98/ 256 (VTD 16443).*

61.84   **Business transferred as going concern but conditions of Sch 1 para 1(2)(a) not satisfied.**   A restaurant was transferred as a going concern on 1 July 1995. The previous proprietors had been registered for VAT, but the new proprietor did not register. The Commissioners issued a ruling that he was required to register from 1 July. He appealed, contending that he was not required to register because the previous owners' turnover during the previous year had been less than £46,000 (which was the then figure in *Sch 1 para 1(2)*). The tribunal accepted this contention and allowed the appeal, observing that the previous proprietors' turnover, as declared on their VAT returns, had been £50,980 including VAT but only £43,389 excluding VAT. The tribunal held that, by virtue of *VATA 1994, s 19(2)*, 'the value of a supply is the tax-exclusive figure. The fact that the Commissioners may have regard to the tax-inclusive figure when considering deregistration under *Sch 1 para 4* or non-registration under *Sch 1 para 1(3)* does not mean that a tax-inclusive figure is to be taken to determine the value of taxable supplies under *Sch 1 para 1(2)(a)*. The tax-inclusive figure is merely evidence which the Commissioners are entitled to consider when seeking to establish what will be a tax-exclusive figure, after deregistration or non-registration.' *M Ahmed, MAN/96/939 (VTD 15399)*.

61.85   **Business held not to be transferred as going concern.**   A public house closed in September 1993 because the company which had operated it became insolvent. The tenancy was transferred to the former manager in December 1993. The Commissioners issued a ruling that he had acquired the public house as a going concern, so that he was required to register for VAT from December 1993. He appealed, contending that *VATA 1994, Sch 1 para 1(2)* did not apply and he was not required to register until March 1994. The tribunal accepted this contention and allowed the appeal, observing that 'the gap in trading was not associated with refurbishment and the customers might well have wondered whether as rumours go the financial difficulties experienced by one tenant might put off others', and held that 'the previous business which had been carried on at the premises ... had ceased entirely'. *Harber*, 61.79 above, and *Andrews*, 61.80 above, distinguished. *A Hulse, MAN/95/1726 (VTD 13896)*.

61.86   A company operated a public house. The business included a restaurant on the upper floor of the premises. The company closed the restaurant at the end of 1995 and leased the relevant part of the premises to a woman (W), who used the premises to operate a smaller restaurant under a different trading name. This venture was not a success and W ceased trading after six months. The Commissioners issued an assessment on the basis that W had taken over part of the company's business as a going concern, and had therefore been liable to register for VAT. The tribunal allowed W's appeal, holding on the evidence that 'there was no transfer of a part of a business as a going concern'. *Mrs S Watt, EDN/98/4 (VTD 15800)*.

61.87   In a Scottish case, a Japanese restaurant, run by three people in partnership, ceased to trade on 27 April 1996. The premises re-opened as a Thai restaurant on 16 June 1996. The new business was run by a partnership of two people, one of whom had been a member of the previous partnership. The Commissioners issued a ruling that the business had been transferred as a going concern, so that the new partnership was required to register for VAT accordingly. The partnership appealed. The tribunal allowed the appeal, holding on the evidence that the business had not been transferred as a going concern. The tribunal specifically declined to follow the QB decision in *Dearwood Ltd*, 61.12 above, holding that 'the case of *Dearwood*, being a decision of a single judge in England, is not binding on a tribunal in Scotland. It has persuasive authority. However, the reasoning in it fails wholly to persuade. The test in the view of this tribunal is not whether the business "could be" carried on without interruption but is properly to be found in the words of the statute and the context of VAT legislation whether the transferred matters, if any, "are to be" carried on as a business. The trenchant criticism of *Dearwood* in *Hartley Engineering Ltd* (see 61.48 above), with which this tribunal agrees, plainly points the error of the test "could be carried on" and adverts to a consideration of the intention of the transferee as one of the matters which requires to be taken into account'. *Dicta* of Schiemann LJ in *Padglade Ltd*, 61.47 above, applied; *Tahmassebi*, 61.81 above, distinguished. *Sawadee Restaurant, EDN/98/43 (VTD 15933).*

61.88   A hairdresser, who traded from a salon in Glasgow and was registered for VAT, suffered from ill-health and financial problems. In July 1995 his wife (W), who was not a hairdresser, took over the premises. She arranged for three stylists, one of whom had previously been employed by her husband, to work at the salon on a self-employed basis, paying her a percentage of their gross takings. Her husband also continued to work at the salon on a self-employed basis (and subsequently cancelled his VAT registration in view of the decline in his turnover). The other hairdressers who had previously been employed by her husband ceased to work at the salon. These arrangements lasted for just over a year, following which she and her husband (whose health had improved) entered into partnership and registered for VAT. Subsequently the Commissioners issued a ruling that W had taken over her husband's business as a going concern, and was therefore required to register for VAT under *Sch 1 para 1(2)*. She appealed, contending that she had not taken over her husband's business as a going concern, but had begun 'a new and separate business of property rental or facility services'. The tribunal accepted this contention and allowed her appeal. W was not herself a hairdresser, and 'the substance of her business was to provide facilities'. There had been 'a legitimate separation of (her husband's) business for administrative purposes'. On the evidence, W 'had no intention of becoming a hairdresser or of employing hairdressers. Her intention was to manage a business making available facilities to self-employed hairdressing stylists.' *E Woods, EDN/97/111 & 122 (VTD 15485).*

61.89   **Business transferred as going concern—whether Sch 1 para 1(3) applicable.**   See *Nash & Nash*, 53.33 REGISTRATION.

LIABILITY TO ACCOUNT FOR TAX (VAT Regulations 1995, reg 6)

61.90   **Business taken over as going concern—whether transferee liable for tax arising before date of transfer.**   A married couple took over as a going concern the business of a company which they had controlled. The company's VAT affairs were in arrears, but the couple were allowed to keep the same VAT registration number on condition that they would submit a return which was outstanding, and would pay the VAT due in respect of the supplies made by the company before the date of transfer. The couple accepted these conditions but did not submit the outstanding return, and appealed against a subsequent assessment charging tax on supplies made by the company. The tribunal dismissed the appeal, finding that the couple had agreed to take over the company's liabilities and holding that the liability to furnish returns and to pay the tax due had passed from the company to the couple as partners. The QB upheld this decision, holding on the evidence that the couple had accepted liability to furnish returns and account for tax. *WH & AJ Ponsonby v C & E Commrs, QB 1987, [1988] STC 28.*

61.91   A similar decision was reached in *CV Todd (t/a Sweeney Todd's Plumbing Squad), LON/95/1060 (VTD 14341).*

61.92   The decision in *Ponsonby*, 61.90 above, was applied in *Bjellica*, 53.21 REGISTRATION.

61.93   In a similar case, a restaurant proprietor who had previously been in partnership with his wife was held to be personally liable for tax due in respect of the partnership, because he had taken over the liabilities in question under what is now *VAT Regulations, reg 6. BA Choudhury, LON/87/16 (VTD 2490).*

61.94   A publican and his wife separated in July 1987. The publican had previously been registered for VAT as a sole trader. Following the separation, the wife took over the licence and the running of the public house. She completed a form VAT 1 indicating that the business had been transferred as a going concern, and stating that she wished to retain the previous registration number. Subsequently, a VAT officer on a control visit formed the view that there had been an underdeclaration of tax, and the Commissioners issued an assessment on the wife, charging tax for periods both before and after the transfer. The wife appealed, contending that she was not liable for tax arising before the date on which she took over the business. The tribunal accepted this contention and allowed the appeal in part, finding that, despite the statement on the form VAT 1, the business had not in fact been transferred as a going concern, and holding that the assessment was not valid with regard to supplies made before the wife acquired the business from her husband. *L MacLean, LON/89/1362 (VTD 5350). (Note.* Compare *Ponsonby & Ponsonby,* 61.90 above, and *Choudhury,* 61.93 above, neither of which were referred to in this decision.)

61.95   A partnership operated a pet shop. It suffered financial difficulties and transferred its business as a going concern to a company of which the partners were directors. The Commissioners discovered that the partnership had overclaimed input tax and issued an assessment in July 1994. The partners were declared bankrupt and did not pay the tax charged by the assessment. In October 1994 the Commissioners withdrew the assessment on the partnership and issued an assessment on the company to recover the tax in question. The company appealed, contending that it should not be held liable for the tax in question. The tribunal accepted this contention and allowed the appeal, distinguishing *Ponsonby & Ponsonby,* 61.90 above, because in that case there had been no previous assessment. The tribunal chairman held that the relevant provisions of the *VAT Regulations* did not 'entitle the Commissioners to recover from the transferee tax on an assessment which has been validly made on the transferor and has, to borrow words from direct tax legislation, become final and conclusive'. *Pets Place (UK) Ltd, [1996] VATDR 418 (VTD 14642).*

61.96   **Business transferred as going concern following bankruptcy—deposits taken before bankruptcy but supplies made following transfer.** See *Camford Ltd,* 35.7 INSOLVENCY.

62 Transport

The cases in this chapter are arranged under the following headings.

Supply and maintenance of ships (VATA 1994, Sch 8, Group 8, Item 1)
62.1–62.4
Transport of passengers (VATA 1994, Sch 8, Group 8, Item 4)
Cases held to qualify for zero-rating 62.5–62.14
Cases where the consideration was apportioned 62.15–62.18
Cases held not to qualify for zero-rating 62.19–62.26
Transport of goods (VATA 1994, Sch 8, Group 8, Item 5) 62.27
Handling services (VATA 1994, Sch 8, Group 8, Item 6) 62.28
The 'making of arrangements' (VATA 1994, Sch 8, Group 8, Item 10)
62.29–62.30

SUPPLY AND MAINTENANCE OF SHIPS (VATA 1994, Sch 8, Group 8, Item 1)

62.1 **42–ton ketch.** A 42–ton, two-masted ketch was held to be 'designed for use for recreation or pleasure', and thus not eligible for zero-rating, in *BR Callison, EDN/78/34 (VTD 810)*.

62.2 **Work on tug intended as support vessel for racing yachts.** A company which carried on the business of ship-repairing undertook substantial work on a 209–ton tug, which was intended as a support vessel for British yachts competing in the America's Cup. In the event, the tug was not used for this purpose, as the company for which the work was carried out did not compete in the Cup. The company did not charge VAT on the work done, and the Commissioners issued an assessment charging tax on the amounts invoiced. The company appealed, contending that the work should be zero-rated under what is now *VATA 1994, Sch 8, Group 8, Item 1*. The tribunal rejected this contention and dismissed the appeal. The work carried out went far beyond 'repair or maintenance', and resulted in the tug becoming 'substantially more luxurious' and 'adapted to enable it to perform a different task'. Furthermore, the tug was not intended to be used for commercial activities, but was intended to be used for 'recreation or pleasure'. Accordingly, the work did not qualify for zero-rating. *A & P Appledore (Falmouth) Ltd, [1992] VATTR 22 (VTD 7308)*.

62.3 **Conversion of barges into houseboats—whether within Group 8, Item 1(b).** Two companies converted barges into houseboats, to be used as permanent residences but remaining capable of self-propulsion. The Commissioners issued rulings that VAT was chargeable on the work, considering that it was excluded from zero-rating by what is now *VATA 1994, Sch 8, Group 8, Item 1(b)*, on the basis that the barges were 'designed or adapted for use for recreation or pleasure'. One of the companies, and a customer of the second company, appealed. (The second company had gone into liquidation by the time the appeal was heard.) The tribunal allowed the appeals, observing that the barges had not originally been designed for 'recreation or pleasure' and holding that 'it stretches the ordinary meaning of the words recreation or pleasure well beyond their natural meaning to say that this encompasses a home or place of permanent habitation'. The barges remained 'ships' within *Group 8, Item 1*, and were not excluded from zero-rating by *Item 1(b)*. *Callison*, 62.1 above, and *A&P Appledore (Falmouth)*, 62.2 above, distinguished. *DG Everett, LON/92/1911A; The London Tideway Harbour Co Ltd, LON/92/1912A (VTD 11736)*.

62.4 **Design work related to modifications of ships.** In an Isle of Man case, a company did not account for output tax on design work relating to modifications of ships. The Isle of Man Treasury issued an assessment charging tax on the work, and the company appealed, contending that it should be treated as zero-rated. The tribunal accepted this contention and allowed the appeal, holding that the design work 'forms an integral part of the modifications themselves and is zero-rated as services of the repair or maintenance of a ship'. The tribunal also held that the question of whether the supplies were made to the owners of the ships, or to their operating agents, was immaterial. *Cholerton Ltd v The Isle of Man Treasury, MAN/94/799 (VTD 13387)*. (*Note.* For the Commissioners' practice following this decision, see Business Brief 5/99, issued on 24 February 1999. Customs state that they 'consider that the tribunal failed to take into account that Cholerton was contracted to supply only design services and therefore made no supply of modification services to which the design services could be integral. Accordingly, with effect from 1 July 1999, Customs will treat design services supplied in the UK as integral to the supply, modification or conversion of a qualifying ship only where a supplier specifically contracts with a customer to design *and* supply, modify or convert a qualifying ship.')

TRANSPORT OF PASSENGERS (VATA 1994, Sch 8, Group 8, Item 4)

Note. The scope of *VATA 1994, Sch 8, Group 8, Item 4* is now restricted by *Note 4A*, which was introduced by the *VAT (Transport) Order 1994 (SI 1994 No 3014)* with effect from 1 April 1995. Cases relating to periods before 1 April 1995 should be read in the light of this change.

Cases held to qualify for zero-rating

62.5   **Payment for railcard enabling holder to travel at half-fare.**   The British Railways Board instituted a scheme whereby students could travel at half-fare. Students wishing to take advantage of the scheme were required to pay £1.50 for a railcard, valid for six months. The Commissioners issued an assessment charging VAT on these supplies, and the Board appealed, contending that they should be zero-rated under what is now *VATA 1994, Sch 8, Group 8, Item 4*. The CA accepted this contention and allowed the Board's appeal. Lord Denning held that the payments of £1.50 were 'part and parcel of the payment which the student made for travelling on the railway. Just as a season ticket is payment in full in advance for travelling on the railway (whether the passenger uses it or not) so also this £1.50 is part payment in advance'. Browne LJ held that 'the transaction should be looked at as a whole, including both the issue of the card and the later taking of a ticket ... the £1.50 should be regarded as part payment in advance for the supply of transport by rail'. *British Railways Board v C & E Commrs, CA [1977] STC 221; [1977] 2 All ER 873*. (*Note.* Sir John Pennycuick also observed that the supply would appear to qualify for zero-rating under what is now *VATA 1994, Sch 8, Group 8, Item 10*.)

62.6   **Air transport including catering—whether consideration apportionable.**   A company which operated air transport services within the UK supplied passengers with free in-flight catering. The Commissioners issued an assessment on the basis that part of the price paid by the passengers should be attributed to the catering, and was therefore standard-rated. The company appealed, contending that the sums paid by the passengers were for the provision of transport and should be wholly zero-rated. The QB accepted this contention and allowed the appeal, and the CA upheld this decision, holding that the provision of in-flight catering on domestic passenger flights was an integral part of the supply of air transport, which was zero-rated. *British Airways plc v C & E Commrs (No 1), CA [1990] STC 643*.

62.7   **Chauffeur-driven car service supplied to airline passengers—whether zero-rated under Sch 8, Group 8, Item 4.**   A company which operated an airline supplied a chauffeur–driven car service to some of its customers (whom it described as 'Upper Class Passengers') on international flights. It did not account for VAT in respect of these services. The Commissioners issued a ruling that the supplies of limousine services were a standard-rated supply on which VAT was chargeable. The company appealed, contending that they were a part of a single composite supply of air transport, which was zero-rated under what is now *VATA 1994, Sch 8, Group 8, Item 4*. The QB accepted this contention and allowed the company's appeal. Turner J held that the word 'place' in *Item 4* was not confined to the airport where the flight began or ended, but could mean the place where the passenger began his or her journey, i.e. his or her home. Since the company did not charge a separate price for the limousine service, it formed part of a single supply which qualified for zero-rating. *Virgin Atlantic Airways Ltd v C & E Commrs, QB [1995] STC 341*. (*Notes*. (1) For another issue in this case, not taken to the QB, see 59.7 TOUR OPERATORS AND TRAVEL AGENTS. (2) For the Commissioners' practice following this decision, see Business Brief 4/96, issued on 13 March 1996.)

62.8   A similar decision was reached in a case which the QB heard with *Virgin Atlantic Airways Ltd*, 62.7 above. *Canadian Airlines International Ltd v C & E Commrs, QB [1995] STC 341*.

62.9   **Railway ticket also giving admission to museum and engine shed—whether wholly zero-rated.**   A company operated a steam railway from Loughborough to Leicester via Quorn and Rothley, on track which had previously been owned by British Rail. It did not account for VAT on its fares, considering that they were zero-rated under what is now *VATA 1994, Sch 8, Group 8, Item 4*. In its publicity material, the company advertised the fact that, at the Loughborough terminus, there were a museum and an engine shed, which passengers could visit without any further charge. (Anyone not travelling on the railway could only visit the museum and engine shed by paying £1 for a platform ticket, although at other stations a platform ticket cost only 25p. Both parties accepted that the platform tickets were standard-rated.) The Commissioners formed the opinion that part of the amounts paid by passengers should be attributed to the right to visit the museum and engine shed, and should therefore be treated as standard-rated. The company appealed, contending that its only supply was a supply of transport which was zero-rated. The tribunal allowed the company's appeal, holding that, since the fare for travelling to Loughborough from the nearest station was the same as the fare for travelling to Leicester, Quorn or Rothley from the nearest station, none of the consideration paid by the passengers was specifically attributable to the right to visit the museum or the engine shed, and the whole of the fares were zero-rated. *Great Central Railway (1976) plc, MAN/90/1071 (VTD 11402)*.

62.10   **Membership fees for travel club—whether advance payments for zero-rated supplies of transport.**   A company which traded as a tour operator operated a 'travel club'. Membership of the club was only open to people who were employed by travel agents and dealt directly with the public. Members were entitled to tours, airline flights, hotel accommodation and car hire at reduced rates. The company did not account for output tax on the subscriptions which it received from its members, treating them as advance payments for zero-rated supplies of transport. The Commissioners issued a ruling that the membership fees did not qualify for zero-rating (with the exception of a small proportion which the Commissioners accepted as attributable to a zero-rated publication). The company appealed. The tribunal allowed the appeal, holding on the evidence that the whole of the membership fee was 'attributable to the supply of reduced rate travel products'. The membership card was 'an integral part of the consideration for which the travel product is supplied'. The company was acting as an independent principal, rather than as an agent. Accordingly, the membership fees qualified for zero-rating. *The UK Travel Agent Ltd, LON/94/432A (VTD 12861)*.

62.11   **Narrowboats—whether 'designed or adapted to carry not less than 12 passengers'.**   A trader provided cruising holidays along canals and navigable rivers, using two narrowboats. Only one of the narrowboats had an engine and it towed the other boat. Together the narrowboats provided sleeping accommodation for a maximum of nine guests and four crew. The trader treated his supplies of transport as zero-rated. The Commissioners accepted that the crew could be treated as 'passengers' for the purposes of *Item 4*, but issued a ruling that the supplies failed to qualify for zero-rating, on the basis that the narrowboats had to be treated individually and were not 'designed or adapted to carry not less than 12 passengers', as required by *VATA 1994, Sch 8, Group 8, Item 4(a)*. The trader appealed, contending that since twelve people (including three of the crew) could travel on either narrowboat at any time, each of the narrowboats should be treated as within *Item 4(a)* even though some of the passengers would have to transfer to the other narrowboat in order to sleep. The tribunal accepted this contention and allowed the trader's appeal, holding on the evidence that there was ample space on each of the narrowboats to transport twelve people and noting that 'the carrying capacity of each boat is greater than its capacity to provide sleeping accommodation'. The fact that neither of the narrowboats could provide sleeping accommodation for twelve people was not conclusive. *GL Ashton (t/a Country Hotel Narrowboats), MAN/95/1587 (VTD 14197)*.

62.12   **Holiday cruises—whether whole consideration zero-rated.**   A company supplied holiday cruises. It treated the consideration which it received for such cruises as wholly zero-rated. The Commissioners issued a ruling that the cruises were not simply a supply of transport, since the passengers also received accommodation, food and entertainment, so that not all the consideration qualified for zero-rating. The company appealed, contending that each cruise was a single supply of transport which qualified for zero-rating under *VATA 1994, Sch 8, Group 8, Item 4*, and that the services of arranging passenger transport within the EC were also zero-rated when supplied to a person registered for VAT in the UK. The tribunal allowed the appeal, holding that a holiday cruise was a single supply of the transport of passengers. 'The elements of accommodation, entertainment, catering, sightseeing, etc., which the Commissioners suggest to be a multiple supply of goods and services additional to a supply of passenger transport are in fact integral to the cruises and incidental to their main purpose.' *British Airways plc*, 62.6 above, applied. The fact that the cruise was a journey of a 'leisurely nature' did not prevent it from constituting the supply of transport of passengers. *River Barge Holidays Ltd*, 63.98 VALUATION, was distinguished on the grounds that 'the river barge appears to have been used more as a place in which to sleep and eat than as a means of transportation'. The QB upheld this decision as one of fact. On the evidence, the tribunal was entitled to find that the main purpose of the cruise was the supply of passenger transport. *C & E Commrs v The Peninsular & Oriental Steam Navigation Co (No 2), QB [1996] STC 698*. (*Note*. For the Commissioners' practice following this decision, see Business Brief 14/96, issued on 15 July 1996.)

62.13   **River trip including catering—whether separate supplies of transport and catering.**   A couple supplied canal boat trips on the Leeds and Liverpool Canal. They provided food for parties of 30 or more people. The Commissioners issued a ruling that, in such cases, they were making a separate standard-rated supply of catering as well as a zero-rated supply of transport. The couple appealed, contending that they were making a single supply of transport which was zero-rated. The tribunal accepted this contention and allowed the appeal, holding on the evidence that 'the substance and reality of the appellants' activities are "a day out on the river"', and that the provision of food was incidental to the supply of passenger transport. *British Airways plc*, 62.6 above, and *The Peninsular & Oriental Navigation Co*, 62.12 above, applied; *Virgin Atlantic Airways Ltd (No 2)*, 62.15 below, was distinguished on the grounds that in that case functions such as wedding receptions and corporate entertaining were a 'primary purpose' of the hiring out of the vessel. *A & J Hughes (t/a Pennine Boat Trips of Skipton), MAN/97/1027 (VTD 15680)*. (*Note.* For the Commissioners' interpretation of this decision, see Business Brief 5/99, issued on 24 February 1999, and Business Brief 10/99, issued on 22 April 1999 following the decision in *Sea Containers Services Ltd*, 62.16 below. Customs state that they consider that the decision in *Hughes* 'is confined to that case' and 'will not accept claims seeking refunds of VAT on the basis of this decision from operators of boat trips or providers of other transport services with catering'.)

62.14   **Narrow-gauge railway in country park.**   A company operated a narrow-gauge railway in a country park in Hampshire. The railway consisted of a single loop which was slightly more than a mile in length. There were two stations, although the smaller station was only 375 yards away from the main station. The Commissioners issued a ruling that the company was required to account for output tax on its fares from the railway. The company appealed, contending that the fares qualified for zero-rating. The tribunal accepted this contention and allowed the appeal. The railway was not within *VATA 1994, Sch 8, Group 8, Note 4A* because the company did not provide any right of admission to the country park in which the railway was situated. The tribunal held that, despite the short distance between the two stations, the company was making supplies of transport which qualified for zero-rating. *Blackpool Pleasure Beach Co*, 62.22 above, distinguished. *Narogauge Ltd, LON/95/1867 (VTD 14680)*.

Cases where the consideration was apportioned

62.15   **River trip including catering—whether separate supplies of transport and catering.**   A company operated a paddle-steamer ship which was based on the River Thames. It hired the ship out for functions such as wedding receptions and summer balls, during which catering services were supplied. In accounting for tax, the company treated part of the consideration which it received as attributable to zero-rated supplies of transport and part as attributable to standard-rated supplies of catering. The Commissioners issued an assessment on the basis that the whole of the consideration should be attributed to the standard-rated supplies of catering, and that the transport should be treated as incidental. The company appealed. The tribunal allowed the appeal, holding that 'in substance and reality' the company was making separate supplies, and the supply of transport was neither incidental to, nor a part of, the supply of catering. The fact that the passengers were transported 'to a certain degree of comfort' did not prevent the supply from qualifying as a supply of transport. *Dicta* in *Rayner & Keeler*, 34.473 INPUT TAX, applied; *British Airways plc*, 62.6 above, and *The Peninsular & Oriental Navigation Co*, 62.12 above, distinguished. *Virgin Atlantic Airways Ltd (No 2), LON/94/1530 (VTD 13840)*. (*Notes.* (1) For the Commissioners' practice following this decision, see Business Brief 14/96, issued on 15 July 1996. (2) For a case in which this decision was distinguished, see *Hughes (t/a Pennine Boat Trips of Skipton)*, 62.13 above.)

62.16   **Rail transport including catering—whether separate supply of catering.**   A company operated a luxury train, which was also available for charter within the UK. Passengers were supplied with catering. The company initially accounted for VAT on part of its receipts which was attributed to catering services. However, following the decision in *The Peninsular & Oriental Steam Navigation Co (No 2)*, 62.12 above, the company claimed a repayment on the basis that it was making single supplies of transport which qualified for zero-rating. The Commissioners accepted that, where the train was used for transport to Continental destinations such as Venice, there was a single supply of transport, but rejected the repayment claim with regard to the UK charters, considering that the company was making separate supplies of transport and catering. The tribunal dismissed the company's appeal and the QB upheld this decision. Keene J held that, as a matter of commercial reality, the provision of catering was clearly a distinct and separate supply. *British Airways plc*, 62.6 above, distinguished. *Sea Containers Services Ltd v C & E Commrs, QB 1999, [2000] STC 82*. (*Note*. For the Commissioners' practice following the tribunal decision, see Business Brief 10/99, issued on 22 April 1999.)

62.17   **Apportionment of consideration for holiday including provision of transport.**   See *River Barge Holidays Ltd*, 63.98 VALUATION.

62.18   **Railway company offering combined ticket also applying entrance to 'Camera Obscura'.**   See *Aberystwyth Cliff Railway Co Ltd*, 63.101 VALUATION.

Cases held not to qualify for zero-rating

62.19   **Cabinlift—whether 'designed or adapted to carry not less than 12 passengers'.**   A company operated a cabinlift to a scenic headland. The cabinlift comprised 41 cabins, each of which was designed to hold up to four passengers, and was hauled by a continuous cable with a device for detaching the cabins at the terminals. The Commissioners issued a ruling that the supplies made by the company did not qualify for zero-rating. The company appealed, contending that the cabinlift should be viewed as a whole for the purpose of what is now *VATA 1994, Sch 8, Group 8, Item 4(a)*, so that it was making zero-rated supplies of transport. The tribunal rejected this contention and dismissed the appeal, holding that each cabin was a separate vehicle, and that as each cabin carried fewer than twelve people, the supplies did not qualify for zero-rating. *Llandudno Cabinlift Co Ltd, [1973] VATTR 1 (VTD 1)*.

62.20   *Llandudno Cabinlift Co Ltd*, 62.19 above, was applied in the similar case of *Needles Chairlift Co Ltd, LON/73/168 (VTD 90)*.

62.21   **Transport in cable cars—whether 'designed or adapted to carry not less than 12 passengers'.**   A company operated a cable car system to carry passengers from a railway station to a nearby pleasure garden. The system provided twelve gondolas, each of which could carry up to six passengers. The Commissioners issued a ruling that the company's supplies did not qualify for zero-rating. The company appealed, contending that the system should be viewed as a whole for the purpose of what is now *VATA 1994, Sch 8, Group 8, Item 4(a)*, so that it was making zero-rated supplies of transport. The tribunal rejected this contention and dismissed the appeal, holding that each of the gondolas had to be regarded as a separate vehicle, and that as each gondola carried fewer than twelve people, the supplies did not qualify for zero-rating. *Heights of Abraham (Matlock Bath) Ltd, MAN/85/51 (VTD 1914)*.

62.22   **'Big Dipper'—whether a form of transport.**   A company operated a 'Big Dipper' at Blackpool. It did not account for VAT on its receipts from the 'Big Dipper', and the Commissioners issued an assessment charging tax on them. The company appealed, contending that the 'Big Dipper' was a form of transport so that its supplies were zero-rated. The QB rejected this contention and upheld the assessment, holding that 'transport' involved the movement of passengers from one place to another, so that the 'Big Dipper' was not a form of transport. Lord Widgery CJ observed that 'the essence ... of transport of passengers is that the passenger is taken from A to B because he wants to be at B or because there is some purpose in being at B'. A person 'who in effect remains on one spot all the time' was not 'being transported as a passenger'. *C & E Commrs v Blackpool Pleasure Beach Co, QB [1974] STC 138; [1974] 1 WLR 540; [1974] 1 All ER 1011*.

62.23   **Miniature railway in 'theme park'.**   A company operated an indoor 'theme park' within a large shopping centre. The 'theme park' included carousels, dodgems, and a miniature railway track, comprising a single loop. The company charged £1 for rides on the railway (which lasted about two minutes). The Commissioners issued a ruling that output tax was chargeable on the fares, and the company appealed, contending that they should be treated as zero-rated passenger transport. The tribunal rejected this contention and dismissed the appeal. Applying *dicta* of Lord Widgery in *Blackpool Pleasure Beach Co*, 62.22 above, the miniature railway was not within the definition of 'transport'. *Metroland Ltd, MAN/95/2709 (VTD 14550)*. (*Note.* Costs were awarded to the Commissioners.)

62.24   A company owned and operated a 200–acre 'theme park', on the site of a former colliery, in Derbyshire. The park included a lake, covering about 37 acres, and a circular railway track, of about one mile in length, which ran around the lake. Visitors to the 'theme park' paid a single entrance fee which entitled them to use the railway. The company accounted for output tax on the entrance fees, but subsequently submitted a repayment claim, contending that, for periods up to 1 April 1995 (when what is now *VATA 1994, Sch 8, Group 8, Note 4A* was introduced by *SI 1994 No 3014*) some of the fees should be treated as being attributable to zero-rated supplies of transport. The Commissioners rejected the claim and the tribunal dismissed the company's appeal. On the evidence, the company was making a single supply of admission to the park which was subject to VAT at the standard rate. *Granada Group plc, MAN/95/2573 (VTD 14803)*.

62.25   **Guided tour around disused mine including transport in miners' cage.**   A company which owned a disused coal mine charged visitors £4 for a guided tour of the mine. The visitors were transported to and from the mine in a mechanically operated miners' cage, the journey taking about two minutes and the distance between the top and bottom of the shaft being about 300 feet. The Commissioners issued an assessment charging tax on the full amount charged for the guided tour, and the company appealed, contending that part of the £4 should be zero-rated as being paid for the transport to and from the bottom of the shaft. The tribunal dismissed the company's appeal, holding that the £4 was paid for the single supply of a guided tour, and that the time spent in the miners' cage was an integral part of the tour, rather than a separate supply of transport. *Big Pit (Blaenafon) Trust Ltd, LON/90/1767 (VTD 6705)*.

62.26   **Subscription paid by airline customers for pre-flight and post-flight facilities—whether zero-rated.**   A company which operated an airline established a club, whereby potential customers would receive additional pre-flight and post-flight facilities in return for their subscriptions. These facilities included priority seat reservations and the use of VIP lounges at certain airports. It did not account for VAT on the club subscriptions. The Commissioners issued an assessment charging tax on these, and the company appealed, contending that the subscriptions should be treated as zero-rated under what is now *VATA 1994, Sch 8, Group 8, Item 4*. The tribunal dismissed the appeal, holding that the club subscriptions could not be regarded as an integral part of the supply of transport, and did not qualify for zero-rating. *El Al Israel Airlines Ltd, LON/93/3037A (VTD 12750)*.

TRANSPORT OF GOODS (VATA 1994, Sch 8, Group 8, Item 5)

62.27   **Carriage of household goods to UK port.**   An individual (B) emigrated from the UK to South Africa, and arranged for a company to collect and pack his furniture and personal effects into packing cases, and transport the cases to a quay at Southampton, alongside the ship in which he and his family were travelling to South Africa. The company accounted for VAT on its services. B lodged an appeal, contending that the services should be treated as zero-rated under what is now *VATA 1994, Sch 8, Group 8, Item 5*. The tribunal rejected this contention and dismissed his appeal. The company's services had been wholly within the UK, so that they did not qualify for zero-rating. *JD Bevington, LON/76/85 (VTD 282)*.

HANDLING SERVICES (VATA 1994, Sch 8, Group 8, Item 6)

62.28   **Facilities at airport.** The British Airports Authority granted an airline company the use of check-in desks and information desks at an airport, together with the rights to use the Authority's scales and conveyor belts for weighing and transporting passengers' luggage. The tribunal held that payments for the use of the scales and conveyor belts were zero-rated under what is now *VATA 1994, Sch 8, Group 8, Item 6*, but that payments for the use of the check-in and information desks did not qualify for zero-rating. *British Airports Authority (No 4), LON/74/154 (VTD 148)*.

THE 'MAKING OF ARRANGEMENTS' (VATA 1994, Sch 8, Group 8, Item 10)

62.29   **Payment for railcard enabling holder to travel at half-fare.** See *British Railways Board v C & E Commrs*, 62.5 above.

62.30   **Flight vouchers.** A company (F) supplied and sold books of 'flight vouchers' to retailers for use in business promotion schemes. The vouchers entitled customers to claim free return flights to the USA on condition that they booked and paid for accommodation at an expensive hotel with which F had entered into an agreement. F did not account for VAT on the payments it received from retailers, and the Commissioners issued a ruling that VAT should have been charged on the payments. The tribunal allowed F's appeal against this decision. Applying *British Railways Board*, 62.5 above, the voucher was provided as part of the making of arrangements for the supply of space in an aircraft. This was a zero-rated supply under what is now *VATA 1994, Sch 8, Group 8, Item 10. Facthaven Incentive Marketing Ltd, LON/90/1340Z (VTD 6443)*. (*Note.* A subsequent application by the Commissioners to make a late appeal against this decision was rejected—see 2.157 APPEALS.)

63   Valuation

The cases in this chapter are arranged under the following headings.

TRANSACTIONS BETWEEN CONNECTED PERSONS (VATA 1994, Sch 6 para 1)

63.1   **Direction under VATA 1994, Sch 6 para 1—whether valid.**   A company (L) was the holding company of a group. One of its subsidiaries (H) carried on an insurance business and was not registered for VAT. L carried on business as a shipping and freight-forwarding agent and was registered. In March 1980 the holding company bought a computer, in which data relating to H was stored. Although it was originally intended that data relating to other companies in the group should be similarly stored, in fact the computer was only used by H. At first L made no charge to H for the use of the computer but from 1983 a charge of £300 per month plus VAT was made. Following a further visit in 1986, the Commissioners discovered that the computer had been used exclusively by H, and took the view that this amounted to a supply of services, the value of which was to be taken to be the full cost to L. Accordingly in April 1987 the Commissioners issued a notice to L under what is now *VATA 1994, Sch 6 para 1*, directing that the value of any supply made between 28 April 1984 and the date of the notice to any connected person for a consideration less than the open market value, should be treated as being made at the open market value, and further directing that any future supplies to connected persons should be subject to VAT at the open market value. Accompanying the direction was a letter which stated that, since the computer had been used exclusively by H, the entire tax-exclusive costs of depreciation, maintenance, manning, etc. incurred by the holding company would constitute the tax-exclusive value for VAT. L appealed, contending that the direction was void for uncertainty. The tribunal rejected this contention, holding that the direction was valid with regard to previous supplies of the use of the computer by L to H and with regard to all future supplies in relation to which the three conditions in what is now *VATA 1994, Sch 6 para 1* were satisfied (but was void with regard to any other previous supplies). *Oughtred & Harrison Ltd, [1988] VATTR 140 (VTD 3174).*

63.2   Valuation

63.2   A bank (which was partly exempt, and could only recover 10% of its input tax) sold various assets to four associated companies, which were not members of its VAT group. The companies then leased the assets back to the bank. The Commissioners issued a direction under *VATA 1994, Sch 6 para 1*. The four companies appealed, contending that the direction was invalid. The tribunal rejected this contention and dismissed the appeals. The provisions of *Sch 6 para 1* were authorised by *Article 27* of the *EC Sixth Directive*. The relevant derogation under *Article 27* covered tax avoidance as well as tax evasion. The bank had 'deliberately implemented a scheme for VAT avoidance'. *Finanzamt Bergisch Gladbach v Skripalle*, 21.234 EUROPEAN COMMUNITY LAW, distinguished. The decision to issue the direction had not been unreasonable, and the leases had been made for consideration which was less than their open market value. *RBS Leasing & Services (No 1) Ltd (and related appeals), [2000] VATDR 33 (VTD 16569)*. (*Note*. For a preliminary issue in this case, see 2.25 APPEALS.)

WHETHER AGREED PRICE TO BE TREATED AS EXCLUSIVE OR INCLUSIVE OF VAT

63.3   **Work carried out by builder—whether quoted price inclusive or exclusive of VAT.**   A farmer engaged a builder to supply and erect a shed and to build a stable block at his farm. He subsequently formed the opinion that he had paid the builder more than the true value of the work, and took legal proceedings against the builder in the Carlisle County Court. The court gave judgment for the farmer and ordered the builder to pay the farmer £4,367 including interest. The court held, *inter alia*, that although the builder had been entitled to charge VAT in respect of the supply of the shed, he was not entitled to add VAT to the agreed price for the stable block. The builder applied to the CA for leave to appeal against this decision, contending *inter alia* that the court had erred in law in holding that the price for the stable block should be treated as VAT-inclusive. The CA rejected this contention and dismissed the builder's application. Chadwick LJ observed that this 'was a contract under which the defendant stipulated for payment in cash, and was paid in cash'. The question of 'whether or not the price for a building contract is inclusive or exclusive of VAT must turn on the terms of the particular contract . . . if the builder fails to make it plain to the employer (*sic*) that he is stipulating for payment of VAT in addition to the contract price, he will be left to account to the revenue (*sic*) for the VAT out of what he receives'. Chadwick LJ accepted that 'there may well be a custom in the construction industry that prices quoted are exclusive of VAT'. However, there was no evidence 'that, on a contract between a small builder seeking to be paid in cash and a part-time farmer, it was an implied custom that VAT would be paid on top of the cash payments'. It would appear most unlikely that 'the parties to such a transaction intended that VAT should be paid on top of the cash payments'. *Lancaster v Bird, CA 19 November 1998 unreported.*

63.4   **Sale of freehold property—whether quoted price inclusive or exclusive of VAT.**   A company purchased a freehold property. The supply was subject to VAT, as an election under *VATA 1994, Sch 10* (see 6.6 BUILDINGS AND LAND *et seq.*) had been made in respect of the property. The contract stated that the purchase price was £400,000 and that 'sums payable under this agreement . . . are exclusive of VAT'. The purchaser paid £400,000. The vendor demanded an additional £70,000 as VAT, and took proceedings to recover this amount. The Ch D gave judgment for the vendor. Under *VATA 1994, s 19(2)*, if a supply was for a monetary consideration, its value was to be taken to be such amount as, with the addition of VAT chargeable, was equal to the consideration. Thus, if a VAT-registered supplier simply charged £100 to a customer, while the VAT rate was 17.5%, he was obliged to treat 7/47 of that sum as VAT, and pay it to the Commissioners. In order to obtain £100 net of VAT, the supplier would be obliged to charge £117.50 to the customer. However, where, as here, a contract specifically stated that a price was VAT-exclusive, it was commonly understood that the purchaser would have to pay the VAT in addition to the quoted price. Accordingly the purchaser was required to pay £70,000 to the vendor, which in return was required to account for that £70,000 to the Commissioners. *Hostgilt Ltd v Megahart Ltd, Ch D 1998, [1999] STC 141.*

63.5   A company (W) sold a property to another company (V). The contract provided that the price was 'exclusive of VAT'. Both companies had assumed that the sale was exempt from VAT. However, the building was a 'new' building as defined by *VATA 1994, Sch 9, Group 1, Note 4*, so that VAT was chargeable. The Commissioners issued an assessment on W, charging tax of £107,250. W paid the tax charged, and sought to recover the tax from V. The CA gave judgment for W. Morritt LJ observed that the effect of the contract was that, if VAT was payable, the price provided by the contract was exclusive of it. *Wynn Realisations Ltd v Vogue Holdings Inc, CA [1999] STC 524.*

63.6   See also *Jaymarke Developments Ltd v Elinacre Ltd*, 6.22 BUILDINGS AND LAND.

SUPPLIES OF GOODS

Deemed supplies under VATA 1994, Sch 4 para 5

63.7   **Deemed supply under VATA 1994, Sch 4 para 5(1)—valuation of deemed supply.** In March 1988 a partnership purchased two JCBs for £26,000. The JCBs were not in good condition, and after a few months they both required repairs which the partnership could not afford to pay for. They were temporarily parked in a field, but the local council demanded that they should be moved. An acquaintance of one of the partners offered to dispose of the JCBs for scrap. The partnership accepted this offer. The Commissioners issued an assessment on the basis that the JCBs had depreciated by 25% during the period in which they were owned by the partnership, and that by virtue of what is now *VATA 1994, Sch 4 para 5(1)*, the partnership should account for VAT on their value at the time they were disposed of. The tribunal upheld the assessment in principle but reduced it in amount, holding on the evidence that the JCBs should be treated as having halved in value on account of their heavy use, and that a further £2,000 should be deducted from their value in respect of necessary repairs, so that their deemed value for VAT purposes at the date of disposal was £11,000. *CR Construction, LON/91/2661Z (VTD 7737).*

63.8   **Footballers' presentation dinner—valuation of supply of trophies.** A company organised a presentation dinner for the Professional Footballers' Association. The company accounted for VAT on the price of the tickets. At the dinner various trophies, which had cost about £3,000, were presented. The Commissioners issued an assessment charging VAT on the cost of the trophies, on the basis that they had been supplied to the recipients without consideration. The company appealed, accepting that there was a deemed supply under *VATA 1994, Sch 4 para 5*, but contending that the awards of the trophies were an integral part of the dinner, and that the price of the tickets included consideration for the presentation of the trophies. The tribunal allowed the appeal, holding that the company supplied the purchasers of the tickets with the right to attend a function at which they would be given dinner and would see the presentation of the awards, the awards ceremony being an integral part of the supply. The consideration for the trophies was included in the price of the tickets, and the fact that the consideration was paid by people other than the recipients of the trophies was irrelevant, applying a *dictum* of Lord Cameron in *Lord Advocate v Largs Golf Club*, 13.9 CLUBS,

ASSOCIATIONS AND ORGANISATIONS. The HL upheld this decision. The awards were made for sound commercial reasons, and their cost was borne by the diners and by the sponsors of the dinner. The fact that it was impossible to identify what part of the ticket price was consideration for the supply to the award winners was irrelevant. There was a direct link between the payment of the ticket price and the supply. *C & E Commrs v Professional Footballers' Association (Enterprises) Ltd, HL [1993] STC 86; [1993] 1 WLR 153.*

63.9 **Caps presented to international footballers.** The Scottish Football Association (SFA) awarded commemorative caps to players who represented its team. The Commissioners issued an assessment on the basis that the SFA was required to account for output tax on the supply of the caps. The SFA appealed, accepting that there was a deemed supply under *VATA 1994, Sch 4 para 5*, but contending that no additional output tax was due because the consideration for the supply of the caps was part of the admission fees paid by the spectators. The tribunal accepted this contention and allowed the appeal, applying *Professional Footballers' Association (Enterprises) Ltd*, 63.8 above. *Scottish Football Association Ltd, EDN/96/127 (VTD 14895).*

63.10 **Videotapes supplied free of charge to doctors.** A company produced videotapes containing programmes of interest to doctors, interspersed with advertisements of pharmaceutical products. The company distributed the videotapes to doctors free of charge, but charged the advertisers for the inclusion of their advertisements. The Commissioners considered that the tapes were supplied for no consideration, so that, by virtue of what is now *VATA 1994, Sch 6 para 6*, the company should account for VAT on the cost of producing the videotapes as well as on the payments received from the advertisers. The company appealed, accepting that there was a deemed supply under *VATA 1994, Sch 4 para 5*, but contending that the consideration it received for the videotapes comprised the sums received by it from the advertisers. The tribunal allowed the company's appeal, holding that it was not necessary for the consideration for goods or services to be paid by the actual recipient, applying *dicta* of Lord Cameron in *Lord Advocate v Largs Golf Club*, 13.9 CLUBS, ASSOCIATIONS AND ORGANISATIONS. The QB upheld the tribunal decision. The company received consideration from the advertisers in return for supplying the tapes to the doctors. The supply of the tapes was, therefore, outside the scope of *Sch 6 para 6. C & E Commrs v Telemed Ltd, QB 1991, [1992] STC 89.*

63.11 **Supply of mobile telephones.** A company (T) supplied mobile telephones to customers under a promotion scheme, under which no charge was made to the customer for the supply of the telephone, provided that the customer agreed to rent a telephone line from another company (V) for a minimum period of twelve months. V paid T £190 for each new customer who entered into such an agreement under the scheme. The Commissioners issued an assessment on T, charging output tax on the cost of the telephones, on the basis that they had been supplied to the customers 'otherwise than for consideration'. T appealed, accepting that there was a deemed supply under *VATA 1994, Sch 4 para 5*, but contending that the payments which it received from V represented consideration for its supply of the telephones. The tribunal accepted this contention and allowed the appeal. There was 'a contractual link between the supply of the mobile phone to the customer and (V's) payment to (T)'. *Professional Footballers' Association (Enterprises) Ltd*, 63.8 above, applied. *Thorn plc, [1998] VATDR 383 (VTD 15284). (Notes.* (1) For a preliminary issue in this case, see 30.18 GROUPS OF COMPANIES. (2) For the Commissioners' practice following this decision, see Business Brief 23/98, issued on 17 November 1998.)

Deemed supplies under VATA 1994, Sch 4 para 8

63.12 In June 1979 a trader had acquired an aircraft for the purposes of his business at a cost of more than £73,000, and had reclaimed input tax on the purchase. He ceased trading some months later and his registration was cancelled on 1 November 1980, at which date he still owned the aircraft. The Commissioners issued an assessment on the basis that the value of the aircraft at that time was £35,000, and that tax should be accounted for on this value under what is now *VATA 1994, Sch 4 para 8*. The tribunal upheld the assessment in principle but directed that it should be recomputed on the basis that the aircraft should be valued at £27,500. *B Mendes, LON/81/259 (VTD 1192)*.

63.13   A company which operated a private ambulance service ceased to be liable to register for VAT from 1 January 1990, when its supplies became exempt by virtue of the *VAT (Finance, Health & Welfare) Order 1989 (SI 1989 No 2272)*. The company owned an ambulance, purchased in 1989, on which it had reclaimed input tax. The Commissioners issued an assessment to charge tax on the deemed supply of the vehicle under what is now *VATA 1994, Sch 4 para 8*. The assessment was computed on the basis that the value of the ambulance had decreased by 30% in the period since its purchase. The tribunal upheld the assessment and dismissed the company's appeal. *Ambu-Medics Ltd, MAN/90/447 (VTD 5697)*.

63.14   A trader had registered for VAT as distributor of a product to be used for the valeting of motor vehicles. The product was not successful, and the trader deregistered with effect from 31 December 1988. At that time he had 300 unsold kits of the product. The Commissioners issued an assessment under what is now *VATA 1994, Sch 4 para 8*, considering that the stock should be valued at its cost price of £9 per item. The trader appealed, contending that the stock was unsaleable and worthless. The tribunal accepted this contention and allowed the appeal, holding that 'the value of the deemed supply must be based on the value of the goods at the time of deregistration'. *A McCormick, [1991] VATTR 196 (VTD 5724)*. (*Note*. The decision here was disapproved in the subsequent case of *Rowledge*, 63.119 below. Customs consider that the decision in *Rowledge* is no longer good law—see Customs' VAT Manual, Part 12, chapter 2, para 4.14. The 'appropriate valuation provision' is now *VATA 1994, Sch 6 para 6*.)

63.15   An aircraft maintenance engineer ceased trading and applied for deregistration. The Commissioners issued an assessment charging output tax on items of equipment which he held, valuing them at cost less depreciation. The trader appealed, contending that the equipment was worthless. The tribunal accepted the trader's evidence and allowed the appeal. *F Hadi (t/a Avionics Maintenance), EDN/96/115 (VTD 14677)*. (*Note*. Compare the decision in *Rowledge*, 63.119 below, which was not referred to in this decision.)

63.16   In the case noted at 53.66 REGISTRATION, a company had purchased some land in 1995 for £100,000 plus VAT of £17,500. It failed to make any subsequent supplies, and was deregistered in 1999. The Commissioners issued an assessment charging VAT of £18,680, on the basis that the value of the land had increased by 2.2% pa. The company appealed, contending that the land had proved to be almost worthless and should be valued at only £1,250. The tribunal rejected this contention and dismissed the appeal, holding that the assessment had been made to the best of the Commissioners' judgment and observing that the company had failed to submit a professional valuation. *DCM Leisure Ltd, MAN/00/323 (VTD 16966)*.

Supplies to non-taxable persons for retail sale (VATA 1994, Sch 6 para 2)

63.17   **School photographs supplied to school for sale to parents.**   A company supplied school photographs. It sent these to the head teachers of schools on a sale or return basis. The company stipulated the prices at which the photographs were to be sold by the head teachers, and permitted the head teachers to retain up to 30% of the sale price. The company only accounted for VAT on the amount which it received from the teachers, and the Commissioners issued a direction under what is now *VATA 1994, Sch 6 para 2*, requiring the company to account for VAT on the price paid by the parents. The tribunal dismissed the company's appeal, holding that the sales to the parents were 'by retail', notwithstanding that the head teacher was not carrying on a business of supplying photographs. *H Tempest Ltd, [1975] VATTR 161 (VTD 201)*.

63.18   The company in the case noted at 63.17 above, and an associated company, appealed against subsequent directions under what is now *VATA 1994, Sch 6 para 2*, contending that the directions were invalid since they were making their supplies to local education authorities which were taxable persons, whereas the provisions of *Sch 6 para 2* were confined to cases where supplies were made to non-taxable persons. The tribunal accepted this contention and held that the directions were invalid in so far as they related to supplies made to schools (rather than to supplies made directly to parents), since any schools which received supplies of photographs were acting as agents of the local education authorities. *H Tempest Ltd (No 2); H Tempest (Cardiff) Ltd, [1993] VATTR 482 (VTD 11210)*. (*Notes.* (1) For appeals against assessments raised on the basis that the companies were supplying photographs directly to parents, see 63.41 below. (2) For a subsequent case in which the decision here was not followed, and where it was held that the effect of the *Education Act 1993* was that schools were no longer acting as agents of local education authorities, see *Lancashire County Council*, 58.279 SUPPLY. The Commissioners now accept that the tribunal's findings in the *Tempest* case have been overtaken by the *Education Act 1993*—see Business Brief 11/97, issued on 9 May 1997.)

63.19   See also *Laughtons Photographs Ltd*, 21.232 EUROPEAN COMMUNITY LAW.

63.20   **Cosmetics supplied to agents for resale.** See *Direct Cosmetics Ltd (No 2)*, 21.232 EUROPEAN COMMUNITY LAW.

63.21   **Sales of lingerie—definition of open market value.** A company supplied lingerie and 'marital aids' to women who acted as demonstrators of its products. These demonstrators were not registered for VAT, since their turnover was below the registration threshold. The demonstrators effected sales to the public by attending parties arranged by hostesses, and displaying samples of goods and copies of catalogues at the parties. After each party the demonstrators placed orders with the company by telephone, and the company supplied the goods to the demonstrators with invoices which included a 30% discount for prompt payment. In cases where the demonstrators were unable to obtain payment from customers who had ordered goods, they could return the goods to the company and would receive a credit note. In accounting for output tax, the company deducted the 30% discount from the sale price. The Commissioners issued a direction under what is now *VATA 1994, Sch 6 para 2*, requiring the company to account for tax on the market value of the goods. The company continued to account for tax as before, and the Commissioners issued an assessment charging tax on the basis that the market value of the goods was the full undiscounted price. The company appealed, contending that the market value was the discounted price. The tribunal dismissed the company's appeal, holding that the 'discount' was in fact a commission. The company was a wholesaler and the demonstrators were retailers. Consequently, the market value of the goods was the undiscounted price, and the company was obliged to account for VAT on that basis. The QB upheld this decision. The 'open market value' for the purposes of *VATA 1994, Sch 6 para 2* was the price paid by the ultimate customer to the demonstrator, not the price paid by the demonstrator to the company. *Gold Star Publications Ltd v C & E Commrs, QB [1992] STC 365*.

63.22 **Tupperware distributors—whether direction under VATA 1994, Sch 6 para 2 unreasonable.** A married couple traded as distributors of Tupperware products. They sold these products through a number of sub-distributors, who were usually housewives and were not registered for VAT. The sub-distributors retained 30% of the price paid by the customers, and the distributors received the remaining 70%. The Commissioners issued a direction under what is now *VATA 1994, Sch 6 para 2*, requiring the distributors to account for VAT on the full recommended retail price paid by the customers. The distributors failed to comply with the direction, and the Commissioners issued an assessment to recover the undeclared tax. The husband lodged an appeal against the assessment, contending that the direction was unfair and unreasonable because he knew of two other Tupperware distributors who had not received directions. The tribunal dismissed the appeal. The Commissioners had a wide managerial discretion, and although it might not have been possible for them to take simultaneous steps against every trader who was avoiding tax, it did not follow that their conduct was unreasonable. *JK Moore, [1989] VATTR 276 (VTD 4474).*

63.23 **Mail order business—whether direction under VATA 1994, Sch 6 para 2 unreasonable.** A company which carried on a mail order business sent catalogues to more than 800,000 'agents', most of whom were housewives. None of the agents were registered for VAT. Agents were allowed commission on orders taken, and in some cases were allowed to purchase goods at a price less than the normal catalogue price. Where commission was allowed, the company deducted the commission in accounting for VAT. The Commissioners issued a direction under what is now *VATA 1994, Sch 6 para 2*, requiring the company to account for tax on the open market value of the goods, and the company appealed. The HL upheld the direction, holding that the 'agents' were not strictly agents of the company, but were acting as independent principals. The fact that the company did not know whether the 'agents' were ordering its goods for resale or for their own use did not render the direction invalid. Part of the company's business consisted of supplying goods to non-taxable persons for retail sale. The direction was applicable to such supplies, and did not contravene European Community law. *Dicta* of Advocate-General Da Cruz Vilaça in *Direct Cosmetics Ltd (No 2)*, 21.232 EUROPEAN COMMUNITY LAW, applied. *Fine Art Developments plc v C & E Commrs, HL [1996] STC 246; [1996] 1 WLR 1054; [1996] 1 All ER 888.*

63.24 **Company selling goods through door-to-door salesmen.** A company sold an assortment of low-priced goods such as pocket calculators, manufactured overseas, through door-to-door salesmen. The goods were supplied to the salesmen on a 'sale or return' basis. The company accounted for VAT only on the amounts which it charged the salesmen, rather than on the amounts which the salesmen charged the ultimate purchasers. The Commissioners issued a direction under what is now *VATA 1994, Sch 6 para 2*, requiring the company to account for tax on the retail market value of the goods. The company appealed, contending that the direction was unreasonable, since the company did not fix a recommended retail price and frequently charged its salesmen different prices for identical goods. Most salesmen only worked for the company for less than two months, and the company had no way of knowing how much the salesmen charged the customers for the goods. The tribunal allowed the company's appeal, holding on the evidence that it was not possible for the company to ascertain the open market value of the goods which it sold. *Beckbell Ltd, [1993] VATTR 212 (VTD 9847).*

63.25 **Outdoor toys—whether direction under VATA 1994, Sch 6 para 2 unreasonable.** A company (T) manufactured outdoor toys such as garden swings, climbing frames, trampolines, etc. Most of its sales were to registered traders, but it also had about 20 customers who carried on small retail businesses on a part-time basis and were not registered for VAT because their turnover was below the threshold. The Commissioners issued a direction under *VATA 1994, Sch 6 para 2* in respect of such sales, requiring T to account for output tax on the recommended retail price. T appealed, contending that the requirement was unreasonable in view of the small number of such sales. The tribunal rejected this contention and dismissed the appeal. It was arguable that occasional sales to unregistered retailers could be ignored, but in this case, T's sales to unregistered retailers exceeded £250,000 p.a., so that the direction was not unreasonable. *TP Activity Toys Ltd, MAN/96/142 (VTD 14377).*

Supplies of goods to agents for own use

63.26 **Goods supplied to hostesses under 'party plan' system—value of consideration for goods supplied to hostess.** A company sold women's and children's clothing under the 'party plan' system, under which its agents arranged meetings of potential customers in private houses to demonstrate its products and secure orders. The customer whose house was allowed as the venue was allowed a commission on the orders placed. She could take commission in cash, or alternatively could take goods produced by the company up to a prescribed retail price, which was considerably greater than the cash commission. Thus, in lieu of cash commission of £4.57, she could take clothing with a retail price of £11.67, paying cash for the excess if the price exceeded the £11.67. The Commissioners issued an assessment on the basis that the company should account for VAT on the retail price of goods supplied in this way. The company appealed, contending that it should only be required to account for VAT on the cash commission. The QB rejected this contention and upheld the assessment. By virtue of what is now *VATA 1994, s 19(3)*, the company was required to account for VAT on the market value of the goods, and this was equivalent to the retail price. *C & E Commrs v Pippa-Dee Parties Ltd, QB [1981] STC 495.*

63.27 In a subsequent case where the facts were similar to those in *Pippa-Dee Parties Ltd*, 63.26 above, the appellant company contended that *Pippa-Dee Parties Ltd* should not be followed on the grounds that Ralph Gibson J had not considered the application of the *EC Sixth Directive*. The tribunal rejected this contention and dismissed the appeal, holding that output tax was chargeable on the normal retail price of the goods supplied to the agent. The CA upheld this decision. There was a direct link between the hostess's services in arranging parties and the supply of the goods to the hostess. Therefore, the supply was 'for a consideration ... not wholly consisting of money', within what is now *VATA 1994, s 19(3)*. On the evidence, the value of the service rendered by the agent was the difference between the normal retail price and the price actually paid. The facts that the price actually paid for the goods exceeded their cost, and that the hostess could have taken cash instead, were immaterial. *Naturally Yours Cosmetics Ltd (No 2)*, 21.128 EUROPEAN COMMUNITY LAW, applied. *Empire Stores Ltd*, 21.129 EUROPEAN COMMUNITY LAW, was distinguished, on the grounds that the goods supplied as inducements in that case were not in the company's current catalogue and thus had no 'usual retail price'. *Rosgill Group Ltd v C & E Commrs, CA [1997] STC 811; [1997] 3 All ER 1012.*

63.28 The Commissioners issued an assessment on a company which sold wickerwork goods under the 'party plan' system. The company appealed against the assessment, contending that, in ascertaining the 'market value' of goods it supplied to its hostesses, discounts which it gave to staff and agents should be taken into account. The tribunal dismissed the appeal, holding that the market value was the price which a member of the public would pay in a retail shop. *Churchway Crafts Ltd (No 2), LON/80/204 (VTD 1186).*

63.29   Two companies which sold cosmetics supplied some of their goods to agents at greatly reduced prices. The agents were expected to arrange 'party plan' sales of the companies' goods, and give the goods which they had obtained cheaply to the hostesses of the parties. The companies accounted for VAT on the price charged to the agents, and the Commissioners issued an assessment on the basis that the companies should have accounted for VAT on the normal wholesale price. The tribunal dismissed the companies' appeals, holding that the companies were required to account for tax on the market value of the goods. *Naturally Yours Cosmetics Ltd; Miss Mary of Sweden Cosmetics Ltd, [1985] VATTR 159 (VTD 1921)*. (*Note*. For a subsequent appeal by one of the companies in this case, see 21.128 EUROPEAN COMMUNITY LAW.)

63.30   **Mail order company offering goods as inducements to new customers—valuation of supply.**   See *Empire Stores Ltd*, 21.129 EUROPEAN COMMUNITY LAW.

63.31   **Mail order company—supplies of goods to agents for own use.**   A company sold goods by mail order, through agents. It allowed its agents commission on payments received. This commission was allowed at 10% in cash or as a part payment for goods which the agents had already ordered, or at 12.5% as a part payment for future orders. When an agent ordered goods for her own use, the company contemplated that she would earn 10% commission on those goods, and therefore treated the commission as a 10% discount on the catalogue price of the goods in question. When an agent ordered goods for customers, the company accounted for output tax on the sale price. When an agent used commission credited to her to buy further goods, the company treated the full 12.5% commission as a discount on the catalogue price. The Commissioners issued an assessment on the basis that only the standard 10% commission could be treated as deductible from the consideration for VAT purposes, and that the additional 2.5% was not deductible. The company appealed, contending that it had accounted for VAT on the correct basis. The Ch D rejected this contention and upheld the assessment, applying the CA decision in *Rosgill Group Ltd*, 63.27 above. Lightman J held that there were two distinct contracts, namely a contract of agency and a contract for the purchase of further goods. There was a direct link between the supply of services under the agency contract and the purchase of the goods, so that the supply of the agent's services formed part of the consideration for the purchase. The 2.5% was not a discount, but part of the consideration for the agent's services. *C & E Commrs v The Littlewoods Organisation plc, Ch D [2000] STC 588*.

Whether commission deductible

63.32   **Retail sales under concession with holiday camp.**   A company (P), which sold toys and fancy goods, had a concession agreement with another company (L) to sell its goods in the general shop of a holiday camp controlled by L, paying L a prescribed percentage of the proceeds of such sales. The goods were sold by P's employees, but the proceeds were banked by L. L accounted to P for the net amount after deducting the agreed percentage. P accounted for tax on the net amount received from L, and appealed against an assessment made on the basis that it should have accounted for tax on the gross takings. The tribunal dismissed the appeal. The consideration for the sale of P's goods in the shop was the gross amount. The percentage deducted by L was not deductible. *P & M Marketing (UK) Ltd, LON/82/328 (VTD 1385)*.

63.33   **Sale of cars—interest on loan paid by vendor.**   Two companies which sold cars arranged for purchasers of the cars to obtain finance from a finance company, under a scheme whereby they paid the interest on the loans by way of a deduction from the amounts payable to them by the finance company in respect of the cars. The companies only accounted for tax on the net amounts which they received from the finance company, and the Commissioners issued assessments to charge tax on the full sale price of the cars. The tribunal dismissed the companies' appeals, holding that the deduction made by the finance company as part of the arrangement with the vendors could not affect the consideration for the supply previously agreed between the vendors and the purchasers. *Grant Melrose & Tennant Ltd; Arnold Clark Automobiles Ltd (No 2), [1985] VATTR 90 (VTD 1858).*

63.34 **Sale of cars under '0% hire-purchase scheme'.** A company (N) sold cars. It arranged with the manufacturers of the cars, and with a finance company (F) associated with the manufacturers, for customers to be able to purchase the cars under a '0% hire-purchase scheme'. Under this scheme N sold the cars to F and made out invoices to F accordingly. F then entered into agreements with the purchasers of the cars for the repayment of the purchase price. The price paid by F to N was reduced by an amount described in the agreement as a 'subsidy', and N deducted this subsidy from the sale price in computing its VAT liability. The Commissioners issued an assessment on the basis that VAT was chargeable on the full sale price. The tribunal upheld the assessment and dismissed N's appeal. On the evidence, the subsidy was consideration for the services provided by F, and was not simply a discount. *North Kent Motor Company, LON/87/633Z (VTD 3735).*

63.35 **Goods sold on credit—whether 'commission' allowed to associated company providing credit deductible in computing consideration.** Two associated companies, not registered as a group for VAT purposes at the relevant time, co-operated in selling goods to members of the public on credit. The goods were supplied by one of the companies (S), and credit facilities were supplied by the other company (C). Part of the consideration paid by customers was allocated to C as consideration for the supply of credit, and a further part was allocated to C as 'commission'. Thus, for example, where goods were advertised for sale at £100, and a further £35 was charged to the customer for the supply for credit, the customer would pay £135 but, in accounting for VAT, S not only deducted the £35 which was expressed to be for the supply of credit but also deducted a further £10 as 'commission' allocated to C, and only accounted for VAT on £90 of the £135 paid. The Commissioners issued a ruling that S should only have deducted the amount specifically expressed to be for the supply of credit, so that, in the above example, it should have accounted for VAT on £100 rather than on £90. S appealed, contending that it supplied the goods to C which in turn supplied them to the ultimate customers, so that it was only required to account for VAT on the net amount received after deducting the amounts allocated to C. The tribunal rejected this contention and dismissed the appeal, finding that the goods were supplied to the customers by S, so that, in accounting for VAT, S was only entitled to deduct the amount specifically attributable to the exempt supply of credit, and was not also entitled to deduct the amounts described as 'commission'. *Provident Financial plc, MAN/91/1114 (VTD 10215).*

63.36 **Commission paid to finance company—whether deductible from consideration.** A company (T) which sold television products arranged with a finance company to provide credit to its customer for periods of up to twelve months. In accounting for output tax, T deducted the commission which it paid to the finance company. The Commissioners issued an assessment charging tax on the full amounts which T charged to its customers, and the tribunal dismissed T's appeal. *A5 Television Ltd, LON/88/1358Y (VTD 12181).*

63.37 **Amount paid to finance company under sales promotion scheme.** A company (C) sold concrete driveways. It entered into a sales promotion scheme with a finance company (ICL), whereby it paid ICL 12.5% of the amount paid by its customers. In return, ICL supplied C with postdated cheques, payable over a five-year period, made out to the customers. C failed to account for output tax on the amounts paid by its customers which it passed to ICL. The Commissioners issued an assessment charging tax on the payments and C appealed, contending that it was acting as an agent for ICL and was not required to account for tax on these amounts. The tribunal rejected this contention and dismissed the appeal. *Classic Driveways (UK) Ltd, MAN/97/834 (VTD 15521)*.

63.38   **Interest-free credit granted to customers by finance company—amount of consideration.**   See *Primback Ltd*, 54.39 RETAILERS' SPECIAL SCHEMES.

63.39   **Import of fish meal from Chile—whether commission paid to Chilean company deductible.**   A company (D) imported fish meal into the UK from Chile, under an agreement with a Chilean company under which it paid one-third of its commission to the Chilean company. The Commissioners assessed D on the full amount of the commission, and D appealed, contending that it should only have to account for VAT on the two-thirds share which it retained, and not on the one-third which it was obliged to pay the Chilean company. The tribunal accepted this contention and allowed the appeal. *David Geddes (Commodities) Ltd, LON/87/573 (VTD 2664)*.

63.40   **School photographs—whether commission to schools deductible.**   A company supplied school photographs. It paid part of the price of the photographs to the headmasters of the schools as commission, and only accounted for output tax on the amounts which it retained. The Commissioners issued an assessment charging tax on the full amounts paid by the purchasers of the photographs, and the tribunal dismissed the company's appeal. *Paget*, 1.50 AGENTS, was distinguished on the grounds that the prices at which the photographs were to be sold were stipulated by the company, and most parents made their cheques payable to the company, whereas in *Paget* parents had made their cheques payable to the schools. Any bad debts were borne by the company, rather than by the schools. It followed that the company was obliged to account for VAT on the whole of the amounts paid by the parents, including the amounts which it passed to the schools as commission. *Flashlight Photography Ltd, LON/91/207Z (VTD 9088)*.

63.41   *Flashlight Photography Ltd*, 63.40 above, was applied in a similar subsequent case where *Paget*, 1.50 AGENTS, was distinguished. The tribunal held that the appellant companies was supplying photographs directly to the parents of the pupils whom it photographed, rather than to the school. Accordingly the companies were liable to account for output tax on the full amounts paid by the parents. *H Tempest Ltd (No 2); H Tempest (Cardiff) Ltd, [1993] VATTR 482 (VTD 11210)*. (*Notes*. (1) The appeals were adjourned to enable the parties to consider whether the companies could reclaim input tax on amounts which it paid to the schools in return for the use of the school facilities. However, there was no further public hearing of the appeal. (2) For another issue in this case, see 63.18 above. (3) This case was decided before the enactment of the *Education Act 1993*. For the effects of that enactment, see *Lancashire County Council*, 58.279 SUPPLY. The Commissioners now accept that the tribunal's findings in the *Tempest* case have been overtaken by the *Education Act 1993*—see Business Brief 11/97, issued on 9 May 1997.)

63.42   **Sales of carpets—commission paid to fitter.**   A carpet retailer arranged for carpets which he sold to be fitted by a self-employed contractor, whom he paid accordingly. He claimed that the amounts which he paid to the fitter should not be treated as part of his turnover and that he should not be required to account for output tax on them. The tribunal rejected this contention and dismissed his appeal, holding on the evidence that there was a single supply of a fitted carpet and that output tax was due on the full amount paid by the customer. *T Lynam (t/a Victoria Road Carpets), EDN/97/53 (VTD 15585).*

Tokens, stamps and vouchers (VATA 1994, Sch 6 para 5)

Note. Following the removal of regulations on the VAT treatment of trading stamps and voucher schemes with effect from 1 June 1996, the Commissioners accepted, in Business Brief 10/96 issued on 5 June 1996, there was no longer any distinction between trading stamps and other forms of vouchers/coupons, and that consideration for any reward goods was included in the payment made for the stamps and/or premium goods. They stated that they did not therefore intend to treat reward goods as gifts. However, following the CJEC decision in *Kuwait (Petroleum) Ltd*, 21.89 EUROPEAN COMMUNITY LAW, the Commissioners withdrew this concessionary treatment with effect from 1 January 1999: see Business Brief 17/99, issued on 6 August 1999. From that date output tax is due under the normal rules for business gifts. The cases in this section should be read in the light of the changes in the Commissioners' practice.

63.43 **Vouchers exchanged for goods.** A company (P) issued vouchers which could be exchanged for goods of a retail value equal for the face value of the voucher. Where traders accepted such vouchers, P did not reimburse the full face value, but deducted 13¾% as its 'commission'. A draper who accepted such vouchers only accounted for output tax on the amounts which P reimbursed him, and the Commissioners issued an assessment charging tax on the full face value of the vouchers. The tribunal dismissed the trader's appeal and the QB upheld this decision. Lord Widgery CJ observed that customers who presented the vouchers were 'paying cash and not consideration other than cash'. *JJ Davies v C & E Commrs, QB 1974, [1975] STC 28; [1975] 1 WLR 204; [1975] 1 All ER 309.*

63.44 In a subsequent case which concerned vouchers issued by the same company (P) as in *Davies*, 63.43 above, a large retail company (K) had accounted for tax on the full face value of P's vouchers, in accordance with the decision in *Davies*. However, K subsequently submitted a substantial repayment claim, contending that the amount (10%) deducted by P as commission should not be treated as part of its consideration. The Commissioners rejected the claim and the tribunal dismissed K's appeal, holding that the vouchers were 'to be regarded as the equivalent of the shelf price of the goods sold by (K), which price (P) is to be regarded as paying on behalf of the customer'. The Ch D upheld this decision, holding that P was providing a service to K, and that K benefited from being able to advertise its acceptance of P's vouchers. *Chaussures Bally SA v Belgian Ministry of Finance*, 21.132 EUROPEAN COMMUNITY LAW, and *Davies*, 63.43 above, applied. *Elida Gibbs Ltd*, 21.130 EUROPEAN COMMUNITY LAW, and *Argos Distributors Ltd*, 21.131 EUROPEAN COMMUNITY LAW, were distinguished, on the grounds that in those cases there was no third party involved, and the relevant scheme 'was that of the retailer itself'. *Kingfisher plc v C & E Commrs, Ch D [2000] STC 992.* (*Note.* The Ch D also held that the discount given by K to P on redemption of the voucher was consideration for a separate supply of services by P to K, which was exempt from VAT under *VATA 1994, Sch 9, Group 5, Item 1.*)

63.45 A company which traded as a retailer issued vouchers to customers at the rate of £1 for every £20 worth of goods purchased. The vouchers could be redeemed against goods supplied by the company, including some types of goods which it did not normally stock but had purchased for the purposes of the sales promotion scheme. The company did not account for VAT on the redeemed vouchers and the Commissioners issued an assessment charging tax on the market value of the goods supplied in exchange. The tribunal dismissed the company's appeal, holding that, as the vouchers were not money, the goods supplied in exchange for them had to be treated as being supplied at market value. *Body Shop Supply Services Ltd, [1984] VATTR 233 (VTD 1752).*

63.46   A company presented hamburgers to readers of a tabloid newspaper under a sales promotion scheme. The newspaper's readers had to present a voucher and four tokens cut out of editions of the newspaper. The voucher and tokens had to be presented within a period of nine days, and the offer was limited to one hamburger per person. No payment changed hands between the company and the newspaper. The Commissioners issued an assessment on the basis that VAT was chargeable on the supply of the hamburgers. The company appealed, contending that the hamburgers were gifts and were therefore not a supply of goods by virtue of what is now *VATA 1994, Sch 4 para 5(2)(a)*. The tribunal rejected this contention, holding that the production of the completed voucher was consideration for the hamburger, applying *Chappell & Co Ltd v Nestlé Co Ltd, HL 1959, [1960] AC 87; [1959] 2 All ER 701* (a case in which the HL held, by a 3–2 majority, that where a company manufacturing chocolate offered gramophone records at a reduced price to members of the public who submitted three wrappers from packets of its milk chocolate, the acquisition and delivery of the wrappers formed part of the consideration for the records). Accordingly, the hamburgers were not gifts. *McDonald's Restaurants Ltd, LON/88/1190Y (VTD 3884)*. (*Note.* The appeal was adjourned to enable consideration of other issues to be deferred until the CJEC had issued its decision in *The Boots Co plc*, 21.136 EUROPEAN COMMUNITY LAW. However, there was no further public hearing of the appeal.)

63.47   A company which sold motor fuel distributed vouchers which entitled purchasers of its fuel to discounts. Some of the company's sales were directly to the public at sites which it owned, but it also supplied some fuel to dealers who then resold the fuel to members of the public. When a dealer submitted such vouchers for redemption, the company credited the dealer with an amount equal to the face value of the voucher. In accounting for output tax, it deducted the amount of such vouchers from its gross takings. The Commissioners issued an assessment on the basis that the company should have accounted on the full amount of its takings without deducting the amounts of the vouchers. The company appealed, contending that the taxable consideration should be reduced by the amount of the vouchers. The tribunal initially directed that the case should be referred to the CJEC for a ruling on whether the taxable amount was the amount originally charged for the fuel, or whether the taxable amount should be reduced by the amount of the vouchers. Subsequently the CJEC issued a ruling in the case of *Elida Gibbs Ltd*, 21.130 EUROPEAN COMMUNITY LAW. The Registrar of the CJEC asked the tribunal if it wished to maintain the reference in view of that decision. At a further hearing the tribunal allowed the company's appeal, applying the CJEC decision in *Elida Gibbs Ltd* and holding that the amounts shown on the vouchers submitted by the dealers were a reduction in the value of the original supply of motor fuel. *Conoco Ltd, [1997] VATDR 47 (VTD 14679).* (*Note.* For the award of costs in this case, see 2.286 APPEALS.)

63.48   A company which manufactured cigarettes operated a promotion scheme whereby it supplied vouchers with packets of cigarettes. When customers had collected a certain number of such vouchers, they could be exchanged for goods. The Commissioners issued a ruling that the company was liable to account for output tax on the cost of the goods it supplied in this way, and the company appealed. The tribunal dismissed the company's appeal. Applying the CJEC decision in *Kuwait Petroleum (GB) Ltd*, 21.89 EUROPEAN COMMUNITY LAW, the vouchers 'were supplied free of charge' for the purposes of *Article 5(6)* of the *EC Sixth Directive*, so that the company was required to account for output tax on the cost of the goods for which the customers exchanged the vouchers. *Gallaher Ltd, LON/96/1928 (VTD 14827, 16395).*

63.49   A company operated a number of retail shops. It accepted vouchers issued by manufacturers as part-payment for the goods which it sold. In such cases it was reimbursed by the manufacturer and accounted for output tax on the full sale price of the goods, including the amounts for which it had accepted vouchers. Subsequently it submitted a repayment claim on the basis that the effect of the CJEC decision in *Elida Gibbs Ltd*, 21.130 EUROPEAN COMMUNITY LAW, was that the amounts of the vouchers, for which it had been reimbursed by the manufacturers, were not 'consideration' and that output tax was not due. The Commissioners rejected the claim on the basis that the reimbursements which the company received from the manufacturers was further consideration for the supplies of the goods to its customers. The company appealed. The tribunal reviewed the CJEC decision in *Elida Gibbs Ltd* and expressed the view that 'the reduction of the taxable amount was not intended by the Court to affect the price at which the manufacturer sold the article to the retailer'. However, the tribunal directed that the appeal should be referred to the CJEC for clarification of the application of the decision in *Elida Gibbs*. *Yorkshire Co-Operatives Ltd, MAN/97/207 (VTD 15821)*. (*Note.* The CJEC has registered the case as *Case C-398/99*. The Advocate General has not yet delivered his Opinion.)

63.50   See also *Kuwait (Petroleum) Ltd*, 21.89 EUROPEAN COMMUNITY LAW; *Elida Gibbs Ltd*, 21.130 EUROPEAN COMMUNITY LAW, and *Boots Co plc*, 21.136 EUROPEAN COMMUNITY LAW.

63.51   **Vouchers repurchased by issuing company after use—amount of consideration.**   A company (H) produced and sold vouchers for a limited number of large retail companies. No VAT was chargeable on the initial sale of these vouchers to the companies by virtue of what is now *VATA 1994, Sch 6 para 5*. The companies to which the vouchers were sold distributed them to members of the public, either for payment or as prizes in competitions. The retailers to whom the vouchers were presented redeemed them after use at a discount which was generally about 9%. The main commercial advantage to the retailers was the hope of increased sales by accepting the vouchers. No change was given to customers who presented the vouchers, and the retailers hoped that some customers might thereby be encouraged to spend more than they would otherwise have done. The Commissioners issued an assessment on the basis that the difference between the face value of the vouchers and the price at which H repurchased them constituted consideration received by H, chargeable to VAT. H appealed, contending that the vouchers were supplied otherwise than for consideration. The QB rejected this contention and upheld the assessment. The amount of the discount forgone by the retailers constituted the consideration paid by the retailers for the services provided by H. *Naturally Yours Cosmetics Ltd (No 2)*, 21.128 EUROPEAN COMMUNITY LAW, and *Diners Club Ltd*, 26.11 FINANCE, applied. *C & E Commrs v High Street Vouchers Ltd, QB [1990] STC 575*.

63.52   **Sales of vouchers to retailers—whether Sch 6 para 5 applicable.**   A company distributed vouchers with a nominal value of £5 or £10, which it sold to retailers for use in sales promotions. The company did not account for output tax on the sales of the vouchers, and the Commissioners issued an assessment charging tax on them. The company appealed, contending that, by virtue of what is now *VATA 1994, Sch 6 para 5*, no tax was chargeable. The QB rejected this contention and upheld the assessment, holding that *Sch 6 para 5* did not apply since the retailers did not have any right to receive goods or services for the amounts stated on the vouchers. The right to receive goods or services was granted to the customers of the retailers to whom the vouchers were sold, rather than to the retailers themselves. *C & E Commrs v Showmarch Marketing Ltd, QB 1993, [1994] STC 19*.

63.53   **Restaurant 'discount cards'—whether Sch 6 para 5 applicable.**   Two companies issued 'discount cards', with a face value of £14.99, entitling the holder to obtain a free course on up to twelve occasions at a stated restaurant. The Commissioners issued a ruling that output tax was payable on the supplies of the cards, and the companies appealed, contending that the cards were within what is now *VATA 1994, Sch 6 para 5*. The CA rejected this contention and dismissed the appeals. The discount cards conferred a right to pay a reduced price for certain supplies but did not confer any rights to goods or services and thus were not within what is now *VATA 1994, Sch 6 para 5*. *C & E Commrs v Granton Marketing Ltd; C & E Commrs v Wentwalk Ltd, CA [1996] STC 1049*. (*Notes.* (1) For a subsequent case in which it was held that the 'discount cards' were not zero-rated brochures, see 5.65 BOOKS, ETC. (2) For another subsequent case concerning the time of the supply of the vouchers, see 58.313 SUPPLY.)

63.54   **Sales of vouchers by car dealers—whether Sch 6 para 5 applicable.**   A company (F) sold books of vouchers to car dealers, who then passed the books of vouchers to the purchasers of second-hand cars. F accounted for output tax on the amounts which it received from the car dealers for the vouchers, but the car dealers did not account for tax on their onward supply of the vouchers to their customers. In March 1998 a local VAT officer ruled that no tax was chargeable on these onward supplies, on the basis that they fell within *Sch 6 para 5*. However, the scheme came to the attention of a regional office, and in June 1998 the Commissioners withdrew the first ruling and ruled that the sale of the vouchers was not within *Sch 6 para 5*, so that VAT was chargeable. F appealed, contending that the initial ruling had been correct and that the supplies were within *Sch 6 para 5*. The tribunal rejected this contention and dismissed the appeal, and the QB upheld this decision. Carnwath J observed that the vouchers in question did 'not entitle the bearer to any particular goods, but simply to a reduction in the price'. *Granton Marketing Ltd*, 63.53 above, applied. Furthermore, the vouchers could not be treated as a part payment. *F & I Services Ltd v C & E Commrs, QB [2000] STC 364*. (*Notes.* (1) The QB also held that the vouchers were not exempt under either *VATA 1994, Sch 9, Group 5, Item 5* or *Article 13B(d)* of the *EC Sixth Directive*. See 26.9 *et seq.* FINANCE and 21.174 *et seq.* EUROPEAN COMMUNITY LAW respectively for cases concerning these provisions. (2) For the Commissioners' view of the scheme, see Business Brief 18/98, issued on 11 September 1998. (3) The company also applied for judicial review of the Commissioners' decision to withdraw their original ruling—see 2.232 APPEALS.)

63.55   **Vouchers sold at discount to persons other than purchasers of goods— calculation of part of consideration represented by vouchers.**   See *Argos Distributors Ltd*, 21.131 EUROPEAN COMMUNITY LAW.

63.56   **Football club—sale of vouchers for admission to matches.**   See *Celtic plc*, 58.337 SUPPLY.

63.57   **Retailers—payments made to company operating promotion scheme— whether deductible from gross takings.**   See *Allied Carpets Group plc*, 54.40 RETAILERS' SPECIAL SCHEMES.

Miscellaneous

63.58   **Sale of old jewellery using jewellery supplied by customer.**   A partnership manufactured gold jewellery to customers' specifications. In some cases the customer provided pieces of old jewellery for adaptation or for re-use of the gold contained therein. The partnership charged its customers for the work done plus the cost of the gold used in excess of the gold content of the old jewellery handed in. It did not account for VAT on the value of the gold handed in for re-use. The Commissioners issued an assessment on the basis that the partnership should have accounted for VAT on the value of all the gold used in the new jewellery supplied to the customers. The tribunal allowed the partnership's appeal, holding that the partnership had accounted for tax on the correct basis. *Sharuna Jewellers, [1979] VATTR 14 (VTD 709).*

63.59   *Sharuna Jewellers,* 63.58 above, was not followed in a subsequent case where the tribunal held that the old articles which the trader melted down became part of his trading stock, so that he was required to account for output tax on all the gold in the new item, rather than only on the excess gold. *HR Babber (t/a Ram Parkash Sunderdass & Sons), [1992] VATTR 268 (VTD 5958). (Note.* For another issue in this case, see 3.51 ASSESSMENT.)

63.60   In a case where the facts were broadly similar to those in *Sharuna Jewellers,* 63.59 above, the tribunal held that the important question was 'whether the appellants and their customers must be taken as having agreed that the new ornament be made using the gold provided by the customer but with the addition of any necessary gold or as having agreed that the old ornament be given in part exchange for a new ornament to be fashioned from no specific gold'. On the evidence, the tribunal found that 'the agreement with some customers was on the basis that their gold was to be refashioned and not mixed, but that the agreements with others was (*sic*) for part exchange'. The tribunal held that transactions where additional gold amounted to 25% or less of the finished article should be treated as refashioning, but that transactions where additional gold amounted to more than 25% of the finished article should be treated as part exchange, and directed that the assessment should be reduced accordingly. Both parties appealed to the QB, which upheld the tribunal decision as one of fact. *Edwards v Bairstow & Harrison, HL 1955, 36 TC 207 (TTC 2001, 4.148)* applied. *C & E Commrs v SAI Jewellers (and cross-appeal), QB [1996] STC 269. (Note.* An alternative contention by the partnership, that the Commissioners were estopped from raising the assessment, was rejected by the tribunal and was not pursued in the QB. For cases concerning estoppel, see 2.72 *et seq.* APPEALS.)

63.61   **Payments made to members of co-operative and described as 'dividends'— whether deductible in computing consideration.**   A company incorporated under the *Industrial & Provident Societies Acts* made payments, which it described as 'dividends', to some of its members who had purchased goods from it. These dividends were calculated as a percentage of the aggregate amount of the members' purchases, using a credit card issued by a bank associated with the company, during a prescribed period. The payments were made only once each year, and were only made to members who had invested at least £50 with the company. For the purposes of direct tax, they were treated as co-operative dividends within *ICTA 1988, s 486(10).* The company deducted the amount of these payments in accounting for VAT, and the Commissioners issued an assessment to charge output tax on them, considering that the dividends were distributions of profit and could not be taken into account in computing the consideration. The company appealed, contending that the amounts were 'price discounts and rebates' within *Article 11A3(b)* of the *EC Sixth Directive.* The tribunal allowed the company's appeal, holding that 'the use of the word "dividend" to describe the payments is of no significance'. The facts that the payments were deferred, and were dependent upon a contingency, did not transform them from discounts into distributions of profit. *Co-Operative Retail Services Ltd, [1992] VATTR 60 (VTD 7527).*

63.62   **Unsold stock considered worthless and returned to supplier—valuation of stock at time of return.**   A company was unable to sell a quantity of stock and returned it to its supplier. The Commissioners issued an assessment on the basis that the stock should be valued at cost, and that tax should be accounted for accordingly.

The tribunal allowed the company's appeal, holding on the evidence that the stock was worthless at the time of its return. *Montessori Teachers Supplies Ltd, LON/91/2421Z (VTD 8825)*. (*Note*. Customs state in their VAT Manual, Part 12, chapter 2, para 4.14, that they consider that this case was wrongly decided, because their representative failed to draw the tribunal's attention 'to the appropriate valuation provision'; see now *VATA 1994, Sch 6 para 6*.)

63.63   **Unsold furniture returned by retailer to wholesaler—whether payments from wholesaler consideration for separate supply by retailer.**   A furniture retailer, who was not registered for VAT, returned quantities of unsold furniture to the wholesaler from whom he had obtained them. The Commissioners issued an assessment on the basis that the amounts paid by the wholesaler were consideration for a separate supply of furniture by the retailer to the wholesaler, with the result that the retailer's supplies exceeded the registration threshold and that he was required to account for output tax. The retailer appealed, contending that he had obtained the furniture on a 'sale or return' basis and that the amounts which he received from the wholesaler should be treated as deductible from the amounts which he had previously paid to the wholesaler for the furniture, rather than as consideration for a separate supply, with the result that his turnover for the period in question was below the registration threshold. The tribunal accepted the retailer's evidence and allowed his appeal. *K Hussain, MAN/97/131 (VTD 15830)*.

63.64   **Repossession of goods—whether a 'decrease in consideration'—VAT Regulations 1995, reg 38*.**   See *Morley Electronic Fire Systems Ltd*, 38.89 INVOICES AND CREDIT NOTES.

63.65   **Computer games supplied by barter—amount of consideration for supply.**   A retailer sold computer games and accessories. He also began a scheme whereby people who had computer games which they no longer wished to use could exchange them for others at his shop. Customers were charged £5 to join this scheme, and could then, after paying a £3 handling fee, exchange games which they no longer wanted for others from a stock of old games kept by the retailer. The retailer accounted for output tax on the £5 joining fees and the £3 handling charges. The Commissioners issued an assessment on the basis that he should also have accounted for output tax on the market value of the games which he passed to the customers under the scheme. The assessment was computed on the basis that the average value of such games was £27.50. The tribunal upheld the assessment in principle, holding that 'for tax purposes there was a supply by barter which is to be taken as a supply at open market value', but reduced the amount of the assessment, holding that the value of each of the second-hand games should be treated as £15. *TC Antoniou-Savva (t/a Game Atronics), LON/93/2225A (VTD 11982)*.

63.66   **Sale of painting at auction—50% of proceeds allocated to charity—whether artist accountable on full amount of sale proceeds.**   An artist sold a painting at an auction. The sale price of the painting was £13,000, but the artist only received £6,500 of this, the remaining £6,500 being paid to the charity which had organised the auction. The artist accounted for output tax on the £6,500 which she had retained. The Commissioners issued an assessment requiring her to account for tax on the £6,500 which had been retained by the charity. She appealed, contending that, because the bidders were aware that the charity would retain 50% of the total price, the £6,500 which the charity retained should be deemed to have been paid by the buyer of the painting, rather than by her. The tribunal allowed her appeal, holding that, under *Article 11A1(a)* of the *EC Sixth Directive*, the taxable amount was 'everything which constitutes the consideration which has been or is to be obtained by the supplier'. The £6,500 which the charity retained was never 'obtained by the supplier', and accordingly she was only required to account for output tax on the £6,500 which she actually retained. *E Patrick, [1994] VATTR 247 (VTD 12354).*

63.67   **Supplies of diaries.**   A number of associated companies produced diaries for various organisations such as local charities. They were entitled to sell advertising space in the diaries, and to retain the advertising revenue which they received. They undertook to provide a specified number of the diaries free of charge to the organisations for whom they produced them. In 1981 the Commissioners issued a ruling that the companies should account for output tax on the cost of producing the diaries and on a notional 30% mark-up, as well as on the advertising revenue. Initially the companies accepted this, but in 1993 they formed the opinion that they should only be required to account for tax on the advertising revenue, and claimed a repayment of tax which they considered that they had overdeclared. In 1995 the Commissioners agreed to repay the tax relating to the notional 30% mark-up, but rejected the claim to repay the output tax on the cost of the diaries. The companies appealed, contending that the only consideration which they obtained was the revenue paid by the advertisers. The tribunal accepted this contention and allowed the appeals. The advertising charges were the consideration for the supply of the diaries to the recipient organisations. The fact that the consideration was paid by a third party did not require any additional value to be attributed to the supplies. *Seaton Sands Ltd & Others, LON/95/2609A (VTD 13879).* (*Note.* For subsequent developments in this case, see 2.353 APPEALS.)

63.68   **Supplies of videocassettes—old videocassette accepted in part-exchange.**   A trader (B) sold videocassettes for £20. However, where a customer offered a videocassette which he had previously purchased from B in part-exchange, B only charged the customer £10 for the new videocassette. The Commissioners issued an assessment on the basis that B was required to account for output tax on the basis that the consideration for each of his supplies was £20. B appealed, contending that, where he accepted an old videocassette in part-exchange, he should only be required to account for output tax on the £10 cash payment which he received. The tribunal accepted this contention but the QB remitted the case for rehearing. Carnwath J held that the consideration consisted partly of the £10 in cash, and partly of the second-hand videocassette. On the evidence, B purchased videocassettes for between £2 and £3, so that the subjective value of the second-hand videocassette could not be more than this. *Naturally Yours Cosmetics Ltd v C & E Commrs (No 2),* 21.128 EUROPEAN COMMUNITY LAW, applied. *C & E Commrs v A Bugeja, QB 1999, [2000] STC 1.*

63.69   **Sales of golf clubs—old golf clubs accepted in part-exchange.**   A company (P) sold golf clubs. In 1990 the Royal & Ancient Golf Club of St Andrews declared that some of P's clubs did not comply with the Rules of Golf, so that they could not be used for golf competitions in the UK after March 1996. P announced that it would supply a new club for £22 to anyone surrendering one of the 'illegal' clubs in part-exchange. These new clubs had a normal wholesale price of £49.99 and a normal retail price of £72. The Commissioners issued a ruling that the 'illegal' clubs had a part-exchange value of £27.99, so that P was required to account for output tax on the normal wholesale price of £49.99. P appealed, contending that the 'illegal' clubs had no value, so that it should only be required to account for output tax on the consideration of £22 which it actually received. The tribunal accepted this contention and allowed the appeal, holding that the scrap value of the old clubs could be ignored, and that 'the value of the non-monetary consideration involved in the present case is nil'. *Ping (Europe) Ltd, MAN/99/74 (VTD 17001).*

63.70   **Sale of asset partly used privately.**   A trader had purchased a glider and had accepted that he was only entitled to reclaim 80% of the relevant input tax, on the basis that the glider was partly used for private purposes. Subsequently he sold the glider at a profit, and only accounted for output tax on 80% of the proceeds. The Commissioners issued a ruling that he was required to account for output tax on the full amount of the proceeds. The tribunal dismissed the trader's appeal, holding that 'there is no applicable provision in the VAT legislation which gives a taxable person who makes a supply of goods in the course or furtherance of any business carried on by him (even if there is a personal element in the use of such goods) any right to deduct and withhold from Customs & Excise any output VAT attributable to that supply'. *DA Smith (t/a Varcom Sailplane Computers), LON/95/2353 (VTD 14196).*

63.71 *Smith,* 63.70 above, was applied in a similar subsequent case involving the sale of a yacht. *D Seward, LON/96/213 (14706).*

63.72 **Valuation of transfer of land.** The Cumbernauld Development Corporation, which had begun the development of the Cumbernauld area in 1956, transferred some of its remaining land to a local golf club in exchange for some land owned by the club. Under the agreement, there was no monetary consideration for either transfer, but the Corporation had to pay for work to be carried out on the golf club's course and for a new clubhouse. The total cost to the Corporation was about £3,000,000, although the land which it obtained by the golf club had been valued at only £120,000. The Commissioners issued a ruling that the supply made by the Corporation should be valued at the subjective cost of £3,000,000. The Corporation appealed, contending that the supply should be valued at £120,000, being the valuation of the land which it had received in exchange. The tribunal rejected this contention, holding that the value had to be determined subjectively, but also held that the Commissioners' valuation was excessive, since, on the evidence, 'the costs of the additional 18 holes for the golf club would not truly form part of the subjective value for the transfer of the old club house'. The tribunal adjourned the appeal in the hope that an 'appropriate value' could be agreed. *Cumbernauld Development Corporation, EDN/96/92 (VTD 14630).* (*Note.* Following the hearing, the parties agreed that the supply should be valued at £1,505,000. For subsequent developments in this case, see 58.297 SUPPLY.)

63.73 **Valuation of new cars supplied under hire-purchase agreements.** A car-dealing company (N) made arrangements with finance companies to enable it to sell cars by hire-purchase, and accepted second-hand cars from its customers in part-exchange, treating the part-exchange value as the deposit required by the finance companies. Since the finance companies required a minimum deposit before they would agree to make loans to the customers, N frequently offered to inflate the allowance which it offered for the used cars which it took in part-exchange. To maintain its profit levels, it inflated the nominal sale price of the cars which it was selling to the finance companies by a similar amount (a practice known as 'bumping'). However, it only accounted for output tax on what it considered to be the true value of the cars, rather than on their inflated price. The Commissioners issued an assessment on the basis that output tax was chargeable on the price shown in the hire-purchase agreement with the finance company. The tribunal upheld the assessment and dismissed N's appeal. As a matter of law, N was supplying the cars to the finance companies. Accordingly, there was 'no room for any other value than that attributed by the parties in the document sent or which is prepared for the purposes of the finance house'. The chairman observed that 'that analysis removes the necessity to have regard to a wholly artificial, if not dishonest, method of securing finance. If, in order to do so, the appellants have manipulated figures, then they can scarcely complain if a value they have promulgated for a vehicle for their own purposes is accepted as its value for the particular transaction. As a matter of principle the appellants should not be entitled to benefit from ... false attribution of value.' The CS upheld the tribunal decision. Earlsferry LJ held that the 'central question' was the value which the parties to the supply treated as the consideration. On the evidence, the only value which could be attributed to the transaction was the amount stated in the finance documents. *North Anderson Cars Ltd v C & E Commrs, CS [1999] STC 1431.*

63.74   **Valuation of second-hand cars.**   See the cases noted at 9.70 to 9.72 CARS.

63.75   **Spectacles dispensed by optician.**   See *Green,* 45.5 PAYMENT OF TAX.

63.76   **Supplies paid for by issue of shares in company—valuation of shares.**   See *A-Z Electrical,* 10.9 CASH ACCOUNTING SCHEME.

SUPPLIES OF SERVICES

Supplies of accommodation (VATA 1994, Sch 6 para 9)

63.77   **Block hotel bookings by tour operators.**   Two companies each owned a hotel used by tour operators, with whom arrangements were made for advance block bookings of the hotel accommodation. The arrangements varied in detail from operator to operator, but in a typical contract, the tour operator booked 30 double and four single rooms at specified prices for the seven months to 31 October. The contract provided a 'release date' six days in advance, which enabled the operator to release rooms which would not be required for a tour due to start a week ahead. The operator was not required to make any payment for the rooms released. He made no payment in advance, and normally paid for the rooms not released after each tour. The companies accounted for VAT on the basis that the reduced rate of what is now *VATA 1994, Sch 6 para 9* applied to all the accommodation booked by the tour operators for the required four-week period, even where this accommodation was subsequently released and not occupied. The Commissioners issued an assessment on the basis that the provisions of *VATA 1994, Sch 6 para 9* applied only to the accommodation actually used. The tribunal upheld the assessment and the QB dismissed the companies' appeals. The reduced rate of *Sch 6 para 9* could only apply to accommodation actually supplied for more than four weeks. *Elga & Askar Co Ltd and Another v C & E Commrs, QB [1983] STC 628.*

63.78   **Hotel accommodation supplied to US Air Force personnel.**   A married couple owned and managed a hotel in Suffolk. Most of their customers were members of the US Air Force. Where they provided accommodation to US service personnel for more than four weeks, the couple only charged VAT at 3%. The Commissioners issued an assessment on the basis that the conditions for the application of the reduced rate under what is now *VATA 1994, Sch 6 para 9* were not satisfied, and that VAT should have been accounted for at 15%. The tribunal dismissed the couple's appeal, finding that the couple had not produced the evidence required to prove that the conditions of *Sch 6 para 9(1)* were satisfied. *BE & CS Rey (t/a Wood Hall Hotel & Country Club), LON/89/653Y (VTD 5676).*

63.79   **VATA 1994, Sch 6 para 9(2)—treatment of payments for meals.**   A company operated a hotel in Northern Ireland. In accounting for output tax on income from long-stay guests, it failed to account for tax on the price it charged for breakfasts. The Commissioners issued an assessment on the basis that the price charged for breakfast was liable to VAT. The company appealed, contending that its provision of breakfast was an integral part of its provision of accommodation. The tribunal rejected this contention and dismissed the appeal, holding that there was a distinction between 'accommodation' and 'board'. 'Accommodation' had to be interpreted as 'sleeping accommodation' or as 'accommodation of rooms'. The provision of breakfast was a supply of catering, not a supply of accommodation. The payments for breakfast were therefore 'attributable to facilities other than the right to occupy the accommodation', within *VATA 1994, Sch 6 para 9(2)(a)*, and were therefore liable to VAT. *Hospitality Resource Ltd, LON/98/582 (VTD 16526)*.

Whether commission deductible

63.80   **Escort agency.**   The proprietors of an escort agency appealed against two assessments, contending that the amounts which they paid to the escorts should not be included as part of their turnover. The tribunal dismissed their appeal, holding that the whole of the amounts paid by customers to the agency were consideration for the services which the agency provided. *Marlow & Hind, LON/77/14 & LON/77/99 (VTD 407)*.

63.81   **Massage parlour—commission retained by masseuses.**   The proprietor of a sauna and massage parlour charged customers for services provided at the parlour by masseuses. The masseuses were treated as self-employed and the proprietor paid the masseuses commission. She deducted such commissions from her takings in accounting for VAT, and the Commissioners issued an assessment to charge tax on the full fees charged to customers. The tribunal dismissed the proprietor's appeal against the assessment, holding that the proprietor should account for VAT on the full amount charged to the customers. *Y Niven, EDN/87/62 (VTD 2591)*.

63.82   See also *Rudd*, 58.253 SUPPLY.

63.83   **Supplies by company providing coach tours—commission paid to Bermudan holding company.**   A company (T), which was a subsidiary of a Bermudan holding company, provided coach tours in Europe from premises in London. The Bermudan company arranged for brochures describing the tours to be published and distributed, and determined the tour prices in local currencies. Payments for the tours were made to the Bermudan company, which deducted a percentage as commission and paid the balance to T. T only accounted for VAT on the net amount it received, and did not account for tax on the commission retained by the Bermudan company. The Commissioners considered that the value of the supplies for tax purposes was the price advertised in the brochures and paid by the customers. T appealed, contending that it supplied the tours to the Bermudan company which in turn supplied those tours to the actual customers. The tribunal dismissed T's appeal, holding that the tours were clearly supplied to the passengers and the Bermudan company was acting as an agent. The Bermudan company was incapable of physically enjoying the services supplied. The consideration was the amount paid by the passengers to the travel agents through whom they booked. The CA upheld this decision. The tribunal was clearly entitled, on the evidence, to regard the detailed arrangements as a facade, designed to conceal the fact that the supply was made to the passengers rather than to the Bermudan company. The consideration for the supply was the total amount paid by the passengers. The fact that T did not receive this total amount was irrelevant; it only failed to receive this amount because it had authorised the Bermudan company and other overseas companies to deduct sums as commission. *Trafalgar Tours Ltd v C & E Commrs, CA 1989, [1990] STC 127*.

63.84   **Language school paying commission to overseas schools—whether commission deductible from consideration.**   A company which operated a language school paid commission to overseas schools which introduced students to it. The company sought to deduct this commission from the consideration it received from the students. The tribunal held that the commission was not deductible. *Butler Question Method School of Languages Ltd, LON/91/1239X (VTD 7178)*.

63.85 **Company operating cab hire business—whether amounts paid to 'controllers' deductible.** A company operated a cab hire business. It had about 40 drivers, who paid a fixed weekly charge of £50, described as a 'circuit fee', to the company. The company engaged staff (whom it treated as self-employed) to act as controllers, and paid them a weekly amount of £15 per driver. Initially the company accounted for tax on the full amounts which it received from the drivers, but subsequently it submitted a repayment claim on the basis that the amounts which it paid to the controllers should not have been included as part of its consideration. The Commissioners rejected the claim and the tribunal dismissed the company's appeal. The company received the 'circuit fees' as an independent principal and was obliged to account for output tax on the full amounts of the fees. *Crayford & Bexleyheath (Motors) Ltd, LON/95/1469A (VTD 13620).*

63.86 A similar decision was reached in *CA Wharmby, MAN/97/1036 (VTD 16436).*

Sponsorship payments

63.87 **Benefits supplied by charity in return for sponsorship—valuation of benefits—whether full amount paid by sponsors constituting 'consideration'.** A company was registered as a charity with the object of promoting drama. It issued a brochure requesting potential supporters to sponsor seats in its theatre by paying it £150. In return for their sponsorship, sponsors were entitled to priority bookings for two gala evenings, and their sponsorship was acknowledged by personalised brass plaques on the seats, and by an acknowledgement on a board in the theatre foyer. The company did not account for VAT on the sponsorship payments, and the Commissioners issued an assessment charging tax on the full amount paid. The CS upheld the assessment. The company would not have provided the goods and services in question for less than the £150 which the sponsors paid. Accordingly, the whole of the £150 was 'consideration in money' within what is now *VATA 1994, s 19(2)*, and VAT was chargeable accordingly. *C & E Commrs v Tron Theatre Ltd, CS 1993, [1994] STC 177.*

63.88 The CS decision in *Tron Theatre Ltd*, 63.87 above, was applied in the similar subsequent case of *High Peak Theatre Trust Ltd, MAN/95/1108 (VTD 13678).*

63.89 **Publishing company making cash awards to scientists—awards financed by sponsors—whether consideration for supply of services to sponsors.** A company (E) published a scientific periodical. It organised cash awards to scientists. The cost of the awards was met by sponsors. In return for their sponsorship, the sponsors received publicity in the periodical and tickets to attend the annual award. The Commissioners issued a ruling that E should account for output tax on the payments from the sponsors. E appealed. The tribunal allowed the appeal, holding that the sponsorship payments 'did not form part of the turnover of the organisers' and 'were not consideration obtained in return for the supply of benefits to sponsors'. The QB upheld this decision. *HJ Glawe Spiel und Unterhaltungsgeräte Aufstellungsgesellschaft mbH & Co KG v Finanzamt Hamburg-Barmbek-Uhlenhorst,* 21.133 EUROPEAN COMMUNITY LAW, applied; *Tron Theatre Ltd*, 63.87 above, and *High Peak Theatre Trust Ltd*, 63.88 above, distinguished. *C & E Commrs v EMAP MacLaren Ltd, QB [1997] STC 490.*

Voluntary payments

63.90 **Tips received by taxi driver.** Tips received by the owner of a taxi were held to be chargeable to VAT, as part of the consideration paid for his services, in *P Kenealy, LON/77/208 (VTD 466).*

63.91   **Optional service charge in restaurant.**   A company operated a restaurant. A suggested 'service charge' was included on its menu and on bills which it gave to customers, but it was stated both on the menu and on the bills that the 'service charge' was optional. The Commissioners issued an assessment on the basis that the service charge formed part of the consideration for meals consumed. The company appealed, contending that the payments for service were voluntary. The tribunal allowed the appeal, holding that under the contract between the company and the customers there was no liability to pay anything for service. Any payments made for service were not part of the consideration for the supplies made by the company, and accordingly were not chargeable to VAT. *Potters Lodge Restaurant Ltd*, 63.110 below, distinguished. *NDP Co Ltd, [1988] VATTR 40 (VTD 2653)*.

63.92   The decision in *NDP Co Ltd*, 63.91 above, was applied in the similar subsequent case of *JD Joyce, LON/95/2747A (VTD 14573)*.

63.93   **Additional ex gratia payment made more than two years after supplies to which it related—whether taxable consideration.**   A veterinary surgeon (P) had practised for several years without registering for VAT, although his turnover exceeded the statutory threshold. When the Commissioners discovered this, they imposed a penalty for non-registration and issued an assessment for the tax due, both of which P paid. P subsequently sought to recover VAT from some of his customers, whom he had not charged VAT during the period in which he had not been registered. One of these customers was the Department of Agriculture for Northern Ireland, which made an ex gratia payment in July 1988, representing the VAT at 15% on supplies made up to July 1986, on which VAT had not originally been charged. P did not account for VAT on the ex gratia payment. A VAT officer discovered this at a control visit in May 1989, and the Commissioners subsequently issued an assessment charging VAT on the amount P had received from the Department of Agriculture. P appealed, contending that the payment was not chargeable to VAT since it was voluntary. The tribunal dismissed P's appeal, holding that the payment related to taxable supplies which P had made to the Department, and was taxable consideration which had not previously been assessed. *AD Pottie, BEL/90/31X (VTD 5460)*.

63.94   **Insulation services—whether Government grants subject to VAT.**   A company supplied insulation services. Where such services were supplied to people on low incomes or aged over 60, grants were paid under a scheme initiated by the Department of the Environment. The company failed to account for output tax on the grants. The Commissioners issued a ruling that the grants were taxable, and the tribunal dismissed the company's appeal, holding that the grants were consideration for the services which the company supplied. The chairman observed that there was 'the clearest possible link' between the grant and the services supplied to the customer, and that the fact that the customer did not know the amount of the grant was irrelevant. *Anglia Energy Conservation Ltd, LON/96/1228 (VTD 14620)*.

63.95   *Anglia Energy Conservation Ltd*, 63.94 above, was applied in the similar subsequent case of *Interglow Ltd, LON/97/114 (VTD 15200)*.

63.96   A network installer, within the *Energy Efficiency Grants Regulations 1992*, received grants from the Energy Grants Action Agency in respect of energy advice which it gave to householders. It initially accounted for VAT in respect of such grants, but subsequently claimed repayment, on the basis that the grants were not consideration for any supplies. The Commissioners rejected the claim, considering that the grants were liable to VAT. The tribunal upheld the Commissioners' ruling, applying *Anglia Energy Conservation Ltd*, 63.94 above, but the QB directed that the case should be referred to the CJEC for a ruling on the interpretation of the words 'including subsidies directly linked to the price of such supplies' in *Article 11A1(a)* of the *EC Sixth Directive. Keeping Newcastle Warm v C & E Commrs, QB [2000] STC 454.*

63.97 **Fund-raising ball—whether part of payment voluntary.** See *Glasgow's Miles Better Mid-Summer 5th Anniversary Ball*, 63.114 below.

Multiple supplies

63.98 **Inclusive charge for river cruise holiday—method of apportionment.** A company provided holiday cruises on the Thames between Windsor and Oxford, using converted river barges for the purpose. The customer paid an inclusive charge to cover his cabin accommodation on the barge, meals, sightseeing tours in places called at en route and transport to and from the barge at the beginning and end of the cruise. The tribunal held that, in apportioning the consideration between cabin accommodation and catering (standard-rated) and the road and river transport (zero-rated), and the apportionment should be by reference to the cost of the supplies including overheads but disregarding capital expenditure. *River Barge Holidays Ltd, LON/77/345 (VTD 572).*

63.99 **Social club providing bingo and live entertainment—apportionment of consideration.** In the case noted at 23.7 EXEMPTIONS: MISCELLANEOUS, a social club provided live entertainment and bingo, for a combined admission fee. The tribunal had originally held that the consideration could not be apportioned and had to be treated as taxable in full, but the QB reversed this decision and remitted the case for reconsideration. Forbes J observed that the apportionment 'should take account of the profit element by ensuring that the part of the payment attributable to the facilities for bingo included a due proportion of the profit for the club from this part of the enterprise'. The tribunal directed that 15% of the consideration should be attributed to bingo (which was exempt from VAT) and 85% should be attributed to the taxable live entertainment. *Tynewydd Labour Working Men's Club & Institute Ltd, [1980] VATTR 165 (VTD 1089).*

63.100 **Coach tours—apportionment of consideration.** A company sold coach tours which included zero-rated transport and standard-rated meals and hotel accommodation. It accounted for tax on the basis that claimed that it was charging its customers for the meals and accommodation at cost, and making all its profit on the transport supplies. The Commissioners issued an assessment on the basis that the profit should be apportioned. The tribunal upheld the assessment and dismissed the company's appeal, observing that 'in arriving at the proportion of a single price which reflects the zero-rated element and the standard-rated elements making up the whole, it is not proper for the appellant company to affect to charge a profit cost on the zero-rated supply of transport and to pass on at cost the standard-rated supplies'. *Waterhouse Coaches Ltd, LON/82/378 (VTD 1417).* (*Note.* The substantive issue has been overtaken by the introduction of the Tour Operators' Margin Scheme, but the case remains an authority on the principles of apportionment. For the Commissioners' interpretation of the decision, see Customs' VAT Manual, Part 12, chapter 2, section 3.10.)

63.101 **Railway company offering combined ticket also allowing entrance to 'Camera Obscura'.** A company owned and operated a funicular railway. In 1985 it also opened a tourist attraction called a 'Camera Obscura', at the top of the cliff served by the railway. It sold tickets allowing both use of the railway and entrance to the Camera Obscura. During 1988 such a combined ticket was priced at £1.65, whereas a ticket allowing use of the railway only was priced at £1, as was a ticket allowing entry to the Camera Obscura but not use of the railway. The Commissioners issued an assessment on the basis that, since travel on the railway was zero-rated but entry to the

Camera Obscura was standard-rated, 50% of the amounts paid for combined tickets should be treated as liable to VAT at the standard rate. The company appealed, contending that the railway was more popular than the Camera, and that the price paid for a combined ticket should be apportioned as £1 for the railway and 65p for the Camera. At the relevant time, more than 50% of the tickets sold by the company were for the railway only, whereas fewer than 10% were for the Camera only, the remainder being combined tickets. The tribunal accepted the company's contentions and allowed the appeal, holding that the price of the combined tickets should be apportioned as £1 to the zero-rated supply of transport and only 65p to the standard-rated supply of admission to the Camera. *Aberystwyth Cliff Railway Co Ltd, MAN/90/1102 (VTD 6449)*.

63.102   **Programmes included with admission charge to greyhound stadium.**   In the case noted at 5.53 BOOKS, ETC. (where admission to a greyhound stadium included the provision of a programme), the tribunal found that 10% of the proprietor's costs related to zero-rated supplies, and held that an uplift of 50% should be allowed for the compilation and distribution of the material. Accordingly, the tribunal directed that 15% of the appellant's supplies should be treated as zero-rated and 85% as standard-rated. *IC Thomas, [1985] VATTR 67 (VTD 1862)*.

63.103   **Introduction agency.**   The proprietor of an introduction agency supplied clients with bulletins and a handbook, which were accepted as zero-rated. These items were not charged for separately, but formed part of the services provided in return for members' subscriptions. The Commissioners directed the proprietor to apportion her supplies on the basis of their relevant value. She appealed, contending that the apportionment should be based on the relevant cost. The tribunal allowed her appeal, holding that the Commissioners had not put forward any basis on which the value of the services could be calculated and that an apportionment between standard-rated and zero-rated services should be made by reference to the cost of supplying those services. The parties were unable to agree on the ratio to be adopted, and the proprietor applied to the tribunal for a determination of the issue. The tribunal found that 95% of the proprietor's printing costs related to zero-rated supplies, and held that an uplift of 100% should be allowed for the compilation and distribution of the material. On the evidence, the tribunal directed that 33.5% of the appellant's supplies should be treated as zero-rated and 66.5% as standard-rated. *BH Bright, LON/88/1383X (VTD 4577)*. (*Note*. For a subsequent application for costs, see 2.277 APPEALS.)

63.104   **Correspondence   courses   in   computer   training—amount   of consideration.**   A company supplied correspondence courses in computer training. The Commissioners agreed that 30% of the consideration was for manuals which qualified for zero-rating. In June 1991 the company claimed that part of the consideration was paid for examination fees, society membership fees and accommodation costs, and should be treated as disbursements which were outside the scope of VAT, thus reducing the amount of output tax payable. The Commissioners rejected the claim, and issued an assessment charging output tax on accommodation costs charged to students in 1992, on which the company had failed to account for tax. The company appealed. The tribunal dismissed the appeal, holding that the company was making a single supply of computer tuition. Output tax was chargeable on the whole of the amounts paid by the students, and the fact that the company spent some of its income on examination fees, subscriptions to professional bodies, and accommodation costs for students, did not reduce the taxable consideration. (The tribunal described the Commissioners' acceptance that 30% of the gross consideration should be treated as paid for the supply of zero-rated manuals as a 'concession'.) *Computeach International Ltd, [1994] VATTR 237 (VTD 12115)*.

Car hire and minicab businesses

63.105 **Minicab business—valuation of supplies of services to drivers.** A partnership operated a minicab business. The drivers who worked for it provided their own vehicles, but the partnership supplied the drivers with two-way radios and introductions to customers, and paid the drivers agreed rates for carrying accounts customers (0.05p per mile for the first 100 miles and not less than 0.65p per mile thereafter). Full-time drivers who failed to reach a 'target mileage' of 100 miles each week in relation to accounts customers were required to pay a 'penalty' of up to £70 for the use of the radio. The drivers were allowed to retain all fares received from cash customers. The partnership accounted for tax on the actual amounts which it received. The Commissioners issued an assessment on the basis that the partnership was making taxable supplies of services to the drivers, and that such services should be valued at £70 per week (i.e. the maximum amount which the partnership charged for the use of its radios). The tribunal upheld the assessment and dismissed the partnership's appeal, holding that there was a 'direct link' between the services which the partnership supplied to the drivers and the drivers' obligation either to provide driving services to the partnership or to pay the partnership cash for the use of the radios. *Staatssecretaris van Financien v Cooperatieve Vereniging 'Cooperatieve Aardappelenbewaarplaats GA'*, 21.45 EUROPEAN COMMUNITY LAW, applied. *RJ & CA Blanks, LON/95/3117 (VTD 14099)*.

63.106 *Blanks*, 63.105 above, was distinguished in a subsequent case where a partnership which operated a minicab business using self-employed drivers had a number of accounts customers. The partnership paid the drivers 90% of the amounts which it charged the accounts customers, less a deduction which it described as a 'contract levy'. (The partnership's other source of income was payments made by the drivers for the hire of radios.) The Commissioners issued an assessment on the basis that the 'contract levy' represented consideration paid by the drivers for a supply of services by the partnership. The partnership appealed, contending that the 'contract levy' was not consideration for a supply, but was simply an amount taken into account in determining the amount payable to the drivers for the services which they provided. The tribunal accepted this contention and allowed the appeal, holding on the evidence that the consideration for the services which the partnership supplied consisted of the amounts paid by the drivers for the hire of radios. Since the partnership was receiving consideration from the drivers for the services which it provided, it followed that there were no grounds for treating the 'contract levy' as additional consideration. On the evidence, the 'contract levy' was simply 'an attempt at creating fairness between drivers who may do more or less contract work' and 'its true nature is an adjustment to the ... 90% paid to drivers for client work'. *A2B Radio Cars, LON/96/933 (VTD 15145)*.

63.107 A company (C) carried on a radio-controlled minicab business, under which it acted as an agent for a number of self-employed owner-drivers, supplying them with radio equipment, providing advertising and putting them in touch with prospective passengers. The drivers paid C for the services which it provided. The normal weekly rates were £73 for part-time drivers and £88 for full-time drivers, but these amounts were frequently reduced if C had been unable to supply sufficient work for a driver during any particular week. On occasions some of the drivers worked for a company associated with C. That company paid the drivers a mileage rate lower than usual for the first 100 miles (as in *Blanks*, 63.105 above) and in such cases, C reduced its weekly charges by a corresponding amount. C accounted for output tax on the amounts which it received from the drivers. The Commissioners issued assessments on the basis that the effect of the arrangements with the drivers who worked for the associated company was that the cash consideration did not fully reflect the value of the services which C provided, and that output tax should be charged on the normal weekly charges, without taking account of the reduction in the rates. C appealed, contending that the rates which it charged the drivers were proportionate to the amount of work which they performed for C and therefore proportionate to the extent to which they used C's services. The tribunal accepted this contention and allowed C's appeal, holding on the evidence that the cash payments 'represented the entirety of the consideration moving to (C) from the drivers for the services supplied to them by (C)'. *Blanks*, 63.105 above, distinguished. *Computer Minicabs Ltd, LON/97/1541 (VTD 15614)*.

Repair services

63.108   **Valuation of repairs carried out under contract.**   A company (M), which was a member of a group, carried on the business of repairing electrical goods sold by other members of the group. To have goods repaired by M, the purchasers of the goods had to have taken out an insurance policy at the time of purchase. These policies were underwritten by an insurance company, which reimbursed M for repairs at an agreed rate. M accounted for tax on the amounts it received from the insurance company. However, the Commissioners formed the opinion that M was making its supplies to the purchasers of the goods, that these supplies should be valued at market value, and that the amounts which M received from the insurance company were significantly less than market value. They issued an assessment accordingly, charging tax of more than £270,000. M appealed, contending that the supplies should be valued at the rate agreed between M and the insurance company, so that there had been no underdeclaration of tax. The tribunal allowed the appeal, holding that M was making the relevant supplies to the insurance company, rather than to the purchasers of the goods. The consideration paid by the insurance company was the agreed rate of reimbursement, and there were no grounds for seeking to charge tax on the supposed market value of the work. *Dixons Group plc, LON/91/2716Y & LON/92/2730A (VTD 9604)*. (*Note*. The tribunal also held that certain credit notes issued by M to the insurance company had been issued *bona fide* and were effective for tax purposes.)

63.109   **Call-out charges for repairs of electrical appliances—charges refunded to purchasers of replacement appliances—valuation of repairs.**   A company sold electrical appliances. It employed a number of engineers to repair and service these appliances. When customers requested repairs, the company charged a call-out fee of between £30 and £40 in addition to its charges for parts and labour. However, the company informed customers that the call-out charge would be refunded if they purchased a replacement appliance from the company within three months. The company accounted for VAT on the amounts of the call-out charges when they were invoiced, but deducted the VAT element of any refunds made or credit notes issued during each accounting period. The Commissioners issued an assessment on the basis that the company was obliged to account for VAT on the full amounts of the call-out charges and was not entitled to deduct the VAT element of any refunds or credit notes from the amount payable. The company appealed, contending that there was in effect a single transaction and that VAT should not be charged on any call-out charges that were subsequently refunded. The tribunal allowed the appeal, holding that the effect of *Article 11C1* of the *EC Sixth Directive* was that the taxable amount was to be reduced by the amount of the refund or credit note. *ME Braine (Boatbuilders) Ltd* and *Castle Associates Ltd*, 38.78 INVOICES AND CREDIT NOTES, distinguished. *AEG (UK) Ltd, LON/93/589A (VTD 10944)*.

Miscellaneous

63.110   **Service charges by restaurant.**   A company carried on a restaurant business. The bills rendered to customers included a 10% service charge and the total, including the service charge, was stated to be tax inclusive. The total of the service charges was paid to the waiters at the end of each day, to be shared between themselves as they agreed. In its returns the company did not account for tax on the service charges. The Commissioners issued an assessment charging tax on them and the tribunal dismissed the company's appeal. The service charge was part of the consideration paid by the customer, and the company's liability to account for the tax on this consideration could not be affected by an arrangement between the company and its employees under which part of the consideration was paid over to the employees. *Potters Lodge Restaurant Ltd, LON/79/286 (VTD 905).*

63.111 **'Touring Allowance' to actress.** An actress, registered for VAT, was engaged by a company to take a part in a play being taken on tour in theatres in various parts of the country. For this purpose she entered into a 'standard contract' under which the company agreed to pay her specified amounts when rehearsing for or performing in the play, together with a weekly 'touring allowance' when rehearsing or performing more than 25 miles away from her address. She did not account for tax on the 'touring allowance', and the Commissioners issued an assessment charging tax on it. The tribunal upheld the assessment and dismissed the actress's appeal. *AC Twigg, [1983] VATTR 17 (VTD 1329).*

63.112 **Use of company yacht by employees.** A company purchased a yacht for use by its employees. The yacht was also used to entertain customers. The Commissioners issued an assessment to charge tax on the supply of the yacht to the employees. The running costs of the yacht, and depreciation at an annual rate of 20%, were apportioned between days when the yacht was used by employees and days when it was used to entertain customers. Thus, in a year where the yacht was used on 51 days by employees and on 9 days for entertaining customers, tax was charged on $\frac{51}{60}$ of the depreciation and running costs. The company appealed, contending that the amount charged should be $\frac{51}{365}$ of the depreciation. The QB rejected this contention and upheld the assessment. It was not permissible to avoid tax on depreciation by allocating most of the charge for depreciation to days on which the yacht was not in use. On the facts found by the tribunal, tax should be charged on $\frac{51}{60}$ of the depreciation for the year. *C & E Commrs v Teknequip Ltd, QB [1987] STC 664.*

63.113 **Gaming machines hired by company owning shop—amount of consideration.** A company (B) owned a shop which sold fishing tackle. It hired two amusement machines for installation in the shop, under a verbal agreement whereby the company which owned the machines (S) would service and empty them, and the takings would be split equally. S treated its 50% of the takings as a hire charge, and retained a further 7.5% of the takings as VAT thereon (the rate of VAT was 15% at the relevant time). S paid this 7.5% to the Commissioners and B reclaimed it as input tax. B accounted for output tax on the 42.5% of the takings which it retained. When the Commissioners discovered this, they issued an assessment on the basis that, since B was hiring the machines from S, B was supplying the use of the machines to its customers and should have accounted for output tax on the full amount of the takings. The tribunal upheld the assessment and dismissed B's appeal. *Bennetts of Sheffield Ltd, [1986] VATTR 253 (VTD 2219).*

63.114 **Fund-raising ball—whether part of ticket price not paid as 'consideration'.** An association organised a fund-raising ball. It printed application forms showing the ticket price as £50. In small print at the foot of the form it was stated that 'for VAT purposes the entrance fee is £20. The balance of £30 represents a minimum voluntary donation in aid of hospice funds.' Similar wording appeared on the tickets. The association accounted for VAT on only £20 per ticket, and the Commissioners issued an assessment on the basis that VAT was chargeable on the full price of £50. The tribunal dismissed the appeal. The statement that £30 was a 'minimum voluntary donation' indicated 'an element of compulsion'. The application forms and tickets clearly stated that the purchase price of the tickets was £50, and indicated that admission could not be obtained for less. Accordingly, the full price of £50 represented consideration for the tickets. *Glasgow's Miles Better Mid-Summer 5th Anniversary Ball, EDN/89/95 (VTD 4460).*

63.115 **Removal   of   asbestos—whether   contribution   from   CEGB 'consideration'.**   A company agreed to purchase the Battersea Power Station from the CEGB. It also agreed to remove asbestos and asbestos-related plant from the site. The CEGB paid the company more than £2 million as a contribution towards the costs of the removal of the asbestos. The Commissioners issued an assessment charging tax on this payment, on the basis that the removal of the asbestos was a service supplied by the company and the payment represented consideration for this service. The company appealed, contending that the payment should not be regarded as consideration for VAT purposes. The QB rejected this contention and upheld the assessment. 'Consideration' meant everything which the supplier had received or was to receive from the purchaser for the relevant supply. The payment by the CEGB was directly linked to the services to be supplied by the company, and was therefore within the definition of 'consideration'. The fact that the CEGB was motivated by a sense of public duty, rather than by commercial motives, did not alter the objective nature of the supply. *C & E Commrs v Battersea Leisure Ltd, QB [1992] STC 213.*

63.116 **Video hire—whether fines for late return of videos chargeable to VAT as consideration for a supply.**   The proprietor of a video club imposed fines on customers who returned videos later than agreed. He did not account for VAT on these fines. The Commissioners issued a decision that the fines were chargeable to VAT as part of the consideration for the supply of the films. The tribunal upheld the Commissioners' decision and dismissed the trader's appeal. *JG Leigh (t/a Moor Lane Video), [1990] VATTR 59 (VTD 5098).*

63.117 **Payphones—whether full amount of coins deposited by customers representing consideration for supplies.**   A company provided telephone services through a number of coin-operated payphones. In some cases, customers paid more than the amount which the company charged for the calls made (e.g. by inserting a £1 coin for a call which only cost 40p). In such cases, the machines did not give the customer any change, and the company retained the full amounts paid into the machines. The Commissioners issued a ruling that the company should account for output tax on the full amounts paid by customers. The company appealed, contending that output tax was only chargeable on the amounts which it charged, and that excess payments received from customers were outside the scope of VAT. The tribunal rejected this contention and dismissed the appeal, holding that the customers had purchased 'the possibility of making telephone calls up to the amount of the coins inserted. The length of the telephone call made does not convert the credit purchased by those coins into a surplus or gift.' *British Telecommunications plc,* 58.355 SUPPLY, distinguished. *New World Payphones Ltd, LON/98/712 (VTD 15964).*

63.118 **Building of work—valuation of consideration where contract price not payable for five years.**   In the case noted at 58.311 SUPPLY, the contract price for certain building work was not payable until five years after completion of the work. The tribunal had held that the supply took place when the work was carried out, but that the value of the consideration should be reduced to take account of the delay in reaching the due date for payment and the possibility of the final price being reduced to allow for any defects in the work. The agreed price of the work had been £72,500, but the company had to pay £5,900 to remedy defects in the work. The company had received £52,500 in the form of an interest-free loan, and the tribunal held that the balance of £20,000 should be discounted at 16% p.a. for five years, the total discount being computed as £10,844. The tribunal's decision therefore was that the original price of £72,500 should be reduced by £10,844 in respect of discounting and by £5,900 in respect of the necessary remedial work, so that VAT was only chargeable on the balance of £55,756. *Mercantile Contracts Ltd, LON/88/786Y (VTD 5266)*.

63.119   **Computer software licences.**   A computer software consultant (R) registered for VAT from January 1991 and deregistered in October 1991. While registered, he had purchased, and reclaimed input tax on, 50 software licences. He had only sold one of these. The Commissioners therefore issued an assessment under what is now *VATA 1994, Sch 4 para 8*, charging tax on the cost of the 49 licences which he still held at deregistration. He appealed, contending that the licences were worth substantially less than their cost, and that they should be valued at their market value. The tribunal allowed the appeal, holding that what R had purchased was 'a software program with the rights to use, make 50 copies and distribute'. Accordingly the supply to R was a supply of services, rather than a supply of goods, and *VATA 1994, Sch 4 para 8* did not apply. The tribunal also observed that, even if the supply had been a supply of goods, the supply would have been valued at cost, rather than at market value, specifically disapproving the decision in *McCormick*, 63.14 above. *TP Rowledge, LON/93/237A (VTD 12590)*.

63.120   **Football club—supplies of season tickets to bondholders.**   A football club wished to raise funds to finance a new stand. It issued bonds which carried no interest, but which guaranteed the holders the right to buy, or to allow a nominated person to buy, a season ticket in the new stand. It did not account for output tax on the issue of the bonds (which it treated as exempt from VAT under *VATA 1994, Sch 9, Group 5*) and accounted for output tax on the sale price of the season tickets. The Commissioners issued an assessment on the basis that the consideration for such season tickets was not solely the amount paid by the bondholders for the tickets, but included an amount representing the interest forgone by the bondholders. The club appealed, contending that the only consideration for the season tickets was the money specifically paid for them. The tribunal accepted this contention and allowed the appeal, holding that the two transactions were separate and that the interest-free loans could not be regarded as consideration for the season tickets. The tribunal observed that 'the most significant feature of the whole arrangement that, in our view, severs the subscription transaction from the subsequent season ticket purchase transaction is that subscriber and purchaser may, and as time goes by inevitably will, be different people'. *Exeter Golf & Country Club Ltd*, 13.31 CLUBS, ASSOCIATIONS AND ORGANISATIONS, distinguished. *The Arsenal Football Club plc, [1996] VATDR 5 (VTD 14011)*.

63.121   **Golf club—sale of debentures to members.**   In the case noted at 26.31 FINANCE, in which the tribunal held that the purchase of debentures in a company formed to operate a golf club represented 'non-monetary consideration for the supply of services, namely the grant of membership rights', the valuation of the consideration was in dispute. The tribunal held that the taxable amount should be taken as the interest which the company would otherwise have been obliged to pay on the amount borrowed, calculated at the minimum lending rate. The tribunal declined to follow *obiter dicta* of Cumming-Bruce LJ in *Exeter Golf & Country Club Ltd*, 13.31 CLUBS, ASSOCIATIONS AND ORGANISATIONS, on the grounds that they were inconsistent with the subsequent CJEC decisions in *Naturally Yours Cosmetics Ltd (No 2)*, 21.128 EUROPEAN COMMUNITY LAW, and *Empire Stores Ltd*, 21.129 EUROPEAN COMMUNITY LAW. *Harleyford Golf Club plc, LON/95/3076 (VTD 14466)*.

63.122   **Free meals supplied to coach drivers.**   A company operated a motorway service station. In an attempt to induce coach drivers to stop at its premises, it offered a free meal to any coach driver with at least 20 passengers who stopped at its premises for at least 30 minutes. The Commissioners issued an assessment charging tax on the normal retail price of the meals consumed by the drivers. The company appealed, contending that output tax should only be chargeable on the cost of the meals. The QB rejected this contention and upheld the assessment, and the CA dismissed the company's appeal. Applying the principles laid down by the CJEC in *Naturally Yours Cosmetics Ltd (No 2)*, 21.128 EUROPEAN COMMUNITY LAW, the crucial question was whether there was an agreement between the company and the drivers placing a monetary value on the meals. On the evidence, the parties must be taken to have attributed a specific monetary value, being the normal retail price of the meal chosen by the driver. *Rosgill Group Ltd*, 63.27 above, applied. *Empire Stores Ltd*, 21.129 EUROPEAN COMMUNITY LAW, was distinguished, on the grounds that the goods in that case were not in the company's catalogue and that no specific value had been attributed to them. *Westmorland Motorway Services Ltd v C & E Commrs, CA [1998] STC 431.*

63.123   **Cable television company—inducements to new customers—valuation of supplies.**   A cable television company launched a scheme whereby it offered reduced charges to new customers (£19.99 per month instead of the standard charge of £30.99 per month) who already held a satellite dish if the customers let the company remove the dish. It accounted for tax on the amounts which it actually received. The Commissioners issued assessments on the basis that the price reductions allowed to such customers were consideration for the right to remove the existing satellite dishes, so that output tax was chargeable on the amount of the standard charge. The tribunal allowed the company's appeal. In principle, the customer's undertaking to allow the company to remove his dish was part of the consideration for the supply of cable television services. However, the dishes (which were scrapped) had no monetary value to either party, so that 'no value falls to be attributed to the consideration obtained by the appellant in the form of its right to remove the customer's satellite dish'. *Telewest Communications Group Ltd, [1996] VATDR 566 (VTD 14383).*

63.124   **Competitions—whether prize money deductible.**   In the case noted at 58.161 SUPPLY, a company which organised a number of 'spot-the-ball' competitions submitted a repayment claim on the basis that it should have deducted the amounts which it paid out in prizes. The tribunal rejected this contention, holding that the company was liable to account for tax on the full amount of the entry fees, but the QB held that the question should be referred to the CJEC, to consider whether *HJ Glawe Spiel und Unterhaltungsgeräte Aufstellungsgesellschaft mbH & Co KG v Finanzamt Hamburg-Barmbek-Uhlenhorst*, 21.133 EUROPEAN COMMUNITY LAW, should be applied or distinguished. *Town & County Factors Ltd v C & E Commrs (and cross-appeal), QB [1998] STC 225.* (*Note.* The CJEC has registered the case as *C-498/99*. However, the Advocate-General has not yet delivered an Opinion.)

63.125   **Management services—set-offs between accountancy partnership and associated service company.**   See *Smith & Williamson*, 41.12 MANAGEMENT SERVICES.

63.126   **Valuation of stock-lending transactions.**   See *Scottish Eastern Investment Trust plc*, 43.101 PARTIAL EXEMPTION.

64   Warehoused Goods and Free Zones

64.1   An individual (C) purchased consignments of alcohol while they were in bonded warehouses. He was subsequently convicted of being knowingly concerned in the fraudulent evasion of duty, and sentenced to four years' imprisonment. In addition the Commissioners issued an assessment charging VAT in respect of the consignments. The tribunal upheld the assessment in principle (while reducing the amount in respect of a consignment which was still in a lorry when he was arrested). The tribunal observed that where goods were removed from a warehouse in the UK, a liability to VAT arose by virtue of *VATA 1994, s 18(3)*. The process used for removing goods for export involved the issue of a C88 which had to be stamped at the port through which the goods were exported. C had not submitted a stamped C88 in respect of any of the goods covered by the assessment. The Commissioners had produced evidence linking C 'with the diversion of the goods to the home market'. *DL Chitolie, LON/96/794 (VTD 16705)*.

65 Zero-Rating: Miscellaneous

Cross-references.

For zero-rating under *VATA 1994, Sch 8, Group 1*, see 27 FOOD. For zero-rating under *VATA 1994, Sch 8, Group 3*, see 5 BOOKS, ETC. For zero-rating under *VATA 1994, Sch 8, Groups 5 and 6*, see 15 CONSTRUCTION OF BUILDINGS, ETC. and 52 PROTECTED BUILDINGS. For zero-rating under *VATA 1994, Sch 8, Group 7*, see 37 INTERNATIONAL SERVICES. For zero-rating under *VATA 1994, Sch 8, Group 8*, see 62 TRANSPORT. For zero-rating under *VATA 1994, Sch 8, Group 12*, see 19 DRUGS, MEDICINES, AIDS FOR THE HANDICAPPED, ETC. For the zero-rating of exports see 24 EXPORTS. For zero-rating under *VATA 1994, Sch 8, Group 15*, see 11 CHARITIES. For zero-rating under *VATA 1994, Sch 8, Group 16*, see 12 CLOTHING.

The cases in this chapter are arranged under the following headings.

> **Group 2—Sewerage services and water** 65.1–65.2
> **Group 9—Caravans and houseboats** 65.3–65.8

GROUP 2—SEWERAGE SERVICES AND WATER

65.1 **Coin-operated washing machines in launderette.** A company owned a number of self-service launderettes. The Commissioners issued a ruling that the company was required to account for output tax on the full amount of its takings. The company appealed, contending that part of the charge was for the supply of water and should be treated as zero-rated under what is now *VATA 1994, Sch 8, Group 2, Item 2*. The tribunal rejected this contention and dismissed the appeal, holding that the whole of the charge was standard-rated. *Mander Laundries Ltd, [1973] VATTR 136 (VTD 31).*

65.2 **Saline solution imported for research—whether water.** The proprietor of an acupuncture clinic imported a large number of ampoules of water described as 'distilled water', but which in fact contained a saline solution with about 0.9% of salt. The Commissioners issued a ruling that tax was chargeable on the importation, and the proprietor appealed, contending that the solution should be treated as water and should be zero-rated under what is now *VATA 1994, Sch 8, Group 2, Item 2*. The tribunal rejected this contention and dismissed the appeal, holding that the solution was not 'water'. *AJ Scott-Morley, LON/80/297 (VTD 1097).*

GROUP 9—CARAVANS AND HOUSEBOATS

65.3 **Scanner—whether a caravan.** A company failed to account for output tax on the supply of a mobile body scanner on an articulated chassis. The Commissioners issued an assessment charging tax on the scanner, and the company appealed, contending that the scanner was a caravan and should be treated as zero-rated. The tribunal rejected this contention and dismissed the appeal, holding that the scanner was not a caravan since it was not designed for human habitation. *Elscint (GB) Ltd, LON/83/337 (VTD 1654).*

65.4 **'Park homes'—whether 'caravans' within VATA 1994, Sch 8, Group 9.** A company which owned a caravan site arranged for structures, described as 'park homes', to be erected on the site. It did not account for output tax on the sale of these 'park homes', and reclaimed the input tax attributable to their construction. The Commissioners issued an assessment to recover the tax, considering that it related to licences to occupy land, which were exempt supplies. The company appealed, contending that the sale of the 'park homes' was zero–rated under what is now either *VATA 1994, Sch 8, Group 5* or *Sch 8, Group 9*. The tribunal held firstly that the 'park homes' were buildings, but that their sale did not qualify for zero–rating under *Sch 8, Group 5* (see 15.72 CONSTRUCTION OF DWELLINGS, ETC.), and secondly that their sale qualified for zero–rating under *Sch 8, Group 9*. The fact that the 'park homes' were within the definition of a 'building' did not prevent them from being within the definition of a 'caravan', since 'the two categories are not necessarily exclusive'. *Stonecliff Caravan Park, [1993] VATTR 464 (VTD 11097)*. (*Note.* The tribunal held that most of the company's input tax was attributable to exempt supplies but that the tax relating to the provision of brick skirtings was directly attributable to the sale of the 'park homes', and adjourned the hearing for the parties to reach agreement on the amount of the allowable input tax. There was no further public hearing of the appeal.)

65.5   **Sale of caravans—apportionment of consideration to fixtures and fittings.**   The owner of a caravan site sold furnished caravans on the site. He did not account for output tax on the sale of the caravans, but did account for output tax on a proportion of the consideration which he treated as being for fixtures and fittings. In a case where he sold a furnished caravan (the cost of which was £26,500) for £56,000, he treated £4,400 of this as being for fixtures and fittings, and accounted for output tax accordingly. The Commissioners issued an assessment on the basis that he should have accounted for output tax on a greater proportion of the consideration (in the above example, on £6,975 rather than on £4,400), in accordance with the method laid down by *Notice 701/20/89*. The tribunal allowed the owner's appeal in part, holding that the consideration of £56,000 included an element in respect of work carried out on the site, which was zero–rated under what is now *VATA 1994, Sch 8, Group 5*, and directing that the assessment should be recomputed accordingly. The Commissioners appealed to the QB, which remitted the case to the tribunal for rehearing, finding that the tribunal had failed to consider the terms of the invoice between the owner and the purchaser. *C & E Commrs v DR Barratt, QB [1995] STC 661*. (*Note.* There was no further public hearing of the appeal.)

65.6   A company which sold furnished caravans submitted a repayment claim on the basis that it had attributed an excessive proportion of the consideration to the standard–rated contents of the caravans. The Commissioners rejected the claim on the basis that it did not conform with the guidelines laid down in *Notice 701/20/89*. The company appealed, contending that the method of apportionment set out in the *Notice* was inappropriate, because it assumed that the manufacturers' apportionment was correct, and that the trader made the same profit margin on the removable contents as on the caravan itself. The tribunal dismissed the appeal, holding that the method of apportionment must give 'a fair and reasonable result', and finding that the method laid down in the *Notice* 'is much more likely to produce such a result than that advanced by the appellant'. *Haulfryn Estates Co Ltd, MAN/97/244 (VTD 16145)*.

65.7   **Caravan used as office—whether input tax reclaimable.**   A trader reclaimed input tax on the purchase of a caravan which he used as an office, although the purchase price was exclusive of VAT. The Commissioners issued an assessment to recover the tax, considering that the caravan was zero–rated so that no input tax was reclaimable. The trader appealed, contending that the input tax should be treated as reclaimable since the caravan was purchased for business use rather than as domestic accommodation. The tribunal dismissed the appeal, holding that the caravan was within what is now *VATA 1994, Sch 8, Group 9, Item 1* and was therefore zero–rated. *MJ Rooke, MAN/91/1566 (VTD 9819)*.

65.8   **Yacht used as permanent residence—whether a 'houseboat'.**   In the case noted at 39.116 LAND, the tribunal held that a yacht was not within the definition of a 'houseboat', even though the appellants used it as their permanent residence. *DM & PJ Roberts, [1992] VATTR 30 (VTD 7516)*.

Table of Cases

The table is referenced to the paragraph number.

A

Table of Cases

Table of Cases

Table of Cases

Table of Cases

Table of Cases

Table of Cases

Table of Cases

Table of Cases

Table of Cases

Table of Cases

Table of Cases

Table of Cases

Table of Cases

Table of Cases

Table of Cases

Table of Cases

Table of Cases

Table of Cases

Table of Cases

Table of Cases

Table of Cases

Table of Cases

Table of Cases

Table of Cases

Table of Cases

Table of Cases

H

Table of Cases

Table of Cases

Table of Cases

Table of Cases

Table of Cases

Table of Cases

J

Table of Cases

Table of Cases

Table of Cases

Table of Cases

Table of Cases

Table of Cases

M

Table of Cases

Table of Cases

Table of Cases

Table of Cases

Table of Cases

Table of Cases

Table of Cases

Table of Cases

P

Table of Cases

Table of Cases

Table of Cases

Table of Cases

Table of Cases

Table of Cases

Table of Cases

Table of Cases

Table of Cases

Table of Cases

Table of Cases

Table of Cases

Table of Cases

Table of Cases

Table of Cases

Table of Cases

Table of Cases

Table of Cases

Table of Cases

Table of Cases

Table of Cases

Table of Statutes

Table of Statutes

Table of Statutes

Table of Statutory Instruments

Table of European Community Directives

Table of European Community Directives

Index

This index is referenced to the paragraph number.
The entries printed in bold capitals are chapter headings in the text.

Index

Index

Index

BUILDINGS AND LAND—*continued*

Index

Index

Index

Index

Index

Index

Index

Index

Index

Index

Index

Index

Index

Index

Index

Index

Index

Index

Index

Index

R

Index

Index

Index

REGISTRATION,

antedated by Commissioners,	53.20–53.25
appealable matters,	55.1, 55.2
associated persons as a single taxable person,	53.95–53.132
—accountancy,	53.99, 53.100
—café and bread shop,	53.101
—car hire,	53.113
—car sales and car wash,	53.117
—catering at public house,	53.107–53.110, 53.123
—cohabitation, relevance of,	53.109, 53.120
—computer supplies,	53.119
—dry-cleaning and ironing,	53.97, 53.98
—failure to comply with direction,	49.285
—fairground amusements,	53.118
—farming and bed and breakfast,	53.128
—farming and pony trekking,	53.127
—fencing contractors,	53.124
—fish and chip shop,	53.102
—fitness club and beauty salon,	53.106
—hairdressers,	53.103, 53.125, 53.126
—health studio,	53.104, 53.105
—holiday cottages and restaurant,	53.114
—ice-cream vendors,	53.115
—jewellers,	53.131
—launderettes operated by associated companies,	53.95, 53.96
—market traders,	53.120
—model aircraft, sale of,	53.112
—public house,	53.107–53.110, 53.123
—restaurant and gift shop,	53.116
—service station and video club,	53.111
—tax consultancy,	53.99, 53.100
—tea room at furniture shop,	53.122
—whether direction may be retrospective,	53.132
cancellation,	53.62–53.91
—duplicated registration,	53.62
—no business carried on,	53.65, 53.66
—supplies exempt,	53.69–53.71
—whether input tax repayable,	53.78, 53.79
cessation of liability to register,	53.41–53.45
conditional,	34.446
date from which effective,	53.13–53.36, 53.57–53.59
entitlement to be registered,	53.51–53.61
exemption from, application for,	53.92–53.94
future turnover,	53.37–53.39
group,	30.1–30.15
—whether group registration may be retrospective,	30.2–30.5
input tax incurred before,	34.472–34.489
'intending trader', as,	34.446, 53.51–53.55
liability to be registered,	53.1–53.40
partnerships,	53.1–53.5

Index

Index

Index

Index

Index

Index

Index

Index

Index

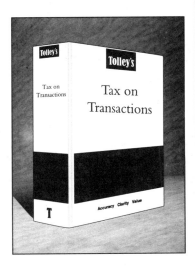